D0042897

HARRAP'S

MINI

French-English

DICTIONARY

DICTIONNAIRE

Anglais-Français

Michael Janes

HARRAP

London and Paris

French Consultant
Fabrice Antoine

English Consultants
Hazel Curties
Stuart Fortey

First published in Great Britain 1988
by HARRAP Ltd
19–23 Ludgate Hill, London EC4M 7PD

© Harrap Limited 1988

Reprinted with amendments 1988

Dépôt légal pour cette édition: avril 1988

Printed in Great Britain by
Richard Clay Ltd, Bungay, Suffolk

Contents/Table des matières

Preface

This dictionary is an entirely new publication designed to provide an up-to-date, practical and concise work of reference giving translations of the most useful French and English vocabulary.

The aim has been to achieve a work of great clarity of equal value to French and to English speakers, whether students, tourists, businessmen or -women or general readers, and to produce a text offering the maximum amount of guidance in pinpointing and understanding translations. Equal importance has been given to the presentation of French and English. Different translations of the same word or phrase are clearly labelled by means of bracketed context indicators and/or style and field labels. A single translation of a word is also often labelled as an additional aid to the user (e.g. **hedgehog** n (animal) hérisson m; **ungainly** a (clumsy) gauche; **béotien, -ienne** nmf (inculte) philistine). The user is helped by having indicators and labels in French in the French section and in English in the English section of the dictionary.

Style and field labels follow bracketed indicators (e.g. **grid** n . . . (system) El réseau m; **bidule** nm (chose) Fam thingummy). In the event of more than one translation within a grammatical category being qualified by the same style or field label, the label may then precede (e.g. **calé, liquidizer, trucker**).

The user will find in the text important abbreviations, useful geographical information such as names of countries, and a wide coverage of American words and usage. The vocabulary treated includes French and English colloquialisms and slang, and important technical jargon. Comparatives and superlatives of English adjectives are also indicated.

In order to save space, derived words are usually included within the entry of a headword. All such words are highlighted by means of a lozenge. Derivatives may be written in full or abbreviated, as is usually the case for important derived forms (such as English **-ly** or French **-ment**).

An oblique stroke in bold is used to mark the stem of a headword at which point the derived ending is added. A bold dash stands for a headword or the portion of a headword to the left of the oblique stroke (e.g. **awkward** a . . . ◆**-ly** adv . . . ◆**-ness** n . . . ; **boulevers/er** vt . . . ◆**-ant** a . . . ◆**-ement** nm).

An oblique stroke within an entry is another space-saving device. It is used to separate non equivalent alternative parts of a phrase or expression matched exactly in French and English (e.g. **les basses/hautes classes** the lower/upper classes is to be understood as: **les basses classes** the lower classes and **les hautes classes** the upper classes; **to give s.o./sth a push** pousser qn/qch as: **to give s.o. a push** pousser qn and **to give sth a push** pousser qch).

A further typographical device, a filled square, may be used to introduce a string of English phrasal verbs (see **come, take**).

In common with other Harrap dictionaries, when a headword appears in an example in the same form, it is represented by its initial letter. This applies whether the headword starts a new line (e.g. **advance** n **in a. of s.o.** avant qn) or appears within an entry, either in full form (e.g. ◆**arterial** a a. **road** route f principale), or in abbreviated form (e.g. (where ◆**-ed** stands for **advanced**) ◆**-ed a a. in years** âgé).

The pronunciation of both English and French is shown using the latest symbols of the International Phonetic Alphabet. Pronunciation is given for headwords at the start of an entry, and, as an additional help to the user, for a word within an entry where the correct pronunciation may be difficult to derive from the form of the word (e.g. ◆**aristocratie** [-asi]; ◆**aoûtien, -ienne** [ausjε̃, -jεn]; ◆**rabid** [ˈræbɪd]; ◆**prayer** [prεər]).

Stress in English is indicated for headwords and for derived words in which stress differs from that of a headword (e.g. **civilize** [ˈsɪvɪlaɪz] and ◆**civili'zation**). American English pronunciation is listed wherever it is considered to differ substantially from that of British English (e.g. **aristocrat** [ˈærɪstəkræt, Am əˈrɪstəkræt]; **quinine** [ˈkwɪniːn, Am ˈkwaɪnaɪn]). American spelling is also given if considered sufficiently different (e.g. **tire** and **tyre, plow** and **plough**).

An original feature of this dictionary is its semantic approach to the order and arrangement of entries. An approach whereby the meaning of words is allowed to

iv

influence the structure of entries is felt to be of particular benefit to the user in his or her understanding of language.

Important semantic categories have been indicated by bold Arabic numerals within an entry (see **bolt**, **tail**, **général**) or have been entered as separate headwords (see **bug¹** and **bug²**, **draw¹** and **draw²**, **start¹** and **start²**). Note that grammatical categories, apart from the first, have been marked by a dash.

Words are entered under the headword from which they are considered to derive (e.g. **approfondi**, abbreviated as ◆—i follows **approfond/ir**; ◆**astronomer** and ◆**astro'no-mical** follow **astronomy**). Present and past participles (used adjectivally) are felt to be closely associated in meaning and form with the infinitive from which they derive. They are entered, usually in abbreviated form, within an entry immediately after the infinitive, any other derivatives there may be following in alphabetical order (e.g. **exalt/er** *vt* ... ◆—**ant** *a* ... ◆—**é** *a* ... ◆**exaltation** *nf*; **accommodat/e** *vt* ... ◆—**ing** *a* ... ◆**accommo'dation** *n*: **expir/e** *vi* ... ◆—**ed** *a* ... ◆**expi'ration** *n* ... ◆**expiry** *n*).

Derived words and compounds are felt to be semantically distinct and are, wherever possible, grouped together alphabetically and listed separately from each other (e.g. **base** *n* ... ◆—**less** *a* ... ◆—**ness** *n* ... ◆**baseball** *n* ... ◆**baseboard** *n*; **bouton** *nm* ... ◆**b.-d'or** *nm* ... ◆**b.-pression** *nm* ... ◆**boutonner** *vt* ... ◆**boutonneux**, **-euse** *a* ... ◆**boutonnière** *nf*). Compounds may be listed in the place within an entry where they are felt best to belong by virtue of meaning.

The author wishes to express his gratitude to Monsieur F. Antoine, Mrs H. Curties and Mr S. Fortey for their advice and help, to Mrs R. Hillmore for her assistance with proofreading, and to Mr J.-L. Barbanneau for his support and encouragement.

M. Janes
London, 1988

Préface

Ce dictionnaire entièrement nouveau a pour ambition d'être un ouvrage de référence moderne, pratique et compact, offrant les traductions des termes les plus courants du français comme de l'anglais.

Il veut être un ouvrage qui, par sa grande clarté, soit utile autant au francophone qu'à l'anglophone, pour les études, le tourisme, les affaires aussi bien que pour l'usage courant: il tente de fournir le plus d'indications possible pour aider l'utilisateur à cerner et à comprendre les traductions proposées. On a accordé la même importance à la présentation du français qu'à celle de l'anglais. Les différentes traductions d'un même mot ou d'une même expression sont clairement définies à l'aide d'indications de contexte entre parenthèses et/ou de symboles indiquant le niveau de langue et le domaine d'utilisation. Lorsqu'un mot est accompagné d'une seule traduction, celle-ci est également souvent précédée d'une indication destinée à fournir à l'utilisateur une aide supplémentaire (par exemple **hedgehog** *n* (*animal*) hérisson *m*; **ungainly** *a* (*clumsy*) gauche; **béotien**, **-ienne** *nmf* (*inculte*) philistine). L'accès à cet ouvrage est facilité par l'utilisation d'indications en français dans la partie français-anglais et en anglais dans la partie anglais-français.

Les indications de niveau de langue et de domaine d'utilisation viennent à la suite de celles entre parenthèses (par exemple **grid** *n* ... (*system*) *El* réseau *m*; **bidule** *nm* (*chose*) *Fam* thingummy). Lorsque plusieurs traductions dans la même catégorie grammaticale sont définies par la même indication, celle-ci peut alors venir en tête (voir **calé**, **liquidizer**, **trucker**).

L'utilisateur trouvera dans cet ouvrage des abréviations importantes, de précieux éléments de géographie tels que des noms de pays, ainsi qu'une large sélection d'américanismes. Le lexique retenu comprend des mots et des expressions familiers et argotiques, tant en français qu'en anglais, et des termes techniques courants. De plus, les comparatifs et superlatifs des adjectifs anglais sont donnés.

Par souci de concision, les mots dérivés sont généralement donnés dans le corps des articles. Tous ces mots sont repérés par un losange. Les dérivés sont donnés soit sous la forme complète, soit en abrégé, ce qui est généralement le cas pour les formes les plus courantes (telles que celles en **-ly** en anglais ou en **-ment** en français).

On utilise une barre oblique pour indiquer le radical d'une entrée à la suite duquel la terminaison d'un dérivé sera ajoutée. Un tiret en gras remplace le mot d'entrée ou la partie de ce mot qui précède la barre oblique (par exemple **awkward** *a* . . . ◆**-ly** *adv* . . . ◆**-ness** *n* . . . ; **boulevers/er** *vt* . . . ◆**-ant** *a* . . . ◆**-ement** *nm*).

Toujours par souci de concision, une barre oblique est utilisée dans un article pour éviter la répétition d'un même élément de phrase (par exemple **les basses/hautes classes** the lower/upper classes se lira: **les basses classes** the lower classes et **les hautes classes** the upper classes; **to give s.o./sth a push** pousser qn/qch se lira: **to give s.o. a push** pousser qn et **to give sth a push** pousser qch).

Enfin, un carré plein peut être utilisé pour introduire une série de verbes à particule en anglais (voir **come**, **take**).

Comme il est d'usage dans les autres dictionnaires Harrap, lorsqu'un mot d'entrée est repris sous la même forme dans un exemple, il est remplacé par sa première lettre. Cela est le cas aussi bien lorsque le mot est au début d'un article (par exemple **advance** *n* in a. of s.o. avant qn) qu'apparaît dans un article, sous sa forme complète (par exemple ◆**arterial** *a* a. road route *f* principale) ou en abrégé (par exemple ◆**-ed** remplaçant **advanced**) ◆**-ed a** a. in years âgé).

La prononciation de l'anglais comme du français est fournie; elle utilise la notation la plus moderne de l'Alphabet Phonétique International. La phonétique est donnée pour les mots d'entrée au début de l'article et, pour aider l'utilisateur, pour tout mot dans un article dont il pourrait être difficile de déduire la prononciation à partir de l'orthographe (par exemple ◆**aristocratie** [-asi]; ◆**soûtien**, **-ienne** [ausjɛ̃, -jɛn]; ◆**rabid** ['ræbid]; ◆**prayer** [preər]).

En anglais, l'accent tonique est indiqué pour les mots d'entrée et pour les dérivés chaque fois que l'accentuation diffère de celle de l'entrée (par exemple **civilize** et ◆**civili'zation**). Les prononciations américaines sont indiquées chaque fois qu'elles diffèrent de façon substantielle de celles de l'anglais britannique (par exemple **aristocrat** ['æristəkræt, *Am* ə'ristəkræt], **quinine** ['kwinin, *Am* 'kwainain]). On indique également l'orthographe américaine lorsqu'elle est suffisamment différente de celle de l'anglais britannique (par exemple **tire** et **tyre**, **plow** et **plough**).

Une des caractérisques originales de ce dictionnaire est son approche sémantique du classement et de l'organisation des articles. On a considéré que cette approche, où le sens des mots détermine pour une part l'organisation des articles, serait d'un grand secours à l'utilisateur en ce qui concerne sa compréhension de la langue.

Les catégories sémantiques importantes sont indiquées dans un article par des chiffres arabes en gras (voir **bolt**, **tail**, **général**) ou sont présentées comme des mots distincts (voir **bug**[1] et **bug**[2], **draw**[1] et **draw**[2], **start**[1] et **start**[2]). Les catégories grammaticales autres que la première traitée sont indiquées par un tiret.

Les mots apparaissent sous les mots d'entrée dont ils sont dérivés (par exemple **approfondi**, abrégé en ◆**-i** suit **approfond/ir**; ◆**astronomer** et ◆**astro'nomical** suivent **astronomy**). Les participes présents et passés (utilisés comme adjectifs) sont considérés comme étant étroitement associés par le sens et par la forme à l'infinitif dont ils sont dérivés. Ils sont placés dans l'article, généralement en abrégé, immédiatement après l'infinitif; tous les autres dérivés éventuels apparaissent ensuite par ordre alphabétique (par exemple **exalt/er** *vt* . . . ◆**-ant** *a* . . . ◆**-é a** . . . ◆**exaltation** *nf*; **accommodat/e** *vt* . . . ◆**-ing** *a* . . . ◆**accommo'dation** *n*; **expir/e** *vi* . . . ◆**-ed a** . . . ◆**expi'ration** *n* . . . ◆**expiry** *n*).

Les mots dérivés et les mots composés sont considérés comme étant distincts, du point de vue du sens, et sont, chaque fois que possible, regroupés séparément (par exemple **base** *n* . . . ◆**-less** *a* . . . ◆**-ness** *n* . . . ◆**baseball** *n*; ◆**baseboard** *n*; **bouton** *nm* . . . ◆**b.-d'or** *nm* . . . ◆**b.-pression** *nm* . . . ◆**boutonner** *vt* . . . ◆**boutonneux**, **-euse** *a* . . . ◆**boutonnière** *nf*). Les composés se trouvent placés dans les articles là où leur sens a semblé devoir les appeler.

L'auteur tient à exprimer sa gratitude à Monsieur F. Antoine, à Mrs H. Curties et à Mr S. Fortey pour leurs conseils et leur collaboration, à Mrs R. Hillmore qui a bien voulu nous aider à relire les épreuves, et à Monsieur J.-L. Barbanneau pour son soutien et ses encouragements.

M. Janes
Londres, 1988

Grammar notes

In French, the feminine of an adjective is formed as a rule by adding **e** to the masculine form (e.g. grand, grande; carré, carrée; chevalin, chevaline). If the masculine already ends in **e**, the feminine is the same as the masculine (e.g. utile). Irregular feminine forms of adjectives (e.g. généreux, généreuse; léger, légère; doux, douce) are given in the French-English side of the dictionary. In the English-French side, French adjectives are shown in the masculine form only. Irregular feminines of adjectives are listed in the following way: généreux, -euse; léger, -ère; doux, douce.

To form the plural of a French noun or adjective **s** is usually added to the singular (e.g. arbre, arbres; taxi, taxis; petit, petits). The plural form of a noun ending in **s**, **x** or **z** (e.g. pois, croix, nez) is the same as that of the singular. Plurals of nouns and adjectives which do not follow these general rules are listed in the French section, including the plurals of French compounds where the formation of the plural involves a change other than the addition of final **s** (e.g. arc-en-ciel, arcs-en-ciel). Those nouns and adjectives where **x** or **aux** is added in the plural are shown in the following way: cerveau, -x; général, -aux.

In English also, **s** is added to form the plural of a noun (e.g. cat, cats; taxi, taxis) but a noun ending in **ch**, **s**, **sh**, **x** or **z** forms its plural by the addition of **es** (e.g. glass, glasses; match, matches). (Note that when **ch** is pronounced [k], the plural is in **s**, e.g. monarch, monarchs.) When a noun ends in **y** preceded by a consonant, **y** is changed to **ies** to form the plural (e.g. army, armies). Irregular English plurals are given in the English-French side, including the plurals of English compounds where the formation of the plural involves a change other than the addition of final **s** (e.g. brother-in-law, brothers-in-law).

English nouns may be used as adjectives. When a French adjective is translated in this way, this use is made clear by the addition of a hyphen following the noun translation (e.g. farm- as a translation of **agricole**).

Most French verbs have regular conjugations though some display spelling anomalies (see French verb conjugations on p (i)). In the French section an asterisk is used to mark an irregular verb, and refers the user to the table of irregular verbs on p (ii).

Most English verbs form their past tense and past participle by adding **ed** to the infinitive (e.g. look, looked) or **d** to an infinitive already ending in **e** (e.g. love, loved). When a verb ends in **y** preceded by a consonant, **y** becomes **ied** (e.g. satisfy, satisfied). To form the third person singular of a verb in the present tense **s** is added to the infinitive (e.g. know, knows) but an infinitive in **ch**, **s**, **sh**, **x** or **z** forms its third person singular by the addition of **es** (e.g. dash, dashes). When an infinitive ends in **y** preceded by a consonant, **y** is changed to **ies** to form the third person singular (e.g. satisfy, satisfies).

The English present participle is formed by the addition of **ing** to the infinitive (e.g. look, looking) but final **e** is omitted when an infinitive ends in **e** (e.g. love, loving). When the infinitive ends in a single consonant preceded by a vowel (e.g. tug), the final consonant is usually doubled in the past tense, past and present participles (e.g. tug, tugged, tugging).

Irregular English verb conjugations are given in the English headword list, and a summary of the most important irregular verbs may also be found on p (vii). The doubling of consonants in English verbs is indicated in the text. The latter is shown in the following way: **tug** . . . *vt* (**-gg-**).

Notes sur la grammaire

En français, le féminin d'un adjectif se forme en général en ajoutant **e** au masculin (par exemple grand, grande; carré, carrée; chevalin, chevaline). Lorsque le masculin se termine déjà par **e**, le féminin est identique (par exemple utile). Les féminins d'adjectifs qui ne se conforment pas à ces règles (par exemple généreux, généreuse; léger, légère; doux, douce) sont donnés dans la partie français-anglais où ils sont notés comme suit: généreux, -euse; léger, -ère; doux, douce. Dans la partie anglais-français, on ne donne que la forme masculine des adjectifs.

On forme en général le pluriel d'un nom ou d'un adjectif français en ajoutant **s** au singulier (par exemple arbre, arbres; taxi, taxis; petit, petits). Le pluriel d'un nom se terminant par **s**, **x** ou **z** (par exemple pois, croix, nez) est identique au singulier. Les pluriels des noms et adjectifs qui font exception à ces règles générales sont signalés dans la partie français-anglais, de même que les pluriels des mots composés français dont le passage au pluriel appelle une modification autre que le simple ajout d'un **s** final (par exemple arc-en-ciel, arcs-en-ciel). Les noms et adjectifs dont le pluriel se forme à l'aide d'un **x** ou de **aux** sont notés comme suit: cerveau, -x; général, -aux.

De la même façon, en anglais, on forme le pluriel des noms en ajoutant **s** (par exemple cat, cats; taxi, taxis) mais on ajoutera **es** aux noms qui se terminent par **ch**, **s**, **sh**, **x** ou **z** (par exemple glass, glasses; match, matches). (Noter cependant que lorsque **ch** se prononce [k], le pluriel est en **s**, comme dans monarch, monarchs.) Lorsqu'un nom se termine par un **y** précédé d'une consonne, le **y** devient **ies** au pluriel (par exemple army, armies). Les pluriels irréguliers de l'anglais sont signalés dans la partie anglais-français, de même que les pluriels des mots composés anglais dont le passage au pluriel entraîne une modification autre que le simple ajout d'un **s** final (par exemple brother-in-law, brothers-in-law).

Les noms anglais peuvent s'utiliser comme adjectifs. Lorsqu'un adjectif français est traduit par un nom, cela est signalé par l'ajout d'un trait d'union à la suite de ce nom (par exemple farm- comme traduction de **agricole**).

La plupart des verbes français ont des conjugaisons régulières; cependant, certains subissent des variations orthographiques (voir: Conjugaisons des verbes français à la page (i)) Dans la partie français-anglais, un astérisque signale un verbe irrégulier et renvoie à la table des verbes irréguliers donnée en page (ii).

En anglais, le passé et le participe passé des verbes se forment dans la plupart des cas en ajoutant **ed** à l'infinitif (par exemple look, looked) ou seulement **d** lorsque l'infinitif se termine par un **e** (par exemple love, loved). Lorsqu'un verbe se termine par un **y** précédé d'une consonne, le **y** devient **ied** (par exemple satisfy, satisfied). La troisième personne du singulier d'un verbe au présent se forme en ajoutant **s** à l'infinitif (par exemple know, knows), mais on ajoutera **es** aux infinitifs qui se terminent par **ch**, **s**, **sh**, **x** ou **z** (par exemple dash, dashes). Enfin, lorsqu'un verbe se termine par un **y** précédé d'une consonne, ce **y** devient **ies** à la troisième personne du singulier (par exemple satisfy, satisfies).

Le participe présent en anglais se forme en ajoutant la désinence **ing** à l'infinitif (par exemple look, looking); lorsqu'un infinitif comporte un **e** final, celui-ci disparaît (par exemple love, loving). Lorsque l'infinitif se termine par une seule consonne précédée d'une voyelle (par exemple tug), la consonne finale est le plus souvent doublée au passé et aux participes passé et présent (par exemple tug, tugged, tugging).

Les formes des verbes irréguliers anglais sont données dans la partie anglais-français et une liste récapitulative des verbes irréguliers usuels figure en page (vii). Le doublement des consonnes dans les verbes irréguliers est signalé dans le corps de l'ouvrage; il est noté comme suit: **tug** . . . *vt* (**-gg-**).

Abbreviations / Abréviations

adjective	*a*	adjectif
abbreviation	*abbr, abrév*	abréviation
adverb	*adv*	adverbe
agriculture	*Agr*	agriculture
American	*Am*	américain
anatomy	*Anat*	anatomie
architecture	*Archit*	architecture
slang	*Arg*	argot
article	*art*	article
cars, motoring	*Aut*	automobile
auxiliary	*aux*	auxiliaire
aviation, aircraft	*Av*	aviation
biology	*Biol*	biologie
botany	*Bot*	botanique
British	*Br*	britannique
Canadian	*Can*	canadien
carpentry	*Carp*	menuiserie
chemistry	*Ch*	chimie
cinema	*Cin*	cinéma
commerce	*Com*	commerce
conjunction	*conj*	conjonction
cookery	*Culin*	cuisine
definite	*def, déf*	défini
demonstrative	*dem, dém*	démonstratif
economics	*Econ, Écon*	économie
electricity	*El, Él*	électricité
et cetera	*etc*	et cetera
feminine	*f*	féminin
familiar	*Fam*	familier
football	*Fb*	football
figurative	*Fig*	figuré
finance	*Fin*	finance
feminine plural	*fpl*	féminin pluriel
French	*Fr*	français
geography	*Geog, Géog*	géographie
geology	*Geol, Géol*	géologie
geometry	*Geom, Géom*	géométrie
grammar	*Gram*	grammaire
history	*Hist*	histoire
humorous	*Hum*	humoristique
indefinite	*indef, indéf*	indéfini
indicative	*indic*	indicatif
infinitive	*inf*	infinitif
interjection	*int*	interjection
invariable	*inv*	invariable
ironic	*Iron*	ironique
journalism	*Journ*	journalisme
legal, law	*Jur*	juridique
linguistics	*Ling*	linguistique
literary	*Lit, Litt*	littéraire
literature	*Liter, Littér*	littérature

masculine	*m*	masculin
mathematics	*Math*	mathématique
medicine	*Med, Méd*	médecine
carpentry	*Menuis*	menuiserie
meteorology	*Met, Mét*	météorologie
military	*Mil*	militaire
masculine plural	*mpl*	masculin pluriel
music	*Mus*	musique
noun	*n*	nom
nautical	*Nau*	nautique
noun feminine	*nf*	nom féminin
noun masculine	*nm*	nom masculin
noun masculine and feminine	*nmf*	nom masculin et féminin
pejorative	*Pej, Péj*	péjoratif
philosophy	*Phil*	philosophie
photography	*Phot*	photographie
physics	*Phys*	physique
plural	*pl*	pluriel
politics	*Pol*	politique
possessive	*poss*	possessif
past participle	*pp*	participe passé
prefix	*pref, préf*	préfixe
preposition	*prep, prép*	préposition
present participle	*pres p*	participe présent
present tense	*pres t*	temps présent
pronoun	*pron*	pronom
psychology	*Psy*	psychologie
past tense	*pt*	prétérit
	qch	quelque chose
	qn	quelqu'un
registered trademark	®	marque déposée
radio	*Rad*	radio
railway, *Am* railroad	*Rail*	chemin de fer
relative	*rel*	relatif
religion	*Rel*	religion
school	*Sch, Scol*	école
singular	*sing*	singulier
slang	*Sl*	argot
someone	*s.o.*	
sport	*Sp*	sport
something	*sth*	
subjunctive	*sub*	subjonctif
technical	*Tech*	technique
telephone	*Tel, Tél*	téléphone
textiles	*Tex*	industrie textile
theatre	*Th*	théâtre
television	*TV*	télévision
typography, printing	*Typ*	typographie
university	*Univ*	université
United States	*US*	États-Unis
auxiliary verb	*v aux*	verbe auxiliaire
intransitive verb	*vi*	verbe intransitif
impersonal verb	*v imp*	verbe impersonnel
pronominal verb	*vpr*	verbe pronominal
transitive verb	*vt*	verbe transitif
transitive and intransitive verb	*vti*	verbe transitif et intransitif

Pronunciation of French

TABLE OF PHONETIC SYMBOLS

Vowels

[i]	vite, cygne	[y]	cru, sûr
[e]	été, donner	[ø]	feu, meule
[ɛ]	elle, mais	[œ]	œuf, jeune
[a]	chat, fameux	[ə]	le, refaire
[ɑ]	pas, âgé	[ɛ̃]	vin, plein, faim
[ɔ]	donne, fort	[ɑ̃]	enfant, temps
[o]	dos, chaud, peau	[ɔ̃]	mon, nombre
[u]	tout, cour	[œ̃]	lundi, humble

Consonants

[p]	pain, absolu	[z]	cousin, zéro
[b]	beau, abbé	[ʃ]	chose, schéma
[t]	table, nette	[ʒ]	gilet, jeter
[d]	donner, sud	[l]	lait, facile
[k]	camp, képi	[r]	rare, rhume
[g]	garde, second	[m]	mon, flamme
[f]	feu, phrase	[n]	né, canne
[v]	voir, wagon	[ɲ]	campagne
[s]	sou, cire	[ŋ]	jogging
		[']	hanche (*i.e. no liaison or elision*)

Semi-consonants

[j]	piano, voyage
[w]	ouest, noir
[ɥ]	muet, lui

Prononciation de l'anglais

TABLEAU DES SIGNES PHONÉTIQUES

Voyelles et diphtongues

[iː]	bee, police	[ɒ]	lot, what
[ɪə]	beer, real	[ɔː]	all, saw
[ɪ]	bit, added	[ɔɪ]	boil, toy
[e]	bet, said	[əʊ]	low, soap
[eɪ]	date, nail	[ʊ]	put, wool
[eə]	bear, air	[uː]	shoe, too
[æ]	bat, plan	[ʊə]	poor, sure
[aɪ]	fly, life	[ʌ]	cut, some
[ɑː]	art, ask	[ɜː]	burn, learn
[aʊ]	fowl, house	[ə]	china, annoy
		[(ə)]	relation

Consonnes

[p]	pat, top	[ð]	that, breathe
[b]	but, tab	[h]	hat, rehearse
[t]	tap, patter	[l]	lad, all
[d]	dab, sadder	[r]	red, barring
[k]	cat, kite	[r]	better, here (*représente un r*
[g]	go, rogue		*final qui se prononce en*
[f]	fat, phrase		*liaison devant une voyelle,*
[v]	veal, rave		*par exemple* 'here is' [hɪərɪz])
[s]	sat, ace	[m]	mat, hammer
[z]	zero, houses	[n]	no, banner
[ʃ]	dish, pressure	[ŋ]	singing, link
[ʒ]	pleasure	[j]	yet, onion
[tʃ]	charm, rich	[w]	wall, quite
[dʒ]	judge, rage	[']	*marque l'accent tonique;*
[θ]	thatch, breath		*précède la syllable accentuée*

A

A, a [a] *nm* A, a.

a [a] *voir* avoir.

à [a] *prép* (à + le = **au** [o], à + les = **aux** [o]) **1** (*direction*: *lieu*) to; (*temps*) till, to; **aller à Paris** to go to Paris; **de 3 à 4 h** from 3 till *ou* to 4 (o'clock). **2** (*position*: *lieu*) at, in; (*surface*) on; (*temps*) at; **être au bureau/à la ferme/au jardin/à Paris** to be at *ou* in the office/on *ou* at the farm/in the garden/in Paris; **à la maison** at home; **à l'horizon** on the horizon; **à 8 h** at 8 (o'clock); **à mon arrivée** on (my) arrival; **à lundi!** see you (on) Monday! **3** (*description*) **l'homme à la barbe** the man with the beard; **verre à liqueur** liqueur glass. **4** (*attribution*) **donner qch à qn** to give sth to s.o., give s.o. sth. **5** (*devant inf*) **apprendre à lire** to learn to read; **travail à faire** work to do; **maison à vendre** house for sale; **prêt à partir** ready to leave. **6** (*appartenance*) **c'est** (son livre) **à lui** it's his (book); **c'est à vous de** (*décider, protester etc*) it's up to you to; (*lire, jouer etc*) it's your turn to. **7** (*prix*) for; **pain à 2F** loaf for 2F. **8** (*poids*) by; **vendre au kilo** to sell by the kilo. **9** (*moyen, manière*) **à bicyclette** by bicycle; **à la main** by hand; **à pied** on foot; **au crayon** with a pencil, in pencil; **au galop** at a gallop; **à la française** in the French style *ou* way; **deux à deux** two by two. **10** (*appel*) **au voleur!** (stop) thief!

abaiss/er [abese] *vt* to lower; **a. qn** to humiliate s.o.; **— s'a.** *vpr* (*barrière*) to lower; (*température*) to drop; **s'a. à faire** to stoop to doing. **◆—ement** [-esmã] *nm* (*chute*) drop.

abandon [abãdɔ̃] *nm* abandonment; surrender; desertion; *Sp* withdrawal; (*naturel*) abandon; (*confiance*) lack of restraint; **à l'a.** in a neglected state. **◆abandonner** *vt* (*renoncer à*) to give up, abandon; (*droit*) to surrender; (*quitter*) to desert, abandon; **— vi** to give up; *Sp* to withdraw; **— s'a.** *vpr* (*se détendre*) to let oneself go; (*se confier*) to open up; **s'a. à** to give oneself up to, abandon oneself to.

abasourdir [abazurdir] *vt* to stun, astound.

abat-jour [abaʒur] *nm inv* lampshade.

abats [aba] *nmpl* offal; (*de volaille*) giblets.

abattant [abatã] *nm* leaf, flap.

abattis [abati] *nmpl* giblets.

abatt/re [abatr] *vt* (*mur*) to knock down; (*arbre*) to cut down, fell; (*animal etc*) to slaughter; (*avion*) to shoot down; (*déprimer*) to demoralize; (*épuiser*) to exhaust; **— s'a.** *vpr* (*tomber*) to collapse; (*oiseau*) to swoop down; (*pluie*) to pour down. **◆—u** *a* (*triste*) dejected, demoralized; (*faible*) at a low ebb. **◆—age** *nm* felling; slaughter(ing). **◆—ement** *nm* (*faiblesse*) exhaustion; (*désespoir*) dejection. **◆abattoir** *nm* slaughterhouse.

abbaye [abei] *nf* abbey.

abbé [abe] *nm* (*chef d'abbaye*) abbot; (*prêtre*) priest. **◆abbesse** *nf* abbess.

abcès [apsɛ] *nm* abscess.

abdiquer [abdike] *vti* to abdicate. **◆abdication** *nf* abdication.

abdomen [abdɔmɛn] *nm* abdomen. **◆abdominal, -aux** *a* abdominal.

abeille [abej] *nf* bee.

aberrant [aberã] *a* (*idée etc*) ludicrous, absurd. **◆aberration** *nf* (*égarement*) aberration; (*idée*) ludicrous idea; **dire des aberrations** to talk sheer nonsense.

abhorrer [abɔre] *vt* to abhor, loathe.

abîme [abim] *nm* abyss, chasm, gulf.

abîmer [abime] *vt* to spoil, damage; **— s'a.** *vpr* to get spoilt; **s'a. dans ses pensées** *Litt* to lose oneself in one's thoughts.

abject [abʒɛkt] *a* abject, despicable.

abjurer [abʒyre] *vti* to abjure.

ablation [ablasjɔ̃] *nf* (*d'organe*) removal.

ablutions [ablysjɔ̃] *nfpl* ablutions.

abnégation [abnegasjɔ̃] *nf* self-sacrifice, abnegation.

abois (aux) [ozabwa] *adv* at bay.

abolir [abɔlir] *vt* to abolish. **◆abolition** *nf* abolition.

abominable [abɔminabl] *a* abominable, obnoxious. **◆abomination** *nf* abomination.

abondant [abɔ̃dã] *a* abundant, plentiful. **◆abondamment** *adv* abundantly. **◆abondance** *nf* abundance (**de** of); **en a.** in abundance; **années d'a.** years of plenty. **◆abonder** *vi* to abound (**en** in).

abonné, -ée [abɔne] *nmf* (*à un journal, au téléphone*) subscriber; *Rail Sp Th* season ticket holder; (*du gaz etc*) consumer.

◆**abonnement** *nm* subscription; (*carte d'*)a. season ticket. ◆**s'abonner** *vpr* to subscribe (à to); to buy a season ticket.

abord [abɔr] 1 *nm* (*accès*) d'un a. facile easy to approach. 2 *nm* (*vue*) au premier a. at first sight. ◆**abords** *nmpl* (*environs*) surroundings; aux abords de around, nearby. ◆**abordable** *a* (*personne*) approachable; (*prix, marchandises*) affordable.

abord (d') [dabɔr] *adv* (*avant tout*) first; (*au début*) at first.

aborder [abɔrde] *vi* to land; – *vt* (*personne*) to approach, accost; (*lieu*) to approach, reach; (*problème*) to tackle, approach; (*attaquer*) Nau to board; (*heurter*) Nau to run foul of. ◆**abordage** *nm* (*assaut*) Nau boarding; (*accident*) Nau collision.

aborigène [abɔriʒɛn] *a & nm* aboriginal.

about/ir [abutir] *vi* to succeed; a. à to end at, lead to, end up in; n'a. à rien to come to nothing. ◆**—issants** *nmpl voir* tenants. ◆**—issement** *nm* (*résultat*) outcome; (*succès*) success.

aboyer [abwaje] *vi* to bark. ◆**aboiement** *nm* bark; *pl* barking.

abrasif, -ive [abrazif, -iv] *a & nm* abrasive.

abrég/er [abreʒe] *vt* (*récit*) to shorten, abridge; (*mot*) to abbreviate. ◆**—é** *nm* summary; en a. (*phrase*) in shortened form; (*mot*) in abbreviated form.

abreuver [abrœve] *vt* (*cheval*) to water; – s'a. *vpr* to drink. ◆**abreuvoir** *nm* (*récipient*) drinking trough; (*lieu*) watering place.

abréviation [abrevjɑsjɔ̃] *nf* abbreviation.

abri [abri] *nm* shelter; à l'a. de (*vent*) sheltered from; (*besoin*) safe from; sans a. homeless. ◆**abriter** *vt* (*protéger*) to shelter; (*loger*) to house; – s'a. *vpr* to (take) shelter.

abricot [abriko] *nm* apricot. ◆**abricotier** *nm* apricot tree.

abroger [abrɔʒe] *vt* to abrogate.

abrupt [abrypt] *a* (*versant*) sheer; (*sentier*) steep, abrupt; (*personne*) abrupt.

abrut/ir [abrytir] *vt* (*alcool*) to stupefy (*s.o.*); (*propagande*) to brutalize (*s.o.*); (*travail*) to leave (*s.o.*) dazed, wear (*s.o.*) out. ◆**—i, -ie** *nmf* idiot; – *a* idiotic.

absence [apsɑ̃s] *nf* absence. ◆**absent, -e** *a* (*personne*) absent, away; (*chose*) missing; air a. faraway look; – *nmf* absentee. ◆**absentéisme** *nm* absenteeism. ◆**s'absenter** *vpr* to go away.

abside [apsid] *nf* (*d'une église*) apse.

absolu [apsɔly] *a & nm* absolute. ◆**—ment** *adv* absolutely.

absolution [apsɔlysjɔ̃] *nf* absolution.

absorb/er [apsɔrbe] *vt* to absorb. ◆**—ant** *a* absorbent; travail a. absorbing job. ◆**absorption** *nf* absorption.

absoudre* [apsudr] *vt* to absolve.

abstenir* (s') [sapstənir] *vpr* to abstain; s'a. de to refrain *ou* abstain from. ◆**abstention** *nf* abstention.

abstinence [apstinɑ̃s] *nf* abstinence.

abstraire* [apstrɛr] *vt* to abstract. ◆**abstrait** *a & nm* abstract. ◆**abstraction** *nf* abstraction; faire a. de to disregard, leave aside.

absurde [apsyrd] *a & nm* absurd. ◆**absurdité** *nf* absurdity; dire des absurdités to talk nonsense.

abus [aby] *nm* abuse, misuse; overindulgence; (*injustice*) abuse. ◆**abuser** 1 *vi* to go too far; a. de (*situation, personne*) to take unfair advantage of; (*autorité*) to abuse, misuse; (*friandises*) to over-indulge in. 2 s'a. *vpr* to be mistaken.

abusi/f, -ive [abyzif, -iv] *a* excessive; emploi a. *Ling* improper use, misuse. ◆**—vement** *adv* Ling improperly.

acabit [akabi] *nm* de cet a. *Péj* of that ilk *ou* sort.

acacia [akasja] *nm* (*arbre*) acacia.

académie [akademi] *nf* academy; Univ = (regional) education authority. ◆**académicien, -ienne** *nmf* academician. ◆**académique** *a* academic.

acajou [akaʒu] *nm* mahogany; cheveux a. auburn hair.

acariâtre [akarjɑtr] *a* cantankerous.

accabl/er [akable] *vt* to overwhelm, overcome; a. d'injures to heap insults upon; accablé de dettes (over)burdened with debt. ◆**—ement** *nm* dejection.

accalmie [akalmi] *nf* lull.

accaparer [akapare] *vt* to monopolize; (*personne*) Fam to take up all the time of.

accéder [aksede] *vi* a. à (*lieu*) to have access to, reach; (*pouvoir, trône, demande*) to accede to.

accélérer [akselere] *vi* Aut to accelerate; – *vt* (*travaux etc*) to speed up; (*allure, pas*) to quicken, speed up; – s'a. *vpr* to speed up. ◆**accélérateur** *nm* Aut accelerator. ◆**accélération** *nf* acceleration; speeding up.

accent [aksɑ̃] *nm* accent; (*sur une syllabe*) stress; mettre l'a. sur to stress. ◆**accentuation** *nf* accentuation. ◆**accentuer** *vt* to emphasize, accentuate, stress; – s'a. *vpr* to become more pronounced.

accepter [aksɛpte] *vt* to accept; a. de faire

to agree to do. ◆**acceptable** a acceptable.
◆**acceptation** nf acceptance.

acception [aksɛpsjɔ̃] nf sense, meaning.

accès [aksɛ] nm access (à to); (de folie,
colère, toux) fit; (de fièvre) attack, bout; pl
(routes) approaches. ◆**accessible** a
accessible; (personne) approachable.
◆**accession** nf accession (à to; à un
traité) adherence; **a. à la propriété** home
ownership.

accessoire [aksɛswar] a secondary; – nmpl
Th props; (de voiture etc) accessories;
accessoires de toilette toilet requisites.

accident [aksidɑ̃] nm accident; **a.
d'avion/de train** plane/train crash; **par a.**
by accident, by chance. ◆**accidenté, -ée**
a (terrain) uneven; (région) hilly; (voiture)
damaged (in an accident); – nmf accident
victim, casualty. ◆**accidentel, -elle** a
accidental. ◆**accidentellement** adv accidentally, unintentionally.

acclamer [aklame] vt to cheer, acclaim.
◆**acclamations** nfpl cheers, acclamations.

acclimater [aklimate] vt, – **s'a.** vpr to acclimatize, Am acclimate. ◆**acclimatation** nf
acclimatization, Am acclimation.

accointances [akwɛ̃tɑ̃s] nfpl Péj contacts.

accolade [akɔlad] nf (embrassade) embrace; Typ brace, bracket.

accoler [akɔle] vt to place (side by side) (à
against).

accommod/er [akɔmɔde] vt to adapt;
Culin to prepare; **s'a.** à to adapt (oneself)
to; **s'a. de** to make the best of. ◆—**ant** a
accommodating, easy to please.
◆—**ement** nm arrangement, compromise.

accompagner [akɔ̃paɲe] vt (personne) to
accompany, go ou come with, escort;
(chose) & Mus to accompany; **s'a. de** to be
accompanied by, go with. ◆**accompagnateur, -trice** nmf Mus accompanist;
(d'un groupe) guide. ◆**accompagnement**
nm Mus accompaniment.

accompl/ir [akɔ̃plir] vt to carry out, fulfil,
accomplish. ◆—**i** a accomplished.
◆—**issement** nm fulfilment.

accord [akɔr] nm agreement; (harmonie)
harmony; Mus chord; **être d'a.** to agree, be
in agreement (avec with); **d'a.!** all right!
◆**accorder** vt (donner) to grant; Mus to
tune; Gram to make agree; – **s'a.** vpr to
agree; (s'entendre) to get along.

accordéon [akɔrdeɔ̃] nm accordion; **en a.**
(chaussette etc) wrinkled.

accoster [akɔste] vt to accost; Nau to come
alongside; – vi Nau to berth.

accotement [akɔtmɑ̃] nm roadside, verge.

accouch/er [akuʃe] vi to give birth (de to);
– vt (enfant) to deliver. ◆—**ement** nm
delivery. ◆—**eur** nm (médecin) a. obstetri-
cian.

accouder (s') [sakude] vpr **s'a.** à ou sur to
lean on (with one's elbows). ◆**accoudoir**
nm armrest.

accoupl/er [akuple] vt to couple; – **s'a.**
vpr (animaux) to mate (à with). ◆—**ement**
nm coupling; mating.

accourir* [akurir] vi to come running, run
over.

accoutrement [akutrəmɑ̃] nm Péj garb,
dress.

accoutumer [akutyme] vt to accustom; –
s'a. vpr to get accustomed (à to); **comme à
l'accoutumée** as usual. ◆**accoutumance**
nf familiarization (à with); Méd addiction.

accréditer [akredite] vt (ambassadeur) to
accredit; (rumeur) to lend credence to.

accroc [akro] nm (déchirure) tear;
(difficulté) hitch, snag.

accroch/er [akrɔʃe] vt (déchirer) to catch;
(fixer) to hook; (suspendre) to hang up (on
a hook); (heurter) to hit, knock; – vi
(affiche etc) to grab one's attention; – **s'a.**
vpr (ne pas céder) to persevere; (se disputer)
Fam to clash; **s'a.** à (se cramponner etc) to
cling to; (s'écorcher) to catch oneself on.
◆—**age** nm Aut knock, slight hit; (friction) Fam clash. ◆—**eur, -euse** a
(personne) tenacious; (affiche etc)
eyecatching, catchy.

accroître* [akrwatr] vt to increase; – **s'a.**
vpr to increase, grow. ◆**accroissement**
nm increase; growth.

accroup/ir (s') [sakrupir] vpr to squat ou
crouch (down). ◆—**i** a squatting, crouching.

accueil [akœj] nm reception, welcome.
◆**accueill/ir*** vt to receive, welcome,
greet. ◆—**ant** a welcoming.

acculer [akyle] vt **a. qn à qch** to drive s.o. to
ou against sth.

accumuler [akymyle] vt, – **s'a.** vpr to pile
up, accumulate. ◆**accumulateur** nm
accumulator, battery. ◆**accumulation** nf
accumulation.

accus/er [akyze] vt (dénoncer) to accuse;
(rendre responsable) to blame (de for);
(révéler) to show; (faire ressortir) to bring
out; **a. réception** to acknowledge receipt
(de of); **a. le coup** to stagger under the
blow. ◆—**é, -ée 1** nmf accused; (cour
d'assises) defendant. **2** a prominent.
◆**accusateur, -trice** a (regard) accusing;

(*document*) incriminating; – *nmf* accuser. ◆**accusation** *nf* accusation; *Jur* charge.

acerbe [asɛrb] *a* bitter, caustic.

acéré [asere] *a* sharp.

acétate [asetat] *nm* acetate. ◆**acétique** *a* acetic.

achalandé [aʃalɑ̃de] *a* **bien a.** (*magasin*) well-stocked.

acharn/er (s') [aʃarne] *vpr* **s'a. sur** (*attaquer*) to set upon, lay into; **s'a. contre** (*poursuivre*) to pursue (relentlessly); **s'a. à faire** to struggle to do, try desperately to do. ◆**–é, –ée** *a* relentless; – *nmf* (*du jeu etc*) fanatic. ◆**–ement** *nm* relentlessness.

achat [aʃa] *nm* purchase; *pl* shopping.

acheminer [aʃmine] *vt* to dispatch; – **s'a.** *vpr* to proceed (**vers** towards).

achet/er [aʃte] *vti* to buy, purchase; **a. à qn** (*vendeur*) to buy from s.o.; (*pour qn*) to buy for s.o. ◆**–eur, –euse** *nmf* buyer, purchaser; (*dans un magasin*) shopper.

achever [aʃve] *vt* to finish (off); **a. de faire qch** (*personne*) to finish doing sth; **a. qn** (*tuer*) to finish s.o. off; – **s'a.** *vpr* to end, finish. ◆**achèvement** *nm* completion.

achoppement [aʃɔpmɑ̃] *nm* **pierre d'a.** stumbling block.

acide [asid] *a* acid, sour; – *nm* acid. ◆**acidité** *nf* acidity.

acier [asje] *nm* steel. ◆**aciérie** *nf* steelworks.

acné [akne] *nf* acne.

acolyte [akɔlit] *nm* *Péj* confederate, associate.

acompte [akɔ̃t] *nm* part payment, deposit.

à-côté [akote] *nm* (*d'une question*) side issue; *pl* (*gains*) little extras.

à-coup [aku] *nm* jerk, jolt; **sans à-coups** smoothly; **par à-coups** in fits and starts.

acoustique [akustik] *a* acoustic; – *nf* acoustics.

acquérir* [akerir] *vt* to acquire, gain; (*par achat*) to purchase; **s'a. une réputation/etc** to win a reputation/*etc*; **être acquis à** (*idée, parti*) to be a supporter of ◆**acquéreur** *nm* purchaser. ◆**acquis** *nm* experience. ◆**acquisition** *nf* acquisition; purchase.

acquiesc/er [akjese] *vi* to acquiesce (**à** to). ◆**–ement** *nm* acquiescence.

acquit [aki] *nm* receipt; **'pour a.'** 'paid'; **par a. de conscience** for conscience sake. ◆**acquitt/er** *vt* to clear, pay; (*accusé*) to acquit; **s'a. de** (*devoir, promesse*) to discharge; **s'a. envers qn** to repay s.o. ◆**–ement** *nm* payment; acquittal; discharge.

âcre [akr] *a* bitter, acrid, pungent.

acrobate [akrɔbat] *nmf* acrobat. ◆**acrobatie(s)** *nf*(*pl*) acrobatics. ◆**acrobatique** *a* acrobatic.

acrylique [akrilik] *a* & *nm* acrylic.

acte [akt] *nm* act, deed; *Th* act; **un a.** de act of; **a. de naissance** birth certificate; **prendre a. de** to take note of.

acteur, -trice [aktœr, -tris] *nmf* actor, actress.

actif, -ive [aktif, -iv] *a* active; – *Fin* assets; **à son a.** to one's credit; (*vols, meurtres*) *Hum* to one's name.

action [aksjɔ̃] *nf* action; *Fin* share. ◆**actionnaire** *nmf* shareholder. ◆**actionner** *vt* to set in motion, activate, actuate.

activer [aktive] *vt* to speed up; (*feu*) to boost; – **s'a.** *vpr* to bustle about; (*se dépêcher*) *Fam* to get a move on.

activiste [aktivist] *nmf* activist.

activité [aktivite] *nf* activity; **en a.** (*personne*) fully active; (*volcan*) active.

actuaire [aktyɛr] *nmf* actuary.

actualité [aktyalite] *nf* (*d'un problème*) topicality; (*événements*) current events; *pl* TV *Cin* news; **d'a.** topical.

actuel, -elle [aktyɛl] *a* (*présent*) present; (*contemporain*) topical. ◆**actuellement** *adv* at present, at the present time.

acuité [akyite] *nf* (*de douleur*) acuteness; (*de vision*) keenness.

acupuncture [akypɔ̃ktyr] *nf* acupuncture. ◆**acupuncteur, -trice** *nmf* acupuncturist.

adage [adaʒ] *nm* (*maxime*) adage.

adapter [adapte] *vt* to adapt; (*ajuster*) to fit (**à** to); **s'a. à** (*s'habituer*) to adapt to; (*tuyau etc*) to fit. ◆**adaptable** *a* adaptable. ◆**adaptateur, -trice** *nmf* adapter. ◆**adaptation** *nf* adaptation.

additif [aditif] *nm* additive.

addition [adisjɔ̃] *nf* addition; (*au restaurant*) bill, *Am* check. ◆**additionnel, -elle** *a* additional. ◆**additionner** *vt* to add (**à** to); (*nombres*) to add up.

adepte [adɛpt] *nmf* follower.

adéquat [adekwa] *a* appropriate.

adhérer [adere] *vi* **a. à** (*coller*) to adhere ou stick to; (*s'inscrire*) to join; (*pneu*) to grip. ◆**adhérence** *nf* (*de pneu*) grip. ◆**adhérent, -ente** *nmf* member.

adhésif, -ive [adezif, -iv] *a* & *nm* adhesive. ◆**adhésion** *nf* membership; (*accord*) support.

adieu, -x [adjø] *int* & *nm* farewell, goodbye.

adipeux, -euse [adipø, -øz] *a* (*tissu*) fatty; (*visage*) fat.

adjacent [adʒasɑ̃] *a* (*contigu*) & *Géom* adjacent.

adjectif [adʒɛktif] *nm* adjective.

adjoindre* [adʒwɛ̃dr] *vt* (*associer*) to appoint (*s.o.*) as an assistant (**à** to); (*ajouter*) to add; **s'a. qn** to appoint s.o. ◆**adjoint, -ointe** *nmf* & *a* assistant; **a. au maire** deputy mayor.

adjudant [adʒydɑ̃] *nm* warrant officer.

adjuger [adʒyʒe] *vt* (*accorder*) to award; **s'a. qch** *Fam* to grab sth for oneself.

adjurer [adʒyre] *vt* to beseech, entreat.

admettre* [admɛtr] *vt* (*laisser entrer, accueillir, reconnaître*) to admit; (*autoriser, tolérer*) to allow; (*supposer*) to admit, grant; (*candidat*) to pass; **être admis à** (*examen*) to have passed.

administrer [administre] *vt* (*gérer, donner*) to administer. ◆**administrateur, -trice** *nmf* administrator. ◆**administratif, -ive** *a* administrative. ◆**administration** *nf* administration; l'A. (*service public*) government service, the Civil Service.

admirer [admire] *vt* to admire. ◆**admirable** *a* admirable. ◆**admirateur, -trice** *nmf* admirer. ◆**admiratif, -ive** *a* admiring. ◆**admiration** *nf* admiration.

admissible [admisibl] *a* acceptable, admissible; (*après un concours*) eligible (**à** for). ◆**admission** *nf* admission.

adolescent, -ente [adɔlesɑ̃, -ɑ̃t] *nmf* adolescent, teenager; — *a* teenage. ◆**adolescence** *nf* adolescence.

adonner (s') [sadɔne] *vpr* **s'a. à** (*boisson*) to take to; (*étude*) to devote oneself to.

adopter [adɔpte] *vt* to adopt. ◆**adoptif, -ive** *a* (*fils, patrie*) adopted. ◆**adoption** *nf* adoption; **suisse d'a.** Swiss by adoption.

adorer [adɔre] *vt* (*personne*) & *Rel* to worship, adore; (*chose*) *Fam* to adore, love; **a. faire** to adore *ou* love doing. ◆**adorable** *a* adorable. ◆**adoration** *nf* adoration, worship.

adosser [adose] *vt* **a. qch à** to lean sth back against; **s'a. à** to lean back against.

adouc/ir [adusir] *vt* (*voix, traits etc*) to soften; (*boisson*) to sweeten; (*chagrin*) to mitigate, ease; — **s'a.** *vpr* (*temps*) to turn milder; (*caractère*) to mellow. ◆**—issement** *nm* **a. de la température** milder weather.

adrénaline [adrenalin] *nf* adrenalin(e).

adresse [adrɛs] *nf* **1** (*domicile*) address. **2** (*habileté*) skill. ◆**adresser** *vt* (*lettre*) to send; (*compliment, remarque etc*) to address; (*coup*) to direct, aim; (*personne*) to direct (**à** to); **a. la parole à** to speak to;

s'a. à to speak to; (*aller trouver*) to go and see; (*bureau*) to enquire at; (*être destiné à*) to be aimed at.

Adriatique [adriatik] *nf* l'A. the Adriatic.

adroit [adrwa] *a* skilful, clever.

adulation [adylasjɔ̃] *nf* adulation.

adulte [adylt] *a* & *nmf* adult, grown-up.

adultère [adyltɛr] *a* adulterous; — *nm* adultery.

advenir [advǝnir] *v imp* to occur; **a. de** (*devenir*) to become of; **advienne que pourra** come what may.

adverbe [advɛrb] *nm* adverb. ◆**adverbial, -aux** *a* adverbial.

adversaire [advɛrsɛr] *nmf* opponent, adversary. ◆**adverse** *a* opposing.

adversité [advɛrsite] *nf* adversity.

aérer [aere] *vt* (*chambre*) to air (out), ventilate; (*lit*) to air (out); — **s'a.** *vpr Fam* to get some air. ◆**aéré** *a* airy. ◆**aération** *nf* ventilation. ◆**aérien, -ienne** *a* (*ligne, attaque etc*) air-; (*photo*) aerial; (*câble*) overhead; (*léger*) airy.

aérobic [aerɔbik] *nf* aerobics.

aéro-club [aerɔklœb] *nm* flying club. ◆**aérodrome** *nm* aerodrome. ◆**aérodynamique** *a* streamlined, aerodynamic. ◆**aérogare** *nf* air terminal. ◆**aéroglisseur** *nm* hovercraft. ◆**aérogramme** *nm* air letter. ◆**aéromodélisme** *nm* model aircraft building and flying. ◆**aéronautique** *nf* aeronautics. ◆**aéronavale** *nf* = *Br* Fleet Air Arm, = *Am* Naval Air Force. ◆**aéroport** *nm* airport. ◆**aéroporté** *a* airborne. ◆**aérosol** *nm* aerosol.

affable [afabl] *a* affable.

affaiblir [afeblir] *vt*, — **s'a.** *vpr* to weaken.

affaire [afɛr] *nf* (*question*) matter, affair; (*marché*) deal; (*firme*) concern, business; (*scandale*) affair; (*procès*) Jur case; pl Com business; (*d'intérêt public, personnel*) affairs; (*effets*) belongings, things; **avoir a. à** to have to deal with; **c'est mon a.** that's my business *ou* affair *ou* concern; **faire une bonne a.** to get a good deal, get a bargain; **ça fera l'a.** that will do nicely; **toute une a.** (*histoire*) quite a business.

affair/er (s') [safere] *vpr* to busy oneself, run *ou* bustle about. ◆**—é** *a* busy. ◆**affairiste** *nm* (political) racketeer.

affaiss/er (s') [safese] *vpr* (*personne*) to collapse; (*plancher*) to cave in, give way; (*sol*) to subside, sink. ◆**—ement** [afesmɑ̃] *nm* (*du sol*) subsidence.

affaler (s') [safale] *vpr* to flop down, collapse.

affamé [afame] a starving; **a. de** Fig hungry for.

affect/er [afɛkte] vt (destiner) to earmark, assign; (nommer à un poste) to post; (feindre, émouvoir) to affect. ◆—é a (manières, personne) affected. ◆**affectation** nf assignment; posting; (simulation) affectation.

affectif, -ive [afɛktif, -iv] a emotional.

affection [afɛksjɔ̃] nf (attachement) affection; (maladie) ailment. ◆**affectionn/er** vt to be fond of. ◆—é a loving. ◆**affectueux, -euse** a affectionate.

affermir [afɛrmir] vt (autorité) to strengthen; (muscles) to tone up; (voix) to steady.

affiche [afiʃ] nf poster; Th bill. ◆**affich/er** vt (affiche etc) to post ou stick up; Th to bill; (sentiment) Péj to display; **a. qn** Péj to parade s.o., flaunt s.o. ◆—**age** nm (bill-)posting; **panneau d'a.** hoarding, Am billboard.

affilée (d') [dafile] adv (à la suite) in a row, at a stretch.

affiler [afile] vt to sharpen.

affilier (s') [safilje] vpr **s'a.** à to join, become affiliated to. ◆**affiliation** nf affiliation.

affiner [afine] vt to refine.

affinité [afinite] nf affinity.

affirmatif, -ive [afirmatif, -iv] a (ton) assertive, positive; (proposition) affirmative; **il a été a.** he was quite positive; − nf **répondre par l'affirmative** to reply in the affirmative.

affirmer [afirme] vt to assert; (proclamer solennellement) to affirm. ◆**affirmation** nf assertion.

affleurer [aflœre] vi to appear on the surface.

affliger [afliʒe] vt to distress; **affligé de** stricken ou afflicted with.

affluence [aflyɑ̃s] nf crowd; **heures d'a.** rush hours.

affluent [aflyɑ̃] nm tributary.

affluer [aflye] vi (sang) to flow, rush; (gens) to flock. ◆**afflux** nm flow; (arrivée) influx.

affol/er [afɔle] vt to drive out of one's mind; (effrayer) to terrify; − **s'a.** vpr to panic. ◆—**ement** nm panic.

affranch/ir [afrɑ̃ʃir] vt (timbre) to stamp; (émanciper) to free. ◆—**issement** nm tarifs **d'a.** postage.

affréter [afrete] vt (avion) to charter; (navire) to freight.

affreux, -euse [afrø, -øz] a hideous, dreadful, ghastly. ◆**affreusement** adv dreadfully.

affriolant [afriɔlɑ̃] a enticing.

affront [afrɔ̃] nm insult, affront; **faire un a. à** to insult.

affronter [afrɔ̃te] vt to confront, face; (mauvais temps, difficultés etc) to brave. ◆—**ement** nm confrontation.

affubler [afyble] vt Péj to dress, rig out (**de** in).

affût [afy] nm à **l'a. de** Fig on the look-out for.

affûter [afyte] vt (outil) to sharpen, grind.

Afghanistan [afganistɑ̃] nm Afghanistan.

afin [afɛ̃] prép **a. de** (+ inf) in order to; − conj **a. que** (+ sub) so that.

Afrique [afrik] nf Africa. ◆**africain, -aine** a & nmf African.

agac/er [agase] vt (personne) to irritate, annoy. ◆—**ement** nm irritation.

âge [ɑʒ] nm age; **quel â. as-tu?** how old are you?; **avant l'â.** before one's time; **d'un certain â.** middle-aged; **l'â. adulte** adulthood; **la force de l'â.** the prime of life; **le moyen â.** the Middle Ages. ◆**âgé** a elderly; **â. de six ans** six years old; **un enfant â. de six ans** a six-year-old child.

agence [aʒɑ̃s] nf agency; (succursale) branch office; **a. immobilière** estate agent's office, Am real estate office.

agenc/er [aʒɑ̃se] vt to arrange; **bien agencé** (maison etc) well-laid-out; (phrase) well put-together. ◆—**ement** nm (de maison etc) lay-out.

agenda [aʒɛ̃da] nm diary, Am datebook.

agenouiller (s') [saʒnuje] vpr to kneel (down); **être agenouillé** to be kneeling (down).

agent [aʒɑ̃] nm agent; **a. (de police)** policeman; **a. de change** stockbroker; **a. immobilier** estate agent, Am real estate agent.

aggloméré [aglɔmere] nm & a (bois) chipboard, fibreboard.

agglomérer (s') [saglɔmere] vpr (s'entasser) to conglomerate. ◆**agglomération** nf conglomeration; (habitations) built-up area; (ville) town.

aggraver [agrave] vt to worsen, aggravate; − **s'a.** vpr to worsen. ◆**aggravation** nf worsening.

agile [aʒil] a agile, nimble. ◆**agilité** nf agility, nimbleness.

agir [aʒir] **1** vi to act; **a. auprès de** to intercede with. **2 s'agir** v imp **il s'agit d'argent/etc** it's a question ou matter of money/etc, it concerns money/etc; **de quoi s'agit-il?** what is it?, what's it about?; **il s'agit de se dépêcher/etc** we have to

hurry/*etc*. ◆**agissant** *a* active, effective.
◆**agissements** *nmpl Péj* dealings.

agit/er [aʒite] *vt* (*remuer*) to stir; (*secouer*) to shake; (*brandir*) to wave; (*troubler*) to agitate; (*discuter*) to debate; — **s'a.** *vpr* (*enfant*) to fidget; (*peuple*) to stir. ◆—**é** *a* (*mer*) rough; (*malade*) restless, agitated; (*enfant*) fidgety, restless. ◆**agitateur, -trice** *nmf* (*political*) agitator. ◆**agitation** *nf* (*de la mer*) roughness; (*d'un malade etc*) restlessness; (*nervosité*) agitation; (*de la rue*) bustle; *Pol* unrest.

agneau, -x [aɲo] *nm* lamb.

agonie [agɔni] *nf* death throes; **être à l'a.** to be suffering the pangs of death. ◆**agoniser** *vi* to be dying.

agrafe [agraf] *nf* hook; (*pour papiers*) staple. ◆**agrafer** *vt* to fasten, hook, do up; (*papiers*) to staple. ◆**agrafeuse** *nf* stapler.

agrand/ir [agrɑdir] *vt* to enlarge; (*grossir*) to magnify; — **s'a.** *vpr* to expand, grow. ◆—**issement** *nm* (*de ville*) expansion; (*de maison*) extension; (*de photo*) enlargement.

agréable [agreabl] *a* pleasant, agreeable, nice. ◆—**ment** [-əmɑ] *adv* pleasantly.

agré/er [agree] *vt* to accept; **veuillez a. mes salutations distinguées** (*dans une lettre*) yours faithfully. ◆—**é** *a* (*fournisseur, centre*) approved.

agrégation [agregasjɔ] *nf* competitive examination for recruitment of *lycée* teachers. ◆**agrégé, -ée** *nmf* teacher who has passed the *agrégation*.

agrément [agremɑ] *nm* (*attrait*) charm; (*accord*) assent; **voyage d'a.** pleasure trip. ◆**agrémenter** *vt* to embellish; **a. un récit d'anecdotes** to pepper a story with anecdotes.

agrès [agrɛ] *nmpl Nau* tackle, rigging; (*de gymnastique*) apparatus.

agresser [agrese] *vt* to attack. ◆**agresseur** *nm* attacker; (*dans la rue*) mugger; (*dans un conflit*) aggressor. ◆**agressif, -ive** *a* aggressive. ◆**agression** *nf* (*d'un État*) aggression; (*d'un individu*) attack. ◆**agressivité** *nf* aggressiveness.

agricole [agrikɔl] *a* (*peuple*) agricultural, farming; (*ouvrier, machine*) farm-. ◆**agriculteur** [agrikyltœr] *nm* farmer. ◆**agriculture** *nf* agriculture, farming.

agripper [agripe] *vt* to clutch, grip; **s'a. à** to cling to, clutch, grip.

agronomie [agrɔnɔmi] *nf* agronomics.

agrumes [agrym] *nmpl* citrus fruit(s).

aguerri [ageri] *a* seasoned, hardened.

aguets (aux) [ozagɛ] *adv* on the look-out.

aguich/er [agiʃe] *vt* to tease, excite. ◆—**ant** *a* enticing.

ah! [a] *int* ah!, oh!

ahur/ir [ayrir] *vt* to astound, bewilder. ◆—**i, -ie** *nmf* idiot.

ai [e] *voir* **avoir.**

aide [ɛd] *nf* help, assistance, aid; — *nmf* (*personne*) assistant; **à l'a. de** with the help ou aid of. ◆**a.-électricien** *nm* electrician's mate. ◆**a.-familiale** *nf* home help. ◆**a.-mémoire** *nm inv Scol* handbook (*of facts etc*).

aider [ede] *vt* to help, assist, aid (**à faire** to do); **s'a. de** to make use of.

aïe! [aj] *int* ouch!, ow!

aïeul, -e [ajœl] *nmf* grandfather, grandmother.

aïeux [ajø] *nmpl* forefathers, forebears.

aigle [ɛgl] *nmf* eagle. ◆**aiglon** *nm* eaglet.

aiglefin [ɛglafɛ] *nm* haddock.

aigre [ɛgr] *a* (*acide*) sour; (*voix, vent, parole*) sharp, cutting. ◆**a.-doux, -douce** *a* bitter-sweet. ◆**aigreur** *nf* sourness; (*de ton*) sharpness; *pl* heartburn.

aigrette [ɛgrɛt] *nf* (*de plumes*) tuft.

aigr/ir (s') [segrir] *vpr* (*vin*) to turn sour; (*caractère*) to sour. ◆—**i** [egri] *a* (*personne*) embittered, bitter.

aigu, -uë [egy] *a* (*crise etc*) acute; (*dents*) sharp, pointed; (*voix*) shrill.

aiguille [egɥij] *nf* (*à coudre, de pin*) needle; (*de montre*) hand; (*de balance*) pointer; **a.** (*rocheuse*) peak.

aiguill/er [egɥije] *vt* (*train*) to shunt, *Am* switch; *Fig* to steer, direct. ◆—**age** *nm* (*appareil*) *Rail* points, *Am* switches. ◆—**eur** *nm Rail* pointsman, *Am* switchman; **a. du ciel** air traffic controller.

aiguillon [egɥijɔ] *nm* (*dard*) sting; (*stimulant*) spur. ◆**aiguillonner** *vt* to spur (on), goad.

aiguiser [eg(ɥ)ize] *vt* (*affiler*) to sharpen; (*appétit*) to whet.

ail [aj] *nm* garlic.

aile [ɛl] *nf* wing; (*de moulin à vent*) sail; *Aut* wing, *Am* fender; **battre de l'a.** to be in a bad way; **d'un coup d'a.** (*avion*) in continuous flight. ◆**ailé** [ele] *a* winged. ◆**aileron** *nm* (*de requin*) fin; (*d'avion*) aileron; (*d'oiseau*) pinion. ◆**ailier** [elje] *nm Fb* wing(er).

ailleurs [ajœr] *adv* somewhere else, elsewhere; **partout a.** everywhere else; **d'a.** (*du reste*) besides, anyway; **par a.** (*en outre*) moreover; (*autrement*) otherwise.

ailloli [ajɔli] *nm* garlic mayonnaise.

aimable [ɛmabl] *a* (*complaisant*) kind;

(*sympathique*) likeable, amiable; (*agréable*) pleasant. ◆**—ment** [-amã] *adv* kindly.

aimant [emã] **1** *nm* magnet. **2** *a* loving. ◆**aimanter** *vt* to magnetize.

aimer [eme] *vt* (*chérir*) to love; **a. (bien)** (*apprécier*) to like, be fond of; **a. faire** to like doing *ou* to do; **a. mieux** to prefer; **ils s'aiment** they're in love.

aine [ɛn] *nf* groin.

aîné, -e [ene] *a* (*de deux frères etc*) elder, older; (*de plus de deux*) eldest, oldest; — *nmf* (*enfant*) elder *ou* older (child); eldest *ou* oldest (child); **c'est mon a.** he's my senior.

ainsi [ɛ̃si] *adv* (*comme ça*) (in) this *ou* that way, thus; (*alors*) so; **a. que** as well as; **et a. de suite** and so on; **pour a. dire** so to speak.

air [ɛr] *nm* **1** air; **en plein a.** in the open (air), outdoors; **ficher** *ou* **flanquer en l'a.** *Fam* (*jeter*) to chuck away; (*gâcher*) to mess up, upset; **en l'a.** (*jeter*) (up) in the air; (*paroles, menaces*) empty; (*projets*) uncertain, (up) in the air; **dans l'a.** (*grippe, idées*) about, around. **2** (*expression*) look, appearance; **avoir l'a.** to look, seem; **avoir l'a. de** to look like; **a. de famille** family likeness. **3** (*mélodie*) tune; **a. d'opéra** aria.

aire [ɛr] *nf* (*de stationnement etc*) & *Math* area; (*d'oiseau*) eyrie; **a. de lancement** launching site.

airelle [ɛrɛl] *nf* bilberry. *Am* blueberry.

aisance [ɛzɑ̃s] *nf* (*facilité*) ease; (*prospérité*) easy circumstances, affluence.

aise [ɛz] *nf* **à l'a.** (*dans un vêtement etc*) comfortable; (*dans une situation*) at ease; (*fortuné*) comfortably off; **aimer ses aises** to like one's comforts; **mal à l'a.** uncomfortable, ill at ease. ◆**aisé** [eze] *a* (*fortuné*) comfortably off; (*naturel*) free and easy; (*facile*) easy. ◆**aisément** *adv* easily.

aisselle [ɛsɛl] *nf* armpit.

ait [ɛ] *voir* **avoir**.

ajonc(s) [aʒɔ̃] *nm(pl)* gorse, furze.

ajouré [aʒure] *a* (*dentelle etc*) openwork.

ajourn/er [aʒurne] *vt* to postpone, adjourn. ◆**—ement** *nm* postponement, adjournment.

ajout [aʒu] *nm* addition. ◆**ajouter** *vti* to add (à to); **s'a.** à to add to.

ajust/er [aʒyste] *vt* (*pièce, salaires*) to adjust; (*coiffure*) to arrange; (*coup*) to aim; **a. à** (*adapter*) to fit to. ◆**—é** *a* (*serré*) close-fitting. ◆**—ement** *nm* adjustment. ◆**—eur** *nm* (*ouvrier*) fitter.

alaise [alɛz] *nf* (*waterproof*) undersheet.

alambic [alɑ̃bik] *nm* still.

alambiqué [alɑ̃bike] *a* convoluted, over-subtle.

alanguir [alɑ̃gir] *vt* to make languid.

alarme [alarm] *nf* (*signal, inquiétude*) alarm; **jeter l'a.** to cause alarm. ◆**alarmer** *vt* to alarm; **s'a. de** to become alarmed at.

Albanie [albani] *nf* Albania. ◆**albanais, -aise** *a & nmf* Albanian.

albâtre [albatr] *nm* alabaster.

albatros [albatros] *nm* albatross.

albinos [albinos] *nmf & a inv* albino.

album [albɔm] *nm* (*de timbres etc*) album; (*de dessins*) sketchbook.

alcali [alkali] *nm* alkali. ◆**alcalin** *a* alkaline.

alchimie [alʃimi] *nf* alchemy.

alcool [alkɔl] *nm* alcohol; (*spiritueux*) spirits; **a. à brûler** methylated spirit(s); **lampe à a.** spirit lamp. ◆**alcoolique** *a & nmf* alcoholic. ◆**alcoolisé** *a* (*boisson*) alcoholic. ◆**alcoolisme** *nm* alcoholism. ◆**alcootest®** *nm* breath test; (*appareil*) breathalyzer.

alcôve [alkov] *nf* alcove.

aléas [alea] *nmpl* hazards, risks. ◆**aléatoire** *a* chancy, uncertain; (*sélection*) random.

alentour [alɑ̃tur] *adv* round about, around; **d'a.** surrounding; — *nmpl* surroundings, vicinity; **aux alentours de** in the vicinity of.

alerte [alɛrt] **1** *a* (*leste*) agile, spry; (*éveillé*) alert. **2** *nf* alarm; **en état d'a.** on the alert; **a. aérienne** air-raid warning. ◆**alerter** *vt* to warn, alert.

alezan, -ane [alzɑ̃ -an] *a & nmf* (*cheval*) chestnut.

algarade [algarad] *nf* (*dispute*) altercation.

algèbre [alʒɛbr] *nf* algebra. ◆**algébrique** *a* algebraic.

Alger [alʒe] *nm ou f* Algiers.

Algérie [alʒeri] *nf* Algeria. ◆**algérien, -ienne** *a & nmf* Algerian.

algue(s) [alg] *nf(pl)* seaweed.

alias [aljas] *adv* alias.

alibi [alibi] *nm* alibi.

alién/er [aljene] *vt* to alienate; **s'a. qn** to alienate s.o. ◆**—é, -ée** *nmf* insane person; *Péj* lunatic. ◆**aliénation** *nf* alienation; *Méd* derangement.

align/er [aline] *vt* to align, line up; **les a.** *Arg* to fork out, pay up; — **s'a.** (*personnes*) to fall into line, line up; *Pol* to align oneself (**sur** with). ◆**—ement** *nm* alignment.

aliment [alimã] *nm* food. ◆**alimentaire** *a* (*industrie, produit etc*) food-. ◆**alimentation** *nf* feeding; supply(ing); (*régime*) diet, nutrition; (*nourriture*) food; **magasin d'a.** grocer's, grocery store. ◆**alimenter** *vt* (*nourrir*) to feed; (*fournir*) to supply (**en** with); (*débat, feu*) to fuel.

alinéa [alinea] *nm* paragraph.

alité [alite] *a* bedridden.

allaiter [alete] *vti* to (breast)feed.

allant [alɑ̃] *nm* drive, energy, zest.

allécher [alefe] *vt* to tempt, entice.

allée [ale] *nf* path, walk, lane; (*de cinéma*) aisle; **allées et venues** comings and goings, running about.

allégation [alegasjɔ̃] *nf* allegation.

alléger [aleʒe] *vt* to alleviate, lighten.

allégorie [alegɔri] *nf* allegory.

allègre [alɛgr] *a* gay, lively, cheerful. ◆**allégresse** *nf* gladness, rejoicing.

alléguer [alege] *vt* (*excuse etc*) to put forward.

alléluia [aleluja] *nm* hallelujah.

Allemagne [alman] *nf* Germany. ◆**allemand, -ande** *a & nmf* German; — *nm* (*langue*) German.

aller* [ale] **1** *vi* (*aux être*) to go; (*montre etc*) to work, go; **a. à** (*convenir à*) to suit; **a. avec** (*vêtement*) to go with, match; **a. bien/mieux** (*personne*) to be well/better; **il va savoir/venir**/*etc* he'll know/come/*etc*, he's going to know/come/*etc*; **il va partir** he's about to leave, he's going to leave; **va voir!** go and see!; **comment vas-tu?, (comment) ça va?** how are you?; **ça va!** all right!, fine!; **ça va (comme ça)?** that's enough!; **allez-y** go on, go ahead; **j'y vais** I'm coming; **allons (donc)!** come on!, come off it!; **allez au lit!** come on *ou* go on to bed!; **ça va de soi** that's obvious; — **s'en aller** *vpr* to go away; (*tache*) to come out. **2** *nm* outward journey; **a. (simple)** single (ticket), *Am* one-way (ticket); **a. (et) retour** return (ticket), *Am* round-trip (ticket).

allergie [alɛrʒi] *nf* allergy. ◆**allergique** *a* allergic (**à** to).

alliage [aljaʒ] *nm* alloy.

alliance [aljɑ̃s] *nf* (*anneau*) wedding ring; *Pol* alliance; *Rel* covenant; (*mariage*) marriage.

alli/er [alje] *vt* (*associer*) to combine (**à** with); (*pays*) to ally (**à** with); — **s'a.** *vpr* (*couleurs*) to combine; (*pays*) to become allied (**à** with, to); **s'a. à** (*famille*) to ally oneself with. ◆**-é, -ée** *nmf* ally.

alligator [aligatɔr] *nm* alligator.

allô! [alo] *int Tél* hullo!, hallo!, hello!

allocation [alɔkasjɔ̃] *nf* (*somme*) allowance; **a. (de) chômage** unemployment benefit. ◆**allocataire** *nmf* claimant.

allocution [alɔkysjɔ̃] *nf* (short) speech, address.

allong/er [alɔ̃ʒe] *vt* (*bras*) to stretch out; (*jupe*) to lengthen; (*sauce*) to thin; — *vi* (*jours*) to get longer; — **s'a.** *vpr* to stretch out. ◆**-é** *a* (*oblong*) elongated.

allouer [alwe] *vt* to allocate.

allum/er [alyme] *vt* (*feu, pipe etc*) to light; (*électricité*) to turn *ou* switch on; (*désir, colère*) *Fig* to kindle; — **s'a.** *vpr* to light up; (*feu, guerre*) to flare up. ◆**-age** *nm* lighting; *Aut* ignition. ◆**allume-gaz** *nm inv* gas lighter. ◆**allumeuse** *nf* (*femme*) teaser.

allumette [alymɛt] *nf* match.

allure [alyr] *nf* (*vitesse*) pace; (*de véhicule*) speed; (*démarche*) gait, walk; (*maintien*) bearing; (*air*) look; (*de conduite*) ways.

allusion [alyzjɔ̃] *nf* allusion; (*voilée*) hint; **faire a. à** to refer *ou* allude to; to hint at.

almanach [almana] *nm* almanac.

aloi [alwa] *nm* **de bon a.** genuine, worthy.

alors [alɔr] *adv* (*en ce temps-là*) then; (*en ce cas-là*) so, then; **a. que** (*lorsque*) when; (*tandis que*) whereas.

alouette [alwɛt] *nf* (sky)lark.

alourd/ir [alurdir] *vt* to weigh down; — **s'a.** *vpr* to become heavy *ou* heavier. ◆**-i** *a* heavy.

aloyau [alwajo] *nm* sirloin.

alpaga [alpaga] *nm* (*tissu*) alpaca.

alpage [alpaʒ] *nm* mountain pasture. ◆**Alpes** *nfpl* **les A.** the Alps. ◆**alpestre** *a*, ◆**alpin** *a* alpine. ◆**alpinisme** *nm* mountaineering. ◆**alpiniste** *nmf* mountaineer.

alphabet [alfabɛ] *nm* alphabet. ◆**alphabétique** *a* alphabetic(al). ◆**alphabétiser** *vt* to teach to read and write.

altercation [altɛrkasjɔ̃] *nf* altercation.

altér/er [altere] *vt* (*denrée, santé*) to impair, spoil; (*voix, vérité*) to distort; (*monnaie, texte*) to falsify; (*donner soif à*) to make thirsty; — **s'a.** *vpr* (*santé, relations*) to deteriorate. ◆**altération** *nf* deterioration, change (**de** in); (*de visage*) distortion.

alternat/if, -ive [altɛrnatif, -iv] *a* alternating. ◆**alternative** *nf* alternative; *pl* alternate periods. ◆**alternativement** *adv* alternately.

altern/er [altɛrne] *vti* to alternate. ◆**-é** *a* alternate. ◆**alternance** *nf* alternation.

altesse [altɛs] *nf* (*titre*) Highness.

altier, -ière [altje, -jɛr] *a* haughty.

altitude [altityd] *nf* altitude, height.

alto [alto] *nm* (*instrument*) viola.

aluminium [alyminjɔm] *nm* aluminium, *Am*

aluminum; *papier a.*, *Fam* **papier alu** tin foil.

alunir [alynir] *vi* to land on the moon.

alvéole [alveɔl] *nf* (*de ruche*) cell; (*dentaire*) socket. ◆**alvéolé** *a* honeycombed.

amabilité [amabilite] *nf* kindness; **faire des amabilités à** to show kindness to.

amadouer [amadwe] *vt* to coax, persuade.

amaigr/ir [amegrir] *vt* to make thin(ner). ◆**—i** *a* thin(ner). ◆**—issant** *a* (*régime*) slimming.

amalgame [amalgam] *nm* amalgam, mixture. ◆**amalgamer** *vt*, **— s'a.** *vpr* to blend, mix, amalgamate.

amande [amɑ̃d] *nf* almond.

amant [amɑ̃] *nm* lover.

amarre [amar] *nf* (mooring) rope, hawser; *pl* moorings. ◆**amarrer** *vt* to moor; *Fig* to tie down, make fast.

amas [amɑ] *nm* heap, pile. ◆**amasser** *vt* to pile up; (*richesse*, *preuves*) to amass, gather; **— s'a.** *vpr* to pile up; (*gens*) to gather.

amateur [amatœr] *nm* (*d'art etc*) lover; *Sp* amateur; (*acheteur*) *Fam* taker; **d'a.** (*talent*) amateur; (*travail*) *Péj* amateurish; **une équipe a.** an amateur team. ◆**amateurisme** *nm Sp* amateurism; *Péj* amateurishness.

amazone [amazon] *nf* horsewoman; **monter en a.** to ride sidesaddle.

ambages (sans) [sɑ̃zabaʒ] *adv* to the point, in plain language.

ambassade [ɑ̃basad] *nf* embassy. ◆**ambassadeur, -drice** *nmf* ambassador.

ambiance [ɑ̃bjɑ̃s] *nf* atmosphere. ◆**ambiant** *a* surrounding.

ambigu, -guë [ɑ̃bigy] *a* ambiguous. ◆**ambiguïté** [-gɥite] *nf* ambiguity.

ambitieux, -euse [ɑ̃bisjø, -øz] *a* ambitious. ◆**ambition** *nf* ambition. ◆**ambitionner** *vt* to aspire to; **il ambitionne de** his ambition is to.

ambre [ɑ̃br] *nm* (*jaune*) amber; (*gris*) ambergris.

ambulance [ɑ̃bylɑ̃s] *nf* ambulance. ◆**ambulancier, -ière** *nmf* ambulance driver.

ambulant [ɑ̃bylɑ̃] *a* itinerant, travelling.

âme [ɑm] *nf* soul; **â. qui vive** a living soul; **état d'â.** state of mind; **â. sœur** soul mate; **â. damnée** evil genius, henchman; **avoir charge d'âmes** to be responsible for human life.

améliorer [ameljɔre] *vt*, **— s'a.** *vpr* to

improve. ◆**amélioration** *nf* improvement.

amen [amen] *adv* amen.

aménag/er [amenaʒe] *vt* (*arranger*, *installer*) to fit up, fit out (**en** as); (*bateau*) to fit out; (*transformer*) to convert (**en** into); (*construire*) to set up; (*ajuster*) to adjust. ◆**—ement** *nm* fitting up; fitting out; conversion; setting up; adjustment.

amende [amɑ̃d] *nf* fine; **frapper d'une a.** to impose a fine on; **faire a. honorable** to make an apology.

amender [amɑ̃de] *vt Pol* to amend; (*terre*) to improve; **— s'a.** *vpr* to mend *ou* improve one's ways.

amener [amne] *vt* to bring; (*causer*) to bring about; **— s'a.** *vpr Fam* to come along, turn up.

amenuiser (s') [samənɥize] *vpr* to grow smaller, dwindle.

amer, -ère [amer] *a* bitter. ◆**amèrement** *adv* bitterly.

Amérique [amerik] *nf* America; **A. du Nord/du Sud** North/South America. ◆**américain, -aine** *a & nmf* American.

amerrir [amerir] *vi* to make a sea landing; (*cabine spatiale*) to splash down.

amertume [amertym] *nf* bitterness.

améthyste [ametist] *nf* amethyst.

ameublement [amœbləmɑ̃] *nm* furniture.

ameuter [amøte] *vt* (*soulever*) to stir up; (*attrouper*) to gather, muster; (*voisins*) to bring out; **— s'a.** *vpr* to gather, muster.

ami, -e [ami] *nmf* friend; (*des livres, de la nature etc*) lover (**de** of); **petit a.** boyfriend; **petite amie** girlfriend; **— a.** a friendly.

amiable (à l') [alamjabl] *a* amicable; **— adv** amicably.

amiante [amjɑ̃t] *nm* asbestos.

amical, -aux [amikal, -o] *a* friendly. ◆**—ement** *adv* in a friendly manner.

amicale [amikal] *nf* association.

amidon [amidɔ̃] *nm* starch. ◆**amidonner** *vt* to starch.

amincir [amɛ̃sir] *vt* to make thin(ner); **— vi** (*personne*) to slim; **— s'a.** *vpr* to become thinner.

amiral, -aux [amiral, -o] *nm* admiral. ◆**amirauté** *nf* admiralty.

amitié [amitje] *nf* friendship; (*amabilité*) kindness; *pl* kind regrds; **prendre en a.** to take a liking to.

ammoniac [amɔnjak] *nm* (*gaz*) ammonia. ◆**ammoniaque** *nf* (*liquide*) ammonia.

amnésie [amnezi] *nf* amnesia.

amnistie [amnisti] *nf* amnesty.

amocher [amɔʃe] *vt Arg* to mess up, bash.

amoindrir [amwɛ̃drir] *vt*, **— s'a.** *vpr to* decrease, diminish.

amoll/ir [amɔlir] *vt to* soften; (*affaiblir*) to weaken. ◆**—issant** *a* enervating.

amonceler [amɔ̃sle] *vt*, **— s'a.** *vpr to* pile up. ◆**amoncellement** *nm* heap, pile.

amont (en) [ãnamɔ̃] *adv* upstream.

amoral, -aux [amɔral, -o] *a* amoral.

amorce [amɔrs] *nf* (*début*) start; *Pêche* bait; (*détonateur*) fuse, detonator; (*de pistolet d'enfant*) cap. ◆**amorcer** *vt to* start; (*hameçon*) to bait; (*pompe*) to prime; **— s'a.** *vpr to* start.

amorphe [amɔrf] *a* listless, apathetic.

amort/ir [amɔrtir] *vt* (*coup*) to cushion, absorb; (*bruit*) to deaden; (*dette*) to pay off; **il a vite amorti sa voiture** his car has been made to pay for itself quickly. ◆**—issement** *nm Fin* redemption. ◆**—isseur** *nm* shock absorber.

amour [amur] *nm* love; (*liaison*) romance, love; (*Cupidon*) Cupid; **pour l'a. de** for the sake of; **mon a.** my darling, my love. ◆**a.-propre** *nm* self-respect, self-esteem. ◆**s'amouracher** *vpr Péj* to become infatuated (**de** with). ◆**amoureux, -euse** *nmf* lover; **— a.** amorous, loving; **a. de** (*personne*) in love with; (*gloire*) *Fig* enamoured of.

amovible [amɔvibl] *a* removable, detachable.

ampère [ãper] *nm Él* amp(ere).

amphi [ãfi] *nm Univ Fam* lecture hall.

amphibie [ãfibi] *a* amphibious; **— nm** amphibian.

amphithéâtre [ãfiteɑtr] *nm Hist* amphitheatre; *Univ* lecture hall.

ample [ãpl] *a* (*vêtement*) ample, roomy; (*provision*) full; (*vues*) broad. ◆**amplement** *adv* amply, fully; **a. suffisant** ample. ◆**ampleur** *nf* (*de robe*) fullness; (*importance, étendue*) scale, extent; **prendre de l'a.** to grow.

amplifier [ãplifje] *vt* (*accroître*) to develop; (*exagérer*) to magnify; (*son, courant*) to amplify; **— s'a.** *vpr* to increase. ◆**amplificateur** *nm* amplifier. ◆**amplification** *nf* (*extension*) increase.

amplitude [ãplityd] *nf Fig* magnitude.

ampoule [ãpul] *nf* (*électrique*) (light) bulb; (*aux pieds etc*) blister; (*de médicament*) phial.

ampoulé [ãpule] *a* turgid.

amputer [ãpyte] *vt* **1** (*membre*) to amputate; **a. qn de la jambe** to amputate s.o.'s leg. **2** (*texte*) to curtail, cut (**de** by).

◆**amputation** *nf* amputation; curtailment.

amuse-gueule [amyzgœl] *nm inv* cocktail snack, appetizer.

amus/er [amyze] *vt* (*divertir*) to amuse, entertain; (*occuper*) to divert the attention of; **— s'a.** *vpr* to enjoy oneself, have fun; (*en chemin*) to dawdle, loiter; **s'a. avec** to play with; **s'a. à faire** to amuse oneself doing. ◆**—ant** *a* amusing. ◆**—ement** *nm* amusement; (*jeu*) game. ◆**amusette** *nf* frivolous pursuit.

amygdale [amidal] *nf* tonsil.

an [ã] *nm* year; **il a dix ans** he's ten (years old); **par a.** per annum, per year; **bon a., mal a.** putting the good years and the bad together; **Nouvel A.** New Year.

anachronisme [anakrɔnism] *nm* anachronism.

anagramme [anagram] *nf* anagram.

analogie [analɔʒi] *nf* analogy. ◆**analogue** *a* similar; **— nm** analogue.

analphabète [analfabet] *a & nmf* illiterate. ◆**analphabétisme** *nm* illiteracy.

analyse [analiz] *nf* analysis; **a. grammaticale** parsing. ◆**analyser** *vt* to analyse; (*phrase*) to parse. ◆**analytique** *a* analytic(al).

ananas [anana(s)] *nm* pineapple.

anarchie [anarʃi] *nf* anarchy. ◆**anarchique** *a* anarchic. ◆**anarchiste** *nmf* anarchist; **— a.** anarchistic.

anathème [anatem] *nm Rel* anathema.

anatomie [anatɔmi] *nf* anatomy. ◆**anatomique** *a* anatomical.

ancestral, -aux [ãsestral, -o] *a* ancestral.

ancêtre [ãsetr] *nm* ancestor.

anche [ãʃ] *nf Mus* reed.

anchois [ãʃwa] *nm* anchovy.

ancien, -ienne [ãsjɛ̃, -jɛn] *a* (*vieux*) old; (*meuble*) antique; (*qui n'est plus*) former, ex-, old; (*antique*) ancient; (*dans une fonction*) senior; **a. élève** old boy, *Am* alumnus; **a. combattant** ex-serviceman, *Am* veteran; **— nmf** (*par l'âge*) elder; (*dans une fonction*) senior; **les anciens** (*auteurs, peuples*) the ancients. ◆**anciennement** *adv* formerly. ◆**ancienneté** *nf* age; (*dans une fonction*) seniority.

ancre [ãkr] *nf* anchor; **jeter l'a.** to (cast) anchor; **lever l'a.** to weigh anchor. ◆**ancrer** *vt Nau* to anchor; (*idée*) *Fig* to root, fix; **ancré dans** rooted in.

andouille [ãduj] *nf* sausage (*made from chitterlings*); **espèce d'a.!** *Fam* (you) nitwit!

âne [ãn] *nm* (*animal*) donkey, ass; (*personne*) *Péj* ass; **bonnet d'â.** dunce's cap; **dos d'â.** (*d'une route*) hump; **pont en dos d'â.** humpback bridge.

anéant/ir [aneɑ̃tir] *vt* to annihilate, wipe out, destroy; — **s'a.** *vpr* to vanish. ◆—**i** *a* (*épuisé*) exhausted; (*stupéfait*) dismayed; (*accablé*) overwhelmed. ◆—**issement** *nm* annihilation; (*abattement*) dejection.

anecdote [anɛkdɔt] *nf* anecdote. ◆**anecdotique** *a* anecdotal.

anémie [anemi] *nf* an(a)emia. ◆**anémique** *a* an(a)emic. ◆**s'anémier** *vpr* to become an(a)emic.

anémone [anemɔn] *nf* anemone.

ânerie [ɑnri] *nf* stupidity; (*action etc*) stupid thing. ◆**ânesse** *nf* she-ass.

anesthésie [anɛstezi] *nf* an(a)esthesia; **a. générale/locale** general/local an(a)esthetic. ◆**anesthésier** *vt* to an(a)esthetize. ◆**anesthésique** *nm* an(a)esthetic.

anfractuosité [ɑ̃fraktyɔzite] *nf* crevice, cleft.

ange [ɑ̃ʒ] *nm* angel; **aux anges** in seventh heaven. ◆**angélique** *a* angelic.

angélus [ɑ̃ʒelys] *nm Rel* angelus.

angine [ɑ̃ʒin] *nf* sore throat; **a. de poitrine** angina (pectoris).

anglais, -aise [ɑ̃glɛ, -ɛz] *a* English; — *nmf* Englishman, Englishwoman; — *nm* (*langue*) English; **filer à l'anglaise** to take French leave.

angle [ɑ̃gl] *nm* (*point de vue*) & *Géom* angle; (*coin*) corner.

Angleterre [ɑ̃glətɛr] *nf* England.

anglican, -ane [ɑ̃glikɑ̃, -an] *a* & *nmf* Anglican.

anglicisme [ɑ̃glisism] *nm* Anglicism. ◆**angliciste** *nmf* English specialist.

anglo- [ɑ̃glɔ] *préf* Anglo-. ◆**anglo-normand** *a* Anglo-Norman; **îles a.-normandes** Channel Islands. ◆**anglophile** *a* & *nmf* anglophile. ◆**anglophone** *a* English-speaking; — *nmf* English speaker. ◆**anglo-saxon, -onne** *a* & *nmf* Anglo-Saxon.

angoisse [ɑ̃gwas] *nf* anguish. ◆**angoissant** *a* distressing. ◆**angoissé** *a* (*personne*) in anguish; (*geste, cri*) anguished.

angora [ɑ̃gɔra] *nm* (*laine*) angora.

anguille [ɑ̃gij] *nf* eel.

angulaire [ɑ̃gylɛr] *a* **pierre a.** cornerstone. ◆**anguleux, -euse** *a* (*visage*) angular.

anicroche [anikrɔʃ] *nf* hitch, snag.

animal, -aux [animal, -o] *nm* animal; (*personne*) *Péj* brute, animal; — *a* animal.

animer [anime] *vt* (*inspirer*) to animate; (*encourager*) to spur on; (*débat, groupe*) to

lead; (*soirée*) to enliven; (*regard*) to light up, brighten up; (*mécanisme*) to actuate, drive; **a. la course** *Sp* to set the pace; **animé de** (*sentiment*) prompted by; — **s'a.** *vpr* (*rue etc*) to come to life; (*yeux*) to light up, brighten up. ◆**animé** *a* (*rue*) lively; (*conversation*) animated, lively; (*doué de vie*) animate. ◆**animateur, -trice** *TV* compere, *Am* master of ceremonies, emcee; (*de club*) leader, organizer; (*d'entreprise*) driving force, spirit. ◆**animation** *nf* (*des rues*) activity; (*de réunion*) liveliness; (*de visage*) brightness; *Cin* animation.

animosité [animozite] *nf* animosity.

anis [ani(s)] *nm* (*boisson, parfum*) aniseed. ◆**anisette** *nf* (*liqueur*) anisette.

ankylose [ɑ̃kiloz] *nf* stiffening. ◆**s'ankylos/er** *vpr* to stiffen up. ◆—**é** *a* stiff.

annales [anal] *nfpl* annals.

anneau, -x [ano] *nm* ring; (*de chaîne*) link.

année [ane] *nf* year; **bonne a.!** Happy New Year!

annexe [anɛks] *nf* (*bâtiment*) annex(e); — *a* (*pièces*) appended; **bâtiment a.** annex(e). ◆**annexer** *vt* (*pays*) to annex; (*document*) to append. ◆**annexion** *nf* annexation.

annihiler [aniile] *vt* to destroy, annihilate.

anniversaire [aniverser] *nm* (*d'événement*) anniversary; (*de naissance*) birthday; — *a* anniversary.

annonce [anɔ̃s] *nf* (*avis*) announcement; (*publicitaire*) advertisement; (*indice*) sign; **petites annonces** classified advertisements, small ads. ◆**annoncer** *vt* (*signaler*) to announce, report; (*être l'indice de*) to indicate; (*vente*) to advertise; **a. le printemps** to herald spring; **s'a. pluvieux/difficile**/*etc* to look like being rainy/difficult/*etc*. ◆**annonceur** *nm* advertiser; *Rad TV* announcer.

annonciation [anɔ̃sjasjɔ̃] *nf* Annunciation.

annoter [anɔte] *vt* to annotate. ◆**annotation** *nf* annotation.

annuaire [anɥer] *nm* yearbook; (*téléphonique*) directory, phone book.

annuel, -elle [anɥel] *a* annual, yearly. ◆**annuellement** *adv* annually. ◆**annuité** *nf* annual instalment.

annulaire [anɥler] *nm* ring *ou* third finger.

annuler [anɥle] *vt* (*visite etc*) to cancel; (*mariage*) to annul; (*jugement*) to quash; — **s'a.** *vpr* to cancel each other out. ◆**annulation** *nf* cancellation; annulment; quashing.

anoblir [anɔblir] *vt* to ennoble.

anodin [anɔdɛ̃] a harmless; (remède) ineffectual.

anomalie [anɔmali] nf (irrégularité) anomaly; (difformité) abnormality.

ânonner [ɑnɔne] vt (en hésitant) to stumble through; (d'une voix monotone) to drone out.

anonymat [anɔnima] nm anonymity; **garder l'a.** to remain anonymous. ◆**anonyme** a & nmf anonymous (person).

anorak [anɔrak] nm anorak.

anorexie [anɔreksi] nf anorexia.

anormal, -aux [anɔrmal, -o] a abnormal; (enfant) educationally subnormal.

anse [ɑ̃s] nf (de tasse etc) handle; (baie) cove.

antagonisme [ɑ̃tagɔnism] nm antagonism. ◆**antagoniste** a antagonistic; – nmf antagonist.

antan (d') [dɑ̃tɑ̃] a Litt of yesteryear.

antarctique [ɑ̃tarktik] a antarctic; – nm **l'A.** the Antarctic, Antarctica.

antécédent [ɑ̃tesedɑ̃] nm Gram antecedent; pl past history, antecedents.

antenne [ɑ̃tɛn] nf TV Rad aerial, Am antenna; (station) station; (d'insecte) antenna, feeler; **a. chirurgicale** surgical outpost; Aut emergency unit; **sur** ou **à l'a.** on the air.

antérieur [ɑ̃terjœr] a (précédent) former, previous, earlier; (placé devant) front; **membre a.** forelimb; **a. à** prior to. ◆**antérieurement** adv previously. ◆**antériorité** nf precedence.

anthologie [ɑ̃tɔlɔʒi] nf anthology.

anthropologie [ɑ̃trɔpɔlɔʒi] nf anthropology.

anthropophage [ɑ̃trɔpɔfaʒ] nm cannibal. ◆**anthropophagie** nf cannibalism.

antiaérien, -ienne [ɑ̃tiaerjɛ̃, -jɛn] a (canon) antiaircraft; (abri) air-raid.

antiatomique [ɑ̃tiatɔmik] a **abri a.** fallout shelter.

antibiotique [ɑ̃tibjɔtik] a & nm antibiotic.

antibrouillard [ɑ̃tibrujar] a & nm (phare) a. fog lamp.

anticancéreux, -euse [ɑ̃tikɑ̃serø, -øz] a **centre a.** cancer hospital.

antichambre [ɑ̃tiʃɑ̃br] nf antechamber, anteroom.

antichoc [ɑ̃tiʃɔk] a inv shockproof.

anticip/er [ɑ̃tisipe] vti **a. (sur)** to anticipate. ◆**—é** a (retraite etc) early; (paiement) advance; **avec mes remerciements anticipés** thanking you in advance. ◆**anticipation** nf anticipation; **par a.** in advance; **d'a.** (roman) science-fiction.

anticlérical, -aux [ɑ̃tiklerikal, -o] a anticlerical.

anticonformiste [ɑ̃tikɔ̃fɔrmist] a & nmf nonconformist.

anticonstitutionnel, -elle [ɑ̃tikɔ̃stitysjɔnɛl] a unconstitutional.

anticorps [ɑ̃tikɔr] nm antibody.

anticyclone [ɑ̃tisiklɔn] nm anticyclone.

antidater [ɑ̃tidate] vt to backdate, antedate.

antidémocratique [ɑ̃tidemɔkratik] a undemocratic.

antidérapant [ɑ̃tiderapɑ̃] a non-skid.

antidote [ɑ̃tidɔt] nm antidote.

antigel [ɑ̃tiʒɛl] nm antifreeze.

Antilles [ɑ̃tij] nfpl **les A.** the West Indies. ◆**antillais, -aise** a & nmf West Indian.

antilope [ɑ̃tilɔp] nf antelope.

antimite [ɑ̃timit] a mothproof; – nm mothproofing agent.

antiparasite [ɑ̃tiparazit] a **dispositif a.** Rad suppressor.

antipathie [ɑ̃tipati] nf antipathy. ◆**antipathique** a disagreeable.

antipodes [ɑ̃tipɔd] nmpl **aux a.** (partir) to the antipodes; **aux a. de** at the opposite end of the world from; Fig poles apart from.

antique [ɑ̃tik] a ancient. ◆**antiquaire** nmf antique dealer. ◆**antiquité** nf (temps, ancienneté) antiquity; (objet ancien) antique; pl (monuments etc) antiquities.

antirabique [ɑ̃tirabik] a (anti-)rabies.

antisémite [ɑ̃tisemit] a anti-Semitic. ◆**antisémitisme** nm anti-Semitism.

antiseptique [ɑ̃tiseptik] a & nm antiseptic.

antisudoral, -aux [ɑ̃tisydɔral, -o] nm antiperspirant.

antithèse [ɑ̃titɛz] nf antithesis.

antivol [ɑ̃tivɔl] nm anti-theft lock ou device.

antonyme [ɑ̃tɔnim] nm antonym.

antre [ɑ̃tr] nm (de lion etc) den.

anus [anys] nm anus.

Anvers [ɑ̃vɛr(s)] nm ou f Antwerp.

anxiété [ɑ̃ksjete] nf anxiety. ◆**anxieux, -euse** a anxious; – nmf worrier.

août [u(t)] nm August. ◆**aoûtien, -ienne** [ausjɛ̃, -jɛn] nmf August holidaymaker ou Am vacationer.

apais/er [apeze] vt (personne) to appease, calm; (scrupules, faim) to appease; (douleur) to allay; – **s'a.** vpr (personne) to calm down. ◆**—ant** a soothing. ◆**—ements** nmpl reassurances.

apanage [apanaʒ] nm privilege, monopoly (de of).

aparté [aparte] nm Th aside; (dans une réunion) private exchange; **en a.** in private.

apartheid [aparted] nm apartheid.

apathie [apati] *nf* apathy. ◆**apathique** *a* apathetic, listless.

apatride [apatrid] *nmf* stateless person.

apercevoir* [apɛrsəvwar] *vt* to see, perceive; (*brièvement*) to catch a glimpse of; **s'a. de** to notice, realize. ◆**aperçu** *nm* overall view, general outline; (*intuition*) insight.

apéritif [aperitif] *nm* aperitif. ◆**apéro** *nm Fam* aperitif.

apesanteur [apəzɑ̃tœr] *nf* weightlessness.

à-peu-près [apøprɛ] *nm inv* vague approximation.

apeuré [apœre] *a* frightened, scared.

aphone [afɔn] *a* voiceless.

aphorisme [afɔrism] *nm* aphorism.

aphrodisiaque [afrɔdizjak] *a* & *nm* aphrodisiac.

aphte [aft] *nm* mouth ulcer. ◆**aphteuse** *af* **fièvre a.** foot-and-mouth disease.

apiculture [apikyltyr] *nf* beekeeping.

apit/oyer [apitwaje] *vt* to move (to pity); **s'a. sur** to pity. ◆**―oiement** *nm* pity, commiseration.

aplanir [aplanir] *vt* (*terrain*) to level; (*difficulté*) to iron out, smooth out.

aplat/ir [aplatir] *vt* to flatten (out); **― s'a.** *vpr* (*s'étendre*) to lie flat; (*s'humilier*) to grovel; (*tomber*) *Fam* to fall flat on one's face; **s'a. contre** to flatten oneself against. ◆**―i** *a* flat. ◆**―issement** *nm* (*état*) flatness.

aplomb [aplɔ̃] *nm* self-possession, self-assurance; *Péj* impudence; **d'a.** (*équilibré*) well-balanced; (*sur ses jambes*) steady; (*bien portant*) in good shape; **tomber d'a.** (*soleil*) to beat down.

apocalypse [apɔkalips] *nf* apocalypse. ◆**apocalyptique** *a* apocalyptic.

apogée [apɔʒe] *nm* apogee; *Fig* peak, apogee.

apolitique [apɔlitik] *a* apolitical.

Apollon [apɔlɔ̃] *nm* Apollo.

apologie [apɔlɔʒi] *nf* defence, vindication. ◆**apologiste** *nmf* apologist.

apoplexie [apɔplɛksi] *nf* apoplexy. ◆**apoplectique** *a* apoplectic.

apostolat [apɔstɔla] *nm* (*prosélytisme*) proselytism; (*mission*) *Fig* calling. ◆**apostolique** *a* apostolic.

apostrophe [apɔstrɔf] *nf* **1** (*signe*) apostrophe. **2** (*interpellation*) sharp *ou* rude remark. ◆**apostropher** *vt* to shout at.

apothéose [apɔteoz] *nf* final triumph, apotheosis.

apôtre [apotr] *nm* apostle.

apparaître* [aparɛtr] *vi* (*se montrer, sembler*) to appear.

apparat [apara] *nm* pomp; **d'a.** (*tenue etc*) ceremonial, formal.

appareil [aparɛj] *nm* (*instrument etc*) apparatus; (*électrique*) appliance; *Anat* system; *Tél* telephone; (*avion*) aircraft; (*législatif etc*) *Fig* machinery; **a. (photo)** camera; **a. (auditif)** hearing aid; **a. (dentier)** brace; **qui est à l'a.?** *Tél* who's speaking?

appareiller [apareje] **1** *vi Nau* to get under way. **2** *vt* (*assortir*) to match (up).

apparence [aparɑ̃s] *nf* appearance; (*vestige*) semblance; **en a.** outwardly; **sous l'a. de** under the guise of; **sauver les apparences** to keep up appearances. ◆**apparemment** [-amɑ̃] *adv* apparently. ◆**apparent** *a* apparent; (*ostensible*) conspicuous.

apparent/er (s') [saparɑ̃te] *vpr* (*ressembler*) to be similar *ou* akin (à to). ◆**―é** *a* (*allié*) related; (*semblable*) similar.

appariteur [aparitœr] *nm Univ* porter.

apparition [aparisjɔ̃] *nf* appearance; (*spectre*) apparition.

appartement [apartəmɑ̃] *nm* flat, *Am* apartment.

appartenir* [apartənir] **1** *vi* to belong (à to); **il vous appartient de** it's your responsibility to. **2 s'a.** *vpr* to be one's own master. ◆**appartenance** *nf* membership (à of).

appât [apɑ] *nm* (*amorce*) bait; (*attrait*) lure. ◆**appâter** *vt* (*attirer*) to lure.

appauvrir [apovrir] *vt* to impoverish; **― s'a.** *vpr* to become impoverished *ou* poorer.

appel [apɛl] *nm* (*cri, attrait etc*) call; (*demande pressante*) & *Jur* appeal; *Mil* call-up; **faire l'a.** *Scol* to take the register; *Mil* to have a roll call; **faire a. à** to appeal to, call upon; (*requérir*) to call for.

appel/er [aple] *vt* (*personne, nom etc*) to call; (*en criant*) to call out to; *Mil* to call up; (*nécessiter*) to call for; **a. à l'aide** to call for help; **en a. à** to appeal to; **il est appelé à** (*de hautes fonctions*) he is marked out for; (*témoigner etc*) he is called upon to; **― s'a.** *vpr* to be called; **il s'appelle Paul** his name is Paul. ◆**―é** *nm Mil* conscript. ◆**appellation** *nf* (*nom*) term; **a. contrôlée** *trade name guaranteeing quality of wine*.

appendice [apɛ̃dis] *nm* appendix; (*d'animal*) appendage. ◆**appendicite** *nf* appendicitis.

appentis [apɑ̃ti] *nm* (*bâtiment*) lean-to.

appesantir (s') [sapəzɑ̃tir] *vpr* to become heavier; **s'a. sur** (*sujet*) to dwell upon.

appétit [apeti] *nm* appetite (de for); **mettre**

qn en a. to whet s.o.'s appetite; **bon a.!** enjoy your meal! ◆**appétissant** *a* appetizing.

applaud/ir [aplodir] *vti* to applaud, clap; **a. à** (*approuver*) to applaud. ◆—**issements** *nmpl* applause.

applique [aplik] *nf* wall lamp.

appliqu/er [aplike] *vt* to apply (à to); (*surnom, baiser, gifle*) to give; (*loi, décision*) to put into effect; **s'a. à** (*un travail*) to apply oneself to; (*concerner*) to apply to; **s'a. à faire** to take pains to do. ◆—**é** *a* (*travailleur*) painstaking; (*sciences*) applied. ◆**applicable** *a* applicable. ◆**application** *nf* application.

appoint [apwɛ̃] *nm* contribution; **faire l'a.** to give the correct money *ou* change.

appointements [apwɛ̃tmɑ̃] *nmpl* salary.

appontement [apɔ̃tmɑ̃] *nm* landing stage.

apport [apɔr] *nm* contribution.

apporter [apɔrte] *vt* to bring.

apposer [apoze] *vt Jur* to affix. ◆**apposition** *nf Gram* apposition.

apprécier [apresje] *vt* (*évaluer*) to appraise; (*aimer, percevoir*) to appreciate. ◆**appréciable** *a* appreciable. ◆**appréciation** *nf* appraisal; appreciation.

appréhender [apreɑ̃de] *vt* (*craindre*) to fear; (*arrêter*) to apprehend. ◆**appréhension** *nf* apprehension.

apprendre* [aprɑ̃dr] *vti* (*étudier*) to learn; (*événement, fait*) to hear of, learn of; (*nouvelle*) to hear; **a. à faire** to learn to do; **a. qch à qn** (*enseigner*) to teach s.o. sth; (*informer*) to tell s.o. sth; **a. à qn à faire** to teach s.o. to do; **a. que** to learn that; (*être informé*) to hear that.

apprenti, -ie [aprɑ̃ti] *nmf* apprentice; (*débutant*) novice. ◆**apprentissage** *nm* apprenticeship; **faire l'a. de** *Fig* to learn the experience of.

apprêt/er [aprete] *vt*, **— s'a.** *vpr* to prepare. ◆—**é** *a Fig* affected.

apprivois/er [aprivwaze] *vt* to tame; **— s'a.** *vpr* to become tame. ◆—**é** *a* tame.

approbation [aprɔbasjɔ̃] *nf* approval. ◆**approbateur, -trice** *a* approving.

approche [aprɔʃ] *nf* approach. ◆**approch/er** *vt* (*chaise etc*) to bring up, draw up (**de** to, close to); (*personne*) to approach, come close to; **— vi** to approach, draw near(er); **a. de, s'a. de** to approach, come close(r) *ou* near(er) to. ◆—**ant** *a* similar. ◆—**é** *a* approximate. ◆—**able** *a* approachable.

approfond/ir [aprɔfɔ̃dir] *vt* (*trou etc*) to deepen; (*question*) to go into thoroughly;

(*mystère*) to plumb the depths of. ◆—**i** *a* thorough. ◆—**issement** *nm* deepening; (*examen*) thorough examination.

approprié [aprɔprije] *a* appropriate.

approprier (s') [saprɔprije] *vpr* **s'a. qch** to appropriate sth.

approuver [apruve] *vt* (*autoriser*) to approve; (*apprécier*) to approve of.

approvisionn/er [aprɔvizjɔne] *vt* (*ville etc*) to supply (with provisions); (*magasin*) to stock; **— s'a.** *vpr* to stock up (**de** with), get one's supplies (**de** of). ◆—**ements** *nmpl* stocks, supplies.

approximat/if, -ive [aprɔksimatif, -iv] *a* approximate. ◆—**ivement** *adv* approximately. ◆**approximation** *nf* approximation.

appui [apɥi] *nm* support; (*pour coude etc*) rest; (*de fenêtre*) sill; **à hauteur d'a.** breast-high. ◆**appuie-tête** *nm inv* headrest. ◆**appuyer** *vt* (*soutenir*) to support; (*accentuer*) to stress; **a. qch sur** (*poser*) to lean *ou* rest sth on; (*presser*) to press sth on; **— vi a. sur** to rest on; (*bouton etc*) to press (on); (*mot, élément etc*) to stress; **s'a. sur** to lean on, rest on; (*compter*) to rely on; (*se baser*) to base oneself on.

âpre [ɑpr] *a* harsh, rough; **a. au gain** grasping.

après [apre] *prép* (*temps*) after; (*espace*) beyond; **a. un an** after a year; **a. le pont** beyond the bridge; **a. coup** after the event; **a. avoir mangé** after eating; **a. qu'il t'a vu** after he saw you; **d'a.** (*selon*) according to, from; **— adv** after(wards); **l'année d'a.** the following year; **et a.?** and then what?

après-demain [apredmɛ̃] *adv* the day after tomorrow. ◆**a.-guerre** *nm* post-war period; **d'a.-guerre** post-war. ◆**a.-midi** *nm ou f inv* afternoon. ◆**a.-shampooing** *nm* (hair) conditioner. ◆**a.-ski** *nm* ankle boot, snow boot.

a priori [aprijɔri] *adv* at the very outset, without going into the matter; **— nm inv** premiss.

à-propos [apropo] *nm* timeliness, aptness.

apte [apt] *a* suited (à to), capable (à of). ◆**aptitude** *nf* aptitude, capacity (à, **pour** for).

aquarelle [akwarɛl] *nf* watercolour, aquarelle.

aquarium [akwarjɔm] *nm* aquarium.

aquatique [akwatik] *a* aquatic.

aqueduc [akdyk] *nm* aqueduct.

aquilin [akilɛ̃] *a* aquiline.

arabe [arab] *a & nmf* Arab; **— a & nm** (*langue*) Arabic; **chiffres arabes** Arabic

numerals; **désert a.** Arabian desert.
◆**Arabie** nf Arabia; **A. Séoudite** Saudi
Arabia.

arabesque [arabɛsk] nf arabesque.

arable [arabl] a arable.

arachide [araʃid] nf peanut, groundnut.

araignée [arene] nf spider.

arbalète [arbalɛt] nf crossbow.

arbitraire [arbitrɛr] a arbitrary.

arbitre [arbitr] nm Jur arbitrator; (maître
absolu) arbiter; Fb referee; Tennis umpire;
libre a. free will. ◆**arbitr/er** vt to arbi-
trate; to referee; to umpire. ◆**—age** nm
arbitration; refereeing; umpiring.

arborer [arbɔre] vt (insigne, vêtement) to
sport, display.

arbre [arbr] nm tree; Aut shaft, axle.
◆**arbrisseau, -x** nm shrub. ◆**arbuste**
nm (small) shrub, bush.

arc [ark] nm (arme) bow; (voûte) arch; Math
arc; **tir à l'a.** archery. ◆**arcade** nf
arch(way); pl arcade.

arc-boutant [arkbutɑ̃] nm (pl
arcs-boutants) flying buttress.
◆**s'arc-bouter** vpr **s'a. à** ou **contre** to
brace oneself against.

arceau, -x [arso] nm (de voûte) arch.

arc-en-ciel [arkɑ̃sjɛl] nm (pl arcs-en-ciel)
rainbow.

archaïque [arkaik] a archaic.

archange [arkɑ̃ʒ] nm archangel.

arche [arʃ] nf (voûte) arch; **l'a. de Noé**
Noah's ark.

archéologie [arkeɔlɔʒi] nf arch(a)eology.
◆**archéologue** nmf arch(a)eologist.

archer [arʃe] nm archer, bowman.

archet [arʃe] nm Mus bow.

archétype [arketip] nm archetype.

archevêque [arʃəvɛk] nm archbishop.

archicomble [arʃikɔ̃bl] a jam-packed.

archipel [arʃipɛl] nm archipelago.

archiplein [arʃiplɛ̃] a chock-full,
chock-a-block.

architecte [arʃitɛkt] nmf architect.
◆**architecture** nf architecture.

archives [arʃiv] nfpl archives, records.
◆**archiviste** nmf archivist.

arctique [arktik] a arctic; — nm **l'A.** the
Arctic.

ardent [ardɑ̃] a (chaud) burning, scorching;
(actif, passionné) ardent, fervent;
(empressé) eager. ◆**ardemment** [-amɑ̃]
adv eagerly, fervently. ◆**ardeur** nf heat;
(énergie) ardour, fervour.

ardoise [ardwaz] nf slate.

ardu [ardy] a arduous, difficult.

are [ar] nm (mesure) 100 square metres.

arène [arɛn] nf Hist arena; (pour taureaux)
bullring; pl Hist amphitheatre; bullring.

arête [arɛt] nf (de poisson) bone; (de cube
etc) & Géog ridge.

argent [arʒɑ̃] nm (métal) silver; (monnaie)
money; **a. comptant** cash. ◆**argenté** a
(plaqué) silver-plated; (couleur) silvery.
◆**argenterie** nf silverware.

Argentine [arʒɑ̃tin] nf Argentina. ◆**argentin, -ine** a & nmf Argentinian.

argile [arʒil] nf clay. ◆**argileux, -euse** a
clayey.

argot [argo] nm slang. ◆**argotique** a
(terme) slang.

arguer [argɥe] vi **a. de qch** to put forward
sth as an argument; **a. que** (protester) to
protest that. ◆**argumentation** nf argumentation, arguments. ◆**argumenter** vi
to argue.

argument [argymɑ̃] nm argument.

argus [argys] nm guide to secondhand cars.

argutie [argysi] nf specious argument, quibble.

aride [arid] a arid, barren.

aristocrate [aristɔkrat] nmf aristocrat.
◆**aristocratie** [-asi] nf aristocracy.
◆**aristocratique** a aristocratic.

arithmétique [aritmetik] nf arithmetic; — a
arithmetical.

arlequin [arləkɛ̃] nm harlequin.

armateur [armatœr] nm shipowner.

armature [armatyr] nf (charpente) framework; (de lunettes, tente) frame.

arme [arm] nf arm, weapon; **a. à feu** firearm; **carrière des armes** military career.
◆**arm/er** vt (personne etc) to arm (de
with); (fusil) to cock; (appareil photo) to
wind on; (navire) to equip; (béton) to reinforce; — **s'a.** vpr to arm oneself (de with).
◆**—ement(s)** nm(pl) arms.

armée [arme] nf army; **a. active/de métier**
regular/professional army; **a. de l'air** air
force.

armistice [armistis] nm armistice.

armoire [armwar] nf cupboard, Am closet;
(penderie) wardrobe, Am closet; **a. à
pharmacie** medicine cabinet.

armoiries [armwari] nfpl (coat of) arms.

armure [armyr] nf armour.

armurier [armyrje] nm gunsmith.

arôme [arom] nm aroma. ◆**aromate** nm
spice. ◆**aromatique** a aromatic.

arpent/er [arpɑ̃te] vt (terrain) to survey;
(trottoir etc) to pace up and down. ◆**—eur**
nm (land) surveyor.

arqué [arke] a arched, curved; (jambes)
bandy.

arrache-pied (d') [daraʃpje] *adv* unceasingly, relentlessly.

arrach/er [araʃe] *vt* (*clou, dent etc*) to pull out; (*cheveux, page*) to tear out, pull out; (*plante*) to pull up; (*masque*) to tear off, pull off; **a. qch à qn** to snatch sth from s.o.; (*aveu, argent*) to force sth out of s.o.; **a. un bras à qn** (*obus etc*) to blow s.o.'s arm off; **a. qn de son lit** to drag s.o. out of bed. ◆**—age** *nm* (*de plante*) pulling up.

arraisonner [arɛzɔne] *vt* (*navire*) to board and examine.

arrang/er [arɑ̃ʒe] *vt* (*chambre, visite etc*) to arrange, fix up; (*voiture, texte*) to put right; (*différend*) to settle; **a. qn** (*maltraiter*) *Fam* to fix s.o.; **ça m'arrange** that suits me (fine); **— s'a.** *vpr* (*se réparer*) to be put right; (*se mettre d'accord*) to come to an agreement *ou* arrangement; (*finir bien*) to turn out fine; **s'a. pour faire** to arrange to do, manage to do. ◆**—eant** *a* accommodating. ◆**—ement** *nm* arrangement.

arrestation [arɛstasjɔ̃] *nf* arrest.

arrêt [arɛ] *nm* (*halte, endroit*) stop; (*action*) stopping; *Méd* arrest; *Jur* decree; **temps d'a.** pause; **à l'a.** stationary; **a. de travail** (*grève*) stoppage; (*congé*) sick leave; **sans a.** constantly, non-stop.

arrêté [arɛte] *nm* order, decision.

arrêt/er [arɛte] *vt* to stop; (*appréhender*) to arrest; (*regard, jour*) to fix; (*plan*) to draw up; **— vi** to stop; **il n'arrête pas de critiquer/etc** he doesn't stop criticizing/etc, he's always criticizing/etc; **— s'a.** *vpr* to stop; **s'a. de faire** to stop doing. ◆**—é** *a* (*projet*) fixed; (*volonté*) firm.

arrhes [ar] *nfpl Fin* deposit.

arrière [arjɛr] *adv* **en a.** (*marcher*) backwards; (*rester*) behind; (*regarder*) back; **en a. de qn/qch** behind s.o./sth; **— nm & a inv** rear, back; (*— nm Fb*) (full) back; **faire marche a.** to reverse, back.

arrière-boutique [arjɛrbutik] *nm* back room (*of a shop*). ◆**a.-garde** *nf* rearguard. ◆**a.-goût** *nm* aftertaste. ◆**a.-grand-mère** *nf* great-grand-mother. ◆**a.-grand-père** *nm* (*pl* **arrière-grands-pères**) great-grand-father. ◆**a.-pays** *nm* hinterland. ◆**a.-pensée** *nf* ulterior motive. ◆**a.-plan** *nm* background. ◆**a.-saison** *nf* end of season, (late) autumn. ◆**a.-train** *nm* hindquarters.

arriéré [arjere] **1** *a* (*enfant*) (mentally) retarded; (*idée*) backward. **2** *nm* (*dette*) arrears.

arrimer [arime] *vt* (*fixer*) to rope down, secure.

arriv/er [arive] *vi* (*aux être*) (*venir*) to arrive, come; (*réussir*) to succeed; (*survenir*) to happen; **a. à** (*atteindre*) to reach; **a. à faire** to manage to do, succeed in doing; **a. à qn** to happen to s.o.; **il m'arrive d'oublier/etc** I happen (sometimes) to forget/etc, I (sometimes) forget/etc; **en a. à faire** to get to the point of doing. ◆**—ant, -ante** *nmf* new arrival. ◆**—ée** *nf* arrival; *Sp* (*winning*) post. ◆**—age** *nm* consignment. ◆**arriviste** *nmf Péj* social climber, self-seeker.

arrogant [arɔgɑ̃] *a* arrogant. ◆**arrogance** *nf* arrogance.

arroger (s') [sarɔʒe] *vpr* (*droit etc*) to assume (falsely).

arrond/ir [arɔ̃dir] *vt* to make round; (*somme, chiffre*) to round off. ◆**—i** *a* rounded.

arrondissement [arɔ̃dismɑ̃] *nm* (*d'une ville*) district.

arros/er [aroze] *vt* (*terre*) to water; (*repas*) to wash down; (*succès*) to drink to. ◆**—age** *nm* watering; *Fam* booze-up, celebration. ◆**arrosoir** *nm* watering can.

arsenal, -aux [arsənal, -o] *nm Nau* dockyard; *Mil* arsenal.

arsenic [arsənik] *nm* arsenic.

art [ar] *nm* art; **film/critique d'a.** film/critic; **arts ménagers** domestic science.

artère [arter] *nf Anat* artery; *Aut* main road. ◆**artériel, -elle** *a* arterial.

artichaut [artiʃo] *nm* artichoke.

article [artikl] *nm* (*de presse, de commerce*) & *Gram* article; (*dans un contrat, catalogue*) item; **a. de fond** feature (article); **articles de toilette/de voyage** toilet/travel requisites; **à l'a. de la mort** at death's door.

articuler [artikyle] *vt* (*mot etc*) to articulate; **— s'a.** *vpr Anat* to articulate; *Fig* to connect. ◆**articulation** *nf Ling* articulation; *Anat* joint; **a. du doigt** knuckle.

artifice [artifis] *nm* trick, contrivance; **feu d'a.** (*spectacle*) fireworks, firework display.

artificiel, -elle [artifisjɛl] *a* artificial. ◆**artificiellement** *adv* artificially.

artillerie [artijri] *nf* artillery. ◆**artilleur** *nm* gunner.

artisan [artizɑ̃] *nm* craftsman, artisan. ◆**artisanal, -aux** *a* (*métier*) craftsman's. ◆**artisanat** *nm* (*métier*) craftsman's trade; (*classe*) artisan class.

artiste [artist] *nmf* artist; *Th Mus Cin* performer, artist. ◆**artistique** *a* artistic.

as [as] *nm* (*carte, champion*) ace; **a. du volant** crack driver.

ascendant [asɑ̃dɑ̃] *a* ascending, upward; – *nm* ascendancy, power; *pl* ancestors. ◆**ascendance** *nf* ancestry.

ascenseur [asɑ̃sœr] *nm* lift, *Am* elevator.

ascension [asɑ̃sjɔ̃] *nf* ascent; **l'A.** Ascension Day.

ascète [asɛt] *nmf* ascetic. ◆**ascétique** *a* ascetic. ◆**ascétisme** *nm* asceticism.

Asie [azi] *nf* Asia. ◆**Asiate** *nmf* Asian. ◆**asiatique** *a* & *nmf* Asian, Asiatic.

asile [azil] *nm* (*abri*) refuge, shelter; (*pour vieillards*) home; *Pol* asylum; **a. (d'aliénés)** *Péj* (lunatic) asylum; **a. de paix** haven of peace.

aspect [aspɛ] *nm* (*vue*) sight; (*air*) appearance; (*perspective*) & *Gram* aspect.

asperge [aspɛrʒ] *nf* asparagus.

asperger [aspɛrʒe] *vt* to spray, sprinkle (**de** with).

aspérité [asperite] *nf* rugged edge, bump.

asphalte [asfalt] *nm* asphalt.

asphyxie [asfiksi] *nf* suffocation. ◆**asphyxier** *vt* to suffocate, asphyxiate.

aspic [aspik] *nm* (*vipère*) asp.

aspirant [aspirɑ̃] *nm* (*candidat*) candidate.

aspirateur [aspiratœr] *nm* vacuum cleaner, hoover®; **passer** (**à**) **l'a.** to vacuum, hoover.

aspir/er [aspire] *vt* (*respirer*) to breathe in, inhale; (*liquide*) to suck up; **a. à** to aspire to. ◆**-é a** *Ling* aspirate(d). ◆**aspiration** *nf* inhaling; suction; (*ambition*) aspiration.

aspirine [aspirin] *nf* aspirin.

assagir (s') [sasaʒir] *vpr* to sober (down), settle down.

assaill/ir [asajir] *vt* to assault, attack; **a. de** (*questions etc*) to assail with. ◆**-ant** *nm* assailant, attacker.

assainir [asenir] *vt* (*purifier*) to clean up; *Fin* to stabilize.

assaisonn/er [asɛzɔne] *vt* to season. ◆**-ement** *nm* seasoning.

assassin [asasɛ̃] *nm* murderer; assassin. ◆**assassinat** *nm* murder; assassination. ◆**assassiner** *vt* to murder; (*homme politique etc*) to assassinate.

assaut [aso] *nm* assault, onslaught; **prendre d'a.** to (take by) storm.

assécher [aseʃe] *vt* to drain.

assemblée [asɑ̃ble] *nf* (*personnes réunies*) gathering; (*réunion*) meeting; *Pol Jur* assembly; (*de fidèles*) *Rel* congregation.

assembl/er [asɑ̃ble] *vt* to assemble, put together; – **s'a.** *vpr* to assemble, gather. ◆**-age** *nm* (*montage*) assembly; (*réunion d'objets*) collection.

asséner [asene] *vt* (*coup*) to deal, strike.

assentiment [asɑ̃timɑ̃] *nm* assent, consent.

asseoir* [aswar] *vt* (*personne*) to sit (down), seat (**sur** on); (*fondations*) to lay; (*autorité, réputation*) to establish; **a. sur** (*théorie etc*) to base on; – **s'a.** *vpr* to sit (down).

assermenté [asɛrmɑ̃te] *a* sworn.

assertion [asɛrsjɔ̃] *nf* assertion.

asserv/ir [asɛrvir] *vt* to enslave. ◆**-issement** *nm* enslavement.

assez [ase] *adv* enough; **a. de pain/de gens** enough bread/people; **j'en ai a.** I've had enough; **a. grand/intelligent/etc** (*suffisamment*) big/clever/etc enough (**pour** to); **a. fatigué/etc** (*plutôt*) fairly *ou* rather *ou* quite tired/etc.

assidu [asidy] *a* (*appliqué*) assiduous, diligent; **a. auprès de** attentive to. ◆**assiduité** *nf* assiduousness, diligence; *pl* (*empressement*) attentiveness. ◆**assidûment** *adv* assiduously.

assiég/er [asjeʒe] *vt* (*ville*) to besiege; (*guichet*) to mob, crowd round; (*importuner*) to pester, harry; **assiégé de** (*demandes*) besieged with; (*maux*) beset by. ◆**-eant, -eante** *nmf* besieger.

assiette [asjɛt] *nf* **1** (*récipient*) plate; **a. anglaise** *Culin* (assorted) cold meats, *Am* cold cuts. **2** (*à cheval*) seat; **il n'est pas dans son a.** he's feeling out of sorts.

assigner [asiɲe] *vt* (*attribuer*) to assign; *Jur* to summon, subpoena. ◆**assignation** *nf* *Jur* subpoena, summons.

assimiler [asimile] *vt* to assimilate; – **s'a.** *vpr* (*immigrants*) to assimilate, become assimilated (**à** with). ◆**assimilation** *nf* assimilation.

assis [asi] *a* (*personne*) seated; (*caractère*) settled; (*situation*) stable, secure.

assise [asiz] *nf* (*base*) *Fig* foundation; *pl* assizes; *Pol* congress; **cour d'assises** court of assizes.

assistance [asistɑ̃s] *nf* **1** (*assemblée*) audience; (*nombre de personnes présentes*) attendance, turn-out. **2** (*aide*) assistance; **l'A. (publique)** the child care service; **enfant de l'A.** child in care. ◆**assist/er 1** *vt* (*aider*) to assist, help. **2** *vi* **a. à** (*réunion, cours etc*) to attend, be present at; (*accident*) to witness. ◆**-ant, -ante** *nmf* assistant; – *nmpl* (*spectateurs*) members of the audience; (*témoins*) those present; **assistante sociale** social worker; **assistante maternelle** mother's help.

associ/er [asɔsje] *vt* to associate (**à** with); **a. qn à** (*ses travaux, profits*) to involve s.o. in; **s'a. à** (*collaborer*) to associate with, become associated with; (*aux vues ou au chagrin de qn*) to share; (*s'harmoniser*) to combine with. ◆**—é, -ée** *nmf* partner, associate; — *a* associate. ◆**association** *nf* association; (*amitié, alliance*) partnership, association.

assoiffé [aswafe] *a* thirsty (**de** for).

assombrir [asɔ̃brir] *vt* (*obscurcir*) to darken; (*attrister*) to cast a cloud over, fill with gloom; — **s'a.** *vpr* to darken; to cloud over.

assomm/er [asɔme] *vt* (*animal*) to stun, brain; (*personne*) to knock unconscious; (*ennuyer*) to bore stiff. ◆**—ant** *a* tiresome, boring.

assomption [asɔ̃psjɔ̃] *nf* Rel Assumption.

assort/ir [asɔrtir] *vt*, — **s'a.** *vpr* to match. ◆**—i** *a* **bien a.** (*magasin*) well-stocked; — *apl* (*objets semblables*) matching; (*fromages etc variés*) assorted; **époux bien assortis** well-matched couple. ◆**—iment** *nm* assortment.

assoup/ir [asupir] *vt* (*personne*) to make drowsy; (*douleur, sentiment etc*) Fig to dull; — **s'a.** *vpr* to doze off; Fig to subside. ◆**—i** *a* (*personne*) drowsy. ◆**—issement** *nm* drowsiness.

assoupl/ir [asuplir] *vt* (*étoffe, muscles*) to make supple; (*corps*) to limber up; (*caractère*) to soften; (*règles*) to ease, relax. ◆**—issement** *nm* **exercices d'a.** limbering up exercises.

assourd/ir [asurdir] *vt* (*personne*) to deafen; (*son*) to muffle. ◆**—issant** *a* deafening.

assouvir [asuvir] *vt* to appease, satisfy.

assujett/ir [asyʒetir] *vt* (*soumettre*) to subject (**à** to); (*peuple*) to subjugate; (*fixer*) to secure; **s'a.** **à** to subject oneself to, submit to. ◆**—issant** *a* (*travail*) constraining. ◆**—issement** *nm* subjection; (*contrainte*) constraint.

assumer [asyme] *vt* (*tâche, rôle*) to assume, take on; (*emploi*) to take up, assume; (*remplir*) to fill, hold.

assurance [asyrɑ̃s] *nf* (*aplomb*) (self-)assurance; (*promesse*) assurance; (*contrat*) insurance; **a. au tiers/tous risques** third-party/comprehensive insurance; **assurances sociales** = national insurance, *Am* = social security.

assur/er [asyre] *vt* (*rendre sûr*) to ensure, *Am* insure; (*par un contrat*) to insure; (*travail etc*) to carry out; (*fixer*) to secure; **a. à qn que** to assure s.o. that; **a. qn de qch, a. qch à qn** to assure s.o. of sth; — **s'a.** *vpr* (*se procurer*) to ensure, secure; (*par un contrat*) to insure oneself, get insured (**contre** against); **s'a. que/de** to make sure that/of. ◆**—é, -ée** *a* (*succès*) assured, certain; (*pas*) firm, secure; (*air*)

(self-)assured, (self-)confident; — *nmf* policyholder, insured person. ◆**—ément** *adv* certainly, assuredly. ◆**assureur** *nm* insurer.

astérisque [asterisk] *nm* asterisk.

asthme [asm] *nm* asthma. ◆**asthmatique** *a* & *nmf* asthmatic.

asticot [astiko] *nm* maggot, worm.

astiquer [astike] *vt* to polish.

astre [astr] *nm* star.

astreindre[*] [astrɛ̃dr] *vt* **a. à** (*discipline*) to compel to accept; **a. à faire** to compel to do. ◆**astreignant** *a* exacting ◆**astreinte** *nf* constraint.

astrologie [astrɔlɔʒi] *nf* astrology. ◆**astrologue** *nm* astrologer.

astronaute [astronot] *nmf* astronaut. ◆**astronautique** *nf* space travel.

astronomie [astronɔmi] *nf* astronomy. ◆**astronome** *nm* astronomer. ◆**astronomique** *a* astronomical.

astuce [astys] *nf* (*pour faire qch*) knack, trick; (*invention*) gadget; (*plaisanterie*) clever joke, wisecrack; (*finesse*) astuteness; **les astuces du métier** the tricks of the trade. ◆**astucieux, -euse** *a* clever, astute.

atelier [atəlje] *nm* (*d'ouvrier*) workshop; (*de peintre*) studio.

atermoyer [atermwaje] *vi* to procrastinate.

athée [ate] *a* atheistic; — *nmf* atheist. ◆**athéisme** *nm* atheism.

Athènes [atɛn] *nm ou f* Athens.

athlète [atlɛt] *nmf* athlete. ◆**athlétique** *a* athletic. ◆**athlétisme** *nm* athletics.

atlantique [atlɑ̃tik] *a* Atlantic; — *nm* **l'A.** the Atlantic.

atlas [atlas] *nm* atlas.

atmosphère [atmɔsfɛr] *nf* atmosphere. ◆**atmosphérique** *a* atmospheric.

atome [atom] *nm* atom. ◆**atomique** [atomik] *a* atomic; **bombe a.** atom ou atomic bomb.

atomis/er [atɔmize] *vt* (*liquide*) to spray; (*région*) to destroy (*by atomic weapons*). ◆**—eur** *nm* spray.

atone [atɔn] *a* (*personne*) lifeless; (*regard*) vacant.

atours [atur] *nmpl* Hum finery.

atout [atu] *nm* trump (card); (*avantage*) Fig trump card, asset; **l'a. est cœur** hearts are trumps.

âtre [atr] *nm* (*foyer*) hearth.

atroce [atrɔs] *a* atrocious; (*crime*) heinous, atrocious. ◆**atrocité** *nf* atrociousness; *pl* (*actes*) atrocities.

atrophie [atrɔfi] *nf* atrophy. ◆**atrophié** *a* atrophied.

attabl/er (s') [satable] *vpr* to sit down at the table. ◆**—é** *a* (seated) at the table.

attache [ataʃ] *nf* (objet) attachment, fastening; *pl* (liens) links.

attach/er [ataʃe] *vt* (lier) to tie (up), attach (à to); (boucler, fixer) to fasten; **a. du prix/un sens à qch** to attach great value/a meaning to sth; **cette obligation m'attache à lui** this obligation binds me to him; **s'a. à** (adhérer) to stick to; (se lier) to become attached to; (se consacrer) to apply oneself to. ◆**—ant** *a* (enfant etc) engaging, appealing. ◆**—é, -ée** *nmf* (personne) Pol Mil attaché. ◆**—ement** *nm* attachment, affection.

attaque [atak] *nf* attack; **a. aérienne** air raid; **d'a.** in tip-top shape, on form. ◆**attaqu/er** *vt*, **s'a. à** to attack; (difficulté, sujet) to tackle; – *vi* to attack. ◆**—ant, -ante** *nmf* attacker.

attard/er (s') [satarde] *vpr* (chez qn) to linger (on), stay on; (en chemin) to loiter, dawdle; **s'a. sur** ou **à** (détails etc) to linger over; **s'a. derrière qn** to lag behind s.o. ◆**—é** *a* (enfant etc) backward; (passant) late.

atteindre* [atɛ̃dr] *vt* (parvenir à) to reach; (idéal) to attain; (blesser) to hit, wound; (toucher) to affect; (offenser) to hurt, wound; **être atteint de** (maladie) to be suffering from.

atteinte [atɛ̃t] *nf* attack; **porter a. à** to attack, undermine; **a. à** (honneur) slur on; **hors d'a.** (objet, personne) out of reach; (réputation) unassailable.

attel/er [atle] *vt* (bêtes) to harness, hitch up; (remorque) to couple; **s'a. à** (travail etc) to apply oneself to. ◆**—age** *nm* harnessing; coupling; (bêtes) team.

attenant [atnɑ̃] *a* **a.** (à) adjoining.

attend/re [atɑ̃dr] *vt* to wait for, await; (escompter) to expect (de of, from); **elle attend un bébé** she's expecting a baby; – *vi* to wait; **s'a. à** to expect, **s'a. à être informé** to expect to be informed; **a. que qn vienne** to wait for s.o. to come, wait until s.o. comes; **faire a. qn** to keep s.o. waiting; **se faire a.** (réponse, personne etc) to be a long time coming; **attends voir** Fam let me see; **en attendant** meanwhile; **en attendant que** (+ sub) until. ◆**—u** *a* (avec joie) eagerly-awaited; (prévu) expected; – *prép* considering; **a. que** considering that.

attendr/ir [atɑ̃drir] *vt* (émouvoir) to move (to compassion); (viande) to tenderize; – **s'a.** *vpr* to be moved (sur by). ◆**—i** *a*

compassionate. ◆**—issant** *a* moving. ◆**—issement** *nm* compassion.

attentat [atɑ̃ta] *nm* attempt (on s.o.'s life); murder attempt; Fig crime, outrage (à against); **a. (à la bombe)** (bomb) attack. ◆**attenter** *vi* **a. à** (la vie de qn) to make an attempt on; Fig to attack.

attente [atɑ̃t] *nf* (temps) wait(ing); (espérance) expectation(s); **une a. prolongée** a long wait; **être dans l'a. de** to be waiting for; **salle d'a.** waiting room.

attentif, -ive [atɑ̃tif, -iv] *a* (personne) attentive; (travail, examen) careful; **a. à** (plaire etc) anxious to; (ses devoirs etc) mindful of. ◆**attentivement** *adv* attentively.

attention [atɑ̃sjɔ̃] *nf* attention; *pl* (égards) consideration; **faire** ou **prêter a. à** (écouter, remarquer) to pay attention to; **faire a. à/que** (prendre garde) to be careful of/that; **a.!** look out!, be careful!; **a. à la voiture!** mind ou watch the car! ◆**attentionné** *a* considerate.

atténu/er [atenɥe] *vt* to attenuate, mitigate; – **s'a.** *vpr* to subside. ◆**—antes** *afpl* **circonstances a.** extenuating circumstances.

atterrer [atere] *vt* to dismay.

atterr/ir [aterir] *vi* Av to land. ◆**—issage** *nm* Av landing; **a. forcé** crash ou emergency landing.

attester [ateste] *vt* to testify to; **a. que** to testify that. ◆**attestation** *nf* (document) declaration, certificate.

attifer [atife] *vt* Fam Péj to dress up, rig out.

attirail [atiraj] *nm* (équipement) Fam gear.

attir/er [atire] *vt* (faire venir) to attract, draw; (plaire à) to attract; (attention) to draw (sur on); **a. qch à qn** (causer) to bring s.o. sth; (gloire etc) to win ou earn s.o. sth; **a. dans** (coin, guet-apens) to draw into; – **s'a.** *vpr* (ennuis etc) to bring upon oneself; (sympathie de qn) to win; **a. sur soi** (colère de qn) to bring down upon oneself. ◆**—ant** *a* attractive. ◆**attirance** *nf* attraction.

attiser [atize] *vt* (feu) to poke; (sentiment) Fig to rouse.

attitré [atitre] *a* (représentant) appointed; (marchand) regular.

attitude [atityd] *nf* attitude; (maintien) bearing.

attraction [atraksjɔ̃] *nf* attraction.

attrait [atrɛ] *nm* attraction.

attrape [atrap] *nf* trick. ◆**a.-nigaud** *nm* con, trick.

attraper [atrape] *vt* (ballon, maladie, voleur, train etc) to catch; (accent, contravention etc) to pick up; **se laisser a.** (duper) to get taken in *ou* tricked; **se faire a.** (*gronder*) *Fam* to get a telling off. **◆attrapade** *nf* (*gronderie*) *Fam* telling off.

attrayant [atrejɑ̃] *a* attractive.

attribuer [atribɥe] *vt* (*donner*) to assign, allot (**à** to); (*imputer, reconnaître*) to attribute, ascribe (**à** to); (*décerner*) to grant, award (**à** to). **◆attribuable** *a* attributable. **◆attribution** *nf* assignment; attribution; (*de prix*) awarding; *pl* (*compétence*) powers.

attribut [atriby] *nm* attribute.

attrister [atriste] *vt* to sadden.

attroup/er [atrupe] *vt*, **— s'a.** *vpr* to gather. **◆—ement** *nm* gathering, (disorderly) crowd.

au [o] *voir* à.

aubaine [oben] *nf* (**bonne**) **a.** stroke of good luck, godsend.

aube [ob] *nf* dawn; **dès l'a.** at the crack of dawn.

aubépine [obepin] *nf* hawthorn.

auberge [oberʒ] *nf* inn; **a. de jeunesse** youth hostel. **◆aubergiste** *nmf* innkeeper.

aubergine [oberʒin] *nf* aubergine, eggplant.

aucun, -une [okœ̃, -yn] *a* no, not any; **il n'a a. talent** he has no talent, he doesn't have any talent; **a. professeur n'est venu** no teacher has come; — *pron* none, not any; **il n'en a a.** he has none (at all), he doesn't have any (at all); **plus qu'a.** more than any(one); **d'aucuns** some (people). **◆aucunement** *adv* not at all.

audace [odas] *nf* (*courage*) daring, boldness; (*impudence*) audacity; *pl* daring innovations. **◆audacieux, -euse** *a* daring, bold.

au-dedans, au-dehors, au-delà *voir* dedans *etc.*

au-dessous [odsu] *adv* (*en bas*) (down) below, underneath; (*moins*) below, under; (*à l'étage inférieur*) downstairs; — *prép* **au-d. de** (*arbre etc*) below, under, beneath; (*âge, prix*) under; (*température*) below; **au-d. de sa tâche** not up to *ou* unequal to one's task.

au-dessus [odsy] *adv* above; over; on top; (*à l'étage supérieur*) upstairs; — *prép* **au-d. de** above; (*âge, température, prix*) over; (*posé sur*) on top of.

au-devant de [odvɑ̃də] *prép* **aller au-d. de** (*personne*) to go to meet; (*danger*) to court; (*désirs de qn*) to anticipate.

audible [odibl] *a* audible.

audience [odjɑ̃s] *nf Jur* hearing; (*entretien*) audience.

audio [odjo] *a inv* (*cassette etc*) audio.

◆audiophone *nm* hearing aid.
◆audio-visuel, -elle *a* audio-visual.

auditeur, -trice [oditœr, -tris] *nmf Rad* listener; **les auditeurs** the audience; **a. libre** *Univ* auditor, *student allowed to attend classes but not to sit examinations.* **◆auditif, -ive** *a* (*nerf*) auditory. **◆audition** *nf* (*ouïe*) hearing; (*séance d'essai*) *Th* audition; (*séance musicale*) recital. **◆auditionner** *vti* to audition. **◆auditoire** *nm* audience. **◆auditorium** *nm Rad* recording studio (*for recitals*).

auge [oʒ] *nf* (feeding) trough.

augmenter [ɔgmɑ̃te] *vt* to increase (**de** by); (*salaire, prix, impôt*) to raise, increase; **a. qn** to give s.o. a rise *ou Am* raise; — *vi* to increase (**de** by); (*prix, population*) to rise, go up. **◆augmentation** *nf* increase (**de** in, of); **a. de salaire** (pay) rise, *Am* raise; **a. de prix** price rise *ou* increase.

augure [ɔgyr] *nm* (*présage*) omen; (*devin*) oracle; **être de bon/mauvais a.** to be a good/bad omen. **◆augurer** *vt* to augur, predict.

auguste [ɔgyst] *a* august.

aujourd'hui [oʒurdɥi] *adv* today; (*actuellement*) nowadays, today; **a. en quinze** two weeks today.

aumône [omon] *nf* alms.

aumônier [omonje] *nm* chaplain.

auparavant [oparavɑ̃] *adv* (*avant*) before(hand); (*d'abord*) first.

auprès de [opredə] *prép* (*assis, situé etc*) by, close to, next to; (*en comparaison de*) compared to; **agir a. de** (*ministre etc*) to use one's influence with; **accès a. de qn** access to s.o.

auquel [okel] *voir* lequel.

aura, aurait [ora, ore] *voir* avoir.

auréole [oreɔl] *nf* (*de saint etc*) halo; (*trace*) ring.

auriculaire [orikyler] *nm* **l'a.** the little finger.

aurore [ɔrɔr] *nf* dawn, daybreak.

ausculter [oskylte] *vt* (*malade*) to examine (*with a stethoscope*); (*cœur*) to listen to. **◆auscultation** *nf Méd* auscultation.

auspices [ospis] *nmpl* **sous les a.** de under the auspices of.

aussi [osi] *adv* **1** (*comparaison*) as; **a. sage que** as wise as. **2** (*également*) too, also, as well; **moi a.** so do, can, am etc I; **a. bien que** as well as. **3** (*tellement*) so; **un repas a. délicieux** so delicious a meal, such a delicious meal. **4** *conj* (*donc*) therefore.

aussitôt [osito] *adv* immediately, at once; **a. que** as soon as; **a. levé, il partit** as soon as he was up, he left; **a. dit, a. fait** no sooner said than done.

austère [ɔster] *a* austere. ◆**austérité** *nf* austerity.

austral, mpl -als [ɔstral] *a* southern.

Australie [ɔstrali] *nf* Australia. ◆**australien, -ienne** *a* & *nmf* Australian.

autant [otɑ̃] *adv* **1 a. de . . . que** (*quantité*) as much . . . as; (*nombre*) as many . . . as; **il a a. d'argent/de pommes que vous** he has as much money/as many apples as you. **2 a. de** (*tant de*) so much; (*nombre*) so many; **je n'ai jamais vu a. d'argent/de pommes** I've never seen so much money/so many apples; **pourquoi manges-tu a.?** why are you eating so much? **3 a. que** (*souffrir, lire etc*) as much as; **il lit a. que vous/que possible** he reads as much as you/as possible; **il n'a jamais souffert a.** he's never suffered as *ou* so much; **a. que je sache** as far as I know; **d'a. (plus) que** all the more (so) since; **d'a. moins que** even less since; **a. avouer/etc** we, you *etc* might as well confess/*etc*; **en faire/dire a.** to do/say the same; **j'aimerais a. aller au cinéma** I'd just as soon go to the cinema.

autel [otel] *nm* altar.

auteur [otœr] *nm* (*de livre*) author, writer; (*de chanson*) composer; (*de procédé*) originator; (*de crime*) perpetrator; (*d'accident*) cause; **droit d'a.** copyright; **droits d'a.** royalties.

authenticité [otɑ̃tisite] *nf* authenticity. ◆**authentifier** *vt* to authenticate. ◆**authentique** *a* genuine, authentic.

autiste [otist] *a*, **autistique** *a* autistic.

auto [oto] *nf* car; **autos tamponneuses** bumper cars, dodgems.

auto- [oto] *préf* self-.

autobiographie [otobjɔgrafi] *nf* autobiography.

autobus [otobys] *nm* bus.

autocar [otokar] *nm* coach, bus.

autochtone [otɔktɔn] *a* & *nmf* native, indigenous.

autocollant [otokɔlɑ̃] *nm* sticker.

autocrate [otokrat] *nm* autocrat. ◆**autocratique** *a* autocratic.

autocuiseur [otokɥizœr] *nm* pressure cooker.

autodéfense [otodefɑ̃s] *nf* self-defence.

autodestruction [otodestryksjɔ̃] *nf* self-destruction.

autodidacte [otodidakt] *a* & *nmf* self-taught (person).

autodrome [otodrom] *nm* motor-racing track.

auto-école [otoekɔl] *nf* driving school, school of motoring.

autographe [otograf] *nm* autograph.

automate [otɔmat] *nm* automaton. ◆**automation** *nf* automation. ◆**automatisation** *nf* automation. ◆**automatiser** *vt* to automate.

automatique [otɔmatik] *a* automatic; – *nm* **l'a.** *Tél* direct dialling. ◆**—ment** *adv* automatically.

automne [otɔn] *nm* autumn, *Am* fall. ◆**automnal, -aux** *a* autumnal.

automobile [otɔmɔbil] *nf* & *a* (motor)car, *Am* automobile; **l'a.** *Sp* motoring; **Salon de l'a.** Motor Show; **canot a.** motor boat. ◆**automobiliste** *nmf* motorist.

autonome [otonɔm] *a* (*région etc*) autonomous, self-governing; (*personne*) *Fig* independent. ◆**autonomie** *nf* autonomy.

autopsie [otɔpsi] *nf* autopsy, post-mortem.

autoradio [otoradjo] *nm* car radio.

autorail [otoraj] *nm* railcar.

autoris/er [otɔrize] *vt* (*habiliter*) to authorize (**à faire** to do); (*permettre*) to permit (**à faire** to do). ◆**—é** *a* (*qualifié*) authoritative. ◆**autorisation** *nf* authorization; permission.

autorité [otɔrite] *nf* authority. ◆**autoritaire** *a* authoritarian; (*homme, ton*) authoritative.

autoroute [otorut] *nf* motorway, *Am* highway, freeway.

auto-stop [otostɔp] *nm* hitchhiking; **faire de l'a.** to hitchhike. ◆**autostoppeur, -euse** *nmf* hitchhiker.

autour [otur] *adv* around; – *prép* **a. de** around.

autre [otr] *a* & *pron* other; **un a. livre** another book; **un a.** another (one); **d'autres** others; **as-tu d'autres questions?** have you any other *ou* further questions?; **qn/personne/rien d'a.** s.o./no one/nothing else; **a. chose/part** sth/somewhere else; **qui/quoi d'a.?** who/what else?; **l'un l'a., les uns les autres** each other; **l'un et l'a.** both (of them); **l'un ou l'a.** either (of them); **ni l'un ni l'a.** neither (of them); **les uns . . . les autres** some . . . others; **nous/vous autres Anglais** we/you English; **d'un moment à l'a.** any moment (now); **. . . et autres . . .** and so on. ◆**autrement** *adv* (*différemment*) differently; (*sinon*) otherwise; (*plus*) far more (**que** than); **pas a. satisfait/etc** not particularly satisfied/*etc*.

autrefois [otrəfwa] *adv* in the past, in days gone by.

Autriche [otriʃ] *nf* Austria. ◆**autrichien, -ienne** *a* & *nmf* Austrian.

autruche [otryʃ] *nf* ostrich.

autrui [otrɥi] *pron* others, other people.

auvent [ovã] *nm* awning, canopy.

aux [o] *voir* à.

auxiliaire [ɔksiljɛr] *a* auxiliary; – *nm Gram* auxiliary; – *nmf* (*aide*) helper, auxiliary.

auxquels, -elles [okɛl] *voir* lequel.

avachir (s') [savaʃir] *vpr* (*soulier, personne*) to become flabby *ou* limp.

avait [avɛ] *voir* avoir.

aval (en) [ɑ̃naval] *adv* downstream (**de** from).

avalanche [avalɑ̃ʃ] *nf* avalanche; *Fig* flood, avalanche.

avaler [avale] *vt* to swallow; (*livre*) to devour; (*mots*) to mumble; – *vi* to swallow.

avance [avɑ̃s] *nf* (*marche, acompte*) advance; (*de coureur, chercheur etc*) lead; *pl* (*galantes*) advances; **à l'a., d'a., par a.** in advance; **en a.** (*arriver, partir*) early; (*avant l'horaire prévu*) ahead (of time); (*dans son développement*) ahead, in advance; (*montre etc*) fast; **en a. sur** (*qn, son époque etc*) ahead of, in advance of; **avoir une heure d'a.** (*train etc*) to be an hour early.

avanc/er [avɑ̃se] *vt* (*thèse, argent*) to advance; (*date*) to bring forward; (*main, chaise*) to move forward; (*travail*) to speed up; – *vi* to advance, move forward; (*montre*) to be fast; (*faire saillie*) to jut out (**sur** over); **a. en âge** to be getting on (in years); – **s'a.** *vpr* to advance, move forward; (*faire saillie*) to jut out. ◆**–é** *a* advanced; (*saison*) well advanced. ◆**–ée** *nf* projection, overhang. ◆**–ement** *nm* advancement.

avanie [avani] *nf* affront, insult.

avant [avɑ̃] *prép* before; **a. de voir** before seeing; **a. qu'il (ne) parte** before he leaves; **a. huit jours** within a week; **a. tout** above all; **a. toute chose** first and foremost; **a. peu** before long; – *adv* before; **en a.** (*mouvement*) forward; (*en tête*) ahead; **en a. de** in front of; **bien a. dans** (*creuser etc*) very deep(ly) into; **la nuit d'a.** the night before; – *nm* & *a inv* front; – *nm* (*joueur*) *Sp* forward.

avantage [avɑ̃taʒ] *nm* advantage; (*bénéfice*) *Fin* benefit; **tu as a. à le faire** it's worth your while to do it; **tirer a. de** to benefit from. ◆**avantager** *vt* (*favoriser*) to favour; (*faire valoir*) to show off to advantage. ◆**avantageux, -euse** *a* worthwhile, attractive; (*flatteur*) flattering; *Péj* conceited; **a. pour qn** advantageous to s.o.

avant-bras [avɑ̃bra] *nm inv* forearm. ◆**a.-centre** *nm Sp* centre-forward. ◆**a.-coureur** *am* ◆**a.-coureur de** (*signe*) heralding. ◆**a.-dernier, -ière** *a* & *nmf* last but one. ◆**a.-garde** *nf Mil* advance guard; **d'a.-garde** (*idée, film etc*) avant-garde. ◆**a.-goût** *nm* foretaste. ◆**a.-guerre** *nm ou f* pre-war period; **d'a.-guerre** pre-war. ◆**a.-hier** [avɑ̃tjɛr] *adv* the day before yesterday. ◆**a.-poste** *nm* outpost. ◆**a.-première** *nf* preview. ◆**a.-propos** *nm inv* foreword. ◆**a.-veille** *nf* **l'a.-veille (de)** two days before.

avare [avar] *a* miserly; **a. de** (*compliments etc*) sparing of; – *nmf* miser. ◆**avarice** *nf* avarice.

avarie(s) [avari] *nf(pl)* damage. ◆**avarié** *a* (*aliment*) spoiled, rotting.

avatar [avatar] *nm Péj Fam* misadventure.

avec [avɛk] *prép* with; (*envers*) to(wards); et **a. ça?** (*dans un magasin*) *Fam* anything else?; – *adv* **il est venu a.** (*son chapeau etc*) *Fam* he came with it.

avenant [avnã] *a* pleasing, attractive; **à l'a.** in keeping (**de** with).

avènement [avɛnmã] *nm* **l'a. de** the coming *ou* advent of; (*roi*) the accession of.

avenir [avnir] *nm* future; **d'a.** (*personne, métier*) with future prospects; **à l'a.** (*désormais*) in future.

aventure [avɑ̃tyr] *nf* adventure; (*en amour*) affair; **à l'a.** (*marcher etc*) aimlessly; **dire la bonne a. à qn** to tell s.o.'s fortune. ◆**aventur/er** *vt* to risk; (*remarque*) to venture; (*réputation*) to risk; – **s'a.** *vpr* to venture (**sur** on to, **à faire** to do). ◆**–é** *a* risky. ◆**aventureux, -euse** *a* (*personne, vie*) adventurous; (*risqué*) risky. ◆**aventurier, -ière** *nmf Péj* adventurer.

avenue [avny] *nf* avenue.

avér/er (s') [savere] *vpr* (*juste etc*) to prove (to be); **il s'avère que** it turns out that. ◆**–é** *a* established.

averse [avɛrs] *nf* shower, downpour.

aversion [avɛrsjɔ̃] *nf* aversion (**pour** to).

avert/ir [avɛrtir] *vt* (*mettre en garde, menacer*) to warn; (*informer*) to notify, inform. ◆**–i** *a* informed. ◆**–issement** *nm* warning; notification; (*dans un livre*) foreword. ◆**–isseur** *nm Aut* horn; **a. d'incendie** fire alarm.

aveu, -x [avø] *nm* confession; **de l'a.** de by the admission of.

aveugle [avœgl] *a* blind; – *nmf* blind man, blind woman; **les aveugles** the blind. ◆**aveuglément** [-emã] *adv* blindly.

◆**aveugl/er** *vt* to blind. ◆**—ement** [-əmɑ̃] *nm* (*égarement*) blindness.

aveuglette (à l') [alavœglɛt] *adv* blindly; **chercher qch à l'a.** to grope for sth.

aviateur, -trice [avjatœr, -tris] *nmf* airman, airwoman. ◆**aviation** *nf* (*industrie, science*) aviation; (*armée de l'air*) air force; (*avions*) aircraft; **l'a.** *Sp* flying; **d'a.** (*terrain, base*) air-.

avide [avid] *a* (*rapace*) greedy (**de** for); **a. d'apprendre/etc** (*désireux*) eager to learn/*etc*. ◆**—ment** *adv* greedily. ◆**avidité** *nf* greed.

avilir [avilir] *vt* to degrade, debase.

avion [avjɔ̃] *nm* aircraft, (aero)plane, *Am* airplane; **a. à réaction** jet; **a. de ligne** airliner; **par a.** (*lettre*) airmail; **en a., par a.** (*voyager*) by plane, by air; **aller en a.** to fly.

aviron [avirɔ̃] *nm* oar; **faire de l'a.** to row, practise rowing.

avis [avi] *nm* opinion; *Pol Jur* judgement; (*communiqué*) notice; (*conseil*) & *Fin* advice; **à mon a.** in my opinion, to my mind; **changer d'a.** to change one's mind.

avis/er [avize] *vt* to advise, inform; (*voir*) to notice; **s'a. de qch** to realize sth suddenly; **s'a. de faire** to venture to do. ◆**—é** *a* prudent, wise; **bien/mal a.** well-/ill-advised.

aviver [avive] *vt* (*couleur*) to bring out; (*douleur*) to sharpen.

avocat, -ate [avɔka, -at] **1** *nmf* barrister, counsel, *Am* attorney, counselor; (*d'une cause*) *Fig* advocate. **2** *nm* (*fruit*) avocado (pear).

avoine [avwan] *nf* oats; **farine d'a.** oatmeal.

avoir * [avwar] **1** *v aux* to have; **je l'ai vu** I've seen him. **2** *vt* (*posséder*) to have; (*obtenir*) to get; (*tromper*) *Fam* to take for a ride; **il a** he has, he's got; **qu'est-ce que tu as?** what's the matter with you?, what's wrong with you?; **j'ai à lui parler** I have to speak

to her; **il n'a qu'à essayer** he only has to try; **a. faim/chaud/etc** to be *ou* feel hungry/hot/*etc*; **a. cinq ans/etc** to be five (years old)/*etc*; **en a. pour longtemps** to be busy for quite a while; **j'en ai pour dix minutes** this will take me ten minutes; (*ne bougez pas*) I'll be with you in ten minutes; **en a. pour son argent** to get *ou* have one's money's worth; **en a. après** *ou* **contre** to have a grudge against. **3** *v imp* **il y a** there is, *pl* there are; **il y a six ans** six years ago; **il n'y a pas de quoi!** don't mention it!; **qu'est-ce qu'il y a?** what's the matter?, what's wrong? **4** *nm* assets, property; (*d'un compte*) *Fin* credit.

avoisin/er [avwazine] *vt* to border on. ◆**—ant** *a* neighbouring, nearby.

avort/er [avɔrte] *vi* (*projet etc*) *Fig* to miscarry, fail; **(se faire) a.** (*femme*) to have *ou* get an abortion. ◆**—ement** *nm* abortion; *Fig* failure. ◆**avorton** *nm* *Péj* runt, puny shrimp.

avou/er [avwe] *vt* to confess, admit (**que** that); **s'a. vaincu** to admit defeat; — *vi* (*coupable*) to confess. ◆**—é** *a* (*ennemi, but*) avowed; — *nm* solicitor, *Am* attorney.

avril [avril] *nm* April; **un poisson d'a.** (*farce*) an April fool joke.

axe [aks] *nm* *Math* axis; (*essieu*) axle; (*d'une politique*) broad direction; **grands axes** (*routes*) main roads. ◆**axer** *vt* to centre; **il est axé sur** his mind is drawn towards.

axiome [aksjom] *nm* axiom.

ayant [ɛjɑ̃] *voir* **avoir.**

azalée [azale] *nf* (*plante*) azalea.

azimuts [azimyt] *nmpl* **dans tous les a.** *Fam* all over the place, here there and everywhere; **tous a.** (*guerre, publicité etc*) all-out.

azote [azot] *nm* nitrogen.

azur [azyr] *nm* azure, (sky) blue; **la Côte d'A.** the (French) Riviera.

azyme [azim] *a* (*pain*) unleavened.

B

B, b [be] *nm* B, b.

babeurre [babœr] *nm* buttermilk.

babill/er [babije] *vi* to prattle, babble. ◆**—age** *nm* prattle, babble.

babines [babin] *nfpl* (*lèvres*) chops, chaps.

babiole [babjɔl] *nf* (*objet*) knick-knack; (*futilité*) trifle.

bâbord [babɔr] *nm* *Nau Av* port (side).

babouin [babwɛ̃] *nm* baboon.

baby-foot [babifut] *nm inv* table *ou* miniature football.

bac [bak] *nm* **1** (*bateau*) ferry(boat). **2** (*cuve*) tank; **b. à glace** ice tray; **b. à laver** washtub. **3** *abrév* = **baccalauréat.**

baccalauréat [bakalɔrea] *nm* school leaving certificate.

bâche [baʃ] *nf* (*toile*) tarpaulin. ◆**bâcher** *vt* to cover over (*with a tarpaulin*).

bachelier, -ière [baʃəlje, -jɛr] *nmf* holder of the baccalauréat.

bachot [baʃo] *nm abrév* = **baccalauréat.** ◆**bachoter** *vi* to cram (*for an exam*).

bacille [basil] *nm* bacillus, germ.

bâcler [bakle] *vt* (*travail*) to dash off carelessly, botch (up).

bactéries [bakteri] *nfpl* bacteria. ◆**bactériologique** *a* bacteriological; **la guerre b.** germ warfare.

badaud, -aude [bado, -od] *nmf* (inquisitive) onlooker, bystander.

baderne [badern] *nf* **vieille b.** *Péj* old fogey, old fuddy-duddy.

badigeon [badiʒɔ̃] *nm* whitewash. ◆**badigeonner** *vt* (*mur*) to whitewash, distemper; (*écorchure*) *Méd* to paint, coat.

badin [badɛ̃] *a* (*peu sérieux*) light-hearted, playful. ◆**badin/er** *vi* to jest, joke; **b. avec** (*prendre à la légère*) to trifle with. ◆**—age** *nm* banter, jesting.

badine [badin] *nf* cane, switch.

bafouer [bafwe] *vt* to mock *ou* scoff at.

bafouiller [bafuje] *vti* to stammer, splutter.

bâfrer [bafre] *vi Fam* to stuff oneself (with food).

bagage [bagaʒ] *nm* (*valise etc*) piece of luggage *ou* baggage; (*connaissances*) *Fig* (fund of) knowledge; *pl* (*ensemble des valises*) luggage, baggage. ◆**bagagiste** *nm* baggage handler.

bagarre [bagar] *nf* brawl. ◆**bagarrer** *vi Fam* to fight, struggle; **— se b.** *vpr* to fight, brawl; (*se disputer*) to fight, quarrel.

bagatelle [bagatel] *nf* trifle, mere bagatelle; **la b. de** *Iron* the trifling sum of.

bagne [baɲ] *nm* convict prison; **c'est le b. ici** *Fig* this place is a real hell hole *ou* workhouse. ◆**bagnard** *nm* convict.

bagnole [baɲɔl] *nf Fam* car; **vieille b.** *Fam* old banger.

bagou(t) [bagu] *nm Fam* glibness; **avoir du b.** to have the gift of the gab.

bague [bag] *nf* (*anneau*) ring; (*de cigare*) band. ◆**bagué** *a* (*doigt*) ringed.

baguenauder [bagnode] *vi*, **— se b.** *vpr* to loaf around, saunter.

baguette [baget] *nf* (*canne*) stick; (*de chef d'orchestre*) baton; (*pain*) (long thin) loaf, stick of bread; *pl* (*de tambour*) drumsticks; (*pour manger*) chopsticks; **b.** (*magique*) (magic) wand; **mener à la b.** to rule with an iron hand.

bah! [ba] *int* really!, bah!

bahut [bay] *nm* (*meuble*) chest, cabinet; (*lycée*) *Fam* school.

baie [bɛ] *nf* **1** *Géog* bay. **2** *Bot* berry. **3** (*fenêtre*) picture window.

baignade [bɛɲad] *nf* (*bain*) bathe, bathing; (*endroit*) bathing place. ◆**baign/er** *vt* (*immerger*) to bathe; (*enfant*) to bath. *Am* bathe; **b. les rivages** (*mer*) to wash the shores; **baigné de** (*sueur, lumière*) bathed in; (*sang*) soaked in; **— vi b. dans** (*tremper*) to soak in; (*être imprégné de*) to be steeped in; **— se b.** *vpr* to go swimming *ou* bathing; (*dans une baignoire*) to have *ou* take a bath. ◆**—eur, -euse 1** *nmf* bather. **2** *nm* (*poupée*) baby doll. ◆**baignoire** *nf* bath (tub).

bail, pl baux [baj, bo] *nm* lease. ◆**bailleur** *nm Jur* lessor; **b. de fonds** financial backer.

bâill/er [baje] *vi* to yawn; (*chemise etc*) to gape; (*porte*) to stand ajar. ◆**—ement** *nm* yawn; gaping.

bâillon [bajɔ̃] *nm* gag. ◆**bâillonner** *vt* (*victime, presse etc*) to gag.

bain [bɛ̃] *nm* bath; (*de mer*) swim, bathe; **salle de bain(s)** bathroom; **être dans le b.** (*au courant*) *Fam* to have got into the swing of things; **petit/grand b.** (*piscine*) shallow/deep end; **b. de bouche** mouthwash. ◆**b.-marie** *nm* (*pl* **bains-marie**) *Culin* double boiler.

baïonnette [bajɔnɛt] *nf* bayonet.

baiser [beze] **1** *vt* **b. au front/sur la joue** to kiss on the forehead/cheek; **— nm** kiss; **bons baisers** (*dans une lettre*) (with) love. **2** *vt* (*duper*) *Fam* to con.

baisse [bɛs] *nf* fall, drop (**de** in); **en b.** (*température*) falling.

baisser [bese] *vt* (*voix, prix etc*) to lower, drop; (*tête*) to bend; (*radio, chauffage*) to turn down; **— vi** (*prix, niveau etc*) to go down, go down; (*soleil*) to go down, sink; (*marée*) to go out, ebb; (*santé, popularité*) to decline; **— se b.** *vpr* to bend down, stoop.

bajoues [baʒu] *nfpl* (*d'animal, de personne*) chops.

bal, pl bals [bal] *nm* (*réunion de grand apparat*) ball; (*populaire*) dance; (*lieu*) dance hall.

balade [balad] *nf Fam* walk; (*en auto*) drive; (*excursion*) tour. ◆**balader** *vt* (*enfant etc*) to take for a walk *ou* drive; (*objet*) to trail around; **— se b.** *vpr* (*à pied*) to go for a walk; (*excursionner*) to tour (around); **se b.** (*en voiture*) to go for a drive. ◆**baladeur** *nm* Walkman®. ◆**baladeuse** *nf* inspection lamp.

balafre [balafr] *nf* (*blessure*) gash, slash;

(*cicatrice*) scar. ◆**balafrer** *vt* to gash, slash; to scar.

balai [balε] *nm* broom; **b. mécanique** carpet sweeper; **manche à b.** broomstick; *Av* joystick. ◆**b.-brosse** *nm* (*pl* **balais-brosses**) garden brush *ou* broom (*for scrubbing paving stones*).

balance [balãs] *nf* (*instrument*) (pair of) scales; (*équilibre*) *Pol Fin* balance; **la B.** (*signe*) Libra; **mettre en b.** to balance, weigh up.

balanc/er [balãse] *vt* (*bras*) to swing; (*hanches, tête, branches*) to sway; (*lancer*) *Fam* to chuck; (*se débarrasser de*) *Fam* to chuck out; **b. un compte** *Fin* to balance an account; — **se b.** *vpr* (*personne*) to swing (from side to side); (*arbre, bateau etc*) to sway; **je m'en balance!** I couldn't care less! ◆**-é** *a* **bien b.** (*phrase*) well-balanced; (*personne*) *Fam* well-built. ◆**-ement** *nm* swinging; swaying. ◆**balancier** *nm* (*d'horloge*) pendulum; (*de montre*) balance wheel. ◆**balançoire** *nf* (*escarpolette*) swing; (*bascule*) seesaw.

balayer [baleje] *vt* (*chambre, rue*) to sweep (out *ou* up); (*enlever, chasser*) to sweep away; **le vent balayait la plaine** the wind swept the plain. ◆**balayette** [balεjεt] *nf* (hand) brush; (*balai*) short-handled broom. ◆**balayeur, -euse** [balεjœr, -øz] *nmf* roadsweeper.

balbutier [balbysje] *vti* to stammer.

balcon [balkɔ̃] *nm* balcony; *Th Cin* dress circle.

baldaquin [baldakɛ̃] *nm* (*de lit etc*) canopy.

baleine [balεn] *nf* (*animal*) whale; (*fanon*) whalebone; (*de parapluie*) rib. ◆**baleinier** *nm* (*navire*) whaler. ◆**baleinière** *nf* whaleboat.

balise [baliz] *nf* *Nau* beacon; *Av* (ground) light; *Aut* road sign. ◆**balis/er** *vt* to mark with beacons *ou* lights; (*route*) to signpost. ◆**-age** *nm* *Nau* beacons; *Av* lighting; *Aut* signposting.

balistique [balistik] *a* ballistic.

balivernes [balivεrn] *nfpl* balderdash, nonsense.

ballade [balad] *nf* (*légende*) ballad; (*poème court*) &-*Mus* ballade.

ballant [balã] *a* (*bras, jambes*) dangling.

ballast [balast] *nm* ballast.

balle [bal] *nf* (*de tennis, golf etc*) ball; (*projectile*) bullet; (*paquet*) bale; *pl* (*francs*) *Fam* francs; **se renvoyer la b.** to pass the buck (to each other).

ballet [balε] *nm* ballet. ◆**ballerine** *nf* ballerina.

ballon [balɔ̃] *nm* (*jouet d'enfant*) & *Av* balloon; (*sport*) ball; **b. de football** football; **lancer un b. d'essai** *Fig* to put out a feeler. ◆**ballonné** *a* (*ventre*) bloated, swollen. ◆**ballot** *nm* (*paquet*) bundle; (*imbécile*) *Fam* idiot.

ballottage [balɔtaʒ] *nm* (*scrutin*) second ballot (*no candidate having achieved the required number of votes*).

ballotter [balɔte] *vti* to shake (about); **ballotté entre** (*sentiments contraires*) torn between.

balnéaire [balneεr] *a* **station b.** seaside resort.

ba‌ourd, -ourde [balur, -urd] *nmf* (clumsy) oaf. ◆**balourdise** *nf* clumsiness, oafishness; (*gaffe*) blunder.

Baltique [baltik] *nf* **la B.** the Baltic.

balustrade [balystrad] *nf* (hand)rail, railing(s).

bambin [bãbɛ̃] *nm* tiny tot, toddler.

bambou [bãbu] *nm* bamboo.

ban [bã] *nm* (*de tambour*) roll; (*applaudissements*) round of applause; *pl* (*de mariage*) banns; **mettre qn au b. de** to cast s.o. out from, outlaw s.o. from; **un b. pour . . .** three cheers for . . . .

banal, mpl -als [banal] *a* (*fait, accident etc*) commonplace, banal; (*idée, propos*) banal, trite. ◆**banalisé** *a* (*voiture de police*) unmarked. ◆**banalité** *nf* banality; *pl* (*propos*) banalities.

banane [banan] *nf* banana.

banc [bã] *nm* (*siège, établi*) bench; (*de poissons*) shoal; **b. d'église** pew; **b. d'essai** *Fig* testing ground; **b. de sable** sandbank; **b. des accusés** *Jur* dock.

bancaire [bãkεr] *a* (*opération*) banking-; (*chèque*) bank-.

bancal, mpl -als [bãkal] *a* (*personne*) bandy, bow-legged; (*meuble*) wobbly; (*idée*) shaky.

bande [bãd] *nf* **1** (*de terrain, papier etc*) strip; (*de film*) reel; (*de journal*) wrapper; (*rayure*) stripe; (*de fréquences*) *Rad* band; (*pansement*) bandage; (*sur la chaussée*) line; **b.** (**magnétique**) tape; **b. vidéo** videotape; **b. sonore** sound track; **b. dessinée** comic strip, strip cartoon; **par la b.** indirectly. **2** (*groupe*) gang, troop, band; (*de chiens*) pack; (*d'oiseaux*) flock; **on a fait b. à part** we split into our own group; **b. d'idiots!** you load of idiots! ◆**bandeau, -x** *nm* (*sur les yeux*) blindfold; (*pour la tête*) headband; (*pansement*) head bandage. ◆**band/er** *vt* (*blessure etc*) to bandage; (*yeux*) to blindfold; (*arc*) to bend; (*muscle*) to tense. ◆**—age** nm (*pansement*) bandage.

banderole [bɑ̃drɔl] nf (*sur mât*) pennant, streamer; (*sur montants*) banner.

bandit [bɑ̃di] nm robber, bandit; (*enfant*) Fam rascal. ◆**banditisme** nm crime.

bandoulière [bɑ̃duljɛr] nf shoulder strap; **en b.** slung across the shoulder.

banjo [bɑ̃(d)ʒo] nm Mus banjo.

banlieue [bɑ̃ljø] nf suburbs, outskirts; **la grande b.** the outer suburbs; **de b.** (*magasin etc*) suburban; (*train*) commuter-. ◆**banlieusard, -arde** nmf (*habitant*) suburbanite; (*voyageur*) commuter.

banne [ban] nf (*de magasin*) awning.

bannière [banjɛr] nf banner.

bann/ir [banir] vt (*exiler*) to banish; (*supprimer*) to ban, outlaw. ◆**—issement** nm banishment.

banque [bɑ̃k] nf bank; (*activité*) banking.

banqueroute [bɑ̃krut] nf (*fraudulent*) bankruptcy.

banquet [bɑ̃kɛ] nm banquet.

banquette [bɑ̃kɛt] nf (bench) seat.

banquier [bɑ̃kje] nm banker.

banquise [bɑ̃kiz] nf ice floe ou field.

baptême [batɛm] nm christening, baptism; **b. du feu** baptism of fire; **b. de l'air** first flight. ◆**baptiser** vt (*enfant*) to christen, baptize; (*appeler*) Fig to christen.

baquet [bakɛ] nm tub, basin.

bar [bar] nm 1 (*lieu, comptoir, meuble*) bar. 2 (*poisson marin*) bass.

baragouin [baragwɛ̃] nm gibberish, gabble. ◆**baragouiner** vt (*langue*) to gabble (a few words of); – vi to gabble away.

baraque [barak] nf hut, shack; (*maison*) Fam house, place; Péj hovel; (*de forain*) stall. ◆**—ment** nm (makeshift) huts.

baratin [baratɛ̃] nm Fam sweet talk; Com patter. ◆**baratiner** vt to chat up; Am sweet-talk.

barbare [barbar] a (*manières, crime*) barbaric; (*peuple, invasions*) barbarian; – nmf barbarian. ◆**barbarie** nf (*cruauté*) barbarity. ◆**barbarisme** nm Gram barbarism.

barbe [barb] nf beard; **une b. de trois jours** three days' growth of beard; **se faire la b.** to shave; **à la b. de** under the nose(s) of; **rire dans sa b.** to laugh up one's sleeve; **la b.!** enough!; **quelle b.!** what a drag!; **b. à papa** candyfloss, Am cotton candy.

barbecue [barbəkju] nm barbecue.

barbelé [barbəle] a barbed; – nmpl barbed wire.

barb/er [barbe] vt Fam to bore (stiff); — **se**

b. vpr to be ou get bored (stiff). ◆**—ant** a Fam boring.

barbiche [barbiʃ] nf goatee (beard).

barbiturique [barbityrik] nm barbiturate.

barbot/er [barbote] 1 vi (*s'agiter*) to splash about, paddle. 2 vt (*voler*) Fam to filch. ◆**—euse** nf (*de bébé*) rompers.

barbouill/er [barbuje] vt (*salir*) to smear; (*peindre*) to daub; (*gribouiller*) to scribble; **avoir l'estomac barbouillé** Fam to feel queasy. ◆**—age** nm smear; daub; scribble.

barbu [barby] a bearded.

barda [barda] nm Fam gear; (*de soldat*) kit.

bardé [barde] a **b. de** (*décorations etc*) covered with.

barder [barde] v imp ça va b.! Fam there'll be fireworks!

barème [barɛm] nm (*des tarifs*) table; (*des salaires*) scale; (*livre de comptes*) ready reckoner.

baril [bari(l)] nm barrel; **b. de poudre** powder keg.

bariolé [barjɔle] a brightly-coloured.

barman, pl **-men** ou **-mans** [barman, -mɛn] nm barman, Am bartender.

baromètre [barɔmɛtr] nm barometer.

baron, -onne [barɔ̃, -ɔn] nm baron; – nf baroness.

baroque [barɔk] 1 a (*idée etc*) bizarre, weird. 2 a & nm Archit Mus etc baroque.

baroud [barud] nm **b. d'honneur** Arg gallant last fight.

barque [bark] nf (small) boat.

barre [bar] nf bar; (*trait*) line, stroke; Nau helm; **b. de soustraction** minus sign; **b. fixe** Sp horizontal bar. ◆**barreau, -x** nm (*de fenêtre etc*) & Jur bar; (*d'échelle*) rung.

barr/er [bare] **1** vt (*route etc*) to block (off), close (off); (*porte*) to bar; (*chèque*) to cross; (*phrase*) to cross out; Nau to steer; **b. la route à qn, b. qn** to bar s.o.'s way; 'rue barrée' 'road closed'. **2 se b.** vpr Fam to hop it, make off. ◆**—age** nm (*sur une route*) roadblock; (*barrière*) barrier; (*ouvrage hydraulique*) dam; (*de petite rivière*) weir; **le b. d'une rue** the closure of a street; **tir de b.** barrage fire; **b. d'agents** cordon of police. ◆**—eur** nm Sp Nau cox.

barrette [barɛt] nf (*pince*) (hair)slide, Am barrette.

barricade [barikad] nf barricade. ◆**barricader** vt to barricade; — **se b.** vpr to barricade oneself.

barrière [barjɛr] nf (*porte*) gate; (*clôture*) fence; (*obstacle, mur*) barrier.

barrique [barik] nf (large) barrel.

baryton [baritɔ̃] *nm* baritone.
bas [1], **basse** [bɑ, bas] *a* (*table, prix etc*) low; (*âme, action*) base, mean; (*partie de ville etc*) lower; (*origine*) lowly; **au b. mot** at the very least; **enfant en b. âge** young child; **avoir la vue basse** to be short-sighted; **le b. peuple** *Péj* the lower orders; **coup b.** *Boxe* blow below the belt; **– *adv* low; (*parler*) in a whisper, softly; **mettre b.** (*animal*) to give birth; **mettre b. les armes** to lay down one's arms; **jeter b.** to overthrow; **plus b.** further *ou* lower down; **en b.** down (below); (*par l'escalier*) downstairs, down below; **en *ou* au b.** de at the foot *ou* bottom of; **de haut en b.** from top to bottom; **sauter à b. du lit** to jump out of bed; **à b. les dictateurs/*etc*!** down with dictators/*etc*! *– nm* (*de côté, page etc*) bottom, foot; **du b.** (*tiroir, étagère*) bottom.
bas [2] *nm* (*chaussette*) stocking; **b. de laine** *Fig* nest egg.
basané [bazane] *a* (*visage etc*) tanned.
bas-bleu [bablø] *nm Péj* bluestocking.
bas-côté [bakote] *nm* (*de route*) roadside, shoulder.
bascule [baskyl] *nf* (*jeu de*) **b.** (game of) seesaw; (*balance à*) **b.** weighing machine; **cheval/fauteuil à b.** rocking horse/chair. ◆**basculer** *vti* (*personne*) to topple over; (*benne*) to tip up.
base [baz] *nf* base; (*principe fondamental*) basis, foundation; **de b.** (*salaire etc*) basic; **produit à b. de lait** milk-based product; **militant de b.** rank-and-file militant. ◆**baser** *vt* to base; **se b. sur** to base oneself on.
bas-fond [bafɔ̃] *nm* (*eau*) shallows; (*terrain*) low ground; *pl* (*population*) *Péj* dregs.
basilic [bazilik] *nm Bot Culin* basil.
basilique [bazilik] *nf* basilica.
basket(-ball) [basket(bol)] *nm* basketball.
basque [bask] **1** *a & nmf* Basque. **2** *nfpl* (*pans de veste*) skirts.
basse [bas] **1** *voir* **bas** [1]. **2** *nf Mus* bass.
basse-cour [baskur] *nf* (*pl* **basses-cours**) farmyard.
bassement [basmɑ̃] *adv* basely, meanly. ◆**bassesse** *nf* baseness, meanness; (*action*) base *ou* mean act.
bassin [basɛ̃] *nm* (*pièce d'eau*) pond; (*piscine*) pool; (*cuvette*) bowl, basin; (*rade*) dock; *Anat* pelvis; *Géog* basin; **b. houiller** coalfield. ◆**bassine** *nf* bowl.
basson [basɔ̃] *nm* (*instrument*) bassoon; (*musicien*) bassoonist.
bastingage [bastɛ̃gaʒ] *nm Nau* bulwarks, rail.

bastion [bastjɔ̃] *nm* bastion.
bastringue [bastrɛ̃g] *nm* (*bal*) *Fam* popular dance hall; (*tapage*) *Arg* shindig, din; (*attirail*) *Arg* paraphernalia.
bas-ventre [bavɑ̃tr] *nm* lower abdomen.
bat [ba] *voir* **battre**.
bât [ba] *nm* packsaddle.
batacian [bataklɑ̃] *nm Fam* paraphernalia; **et tout le b.** *Fam* and the whole caboodle.
bataille [bataj] *nf* battle; *Cartes* beggar-my-neighbour. ◆**bataill/er** *vi* to fight, battle. ◆**–eur, -euse** *nmf* fighter; *– a* belligerent. ◆**bataillon** *nm* battalion.
bâtard, -arde [batar, -ard] *a & nmf* bastard; **chien b.** mongrel; **œuvre bâtarde** hybrid work.
bateau, -x [bato] *nm* boat; (*grand*) ship. ◆**b.-citerne** *nm* (*pl* **bateaux-citernes**) tanker. ◆**b.-mouche** *nm* (*pl* **bateaux-mouches**) (*sur la Seine*) pleasure boat.
batifoler [batifɔle] *vi Hum* to fool *ou* lark about.
bâtiment [batimɑ̃] *nm* (*édifice*) building; (*navire*) vessel; **le b., l'industrie du b.** the building trade; **ouvrier du b.** building worker. ◆**bât/ir** *vt* (*construire*) to build; (*coudre*) to baste, tack; **terrain à b.** building site. ◆**–i** *a* **bien b.** well-built; *– nm Menuis* frame, support. ◆**bâtisse** *nf Péj* building. ◆**bâtisseur, -euse** *nmf* builder (**de** *of*).
bâton [batɔ̃] *nm* (*canne*) stick; (*de maréchal, d'agent*) baton; **b. de rouge** lipstick; **donner des coups de b. à qn** to beat s.o. (with a stick); **parler à bâtons rompus** to ramble from one subject to another; **mettre des bâtons dans les roues à qn** to put obstacles in s.o.'s way.
batterie [batri] *nf Mil Aut* battery; **la b.** *Mus* the drums; **b. de cuisine** set of kitchen utensils.
batt/re* [batr] **1** *vt* (*frapper, vaincre*) to beat; (*blé*) to thresh; (*cartes*) to shuffle; (*pays, chemins*) to scour; (*à coups redoublés*) to batter, pound; **b. la mesure** to beat time; **à mort** to batter *ou* beat to death; **b. pavillon** to fly a flag; *– vi* to beat; (*porte*) to bang; **b. des mains** to clap (one's hands); **b. des paupières** to blink; **b. des ailes** (*oiseau*) to flap its wings; **le vent fait b. la porte** the wind bangs the door. **2 se b.** *vpr* to fight. ◆**–ant -a** (*pluie*) driving; (*porte*) swing- **2** *nm* (*de cloche*) tongue; (*vantail de porte etc*) flap; **porte à deux battants** double door. **3** *nm* (*personne*) fighter. ◆**–u a chemin *ou* sentier b.** beaten track. ◆**–age** *nm* (*du blé*) threshing; (*publicité*) *Fam*

publicity, hype, ballyhoo. ◆—**ement** nm
(de cœur, de tambour) beat; (délai) interval;
battements de cœur palpitations. ◆—**eur**
nm (musicien) percussionist; **b. à œufs** egg
beater.

baudet [bode] nm donkey.

baume [bom] nm (résine) & Fig balm.

baux [bo] voir **bail**.

bavard, -arde [bavar, -ard] a (loquace) talkative; (cancanier) gossip; – nmf chatterbox; gossip. ◆**bavarder** vi to chat, chatter; (papoter) to gossip; (divulguer) to blab.
◆—**age** nm chatting, chatter(ing);
gossip(ing).

bave [bav] nf dribble, slobber; foam; (de
limace) slime. ◆**baver** vi to dribble, slobber; (chien enragé) to foam; (encre) to
smudge; **en b.** Fam to have a rough time of
it. ◆**bavette** nf bib. ◆**baveux, -euse** a
(bouche) slobbery; (omelette) runny.
◆**bavoir** nm bib. ◆**bavure** nf smudge;
(erreur) blunder; **sans b.** perfect(ly), flaw-
less(ly).

bazar [bazar] nm (magasin, marché) bazaar;
(désordre) mess, clutter; (attirail) Fam
stuff, gear. ◆**bazarder** vt Fam to sell off,
get rid of.

bazooka [bazuka] nm bazooka.

béant [beᾶ] a (plaie) gaping; (gouffre)
yawning.

béat [bea] a Péj smug; (heureux) Hum blissf-
ful. ◆**béatitude** nf Hum bliss.

beau (or **bel** before vowel or mute h), **belle**,
pl **beaux, belles** [bo, bel] a (femme, fleur
etc) beautiful, attractive; (homme) handsome, good-looking; (voyage, temps etc)
fine, lovely; **au b. milieu** right in the
middle; **j'ai b. crier/essayer/etc** it's no use
(my) shouting/trying/etc; **un b. morceau** a
good or sizeable bit; **de plus belle** (recommencer etc) worse than ever; **bel et bien**
really; – nm **le b.** the beautiful; **faire le b.**
(chien) to sit up and beg; **le plus b. de
l'histoire** the best part of the story; – nf
(femme) beauty; Sp deciding game.

beaucoup [boku] adv (lire etc) a lot, a great
deal; **aimer b.** to like very much;
s'intéresser b. à to be very interested in; **b.
de** (livres etc) many, a lot ou a great deal of;
(courage etc) a lot of, a great deal of;
pas b. d'argent/etc not much money/etc;
j'en ai b. (quantité) I have a lot; (nombre) I
have many; **b. plus/moins** much
more/less; many more/fewer; **b. trop**
much too much; much too many; **de b.** by
far; **b. sont . . .** many are . . . .

beau-fils [bofis] nm (pl **beaux-fils**) (d'un

précédent mariage) stepson; (gendre)
son-in-law. ◆**b.-frère** nm (pl
beaux-frères) brother-in-law. ◆**b.-père**
nm (pl **beaux-pères**) father-in-law; (parâ-
tre) stepfather.

beauté [bote] nf beauty; **institut** ou **salon de
b.** beauty parlour; **en b.** (gagner etc)
magnificently; **être en b.** to look one's very
best; **de toute b.** beautiful.

beaux-arts [bozar] nmpl fine arts.
◆**b.-parents** nmpl parents-in-law.

bébé [bebe] nm baby; **b.-lion**/etc (pl
bébés-lions/etc) baby lion/etc.

bébête [bebet] a Fam silly.

bec [bɛk] nm (d'oiseau) beak, bill; (de
cruche) lip, spout; (de plume) nib; (bouche)
Fam mouth; Mus mouthpiece; **coup de b.**
peck; **b. de gaz** gas lamp; **clouer le b. à qn**
Fam to shut s.o. up; **tomber sur un b.** Fam
to come up against a serious snag.
◆**b.-de-cane** nm (pl **becs-de-cane**) door
handle.

bécane [bekan] nf Fam bike.

bécarre [bekar] nm Mus natural.

bécasse [bekas] nf (oiseau) woodcock;
(personne) Fam simpleton.

bêche [bɛʃ] nf spade. ◆**bêcher** vt **1**
(cultiver) to dig. **2** Fig to criticize; (snober)
to snub. ◆**bêcheur, -euse** nmf snob.

bécot [beko] nm Fam kiss. ◆**bécoter** vt, –
se b. vpr Fam to kiss.

becquée [beke] nf beakful; **donner la b. à**
(oiseau, enfant) to feed. ◆**becqueter** vt
(picorer) to peck (at); (manger) Fam to eat.

bedaine [bədɛn] nf Fam paunch, potbelly.

bedeau, -x [bado] nm beadle, verger.

bedon [bədɔ̃] nm Fam paunch. ◆**bedonnant** a paunchy, potbellied.

bée [be] a **bouche b.** open-mouthed.

beffroi [befrwa] nm belfry.

bégayer [begeje] vi to stutter, stammer.
◆**bègue** [beg] nmf stutterer, stammerer;
– a **être b.** to stutter, stammer.

bégueule [begœl] a prudish; – nf prude.

béguin [begɛ̃] nm **avoir le b. pour qn** Fam to
have taken a fancy to s.o.

beige [bɛʒ] a & nm beige.

beignet [bɛɲɛ] nm Culin fritter.

bel [bɛl] voir **beau**.

bêler [bele] vi to bleat.

belette [bəlɛt] nf weasel.

Belgique [bɛlʒik] nf Belgium. ◆**belge** a &
nmf Belgian.

bélier [belje] nm (animal, machine) ram; **le
B.** (signe) Aries.

belle [bɛl] voir **beau**.

belle-fille [bɛlfij] nf (pl **belles-filles**) (d'un

précédent mariage) stepdaughter; (*bru*) daughter-in-law. ◆**b.-mère** *nf* (*pl belles-mères*) mother-in-law; (*marâtre*) stepmother. ◆**b.-sœur** *nf* (*pl belles-sœurs*) sister-in-law.

belligérant [beliʒerɑ̃] *a & nm* belligerent.

belliqueux, -euse [belikø, -øz] *a* warlike; *Fig* aggressive.

belvédère [belveder] *nm* (*sur une route*) viewpoint.

bémol [bemɔl] *nm Mus* flat.

bénédiction [benediksjɔ̃] *nf* blessing, benediction.

bénéfice [benefis] *nm* (*gain*) profit; (*avantage*) benefit; **b.** (**ecclésiastique**) living, benefice. ◆**bénéficiaire** *nmf* beneficiary; – *a* (*marge, solde*) profit-. ◆**bénéficier** *vi* **b. de** to benefit from, have the benefit of. ◆**bénéfique** *a* beneficial.

Bénélux [benelyks] *nm* Benelux.

benêt [bənɛ] *nm* simpleton; – *a* simple-minded.

bénévole [benevɔl] *a* voluntary, unpaid.

bénin, -igne [benɛ̃, -iɲ] *a* (*tumeur, critique*) benign; (*accident*) minor.

bénir [benir] *vt* to bless; (*exalter, remercier*) to give thanks to. ◆**bénit** *a* (*pain*) consecrated; **eau bénite** holy water. ◆**bénitier** [-itje] *nm* (holy-water) stoup.

benjamin, -ine [bɛ̃ʒamɛ̃, -in] *nmf* youngest child; *Sp* young junior.

benne [bɛn] *nf* (*de grue*) scoop; (*à charbon*) tub, skip; (*de téléphérique*) cable car; **camion à b. basculante** dump truck; **b. à ordures** skip.

béotien, -ienne [beɔsjɛ̃, -jɛn] *nmf* (*inculte*) philistine.

béquille [bekij] *nf* (*canne*) crutch; (*de moto*) stand.

bercail [berkaj] *nm* (*famille etc*) *Hum* fold.

berceau, -x [bersо] *nm* cradle.

berc/er [berse] *vt* (*balancer*) to rock; (*apaiser*) to lull; (*leurrer*) to delude (de with); **se b. d'illusions** to delude oneself. ◆**—euse** *nf* lullaby.

béret [berɛ] *nm* beret.

berge [berʒ] *nf* (*rivage*) (raised) bank.

berger, -ère [berʒe, -ɛr] **1** *nm* shepherd; **chien (de) b.** sheepdog; – *nf* shepherdess. **2** *nm* **b. allemand** Alsatian (dog), *Am* German shepherd. ◆**bergerie** *nf* sheepfold.

berline [berlin] *nf Aut* (four-door) saloon, *Am* sedan.

berlingot [berlɛ̃go] *nm* (*bonbon aux fruits*) boiled sweet; (*à la menthe*) mint; (*emballage*) (milk) carton.

berlue [berly] *nf* **avoir la b.** to be seeing things.

berne (en) [(ɑ̃)bern] *adv* at half-mast.

berner [berne] *vt* to fool, hoodwink.

besogne [bəzɔɲ] *nf* work, job, task. ◆**besogneux, -euse** *a* needy.

besoin [bəzwɛ̃] *nm* need; **avoir b. de** to need; **au b.** if necessary, if need(s) be; **dans le b.** in need, needy.

bestial, -aux [bestjal, -o] *a* bestial, brutish. ◆**bestiaux** *nmpl* livestock; (*bovins*) cattle. ◆**bestiole** *nf* (*insecte*) creepy-crawly, bug.

bétail [betaj] *nm* livestock; (*bovins*) cattle.

bête ¹ [bɛt] *nf* animal; (*bestiole*) bug, creature; **b. de somme** beast of burden; **b. à bon dieu** ladybird, *Am* ladybug; **b. noire** pet hate, pet peeve; **chercher la petite b.** (*critiquer*) to pick holes.

bête ² [bɛt] *a* silly, stupid. ◆**bêtement** *adv* stupidly; **tout b.** quite simply. ◆**bêtise** [betiz] *nf* silliness, stupidity; (*action, parole*) silly *ou* stupid thing; (*bagatelle*) mere trifle.

béton [betɔ̃] *nm* concrete; **en b.** concrete-; **b. armé** reinforced concrete. ◆**bétonnière** *nf*, ◆**bétonneuse** *nf* cement *ou* concrete mixer.

betterave [betrav] *nf Culin* beetroot, *Am* beet; **b. sucrière** *ou* **à sucre** sugar beet.

beugler [bøgle] *vi* (*taureau*) to bellow; (*vache*) to moo; (*radio*) to blare (out).

beurre [bœr] *nm* butter; **b. d'anchois** anchovy paste. ◆**beurrer** *vt* to butter. ◆**beurrier** *nm* butter dish.

beuverie [bøvri] *nf* drinking session, booze-up.

bévue [bevy] *nf* blunder, mistake.

biais [bjɛ] *nm* (*moyen détourné*) device, expedient; (*aspect*) angle; **regarder de b.** to look at sidelong; **traverser en b.** to cross at an angle. ◆**biaiser** [bjeze] *vi* to prevaricate, hedge.

bibelot [biblo] *nm* curio, trinket.

biberon [bibrɔ̃] *nm* (feeding) bottle.

bible [bibl] *nf* bible; **la B.** the Bible. ◆**biblique** *a* biblical.

bibliobus [biblijɔbys] *nm* mobile library.

bibliographie [biblijɔgrafi] *nf* bibliography.

bibliothèque [biblijɔtɛk] *nf* library; (*meuble*) bookcase; (*à la gare*) bookstall. ◆**bibliothécaire** *nmf* librarian.

bic® [bik] *nm* ballpoint, biro®.

bicarbonate [bikarbɔnat] *nm* bicarbonate.

bicentenaire [bisɑ̃tner] *nm* bicentenary, bicentennial.

biceps [bisɛps] *nm Anat* biceps.

biche [biʃ] *nf* doe, hind; **ma b.** *Fig* my pet.

bichonner [biʃɔne] vt to doll up.

bicoque [bikɔk] nf Péj shack, hovel.

bicyclette [bisiklɛt] nf bicycle, cycle; **la b.** Sp cycling; **aller à b.** to cycle.

bide [bid] nm (ventre) Fam belly; **faire un b.** Arg to flop.

bidet [bide] nm (cuvette) bidet.

bidon [bidɔ̃] **1** nm (d'essence) can; (pour boissons) canteen; (ventre) Fam belly. **2** nm **du b.** Fam rubbish, bluff; – a inv (simulé) Fam fake, phoney. ◆**se bidonner** vpr Fam to have a good laugh.

bidonville [bidɔ̃vil] nf shantytown.

bidule [bidyl] nm (chose) Fam thingummy, whatsit.

bielle [bjɛl] nf Aut connecting rod.

bien [bjɛ̃] adv well; **il joue b.** he plays well; **je vais b.** I'm fine ou well; **b. fatigué/souvent/etc** (très) very tired/often/etc; **merci b.!** thanks very much!; **b.! fine!**, right!; **b. du courage/etc** a lot of courage/etc; **b. des fois/des gens/etc** lots of ou many times/people/etc; **je l'ai b. dit** (intensif) I did say so; **c'est b. compris?** is that quite understood?; **c'est b. toi?** is it really you?; **tu as b. fait** you did right; **c'est b. fait (pour lui)** it serves him right; – a inv (convenable) all right, fine; (compétent, bon) good, fine; (à l'aise) comfortable, fine; (beau) attractive; (en forme) well; (moralement) nice; **une fille b.** a nice ou respectable girl; – nm (avantage) good; (capital) possession; **ça te fera du b.** it will do you good; **le b. et le mal** good and evil; **biens de consommation** consumer goods. ◆**b.-aimé, -ée** a & nmf beloved. ◆**b.-être** nm wellbeing. ◆**b.-fondé** nm validity, soundness.

bienfaisance [bjɛ̃fəzɑ̃s] nf benevolence, charity; **de b.** (société etc) benevolent, charitable. ◆**bienfaisant** a beneficial.

bienfait [bjɛ̃fɛ] nm (générosité) favour; pl benefits, blessings. ◆**bienfaiteur, -trice** nmf benefactor, benefactress.

bienheureux, -euse [bjɛ̃nœrø, -øz] a blessed, blissful.

biennal, -aux [bjenal, -o] a biennial.

bien que [bjɛ̃k(ə)] conj although.

bienséant [bjɛ̃seɑ̃] a proper. ◆**bienséance** nf propriety.

bientôt [bjɛ̃to] adv soon; **à b.!** see you soon!; **il est b. dix heures/etc** it's nearly ten o'clock/etc.

bienveillant [bjɛ̃vejɑ̃] a kindly. ◆**bienveillance** nf kindliness.

bienvenu, -ue [bjɛ̃vny] a welcome; – nmf **soyez le b.!** welcome!; – nf welcome; **souhaiter la bienvenue à** to welcome.

bière [bjɛr] nf **1** (boisson) beer; **b. pression** draught beer. **2** (cercueil) coffin.

biffer [bife] vt to cross ou strike out.

bifteck [biftɛk] nm steak; **gagner son b.** Fam to earn one's (daily) bread.

bifurquer [bifyrke] vi to branch off, fork. ◆**bifurcation** nf fork, junction.

bigame [bigam] a bigamous; – nmf bigamist. ◆**bigamie** nf bigamy.

bigarré [bigare] a (bariolé) mottled; (hétéroclite) motley, mixed.

bigler [bigle] vi (loucher) Fam to squint; – vti **b. (sur)** (lorgner) Fam to leer at. ◆**bigleux, -euse** a Fam cock-eyed.

bigorneau, -x [bigɔrno] nm (coquillage) winkle.

bigot, -ote [bigo, -ɔt] nmf Péj religious bigot; – a over-devout, fanatical.

bigoudi [bigudi] nm (hair)curler ou roller.

bigrement [bigrəmɑ̃] adv Fam awfully.

bijou, -x [biʒu] nm jewel; (ouvrage élégant) Fig gem. ◆**bijouterie** nf (commerce) jeweller's shop; (bijoux) jewellery. ◆**bijoutier, -ière** nmf jeweller.

bikini [bikini] nm bikini.

bilan [bilɑ̃] nm Fin balance sheet; (résultat) outcome; (d'un accident) (casualty) toll; **b. de santé** checkup; **faire le b.** to make an assessment (**de** of).

bilboquet [bilbɔkɛ] nm cup-and-ball (game).

bile [bil] nf bile; **se faire de la b.** Fam to worry, fret. ◆**bilieux, -euse** a bilious.

bilingue [bilɛ̃g] a bilingual.

billard [bijar] nm (jeu) billiards; (table) billiard table; Méd Fam operating table; **c'est du b.** Fam it's a cinch.

bille [bij] nf (d'un enfant) marble; (de billard) billiard ball; **stylo à b.** ballpoint pen, biro®.

billet [bijɛ] nm ticket; **b. (de banque)** (bank)note, Am bill; **b. aller, b. simple** single ticket, Am one-way ticket; **b. (d')aller et retour** return ticket, Am round trip ticket; **b. doux** love letter.

billion [biljɔ̃] nm billion, Am trillion.

billot [bijo] nm (de bois) block.

bimensuel, -elle [bimɑ̃sɥɛl] a bimonthly, fortnightly.

bimoteur [bimɔtœr] a twin-engined.

binaire [binɛr] a binary.

biner [bine] vt to hoe. ◆**binette** nf hoe; (visage) Arg mug, face.

biochimie [bjɔʃimi] nf biochemistry.

biodégradable [bjɔdegradabl] *a* biode-gradable.

biographie [bjɔgrafi] *nf* biography. ◆**biographe** *nmf* biographer.

biologie [bjɔlɔʒi] *nf* biology. ◆**biologique** *a* biological.

bip-bip [bipbip] *nm* bleeper.

bipède [biped] *nm* biped.

bique [bik] *nf Fam* nanny-goat.

Birmanie [birmani] *nf* Burma. ◆**birman, -ane** *a & nmf* Burmese.

bis¹ [bis] *adv* (*cri*) *Th* encore; *Mus* repeat; **4 bis** (*numéro*) 4A; – *nm Th* encore.

bis², bise [bi, biz] *a* greyish-brown.

bisbille [bisbij] *nf* squabble; **en b. avec** *Fam* at loggerheads with.

biscornu [biskɔrny] *a* (*objet*) distorted, misshapen; (*idée*) cranky.

biscotte [biskɔt] *nf* (*pain*) Melba toast; (*biscuit*) rusk, *Am* zwieback.

biscuit [biskɥi] *nm* (*salé*) biscuit, *Am* cracker; (*sucré*) biscuit, *Am* cookie; **b. de Savoie** sponge (cake). ◆**biscuiterie** *nf* biscuit factory.

bise [biz] *nf* **1** (*vent*) north wind. **2** (*baiser*) *Fam* kiss.

biseau, -x [bizo] *nm* bevel.

bison [bizɔ̃] *nm* bison, (American) buffalo.

bisou [bizu] *nm Fam* kiss.

bisser [bise] *vt* (*musicien, acteur*) to encore.

bissextile [bisɛkstil] *af* **année b.** leap year.

bistouri [bisturi] *nm* scalpel, lancet.

bistre [bistr] *a inv* bistre, dark-brown.

bistro(t) [bistro] *nm* bar, café.

bitume [bitym] *nm* (*revêtement*) asphalt.

bivouac [bivwak] *nm Mil* bivouac.

bizarre [bizar] *a* peculiar, odd, bizarre. ◆**-ment** *adv* oddly. ◆**bizarrerie** *nf* peculiarity.

blabla(bla) [blabla(bla)] *nm* claptrap, bunkum.

blafard [blafar] *a* pale, pallid.

blague [blag] *nf* **1** (*à tabac*) pouch. **2** (*plaisanterie, farce*) *Fam* joke; *pl* (*absurdités*) *Fam* nonsense; **sans b.!** you're joking! ◆**blagu/er** *vi* to be joking; – *vt* to tease. ◆**-eur, -euse** *nmf* joker.

blair [blɛr] *nm* (*nez*) *Arg* snout, conk. ◆**blairer** *vt Arg* to stomach.

blaireau, -x [blɛro] *nm* **1** (*animal*) badger. **2** (*brosse*) (shaving) brush.

blâme [blɑm] *nm* (*réprimande*) rebuke; (*reproche*) blame. ◆**blâmable** *a* blame-worthy. ◆**blâmer** *vt* to rebuke; to blame.

blanc, blanche [blɑ̃, blɑ̃ʃ] **1** *a* white; (*page etc*) blank; **nuit blanche** sleepless night; **voix blanche** expressionless voice; – *nmf*

(*personne*) white (man *ou* woman); – *nm* (*couleur*) white; (*de poulet*) white meat, breast; (*espace, interligne*) blank; **b. (d'œuf)** (egg) white; **le b.** (*linge*) whites; **magasin de b.** linen shop; **laisser en b.** to leave blank; **chèque en b.** blank cheque; **cartouche à b.** blank (cartridge); **saigner à b.** to bleed white. **2** *nf Mus* minim, *Am* half-note. ◆**blanchâtre** *a* whitish. ◆**blancheur** *nf* whiteness.

blanchir [blɑ̃ʃir] *vt* to whiten; (*draps*) to launder; (*mur*) to whitewash; *Culin* to blanch; (*argent*) *Fig* to launder; **b. qn** (*disculper*) to clear s.o.; – *vi* to turn white, whiten. ◆**blanchissage** *nm* laundering. ◆**blanchisserie** *nf* (*lieu*) laundry. ◆**blanchisseur, -euse** *nmf* laundryman, laundrywoman.

blanquette [blɑ̃kɛt] *nf* **b. de veau** veal stew in white sauce.

blasé [blaze] *a* blasé.

blason [blazɔ̃] *nm* (*écu*) coat of arms; (*science*) heraldry.

blasphème [blasfɛm] *nf* blasphemy. ◆**blasphématoire** *a* (*propos*) blasphe-mous. ◆**blasphémer** *vti* to blaspheme.

blatte [blat] *nf* cockroach.

blazer [blazœr] *nm* blazer.

blé [ble] *nm* wheat; (*argent*) *Arg* bread.

bled [blɛd] *nm Péj Fam* (dump of a) village.

blême [blɛm] *a* sickly pale, wan; **b. de colère** livid with anger.

bless/er [blese] *vt* to injure, hurt; (*avec un couteau, une balle etc*) to wound; (*offenser*) to hurt, offend, wound; **se b. le** *ou* **au bras/etc** to hurt one's arm/etc. ◆**-ant** [blesɑ̃] *a* (*parole, personne*) hurtful. ◆**-é, -ée** *nmf* casualty, injured *ou* wounded person. ◆**blessure** *nf* injury; wound.

blet, blette [blɛ, blɛt] *a* (*fruit*) overripe.

bleu [blø] *a* blue; **b. de colère** blue in the face; **steak b.** *Culin* very rare steak; – *nm* (*couleur*) blue; (*contusion*) bruise; (*vêtement*) overalls; (*conscrit*) raw recruit; **bleus de travail** overalls. ◆**bleuir** *vti* to turn blue.

bleuet [bløɛ] *nm* cornflower.

blind/er [blɛ̃de] *vt Mil* to armour(-plate). ◆**-é** *a* (*train etc*) *Mil* armoured; **porte blindée** reinforced steel door; – *nm Mil* armoured vehicle.

bloc [blɔk] *nm* block; (*de pierre*) lump, block; (*de papier*) pad; (*masse compacte*) unit; *Pol* bloc; **en b.** all together; **à b.** (*serrer etc*) tight, hard; **travailler à b.** *Fam* to work flat out. ◆**b.-notes** *nm* (*pl* **blocs-notes**) writing pad.

blocage [blɔkaʒ] nm (des roues) locking; Psy mental block; **b. des prix** price freeze.

blocus [blɔkys] nm blockade.

blond, -onde [blɔ̃, -ɔ̃d] a fair(-haired), blond; — nm fair-haired man; (couleur) blond; — nf fair-haired woman, blonde; **(bière) blonde** lager, pale ou light ale. ◆**blondeur** nf fairness, blondness.

bloquer [blɔke] vt (obstruer) to block; (coincer) to jam; (grouper) to group together; (ville) to blockade; (freins) to slam ou jam on; (roue) to lock; (salaires, prix) to freeze; **bloqué par la neige/la glace** snowbound/icebound; — **se b.** vpr to stick, jam; (roue) to lock.

blottir (se) [səblɔtir] vpr (dans un coin etc) to crouch; (dans son lit) to snuggle down; **se b. contre** to huddle ou snuggle up to.

blouse [bluz] nf (tablier) overall, smock; (corsage) blouse. ◆**blouson** nm (waist-length) jacket.

blue-jean [bludʒin] nm jeans, denims.

bluff [blœf] nm bluff. ◆**bluffer** vti to bluff.

boa [bɔa] nm (serpent, tour de cou) boa.

bobard [bɔbar] nm Fam fib, yarn, tall story.

bobine [bɔbin] nf (de fil, film etc) reel, spool; (pour machine à coudre) bobbin, spool.

bobo [bɔbo] nm (langage enfantin) pain; **j'ai b., ça fait b.** it hurts.

bocage [bɔkaʒ] nm copse.

bocal, -aux [bɔkal, -o] nm glass jar; (à poissons) bowl.

bock [bɔk] nm (récipient) beer glass; (contenu) glass of beer.

bœuf, pl **-fs** [bœf, bø] nm (animal) ox (pl oxen), bullock; (viande) beef.

bohème [bɔɛm] a & nmf bohemian. ◆**bohémien, -ienne** a & nmf gipsy.

boire* [bwar] vt to drink; (absorber) to soak up; (paroles) Fig to take ou drink in; **b. un coup** to have a drink; **offrir à b. à qn** to offer s.o. a drink; **b. à petits coups** to sip; — vi to drink.

bois¹ [bwa] voir **boire.**

bois² [bwa] nm (matière, forêt) wood; (de construction) timber; (gravure) woodcut; pl (de cerf) antlers; Mus woodwind instruments; **en ou de b.** wooden; **b. de chauffage** firewood; **b. de lit** bedstead. ◆**boisé** a wooded. ◆**boiserie(s)** nf(pl) panelling.

boisson [bwasɔ̃] nf drink, beverage.

boit [bwa] voir **boire.**

boîte [bwat] nf box; (de conserve) tin, Am can; (lieu de travail) Fam firm; **b. aux ou à lettres** letterbox; **b. de nuit** nightclub; **mettre qn en b.** Fam to pull s.o.'s leg. ◆**boîtier** nm (de montre etc) case.

boiter [bwate] vi (personne) to limp. ◆**boiteux, -euse** a lame; (meuble) wobbly; (projet etc) Fig shaky.

bol [bɔl] nm (récipient) bowl; **prendre un b. d'air** to get a breath of fresh air; **avoir du b.** Fam to be lucky.

bolide [bɔlid] nm (véhicule) racing car.

Bolivie [bɔlivi] nf Bolivia. ◆**bolivien, -ienne** a & nmf Bolivian.

bombard/er [bɔ̃barde] vt (ville etc) to bomb; (avec des obus) to shell; **b. qn** Fam (nommer) to pitchfork s.o. (à un poste into a job); **b. de** (questions) to bombard with; (objets) to pelt with. ◆**-ement** nm bombing; shelling. ◆**bombardier** nm (avion) bomber.

bombe [bɔ̃b] nf (projectile) bomb; (atomiseur) spray; **tomber comme une b.** Fig to be a bombshell, be quite unexpected; **faire la b.** Fam to have a binge.

bomb/er [bɔ̃be] vi (gonfler) to bulge; — vt **b. la poitrine** to throw out one's chest. **2** vi (véhicule etc) Fam to bomb ou belt along. ◆**-é** a (verre etc) rounded; (route) cambered.

bon¹, bonne¹ [bɔ̃, bɔn] a **1** (satisfaisant etc) good. **2** (charitable) kind, good. **3** (agréable) nice, good; **il fait b. se reposer** it's nice ou good to rest; **b. anniversaire!** happy birthday! **4** (qui convient) right; **c'est le b. clou** it's the right nail. **5** (approprié, apte) fit; **b. à manger** fit to eat; **b. pour le service** fit for service; **ce n'est b. à rien** it's useless; **comme b. te semble** as you think fit ou best; **c'est b. à savoir** it's worth knowing. **6** (prudent) wise, good; **croire b. de** to think it wise ou good to. **7** (compétent) good; **b. en français** good at French. **8** (valable) good; **ce billet est encore b.** this ticket's still good. **9** (intensif) **un b. moment** a good while. **10** **à quoi b.?** what's the use ou point ou good?; **pour de b.** in earnest; **tenir b.** to stand firm; **ah b.?** is that so? **11** nm **du b.** some good; **les bons** the good.

bon² [bɔ̃] nm (billet) coupon, voucher; (titre) Fin bond; (formulaire) slip.

bonasse [bɔnas] a feeble, soft.

bonbon [bɔ̃bɔ̃] nm sweet, Am candy. ◆**bonbonnière** nf sweet box, Am candy box.

bonbonne [bɔ̃bɔn] nf (récipient) demijohn.

bond [bɔ̃] nm leap, bound; (de balle) bounce; **faire faux b. à qn** to stand s.o. up, let s.o. down (by not turning up). ◆**bondir** vi to leap, bound.

bonde [bɔ̃d] nf (bouchon) plug; (trou) plughole.

bondé [bɔ̃de] *a* packed, crammed.

bonheur [bɔnœr] *nm* (*chance*) good luck, good fortune; (*félicité*) happiness; **par b.** luckily; **au petit b.** haphazardly.

bonhomie [bɔnɔmi] *nf* good-heartedness.

bonhomme, *pl* **bonshommes** [bɔnɔm, bɔ̃zɔm] **1** *nm* fellow, guy; **b. de neige** snowman; **aller son petit b. de chemin** to go on in one's own sweet way. **2** *a inv* good-hearted.

boniment(s) [bɔnimɑ̃] *nm*(*pl*) (*bobard*) claptrap; (*baratin*) patter.

bonjour [bɔ̃ʒur] *nm* & *int* good morning; (*après-midi*) good afternoon; **donner le b. à**, **dire b. à** to say hello to.

bonne[2] [bɔn] *nf* (*domestique*) maid; **b. d'enfants** nanny.

bonnement [bɔnmɑ̃] *adv* **tout b.** simply.

bonnet [bɔnɛ] *nm* cap; (*de femme, d'enfant*) bonnet; (*de soutien-gorge*) cup; **gros b.** *Fam* bigshot, bigwig. **◆bonneterie** *nf* hosiery.

bonsoir [bɔ̃swar] *nm* & *int* (*en rencontrant qn*) good evening; (*en quittant qn*) goodbye; (*au coucher*) good night.

bonté [bɔ̃te] *nf* kindness, goodness.

bonus [bɔnys] *nm* no claims bonus.

bonze [bɔ̃z] *nm Péj Fam* bigwig.

boom [bum] *nm Écon* boom.

bord [bɔr] *nm* (*rebord*) edge; (*rive*) bank; (*de vêtement*) border; (*de chapeau*) brim; (*de verre*) rim, brim, edge; **au b. de la mer/route** at *ou* by the seaside/roadside; **b. du trottoir** kerb, *Am* curb; **au b. de** (*précipice*) on the brink of; **au b. des larmes** on the verge of tears; **à bord (de)** *Nau Av* on board; **jeter par-dessus b.** to throw overboard. **◆border** *vt* (*vêtement*) to border, edge; (*lit, personne*) to tuck in; **la b. la rue/etc** (*maisons, arbres etc*) to line the street/etc. **◆bordure** *nf* border; **en b. de** bordering on.

bordeaux [bɔrdo] *a inv* maroon.

bordée [bɔrde] *nf* (*salve*) *Nau* broadside; (*d'injures*) *Fig* torrent, volley.

bordel [bɔrdel] *nm* **1** *Fam* brothel. **2** (*désordre*) *Fam* mess.

bordereau, -x [bɔrdəro] *nm* (*relevé*) docket, statement; (*formulaire*) note.

borgne [bɔrɲ] *a* (*personne*) one-eyed, blind in one eye; (*hôtel etc*) *Fig* shady.

borne [bɔrn] *nf* (*pierre*) boundary mark; *Él* terminal; *pl* (*limites*) *Fig* bounds; **b. kilométrique** = milestone; **dépasser** *ou* **franchir les bornes** to go too far. **◆born/er** *vt* (*limiter*) to confine; **se b. à** to confine oneself to. **◆-é** *a* (*personne*) narrow-minded; (*intelligence*) narrow, limited.

bosquet [bɔskɛ] *nm* grove, thicket, copse.

bosse [bɔs] *nf* (*grosseur dorsale*) hump; (*enflure*) bump, lump; (*de terrain*) bump; **avoir la b. de** *Fam* to have a flair for; **rouler sa b.** *Fam* to knock about the world. **◆bossu, -ue** *a* hunchbacked; **dos b.** hunchback; – *nmf* (*personne*) hunchback.

bosseler [bɔsle] *vt* (*orfèvrerie*) to emboss; (*déformer*) to dent.

bosser [bɔse] *vi Fam* to work (hard).

bot [bo] *am* **pied b.** club foot.

botanique [bɔtanik] *a* botanical; – *nf* botany.

botte [bɔt] *nf* (*chaussure*) boot; (*faisceau*) bunch, bundle. **◆botter** *vt* (*ballon etc*) *Fam* to boot. **◆bottier** *nm* bootmaker. **◆bottillon** *nm*, **◆bottine** *nf* (*ankle*) boot.

Bottin® [bɔtɛ̃] *nm* telephone book.

bouc [buk] *nm* billy goat; (*barbe*) goatee; **b. émissaire** scapegoat.

boucan [bukɑ̃] *nm Fam* din, row, racket.

bouche [buʃ] *nf* mouth; **faire la petite** *ou* **fine b.** *Péj* to turn up one's nose; **une fine b.** a gourmet; **b. de métro** métro entrance; **b. d'égout** drain opening, manhole; **b. d'incendie** fire hydrant; **le b.-à-b.** the kiss of life. **◆bouchée** *nf* mouthful.

bouch/er[1] [buʃe] **1** *vt* (*évier, nez etc*) to block (up), stop up; (*bouteille*) to close, cork; (*vue, rue etc*) to block; **se b. le nez** to hold one's nose. **◆-é** *a* (*vin*) bottled; (*temps*) overcast; (*personne*) *Fig* stupid, dense. **◆bouche-trou** *nm* stopgap. **◆bouchon** *nm* stopper, top; (*de liège*) cork; (*de tube, bidon*) cap, top; *Pêche* float; (*embouteillage*) *Fig* traffic jam.

boucher[2] [buʃe] *nm* butcher. **◆boucherie** *nf* butcher's (shop); (*carnage*) butchery.

boucle [bukl] *nf* **1** (*de ceinture*) buckle; (*de fleuve etc*) & *Av* loop; (*de ruban*) bow; **b. d'oreille** earring. **2 b.** (*de cheveux*) curl. **◆boucl/er** *vt* **1** to fasten, buckle; (*travail etc*) to finish off; (*enfermer, fermer*) *Fam* to lock up; (*budget*) to balance; (*circuit*) to lap; (*encercler*) to surround, cordon off; **la boucle** *Av* to loop the loop; **la b.** *Fam* to shut up. **2** *vt* (*cheveux*) to curl; – *vi* to be curly. **◆-é** *a* (*cheveux*) curly.

bouclier [buklije] *nm* shield.

bouddhiste [budist] *a* & *nmf* Buddhist.

bouder [bude] *vi* to sulk; – *vt* (*personne, plaisirs etc*) to steer clear of. **◆bouderie** *nf* sulkiness. **◆boudeur, -euse** *a* sulky, moody.

boudin [budɛ̃] *nm* black pudding, *Am* blood pudding.

boue [bu] *nf* mud. **◆boueux, -euse 1** *a*

muddy. **2** *nm* dustman, *Am* garbage collector.

bouée [bwe] *nf* buoy; **b. de sauvetage** life-buoy.

bouffe [buf] *nf Fam* food, grub, nosh.

bouffée [bufe] *nf* (*de fumée*) puff; (*de parfum*) whiff; (*d'orgueil*) fit; **b. de chaleur** *Méd* hot flush. ◆**bouff/er 1** *vi* to puff out. **2** *vti* (*manger*) *Fam* to eat. ◆**—ant** *a* (*manche*) puff(ed). ◆**bouffi** *a* puffy, bloated.

bouffon, -onne [bufɔ̃, -ɔn] *a* farcical; — *nm* buffoon. ◆**bouffonneries** *nfpl* antics, buffoonery.

bouge [buʒ] *nm* (*bar*) dive; (*taudis*) hovel.

bougeotte [buʒɔt] *nf* **avoir la b.** *Fam* to have the fidgets.

bouger [buʒe] *vi* to move; (*agir*) to stir; (*rétrécir*) to shrink; – *vt* to move; — **se b.** *vpr Fam* to move.

bougie [buʒi] *nf* candle; *Aut* spark(ing) plug. ◆**bougeoir** *nm* candlestick.

bougon, -onne [bugɔ̃, -ɔn] *a Fam* grumpy; – *nmf* grumbler, grouch. ◆**bougonner** *vi Fam* to grumble, grouch.

bougre [bugr] *nm* fellow, bloke; (*enfant*) *Péj* (little) devil. ◆**bougrement** *adv Arg* damned.

bouillabaisse [bujabes] *nf* fish soup.

bouillie [buji] *nf* porridge; **en b.** in a mush, mushy.

bouill/ir* [bujir] *vi* to boil; **b. à gros bouillons** to bubble, boil hard; **faire b. qch** to boil sth. ◆**—ant** *a* boiling; **b. de colère**/*etc* seething with anger/*etc*. ◆**bouilloire** *nf* kettle. ◆**bouillon** *nm* (*eau*) broth, stock; (*bulle*) bubble. ◆**bouillonner** *vi* to bubble. ◆**bouillotte** *nf* hot water bottle.

boulanger, -ère [bulɑ̃ʒe, -er] *nmf* baker. ◆**boulangerie** *nf* baker's (shop).

boule [bul] *nf* (*sphère*) ball; *pl* (*jeu*) bowls; **b. de neige** snowball; **faire b. de neige** to snowball; **perdre la b.** *Fam* to go out of one's mind; **se mettre en b.** (*chat etc*) to curl up into a ball; **boules Quiès®** earplugs. ◆**boulet** *nm* (*de forçat*) ball and chain; **b. de canon** cannonball. ◆**boulette** *nf* (*de papier*) pellet; (*de viande*) meatball; (*gaffe*) *Fam* blunder.

bouleau, -x [bulo] *nm* (silver) birch.

bouledogue [buldɔg] *nm* bulldog.

boulevard [bulvar] *nm* boulevard.

boulevers/er [bulverse] *vt* (*déranger*) to turn upside down; (*émouvoir*) to upset deeply, distress; (*vie de qn, pays*) to disrupt. ◆**—ant** *a* upsetting, distressing. ◆**—ement** *nm* upheaval.

boulon [bulɔ̃] *nm* bolt.

boulot, -otte [bulo, -ɔt] *a* dumpy. **2** *nm* (*travail*) *Fam* work.

boum [bum] **1** *int* & *nm* bang. **2** *nf* (*surprise-partie*) *Fam* party.

bouquet [buke] *nm* (*de fleurs*) bunch, bouquet; (*d'arbres*) clump; (*de vin*) bouquet; (*crevette*) prawn; **c'est le b.!** that's the last straw!

bouquin [bukɛ̃] *nm Fam* book. ◆**bouquiner** *vti Fam* to read. ◆**bouquiniste** *nmf* second-hand bookseller.

bourbeux, -euse [burbø, -øz] *a* muddy. ◆**bourbier** *nm* (*lieu, situation*) quagmire, morass.

bourde [burd] *nf* blunder, bloomer.

bourdon [burdɔ̃] *nm* (*insecte*) bumblebee. ◆**bourdonn/er** *vi* to buzz, hum. ◆**—ement** *nm* buzzing, humming.

bourg [bur] *nm* (small) market town. ◆**bourgade** *nf* (large) village.

bourgeois, -oise [burʒwa, -waz] *a* & *nmf* middle-class (person); *Péj* bourgeois. ◆**bourgeoisie** *nf* middle class, bourgeoisie.

bourgeon [burʒɔ̃] *nm* bud. ◆**bourgeonner** *vi* to bud; (*nez*) *Fam* to be pimply.

bourgmestre [burgmestr] *nm* (*en Belgique, Suisse*) burgomaster.

bourgogne [burgɔɲ] *nm* (*vin*) Burgundy.

bourlinguer [burlɛ̃ge] *vi* (*voyager*) *Fam* to knock about.

bourrade [burad] *nf* (*du coude*) poke.

bourrasque [burask] *nf* squall.

bourratif, -ive [buratif, -iv] *a* (*aliment*) *Fam* filling, stodgy.

bourreau, -x [buro] *nm* executioner; **b. d'enfants** child batterer; **b. de travail** workaholic.

bourrelet [burle] *nm* weather strip; **b. de graisse** roll of fat, spare tyre.

bourr/er [bure] **1** *vt* to stuff, cram (full) (*de* with); (*pipe, coussin*) to fill; **b. de coups** to thrash; **b. le crâne à qn** to brainwash s.o. **2 se b.** *vpr* (*s'enivrer*) *Fam* to get plastered. ◆**—age** *nm* **b. de crâne** brainwashing.

bourrique [burik] *nf* ass.

bourru [bury] *a* surly, rough.

bourse [burs] *nf* (*sac*) purse; *Scol Univ* grant, scholarship; **la B.** the Stock Exchange; **sans b. délier** without spending a penny. ◆**boursier, -ière 1** *a* **la B.** Stock Exchange-. **2** *nmf Scol Univ* grant holder, scholar.

boursouflé [bursufle] *a* (*visage etc*) puffy; (*style*) *Fig* inflated.

bousculer [buskyle] *vt* (*heurter, pousser*) to

jostle; (*presser*) to rush, push; **b. qch** (*renverser*) to knock sth over; **b. les habitudes**/*etc* to turn one's habits/*etc* upside down. ◆**bousculade** *nf* rush, jostling.

bouse [buz] *nf* **b. de vache** cow dung.

bousiller [buzije] *vt Fam* to mess up, wreck.

boussole [busɔl] *nf* compass.

bout [bu] *nm* end; (*de langue, canne, doigt*) tip; (*de papier, pain, ficelle*) bit; **un b. de temps/chemin** a little while/way; **au b. d'un moment** after a moment; **à b.** exhausted; **à b. de souffle** out of breath; **à b. de bras** at arm's length; **venir à b. de** (*travail*) to get through; (*adversaire*) to get the better of; **à tout b. de champ** at every turn, every minute; **à b. portant** point-blank.

boutade [butad] *nf* (*plaisanterie*) quip, witticism.

boute-en-train [butɑ̃trɛ̃] *nm inv* (*personne*) live wire.

bouteille [butɛj] *nf* bottle; (*de gaz*) cylinder.

bouteur [butœr] *nm* bulldozer.

boutique [butik] *nf* shop; (*d'un grand couturier*) boutique. ◆**boutiquier, -ière** *nmf Péj* shopkeeper.

boutoir [butwar] *nm* **coup de b.** staggering blow.

bouton [butɔ̃] *nm* (*bourgeon*) bud; (*pustule*) pimple, spot; (*de vêtement*) button; (*poussoir*) (push-)button; (*de porte, de télévision*) knob; **b. de manchette** cuff link. ◆**b.-d'or** *nm* (*pl* **boutons-d'or**) buttercup. ◆**b.-pression** *nm* (*pl* **boutons-pression**) press-stud, *Am* snap. ◆**boutonner** *vt*, — **se b.** *vpr* to button (up). ◆**boutonneux, -euse** *a* pimply, spotty. ◆**boutonnière** *nf* buttonhole.

bouture [butyr] *nf* (*plante*) cutting.

bouvreuil [buvrœj] *nm* (*oiseau*) bullfinch.

bovin [bɔvɛ̃] *a* bovine; – *nmpl* cattle.

bowling [bolin] *nm* (tenpin) bowling; (*lieu*) bowling alley.

box, *pl* **boxes** [bɔks] *nm* (*d'écurie*) (loose) box; (*de dortoir*) cubicle; *Jur* dock; *Aut* lockup *ou* individual garage.

boxe [bɔks] *nf* boxing. ◆**boxer** *vi Sp* to box; – *vt Fam* to whack, punch. ◆**boxeur** *nm* boxer.

boyau, -x [bwajo] *nm Anat* gut; (*corde*) catgut; (*de bicyclette*) (racing) tyre *ou Am* tire.

boycott/er [bɔjkɔte] *vt* to boycott. ◆**-age** *nm* boycott.

BP [bepe] *abrév* (*boîte postale*) PO Box.

bracelet [braslɛ] *nm* bracelet, bangle; (*de montre*) strap.

braconner [brakɔne] *vi* to poach. ◆**braconnier** *nm* poacher.

brader [brade] *vt* to sell off cheaply. ◆**braderie** *nf* open-air (clearance) sale.

braguette [bragɛt] *nf* (*de pantalon*) fly, flies.

braille [braj] *nm* Braille.

brailler [braje] *vti* to bawl. ◆**braillard** *a* bawling.

braire* [brɛr] *vi* (*âne*) to bray.

braise(s) [brɛz] *nf(s)* embers, live coals. ◆**braiser** [brɛze] *vt* Culin to braise.

brancard [brɑ̃kar] *nm* (*civière*) stretcher; (*de charrette*) shaft. ◆**brancardier** *nm* stretcher-bearer.

branche [brɑ̃ʃ] *nf* (*d'un arbre, d'une science etc*) branch; (*de compas*) leg; (*de lunettes*) side piece. ◆**branchages** *nmpl* (cut *ou* fallen) branches.

branch/er [brɑ̃ʃe] *vt El* to plug in; (*installer*) to connect. ◆**-é** *a* (*informé*) *Fam* with it. ◆**-ement** *nm El* connection.

brandir [brɑ̃dir] *vt* to brandish, flourish.

brandon [brɑ̃dɔ̃] *nm* (*paille, bois*) firebrand.

branle [brɑ̃l] *nm* impetus; **mettre en b.** to set in motion. ◆**b.-bas** *nm inv* turmoil. ◆**branl/er** *vi* to be shaky, shake. ◆**-ant** *a* shaky.

braqu/er [brake] **1** *vt* (*arme etc*) to point, aim; (*yeux*) to fix; **b. qn contre qn** to set *ou* turn s.o. against s.o. **2** *vti Aut* to steer, turn. ◆**-age** *nm Aut* steering; **rayon de b.** turning circle.

bras [bra] *nm* arm; **en b. de chemise** in one's shirtsleeves; **b. dessus b. dessous** arm in arm; **sur les b.** Fig on one's hands; **son b. droit** Fig his right-hand man; **à b. ouverts** with open arms; **à tour de b.** with all one's might; **faire le b. d'honneur** Fam to make an obscene gesture; **à b.-le-corps** round the waist. ◆**brassard** *nm* armband. ◆**brassée** *nf* armful. ◆**brassière** *nf* (*de bébé*) vest, *Am* undershirt.

brasier [brazje] *nm* inferno, blaze.

brasse [bras] *nf* (*nage*) breaststroke; (*mesure*) fathom; **b. papillon** butterfly stroke.

brasser [brase] *vt* to mix; (*bière*) to brew. ◆**brassage** *nm* mixture; brewing. ◆**brasserie** *nf* (*usine*) brewery; (*café*) brasserie. ◆**brasseur** *nm* **b. d'affaires** *Péj* big businessman.

bravache [bravaʃ] *nm* braggart.

bravade [bravad] *nf* **par b.** out of bravado.

brave [brav] *a & nm* (*hardi*) brave (man); (*honnête*) good (man). ◆**bravement** *adv* bravely. ◆**braver** *vt* to defy; (*danger*) to brave. ◆**bravoure** *nf* bravery.

bravo [bravo] *int* well done, bravo, good show; – *nm* cheer.

break [brɛk] *nm* estate car, *Am* station wagon.

brebis [brəbi] *nf* ewe; **b. galeuse** black sheep.

brèche [brɛʃ] *nf* breach, gap; **battre en b.** (*attaquer*) to attack (mercilessly).

bredouille [brəduj] *a* **rentrer b.** to come back empty-handed.

bredouiller [brəduje] *vti* to mumble.

bref, brève [brɛf, brɛv] *a* brief, short; – *adv* (*enfin*) in a word.

breloque [brələk] *nf* charm, trinket.

Brésil [brezil] *nm* Brazil. ◆**brésilien, -ienne** *a & nmf* Brazilian.

Bretagne [brətaɲ] *nf* Brittany. ◆**breton, -onne** *a & nmf* Breton.

bretelle [brətɛl] *nf* strap; (*voie de raccordement*) *Aut* access road; *pl* (*pour pantalon*) braces, *Am* suspenders.

breuvage [brœvaʒ] *nm* drink, brew.

brève [brɛv] *voir* **bref.**

brevet [brəvɛ] *nm* diploma; **b.** (**d'invention**) patent. ◆**brevet/er** *vt* to patent. ◆**-é a** (*technicien*) qualified.

bréviaire [brevjɛr] *nm* breviary.

bribes [brib] *nfpl* scraps, bits.

bric-à-brac [brikabrak] *nm inv* bric-à-brac, jumble, junk.

brick [brik] *nm* (*de lait, jus d'orange etc*) carton.

bricole [brikɔl] *nf* (*objet, futilité*) trifle. ◆**bricol/er** *vi* to do odd jobs; – *vt* (*réparer*) to patch up; (*fabriquer*) to put together. ◆**-age** *nm* (*petits travaux*) odd jobs; (*passe-temps*) do-it-yourself; **salon/rayon du b.** do-it-yourself exhibition/department. ◆**-eur, -euse** *nmf* handyman, handywoman.

bride [brid] *nf* (*de cheval*) bridle; **à b. abattue** at full gallop. ◆**brider** *vt* (*cheval*) to bridle; (*personne, désir*) to curb; *Culin* to truss; **avoir les yeux bridés** to have slit eyes.

bridge [bridʒ] *nm* (*jeu*) bridge.

brièvement [brivmɑ̃] *adv* briefly. ◆**brièveté** *nf* brevity.

brigade [brigad] *nf* (*de gendarmerie*) squad; *Mil* brigade; **b. des mœurs** vice squad. ◆**brigadier** *nm* police sergeant; *Mil* corporal.

brigand [brigɑ̃] *nm* robber; (*enfant*) rascal.

briguer [brige] *vt* to covet; (*faveurs, suffrages*) to court.

brillant [brijɑ̃] *a* (*luisant*) shining; (*astiqué*) shiny; (*couleur*) bright; (*magnifique*) *Fig* brilliant; – *nm* shine; brightness; *Fig* bril-

liance; (*diamant*) diamond. ◆**brillamment** *adv* brilliantly.

briller [brije] *vi* to shine; **faire b.** (*meuble*) to polish (up).

brimer [brime] *vt* to bully. ◆**brimade** *nm Scol* bullying, ragging, (*hazing*) *Fig* vexation.

brin [brɛ̃] *nm* (*d'herbe*) blade; (*de corde, fil*) strand; (*de muguet*) spray; **un b. de** *Fig* a bit of.

brindille [brɛ̃dij] *nf* twig.

bringue [brɛ̃g] *nf* **faire la b.** *Fam* to have a binge.

bringuebaler [brɛ̃gbale] *vi* to wobble about.

brio [brijo] *nm* (*virtuosité*) brilliance.

brioche [brijɔʃ] *nf* **1** brioche (*light sweet bun*). **2** (*ventre*) *Fam* paunch.

brique [brik] *nf* brick. ◆**briquette** *nf* (*aggloméré*) breezeblock.

briquer [brike] *vt* to polish (up).

briquet [brikɛ] *nm* (*cigarette*) lighter.

brise [briz] *nf* breeze.

bris/er [brize] *vt* to break; (*en morceaux*) to smash, break; (*espoir, carrière*) to shatter; (*fatiguer*) to exhaust; — **se b.** *vpr* to break. ◆**—ants** *nmpl* reefs. ◆**brise-lames** *inv* breakwater.

britannique [britanik] *a* British; – *nmf* Briton; **les Britanniques** the British.

broc [bro] *nm* pitcher, jug.

brocanteur, -euse [brɔkɑ̃tœr, -øz] *nmf* secondhand dealer (*in furniture etc*).

broche [brɔʃ] *nf Culin* spit; (*bijou*) brooch; *Méd* pin. ◆**brochette** *nf* (*tige*) skewer; (*plat*) kebab.

broché [brɔʃe] *a* **livre b.** paperback.

brochet [brɔʃɛ] *nm* (*poisson*) pike.

brochure [brɔʃyr] *nf* brochure, booklet, pamphlet.

broder [brɔde] *vt* to embroider (**de** with). ◆**broderie** *nf* embroidery.

broncher [brɔ̃ʃe] *vi* (*bouger*) to budge; (*reculer*) to flinch; (*regimber*) to balk.

bronches [brɔ̃ʃ] *nfpl* bronchial tubes. ◆**bronchite** *nf* bronchitis.

bronze [brɔ̃z] *nm* bronze.

bronz/er [brɔ̃ze] *vt* to tan; – *vi*, — **se b.** *vpr* to get (sun)tanned; **se (faire) b.** to sunbathe. ◆**—age** *nm* (sun)tan, sunburn.

brosse [brɔs] *nf* brush; **b. à dents** toothbrush; **cheveux en b.** crew cut. ◆**brosser** *vt* to brush; **b. un tableau de** to give an outline of; **se b. les dents/les cheveux** to brush one's teeth/one's hair.

brouette [bruɛt] *nf* wheelbarrow.

brouhaha [bruaa] *nm* hubbub.

broullard [brujar] *nm* fog; **il fait du b.** it's foggy.

brouille [bruj] *nf* disagreement, quarrel. ◆**brouiller 1** *vt* (*papiers, idées etc*) to mix up; (*vue*) to blur; (*œufs*) to scramble; **Rad** to jam; — **se b.** *vpr* (*idées*) to be *ou* get confused; (*temps*) to cloud over; (*vue*) to blur. **2** *vt* (*amis*) to cause a split between; — **se b.** *vpr* to fall out (**avec** with). ◆**brouillon, -onne 1** *a* confused. **2** *nm* rough draft.

broussailles [brusɑj] *nfpl* brushwood.

brousse [brus] *nf* **la b.** the bush.

brouter [brute] *vti* to graze.

broyer [brwaje] *vt* to grind; (*doigt, bras*) to crush; **b. du noir** to be (down) in the dumps.

bru [bry] *nf* daughter-in-law.

brugnon [bryɲɔ̃] *nm* (*fruit*) nectarine.

bruine [bryin] *nf* drizzle. ◆**bruiner** *v imp* to drizzle.

bruissement [bryismɑ̃] *nm* (*de feuilles*) rustle, rustling.

bruit [brɥi] *nm* noise, sound; (*nouvelle*) rumour; **faire du b.** to be noisy, make a noise. ◆**bruitage** *nm Cin* sound effects.

brûle-pourpoint (à) [abrylpurpwɛ̃] *adv* point-blank.

brûl/er [bryle] *vt* to burn; (*consommer*) to use up, burn; (*signal, station*) to go through (without stopping); **b. un feu (rouge)** to jump *ou* go through the lights; **ce désir le brûlait** this desire consumed him; — *vi* to burn; **b. (d'envie) de faire** to be burning to do; **ça brûle** (*temps*) it's baking *ou* scorching; — **se b.** *vpr* to burn oneself. ◆**—ant** *a* (*objet, soleil*) burning (hot); (*sujet*) *Fig* red-hot. ◆**—é 1** *nm* **odeur de b.** smell of burning. **2** *a* **cerveau b.,** **tête brûlée** hothead. ◆**brûlure** *nf* burn; **brûlures d'estomac** heartburn.

brume [brym] *nf* mist, haze. ◆**brumeux, -euse** *a* misty, hazy; (*obscur*) *Fig* hazy.

brun, brune [brœ̃, bryn] *a* brown; (*cheveux*) dark, brown; (*personne*) dark-haired; — *nm* (*couleur*) brown; — *nmf* dark-haired person. ◆**brunette** *nf* brunette. ◆**brunir** *vt* (*peau*) to tan; — *vi* to turn brown; (*cheveux*) to go darker.

brushing [brœʃiŋ] *nm* blow-dry.

brusque [brysk] *a* (*manière etc*) abrupt, blunt; (*subit*) sudden, abrupt. ◆**brusquement** *adv* suddenly, abruptly. ◆**brusquer** *vt* to rush. ◆**brusquerie** *nf* abruptness, bluntness.

brut [bryt] *a* (*pétrole*) crude; (*diamant*) rough; (*sucre*) unrefined; (*soie*) raw; (*poids*) & *Fin* gross.

brutal, -aux [brytal, -o] *a* (*violent*) savage, brutal; (*franchise, réponse*) crude, blunt; (*fait*) stark. ◆**brutaliser** *vt* to ill-treat. ◆**brutalité** *nf* (*violence, acte*) brutality. ◆**brute** *nf* brute.

Bruxelles [brysɛl] *nm ou f* Brussels.

bruyant [brɥijɑ̃] *a* noisy. ◆**bruyamment** *adv* noisily.

bruyère [bryjɛr] *nf* (*plante*) heather; (*terrain*) heath.

bu [by] *voir* **boire.**

buanderie [bɥɑ̃dri] *nf* (*lieu*) laundry.

bûche [byʃ] *nf* log; **ramasser une b.** *Fam* to come a cropper, *Am* take a spill. ◆**bûcher 1** *nm* (*local*) woodshed; (*supplice*) stake. **2** *vt* (*étudier*) *Fam* to slog away at. ◆**bûcheron** *nm* woodcutter, lumberjack.

budget [bydʒɛ] *nm* budget. ◆**budgétaire** *a* budgetary; (*année*) financial.

buée [bɥe] *nf* condensation, mist.

buffet [byfɛ] *nm* (*armoire*) sideboard; (*table, restaurant, repas*) buffet.

buffle [byfl] *nm* buffalo.

buis [bɥi] *nm* (*arbre*) box; (*bois*) boxwood.

buisson [bɥisɔ̃] *nm* bush.

buissonnière [bɥisɔnjɛr] *af* **faire l'école b.** to play truant *ou Am* hookey.

bulbe [bylb] *nm* bulb. ◆**bulbeux, -euse** *a* bulbous.

Bulgarie [bylgari] *nf* Bulgaria. ◆**bulgare** *a* & *nmf* Bulgarian.

bulldozer [byldozœr] *nm* bulldozer.

bulle [byl] *nf* **1** bubble; (*de bande dessinée*) balloon. **2** (*décret du pape*) bull.

bulletin [byltɛ̃] *nm* (*communiqué, revue*) bulletin; (*de la météo*) & *Scol* report; (*de bagages*) ticket, *Am* check; **b. de paie** pay slip; **b. de vote** ballot paper.

buraliste [byralist] *nmf* (*à la poste*) clerk; (*au tabac*) tobacconist.

bureau, -x [byro] *nm* **1** (*table*) desk. **2** (*lieu*) office; (*comité*) board; **b. de change** bureau de change; **b. de location** *Th Cin* box office; **b. de tabac** tobacconist's (shop). ◆**bureaucrate** *nmf* bureaucrat. ◆**bureaucratie** [-asi] *nf* bureaucracy. ◆**bureautique** *nf* office automation.

burette [byrɛt] *nf* oilcan; *Culin* cruet.

burlesque [byrlɛsk] *a* (*idée etc*) ludicrous; (*genre*) burlesque.

bus¹ [bys] *nm Fam* bus.

bus² [by] *voir* **boire.**

busqué [byske] *a* (*nez*) hooked.

buste [byst] *nm* (*torse, sculpture*) bust. ◆**bustier** *nm* long-line bra(ssiere).

but¹ [by(t)] *nm* (*dessein, objectif*) aim, goal;

(cible) target; *Fb* goal; **de b. en blanc** point-blank; **aller droit au b.** to go straight to the point; **j'ai pour b. de ...** my aim is to ...

but² [by] *voir* **boire.**

butane [bytan] *nm (gaz)* butane.

but/er [byte] **1** *vi* **b. contre** to stumble over; *(difficulté) Fig* to come up against. **2 se b.** *vpr (s'entêter)* to get obstinate. **◆—é** *a* obstinate.

butin [bytɛ̃] *nm* loot, booty.

butiner [bytine] *vi (abeille)* to gather nectar.

butoir [bytwar] *nm Rail* buffer; *(de porte)* stop(per).

butor [bytɔr] *nm Péj* lout, oaf, boor.

butte [byt] *nf* hillock, mound; **en b. à** *(calomnie etc)* exposed to.

buvable [byvabl] *a* drinkable. **◆buveur, -euse** *nmf* drinker.

buvard [byvar] *a & nm (papier)* **b.** blotting paper.

buvette [byvɛt] *nf* refreshment bar.

C

C, c [se] *nm* C, c

c *abrév* centime.

c' [s] *voir* **ce¹.**

ça [sa] *pron dém (abrév de cela) (pour désigner)* that; *(plus près)* this; *(sujet indéfini)* it, that; **ça m'amuse que ...** it amuses me that ...; **où/quand/ comment/etc ça?** where?/when?/how?/ etc; **ça va (bien)?** how's it going?; **ça va fine!, OK!; ça alors!** *(surprise, indignation)* well I never!, how about that!; **c'est ça** that's right; **et avec ça?** *(dans un magasin)* anything else?

çà [sa] *adv* **çà et là** here and there.

caban [kabɑ̃] *nm (veste)* reefer.

cabane [kaban] *nf* hut, cabin; *(à outils)* shed; *(à lapins)* hutch.

cabaret [kabarɛ] *nm* night club, cabaret.

cabas [kabɑ] *nm* shopping bag.

cabillaud [kabijo] *nm* (fresh) cod.

cabine [kabin] *nf Nau Av* cabin; *Tél* phone booth, phone box; *(de camion)* cab; *(d'ascenseur)* car, cage; **c. (de bain)** beach hut; *(à la piscine)* cubicle; **c. (de pilotage)** cockpit; *(d'un grand avion)* flight deck; **c. d'essayage** fitting room; **c. d'aiguillage** signal box.

cabinet [kabinɛ] *nm (local) Méd* surgery, *Am* office; *(d'avocat)* office, chambers; *(clientèle de médecin ou d'avocat)* practice; *Pol* cabinet; *pl (toilettes)* toilet; **c. de toilette** bathroom, toilet; **c. de travail** study.

câble [kɑbl] *nm* cable; *(cordage)* rope; **la télévision par c.** cable television; **le c.** *TV* cable. **◆câbler** *vt (message)* to cable; **être câblé** *TV* to have cable.

caboche [kabɔʃ] *nf (tête) Fam* nut, noddle.

cabosser [kabɔse] *vt* to dent.

caboteur [kabotœr] *nm (bateau)* coaster.

cabotin, -ine [kabotɛ̃, -in] *nmf Th* ham actor, ham actress; *Fig* play-actor. **◆cabotinage** *nm* histrionics, play-acting.

cabrer (se) [səkabre] *vpr (cheval)* to rear (up); *(personne)* to rebel.

cabri [kabri] *nm (chevreau)* kid.

cabrioles [kabriɔl] *nfpl* **faire des c.** *(sauts)* to cavort, caper.

cabriolet [kabriɔlɛ] *nm Aut* convertible.

cacah(o)uète [kakawɛt] *nf* peanut.

cacao [kakao] *nm (boisson)* cocoa.

cacatoès [kakatoɛs] *nm* cockatoo.

cachalot [kaʃalo] *nm* sperm whale.

cache-cache [kaʃkaʃ] *nm inv* hide-and-seek. **◆c.-col** *nm inv*, **◆c.-nez** *nm inv* scarf, muffler. **◆c.-sexe** *nm inv* G-string.

cachemire [kaʃmir] *nm (tissu)* cashmere.

cacher [kaʃe] *vt* to hide, conceal *(à* from*)*; **je ne cache pas que ...** I don't hide the fact that ...; **c. la lumière à qn** to stand in s.o.'s light; **— se c.** *vpr* to hide. **◆cachette** *nf* hiding place; **en c.** in secret; **en c. de qn** without s.o. knowing.

cachet [kaʃɛ] *nm (sceau)* seal; *(de la poste)* postmark; *(comprimé)* tablet; *(d'acteur etc)* fee; *Fig* distinctive character. **◆cacheter** *vt* to seal.

cachot [kaʃo] *nm* dungeon.

cachotteries [kaʃɔtri] *nfpl* secretiveness; *(petits secrets)* little mysteries. **◆cachottier, -ière** *a & nmf* secretive (person).

cacophonie [kakɔfɔni] *nf* cacophony.

cactus [kaktys] *nm* cactus.

cadastre [kadastr] *nm (registre)* land register.

cadavre [kadavr] *nm* corpse. **◆cadavéri-**

que a (*teint etc*) cadaverous; **rigidité c.** rigor mortis.

caddie® [kadi] *nm* supermarket trolly *ou Am* cart.

cadeau, -x [kado] *nm* present, gift.

cadenas [kadnɑ] *nm* padlock. ◆**cadenasser** *vt* to padlock.

cadence [kadɑ̃s] *nf* rhythm; *Mus* cadence; (*taux, vitesse*) rate; **en c.** in time. ◆**cadencé** a rhythmical.

cadet, -ette [kade, -et] a (*de deux frères etc*) younger; (*de plus de deux*) youngest; – *nmf* (*enfant*) younger (child); youngest (child); *Sp* junior; **c'est mon c.** he's my junior.

cadran [kadrɑ̃] *nm* (*de téléphone etc*) dial; (*de montre*) face; **c. solaire** sundial; **faire le tour du c.** to sleep round the clock.

cadre [kadr] *nm* **1** (*de photo, vélo etc*) frame; (*décor*) setting; (*sur un imprimé*) box; **dans le c. de** (*limites, contexte*) within the framework *ou* scope of, as part of. **2** (*chef*) *Com* executive, manager; *pl* (*personnel*) *Mil* officers; *Com* management, managers.

cadr/er [kadre] *vi* to tally (**avec** with); – *vt* (*image*) *Cin Phot* to centre. ◆**—eur** *nm* cameraman.

caduc, -uque [kadyk] a (*usage*) obsolete; *Bot* deciduous; *Jur* null and void.

cafard, -arde [kafar, -ard] **1** *nmf* (*espion*) sneak. **2** *nm* (*insecte*) cockroach; **avoir le c.** to be in the dumps; **ça me donne le c.** it depresses me. ◆**cafardeux, -euse** a (*personne*) in the dumps; (*qui donne le cafard*) depressing.

café [kafe] *nm* coffee; (*bar*) café; **c. au lait, c. crème** white coffee, coffee with milk; **c. noir, c. nature** black coffee; **tasse de c.** cup of black coffee. ◆**caféine** *nf* caffeine. ◆**cafétéria** *nf* cafeteria. ◆**cafetier** *nm* café owner. ◆**cafetière** *nf* percolator, coffeepot.

cafouiller [kafuje] *vi Fam* to make a mess (of things). ◆**cafouillage** *nm Fam* mess, muddle, snafu.

cage [kaʒ] *nf* cage; (*d'escalier*) well; (*d'ascenseur*) shaft; **c. des buts** *Fb* goal (area).

cageot [kaʒo] *nm* crate.

cagibi [kaʒibi] *nm* (storage) room, cubbyhole.

cagneux, -euse [kaɲø, -øz] a knock-kneed.

cagnotte [kaɲɔt] *nf* (*tirelire*) kitty.

cagoule [kagul] *nf* (*de bandit, pénitent*) hood.

cahier [kaje] *nm* (*carnet*) (note)book; *Scol* exercise book.

cahin-caha [kaɛ̃kaa] *adv* **aller c.-caha** to jog along (with ups and downs).

cahot [kao] *nm* jolt, bump. ◆**cahot/er** *vt* to jolt, bump; – *vi* (*véhicule*) to jolt along. ◆**—ant** a, ◆**cahoteux, -euse** a bumpy.

caïd [kaid] *nm Fam* big shot, leader.

caille [kɑj] *nf* (*oiseau*) quail.

cailler [kɑje] *vti*, – **se c.** *vpr* (*sang*) to clot, congeal; (*lait*) to curdle; **faire c.** (*lait*) to curdle; **ça caille** *Fam* it's freezing cold. ◆**caillot** *nm* (blood) clot.

caillou, -x [kɑju] *nm* stone; (*galet*) pebble. ◆**caillouté** a gravelled. ◆**caillouteux, -euse** a stony.

caisse [kes] *nf* (*boîte*) case, box; (*cageot*) crate; (*guichet*) cash desk, pay desk; (*de supermarché*) checkout; (*fonds*) fund; (*bureau*) (paying-in) office; *Mus* drum; *Aut* body; **c. (enregistreuse)** cash register, till; **c. d'épargne** savings bank; **de c.** (*livre, recettes*) cash-. ◆**caissier, -ière** *nmf* cashier; (*de supermarché*) checkout assistant.

caisson [kesɔ̃] *nm* (*de plongeur*) & *Mil* caisson.

cajoler [kaʒɔle] *vt* (*câliner*) to pamper, pet, cosset. ◆**cajolerie(s)** *nf(pl)* pampering.

cajou [kaʒu] *nm* (*noix*) cashew.

cake [kɛk] *nm* fruit cake.

calamité [kalamite] *nf* calamity.

calandre [kalɑ̃dr] *nf Aut* radiator grille.

calcaire [kalkɛr] a (*terrain*) chalky; (*eau*) hard; – *nm Géol* limestone.

calciné [kalsine] a charred, burnt to a cinder.

calcium [kalsjɔm] *nm* calcium.

calcul [kalkyl] *nm* **1** calculation; (*estimation*) calculation, reckoning; (*discipline*) arithmetic; (*différentiel*) calculus. **2** *Méd* stone. ◆**calcul/er** *vt* (*compter*) to calculate, reckon; (*évaluer, combiner*) to calculate. ◆**—é** a (*risque etc*) calculated. ◆**calculateur** *nm* calculator, computer. ◆**calculatrice** *nf* (*ordinateur*) calculator.

cale [kal] *nf* **1** (*pour maintenir*) wedge. **2** *Nau* hold; **c. sèche** dry dock.

calé [kale] a *Fam* (*instruit*) clever (**en qch** at sth); (*difficile*) tough.

caleçon [kalsɔ̃] *nm* underpants; **c. de bain** bathing trunks.

calembour [kalɑ̃bur] *nm* pun.

calendrier [kalɑ̃drije] *nm* (*mois et jours*) calendar; (*programme*) timetable.

cale-pied [kalpje] *nm* (*de bicyclette*) toeclip.

calepin [kalpɛ̃] *nm* (pocket) notebook.

caler [kale] **1** *vt* (*meuble etc*) to wedge (up); (*appuyer*) to prop (up). **2** *vt* (*moteur*) to stall; – *vi* to stall; *(abandonner)* *Fam* give up.

calfeutrer [kalføtre] *vt (avec du bourrelet)* to draughtproof; **se c. (chez soi)** to shut oneself away, hole up.

calibre [kalibr] *nm (diamètre)* calibre; *(d'œuf)* grade; **de ce c.** *(bêtise etc)* of this degree. ◆**calibrer** *vt (œufs)* to grade.

calice [kalis] *nm (vase) Rel* chalice.

calicot [kaliko] *nm (tissu)* calico.

califourchon (à) [akalifurʃɔ̃] *adv* astride; **se mettre à c. sur** to straddle.

câlin [kalɛ̃] *a* endearing, cuddly. ◆**câliner** *vt (cajoler)* to make a fuss of; *(caresser)* to cuddle. ◆**câlineries** *nfpl* endearing ways.

calleux, -euse [kalø, -øz] *a* callous, horny.

calligraphie [kaligrafi] *nf* calligraphy.

calme [kalm] *a* calm; *(flegmatique)* calm, cool; *(journée etc)* quiet, calm; – *nm* calm(ness); **du c.!** keep quiet!; *(pas de panique)* keep calm!; **dans le c.** *(travailler, étudier)* in peace and quiet. ◆**calm/er** *vt (douleur)* to soothe; *(inquiétude)* to calm; *(ardeur)* to damp(en); **c. qn** to calm s.o. (down); – **se c.** *vpr* to calm down. ◆**-ant** *nm* sedative; **sous calmants** under sedation.

calomnie [kalɔmni] *nf* slander; *(par écrit)* libel. ◆**calomnier** *vt* to slander; to libel. ◆**calomnieux, -euse** *a* slanderous; libellous.

calorie [kalɔri] *nf* calorie.

calorifère [kalɔrifɛr] *nm* stove.

calorifuge [kalɔrifyʒ] *a* (heat-)insulating. ◆**calorifuger** *vt* to lag.

calot [kalo] *nm Mil* forage cap.

calotte [kalɔt] *nf Rel* skull cap; *(gifle) Fam* slap; **c. glaciaire** icecap.

calque [kalk] *nm (dessin)* tracing; *(imitation)* (exact *ou* carbon) copy; **(papier-)c.** tracing paper. ◆**calquer** *vt* to trace; to copy; **c. sur** to model on.

calumet [kalymɛ] *nm* **c. de la paix** peace pipe.

calvaire [kalvɛr] *nm Rel* calvary; *Fig* agony.

calvitie [kalvisi] *nf* baldness.

camarade [kamarad] *nmf* friend, chum; *Pol* comrade; **c. de jeu** playmate; **c. d'atelier** workmate. ◆**camaraderie** *nf* friendship, companionship.

cambouis [kɑ̃bwi] *nm* grease, (engine) oil.

cambrer [kɑ̃bre] *vt* to arch; **c. les reins** *ou* **le buste** to throw out one's chest; – **se c.** *vpr* to throw back one's shoulders. ◆**cambrure** *nf* curve; *(de pied)* arch, instep.

cambriol/er [kɑ̃brijɔle] *vt* to burgle, *Am* burglarize. ◆**-age** *nm* burglary. ◆**-eur, -euse** *nmf* burglar.

came [kam] *nf Tech* cam; **arbre à cames** camshaft.

camée [kame] *nm (pierre)* cameo.

caméléon [kameleɔ̃] *nm (reptile)* chameleon.

camélia [kamelja] *nm Bot* camellia.

camelot [kamlo] *nm* street hawker. ◆**camelote** *nf* cheap goods, junk.

camembert [kamɑ̃bɛr] *nm* Camembert (cheese).

camer (se) [səkame] *vpr Fam* to get high (on drugs).

caméra [kamera] *nf (TV ou film)* camera. ◆**caméraman** *nm (pl -mans ou -men)* cameraman.

camion [kamjɔ̃] *nm* lorry, *Am* truck. ◆**c.-benne** *nm (pl camions-bennes)* dustcart, *Am* garbage truck. ◆**c.-citerne** *nm (pl camions-citernes)* tanker, *Am* tank truck. ◆**camionnage** *nm* (road) haulage, *Am* trucking. ◆**camionnette** *nf* van. ◆**camionneur** *nm (entrepreneur)* haulage contractor, *Am* trucker; *(conducteur)* lorry *ou Am* truck driver.

camisole [kamizɔl] *nf* **c. de force** straitjacket.

camomille [kamɔmij] *nf Bot* camomile; *(tisane)* camomile tea.

camoufl/er [kamufle] *vt* to camouflage. ◆**-age** *nm* camouflage.

camp [kɑ̃] *nm* camp; **feu de c.** campfire; **lit de c.** camp bed; **c. de concentration** concentration camp; **dans mon c.** *(jeu)* on my side; **ficher** *ou* **foutre le c.** *Arg* to clear off. ◆**camp/er** *vi* to camp; – *vt (personnage)* to portray (boldly); *(chapeau etc)* to plant boldly; – **se c.** *vpr* to plant oneself (boldly) **(devant** in front of). ◆**-ement** *nm* encampment, camp. ◆**-eur, -euse** *nmf* camper. ◆**camping** *nm* camping; *(terrain)* camp(ing) site. ◆**camping-car** *nm* camper.

campagne [kɑ̃paɲ] *nf* **1** country(side); **à la c.** in the country. **2** *(électorale, militaire etc)* campaign. ◆**campagnard, -arde** *a* country-; – *nm* countryman; – *nf* countrywoman.

campanile [kɑ̃panil] *nm* belltower.

camphre [kɑ̃fr] *nm* camphor.

campus [kɑ̃pys] *nm Univ* campus.

camus [kamy] *a (personne)* snub-nosed; **nez c.** snub nose.

Canada [kanada] *nm* Canada. ◆**canadien, -ienne** *a & nmf* Canadian; – *nf* fur-lined jacket.

canaille [kanɑj] *nf* rogue, scoundrel; – *a* vulgar, cheap.

canal, -aux [kanal, -o] *nm* (*artificiel*) canal; (*bras de mer*) & *TV* channel; (*conduite*) & *Anat* duct; **par le c. de** via, through. ◆**canalisation** *nf* (*de gaz etc*) mains. ◆**canaliser** *vt* (*rivière etc*) to canalize; (*diriger*) *Fig* to channel.

canapé [kanape] *nm* **1** (*siège*) sofa, couch, settee. **2** (*tranche de pain*) canapé.

canard [kanar] *nm* **1** duck; (*mâle*) drake. **2** *Mus* false note. **3** (*journal*) *Péj* rag. ◆**canarder** *vt* (*faire feu sur*) to fire at ou on.

canari [kanari] *nm* canary.

cancans [kãkã] *nmpl* (malicious) gossip. ◆**cancaner** *vi* to gossip. ◆**cancanier, -ière** *a* gossipy.

cancer [kãsɛr] *nm* cancer; **le C.** (*signe*) Cancer. ◆**cancéreux, -euse** *a* cancerous; – *nmf* cancer patient. ◆**cancérigène** *a* carcinogenic. ◆**cancérologue** *nmf* cancer specialist.

cancre [kãkr] *nm Scol Péj* dunce.

cancrelat [kãkrəla] *nm* cockroach.

candélabre [kãdelabr] *nm* candelabra.

candeur [kãdœr] *nf* innocence, artlessness. ◆**candide** *a* artless, innocent.

candidat, -ate [kãdida, -at] *nmf* candidate; (*à un poste*) applicant, candidate; **être** ou **se porter c.** à to apply for. ◆**candidature** *nf* application; *Pol* candidacy; **poser sa c.** to apply (à for).

cane [kan] *nf* (female) duck. ◆**caneton** *nm* duckling.

canette [kanɛt] *nf* **1** (*de bière*) (small) bottle. **2** (*bobine*) spool.

canevas [kanva] *nm* (*toile*) canvas; (*ébauche*) framework, outline.

caniche [kaniʃ] *nm* poodle.

canicule [kanikyl] *nf* scorching heat; (*période*) dog days.

canif [kanif] *nm* penknife.

canine [kanin] **1** *a* (*espèce, race*) canine; **exposition c.** dog show. **2** *nf* (*dent*) canine.

caniveau, -x [kanivo] *nm* gutter (*in street*).

canne [kan] *nf* (walking) stick; (*à sucre, de bambou*) cane; (*de roseau*) reed; **c. à pêche** fishing rod.

cannelle [kanɛl] *nf Bot Culin* cinnamon.

cannelure [kanlyr] *nf* groove; *Archit* flute.

cannette [kanɛt] *nf* = **canette**.

cannibale [kanibal] *nmf* & *a* cannibal. ◆**cannibalisme** *nm* cannibalism.

canoë [kanɔe] *nm* canoe; *Sp* canoeing. ◆**canoéiste** *nmf* canoeist.

canon [kanɔ̃] *nm* **1** (big) gun; *Hist* cannon; (*de fusil etc*) barrel; **c. lisse** smooth bore; **chair à c.** cannon fodder. **2** (*règle*) canon.

◆**canoniser** *vt* to canonize. ◆**canonnade** *nf* gunfire. ◆**canonnier** *nm* gunner.

cañon [kanɔ̃] *nm* canyon.

canot [kano] *nm* boat; **c. de sauvetage** lifeboat; **c. pneumatique** rubber dinghy. ◆**canot/er** *vi* to boat, go boating. ◆**—age** *nm* boating.

cantaloup [kãtalu] *nm* (*melon*) cantaloup(e).

cantate [kãtat] *nf Mus* cantata.

cantatrice [kãtatris] *nf* opera singer.

cantine [kãtin] *nf* **1** (*réfectoire*) canteen; **manger à la c.** *Scol* to have school dinners. **2** (*coffre*) tin trunk.

cantique [kãtik] *nm* hymn.

canton [kãtɔ̃] *nm* (*en France*) district (*division of arrondissement*); (*en Suisse*) canton. ◆**cantonal, -aux** *a* divisional; cantonal.

cantonade (à la) [alakãtonad] *adv* (*parler etc*) to all and sundry, to everyone in general.

cantonn/er [kãtone] *vt Mil* to billet; (*confiner*) to confine; – *vi Mil* to be billeted; – **se c.** *vpr* to confine oneself (**dans** to). ◆**—ement** *nm* (*lieu*) billet, quarters.

cantonnier [kãtonje] *nm* road mender.

canular [kanylar] *nm* practical joke, hoax.

canyon [kanɔ̃] *nm* canyon.

caoutchouc [kautʃu] *nm* rubber; (*élastique*) rubber band; *pl* (*chaussures*) galoshes; **en c.** (*balle etc*) rubber-; **c. mousse** foam. ◆**caoutchouter** *vt* to rubberize. ◆**caoutchouteux, -euse** *a* rubbery.

CAP [seape] *nm abrév* (*certificat d'aptitude professionnelle*) technical and vocational diploma.

cap [kap] *nm Géog* cape, headland; *Nau* course; **mettre le c. sur** to steer a course for; **franchir** ou **doubler le c. de** (*difficulté*) to get over the worst of; **franchir** ou **doubler le c. de la trentaine**/*etc* to turn thirty/*etc*.

capable [kapabl] *a* capable, able; **c. de faire** able to do, capable of doing. ◆**capacité** *nf* ability, capacity; (*contenance*) capacity.

cape [kap] *nf* cape, (*grande*) cloak.

CAPES [kapes] *nm abrév* (*certificat d'aptitude professionnelle à l'enseignement secondaire*) teaching diploma.

capillaire [kapilɛr] *a* (*huile, lotion*) hair-.

capitaine [kapitɛn] *nm* captain.

capital, -ale, -aux [kapital, -o] **1** *a* major, fundamental, capital; (*peine*) capital; (*péché*) deadly. **2** *nf* (*lettre*) capital; (*lettre, ville*) capital. **3** *nm* & *nmpl Fin* capital. ◆**capitaliser** *vt* (*accumuler*) to build up; – *vi* to save up. ◆**capitalisme** *nm* capitalism. ◆**capitaliste** a & nmf capitalist.

capiteux, -euse [kapitø, -øz] a (vin, parfum) heady.

capitonn/er [kapitɔne] vt to pad, upholster. ◆**-age** nm (garniture) padding, upholstery.

capituler [kapityle] vi to surrender, capitulate. ◆**capitulation** nf surrender, capitulation.

caporal, -aux [kapɔral, -o] nm corporal.

capot [kapo] nm Aut bonnet, Am hood.

capote [kapɔt] nf Aut hood, Am (convertible) top; Mil greatcoat; **c. (anglaise)** (préservatif) Fam condom. ◆**capoter** vi Aut Av to overturn.

câpre [kɑpr] nf Bot Culin caper.

caprice [kapris] nm (passing) whim, caprice. ◆**capricieux, -euse** a capricious.

Capricorne [kaprikɔrn] nm le **C.** (signe) Capricorn.

capsule [kapsyl] nf (spatiale) & Méd etc capsule; (de bouteille, pistolet d'enfant) cap.

capter [kapte] vt (faveur etc) to win; (attention) to capture, win; (eau) to draw off; Rad to pick up.

captif, -ive [kaptif, -iv] a & nmf captive. ◆**captiver** vt to captivate, fascinate. ◆**captivité** nf captivity.

capture [kaptyr] nf capture; catch. ◆**capturer** vt (criminel, navire) to capture; (animal) to catch, capture.

capuche [kapyʃ] nf hood. ◆**capuchon** nm hood; (de moine) cowl; (pèlerine) hooded (rain)coat; (de stylo) cap, top.

capucine [kapysin] nf (plante) nasturtium.

caquet [kake] nm (bavardage) cackle. ◆**caquet/er** vi (poule, personne) to cackle. ◆**-age** nm cackle.

car [kar] 1 conj because, for. 2 nm coach, bus, Am bus; **c. de police** police van.

carabine [karabin] nf rifle, carbine; **c. à air comprimé** airgun.

carabiné [karabine] a Fam violent; (punition, amende) very stiff.

caracoler [karakɔle] vi to prance, caper.

caractère [karaktɛr] nm 1 (lettre) Typ character; **en petits caractères** in small print; **caractères d'imprimerie** block capitals ou letters; **caractères gras** bold type ou characters. 2 (tempérament, nature) character, nature; (attribut) characteristic; **aucun c. de gravité** no serious element; **son ou** her uneven temper; **avoir bon c.** to be good-natured. ◆**caractériel, -ielle** a (trait, troubles) character-; — a & nmf

disturbed (child). ◆**caractériser** vt to characterize; **se c. par** to be characterized by. ◆**caractéristique** a & nf characteristic.

carafe [karaf] nf decanter, carafe.

carambol/er [karɑ̃bɔle] vt Aut to smash into. ◆**-age** nm pileup, multiple smash-up.

caramel [karamɛl] nm caramel; (bonbon dur) toffee.

carapace [karapas] nf (de tortue etc) & Fig shell.

carat [kara] nm carat.

caravane [karavan] nf (dans le désert) caravan; Aut caravan, Am trailer; **c. publicitaire** publicity convoy. ◆**caravaning** n, ◆**caravanage** n caravanning.

carbone [karbɔn] nm carbon; **(papier) c.** carbon (paper). ◆**carboniser** vt to burn (to ashes), char; (substance) Ch to carbonize; **être mort carbonisé** to be burned to death.

carburant [karbyrɑ̃] nm Aut fuel. ◆**carburateur** nm carburettor, Am carburetor.

carcan [karkɑ̃] nm Hist iron collar; (contrainte) Fig yoke.

carcasse [karkas] nf Anat carcass; (d'immeuble etc) frame, shell.

cardiaque [kardjak] a (trouble etc) heart-; **crise c.** heart attack; **arrêt c.** cardiac arrest; — nmf heart patient.

cardinal, -aux [kardinal, -o] 1 a (nombre, point) cardinal. 2 nm Rel cardinal.

Carême [karɛm] nm Lent.

carence [karɑ̃s] nf inadequacy, incompetence; Méd deficiency.

carène [karɛn] nf Nau hull. ◆**caréné** a Aut Av streamlined.

caresse [karɛs] nf caress. ◆**caress/er** [karese] vt (animal, enfant etc) to stroke, pat, fondle; (femme, homme) to caress; (espoir) to cherish. ◆**-ant** a endearing, loving.

cargaison [kargɛzɔ̃] nf cargo, freight. ◆**cargo** nm freighter, cargo boat.

caricature [karikatyr] nf caricature. ◆**caricatural, -aux** a ludicrous; **portrait c.** portrait in caricature. ◆**caricaturer** vt to caricature.

carie [kari] nf **la c. (dentaire)** tooth decay; **une c.** a cavity. ◆**carié** a (dent) decayed, bad.

carillon [karijɔ̃] nm (cloches) chimes, peal; (horloge) chiming clock. ◆**carillonner** vi to chime, peal.

carlingue [karlɛ̃g] nf (fuselage) Av cabin.

carnage [karnaʒ] nm carnage.

carnassier, -ière [karnasje, -jɛr] a carnivorous; — nm carnivore.

carnaval, pl -als [karnaval] nm carnival.

carné [karne] a (régime) meat-.

carnet [karnɛ] nm notebook; (de timbres, chèques, adresses etc) book; **c. de notes** school report; **c. de route** logbook; **c. de vol** Av logbook.

carnivore [karnivɔr] a carnivorous; — nm carnivore.

carotte [karɔt] nf carrot.

carotter [karɔte] vt Arg to wangle, cadge (à qn from s.o.).

carpe [karp] nf carp.

carpette [karpɛt] nf rug.

carquois [karkwa] nm (étui) quiver.

carré [kare] a (en affaires) Fig plain-dealing; — nm square; (de jardin) patch; Nau messroom; **c. de soie** (square) silk scarf.

carreau, -x [karo] nm (vitre) (window) pane; (pavé) tile; (sol) tiled floor; Cartes diamonds; **à carreaux** (nappe etc) check(ed); **se tenir à c.** to watch one's step; **rester sur le c.** to be left for dead; (candidat) Fig to be left out in the cold. ◆**carrel/er** vt to tile. ◆**—age** nm (sol) tiled floor; (action) tiling.

carrefour [karfur] nm crossroads.

carrelet [karlɛ] nm (poisson) plaice, Am flounder.

carrément [karemã] adv (dire etc) straight out, bluntly; (complètement) downright, well and truly.

carrer (se) [səkare] vpr to settle down firmly.

carrière [karjɛr] nf 1 (terrain) quarry. 2 (métier) career.

carrosse [karɔs] nm Hist (horse-drawn) carriage. ◆**carrossable** a suitable for vehicles. ◆**carrosserie** nf Aut body(work).

carrousel [karuzɛl] nm (tourbillon) Fig whirl, merry-go-round.

carrure [karyr] nf breadth of shoulders, build; Fig calibre.

cartable [kartabl] nm Scol satchel.

carte [kart] nf card; (de lecteur) ticket; Géog map; Nau Mét chart; pl (jeu) cards; **c. (postale)** (post)card; **c. à jouer** playing card; **c. de crédit** credit card; **c. des vins** wine list; **c. grise** Aut vehicle registration; **c. blanche** Fig free hand.

cartel [kartɛl] nm Écon Pol cartel.

carter [kartɛr] nm (de moteur) Aut crankcase; (de bicyclette) chain guard.

cartilage [kartilaʒ] nm cartilage.

carton [kartɔ̃] nm cardboard; (boîte) cardboard box, carton; **c. à dessin** portfolio; **en c.-pâte** (faux) Péj pasteboard; **faire un c. sur** Fam to take a potshot at. ◆**cartonn/er** vt (livre) to case; livre **cartonné** hardback. ◆**—age** nm (emballage) cardboard package.

cartouche [kartuʃ] nf cartridge; (de cigarettes) carton; Phot cassette. ◆**cartouchière** nf (ceinture) cartridge belt.

cas [ka] nm case; **en tout c.** in any case or event; **en aucun c.** on no account; **en c. de besoin** if need(s) be; **en c. d'accident** in the event of an accident; **en c. d'urgence** in (case of) an emergency; **faire c. de/peu de c. de** to set great/little store by; **au c. où elle tomberait** if she should fall; **pour le c. où il pleuvrait** in case it rains.

casanier, -ière [kazanje, -jɛr] a & nmf home-loving (person); (pantouflard) Péj stay-at-home (person).

casaque [kazak] nf (de jockey) shirt, blouse.

cascade [kaskad] nf 1 waterfall; (série) Fig spate; **en c.** in succession. 2 Cin stunt. ◆**cascadeur, -euse** nmf Cin stunt man, stunt woman.

case [kaz] nf 1 pigeonhole; (de tiroir) compartment; (d'échiquier etc) square; (de formulaire) box. 2 (hutte) hut, cabin.

caser [kaze] vt Fam (ranger) to park, place; **c. qn** (dans un logement ou un travail) to find a place for s.o.; (marier) to marry s.o. off; — **se c.** vpr to settle down.

caserne [kazɛrn] nf Mil barracks; **c. de pompiers** fire station.

casier [kazje] nm pigeonhole, compartment; (meuble à tiroirs) filing cabinet; (fermant à clef, à consigne automatique) locker; **c. à bouteilles/à disques** bottle/record rack; **c. judiciaire** criminal record.

casino [kazino] nm casino.

casque [kask] nm helmet; (pour cheveux) (hair) dryer; **c. (à écouteurs)** headphones; **les Casques bleus** the UN peace-keeping force. ◆**casqué** a helmeted, wearing a helmet.

casquer [kaske] vi Fam to pay up, cough up.

casquette [kaskɛt] nf (coiffure) cap.

cassation [kasasjɔ̃] nf Cour de c. supreme court of appeal.

casse¹ [kas] nf 1 (action) breakage; (objets) breakages; (grabuge) Fam trouble; **mettre à la c.** to scrap; **vendre à la c.** to sell for scrap. **2** *Typ* case; **bas/haut de c.** lower/upper case.

casse² [kas] *nm* (*cambriolage*) *Arg* break-in.

casse-cou [kɑsku] *nmf inv* (*personne*) *Fam* daredevil. ◆**c.-croûte** *nm inv* snack. ◆**c.-gueule** *nm inv Fam* death trap; *– a inv* perilous. ◆**c.-noisettes** *nm inv* nut-cracker(s). ◆**c.-noix** *nm inv* nut-cracker(s). ◆**c.-pieds** *nmf inv* (*personne*) *Fam* pain in the neck. ◆**c.-tête** *nm inv* **1** (*massue*) club. **2** (*problème*) headache; (*jeu*) puzzle, brain teaser.

cass/er [kɑse] *vt* to break; (*noix*) to crack; (*annuler*) *Jur* to annul; (*dégrader*) *Mil* to cashier; *– vi*, *– se c. vpr* to break; **il me casse la tête** *Fam* he's giving me a headache; **elle me casse les pieds** *Fam* she's getting on my nerves; **se c. la tête** *Fam* to rack one's brains; **c. la figure à qn** *Fam* to smash s.o.'s face in; **se c. la figure** (*tomber*) *Fam* to come a cropper; *Am* take a spill; **ça ne casse rien** *Fam* it's nothing special; **ça vaut 50F à tout c.** *Fam* it's worth 50F at the very most; **il ne s'est pas cassé** *Iron Fam* he didn't bother himself *ou* exhaust himself. ◆**–ant** *a* (*fragile*) brittle; (*brusque*) curt, imperious; (*fatigant*) *Fam* exhausting. ◆**–eur** *nm Aut* breaker, scrap merchant; (*manifestant*) demonstrator who damages property.

casserole [kasrɔl] *nf* (sauce)pan.

cassette [kaset] *nf* (*pour magnétophone ou magnétoscope*) cassette; **sur c.** (*film*) on video; **faire une c. de** (*film*) to make a video of.

cassis 1 [kasis] *nm Bot* blackcurrant; (*boisson*) blackcurrant liqueur. **2** [kasi] *nm Aut* dip (across road).

cassoulet [kasulɛ] *nm* stew (*of meat and beans*).

cassure [kasyr] *nf* (*fissure, rupture*) break; *Géol* fault.

castagnettes [kastaɲɛt] *nfpl* castanets.

caste [kast] *nf* caste; **esprit de c.** class consciousness.

castor [kastɔr] *nm* beaver.

castrer [kastre] *vt* to castrate. ◆**castration** *nf* castration.

cataclysme [kataklism] *nm* cataclysm.

catacombes [katakɔ̃b] *nfpl* catacombs.

catalogue [katalɔg] *nm* catalogue. ◆**cataloguer** *vt* (*livres etc*) to catalogue; **c. qn** *Péj* to categorize s.o.

catalyseur [katalizœr] *nm Ch & Fig* catalyst.

cataphote® [katafɔt] *nm Aut* reflector.

cataplasme [kataplasm] *nm Méd* poultice.

catapulte [katapylt] *nf Hist Av* catapult. ◆**catapulter** *vt* to catapult.

cataracte [katarakt] *nf* **1** *Méd* cataract. **2** (*cascade*) falls, cataract.

catastrophe [katastrɔf] *nf* disaster, catastrophe; **atterrir en c.** to make an emergency landing. ◆**catastrophique** *a* disastrous, catastrophic.

catch [katʃ] *nm* (all-in) wrestling. ◆**catcheur, -euse** *nmf* wrestler.

catéchisme [kateʃism] *nm Rel* catechism.

catégorie [kategɔri] *nf* category. ◆**catégorique** *a* categorical.

cathédrale [katedral] *nf* cathedral.

catholicisme [katɔlisism] *nm* Catholicism. ◆**catholique** *a & nmf* Catholic; **pas (très) c.** (*affaire, personne*) *Fig* shady, doubtful.

catimini (en) [ɑ̃katimini] *adv* on the sly.

cauchemar [koʃmar] *nm* nightmare.

cause [koz] *nf* cause; *Jur* case; **à c. de** because of, on account of; **et pour c.!** for a very good reason!; **pour c. de** on account of; **en connaissance de c.** in full knowledge of the facts; **mettre en c.** (*la bonne foi de qn etc*) to (call into) question; (*personne*) to implicate; **en c.** involved, in question.

caus/er [koze] **1** *vt* (*provoquer*) to cause. **2** *vi* (*bavarder*) to chat (*de* about); (*discourir*) to talk; (*jaser*) to blab. ◆**–ant** *a Fam* chatty, talkative. ◆**causerie** *nf* talk. ◆**causette** *nf* **faire la c.** *Fam* to have a little chat.

caustique [kostik] *a* (*substance, esprit*) caustic.

cauteleux, -euse [kotlø, -øz] *a* wily, sly.

cautériser [koterize] *vt Méd* to cauterize.

caution [kosjɔ̃] *nf* surety; (*pour libérer qn*) *Jur* bail; **sous c.** on bail; **sujet à c.** (*nouvelle etc*) very doubtful. ◆**cautionn/er** *vt* (*approuver*) to sanction. ◆**–ement** *nm* (*garantie*) surety.

cavalcade [kavalkad] *nf Fam* stampede; (*défilé*) cavalcade. ◆**cavale** *nf* **en c.** *Arg* on the run. ◆**cavaler** *vi Fam* to run, rush.

cavalerie [kavalri] *nf Mil* cavalry; (*de cirque*) horses. ◆**cavalier, -ière 1** *nmf* rider; *– nm Mil* trooper, cavalryman; *Échecs* knight; *– af* **allée cavalière** bridle path. **2** *nmf* (*pour danser*) partner, escort. **3** *a* (*insolent*) offhand.

cave [kav] *nf* **1** cellar, vault. **2** *a* sunken, hollow. ◆**caveau, -x** *nm* (*sépulture*) (burial) vault.

caverne [kavɛrn] *nf* cave, cavern; **homme**

des **cavernes** caveman. ◆**caverneux, -euse** a (voix, rire) hollow, deep-sounding.
caviar [kavjar] nm caviar(e).
cavité [kavite] nf cavity.
CCP [sesepe] nm abrév (Compte chèque postal) PO Giro account, Am Post Office checking account.
ce [s(ə)] (c' before e and é) pron dém **1** it, that; **c'est toi/bon/demain**/etc it's ou that's you/good/tomorrow/etc; **c'est mon médecin** he's my doctor; **ce sont eux qui ...** they are the ones who ... ; **c'est à elle de jouer** it's her turn to play; **est-ce que tu viens?** are you coming? **sur ce** at this point, thereupon. **2 ce que, ce qui** what; **je sais ce qui est bon/ce que tu veux** I know what is good/what you want; **ce que c'est beau!** how beautiful it is!
ce², **cette**, pl **ces** [s(ə), sɛt, se] (ce becomes **cet** before a vowel or mute h) a dém this, that, pl these, those; (+ -ci) this, pl these; (+ -là) that, pl those; **cet homme** this ou that man; **cet homme-ci** this man; **cet homme-là** that man.
ceci [səsi] pron dém this; **écoutez bien c.** listen to this.
cécité [sesite] nf blindness.
céder [sede] vt to give up (à to); Jur to transfer; **le pas à** to give way ou precedence to; – vi (personne) to give way, give in, yield (à to); (branche, chaise etc) to give way.
cédille [sedij] nf Gram cedilla.
cèdre [sɛdr] nm (arbre, bois) cedar.
CEE [seəə] nf abrév (Communauté économique européenne) EEC.
ceindre [sɛdr] vt (épée) Lit to gird on.
ceinture [sɛtyr] nf belt; (de robe de chambre) cord; (taille) Anat waist; (de remparts) Hist girdle; **petite/grande c.** Rail inner/outer circle; **c. de sécurité** Aut Av seatbelt; **c. de sauvetage** lifebelt. ◆**ceinturer** vt to seize round the waist; Rugby to tackle; (ville) to girdle, surround.
cela [s(ə)la] pron dém (pour désigner) that; (sujet indéfini) it, that; **c. m'attriste que ...** it saddens me that ... ; **quand/comment**/etc **c.?** when?/how?/etc; **c'est c.** that is so.
célèbre [selebr] a famous. ◆**célébrité** nf fame; (personne) celebrity.
célébrer [selebre] vt to celebrate. ◆**célébration** nf celebration (de of).
céleri [sɛlri] nm (en branches) celery.
céleste [selɛst] a celestial, heavenly.
célibat [seliba] nm celibacy. ◆**célibataire** a (non marié) single, unmarried; (chaste)

celibate; – nm bachelor; – nf unmarried woman, spinster.
celle voir celui.
cellier [selje] nm storeroom (for wine etc).
cellophane® [sɛlɔfan] nf cellophane®.
cellule [selyl] nf cell. ◆**cellulaire** a (tissu etc) Biol cell-; **voiture c.** prison van.
celluloïd [selyloid] nm celluloid.
cellulose [selyloz] nf cellulose.
celtique ou **celte** [sɛltik, sɛlt] a Celtic.
celui, celle, pl **ceux, celles** [səlɥi, sɛl, sø, sel] pron dém **1** the one, pl those, the ones; **c. de Jean** John's (one); **ceux de Jean** John's (ones), those of John. **2** (+ -ci) this one, pl these (ones); (dont on vient de parler) the latter; (+ -là) that one, pl those (ones); the former; **ceux-ci sont gros** these (ones) are big.
cendre [sɑdr] nf ash. ◆**cendré** a ash(-coloured), ashen. ◆**cendrée** nf Sp cinder track.
Cendrillon [sɑdrijɔ] nm Cinderella.
censé [sɑse] a supposed; **il n'est pas c. le savoir** he's not supposed to know.
censeur [sɑsœr] nm censor; Scol assistant headmaster, vice-principal. ◆**censure** nf la **c.** (examen) censorship; (comité, service) the censor; **motion de c.** Pol censure motion. ◆**censurer** vt (film etc) to censor; (critiquer) & Pol to censure.
cent [sɑ] ([sɑt] pl [sɑz] before vowel and mute h except un and onze) a & nm hundred; **c. pages** a ou one hundred pages; **deux cents pages** two hundred pages; **deux c. trois pages** two hundred and three pages; **cinq pour c.** five per cent. ◆**centaine** nf une **c.** a hundred (or so); **des centaines de** hundreds of. ◆**centenaire** a & nmf centenarian; – nm (anniversaire) centenary. ◆**centième** a & nmf hundredth; **un c.** a hundredth. ◆**centigrade** a centigrade. ◆**centime** nm centime. ◆**centimètre** nm centimetre; (ruban) tape measure.
central, -aux [sɑtral, -o] **1** a central; **pouvoir c.** (power of) central government. **2** nm **c.** (téléphonique) (telephone) exchange. ◆**centrale** nf (usine) power station. ◆**centraliser** vt to centralize. ◆**centre** nm centre; **c. commercial** shopping centre. ◆**c.-ville** nm inv city ou town centre. ◆**centrer** vt to centre. ◆**centrifuge** a centrifugal. ◆**centrifugeuse** nf liquidizer, juice extractor.
centuple [sɑtypl] nm hundredfold; **au c.** a hundredfold. ◆**centupler** vti to increase a hundredfold. ◆

cep [sɛp] *nm* vine stock. ◆**cépage** *nm* vine (plant).

cependant [səpɑ̃dɑ̃] *conj* however, yet.

céramique [seramik] *nf* (*art*) ceramics; (*matière*) ceramic, de ou en c. ceramic.

cerceau, -x [sɛrso] *nm* hoop.

cercle [sɛrkl] *nm* (*forme, groupe, étendue*) circle; **les yeux cernés** vicious circle.

cercueil [sɛrkœj] *nm* coffin.

céréale [sereal] *nf* cereal.

cérébral, -aux [serebral, -o] *a* cerebral.

cérémonie [seremɔni] *nf* ceremony; de c. (*tenue etc*) ceremonial; **sans c.** (*inviter, manger*) informally; **faire des cérémonies** *Fam* to make a lot of fuss. ◆**cérémonial**, *pl* **-als** *nm* ceremonial. ◆**cérémonieux, -euse** *a* ceremonious.

cerf [sɛr] *nm* deer; (*mâle*) stag. ◆**cerf-volant** *nm* (*pl* **cerfs-volants**) (*jouet*) kite.

cerise [s(ə)riz] *nf* cherry. ◆**cerisier** *nm* cherry tree.

cerne [sɛrn] *nm* (*cercle, marque*) ring. ◆**cerner** *vt* to surround; (*problème*) to define; **les yeux cernés** with rings under one's eyes.

certain [sɛrtɛ̃] **1** *a* (*sûr*) certain, sure; **il est ou c'est sûr que tu réussiras** you're certain ou sure to succeed; **je suis c. de réussir** I'm certain ou sure I'll succeed; **être c. de qch** to be certain ou sure of sth. **2** *a* (*imprécis, difficile à fixer*) certain; *pl* certain, some; **un c. temps** a certain (amount of) time; – *pron pl* some (people), certain people; (*choses*) some. ◆**certainement** *adv* certainly. ◆**certes** *adv* indeed.

certificat [sɛrtifika] *nm* certificate. ◆**certifi/er** *vt* to certify; **je vous certifie que** I assure you that. ◆**-é** *a* (*professeur*) qualified.

certitude [sɛrtityd] *nf* certainty; **avoir la c.** que to be certain that.

cerveau, -x [sɛrvo] *nm* (*organe*) brain; (*intelligence*) mind, brain(s); **rhume de c.** head cold; **fuite des cerveaux** brain drain.

cervelas [sɛrvəla] *nm* saveloy.

cervelle [sɛrvɛl] *nf* (*substance*) brain; *Culin* brains; **tête sans c.** scatterbrain.

ces *voir* ce².

CES [seɛs] *nm abrév* (*collège d'enseignement secondaire*) comprehensive school, *Am* high school.

césarienne [sezarjɛn] *nf* *Méd* Caesarean (section).

cessation [sɛsɑsjɔ̃] *nf* (*arrêt, fin*) suspension.

cesse [sɛs] *nf* **sans c.** incessantly; **elle n'a**

(**pas**) **eu de c. que je fasse** ... she had no rest until I did ....

cesser [sese] *vti* to stop; **faire c.** to put a stop ou halt to; **il ne cesse (pas) de parler** he doesn't stop talking. ◆**cessez-le-feu** *nm inv* ceasefire.

cession [sɛsjɔ̃] *nf* *Jur* transfer.

c'est-à-dire [sɛtadir] *conj* that is (to say), in other words.

cet, cette *voir* ce².

ceux *voir* celui.

chacal, *pl* **-als** [ʃakal] *nm* jackal.

chacun, -une [ʃakœ̃, -yn] *pron* each (one), every one; (*tout le monde*) everyone.

chagrin [ʃagrɛ̃] **1** *nm* sorrow, grief; **avoir du c.** to be very upset. **2** *a* *Lit* doleful. ◆**chagriner** *vt* to upset, distress.

chahut [ʃay] *nm* racket, noisy disturbance. ◆**chahut/er** *vi* to create a racket ou a noisy disturbance; – *vt* (*professeur*) to be rowdy with, play up. ◆**—eur, -euse** *nmf* rowdy.

chai [ʃɛ] *nm* wine and spirits storehouse.

chaîne [ʃɛn] *nf* chain; *TV* channel, network; *Géog* chain, range; *Nau* cable; *Tex* warp; *pl* (*liens*) *Fig* shackles, chains; **c. de montage** assembly line; **travail à la c.** production-line work; **c. haute fidélité, c. hi-fi** hi-fi system; **c. de magasins** chain of shops ou *Am* stores; **collision en c.** multiple collision; **réaction en c.** chain reaction. ◆**chaînette** *nf* (small) chain. ◆**chaînon** *nm* (*anneau, lien*) link.

chair [ʃɛr] *nf* flesh; (*couleur*) **c.** flesh-coloured; **en c. et en os** in the flesh; **la c. de poule** goose pimples, gooseflesh; **bien en c.** plump; **c. à saucisses** sausage meat.

chaire [ʃɛr] *nf* *Univ* chair; *Rel* pulpit.

chaise [ʃɛz] *nf* chair, seat; **c. longue** (*siège pliant*) deckchair; **c. d'enfant, c. haute** high-chair.

chaland [ʃalɑ̃] *nm* barge, lighter.

châle [ʃal] *nm* shawl.

chalet [ʃalɛ] *nm* chalet.

chaleur [ʃalœr] *nf* heat; (*douce*) warmth; (*d'un accueil, d'une voix etc*) warmth; (*des convictions*) ardour; (*d'une discussion*) heat. ◆**chaleureux, -euse** *a* warm.

challenge [ʃalɑ̃ʒ] *nm* *Sp* contest.

chaloupe [ʃalup] *nf* launch, long boat.

chalumeau, -x [ʃalymo] *nm* blowlamp, *Am* blowtorch; *Mus* pipe.

chalut [ʃaly] *nm* trawl net, drag net. ◆**chalutier** *nm* (*bateau*) trawler.

chamailler (se) [səʃamɑje] *vpr* to squabble, bicker. ◆**chamailleries** *nfpl* squabbling, bickering.

chamarré [ʃamare] a (robe etc) richly coloured; **c. de** (décorations etc) Péj bedecked with.

chambard [ʃɑ̃bar] nm Fam (tapage) rumpus, row. **◆chambarder** vt Fam to turn upside down; **il a tout chambardé dans** he's turned everything upside down in.

chambouler [ʃɑ̃bule] vt Fam to make topsy-turvy, turn upside down.

chambre [ʃɑ̃br] nf (bed)room; c. à coucher bedroom; (mobilier) bedroom suite; c. à air (de pneu) inner tube; **C. des Communes** Pol House of Commons; **c. d'ami** guest ou spare room; **c. forte** strongroom; **c. noire** Phot darkroom; **garder la c.** to stay indoors. **◆chambrée** nf Mil barrack room. **◆chambrer** vt (vin) to bring to room temperature.

chameau, -x [ʃamo] nm camel.

chamois [ʃamwa] **1** nm (animal) chamois; peau de c. chamois (leather), shammy. **2** a inv buff(-coloured).

champ [ʃɑ̃] nm field; (domaine) Fig scope, range; **c. de bataille** battlefield; **c. de courses** racecourse, racetrack; **c. de foire** fairground; **c. de tir** (terrain) rifle range; **laisser le c. libre à qn** to leave the field open for s.o. **◆champêtre** a rustic, rural.

champagne [ʃɑ̃paɲ] nm champagne; c. brut extra-dry champagne.

champignon [ʃɑ̃piɲɔ̃] nm **1** Bot mushroom; **c. vénéneux** toadstool, poisonous mushroom; **c. atomique** mushroom cloud. **2** Aut Fam accelerator pedal.

champion [ʃɑ̃pjɔ̃] nm champion. **◆championnat** nm championship.

chance [ʃɑ̃s] nf luck; (probabilité de réussir, occasion) chance; **avoir de la c.** to be lucky; **tenter ou courir sa c.** to try one's luck; **c'est une c. que** . . . it's a stroke of luck that . . . ; **mes chances de succès** my chances of success. **◆chanceux, -euse** a lucky.

chancel/er [ʃɑ̃sle] vi to stagger, totter; (courage) Fig to falter. **◆—ant** a (pas, santé) faltering, shaky.

chancelier [ʃɑ̃səlje] nm chancellor. **◆chancellerie** nf chancellery.

chancre [ʃɑ̃kr] nm Méd & Fig canker.

chandail [ʃɑ̃daj] nm (thick) sweater, jersey.

chandelier [ʃɑ̃dəlje] nm candlestick.

chandelle [ʃɑ̃dɛl] nf candle; **voir trente-six chandelles** Fig to see stars; **en c.** Av Sp straight into the air.

change [ʃɑ̃ʒ] nm Fin exchange; **le contrôle des changes** exchange control; **donner le c. à qn** to deceive s.o. **◆chang/er** vt (modifier, remplacer, échanger) to change; **c. qn**

en to change s.o. into; **ça la changera de ne pas travailler** it'll be a change for her not to be working; **– vi** to change; **c. de voiture/d'adresse/etc** to change one's car/address/etc; **c. de train/de place** to change trains/places; **c. de vitesse/de cap** to change gear/course; **c. de sujet** to change the subject; **– se c.** vpr to change (one's clothes). **◆—eant** a (temps) changeable; (humeur) fickle; (couleurs) changing. **◆—ement** nm change; **aimer le c.** to like change. **◆—eur** nm moneychanger; **c. de monnaie** change machine.

chanoine [ʃanwan] nm (personne) Rel canon.

chanson [ʃɑ̃sɔ̃] nf song. **◆chant** nm singing; (chanson) song; (hymne) chant; **c. de Noël** Christmas carol. **◆chant/er** vi to sing; (psalmodier) to chant; (coq) to crow; **si ça te chante** Fam if you feel like it; **faire c. qn** to blackmail s.o.; **– vt** to sing; (glorifier) to sing of; (dire) Fam to say. **◆—ant** a (air, voix) melodious. **◆—age** nm blackmail. **◆—eur, -euse** nm singer.

chantier [ʃɑ̃tje] nm (building) site; (entrepôt) builder's yard; **c. naval** shipyard; **mettre un travail en c.** to get a task under way.

chantonner [ʃɑ̃tɔne] vti to hum.

chantre [ʃɑ̃tr] nm Rel cantor.

chanvre [ʃɑ̃vr] nm hemp; **c. indien** (plante) cannabis.

chaos [kao] nm chaos. **◆chaotique** a chaotic.

chaparder [ʃaparde] vt Fam to filch, pinch (à from).

chapeau, -x [ʃapo] nm hat; (de champignon, roue) cap; **c.!** well done!; donner un coup de c. (pour saluer etc) to raise one's hat; **c. mou** trilby, Am fedora. **◆chapelier** nm hatter.

chapelet [ʃaplɛ] nm rosary; **dire son c.** to tell one's beads; **un c. de** (saucisses, injures etc) a string of.

chapelle [ʃapɛl] nf chapel; **c. ardente** chapel of rest.

chaperon [ʃaprɔ̃] nm chaperon(e). **◆chaperonner** vt to chaperon(e).

chapiteau, -x [ʃapito] nm (de cirque) big top; (pour expositions etc) marquee, tent; (de colonne) Archit capital.

chapitre [ʃapitr] nm chapter; **sur le c. de** on the subject of. **◆chapitrer** vt to scold, lecture.

chaque [ʃak] a each, every.

char [ʃar] nm Hist chariot; (de carnaval)

float; *Can Fam* car; **c. à bœufs** oxcart; **c. (d'assaut)** *Mil* tank.

charabia [ʃarabja] *nm Fam* gibberish.

charade [ʃarad] *nf (énigme)* riddle; *(mimée)* charade.

charbon [ʃarbɔ̃] *nm* coal; *(fusain)* charcoal; **c. de bois** charcoal; **sur des charbons ardents** like a cat on hot bricks. ◆**charbonnages** *nmpl* coalmines, collieries. ◆**charbonnier, -ière** *a* coal-; – *nm* coal merchant.

charcuter [ʃarkyte] *vt (opérer) Fam Péj* to cut up (badly).

charcuterie [ʃarkytri] *nf* pork butcher's shop; *(aliment)* cooked (pork) meats. ◆**charcutier, -ière** *nmf* pork butcher.

chardon [ʃardɔ̃] *nm Bot* thistle.

chardonneret [ʃardɔnrɛ] *nm (oiseau)* goldfinch.

charge [ʃarʒ] *nf (poids)* load; *(fardeau)* burden; *Jur Él Mil* charge; *(fonction)* office; *pl Fin* financial obligations; *(dépenses)* expenses; *(de locataire)* (maintenance) charges; **charges sociales** national insurance contributions, *Am* Social Security contributions; **à c.** *(enfant, parent)* dependent; **être à c.** to be a burden to s.o.; **à la c. de qn** *(personne)* dependent on s.o.; *(frais)* payable by s.o.; **prendre en c.** to take charge of, take responsibility for.

charg/er [ʃarʒe] *vt* to load; *Él Mil* to charge; *(passager) Fam* to pick up; **se c. de** *(enfant, tâche etc)* to take charge of; **c. qn de** *(impôts etc)* to burden s.o. with; *(paquets etc)* to load s.o. with; *(tâche etc)* to entrust s.o. with; **c. qn de faire** to instruct s.o. to do. ◆**—é, -ée** *a (personne, véhicule, arme etc)* loaded; *(journée etc)* heavy, busy; *(langue)* coated; **c. de** *(arbre, navire etc)* laden with; – *nmf* **c. de cours** *Univ* (temporary) lecturer. ◆**—ement** *nm (action)* loading; *(objet)* load. ◆**—eur** *nm (de piles)* charger.

chariot [ʃarjo] *nm (à bagages etc)* trolley, *Am* cart; *(de ferme)* waggon; *(de machine à écrire)* carriage.

charité [ʃarite] *nf (vertu, secours)* charity; *(acte)* act of charity; **faire la c.** to give to charity; **faire la c. à** *(mendiant)* to give to. ◆**charitable** *a* charitable.

charivari [ʃarivari] *nm Fam* hubbub, hullabaloo.

charlatan [ʃarlatɑ̃] *nm* charlatan, quack.

charme [ʃarm] *nm* **1** charm; *(magie)* spell. **2** *(arbre)* hornbeam. ◆**charm/er** *vt* to charm; **je suis charmé de vous voir** I'm delighted to see you. ◆**—ant** *a* charming.

◆**—eur, -euse** *nmf* charmer; – *a* engaging.

charnel, -elle [ʃarnɛl] *a* carnal.

charnier [ʃarnje] *nm* mass grave.

charnière [ʃarnjɛr] *nf* hinge; *Fig* meeting point (**de** between).

charnu [ʃarny] *a* fleshy.

charogne [ʃarɔɲ] *nf* carrion.

charpente [ʃarpɑ̃t] *nf* frame(work); *(de personne)* build. ◆**charpenté** *a* **bien c.** solidly built. ◆**charpenterie** *nf* carpentry. ◆**charpentier** *nm* carpenter.

charpie [ʃarpi] *nf* **mettre en c.** *(déchirer)* & *Fig* to tear to shreds.

charrette [ʃarɛt] *nf* cart. ◆**charretier** *nm* carter. ◆**charrier 1** *vt (transporter)* to cart; *(rivière)* to carry along, wash down *(sand etc)*. **2** *vti (taquiner) Fam* to tease.

charrue [ʃary] *nf* plough, *Am* plow.

charte [ʃart] *nf Pol* charter.

charter [ʃarter] *nm Av* charter (flight).

chas [ʃa] *nm* eye *(of a needle)*.

chasse [ʃas] *nf* **1** hunting, hunt; *(poursuite)* chase; *Av* fighter forces; **de c.** *(pilote, avion)* fighter-; **c. sous-marine** underwater (harpoon) fishing; **c. à courre** hunting; **tableau de c.** *(animaux abattus)* bag; **faire la c. à** to hunt down, hunt for; **donner la c. à** to give chase to; **c. à l'homme** manhunt. **2** **c. d'eau** toilet flush; **tirer la c.** to flush the toilet.

châsse [ʃas] *nf* shrine.

chassé-croisé [ʃasekrwaze] *nm (pl chassés-croisés)* *Fig* confused coming(s) and going(s).

chass/er [ʃase] *vt (animal)* to hunt; *(papillon)* to chase; *(faire partir)* to drive out *ou* off; *(employé)* to dismiss; *(mouche)* to brush away; *(odeur)* to get rid of; – *vi* to hunt; *Aut* to skid. ◆**—eur, -euse** *nmf* hunter; – *nm (domestique)* pageboy, bellboy; *Av* fighter; **c. à pied** infantryman. ◆**chasse-neige** *nm inv* snowplough, *Am* snowplow.

châssis [ʃasi] *nm* frame; *Aut* chassis.

chaste [ʃast] *a* chaste, pure. ◆**chasteté** *nf* chastity.

chat, chatte [ʃa, ʃat] *nmf* cat; **un c. dans la gorge** a frog in one's throat; **d'autres chats à fouetter** other fish to fry; **pas un c.** not a soul; **ma (petite) chatte** my darling; **c. perché** *(jeu)* tag.

châtaigne [ʃatɛɲ] *nf* chestnut. ◆**châtaignier** *nm* chestnut tree. ◆**châtain** *a inv* (chestnut) brown.

château, -x [ʃato] *nm (forteresse)* castle; *(palais)* palace, stately home; **c. fort** fortified castle; **châteaux en Espagne** *Fig* castles in the air; **c. d'eau** water tower; **c. de cartes** house of cards. ◆**châtelain, -aine** *nmf* lord of the manor, lady of the manor.

châtier [ʃɑtje] *vt Litt* to chastise, castigate; *(style)* to refine.

châtiment [ʃɑtimɑ̃] *nm* punishment.

chaton [ʃatɔ̃] *nm* **1** *(chat)* kitten. **2** *(de bague)* setting, mounting. **3** *Bot* catkin.

chatouill/er [ʃatuje] *vt (pour faire rire)* to tickle; *(exciter, plaire à) Fig* to titillate. ◆**—ement** *nm* tickle; *(action)* tickling. ◆**chatouilleux, -euse** *a* ticklish; *(irritable)* touchy.

chatoyer [ʃatwaje] *vi* to glitter, sparkle.

châtrer [ʃɑtre] *vt* to castrate.

chatte [ʃat] *voir* **chat**.

chatteries [ʃatri] *nfpl* cuddles; *(friandises)* delicacies.

chatterton [ʃatɛrtɔn] *nm* adhesive insulating tape.

chaud [ʃo] *a* hot; *(doux)* warm; *(fervent) Fig* warm; **pleurer à chaudes larmes** to cry bitterly; *— nm* heat; warmth; **avoir c.** to be hot; to be warm; **il fait c.** it's hot; it's warm; **être au c.** to be in the warm(th); **ça ne me fait ni c. ni froid** it leaves me indifferent. ◆**chaudement** *adv* warmly; *(avec passion)* hotly.

chaudière [ʃodjɛr] *nf* boiler.

chaudron [ʃodrɔ̃] *nm* cauldron.

chauffard [ʃofar] *nm* road hog, reckless driver.

chauff/er [ʃofe] *vt* to heat up, warm up; *(métal etc) Tech* to heat; *— vi* to heat up, warm up; *Aut* to overheat; **ça va c.** *Fam* things are going to hot up; *— se c. vpr* to warm oneself up. ◆**—ant** *a (couverture)* electric; *(plaque)* hot-; *(surface)* heating. ◆**—age** *nm* heating. ◆**—eur** *nm* **1** *(de chaudière)* stoker. **2** *Aut* driver; *(employé, domestique)* chauffeur. ◆**chauffe-bain** *nm*, ◆**chauffe-eau** *nm inv* water heater. ◆**chauffe-plats** *nm inv* hotplate.

chaume [ʃom] *nm (tiges coupées)* stubble, straw; *(pour toiture)* thatch; **toit de c.** thatched roof. ◆**chaumière** *nf* thatched cottage.

chaussée [ʃose] *nf* road(way).

chausser [ʃose] *vt (chaussures)* to put on; *(fournir)* to supply in footwear; **c. qn** to put shoes on (to) s.o.; **c. du 40** to take a size 40 shoe; **ce soulier te chausse bien** this shoe fits (you) well; *— se c. vpr* to put on one's shoes. ◆**chausse-pied** *nm* shoehorn. ◆**chausson** *nm* slipper; *(de danse)* shoe; **c. (aux pommes)** apple turnover. ◆**chaus-**

-sure *nf* shoe; *pl* shoes, footwear; **chaussures à semelles compensées** platform shoes.

chaussette [ʃosɛt] *nf* sock.

chauve [ʃov] *a & nmf* bald (person).

chauve-souris [ʃovsuri] *nf (pl chauves-souris) (animal)* bat.

chauvin, -ine [ʃovɛ̃, -in] *a & nmf* chauvinist.

chaux [ʃo] *nf* lime; **blanc de c.** whitewash.

chavirer [ʃavire] *vti Nau* to capsize.

chef [ʃɛf] *nm* **1 de son propre c.** on one's own authority. **2** leader; head; *(de tribu)* chief; *Culin* chef; en c. *(commandant, rédacteur)* in chief; **c'est un c.!** *(personne remarquable)* he's an ace!; **c. d'atelier** *(shop)* foreman; **c. de bande** ringleader, gang leader; **c. d'entreprise** company head; **c. d'équipe** foreman; **c. d'État** head of state; **c. d'état-major** chief of staff; **c. de famille** head of the family; **c. de file** leader; **c. de gare** stationmaster; **c. d'orchestre** conductor. ◆**chef-lieu** *nm (pl chefs-lieux)* chief town *(d'un département)*.

chef-d'œuvre [ʃɛdœvr] *nm (pl chefs-d'œuvre)* masterpiece.

chemin [ʃ(ə)mɛ̃] *nm* **1** road, path; *(trajet, direction)* way; **beaucoup de c. à faire** a long way to go; **dix minutes de c.** ten minutes' walk; **se mettre en c.** to start out, set out; **faire du c.** to come a long way; *(idée)* to make considerable headway; **c. faisant** on the way; **à mi-c.** half-way. **2 c. de fer** railway, *Am* railroad. ◆**chemin/er** *vi* to proceed; *(péniblement)* to trudge (along) on foot; *(évoluer) Fig* to progress. ◆**—ement** *nm Fig* progress. ◆**cheminot** *nm* railway *ou Am* railroad employee.

cheminée [ʃ(ə)mine] *nf (sur le toit)* chimney; *(de navire)* funnel; *(âtre)* fireplace; *(encadrement)* mantelpiece.

chemise [ʃ(ə)miz] *nf* shirt; *(couverture cartonnée)* folder; **c. de nuit** nightdress. ◆**chemiserie** *nf* men's shirt (and underwear) shop. ◆**chemisette** *nf* short-sleeved shirt. ◆**chemisier** *nm (vêtement)* blouse.

chenal, -aux [ʃənal, -o] *nm* channel.

chenapan [ʃ(ə)napɑ̃] *nm Hum* rogue, scoundrel.

chêne [ʃɛn] *nm (arbre, bois)* oak.

chenet [ʃ(ə)nɛ] *nm* firedog, andiron.

chenil [ʃ(ə)ni(l)] *nm* kennels.

chenille [ʃ(ə)nij] *nf* caterpillar; *(de char) Mil* caterpillar track.

cheptel [ʃɛptɛl] *nm* livestock.

chèque [ʃɛk] *nm* cheque, *Am* check; **c. de voyage** traveller's cheque, *Am* traveler's check. ◆**c.-repas** nm (pl **chèques-repas**) luncheon voucher. ◆**chéquier** nm cheque book, Am checkbook.

cher, chère [ʃɛr] 1 a (aimé) dear (à to); − nmf **mon c.** my dear fellow; **ma chère** my dear (woman). 2 a (coûteux) dear, expensive; (quartier, hôtel etc) expensive; **la vie chère** the high cost of living; **payer c.** (objet) to pay a lot for; (erreur) Fig to pay dearly for. ◆**chèrement** adv dearly.

cherch/er [ʃɛrʃe] vt to look for, search for; (du secours, la paix etc) to seek; (dans un dictionnaire) to look up; **c. ses mots** to fumble for one's words; **aller c.** to (go and) fetch ou get; **c. à faire** to attempt to do; **tu l'as bien cherché!** it's your own fault!, you asked for it! ◆**—eur, -euse** nmf research worker; **c. d'or** gold-digger.

chér/ir [ʃerir] vt to cherish. ◆**—i, -ie** a dearly loved, beloved; − nmf darling.

chérot [ʃero] am Fam pricey.

cherté [ʃɛrte] nf high cost, expensiveness.

chétif, -ive [ʃetif, -iv] a puny; (dérisoire) wretched.

cheval, -aux [ʃ(ə)val, -o] nm horse; **c.** (vapeur) Aut horsepower; **à c.** on horse-back; **faire du c.** to go horse riding; **à c. sur** straddling; **à c. sur les principes** a stickler for principle; **monter sur ses grands chevaux** to get excited; **c. à bascule** rocking horse; **c. d'arçons** Sp vaulting horse; **c. de bataille** (dada) hobbyhorse; **chevaux de bois** (manège) merry-go-round. ◆**chevaleresque** a chivalrous. ◆**chevalier** nm knight. ◆**chevalin** a equine; (boucherie) horse-.

chevalet [ʃ(ə)valɛ] nm easel; Mus trestle.

chevalière [ʃ(ə)valjɛr] nf signet ring.

chevauchée [ʃ(ə)voʃe] nf (horse) ride.

chevaucher [ʃ(ə)voʃe] vt to straddle; − vi, − **se c.** vpr to overlap.

chevet [ʃ(ə)vɛ] nm bedhead; **table/livre de c.** bedside table/book; **au c. de** at the bedside of.

cheveu, -x [ʃ(ə)vø] nm **un c.** a hair; **les cheveux** hair; **couper les cheveux en quatre** Fig to split hairs; **tiré par les cheveux** (argument) far-fetched. ◆**chevelu** a hairy. ◆**chevelure** nf (head of) hair.

cheville [ʃ(ə)vij] nf Anat ankle; Menuis peg, pin; (pour vis) (wall)plug; **c. ouvrière** Aut et Fig linchpin; **en c. avec** Fam in cahoots with. ◆**cheviller** vt Menuis to pin, peg.

chèvre [ʃɛvr] nf goat; (femelle) nanny-goat. ◆**chevreau, -x** nm kid.

chèvrefeuille [ʃɛvrəfœj] nm honeysuckle.

chevreuil [ʃəvrœj] nm roe deer; Culin venison.

chevron [ʃəvrɔ̃] nm (poutre) rafter; Mil stripe, chevron; **à chevrons** (tissu, veste etc) herringbone.

chevronné [ʃəvrɔne] a seasoned, experienced.

chevroter [ʃəvrɔte] vi to quaver, tremble.

chez [ʃe] prép **c. qn** at s.o.'s house, flat etc; **il est c. Jean/c. l'épicier** he's at John's (place)/at the grocer's; **il va c. Jean/c. l'épicier** he's going to John's (place)/to the grocer's; **je vais c. moi/c. nous** at home; **je vais c. moi** I'm going home; **c. les Suisses/les jeunes** among the Swiss/the young; **c. Camus** in Camus; **c. l'homme** in man; **une habitude c. elle** a habit with her; **c. Mme Dupont** (adresse) care of ou c/o Mme Dupont. ◆**c.-soi** nm inv **un c.-soi** a home (of one's own).

chialer [ʃjale] vi (pleurer) Fam to cry.

chic [ʃik] 1 a inv stylish, smart; (gentil) Fam decent, nice; − int **c. (alors)!** great!; − nm style, elegance. 2 nm **avoir le c. pour faire** to have the knack of doing.

chicane [ʃikan] 1 nf (querelle) quibble. 2 nfpl (obstacles) zigzag barriers. ◆**chicaner** vt to quibble with (s.o.); − vi to quibble.

chiche [ʃiʃ] 1 a mean, niggardly; **c. de** sparing of. 2 int (défi) Fam I bet you I do, can etc; **c. que je parte sans lui** I bet I leave without him.

chichis [ʃiʃi] nmpl **faire des c.** to make a lot of fuss.

chicorée [ʃikɔre] nf (à café) chicory; (pour salade) endive.

chien [ʃjɛ̃] nm dog; **c. d'arrêt** pointer, retriever; **un mal de c.** a hell of a job; **temps de c.** filthy weather; **vie de c.** Fig dog's life; **entre c. et loup** at dusk, in the gloaming. ◆**c.-loup** nm (pl **chiens-loups**) wolfhound. ◆**chienne** nf dog, bitch.

chiendent [ʃjɛ̃dɑ̃] nm Bot couch grass.

chiffon [ʃifɔ̃] nm rag; **c. (à poussière)** duster. ◆**chiffonner** vt to crumple; (ennuyer) Fig to bother, distress. ◆**chiffonnier** nm ragman.

chiffre [ʃifr] nm figure, number; (romain, arabe) numeral; (code) cipher; **c. d'affaires** Fin turnover. ◆**chiffrer** vt (montant) to assess, work out; (message) to cipher, code; − vi to mount up; **se c. à** to amount to, work out at.

chignon [ʃiɲɔ̃] nm bun, chignon.

Chili [ʃili] nm Chile. ◆**chilien, -ienne** a & nmf Chilean.

chimère [ʃimɛr] nf fantasy, (wild) dream. ◆chimérique a fanciful.

chimie [ʃimi] nf chemistry. ◆chimique a chemical. ◆chimiste nmf (research) chemist.

chimpanzé [ʃɛ̃pɑ̃ze] nm chimpanzee.

Chine [ʃin] nf China. ◆chinois, -oise a & nmf Chinese; – nm (langue) Chinese. ◆chinoiser vi to quibble. ◆chinoiserie nf (objet) Chinese curio; pl (bizarreries) Fig weird complications.

chiner [ʃine] vi (brocanteur etc) to hunt for bargains.

chiot [ʃjo] nm pup(py).

chiper [ʃipe] vt Fam to swipe, pinch (à from).

chipie [ʃipi] nf vieille c. (femme) Péj old crab.

chipoter [ʃipɔte] vi 1 (manger) to nibble. 2 (chicaner) to quibble.

chips [ʃips] nmpl (potato) crisps, Am chips.

chiquenaude [ʃiknod] nf flick (of the finger).

chiromancie [kirɔmɑ̃si] nf palmistry.

chirurgie [ʃiryrʒi] nf surgery. ◆chirurgical, -aux a surgical. ◆chirurgien nm surgeon.

chlore [klɔr] nm chlorine. ◆chloroforme nm chloroform. ◆chlorure nm chloride.

choc [ʃɔk] nm (heurt) impact, shock; (émotion) & Méd shock; (collision) crash; (des opinions, entre manifestants etc) clash.

chocolat [ʃɔkɔla] nm chocolate; c. à croquer plain ou Am bittersweet chocolate; c. au lait milk chocolate; c. glacé choc-ice; – a inv chocolate(-coloured). ◆chocolaté a chocolate-flavoured.

chœur [kœr] nm (chanteurs, nef) Rel choir; (composition musicale) & Fig chorus; en c. (all) together, in chorus.

choir [ʃwar] vi laisser c. qn Fam to turn one's back on s.o.

chois/ir [ʃwazir] vt to choose, pick, select. ◆—i a (œuvres) selected; (terme, langage) well-chosen; (public) select. ◆choix nm choice; (assortiment) selection; morceau de c. choice piece; au c. du client according to choice.

choléra [kɔlera] nm cholera.

cholestérol [kɔlesterɔl] nm cholesterol.

chôm/er [ʃome] vi (ouvrier etc) to be unemployed; jour chômé (public) holiday. ◆—age nm unemployment; en ou au c. unemployed; mettre en c. technique to lay off, dismiss.

chope [ʃɔp] nf beer mug, tankard; (contenu) pint.

choqu/er [ʃoke] vt to offend, shock; (verres) to clink; (commotionner) to shake up. ◆—ant a shocking, offensive.

choral, mpl -als [kɔral] a choral. ◆chorale nf choral society. ◆choriste nmf chorister.

chorégraphe [kɔregraf] nmf choreographer. ◆chorégraphie nf choreography.

chose [ʃoz] nf thing; état de choses state of affairs; par la force des choses through force of circumstance; dis-lui bien des choses de ma part remember me to him ou her; ce monsieur C. that Mr What's-his-name; se sentir tout c. Fam (décontenancé) to feel all funny; (malade) to feel out of sorts.

chou, -x [ʃu] nm cabbage; choux de Bruxelles Brussels sprouts; mon c.! my pet!; c. à la crème cream puff. ◆c.-fleur nm (pl choux-fleurs) cauliflower.

choucas [ʃuka] nm jackdaw.

chouchou, -oute [ʃuʃu, -ut] nmf (favori) Fam pet, darling. ◆chouchouter vt to pamper.

choucroute [ʃukrut] nf sauerkraut.

chouette [ʃwɛt] 1 nf (oiseau) owl. 2 a (chic) Fam super, great.

choyer [ʃwaye] vt to pet, pamper.

chrétien, -ienne [kretjɛ̃, -jɛn] a & nmf Christian. ◆chrétienté nf Christendom. ◆Christ [krist] nm Christ. ◆christianisme nm Christianity.

chrome [krom] nm chromium, chrome. ◆chromé a chromium-plated.

chromosome [krɔmozom] nm chromosome.

chronique [krɔnik] 1 a (malade, chômage etc) chronic. 2 nf (annales) chronicle; Journ report, news; (rubrique) column. ◆chroniqueur nm chronicler; Journ reporter, columnist.

chronologie [krɔnɔlɔʒi] nf chronology. ◆chronologique a chronological.

chronomètre [krɔnɔmɛtr] nm stopwatch. ◆chronométr/er vt Sp to time. ◆—eur nm Sp timekeeper.

chrysanthème [krizɑ̃tɛm] nm chrysanthemum.

chuchot/er [ʃyʃɔte] vti to whisper. ◆—ement nm whisper(ing). ◆chuchoteries nfpl Fam whispering.

chuinter [ʃɥɛ̃te] vi (vapeur) to hiss.

chut! [ʃyt] int sh!, hush!

chute [ʃyt] nf fall; (défaite) (down)fall; c. d'eau waterfall; c. de neige snowfall; c. de pluie rainfall; c. des cheveux hair loss. ◆chuter vi Fam to fall.

Chypre [ʃipr] *nf* Cyprus. ◆**chypriote** *a* & *nmf* Cypriot.

ci [si] **1** *adv* **par-ci par-là** here and there. **2** *pron détem* **celui ci comme ça** so so. **3** *voir* **ce²**, **celui**.

ci-après [siapʀɛ] *adv* below, hereafter. ◆**ci-contre** *adv* opposite. ◆**ci-dessous** *adv* below. ◆**ci-dessus** *adv* above. ◆**ci-gît** here lies (*on gravestones*). ◆**ci-inclus** *a*, ◆**ci-joint** *a* (*inv before n*) (*dans une lettre*) enclosed (herewith).

cible [sibl] *nf* target.

ciboulette [sibulɛt] *nf* Culin chives.

cicatrice [sikatris] *nf* scar. ◆**cicatriser** *vt*, **— se c.** *vpr* to heal up (*leaving a scar*).

cidre [sidr] *nm* cider.

Cie *abrév* (*compagnie*) Co.

ciel [sjɛl] *nm* **1** (*pl* **ciels**) sky; **à c. ouvert** (*piscine etc*) open-air; **c. de lit** canopy. **2** (*pl* **cieux** [sjø]) *Rel* heaven; **juste c.!** good heavens!; **sous d'autres cieux** *Hum* in other climes.

cierge [sjɛrʒ] *nm* *Rel* candle.

cigale [sigal] *nf* (*insecte*) cicada.

cigare [sigar] *nm* cigar. ◆**cigarette** *nf* cigarette.

cigogne [sigɔɲ] *nf* stork.

cil [sil] *nm* (eye)lash.

cime [sim] *nf* (*d'un arbre*) top; (*d'une montagne*) summit; & *Fig* peak.

ciment [simã] *nm* cement. ◆**cimenter** *vt* to cement.

cimetière [simtjɛr] *nm* cemetery, graveyard; **c. de voitures** scrapyard, breaker's yard, *Am* auto graveyard.

ciné [sine] *nm* *Fam* cinema. ◆**c.-club** *nm* film society. ◆**cinéaste** *nm* film maker. ◆**cinéphile** *nmf* film buff.

cinéma [sinema] *nm* cinema; **faire du c.** to make films. ◆**cinémascope** *nm* cinemascope. ◆**cinémathèque** *nf* film library; (*salle*) film theatre. ◆**cinématographique** *a* cinema-.

cinglé [sɛ̃gle] *a* *Fam* crazy.

cingl/er [sɛ̃gle] *vt* to lash. ◆**—ant** *a* (*vent, remarque*) cutting, biting.

cinoche [sinɔʃ] *nm* *Fam* cinema.

cinq [sɛ̃k] *nm* five; *– a* ([sɛ̃] *before consonant*) five. ◆**cinquième** *a* & *nmf* fifth; **un c. a** fifth.

cinquante [sɛ̃kɑ̃t] *a* & *nm* fifty. ◆**cinquantaine** *nf* about fifty. ◆**cinquantenaire** *a* & *nmf* fifty-year-old (person); *– nm* fiftieth anniversary. ◆**cinquantième** *a* & *nmf* fiftieth.

cintre [sɛ̃tr] *nm* coathanger; *Archit* arch. ◆**cintré** *a* arched; (*veste etc*) tailored, slim-fitting.

cirage [siraʒ] *nm* (shoe) polish.

circoncis [sirkɔ̃si] *a* circumcised. ◆**circoncision** *nf* circumcision.

circonférence [sirkɔ̃feʀɑ̃s] *nf* circumference.

circonflexe [sirkɔ̃flɛks] *a* *Gram* circumflex.

circonlocution [sirkɔ̃lɔkysjɔ̃] *nf* circumlocution.

circonscrire [sirkɔ̃skrir] *vt* to circumscribe. ◆**circonscription** *nf* division; **c.** (**électorale**) constituency.

circonspect, -ecte [sirkɔ̃spɛ(kt), -ɛkt] *a* cautious, circumspect. ◆**circonspection** *nf* caution.

circonstance [sirkɔ̃stɑ̃s] *nf* circumstance; **pour/en la c.** for/on this occasion; **de c.** (*habit, parole etc*) appropriate. ◆**circonstancié** *a* detailed. ◆**circonstanciel, -ielle** *a* *Gram* adverbial.

circonvenir [sirkɔ̃vnir] *vt* to circumvent.

circuit [sirkɥi] *nm* *Sp* *Él* *Fin* circuit; (*périple*) tour, trip; (*détour*) roundabout way; *pl* *Él* circuitry, circuits.

circulaire [sirkylɛr] *a* circular; *– nf* (*lettre*) circular. ◆**circulation** *nf* circulation; *Aut* traffic. ◆**circuler** *vi* to circulate; (*véhicule, train*) to move, travel; (*passant*) to walk about; (*rumeur*) to go round, circulate; **faire c.** to circulate; (*piétons etc*) to move on; **circulez!** keep moving!

cire [sir] *nf* wax; (*pour meubles*) polish, wax. ◆**cir/er** *vt* to polish, wax. ◆**—é** *nm* (*vêtement*) oilskin(s). ◆**—eur** *nm* bootblack. ◆**—euse** *nf* (*appareil*) floor polisher. ◆**cireux, -euse** *a* waxy.

cirque [sirk] *nm* *Th* *Hist* circus.

cirrhose [siroz] *nf* *Méd* cirrhosis.

cisaille(s) [sizaj] *nf*(*pl*) shears. ◆**ciseau, -x** *nm* chisel; *pl* scissors. ◆**ciseler** *vt* to chisel.

citadelle [sitadɛl] *nf* citadel.

cité [site] *nf* city; **c.** (**ouvrière**) housing estate (*for workers*), *Am* housing project *ou* development; **c. universitaire** (students') halls of residence. ◆**citadin, -ine** *nmf* city dweller; *– a* city-, urban.

citer [site] *vt* to quote; *Jur* to summon; *Mil* to mention, cite. ◆**citation** *nf* quotation; *Jur* summons; *Mil* mention, citation.

citerne [sitɛrn] *nf* (*réservoir*) tank.

cithare [sitar] *nf* zither.

citoyen, -enne [sitwajɛ̃, -ɛn] *nmf* citizen. ◆**citoyenneté** *nf* citizenship.

citron [sitrɔ̃] *nm* lemon; **c. pressé** (fresh)

lemon juice. ◆**citronnade** *nf* lemon drink, (still) lemonade.

citrouille [sitruj] *nf* pumpkin.

civet [sive] *nm* stew; **c. de lièvre** jugged hare.

civière [sivjεr] *nf* stretcher.

civil [sivil] **1** *a* (*droits, guerre, mariage etc*) civil; (*non militaire*) civilian; (*courtois*) civil; **année civile** calendar year. **2** *nm* civilian; **dans le c.** in civilian life; **en c.** (*policier*) in plain clothes; (*soldat*) in civilian clothes. ◆**civilité** *nf* civility.

civiliser [sivilize] *vt* to civilize; **— se c.** *vpr* to become civilized. ◆**civilisation** *nf* civilization.

civique [sivik] *a* civic; **instruction c.** *Scol* civics. ◆**civisme** *nm* civic sense.

clair [klεr] *a* (*distinct, limpide, évident*) clear; (*éclairé*) light; (*pâle*) light(-coloured); (*sauce, chevelure*) thin; **bleu/vert c.** light blue/green; **il fait c.** it's light *ou* bright; **— *adv* (*voir*) clearly; **— *nm* **c. de lune** moonlight; **le plus c. de** the major *ou* greater part of; **tirer au c.** (*question etc*) to clear up. ◆**—ement** *adv* clearly. ◆**claire-voie** *nf* à **c.-voie** (*barrière*) lattice-; (*caisse*) openwork; (*porte*) louvre(d).

clairière [klεrjεr] *nf* clearing, glade.

clairon [klεrɔ̃] *nm* bugle; (*soldat*) bugler. ◆**claironner** *vt* (*annoncer*) to trumpet forth.

clairsemé [klεrsəme] *a* sparse.

clairvoyant [klεrvwajɑ̃] *a* (*perspicace*) clear-sighted. ◆**clairvoyance** *nf* clear-sightedness.

clam/er [klame] *vt* to cry out. ◆**—eur** *nf* clamour, outcry.

clan [klɑ̃] *nm* clan, clique, set.

clandestin [klɑ̃dεstε̃] *a* secret, clandestine; (*journal, mouvement*) underground; **passager c.** stowaway.

clapet [klapε] *nm Tech* valve; (*bouche*) *Arg* trap.

clapier [klapje] *nm* (rabbit) hutch.

clapot/er [klapɔte] *vi* (*vagues*) to lap. ◆**—ement** *nm*, ◆**clapotis** *nm* lap(ping).

claque [klak] *nf* smack, slap. ◆**claquer** *vt* (*porte*) to slam, bang; (*gifler*) to smack, slap; (*fouet*) to crack; (*fatiguer*) *Fam* to tire out; (*dépenser*) *Arg* to blow; **se c. un muscle** to tear a muscle; **faire c.** (*doigts*) to snap; (*langue*) to click; (*fouet*) to crack; **— *vi* (*porte*) to slam, bang; (*drapeau*) to flap; (*coup de revolver*) to ring out; (*mourir*) *Fam* to die; (*tomber en panne*) *Fam* to break down; **c. des mains** to clap one's hands; **elle claque des dents** her teeth are chattering.

claquemurer (se) [səklakmyre] *vpr* to shut oneself up, hole up.

claquettes [klakεt] *nfpl* tap dancing.

clarifier [klarifje] *vt* to clarify. ◆**clarification** *nf* clarification.

clarinette [klarinεt] *nf* clarinet.

clarté [klarte] *nf* light, brightness; (*précision*) clarity, clearness.

classe [klɑs] *nf* class; **aller en c.** to go to school; **c. ouvrière/moyenne** working/middle class; **avoir de la c.** to have class.

class/er [klɑse] *vt* to classify, class; (*papiers*) to file; (*candidats*) to grade; (*affaire*) to close; **se c. parmi** to rank *ou* be classed among; **se c. premier** to come first. ◆**—ement** *nm* classification; filing; grading; (*rang*) place; *Sp* placing. ◆**—eur** *nm* (*meuble*) filing cabinet; (*portefeuille*) (loose leaf) file. ◆**classification** *nf* classification. ◆**classifier** *vt* to classify.

classique [klasik] *a* classical; (*typique*) classic; **— *nm* (*œuvre, auteur*) classic. ◆**classicisme** *nm* classicism.

clause [kloz] *nf* clause.

claustrophobie [klostrɔfɔbi] *nf* claustrophobia. ◆**claustrophobe** *a* claustrophobic.

clavecin [klavsε̃] *nm Mus* harpsichord.

clavicule [klavikyl] *nf* collarbone.

clavier [klavje] *nm* keyboard.

clé, clef [kle] *nf* key; (*outil*) spanner, wrench; *Mus* clef; **fermer à c.** to lock; **sous c.** under lock and key; **c. de contact** ignition key; **c. de voûte** keystone; **poste/industrie c.** key post/industry; **clés en main** (*acheter une maison etc*) ready to move in; **prix clés en main** (*voiture*) on the road price.

clément [klemɑ̃] *a* (*temps*) mild, clement; (*juge*) lenient, clement. ◆**clémence** *nf* mildness; leniency; clemency.

clémentine [klemɑ̃tin] *nf* clementine.

clerc [klεr] *nm Rel* cleric; (*notaire*) clerk. ◆**clergé** *nm* clergy. ◆**clérical, -aux** *a Rel* clerical.

cliché [kliʃe] *nm Phot* negative; *Typ* plate; (*idée*) cliché.

client, -ente [klijɑ̃, -ɑ̃t] *nmf* (*de magasin etc*) customer; (*d'un avocat etc*) client; (*d'un médecin*) patient; (*d'hôtel*) guest. ◆**clientèle** *nf* customers, clientele; (*d'un avocat*) practice, clientele; (*d'un médecin*) practice, patients; **accorder sa c. à** to give one's custom to.

cligner [kliɲe] *vi* **c. des yeux** (*ouvrir et fermer*) to blink; (*fermer à demi*) to screw up one's eyes; **c. de l'œil** to wink.

◆**clignot/er** vi to blink; (lumière) to flicker; Aut to flash; (étoile) to twinkle. ◆**—ant** nm Aut indicator, Am directional signal.

climat [klima] nm Mét & Fig climate. ◆**climatique** a climatic. ◆**climatisation** nf air-conditioning. ◆**climatiser** vt to air-condition.

clin d'œil [klɛ̃dœj] nm wink; **en un c. d'œil** in the twinkling of an eye.

clinique [klinik] a clinical; – nf (hôpital) (private) clinic.

clinquant [klɛ̃kɑ̃] a tawdry.

clique [klik] nf Péj clique; Mus Mil (drum and bugle) band.

cliqueter [klikte] vi to clink. ◆**cliquetis** nm clink(ing).

clivage [klivaʒ] nm split, division (de in).

cloaque [klɔak] nm cesspool.

clochard, -arde [klɔʃar, -ard] nmf tramp, vagrant.

cloche [klɔʃ] nf 1 bell; **c. à fromage** cheese cover. **2** (personne) Fam idiot, oaf. ◆**clocher 1** nm bell tower; (en pointe) steeple; **de c.** Fig parochial; **esprit de c.** parochialism. **2** vi to be wrong ou amiss. ◆**clochette** nf (small) bell.

cloche-pied (à) [aklɔʃpje] adv **sauter à c.-pied** to hop on one foot.

cloison [klwazɔ̃] nf partition; Fig barrier. ◆**cloisonner** vt to partition; (activités etc) Fig to compartmentalize.

cloître [klwatr] nm cloister. ◆**se cloître** vpr to shut oneself away, cloister oneself.

clopin-clopant [klɔpɛ̃klɔpɑ̃] adv **aller c.-clopant** to hobble.

cloque [klɔk] nf blister.

clore [klɔr] vt (débat, lettre) to close. ◆**clos** a (incident etc) closed; (espace) enclosed; – nm (enclosed) field.

clôture [klotyr] nf (barrière) enclosure, fence; (fermeture) closing. ◆**clôturer** vt to enclose; (compte, séance etc) to close.

clou [klu] nm nail; (furoncle) boil; **le c.** (du spectacle) Fam the star attraction; **les clous** (passage) pedestrian crossing; **des clous!** Fam nothing at all! ◆**clouer** vt to nail; **cloué au lit** confined to (one's) bed; **cloué sur place** nailed to the spot; **c. le bec à qn** Fam to shut s.o. up. ◆**clouté** a (chaussures) hobnailed; (ceinture, pneus) studded; **passage c.** pedestrian crossing, Am crosswalk.

clown [klun] nm clown.

club [klœb] nm (association) club.

cm abrév (centimètre) cm.

co- [kɔ] préf co-.

coaguler (se) [kɔagyle] vti, – **se c.** vpr to coagulate.

coaliser (se) [kɔalize] vpr to form a coalition, join forces. ◆**coalition** nf coalition.

coasser [kɔase] vi (grenouille) to croak.

cobaye [kɔbaj] nm (animal) & Fig guinea pig.

cobra [kɔbra] nm (serpent) cobra.

coca [kɔka] nm (Coca-Cola®) coke.

cocagne [kɔkaɲ] nf **pays de c.** dreamland, land of plenty.

cocaïne [kɔkain] nf cocain.

cocarde [kɔkard] nf rosette, cockade; Av roundel. ◆**cocardier, -ière** a Péj flag-waving.

cocasse [kɔkas] a droll, comical. ◆**cocasserie** nf drollery.

coccinelle [kɔksinel] nf ladybird, Am ladybug.

cocher[1] [kɔʃe] vt to tick (off), Am to check (off).

cocher[2] [kɔʃe] nm coachman. ◆**cochère** af **porte c.** main gateway.

cochon, -onne [kɔʃɔ̃, -ɔn] **1** nm pig; (mâle) hog; **c. d'Inde** guinea pig. **2** nmf (personne sale) (dirty) pig; (salaud) swine; – a (histoire, film) dirty, filthy. ◆**cochonnerie(s)** nf(pl) (obscénité(s)) filth; (pacotille) Fam rubbish.

cocktail [kɔktel] nm (boisson) cocktail; (réunion) cocktail party.

coco [kɔko] nm **noix de c.** coconut. ◆**cocotier** nm coconut palm.

cocon [kɔkɔ̃] nm cocoon.

cocorico [kɔkɔriko] int & nm cock-a-doodle-doo; **faire c.** (crier victoire) Fam to give three cheers for France, wave the flag.

cocotte [kɔkɔt] nf (marmite) casserole; **c. minute®** pressure cooker.

cocu [kɔky] nm Fam cuckold.

code [kɔd] nm code; **codes, phares c.** Aut dipped headlights, Am low beams; **C. de la route** Highway Code. ◆**coder** vt to code. ◆**codifier** vt to codify.

coefficient [kɔefisjɑ̃] nm Math coefficient; (d'erreur, de sécurité) Fig margin.

coéquipier, -ière [kɔekipje, -jɛr] nmf team mate.

cœur [kœr] nm heart; Cartes hearts; **au c.** (de ville, hiver etc) in the heart of; **par c.** by heart; **ça me (sou)lève le c.** that turns my stomach; **à c. ouvert** (opération) open-heart; (parler) freely; **avoir mal au c.** to feel sick; **avoir le c. gros ou serré** to have a heavy heart; **ça me tient à c.** that's close to my heart; **avoir bon c.** to be kind-hearted; **de bon c.** (*offrir*) with a good heart, willingly; (*rire*) heartily; **si le c. vous en dit** if you so desire.

coexister [kɔɛɡziste] *vi* to coexist. ◆**coexistence** *nf* coexistence.

coffre [kɔfr] *nm* chest, (*de banque*) safe; (*de voiture*) boot, *Am* trunk; (*d'autocar*) luggage *ou Am* baggage compartment. ◆**c.-fort** *nm* (*pl* coffres-forts) safe. ◆**coffret** *nm* casket, box.

cogiter [kɔʒite] *vi Iron* to cogitate.

cognac [kɔɲak] *nm* cognac.

cogner [kɔɲe] *vti* to knock; **c. qn** *Arg* (*frapper*) to thump s.o.; (*tabasser*) to beat s.o. up; **se c. la tête**/*etc* to knock one's head/*etc*.

cohabiter [kɔabite] *vi* to live together. ◆**cohabitation** *nf* living together; *Pol Fam* power sharing.

cohérent [kɔerɑ̃] *a* coherent. ◆**cohérence** *nf* coherence. ◆**cohésion** *nf* cohesion, cohesiveness.

cohorte [kɔɔrt] *nf* (*groupe*) troop, band, cohort.

cohue [kɔy] *nf* crowd, mob.

coiffe [kwaf] *nf* headdress.

coiff/er [kwafe] *vt* (*chapeau*) to put on, wear; (*surmonter*) *Fig* to cap; (*être à la tête de*) to head; **c. qn** to do s.o.'s hair; **c. qn d'un chapeau** to put a hat on s.o.; — **se c.** *vpr* to do one's hair; **se c. d'un chapeau** to put on a hat. ◆**—eur, -euse**[1] *nmf* (*pour hommes*) barber, hairdresser; (*pour dames*) hairdresser. ◆**—euse**[2] *nf* dressing table. ◆**coiffure** *nf* headgear, hat; (*arrangement*) hairstyle; (*métier*) hairdressing.

coin [kwɛ̃] *nm* (*angle*) corner; (*endroit*) spot; (*de terre, de ciel*) patch; (*cale*) wedge; **du c.** (*magasin etc*) local; **dans le c.** in the (local) area; **au c. du feu** by the fireside; **petit c.** *Fam* loo, *Am* john.

coinc/er [kwɛ̃se] *vt* (*mécanisme, tiroir*) to jam; (*caler*) to wedge; **c. qn** *Fam* to catch s.o., corner s.o.; — **se c.** *vpr* (*mécanisme etc*) to get jammed *ou* stuck. ◆**—é** *a* (*tiroir etc*) stuck, jammed; (*personne*) *Fam* stuck.

coïncider [kɔɛ̃side] *vi* to coincide. ◆**coïncidence** *nf* coincidence.

coin-coin [kwɛ̃kwɛ̃] *nm inv* (*de canard*) quack.

coing [kwɛ̃] *nm* (*fruit*) quince.

coke [kɔk] *nm* (*combustible*) coke.

col [kɔl] *nm* (*de chemise*) collar; (*de bouteille, & Anat*) neck; *Géog* pass; **c. roulé** polo neck, *Am* turtleneck.

colère [kɔlɛr] *nf* anger; **une c.** (*accès*) a fit of anger; **en c.** angry (**contre** with); **se mettre**

en c. to lose one's temper. ◆**coléreux, -euse** *a*, ◆**colérique** *a* quick-tempered.

colibri [kɔlibri] *nm* hummingbird.

colifichet [kɔlifiʃɛ] *nm* trinket.

colimaçon (en) [ɑ̃kɔlimasɔ̃] *adv* **escalier en c.** spiral staircase.

colin [kɔlɛ̃] *nm* (*poisson*) hake.

colique [kɔlik] *nf* diarrh(o)ea; (*douleur*) stomach pain, colic.

colis [kɔli] *nm* parcel, package.

collaborer [kɔlabɔre] *vi* to collaborate (**avec** with, **à** on); **c. à** (*journal*) to contribute to. ◆**collaborateur, -trice** *nmf* collaborator; contributor. ◆**collaboration** *nf* collaboration; contribution.

collage [kɔlaʒ] *nm* (*œuvre*) collage.

collant [kɔlɑ̃] **1** *a* (*papier*) sticky; (*vêtement*) skin-tight; **être c.** (*importun*) *Fam* to be a pest. **2** *nm* (pair of) tights; (*de danse*) leotard.

collation [kɔlasjɔ̃] *nf* (*repas*) light meal.

colle [kɔl] *nf* (*transparente*) glue; (*blanche*) paste; (*question*) *Fam* poser, teaser; (*interrogation*) *Scol Arg* oral; (*retenue*) *Scol Arg* detention.

collecte [kɔlɛkt] *nf* (*quête*) collection. ◆**collect/er** *vt* to collect. ◆**—eur** *nm* collector; (*égout*) **c. main** sewer.

collectif, -ive [kɔlɛktif, -iv] *a* collective; (*hystérie, démission*) mass-; **billet c.** group ticket. ◆**collectivement** *adv* collectively. ◆**collectivisme** *nm* collectivism. ◆**collectivité** *nf* community, collectivity.

collection [kɔlɛksjɔ̃] *nf* collection. ◆**collectionn/er** *vt* (*timbres etc*) to collect. ◆**—eur, -euse** *nmf* collector.

collège [kɔlɛʒ] *nm* (secondary) school, *Am* (high) school; (*électoral, sacré*) college. ◆**collégien** *nm* schoolboy. ◆**collégienne** *nf* schoolgirl.

collègue [kɔlɛg] *nmf* colleague.

coller [kɔle] *vt* (*timbre etc*) to stick; (*à la colle transparente*) to glue; (*à la colle blanche*) to paste; (*affiche*) to stick up; (*papier peint*) to hang; (*mettre*) *Fam* to stick, shove; **c. contre** (*nez, oreille etc*) to press against; **c. qn** (*embarrasser*) *Fam* to stump s.o., catch s.o. out; (*consigner*) *Scol* to keep s.o. in; **être collé à** (*examen*) *Fam* to fail, flunk; **se c. contre** to cling (close) to; **se c. qn/qch** *Fam* to get stuck with s.o./sth.; — *vi* to stick, cling; **c. à** (*s'adapter*) to fit, correspond to; **ça colle!** *Fam* everything's just fine! ◆**colleur, -euse** *nmf* **c. d'affiches** billsticker.

collet [kɔlɛ] *nm* (*lacet*) snare; **prendre qn au c.** to grab s.o. by the scruff of the neck; **elle**

est/ils sont c. monté she is/they are prim and proper *ou* straight-laced.

collier [kɔlje] *nm* (*bijou*) necklace; (*de chien, cheval*) & *Tech* collar.

colline [kɔlin] *nf* hill.

collision [kɔlizjɔ̃] *nf* (*de véhicules*) collision; (*bagarre, conflit*) clash; **entrer en c. avec** to collide with.

colloque [kɔlɔk] *nm* symposium.

collusion [kɔlyzjɔ̃] *nf* collusion.

colmater [kɔlmate] *vt* (*fuite, fente*) to seal; (*trou*) to fill in; (*brèche*) *Mil* to close, seal.

colombe [kɔlɔ̃b] *nf* dove.

colon [kɔlɔ̃] *nm* settler, colonist; (*enfant*) child taking part in a holiday camp. ◆**colonial, -aux** *a* colonial. ◆**colonie** *nf* colony; **c. de vacances** (children's) holiday camp *ou Am* vacation camp.

coloniser [kɔlɔnize] *vt Pol* to colonize; (*peupler*) to settle. ◆**colonisateur, -trice** *a* colonizing; *nmf* colonizer. ◆**colonisation** *nf* colonization.

côlon [kɔlɔ̃] *nm Anat* colon.

colonel [kɔlɔnɛl] *nm* colonel.

colonne [kɔlɔn] *nf* column; **c. vertébrale** spine. ◆**colonnade** *nf* colonnade.

color/er [kɔlɔre] *vt* to colour. ◆**-ant** *a* & *nm* colouring. ◆**-é** *a* (*verre etc*) coloured; (*teint*) ruddy; (*style, foule*) colourful. ◆**coloration** *nf* colouring, colour. ◆**coloriage** *nm* colouring; (*dessin*) coloured drawing. ◆**colorier** *vt* (*dessin etc*) to colour (in). ◆**coloris** *nm* (*effet*) colouring; (*nuance*) shade.

colosse [kɔlɔs] *nm* giant, colossus. ◆**colossal, -aux** *a* colossal, gigantic.

colporter [kɔlpɔrte] *vt* to peddle, hawk.

coltiner [kɔltine] *vt* (*objet lourd*) *Fam* to lug, haul; — **se c.** *vpr* (*tâche pénible*) *Fam* to take on, tackle.

coma [kɔma] *nm* coma; **dans le c.** in a coma.

combat [kɔ̃ba] *nm* fight; *Mil* combat. ◆**combatif, -ive** *a* (*personne*) eager to fight; (*instinct, esprit*) fighting. ◆**combat-tre*** *vt* to fight; (*maladie, inflation etc*) to combat, fight; — *vi* to fight. ◆**-ant** *nm Mil* combattant; (*bagarreur*) *Fam* brawler; — *a* (*unité*) fighting.

combien [kɔ̃bjɛ̃] **1** *adv* (*quantité*) how much; (*nombre*) how many; **c. de** (*temps, argent etc*) how much; (*gens, livres etc*) how many. **2** *adv* (*à quel point*) how; **tu verras c. il est bête** you'll see how silly he is. **3** *adv* (*distance*) **c. y a-t-il d'ici à . . . ?** how far is it to . . . ? **4** *nm inv* **le c. sommes-nous?** (*date*) *Fam* what date is it?; **tous les c.?** (*fréquence*) *Fam* how often?

combine [kɔ̃bin] *nf* (*truc, astuce*) *Fam* trick.

combin/er [kɔ̃bine] *vt* (*disposer*) to combine; (*calculer*) to devise, plan (out). ◆**-é** *nm* (*de téléphone*) receiver. ◆**combinaison** *nf* **1** combination; (*manœuvre*) scheme. **2** (*vêtement de femme*) slip; (*de mécanicien*) boiler suit, *Am* overalls; (*de pilote*) flying suit; **c. de ski** ski suit.

comble [kɔ̃bl] **1** *nm* **le c. de** (*la joie etc*) the height of; **pour c. (de malheur)** to crown *ou* cap it all; **c'est un** *ou* **le c.!** that's the limit! **2** *nmpl* (*mansarde*) attic, loft; **sous les combles** beneath the roof, in the loft *ou* attic. **3** *a* (*bondé*) packed, full.

combler [kɔ̃ble] *vt* (*trou, lacune etc*) to fill; (*retard, perte*) to make good; (*vœu*) to fulfil; **c. qn de** (*cadeaux etc*) to lavish on s.o.; (*joie*) to fill s.o. with; **je suis comblé** I'm completely satisfied; **vous me comblez!** you're too good to me!

combustible [kɔ̃bystibl] *nm* fuel; — *a* combustible. ◆**combustion** *nf* combustion.

comédie [kɔmedi] *nf* comedy; (*complication*) *Fam* fuss, palaver; **c. musicale** musical; **jouer la c.** *Fig* to put on an act, play-act; **c'est de la c.** (*c'est faux*) it's a sham. ◆**comédien** *nm Th* & *Fig* actor. ◆**comédienne** *nf Th* & *Fig* actress.

comestible [kɔmɛstibl] *a* edible; — *nmpl* foods.

comète [kɔmɛt] *nf* comet.

comique [kɔmik] *a* (*style etc*) *Th* comic; (*amusant*) *Fig* comical, funny; (*auteur*) **c.** comedy writer; — *nm* (*genre*) (*acteur*) comic (actor); **le c.** (*genre*) comedy; *Fig* the comical side of (*de*).

comité [kɔmite] *nm* committee; **c. de gestion** board (of management); **en petit c.** in a small group.

commande [kɔmɑ̃d] **1** *nf* (*achat*) order; **sur c.** to order. **2** *nfpl* **les commandes** *Av Tech* the controls; **tenir les commandes** (*diriger*) *Fig* to have control.

command/er [kɔmɑ̃de] *vt* **1** (*diriger, exiger, dominer*) to command; (*faire fonctionner*) to control; — *vi* **c. à** (*ses passions etc*) to have control over; **c. à qn de faire** to command s.o. to do. **2** (*acheter*) to order. ◆**-ant** *nm Nau* captain; (*grade*) *Mil* major; (*grade*) *Av* squadron leader; **c. de bord** *Av* captain. ◆**-ement** *nm* (*autorité*) command; *Rel* commandment. ◆**commando** *nm* commando.

commanditaire [kɔmɑ̃ditɛr] *nm Com* sleeping *ou* limited partner, *Am* silent partner.

comme [kɔm] **1** *adv* & *conj* as, like; **un peu**

c. a bit like; **c. moi** like me; **c. cela** like that; **blanc c. neige** (as) white as snow; **c. si** as if; **c. pour faire** as if to do; **c. par hasard** as if by chance; **joli c. tout** *Fam* ever so pretty; **c. ami** as a friend; **c. quoi** (*disant que*) to the effect that; (*ce qui prouve que*) so, which goes to show that; **qu'as-tu c. diplômes?** what do you have in the way of certificates? **2** *adv* (*exclamatif*) **regarde c. il pleut!** look how it's raining!; **c'est petit!** isn't it small! **3** *conj* (*temps*) as; (*cause*) as, since; **je pars** as I'm leaving; **c. elle entrait** (just) as she was coming in.

commémorer [kɔmemɔre] *vt* to commemorate. ◆**commémoratif, -ive** *a* commemorative. ◆**commémoration** *nf* commemoration.

commenc/er [kɔmɑ̃se] *vti* to begin, start (**à faire** to do, doing; **par** with; **par faire** by doing); **pour c.** to begin with. ◆**—ement** *nm* beginning, start.

comment [kɔmɑ̃] *adv* how; **c. le sais-tu?** how do you know?; **et c.!** and how!; **c.?** (*répétition, surprise*) what?; **c.!** (*indignation*) what!; **c. est-il?** what is he like?; **c. faire?** what's to be done?; **c. t'appelles-tu?** what's your name?; **c. allez-vous?** how are you?

commentaire [kɔmɑ̃tɛr] *nm* (*explications*) commentary; (*remarque*) comment. ◆**commentateur, -trice** *nmf* commentator. ◆**commenter** *vt* to comment (up)on.

commérage(s) [kɔmeraʒ] *nm(pl)* gossip.

commerce [kɔmɛrs] *nm* trade, commerce; (*magasin*) shop, business; **de c.** (*voyageur, maison, tribunal*) commercial; (*navire*) trading; **chambre de c.** chamber of commerce; **faire du c.** to trade; **dans le c.** (*objet*) (on sale) in the shops. ◆**commercer** *vi* to trade. ◆**commerçant, -ante** *nmf* shopkeeper; **c. en gros** wholesale dealer; *a* (*nation*) trading, mercantile; (*rue, quartier*) shopping-; (*personne*) business-minded. ◆**commercial, -aux** *a* commercial, business-. ◆**commercialiser** *vt* to market.

commère [kɔmɛr] *nf* (*femme*) gossip.

commettre* [kɔmɛtr] *vt* (*délit etc*) to commit; (*erreur*) to make.

commis [kɔmi] *nm* (*de magasin*) assistant, *Am* clerk; (*de bureau*) clerk, *Am* clerical worker.

commissaire [kɔmisɛr] *nm* *Sp* steward; **c. (de police)** police superintendent *ou Am* chief; **c. aux comptes** auditor; **c. du bord** *Nau* purser. ◆**c.-priseur** *nm* (*pl* commissaires-priseurs*) auctioneer. ◆**commis-**

sariat *nm* **c. (de police)** (central) police station.

commission [kɔmisjɔ̃] *nf* (*course*) errand; (*message*) message; (*réunion*) commission, committee; (*pourcentage*) *Com* commission (**sur** on); **faire les commissions** to do the shopping. ◆**commissionnaire** *nm* messenger; (*d'hôtel*) commissionaire; *Com* agent.

commod/e [kɔmɔd] **1** *a* (*pratique*) handy; (*simple*) easy; **il n'est pas c.** (*pas aimable*) he's unpleasant; (*difficile*) he's a tough one. **2** *nf* chest of drawers, *Am* dresser. ◆**—ément** *adv* comfortably. ◆**commodité** *nf* convenience.

commotion [kɔmosjɔ̃] *nf* shock; **c. (cérébrale)** concussion. ◆**commotionner** *vt* to shake up.

commuer [kɔmɥe] *vt* (*peine*) *Jur* to commute (**en** to).

commun [kɔmœ̃] **1** *a* (*collectif, comparable, habituel*) common; (*frais, cuisine etc*) shared; (*action, démarche etc*) joint; **ami c.** mutual friend; **peu c.** uncommon; **en c.** in common; **transports en c.** public transport; **avoir** *ou* **mettre en c.** to share; **vivre en c.** to live together; **il n'a rien de c. avec** he has nothing in common with. **2** *nm* **le c. des mortels** ordinary mortals. ◆**—ément** [kɔmynemɑ̃] *adv* commonly.

communauté [kɔmynote] *nf* community. ◆**communautaire** *a* community-.

commune [kɔmyn] *nf* (*municipalité française*) commune; **les Communes** *Br Pol* the Commons. ◆**communal, -aux** *a* communal, local, municipal.

communi/er [kɔmynje] *vi* to receive Holy Communion, communicate. ◆**—ant, -ante** *nmf* *Rel* communicant. ◆**communion** *nf* communion; *Rel* (Holy) Communion.

communiqu/er [kɔmynike] *vt* to communicate, pass on; (*mouvement*) to impart, communicate; **se c. à** (*feu, rire*) to spread to; *– vi* (*personne, pièces etc*) to communicate. ◆**—é** *nm* (*avis*) *Pol* communiqué; (*publicitaire*) message; **c. de presse** press release. ◆**communicatif, -ive** *a* communicative; (*contagieux*) infectious. ◆**communication** *nf* communication; **c. (téléphonique)** (telephone) call; **mauvaise c.** *Tél* bad line.

communisme [kɔmynism] *nm* communism. ◆**communiste** *a & nmf* communist.

communs [kɔmœ̃] *nmpl* (*bâtiments*) outbuildings.

commutateur [kɔmytatœr] nm (bouton) Él switch.

compact [kɔ̃pakt] a dense; (mécanisme, disque, véhicule) compact.

compagne [kɔ̃paɲ] nf (camarade) friend; (épouse, maîtresse) companion. ◆**compagnie** nf (présence, société) & Com Mil company; **tenir c. à qn** to keep s.o. company. ◆**compagnon** nm companion; (ouvrier) workman; **c. de route** travelling companion, fellow traveller; **c. de jeu/de travail** playmate/workmate.

comparaître* [kɔ̃parɛtr] vi Jur to appear (in court) (devant before).

compar/er [kɔ̃pare] vt to compare; — **se c.** vpr to be compared (à to). ◆**—é** a (science etc) comparative. ◆**—able** a comparable. ◆**comparaison** nf comparison; Littér simile. ◆**comparatif, -ive** a (méthode etc) comparative; — nm Gram comparative.

comparse [kɔ̃pars] nmf Jur minor accomplice, stooge.

compartiment [kɔ̃partimɑ̃] nm compartment. ◆**compartimenter** vt to compartmentalize, divide up.

comparution [kɔ̃parysjɔ̃] nf Jur appearance (in court).

compas [kɔ̃pa] nm **1** (pour mesurer etc) (pair of) compasses, Am compass. **2** (boussole) Nau compass.

compassé [kɔ̃pase] a (affecté) starchy, stiff.

compassion [kɔ̃pasjɔ̃] nf compassion.

compatible [kɔ̃patibl] a compatible. ◆**compatibilité** nf compatibility.

compat/ir [kɔ̃patir] vi to sympathize; **c. à** (la douleur etc de qn) to share in. ◆**—issant** a sympathetic.

compatriote [kɔ̃patrijɔt] nmf compatriot.

compenser [kɔ̃pɑ̃se] vt to make up for, compensate for; — vi to compensate. ◆**compensation** nf compensation; **en c. de** in compensation for.

compère [kɔ̃pɛr] nm accomplice.

compétent [kɔ̃petɑ̃] a competent. ◆**compétence** nf competence.

compétition [kɔ̃petisjɔ̃] nf competition; (épreuve) Sp event; **de c.** (esprit, sport) competitive. ◆**compétitif, -ive** a competitive. ◆**compétitivité** nf competitiveness.

compiler [kɔ̃pile] vt (documents) to compile.

complainte [kɔ̃plɛ̃t] nf (chanson) lament.

complaire (se) [sakɔ̃plɛr] vpr **se c. dans qch/à faire** to delight in sth/in doing.

complaisant [kɔ̃plɛzɑ̃] a kind, obliging; (indulgent) self-indulgent, complacent. ◆**complaisance** nf kindness, obligingness; self-indulgence, complacency.

complément [kɔ̃plemɑ̃] nm complement; **le c.** (le reste) the rest; **un c. d'information** additional information. ◆**complémentaire** a complementary; (détails) additional.

complet, -ète [kɔ̃plɛ, -ɛt] **1** a complete; (train, hôtel, examen etc) full; (aliment) whole; **au (grand) c.** in full strength. **2** nm (costume) suit. ◆**complètement** adv completely. ◆**compléter** vt to complete; (ajouter à) to complement; (somme) to make up; — **se c.** vpr (caractères) to complement each other.

complexe [kɔ̃plɛks] **1** a complex. **2** nm (sentiment, construction) complex. ◆**complexé** a Fam hung up, inhibited. ◆**complexité** nf complexity.

complication [kɔ̃plikasjɔ̃] nf complication; (complexité) complexity.

complice [kɔ̃plis] nm accomplice; — a (regard) knowing; (silence, attitude) conniving; **c. de** Jur a party to. ◆**complicité** nf complicity.

compliment [kɔ̃plimɑ̃] nm compliment; pl (éloges) compliments; (félicitations) congratulations. ◆**complimenter** vt to compliment (sur, pour on).

compliqu/er [kɔ̃plike] vt to complicate; — **se c.** vpr (situation) to get complicated. ◆**—é** a complicated; (mécanisme etc) intricate; complicated; (histoire, problème etc) involved, complicated.

complot [kɔ̃plo] nm plot, conspiracy. ◆**comploter** [kɔ̃plɔte] vti to plot (**de faire** to do).

comport/er [kɔ̃pɔrte] vt **1** (impliquer) to involve, contain; (comprendre en soi, présenter) to contain, comprise, have. **2 se c.** vpr to behave; (joueur, voiture) to perform. ◆**—ement** nm behaviour; (de joueur etc) performance.

compos/er [kɔ̃poze] vt (former, constituer) to compose, make up; (musique, visage) to compose; (numéro) Tél to dial; (texte) Typ to set (up); **se c. de**, **être composé de** to be composed of; — vi Scol to take an examination; **c. avec** to come to terms with. ◆**—ant** nm (chimique, électronique) component. ◆**—ante** nf (d'une idée etc) component. ◆**—é** a & nm compound. ◆**compositeur, -trice** nmf Mus composer; Typ typesetter. ◆**composition** nf (action) composing, making up; Typ typesetting; Mus Littér Ch composition; Scol test, class exam; **c. française** Scol French essay ou composition.

composter [kɔ̃pɔste] vt (billet) to cancel, punch.

compote [kɔ̃pɔt] nf stewed fruit; **c. de pommes** stewed apples, apple sauce. ◆**compotier** nm fruit dish.

compréhensible [kɔ̃preɑ̃sibl] a understandable, comprehensible. ◆**compréhensif, -ive** a (personne) understanding. ◆**compréhension** nf understanding, comprehension.

comprendre* [kɔ̃prɑ̃dr] vt to understand, comprehend; (comporter) to include, comprise; **je n'y comprends rien** I don't understand anything about it; **ça se comprend** that's understandable. ◆**compris** a (inclus) included (dans in); **frais c.** including expenses; **tout c.** (all) inclusive; **y c.** including; **c. entre** (situated) between; **(c'est) c.!** it's agreed!

compresse [kɔ̃pres] nf Méd compress.

compresseur [kɔ̃presœr] a **rouleau c.** steam roller.

comprim/er [kɔ̃prime] vt to compress; (colère etc) to repress; (dépenses) to reduce. ◆**—é** nm Méd tablet. ◆**compression** nf compression; (du personnel etc) reduction.

compromettre* [kɔ̃prɔmetr] vt to compromise. ◆**compromis** nm compromise. ◆**compromission** nf compromising action, compromise.

comptable [kɔ̃tabl] a (règles etc) bookkeeping-; — nmf bookkeeper; (expert) accountant. ◆**comptabilité** nf (comptes) accounts; (science) bookkeeping, accountancy; (service) accounts department.

comptant [kɔ̃tɑ̃] a **argent c.** (hard) cash; — adv **payer c.** to pay (in) cash; **(au) c.** (acheter, vendre) for cash.

compte [kɔ̃t] nm (comptabilité) account; (calcul) count; (nombre) (right) number; **avoir un c. en banque** to have a bank(ing) account; **c. chèque** cheque account, Am checking account; **tenir c. de** to take into account; **c. tenu de** considering; **entrer en ligne de c.** to be taken into account; **se rendre c. de** to realize; **rendre c. de** (exposer) to report on; (justifier) to account for; **c. rendu** report; (de livre, film) review; **demander des comptes à** to call to account; **faire le c. de** to count; **à son c.** (travailler) for oneself; (s'installer) on one's own; **pour le c. de** on behalf of; **pour mon c.** for my part; **sur le c. de qn** about s.o.; **en fin de c.** all things considered; **à bon c.** (acheter) cheap(ly); **s'en tirer à bon c.** to get off lightly; **avoir un c. à régler avec qn** to have a score to settle with s.o.; **c. à rebours**

countdown. ◆**c.-gouttes** nm inv Méd dropper; **au c.-gouttes** very sparingly. ◆**c.-tours** nm inv Aut rev counter.

compt/er [kɔ̃te] vt (calculer) to count; (prévoir) to reckon, allow; (considérer) to consider; (payer) to pay; **c. faire** to expect to do; (avoir l'intention de) to intend to do; **c. qch à qn** (facturer) to charge s.o. for sth; **il compte deux ans de service** he has two years' service; **ses jours sont comptés** his ou her days are numbered; — vi (calculer, avoir de l'importance) to count; **c. sur** to rely on; **c. avec** to reckon with; **c. parmi** to be (numbered) among. ◆**—eur** nm Él meter; **c. de vitesse** Aut speedometer; **c. (kilométrique)** milometer, clock; **c. Geiger** Geiger counter.

comptoir [kɔ̃twar] nm **1** (de magasin) counter; (de café) bar; (de bureau) (reception) desk. **2** Com branch, agency.

compulser [kɔ̃pylse] vt to examine.

comte [kɔ̃t] nm (noble) count; Br earl. ◆**comté** nm county. ◆**comtesse** nf countess.

con, conne [kɔ̃, kɔn] a (idiot) Fam stupid; — nmf Fam stupid fool.

concave [kɔ̃kav] a concave.

concéder [kɔ̃sede] vt to concede, grant (à to, que that).

concentr/er [kɔ̃sɑ̃tre] vt to concentrate; (attention etc) to focus, concentrate; — **se c.** vpr (réfléchir) to concentrate. ◆**—é** a (solution) concentrated; (lait) condensed; (attentif) in a state of concentration; — nm Ch concentrate; **c. de tomates** tomato purée. ◆**concentration** nf concentration.

concentrique [kɔ̃sɑ̃trik] a concentric.

concept [kɔ̃sept] nm concept. ◆**conception** nf (idée) & Méd conception.

concern/er [kɔ̃serne] vt to concern; **en ce qui me concerne** as far as I'm concerned. ◆**—ant** prép concerning.

concert [kɔ̃ser] nm Mus concert; (de louanges) chorus; **de c.** (agir) together, in concert.

concert/er [kɔ̃serte] vt to arrange, devise (in agreement); — **se c.** vpr to consult together. ◆**—é** a (plan) concerted. ◆**concertation** nf (dialogue) dialogue.

concession [kɔ̃sesjɔ̃] nf concession (à to); (terrain) plot (of land). ◆**concessionnaire** nmf Com (authorized) dealer, agent.

concev/oir* [kɔ̃səvwar] **1** vt (imaginer, éprouver, engendrer) to conceive; (comprendre) to understand; **ainsi conçu** (dépêche etc) worded as follows. **2** vi (femme) to conceive. ◆**—able** a conceivable.

concierge [kɔ̃sjɛrʒ] *nmf* caretaker, *Am* janitor.

concile [kɔ̃sil] *nm Rel* council.

concili/er [kɔ̃silje] *vt* (*choses*) to reconcile; **se c. l'amitié/etc de qn** to win (over) s.o.'s friendship/*etc*. ◆—**ant** *a* conciliatory. ◆**conciliateur, -trice** *nmf* conciliator. ◆**conciliation** *nf* conciliation.

concis [kɔ̃si] *a* concise, terse. ◆**concision** *nf* concision.

concitoyen, -enne [kɔ̃sitwajɛ̃, -ɛn] *nmf* fellow citizen.

conclu/re [kɔ̃klyr] *vt* (*terminer, régler*) to conclude; **c. que** (*déduire*) to conclude that; – *vi* (*orateur etc*) to conclude; **c. à** to conclude in favour of. ◆—**ant** *a* conclusive. ◆**conclusion** *nf* conclusion.

concombre [kɔ̃kɔ̃br] *nm* cucumber.

concorde [kɔ̃kɔrd] *nf* concord, harmony. ◆**concord/er** *vi* (*faits etc*) to agree; (*caractères*) to match; **c. avec** to match. ◆—**ant** *a* in agreement. ◆**concordance** *nf* agreement; (*de situations, résultats*) similarity; **c. des temps** *Gram* sequence of tenses.

concourir* [kɔ̃kurir] *vi* (*candidat*) to compete (**pour** for); (*directions*) to converge; **c. à** (*un but*) to contribute to. ◆**concours** *nm Scol Univ* competitive examination; (*jeu*) competition; (*aide*) assistance; (*de circonstances*) combination; **c. hippique** horse show.

concret, -ète [kɔ̃krɛ, -ɛt] *a* concrete. ◆**concrétiser** *vt* to give concrete form to; – **se c.** *vpr* to materialize.

conçu [kɔ̃sy] *voir* **concevoir**; – *a* **c. pour faire** designed to do; **bien c.** (*maison etc*) well-designed.

concubine [kɔ̃kybin] *nf* (*maîtresse*) concubine. ◆**concubinage** *nm* cohabitation; **en c.** as husband and wife.

concurrent, -ente [kɔ̃kyrɑ̃, -ɑ̃t] *nmf* competitor; *Scol Univ* candidate. ◆**concurrence** *nf* competition; **faire c. à** to compete with; **jusqu'à c. de** up to the amount of. ◆**concurrencer** *vt* to compete with. ◆**concurrentiel, -ielle** *a* (*prix etc*) competitive.

condamn/er [kɔ̃dane] *vt* to condemn; *Jur* to sentence (**à** to); (*porte*) to block up, bar; (*pièce*) to keep locked; **c. à une amende** to fine. ◆—**é, -ée** *nmf Jur* condemned man, condemned woman; **être c.** (*malade*) to be doomed, be a hopeless case. ◆**condamnation** *nf Jur* sentence; (*censure*) condemnation.

condenser [kɔ̃dɑ̃se] *vt*, – **se c.** *vpr* to condense. ◆**condensateur** *nm El* condenser. ◆**condensation** *nf* condensation.

condescendre [kɔ̃desɑ̃dr] *vi* to condescend (**à** to). ◆**condescendance** *nf* condescension.

condiment [kɔ̃dimɑ̃] *nm* condiment.

condisciple [kɔ̃disipl] *nm Scol* classmate, schoolfellow; *Univ* fellow student.

condition [kɔ̃disjɔ̃] *nf* (*état, stipulation, rang*) condition; *pl* (*clauses, tarifs*) *Com* terms; **à c. de faire**, **à c. que l'on fasse** providing *ou* provided (that) one does; **mettre en c.** (*endoctriner*) to condition; **sans c.** (*se rendre*) unconditionally. ◆**conditionnel, -elle** *a* conditional. ◆**conditionn/er** *vt* **1** (*influencer*) to condition. **2** (*article*) *Com* to package. ◆—**é** *a* (*réflexe*) conditioned; **à air c.** (*pièce etc*) air-conditioned. ◆—**ement** *nm* conditioning; packaging.

condoléances [kɔ̃dɔleɑ̃s] *nfpl* condolences.

conducteur, -trice [kɔ̃dyktœr, -tris] **1** *nmf Aut Rail* driver. **2** *a* & *nm* (**corps**) **c.** *El* conductor; (**fil**) **c.** *El* lead (wire).

conduire* [kɔ̃dɥir] **1** *vt* to lead; *Aut* to drive; (*affaire etc*) & *El* to conduct; (*eau*) to carry; **c. qn à** (*accompagner*) to take s.o. to. **2 se c.** *vpr* to behave. ◆**conduit** *nm* duct. ◆**conduite** *nf* conduct, behaviour; *Aut* driving (**de** of); (*d'entreprise etc*) conduct; (*d'eau, de gaz*) main; **c. à gauche** (*volant*) left-hand drive; **faire un bout de c. à qn** to go with s.o. part of the way; **sous la c. de** under the guidance of.

cône [kon] *nm* cone.

confection [kɔ̃fɛksjɔ̃] *nf* making (**de** of); **vêtements de c.** ready-made clothes; **magasin de c.** ready-made clothing shop. ◆**confectionner** *vt* (*gâteau, robe*) to make.

confédération [kɔ̃federasjɔ̃] *nf* confederation. ◆**confédéré** *a* confederate.

conférence [kɔ̃ferɑ̃s] *nf* conference; (*exposé*) lecture. ◆**conférencier, -ière** *nmf* lecturer. ◆**conférer** *vt* (*attribuer, donner*) to confer (**à** on).

confess/er [kɔ̃fese] *vt* to confess; – **se c.** *vpr Rel* to confess (**à** to). ◆—**eur** *nm* (*prêtre*) confessor. ◆**confession** *nf* confession. ◆**confessionnal, -aux** *nm Rel* confessional. ◆**confessionnel, -elle** *a* (*école*) *Rel* denominational.

confetti [kɔ̃feti] *nmpl* confetti.

confiance [kɔ̃fjɑ̃s] *nf* trust, confidence; **faire c. à qn, avoir c. en qn** to trust s.o.; **c. en soi** (self-)confidence; **poste/abus de c.** position/breach of trust; **homme de c.** reliable man; **en toute c.** (*acheter*) quite confidently; **poser la question de c.** Pol to ask for a vote of confidence. ◆**confiant** a trusting; (*sûr de soi*) confident; **être c. en** ou **dans** to have confidence in.

confidence [kɔ̃fidɑ̃s] nf (*secret*) confidence; **en c.** in confidence; **il m'a fait une c.** he confided in me. ◆**confident** nm confidant. ◆**confidente** nf confidante. ◆**confidentiel, -ielle** a confidential.

confier [kɔ̃fje] vt **c. à qn** (*enfant, objet*) to give s.o. to look after, entrust s.o. with; **c. un secret/etc à qn** to confide a secret/etc to s.o.; **— se c.** vpr to confide (**à qn** in s.o.).

configuration [kɔ̃figyrasjɔ̃] nf configuration.

confin/er [kɔ̃fine] vt to confine; **— vi c. à** to border on; **— se c.** vpr to confine oneself (**dans** to). ◆**-é** a (*atmosphère*) stuffy.

confins [kɔ̃fɛ̃] nmpl confines.

confire [kɔ̃fir] vt (*cornichon*) to pickle; (*fruit*) to preserve.

confirmer [kɔ̃firme] vt to confirm (**que** that); **c. qn dans sa résolution** to confirm s.o.'s resolve. ◆**confirmation** nf confirmation.

confiserie [kɔ̃fizri] nf (*magasin*) sweet shop, *Am* candy store; pl (*produits*) confectionery, sweets, *Am* candy. ◆**confiseur, -euse** nmf confectioner.

confisquer [kɔ̃fiske] vt to confiscate (**à qn** from s.o.). ◆**confiscation** nf confiscation.

confit [kɔ̃fi] a **fruits confits** crystallized ou candied fruit. ◆**confiture** nf jam, preserves.

conflit [kɔ̃fli] nm conflict. ◆**conflictuel, -elle** a Psy conflict-provoking.

confluent [kɔ̃flyɑ̃] nm (*jonction*) confluence.

confondre [kɔ̃fɔ̃dr] vt (*choses, personnes*) to confuse, mix up; (*consterner, étonner*) to confound; (*amalgamer*) to fuse; **c. avec** to mistake for; **— se c.** vpr (*s'unir*) to merge; **se c. en excuses** to be very apologetic.

conforme [kɔ̃fɔrm] a **c. à** in accordance with; **c. (à l'original)** (*copie*) true (to the original). ◆**conform/er** vt to model, adapt; **— se c.** vpr to conform (**à** to). ◆**-ément** adv **c. à** in accordance with. ◆**conformisme** nm conformity, conformism. ◆**conformiste** a & nmf conformist. ◆**conformité** nf conformity.

confort [kɔ̃fɔr] nm comfort. ◆**confortable** a comfortable.

confrère [kɔ̃frɛr] nm colleague. ◆**confrérie** nf Rel brotherhood.

confronter [kɔ̃frɔ̃te] vt Jur etc to confront

(**avec** with); (*textes*) to collate; **confronté à** confronted with. ◆**confrontation** nf confrontation; collation.

confus [kɔ̃fy] a (*esprit, situation, bruit*) confused; (*idée, style*) confused, jumbled, hazy; (*gêné*) embarrassed; **je suis c.!** (*désolé*) I'm terribly sorry!; (*comblé de bienfaits*) I'm overwhelmed! ◆**confusément** adv indistinctly, vaguely. ◆**confusion** nf confusion; (*gêne, honte*) embarrassment.

congé [kɔ̃ʒe] nm leave (of absence); (*avis pour locataire*) notice (to quit); (*pour salarié*) notice (of dismissal); (*vacances*) holiday, *Am* vacation; **c. de maladie** sick leave; **congés payés** holidays with pay, paid holidays; **donner son c. à** (*employé, locataire*) to give notice to; **prendre c. de** to take leave of. ◆**congédier** vt (*domestique etc*) to dismiss.

congeler [kɔ̃ʒle] vt to freeze. ◆**congélateur** nm freezer, deep-freeze. ◆**congélation** nf freezing.

congénère [kɔ̃ʒener] nmf fellow creature. ◆**congénital, -aux** a congenital.

congère [kɔ̃ʒer] nf snowdrift.

congestion [kɔ̃ʒɛstjɔ̃] nf congestion; **c. cérébrale** Méd stroke. ◆**congestionn/er** vt to congest. ◆**-é** a (*visage*) flushed.

Congo [kɔ̃go] nm Congo. ◆**congolais, -aise** a & nmf Congolese.

congratuler [kɔ̃gratyle] vt Iron to congratulate.

congrégation [kɔ̃gregasjɔ̃] nf (*de prêtres etc*) congregation.

congrès [kɔ̃grɛ] nm congress. ◆**congressiste** nmf delegate (to a congress).

conifère [kɔnifɛr] nm conifer.

conique [kɔnik] a conic(al), cone-shaped.

conjecture [kɔ̃ʒɛktyr] nf conjecture. ◆**conjectural, -aux** a conjectural. ◆**conjecturer** vt to conjecture, surmise.

conjoint [kɔ̃ʒwɛ̃] **1** a (*problèmes, action etc*) joint. **2** nm spouse; pl husband and wife. ◆**conjointement** adv jointly.

conjonction [kɔ̃ʒɔ̃ksjɔ̃] nf Gram conjunction.

conjoncture [kɔ̃ʒɔ̃ktyr] nf circumstances; Écon economic situation. ◆**conjoncturel, -elle** a (*prévisions etc*) economic.

conjugal, -aux [kɔ̃ʒygal, -o] a conjugal.

conjuguer [kɔ̃ʒyge] vt (*verbe*) to conjugate; (*efforts*) to combine; **— se c.** vpr (*verbe*) to be conjugated. ◆**conjugaison** nf Gram conjugation.

conjur/er [kɔ̃ʒyre] vt (*danger*) to avert; (*mauvais sort*) to ward off; **c. qn** (*implorer*) to entreat s.o. (**de faire** to do). ◆**—é, -ée** *nmf* conspirator. ◆**conjuration** *nf* (*complot*) conspiracy.

connaissance [kɔnɛsɑ̃s] *nf* knowledge; (*personne*) acquaintance; *pl* (*science*) knowledge (**en** of); **faire la c. de qn, faire c. avec qn** to make s.o.'s acquaintance, meet s.o.; (*ami, époux etc*) to get to know s.o.; **à ma c.** as far as I know; **avoir c. de** to be aware of; **perdre c.** to lose consciousness, faint; **sans c.** unconscious. ◆**connaisseur** *nm* connoisseur.

connaître* [kɔnɛtr] *vt* to know; (*rencontrer*) to meet; (*un succès etc*) to have; (*un malheur etc*) to experience; **faire c.** to make known; **— se c.** *vpr* (*amis etc*) to get to know each other; **nous nous connaissons déjà** we've met before; **s'y c. à** *ou* **en qch** to know (all) about sth; **il ne se connaît plus** he's losing his cool.

connecter [kɔnɛkte] *vt* Él to connect. ◆**connexe** *a* (*matières*) allied. ◆**connexion** *nf* Él connection.

connerie [kɔnri] *nf* Fam (*bêtise*) stupidity; (*action*) stupid thing; *pl* (*paroles*) stupid nonsense.

connivence [kɔnivɑ̃s] *nf* connivance.

connotation [kɔnɔtasjɔ̃] *nf* connotation.

connu *voir* **connaître;** *— a* (*célèbre*) well-known.

conquér/ir* [kɔ̃kerir] *vt* (*pays, marché etc*) to conquer. ◆**—ant, -ante** *nmf* conqueror. ◆**conquête** *nf* conquest; **faire la c. de** (*pays, marché etc*) to conquer.

consacrer [kɔ̃sakre] *vt* (*temps, vie etc*) to devote (**à** to); (*église etc*) Rel to consecrate; (*coutume etc*) to establish, sanction, consecrate; **se c. à** to devote oneself to.

conscience [kɔ̃sjɑ̃s] *nf* 1 (*psychologique*) consciousness; **la c. de qch** the awareness *ou* consciousness of sth; **c. de soi** self-awareness; **avoir/prendre c. de** to be/become aware *ou* conscious of; **perdre c.** to lose consciousness. 2 (*morale*) conscience; **avoir mauvaise c.** to have a guilty conscience; **c. professionnelle** conscientiousness. ◆**consciemment** [kɔ̃sjamɑ̃] *adv* consciously. ◆**conscienceux, -euse** *a* conscientious. ◆**conscient** *a* conscious; **c. de** aware *ou* conscious of.

conscrit [kɔ̃skri] *nm* Mil conscript. ◆**conscription** *nf* conscription.

consécration [kɔ̃sekrasjɔ̃] *nf* Rel consecration; (*confirmation*) sanction, consecration.

consécuti/f, -ive [kɔ̃sekytif, -iv] *a* consecu-

tive; **c. à** following upon. ◆**—vement** *adv* consecutively.

conseil [kɔ̃sɛj] *nm* 1 **un c.** a piece of advice, some advice; **des conseils** advice; (**expert-**)**c.** consultant. 2 (*assemblée*) council, committee; **c. d'administration** board of directors; **C. des ministres** Pol Cabinet; (*réunion*) Cabinet meeting. ◆**conseiller[1]** *vt* (*guider, recommander*) to advise; **c. qch à qn** to recommend sth to s.o.; **c. à qn de faire** to advise s.o. to do. ◆**conseiller[2], -ère** *nmf* (*expert*) consultant; (*d'un conseil*) councillor.

consent/ir* [kɔ̃sɑ̃tir] *vi* **c. à** to consent to; *— vt* to grant (**à** to). ◆**—ement** *nm* consent.

conséquence [kɔ̃sekɑ̃s] *nf* consequence; (*conclusion*) conclusion; **en c.** accordingly; **sans c.** (*importance*) of no importance. ◆**conséquent** *a* logical; (*important*) Fam important; **par c.** consequently.

conservatoire [kɔ̃sɛrvatwar] *nm* academy, school (*of music, drama*).

conserve [kɔ̃sɛrv] *nf* **conserves** tinned *ou* canned food; **de ou en c.** tinned, canned; **mettre en c.** to tin, can.

conserv/er [kɔ̃sɛrve] *vt* (*ne pas perdre*) to retain, keep; (*fruits, vie, tradition etc*) to preserve; **— se c.** *vpr* (*aliment*) to keep. ◆**—é a bien c.** (*vieillard*) well-preserved. ◆**conservateur, -trice 1** *a* & *nmf* Pol Conservative. **2** *nm* (*de musée*) curator; (*de bibliothèque*) (chief) librarian. **3** *nm* (*produit*) Culin preservative. ◆**conservation** *nf* preservation; **instinct de c.** survival instinct. ◆**conservatisme** *nm* conservatism.

consider/er [kɔ̃sidere] *vt* to consider (**que** that); **c. qn** (*faire cas de*) to respect s.o.; **c. comme** to consider to be, regard as; **tout bien considéré** all things considered. ◆**—able** *a* considerable. ◆**considération** *nf* (*motif, examen*) consideration; (*respect*) regard, esteem; *pl* (*remarques*) observations; **prendre en c.** to take into consideration.

consigne [kɔ̃siɲ] *nf* (*instruction*) orders; Rail left-luggage office, Am baggage checkroom; Scol detention; Mil confinement to barracks; (*somme*) deposit; **c. automatique** Rail luggage lockers, Am baggage lockers. ◆**consignation** *nf* (*somme*) deposit. ◆**consigner** *vt* (*écrire*) to record; (*bouteille etc*) to charge a deposit on; (*bagages*) to deposit in the left-luggage office, Am to check; (*élève*) Scol to keep in;

(*soldat*) *Mil* to confine (to barracks); (*salle*) to seal off, close.

consistant [kɔ̃sistɑ̃] *a* (*sauce, bouillie*) thick; (*argument, repas*) solid. ◆**consistance** *nf* (*de liquide*) consistency; **sans c.** (*rumeur*) unfounded; (*esprit*) irresolute.

consister [kɔ̃siste] *vi* **c. en/dans** to consist of/in; **c. à faire** to consist in doing.

consistoire [kɔ̃sistwar] *nm Rel* council.

console [kɔ̃sɔl] *nf Tech El* console.

consoler [kɔ̃sɔle] *vt* to console, comfort (**de** for); **se c. de** (*la mort de qn etc*) to get over. ◆**consolation** *nf* consolation, comfort.

consolider [kɔ̃sɔlide] *vt* to strengthen, consolidate. ◆**consolidation** *nf* strengthening, consolidation.

consomm/er [kɔ̃sɔme] *vt* (*aliment, carburant etc*) to consume; (*crime, œuvre*) *Litt* to accomplish; – *vi* (*au café*) to drink; **c. beaucoup/peu** (*véhicule*) to be heavy/light on petrol *ou Am* gas. ◆**–é** 1 *a* (*achevé*) consummate. 2 *nm* clear meat soup, consommé. ◆**consommateur, -trice** *nmf Com* consumer; (*au café*) customer. ◆**consommation** *nf* consumption; drink; **biens/société de c.** consumer goods/society.

consonance [kɔ̃sɔnɑ̃s] *nf Mus* consonance; *pl* (*sons*) sounds.

consonne [kɔ̃sɔn] *nf* consonant.

consortium [kɔ̃sɔrsjɔm] *nm Com* consortium.

consorts [kɔ̃sɔr] *nmpl* **et c.** *Péj* and people of that ilk.

conspirer [kɔ̃spire] *vi* 1 to conspire, plot (**contre** against). 2 **c. à faire** (*concourir*) to conspire to do. ◆**conspirateur, -trice** *nmf* conspirator. ◆**conspiration** *nf* conspiracy.

conspuer [kɔ̃spɥe] *vt* (*orateur etc*) to boo.

constant, -ante [kɔ̃stɑ̃, -ɑ̃t] *a* constant; – *nf Math* constant. ◆**constamment** *adv* constantly. ◆**constance** *nf* constancy.

constat [kɔ̃sta] *nm* (official) report; **dresser un c. d'échec** to acknowledge one's failure.

constater [kɔ̃state] *vt* to note, observe (**que** that); (*vérifier*) to establish; (*enregistrer*) to record; **je ne fais que c.** I'm merely stating a fact. ◆**constatation** *nf* (*remarque*) observation.

constellation [kɔ̃stelasjɔ̃] *nf* constellation. ◆**constellé** *a* **c. de** (*étoiles, joyaux*) studded with.

consterner [kɔ̃sterne] *vt* to distress, dismay. ◆**consternation** *nf* distress, (profound) dismay.

constip/er [kɔ̃stipe] *vt* to constipate. ◆**–é**

a constipated; (*gêné*) *Fam* embarrassed, stiff. ◆**constipation** *nf* constipation.

constitu/er [kɔ̃stitɥe] *vt* (*composer*) to make up, constitute; (*être, représenter*) to constitute; (*organiser*) to form; (*instituer*) *Jur* to appoint; **constitué de** made up of; **se c. prisonnier** to give oneself up. ◆**–ant** *a* (*éléments*) component, constituent; (*assemblée*) *Pol* constituent. ◆**constitutif, -ive** *a* constituent. ◆**constitution** *nf* (*santé*) & *Pol* constitution; (*fondation*) formation (**de** of); (*composition*) composition. ◆**constitutionnel, -elle** *a* constitutional.

constructeur [kɔ̃stryktœr] *nm* builder; (*fabricant*) maker (**de** of). ◆**constructif, -ive** *a* constructive. ◆**construction** *nf* (*de pont etc*) building, construction (**de** of); (*édifice*) building, structure; (*de théorie etc*) & *Gram* construction; **de c.** (*matériaux, jeu*) building-.

construire* [kɔ̃strɥir] *vt* (*maison, route etc*) to build, construct; (*phrase, théorie etc*) to construct.

consul [kɔ̃syl] *nm* consul. ◆**consulaire** *a* consular. ◆**consulat** *nm* consulate.

consulter [kɔ̃sylte] 1 *vt* to consult; – **se c.** *vpr* to consult (each other), confer. 2 *vi* (*médecin*) to hold surgery, *Am* hold office hours. ◆**consultatif, -ive** *a* consultative, advisory. ◆**consultation** *nf* consultation; **cabinet de c.** *Méd* surgery, *Am* office; **heures de c.** *Méd* surgery hours, *Am* office hours.

consumer [kɔ̃syme] *vt* (*détruire, miner*) to consume.

contact [kɔ̃takt] *nm* contact; (*toucher*) touch; *Aut* ignition; **être en c. avec** to be in touch *ou* contact with; **prendre c.** to get in touch (**avec** with); **entrer en c. avec** to come into contact with; **prise de c.** first meeting; **mettre/couper le c.** *Aut* to switch on/off the ignition. ◆**contacter** *vt* to contact.

contagieux, -euse [kɔ̃taʒjø, -øz] *a* (*maladie, rire*) contagious, infectious; **c'est c.** it's catching *ou* contagious. ◆**contagion** *nf Méd* contagion, infection; (*de rire etc*) contagiousness.

contaminer [kɔ̃tamine] *vt* to contaminate. ◆**contamination** *nf* contamination.

conte [kɔ̃t] *nm* tale; **c. de fée** fairy tale.

contempler [kɔ̃tɑ̃ple] *vt* to contemplate, gaze at. ◆**contemplatif, -ive** *a* contemplative. ◆**contemplation** *nf* contemplation.

contemporain, -aine [kɔ̃tɑ̃pɔrɛ̃, -ɛn] *a* & *nmf* contemporary.

contenance [kɔ̃tnɑ̃s] nf 1 (contenu) capacity. 2 (allure) bearing; **perdre c.** to lose one's composure.

conten/ir° [kɔ̃tnir] vt (renfermer) to contain; (avoir comme capacité) to hold; (contrôler) to hold back, contain; — **se c.** vpr to contain oneself. ◆—ant nm container. ◆—eur nm (freight) container.

content [kɔ̃tɑ̃] 1 a pleased, happy, glad (**de faire** to do); **c. de qn/qch** pleased ou happy with s.o./sth; **c. de soi** self-satisfied; **non c. d'avoir fait** not content with having done. 2 nm **avoir son c.** to have had one's fill (**de** of). ◆**content/er** vt to satisfy, please; **se c. de** to be content with, content oneself with. ◆—ement nm contentment, satisfaction.

contentieux [kɔ̃tɑ̃sjø] nm (affaires) matters in dispute; (service) legal ou claims department.

contenu [kɔ̃tny] nm (de récipient) contents; (de texte, film etc) content.

cont/er [kɔ̃te] vt (histoire etc) to tell, relate. ◆—eur, -euse nmf storyteller.

conteste (sans) [sɑ̃kɔ̃test] adv indisputably.

contest/er [kɔ̃teste] 1 vt (fait etc) to dispute, contest. 2 vi (étudiants etc) to protest; — vt to protest against. ◆—é a (théorie etc) controversial. ◆—able a debatable. ◆**contestataire** a étudiant/ouvrier c. student/worker protester; — nmf protester. ◆**contestation** nf (discussion) dispute; **faire de la c.** to protest (against the establishment).

contexte [kɔ̃tekst] nm context.

contigu, -uë [kɔ̃tigy] a c. (**à**) (maisons etc) adjoining. ◆**contiguïté** nf close proximity.

continent [kɔ̃tinɑ̃] nm continent; (opposé à une île) mainland. ◆**continental, -aux** a continental.

contingent [kɔ̃tɛ̃ʒɑ̃] 1 a (accidentel) contingent. 2 nm Mil contingent; (part, quota) quota. ◆**contingences** nfpl contingencies.

continu [kɔ̃tiny] a continuous. ◆**continuel, -elle** a continual, unceasing. ◆**continuellement** adv continually.

continuer [kɔ̃tinɥe] vt to continue, carry on (**à** ou **de faire** doing); (prolonger) to continue; — vi to continue, go on. ◆**continuation** nf continuation; **bonne c.!** Fam I hope the rest of it goes well, keep up the good work! ◆**continuité** nf continuity.

contondant [kɔ̃tɔ̃dɑ̃] a **instrument c.** Jur blunt instrument.

contorsion [kɔ̃tɔrsjɔ̃] nf contortion. ◆**se**

contorsionner vpr to contort oneself. ◆**contorsionniste** nmf contortionist.

contour [kɔ̃tur] nm outline, contour; pl (de route, rivière) twists, bends. ◆**contourn/er** vt (colline etc) to go round, skirt; (difficulté, loi) to get round. ◆—é a (style) convoluted, tortuous.

contraception [kɔ̃trasɛpsjɔ̃] nf contraception. ◆**contraceptif, -ive** a & nm contraceptive.

contract/er [kɔ̃trakte] vt (muscle, habitude, dette etc) to contract; — **se c.** vpr (cœur etc) to contract. ◆—é a (inquiet) tense. ◆**contraction** nf contraction.

contractuel, -elle [kɔ̃traktɥel] 1 nmf traffic warden; — nf Am meter maid. 2 a contractual.

contradicteur [kɔ̃tradiktœr] nm contradictor. ◆**contradiction** nf contradiction. ◆**contradictoire** a (propos etc) contradictory; (rapports, théories) conflicting; **débat c.** debate.

contraindre° [kɔ̃trɛ̃dr] vt to compel, force (**à faire** to do); — **se c.** vpr to compel ou force oneself; (se gêner) to restrain oneself. ◆**contraignant** a constraining, restricting. ◆**contraint** a (air etc) forced, constrained. ◆**contrainte** nf compulsion, constraint; (gêne) constraint, restraint.

contraire [kɔ̃trer] a opposite; (défavorable) contrary; **c. à** contrary to; — nm opposite; (**bien**) **au c.** on the contrary. ◆—ment adv **c. à** contrary to.

contrari/er [kɔ̃trarje] vt (projet, action) to thwart; (personne) to annoy. ◆—ant a (action etc) annoying; (personne) difficult, perverse. ◆**contrariété** nf annoyance.

contraste [kɔ̃trast] nm contrast. ◆**contraster** vi to contrast (**avec** with); **faire c.** (mettre en contraste) to contrast.

contrat [kɔ̃tra] nm contract.

contravention [kɔ̃travɑ̃sjɔ̃] nf (amende) Aut fine; (pour stationnement interdit) (parking) ticket; **en c.** contravening the law; **en c. à** in contravention of.

contre [kɔ̃tr] 1 prép & adv against; (en échange de) (in exchange) for; **échanger c.** to exchange for; **fâché c.** angry with; **s'abriter c.** to shelter from; **il va s'appuyer c.** he's going to lean against it; **six voix c. deux** six votes to two; **Nîmes c. Arras** Sp Nîmes versus Arras; **un médicament c.** (toux, grippe etc) a medicine for; **par c.** on the other hand; **tout c.** close to ou by. 2 nm (riposte) Sp counter.

contre- [kɔ̃tr] préf counter-.

contre-attaque [kɔ̃tratak] *nf* counterattack.
◆**contre-attaquer** *vt* to counterattack.

contrebalancer [kɔ̃trəbalɑ̃se] *vt* to counterbalance.

contrebande [kɔ̃trəbɑ̃d] *nf* (*fraude*) smuggling, contraband; (*marchandise*) contraband; **de c.** (*tabac etc*) contraband, smuggled; **faire de la c.** to smuggle; **passer qch en c.** to smuggle sth. ◆**contrebandier, -ière** *nmf* smuggler.

contrebas (en) [ɑ̃kɔ̃trəba] *adv* & *prép* **en c. (de)** down below.

contrebasse [kɔ̃trəbas] *nf* Mus double-bass.

contrecarrer [kɔ̃trəkare] *vt* to thwart, frustrate.

contrecœur (à) [akɔ̃trəkœr] *adv* reluctantly.

contrecoup [kɔ̃trəku] *nm* (indirect) effect *ou* consequence; **par c.** as an indirect consequence.

contre-courant (à) [akɔ̃trəkurɑ̃] *adv* against the current.

contredanse [kɔ̃trədɑ̃s] *nf* (*amende*) Aut Fam ticket.

contredire* [kɔ̃trədir] *vt* to contradict; — **se c.** *vpr* to contradict oneself.

contrée [kɔ̃tre] *nf* region, land.

contre-espionnage [kɔ̃trɛspjɔnaʒ] *nm* counterespionage.

contrefaçon [kɔ̃trəfasɔ̃] *nf* counterfeiting, forgery; (*objet imité*) counterfeit, forgery. ◆**contrefaire** *vt* (*parodier*) to mimic; (*déguiser*) to disguise; (*monnaie etc*) to counterfeit, forge.

contreforts [kɔ̃trəfɔr] *nmpl* Géog foothills.

contre-indiqué [kɔ̃trɛ̃dike] *a* (*médicament*) dangerous, not recommended.

contre-jour (à) [akɔ̃trəʒur] *adv* against the (sun)light.

contremaître [kɔ̃trəmɛtr] *nm* foreman.

contre-offensive [kɔ̃trɔfɑ̃siv] *nf* counteroffensive.

contrepartie [kɔ̃trəparti] *nf* compensation; **en c.** in exchange.

contre-performance [kɔ̃trəpɛrfɔrmɑ̃s] *nf* Sp bad performance.

contre-pied [kɔ̃trəpje] *nm* **le c.-pied d'une opinion/attitude** the (exact) opposite view/attitude; **à c.-pied** Sp on the wrong foot.

contre-plaqué [kɔ̃trəplake] *nm* plywood.

contrepoids [kɔ̃trəpwa] *nm* Tech & Fig counterbalance; **faire c. (à)** to counterbalance.

contrepoint [kɔ̃trəpwɛ̃] *nm* Mus counterpoint.

contrer [kɔ̃tre] *vt* (*personne, attaque*) to counter.

contre-révolution [kɔ̃trərevɔlysjɔ̃] *nf* counter-revolution.

contresens [kɔ̃trəsɑ̃s] *nm* misinterpretation; (*en traduisant*) mistranslation; (*non-sens*) absurdity; **à c.** the wrong way.

contresigner [kɔ̃trəsiɲe] *vt* to countersign.

contretemps [kɔ̃trətɑ̃] *nm* hitch, mishap; **à c.** (*arriver etc*) at the wrong moment.

contre-torpilleur [kɔ̃trətɔrpijœr] *nm* (*navire*) destroyer, torpedo boat.

contrevenir [kɔ̃trəvnir] *vi* **c. à** (*loi etc*) to contravene.

contre-vérité* [kɔ̃traverite] *nf* untruth.

contribu/er [kɔ̃tribɥe] *vi* to contribute (**à** to). ◆**—able** *nmf* taxpayer. ◆**contribution** *nf* contribution; (*impôt*) tax; *pl* (*administration*) tax office; **mettre qn à c.** to use s.o.'s services.

contrit [kɔ̃tri] *a* (*air etc*) contrite. ◆**contrition** *nf* contrition.

contrôle [kɔ̃trol] *nm* (*vérification*) inspection, check(ing) (**de** of); (*des prix, de la qualité*) control; (*maîtrise*) control; (*sur bijou*) hallmark; **un c.** (*examen*) a check (sur on); **le c. de soi(-même)** self-control; **le c. des naissances** birth control; **un c. d'identité** an identity check. ◆**contrôl/er** *vt* (*examiner*) to inspect, check; (*maîtriser, surveiller*) to control; — **se c.** *vpr* (*se maîtriser*) to control oneself. ◆**—eur, -euse** *nmf* (*de train*) (ticket) inspector; (*au quai*) ticket collector; (*de bus*) conductor, conductress.

contrordre [kɔ̃trɔrdr] *nm* change of orders.

controverse [kɔ̃trɔvɛrs] *nf* controversy. ◆**controversé** *a* controversial.

contumace (par) [parkɔ̃tymas] *adv* Jur in one's absence, in absentia.

contusion [kɔ̃tyzjɔ̃] *nf* bruise. ◆**contusionner** *vt* to bruise.

convainc/re* [kɔ̃vɛ̃kr] *vt* to convince (**de** of); (*accusé*) to prove guilty (**de** of); **c. qn de faire** to persuade s.o. to do. ◆**—ant** *a* convincing. ◆**—u** *a* (*certain*) convinced (**de** of).

convalescent, -ente [kɔ̃valesɑ̃, -ɑ̃t] *nmf* convalescent; — *a* **être c.** to convalesce. ◆**convalescence** *nf* convalescence; **être en c.** to convalesce; **maison de c.** convalescent home.

conven/ir* [kɔ̃vnir] *vi* **c. à** (*être approprié à*) to be suitable for; (*plaire à, aller à*) to suit; **ça convient** (*date etc*) that's suitable; **de** (*lieu etc*) to agree upon; (*erreur*) to admit; **c. que** to admit that; **il convient de** it's advisable to; (selon les usages) it is proper ou fitting to. ◆—u a (prix etc) agreed. ◆—able a (approprié, acceptable) suitable; (correct) decent, proper. ◆—ablement adv suitably; decently. ◆convenance nf convenances (usages) convention(s), proprieties; à sa c. to one's satisfaction ou taste.

convention [kɔ̃vɑ̃sjɔ̃] nf (accord) agreement, convention; (règle) & Am Pol convention; c. collective collective bargaining; de c. (sentiment etc) conventional. ◆conventionné a (prix, tarif) regulated (by voluntary agreement); médecin c. = National Health Service doctor (bound by agreement with the State). ◆conventionnel, -elle a conventional.

convergent [kɔ̃vɛrʒɑ̃] a converging, convergent. ◆convergence nf convergence. ◆converger vi to converge.

converser [kɔ̃vɛrse] vi to converse. ◆conversation nf conversation.

conversion [kɔ̃vɛrsjɔ̃] nf conversion. ◆convert/ir vt to convert (à to, en into); — se c. vpr to be converted, convert. ◆—i, -ie nmf convert. ◆convertible a convertible; — nm (canapé) c. bed settee.

convexe [kɔ̃vɛks] a convex.

conviction [kɔ̃viksjɔ̃] nf (certitude, croyance) conviction; pièce à c. Jur exhibit.

convier [kɔ̃vje] vt to invite (à une soirée/etc to a party/etc, à faire to do).

convive [kɔ̃viv] nmf guest (at table).

convoi [kɔ̃vwa] nm (véhicules, personnes etc) convoy; Rail train; c. (funèbre) funeral procession. ◆convoy/er vt to escort. ◆—eur nm Nau escort ship; c. de fonds security guard.

convoiter [kɔ̃vwate] vt to desire, envy, covet. ◆convoitise nf desire, envy.

convoquer [kɔ̃vɔke] vt (candidats, membres etc) to summon ou invite (to attend); (assemblée) to convene, summon; c. à to summon ou invite to. ◆convocation nf (action) summoning; convening; (ordre) summons (to attend); (lettre) (written) notice (to attend).

convulser [kɔ̃vylse] vt to convulse. ◆convulsif, -ive a convulsive. ◆convulsion nf convulsion.

coopérer [kɔɔpere] vi to co-operate (à in, avec with). ◆coopératif, -ive a co-operative; — nf co-operative (society). ◆coopération nf co-operation.

coopter [kɔɔpte] vt to co-opt.

coordonn/er [kɔɔrdɔne] vt to co-ordinate. ◆—ées nfpl Math co-ordinates; (adresse,

téléphone) Fam particulars, details. ◆coordination nf co-ordination.

copain [kɔpɛ̃] nm Fam (camarade) pal; (petit ami) boyfriend; être c. avec to be pals with.

copeau, -x [kɔpo] nm (de bois) shaving.

copie [kɔpi] nf copy; (devoir, examen) Scol paper. ◆copier vti to copy; Scol to copy, crib (sur from). ◆copieur, -euse nmf (élève etc) copycat, copier.

copieux, -euse [kɔpjø, -øz] a copious, plentiful.

copilote [kɔpilɔt] nm co-pilot.

copine [kɔpin] nf Fam (camarade) pal; (petite amie) girlfriend; être c. avec to be pals with.

copropriété [kɔprɔprijete] nf joint ownership; (immeuble en) c. block of flats in joint ownership, Am condominium.

copulation [kɔpylasjɔ̃] nf copulation.

coq [kɔk] nm cock, rooster; c. au vin coq au vin (chicken cooked in wine); passer du c. à l'âne to jump from one subject to another.

coque [kɔk] nf 1 (de noix) shell; (mollusque) cockle; œuf à la c. boiled egg. 2 Nau hull.

coquelicot [kɔkliko] nm poppy.

coqueluche [kɔklyʃ] nf Méd whooping-cough; la c. de Fig the darling of.

coquet, -ette [kɔkɛ, -ɛt] a (chic) smart; (joli) pretty; (provocant) coquettish, flirtatious; (somme) Fam tidy; — nf coquette, flirt. ◆coquetterie nf (élégance) smartness; (goût de la toilette) dress sense; (galanterie) coquetry.

coquetier [kɔktje] nm egg cup.

coquille [kɔkij] nf shell; Typ misprint; c. Saint-Jacques scallop. ◆coquillage nm (mollusque) shellfish; (coquille) shell.

coquin, -ine [kɔkɛ̃, -in] nmf rascal; — a mischievous, rascally; (histoire etc) naughty.

cor [kɔr] nm Mus horn; c. (au pied) corn; réclamer ou demander à c. et à cri to clamour for.

corail, -aux [kɔraj, -o] nm coral.

Coran [kɔrɑ̃] nm le C. the Koran.

corbeau, -x [kɔrbo] nm crow; (grand) c. raven.

corbeille [kɔrbɛj] nf basket; c. à papier waste paper basket.

corbillard [kɔrbijar] nm hearse.

corde [kɔrd] nf rope; (plus mince) (fine) cord; (de raquette, violon etc) string; c. (raide) (d'acrobate) tightrope; instrument à cordes Mus string(ed) instrument; c. à linge (washing ou clothes) line; c. à sauter skipping rope, Am jump rope; usé jusqu'à la c. threadbare; **cordes vocales** vocal cords; **prendre un virage à la c.** *Aut* to hug a bend; **pas dans mes cordes** *Fam* not my line. ◆**cordage** *nm Nau* rope. ◆**cordée** *nf* roped (climbing) party. ◆**cordelette** *nf* (fine) cord. ◆**corder** *vt* (*raquette*) to string. ◆**cordon** *nm* (*de tablier, sac etc*) string; (*de soulier*) lace; (*de rideau*) cord, rope; (*d'agents de police*) cordon; (*décoration*) ribbon, sash; (*ombilical*) *Anat* cord. ◆**c.-bleu** *nm* (*pl* cordons-bleus) cordon bleu (cook), first-class cook.

cordial, -aux [kɔrdjal, -o] *a* cordial, warm; – *nm Méd* cordial. ◆**cordialité** *nf* cordiality.

cordonnier [kɔrdɔnje] *nm* shoe repairer, cobbler. ◆**cordonnerie** *nf* shoe repairer's shop.

Corée [kɔre] *nf* Korea. ◆**coréen, -enne** *a* & *nmf* Korean.

coriace [kɔrjas] *a* (*aliment, personne*) tough.

corne [kɔrn] *nf* (*de chèvre etc*) horn; (*de cerf*) antler; (*matière, instrument*) horn; (*angle, pli*) corner.

cornée [kɔrne] *nf Anat* cornea.

corneille [kɔrnɛj] *nf* crow.

cornemuse [kɔrnəmyz] *nf* bagpipes.

corner [kɔrne] **1** *vt* (*page*) to turn down the corner of, dog-ear. **2** *vi* (*véhicule*) to sound its horn. **3** [kɔrnɛr] *nm Fb* corner.

cornet [kɔrnɛ] *nm* **1 c.** (**à pistons**) *Mus* cornet. **2** (*de glace*) cornet, cone; **c.** (**de papier**) (paper) cone.

corniaud [kɔrnjo] *nm* (*chien*) mongrel; (*imbécile*) *Fam* drip, twit.

corniche [kɔrniʃ] *nf Archit* cornice; (*route*) cliff road.

cornichon [kɔrniʃɔ̃] *nm* (*concombre*) gherkin; (*niais*) *Fam* clot, twit.

cornu [kɔrny] *a* (*diable etc*) horned.

corollaire [kɔrɔlɛr] *nm* corollary.

corporation [kɔrpɔrasjɔ̃] *nf* trade association, professional body.

corps [kɔr] *nm Anat Ch Fig etc* body; *Mil Pol* corps; **c. électoral** electorate; **c. enseignant** teaching profession; **c. d'armée** army corps; **garde du c.** bodyguard; **un c. de bâtiment** a main building; **c. et âme** body and soul; **lutter c. à c.** to fight hand-to-hand; **à son c. défendant** under protest; **prendre c.** (*projet*) to take shape; **donner c. à** (*rumeur, idée*) to give substance to; **faire c. avec** to form a part of, belong with; **perdu c. et biens** *Nau* lost with all hands; **esprit de c.** corporate spirit. ◆**corporel, -elle** *a* bodily; (*châtiment*) corporal.

corpulent [kɔrpylɑ̃] *a* stout, corpulent. ◆**corpulence** *nf* stoutness, corpulence.

corpus [kɔrpys] *nm Ling* corpus.

correct [kɔrɛkt] *a* (*exact*) correct; (*bienséant, honnête*) proper, correct; (*passable*) adequate. ◆**-ement** *adv* correctly; properly; adequately. ◆**correcteur, -trice 1** *a* (*verres*) corrective. **2** *nmf Scol* examiner; *Typ* proofreader. ◆**correctif, -ive** *a* & *nm* corrective.

correction [kɔrɛksjɔ̃] *nf* (*rectification etc*) correction; (*punition*) thrashing; (*exactitude, bienséance*) correctness; **la c. de** (*devoirs, examen*) the marking of; **c. d'épreuves** *Typ* proofreading. ◆**correctionnel, -elle** *a* **tribunal c.,** – *nf* magistrates' court, *Am* police court.

corrélation [kɔrelasjɔ̃] *nf* correlation.

correspond/re [kɔrɛspɔ̃dr] **1** *vi* (*s'accorder*) to correspond (**à** to, with); (*chambres etc*) to communicate; **c. avec** *Rail* to connect with; **– se c.** *vpr* (*idées etc*) to correspond; (*chambres etc*) to communicate. **2** *vi* (*écrire*) to correspond (**avec** with). ◆**-ant, -ante** *a* corresponding; – *nmf* correspondent; (*d'un élève, d'un adolescent*) pen friend; *Tél* caller. ◆**correspondance** *nf* correspondence; (*de train, d'autocar*) connection, *Am* transfer.

corrida [kɔrida] *nf* bullfight.

corridor [kɔridɔr] *nm* corridor.

corrig/er [kɔriʒe] *vt* (*texte, injustice etc*) to correct; (*épreuve*) *Typ* to read; (*devoir*) *Scol* to mark, correct; (*châtier*) to beat, punish; **c. qn de** (*défaut*) to cure s.o. of; **se c. de** to cure oneself of. ◆**-é** *nm Scol* model (answer), correct version, key.

corroborer [kɔrɔbɔre] *vt* to corroborate.

corroder [kɔrɔde] *vt* to corrode. ◆**corrosif, -ive** *a* corrosive. ◆**corrosion** *nf* corrosion.

corromp/re [kɔrɔ̃pr] *vt* to corrupt; (*soudoyer*) to bribe; (*aliment, eau*) to taint. ◆**-u** *a* corrupt; (*altéré*) tainted. ◆**corruption** *nf* (*dépravation*) corruption; (*de juge etc*) bribery.

corsage [kɔrsaʒ] *nm* (*chemisier*) blouse; (*de robe*) bodice.

corsaire [kɔrsɛr] *nm* (*marin*) *Hist* privateer.

Corse [kɔrs] *nf* Corsica. ◆**corse** *a* & *nmf* Corsican.

cors/er [kɔrse] *vt* (*récit, action*) to heighten; **l'affaire se corse** things are hotting up. ◆**-é** *a* (*vin*) full-bodied; (*café*) strong; (*sauce, histoire*) spicy; (*problème*) tough; (*addition de restaurant*) steep.

corset [kɔrsɛ] *nm* corset.

cortège [kɔrtɛʒ] *nm* (*défilé*) procession; (*suite*) retinue; **c. officiel** (*automobiles*) motorcade.

corvée [kɔrve] *nf* chore, drudgery; *Mil* fatigue (duty).

cosaque [kɔzak] *nm* Cossack.

cosmopolite [kɔsmɔpɔlit] *a* cosmopolitan.

cosmos [kɔsmɔs] *nm* (*univers*) cosmos; (*espace*) outer space. ◆**cosmique** *a* cosmic. ◆**cosmonaute** *nmf* cosmonaut.

cosse [kɔs] *nf* (*de pois etc*) pod.

cossu [kɔsy] *a* (*personne*) well-to-do; (*maison etc*) opulent.

costaud [kɔsto] *a Fam* brawny, beefy; – *nm Fam* strong man.

costume [kɔstym] *nm* (*pièces d'habillement*) costume, dress; (*complet*) suit. ◆**costum/er** *vt* **c. qn** to dress s.o. up (**en** as). ◆**-é** **a bal c.** fancy-dress ball.

cote [kɔt] *nf* (*marque de classement*) mark, letter, number; (*tableau des valeurs*) (official) listing; (*des valeurs boursières*) quotation; (*évaluation, popularité*) rating; (*de cheval*) odds (**de** on); **c. d'alerte** danger level.

côte [kot] *nf* **1** *Anat* rib; (*de mouton*) chop; (*de veau*) cutlet; **à côtes** (*étoffe*) ribbed; **c. à c.** side by side, **se tenir les côtes** to split one's sides (laughing). **2** (*montée*) hill; (*versant*) hillside. **3** (*littoral*) coast.

côté [kote] *nm* side; (*direction*) way; **de l'autre c.** on the other side (**de** of); (*direction*) the other way; **de ce c.** (*passer*) this way; **du c. de** (*vers, près de*) towards; **de c.** (*se jeter, mettre de l'argent etc*) to one side; (*regarder*) sideways, to one side; **à c.** close by, nearby; (*pièce*) in the other room; (*maison*) next door; **la maison (d')à c.** the house next door; **à c. de** next to, beside; (*comparaison*) compared to; **passer à c.** (*balle*) to fall wide (**de** of); **venir de tous côtés** to come from all directions; **d'un c.** on the one hand; **de mon c.** for my part; **à mes côtés** by my side; **laisser de c.** (*travail*) to neglect; (**du**) **c. argent**/*etc Fam* as regards money/*etc*, moneywise/*etc*; **le bon c.** (*d'une affaire*) the bright side (**de** of).

coteau, -x [kɔto] *nm* (small) hill; (*versant*) hillside.

côtelé [kotle] *a* (*étoffe*) ribbed; **velours c.** cord(uroy).

côtelette [kotlɛt] *nf* (*d'agneau, de porc*) chop; (*de veau*) cutlet.

cot/er [kɔte] *vt* (*valeur boursière*) to quote. ◆**-é a bien c.** highly rated.

coterie [kɔtri] *nf Péj* set, clique.

côtier, -ière [kotje, -jɛr] *a* coastal; (*pêche*) inshore.

cotiser [kɔtize] *vi* to contribute (**à** to, **pour** towards); **c. (à)** to subscribe (to); – **se c.** *vpr* to club together (**pour acheter** to buy). ◆**cotisation** *nf* (*de club*) dues, subscription; (*de pension etc*) contribution(s).

coton [kɔtɔ̃] *nm* cotton; **c. (hydrophile)** cottonwool, *Am* (absorbent) cotton. ◆**cotonnade** *nf* cotton (fabric). ◆**cotonnier, -ière** *a* (*industrie*) cotton-.

côtoyer [kotwaje] *vt* (*route, rivière*) to run along, skirt; (*la misère, la folie etc*) *Fig* to be ou come close to; **c. qn** (*fréquenter*) to rub shoulders with s.o.

cotte [kɔt] *nf* (*de travail*) overalls.

cou [ku] *nm* neck; **sauter au c. de qn** to throw one's arms around s.o.; **jusqu'au c.** *Fig* up to one's eyes ou ears.

couche [kuʃ] *nf* **1** (*épaisseur*) layer; (*de peinture*) coat; *Géol* stratum; **couches sociales** social strata. **2** (*linge de bébé*) nappy, *Am* diaper. **3** **faire une fausse c.** *Méd* to have a miscarriage; **les couches** *Méd* confinement.

couch/er [kuʃe] *vt* to put to bed; (*héberger*) to put up; (*allonger*) to lay (down ou out); (*blé*) to flatten; **c. (par écrit)** to put down (in writing); **c. qn en joue** to aim at s.o.; – *vi* to sleep (**avec** with); – **se c.** *vpr* to go to bed; (*s'allonger*) to lie flat ou down; (*soleil*) to set, go down; – *nm* (*moment*) bedtime; **c. de soleil** sunset. ◆**-ant** *a* (*soleil*) setting; – *nm* (*aspect*) sunset; **le c.** (*ouest*) west. ◆**-é a être c.** to be in bed; (*étendu*) to be lying (down). ◆**-age** *nm* sleeping (situation); (*matériel*) bedding; **sac de c.** sleeping bag. ◆**couchette** *nf Rail* sleeping berth, couchette; *Nau* bunk.

couci-couça [kusikusa] *adv Fam* so-so.

coucou [kuku] *nm* (*oiseau*) cuckoo; (*pendule*) cuckoo clock; *Bot* cowslip.

coude [kud] *nm* elbow; (*de chemin, rivière*) bend; **se serrer** ou **se tenir les coudes** to help one another, stick together; **c. à c.** side by side; **coup de c.** poke ou dig (with one's elbow), nudge; **pousser du c.** to nudge. ◆**coudoyer** *vt* to rub shoulders with.

cou-de-pied [kudpje] *nm* (*pl* cous-de-pied) instep.

coudre* [kudr] *vti* to sew.

couenne [kwan] *nf* (pork) crackling.

couette [kwɛt] *nf* (*édredon*) duvet, continental quilt.

couffin [kufɛ̃] *nm* (*de bébé*) Moses basket, *Am* bassinet.

couic! [kwik] *int* eek!, squeak! ◆**couiner** *vi*
Fam to squeal; (*pleurer*) to whine.

couillon [kujɔ̃] *nm* (*idiot*) *Arg* drip, cretin.

coul/er[1] [kule] *vi* (*eau etc*) to flow; (*robinet,
nez, sueur*) to run; (*fuir*) to leak; **c. de
source** *Fig* to follow naturally; **faire c. le
sang** to cause bloodshed; – *vt* (*métal,
statue*) to cast; (*vie*) *Fig* to pass, lead;
(*glisser*) to slip; **se c. dans** (*passer*) to slip
into; **se la c. douce** (*passer*) to have things easy.
◆**—ant** *a* (*style*) flowing; (*caractère*)
easygoing. ◆**—ée** *nf* (*de métal*) casting; **c.
de lave** lava flow. ◆**—age** *nm* (*de métal,
statue*) casting; (*gaspillage*) *Fam* wastage.

couler[2] [kule] *vi* (*bateau, nageur*) to sink; **c.
à pic** to sink to the bottom; – *vt* to sink;
(*discréditer*) *Fig* to discredit.

couleur [kulœr] *nf* colour; (*colorant*) paint;
Cartes suit; *pl* (*teint, carnation*) colour; **c.
chair** flesh-coloured; **de c.** (*homme, habit
etc*) coloured; **en couleurs** (*photo, télévision*) colour-; **téléviseur c.** colour TV set;
haut en c. colourful; **sous c. de** faire while
pretending to do.

couleuvre [kulœvr] *nf* (grass) snake.

coulisse [kulis] *nf* **1** (*de porte*) runner; **à c.**
(*porte etc*) sliding. **2 dans les coulisses** Th
in the wings, backstage; **dans la c.** (*caché*)
Fig behind the scenes. ◆**coulissant** *a*
(*porte etc*) sliding.

couloir [kulwar] *nm* corridor; (*de circulation*) & *Sp* lane; (*dans un bus*) gangway.

coup [ku] *nm* blow, knock; (*léger*) tap,
touch; (*choc moral*) blow; (*de fusil etc*)
shot; (*de crayon, d'horloge*) & *Sp* stroke;
(*aux échecs etc*) move; (*fois*) *Fam* time;
donner des coups à to hit; **c. de brosse**
brush(-up); **c. de chiffon** wipe (with a rag);
c. de sonnette ring (on a bell); **c. de dents**
bite; **c. de chance** stroke of luck; **c. d'État**
coup; **c. dur** nasty blow; **sale c.** dirty
trick; **mauvais c.** piece of mischief; **c. franc**
Fb free kick; **tenter le c.** *Fam* to have a go
ou try; **réussir son c.** to bring it off; **faire les
quatre cents coups** to get into all kinds of
mischief; **tenir le c.** to hold out;
avoir/attraper le c. to have/get the knack;
sous le c. de (*émotion etc*) under the influence of; **il est dans le c.** *Fam* he's in the
know; **après c.** after the event, afterwards;
sur le c. de midi on the stroke of twelve; **sur
le c.** (*alors*) at the time; **tué sur le c.** killed
outright; **à c. sûr** for sure; **sur le c.** (*à la
suite*) one after the other, in quick succession; **tout à c., tout d'un c.** suddenly; **à tout
c.** at every go; **d'un seul c.** in one go; **du
premier c.** *Fam* (at the) first go; **du c.**

suddenly; (*de ce fait*) as a result; **pour le c.**
this time. ◆**c.-de-poing** *nm* (*pl
coups-de-poing*) **c.-de-poing** (**américain**)
knuckle-duster.

coupable [kupabl] *a* guilty (**de** of); (*plaisir,
désir*) sinful; **déclarer c.** *Jur* to convict; –
nmf guilty person, culprit.

coupe [kup] *nf* **1** *Sp* cup; (*à fruits*) dish; (*à
boire*) goblet, glass. **2** (*de vêtement etc*) cut;
Géom section; **c. de cheveux** haircut.
◆**coup/er** *vt* to cut; (*arbre*) to cut down;
(*vivres etc*) & *Tél* to cut off; (*courant etc*) to
switch (off); (*voyage*) to break (off); (*faim,
souffle etc*) to take away; (*vin*) to water
down; (*morceler*) to cut up; (*croiser*) to cut
across; **c. la parole à** to cut short; – *vi* to
cut; **c. à** (*corvée*) *Fam* to get out of; **ne
coupez pas!** *Tél* hold the line! **— se c.** *vpr*
(*routes*) to intersect; (*se trahir*) to give
oneself away; **se c. au doigt** to cut one's
finger. ◆**—ant** *a* sharp; – *nm* (cutting)
edge. ◆**—é** *nm* *Aut* coupé.

coupe-circuit [kupsirkɥi] *nm inv* Él cutout,
circuit breaker. ◆**c.-file** *nm inv* (*carte*)
official pass. ◆**c.-gorge** *nm inv* cut-throat
alley. ◆**c.-ongles** *nm inv* (finger nail)
clippers. ◆**c.-papier** *nm inv* paper knife.

couperet [kupre] *nm* (meat) chopper; (*de
guillotine*) blade.

couperosé [kuproze] *a* (*visage*) blotchy.

couple [kupl] *nm* pair, couple. ◆**coupler**
vt to couple, connect.

couplet [kuplε] *nm* verse.

coupole [kupɔl] *nf* dome.

coupon [kupɔ̃] *nm* (*tissu*) remnant,
oddment; (*pour la confection d'un vêtement*) length; (*ticket, titre*) coupon; **c.
réponse** reply coupon.

coupure [kupyr] *nf* cut; (*de journal*)
cutting, *Am* clipping; (*billet*) banknote.

cour [kur] *nf* **1** court(yard); (*de gare*)
forecourt; **c. (de récréation)** *Scol* playground. **2** (*de roi*) & *Jur* court. **3** (*de femme,
d'homme*) courtship; **faire la c. à qn** to court
s.o., woo s.o.

courage [kuraʒ] *nm* courage; (*zèle*) spirit;
perdre c. to lose heart *ou* courage; **s'armer
de c.** to pluck up courage; **bon c.!** keep your
chin up! ◆**courageux, -euse** *a* courageous; (*énergique*) spirited.

couramment [kuramɑ̃] *adv* (*parler*)
fluently; (*souvent*) frequently.

courant [kurɑ̃] **1** *a* (*fréquent*) common;
(*compte, année, langage*) current; (*eau*)
running; (*modèle, taille*) standard;
(*affaires*) routine; **le dix/etc c.** *Com* the
tenth/etc inst(ant). **2** *nm* (*de l'eau, élec-*

trique) current; **c. d'air** draught; **coupure de c.** *Él* power cut; **dans le c. de** (*mois etc*) during the course of; **être/mettre au c.** to know/tell (**de** about); **au c.** (**à jour**) up to date.

courbature [kurbatyr] *nf* (muscular) ache. ◆**courbaturé** *a* aching (all over).

courbe [kurb] *a* curved; — *nf* curve. ◆**courber** *vti* to bend; — **se c.** *vpr* to bend (over).

courge [kurʒ] *nf* marrow, *Am* squash. ◆**courgette** *nf* courgette, *Am* zucchini.

cour/ir* [kurir] *vi* to run; (*se hâter*) to rush; (*à bicyclette, en auto*) to race; **en courant** (*vite*) in a rush; **le bruit court que...** there's a rumour going around that...; **faire c.** (*nouvelle*) to spread; **il court encore** (*voleur*) he's still at large; — *vt* (*risque*) to run; (*épreuve sportive*) to run (in); (*danger*) to face, court; (*rues, monde*) to roam; (*magasins, cafés*) to go round; (*filles*) to run after. ◆**—eur** *nm Sp etc* runner; (*cycliste*) cyclist; *Aut* racing driver; (*galant*) *Péj* womanizer.

couronne [kurɔn] *nf* (*de roi, dent*) crown; (*funéraire*) wreath. ◆**couronn/er** *vt* to crown; (*auteur, ouvrage*) to award a prize to. ◆**—é** *a* (*tête*) crowned; (*ouvrage*) prize-. ◆**—ement** *nm* (*sacre*) coronation; *Fig* crowning achievement.

courrier [kurje] *nm* post, mail; (*transport*) postal *ou* mail service; (*article*) *Journ* column; **par retour du c.** by return of post, *Am* by return mail.

courroie [kurwa] *nf* (*attache*) strap; (*de transmission*) *Tech* belt.

courroux [kuru] *nm Litt* wrath.

cours [kur] *nm* **1** (*de maladie, rivière, astre, pensées etc*) course; (*cote*) rate, price; **c. d'eau** river, stream; **suivre son c.** (*déroulement*) to follow its course; **avoir c.** (*monnaie*) to be legal tender; (*théorie*) to be current; **en c.** (*travail*) in progress; (*année*) current; (*affaires*) outstanding; **en c. de route** on the way; **au c. de** during; **donner libre c. à** to give free rein to. **2** (*leçon*) class; (*série de leçons*) course; (*conférence*) lecture; (*établissement*) school; (*manuel*) textbook; **c. magistral** lecture. **3** (*allée*) avenue.

course [kurs] *nf* **1** (*action*) run(ning); (*épreuve de vitesse*) & *Fig* race; (*trajet*) journey, run; (*excursion*) hike; (*de projectile etc*) path, flight; *pl* (*de chevaux*) races; **il n'est plus dans la c.** *Fig* he's out of touch; **cheval de c.** racehorse; **voiture de c.** racing car. **2** (*commission*) errand; *pl* (*achats*)

shopping; **faire une c.** to run an errand; **faire les courses** to do the shopping.

coursier, -ière [kursje, -jɛr] *nmf* messenger.

court [kur] **1** *a* short; **c'est un peu c.** *Fam* that's not very much; — *adv* short; **couper c. à** (*entretien*) to cut short; **tout c.** quite simply; **à c. de** (*argent etc*) short of; **pris de c.** caught unawares. **2** *nm* Tennis court. ◆**c.-bouillon** *nm* (*pl* **courts-bouillons**) court-bouillon (*spiced water for cooking fish*). ◆**c.-circuit** *nm* (*pl* **courts-circuits**) *Él* short circuit. ◆**c.-circuiter** *vt* to short-circuit.

courtier, -ière [kurtje, -jɛr] *nmf* broker. ◆**courtage** *nm* brokerage.

courtisan [kurtizɑ̃] *nm Hist* courtier. ◆**courtisane** *nf Hist* courtesan. ◆**courtiser** *vt* to court.

courtois [kurtwa] *a* courteous. ◆**courtoisie** *nf* courtesy.

couru [kury] *a* (*spectacle, lieu*) popular; **c'est c.** (**d'avance**) *Fam* it's a sure thing.

couscous [kuskus] *nm Culin* couscous.

cousin, -ine [kuzɛ̃, -in] **1** *nmf* cousin. **2** *nm* (*insecte*) gnat, midge.

coussin [kusɛ̃] *nm* cushion.

cousu [kuzy] *a* sewn; **c. main** handsewn.

coût [ku] *nm* cost. ◆**coût/er** *vti* to cost; **ça coûte combien?** how much is it?, how much does it cost?; **ça lui en coûte de faire** it pains him *ou* her to do; **coûte que coûte** at all costs; **c. les yeux de la tête** to cost the earth. ◆**—ant** *a* **à prix c.** cost price. ◆**coûteux, -euse** *a* costly, expensive.

couteau, -x [kuto] *nm* knife; **coup de c.** stab; **à couteaux tirés** at daggers drawn (**avec** with); **visage en lame de c.** hatchet face; **retourner le c. dans la plaie** *Fig* to rub it in.

coutume [kutym] *nf* custom; **avoir c. de faire** to be accustomed to doing; **comme de c.** as usual; **plus que de c.** more than is customary. ◆**coutumier, -ière** *a* customary.

couture [kutyr] *nf* sewing, needlework; (*métier*) dressmaking; (*raccord*) seam; **maison de c.** fashion house. ◆**couturier** *nm* fashion designer. ◆**couturière** *nf* dressmaker.

couvent [kuvɑ̃] *nm* (*pour religieuses*) convent; (*pour moines*) monastery; (*pensionnat*) convent school.

couv/er [kuve] *vt* (*œufs*) to sit on, hatch; (*projet*) *Fig* to hatch; (*personne*) to be getting; **c. qn** to pamper s.o.; **c. des yeux** (*convoiter*) to look at enviously; — *vi* (*poule*) to brood; (*mal*) to be brewing;

(*feu*) to smoulder. ◆—ée *nf* (*petits*) brood; (*œufs*) clutch. ◆couveuse *nf* (*pour nouveaux-nés, œufs*) incubator.

couvercle [kuvɛrkl] *nm* lid, cover.

couvert [kuvɛr] 1 *nm* (*cuiller, fourchette, couteau*) (set of) cutlery; (*au restaurant*) cover charge; mettre le c. to lay the table; table de cinq couverts table set for five. 2 *nm* sous (le) c. de (*apparence*) under cover of; se mettre à c. to take cover. 3 *a* covered (de with, in); (*ciel*) overcast. ◆couverture *nf* (*de lit*) blanket, cover; (*de livre etc*) & *Fin Mil* cover; (*de toit*) roofing; c. chauffante electric blanket; c. de voyage travelling rug.

couvre-chef [kuvrǝʃɛf] *nm Hum* headgear. ◆c.-feu *nm* (*pl -x*) curfew. ◆c.-lit *nm* bedspread. ◆c.-pied *nm* quilt.

couvr/ir* [kuvrir] *vt* to cover (de with); (*voix*) to drown; — se c. *vpr* (*se vêtir*) to cover up, wrap up; (*se coiffer*) to cover one's head; (*ciel*) to cloud over. ◆—eur *nm* roofer.

cow-boy [kɔbɔj] *nm* cowboy.

crabe [krab] *nm* crab.

crac! [krak] *int* (*rupture*) snap!; (*choc*) bang!, smash!

crach/er [kraʃe] *vi* to spit; (*stylo*) to splutter; (*radio*) to crackle; — *vt* to spit (out); c. sur qch (*dédaigner*) *Fam* to turn one's nose up at sth. ◆—é a c'est son portrait tout c. *Fam* that's the spitting image of him *ou* her. ◆crachat *nm* spit, spittle.

crachin [kraʃɛ̃] *nm* (fine) drizzle.

crack [krak] *nm Fam* ace, wizard, real champ.

craie [krɛ] *nf* chalk.

craindre* [krɛ̃dr] *vt* (*personne, mort, douleur etc*) to be afraid of, fear, dread; (*chaleur etc*) to be sensitive to; c. de faire to be afraid of doing, dread doing; je crains qu'elle ne vienne I'm afraid *ou* I fear *ou* I dread (that) she might come; c. pour qch to fear for sth; ne craignez rien have no fear. ◆crainte *nf* fear, dread; de c. de faire for fear of doing; de c. que (+ *sub*) for fear that. ◆craintif, -ive *a* timid.

cramoisi [kramwazi] *a* crimson.

crampe [krɑ̃p] *nf Méd* cramp.

crampon [krɑ̃pɔ̃] 1 *nm* (*personne*) *Fam* leech, hanger-on. 2 *nmpl* (*de chaussures*) studs.

cramponner (se) [səkrɑ̃pɔne] *vpr* se c. à to hold on to, cling to.

cran [krɑ̃] *nm* 1 (*entaille*) notch; (*de ceinture*) hole; c. d'arrêt catch; couteau à c. d'arrêt flick-knife, *Am* switchblade; c. de

sûreté safety catch. 2 (*de cheveux*) wave. 3 (*audace*) *Fam* pluck, guts. 4 à c. (*excédé*) *Fam* on edge.

crâne [krɑn] *nm* skull; (*tête*) *Fam* head. ◆crânienne *af* boîte c. cranium, brain pan.

crâner [krɑne] *vi Péj* to show off, swagger.

crapaud [krapo] *nm* toad.

crapule [krapyl] *nf* villain, (filthy) scoundrel. ◆crapuleux, -euse *a* vile, sordid.

craqueler [krakle] *vt*, — se c. *vpr* to crack.

craqu/er [krake] *vi* (*branche*) to snap; (*chaussure*) to creak; (*bois sec*) to crack; (*sous la dent*) to crunch; (*se déchirer*) to split, rip; (*projet, entreprise etc*) to come apart at the seams, crumble; (*personne*) to break down, reach breaking point; — *vt* (*faire*) c. (*allumette*) to strike. ◆—ement *nm* snapping *ou* creaking *ou* cracking (sound).

crasse [kras] 1 *a* (*ignorance*) crass. 2 *nf* filth. ◆crasseux, -euse *a* filthy.

cratère [krater] *nm* crater.

cravache [kravaʃ] *nf* horsewhip, riding crop.

cravate [kravat] *nf* (*autour du cou*) tie. ◆cravaté *a* wearing a tie.

crawl [krol] *nm* (*nage*) crawl. ◆crawlé *a* dos c. backstroke.

crayeux, -euse [krɛjø, -øz] *a* chalky.

crayon [krɛjɔ̃] *nm* (*en bois*) pencil; (*de couleur*) crayon; c. à bille ballpoint (pen). ◆crayonner *vt* to pencil.

créance [kreɑ̃s] *nf* 1 *Fin Jur* claim (for money). 2 lettres de c. *Pol* credentials. ◆créancier, -ière *nmf* creditor.

créateur, -trice [kreatœr, -tris] *nmf* creator; – *a* creative; esprit c. creativeness. ◆créatif, -ive *a* creative. ◆création *nf* creation. ◆créativité *nf* creativity. ◆créature *nf* (*être*) creature.

crécelle [kresɛl] *nf* (*de supporter*) rattle.

crèche [krɛʃ] *nf* (*de Noël*) *Rel* crib, manger; *Scol* day nursery, crèche. ◆crécher *vi* (*loger*) *Arg* to bunk down, hang out.

crédible [kredibl] *a* credible. ◆crédibilité *nf* credibility.

crédit [kredi] *nm* (*influence*) & *Fin* credit; *pl* (*sommes*) funds; à c. (*acheter*) on credit, on hire purchase; faire c. *Fin* to give credit (à to). ◆créditer *vt Fin* to credit (de with). ◆créditeur, -euse *a* (*solde, compte*) crédit-; son compte est c. his account is in credit, he is in credit.

credo [kredo] *nm* creed.

crédule [kredyl] *a* credulous. ◆crédulité *nf* credulity.

créer [kree] *vt* to create.

crémaillère [kremajɛr] *nf* **pendre la c.** to have a house-warming (party).

crématoire [krematwar] *a* **four c.** crematorium. ◆**crémation** *nf* cremation.

crème [krɛm] *nf* cream; (*dessert*) cream dessert; **café c.** white coffee, coffee with cream *ou* milk; **c. Chantilly** whipped cream; **c. glacée** ice cream; **c. à raser** shaving cream; **c. anglaise** custard; – *a inv* cream(-coloured); – *nm* (*café*) white coffee. ◆**crémerie** *nf* (*magasin*) dairy (shop). ◆**crémeux, -euse** *a* creamy. ◆**crémier, -ière** *nmf* dairyman, dairywoman.

créneau, -x [kreno] *nm Hist* crenellation; (*trou*) *Fig* slot, gap; *Écon* market opportunity, niche; **faire un c.** *Aut* to park between two vehicles.

créole [kreɔl] *nmf* Creole; – *nm Ling* Creole.

crêpe [krɛp] **1** *nf Culin* pancake. **2** *nm* (*tissu*) crepe; (*caoutchouc*) crepe (rubber). ◆**crêperie** *nf* pancake bar.

crépi [krepi] *a & nm* roughcast.

crépit/er [krepite] *vi* to crackle. ◆**—ement** *nm* crackling (sound).

crépu [krepy] *a* (*cheveux, personne*) frizzy.

crépuscule [krepyskyl] *nm* twilight, dusk. ◆**crépusculaire** *a* (*lueur etc*) twilight-, dusk-.

crescendo [kreʃɛndo] *adv & nm inv* crescendo.

cresson [kresɔ̃] *nm* (water) cress.

crête [krɛt] *nf* (*d'oiseau, de vague, de montagne*) crest; **c. de coq** cockscomb.

Crète [krɛt] *nf* Crete.

crétin, -ine [kretɛ̃, -in] *nmf* cretin; – *a* cretinous.

creus/er [krøze] **1** *vt* (*terre, sol*) to dig (a hole *ou* holes in); (*trou, puits*) to dig; (*évider*) to hollow (out); (*idée*) *Fig* to go deeply into; **c. l'estomac** to whet the appetite. **2 se c.** *vpr* (*joues etc*) to become hollow; (*abîme*) *Fig* to form; **se c. la tête** *ou* **la cervelle** to rack one's brains. ◆**—é** *a* **c. de rides** (*visage*) furrowed with wrinkles.

creuset [krøzɛ] *nm* (*récipient*) crucible; (*lieu*) *Fig* melting pot.

creux, -euse [krø, -øz] *a* (*tube, joues, paroles etc*) hollow; (*estomac*) empty; (*sans activité*) slack; **assiette creuse** soup plate; – *nm* hollow; (*de l'estomac*) pit; (*moment*) slack period; **c. des reins** small of the back.

crevaison [krəvɛzɔ̃] *nf* puncture.

crevasse [krəvas] *nf* crevice, crack; (*de glacier*) crevasse; *pl* (*aux mains*) chaps. ◆**crevasser** *vt*, **– se c.** *vpr* to crack; (*peau*) to chap.

crève [krɛv] *nf* (*rhume*) *Fam* bad cold.

crev/er [krəve] *vi* (*bulle etc*) to burst; (*pneu*) to puncture, burst; (*mourir*) *Fam* to die, drop dead; **c. d'orgueil** to be bursting with pride; **c. de rire** *Fam* to split one's sides; **c. d'ennui/de froid** *Fam* to be bored/ou freeze to death; **c. de faim** *Fam* to be starving; – *vt* to burst; (*œil*) to put ou knock out; **c. qn** *Fam* to wear ou knock s.o. out; **ça (vous) crève les yeux** *Fam* it's staring you in the face; **c. le cœur** to be heartbreaking. ◆**—ant** *a* (*fatigant*) *Fam* exhausting; (*drôle*) *Fam* hilarious, killing. ◆**—é** *a* (*fatigué*) *Fam* worn ou knocked out; (*mort*) *Fam* dead. ◆**crève-cœur** *nm inv* heartbreak.

crevette [krəvɛt] *nf* (*grise*) shrimp; (*rose*) prawn.

cri [kri] *nm* (*de joie, surprise*) cry, shout; (*de peur*) scream; (*de douleur, d'alarme*) cry; (*appel*) call, cry; **c. de guerre** war cry; **un chapeau/etc dernier c.** the latest hat/etc. ◆**criard** *a* (*enfant*) bawling; (*son*) screeching; (*couleur*) gaudy, showy.

criant [krijã] *a* (*injustice etc*) glaring.

crible [kribl] *nm* sieve, riddle. ◆**cribler** *vt* to sift; **criblé de** (*balles, dettes etc*) riddled with.

cric [krik] *nm* (*instrument*) *Aut* jack.

cricket [krikɛt] *nm Sp* cricket.

crier [krije] *vi* to shout (out), cry (out); (*de peur*) to scream; (*oiseau*) to chirp; (*grincer*) to creak, squeak; **c. au scandale/etc** to proclaim sth to be a scandal/etc; **c. après qn** *Fam* to shout at s.o.; – *vt* (*injure, ordre*) to shout (out); (*son innocence etc*) to proclaim; **c. vengeance** to cry out for vengeance. ◆**crieur, -euse** *nmf* **c. de journaux** newspaper seller.

crime [krim] *nm* crime; (*assassinat*) murder. ◆**criminalité** *nf* crime (in general), criminal practice. ◆**criminel, -elle** *a* criminal; – *nmf* criminal; (*assassin*) murderer.

crin [krɛ̃] *nm* horsehair; **c. végétal** vegetable fibre; **à tous crins** (*pacifiste etc*) out-and-out. ◆**crinière** *nf* mane.

crique [krik] *nf* creek, cove.

criquet [krikɛ] *nm* locust.

crise [kriz] *nf* crisis; (*accès*) attack; (*de colère etc*) fit; (*pénurie*) shortage; **c. de conscience** (moral) dilemma.

crisp/er [krispe] *vt* (*muscle*) to tense; (*visage*) to make tense; (*poing*) to clench; **c. qn** *Fam* to aggravate s.o.; **se c. sur** (*main*) to grip tightly. ◆**—ant** *a* aggravating. ◆**—é**

a (*personne*) tense. ◆**crispation** *nf* (*agacement*) aggravation.

crisser [krise] *vi* (*pneu, roue*) to screech; (*neige*) to crunch.

cristal, -aux [kristal, -o] *nm* crystal; (*objets*) crystal(ware); (*pour nettoyer*) washing soda. ◆**cristallin** *a* (*eau, son*) crystal-clear. ◆**cristalliser** *vti*, **— se c.** *vpr* to crystallize.

critère [kriter] *nm* criterion.

critérium [kriterjɔm] *nm* (*épreuve*) *Sp* eliminating heat.

critique [kritik] *a* critical; — *nf* (*reproche*) criticism; (*analyse de film, livre etc*) review; (*de texte*) critique; **faire la c. de** (*film etc*) to review; **affronter la c.** to confront the critics; — *nm* critic. ◆**critiqu/er** *vt* to criticize. ◆**—able** *a* open to criticism.

croasser [krɔase] *vi* (*corbeau*) to caw.

croc [kro] *nm* (*crochet*) hook; (*dent*) fang. ◆**c.-en-jambe** *nm* (*pl* crocs-en-jambe) = **croche-pied**.

croche [krɔʃ] *nf* *Mus* quaver, *Am* eighth (note).

croche-pied [krɔʃpje] *nm* **faire un c.-pied à qn** to trip s.o. up.

crochet [krɔʃɛ] *nm* (*pour accrocher*) & *Boxe* hook; (*aiguille*) crochet hook; (*travail*) crochet; (*clef*) picklock; *Typ* (*square*) bracket; **faire qch au c.** to crochet sth; **faire un c.** (*route*) to make a sudden turn; (*personne*) to make a detour *ou* side trip; (*pour éviter*) to swerve; **vivre aux crochets de qn** *Fam* to sponge off *ou* on s.o. ◆**crocheter** *vt* (*serrure*) to pick. ◆**crochu** *a* (*nez*) hooked.

crocodile [krɔkɔdil] *nm* crocodile.

crocus [krɔkys] *nm* *Bot* crocus.

croire* [krwar] *vt* to believe; (*estimer*) to think, believe (**que** that); **j'ai cru la voir** I thought I saw her; **je crois que oui** I think *ou* believe so; **je n'en crois pas mes yeux** I can't believe my eyes; **à l'en c.** according to him; **il se croit malin/quelque chose** he thinks he's smart/quite something; — *vi* to believe (**à, en** in).

croisé¹ [krwaze] *nm* *Hist* crusader. ◆**croisade** *nf* crusade.

crois/er [krwaze] *vt* to cross; (*bras*) to fold, cross; **c. qn** to pass *ou* meet s.o.; — *vi* (*veston*) to fold over; *Nau* to cruise; **— se c.** *vpr* (*voitures etc*) to pass *ou* meet each other; (*routes*) to intersect; (*lettres*) to cross in the post. ◆**—é², -ée** *a* (*bras*) folded, crossed; (*veston*) double-breasted; **mots croisés** crossword; **tirs croisés** crossfire; **race croisée** crossbreed; — *nf* (*fenêtre*)

casement; **croisée des chemins** crossroads. ◆**—ement** *nm* (*action*) crossing; (*de routes*) crossroads, intersection; (*de véhicules*) passing. ◆**—eur** *nm* (*navire de guerre*) cruiser. ◆**croisière** *nf* cruise; **vitesse de c.** *Nau Av* & *Fig* cruising speed.

croître* [krwatr] *vi* (*plante etc*) to grow; (*augmenter*) to grow, increase; (*lune*) to wax. ◆**croissant 1** *a* (*nombre etc*) growing. **2** *nm* crescent; (*pâtisserie*) croissant. ◆**croissance** *nf* growth.

croix [krwa] *nf* cross.

croque-mitaine [krɔkmiten] *nm* bogeyman. ◆**c.-monsieur** *nm inv* toasted cheese and ham sandwich. ◆**c.-mort** *Fam* undertaker's assistant.

croqu/er [krɔke] **1** *vt* (*manger*) to crunch; — *vi* (*fruit etc*) to be crunchy, crunch. **2** *vt* (*peindre*) to sketch; **joli à c.** pretty as a picture. ◆**—ant** *a* (*biscuit etc*) crunchy. ◆**croquette** *nf* *Culin* croquette.

croquet [krɔkɛ] *nm* *Sp* croquet.

croquis [krɔki] *nm* sketch.

crosse [krɔs] *nf* (*d'évêque*) crook; (*de fusil*) butt; (*de hockey*) stick.

crotte [krɔt] *nf* (*de lapin etc*) mess, droppings. ◆**crottin** *nm* (*horse*) dung.

crotté [krɔte] *a* (*bottes etc*) muddy.

croul/er [krule] *vi* (*édifice, projet etc*) to crumble, collapse; **c. sous une charge** (*porteur etc*) to totter beneath a burden; **faire c.** (*immeuble etc*) to bring down. ◆**—ant** *a* (*mur etc*) tottering; — *nm* (*vieux*) *Fam* old-timer.

croupe [krup] *nf* (*de cheval*) rump; **monter en c.** (*à cheval*) to ride pillion. ◆**croupion** *nm* (*de poulet*) parson's nose.

croupier [krupje] *nm* (*au casino*) croupier.

croupir [krupir] *vi* (*eau*) to stagnate, become foul; **c. dans** (*le vice etc*) to wallow in; **eau croupie** stagnant water.

croustill/er [krustije] *vi* to be crusty; to be crunchy. ◆**—ant** *a* (*pain*) crusty; (*biscuit*) crunchy; (*histoire*) *Fig* spicy, juicy.

croûte [krut] *nf* (*de pain etc*) crust; (*de fromage*) rind; (*de plaie*) scab; **casser la c.** *Fam* to have a snack; **gagner sa c.** *Fam* to earn one's bread and butter. ◆**croûton** *nm* crust (*at end of loaf*); *pl* (*avec soupe*) croûtons.

croyable [krwajabl] *a* credible, believable. ◆**croyance** *nf* belief (**à, en** in). ◆**croyant, -ante** *a* **être c.** to be a believer; — *nmf* believer.

CRS [seeres] *nmpl abrév* (*Compagnies républicaines de sécurité*) French state security police, riot police.

cru¹ [kry] *voir* croire.

cru² [kry] 1 *a* (*aliment etc*) raw; (*lumière*) glaring; (*propos*) crude; monter à c. to ride bareback. 2 *nm* (*vignoble*) vineyard; un grand c. (*vin*) a vintage wine; vin du c. local wine.

cruauté [kryote] *nf* cruelty (envers to).

cruche [kryʃ] *nf* pitcher, jug.

crucial, -aux [krysjal, -o] *a* crucial.

crucifier [krysifje] *vt* to crucify. ◆crucifix [krysifi] *nm* crucifix. ◆crucifixion *nf* crucifixion.

crudité [krydite] *nf* (*grossièreté*) crudeness; *pl* Culin assorted raw vegetables.

crue [kry] *nf* (*de cours d'eau*) swelling, flood; en c. in spate.

cruel, -elle [kryɛl] *a* cruel (envers, avec to).

crûment [krymɑ̃] *adv* crudely.

crustacés [krystase] *nmpl* shellfish, crustaceans.

crypte [kript] *nf* crypt.

Cuba [kyba] *nm* Cuba. ◆cubain, -aine *a* & *nmf* Cuban.

cube [kyb] *nm* cube; *pl* (*jeu*) building blocks; − *a* (*mètre etc*) cubic. ◆cubique *a* cubic.

cueillir* [kœjir] *vt* to gather, pick; (*baiser*) to snatch; (*voleur*) Fam to pick up, run in ◆cueillette *nf* gathering, picking; (*fruits cueillis*) harvest.

cuiller, cuillère [kyijɛr] *nf* spoon; petite c., c. à café teaspoon; c. à soupe table spoon. ◆cuillerée *nf* spoonful.

cuir [kyir] *nm* leather; (*peau épaisse d'un animal vivant*) hide; c. chevelu scalp.

cuirasse [kyiras] *nf* Hist breastplate. ◆se cuirass/er *vpr* to steel oneself (contre against). ◆-é *nm* battleship.

cuire* [kyir] *vt* to cook; (à l'eau) to boil; (*porcelaine*) to bake, fire; − *vi* (au four) to bake; (*viande*) to roast; − *vi* to cook; to bake; (*soleil*) to bake, boil; faire c. to cook. ◆cuisant *a* (*affront, blessure etc*) stinging. ◆cuisson *nm* cooking; (*de porcelaine*) baking, firing.

cuisine [kyizin] *nf* (*pièce*) kitchen; (*art*) cooking, cuisine, cookery; (*aliments*) cooking; (*intrigues*) Péj scheming; faire la c. to cook, do the cooking; livre de c. cook(ery) book; haute c. high-class cooking. ◆cuisiner *vti* to cook; (*qn*) (*interroger*) Fam to grill s.o. ◆cuisinier, -ière *nmf* cook; − *nf* (*appareil*) cooker, stove, Am range.

cuisse [kyis] *nf* thigh; (*de poulet, mouton*) leg.

cuit [kyi] 1 *voir* cuire; − *a* cooked; bien c. well done *ou* cooked. 2 *a* (*pris*) Fam done for.

cuite [kyit] *nf* prendre une c. Fam to get plastered *ou* drunk.

cuivre [kyivr] *nm* (*rouge*) copper; (*jaune*) brass; *pl* (*ustensiles*) & Mus brass. ◆cuivré *a* a copper-coloured, coppery.

cul [ky] *nm* (*derrière*) Fam backside; (*de bouteille etc*) bottom. ◆c.-de-jatte *nm* (*pl* culs-de-jatte) legless cripple. ◆c.-de-sac *nm* (*pl* culs-de-sac) dead end, cul-de-sac.

culasse [kylas] *nf* Aut cylinder head; (*d'une arme à feu*) breech.

culbute [kylbyt] *nf* (*cabriole*) sommersault; (*chute*) (backward) tumble; faire une c. to sommersault; to tumble. ◆culbuter *vi* to tumble over (backwards); − *vt* (*personne, chaise*) to knock over.

culinaire [kyliner] *a* (*art*) culinary; (*recette*) cooking.

culmin/er [kylmine] *vi* (*montagne*) to reach its highest point, peak (à at); (*colère*) Fig to reach a peak. ◆—ant *a* point c. (*de réussite, montagne etc*) peak.

culot [kylo] *nm* 1 (*aplomb*) Fam nerve, cheek. 2 (*d'ampoule, de lampe etc*) base. ◆culotté *a* être c. Fam to have plenty of nerve *ou* cheek.

culotte [kylɔt] *nf* Sp (pair of) shorts; (*de femme*) (pair of) knickers *ou* Am panties; culottes (courtes) (*de jeune garçon*) short trousers *ou* Am pants; c. de cheval riding breeches.

culpabilité [kylpabilite] *nf* guilt.

culte [kylt] *nm* (*hommage*) Rel worship, cult; (*pratique*) Rel religion; (*service protestant*) service; (*admiration*) Fig cult.

cultiv/er [kyltive] *vt* (*terre*) to farm, cultivate; (*plantes*) to grow, cultivate; (*goût, relations etc*) to cultivate; − se c. *vpr* to cultivate one's mind. ◆—é *a* (*esprit, personne*) cultured, cultivated. ◆cultivateur, -trice *nmf* farmer. ◆culture *nf* (*action*) farming, cultivation; (*agriculture*) farming; (*horticulture*) growing, cultivation; (*éducation, civilisation*) culture; *pl* (*terres*) fields (under cultivation); (*plantes*) crops; c. générale general knowledge. ◆culturel, -elle *a* cultural.

cumin [kymɛ̃] *nm* Bot Culin caraway.

cumul [kymyl] *nm* c. de fonctions plurality of offices. ◆cumulatif, -ive *a* cumulative. ◆cumuler *vt* c. deux fonctions to hold two offices (at the same time).

cupide [kypid] *a* avaricious. ◆cupidité *nf* avarice, cupidity.

Cupidon [kypidɔ̃] *nm* Cupid.

cure [kyr] *nf* **1** (course of) treatment, cure. **2** (*fonction*) office (of a parish priest); (*résidence*) presbytery. **◆curable** *a* curable. **◆curatif, -ive** *a* curative. **◆curé** *nm* (parish) priest.

curer [kyre] *vt* to clean out; **se c. le nez/ les dents** to pick one's nose/ teeth. **◆curedent** *nm* toothpick. **◆cure-ongles** *nm inv* nail cleaner. **◆cure-pipe** *nm* pipe cleaner.

curieux, -euse [kyrjø, -øz] *a* (*bizarre*) curious; (*indiscret*) inquisitive, curious (**de** about); **c. de savoir** curious to know; – *nmf* inquisitive *ou* curious person; (*badaud*) onlooker. **◆curieusement** *adv* curiously. **◆curiosité** *nf* (*de personne, forme etc*) curiosity; (*chose*) curiosity; (*spectacle*) unusual sight.

curriculum (vitæ) [kyrikylɔm(vite)] *nm inv* curriculum (vitae), *Am* résumé.

curseur [kyrsœr] *nm* (*d'un ordinateur*) cursor.

cutané [kytane] *a* (*affection etc*) skin-. **◆cuti(-réaction)** *nf* skin test.

cuve [kyv] *nf* vat; (*réservoir*) & *Phot* tank. **◆cuvée** *nf* (*récolte de vin*) vintage.

◆cuver *vt* **c. son vin** *Fam* to sleep it off.
◆cuvette *nf* (*récipient*) & *Géog* basin, bowl; (*des cabinets*) pan, bowl.

cyanure [sjanyr] *nm* cyanide.

cybernétique [sibɛrnetik] *nf* cybernetics.

cycle [sikl] *nm* **1** (*série, révolution*) cycle. **2** (*bicyclette*) cycle. **◆cyclable** *a* (*piste*) cycle-. **◆cyclique** *a* cyclic(al). **◆cyclisme** *nm Sp* cycling. **◆cycliste** *nmf* cyclist; – *a* (*course*) cycle-; (*champion*) cycling; **coureur c.** racing cyclist. **◆cyclomoteur** *nm* moped.

cyclone [siklon] *nm* cyclone.

cygne [siɲ] *nm* swan; **chant du c.** *Fig* swan song.

cylindre [silɛ̃dr] *nm* cylinder; (*de rouleau compresseur*) roller. **◆cylindrée** *nf Aut* (engine) capacity. **◆cylindrique** *a* cylindrical.

cymbale [sɛbal] *nf* cymbal.

cynique [sinik] *a* cynical; – *nmf* cynic. **◆cynisme** *nm* cynicism.

cyprès [siprɛ] *nm* (*arbre*) cypress.

cypriote [siprijɔt] *a* & *nmf* Cypriot.

cytise [sitiz] *nf Bot* laburnum.

D

D, d [de] *nm* D, d.

d' [d] *voir de* 1,2.

d'abord [dabɔr] *adv* (*en premier lieu*) first; (*au début*) at first.

dactylo [daktilo] *nf* (*personne*) typist; (*action*) typing. **◆dactylographie** *nf* typing. **◆dactylographier** *vt* to type.

dada [dada] *nm* (*manie*) hobby horse, pet subject.

dadais [dadɛ] *nm* (**grand**) **d.** big oaf.

dahlia [dalja] *nm* dahlia.

daigner [deɲe] *vt* **d. faire** to condescend *ou* deign to do.

daim [dɛ̃] *nm* fallow deer; (*mâle*) buck; (*cuir*) suede.

dais [dɛ] *nm* (*de lit, feuillage etc*) canopy.

dalle [dal] *nf* paving stone; (*funèbre*) (flat) gravestone. **◆dallage** *nm* (*action, surface*) paving. **◆dallé** *a* (*pièce, cour etc*) paved.

daltonien, -ienne [daltɔnjɛ̃, -jɛn] *a* & *n* colour-blind (person). **◆daltonisme** *nm* colour blindness.

dame [dam] *nf* **1** lady; (*mariée*) married lady. **2** *Échecs Cartes* queen; (*au jeu de dames*) king; (**jeu de**) **dames** draughts, *Am*

checkers. **◆damer** *vt* (*au jeu de dames*) to crown; **d. le pion à qn** to outsmart s.o. **◆damier** *nm* draughtboard, *Am* checkerboard.

damner [dane] *vt* to damn; **faire d.** *Fam* to torment, drive mad; – **se d.** *vpr* to be damned. **◆damnation** *nf* damnation.

dancing [dɑ̃siŋ] *nm* dance hall.

dandiner (se) [sədɑ̃dine] *vpr* to waddle.

dandy [dɑ̃di] *nm* dandy.

Danemark [danmark] *nm* Denmark. **◆danois, -oise** *a* Danish; – *nmf* Dane; – *nm* (*langue*) Danish.

danger [dɑ̃ʒe] *nm* danger; **en d.** in danger *ou* jeopardy; **mettre en d.** to endanger, jeopardize; **en cas de d.** in an emergency; **en d. de mort** in peril of death; **'d. de mort'** (*panneau*) 'danger'; **sans d.** (*se promener*) safely; **être sans d.** to be safe; **pas de d.!** *Fam* no way!, no fear! **◆dangereux, -euse** *a* dangerous (**pour** to). **◆dangereusement** *adv* dangerously.

dans [dɑ̃] *prép* in; (*changement de lieu*) into; (*à l'intérieur de*) inside, within; **entrer d.** to go in(to); **d. Paris** in Paris, within Paris;

d. un rayon de within (a radius of); **boire/prendre**/*etc* **d.** to drink/take/*etc* from *ou* out of; **marcher d. les rues** (*à travers*) to walk through *ou* about the streets; **d. ces circonstances** under *ou* in these circumstances; **d. deux jours**/*etc* (*temps futur*) in two days/*etc*, in two days'/*etc* time; **d. les dix francs**/*etc* (*quantité*) about ten francs/*etc*.

danse [dɑ̃s] *nf* dance; (*art*) dancing. ◆**dans/er** *vti* to dance; **faire d. l'anse du panier** (*domestique*) to fiddle on the shopping money. ◆—**eur, -euse** *nmf* dancer; (*cycliste*) standing on the pedals.

dard [dar] *nm* (*d'abeille etc*) sting; (*de serpent*) tongue. ◆**darder** *vt Litt* (*flèche*) to shoot; (*regard*) to flash, dart; **le soleil dardait ses rayons** the sun cast down its burning rays.

dare-dare [dardar] *adv Fam* at *ou* on the double.

date [dat] *nf* date; **de vieille d.** (*amitié etc*) (of) long-standing; **faire d.** (*événement*) to mark an important date, be epoch-making; **en d. du ...** dated the ...; **d. limite** deadline. ◆**datation** *nf* dating. ◆**dater** *vt* (*lettre etc*) to date; – *vi* (*être dépassé*) to date, be dated; **d. de** to date back to, date from; **à d. de** as from. ◆**dateur** *nm* (*de montre*) date indicator; – *a & nm* (*tampon*) date stamp.

datte [dat] *nf* (*fruit*) date. ◆**dattier** *nm* date palm.

daube [dob] *nf* **bœuf en d.** braised beef stew.

dauphin [dofɛ̃] *nm* (*mammifère marin*) dolphin.

davantage [davɑ̃taʒ] *adv* (*quantité*) more; (*temps*) longer; **d. de temps**/*etc* more time/*etc*; **d. que** more than; longer than.

de[1] [d(ə)] (**d'** *before a vowel or mute h*; **de** + **le** = **du**, **de** + **les** = **des**) *prép* **1** (*complément d'un nom*) of; **les rayons du soleil** the rays of the sun, the sun's rays; **la ville de Paris** the town of Paris; **le livre de Paul** Paul's book; **un pont de fer** an iron bridge; **le train de Londres** the London train; **une augmentation/diminution de** an increase/decrease in. **2** (*complément d'un adjectif*) **digne de** worthy of; **heureux de partir** happy to leave; **content de qch** pleased with sth. **3** (*complément d'un verbe*) **parler de** to speak of *ou* about; **se souvenir de** to remember; **décider de faire** to decide to do; **traiter de lâche** to call a coward. **4** (*provenance: lieu & temps*) from; **venir/dater de** to come/date from; **mes**

amis du village my friends from the village, my village friends; **le train de Londres** the train from London. **5** (*agent*) **accompagné de** accompanied by. **6** (*moyen*) **armé de** armed with; **se nourrir de** to live on. **7** (*manière*) **d'une voix douce** in *ou* with a gentle voice. **8** (*cause*) **puni de** punished for; **mourir de faim** to die of hunger. **9** (*temps*) **travailler de nuit** to work by night; **six heures du matin** six o'clock in the morning. **10** (*mesure*) **avoir six mètres de haut**, **être haut de six mètres** to be six metres high; **retarder de deux heures** to delay by two hours; **homme de trente ans** thirty-year-old man; **gagner cent francs de l'heure** to earn one hundred francs an hour.

de[2] [d(ə)] *art partitif* some; **elle boit du vin** she drinks (some) wine; **il ne boit pas de vin** (*négation*) he doesn't drink (any) wine; **des fleurs** (some) flowers; **de jolies fleurs** (some) pretty flowers; **d'agréables soirées** (some) pleasant evenings; **il y en a six de tués** (*avec un nombre*) there are six killed.

dé [de] *nm* (*à jouer*) dice; (*à coudre*) thimble; **les dés** the dice; (*jeu*) dice; **les dés sont jetés** *Fig* the die is cast; **couper en dés** *Culin* to dice.

déambuler [deɑ̃byle] *vi* to stroll, saunter.

débâcle [debɑkl] *nf Mil* rout; (*ruine*) *Fig* downfall; (*des glaces*) *Géog* breaking up.

déball/er [debale] *vt* to unpack; (*étaler*) to display. ◆—**age** *nm* unpacking; display.

débandade [debɑ̃dad] *nf* (*mad*) rush, stampede; *Mil* rout; **à la d.** in confusion; **tout va à la d.** everything's going to rack and ruin.

débaptiser [debatize] *vt* (*rue*) to rename.

débarbouiller [debarbuje] *vt* **d. qn** to wash s.o.'s face; **se d.** to wash one's face.

débarcadère [debarkader] *nm* landing stage, quay.

débardeur [debardœr] *nm* **1** (*docker*) stevedore. **2** (*vêtement*) slipover, *Am* (*sweater*) vest.

débarqu/er [debarke] *vt* (*passagers*) to land; (*marchandises*) to unload; (*qn congédier*) *Fam* to sack s.o.; – *vi* (*passagers*) to disembark, land; (*être naïf*) *Fam* not to be aware of sth; **d. chez qn** *Fam* to turn up suddenly at s.o.'s place. ◆—**ement** *nm* landing; unloading; *Mil* landing.

débarras [debara] *nm* lumber room, *Am* storeroom; **bon d.!** *Fam* good riddance! ◆**débarrasser** *vt* (*voie, table etc*) to clear (**de** of); **d. qn de** (*ennemi, soucis etc*) to rid s.o. of; (*manteau etc*) to relieve s.o. of; **se d. de** to get rid of, rid oneself of.

débat [deba] *nm* discussion, debate; *pl* Pol Jur proceedings. ◆**débattre*** *vt* to discuss, debate; — **se d.** *vpr* to struggle *ou* fight (to get free), put up a fight.

débauche [deboʃ] *nf* debauchery; **une d. de** Fig a wealth *ou* profusion of. ◆**débauch/er** *vt* **d. qn** (*détourner*) Fam to entice s.o. away from his work; (*licencier*) to dismiss s.o., lay s.o. off. ◆**-é, -ée** a (*libertin*) debauched, profligate; — *nmf* debauchee, profligate.

débile [debil] a (*esprit, enfant etc*) weak, feeble; *Péj* Fam idiotic; — *nmf* Péj Fam idiot, moron. ◆**débilité** *nf* debility, weakness; *pl* (*niaiseries*) Fam sheer nonsense. ◆**débiliter** *vt* to debilitate, weaken.

débiner [debine] **1** *vt* (*décrier*) Fam to run down. **2 se d.** *vpr* (*s'enfuir*) Arg to hop it, bolt.

débit [debi] *nm* **1** (*vente*) turnover, sales; (*de fleuve*) (rate of) flow; (*d'un orateur*) delivery; **d. de tabac** tobacconist's shop, *Am* tobacco store; **d. de boissons** bar, café. **2** (*compte*) Fin debit. ◆**débiter** *vt* **1** (*découper*) to cut up, slice up (*en into*); (*vendre*) to sell; (*fournir*) to yield; (*dire*) Péj to utter, spout. **2** Fin to debit. ◆**débiteur, -trice** *nmf* debtor; — a (*solde, compte*) debit-; **son compte est d.** his account is in debit, he is in debit.

déblais [deble] *nmpl* (*terre*) earth; (*décombres*) rubble. ◆**déblayer** *vt* (*terrain, décombres*) to clear.

débloquer [debloke] **1** *vt* (*machine*) to unjam; (*crédits, freins, compte*) to release; (*prix*) to decontrol. **2** *vi* (*divaguer*) Fam to talk through one's hat, talk nonsense.

déboires [debwar] *nmpl* disappointments, setbacks.

déboît/er [debwate] **1** *vt* (*tuyau*) to disconnect; (*os*) Méd to dislocate. **2** *vi* Aut to pull out, change lanes. ◆**-ement** *nm* Méd dislocation.

débonnaire [deboner] a good-natured, easy-going.

débord/er [deborde] *vi* (*fleuve, liquide*) to overflow; (*en bouillant*) to boil over; **d. de** (*vie, joie etc*) Fig to be overflowing *ou* bubbling over with; **l'eau déborde du vase** the water is running over the top of the vase, the water is overflowing the vase; — *vt* (*dépasser*) to go *ou* extend beyond; (*faire saillie*) to stick out from; *Mil Sp* to outflank; **débordé de travail/de visites** snowed under with work/visits.

◆**-ement** *nm* overflowing; (*de joie, activité*) outburst.

débouch/er [debuʃe] **1** *vt* (*bouteille*) to open, uncork; (*lavabo, tuyau*) to clear, unblock. **2** *vi* (*surgir*) to emerge, come out (*de from*); **d. sur** (*rue*) to lead out onto, lead into; Fig to lead up to. ◆**-é** *nm* (*carrière*) & Géog opening; (*de rue*) exit; (*marché*) Com outlet.

débouler [debule] *vi* (*arriver*) Fam to burst in, turn up.

déboulonner [debulone] *vt* to unbolt; **d. qn** Fam (*renvoyer*) to sack *ou* fire s.o.; (*discréditer*) to bring s.o. down.

débours [debur] *nmpl* expenses. ◆**débourser** *vt* to pay out.

debout [d(ə)bu] adv standing (up); **mettre d.** (*planche etc*) to stand up, put upright; **se mettre d.** to stand *ou* get up; **se tenir** *ou* **rester d.** (*personne*) to stand (up), remain standing (up); **rester d.** (*édifice etc*) to remain standing; **être d.** (*levé*) to be up (and about); **d.!** get up!; **ça ne tient pas d.** (*théorie etc*) that doesn't hold water *ou* make sense.

déboutonner [debutone] *vt* to unbutton, undo; — **se d.** *vpr* (*personne*) to undo one's buttons.

débraillé [debraje] a (*tenue etc*) slovenly, sloppy; — *nm* slovenliness, sloppiness.

débrancher [debrãʃe] *vt* Él to unplug, disconnect.

débrayer [debreje] *vi* **1** Aut to declutch, release the clutch. **2** (*se mettre en grève*) to stop work. ◆**débrayage** (*grève*) strike, walk-out.

débridé [debride] a (*effréné*) unbridled.

débris [debri] *nmpl* fragments, scraps; (*restes*) remains; (*détritus*) rubbish, debris.

débrouiller [debruje] **1** *vt* (*écheveau etc*) to unravel, disentangle; (*affaire*) to sort out. **2 se d.** *vpr* to manage, get by, make out; **se d. pour faire** to manage (somehow) to do. ◆**débrouillard** a smart, resourceful. ◆**débrouillardise** *nf* smartness, resourcefulness.

débroussailler [debrusaje] *vt* (*chemin*) to clear (of brushwood); (*problème*) Fig to clarify.

débusquer [debyske] *vt* (*gibier, personne*) to drive out, dislodge.

début [deby] *nm* start, beginning; **au d.** at the beginning; **faire ses débuts** (*sur la scène etc*) to make one's debut. ◆**début/er** *vi* to start, begin; (*dans une carrière*) to start out in life; (*sur la scène etc*) to make one's debut. ◆—**ant, -ante** *nmf* beginner; — *a* novice.

déca [deka] *nm Fam* decaffeinated coffee.

deçà (en) [ɑ̃d(ə)sa] *adv* (on) this side; — *prép* **en d. de** (on) this side of; (*succès, prix etc*) *Fig* short of.

décacheter [dekaʃte] *vt* (*lettre etc*) to open, unseal.

décade [dekad] *nf* (*dix jours*) period of ten days; (*décennie*) decade.

décadent [dekadɑ̃] *a* decadent. ◆**décadence** *nf* decay, decadence.

décaféiné [dekafeine] *a* decaffeinated.

décalaminer [dekalamine] *vt* (*moteur*) *Aut* to decoke, decarbonize.

décal/er [dekale] *vt* **1** (*avancer*) to shift; (*départ, repas*) to shift (the time of). **2** (*ôter les cales de*) to unwedge. ◆—**age** *nm* (*écart*) gap, discrepancy; **d. horaire** time difference.

décalque [dekalk] *nm* tracing. ◆**décalquer** *vt* (*dessin*) to trace.

décamper [dekɑ̃pe] *vi* to make off, clear off.

décanter [dekɑ̃te] *vt* (*liquide*) to settle, clarify; **d. ses idées** to clarify one's ideas; — **se d.** *vpr* (*idées, situation*) to become clearer, settle.

décap/er [dekape] *vt* (*métal*) to clean, scrape down; (*surface peinte*) to strip. ◆—**ant** *nm* cleaning agent; (*pour enlever la peinture*) paint stripper. ◆—**eur** *nm* **d. thermique** hot-air paint stripper.

décapiter [dekapite] *vt* to decapitate, behead.

décapotable [dekapɔtabl] *a* (*voiture*) convertible.

décapsul/er [dekapsyle] *vt* **d. une bouteille** to take the cap *ou* top off a bottle. ◆—**eur** *nm* bottle-opener.

décarcasser (se) [sədekarkase] *vpr Fam* to flog oneself to death (**pour faire** doing).

décathlon [dekatlɔ̃] *nm Sp* decathlon.

décati [dekati] *a* worn out, decrepit.

décavé [dekave] *a Fam* ruined.

décéd/er [desede] *vi* to die. ◆—**é** *a* deceased.

déceler [desle] *vt* (*trouver*) to detect, uncover; (*révéler*) to reveal.

décembre [desɑ̃br] *nm* December.

décennie [deseni] *nf* decade.

décent [desɑ̃] *a* (*bienséant, acceptable*) decent. ◆**décemment** [-amɑ̃] *adv* decently. ◆**décence** *nf* decency.

décentraliser [desɑ̃tralize] *vt* to decentral-

ize. ◆**décentralisation** *nf* decentralization.

déception [desɛpsjɔ̃] *nf* disappointment. ◆**décevoir*** *vt* to disappoint. ◆**décevant** *a* disappointing.

décerner [deserne] *vt* (*prix etc*) to award; (*mandat d'arrêt etc*) *Jur* to issue.

décès [desɛ] *nm* death.

déchaîn/er [deʃene] *vt* (*colère, violence*) to unleash, let loose; **d. l'enthousiasme/les rires** to set off wild enthusiasm/a storm of laughter; — **se d.** *vpr* (*tempête, rires*) to break out; (*foule*) to run amok *ou* riot; (*colère, personne*) to explode. ◆—**é** *a* (*foule, flots*) wild, raging. ◆—**ement** [-ɛnmɑ̃] *nm* (*de rires, de haine etc*) outburst; (*de violence*) outbreak, eruption; **le d. de la tempête** the raging of the storm.

déchanter [deʃɑ̃te] *vi Fam* to become disillusioned; (*changer de ton*) to change one's tune.

décharge [deʃarʒ] *nf Jur* discharge; **d. (publique)** (rubbish) dump *ou* tip, *Am* (garbage) dump; **d. (électrique)** (electrical) discharge, shock; **recevoir une d. (électrique)** to get a shock; **à la d. de qn** in s.o.'s defence. ◆**décharg/er** *vt* to unload; (*batterie*) *Él* to discharge; (*accusé*) *Jur* to discharge, exonerate; **d. qn de** (*travail etc*) to relieve s.o. of; **d. sur qn** (*son arme*) to fire at s.o.; (*sa colère*) to vent on s.o.; — **se d.** *vpr* (*batterie*) to go flat; **se d. sur qn du soin de faire qch** to unload onto s.o. the job of doing sth. ◆—**ement** *nm* unloading.

décharné [deʃarne] *a* skinny, bony.

déchauss/er [deʃose] *vt* **d. qn** to take s.o.'s shoes off; **se d.** to take one's shoes off; (*dent*) to get loose.

dèche [dɛʃ] *nf* **être dans la d.** *Arg* to be flat broke.

déchéance [deʃeɑ̃s] *nf* (*déclin*) decline, decay, degradation.

déchet [deʃɛ] *nm* **déchets** (*résidus*) scraps, waste; **il y a du d.** there's some waste *ou* wastage.

déchiffrer [deʃifre] *vt* (*message*) to decipher; (*mauvaise écriture*) to make out, decipher.

déchiquet/er [deʃikte] *vt* to tear to shreds, cut to bits. ◆—**é** *a* (*drapeau etc*) (all) in shreds; (*côte*) jagged.

déchir/er [deʃire] *vt* to tear (up), rip (up); (*vêtement*) to tear, rip; (*ouvrir*) to tear *ou* rip open; (*pays, groupe*) to tear apart; **d. l'air** (*bruit*) to rend the air; **ce bruit me déchire les oreilles** this noise is ear-splitting; — **se d.** *vpr* (*robe etc*) to tear, rip. ◆—ant a (navrant) heart-breaking; (aigu) ear-splitting. ◆—ement nm (souffrance) heartbreak; pl (divisions) Pol deep rifts. ◆**déchirure** nf tear, rip; d. musculaire torn muscle.

déchoir [deʃwar] vi to lose prestige. ◆**déchu** a (ange) fallen; être d. de (ses droits etc) to have forfeited.

décibel [desibɛl] nm decibel.

décid/er [deside] vt (envoi, opération) to decide on; d. que to decide that; d. qn à faire to persuade s.o. to do; — vi de (destin de qn) to decide; (voyage etc) to decide on; d. de faire to decide to do; — se d. vpr (question) to be decided; se d. à faire to make up one's mind to do; se d. pour qch to decide on sth ou in favour of sth. ◆—é a (air, ton) determined, decided; (net, pas douteux) decided; (net) it's settled; être d. à faire to be decided about doing ou determined to do. ◆—ément adv undoubtedly

décilitre [desilitr] nm decilitre.

décimal, -aux [desimal, -o] a decimal. ◆**décimale** nf decimal.

décimer [desime] vt to decimate.

décimètre [desimetr] nm decimetre; double d. ruler.

décisif, -ive [desizif, -iv] a decisive; (moment) crucial. ◆**décision** nf decision; (fermeté) determination.

déclamer [deklame] vt to declaim; Péj to spout. ◆**déclamatoire** a Péj bombastic.

déclarer [deklare] vt to declare (que that); (décès, vol etc) to notify; d. coupable to convict, find guilty; d. la guerre to declare war (à on); — se d. vpr (s'expliquer) to declare one's views; (incendie, maladie) to break out; se d. contre to come out against. ◆**déclaration** nf declaration; (de décès etc) notification; (commentaire) statement, comment; d. de revenus tax return.

déclasser [deklase] vt (livres etc) to put out of order; (hôtel etc) to downgrade; d. qn Sp to relegate to s.o. (in the placing).

déclench/er [deklɑ̃ʃe] vt (mécanisme) to set ou trigger off, release; (attaque) to launch; (provoquer) to trigger off, spark off; d. le travail Méd to induce labour; — se d. vpr (sonnerie) to go off; (attaque, grève) to start. ◆—ement nm (d'un appareil) release.

déclic [deklik] nm (mécanisme) catch, trigger; (bruit) click.

déclin [deklɛ̃] nm decline; (du jour) close; (de la lune) wane. ◆**décliner** 1 vt (refuser) to decline. 2 vt (réciter) to state. 3 vi (forces etc) to decline, wane; (jour) to draw to a close.

déclivité [deklivite] nf slope.

décocher [dekɔʃe] vt (flèche) to shoot, fire; (coup) to let fly, aim; (regard) to flash.

décoder [dekɔde] vt (message) to decode.

décoiffer [dekwafe] vt d. qn to mess up s.o.'s hair.

décoincer [dekwɛ̃se] vt (engrenage) to unjam.

décoll/er [dekɔle] 1 vi (avion etc) to take off; elle ne décolle pas d'ici Fam she won't leave ou budge. 2 vt (timbre etc) to unstick; — se d. vpr to come unstuck. ◆—age nm Av takeoff.

décolleté [dekɔlte] a (robe) low-cut; — nm (de robe) low neckline; (de femme) bare neck and shoulders.

décoloniser [dekɔlɔnize] vt to decolonize. ◆**décolonisation** nf decolonization.

décolor/er [dekɔlɔre] vt to discolour, fade; (cheveux) to bleach. ◆—ant nm bleach. ◆**décoloration** nf discolo(u)ration; bleaching.

décombres [dekɔ̃br] nmpl ruins, rubble, debris.

décommander [dekɔmɑ̃de] vt (marchandises, invitation) to cancel; (invités) to put off; — se d. vpr to cancel (one's appointment).

décomposer [dekɔ̃poze] vt to decompose; (visage) to distort; — se d. vpr (pourrir) to decompose; (visage) to become distorted. ◆**décomposition** nf decomposition.

décompresser [dekɔ̃prese] vi Psy Fam to unwind.

décompression [dekɔ̃presjɔ̃] nf decompression.

décompte [dekɔ̃t] nm deduction; (détail) breakdown. ◆**décompter** vt to deduct.

déconcerter [dekɔ̃sɛrte] vt to disconcert.

déconfit [dekɔ̃fi] a downcast. ◆**déconfiture** nf (state of) collapse ou defeat; (faillite) Fam financial ruin.

décongeler [dekɔ̃ʒle] vt (aliment) to thaw, defrost.

décongestionner [dekɔ̃ʒɛstjɔne] vt (rue) & Méd to relieve congestion in.

déconnecter [dekɔnɛkte] vt El & Fig to disconnect.

déconner [dekɔne] vi (divaguer) Fam to talk nonsense.

déconseiller [dekɔ̃seje] vt d. qch à qn to advise s.o. against sth; d. à qn de faire to advise s.o. against doing; c'est déconseillé it is inadvisable.

déconsidérer [dekɔ̃sidere] vt to discredit.

décontaminer [dekɔ̃tamine] vt to decontaminate.

décontenancer [dekɔ̃tnɑ̃se] vt to disconcert; — **se d.** vpr to lose one's composure, become flustered.

décontracter [dekɔ̃trakte] vt, — **se d.** vpr to relax. ◆**décontraction** nf relaxation.

déconvenue [dekɔ̃vny] nf disappointment.

décor [dekɔr] nm Th scenery, decor; Cin set; (paysage) scenery; (d'intérieur) decoration; (cadre, ambiance) setting; **entrer dans le d.** (véhicule) Fam to run off the road.

décorer [dekɔre] vt (maison, soldat etc) to decorate (de with). ◆**décorateur, -trice** nmf (interior) decorator; Cin set designer; Cin set designer. ◆**décoratif, -ive** a decorative. ◆**décoration** nf decoration.

décortiquer [dekɔrtike] vt (graine) to husk; (homard etc) to shell; (texte) Fam to take to pieces, dissect.

découcher [dekuʃe] vi to stay out all night.

découdre [dekudr] vt to unstitch; — vi **en d.** Fam to fight it out; — **se d.** vpr to come unstitched.

découler [dekule] vi **d. de** to follow from.

découp/er [dekupe] vt (poulet etc) to carve; (article etc) Journ to cut out; **se d. sur** to stand out against. ◆**-é a** (côte) jagged. ◆**-age** nm carving; cutting out; (image) cut-out. ◆**découpure** nf (contour) jagged outline; (morceau) piece cut out, cut-out.

découplé [dekuple] a **bien d.** (personne) well-built, strapping.

décourag/er [dekuraʒe] vt (dissuader) to discourage (de from); (démoraliser) to dishearten, discourage; — **se d.** vpr to get discouraged ou disheartened. ◆**-ement** nm discouragement.

décousu [dekuzy] a (propos, idées) disconnected.

découvrir* [dekuvrir] vt (trésor, terre etc) to discover; (secret, vérité etc) to find out, discover; (casserole etc) to take the lid off; (dévoiler) to disclose (à to); (dénuder) to uncover, expose; (voir) to perceive; **d. que** to discover ou find out that; — **se d.** vpr (se dénuder) to uncover oneself; (enlever son chapeau) to take one's hat off; (ciel) to clear (up). ◆**découvert 1** a (terrain) open; (tête etc) bare; **à d.** exposed, unprotected; **agir à d.** to act openly. **2** nm (d'un compte) Fin overdraft. ◆**découverte** nf discovery; **partir** ou **aller à la d. de** to go in search of.

décrasser [dekrase] vt (éduquer) to take the rough edges off.

décrépit [dekrepi] a (vieillard) decrepit.

◆**décrépitude** nf (des institutions etc) decay.

décret [dekre] nm decree. ◆**décréter** vt to order, decree.

décrier [dekrije] vt to run down, disparage.

décrire* [dekrir] vt to describe.

décroch/er [dekrɔʃe] **1** vt (détacher) to unhook; (tableau) to take down; (obtenir) Fam to get, land; (le téléphone) to pick up the phone. **2** vi Fam (abandonner) to give up; (perdre le fil) to be unable to follow, lose track. ◆**-é a** (téléphone) off the hook.

décroître* [dekrwatr] vi (mortalité etc) to decrease, decline; (eaux) to subside; (jours) to draw in. ◆**décroissance** nf decrease, decline (de in, of).

décrotter [dekrɔte] vt (chaussures) to clean ou scrape (the mud off). ◆**décrottoir** nm shoe scraper.

décrypter [dekripte] vt (message) to decipher, decode.

déçu [desy] voir **décevoir**; – a disappointed.

déculotter (se) [sədekylɔte] vpr to take off one's trousers ou Am pants. ◆**déculottée** nf Fam thrashing.

décupler [dekyple] vti to increase tenfold.

dédaigner [dedeɲe] vt (personne, richesse etc) to scorn, despise; (repas) to turn up one's nose at; (offre) to spurn; (ne pas tenir compte de) to disregard. ◆**dédaigneux, -euse** a scornful, disdainful (de of). ◆**dédain** nm scorn, disdain (pour, de for).

dédale [dedal] nm maze, labyrinth.

dedans [d(ə)dɑ̃] adv inside; **de d.** from (the) inside, from within; **en d.** on the inside; **au-d. (de), au d. (de)** inside; **au-d.** ou **au d. de lui-même** inwardly; **tomber d.** (trou) to fall in (it); **donner d.** (être dupé) Fam to fall in; **mettre d.** Fam (en prison) to put inside; (tromper) to take in; **je me suis fait rentrer d.** (accident de voiture) Fam someone went ou crashed into me; — nm **le d.** the inside.

dédicace [dedikas] nf dedication, inscription. ◆**dédicacer** vt (livre etc) to dedicate, inscribe (à to).

dédier [dedje] vt to dedicate.

dédire (se) [sədedir] vpr to go back on one's word; **se d. de** (promesse etc) to go back on. ◆**dédit** nm (somme) Com forfeit, penalty.

dédommag/er [dedomaʒe] vt to compensate (de for). ◆**-ement** nm compensation.

dédouaner [dedwane] vt (marchandises) to clear through customs; **d. qn** to restore s.o.'s prestige.

dédoubl/er [deduble] vt (classe etc) to split into two; **d. un train** to run an extra train; **– se d.** vpr to be in two places at once. **◆—ement** nm **d. de la personnalité** Psy split personality.

déduire* [dedɥir] vt (retirer) to deduct (de from); (conclure) to deduce (de from). **◆déductible** à (frais) deductible, allowable. **◆déduction** nf (raisonnement) & Com deduction.

déesse [dees] nf goddess.

défaill/ir* [defajir] vi (s'évanouir) to faint; (forces) to fail, flag; **sans d.** without flinching. **◆—ant** à (personne) faint; (témoin) Jur defaulting. **◆défaillance** nf (évanouissement) fainting fit; (faiblesse) weakness; (panne) fault; **une d. de mémoire** a lapse of memory.

défaire* [defer] vt (nœud etc) to undo, untie; (bagages) to unpack; (installation) to take down; (coiffure) to mess up; **d. qn de** to rid s.o. of; **– se d.** vpr (nœud etc) to come undone ou untied; **se d. de** to get rid of. **◆défait** à (lit) unmade; (visage) drawn; (armée) defeated. **◆défaite** nf defeat. **◆défaitisme** nm defeatism.

défalquer [defalke] vt (frais etc) to deduct (de from).

défaut [defo] nm (faiblesse) fault, shortcoming, failing, defect; (de diamant etc) flaw; (désavantage) drawback; (contumace) Jur default; **le d. de la cuirasse** the chink in the armour; **faire d.** to be lacking; **le temps me fait d.** I lack time; **à d. de** for want of; **en d.** at fault; **prendre qn en d.** to catch s.o. out; **ou, à d. . . .** or, failing that . . .

défaveur [defavœr] nf disfavour. **◆défavorable** à unfavourable (à to). **◆défavoriser** vt to put at a disadvantage, be unfair to.

défection [defeksjɔ̃] nf defection, desertion; **faire d.** to desert; (ne pas venir) to fail to turn up.

défectueux, -euse [defektɥø, -øz] à faulty, defective. **◆défectuosité** nf defectiveness; (défaut) defect (de in).

défendre [defɑ̃dr] **1** vt (protéger) to defend; **– se d.** vpr to defend oneself; **se d. de** (pluie etc) to protect oneself from; **se d. de faire** (s'empêcher de) to refrain from doing; **je me défends (bien)** Fam I can hold my own. **2** vt **d. à qn de faire** (interdire) to forbid s.o. to do, not allow s.o. to; **d. qch à qn** to forbid s.o. sth. **◆défendable** à defensible.

défense [defɑ̃s] nf **1** (protection) defence, Am defense; **sans d.** defenceless. **2** (interdiction) **'d. de fumer'** 'no smoking'; **'d. d'entrer'** 'no entry', 'no admittance'. **3** (d'éléphant) tusk. **◆défenseur** nm defender; (des faibles) protector, defender. **◆défensif, -ive** à defensive; **– nf sur la défensive** on the defensive.

déférent [deferɑ̃] à deferential. **◆déférence** nf deference.

déférer [defere] **1** vt (coupable) Jur to refer (à to). **2** vi **d. à l'avis de qn** to defer to s.o.'s opinion.

déferler [deferle] vi (vagues) to break; (haine etc) to erupt; **d. dans ou sur** (foule) to surge ou sweep into.

défi [defi] nm challenge; **lancer un d. à qn** to challenge s.o.; **mettre qn au d. de faire** to defy ou dare ou challenge s.o. to do.

déficient [defisjɑ̃] à Méd deficient. **◆déficience** nf Méd deficiency.

déficit [defisit] nm deficit. **◆déficitaire** à (budget etc) in deficit; (récolte etc) Fig short, insufficient.

défier¹ [defje] vt (provoquer) to challenge (à to); (braver) to defy; **d. qn de faire** to defy ou challenge s.o. to do.

défier² (se) [sədefje] vpr **se d. de** Litt to distrust. **◆défiance** nf distrust (de of). **◆défiant** à distrustful (à l'égard de of).

défigur/er [defigyre] vt (visage) to disfigure; (vérité etc) to distort. **◆—ement** nm disfigurement; distortion.

défil/er [defile] vi (manifestants) to march (devant past); Mil to march ou file past; (paysage, jours) to pass by; (visiteurs) to keep coming and going, stream in and out; (images) Cin to flash by (on the screen); **– se d.** vpr Fam (s'éloigner) to sneak off; (éviter d'agir) to cop out. **◆—é** nm **1** (cortège) procession; (de manifestants) march; Mil parade, march past; (de visiteurs) stream, succession. **2** Géog gorge, pass.

défin/ir [definir] vt to define. **◆—i** à (article) Gram definite. **◆définition** nf definition; (de mots croisés) clue.

définitif, -ive [definitif, -iv] à final, definitive; **– nf en définitive** in the final analysis, finally. **◆définitivement** adv (partir) permanently, for good; (exclure) definitively.

déflagration [deflagrasjɔ̃] nf explosion.

déflation [deflasjɔ̃] nf Écon deflation.

déflorer [deflore] vt (idée, sujet) to spoil the freshness of.

défonc/er [defɔ̃se] **1** vt (porte, mur etc) to smash in ou down; (trottoir, route etc) to dig up, break up. **2 se d.** vpr (drogué) Fam to get high (à on). ◆—é a 1 (route) full of potholes, bumpy. 2 (drogué) Fam high.

déform/er [deforme] vt (objet) to put ou knock out of shape; (doigt, main) to deform; (faits, image etc) to distort; (goût) to corrupt; — **se d.** vpr to lose its shape. ◆—é a (objet) misshapen; (corps etc) deformed, misshapen; **chaussée déformée** uneven road surface. ◆**déformation** nf distortion; corruption; (de membre) deformity; **c'est de la d. professionnelle** it's an occupational hazard, it's a case of being conditioned by one's job.

défouler (se) [sədefule] vpr Fam to let off steam.

défraîchir (se) [sədefreʃir] vpr (étoffe etc) to lose its freshness, become faded.

défrayer [defreje] vt d. qn to pay ou defray s.o.'s expenses; **d. la chronique** to be the talk of the town.

défricher [defriʃe] vt (terrain) to clear (for cultivation); (sujet etc) Fig to open up.

défriser [defrize] vt (cheveux) to straighten; **d. qn** (contrarier) Fam to ruffle ou annoy s.o.

défroisser [defrwase] vt (papier) to smooth out.

défroqué [defrɔke] a (prêtre) defrocked.

défunt, -unte [defœ̃, -œ̃t] a (mort) departed; **son d. mari** her late husband; — nmf **le d., la défunte** the deceased, the departed.

dégag/er [degaʒe] vt (lieu, table) to clear (de of); (objet en gage) to redeem; (odeur) to give off; (chaleur) to give out; (responsabilité) to disclaim; (idée, conclusion) to bring out; **d. qn de** (promesse) to release s.o. from; (décombres) to free s.o. from, pull s.o. out of; **cette robe dégage la taille** this dress leaves the waist free and easy; — vi Fb to clear the ball (down the pitch); **d.!** clear the way!; — **se d.** vpr (rue, ciel) to clear; **se d. de** (personne) to release oneself from (promise); to get free from, free oneself from (rubble); **se d. de** (odeur) to issue ou emanate from; (vérité, impression) to emerge from. ◆—é a (ciel) clear; (ton, allure) easy-going, casual; (vue) open. ◆—**ement** nm 1 (action) clearing; redemption; (d'odeur) emanation; (de chaleur) emission; release; freeing; Fb clearance, kick; **itinéraire de d.** Aut relief road. 2 (espace libre) clearing; (de maison) passage.

dégainer [degene] vti (arme) to draw.

dégarn/ir [degarnir] vt to clear, empty; (arbre, compte) to strip; — **se d.** vpr (crâne) to go bald; (salle) to clear, empty. ◆—i a

(salle) empty, bare; (tête) balding; **front d.** receding hairline.

dégâts [dega] nmpl damage; **limiter les d.** Fig to prevent matters getting worse.

dégel [deʒɛl] nm thaw. ◆**dégeler** vt to thaw (out); (crédits) to unfreeze; — vi to thaw (out); — v imp to thaw; — **se d.** vpr (personne, situation) to thaw (out).

dégénér/er [deʒenere] vi to degenerate (en into). ◆—é, -ée a & nmf degenerate. ◆**dégénérescence** nf degeneration.

dégingandé [deʒɛ̃gɑ̃de] a gangling, lanky.

dégivrer [deʒivre] vt Aut Av to de-ice; (réfrigérateur) to defrost.

déglingu/er (se) [sədeglɛ̃ge] vpr Fam to fall to bits. ◆—é a falling to bits, in bits.

dégobiller [degɔbije] vt Fam to spew up.

dégonfl/er [degɔ̃fle] vt (pneu etc) to deflate, let down; — **se d.** vpr (flancher) Fam to chicken out, get cold feet. ◆—é, -ée a (pneu) flat; (lâche) Fam chicken, yellow; — nmf Fam yellow belly.

dégorger [degɔrʒe] vi (se déverser) to discharge (dans into); **faire d.** (escargots) Culin to cover with salt.

dégot(t)er [degɔte] vt Fam to find, turn up.

dégouliner [deguline] vi to trickle, drip, run.

dégourd/ir [degurdir] vt (doigts etc) to take the numbness out of; **d. qn** Fig to smarten ou wise s.o. up, sharpen s.o.'s wits; — **se d.** vpr to smarten up, wise up; **se d. les jambes** to stretch one's legs. ◆—i a (malin) smart, sharp.

dégoût [degu] nm disgust; **le d. de** (la vie, des gens etc) disgust for; **avoir un ou du d. pour qch** to have a (strong) dislike ou distaste for sth. ◆**dégoût/er** vt to disgust; **d. qn de qch** to put s.o. off sth; **se d. de** to take a (strong) dislike to, become disgusted with. ◆—**ant** a disgusting. ◆—é a disgusted; **être d. de** to be sick of ou disgusted with ou by ou at; **elle est partie dégoûtée** she left in disgust; **il n'est pas d.** (difficile) he's not too fussy; **faire le d.** to be fussy.

dégrad/er [degrade] vt 1 (avilir) to degrade; (mur etc) to deface, damage; — **se d.** vpr (s'avilir) to degrade oneself; (édifice, situation) to deteriorate. 2 vt (couleur) to shade off. ◆—**ant** a degrading. ◆—é nm (de couleur) shading off, gradation. ◆**dégradation** nf (de drogué etc) & Ch degradation; (de situation etc) deterioration; pl (dégâts) damage.

dégrafer [degrafe] vt (vêtement) to unfasten, unhook.

dégraisser [degrese] vt 1 (bœuf) to take the

fat off; *(bouillon)* to skim. **2** *(entreprise)* *Fam* to slim down, trim down the size of *(by laying off workers)*.

degré [dəgre] *nm* **1** degree; **enseignement du premier/second d.** primary/secondary education; **au plus haut d.** *(avare etc)* extremely. **2** *(gradin) Litt* step.

dégrever [degrəve] *vt (contribuable)* to reduce the tax burden on.

dégriffé [degrife] *a* **vêtement d.** unlabelled designer garment.

dégringoler [degrɛ̃gɔle] *vi* to tumble (down); **faire d. qch** to topple sth over; — *vt (escalier)* to rush down. ◆**dégringolade** *nf* tumble.

dégriser [degrize] *vt* **d. qn** to sober s.o. (up).

dégrossir [degrosir] *vt (travail)* to rough out; **d. qn** to refine s.o.

déguerpir [degerpir] *vi* to clear off *ou* out.

dégueulasse [degœlas] *a Fam* lousy, disgusting.

dégueuler [degœle] *vi (vomir) Arg* to puke.

déguis/er [degize] *vt (pour tromper)* to disguise; **d. qn en** *(costumer)* to dress s.o. up as, disguise s.o. as; — **se d.** *vpr* to dress oneself up, disguise oneself (en as). ◆**—ement** *nm* disguise; *(de bal costumé etc)* fancy dress.

déguster [degyste] **1** *vt (goûter)* to taste, sample; *(apprécier)* to relish. **2** *vi (subir des coups) Fam* to cop it, get a good hiding. ◆**dégustation** *nf* tasting, sampling.

déhancher (se) [sədeɑ̃ʃe] *vpr (femme etc)* to sway *ou* wiggle one's hips; *(boiteux)* to walk lop-sided.

dehors [dəɔr] *adv* out(side); *(à l'air)* outdoors, outside; **en d.** on the outside; **en d. de** outside; *(excepté)* apart from; **en d. de la ville/fenêtre** out of town/the window; **au-d. (de), au d. (de)** outside; **déjeuner/jeter/etc** to lunch/throw/etc out; — *nm (extérieur)* outside; *pl (aspect)* outward appearance.

déjà [deʒa] *adv* already; **est-il d. parti?** has he left yet *ou* already?; **elle l'a d. vu** she's seen it before, she's already seen it; **c'est d. pas mal** that's not bad at all; **quand partez-vous, d.?** when are you leaving, again?

déjeuner [deʒœne] *vi (à midi)* to (have) lunch; *(le matin)* to (have) breakfast; — *nm* lunch; **petit d.** breakfast.

déjouer [deʒwe] *vt (intrigue etc)* to thwart, foil.

déjuger (se) [sədeʒyʒe] *vpr* to go back on one's opinion *ou* decision.

delà [d(ə)la] *adv* **au-d. (de), au d. (de), par-d.,**

par d. beyond; **au-d. du pont/etc** beyond *ou* past the bridge/etc; — *nm* **l'au-d.** the (world) beyond.

délabr/er (se) [sədelabre] *vpr (édifice)* to become dilapidated, fall into disrepair; *(santé)* to become impaired. ◆**—ement** *nm* dilapidation, disrepair; impaired state.

délacer [delase] *vt (chaussures)* to undo.

délai [dele] *nm* time limit; *(répit, sursis)* extra time, extension; **dans un d. de dix jours** within ten days; **sans d.** without delay; **à bref d.** at short notice; **dans les plus brefs délais** as soon as possible; **dernier d.** final date.

délaisser [delese] *vt* to forsake, desert, abandon; *(négliger)* to neglect.

délass/er [delase] *vt*, — **se d.** *vpr* to relax. ◆**—ement** *nm* relaxation, diversion.

délateur, -trice [delatœr, -tris] *nmf* informer.

délavé [delave] *a (tissu, jean)* faded; *(ciel)* watery; *(terre)* waterlogged.

délayer [deleje] *vt (mélanger)* to mix (with liquid); *(discours, texte) Fig* to pad out, drag out.

delco [delko] *nm Aut* distributor.

délect/er (se) [sədelekte] *vpr* **se d. de qch/à faire** to (take) delight in sth/in doing. ◆**—able** *a* delectable. ◆**délectation** *nf* delight.

délégu/er [delege] *vt* to delegate (à to). ◆**-é, -ée** *nmf* delegate. ◆**délégation** *nf* delegation.

délest/er [deleste] *vt Él* to cut the power from; **d. qn de** *(voler à qn) Fam* to relieve s.o. of. ◆**—age** *nm Aut* relief; **itinéraire de d.** alternative route *(to relieve congestion)*.

délibér/er [delibere] *vi (réfléchir)* to deliberate (**sur** upon); *(se consulter)* to confer, deliberate (**de** about). ◆**-é** *a (résolu)* determined; *(intentionnel)* deliberate; **de propos d.** deliberately. ◆**—ément** *adv (à dessein)* deliberately. ◆**délibération** *nf* deliberation.

délicat [delika] *a (santé, travail etc)* delicate; *(question)* tricky, delicate; *(geste)* tactful; *(conscience)* scrupulous; *(exigeant)* particular. ◆**délicatement** *adv* delicately; tactfully. ◆**délicatesse** *nf* delicacy; tact(fulness); scrupulousness.

délice [delis] *nm* delight; — *nfpl* delights. ◆**délicieux, -euse** *a (mets, fruit etc)* delicious; *(endroit, parfum etc)* delightful.

délié [delje] **1** *a (esprit) (doigts)* nimble; *(mince)* slender. **2** *nm (d'une lettre)* (thin) upstroke.

délier [delje] *vt* to untie, undo; *(langue) Fig*

délimiter

85

démettre

to loosen; **d. qn de** to release s.o. from; **— se d.** *vpr* (*paquet etc*) to come undone *ou* untied.

délimiter [delimite] *vt* to mark off, delimit; (*définir*) to define. ◆**délimitation** *nf* demarcation, delimitation; definition.

délinquant, -ante [delɛ̃kɑ̃, -ɑ̃t] *a & nmf* delinquent. ◆**délinquance** *nf* delinquency.

délire [delir] *nm* Méd delirium; (*exaltation*) Fig frenzy. ◆**délir/er** *vi* Méd to be delirious; (*dire n'importe quoi*) Fig to rave; **d. de** (*joie etc*) to be wild with. ◆**—ant a** (*malade*) delirious; (*joie*) frenzied, wild; (*déraisonnable*) utterly absurd.

délit [deli] *nm* offence, misdemeanour.

délivrer [delivre] *vt* **1** (*prisonnier*) to release, deliver; (*ville*) to deliver; **d. qn de** (*souci etc*) to rid s.o. of. **2** (*billet, diplôme etc*) to issue. ◆**délivrance** *nf* release; deliverance; issue; (*soulagement*) relief.

déloger [deloʒe] *vi* to move out; **— vt** to force *ou* drive out; Mil to dislodge.

déloyal, -aux [delwajal, -o] *a* disloyal; (*concurrence*) unfair. ◆**déloyauté** *nf* disloyalty; unfairness; (*action*) disloyal act.

delta [dɛlta] *nm* (*de fleuve*) delta.

deltaplane® [deltaplan] *nm* (*engin*) hang-glider; **faire du d.** to practise hang-gliding.

déluge [delyʒ] *nm* flood; (*de pluie*) downpour; (*de compliments, coups*) shower.

déluré [delyre] *a* (*malin*) smart, sharp; (*fille*) Péj brazen.

démagogie [demagɔʒi] *nf* demagogy. ◆**démagogue** *nmf* demagogue.

demain [d(ə)mɛ̃] *adv* tomorrow; **à d.!** see you tomorrow!; **ce n'est pas d. la veille** Fam that won't happen for a while yet.

demande [d(ə)mɑ̃d] *nf* request; (*d'emploi*) application; (*de renseignements*) inquiry; Écon demand; (*question*) question; **d. (en mariage)** proposal (of marriage); **demandes d'emploi** Journ situations wanted. ◆**demander** *vt* to ask for; (*emploi*) to apply for; (*autorisation*) to request, ask for; (*charité*) to beg for; (*prix*) to charge; (*nécessiter, exiger*) to require; **d. un nom/le chemin/l'heure** to ask a name/the way/the time; **d. qch à qn** to ask s.o. for sth; **d. à qn de faire** to ask s.o. to do; **d. si/où** to ask *ou* inquire whether/where; **on te demande!** you're wanted!; **ça demande du temps/une heure** it takes time/an hour; **d. en mariage** to propose (marriage) to; **— se d.** *vpr* to wonder, ask oneself (*pourquoi* why, *si* if).

démanger [demɑ̃ʒe] *vti* to itch; **son bras le**

ou **lui démange** his arm itches; **ça me démange de ...** Fig I'm itching to .... ◆**démangeaison** *nf* itch; **avoir des démangeaisons** to be itching; **j'ai une d. au bras** my arm's itching.

démanteler [demɑ̃tle] *vt* (*bâtiment*) to demolish; (*organisation etc*) to break up.

démantibuler [demɑ̃tibyle] *vt* (*meuble etc*) Fam to pull to pieces.

démaquill/er (se) [sədemakije] *vpr* to take off one's make-up. ◆**—ant** *nm* make-up remover.

démarcation [demarkasjɔ̃] *nf* demarcation.

démarche [demarʃ] *nf* walk, step, gait; (*de pensée*) process; **faire des démarches** to take the necessary steps (**pour faire** to do).

démarcheur, -euse [demarʃœr, -øz] *nmf* Pol canvasser; Com door-to-door salesman *ou* saleswoman.

démarquer [demarke] *vt* (*prix*) to mark down; **se d. de** Fig to dissociate oneself from.

démarr/er [demare] *vi* (*moteur*) Aut to start (up); (*partir*) Aut to move *ou* drive off; (*entreprise etc*) Fig to get off the ground; **— vt** (*commencer*) Fam to start. ◆**—age** *nm* Aut start; **d. en côte** hill start. ◆**—eur** *nm* Aut starter.

démasquer [demaske] *vt* to unmask.

démêl/er [demele] *vt* to disentangle; (*discerner*) to fathom. ◆**—é** *nm* (*dispute*) squabble; *pl* (*ennuis*) trouble (**avec** with).

démembrer [demɑ̃bre] *vt* (*pays etc*) to dismember.

déménag/er [demenaʒe] *vi* to move (out), move house; **— vt** (*meubles*) to (re)move. ◆**—ement** *nm* move, moving (house); (*de meubles*) removal, moving (de of); **voiture de d.** removal van, Am moving van. ◆**—eur** *nm* removal man, Am (furniture) mover.

démener (se) [sədemne] *vpr* to fling oneself about; **se d. pour faire** to spare no effort to do.

dément, -ente [demɑ̃, -ɑ̃t] *a* insane; (*génial*) Iron fantastic; **— nmf** lunatic. ◆**démence** *nf* insanity. ◆**démentiel, -ielle** *a* insane.

dément/ir [demɑ̃tir] *vt* (*infirmer*) to belie; (*nouvelle, faits etc*) to deny; **d. qn** to give the lie to s.o. ◆**—i** *nm* denial.

démerder (se) [sədemɛrde] *vpr* (*se débrouiller*) Arg to manage (by oneself).

démesure [deməzyr] *nf* excess. ◆**démesuré** *a* excessive, inordinate.

démettre [demɛtr] *vt* **1** (*os*) to dislocate; **se d. le pied** to dislocate one's foot. **2 d. qn de**

to dismiss s.o. from; **se d. de ses fonctions** to resign one's office.

demeurant (au) [odəmœrɑ̃] *adv* for all that, after all.

demeure [dəmœr] *nf* **1** dwelling (place), residence. **2 mettre qn en d. de faire** to summon *ou* instruct s.o. to do. ◆**demeur/er** *vi* **1** (*aux être*) (*rester*) to remain; **en d. là** (*affaire etc*) to rest there. **2** (*aux avoir*) (*habiter*) to live, reside. ◆**—é** *a Fam* (mentally) retarded.

demi, -ie [d(ə)mi] *a* half; **d.-journée** half-day; **une heure et demie** an hour and a half; (*horloge*) half past one; – *adv* (**à**) **d. plein** half-full; **à d. nu** half-naked; **ouvrir à d.** to open halfway; **faire les choses à d.** to do things by halves; – *nmf* (*moitié*) half; – *nm* (*verre*) (half-pint) glass of beer; *Fb* half-back; – *nf* (*à l'horloge*) half-hour.

demi-cercle [d(ə)miserkl] *nm* semicircle. ◆**d.-douzaine** *nf* **une d.-douzaine (de)** a half-dozen, half a dozen. ◆**d. finale** *nf Sp* semifinal. ◆**d.-frère** *nm* stepbrother. ◆**d.-heure** *nf* **une d.-heure** a half-hour, half an hour. ◆**d.-mesure** *nf* half-measure. ◆**d.-mot** *nm* **tu comprendras à d.-mot** you'll understand without my having to spell it out. ◆**d.-pension** *nf* half-board. ◆**d.-pensionnaire** *nmf* day boarder, *Am* day student. ◆**d.-saison** *nf* **de d.-saison** (*vêtement*) between seasons. ◆**d.-sel** *a inv* (*beurre*) slightly salted; (*fromage*) **d.-sel** cream cheese. ◆**d.-sœur** *nf* stepsister. ◆**d.-tarif** *nm* & *a inv* (*billet*) (**à**) **d.-tarif** half-price. ◆**d.-tour** *nm* about turn, *Am* about face; *Aut* U-turn; **faire d.-tour** to turn back.

démission [demisjɔ̃] *nf* resignation. ◆**démissionnaire** *a* (*ministre etc*) outgoing. ◆**démissionner** *vi* to resign.

démobiliser [demɔbilize] *vt* to demobilize. ◆**démobilisation** *nf* demobilization.

démocrate [demɔkrat] *nmf* democrat; – *a* democratic. ◆**démocratie** [-asi] *nf* democracy. ◆**démocratique** *a* democratic.

démod/er (se) [sədemɔde] *vpr* to go out of fashion. ◆**—é** *a* old-fashioned.

démographie [demɔgrafi] *nf* demography.

demoiselle [dəmwazel] *nf* (*célibataire*) spinster, single woman; (*jeune fille*) young lady; **d. d'honneur** (*à un mariage*) bridesmaid; (*de reine*) maid of honour.

démolir [demɔlir] *vt* (*maison, jouet etc*) to demolish; (*projet etc*) to shatter; **d. qn** (*battre, discréditer*) *Fam* to tear s.o. to

pieces. ◆**démolition** *nf* demolition; **en d.** being demolished.

démon [demɔ̃] *nm* demon; **petit d.** (*enfant*) little devil. ◆**démoniaque** *a* devilish, fiendish.

démonstrateur, -trice [demɔ̃stratœr, -tris] *nmf* (*dans un magasin etc*) demonstrator. ◆**démonstratif, -ive** *a* demonstrative. ◆**démonstration** *nf* demonstration; **d. de force** show of force.

démonter [demɔ̃te] *vt* (*assemblage*) to dismantle, take apart; (*installation*) to take down; **d. qn** (*troubler*) *Fig* to disconcert s.o.; **une mer démontée** a stormy sea; – **se d.** *vpr* to come apart; (*installation*) to come down; (*personne*) to be put out *ou* disconcerted.

démontrer [demɔ̃tre] *vt* to demonstrate, show.

démoraliser [demɔralize] *vt* to demoralize; – **se d.** *vpr* to become demoralized. ◆**démoralisation** *nf* demoralization.

démordre [demɔrdr] *vi* **il ne démordra pas de** (*son opinion etc*) he won't budge from.

démouler [demule] *vt* (*gâteau*) to turn out (*from its mould*).

démunir [demynir] *vt* **d. qn de** to deprive s.o. of; **se d. de** to part with.

démystifier [demistifje] *vt* (*public etc*) to disabuse; (*idée etc*) to debunk.

dénationaliser [denasjɔnalize] *vt* to denationalize.

dénatur/er [denatyre] *vt* (*propos, faits etc*) to misrepresent, distort. ◆**—é** (*goût, père etc*) unnatural.

dénégation [denegasjɔ̃] *nf* denial.

déneiger [deneʒe] *vt* to clear of snow.

dénicher [denife] *vt* (*trouver*) to dig up, turn up; (*ennemi, fugitif*) to hunt out, flush out.

dénier [denje] *vt* to deny; (*responsabilité*) to disclaim, deny; **d. qch à qn** to deny s.o. sth.

dénigr/er [denigre] *vt* to denigrate, disparage. ◆**—ement** *nm* denigration, disparagement.

dénivellation [denivelasjɔ̃] *nf* unevenness; (*pente*) gradient; *pl* (*accidents*) bumps.

dénombrer [denɔ̃bre] *vt* to count, number.

dénomm/er [denɔme] *vt* to name. ◆**—é, -ée** *nmf* **un d. Dupont** a man named Dupont. ◆**dénomination** *nf* designation, name.

dénonc/er [denɔ̃se] *vt* (*injustice etc*) to denounce (**à** to); **d. qn** to inform on s.o., denounce s.o. (**à** to); *Scol* to tell on s.o. (**à** to); – **se d.** *vpr* to give oneself up (**à** to). ◆**dénonciateur, -trice** *nmf* informer. ◆**dénonciation** *nf* denunciation.

dénoter [denɔte] vt to denote.

dénouer [denwe] vt (nœud, corde) to undo, untie; (cheveux) to undo; (situation, intrigue) to unravel; (problème, crise) to clear up; — **se d.** vpr (nœud) to come undone ou untied; (cheveux) to come undone. ◆**dénouement** nm outcome, ending; Th dénouement.

dénoyauter [denwajote] vt (prune etc) to stone, Am to pit.

denrée [dɑ̃re] nf food(stuff); **denrées alimentaires** foodstuffs.

dense [dɑ̃s] a dense. ◆**densité** nf density.

dent [dɑ̃] nf tooth; (de roue) cog; (de fourche) prong; (de timbre-poste) perforation; **d. de sagesse** wisdom tooth; **rien à se mettre sous la d.** nothing to eat; **manger à belles dents/du bout des dents** to eat whole-heartedly/half-heartedly; **faire ses dents** (enfant) to be teething; **coup de d.** bite; **sur les dents** (surmené) exhausted; (énervé) on edge; **avoir une d. contre qn** to have it in for s.o. ◆**dentaire** a dental. ◆**dentée** af roue d. cogwheel. ◆**dentier** nm denture(s), (set of) false teeth. ◆**dentifrice** nm toothpaste. ◆**dentiste** nmf dentist; **chirurgien d.** dental surgeon. ◆**dentition** nf (dents) (set of) teeth.

dentelé [dɑ̃tle] a (côte) jagged; (feuille) serrated. ◆**dentelure** nf jagged outline ou edge.

dentelle [dɑ̃tɛl] nf lace.

dénud/er [denyde] vt to (lay) bare. ◆—**é** a bare.

dénué [denɥe] a **d. de** devoid of, without.

dénuement [denymɑ̃] nm destitution; **dans le d.** poverty-stricken.

déodorant [deɔdɔrɑ̃] nm deodorant.

dépann/er [depane] vt (mécanisme) to get going (again), repair; **d. qn** Fam to help s.o. out. ◆—**age** nm (emergency) repair; **voiture/service de d.** breakdown vehicle/service. ◆—**eur** nm repairman; Aut breakdown mechanic. ◆—**euse** nf (voiture) Aut breakdown lorry, Am wrecker, tow truck.

dépareillé [depareje] a (chaussure etc) odd, not matching; (collection) incomplete.

déparer [depare] vt to mar, spoil.

départ [depar] nm departure; (début) start, beginning; Sp start; **point/ligne de d.** starting point/post; **au d.** at the outset, at the start; **au d. de Paris/etc** (excursion etc) departing from Paris/etc.

départager [departaʒe] vt (concurrents) to decide between; **d. les votes** to give the casting vote.

département [departəmɑ̃] nm department.

◆**départemental, -aux** a departmental; **route départementale** secondary road.

départir (se) [sədepartir] vpr **se d. de** (attitude) to depart from, abandon.

dépass/er [depase] vt (durée, attente etc) to go beyond, exceed; (endroit) to go past, go beyond; (véhicule, bicyclette etc) to overtake, pass; (pouvoir) to go beyond, overstep; **d. qn** (en hauteur) to be taller than s.o.; (surclasser) to be ahead of s.o.; **ça me dépasse** Fig that's (quite) beyond me; — vi (jupon, clou etc) to stick out, show. ◆—**é** a (démodé) outdated; (incapable) unable to cope. ◆—**ement** nm Aut overtaking, passing.

dépays/er [depeize] vt to disorientate, Am disorient. ◆—**ement** nm disorientation; (changement) change of scenery.

dépecer [depəse] vt (animal) to cut up, carve up.

dépêche [depɛʃ] nf telegram; (diplomatique) dispatch. ◆**dépêcher** vt to dispatch; — **se d.** vpr to hurry (up).

dépeigner [depene] vt to make s.o.'s hair untidy. ◆—**é** a **être d.** to have untidy hair; **sortir d.** to go out with untidy hair.

dépeindre* [depɛ̃dr] vt to depict, describe.

dépenaillé [depənaje] a in tatters ou rags.

dépend/re [depɑ̃dr] 1 vi to depend (de on); **d. de** (appartenir à) to belong to; (être soumis à) to be dependent on; **ça dépend de toi** that depends on you, that's up to you. 2 vt (décrocher) to take down. ◆—**ant** a dependent (de on). ◆**dépendance** 1 nf dependence; **sous la d. de qn** under s.o.'s domination. 2 nfpl (bâtiments) outbuildings.

dépens [depɑ̃] nmpl Jur costs; **aux d. de** at the expense of; **apprendre à ses d.** to learn to one's cost.

dépense [depɑ̃s] nf (action) spending; (frais) expense, expenditure; (d'électricité etc) consumption; (physique) exertion.

◆**dépenser** vt (argent) to spend; (électricité etc) to use; (forces) to exert; (énergie) to expend; — **se d.** vpr to exert oneself. ◆**dépensier, -ière** a wasteful, extravagant.

déperdition [deperdisjɔ̃] nf (de chaleur etc) loss.

dépér/ir [deperir] vi (personne) to waste away; (plante) to wither; (santé etc) to decline. ◆—**issement** nm (baisse) decline.

dépêtrer [depetre] vt to extricate; — **se d.** vpr to extricate oneself (de from).

dépeupl/er [depœple] vt to depopulate.

◆—**ement** nm depopulation.

dépilatoire [depilatwar] *nm* hair-remover.

dépist/er [depiste] *vt* (*criminel etc*) to track down; (*maladie, fraude*) to detect. ◆**—age** *nm Méd* detection.

dépit [depi] *nm* resentment, chagrin; **en d.** de in spite of. ◆**dépiter** *vt* to vex, chagrin; **— se d.** *vpr* to feel resentment *ou* chagrin.

déplac/er [deplase] *vt* to shift, move; (*fonctionnaire*) to transfer; **— se d.** *vpr* to move (about); (*voyager*) to get about, travel (about). ◆**—é** *a* (*mal à propos*) out of place; **personne déplacée** (*réfugié*) displaced person. ◆**—ement** *nm* (*voyage*) (business *ou* professional) trip; (*d'ouragan, de troupes*) movement; **les déplacements** (*voyages*) travel(ling); **frais de d.** travelling expenses.

déplaire* [depler] *vi* **d. à qn** to displease s.o.; **cet aliment lui déplaît** he *ou* she dislikes this food; **n'en déplaise à** *Iron* with all due respect to; **– v imp il me déplaît de faire** I dislike doing, it displeases me to do; **— se d.** *vpr* to dislike it. ◆**déplaisant** *a* unpleasant, displeasing. ◆**déplaisir** *nm* displeasure.

dépli/er [deplije] *vt* to open out, unfold. ◆**—ant** *nm* (*prospectus*) leaflet.

déplor/er [deplore] *vt* (*regretter*) to deplore; (*la mort de qn*) to mourn (over), lament (over); **d. qn** to mourn (for) s.o.; **d. que** (+ *sub*) to deplore the fact that, regret that. ◆**—able** *a* deplorable, lamentable.

déployer [deplwaje] *vt* (*ailes*) to spread; (*journal, carte etc*) to unfold, spread (out); (*objets, courage etc*) to display; (*troupes*) to deploy; **— se d.** *vpr* (*drapeau*) to unfurl. ◆**déploiement** *nm* (*démonstration*) display; *Mil* deployment.

dépoli [depoli] *a* **verre d.** frosted glass.

déport/er [deporte] *vt* **1** (*exiler*) *Hist* to deport (to a penal colony); (*dans un camp de concentration*) *Hist* to send to a concentration camp, deport. **2** (*dévier*) to veer *ou* carry (off course). ◆**—é, -ée** *nmf* deportee; (*concentration camp*) inmate. ◆**déportation** *nf* deportation; internment (in a concentration camp).

dépos/er [depoze] *vt* (*poser*) to put down; (*laisser*) to leave; (*argent, lie*) to deposit; (*plainte*) to lodge; (*armes*) to lay down; (*gerbe*) to lay; (*ordures*) to dump; (*marque de fabrique*) to register; (*projet de loi*) to introduce; (*souverain*) to depose; **d. qn** *Aut* to drop s.o. (off), put s.o. off; **d. son bilan** *Fin* to go into liquidation, file for bankruptcy; **– vi** *Jur* to testify; (*liquide*) to leave a deposit; **— se d.** *vpr* (*poussière, lie*) to

settle. ◆**dépositaire** *nmf Fin* agent; (*de secret*) custodian. ◆**déposition** *nf Jur* statement; (*de souverain*) deposing.

déposséder [deposede] *vt* to deprive, dispossess (**de** of).

dépôt [depo] *nm* (*d'ordures etc*) dumping, (*lieu*) dump; (*de gerbe*) laying; (*d'autobus, de trains*) depot; (*entrepôt*) warehouse; (*argent*) deposit; (*de vin*) deposit, sediment; **d.** (*calcaire*) (*de chaudière etc*) deposit; **laisser qch à qn en d.** to give s.o. sth for safekeeping *ou* in trust.

dépotoir [depotwar] *nm* rubbish dump, *Am* garbage dump.

dépouille [depuj] *nf* hide, skin; (*de serpent*) slough; *pl* (*butin*) spoils; **d.** (**mortelle**) mortal remains. ◆**dépouill/er** *vt* (*animal*) to skin, flay; (*analyser*) to go through, analyse; **d. de** (*dégarnir*) to strip of; (*déposséder*) to deprive of; **se d. de** to rid *ou* divest oneself of, cast off; **d. un scrutin** to count votes. ◆**—é** *a* (*arbre*) bare; (*style*) austere, spare; **d. de** bereft of. ◆**—ement** *nm* (*de document etc*) analysis; (*privation*) deprivation; (*sobriété*) austerity; **d. du scrutin** counting of the votes.

dépourvu [depurvy] *a* **d. de** devoid of; **prendre qn au d.** to catch s.o. unawares *ou* off his guard.

dépraver [deprave] *vt* to deprave. ◆**dépravation** *nf* depravity.

dépréci/er [depresje] *vt* (*dénigrer*) to disparage; (*monnaie, immeuble etc*) to depreciate; **— se d.** *vpr* (*baisser*) to depreciate, lose (its) value. ◆**dépréciation** *nf* depreciation.

déprédations [depredasjɔ̃] *nfpl* damage, ravages.

dépression [depresjɔ̃] *nf* depression; **zone de d.** trough of low pressure; **d. nerveuse** nervous breakdown; **d. économique** slump. ◆**dépressif, -ive** *a* depressive. ◆**déprime** *nf* **la d.** (*dépression*) *Fam* the blues. ◆**déprim/er** *vt* to depress. ◆**—é** *a* depressed.

depuis [dəpɥi] *prép* since; **d. lundi** since Monday; **d. qu'elle est partie** since she left; **j'habite ici d. un mois** I've been living here for a month; **d. quand êtes-vous là?** how long have you been here?; **d. peu/longtemps** for a short/long time; **d. Paris jusqu'à Londres** from Paris to London; **– adv** since (then), ever since.

députation [depytasjɔ̃] *nf* (*groupe*) deputation, delegation; **candidat à la d.** parliamentary candidate. ◆**député** *nm* delegate, deputy; (*au parlement*) deputy, = *Br* MP, = *Am* congressman, congresswoman.

déracin/er [derasine] *vt* (*personne, arbre etc*) to uproot; (*préjugés etc*) to eradicate, root out. **◆—ement** *nm* uprooting; eradication.

déraill/er [deraje] *vi* 1 (*train*) to jump the rails, be derailed; **faire d.** to derail. 2 (*divaguer*) *Fam* to drivel, talk through one's hat. **◆—ement** *nm* (*de train*) derailment. **◆—eur** *nm* (*de bicyclette*) derailleur (gear change).

déraisonnable [derezonabl] *a* unreasonable. **◆déraisonner** *vi* to talk nonsense.

dérang/er [derãʒe] *vt* (*affaires*) to disturb, upset; (*estomac*) to upset; (*projets*) to mess up, upset; (*vêtements*) to mess up; (*cerveau, esprit*) to derange; **d. qn** to disturb ou bother ou trouble s.o.; **je viendrai si ça ne te dérange pas** I'll come if that doesn't put you out ou if that's not imposing; **ça vous dérange si je fume?** do you mind if I smoke?; **— se d.** *vpr* to put oneself to a lot of trouble (**pour faire** to do), (*se déplacer*) to move; **ne te dérange pas!** don't trouble yourself!, don't bother! **◆—ement** *nm* (*gêne*) bother, inconvenience; (*désordre*) disorder; **en d.** (*téléphone etc*) out of order.

dérap/er [derape] *vi* to skid. **◆—age** *nm* skid; (*des prix, de l'inflation*) *Fig* loss of control ou (over).

dératé [derate] *nm* **courir comme un d.** to run like mad.

dérégl/er [deregle] *vt* (*mécanisme*) to put out of order; (*estomac, habitudes*) to upset; (*esprit*) to unsettle; **— se d.** *vpr* (*montre, appareil*) to go wrong. **◆—é** *a* out of order; (*vie, mœurs*) dissolute, wild; (*imagination*) wild. **◆dérèglement** *nm* (*de mécanisme*) breakdown; (*d'esprit*) disorder; (*d'estomac*) upset.

dérider [deride] *vt*, **— se d.** *vpr* to cheer up.

dérision [derizjɔ̃] *nf* derision, mockery; **tourner en d.** to mock, deride; **par d.** derisively; **de d.** derisive. **◆dérisoire** *a* ridiculous, derisory, derisive.

dérive [deriv] *nf* *Nau* drift; **partir à la d.** (*navire*) to drift out to sea; **aller à la d.** (*navire*) to go adrift; (*entreprise etc*) *Fig* to drift (towards ruin). **◆dériv/er** *vi* *Nau Av* to drift; **d. de** (*venir*) to derive from, be derived from; **— *vt* (*cours d'eau*) to divert; *Ling* to derive (**de** from). **◆—é** *nm* *Ling Ch* derivative; (*produit*) by-product. **◆dérivatif** *nm* distraction (**à** from). **◆dérivation** *nf* (*de cours d'eau*) diversion; *Ling* derivation; (*déviation routière*) bypass.

dermatologie [dɛrmatɔlɔʒi] *nf* dermatology.

dernier -ière [dɛrnje, -jɛr] *a* last; (*nouvelles, mode*) latest; (*étage*) top; (*degré*) highest; (*qualité*) lowest; **le d. rang** the back ou last row; **ces derniers mois** these past few months, these last ou final months; **de la dernière importance** of (the) utmost importance; **en d.** last; **— *nmf* last** (person ou one); **ce d.** (*de deux*) the latter; (*de plusieurs*) the last-mentioned; **être le d. de la classe** to be (at) the bottom of the class; **le d. des derniers** the lowest of the low; **le d. de mes soucis** the least of my worries. **◆d.-né, ◆dernière-née** *nmf* youngest (child). **◆dernièrement** *adv* recently.

dérob/er [derɔbe] *vt* (*voler*) to steal (**à** from); (*cacher*) to hide (**à** from); **— se d.** *vpr* to get out of one's obligations; (*s'éloigner*) to slip away; (*éviter de répondre*) to dodge the issue; **se d. à** (*obligations*) to shirk, get out of; (*regards*) to hide from; **ses jambes se sont dérobées sous lui** his legs gave way beneath him. **◆—é** *a* (*porte etc*) hidden, secret; **à la dérobée** *adv* on the sly, stealthily. **◆dérobade** *nf* dodge, evasion.

déroger [derɔʒe] *vi* **d. à une règle/etc** to depart from a rule/etc. **◆dérogation** *nf* exemption, (special) dispensation.

dérouiller [deruje] *vt* **d. qn** (*battre*) *Arg* to thrash ou trounce s.o.; **se d. les jambes** *Fam* to stretch one's legs.

déroul/er [derule] *vt* (*carte etc*) to unroll; (*film*) to unwind; **— se d.** *vpr* (*événement*) to take place, pass off; (*paysage, souvenirs*) to unfold; (*récit*) to develop. **◆—ement** *nm* (*d'une action*) unfolding, development; (*cours*) course;

dérouter [derute] *vt* (*avion, navire*) to divert, reroute; (*candidat etc*) to baffle; (*poursuivant*) to throw off the scent.

derrick [dɛrik] *nm* derrick.

derrière [dɛrjɛr] *prép & adv* behind; **d. moi** behind me, *Am* in back of me; **assis d.** (*dans une voiture*) sitting in the back; **de d.** (*roue*) back, rear; (*pattes*) hind; **par d.** (*attaquer*) from behind, from the rear; **—** *nm* (*de maison etc*) back, rear; (*fesses*) behind, bottom.

des [de] *voir* **de** 1,2, **le**.

dès [dɛ] *prép* from; **d. cette époque** (as) from that time, from that time on; **d. le début** (right) from the start; **d. son enfance** since ou from (his ou her) childhood; **d. le**

désabusé	90	désespérer

sixième siècle as early as *ou* as far back as the sixth century; **d. l'aube** at (the crack of) dawn; **d. qu'elle viendra** as soon as she comes.

désabusé [dezabyze] *a* disenchanted, disillusioned.

désaccord [dezakɔr] *nm* disagreement. ◆**désaccordé** *a Mus* out of tune.

désaccoutumer (se) [sǝdezakutyme] *vpr* **se d. de** to lose the habit of.

désaffecté [dezafɛkte] *a* (école etc) disused.

désaffection [dezafɛksjɔ̃] *nf* loss of affection, disaffection (**pour** for).

désagréable [dezagreabl] *a* unpleasant, disagreeable. ◆**—ment** [-ǝmɑ̃] *adv* unpleasantly.

désagréger [dezagreʒe] *vt*, — **se d.** *vpr* to disintegrate, break up. ◆**désagrégation** *nf* disintegration.

désagrément [dezagremɑ̃] *nm* annoyance, trouble.

désaltérer [dezaltere] *vt* **d. qn** to quench s.o.'s thirst; **se d.** to quench one's thirst. ◆**—ant** a thirst-quenching.

désamorcer [dezamɔrse] *vt* (obus, situation) to defuse.

désappointer [dezapwɛ̃te] *vt* to disappoint.

désapprouver [dezapruve] *vt* to disapprove of; — *vi* to disapprove. ◆**désapprobateur, -trice** *a* disapproving. ◆**désapprobation** *nf* disapproval.

désarçonner [dezarsɔne] *vt* (jockey) to throw, unseat; (déconcerter) *Fig* to nonpluss, throw.

désarmer [dezarme] *vt* (émouvoir) & *Mil* to disarm; — *vi Mil* to disarm; (céder) to let up. ◆**—ant** a (charme etc) disarming. ◆**—é** a (sans défense) unarmed; *Fig* helpless. ◆**—ement** *nm* (de nation) disarmament.

désarroi [dezarwa] *nm* (angoisse) distress.

désarticuler [dezartikyle] *vt* (membre) to dislocate.

désastre [dezastr] *nm* disaster. ◆**désastreux, -euse** *a* disastrous.

désavantage [dezavɑ̃taʒ] *nm* disadvantage, handicap; (inconvénient) drawback, disadvantage. ◆**désavantager** *vt* to put at a disadvantage, handicap. ◆**désavantageux, -euse** *a* disadvantageous.

désaveu, -x [dezavø] *nm* repudiation. ◆**désavouer** *vt* (livre, personne) to disown, repudiate.

désaxé, -ée [dezakse] *a* & *nmf* unbalanced (person).

desceller [desele] *vt* (pierre etc) to loosen; — **se d.** *vpr* to come loose.

descendre [desɑ̃dr] *vi* (aux être) to come *ou* go down, descend (**de** from); (d'un train etc) to get off *ou* out, alight (**de** from); (d'un arbre) to climb down (**de** from); (nuit, thermomètre) to fall; (marée) to go out; **d. à** (une bassesse) to stoop to; **d. à l'hôtel** to put up at a hotel; **d. de** (être issu de) to be descended from; **d. de cheval** to dismount; **d. en courant/flânant/etc** to run/stroll/etc down; — *vt* (aux avoir) (escalier) to come *ou* go down, descend; (objets) to bring *ou* take down; (avion) to bring *ou* shoot down; **d. qn** (tuer) *Fam* to bump s.o. off. ◆**—ant, -ante 1** *a* descending; (marée) outgoing. **2** *nmf* (personne) descendant. ◆**descendance** *nf* (enfants) descendants; (origine) descent.

descente [desɑ̃t] *nf* (action) descent; (irruption) raid (**dans** upon); (en parachute) drop; (pente) slope; **la d. des bagages** bringing *ou* taking down the luggage; **il fut accueilli à sa d. d'avion** he was met as he got off the plane; **d. à skis** downhill run; **d. de lit** (tapis) bedside rug.

descriptif, -ive [dɛskriptif, -iv] *a* descriptive. ◆**description** *nf* description.

déségrégation [desegregasjɔ̃] *nf* desegregation.

désemparé [dezɑ̃pare] *a* distraught, at a loss; (navire) crippled.

désemplir [dezɑ̃plir] *vi* **ce magasin/etc ne désemplit pas** this shop/etc is always crowded.

désenchanter [dezɑ̃ʃɑ̃te] *vt* to disenchant. ◆**—ement** *nm* disenchantment.

désencombrer [dezɑ̃kɔ̃bre] *vt* (passage etc) to clear.

désenfler [dezɑ̃fle] *vi* to go down, become less swollen.

déséquilibre [dezekilibr] *nm* (inégalité) imbalance; (mental) unbalance; **en d.** (meuble etc) unsteady. ◆**déséquilibrer** *vt* to throw off balance; (esprit, personne) *Fig* to unbalance.

désert [dezɛr] *a* deserted; **île déserte** desert island; — *nm* desert, wilderness. ◆**désertique** *a* (région etc) desert-.

déserter [dezɛrte] *vti* to desert. ◆**déserteur** *nm Mil* deserter. ◆**désertion** *nf* desertion.

désespérer [dezɛspere] *vi* to despair (**de** of); — *vt* to drive to despair; — **se d.** *vpr* to (be in) despair. ◆**—ant** *a* (enfant etc) that drives one to despair, hopeless. ◆**—é, -ée** *a* (personne) in despair, despairing; (cas, situation) desperate, hopeless; (efforts, cris) desperate; — *nmf* (suicidé) person driven to despair *ou* desperation. ◆**—ément** *adv* desperately. ◆**désespoir** *nm* despair; **au d.** in despair; **en d. de cause** in desperation, as a (desperate) last resort.

déshabiller [dezabije] *vt* to undress, strip; **— se d.** *vpr* to get undressed, undress.

déshabituer [dezabitɥe] *vt* **d. qn de** to break s.o. of the habit of.

désherb/er [dezɛrbe] *vti* to weed. ◆**—ant** *nm* weed killer.

déshérit/er [dezerite] *vt* to disinherit. ◆**—é** *a* (*pauvre*) underprivileged; (*laid*) ill-favoured.

déshonneur [dezɔnœr] *nm* dishonour, disgrace. ◆**déshonor/er** *vt* to disgrace, dishonour. ◆**—ant** *a* dishonourable.

déshydrater [dezidrate] *vt* to dehydrate; **— se d.** *vpr* to become dehydrated.

désigner [dezine] *vt* (*montrer*) to point to, point out; (*élire*) to appoint, designate; (*signifier*) to indicate, designate; **ses qualités le désignent pour** his qualities mark him out for. ◆**désignation** *nf* designation.

désillusion [dezilyzjɔ̃] *nf* disillusion(ment). ◆**désillusionner** *vt* to disillusion.

désincarné [dezɛ̃karne] *a* (*esprit*) disembodied.

désinence [dezinɑ̃s] *nf* *Gram* ending.

désinfect/er [dezɛ̃fɛkte] *vt* to disinfect. ◆**—ant** *nm* & *a* disinfectant. ◆**désinfection** *nf* disinfection.

désinformation [dezɛ̃fɔrmasjɔ̃] *nf* *Pol* misinformation.

désintégrer (se) [sɔdezɛ̃tegre] *vpr* to disintegrate. ◆**désintégration** *nf* disintegration.

désintéress/er (se) [sɔdezɛ̃terese] *vpr* **se d. de** to lose interest in, take no further interest in. ◆**—é** *a* (*altruiste*) disinterested. ◆**—ement** [-ɛsmɑ̃] *nm* (*altruisme*) disinterestedness. ◆**désintérêt** *nm* lack of interest.

désintoxiquer [dezɛ̃tɔksike] *vt* (*alcoolique, drogué*) to cure.

désinvolte [dezɛ̃vɔlt] *a* (*dégagé*) easy-going, casual; (*insolent*) offhand, casual. ◆**désinvolture** *nf* casualness; offhandedness.

désir [dezir] *nm* desire, wish. ◆**désirable** *a* desirable. ◆**désirer** *vt* to want, desire; (*convoiter*) to desire; **je désire venir** I would like to come, I wish *ou* want to come; **je désire que tu viennes** I want you to come; **ça laisse à d.** it leaves something *ou* a lot to be desired. ◆**désireux, -euse** *a* **d. de faire** anxious *ou* eager to do, desirous of doing.

désist/er (se) [sɔdeziste] *vpr* (*candidat etc*) to withdraw. ◆**—ement** *nm* withdrawal.

désobé/ir [dezɔbeir] *vi* to disobey; **d. à qn** to disobey s.o. ◆**—issant** *a* disobedient. ◆**désobéissance** *nf* disobedience (à to).

désobligeant [dezɔbliʒɑ̃] *a* disagreeable, unkind.

désodorisant [dezɔdɔrizɑ̃] *nm* air freshener.

désœuvré [dezœvre] *a* idle, unoccupied. ◆**désœuvrement** *nm* idleness.

désol/er [dezɔle] *vt* to distress, upset (very much); **— se d.** *vpr* to be distressed *ou* upset (**de** at). ◆**—ant** *a* distressing, upsetting. ◆**—é** *a* (*région*) desolate; (*affligé*) distressed; **être d.** (*navré*) to be sorry (**que** (+ *sub*) that, **de faire** to do). ◆**désolation** *nf* (*peine*) distress, grief.

désolidariser (se) [sɔdesɔlidarize] *vpr* to dissociate oneself (**de** from).

désopilant [dezɔpilɑ̃] *a* hilarious, screamingly funny.

désordre [dezɔrdr] *nm* (*de papiers, affaires, idées*) mess, muddle, disorder; (*de cheveux, pièce*) untidiness; *Méd* disorder; *pl* (*émeutes*) disorder, unrest; **en d.** untidy, messy. ◆**désordonné** *a* (*personne, chambre*) untidy, messy.

désorganiser [dezɔrganize] *vt* to disorganize. ◆**désorganisation** *nf* disorganization.

désorienter [dezɔrjɑ̃te] *vt* **d. qn** to disorientate *ou* *Am* disorient s.o., make s.o. lose his bearings; (*déconcerter*) to bewilder s.o. ◆**désorientation** *nf* disorientation.

désormais [dezɔrmɛ] *adv* from now on, in future, henceforth.

désosser [dezɔse] *vt* (*viande*) to bone.

despote [dɛspɔt] *nm* despot. ◆**despotique** *a* despotic. ◆**despotisme** *nm* despotism.

desquels, desquelles [dekɛl] *voir* lequel.

dessaisir (se) [sɔdesezir] *vpr* **se d. de qch** to part with sth, relinquish sth.

dessaler [desale] *vt* (*poisson etc*) to remove the salt from (*by smoking*).

dessécher [desefe] *vt* (*végétation*) to dry up, wither; (*gorge, bouche*) to dry, parch; (*fruits*) to desiccate, dry; (*cœur*) to harden; **— se d.** *vpr* (*plante*) to wither, dry up; (*peau*) to dry (up), get dry; (*maigrir*) to waste away.

dessein [desɛ̃] *nm* aim, design; **dans le d. de faire** with the aim of doing; **à d.** intentionally.

desserrer [desere] *vt* (*ceinture etc*) to loosen, slacken; (*poing*) to open, unclench;

(frein) to release; **il n'a pas desserré les dents** he didn't open his mouth; **— se d.** *vpr* to come loose.

dessert [desɛr] *nm* dessert, sweet.

desserte [desɛrt] *nf* **assurer la d. de** *(village etc)* to provide a (bus *ou* train) service to. ◆**desservir** *vt* **1** *(table)* to clear (away). **2 d. qn** to harm s.o., do s.o. a disservice. **3 l'autobus/etc dessert ce village** the bus/*etc* provides a service to *ou* stops at this village; **ce quartier est bien desservi** this district is well served by public transport.

dessin [desɛ̃] *nm* drawing; *(rapide)* sketch; *(motif)* design, pattern; *(contour)* outline; **d. animé** *Cin* cartoon; **d. humoristique** *Journ* cartoon; **école de d.** art school; **planche à d.** drawing board. ◆**dessinateur, -trice** *nmf* drawer; sketcher; **d. humoristique** cartoonist; **d. de modes** dress designer; **d. industriel** draughtsman, *Am* draftsman. ◆**dessiner** *vt* to draw; *(rapidement)* to sketch; *(meuble, robe etc)* to design; *(indiquer)* to outline, trace; **(bien) la taille** *(vêtement)* to show off the figure; **— se d.** *vpr (colline etc)* to stand out, be outlined; *(projet)* to take shape.

dessoûler [desule] *vti Fam* to sober up.

dessous [d(ə)su] *adv* under(neath), beneath, below; **en d.** *(sous)* under(neath); *(agir)* Fig in an underhand way; **vêtement de d.** undergarment; **drap de d.** bottom sheet; **— *nm* underneath; *pl (vêtements)* underclothes; **d. de table** backhander, bribe; **les gens du d.** the people downstairs *ou* below; **avoir le d.** to be defeated, get the worst of it. ◆**d.-de-plat** *nm inv* table mat.

dessus [d(ə)sy] *adv (marcher, écrire)* on it; *(monter)* on top (of it), on it; *(lancer, passer)* over it; **de d. la table** off *ou* from the table; **vêtement de d.** outer garment; **drap de d.** top sheet; **par-d.** *(sauter etc)* over (it); **par-d. tout** above all; **— *nm* top; *(de chaussure)* upper; **avoir le d.** to have the upper hand, get the best of it; **les gens du d.** the people upstairs *ou* above. ◆**d.-de-lit** *inv* bedspread.

déstabiliser [destabilize] *vt* to destabilize.

destin [destɛ̃] *nm* fate, destiny. ◆**destinée** *nf* fate, destiny *(of an individual)*.

destin/er [destine] *vt* **d. qch à qn** to intend *ou* mean sth for s.o.; **d. qn à** *(carrière, fonction)* to intend *ou* destine s.o. for; **se d. à** *(carrière)* to intend *ou* mean to take up; **destiné à mourir/etc** *(condamné)* destined *ou* fated to die/*etc.* ◆**destinataire** *nmf* addressee. ◆**destination** *nf (usage)*

purpose; *(lieu)* destination; **à d. de** *(train etc)* (going) to, (bound) for.

destituer [destitɥe] *vt (fonctionnaire etc)* to dismiss (from office). ◆**destitution** *nf* dismissal.

destructeur, -trice [dɛstryktœr, -tris] *a* destructive; **— *nmf (personne)* destroyer. ◆**destructif, -ive** *a* destructive. ◆**destruction** *nf* destruction.

désuet, -ète [desɥɛ, -ɛt] *a* antiquated, obsolete.

désunir [dezynir] *vt (famille etc)* to divide, disunite. ◆**désunion** *nf* disunity, dissension.

détach/er¹ [detaʃe] *vt (ceinture, vêtement)* to undo; *(nœud)* to untie, undo; *(personne, mains)* to untie; *(ôter)* to take off, detach; *(mots)* to pronounce clearly; **d. qn** *(libérer)* to let s.o. loose; *(affecter)* to transfer s.o. (on assignment) (à to); **d. les yeux de qn/qch** to take one's eyes off s.o./sth; **— se d.** *vpr (chien, prisonnier)* to break loose; *(se dénouer)* to come undone; **se d. (de qch)** *(fragment)* to come off (sth); **se d. (de amis)** to break away from, grow apart from; **se d. (sur)** *(ressortir)* to stand out (against). ◆**—é à 1** *(nœud* loose, undone. **2** *(air, ton etc)* detached. ◆**—ement** *nm* **1** *(indifférence)* detachment. **2** *(de fonctionnaire)* (temporary) transfer; *Mil* detachment.

détach/er² [detaʃe] *vt (linge etc)* to remove the spots *ou* stains from. ◆**—ant** *nm* stain remover.

détail [detaj] *nm* **1** detail; **en d.** in detail; **le d. de** *(dépenses etc)* a detailing *ou* breakdown of. **2 de d.** *(magasin, prix)* retail; **vendre au d.** to sell retail; *(par petites quantités)* to sell separately; **faire le d.** to retail to the public. ◆**détaill/er** *vt* **1** *(vendre)* to sell in small quantities *ou* separately; *(au détail)* to (sell) retail. **2** *(énumérer)* to detail. ◆**—ant, -ante** *nmf* retailer. ◆**—é** *a (récit etc)* detailed.

détaler [detale] *vi Fam* to run off, make tracks.

détartrer [detartre] *vt (chaudière, dents etc)* to scale.

détaxer [detakse] *vt (denrée etc)* to reduce the tax on; *(supprimer)* to take the tax off; **produit détaxé** duty-free article.

détecter [detɛkte] *vt* to detect. ◆**détecteur** *(appareil)* detector. ◆**détection** *nf* detection.

détective [detɛktiv] *nm* **d. (privé)** (private) detective.

déteindre* [detɛ̃dr] *vi (couleur ou étoffe au lavage)* to run; *(au soleil)* to fade; **ton**

tablier bleu a déteint sur ma chemise the blue of your apron has come off on(to) my shirt; **d. sur qn** (*influencer*) to leave one's mark on s.o.

dételer [detle] *vt* (*chevaux*) to unhitch, unharness.

détend/re [detɑ̃dr] *vt* (*arc etc*) to slacken, relax; (*situation, atmosphère*) to ease; **d. qn** to relax s.o.; — **se d.** *vpr* to slacken, get slack; to ease; (*se reposer*) to relax; (*rapports*) to become less strained. ◆—**u** *a* (*visage, atmosphère*) relaxed; (*ressort, câble*) slack. ◆**détente** *nf* 1 (*d'arc*) slackening; (*de relations*) easing of tension, *Pol* détente; (*repos*) relaxation; (*saut*) leap, spring. **2** (*gâchette*) trigger.

déten/ir° [detnir] *vt* to hold; (*secret, objet volé*) to be in possession of; (*prisonnier*) to hold, detain. ◆—**u, -ue** *nmf* prisoner. ◆**détenteur, -trice** *nmf* (*de record etc*) holder. ◆**détention** *nf* (*d'armes*) possession; (*captivité*) detention; **d. préventive** *Jur* custody.

détergent [detɛrʒɑ̃] *nm* detergent.

détériorer [deterjore] *vt* (*abîmer*) to damage; — **se d.** *vpr* (*empirer*) to deteriorate. ◆**détérioration** *nf* damage (de to); (*d'une situation etc*) deterioration (de in).

détermin/er [detɛrmine] *vt* (*préciser*) to determine; (*causer*) to bring about; **d. qn à faire** to induce s.o. to do, make s.o. do; **se d. à faire** to resolve *ou* determine to do. ◆—**ant** *a* (*motif*) determining, deciding; (*rôle*) decisive. ◆—**é** *a* (*précis*) specific; (*résolu*) determined. ◆**détermination** *nf* (*fermeté*) determination; (*résolution*) resolve.

déterrer [detere] *vt* to dig up, unearth.

détest/er [detɛste] *vt* to hate, detest; **d. faire** to hate doing *ou* to do, detest doing. ◆—**able** *a* awful, foul.

détonateur [detɔnatœr] *nm* detonator. ◆**détonation** *nf* explosion, blast.

détonner [detɔne] *vi* (*contraster*) to jar, be out of place.

détour [detur] *nm* (*de route etc*) bend, curve; (*crochet*) detour; **sans d.** (*parler*) without beating about the bush; **faire des détours** (*route*) to wind.

détourn/er [deturne] *vt* (*fleuve, convoi etc*) to divert; (*tête*) to turn (away); (*coups*) to ward off; (*conversation, sens*) to change; (*fonds*) to embezzle, misappropriate; (*avion*) to hijack; **d. qn de** (*son devoir, ses amis*) to take *ou* turn s.o. away from; (*sa route*) to lead s.o. away from; (*projet*) to talk s.o. out of; **d. les yeux** to look away,

avert one's eyes; — **se d.** *vpr* to turn aside *ou* away; **se d. de** (*chemin*) to wander *ou* stray from. ◆—**é a** (*chemin, moyen*) roundabout, indirect. ◆—**ement** *nm* (*de cours d'eau*) diversion; **d.** (**d'avion**) hijack(ing); **d. (de fonds)** embezzlement.

détraqu/er [detrake] *vt* (*mécanisme*) to break, put out of order; — **se d.** *vpr* (*machine*) to go wrong; **se d. l'estomac** to upset one's stomach; **se d. la santé** to ruin one's health. ◆—**é, -ée** *a* out of order; (*cerveau*) deranged; — *nmf* crazy *ou* deranged person.

détremper [detrɑ̃pe] *vt* to soak, saturate.

détresse [detrɛs] *nf* distress; **en d.** (*navire, âme*) in distress; **dans la d.** (*misère*) in (great) distress.

détriment de (au) [detrimɑ̃də] *prép* to the detriment of.

détritus [detritys] *nmpl* refuse, rubbish.

détroit [detrwa] *nm* *Géog* strait(s), sound.

détromper [detrɔ̃pe] *vt* **d. qn** to undeceive s.o., put s.o. right; **détrompez-vous!** don't you believe it!

détrôner [detrone] *vt* (*souverain*) to dethrone; (*supplanter*) to supersede, oust.

détrousser [detruse] *vt* (*voyageur etc*) to rob.

détruire° [detrɥir] *vt* (*ravager, tuer*) to destroy; (*projet, santé*) to ruin, wreck, destroy.

dette [dɛt] *nf* debt; **faire des dettes** to run *ou* get into debt; **avoir des dettes** to be in debt.

deuil [dœj] *nm* (*affliction, vêtements*) mourning; (*mort de qn*) bereavement; **porter le d.**, **être en d.** to be in mourning.

deux [dø] *a* & *nm* two; **d. fois** twice, two times; **tous (les) d.** both; **en moins de d.** *Fam* in no time. ◆**d.-pièces** *nm inv* (*vêtement*) two-piece; (*appartement*) two-roomed flat *ou* *Am* apartment. ◆**d.-points** *nm inv* *Gram* colon. ◆**d.-roues** *nm inv* two-wheeled vehicle. ◆**d.-temps** *nm inv* two-stroke (engine).

deuxième [døzjɛm] *a* & *nmf* second. ◆—**ment** *adv* secondly.

dévaler [devale] *vt* (*escalier etc*) to hurtle *ou* race *ou* rush down; — *vi* (*tomber*) to tumble down, come tumbling down.

dévaliser [devalize] *vt* (*détrousser*) to clean out, strip, rob (of everything).

dévaloris/er [devalɔrize] **1** *vt*, — **se d.** *vpr* (*monnaie*) to depreciate. **2** *vt* (*humilier etc*) to devalue, disparage. ◆**dévalorisation** *nf* (*de monnaie*) depreciation.

dévaluer [devalɥe] *vt* (*monnaie*) & *Fig* to devalue. ◆**dévaluation** *nf* devaluation.

devancer [d(ə)vɑ̃se] vt to get ou be ahead of; (question etc) to anticipate, forestall; (surpasser) to outstrip; **tu m'as devancé** (action) you did it before me; (lieu) you got there before me. ◆**devancier, -ière** nmf predecessor.

devant [d(ə)vɑ̃] prép & adv in front (of); **d. (l'hôtel etc)** in front (of the hotel/etc); **marcher d. (qn)** to walk in front (of s.o.) ou ahead (of s.o.); **passer d. (l'église/etc)** to go past the church/etc; **assis d.** (dans une voiture) sitting in the front; **l'avenir est d. toi** the future is ahead of you; **loin d.** a long way ahead ou in front; **d. le danger** (confronté à) in the face of danger; **d. mes yeux/la loi** before my eyes/the law; – nm front; **de d.** (roue, porte) front; **patte de d.** foreleg; **par d.** from ou at the front; **prendre les devants** (action) to take the initiative. ◆**devanture** nf (vitrine) shop window; (façade) shop front.

dévaster [devaste] vt (ruiner) to devastate. ◆**dévastation** nf devastation.

déveine [devɛn] nf Fam tough ou bad luck.

développ/er [devlope] vt to develop; Phot to develop, process; – **se d.** vpr to develop. ◆**-ement** nm development; Phot developing, processing; **les pays en voie de d.** the developing countries.

devenir* [dəvnir] vi (aux être) to become; (vieux, difficile etc) to get, grow, become; (rouge, bleu etc) to turn, go, become; **d. un papillon/un homme/etc** to grow into a butterfly/a man/etc; **qu'est-il devenu?** what's become of him ou it?, where's he ou it got to?; **qu'est-ce que tu deviens?** Fam how are you doing?

dévergond/er (se) [sədevergɔ̃de] vpr to fall into dissolute ways. ◆**-é** a dissolute, licentious.

déverser [deverse] vt (liquide, rancune) to pour out; (bombes, ordures) to dump; – **se d.** vpr (liquide) to empty, pour out (dans into).

dévêtir [devetir] vt, – **se d.** vpr Litt to undress.

dévier [devje] vt (circulation, conversation) to divert; (coup, rayons) to deflect; – vi (de ses principes etc) to deviate (de from); (de sa route) to veer (off course). ◆**déviation** nf deflection; deviation; (chemin) bypass; (itinéraire provisoire) diversion.

deviner [d(ə)vine] vt to guess (que that); (avenir) to predict; **d. (le jeu de) qn** to see through s.o. ◆**devinette** nf riddle.

devis [d(ə)vi] nm estimate (of cost of work to be done).

dévisager [devizaʒe] vt **d. qn** to stare at s.o.

devise [d(ə)viz] nf (légende) motto; pl (monnaie) (foreign) currency.

dévisser [devise] vt to unscrew, undo; – **se d.** vpr (bouchon etc) to come undone.

dévoiler [devwale] vt (révéler) to disclose; (statue) to unveil; – **se d.** vpr (mystère) to come to light.

devoir* [d(ə)vwar] v aux 1 (nécessité) **je dois refuser** I must refuse, I have (got) to refuse; **j'ai dû refuser** I had to refuse. 2 (forte probabilité) **il doit être tard** it must be late; **elle a dû oublier** she must have forgotten; **il ne doit pas être bête** he can't be stupid. 3 (obligation) **tu dois l'aider** you should help her, you ought to help her; **il aurait dû venir** he should have come, he ought to have come; **vous devriez rester** you should stay, you ought to stay. 4 (supposition) **elle doit venir** she should be coming, she's supposed to be coming; **le train devait arriver à midi** the train was due (to arrive) at noon; **je devais le voir** I was (due) to see him.

devoir* [d(ə)vwar] 1 vt to owe; **d. qch à qn** to owe s.o. sth, owe sth to s.o.; **l'argent qui m'est dû** the money due to ou owing to me, the money owed (to) me; **se d. à** to have to devote oneself to; **comme il se doit** as is proper. 2 nm duty; Scol exercise; **devoir(s)** (travail à faire à la maison) Scol homework; **présenter ses devoirs à qn** to pay one's respects to s.o.

dévolu [devɔly] 1 a **d. à qn** (pouvoirs, tâche) vested in s.o., allotted to s.o. 2 nm **jeter son d. sur** to set one's heart on.

dévor/er [devɔre] vt (manger) to gobble up, devour; (incendie) to engulf, devour; (tourmenter, lire) to devour. ◆**-ant** a (faim) ravenous; (passion) devouring.

dévot, -ote [devo, -ɔt] a & nmf devout ou pious (person). ◆**dévotion** nf devotion.

dévou/er (se) [sədevwe] vpr (à une tâche) to dedicate oneself, devote oneself (à to); **se d. (pour qn)** (se sacrifier) to sacrifice oneself (for s.o.). ◆**-é** a (ami, femme etc) devoted (à qn to s.o.); (domestique, soldat etc) dedicated. ◆**-ement** [-umɑ̃] nm devotion, dedication; (de héros) devotion to duty.

dévoyé, -ée [devwaje] a & nmf delinquent.

dextérité [dɛksterite] nf dexterity, skill.

diabète [djabɛt] nm Méd diabetes. ◆**diabétique** a & nmf diabetic.

diable [djabl] nm devil; **d.!** heavens!; **où/pourquoi/que d.?** where/why/what the devil?; **un bruit/vent/etc du d.** the devil of a noise/wind/*etc*; **à la d.** anyhow; **habiter au d.** to live miles from anywhere. ◆**diablerie** *nf* devilment, mischief. ◆**diablesse** *nf* c'est une d. *Fam* she's a devil. ◆**diablotin** *nm* (*enfant*) little devil. ◆**diabolique** *a* diabolical, devilish.

diabolo [djabɔlo] *nm* (*boisson*) lemonade *ou* Am lemon soda flavoured with syrup.

diacre [djakr] *nm Rel* deacon.

diadème [djadɛm] *nm* diadem.

diagnostic [djagnɔstik] *nm* diagnosis. ◆**diagnostiquer** *vt* to diagnose.

diagonal, -aux [djagɔnal, -o] *a* diagonal. ◆**diagonale** *nf* diagonal (line); **en d.** diagonally.

diagramme [djagram] *nm* (*schéma*) diagram; (*courbe*) graph.

dialecte [djalɛkt] *nm* dialect.

dialogue [djalɔg] *nm* conversation; *Pol Cin Th Littér* dialogue. ◆**dialoguer** *vi* to have a conversation *ou* dialogue.

dialyse [djaliz] *nf Méd* dialysis.

diamant [djamɑ̃] *nm* diamond.

diamètre [djamɛtr] *nm* diameter. ◆**diamétralement** *adv* **d. opposés** (*avis etc*) diametrically opposed, poles apart.

diapason [djapazɔ̃] *nm Mus* tuning fork; **être/se mettre au d. de** *Fig* to be/get in tune with.

diaphragme [djafragm] *nm* diaphragm.

diapositive, *Fam* **diapo** [djapozitiv, djapo] *nf* (*colour*) slide, transparency.

diarrhée [djare] *nf* diarrh(o)ea.

diatribe [djatrib] *nf* diatribe.

dictateur [diktatœr] *nm* dictator. ◆**dictatorial, -aux** *a* dictatorial. ◆**dictature** *nf* dictatorship.

dict/er [dikte] *vt* to dictate (à to). ◆**—ée** *nf* dictation. ◆**dictaphone**® *nm* dictaphone®.

diction [diksjɔ̃] *nf* diction, elocution.

dictionnaire [diksjɔnɛr] *nm* dictionary.

dicton [diktɔ̃] *nm* saying, adage, dictum.

didactique [didaktik] *a* didactic.

dièse [djɛz] *a & nm Mus* sharp.

diesel [djezɛl] *a & nm* (**moteur**) **d.** diesel (engine).

diète [djɛt] *nf* (*jeûne*) starvation diet; **à la d.** on a starvation diet. ◆**diététicien, -ienne** *nmf* dietician. ◆**diététique** *nf* dietetics; — *a* (*magasin etc*) health-; **aliment** *ou* **produit d.** health food.

dieu, -x [djø] *nm* god; **D.** God; **D. merci!** thank God!, thank goodness!

diffamer [difame] *vt* (*en paroles*) to slander; (*par écrit*) to libel. ◆**diffamation** *nf* defamation; (*en paroles*) slander; (*par écrit*)

libel; **campagne de d.** smear campaign. ◆**diffamatoire** *a* slanderous; libellous.

différent [diferɑ̃] *a* different; *pl* (*divers*) different, various; **d. de** different from *ou* to, unlike. ◆**différemment** [-amɑ̃] *adv* differently (**de** from, to). ◆**différence** *nf* difference (**de** in); **à la d. de** unlike; **faire la d. entre** to make a distinction between.

différencier [diferɑ̃sje] *vt* to differentiate (**de** from); — **se d.** *vpr* to differ (**de** from).

différend [diferɑ̃] *nm* difference (of opinion).

différentiel, -ielle [diferɑ̃sjɛl] *a* differential.

différ/er [difere] **1** *vi* to differ (**de** from). **2** *vt* (*remettre*) to postpone, defer. ◆**—é en d.** (*émission*) (pre)recorded.

difficile [difisil] *a* difficult; (*exigeant*) fussy, particular, hard *ou* difficult to please; **c'est d. à faire** it's hard *ou* difficult to do; **il (nous) est d. de faire ça** it's hard *ou* difficult (for us) to do that. ◆**—ment** *adv* with difficulty; **d. lisible** not easily read. ◆**difficulté** *nf* difficulty (**à faire** in doing); **en d.** in a difficult situation.

difforme [difɔrm] *a* deformed, misshapen. ◆**difformité** *nf* deformity.

diffus [dify] *a* (*lumière, style*) diffuse.

diffuser [difyze] *vt* (*émission, nouvelle etc*) to broadcast; (*lumière, chaleur*) *Phys* to diffuse; (*livre*) to distribute. ◆**diffusion** *nf* broadcasting; (*de connaissances*) & *Phys* diffusion; (*de livre*) distribution.

digérer [diʒere] *vt* to digest; (*endurer*) *Fam* to stomach; — *vi* to digest. ◆**digeste** *a*, ◆**digestible** *a* digestible. ◆**digestif, -ive** *a* digestive; — *nm* after-dinner liqueur. ◆**digestion** *nf* digestion.

digitale [diʒital] *af* **empreinte d.** fingerprint.

digne [diɲ] *a* (*fier*) dignified; (*honnête*) worthy; **d. de** qn worthy of s.o.; **d. d'admiration**/*etc* worthy of *ou* deserving of admiration/*etc*; **d. de foi** reliable. ◆**dignement** *adv* with dignity. ◆**dignitaire** *nm* dignitary. ◆**dignité** *nf* dignity.

digression [digresjɔ̃] *nf* digression.

digue [dig] *nf* dyke, dike.

dilapider [dilapide] *vt* to squander, waste.

dilater [dilate] *vt*, — **se d.** *vpr* to dilate, expand. ◆**dilatation** *nf* dilation, expansion.

dilatoire [dilatwar] *a* **manœuvre** *ou* **moyen d.** delaying tactic.

dilemme [dilɛm] *nm* dilemma.

dilettante [diletɑ̃t] *nmf Péj* dabbler, amateur.

diligent [diliʒɑ̃] *a* (*prompt*) speedy and effi-

cient; (*soin*) diligent. ◆**diligence** *nf* **1**
(*célérité*) speedy efficiency; **faire d.** to make
haste. **2** (*véhicule*) *Hist* stagecoach.

diluer [dilɥe] *vt* to dilute. ◆**dilution** *nf*
dilution.

diluvienne [dilyvjɛn] *af* **pluie d.** torrential
rain.

dimanche [dimɑ̃ʃ] *nm* Sunday.

dimension [dimɑ̃sjɔ̃] *nf* dimension; **à deux
dimensions** two-dimensional.

diminuer [diminɥe] *vt* to reduce, decrease;
(*frais*) to cut down (on), reduce; (*mérite,
forces*) to diminish, lessen, reduce; **d. qn**
(*rabaisser*) to diminish s.o., lessen s.o.'s; – *vi*
(*réserves, nombre*) to decrease, diminish;
(*jours*) to get shorter, draw in; (*prix*)
to drop, decrease. ◆**diminutif, -ive** *a* &
nm Gram diminutive; – *nm* (*prénom*)
nickname. ◆**diminution** *nf* reduction,
decrease (**de** in).

dinde [dɛ̃d] *nf* turkey (hen), *Culin* turkey.
◆**dindon** *nm* turkey (cock).

dîner [dine] *vi* to have dinner, dine; (*au
Canada, en Belgique etc*) to (have) lunch; –
nm dinner; lunch; (*soirée*) dinner party.
◆**dinette** *nf* (*jouet*) doll's dinner service;
(*jeu*) doll's dinner party. ◆**dîneur, -euse**
nmf diner.

dingue [dɛ̃g] *a Fam* nuts, screwy, crazy; –
nmf Fam nutcase.

dinosaure [dinozɔr] *nm* dinosaur.

diocèse [djɔsɛz] *nm Rel* diocese.

diphtérie [difteri] *nf* diphtheria.

diphtongue [diftɔ̃g] *nf Ling* diphthong.

diplomate [diplɔmat] *nm Pol* diplomat; –
nmf (*négociateur*) diplomatist; – *a* (*habile,
plein de tact*) diplomatic. ◆**diplomatie**
[-asi] *nf* (*tact*) & *Pol* diplomacy; (*carrière*)
diplomatic service. ◆**diplomatique** *a Pol*
diplomatic.

diplôme [diplom] *nm* certificate, diploma;
Univ degree. ◆**diplômé, -ée** *a* & *nmf*
qualified (person); **être d. (de)** *Univ* to be a
graduate (of).

dire* [dir] *vt* (*mot, avis etc*) to say; (*vérité,
secret, heure etc*) to tell; (*penser*) to think
(**de** of, about); **d. des bêtises** to talk
nonsense; **elle dit que tu mens** she says
(that) you're lying; **d. qch à qn** to tell s.o.
sth, say sth to s.o.; **d. à qn que** to tell s.o.
that, say to s.o. that; **d. à qn de faire** to tell
s.o. to do; **dit-il** he said; **dit-on** they say; **d.
que oui/non** to say yes/no; **d. du mal/du
bien de** to speak ill/well of; **on dirait un
château** it looks like a castle; **on dirait du
Mozart** it sounds like Mozart; **on dirait du
cabillaud** it tastes like cod; **on dirait que il**

would seem that; **ça ne me dit rien** (*envie*) I
don't feel like *ou* fancy that; (*souvenir*) it
doesn't ring a bell; **ça vous dit de rester?** do
you feel like staying?; **dites donc!** I say!; **ça
va sans d.** that goes without saying; **autrement dit** in other words; **c'est beaucoup d.**
that's going too far; **à l'heure dite** at the
agreed time; **à vrai d.** to tell the truth; **il se
dit malade/etc** he says he's ill/etc; **ça ne se
dit pas** that's not said; – *nm* **au d. de**
according to; **les dires de** (*déclarations*) the
statements of.

direct [dirɛkt] *a* direct; (*chemin*) straight,
direct; (*manière*) straightforward, direct;
train d. through train, non-stop train; – *nm*
en d. (*émission*) live; **un d. du gauche** *Boxe*
a straight left. ◆**-ement** *adv* directly;
(*immédiatement*) straight (away), directly.

directeur, -trice [dirɛktœr, -tris] *nmf* director; (*d'entreprise*) manager(ess), director;
(*de journal*) editor; *Scol* headmaster, headmistress; – *a* (*principe*) guiding; **idées** *ou*
lignes directrices guidelines.

direction [dirɛksjɔ̃] *nf* **1** (*de société*) running, management; (*de club*) leadership,
running; (*d'études*) supervision; (*mécanisme*) *Aut* steering; **avoir la d. de** to be in
charge of; **sous la d. de** (*orchestre*)
conducted by; **la d.** (*équipe dirigeante*) the
management; **une d.** (*fonction*) *Com* a
directorship; *Journ* an editorship. **2** (*sens*) direction; **en d. de**
(*train*) (going) to, for.

directive [dirɛktiv] *nf* directive, instruction.

dirig/er [diriʒe] *vt* (*société*) to run, manage,
direct; (*débat, cheval*) to lead; (*véhicule*) to
steer; (*orchestre*) to conduct; (*études*) to
supervise, direct; (*conscience*) to guide;
(*orienter*) to turn (**vers** towards); (*arme,
lumière*) to point, direct (**vers** towards); **se
d. vers** (*lieu, objet*) to make one's way
towards, head *ou* make for; (*dans une
carrière*) to turn towards. ◆**—eant** *a*
(*classe*) ruling; – *nm* (*de pays, club*) leader;
(*d'entreprise*) manager. ◆**—é** *a* (*économie*)
planned. ◆**—eable** *a* & *nm* (*ballon*) d.
airship. ◆**dirigisme** *nm Écon* state
control.

dis [di] *voir* **dire**.

discern/er [disɛrne] *vt* (*voir*) to make out,
discern; (*différencier*) to distinguish.
◆**—ement** *nm* discernment, discrimination.

disciple [disipl] *nm* disciple, follower.

discipline [disiplin] *nf* (*règle, matière*) discipline. ◆**disciplinaire** *a* disciplinary.
◆**disciplin/er** *vt* (*contrôler, éduquer*) to

discipline; **— se d.** *vpr* to discipline oneself. **◆—é** *a* well-disciplined.

disco [disko] *nf Fam* disco; **aller en d.** to go to a disco.

discontinu [diskɔtiny] *a* (*ligne*) discontinuous; (*bruit etc*) intermittent. **◆discontinuer** *vi* **sans d.** without stopping.

disconvenir [diskɔ̃vnir] *vi* **je n'en disconviens pas** I don't deny it.

discorde [diskɔrd] *nf* discord. **◆discordance** *nf* (*de caractères*) clash, conflict; (*de son*) discord. **◆discordant** *a* (*son*) discordant; (*témoignages*) conflicting; (*couleurs*) clashing.

discothèque [diskɔtɛk] *nf* record library; (*club*) discotheque.

discours [diskur] *nm* speech; (*écrit littéraire*) discourse. **◆discourir** *vi Péj* to speechify, ramble on.

discourtois [diskurtwa] *a* discourteous.

discrédit [diskredi] *nm* disrepute, discredit. **◆discréditer** *vt* to discredit, bring into disrepute; **— se d.** *vpr* (*personne*) to become discredited.

discret, -ète [diskrɛ, -ɛt] *a* (*personne, manière etc*) discreet; (*vêtement*) simple. **◆discrètement** *adv* discreetly; (*s'habiller*) simply. **◆discrétion** *nf* discretion; **vin/etc à d.** as much wine/etc as one wants. **◆discrétionnaire** *a* discretionary.

discrimination [diskriminasjɔ̃] *nf* (*ségrégation*) discrimination. **◆discriminatoire** *a* discriminatory.

disculper [diskylpe] *vt* to exonerate (**de** from).

discussion [diskysjɔ̃] *nf* discussion; (*conversation*) talk; (*querelle*) argument; **pas de d.!** no argument! **◆discuter/er** *vt* to discuss; (*familièrement*) to talk over; (*contester*) to question; **ça peut se d., ça se discute** that's arguable; **— vi** (*parler*) to talk (**de** about, **avec** with); (*répliquer*) to argue; **d. de** *ou* **sur qch** to discuss sth. **◆—é** *a* (*auteur*) much discussed *ou* debated; (*théorie, question*) disputed, controversial. **◆—able** *a* arguable, debatable.

disette [dizɛt] *nf* food shortage.

diseuse [dizœz] *nf* **d. de bonne aventure** fortune-teller.

disgrâce [disgras] *nf* disgrace, disfavour. **◆disgracier** *vt* to disgrace.

disgracieux, -euse [disgrasjø, -øz] *a* ungainly.

disjoindre [disʒwɛ̃dr] *vt* (*questions*) to treat separately. **◆disjoint** *a* (*questions*) unconnected, separate. **◆disjoncteur** *nm* *Él* circuit breaker.

disloquer [dislɔke] *vt* (*membre*) to dislocate; (*meuble, machine*) to break; **— se d.** *vpr* (*cortège*) to break up; (*meuble etc*) to fall apart; **se d. le bras** to dislocate one's arm. **◆dislocation** *nf* (*de membre*) dislocation.

dispar/aître* [disparɛtr] *vi* to disappear; (*être porté manquant*) to be missing; (*mourir*) to die; **d. en mer** to be lost at sea; **faire d.** to remove, get rid of. **◆—u, -ue** *a* (*soldat etc*) missing, lost; *nmf* (*absent*) missing person; (*mort*) departed; **être porté d.** to be reported missing. **◆disparition** *nf* disappearance; (*mort*) death.

disparate [disparat] *a* ill-assorted.

disparité [disparite] *nf* disparity (**entre, de** between).

dispendieux, -euse [dispɑ̃djø, -øz] *a* expensive, costly.

dispensaire [dispɑ̃sɛr] *nm* community health centre.

dispense [dispɑ̃s] *nf* exemption; **d. d'âge** waiving of the age limit. **◆dispenser** *vt* (*soins, bienfaits etc*) to dispense; **d. qn de** (*obligation*) to exempt *ou* excuse s.o. from; **je vous dispense de** (*vos réflexions etc*) I can dispense with; **se d. de faire** to spare oneself the bother of doing.

disperser [dispɛrse] *vt* to disperse, scatter; (*efforts*) to dissipate; **— se d.** *vpr* (*foule*) to disperse; **elle se disperse trop** she tries to do too many things at once. **◆dispersion** *nf* (*d'une armée etc*) dispersal, dispersion.

disponible [disponibl] *a* available; (*place*) spare, available; (*esprit*) alert. **◆disponibilité** *nf* availability; *pl Fin* available funds.

dispos [dispo] *a* **frais et d.** refreshed.

dispos/er [dispoze] *vt* to arrange; (*troupes*) *Mil* to dispose; **d. qn à** (*la bonne humeur etc*) to dispose *ou* incline s.o. towards; **se d. à faire** to prepare to do; **— vi d. de qch** to have sth at one's disposal; (*utiliser*) to make use of sth; **d. de qn** *Péj* to take advantage of s.o., abuse s.o. **◆—é** *a* **bien/mal d.** in a good/bad mood; **bien d. envers** well-disposed towards; **d. à faire** prepared *ou* disposed to do. **◆disposition** *nf* arrangement; (*de troupes*) disposition; (*de maison, page*) layout; (*humeur*) frame of mind; (*tendance*) tendency, (pre)disposition (**à** to); (*clause*) *Jur* provision; *pl* (*aptitudes*) ability, aptitude (**pour** for); **à la d. de qn** at s.o.'s disposal; **prendre ses** *ou* **des dispositions** (*préparatifs*) to make arrangements, prepare; (*pour l'avenir*) to

make provision; **dans de bonnes dispositions à l'égard de** well-disposed towards.
dispositif [dispozitif] *nm* (*mécanisme*)
device; **d. de défense** *Mil* defence system;
d. antiparasite *Él* suppressor.
disproportion [disproporsjɔ̃] *nf* disproportion. ◆**disproportionné** *a* disproportionate.
dispute [dispyt] *nf* quarrel. ◆**disputer** *vt*
(*match*) to play; (*terrain, droit etc*) to
contest, dispute; (*rallye*) to compete in; **d.
qch à qn** (*prix, première place etc*) to fight
with s.o. for *ou* over sth, contend with s.o.
for sth; **d. qn** (*gronder*) *Fam* to tell s.o. off;
— se d. *vpr* to quarrel (**avec** with); (*match*)
to take place; **se d. qch** to fight over sth.
disqualifier [diskalifje] *vt Sp* to disqualify;
— se d. *vpr Fig* to become discredited.
◆**disqualification** *nf Sp* disqualification.
disque [disk] *nm Mus* record; *Sp* discus;
(*cercle*) disc, *Am* disk; (*pour ordinateur*)
disk. ◆**disquaire** *nmf* record dealer.
◆**disquette** *nf* (*pour ordinateur*) floppy
disk.
dissection [disɛksjɔ̃] *nf* dissection.
dissemblable [disɑ̃blabl] *a* dissimilar (**à**
to).
disséminer [disemine] *vt* (*graines, mines
etc*) to scatter; (*idées*) *Fig* to disseminate.
◆**dissémination** *nf* scattering; (*d'idées*)
Fig dissemination.
dissension [disɑ̃sjɔ̃] *nf* dissension.
disséquer [diseke] *vt* to dissect.
disserter [disɛrte] *vi* **d. sur** to comment
upon, discuss. ◆**dissertation** *nf Scol*
essay.
dissident, -ente [disidɑ̃, -ɑ̃t] *a & nmf* dissident. ◆**dissidence** *nf* dissidence.
dissimuler [disimyle] *vt* (*cacher*) to
conceal, hide (**à** from); **— vi** (*feindre*) to
pretend; **— se d.** *vpr* to hide, conceal
oneself. ◆**-é** *a* (*enfant*) *Péj* secretive.
◆**dissimulation** *nf* concealment; (*duplicité*) deceit.
dissiper [disipe] *vt* (*brouillard, craintes*) to
dispel; (*fortune*) to squander, dissipate; **d.
qn** to lead s.o. astray, distract s.o.; **— se d.**
vpr (*brume*) to clear, lift; (*craintes*) to
disappear; (*élève*) to misbehave. ◆**-é** *a*
(*élève*) unruly; (*vie*) dissipated. ◆**dissipation** *nf* (*de brouillard*) clearing; (*indiscipline*) misbehaviour; (*débauche*) *Litt*
dissipation.
dissocier [disosje] *vt* to dissociate (**de**
from).
dissolu [disoly] *a* (*vie etc*) dissolute.
dissoudre* [disudr] *vt*, **— se d.** *vpr* to

dissolve. ◆**dissolution** *nf* dissolution.
◆**dissolvant** *a & nm* solvent; (*pour vernis
à ongles*) nail polish remover.
dissuader [disɥade] *vt* to dissuade, deter
(**de qch** from sth, **de faire** from doing).
◆**dissuasif, -ive** *a* (*effet*) deterrent; **être
d.** *Fig* to be a deterrent. ◆**dissuasion** *nf*
dissuasion; **force de d.** *Mil* deterrent.
distant [distɑ̃] *a* distant; (*personne*) aloof,
distant; **d. de dix kilomètres** (*éloigné*) ten
kilometres away; (*à intervalles*) ten kilometres apart. ◆**distance** *nf* distance; **à deux
mètres de d.** two metres apart; **à d.** at *ou*
from a distance; **garder ses distances** to
keep one's distance. ◆**distancer** *vt* to
leave behind, outstrip.
distendre [distɑ̃dr] *vt*, **— se d.** *vpr* to
distend.
distiller [distile] *vt* to distil. ◆**distillation**
nf distillation. ◆**distillerie** *nf* (*lieu*) distillery.
distinct, -incte [distɛ̃, -ɛ̃kt] *a* (*différent*)
distinct, separate (**de** from); (*net*) clear,
distinct. ◆**distinctement** *adv* distinctly,
clearly. ◆**distinctif, -ive** *a* distinctive.
◆**distinction** *nf* (*différence, raffinement*)
distinction.
distinguer [distɛ̃ge] *vt* (*différencier*) to
distinguish; (*voir*) to make out; (*choisir*) to
single out; **d. le blé de l'orge** to tell wheat
from barley, distinguish between wheat
and barley; **— se d.** *vpr* (*s'illustrer*) to
distinguish oneself; **se d. de** (*différer*) to be
distinguishable from; **se d. par** (*sa gaieté,
beauté etc*) to be conspicuous for. ◆**-é** *a*
(*bien élevé, éminent*) distinguished; **sentiments distingués** (*formule épistolaire*) Com
yours faithfully.
distorsion [distorsjɔ̃] *nf* (*du corps, d'une
image etc*) distortion.
distraction [distraksjɔ̃] *nf* amusement,
distraction; (*étourderie*) (fit of)
absent-mindedness. ◆**distraire*** *vt* (*divertir*) to entertain, amuse; **d. qn** (**de**)
(*détourner*) to distract s.o. (from); **— se d.**
vpr to amuse oneself, enjoy oneself. ◆**distrait** *a* absent-minded. ◆**distraitement**
adv absent-mindedly. ◆**distrayant** *a*
entertaining.
distribuer [distribɥe] *vt* (*répartir*) to
distribute; (*donner*) to give *ou* hand out,
distribute; (*courrier*) to deliver; (*eau*) to
supply; (*cartes*) to deal; **bien distribué**
(*appartement*) well-arranged. ◆**distributeur** *nm Aut Cin* distributor; **d. (automatique)** vending machine; **d. de billets** *Rail*
ticket machine; (*de billets de banque*) cash

dispenser *ou* machine. ◆**distribution** *nf* distribution; (*du courrier*) delivery; (*de l'eau*) supply; (*acteurs*) *Th Cin* cast; **d. des prix** prize giving.

district [distrikt] *nm* district.

dit [di] *voir* **dire**; — *a* (*convenu*) agreed; (*surnommé*) called.

dites [dit] *voir* **dire**.

divaguer [divage] *vi* (*dérailler*) to rave, talk drivel. ◆**divagations** *nfpl* ravings.

divan [divā] *nm* divan, couch.

divergent [diverɜā] *a* diverging, divergent. ◆**divergence** *nf* divergence. ◆**diverger** *vi* to diverge (**de** from).

divers, -erses [diver, -ɛrs] *apl* (*distincts*) varied, diverse; **d. groupes** (*plusieurs*) various *ou* sundry groups. ◆**diversement** *adv* in various ways. ◆**diversifier** *vt* to diversify; — **se d.** *vpr Écon* to diversify. ◆**diversité** *nf* diversity.

diversion [diversjɔ̃] *nf* diversion.

divert/ir [divertir] *vt* to amuse, entertain; — **se d.** *vpr* to enjoy oneself, amuse oneself. ◆**—issement** *nm* amusement, entertainment.

dividende [dividãd] *nm Math Fin* dividend.

divin [divɛ̃] *a* divine. ◆**divinité** *nf* divinity.

diviser [divize] *vt,* — **se d.** *vpr* to divide (**en** into). ◆**divisible** *a* divisible. ◆**division** *nf* division.

divorce [divɔrs] *nm* divorce. ◆**divorc/er** *vi* to get *ou* be divorced, divorce; **d. d'avec qn** to divorce s.o. ◆**—é, -ée** *a* divorced (**d'avec** from); — *nmf* divorcee.

divulguer [divylge] *vt* to divulge. ◆**divulgation** *nf* divulgence.

dix [dis] ([di] *before consonant,* [diz] *before vowel*) *a & nm* ten. ◆**dixième** [dizjɛm] *a & nmf* tenth; **un d.** a tenth. ◆**dix-huit** [dizɥit] *a & nm* eighteen. ◆**dix-huitième** *a & nmf* eighteenth. ◆**dix-neuf** [diznœf] *a & nm* nineteen. ◆**dix-neuvième** *a & nmf* nineteenth. ◆**dix-sept** [disset] *a & nm* seventeen. ◆**dix-septième** *a & nmf* seventeenth.

dizaine [dizɛn] *nf* about ten.

docile [dɔsil] *a* submissive, docile. ◆**docilité** *nf* submissiveness, docility.

dock [dɔk] *nm Nau* dock. ◆**docker** [dɔkɛr] *nm* docker.

docteur [dɔktœr] *nm Méd Univ* doctor (**ès,** **en** *of*). ◆**doctorat** *nm* doctorate, = PhD (**ès, en** in).

doctrine [dɔktrin] *nf* doctrine. ◆**doctrinaire** *a & nmf Péj* doctrinaire.

document [dɔkymã] *nm* document. ◆**documentaire** *a* documentary; — *nm*

(*film*) documentary. ◆**documentaliste** *nmf* information officer.

document/er [dɔkymãte] *vt* (*informer*) to document; — **se d.** *vpr* to collect material *ou* information. ◆**—é a** (**bien** *ou* **très**) **d.** (*personne*) well-informed. ◆**documentation** *nf* (*documents*) documentation, *Com* literature; (*renseignements*) information.

dodeliner [dɔdline] *vi* **d. de la tête** to nod (one's head).

dodo [dɔdo] *nm* (*langage enfantin*) **faire d.** to sleep; **aller au d.** to go to bye-byes.

dodu [dɔdy] *a* chubby, plump.

dogme [dɔgm] *nm* dogma. ◆**dogmatique** *a* dogmatic. ◆**dogmatisme** *nm* dogmatism.

dogue [dɔg] *nm* (*chien*) mastiff.

doigt [dwa] *nm* finger; **d. de pied** toe; **à deux doigts de** within an ace of; **montrer du d.** to point (to); **savoir sur le bout du d.** to have at one's finger tips. ◆**doigté** *nm Mus* fingering, touch; (*savoir-faire*) tact, expertise. ◆**doigtier** *nm* fingerstall.

dois, doit [dwa] *voir* **devoir** [1,2].

doléances [dɔleɑ̃s] *nfpl* (*plaintes*) grievances.

dollar [dɔlar] *nm* dollar.

domaine [dɔmɛn] *nm* (*terres*) estate, domain; (*sphère*) province, domain.

dôme [dom] *nm* dome.

domestique [dɔmɛstik] *a* (*animal*) domestic(ated); (*de la famille*) family-, domestic; (*ménager*) domestic, household; — *nmf* servant. ◆**domestiquer** *vt* to domesticate.

domicile [dɔmisil] *nm* home; *Jur* abode; **travailler à d.** to work at home; **livrer à d.** (*pain etc*) to deliver (to the house). ◆**domicilié** *a* resident (**à, chez** at).

domin/er [dɔmine] *vt* to dominate; (*situation, sentiment*) to master, dominate; (*être supérieur à*) to surpass, outclass; (*tour, rocher*) to tower above, dominate (*valley, building etc*); — *vi* (*être le plus fort*) to be dominant, dominate; (*être le plus important*) to predominate; — **se d.** *vpr* to control oneself. ◆**—ant** *a* dominant. ◆**—ante** *nf* dominant feature; *Mus* dominant. ◆**dominateur, -trice** *a* domineering. ◆**domination** *nf* domination.

dominicain, -aine [dɔminikɛ̃, -ɛn] *a & nmf Rel* Dominican.

dominical, -aux [dɔminikal, -o] *a* (*repos*) Sunday-.

domino [dɔmino] *nm* domino; *pl* (*jeu*) dominoes.

dommage [dɔmaʒ] *nm* **1** (**c'est**) **d.!** it's a

pity *ou* a shame! (*que* that); **quel d.!** what a pity *ou* a shame! **2** (*tort*) prejudice, harm; *pl* (*dégâts*) damage; **dommages-intérêts** *Jur* damages.

dompt/er [dɔ̃te] *vt* (*animal*) to tame; (*passions, rebelles*) to subdue. **◆—eur, -euse** *nmf* (*de lions*) lion tamer.

don [dɔ̃] *nm* (*cadeau, aptitude*) gift; (*aumône*) donation; **le d. du sang**/*etc* (the) giving of blood/*etc*; **faire d.** de to give; **avoir le d.** de (*le chic pour*) to have the knack of. **◆donateur, -trice** *nmf Jur* donor. **◆donation** *nf Jur* donation.

donc [dɔ̃(k)] *conj* so, then; (*par conséquent*) so, therefore; **asseyez-vous d.!** (*intensif*) will you sit down!, sit down then!; **qui/quoi d.?** who?/what?; **allons d.!** come on!

donjon [dɔ̃ʒɔ̃] *nm* (*de château*) keep.

donne [dɔn] *nf Cartes* deal.

donner [dɔne] *vt* to give; (*récolte, résultat*) to produce; (*sa place*) to give up; (*pièce, film*) to put on; (*cartes*) to deal; **d. un coup à** to hit, give a blow to; **d. le bonjour à qn** to say hello to s.o.; **d. à réparer** to take (in) to be repaired; **d. raison à qn** to say s.o. is right; **ça donne soif/faim** it makes you thirsty/hungry; **je lui donne trente ans** I'd say *ou* guess he *ou* she was thirty; **ça n'a rien donné** (*efforts*) it hasn't got us anywhere; **c'est donné** *Fam* it's dirt cheap; **étant donné** (*la situation etc*) considering, in view of; **étant donné que** seeing (that), considering (that); **à un moment donné** at some stage; **— vi d. sur** (*fenêtre*) to look out onto, overlook; (*porte*) to open onto; **d. dans** (*piège*) to fall into; **d. de la tête contre** to hit one's head against; **— se d.** *vpr* (*se consacrer*) to devote oneself (à to); **se d. du mal** to go to a lot of trouble (**pour faire** to do); **s'en d. à cœur joie** to have a whale of a time, enjoy oneself to the full. **◆données** *nfpl* (*information*) data; (*de problème*) (known) facts; (*d'un roman*) basic elements. **◆donneur, -euse** *nmf* giver; (*de sang, d'organe*) donor; *Cartes* dealer.

dont [dɔ̃] *pron rel* (= **de qui, duquel, de quoi** *etc*) (*personne*) of whom; (*chose*) of which; (*appartenance: personne*) whose, of whom; (*appartenance: chose*) of which, whose; **une mère d. le fils est malade** a mother whose son is ill; **la fille d. il est fier** the daughter he is proud of *ou* of whom he is proud; **les outils d. j'ai besoin** the tools I need; **la façon d. elle joue** the way (in which) she plays; **voici ce d. il s'agit** here's what it's about.

doper [dɔpe] *vt* (*cheval, sportif*) to dope; —

se d. *vpr* to dope oneself. **◆doping** *nm* (*action*) doping; (*substance*) dope.

dorénavant [dɔrenavɑ̃] *adv* henceforth.

dor/er [dɔre] *vt* (*objet*) to gild; **d. la pilule** *Fig* to sugar the pill; **se (faire) d. au soleil** to bask in the sun; — *vi Culin* to brown. **◆—é** *a* (*objet*) gilt; (*couleur*) golden; **—** *nm* (*couche*) gilt. **◆dorure** *nf* gilding.

dorloter [dɔrlɔte] *vt* to pamper, coddle.

dormir * [dɔrmir] *vi* to sleep; (*être endormi*) to be asleep; (*argent*) to lie idle; **histoire à d. debout** tall story, cock-and-bull story; **eau dormante** stagnant water. **◆dortoir** *nm* dormitory.

dos [do] *nm* back; (*de nez*) bridge; (*de livre*) spine; **voir qn de d.** to have a back view of s.o.; **à d. de chameau** (riding) on a camel; **'voir au d.'** (*verso*) 'see over'; **j'en ai plein le d.** *Fam* I'm sick of it; **mettre qch sur le d. de qn** (*accusation*) to pin sth on s.o. **◆dossard** *nm Sp* number (*fixed on back*). **◆dossier** *nm* **1** (*de siège*) back. **2** (*papiers, compte rendu*) file, dossier; (*classeur*) folder, file.

dose [doz] *nf* dose; (*quantité administrée*) dosage. **◆dos/er** *vt* (*remède*) to measure out the dose of; (*équilibrer*) to strike the correct balance between. **◆—age** *nm* measuring out (*of dose*); (*équilibre*) balance; **faire le d. de** = **doser**. **◆—eur** *nm* **bouchon d.** measuring cap.

dot [dɔt] *nf* dowry.

doter [dɔte] *vt* (*hôpital etc*) to endow; **d. de** (*matériel*) to equip with; (*qualité*) *Fig* to endow with. **◆dotation** *nf* endowment; equipping.

douane [dwan] *nf* customs. **◆douanier, -ière** *nm* customs officer; — *a* (*union etc*) customs-.

double [dubl] *a* double; (*rôle, avantage etc*) twofold; — *adv* double; — *nm* (*de personne*) double; (*copie*) copy, duplicate; (*de timbre*) swap, duplicate; **le d. (de)** (*quantité*) twice as much (as). **◆doublage** *nm* (*de film*) dubbing. **◆doublement** *adv* doubly; — *nm* doubling. **◆doubler 1** *vt* (*augmenter*) to double; (*vêtement*) to line; (*film*) to dub; (*acteur*) to stand in for; (*classe*) *Scol* to repeat; (*cap*) *Nau* to round; **se d.** de to be coupled with; — *vi* (*augmenter*) to double. **2** *vti Aut* to overtake, pass. **◆doublure** *nf* (*étoffe*) lining; *Th* understudy; *Cin* stand-in, double.

douce [dus] *voir* **doux**. **◆doucement** *adv* (*délicatement*) gently; (*à voix basse*) softly; (*sans bruit*) quietly; (*lentement*) slowly; (*sans à-coups*) smoothly; (*assez bien*) *Fam* so-so. ◆**douceur** nf (de miel etc) sweetness; (de personne, pente etc) gentleness; (de peau etc) softness; (de temps) mildness; pl (sucreries) sweets, Am candies; **en d.** (démarrer etc) smoothly.

douche [duʃ] nf shower. ◆**doucher** vt **qn** to give s.o. a shower; **— se d.** vpr to take ou have a shower.

doué [dwe] a gifted, talented (**en at**); (intelligent) clever; **d. de** gifted with; **il est d. pour** he has a gift ou talent for.

douille [duj] nf (d'ampoule) Él socket; (de cartouche) case.

douillet, -ette [dujɛ, -ɛt] a (lit etc) soft, cosy, snug; **il est d.** (délicat) Péj he's soft.

douleur [dulœr] nf (mal) pain; (chagrin) sorrow, grief. ◆**douloureux, -euse** a (maladie, membre, décision, perte etc) painful.

doute [dut] nm doubt; pl (méfiance) doubts, misgivings; **sans d.** no doubt, probably; **sans aucun d.** without (any ou a) doubt; **mettre en d.** to cast doubt on; **dans le d.** uncertain, doubtful; **ça ne fait pas de d.** there is no doubt about it. ◆**douter** vi to doubt; **d. de qch/qn** to doubt sth/s.o.; **d. que** (+ sub) to doubt whether ou that; **se d. de qch** to suspect sth; **je m'en doute** I suspect so, I would think so. ◆**douteux, -euse** a doubtful; (louche, médiocre) dubious; **il est d. que** (+ sub) it's doubtful whether ou that.

douve(s) [duv] nf(pl) (de château) moat.

Douvres [duvr] nm ou f Dover.

doux, douce [du, dus] a (miel, son etc) sweet; (personne, pente etc) gentle; (peau, lumière, drogue etc) soft; (émotion, souvenir etc) pleasant; (temps, climat) mild; **en douce** on the quiet.

douze [duz] a & nm twelve. ◆**douzaine** nf (douze) dozen; (environ) about twelve; **une d. d'œufs/etc** a dozen eggs/etc. ◆**douzième** a & nmf twelfth; **un d.** a twelfth.

doyen, -enne [dwajɛ̃, -ɛn] nmf Rel Univ dean; **d.** (d'âge) oldest person.

draconien, -ienne [drakɔnjɛ̃, -jɛn] a (mesures) drastic.

dragée [draʒe] nf sugared almond; **tenir la d. haute à qn** (tenir tête à qn) to stand up to s.o.

dragon [dragɔ̃] nm (animal) dragon; Mil Hist dragoon.

drague [drag] nf (appareil) dredge; (filet) drag net. ◆**draguer** vt **1** (rivière etc) to dredge. **2** Arg (racoler) to try and pick up;

(faire du baratin à) to chat up, Am smooth-talk.

drainer [drene] vt to drain.

drame [dram] nm drama; (catastrophe) tragedy. ◆**dramatique** a dramatic; **critique d.** drama critic; **auteur d.** playwright, dramatist; **film d.** drama. ◆**dramatiser** vt (exagérer) to dramatize. ◆**dramaturge** nmf dramatist.

drap [dra] nm (de lit) sheet; (tissu) cloth; **dans de beaux draps** Fig in a fine mess.

drapeau, -x [drapo] nm flag; **être sous les drapeaux** Mil to be in the services.

draper [drape] vt to drape (**de** with). ◆**draperie** nf (étoffe) drapery.

dresser [drese] **1** vt (échelle, statue) to put up, erect; (piège) to lay, set; (oreille) to prick up; (liste) to draw up, make out; **— se d.** vpr (personne) to stand up; (statue, montagne) to rise up, stand; **se d. contre** (abus) to stand up against. **2** vt (animal) to train; (personne) Péj to drill, teach. ◆**dressage** nm training. ◆**dresseur, -euse** nmf trainer.

dribbler [drible] vti Fb to dribble.

drogue [drɔg] nf (médicament) Péj drug; **une d.** (stupéfiant) a drug; **les d.** drugs, dope. ◆**drogu/er** vt (victime) to drug; (malade) to dose up; **— se d.** vpr to take drugs, be on drugs; (malade) to dose oneself up. ◆**-é, -ée** nmf drug addict.

droguerie [drɔgri] nf hardware shop ou Am store. ◆**droguiste** nmf owner of a droguerie.

droit¹ [drwa] nm (privilège) right; (d'inscription etc) fee(s), dues; pl (de douane) duty; **le d.** (science juridique) law; **avoir d.** to be entitled to; **avoir le d. de faire** to be entitled to do, have the right to do; **à bon d.** rightly; **d. d'entrée** entrance fee.

droit² [drwa] a (ligne, route etc) straight; (personne, mur etc) upright, straight; (angle) right; (veston) single-breasted; (honnête) Fig upright; **— adv** straight; **tout d.** straight ou right ahead. ◆**droite¹** nf (ligne) straight line.

droit³ [drwa] a (côté, bras etc) right; **— nm** (coup) Boxe right. ◆**droite²** nf la d. (côté) the right (side); Pol the right (wing); **à d.** (tourner) to the right; (rouler, se tenir) on the right(-hand) side; **de d.** (fenêtre etc) right-hand; (politique, candidat) right-wing; **à d. de** on ou to the right of; **à d. et à gauche** (voyager etc) here, there and everywhere. ◆**droitier, -ière** a & nmf right-handed (person). ◆**droiture** nf uprightness.

drôle [drol] a funny; **d. d'air/de type** funny look/fellow. ◆**—ment** adv funnily; (extrêmement) Fam dreadfully.

dromadaire [drɔmadɛr] nm dromedary.

dru [dry] a (herbe etc) thick, dense; – adv **tomber d.** (pluie) to pour down heavily; **pousser d.** to grow thick(ly).

du [dy] = **de + le**.

dû, due [dy] a **d. à** (accident etc) due to; – nm due; (argent) dues.

dualité [dɥalite] nf duality.

dubitatif, -ive [dybitatif, -iv] a (regard etc) dubious.

duc [dyk] nm duke. ◆**duché** nm duchy. ◆**duchesse** nf duchess.

duel [dɥɛl] nm duel.

dûment [dymã] adv duly.

dune [dyn] nf (sand) dune.

duo [dɥo] nm Mus duet; (couple) Hum duo.

dupe [dyp] nf dupe, fool; – a **d. de** duped by, fooled by. ◆**duper** vt to fool, dupe.

duplex [dypleks] nm split-level flat, Am duplex; (émission e) nd. Tél link-up.

duplicata [dyplikata] nm inv duplicate.

duplicateur [dyplikatœr] nm (machine) duplicator.

duplicité [dyplisite] nf duplicity, deceit.

dur [dyr] a (substance) hard; (difficile) hard, tough; (viande) tough; (hiver, leçon, ton) harsh; (personne) hard, harsh; (brosse, carton) stiff; (œuf) hard-boiled; **d. d'oreille** hard of hearing; **d. à cuire** Fam hard-bitten, tough; – adv (travailler) hard; – nm Fam tough guy. ◆**durement** adv harshly. ◆**dureté** nf hardness; harshness; toughness.

durant [dyrã] prép during.

durc/ir [dyrsir] vti, – **se d.** vpr to harden. ◆**—issement** nm hardening.

durée [dyre] nf (de film, évènement etc) length; (période) duration; (de pile) Él life; **de longue d.** (disque) long-playing. ◆**dur/er** vi to last; **ça dure depuis . . .** it's been going on for . . . . ◆**—able** a durable, lasting.

durillon [dyrijɔ̃] nm callus.

duvet [dyvɛ] nm **1** (d'oiseau, de visage) down. **2** (sac) sleeping bag. ◆**duveté** a, ◆**duveteux, -euse** a downy.

dynamique [dinamik] a dynamic; – nf (force) Fig dynamic force, thrust. ◆**dynamisme** nm dynamism.

dynamite [dinamit] nf dynamite. ◆**dyna-miter** vt to dynamite.

dynamo [dinamo] nf dynamo.

dynastie [dinasti] nf dynasty.

dysenterie [disãtri] nf Méd dysentery.

dyslexique [dislɛksik] a & nmf dyslexic.

E

E, e [ə, ø] nm E, e.

eau, -x [o] nf water; **il est tombé beaucoup d'e.** a lot of rain fell; **e. douce** (non salée) fresh water; (du robinet) soft water; **e. salée** salt water; **e. de Cologne** eau de Cologne; **e. de toilette** toilet water; **grandes eaux** (d'un parc) ornamental fountains; **tomber à l'e.** (projet) to fall through; **ça lui fait venir l'e. à la bouche** it makes his ou her mouth water; **tout en e.** sweating; **prendre l'e.** (chaussure) to take water, leak. ◆**e.-de-vie** nf (pl eaux-de-vie) brandy. ◆**e.-forte** nf (pl eaux-fortes) (gravure) etching.

ébah/ir [ebair] vt to astound, dumbfound, amaze. ◆**—issement** nm amazement.

ébattre (s') [sebatr] vpr to frolic, frisk about. ◆**ébats** nmpl frolics.

ébauche [ebof] nf (esquisse) (rough) outline, (rough) sketch; (début) beginnings. ◆**ébaucher** vt (projet, tableau, œuvre) to sketch out, outline; **e. un sourire** to give a faint smile; – **s'é.** vpr to take shape.

ébène [ebɛn] nf (bois) ebony.

ébéniste [ebenist] nm cabinet-maker. ◆**ébénisterie** nf cabinet-making.

éberlué [ebɛrlɥe] a Fam dumbfounded.

éblou/ir [ebluir] vt to dazzle. ◆**—isse-ment** nm (aveuglement) dazzling, dazzle; (émerveillement) feeling of wonder; (malaise) fit of dizziness.

ébouer [ebwœr] nm dustman, Am garbage collector.

ébouillanter [ebujãte] vt to scald; – **s'é.** vpr to scald oneself.

éboul/er (s') [sebule] vpr (falaise etc) to crumble; (terre, roches) to fall. ◆**—ement** nm landslide. ◆**éboulis** nm (mass of) fallen debris.

ébouriffant [eburifã] a Fam astounding.

ébouriffer [eburife] vt (cheveux) to dishevel, ruffle, tousle.

ébranl/er [ebrɑ̃le] vt (mur, confiance etc) to shake; (santé) to weaken, affect; (personne) to shake, shatter; **— s'é.** vpr (train, cortège etc) to move off. **◆—ement** nm (secousse) shaking, shock; (nerveux) shock.

ébrécher [ebreʃe] vt (assiette) to chip; (lame) to nick. **◆ébréchure** nf chip; nick.

ébriété [ebrijete] nf drunkenness.

ébrouer (s') [sebrue] vpr (cheval) to snort; (personne) to shake oneself (about).

ébruiter [ebrɥite] vt (nouvelle etc) to make known, divulge.

ébullition [ebylisjɔ̃] nf boiling; **être en é.** (eau) to be boiling; (ville) Fig to be in turmoil.

écaille [ekaj] nf **1** (de poisson) scale; (de tortue, d'huître) shell; (résine synthétique) tortoise-shell. **2** (de peinture) flake. **◆écailler 1** vt (poisson) to scale; (huître) to shell. **2 s'é.** vpr (peinture) to flake (off), peel.

écarlate [ekarlat] a & nf scarlet.

écarquiller [ekarkije] vt **é. les yeux** to open one's eyes wide.

écart [ekar] nm (intervalle) gap, distance; (mouvement, embardée) swerve; (différence) difference (de in, entre between); **écarts de** (conduite, langage etc) lapses in; **le grand é.** (de gymnaste) the splits; **à l'é.** out of the way; **tenir qn à l'é.** Fig to keep s.o. out of things; **à l'é. de** away from, clear of. **◆écart/er** vt (objets) to move away from each other, move apart; (jambes) to spread, open; (rideaux) to draw (aside), open; (crainte, idée) to brush aside, dismiss; (carte) to discard; **é. qch de qch** to move sth away from sth; **é. qn de** (éloigner) to keep ou take s.o. away from; (exclure) to keep s.o. out of; **— s'é.** vpr (s'éloigner) to move away (de from); (se séparer) to move aside (de from); **s'é. de** (sujet, bonne route) to stray ou deviate from. **◆—é** a (endroit) remote; **les jambes écartées** with legs (wide) apart. **◆—ement** nm (espace) gap, distance (de between).

écartelé [ekartəle] a **é. entre** (tiraillé) torn between.

ecchymose [ekimoz] nf bruise.

ecclésiastique [eklezjastik] a ecclesiastical; **—** nm ecclesiastic, clergyman.

écervelé, -ée [esɛrvəle] a scatterbrained; **—** nmf scatterbrain.

échafaud [eʃafo] nm (pour exécution) scaffold.

échafaudage [eʃafodaʒ] nm (construction) scaffold(ing); (tas) heap; (système) Fig fabric. **◆échafauder** vi to put up scaf-

folding ou a scaffold; **—** vt (projet etc) to put together, think up.

échalas [eʃala] nm grand é. tall skinny person.

échalote [eʃalɔt] nf Bot Culin shallot, scallion.

échancré [eʃɑ̃kre] a (encolure) V-shaped, scooped. **◆échancrure** nf (de robe) opening.

échange [eʃɑ̃ʒ] nm exchange; **en é.** in exchange (**de** for). **◆échanger** vt to exchange (**contre** for). **◆échangeur** nm (intersection) Aut interchange.

échantillon [eʃɑ̃tijɔ̃] nm sample. **◆échantillonnage** nm (collection) range (of samples).

échappatoire [eʃapatwar] nf evasion, way out.

échapp/er [eʃape] vi **é. à qn** to escape from s.o.; **é. à la mort/un danger/etc** to escape death/a danger/etc; **ce nom m'échappe** that name escapes me; **ça lui a échappé (des mains)** it slipped out of his ou her hands; **laisser é.** (cri) to let out; (objet, occasion) to let slip; **l'é. belle** to have a close shave; **ça m'a échappé** (je n'ai pas compris) I didn't catch it; **— s'é.** vpr (s'enfuir) to escape (de from); (s'éclipser) to slip away; Sp to break away; (gaz, eau) to escape, come out. **◆—é, -ée** nmf runaway. **◆—ée** nf Sp breakaway; (vue) vista. **◆—ement** nm **tuyau d'é.** Aut exhaust pipe; **pot d'é.** Aut silencer, Am muffler.

écharde [eʃard] nf (de bois) splinter.

écharpe [eʃarp] nf scarf; (de maire) sash; **en é.** (bras) in a sling; **prendre en é.** Aut to hit sideways.

écharper [eʃarpe] vt **é. qn** to cut s.o. to bits.

échasse [eʃas] nf (bâton) stilt. **◆échassier** nm wading bird.

échauder [eʃode] vt **être échaudé, se faire é.** (déçu) Fam to be taught a lesson.

échauffer [eʃofe] vt (moteur) to overheat; (esprit) to excite; **— s'é.** vpr (discussion) & Sp to warm up.

échauffourée [eʃofure] nf (bagarre) clash, brawl, skirmish.

échéance [eʃeɑ̃s] nf Com date (due), expiry ou Am expiration date; (paiement) payment (due); (obligation) commitment; **à brève/longue é.** (projet, emprunt) short-/long-term.

échéant (le cas) [ləkazeʃeɑ̃] adv if the occasion should arise, possibly.

échec [eʃɛk] nm **1** (insuccès) failure; **faire é. à** (inflation etc) to hold in check. **2 les**

échecs (*jeu*) chess; **en é.** in check; **é.!** check!; **é. et mat!** checkmate!

échelle [eʃɛl] *nf* **1** (*marches*) ladder; **faire la courte é. à qn** to give s.o. a leg up. **2** (*mesure, dimension*) scale; **à l'é. nationale** on a national scale. ◆**échelon** *nm* (*d'échelle*) rung; (*de fonctionnaire*) grade; (*dans une organisation*) echelon; **à l'é. régional/national** on a regional/national level. ◆**échelonner** *vt* (*paiements*) to spread out, space out; **— s'é.** *vpr* to be spread out.

écheveau, -x [eʃvo] *nm* (*de laine*) skein; *Fig* muddle, tangle.

échevelé [eʃəvle] *a* (*ébouriffé*) dishevelled; (*course, danse etc*) *Fig* wild.

échine [eʃin] *nf Anat* backbone, spine.

échiner (s') [seʃine] *vpr* (*s'évertuer*) *Fam* to knock oneself out (**à** to faire doing).

échiquier [eʃikje] *nm* (*tableau*) chessboard.

écho [eko] *nm* (*d'un son*) echo; (*réponse*) response; *pl Journ* gossip (items), local news; **avoir des échos de** to hear some news about; **se faire l'é. de** (*opinions etc*) to echo. ◆**échotier, -ière** *nmf Journ* gossip columnist.

échographie [ekografi] *nf* (ultrasound) scan; **passer une é.** (*femme enceinte*) to have a scan.

échoir* [eʃwar] *vi* (*terme*) to expire; **é. à qn** (*part*) to fall to s.o.

échouer [eʃwe] **1** *vi* to fail; **é. à** (*examen*) to fail. **2** *vi*, **— s'é.** *vpr* (*navire*) to run aground.

éclabousser [eklabuse] *vt* to splash, spatter (**de** with); (*salir*) *Fig* to tarnish the image of. ◆**éclaboussure** *nf* splash, spatter.

éclair [eklɛr] **1** *nm* (*lumière*) flash; **un é.** Mét a flash of lightning. **2** *nm* (*gâteau*) éclair. **3** *a inv* (*visite, raid*) lightning.

éclaircir [eklɛrsir] *vt* (*couleur etc*) to lighten, make lighter; (*sauce*) to thin out; (*question, mystère*) to clear up, clarify; **— s'é.** *vpr* (*temps*) to clear (up); (*idées*) to become clear(er); (*devenir moins dense*) to thin out; **s'é. la voix** to clear one's throat. ◆**-ie** *nf* (*dans le ciel*) clear patch; (*durée*) sunny spell. ◆**-issement** *nm* (*explication*) clarification.

éclair/er [eklere] *vt* (*pièce etc*) to light (up); (*situation*) *Fig* to throw light on; **é. qn** (*avec une lampe etc*) to give s.o. some light; (*informer*) *Fig* to enlighten s.o.; **– vi** (*lampe*) to give light; **– s'é.** *vpr* (*visage*) to light up, brighten up; (*question, situation*) *Fig* to become clear(er); **s'é. à la bougie** to use candlelight. ◆**-é** *a* (*averti*) enlightened; **bien/mal é.** (*illuminé*) well/badly lit.

éclaireur, -euse [eklɛrœr, -øz] *nm Mil* scout; **–** *nmf* (boy) scout, (girl) guide.

éclat [ekla] *nm* **1** (*de la lumière*) brightness; (*de phare*) *Aut* glare; (*du feu*) blaze; (*splendeur*) brilliance, radiance; (*de la jeunesse*) bloom; (*de diamant*) glitter, sparkle. **2** (*fragment de verre ou de bois*) splinter; (*de rire, colère*) (out)burst; **é. d'obus** shrapnel; **éclats de voix** noisy outbursts, shouts. ◆**éclat/er** *vi* (*pneu, obus etc*) to burst; (*pétard, bombe*) to go off, explode; (*verre*) to shatter, break into pieces; (*guerre, incendie*) to break out; (*orage, scandale*) to break; (*parti*) to break up; **é. de rire** to burst out laughing; **é. en sanglots** to burst into tears. ◆**-ant** *a* (*lumière, couleur, succès*) brilliant; (*bruit*) thunderous; (*vérité*) blinding; (*beauté*) radiant. ◆**-ement** *nm* (*de pneu etc*) bursting; (*de bombe etc*) explosion; (*de parti*) break up.

éclectique [eklɛktik] *a* eclectic.

éclipse [eklips] *nf* (*du soleil*) & *Fig* eclipse. ◆**éclipser** *vt* to eclipse; **— s'é.** *vpr* (*soleil*) to be eclipsed; (*partir*) *Fam* to slip away.

éclopé, -ée [eklɔpe] *a* & *nmf* limping *ou* lame (person).

éclore [eklɔr] *vi* (*œuf*) to hatch; (*fleur*) to open (out), blossom. ◆**éclosion** *nf* hatching; opening, blossoming.

écluse [eklyz] *nf Nau* lock.

écœur/er [ekœre] *vt* (*aliment etc*) to make (s.o.) feel sick; (*au moral*) to sicken, nauseate. ◆**-ement** *nm* (*répugnance*) nausea, disgust.

école [ekɔl] *nf* school; (*militaire*) academy; **aller à l'é.** to go to school; **é. de danse/dessin** dancing/art school; **faire é.** to gain a following; **les grandes écoles** university establishments giving high-level professional training; **é. normale** teachers' training college. ◆**écolier, -ière** *nmf* schoolboy, schoolgirl.

écologie [ekɔlɔʒi] *nf* ecology. ◆**écologique** *a* ecological. ◆**écologiste** *nmf Pol* environmentalist.

éconduire [ekɔ̃dɥir] *vt* (*repousser*) to reject.

économe [ekɔnɔm] *a* **1** thrifty, economical. **2** *nmf* (*de collège etc*) bursar, steward. ◆**économie** *nf* (*activité économique, vertu*) economy; *pl* (*pécule*) savings; **une é. de** (*gain*) a saving of; **faire une é. de temps** to save time; **faire des économies** to save (up); **é. politique** economics. ◆**économique** *a* **1** (*doctrine etc*) economic; **science é.** economics. **2** (*bon marché*, *avantageux*) economical. ◆**économique-ment** *adv* economically. ◆**économiser** *vt* (*forces, argent, énergie etc*) to save; — *vi* to economize (**sur** on). ◆**économiste** *nmf* economist.

écoper [ekɔpe] **1** *vt* (*bateau*) to bail out, bale out. **2** *vi Fam* to cop it; **é.** (**de**) (*punition*) to cop, get.

écorce [ekɔrs] *nf* (*d'arbre*) bark; (*de fruit*) peel, skin; **l'é. terrestre** the earth's crust.

écorcher [ekɔrʃe] *vt* (*animal*) to skin, flay; (*érafler*) to graze; (*client*) *Fam* to fleece; (*langue étrangère*) *Fam* to murder; **é. les oreilles** to grate on one's ears; — **s'é.** *vpr* to graze oneself. ◆**écorchure** *nf* graze.

Écosse [ekɔs] *nf* Scotland. ◆**écossais, -aise** *a* Scottish; (*tissu*) tartan; (*whisky*) Scotch; — *nmf* Scot.

écosser [ekɔse] *vt* (*pois*) to shell.

écot [eko] *nm* (*quote-part*) share.

écoul/er [ekule] **1** *vt* (*se débarrasser de*) to dispose of; (*produits*) *Com* to sell (off), clear. **2 s'é.** *vpr* (*eau*) to flow out, run out; (*temps*) to pass, elapse; (*foule*) to disperse. ◆**—é a** (*années etc*) past. ◆**—ement** *nm* **1** (*de liquide, véhicules*) flow; (*de temps*) passage. **2** (*débit*) *Com* sale, selling.

écourter [ekurte] *vt* (*séjour, discours etc*) to cut short; (*texte, tige etc*) to shorten.

écoute [ekut] *nf* listening; **à l'é.** *Rad* tuned in, listening in (**de** to); **être aux écoutes** (*attentif*) to keep one's ears open (**de** for). ◆**écout/er** *vt* to listen to; (*radio*) to listen (in) to; — *vi* to listen; (*aux portes etc*) to eavesdrop, listen; **si je m'écoutais** if I did what I wanted. ◆**—eur** *nm* (*de téléphone*) earpiece; *pl* (*casque*) headphones, earphones.

écrabouiller [ekrabuje] *vt Fam* to crush to a pulp.

écran [ekrɑ̃] *nm* screen; **le petit é.** television.

écras/er [ekraze] *vt* (*broyer*) to crush; (*fruit, insecte*) to squash, crush; (*cigarette*) to put out; (*tuer*) *Aut* to run over; (*vaincre*) to beat (hollow), crush; (*dominer*) to outstrip; **écrasé de** (*travail, douleur*) overwhelmed with; **se faire é.** *Aut* to get run over; — **s'é.** *vpr* (*avion, voiture*) to crash (**contre** into); **s'é. dans** (*foule*) to crush *ou* squash into. ◆**—ant** *a* (*victoire, nombre, chaleur*) overwhelming. ◆**—é a** (*nez*) snub. ◆**—ement** *nm* crushing.

écrémer [ekreme] *vt* (*lait*) to skim, cream; (*collection etc*) *Fig* to cream off the best from.

écrevisse [ekrəvis] *nf* (*crustacé*) crayfish.

écrier (s') [sekrije] *vpr* to cry out, exclaim (**que** that).

écrin [ekrɛ̃] *nm* (*jewel*) case.

écrire* [ekrir] *vt* to write; (*noter*) to write (down); (*orthographier*) to spell; **é. à la machine** to type; — *vi* to write; — **s'é.** *vpr* (*mot*) to be spelt. ◆**écrit** *nm* written document, paper; (*examen*) *Scol* written paper; *pl* (*œuvres*) writings; **par é.** in writing. ◆**écriteau, -x** *nm* notice, sign. ◆**écriture** *nf* (*système*) writing; (*personnelle*) (hand)writing; *pl Com* accounts; **l'É. Rel** the Scripture(s). ◆**écrivain** *nm* author, writer.

écrou [ekru] *nm Tech* nut.

écrouer [ekrue] *vt* to imprison.

écroul/er (s') [sekrule] *vpr* (*édifice, projet etc*) to collapse; (*blessé etc*) to slump down, collapse. ◆**—ement** *nm* collapse.

écru [ekry] *af* **toile é.** unbleached linen; **soie é.** raw silk.

écueil [ekœj] *nm* (*rocher*) reef; (*obstacle*) *Fig* pitfall.

écuelle [ekɥɛl] *nf* (*bol*) bowl.

éculé [ekyle] *a* (*chaussure*) worn out at the heel; *Fig* hackneyed.

écume [ekym] *nf* (*de mer, bave d'animal etc*) foam; *Culin* scum. ◆**écumer** *vt Culin* to skim; (*piller*) to plunder; — *vi* to foam (**de rage** with anger). ◆**écumoire** *nf Culin* skimmer.

écureuil [ekyrœj] *nm* squirrel.

écurie [ekyri] *nf* stable.

écusson [ekysɔ̃] *nm* (*emblème d'étoffe*) badge.

écuyer, -ère [ekɥije, -ɛr] *nmf* (*cavalier*) (horse) rider, equestrian.

eczéma [egzema] *nm Méd* eczema.

édenté [edɑ̃te] *a* toothless.

édicter [edikte] *vt* to enact, decree.

édifice [edifis] *nm* building, edifice; (*ensemble organisé*) *Fig* edifice. ◆**édification** *nf* construction; edification; enlightenment. ◆**édifier** *vt* (*bâtiment*) to construct, erect; (*théorie*) to construct; **é. qn** (*moralement*) to edify s.o.; (*détromper*) *Iron* to enlighten s.o.

Édimbourg [edɛ̃bur] *nm ou f* Edinburgh.

édit [edi] *nm Hist* edict.

éditer [edite] *vt* (*publier*) to publish; (*annoter*) to edit. ◆**éditeur, -trice** *nmf* publisher; editor. ◆**édition** *nf* (*livre, journal*) edition; (*diffusion, métier*) publishing. ◆**éditorial, -aux** *nm* (*article*) editorial.

édredon [edrədɔ̃] *nm* eiderdown.

éducation [edykasjɔ̃] *nf* (*enseignement*) education; *(façon d'élever)* upbringing, education; **avoir de l'é.** to have good manners, be well-bred. ◆**éducateur, -trice** *nmf* educator. ◆**éducatif, -ive** *a* educational. ◆**éduquer** *vt (à l'école)* to educate *(s.o.)*; *(à la maison)* to bring *(s.o.)* up, educate *(s.o.)* **(à faire** to do); *(esprit)* to educate, train.

effac/er [efase] *vt (gommer)* to rub out, erase; *(en lavant)* to wash out; *(avec un chiffon)* to wipe away; *(souvenir)* Fig to blot out, erase; **— s'e.** *vpr (souvenir, couleur etc)* to fade; *(se placer en retrait)* to step ou draw aside. ◆**—é** *a (modeste)* self-effacing. ◆**—ement** *nm (modestie)* self-effacement.

effar/er [efare] *vt* to scare, alarm. ◆**—ement** *nm* alarm.

effaroucher [efaruʃe] *vt* to scare away, frighten away.

effectif, -ive [efektif, -iv] **1** *a (réel)* effective, real. **2** *nm (nombre)* (total) strength; *(de classe)* Scol size, total number; *pl (employés)* ou Mil manpower. ◆**effectivement** *adv (en effet)* actually, effectively, indeed.

effectuer [efektɥe] *vt (expérience etc)* to carry out; *(paiement, trajet etc)* to make.

efféminé [efemine] *a* effeminate.

effervescent [efervesɑ̃] *a (mélange, jeunesse)* effervescent. ◆**effervescence** *nf (exaltation)* excitement, effervescence; *(de liquide)* effervescence.

effet [efe] *nm* **1** *(résultat)* effect; *(impression)* impression, effect **(sur** on); **faire de l'e.** *(remède etc)* to be effective; **rester sans e.** to have no effect; **à cet e.** to this end, for this purpose; **en e.** indeed, in fact; **il me fait l'e. d'être fatigué** he seems to me to be tired; **sous l'e. de la colère** *(agir)* in anger, out of anger. **2 e. de commerce** bill, draft.

effets [efe] *nmpl (vêtements)* clothes, things.

efficace [efikas] *a (mesure etc)* effective; *(personne)* efficient. ◆**efficacité** *nf* effectiveness; efficiency.

effigie [efiʒi] *nf* effigy.

effilé [efile] *a* tapering, slender.

effilocher (s') [sefiloʃe] *vpr* to fray.

efflanqué [eflɑ̃ke] *a* emaciated.

effleurer [eflœre] *vt (frôler)* to skim, touch lightly; *(égratigner)* to graze; *(question)* Fig to touch on; **e. qn** *(pensée etc)* to cross s.o.'s mind.

effondr/er (s') [sefɔ̃dre] *vpr (projet, édifice, personne)* to collapse; *(toit)* to cave in, collapse. ◆**—ement** *nm* collapse; Com slump; *(abattement)* dejection.

efforcer (s') [seforse] *vpr* **s'e. de faire** to try (hard) ou endeavour ou strive to do.

effort [efor] *nm* effort; **sans e.** *(réussir etc)* effortlessly; *(réussite etc)* effortless.

effraction [efraksjɔ̃] *nf* **entrer par e.** *(cambrioleur)* to break in; **vol avec e.** housebreaking.

effranger (s') [sefrɑ̃ʒe] *vpr* to fray.

effray/er [efreje] *vt* to frighten, scare; **— s'e.** *vpr* to be frightened ou scared. ◆**—ant** *a* frightening, scary.

effréné [efrene] *a* unrestrained, wild.

effriter [efrite] *vt,* **— s'e.** *vpr* to crumble (away).

effroi [efrwa] *nm (frayeur)* dread. ◆**effroyable** *a* dreadful, appalling. ◆**effroyablement** *adv* dreadfully.

effronté [efrɔ̃te] *a (enfant etc)* cheeky, brazen; *(mensonge)* shameless. ◆**effronterie** *nf* effrontery.

effusion [efyzjɔ̃] *nf* **1 e. de sang** bloodshed. **2** *(manifestation)* effusion; **avec e.** effusively.

égailler (s') [segaje] *vpr* to disperse.

égal, -ale, -aux [egal, -o] *a* equal **(à** to); *(uniforme, régulier)* even; **ça m'est é.** I don't care, it's all the same to me; **— nmf** *(personne)* equal; **traiter qn d'é. à é.** ou **en é.** to treat s.o. as an equal; **sans é.** without match. ◆**—ement** *adv (au même degré)* equally; *(aussi)* also, as well. ◆**égaler** *vt* to equal, match **(en** in); *(en quantité)* Math to equal. ◆**égalisation** *nf* Sp equalization; levelling. ◆**égaliser** *vt* to equalize; *(terrain)* to level; **— vi** Sp to equalize. ◆**égalitaire** *a* egalitarian. ◆**égalité** *nf* equality; *(régularité)* evenness; **à é. (de score)** Sp equal (on points); **signe d'é.** Math equals sign.

égard [egar] *nm* **à l'é. de** *(concernant)* with respect ou regard to; *(envers)* towards; **avoir des égards pour** to have respect ou consideration for; **à cet é.** in this respect; **à certains égards** in some respects.

égarer [egare] *vt (objet)* to mislay; **é. qn** *(dérouter)* to mislead s.o.; *(aveugler, troubler)* to lead s.o. astray, misguide s.o.; **— s'é.** *vpr* to lose one's way, get lost; *(objet)* to get mislaid, go astray; *(esprit)* to wander.

égayer [egeje] *vt (pièce)* to brighten up; **é. qn** *(réconforter, amuser)* to cheer s.o. up; **— s'é.** *vpr (par la moquerie)* to be amused.

égide [eʒid] *nf* **sous l'é. de** under the aegis of.

églantier [eglɑ̃tje] *nm (arbre)* wild rose. ◆**églantine** *nf (fleur)* wild rose.

église [egliz] *nf* church.

égocentrique [egɔsɑ̃trik] *a* egocentric.

égoïne [egɔin] *nf* (**scie**) **é.** hand saw.

égoïsme [egɔism] *nm* selfishness, egoism. ◆**égoïste** *a* selfish, egoistic(al); – *nmf* egoist.

égorger [egɔrʒe] *vt* to cut *ou* slit the throat of.

égosiller (s') [segɔzije] *vpr* to scream one's head off, bawl out.

égotisme [egɔtism] *nm* egotism.

égout [egu] *nm* sewer; **eaux d'é.** sewage. ◆**égoutter** [egute] *vt* (*vaisselle*) to drain; (*légumes*) to strain, drain; – *vi*, – **s'é.** *vpr* to drain; to strain; (*linge*) to drip. ◆**égouttoir** *nm* (*panier*) (dish) drainer.

égratigner [egratine] *vt* to scratch. ◆**égratignure** *nf* scratch.

égrener [egrəne] *vt* (*raisins*) to pick off; (*épis*) to shell; **é. son chapelet** *Rel* to count one's beads.

Égypte [eʒipt] *nf* Egypt. ◆**égyptien, -ienne** [-sjɛ̃, -sjɛn] *a* & *nmf* Egyptian.

eh! [e] *int* hey!; **eh bien!** well!

éhonté [eɔ̃te] *a* shameless; **mensonge é.** barefaced lie.

éjecter [eʒɛkte] *vt* to eject. ◆**éjectable** *a* **siège é.** *Av* ejector seat. ◆**éjection** *nf* ejection.

élaborer [elabɔre] *vt* (*système etc*) to elaborate. ◆**élaboration** *nf* elaboration.

élaguer [elage] *vt* (*arbre, texte etc*) to prune.

élan [elɑ̃] *nm* **1** (*vitesse*) momentum, impetus; (*impulsion*) impulse; (*fougue*) fervour, spirit; **prendre son é.** *Sp* to take a run (up); **d'un seul é.** in one bound. **2** (*animal*) elk.

élanc/er [elɑ̃se] **1** *vi* (*dent etc*) to give shooting pains. **2 s'é.** *vpr* (*bondir*) to leap *ou* rush (forward); **s'é. vers le ciel** (*tour*) to soar up (high) into the sky. ◆**—é** *a* (*personne, taille etc*) slender. ◆**—ement** *nm* shooting pain.

élargir [elarʒir] **1** *vt* (*chemin*) to widen; (*esprit, débat*) to broaden; – **s'é.** *vpr* (*sentier etc*) to widen out. **2** *vt* (*prisonnier*) to free.

élastique [elastik] *a* (*objet, caractère*) elastic; (*règlement, notion*) flexible, supple; – *nm* (*tissu*) elastic; (*lien*) elastic *ou* rubber band. ◆**élasticité** *nf* elasticity.

élection [elɛksjɔ̃] *nf* election; **é. partielle** by-election. ◆**électeur, -trice** *nmf* voter, elector. ◆**électoral, -aux** *a* (*campagne, réunion*) election-; **collège é.** electoral college. ◆**électorat** *nm* (*électeurs*) electorate, voters.

électricien [elɛktrisjɛ̃] *nm* electrician. ◆**électricité** *nf* electricity; **coupure d'é.** power cut. ◆**électrifier** *vt* *Rail* to electrify. ◆**électrique** *a* (*pendule, décharge*) electric; (*courant, fil*) electric(al); (*phénomène, effet*) *Fig* electric. ◆**électriser** *vt* (*animer*) *Fig* to electrify. ◆**électrocuter** *vt* to electrocute.

électrode [elɛktrɔd] *nf* *Él* electrode.

électrogène [elɛktrɔʒɛn] *a* **groupe é.** *Él* generator.

électroménager [elɛktrɔmenaʒe] *am* appareil é. household electrical appliance.

électron [elɛktrɔ̃] *nm* electron. ◆**électronicien, -ienne** *nmf* electronics engineer. ◆**électronique** *a* electronic; (*microscope*) electron-; – *nf* electronics.

électrophone [elɛktrɔfɔn] *nm* record player.

élégant [elegɑ̃] *a* (*style, mobilier, solution etc*) elegant; (*bien habillé*) smart, elegant. ◆**élégamment** *adv* elegantly; smartly. ◆**élégance** *nf* elegance.

élégie [eleʒi] *nf* elegy.

élément [elemɑ̃] *nm* (*composante, personne*) & *Ch* element; (*de meuble*) unit; (*d'ensemble*) *Math* member; *pl* (*notions*) rudiments, elements; **dans son é.** (*milieu*) in one's element. ◆**élémentaire** *a* elementary.

éléphant [elefɑ̃] *nm* elephant. ◆**éléphantesque** *a* (*énorme*) *Fam* elephantine.

élévateur [elevatœr] *am* **chariot é.** forklift truck.

élévation [elevasjɔ̃] *nf* raising; *Géom* elevation; **é. de** (*hausse*) rise in.

élève [elɛv] *nmf* *Scol* pupil.

élev/er [elve] *vt* (*prix, objection, voix etc*) to raise; (*enfant*) to bring up, raise; (*animal*) to breed, rear; (*âme*) to uplift, raise; – **s'é.** *vpr* (*prix, montagne, ton, avion etc*) to rise; **s'é. à** (*prix etc*) to amount to; **s'é. contre** to rise up against. ◆**—é** *a* (*haut*) high; (*noble*) noble; **bien/mal é.** well-/bad-mannered. ◆**—age** *nm* (*de bovins*) cattle rearing; **l'é. de** the breeding *ou* rearing of. ◆**—eur, -euse** *nmf* breeder.

élider [elide] *vt* *Ling* to elide.

éligible [eliʒibl] *a* *Pol* eligible (à for).

élimé [elime] *a* (*tissu*) threadbare, worn thin.

éliminer [elimine] *vt* to eliminate. ◆**élimination** *nf* elimination. ◆**éliminatoire** *a* & *nf* (*épreuve*) é. *Sp* heat, qualifying round.

élire* [elir] *vt* *Pol* to elect (à to).

élision [elizjɔ̃] *nf* *Ling* elision.

élite [elit] *nf* elite (**de** of); **d'é.** (*chef, sujet etc*) top-notch.

elle [ɛl] *pron* **1** (*sujet*) she; (*chose, animal*) it;

pl they; **e. est** she is; it is; **elles sont** they are. **2** (*complément*) her; (*chose, animal*) it; *pl* them; **pour e.** for her; **pour elles** for them; **plus grande qu'e./qu'elles** taller than her/them. **◆e.-même** *pron* herself; (*chose, animal*) itself; *pl* themselves.

ellipse [elips] *nf Géom* ellipse. **◆elliptique** *a* elliptical.

élocution [elɔkysjɔ̃] *nf* diction; **défaut d'é.** speech defect.

éloge [elɔʒ] *nm* praise; (*panégyrique*) eulogy; **faire l'é. de** to praise. **◆élogieux, -euse** *a* laudatory.

éloign/er [elwaɲe] *vt* (*chose, personne*) to move *ou* take away (**de**); (*clients*) to keep away; (*crainte, idée*) to get rid of, banish; (*date*) to put off; **é. qn de** (*sujet, but*) to take *ou* get s.o. away from; **— s'é.** *vpr* (*partir*) to move *ou* go away (**de** from); (*dans le passé*) to become (more) remote; **s'é. de** (*sujet, but*) to get away from. **◆—é** *a* far-off, remote, distant; (*parent*) distant; **é. de** (*village, maison etc*) far (away) from; (*très différent*) far removed from. **◆—ement** *nm* remoteness, distance; (*absence*) separation (**de** from); **avec l'é.** (*avec le recul*) with time.

élongation [elɔ̃gasjɔ̃] *nf Méd* pulled muscle.

éloquent [elɔkɑ̃] *a* eloquent. **◆éloquence** *nf* eloquence.

élu, -ue [ely] *voir* **élire**; **—** *nmf Pol* elected member *ou* representative; **les élus** *Rel* the chosen, the elect.

élucider [elyside] *vt* to elucidate. **◆élucidation** *nf* elucidation.

éluder [elyde] *vt* to elude, evade.

émacié [emasje] *a* emaciated.

émail, -aux [emaj, -o] *nm* enamel; **en é.** enamel-. **◆émailler** *vt* to enamel.

émaillé [emaje] *a* **é. de fautes/***etc* (*texte*) peppered with errors/*etc.*

émanciper [emɑ̃sipe] *vt* (*femmes*) to emancipate; **— s'é.** *vpr* to become emancipated. **◆émancipation** *nf* emancipation.

émaner [emane] *vi* to emanate. **◆émanation** *nf* emanation; **une é. de** *Fig* a product of.

emball/er [ɑ̃bale] **1** *vt* (*dans une caisse etc*) to pack; (*dans du papier*) to wrap (up). **2** *vt* (*moteur*) to race; **e. qn** (*passionner*) *Fam* to enthuse s.o., thrill s.o.; **— s'e.** *vpr* (*personne*) *Fam* to get carried away; (*cheval*) to bolt; (*moteur*) to race. **◆—é** *a Fam* enthusiastic. **◆—age** *nm* (*action*) ∮ packing; wrapping; (*caisse*) packaging; (*papier*) wrapping (paper). **◆—ement** *nm Fam* (sudden) enthusiasm.

embarcadère [ɑ̃barkadɛr] *nm* landing place, quay.

embarcation [ɑ̃barkasjɔ̃] *nf* (small) boat.

embardée [ɑ̃barde] *nf Aut* (sudden) swerve; **faire une e.** to swerve.

embargo [ɑ̃bargo] *nm* embargo.

embarqu/er [ɑ̃barke] *vt* (*passagers*) to embark, take on board; (*marchandises*) to load (up); (*voler*) *Fam* to walk off with; (*prisonnier*) *Fam* to cart off; **e. qn dans** (*affaire*) *Fam* to involve s.o. in, launch s.o. into; **— vi, — s'e.** *vpr* to embark, (go on) board; **s'e. dans** (*aventure etc*) *Fam* to embark on. **◆—ement** *nm* (*de passagers*) boarding.

embarras [ɑ̃bara] *nm* (*malaise, gêne*) embarrassment; (*difficulté*) difficulty, trouble; (*obstacle*) obstacle; **dans l'e.** in difficulty; **faire des e.** (*chichis*) to make a fuss. **◆embarrass/er** *vt* (*obstruer*) to clutter, encumber; **e. qn** to be in s.o.'s way; (*déconcerter*) to embarrass s.o., bother s.o.; **s'e. de** to burden oneself with; (*se soucier*) to bother oneself about. **◆—ant** *a* (*paquet*) cumbersome; (*question*) embarrassing.

embauche [ɑ̃boʃ] *nf* (*action*) hiring; (*travail*) work. **◆embaucher** *vt* (*ouvrier*) to hire, take on.

embaumer [ɑ̃bome] **1** *vt* (*cadavre*) to embalm. **2** *vt* (*parfumer*) to give a sweet smell to; **— vi** to smell sweet.

embell/ir [ɑ̃belir] *vt* (*texte, vérité*) to embellish; **e. qn** to make s.o. attractive. **◆—issement** *nm* (*de ville etc*) improvement, embellishment.

embêt/er [ɑ̃bɛte] *vt Fam* (*contrarier, taquiner*) to annoy, bother; (*raser*) to bore; **— s'e.** *vpr Fam* to get bored. **◆—ant** *a Fam* annoying; boring. **◆—ement** [-ɛtmã] *nm Fam* **un e.** (some) trouble *ou* bother; **des embêtements** trouble(s), bother.

emblée (d') [dɑ̃ble] *adv* right away.

emblème [ɑ̃blɛm] *nm* emblem.

embobiner [ɑ̃bɔbine] *vt* (*tromper*) *Fam* to hoodwink.

emboîter [ɑ̃bwate] *vt, — s'e.* *vpr* (*pièces*) to fit into each other, fit together; **e. le pas à qn** to follow on s.o.'s heels; (*imiter*) *Fig* to follow in s.o.'s footsteps.

embonpoint [ɑ̃bɔ̃pwɛ̃] *nm* plumpness.

embouchure [ɑ̃buʃyr] *nf* (*de cours d'eau*) mouth; *Mus* mouthpiece.

embourber (s') [sɑ̃burbe] *vpr* (*véhicule*) & *Fig* to get bogged down.

embourgeoiser (s') [sɑ̃burʒwaze] *vpr* to become middle-class.

embout [ãbu] nm (de canne) tip, end piece; (de seringue) nozzle.

embouteill/er [ãbuteje] vt Aut to jam, congest. ◆—age nm traffic jam.

emboutir [ãbutir] vt (voiture) to bash ou crash into; (métal) to stamp, emboss.

embranch/er (s') [sãbrãʃe] vpr (voie) to branch off. ◆—ement nm (de voie) junction, fork; (de règne animal) branch.

embras/er [ãbraze] vt to set ablaze; — s'e. vpr (prendre feu) to flare up. ◆—ement nm (troubles) flare-up.

embrasser [ãbrase] vt (adopter, contenir) to embrace; e. qn to kiss s.o.; (serrer) to embrace ou hug s.o.; — s'e. vpr to kiss (each other). ◆embrassade nf embrace, hug.

embrasure [ãbrazyr] nf (de fenêtre, porte) opening.

embray/er [ãbreje] vi to let in ou engage the clutch. ◆—age nm (mécanisme, pédale) Aut clutch.

embrigader [ãbrigade] vt to recruit.

embrocher [ãbrɔʃe] vt Culin & Fig to skewer.

embrouiller [ãbruje] vt (fils) to tangle (up); (papiers etc) to muddle (up), mix up; e. qn to confuse s.o., get s.o. muddled; — s'e. vpr to get confused ou muddled (dans in, with). ◆embrouillamini nm Fam muddle, mix-up. ◆embrouillement nm confusion, muddle.

embroussaillé [ãbrusaje] a (barbe, chemin) bushy.

embruns [ãbrœ̃] nmpl (sea) spray.

embryon [ãbrijɔ̃] nm embryo. ◆embryonnaire a Méd & Fig embryonic.

embûches [ãbyʃ] nfpl (difficultés) traps, pitfalls.

embuer [ãbɥe] vt (vitre, yeux) to mist up.

embusquer (s') [sãbyske] vpr to lie in ambush. ◆embuscade nf ambush.

éméché [emeʃe] a (ivre) Fam tipsy.

émeraude [emrod] nf emerald.

émerger [emerʒe] vi to emerge (de from).

émeri [emri] nm toile (d')é. emery cloth.

émerveill/er [emerveje] vt to amaze; — s'é. vpr to marvel, be filled with wonder (de at). ◆—ement nm wonder, amazement.

émett/re [emetr] vt (lumière, son etc) to give out, emit; Rad to transmit, broadcast; (cri) to utter; (opinion, vœu) to express; (timbre-poste, monnaie) to issue; (chèque) to draw; (emprunt) Com to float. ◆—eur nm (poste) é. Rad transmitter.

émeute [emøt] nf riot. ◆émeutier, -ière nmf rioter.

émietter [emjete] vt, — s'é. vpr (pain etc) to crumble.

émigr/er [emigre] vi (personne) to emigrate. ◆—ant, -ante nmf emigrant. ◆—é, -ée nmf exile, émigré. ◆émigration nf emigration.

éminent [eminã] a eminent. ◆éminemment [-amã] adv eminently. ◆éminence nf 1 (colline) hillock. 2 son É. Rel his Eminence.

émissaire [emiser] nm emissary.

émission [emisjɔ̃] nf (programme) TV broadcast; (action) emission (de of); (de programme) TV Rad transmission; (de timbre-poste, monnaie) issue.

emmagasiner [ãmagazine] vt to store (up).

emmanchure [ãmãʃyr] nf (de vêtement) arm hole.

emmêler [ãmele] vt to tangle (up).

emménag/er [ãmenaʒe] vi (dans un logement) to move in; e. dans to move into. ◆—ement nm moving in.

emmener [ãmne] vt to take (à to); (prisonnier) to take away; e. qn faire une promenade to take s.o. for a walk.

emmerd/er [ãmerde] vt Arg to annoy, bug; (raser) to bore stiff; — s'e. vpr Arg to get bored stiff. ◆—ement nm Arg bother, trouble. ◆—eur, -euse nmf (personne) Arg pain in the neck.

emmitoufler (s') [sãmitufle] vpr to wrap (oneself) up.

emmurer [ãmyre] vt (personne) to wall in.

émoi [emwa] nm excitement; en é. agog, excited.

émoluments [emɔlymã] nmpl remuneration.

émotion [emosjɔ̃] nf (trouble) excitement; (sentiment) emotion; une é. (peur) a scare. ◆émotif, -ive a emotional. ◆émotionné a Fam upset.

émouss/er [emuse] vt (pointe) to blunt; (sentiment) to dull. ◆—é a (pointe) blunt; (sentiment) dulled.

émouv/oir* [emuvwar] vt (affecter) to move, touch; — s'é. vpr to be moved ou touched. ◆—ant, -a moving, touching.

empailler [ãpaje] vt (animal) to stuff.

empaler (s') [sãpale] vpr to impale oneself.

empaqueter [ãpakte] vt to pack(up).

emparer (s') [sãpare] vpr s'e. de to seize, take hold of.

empât/er (s') [sãpɑte] vpr to fill out, get fat(ter). ◆—é a fleshy, fat.

empêch/er [ãpeʃe] vt to prevent, stop; e. qn de faire to prevent ou stop s.o. (from) doing; n'empêche qu'elle a raison Fam all the same she's right; **n'empêche!** *Fam* all the same!; **elle ne peut pas s'e. de rire** she can't help laughing. ◆**—ement** [-ɛʃmɑ̃] *nm* difficulty, hitch; **avoir un e.** to be unavoidably held up.

empereur [ɑ̃prœr] *nm* emperor.

empeser [ɑ̃pəze] *vt* to starch.

empester [ɑ̃pɛste] *vt* (*pièce*) to make stink, stink out; (*tabac etc*) to stink of; **e. qn** to stink s.o. out; — *vi* to stink.

empêtrer (s') [sɑ̃petre] *vpr* to get entangled (**dans** in).

emphase [ɑ̃faz] *nf* pomposity. ◆**emphatique** *a* pompous.

empiéter [ɑ̃pjete] *vi* **e. sur** to encroach upon. ◆**empiétement** *nm* encroachment.

empiffrer (s') [sɑ̃pifre] *vpr Fam* to gorge ou stuff oneself (**de** with).

empil/er [ɑ̃pile] *vt*, — **s'e.** *vpr* to pile up (**sur** on); **s'e. dans** (*personnes*) to pile into (*building, car etc*). ◆**—ement** *nm* (*tas*) pile.

empire [ɑ̃pir] *nm* (*territoires*) empire; (*autorité*) hold, influence; **sous l'e. de** (*peur etc*) in the grip of.

empirer [ɑ̃pire] *vi* to worsen, get worse.

empirique [ɑ̃pirik] *a* empirical. ◆**empirisme** *nm* empiricism.

emplacement [ɑ̃plasmɑ̃] *nm* site, location; (*de stationnement*) place.

emplâtre [ɑ̃platr] *nm* (*onguent*) *Méd* plaster.

emplette [ɑ̃plɛt] *nf* purchase; *pl* shopping.

emplir [ɑ̃plir] *vt*, — **s'e.** *vpr* to fill (**de** with).

emploi [ɑ̃plwa] *nm* **1** (*usage*) use; **e. du temps** timetable; **mode d'e.** directions (for use). **2** (*travail*) job, position, employment; **l'e.** (*travail*) *Écon Pol* employment; **sans e.** unemployed. ◆**employ/er** *vt* (*utiliser*) to use; (*personne*) to employ; **e. qn** (*occuper*) to employ s.o.; — **s'e.** *vpr* (*expression etc*) to be used; **s'e. à faire** to devote oneself to doing. ◆**—é, -ée** *nmf* employee; (*de bureau, banque*) clerk, employee; **e. des postes/etc** postal/etc worker; **e. de magasin** shop assistant, *Am* sales clerk. ◆**employeur, -euse** *nmf* employer.

empocher [ɑ̃pɔʃe] *vt* (*argent*) to pocket.

empoigner [ɑ̃pwaɲe] *vt* (*saisir*) to grab, grasp; — **s'e.** *vpr* to come to blows, fight. ◆**empoignade** *nf* (*querelle*) fight.

empoisonn/er [ɑ̃pwazɔne] *vt* (*personne, aliment, atmosphère*) to poison; (*empester*) to stink out; (*gâter, altérer*) to trouble, bedevil; **e. qn** (*embêter*) *Fam* to get on s.o.'s nerves; — **s'e.** *vpr* (*par accident*) to be poisoned; (*volontairement*) to poison oneself. ◆**—ant** *a* (*embêtant*) *Fam* irritating.

◆**—ement** *nm* poisoning; (*ennui*) *Fam* problem, trouble.

emport/er [ɑ̃pɔrte] *vt* (*prendre*) to take (away) (**avec soi** with one); (*enlever*) to take away; (*prix, trophée*) to carry off; (*décision*) to carry; (*entraîner*) to carry along ou away; (*par le vent*) to blow off ou away; (*par les vagues*) to sweep away; (*par la maladie*) to carry off; **l'e. sur qn** to get the upper hand over s.o.; **se laisser e.** *Fig* to get carried away (**par** by); — **s'e.** *vpr* to lose one's temper (**contre** with). ◆**—é** *a* (*caractère*) hot-tempered. ◆**—ement** *nm* anger; *pl* fits of anger.

empoté [ɑ̃pɔte] *a Fam* clumsy.

empourprer (s') [sɑ̃purpre] *vpr* to turn crimson.

empreint [ɑ̃prɛ̃] *a* **e. de** stamped with, heavy with.

empreinte [ɑ̃prɛ̃t] *nf* (*marque*) & *Fig* mark, stamp; **e. digitale** fingerprint; **e. des pas** footprint.

empress/er (s') [sɑ̃prese] *vpr* **s'e. de faire** to hasten to do; **s'e. auprès de qn** to busy oneself with s.o.; **s'e.** to be attentive to s.o.; **s'e. autour de qn** to rush around s.o. ◆**—é** *a* eager, attentive; **e. à faire** eager to do. ◆**—ement** [-ɛsmɑ̃] *nm* (*hâte*) eagerness; (*auprès de qn*) attentiveness.

emprise [ɑ̃priz] *nf* ascendancy, hold (**sur** over).

emprisonn/er [ɑ̃prizɔne] *vt Jur* to imprison; (*enfermer*) *Fig* to confine. ◆**—ement** *nm* imprisonment.

emprunt [ɑ̃prœ̃] *nm* (*argent*) *Com* loan; (*mot*) *Ling* borrowed word; **un e. à** *Ling* a borrowing from; **l'e. de qch** the borrowing of sth; **d'e.** borrowed; **nom d'e.** assumed name. ◆**emprunt/er** *vt* (*obtenir*) to borrow (**à qn** from s.o.); (*route etc*) to use; (*nom*) to assume; **e. à** (*tirer de*) to derive ou borrow from. ◆**—é** *a* (*gêné*) ill-at-ease.

empuantir [ɑ̃pɥɑ̃tir] *vt* to make stink, stink out.

ému [emy] *voir* **émouvoir**; — *a* (*attendri*) moved; (*apeuré*) nervous; (*attristé*) upset; **une voix émue** a voice charged with emotion.

émulation [emylasjɔ̃] *nf* emulation.

émule [emyl] *nmf* imitator, follower.

en¹ [ɑ̃] *prép* **1** (*lieu*) in; (*direction*) to; **être en ville/en France** to be in town/in France; **aller en ville/en France** to go (in)to town/to France. **2** (*temps*) in; **en été** in summer; **en février** in February; **d'heure en heure** from hour to hour. **3** (*moyen, état etc*) by; in; at; on; **en avion** by plane; **en groupe**

in a group; **en mer** at sea; **en guerre** at war; **en fleur** in flower; **en congé** on leave; **en vain** in vain. **4** (*matière*) in; **en bois** wooden, in wood; **chemise en nylon** nylon shirt; **c'est en or** it's (made of) gold. **5** (*comme*) **en cadeau** as a present; **en ami** as a friend. **6** (+ *participe présent*) **en mangeant/chantant/etc** while eating/singing/etc; **en apprenant que...** on hearing that...; **en souriant** smiling, with a smile; **en ne disant rien** by saying nothing; **sortir en courant** to run out. **7** (*transformation*) into; **traduire en** to translate into.

en² [ɑ̃] *pron & adv* **1** (= *de là*) from there; **j'en viens** I've just come from there. **2** (= *de ça, lui, eux etc*) **il en est content** he's pleased with it *ou* him *ou* them; **en parler** to talk about it; **en mourir** to die of *ou* from it; **elle m'en frappa** she struck me with it. **3** (*partitif*) some; **j'en ai** I have some; **en veux-tu?** do you want some *ou* any?; **je t'en supplie** I beg you (to).

encadr/er [ɑ̃kadre] *vt* (*tableau*) to frame; (*entourer d'un trait*) to box in; (*troupes, étudiants*) to supervise, train; (*prisonnier, accusé*) to flank. ◆**—ement** *nm* (*action*) framing; supervision; (*de porte, photo*) frame; (*décor*) setting; (*personnel*) training and supervisory staff.

encaissé [ɑ̃kese] *a* (*vallée*) deep.

encaiss/er [ɑ̃kese] *vt* (*argent, loyer etc*) to collect; (*effet, chèque*) Com to cash; (*coup*) Fam to take; **je ne peux pas l'e.** Fam I can't stand him *ou* her. ◆**encaissement** *nm* (*de loyer etc*) collection; (*de chèque*) cashing.

encapuchonné [ɑ̃kapyʃɔne] *a* hooded.

encart [ɑ̃kar] *nm* (*feuille*) insert. ◆**encarter** *vt* to insert.

en-cas [ɑ̃kɑ] *nm inv* (*repas*) snack.

encastrer [ɑ̃kastre] *vt* to build in (**dans** in), embed (**dans** into).

encaustique [ɑ̃kostik] *nf* (*wax*) polish. ◆**encaustiquer** *vt* to wax, polish.

enceinte [ɑ̃sɛ̃t] **1** *af* (*femme*) pregnant; **e. de six mois/etc** six months/etc pregnant. **2** *nf* (*muraille*) surrounding wall; (*espace*) enclosure; **e. acoustique** (loud)speakers.

encens [ɑ̃sɑ̃] *nm* incense. ◆**encensoir** *nm* Rel censer.

encercler [ɑ̃sɛrkle] *vt* to surround, encircle.

enchaîner [ɑ̃ʃene] *vt* (*animal*) to chain (up); (*prisonnier*) to put in chains, chain (up); (*assembler*) to link (up), connect; — *vi* (*continuer à parler*) to continue; — **s'e.** *vpr* (*idées etc*) to be linked (up). ◆**enchaînement** *nm* (*succession*) chain, series; (*liaison*) link(ing) (**de** of).

enchant/er [ɑ̃ʃɑ̃te] *vt* (*ravir*) to delight, enchant; (*ensorceler*) to bewitch, enchant. ◆**—é** *a* (*ravi*) delighted (**de** with, **que** + *sub*) that); **e. de faire votre connaissance!** pleased to meet you! ◆**—ement** *nm* delight; enchantment; **comme par e.** as if by magic. ◆**—eur** *a* delightful, enchanting; — *nm* (*sorcier*) magician.

enchâsser [ɑ̃ʃɑse] *vt* (*diamant*) to set, embed.

enchère [ɑ̃ʃɛr] *nf* (*offre*) bid; **vente aux enchères** auction; **mettre aux enchères** (put up for) auction. ◆**enchér/ir** *vi* **e. sur qn** to outbid s.o. ◆**—isseur** *nm* bidder.

enchevêtrer [ɑ̃ʃvetre] *vt* to (en)tangle; — **s'e.** *vpr* to get entangled (**dans** in). ◆**enchevêtrement** *nm* tangle, entanglement.

enclave [ɑ̃klav] *nf* enclave. ◆**enclaver** *vt* to enclose (completely).

enclencher [ɑ̃klɑ̃ʃe] *vt* Tech to engage.

enclin [ɑ̃klɛ̃] *am* **e. à** inclined *ou* prone to.

enclore [ɑ̃klɔr] *vt* (*terrain*) to enclose. ◆**enclos** *nm* (*terrain, clôture*) enclosure.

enclume [ɑ̃klym] *nf* anvil.

encoche [ɑ̃kɔʃ] *nf* notch, nick (**à** in).

encoignure [ɑ̃kwaɲyr] *nf* corner.

encoller [ɑ̃kɔle] *vt* to paste.

encolure [ɑ̃kɔlyr] *nf* (*de cheval, vêtement*) neck; (*tour du cou*) collar (size).

encombre (sans) [sɑ̃zɑ̃kɔ̃br] *adv* without a hitch.

encombr/er [ɑ̃kɔ̃bre] *vt* (*couloir, pièce etc*) to clutter up (**de** with); (*rue*) to congest, clog (**de** with); **e. qn** to hamper s.o.; **s'e.** **de** to burden *ou* saddle oneself with. ◆**—ant** *a* (*paquet*) bulky, cumbersome; (*présence*) awkward. ◆**—é** *a* (*profession, marché*) overcrowded, saturated. ◆**—ement** *nm* (*embarras*) clutter; Aut traffic jam; (*volume*) bulk(iness).

encontre de (à l') [alɑ̃kɔ̃trədə] *adv* against; (*contrairement à*) contrary to.

encore [ɑ̃kɔr] *adv* **1** (*toujours*) still; **tu es e. là?** are you still here? **2** (*avec négation*) yet; **pas e.** not yet; **ne pars pas e.** don't go yet; **je ne suis pas e. prêt** I'm not ready yet, I'm still not ready. **3** (*de nouveau*) again; **essaie e.** try again. **4** (*de plus*) **e. un café** another coffee, one more coffee; **e. une fois** (once) again, once more; **e. un** another (one), one more; **e. du pain** (some) more bread; **que veut-il e.?** what else *ou* more does he want?; **e. quelque chose** something else; **qui/quoi e.?** who/what else?; **chante e.** sing some more. **5** (*avec comparatif*) even, still; **e. mieux** even better, better still. **6** (*aussi*) also. **7 si e.** (*si seulement*) if only; **et e.!** (*à peine*) if that!, only just! **8 e. que** (+ *sub*) although.

encourag/er [ɑ̃kuraʒe] *vt* to encourage (à faire to do). ◆**—eant** *a* encouraging. ◆**—ement** *nm* encouragement.

encourir* [ɑ̃kurir] *vt* (*amende etc*) to incur.

encrasser [ɑ̃krase] *vt* to clog up (with dirt).

encre [ɑ̃kr] *nf* ink; **e. de Chine** Indian ink; **e. sympathique** invisible ink. ◆**encrier** *nm* inkwell, inkpot.

encroûter (s') [sɑ̃krute] *vpr Péj* to get set in one's ways; **s'e. dans** (*habitude*) to get stuck in.

encyclique [ɑ̃siklik] *nf Rel* encyclical.

encyclopédie [ɑ̃siklɔpedi] *nf* encyclop(a)edia. ◆**encyclopédique** *a* encyclop(a)edic.

endémique [ɑ̃demik] *a* endemic.

endetter [ɑ̃dete] *vt* **e. qn** to get s.o. into debt; **— s'e.** *vpr* to get into debt. ◆**endettement** *nm* (*dettes*) debts.

endeuiller [ɑ̃dœje] *vt* to plunge into mourning.

endiablé [ɑ̃djable] *a* (*rythme etc*) frantic, wild.

endiguer [ɑ̃dige] *vt* (*fleuve*) to dam (up); (*réprimer*) Fig to stem.

endimanché [ɑ̃dimɑ̃ʃe] *a* in one's Sunday best.

endive [ɑ̃div] *nf* chicory, endive.

endoctrin/er [ɑ̃dɔktrine] *vt* to indoctrinate. ◆**—ement** *nm* indoctrination.

endolori [ɑ̃dɔlɔri] *a* painful, aching.

endommager [ɑ̃dɔmaʒe] *vt* to damage.

endorm/ir* [ɑ̃dɔrmir] *vt* (*enfant, patient*) to put to sleep; (*ennuyer*) to send to sleep; (*soupçons etc*) to lull; (*douleur*) to deaden; **— s'e.** *vpr* to fall asleep, go to sleep. ◆**—i** *a* asleep, sleeping; (*indolent*) Fam sluggish.

endosser [ɑ̃dose] *vt* (*vêtement*) to put on, don; (*responsabilité*) to assume; (*chèque*) to endorse.

endroit [ɑ̃drwa] *nm* **1** place, spot; (*de film, livre*) part, place. **2** (*de tissu*) right side; **à l'e.** (*vêtement*) right side out, the right way round.

enduire* [ɑ̃dɥir] *vt* to smear, coat (**de** with). ◆**enduit** *nm* coating; (*de mur*) plaster.

endurant [ɑ̃dyrɑ̃] *a* hardy, tough. ◆**endurance** *nf* endurance.

endurc/ir [ɑ̃dyrsir] *vt* to harden; **s'e. à** (*personne*) to become hardened to (*pain etc*). ◆**—i** *a* hardened; (*célibataire*) confirmed. ◆**—issement** *nm* hardening.

endurer [ɑ̃dyre] *vt* to endure, bear.

énergie [enɛrʒi] *nf* energy; **avec é.** (*protester etc*) forcefully. ◆**énergétique** *a* (*ressources etc*) energy-. ◆**énergique** *a* (*dynamique*) energetic; (*remède*) powerful; (*mesure, ton*) forceful. ◆**énergiquement** *adv* (*protester etc*) energetically.

énergumène [enɛrgymɛn] *nmf Péj* rowdy character.

énerv/er [enɛrve] *vt* **é. qn** (*irriter*) to get on s.o.'s nerves; (*rendre énervé*) to make s.o. nervous; **— s'é.** *vpr* to get worked up. ◆**—é** *a* on edge, irritated. ◆**—ement** *nm* irritation, nervousness.

enfant [ɑ̃fɑ̃] *nmf* child (*pl* children); **e. en bas âge** infant; **un e. de** (*originaire*) a native of; **attendre un e.** to expect a baby or a child; **e. trouvé** foundling; **e. de chœur** Rel altar boy; **e. prodige** child prodigy; **e. prodigue** prodigal son; **bon e.** (*caractère*) good natured. ◆**enfance** *nf* childhood; **première e.** infancy, early childhood; **dans son e.** (*science etc*) in its infancy. ◆**enfanter** *vt* to give birth to; **— vi** to give birth. ◆**enfantillage** *nm* childishness. ◆**enfantin** *a* (*voix, joie*) childlike; (*langage, jeu*) children's; (*puéril*) childish; (*simple*) easy.

enfer [ɑ̃fɛr] *nm* hell; **d'e.** (*vision, bruit*) infernal; **feu d'e.** roaring fire; **à un train d'e.** at breakneck speed.

enfermer [ɑ̃fɛrme] *vt* (*personne etc*) to shut up, lock up; (*objet précieux*) to lock up, shut away; (*jardin*) to enclose; **s'e. dans** (*chambre etc*) to shut ou lock oneself (up) in; (*attitude etc*) Fig to maintain stubbornly.

enferrer (s') [sɑ̃fɛre] *vpr* **s'e. dans** to get caught up in.

enfiévré [ɑ̃fjevre] *a* (*surexcité*) feverish.

enfiler [ɑ̃file] *vt* (*aiguille*) to thread; (*perles etc*) to string; (*vêtement*) Fam to slip on, pull on; (*rue, couloir*) to take; (*rue etc*) to take. ◆**enfilade** *nf* (*série*) row, string.

enfin [ɑ̃fɛ̃] *adv* (*à la fin*) finally, at last; (*en dernier lieu*) lastly; (*en somme*) in a word; (*conclusion résignée*) well; **e. bref** (*en somme*) Fam in a word; **il est grand, e. pas trop petit** he's tall — well, not too short anyhow; **mais e.** but; (*mais*) **e.!** for heaven's sake!

enflamm/er [ɑ̃flame] *vt* to set fire to, ignite; (*allumette*) to light; (*irriter*) Méd to inflame; (*imagination, colère*) to excite, inflame; **— s'e.** *vpr* to catch fire, ignite; **s'e. de colère** to flare up. ◆**—é** *a* (*discours*) fiery.

enfler [ɑ̃fle] vt to swell; (voix) to raise; — vi Méd to swell (up). ◆**enflure** nf swelling.

enfonc/er [ɑ̃fɔ̃se] vt (clou etc) to knock in, drive in; (chapeau) to push ou force down; (porte, voiture) to smash in; **e. dans** (couteau, mains etc) to plunge into; — vi, — **s'e.** vpr (s'enliser) to sink (dans into); **s'e. dans** (pénétrer) to plunge into, disappear (deep) into. ◆—**é** a (yeux) sunken.

enfouir [ɑ̃fwir] vt to bury.

enfourcher [ɑ̃furʃe] vt (cheval etc) to mount, bestride.

enfourner [ɑ̃furne] vt to put in the oven.

enfreindre* [ɑ̃frɛ̃dr] vt to infringe.

enfuir* (s') [sɑ̃fɥir] vpr to run away ou off, flee (de from).

enfumer [ɑ̃fyme] vt (pièce) to fill with smoke; (personne) to smoke out.

engag/er [ɑ̃gaʒe] vt (bijou etc) to pawn; (parole) to pledge; (discussion, combat) to start; (clef etc) to insert (dans into); (capitaux) to tie up, invest; **e. la bataille avec** to join battle with; **e. qn** (lier) to bind s.o., commit s.o.; (embaucher) to hire s.o., engage s.o.; **e. qn dans** (affaire etc) to involve s.o. in; **e. qn à faire** (exhorter) to urge s.o. to do; — **s'e.** vpr (s'inscrire) Mil to enlist; Sp to enter; (au service d'une cause) to commit oneself; (action) to start; **s'e. à faire** to commit oneself to doing, undertake to do; **s'e. dans** (voie) to enter; (affaire etc) to get involved in. ◆—**eant** a (écrivain etc) engaging, inviting. ◆—**é** a (écrivain etc) committed. ◆—**ement** nm (promesse) commitment; (commencement) start; (de recrues) Mil enlistment; (inscription) Sp entry; (combat) Mil engagement; **prendre l'e. de** to undertake to.

engelure [ɑ̃ʒlyr] nf chilblain.

engendrer [ɑ̃ʒɑ̃dre] vt (procréer) to beget; (causer) to generate, engender.

engin [ɑ̃ʒɛ̃] nm machine, device; (projectile) missile; **e. explosif** explosive device.

englober [ɑ̃glɔbe] vt to include, embrace.

engloutir [ɑ̃glutir] vt (avaler) to wolf (down), gobble (up); (faire sombrer ou disparaître) to engulf.

engorger [ɑ̃gɔrʒe] vt to block up, clog.

engouement [ɑ̃gumɑ̃] nm craze.

engouffrer [ɑ̃gufre] vt (avaler) to wolf (down); (fortune) to consume; **s'e. dans** to sweep ou rush into.

engourd/ir [ɑ̃gurdir] vt (membre) to numb; (esprit) to dull; — **s'e.** vpr to go numb; to become dull. ◆—**issement** nm numbness; dullness.

engrais [ɑ̃grɛ] nm (naturel) manure; (chimique) fertilizer.

engraisser [ɑ̃grese] vt (animal) to fatten (up); — vi, — **s'e.** vpr to get fat, put on weight.

engrenage [ɑ̃grənaʒ] nm Tech gears; Fig mesh, chain, web.

engueuler [ɑ̃gœle] vt **e. qn** Fam to swear at s.o., give s.o. hell. ◆**engueulade** nf Fam (réprimande) dressing-down, severe talking-to; (dispute) slanging match, row.

enhardir [ɑ̃ardir] vt to make bolder; **s'e. à faire** to make bold to do.

énième [ɛnjɛm] a Fam umpteenth, nth.

énigme [enigm] nf enigma, riddle. ◆**énigmatique** a enigmatic.

enivrer [ɑ̃nivre] vt (soûler, troubler) to intoxicate; — **s'e.** vpr to get drunk (de on).

enjamber [ɑ̃ʒɑ̃be] vt to step over; (pont etc) to span (river etc). ◆**enjambée** nf stride.

enjeu, -x [ɑ̃ʒø] nm (mise) stake(s).

enjoindre [ɑ̃ʒwɛ̃dr] vt **e. à qn de faire** Litt to order s.o. to do.

enjôler [ɑ̃ʒole] vt to wheedle, coax.

enjoliv/er [ɑ̃ʒɔlive] vt to embellish. ◆—**eur** nm Aut hubcap.

enjoué [ɑ̃ʒwe] a playful. ◆**enjouement** nm playfulness.

enlacer [ɑ̃lase] vt to entwine; (serrer dans ses bras) to clasp.

enlaidir [ɑ̃ledir] vt to make ugly; — vi to grow ugly.

enlev/er [ɑ̃lve] vt to take away ou off, remove (à qn from s.o.); (ordures) to collect; (vêtement) to take off, remove; (tache) to take out, lift, remove; (enfant etc) to kidnap, abduct; — **s'e.** vpr (tache) to come out; (vernis) to come off. ◆—**é** a (scène, danse etc) well-rendered. ◆**enlèvement** nm kidnapping, abduction; (d'un objet) removal; (des ordures) collection.

enliser (s') [sɑ̃lize] vpr (véhicule) & Fig to get bogged down (dans in).

enneigé [ɑ̃neʒe] a snow-covered. ◆**enneigement** nm snow coverage; **bulletin d'e.** snow report.

ennemi, -ie [ɛnmi] nmf enemy; — a (personne) hostile (de to); (pays etc) enemy-.

ennui [ɑ̃nɥi] nm boredom; (mélancolie) weariness; **un e.** (tracas) (some) trouble ou bother; **des ennuis** trouble(s), bother; **l'e., c'est que ...** the annoying thing is that . . . .

ennuy/er [ɑ̃nɥije] vt (agacer) to annoy, bother; (préoccuper) to bother; (fatiguer) to bore; — **s'e.** vpr to get bored. ◆—**é**

a (*air*) bored; **je suis e.** that annoys *ou* bothers me. ◆**ennuyeux, -euse** *a* (*fastidieux*) boring; (*contrariant*) annoying.

énonc/er [enɔse] *vt* to state, express. ◆**-é** *nm* (*de texte*) wording, terms; (*phrase*) Ling utterance.

enorgueillir [ɑnɔrgœjir] *vt* to make proud; **s'e. de** to pride oneself on.

énorme [enɔrm] *a* enormous, huge, tremendous. ◆**énormément** *adv* enormously, tremendously; **e. de** an enormous *ou* tremendous amount of. ◆**énormité** *nf* (*dimension*) enormity; (*faute*) enormous blunder.

enquérir (s') [sɑkerir] *vpr* **s'e. de** to inquire about.

enquête [ɑket] *nf* (*de police etc*) investigation; (*judiciaire, administrative*) inquiry; (*sondage*) survey. ◆**enquêter** *vi* (*police etc*) to investigate; **e. sur** (*crime*) to investigate. ◆**enquêteur, -euse** *nmf* investigator.

enquiquiner [ɑkikine] *vt* Fam to annoy, bug.

enraciner (s') [sɑrasine] *vpr* to take root; **enraciné dans** (*personne, souvenir*) rooted in; **bien enraciné** (*préjugé etc*) deep-rooted.

enrag/er [ɑraʒe] *vi* **e. de faire** to be furious about doing; **faire e. qn** to get on s.o.'s nerves. ◆**-eant** *a* infuriating. ◆**-é** *a* (*chien*) rabid, mad; (*joueur etc*) Fam fanatical (**de** about); **rendre/devenir e.** (*furieux*) to make/become furious.

enrayer [ɑreje] *vt* (*maladie etc*) to check; — **s'e.** *vpr* (*fusil*) to jam.

enregistr/er [ɑrʒistre] *vt* **1** (*inscrire*) to record; (*sur registre*) to register; (*constater*) to note, register; (*faire*) **e.** (*bagages*) to register, Am check. **2** (*musique, émission etc*) to record. ◆**-ement** *nm* (*de bagages*) registration, Am checking; (*d'un acte*) registration; (*sur bande etc*) recording. ◆**-eur, -euse** *a* (*appareil*) recording; **caisse enregistreuse** cash register.

enrhumer [ɑryme] *vt* **e. qn** to give s.o. a cold; **être enrhumé** to have a cold; — **s'e.** *vpr* to catch a cold.

enrich/ir [ɑriʃir] *vt* to enrich (**de** with); — **s'e.** *vpr* (*personne*) to get rich. ◆**-issement** *nm* enrichment.

enrober [ɑrɔbe] *vt* to coat (**de** in); **enrobé de chocolat** chocolate-coated.

enrôl/er [ɑrole] *vt*, — **s'e.** *vpr* to enlist. ◆**-ement** *nm* enlistment.

enrou/er (s') [sɑrwe] *vpr* to get hoarse. ◆**-é** *a* hoarse. ◆**-ement** [ɑrumɑ] *nm* hoarseness.

enrouler [ɑrule] *vt* (*fil etc*) to wind; (*tapis, cordage*) to roll up; **s'e. dans** (*couvertures*) to roll *ou* wrap oneself up in; **s'e. sur** *ou* **autour de qch** to wind round sth.

ensabler [ɑsable] *vt*, — **s'e.** *vpr* (*port*) to silt up.

ensanglanté [ɑsɑglɑte] *a* bloodstained.

enseigne [ɑsɛɲ] **1** *nf* (*de magasin etc*) sign; **e. lumineuse** neon sign; **logés à la même e.** Fig in the same boat. **2** *nm* **e. de vaisseau** lieutenant, Am ensign.

enseign/er [ɑsɛɲe] *vt* to teach; **e. qch à qn** to teach s.o. sth; — *vi* to teach. ◆**-ant, -ante** [-ɑ̃, -ɑ̃t] *a* (*corps*) teaching; — *nmf* teacher. ◆**-ement** [-ɛɲmɑ] *nm* education; (*action, métier*) teaching.

ensemble [ɑsɑbl] **1** *adv* together. **2** *nm* (*d'objets*) group, set; Math set; Mus ensemble; (*mobilier*) suite; (*vêtement féminin*) outfit; (*harmonie*) unity; **l'e. du personnel** (*totalité*) the whole (of the) staff; **l'e. des enseignants** all (of) the teachers; **dans l'e.** on the whole; **d'e.** (*vue etc*) general; **grand e.** (*quartier*) housing complex *ou* Am development; (*ville*) = new town; = Am planned community. ◆**ensemblier** *nm* (interior) decorator.

ensemencer [ɑsmɑse] *vt* (*terre*) to sow.

ensevelir [ɑsəvlir] *vt* to bury.

ensoleillé [ɑsoleje] *a* (*endroit, journée*) sunny.

ensommeillé [ɑsomeje] *a* sleepy.

ensorceler [ɑsɔrsəle] *vt* (*envoûter, séduire*) to bewitch. ◆**ensorcellement** *nm* (*séduction*) spell.

ensuite [ɑsɥit] *adv* (*puis*) next, then; (*plus tard*) afterwards.

ensuivre° (s') [sɑsɥivr] *vpr* to follow, ensue; — *v imp* **il s'ensuit que** it follows that.

entacher [ɑtaʃe] *vt* (*honneur etc*) to sully, taint.

entaille [ɑtaj] *nf* (*fente*) notch; (*blessure*) gash, slash. ◆**entailler** *vt* to notch; to gash, slash.

entame [ɑtam] *nf* first slice.

entamer [ɑtame] *vt* (*pain, peau etc*) to cut (into); (*bouteille, boîte etc*) to start (on); (*négociations etc*) to enter into, start; (*sujet*) to broach; (*capital*) to break *ou* eat into; (*métal, plastique*) to damage; (*résolution, réputation*) to shake.

entass/er [ɑtase] *vt*, — **s'e.** *vpr* (*objets*) to pile up, heap up; (*s')e. dans** (*passagers etc*) to crowd *ou* pack into; pile into; **ils s'entassaient sur la plage** they were crowded *ou* packed (together) on the beach.

◆—ement nm (tas) pile, heap; (de gens) crowding.

entend/re [ɑ̃tɑ̃dr] vt to hear; (comprendre) to understand; (vouloir) to intend, mean; e. parler de to hear of; e. dire que to hear (it said) that; e. raison to listen to reason; laisser e. à qn que to give s.o. to understand that; — s'e. vpr (être entendu) to be heard; (être compris) to be understood; s'e. (sur) (être d'accord) to agree (on); s'e. (avec qn) (s'accorder) to get on (with s.o.); on ne s'entend plus! (à cause du bruit etc) we can't hear ourselves speak!; il s'y entend (est expert) he knows all about that. ◆—u a (convenu) agreed; (compris) understood; (sourire, air) knowing; e.! all right!; bien e. of course. ◆—ement nm (faculté) understanding. ◆entente nf (accord) agreement, understanding; (bonne) e. (amitié) good relationship, harmony.

entériner [ɑ̃terine] vt to ratify.

enterrer [ɑ̃tere] vt (mettre en ou sous terre) to bury; (projet) Fig to scrap. ◆enterrement nm burial; (funérailles) funeral.

entêtant [ɑ̃tetɑ̃] a (enivrant) heady.

en-tête [ɑ̃tɛt] nm (de papier) heading; papier à en-tête headed paper.

entêt/er (s') [ɑ̃tete] vpr to persist (à faire in doing). ◆—é a (têtu) stubborn; (persévérant) persistent. ◆—ement [ɑ̃tɛtmɑ̃] nm stubbornness; (à faire qch) persistence.

enthousiasme [ɑ̃tuzjasm] nm enthusiasm. ◆enthousiasmer vt to fill with enthusiasm, enthuse; s'e. pour to be ou get enthusiastic over, enthuse over. ◆enthousiaste a enthusiastic.

enticher (s') [ɑ̃tiʃe] vpr s'e. de to become infatuated with.

entier, -ière [ɑ̃tje, -jɛr] 1 a (total) whole, entire; (absolu) absolute, complete, entire; (intact) intact; payer place entière to pay full price; le pays tout e. the whole ou entire country; — nm (unité) whole; en e., dans son e. in its entirety, completely. 2 a (caractère, personne) unyielding. ◆entièrement adv entirely.

entité [ɑ̃tite] nf entity.

entonner [ɑ̃tɔne] vt (air) to start singing.

entonnoir [ɑ̃tɔnwar] nm (ustensile) funnel.

entorse [ɑ̃tɔrs] nf Méd sprain; e. à (règlement) infringement of.

entortill/er [ɑ̃tɔrtije] vt e. qch autour de qch (papier etc) to wrap sth around sth; e. qn Fam to dupe s.o., get round s.o.; — s'e. vpr (lierre etc) to wind, twist. ◆—é a (phrase etc) convoluted.

entour/er [ɑ̃ture] vt to surround (de with;

(envelopper) to wrap (de in); e. qn de ses bras to put one's arms round s.o.; s'e. de to surround oneself with. ◆—age nm (proches) circle of family and friends.

entourloupette [ɑ̃turlupɛt] nf Fam nasty trick.

entracte [ɑ̃trakt] nm Th interval, Am intermission.

entraide [ɑ̃trɛd] nf mutual aid. ◆s'entraider [sɑ̃trede] vpr to help each other.

entrailles [ɑ̃traj] nfpl entrails.

entrain [ɑ̃trɛ̃] nm spirit, liveliness; plein d'e. lively.

entraîn/er [ɑ̃trene] 1 vt (charrier) to sweep ou carry away; (roue) Tech to drive; (causer) to bring about; (impliquer) to entail, involve; e. qn (emmener) to lead ou draw s.o. (away); (de force) to drag s.o. (away); (attirer) Péj to lure s.o.; (charmer) to carry s.o. away; e. qn à faire (amener) to lead s.o. to do. 2 vt (athlète, cheval etc) to train (à for); — s'e. vpr to train oneself; Sp to train. ◆—ant [-nɑ̃] a (musique) captivating. ◆—ement [-nmɑ̃] nm 1 Sp training. 2 Tech drive; (élan) impulse. ◆—eur [-nœr] nm (instructeur) Sp trainer, coach; (de cheval) trainer.

entrave [ɑ̃trav] nf (obstacle) Fig hindrance (à to). ◆entraver vt to hinder, hamper.

entre [ɑ̃tr(ə)] prép between; (parmi) among(st); l'un d'e. vous one of you; (soit dit) e. nous between you and me; se dévorer e. eux (réciprocité) to devour each other; e. deux âges middle-aged; e. autres among other things; e. les mains de in the hands of.

entrebâill/er [ɑ̃trəbaje] vt (porte) to open slightly. ◆—é a ajar, slightly open. ◆—eur nm e. de (porte) door chain.

entrechoquer (s') [ɑ̃trəʃɔke] vpr (bouteilles etc) to knock against each other, chink.

entrecôte [ɑ̃trəkot] nf (boned) rib steak.

entrecouper [ɑ̃trəkupe] vt (entremêler) to punctuate (de with), intersperse.

entrecroiser [ɑ̃trəkrwaze] vt, — s'e. vpr (fils) to interlace; (routes) to intersect.

entre-deux-guerres [ɑ̃trədøgɛr] nm inv inter-war period.

entrée [ɑ̃tre] nf (action) entry, entrance; (porte) entrance; (accès) entry, admission (de to); (vestibule) entrance hall, entry; (billet) ticket (of admission); Culin first course, entrée; (mot dans un dictionnaire etc) entry; (processus informatique) input; à son e. as he ou she came in; 'e. interdite' 'no entry', 'no admittance'; 'e. libre' 'admission free'; **e. en matière** (*d'un discours*) opening.

entrefaites (sur ces) [syrsezãtrəfɛt] *adv* at that moment.

entrefilet [ãtrəfilɛ] *nm Journ* (news) item.

entrejambes [ãtrəʒãb] *nm inv* (*de pantalon*) crutch, crotch.

entrelacer [ãtrəlase] *vt*, **— s'e.** *vpr* to intertwine.

entremêler [ãtrəmele] *vt*, **— s'e.** *vpr* to intermingle.

entremets [ãtrəmɛ] *nm* (*plat*) sweet, dessert.

entremetteur, -euse [ãtrəmɛtœr, -øz] *nmf Péj* go-between.

entremise [ãtrəmiz] *nf* intervention; **par l'e. de qn** through s.o.

entreposer [ãtrəpoze] *vt* to store; *Jur* to bond. ◆**entrepôt** *nm* warehouse; (*de la douane*) *Jur* bonded warehouse.

entreprendre° [ãtrəprãdr] *vt* (*travail, voyage etc*) to start on, undertake; **e. de faire** to undertake to do. ◆**entreprenant** *a* enterprising; (*galant*) brash, forward. ◆**entrepreneur** *nm* (*en bâtiment*) (building) contractor. ◆**entreprise** *nf* **1** (*opération*) undertaking. **2** (*firme*) company, firm.

entrer [ãtre] *vi* (*aux* être) (*aller*) to go in, enter; (*venir*) to come in, enter; **e. dans** to go into; (*carrière*) to enter, go into; (*club*) to join, enter; (*détail, question*) to go ou enter into; (*pièce*) to come ou go into, enter; (*arbre etc*) *Aut* to crash into; **e. en action** to go ou get into action; **e. en ébullition** to start boiling; **entrez!** come in!; **faire/laisser e. qn** to show/let s.o. in.

entresol [ãtrəsɔl] *nm* mezzanine (floor).

entre-temps [ãtrətã] *adv* meanwhile.

entretenir/ir° [ãtrətnir] *vt* **1** (*voiture, maison etc*) to maintain; (*relations, souvenir*) to keep up; (*famille*) to keep, maintain; (*sentiment*) to entertain; **e. sa forme/sa santé** to keep fit/healthy. **2 e. qn de** to talk to s.o. about; **s'e. de** to talk about (avec with). ◆**—u** *a* (*femme*) kept. ◆**entretien** *nm* **1** (*de route, maison etc*) maintenance, upkeep; (*substance*) keep. **2** (*dialogue*) conversation; (*entrevue*) interview.

entre-tuer (s') [sãtrətɥe] *vpr* to kill each other.

entrevoir° [ãtrəvwar] *vt* (*rapidement*) to catch a glimpse of; (*pressentir*) to (fore)see.

entrevue [ãtrəvy] *nf* interview.

entrouvrir° [ãtruvrir] *vt*, **— s'e.** *vpr* to half-open. ◆**entrouvert** *a* (*porte, fenêtre*) ajar, half-open.

énumérer [enymere] *vt* to enumerate, list. ◆**énumération** *nf* enumeration.

envah/ir [ãvair] *vt* to invade; (*herbe etc*) to overrun; **e. qn** (*doute, peur etc*) to overcome s.o. ◆**—issant** *a* (*voisin etc*) intrusive. ◆**—issement** *nm* invasion. ◆**—isseur** *nm* invader.

enveloppe [ãvlɔp] *nf* (*pli*) envelope; (*de colis*) wrapping; (*de pneu*) casing; (*d'oreiller*) cover; (*apparence*) *Fig* exterior; **mettre sous e.** to put into an envelope. ◆**envelopp/er** *vt* to wrap (up); **e. la ville** (*brouillard etc*) to envelop the town; **enveloppé de mystère** shrouded ou enveloped in mystery; **s'e.** to wrap oneself (up) (dans in). ◆**—ant** *a* (*séduisant*) captivating.

envenimer [ãvnime] *vt* (*plaie*) to make septic; (*querelle*) *Fig* to envenom; **— s'e.** *vpr* to turn septic; *Fig* to become envenomed.

envergure [ãvɛrgyr] *nf* **1** (*d'avion, d'oiseau*) wingspan. **2** (*de personne*) calibre; (*ampleur*) scope, importance; **de grande e.** wide-ranging, far-reaching.

envers [ãvɛr] **1** *prep* towards, *Am* toward(s). **2** *nm* (*de tissu*) wrong side; (*de médaille*) reverse side; **à l'e.** (*chaussette*) inside out; (*pantalon*) back to front; (*à contresens, de travers*) the wrong way; (*en désordre*) upside down.

envie [ãvi] *nf* **1** (*jalousie*) envy; (*désir*) longing, desire; **avoir e. de qch** to want sth; **j'ai e. de faire** I feel like doing, I would like to do; **elle meurt d'e. de faire** she's dying ou longing to do. **2** (*peau autour des ongles*) hangnail. ◆**envier** *vt* to envy (**qch à qn** s.o. sth). ◆**envieux, -euse** *a & nmf* envious (person); **faire des envieux** to cause envy.

environ [ãvirõ] *adv* (*à peu près*) about; — *nmpl* outskirts, surroundings; **aux environs de** (*Paris, Noël, dix francs etc*) around, in the vicinity of. ◆**environn/er** *vt* to surround. ◆**—ant** *a* surrounding. ◆**—ement** *nm* environment.

envisag/er [ãvizaʒe] *vt* to consider; (*imaginer comme possible*) to envisage, *Am* envision, consider; **e. de faire** to consider ou contemplate doing. ◆**—eable** *a* thinkable.

envoi [ãvwa] *nm* (*action*) dispatch, sending; (*paquet*) consignment; **coup d'e.** *Fb* kick-off.

envol [ãvɔl] *nm* (*d'oiseau*) taking flight; (*d'avion*) take-off; **piste d'e.** *Av* runway. ◆**s'envol/er** *vpr* (*oiseau*) to fly away; (*avion*) to take off; (*emporté par le vent*) to blow away; (*espoir*) *Fig* to vanish. ◆—ée *nf* (*élan*) *Fig* flight.

envoût/er [ɑ̃vute] *vt* to bewitch. ◆—ement *nm* bewitchment.

envoy/er* [ɑ̃vwaje] *vt* to send; (*pierre*) to throw; (*gifle*) to give; **e. chercher qn** to send for s.o.; — **s'e.** *vpr Fam* (*travail etc*) to take on, do; (*repas etc*) to put ou stash away. ◆—é, -ée *nmf* envoy; *Journ* correspondent. ◆—eur *nm* sender.

épagneul, -eule [epaɲœl] *nmf* spaniel.

épais, -aisse [epɛ, -ɛs] *a* thick; (*personne*) thick-set; (*esprit*) dull. ◆**épaisseur** *nf* thickness; (*dimension*) depth. ◆**épaissir** *vt* to thicken; — *vi*, — **s'é.** *vpr* to thicken; (*grossir*) to fill out; **le mystère s'épaissit** the mystery is deepening.

épanch/er [epɑ̃ʃe] *vt* (*cœur*) *Fig* to pour out; — **s'é.** *vpr* (*parler*) to pour out one's heart, unbosom oneself. ◆—ement *nm* (*aveu*) outpouring; *Méd* effusion.

épanou/ir (s') [sepanwir] *vpr* (*fleur*) to open out; (*personne*) *Fig* to fulfil oneself, blossom (out); (*visage*) to beam. ◆—i *a* (*fleur, personne*) in full bloom; (*visage*) beaming. ◆—issement *nm* (*éclat*) full bloom; (*de la personnalité*) fulfilment.

épargne [eparɲ] *nf* saving (**de** of); (*qualité, vertu*) thrift; (*sommes d'argent*) savings. ◆**épargn/er** *vt* (*ennemi etc*) to spare; (*denrée rare etc*) to be sparing with; (*argent, temps*) to save; **e. qch à qn** (*ennuis, chagrin etc*) to spare s.o. sth. ◆—ant, -ante *nmf* saver.

éparpiller [eparpije] *vt*, — **s'é.** *vpr* to scatter; (*efforts*) to dissipate. ◆**épars** *a* scattered.

épaté [epate] *a* (*nez*) flat. ◆**épatement** *nm* flatness.

épat/er [epate] *vt Fam* to stun, astound. ◆—ant *a Fam* stunning, marvellous.

épaule [epol] *nf* shoulder. ◆**épauler** *vt* (*fusil*) to raise (to one's shoulder); **é. qn** (*aider*) to back s.o. up.

épave [epav] *nf* (*bateau, personne*) wreck; *pl* (*débris*) *Nau* (pieces of) wreckage.

épée [epe] *nf* sword; **un coup d'é.** a sword thrust.

épeler [eple] *vt* (*mot*) to spell.

éperdu [eperdy] *a* frantic, wild (**de** with); (*regard*) distraught. ◆—ment *adv* (*aimer*) madly; **elle s'en moque e.** she couldn't care less.

éperon [eprɔ̃] *nm* (*de cavalier, coq*) spur. ◆**éperonner** (*cheval, personne*) to spur (on).

épervier [epervje] *nm* sparrowhawk.

éphémère [efemɛr] *a* short-lived, ephemeral, transient.

épi [epi] *nm* (*de blé etc*) ear; (*mèche de cheveux*) tuft of hair.

épice [epis] *nf Culin* spice. ◆**épic/er** *vt* to spice. ◆—é *a* (*plat, récit etc*) spicy.

épicier, -ière [episje, -jɛr] *nmf* grocer. ◆**épicerie** (*magasin*) grocer's (shop); (*produits*) groceries.

épidémie [epidemi] *nf* epidemic. ◆**épidémique** *a* epidemic.

épiderme [epiderm] *nm Anat* skin.

épier [epje] *vt* (*observer*) to watch closely; (*occasion*) to watch out for; **é. qn** to spy on s.o.

épilepsie [epilɛpsi] *nf* epilepsy. ◆**épileptique** *a* & *nmf* epileptic.

épiler [epile] *vt* (*jambe*) to remove unwanted hair from; (*sourcil*) to pluck.

épilogue [epilɔg] *nm* epilogue.

épinard [epinar] *nm* (*plante*) spinach; *pl* (*feuilles*) *Culin* spinach.

épine [epin] *nf* **1** (*de buisson*) thorn; (*d'animal*) spine, prickle. **2 é. dorsale** *Anat* spine. ◆**épineux, -euse** (*tige, question*) thorny.

épingle [epɛ̃gl] *nf* pin; **é. de nourrice, é. de sûreté** safety pin; **é. à linge** clothes peg, *Am* clothes pin; **virage en é. à cheveux** hairpin bend; **tiré à quatre épingles** very spruce. ◆**épingler** *vt* to pin; **é. qn** (*arrêter*) *Fam* to nab s.o.

épique [epik] *a* epic.

épiscopal, -aux [episkɔpal, -o] *a* episcopal.

épisode [epizod] *nm* episode; **film à épisodes** serial. ◆**épisodique** *a* occasional, episodic; (*accessoire*) minor.

épitaphe [epitaf] *nf* epitaph.

épithète [epitɛt] *nf* epithet; *Gram* attribute.

épître [epitr] *nf* epistle.

éploré [eplore] *a* (*personne, air*) tearful.

éplucher [eplyʃe] *vt* (*pommes de terre*) to peel; (*salade*) to clean, pare; (*texte*) *Fig* to dissect. ◆**épluchure** *nf* peeling.

éponge [epɔ̃ʒ] *nf* sponge. ◆**éponger** *vt* (*liquide*) to sponge up, mop up; (*carrelage*) to sponge (down), mop; (*dette etc*) *Fin* to absorb; **s'é. le front** to mop one's brow.

épopée [epope] *nf* epic.

époque [epɔk] *nf* (*date*) time, period; (*historique*) age; **meubles d'é.** period furniture; **à l'é.** at the *ou* that time.

épouse [epuz] *nf* wife; *Jur* spouse.

épouser [epuze] *vt* **1 é. qn** to marry s.o. **2** (*opinion etc*) to espouse; (*forme*) to assume, adopt.

épousseter [epuste] *vt* to dust.

époustoufler [epustufle] vt Fam to astound.

épouvantail [epuvɑ̃taj] nm (à oiseaux) scarecrow.

épouvante [epuvɑ̃t] nf (peur) terror; (appréhension) dread; **d'é.** (film etc) horror-. ◆**épouvant/er** vt to terrify. ◆**—able** a terrifying; (très mauvais) appalling.

époux [epu] nm husband, Jur spouse; pl husband and wife.

éprendre* **(s')** [seprɑ̃dr] vpr **s'é. de qn** to fall in love with s.o. ◆**épris** a in love (**de** with).

épreuve [eprœv] nf (essai, examen) test; Sp event, heat; Phot print; Typ proof; (malheur) ordeal, trial; **mettre à l'é.** to put to the test. ◆**éprouv/er** vt to test, try; (sentiment etc) to experience, feel; **é. qn** (mettre à l'épreuve) to put s.o. to the test; (faire souffrir) to distress s.o. ◆**—é** a (pénible) trying. ◆**—é** a (sûr) well-tried.

éprouvette [epruvɛt] nf test tube; **bébé é.** test tube baby.

épuis/er [epɥize] vt (personne, provisions, sujet) to exhaust; — **s'é.** vpr (réserves, patience) to run out; **s'é. à faire** to exhaust oneself doing. ◆**—é** a exhausting. ◆**—é** a exhausted; (édition) out of print; (marchandise) out of stock. ◆**—ement** nm exhaustion.

épuisette [epɥizɛt] nf fishing net (on pole).

épurer [epyre] vt to purify; (personnel etc) to purge; (goût) to refine. ◆**épuration** nf purification; purging; refining.

équateur [ekwatœr] nm equator; **sous l'é.** at ou on the equator. ◆**équatorial, -aux** a equatorial.

équation [ekwasjɔ̃] nf Math equation.

équerre [ekɛr] nf **é.** (à dessiner) setsquare, Am triangle; **d'é.** straight, square.

équestre [ekɛstr] a (figure etc) equestrian; (exercices etc) horseriding-.

équilibre [ekilibr] nm balance; **tenir** ou **mettre en é.** to balance (**sur** on); **se tenir en é.** to balance; **perdre l'é.** to lose one's balance. ◆**équilibrer** vt (charge, budget etc) to balance; — **s'é.** vpr (équipes etc) to (counter)balance each other; (comptes) to balance.

équinoxe [ekinɔks] nm equinox.

équipage [ekipaʒ] nm Nau Av crew.

équipe [ekip] nf team; (d'ouvriers) gang; **é. de nuit** night shift; **é. de secours** search party; **faire é. avec** to team up with. ◆**équipier, -ière** nf team member.

équipée [ekipe] nf escapade.

équip/er [ekipe] vt to equip (**de** with); — **s'é.** vpr to equip oneself. ◆**—ement** nm

equipment; (de camping, ski etc) gear, equipment.

équitation [ekitasjɔ̃] nf (horse) riding.

équité [ekite] nf fairness. ◆**équitable** a fair, equitable. ◆**équitablement** adv fairly.

équivalent [ekivalɑ̃] a & nm equivalent. ◆**équivalence** nf equivalence. ◆**équivaloir** vi **é.** à to be equivalent to.

équivoque [ekivɔk] a (ambigu) equivocal; (douteux) dubious; — nf ambiguity.

érable [erabl] nm (arbre, bois) maple.

érafler [erafle] vt to graze, scratch. ◆**éraflure** nf graze, scratch.

éraillée [eraje] a (voix) rasping.

ère [ɛr] nf era.

érection [erɛksjɔ̃] nf (de monument etc) erection.

éreinter [erɛ̃te] vt (fatiguer) to exhaust; (critiquer) to tear to pieces, slate, slam.

ergot [ergo] nm (de coq) spur.

ergoter [ergɔte] vi to quibble, cavil.

ériger [eriʒe] vt to erect; **s'é. en** to set oneself up as.

ermite [ermit] nm hermit.

érosion [erozjɔ̃] nf erosion. ◆**éroder** vt to erode.

érotique [erɔtik] a erotic. ◆**érotisme** nm eroticism.

err/er [ere] vi to wander, roam. ◆**—ant** a a wandering, roving; (animal) stray.

erreur [erœr] nf (faute) error, mistake; (action blâmable, opinion fausse) error; **par e.** by mistake, in error; **dans l'e.** mistaken. ◆**erroné** a erroneous.

ersatz [ɛrzats] nm substitute.

éructer [erykte] vi Litt to belch.

érudit, -ite [erydi, -it] a scholarly, erudite; — nmf scholar. ◆**érudition** nf scholarship, erudition.

éruption [erypsjɔ̃] nf (de volcan, colère) eruption (de of); Méd rash.

es voir **être**.

ès [ɛs] prép of; **licencié/docteur ès lettres** = BA/PhD.

escabeau, -x [ɛskabo] nm stepladder, (pair of) steps; (tabouret) stool.

escadre [ɛskadr] nf Nau Av fleet, squadron. ◆**escadrille** nf (unité) Av flight. ◆**escadron** nm squadron.

escalade [ɛskalad] nf climbing; (de prix) & Mil escalation. ◆**escalader** vt to climb, scale.

escale [ɛskal] nf Av stop(over); Nau port of call; **faire e. à** Av to stop (over) at; Nau to put in at; **vol sans e.** non-stop flight.

escalier [ɛskalje] nm staircase, stairs; **e. mé-**

canique *ou* **roulant** escalator; **e. de secours** fire escape.

escalope [ɛskalɔp] *nf Culin* escalope.

escamot/er [ɛskamɔte] *vt* (*faire disparaître*) to make vanish; (*esquiver*) to dodge. ◆**—able** *a Av Tech* retractable.

escapade [ɛskapad] *nf* (*excursion*) jaunt; **faire une e.** to run off.

escargot [ɛskargo] *nm* snail.

escarmouche [ɛskarmuʃ] *nf* skirmish.

escarpé [ɛskarpe] *a* steep. ◆**escarpement** *nm* (*côte*) steep slope.

escarpin [ɛskarpɛ̃] *nm* (*soulier*) pump, court shoe.

escient [ɛsjɑ̃] *nm* **à bon e.** discerningly, wisely.

esclaffer (s') [ɛsklafe] *vpr* to roar with laughter.

esclandre [ɛsklɑ̃dr] *nm* (noisy) scene.

esclave [ɛsklav] *nmf* slave; **être l'e. de** to be a slave to. ◆**esclavage** *nm* slavery.

escompte [ɛskɔ̃t] *nm* discount; **taux d'e.** bank rate. ◆**escompter** *vt* 1 (*espérer*) to anticipate (**faire doing**), expect (**faire** to do). 2 *Com* to discount.

escorte [ɛskɔrt] *nf Mil Nau etc* escort. ◆**escorter** *vt* to escort.

escouade [ɛskwad] *nf* (*petite troupe*) squad.

escrime [ɛskrim] *nf Sp* fencing. ◆**escrimeur, -euse** *nmf* fencer.

escrimer (s') [ɛskrime] *vpr* to slave away (**à faire** at doing).

escroc [ɛskro] *nm* swindler, crook. ◆**escroquer** *vt* **e. qn** to swindle s.o.; **e. qch à qn** to swindle s.o. out of sth. ◆**escroquerie** *nf* swindling; **une e.** a swindle.

espace [ɛspas] *nm* space; **e. vert** garden, park. ◆**espacer** *vt* to space out; **espacés d'un mètre** (spaced out) one metre apart; **— s'e.** (*maisons, visites etc*) to become less frequent.

espadon [ɛspadɔ̃] *nm* swordfish.

espadrille [ɛspadrij] *nf* rope-soled sandal.

Espagne [ɛspaɲ] *nf* Spain. ◆**espagnol, -ole** *a* Spanish; *— nmf* Spaniard; *— nm* (*langue*) Spanish.

espèce [ɛspɛs] 1 *nf* (*race*) species; (*genre*) kind, sort; **c'est une e. d'idiot** he's a silly fool; **e. d'idiot!/de maladroit!/*etc* (you) silly fool!/oaf!/*etc.* 2 *nfpl* (*argent*) **en espèces** in cash.

espérance [ɛsperɑ̃s] *nf* hope; **avoir des espérances** to have expectations; **e. de vie** life expectancy. ◆**espérer** *vt* to hope for; **e. que** to hope that; **e. faire** to hope to do; *— vi* to hope; **e. en qn/qch** to trust in s.o./sth.

espiègle [ɛspjɛgl] *a* mischievous. ◆**es-**

pièglerie *nf* mischievousness; (*farce*) mischievous trick.

espion, -onne [ɛspjɔ̃, -ɔn] *nmf* spy. ◆**espionnage** *nm* espionage, spying. ◆**espionner** *vt* to spy on; *— vi* to spy.

esplanade [ɛsplanad] *nf* esplanade.

espoir [ɛspwar] *nm* hope; **avoir de l'e.** to have hope(s); **sans e.** (*cas etc*) hopeless.

esprit [ɛspri] *nm* (*attitude, fantôme*) spirit; (*intellect*) mind; (*humour*) wit; (*être humain*) person; **avoir de l'e.** to be witty; **cette idée m'est venue à l'e.** this idea crossed my mind.

esquimau, -aude, -aux [ɛskimo, -od, -o] 1 *a & nm* **E**skimo. 2 *nm* (*glace*) choc-ice (*on a stick*).

esquinter [ɛskɛ̃te] *vt Fam* (*voiture etc*) to damage, bash; (*critiquer*) to slam, pan (*author, film etc*); **s'e.** to damage to one's health; **s'e. à faire** (*se fatiguer*) to wear oneself out doing.

esquisse [ɛskis] *nf* (*croquis, plan*) sketch. ◆**esquisser** *vt* to sketch; **e. un geste** to make a (slight) gesture.

esquive [ɛskiv] *nf Boxe* dodge; **e. de** (*question*) dodging of, evasion of. ◆**esquiver** *vt* (*coup, problème*) to dodge; *— s'e.* *vpr* to slip away.

essai [ɛsɛ] *nm* (*épreuve*) test, trial; (*tentative*) try, attempt; *Rugby* try; *Littér* essay; **à l'e.** (*objet*) *Com* on trial, on approval; **pilote d'e.** test pilot; **période d'e.** trial period.

essaim [ɛsɛ̃] *nm* swarm (*of bees etc*).

essayer [ɛseje] *vt* to try (**de faire** to do); (*vêtement*) to try on; (*méthode*) to try (*out*); **s'e. à qch/à faire** to try one's hand at sth/at doing. ◆**essayage** *nm* (*de costume*) fitting.

essence [ɛsɑ̃s] *nf* 1 (*extrait*) *Ch Culin* essence; *Aut* petrol, *Am* gas; **poste d'e.** filling station. 2 *Phil* essence. 3 (*d'arbres*) species. ◆**essentiel, -ielle** *a* essential (**à, pour** for); *— nm* **l'e.** the main thing *ou* point; (*quantité*) the main part (**de** of). ◆**essentiellement** *adv* essentially.

essieu, -x [ɛsjø] *nm* axle.

essor [ɛsɔr] *nm* (*de pays, d'entreprise etc*) development, rise, expansion; **en plein e.** (*industrie etc*) booming.

essor/er [ɛsɔre] *vt* (*linge*) to wring; (*dans une essoreuse*) to spin-dry; (*dans une machine à laver*) to spin. ◆**—euse** *nf* (*à main*) wringer; (*électrique*) spin dryer.

essouffler [ɛsufle] *vt* to make (*s.o.*) out of breath; *— s'e.* *vpr* to get out of breath.

essuyer [ɛsɥije] 1 *vt* to wipe; *— s'e.* *vpr* to wipe oneself. 2 *vt* (*subir*) to suffer. ◆**es-**

suie-glace *nm inv* windscreen wiper, *Am* windshield wiper. ◆**essuie-mains** *nm inv* (hand) towel.

est¹ [ɛ] *voir* être.

est² [ɛst] *nm* east; — *a inv* (*côte*) east(ern); **d'e.** (*vent*) east(erly); **de l'e.** eastern; **l'Allemagne de l'E.** East Germany. ◆**e.-allemand, -ande** *a* & *nmf* East German.

estafilade [ɛstafilad] *nf* gash, slash.

estampe [ɛstɑ̃p] *nf* (*gravure*) print.

estamper [ɛstɑ̃pe] *vt* (*rouler*) *Fam* to swindle.

estampille [ɛstɑ̃pij] *nf* mark, stamp.

esthète [ɛstɛt] *nmf* aesthete, *Am* esthete. ◆**esthétique** *a* aesthetic, *Am* esthetic.

esthéticienne [ɛstetisjɛn] *nf* beautician.

estime [ɛstim] *nf* esteem, regard. ◆**estim/er** *vt* (*objet*) to value; (*juger*) to consider (que that); (*calculer*) to estimate; (*apprécier*) to appreciate; **e. qn** to have high regard for s.o., esteem s.o.; **s'e. heureux**/*etc* to consider oneself happy/*etc*. ◆**-able** *a* respectable. ◆**estimation** *nf* (*de mobilier etc*) valuation; (*calcul*) estimation.

estival, -aux [ɛstival, -o] *a* (*période etc*) summer-. ◆**estivant, -ante** *nmf* holidaymaker, *Am* vacationer.

estomac [ɛstɔma] *nm* stomach.

estomaquer [ɛstɔmake] *vt* *Fam* to flabbergast.

estomper [ɛstɔ̃pe] *vt* (*rendre flou*) to blur; — **s'e.** *vpr* to become blurred.

estrade [ɛstrad] *nf* (*tribune*) platform.

estropi/er [ɛstrɔpje] *vt* to cripple, maim. ◆**-é, -ée** *nmf* cripple.

estuaire [ɛstɥɛr] *nm* estuary.

esturgeon [ɛstyrʒɔ̃] *nm* (*poisson*) sturgeon.

et [e] *conj* and; **vingt et un**/*etc* twentyone/*etc*.

étable [etabl] *nf* cowshed.

établi [etabli] *nm* *Menuis* (work)bench.

établ/ir [etablir] *vt* to establish; (*installer*) to set up; (*plan, chèque, liste*) to draw up; — **s'é.** *vpr* (*habiter*) to settle; (*épicier etc*) to set up shop as, set (oneself) up as. ◆**-issement** *nm* (*action, bâtiment, institution*) establishment; *Com* firm, establishment; **é. scolaire** school.

étage [etaʒ] *nm* (*d'immeuble*) floor, storey, *Am* story; (*de fusée etc*) stage; **à l'é.** upstairs; **au premier é.** on the first *ou Am* second floor. ◆**étager** *vt*, — **s'é.** *vpr* (*rochers, maisons etc*) to range above one another.

étagère [etaʒɛr] *nf* shelf; (*meuble*) shelving unit.

étai [etɛ] *nm* *Tech* prop, stay.

étain [etɛ̃] *nm* (*métal*) tin; (*de gobelet etc*) pewter.

était [etɛ] *voir* être.

étal, pl étals [etal] *nm* (*au marché*) stall.

étalage [etalaʒ] *nm* display; (*vitrine*) display window; **faire é. de** to make a show *ou* display of. ◆**étalagiste** *nmf* window dresser.

étaler [etale] *vt* (*disposer*) to lay out; (*luxe etc*) & *Com* to display; (*crème, beurre etc*) to spread; (*vacances*) to stagger; — **s'é.** *vpr* (*s'affaler*) to sprawl; (*tomber*) *Fam* to fall flat; **s'é. sur** (*congés, paiements etc*) to be spread over.

étalon [etalɔ̃] *nm* **1** (*cheval*) stallion. **2** (*modèle*) standard.

étanche [etɑ̃ʃ] *a* watertight; (*montre*) waterproof.

étancher [etɑ̃ʃe] *vt* (*sang*) to stop the flow of; (*soif*) to quench, slake.

étang [etɑ̃] *nm* pond.

étant [etɑ̃] *voir* être.

étape [etap] *nf* (*de voyage etc*) stage; (*lieu*) stop(over); **faire é. à** to stop off *ou* over at.

état [eta] *nm* **1** (*condition, manière d'être*) state; (*registre, liste*) statement, list; **en bon é.** in good condition; **en é. de faire** in a position to do; **é. d'esprit** state *ou* frame of mind; **é. d'âme** mood; **é. civil** civil status (*birth, marriage, death etc*); **é. de choses** situation, state of affairs; **à l'é. brut** in a raw state; **de son é.** (*métier*) by trade; **faire é. de** (*mention*) to mention, put forward. **2** É. (*nation*) State; **homme d'É.** statesman. ◆**étatisé** *a* state-controlled, state-owned.

état-major [etamaʒɔr] *nm* (*pl* états-majors) (*d'un parti etc*) senior staff.

États-Unis [etazyni] *nmpl* É.-Unis (d'Amérique) United States (of America).

étau, -x [eto] *nm* *Tech* vice, *Am* vise.

étayer [eteje] *vt* to prop up, support.

été¹ [ete] *nm* summer.

été² [ete] *voir* être.

éteindre [etɛ̃dr] *vt* (*feu, cigarette etc*) to put out, extinguish; (*lampe etc*) to turn *ou* switch off; (*dette, espoir*) to extinguish; — *vi* to switch off; — **s'é.** *vpr* (*feu*) to go out; (*personne*) to pass away; (*race*) to die out. ◆**éteint** *a* (*feu*) out; (*volcan, race, amour*) extinct; (*voix*) faint.

étendard [etɑ̃dar] *nm* (*drapeau*) standard.

étend/re [etɑ̃dr] *vt* (*nappe*) to spread (out); (*beurre*) to spread; (*linge*) to hang out; (*agrandir*) to extend; **é. le bras**/*etc* to stretch out one's arm/*etc*; **é. qn** to stretch s.o. out; — **s'é.** *vpr* (*personne*) to stretch (oneself) out; (*plaine etc*) to stretch; (*feu*) to spread; (*pouvoir*) to extend; **s'é. sur** (*sujet*) to dwell on. ◆**—u** *a* (*forêt, vocabulaire etc*) extensive; (*personne*) stretched out. ◆**-ue** *nf* (*importance*) extent; (*surface*) area; (*d'eau*) expanse, stretch.

éternel, -elle [etɛrnɛl] *a* eternal. ◆**éternellement** *adv* eternally, for ever. ◆**éterniser** *vt* to perpetuate; **— s'é.** *vpr* (*débat etc*) to drag on endlessly; (*visiteur etc*) to stay for ever. ◆**éternité** *nf* eternity.

éternu/er [etɛrnɥe] *vi* to sneeze. ◆**-ement** [-ymɑ̃] *nm* sneeze.

êtes [ɛt] *voir* **être**.

éther [etɛr] *nm* ether.

Éthiopie [etjɔpi] *nf* Ethiopia. ◆**éthiopien, -ienne** *a & nmf* Ethiopian.

éthique [etik] *a* ethical; *— nf Phil* ethics; **l'é. puritaine/***etc* the Puritan/*etc* ethic.

ethnie [etni] *nf* ethnic group. ◆**ethnique** *a* ethnic.

étinceler [etɛ̃sle] *vi* to sparkle. ◆**étincelle** *nf* spark. ◆**étincellement** *nm* sparkle.

étioler (s') [setjɔle] *vpr* to wilt, wither.

étiqueter [etikte] *vt* to label. ◆**étiquette** *nf* **1** (*marque*) label. **2** (*protocole*) (diplomatic *ou* court) etiquette.

étirer [etire] *vt* to stretch; **— s'é.** *vpr* to stretch (oneself).

étoffe [etɔf] *nf* material, cloth, fabric; (*de héros etc*) Fig stuff (**de** of).

étoffer [etɔfe] *vt*, **— s'é.** *vpr* to fill out.

étoile [etwal] *nf* **1** star; **à la belle é.** in the open. **2 é. de mer** starfish. ◆**étoilé** *a* (*ciel, nuit*) starry; (*vitre*) cracked (*star-shaped*); **é. de** (*rubis etc*) studded with; **la bannière étoilée** *Am* the Star-Spangled Banner.

étonn/er [etɔne] *vt* to surprise, astonish; **— s'é.** *vpr* to be surprised *ou* astonished (**de qch** at sth, **que** (+ *sub*) that). ◆**-ant** *a* (*ahurissant*) surprising; (*remarquable*) amazing. ◆**-ement** *nm* surprise, astonishment.

étouff/er [etufe] *vt* (*tuer*) to suffocate, smother; (*bruit*) to muffle; (*feu*) to smother; (*révolte, sentiment*) to stifle; (*scandale*) to hush up; **é. qn** (*chaleur*) to stifle s.o.; (*aliment, colère*) to choke s.o.; *— vi* to suffocate; **on étouffe!** it's stifling!; **é. de colère** to choke with anger. **— s'é.** *vpr* (*en mangeant*) to choke, gag (**sur, avec** on); (*mourir*) to suffocate. ◆**-ant** *a* (*air*) stifling. ◆**-ement** *nm Méd* suffocation.

étourdi, -ie [eturdi] *a* thoughtless; *— nmf* scatterbrain. ◆**étourderie** *nf* thoughtlessness; **une é.** (*faute*) a thoughtless blunder.

étourd/ir [eturdir] *vt* to stun, daze; (*vertige,*

vin) to make dizzy; (*abrutir*) to deafen. ◆**—issant** *a* (*bruit*) deafening; (*remarquable*) stunning. ◆**—issement** *nm* dizziness; (*syncope*) dizzy spell.

étourneau, -x [eturno] *nm* starling.

étrange [etrɑ̃ʒ] *a* strange, odd. ◆**—ment** *adv* strangely, oddly. ◆**étrangeté** *nf* strangeness, oddness.

étranger, -ère [etrɑ̃ʒe, -ɛr] *a* (*d'un autre pays*) foreign; (*non familier*) strange (**à** to); **il m'est é.** he's unknown to me; *— nmf* foreigner; (*inconnu*) stranger; **à l'é.** abroad; **de l'é.** from abroad.

étrangl/er [etrɑ̃gle] *vt* **é. qn** (*tuer*) to strangle s.o.; (*col, aliment*) to choke s.o.; **— s'é.** *vpr* (*de colère, en mangeant etc*) to choke. ◆**—é** *a* (*voix*) choking; (*passage*) constricted. ◆**—ement** *nm* (*d'une victime*) strangulation. ◆**—eur, -euse** *nmf* strangler.

être* [ɛtr] **1** *vi* to be; **il est tailleur** he's a tailor; **est-ce qu'elle vient?** is she coming?; **il vient, n'est-ce pas?** he's coming, isn't he?; **est-ce qu'il aime le thé?** does he like tea?; **nous sommes dix** there are ten of us; **nous sommes le dix** today is the tenth (of the month); **où en es-tu?** how far have you got?; **il a été à Paris** (*est allé*) he's been to Paris; **elle est de Paris** she's from Paris; **elle est de la famille** she's one of the family; **c'est à faire tout de suite** it must be done straight away; **c'est à lui** it's his; **cela étant** that being so. **2** *v aux* (*avec venir, partir etc*) to have; **elle est déjà arrivée** she has already arrived. **3** *nm* (*personne*) being; **ê. humain** human being; **les êtres chers** the loved ones.

étreindre [etrɛ̃dr] *vt* to grip; (*ami*) to embrace. ◆**étreinte** *nf* grip; (*amoureuse etc*) embrace.

étrenner [etrene] *vt* to use *ou* wear for the first time.

étrennes [etrɛn] *nfpl* New Year gift; (*gratification*) = Christmas box *ou* tip.

étrier [etrije] *nm* stirrup.

étriper (s') [setripe] *vpr Fam* to fight (each other) to the kill.

étriqué [etrike] *a* (*vêtement*) tight, skimpy; (*esprit, vie*) narrow.

étroit [etrwa] *a* narrow; (*vêtement*) tight; (*parenté, collaboration etc*) close; (*discipline*) strict; **être à l'é.** to be cramped. ◆**étroitement** *adv* (*surveiller etc*) closely. ◆**étroitesse** *nf* narrowness; closeness; **é. d'esprit** narrow-mindedness.

étude [etyd] *nf* **1** (*action, ouvrage*) study; (*salle*) *Scol* study room; **à l'é.** (*projet*) under consideration; **faire des études de** (*médecine etc*) to study. **2** (*de notaire etc*) office. ◆**étudiant, -ante** *nmf* & a student. ◆**étudier** *vti* to study.

étui [etɥi] *nm* (*à lunettes, à cigarettes etc*) case; (*de revolver*) holster.

étymologie [etimɔlɔʒi] *nf* etymology.

eu, eue [y] *voir* **avoir.**

eucalyptus [økaliptys] *nm* (*arbre*) eucalyptus.

Eucharistie [økaristi] *nf* Rel Eucharist.

euh! [ø] *int* hem!, er!, well!

euphémisme [øfemism] *nm* euphemism.

euphorie [øfɔri] *nf* euphoria.

eurent [yr] *voir* **avoir.**

euro- [øro] *préf* Euro-.

Europe [ørɔp] *nf* Europe. ◆**européen, -enne** *a* & *nmf* European.

eut [y] *voir* **avoir.**

euthanasie [øtanazi] *nf* euthanasia.

eux [ø] *pron* (*sujet*) they; (*complément*) them; (*réfléchi, emphase*) themselves. ◆**eux-mêmes** *pron* themselves.

évacuer [evakɥe] *vt* to evacuate; (*liquide*) to drain off. ◆**évacuation** *nf* evacuation.

évad/er (s') [sevade] *vpr* to escape (*de* from). ◆**-é, -ée** *nmf* escaped prisoner.

évaluer [evalɥe] *vt* (*chiffre, foule etc*) to estimate; (*meuble etc*) to value. ◆**évaluation** *nf* estimation; valuation.

évangile [evãʒil] *nm* gospel; É. Gospel. ◆**évangélique** *a* evangelical.

évanou/ir (s') [sevanwir] *vpr* Méd to black out, faint; (*espoir, crainte etc*) to vanish. ◆**-i** *a* Méd unconscious. ◆**-issement** *nm* (*syncope*) blackout, fainting fit; (*disparition*) vanishing.

évaporer (s') [sevapɔre] *vpr* Ch to evaporate; (*disparaître*) Fam to vanish into thin air. ◆**évaporation** *nf* evaporation.

évasif, -ive [evazif, -iv] *a* evasive.

évasion [evazjɔ̃] *nf* escape (**d'un lieu** from a place, **devant un danger**/*etc* from a danger/*etc*); (*hors de la réalité*) escapism; é. fiscale tax evasion.

évêché [eveʃe] *nm* (*territoire*) bishopric, see.

éveil [evɛj] *nm* awakening; **en é.** on the alert; **donner l'é. à** to alert.

éveill/er [eveje] *vt* (*susciter*) to arouse; é. **qn** to awake(n) s.o.; **– s'é.** *vpr* to awake(n) (à to); (*sentiment, idée*) to be aroused. ◆**-é** *a* awake; (*vif*) lively, alert.

événement [evɛnmã] *nm* event.

éventail [evãtaj] *nm* **1** (*instrument portatif*) fan; **en é.** (*orteils*) spread out. **2** (*choix*) range.

évent/er [evãte] *vt* **1** (*secret*) to discover. **2**

é. **qn** to fan s.o. **3 s'é.** *vpr* (*bière, vin etc*) to turn stale. ◆**-é** *a* (*bière, vin etc*) stale.

éventrer [evãtre] *vt* (*animal etc*) to disembowel; (*sac*) to rip open.

éventuel, -elle [evãtɥɛl] *a* possible. ◆**éventuellement** *adv* possibly. ◆**éventualité** *nf* possibility; **dans l'é. de** in the event of.

évêque [evɛk] *nm* bishop.

évertuer (s') [severtɥe] *vpr* **s'é. à faire** to do one's utmost to do, struggle to do.

éviction [eviksjɔ̃] *nf* (*de concurrent etc*) & Pol ousting.

évident [evidã] *a* obvious, evident (**que** that). ◆**évidemment** [-amã] *adv* certainly, obviously. ◆**évidence** *nf* obviousness; **une é.** an obvious fact; **nier l'é.** to deny the obvious; **être en é.** to be conspicuous *ou* in evidence; **mettre en é.** (*fait*) to underline.

évider [evide] *vt* to hollow out.

évier [evje] *nm* (kitchen) sink.

évincer [evɛ̃se] *vt* (*concurrent etc*) & Pol to oust.

éviter [evite] *vt* to avoid (**de faire** doing); é. **qch à qn** to spare *ou* save s.o. sth.

évolu/er [evolɥe] *vi* **1** (*changer*) to develop, change; (*société, idée, situation*) to evolve. **2** (*se déplacer*) to move; Mil to manœuvre, Am maneuver. ◆**-é** *a* (*pays*) advanced; (*personne*) enlightened. ◆**évolution** *nf* **1** (*changement*) development; evolution. **2** (*d'un danseur etc*) & Mil movement.

évoquer [evɔke] *vt* to evoke, call to mind. ◆**évocateur, -trice** *a* evocative. ◆**évocation** *nf* evocation, recalling.

ex [ɛks] *nmf* (*mari, femme*) Fam ex.

ex- [ɛks] *préf* ex-; **ex-mari** ex-husband.

exacerber [ɛgzaserbe] *vt* (*douleur etc*) to exacerbate.

exact [ɛgzakt] *a* (*précis*) exact, accurate; (*juste, vrai*) correct, exact, right; (*ponctuel*) punctual. ◆**exactement** *adv* exactly. ◆**exactitude** *nf* exactness; accuracy; correctness; punctuality.

exaction [ɛgzaksjɔ̃] *nf* exaction.

ex aequo [ɛgzeko] *adv* **être classés ex ae.** Sp to tie, be equally placed.

exagér/er [ɛgzaʒere] *vt* to exaggerate; **– vi** (*parler*) to exaggerate; (*agir*) to overdo it, go too far. ◆**-é** *a* excessive. ◆**-ément** *adv* excessively. ◆**exagération** *nf* exaggeration; (*excès*) excessiveness.

exalt/er [ɛgzalte] *vt* (*glorifier*) to exalt; (*animer*) to fire, stir. ◆**-ant** *a* stirring. ◆**-é, -ée** *a* (*sentiment*) impassioned.

wild; — *nmf Péj* fanatic. ◆**exaltation** *nf* (*délire*) elation, excitement.

examen [ɛgzamɛ̃] *nm* examination; *Scol* exam(ination); **e. blanc** *Scol* mock exam(ination). ◆**examinateur, -trice** *nmf* *Scol* examiner. ◆**examiner** *vt* (*considérer, regarder*) to examine.

exaspérer [ɛgzaspere] *vt* (*énerver*) to aggravate, exasperate. ◆**exaspération** *nf* exasperation, aggravation.

exaucer [ɛgzose] *vt* (*désir*) to grant; **e. qn** to grant s.o.'s wish(es).

excavation [ɛkskavɑsjɔ̃] *nf* (*trou*) hollow.

excéder [ɛksede] *vt* **1** (*dépasser*) to exceed. **2 é. qn** (*fatiguer, énerver*) to exasperate s.o. ◆**excédent** *nm* surplus, excess; **e. de bagages** excess luggage *ou Am* baggage. ◆**excédentaire** *a* (*poids etc*) excess-.

excellent [ɛksɛlɑ̃] *a* excellent. ◆**excellence** *nf* **1** excellence; **par e.** above all else *ou* all others. **2 E.** (*titre*) Excellency. ◆**exceller** *vi* to excel (**en qch** in sth, **à faire** in doing).

excentrique [ɛksɑ̃trik] **1** *a & nmf* (*original*) eccentric. **2** *a* (*quartier*) remote. ◆**excentricité** *nf* (*bizarrerie*) eccentricity.

excepté [ɛksɛpte] *prép* except. ◆**excepter** *vt* to except. ◆**exception** *nf* exception; **à l'e. de** except (for), with the exception of; **faire e.** to be an exception. ◆**exceptionnel, -elle** *a* exceptional. ◆**exceptionnellement** *adv* exceptionally.

excès [ɛksɛ] *nm* excess; (*de table*) over-eating; **e. de vitesse** *Aut* speeding. ◆**excessif, -ive** *a* excessive. ◆**excessivement** *adv* excessively.

excit/er [ɛksite] *vt* (*faire naître*) to excite, rouse, stir; **e. qn** (*mettre en colère*) to provoke s.o.; (*agacer*) to annoy s.o.; (*enthousiasmer*) to thrill s.o., excite s.o.; **e. qn à faire** to incite s.o. to do; — **s'e.** *vpr* (*nerveux, enthousiaste*) to get excited. ◆**—ant** *a* exciting; — *nm* stimulant. ◆**—é** *a* excited. ◆**—able** *a* excitable. ◆**excitation** *nf* (*agitation*) excitement; **e. à** (*haine etc*) incitement to.

exclamer (s') [ɛksklame] *vpr* to exclaim. ◆**exclamatif, -ive** *a* exclamatory. ◆**exclamation** *nf* exclamation.

excl/ure* [ɛksklyr] *vt* (*écarter*) to exclude (**de** from); (*chasser*) to expel (**de** from); **e. qch** (*rendre impossible*) to preclude sth. ◆**—u** *a* (*solution etc*) out of the question; (*avec une date*) exclusive. ◆**exclusif, -ive** *a* (*droit, modèle, préoccupation*) exclusive. ◆**exclusion** *nf* exclusion. ◆**exclusivement** *adv* exclusively. ◆**exclusivité** *nf*

Com exclusive rights; **en e.** (*film*) having an exclusive showing (**à** at).

excommunier [ɛkskɔmynje] *vt* to excommunicate. ◆**excommunication** *nf* excommunication.

excrément(s) [ɛkskremɑ̃] *nm(pl)* excrement.

excroissance [ɛkskrwasɑ̃s] *nf* (out)growth.

excursion [ɛkskyrsjɔ̃] *nf* outing, excursion, tour; (*à pied*) hike.

excuse [ɛkskyz] *nf* (*prétexte*) excuse; *pl* (*regrets*) apology; **des excuses** an apology; **faire des excuses** to apologize (**à** to); **toutes mes excuses** (my) sincere apologies. ◆**excuser** *vt* (*justifier, pardonner*) to excuse (**qn d'avoir fait, qn de faire** s.o. for doing); — **s'e.** *vpr* to apologize (**de** for, **auprès de** to); **excusez-moi!, je m'excuse!** excuse me!

exécrer [ɛgzekre] *vt* to loathe. ◆**exécrable** *a* atrocious.

exécut/er [ɛgzekyte] *vt* **1** (*projet, tâche etc*) to carry out, execute; (*statue, broderie etc*) to produce; (*jouer*) *Mus* to perform. **2 e. qn** (*tuer*) to execute s.o. **3 s'e.** *vpr* to comply. ◆**—ant, -ante** *nmf Mus* performer. ◆**—able** *a* practicable. ◆**exécutif** *am* (*pouvoir*) executive; — *nm* **l'e.** *Pol* the executive. ◆**exécution** *nf* **1** carrying out, execution; production; performance. **2** (*mise à mort*) execution.

exemple [ɛgzɑ̃pl] *nm* example; **par e.** for example, for instance; **(ça) par e.!** *Fam* good heavens!; **donner l'e.** to set an example (**à** to). ◆**exemplaire 1** *a* exemplary. **2** *nm* (*livre etc*) copy.

exempt [ɛgzɑ̃] *a* **e. de** (*dispensé de*) exempt from; (*sans*) free from. ◆**exempter** *vt* to exempt (**de** from). ◆**exemption** *nf* exemption.

exercer [ɛgzɛrse] *vt* (*muscles, droits*) to exercise; (*autorité, influence*) to exert (**sur** over); (*métier*) to carry on, work at; (*profession*) to practise; **e. qn à** (*couture etc*) to train s.o. in; **e. qn à faire** to train s.o. to do; — *vi* (*médecin*) to practise; — **s'e.** *vpr* (*influence etc*) to be exerted; **s'e.** (**à qch**) (*sportif etc*) to practise (sth); **s'e. à faire** to practise doing. ◆**exercice** *nm* (*physique etc*) & *Scol* exercise; *Mil* drill, exercise; (*de métier*) practice; **l'e. de** (*pouvoir etc*) the exercise of; **en e.** (*fonctionnaire*) in office; (*médecin*) in practice; **faire de l'e., prendre de l'e.** to (take) exercise.

exhaler [ɛgzale] *vt* (*odeur etc*) to give off.

exhaustif, -ive [ɛgzostif, -iv] *a* exhaustive.

exhiber [ɛgzibe] *vt* to exhibit, show.

◆**exhibition** nf exhibition. ◆**exhibitionniste** nmf exhibitionist.

exhorter [ɛgzɔrte] vt to urge, exhort (**à faire** to do).

exhumer [ɛgzyme] vt (cadavre) to exhume; (vestiges) to dig up.

exiger [ɛgziʒe] vt to demand, require (**de** from, que (+ sub) that). ◆**exigeant** a demanding, exacting. ◆**exigence** nf demand, requirement; **d'une grande e.** very demanding.

exigu, -uë [ɛgzigy] a (appartement etc) cramped, tiny. ◆**exiguïté** nf crampedness.

exil [ɛgzil] nm (expulsion) exile. ◆**exil/er** vt to exile; — **s'e.** vpr to go into exile. ◆**-é, -ée** nmf (personne) exile.

existence [ɛgzistɑ̃s] nf existence. ◆**existentialisme** nm existentialism. ◆**exist/er** vi to exist; – v imp **il existe** . . . (sing) there is . . . ; (pl) there are . . . . ◆**-ant** a existing.

exode [ɛgzɔd] nm exodus.

exonérer [ɛgzɔnere] vt to exempt (**de** from). ◆**exonération** nf exemption.

exorbitant [ɛgzɔrbitɑ̃] a exorbitant.

exorciser [ɛgzɔrsize] vt to exorcize. ◆**exorcisme** nm exorcism.

exotique [ɛgzɔtik] a exotic. ◆**exotisme** nm exoticism.

expansif, -ive [ɛkspɑ̃sif, -iv] a expansive, effusive.

expansion [ɛkspɑ̃sjɔ̃] nf Com Phys Pol expansion; **en (pleine) e.** (fast ou rapidly) expanding.

expatri/er (s') [ɛkspatrije] vpr to leave one's country. ◆**-é, -ée** a & nmf expatriate.

expectative [ɛkspɛktativ] nf **être dans l'e.** to be waiting to see what happens.

expédient [ɛkspedjɑ̃] nm (moyen) expedient.

expédier [ɛkspedje] vt 1 (envoyer) to send off. 2 (affaires, client) to dispose of quickly, dispatch. ◆**expéditeur, -trice** nmf sender. ◆**expéditif, -ive** a expeditious, quick. ◆**expédition** nf 1 (envoi) dispatch. 2 (voyage) expedition.

expérience [ɛksperjɑ̃s] nf (pratique, connaissance) experience; (scientifique) experiment; **faire l'e. de qch** to experience sth. ◆**expérimental, -aux** a experimental. ◆**expérimentation** nf experimentation. ◆**expériment/er** vt Phys Ch to try out, experiment with; – vi to experiment. ◆**-é** a experienced.

expert [ɛkspɛr] a expert, skilled (**en** in); –

nm expert; (d'assurances) valuer. ◆**e.-comptable** nm (pl **experts-comptables**) = chartered accountant, = Am certified public accountant. ◆**expertise** nf (évaluation) (expert) appraisal; (compétence) expertise.

expier [ɛkspje] vt (péchés, crime) to expiate, atone for. ◆**expiation** nf expiation (**de** of).

expir/er [ɛkspire] 1 vti to breathe out. 2 vi (mourir) to pass away; (finir, cesser) to expire. ◆**-ant** a dying. ◆**expiration** nf (échéance) expiry, Am expiration.

explicite [ɛksplisit] a explicit. ◆**-ment** adv explicitly.

expliquer [ɛksplike] vt to explain (**à** to); – **s'e.** vpr to explain oneself; (discuter) to talk things over, have it out (**avec** with); **s'e. qch** (comprendre) to understand sth; **ça s'explique** that is understandable. ◆**explicable** a understandable. ◆**explicatif, -ive** a explanatory. ◆**explication** nf explanation; (mise au point) discussion.

exploit [ɛksplwa] nm exploit, feat.

exploit/er [ɛksplwate] vt 1 (champs) to farm; (ferme, entreprise) to run; (mine) to work; (situation) Fig to exploit. 2 (abuser de) Péj to exploit (s.o.). ◆**-ant, -ante** nmf farmer. ◆**exploitation** nf 1 Péj exploitation. 2 farming; running; working; (entreprise) concern; (agricole) farm.

explorer [ɛksplɔre] vt to explore. ◆**explorateur, -trice** nmf explorer. ◆**exploration** nf exploration.

exploser [ɛksploze] vi (gaz etc) to explode; (bombe) to blow up, explode; **e. (de colère)** Fam to explode, blow up; **faire e. (bombe)** to explode. ◆**explosif, -ive** a & nm explosive. ◆**explosion** nf explosion; (de colère, joie) outburst.

exporter [ɛksporte] vt to export (**vers** to, **de** from). ◆**exportateur, -trice** nmf exporter; – a exporting. ◆**exportation** nf (produit) export; (action) export(ation), exporting.

expos/er [ɛkspoze] vt (présenter, soumettre) & Phot to expose (**à** to); (marchandises) to display; (tableau etc) to exhibit; (idée, théorie) to set out; (vie, réputation) to risk, endanger; **s'e. à** to expose oneself to. ◆**-ant, -ante** nmf exhibitor. ◆**-é 1** a **bien e.** (édifice) having a good exposure; **e. au sud** facing south. 2 nm (compte rendu) account (**de** of); (discours) talk; Scol paper. ◆**exposition** nf (de marchandises etc) display; (salon) exhibition; (au danger etc) &

Phot exposure (à to); (*de maison etc*) aspect.

exprès[1] [ɛkspre] *adv* on purpose, intentionally; (*spécialement*) specially.

exprès[2], **-esse** [ɛkspres] **1** *a* (*ordre, condition*) express. **2** *a inv* **lettre/colis** e. express letter/parcel. **◆expressément** *adv* expressly.

express [ɛkspres] *a* & *nm inv* (*train*) express; (*café*) espresso.

expressif, -ive [ɛkspresif, -iv] *a* expressive. **◆expression** *nf* (*phrase, mine etc*) expression. **◆exprimer** *vt* to express; **— s'e.** *vpr* to express oneself.

exproprier [ɛksprɔprije] *vt* to seize the property of by compulsory purchase.

expulser [ɛkspylse] *vt* to expel (de from); (*joueur*) *Sp* to send off; (*locataire*) to evict. **◆expulsion** *nf* expulsion; eviction; sending off.

expurger [ɛkspyrʒe] *vt* to expurgate.

exquis [ɛkski] *a* exquisite.

extase [ɛkstɑz] *nf* ecstasy, rapture. **◆s'extasi/er** *vpr* to be in raptures (**sur** over, about). **◆—é** *a* ecstatic.

extensible [ɛkstɑ̃sibl] *a* expandable. **◆extension** *nf* extension; (*essor*) expansion.

exténuer [ɛkstenɥe] *vt* (*fatiguer*) to exhaust. **◆exténuation** *nf* exhaustion.

extérieur [ɛksterjœr] *a* (*monde etc*) outside; (*surface*) outer; (*signe*) outward, external; (*politique*) foreign; **e. à** external to; **—** *nm* outside, exterior; **à l'e. (de)** outside; **à l'e.** (*match*) away; **en e.** *Cin* on location. **◆—ement** *adv* outwardly; (*en apparence*) outwardly. **◆extérioriser** *vt* to express.

exterminer [ɛkstɛrmine] *vt* to exterminate,

wipe out. **◆extermination** *nf* extermination.

externe [ɛkstɛrn] **1** *a* external. **2** *nmf Scol* day pupil; *Méd* non-resident hospital doctor, *Am* extern.

extincteur [ɛkstɛ̃ktœr] *nm* fire extinguisher. **◆extinction** *nf* (*de feu*) extinguishing; (*de voix*) loss; (*de race*) extinction.

extirper [ɛkstirpe] *vt* to eradicate.

extorquer [ɛkstɔrke] *vt* to extort (à from). **◆extorsion** *nf* extortion.

extra [ɛkstra] **1** *a inv* (*très bon*) *Fam* top-quality. **2** *nm inv Culin* (extra-special) treat; (*serviteur*) extra hand *ou* help.

extra- [ɛkstra] *préf* extra-. **◆e.-fin** *a* extra-fine. **◆e.-fort** *a* extra-strong.

extradition [ɛkstradisjɔ̃] *nf* extradition. **◆extrader** *vt* to extradite.

extraire* [ɛkstrɛr] *vt* to extract (de from); (*charbon*) to mine. **◆extraction** *nf* extraction. **◆extrait** *nm* extract; **un e. de naissance** a (copy of one's) birth certificate.

extraordinaire [ɛkstraɔrdinɛr] *a* extraordinary. **◆—ment** *adv* exceptionally; (*très, bizarrement*) extraordinarily.

extravagant [ɛkstravagɑ̃] *a* extravagant. **◆extravagance** *nf* extravagance.

extrême [ɛkstrɛm] *a* extreme; **—** *nm* extreme; **pousser à l'e.** to take *ou* carry to extremes. **◆—ment** *adv* extremely. **◆extrémiste** *a* & *nmf* extremist. **◆extrémité** *nf* (*bout*) extremity, end; *pl* (*excès*) extremes.

exubérant [ɛgzyberɑ̃] *a* exuberant. **◆exubérance** *nf* exuberance.

exulter [ɛgzylte] *vi* to exult, rejoice. **◆exultation** *nf* exultation.

F

F, f [ɛf] *nm* F, f.

F *abrév* **franc(s)**.

fable [fɑbl] *nf* fable.

fabrique [fabrik] *nf* factory; **marque de f.** trade mark.

fabriquer [fabrike] *vt* (*objet*) to make; (*industriellement*) to manufacture; (*récit*) *Péj* to fabricate, make up; **qu'est-ce qu'il fabrique?** *Fam* what's he up to? **◆fabricant, -ante** *nmf* manufacturer. **◆fabrication** *nf* manufacture; (*artisanale*) making; **de f. française** of French make.

fabuleux, -euse [fabylø, -øz] *a* (*légendaire, incroyable*) fabulous.

fac [fak] *nf Univ Fam* = **faculté 2**.

façade [fasad] *nf* (*de bâtiment*) front, façade; (*apparence*) *Fig* pretence, façade; **de f.** (*luxe etc*) sham.

face [fas] *nf* face; (*de cube etc*) side;(*de monnaie*) head; **de f.** (*photo*) full-face; (*vue*) front; **faire f. à** (*situation etc*) to face, face up to; **en f.** opposite; **en f. de** opposite, facing; (*en présence de*) in front of; **en f. d'un problème, f. à un problème** in the face of a problem, faced with a problem; **f. à** (*vis-à-vis de*) facing; **regarder qn en f.** to look s.o. in the face; **f. à f.** face to face; **un f. à f.** TV a face to face encounter; **sauver/perdre la f.** to save/lose face.

facétie [fasesi] *nf* joke, jest. ◆**facétieux, -euse** [-esjø, -øz] *a* (*personne*) facetious.

facette [faset] *nf* (*de diamant, problème etc*) facet.

fâch/er [faʃe] *vt* to anger; **se f.** *vpr* to get angry *ou* annoyed (**contre** with); **se f. avec qn** (*se brouiller*) to fall out with s.o. ◆**—é a** (*air*) angry; (*amis*) on bad terms; **f. avec** *ou* **contre qn** angry *ou* annoyed with s.o.; **f. de qch** sorry about sth. ◆**fâcherie** *nf* quarrel. ◆**fâcheux, -euse** *a* (*nouvelle etc*) unfortunate.

facho [faʃo] *a & nmf* Fam fascist.

facile [fasil] *a* easy; (*caractère, humeur*) easygoing; (*banal*) *Péj* facile; **c'est f. à faire** it's easy to do; **il est f. de faire ça** it's easy to do that; **f. à vivre** easy to get along with, easygoing. ◆**—ment** *adv* easily. ◆**facilité** *nf* (*simplicité*) easiness; (*aisance*) ease; **facilités de paiement** Com easy terms; **avoir de la f.** to be gifted; **avoir toutes facilités pour** to have every facility *ou* opportunity to. ◆**faciliter** *vt* to facilitate, make easier.

façon [fasõ] *nf* 1 way; **la f. dont elle parle** the way (in which) she talks; **f. (d'agir)** behaviour; **je n'aime pas ses façons** I don't like his *ou* her manners *ou* ways; **une f. de parler** a manner of speaking; **à la f. de** in the fashion of; **de toute f.** anyway, anyhow; **de f.** à so as to; **de f. générale** generally speaking; **à ma f.** my way, (in) my own way; **faire des façons** to make a fuss; **table f. chêne** imitation oak table. 2 (*coupe de vêtement*) cut, style. ◆**façonner** *vt* (*travailler, former*) to fashion, shape; (*fabriquer*) to manufacture.

facteur [faktœr] *nm* 1 postman, Am mailman. 2 (*élément*) factor. ◆**factrice** *nf* Fam postwoman.

factice [faktis] *a* false, artificial; (*diamant*) imitation-.

faction [faksjõ] *nf* 1 (*groupe*) Pol faction. 2 **de f.** Mil on guard (duty), on sentry duty.

facture [faktyr] *nf* Com invoice, bill. ◆**facturer** *vt* to invoice, bill.

facultatif, -ive [fakyltatif, -iv] *a* optional; **arrêt f.** request stop.

faculté [fakylte] *nf* 1 (*aptitude*) faculty; (*possibilité*) freedom (**de faire** to do); **une f. de travail** a capacity for work. 2 Univ faculty; **à la f.** Fam at university, Am at school.

fadaises [fadɛz] *nfpl* twaddle, nonsense.

fade [fad] *a* insipid. ◆**fadasse** *a* Fam wishy-washy.

fagot [fago] *nm* bundle (of firewood).

fagoter [fagɔte] *vt* Péj to dress, rig out.

faible [fɛbl] *a* weak, feeble; (*bruit, voix*) faint; (*vent, quantité, chances*) slight; (*revenus*) small; **f. en anglais**/*etc* poor at English/*etc*; – *nm* (*personne*) weakling; **les faibles** the weak; **avoir un f. pour** to have a weakness *ou* a soft spot for. ◆**faiblement** *adv* weakly; (*légèrement*) slightly; (*éclairer, parler*) faintly. ◆**faiblesse** *nf* weakness, feebleness; faintness; slightness; smallness; (*défaut, syncope*) weakness. ◆**faiblir** *vi* (*forces*) to weaken; (*courage, vue*) to fail; (*ralentir*) to slacken.

faïence [fajãs] *nf* (*matière*) earthenware; *pl* (*objets*) crockery, earthenware.

faille [faj] *nf* Géol fault; Fig flaw.

faillible [fajibl] *a* fallible.

faillir⋆ [fajir] *vi* 1 **il a failli tomber** he almost *ou* nearly fell. 2 **f. à** (*devoir*) to fail in.

faillite [fajit] *nf* Com bankruptcy; Fig failure; **faire f.** to go bankrupt.

faim [fɛ̃] *nf* hunger; **avoir f.** to be hungry; **donner f. à qn** to make s.o. hungry; **manger à sa f.** to eat one's fill; **mourir de f.** to die of starvation; (*avoir très faim*) Fig to be starving.

fainéant, -ante [feneã, -ãt] *a* idle; – *nmf* idler. ◆**fainéanter** *vi* to idle. ◆**fainéantise** *nf* idleness.

faire⋆ [fɛr] 1 *vt* (*bruit, pain, faute etc*) to make; (*devoir, dégâts, ménage etc*) to do; (*rêve, chute*) to have; (*sourire, grognement*) to give; (*promenade, sieste*) to have, take; (*guerre*) to wage, make; **ça fait dix mètres de large** (*mesure*) it's ten metres wide; **2 et 2 font 4** 2 and 2 are 4; **ça fait dix francs** that is *ou* comes to ten francs; **qu'a-t-il fait (de)?** what's he done (with)?; **que f.?** what's to be done?; **f. du tennis/du piano**/*etc* to play tennis/the piano/*etc*; **f. l'idiot** to act *ou* play the fool; **ça ne fait rien** that doesn't matter; **comment as-tu fait pour . . . ?** how did you manage to . . . ?; **il ne fait que travailler** he does nothing but work, he keeps on working; **je ne fais que d'arriver** I've just arrived; **oui, fit-elle** yes, she said. 2 *vi* (*agir*) to do; (*paraître*) to look; **il fait vieux** he looks old; **il fera un bon médecin** he'll be *ou* make a good doctor; **elle ferait bien de partir** she'd do well to leave; – 3 *v imp* **il fait beau/froid**/*etc* it's fine/cold/*etc*; **quel temps fait-il?** what's the weather like?; **ça fait deux ans que je ne l'ai pas vu** I haven't seen him for two years, it's (been) two years since I saw him. **4** *v aux* (+ *inf*): f. construire une maison to have *ou* get a house built (à qn, par qn by s.o.); f. crier/souffrir/*etc* qn to make s.o. shout/suffer/*etc*; se f. couper les cheveux to have one's hair cut; se f. craindre/obéir/*etc* to make oneself feared/obeyed/*etc*; se f. tuer/renverser/*etc* to get *ou* be killed/knocked down/*etc*. **5** se f. *vpr* (*fabrication*) to be made; (*activité*) to be done; se f. des illusions to have illusions; se f. des amis to make friends; se f. vieux/*etc* (*devenir*) to get old/*etc*; il se fait tard it's getting late; comment se fait-il que? how is it that?; se f. à to get used to, adjust to; ne t'en fais pas! don't worry!

faire-part [ferpar] *nm inv* (*de mariage etc*) announcement.

faisable [fəzabl] *a* feasible.

faisan [fəzɑ̃] *nm* (*oiseau*) pheasant.

faisandé [fəzɑ̃de] *a* (*gibier*) high.

faisceau, -x [feso] *nm* (*lumineux*) beam; (*de tiges etc*) bundle.

fait [fe] **1** *voir* faire; − *a* (*fromage*) ripe; (*homme*) grown; (*yeux*) made up; (*ongles*) polished; tout f. ready made; bien f. (*jambes, corps etc*) shapely; c'est bien f.! it serves you right! **2** *nm* event, occurrence; (*donnée, réalité*) fact; prendre sur le f. *Jur* to catch in the act; du f. de on account of; f. divers *Journ* (miscellaneous) news item; au f. (*à propos*) by the way; aller au f. to get to the point; faits et gestes actions; en f. in fact; en f. de in the matter of.

faîte [fet] *nm* (*haut*) top; (*apogée*) *Fig* height.

faites [fet] *voir* faire.

faitout [fetu] *nm* stewing pot, casserole.

falaise [falez] *nf* cliff.

falloir* [falwar] **1** *v imp* il faut qch/qn I, you, we *etc* need sth/s.o.; il lui faut un stylo he *ou* she needs a pen; il faut partir/*etc* I, you, we *etc* have to go/*etc*; il faut que je parte I have to go; il faudrait qu'elle reste she ought to stay; il faut un jour it takes a day (pour faire to do); comme il faut proper(ly); s'il le faut if need be. **2** s'en f. *v imp* peu s'en est fallu qu'il ne pleure he almost cried; tant s'en faut far from it.

falsifier [falsifje] *vt* (*texte etc*) to falsify. ◆falsification *nf* falsification.

famé (mal) [malfame] *a* of ill repute.

famélique [famelik] *a* ill-fed, starving.

fameux, -euse [famø, -øz] *a* famous; (*excellent*) *Fam* first-class; pas f. *Fam* not much good.

familial, -aux [familjal, -o] *a* family-.

familier, -ière [familje, -jɛr] *a* (*bien connu*) familiar (à to); (*amical*) friendly, informal; (*locution*) colloquial, familiar; f. avec qn (over)familiar with s.o.; − *nm* (*de club etc*) regular visitor. ◆familiariser *vt* to familiarize (avec with); − se f. *vpr* to familiarize oneself (avec with). ◆familiarité *nf* familiarity; *pl Péj* liberties. ◆familièrement *adv* familiarly; (*parler*) informally.

famille [famij] *nf* family; en f. (*dîner etc*) with one's family; un père de f. a family man.

famine [famin] *nf* famine.

fan [fã] *nm* (*admirateur*) *Fam* fan.

fana [fana] *nmf Fam* fan; être f. de to be crazy about.

fanal, -aux [fanal, -o] *nm* lantern, light.

fanatique [fanatik] *a* fanatical; − *nmf* fanatic. ◆fanatisme *nm* fanaticism.

faner (se) [səfane] *vpr* (*fleur, beauté*) to fade. ◆−é *a* faded.

fanfare [fɑ̃far] *nf* (*orchestre*) brass band; (*air, musique*) fanfare.

fanfaron, -onne [fɑ̃farɔ̃, -ɔn] *a* boastful; − *nmf* braggart.

fange [fɑ̃ʒ] *nf Litt* mud, mire.

fanion [fanjɔ̃] *nm* (*drapeau*) pennant.

fantaisie [fɑ̃tezi] *nf* (*caprice*) fancy, whim; (*imagination*) imagination, fantasy; (de) f. (*bouton etc*) fancy. ◆fantaisiste *a* (*pas sérieux*) fanciful; (*irrégulier*) unorthodox.

fantasme [fɑ̃tasm] *nm* *Psy* fantasy. ◆fantasmer *vi* to fantasize (sur about).

fantasque [fɑ̃task] *a* whimsical.

fantassin [fɑ̃tasɛ̃] *nm* *Mil* infantryman.

fantastique [fɑ̃tastik] *a* (*imaginaire, excellent*) fantastic.

fantoche [fɑ̃tɔʃ] *nm & a* puppet.

fantôme [fɑ̃tom] *nm* ghost, phantom; − *a* (*ville, train*) ghost-; (*firme*) bogus.

faon [fã] *nm* (*animal*) fawn.

faramineux, -euse [faraminø, -øz] *a Fam* fantastic.

farce[1] [fars] *nf* practical joke, prank; *Th* farce; magasin de farces et attrapes joke shop. ◆farceur, -euse *nmf* (*blagueur*) wag, joker.

farce[2] [fars] *nf Culin* stuffing. ◆farcir *vt* 1 *Culin* to stuff. 2 se f. qn/qch *Fam* to put up with s.o./sth.

fard [far] *nm* make-up. ◆farder *vt* (*vérité*) to camouflage; − se f. *vpr* (*se maquiller*) to make up.

fardeau, -x [fardo] *nm* burden, load.

farfelu, -ue [farfəly] *a Fam* crazy, bizarre; − *nmf Fam* weirdo.

farine [farin] *nf* (*de blé*) flour; f. d'avoine

oatmeal. ◆**farineux, -euse** *a Péj* floury, powdery.

farouche [faruʃ] *a* **1** (*timide*) shy, unsociable; (*animal*) easily scared. **2** (*violent, acharné*) fierce. ◆**—ment** *adv* fiercely.

fart [far(t)] *nm* (ski) wax. ◆**farter** *vt* (skis) to wax.

fascicule [fasikyl] *nm* volume.

fasciner [fasine] *vt* to fascinate. ◆**fascination** *nf* fascination.

fascisme [faʃism] *nm* fascism. ◆**fasciste** *a & nmf* fascist.

fasse(nt) [fas] *voir* **faire.**

faste [fast] *nm* ostentation, display.

fastidieux, -euse [fastidjø, -øz] *a* tedious, dull.

fatal, mpl -als [fatal] *a* (*mortel*) fatal; (*inévitable*) inevitable; (*moment, ton*) fateful; **c'était f.!** it was bound to happen! ◆**—ement** *adv* inevitably. ◆**fataliste** *a* fatalistic; — *nmf* fatalist. ◆**fatalité** *nf* (*destin*) fate. ◆**fatidique** *a* (*jour, date*) fateful.

fatigue [fatig] *nf* tiredness, fatigue, weariness. ◆**fatigant** *a* (*épuisant*) tiring; (*ennuyeux*) tiresome. ◆**fatigu/er** *vt* to tire, fatigue; (*yeux*) to strain; (*importuner*) to annoy; (*raser*) to bore; — *vi* (*moteur*) to strain; — **se f.** *vpr* (*se lasser*) to get tired, tire (**de** *of*); (*travailler*) to tire oneself out (**à faire** doing). ◆**—é** *a* tired, weary (**de** *of*).

fatras [fatra] *nm* jumble, muddle.

faubourg [fobur] *nm* suburb. ◆**faubourien, -ienne** *a* (*accent etc*) suburban, common.

fauché [foʃe] *a* (*sans argent*) *Fam* broke.

fauch/er [foʃe] *vt* **1** (*herbe*) to mow; (*blé*) to reap; (*abattre, renverser*) *Fig* to mow down. **2** (*voler*) *Fam* to snatch, pinch. ◆**—euse** *nf* (*machine*) reaper.

faucille [fosij] *nf* (*instrument*) sickle.

faucon [fokɔ̃] *nm* (*oiseau*) falcon, hawk; (*personne*) *Fig* hawk.

faudra, faudrait [fodra, fodrɛ] *voir* **falloir.**

faufiler (se) [safofile] *vpr* to edge *ou* inch one's way (**dans** through, into; **entre** between).

faune [fon] *nf* wildlife, fauna; (*gens*) *Péj* set.

faussaire [fosɛr] *nm* (*faux-monnayeur*) forger.

fausse [fos] *voir* **faux** [1]. ◆**faussement** *adv* falsely.

fausser [fose] *vt* (*sens, réalité etc*) to distort; (*clé etc*) to buckle; **f. compagnie à qn** to give s.o. the slip.

fausseté [foste] *nf* (*d'un raisonnement etc*) falseness; (*hypocrisie*) duplicity.

faut [fo] *voir* **falloir.**

faute [fot] *nf* (*erreur*) mistake; (*responsabilité*) fault; (*délit*) offence; (*péché*) sin; *Fb* foul; **c'est sa f.** it's your fault, you're to blame; **f. de temps/etc** for lack of time/*etc*; **f. de mieux** for want of anything better; **en f.** at fault; **sans f.** without fail. ◆**fautif, -ive** *a* (*coupable*) in the wrong; (*erroné*) faulty.

fauteuil [fotœj] *nm* armchair; (*de président*) chair; **f. d'orchestre** *Th* seat in the stalls; **f. roulant** wheelchair; **f. pivotant** swivel chair.

fauteur [fotœr] *nm* **f. de troubles** troublemaker.

fauve [fov] **1** *a & nm* (*couleur*) fawn. **2** *nm* wild beast; **chasse aux fauves** big game hunting.

faux [1], **fausse** [fo, fos] *a* (*inauthentique*) false; (*pas vrai*) untrue, false; (*pas exact*) wrong; (*monnaie*) counterfeit, forged; (*bijou, marbre*) imitation-, fake; (*voix*) out of tune; (*col*) detachable; — *adv* (*chanter*) out of tune; — *nm* (*contrefaçon*) forgery; **le f.** the false, the untrue. ◆**f.-filet** *nm Culin* sirloin. ◆**f.-fuyant** *nm* subterfuge. ◆**f.-monnayeur** *nm* counterfeiter.

faux [2] [fo] *nf* (*instrument*) scythe.

faveur [favœr] *nf* favour; **en f. de** (*au profit de*) in favour of; **de f.** (*billet*) complimentary; (*traitement, régime*) preferential. ◆**favorable** *a* favourable (**à** to). ◆**favori, -ite** *a & nmf* favourite. ◆**favoriser** *vt* to favour. ◆**favoritisme** *nm* favouritism.

favoris [favori] *nmpl* sideburns, side whiskers.

fébrile [febril] *a* feverish. ◆**fébrilité** *nf* feverishness.

fécond [fekɔ̃] *a* (*femme, idée etc*) fertile. ◆**féconder** *vt* to fertilize. ◆**fécondité** *nf* fertility.

fécule [fekyl] *nf* starch. ◆**féculents** *nmpl* (*aliments*) carbohydrates.

fédéral, -aux [federal, -o] *a* federal. ◆**fédération** *nf* federation. ◆**fédérer** *vt* to federate.

fée [fe] *nf* fairy. ◆**féerie** *nf Th* fantasy extravaganza; *Fig* fairy-like spectacle. ◆**féerique** *a* fairy-like), magical.

feindre* [fɛ̃dr] *vt* to feign, sham; **f. de faire** to pretend to do. ◆**feint** *a* feigned, sham. ◆**feinte** *nf* sham, pretence; *Boxe Mil* feint.

fêler [fele] *vt*, — **se f.** *vpr* (*tasse*) to crack. ◆**fêlure** *nf* crack.

félicité [felisite] *nf* bliss, felicity.

féliciter [felisite] *vt* to congratulate (**qn de** *ou* **sur** s.o. on); **se f. de** to congratulate oneself

on. ◆**félicitations** *nfpl* congratulations
(**pour** on).

félin [felɛ̃] *a* & *nm* feline.

femelle [fəmɛl] *a* & *nf* (*animal*) female.

féminin [feminɛ̃] *a* (*prénom, hormone etc*)
female; (*trait, intuition etc*) & *Gram* feminine; (*mode, revue, équipe etc*) women's.
◆**féministe** *a* & *nmf* feminist. ◆**féminité**
nf femininity.

femme [fam] *nf* woman; (*épouse*) wife; **f.
médecin** woman doctor; **f. de chambre**
(chamber)maid; **f. de ménage** cleaning
lady, maid; **bonne f. Fam** woman.

fémur [femyr] *nm* thighbone, femur.

fendiller (se) [səfɑ̃dije] *vpr* to crack.

fendre [fɑ̃dr] *vt* (*bois etc*) to split; (*foule*) to
force one's way through; (*onde, air*) to
cleave; (*cœur*) *Fig* to break, rend; — **se f.**
vpr (*se fissurer*) to crack.

fenêtre [f(ə)nɛtr] *nf* window.

fenouil [fənuj] *nm Bot Culin* fennel.

fente [fɑ̃t] *nf* (*de tirelire, palissade, jupe etc*)
slit; (*de rocher*) split, crack.

féodal, -aux [feɔdal, -o] *a* feudal.

fer [fɛr] *nm* iron; (*partie métallique de qch*)
metal (part); **de f., en f.** (*outil etc*) iron-;
fil de f. wire; **f. à cheval** horseshoe; **f.**
(**à repasser**) iron; **f. à friser** curling tongs;
f. de lance *Fig* spearhead; **de f.** (*santé*) *Fig*
cast-iron; (*main, volonté*) *Fig* iron-. ◆**fer-
blanc** *nm* (*pl* **fers-blancs**) tin(-plate).

fera, ferait [fəra, fərɛ] *voir* **faire**.

férié [ferje] *a* **jour f.** (public) holiday.

ferme¹ [fɛrm] *nf* farm; (*maison*)
farm(house).

ferme² [fɛrm] *a* (*beurre, décision etc*) firm;
(*autoritaire*) firm (**avec** with); (*pas, voix*)
steady; (*pâte*) stiff; — *adv* (*travailler, boire*)
hard; (*discuter*) keenly; **tenir f.** to stand
firm *ou* fast. ◆**—ment** [-əmɑ̃] *adv* firmly.

ferment [fɛrmɑ̃] *nm* ferment. ◆**fermentation** *nf* fermentation. ◆**fermenter** *vi* to
ferment.

ferm/er [fɛrme] *vt* to close, shut; (*gaz, radio
etc*) to turn *ou* switch off; (*passage*) to
block; (*vêtement*) to do up; **f. (à clef)** to
lock; **f. la marche** to bring up the rear; — *vi*,
— **se f.** *vpr* to close, shut. ◆—**é** *a* (*porte,
magasin etc*) closed, shut; (*route, circuit etc*)
closed; (*gaz etc*) off. ◆**fermeture** *nf* closing, closure; (*heure*) closing time; (*mécanisme*) catch; **f. éclair®** zip (fastener), *Am*
zipper. ◆**fermoir** *nm* clasp, (snap) fastener.

fermeté [fɛrməte] *nf* firmness; (*de geste,
voix*) steadiness.

fermier, -ière [fɛrmje, -jɛr] *nmf* farmer; — *a*
(*poulet, produit*) farm-.

féroce [ferɔs] *a* fierce, ferocious. ◆**férocité**
nf ferocity, fierceness.

ferraille [fɛrɑj] *nf* scrap-iron; **mettre à la
f.** to scrap. ◆**ferrailleur** *nm* scrap-iron
merchant.

ferré [fɛre] *a* **1** (*canne*) metal-tipped; **voie
ferrée** railway, *Am* railroad; (*rails*) track. **2**
(*calé*) *Fam* well up (**en** in, **sur** on).

ferrer [fɛre] *vt* (*cheval*) to shoe.

ferronnerie [fɛrɔnri] *nf* ironwork.

ferroviaire [fɛrɔvjɛr] *a* (*compagnie etc*) rail-
way-, *Am* railroad-.

ferry-boat [fɛribot] *nm* ferry.

fertile [fɛrtil] *a* (*terre, imagination*) fertile; **f.
en incidents** eventful. ◆**fertiliser** *vt* to fertilize. ◆**fertilité** *nf* fertility.

fervent, -ente [fɛrvɑ̃, -ɑ̃t] *a* fervent; — *nmf*
devotee (**de** of). ◆**ferveur** *nf* fervour.

fesse [fɛs] *nf* buttock; **les fesses** one's behind. ◆**fessée** *nf* spanking.

festin [fɛstɛ̃] *nm* (*banquet*) feast.

festival, *pl* -als [fɛstival] *nm Mus Cin* festival.

festivités [fɛstivite] *nfpl* festivities.

festoyer [fɛstwaje] *vi* to feast, carouse.

fête [fɛt] *nf* (*civile*) holiday; *Rel* festival,
feast; (*entre amis*) party; **f. du village** village fair *ou* fête; **f. de famille** family celebration; **c'est sa f.** it's his *ou* her saint's
day; **f. des Mères** Mother's Day; **jour de f.**
(public) holiday; **faire la f.** to make merry,
revel; **air de f.** festive air. ◆**fêter** *vt* (*événement*) to celebrate.

fétiche [fetiʃ] *nm* (*objet de culte*) fetish;
(*mascotte*) *Fig* mascot.

fétide [fetid] *a* fetid, stinking.

feu¹, -x [fø] *nm* fire; (*lumière*) *Aut Nau Av*
light; (*de réchaud*) burner; (*de dispute*) *Fig*
heat; *pl* (*de signalisation*) traffic lights; **feux
de position** *Aut* parking lights; **feux de
croisement** *Aut* dipped headlights, *Am* low
beams; **f. rouge** *Aut* (*lumière*) red light;
(*objet*) traffic lights; **tous feux éteints** *Aut*
without lights; **mettre le f. à** to set fire to;
en f. on fire, ablaze; **avez-vous du f.?** have
you got a light?; **donner le f. vert** to give the
go-ahead (**à** to); **ne pas faire long f.** not to
last very long; **à f. doux** *Culin* on a low
light; **au f.!** (there's a) fire!; **f.! Mil** fire!;
coup de f. (*bruit*) gunshot; **feux croisés** *Mil*
crossfire.

feu², -e [fø] *a inv* late; **f. ma tante** my late aunt.

feuille [fœj] *nf* leaf; (*de papier etc*) sheet; (*de
température*) chart; *Journ* newssheet; **f.
d'impôt** tax form *ou* return; **f. de paye** pay

slip. ◆**feuillage** nm foliage. ◆**feuillet** nm (de livre) leaf. ◆**feuilleter** vt (livre) to flip ou leaf through; **pâte feuilletée** puff ou flaky pastry. ◆**feuilleton** nm (roman, film etc) serial. ◆**feuillu** a leafy.

feutre [føtr] nm felt; (chapeau) felt hat; **crayon f.** felt-tip(ped) pen. ◆**feutré** a (bruit) muffled; **à pas feutrés** silently.

fève [fɛv] nf bean.

février [fevrije] nm February.

fiable [fjabl] a reliable. ◆**fiabilité** nf reliability.

fiacre [fjakr] nm Hist hackney carriage.

fianc/er (se) [səfjɑ̃se] vpr to become engaged (avec to). ◆—**é** nm fiancé; en engaged couple. ◆—**ée** nf fiancée. ◆**fiançailles** nfpl engagement.

fiasco [fjasko] nm fiasco; **faire f.** to be a fiasco.

fibre [fibr] nf fibre; **f. (alimentaire)** roughage, (dietary) fibre; **f. de verre** fibreglass.

ficelle [fisɛl] nf 1 string; **connaître les ficelles** (d'un métier etc) to known the ropes. 2 (pain) long thin loaf. ◆**ficeler** vt to tie up.

fiche [fiʃ] nf 1 (carte) index ou record card; (papier) slip, form; **f. technique** data record. 2 Él (broche) pin; (prise) plug. ◆**fichier** nm card index, file.

fiche(r) [fiʃ(e)] vt (pp fichu) Fam (faire) to do; (donner) to give; (jeter) to throw; (mettre) to put; **f. le camp** to shove off; **fiche-moi la paix!** leave me alone!; **se f. de qn** to make fun of s.o.; **je m'en fiche!** I don't give a damn!

ficher [fiʃe] vt 1 (enfoncer) to drive in. 2 (renseignement, personne) to put on file.

fichu [fiʃy] 1 a Fam (mauvais) lousy, rotten; (capable) able (**de faire** to do); **il est f.** he's had it, he's done for; **mal f.** (malade) not well. 2 nm (head) scarf.

fictif, -ive [fiktif, -iv] a fictitious. ◆**fiction** nf fiction.

fidèle [fidɛl] a faithful (à to); – nmf faithful supporter; (client) regular (customer); **les fidèles** (croyants) the faithful; (à l'église) the congregation. ◆—**ment** adv faithfully. ◆**fidélité** nf fidelity, faithfulness.

fief [fjɛf] nm (spécialité, chasse gardée) domain.

fiel [fjɛl] nm gall.

fier (se) [səfje] vpr **se f. à** to trust.

fier, fière [fjɛr] a proud (**de** of); **un f. culot** Péj a rare cheek. ◆**fièrement** adv proudly. ◆**fierté** nf pride.

fièvre [fjɛvr] nf (maladie) fever; (agitation) frenzy; **avoir de la f.** to have a temperature ou a fever. ◆**fiévreux, -euse** a feverish.

fig/er [fiʒe] vt (sang, sauce etc) to congeal; **f. qn** (paralyser) Fig to freeze s.o.; – vi (liquide) to congeal; – **se f.** qn (liquide) to congeal; (sourire, personne) Fig to freeze. ◆—**é** a (locution) set, fixed; (regard) frozen; (société) petrified.

fignol/er [finɔle] vt Fam to round off meticulously, refine. ◆—**é** a Fam meticulous.

figue [fig] nf fig; **mi-f., mi-raisin** (accueil etc) neither good nor bad, mixed. ◆**figuier** nm fig tree.

figurant, -ante [figyrã, -ãt] nmf Cin Th extra.

figure [figyr] nf 1 (visage) face. 2 (personnage) & Géom figure; (de livre) figure, illustration; **faire f. de riche/d'imbécile**/etc to look rich/a fool/etc. ◆**figurine** nf statuette.

figur/er [figyre] vt to represent; – vi to appear, figure; – **se f.** vpr to imagine; **figurez-vous que . . .?** would you believe that . . .? ◆—**é** a (sens) figurative; – nm **au f.** figuratively.

fil [fil] nm 1 (de coton, pensée etc) thread; (lin) linen; **f. dentaire** dental floss; **de f. en aiguille** bit by bit. 2 (métallique) wire; **f. de fer** wire; **f. à plomb** plumbline; **au bout du f.** Tél on the line; **passer un coup de f. à qn** Tél to give s.o. a ring ou a call. 3 (de couteau) edge. 4 **au f. de l'eau/des jours** with the current/the passing of time.

filament [filamã] nm Él filament.

filandreux, -euse [filãdrø, -øz] a (phrase) long-winded.

filante [filãt] a **f. étoile f.** shooting star.

file [fil] nf line; (couloir) Aut lane; **f. d'attente** queue, Am line; **en f. (indienne)** in single file; **chef de f.** leader; **(se) mettre en f.** to line up.

fil/er [file] 1 vt (coton etc) to spin. 2 vt **f. qn** (suivre) to shadow s.o., tail s.o. 3 vt Fam **f. qch à qn** (objet) to slip s.o. sth; **f. un coup de pied**/etc à qn to give s.o. a kick/etc. 4 vi (partir) to shoot off, bolt; (aller vite) to speed along; (temps) to fly; (bas, collant) to ladder, run; (liquide) to trickle, run; **filez!** hop it!; **f. entre les doigts de qn** to slip through s.o.'s fingers; **f. doux** to be obedient. ◆**filature** nf 1 (usine) textile mill. 2 (de policiers etc) shadowing; **prendre en f.** to shadow.

filet [file] nm 1 (de pêche) & Sp net; (à bagages) Rail (luggage) rack; **f. (à provisions)** string ou net bag (for shopping). 2 (d'eau) trickle. 3 (de poisson, viande) fillet.

filial, -aux [filjal, -o] a filial.

filiale [filjal] nf subsidiary (company).

filiation [filjɑsjɔ̃] *nf* relationship.

filière [filjɛr] *nf* (*de drogue*) network; **suivre la f.** (*pour obtenir qch*) to go through the official channels; (*employé*) to work one's way up.

filigrane [filigran] *nm* (*de papier*) watermark.

filin [filɛ̃] *nm* Nau rope.

fille [fij] *nf* 1 girl; **petite f.** (little *ou* young) girl; **jeune f.** girl, young lady; **vieille f.** Péj old maid; **f. (publique)** Péj prostitute. 2 (*parenté*) daughter, girl. ◆**f.-mère** *nf* (*pl* **filles-mères**) Péj unmarried mother. ◆**fillette** *nf* little girl.

filleul [fijœl] *nm* godson. ◆**filleule** *nf* goddaughter.

film [film] *nm* film, movie; (*pellicule*) film; **f. muet/parlant** silent/talking film *ou* movie; **le f. des événements** the sequence of events. ◆**filmer** *vt* (*personne, scène*) to film.

filon [filɔ̃] *nm* Géol seam; **trouver le (bon) f.** to strike it lucky.

filou [filu] *nm* rogue, crook.

fils [fis] *nm* son; **Dupont f.** Dupont junior.

filtre [filtr] *nm* filter; (**à bout**) **f.** (*cigarette*) (filter-)tipped; (**bout**) **f.** filter tip. ◆**filtrer** *vt* to filter; (*personne, nouvelles*) to scrutinize; – *vi* to filter (through).

fin [fɛ̃] 1 *nf* end; (*but*) end, aim; **mettre f. à** to put an end *ou* a stop to; **prendre f.** to come to an end; **tirer à sa f.** to draw to an end *ou* a close; **sans f.** endless; **à la f.** in the end; **arrêtez, à la f.!** stop, for heaven's sake!; **f. de semaine** weekend; **f. mai** at the end of May; **à cette f.** to this end. 2 *a* (*pointe, travail, tissu etc*) fine; (*taille, tranche*) thin; (*plat*) delicate, choice; (*esprit, oreille*) sharp; (*observation*) sharp, fine; (*gourmet*) discerning; (*rusé*) shrewd; (*intelligent*) clever; **au f. fond de** in the depths of; – *adv* (*couper, moudre*) finely; (*écrire*) small.

final, -aux *ou* **-als** [final, -o] *a* final; – *nm* Mus finale. ◆**finale** *nf* Sp final; Gram final syllable; – *nm* Mus finale. ◆**finalement** *adv* finally; (*en somme*) after all. ◆**finaliste** *nmf* Sp finalist.

finance [finɑ̃s] *nf* finance. ◆**financer** *vt* to finance. ◆—**ement** *nm* financing. ◆**financier, -ière** *a* financial; – *nm* financier. ◆**financièrement** *adv* financially.

fine [fin] *nf* liqueur brandy.

finement [finmɑ̃] *adv* (*broder, couper etc*) finely; (*agir*) cleverly.

finesse [finɛs] *nf* (*de pointe etc*) fineness; (*de taille etc*) thinness; (*de plat*) delicacy; (*d'esprit, de goût*) finesse; *pl* (*de langue*) niceties.

fin/ir [finir] *vt* to finish; (*discours, vie*) to end, finish; – *vi* to finish, end; **f. de faire** to finish doing; (*cesser*) to stop doing; **f. par faire** to end up *ou* finish up doing; **f. par qch** to finish (up) *ou* end (up) with sth; **en f. avec** to put an end to, finish with; **elle n'en finit pas** there's no end to it, she goes on and on. ◆—**i** *a* (*produit*) finished; (*univers etc*) & Math finite; **c'est f.** it's over *ou* finished; **il est f.** (*fichu*) he's done for *ou* finished; – *nm* (*poli*) finish. ◆—**issant** *a* (*siècle*) declining. ◆**finish** *nm* Sp finish. ◆**finition** *nf* (*action*) Tech finishing; (*résultat*) finish.

Finlande [fɛ̃lɑ̃d] *nf* Finland. ◆**finlandais, -aise** *a* Finnish; – *nmf* Finn. ◆**finnois, -oise** *a* Finnish; – *nmf* Finn; – *nm* (*langue*) Finnish.

fiole [fjɔl] *nf* phial, flask.

firme [firm] *nf* (*entreprise*) Com firm.

fisc [fisk] *nm* tax authorities, = Inland Revenue, = An Internal Revenue. ◆**fiscal, -aux** *a* fiscal, tax-. ◆**fiscalité** *nf* tax system; (*charges*) taxation.

fission [fisjɔ̃] *nf* Phys fission.

fissure [fisyr] *nf* split, crack, fissure. ◆**se fissurer** *vpr* to split, crack.

fiston [fistɔ̃] *nm* Fam son, sonny.

fixe [fiks] *a* fixed; (*prix, heure*) set, fixed; **idée f.** obsession; **regard f.** stare; **être au beau f.** Mét to be set fair; – *nm* (*paie*) fixed salary. ◆—**ment** [-əmɑ̃] *adv* **regarder f.** to stare at. ◆**fixer** *vt* (*attacher*) to fix (à to); (*choix*) to settle; (*règle, date etc*) to decide, fix; **f.** (**du regard**) to stare at; **f. qn sur** to inform s.o. clearly about; **être fixé** (*décidé*) to be decided; **comme ça on est fixé!** (*renseigné*) we've got the picture!; – **se f.** *vpr* (*regard*) to become fixed; (*s'établir*) to settle. ◆**fixateur** *nm* Phot fixer; (*pour cheveux*) setting lotion. ◆**fixation** *nf* (*action*) fixing; (*dispositif*) fastening, binding; Psy fixation.

flacon [flakɔ̃] *nm* bottle, flask.

flageoler [flaʒɔle] *vi* to shake, tremble.

flageolet [flaʒɔlɛ] *nm* Bot Culin (dwarf) kidney bean.

flagrant, -ante [flagrɑ̃, -ɑ̃t] *a* (*injustice etc*) flagrant, glaring; **pris en f. délit** caught in the act *ou* red-handed.

flair [flɛr] *nm* 1 (*d'un chien etc*) (sense of) smell, scent. 2 (*clairvoyance*) intuition, flair. ◆**flairer** *vt* to sniff at, smell; (*discerner*) Fig to smell, sense.

flamand, -ande [flamɑ̃, -ɑ̃d] *a* Flemish; – *nmf* Fleming; – *nm* (*langue*) Flemish.

flamant [flamɑ̃] *nm* (*oiseau*) flamingo.

flambant [flɑ̃bɑ̃] adv **f. neuf** brand new.
flambeau, -x [flɑ̃bo] nm torch.
flamb/er [flɑ̃be] vi to burn, blaze; — vt (aiguille) Méd to sterilize; (poulet) to singe. **2** vi (jouer) Fam to gamble for big money. ◆**—é** a (ruiné) Fam done for. ◆**—ée** nf blaze; (de colère, des prix etc) Fig surge; (de violence) flare-up, eruption. ◆**—eur** nm Fam big gambler. ◆**flamboyer** vi to blaze, flame.
flamme [flam] nf flame; (ardeur) Fig fire; **en flammes** on fire. ◆**flammèche** nf spark.
flan [flɑ̃] nm Culin custard tart ou pie. **2 au f.** Fam on the off chance, on the spur of the moment.
flanc [flɑ̃] nm side; (d'une armée, d'un animal) flank; **tirer au f.** Arg to shirk, idle.
flancher [flɑ̃ʃe] vi Fam to give in, weaken.
Flandre(s) [flɑ̃dr] nf(pl) Flanders.
flanelle [flanɛl] nf (tissu) flannel.
flâner [flɑne] vi to stroll, dawdle. ◆**flânerie** nf (action) strolling; (promenade) stroll.
flanquer [flɑ̃ke] vt **1** to flank (de with). **2** Fam (jeter) to chuck; (donner) to give; **f. qn à la porte** to throw s.o. out.
flaque [flak] nf puddle, pool.
flash, pl **flashes** [flaʃ] nm **1** Phot (éclair) flashlight; (dispositif) flash(gun). **2** TV Rad (news)flash.
flasque [flask] a flabby, floppy.
flatt/er [flate] vt to flatter; **se f. d'être malin/de réussir** to flatter oneself on being smart/on being able to succeed. ◆**—é** a flattered (**de qch** by sth, **de faire** to do, **que** that). ◆**flatterie** nf flattery. ◆**flatteur, -euse** nmf flatterer. ◆a flattering.
fléau, -x [fleo] nm **1** (calamité) scourge; (personne, chose) bane, plague. **2** Agr flail.
flèche [flɛʃ] nf arrow; (d'église) spire; **monter en f.** (prix) to (sky)rocket, shoot ahead. ◆**flécher** [fleʃe] vt to signpost (with arrows). ◆**fléchette** nf dart; pl (jeu) darts.
fléchir [fleʃir] vt (membre) to flex, bend; **f. qn** Fig to move s.o., persuade s.o.; — vi (membre) to bend; (poutre) to sag; (faiblir) to give way; (baisser) to fall off.
flegme [flɛgm] nm composure. ◆**flegmatique** a phlegmatic, stolid.
flemme [flɛm] nf Fam laziness; **il a la f.** he can't be bothered, he's just too lazy. ◆**flemmard, -arde** a Fam lazy; — nmf Fam lazybones.
flétrir [fletrir] **1** vt — **se f.** vpr to wither. **2** vt (blâmer) to stigmatize, brand.
fleur [flœr] nf flower; (d'arbre, d'arbuste) blossom; **en f.** in flower, in bloom; in blos-

som; **à** ou **dans la f. de l'âge** in the prime of life; **à f. d'eau** just above the water; **à fleurs** (tissu) floral. ◆**fleur/ir** vi to flower, bloom; (arbre etc) to blossom; (art, commerce etc) Fig to flourish; — vt (table etc) to decorate with flowers. ◆**—i** a (fleur, jardin) in bloom; (tissu) flowered, floral; (teint) florid; (style) flowery, florid. ◆**fleuriste** nmf florist.
fleuve [flœv] nm river.
flexible [flɛksibl] a flexible, pliable. ◆**flexibilité** nf flexibility.
flexion [flɛksjɔ̃] nf **1** Anat flexion, flexing. **2** Gram inflexion.
flic [flik] nm Fam cop, policeman.
flinguer [flɛ̃ge] vt **f. qn** Arg to shoot s.o.
flipper [flipœr] nm (jeu) pinball.
flirt [flœrt] nm (rapports) flirtation; (personne) flirt. ◆**flirter** vi to flirt (**avec** with). ◆**flirteur, -euse** a flirtatious; — nmf flirt.
flocon [flɔkɔ̃] nm (de neige) flake; (de laine) flock; **flocons d'avoine** Culin porridge oats. ◆**floconneux, -euse** a fluffy.
floraison [flɔrɛzɔ̃] nf flowering; **en pleine f.** in full bloom. ◆**floral, -aux** a floral. ◆**floralies** nfpl flower show.
flore [flɔr] nf flora.
florissant [flɔrisɑ̃] a flourishing.
flot [flo] nm (de souvenirs, larmes) flood, stream; (marée) floodtide; pl (de mer) waves; (de lac) waters; **à flots** in abundance; **à f.** (bateau, personne) afloat; **mettre à f.** (bateau, firme) to launch; **remettre qn à f.** to restore s.o.'s fortunes.
flotte [flɔt] nf **1** Nau Av fleet. **2** Fam (pluie) rain; (eau) water. ◆**flottille** nf Nau flotilla.
flott/er [flɔte] vi to float; (drapeau) to fly; (cheveux) to flow; (pensées) to drift; (pleuvoir) Fam to rain. ◆**—ant** a **1** (bois, dette etc) floating; (vêtement) flowing, loose. **2** (esprit) indecisive. ◆**—ement** nm (hésitation) indecision. ◆**—eur** nm Pêche etc float.
flou [flu] a (photo) fuzzy, blurred; (idée) hazy, fuzzy; — nm fuzziness.
fluctuant [flyktɥɑ̃] a (prix, opinions) fluctuating. ◆**fluctuations** nfpl fluctuation(s) (**de** in).
fluet, -ette [flɥɛ, -ɛt] a thin, slender.
fluide [flɥid] a (liquide) & Fig fluid; — nm (liquide) fluid. ◆**fluidité** nf fluidity.
fluorescent [flyɔrɛsɑ̃] a fluorescent.
flûte [flyt] **1** nf Mus flute. **2** nf (verre) champagne glass. **3** int heck!, darn!, dash it! ◆**flûté** a (voix) piping. ◆**flûtiste** nmf flautist, Am flutist.
fluvial, -aux [flyvjal, -o] a river-, fluvial.

flux [fly] nm (abondance) flow; **f. et reflux** ebb and flow.

focal, -aux [fɔkal, -o] a focal. ◆**focaliser** vt (intérêt etc) to focus.

fœtus [fetys] nm foetus, Am fetus.

foi [fwa] nf faith; **sur la f. de** on the strength of; **agir de bonne/mauvaise f.** to act in good/bad faith; **ma f., oui!** yes, indeed!

foie [fwa] nm liver.

foin [fwɛ̃] nm hay; **faire du f.** (scandale) Fam to make a stink.

foire [fwar] nf fair; **faire la f.** Fam to go on a binge, have a ball.

fois [fwa] nf time; **une f.** once; **deux f.** twice, two times; **chaque f. que** each time (that), whenever; **une f. qu'il sera arrivé** (dès que) once he has arrived; **à la f.** at the same time, at once; **à la f. riche et heureux** both rich and happy; **une autre f.** (elle fera attention etc) next time; **des f.** Fam sometimes; **non mais des f.!** Fam you must be joking!; **une f. pour toutes, une bonne f.** once and for all.

foison [fwazɔ̃] nf **à f.** in plenty. ◆**foisonn/er** vi to abound (de, en in). ◆**—ement** nm abundance.

fol [fɔl] voir **fou**.

folâtre [fɔlɑtr] a playful. ◆**folâtrer** vi to romp, frolic.

folichon, -onne [fɔliʃɔ̃, -ɔn] a pas **f.** not very funny, not much fun.

folie [fɔli] nf madness, insanity; **faire une f.** to do a foolish thing; (dépense) to be wildly extravagant; **aimer qn à la f.** to be madly in love with s.o..

folklore [fɔlklɔr] nm folklore. ◆**folklorique** a (danse etc) folk-; (pas sérieux) Fam lightweight, trivial, silly.

folle [fɔl] voir **fou**. ◆**follement** adv madly.

fomenter [fɔmɑ̃te] vt (révolte etc) to foment.

foncé [fɔ̃se] a (couleur) dark.

foncer [fɔ̃se] **1** vi (aller vite) to tear ou charge along; **f. sur qn** to charge into ou at s.o. **2** vti (couleur) to darken.

foncier, -ière [fɔ̃sje, -jɛr] a **1** fundamental, basic. **2** (propriété) landed. ◆**foncièrement** adv fundamentally.

fonction [fɔ̃ksjɔ̃] nf (rôle) & Math function; (emploi) office, function, duty; **f. publique** civil service; **faire f. de** (personne) to act as; (objet) to serve ou act as; **en f. de** according to. ◆**fonctionnaire** nmf civil servant. ◆**fonctionnel, -elle** a functional. ◆**fonctionn/er** vi (machine etc) to work, operate, function; (organisation) to function; **faire f.** to operate, work. ◆**—ement** nm working.

fond [fɔ̃] nm (de boîte, jardin, vallée etc) bottom; (de salle, armoire etc) back; (de culotte) seat; (de problème, débat etc) essence; (arrière-plan) background; (contenu) content; (du désespoir) Fig depths; **au f. de** at the bottom of; at the back of; **fonds de verre** dregs; **f. de teint** foundation cream; **f. sonore** background music; **un f. de bon sens** a stock of good sense; **au f.** basically, in essence; **à f.** (connaître etc) thoroughly; **de f. en comble** from top to bottom; **de f.** (course) long-distance; (bruit) background-.

fondamental, -aux [fɔ̃damɑ̃tal, -o] a fundamental, basic.

fond/er [fɔ̃de] vt (ville etc) to found; (commerce) to set up; (famille) to start; (se) **f. sur** to base (oneself) on; **être fondé à croire/etc** to be justified in thinking/etc; **bien fondé** well-founded. ◆**—ement** nm foundation. ◆**fondateur, -trice** nmf founder; – a (membre) founding, founder-. ◆**fondation** nf (création, œuvre) foundation (de of).

fond/re [fɔ̃dr] vt to melt; (métal) to smelt; (cloche) to cast; (amalgamer) Fig to fuse (avec with); **faire f.** (dissoudre) to dissolve; – vi to melt; (se dissoudre) to dissolve; **f. en larmes** to burst into tears; **f. sur** to swoop on; – **se f.** vpr to merge, fuse. ◆**—ant** a (fruit) which melts in the mouth. ◆**—ue** nf Culin fondue. ◆**fonderie** nf (usine) smelting works, foundry.

fonds [fɔ̃] **1** nm **un f. (de commerce)** a business. **2** nmpl (argent) funds. **3** nm (culturel etc) Fig fund.

font [fɔ̃] voir **faire**.

fontaine [fɔ̃tɛn] nf (construction) fountain; (source) spring.

fonte [fɔ̃t] nf **1** (des neiges) melting; (d'acier) smelting. **2** (fer) cast iron; **en f.** (poêle etc) cast-iron.

fonts [fɔ̃] nmpl **f. baptismaux** Rel font.

football [futbol] nm football, soccer. ◆**footballeur, -euse** nmf footballer.

footing [futiŋ] nm Sp jogging, jog-trotting.

forage [fɔraʒ] nm drilling, boring.

forain [fɔrɛ̃] a (marchand) itinerant; **fête foraine** (fun)fair.

forçat [fɔrsa] nm (prisonnier) convict.

force [fɔrs] nf force; (physique, morale) strength; (atomique etc) power; **de toutes ses forces** with all one's strength; **les forces armées** the armed forces; **de f.** by force, forcibly; **en f.** (attaquer, venir) in force; **cas de f. majeure** circumstances beyond one's control; **dans la f. de l'âge** in the prime of life; **à f. de** through sheer force of, by dint of. ◆**forc/er** vt (porte, fruits etc) to force; (attention) to force, compel; (voix) to strain; (sens) to stretch; **f. qn à faire** to force ou compel s.o. to do; – vi (y aller trop fort) to overdo it; – **se f.** vpr to force oneself (à faire to do). ◆**—é** a forced (de faire to do); **un sourire f.** a forced smile; **c'est f.** Fam it's inevitable ou obvious. ◆**—ément** adv inevitably, obviously; **pas f.** not necessarily.

forcené, -ée [fɔrsəne] a frantic, frenzied; – nmf madman, madwoman.

forceps [fɔrsɛps] nm forceps.

forcir [fɔrsir] vi (grossir) to fill out.

forer [fɔre] vt to drill, bore. ◆**foret** nm drill.

forêt [fɔre] nf forest. ◆**forestier, -ière** a forest-; – nm (garde) forester, Am (forest) ranger.

forfait [fɔrfɛ] nm 1 (prix) all-inclusive price; **travailler à f.** to work for a lump sum. 2 **déclarer f.** Sp to withdraw from the game. 3 (crime) Litt heinous crime. ◆**forfaitaire** a prix f. all-inclusive price.

forge [fɔrʒ] nf forge. ◆**forg/er** vt (métal, liens etc) to forge; (inventer) to make up. ◆**—é** a **fer f.** wrought iron. ◆**forgeron** nm (black)smith.

formaliser (se) [səfɔrmalize] vpr to take offence (de at).

formalité [fɔrmalite] nf formality.

format [fɔrma] nm format, size.

forme [fɔrm] nf (contour) shape, form; (manière, genre) form; pl (de femme, d'homme) figure; **en f. de** in the form of; **en f. d'aiguille/de poire/**etc needle-/pear-/etc shaped; **dans les formes** in due form; **en (pleine) f.** in good shape ou form, on form; **prendre f.** to take shape. ◆**formateur, -trice** a formative. ◆**formation** nf formation; (éducation) education, training. ◆**formel, -elle** a (structure, logique etc) formal; (démenti) categorical, formal; (preuve) positive, formal. ◆**formellement** adv (interdire) strictly. ◆**form/er** vt (groupe, caractère etc) to form; (apprenti etc) to train; – **se f.** vpr (apparaître) to form; (institution) to be formed. ◆**—é** a (personne) fully-formed.

formidable [fɔrmidabl] a tremendous.

formule [fɔrmyl] nf 1 formula; (phrase) (set) expression; (méthode) method; **f. de politesse** polite expression. 2 (feuille) form. ◆**formulaire** nm (feuille) form. ◆**formulation** nf formulation. ◆**formuler** vt to formulate.

fort¹ [fɔr] a strong; (pluie, mer) heavy;

(voix) loud; (fièvre) high; (femme, homme) large; (élève) bright; (pente) steep; (ville) fortified; (chances) good; **f. en** (maths etc) good at; **c'est plus f. qu'elle** she can't help it; **c'est un peu f.** Fam that's a bit much; **à plus forte raison** all the more reason; – adv **1** (frapper) hard; (pleuvoir) hard, heavily; (parler) loud; (serrer) tight; **sentir f.** to have a strong smell. **2** (très) Vieilli very; (beaucoup) Litt very much; – nm **son f.** one's strong point; **les forts** the strong; **au plus f. de** in the thick of. ◆**fortement** adv greatly; (frapper) hard.

fort² [fɔr] nm Hist Mil fort. ◆**forteresse** nf fortress.

fortifi/er [fɔrtifje] vt to strengthen, fortify; – **se f.** vpr (malade) to fortify oneself. ◆**—ant** nm Méd tonic. ◆**—é** a (ville, camp) fortified. ◆**fortification** nf fortification.

fortuit [fɔrtɥi] a (rencontre etc) chance-, fortuitous. ◆**fortuitement** adv by chance.

fortune [fɔrtyn] nf (argent, hasard) fortune; **avoir de la f.** to have (private) means; **faire f.** to make one's fortune; **de f.** (moyens etc) makeshift; **dîner à la f. du pot** to take pot luck. ◆**fortuné** a (riche) well-to-do.

forum [fɔrɔm] nm forum.

fosse [fos] nf (trou) pit; (tombe) grave; **f. d'aisances** cesspool.

fossé [fose] nm ditch; (douve) moat; (dissentiment) Fig gulf, gap.

fossette [fosɛt] nf dimple.

fossile [fɔsil] nm & a fossil.

fossoyeur [foswajœr] nm gravedigger.

fou (or **fol** before vowel or mute h), **folle** [fu, fɔl] a (personne, projet etc) mad, insane, crazy; (envie) wild, mad; (espoir) foolish; (rire) uncontrollable; (cheval, camion) runaway; (succès, temps) tremendous; **f. à lier** raving mad; **f. de** (musique, personne etc) mad ou wild ou crazy about; **f. de joie** wild with joy; – nmf madman, madwoman; – nm (bouffon) jester; Échecs bishop; **faire le f.** to play the fool.

foudre [fudr] nf la f. lightning; **coup de f.** Fig love at first sight. ◆**foudroy/er** vt to strike by lightning; Él to electrocute; (malheur etc) Fig to strike (s.o.) down. ◆**—ant** a (succès, vitesse etc) staggering. ◆**—é** a (stupéfait) thunderstruck.

fouet [fwe] nm whip; Culin (egg) whisk. ◆**fouetter** vt to whip; (œufs) to whisk; (pluie etc) to lash (face, windows etc); **crème fouettée** whipped cream.

fougère [fuʒɛr] nf fern.

fougue [fug] *nf* fire, ardour. ◆**fougueux, -euse** *a* fiery, ardent.

fouille [fuj] *nf* **1** (*archéologique*) excavation, dig. **2** (*de personne, bagages etc*) search. ◆**fouiller 1** *vti* (*creuser*) to dig. **2** *vt* (*personne, maison etc*) to search; — *vi* **f. dans** (*tiroir etc*) to rummage *ou* search through. **fouillis** [fuji] *nm* jumble.

fouine [fwin] *nf* (*animal*) stone marten. ◆**fouiner** *vi Fam* to nose about. ◆**-eur, -euse** *a Fam* nosy; – *nmf Fam* nosy parker.

foulard [fular] *nm* (head) scarf.

foule [ful] *nf* crowd; **en f.** in mass; **une f. de** (*objets etc*) a mass of; **un bain de f.** a walkabout.

foulée [fule] *nf Sp* stride; **dans la f.** *Fam* at one and the same time.

fouler [fule] *vt* to press; (*sol*) to tread; **f. aux pieds** to trample on; **se f. la cheville**/*etc* to sprain one's ankle/*etc*; **il ne se foule pas (la rate)** *Fam* he doesn't exactly exert himself. ◆**foulure** *nf* sprain.

four [fur] *nm* **1** oven; (*de potier etc*) kiln. **2 petit f.** (*gâteau*) (small) fancy cake. **3** *Th Cin* flop; **faire un f.** to flop.

fourbe [furb] *a* deceitful; – *nmf* cheat. ◆**fourberie** *nf* deceit.

fourbi [furbi] *nm* (*choses*) *Fam* stuff, gear, rubbish.

fourbu [furby] *a* (*fatigué*) dead beat.

fourche [furʃ] *nf* fork; **f. à foin** pitchfork. ◆**fourchette** *nf* **1** Culin fork. **2** (*de salaires etc*) Écon bracket. ◆**fourchu** *a* forked.

fourgon [furgɔ̃] *nm* (*camion*) van; (*mortuaire*) hearse; *Rail* luggage van, *Am* baggage car. ◆**fourgonnette** *nf* (small) van.

fourmi [furmi] *nf* **1** (*insecte*) ant. **2 avoir des fourmis** *Méd* to have pins and needles (**dans** in). ◆**fourmilière** *nf* anthill. ◆**fourmiller** *vi* **1** to teem, swarm (**de** with). **2** *Méd* to tingle.

fournaise [furnɛz] *nf* (*chambre etc*) *Fig* furnace.

fourneau, -x [furno] *nm* (*poêle*) stove; (*four*) furnace; **haut f.** blast furnace.

fournée [furne] *nf* (*de pain, gens*) batch.

fourn/ir [furnir] *vt* to supply, provide; (*effort*) to make; **f. qch à qn** to supply s.o. with sth; – *vi* **f. à** (*besoin etc*) to provide for; – **se f.** *vpr* to get one's supplies (**chez** from), shop (**chez** at). ◆**-i** *a* (*barbe*) bushy; **bien f.** (*boutique*) well-stocked. ◆**fournisseur** *nm* (*commerçant*) supplier. ◆**fourniture** *nf* (*action*) supply(ing) (**de** of); *pl* (*objets*) supplies.

fourrage [furaʒ] *nm* fodder.

fourrager [furaʒe] *vi Fam* to rummage (**dans** in, through).

fourreau, -x [furo] *nm* (*gaine*) sheath.

fourr/er [fure] **1** *vt* Culin to fill, stuff; (*vêtement*) to fur-line. **2** *vt Fam* (*mettre*) to stick; (*flanquer*) to chuck; **f. qch dans la tête de qn** to knock sth into s.o.'s head; **f. son nez dans** to poke one's nose into; – **se f.** *vpr* to put *ou* stick oneself (**dans** in). ◆**-é 1** *a* (*gant etc*) fur-lined; (*gâteau*) jam- *ou* cream-filled; **coup f.** (*traîtrise*) stab in the back. **2** *nm Bot* thicket. ◆**-eur** *nm* furrier. ◆**fourrure** *nf* (*pour vêtement etc, de chat etc*) fur.

fourre-tout [furtu] *nm inv* (*pièce*) junk room; (*sac*) holdall, *Am* carryall.

fourrière [furjɛr] *nf* (*lieu*) pound.

fourvoyer (se) [səfurvwaje] *vpr* to go astray.

foutre* [futr] *vt Arg* = **fiche(r)**. ◆**foutu** *a Arg* = **fichu 1.** ◆**foutaise** *nf Arg* rubbish, rot.

foyer [fwaje] *nm* (*domicile*) home; (*d'étudiants etc*) hostel; (*âtre*) hearth; (*lieu de réunion*) club; *Th* foyer; *Géom Phys* focus; **f. de** (*maladie etc*) seat of; (*énergie, lumière*) source of; **fonder un f.** to start a family.

fracas [fraka] *nm* din; (*d'un objet qui tombe*) crash. ◆**fracass/er** *vt*, — **se f.** *vpr* to smash. ◆**-ant** *a* (*nouvelle, film etc*) sensational.

fraction [fraksjɔ̃] *nf* fraction. ◆**fractionner** *vt*, — **se f.** *vpr* to split (up).

fracture [fraktyr] *nf* fracture; **se faire une f. au bras**/*etc* to fracture one's arm/*etc*. ◆**fracturer** *vt* (*porte etc*) to break (open); **se f. la jambe**/*etc* to fracture one's leg/*etc*.

fragile [fraʒil] *a* (*verre, santé etc*) fragile; (*enfant etc*) frail; (*équilibre*) shaky. ◆**fragilité** *nf* fragility; (*d'un enfant etc*) frailty.

fragment [fragmɑ̃] *nm* fragment. ◆**fragmentaire** *a* fragmentary, fragmented. ◆**fragmentation** *nf* fragmentation. ◆**fragmenter** *vt* to fragment, divide.

frais, fraîche [frɛ, frɛʃ] *a* (*poisson, souvenir etc*) fresh; (*temps*) cool, fresh, (*plutôt désagréable*) chilly; (*œufs*) new-laid, fresh; (*boisson*) cold, cool; (*peinture*) wet; (*date*) recent; **boire f.** to drink something cold *ou* cool; **servir f.** to serve chilled; – *nm* **prendre le f.** to get some fresh air; **il fait f.** it's cool; (*froid*) it's chilly; **mettre au f.** to put in a cool place. ◆**fraîchement** *adv* **1** (*récemment*) freshly. **2** (*accueillir etc*) coolly. ◆**fraîcheur** *nf* freshness; coolness;

chilliness. **fraîchir** vi (temps) to get cooler ou chillier, freshen.

frais [fre] nmpl expenses; (droits) fees; à mes f. at my expense; **faire des f.** to go to some expense; **faire les f.** to bear the cost (de of); j'en ai été pour mes f. I wasted my time and effort; **faux f.** incidental expenses; **f. généraux** running expenses, overheads.

fraise [frez] nf 1 (fruit) strawberry. 2 (de dentiste) drill. **fraisier** nm (plante) strawberry plant.

framboise [frɑ̃bwaz] nf raspberry. **framboisier** nm raspberry cane.

franc¹, franche [frɑ̃, frɑ̃ʃ] a 1 (personne, réponse etc) frank; (visage, gaieté) open; (net) clear; (cassure, coupe) clean; (vrai) Péj downright. 2 (zone) free; **coup f.** Fb free kick; **f. de port** carriage paid. **franchement** adv (honnêtement) frankly; (sans ambiguïté) clearly; (vraiment) really. **franchise** nf 1 frankness; openness; **en toute f.** quite frankly. 2 (exemption) Com exemption; **en f.** (produit) duty-free; '**f. postale**' 'official paid'. 3 (permis de vendre) Com franchise.

franc² [frɑ̃] nm (monnaie) franc.

France [frɑ̃s] nf France. **français, -aise** a French; – nmf Frenchman, Frenchwoman; **les F.** the French; – nm (langue) French.

franch/ir [frɑ̃ʃir] vt (fossé) to jump (over), clear; (frontière, seuil etc) to cross; (porte) to go through; (distance) to cover; (limites) to exceed; (mur du son) to break (through), go through. **issable** a (rivière, col) passable.

franc-maçon [frɑ̃masɔ̃] nm (pl francs-maçons) Freemason. **franc-maçonnerie** nf Freemasonry.

franco [frɑ̃ko] adv carriage paid.

franco- [frɑ̃ko] préf Franco-.

francophile [frɑ̃kɔfil] a & nmf francophile. **francophone** a French-speaking; – nmf French speaker. **francophonie** nf la f. the French-speaking community.

frange [frɑ̃ʒ] nf (de vêtement etc) fringe; (de cheveux) fringe, Am bangs.

frangin [frɑ̃ʒɛ̃] nm Fam brother. **frangine** nf Fam sister.

franquette (à la bonne) [alabɔnfrɑ̃kɛt] adv without ceremony.

frappe [frap] nf 1 (dactylographie) typing; (de dactylo etc) touch; **faute de f.** typing error. 2 **force de f.** Mil strike force. **frapp/er** vt (battre) to strike, hit; (monnaie) to mint; **f. qn** (surprendre, affecter) to

strike s.o.; (impôt, mesure etc) to hit s.o.; **frappé de** (horreur etc) stricken with; **frappé de panique** panic-stricken; – vi (à la porte etc) to knock, bang (à at); **f. du pied** to stamp (one's foot); – **se f.** vpr (se tracasser) to worry. **ant** a striking. **é** a (vin) chilled.

frasque [frask] nf prank, escapade.

fraternel, -elle [fratɛrnɛl] a fraternal, brotherly. **fraterniser** vi to fraternize (avec with). **fraternité** nf fraternity, brotherhood.

fraude [frod] nf Jur fraud; (à un examen) cheating; **passer qch en f.** to smuggle sth; **prendre qn en f.** to catch s.o. cheating. **fraud/er** vt to defraud; – vi Jur to commit fraud; (à un examen) to cheat (à in); **f. sur** (poids etc) to cheat on ou over. **eur, -euse** nmf Jur defrauder. **frauduleux, -euse** a fraudulent.

frayer [freje] vt (voie etc) to clear; **se f. un passage** to clear a way, force one's way (à travers, dans through).

frayeur [frejœr] nf fear, fright.

fredaine [frədɛn] nf prank, escapade.

fredonner [frədɔne] vt to hum.

freezer [frizœr] nm (de réfrigérateur) freezer.

frégate [fregat] nf (navire) frigate.

frein [frɛ̃] nm brake; **donner un coup de f.** to brake; **mettre un f. à** Fig to put a curb on. **frein/er** vi Aut to brake; – vt (gêner) Fig to check, curb. **age** nm Aut braking.

frelaté [frəlate] a (vin etc) Fig adulterated.

frêle [frɛl] a frail, fragile.

frelon [frəlɔ̃] nm (guêpe) hornet.

frémir [fremir] vi to shake, shudder (de with); (feuille) to quiver; (eau chaude) to simmer.

frêne [frɛn] nm (arbre, bois) ash.

frénésie [frenezi] nf frenzy. **frénétique** a frenzied, frantic.

fréquent [frekɑ̃] a frequent. **fréquemment** [-amɑ̃] adv frequently. **fréquence** nf frequency.

fréquent/er [frekɑ̃te] vt (lieu) to visit, frequent; (école, église) to attend; **f. qn** to see ou visit s.o.; – **se f.** vpr (fille et garçon) to see each other, go out together; (voisins) to see each other (mutually). **é** a très f. (lieu) very busy. **fréquentable** a peu f. (personne, endroit) not very commendable. **fréquentation** nf visiting; pl (personnes) company.

frère [frɛr] nm brother.

fresque [frɛsk] nf (œuvre peinte) fresco.

fret [frɛ] nm freight.

frétiller [fretije] vi (poisson) to wriggle; **f. de** (impatience) to quiver with; **f. de joie** to tingle with excitement.

fretin [frətɛ̃] nm menu **f**. small fry.

friable [frijabl] a crumbly.

friand [frijɑ̃] a **f. de** fond of, partial to. ◆**friandises** nfpl sweet stuff, sweets, Am candies.

fric [frik] nm (argent) Fam cash, dough.

fric-frac [frikfrak] nm (cambriolage) Fam break-in.

friche (en) [ɑ̃friʃ] adv fallow.

friction [friksjɔ̃] nf **1** massage, rub(-down); (de cheveux) friction. **2** (désaccord) friction. ◆**frictionner** vt to rub (down).

frigidaire® [friʒidɛr] nm fridge. ◆**frigo** nm Fam fridge. ◆**frigorifié** a (personne) Fam very cold. ◆**frigorifique** a (vitrine) refrigerated; (wagon) refrigerator-.

frigide [friʒid] a frigid. ◆**frigidité** nf frigidity.

frileux, -euse [frilø, -øz] a sensitive to cold, chilly.

frime [frim] nf Fam sham, show.

frimousse [frimus] nf Fam little face.

fringale [frɛ̃gal] nf Fam raging appetite.

fringant [frɛ̃gɑ̃] a (allure etc) dashing.

fringues [frɛ̃g] nfpl (vêtements) Fam togs, clothes.

frip/er [fripe] vt to crumple; — **se f.** vpr to get crumpled. ◆**—é** a (visage) crumpled, wrinkled.

fripier, -ière [fripje, -jɛr] nmf secondhand clothes dealer.

fripon, -onne [fripɔ̃, -ɔn] nmf rascal; — a rascally.

fripouille [fripuj] nf rogue, scoundrel.

frire* [frir] vti to fry; **faire f.** to fry.

frise [friz] nf Archit frieze.

fris/er [frize] **1** vti (cheveux) to curl, wave; **f. qn** to curl ou wave s.o.'s hair. **2** vt (effleurer) to skim; (accident etc) to be within an ace of; **f. la trentaine** to be close on thirty. ◆**—é** a curly. ◆**frisette** nf ringlet, little curl.

frisquet [friskɛ] am chilly, coldish.

frisson [frisɔ̃] nm shiver; shudder; **donner le f. à qn** to give s.o. the creeps ou shivers. ◆**frissonner** vi (de froid) to shiver; (de peur etc) to shudder (de with).

frit [fri] voir **frire** — a (poisson etc) fried. ◆**frites** nfpl chips, Am French fries. ◆**friteuse** nf (deep) fryer. ◆**friture** nf (matière) (frying) oil ou fat; (aliment) fried fish; (bruit) Rad Tél crackling.

frivole [frivɔl] a frivolous. ◆**frivolité** nf frivolity.

froid [frwa] a cold; **garder la tête froide** to keep a cool head; — nm cold; **avoir/prendre f.** to be/catch cold; **il fait f.** it's cold; **coup de f.** Méd chill; **jeter un f.** to cast a chill (dans over); **démarrer à f.** Aut to start (from) cold; **être en f.** to be on bad terms (avec with). ◆**froidement** adv coldly. ◆**froideur** nf (de sentiment, personne etc) coldness.

froisser [frwase] **1** vt, — **se f.** vpr (tissu etc) to crumple, rumple; **se f. un muscle** to strain a muscle. **2** vt **f. qn** to offend s.o.; **se f.** to take offence (de at).

frôler [frole] vt (toucher) to brush against, touch lightly; (raser) to skim; (la mort etc) to come within an ace of.

fromage [frɔmaʒ] nm cheese; **f. blanc** soft white cheese. ◆**fromager, -ère** a (industrie) cheese-; — nm (fabricant) cheesemaker. ◆**fromagerie** nf cheese dairy.

froment [frɔmɑ̃] nm wheat.

fronce [frɔ̃s] nf (pli dans un tissu) gather, fold. ◆**fronc/er** vt **1** (étoffe) to gather. **2 f. les sourcils** to frown. ◆**—ement** nm f. de sourcils frown.

fronde [frɔ̃d] nf **1** (arme) sling. **2** (sédition) revolt.

front [frɔ̃] nm forehead, brow; Mil Pol front; **de f.** (heurter) head-on; (côte à côte) abreast; (à la fois) (all) at once; **faire f. à** to face.

frontière [frɔ̃tjɛr] nf border, frontier; — a inv **ville/**etc **f.** border town/etc. ◆**frontalier, -ière** a border-, frontier-.

fronton [frɔ̃tɔ̃] nm Archit pediment.

frott/er [frɔte] vt to rub; (astiquer) to rub (up), shine; (plancher) to scrub; (allumette) to strike; **se f. à qn** (défier) to meddle with s.o., provoke s.o.; — vi to rub; (nettoyer, laver) to scrub. ◆**—ement** nm rubbing, Tech friction.

froufrou(s) [frufru] nm(pl) (bruit) rustling.

frousse [frus] nf Fam funk, fear; **avoir la f.** to be scared. ◆**froussard, -arde** nmf Fam coward.

fructifier [fryktifje] vi (arbre, capital) to bear fruit. ◆**fructueux, -euse** a (profitable) fruitful.

frugal, -aux [frygal, -o] a frugal. ◆**frugalité** nf frugality.

fruit [frɥi] nm fruit; **des fruits, les fruits** fruit; **porter f.** to bear fruit; **fruits de mer** seafood; **avec f.** fruitfully. ◆**fruité** a fruity. ◆**fruitier, -ière** a (arbre) fruit-; — nmf fruiterer.

frusques [frysk] nfpl (vêtements) Fam togs, clothes.

fruste [fryst] a (*personne*) rough.

frustr/er [frystre] vt f. qn to frustrate s.o.; f. qn de to deprive s.o. of. ◆—é a frustrated. ◆**frustration** nf frustration.

fuel [fjul] nm (fuel) oil.

fugace [fygas] a fleeting.

fugitif, -ive [fyʒitif, -iv] 1 nmf runaway, fugitive. 2 a (*passager*) fleeting.

fugue [fyg] nf 1 Mus fugue. 2 (*absence*) flight; **faire une f.** to run away.

fuir* [fɥir] vi to flee, run away; (*temps*) to fly; (*gaz, robinet, stylo etc*) to leak; — vt (*éviter*) to shun, avoid. ◆**fuite** nf (*évasion*) flight (de from); (*de gaz etc*) leak(age); (*de documents*) leak; **en f.** on the run; **prendre la f.** to take flight; **f. des cerveaux** brain drain; **délit de f.** Aut hit-and-run offence.

fulgurant [fylgyrã] a (*regard*) flashing; (*vitesse*) lightning-; (*idée*) spectacular, striking.

fulminer [fylmine] vi (*personne*) to thunder forth (contre against).

fumée [fyme] nf smoke; (*vapeur*) steam, fumes; pl (de vin) fumes. ◆**fum/er** vi to smoke; (*liquide brûlant*) to steam; (*rager*) Fam to fume; — vt to smoke. ◆—é a (*poisson, verre etc*) smoked. ◆—eur, -euse nmf smoker; **compartiment fumeurs** Rail smoking compartment. ◆**fume-cigarette** nm inv cigarette holder.

fumet [fyme] nm aroma, smell.

fumeux, -euse [fymø, -øz] a (*idée etc*) hazy, woolly.

fumier [fymje] nm manure, dung; (*tas*) dunghill.

fumigation [fymigasjɔ̃] nf fumigation.

fumigène [fymiʒɛn] a (*bombe, grenade etc*) smoke-.

fumiste [fymist] nmf (*étudiant etc*) time-waster, good-for-nothing. ◆**fumisterie** nf Fam farce, con.

funambule [fynãbyl] nmf tightrope walker.

funèbre [fynɛbr] a (*service, marche etc*) funeral-; (*lugubre*) gloomy. ◆**funérailles** nfpl funeral. ◆**funéraire** a (*frais, salon etc*) funeral-.

funeste [fynɛst] a (*désastreux*) catastrophic.

funiculaire [fynikylɛr] nm funicular.

fur et à mesure (au) [ofyreamzyr] adv as one goes along, progressively; **au f. et à m. que** as.

furent [fyr] voir être.

furet [fyrɛ] nm (*animal*) ferret. ◆**furet/er** vi to pry ou ferret about. ◆—eur, -euse a inquisitive, prying; — nmf inquisitive person.

fureur [fyrœr] nf (*violence*) fury; (*colère*) rage, fury; (*passion*) passion (de for); en f. furious; **faire f.** (*mode etc*) to be all the rage. ◆**furibond** a furious. ◆**furie** nf (*colère, mégère*) fury. ◆**furieux, -euse** a (*violent, en colère*) furious (contre with, at); (*vent*) raging; (*coup*) Fig tremendous.

furoncle [fyrɔ̃kl] nm Méd boil.

furtif, -ive [fyrtif, -iv] a furtive, stealthy.

fusain [fyzɛ̃] nm 1 (*crayon, dessin*) charcoal. 2 Bot spindle tree.

fuseau, -x [fyzo] nm 1 Tex spindle; **en f.** (*jambes*) spindly. 2 **f. horaire** time zone. 3 (*pantalon*) ski pants. ◆**fuselé** a slender.

fusée [fyze] nf rocket; (*d'obus*) fuse; **f. éclairante** flare.

fuselage [fyzlaʒ] nm Av fuselage.

fuser [fyze] vi (*rires etc*) to burst forth.

fusible [fyzibl] nm Él fuse.

fusil [fyzi] nm rifle, gun; (*de chasse*) shotgun; **coup de f.** gunshot, report; **un bon f.** (*personne*) a good shot. ◆**fusillade** nf (*tirs*) gunfire; (*exécution*) shooting. ◆**fusiller** vt (*exécuter*) to shoot; **f. qn du regard** to glare at s.o.

fusion [fyzjɔ̃] nf 1 melting; Phys Biol fusion; **point de f.** melting point; **en f.** (*métal*) molten. 2 (*union*) fusion; Com merger. ◆**fusionner** vti Com to merge.

fut [fy] voir être.

fût [fy] nm 1 (*tonneau*) barrel, cask. 2 (*d'arbre*) trunk. ◆**futaie** nf timber forest.

futé [fyte] a cunning, smart.

futile [fytil] a (*propos, prétexte etc*) frivolous, futile; (*personne*) frivolous; (*tentative, action*) futile. ◆**futilité** nf futility; pl (*bagatelles*) trifles.

futur, -ure [fytyr] a future; **future mère** mother-to-be; — nmf **f.** (mari) husband-to-be; **future (épouse)** wife-to-be; — nm future.

fuyant [fɥijɑ̃] voir **fuir**; — a (*front, ligne*) receding; (*personne*) evasive. ◆**fuyard** nm (*soldat*) runaway, deserter.

G

G, g [ʒe] nm G, g.
gabardine [gabardin] nf (tissu, imperméable) gabardine.
gabarit [gabari] nm (de véhicule etc) size, dimension.
gâcher [gɑʃe] vt 1 (gâter) to spoil; (occasion, argent) to waste; (vie, travail) to mess up. 2 (plâtre) to mix. ◆**gâchis** nm (désordre) mess; (gaspillage) waste.
gâchette [gɑʃɛt] nf (d'arme à feu) trigger; **une fine g.** (personne) Fig a marksman.
gadget [gadʒɛt] nm gadget.
gadoue [gadu] nf (boue) dirt, sludge; (neige) slush.
gaffe [gaf] nf (bévue) Fam blunder, gaffe.
◆**gaff/er** vi to blunder. ◆**—eur, -euse** nmf blunderer.
gag [gag] nm (effet comique) Cin Th (sight) gag.
gaga [gaga] a Fam senile, gaga.
gage [gaʒ] 1 nm (promesse) pledge; (témoignage) proof; (caution) security; **mettre en g.** to pawn. 2 nmpl (salaire) pay; **tueur à gages** hired killer, hitman.
gager [gaʒe] vt **g. que** Litt to wager that.
◆**gageure** [gaʒyr] nf Litt (impossible) wager.
gagn/er [gɑɲe] vt 1 (par le travail) to earn; (mériter) Fig to earn. 2 vt (par le jeu) to win; (réputation, estime etc) Fig to win, gain; **g. qn** to win s.o. over (à to); **g. une heure/etc** (économiser) to save an hour/etc; **g. du temps** (temporiser) to gain time; **g. du terrain/du poids** to gain ground/weight; – vi (être vainqueur) to win; **g. à être connu** to be well worth getting to know. 3 vt (atteindre) to reach; **g. qn** (sommeil, faim etc) to overcome s.o.; – vi (incendie etc) to spread, gain. ◆**—ant, -ante** a (billet, cheval) winning; – nmf winner. ◆**gagne-pain** nm inv (emploi) job, livelihood.
gai [ge] a (personne, air etc) cheerful, gay, jolly; (ivre) merry, tipsy; (couleur, pièce) bright, cheerful. ◆**gaiement** adv cheerfully, gaily. ◆**gaieté** nf (de personne etc) gaiety, cheerfulness, jollity.
gaillard [gajar] a vigorous; (grivois) coarse; – nm (robuste) strapping fellow; (type) Fam fellow. ◆**gaillarde** nf Péj brazen wench.

gain [gɛ̃] nm (profit) gain, profit; (avantage) Fig advantage; pl (salaire) earnings; (au jeu) winnings; **un g. de temps** a saving of time.
gaine [gɛn] nf 1 (sous-vêtement) girdle. 2 (étui) sheath.
gala [gala] nm official reception, gala.
galant [galɑ̃] a (homme) gallant; (ton, propos) Hum amorous; – nm suitor. ◆**galanterie** nf (courtoisie) gallantry.
galaxie [galaksi] nf galaxy.
galbe [galb] nm curve, contour. ◆**galbé** a (jambes) shapely.
gale [gal] nf **la g.** Méd the itch, scabies; (d'un chien) mange; **une (mauvaise) g.** (personne) Fam a pest.
galère [galɛr] nf (navire) Hist galley.
◆**galérien** nm Hist & Fig galley slave.
galerie [galri] nf 1 (passage, magasin etc) gallery; Th balcony. 2 Aut roof rack.
galet [galɛ] nm pebble, stone; pl shingle, pebbles.
galette [galɛt] nf 1 round, flat, flaky cake; (crêpe) pancake. 2 (argent) Fam dough, money.
galeux, -euse [galø, -øz] a (chien) mangy.
galimatias [galimatja] nm gibberish.
Galles [gal] nfpl **pays de G.** Wales. ◆**gallois, -oise** a Welsh; – nm (langue) Welsh; – nmf Welshman, Welshwoman.
gallicisme [galisism] nm (mot etc) gallicism.
galon [galɔ̃] nm (ruban) braid; (signe) Mil stripe; **prendre du g.** Mil & Fig to get promoted.
galop [galo] nm gallop; **aller au g.** to gallop; **g. d'essai** Fig trial run. ◆**galopade** nf (ruée) stampede. ◆**galop/er** vi (cheval) to gallop; (personne) to rush. ◆**—ant** a (inflation etc) Fig galloping.
galopin [galopɛ̃] nm urchin, rascal.
galvaniser [galvanize] vt (métal) & Fig to galvanize.
galvauder [galvode] vt (talent, avantage etc) to debase, misuse.
gambade [gɑ̃bad] nf leap, caper.
◆**gambader** vi to leap up ou frisk about.
gambas [gɑ̃bas] nfpl scampi.
gamelle [gamɛl] nf (de soldat) mess tin; (de campeur) billy(can).
gamin, -ine [gamɛ̃, -in] nmf (enfant) Fam

kid; – a playful, naughty. ◆**gaminerie** nf playfulness; (acte) naughty prank.

gamme [gam] nf Mus scale; (série) range.

gammée [game] af **croix g.** swastika.

gang [gɑ̃g] nm (de malfaiteurs) gang. ◆**gangster** nm gangster.

gangrène [gɑ̃grɛn] nf gangrene. ◆**se gangrener** [sɔgɑ̃grəne] vpr Méd to become gangrenous.

gangue [gɑ̃g] nf (enveloppe) Fig Péj outer crust.

gant [gɑ̃] nm glove; **g. de toilette** face cloth, cloth glove (for washing); **jeter/relever le g.** Fig to throw down/take up the gauntlet; **boîte à gants** glove compartment. ◆**ganté** a (main) gloved; (personne) wearing gloves.

garage [garaʒ] nm Aut garage; **voie de g.** Rail siding; Fig dead end. ◆**garagiste** nmf garage owner.

garant, -ante [garɑ̃, -ɑ̃t] nmf (personne) Jur guarantor; **se porter g. de** to guarantee, vouch for; – nm (garantie) guarantee. ◆**garantie** nf guarantee; (caution) security; (protection) Fig safeguard; **garantie(s)** (de police d'assurance) cover. ◆**garantir** vt to guarantee (**contre** against); **g. (à qn) que** to guarantee (s.o.) that; **g. de** (protéger) to protect from.

garce [gars] nf Péj Fam bitch.

garçon [garsõ] nm boy, lad; (jeune homme) young man; (célibataire) bachelor; **g. (de café)** waiter; **g. d'honneur** (d'un mariage) best man; **g. manqué** tomboy; de **g.** (comportement) boyish. ◆**garçonnet** nm little boy. ◆**garçonnière** nf bachelor flat ou Am apartment.

garde [gard] **1** nm (gardien) guard; Mil guardsman; **g. champêtre** rural policeman; **g. du corps** bodyguard; **G. des Sceaux** Justice Minister. **2** nf (d'enfants, de bagages etc) care, custody (**de** of); **avoir la g. de** to be in charge of; **faire bonne g.** to keep a close watch; **prendre g.** to pay attention (**à qch** to sth), be careful (**à qch** of sth); **prendre g. de ne pas faire** to be careful not to do; **mettre en g.** to warn (**contre** against); **mise en g.** warning; **de g.** on duty; (soldat) on guard duty; **monter la g.** to stand ou mount guard; **sur ses gardes** on one's guard; **g. à vue** (police) custody; **chien de g.** watchdog. **3** nf (escorte, soldats) guard.

garde-à-vous [gardavu] nm inv Mil (position of) attention. ◆**g.-boue** nm inv mudguard, Am fender. ◆**g.-chasse** nm (pl **gardes-chasses**) gamekeeper. ◆**g.-côte** nm (personne) coastguard. ◆**g.-fou** nm railing(s), parapet. ◆**g.-malade** nmf (pl

gardes-malades) nurse. ◆**g.-manger** nm inv (armoire) food safe; (pièce) larder. ◆**g.-robe** nf (habits, armoire) wardrobe.

garder [garde] vt (maintenir, conserver, mettre de côté) to keep; (vêtement) to keep on; (surveiller) to watch (over); (défendre) to guard; (enfant) to look after, watch; (habitude) to keep up; **g. qn** (retenir) to keep s.o.; **g. la chambre** to keep to one's room; **g. le lit** to stay in bed; – **se g.** vpr (aliment) to keep; **se g. de qch** (éviter) to beware of sth; **se g. de faire** to take care not to do. ◆**garderie** nf day nursery. ◆**gardeuse** nf **g. d'enfants** babysitter.

gardien, -ienne [gardjɛ̃, -jɛn] nmf (d'immeuble, d'hôtel) caretaker; (de prison) (prison) guard, warder; (de zoo, parc) keeper; (de musée) attendant; **g. de but** Fb goalkeeper; **gardienne d'enfants** child minder; **g. de nuit** night watchman; **g. de la paix** policeman; **g. de (libertés etc)** Fig guardian of; – am **ange g.** guardian angel.

gare [gar] **1** nf Rail station; **g. routière** bus ou coach station. **2** int **g. à** watch ou look out for; **g. à toi!** watch ou look out!; **sans crier g.** without warning.

garer [gare] vt (voiture etc) to park; (au garage) to garage; – **se g.** vpr (se protéger) to get out of the way (**de** of); Aut to park.

gargariser (se) [sɔgargarize] vpr to gargle. ◆**gargarisme** nm gargle.

gargote [gargɔt] nf cheap eating house.

gargouille [garguj] nf Archit gargoyle.

gargouiller [garguje] vi (fontaine, eau) to gurgle; (ventre) to rumble. ◆**gargouillis** nm gurgling; rumbling.

garnement [garnəmɑ̃] nm rascal, urchin.

garn/ir [garnir] vt (équiper) to furnish, fit out (**de** with); (magasin) to stock; (tissu) to line; (orner) to adorn (**de** with); (enjoliver) to trim (**de** with); (couvrir) to cover; Culin to garnish; – **se g.** vpr (lieu) to fill (up) (**de** with). ◆**-i** a (plat) served with vegetables; **bien g.** (portefeuille) Fig well-lined. ◆**garniture** nf Culin garnish, trimmings; pl Aut fittings, upholstery; **g. de lit** bed linen.

garnison [garnizõ] nf Mil garrison.

gars [gɑ] nm Fam fellow, guy.

gas-oil [gazwal] nm diesel (oil).

gaspill/er [gaspije] vt to waste. ◆**-age** nm waste.

gastrique [gastrik] a gastric. ◆**gastronome** nmf gourmet. ◆**gastronomie** nf gastronomy.

gâteau, -x [gɑto] nm cake; **g. de riz** rice pudding; **g. sec** (sweet) biscuit, Am cookie;

c'était du g. (facile) Fam it was a piece of cake.

gât/er [gɑte] vt to spoil; (plaisir, vue) to mar, spoil; — **se g.** vpr (aliment, dent) to go bad; (temps, situation) to get worse; (relations) to turn sour. ◆—**é** a (dent, fruit etc) bad. ◆**gâteries** nfpl (cadeaux) treats.

gâteux, -euse [gɑtø, -øz] a senile, soft in the head.

gauche[1] [goʃ] a (côté, main etc) left; — nf la g. (côté) the left (side); (Pol the left (wing); à g. (tourner etc) (to the) left; (marcher, se tenir) on the left(-hand) side; **de g.** (fenêtre etc) left-hand; (parti, politique etc) left-wing; à g. **de** on ou to the left of. ◆**gaucher, -ère** a & nmf left-handed (person). ◆**gauchisant** a Pol leftish. ◆**gauchiste** a & nmf Pol (extreme) leftist.

gauche[2] [goʃ] a (maladroit) awkward. ◆—**ment** adv awkwardly. ◆**gaucherie** nf awkwardness; (acte) blunder.

gauchir [goʃir] vti to warp.

gaufre [gofr] nf Culin waffle. ◆**gaufrette** nf wafer (biscuit).

gaule [gol] nf long pole; Pêche fishing rod.

Gaule [gol] nf (pays) Hist Gaul. ◆**gaulois** a Gallic; (propos etc) Fig broad, earthy; — nmpl les G. Hist the Gauls. ◆**gauloiserie** nf broad joke.

gausser (se) [sagose] vpr Litt to poke fun (de at).

gaver [gave] vt (animal) to force-feed; (personne) Fig to cram (de with); — **se g.** vpr to gorge ou stuff oneself (de with).

gaz [gɑz] nm inv gas; usine à g. gasworks; chambre/réchaud à g. gas chamber/stove; **avoir des g.** to have wind ou flatulence.

gaze [gɑz] nf (tissu) gauze.

gazelle [gɑzɛl] nf (animal) gazelle.

gazer [gɑze] **1** vi Aut Fam to whizz along; ça gaze! everything's just fine! **2** vt Mil to gas.

gazette [gɑzɛt] nf Journ newspaper.

gazeux, -euse [gɑzø, -øz] a (état) gaseous; (boisson, eau) fizzy. ◆**gazomètre** nm gasometer.

gazinière [gɑzinjɛr] nf gas cooker ou Am stove.

gazole [gɑzɔl] nm diesel (oil).

gazon [gɑzɔ̃] nm grass, lawn.

gazouiller [gɑzuje] vi (oiseau) to chirp; (bébé, ruisseau) to babble. ◆**gazouillis** nm chirping; babbling.

geai [ʒɛ] nm (oiseau) jay.

géant, -ante [ʒeɑ̃, -ɑ̃t] a & nmf giant.

Geiger [ʒɛʒɛr] nm compteur G. Geiger counter.

geindre [ʒɛ̃dr] vi to whine, whimper.

gel [ʒɛl] nm **1** (temps, glace) frost; (de crédits) Écon freezing. **2** (substance) gel. ◆**gel/er** vti to freeze; on gèle it's freezing here; — v imp il gèle it's freezing. ◆—**é** a frozen; (doigts) Méd frostbitten. ◆—**ée** nf frost; Culin jelly, Am jello; g. blanche ground frost.

gélatine [ʒelatin] nf gelatin(e).

gélule [ʒelyl] nf (médicament) capsule.

Gémeaux [ʒemo] nmpl les G. (signe) Gemini.

gém/ir [ʒemir] vi to groan, moan. ◆—**issement** nm groan, moan.

gencive [ʒɑ̃siv] nf Anat gum.

gendarme [ʒɑ̃darm] nm gendarme, policeman (soldier performing police duties). ◆**gendarmerie** nf police force; (local) police headquarters.

gendre [ʒɑ̃dr] nm son-in-law.

gène [ʒɛn] nm Biol gene.

gêne [ʒɛn] nf (trouble physique) discomfort; (confusion) embarrassment; (dérangement) bother, trouble; **dans la g.** Fin in financial difficulties. ◆**gên/er** vt (déranger, irriter) (troubler) to embarrass; (mouvement, action) to hamper, hinder; (circulation) Aut to hold up, block; **g. qn** (vêtement) to be uncomfortable on s.o.; (par sa présence) to be in s.o.'s way; **ça me gêne pas** I don't mind (si if); — **se g.** vpr (se déranger) to put oneself out; **ne te gêne pas pour moi!** don't mind me! ◆—**ant** a (objet) cumbersome; (présence, situation) awkward; (personne) annoying. ◆—**é** a (intimidé) embarrassed; (mal à l'aise) uneasy, awkward; (silence, sourire) awkward; (sans argent) short of money.

généalogie [ʒenealɔʒi] nf genealogy. ◆**généalogique** a genealogical; **arbre g.** family tree.

général, -aux [ʒeneral, -o] **1** a (global, commun) general; **en g.** in general. **2** nm (officier) Mil general. ◆**générale** nf Th dress rehearsal. ◆**généralement** adv generally; **g. parlant** broadly ou generally speaking. ◆**généralisation** nf generalization. ◆**généraliser** vti to generalize; — **se g.** vpr to become general ou widespread. ◆**généraliste** nmf Méd general practitioner, GP. ◆**généralité** nf generality; **la g. de** the majority of.

générateur [ʒeneratœr] nm, ◆**génératrice** nf Él generator.

génération [ʒenerasjɔ̃] nf generation.

généreux, -euse [ʒenerø, -øz] a generous (de with). ◆**généreusement** adv generously. ◆**générosité** nf generosity.

générique [ʒenerik] *nm Cin* credits.

genèse [ʒənɛz] *nf* genesis.

genêt [ʒənɛ] *nm* (*arbrisseau*) broom.

génétique [ʒenetik] *nf* genetics; – *a* genetic.

Genève [ʒənɛv] *nm ou f* Geneva.

génie [ʒeni] *nm* **1** (*aptitude, personne*) genius; **avoir le g. pour faire/de qch** to have a genius for doing/for sth. **2** (*lutin*) genie, spirit. **3 g. civil** civil engineering; **g. militaire** engineering corps. ◆**génial, -aux** *a* (*personne, invention*) brilliant; (*formidable*) *Fam* fantastic.

génisse [ʒenis] *nf* (*vache*) heifer.

génital, -aux [ʒenital, -o] *a* genital; **organes génitaux** genitals.

génocide [ʒenɔsid] *nm* genocide.

genou, -x [ʒ(ə)nu] *nm* knee; **être à genoux** to be kneeling (down); **se mettre à genoux** to kneel (down); **prendre qn sur ses genoux** to take s.o. on one's lap *ou* knee. ◆**genouillère** *nf Fb etc* knee pad.

genre [ʒɑr] *nm* **1** (*espèce*) kind, sort; (*attitude*) manner, way; **g. humain** mankind; **g. de vie** way of life. **2** *Littér Cin* genre; *Gram* gender; *Biol* genus.

gens [ʒɑ] *nmpl ou nfpl* people; **jeunes g.** young people; (*hommes*) young men.

gentil, -ille [ʒɑti, -ij] *a* (*agréable*) nice, pleasant; (*aimable*) kind, nice; (*mignon*) pretty; **g. avec qn** nice *ou* kind to s.o.; **sois g.** (*sage*) be good. ◆**gentillesse** *nf* kindness; **avoir la g. de faire** to be kind enough to do. ◆**gentiment** *adv* (*aimablement*) kindly; (*sagement*) nicely.

gentilhomme, *pl* **gentilshommes** [ʒɑtijɔm, ʒɑtizɔm] *nm* (*noble*) *Hist* gentleman.

géographie [ʒeɔgrafi] *nf* geography. ◆**géographique** *a* geographical.

geôlier, -ière [ʒolje, -jɛr] *nmf* jailer, gaoler.

géologie [ʒeɔlɔʒi] *nf* geology. ◆**géologique** *a* geological. ◆**géologue** *nmf* geologist.

géomètre [ʒeɔmɛtr] *nm* (*arpenteur*) surveyor.

géométrie [ʒeɔmetri] *nf* geometry. ◆**géométrique** *a* geometric(al).

géranium [ʒeranjɔm] *nm Bot* geranium.

gérant, -ante [ʒerɑ, -ɑt] *nmf* manager, manageress; **g. d'immeubles** landlord's agent. ◆**gérance** *nf* (*gestion*) management.

gerbe [ʒɛrb] *nf* (*de blé*) sheaf; (*de fleurs*) bunch; (*d'eau*) spray; (*d'étincelles*) shower.

gercer [ʒɛrse] *vti*, **— se g.** *vpr* (*peau, lèvres*) to chap, crack. ◆**gerçure** *nf* chap, crack.

gérer [ʒere] *vt* (*fonds, commerce etc*) to manage.

germain [ʒɛrmɛ̃] *a* **cousin g.** first cousin.

germanique [ʒɛrmanik] *a* Germanic.

germe [ʒɛrm] *nm Méd Biol* germ; *Bot* shoot; (*d'une idée*) *Fig* seed, germ. ◆**germer** *vi Bot & Fig* to germinate.

gésir [ʒezir] *vi* (*être étendu*) *Litt* to be lying; **il gît/gisait** he is/was lying; **ci-gît** here lies.

gestation [ʒɛstasjɔ̃] *nf* gestation.

geste [ʒɛst] *nm* gesture; **ne pas faire un g.** (*ne pas bouger*) not to make a move. ◆**gesticuler** *vi* to gesticulate.

gestion [ʒɛstjɔ̃] *nf* (*action*) management, administration. ◆**gestionnaire** *nmf* administrator.

geyser [ʒezɛr] *nm Géol* geyser.

ghetto [ɡeto] *nm* ghetto.

gibecière [ʒibsjɛr] *nf* shoulder bag.

gibier [ʒibje] *nm* (*animaux, oiseaux*) game.

giboulée [ʒibule] *nf* shower, downpour.

gicl/er [ʒikle] *vi* (*liquide*) to spurt, squirt; (*boue*) to splash; **faire g.** to spurt, squirt. ◆**—ée** *nf* jet, spurt. ◆**—eur** *nm* (*de carburateur*) *Aut* jet.

gifle [ʒifl] *nf* slap (in the face). ◆**gifler** *vt* **g. qn** to slap s.o., slap s.o.'s face.

gigantesque [ʒiɡɑtɛsk] *a* gigantic.

gigogne [ʒiɡɔɲ] *a* **table g.** nest of tables.

gigot [ʒiɡo] *nm* leg of mutton *ou* lamb.

gigoter [ʒiɡote] *vi Fam* to kick, wriggle.

gilet [ʒile] *nm* waistcoat, *Am* vest; (*cardigan*) cardigan; **g. (de corps)** vest, *Am* undershirt; **g. pare-balles** bulletproof jacket *ou Am* vest; **g. de sauvetage** life jacket.

gin [dʒin] *nm* (*eau-de-vie*) gin.

gingembre [ʒɛʒɑbr] *nm Bot Culin* ginger.

girafe [ʒiraf] *nf* giraffe.

giratoire [ʒiratwar] *a* **sens g.** *Aut* roundabout, *Am* traffic circle.

girl [ɡœrl] *nf* (*danseuse*) chorus girl.

girofle [ʒirɔfl] *nm* **clou de g.** *Bot* clove.

giroflée [ʒirɔfle] *nf Bot* wall flower.

girouette [ʒirwɛt] *nf* weathercock, weather vane.

gisement [ʒizmɑ] *nm* (*de minerai, pétrole*) *Géol* deposit.

gitan, -ane [ʒitɑ, -an] *nmf* (*Spanish*) gipsy.

gîte [ʒit] *nm* (*abri*) resting place.

giter [ʒite] *vi* (*navire*) to list.

givre [ʒivr] *nm* (hoar)frost. ◆**se givrer** *vpr* (*pare-brise etc*) to ice up, frost up. ◆**givré** *a* frost-covered.

glabre [ɡlabr] *a* (*visage*) smooth.

glace [ɡlas] *nf* **1** (*eau gelée*) ice; (*crème glacée*) ice cream. **2** (*vitre*) window; (*miroir*) mirror; (*verre*) plate glass.

glacer [glase] **1** vt (sang) Fig to chill; **g. qn** (transir, paralyser) to chill s.o.; **– se g.** vpr (eau) to freeze. **2** vt (gâteau) to ice, (au jus) to glaze; (papier) to glaze. **◆glaçant** a (attitude etc) chilling, icy. **◆glacé** a **1** (eau, main, pièce) ice-cold, icy; (vent) freezing, icy; (accueil) Fig icy, chilly. **2** (thé) iced; (fruit, marron) candied; (papier) glazed. **◆glaçage** nm (de gâteau etc) icing. **◆glacial, -aux** a icy. **◆glacier** nm **1** Géol glacier. **2** (vendeur) ice-cream man. **◆glacière** nf (boîte, endroit) icebox. **◆glaçon** nm Culin ice cube; Géol block of ice; (sur le toit) icicle.

glaïeul [glajœl] nm Bot gladiolus.

glaires [glɛr] nfpl Méd phlegm.

glaise [glɛz] nf clay.

gland [glɑ̃] nm **1** Bot acorn. **2** (pompon) Tex tassel.

glande [glɑ̃d] nf gland.

glander [glɑ̃de] vi Arg to fritter away one's time.

glaner [glane] vt (blé, renseignement etc) to glean.

glapir [glapir] vi to yelp, yap.

glas [glɑ] nm (de cloche) knell.

glauque [glok] a sea-green.

gliss/er [glise] vi (involontairement) to slip; (patiner, coulisser) to slide; (sur l'eau) to glide; **g. sur** (sujet) to slide ou gloss over; **ça glisse** it's slippery; **– vt** (introduire) to slip (dans into); (murmurer) to whisper; **se g. dans/sous** to slip into/under. **◆–ant** a slippery. **◆glissade** nf (involontaire) slip; (volontaire) slide. **◆glissement** nm (de sens) Ling shift; **g. à gauche** Pol swing ou shift to the left; **g. de terrain** Géol landslide. **◆glissière** nf groove; **porte à g.** sliding door; **fermeture à g.** zip (fastener), Am zipper.

global, -aux [global, -o] a total, global; **somme globale** lump sum. **◆–ement** adv collectively, as a whole.

globe [glɔb] nm globe; **g. de l'œil** eyeball.

globule [glɔbyl] nm (du sang) corpuscle.

gloire [gwar] nf (renommée, louange, mérite) glory; (personne célèbre) celebrity; **se faire g. de** to glory in; **à la g. de** in praise of. **◆glorieux, -euse** a (plein de gloire) glorious. **◆glorifier** vt to glorify; **se g. de** to glory in.

glossaire [glɔsɛr] nm glossary.

glouglou [gluglu] nm (de liquide) gurgle. **◆glouglouter** vi to gurgle.

glouton, -onne [glutɔ̃, -ɔn] a greedy, gluttonous; **– nmf** glutton. **◆gloutonnerie** nf gluttony.

gluant [glyɑ̃] a sticky.

glucose [glykoz] nm glucose.

glycérine [gliserin] nf glycerin(e).

glycine [glisin] nf Bot wisteria.

gnome [gnom] nm (nain) gnome.

gnon [ɲɔ̃] nm Arg blow, punch.

goal [gol] nm Fb goalkeeper.

gobelet [gɔblɛ] nm tumbler; (de plastique, papier) cup.

gober [gɔbe] vt (œuf, mouche etc) to swallow (whole); (propos) Fig to swallow.

godasse [gɔdas] nf Fam shoe.

godet [gɔdɛ] nm (récipient) pot; (verre) Arg drink.

goéland [gɔelɑ̃] nm (sea)gull.

gogo [gogo] nm (homme naïf) Fam sucker.

gogo (à) [agogo] adv Fam galore.

goguenard [gɔgnar] a mocking.

goguette (en) [ɑ̃gɔgɛt] adv Fam on the spree.

goinfre [gwɛ̃fr] nm (glouton) Fam pig, guzzler. **◆se goinfrer** vpr Fam to stuff oneself (de with).

golf [gɔlf] nm golf; (terrain) golf course. **◆golfeur, -euse** nmf golfer.

golfe [gɔlf] nm gulf, bay.

gomme [gɔm] nf **1** (substance) gum. **2** (à effacer) rubber, Am eraser. **◆gommé** a (papier) gummed. **◆gommer** vt (effacer) to rub out, erase.

gomme (à la) [alagɔm] adv Fam useless.

gond [gɔ̃] nm (de porte etc) hinge.

gondole [gɔ̃dɔl] nf (bateau) gondola. **◆gondolier** nm gondolier.

gondoler [gɔ̃dɔle] **1** vi, **– se g.** vpr (planche) to warp. **2 se g.** vpr (rire) Fam to split one's sides.

gonfl/er [gɔ̃fle] vt to swell; (pneu) to inflate, pump up; (en soufflant) to blow up; (poitrine) to swell out; (grossir) Fig to inflate; **– vi, – se g.** vpr to swell; **se g. de** (orgueil, émotion) to swell with. **◆–é** a swollen; **être g.** Fam (courageux) to have plenty of pluck; (insolent) to have plenty of nerve. **◆–able** a inflatable. **◆–ement** nm swelling. **◆–eur** nm (air) pump.

gong [gɔ̃g] nm gong.

gorge [gɔrʒ] nf **1** throat; (seins) Litt bust. **2** Géog gorge. **◆gorg/er** vt (remplir) to stuff (de with); **se g.** to stuff ou gorge oneself with. **◆–é** a **g. de** (saturé) gorged with. **◆–ée** nf mouthful; **petite g.** sip; **d'un seule g.** ou at one gulp.

gorille [gɔrij] nm 1 (animal) gorilla. 2 (garde du corps) Fam bodyguard.

gosier [gozje] nm throat, windpipe.

gosse [gɔs] nmf (enfant) Fam kid, youngster.

gothique [gɔtik] a & nm Gothic.

gouache [gwaʃ] nf (peinture) gouache.

goudron [gudrɔ̃] nm tar. ◆**goudronner** vt to tar.

gouffre [gufr] nm gulf, chasm.

goujat [guʒa] nm churl, lout.

goulasch [gulaʃ] nf Culin goulash.

goulot [gulo] nm (de bouteille) neck; **boire au g.** to drink from the bottle.

goulu, -ue [guly] a greedy; — nmf glutton. ◆**goulûment** adv greedily.

goupille [gupij] nf (cheville) pin.

goupiller [gupije] vt (arranger) Fam to work out, arrange.

gourde [gurd] nf 1 (à eau) water bottle, flask. 2 (personne) Péj Fam chump, oaf.

gourdin [gurdɛ̃] nm club, cudgel.

gourer (se) [sagure] vpr Fam to make a mistake.

gourmand, -ande [gurmã, -ãd] a fond of eating, Péj greedy; **g. de** fond of (sucreries) to have a sweet tooth; — nmf hearty eater, Péj glutton. ◆**gourmandise** nf good eating, Péj gluttony; pl (mets) delicacies.

gourmet [gurme] nm gourmet, epicure.

gourmette [gurmet] nf chain ou identity bracelet.

gousse [gus] nf g. **d'ail** clove of garlic.

goût [gu] nm taste; **de bon g.** in good taste; **prendre g. à qch** to take a liking to sth; **par g.** from ou by choice; **sans g.** tasteless. ◆**goûter** vt (aliment) to taste; (apprécier) to relish, enjoy; **g. à qch** to taste (a little of) sth; **g. de** (pour la première fois) to try out, taste; — vi to have a snack, have tea; — nm snack, tea.

goutte [gut] nf 1 drop. **couler g. à g.** to drip. 2 (maladie) gout. ◆**g.-à-goutte** nm inv Méd drip. ◆**gouttelette** nf droplet. ◆**goutter** vi (eau, robinet, nez) to drip (**de** from).

gouttière [gutjɛr] nf (d'un toit) gutter.

gouvernail [guvernaj] nm (pale) rudder; (barre) helm.

gouvernante [guvernɑ̃t] nf governess.

gouvernement [guvernəmã] nm government. ◆**gouvernemental, -aux** a (parti, politique etc) government.

gouvern/er [guverne] vti Pol & Fig to govern, rule. ◆**-ants** nmpl rulers. ◆**-eur** nm governor.

grabuge [grabyʒ] nm **du g.** (querelle) Fam a rumpus.

grâce [grɑs] nf (charme) & Rel grace; (avantage) favour; (miséricorde) mercy; **crier g.** to cry for mercy; **de bonne/mauvaise g.** with good/bad grace; **donner le coup de g. à** to finish off; **faire g. de qch à qn** to spare s.o. sth. 2 prép **g. à** thanks to. ◆**gracier** vt (condamné) to pardon.

gracieux, -euse [grasjø, -øz] a 1 (élégant) graceful; (aimable) gracious. 2 (gratuit) gratuitous; **à titre g.** free (of charge). ◆**gracieusement** adv gracefully; graciously; free (of charge).

gracile [grasil] a Litt slender.

gradation [gradɑsjɔ̃] nf gradation.

grade [grad] nm Mil rank; **monter en g.** to be promoted. ◆**gradé** nm Mil noncommissioned officer.

gradin [gradɛ̃] nm Th etc row of seats, tier.

graduel, -elle [graduɛl] a gradual.

graduer [gradue] vt (règle) to graduate; (exercices) to grade, make gradually more difficult.

graffiti [grafiti] nmpl graffiti.

grain [grɛ̃] nm 1 (de blé etc) & Fig grain; (de café) bean; (de chapelet) bead; (de poussière) speck; pl (céréales) grain; **le g.** (de cuir, papier) the grain; **g. de beauté** mole; (sur le visage) beauty spot; **g. de raisin** grape. 2 Mét shower.

graine [grɛn] nf seed; **mauvaise g.** (enfant) Péj bad lot, rotten egg.

graisse [grɛs] nf fat; (lubrifiant) grease. ◆**graissage** nm Aut lubrication. ◆**graisser** vt to grease. ◆**graisseux, -euse** a (vêtement etc) greasy, oily; (bourrelets, tissu) fatty.

grammaire [gramer] nf grammar. ◆**grammatical, -aux** a grammatical.

gramme [gram] nm gram(me).

grand, grande [grɑ̃, grɑ̃d] a big, large; (en hauteur) tall; (mérite, âge, chaleur, ami etc) great; (bruit) loud; (différence) wide, great, big; (adulte, mûr, plus âgé) grown up, big; (officier, maître) great; (âme) noble; le **g. air** the open air; **il est g. temps** it's high time (**que** that); — adv **g. ouvert** (yeux, fenêtre) wide-open; **ouvrir g.** to open wide; **en g.** on a grand ou large scale; — nmf Scol senior; (adulte) grown-up; **les quatre Grands** Pol the Big Four. ◆**grandement** adv (beaucoup) greatly (généreusement) grandly; **avoir g. de quoi vivre** to have plenty to live on. ◆**grandeur** nf (importance, gloire) greatness; (dimension) size, magni-

tude; (*majesté, splendeur*) grandeur; **g. nature** life-size; **g. d'âme** generosity.
grand-chose [grɑ̃ʃoz] *pron* **pas g.**-chose not
much. ◆**g.-mère** *nf* (*pl* **grands-mères**)
grandmother. ◆**grands-parents** *nmpl*
grandparents. ◆**g.-père** *nm* (*pl* **grands-
pères**) grandfather.
Grande-Bretagne [grɑ̃dbrətaɲ] *nf* Great
Britain.
grandiose [grɑ̃djoz] *a* grandiose, grand.
grandir [grɑ̃dir] *vi* to grow; (*bruit*) to grow
louder; — *vt* (*grossir*) to magnify; **g. qn**
(*faire paraître plus grand*) to make s.o.
seem taller.
grange [grɑ̃ʒ] *nf* barn.
granit(e) [granit] *nm* granite.
graphique [grafik] *a* (*signe, art*) graphic; —
nm graph.
grappe [grap] *nf* (*de fruits etc*) cluster; **g. de
raisin** bunch of grapes.
grappin [grapɛ̃] *nm* **mettre le g. sur** *Fam* to
grab hold of.
gras, grasse [grɑ, grɑs] *a* (*personne, ventre
etc*) fat; (*aliment*) fatty; (*graisseux*) greasy,
oily; (*caractère*) *Typ* bold, heavy; (*plante,
contour*) thick; (*rire*) throaty, deep; (*toux*)
loose, phlegmy; (*récompense*) rich; **matières grasses** fat; **foie g.** *Culin* foie gras, fatted
goose liver; — *nm* (*de viande*) fat. ◆**gras-
sement** *adv* (*abondamment*) handsomely.
◆**grassouillet, -ette** *a* plump.
gratifier [gratifje] *vt* **g. qn de** to present
ou favour s.o. with. ◆**gratification** *nf*
(*prime*) bonus.
gratin [gratɛ̃] *nm* **1 au g.** *Culin* baked with
breadcrumbs and grated cheese. **2** (*élite*)
Fam upper crust.
gratis [gratis] *adv* *Fam* free (of charge), gratis.
gratitude [gratityd] *nf* gratitude.
gratte-ciel [gratsjel] *nm inv* skyscraper.
gratte-papier [gratpapje] *nm* (*employé*) *Péj*
pen-pusher.
gratter [grate] *vt* (*avec un outil etc*) to scrape;
(*avec les ongles, les griffes etc*) to scratch;
(*boue*) to scrape off; (*effacer*) to scratch
out; **ça me gratte** *Fam* it itches, I have an
itch; — *vi* (*à la porte etc*) to scratch; (*tissu*)
to be scratchy; — **se g.** *vpr* to scratch oneself. ◆**grattoir** *nm* scraper.
gratuit [gratɥi] *a* (*billet etc*) free; (*hypothèse,
acte*) gratuitous. ◆**gratuité** *nf* **la g. de
l'enseignement**/*etc* free education/*etc*.
◆**gratuitement** *adv* free (of charge); gra-
tuitously.
gravats [grava] *nmpl* rubble, debris.
grave [grav] *a* serious; (*juge, visage*) grave,

solemn; (*voix*) deep, low; (*accent*) *Gram*
grave; **ce n'est pas g.!** it's not important!
◆**—ment** *adv* (*malade, menacé*) seriously;
(*dignement*) gravely.
grav/er [grave] *vt* (*sur métal etc*) to engrave;
(*sur bois*) to carve; (*disque*) to cut; (*dans sa
mémoire*) to imprint, engrave. ◆**—eur** *nm*
engraver.
gravier [gravje] *nm* gravel. ◆**gravillon** *nm*
gravel; *pl* gravel, (loose) chippings.
gravir [gravir] *vt* to climb (*with effort*).
gravité [gravite] *nf* **1** (*de la situation etc*) seriousness; (*solennité*) gravity. **2** *Phys* gravity.
graviter [gravite] *vi* to revolve (*autour de*
around). ◆**gravitation** *nf* gravitation.
gravure [gravyr] *nf* (*action, art*) engraving;
(*à l'eau forte*) etching; (*estampe*) print; (*de
disque*) recording; **g. sur bois** (*objet*) woodcut.
gré [gre] *nm* **à son g.** (*goût*) to his *ou* her
taste; (*désir*) as he *ou* she pleases; **de bon g.**
willingly; **contre le g. de** against the will of;
bon g. mal g. willy-nilly; **au g. de** (*vent etc*)
at the mercy of.
Grèce [gres] *nf* Greece. ◆**grec, grecque** *a*
& *nmf* Greek; — *nm* (*langue*) Greek.
greffe [gref] **1** *nf* (*de peau*) & *Bot* graft;
(*d'organe*) transplant. **2** *nm* *Jur* record office. ◆**greffer** *vt* (*peau etc*) & *Bot* to graft
(à on to); (*organe*) to transplant. ◆**greffier** *nm* clerk (of the court). ◆**greffon** *nm*
(*de peau*) & *Bot* graft.
grégaire [greger] *a* (*instinct*) gregarious.
grêle [grel] **1** *nf* *Mét* & *Fig* hail. **2** *a* (*fin*)
spindly, (very) slender *ou* thin. ◆**grêler** *v
imp* to hail. ◆**grêlon** *nm* hailstone.
grêlé [grele] *a* (*visage*) pockmarked.
grelot [grəlo] *nm* (small round) bell.
grelotter [grəlote] *vi* to shiver (**de** with).
grenade [grənad] *nf* **1** *Bot* pomegranate. **2**
(*projectile*) *Mil* grenade. ◆**grenadine** *nf*
pomegranate syrup, grenadine.
grenat [grəna] *a inv* (*couleur*) dark red.
grenier [grənje] *nm* attic; *Agr* granary.
grenouille [grənuj] *nf* frog.
grès [gre] *nm* (*roche*) sandstone; (*poterie*)
stoneware.
grésiller [grezije] *vi* *Culin* to sizzle; *Rad* to
crackle.
grève [grev] *nf* **1** strike; **g. de la faim** hunger
strike; **g. du zèle** work-to-rule, *Am*
rule-book slow-down; **g. perlée** go-slow,
Am slow-down (strike); **g. sauvage/sur le
tas** wildcat/sit-down strike; **g. tournante**
strike by rota. **2** (*de mer*) shore; (*de rivière*)
bank. ◆**gréviste** *nmf* striker.

gribouiller [gribuje] *vti* to scribble. ◆**gribouillis** *nm* scribble.

grief [grijɛf] *nm* (*plainte*) grievance.

grièvement [grijɛvmɑ̃] *adv* g. blessé seriously *ou* badly injured.

griffe [grif] *nf* **1** (*ongle*) claw; **sous la g. de qn** (*pouvoir*) in s.o.'s clutches. **2** (*de couturier*) (designer) label; (*tampon*) printed signature; (*d'auteur*) Fig mark, stamp. ◆**griffé** *a* (*vêtement*) designer-. ◆**griffer** *vt* to scratch, claw.

griffonn/er [grifɔne] *vt* to scrawl, scribble. ◆**-age** *nm* scrawl, scribble.

grignoter [griɲɔte] *vti* to nibble.

gril [gril] *nm* Culin grill, grid(iron). ◆**grillade** [grijad] *nf* (*viande*) grill. ◆**grille-pain** *nm inv* toaster. ◆**griller** *vt* (*viande*) to grill, broil; (*pain*) to toast; (*café*) to roast; (*ampoule*) El to blow; (*brûler*) to scorch; (*cigarette*) Fam to smoke; **un feu rouge** Aut Fam to drive through *ou* jump a red light; *– vi* **mettre à g.** to put on the grill; **on grille ici** Fam it's scorching; **g. de faire** to be itching to do.

grille [grij] *nf* (*clôture*) railings; (*porte*) (iron) gate; (*de fourneau, foyer*) grate; (*de radiateur*) Aut grid, grille; (*des salaires*) Fig scale; *pl* (*de fenêtre*) bars, grating; **g.** (**des horaires**) schedule. ◆**grillage** *nm* wire netting.

grillon [grijɔ̃] *nm* (*insecte*) cricket.

grimace [grimas] *nf* (*pour faire rire*) (funny) face, grimace; (*de dégoût, douleur*) grimace. ◆**grimacer** *vi* to grimace (de with).

grimer [grime] *vt*, **– se g.** *vpr* (*acteur*) to make up.

grimp/er [grɛpe] *vi* to climb (à qch up sth); (*prix*) Fam to rocket; *– vt* to climb. ◆**-ant** *a* (*plante*) climbing.

grinc/er [grɛse] *vi* to grate, creak; **g. des dents** to grind *ou* gnash one's teeth. ◆**-ement** *nm* grating; grinding.

grincheux, -euse [grɛ̃ʃø, -øz] *a* grumpy, peevish.

gringalet [grɛ̃galɛ] *nm* (*homme*) Péj puny runt, weakling.

grippe [grip] *nf* **1** (*maladie*) flu, influenza. **2 prendre qch/qn en g.** to take a strong dislike to sth/s.o. ◆**grippé** *a* **être g.** to have (the) flu.

gripper [gripe] *vi*, **– se g.** *vpr* (*moteur*) to seize up.

grippe-sou [gripsu] *nm* skinflint, miser.

gris [gri] *a* grey, Am gray; (*temps*) dull, grey; (*ivre*) tipsy; *– nm* grey. ◆**grisaille** *nf* (*de vie*) dullness, greyness, Am grayness. ◆**grisâtre** *a* greyish, Am grayish.

◆**griser** *vt* (*vin etc*) to make (s.o.) tipsy, intoxicate (s.o.); (*air vif, succès*) to exhilarate (s.o.). ◆**griserie** *nf* intoxication; exhilaration. ◆**grisonn/er** *vi* (*cheveux, personne*) to go grey. ◆**-ant** *a* greying.

grisou [grizu] *nm* (*gaz*) firedamp.

grive [griv] *nf* (*oiseau*) thrush.

grivois [grivwa] *a* bawdy. ◆**grivoiserie** *nf* (*propos*) bawdy talk.

Groenland [grɔɛnlɑ̃d] *nm* Greenland.

grog [grɔg] *nm* (*boisson*) grog, toddy.

grogn/er [grɔɲe] *vi* to growl, grumble (contre at); (*cochon*) to grunt. ◆**-ement** *nm* growl, grumble; grunt. ◆**grognon, -onne** *a* grumpy, peevish.

grommeler [grɔmle] *vti* to grumble, mutter.

gronder [grɔ̃de] *vi* (*chien*) to growl; (*tonnerre*) to rumble; *– vt* (*réprimander*) to scold. ◆**grondement** *nm* growl; rumble. ◆**gronderie** *nf* scolding.

gros, grosse [gro, gros] *a* big; (*gras*) fat; (*épais*) thick; (*effort, progrès*) great; (*fortune, somme*) large; (*bruit*) loud; (*averse, mer, rhume*) heavy; (*faute*) serious, gross; (*traits, laine, fil*) coarse; **g. mot** swear word; *– adv* **gagner g.** to earn big money; **risquer g.** to take a big risk; **en g.** (*globalement*) roughly; (*écrire*) in big letters; (*vendre*) in bulk, wholesale; *– nmf* (*personne*) fat man, fat woman; *– nm* **le g. de** the bulk of; **de g.** (*maison, prix*) wholesale.

groseille [grozɛj] *nf* (white *ou* red) currant; **g. à maquereau** gooseberry.

grossesse [grosɛs] *nf* pregnancy.

grosseur [grosœr] *nf* **1** (*volume*) size; (*obésité*) weight. **2** (*tumeur*) Méd lump.

grossier, -ière [grosje, -jɛr] *a* (*matière, tissu, traits*) coarse, rough; (*idée, solution*) rough, crude; (*instrument*) crude; (*erreur*) gross; (*personne, manières*) coarse, uncouth, rude; **être g. envers** (*insolent*) to be rude to s.o. ◆**grossièrement** *adv* (*calculer*) roughly; (*se tromper*) grossly; (*répondre*) coarsely, rudely. ◆**grossièreté** *nf* coarseness; roughness; (*insolence*) rudeness; (*mot*) rude word.

gross/ir [grosir] *vi* (*personne*) to put on weight; (*fleuve*) to swell; (*nombre, bosse, foule*) to swell, get bigger; (*bruit*) to get louder; *– vt* to swell; (*exagérer*) Fig to magnify; *– vti* (*verre, loupe etc*) to magnify; **verre grossissant** magnifying glass. ◆**-issement** *nm* increase in weight; swelling, increase in size; (*de microscope etc*) magnification.

grossiste [grosist] *nmf* Com wholesaler.

grosso modo [grosomɔdo] *adv* (*en gros*) roughly.

grotesque [grɔtɛsk] *a* (*risible*) ludicrous, grotesque.

grotte [grɔt] *nf* grotto.

grouill/er [gruje] **1** *vi* (*rue, fourmis, foule etc*) to be swarming (**de** with). **2 se g.** *vpr* (*se hâter*) *Arg* to step on it. ◆**—ant** *a* swarming (**de** with).

groupe [grup] *nm* group; **g. scolaire** (*bâtiments*) school block. ◆**groupement** *nm* (*action*) grouping; (*groupe*) group. ◆**grouper** *vt* to group (together); — **se g.** *vpr* to band together, group (together).

grue [gry] *nf* (*machine, oiseau*) crane.

grumeau, -x [grymo] *nm* (*dans une sauce etc*) lump. ◆**grumeleux, -euse** *a* lumpy.

gruyère [gryjɛr] *nm* gruyère (cheese).

gué [ge] *nm* ford; **passer à g.** to ford.

guenilles [gənij] *nfpl* rags (and tatters).

guenon [gənɔ̃] *nf* female monkey.

guépard [gepar] *nm* cheetah.

guêpe [gɛp] *nf* wasp. ◆**guêpier** *nm* (*nid*) wasp's nest; (*piège*) *Fig* trap.

guère [gɛr] *adv* (**ne**) ... **g.** hardly, scarcely; **il ne sort g.** he hardly *ou* scarcely goes out.

guéridon [geridɔ̃] *nm* pedestal table.

guérilla [gerija] *nf* guerrilla warfare. ◆**guérillero** *nm* guerrilla.

guér/ir [gerir] *vt* (*personne, maladie*) to cure (**de** of); (*blessure*) to heal; — *vi* to recover; (*blessure*) to heal; (*rhume*) to get better; **g. de** (*fièvre etc*) to get over, recover from. ◆**—i** *a* cured, better, well. ◆**guérison** *nf* (*de personne*) recovery; (*de maladie*) cure; (*de blessure*) healing. ◆**guérisseur, -euse** *nmf* faith healer.

guérite [gerit] *nf* *Mil* sentry box.

guerre [gɛr] *nf* war; (*chimique etc*) warfare; **en g.** at war (**avec** with); **faire la g.** to wage *ou* make war (**à** on, against); **g. d'usure** war of attrition; **conseil de g.** court-martial. ◆**guerrier, -ière** *a* (*chant, danse*) war-; (*nation*) war-like; — *nmf* warrior. ◆**guerroyer** *vi* *Litt* to war.

guet [gɛ] *nm* **faire le g.** to be on the look-out. ◆**guett/er** *vt* to be on the look-out for,

watch (out) for; (*gibier*) to lie in wait for. ◆**—eur** *nm* (*soldat*) look-out.

guet-apens [gɛtapɑ̃] *nm inv* ambush.

guêtre [gɛtr] *nf* gaiter.

gueule [gœl] *nf* (*d'animal, de canon*) mouth; (*de personne*) *Fam* mouth; (*figure*) *Fam* face; **avoir la g. de bois** *Fam* to have a hangover; **faire la g.** *Fam* to sulk. ◆**gueuler** *vti* to bawl (out). ◆**gueuleton** *nm* (*repas*) *Fam* blow-out, feast.

gui [gi] *nm* *Bot* mistletoe.

guichet [giʃɛ] *nm* (*de gare, cinéma etc*) ticket office; (*de banque etc*) window; *Th* box office, ticket office; **à guichets fermés** *Th Sp* with all tickets sold in advance. ◆**guichetier, -ière** *nmf* (*à la poste etc*) counter clerk; (*à la gare*) *Rail* ticket office clerk.

guide [gid] **1** *nm* (*personne, livre etc*) guide. **2** *nf* (*éclaireuse*) (girl) guide. **3** *nfpl* (*rênes*) reins. ◆**guider** *vt* to guide; **se g. sur** to guide oneself by.

guidon [gidɔ̃] *nm* (*de bicyclette etc*) handlebar(s).

guigne [giɲ] *nf* (*malchance*) *Fam* bad luck.

guignol [giɲɔl] *nm* (*spectacle*) = Punch and Judy show.

guillemets [gijmɛ] *nmpl* *Typ* inverted commas, quotation marks.

guilleret, -ette [gijrɛ, -ɛt] *a* lively, perky.

guillotine [gijɔtin] *nf* guillotine.

guimauve [gimov] *nf* *Bot Culin* marshmallow.

guimbarde [gɛ̃bard] *nf* (*voiture*) *Fam* old banger, *Am* (old) wreck.

guindé [gɛ̃de] *a* (*affecté*) stiff, stilted, stuck-up.

guingois (de) [dəgɛ̃gwa] *adv* askew.

guirlande [girlɑ̃d] *nf* garland, wreath.

guise [giz] *nf* **n'en faire qu'à sa g.** to do as one pleases; **en g. de** by way of.

guitare [gitar] *nf* guitar. ◆**guitariste** *nmf* guitarist.

guttural, -aux [gytyral, -o] *a* guttural.

gymnase [ʒimnɑz] *nm* gymnasium. ◆**gymnaste** *nmf* gymnast. ◆**gymnastique** *nf* gymnastics.

gynécologie [ʒinekɔlɔʒi] *nf* gynaecology, *Am* gynecology. ◆**gynécologue** *nmf* gynaecologist, *Am* gynecologist.

H

H, h [aʃ] *nm* H, h; **l'heure H** zero hour; **bombe H** H-bomb.

ha! [ʼa] *int* ah!, oh!; **ha, ha!** (*rire*) ha-ha!

habile [abil] *a* clever, skilful (à qch at sth, à faire at doing). ◆**habilement** *adv* cleverly, skilfully. ◆**habileté** *nf* skill, ability.

habill/er [abije] *vt* to dress (de in); (*fournir en vêtements*) to clothe; (*couvrir*) to cover (de with); **h. qn en soldat**/*etc* (*déguiser*) to dress s.o. up as a soldier/*etc*; **— s'h.** *vpr* to dress (oneself), get dressed; (*avec élégance, se déguiser*) to dress up. ◆**—é** *a* dressed (de in); (*costume, robe*) smart, dressy. ◆**—ement** *nm* (*vêtements*) clothing, clothes.

habit [abi] *nm* costume, outfit; (*tenue de soirée*) evening dress, tails; *pl* (*vêtements*) clothes.

habit/er [abite] *vi* to live (à, en, dans in); — *vt* (*maison, région*) to live in; (*planète*) to inhabit. ◆**—ant, -ante** *nmf* (*de pays etc*) inhabitant; (*de maison*) resident, occupant. ◆**—é** *a* (*région*) inhabited; (*maison*) occupied. ◆**—able** *a* (in)habitable. ◆**habitat** *nm* (*d'animal, de plante*) habitat; (*conditions*) housing, living conditions. ◆**habitation** *nf* house, dwelling; (*action de résider*) living.

habitude [abityd] *nf* habit; **avoir l'h. de qch** to be used to sth; **avoir l'h. de faire** to be used to doing, be in the habit of doing; **prendre l'h. de faire** to get into the habit of doing; **d'h.** usually; **comme d'h.** as usual. ◆**habituel, -elle** *a* usual, customary. ◆**habituellement** *adv* usually. ◆**habitu/er** *vt* **h. qn à** to accustom s.o. to; **être habitué à** to be used *ou* accustomed to; **— s'h.** *vpr* to get accustomed (à to). ◆**—é, -ée** *nmf* regular (customer *ou* visitor).

hache [ʼaʃ] *nf* axe, *Am* ax. ◆**hachette** *nf* hatchet.

hach/er [ʼaʃe] *vt* (*au couteau*) to chop (up); (*avec un appareil*) to mince, *Am* grind; (*déchiqueter*) to cut to pieces. ◆**—é** *a* **1** (*viande*) minced, *Am* ground; chopped. **2** (*style*) staccato, broken. ◆**hachis** *nm* (*viande*) mince, minced *ou Am* ground meat. ◆**hachoir** *nm* (*couteau*) chopper; (*appareil*) mincer, *Am* grinder.

hagard [ʼagar] *a* wild-looking, frantic.

haie [ʼɛ] *nf* (*clôture*) *Bot* hedge; (*rangée*) row; (*de coureur*) *Sp* hurdle; (*de chevaux*) *Sp* fence, hurdle; **course de haies** (*coureurs*) hurdle race; (*chevaux*) steeplechase.

haillons [ʼajɔ̃] *nmpl* rags (and tatters).

haine [ʼɛn] *nf* hatred, hate. ◆**haineux, -euse** *a* full of hatred.

haïr [ʼair] *vt* to hate. ◆**haïssable** *a* hateful, detestable.

hâle [ʼal] *nm* suntan. ◆**hâlé** *a* (*par le soleil*) suntanned; (*par l'air*) weather-beaten.

haleine [alɛn] *nf* breath; **hors d'h.** out of breath; **perdre h.** to get out of breath; **reprendre h.** to get one's breath back, catch one's breath; (*de longue h.* (*travail*) long-term; **tenir en h.** to hold in suspense.

hal/er [ʼale] *vt Nau* to tow. ◆**—age** *nm* towing; **chemin de h.** towpath.

halet/er [ʼalte] *vi* to pant, gasp. ◆**—ant** *a* panting, gasping.

hall [ʼol] *nm* (*de gare*) main hall, concourse; (*d'hôtel*) lobby, hall; (*de maison*) hall(way).

halle [ʼal] *nf* (covered) market; **les halles** the central food market.

hallucination [alysinasjɔ̃] *nf* hallucination. ◆**hallucinant** *a* extraordinary.

halo [ʼalo] *nm* (*auréole*) halo.

halte [ʼalt] *nf* (*arrêt*) stop, *Mil* halt; (*lieu*) stopping place, *Mil* halting place; **faire h.** to stop; — *int* stop!, *Mil* halt!

haltère [altɛr] *nm* (*poids*) *Sp* dumbbell. ◆**haltérophilie** *nf* weight lifting.

hamac [ʼamak] *nm* hammock.

hameau, -x [ʼamo] *nm* hamlet.

hameçon [amsɔ̃] *nm* (*fish*) hook; **mordre à l'h.** *Pêche* & *Fig* to rise to *ou* swallow the bait.

hamster [ʼamster] *nm* hamster.

hanche [ʼɑ̃ʃ] *nf Anat* hip.

hand(-)ball [ʼɑdbal] *nm Sp* handball.

handicap [ʼɑ̃dikap] *nm* (*désavantage*) & *Sp* handicap. ◆**handicap/er** *vt* to handicap. ◆**—é, -ée** *a* & *nmf* handicapped (person); **h. moteur** spastic.

hangar [ʼɑ̃gar] *nm* (*entrepôt*) shed; (*pour avions*) hangar.

hanneton [ʼantɔ̃] *nm* (*insecte*) cockchafer.

hanter [ʼɑ̃te] *vt* to haunt.

hantise [ʼɑ̃tiz] *nf* **la h. de** an obsession with.

happer ['ape] *vt* (*saisir*) to catch, snatch; (*par la gueule*) to snap up.

haras ['ɑrɑ] *nm* stud farm.

harasser ['arase] *vt* to exhaust.

harceler ['arsəle] *vt* to harass, torment (**de** with). ◆**harcèlement** *nm* harassment.

hardi ['ardi] *a* bold, daring. ◆**—ment** *adv* boldly. ◆**hardiesse** *nf* boldness, daring; **une h.** (*action*) *Litt* an audacity.

harem ['arɛm] *nm* harem.

hareng ['arɑ̃] *nm* herring.

hargne ['arɲ] *nf* aggressive bad temper. ◆**hargneux, -euse** *a* bad-tempered, aggressive.

haricot ['ariko] *nm* (*blanc*) (haricot) bean; (*vert*) French bean, green bean.

harmonica [armɔnika] *nm* harmonica, mouthorgan.

harmonie [armɔni] *nf* harmony. ◆**harmonieux, -euse** *a* harmonious. ◆**harmonique** *a* & *nm* *Mus* harmonic. ◆**harmoniser** *vt*, — **s'h.** *vpr* to harmonize. ◆**harmonium** *nm* *Mus* harmonium.

harnacher ['arnaʃe] *vt* (*cheval etc*) to harness. ◆**harnais** (*de cheval, bébé*) harness.

harpe ['arp] *nf* harp. ◆**harpiste** *nmf* harpist.

harpon ['arpɔ̃] *nm* harpoon. ◆**harponner** *vt* (*baleine*) to harpoon; **h. qn** (*arrêter*) *Fam* to waylay s.o.

hasard ['azar] *nm* **le h.** chance; **un h.** (*coïncidence*) a coincidence; **un heureux h.** a stroke of luck; **un malheureux h.** a rotten piece of luck; **par h.** by chance; **si par h.** if by any chance; **au h.** at random, haphazardly; **à tout h.** just in case; **les hasards de** (*risques*) the hazards of. ◆**hasard/er** *vt* (*remarque, démarche*) to venture, hazard; (*vie, réputation*) to risk; **se h. dans** to venture into; **se h. à faire** to risk doing, venture to do. ◆**—é** *a*, ◆**hasardeux, -euse** *a* risky, hazardous.

haschisch ['aʃiʃ] *nm* hashish.

hâte ['at] *nf* haste, speed; (*impatience*) eagerness; **en h., à la h.** hurriedly, in a hurry, in haste; **avoir h. de faire** (*désireux*) to be eager to do, be in a hurry to do. ◆**hâter** *vt* (*pas, départ*) to hasten; — **se h.** *vpr* to hurry, make haste (**de faire** to do). ◆**hâtif, -ive** *a* hasty, hurried; (*développement*) precocious; (*fruit*) early.

hausse ['os] *nf* rise (**de** in); **en h.** rising. ◆**hausser** *vt* (*prix, voix etc*) to raise; (*épaules*) to shrug; **se h. sur la pointe des pieds** to stand on tip-toe.

haut ['o] *a* high; (*de taille*) tall; (*classes*) upper, higher; (*fonctionnaire etc*) high-ranking; **le h. Rhin** the upper Rhine; **la haute couture** high fashion; **à haute voix** aloud, in a loud voice; **h. de 5 mètres** metres high *ou* tall; — *adv* (*voler, viser etc*) high (up); (*estimer*) highly; (*parler*) loud, loudly; **tout h.** (*lire, penser*) aloud, out loud; **h. placé** (*personne*) in a high position; **plus h.** (*dans un texte*) above, further back; — *nm* (*partie haute*) top; **en h. de** at the top of; **en h.** (*loger*) upstairs; (*regarder*) up; (*mettre*) on (the) top; **d'en h.** (*de la partie haute, du ciel etc*) from high up, from up above; **avoir 5 mètres de h.** to be 5 metres high *ou* tall; **des hauts et des bas** *Fig* ups and downs.

hautain ['otɛ̃] *a* haughty.

hautbois ['obwa] *nm* *Mus* oboe.

haut-de-forme ['odfɔrm] *nm* (*pl* **hauts-de-forme**) top hat.

hautement ['otmɑ̃] *adv* (*tout à fait, très*) highly. ◆**hauteur** *nf* height; *Géog* hill; (*orgueil*) *Péj* haughtiness; *Mus* pitch; **à la h. de** (*objet*) level with; (*rue*) opposite; (*situation*) *Fig* equal to; **il n'est pas à la h.** he isn't up to it; **saut en h.** *Sp* high jump.

haut-le-cœur ['olkœr] *nm inv* **avoir des h.-le-cœur** to reach, gag.

haut-le-corps ['olkɔr] *nm inv* (*sursaut*) sudden start, jump.

haut-parleur ['oparlœr] *nm* loudspeaker.

hâve ['av] *a* gaunt, emaciated.

havre ['avr] *nm* (*refuge*) *Litt* haven.

Haye (La) [la'ɛ] *nf* The Hague.

hayon ['ɛjɔ̃] *nm* (*porte*) *Aut* tailgate, hatchback.

hé! [e] *int* **h.** (*là*) (*appel*) hey!; **hé! hé!** well, well!

hebdomadaire [ɛbdɔmadɛr] *a* weekly; — *nm* (*publication*) weekly.

héberg/er [ebɛrʒe] *vt* to put up, accommodate. ◆**—ement** *nm* accommodation; **centre d'h.** shelter.

hébété [ebete] *a* dazed, stupefied.

hébreu, -x [ebrø] *am* Hebrew; — *nm* (*langue*) Hebrew. ◆**hébraïque** *a* Hebrew.

hécatombe [ekatɔ̃b] *nf* (*great*) slaughter.

hectare [ɛktar] *nm* hectare (= 2.47 acres).

hégémonie [eʒemɔni] *nf* hegemony, supremacy.

hein! [ɛ̃] *int* (*surprise, interrogation etc*) eh!

hélas! ['elas] *int* alas!, unfortunately.

héler [ele] *vt* (*taxi etc*) to hail.

hélice [elis] *nf* *Av Nau* propeller.

hélicoptère [elikɔptɛr] *nm* helicopter. ◆**héliport** *nm* heliport.

hellénique [elenik] *a* Hellenic, Greek.

helvétique [elvetik] *a* Swiss.

hem! ['ɛm] *int* (a)hem!, hm!

hémicycle [emisikl] *nm* semicircle; *Pol Fig* French National Assembly.

hémisphère [emisfɛr] *nm* hemisphere.

hémorragie [emɔraʒi] *nf Méd* h(a)emorrhage; (*de capitaux*) *Com* outflow, drain.

hémorroïdes [emɔrɔid] *nfpl* piles, h(a)emorrhoids.

henn/ir ['enir] *vi* (*cheval*) to neigh. ◆—**issement** *nm* neigh.

hep! ['ɛp] *int* hey!, hey there!

hépatite [epatit] *nf* hepatitis.

herbe [ɛrb] *nf* grass; (*médicinale etc*) herb; mauvaise h. weed; fines herbes *Culin* herbs; en h. (*blés*) green; (*poète etc*) *Fig* budding. ◆**herbage** *nm* grassland. ◆**herbeux, -euse** *a* grassy. ◆**herbicide** *nm* weed killer. ◆**herbivore** *a* grass-eating, herbivorous. ◆**herbu** *a* grassy.

hercule [ɛrkyl] *nm* Hercules, strong man. ◆**herculéen, -enne** *a* herculean.

hérédité [eredite] *nf* heredity. ◆**héréditaire** *a* hereditary.

hérésie [erezi] *nf* heresy. ◆**hérétique** *a* heretical; — *nmf* heretic.

hériss/er ['erise] *vt* (*poils*) to bristle (up); h. qn (*irriter*) to ruffle s.o.'s feathers; — **se h.** *vpr* to bristle (up); to get ruffled. ◆—**é** *a* (*cheveux*) bristly; (*cactus*) prickly; h. de bristling with.

hérisson ['erisɔ̃] *nm* (*animal*) hedgehog.

hérit/er [erite] *vti* to inherit (**qch de qn** sth from s.o.); **h. de qch** to inherit sth. ◆—**age** *nm* (*biens*) inheritance; (*culturel, politique etc*) *Fig* heritage. ◆**héritier** *nm* heir. ◆**héritière** *nf* heiress.

hermétique [ɛrmetik] *a* hermetically sealed, airtight; (*obscur*) *Fig* impenetrable. ◆—**ment** *adv* hermetically.

hermine [ɛrmin] *nf* (*animal, fourrure*) ermine.

hernie ['ɛrni] *nf Méd* hernia, rupture; (*de pneu*) swelling.

héron ['erɔ̃] *nm* (*oiseau*) heron.

héros ['ero] *nm* hero. ◆**héroïne** [erɔin] *nf* **1** (*femme*) heroine. **2** (*stupéfiant*) heroin. ◆**héroïque** [erɔik] *a* heroic. ◆**héroïsme** [erɔism] *nm* heroism.

hésit/er [ezite] *vi* to hesitate (**sur** over, about; **à faire** to do); (*en parlant*) to falter, hesitate. ◆—**ant** *a* (*personne*) hesitant; (*pas, voix*) faltering, unsteady, wavering. ◆**hésitation** *nf* hesitation; **avec h.** hesitantly.

hétéroclite [eterɔklit] *a* (*disparate*) motley.

hétérogène [eterɔʒɛn] *a* heterogeneous.

hêtre ['ɛtr] *nm* (*arbre, bois*) beech.

heu! [ø] *int* (*hésitation*) er!

heure [œr] *nf* (*mesure*) hour; (*moment*) time; **quelle h. est-il?** what time is it?; **il est six heures** it's six (o'clock); (*expression, choix*) **six heures moins cinq** five to six; **six heures cinq** five past *ou Am* after six; **à l'h.** (*arriver*) on time; (*être payé*) by the hour; **dix kilomètres à l'h.** ten kilometres an hour; **à l'h. qu'il est** (by) now; **de dernière h.** (*nouvelle*) last minute; **de bonne h.** early; **à une h. avancée** at a late hour, late at night; **tout à l'h.** (*futur*) in a few moments, later; (*passé*) a moment ago; **à toute h.** (*continuellement*) at all hours; **faire des heures supplémentaires** to work *ou* do overtime; **heures creuses** off-peak *ou* slack periods; **l'h. d'affluence, l'h. de pointe** (*circulation etc*) rush hour; (*dans les magasins*) peak period; **l'h. de pointe** (*électricité etc*) peak period.

heureux, -euse [œrø, -øz] *a* happy; (*chanceux*) lucky, fortunate; (*issue, changement*) successful; (*expression, choix*) apt; **h. de qch/de voir qn** (*satisfait*) happy *ou* pleased *ou* glad about sth/to see s.o.; — *adv* (*vivre, mourir*) happily. ◆**heureusement** *adv* (*par chance*) fortunately, luckily, happily (**pour** for); (*avec succès*) successfully; (*exprimer*) aptly.

heurt [œr] *nm* bump, knock; (*d'opinions etc*) *Fig* clash; **sans heurts** smoothly. ◆**heurt/er** *vt* (*cogner*) to knock, bump, hit (**contre** against); (*mur, piéton*) to bump into, hit; **h. qn** (*choquer*) to offend s.o., upset s.o.; **se h. à** to bump into, hit; (*difficultés*) *Fig* to come up against. ◆—**é** *a* (*couleurs, tons*) clashing; (*style, rythme*) jerky. ◆**heurtoir** *nm* (*door*) knocker.

hexagone [ɛgzagɔn] *nm* hexagon; **l'H.** *Fig* France. ◆**hexagonal, -aux** *a* hexagonal; *Fig Fam* French.

hiatus [jatys] *nm Fig* hiatus, gap.

hiberner [iberne] *vi* to hibernate. ◆**hibernation** *nf* hibernation.

hibou, -x ['ibu] *nm* owl.

hic ['ik] *nm* **voilà le h.** *Fam* that's the snag.

hideux, -euse ['idø, -øz] *a* hideous.

hier [(i)jɛr] *adv & nm* yesterday; **h. soir** last *ou* yesterday night, yesterday evening; **elle n'est pas née d'h.** *Fig* she wasn't born yesterday.

hiérarchie ['jerarʃi] *nf* hierarchy. ◆**hiérarchique** *a* (*ordre*) hierarchical; **par la voie h.** through (the) official channels. ◆**hiérarchiser** *vt* (*emploi, valeurs*) to grade.

hi-fi ['ifi] *a inv & nf inv Fam* hi-fi.

hilare [ilar] a merry. ◆hilarant a (drôle) hilarious. ◆hilarité nf (sudden) laughter.

hindou, -oue [ɛ̃du] a & nmf Hindu.

hippie ['ipi] nmf hippie.

hippique [ipik] a un concours h. a horse show, a show-jumping event. ◆hippodrome nm racecourse, racetrack (for horses).

hippopotame [ipɔpɔtam] nm hippopotamus.

hirondelle [irɔ̃dɛl] nf (oiseau) swallow.

hirsute [irsyt] a (personne, barbe) unkempt, shaggy.

hispanique [ispanik] a Spanish, Hispanic.

hisser ['ise] vt (voile, fardeau etc) to hoist, raise; — se h. vpr to raise oneself (up).

histoire [istwar] nf (science, évènements) history; (récit, mensonge) story; (affaire) Fam business, matter; pl (ennuis) trouble; (façons, chichis) fuss; toute une h. (problème) quite a lot of trouble; (chichis) quite a lot of fuss; h. de voir/etc (so as) to see/etc; h. de rire for (the sake of) a laugh; sans histoires (voyage etc) uneventful. ◆historien, -ienne nmf historian. ◆historique a historical; (lieu, évènement) historic; — nm faire l'h. de to give an historical account of.

hiver [iver] nm winter. ◆hivernal, -aux a (froid etc) winter-.

HLM ['aʃɛlɛm] nm ou f abrév (habitation à loyer modéré) = council flats, Am = low-rent apartment building (sponsored by government).

hoch/er ['ɔʃe] vt h. la tête (pour dire oui) to nod one's head; (pour dire non) to shake one's head. ◆—ement nm h. de tête nod; shake of the head.

hochet ['ɔʃɛ] nm (jouet) rattle.

hockey ['ɔke] nm hockey; h. sur glace ice hockey.

holà! ['ɔla] int (arrêtez) hold on!, stop!; (pour appeler) hallo!; — nm inv mettre le h. à to put a stop to.

hold-up ['ɔldœp] nm inv (attaque) holdup, stick-up.

Hollande ['ɔlɑ̃d] nf Holland. ◆hollandais, -aise a Dutch; — nmf Dutchman, Dutchwoman; — nm (langue) Dutch.

holocauste [ɔlɔkost] nm (massacre) holocaust.

homard [ɔmar] nm lobster.

homélie [ɔmeli] nf homily.

homéopathie [ɔmeɔpati] nf hom(o)eopathy.

homicide [ɔmisid] nm murder, homicide; h. involontaire manslaughter.

hommage [ɔmaʒ] nm tribute, homage (à to); pl (civilités) respects; rendre h. à to pay (a) tribute to, pay homage to.

homme [ɔm] nm man; l'h. (espèce) man(kind); des vêtements d'h. men's clothes; d'h. à h. man to man; l'h. de la rue Fig the man in the street; h. d'affaires businessman. ◆h.-grenouille nm (pl hommes-grenouilles) frogman.

homogène [ɔmɔʒɛn] a homogeneous. ◆homogénéité nf homogeneity.

homologue [ɔmɔlɔg] nm an equivalent (de to); — nmf counterpart, opposite number.

homologuer [ɔmɔlɔge] vt to approve ou recognize officially, validate.

homonyme [ɔmɔnim] nm (personne, lieu) namesake.

homosexuel, -elle [ɔmɔsɛksɥɛl] a & nmf homosexual. ◆homosexualité nf homosexuality.

Hongrie ['ɔ̃gri] nf Hungary. ◆hongrois, -oise a & nmf Hungarian; — nm (langue) Hungarian.

honnête [ɔnɛt] a (intègre) honest; (satisfaisant, passable) decent, fair. ◆honnêtement adv honestly; decently. ◆honnêteté nf honesty.

honneur [ɔnœr] nm (dignité, faveur) honour; (mérite) credit; en l'h. de in honour of; faire h. à (sa famille etc) to be a credit to; (par sa présence) to do honour to; (promesse etc) to honour; (repas) to do justice to; en h. (roman etc) in vogue; invité d'h. guest of honour; membre d'h. honorary member; avoir la place d'h. to have pride of place ou the place of honour. ◆honorabilité nf respectability. ◆honorable a honourable; (résultat, salaire etc) Fig respectable. ◆honoraire 1 a (membre) honorary. 2 nmpl (d'avocat etc) fees. ◆honorer vt to honour (de with); h. qn (conduite etc) to do credit to s.o.; s'h. d'être to pride oneself ou itself on being. ◆honorifique a (titre) honorary.

honte ['ɔ̃t] nf shame; avoir h. to be ou feel ashamed (de qch/de faire of sth/to do, of doing); faire h. à to put to shame; fausse h. self-consciousness. ◆honteux, -euse a (déshonorant) shameful; (penaud) ashamed, shamefaced; être h. de to be ashamed of. ◆honteusement adv shamefully.

hop! ['ɔp] int allez, h.! jump!, move!

hôpital, -aux [ɔpital, -o] nm hospital; à l'h. in hospital, Am in the hospital.

hoquet ['ɔkɛ] nm hiccup; le h. (the) hiccups. ◆hoqueter vi to hiccup.

horaire [ɔrɛr] a (salaire etc) hourly; (vitesse) per hour; — nm timetable, schedule.

horde ['ɔrd] nf (troupe) Péj horde.

horizon [ɔrizɔ̃] nm horizon; (vue, paysage) view; à l'h. on the horizon.

horizontal, -aux [ɔrizɔ̃tal, -o] a horizontal. ◆—**ement** adv horizontally.

horloge [ɔrlɔʒ] nf clock. ◆**horloger, -ère** nmf watchmaker. ◆**horlogerie** nf (magasin) watchmaker's (shop); (industrie) watchmaking.

hormis ['ɔrmi] prép Litt save, except (for).

hormone [ɔrmɔn] nf hormone. ◆**hormonal, -aux** a (traitement etc) hormone-.

horoscope [ɔrɔskɔp] nm horoscope.

horreur [ɔrœr] nf horror; pl (propos) horrible things; faire h. à to disgust; avoir h. de to hate, loathe. ◆**horrible** a horrible, awful. ◆**horriblement** adv horribly. ◆**horrifiant** a horrifying, horrific. ◆**horrifié** a horrified.

horripiler [ɔripile] vt to exasperate.

hors ['ɔr] prép h. de (maison, boîte etc) outside, out of; (danger, haleine etc) Fig out of; h. de doute beyond doubt; h. de soi (furieux) beside oneself; être h. jeu Fb to be offside. ◆**h.-bord** nm inv speedboat; moteur h.-bord outboard motor. ◆**h.-concours** a inv non-competing. ◆**h.-d'œuvre** nm inv Culin starter, hors-d'œuvre. ◆**h.-jeu** nm inv Fb offside. ◆**h.-la-loi** nm inv outlaw. ◆**h.-taxe** a inv (magasin, objet) duty-free.

hortensia [ɔrtɑ̃sja] nm (arbrisseau) hydrangea.

horticole [ɔrtikɔl] a horticultural. ◆**horticulteur, -trice** nmf horticulturalist. ◆**horticulture** nf horticulture.

hospice [ɔspis] nm (pour vieillards) geriatric hospital.

hospitalier, -ière [ɔspitalje, -jɛr] a 1 (accueillant) hospitable. 2 (personnel etc) Méd hospital-. ◆**hospitaliser** vt to hospitalize. ◆**hospitalité** nf hospitality.

hostie [ɔsti] nf (pain) Rel host.

hostile [ɔstil] a hostile (à to, towards). ◆**hostilité** nf hostility (envers to, towards); pl Mil hostilities.

hôte [ot] 1 nm (maître) host. 2 nmf (invité) guest. ◆**hôtesse** nf hostess; h. de (de l'air) (air) hostess.

hôtel [otɛl] nm hotel; h. particulier mansion, town house; h. de ville town hall; h. des ventes auction rooms. ◆**hôtelier, -ière** nmf hotel-keeper, hotelier; — a (industrie etc) hotel-. ◆**hôtellerie** nf 1 (auberge) inn, hostelry. 2 (métier) hotel trade.

hotte ['ɔt] nf 1 (panier) basket (carried on back). 2 (de cheminée etc) hood.

houblon ['ublɔ̃] nm le h. Bot hops.

houille ['uj] nf coal; h. blanche hydro-electric power. ◆**houiller, -ère** a (bassin, industrie) coal-; — nf coalmine, colliery.

houle ['ul] nf (de mer) swell, surge. ◆**houleux, -euse** a (mer) rough; (réunion etc) Fig stormy.

houppette ['upɛt] nf powder puff.

hourra ['ura] nm & int hurray, hurrah.

houspiller ['uspije] vt to scold, upbraid.

housse ['us] nf (protective) cover.

houx ['u] nm holly.

hublot ['yblo] nm Nau Av porthole.

huche ['yʃ] nf h. à pain bread box ou chest.

hue! ['y] int gee up! (to horse).

huer ['ɥe] vt to boo. ◆**huées** nfpl boos.

huile [ɥil] nf 1 oil; peinture à l'h. oil painting. 2 (personnage) Fam big shot. ◆**huiler** vt to oil. ◆**huileux, -euse** a oily.

huis [ɥi] nm à h. clos Jur in camera.

huissier [ɥisje] nm (introducteur) usher; (officier) Jur bailiff.

huit ['ɥit] a (['ɥi] before consonant) eight; h. jours a week; — nm eight. ◆**huitaine** nf (about) eight; (semaine) week. ◆**huitième** a & nmf eighth; un h. an eighth.

huître [ɥitr] nf oyster.

hululer ['ylyle] vi (hibou) to hoot.

humain [ymɛ̃] a human; (compatissant) humane; — nmpl humans. ◆**humainement** adv (possible etc) humanly; (avec humanité) humanely. ◆**humaniser** vt (prison, ville etc) to humanize, make more humane. ◆**humanitaire** a humanitarian. ◆**humanité** nf (genre humain, sentiment) humanity.

humble [œbl] a humble. ◆**humblement** adv humbly.

humecter [ymɛkte] vt to moisten, damp(en).

humer ['yme] vt (respirer) to breathe in; (sentir) to smell.

humeur [ymœr] nf (caprice) mood, humour; (caractère) temperament; (irritation) bad temper; bonne h. (gaieté) good humour; de bonne/mauvaise h. in a good/bad mood ou humour; égalité d'h. evenness of temper.

humide [ymid] a damp, wet; (saison, route) wet; (main, yeux) moist; climat/temps h. (chaud) humid climate/weather; (froid, pluvieux) damp ou wet climate/weather. ◆**humidifier** vt to humidify. ◆**humidité** nf humidity; (plutôt froide) damp(ness); (vapeur) moisture.

humili/er [ymilje] vt to humiliate, humble

◆—**ant** a humiliating. ◆**humiliation** nf humiliation. ◆**humilité** nf humility.

humour [ymur] nm humour; **avoir de l'h.** ou **beaucoup d'h.** ou **le sens de l'h.** to have a sense of humour. ◆**humoriste** nmf humorist. ◆**humoristique** a (livre, ton etc) humorous.

huppé ['ype] a (riche) Fam high-class, posh.

hurl/er ['yrle] vi (loup, vent) to howl; (personne) to scream, yell; — vt (slogans, injures etc) to scream. ◆—**ement** nm howl; scream, yell.

hurluberlu [yrlyberly] nm (personne) scatterbrain.

hutte ['yt] nf hut.

hybride [ibrid] a & nm hybrid.

hydrater [idrate] vt (peau) to moisturize; **crème hydratante** moisturizing cream.

hydraulique [idrolik] a hydraulic.

hydravion [idravjɔ̃] nm seaplane.

hydro-électrique [idrɔelektrik] a hydroelectric.

hydrogène [idrɔʒɛn] nm Ch hydrogen.

hydrophile [idrɔfil] a **coton h.** cotton wool, Am (absorbent) cotton.

hyène [jɛn] nf (animal) hyena.

hygiaphone [iʒjafon] nm (hygienic) grill.

hygiène [iʒjɛn] nf hygiene. ◆**hygiénique** a hygienic; (promenade) healthy; (serviette, conditions) sanitary; **papier h.** toilet paper.

hymne [imn] nm Rel Littér hymn; **h. national** national anthem.

hyper- [iper] préf hyper-.

hypermarché [ipermarʃe] nm hypermarket.

hypertension [ipertɑ̃sjɔ̃] nf high blood pressure.

hypnose [ipnoz] nf hypnosis. ◆**hypnotique** a hypnotic. ◆**hypnotiser** vt to hypnotize. ◆**hypnotiseur** nm hypnotist. ◆**hypnotisme** nm hypnotism.

hypocrisie [ipɔkrizi] nf hypocrisy. ◆**hypocrite** a hypocritical; — nmf hypocrite.

hypodermique [ipɔdermik] a hypodermic.

hypothèque [ipɔtɛk] nf mortgage. ◆**hypothéquer** (maison, avenir) to mortgage.

hypothèse [ipɔtɛz] nf assumption; (en sciences) hypothesis; **dans l'h. où . . .** supposing (that) . . . . ◆**hypothétique** a hypothetical.

hystérie [isteri] nf hysteria. ◆**hystérique** a hysterical.

I

I, i [i] nm I, i.

iceberg [isberg] nm iceberg.

ici [isi] adv here; **par i.** (passer) this way; (habiter) around here, hereabouts; **jusqu'i.** (temps) up to now; (lieu) as far as this ou here; **d'i. à mardi** by Tuesday, between now and Tuesday; **d'i. à une semaine** within a week; **d'i. peu** before long; **i. Dupont** Tél this is Dupont, Dupont here; **je ne suis pas d'i.** I'm a stranger around here; **les gens d'i.** the people (from) around here, the locals. ◆**i.-bas** adv on earth.

icône [ikon] nf Rel icon.

idéal, -aux [ideal, -o] a & nm ideal; **l'i.** (valeurs spirituelles) ideals; **c'est l'i.** Fam that's the ideal thing. ◆**idéalement** adv ideally. ◆**idéaliser** vt to idealize. ◆**idéalisme** nm idealism. ◆**idéaliste** a idealistic; — nmf idealist.

idée [ide] nf idea (**de** of, que that); **changer d'i.** to change one's mind; **il m'est venu à l'i. que** it occurred to me that; **se faire une i. de** (rêve) to imagine; (concept) to get ou have

an idea of; **avoir dans l'i. de faire** to have it in mind to do; **i. fixe** obsession.

idem [idem] adv ditto.

identifier [idɑ̃tifje] vt to identify (**à, avec** with). ◆**identification** nf identification. ◆**identique** a identical (**à** to, with). ◆**identité** nf identity; **carte d'i** identity card.

idéologie [ideɔlɔʒi] nf ideology. ◆**idéologique** a ideological.

idiome [idjom] nm (langue) idiom. ◆**idiomatique** a idiomatic.

idiot, -ote [idjo, -ɔt] a idiotic, silly; — nmf idiot. ◆**idiotement** adv idiotically. ◆**idiotie** [-ɔsi] nf (état) idiocy; **une i.** an idiotic ou silly thing.

idole [idɔl] nm idol. ◆**idolâtrer** vt to idolize.

idylle [idil] nf (amourette) romance.

idyllique [idilik] a (merveilleux) idyllic.

if [if] nm yew (tree).

igloo [iglu] nm igloo.

ignare [iɲar] a Péj ignorant; — nmf ignoramus.

ignifugé [iɲifyʒe] a fireproof(ed).

ignoble [iɲɔbl] a vile, revolting.

ignorant [iɲɔrɑ̃] a ignorant (**de** of). ◆**ignorance** nf ignorance. ◆**ignor/er** vt not to know, be ignorant of; **j'ignore si** I don't know if; **i. qn** (être indifférent à) to ignore s.o., cold-shoulder s.o. ◆**—é** a (inconnu) unknown.

il [il] pron (personne) he; (chose, animal) it; **il est he is; it is; il pleut** it's raining; **il est vrai que** it's true that; **il y a** there is; pl there are; **il y a six ans** (temps écoulé) six years ago; **il y a une heure qu'il travaille** (durée) he's been working for an hour; **qu'est-ce qu'il y a?** what's the matter?, what's wrong?; **il n'y a pas de quoi!** don't mention it!; **il doit/peut y avoir** there must/may be.

île [il] nf island; **les îles Britanniques** the British Isles.

illégal, -aux [ilegal, -o] a illegal. ◆**illégalité** nf illegality.

illégitime [ileʒitim] a (enfant, revendication) illegitimate; (non fondé) unfounded.

illettré, -ée [iletre] a & nmf illiterate.

illicite [ilisit] a unlawful, illicit.

illico [iliko] adv **i.** (presto) Fam straightaway.

illimité [ilimite] a unlimited.

illisible [ilizibl] a (écriture) illegible; (livre) unreadable.

illogique [ilɔʒik] a illogical.

illumin/er [ilymine] vt to light up, illuminate; — **s'i.** vpr (visage, personne, ciel) to light up. ◆**—é** a (monument) floodlit, lit up. ◆**illumination** nf (action, lumière) illumination.

illusion [ilyzjɔ̃] nf illusion (**sur** about); **se faire des illusions** to delude oneself. ◆**s'illusionner** vpr to delude oneself (**sur** about). ◆**illusionniste** nmf conjurer. ◆**illusoire** a illusory, illusive.

illustre [ilystr] a famous, illustrious.

illustr/er [ilystre] vt (d'images, par des exemples) to illustrate (**de** with); — **s'i.** vpr to become famous. ◆**—é** a (livre, magazine) illustrated; — nm (périodique) comic. ◆**illustration** nf illustration.

îlot [ilo] nm **1** (île) small island. **2** (maisons) block.

ils [il] pron they; **ils sont** they are.

image [imaʒ] nf picture; (ressemblance, symbole) image; (dans une glace) reflection; **i. de marque** (de firme etc) (public) image. ◆**imagé** a (style) colourful, full of imagery.

imagination [imaʒinasjɔ̃] nf imagination; pl (chimères) imaginings.

imaginer [imaʒine] vt (envisager, supposer) to imagine; (inventer) to devise; — **s'i.** vpr (se figurer) to imagine (**que** that); (se voir) to imagine oneself. ◆**imaginable** a imaginable. ◆**imaginaire** a imaginary. ◆**imaginatif, -ive** a imaginative.

imbattable [ɛ̃batabl] a unbeatable.

imbécile [ɛ̃besil] a idiotic; — nmf imbecile, idiot. ◆**imbécillité** nf (état) imbecility; **une i.** (action, parole) an idiotic thing.

imbiber [ɛ̃bibe] vt to soak (**de** with, in); — **s'i.** vpr to become soaked.

imbriquer (s') [ɛ̃brike] vpr (questions etc) to overlap, be bound up with each other.

imbroglio [ɛ̃brɔljo] nm muddle, foul-up.

imbu [ɛ̃by] a **i. de** imbued with.

imbuvable [ɛ̃byvabl] a undrinkable; (personne) Fig insufferable.

imiter [imite] vt to imitate; (contrefaire) to forge; **i. qn** (pour rire) to mimic s.o., take s.o. off; (faire comme) to do the same as s.o., follow suit. ◆**imitateur, -trice** nmf imitator; (artiste) Th impersonator, mimic. ◆**imitatif, -ive** a imitative. ◆**imitation** nf imitation.

immaculé [imakyle] a (sans tache, sans péché) immaculate.

immangeable [ɛ̃mɑ̃ʒabl] a inedible.

immanquable [ɛ̃mɑ̃kabl] a inevitable.

immatriculer [imatrikyle] vt to register; se **faire i.** to register. ◆**immatriculation** nf registration.

immédiat [imedja] a immediate; — nm **dans l'i.** for the time being. ◆**immédiatement** adv immediately.

immense [imɑ̃s] a immense, vast. ◆**immensément** adv immensely. ◆**immensité** nf immensity, vastness.

immerger [imerʒe] vt to immerse, put under water; — **s'i.** vpr (sous-marin) to submerge. ◆**immersion** nf immersion; submersion.

immettable [ɛ̃metabl] a (vêtement) unfit to be worn.

immeuble [imœbl] nm building; (d'habitation) block of flats, Am apartment building; (de bureaux) office block.

immigr/er [imigre] vi to immigrate. ◆**—ant, -ante** nmf immigrant. ◆**—é, -ée** a & nmf immigrant. ◆**immigration** nf immigration.

imminent [iminɑ̃] a imminent. ◆**imminence** nf imminence.

immiscer (s') [simise] vpr to interfere (**dans** in).

immobile [imɔbil] a still, motionless. ◆**immobiliser** vt to immobilize; (arrêter) to stop; — **s'i.** *vpr* to stop, come to a standstill. ◆**immobilité** *nf* stillness; *(inactivité)* immobility.

immobilier, -ière [imɔbilje, -jɛr] *a (vente)* property-; *(société)* construction-; **agent i.** estate agent, *Am* real estate agent.

immodéré [imɔdere] *a* immoderate.

immonde [imɔ̃d] *a* filthy. ◆**immondices** *nfpl* refuse, rubbish.

immoral, -aux [imɔral, -o] *a* immoral. ◆**immoralité** *nf* immorality.

immortel, -elle [imɔrtɛl] *a* immortal. ◆**immortaliser** *vt* to immortalize. ◆**immortalité** *nf* immortality.

immuable [imɥabl] *a* immutable, unchanging.

immuniser [imynize] *vt* to immunize (contre against); **immunisé contre** *(à l'abri de) Méd & Fig* immune to *ou* from. ◆**immunitaire** *a (déficience etc) Méd* immune. ◆**immunité** *nf* immunity.

impact [ɛ̃pakt] *nm* impact (sur on).

impair [ɛ̃pɛr] **1** *a (nombre)* odd, uneven. **2** *nm (gaffe)* blunder.

imparable [ɛ̃parabl] *a (coup etc)* unavoidable.

impardonnable [ɛ̃pardɔnabl] *a* unforgivable.

imparfait [ɛ̃parfɛ] **1** *a (connaissance etc)* imperfect. **2** *nm (temps) Gram* imperfect.

impartial, -aux [ɛ̃parsjal, -o] *a* impartial, unbiased. ◆**impartialité** *nf* impartiality.

impartir [ɛ̃partir] *vt* to grant (à to).

impasse [ɛ̃pɑs] *nf (rue)* dead end, blind alley; *(situation) Fig* impasse; **dans l'i.** *(négociations)* in deadlock.

impassible [ɛ̃pasibl] *a* impassive, unmoved. ◆**impassibilité** *nf* impassiveness.

impatient [ɛ̃pasjɑ̃] *a* impatient; **i. de faire** eager *ou* impatient to do. ◆**impatiemment** [-amɑ̃] *adv* impatiently. ◆**impatience** *nf* impatience. ◆**impatienter** *vt* to annoy, make impatient; — **s'i.** *vpr* to get impatient.

impayable [ɛ̃pɛjabl] *a (comique) Fam* hilarious, priceless.

impayé [ɛ̃peje] *a* unpaid.

impeccable [ɛ̃pekabl] *a* impeccable, immaculate. ◆**—ment** [-əmɑ̃] *adv* impeccably, immaculately.

impénétrable [ɛ̃penetrabl] *a (forêt, mystère etc)* impenetrable.

impénitent [ɛ̃penitɑ̃] *a* unrepentant.

impensable [ɛ̃pɑ̃sabl] *a* unthinkable.

imper [ɛ̃pɛr] *nm Fam* raincoat, mac.

impératif, -ive [ɛ̃peratif, -iv] *a (consigne,*

ton) imperative; — *nm (mode) Gram* imperative.

impératrice [ɛ̃peratris] *nf* empress.

imperceptible [ɛ̃pɛrsɛptibl] *a* imperceptible (à to).

imperfection [ɛ̃pɛrfɛksjɔ̃] *nf* imperfection.

impérial, -aux [ɛ̃perjal, -o] *a* imperial. ◆**impérialisme** *nm* imperialism.

impériale [ɛ̃perjal] *nf (d'autobus)* top deck.

impérieux, -euse [ɛ̃perjø, -øz] *a (autoritaire)* imperious; *(besoin)* pressing, imperative.

imperméable [ɛ̃pɛrmeabl] **1** *a* impervious (à to); *(manteau, tissu)* waterproof. **2** *nm* raincoat, mackintosh. ◆**imperméabilisé** *a* waterproof.

impersonnel, -elle [ɛ̃pɛrsɔnɛl] *a* impersonal.

impertinent [ɛ̃pɛrtinɑ̃] *a* impertinent (envers to). ◆**impertinence** *nf* impertinence.

imperturbable [ɛ̃pɛrtyrbabl] *a* unruffled, imperturbable.

impétueux, -euse [ɛ̃petɥø, -øz] *a* impetuous. ◆**impétuosité** *nf* impetuosity.

impitoyable [ɛ̃pitwajabl] *a* ruthless, pitiless, merciless.

implacable [ɛ̃plakabl] *a* implacable, relentless.

implanter [ɛ̃plɑ̃te] *vt (industrie, mode etc)* to establish; — **s'i.** *vpr* to become established. ◆**implantation** *nf* establishment.

implicite [ɛ̃plisit] *a* implicit. ◆**—ment** *adv* implicitly.

impliquer [ɛ̃plike] *vt (entraîner)* to imply; **i. que** *(supposer)* to imply that; **i. qn** *(engager)* to implicate s.o. (dans in). ◆**implication** *nf (conséquence, participation)* implication.

implorer [ɛ̃plɔre] *vt* to implore (qn de faire s.o. to do).

impoli [ɛ̃pɔli] *a* impolite, rude. ◆**impolitesse** *nf* impoliteness, rudeness; **une i.** an act of rudeness.

impopulaire [ɛ̃pɔpylɛr] *a* unpopular.

important [ɛ̃pɔrtɑ̃] *a (personnage, événement etc)* important; *(quantité, somme etc)* considerable, big, great; — *nm* **l'i., c'est de ...** the important thing is to.... ◆**importance** *nf* importance, significance; *(taille)* size; *(de dégâts)* extent; **ça n'a pas d'i.** it doesn't matter.

importer [ɛ̃pɔrte] **1** *v imp* to matter, be important (à to); **il importe de faire** it's important to do; **peu importe, n'importe** it doesn't matter; **n'importe qui/quoi/où/quand/comment** anyone/anything/anywhere/any time/anyhow. **2** *vt (marchandises etc)* to import (de from). ◆**im-**

portateur, -trice nmf importer; – a importing. **◆importation** nf (objet) import; (action) import(ing), imports; **d'i.** (article) imported.

importun, -une [ɛ̃pɔrtœ̃, -yn] a troublesome, intrusive; – nmf nuisance, intruder. **◆importuner** vt to inconvenience, trouble.

impos/er [ɛ̃poze] **1** vt to impose, enforce (à on); (exiger) to demand; (respect) to command; – vi en i. à qn to impress s.o., command respect from s.o.; – **s'i.** vpr (chez qn) Péj to impose; (s'affirmer) to assert oneself, compel recognition; (aller de soi) to stand out; (être nécessaire) to be essential. **2** vt Fin to tax. **◆—ant** a imposing. **◆—able** a Fin taxable. **◆imposition** nf Fin taxation.

impossible [ɛ̃pɔsibl] a impossible (à faire to do); **il (nous) est i. de faire** it is impossible (for us) to do; **il est i. que** (+ sub) it is impossible that; **ça m'est i.** I cannot possibly; – nm faire l'i. to do the impossible. **◆impossibilité** nf impossibility.

imposteur [ɛ̃pɔstœr] nm impostor. **◆imposture** nf deception.

impôt [ɛ̃po] nm tax; pl (contributions) (income) tax, taxes; **i. sur le revenu** income tax.

impotent, -ente [ɛ̃pɔtɑ̃, -ɑ̃t] a crippled, disabled; – nmf cripple, invalid.

impraticable [ɛ̃pratikabl] a (projet etc) impracticable; (chemin etc) impassable.

imprécis [ɛ̃presi] a imprecise. **◆imprécision** nf lack of precision.

imprégner [ɛ̃preɲe] vt to saturate, impregnate (de with); – **s'i.** vpr to become saturated ou impregnated (de with); **imprégné de** (idées) imbued ou infused with. **◆imprégnation** nf saturation.

imprenable [ɛ̃prənabl] a Mil impregnable.

impresario [ɛ̃presarjo] nm (business) manager, impresario.

impression [ɛ̃presjɔ̃] nf **1** impression; **avoir l'i. que** to have the feeling ou impression that; **be under the impression that; faire une bonne i. à qn** to make a good impression on s.o. **2** Typ printing.

impressionn/er [ɛ̃presjɔne] vt (influencer) to impress; (émouvoir, troubler) to make a strong impression on. **◆—ant** a impressive. **◆—able** a impressionable.

imprévisible [ɛ̃previzibl] a unforeseeable. **◆imprévoyance** nf lack of foresight. **◆imprévoyant** a shortsighted. **◆imprévu** a unexpected, unforeseen; – nm **en cas d'i.** in case of anything unexpected.

imprim/er [ɛ̃prime] vt **1** (livre etc) to print;

(trace) to impress (dans in); (cachet) to stamp. **2** (communiquer) Tech to impart (à to). **◆—ante** nf (d'ordinateur) printer. **◆—é** nm (formulaire) printed form; – nm(pl) (par la poste) printed matter. **◆imprimerie** nf (technique) printing; (lieu) printing works. **◆imprimeur** nm printer.

improbable [ɛ̃prɔbabl] a improbable, unlikely. **◆improbabilité** nf improbability, unlikelihood.

impromptu [ɛ̃prɔ̃pty] a & adv impromptu.

impropre [ɛ̃prɔpr] a inappropriate; **i. à qch** unfit for sth. **◆impropriété** nf (incorrection) Ling impropriety.

improviser [ɛ̃prɔvize] vti to improvise. **◆improvisation** nf improvisation.

improviste (à l') [alɛ̃prɔvist] adv unexpectedly; **une visite à l'i.** an unexpected visit; **prendre qn à l'i.** to catch s.o. unawares.

imprudent [ɛ̃prydɑ̃] a (personne, action) careless, rash; **il est i. de** it is unwise to. **◆imprudemment** [-amɑ̃] adv carelessly. **◆imprudence** nf carelessness; **une i.** an act of carelessness.

impudent [ɛ̃pydɑ̃] a impudent **◆impudence** nf impudence.

impudique [ɛ̃pydik] a lewd.

impuissant, -ante [ɛ̃pɥisɑ̃, -ɑ̃t] a helpless; Méd impotent; **i. à faire** powerless to do. **◆impuissance** nf helplessness; Méd impotence.

impulsif, -ive [ɛ̃pylsif, -iv] a impulsive. **◆impulsion** nf impulse; **donner une i. à** (élan) Fig to give an impetus ou impulse to.

impunément [ɛ̃pynemɑ̃] adv with impunity. **◆impuni** a unpunished.

impur [ɛ̃pyr] a impure. **◆impureté** nf impurity.

imputer [ɛ̃pyte] vt to attribute, impute (à to); (affecter) Fin to charge (à to). **◆imputable** a attributable (à to). **◆imputation** nf Jur accusation.

inabordable [inabɔrdabl] a (lieu) inaccessible; (personne) unapproachable; (prix) prohibitive.

inacceptable [inaksɛptabl] a unacceptable.

inaccessible [inaksesibl] a inaccessible.

inaccoutumé [inakutyme] a unusual, unaccustomed.

inachevé [inaʃve] a unfinished.

inactif, -ive [inaktif, -iv] a inactive. **◆inaction** nf inactivity, inaction. **◆inactivité** nf inactivity.

inadapté, -ée [inadapte] a & nmf maladjusted (person). **◆inadaptation** nf maladjustment.

inadmissible [inadmisibl] *a* unacceptable, inadmissible.

inadvertance (par) [parinadvertɑ̃s] *adv* inadvertently.

inaltérable [inalterabl] *a* (*couleur*) fast; (*sentiment*) unchanging.

inamical, -aux [inamikal, -o] *a* unfriendly.

inanimé [inanime] *a* (*mort*) lifeless; (*évanoui*) unconscious; (*matière*) inanimate.

inanité [inanite] *nf* (*vanité*) futility.

inanition [inanisjɔ̃] *nf* **mourir d'i.** to die of starvation.

inaperçu [inapɛrsy] *a* **passer i.** to go unnoticed.

inapplicable [inaplikabl] *a* inapplicable (à to).

inappliqué [inaplike] *a* (*élève etc*) inattentive.

inappréciable [inapresjabl] *a* invaluable.

inapte [inapt] *a* unsuited (**à qch** to sth), inept (**à qch** at sth); *Mil* unfit **◆inaptitude** *nf* ineptitude, incapacity.

inarticulé [inartikyle] *a* (*son*) inarticulate.

inattaquable [inatakabl] *a* unassailable.

inattendu [inatɑ̃dy] *a* unexpected.

inattentif, -ive [inatɑ̃tif, -iv] *a* inattentive, careless; **à** (*soucis, danger etc*) heedless of. **◆inattention** *nf* lack of attention; **dans un moment d'i.** in a moment of distraction.

inaudible [inodibl] *a* inaudible.

inaugurer [inogyre] *vt* (*politique, édifice*) to inaugurate; (*école, congrès*) to open, inaugurate; (*statue*) to unveil. **◆inaugural, -aux** *a* inaugural. **◆inauguration** *nf* inauguration; opening; unveiling.

inauthentique [inotɑ̃tik] *a* not authentic.

inavouable [inavwabl] *a* shameful.

incalculable [ɛ̃kalkylabl] *a* incalculable.

incandescent [ɛ̃kɑ̃desɑ̃] *a* incandescent.

incapable [ɛ̃kapabl] *a* incapable; **i. de faire** unable to do, incapable of doing; — *nmf* (*personne*) incompetent. **◆incapacité** *nf* incapacity, inability (**de faire** to do); *Méd* disability, incapacity.

incarcérer [ɛ̃karsere] *vt* to incarcerate. **◆incarcération** *nf* incarceration.

incarné [ɛ̃karne] *a* (*ongle*) ingrown.

incarner [ɛ̃karne] *vt* to embody, incarnate. **◆incarnation** *nf* embodiment, incarnation.

incartade [ɛ̃kartad] *nf* indiscretion, prank.

incassable [ɛ̃kasabl] *a* unbreakable.

incendie [ɛ̃sɑ̃di] *nm* fire; (*guerre*) *Fig* conflagration. **◆incendiaire** *nmf* arsonist; — *a* (*bombe*) incendiary; (*discours*) inflammatory. **◆incendier** *vt* to set fire to, set on fire.

incertain [ɛ̃sɛrtɛ̃] *a* uncertain; (*temps*) unsettled; (*entreprise*) chancy; (*contour*) indistinct. **◆incertitude** *nf* uncertainty.

incessamment [ɛ̃sesamɑ̃] *adv* without delay, shortly.

incessant [ɛ̃sesɑ̃] *a* incessant.

inceste [ɛ̃sɛst] *nm* incest. **◆incestueux, -euse** *a* incestuous.

inchangé [ɛ̃ʃɑ̃ʒe] *a* unchanged.

incidence [ɛ̃sidɑ̃s] *nf* (*influence*) effect.

incident [ɛ̃sidɑ̃] *nm* incident; (*accroc*) hitch.

incinérer [ɛ̃sinere] *vt* (*ordures*) to incinerate; (*cadavre*) to cremate. **◆incinération** *nf* incineration; cremation.

inciser [ɛ̃size] *vt* to make an incision in. **◆incision** *nf* (*entaille*) incision.

incisif, -ive[1] [ɛ̃sizif, -iv] *a* incisive, sharp.

incisive[2] [ɛ̃siziv] *nf* (*dent*) incisor.

inciter [ɛ̃site] *vt* to urge, incite (**à faire** to do). **◆incitation** *nf* incitement (**à** to).

incliner [ɛ̃kline] *vt* (*courber*) to bend; (*pencher*) to tilt, incline; **i. la tête** (*approuver*) to nod one's head; (*révérence*) to bow (one's head); **i. qn à faire** to make s.o. inclined to do, incline s.o. to do; — *vi* **i. à** to be inclined towards; — **s'i.** *vpr* (*se courber*) to bow (down); (*s'avouer vaincu*) to admit defeat; (*chemin*) to slope down. **◆inclinaison** *nf* incline, slope. **◆inclination** *nf* (*goût*) inclination; (*de tête*) nod, (*révérence*) bow.

incl/ure* [ɛ̃klyr] *vt* to include; (*enfermer*) to enclose. **◆—us** *a* inclusive; **du quatre jusqu'au dix mai i.** from the fourth to the tenth of May inclusive; **jusqu'à lundi i.** up to and including (next) Monday. **◆inclusion** *nf* inclusion. **◆inclusivement** *adv* inclusively.

incognito [ɛ̃kɔɲito] *adv* incognito.

incohérent [ɛ̃kɔerɑ̃] *a* incoherent. **◆incohérence** *nf* incoherence.

incollable [ɛ̃kɔlabl] *a* *Fam* infallible, unable to be caught out.

incolore [ɛ̃kɔlɔr] *a* colourless; (*verre, vernis*) clear.

incomber [ɛ̃kɔbe] *vi* **i. à qn** (*devoir*) to fall to s.o.; **il lui incombe de faire** it's his *ou* her duty *ou* responsiblity to do.

incommode [ɛ̃kɔmɔd] *a* awkward. **◆incommodité** *nf* awkwardness.

incommod/er [ɛ̃kɔmɔde] *vt* to bother, annoy. **◆—ant** *a* annoying.

incomparable [ɛ̃kɔparabl] *a* incomparable.

incompatible [ɛ̃kɔpatibl] *a* incompatible, inconsistent (**avec** with). **◆incompatibilité** *nf* incompatibility, inconsistency.

incompétent [ɛ̃kɔ̃petã] a incompetent. ◆**incompétence** nf incompetence.
incomplet, -ète [ɛ̃kɔ̃plɛ, -ɛt] a incomplete; (fragmentaire) scrappy, sketchy.
incompréhensible [ɛ̃kɔ̃preãsibl] a incomprehensible. ◆**incompréhensif, -ive** a uncomprehending, lacking understanding. ◆**incompréhension** nf lack of understanding. ◆**incompris** a misunderstood.
inconcevable [ɛ̃kɔ̃svabl] a inconceivable.
inconciliable [ɛ̃kɔ̃siljabl] a irreconcilable.
inconditionnel, -elle [ɛ̃kɔ̃disjɔnɛl] a unconditional.
inconfort [ɛ̃kɔ̃fɔr] nm lack of comfort. ◆**inconfortable** a uncomfortable.
incongru [ɛ̃kɔ̃gry] a unseemly, incongruous.
inconnu, -ue [ɛ̃kɔny] a unknown (à to); – nmf (étranger) stranger; (auteur) unknown; – nm l'i. the unknown; – nf Math unknown (quantity).
inconscient [ɛ̃kɔ̃sjã] a unconscious (de of); (irréfléchi) thoughtless, senseless; – nm l'i. Psy the unconscious. ◆**inconsciemment** [-amã] adv unconsciously. ◆**inconscience** nf (physique) unconsciousness; (irréflexion) utter thoughtlessness.
inconséquence [ɛ̃kɔ̃sekãs] nf inconsistency.
inconsidéré [ɛ̃kɔ̃sidere] a thoughtless.
inconsolable [ɛ̃kɔ̃sɔlabl] a inconsolable.
inconstant [ɛ̃kɔ̃stã] a fickle. ◆**inconstance** nf fickleness.
incontestable [ɛ̃kɔ̃tɛstabl] a undeniable, indisputable. ◆**incontesté** a undisputed.
incontinent [ɛ̃kɔ̃tinã] a incontinent.
incontrôlé [ɛ̃kɔ̃trole] a unchecked. ◆**incontrôlable** a unverifiable.
inconvenant [ɛ̃kɔ̃vnã] a improper. ◆**inconvenance** nf impropriety.
inconvénient [ɛ̃kɔ̃venjã] nm (désavantage) drawback; (risque) risk; (objection) objection.
incorporer [ɛ̃kɔrpɔre] vt (introduire, admettre) to incorporate (dans into); (ingrédient) to blend (à with); Mil to enrol. ◆**incorporation** nf incorporation (de of); Mil enrolment.
incorrect [ɛ̃kɔrɛkt] a (inexact) incorrect; (inconvenant) improper; (grossier) impolite. ◆**incorrection** nf (faute) impropriety, error; (inconvenance) improper; une i. (grossièreté) an impolite word ou act.
incorrigible [ɛ̃kɔriʒibl] a incorrigible.
incorruptible [ɛ̃kɔryptibl] a incorruptible.
incrédule [ɛ̃kredyl] a incredulous. ◆**incrédulité** nf disbelief, incredulity.

increvable [ɛ̃krəvabl] a (robuste) Fam tireless.
incriminer [ɛ̃krimine] vt to incriminate.
incroyable [ɛ̃krwajabl] a incredible, unbelievable. ◆**incroyablement** adv incredibly. ◆**incroyant, -ante** a unbelieving; – nmf unbeliever.
incrusté [ɛ̃kryste] a (de tartre) encrusted; i. de (orné) inlaid with. ◆**incrustation** nf (ornement) inlay; (action) inlaying.
incruster (s') [sɛ̃kryste] vpr (chez qn) Fig to dig oneself in, be difficult to get rid of.
incubation [ɛ̃kybasjɔ̃] nf incubation.
inculper [ɛ̃kylpe] vt Jur to charge (de with), indict (de for). ◆**-é, -ée** nmf l'i. the accused. ◆**inculpation** nf charge, indictment.
inculquer [ɛ̃kylke] vt to instil (à into).
inculte [ɛ̃kylt] a (terre) uncultivated; (personne) uneducated.
incurable [ɛ̃kyrabl] a incurable.
incursion [ɛ̃kyrsjɔ̃] nf incursion, inroad (dans into).
incurver [ɛ̃kyrve] vt to curve.
Inde [ɛ̃d] nf India.
indécent [ɛ̃desã] a indecent. ◆**indécemment** [-amã] adv indecently. ◆**indécence** nf indecency.
indéchiffrable [ɛ̃deʃifrabl] a undecipherable.
indécis [ɛ̃desi] a (victoire, résultat) undecided; (indistinct) vague; être i. (hésiter) to be undecided; (de tempérament) to be indecisive ou irresolute. ◆**indécision** nf indecisiveness, indecision.
indéfectible [ɛ̃defɛktibl] a unfailing.
indéfendable [ɛ̃defãdabl] a indefensible.
indéfini [ɛ̃defini] a (indéterminé) indefinite; (imprécis) undefined. ◆**indéfiniment** adv indefinitely. ◆**indéfinissable** a indefinable.
indéformable [ɛ̃defɔrmabl] a (vêtement) which keeps its shape.
indélébile [ɛ̃delebil] a (encre, souvenir) indelible.
indélicat [ɛ̃delika] a (grossier) indelicate; (malhonnête) unscrupulous.
indemne [ɛ̃dɛmn] a unhurt, unscathed.
indemniser [ɛ̃dɛmnize] vt to indemnify, compensate (de for). ◆**indemnisation** nf compensation. ◆**indemnité** nf (dédommagement) indemnity; (allocation) allowance.
indémontable [ɛ̃demɔ̃tabl] a that cannot be taken apart.
indéniable [ɛ̃denjabl] a undeniable.
indépendant [ɛ̃depãdã] a independent (de

of); (*chambre*) self-contained; (*journaliste*) freelance. ◆**indépendamment** *adv* independently (**de** of); **i. de** (*sans aucun égard à*) apart from. ◆**indépendance** *nf* independence.

indescriptible [ɛ̃dɛskriptibl] *a* indescribable.

indésirable [ɛ̃dezirabl] *a* & *nmf* undesirable.

indestructible [ɛ̃dɛstryktibl] *a* indestructible.

indéterminé [ɛ̃detɛrmine] *a* indeterminate. ◆**indétermination** *nf* (*doute*) indecision.

index [ɛ̃dɛks] *nm* (*liste*) index; *Anat* forefinger, index finger.

indexer [ɛ̃dɛkse] *vt* *Écon* to index-link, tie (**sur** to).

indicateur, -trice [ɛ̃dikatœr, -tris] **1** *nmf* (*espion*) (*police*) informer. **2** *nm* *Rail* guide, timetable; *Tech* indicator, gauge. **3** *a* poteau **i.** signpost. ◆**indicatif, -ive 1** *a* indicative (**de** of); – *nm* *Mus* signature tune; *Tél* dialling code, *Am* area code. **2** *nm* (*mode*) *Gram* indicative. ◆**indication** *nf* indication (**de** of); (*renseignement*) (piece of) information; (*directive*) instruction.

indice [ɛ̃dis] *nm* (*indication*) sign; (*dans une enquête*) *Jur* clue; (*des prix*) index; (*de salaire*) rating; **i. d'écoute** *TV Rad* rating.

indien, -ienne [ɛ̃djɛ̃, -jɛn] *a* & *nmf* Indian.

indifférent, -ente [ɛ̃difera] *a* indifferent (**à** to); **ça m'est i.** that's all the same to me. ◆**indifféremment** [-amã] *adv* indifferently. ◆**indifférence** *nf* indifference (**à** to).

indigène [ɛ̃diʒɛn] *a* & *nmf* native.

indigent [ɛ̃diʒa] *a* (very) poor. ◆**indigence** *nf* poverty.

indigeste [ɛ̃diʒɛst] *a* indigestible. ◆**indigestion** *nf* (attack of) indigestion.

indigne [ɛ̃diɲ] *a* (*personne*) unworthy; (*chose*) shameful; **i. de qn/qch** unworthy of s.o./sth. ◆**indignité** *nf* unworthiness; **une i.** (*honte*) an indignity.

indigner [ɛ̃diɲe] *vt* **i. qn** to make s.o. indignant; – **s'i.** *vpr* to be *ou* become indignant (**de** at). ◆**indignation** *nf* indignation.

indigo [ɛ̃digo] *nm* & *a inv* (*couleur*) indigo.

indiqu/er [ɛ̃dike] *vt* (*montrer*) to show, indicate; (*dire*) to point out, tell; (*recommander*) to recommend; **i. du doigt** to point to *ou* at. ◆**-é** *a* (*heure*) appointed; (*conseillé*) recommended; (*adéquat*) appropriate.

indirect [ɛ̃dirɛkt] *a* indirect. ◆**-ement** *adv* indirectly.

indiscipline [ɛ̃disiplin] *nf* lack of discipline. ◆**indiscipliné** *a* unruly.

indiscret, -ète [ɛ̃diskrɛ, -ɛt] *a* (*indélicat*) indiscreet, tactless; (*curieux*) *Péj* inquisitive, prying. ◆**indiscrétion** *nf* indiscretion.

indiscutable [ɛ̃diskytabl] *a* indisputable.

indispensable [ɛ̃dispãsabl] *a* indispensable, essential.

indispos/er [ɛ̃dispoze] *vt* (*incommoder*) to make unwell, upset; **i. qn** (*contre soi*) (*mécontenter*) to antagonize s.o. ◆**-é** *a* (*malade*) indisposed, unwell. ◆**indisposition** *nf* indisposition.

indissoluble [ɛ̃disɔlybl] *a* (*liens etc*) solid, indissoluble.

indistinct, -incte [ɛ̃distɛ̃(kt), -ɛ̃kt] *a* indistinct. ◆**-ement** [-ɛ̃ktəmã] *adv* indistinctly; (*également*) without distinction.

individu [ɛ̃dividy] *nm* individual. ◆**individualiser** *vt* to individualize. ◆**individualiste** *a* individualistic; – *nmf* individualist. ◆**individualité** *nf* (*originalité*) individuality. ◆**individuel, -elle** *a* individual. ◆**individuellement** *adv* individually.

indivisible [ɛ̃divizibl] *a* indivisible.

Indochine [ɛ̃dɔʃin] *nf* Indo-China.

indolent [ɛ̃dɔlã] *a* indolent. ◆**indolence** *nf* indolence.

indolore [ɛ̃dɔlɔr] *a* painless.

indomptable [ɛ̃dɔ̃tabl] *a* (*énergie, volonté*) indomitable. ◆**indompté** *a* (*animal*) untamed.

Indonésie [ɛ̃dɔnezi] *nf* Indonesia.

indubitable [ɛ̃dybitabl] *a* beyond doubt.

indue [ɛ̃dy] *af* **à une heure i.** at an ungodly hour.

induire* [ɛ̃dɥir] *vt* **i. qn en erreur** to lead s.o. astray.

indulgent [ɛ̃dylʒã] *a* indulgent (**envers** to, **avec** with). ◆**indulgence** *nf* indulgence.

industrie [ɛ̃dystri] *nf* industry. ◆**industrialisé** *a* industrialized. ◆**industriel, -elle** *a* industrial; – *nmf* industrialist.

inébranlable [inebrãlabl] *a* (*certitude, personne*) unshakeable, unwavering.

inédit [inedi] *a* (*texte*) unpublished; (*nouveau*) *Fig* original.

ineffable [inefabl] *a* *Litt* inexpressible, ineffable.

inefficace [inefikas] *a* (*mesure, effort etc*) ineffective, ineffectual; (*personne*) inefficient. ◆**inefficacité** *nf* ineffectiveness; inefficiency.

inégal, -aux [inegal, -o] *a* unequal; (*sol, humeur*) uneven. ◆**inégalable** *a* incomparable. ◆**inégalé** *a* unequalled. ◆**inégalité** *nf* (*morale*) inequality; (*physique*) difference; (*irrégularité*) unevenness; *pl* (*bosses*) bumps.

inélégant [inelegɑ̃] *a* coarse, inelegant.

inéligible [ineliʒibl] *a* (*candidat*) ineligible.

inéluctable [inelyktabl] *a* inescapable.

inepte [inɛpt] *a* absurd, inept. ◆**ineptie** [-si] *nf* absurdity, ineptitude.

inépuisable [inepɥizabl] *a* inexhaustible.

inerte [inɛrt] *a* inert; (*corps*) lifeless. ◆**inertie** [-si] *nf* inertia.

inespéré [inespere] *a* unhoped-for.

inestimable [inestimabl] *a* priceless.

inévitable [inevitabl] *a* inevitable, unavoidable.

inexact [inɛgzakt] *a* (*erroné*) inaccurate, inexact; **c'est i.!** it's incorrect! ◆**inexactitude** *nf* inaccuracy, inexactitude; (*manque de ponctualité*) lack of punctuality.

inexcusable [inɛkskyzabl] *a* inexcusable.

inexistant [inɛgzistɑ̃] *a* non-existent.

inexorable [inɛgzɔrabl] *a* inexorable.

inexpérience [inɛksperjɑ̃s] *nf* inexperience. ◆**inexpérimenté** *a* (*personne*) inexperienced; (*machine, arme*) untested.

inexplicable [inɛksplikabl] *a* inexplicable. ◆**inexpliqué** *a* unexplained.

inexploré [inɛksplɔre] *a* unexplored.

inexpressif, -ive [inɛkspresif, -iv] *a* expressionless.

inexprimable [inɛksprimabl] *a* inexpressible.

inextricable [inɛkstrikabl] *a* inextricable.

infaillible [ɛ̃fajibl] *a* infallible. ◆**infaillibilité** *nf* infallibility.

infaisable [ɛ̃fəzabl] *a* (*travail etc*) that cannot be done.

infamant [ɛ̃famɑ̃] *a* ignominious.

infâme [ɛ̃fam] *a* (*odieux*) vile, infamous; (*taudis*) squalid. ◆**infamie** *nf* infamy.

infanterie [ɛ̃fɑ̃tri] *nf* infantry.

infantile [ɛ̃fɑ̃til] *a* (*maladie, réaction*) infantile.

infarctus [ɛ̃farktys] *nm* **un i.** *Méd* a coronary.

infatigable [ɛ̃fatigabl] *a* tireless, indefatigable.

infect [ɛ̃fɛkt] *a* (*puant*) foul; (*mauvais*) lousy, vile.

infecter [ɛ̃fɛkte] **1** *vt* (*air*) to contaminate, foul. **2** *vt Méd* to infect; — **s'i.** *vpr* to get infected. ◆**infectieux, -euse** *a* infectious. ◆**infection** *nf* **1** *Méd* infection. **2** (*odeur*) stench.

inférer [ɛ̃fere] *vt* (*conclure*) to infer (**de** from, **que** that).

inférieur, -eure [ɛ̃ferjœr] *a* (*partie*) lower; (*qualité, personne*) inferior; **à l'étage i.** on the floor below; **i. à** inferior to; (*plus petit que*) smaller than; — *nmf* (*personne*) *Péj* inferior. ◆**infériorité** *nf* inferiority.

infernal, -aux [ɛ̃fɛrnal, -o] *a* infernal.

infester [ɛ̃fɛste] *vt* to infest, overrun (**de** with). ◆—**é** *a* **i. de** **requins/de fournis**/*etc* shark-/ant-/*etc* infested.

infidèle [ɛ̃fidɛl] *a* unfaithful (**à** to). ◆**infidélité** *nf* unfaithfulness; **une i.** (*acte*) an infidelity.

infiltrer (s') [sɛ̃filtre] *vpr* (*liquide*) to seep *ou* percolate (through) (**dans** into); (*lumière*) to filter (through) (**dans** into); **s'i. dans** (*groupe, esprit*) *Fig* to infiltrate. ◆**infiltration** *nf* (*de personne, idée, liquide*) infiltration.

infime [ɛ̃fim] *a* (*très petit*) tiny; (*personne*) *Péj* lowly.

infini [ɛ̃fini] *a* infinite; — *nm Math Phot* infinity; *Phil* infinite; **à l'i.** (*beaucoup*) *ad* infinitum, endlessly; *Math* to infinity. ◆**infiniment** *adv* infinitely; (*regretter, remercier*) very much. ◆**infinité** *nf* **une i. de** an infinite amount of.

infinitif [ɛ̃finitif] *nm Gram* infinitive.

infirme [ɛ̃firm] *a* disabled, crippled; — *nmf* disabled person. ◆**infirmité** *nf* disability.

infirmer [ɛ̃firme] *vt* to invalidate.

infirmerie [ɛ̃firmari] *nf* infirmary, sickbay. ◆**infirmier** *nm* male nurse. ◆**infirmière** *nf* nurse.

inflammable [ɛ̃flamabl] *a* (in)flammable.

inflammation [ɛ̃flamasjɔ̃] *nf Méd* inflammation.

inflation [ɛ̃flasjɔ̃] *nf Écon* inflation. ◆**inflationniste** *a Écon* inflationary.

infléchir [ɛ̃fleʃir] *vt* (*courber*) to inflect, bend; (*modifier*) to shift. ◆**inflexion** *nf* bend; (*de voix*) tone, inflexion; **une i. de la tête** a nod.

inflexible [ɛ̃flɛksibl] *a* inflexible.

infliger [ɛ̃fliʒe] *vt* to inflict (**à** on); (*amende*) to impose (**à** on).

influence [ɛ̃flyɑ̃s] *nf* influence. ◆**influencer** *vt* to influence. ◆**influençable** *a* easily influenced. ◆**influent** *a* influential. ◆**influer** *vi* **i. sur** to influence.

information [ɛ̃fɔrmasjɔ̃] *nf* information; (*nouvelle*) piece of news; (*enquête*) *Jur* inquiry; *pl* information; *Journ Rad TV* news.

informatique [ɛ̃fɔrmatik] *nf* (*science*) computer science; (*technique*) data processing. ◆**informaticien, -ienne** *nmf* computer scientist. ◆**informatiser** *vt* to computerize.

informe [ɛ̃fɔrm] *a* shapeless.

informer [ɛ̃fɔrme] *vt* to inform (**de** of, about;

que that); — s'i. *vpr* to inquire (de about; si if, whether). ◆**informateur, -trice** *nmf* informant.

infortune [ɛ̃fɔrtyn] *nf* misfortune. ◆**infortuné** *a* ill-fated, hapless.

infraction [ɛ̃fraksjɔ̃] *nf* (*délit*) offence; **i. à** breach of, infringement of.

infranchissable [ɛ̃frɑ̃ʃisabl] *a* (*mur, fleuve*) impassable; (*difficulté*) *Fig* insuperable.

infrarouge [ɛ̃fraruʒ] *a* infrared.

infroissable [ɛ̃frwasabl] *a* crease-resistant.

infructueux, -euse [ɛ̃fryktɥø, -øz] *a* fruitless.

infuser [ɛ̃fyze] *vt* (faire) **i.** (*thé*) to infuse. ◆**infusion** *nf* (*tisane*) (herb *ou* herbal) tea, infusion.

ingénier (s') [sɛ̃ʒenje] *vpr* to exercise one's wits (**à faire** in order to do).

ingénieur [ɛ̃ʒenjœr] *nm* engineer. ◆**ingénierie** [-iri] *nf* engineering.

ingénieux, -euse [ɛ̃ʒenjø, -øz] *a* ingenious. ◆**ingéniosité** *nf* ingenuity.

ingénu [ɛ̃ʒeny] *a* artless, naïve.

ingérer (s') [sɛ̃ʒere] *vpr* to interfere (**dans** in). ◆**ingérence** *nf* interference.

ingrat [ɛ̃gra] *a* (*personne*) ungrateful (**envers** to); (*sol*) barren; (*tâche*) thankless; (*visage, physique*) unattractive; (*âge*) awkward. ◆**ingratitude** *nf* ingratitude.

ingrédient [ɛ̃gredjɑ̃] *nm* ingredient.

inguérissable [ɛ̃gerisabl] *a* incurable.

ingurgiter [ɛ̃gyrʒite] *vt* to gulp down.

inhabitable [inabitabl] *a* uninhabitable. ◆**inhabité** *a* uninhabited.

inhabituel, -elle [inabitɥɛl] *a* unusual.

inhalateur [inalatœr] *nm* *Méd* inhaler. ◆**inhalation** *nf* inhalation; **faire des inhalations** to inhale.

inhérent [inerɑ̃] *a* inherent (**à** in).

inhibé [inibe] *a* inhibited. ◆**inhibition** *nf* inhibition.

inhospitalier, -ière [inɔspitalje, -jɛr] *a* inhospitable.

inhumain [inymɛ̃] *a* (*cruel, terrible*) inhuman.

inhumer [inyme] *vt* to bury, inter. ◆**inhumation** *nf* burial.

inimaginable [inimaʒinabl] *a* unimaginable.

inimitable [inimitabl] *a* inimitable.

inimitié [inimitje] *nf* enmity.

ininflammable [inɛ̃flamabl] *a* (*tissu etc*) non-flammable.

inintelligent [inɛ̃teliʒɑ̃] *a* unintelligent.

inintelligible [inɛ̃teliʒibl] *a* unintelligible.

inintéressant [inɛ̃teresɑ̃] *a* uninteresting.

ininterrompu [inɛ̃terɔ̃py] *a* uninterrupted, continuous.

inique [inik] *a* iniquitous. ◆**iniquité** *nf* iniquity.

initial, -aux [inisjal, -o] *a* initial. ◆**initiale** *nf* (*lettre*) initial. ◆**initialement** *adv* initially.

initiative [inisjativ] *nf* **1** initiative. **2 syndicat d'i.** tourist office.

initi/er [inisje] *vt* to initiate (**à** into); **s'i. à** (*art, science*) to become acquainted with *ou* initiated into. ◆**-é, -ée** *nmf* initiate; **les initiés** the initiated. ◆**initiateur, -trice** *nmf* initiator. ◆**initiation** *nf* initiation.

injecter [ɛ̃ʒɛkte] *vt* to inject; **injecté de sang** bloodshot. ◆**injection** *nf* injection.

injonction [ɛ̃ʒɔ̃ksjɔ̃] *nf* order, injunction.

injure [ɛ̃ʒyr] *nf* insult; *pl* abuse, insults. ◆**injurier** *vt* to abuse, insult, swear at. ◆**injurieux, -euse** *a* abusive, insulting (**pour** to).

injuste [ɛ̃ʒyst] *a* (*contraire à la justice*) unjust; (*partial*) unfair. ◆**injustice** *nf* injustice.

injustifiable [ɛ̃ʒystifjabl] *a* unjustifiable. ◆**injustifié** *a* unjustified.

inlassable [ɛ̃lasabl] *a* untiring.

inné [ine] *a* innate, inborn.

innocent, -ente [inɔsɑ̃, -ɑ̃t] *a* innocent (**de** of); — *nmf Jur* innocent person; (*idiot*) simpleton. ◆**innocemment** [-amɑ̃] *adv* innocently. ◆**innocence** *nf* innocence. ◆**innocenter** *vt* **i. qn** to clear s.o. (**de** of).

innombrable [inɔ̃brabl] *a* innumerable.

innommable [inɔmabl] *a* (*dégoûtant*) unspeakable, foul.

innover [inɔve] *vi* to innovate. ◆**innovateur, -trice** *nmf* innovator. ◆**innovation** *nf* innovation.

inoccupé [inɔkype] *a* unoccupied.

inoculer [inɔkyle] *vt* **i. qch à qn** to infect *ou* inoculate s.o. with sth. ◆**inoculation** *nf* (*vaccination*) inoculation.

inodore [inɔdɔr] *a* odourless.

inoffensif, -ive [inɔfɑ̃sif, -iv] *a* harmless, inoffensive.

inonder [inɔ̃de] *vt* to flood, inundate; (*mouiller*) to soak; **inondé de** (*envahi*) inundated with; **inondé de soleil** bathed in sunlight. ◆**inondable** *a* (*chaussée etc*) liable to flooding. ◆**inondation** *nf* flood; (*action*) flooding (**de** of).

inopérant [inɔperɑ̃] *a* inoperative.

inopiné [inɔpine] *a* unexpected.

inopportun [inɔpɔrtœ̃] *a* inopportune.

inoubliable [inublijabl] *a* unforgettable.

inouï [inwi] *a* incredible, extraordinary.

inox [inɔks] nm stainless steel; **en i.** (couteau etc) stainless-steel. ◆**inoxydable** a (couteau etc) stainless-steel; **acier i.** stainless steel.

inqualifiable [ɛ̃kalifjabl] a (indigne) unspeakable.

inquiet, -iète [ɛ̃kjɛ, -jɛt] a anxious, worried (de about). ◆**inquiéter** vt (préoccuper) to worry; (police) to bother, harass (suspect etc); — **s'i.** vpr to worry (de about). ◆**-ant** a worrying. ◆**inquiétude** nf anxiety, concern, worry.

inquisiteur, -trice [ɛ̃kizitœr, -tris] a (regard) Péj inquisitive. ◆**inquisition** nf inquisition.

insaisissable [ɛ̃sezisabl] a elusive.

insalubre [ɛ̃salybr] a unhealthy, insalubrious.

insanités [ɛ̃sanite] nfpl (idioties) absurdities.

insatiable [ɛ̃sasjabl] a insatiable.

insatisfait [ɛ̃satisfɛ] a unsatisfied, dissatisfied.

inscrire* [ɛ̃skrir] vt to write ou put down; (sur un registre) to register; (graver) to inscribe; **i. qn** to enrol s.o.; — **s'i.** vpr to enrol (à at); **s'i. à** (parti, club) to join, enrol in; (examen) to enter ou enrol ou register for; **s'i. dans** (le cadre de) to be part of; **s'i. en faux contre** to deny absolutely. ◆**inscription** nf writing down; enrolment; registration; (de médaille, sur écriteau etc) inscription; **frais d'i.** Univ tuition fees.

insecte [ɛ̃sɛkt] nm insect. ◆**insecticide** nm insecticide.

insécurité [ɛ̃sekyrite] nf insecurity.

insémination [ɛ̃seminasjɔ̃] nf Méd insemination.

insensé [ɛ̃sɑ̃se] a senseless, absurd.

insensible [ɛ̃sɑ̃sibl] a (indifférent) insensitive (à to); (graduel) imperceptible, very slight. ◆**insensiblement** adv imperceptibly. ◆**insensibilité** nf insensitivity.

inséparable [ɛ̃separabl] a inseparable (de from).

insérer [ɛ̃sere] vt to insert (dans into, in); **s'i. dans** (programme etc) to be part of. ◆**insertion** nf insertion.

insidieux, -euse [ɛ̃sidjø, -øz] a insidious.

insigne [ɛ̃siɲ] nm badge, emblem; pl (de maire etc) insignia.

insignifiant [ɛ̃siɲifjɑ̃] a insignificant, unimportant. ◆**insignifiance** nf insignificance.

insinuer [ɛ̃sinɥe] vt Péj to insinuate (que that); — **s'i.** vpr to insinuate oneself (dans into). ◆**insinuation** nf insinuation.

insipide [ɛ̃sipid] a insipid.

insist/er [ɛ̃siste] vi to insist (pour faire on doing); (continuer) Fam to persevere; **i. sur** (détail, syllabe etc) to stress; **i. pour que** (+ sub) to insist that. ◆**-ant** a insistent, persistent. ◆**insistance** nf insistence, persistence.

insolation [ɛ̃sɔlasjɔ̃] nf Méd sunstroke.

insolent [ɛ̃sɔlɑ̃] a (impoli) insolent; (luxe) indecent. ◆**insolence** nf insolence.

insolite [ɛ̃sɔlit] a unusual, strange.

insoluble [ɛ̃sɔlybl] a insoluble.

insolvable [ɛ̃sɔlvabl] a Fin insolvent.

insomnie [ɛ̃sɔmni] nf insomnia; pl (periods of) insomnia; **nuit d'i.** sleepless night. ◆**insomniaque** nmf insomniac.

insondable [ɛ̃sɔ̃dabl] a unfathomable.

insonoriser [ɛ̃sɔnɔrize] vt to soundproof, insulate. ◆**insonorisation** nf soundproofing, insulation.

insouciant [ɛ̃susjɑ̃] a carefree; **i. de** unconcerned about. ◆**insouciance** nf carefree attitude, lack of concern.

insoumis [ɛ̃sumi] a rebellious. ◆**insoumission** nf rebelliousness.

insoupçonnable [ɛ̃supsɔnabl] a beyond suspicion. ◆**insoupçonné** a unsuspected.

insoutenable [ɛ̃sutnabl] a unbearable; (théorie) untenable.

inspecter [ɛ̃spɛkte] vt to inspect. ◆**inspecteur, -trice** nmf inspector. ◆**inspection** nf inspection.

inspir/er [ɛ̃spire] 1 vt to inspire; **i. qch à qn** to inspire s.o. with sth; **s'i. de** to take one's inspiration from. 2 vi Méd to breathe in. ◆**-é** a inspired; **être bien i. de faire** to have the good idea to do. ◆**inspiration** nf 1 inspiration. 2 Méd breathing in.

instable [ɛ̃stabl] a (meuble) unsteady, shaky; (temps) unsettled; (caractère, situation) unstable. ◆**instabilité** nf unsteadiness; instability.

installer [ɛ̃stale] vt (équiper) to fit out, fix up; (appareil, meuble etc) to install, put in; (étagère) to put up; **i. qn** (dans une fonction, un logement) to install s.o. (dans in); — **s'i.** vpr (s'asseoir, s'établir) to settle (down); (médecin etc) to set oneself up; **s'i. dans** (maison, hôtel) to move into. ◆**installateur** nm fitter. ◆**installation** nf fitting out; installation; putting in; moving in; pl (appareils) fittings; (bâtiments) facilities.

instance [ɛ̃stɑ̃s] 1 nf (juridiction, autorité) authority; **tribunal de première i.** = magistrates' court; **en i. de** (divorce, départ) in the

process of. **2** *nfpl* (*prières*) insistence, entreaties.
instant [ɛ̃stɑ̃] *nm* moment, instant; **à l'i.** a moment ago; **pour l'i.** for the moment. ◆**instantané** *a* instantaneous; **café i.** instant coffee; — *nm Phot* snapshot.
instaurer [ɛ̃stɔre] *vt* to found, set up.
instigateur, -trice [ɛ̃stigatœr, -tris] *nmf* instigator. ◆**instigation** *nf* instigation.
instinct [ɛ̃stɛ̃] *nm* instinct; **d'i.** instinctively, by instinct. ◆**instinctif, -ive** *a* instinctive.
instituer [ɛ̃stitɥe] *vt* (*règle, régime*) to establish, institute.
institut [ɛ̃stity] *nm* institute; **i. de beauté** beauty salon *ou* parlour; **i. universitaire de technologie** polytechnic, technical college.
instituteur, -trice [ɛ̃stitytœr, -tris] *nmf* primary school teacher.
institution [ɛ̃stitysjɔ̃] *nf* (*règle, organisation, structure etc*) institution; *Scol* private school. ◆**institutionnel, -elle** *a* institutional.
instructif, -ive [ɛ̃stryktif, -iv] *a* instructive.
instruction [ɛ̃stryksjɔ̃] *nf* education, schooling; *Mil* training; *Jur* investigation; (*document*) directive; *pl* (*ordres*) instructions. ◆**instructeur** *nm* (*moniteur*) & *Mil* instructor.
instruire* [ɛ̃strɥir] *vt* to teach, educate; *Mil* to train; *Jur* to investigate; **i. qn de** to inform *ou* instruct s.o. of; — **s'i.** *vpr* to educate oneself; **s'i. de** to inquire about. ◆**instruit** *a* educated.
instrument [ɛ̃strymɑ̃] *nm* instrument; (*outil*) implement, tool. ◆**instrumental, -aux** *a Mus* instrumental. ◆**instrumentiste** *nmf Mus* instrumentalist.
insu de (à l') [alɛ̃syd(ə)] *prép* without the knowledge of.
insuccès [ɛ̃syksɛ] *nm* failure.
insuffisant [ɛ̃syfizɑ̃] *a* (*en qualité*) inadequate; (*en quantité*) insufficient, inadequate. ◆**insuffisance** *nf* inadequacy.
insulaire [ɛ̃sylɛr] *a* insular; — *nmf* islander.
insuline [ɛ̃sylin] *nf Méd* insulin.
insulte [ɛ̃sylt] *nf* insult (à to). ◆**insulter** *vt* to insult.
insupportable [ɛ̃syportabl] *a* unbearable.
insurg/er (s') [sɛ̃syrʒe] *vpr* to rise (up), rebel (contre against). ◆**-é, -ée** *nmf* a insurgent, rebel. ◆**insurrection** *nf* insurrection, uprising.
insurmontable [ɛ̃syrmɔ̃tabl] *a* insurmountable, insuperable.
intact [ɛ̃takt] *a* intact.
intangible [ɛ̃tɑ̃ʒibl] *a* intangible.
intarissable [ɛ̃tarisabl] *a* inexhaustible.

intégral, -aux [ɛ̃tegral, -o] *a* full, complete; (*édition*) unabridged. ◆**intégralement** *adv* in full, fully. ◆**intégralité** *nf* whole (de of); **dans son i.** in full.
intègre [ɛ̃tɛgr] *a* upright, honest. ◆**intégrité** *nf* integrity.
intégr/er [ɛ̃tegre] *vt* to integrate (dans in); — **s'i.** *vpr* to become integrated, adapt. ◆**—ante** *af* **faire partie i. de** to be part and parcel of. ◆**intégration** *nf* integration.
intellectuel, -elle [ɛ̃telɛktɥel] *a* & *nmf* intellectual.
intelligent [ɛ̃teliʒɑ̃] *a* intelligent, clever. ◆**intelligemment** [-amɑ̃] *adv* intelligently. ◆**intelligence** *nf* (*faculté*) intelligence; *pl Mil Pol* secret relations; **avoir l'i. de qch** (*compréhension*) to have an understanding of sth; **d'i. avec qn** in complicity with s.o. ◆**intelligentsia** [-dʒentsja] *nf* intelligentsia.
intelligible [ɛ̃teliʒibl] *a* intelligible. ◆**intelligibilité** *nf* intelligibility.
intempérance [ɛ̃tɑ̃perɑ̃s] *nf* intemperance.
intempéries [ɛ̃tɑ̃peri] *nfpl* **les i.** the elements, bad weather.
intempestif, -ive [ɛ̃tɑ̃pɛstif, -iv] *a* untimely.
intenable [ɛ̃tnabl] *a* (*position*) untenable; (*enfant*) unruly, uncontrollable.
intendant, -ante [ɛ̃tɑ̃dɑ̃, -ɑ̃t] *nmf Scol* bursar. ◆**intendance** *nf Scol* bursar's office.
intense [ɛ̃tɑ̃s] *a* intense; (*circulation, trafic*) heavy. ◆**intensément** *adv* intensely. ◆**intensif, -ive** *a* intensive. ◆**intensifier** *vt*, — **s'i.** *vpr* to intensify. ◆**intensité** *nf* intensity.
intenter [ɛ̃tɑ̃te] *vt* **i. un procès à** *Jur* to institute proceedings against.
intention [ɛ̃tɑ̃sjɔ̃] *nf* intention; *Jur* intent; **avoir l'i. de faire** to intend to do; **à l'i. de** for s.o.; **à votre i.** for you. ◆**intentionné** *a* **bien i.** well-intentioned. ◆**intentionnel, -elle** *a* intentional, wilful. ◆**intentionnellement** *adv* intentionally.
inter- [ɛ̃ter] *préf* inter-.
interaction [ɛ̃teraksjɔ̃] *nf* interaction.
intercaler [ɛ̃terkale] *vt* to insert.
intercéder [ɛ̃tersede] *vt* to intercede (auprès de with).
intercepter [ɛ̃tersepte] *vt* to intercept. ◆**interception** *nf* interception.
interchangeable [ɛ̃terʃɑ̃ʒabl] *a* interchangeable.
interclasse [ɛ̃terklɑs] *nm Scol* break (between classes).
intercontinental, -aux [ɛ̃terkɔ̃tinɑ̃tal, -o] *a* intercontinental.

interdépendant [ɛ̃tɛrdepɑ̃dɑ̃] *a* interdependent.

interdire/ire* [ɛ̃tɛrdir] *vt* to forbid, not to allow (**qch à qn** s.o. sth); (*meeting, film etc*) to ban; **i. à qn de faire** (*médecin, père etc*) not to allow s.o. to do, forbid s.o. to do; (*attitude, santé etc*) to prevent s.o. from doing, not allow s.o. to do. ◆**—it a 1** forbidden, not allowed; **il est i. de** it is forbidden to; **'stationnement i.'** 'no parking'. **2** (*étonné*) nonplussed. ◆**interdiction** *nf* ban (**de** on); **'i. de fumer'** 'no smoking'.

intéress/er [ɛ̃terese] *vt* to interest; (*concerner*) to concern; **s'i. à** to take an interest in, be interested in. ◆**—ant** *a* (*captivant*) interesting; (*affaire, prix etc*) attractive, worthwhile. ◆**—é, -ée** *a* (*avide*) self-interested; (*motif*) selfish; (*concerné*) concerned; – *nmf* **l'i.** the interested party.

intérêt [ɛ̃terɛ] *nm* interest; *Péj* self-interest; *pl Fin* interest; **tu as i. à faire** it would pay you to do, you'd do well to do; **des intérêts dans** *Com* an interest *ou* stake in.

interface [ɛ̃terfas] *nf Tech* interface.

intérieur [ɛ̃terjœr] *a* (*cour, paroi*) inner, interior; (*poche*) inside; (*vie, sentiment*) inner, inward; (*mer*) inland; (*politique, vol*) internal, domestic; – *nm* (*de boîte etc*) inside (**de** of); (*de maison*) interior, inside; (*de pays*) interior; **à l'i. (de)** inside; **d'i.** (*vêtement, jeux*) indoor; **femme d'i.** home-loving woman; **ministère de l'I.** Home Office, *Am* Department of the Interior. ◆**—ement** *adv* (*dans le cœur*) inwardly.

intérim [ɛ̃terim] *nm* **pendant l'i.** in the interim; **assurer l'i.** to deputize (**de** for); **ministre/etc par i.** acting minister/etc. ◆**intérimaire** *a* temporary, interim; – *nmf* (*fonctionnaire*) deputy; (*secrétaire*) temporary.

interligne [ɛ̃terliɲ] *nm Typ* space (between the lines).

interlocuteur, -trice [ɛ̃terlɔkytœr, -tris] *nmf Pol* negotiator; **mon i.** the person I am, was *etc* speaking to.

interloqué [ɛ̃terlɔke] *a* dumbfounded.

interlude [ɛ̃terlyd] *nm Mus TV* interlude.

intermède [ɛ̃termɛd] *nm* (*interruption*) & *Th* interlude.

intermédiaire [ɛ̃termedjɛr] *a* intermediate; – *nmf* intermediary; **par l'i. de** through (the medium of).

interminable [ɛ̃terminabl] *a* endless, interminable.

intermittent [ɛ̃termitɑ̃] *a* intermittent. ◆**intermittence** *nf* **par i.** intermittently.

international, -aux [ɛ̃ternasjɔnal, -o] *a* in-

ternational; – *nm* (*joueur*) *Sp* international.

interne [ɛ̃tɛrn] **1** *a* (*douleur etc*) internal; (*oreille*) inner. **2** *nmf Scol* boarder; **i.** (**des hôpitaux**) houseman, *Am* intern. ◆**internat** *nm* (*école*) boarding school.

intern/er [ɛ̃tɛrne] *vt* (*réfugié*) to intern; (*aliéné*) to confine. ◆**—ement** *nm* internment; confinement.

interpeller [ɛ̃tɛrpele] *vt* to shout at, address sharply; (*dans une réunion*) to question, (*interrompre*) to heckle; (*arrêter*) *Jur* to take in for questioning. ◆**interpellation** *nf* sharp address; questioning; heckling; (*de police*) arrest.

interphone [ɛ̃tɛrfɔn] *nm* intercom.

interplanétaire [ɛ̃tɛrplaneter] *a* interplanetary.

interpoler [ɛ̃tɛrpɔle] *vt* to interpolate.

interposer (s') [sɛ̃tɛrpoze] *vpr* (*dans une dispute etc*) to intervene (**dans** in); **s'i. entre** to come between.

interprète [ɛ̃tɛrprɛt] *nmf Ling* interpreter; (*chanteur*) singer; *Th Mus* performer; (*porte-parole*) spokesman, spokeswoman; **faire l'i.** *Ling* to interpret. ◆**interprétariat** *nm* (*métier*) *Ling* interpreting. ◆**interprétation** *nf* interpretation; *Th Mus* performance. ◆**interpréter** *vt* (*expliquer*) to interpret; (*chanter*) to sing; (*jouer*) *Th* to play, perform; (*exécuter*) *Mus* to perform.

interroger [ɛ̃terɔʒe] *vt* to question; *Jur* to interrogate; (*faits*) to examine. ◆**interrogateur, -trice** *a* (*air*) questioning; – *nmf Scol* examiner. ◆**interrogatif, -ive** *a* & *nm Gram* interrogative. ◆**interrogation** *nf* question; (*action*) questioning; (*épreuve*) *Scol* test. ◆**interrogatoire** *nm Jur* interrogation.

interrompre* [ɛ̃terɔ̃pr] *vt* to interrupt, break off; **i. qn** to interrupt s.o.; – **s'i.** *vpr* (*personne*) to break off, stop. ◆**interrupteur** *nm* (*bouton*) *Él* switch. ◆**interruption** *nf* interruption; (*des hostilités, du courant*) break (**de** in).

intersection [ɛ̃tɛrsɛksjɔ̃] *nf* intersection.

interstice [ɛ̃tɛrstis] *nm* crack, chink.

interurbain [ɛ̃teryrbɛ̃] *a* & *nm* (*téléphone*) **i.** long-distance telephone service.

intervalle [ɛ̃terval] *nm* (*écart*) space, gap; (*temps*) interval; **dans l'i.** (*entretemps*) in the meantime.

intervenir* [ɛ̃tervənir] *vi* (*s'interposer, agir*) to intervene; (*survenir*) to occur; (*opérer*) *Méd* to operate; **être intervenu** (*accord*) to be reached. ◆**intervention** *nf* intervention; **i. (chirurgicale)** operation.

intervertir [ɛ̃tɛrvɛrtir] vt to invert. ◆**interversion** nf inversion.

interview [ɛ̃tɛrvju] nf Journ TV interview. ◆**interviewer** [-vjuve] vt to interview.

intestin [ɛ̃tɛstɛ̃] nm intestine, bowel. ◆**intestinal, -aux** a intestinal, bowel-.

intime [ɛ̃tim] a intimate; (ami) close, intimate; (vie, fête, journal) private; (pièce, coin) cosy; (cérémonie) quiet; — nmf close ou intimate friend. ◆**—ment** adv intimately. ◆**intimité** nf intimacy; privacy; cosiness; **dans l'i.** (mariage etc) in private.

intimider [ɛ̃timide] vt to intimidate, frighten. ◆**intimidation** nf intimidation.

intituler [ɛ̃tityle] vt to entitle; — **s'i.** vpr to be entitled.

intolérable [ɛ̃tɔlerabl] a intolerable (que that). ◆**intolérance** nf intolerance. ◆**intolérant** a intolerant (de of).

intonation [ɛ̃tɔnɑsjɔ̃] nf Ling intonation; (ton) tone.

intoxiqu/er [ɛ̃tɔksike] vt (empoisonner) to poison; Psy Pol to brainwash; — **s'i.** vpr to be ou become poisoned. ◆**—é, -ée** nmf addict. ◆**intoxication** nf poisoning; Psy Pol brainwashing.

intra- [ɛ̃tra] préf intra-.

intraduisible [ɛ̃tradɥizibl] a untranslatable.

intraitable [ɛ̃trɛtabl] a uncompromising.

intransigeant [ɛ̃trɑ̃ziʒɑ̃] a intransigent. ◆**intransigeance** nf intransigence.

intransitif, -ive [ɛ̃trɑ̃zitif, -iv] a & nm Gram intransitive.

intraveineux, -euse [ɛ̃travɛnø, -øz] a Méd intravenous.

intrépide [ɛ̃trepid] a (courageux) fearless, intrepid; (obstiné) headstrong. ◆**intrépidité** nf fearlessness.

intrigue [ɛ̃trig] nf intrigue; Th Cin Littér plot. ◆**intrigant, -ante** nmf schemer. ◆**intriguer** 1 vi to scheme, intrigue. 2 vt **i. qn** (intéresser) to intrigue s.o., puzzle s.o.

intrinsèque [ɛ̃trɛ̃sɛk] a intrinsic. ◆**—ment** adv intrinsically.

introduire* [ɛ̃trɔdɥir] vt (présenter) to introduce, bring in; (insérer) to insert (dans into), put in (dans to); (faire entrer) to show (s.o.) in; **s'i. dans** to get into. ◆**introduction** nf (texte, action) introduction.

introspectif, -ive [ɛ̃trɔspɛktif, -iv] a introspective. ◆**introspection** nf introspection.

introuvable [ɛ̃truvabl] a that cannot be found anywhere.

introverti, -ie [ɛ̃trɔverti] nmf introvert.

intrus, -use [ɛ̃try, -yz] nmf intruder. ◆**intrusion** nf intrusion (dans into).

intuition [ɛ̃tɥisjɔ̃] nf intuition. ◆**intuitif, -ive** a intuitive.

inusable [inyzabl] a Fam hard-wearing.

inusité [inyzite] a Gram unused.

inutile [inytil] a unnecessary, useless; **c'est i. de crier** it's pointless ou useless to shout. ◆**inutilement** adv (vainement) needlessly. ◆**inutilité** nf uselessness.

inutilisable [inytilizabl] a unusable. ◆**inutilisé** a unused.

invalider [ɛ̃valide] vt to invalidate.

invariable [ɛ̃varjabl] a invariable. ◆**—ment** [-amɑ̃] adv invariably.

invasion [ɛ̃vɑzjɔ̃] nf invasion.

invective [ɛ̃vɛktiv] nf invective. ◆**invectiver** vt to abuse; — vi **i. contre** to inveigh against.

invendable [ɛ̃vɑ̃dabl] a unsaleable. ◆**invendu** a unsold.

inventaire [ɛ̃vɑ̃tɛr] nm (liste) Com inventory; (étude) Fig survey; **faire l'i.** Com to do the stocktaking (**de** of).

inventer [ɛ̃vɑ̃te] vt (découvrir) to invent; (imaginer) to make up. ◆**inventeur, -trice** nmf inventor. ◆**inventif, -ive** a inventive. ◆**invention** nf invention.

inverse [ɛ̃vɛrs] a (sens) opposite; (ordre) reverse; Math inverse; — nm **l'i.** the reverse, the opposite. ◆**inversement** adv conversely. ◆**inverser** vt (ordre) to reverse. ◆**inversion** nf Gram Anat etc inversion.

investigation [ɛ̃vɛstigɑsjɔ̃] nf investigation.

invest/ir [ɛ̃vɛstir] 1 vti Com to invest (dans in). 2 vt **i. qn de** (fonction etc) to invest s.o. with. ◆**—issement** nm Com investment. ◆**investiture** nf Pol nomination.

invétéré [ɛ̃vetere] a inveterate.

invincible [ɛ̃vɛ̃sibl] a invincible.

invisible [ɛ̃vizibl] a invisible.

invit/er [ɛ̃vite] vt to invite; **i. qn à faire** to invite ou ask s.o. to do; (inciter) to tempt s.o. to do. ◆**—é, -ée** nmf guest. ◆**invitation** nf invitation.

invivable [ɛ̃vivabl] a unbearable.

involontaire [ɛ̃vɔlɔ̃tɛr] a involuntary. ◆**—ment** adv accidentally, involuntarily.

invoquer [ɛ̃vɔke] vt (argument etc) to put forward; (appeler) to invoke, call upon. ◆**invocation** nf invocation (à to).

invraisemblable [ɛ̃vrɛsɑ̃blabl] a incredible; (improbable) improbable. ◆**invraisemblance** nf improbability.

invulnérable [ɛ̃vylnerabl] a invulnerable.

iode [jɔd] nm **teinture d'i.** Méd iodine.

ira, irait [ira, irɛ] voir aller 1.

Irak [irak] nm Iraq. ◆**irakien, -ienne** a & nmf Iraqi.

Iran [irɑ̃] nm Iran. ◆**iranien, -ienne** a & nmf Iranian.

irascible [irasibl] a irascible.

iris [iris] nm Anat Bot iris.

Irlande [irlɑ̃d] nf Ireland. ◆**irlandais, -aise** a Irish; — nmf Irishman, Irishwoman; — nm (langue) Irish.

ironie [irɔni] nf irony. ◆**ironique** a ironic(al).

irradier [iradje] vt to irradiate.

irraisonné [irɛzɔne] a irrational.

irréconciliable [irekɔ̃siljabl] a irreconcilable.

irrécusable [irekyzabl] a irrefutable.

irréel, -elle [ireɛl] a unreal.

irréfléchi [irefleʃi] a thoughtless, unthinking.

irréfutable [irefytabl] a irrefutable.

irrégulier, -ière [iregylje, -jɛr] a irregular. ◆**irrégularité** nf irregularity.

irrémédiable [iremedjabl] a irreparable.

irremplaçable [irɑ̃plasabl] a irreplaceable.

irréparable [ireparabl] a (véhicule etc) beyond repair; (tort, perte) irreparable.

irrépressible [irepresibl] a (rires etc) irrepressible.

irréprochable [ireprɔʃabl] a beyond reproach, irreproachable.

irrésistible [irezistibl] a (personne, charme etc) irresistible.

irrésolu [irezɔly] a irresolute.

irrespirable [irespirabl] a unbreathable; Fig stifling.

irresponsable [irespɔ̃sabl] a (personne) irresponsible.

irrévérencieux, -euse [ireverɑ̃sjø, -øz] a irreverent.

irréversible [ireversibl] a irreversible.

irrévocable [irevɔkabl] a irrevocable.

irriguer [irige] vt to irrigate. ◆**irrigation** nf irrigation.

irrit/er [irite] vt to irritate; — **s'i.** vpr to get angry (de, contre at). ◆**—ant** a irritating; — nm irritant. ◆**—able** a irritable. ◆**irritation** nf (colère) & Méd irritation.

irruption [irypsjɔ̃] nf faire i. dans to burst into.

islam [islam] nm Islam. ◆**islamique** a Islamic.

Islande [islɑ̃d] nf Iceland. ◆**islandais, -aise** a Icelandic.

isol/er [izɔle] vt to isolate (de from); (contre le froid etc) & Él to insulate; — **s'i.** vpr to cut oneself off, isolate oneself. ◆**—ant** a insulating; — nm insulating material. ◆**—é** a isolated; (écarté) remote, isolated; i. de cut off ou isolated from. ◆**isolation** nf insulation. ◆**isolement** nm isolation. ◆**isolément** adv in isolation, singly. ◆**isoloir** nm polling booth.

isorel® [izɔrɛl] nm hardboard.

Israël [israɛl] nm Israel. ◆**israélien, -ienne** a & nmf Israeli. ◆**israélite** a Jewish; — nm Jew; — nf Jewess.

issu [isy] a être i. de to come from.

issue [isy] nf (sortie) exit, way out; (solution) Fig way out; (résultat) outcome; à l'i. de at the close of; rue etc sans i. dead end; situation etc sans i. Fig dead end.

isthme [ism] nm Géog isthmus.

Italie [itali] nf Italy. ◆**italien, -ienne** a & nmf Italian; — nm (langue) Italian.

italique [italik] a Typ italic; — nm italics.

itinéraire [itinerɛr] nm itinerary, route.

itinérant [itinerɑ̃] a itinerant.

IVG [iveʒe] nf abrév (interruption volontaire de grossesse) (voluntary) abortion.

ivoire [ivwar] nm ivory.

ivre [ivr] a drunk (de with). ◆**ivresse** nf drunkenness; en état d'i. under the influence of drink. ◆**ivrogne** nmf drunk(ard).

J

J, j [ʒi] nm J, j; le jour J. D-day.

j' [ʒ] voir je.

jacasser [ʒakase] vi (personne, pie) to chatter.

jachère (en) [ɑ̃ʒaʃɛr] adv (champ etc) fallow.

jacinthe [ʒasɛ̃t] nf hyacinth.

jacousi [ʒakuzi] nm (baignoire, piscine) jacuzzi.

jade [ʒad] nm (pierre) jade.

jadis [ʒadis] adv at one time, once.

jaguar [ʒagwar] nm (animal) jaguar.

jaill/ir [ʒajir] vi (liquide) to spurt (out), gush (out); (lumière) to flash, stream; (cri) to burst out; (vérité) to burst forth; (étincelle) to fly out. ◆**—issement** nm (de liquide) gush.

jais [ʒɛ] nm (noir) de j. jet-black.

jalon [ʒalɔ̃] nm (*piquet*) marker; **poser les jalons** *Fig* to prepare the way (**de** for). ◆**jalonner** vt to mark (out); (*border*) to line.

jaloux, -ouse [ʒalu, -uz] a jealous (**de** of). ◆**jalouser** vt to envy. ◆**jalousie** nf **1** jealousy. **2** (*persienne*) venetian blind.

Jamaïque [ʒamaik] nf Jamaica.

jamais [ʒamɛ] adv **1** (*négatif*) never; **sans j. sortir** without ever going out; **elle ne sort j.** she never goes out. **2** (*positif*) ever; **à (tout) j.** for ever; **si j.** if ever.

jambe [ʒɑ̃b] nf leg; **à toutes jambes** as fast as one can; **prendre ses jambes à son cou** to take to one's heels.

jambon [ʒɑ̃bɔ̃] nm *Culin* ham. ◆**jambonneau, -x** nm knuckle of ham.

jante [ʒɑ̃t] nf (*de roue*) rim.

janvier [ʒɑ̃vje] nm January.

Japon [ʒapɔ̃] nm Japan. ◆**japonais, -aise** a nmf Japanese; – & nm (*langue*) Japanese.

japp/er [ʒape] vi (*chien etc*) to yap, yelp. ◆**-ement** nm yap, yelp.

jaquette [ʒakɛt] nf (*d'homme*) tailcoat, morning coat; (*de femme, livre*) jacket.

jardin [ʒardɛ̃] nm garden; **j. d'enfants** kindergarten, playschool; **j. public** park; (*plus petit*) gardens. ◆**jardinage** nm gardening. ◆**jardiner** vi to do the garden, be gardening. ◆**jardinerie** nf garden centre. ◆**jardinier** nm gardener. ◆**jardinière** nf (*personne*) gardener; (*caisse à fleurs*) window-box; **j. (de légumes)** *Culin* mixed vegetable dish; **j. d'enfants** kindergarten teacher.

jargon [ʒargɔ̃] nm jargon.

jarret [ʒarɛ] nm *Anat* back of the knee.

jarretelle [ʒartɛl] nf (*de gaine*) suspender, *Am* garter. ◆**jarretière** nf (*autour de la jambe*) garter.

jaser [ʒaze] vi (*bavarder*) to jabber.

jasmin [ʒasmɛ̃] nm *Bot* jasmine.

jatte [ʒat] nf (*bol*) bowl.

jauge [ʒoʒ] nf **1** (*instrument*) gauge. **2** (*capacité*) capacity; *Nau* tonnage. ◆**jauger** vt (*personne*) *Litt* to size up.

jaune [ʒon] a **1** yellow; – nm (*couleur*) yellow; **j. d'œuf** (egg) yolk. **2** nm (*ouvrier*) *Péj* blackleg, scab. ◆**jaunâtre** a yellowish. ◆**jaunir** vti to (turn) yellow. ◆**jaunisse** nf *Méd* jaundice.

Javel (eau de) [odʒavɛl] nf bleach. ◆**javelliser** vt to chlorinate.

javelot [ʒavlo] nm javelin.

jazz [dʒaz] nm jazz.

je [ʒ(ə)] pron (**j'** before vowel or mute h) I; **je suis** I am.

jean [dʒin] nm (pair of) jeans.

jeep [dʒip] nf jeep.

je-m'en-fichisme [ʒmɑ̃fiʃism] nm inv *Fam* couldn't-care-less attitude.

jérémiades [ʒeremjad] nfpl *Fam* lamentations.

jerrycan [(d)ʒerikan] nm jerry can.

jersey [ʒɛrze] nm (*tissu*) jersey.

Jersey [ʒɛrze] nf Jersey.

jésuite [ʒezɥit] nm Jesuit.

Jésus [ʒezy] nm Jesus; **J.-Christ** Jesus Christ.

jet [ʒɛ] nm throw; (*de vapeur*) burst, gush; (*de lumière*) flash; **j. d'eau** fountain; **premier j.** (*ébauche*) first draft; **d'un seul j.** in one go.

jetée [ʒ(ə)te] nf pier, jetty.

jeter [ʒ(ə)te] vt to throw (**à** to, **dans** into); (*mettre à la poubelle*) to throw away; (*ancre, regard, sort*) to cast; (*bases*) to lay; (*cri, son*) to let out, utter; (*éclat, lueur*) to throw out, give out; (*noter*) to jot down; **j. un coup d'œil sur ou à** to have *ou* take a look at; (*rapidement*) to glance at; – **se j.** vpr to throw oneself; **se j. sur** to fall on, pounce on; **se j. contre** (*véhicule*) to crash into; **se j. dans** (*fleuve*) to flow into. ◆**jetable** a (*rasoir etc*) disposable.

jeton [ʒ(ə)tɔ̃] nm (*pièce*) token; (*pour compter*) counter; (*à la roulette*) chip.

jeu, -x [ʒø] nm **1** game; (*amusement*) play; (*d'argent*) gambling; *Th* acting; *Mus* playing; **j. de mots** play on words, pun; **jeux de société** parlour *ou* party games; **j. télévisé** television quiz; **maison de jeux** gambling club; **en j.** (*en cause*) at stake; (*forces etc*) at work; **entrer en j.** to come into play. **2** (*série complète*) set; (*de cartes*) pack, deck, *Am* deck; (*cartes en main*) hand; **j. d'échecs** (*boîte, pièces*) chess set. **3** (*de ressort, verrou*) *Tech* play.

jeudi [ʒødi] nm Thursday.

jeun (à) [aʒœ̃] adv on an empty stomach; **être à j.** to have eaten no food.

jeune [ʒœn] a young; (*inexpérimenté*) inexperienced; **Dupont j.** Dupont junior; **d'allure j.** young-looking; **jeunes gens** young people; – nmf young person; **les jeunes** young people. ◆**jeunesse** nf youth; (*apparence*) youthfulness; **la j.** (*jeunes*) the young, youth.

jeûne [ʒøn] nm fast; (*action*) fasting. ◆**jeûner** vi to fast.

joaillier, -ière [ʒɔaje, -jɛr] nmf jeweller.

◆**joaillerie** *nf* jewellery; (*magasin*) jewellery shop.

jockey [ʒɔkɛ] *nm* jockey.

jogging [dʒɔgiŋ] *nm Sp* jogging; (*chaussure*) running *ou* jogging shoe; **faire du j.** to jog.

joie [ʒwa] *nf* joy, delight; **feu de j.** bonfire.

joindre* [ʒwɛ̃dr] *vt* (*mettre ensemble, relier*) to join; (*efforts*) to combine; (*insérer dans une enveloppe*) to enclose (**à** with); (*ajouter*) to add (**à** to); **j. qn** (*contacter*) to get in touch with s.o.; **j. les deux bouts** *Fig* to make ends meet; **se j. à** (*se mettre avec, participer à*) to join. ◆**joint** *a* (*efforts*, combined); **à pieds joints** with feet together; – *nm Tech* joint; (*de robinet*) washer. ◆**jointure** *nf Anat* joint.

joker [ʒɔkɛr] *nm Cartes* joker.

joli [ʒɔli] *a* nice, lovely; (*femme, enfant*) pretty. ◆**—ment** *adv* nicely; (*très, beaucoup*) awfully.

jonc [ʒɔ̃] *nm Bot* (bul)rush.

joncher [ʒɔ̃ʃe] *vt* to litter (**de** with); **jonché de** strewn *ou* littered with.

jonction [ʒɔ̃ksjɔ̃] *nf* (*de tubes, routes etc*) junction.

jongl/er [ʒɔ̃gle] *vi* to juggle. ◆**—eur, -euse** *nmf* juggler.

jonquille [ʒɔ̃kij] *nf* daffodil.

Jordanie [ʒɔrdani] *nf* Jordan.

joue [ʒu] *nf Anat* cheek; **coucher qn en j.** to aim (a gun) at s.o.

jouer [ʒwe] *vi* to play; *Th* to act; (*au tiercé etc*) to gamble, bet; (*à la Bourse*) to gamble; (*entrer en jeu*) to come into play; (*être important*) to count; (*fonctionner*) to work; **j. au tennis/aux cartes/***etc* to play tennis/cards/*etc*; **j. du piano/du violon/***etc* to play the piano/violin/*etc*; **j. des coudes** to use one's elbows; – *vt* (*musique, tour, jeu*) to play; (*risquer*) to gamble, bet (**sur** on); (*cheval*) to bet on; (*personnage, rôle*) *Th* to play; (*pièce*) *Th* to perform, put on; (*film*) to show, put on; **j. gros jeu** to play for high stakes; **se j. de** to scoff at; (*difficultés*) to make light of. ◆**jouet** *nm* toy; **être le j. de qn** *Fig* s.o.'s plaything. ◆**joueur, -euse** *nmf* player; (*au tiercé etc*) gambler; **beau j., bon j.,** good loser.

joufflu [ʒufly] *a* (*visage*) chubby; (*enfant*) chubby-cheeked.

joug [ʒu] *nm Agr & Fig* yoke.

jouir [ʒwir] *vi* **1 j. de** (*savourer, avoir*) to enjoy. **2** (*éprouver le plaisir sexuel*) to come. ◆**jouissance** *nf* enjoyment; (*usage*) *Jur* use.

joujou, -x [ʒuʒu] *nm Fam* toy.

jour [ʒur] *nm* day; (*lumière*) (day)light; (*ouverture*) gap, opening; (*aspect*) *Fig* light; **il fait j.** it's (day)light; **grand j., plein j.** broad daylight; **de nos jours** nowadays, these days; **au j. le j.** from day to day; **du j. au lendemain** overnight; **mettre à j.** to bring up to date; **mettre au j.** to bring into the open; **se faire j.** to come to light; **donner le j. à** to give birth to; **le j. de l'An** New Year's day. ◆**journalier, -ière** *a* daily. ◆**journée** *nf* day; **pendant la j.** during the day(time); **toute la j.** all day (long). ◆**journellement** *adv* daily.

journal, -aux [ʒurnal, -o] *nm* (news)paper; (*spécialisé*) journal; (*intime*) diary; (*parlé*) *Rad* news bulletin; **j. de bord** *Nau* logbook. ◆**journalisme** *nm* journalism. ◆**journaliste** *nmf* journalist. ◆**journalistique** *a* (*style etc*) journalistic.

jovial, -aux [ʒɔvjal, -o] *a* jovial, jolly. ◆**jovialité** *nf* jollity.

joyau, -aux [ʒwajo] *nm* jewel.

joyeux, -euse [ʒwajø, -øz] *a* merry, happy, joyful; **j. anniversaire!** happy birthday!; **j. Noël!** merry *ou* happy Christmas!

jubilé [ʒybile] *nm* (golden) jubilee.

jubiler [ʒybile] *vi* to be jubilant. ◆**jubilation** *nf* jubilation.

jucher [ʒyʃe] *vt,* — **se j.** *vpr* to perch (**sur** on).

judaïque [ʒydaik] *a* Jewish. ◆**judaïsme** *nm* Judaism.

judas [ʒyda] *nm* (*de porte*) peephole, spy hole.

judiciaire [ʒydisjɛr] *a* judicial, legal.

judicieux, -euse [ʒydisjø, -øz] *a* sensible, judicious.

judo [ʒydo] *nm* judo. ◆**judoka** *nmf* judo expert.

juge [ʒyʒ] *nm* judge; *Sp* referee, umpire; **j. d'instruction** examining magistrate; **j. de paix** Justice of the Peace; **j. de touche** *Fb* linesman. ◆**juger** *vt* (*personne, question etc*) to judge; (*affaire*) *Jur* to try; (*estimer*) to consider (**que** that); **j. qn** *Jur* to try s.o.; – *vi* **j.** de to judge; **jugez de ma surprise/***etc* imagine my surprise/*etc*. ◆**jugement** *nm.* judg(e)ment; (*verdict*) *Jur* sentence; **passer en j.** *Jur* to stand trial. ◆**jugeote** *nf Fam* commonsense.

jugé (au) [oʒyʒe] *adv* by guesswork.

juguler [ʒygyle] *vt* to check, suppress.

juif, juive [ʒɥif, ʒɥiv] *a* Jewish; – *nm* Jew; – *nf* Jew(ess).

juillet [ʒɥijɛ] *nm* July.

juin [ʒɥɛ̃] *nm* June.

jumeau, -elle, *pl* **-eaux, -elles** [ʒymo, -ɛl] *a* (*frères, lits etc*) twin; – *nmf* twin. **2** *nfpl* (*longue-vue*) binoculars; **jumelles de théâtre** opera glasses. ◆**jumel/er** *vt* (*villes*) to twin. ◆**–age** *nm* twinning.

jument [ʒymɑ̃] *nf* (*cheval*) mare.

jungle [ʒœ̃gl] *nf* jungle.

junior [ʒynjɔr] *nm* & *a* (*inv an sing*) *Sp* junior.

junte [ʒœ̃t] *nf Pol* junta.

jupe [ʒyp] *nf* skirt. ◆**jupon** *nm* petticoat.

jurer [ʒyre] **1** *vi* (*blasphémer*) to swear. **2** *vt* (*promettre*) to swear (**que** that, **de faire** to do); – *vi* **j. de qch** to swear to sth. **3** *vi* (*contraster*) to clash (**avec** with). ◆**juré** *a* (*ennemi*) sworn; – *nm Jur* juror. ◆**juron** *nm* swearword, oath.

juridiction [ʒyridiksjɔ̃] *nf* jurisdiction.

juridique [ʒyridik] *a* legal. ◆**juriste** *nmf* legal expert, jurist.

jury [ʒyri] *nm Jur* jury; (*de concours*) panel (of judges), jury.

jus [ʒy] *nm* (*des fruits etc*) juice; (*de viande*) gravy; (*café*) *Fam* coffee; (*électricité*) *Fam* power.

jusque [ʒysk] *prép* **jusqu'à** (*espace*) as far as, (right) up to; (*temps*) until, (up) till, to; (*même*) even; **jusqu'à dix francs**/*etc* (*limite*) up to ten francs/*etc*; **jusqu'en mai**/*etc* until May/*etc*; **jusqu'où?** how far?; **j. dans**/**sous**/*etc* right into/under/*etc*; **j. chez moi** as far as my place; **jusqu'ici** as far as this; (*temps*) up till now; **en avoir j.-là** *Fam* to be fed up; – *conj* **jusqu'à ce qu'il vienne** until he comes.

juste [ʒyst] *a* (*équitable*) fair, just; (*légitime*) just; (*calcul, heure, réponse*) correct, right, accurate; (*remarque*) sound; (*oreille*) good; (*voix*) *Mus* true; (*vêtement*) tight; **un peu j.** (*quantité, repas etc*) barely enough; **très j.!** quite so *ou* right!; **à 3 heures j.** on the stroke of 3; – *adv* (*deviner, compter*) correctly, right, accurately; (*chanter*) in tune; (*exactement, seulement*) just; **au j.** exactly; **tout j.** (*à peine, seulement*) only just; **c'était j.!** (*il était temps*) it was a near thing!; **un peu j.** (*mesurer, compter*) a bit on the short side; – *nm* (*homme*) just man. ◆**justement** *adv* precisely, exactly, just; (*avec justesse ou justice*) justly. ◆**justesse** *nf* (*exactitude*) accuracy; **de j.** (*éviter, gagner etc*) just.

justice [ʒystis] *nf* justice; (*organisation, autorités*) law; **en toute j.** in all fairness; **rendre j. à** to do justice to. ◆**justicier, -ière** *nmf* dispenser of justice.

justifier [ʒystifje] *vt* to justify; – *vi* **j. de** to prove; – **se j.** *vpr Jur* to clear oneself (**de** of); (*attitude etc*) to be justified. ◆**justifiable** *a* justifiable. ◆**justificatif, -ive** *a* **document j.** supporting document, proof. ◆**justification** *nf* justification; (*preuve*) proof.

jute [ʒyt] *nm* (*fibre*) jute.

juteux, -euse [ʒytø, -øz] *a* juicy.

juvénile [ʒyvenil] *a* youthful.

juxtaposer [ʒykstapoze] *vt* to juxtapose. ◆**juxtaposition** *nf* juxtaposition.

K

K, k [kɑ] *nm* K, k.

kaki [kaki] *a inv* & *nm* khaki.

kaléidoscope [kaleidɔskɔp] *nm* kaleidoscope.

kangourou [kɑ̃guru] *nm* **1** (*animal*) kangaroo. **2**® (*porte-bébé*) baby sling.

karaté [karate] *nm Sp* karate.

kart [kart] *nm Sp* (go-)kart, go-cart. ◆**karting** [-iŋ] *nm Sp* (go-)karting.

kascher [kaʃɛr] *a inv Rel* kosher.

kayac [kajak] *nm* (*bateau*) *Sp* canoe.

képi [kepi] *nm* (*coiffure*) *Mil* kepi.

kermesse [kermɛs] *nf* charity fête; (*en Belgique etc*) village fair.

kérosène [kerozɛn] *nm* kerosene, aviation fuel.

kibboutz [kibuts] *nm* kibbutz.

kidnapp/er [kidnape] *vt* to kidnap. ◆**–eur, -euse** *nmf* kidnapper.

kilo(gramme) [kilo, kilɔgram] *nm* kilo(gramme).

kilomètre [kilɔmɛtr] *nm* kilometre. ◆**kilométrage** *nm Aut* = mileage. ◆**kilométrique** *a* **borne k.** = milestone.

kilowatt [kilɔwat] *nm* kilowatt.

kimono [kimɔno] *nm* (*tunique*) kimono.

kinésithérapie [kineziterapi] *nf* physiotherapy. ◆**kinésithérapeute** *nmf* physiotherapist.

kiosque [kjɔsk] *nm* (*à journaux*) kiosk, stall; **k. à musique** bandstand.

kit [kit] *nm* (*meuble etc prêt à monter*) kit; **en k.** in kit form, ready to assemble.

klaxon® [klaksɔn] *nm Aut* horn. ◆**klaxonner** *vi* to hoot, *Am* honk.

km *abrév (kilomètre)* km.

k.-o. [kao] *a inv* mettre k.-o. *Boxe* to knock out.

kyrielle [kirjɛl] *nf* une k. de a long string of.

kyste [kist] *nm Méd* cyst.

L

L, l [ɛl] *nm* L, l.

l', la [l, la] *voir* le.

là [la] **1** *adv* there; *(chez soi)* in, home; je reste là I'll stay here; c'est là que *ou* où that's where; c'est là ton erreur that's *ou* there's your mistake; là où il est where he is; à cinq mètres de là five metres away; de là son échec *(cause)* hence his *ou* her failure; jusque-là *(lieu)* as far as that; passe par là go that way. **2** *adv (temps)* then; jusque-là up till then. **3** *int* là, là! *(pour rassurer)* there, there!; alors là! well!; oh là là! oh dear! **4** *voir* ce², celui.

là-bas [labɑ] *adv* over there.

label [labɛl] *nm Com* label, mark *(of quality, origin etc)*.

labeur [labœr] *nm Litt* toil.

labo [labo] *nm Fam* lab. ◆**laboratoire** *nm* laboratory; l. de langues language laboratory.

laborieux, -euse [labɔrjø, -øz] *a (pénible)* laborious; *(personne)* industrious; les classes laborieuses the working classes.

labour [labur] *nm* ploughing, *Am* plowing, digging over. ◆**labour/er** *vt (avec charrue)* to plough, *Am* plow; *(avec bêche)* to dig over; *(visage etc) Fig* to furrow. ◆**—eur** *nm* ploughman, *Am* plowman.

labyrinthe [labirɛ̃t] *nm* maze, labyrinth.

lac [lak] *nm* lake.

lacer [lase] *vt* to lace (up). ◆**lacet** *nm* **1** *(shoe- ou boot-)*lace. **2** *(de route)* twist, zigzag; route en s. winding *ou* zigzag road.

lacérer [lasere] *vt (papier etc)* to tear; *(visage etc)* to lacerate.

lâche [lɑʃ] **1** *a* cowardly; *– nmf* coward. **2** *a (détendu)* loose, slack. ◆**lâchement** *adv* in a cowardly manner. ◆**lâcheté** *nf* cowardice; une l. *(action)* a cowardly act.

lâch/er [lɑʃe] *vt (main, objet etc)* to let go of; *(bombe, pigeon)* to release; *(place, études)* to give up; *(juron)* to utter, let slip; *(secret)* to let out; l. qn *(laisser tranquille) Fam* to leave s.o. (alone); *(abandonner) Fam* to drop s.o.; l. prise to let go; *– vi (corde)* to give way; *– nm* release. ◆**—eur, -euse** *nmf Fam* deserter.

laconique [lakɔnik] *a* laconic.

lacrymogène [lakrimɔʒɛn] *a* gaz l. tear gas.

lacté [lakte] *a (régime)* milk-; la Voie lactée the Milky Way.

lacune [lakyn] *nf* gap, deficiency.

lad [lad] *nm* stable boy, groom.

là-dedans [lad(ə)dɑ̃] *adv (lieu)* in there, inside. ◆**là-dessous** *adv* underneath. ◆**là-dessus** *adv* on it, on that; *(monter)* on top; *(alors)* thereupon. ◆**là-haut** *adv* up there; *(à l'étage)* upstairs.

lagon [lagɔ̃] *nm (small)* lagoon. ◆**lagune** *nf* lagoon.

laid [lɛ] *a* ugly; *(ignoble)* wretched. ◆**laideur** *nf* ugliness.

laine [lɛn] *nf* wool; de l., en l. woollen. ◆**lainage** *nm (vêtement)* woollen garment, woolly; *(étoffe)* woollen material; *pl (vêtements, objets fabriqués)* woollens. ◆**laineux, -euse** *a* woolly.

laïque [laik] *a (vie)* secular; *(habit, tribunal)* lay; *– nmf (non-prêtre)* layman, laywoman.

laisse [lɛs] *nf* lead, leash; en l. on a lead *ou* leash.

laisser [lese] *vt* to leave; l. qn partir/entrer/etc *(permettre)* to let s.o. go/come in/etc; l. qch à qn *(confier, donner)* to let s.o. have sth, leave sth with s.o.; *(vendre)* to let s.o. have sth; laissez-moi le temps de le faire give me *ou* leave me time to do it; se l. aller/faire to let oneself go/be pushed around. ◆**laissé(e)-pour-compte** *nmf (personne)* misfit, reject. ◆**laisser-aller** *nm inv* carelessness, slovenliness; ◆**laissez-passer** *nm inv (sauf-conduit)* pass.

lait [lɛ] *nm* milk; frère/sœur de l. foster-brother/-sister; dent de l. milk tooth. ◆**laitage** *nm* milk product *ou* food. ◆**laiterie** *nf* dairy. ◆**laiteux, -euse** *a* milky. ◆**laitier, -ière** *a (produits)* dairy-; *– nm (livreur)* milkman; *(vendeur)* dairyman; *– nf* dairywoman.

laiton [lɛtɔ̃] *nm* brass.

laitue [lety] nf lettuce.

laïus [lajys] nm Fam speech.

lama [lama] nm (animal) llama.

lambeau, -x [lãbo] nm shred, bit; mettre en lambeaux to tear to shreds; tomber en lambeaux to fall to bits.

lambin, -ine [lãbẽ, -in] nmf dawdler. ◆lambiner vi to dawdle.

lambris [lãbri] nm panelling. ◆lambrisser vt to panel.

lame [lam] nf 1 (de couteau, rasoir etc) blade; (de métal) strip, plate; l. de parquet floorboard. 2 (vague) wave; l. de fond ground swell.

lamelle [lamɛl] nf thin strip; l. de verre (pour microscope) slide.

lamenter (se) [salamãte] vpr to moan, lament; se l. sur to lament (over). ◆lamentable a (mauvais) deplorable; (voix, cri) mournful. ◆lamentation nf lament(ation).

laminé [lamine] a (métal) laminated.

lampadaire [lãpadɛr] nm standard lamp; (de rue) street lamp.

lampe [lãp] nf lamp; (au néon) light; (de vieille radio) valve, Am (vacuum) tube; l. de poche torch, Am flashlight.

lampée [lãpe] nf Fam gulp.

lampion [lãpjɔ̃] nm Chinese lantern.

lance [lãs] nf spear; (de tournoi) Hist lance; (extrémité de tuyau) nozzle; l. d'incendie fire hose. ◆l.-flammes [lãsflam] nm inv flame thrower. ◆l.-pierres nm inv catapult. ◆l.-roquettes nm inv rocket launcher.

lanc/er [lãse] vt (jeter) to throw (à to); (avec force) to hurl; (navire, mode, acteur, idée) to launch; (regard) to cast (à at); (moteur) to start; (ultimatum) to issue; (bombe) to drop; (gifle) to give; (cri) to utter; — se l. vpr (se précipiter) to rush; se l. dans (aventure, discussion) to launch into; — nm un l. a throw; le l. de the throwing of. ◆—ée nf momentum. ◆—ement nm Sp throwing; (de fusée, navire etc) launch(ing).

lancinant [lãsinã] a (douleur) shooting; (obsédant) haunting.

landau [lãdo] nm (pl -s) pram, Am baby carriage.

lande [lãd] nf moor, heath.

langage [lãgaʒ] nm (système, faculté d'expression) language; l. machine computer language.

lange [lãʒ] nm (baby) blanket. ◆langer vt (bébé) to change.

langouste [lãgust] nf (spiny) lobster.

◆langoustine nf (Dublin) prawn, Norway lobster.

langue [lãg] nf Anat tongue; Ling language; de l. anglaise/française English-/French-speaking; l. maternelle mother tongue; mauvaise l. (personne) gossip. ◆languette nf (patte) tongue.

langueur [lãgœr] nf languor. ◆langu/ir vi to languish (après for, after); (conversation) to flag. ◆—issant a languid; (conversation) flagging.

lanière [lanjɛr] nf strap; (d'étoffe) strip.

lanterne [lãtɛrn] nf lantern; (électrique) lamp; pl Aut sidelights.

lanterner [lãtɛrne] vi to loiter.

lapalissade [lapalisad] nf statement of the obvious, truism.

laper [lape] vt (boire) to lap up; — vi to lap.

lapider [lapide] vt to stone.

lapin [lapẽ] nm rabbit; mon (petit) l.! my dear!; poser un l. à qn Fam to stand s.o. up.

laps [laps] nm un l. de temps a lapse of time.

lapsus [lapsys] nm slip (of the tongue).

laquais [lakɛ] nm Hist & Fig lackey.

laque [lak] nf lacquer; l. à cheveux hair spray, (hair) lacquer. ◆laquer vt to lacquer.

laquelle [lakɛl] voir lequel.

larbin [larbẽ] nm Fam flunkey.

lard [lar] nm (fumé) bacon; (gras) (pig's) fat. ◆lardon nm Culin strip of bacon ou fat.

large [larʒ] a wide, broad; (vêtement) loose; (idées, esprit) broad; (grand) large; (généreux) liberal; l. d'esprit broad-minded; l. de six mètres six metres wide; — adv (calculer) liberally, broadly; — nm breadth, width; avoir six mètres de l. to be six metres wide; le l. (mer) the open sea; au l. de Cherbourg Nau off Cherbourg; être au l. to have lots of room. ◆—ment adv widely; (ouvrir) wide; (servir, payer) liberally; (au moins) easily; avoir l. le temps to have plenty of time, have ample time. ◆largesse nf liberality. ◆largeur nf width, breadth; (d'esprit) breadth.

larguer [large] vt (bombe, parachutiste) to drop; l. qn (se débarrasser de) to drop s.o.; l. les amarres Nau to cast off.

larme [larm] nf tear; (goutte) Fam drop; en larmes in tears; rire aux larmes to laugh till one cries. ◆larmoyer vi (yeux) to water.

larve [larv] nf (d'insecte) larva, grub.

larvé [larve] a latent, underlying.

larynx [larẽks] nm Anat larynx ◆laryngite nf Méd laryngitis.

las, lasse [lɑ, lɑs] a tired, weary (de of).

◆**lasser** vt to tire, weary; **se l. de** to tire of.

◆**lassitude** nf tiredness, weariness.

lascar [laskar] nm Fam (clever) fellow.

lascif, -ive [lasif, -iv] a lascivious.

laser [lazɛr] nm laser.

lasso [laso] nm lasso.

latent, -ente [latɑ̃] a latent.

latéral, -aux [lateral, -o] a lateral, side-.

latin, -ine [latɛ̃, -in] a & nmf Latin; — nm (langue) Latin.

latitude [latityd] nf Géog & Fig latitude.

latrines [latrin] nfpl latrines.

latte [lat] nf slat, lath; (de plancher) board.

lauréat, -ate [lorea, -at] nmf (prize)winner; — a prize-winning.

laurier [lɔrje] nm Bot laurel, bay; **du l.** Culin bay leaves.

lavabo [lavabo] nm washbasin, sink; pl (cabinet) toilet(s), Am washroom.

lavande [lavɑ̃d] nf lavender.

lave [lav] nf Géol lava.

lave-auto [lavoto] nm car wash. ◆**l.-glace** nm windscreen ou Am windshield washer. ◆**l.-linge** nm washing machine. ◆**l.-vaisselle** nm dishwasher.

laver [lave] vt to wash; **l. qn de** (soupçon etc) to clear s.o. of; — **se l.** vpr to wash (oneself), Am wash up; **se l. les mains** to wash one's hands (Fig de of). ◆**lavable** a washable. ◆**lavage** nm washing; **l. de cerveau** Psy brainwashing. ◆**laverie** nf (automatique) launderette, Am laundromat. ◆**lavette** nf (dish) cloth; (homme) Péj drip. ◆**laveur** nm **l. de carreaux** window cleaner ou Am washer. ◆**lavoir** nm (bâtiment) washhouse.

laxatif, -ive [laksatif, -iv] nm & a Méd laxative.

laxisme [laksism] nm permissiveness, laxity. ◆**laxiste** a permissive.

layette [lɛjet] nf baby clothes, layette.

le, la, pl **les** [l(ə), la, le] (le & la become l' before a vowel or mute h) **1** art déf (à = le = au, à + les = aux; de + le = du, de + les = des) the; **le garçon** the boy; **la fille** the girl; **venez, les enfants!** come children!; **les petits/rouges/etc** the little ones/red ones/etc; **mon ami le plus intime** my closest friend. **2** (généralisation, abstraction) **la beauté** beauty; **la France** France; **les Français** the French; **les hommes** men; **aimer le café** to like coffee. **3** (possession) **il ouvrit la bouche** he opened his mouth; **se blesser au pied** to hurt one's foot; **avoir les cheveux blonds** to have blond hair. **4** (mesure) **dix francs le kilo** ten francs a kilo. **5** (temps) **elle vient le lundi** she comes on Monday(s);

elle passe le soir she comes over in the evening(s); **l'an prochain** next year; **une fois l'an** once a year. **6** pron (homme) him; (femme) her; (chose, animal) it; pl them; **je la vois** I see her; I see it; **je le vois** I see him; I see it; **je les vois** I see them; **je te fatigue? – je le suis** are you tired? – I am; **je le crois** I think so.

leader [lidœr] nm Pol leader.

lécher [leʃe] vt to lick; **se l. les doigts** to lick one's fingers. ◆**lèche-vitrines** nm **faire du l.-vitrines** to go window-shopping.

leçon [ləsɔ̃] nf lesson; **faire la l. à qn** to lecture s.o.

lecteur, -trice [lɛktœr, -tris] nmf reader; Univ (foreign language) assistant; **l. de cassettes** cassette player. ◆**lecture** nf reading; pl (livres) books; **faire de la l. à qn** to read to s.o.; **de la l.** some reading matter.

légal, -aux [legal, -o] a legal; (médecine) forensic. ◆**légalement** adv legally. ◆**légaliser** vt to legalize. ◆**légalité** nf legality (de of); **respecter la l.** to respect the law.

légation [legasjɔ̃] nf Pol legation.

légende [leʒɑ̃d] nf **1** (histoire, fable) legend. **2** (de plan, carte) key, legend; (de photo) caption. ◆**légendaire** a legendary.

léger, -ère [leʒe, -ɛr] a light; (bruit, faute, fièvre etc) slight; (café, thé, argument) weak; (bière, tabac) mild; (frivole) frivolous; (irréfléchi) careless; **à la légère** (agir) rashly. ◆**légèrement** adv lightly; (un peu) slightly; (à la légère) rashly. ◆**légèreté** nf lightness; frivolity.

légiférer [leʒifere] vi to legislate.

légion [leʒjɔ̃] nf Mil & Fig legion. ◆**légionnaire** nm (de la Légion étrangère) legionnaire.

législatif, -ive [leʒislatif, -iv] a legislative; (élections) parliamentary. ◆**législation** nf legislation. ◆**législature** nf (période) Pol term of office.

légitime [leʒitim] a (action, enfant etc) legitimate; **en état de l. défense** acting in self-defence. ◆**légitimité** nf legitimacy.

legs [leg] nm Jur legacy, bequest; (héritage) Fig legacy. ◆**léguer** vt to bequeath (à to).

légume [legym] **1** nm vegetable. **2** nf **grosse l.** (personne) Fam bigwig.

lendemain [lɑ̃dmɛ̃] nm **le l.** the next day; (avenir) Fig the future; **le l. de** the day after; **le l. matin** the next morning.

lent [lɑ̃] a slow. ◆**lentement** adv slowly. ◆**lenteur** nf slowness.

lentille [lɑ̃tij] nf **1** Bot Culin lentil. **2** (verre) lens.

léopard [leɔpar] nm leopard.

lèpre [lɛpr] nf leprosy. ◆**lépreux, -euse** a leprous; − nmf leper.

lequel, laquelle, pl **lesquels, lesquelles** [ləkɛl, lakɛl, lekɛl] (+ à = **auquel,** à **laquelle, auxquel(le)s;** + de = **duquel,** de **laquelle, desquel(le)s**) pron (chose, animal) which; (personne) who, (indirect) whom; (interrogatif) which (one); **dans l.** into which; **parmi lesquels** (choses, animaux) among which; (personnes) among whom; **l. préférez-vous?** which (one) do you prefer?

les [le] voir **le.**

lesbienne [lɛsbjɛn] nf & af lesbian.

léser [leze] vt (personne) Jur to wrong.

lésiner [lezine] vi to be stingy (**sur** with).

lésion [lezjɔ̃] nf Méd lesion.

lessive [lesiv] nf (produit) washing powder; (linge) washing; **faire la l.** to do the wash(ing). ◆**lessiver** vt to scrub, wash. ◆**−é** a Fam (fatigué) washed-out; (ruiné) washed-up. ◆**−euse** nf (laundry) boiler.

lest [lɛst] nm ballast. ◆**lester** vt to ballast, weight down; (remplir) Fam to overload.

leste [lɛst] a (agile) nimble; (grivois) coarse.

léthargie [letarʒi] nf lethargy. ◆**léthargique** a lethargic.

lettre [lɛtr] nf (missive, caractère) letter; **en toutes lettres** (mot) in full; (nombre) in words; **les lettres** (discipline) Univ arts; **homme de lettres** man of letters. ◆**lettré, -ée** a well-read; − nmf scholar.

leucémie [løsemi] nf leuk(a)emia.

leur [lœr] **1** a poss their; **l.** chat the cat; **leurs voitures** their cars; − pron poss **le l., la l., les leurs** theirs. **2** pron inv (indirect) (to) them; **il l. est facile de . . .** it's easy for them to . . . .

leurre [lœr] nm illusion; (tromperie) trickery. ◆**leurrer** vt to delude.

lev/er [l(ə)ve] vt to lift (up), raise; (blocus, interdiction) to lift; (séance) to close; (camp) to strike; (plan) to draw up; (impôts, armée) to levy; **l. les yeux** to look up; − vi (pâte) to rise; (blé) to come up; − **se l.** vpr to get up; (soleil, rideau) to rise; (jour) to break; (brume) to clear, lift; − nm **le l. du soleil** sunrise; **le l. du rideau** Th the curtain. ◆**−ant** a (soleil) rising; − nm **le l.** the east. ◆**−é** a être **l.** (debout) to be up. ◆**−ée** nf (d'interdiction) lifting; (d'impôts) levying; (du courrier) collection; **l. de boucliers** public outcry.

levier [ləvje] nm lever; (pour soulever) crowbar.

lèvre [lɛvr] nf lip; **du bout des lèvres** half-heartedly, grudgingly.

lévrier [levrije] nm greyhound.

levure [ləvyr] nf yeast.

lexique [lɛksik] nm vocabulary, glossary.

lézard [lezar] nm lizard.

lézarde [lezard] nf crack, split. ◆**lézarder** **1** vi Fam to bask in the sun. **2 se l.** vpr to crack, split.

liaison [ljɛzɔ̃] nf (rapport) connection; (routière etc) link; Gram Mil liaison; **l.** (amoureuse) love affair; **en l. avec qn** in contact with s.o.

liane [ljan] nf Bot jungle vine.

liant [ljɑ̃] a sociable.

liasse [ljas] nf bundle.

Liban [libɑ̃] nm Lebanon. ◆**libanais, -aise** a & nmf Lebanese.

libell/er [libele] vt (contrat etc) to word, draw up; (chèque) to make out. ◆**−é** nm wording.

libellule [libelyl] nf dragonfly.

libéral, -ale, -aux [liberal, -o] a & nmf liberal. ◆**libéraliser** vt to liberalize. ◆**libéralisme** nm liberalism. ◆**libéralité** nf liberality; (don) liberal gift.

libérer [libere] vt (prisonnier etc) to (set) free, release; (pays, esprit) to liberate (**de** from); **l. qn de** to free s.o. of (from); − **se l.** vpr to get free, free oneself (**de** of, from). ◆**libérateur, -trice** a (sentiment etc) liberating; − nmf liberator. ◆**libération** nf freeing, release; liberation; **l. conditionnelle** Jur parole. ◆**liberté** nf freedom, liberty; **en l. provisoire** Jur on bail; **mettre en l.** to free, release; **mise en l.** release.

libraire [librɛr] nmf bookseller. ◆**librairie** nf (magasin) bookshop.

libre [libr] a free (**de qch** from sth, **de faire** to do); (voie, route) clear; (place) vacant, free; (école) private (and religious); **l. penseur** freethinker. ◆**l.-échange** nm Écon free trade. ◆**l.-service** nm (pl **libres-services**) (système, magasin etc) self-service. ◆**librement** adv freely.

Libye [libi] nf Libya. ◆**libyen, -enne** a & nmf Libyan.

licence [lisɑ̃s] nf Sp Com Littér licence; Univ (bachelor's) degree; **l. ès lettres/sciences** arts/science degree, = BA/BSc, = Am BA/BS. ◆**licencié, -ée** a & nmf graduate; **l. ès lettres/sciences** bachelor of arts/science, = BA/BSc, = Am BA/BS.

licencier [lisɑ̃sje] vt (ouvrier) to lay off, dismiss. ◆**licenciement** nm dismissal.

licite [lisit] a licit, lawful.

licorne [likɔrn] nf unicorn.

lie [li] nf dregs.

liège [ljɛʒ] nm (matériau) cork.

lien [ljɛ̃] nm (rapport) link, connection; (de

parenté) tie, bond; (*attache, ficelle*) tie.
◆**lier** *vt* (*attacher*) to tie (up); bind; (*relier*) to link (up), connect; (*conversation, amitié*) to strike up; **l. qn** (*unir, engager*) to bind s.o.; **— se l.** *vpr* (*idées etc*) to connect, link together; **se l. avec qn** to make friends with s.o.; **amis très liés** very close friends.

lierre [ljɛr] *nm* ivy.

lieu, -x [ljø] *nm* place; (*d'un accident*) scene; **les lieux** (*locaux*) the premises; **sur les lieux** on the spot; **avoir l.** to take place, be held; **au l. de** instead of; **avoir l. de faire** (*des raisons*) to have good reason to do; **en premier l.** in the first place, firstly; **en dernier l.** lastly; **l. commun** commonplace. ◆**l.-dit** *nm* (*pl* **lieux-dits**) *Géog* locality.

lieue [ljø] *nf* (*mesure*) *Hist* league.

lieutenant [ljøtnɑ̃] *nm* lieutenant.

lièvre [ljɛvr] *nm* hare.

ligament [ligamɑ̃] *nm* ligament.

ligne [liɲ] *nf* (*trait, règle, contour, transport*) line; (*belle silhouette de femme etc*) figure; (*rangée*) row, line; **(se) mettre en l.** to line up; **en l.** *Tél* connected, through; **entrer en l. de compte** to be of consequence, count; **faire entrer en l. de compte** to take into account; **grande l.** *Rail* main line; **les grandes lignes** *Fig* the broad outline; **pilote de l.** airline pilot; **à la l.** *Gram* new paragraph.

lignée [liɲe] *nf* line, ancestry.

ligoter [ligɔte] *vt* to tie up.

ligue [lig] *nf* (*alliance*) league. ◆**se liguer** *vpr* to join together, gang up (**contre** against).

lilas [lila] *nm* lilac; — *a inv* (*couleur*) lilac.

limace [limas] *nf* (*mollusque*) slug.

limaille [limaj] *nf* filings.

limande [limɑ̃d] *nf* (*poisson*) dab.

lime [lim] *nf* (*outil*) file. ◆**limer** *vt* to file.

limier [limje] *nm* (*chien*) bloodhound.

limite [limit] *nf* limit; (*de propriété, jardin etc*) boundary; *pl Fb* boundary lines; **dépasser la l.** to go beyond the bounds; — *a* (*cas*) extreme; (*vitesse, prix, âge etc*) maximum; **date l.** latest date, deadline; **date l. de vente** *Com* sell-by date. ◆**limitatif, -ive** *a* restrictive. ◆**limitation** *nf* limitation; (*de vitesse*) limit. ◆**limiter** *vt* to limit, restrict; (*délimiter*) to border; **se l. à faire** to limit *ou* restrict oneself to doing.

limoger [limɔʒe] *vt* (*destituer*) to dismiss.

limonade [limɔnad] *nf* (*fizzy*) lemonade.

limpide [lɛ̃pid] *a* (*eau, explication*) (crystal) clear. ◆**limpidité** *nf* clearness.

lin [lɛ̃] *nm Bot* flax; (*tissu*) **huile de l.** linseed oil.

linceul [lɛ̃sœl] *nm* shroud.

linéaire [lineɛr] *a* linear.

linge [lɛ̃ʒ] *nm* (*pièces de tissu*) linen; (*à laver*) washing, linen; (*torchon*) cloth; **l. (de corps)** underwear. ◆**lingerie** *nf* (*de femmes*) underwear; (*local*) linen room.

lingot [lɛ̃go] *nm* ingot.

linguiste [lɛ̃gɥist] *nmf* linguist. ◆**linguistique** *a* linguistic; — *nf* linguistics.

lino [lino] *nm* lino. ◆**linoléum** *nm* linoleum.

linotte [linɔt] *nf* (*oiseau*) linnet; **tête de l.** *Fig* scatterbrain.

lion [ljɔ̃] *nm* lion. ◆**lionceau, -x** *nm* lion cub. ◆**lionne** *nf* lioness.

liquéfier [likefje] *vt*, **— se l.** *vpr* to liquefy.

liqueur [likœr] *nf* liqueur.

liquide [likid] *a* liquid; **argent l.** ready cash; **— nm** liquid; **du l.** (*argent*) ready cash.

liquider [likide] *vt* (*dette, stock etc*) to liquidate; (*affaire, travail*) to wind up, finish off; **l. qn** (*tuer*) *Fam* to liquidate s.o. ◆**liquidation** *nf* liquidation; winding up; (*vente*) (clearance) sale.

lire[1] [lir] *vti* to read.

lire[2] [lir] *nf* (*monnaie*) lira.

lis[1] [lis] *nm* (*plante, fleur*) lily.

lis[2], lisent [li, liz] *voir* **lire[1]**.

liseron [lizrɔ̃] *nm Bot* convolvulus.

lisible [lizibl] *a* (*écriture*) legible; (*livre*) readable. ◆**lisiblement** *adv* legibly.

lisière [lizjɛr] *nf* edge, border.

lisse [lis] *a* smooth. ◆**lisser** *vt* to smooth; (*plumes*) to preen.

liste [list] *nf* list; **l. électorale** register of electors, electoral roll; **sur la l. rouge** *Tél* ex-directory, *Am* unlisted.

lit[1] [li] *nm* bed; **l. d'enfant** cot, *Am* crib; **lits superposés** bunk beds; **garder le l.** to stay in bed. ◆**literie** *nf* bedding, bed clothes.

lit[2] [li] *voir* **lire[1]**.

litanie [litani] **1** *nf* (*énumération*) long list (de of). **2** *nfpl* (*prière*) *Rel* litany.

litière [litjɛr] *nf* (*couche de paille*) litter.

litige [litiʒ] *nm* dispute; *Jur* litigation. ◆**litigieux, -euse** *a* contentious.

litre [litr] *nm* litre.

littéraire [literɛr] *a* literary. ◆**littérature** *nf* literature.

littéral, -aux [literal, -o] *a* literal. ◆**—ement** *adv* literally.

littoral, -aux [litɔral, -o] *a* coastal; — *nm* coast(line).

liturgie [lityrʒi] *nf* liturgy. ◆**liturgique** *a* liturgical.

livide [livid] *a* (*bleuâtre*) livid; (*pâle*) (ghastly) pale, pallid.

livre[1] [livr] **1** *nm* book; **l. de bord** *Nau* logbook; **l. de poche** paperback (book); **le l., l'industrie du l.** the book industry. **2** *nf* (*monnaie, poids*) pound. ◆**livresque** *a* (*savoir*) *Péj* bookish. ◆**livret** *nm* (*registre*) book; *Mus* libretto; **l. scolaire** school report book; **l. de famille** family registration book; **l. de caisse d'épargne** bankbook, passbook.

livrée [livre] *nf* (*uniforme*) livery.

livrer [livre] *vt* (*marchandises*) to deliver (à to); (*secret*) to give away; **l. qn à** (*la police etc*) to give s.o. up *ou* over to; **l. bataille** to do *ou* join battle; **— se l.** *vpr* (*se rendre*) to give oneself up (à to); (*se confier*) to confide (à in); **se l. à** (*habitude, excès etc*) to indulge in; (*tâche*) to devote oneself to; (*désespoir, destin*) to abandon oneself to. ◆**livraison** *nf* delivery. ◆**livreur, -euse** *nmf* delivery man, delivery woman.

lobe [lɔb] *nm Anat* lobe.

local, -aux [lɔkal, -o] **1** *a* local. **2** *nm & nmpl* (*pièce, bâtiment*) premises. ◆**localement** *adv* locally. ◆**localiser** *vt* (*déterminer*) to locate; (*limiter*) to localize. ◆**localité** *nf* locality.

locataire [lɔkatɛr] *nmf* tenant; (*hôte payant*) lodger.

location [lɔkasjɔ̃] *nf* (*de maison etc*) renting; (*à bail*) leasing; (*de voiture*) hiring; (*réservation*) booking; (*par propriétaire*) renting (out), letting; leasing (out); hiring (out); (*loyer*) rental; (*bail*) lease; **bureau de l.** booking office; **en l.** on hire.

lock-out [lɔkawt] *nm inv* (*industriel*) lock-out.

locomotion [lɔkɔmɔsjɔ̃] *nf* locomotion. ◆**locomotive** *nf* locomotive, engine.

locuteur [lɔkytœr] *nm Ling* speaker. ◆**locution** *nf* phrase, idiom; *Gram* phrase.

logarithme [lɔgaritm] *nm* logarithm.

loge [lɔʒ] *nf* (*de concierge*) lodge; (*d'acteur*) dressing-room; (*de spectateur*) *Th* box.

log/er [lɔʒe] *vt* (*recevoir, mettre*) to accommodate, house; (*héberger*) to put up; **être logé et nourri** to have board and lodging; **—** *vi* (à l'hôtel etc) to put up, lodge; (*habiter*) to live; (*trouver à*) **se l.** to find somewhere to stay; **se l. dans** (*balle*) to lodge (itself) in. ◆**—eable** *a* habitable. ◆**—ement** *nm* accommodation, lodging; (*habitat*) housing; (*appartement*) lodgings, flat, *Am* apartment; (*maison*) dwelling. ◆**—eur, -euse** *nmf* landlord, landlady.

logiciel [lɔʒisjɛl] *nm* (*d'un ordinateur*) software *inv*.

logique [lɔʒik] *a* logical; **—** *nf* logic. ◆**—ment** *adv* logically.

logistique [lɔʒistik] *nf* logistics.

logo [lɔgo] *nm* logo.

loi [lwa] *nf* law; *Pol* act; **projet de l.** *Pol* bill; **faire la l.** to lay down the law (à to).

loin [lwɛ̃] *adv* far (away *ou* off); **Boston est l. (de Paris)** Boston is a long way away (from Paris); **plus l.** further, farther; (*ci-après*) further on; **l. de là** *Fig* far from it; **au l.** in the distance, far away; **de l.** from a distance; (*de beaucoup*) by far; **de l. en l.** every so often. ◆**lointain** *a* distant, far-off; **—** *nm* **dans le l.** in the distance.

loir [lwar] *nm* (*animal*) dormouse.

loisir [lwazir] *nm* **le l. de faire** the time to do; **moment de l.** moment of leisure; **loisirs** (*temps libre*) spare time, leisure (time); (*distractions*) spare-time *ou* leisure activities.

Londres [lɔ̃dr] *nm ou f* London. ◆**londonien, -ienne** *a* London-; **—** *nmf* Londoner.

long, longue [lɔ̃, lɔ̃g] *a* long; **être l. (à faire)** to be a long time *ou* slow (in doing); **l. de deux mètres** two metres long; **—** *nm* **avoir deux mètres de l.** to be two metres long; **tomber de tout son l.** to fall flat; **(tout) le l. de** (*espace*) (all) along; **tout le l. de** (*temps*) throughout; **de l. en large** (*marcher etc*) up and down; **en l. et en large** thoroughly; **en l.** lengthwise; **à la longue** in the long run. ◆**l.-courrier** *nm Av* long-distance airliner. ◆**longue-vue** *nf* (*pl* **longues-vues**) telescope.

longer [lɔ̃ʒe] *vt* to pass *ou* go along; (*forêt, mer*) to skirt; (*mur*) to hug.

longévité [lɔ̃ʒevite] *nf* longevity.

longitude [lɔ̃ʒityd] *nf* longitude.

longtemps [lɔ̃tɑ̃] *adv* (for) a long time; **trop/avant l.** too/before long; **aussi l. que** as long as.

longue [lɔ̃g] *voir* **long**. ◆**longuement** *adv* at length. ◆**longuet, -ette** *a Fam* (fairly) lengthy. ◆**longueur** *nf* length; *pl* (*de texte, film*) over-long passages; **saut en l.** *Sp* long jump; **à l. de journée** all day long; **l. d'onde** *Rad & Fig* wavelength.

lopin [lɔpɛ̃] *nm* **l. de terre** plot *ou* patch of land.

loquace [lɔkas] *a* loquacious.

loque [lɔk] **1** *nfpl* rags. **2** *nf* **l. (humaine)** (*personne*) human wreck.

loquet [lɔkɛ] *nm* latch.

lorgner [lɔrɲe] *vt* (*regarder, convoiter*) to eye.

lors [lɔr] *adv* **l. de** at the time of; **depuis l.,**

dès l. from then on; **dès l. que** (*puisque*) since.

losange [lɔzɑ̃ʒ] *nm Géom* diamond, lozenge.

lot [lo] *nm* **1** (*de loterie*) prize; **gros l.** top prize, jackpot. **2** (*portion, destin*) lot. ◆**loterie** *nf* lottery, raffle. ◆**lotir** *vt* (*terrain*) to divide into lots; **bien loti** Fig favoured by fortune. ◆**lotissement** *nm* (*terrain*) building plot; (*habitations*) housing estate *ou* development.

lotion [losjɔ̃] *nf* lotion.

loto [loto] *nm* (*jeu*) lotto.

louche [luʃ] **1** *a* (*suspect*) shady, fishy. **2** *nf* Culin ladle.

loucher [luʃe] *vi* to squint; **l. sur** Fam to eye.

louer [lwe] *vt* **1** (*prendre en location*) to rent (*house, flat etc*); (*à bail*) to lease; (*voiture*) to hire, rent; (*réserver*) to book; (*donner en location*) to rent (out), let; to lease (out); to hire (out); **maison/chambre à l.** house/room to let. **2** (*exalter*) to praise (**de** for); **se l. de** to be highly satisfied with. ◆**louable** *a* praiseworthy, laudable. ◆**louange** *nf* praise; **à la l. de** in praise of.

loufoque [lufɔk] *a* (*fou*) Fam nutty, crazy.

loukoum [lukum] *nm* Turkish delight.

loup [lu] *nm* wolf; **avoir une faim de l.** to be ravenous. ◆**l.-garou** *nm* (*pl* loups-garous) werewolf.

loupe [lup] *nf* magnifying glass.

louper [lupe] *vt* Fam (*train etc*) to miss; (*examen*) to fail; (*travail*) to mess up.

lourd [lur] *a* heavy (Fig **de** with); (*temps, chaleur*) close, sultry; (*faute*) gross; (*tâche*) arduous; (*esprit*) dull; – *adv* **peser l.** (*malle etc*) to be heavy. ◆**lourdaud, -aude** *a* loutish, oafish; – *nmf* lout, oaf. ◆**lourdement** *adv* heavily. ◆**lourdeur** *nf* heaviness; (*de temps*) closeness; (*d'esprit*) dullness.

loutre [lutr] *nf* otter.

louve [luv] *nf* she-wolf. ◆**louveteau, -x** *nm* (*scout*) cub (scout).

louvoyer [luvwaje] *vi* (*tergiverser*) to hedge, be evasive.

loyal, -aux [lwajal, -o] *a* (*fidèle*) loyal (**envers** to); (*honnête*) honest, fair (**envers** to). ◆**loyalement** *adv* loyally; fairly. ◆**loyauté** *nf* loyalty; honesty, fairness.

loyer [lwaje] *nm* rent.

lu [ly] *voir* lire [1].

lubie [lybi] *nf* whim.

lubrifi/er [lybrifje] *vt* to lubricate. ◆**—ant** *nm* lubricant.

lubrique [lybrik] *a* lewd, lustful.

lucarne [lykarn] *nf* (*ouverture*) skylight; (*fenêtre*) dormer window.

lucide [lysid] *a* lucid. ◆**lucidité** *nf* lucidity.

lucratif, -ive [lykratif, -iv] *a* lucrative.

lueur [lɥœr] *nf* (*lumière*) & Fig glimmer.

luge [lyʒ] *nf* toboggan, sledge.

lugubre [lygybr] *a* gloomy, lugubrious.

lui [lɥi] **1** *pron mf* (*complément indirect*) (to) him; (*femme*) (to) her; (*chose, animal*) (to) it; **je le lui ai montré** I showed it to him *ou* to her, I showed him it *ou* her it; **il lui est facile de . . .** it's easy for him *ou* her to . . . . **2** *pron m* (*complément direct*) him; (*chose, animal*) it; (*sujet emphatique*) he; **pour lui** for him; **plus grand que lui** taller than him; **il ne pense qu'à lui** he only thinks of himself. ◆**lui-même** *pron* himself; (*chose, animal*) itself.

luire* [lɥir] *vi* to shine, gleam. ◆**luisant** *a* (*métal etc*) shiny.

lumbago [lɔ̃bago] *nm* lumbago.

lumière [lymjɛr] *nf* light; **à la l. de** by the light of; (*grâce à*) Fig in the light of; **faire toute la l. sur** Fig to clear up; **mettre en l.** to bring to light. ◆**luminaire** *nm* (*appareil*) lighting appliance. ◆**lumineux, -euse** *a* (*idée, ciel etc*) bright, brilliant; (*ondes, source etc*) light-; (*cadran, corps etc*) Tech luminous.

lunaire [lynɛr] *a* lunar; **clarté l.** light *ou* brightness of the moon.

lunatique [lynatik] *a* temperamental.

lunch [lœ̃ʃ, lœ̃tʃ] *nm* buffet lunch, snack.

lundi [lœ̃di] *nm* Monday.

lune [lyn] *nf* moon; **l. de miel** honeymoon.

lunette [lynɛt] *nf* **1 lunettes** glasses, spectacles; (*de protection, de plongée*) goggles; **lunettes de soleil** sunglasses. **2** (*astronomique*) telescope; **l. arrière** Aut rear window.

lurette [lyrɛt] *nf* **il y a belle l.** a long time ago.

luron [lyrɔ̃] *nm* **gai l.** gay fellow.

lustre [lystr] *nm* (*éclairage*) chandelier; (*éclat*) lustre. ◆**lustré** *a* (*par l'usure*) shiny.

luth [lyt] *nm* Mus lute.

lutin [lytɛ̃] *nm* elf, imp, goblin.

lutte [lyt] *nf* fight, struggle; Sp wrestling; **l. des classes** class warfare *ou* struggle. ◆**lutter** *vi* to fight, struggle; Sp to wrestle. ◆**lutteur, -euse** *nmf* fighter; Sp wrestler.

luxe [lyks] *nm* luxury; **un l. de** a wealth of; **de l.** (*article*) luxury-; (*modèle*) de luxe. ◆**luxueux, -euse** *a* luxurious.

Luxembourg [lyksãbur] *nm* Luxembourg.

luxure [lyksyr] *nf* lewdness, lust.

luxuriant [lyksyrjɑ̃] *a* luxuriant.

luzerne [lyzɛrn] *nf Bot* lucerne, *Am* alfalfa.

lycée [lise] *nm* (secondary) school, *Am* high school. ◆**lycéen, -enne** *nmf* pupil (*at lycée*).

lymphatique [lɛ̃fatik] *a* (*apathique*) sluggish.

lynch/er [lɛ̃ʃe] *vt* to lynch. ◆**—age** *nm* lynching.

lynx [lɛ̃ks] *nm* (*animal*) lynx.

lyre [lir] *nf Mus Hist* lyre.

lyrique [lirik] *a* (*poème etc*) lyric; (*passionné*) *Fig* lyrical. ◆**lyrisme** *nm* lyricism.

lys [lis] *nm* (*plante, fleur*) lily.

M

M, m [ɛm] *nm* M, m.

m *abrév* (*mètre*) metre.

M [məsjø] *abrév* = **Monsieur**.

m' [m] *voir* **me.**

ma [ma] *voir* **mon.**

macabre [makabr] *a* macabre, gruesome.

macadam [makadam] *nm* (*goudron*) tarmac.

macaron [makarɔ̃] *nm* (*gâteau*) macaroon; (*insigne*) (round) badge.

macaroni(s) [makarɔni] *nm*(*pl*) macaroni.

macédoine [masedwan] *nf* **m.** (**de légumes**) mixed vegetables; **m.** (**de fruits**) fruit salad.

macérer [masere] *vti Culin* to soak. ◆**macération** *nf* soaking.

mâcher [maʃe] *vt* to chew; **il ne mâche pas ses mots** he doesn't mince matters *ou* his words.

machiavélique [makjavelik] *a* Machiavellian.

machin [maʃɛ̃] *nm Fam* (*chose*) thing, what's-it; (*personne*) what's-his-name.

machinal, -aux [maʃinal, -o] *a* (*involontaire*) unconscious, mechanical. ◆**—ement** *adv* unconsciously, mechanically.

machination [maʃinɑsjɔ̃] *nf* machination.

machine [maʃin] *nf* (*appareil, avion, système etc*) machine; (*locomotive, moteur*) engine; *pl Tech* machines, (heavy) machinery; **m. à coudre** sewing machine; **m. à écrire** typewriter; **m. à laver** washing machine. ◆**machinerie** *nf Nau* engine room. ◆**machiniste** *nm Th* stage-hand.

macho [matʃo] *nm* macho *m*; – *a* (*f inv*) (*attitude etc*) macho.

mâchoire [maʃwar] *nf* jaw.

mâchonner [maʃɔne] *vt* to chew, munch.

maçon [masɔ̃] *nm* builder; bricklayer; mason. ◆**maçonnerie** *nf* (*travaux*) building work; (*ouvrage de briques*) brickwork; (*de pierres*) masonry, stonework.

maculer [makyle] *vt* to stain (**de** with).

Madagascar [madagaskar] *nf* Madagascar.

madame, *pl* **mesdames** [madam, medam] *nf* madam; **oui m.** yes (madam); **bonjour mesdames** good morning (ladies); **Madame** *ou* **Mme Legras** Mrs Legras; **Madame** (*sur une lettre*) *Com* Dear Madam.

madeleine [madlɛn] *nf* (small) sponge cake.

mademoiselle, *pl* **mesdemoiselles** [madmwazɛl, medmwazɛl] *nf* miss; **oui m.** yes (miss); **bonjour mesdemoiselles** good morning (ladies); **Mademoiselle** *ou* **Mlle Legras** Miss Legras; **Mademoiselle** (*sur une lettre*) *Com* Dear Madam.

madère [madɛr] *nm* (*vin*) Madeira.

madone [madɔn] *nf Rel* madonna.

madrier [madrije] *nm* (*poutre*) beam.

maestro [maestro] *nm Mus* maestro.

maf(f)ia [mafja] *nf* Mafia.

magasin [magazɛ̃] *nm* shop, *Am* store; (*entrepôt*) warehouse; (*d'arme*) & *Phot* magazine; **grand m.** department store. ◆**magasinier** *nm* warehouseman.

magazine [magazin] *nm* (*revue*) magazine.

magie [maʒi] *nf* magic. ◆**magicien, -ienne** *nmf* magician. ◆**magique** *a* (*baguette, mot*) magic; (*mystérieux, enchanteur*) magical.

magistral, -aux [maʒistral, -o] *a* masterly, magnificent. ◆**—ement** *adv* magnificently.

magistrat [maʒistra] *nm* magistrate. ◆**magistrature** *nf* judiciary, magistracy.

magnanime [maɲanim] *a* magnanimous.

magnat [magna] *nm* tycoon, magnate.

magner (se) [səmaɲe] *vpr Fam* to hurry up.

magnésium [maɲezjɔm] *nm* magnesium.

magnétique [maɲetik] *a* magnetic. ◆**magnétiser** *vt* to magnetize. ◆**magnétisme** *nm* magnetism.

magnétophone [maɲetɔfɔn] *nm* (*Fam* **magnéto**) tape recorder; **m. à cassettes** cassette recorder. ◆**magnétoscope** *nm* video (cassette) recorder.

magnifique [manifik] *a* magnificent. **◆magnificence** *nf* magnificence. **◆magnifiquement** *adv* magnificently.

magnolia [manɔlja] *nm (arbre)* magnolia.

magot [mago] *nm (économies)* nest egg, hoard.

magouille(s) [maguj] *nf(pl) Pol Fam* fiddling, graft.

mai [mɛ] *nm* May.

maigre [mɛgr] *a* thin, lean; *(viande)* lean; *(fromage, yaourt)* low-fat; *(repas, salaire, espoir)* meagre; **faire m.** to abstain from meat **◆maigrement** *adv (chichement)* meagrely. **◆maigreur** *nf* thinness; *(de viande)* leanness; *(médiocrité) Fig* meagreness. **◆maigrichon, -onne** *a* & *nmf* skinny (person). **◆maigrir** *vi* to get thin(ner); – *vt* to make thin(ner).

maille [maj] *nf (de tricot)* stitch; *(de filet)* mesh; **m. filée** *(de bas)* run, ladder. **◆maillon** *nm (de chaîne)* link.

maillet [majɛ] *nm (outil)* mallet.

maillot [majo] *nm (de sportif)* jersey; *(de danseur)* leotard, tights; **m. (de corps)** vest, *Am* undershirt; **m. (de bain)** *(de femme)* swimsuit; *(d'homme)* (swimming) trunks.

main [mɛ̃] *nf* hand; **tenir à la m.** to hold in one's hand; **à la m.** *(livrer, faire etc)* by hand; **la m. dans la m.** hand in hand; **haut les mains!** hands up!; **donner un coup de m. à qn** to lend s.o. a (helping) hand; **coup de m.** *(habileté)* knack; **sous la m.** at hand, handy; **en venir aux mains** to come to blows; **avoir la m. heureuse** to be lucky, have a lucky streak; **mettre la dernière m. à** to put the finishing touches to; **en m. propre** *(remettre qch)* in person; **attaque/vol à m. armée** armed attack/robbery; **homme de m.** henchman, hired man; **m. courante** handrail; **prêter m.-forte à** to lend assistance to. **◆m.-d'œuvre** *nf (pl* mains-d'œuvre) *(travail)* manpower, labour; *(salariés)* labour *ou* work force.

maint [mɛ̃] *a Litt* many a; **maintes fois, à maintes reprises** many a time.

maintenant [mɛ̃tnɑ̃] *adv* now; *(de nos jours)* nowadays; **m. que** now that; **dès m.** from now on.

maintenir* [mɛ̃tnir] *vt (conserver)* to keep, maintain; *(retenir)* to hold, keep; *(affirmer)* to maintain (que that); – **se m.** *vpr (durer)* to be maintained; *(rester)* to keep; *(malade, vieillard)* to hold one's own. **◆maintien** *nm (action)* maintenance (de of); *(allure)* bearing.

maire [mɛr] *nm* mayor. **◆mairie** *nf* town hall; *(administration)* town council.

mais [mɛ] *conj* but; **m. oui, m. si** yes of course; **m. non** definitely not.

maïs [mais] *nm (céréale)* maize, *Am* corn; **farine de m.** cornflour, *Am* cornstarch.

maison [mɛzɔ̃] *nf (bâtiment)* house; *(immeuble)* building; *(chez-soi, asile)* home; *Com* firm; *(famille)* household; **à la m.** (être) at home; *(rentrer, aller)* home; – *a inv (pâté, tartes etc)* homemade; **m. de la culture** arts *ou* cultural centre; **m. d'étudiants** student hostel; **m. des jeunes** youth club; **m. de repos** rest home; **m. de retraite** old people's home. **◆maisonnée** *nf* household. **◆maisonnette** *nf* small house.

maître [mɛtr] *nm* master; **se rendre m. de** *(incendie)* to master, control; *(pays)* to conquer; **être m. de** *(situation etc)* to be in control of, be master of; **m. de soi** in control of oneself; **m. d'école** teacher; **m. d'hôtel** *(restaurant)* head waiter; **m. de maison** host; **m. chanteur** blackmailer; **m. nageur** (sauveteur) swimming instructor (and lifeguard). **◆maîtresse** *nf* mistress; **m. d'école** teacher; **m. de maison** hostess; *(ménagère)* housewife; **être m. de** *(situation etc)* to be in control of; – *af (idée, poutre)* main; *(carte)* master.

maîtrise [mɛtriz] *nf (habileté, contrôle)* mastery (de of); *(grade) Univ* master's degree (de in); **m. (de soi)** self-control. **◆maîtriser** *vt (émotion)* to master, control; *(sujet)* to master; *(incendie)* to (bring under) control; **m. qn** to subdue s.o.; – **se m.** *vpr* to control oneself.

majesté [maʒeste] *nf* majesty; **Votre M.** *(titre)* Your Majesty. **◆majestueux, -euse** *a* majestic, stately.

majeur [maʒœr] **1** *a (primordial)* & *Mus* major; **être m.** *Jur* to be of age; **la majeure partie de** most of; **en majeure partie** for the most part. **2** *nm (doigt)* middle finger.

majorer [maʒɔre] *vt* to raise, increase. **◆majoration** *nf (hausse)* increase (de in).

majorette [maʒɔrɛt] *nf (drum)* majorette.

majorité [maʒɔrite] *nf* majority (de of); *(âge) Jur* coming of age, majority; *(gouvernement)* party in office, government; **en m.** in the *ou* a majority; *(pour la plupart)* in the main. **◆majoritaire** *a (vote etc)* majority-; **être m.** to be in the *ou* a majority; **être m. aux élections** to win the elections.

Majorque [maʒɔrk] *nf* Majorca.

majuscule [maʒyskyl] *a* capital; – *nf* capital letter.

mal, maux [mal, mo] **1** *nm Phil Rel* evil;

(*dommage*) harm; (*douleur*) pain; (*maladie*) illness; (*malheur*) misfortune; **dire du m. de** to speak ill of; **m. de dents** toothache; **m. de gorge** sore throat; **m. de tête** headache; **m. de ventre** stomachache; **m. de mer** seasickness; **m. du pays** homesickness; **avoir le m. du pays/***etc* to be homesick/*etc*; **avoir m. à la tête/à la gorge/***etc* to have a headache/sore throat/*etc*; **ça (me) fait m., j'ai m.** it hurts (me); **faire du m. à** to harm, hurt; **avoir du m. à faire** to have trouble (in) doing; **se donner du m. pour faire** to go to a lot of trouble to do. **2** *adv* (*travailler etc*) badly; (*entendre, comprendre*) not too well; **aller m.** (*projet etc*) to be going badly; (*personne*) *Méd* to be bad or ill; **m. (à l'aise)** uncomfortable; **se trouver m.** to feel faint; **(ce n'est) pas m.** (*mauvais*) (that's) not bad; **pas m.** (*beaucoup*) *Fam* quite a lot (de of); **c'est m. de jurer/***etc* (*moralement*) it's wrong to swear/*etc*; **de m. en pis** from bad to worse; **m. renseigner/misinterpréter/** *etc* to misinform/misinterpret/*etc*.

malade [malad] *a* ill, sick; (*arbre, dent*) diseased; (*estomac, jambe*) bad; **être m. du foie/cœur** to have a bad liver/heart; − *nmf* sick person; (*à l'hôpital, d'un médecin*) patient; **les malades** the sick. ◆**maladie** *nf* illness, sickness, disease. ◆**maladif, -ive** *a* (*personne*) sickly; (*morbide*) morbid.

maladroit [maladrwa] *a* (*malhabile*) clumsy, awkward; (*indélicat*) tactless. ◆**maladresse** *nf* clumsiness, awkwardness; tactlessness; (*bévue*) blunder.

malaise [malɛz] *nm* (*angoisse*) uneasiness, malaise; (*indisposition*) faintness, dizziness; **avoir un m.** to feel faint *ou* dizzy.

malaisé [malɛze] *a* difficult.

Malaisie [malɛzi] *nf* Malaysia.

malaria [malarja] *nf* malaria.

malavisé [malavize] *a* ill-advised (**de faire** to do).

malax/er [malakse] *vt* (*pétrir*) to knead; (*mélanger*) to mix. ◆**−eur** *nm* *Tech* mixer.

malchance [malʃɑ̃s] *nf* bad luck; **une m.** (*mésaventure*) a mishap. ◆**malchanceux, -euse** *a* unlucky.

malcommode [malkɔmɔd] *a* awkward.

mâle [mal] *a* male; (*viril*) manly; − *nm* male.

malédiction [malediksjɔ̃] *nf* curse.

maléfice [malefis] *nm* evil spell. ◆**maléfique** *a* baleful, evil.

malencontreux, -euse [malɑ̃kɔ̃trø, -øz] *a* unfortunate.

malentendant, -ante [malɑ̃tɑ̃dɑ̃, -ɑ̃t] *nmf* person who is hard of hearing.

malentendu [malɑ̃tɑ̃dy] *nm* misunderstanding.

malfaçon [malfasɔ̃] *nf* defect.

malfaisant [malfəzɑ̃] *a* evil, harmful.

malfaiteur [malfɛtœr] *nm* criminal.

malformation [malfɔrmasjɔ̃] *nf* malformation.

malgré [malgre] *prép* in spite of; **m. tout** for all that, after all; **m. soi** (*à contrecœur*) reluctantly.

malhabile [malabil] *a* clumsy.

malheur [malœr] *nm* (*évènement*) misfortune; (*accident*) mishap; (*malchance*) bad luck, misfortune; **par m.** unfortunately. ◆**malheureusement** *adv* unfortunately. ◆**malheureux, -euse** *a* (*misérable, insignifiant*) wretched, miserable; (*fâcheux*) unfortunate; (*malchanceux*) unlucky, unfortunate; − *nmf* (*infortuné*) (poor) wretch; (*indigent*) needy person.

malhonnête [malɔnɛt] *a* dishonest. ◆**malhonnêteté** *nf* dishonesty; **une m.** (*action*) a dishonest act.

malice [malis] *nf* mischievousness. ◆**malicieux, -euse** *a* mischievous.

malin, -igne [malɛ̃, -iɲ] *a* (*astucieux*) smart, clever; (*plaisir*) malicious; (*tumeur*) *Méd* malignant. ◆**malignité** *nf* (*méchanceté*) malignity; *Méd* malignancy.

malingre [malɛ̃gr] *a* puny, sickly.

malintentionné [malɛ̃tɑ̃sjɔne] *a* ill-intentioned (**à l'égard de** towards).

malle [mal] *nf* (*coffre*) trunk; (*de véhicule*) boot, *Am* trunk. ◆**mallette** *nf* small suitcase; (*pour documents*) attaché case.

malléable [maleabl] *a* malleable.

malmener [malməne] *vt* to manhandle, treat badly.

malodorant [malɔdɔrɑ̃] *a* smelly.

malotru, -ue [malɔtry] *nmf* boor, lout.

malpoli [malpɔli] *a* impolite.

malpropre [malprɔpr] *a* (*sale*) dirty. ◆**malpropreté** *nf* dirtiness.

malsain [malsɛ̃] *a* unhealthy, unwholesome.

malséant [malseɑ̃] *a* unseemly.

malt [malt] *nm* malt.

Malte [malt] *nf* Malta. ◆**maltais, -aise** *a* nmf Maltese.

maltraiter [maltrete] *vt* to ill-treat.

malveillant [malvɛjɑ̃] *a* malevolent. ◆**malveillance** *nf* malevolence, ill will.

malvenu [malvəny] *a* (*déplacé*) uncalled-for.

maman [mamɑ̃] *nf* mum(my), *Am* mom(my).

mamelle [mamɛl] *nf* (*d'animal*) teat; (*de*

vache) udder. ◆**mamelon** *nm* **1** (*de femme*) nipple. **2** (*colline*) hillock.

mamie [mami] *nf Fam* granny, grandma.

mammifère [mamifɛr] *nm* mammal.

manche [mɑ̃ʃ] **1** *nf* (*de vêtement*) sleeve; *Sp Cartes* round; **la M.** *Géog* the Channel. **2** *nm* (*d'outil etc*) handle; **m. à balai** broomstick; (*d'avion, d'ordinateur*) joystick. ◆**manchette** *nf* **1** (*de chemise etc*) cuff. **2** *Journ* headline. ◆**manchon** *nm* (*fourrure*) muff.

manchot, -ote [mɑ̃ʃo, -ɔt] **1** *a & nmf* one-armed *ou* one-handed (person). **2** *nm* (*oiseau*) penguin.

mandarin [mɑ̃darɛ̃] *nm* (*lettré influent*) *Univ Péj* mandarin.

mandarine [mɑ̃darin] *nf* (*fruit*) tangerine, mandarin (orange).

mandat [mɑ̃da] *nm* **1** (*postal*) money order. **2** *Pol* mandate; *Jur* power of attorney; **m. d'arrêt** warrant (**contre qn** for s.o.'s arrest). ◆**mandataire** *nmf* (*délégué*) representative, proxy. ◆**mandater** *vt* to delegate; *Pol* to give a mandate to.

manège [manɛʒ] *nm* **1** (*à la foire*) merry-go-round, roundabout; (*lieu*) riding-school; (*piste*) ring, manège; (*exercice*) horsemanship. **2** (*intrigue*) wiles, trickery.

manette [manɛt] *nf* lever, handle.

manger [mɑ̃ʒe] *vt* to eat; (*essence, électricité*) *Fig* to guzzle; (*fortune*) to eat up; (*corroder*) to eat into; **donner à m.** to feed; — *vi* to eat; **on mange bien ici** the food is good here; **m. à sa faim** to have enough to eat; — *nm Fam* food. ◆**mangeable** *a* eatable. ◆**mangeaille** *nf Péj* (bad) food. ◆**mangeoire** *nf* (feeding) trough. ◆**mangeur, -euse** *nmf* eater.

mangue [mɑ̃g] *nf* (*fruit*) mango.

manie [mani] *nf* mania, craze (**de** for). ◆**maniaque** *a* a finicky, fussy; — *nmf* fusspot, *Am* fussbudget; **un m. de la propreté** a maniac for cleanliness/*etc*.

manier [manje] *vt* to handle; **se m. bien** (*véhicule etc*) to handle well. ◆**maniabilité** *nf* (*de véhicule etc*) manoeuvrability. ◆**maniable** *a* easy to handle. ◆**maniement** *nm* handling; **m. d'armes** *Mil* drill.

manière [manjɛr] *nf* way, manner; *pl* (*politesse*) manners; **de toute m.** anyway, anyhow; **de m. à faire** so as to do; **à ma m.** my way, (in) my own way; **de cette m.** (in) this way; **la m. dont elle parle** the way (in which) she talks; **faire des manières** (*chichis*) to make a fuss; (*être affecté*) to put on airs. ◆**maniéré** *a* affected; (*style*) mannered.

manif [manif] *nf Fam* demo.

manifeste [manifɛst] **1** *a* (*évident*) manifest, obvious. **2** *nm Pol* manifesto.

manifester [manifɛste] **1** *vt* to show, manifest; — **se m.** *vpr* (*apparaître*) to appear; (*sentiment, maladie etc*) to show *ou* manifest itself. **2** *vi Pol* to demonstrate. ◆**manifestant, -ante** *nmf* demonstrator. ◆**manifestation** *nf* **1** (*expression*) expression, manifestation; (*apparition*) appearance. **2** *Pol* demonstration; (*réunion, fête*) event.

manigance [manigɑ̃s] *nf* little scheme. ◆**manigancer** *vt* to plot.

manipuler [manipyle] *vt* (*manier*) to handle; (*faits, électeurs*) *Péj* to manipulate. ◆**manipulation** *nf* handling; *Péj* manipulation (**de** of); *pl Pol Péj* manipulation.

manivelle [manivɛl] *nf* *Aut* crank.

mannequin [mankɛ̃] *nm* (*femme, homme*) (fashion) model; (*statue*) dummy.

manœuvre [manœvr] **1** *nm* (*ouvrier*) labourer. **2** *nf* (*opération*) & *Mil* manoeuvre, *Am* maneuver; (*action*) manoeuvring; (*intrigue*) scheme. ◆**manœuvrer** *vt* (*véhicule, personne etc*) to manoeuvre, *Am* maneuver; (*machine*) to operate; — *vi* to manoeuvre, *Am* maneuver.

manoir [manwar] *nm* manor house.

manque [mɑ̃k] *nm* lack (**de** of); (*lacune*) gap; *pl* (*défauts*) shortcomings; **m. à gagner** loss of profit. ◆**manqu/er** *vt* (*chance, cible etc*) to miss; (*ne pas réussir*) to make a mess of, ruin; (*examen*) to fail; — *vi* (*faire défaut*) to be short *ou* lacking; (*être absent*) to be absent (**à** from); (*être en moins*) to be missing *ou* short; (*défaillir, échouer*) to fail. **m. de** (*pain, argent etc*) to be short of; (*attention, cohérence*) to lack; **ça manque de sel**/*etc* it lacks salt/*etc*, there isn't any salt/*etc*; **m. à** (*son devoir*) to fail in; (*sa parole*) to break; **le temps lui manque** he's short of time, he has no time; **elle/cela lui manque** he misses her/that; **je ne manquerai pas de venir** I won't fail to come; **ne manquez pas de venir** don't forget to come; **elle a manqué (de) tomber** (*faillir*) she nearly fell; — *v imp* **il manque/il nous manque dix tasses** there are/we are ten cups short. ◆**—ant** *a* missing. ◆**—é** *a* (*médecin, pilote etc*) failed; (*livre*) unsuccessful. ◆**—ement** *nm* breach (**à** of).

mansarde [mɑ̃sard] *nf* attic.

manteau, -x [mɑ̃to] *nm* coat.

manucure [manykyr] *nmf* manicurist. ◆**manucurer** *vt Fam* to manicure.

manuel, -elle [manɥɛl] **1** *a (travail etc)* manual. **2** *nm (livre)* handbook, manual.

manufacture [manyfaktyr] *nf* factory. ◆**manufacturé** *a (produit)* manufactured.

manuscrit [manyskri] *nm* manuscript; *(tapé à la machine)* typescript.

manutention [manytɑ̃sjɔ̃] *nf Com* handling *(of stores)*. ◆**manutentionnaire** *nmf* packer.

mappemonde [mapmɔ̃d] *nf* map of the world; *(sphère)* Am globe.

maquereau, -x [makro] *nm (poisson)* mackerel.

maquette [makɛt] *nf (scale)* model.

maquill/er [makije] *vt (visage)* to make up; *(voiture etc) Péj* to tamper with; *(vérité etc) Péj* to fake; **— se m.** to make (oneself) up. ◆**-age** *nm (fard)* make-up.

maquis [maki] *nm Bot* scrub, bush; *Mil Hist* maquis.

maraîcher, -ère [mareʃe, -ɛʃɛr] *nmf* market gardener, *Am* truck farmer.

marais [mare] *nm* marsh, bog; **m. salant** saltworks, saltern.

marasme [marasm] *nm Écon* stagnation.

marathon [maratɔ̃] *nm* marathon.

maraudeur, -euse [marodœr, -øz] *nmf* petty thief.

marbre [marbr] *nm* marble. ◆**marbrier** *nm (funéraire)* monumental mason.

marc [mar] *nm (eau-de-vie)* marc, brandy; **m. (de café)** coffee grounds.

marchand, -ande [marʃɑ̃, -ɑ̃d] *nmf* trader, shopkeeper; *(de vins, charbon)* merchant; *(de cycles, meubles)* dealer; **m. de bonbons** confectioner; **m. de couleurs** hardware merchant *ou* dealer; **m. de journaux** *(dans la rue)* newsvendor; *(dans un magasin)* newsagent, *Am* news dealer; **m. de légumes** greengrocer; **m. de poissons** fishmonger; *— a (valeur)* market; *(prix)* trade-. ◆**marchandise(s)** *nf(pl)* goods, merchandise.

marchand/er [marʃɑ̃de] *vi* to haggle, bargain; *— vt (objet)* to haggle over. ◆**-age** *nm* haggling, bargaining.

marche [marʃ] *nf* **1** *(d'escalier)* step, stair. **2** *(démarche, trajet)* walk; *Mil Mus* march; *(pas)* pace; *(de train, véhicule)* movement; *(de maladie, d'événement)* progress, course; **la m.** *(action) Sp* walking; **faire m. arrière** *Aut* to reverse; **la bonne m. de** *(opération, machine)* the smooth running of; **un train/véhicule en m.** a moving train/vehicle; **mettre qch en m.** to start sth (up). ◆**marcher** *vi (à pied)* to walk; *Mil* to

march; *(poser le pied)* to tread; step; *(train, véhicule etc)* to run, go, move; *(fonctionner)* to go, work, run; *(prospérer)* to go well; **faire m.** *(machine)* to work; *(entreprise)* to run; *(personne) Fam* to kid; **ça marche?** *Fam* how's it going?; **elle va m.** *(accepter) Fam* she'll go along (with it). ◆**marcheur, -euse** *nmf* walker.

marché [marʃe] *nm (lieu)* market; *(contrat)* deal; **faire son** *ou* **le m.** to do one's shopping *(in the market)*; **être bon m.** to be cheap; **voiture(s)/etc bon m.** cheap car(s)/ *etc*; **vendre (à) bon m.** to sell cheap(ly); **c'est meilleur m.** it's cheaper; **par-dessus le m.** *Fig* into the bargain; **au m. noir** on the black market; **le M. commun** the Common Market.

marchepied [marʃəpje] *nm (de train, bus)* step(s); *(de voiture)* running board.

mardi [mardi] *nm* Tuesday; **M. gras** Shrove Tuesday.

mare [mar] *nf (flaque)* pool; *(étang)* pond.

marécage [mareka3] *nm* swamp, marsh. ◆**marécageux, -euse** *a* marshy, swampy.

maréchal, -aux [mareʃal, -o] *nm Fr Mil* marshal. ◆**m.-ferrant** *nm (pl* maréchaux-ferrants*)* blacksmith.

marée [mare] *nf* tide; *(poissons)* fresh (sea) fish; **m. noire** oil slick.

marelle [marɛl] *nf (jeu)* hopscotch.

margarine [margarin] *nf* margarine.

marge [mar3] *nf* margin; **en m. de** *(en dehors de)* on the periphery of, on the fringe(s) of; **m. de sécurité** safety margin. ◆**marginal, -ale, -aux** *a (secondaire, asocial)* marginal; *— nmf* misfit, dropout; *(bizarre)* weirdo.

marguerite [margərit] *nf (fleur)* marguerite, daisy.

mari [mari] *nm* husband.

mariage [marja3] *nm* marriage; *(cérémonie)* wedding; *(mélange) Fig* blend, marriage; **demande en m.** proposal (of marriage). ◆**mari/er** *vt (couleurs)* to blend; *(maire, prêtre etc)* to marry s.o.; **m. qn avec** to marry s.o. (off) to; **— se m.** *vpr* to get married, marry; **se m. avec qn** to marry s.o., get married to s.o. ◆**-é** *a* married; *— nm* (bride)groom; **les mariés** the bride and (bride)groom; **les jeunes mariés** the newly-weds. ◆**-ée** *nf* bride.

marijuana [mariʒɥana] *nf* marijuana.

marin [marɛ̃] *a (air, sel etc)* sea-; *(flore)* marine; *(mille)* nautical; *(costume)* sailor-; *— nm* seaman, sailor. ◆**marine** *nf* **m.** (de guerre) navy; **m. marchande** merchant navy; **(bleu) m.** *(couleur)* navy (blue).

marina [marina] *nf* marina.

mariner [marine] *vti Culin* to marinate.

marionnette [marjɔnɛt] *nf* puppet; (*à fils*) marionette.

maritalement [maritalmɑ̃] *adv* vivre m. to live together (as husband and wife).

maritime [maritim] *a* (*droit, province, climat etc*) maritime; (*port*) sea-; (*chantier*) naval; (*agent*) shipping-.

marjolaine [marʒɔlɛn] *nf* (*aromate*) marjoram.

mark [mark] *nm* (*monnaie*) mark.

marmaille [marmaj] *nf* (*enfants*) *Fam* kids.

marmelade [marmǝlad] *nf* m. (de fruits) stewed fruit; en m. *Culin Fig* in a mush.

marmite [marmit] *nf* (cooking) pot.

marmonner [marmɔne] *vti* to mutter.

marmot [marmo] *nm* (*enfant*) *Fam* kid.

marmotter [marmɔte] *vti* to mumble.

Maroc [marɔk] *nm* Morocco. ◆**marocain, -aine** *a* & *nmf* Moroccan.

maroquinerie [marɔkinri] *nf* (*magasin*) leather goods shop. ◆**maroquinier** *nm* leather dealer.

marotte [marɔt] *nf* (*dada*) *Fam* fad, craze.

marque [mark] *nf* (*trace, signe*) mark; (*de fabricant*) make, brand; (*points*) Sp score; **m. de fabrique** trademark; **m. déposée** registered trademark; **la m. de** (*preuve*) the stamp of; **de m.** (*hôte, visiteur*) distinguished; (*produit*) of quality. ◆**marqu/er** *vt* (*par une marque etc*) to mark; (*écrire*) to note down; (*indiquer*) to show, mark; (*point, but*) Sp to score; **m. qn** Sp to mark s.o.; **m. les points** Sp to keep (the) score; **m. le coup** to mark the event; – *vi* (*trace*) to leave a mark; (*date, événement*) to stand out; Sp to score. ◆**—ant** *a* (*remarquable*) outstanding. ◆**—é** *a* (*différence, accent etc*) marked, pronounced. ◆**—eur** *nm* (*crayon*) marker.

marquis [marki] *nm* marquis. ◆**marquise** *nf* 1 marchioness. 2 (*auvent*) glass canopy.

marraine [marɛn] *nf* godmother.

marre [mar] *nf* en avoir m. *Fam* to be fed up (de with).

marr/er (se) [sǝmare] *vpr Fam* to have a good laugh. ◆**—ant** *a Fam* hilarious, funny.

marron¹ [marɔ̃] 1 *nm* chestnut; (*couleur*) (chestnut) brown; **m. (d'Inde)** horse chestnut; – *a inv* (*couleur*) (chestnut) brown. 2 *nm* (*coup*) *Fam* punch, clout. ◆**marronnier** *nm* (horse) chestnut tree.

marron², -onne [marɔ̃, -ɔn] *a* (*médecin etc*) bogus.

mars [mars] *nm* March.

marsouin [marswɛ̃] *nm* porpoise.

marteau, -x [marto] *nm* hammer; (de porte) (door)knocker; **m. piqueur, m. pneumatique** pneumatic drill. ◆**marteler** *vt* to hammer. ◆**martèlement** *nm* hammering.

martial, -aux [marsjal, -o] *a* martial; **cour martiale** court-martial; **loi martiale** martial law.

martien, -ienne [marsjɛ̃, -jɛn] *nmf* & *a* Martian.

martinet [martinɛ] *nm* (*fouet*) (small) whip.

martin-pêcheur [martɛ̃pɛʃœr] *nm* (*pl* martins-pêcheurs) (*oiseau*) kingfisher.

martyr, -yre¹ [martir] *nmf* (*personne*) martyr; **enfant m.** battered child. ◆**martyre²** *nm* (*souffrance*) martyrdom. ◆**martyriser** *vt* to torture; (*enfant*) to batter.

marxisme [marksism] *nm* Marxism. ◆**marxiste** *a* & *nmf* Marxist.

mascara [maskara] *nm* mascara.

mascarade [maskarad] *nf* masquerade.

mascotte [maskɔt] *nf* mascot.

masculin [maskylɛ̃] *a* male; (*viril*) masculine, manly; *Gram* masculine; (*vêtement, équipe*) men's; – *nm Gram* masculine. ◆**masculinité** *nf* masculinity.

masochisme [mazoʃism] *nm* masochism. ◆**masochiste** *nmf* masochist; – *a* masochistic.

masque [mask] *nm* mask. ◆**masquer** *vt* (*dissimuler*) to mask (à from); (*cacher à la vue*) to block off.

massacre [masakr] *nm* massacre, slaughter. ◆**massacr/er** *vt* to massacre, slaughter; (*abîmer*) *Fam* to ruin. ◆**—ant** *a* (*humeur*) excruciating.

massage [masaʒ] *nm* massage.

masse [mas] *nf* 1 (*volume*) mass; (*gros morceau, majorité*) bulk (de of); **en m.** (*venir, vendre*) in large numbers; **départ en m.** mass *ou* wholesale departure; **manifestation de m.** mass demonstration; **la m.** (*foule*) the masses; **les masses** (*peuple*) the masses; **une m. de** (*tas*) a mass of; **des masses de** *Fam* masses of. 2 (*outil*) sledgehammer. 3 *Él* earth, *Am* ground. ◆**mass/er** 1 *vt, — se m.* *vpr* (*gens*) to mass. 2 *vt* (*frotter*) to massage. ◆**—eur** *nm* masseur. ◆**—euse** *nf* masseuse.

massif, -ive [masif, -iv] 1 *a* massive; (*départs etc*) mass-; (*or, chêne etc*) solid. 2 *nm* (*d'arbres, de fleurs*) clump; *Géog* massif. ◆**massivement** *adv* (*en masse*) in large numbers.

massue [masy] *nf* (*bâton*) club.

mastic [mastik] *nm* (*pour vitres*) putty; (*pour bois*) filler; **m. (silicone)** mastic.

◆**mastiquer** vt **1** (vitre) to putty; (porte) to mastic; (bois) to fill. **2** (mâcher) to chew, masticate.

mastoc [mastɔk] a inv Péj Fam massive.

mastodonte [mastɔdɔt] nm (personne) Péj monster; (véhicule) juggernaut.

masturber (se) [səmastyrbe] vpr to masturbate. ◆**masturbation** nf masturbation.

masure [mazyr] nf tumbledown house.

mat [mat] **1** a (papier, couleur) mat(t); (bruit) dull. **2** a inv & nm Échecs (check)mate; **faire** ou **mettre m.** to (check)mate.

mât [mɑ] nm (de navire) mast; (poteau) pole.

match [matʃ] nm Sp match, Am game; **m. nul** tie, draw.

matelas [matla] nm mattress; **m. pneumatique** air bed. ◆**matelassé** a (meuble) padded; (tissu) quilted.

matelot [matlo] nm sailor, seaman.

mater [mate] vt (enfant, passion etc) to subdue.

matérialiser [materjalize] vt, — **se m.** vpr to materialize. ◆**matérialisation** nf materialization.

matérialisme [materjalism] nm materialism. ◆**matérialiste** a materialistic; – nmf materialist.

matériaux [materjo] nmpl (building) materials; (de roman, enquête etc) material.

matériel, -ielle [materjɛl] a **1** material; (personne) Péj materialistic; (financier) financial; (pratique) practical. **2** nm equipment, material(s); (d'un ordinateur) hardware inv. ◆**matériellement** adv materially; **m. impossible** physically impossible.

maternel, -elle [matɛrnɛl] a motherly, maternal; (parenté, réprimande) maternal; – nf (école) **maternelle** nursery school. ◆**materner** vt to mother. ◆**maternité** nf (état) motherhood, maternity; (hôpital) maternity hospital ou unit; (grossesse) pregnancy; **de m.** (congé, allocation) maternity-.

mathématique [matematik] a mathematical; – nfpl mathematics. ◆**mathématicien, -ienne** nmf mathematician. ◆**maths** [mat] nfpl Fam maths, Am math.

matière [matjɛr] nf (sujet) & Scol subject; (de livre) subject matter; **une m., la m., des matières** (substance(s)) matter; **en première** raw material; **en m. d'art**/etc as regards art/etc, in art/etc; **s'y connaître en m. de** to be experienced in.

matin [matɛ̃] nm morning; **de grand m., de bon m., au petit m.** very early (in the morn-

ing); **le m.** (chaque matin) in the morning; **à sept heures du m.** at seven in the morning; **tous les mardis m.** every Tuesday morning. ◆**matinal, -aux** a (personne) early; (fleur, soleil etc) morning-. ◆**matinée** nf morning; Th matinée; **faire la grasse m.** to sleep late, lie in.

matou [matu] nm tomcat.

matraque [matrak] nf (de policier) truncheon, Am billy (club); (de malfaiteur) cosh, club. ◆**matraqu/er** vt (frapper) to club; (publicité etc) to plug (away) at. ◆**-age** nm m. (publicitaire) plugging, publicity build-up.

matrice [matris] nf **1** Anat womb. **2** Tech matrix.

matricule [matrikyl] nm (registration) number; – a (livret, numéro) registration.

matrimonial, -aux [matrimɔnjal, -o] a matrimonial.

mâture [matyr] nf Nau masts.

maturité [matyrite] nf maturity. ◆**maturation** nf maturing.

maudire* [modir] vt to curse. ◆**maudit** a (sacré) (ac)cursed, damned.

maugréer [mogree] vi to growl, grumble (contre at).

mausolée [mozole] nm mausoleum.

maussade [mosad] a (personne etc) glum, sullen; (temps) gloomy.

mauvais [movɛ] a bad; (méchant, malveillant) evil, wicked; (mal choisi) wrong; (mer) rough; **plus m.** worse; **le plus m.** the worst; **il fait m.** the weather's bad; **ça sent m.** it smells bad; **être m. en** (anglais etc) to be bad at; **mauvaise santé** ill ou bad ou poor health; – nm **le bon et le m.** the good and the bad.

mauve [mov] a & nm (couleur) mauve.

mauviette [movjɛt] nf personne Péj weakling.

maux [mo] voir **mal**.

maxime [maksim] nf maxim.

maximum [maksimɔm] nm maximum; **le m. de** (force etc) the maximum (amount of); **au m.** as much as possible; (tout au plus) at most; – a maximum; **la température m.** maximum temperature. ◆**maximal, -aux** a maximum.

mayonnaise [majonɛz] nf mayonnaise.

mazout [mazut] nm (fuel) oil.

me [m(ə)] (**m'** before vowel or mute h) pron **1** (complément direct) me; **il me voit** he sees me. **2** (indirect) to me; **elle me parle** she speaks to me; **tu me l'as dit** you told me. **3** (réfléchi) myself; **je me lave** I wash myself.

méandres [meɑ̃dr] nmpl meander(ing)s.

mec [mɛk] *nm* (*individu*) *Arg* guy, bloke.

mécanique [mekanik] *a* mechanical; (*jouet*) clockwork; – *nf* (*science*) mechanics; (*mécanisme*) mechanism. ◆**mécanicien** *nm* mechanic; *Rail* train driver. ◆**mécanisme** *nm* mechanism.

mécaniser [mekanize] *vt* to mechanize. ◆**mécanisation** *nf* mechanization.

mécène [mesɛn] *nm* patron (of the arts).

méchant [meʃɑ̃] *a* (*cruel*) malicious, wicked, evil; (*désagréable*) nasty; (*enfant*) naughty; (*chien*) vicious; **ce n'est pas m.** (*grave*) *Fam* it's nothing much. ◆**méchamment** *adv* (*cruellement*) maliciously; (*très*) *Fam* terribly. ◆**méchanceté** *nf* malice, wickedness; **une m.** (*acte*) a malicious act; (*parole*) a malicious word.

mèche [mɛʃ] *nf* **1** (*de cheveux*) lock; *pl* (*reflets*) highlights. **2** (*de bougie*) wick; (*de pétard*) fuse; (*de perceuse*) drill, bit. **3 de m. avec qn** (*complicité*) *Fam* in collusion *ou* cahoots with s.o.

méconn/aître [mekɔnɛtr] *vt* to ignore; (*méjuger*) to fail to appreciate. ◆**-u** *a* unrecognized. ◆**-aissable** *a* unrecognizable.

mécontent [mekɔ̃tɑ̃] *a* dissatisfied, discontented (**de** with). ◆**mécontent/er** *vt* to displease, dissatisfy. ◆**-ement** *nm* dissatisfaction, discontent.

médaille [medaj] *nf* (*décoration*) *Sp* medal; (*pieuse*) medallion; (*pour chien*) name tag; **être m. d'or/d'argent** *Sp* to be a gold/silver medallist. ◆**médaillé, -ée** *nmf* medal holder. ◆**médaillon** *nm* (*bijou*) locket, medallion; (*ornement*) *Archit* medallion.

médecin [medsɛ̃] *nm* doctor, physician. ◆**médecine** *nf* medicine; **étudiant en m.** medical student. ◆**médical, -aux** *a* medical. ◆**médicament** *nm* medicine. ◆**médicinal, -aux** *a* medicinal. ◆**médico-légal, -aux** *a* (*laboratoire*) forensic.

médias [medja] *nmpl* (*mass*) media. ◆**médiatique** *a* media-.

médiateur, -trice [medjatœr, -tris] *nmf* mediator; – *a* mediating. ◆**médiation** *nf* mediation.

médiéval, -aux [medjeval, -o] *a* medi(a)eval.

médiocre [medjɔkr] *a* mediocre, second-rate. ◆**médiocrement** *adv* (*pas très*) not very; (*pas très bien*) not very well. ◆**médiocrité** *nf* mediocrity.

médire* [medir] *vi* **m. de** to speak ill of, slander. ◆**médisance(s)** *nf*(*pl*) mali-

cious gossip, slander; **une m.** a piece of malicious gossip.

méditer [medite] *vt* (*conseil etc*) to meditate on; **m. de faire** to consider doing; – *vi* to meditate (**sur** on). ◆**méditatif, -ive** *a* meditative. ◆**méditation** *nf* meditation.

Méditerranée [mediterane] *nf* **la M.** the Mediterranean. ◆**méditerranéen, -enne** *a* Mediterranean.

médium [medjɔm] *nm* (*spirite*) medium.

méduse [medyz] *nf* jellyfish.

méduser [medyze] *vt* to stun, dumbfound.

meeting [mitiŋ] *nm* *Pol Sp* meeting, rally.

méfait [mefɛ] *nm* *Jur* misdeed; *pl* (*dégâts*) ravages.

méfi/er (se) [səmefje] *vpr* **se m. de** to distrust, mistrust; (*faire attention à*) to watch out for, beware of; **méfie-toi!** watch out!, beware!; **je me méfie** I'm distrustful *ou* suspicious. ◆**-ant** *a* distrustful, suspicious. ◆**méfiance** *nf* distrust, mistrust.

mégalomane [megaloman] *nmf* megalomaniac. ◆**mégalomanie** *nf* megalomania.

mégaphone [megafɔn] *nm* loudhailer.

mégarde (par) [parmegard] *adv* inadvertently, by mistake.

mégère [meʒɛr] *nf* (*femme*) *Péj* shrew.

mégot [mego] *nm* *Fam* cigarette end *ou* butt.

meilleur, -eure [mejœr] *a* better (**que** than); **le m. moment/résultat/etc** the best moment/result/etc; – *nmf* **le m., la meilleure** the best (one).

mélancolie [melɑ̃kɔli] *nf* melancholy, gloom. ◆**mélancolique** *a* melancholy, gloomy.

mélange [melɑ̃ʒ] *nm* mixture, blend; (*opération*) mixing. ◆**mélanger** *vt* (*mêler*) to mix; (*brouiller*) to mix (up), muddle; – **se m.** *vpr* to mix; (*idées etc*) to get mixed (up) *ou* muddled.

mélasse [melas] *nf* treacle, *Am* molasses.

mêl/er [mele] *vt* to mix, mingle (**à** with); (*qualités, thèmes*) to combine; (*brouiller*) to mix (up), muddle; **m. qn à** (*impliquer*) to involve s.o. in; – **se m.** *vpr* to mix, mingle (**à** with); **se m. à** (*la foule etc*) to join; **se m. de** (*s'ingérer dans*) to meddle in; **mêle-toi de ce qui te regarde!** mind your own business! ◆**-é** *a* mixed (**de** with). ◆**-ée** *nf* (*bataille*) rough-and-tumble; *Rugby* scrum(mage).

méli-mélo [melimelo] *nm* (*pl* **mélis-mélos**) *Fam* muddle.

mélodie [melɔdi] *nf* melody. ◆**mélodieux, -euse** *a* melodious. ◆**mélodique** *a* *Mus* melodic. ◆**mélomane** *nmf* music lover.

mélodrame [melodram] *nm* melodrama. ◆**mélodramatique** *a* melodramatic.

melon [m(ə)lɔ̃] *nm* 1 (*fruit*) melon. 2 (*chapeau*) m. bowler (hat).

membrane [mɑ̃bran] *nf* membrane.

membre [mɑ̃br] *nm* 1 *Anat* limb. 2 (*d'un groupe*) member.

même [mɛm] 1 *a* (*identique*) same; **en m. temps** at the same time (**que** as); **ce livre/ etc m.** (*exact*) this very book/*etc*; **il est la bonté m.** he is kindness itself; **lui-m./vous-m./***etc* himself/ yourself/ *etc*; — *pron* **le m., la m.** the same (one); **j'ai les mêmes** I have the same (ones). 2 *adv* (*y compris, aussi*) even; **m. si** even if; **tout de m., quand m.** all the same; **de m.** likewise; **de m. que** just as; **ici m.** in this very place; **à m. de** in a position to; **à m. le sol** on the ground; **à m. la bouteille** from the bottle.

mémento [meméto] *nm* (*aide-mémoire*) handbook; (*agenda*) notebook.

mémoire [memwar] 1 *nf* memory; **de m. d'homme** in living memory; **à la m. de** in memory of. 2 *nm* (*requête*) petition; *Univ* memoir; *pl Littér* memoirs. ◆**mémorable** *a* memorable. ◆**mémorandum** [memɔrɑ̃dɔm] *nm Pol Com* memorandum. ◆**mémorial, -aux** *nm* (*monument*) memorial.

menace [mənas] *nf* threat, menace. ◆**mena/cer** *vt* to threaten (**de faire** to do). ◆—**çant** *a* threatening.

ménage [menaʒ] *nm* (*entretien*) housekeeping; (*couple*) couple, household; **faire le m.** to do the housework; **faire bon m. avec** to get on happily with. ◆**ménager¹, -ère** *a* (*appareil*) domestic, household-; **travaux ménagers** housework; — *nf* (*femme*) housewife.

ménag/er² [menaʒe] *vt* (*arranger*) to prepare *ou* arrange (carefully); (*épargner*) to use sparingly, be careful with; (*fenêtre, escalier etc*) to build; **m. qn** to treat *ou* handle s.o. gently *ou* carefully. ◆—**ement** *nm* (*soin*) care.

ménagerie [menaʒri] *nf* menagerie.

mendier [mɑ̃dje] *vi* to beg; — *vt* to beg for. ◆**mendiant, -ante** *nmf* beggar. ◆**mendicité** *nf* begging.

menées [məne] *nfpl* schemings, intrigues.

men/er [məne] *vt* (*personne, vie etc*) to lead; (*lutte, enquête, tâche etc*) to carry out; (*affaires*) to run; (*bateau*) to command; **m. qn à** (*accompagner, transporter*) to take s.o. to; **m. à bien** *Fig* to carry through; — *vi Sp* to lead. ◆—**eur, -euse** *nmf* (*de révolte*) (ring)leader.

méningite [menéʒit] *nf Méd* meningitis.

ménopause [menopoz] *nf* menopause.

menottes [mənɔt] *nfpl* handcuffs.

mensonge [mɑ̃sɔ̃ʒ] *nm* lie; (*action*) lying. ◆**mensonger, -ère** *a* untrue, false.

menstruation [mɑ̃stryasjɔ̃] *nf* menstruation.

mensuel, -elle [mɑ̃sɥɛl] *a* monthly; — *nm* (*revue*) monthly. ◆**mensualité** *nf* monthly payment. ◆**mensuellement** *adv* monthly.

mensurations [mɑ̃syrasjɔ̃] *nfpl* measurements.

mental, -aux [mɑ̃tal, -o] *a* mental. ◆**mentalité** *nf* mentality.

menthe [mɑ̃t] *nf* mint.

mention [mɑ̃sjɔ̃] *nf* mention, reference; (*annotation*) comment; **m. bien** *Scol Univ* distinction; **faire m. de** to mention. ◆**mentionner** *vt* to mention.

ment/ir° [mɑ̃tir] *vi* to lie, tell lies *ou* a lie (**à** to). ◆—**eur, -euse** *nmf* liar; — *a* lying.

menton [mɑ̃tɔ̃] *nm* chin.

menu [məny] 1 *a* (*petit*) tiny; (*mince*) slender, fine; (*peu important*) minor, petty; — *adv* (*hacher*) small, finely; — *nm* **par le m.** in detail. 2 *nm* (*carte*) *Culin* menu.

menuisier [mənɥizje] *nm* carpenter, joiner. ◆**menuiserie** *nf* carpentry, joinery; (*ouvrage*) woodwork.

méprendre (se) [səmeprɑ̃dr] *vpr* **se m. sur** to be mistaken about. ◆**méprise** *nf* mistake.

mépris [mepri] *nm* contempt (**de** of, for), scorn (**de** for); **au m. de** without regard to. ◆**mépris/er** *vt* to despise, scorn. ◆—**ant** *a* scornful, contemptuous. ◆—**able** *a* despicable.

mer [mɛr] *nf* sea; (*marée*) tide; **en m.** at sea; **par m.** by sea; **aller à la m.** to go to the seaside; **un homme à la m.!** man overboard!

mercantile [mɛrkɑ̃til] *a Péj* money-grabbing.

mercenaire [mɛrsənɛr] *a* & *nm* mercenary.

mercerie [mɛrsəri] *nf* (*magasin*) haberdasher's, *Am* notions store. ◆**mercier, -ière** *nmf* haberdasher, *Am* notions merchant.

merci [mɛrsi] 1 *int* & *nm* thank you, thanks (**de, pour** for); (**non**) **m.!** no, thank you! 2 *nf* **à la m. de** at the mercy of.

mercredi [mɛrkrədi] *nm* Wednesday.

mercure [mɛrkyr] *nm* mercury.

merde! [mɛrd] *int Fam* (bloody) hell!

mère [mɛr] *nf* mother; **m. de famille** mother (of a family); **la m.** Dubois *Fam* old Mrs Dubois; **maison m.** *Com* parent firm.

méridien [meridjē] *nm* meridian.

méridional, -ale, -aux [meridjonal, -o] *a* southern; – *nmf* southerner.

meringue [mərɛ̃g] *nf* (*gâteau*) meringue.

merisier [mərizje] *nm* (*bois*) cherry.

mérite [merit] *nm* merit; **homme de m.** (*valeur*) man of worth. ◆**mérit/er** *vt* (*être digne de*) to deserve; (*valoir*) to be worth; **m. de réussir**/*etc* to deserve to succeed/*etc*. ◆**—ant** *a* deserving. ◆**méritoire** *a* commendable.

merlan [mɛrlɑ̃] *nm* (*poisson*) whiting.

merle [mɛrl] *nm* blackbird.

merveille [mɛrvɛj] *nf* wonder, marvel; **à m.** wonderfully (well). ◆**merveilleusement** *adv* wonderfully. ◆**merveilleux, -euse** *a* wonderful, marvellous; – *nm* **le m.** (*surnaturel*) the supernatural.

mes [me] *voir* **mon.**

mésange [mezɑ̃ʒ] *nf* (*oiseau*) tit.

mésaventure [mezavɑ̃tyr] *nf* misfortune, misadventure.

mesdames [medam] *voir* **madame.**

mesdemoiselles [medmwazɛl] *voir* **mademoiselle.**

mésentente [mezɑ̃tɑ̃t] *nf* misunderstanding.

mesquin [mɛskɛ̃] *a* mean, petty. ◆**mesquinerie** *nf* meanness, pettiness; **une m.** an act of meanness.

mess [mes] *nm inv Mil* mess.

message [mesaʒ] *nm* message. ◆**messager, -ère** *nmf* messenger.

messageries [mesaʒri] *nfpl Com* courier service.

messe [mes] *nf Rel* mass.

Messie [mesi] *nm* Messiah.

messieurs [mesjø] *voir* **monsieur.**

mesure [mɑzyr] *nf* (*évaluation, dimension*) measurement; (*quantité, disposition*) measure; (*retenue*) moderation; (*cadence*) *Mus* time, beat; **fait sur m.** made to measure; **à m. que** as, as soon *ou* as fast as; **dans la m. où** in so far as; **dans une certaine m.** to a certain extent; **en m. de** able to, in a position to; **dépasser la m.** to exceed the bounds. ◆**mesur/er** *vt* to measure; (*juger, estimer*) to calculate, assess, measure; (*argent, temps*) to ration (out); **m. 1 mètre 83** (*personne*) to be six feet tall; (*objet*) to measure six feet; **se m.** à *ou* avec **qn** *Fig* to pit oneself against s.o. ◆**—é** *a* (*pas, ton*) measured; (*personne*) moderate.

met [mɛ] *voir* **mettre.**

métal, -aux [metal, -o] *nm* metal. ◆**métallique** *a* (*objet*) metal-; (*éclat, reflet, couleur*) metallic. ◆**métallisé** *a* (*peinture*) metallic.

métallo [metalo] *nm Fam* steelworker. ◆**métallurgie** *nf* (*industrie*) steel industry; (*science*) metallurgy. ◆**métallurgique** *a usine* m. steelworks. ◆**métallurgiste** *a* & *nm* (*ouvrier*) m. steelworker.

métamorphose [metamɔrfoz] *nf* metamorphosis. ◆**métamorphoser** *vt*, – **se m.** *vpr* to transform (en into).

métaphore [metafɔr] *nf* metaphor. ◆**métaphorique** *a* metaphorical.

métaphysique [metafizik] *a* metaphysical.

météo [meteo] *nf* (*bulletin*) weather forecast.

météore [meteɔr] *nm* meteor. ◆**météorite** *nm* meteorite.

météorologie [meteɔrɔlɔʒi] *nf* (*science*) meteorology; (*service*) weather bureau. ◆**météorologique** *a* meteorological; (*bulletin, station, carte*) weather-.

méthode [metɔd] *nf* method; (*livre*) course. ◆**méthodique** *a* methodical.

méticuleux, -euse [metikylø, -øz] *a* meticulous.

métier [metje] *nm* **1** (*travail*) job; (*manuel*) trade; (*intellectuel*) profession; (*habileté*) professional skill; **homme de m.** specialist. **2 m.** (**à tisser**) loom.

mètre [mɛtr] *nm* (*mesure*) metre; (*règle*) (metre) rule; **m.** (**à ruban**) tape measure. ◆**métr/er** *vt* (*terrain*) to survey. ◆**—age** *nm* **1** surveying. **2** (*tissu*) length; (*de film*) footage; **long m.** (*film*) full length film; **court m.** (*film*) short (film). ◆**—eur** *nm* quantity surveyor. ◆**métrique** *a* metric.

métro [metro] *nm* underground, *Am* subway.

métropole [metrɔpɔl] *nf* (*ville*) metropolis; (*pays*) mother country. ◆**métropolitain** *a* metropolitan.

mets [mɛ] *nm* (*aliment*) dish.

mett/re* [mɛtr] **1** *vt* to put; (*table*) to lay; (*vêtement, lunettes*) to put on, wear; (*chauffage, radio etc*) to put on, switch on; (*réveil*) to set (à for); (*dépenser*) to spend (**pour une robe**/*etc* on a dress/*etc*); **m. dix heures**/*etc* **à venir** (*consacrer*) to take ten hours/*etc* coming *ou* to come; **m. à l'aise** (*rassurer*) to put *ou* set at ease; (*dans un fauteuil etc*) to make comfortable; **m. en colère** to make angry; **m. en liberté** to free; **m. en bouteille(s)** to bottle; **m. du soin à faire** to take care to do; **mettons que** (+ *sub*) let's suppose that; – **se m.** *vpr* (*se placer*) to put oneself; (*debout*) to stand; (*assis*) to sit; (*objet*) to be put, go; **se m. en short/pyjama**/*etc* to get into one's shorts/pyjamas/*etc*; **se m. en rapport avec** to get in touch with; **se m. à** (*endroit*) to go to; (*travail*) to set oneself to, start; **se m. à faire** to start doing; **se m. à table** to sit (down) at the table; **se m. à l'aise** to make oneself comfortable; **se m. au beau/froid** (*temps*) to turn fine/cold. ◆—**able** *a* wearable. ◆—**eur** *nm* **m. en scène** *Th* producer; **Cin** director.

meuble [mœbl] *nm* piece of furniture; *pl* furniture. ◆**meubl/er** *vt* to furnish; (*remplir*) *Fig* to fill. ◆—**é** *nm* furnished flat *ou* Am apartment.

meugl/er [møgle] *vi* to moo, low. ◆—**ement(s)** *nm(pl)* mooing.

meule [møl] *nf* **1** (*de foin*) haystack. **2** (*pour moudre*) millstone.

meunier, -ière [mønje, -jɛr] *nmf* miller.

meurt [mœr] *voir* **mourir**.

meurtre [mœrtr] *nm* murder. ◆**meurtrier, -ière** *nmf* murderer; – *a* deadly, murderous.

meurtrir [mœrtrir] *vt* to bruise. ◆**meurtrissure** *nf* bruise.

meute [møt] *nf* (*de chiens, de créanciers etc*) pack.

Mexique [mɛksik] *nm* Mexico. ◆**mexicain, -aine** *a* & *nmf* Mexican.

mi- [mi] *préf* **la mi-mars/***etc* mid March/*etc*; **à mi-distance** mid-distance, midway.

miaou [mjau] *int* (*cri du chat*) miaow. ◆**miaul/er** [mjole] *vi* to miaow, mew. ◆—**ement(s)** *nm(pl)* miaowing, mewing.

mi-bas [miba] *nm inv* knee sock.

miche [miʃ] *nf* round loaf.

mi-chemin (à) [amiʃmɛ̃] *adv* halfway.

mi-clos [miklo] *a* half-closed.

micmac [mikmak] *nm* (*manigance*) *Fam* intrigue.

mi-corps (à) [amikɔr] *adv* (up) to the waist.

mi-côte (à) [amikot] *adv* halfway up *ou* down (the hill).

micro [mikro] *nm* microphone, mike. ◆**microphone** *nm* microphone.

micro- [mikro] *préf* micro-.

microbe [mikrɔb] *nm* germ, microbe.

microcosme [mikrɔkɔsm] *nm* microcosm.

microfilm [mikrɔfilm] *nm* microfilm.

micro-onde [mikrɔɔd] *nf* microwave; **four à micro-ondes** microwave oven.

microscope [mikrɔskɔp] *nm* microscope. ◆**microscopique** *a* miscroscopic.

midi [midi] *nm* **1** (*heure*) midday, noon, twelve o'clock; (*heure du déjeuner*) lunchtime. **2** (*sud*) south; **le M.** the south of France.

mie [mi] *nf* soft bread, crumb.

miel [mjɛl] *nm* honey. ◆**mielleux, -euse** *a* (*parole, personne*) unctuous.

mien, mienne [mjɛ̃, mjɛn] *pron poss* **le m., la mienne** mine, my one; **les miens, les miennes** mine, my ones; **les deux miens** my two; – *nmpl* **les miens** (*amis etc*) my (own) people.

miette [mjɛt] *nf* (*de pain, de bon sens etc*) crumb; **réduire en miettes** to smash to pieces.

mieux [mjø] *adv* & *a inv* better (**que** than); (*plus à l'aise*) more comfortable; (*plus beau*) better-looking; **le m., la m., les m.** (*convenir, être etc*).the best; (*de deux*) the better; **le m. serait de . . .** the best thing would be to . . . ; **de m. en m.** better and better; **tu ferais m. de partir** you had better leave; **je ne demande pas m.** there's nothing I'd like better (**que de faire** than to do); – *nm* (*amélioration*) improvement; **faire de son m.** to do one's best.

mièvre [mjɛvr] *a* (*doucereux*) *Péj* mannered, wishy-washy.

mignon, -onne [miɲɔ̃, -ɔn] *a* (*charmant*) cute; (*agréable*) nice.

migraine [migrɛn] *nf* headache; *Méd* migraine.

migration [migrasjɔ̃] *nf* migration. ◆**migrant, -ante** *a* & *nmf* (*travailleur*) **m.** migrant worker, migrant.

mijoter [miʒɔte] *vt* Culin to cook (lovingly); (*lentement*) to simmer; (*complot*) *Fig Fam* to brew; – *vi* to simmer.

mil [mil] *nm inv* (*dans les dates*) **a** *ou* one thousand; **l'an deux m.** the year two thousand.

milice [milis] *nf* militia. ◆**milicien** *nm* militiaman.

milieu, -x [miljø] *nm* (*centre*) middle; (*cadre, groupe social*) environment; (*entre extrêmes*) middle course; (*espace*) *Phys* medium; *pl* (*groupes, littéraires etc*) circles; **au m. de** in the middle of; **au m. du danger** in the midst of danger; **le juste m.** the happy medium; **le m.** (*de malfaiteurs*) the underworld.

militaire [militɛr] *a* military; – *nm* serviceman; (*dans l'armée de terre*) soldier.

milit/er [milite] *vi* (*personne*) to be a militant; (*arguments etc*) to militate (**pour** in favour of). ◆—**ant, -ante** *a* & *nmf* militant.

mille [mil] **1** *a* & *nm inv* thousand; **m. hommes/***etc* a *ou* one thousand men/*etc*; **deux m.** two thousand; **mettre dans le m.** to hit the bull's-eye. **2** *nm* (*mesure*) mile. ◆**m.-pattes** *nm inv* (*insecte*) centipede.

◆**millième** a & nmf thousandth; **un m.** a thousandth. ◆**millier** nm thousand; **un m. (de)** a thousand or so.
millefeuille [milfœj] nm (*gâteau*) cream slice.
millénaire [milener] nm millennium.
millésime [milezim] nm date (*on coins, wine etc*).
millet [mijɛ] nm Bot millet.
milli- [mili] préf milli-.
milliard [miljar] nm thousand million, Am billion. ◆**milliardaire** a & nmf multimillionaire.
millimètre [milimɛtr] nm millimetre.
million [miljɔ̃] nm million; **un m. de livres/etc** a million pounds/*etc*; **deux millions** two million. ◆**millionième** a & nmf millionth. ◆**millionnaire** nmf millionaire.
mime [mim] nm (*acteur*) mime; **le m.** (*art*) mime. ◆**mimer** vti to mime. ◆**mimique** nf (*mine*) (funny) face; (*gestes*) signs, sign language.
mimosa [mimoza] nm (*arbre, fleur*) mimosa.
minable [minabl] a (*médiocre*) pathetic; (*lieu, personne*) shabby.
minaret [minarɛ] nm (*de mosquée*) minaret.
minauder [minode] vi to simper, make a show of affectation.
mince [mɛ̃s] **1** a thin; (*élancé*) slim; (*insignifiant*) slim, paltry. **2** int **m. (alors)!** oh heck!, blast (it)! ◆**minceur** nf thinness; slimness. ◆**mincir** vi to grow slim.
mine [min] nf **1** appearance; (*physionomie*) look; **avoir bonne/mauvaise m.** (*santé*) to look well/ill; **faire m. de faire** to appear to do, make as if to do. **2** (*d'or, de charbon etc*) & Fig mine; **m. de charbon** coalmine. **3** (*de crayon*) lead. **4** (*engin explosif*) mine. ◆**miner** vt **1** (*saper*) to undermine. **2** (*garnir d'explosifs*) to mine.
minerai [minrɛ] nm ore.
minéral, -aux [mineral, -o] a & nm mineral.
minéralogique [mineralɔʒik] a **numéro m.** Aut registration ou Am license number.
minet, -ette [minɛ, -ɛt] nmf **1** (*chat*) puss. **2** (*personne*) Fam fashion-conscious young man ou woman.
mineur, -eure [minœr] **1** nm (*ouvrier*) miner. **2** a (*jeune, secondaire*) & Mus minor; – nmf Jur minor. ◆**minier, -ière** a (*industrie*) mining-.
mini- [mini] préf mini-.
miniature [minjatyr] nf miniature; – a inv (*train etc*) miniature-.
minibus [minibys] nm minibus.

minime [minim] a trifling, minor, minimal. ◆**minimiser** vt to minimize.
minimum [minimɔm] nm minimum; **le m. de** (*force etc*) the minimum (amount of); **au (grand) m.** at the very least; **la température m.** the minimum temperature. ◆**minimal, -aux** a minimal.
ministre [ministr] nm Pol Rel minister; **m. de l'Intérieur** = Home Secretary, Am Secretary of the Interior. ◆**ministère** nm ministry; (*gouvernement*) cabinet; **m. de l'Intérieur** = Home Office, Am Department of the Interior. ◆**ministériel, -ielle** a ministerial; (*crise, remaniement*) cabinet-.
minorer [minɔre] vt to reduce.
minorité [minɔrite] nf minority; **en m.** in the ou a minority. ◆**minoritaire** a (*parti etc*) minority-; **être m.** to be in the ou a minority.
Minorque [minɔrk] nf Minorca.
minuit [minɥi] nm midnight, twelve o'clock.
minus [minys] nm (*individu*) Péj Fam moron.
minuscule [minyskyl] **1** a (*petit*) tiny, minute. **2** a & nf (*lettre*) **m.** small letter.
minute [minyt] nf minute; **à la m.** (*tout de suite*) (this very) minute; **d'une m. à l'autre** any minute (now); – a inv **aliments** ou **plats m.** convenience food(s). ◆**minuter** vt to time. ◆**minuterie** nf time switch.
minutie [minysi] nf meticulousness. ◆**minutieux, -euse** a meticulous.
mioche [mjɔʃ] nmf (*enfant*) Fam kid, youngster.
miracle [mirakl] nm miracle; **par m.** miraculously. ◆**miraculeux, -euse** a miraculous.
mirador [miradɔr] nm Mil watchtower.
mirage [miraʒ] nm mirage.
mirifique [mirifik] a Hum fabulous.
mirobolant [mirɔbɔlɑ̃] a Fam fantastic.
miroir [mirwar] nm mirror. ◆**miroiter** vi to gleam, shimmer.
mis [mi] voir **mettre**; – a **bien m.** (*vêtu*) well dressed.
misanthrope [mizɑ̃trɔp] nmf misanthropist; – a misanthropic.
mise [miz] nf **1** (*action de mettre*) putting; **m. en service** putting into service; **m. en marche** starting up; **m. à la retraite** pensioning off; **m. à feu** (*de fusée*) blast-off; **m. en scène** Th production; Cin direction. **2** (*argent*) stake. **3** (*tenue*) attire. ◆**miser** vt (*argent*) to stake (sur on); – vi **m. sur** (*cheval*) to back; (*compter sur*) to bank on.
misère [mizɛr] nf (*grinding*) poverty; (*malheur*) misery; (*bagatelle*) trifle. ◆**mi-**

sérable a miserable, wretched; (*indigent*) poor, destitute; (*logement, quartier*) seedy, slummy; − *nmf* (poor) wretch; (*indigent*) pauper. ◆**miséreux, -euse** a destitute; − *nmf* pauper.

miséricorde [mizerikɔrd] *nf* mercy. ◆**miséricordieux, -euse** a merciful.

misogyne [mizɔʒin] *nmf* misogynist.

missile [misil] *nm* (*fusée*) missile.

mission [misjɔ̃] *nf* mission; (*tâche*) task. ◆**missionnaire** *nm* & a missionary.

missive [misiv] *nf* (*lettre*) missive.

mistral [mistral] *nm inv* (*vent*) mistral.

mite [mit] *nf* (*clothes*) moth; (*du fromage etc*) mite. ◆**mité** a moth-eaten.

mi-temps [mitɑ̃] *nf* (*pause*) Sp half-time; (*période*) Sp half; **à mi-t.** (*travailler etc*) part-time.

miteux, -euse [mitø, -øz] a shabby.

mitigé [mitiʒe] a (*zèle etc*) moderate, luke-warm; (*mêlé*) Fam mixed.

mitraille [mitrɑj] *nf* gunfire. ◆**mitrailler** vt to machinegun; (*photographier*) Fam to click ou snap away at. ◆**mitraillette** *nf* submachine gun. ◆**mitrailleur** a fusil m. machinegun. ◆**mitrailleuse** *nf* machine-gun.

mi-voix (à) [amivwa] adv in an undertone.

mixe(u)r [miksœr] *nm* (*pour mélanger*) (food) mixer.

mixte [mikst] a mixed; (*école*) co-educational, mixed; (*tribunal*) joint.

mixture [mikstyr] *nf* (*boisson*) Péj mixture.

Mlle [madmwazɛl] abrév = **Mademoiselle**.

MM [mesjø] abrév = **Messieurs**.

mm abrév (*millimètre*) mm.

Mme [madam] abrév = **Madame**.

mobile [mobil] **1** a (*pièce etc*) moving; (*personne*) mobile; (*feuillets*) detachable, loose; (*reflets*) changing; **échelle m.** sliding scale; **fête m.** mov(e)able feast; − *nm* (*œuvre d'art*) mobile. **2** *nm* (*motif*) motive (de for). ◆**mobilité** *nf* mobility.

mobilier [mobilje] *nm* furniture.

mobiliser [mobilize] vti to mobilize. ◆**mobilisation** *nf* mobilization.

mobylette [mobilɛt] *nf* moped.

mocassin [mokasɛ̃] *nm* (*chaussure*) moccasin.

moche [mɔʃ] a Fam (*laid*) ugly; (*mauvais, peu gentil*) lousy, rotten.

modalité [modalite] *nf* method (de of).

mode [mod] **1** *nf* fashion; (*industrie*) fashion trade; **à la m.** in fashion, fashionable; **passé de m.** out of fashion; **à la m. de** in the manner of. **2** *nm* mode, method; **m. d'emploi**

directions (for use); **m. de vie** way of life. **3** *nm* Gram mood.

modèle [modɛl] *nm* (*schéma, exemple, personne*) model; **m. (réduit)** (scale) model; − a (*élève etc*) model-. ◆**model/er** vt to model (sur on); **se m. sur** to model oneself on. ◆**—age** *nm* (*de statue etc*) modelling. ◆**modéliste** *nmf* Tex stylist, designer.

modéré [modere] a moderate. ◆**—ment** adv moderately.

modérer [modere] vt to moderate, restrain; (*vitesse, allure*) to reduce; − **se m.** vpr to restrain oneself. ◆**modérateur, -trice** a moderating; − *nmf* moderator. ◆**modération** *nf* moderation, restraint; reduction; **avec m.** in moderation.

moderne [modɛrn] a modern; − *nm* le m. (*mobilier*) modern furniture. ◆**modernisation** *nf* modernization. ◆**moderniser** vt − **se m.** vpr to modernize. ◆**modernisme** *nm* modernism.

modeste [modɛst] a modest. ◆**modestement** adv modestly. ◆**modestie** *nf* modesty.

modifier [modifje] vt to modify, alter; − **se m.** vpr to alter. ◆**modification** *nf* modification, alteration.

modique [modik] a (*salaire, prix*) modest. ◆**modicité** *nf* modesty.

module [modyl] *nm* module.

moduler [modyle] vt to modulate. ◆**modulation** *nf* modulation.

moelle [mwal] *nf* Anat marrow; **m. épinière** spinal cord.

moelleux, -euse [mwalø, -øz] a soft; (*voix, vin*) mellow.

mœurs [mœr(s)] *nfpl* (*morale*) morals; (*habitudes*) habits, customs.

mohair [mɔɛr] *nm* mohair.

moi [mwa] pron **1** (*complément direct*) me; **laissez-moi** leave me; **pour moi** for me. **2** (*indirect*) (to) me; **montrez-le-moi** show it to me, show me it. **3** (*sujet*) I; **moi, je veux** I want. **4** *nm inv* Psy self, ego. ◆**moi-même** pron myself.

moignon [mwaɲɔ̃] *nm* stump.

moindre [mwɛ̃dr] a **être m.** (*moins grand*) to be less; **le m. doute/etc** the slightest ou least doubt/etc; **le m.** (*de mes problèmes etc*) the least (de of); (*de deux problèmes etc*) the lesser (de of).

moine [mwan] *nm* monk, friar.

moineau, -x [mwano] *nm* sparrow.

moins [mwɛ̃] **1** adv (*before vowel*) less (que than); **m. de** (*temps, zèle etc*) less (que than), not so much (que as); (*gens, livres etc*) fewer (que than), not so many

(que as); (cent francs etc) less than; m.
froid/grand/etc not as cold/big/etc (que
as); de m. en m. less and less; le m., la m.,
les m. (travailler etc) the least; le m. grand
the smallest; au m., du m. at least; de m., en
m. (qui manque) missing; dix ans/etc de m.
ten years/etc less; en m. (personne, objet)
less; (personnes, objets) fewer; les m. de
vingt ans those under twenty, the under-
twenties; à m. que (+ sub) unless. 2 prép
Math minus; deux heures m. cinq five to
two; il fait m. dix (degrés) it's minus ten
(degrees).

mois [mwa] nm month; au m. de juin/etc in
(the month of) June/etc.

mois/ir [mwazir] vi to go mouldy; (attendre) Fig to hang about. ◆—I a mouldy; —
nm mould, mildew; sentir le m. to smell
musty. ◆moisissure nf mould, mildew.

moisson [mwasɔ̃] nf harvest. ◆moisson-
ner vt to harvest. ◆moissonneuse-
batteuse nf (pl moissonneuses-batteuses)
combine-harvester.

moite [mwat] a sticky, moist. ◆moiteur nf
stickiness, moistness.

moitié [mwatje] nf half; la m. de la
pomme/etc half (of) the apple/etc; à m.
(remplir etc) halfway; à m. fermé/cru/etc
half closed/raw/etc; à m. prix (for ou at)
half-price; de m. by half; m.-moitié Fam
so-so; partager m.-moitié Fam to split
fifty-fifty.

moka [mɔka] nm (café) mocha.

mol [mɔl] voir mou.

molaire [mɔlɛr] nf (dent) molar.

molécule [mɔlekyl] nf molecule.

moleskine [mɔlɛskin] nf imitation leather.

molester [mɔlɛste] vt to manhandle.

molette [mɔlɛt] nf clé à m. adjustable
wrench ou spanner.

mollasse [mɔlas] a Péj flabby.

molle [mɔl] voir mou. ◆mollement adv
feebly; (paresseusement) lazily. ◆mol-
lesse nf softness; (faiblesse) feebleness.
◆mollir vi to go soft; (courage) to flag.

mollet [mɔlɛ] 1 a œuf m. soft-boiled egg. 2
nm (de jambe) calf.

mollusque [mɔlysk] nm mollusc.

môme [mom] nmf (enfant) Fam kid.

moment [mɔmɑ̃] nm (instant) moment;
(période) time; en ce m. at the moment; par
moments at times; au m. de partir when just
about to leave; au m. où when, just as; du
m. que (puisque) seeing that. ◆mo-
mentané a momentary. ◆momentané-
ment adv temporarily, for the moment.

momie [mɔmi] nf (cadavre) mummy.

mon, ma, pl mes [mɔ̃, ma, me] (ma becomes
mon [mɔ̃n] before a vowel or mute h) a poss
my; mon père my father; ma mère my
mother; mon ami(e) my friend.

Monaco [mɔnako] nf Monaco.

monarque [mɔnark] nm monarch. ◆mo-
narchie nf monarchy. ◆monarchique a
monarchic.

monastère [mɔnastɛr] nm monastery.

monceau, -x [mɔ̃so] nm heap, pile.

monde [mɔ̃d] nm world; (milieu social) set;
du m. (gens) people; (beaucoup) a lot of
people; un m. fou a tremendous crowd; le
(grand) m. (high) society; le m. entier the
whole world; tout le m. everybody; mettre
au m. to give birth to; pas le moins du m.!
not in the least ou slightest! ◆mondain,
-aine a (vie, réunion etc) society-.
◆mondanités nfpl (évènements) social
events. ◆mondial, -aux a (renommée etc)
world-; (crise) worldwide. ◆mondiale-
ment adv the (whole) world over.

monégasque [mɔnegask] a & nmf Mone-
gasque.

monétaire [mɔnetɛr] a monetary.

mongolien, -ienne [mɔ̃gɔljɛ̃, -jɛn] a & nmf
Méd mongol.

moniteur, -trice [mɔnitœr, -tris] nm 1 instructor; (de colonie de vacances) assistant,
Am camp counselor. 2 (écran) Tech monitor.

monnaie [mɔnɛ] nf (devise) currency, money; (appoint, pièces) change; pièce de m.
coin; (petite) m. (small) change; faire de la
m. to get change; faire la m. à qn to give
s.o. change (sur un billet for a note); c'est
m. courante it's very frequent; Hôtel de la
M. mint. ◆monnayer vt (talent etc) to
cash in on; (bien, titre) Com to convert into
cash.

mono [mɔnɔ] a inv (disque etc) mono.

mono- [mɔnɔ] préf mono-.

monocle [mɔnɔkl] nm monocle.

monologue [mɔnɔlɔg] nm monologue.

monoplace [mɔnɔplas] a & nmf (avion, voiture) single-seater.

monopole [mɔnɔpɔl] nm monopoly.
◆monopoliser vt to monopolize.

monosyllabe [mɔnɔsilab] nm monosyllable. ◆monosyllabique a monosyllabic.

monotone [mɔnɔtɔn] a monotonous.
◆monotonie nf monotony.

monseigneur [mɔ̃sɛɲœr] nm (évêque) His
ou Your Grace; (prince) His ou Your Highness.

monsieur, pl messieurs [məsjø, mesjø] nm
gentleman; oui m. yes; (avec déférence) yes

sir; **oui messieurs** yes (gentlemen); **M. Legras** Mr Legras; **Messieurs** *ou* **MM Legras** Messrs Legras; **tu vois ce m.?** do you see that man *ou* gentleman?; **Monsieur** (*sur une lettre*) *Com* Dear Sir.

monstre [mɔstr] *nm* monster; – *a* (*énorme*) *Fam* colossal. ◆**monstrueux, -euse** *a* (*abominable, énorme*) monstrous. ◆**monstruosité** *nf* (*horreur*) monstrosity.

mont [mɔ̃] *nm* (*montagne*) mount.

montagne [mɔtaɲ] *nf* mountain; **la m.** (*zone*) the mountains; **montagnes russes** *Fig* roller coaster. ◆**montagnard, -arde** *nmf* mountain dweller; – *a* (*peuple*) mountain-. ◆**montagneux, -euse** *a* mountainous.

mont-de-piété [mɔ̃dpjete] *nm* (*pl* **monts-de-piété**) pawnshop.

monte-charge [mɔ̃tʃarʒ] *nm inv* service lift *ou Am* elevator.

mont/er [mɔte] *vi* (*aux être*) (*personne*) to go up, come up; (*s'élever*) to go up; (*grimper*) to climb (up) (**sur** onto); (*prix*) to go up, rise; (*marée*) to come in; (*avion*) to climb; **m. dans un véhicule** to get in(to) a vehicle; **m. dans un train** to get on(to) a train; **m. sur** (*échelle etc*) to climb up; (*trône*) to ascend; **m. en courant**/*etc* to run/*etc* up; **m. (à cheval)** *Sp* to ride (a horse); **m. en graine** (*salade etc*) to go to seed; – *vt* (*aux avoir*) (*côte etc*) to climb (up); (*objets*) to bring *ou* take up; (*cheval*) to ride; (*tente, affaire*) to set up; (*machine*) to assemble; (*bijou*) to set, mount; (*complot, démonstration*) to mount; (*pièce*) *Th* to stage, mount; **m. l'escalier** to go *ou* come upstairs *ou* up the stairs; **faire m.** (*visiteur etc*) to show up; **m. qn contre qn** to set s.o. against s.o.; – **se m.** *vpr* (*s'irriter*) *Fam* to get angry; **se m. à** (*frais*) to amount to. ◆**-ant 1** *a* (*chemin*) uphill; (*mouvement*) upward; (*marée*) rising; (*col*) stand-up; (*robe*) high-necked; **chaussure montante** boot. **2** *nm* (*somme*) amount. **3** *nm* (*de barrière*) post; (*d'échelle*) upright. ◆**-é-e** *nf* (*police*) mounted. ◆**-ée** *nf* ascent, climb; (*de prix, des eaux*) rise; (*chemin*) slope. ◆**-age** *nm Tech* assembling, assembly; *Cin* editing. ◆**-eur, -euse** *nmf Tech* fitter; *Cin* editor.

montre [mɔtr] *nf* **1** watch; **course contre la m.** race against time. **2** **faire m. de** to show. ◆**m.-bracelet** *nf* (*pl* **montres-bracelets**) wristwatch.

Montréal [mɔreal] *nm ou f* Montreal.

montrer [mɔtre] *vt* to show (**à** to); **m. du doigt** to point to; **m. à qn à faire qch** to

show s.o. how to do sth; – **se m.** *vpr* to show oneself, appear; (*s'avérer*) to turn out to be; **se m. courageux**/*etc* (*être*) to be courageous/*etc*.

monture [mɔtyr] *nf* **1** (*cheval*) mount. **2** (*de lunettes*) frame; (*de bijou*) setting.

monument [mɔnymɑ̃] *nm* monument; **m. aux morts** war memorial. ◆**monumental, -aux** *a* (*imposant, énorme etc*) monumental.

moquer (se) [səmɔke] *vpr* **se m. de** (*allure etc*) to make fun of; (*personne*) to make a fool of, make fun of; **je m'en moque!** I couldn't care less! ◆**moquerie** *nf* mockery. ◆**moqueur, -euse** *a* mocking.

moquette [mɔkɛt] *nf* fitted carpet(s), wall-to-wall carpeting.

moral, -aux [mɔral, -o] *a* moral; – *nm* **le m.** spirits, morale. ◆**morale** *nf* (*principes*) morals; (*code*) moral code; (*d'histoire etc*) moral; **faire la m. à qn** to lecture s.o. ◆**moralement** *adv* morally. ◆**moraliser** *vi* to moralize. ◆**moraliste** *nmf* moralist. ◆**moralité** *nf* (*mœurs*) morality; (*de fable, récit etc*) moral.

moratoire [mɔratwar] *nm* moratorium.

morbide [mɔrbid] *a* morbid.

morceau, -x [mɔrso] *nm* piece, bit; (*de sucre*) lump; (*de viande*) *Culin* cut; (*extrait*) *Littér* extract. ◆**morceler** *vt* (*terrain*) to divide up.

mordiller [mɔrdije] *vt* to nibble.

mord/re [mɔrdr] *vti* to bite; **ça mord** *Pêche* I have a bite. ◆**-ant 1** *a* (*voix, manière*) scathing; (*froid*) biting; (*personne, ironie*) caustic. **2** *nm* (*énergie*) punch. ◆**-u, -ue** *nmf* **un m. du jazz**/*etc Fam* a jazz/*etc* fan.

morfondre (se) [səmɔrfɔdr] *vpr* to get bored (waiting), mope (about).

morgue [mɔrg] *nf* (*lieu*) mortuary, morgue.

moribond, -onde [mɔribɔ̃, -ɔ̃d] *a* & *nmf* dying *ou* moribund (person).

morne [mɔrn] *a* dismal, gloomy, dull.

morose [mɔroz] *a* morose, sullen.

morphine [mɔrfin] *nf* morphine.

mors [mɔr] *nm* (*de harnais*) bit.

morse [mɔrs] *nm* **1** Morse (code). **2** (*animal*) walrus.

morsure [mɔrsyr] *nf* bite.

mort¹ [mɔr] *nf* death; **mettre à m.** to put to death; **silence de m.** dead silence. ◆**mortalité** *nf* death rate, mortality. ◆**mortel, -elle** *a* (*hommes, ennemi, danger etc*) mortal; (*accident*) fatal; (*chaleur*) deadly; (*pâleur*) mortal; – *nmf* mortal. ◆**mortellement** *adv* (*blessé*) fatally.

mort², morte [mɔr, mɔrt] *a* (*personne, plante, ville etc*) dead; **m. de fatigue** dead tired; **m. de froid** numb with cold; **m. de peur** frightened to death; − *nmf* dead man, dead woman; **les morts** the dead; **de nombreux morts** (*victimes*) many deaths *ou* casualties; **le jour** *ou* **la fête des Morts** All Souls' Day. ◆**morte-saison** *nf* off season. ◆**mort-né** *a* (*enfant*) & *Fig* stillborn.

mortier [mɔrtje] *nm* mortar.

mortifier [mɔrtifje] *vt* to mortify.

mortuaire [mɔrtɥɛr] *a* (*avis, rites etc*) death-, funeral.

morue [mɔry] *nf* cod.

morve [mɔrv] *nf* (nasal) mucus. ◆**morveux, -euse** *a* (*enfant*) snotty (-nosed).

mosaïque [mɔzaik] *nf* mosaic.

Moscou [mɔsku] *nm ou f* Moscow.

mosquée [mɔske] *nf* mosque.

mot [mo] *nm* word; **envoyer un m.** à to drop a line to; **m. à** *ou* **pour m.** word for word; **bon m.** witticism; **mots croisés** crossword (puzzle); **m. d'ordre** *Pol* resolution, order; (*slogan*) watchword; **m. de passe** password.

motard [mɔtar] *nm Fam* motorcyclist.

motel [mɔtɛl] *nm* motel.

moteur [mɔtœr] *nm* (*de véhicule etc*) engine, motor; *El* motor.

moteur [mɔtœr, -tris] *a* (*force*) driving-; (*nerf, muscle*) motor.

motif [mɔtif] *nm* **1** reason, motive. **2** (*dessin*) pattern.

motion [mɔsjɔ̃] *nf Pol* motion; **on a voté une m. de censure** a vote of no confidence was given.

motiver [mɔtive] *vt* (*inciter, causer*) to motivate; (*justifier*) to justify. ◆**motivation** *nf* motivation.

moto [mɔto] *nf* motorcycle, motorbike. ◆**motocycliste** *nmf* motorcyclist.

motorisé [mɔtɔrize] *a* motorized.

motte [mɔt] *nf* (*de terre*) clod, lump; (*de beurre*) block.

mou (*or* **mol** *before vowel or mute h*), **molle** [mu, mɔl] *a* soft; (*faible, sans énergie*) feeble; − *nm* **avoir du m.** (*cordage*) to be slack.

mouchard, -arde [muʃar, -ard] *nmf Péj* informer. ◆**moucharder** *vt* **m. qn** *Fam* to inform on s.o.

mouche [muʃ] *nf* (*insecte*) fly; **prendre la m.** (*se fâcher*) to go into a huff; **faire m.** to hit the bull's-eye. ◆**moucheron** *nm* (*insecte*) midge.

moucher [muʃe] *vt* **m. qn** to wipe s.o.'s nose; **se m.** to blow one's nose.

moucheté [muʃte] *a* speckled, spotted.

mouchoir [muʃwar] *nm* handkerchief; (*en papier*) tissue.

moudre [mudr] *vt* (*café, blé*) to grind.

moue [mu] *nf* long face, pout; **faire la m.** to pout, pull a (long) face.

mouette [mwɛt] *nf* (sea)gull.

moufle [mufl] *nf* (*gant*) mitt(en).

mouill/er [muje] **1** *vt* to wet, make wet; **se faire m.** to get wet; − **se m.** *vpr* to get (one-self) wet; (*se compromettre*) *Fam* to get involved (*by taking risks*). **2** *vt* **m. l'ancre** *Nau* to (drop) anchor; − *vi* to anchor. ◆**-é** *a* wet (*de* with). ◆**-age** *nm* (*action*) *Nau* anchoring; (*lieu*) anchorage.

moule [mul] *nm* mould, *Am* mold; **m. à gâteaux** cake tin. ◆**moul/er** *vt* to mould, *Am* mold; (*statue*) to cast; **m. qn** (*vêtement*) to fit s.o. tightly. ◆**-ant** *a* (*vêtement*) tight-fitting. ◆**-age** *nm* moulding; casting; (*objet*) cast. ◆**moulure** *nf Archit* moulding.

moule [mul] *nf* (*mollusque*) mussel.

moulin [mulɛ̃] *nm* mill; (*moteur*) *Fam* engine; **m. à vent** windmill; **m. à café** coffee-grinder.

moulinet [mulinɛ] *nm* **1** (*de canne à pêche*) reel. **2** (*de bâton*) twirl.

moulu [muly] *voir* **moudre**; − *a* (*café*) ground; (*éreinté*) *Fam* dead tired.

mour/ir [murir] *vi* (*aux être*) to die (*de* of, from); **m. de froid** to die of exposure; **m. d'ennui/de fatigue** *Fig* to be dead bored/tired; **m. de peur** *Fig* to be frightened to death; **s'ennuyer à m.** to be bored to death; − **se m.** *vpr* to be dying. ◆**-ant, -ante** *a* dying; (*voix*) faint; − *nmf* dying person.

mousquetaire [muskɛtɛr] *nm Mil Hist* musketeer.

mousse [mus] *nf* **1** *Bot* moss. **2** *nf* (*écume*) froth, foam; (*de bière*) froth; (*de savon*) lather; **m. à raser** shaving foam. **3** *nf Culin* mousse. ◆**mousser** *vi* (*bière etc*) to froth; (*savon*) to lather; (*eau savonneuse*) to foam. ◆**mousseux, -euse** *a* frothy; (*vin*) sparkling; − *nm* sparkling wine. ◆**moussu** *a* mossy.

mousseline [muslin] *nf* (*coton*) muslin.

mousson [musɔ̃] *nf* (*vent*) monsoon.

moustache [mustaʃ] *nf* moustache, *Am* mustache; *pl* (*de chat etc*) whiskers. ◆**moustachu** *a* wearing a moustache.

moustique [mustik] *nm* mosquito. ◆**moustiquaire** *nf* mosquito net; (*en métal*) screen.

moutard [mutar] *nm* (*enfant*) *Arg* kid.

moutarde [mutard] *nf* mustard.

mouton [mutɔ̃] *nm* sheep; (*viande*) mutton;

pl (*sur la mer*) white horses; (*poussière*) bits of dust; **peau de m.** sheepskin.

mouvement [muvmã] *nm* (*geste, déplacement, groupe etc*) & *Mus* movement; (*de colère*) outburst; (*impulsion*) impulse; **en m.** in motion. ◆**mouvementé** *a* (*animé*) lively, exciting; (*séance, vie etc*) eventful.

mouv/oir° [muvwar] *vi, — se m.* *vpr* to move; **mû par** (*mécanisme*) driven by. ◆**—ant** *a* (*changeant*) changing; **sables mouvants** quicksands.

moyen[1], **-enne** [mwajẽ, -ɛn] *a* average; (*format, entreprise etc*) medium(-sized); (*solution*) intermediate, middle; — *nf* average; (*dans un examen*) pass mark; (*dans un devoir*) half marks; **la moyenne d'âge** the average age; **en moyenne** on average. ◆**moyennement** *adv* averagely, moderately.

moyen[2] [mwajẽ] *nm* (*procédé, façon*) means, way (**de faire** of doing, to do); *pl* (*capacités*) ability, powers; (*argent, ressources*) means; **au m. de** by means of; **il n'y a pas m. de faire** it's not possible to do; **je n'ai pas les moyens** (*argent*) I can't afford it; **par mes propres moyens** under my own steam.

moyennant [mwajenã] *prép* (*pour*) (in return) for; (*avec*) with.

moyeu, -x [mwajø] *nm* (*de roue*) hub.

mucosités [mykozite] *nfpl* mucus.

mue [my] *nf* moulting; breaking of the voice. ◆**muer** [mɥe] *vi* (*animal*) to moult; (*voix*) to break; **se m. en** to become transformed into.

muet, -ette [mɥe, -ɛt] *a* (*infirme*) dumb; (*de surprise etc*) speechless; (*film, reproche etc*) silent; *Gram* mute; — *nmf* dumb person.

mufle [myfl] *nm* **1** (*d'animal*) nose, muzzle. **2** (*individu*) *Péj* lout.

mug/ir [myʒir] *vi* (*vache*) to moo; (*bœuf*) to bellow; (*vent*) *Fig* to roar. ◆**—issement(s)** *nm*(*pl*) moo(ing); bellowing; roar(ing).

muguet [mygɛ] *nm* lily of the valley.

mule [myl] *nf* **1** (*pantoufle*) mule. **2** (*animal*) (she-)mule. ◆**mulet**[1] *nm* (he-)mule.

mulet[2] [mylɛ] *nm* (*poisson*) mullet.

multi- [mylti] *préf* multi-.

multicolore [myltikɔlɔr] *a* multicoloured.

multinationale [myltinasjɔnal] *nf* multinational.

multiple [myltipl] *a* (*nombreux*) numerous; (*ayant des formes variées*) multiple; — *nm* *Math* multiple. ◆**multiplication** *nf* multiplication; (*augmentation*) increase. ◆**multiplicité** *nf* multiplicity. ◆**multiplier** *vt* to

multiply; **— se m.** *vpr* to increase; (*se reproduire*) to multiply.

multitude [myltityd] *nf* multitude.

municipal, -aux [mynisipal, -o] *a* municipal; **conseil m.** town council. ◆**municipalité** *nf* (*corps*) town council; (*commune*) municipality.

munir [mynir] *vt* **m. de** to provide *ou* equip with; **se m. de** to provide oneself with; **muni de** (*papiers, arme etc*) in possession of.

munitions [mynisjɔ̃] *nfpl* ammunition.

muqueuse [mykøz] *nf* mucous membrane.

mur [myr] *nm* wall; **m. du son** sound barrier; **au pied du m.** *Fig* with one's back to the wall. ◆**muraille** *nf* (high) wall. ◆**mural, -aux** *a* (*carte etc*) wall-; **peinture murale** mural (painting). ◆**murer** *vt* (*porte*) to wall up; **m. qn** to wall s.o. in.

mûr [myr] *a* (*fruit, projet etc*) ripe; (*âge, homme*) mature. ◆**mûrement** *adv* (*réfléchir*) carefully. ◆**mûrir** *vti* (*fruit*) to ripen; (*personne, projet*) to mature.

muret [myrɛ] *nm* low wall.

murmure [myrmyr] *nm* murmur. ◆**murmurer** *vti* to murmur.

musc [mysk] *nm* (*parfum*) musk.

muscade [myskad] *nf* nutmeg.

muscle [myskl] *nm* muscle. ◆**musclé** *a* (*bras*) brawny, muscular. ◆**musculaire** *a* (*tissu, système etc*) muscular. ◆**musculature** *nf* muscles.

museau, -x [myzo] *nm* (*de chien etc*) muzzle; (*de porc*) snout. ◆**museler** *vt* (*animal, presse etc*) to muzzle. ◆**muselière** *nf* (*appareil*) muzzle.

musée [myze] *nm* museum; **m. de peinture** (public) art gallery. ◆**muséum** *nm* (natural history) museum.

musette [myzɛt] *nf* (*d'ouvrier*) duffel bag, kit bag.

music-hall [myzikol] *nm* variety theatre.

musique [myzik] *nf* music; (*fanfare*) *Mil* band. ◆**musical, -aux** *a* musical. ◆**musicien, -ienne** *nmf* musician; — *a* **être très/assez m.** to be very/quite musical.

musulman, -ane [myzylmɑ̃, -an] *a* & *nmf* Moslem, Muslim.

muter [myte] *vt* (*employé*) to transfer. ◆**mutation** *nf* **1** transfer. **2** *Biol* mutation.

mutil/er [mytile] *vt* to mutilate, maim; **être mutilé** to be disabled. ◆**—é, -ée** *nmf* **m. de guerre/du travail** disabled ex-serviceman/ worker. ◆**mutilation** *nf* mutilation.

mutin [mytɛ̃] *a* (*espiègle*) saucy. **2** (*rebelle*) mutineer. ◆**se mutin/er** *vpr* to mutiny. ◆**—é** *a* mutinous. ◆**mutinerie** *nf* mutiny.

mutisme [mytism] nm (stubborn) silence.
mutualité [mytųalite] nf mutual insurance. ◆mutualiste nmf member of a friendly ou Am benefit society. ◆mutuelle¹ nf friendly society, Am benefit society.
mutuel, -elle² [mytųɛl] a (réciproque) mutual. ◆mutuellement adv (l'un l'autre) each other (mutually).
myope [mjɔp] a & nmf shortsighted (person). ◆myopie nf shortsightedness.
myosotis [mjɔzɔtis] nm Bot forget-me-not.
myrtille [mirtij] nf Bot bilberry.

mystère [mistɛr] nm mystery. ◆mystérieux, -euse a mysterious.
mystifier [mistifje] vt to fool, deceive, hoax. ◆mystification nf hoax.
mystique [mistik] a mystic(al); — nmf (personne) mystic; — nf mystique (de of). ◆mysticisme nm mysticism.
mythe [mit] nm myth. ◆mythique a mythical. ◆mythologie nf mythology. ◆mythologique a mythological.
mythomane [mitɔman] nmf compulsive liar.

N

N, n [ɛn] nm N, n.
n' [n] voir ne.
nabot [nabo] nm Péj midget.
nacelle [nasɛl] nf (de ballon) car, gondola; (de landau) carriage, carrycot.
nacre [nakr] nf mother-of-pearl. ◆nacré a pearly.
nage [naʒ] nf (swimming) stroke; n. libre freestyle; traverser à la n. to swim across; en n. Fig sweating. ◆nager vi to swim; (flotter) to float; je nage dans le bonheur my happiness knows no bounds; je nage complètement (je suis perdu) Fam I'm all at sea; — vt (crawl etc) to swim. ◆nageur, -euse nmf swimmer.
nageoire [naʒwar] nf (de poisson) fin; (de phoque) flipper.
naguère [nagɛr] adv Litt not long ago.
naïf, -ïve [naif, -iv] a simple, naïve; — nmf (jobard) simpleton.
nain, naine [nɛ̃, nɛn] nmf dwarf; — a (arbre, haricot) dwarf-.
naissance [nɛsɑ̃s] nf birth; (de bras, cou) base; donner n. à Fig to give rise to; de n. from birth.
naître* [nɛtr] vi to be born; (jour) to dawn; (sentiment, difficulté) to arise (de from); faire n. (soupçon, industrie etc) to give rise to, create. ◆naissant a (amitié etc) incipient.
naïveté [naivte] nf simplicity, naïveté.
nant/ir [nɑ̃tir] vt n. de to provide with. ◆—i a & nmpl (riche) affluent.
naphtaline [naftalin] nf mothballs.
nappe [nap] nf 1 table cloth. 2 (d'eau) sheet; (de gaz, pétrole) layer; (de brouillard) blanket. ◆napperon nm (soft) table mat; (pour vase etc) (soft) mat, cloth.

narcotique [narkɔtik] a & nm narcotic.
narguer [narge] vt to flout, mock.
narine [narin] nf nostril.
narquois [narkwa] a sneering.
narration [narɑsjɔ̃] nf (récit, acte, art) narration. ◆narrateur, -trice nmf narrator.
nasal, -aux [nazal, -o] a nasal.
naseau, -x [nazo] nm (de cheval) nostril.
nasiller [nazije] vi (personne) to speak with a twang; (micro, radio) to crackle. ◆nasillard a (voix) nasal; (micro etc) crackling.
natal, mpl -als [natal] a (pays etc) native; sa maison natale the house where he ou she was born. ◆natalité nf birthrate.
natation [natasjɔ̃] nf swimming.
natif, -ive [natif, -iv] a & nmf native; être n. de to be a native of.
nation [nasjɔ̃] nf nation; les Nations Unies the United Nations. ◆national, -aux a national; ◆nationale nf (route) trunk road, Am highway. ◆nationaliser vt to nationalize. ◆nationaliste a Péj nationalistic; — nmf nationalist. ◆nationalité nf nationality.
nativité [nativite] nf Rel nativity.
natte [nat] nf 1 (de cheveux) plait, Am braid. 2 (tapis) mat, (piece of) matting. ◆natt/er vt to plait, Am braid. ◆—age nm (matière) matting.
naturaliser [natyralize] vt (personne) Pol to naturalize. ◆naturalisation nf naturalization.
nature [natyr] nf (monde naturel, caractère) nature; de toute n. of every kind; être de n. à to be likely to; payer en n. Fin to pay in kind; n. morte (tableau) still life; plus grand que n. larger than life; — a inv (omelette, yaourt etc) plain; (café) black. ◆natura-

liste *nmf* naturalist. ◆**naturiste** *nmf* nudist, naturist.

naturel, -elle [natyrɛl] *a* natural; **mort naturelle** death from natural causes; – *nm* (*caractère*) nature; (*simplicité*) naturalness. ◆**naturellement** *adv* naturally.

naufrage [nofraʒ] *nm* (ship)wreck; (*ruine*) *Litt Fig* ruin; **faire n.** to be (ship)wrecked. ◆**naufragé, -ée** *a & nmf* shipwrecked (person).

nausée [noze] *nf* nausea, sickness. ◆**nauséabond** *a* nauseating, sickening.

nautique [notik] *a* nautical; (*sports, ski*) water-.

naval [naval] *a* naval; **constructions navales** shipbuilding.

navet [navɛ] *nm* **1** *Bot Culin* turnip. **2** (*film etc*) *Péj* flop, dud.

navette [navɛt] *nf* (*transport*) shuttle (service); **faire la n.** (*véhicule, personne etc*) to shuttle back and forth (**entre** between); **n. spatiale** space shuttle.

naviguer [navige] *vi* (*bateau*) to sail; (*piloter, voler*) to navigate. ◆**navigabilité** *nf* (*de bateau*) seaworthiness; (*d'avion*) airworthiness. ◆**navigable** *a* (*fleuve*) navigable. ◆**navigant** *a personnel n. Av Nau* crew. ◆**navigateur** *nm* Av navigator. ◆**navigation** *nf* (*pilotage*) navigation; (*trafic*) Nau shipping.

navire [navir] *nm* ship.

navr/er [navre] *vt* to upset (greatly), grieve. ◆**—ant** *a* upsetting. ◆**—é** *a* (*air*) grieved; **je suis n.** I'm (terribly) sorry (**de faire** to do).

nazi, -ie [nazi] *a & nmf Pol Hist* Nazi.

ne [n(ə)] (**n'** *before vowel or mute h; used to form negative verb with* **pas, jamais, que** *etc*) *adv* **1** (+ *pas*) not; **elle ne boit pas** she does not *ou* doesn't drink; **il n'ose (pas)** he doesn't dare; **n'importe** it doesn't matter. **2** (*with* **craindre, avoir peur** *etc*) **je crains qu'il ne parte** I'm afraid he'll leave.

né [ne] *a* born; **il est né** he was born; **née Dupont** née Dupont.

néanmoins [neɑ̃mwɛ] *adv* nevertheless, nonetheless.

néant [neɑ̃] *nm* nothingness, void; (*sur un formulaire*) = none.

nébuleux, -euse [nebylø, -øz] *a* hazy, nebulous.

nécessaire [neseser] *a* necessary; (*inéluctable*) inevitable; – *nm* **le n.** (*biens*) the necessities; **le strict n.** the bare necessities; **n. de couture** sewing box, workbox; **n. de toilette** sponge bag, dressing case; **faire le n.** to do what's necessary *ou* the necessary. ◆**né-**

cessairement *adv* necessarily; (*échouer etc*) inevitably. ◆**nécessité** *nf* necessity. ◆**nécessiter** *vt* to necessitate, require. ◆**nécessiteux, -euse** *a* needy.

nécrologie [nekrɔlɔʒi] *nf* obituary.

nectarine [nektarin] *nf* (*fruit*) nectarine.

néerlandais, -aise [neerlɑ̃dɛ, -ɛz] *a* Dutch; – *nmf* Dutchman, Dutchwoman; – *nm* (*langue*) Dutch.

nef [nɛf] *nf* (*d'église*) nave.

néfaste [nefast] *a* (*influence etc*) harmful (**à** to).

négatif, -ive [negatif, -iv] *a* negative; – *nm Phot* negative; – *nf* **répondre par la négative** to answer in the negative. ◆**négation** *nf* negation, denial (**de** of); *Gram* negation; (*mot*) negative.

négligeable [negliʒabl] *a* negligible.

négligent [negliʒɑ̃] *a* negligent, careless. ◆**négligemment** [-amɑ̃] *adv* negligently, carelessly. ◆**négligence** *nf* negligence, carelessness; (*faute*) (careless) error.

néglig/er [negliʒe] *vt* (*personne, conseil, travail etc*) to neglect; **n. de faire** to neglect to do; – **se n.** *vpr* (*négliger sa tenue ou sa santé*) to neglect oneself. ◆**—é** *a* (*tenue*) untidy, neglected; (*travail*) careless; – *nm* (*de tenue*) untidiness; (*vêtement*) negligee.

négoci/er [negɔsje] *vti Fin Pol* to negotiate. ◆**—ant, -ante** *nmf* merchant, trader. ◆**—able** *a Fin* negotiable. ◆**négociateur, -trice** *nmf* negotiator. ◆**négociation** *nf* negotiation.

nègre [nɛgr] **1** *a* (*art, sculpture etc*) Negro. **2** *nm* (*écrivain*) ghost writer.

neige [nɛʒ] *nf* snow; **n. fondue** sleet; **n. carbonique** dry ice. ◆**neiger** *v imp* to snow. ◆**neigeux, -euse** *a* snowy.

nénuphar [nenyfar] *nm* water lily.

néo [neɔ] *préf* neo-.

néon [neɔ̃] *nm* (*gaz*) neon; **au n.** (*éclairage etc*) neon-.

néophyte [neɔfit] *nmf* novice.

néo-zélandais, -aise [neozelɑ̃dɛ, -ɛz] *a* (*peuple etc*) New Zealand-; – *nmf* New Zealander.

nerf [nɛr] *nm Anat* nerve; **avoir du n.** (*vigueur*) *Fam* to have guts; **du n.!** buck up!; **un peu de n.!** buck up!; **ça me porte** *ou* **me tape sur les nerfs** it gets on my nerves; **être sur les nerfs** *Fig* to be keyed up *ou* het up. ◆**nerveux, -euse** *a* nervous; (*centre, cellule*) nerve-. ◆**nervosité** *nf* nervousness.

nervure [nervyr] *nf* (*de feuille*) vein.

nescafé [neskafe] *nm* instant coffee.

n'est-ce pas? [nɛspa] *adv* isn't he?, don't

you? *etc*; **il fait beau, n'est-ce pas?** the weather's fine, isn't it?

net, nette [nɛt] *a* (*conscience, idée, image, refus*) clear; (*coupure, linge*) clean; (*soigné*) neat; (*copie*) fair; − *adv* (*s'arrêter*) short, dead; (*tuer*) outright; (*parler*) plainly; (*refuser*) flat(ly); (*casser, couper*) clean. **2** *a* (*poids, prix etc*) Com net(t). ◆**nettement** *adv* clearly, plainly; (*sensiblement*) markedly. ◆**netteté** *nf* clearness; (*de travail*) neatness.

nettoyer [nɛtwaje] *vt* to clean (up); (*plaie*) to cleanse, clean (up); (*vider, ruiner*) *Fam* to clean out. ◆**nettoiement** *nm* cleaning; **service du n.** refuse *ou Am* garbage collection. ◆**nettoyage** *nm* cleaning; **n. à sec** dry cleaning.

neuf¹, neuve [nœf, nœv] *a* new; **quoi de n.?** what's new(s)?; − *nm* **il y a du n.** there's been something new; **remettre à n.** to make as good as new.

neuf² [nœf] *a & nm* [nœv] before **heures** & **ans**) nine. ◆**neuvième** *a & nmf* ninth.

neurasthénie [nørastenik] *a* depressed.

neutre [nøtr] **1** *a* (*pays, personne etc*) neutral; − *nm* El neutral. **2** *a & nm* Gram neuter. ◆**neutraliser** *vt* to neutralize. ◆**neutralité** *nf* neutrality.

neveu, -x [nəvø] *nm* nephew.

névralgie [nevralʒi] *nf* headache; *Méd* neuralgia. ◆**névralgique** *a* **centre n.** *Fig* nerve centre.

névrose [nevroz] *nf* neurosis. ◆**névrosé, -ée** *a & nmf* neurotic.

nez [ne] *nm* nose; **n. à n.** face to face (**avec** with); **au n. de qn** (*rire etc*) in s.o.'s face; **mettre le n. dehors** *Fam* to stick one's nose outside.

ni [ni] *conj* **ni . . . ni** (+ *ne*) neither . . . nor; **il n'a ni faim ni soif** he's neither hungry nor thirsty; **sans manger ni boire** without eating or drinking; **ni l'un(e) ni l'autre** neither (of them).

niais, -aise [njɛ, -ɛz] *a* silly, simple; − *nmf* simpleton. ◆**niaiserie** *nf* silliness; *pl* (*paroles*) nonsense.

niche [niʃ] *nf* (*de chien*) kennel; (*cavité*) niche, recess.

nich/er [niʃe] *vi* (*oiseau*) to nest; (*loger*) *Fam* to hang out; − **se n.** *vpr* (*oiseau*) to nest; (*se cacher*) to hide oneself. ◆**-ée** *nf* (*oiseaux, enfants*) brood; (*chiens*) litter.

nickel [nikɛl] *nm* (*métal*) nickel.

nicotine [nikɔtin] *nf* nicotine.

nid [ni] *nm* nest; **n. de poules** *Aut* pothole.

nièce [njɛs] *nf* niece.

nième [ɛnjɛm] *a* nth.

nier [nje] *vt* to deny (**que** that); − *vi* Jur to deny the charge.

nigaud, -aude [nigo, -od] *a* silly; − *nmf* silly fool.

Nigéria [niʒerja] *nm ou f* Nigeria.

n'importe [nɛ̃pɔrt] *voir* **importer 1**.

nippon, -one *ou* **-onne** [nipɔ̃, -ɔn] *a* Japanese.

niveau, -x [nivo] *nm* (*hauteur*) level; (*degré, compétence*) standard, level; **n. de vie** standard of living; **n. à bulle (d'air)** spirit level; **au n. de qn** (*élève etc*) up to s.o.'s standard. ◆**niveler** *vt* to level; (*fortunes etc*) to even (up).

noble [nɔbl] *a* noble; − *nmf* nobleman, noblewoman. ◆**noblement** *adv* nobly. ◆**noblesse** *nf* (*caractère, classe*) nobility.

noce(s) [nɔs] *nf(pl)* wedding; **faire la noce** *Fam* to have a good time, make merry; **noces d'argent/d'or** silver/golden wedding. ◆**noceur, -euse** *nmf Fam* fast liver, reveller.

nocif, -ive [nɔsif, -iv] *a* harmful. ◆**nocivité** *nf* harmfulness.

noctambule [nɔktɑ̃byl] *nmf* (*personne*) night bird *ou* prowler. ◆**nocturne** *a* nocturnal, night-; − *nm* (*de magasins etc*) late night opening; (**match en**) **n.** *Sp* floodlit match, *Am* night game.

Noël [nɔɛl] *nm* Christmas; **le père N.** Father Christmas, Santa Claus.

nœud [nø] *nm* **1** knot; (*ruban*) bow; **le n. du problème**/*etc* the crux of the problem/*etc*; **n. coulant** noose, slipknot; **n. papillon** bow tie. **2** (*mesure*) Nau knot.

noir, noire [nwar] *a* black; (*nuit, lunettes etc*) dark; (*idées*) gloomy; (*âme, crime*) vile; (*misère*) dire; **roman n.** thriller; **film n.** film noir; **il fait n.** it's dark; − *nm* (*couleur*) black; (*obscurité*) dark; **N.** (*homme*) black; **vendre au n.** to sell on the black market; − *nf Mus* crotchet, *Am* quarter note; **Noire** (*femme*) black. ◆**noirceur** *nf* blackness; (*d'une action etc*) vileness. ◆**noircir** *vt* to blacken; − *vi*, − **se n.** *vpr* to turn black.

noisette [nwazɛt] *nf* hazelnut. ◆**noisetier** *nm* hazel (tree).

noix [nwa] *nf* (*du noyer*) walnut; **n. de coco** coconut; **n. du Brésil** Brazil nut; **n. de beurre** knob of butter; **à la n.** *Fam* trashy, awful.

nom [nɔ̃] *nm* name; *Gram* noun; **n. de famille** surname; **n. de jeune fille** maiden name; **n. propre** proper noun; **au n. de qn** on s.o.'s behalf; **sans n.** (*anonyme*) nameless; (*vil*) vile; **n. d'un chien!** *Fam* oh hell!

nomade [nɔmad] *a* nomadic; – *nmf* nomad.

nombre [nɔ̃br] *nm* number; **ils sont au ou du n. de** (*parmi*) they're among; **ils sont au n. de dix** there are ten of them; **elle est au n. de six** she's one of; **le plus grand n. de** the majority of. ◆**nombreux, -euse** *a* (*amis, livres etc*) numerous; (*famille, collection etc*) large; **peu n.** few; **venir n.** to come in large numbers.

nombril [nɔ̃bri] *nm* navel.

nominal, -aux [nɔminal, -o] *a* nominal. ◆**nomination** *nf* appointment, nomination.

nommer [nɔme] *vt* (*appeler*) to name; **n. qn** (*désigner*) to appoint s.o. (**à un poste**/*etc* to a post/*etc*); **n. qn président/lauréat** to nominate s.o. chairman/prizewinner; – **se n.** *vpr* (*s'appeler*) to be called. ◆**nommément** *adv* by name.

non [nɔ̃] *adv & nm inv* no; **n.!** no!; **tu viens ou n.?** are you coming or not?; **n. seulement** not only; **n. (pas) que** (+ *sub*) . . . not that . . . ; **c'est bien, n.?** *Fam* it's all right, isn't it?; **je crois que n.** I don't think so; (**ni**) **moi n. plus** neither do, am, can *etc* I; **une place n. réservée** an unreserved seat.

non- [nɔ̃] *préf* non-.

nonante [nɔnɑ̃t] *a* (*en Belgique, en Suisse*) ninety.

nonchalant [nɔ̃ʃalɑ̃] *a* nonchalant, apathetic. ◆**nonchalance** *nf* nonchalance, apathy.

non-conformiste [nɔ̃kɔ̃fɔrmist] *a & nmf* nonconformist.

non-fumeur, -euse [nɔ̃fymœr, -øz] *nmf* non-smoker.

non-sens [nɔ̃sɑ̃s] *nm inv* absurdity.

nord [nɔr] *nm* north; **au n. de** north of; **du n.** (*vent, direction*) northerly; (*ville*) northern; (*gens*) from *ou* in the north; **Amérique/Afrique du N.** North America/Africa; **l'Europe du N.** Northern Europe; – *a inv* (*côte*) north(ern). ◆**n.-africain, -aine** *a & nmf* North African. ◆**n.-américain, -aine** *a & nmf* North American. ◆**n.-est** *nm & a inv* north-east. ◆**n.-ouest** *nm & a inv* north-west.

nordique [nɔrdik] *a & nmf* Scandinavian.

normal, -aux [nɔrmal, -o] *a* normal. ◆**normale** *nf* norm, normality; **au-dessus de la n.** above normal. ◆**normalement** *adv* normally. ◆**normaliser** *vt* (*uniformiser*) to standardize; (*relations etc*) to normalize.

normand, -ande [nɔrmɑ̃, -ɑ̃d] *a & nmf* Norman. ◆**Normandie** *nf* Normandy.

norme [nɔrm] *nf* norm.

Norvège [nɔrvɛʒ] *nf* Norway. ◆**norvégien, -ienne** *a & nmf* Norwegian; – *nm* (*langue*) Norwegian.

nos [no] *voir* **notre**.

nostalgie [nɔstalʒi] *nf* nostalgia. ◆**nostalgique** *a* nostalgic.

notable [nɔtabl] *a* (*fait etc*) notable; – *nm* (*personne*) notable. ◆**-ment** [-əmɑ̃] *adv* (*sensiblement*) notably.

notaire [nɔtɛr] *nm* solicitor, notary.

notamment [nɔtamɑ̃] *adv* notably.

note [nɔt] *nf* (*remarque etc & Mus* note; (*chiffrée*) *Scol* mark, *Am* grade; (*compte, facture*) bill, *Am* check; **prendre n. de** to make a note of. ◆**notation** *nf* notation; *Scol* marking. ◆**noter** *vt* (*prendre note de*) to note; (*remarquer*) to notice; (*écrire*) to note down; (*devoir etc*) *Scol* to mark, *Am* grade; **être bien noté** (*personne*) to be highly rated.

notice [nɔtis] *nf* (*résumé, préface*) note; (*mode d'emploi*) instructions.

notifier [nɔtifje] *vt* **n. qch à qn** to notify s.o. of sth.

notion [nɔsjɔ̃] *nf* notion, idea; *pl* (*éléments*) rudiments.

notoire [nɔtwar] *a* (*criminel, bêtise*) notorious; (*fait*) well-known. ◆**notoriété** *nf* (*renom*) fame; (*de fait*) general recognition.

notre, *pl* nos [nɔtr, no] *a poss* our. ◆**nôtre** *pron poss* **le ou la n., les nôtres** ours; – *nmpl* **les nôtres** (*parents etc*) our (own) people.

nouer [nwe] *vt* tie, knot; (*amitié, conversation*) to strike up; **avoir la gorge nouée** to have a lump in one's throat. ◆**noueux, -euse** *a* (*bois*) knotty; (*doigts*) gnarled.

nougat [nuga] *nm* nougat.

nouille [nuj] *nf* (*idiot*) *Fam* drip.

nouilles [nuj] *nfpl* noodles.

nounours [nunurs] *nm* teddy bear.

nourrice [nuris] *nf* (*assistante maternelle*) child minder, nurse; (*qui allaite*) wet nurse; **mettre en n.** to put out to nurse.

nourr/ir [nurir] *vt* (*alimenter, faire vivre*) to feed; (*espoir etc*) *Fig* to nourish; (*esprit*) to enrich; **se n. de** to feed on; – *vi* (*aliment*) to be nourishing. ◆**-issant** *a* nourishing. ◆**nourriture** *nf* food.

nourrisson [nurisɔ̃] *nm* infant.

nous [nu] *pron* **1** (*sujet*) we; **n. sommes** we are. **2** (*complément direct*) us; **il n. connaît** he knows us. **3** (*indirect*) (to) us; **il n. l'a donné** he gave it to us, he gave us it. **4** (*réfléchi*) ourselves; **n. n. lavons** we wash ourselves. **5** (*réciproque*) each other;

n. n. **détestons** we hate each other. ◆**n.-mêmes** pron ourselves.

nouveau (or **nouvel** before vowel or mute h), **nouvelle**[1], pl **nouveaux, nouvelles** [nuvo, nuvel] a new; – nmf Scol new boy, new girl; – nm **du n.** something new; **de n.**, à n. again. ◆**n.-né, -ée** a & nmf new-born (baby). ◆**n.-venu** nm, ◆**nouvelle-venue** nf newcomer. ◆**nouveauté** nf newness, novelty; pl (livres) new books; (disques) new releases; (vêtements) new fashions; **une n.** (objet) a novelty.

nouvelle[2] [nuvɛl] nf **1 nouvelle(s)** news; **une n.** a piece of news. **2** Littér short story.

Nouvelle-Zélande [nuvɛlzelɑ̃d] nf New Zealand.

novateur, -trice [novatœr, -tris] nmf innovator.

novembre [novɑ̃br] nm November.

novice [novis] nmf novice; – a inexperienced.

noyau, -x [nwajo] nm (de fruit) stone, Am pit; (d'atome, de cellule) nucleus; (groupe) group; **un n. d'opposants** a hard core of opponents.

noyaut/er [nwajote] vt Pol to infiltrate. ◆**—age** nm infiltration.

noy/er[1] [nwaje] vt (personne etc) to drown; (terres) to flood; — **se n.** vpr to drown; (se suicider) to drown oneself; **se n. dans le détail** to get bogged down in details. ◆**—é, -ée** nmf (mort) drowned person; — a être n. (perdu) Fig to be out of one's depth. ◆**noyade** nf drowning.

noyer[2] [nwaje] nm (arbre) walnut tree.

nu [ny] a (personne, vérité) naked; (mains, chambre) bare; **tout nu** (stark) naked, (in the) nude; **voir à l'œil nu** to see with the naked eye; **mettre à nu** (exposer) to lay bare; **se mettre nu** to strip off; **tête nue, nu-tête** bare-headed; – nm (femme, homme, œuvre) nude.

nuage [nɥaʒ] nm cloud; **un n. de lait** Fig a dash of milk. ◆**nuageux, -euse** a (ciel) cloudy.

nuance [nɥɑ̃s] nf (de sens) nuance; (de couleurs) shade, nuance; (de regret) tinge, nuance. ◆**nuanc/er** vt (teintes) to blend,

shade; (pensée) to qualify. ◆**—é** a (jugement) qualified.

nucléaire [nykleɛr] a nuclear.

nudisme [nydism] nm nudism. ◆**nudiste** nmf nudist. ◆**nudité** nf nudity, nakedness; (de mur etc) bareness.

nuée [nɥe] nf **une n. de** (foule) a host of; (groupe compact) a cloud of.

nues [ny] nfpl **porter qn aux n.** to praise s.o. to the skies.

nuire [nɥir] vi **n. à** (personne, intérêts etc) to harm. ◆**nuisible** a harmful.

nuit [nɥi] nf night; (obscurité) dark(ness); **il fait n.** it's dark; **avant la n.** before nightfall; **la n.** (se promener etc) at night; **cette n.** (aujourd'hui) tonight; (hier) last night. ◆**nuitée** nf overnight stay (in hotel etc).

nul, nulle [nyl] **1** a (risque etc) non-existent, nil; (médiocre) useless, hopeless; (non valable) Jur null (and void); **faire match n.** Sp to tie, draw. **2** a (aucun) no; **de nulle importance** of no importance; **sans n. doute** without any doubt; **nulle part** nowhere; – pron m (aucun) no one. ◆**nullard, -arde** nmf Fam useless person. ◆**nullement** adv not at all. ◆**nullité** nf (d'un élève etc) uselessness; (personne) useless person.

numéraire [nymerɛr] nm cash, currency.

numéral, -aux [nymeral, -o] a & nm numeral. ◆**numérique** a numerical; (montre etc) digital.

numéro [nymero] nm number; (de journal) issue, number; (au cirque) act; **un n. de danse/de chant** a dance/song number; **quel n.!** (personne) Fam what a character!; **n. vert** Tél = Freefone®, = Am tollfree number. ◆**numérot/er** vt (pages, sièges) to number. ◆**—age** nm numbering.

nu-pieds [nypje] nmpl open sandals.

nuptial, -aux [nypsjal, -o] a (chambre) bridal; (anneau, cérémonie) wedding-.

nuque [nyk] nf back ou nape of the neck.

nurse [nœrs] nf nanny, (children's) nurse.

nutritif, -ive [nytritif, -iv] a nutritious, nutritive. ◆**nutrition** nf nutrition.

nylon [nilɔ̃] nm (fibre) nylon.

nymphe [nɛ̃f] nf nymph. ◆**nymphomane** nf Péj nymphomaniac.

O

O, o [o] *nm* O, o.

oasis [oazis] *nf* oasis.

obédience [ɔbedjɑ̃s] *nf Pol* allegiance.

obé/ir [ɔbeir] *vi* to obey; **o. à qn/qch** to obey s.o./sth; **être obéi** to be obeyed. **◆—issant** *a* obedient. **◆obéissance** *nf* obedience (à to).

obélisque [ɔbelisk] *nm* (*monument*) obelisk.

obèse [ɔbɛz] *a & nmf* obese (person). **◆obésité** *nf* obesity.

objecter [ɔbʒɛkte] *vt* (*prétexte*) to put forward, plead; **o. que** to object that; **on lui objecta son jeune âge** they objected that he *ou* she was too young. **◆objecteur** *nm* **o. de conscience** conscientious objector. **◆objection** *nf* objection.

objectif, -ive [ɔbʒɛktif, -iv] **1** *a* (*opinion etc*) objective. **2** *nm* (*but*) objective, Phot lens. **◆objectivement** *adv* objectively. **◆objectivité** *nf* objectivity.

objet [ɔbʒɛ] *nm* (*chose, sujet, but*) object; (*de toilette*) article; **faire l'o. de** (*étude, critiques etc*) to be the subject of; (*soins, surveillance*) to be given, receive; **objets trouvés** (*bureau*) lost property, *Am* lost and found.

obligation [ɔbligasjɔ̃] *nf* (*devoir, lieu, nécessité*) obligation; *Fin* bond. **◆obligatoire** *a* compulsory, obligatory; (*inévitable*) *Fam* inevitable. **◆obligatoirement** *adv* (*fatalement*) inevitably; **tu dois o. le faire** you have to do it.

oblig/er [ɔbliʒe] *vt* **1** (*contraindre*) to compel, oblige (à faire to do); (*engager*) to bind; **être obligé de faire** to have to do, be compelled *ou* obliged to do. **2** (*rendre service à*) to oblige; **être obligé à qn de qch** to be obliged to s.o. for sth. **◆—eant** *a* obliging, kind. **◆—é** *a* (*obligatoire*) necessary; (*fatal*) *Fam* inevitable. **◆obligeamment** [-amã] *adv* obligingly. **◆obligeance** *nf* kindness.

oblique [ɔblik] *a* oblique; **regard o.** sidelong glance; **en o.** at an (oblique) angle. **◆obliquer** *vi* (*véhicule etc*) to turn off.

oblitérer [ɔblitere] *vt* (*timbre*) to cancel; (*billet, carte*) to stamp; **timbre oblitéré** (*non neuf*) used stamp. **◆oblitération** *nf* cancellation; stamping.

oblong, -ongue [ɔblɔ̃, -ɔ̃g] *a* oblong.

obnubilé [ɔbnybile] *a* (*obsédé*) obsessed (par with).

obscène [ɔpsɛn] *a* obscene. **◆obscénité** *nf* obscenity.

obscur [ɔpskyr] *a* (*noir*) dark; (*peu clair, inconnu, humble*) obscure. **◆obscurcir** *vt* (*chambre etc*) to darken; (*rendre peu intelligible*) to obscure (*text, ideas etc*); — **s'o.** *vpr* (*ciel*) to cloud over, darken; (*vue*) to become dim. **◆obscurément** *adv* obscurely. **◆obscurité** *nf* dark(ness); (*de texte, d'acteur etc*) obscurity.

obséd/er [ɔpsede] *vt* to obsess, haunt. **◆—ant** *a* haunting, obsessive. **◆—é, -ée** *nmf* maniac (de for); **o. sexuel** sex maniac.

obsèques [ɔpsɛk] *nfpl* funeral.

obséquieux, -euse [ɔpsekjø, -øz] *a* obsequious.

observer [ɔpsɛrve] *vt* (*regarder*) to observe, watch; (*remarquer, respecter*) to observe; **faire o. qch à qn** (*signaler*) to point sth out to s.o. **◆observateur, -trice** *a* observant; — *nmf* observer. **◆observation** *nf* (*examen, remarque*) observation; (*reproche*) (critical) remark, rebuke; (*de règle etc*) observance; **en o.** (*malade*) under observation. **◆observatoire** *nm* observatory; (*colline etc*) *Fig & Mil* observation post.

obsession [ɔpsesjɔ̃] *nf* obsession. **◆obsessif, -ive** *a* (*peur etc*) obsessive. **◆obsessionnel, -elle** *a Psy* obsessive.

obstacle [ɔpstakl] *nm* obstacle; **faire o. à** to stand in the way of.

obstétrique [ɔpstetrik] *nf Méd* obstetrics.

obstin/er (s') [ɔpstine] *vpr* to be obstinate *ou* persistent; **s'o. à faire** to persist in doing. **◆—é** *a* stubborn, obstinate, persistent. **◆obstination** *nf* stubbornness, obstinacy, persistence.

obstruction [ɔpstryksjɔ̃] *nf Méd Pol Sp* obstruction; **faire de l'o.** *Pol Sp* to be obstructive. **◆obstruer** *vt* to obstruct.

obtempérer [ɔptãpere] *vi* to obey an injunction; **o. à** to obey.

obtenir* [ɔptənir] *vt* to get, obtain, secure. **◆obtention** *nf* obtaining, getting.

obturer [ɔptyre] *vt* (*trou etc*) to stop *ou* close up. **◆obturateur** *nm Phot* shutter; *Tech* valve.

obtus [ɔpty] *a* (*angle, esprit*) obtuse.

obus [ɔby] nm Mil shell.

occasion [ɔkazjɔ̃] nf 1 (chance) opportunity, chance (de faire to do); (circonstance) occasion; à l'o. on occasion, when the occasion arises; à l'o. de on the occasion of. 2 Com (marché avantageux) bargain; (objet non neuf) second-hand buy; d'o. second-hand, used. ◆**occasionner** vt to cause; o. qch à qn to cause s.o. sth.

occident [ɔksidɑ̃] nm l'O. Pol the West. ◆**occidental, -aux** a Géog Pol western; — nmpl les occidentaux Pol Westerners. ◆**occidentalisé** a Pol Westernized.

occulte [ɔkylt] a occult.

occup/er [ɔkype] vt (maison, pays, usine etc) to occupy; (place, temps) to take up, occupy; (poste) to hold, occupy; o. qn (absorber) to occupy s.o., keep s.o. busy; (ouvrier etc) to employ s.o.; — **s'o.** vpr to keep (oneself) busy (à faire doing); s'o. de (affaire, problème etc) to deal with; (politique) to be engaged in; s'o. de qn (malade etc) to take care of s.o.; (client) to see to s.o., deal with s.o.; **ne t'en occupe pas!** ne t'en fais pas!) don't worry!; (ne t'en mêle pas) mind your own business! ◆**-ant, -ante** a (armée) occupying; — nmf (habitant) occupant; — nm Mil forces of occupation, occupier. ◆**-é** a busy (à faire doing); (place, maison etc) occupied; (ligne) Tél engaged; (taxi) hired. ◆**occupation** nf (activité, travail etc) occupation; l'o. de (action) the occupation of.

occurrence [ɔkyrɑ̃s] nf Ling occurrence; en l'o. in the circumstances, as it happens ou happened.

océan [ɔseɑ̃] nm ocean. ◆**océanique** a oceanic.

ocre [ɔkr] nm & a inv (couleur) ochre.

octave [ɔktav] nf Mus octave.

octobre [ɔktɔbr] nm October.

octogénaire [ɔktɔʒenɛr] nmf octogenarian.

octogone [ɔktɔgɔn] nm octagon. ◆**octogonal, -aux** a octagonal.

octroi [ɔktrwa] nm Litt granting. ◆**octroyer** vt Litt to grant (à to).

oculaire [ɔkylɛr] a témoin o. eyewitness; globe o. eyeball. ◆**oculiste** nmf eye specialist.

ode [ɔd] nf (poème) ode.

odeur [ɔdœr] nf smell, odour; (de fleur) scent. ◆**odorant** a sweet-smelling. ◆**odorat** nm sense of smell.

odieux, -euse [ɔdjø, -øz] a odious, obnoxious.

œcuménique [ekymenik] a Rel (o)ecumenical.

œil, pl **yeux** [œj, jø] nm eye; sous mes yeux before my very eyes; lever/baisser les yeux to look up/down; fermer l'o. (dormir) to shut one's eyes; fermer les yeux sur to turn a blind eye; ouvre l'o.! keep your eyes open!; coup d'o. (regard) glance, look; jeter un coup d'o. sur to (have a) look ou glance at; à vue d'o. visibly; faire les gros yeux à to scowl at; avoir à l'o. (surveiller) to keep an eye on; à l'o. (gratuitement) Fam free; faire de l'o. à Fam to make eyes at; o. au beurre noir Fig black eye; mon o.! Fam (incrédulité) my foot!; (refus) no way!, no chance!

œillade [œjad] nf (clin d'œil) wink.

œillères [œjɛr] nfpl (de cheval) & Fig blinkers, Am blinders.

œillet [œjɛ] nm 1 Bot carnation. 2 (trou de ceinture etc) eyelet.

œuf, pl **œufs** [œf, ø] nm egg; pl (de poisson) (hard) roe; o. sur le plat fried egg; étouffer qch dans l'o. Fig to nip ou stifle sth in the bud.

œuvre [œvr] nf (travail, acte, livre etc) work; o. (de charité) (organisation) charity; l'o. de (production artistique etc) the works of; mettre en o. (employer) to make use of; mettre tout en o. to do everything possible (pour faire to do). ◆**œuvrer** vi Litt to work.

offense [ɔfɑ̃s] nf insult; Rel transgression. ◆**offens/er** vt to offend; s'o. de to take offence at. ◆**-ant** a offensive.

offensif, -ive [ɔfɑ̃sif, -iv] a offensive; — nf (attaque) offensive; (du froid) onslaught.

offert [ɔfɛr] voir offrir.

office [ɔfis] nm 1 (fonction) office; (bureau) office, bureau; d'o. (être promu etc) automatically; faire o. de to serve as; ses bons offices (service) one's good offices. 2 nm Rel service. 3 nm ou f (pièce pour provisions) pantry.

officiel, -ielle [ɔfisjɛl] a (acte etc) official; — nm (personnage) official. ◆**officiellement** adv officially. ◆**officieux, -euse** a unofficial.

officier [ɔfisje] 1 vi Rel to officiate. 2 nm (dans l'armée etc) officer.

offre [ɔfr] nf offer; (aux enchères) bid; l'o. et la demande Écon supply and demand; offres d'emploi Journ situations vacant. ◆**offrande** nf offering.

offr/ir* [ɔfrir] vt (proposer, présenter) to offer (de faire to do); (donner en cadeau) to give; (démission) to tender, offer; je lui ai offert de le loger I offered to put him up; — **s'o.** vpr (cadeau etc) to treat oneself to; (se *proposer*) to offer oneself (**comme** as); **s'o. à faire** to offer *ou* volunteer to do; **s'o. (aux yeux)** (*vue etc*) to present itself. ◆**—ant o.** au plus o. to the highest bidder.

offusquer [ɔfyske] *vt* to offend, shock; **s'o. de** to take offence at.

ogive [ɔʒiv] *nf* (*de fusée*) nose cone; **o. nucléaire** nuclear warhead.

ogre [ɔgr] *nm* ogre.

oh! [o] *int* oh!, o!

ohé! [ɔe] *int* hey (there)!

oie [wa] *nf* goose.

oignon [ɔɲɔ̃] *nm* (*légume*) onion; (*de tulipe, lis etc*) bulb; **occupe-toi de tes oignons!** *Fam* mind your own business!

oiseau, -x [wazo] *nm* bird; **à vol d'o.** as the crow flies; **drôle d'o.** (*individu*) *Péj* odd fish, *Am* oddball; **o. rare** (*personne étonnante*) *Iron* rare bird, perfect gem.

oiseux, -euse [wazø, -øz] *a* (*futile*) idle, vain.

oisif, -ive [wazif, -iv] *a* (*inactif*) idle; — *nmf* idler. ◆**oisiveté** *nf* idleness.

oléoduc [ɔleɔdyk] *nm* oil pipeline.

olive [ɔliv] *nf* (*fruit*) olive; **huile d'o.** olive oil; — *a inv* (*couleur*) (**vert**) **o.** olive (green). ◆**olivier** *nm* (*arbre*) olive tree.

olympique [ɔlɛ̃pik] *a* (*jeux, record etc*) Olympic.

ombilical, -aux [ɔ̃bilikal, -o] *a* (*cordon*) umbilical.

ombrage [ɔ̃braʒ] *nm* **1** (*ombre*) shade. **2 prendre o.** (*jalousie, dépit*) to take umbrage at. ◆**ombrag/er** *vt* to give shade to. ◆**—é** *a* shady. ◆**ombrageux, -euse** *a* (*caractère, personne*) touchy.

ombre [ɔ̃br] *nf* (*d'arbre etc*) shade; (*de personne, objet*) shadow; **l'o. d'un doute** *Fig* the shadow of a doubt; **l'o. de** (*remords, reproche etc*) the trace of; **30° à l'o.** 30° in the shade; **dans l'o.** (*comploter, travailler etc*) in secret.

ombrelle [ɔ̃brɛl] *nf* sunshade, parasol.

omelette [ɔmlɛt] *nf* omelet(te); **o. au fromage/etc** cheese/etc omelet(te).

omettre [ɔmɛtr] *vt* to omit (**de faire** to do). ◆**omission** *nf* omission.

omni- [ɔmni] *préf* omni-. ◆**omnipotent** *a* omnipotent.

omnibus [ɔmnibys] *a* & *nm* (**train**) **o.** slow train (*stopping at all stations*).

omoplate [ɔmɔplat] *nf* shoulder blade.

on [ɔ̃] (*sometimes* **l'on** [lɔ̃]) *pron* (*les gens*) they, people; (*nous*) we, one; (*vous*) you, one; **on dit** they say, people say, it is said; **on frappe** (*quelqu'un*) someone's knocking;

on me l'a donné it was given to me, I was given it.

once [ɔ̃s] *nf* (*mesure*) & *Fig* ounce.

oncle [ɔ̃kl] *nm* uncle.

onctueux, -euse [ɔ̃ktyø, -øz] *a* (*liquide, crème*) creamy; (*manières, paroles*) *Fig* smooth.

onde [ɔ̃d] *nf Phys Rad* wave; **grandes ondes** long wave; **ondes courtes/moyennes** short/medium wave; **sur les ondes** (*sur l'antenne*) on the radio.

ondée [ɔ̃de] *nf* (*pluie*) (sudden) shower.

on-dit [ɔ̃di] *nm inv* rumour, hearsay.

ondoyer [ɔ̃dwaje] *vi* to undulate. ◆**ondulation** *nf* undulation; (*de cheveux*) wave. ◆**ondul/er** *vi* to undulate; (*cheveux*) to be wavy. ◆**—é** *a* wavy.

onéreux, -euse [ɔnerø, -øz] *a* costly.

ongle [ɔ̃gl] *nm* (finger) nail.

onglet [ɔ̃glɛ] *nm* (*entaille de canif etc*) (nail) groove.

ont [ɔ̃] *voir* **avoir**.

ONU [ɔny] *nf abrév* (*Organisation des nations unies*) UN.

onyx [ɔniks] *nm* (*pierre précieuse*) onyx.

onze [ɔ̃z] *a* & *nm* eleven. ◆**onzième** *a* & *nmf* eleventh.

opale [ɔpal] *nf* (*pierre*) opal.

opaque [ɔpak] *a* opaque. ◆**opacité** *nf* opacity.

opéra [ɔpera] *nm* (*ouvrage, art*) opera; (*édifice*) opera house. ◆**opérette** *nf* operetta.

opér/er [ɔpere] *vt* **1** (*exécuter*) to carry out; (*choix*) to make; (*—il y agir*) to work, act; (*procéder*) to proceed; — **s'o.** (*se produire*) to take place. **2** *vt* (*personne, organe*) *Méd* to operate on (**de** for); (*tumeur*) to remove; **cela peut s'o.** this can be removed; **se faire o.** to have an operation; — *vi* (*chirurgien*) to operate. ◆**—ant** *a* (*efficace*) operative. ◆**—é, -ée** *Méd* **pa-**tient (operated on). ◆**opérateur, -trice** *nmf* (*de prise de vues*) *Cin* cameraman; (*sur machine*) operator. ◆**opération** *nf* (*acte*) & *Méd Mil Math etc* operation; *Fin* deal. ◆**opérationnel, -elle** *a* operational. ◆**opératoire** *a Méd* operative; **bloc o.** operating theatre; *Am* surgical wing.

opiner [ɔpine] *vi* **o.** (**de la tête** *ou* **du chef**) to nod assent.

opiniâtre [ɔpinjatr] *a* stubborn, obstinate. ◆**opiniâtreté** *nf* stubbornness, obstinacy.

opinion [ɔpinjɔ̃] *nf* opinion (**sur** about, on).

opium [ɔpjɔm] *nm* opium.

opportun [ɔpɔrtœ̃] *a* opportune, timely. ◆**opportunément** *adv* opportunely.

◆**opportunisme** *nm* opportunism. ◆**opportunité** *nf* timeliness.

oppos/er [ɔpoze] *vt* (*argument, résistance*) to put up (à against); (*équipes, rivaux*) to bring together, set against each other; (*objets*) to place opposite each other; (*couleurs*) to contrast; **o. qch à qch** (*objet*) to place sth opposite sth; **o. qn à qn** to set s.o. against s.o.; **match qui oppose . . .** match between . . . ; **— s'o.** *vpr* (*couleurs*) to contrast; (*équipes*) to confront each other; **s'o. à** (*mesure, personne etc*) to oppose, be opposed to; **je m'y oppose** I'm opposed to it, I oppose. ◆**—ant, -ante** *a* opposing; **—** *nmf* opponent. ◆**—é** *a* (*direction etc*) opposite; (*intérêts, équipe*) opposing; (*opinions*) opposite, opposing; (*couleurs*) contrasting; **être o. à** to be opposed to; **—** *nm* **l'o.** the opposite (**de** of); **à l'o.** (*côté*) on the opposite side (**de** from; to); **à l'o. de** (*contrairement à*) contrary to. ◆**opposition** *nf* opposition; **faire o. à** to oppose; **par o. à** as opposed to.

oppress/er [ɔprese] *vt* (*gêner*) to oppress. ◆**—ant** *a* oppressive. ◆**—eur** *nm* Pol oppressor. ◆**oppressif, -ive** *a* (*loi etc*) oppressive. ◆**oppression** *nf* oppression. ◆**opprim/er** *vt* (*tyranniser*) to oppress. ◆**—és** *nmpl* **les o.** the oppressed.

opter [ɔpte] *vi* **o. pour** to opt for.

opticien, -ienne [ɔptisjɛ̃, -jɛn] *nmf* optician.

optimisme [ɔptimism] *nm* optimism. ◆**optimiste** *a* optimistic; **—** *nmf* optimist.

optimum [ɔptimɔm] *nm & a* optimum; **la température o.** the optimum temperature. ◆**optimal, -aux** *a* optimal.

option [ɔpsjɔ̃] *nf* (*choix*) option; (*chose*) optional extra.

optique [ɔptik] *a* (*verre*) optical; **—** *nf* optics; (*aspect*) Fig perspective; **d'o.** (*illusion, instrument etc*) optical.

opulent [ɔpylɑ̃] *a* opulent. ◆**opulence** *nf* opulence.

or [ɔr] **1** *nm* gold; **en or** (*chaîne etc*) gold-; **d'or** (*cheveux, âge, règle*) golden; (*cœur*) of gold; **mine d'or** *Géol* goldmine; (*fortune*) Fig goldmine; **affaire en or** (*achat*) bargain; (*commerce*) Fig goldmine; **or noir** (*pétrole*) Fig black gold. **2** *conj* (*alors, cependant*) now, well.

oracle [ɔrakl] *nm* oracle.

orage [ɔraʒ] *nm* (thunder)storm. ◆**orageux, -euse** *a* stormy.

oraison [ɔrezɔ̃] *nf* prayer; **o. funèbre** funeral oration.

oral, -aux [ɔral, -o] *a* oral; **—** *nm* (*examen*) *Scol* oral.

orange [ɔrɑ̃ʒ] *nf* (*fruit*) orange; **o. pressée** (fresh) orange juice; **—** *a & nm inv* (*couleur*) orange. ◆**orangé** *a & nm* (*couleur*) orange. ◆**orangeade** *nf* orangeade. ◆**oranger** *nm* orange tree.

orang-outan(g) [ɔrɑ̃utɑ̃] *nm* (*pl* **orangs-outan(g)s**) orang-outang.

orateur [ɔratœr] *nm* speaker, orator.

orbite [ɔrbit] *nf* (*d'astre etc*) & Fig orbit; (*d'œil*) socket; **mettre sur o.** (*fusée etc*) to put into orbit.

orchestre [ɔrkɛstr] *nm* (*classique*) orchestra; (*moderne*) band; (*places*) Th stalls, Am orchestra. ◆**orchestrer** *vt* (*organiser*) & Mus to orchestrate.

orchidée [ɔrkide] *nf* orchid.

ordinaire [ɔrdinɛr] *a* (*habituel, normal*) ordinary, Am regular; (*médiocre*) ordinary, average; **d'o., à l'o.** usually; **comme d'o., comme à l'o.** as usual; **de l'essence o.** two-star (petrol), Am regular. ◆**—ment** *adv* usually.

ordinal, -aux [ɔrdinal, -o] *a* (*nombre*) ordinal.

ordinateur [ɔrdinatœr] *nm* computer.

ordination [ɔrdinasjɔ̃] *nf* Rel ordination.

ordonnance [ɔrdɔnɑ̃s] *nf* **1** (*de médecin*) prescription. **2** (*décret*) Jur order, ruling. **3** (*disposition*) arrangement. **4** (*soldat*) orderly.

ordonn/er [ɔrdɔne] *vt* **1** (*enjoindre*) to order (**que** (+ *sub*) that); **o. à qn de faire** to order s.o. to do. **2** (*agencer*) to arrange, order. **3** (*médicament etc*) to prescribe. **4** (*prêtre*) to ordain. ◆**—é** *a* (*personne, maison etc*) orderly.

ordre [ɔrdr] *nm* (*commandement, structure, association etc*) order; (*absence de désordre*) tidiness (*of room, person etc*); **en o.** (*chambre etc*) tidy; **mettre en o., mettre de l'o. dans** to tidy (up); **de premier o.** first-rate; **o.** (*public*) (law and) order; **par o. d'âge** in order of age; **à l'o. du jour** (*au programme*) on the agenda; (*d'actualité*) of topical interest; **les forces de l'o.** the police; **jusqu'à nouvel o.** until further notice; **de l'o. de** (*environ*) of the order of.

ordure [ɔrdyr] *nf* filth, muck; *pl* (*débris*) refuse, rubbish, Am garbage. ◆**ordurier, -ière** *a* (*plaisanterie etc*) lewd.

oreille [ɔrɛj] *nf* ear; **être tout oreilles** to be all ears; **faire la sourde o.** to turn a deaf ear; **casser les oreilles à qn** to deafen s.o.

oreiller [ɔreje] *nm* pillow.

oreillons [ɔrejɔ̃] *nmpl* Méd mumps.

ores (d') [dɔr] *adv* **d'ores et déjà** [dɔrzedeʒa] henceforth.

orfèvre [ɔrfɛvr] *nm* goldsmith, silversmith. ◆**orfèvrerie** *nf* (*magasin*) goldsmith's *ou* silversmith's shop; (*objets*) gold *ou* silver plate.

organe [ɔrgan] *nm* Anat & Fig organ; (*porte-parole*) mouthpiece. ◆**organique** *a* organic. ◆**organisme** *nm* 1 (*corps*) body; Anat Biol organism. 2 (*bureaux etc*) organization.

organisation [ɔrganizasjɔ̃] *nf* (*arrangement, association*) organization.

organis/er [ɔrganize] *vt* to organize; — **s'o.** *vpr* to organize oneself, get organized. ◆—**é** *a* (*esprit, groupe etc*) organized. ◆**organisateur, -trice** *nmf* organizer.

organiste [ɔrganist] *nmf* Mus organist.

orgasme [ɔrgasm] *nm* orgasm.

orge [ɔrʒ] *nf* barley.

orgie [ɔrʒi] *nf* orgy.

orgue [ɔrg] *nm* Mus organ; **o. de Barbarie** barrel organ; — *nfpl* organ; **grandes orgues** great organ.

orgueil [ɔrgœj] *nm* pride. ◆**orgueilleux, -euse** *a* proud.

orient [ɔrjɑ̃] *nm* l'**O.** the Orient, the East; **Moyen-O., Proche-O.** Middle East; **Extrême-O.** Far East. ◆**oriental, -ale, -aux** *a* eastern; (*de l'Orient*) oriental; — *nmf* oriental.

orient/er [ɔrjɑ̃te] *vt* (*lampe, antenne etc*) to position, direct; (*voyageur, élève etc*) to direct; (*maison*) to orientate, Am orient; — **s'o.** *vpr* to find one's bearings *ou* direction; **s'o. vers** (*carrière etc*) to move towards. ◆—**é** *a* (*ouvrage, film etc*) slanted. ◆**orientable** *a* (*lampe etc*) adjustable, flexible; (*bras de machine*) movable. ◆**orientation** *nf* direction; (*action*) positioning, directing; (*de maison*) aspect, orientation; (*tendance*) Pol Littér etc trend; **o. professionnelle** vocational guidance.

orifice [ɔrifis] *nm* opening, orifice.

originaire [ɔriʒinɛr] *a* **être o. de** (*natif*) to be a native of.

original, -ale, -aux [ɔriʒinal, -o] 1 *a* (*idée, artiste, version etc*) original; — *nm* (*modèle*) original. 2 *a* & *nmf* (*bizarre*) eccentric. ◆**originalité** *nf* originality; eccentricity.

origine [ɔriʒin] *nf* origin; **à l'o.** originally; **d'o.** (*pneu etc*) original; **pays d'o.** country of origin. ◆**originel, -elle** *a* (*sens, péché, habitant etc*) original.

orme [ɔrm] *nm* (*arbre, bois*) elm.

ornement [ɔrnəmɑ̃] *nm* ornament. ◆**ornemental, -aux** *a* ornamental. ◆**ornementation** *nf* ornamentation. ◆**ornementé** *a* adorned, ornamented (**de** with). ◆**orn/er** *vt* to decorate, adorn (**de** with). ◆—**é** *a* (*style etc*) ornate.

ornière [ɔrnjɛr] *nf* (*sillon*) & Fig rut.

orphelin, -ine [ɔrfəlɛ̃, -in] *nmf* orphan; — *a* orphaned. ◆**orphelinat** *nm* orphanage.

orteil [ɔrtɛj] *nm* toe; **gros o.** big toe.

orthodoxe [ɔrtɔdɔks] *a* orthodox; — *nmpl* **les orthodoxes** the orthodox. ◆**orthodoxie** *nf* orthodoxy.

orthographe [ɔrtɔgraf] *nf* spelling. ◆**orthographier** *vt* (*mot*) to spell.

orthopédie [ɔrtɔpedi] *nf* orthop(a)edics.

ortie [ɔrti] *nf* nettle.

os [ɔs, *pl o ou* o] *nm* bone; **trempé jusqu'aux os** soaked to the skin; **tomber sur un os** (*difficulté*) Fam to hit a snag.

OS [ɔɛs] *abrév* = **ouvrier spécialisé.**

oscar [ɔskar] *nm* Cin Oscar.

osciller [ɔsile] *vi* Tech to oscillate; (*se balancer*) to swing, sway; (*hésiter*) to waver; (*varier*) to fluctuate; (*flamme*) to flicker. ◆**oscillation** *nf* Tech oscillation; (*de l'opinion*) fluctuation.

oseille [ozɛj] *nf* 1 Bot Culin sorrel. 2 (*argent*) Arg dough.

os/er [oze] *vti* to dare; **o. faire** to dare (to) do. ◆—**é** *a* bold, daring.

osier [ozje] *nm* (*branches*) wicker.

ossature [ɔsatyr] *nf* (*du corps*) frame; (*de bâtiment*) & Fig framework. ◆**osselets** *nmpl* (*jeu*) jacks, knucklebones. ◆**ossements** *nmpl* (*de cadavres*) bones. ◆**osseux, -euse** *a* (*tissu*) bone-; (*maigre*) bony.

ostensible [ɔstɑ̃sibl] *a* conspicuous.

ostentation [ɔstɑ̃tasjɔ̃] *nf* ostentation.

otage [ɔtaʒ] *nm* hostage; **prendre qn en o.** to take s.o. hostage.

OTAN [ɔtɑ̃] *nf abrév* (*Organisation du traité de l'Atlantique Nord*) NATO.

otarie [ɔtari] *nf* (*animal*) sea lion.

ôter [ote] *vt* to remove, take away (**à qn** from s.o.); (*vêtement*) to take off, remove; (*déduire*) to take (away); **ôte-toi de là!** Fam get out of the way!

otite [ɔtit] *nf* ear infection.

oto-rhino [ɔtorino] *nmf* Méd Fam ear, nose and throat specialist.

ou [u] *conj* or; **ou bien** or else; **ou elle ou moi** either her or me.

où [u] *adv* & *pron* where; **le jour où** the day when, the day on which; **la table où** the table on which; **l'état où** the condition in which; **par où?** which way?; **d'où?** where from?; **d'où ma surprise**/etc (conséquence) hence my surprise/etc; **le pays d'où** the country from which; **où qu'il soit** wherever he may be.

ouate [wat] nf Méd cotton wool, Am absorbent cotton. ·

oubli [ubli] nm (défaut) forgetfulness; **l'o. de qch** forgetting sth; **un o.** a lapse of memory; (omission) an oversight; **tomber dans l'o.** to fall into oblivion. ◆**oublier** vt to forget (**de faire** to do); (faute, problème) to overlook; **— s'o.** vpr (traditions etc) to be forgotten; (personne) Fig to forget oneself. ◆**oublieux, -euse** a forgetful (**de** of).

oubliettes [ublijet] nfpl (de château) dungeon.

ouest [west] nm west; **à l'o. de** west of; **d'o.** (vent) west(erly); **de l'o.** western; **Allemagne de l'O.** West Germany; **l'Europe de l'O.** Western Europe; **— a inv** (côte) west(ern). ◆**o.-allemand, -ande** a & nmf West German.

ouf! [uf] int (soulagement) ah!, phew!

oui [wi] adv & nm inv yes; **o.!** yes!; **les o.** (votes) the ayes; **tu viens, o.?** come on, will you?; **je crois que o.** I think so; **si o.** if so.

ouï-dire [widir] nm inv hearsay.

ouïe [1] [wi] nf hearing; **être tout o.** Fam to be all ears.

ouïe?! [2] [uj] int ouch!

ouïes [wi] nfpl (de poisson) gills.

ouille! [uj] int ouch!

ouragan [uragã] nm hurricane.

ourler [urle] vt to hem. ◆**ourlet** nm hem.

ours [urs] nm bear; **o. blanc/gris** polar/grizzly bear.

oursin [ursɛ̃] nm (animal) sea urchin.

ouste! [ust] int Fam scram!

outil [uti] nm tool. ◆**outill/er** vt to equip. ◆**—age** nm tools; (d'une usine) equipment.

outrage [utraʒ] nm insult (**à** to). ◆**outrag/er** vt to insult, offend. ◆**—eant** a insulting, offensive.

outrance [utrɑ̃s] nf (excès) excess; **à o.** (travailler etc) to excess; **guerre à o.** all-out war. ◆**outrancier, -ière** a excessive.

outre [utr] prép besides; **— adv en o.** besides, moreover; **o. mesure** inordinately; **passer o.** to take no notice (**à** of). ◆**o.-Manche**

adv across the Channel. ◆**o.-mer** adv overseas; **d'o.-mer** (peuple) overseas.

outrepasser [utrapase] vt (limite etc) to go beyond, exceed.

outr/er [utre] vt to exaggerate, overdo; (indigner) to outrage s.o. ◆**—é** a (excessif) exaggerated; (révolté) outraged.

outsider [awtsajder] nm Sp outsider.

ouvert [uver] voir **ouvrir**; **— a** open; (robinet, gaz etc) on; **à bras ouverts** with open arms. ◆**ouvertement** adv openly. ◆**ouverture** nf opening; (trou) hole; (avance) & Mus overture; (d'objectif) Phot aperture; **o. d'esprit** open-mindedness.

ouvrable [uvrabl] a **jour o.** working day.

ouvrage [uvraʒ] nm (travail, objet, livre) work; (couture) (needle)work; **un o.** (travail) a piece of work. ◆**ouvragé** a (bijou etc) finely worked.

ouvreuse [uvrøz] nf Cin usherette.

ouvrier, -ière [uvrije, -jɛr] nmf worker; **o. agricole** farm labourer; **o. qualifié/spécialisé** skilled/unskilled worker; **— a** (législation etc) industrial; (quartier, éducation) working-class; **classe ouvrière** working class.

ouvrir [uvrir] vt to open (up); (gaz, radio etc) to turn on, switch on; (inaugurer) to open; (hostilités) to begin; (appétit) to whet; (liste, procession) to head; **— vi** to open; (ouvrir la porte) to open (up); **— s'o.** vpr (porte, boîte etc) to open (up); **s'o. la jambe** to cut one's leg open; **s'o. à qn** Fig to open one's heart to s.o. (**de qch** about sth). ◆**ouvre-boîtes** nm inv tin opener, Am can-opener. ◆**ouvre-bouteilles** nm inv bottle opener.

ovaire [over] nm Anat ovary.

ovale [oval] a & nm oval.

ovation [ovasjɔ̃] nf (standing) ovation.

OVNI [ɔvni] nm abrév (objet volant non identifié) UFO.

oxyde [ɔksid] nm Ch oxide; **o. de carbone** carbon monoxide. ◆**oxyder** vt, **— s'o.** vpr to oxidize.

oxygène [ɔksiʒɛn] nm oxygen; **à o.** (masque, tente) oxygen-. ◆**oxygén/er** vt (cheveux) to bleach; **— s'o.** vpr Fam to breathe ou get some fresh air. ◆**—ée** af **eau o.** (hydrogen) peroxide.

P

P, p [pe] *nm* P. p.
pachyderme [paʃidɛrm] *nm* elephant.
pacifier [pasifje] *vt* to pacify. ◆**pacification** *nf* pacification. ◆**pacifique 1** *a* (*non violent, non militaire*) peaceful; (*caractère, personne*) peace-loving. **2** *a* (*côte etc*) Pacific; **Océan P.** Pacific Ocean; – *nm* **le P.** the Pacific. ◆**pacifiste** *a* & *nmf* pacifist.
pack [pak] *nm* (*de lait etc*) carton.
pacotille [pakɔtij] *nf* (*camelote*) trash.
pacte [pakt] *nm* pact. ◆**pactiser** *vi* p. avec **qn** *Péj* to be in league with s.o.
paf! [paf] **1** *int* bang!, wallop! **2** *a inv* (*ivre*) *Fam* sozzled, plastered.
pagaie [pagɛ] *nf* paddle. ◆**pagayer** *vi* (*ramer*) to paddle.
pagaïe, pagaille [pagaj] *nf* (*désordre*) *Fam* mess, shambles; **en p.** *Fam* in a mess; **avoir des livres/etc en p.** *Fam* to have loads of books/*etc*.
paganisme [paganism] *nm* paganism.
page [paʒ] **1** *nf* (*de livre etc*) page; **à la p.** (*personne*) *Fig* up-to-date. **2** *nm* (*à la cour*) *Hist* page (boy).
pagne [paɲ] *nm* loincloth.
pagode [pagɔd] *nf* pagoda.
paie [pɛ] *nf* pay, wages. ◆**paiement** *nm* payment.
païen, -enne [pajɛ̃, -ɛn] *a* & *nmf* pagan, heathen.
paillasson [pajasɔ̃] *nm* (door)mat.
paille [paj] *nf* straw; (*pour boire*) (drinking) straw; **homme de p.** *Fig* stooge, man of straw; **tirer à la courte p.** to draw lots; **sur la p.** *Fig* penniless; **feu de p.** *Fig* flash in the pan. ◆**paillasse** *nf* **1** (*matelas*) straw mattress. **2** (*d'un évier*) draining-board.
paillette [pajɛt] *nf* (*d'habit*) sequin; *pl* (*de lessive, savon*) flakes; (*d'or*) *Géol* gold dust.
pain [pɛ̃] *nm* bread; **un p.** a loaf (of bread); **p. grillé** toast; **p. complet** wholemeal bread; **p. d'épice** gingerbread; **petit p.** roll; **p. de savon/cire** bar of soap/wax; **avoir du p. sur la planche** (*travail*) *Fig* to have a lot on one's plate.
pair [pɛr] **1** *a* (*numéro*) even. **2** *nm* (*personne*) peer; hors p., unrivalled, without equal; **aller de p.** to go hand in hand (**avec** with); **au p.** (*étudiante etc*) au pair; **travailler au p.** to work as an au pair.

paire [pɛr] *nf* pair (**de** of).
paisible [pezibl] *a* (*vie etc*) peaceful; (*caractère, personne*) peaceable.
paître* [pɛtr] *vi* to graze; **envoyer p.** *Fig* to send packing.
paix [pɛ] *nf* peace; (*traité*) *Pol* peace treaty; **en p.** in peace; (*avec sa conscience*) at peace (**avec** with); **avoir la p.** to have (some) peace and quiet.
Pakistan [pakistɑ̃] *nm* Pakistan. ◆**pakistanais, -aise** *a* & *nmf* Pakistani.
palabres [palabr] *nmpl* palaver.
palace [palas] *nm* luxury hotel.
palais [palɛ] *nm* **1** (*château*) palace; **P. de justice** law courts; **p. des sports** sports stadium *ou* centre. **2** *Anat* palate.
palan [palɑ̃] *nm* (*de navire etc*) hoist.
pâle [pɑl] *a* pale.
palet [palɛ] *nm* (*hockey sur glace*) puck.
paletot [palto] *nm* (knitted) cardigan.
palette [palɛt] *nf* **1** (*de peintre*) palette. **2** (*support pour marchandises*) pallet.
pâleur [pɑlœr] *nf* paleness, pallor. ◆**pâlir** *vi* to go *ou* turn pale (**de** with).
palier [palje] *nm* **1** (*d'escalier*) landing; **être voisins de p.** to live on the same floor. **2** (*niveau*) level; (*phase de stabilité*) plateau; **par paliers** (*étapes*) in stages.
palissade [palisad] *nf* fence (*of stakes*).
pallier [palje] *vt* (*difficultés etc*) to alleviate. ◆**palliatif** *nm* palliative.
palmarès [palmarɛs] *nm* prize list; (*des chansons*) hit-parade.
palme [palm] *nf* **1** palm (leaf); (*symbole*) *Fig* palm. **2** (*de nageur*) flipper. ◆**palmier** *nm* palm (tree).
palmé [palme] *a* (*patte, pied*) webbed.
palombe [palɔ̃b] *nf* (*mollusque*) wood pigeon.
pâlot, -otte [pɑlo, -ɔt] *a* pale.
palourde [palurd] *nf* (*mollusque*) clam.
palp/er [palpe] *vt* to feel, finger. ◆**—able** *a* tangible.
palpit/er [palpite] *vi* (*frémir*) to quiver; (*cœur*) to palpitate, throb. ◆**—ant** *a* (*film etc*) thrilling. ◆**palpitations** *nfpl* quivering; palpitations.
pâmer (se) [səpame] *vpr* **se p. de** (*joie etc*) to be paralysed *ou* ecstatic with.
pamphlet [pɑ̃flɛ] *nm* lampoon.
pamplemousse [pɑ̃pləmus] *nm* grapefruit.

pan [pã] **1** nm (de chemise) tail; (de ciel) patch; **p. de mur** section of wall. **2** int bang!

pan- [pã, pan] préf Pan-.

panacée [panase] nf panacea.

panache [panaʃ] nm (plumet) plume; **avoir du p.** (fière allure) to have panache; **un p. de fumée** a plume of smoke.

panaché [panaʃe] **1** a (bigarré, hétéroclite) motley. **2** a & nm (demi) p. shandy; **bière panachée** shandy.

pancarte [pãkart] nf sign, notice; (de manifestant) placard.

pancréas [pãkreas] nm Anat pancreas.

panda [pãda] nm (animal) panda.

pané [pane] a Culin breaded.

panier [panje] nm (ustensile, contenu) basket; **p. à salade** salad basket; (voiture) Fam police van, prison van. **◆p.-repas** nm (pl paniers-repas) packed lunch.

panique [panik] nf panic; **pris de p.** panic-stricken; – a **peur p.** panic fear. **◆paniqu/er** vi to panic. **◆-é** a panic-stricken.

panne [pan] nf breakdown; **tomber en p.** to break down; **être en p.** to have broken down; **p. d'électricité** power cut, blackout; **avoir une p. sèche** to run out of petrol ou Am gas.

panneau, -x [pano] nm **1** (écriteau) sign, notice, board; **p. (de signalisation)** traffic ou road sign; **p. (d'affichage)** (publicité) hoarding, Am billboard. **2** (de porte etc) panel. **◆panonceau, -x** nm (enseigne) sign.

panoplie [panɔpli] nf **1** (jouet) outfit. **2** (gamme, arsenal) (wide) range, assortment.

panorama [panɔrama] nm panorama. **◆panoramique** a panoramic.

panse [pãs] nf Fam paunch, belly. **◆pansu** a potbellied.

pans/er [pãse] vt (plaie, main etc) to dress, bandage; (personne) to dress the wound(s) of, bandage (up); (cheval) to groom. **◆-ement** nm (bande) bandage, dressing; **p. adhésif** sticking plaster, Am Band-Aid®.

pantalon [pãtalɔ̃] nm (pair of) trousers ou Am pants; **deux pantalons** two pairs of trousers ou Am pants; **en p.** in trousers, Am in pants.

pantelant [pãtlã] a gasping.

panthère [pãtɛr] nf (animal) panther.

pantin [pãtɛ̃] nm (jouet) jumping jack; (personne) Péj puppet.

pantois [pãtwa] a flabbergasted.

pantoufle [pãtufl] nf slipper. **◆pantou-**

flard, -arde nmf Fam stay-at-home, Am homebody.

paon [pã] nm peacock.

papa [papa] nm dad(dy); **de p.** (désuet) Péj outdated; **fils à p.** Péj rich man's son, daddy's boy.

pape [pap] nm pope. **◆papauté** nf papacy.

paperasse(s) [papras] nf(pl) Péj (official) papers. **◆paperasserie** nf Péj (official) papers; (procédure) red tape.

papeterie [papetri] nf (magasin) stationer's shop; (articles) stationery; (fabrique) paper mill. **◆papetier, -ière** nmf stationer.

papi [papi] nm Fam grand(d)ad.

papier [papje] nm (matière) paper; **un p.** (feuille) a piece ou sheet of paper; (formulaire) a form; Journ an article; **en p.** (sac etc) paper-; **papiers (d'identité)** (identity) papers; **p. à lettres** writing paper; **du p. journal** (some) newspaper; **p. peint** wallpaper; **p. de verre** sandpaper.

papillon [papijɔ̃] nm **1** (insecte) butterfly; (écrou) butterfly nut, Am wing nut; **p. (de nuit)** moth. **2** (contravention) (parking) ticket.

papot/er [papote] vi to prattle. **◆-age(s)** nm(pl) prattle.

paprika [paprika] nm (poudre) Culin paprika.

papy [papi] nm Fam grand(d)ad.

Pâque [pɑk] nf la P. Rel Passover.

paquebot [pakbo] nm Nau liner.

pâquerette [pakrɛt] nf daisy.

Pâques [pɑk] nm & nfpl Easter.

paquet [pakɛ] nm (de sucre, bonbons etc) packet; (colis) package; (de cigarettes) pack(et); (de cartes) pack.

par [par] prép **1** (agent, manière, moyen) by; **choisi/frappé/etc** p. chosen/hit/etc by; **erreur** by mistake; **p. mer** by sea; **p. le train** by train; **p. la force/le travail/etc** by ou through force/work/etc; **apprendre p. un voisin** to learn from ou through a neighbour; **commencer/s'ouvrir p. qch** (récit etc) to begin/open with sth; **p. malchance** unfortunately. **2** (lieu) through; **p. la porte/le tunnel/etc** through ou by the door/tunnel/etc; **regarder/jeter p. la fenêtre** to look/throw out (of) the window; **p. les rues** through the streets; **p. ici/là** (aller) this/that way; (habiter) around here/there. **3** (motif) out of, from; **p. respect/pitié/etc** out of ou from respect/pity/etc. **4** (temps) on; **p. un jour d'hiver/etc** on a winter's day/etc; **p. le passé** in the past; **p. ce froid** in this cold. **5** (distributif) **dix fois p. an** ten times a ou per year; **deux p. deux** two by two; **p. deux fois** twice. **6** (*trop*) p. **trop ai-mable**/*etc* far too kind/*etc*.

para [para] *nm* Mil Fam para(trooper).

para- [para] *préf* para-.

parabole [parabɔl] *nf* **1** (*récit*) parable. **2** *Math* parabola.

parachever [paraʃve] *vt* to perfect.

parachute [paraʃyt] *nf* parachute. ◆**parachuter** *vt* to parachute; (*nommer*) Fam to pitchfork (**à un poste** into a job). ◆**parachutisme** *nm* parachute jumping. ◆**parachutiste** *nmf* parachutist; Mil paratrooper.

parade [parad] *nf* **1** (*étalage*) show, parade; (*spectacle*) & Mil parade. **2** Boxe Escrime parry; (*riposte*) Fig reply. ◆**parader** *vi* to parade, show off.

paradis [paradi] *nm* paradise, heaven. ◆**paradisiaque** *a* (*endroit etc*) Fig heavenly.

paradoxe [paradɔks] *nm* paradox. ◆**paradoxalement** *adv* paradoxically.

parafe [paraf] *voir* **paraphe**. ◆**parafer** *voir* **parapher**.

paraffine [parafin] *nf* paraffin (wax).

parages [paraʒ] *nmpl* region, area (**de** of); **dans ces p.** in these parts.

paragraphe [paragraf] *nm* paragraph.

paraître* [paretr] **1** *vi* (*se montrer*) to appear; (*sembler*) to seem, look, appear; – *v imp* **il paraît qu'il va partir** it appears ou seems (that) he's leaving. **2** *vi* (*livre*) to be published, come out; **faire p.** to bring out.

parallèle [paralɛl] **1** *a* (*comparable*) & Math parallel (**à** with, to); (*marché*) Com unofficial. **2** *nm* (*comparaison*) & Géog parallel. ◆**—ment** *adv* **p. à** parallel to.

paralyser [paralize] *vt* to paralyse, Am paralyze. ◆**paralysie** *nf* paralysis. ◆**paralytique** *a* & *nmf* paralytic.

paramètre [parametr] *nm* parameter.

paranoïa [paranɔja] *nf* paranoia. ◆**paranoïaque** *a* & *nmf* paranoid.

parapet [parapɛ] *nm* parapet.

paraphe [paraf] *nm* initials, signature; (*traits*) flourish. ◆**parapher** *vt* to initial, sign.

paraphrase [parafraz] *nf* paraphrase. ◆**paraphraser** *vt* to paraphrase.

parapluie [paraplɥi] *nm* umbrella.

parasite [parazit] *nm* (*personne, organisme*) parasite; *pl* Rad interference; – *a* parasitic(al).

parasol [parasɔl] *nm* parasol, sunshade.

paratonnerre [paratɔnɛr] *nm* lightning conductor ou Am rod.

paravent [paravɑ̃] *nm* (folding) screen.

parc [park] *nm* **1** park; (*de château*) grounds. **2** (*de bébé*) (play) pen; (*à moutons, à bétail*) pen; **p.** (**de stationnement**) car park, Am parking lot; **p. à huîtres** oyster bed.

parcelle [parsɛl] *nf* fragment, particle; (*terrain*) plot; (*de vérité*) Fig grain.

parce que [parsk(ə)] *conj* because.

parchemin [parʃəmɛ̃] *nm* parchment.

parcimonie [parsimɔni] *nf* **avec p.** parsimoniously. ◆**parcimonieux, -euse** *a* parsimonious.

par-ci par-là [parsiparla] *adv* here, there and everywhere.

parcmètre [parkmɛtr] *nm* parking meter.

parcourir* [parkurir] *vt* (*région*) to travel through, tour, scour; (*distance*) to cover; (*texte*) to glance through. ◆**parcours** *nm* (*itinéraire*) route; (*de fleuve*) & Sp course; (*voyage*) trip, journey.

par-delà [pard(ə)la] *voir* **delà**.

par-derrière [parderjɛr] *voir* **derrière**.

par-dessous [pard(ə)su] *prép* & *adv* under(neath).

pardessus [pard(ə)sy] *nm* overcoat.

par-dessus [pard(ə)sy] *prép* & *adv* over (the top of); **p.-dessus tout** above all.

par-devant [pard(ə)vɑ̃] *voir* **devant**.

pardon [pardɔ̃] *nm* forgiveness, pardon; **p.?** (*pour demander*) excuse me?, Am pardon me?; **p.!** (*je le regrette*) sorry!; **demander p.** to apologize (**à** to). ◆**pardonn/er** *vt* to forgive; **p. qch à qn/à qn d'avoir fait qch** to forgive s.o. for sth/for doing sth. ◆**–able** *a* forgivable.

pare-balles [parbal] *a inv* **gilet p.-balles** bulletproof jacket ou Am vest.

pare-brise [parbriz] *nm inv* Aut windscreen, Am windshield.

pare-chocs [parʃɔk] *nm inv* Aut bumper.

pareil, -eille [parɛj] *a* similar; **p. à** the same as, similar to; **être pareils** to be the same, be similar ou alike; **un p. désordre**/*etc* such a mess/*etc*; **en p. cas** in such a case; – *nmf* (*personne*) equal; **rendre la pareille à qn** to treat s.o. the same way; **sans p.** unparalleled, unique; – *adv* Fam the same. ◆**pareillement** *adv* in the same way; (*aussi*) likewise.

parement [parmɑ̃] *nm* (*de pierre, de vêtement*) facing.

parent, -ente [parɑ̃, -ɑ̃t] *nmf* relation, relative; – *nmpl* (*père et mère*) parents; – *a* related (**de** to). ◆**parenté** *nf* (*rapport*) relationship, kinship.

parenthèse [parɑ̃tɛz] *nf* (*signe*) bracket, parenthesis; (*digression*) digression.

parer [pare] **1** *vt* (*coup*) to parry, ward off; — *vi* **p. à** to be prepared for. **2** *vt* (*orner*) to adorn (**de** with).

paresse [parɛs] *nf* laziness, idleness. ◆**paresser** *vi* to laze (about). ◆**paresseux, -euse** *a* lazy, idle; — *nmf* lazybones.

parfaire [parfɛr] *vt* to perfect. ◆**parfait** *a* perfect; **p.!** excellent!; — *nm* *Gram* perfect (tense). ◆**parfaitement** *adv* perfectly; (*certainement*) certainly.

parfois [parfwa] *adv* sometimes.

parfum [parfœ̃] *nm* (*odeur*) fragrance, scent; (*goût*) flavour; (*liquide*) perfume, scent. ◆**parfum/er** *vt* to perfume, scent; (*glace, crème etc*) to flavour (**de** with). ◆—**é** *a* (*savon, mouchoir*) scented; **p. au café**/*etc* coffee-/*etc* flavoured. ◆**parfumerie** *nf* (*magasin*) perfume shop.

pari [pari] *nm* bet, wager; *pl* *Sp* betting, bets; **p. mutuel urbain** = the tote, *Am* pari-mutuel. ◆**parier** *vti* to bet (**sur** on, **que** that). ◆**parieur, -euse** *nmf* *Sp* better, punter.

Paris [pari] *nm ou f* Paris. ◆**parisien, -ienne** *a* (*accent etc*) Parisian, Paris-; — *nmf* Parisian.

parité [parite] *nf* parity.

parjure [parʒyr] *nm* perjury; — *nmf* perjurer. ◆**se parjurer** *vpr* to perjure oneself.

parka [parka] *nm* parka.

parking [parkiŋ] *nm* (*lieu*) car park, *Am* parking lot.

par-là [parla] *adv voir* **par-ci.**

parlement [parləmã] *nm* parliament. ◆**parlementaire** *a* parliamentary; — *nmf* member of parliament.

parlementer [parləmãte] *vi* to parley, negotiate.

parl/er [parle] *vi* to talk, speak (**de** about, of; **à** to); **tu parles!** *Fam* you must be joking!; **sans p. de . . .** not to mention . . . ; — *vt* (*langue*) to speak; **p. affaires**/*etc* to talk business/*etc*; — **se p.** *vpr* (*langue*) to be spoken; — *nm* speech; (*régional*) dialect. ◆—**ant** *a* (*film*) talking; (*regard etc*) eloquent. ◆—**é** *a* (*langue*) spoken.

parloir [parlwar] *nm* (*de couvent, prison*) visiting room.

parmi [parmi] *prép* among(st).

parodie [parɔdi] *nf* parody. ◆**parodier** *vt* to parody.

paroi [parwa] *nf* wall; (*de maison*) inside wall; (*de rocher*) (rock) face.

paroisse [parwas] *nf* parish. ◆**paroissial,**

-**aux** *a* (*registre, activité etc*) parish-. ◆**paroissien, -ienne** *nmf* parishioner.

parole [parɔl] *nf* (*mot, promesse*) word; (*faculté, langage*) speech; **adresser la p. à** to speak to; **prendre la p.** to speak, make a speech; **demander la p.** to ask to speak; **perdre la p.** to lose one's tongue.

paroxysme [parɔksism] *nm* (*de douleur etc*) height.

parpaing [parpɛ̃] *nm* concrete block, breezeblock.

parquer [parke] *vt* (*bœufs*) to pen; (*gens*) to herd together, confine; (*véhicule*) to park; — **se p.** *vpr* *Aut* to park.

parquet [parke] *nm* **1** (*parquet*) floor(ing). **2** *Jur* Public Prosecutor's office.

parrain [parɛ̃] *nm* *Rel* godfather; (*répondant*) sponsor. ◆**parrain/er** *vt* to sponsor. ◆—**age** *nm* sponsorship.

pars, part[1] [par] *voir* **partir.**

parsemer [parsəme] *vt* to strew, dot (**de** with).

part[2] [par] *nf* (*portion*) share, part; **prendre p. à** (*activité*) to take part in; (*la joie etc de qn*) to share; **de toutes parts** from *ou* on all sides; **de p. et d'autre** on both sides; **d'une p.,...d'autre p.** on the one hand,... on the other hand; **d'autre p.** (*d'ailleurs*) moreover; **pour ma p.** as far as I'm concerned; **de la p. de** (*provenance*) from; **c'est de la p. de qui?** *Tél* who's speaking?; **faire p. de qch à qn** to inform s.o. of sth; **quelque p.** somewhere; **nulle p.** nowhere; **autre p.** somewhere else; **à p.** (*séparément*) apart; (*mettre, prendre*) aside; (*excepté*) apart from; **un cas/une place**/*etc* **à p.** a separate *ou* special case/place/*etc*; **membre à p. entière** full member.

partage [partaʒ] *nm* dividing (up), division; (*participation*) sharing; (*distribution*) sharing out; (*sort*) *Fig* lot. ◆**partag/er** *vt* (*repas, frais, joie etc*) to share (**avec** with); (*diviser*) to divide (up); (*distribuer*) to share out; — **se p.** *vpr* (*bénéfices etc*) to share (between themselves *etc*); **se p. entre** to divide one's time between. ◆—**é** *a* (*avis etc*) divided; **p. entre** (*sentiments*) torn between.

partance (en) [ãpartãs] *adv* (*train etc*) about to depart (**pour** for).

partant [partã] *nm* (*coureur, cheval*) *Sp* starter.

partenaire [partənɛr] *nmf* (*époux etc*) & *Sp* *Pol* partner.

parterre [partɛr] *nm* **1** (*de jardin etc*) flower bed. **2** *Th* stalls, *Am* orchestra.

parti [parti] *nm* *Pol* party; (*époux*) match; **prendre un p.** to make a decision, follow a course; **prendre p. pour** to side with; **tirer p. de** to turn to (good) account; **p. pris** (*préjugé*) prejudice; **être de p. pris** to be prejudiced (contre against).

partial, -aux [parsjal, -o] *a* biased. ◆**partialité** *nf* bias.

participe [partisip] *nm Gram* participle.

particip/er [partisipe] *vi* **p. à** (*activité, jeu etc*) to take part in, participate in; (*frais, joie etc*) to share (in). ◆**-ant, -ante** *nmf* participant. ◆**participation** *nf* participation; sharing; (*d'un acteur*) appearance, collaboration; **p. (aux frais)** (*contribution*) share (in the expenses).

particule [partikyl] *nf* particle.

particulier, -ière [partikylje, -ɛr] *a* (*spécial, spécifique*) particular; (*privé*) private; (*bizarre*) peculiar; **p. à** peculiar to; **en p.** (*surtout*) in particular; (*à part*) in private; − *nm* private individual *ou* citizen. ◆**particularité** *nf* peculiarity. ◆**particulièrement** *adv* particularly; **tout p.** especially.

partie [parti] *nf* part; (*de cartes, de tennis etc*) game; (*de chasse, de plaisir*) & *Jur* party; (*métier*) line, field; **en p.** partly, in part; **en grande p.** mainly; **faire p. de** to be a part of; (*adhérer à*) to belong to; (*comité*) to be on. ◆**partiel, -ielle** *a* partial; − *nm* (*examen*) **p.** *Univ* term exam. ◆**partiellement** *adv* partially.

part/ir* [partir] *vi* (*aux* **être**) (*aller, disparaître*) to go; (*s'en aller*) to leave, go (off); (*se mettre en route*) to set off; (*s'éloigner*) to go (away); (*moteur*) to start; (*fusil, coup de feu*) to go off; (*flèche*) to shoot off; (*bouton*) to come off; (*tache*) to come out; **p. de** (*commencer par*) to start (off) with; **ça part du cœur** it comes from the heart; **p. bien** to get off to a good start; **à p. de** (*date, prix*) from. ◆**-i** **bien p.** off to a good start.

partisan [partizã] *nm* follower, supporter; *Mil* partisan; − *a* (*esprit*) *Péj* partisan; **être p. de qch/de faire** to be in favour of sth/of doing.

partition [partisjɔ̃] *nf Mus* score.

partout [partu] *adv* everywhere; **p. où tu vas ou iras** everywhere *ou* wherever you go; **p. sur la table/etc** all over the table/etc.

paru [pary] *voir* **paraître**. ◆**parution** *nf* (*de livre etc*) publication.

parure [paryr] *nf* (*toilette*) finery; (*bijoux*) jewellery.

parven/ir* [parvənir] *vi* (*aux* **être**) **p. à** (*lieu*) to reach; (*fortune, ses fins*) to achieve; **p. à faire** to manage to do. ◆**-u, -ue** *nmf Péj* upstart.

parvis [parvi] *nm* square (*in front of church etc*).

pas¹ [pa] *adv* (*négatif*) not; (**ne**) ... **p.** not; **je ne sais p.** I do not *ou* don't know; **p. de pain/de café/etc** no bread/coffee/etc; **p. encore** not yet; **p. du tout** not at all.

pas² [pa] *nm* **1** step, pace; (*allure*) pace; (*bruit*) footstep; (*trace*) footprint; **à deux (de)** close by; **revenir sur ses p.** to go back on one's tracks; **au p.** at a walking pace; **rouler au p.** (*véhicule*) to go dead slow(ly); **au p. (cadencé)** in step; **faire les cent p.** to walk up and down; **faux p.** stumble; (*faute*) *Fig* blunder; **le p. de la porte** the doorstep. **2** (*de vis*) thread. **3** *Géog* straits; **le p. de Calais** the Straits of Dover.

pascal [paskal] *a* (*semaine, messe etc*) Easter-.

passable [pasabl] *a* acceptable, tolerable; **mention p.** *Scol Univ* pass. ◆**-ment** [-əmɑ̃] *adv* acceptably; (*beaucoup*) quite a lot.

passage [pasaʒ] *nm* (*action*) passing, passage; (*traversée*) *Nau* crossing, passage; (*extrait*) passage; (*couloir*) passage(way); (*droit*) right of way; (*venue*) arrival; (*chemin*) path; **p. clouté ou pour piétons** (pedestrian) crossing; **obstruer le p.** to block the way; **p. souterrain** subway, *Am* underpass; **p. à niveau** level crossing, *Am* grade crossing; **'p. interdit'** 'no thoroughfare'; **'cédez le p.'** *Aut* 'give way', *Am* 'yield'; **être de p.** to be passing through (**à Paris**/*etc* Paris/*etc*); **hôte de p.** passing guest. ◆**passager, -ère** **1** *nmf* passenger; **p. clandestin** stowaway. **2** *a* (*de courte durée*) passing, temporary. ◆**passagèrement** *adv* temporarily.

passant, -ante [pasã, -ãt] **1** *a* (*rue*) busy; − *nmf* passer-by. **2** *nm* (*de ceinture etc*) loop.

passe [pas] *nf Sp* pass; **mot de p.** password; **en p. de faire** on the road to doing; **une mauvaise p.** *Fig* a bad patch.

passe-montagne [pasmɔ̃taɲ] *nm* balaclava.

passe-partout [paspartu] *nm inv* (*clé*) master key; − *a inv* (*compliment, phrase*) all-purpose.

passe-passe [paspas] *nm inv* **tour de p.-passe** conjuring trick.

passe-plat [paspla] *nm* service hatch.

passeport [paspɔr] *nm* passport.

passer [pase] *vi* (*aux* **être** *ou* **avoir**) (*aller, venir*) to pass (à to); (*facteur, laitier*) to come; (*temps*) to pass (by), go by; (*courant*) to flow; (*film, programme*) to be shown, be on; (*loi*) to be passed; (*douleur, mode*) to pass; (couleur) to fade; **p. devant** (maison etc) to go past ou by, pass (by); **p. à** ou **par Paris** to go through Paris; **p. à la radio** to come ou go on the radio; **p. à l'ennemi/à la caisse** to go over to the enemy/the cash desk; **laisser p.** (personne, lumière) to let in ou through; (occasion) to let slip; **p. prendre** to pick up, fetch; **p. voir qn** to drop in on s.o.; **p. pour** (riche etc) to be taken for; **faire p. qn pour** to pass s.o. off as; **p. sur** (détail etc) to overlook, pass over; **p. capitaine/etc** to be promoted captain/etc; **p. en** (seconde etc) Scol to pass up into; Aut to change up to; **ça passe** (c'est passable) that'll do; **en passant** (dire qch) in passing; – vt (avoir) (frontière etc) to pass, cross; (maison etc) to pass, go past; (donner) to pass, hand (à to); (mettre) to put; (omettre) to overlook; (temps) to spend, pass (à faire doing); (disque) to play, put on; (film, programme) to show, put on; (loi, motion) to pass; (chemise) to slip on; (examen) to take, sit (for); (thé) to strain; (café) to filter; (commande) to place; (accord) to conclude; (colère) to vent (sur on); (limites) to go beyond; (visite médicale) to go through; **p. (son tour)** to pass; **p. qch à qn** (caprice etc) to grant s.o. sth; (pardonner) to excuse s.o. sth; **je vous passe ...** Tél I'm putting you through to ...; **p. un coup d'éponge/etc à qch** to go over sth with a sponge/etc; – **se p.** vpr (se produire) to take place, happen; (douleur) to pass, go (away); **se p. de** to do ou go without; **se p. de commentaires** to need no comment; **ça s'est bien passé** it went off all right. ◆**passé 1** a (temps etc) past; (couleur) faded; **la semaine passée** last week; **dix heures passées** after ou gone ten (o'clock); **être passé** (personne) to have been (and gone); (orage) to be over; **avoir vingt ans passés** to be over twenty; – nm (temps, vie passée) past; Gram past (tense). **2** prép after; **p. huit heures** after eight (o'clock).

passerelle [pɑsrɛl] nf (pont) footbridge; (voie d'accès) Nau Av gangway.

passe-temps [pɑstɑ̃] nm inv pastime.

passeur, -euse [pɑsœr, -øz] nmf 1 Nau ferryman, ferrywoman. 2 (contrebandier) smuggler.

passible [pɑsibl] a **p. de** (peine) Jur liable to.

passif, -ive [pɑsif, -iv] **1** a (rôle, personne etc) passive; – nm Gram passive. **2** nm Com liabilities. ◆**passivité** nf passiveness, passivity.

passion [pɑsjɔ̃] nf passion; **avoir la p. des**

voitures/d'écrire/etc to have a passion ou a great love for cars/writing/etc. ◆**passionnel, -elle** a (crime) of passion. ◆**passionner** vt to thrill, fascinate; **se p. pour** to have a passion for. ◆**-ant** a thrilling. ◆**-é, -ée** a passionate; **p. de qch** passionately fond of sth; – nmf fan (de of). ◆**-ément** adv passionately.

passoire [pɑswar] nf (pour liquides) sieve; (à thé) strainer; (à légumes) colander.

pastel [pastɛl] nm pastel; **au p.** (dessin) pastel-; – a inv (ton) pastel-.

pastèque [pastɛk] nf watermelon.

pasteur [pastœr] nm Rel pastor.

pasteurisé [pastœrize] a (lait, beurre etc) pasteurized.

pastiche [pastiʃ] nm pastiche.

pastille [pastij] nf pastille, lozenge.

pastis [pastis] nm aniseed liqueur, pastis.

pastoral, -aux [pastoral, -o] a pastoral.

patate [patat] nf Fam spud, potato.

patatras! [patatra] int crash!

pataud [pato] a clumsy, lumpish.

patauger [patoʒe] vi (marcher) to wade (in the mud etc); (barboter) to splash about; (s'empêtrer) Fig to flounder. ◆**pataugeoire** nf paddling pool.

patchwork [patʃwœrk] nm patchwork.

pâte [pɑt] nf (substance) paste; (à pain, à gâteau) dough; (à tarte) pastry; **pâtes (alimentaires)** pasta; **p. à modeler** plasticine®, modelling clay; **p. à frire** batter; **p. dentifrice** toothpaste.

pâté [pɑte] nm **1** (charcuterie) pâté; **p. (en croûte)** meat pie. **2 p. (de sable)** sand castle; **p. de maisons** block of houses. **3** (tache d'encre) (ink) blot.

pâtée [pɑte] nf (pour chien, volaille etc) mash.

patelin [patlɛ̃] nm Fam village.

patent [patɑ̃] a patent, obvious.

patère [patɛr] nf (coat) peg.

paternel, -elle [patɛrnɛl] a (amour etc) fatherly, paternal; (parenté, réprimande) paternal. ◆**paternité** nf (état) paternity, fatherhood; (de livre) authorship.

pâteux, -euse [pɑtø, -øz] a (substance) doughy, pasty; (style) woolly; **avoir la bouche** ou **la langue pâteuse** (après s'être enivré) to have a mouth full of cotton wool ou Am cotton.

pathétique [patetik] a moving; – nm pathos.

pathologie [patɔlɔʒi] nf pathology. ◆**pathologique** a pathological.

patient, -ente [pasjɑ̃, -ɑ̃t] **1** a patient. **2** nmf Méd patient. ◆**patiemment** [-amɑ̃] adv patiently. ◆**patience** nf patience; **prendre p.** to have patience; **perdre p.** to lose patience. ◆**patienter** vi to wait (patiently).

patin [patɛ̃] nm skate; (*pour le parquet*) cloth pad (*used for walking*); **p. à glace/à roulettes** ice/roller skate. ◆**patin/er** vi Sp to skate; (*véhicule, embrayage*) to slip. ◆**—age** nm Sp skating; **p. artistique** figure skating. ◆**—eur, -euse** nmf Sp skater. ◆**patinoire** nf (*piste*) & Fig skating rink, ice rink.

patine [patin] nf patina.

patio [patjo] nm patio.

pâtir [pɑtir] vi **p. de** to suffer from.

pâtisserie [pɑtisri] nf pastry, cake; (*magasin*) cake shop; (*art*) cake ou pastry making. ◆**pâtissier, -ière** nmf pastrycook and cake shop owner.

patois [patwa] nm Ling patois.

patraque [patrak] a (*malade*) Fam under the weather.

patriarche [patrijarʃ] nm patriarch.

patrie [patri] nf (*native*) country; (*ville*) birth place. ◆**patriote** nmf patriot; – a (*personne*) patriotic. ◆**patriotique** a (*chant etc*) patriotic. ◆**patriotisme** nm patriotism.

patrimoine [patrimwan] nm (*biens*) & Fig heritage.

patron, -onne [patrɔ̃, -ɔn] 1 nmf (*chef*) employer, boss; (*propriétaire*) owner (**de** of); (*gérant*) manager, manageress; (*de bar*) landlord, landlady. 2 nmf Rel patron saint. 3 nm (*modèle de papier*) Tex pattern. ◆**patronage** nm 1 (*protection*) patronage. 2 (*centre*) youth club. ◆**patronal, -aux** a (*syndicat etc*) employers'. ◆**patronat** nm employers. ◆**patronner** vt to sponsor.

patrouille [patruj] nf patrol. ◆**patrouill/er** vi to patrol. ◆**—eur** nm (*navire*) patrol boat.

patte [pat] nf 1 (*membre*) leg; (*de chat, chien*) paw; (*main*) Fam hand; **à quatre pattes** on all fours. 2 (*de poche*) flap; (*languette*) tongue.

pattes [pat] nfpl (*favoris*) sideboards, Am sideburns.

pause [poz] nf (*arrêt*) break; (*dans le discours etc*) pause.

pauvre [povr] a poor; (*terre*) impoverished, poor; **p. en** (*calories etc*) low in; (*ressources etc*) low on; – nmf (*indigent, malheureux*) poor man, poor woman; **les pauvres** the poor. ◆**pauvrement** adv poorly. ◆**pauvreté** nf (*besoin*) poverty; (*insuffisance*) poorness.

pavaner (se) [səpavane] vpr to strut (about).

pav/er [pave] vt to pave. ◆**—é** nm un p. a paving stone; (*rond, de vieille chaussée*) a cobblestone; **sur le p.** Fig on the streets. ◆**—age** nm (*travail, revêtement*) paving.

pavillon [pavijɔ̃] nm 1 (*maison*) house; (*de chasse*) lodge; (*d'hôpital*) ward; (*d'exposition*) pavilion. 2 (*drapeau*) flag.

pavoiser [pavwaze] vt to deck out with flags; – vi (*exulter*) Fig to rejoice.

pavot [pavo] nm (*cultivé*) poppy.

pay/er [peje] vt (*personne, somme*) to pay; (*service, objet, faute*) to pay for; (*récompenser*) to repay; **p. qch à qn** (*offrir en cadeau*) Fam to treat s.o. to sth; **p. qn pour faire** ou **de faire** to pay s.o. to do ou for doing; – vi (*personne, métier, crime*) to pay; **se p. qch** (*s'acheter*) Fam to treat oneself to sth; **se p. la tête de qn** Fam to make fun of s.o. ◆**—ant** [pejɑ̃] a (*hôte, spectateur*) who pays, paying; (*place, entrée*) that one has to pay for; (*rentable*) worthwhile. ◆**payable** a payable. ◆**paye** nf pay, wages. ◆**payement** nm payment.

pays [pei] nm country; (*région*) region; (*village*) village; **p. des rêves/du soleil** land of dreams/sun; **du p.** (*vin, gens etc*) local.

paysage [peizaʒ] nm landscape, scenery.

paysan, -anne [peizɑ̃, -an] nmf (*small*) farmer; (*rustre*) Péj peasant; – a (*country-/monde*) farming.

Pays-Bas [peiba] nmpl **les P.-Bas** the Netherlands.

PCV [peseve] abrév (*paiement contre vérification*) **téléphoner en PCV** to reverse the charges, Am call collect.

PDG [pedeʒe] abrév = **président directeur général.**

péage [peaʒ] nm (*droit*) toll; (*lieu*) tollgate.

peau, -x [po] nf skin; (*de fruit*) peel, skin; (*cuir*) hide, skin; (*fourrure*) pelt; **dans la p. de qn** Fig in s.o.'s shoes; **faire p. neuve** Fig to turn over a new leaf. ◆**P.-Rouge** nmf (*pl* **Peaux-Rouges**) (Red) Indian.

pêche[1] [pɛʃ] nf (*activité*) fishing; (*poissons*) catch; **p. (à la ligne)** angling; **aller à la p.** to go fishing. ◆**pêcher**[1] vi to fish; – vt (*chercher à prendre*) to fish for; (*attraper*) to

catch; (dénicher) Fam to dig up.
◆**pêcheur** nm fisherman; angler.

pêche² [pɛʃ] nf (fruit) peach. ◆**pêcher²** nm (arbre) peach tree.

péché [peʃe] nm sin. ◆**péch/er** vi to sin; **p. par orgueil**/etc to be too proud/etc. ◆**—eur, -eresse** nmf sinner.

pectoraux [pɛktɔro] nmpl (muscles) chest muscles.

pécule [pekyl] nm **un p.** (économies) (some) savings, a nest egg.

pécuniaire [pekynjɛr] a monetary.

pédagogie [pedagɔʒi] nf (science) education, teaching methods. ◆**pédagogique** a educational. ◆**pédagogue** nmf teacher.

pédale [pedal] nf **1** pedal; **p. de frein** footbrake (pedal). **2** (homosexuel) Péj Fam pansy, queer. ◆**pédaler** vi to pedal.

pédalo [pedalo] nm pedal boat, pedalo.

pédant, -ante [pedɑ̃, -ɑ̃t] nmf pedant; – a pedantic. ◆**pédantisme** nm pedantry.

pédé [pede] nm (homosexuel) Péj Fam queer.

pédiatre [pedjatr] nmf Méd p(a)ediatrician.

pédicure [pedikyr] nmf chiropodist.

pedigree [pedigre] nm (de chien, cheval etc) pedigree.

pègre [pɛgr] nf **la p.** the (criminal) underworld.

peigne [pɛɲ] nm comb; **passer au p. fin** Fig to go through with a fine toothcomb; **un coup de p.** (action) a comb. ◆**peigner** vt (cheveux) to comb; **p. qn** to comb s.o.'s hair; **— se p.** vpr to comb one's hair.

peignoir [pɛɲwar] nm dressing gown, Am bathrobe; **p. (de bain)** bathrobe.

peinard [pɛnar] a Arg quiet (and easy).

peindre* [pɛ̃dr] vt to paint; (décrire) Fig to depict, paint; **p. en bleu**/etc to paint blue/etc; – vi to paint.

peine [pɛn] nf **1** (châtiment) punishment; **p. de mort** death penalty ou sentence; **p. de prison** prison sentence; **'défense d'entrer sous p. d'amende'** 'trespassers will be fined'. **2** (chagrin) sorrow, grief; **avoir de la p.** to be upset ou sad; **faire de la p. à** to upset, cause pain ou sorrow to. **3** (effort, difficulté) trouble; **se donner de la p.** ou **beaucoup de p.** to go to a lot of trouble (**pour faire** to do); **avec p.** with difficulty; **ça vaut la p. d'attendre**/etc it's worth (while) waiting/etc; **ce n'est pas ou ça ne vaut pas la p.** it's not worth while ou worth it ou worth bothering. ◆**peiner 1** vt to upset, grieve. **2** vi to labour, struggle.

peine (à) [apɛn] adv hardly, scarcely.

peintre [pɛ̃tr] nm painter; **p. (en bâtiment)**

(house) painter, (painter and) decorator. ◆**peinture** nf (tableau, activité) painting; (couleur) paint; **'p. fraîche'** 'wet paint'. ◆**peinturlurer** vt Fam to daub with colour; **se p. (le visage)** to paint one's face.

péjoratif, -ive [peʒɔratif, -iv] a pejorative, derogatory.

pékinois [pekinwa] nm (chien) pekin(g)ese.

pelage [pəlaʒ] nm (d'animal) coat, fur.

pelé [pəle] a bare.

pêle-mêle [pɛlmɛl] adv in disorder.

peler [pəle] vt (fruit) to peel; **se p. facilement** (fruit) to peel easily; – vi (peau bronzée) to peel.

pèlerin [pɛlrɛ̃] nm pilgrim. ◆**pèlerinage** nm pilgrimage.

pèlerine [pɛlrin] nf (manteau) cape.

pélican [pelikɑ̃] nm (oiseau) pelican.

pelisse [pəlis] nf fur-lined coat.

pelle [pɛl] nf shovel; (d'enfant) spade; **p. à poussière** dustpan; **ramasser** ou **prendre une p.** (tomber) Fam to come a cropper, Am take a spill; **à la p.** (argent etc) Fam galore. ◆**pelletée** nf shovelful. ◆**pelleteuse** nf Tech mechanical shovel, excavator.

pellicule [pelikyl] nf Phot film; (couche) film, layer; pl Méd dandruff.

pelote [pəlɔt] nf (de laine) ball; (à épingles) pincushion; **p. (basque)** Sp pelota.

peloter [pəlɔte] vt (palper) Péj Fam to paw.

peloton [pəlɔtɔ̃] nm **1** (coureurs) Sp pack, main body. **2** Mil squad; **p. d'exécution** firing squad. **3** (de ficelle) ball.

pelotonner (se) [səpəlɔtɔne] vpr to curl up (into a ball).

pelouse [pəluz] nf lawn; Sp enclosure.

peluche [pəlyʃ] nf (tissu) plush; pl (flocons) fluff, lint; **une p.** (flocon) a bit of fluff ou lint; **jouet en p.** soft toy; **chien**/etc **en p.** (jouet) furry dog/etc; **ours en p.** teddy bear. ◆**pelucher** vi to get fluffy ou linty. ◆**pelucheux, -euse** a fluffy, linty.

pelure [pəlyr] nf (d'épluchure) peeling; **une p.** a (piece of) peeling.

pénal, -aux [penal, -o] a (droit, code etc) penal. ◆**pénalisation** nf Sp penalty. ◆**pénaliser** vt Sp Jur to penalize (**pour** for). ◆**pénalité** nf Jur Rugby penalty.

penalty, pl -ties [penalti, -iz] nm Fb penalty.

penaud [pəno] a sheepish.

penchant [pɑ̃ʃɑ̃] nm (goût) liking (**pour** for); (tendance) inclination (**à qch** towards sth).

pench/er [pɑ̃ʃe] vt (objet) to tilt; (tête) to lean; – vi (arbre etc) to lean (over); **p. pour** Fig to be inclined towards; **— se p.** vpr to lean (forward); **se p. par** (fenêtre) to lean out of; **se p. sur** (*problème etc*) to examine. **◆-é** *a* leaning.

pendaison [pɑ̃dɛzɔ̃] *nf* hanging.

pendant[1] [pɑ̃dɑ̃] *prép* (*au cours de*) during; **p. la nuit** during the night; **p. deux mois** (*pour une période de*) for two months; **p. que** while, whilst.

pendentif [pɑ̃dɑ̃tif] *nm* (*collier*) pendant.

penderie [pɑ̃dri] *nf* wardrobe.

pend/re [pɑ̃dr] *vti* to hang (à from); **— se p.** *vpr* (*se tuer*) to hang oneself; (*se suspendre*) to hang (à from). **◆-ant**[2] *1 a* hanging; (*langue*) hanging out; (*joues*) sagging; (*question*) *Fig* pending. **2** *nm* **p.** (*d'oreille*) drop earring. **3** *nm* **le p.** de the companion piece to. **◆-u, -ue** *a* (*objet*) hanging (à from); **— *nmf*** hanged man, hanged woman.

pendule [pɑ̃dyl] *1 nf* clock. **2** *nm* (*balancier*) & *Fig* pendulum. **◆pendulette** *nf* small clock.

pénétr/er [penetre] *vi* **p. dans** to enter; (*profondément*) to penetrate (into); **— *vt*** (*substance, mystère etc*) to penetrate; **se p. de** (*idée*) to become convinced of. **◆-ant** *a* (*esprit, froid etc*) penetrating, keen. **◆pénétration** *nf* penetration.

pénible [penibl] *a* (*difficile*) difficult; (*douloureux*) painful, distressing; (*ennuyeux*) tiresome; (*agaçant*) annoying. **◆-ment** [-əmɑ̃] *adv* with difficulty; (*avec douleur*) painfully.

péniche [penif] *nf* barge; **p. de débarquement** *Mil* landing craft.

pénicilline [penisilin] *nf* penicillin.

péninsule [penɛ̃syl] *nf* peninsula. **◆péninsulaire** *a* peninsular.

pénis [penis] *nm* penis.

pénitence [penitɑ̃s] *nf* (*punition*) punishment; (*peine*) *Rel* penance; (*regret*) penitence. **◆pénitent, -ente** *nmf Rel* penitent.

pénitencier [penitɑ̃sje] *nm* prison. **◆pénitentiaire** *a* (*régime etc*) prison-.

pénombre [penɔ̃br] *nf* half-light, darkness.

pensée [pɑ̃se] *nf* **1** thought. **2** (*fleur*) pansy. **◆pens/er** *vi* to think (à of, about); **p. à qch/à faire qch** (*ne pas oublier*) to remember sth/to do sth; **p. à tout** (*prévoir*) to think of everything; **penses-tu!** you must be joking!, not at all!; **— *vt*** to think (que that); (*concevoir*) to think out; (*imaginer*) to imagine (que that); **je pensais rester** (*intention*) I was thinking of staying, I thought I'd stay; **je pense réussir** (*espoir*) I hope to succeed; **que pensez-vous de . . . ?** what do you think of *ou* about . . . ?; **p. du bien de** to think highly of. **◆-ant** *a* **bien p.** *Péj* or-

thodox. **◆-eur** *nm* thinker. **◆pensif, -ive** *a* thoughtful, pensive.

pension [pɑ̃sjɔ̃] *nf* **1** boarding school; (*somme, repas*) board; **être en p.** to board, be a boarder (**chez** with); **p.** (**de famille**) guesthouse, boarding house; **p. complète** full board. **2** (*allocation*) pension; **p. alimentaire** maintenance allowance. **◆pensionnaire** *nmf* (*élève*) boarder; (*d'hôtel*) resident; (*de famille*) lodger. **◆pensionnat** *nm* boarding school; (*élèves*) boarders. **◆pensionné, -ée** *nmf* pensioner.

pentagone [pɛ̃tagɔn] *nm* **le P.** *Am Pol* the Pentagon.

pentathlon [pɛ̃tatlɔ̃] *nm Sp* pentathlon.

pente [pɑ̃t] *nf* slope; **être en p.** to slope, be sloping.

Pentecôte [pɑ̃tkot] *nf* Whitsun, *Am* Pentecost.

pénurie [penyri] *nf* scarcity, shortage (**de** of).

pépère [pepɛr] **1** *nm Fam* grand(d)ad. **2** *a* (*tranquille*) *Fam* quiet and easy).

pépier [pepje] *vi* (*oiseau*) to cheep, chirp.

pépin [pepɛ̃] *nm* **1** (*de fruit*) pip, *Am* pit. **2** (*ennui*) *Fam* hitch, bother. **3** (*parapluie*) *Fam* brolly.

pépinière [pepinjɛr] *nf Bot* nursery.

pépite [pepit] *nf* (*gold*) nugget.

péquenaud, -aude [pekno, -od] *nmf Péj Arg* peasant, bumpkin.

perçant [pɛrsɑ̃] *a* (*cri, froid*) piercing; (*yeux*) sharp, keen.

percée [pɛrse] *nf* (*dans une forêt*) opening; (*avance technologique, attaque militaire*) breakthrough.

perce-neige [pɛrsənɛʒ] *nm ou f inv Bot* snowdrop.

perce-oreille [pɛrsɔrɛj] *nm* (*insecte*) earwig.

percepteur [pɛrseptœr] *nm* tax collector. **◆perceptible** *a* perceptible (à to), noticeable. **◆perception** *nf* **1** (*bureau*) tax office; (*d'impôt*) collection. **2** (*sensation*) perception.

perc/er [pɛrse] *vt* (*trouer*) to pierce; (*avec perceuse*) to drill (a hole in); (*trou, ouverture*) to make, drill; (*mystère etc*) to uncover; **p. une dent** (*bébé*) to cut a tooth; **— *vi*** (*soleil, ennemi, sentiment*) to break *ou* come through; (*abcès*) to burst. **◆-euse** *nf* drill.

percevoir* [pɛrsəvwar] *vt* **1** (*sensation*) to perceive; (*son*) to hear. **2** (*impôt*) to collect.

perche [pɛrʃ] *nf* **1** (*bâton*) pole; **saut à la p.** pole-vaulting. **2** (*poisson*) perch.

perch/er [pɛrʃe] *vi* (*oiseau*) to perch; (*volailles*) to roost; (*loger*) *Fam* to hang out; **—**

vt (*placer*) *Fam* to perch; **— se p.** *vpr* (*oiseau, personne*) to perch. ◆**—é a** perched. ◆**perchoir** *nm* perch; (*de volailles*) roost.

percolateur [pɛrkɔlatœr] *nm* (*de restaurant*) percolator.

percussion [pɛrkysjɔ̃] *nf Mus* percussion.

percutant [pɛrkytɑ̃] *a Fig* powerful.

percuter [pɛrkyte] *vt* (*véhicule*) to crash into; **— vi p. contre** to crash into.

perd/re [pɛrdr] *vt* to lose; (*gaspiller*) to waste; (*ruiner*) to ruin; (*habitude*) to get out of; **p. de vue** to lose sight off; **— vi** to lose; (*récipient, tuyau*) to leak; **j'y perds** I lose out, I lose on the deal; **— se p.** *vpr* (*s'égarer*) to get lost; (*dans les détails*) to lose oneself; (*disparaître*) to disappear; **je m'y perds** I'm lost ou confused. ◆**—ant, -ante** *a* (*billet*) losing; **— *nmf* loser. ◆**—u a** lost; wasted; (*malade*) finished; (*lieu*) isolated, in the middle of nowhere; **à ses moments perdus** in one's spare time; **une balle perdue** a stray bullet; **c'est du temps p.** it's a waste of time. ◆**perdition (en)** *adv* (*navire*) in distress.

perdrix [pɛrdri] *nf* partridge. ◆**perdreau, -x** *nm* young partridge.

père [pɛr] *nm* father; **Dupont p.** Dupont senior; **le p. Jean** *Fam* old John.

péremptoire [perɑ̃ptwar] *a* peremptory.

perfection [pɛrfɛksjɔ̃] *nf* perfection. ◆**perfectionn/er** *vt* to improve, perfect; **se p. en anglais**/*etc* to improve one's English/*etc*. ◆**—é a** (*machine etc*) advanced. ◆**—ement** *nm* improvement (**de** in, **par rapport à** on); **cours de p.** advanced ou refresher course. ◆**perfectionniste** *nmf* perfectionist.

perfide [pɛrfid] *a Litt* treacherous, perfidious. ◆**perfidie** *nf Litt* treachery.

perforer [pɛrfɔre] *vt* (*pneu, intestin etc*) to perforate; (*billet, carte*) to punch; **carte perforée** punch card. ◆**perforateur** *nm* (*appareil*) drill. ◆**perforation** *nf* perforation; (*trou*) punched hole. ◆**perforatrice** *nf* (*pour cartes*) *Tech* (*card*) punch. ◆**perforeuse** *nf* (*paper*) punch.

performance [pɛrfɔrmɑ̃s] *nf* (*d'athlète, de machine etc*) performance. ◆**performant** *a* (highly) efficient.

péricliter [periklite] *vi* to go to rack and ruin.

péril [peril] *nm* peril; **à tes risques et périls** at your own risk. ◆**périlleux, -euse** *a* perilous; **saut p.** somersault (*in mid air*).

périm/er [perime] *vi*, **— se p.** *vpr* laisser

(**se**) **p.** (*billet*) to allow to expire. ◆**—é a** expired; (*désuet*) outdated.

périmètre [perimɛtr] *nm* perimeter.

période [perjɔd] *nf* period. ◆**périodique** *a* periodic; **— *nm* (*revue*) periodical.

péripétie [peripesi] *nf* (unexpected) event.

périphérie [periferi] *nf* (*limite*) periphery; (*banlieue*) outskirts. ◆**périphérique** *a* (*quartier*) outlying, peripheral; **— *nm* (**boulevard**) p.** (motorway) ring road, *Am* beltway.

périphrase [perifraz] *nf* circumlocution.

périple [peripl] *nm* trip, tour.

pér/ir [perir] *vi* to perish, die. ◆**—issable** *a* (*denrée*) perishable.

périscope [periskɔp] *nm* periscope.

perle [pɛrl] *nf* (*bijou*) pearl; (*de bois, verre etc*) bead; (*personne*) *Fig* gem, pearl; (*erreur*) *Iron* howler, gem. ◆**perler** *vi* (*sueur*) to form beads; **grève perlée** go-slow, *Am* slow-down strike.

permanent, -ente [pɛrmanɑ̃, -ɑ̃t] **1** *a* permanent; (*spectacle*) *Cin* continuous; (*comité*) standing. **2** *nf* (*coiffure*) perm. ◆**permanence** *nf* permanence; (*service, bureau*) duty office; (*salle*) *Scol* study room; **être de p.** to be on duty; **en p.** permanently.

perméable [pɛrmeabl] *a* permeable.

permettre* [pɛrmɛtr] *vt* to allow, permit; **p. à qn de faire** (*permission, possibilité*) to allow ou permit s.o. to do; **permettez!** excuse me!; **vous permettez?** may I?; **se p. de faire** to allow oneself to do, take the liberty to do; **se p. qch** (*se payer*) to afford sth. ◆**permis** *a* allowed, permitted; **— *nm* (*autorisation*) permit, licence; **p. de conduire** (*carte*) driving licence, *Am* driver's license; **p. de travail** work permit. ◆**permission** *nf* permission; (*congé*) *Mil* leave; **demander la p.** to ask (for) permission (**de faire** to do).

permuter [pɛrmyte] *vt* to change round ou over, permutate. ◆**permutation** *nf* permutation.

pernicieux, -euse [pɛrnisjø, -øz] *a* (*nocif*) & *Méd* pernicious.

pérorer [perɔre] *vi Péj* to speechify.

Pérou [peru] *nm* Peru.

perpendiculaire [pɛrpɑ̃dikylɛr] *a* & *nf* perpendicular (**à** to).

perpétrer [pɛrpetre] *vt* (*crime*) to perpetrate.

perpétuel, -elle [pɛrpetɥɛl] *a* perpetual; (*fonction, rente*) for life. ◆**perpétuellement** *adv* perpetually. ◆**perpétuer** *vt* to

perpetuate. ◆**perpétuité (à)** *adv* in perpetuity; (*condamné*) for life.

perplexe [pɛrplɛks] *a* perplexed, puzzled. ◆**perplexité** *nf* perplexity.

perquisition [pɛrkizisjɔ̃] *nf* (house) search (*by police*). ◆**perquisitionner** *vti* to search.

perron [perɔ̃] *nm* (front) steps.

perroquet [perɔkɛ] *nm* parrot.

perruche [peryʃ] *nf* budgerigar, *Am* parakeet.

perruque [peryk] *nf* wig.

persan [persɑ̃] *a* (*langue, tapis, chat*) Persian; – *nm* (*langue*) Persian.

persécuter [persekyte] *vt* (*tourmenter*) to persecute; (*importuner*) to harass. ◆**persécuteur, -trice** *nmf* persecutor. ◆**persécution** *nf* persecution.

persévér/er [persevere] *vi* to persevere (dans in). ◆**—ant** *a* persevering. ◆**persévérance** *nf* perseverance.

persienne [persjɛn] *nf* (outside) shutter.

persil [pɛrsi] *nm* parsley.

persist/er [persiste] *vi* to persist (à faire in doing). ◆**—ant** *a* persistent; à feuilles persistantes (*arbre etc*) evergreen. ◆**persistance** *nf* persistence.

personnage [persɔnaʒ] *nm* (*célébrité*) (important) person; *Th Littér* character.

personnaliser [persɔnalize] *vt* to personalize; (*voiture*) to customize.

personnalité [persɔnalite] *nf* (*individualité, personnage*) personality.

personne [persɔn] 1 *nf* person; *pl* people; grande p. grown-up, adult; jolie p. pretty girl *ou* woman; en p. in person. 2 *pron* (*négatif*) nobody, no one; ne . . . p. nobody, no one; je ne vois p. I don't see anybody *ou* anyone; mieux que p. better than anybody *ou* anyone.

personnel, -elle [persɔnɛl] *a* personal; (*joueur, jeu*) individualistic. 2 *nm* staff, personnel. ◆**personnellement** *adv* personally.

personnifier [persɔnifje] *vt* to personify. ◆**personnification** *nf* personification.

perspective [perspektiv] *nf* (*art*) perspective; (*point de vue*) view; (*de paysage etc*) view; (*possibilité, espérance*) prospect; en p. *Fig* in view, in prospect.

perspicace [perspikas] *a* shrewd. ◆**perspicacité** *nf* shrewdness.

persuader [persɥade] *vt* to persuade (qn de faire s.o. to do); se p. que to be convinced that. ◆**persuasif, -ive** *a* persuasive.

◆**persuasion** *nf* persuasion; (*croyance*) conviction.

perte [pɛrt] *nf* loss; (*gaspillage*) waste (de temps/d'argent of time/money); (*ruine*) ruin; à p. de vue as far as the eye can see; vendre à p. to sell at a loss.

pertinent [pɛrtinɑ̃] *a* relevant, pertinent. ◆**pertinence** *nf* relevance.

perturb/er [pɛrtyrbe] *vt* (*trafic, cérémonie etc*) to disrupt; (*ordre public, personne*) to disturb. ◆**—é** *a* (*troublé*) *Fam* perturbed. ◆**perturbateur, -trice** *a* (*élément*) disruptive; – *nmf* trouble-maker. ◆**perturbation** *nf* disruption; (*crise*) upheaval.

péruvien, -ienne [peryvjɛ̃, -jɛn] *a & nmf* Peruvian.

pervenche [pɛrvɑ̃ʃ] *nf Bot* periwinkle.

pervers [pɛrvɛr] *a* wicked, perverse; (*dépravé*) perverted. ◆**perversion** *nf* perversion. ◆**perversité** *nf* perversity. ◆**pervert/ir** *vt* to pervert. ◆**—i, -ie** *nmf* pervert.

pesant [pəzɑ̃] *a* heavy, weighty; – *nm* valoir son p. d'or to be worth one's weight in gold. ◆**pesamment** *adv* heavily. ◆**pesanteur** *nf* heaviness; (*force*) *Phys* gravity.

pes/er [pəze] *vt* to weigh; – *vi* to weigh; p. lourd to be heavy; (*argument etc*) *Fig* to carry (a lot of) weight; p. sur (*appuyer*) to bear down upon; (*influer*) to bear upon; p. sur qn (*menace*) to hang over s.o.; p. sur l'estomac to lie (heavily) on the stomach. ◆**—ée** *nf* weighing; *Boxe* weigh-in; (*effort*) pressure. ◆**—age** *nm* weighing. ◆**pèse-bébé** *nm* (baby) scales. ◆**pèse-personne** *nm* (bathroom) scales.

pessimisme [pesimism] *nm* pessimism. ◆**pessimiste** *a* pessimistic; – *nmf* pessimist.

peste [pɛst] *nf Méd* plague; (*personne, enfant*) *Fig* pest.

pester [pɛste] *vi* to curse; p. contre qch/qn to curse sth/s.o.

pestilentiel, -ielle [pɛstilɑ̃sjɛl] *a* fetid, stinking.

pétale [petal] *nm* petal.

pétanque [petɑ̃k] *nf* (*jeu*) bowls.

pétarades [petarad] *nfpl* (*de moto etc*) backfiring. ◆**pétarader** *vi* to backfire.

pétard [petar] *nm* (*explosif*) firecracker, banger.

péter [pete] *vi Fam* (*éclater*) to go bang *ou* pop; (*se rompre*) to snap.

pétill/er [petije] *vi* (*eau, champagne*) to sparkle, fizz; (*bois, feu*) to crackle; (*yeux*) to sparkle. ◆**—ant** *a* (*eau, vin, regard*) sparkling.

petit, -ite [p(ə)ti, -it] *a* small, little; (*de taille*) short; (*bruit, espoir, coup*) slight; (*jeune*) young, small; (*mesquin, insignifiant*) petty; **tout p.** tiny; **un bon p. travail** a nice little job; **un p. Français** a (little) French boy; – *nmf* (little) boy, (little) girl; (*personne*) small person; *Scol* junior; *pl* (*d'animal*) young; (*de chien*) pups, young; (*de chat*) kittens, young; – *adv* **p. à p.** little by little. **◆p.-bourgeois** *a* *Péj* middle-class. **◆p.-suisse** *nm* soft cheese (*for dessert*). **◆petitement** *adv* (*chichement*) shabbily, poorly. **◆petitesse** *nf* (*de taille*) smallness; (*mesquinerie*) pettiness.

petit-fils [p(ə)tifis] *nm* (*pl petits-fils*) grandson, grandchild. **◆petite-fille** *nf* (*pl petites-filles*) granddaughter, grandchild. **◆petits-enfants** *nmpl* grandchildren.

pétition [petisjɔ̃] *nf* petition.

pétrifier [petrifje] *vt* (*de peur, d'émoi etc*) to petrify.

pétrin [petrɛ̃] *nm* (*situation*) *Fam* fix; **dans le p.** in a fix.

pétrir [petrir] *vt* to knead.

pétrole [petrɔl] *nm* oil, petroleum; **p. (lampant)** paraffin, *Am* kerosene; **nappe de p.** (*sur la mer*) oil slick. **◆pétrolier, -ière** *a* (*industrie*) oil-; – *nm* (*navire*) oil tanker. **◆pétrolifère** *a* **gisement p.** oil field.

pétulant [petylɑ̃] *a* exuberant.

pétunia [petynja] *nm* *Bot* petunia.

peu [pø] *adv* (*lire, manger etc*) not much, little; **elle mange p.** she doesn't eat much, she eats little; **un p.** (*lire, surpris etc*) a bit, a little; **p. de sel/de temps**/*etc* not much salt/time/*etc*, little salt/time/*etc*; **un p. de fromage**/*etc* a little cheese/*etc*; **le p. de fromage que j'ai** the little cheese I have; **p. de gens/de livres**/*etc* few people/books/*etc*, not many people/books/*etc*; **p. sont...** few are...; **un (tout) petit p.** a (tiny) little bit; **p. intéressant/souvent**/*etc* not very interesting/often/*etc*; **p. de chose** not much; **p. à p.** gradually, little by little; **à p. près** more or less; **p. après/avant** shortly after/before.

peuplade [pœplad] *nf* tribe.

peuple [pœpl] *nm* (*nation, masse*) people; **les gens du p.** the common people. **◆peupl/er** *vt* to populate, people. **◆–é** *a* (*quartier etc*) populated (**de** with).

peuplier [pøplije] *nm* (*arbre, bois*) poplar.

peur [pœr] *nf* fear; **avoir p.** to be afraid ou frightened ou scared (**de** of); **faire p. à** to frighten; scare; **de p. que** (+ *sub*) for fear that; **de p. de faire** for fear of doing.

◆peureux, -euse *a* fearful, easily frightened.

peut, peux [pø] *voir* **pouvoir 1.**

peut-être [pøtɛtr] *adv* perhaps, maybe; **p.-être qu'il viendra** perhaps ou maybe he'll come.

phallique [falik] *a* phallic. **◆phallocrate** *nm* *Péj* male chauvinist.

phare [far] *nm* *Nau* lighthouse; *Aut* headlight, headlamp; **rouler pleins phares** *Aut* to drive on full headlights; **faire un appel de phares** *Aut* to flash one's lights.

pharmacie [farmasi] *nf* chemist's shop, *Am* drugstore; (*science*) pharmacy; (*armoire*) medicine cabinet. **◆pharmaceutique** *a* pharmaceutical. **◆pharmacien, -ienne** *nmf* chemist, pharmacist, *Am* druggist.

pharynx [farɛ̃ks] *nm* *Anat* pharynx.

phase [faz] *nf* phase.

phénomène [fenɔmɛn] *nm* phenomenon; (*personne*) *Fam* eccentric. **◆phénoménal, -aux** *a* phenomenal.

philanthrope [filɑ̃trɔp] *nmf* philanthropist. **◆philanthropique** *a* philanthropic.

philatélie [filateli] *nf* philately, stamp collecting. **◆philatélique** *a* philatelic. **◆philatéliste** *nmf* philatelist, stamp collector.

philharmonique [filarmɔnik] *a* philharmonic.

philosophe [filozɔf] *nmf* philosopher; – *a* (*sage, résigné*) philosophical. **◆philosopher** *vi* to philosophize (**sur** about). **◆philosophie** *nf* philosophy. **◆philosophique** *a* philosophical.

phobie [fɔbi] *nf* phobia.

phonétique [fɔnetik] *a* phonetic; – *nf* phonetics.

phonographe [fɔnɔgraf] *nm* gramophone, *Am* phonograph.

phoque [fɔk] *nm* (*animal marin*) seal.

phosphate [fɔsfat] *nm* *Ch* phosphate.

phosphore [fɔsfɔr] *nm* *Ch* phosphorus.

photo [fɔto] *nf* photo; (*art*) photography; **prendre une p. de, prendre en p.** to take a photo of; – *a inv* **appareil p.** camera. **◆photocopie** *nf* photocopy. **◆photocopier** *vt* to photocopy. **◆photocopieur** *nm*, **◆photocopieuse** *nf* (*machine*) photocopier. **◆photogénique** *a* photogenic. **◆photographe** *nmf* photographer. **◆photographie** *nf* (*art*) photography; (*image*) photograph. **◆photographier** *vt* to photograph. **◆photographique** *a* photographic. ◆**photomaton**® *nm* (*appareil*) photo booth.

phrase [fraz] *nf* (*mots*) sentence.

physicien, -ienne [fizisjɛ̃, -jɛn] *nmf* physicist.

physiologie [fizjɔlɔʒi] *nf* physiology. ◆**physiologique** *a* physiological.

physionomie [fizjɔnɔmi] *nf* face.

physique [fizik] **1** *a* physical; — *nm* (*corps, aspect*) physique; **au p.** physically. **2** *nf* (*science*) physics. ◆**—ment** *adv* physically.

piaffer [pjafe] *vi* (*cheval*) to stamp; **p. d'impatience** *Fig* to fidget impatiently.

piailler [pjɑje] *vi* (*oiseau*) to cheep; (*enfant*) *Fam* to squeal.

piano [pjano] *nm* piano; **p. droit/à queue** upright/grand piano. ◆**pianiste** *nmf* pianist.

piaule [pjol] *nf* (*chambre*) *Arg* room, pad.

pic [pik] *nm* **1** (*cime*) peak. **2** (*outil*) pick(axe); **p. à glace** ice pick. **3** (*oiseau*) woodpecker.

pic (à) [apik] *adv* (*verticalement*) sheer; **couler à p.** to sink to the bottom; **arriver à p.** *Fig* to arrive in the nick of time.

pichet [piʃɛ] *nm* jug, pitcher.

pickpocket [pikpɔkɛt] *nm* pickpocket.

pick-up [pikœp] *nm inv* (*camionnette*) pick-up truck.

picorer [pikɔre] *vti* to peck.

picoter [pikɔte] *vt* (*yeux*) to make smart; (*jambes*) to make tingle; **les yeux me picotent** my eyes are smarting.

pie [pi] **1** *nf* (*oiseau*) magpie. **2** *a inv* (*couleur*) piebald.

pièce [pjɛs] *nf* **1** (*de maison etc*) room. **2** (*morceau, objet etc*) piece; (*de pantalon*) patch; (*écrit*) *Jur* document; **p. (de monnaie)** coin; **p.** (**de théâtre**) play; (**d'artillerie**) gun; **p. d'identité** proof of identity, identity card; **p. d'eau** pool, pond; **pièces détachées** *ou* **de rechange** (*de véhicule etc*) spare parts; **cinq dollars**/*etc* (**la**) **p.** five dollars/*etc* each; **travailler à la p.** to do piecework.

pied [pje] *nm* foot; (*de meuble*) leg; (*de verre, lampe*) base; *Phot* stand; **p. de salade** a head of lettuce; **à p.** on foot; **aller à p.** to walk, go on foot; **au p. de** at the foot *ou* bottom of; **au p. de la lettre** *Fig* literally; **avoir p.** (*nageur*) to have a footing, touch the bottom; **coup de p.** kick; **donner un coup de p.** to kick (**à qn** s.o.); **sur p.** (*debout, levé*) up and about; **sur ses pieds** (*malade guéri*) up and about; **sur un p. d'égalité** on an equal footing; **comme un p.** (*mal*) *Fam* dreadfully; **faire un p. de nez** to thumb

one's nose (**à** at); **mettre sur p.** (*projet*) to set up. ◆**p.-noir** *nmf* (*pl* **pieds-noirs**) Algerian Frenchman *ou* Frenchwoman.

piédestal, -aux [pjedestal, -o] *nm* pedestal.

piège [pjɛʒ] *nm* (*pour animal*) & *Fig* trap. ◆**piéger** *vt* (*animal*) to trap; (*voiture etc*) to booby-trap; **engin piégé** booby trap; **lettre/colis/voiture piégé(e)** letter/parcel/car bomb.

pierre [pjɛr] *nf* stone; (*précieuse*) gem, stone; **p. à briquet** flint; **geler à p. fendre** to freeze (*rock*) hard. ◆**pierreries** *nfpl* gems, precious stones. ◆**pierreux, -euse** *a* stony.

piété [pjete] *nf* piety.

piétiner [pjetine] *vt* (*fouler aux pieds*) to trample (on); — *vi* to stamp (one's feet); (*marcher sur place*) to mark time; (*ne pas avancer*) *Fig* to make no headway.

piéton¹ [pjetɔ̃] *nm* pedestrian. ◆**piéton², -onne** *a*, ◆**piétonnier, -ière** *a* (*rue etc*) pedestrian-.

piètre [pjɛtr] *a* wretched, poor.

pieu, -x [pjø] *nm* **1** (*piquet*) post, stake. **2** (*lit*) *Fam* bed.

pieuvre [pjœvr] *nf* octopus.

pieux, -euse [pjø, -øz] *a* pious.

pif [pif] *nm* (*nez*) *Fam* nose. ◆**pifomètre (au)** *adv* (*sans calcul*) *Fam* at a rough guess.

pigeon [piʒɔ̃] *nm* pigeon; (*personne*) *Fam* dupe; **p. voyageur** carrier pigeon. ◆**pigeonner** *vt* (*voler*) *Fam* to rip off.

piger [piʒe] *vti Fam* to understand.

pigment [pigmɑ̃] *nm* pigment.

pignon [piɲɔ̃] *nm* (*de maison etc*) gable.

pile [pil] **1** *nf* *El* battery; (*atomique*) pile; **radio à piles** battery radio. **2** *nf* (*tas*) pile; **en p. in a pile. 3** *nf* (*de pont*) pier. **4** *nf* **p. (ou face)?** heads (or tails)?; **jouer à p. ou face** to toss up. **5** *adv* **s'arrêter p.** to stop short *ou* dead; **à deux heures p.** on the dot of two.

piler [pile] **1** *vt* (*amandes*) to grind; (*ail*) to crush. **2** *vi* (*en voiture*) to stop dead. ◆**pilonner** *vt Mil* to bombard, shell.

pilier [pilje] *nm* pillar.

pilon [pilɔ̃] *nm* (*de poulet*) drumstick.

piller [pije] *vti* to loot, pillage. ◆**pillage** *nm* looting, pillage. ◆**pillard, -arde** *nmf* looter.

pilori [pilɔri] *nm* **mettre au p.** *Fig* to pillory.

pilote [pilɔt] *nm* *Av* *Nau* pilot; (*de voiture, char*) driver; (*guide*) *Fig* guide; — *a* **usine(-)/projet(-)p.** pilot factory/plan. ◆**pilot/er** *vt* *Av* to fly, pilot; *Nau* to pilot; **p. qn** to show s.o. around. ◆**—age** *nm* piloting; **école de p.** flying school; **poste de p.** cockpit.

pilotis [piloti] *nm* (*pieux*) *Archit* piles.

pilule [pilyl] *nf* pill; **prendre la p.** (*femme*) to be on the pill; **se mettre à/arrêter la p.** to go on/off the pill.

piment [pimã] *nm* pimento, pepper. ◆**pimenté** *a Culin & Fig* spicy.

pimpant [pɛ̃pã] *a* pretty, spruce.

pin [pɛ̃] *nm* (*bois, arbre*) pine; **pomme de p.** pine cone.

pinailler [pinaje] *vi Fam* to quibble, split hairs.

pinard [pinar] *nm* (*vin*) *Fam* wine.

pince [pɛ̃s] *nf* (*outil*) pliers; *Méd* forceps; (*de cycliste*) clip; (*levier*) crowbar; *pl* (*de crabe*) pincers; **p. (à linge)** (clothes) peg *ou Am* pin; **p. (à épiler)** tweezers; **p. (à sucre)** sugar tongs; **p. à cheveux** hairgrip. ◆**pinc/er** *vt* to pinch; (*corde*) *Mus* to pluck; **p. qn** (*arrêter*) *Jur* to nab s.o., pinch s.o.; **se p. le doigt** to get one's finger caught (**dans** in). ◆**-é** *a* (*air*) stiff, constrained. ◆**-ée** *nf* (*de sel etc*) pinch (**de** of). ◆**pincettes** *nfpl* (*fire*) tongs; (*d'horloger*) tweezers. ◆**pinçon** *nm* pinch (mark).

pinceau, -x [pɛ̃so] *nm* (paint)brush.

pince-sans-rire [pɛ̃ssãrir] *nm inv* person of dry humour.

pinède [pined] *nf* pine forest.

pingouin [pɛ̃gwɛ̃] *nm* auk, penguin.

ping-pong [piŋpɔ̃g] *nm* ping-pong.

pingre [pɛ̃gr] *a* stingy; — *nmf* skinflint.

pinson [pɛ̃sɔ̃] *nm* (*oiseau*) chaffinch.

pintade [pɛ̃tad] *nf* guinea fowl.

pin-up [pinœp] *nf inv* (*fille*) pinup.

pioche [pjɔʃ] *nf* pick(axe). ◆**piocher** *vti* (*creuser*) to dig (with a pick).

pion [pjɔ̃] *nm* **1** (*au jeu de dames*) piece; *Échecs & Fig* pawn. **2** *Scol* master (in charge of discipline).

pionnier [pjɔnje] *nm* pioneer.

pipe [pip] *nf* (*de fumeur*) pipe; **fumer la p.** to smoke a pipe.

pipeau, -x [pipo] *nm* (*flûte*) pipe.

pipe-line [piplin] *nm* pipeline.

pipi [pipi] *nm* **faire p.** *Fam* to go for a pee.

pique [pik] **1** *nm* (*couleur*) *Cartes* spades. **2** *nf* (*arme*) pike. **3** *nf* (*allusion*) cutting remark.

pique-assiette [pikasjɛt] *nmf inv* scrounger.

pique-nique [piknik] *nm* picnic. ◆**pique-niquer** *vi* to picnic.

piqu/er [pike] *vt* (*entamer, percer*) to prick; (*langue, yeux*) to sting; (*curiosité*) to rouse; (*coudre*) to (machine-)stitch; (*édredon, couvre-lit*) to quilt; (*crise de nerfs*) to have;

(*maladie*) to get; **p. qn** (*abeille*) to sting s.o.; (*serpent*) to bite s.o.; *Méd* to give s.o. an injection; **p. qch dans** (*enfoncer*) to stick sth into; **p. qn** (*arrêter*) *Jur* to nab s.o., pinch s.o.; **p. qch** (*voler*) *Fam* to pinch sth; **p. une colère** to fly into a rage; **p. une tête** to plunge headlong; — *vi* (*avion*) to dive; (*moutarde etc*) to prick oneself; **se p. de faire qch** to pride oneself on being able to do sth. ◆**-ant** *a* (*épine*) prickly; (*froid*) biting; (*sauce, goût*) pungent, piquant; (*mot*) cutting; (*détail*) spicy; — *nm Bot* prickle, thorn; (*d'animal*) spine, prickle. ◆**-é** *a* (*meuble*) worm-eaten; (*fou*) *Fam* crazy; — *nm Av* (nose)dive; **descente en p.** *Av* nosedive. ◆**-eur, -euse** *nmf* (*sur machine à coudre*) machinist. ◆**piqûre** *nf* (*d'épingle*) prick; (*d'abeille*) sting; (*de serpent*) bite; (*trou*) hole; *Méd* injection; (*point*) stitch.

piquet [pikɛ] *nm* **1** (*pieu*) stake, picket; (*de tente*) peg. **2 p. (de grève)** picket (line), strike picket. **3 au p.** *Scol* in the corner.

piqueté [pikte] *a* **p.** dotted with.

pirate [pirat] *nm* pirate; **p. de l'air** hijacker; — *a* (*radio, bateau*) pirate-. ◆**piraterie** *nf* piracy; (*acte*) act of piracy; **p. (aérienne)** hijacking.

pire [pir] *a* worse (**que** than); **le p. moment/résultat/etc** the worst moment/ result/etc; — *nmf* **le** *ou* **la p.** the worst (one); **le p. de tout** the worst (thing) of all; **au p.** at (the very) worst; **s'attendre au p.** to expect the (very) worst.

pirogue [pirɔg] *nf* canoe, dugout.

pis [pi] **1** *nm* (*de vache*) udder. **2** *a inv & adv Litt* worse; **de mal en p.** from bad to worse; — *nm* **le p.** *Litt* the worst.

pis-aller [pizale] *nm inv* (*personne, solution*) stopgap.

piscine [pisin] *nf* swimming pool.

pissenlit [pisɑ̃li] *nm* dandelion.

pistache [pistaʃ] *nf* (*fruit, parfum*) pistachio.

piste [pist] *nf* (*trace de personne ou d'animal*) track, trail; *Sp* track, racetrack; (*de magnétophone*) track; *Av* runway; (*de cirque*) ring; (*de patinage*) rink; (*pour chevaux*) racecourse, racetrack; **p. cyclable** cycle track, *Am* bicycle path; **p. de danse** dance floor; **p. de ski** ski run; **tour de p.** *Sp* lap.

pistolet [pistɔlɛ] *nm* gun, pistol; (*de peintre*) spray gun.

piston [pistɔ̃] *nm* **1** *Aut* piston. **2 avoir du p.** (*appui*) to have connections. ◆**pistonner** *vt* (*appuyer*) to pull strings for.

pitié [pitje] *nf* pity; **j'ai p. de lui, il me fait p.** I pity him, I feel sorry for him. ◆**piteux, -euse** *a Iron* pitiful. ◆**pitoyable** *a* pitiful.

piton [pitɔ̃] *nm* **1** (*à crochet*) hook. **2** *Géog* peak.

pitre [pitr] *nm* clown. ◆**pitrerie(s)** *nf(pl)* clowning.

pittoresque [pitɔrɛsk] *a* picturesque.

pivert [piver] *nm* (*oiseau*) woodpecker.

pivoine [pivwan] *nf Bot* peony.

pivot [pivo] *nm* pivot; (*personne*) *Fig* linchpin, mainspring. ◆**pivoter** *vi* (*personne*) to swing round; (*fauteuil*) to swivel; (*porte*) to revolve.

pizza [pidza] *nf* pizza. ◆**pizzeria** *nf* pizza parlour.

placage [plakaʒ] *nm* (*revêtement*) facing; (*en bois*) veneer.

placard [plakar] *nm* **1** (*armoire*) cupboard, *Am* closet. **2** (*pancarte*) poster. ◆**placarder** *vt* (*affiche*) to post (up); (*mur*) to cover with posters.

place [plas] *nf* (*endroit, rang*) & *Sp* place; (*occupée par qn ou qch*) room; (*lieu public*) square; (*siège*) seat, place; (*prix d'un trajet Aut* fare; (*emploi*) job, position; **p. (forte)** *Mil* fortress; **p. (de parking)** (*parking*) space; **p. (financière)** (*money*) market; **à la p.** (*échange*) instead (**de** of); **à votre p.** in your place; **sur p.** on the spot; **en p.** (*objet*) in place; **ne pas tenir en p.** to be unable to keep still; **mettre en p.** to install, set up; **faire p. à** to give way to; **changer qch de p.** to move sth.

plac/er [plase] *vt* (*mettre*) to put, place; (*situer*) to place, position; (*invité, spectateur*) to seat; (*argent*) to invest, place (**dans** in); (*vendre*) to place, sell; **p. un mot** to get a word in edgeways ou *Am* sideways; **— se p.** *vpr* (*personne*) to take up a position, place oneself; (*objet*) to be put ou placed; (*cheval, coureur*) to be placed; **se p. troisième/etc** *Sp* to come ou be third/etc. ◆**—é** *a* (*objet*) & *Sp* placed; **bien/mal p. pour faire** in a good/bad position to do; **les gens haut placés** people in high places. ◆**—ement** *nm* (*d'argent*) investment.

placide [plasid] *a* placid.

plafond [plafɔ̃] *nm* ceiling. ◆**plafonnier** *nm Aut* roof light.

plage [plaʒ] *nf* **1** beach; (*ville*) (*seaside*) resort. **2** (*sur disque*) track. **3 p. arrière** *Aut* parcel shelf.

plagiat [plaʒja] *nm* plagiarism. ◆**plagier** *vt* to plagiarize.

plaid [plɛd] *nm* travelling rug.

plaider [plede] *vti Jur* to plead. ◆**plaideur,**

-euse *nmf* litigant. ◆**plaidoirie** *nf Jur* speech (for the defence). ◆**plaidoyer** *nm* plea.

plaie [plɛ] *nf* (*blessure*) wound; (*coupure*) cut; (*corvée, personne*) *Fig* nuisance.

plaignant, -ante [plɛɲɑ̃, -ɑ̃t] *nmf Jur* plaintiff.

plaindre* [plɛ̃dr] **1** *vt* to feel sorry for, pity. **2 se p.** *vpr* (*protester*) to complain (**de** about, **que** that); **se p. de** (*maux de tête etc*) to complain of ou about. ◆**plainte** *nf* complaint; (*cri*) moan, groan. ◆**plaintif, -ive** *a* sorrowful, plaintive.

plaine [plɛn] *nf Géog* plain.

plaire* [plɛr] *vi & v imp* **p. à** to please; **elle lui plaît** he likes her, she pleases him; **ça me plaît** I like it; **il me plaît de faire** I like doing; **s'il vous** ou **te plaît** please; **— se p.** *vpr* (*à Paris etc*) to like ou enjoy it; (*l'un l'autre*) to like each other.

plaisance [plɛzɑ̃s] *nf* **bateau de p.** pleasure boat; **navigation de p.** yachting.

plaisant [plɛzɑ̃] *a* (*drôle*) amusing; (*agréable*) pleasing; **— nm mauvais p.** *Péj* joker. ◆**plaisanter** *vi* to joke, jest; **p. avec qch** to trifle with sth; **— vt** to tease. ◆**plaisanterie** *nf* joke, jest; (*bagatelle*) trifle; **par p.** for a joke. ◆**plaisantin** *nm Péj* joker.

plaisir [plɛzir] *nm* pleasure; **faire p. à** to please; **faites-moi le p. de . . .** would you be good enough to . . . ; **pour le p.** for fun, for the fun of it; **au p. (de vous revoir)** see you again sometime.

plan [plɑ̃] **1** *nm* (*projet, dessin*) plan; (*de ville*) plan, map; (*niveau*) *Géom* plane; **au premier p.** in the foreground; **gros p.** *Phot Cin* close-up; **sur le p. politique/etc** from the political/etc viewpoint, politically/etc; **de premier p.** (*question etc*) major; **p. d'eau** stretch of water; **laisser en p.** (*abandonner*) to ditch. **2** *a* (*plat*) even, flat.

planche [plɑ̃ʃ] *nf* **1** board, plank; **p. à repasser/à dessin** ironing/drawing board; **p. (à roulettes)** skateboard; **p. (de surf)** surfboard; **p. (à voile)** sailboard; **faire de la p. (à voile)** to go windsurfing; **faire la p.** to float on one's back. **2** (*illustration*) plate. **3** (*de légumes*) bed, plot.

plancher [plɑ̃ʃe] *nm* floor.

plan/er [plane] *vi* (*oiseau*) to glide, hover; (*avion*) to glide; **p. sur qn** (*mystère, danger*) to hang over s.o.; **vol plané** glide. ◆**—eur** *nm* (*avion*) glider.

planète [planɛt] *nf* planet. ◆**planétaire** *a* planetary. ◆**planétarium** *nm* planetarium.

planifier [planifje] *vt Écon* to plan. ◆**pla-**

nification nf Écon planning. ◆**planning** nm (industriel, commercial) planning; **p** familial family planning.

planque [plɑ̃k] nf 1 (travail) Fam cushy job. 2 (lieu) Fam hideout. ◆**planquer** vt, — **se p.** vpr Fam to hide.

plant [plɑ̃] nm (plante) seedling; (de légumes etc) bed.

plante [plɑ̃t] nf 1 Bot plant; **p. d'appartement** house plant; **jardin des plantes** botanical gardens. 2 **p. des pieds** sole (of the foot). ◆**plant/er** vt (arbre, plante etc) to plant; (clou, couteau) to drive in; (tente, drapeau, échelle) to put up; (mettre) to put (sur on, contre against); (regard) to fix (sur on); **p. là** qn to leave s.o. standing; **se p. devant** qn to plant oneself in front of. ◆**—é** a (immobile) standing; **bien p.** (personne) sturdy. ◆**plantation** nf (action) planting; (terrain) bed; (de café, d'arbres etc) plantation. ◆**planteur** nm plantation owner.

planton [plɑ̃tɔ̃] nm Mil orderly.

plantureux, -euse [plɑ̃tyrø, -øz] a (repas etc) abundant.

plaque [plak] nf plate; (de verre, métal) sheet, plate; (de verglas) sheet; (de marbre) slab; (de chocolat) bar; (commémorative) plaque; (tache) Méd blotch; **p. chauffante** Culin hotplate; **p. tournante** (carrefour) Fig centre; **p. minéralogique, p. d'immatriculation** Aut number ou Am license plate; **p. dentaire** (dental) plaque.

plaqu/er [plake] vt (métal, bijou) to plate; (bois) to veneer; (cheveux) to plaster (down); Rugby to tackle; (aplatir) to flatten (contre against); (abandonner) Fam to give (sth) up; **p.** qn Fam to ditch s.o.; **se p. contre** to flatten oneself against. ◆**—é** a (bijou) plated; **p. or** gold-plated; — nm **p. or** gold plate. ◆**—age** nm Rugby tackle.

plasma [plasma] nm Méd plasma.

plastic [plastik] nm plastic explosive. ◆**plastiquer** vt to blow up.

plastique [plastik] a (art, substance) plastic; **matière p.** plastic; — nm (matière) plastic; **en p.** (bouteille etc) plastic.

plastron [plastrɔ̃] nm shirtfront.

plat [pla] 1 a flat; (mer) calm, smooth; (fade) flat, dull; **à fond p.** flat-bottomed; **à p. ventre** flat on one's face; (pneu, batterie) flat; (déprimé, épuisé) Fam low; **poser à p.** to put ou lay (down) flat; **tomber à p.** to fall down flat; **assiette plate** dinner plate; **calme p.** dead calm; — nm (de la main) flat. 2 nm (récipient, mets) dish; (partie du repas) course; '**p. du jour**' (au restaurant) 'today's special'.

platane [platan] nm plane tree.

plateau, -x [plato] nm (pour servir) tray; (de balance) pan; (de tourne-disque) turntable; (plate-forme) Cin TV set; Th stage; Géog plateau; **p. à fromages** cheeseboard.

plate-bande [platbɑ̃d] nf (pl plates-bandes) flower bed.

plate-forme [platfɔrm] nf (pl plates-formes) platform; **p.-forme pétrolière** oil rig.

platine [platin] 1 nm (métal) platinum. 2 nf (d'électrophone) deck. ◆**platiné** a (cheveux) platinum, platinum-blond(e).

platitude [platityd] nf platitude.

plâtre [plɑtr] nm (matière) plaster; **un p.** Méd a plaster cast; **dans le p.** Méd in plaster; **les plâtres** (d'une maison etc) the plasterwork; **p. à mouler** plaster of Paris. ◆**plâtr/er** vt (mur) to plaster; (membre) to put in plaster. ◆**—age** nm plastering. ◆**plâtrier** nm plasterer.

plausible [plozibl] a plausible.

plébiscite [plebisit] nm plebiscite.

plein [plɛ̃] a (rempli, complet) full; (paroi) solid; (ivre) Fam tight; **p. de** full of; **en pleine mer** on the open sea; **en p. visage/etc** right in the middle of the face/etc; **en p. jour** in broad daylight; — prép & adv **des billes p. les poches** pockets full of marbles; **du chocolat p. la figure** chocolate all over one's face; **p. de lettres/d'argent/etc** (beaucoup de) Fam lots of letters/money/etc; **à p.** (travailler) to full capacity; — nm **faire le p.** Aut to fill up (the tank); **battre son p.** (fête) to be in full swing. ◆**pleinement** adv fully.

pléonasme [pleɔnasm] nm (expression) redundancy.

pléthore [pletɔr] nf plethora.

pleurer [plœre] vi to cry, weep (sur over); — vt (regretter) to mourn (for). ◆**pleureur** a **saule p.** weeping willow. ◆**pleurnicher** vi to snivel, grizzle. ◆**pleurs (en)** adv in tears.

pleurésie [plœrezi] nf Méd pleurisy.

pleuvoir* [pløvwar] v imp to rain; **il pleut** it's raining; — vi (coups etc) to rain down (sur on).

pli [pli] nm 1 (de papier etc) fold; (de jupe, robe) pleat; (de pantalon, de bouche) crease; (de bras) bend; (faux) p. crease; **mise en plis** (coiffure) set. 2 (enveloppe) Com envelope, letter; **sous p. séparé** under separate cover. 3 Cartes trick. 4 (habitude) habit; **prendre le p. de faire** to get into the habit of doing. ◆**pli/er** vt to fold; (courber) to bend; **p.** qn à to submit s.o. to; — vi (branche) to bend; — **se p.** vpr (lit, chaise *etc*) to fold (up); **se p. à** to submit to, give in to. ◆**—ant** *a* (*chaise etc*) folding; (*parapluie*) telescopic; — *nm* folding stool. ◆**—able** *a* (*chaise etc*) folding; (*action*) folding.

plinthe [plɛ̃t] *nf* skirting board, *Am* baseboard.

pliss/er [plise] *vt* (*jupe, robe*) to pleat; (*froisser*) to crease; (*lèvres*) to pucker; (*front*) to wrinkle, crease; (*yeux*) to screw up. ◆**—é** *nm* pleating, pleats.

plomb [plɔ̃] *nm* (*métal*) lead; (*fusible*) *Él* fuse; (*poids pour rideau etc*) lead weight; *pl* (*de chasse*) lead shot, buckshot; **de p.** (*tuyau etc*) lead-; (*sommeil*) *Fig* heavy; (*soleil*) blazing; (*ciel*) leaden. ◆**plomb/er** *vt* (*dent*) to fill; (*colis*) to seal (with lead). ◆**—é** *a* (*teint*) leaden. ◆**—age** *nm* (*de dent*) filling.

plombier [plɔ̃bje] *nm* plumber. ◆**plomberie** *nf* (*métier, installations*) plumbing.

plong/er [plɔ̃ʒe] *vi* (*personne, avion etc*) to dive, plunge; (*route, regard*) *Fig* to plunge; — *vt* (*mettre, enfoncer*) to plunge, thrust (**dans** into); **se p. dans** (*lecture etc*) to immerse oneself in. ◆**—eant** *a* (*décolleté*) plunging; (*vue*) bird's eye-. ◆**—é** *a* **dans** (*lecture etc*) immersed *ou* deep in. ◆**—ée** *nf* diving; (*de sous-marin*) submersion; **en p.** (*sous-marin*) submerged. ◆**plongeoir** *nm* diving board. ◆**plongeon** *nm* dive. ◆**plongeur, -euse** *nmf* diver; (*employé de restaurant*) dishwasher.

plouf [pluf] *nm & int* splash.

ployer [plwaje] *vti* to bend.

plu [ply] *voir* **plaire, pleuvoir.**

pluie [plɥi] *nf* rain; **une p.** (*averse*) & *Fig* a shower; **sous la p.** in the rain.

plume [plym] *nf* **1** (*d'oiseau*) feather. **2** (*pour écrire*) *Hist* quill (pen); (*pointe en acier*) (pen) nib; **stylo à p.** (fountain) pen; **vivre de sa p.** *Fig* to live by one's pen. ◆**plumage** *nm* plumage. ◆**plumeau, -x** *nm* feather duster. ◆**plumer** *vt* (*volaille*) to pluck; **p. qn** (*voler*) *Fig* to fleece s.o. ◆**plumet** *nm* plume. ◆**plumier** *nm* pencil box, pen box.

plupart (la) [laplypar] *nf* most; **la p. des cas/etc** most cases/etc; **la p. du temps** most of the time; **la p. d'entre eux** most of them; **pour la p.** mostly.

pluriel, -ielle [plyrjɛl] *a & nm Gram* plural; **au p.** (*nom*) plural, in the plural.

plus¹ [ply] ([plys] *before vowel,* [plys] *in end position*) **1** *adv comparatif* (*travailler etc*) more (**que** than); **p. d'un kilo/de dix/etc** (*quantité, nombre*) more than a kilo/ten/

etc; **p. de thé/etc** (*davantage*) more tea/etc; **p. beau/rapidement/etc** more beautiful/rapidly/etc (**que** than); **p. tard** later; **p. petit** smaller; **de p. en p.** more and more; **de p. en p. vite** quicker and quicker; **p. il crie p. il s'enroue** the more he shouts the more hoarse he gets; **p. ou moins** more or less; **p. in** addition (**de** to); **de p.** more (**que** than); (*en outre*) moreover; **les enfants (âgés) de p. de dix ans** children over ten; **j'ai dix ans de p. qu'elle** I'm ten years older than she is; **il est p. de cinq heures** it's after five (o'clock). **2** *adv superlatif* **le p.** (*travailler etc*) (the) most; **le p. beau/etc** the most beautiful/etc; (*de deux*) the more beautiful/etc; **le p. grand/etc** the biggest/etc; (*de deux*) the bigger/etc; **j'ai le p. de livres** I have (the) most books; **j'en ai le p.** I have (the) most; (*tout*) **au p.** at (the very) most.

plus² [ply] *adv de négation* **p. de** (*pain, argent etc*) no more; **il n'a p. de pain** he has no more bread, he doesn't have any more bread; **tu n'es p. jeune** you're no longer young, you're not young any more *ou* any longer; **elle ne le fait p.** she no longer does it, she doesn't do it any more *ou* any longer; **je ne la reverrai p.** I won't see her again.

plus³ [plys] *prép* plus; **deux p. deux font quatre** two plus two are four; **il fait p. deux (degrés)** it's two degrees above freezing; — *nm* **le signe p.** the plus sign.

plusieurs [plyzjœr] *a & pron* several.

plus-value [plyvaly] *nf* (*bénéfice*) profit.

plutonium [plytɔnjɔm] *nm* plutonium.

plutôt [plyto] *adv* rather (**que** than).

pluvieux, -euse [plyvjø, -øz] *a* rainy, wet.

PMU [peemy] *abrév* = **pari mutuel urbain.**

pneu [pnø] *nm* (*pl* **-s**) **1** (*de roue*) tyre, *Am* tire. **2** (*lettre*) express letter. ◆**pneumatique 1** *a* (*matelas etc*) inflatable; **marteau p.** pneumatic drill. **2** *nm* = **pneu.**

pneumonie [pnømɔni] *nf* pneumonia.

poche [pɔʃ] *nf* pocket; (*de kangourou etc*) pouch; (*sac en papier etc*) bag; *pl* (*sous les yeux*) bags; **livre de p.** paperback; **faire des poches** (*pantalon*) to be baggy; **j'ai un franc en p.** I have one franc on me. ◆**pochette** *nf* (*sac*) bag, envelope; (*d'allumettes*) book; (*de disque*) sleeve, jacket; (*mouchoir*) pocket handkerchief; (*sac à main*) (clutch) bag.

poch/er [pɔʃe] *vt* **1 p. l'œil à qn** to give s.o. a black eye. **2** (*œufs*) to poach. ◆**—é** *a* **œil p.** black eye.

podium [pɔdjɔm] *nm Sp* rostrum, podium.

poêle [pwal] **1** *nm* stove. **2** *nf* **p.** (**à frire**) frying pan.

poème [pɔɛm] *nm* poem. ◆**poésie** *nf* poet-

ry; **une p.** (*poème*) a piece of poetry.
◆**poète** *nm* poet; – *a femme p.* poetess.
◆**poétique** *a* poetic.

pognon [pɔɲ5] *nm* (*argent*) *Fam* dough.

poids [pwa] *nm* weight; **au p.** by weight; **de p.** (*influent*) influential; **p. lourd** (*heavy*) lorry *ou Am* truck; **lancer le p.** *Sp* to put *ou* hurl the shot.

poignant [pwaɲɑ̃] *a* (*souvenir etc*) poignant.

poignard [pwaɲar] *nm* dagger; **coup de p.** stab. ◆**poignarder** *vt* to stab.

poigne [pwaɲ] *nf* (*étreinte*) grip.

poignée [pwaɲe] *nf* (*quantité*) handful (**de** of); (*de porte, casserole etc*) handle; (*d'épée*) hilt; **p. de main** handshake; **donner une p. de main à** to shake hands with.

poignet [pwaɲɛ] *nm* wrist; (*de chemise*) cuff.

poil [pwal] *nm* hair; (*pelage*) coat, fur; (*de brosse*) bristle; (*de tapis*) pile; (*d'étoffe*) nap; **à p.** (*nu*) *Arg* (stark) naked; **au p.** (*travail etc*) *Arg* top-rate; **de bon/mauvais p.** *Fam* in a good/bad mood; **de tout p.** *Fam* of all kinds. ◆**poilu** *a* hairy.

poinçon [pwɛ̃s5] *nm* (*outil*) awl, bradawl; (*marque de bijou etc*) hallmark. ◆**poinçonner** *vt* (*bijou*) to hallmark; (*billet*) to punch. ◆**poinçonneuse** *nf* (*machine*) punch.

poindre [pwɛ̃dr] *vi* (*jour*) *Litt* to dawn.

poing [pwɛ̃] *nm* fist; **coup de p.** punch.

point¹ [pwɛ̃] *nm* (*lieu, question, degré, score etc*) point; (*sur i, à l'horizon etc*) dot; (*tache*) spot; (*note*) *Scol* mark; (*de couture*) stitch; **sur le p. de faire** about to do, on the point of doing; **p.** (*final*) full stop, period; **p. d'exclamation** exclamation mark *ou Am* point; **p. d'interrogation** question mark; **p. de vue** point of view, viewpoint; (*endroit*) viewing point; **à p.** (*nommé*) (*arriver etc*) at the right moment; **à p.** (*rôti etc*) medium (cooked); (*steak*) medium rare; **mal en p.** in bad shape; **mettre au p.** *Phot* to focus; *Aut* to tune; (*technique etc*) to elaborate, perfect; (*éclaircir*) *Fig* to clarify, clear up; **mise au p.** focusing; tuning, tune-up; elaboration; *Fig* clarification; **faire le p.** *Fig* to take stock, sum up; **p. mort** *Aut* neutral; **au p. mort** *Fig* at a standstill; **p. noir** *Aut* (*accident*) black spot; **p. du jour** daybreak; **p. de côté** (*douleur*) stitch (in one's side). ◆**p.-virgule** *nm* (*pl* **points-virgules**) semicolon.

point² [pwɛ̃] *adv Litt* = **pas¹**.

pointe [pwɛ̃t] *nf* (*extrémité*) point, tip; (*pour grille*) spike; (*clou*) nail; *Géog* headland; (*maximum*) *Fig* peak; **une p. de** (*soupçon, nuance*) a touch of; **sur la p. des pieds** on

tiptoe; **en p.** pointed; **de p.** (*technique etc*) latest, most advanced; **à la p. de** (*progrès etc*) *Fig* in *ou* at the forefront of.

point/er [pwɛ̃te] **1** *vt* (*cocher*) to tick (off), *Am* check (off). **2** *vt* (*braquer, diriger*) to point (**sur, vers** at). **3** *vi* (*employé*) to clock in, (*à la sortie*) to clock out; **— se p.** *vpr* (*arriver*) *Fam* to show up. **4** *vi* (*bourgeon etc*) to appear; **p. vers** to point upwards towards. ◆**—age** *nm* (*de personnel*) clocking in; clocking out.

pointillé [pwɛ̃tije] *nm* dotted line; – *a* dotted.

pointilleux, -euse [pwɛ̃tijø, -øz] *a* fussy, particular.

pointu [pwɛ̃ty] *a* (*en pointe*) pointed; (*voix*) shrill.

pointure [pwɛ̃tyr] *nf* (*de chaussure, gant*) size.

poire [pwar] *nf* **1** (*fruit*) pear. **2** (*figure*) *Fam* mug. **3** (*personne*) *Fam* sucker. ◆**poirier** *nm* pear tree.

poireau, -x [pwaro] *nm* leek.

poireauter [pwarote] *vi* (*attendre*) *Fam* to kick one's heels.

pois [pwa] *nm* (*légume*) pea; (*dessin*) (polka) dot; **petits p.** (garden) peas; **p. chiche** chickpea; **à p.** (*vêtement*) spotted, dotted.

poison [pwaz5] *nm* (*substance*) poison.

poisse [pwas] *nf Fam* bad luck.

poisseux, -euse [pwasø, -øz] *a* sticky.

poisson [pwas5] *nm* fish; **p. rouge** goldfish; **les Poissons** (*signe*) Pisces. ◆**poissonnerie** *nf* fish shop. ◆**poissonnier, -ière** *nmf* fishmonger.

poitrine [pwatrin] *nf* *Anat* chest; (*seins*) breast, bosom; (*de veau, mouton*) *Culin* breast.

poivre [pwavr] *nm* pepper. ◆**poivr/er** *vt* to pepper; – *a Culin* peppery; (*plaisanterie*) *Fig* spicy. ◆**poivrier** *nm Bot* pepper plant; (*ustensile*) pepperpot. ◆**poivrière** *nf* pepperpot.

poivron [pwavr5] *nm* pepper, capsicum.

poivrot, -ote [pwavro, -ɔt] *nmf Fam* drunk(ard).

poker [pɔkɛr] *nm Cartes* poker.

polar [pɔlar] *nm* (*roman*) *Fam* whodunit.

polariser [pɔlarize] *vt* to polarize.

pôle [pol] *nm Géog* pole; **p. Nord/Sud** North/South Pole. ◆**polaire** *a* polar.

polémique [pɔlemik] *a* controversial, polemical; – *nf* controversy, polemic.

poli [pɔli] *a* (*courtois*) polite (**avec** to, with). **2** *a* (*lisse, brillant*) polished; – *nm* (*aspect*) polish. ◆**—ment** *adv* politely.

police [pɔlis] *nf* **1** police; **faire** *ou* **assurer la**

p. to maintain order (**dans** in); **p. secours** emergency services; **p. mondaine** *ou* **des mœurs** = vice squad. **2** *p*. (**d'assurance**) (insurance) policy. ◆**policier** *a* (*enquête, état*) police-; **roman p.** detective novel; – *nm* policeman, detective.

polichinelle [pɔliʃinɛl] *nf* **secret de p.** open secret.

polio [pɔljo] *nf* (*maladie*) polio; – *nmf* (*personne*) polio victim. ◆**poliomyélite** *nf* poliomyelitis.

polir [pɔlir] *vt* (*substance dure, style*) to polish.

polisson, -onne [pɔlisɔ̃, -ɔn] *a* naughty; – *nmf* rascal.

politesse [pɔlitɛs] *nf* politeness; **une p.** (*parole*) a polite word; (*action*) an act of politeness.

politique [pɔlitik] *a* political; **homme p.** politician; – *nf* (*science, activité*) politics; (*mesures, manières de gouverner*) *Pol* policies; **une p.** (*tactique*) a policy. ◆**politicien, -ienne** *nmf Péj* politician. ◆**politiser** *vt* to politicize.

pollen [pɔlɛn] *nm* pollen.

polluer [pɔlɥe] *vt* to pollute. ◆**polluant** *nm* pollutant. ◆**pollution** *nf* pollution.

polo [pɔlo] *nm* **1** (*chemise*) sweat shirt. **2** *Sp* polo.

polochon [pɔlɔʃɔ̃] *nm* (*traversin*) *Fam* bolster.

Pologne [pɔlɔɲ] *nf* Poland. ◆**polonais, -aise** *a* Polish; – *nmf* Pole; – *nm* (*langue*) Polish.

poltron, -onne [pɔltrɔ̃, -ɔn] *a* cowardly; – *nmf* coward.

polycopi/er [pɔlikɔpje] *vt* to mimeograph, duplicate. ◆**-é** *nm Univ* mimeographed copy (*of lecture etc*).

polyester [pɔliɛstɛr] *nm* polyester.

Polynésie [pɔlinezi] *nf* Polynesia.

polyvalent [pɔlivalɑ̃] *a* (*rôle*) multi-purpose, varied; (*professeur, ouvrier*) all-round; **école polyvalente, lycée p.** comprehensive school.

pommade [pɔmad] *nf* ointment.

pomme [pɔm] *nf* **1** apple; **p. d'Adam** *Anat* Adam's apple. **2** (*d'arrosoir*) rose. **3 p. de terre** potato; **pommes vapeur** steamed potatoes; **pommes frites** chips, *Am* French fries; **pommes chips** potato crisps *ou Am* chips. ◆**pommier** *nm* apple tree.

pommette [pɔmɛt] *nf* cheekbone.

pompe [pɔ̃p] *nf* **1** pump; **p. à essence** petrol *ou Am* gas station; **p. à incendie** fire engine; **coup de p.** *Fam* tired feeling. **2** *nf* (*chaussure*) *Fam* shoe. **3** *nf* (*en gymnastique*)

press-up. *Am* push-up. **4** *nfpl* **pompes funèbres** undertaker's; **entrepreneur de pompes funèbres** undertaker. **5** *nf* **p.** anti-sèche *Scol* crib. **6** *nf* (*splendeur*) pomp. ◆**pomper** *vt* to pump; (*évacuer*) to pump out (**de** of); (*absorber*) to soak up; (*épuiser*) *Fam* to tire out; – *vi* to pump. ◆**pompeux, -euse** *a* pompous. ◆**pompier 1** *nm* fireman; **voiture des pompiers** fire engine. **2** *a* (*emphatique*) pompous. ◆**pompiste** *nmf Aut* pump attendant.

pompon [pɔ̃pɔ̃] *nm* (*ornement*) pompon.

pomponner [pɔ̃pɔne] *vt* to doll up.

ponce [pɔ̃s] *nf* (**pierre**) **p.** pumice (stone). ◆**poncer** *vt* to rub down, sand. ◆**ponceuse** *nf* (*machine*) sander.

ponctuation [pɔ̃ktɥasjɔ̃] *nf* punctuation. ◆**ponctuer** *vt* to punctuate (**de** with).

ponctuel, -elle [pɔ̃ktɥɛl] *a* (*à l'heure*) punctual; (*unique*) *Fig* one-off, *Am* one-of-a-kind. ◆**ponctualité** *nf* punctuality.

pondéré [pɔ̃dere] *a* level-headed. ◆**pondération** *nf* level-headedness.

pondre [pɔ̃dr] *vt* (*œuf*) to lay; (*livre, discours*) *Péj Fam* to produce; – *vi* (*poule*) to lay.

poney [pɔnɛ] *nm* pony.

pont [pɔ̃] *nm* bridge; (*de bateau*) deck; **p.** (**de graissage**) *Aut* ramp; **faire le p.** *Fig* to take the intervening day(s) off (*between two holidays*); **p. aérien** airlift. ◆**p.-levis** *nm* (*pl* **ponts-levis**) drawbridge.

ponte [pɔ̃t] **1** *nf* (*d'œufs*) laying. **2** *nm* (*personne*) *Fam* bigwig.

pontife [pɔ̃tif] *nm* **1** (*souverain*) **p.** pope. **2** (*ponte*) *Fam* bigshot. ◆**pontifical, -aux** *a* papal, pontifical.

pop [pɔp] *nm* & *a inv Mus* pop.

popote [pɔpɔt] *nf* (*cuisine*) *Fam* cooking.

populace [pɔpylas] *nf Péj* rabble.

populaire [pɔpylɛr] *a* (*personne, tradition, gouvernement etc*) popular; (*quartier, milieu*) lower-class; (*expression*) colloquial; (*art*) folk-. ◆**populariser** *vt* to popularize. ◆**popularité** *nf* popularity (**auprès de** with).

population [pɔpylasjɔ̃] *nf* population. ◆**populeux, -euse** *a* populous, crowded.

porc [pɔr] *nm* pig; (*viande*) pork; (*personne*) *Péj* swine.

porcelaine [pɔrsəlɛn] *nf* china, porcelain.

porc-épic [pɔrkepik] *nm* (*pl* **porcs-épics**) (*animal*) porcupine.

porche [pɔrʃ] *nm* porch.

porcherie [pɔrʃəri] *nf* pigsty.

pore [pɔr] *nm* pore. ◆**poreux, -euse** *a* porous.

pornographie [pɔrnɔgrafi] nf pornography. ◆**pornographique** a (Fam **porno**) pornographic.

port [pɔr] nm **1** port, harbour; **arriver à bon p.** to arrive safely. **2** (d'armes) carrying; (de barbe) wearing; (prix) carriage, postage; (attitude) bearing.

portable [pɔrtabl] a (robe etc) wearable; (portatif) portable.

portail [pɔrtaj] nm (de cathédrale etc) portal.

portant, -ive [pɔrtɑ̃, -iv] a bien p. in good health.

portatif, -ive [pɔrtatif, -iv] a portable.

porte [pɔrt] nf door, (passage) doorway; (de jardin) gate, (passage) gateway; (de ville) entrance, Hist gate; **p. (d'embarquement)** Av (departure) gate; Alger, **p. de . . .** Algiers, gateway to . . . ; **p. d'entrée** front door; **mettre à la p.** (jeter dehors) to throw out; (renvoyer) to sack. ◆**p.-fenêtre** nf (pl **portes-fenêtres**) French window.

porte-à-faux [pɔrtafo] nm inv **en p.-à-faux** (en déséquilibre) unstable.

porte-avions [pɔrtavjɔ̃] nm inv aircraft carrier. ◆**p.-bagages** nm inv luggage rack. ◆**p.-bébé** nm (nacelle) carrycot, Am baby basket; (kangourou®) baby sling. ◆**p.-bonheur** nm inv (fétiche) (lucky) charm. ◆**p.-cartes** nm inv card holder ou case. ◆**p.-clés** nm inv key ring. ◆**p.-documents** nm inv briefcase. ◆**p.-drapeau, -x** nm Mil standard bearer. ◆**p.-jarretelles** nm inv suspender ou Am garter belt. ◆**p.-monnaie** nm inv purse. ◆**p.-parapluie** nm inv umbrella stand. ◆**p.-plume** nm inv pen (for dipping in ink). ◆**p.-revues** nm inv newspaper rack. ◆**p.-savon** nm soapdish. ◆**p.-serviettes** nm inv towel rail. ◆**p.-voix** nm inv megaphone.

portée [pɔrte] nf **1** (de fusil etc) range; **à la p. de qn** within reach of s.o.; (richesse, plaisir etc) Fig within s.o.'s grasp; **à p. de la main** within (easy) reach; **à p. de voix** within earshot; **hors de p.** out of reach. **2** (animaux) litter. **3** (importance, effet) significance, import. **4** Mus stave.

portefeuille [pɔrtəfœj] nm wallet; Pol Com portfolio.

portemanteau, -x [pɔrtmɑ̃to] nm (sur pied) hatstand; (barre) hat ou coat peg.

porte-parole [pɔrtparɔl] nm inv (homme) spokesman; (femme) spokeswoman (**de** for, of).

port/er [pɔrte] vt to carry; (vêtement, lunettes, barbe etc) to wear; (trace, responsabilité, fruits etc) to bear; (regard) to cast; (attaque) to make (**contre** against); (coup) to strike; (sentiment) to have (**à** for); (inscrire) to enter, write down; **p. qch à** (amener) to bring ou take sth to; **p. qn à faire** (pousser) to lead ou prompt s.o. to do; **p. bonheur/malheur** to bring good/bad luck; **se faire p. malade** to report sick; — vi (voix) to carry; (canon) to fire; (vue) to extend; **p. (juste)** (coup) to hit the mark; (mot, reproche) to hit home; **p. sur** (reposer sur) to rest on; (concerner) to bear on; (accent) to fall on; (heurter) to strike; — **se p.** vpr (vêtement) to be worn; **se p. bien/mal** to be well/ill; **comment te portes-tu?** how are you?; **se p. candidat** to stand as a candidate. ◆**-é** a **p. à croire/**etc inclined to believe/etc; **p. sur qch** fond of sth. ◆**-ant, -euse** nm Rail porter; — nmf Méd carrier; (de valeurs, chèque) bearer; **mère porteuse** surrogate mother.

portier [pɔrtje] nm doorkeeper, porter. ◆**portière** nf (de véhicule, train) door. ◆**portillon** nm gate.

portion [pɔrsjɔ̃] nf (part, partie) portion; (de nourriture) helping, portion.

portique [pɔrtik] nm **1** Archit portico. **2** (de balançoire etc) crossbar, frame.

porto [pɔrto] nm (vin) port.

portrait [pɔrtre] nm portrait; **être le p. de** (son père etc) to be the image of; **faire un p.** to paint ou draw a portrait (**de** of); **p. en pied** full-length portrait. ◆**p.-robot** nm (pl **portraits-robots**) identikit (picture), photofit.

portuaire [pɔrtɥer] a (installations etc) harbour-.

Portugal [pɔrtygal] nm Portugal. ◆**portugais, -aise** a & nmf Portuguese; — nm (langue) Portuguese.

pose [poz] nf **1** (installation) putting up; putting in; laying. **2** (attitude de modèle, affectation) pose; (temps) Phot exposure. ◆**pos/er** vt to put (down); (papier peint, rideaux) to put up; (sonnette, chauffage) to put in; (mine, moquette, fondations) to lay; (question) to ask (**à qn** s.o.); (principe, conditions) to lay down; **p. sa candidature** to apply, put in one's application (**à** for); **ça pose la question de . . .** it poses the question of . . . ; — vi (modèle etc) to pose (**pour** for); — **se p.** vpr (oiseau, avion) to land; (problème, question) to arise; **se p. sur** (yeux) to fix on; **se p. en chef/**etc to set oneself up as ou pose as a leader/etc; **la question se pose!** this question should be asked! ◆**-é** a (calme) calm, staid.

◆—**ément** adv calmly. ◆—**eur, -euse** nmf Péj poseur.

positif, -ive [pozitif, -iv] a positive. ◆**positivement** adv positively.

position [pozisjɔ̃] nf (attitude, emplacement, opinion etc) position; **prendre p.** Fig to take a stand (**contre** against); **prise de p.** stand.

posologie [pozɔlɔʒi] nf (de médicament) dosage.

posséder [posede] vt to possess; (maison etc) to own, possess; (bien connaître) to master. ◆**possesseur** nm possessor; owner. ◆**possessif, -ive** a (personne, adjectif etc) possessive; – nm Gram possessive. ◆**possession** nf possession; **en p. de** in possession of; **prendre p. de** to take possession of.

possible [posibl] a possible (**à faire** to do); **il (nous) est p. de le faire** it is possible (for us) to do it; **il est p. que** (+ sub) it is possible that; **si p.** if possible; **le plus tôt/etc p.** as soon/etc as possible; **autant que p.** as much ou as many as possible; – nm **faire son p.** to do one's utmost (**pour faire** to do); **dans la mesure du p.** as far as possible. ◆**possibilité** nf possibility.

post- [pɔst] préf post-.

postdater [pɔstdate] vt to postdate.

poste [pɔst] **1** nf (service) post, mail; (local) post office; **bureau de p.** post office; **Postes (et Télécommunications)** (administration) Post Office; **par la p.** by post, by mail; **par avion** airmail; **mettre à la p.** to post, mail. **2** nm (lieu, emploi) post; **p. de secours** first aid post; **p. de police** police station; **p. d'essence** petrol ou Am gas station; **p. d'incendie** fire hydrant; **p. d'aiguillage** signal box ou Am tower. **3** nm (appareil) Rad TV set; Tél extension (number). ◆**postal, -aux** a postal; **boîte postale** PO Box; **code p.** postcode, Am zip code. ◆**poster 1** vt p. qn (placer) Mil to post s.o. **2** vt (lettre) to post, mail. **3** [pɔster] nm poster.

postérieur [pɔsterjœr] **1** a (document etc) later; **p. à** after. **2** nm (derrière) Fam posterior.

postérité [pɔsterite] nf posterity.

posthume [pɔstym] a posthumous; **à titre p.** posthumously.

postiche [pɔstiʃ] a (barbe etc) false.

postier, -ière [pɔstje, -jɛr] nmf postal worker.

postillonner [pɔstijɔne] vi to sputter.

post-scriptum [pɔstskriptɔm] nm inv postscript.

postul/er [pɔstyle] vt **1** (emploi) to apply

for. **2** (poser) Math to postulate. ◆—**ant, -ante** nmf applicant.

posture [pɔstyr] nf posture.

pot [po] nm **1** pot; (à confiture) jar, pot; (à lait) jug; (à bière) mug; (de crème, yaourt) carton; **p. de chambre** chamber pot; **p. de fleurs** flower pot; **prendre un p.** (verre) Fam to have a drink. **2** (chance) Fam luck; **avoir du p.** to be lucky.

potable [pɔtabl] a drinkable; (passable) Fam tolerable; **'eau p.'** 'drinking water'.

potage [pɔtaʒ] nm soup.

potager, -ère [pɔtaʒe, -ɛr] a (jardin) vegetable-; **plante potagère** vegetable; – nm vegetable garden.

potasser [pɔtase] vt (examen) to cram for; – vi to cram.

pot-au-feu [pɔtofø] nm inv (plat) beef stew.

pot-de-vin [pɔdvɛ̃] nm (pl pots-de-vin) bribe.

pote [pɔt] nm (ami) Fam pal, buddy.

poteau, -x [pɔto] nm post; (télégraphique) pole; **p. d'arrivée** Sp winning post.

potelé [pɔtle] a plump, chubby.

potence [pɔtɑ̃s] nf (gibet) gallows.

potentiel, -ielle [pɔtɑ̃sjɛl] a & nm potential.

poterie [pɔtri] nf (art) pottery; **une p.** a piece of pottery; **des poteries** (objets) pottery. ◆**potier** nm potter.

potin [pɔtɛ̃] **1** nmpl (cancans) gossip. **2** nm (bruit) Fam row.

potion [pɔsjɔ̃] nf potion.

potiron [pɔtirɔ̃] nm pumpkin.

pot-pourri [popuri] nm (pl pots-pourris) Mus medley.

pou, -x [pu] nm louse; **poux** lice.

poubelle [pubɛl] nf dustbin, Am garbage can.

pouce [pus] nm **1** thumb; **un coup de p.** Fam a helping hand. **2** (mesure) Hist & Fig inch.

poudre [pudr] nf powder; **p. (à canon)** (explosif) gunpowder; **en p.** (lait) powdered; (chocolat) drinking; **sucre en p.** castor ou caster sugar. ◆**poudrer** vt to powder; – **se p.** vpr (femme) to powder one's nose. ◆**poudreux, -euse** a powdery, dusty. ◆**poudrier** nm (powder) compact. ◆**poudrière** nf powder magazine; (région) Fig powder keg.

pouf [puf] **1** int thump! **2** nm (siège) pouf(fe).

pouffer [pufe] vi **p. (de rire)** to burst out laughing, guffaw.

pouilleux, -euse [pujø, -øz] a (sordide) miserable; (mendiant) lousy.

poulain [pulɛ̃] nm (cheval) foal; **le p. de qn** Fig s.o.'s protégé.

poule [pul] *nf* **1** hen, *Culin* fowl; **être p. mouillée** (*lâche*) to be chicken; **oui, ma p.!** *Fam* yes, my pet! **2** (*femme*) *Péj* tart. ◆**poulailler** *nm* **1** (hen) coop. **2 le p.** *Th Fam* the gods, the gallery. ◆**poulet** *nm* **1** (*poule, coq*) *Culin* chicken. **2** (*policier*) *Fam* cop.

pouliche [puliʃ] *nf* (*jument*) filly.

poulie [puli] *nf* pulley.

poulpe [pulp] *nm* octopus.

pouls [pu] *nm Méd* pulse.

poumon [pumɔ̃] *nm* lung; **à pleins poumons** (*respirer*) deeply; (*crier*) loudly; **p. d'acier** iron lung.

poupe [pup] *nf Nau* stern, poop.

poupée [pupe] *nf* doll.

poupin [pupɛ̃] *a* **visage p.** baby face.

poupon [pupɔ̃] *nm* (*bébé*) baby; (*poupée*) doll.

pour [pur] **1** *prép* for; **p. toi/moi/***etc* for you/me/*etc*; **faites-le p. lui** do it for him, do it for his sake; **partir p.** (*Paris etc*) to leave for; **elle va partir p. cinq ans** she's leaving for five years; **p. femme/base/***etc* as a wife/basis/*etc*; **p. moi, p. ma part** (*quant à moi*) as for me; **dix p. cent** ten per cent; **gentil p.** kind to; **elle est p.** she's in favour; **p. faire** (*in order*) to do, so as to do; **p. que tu saches** so (that) you may know; **p. quoi faire?** what for?; **trop petit/poli/***etc* **p. faire** too small/polite/*etc* to do; **assez grand/***etc* **p. faire** big/*etc* enough to do; **p. cela** for that reason; **jour p. jour/heure p. heure** to the day/hour; **p. intelligent/***etc* **qu'il soit** however clever/*etc* he may be; **ce n'est pas p. me plaire** it doesn't exactly please me; **acheter p. cinq francs de bonbons** to buy five francs' worth of sweets. **2** *nm* **le p. et le contre** the pros and cons.

pourboire [purbwar] *nm* (*argent*) tip.

pourcentage [pursɑ̃taʒ] *nm* percentage.

pourchasser [purʃase] *vt* to pursue.

pourparlers [purparle] *nmpl* negotiations, talks.

pourpre [purpr] *a & nm* purple.

pourquoi [purkwa] *adv & conj* why; **p. pas?** why not?; – *nm inv* reason (**de** for); **le p. et le comment** the whys and wherefores.

pourra, pourrait [pura, purɛ] *voir* **pouvoir 1.**

pourrir [purir] *vi*, – **se p.** *vpr* to rot; – *vt* to rot; **p. qn** to corrupt s.o. ◆**pourri** *a* (*fruit, temps, personne etc*) rotten. ◆**pourriture** *nf* rot, rottenness; (*personne*) *Péj* swine.

poursuite [pursɥit] **1** *nf* chase, pursuit; (*du bonheur, de créancier*) pursuit (**de** of); (*continuation*) continuation; **se mettre à la p. de** to go in pursuit of. **2** *nfpl Jur* legal proceed-

ings (**contre** against). ◆**poursuiv/re** * *vt* (*courir après*) to chase, pursue; (*harceler, relancer*) to hound, pursue; (*obséder*) to haunt; (*but, idéal etc*) to pursue. **2** *vt* **p. qn** *Jur* (*au criminel*) to prosecute s.o.; (*au civil*) to sue s.o. **3** *vt* (*lecture, voyage etc*) to continue (with), carry on (with), pursue; – *vi*, – **se p.** *vpr* to continue, go on. ◆—**ant, -ante** *nmf* pursuer.

pourtant [purtɑ̃] *adv* yet, nevertheless.

pourtour [purtur] *nm* perimeter.

pourvoir * [purvwar] *vt* to provide (**de** with); **être pourvu de** to have, be provided with; – *vi* **p. à** (*besoins etc*) to provide for. ◆**pourvoyeur, -euse** *nmf* supplier.

pourvu que [purvykə] *conj* (*condition*) provided *ou* providing (that); **p. qu'elle soit là** (*souhait*) I only hope (that) she's there.

pousse [pus] *nf* **1** (*bourgeon*) shoot, sprout. **2** (*croissance*) growth.

pousse-café [puskafe] *nm inv* after-dinner liqueur.

pouss/er [puse] **1** *vt* to push; (*du coude*) to nudge, poke; (*véhicule, machine*) to drive hard; (*recherches*) to pursue; (*cri*) to utter; (*soupir*) to heave; **p. qn à faire** to urge s.o. to do; **p. qn à bout** to push s.o. to his limits; **p. trop loin** (*gentillesse etc*) to carry too far; **p. à la perfection** to bring to perfection; – *vi* to push; **p. jusqu'à Paris/***etc* to push on as far as Paris/*etc*; – **se p.** *vpr* (*se déplacer*) to move up *ou* over. **2** *vi* (*croître*) to grow; **faire p.** (*plante, barbe etc*) to grow. ◆—**é a** (*travail, études*) advanced. ◆—**ée** *nf* (*pression*) pressure; (*coup*) push; (*d'ennemi*) thrust, push; (*de fièvre etc*) outbreak; (*de l'inflation*) upsurge. ◆**poussette** *nf* pushchair, *Am* stroller; **p. canne** (baby) buggy, *Am* (collapsible) stroller; **p. de marché** shopping trolley *ou Am* cart. ◆**poussoir** *nm* (push) button.

poussière [pusjɛr] *nf* dust; **dix francs et des poussières** *Fam* a bit over ten francs. ◆**poussiéreux, -euse** *a* dusty.

poussif, -ive [pusif, -iv] *a* short-winded, puffing.

poussin [pusɛ̃] *nm* (*poulet*) chick.

poutre [putr] *nf* (*en bois*) beam; (*en acier*) girder. ◆**poutrelle** *nf* girder.

pouvoir * [puvwar] **1** *v aux* (*capacité*) to be able, can; (*permission, éventualité*) may, can; **je peux deviner** I can guess, I'm able to guess; **tu peux entrer** you may *ou* can come in; **il peut être malade** he may *ou* might be ill; **elle pourrait/pouvait venir** she might/could come; **j'ai pu l'obtenir** I managed to get it; **j'aurais pu l'obtenir** I could have got it *ou Am* gotten it; **je n'en peux plus** I'm utterly exhausted; − *v imp* **il peut neiger** it may snow; − **se p.** *vpr* **il se peut qu'elle parte** (it's possible that) she might leave. **2** *nm* (*capacité, autorité*) power; (*procuration*) power of attorney; **les pouvoirs publics** the authorities; **au p.** *Pol* in power; **en son p.** in one's power (**de faire** to do).

poux [pu] *voir* **pou**.

pragmatique [pragmatik] *a* pragmatic.

praire [prɛr] *nf* (*mollusque*) clam.

prairie [preri] *nf* meadow.

praline [pralin] *nf* sugared almond. ◆**praliné** *a* (*glace*) praline-flavoured.

praticable [pratikabl] *a* (*projet, chemin*) practicable.

praticien, -ienne [pratisjɛ̃, -jɛn] *nmf* practitioner.

pratique [pratik] **1** *a* (*connaissance, personne, instrument etc*) practical. **2** *nf* (*exercice, procédé*) practice; (*expérience*) practical experience; **la p. de la natation/du golf/etc** swimming/golfing/etc; **mettre en p.** to put into practice; **en p.** (*en réalité*) in practice. ◆**pratiqu/er** *vt* (*art etc*) to practise; (*football*) to play, practise; (*trou, route*) to make; (*opération*) to carry out; **p. la natation** to go swimming; − *vi* to practise. ◆**-ant, -ante** *a Rel* practising; − *nmf* churchgoer.

pratiquement [pratikmɑ̃] *adv* (*presque*) practically, (*en réalité*) in practice.

pré [pre] *nm* meadow.

pré- [pre] *préf* pre-.

préalable [prealabl] *a* previous, preliminary; **p. à** prior to; − *nm* precondition, prerequisite; **au p.** beforehand. ◆**—ment** [-əmɑ̃] *adv* beforehand.

préambule [preɑ̃byl] *nm* (*de loi*) preamble; *Fig* prelude (**à** to).

préau, -x [preo] *nm Scol* covered playground.

préavis [preavi] *nm* (*de congé etc*) (advance) notice (**de** of).

précaire [prekɛr] *a* precarious.

précaution [prekosjɔ̃] *nf* (*mesure*) precaution; (*prudence*) caution; **par p.** as a precaution. ◆**précautionneux, -euse** *a* cautious.

précédent, -ente [presedɑ̃, -ɑ̃t] **1** *a* previous, preceding, earlier; − *nmf* previous one. **2** *nm* **un p.** (*fait, exemple*) a precedent; **sans p.** unprecedented. ◆**précédemment** [-amɑ̃] *adv* previously. ◆**précéder** *vti* to precede; **faire p. qch de qch** to precede sth by sth.

précepte [presɛpt] *nm* precept.

précepteur, -trice [preseptœr, -tris] *nmf* (private) tutor.

prêcher [preʃe] *vti* to preach; **p. qn** *Rel & Fig* to preach to s.o.

précieux, -euse [presjø, -øz] *a* precious.

précipice [presipis] *nm* abyss, chasm.

précipit/er [presipite] *vt* (*jeter*) to throw, hurl; (*plonger*) to plunge (**dans** into); (*hâter*) to hasten; − **se p.** *vpr* (*se jeter*) to throw *ou* hurl oneself; (*foncer*) to rush (**à, sur** on to); (*s'accélérer*) to speed up. ◆**-é** *a* hasty. ◆**précipitamment** *adv* hastily. ◆**précipitation 1** *nf* haste. **2** *nfpl* (*pluie*) precipitation.

précis [presi] **1** *a* precise; (*idée, mécanisme*) accurate, precise; **à deux heures précises** at two o'clock sharp *ou* precisely. **2** *nm* (*résumé*) summary; (*manuel*) handbook. ◆**précisément** *adv* precisely. ◆**préciser** *vt* to specify (**que** that); − **se p.** *vpr* to become clear(er). ◆**précision** *nf* precision; accuracy; (*détail*) detail; (*explication*) explanation.

précoce [prekos] *a* (*fruit, mariage, mort etc*) early; (*personne*) precocious. ◆**précocité** *nf* precociousness; earliness.

préconçu [prekɔ̃sy] *a* preconceived.

préconiser [prekɔnize] *vt* to advocate (**que** that).

précurseur [prekyrsœr] *nm* forerunner, precursor; − *a* **un signe p. de qch** a sign heralding sth.

prédécesseur [predesesœr] *nm* predecessor.

prédestiné [predestine] *a* fated, predestined (**à faire** to do).

prédicateur [predikatœr] *nm* preacher.

prédilection [predileksjɔ̃] *nf* (special) liking; **de p.** favourite.

prédire* [predir] *vt* to predict (**que** that). ◆**prédiction** *nf* prediction.

prédisposer [predispoze] *vt* to predispose (**à qch** to sth, **à faire** to do). ◆**prédisposition** *nf* predisposition.

prédomin/er [predomine] *vi* to predominate. ◆**-ant** *a* predominant. ◆**prédominance** *nf* predominance.

préfabriqué [prefabrike] *a* prefabricated.

préface [prefas] *nf* preface. ◆**préfacer** *vt* to preface.

préfér/er [prefere] *vt* to prefer (**à** to); **p. faire** to prefer to do. ◆**-é, -ée** *a & nmf* favourite. ◆**-able** *a* preferable (**à** to). ◆**préférence** *nf* preference; **de p.** preferably; **de p. à** in preference to. ◆**préférentiel, -ielle** *a* preferential.

préfet [prefε] nm prefect, *chief administrator in a department*; **p. de police** prefect of police, *Paris chief of police*. ◆**préfecture** nf prefecture; **p. de police** Paris police headquarters.

préfixe [prefiks] nm prefix.

préhistoire [preistwar] nf prehistory. ◆**préhistorique** a prehistoric.

préjudice [preʒydis] nm Jur prejudice, harm; **porter p. à** to prejudice, harm. ◆**préjudiciable** a prejudicial (à to).

préjugé [preʒyʒe] nm (parti pris) prejudice; **avoir un p. ou des préjugés** to be prejudiced (**contre** against).

prélasser (se) [səprelɑse] vpr to loll (about), lounge (about).

prélat [prela] nm Rel prelate.

prélever [prelve] vt (échantillon) to take (**sur** from); (somme) to deduct (**sur** from). ◆**prélèvement** nm taking; deduction; **p. de sang** blood sample; **p. automatique** Fin standing order.

préliminaire [preliminεr] a preliminary; — nmpl preliminaries.

prélude [prelyd] nm prelude (à to).

prématuré [prematyre] a premature; — nm (bébé) premature baby. ◆**—ment** adv prematurely, too soon.

préméditer [premedite] vt to premeditate. ◆**préméditation** nf Jur premeditation.

premier, -ière [prəmje, -jεr] a first; (enfance) early; (page) Journ front; first; (qualité, nécessité, importance) prime; (état) original; (notion, cause) basic; (danseuse, rôle) leading; (inférieur) bottom; (supérieur) top; **nombre p.** Math prime number; **le p. rang** the front ou first row; **à la première occasion** at the earliest opportunity; **P. ministre** Prime Minister, Premier; — nmf first (one); **arriver le p. ou en p.** to arrive first; **être le p. de la classe** to be (at) the top of the class; — nm (date) first; (étage) first ou Am second floor; **le p. de l'an** New Year's Day; — nf Th Cin première; Rail first class; Scol = sixth form, Am = twelfth grade; Aut first (gear); (évènement historique) first. ◆**premier-né** nm, ◆**première-née** nf first-born (child). ◆**premièrement** adv firstly.

prémisse [premis] nf premiss.

prémonition [premonisjɔ̃] nf premonition.

prémunir [premynir] vt to safeguard (**contre** against).

prénatal, mpl -als [prenatal] a antenatal, Am prenatal.

prendre* [prɑ̃dr] vt (à qn from s.o.); (attraper) to catch, get; (voyager par) to take, travel by; (acheter) to get; (douche, bain) to take, have; (repas) to have; (nouvelles) to get; (temps, heure) to take (up); (pensionnaire) to take (in); (ton, air) to put on; (engager) to take (s.o.) (on); (chercher) to pick up, get; **p. qn pour** (un autre) to (mis)take s.o. for; (considérer) to take s.o. for; **p. qn** (doute etc) to seize s.o.; **p. feu** to catch fire; **p. de la place** to take up room; **p. du poids/de la vitesse** to put on weight/speed; **à tout p.** on the whole; **qu'est-ce qui te prend?** what's got ou Am gotten into you?; — vi (feu) to catch; (gelée, ciment) to set; (greffe, vaccin) to take; (mode) to catch on; — **se p.** vpr (objet) to be taken; (s'accrocher) to get caught; (eau) to freeze; **se p. pour un génie**/etc to think one is a genius/etc; **s'y p.** to go ou set about it; **s'en p. à** (critiquer, attaquer) to attack; (accuser) to blame; **se p. à faire** to begin to do. ◆**prenant** a (travail, film etc) engrossing; (voix) engaging. ◆**preneur, -euse** nmf taker, buyer.

prénom [prenɔ̃] nm first name. ◆**prénommer** vt to name; **il se prénomme Louis** his first name is Louis.

préoccup/er [preɔkype] vt (inquiéter) to worry; (absorber) to preoccupy; **se p. de** to be worried about; to be preoccupied about. ◆**—ant** a worrying. ◆**—é** a worried. ◆**préoccupation** nf worry; (idée, problème) preoccupation.

préparer [prepare] vt to prepare; (repas etc) to get ready, prepare; (examen) to study for, prepare (for); **p. qch à qn** to prepare sth for s.o.; **p. qn à** (examen) to prepare ou coach s.o. for; — **se p.** vpr to get (oneself) ready, prepare oneself (à qch for sth); (orage) to brew, threaten. ◆**préparatifs** nmpl preparations (de for). ◆**préparation** nf preparation. ◆**préparatoire** a preparatory.

prépondérant [prepɔ̃derɑ̃] a dominant. ◆**prépondérance** nf dominance.

prépos/er [prepoze] vt **p. qn à** to put s.o. in charge of. ◆**—é, -ée** nmf employee; (facteur) postman, postwoman. ◆**préposition** [prepozisjɔ̃] nf preposition.

préretraite [prerətrεt] nf early retirement.

prérogative [prerɔgativ] nf prerogative.

près [prε] adv **p. de** (qn, qch) near (to), close to; (presque) nearly; **p. de deux ans**/etc (presque) nearly two years/etc; **p. de partir**/etc about to leave/etc; **tout p.** nearby (**de qn/qch** s.o./sth), close by (**de qn/qch** s.o./sth); **de p.** (lire, examiner, suivre) closely; **à peu de chose p.** almost; **à cela p.** except for that; **voici le**

chiffre à un franc p. here is the figure give or take a franc; **calculer au franc p.** to calculate to the nearest franc.

présage [preza3] nm omen, foreboding. ◆**présager** vt to forebode.

presbyte [presbit] a & nmf long-sighted (person). ◆**presbytie** [-bisi] nf long-sightedness.

presbytère [presbiter] nm Rel presbytery.

préscolaire [preskɔler] a (âge etc) pre-school.

prescrire* [preskrir] vt to prescribe. ◆**prescription** nf (instruction) & Jur prescription.

préséance [preseãs] nf precedence (**sur** over).

présent¹ [prezã] 1 a (non absent) present; **les personnes présentes** those present. 2 a (actuel) present; – nm (temps) present; Gram present (tense); **à p.** now, at present; **dès à p.** as from now. ◆**présence** nf presence; (à l'école, au bureau etc) attendance (**à** at); **feuille de p.** attendance sheet; **faire acte de p.** to put in an appearance; **en p.** (personnes) face to face; **en p. de** in the presence of; **p. d'esprit** presence of mind.

présent² [prezã] nm (cadeau) present.

présent/er [prezãte] vt (offrir, exposer, animer etc) to present; (montrer) to show, present; **p. qn à qn** to introduce ou present s.o. to s.o.; – **se p.** vpr to introduce ou present oneself (**à** to); (chez qn) to show up; (occasion etc) to arise; **se p. à** (examen) to sit for; (élections) to stand in ou run in; (emploi) to apply for; (autorités) to report to; **ça se présente bien** it looks promising. ◆**-able** a presentable. ◆**présentateur, -trice** nmf TV announcer, presenter. ◆**présentation** nf presentation; introduction. ◆**présentoir** nm (étagère) (display) stand.

préserver [prezerve] vt to protect, preserve (**de** from). ◆**préservatif** nm sheath, condom. ◆**préservation** nf protection, preservation.

présidence [prezidãs] nf (de nation) presidency; (de firme etc) chairmanship. ◆**président, -ente** nmf (de nation) president; (de réunion, firme) chairman, chairwoman; **p. directeur général** chairman and managing director, Am chief executive officer. ◆**présidentiel, -ielle** a presidential.

présider [prezide] vt (réunion) to preside at ou over, chair; – vi to preside.

présomption [prezɔ̃psjɔ̃] nf (conjecture, suffisance) presumption.

présomptueux, -euse [prezɔ̃ptɥø, -øz] a presumptuous.

presque [prɛsk(ə)] adv almost, nearly; **p. jamais/rien** hardly ever/anything.

presqu'île [prɛskil] nf peninsula.

presse [prɛs] nf (journaux, appareil) press; Typ (printing) press; **de p.** (conférence, agence) press-.

presse-citron [prɛssitrɔ̃] nm inv lemon squeezer. ◆**p.-papiers** nm inv paperweight. ◆**p.-purée** nm inv (potato) masher.

pressentir* [presãtir] vt (deviner) to sense (que that). ◆**pressentiment** nm foreboding, presentiment.

press/er [prese] vt (serrer) to squeeze, press; (bouton) to press; (fruit) to squeeze; (départ etc) to hasten; **p. qn** to hurry s.o. (**de** faire to do); (assaillir) to harass s.o. (**de** questions with questions); **p. le pas** to speed up; – vi (temps) to press; (affaire) to be pressing ou urgent; **rien ne presse** there's no hurry; – **se p.** vpr (se grouper) to crowd, swarm; (se serrer) to squeeze (together); (se hâter) to hurry (**de** faire to do); **presse-toi (de partir)** hurry up (and go). ◆**-ant** a pressing, urgent. ◆**-é** a (personne) in a hurry; (air) hurried; (travail) pressing, urgent. ◆**pressing** [-iŋ] nm (magasin) dry cleaner's. ◆**pressoir** nm (wine) press.

pression [presjɔ̃] nf pressure; **faire p. sur qn** to put pressure on s.o., pressurize s.o.; **bière (à la) p.** draught beer; – nm (bouton-)p. press-stud, Am snap.

pressuriser [presyrize] vt Av to pressurize.

prestance [prɛstãs] nf (imposing) presence.

prestation [prɛstasjɔ̃] nf 1 (allocation) allowance, benefit. 2 (performance) performance.

prestidigitateur, -trice [prɛstidiʒitatœr, -tris] nmf conjurer. ◆**prestidigitation** nf conjuring.

prestige [prɛstiʒ] nm prestige. ◆**prestigieux, -euse** a prestigious.

presto [prɛsto] Fam voir **illico**.

présumer [prezyme] vt to presume (**que** that).

présupposer [presypoze] vt to presuppose (que that).

prêt¹ [prɛ] a (préparé, disposé) ready (**à faire** to do, **à qch** for sth). ◆**p.-à-porter** [prɛtaporte] nm inv ready-to-wear clothes.

prêt² [prɛ] nm (emprunt) loan. ◆**p.-logement** nm (pl prêts-logement) mortgage.

prétend/re [pretãdr] vt to claim (**que** that); (vouloir) to intend (**faire** to do); **p.**

être/savoir to claim to be/to know; **elle se prétend riche** she claims to be rich; – *vi* **p. à** (*titre etc*) to lay claim to. ◆**—ant** *nm* (*amoureux*) suitor. ◆**—u** *a* so-called. ◆**—ument** *adv* supposedly.

prétentieux, -euse [pretɑ̃sjø, -øz] *a & nmf* pretentious (person). ◆**prétention** *nf* (*vanité*) pretension; (*revendication, ambition*) claim.

prêt/er [prete] *vt* (*argent, objet*) to lend (à to); (*aide, concours*) to give (à to); (*attribuer*) to attribute (à to); **p. attention** to pay attention (à to); **p. serment** to take an oath; – *vi* **p. à** (*phrase etc*) to lend itself to; **se p. à** (*consentir à*) to agree to; (*sujet etc*) to lend itself to. ◆**—eur, -euse** *nmf* (*d'argent*) lender; **p. sur gages** pawnbroker.

prétexte [pretɛkst] *nm* pretext, excuse; **sous p. de/que** on the pretext of/that. ◆**prétexter** *vt* to plead (**que** that).

prêtre [prɛtr] *nm* priest; **grand p.** high priest.

preuve [prœv] *nf* proof, evidence; **faire p. de** to show; **faire ses preuves** (*personne*) to prove oneself; (*méthode*) to prove itself.

prévaloir [prevalwar] *vi* to prevail (**contre**, **sur** over).

prévenant [prevnɑ̃] *a* considerate. ◆**prévenance(s)** *nf(pl)* (*gentillesse*) consideration.

préven/ir*** [prevnir] *vt* 1 (*avertir*) to warn (**que** that); (*aviser*) to tell, inform (**que** that). 2 (*désir, question*) to anticipate; (*malheur*) to avert. ◆**—u, -ue** 1 *nmf Jur* defendant, accused. 2 *a* prejudiced (**contre** against). ◆**préventif, -ive** *a* preventive. ◆**prévention** *nf* 1 prevention; **p. routière** road safety. 2 (*opinion*) prejudice.

prév/oir*** [prevwar] *vt* (*anticiper*) to foresee (**que** that); (*prédire*) forecast (**que** that); (*temps*) *Mét* to forecast; (*projeter, organiser*) to plan (for); (*réserver, préparer*) to allow, provide. ◆**—u** *a* (*conditions*) laid down; **un repas est p.** a meal is provided; **au moment p.** at the appointed time; **comme p.** as planned, as expected; **p. pour** (*véhicule, appareil etc*) designed for. ◆**prévisible** *a* foreseeable. ◆**prévision** *nf* (*opinion*) & *Mét* forecast; **en p. de** in expectation of.

prévoyant [prevwajɑ̃] *a* (*personne*) provident. ◆**prévoyance** *nf* foresight; **société de p.** provident society.

prier [prije] 1 *vi Rel* to pray; – *vt* **p. Dieu pour qu'il nous accorde qch** to pray (to God) for sth. 2 *vt* **p. qn de faire** to ask *ou* request s.o. to do; (*implorer*) to beg s.o. to do; **je vous en prie** (*faites donc, allez-y*)

please; (*en réponse à 'merci'*) don't mention it; **je vous prie** please; **se faire p.** to wait to be asked. ◆**prière** *nf Rel* prayer; (*demande*) request; **p. de répondre/etc** please answer/etc.

primaire [primɛr] *a* primary.

prime [prim] 1 *nf* (*d'employé*) bonus; (*d'État*) subsidy; (*cadeau*) *Com* free gift; **p. (d'assurance)** (insurance) premium. 2 *a* **de p. abord** at the very first glance.

primé [prime] *a* (*animal*) prize-winning.

primer [prime] *vi* to excel, prevail; – *vt* to prevail over.

primeurs [primœr] *nfpl* early fruit and vegetables.

primevère [primvɛr] *nf* (*à fleurs jaunes*) primrose.

primitif, -ive [primitif, -iv] *a* (*art, société etc*) primitive; (*état, sens*) original; – *nm* (*artiste*) primitive. ◆**primitivement** *adv* originally.

primo [primo] *adv* first(ly).

primordial, -aux [primɔrdjal, -o] *a* vital (**de faire** to do).

prince [prɛ̃s] *nm* prince. ◆**princesse** *nf* princess. ◆**princier, -ière** *a* princely. ◆**principauté** *nf* principality.

principal, -aux [prɛ̃sipal, -o] *a* main, chief, principal; – *nm* (*de collège*) *Scol* principal; **le p.** (*essentiel*) the main *ou* chief thing. ◆**—ement** *adv* mainly.

principe [prɛ̃sip] *nm* principle; **par p.** on principle; **en p.** theoretically, in principle; (*normalement*) as a rule.

printemps [prɛ̃tɑ̃] *nm* (*saison*) spring. ◆**printanier, -ière** *a* (*temps etc*) spring-, spring-like.

priorité [priorite] *nf* priority; **la p.** *Aut* the right of way; **la p. à droite** *Aut* right of way to traffic coming from the right; **'cédez la p.'** *Aut* 'give way', *Am* 'yield'; **en p.** as a matter of priority. ◆**prioritaire** *a* (*industrie etc*) priority-; **être p.** to have priority; *Aut* to have the right of way.

pris [pri] *voir* **prendre**; – *a* (*place*) taken; (*crème, ciment*) set; (*eau*) frozen; (*gorge*) infected; (*nez*) congested; **être (très) p.** (*occupé*) to be (very) busy; **p. de** (*peur, panique*) stricken with.

prise [priz] *voir* **prendre**; – *nf* taking; (*manière d'empoigner*) grip, hold; (*de ville*) capture, taking; (*objet saisi*) catch; (*de tabac*) snuff; **p. (de courant)** *Él* (*mâle*) plug; (*femelle*) socket; **p. multiple** *Él* adaptor; **p. d'air** air vent; **p. de conscience** awareness; **p. de contact** first meeting; **p. de position** *Fig* stand; **p. de sang** blood test; **p.**

de son (sound) recording; **p. de vue(s)** *Cin Phot* (*action*) shooting; (*résultat*) shot; **aux prises avec** at grips with.

priser [prize] **1** *vt* **tabac à p.** snuff; − *vi* to take snuff. **2** *vt* (*estimer*) to prize.

prisme [prism] *nm* prism.

prison [prizɔ̃] *nf* prison, jail, gaol; (*réclusion*) imprisonment; **mettre en p.** to imprison, put in prison. ◆**prisonnier, -ière** *nmf* prisoner; **faire qn p.** to take s.o. prisoner.

privé [prive] *a* private; **en p.** (*seul à seul*) in private; − *nm* **dans le p.** in private life; *Com Fam* in the private sector.

priver [prive] *vt* to deprive (**de** of); **se p. de** to deprive oneself of, do without. ◆**privation** *nf* deprivation (**de** of); *pl* (*sacrifices*) hardships.

privilège [privilɛʒ] *nm* privilege. ◆**privilégié, -ée** *a* & *nmf* privileged (person).

prix [pri] *nm* **1** (*d'un objet, du succès etc*) price; **à tout p.** at all costs; **à aucun p.** on no account; **hors (de) p.** exorbitant; **attacher du p. à** to attach importance to; **menu à p. fixe** set price menu. **2** (*récompense*) prize.

pro- [pro] *préf* pro-.

probable [prɔbabl] *a* probable, likely; **peu p.** unlikely. ◆**probabilité** *nf* probability, likelihood; **selon toute p.** in all probability. ◆**probablement** *adv* probably.

probant [prɔbɑ̃] *a* conclusive.

probité [prɔbite] *nf* (*honnêteté*) integrity.

problème [prɔblɛm] *nm* problem. ◆**problématique** *a* doubtful, problematic.

procéd/er [prɔsede] *vi* (*agir*) to proceed; (*se conduire*) to behave; **p. à** (*enquête etc*) to carry out. ◆**-é** *nm* process; (*conduite*) behaviour. ◆**procédure** *nf* procedure; *Jur* proceedings.

procès [prɔsɛ] *nm* (*criminel*) trial; (*civil*) lawsuit; **faire un p. à** to take to court.

processeur [prɔsesœr] *nm* (*d'ordinateur*) processor.

procession [prɔsesjɔ̃] *nf* procession.

processus [prɔsesys] *nm* process.

procès-verbal, -aux [prɔsevɛrbal, -o] *nm* (*de réunion*) minutes; (*constat*) *Jur* report; (*contravention*) fine, ticket.

prochain, -aine [prɔʃɛ̃, -ɛn] **1** *a* next; (*avenir*) near; (*parent*) close; (*mort, arrivée*) impending; (*mariage*) forthcoming; **un jour p.** one day soon; − *nf* **à la prochaine!** *Fam* see you soon!; **à la prochaine (station)** at the next stop. **2** *nm* (*semblable*) fellow (man). ◆**prochainement** *adv* shortly, soon.

proche [prɔʃ] *a* (*espace*) near, close; (*temps*)

close (at hand); (*parent, ami*) close; (*avenir*) near; **p. de** near (to), close to; **une maison/etc p.** a house/etc nearby ou close by; − *nmpl* close relations.

proclamer [prɔklame] *vt* to proclaim, declare (**que** that); **p. roi** to proclaim king. ◆**proclamation** *nf* proclamation, declaration.

procréer [prɔkree] *vt* to procreate. ◆**procréation** *nf* procreation.

procuration [prɔkyrasjɔ̃] *nf* power of attorney; **par p.** (*voter*) by proxy.

procurer [prɔkyre] *vt* **p. qch à qn** (*personne*) to obtain sth for s.o.; (*occasion etc*) to afford s.o. sth; **se p. qch** to obtain sth.

procureur [prɔkyrœr] *nm* = *Br* public prosecutor, = *Am* district attorney.

prodige [prɔdiʒ] *nm* (*miracle*) wonder; (*personne*) prodigy. ◆**prodigieux, -euse** *a* prodigious, extraordinary.

prodigue [prɔdig] *a* (*dépensier*) wasteful, prodigal. ◆**prodiguer** *vt* to lavish (**à qn** on s.o.).

production [prɔdyksjɔ̃] *nf* production; (*de la terre*) yield. ◆**producteur, -trice** *nmf Com Cin* producer; − *a* producing; **pays p. de pétrole** oil-producing country. ◆**productif, -ive** *a* (*terre, réunion etc*) productive. ◆**productivité** *nf* productivity.

produire* [prɔdɥir] **1** *vt* (*fabriquer, présenter etc*) to produce; (*causer*) to bring about, produce. **2 se p.** *vpr* (*événement etc*) to happen, occur. ◆**produit** *nm* (*article etc*) product; (*pour la vaisselle*) liquid; (*d'une vente, d'une collecte*) proceeds; *pl* (*de la terre*) produce; **p. (chimique)** chemical; **p. de beauté** cosmetic.

proéminent [prɔeminɑ̃] *a* prominent.

prof [prɔf] *nm Fam* = **professeur**.

profane [prɔfan] **1** *nmf* lay person. **2** *a* (*art etc*) secular.

profaner [prɔfane] *vt* to profane, desecrate. ◆**profanation** *nf* profanation, desecration.

proférer [prɔfere] *vt* to utter.

professer [prɔfese] *vt* to profess (**que** that).

professeur [prɔfesœr] *nm* teacher; *Univ* lecturer, *Am* professor; (*titulaire d'une chaire*) *Univ* professor.

profession [prɔfesjɔ̃] *nf* (*occupation*) occupation, vocation; (*libérale*) profession; (*manuelle*) trade; **de p.** (*chanteur etc*) professional, by profession. **2 p. de foi** *Fig* declaration of principles. ◆**professionnel, -elle** *a* professional; (*école*) vocational, trade-; − *nmf* (*non amateur*) professional.

profil [prɔfil] *nm* (*de personne, objet*) profile;

de p. in profile. ◆**profiler** vt to outline, profile; **— se p.** vpr to be outlined ou profiled (**sur** against).

profit [prɔfi] nm profit; (avantage) advantage, profit; **vendre à p.** to sell at a profit; **tirer p. de** to benefit by, profit by; **au p. de** for the benefit of. ◆**profitable** a profitable (à to). ◆**profiter** vi **p. de** to take advantage of; **p. à qn** to profit s.o.; **p. (bien)** (enfant) Fam to thrive. ◆**profiteur, -euse** Péj profiteur.

profond [prɔfɔ̃] a deep; (esprit, joie, erreur etc) profound, great; (cause) underlying; **p. de deux mètres** two metres deep; **—** adv (pénétrer etc) deep; **—** nm **au plus p. de** in the depths of. ◆**profondément** adv deeply; (dormir) soundly; (triste, souhaiter) profoundly; (extrêmement) thoroughly. ◆**profondeur** nf depth; profoundness; pl depths (the of); **en p.** (étudier etc) in depth; **à six mètres de p.** at a depth of six metres.

profusion [prɔfyzjɔ̃] nf profusion; **à p.** in profusion.

progéniture [prɔʒenityr] nf Hum offspring.

progiciel [prɔʒisjɛl] nm (pour ordinateur) (software) package.

programme [prɔgram] nm programme, Am program; (d'une matière) Scol syllabus; (d'ordinateur) program; **p. (d'études)** (d'une école) curriculum. ◆**programmation** nf programming. ◆**programmer** vt Cin Rad TV to programme, Am program; (ordinateur) to program. ◆**programmeur, -euse** nmf (computer) programmer.

progrès [prɔgrɛ] nm & nmpl progress; **faire des p.** to make (good) progress. ◆**progresser** vi to progress. ◆**progressif, -ive** a progressive. ◆**progression** nf progression. ◆**progressiste** a & nmf Pol progressive. ◆**progressivement** adv progressively, gradually.

prohiber [prɔibe] vt to prohibit, forbid. ◆**prohibitif, -ive** a prohibitive. ◆**prohibition** nf prohibition.

proie [prwa] nf prey; **être en p. à** to be (a) prey to, to be tortured by.

projecteur [prɔʒɛktœr] nm (de monument) floodlight; (de prison) & Mil searchlight; Th spot(light); Cin projector.

projectile [prɔʒɛktil] nm missile.

projet [prɔʒɛ] nm plan; (ébauche) draft; (entreprise, étude) project.

projeter [prɔʒte] vt **1** (lancer) to hurl, project. **2** (film, ombre) to project; (lumière) to flash. **3** (voyage, fête etc) to plan; **p. de faire** to plan to do. ◆**projection** nf (lancement)

hurling, projection; (de film, d'ombre) projection; (séance) showing.

prolétaire [prɔleter] nmf proletarian. ◆**prolétariat** nm proletariat. ◆**prolétarien, -ienne** a proletarian.

proliférer [prɔlifere] vi to proliferate. ◆**prolifération** nf proliferation.

prolifique [prɔlifik] a prolific.

prolixe [prɔliks] a verbose, wordy.

prologue [prɔlɔg] nm prologue (**de, à** to).

prolonger [prɔlɔ̃ʒe] vt to prolong, extend; **— se p.** vpr (séance, rue, effet) to continue. ◆**prolongateur** nm (rallonge) El extension cord. ◆**prolongation** nf extension; pl Fb extra time. ◆**prolongement** nm extension.

promenade [prɔmnad] nf (à pied) walk; (en voiture) ride, drive; (en vélo, à cheval) ride; (action) Sp walking; (lieu) walk, promenade; **faire une p. =** se promener. ◆**promener** vt to take for a walk ou ride; (visiteur) to take ou show around; **p. qch sur qch** (main, regard) to run sth over sth; **envoyer p.** Fam to send packing; **— se p.** vpr (à pied) to (go for a) walk; (en voiture) to (go for a) ride ou drive. ◆**promeneur, -euse** nmf walker, stroller.

promesse [prɔmɛs] nf promise. ◆**promett/re**[*] vt to promise (**qch à qn** s.o. sth); **p. de faire** to promise to do; **c'est promis** it's a promise; **—** vi **p. (beaucoup)** Fig to be promising; **se p. qch** to promise oneself sth; **se p. de faire** to resolve to do. ◆**—eur, -euse** a promising.

promontoire [prɔmɔ̃twar] nm Géog headland.

promoteur [prɔmɔtœr] nm **p. (immobilier)** property developer.

promotion [prɔmɔsjɔ̃] nf **1** promotion; **en p.** Com on (special) offer. **2** (candidats) Univ year. ◆**promouvoir**[*] vt (personne, produit etc) to promote; **être promu** (employé) to be promoted (à to).

prompt [prɔ̃] a swift, prompt, quick. ◆**promptitude** nf swiftness, promptness.

promulguer [prɔmylge] vt to promulgate.

prôner [prone] vt (vanter) to extol; (préconiser) to advocate.

pronom [prɔnɔ̃] nm Gram pronoun. ◆**pronominal, -aux** a pronominal.

prononc/er [prɔnɔ̃se] vt (articuler) to pronounce; (dire) to utter; (discours) to deliver; (jugement) Jur to pronounce, pass; **—** vi Jur Ling to pronounce; **— se p.** vpr (mot) to be pronounced; (personne) to reach a decision (**sur** about, on); **se p. pour** to come out in favour of. ◆**—é** a (visible) pronounced, marked. ◆**prononciation** nf pronunciation.

pronostic [prɔnɔstik] nm (*prévision*) & Sp forecast. ◆**pronostiquer** vt to forecast.

propagande [prɔpaɡɑ̃d] nf propaganda. ◆**propagandiste** nmf propagandist.

propager [prɔpaʒe] vt, — **se p.** vpr to spread. ◆**propagation** nf spread(ing).

propension [prɔpɑ̃sjɔ̃] nf propensity (à qch for sth, à faire to do).

prophète [prɔfɛt] nm prophet. ◆**prophétie** [-fesi] nf prophecy. ◆**prophétique** a prophetic. ◆**prophétiser** vti to prophesy.

propice [prɔpis] a favourable (à to).

proportion [prɔpɔrsjɔ̃] nf proportion; Math ratio; **en p. de** in proportion to; **hors de p.** out of proportion (**avec** to). ◆**proportionnel, -elle** a proportional (à to). ◆**proportionn/er** vt to proportion (à to). ◆**—é** a proportionate (à to); **bien p.** well ou nicely proportioned.

propos [prɔpo] **1** nmpl (*paroles*) remarks, utterances. **2** nm (*intention*) purpose. **3** nm (*sujet*) subject; **à p.** de about; **à p. de rien** for no reason; **à tout p.** for no reason, at every turn. **4** adv **à p.** (*arriver etc*) at the right time; **à p.!** by the way!; **juger à p. de faire** to consider it fit to do.

proposer [prɔpoze] vt (*suggérer*) to suggest, propose (qch à qn sth to s.o., que (+ sub) that); (*offrir*) to offer (qch à qn s.o. sth, de faire to do); (*candidat*) to put forward, propose: **je te propose de rester** I suggest (that) you stay; **se p. pour faire** to offer to do; **se p. de faire** to propose ou mean to do. ◆**proposition** nf suggestion, proposal; (*de paix*) proposal, (*affirmation*) proposition; Gram clause.

propre[1] [prɔpr] a clean; (*soigné*) neat; (*honnête*) decent; — nm **mettre qch au p.** to make a fair copy of sth. ◆**proprement**[1] adv (*avec propreté*) cleanly; (*avec netteté*) neatly; (*comme il faut*) decently. ◆**propreté** nf cleanliness; (*netteté*) neatness.

propre[2] [prɔpr] **1** a (à soi) own; **mon p. argent** my own money; **ses propres mots** his very ou his own words. **2** a (*qui convient*) right, proper; **p. à** (*attribut, coutume etc*) peculiar to; (*approprié*) well-suited to; **p. à faire** likely to do; **sens p.** literal meaning; **nom p.** proper noun; — nm **le p. de** (*qualité*) the distinctive quality of sth; **au p.** (*au sens propre*) literally. ◆**proprement**[2] adv (*strictement*) strictly; **à p. parler** strictly speaking; **le village/etc p. dit** the village/etc proper ou itself.

propriété [prɔprijete] nf **1** (*bien*) property;

(*droit*) ownership, property. **2** (*qualité*) property. **3** (*de mot*) suitability. ◆**propriétaire** nmf owner; (*d'hôtel*) proprietor, owner; (*qui loue*) landlord, landlady; **p.** foncier landowner.

propulser [prɔpylse] vt (*faire avancer, projeter*) to propel. ◆**propulsion** nf propulsion.

prosaïque [prɔzaik] a prosaic, pedestrian.

proscrire* [prɔskrir] vt to proscribe, banish. ◆**proscrit, -ite** nmf (*personne*) exile. ◆**proscription** nf banishment.

prose [proz] nf prose.

prospecter [prɔspɛkte] vt (*sol*) to prospect; (*pétrole*) to prospect for; (*région*) Com to canvass. ◆**prospecteur, -trice** nmf prospector. ◆**prospection** nf prospecting; Com canvassing.

prospectus [prɔspɛktys] nm leaflet, prospectus.

prospère [prɔspɛr] a (*florissant*) thriving, prosperous; (*riche*) prosperous. ◆**prospérer** vi to thrive, flourish, prosper. ◆**prospérité** nf prosperity.

prostate [prɔstat] nf Anat prostate (gland).

prostern/er (se) [səprɔstɛrne] vpr to prostrate oneself (**devant** before). ◆**—é** a prostrate. ◆**—ement** nm prostration.

prostituer [prɔstitɥe] vt to prostitute; — **se p.** vpr to prostitute oneself. ◆**prostituée** nf prostitute. ◆**prostitution** nf prostitution.

prostré [prɔstre] a (*accablé*) prostrate. ◆**prostration** nf prostration.

protagoniste [prɔtaɡɔnist] nmf protagonist.

protecteur, -trice [prɔtɛktœr, -tris] nmf protector; (*mécène*) patron; — a (*geste etc*) & Écon protective; (*ton, air*) Péj patronizing. ◆**protection** nf protection; (*mécénat*) patronage (**de** qn etc) protective. ◆**protectionnisme** nm Écon protectionism.

protég/er [prɔteʒe] vt to protect (**de** from, **contre** against); (*appuyer*) Fig to patronize; — **se p.** vpr to protect oneself. ◆**—é** nm protégé. ◆**—ée** nf protégée. ◆**protège-cahier** nm exercise book cover.

protéine [prɔtein] nf protein.

protestant, -ante [prɔtɛstɑ̃, -ɑ̃t] a & nmf Protestant. ◆**protestantisme** nm Protestantism.

protester [prɔtɛste] vi to protest (**contre** against); **p. de** (*son innocence etc*) to protest; — vt to protest (**que** that). ◆**protestation** nf protest (**contre** against); pl (*d'amitié*) protestations (**de** of).

prothèse [prɔtɛz] nf **(appareil de) p.** (membre) artificial limb; (dents) false teeth.

protocole [prɔtɔkɔl] nm protocol.

prototype [prɔtɔtip] nm prototype.

protubérance [prɔtyberɑ̃s] nf protuberance. ◆**protubérant** a (yeux) bulging; (menton) protruding.

proue [pru] nf Nau prow, bow(s).

prouesse [prues] nf feat, exploit.

prouver [pruve] vt to prove (que that).

Provence [prɔvɑ̃s] nf Provence. ◆**provençal, -ale, -aux** a & nmf Provençal.

provenir* [prɔvnir] vi **p. de** to come from. ◆**provenance** nf origin; **en p. de** from.

proverbe [prɔvɛrb] nm proverb. ◆**proverbial, -aux** a proverbial.

providence [prɔvidɑ̃s] nf providence. ◆**providentiel, -ielle** a providential.

province [prɔvɛ̃s] nf province; **la p.** the provinces; **en p.** in the provinces; **de p.** (ville etc) provincial. ◆**provincial, -ale, -aux** a & nmf provincial.

proviseur [prɔvizœr] nm (de lycée) headmaster.

provision [prɔvizjɔ̃] nf 1 (réserve) supply, stock; pl (achats) shopping; (vivres) provisions: **panier/sac à provisions** shopping basket/bag. 2 (acompte) advance payment; **chèque sans p.** dud cheque.

provisoire [prɔvizwar] a temporary, provisional. ◆**—ment** adv temporarily, provisionally.

provoquer [prɔvɔke] vt 1 (causer) to bring about, provoke; (désir) to arouse. 2 (défier) to provoke (s.o.). ◆**provocant** a provocative. ◆**provocateur** nm troublemaker. ◆**provocation** nf provocation.

proxénète [prɔksenɛt] nm pimp.

proximité [prɔksimite] nf closeness, proximity; **à p.** close by; **à p. de** close to.

prude [pryd] a prudish; – nf prude.

prudent [prydɑ̃] a (circonspect) cautious, careful; (sage) sensible. ◆**prudemment** [-amɑ̃] adv cautiously, carefully; (sagement) sensibly. ◆**prudence** nf caution, care, prudence; (sagesse) wisdom; **par p.** as a precaution.

prune [pryn] nf (fruit) plum. ◆**pruneau, -x** nm prune. ◆**prunelle** nf 1 (fruit) sloe. 2 (de l'œil) pupil. ◆**prunier** nm plum tree.

P.-S. [pees] abrév (post-scriptum) PS.

psaume [psom] nm psalm.

pseudo- [psødo] préf pseudo-.

pseudonyme [psødɔnim] nm pseudonym.

psychanalyse [psikanaliz] nf psychoanalysis. ◆**psychanalyste** nmf psychoanalyst.

psychiatre [psikjatr] nmf psychiatrist. ◆**psychiatrie** nf psychiatry. ◆**psychiatrique** a psychiatric.

psychique [psiʃik] a mental, psychic.

psycho [psiko] préf psycho-.

psychologie [psikɔlɔʒi] nf psychology. ◆**psychologique** a psychological. ◆**psychologue** nmf psychologist.

psychose [psikoz] nf psychosis.

PTT [petete] nfpl (Postes, Télégraphes, Téléphones) Post Office, = GPO.

pu [py] voir pouvoir 1.

puant [pyɑ̃] a stinking. ◆**puanteur** nf stink, stench.

pub [pyb] nf Fam (réclame) advertising; (annonce) ad.

puberté [pybɛrte] nf puberty.

public, -ique [pyblik] a public; **dette publique** national debt; – nm public; (de spectacle) audience; **le grand p.** the general public; **en p.** in public. ◆**publiquement** adv publicly.

publication [pyblikasjɔ̃] nf (action, livre etc) publication. ◆**publier** vt to publish.

publicité [pyblisite] nf publicity (pour for); (réclame) advertising, publicity; (annonce) advertisement; Rad TV commercial. ◆**publicitaire** a (agence, film) publicity-, advertising-.

puce [pys] nf 1 flea; **le marché aux puces, les puces** the flea market. 2 (d'un ordinateur) chip, microchip.

puceron [pysrɔ̃] nm greenfly.

pudeur [pydœr] nf (sense of) modesty; **attentat à la p.** Jur indecency. ◆**pudibond** a prudish. ◆**pudique** a modest.

puer [pɥe] vi to stink; – vt to stink of.

puériculture [pɥerikyltyr] nf infant care, child care. ◆**puéricultrice** nf children's nurse.

puéril [pɥeril] a puerile. ◆**puérilité** nf puerility.

puis [pɥi] adv then; **et p. quoi?** and so what?

puiser [pɥize] vt to draw, take (dans from); – vi **p. dans** to dip into.

puisque [pɥisk(ə)] conj since, as.

puissant [pɥisɑ̃] a powerful. ◆**puissamment** adv powerfully. ◆**puissance** nf (force, nation) & Math Tech power; **en p.** (talent, danger etc) potential.

puits [pɥi] nm well; (de mine) shaft.

pull(-over) [pyl(ɔvɛr)] nm pullover, sweater.

pulluler [pylyle] vi Péj to swarm.

pulmonaire [pylmɔnɛr] a (congestion, maladie) of the lungs, lung-.

pulpe [pylp] *nf* (*de fruits*) pulp.

pulsation [pylsasjɔ̃] *nf* (*heart*)beat.

pulvériser [pylverize] *vt* (*broyer*) & *Fig* to pulverize; (*liquide*) to spray. ◆**pulvérisateur** *nm* spray, atomizer. ◆**pulvérisation** *nf* (*de liquide*) spraying.

punaise [pynɛz] *nf* **1** (*insecte*) bug. **2** (*clou*) drawing pin, *Am* thumbtack. ◆**punaiser** *vt* (*fixer*) to pin (up).

punch [pɔ̃ʃ] *nm* **1** (*boisson*) punch. **2** [pœnʃ] (*énergie*) punch.

punir [pynir] *vt* to punish. ◆**punissable** *a* punishable (**de** by). ◆**punition** *nf* punishment.

pupille [pypij] **1** *nf* (*de l'œil*) pupil. **2** *nmf* (*enfant sous tutelle*) ward.

pupitre [pypitr] *nm* (*d'écolier*) desk; (*d'orateur*) lectern; **p. à musique** music stand.

pur [pyr] *a* pure; (*alcool*) neat, straight. ◆**purement** *adv* purely. ◆**pureté** *nf* purity.

purée [pyre] *nf* purée; **p. (de pommes de terre**) mashed potatoes, mash.

purgatoire [pyrgatwar] *nm* purgatory.

purge [pyrʒ] *nf* *Pol Méd* purge.

purger [pyrʒe] *vt* **1** (*conduite*) *Tech* to drain, clear. **2** (*peine*) *Jur* to serve.

purifier [pyrifje] *vt* to purify. ◆**purification** *nf* purification.

purin [pyrɛ̃] *nm* liquid manure.

puriste [pyrist] *nmf Gram* purist.

puritain, -aine [pyritɛ̃, -ɛn] *a* & *nmf* puritan.

pur-sang [pyrsɑ̃] *nm inv* (*cheval*) thoroughbred.

pus[1] [py] *nm* (*liquide*) pus, matter.

pus[2], **put** [py] *voir* **pouvoir 1**.

putain [pytɛ̃] *nf Péj Fam* whore.

putois [pytwa] *nm* (*animal*) polecat.

putréfier [pytrefje] *vt*, **— se p.** *vpr* to putrefy. ◆**putréfaction** *nf* putrefaction.

puzzle [pœzl] *nm* (*jigsaw*) puzzle, jigsaw.

p.-v. [peve] *nm inv* (*procès-verbal*) (*traffic*) fine.

PVC [pevese] *nm* (*plastique*) PVC.

pygmée [pigme] *nm* pygmy.

pyjama [piʒama] *nm* pyjamas, *Am* pajamas; **un p. a pair** of pyjamas *ou Am* pajamas; **de p.** (*veste, pantalon*) pyjama-, *Am* pajama-.

pylône [pilon] *nm* pylon.

pyramide [piramid] *nf* pyramid.

Pyrénées [pirene] *nfpl* **les P.** the Pyrenees.

pyromane [piroman] *nmf* arsonist, firebug.

python [pitɔ̃] *nm* (*serpent*) python.

Q

Q, q [ky] *nm* Q, q.

QI [kyi] *nm inv abrév* (*quotient intellectuel*) IQ.

qu' [k] *voir* **que**.

quadrill/er [kadrije] *vt* (*troupes, police*) to be positioned throughout, comb, cover (*town etc*). ◆**-é** *a* (*papier*) squared. ◆**-age** *nm* (*lignes*) squares.

quadrupède [k(w)adryped] *nm* quadruped.

quadruple [k(w)adrypl] *a* **q. de** fourfold; **—** *nm* **le q. de** four times as much as. ◆**quadrupl/er** *vti* to quadruple. ◆**-és, -ées** *nmfpl* (*enfants*) quadruplets, quads.

quai [ke] *nm Nau* quay; (*pour marchandises*) wharf; (*de fleuve*) embankment, bank; *Rail* platform.

qualification [kalifikasjɔ̃] *nf* **1** description. **2** (*action*) *Sp* qualifying, qualification. ◆**qualificatif** *nm* (*mot*) term. ◆**qualifi/er/ 1** *vt* (*décrire*) to describe (**de** as); **se faire q. de menteur/**etc to be called a liar/etc. **2** *vt* (*rendre apte*) & *Sp* to qualify (**pour qch** for sth, **pour faire** to do); **— se q.** *vpr Sp* to qualify (**pour** for). **3** *vt Gram* to qualify. ◆**-é** *a* qualified (**pour faire** to do); (*ouvrier, main-d'œuvre*) skilled.

qualité [kalite] *nf* quality; (*condition sociale etc*) occupation, status; **produit/**etc **de** high-quality product/etc; **en sa q. de** in one's capacity as. ◆**qualitatif, -ive** *a* qualitative.

quand [kɑ̃] *conj* & *adv* when; **q. je viendrai** when I' come; **c'est pour q.?** (*réunion, mariage*) when is it?; **q. bien même vous le feriez** even if you did it; **q. même** all the same.

quant (à) [kɑ̃ta] *prép* as for.

quantité [kɑ̃tite] *nf* quantity; **une q., des quantités** (*beaucoup*) a lot (**de** of); **en q.** (*abondamment*) in plenty. ◆**quantifier** *vt* to quantify. ◆**quantitatif, -ive** *a* quantitative.

quarante [karɑ̃t] *a* & *nm* forty. ◆**quarantaine** *nf* **1** **une q. (de**) (*nombre*) (about) forty; **avoir la q.** (*âge*) to be about forty. **2** *Méd* quarantine; **mettre en q.** *Méd* to quarantine; *Fig* to send to Coventry, *Am* give the silent treatment to. ◆**quarantième** *a* & *nmf* fortieth.

quart [kar] *nm* **1** quarter; **q.** (**de litre**) quarter litre, quarter of a litre; **q. d'heure** quarter of an hour; **un mauvais q. d'heure** *Fig* a trying time; **une heure et q.** an hour and a quarter; **il est une heure et q.** it's a quarter past *ou Am* after one; **une heure moins le q.** a quarter to one. **2** *Nau* watch; **de q.** on watch.

quartette [kwartɛt] *nm* (jazz) quartet(te).

quartier [kartje] **1** *nm* neighbourhood, district; (*chinois etc*) quarter; **de q.** (*cinéma etc*) local; **les gens du q.** the local people. **2** *nm* (*de pomme, lune*) piece; (*d'orange*) segment. **3** *nm*(*pl*) **quartier(s)** *Mil* quarters; **q. général** headquarters.

quartz [kwarts] *nm* quartz; **montre**/*etc* **à q.** quartz watch/*etc*.

quasi [kazi] *adv* almost. ◆**quasi-** *préf* near; **q.-obscurité** near darkness. ◆**quasiment** *adv* almost.

quatorze [katɔrz] *a* & *nm* fourteen. ◆**quatorzième** *a* & *nmf* fourteenth.

quatre [katr] *a* & *nm* four; **se mettre en q.** to go out of one's way (**pour faire** to do); **son q. heures** (*goûter*) one's afternoon snack; **un de ces q.** *Fam* some day soon. ◆**quatrième** *a* & *nmf* fourth. ◆**quatrièmement** *adv* fourthly.

quatre-vingt(s) [katrəvɛ̃] *a* & *nm* eighty; **q.-vingts ans** eighty years; **q.-vingt-un** eighty-one. ◆**q.-vingt-dix** *a* & *nm* ninety.

quatuor [kwatɥɔr] *nm Mus* quartet(te).

que [k(ə)] (**qu'** before a vowel or mute *h*) **1** *conj* that; **je pense qu'elle restera** I think (that) she'll stay; **qu'elle vienne ou non** whether she comes or not; **qu'il s'en aille!** let him leave!; **ça fait un an q. je suis là** I've been here for a year; **ça fait un an q. je suis parti** I left a year ago. **2** (*ne*) . . . **q.** only; **tu n'as qu'un franc** you only have one franc. **3** (*comparaison*) than; (*avec aussi, même, tel, autant*) as; **plus/moins âgé q. lui** older/younger than him; **aussi sage**/*etc* **q.** as wise/*etc* as; **le même q.** the same as. **4** *adv* (*ce*) **qu'il est bête!** (*comme*) how silly he is!; **q. de gens!** (*combien*) what a lot of people! **5** *pron rel* (*chose*) that, which; (*personne*) that, whom; (*temps*) when; **le livre q. j'ai** the book (that *ou* which) I have; **l'ami q. j'ai** the friend (that *ou* whom) I have; **un jour**/*mois*/*etc* **q.** one day/month/*etc* when. **6** *pron interrogatif* what; **q. fait-il?**,

qu'est-ce qu'il fait? what is he doing?; **qu'est-ce qui est dans ta poche?** what's in your pocket?; **q. préférez-vous?** which do you prefer?

Québec [kebɛk] *nm* le Q. Quebec.

quel, quelle [kɛl] **1** *a interrogatif* what, which; (*qui*) who; **q. livre/acteur?** what *ou* which book/actor?; **q. livre/acteur préférez-vous?** which *ou* what book/actor do you prefer?; **q. est cet homme?** who is that man?; **je sais q. est ton but** I know what your aim is; **q. qu'il soit** (*chose*) whatever it may be; (*personne*) whoever *ou* he may be; – *pron interrogatif* which (one); **q. est le meilleur?** which (one) is the best? **2** *a exclamatif* **q. idiot!** what a fool!; **q. joli bébé!** what a pretty baby!

quelconque [kɛlkɔ̃k] *a* **1** any, some (or other); **une raison q.** any reason (whatever *ou* at all), some reason (or other). **2** (*banal*) ordinary.

quelque [kɛlk(ə)] **1** *a* some; **q. jour** some day; **quelques femmes** a few women, some women; **les quelques amies qu'elle a** the few friends she has. **2** *adv* (*environ*) about, some; **et q.** *Fam* and a bit; **q. grand qu'il soit** however tall he may be; **q. numéro qu'elle choisisse** whichever number she chooses; **q. peu** somewhat. **3** *pron* **q. chose** something; (*interrogation*) anything, something; **il a q. chose** *Fig* there's something the matter with him; **q. chose d'autre** something else; **q. chose de grand**/*etc* something big/*etc*. **4** *adv* **q. part** somewhere; (*interrogation*) anywhere, somewhere.

quelquefois [kɛlkəfwa] *adv* sometimes.

quelques-uns, -unes [kɛlkəzœ̃, -yn] *pron pl* some.

quelqu'un [kɛlkœ̃] *pron* someone, somebody; (*interrogation*) anyone, anybody, someone, somebody; **q. d'intelligent**/*etc* someone clever/*etc*.

quémander [kemɑ̃de] *vt* to beg for.

qu'en-dira-t-on [kɑ̃diratɔ̃] *nm inv* (*propos*) gossip.

quenelle [kənɛl] *nf Culin* quenelle, fish *ou* meat roll.

querelle [kərɛl] *nf* quarrel, dispute. ◆**se quereller** *vpr* to quarrel. ◆**querelleur, -euse** *a* quarrelsome.

question [kɛstjɔ̃] *nf* question (*affaire, problème*) matter, issue, question; **il est q. de** it's a question *ou* question of (**faire** doing); (*on projette de*) there's some question of (**faire** doing); **il n'en est pas q.** there's no question of it, it's out of the question; **en q.** in question; **hors de q.** out of the question;

(re)mettre en q. to (call in) question.
◆**questionner** vt to question (sur about).
quête [kɛt] nf 1 (collecte) collection. 2 (recherche) quest (de for); **en q. de** in quest ou search of. ◆**quêter** vt to seek, beg for; – vi to collect money.

queue [kø] nf 1 (d'animal) tail; (de fleur) stalk, stem; (de fruit) stalk; (de poêle) handle; (de comète) trail; (de robe) train; (de cortège, train) rear; **q. de cheval** (coiffure) ponytail; **faire une q. de poisson** Aut to cut in (à qn in front of s.o.); **à la q.** (de classe) at the bottom of; **à la q. leu leu** (marcher) in single file. 2 (file) queue, Am line; **faire la q.** to queue up. Am line up. 3 (de billard) cue.
◆**q.-de-pie** nf (pl queues-de-pie) (habit) tails.

qui [ki] pron (personne) who, that; (interrogatif) who; (après prép) whom; (chose) which, that; **l'homme q.** the man who ou that; **la maison q.** the house which ou that; **q.?** who?; **q. (est-ce q.) est là?** who's there?; **q. désirez-vous voir?**, **q. est-ce que vous désirez voir?** who(m) do you want to see?; **sans q.** without whom; **la femme de q. je parle** the woman I'm talking about ou about whom I'm talking; **l'ami sur l'aide de q. je compte** the friend on whose help I rely; **q. que vous soyez** whoever you are, whoever you may be; **q. que ce soit** anyone (at all); **à q. est ce livre?** whose book is this?
quiche [kiʃ] nf (tarte) quiche.
quiconque [kikɔ̃k] pron (celui qui) whoever; (n'importe qui) anyone.
quignon [kiɲɔ̃] nm chunk (of bread).
quille [kij] nf 1 (de navire) keel. 2 (de jeu) skittle; pl (jeu) skittles, ninepins. 3 (jambe) Fam leg.
quincaillier, -ière [kɛ̃kaje, -jɛr] nmf hardware dealer, ironmonger. ◆**quincaillerie** nf hardware; (magasin) hardware shop.
quinine [kinin] nf Méd quinine.
quinquennal, -aux [kɛ̃kenal, -o] a (plan) five-year.
quinte [kɛ̃t] nf Méd coughing fit.

quintessence [kɛ̃tesɑ̃s] nf quintessence.
quintette [kɛ̃tɛt] nm Mus quintet(te).
quintuple [kɛ̃typl] a q. de fivefold; – nm le q. de five times as much as. ◆**quintupl**er vti to increase fivefold. ◆**-és**, **-ées** nmfpl (enfants) quintuplets, quins.
quinze [kɛ̃z] a & nm fifteen; **q. jours** two weeks, fortnight. ◆**quinzaine** nf une q. (de) (nombre) (about) fifteen; **q. (de jours)** two weeks, fortnight. ◆**quinzième** a & nmf fifteenth.
quiproquo [kiprɔko] nm misunderstanding.
quittance [kitɑ̃s] nf receipt.
quitte [kit] a quits, even (envers with); **q. à faire** even if it means doing; **en être q. pour une amende**/etc (to be lucky enough to) get off with a fine/etc.
quitter [kite] vt to leave; (ôter) to take off; – vi **ne quittez pas!** Tél hold the line!, hold on!; – **se q.** vpr (se séparer) to part.
qui-vive (sur le) [syrləkiviv] adv on the alert.
quoi [kwa] pron what; (après prép) which; **à q. penses-tu?** what are you thinking about?; **après q.** after which; **ce à q. je m'attendais** what I was expecting; **de q. manger**/etc (assez) enough to eat/etc; **de q. couper/écrire**/etc (instrument) something to cut/write/etc with; **q. que je dise** whatever I say; **q. que ce soit** anything (at all); **q. qu'il en soit** be that as it may; **il n'y a pas de q.!** (en réponse à 'merci') don't mention it!; **q.?** what?; **c'est un idiot, q.!** (non traduit) Fam he's a fool!
quoique [kwak(ə)] conj (+ sub) (al)though.
quolibet [kɔlibɛ] nm Litt gibe.
quorum [k(w)ɔrɔm] nm quorum.
quota [k(w)ɔta] nm quota.
quote-part [kɔtpar] nf (pl quotes-parts) share.
quotidien, -ienne [kɔtidjɛ̃, -jɛn] a (journalier) daily; (banal) everyday; – nm daily (paper). ◆**quotidiennement** adv daily.
quotient [kɔsjɑ̃] nm quotient.

R

R, r [ɛr] nm R, r.
rabâch/er [rabaʃe] vt to repeat endlessly; – vi to repeat oneself ◆**-age** nm endless repetition.
rabais [rabɛ] nm (price) reduction, dis-

count; **au r.** (acheter) cheap, at a reduction.
rabaisser [rabese] vt (dénigrer) to belittle, humble; **r. à** (ravaler) to reduce to.
rabat-joie [rabaʒwa] nm inv killjoy.

rabattre° [rabatr] vt (baisser) to put ou pull down; (refermer) to close (down); (replier) to fold down ou over; (déduire) to take off; **en r.** (prétentieux) Fig to climb down (from one's high horse); **— se r.** vpr (se refermer) to close; (après avoir doublé) Aut to cut in (devant in front of); **se r. sur** Fig to fall back on.

rabbin [rabε̃] nm rabbi; **grand r.** chief rabbi.

rabibocher [rabibɔʃe] vt (réconcilier) Fam to patch it up between; **— se r.** vpr Fam to patch it up.

rabiot [rabjo] nm (surplus) Fam extra (helping); **faire du r.** Fam to work extra time.

râblé [rable] a stocky, thickset.

rabot [rabo] nm (outil) plane. ◆**raboter** vt to plane.

raboteux, -euse [rabotø, -øz] a uneven, rough.

rabougri [rabugri] a (personne, plante) stunted.

rabrouer [rabrue] vt to snub, rebuff.

racaille [rakαj] nf rabble, riffraff.

raccommod/er [rakɔmɔde] 1 vt to mend; (chaussette) to darn. 2 vt (réconcilier) Fam to reconcile; **— se r.** vpr Fam to make it up (avec with). ◆**—age** nm mending; darning.

raccompagner [rakɔ̃paɲe] vt to see ou take back (home); **r. à la porte** to see to the door, see out.

raccord [rakɔr] nm (dispositif) connection; (de papier peint) join; **r. (de peinture)** touch-up. ◆**raccord/er** vt, **— se r.** vpr to connect (up), join (up) (à with, to). ◆**—ement** nm (action, résultat) connection.

raccourc/ir [rakursir] vt to shorten; **— vi** to get shorter; (au lavage) to shrink. ◆**—i** nm 1 (chemin) short cut. 2 **en r.** (histoire etc) in a nutshell.

raccroc (par) [parrakro] adv by (a lucky) chance.

raccrocher [rakrɔʃe] vt to hang back up; (récepteur) Tél to put down; (relier) to connect (à with, to); (client) to accost; **se r. à** to hold on to, cling to; (se rapporter à) to link (up) with; **— vi** Tél to hang up, ring off.

race [ras] nf (groupe ethnique) race; (animale) breed; (famille) stock; (engeance) Péj breed; **de r.** (chien) pedigree-; (cheval) thoroughbred. ◆**racé** a (chien) pedigree-; (cheval) thoroughbred; (personne) distinguished. ◆**racial, -aux** a racial. ◆**racisme** nm racism, racialism. ◆**raciste** a & nmf racist, racialist.

rachat [raʃa] nm Com repurchase; (de firme)

take-over; Rel redemption. ◆**racheter** vt to buy back; (objet d'occasion) to buy; (nouvel article) to buy another; (firme) to take over, buy out; (pécheur, dette) to redeem; (compenser) to make up for; **r. des chaussettes/du pain/etc** to buy (some) more socks/bread/etc; **— se r.** vpr to make amends, redeem oneself.

racine [rasin] nf (de plante, personne etc) & Math root; **prendre r.** (plante) & Fig to take root.

racket [raket] nm (association) racket; (activité) racketeering.

raclée [rakle] nf Fam hiding, thrashing.

racler [rakle] vt to scrape; (enlever) to scrape off; **se r. la gorge** to clear one's throat. ◆**raclette** nf scraper; (à vitres) squeegee. ◆**racloir** nm scraper. ◆**raclures** nfpl (déchets) scrapings.

racol/er [rakole] vt (prostituée) to solicit (s.o.); (vendeur etc) to tout for (s.o.), solicit (s.o.). ◆**—age** nm soliciting; touting. ◆**—eur, -euse** nmf tout.

raconter [rakɔ̃te] vt (histoire) to tell, relate; (décrire) to describe; **r. qch à qn** (vacances etc) to tell s.o. about sth; **r. à qn que** to tell s.o. that, say to s.o. that. ◆**racontars** nmpl gossip, stories.

racornir [rakɔrnir] vt to harden; **— se r.** vpr to get hard.

radar [radar] nm radar; **contrôle r.** (pour véhicules etc) radar control. ◆**radariste** nmf radar operator.

rade [rad] nf 1 Nau (natural) harbour. 2 **laisser en r.** to leave stranded, abandon; **rester en r.** to be left behind.

radeau, -x [rado] nm raft.

radiateur [radjatœr] nm (à eau) & Aut radiator; (électrique, à gaz) heater.

radiation [radjasjɔ̃] nf 1 Phys radiation. 2 (suppression) removal (de from).

radical, -ale, -aux [radikal, -o] a radical; **—** nm Ling stem; **—** nmf Pol radical.

radier [radje] vt to strike ou cross off (de from).

radieux, -euse [radjø, -øz] a (personne, visage) radiant, beaming; (soleil) brilliant; (temps) glorious.

radin, -ine [radε̃, -in] a Fam stingy; **—** nmf Fam skinflint.

radio [radjo] 1 nf radio; (poste) radio (set); **à la r.** on the radio. 2 nf (photo) Méd X-ray; **passer ou faire une r.** to be X-rayed, have an X-ray. 3 nm (opérateur) radio operator. ◆**radioactif, -ive** a radioactive. ◆**radioactivité** nf radioactivity. ◆**radiodiffuser** vt to broadcast (on the radio). ◆**radio-**

diffusion *nf* broadcasting. ◆**radiographie** *nf* (*photo*) X-ray; (*technique*) radiography. ◆**radiographier** *vt* to X-ray. ◆**radiologie** *nf* Méd radiology. ◆**radiologue** *nmf* (*technicien*) radiographer; (*médecin*) radiologist. ◆**radiophonique** *a* (*programme*) radio-. ◆**radiotélévisé** *a* broadcast on radio and television.

radis [radi] *nm* radish; **r. noir** horseradish.

radot/er [radɔte] *vi* to drivel (on), ramble (on). ◆**—age** *nm* (*propos*) drivel.

radouc/ir (se) [saraduir] *vpr* to calm down; (*temps*) to become milder. ◆**—issement** *nm* r. (**du temps**) milder weather.

rafale [rafal] *nf* (*vent*) gust, squall; (*de mitrailleuse*) burst; (*de balles*) hail.

raffermir [rafermir] *vt* to strengthen; (*muscles etc*) to tone up; **— se r.** *vpr* to become stronger.

raffin/er [rafine] *vt* (*pétrole, sucre, manières*) to refine. ◆**—é** *a* refined. ◆**—age** *nm* (*du pétrole, sucre*) refining. ◆**—ement** *nm* (*de personne*) refinement. ◆**raffinerie** *nf* refinery.

raffoler [rafole] *vi* **r. de** (*aimer*) to be very fond of, be mad *ou* wild about.

raffut [rafy] *nm* Fam din, row.

rafiot [rafjo] *nm* (*bateau*) Péj (old) tub.

rafistoler [rafistole] *vt* Fam to patch up.

rafle [rafl] *nf* (*police*) raid.

rafler [rafle] *vt* (*enlever*) Fam to swipe, make off with.

rafraîch/ir [rafreʃir] *vt* to cool (down); (*remettre à neuf*) to brighten up; (*mémoire, personne*) to refresh; — *vi* **mettre à r.** Culin to chill; — **se r.** *vpr* (*boire*) to refresh oneself; (*se laver*) to freshen (oneself) up; (*temps*) to get cooler. ◆**—issant** *a* refreshing. ◆**—issement** *nm* **1** (*de température*) cooling. **2** (*boisson*) cold drink; *pl* (*fruits, glaces etc*) refreshments.

ragaillardir [ragajardir] *vt* to buck up.

rage [raʒ] *nf* **1** (*colère*) rage; **r. de dents** violent toothache; **faire r.** (*incendie, tempête*) to rage. **2** (*maladie*) rabies. ◆**rager** *vi* (*personne*) Fam to rage, fume. ◆**rageant** *a* Fam infuriating. ◆**rageur, -euse** *a* bad-tempered, furious.

ragots [rago] *nmpl* Fam gossip.

ragoût [ragu] *nm* Culin stew.

ragoûtant [ragutɑ̃] *a* **peu r.** (*mets, personne*) unsavory.

raid [rɛd] *nm* (*incursion, attaque*) Mil Av raid.

raide [rɛd] *a* (*rigide, guindé*) stiff; (*côte*) steep; (*cheveux*) straight; (*corde etc*) tight; **c'est r.!** (*exagéré*) Fam it's a bit stiff *ou*

much!; — *adv* (*grimper*) steeply; **tomber r. mort** to drop dead. ◆**raideur** *nf* stiffness; steepness. ◆**raidillon** *nm* (*pente*) short steep rise. ◆**raidir** *vt*, — **se r.** *vpr* to stiffen; (*corde*) to tighten; (*position*) to harden; **se r. contre** Fig to steel oneself against.

raie [rɛ] *nf* **1** (*trait*) line; (*de tissu, zèbre*) stripe; (*de cheveux*) parting, Am part. **2** (*poisson*) skate, ray.

rail [raj] *nm* (*barre*) rail; **le r.** (*transport*) rail.

railler [raje] *vt* to mock, make fun of. ◆**raillerie** *nf* gibe, mocking remark. ◆**railleur, -euse** *a* mocking.

rainure [renyr] *nf* groove.

raisin [rezɛ̃] *nm* **raisin(s)** grapes; **grain de r.** grape; **manger du r.** *ou* **des raisins** to eat grapes; **r. sec** raisin.

raison [rezɔ̃] *nf* **1** (*faculté, motif*) reason; **entendre r.** to listen to reason; **la r. pour laquelle je . . .** the reason (why *ou* that) I . . . ; **pour raisons de famille/de santé**/*etc* for family/health/*etc* reasons; **en r. de** (*cause*) on account of; **à r. de** (*proportion*) at the rate of; **avoir r. de qn/de qch** to get the better of s.o./sth; **mariage de r.** marriage of convenience; **à plus forte r.** all the more so; **r. de plus** all the more reason (**pour faire** to do, for doing). **2** **avoir r.** to be right (**de faire** to do, in doing); **donner r. à qn** to agree with s.o.; (*événement etc*) to prove s.o. right; **avec r.** rightly. ◆**raisonnable** *a* reasonable. ◆**raisonnablement** *adv* reasonably.

raisonn/er [rɛzɔne] *vi* (*penser*) to reason; (*discuter*) to argue; — *vt* **r. qn** to reason with s.o. ◆**—é** *a* (*projet*) well-thought-out. ◆**—ement** *nm* (*faculté, activité*) reasoning; (*propositions*) argument. ◆**—eur, -euse** *a* Péj argumentative; — *nmf* Péj arguer.

rajeun/ir [raʒœnir] *vt* to make (feel *ou* look) younger; (*personnel*) to infuse new blood into; (*moderniser*) to modernize, update; (*personne âgée*) Méd to rejuvenate; — *vi* to get *ou* feel *ou* look younger. ◆**—issant** *a* Méd rejuvenating. ◆**—issement** *nm* Méd rejuvenation; **le r. de la population** the population getting younger.

rajout [raʒu] *nm* addition. ◆**rajouter** *vt* to add (**à** to); **en r.** Fig to overdo it.

rajuster [raʒyste] *vt* (*mécanisme*) to readjust; (*lunettes, vêtements*) to straighten, adjust; (*cheveux*) to rearrange; — **se r.** *vpr* to straighten up *ou* tidy oneself up.

râle [rɑl] *nm* (*de blessé*) groan; (*de mourant*) death rattle. ◆**râler** *vi* (*blessé*) to groan; (*mourant*) to give the death rattle; (*protes-*

er) *Fam* to grouse, moan. ◆**râleur, -euse** *nmf Fam* grouser, moaner.

ralent/ir [ralɑ̃tir] *vti*, — **se r.** *vpr* to slow down. ◆—**i** *nm Cin TV* slow motion; **au r.** (*filmer, travailler*) in slow motion; (*vivre*) at a slower pace; **tourner au r.** (*moteur, usine*) to idle, tick over, *Am* turn over.

rallier [ralje] *vt* (*rassembler*) to rally; (*rejoindre*) to rejoin; **r. qn à** (*convertir*) to win s.o. over to; — **se r.** *vpr* (*se regrouper*) to rally; **se r. à** (*point de vue*) to come over *ou* round to.

rallonge [ralɔ̃ʒ] *nf* (*de table*) extension; (*fil électrique*) extension (lead); **une r. (de)** (*supplément*) *Fam* (some) extra. ◆**rallonger** *vti* to lengthen.

rallumer [ralyme] *vt* to light again, relight; (*lampe*) to switch on again; (*conflit, haine*) to rekindle; — **se r.** *vpr* (*guerre, incendie*) to flare up again.

rallye [rali] *nm Sp Aut* rally.

ramage [ramaʒ] **1** *nm* (*d'oiseaux*) song, warbling. **2** *nmpl* (*dessin*) foliage.

ramass/er [ramase] **1** *vt* (*prendre par terre, réunir*) to pick up; (*ordures, copies*) to collect, pick up; (*fruits, coquillages*) to gather; (*rhume, amende*) *Fam* to pick up, get; **r. une bûche** *ou* **une pelle** *Fam* to come a cropper, *Am* take a spill. **2 se r.** *vpr* (*se pelotonner*) to curl up. ◆—**é** *a* (*trapu*) squat, stocky; (*recroquevillé*) huddled; (*concis*) compact. ◆—**age** *nm* picking up; collection; gathering; **r. scolaire** school bus service.

ramassis [ramasi] *nm* **r. de** (*voyous etc*) *Péj* bunch of.

rambarde [rɑ̃bard] *nf* guardrail.

rame [ram] *nf* **1** (*aviron*) oar. **2** (*de métro*) train. **3** (*de papier*) ream. ◆**ramer** *vi* to row. ◆**rameur, -euse** *nmf* rower.

rameau, -x [ramo] *nm* branch; **les Rameaux** *Rel* Palm Sunday.

ramener [ramne] *vt* to bring *ou* take back; (*paix, calme, ordre etc*) to restore, bring back; (*remettre en place*) to put back; **r. à** (*réduire à*) to reduce to; **r. à la vie** to bring back to life; — **se r.** *vpr* (*arriver*) *Fam* to turn up; **se r. à** (*problème etc*) to boil down to.

ramier [ramje] *nm* (**pigeon**) **r.** wood pigeon.

ramification [ramifikasjɔ̃] *nf* ramification.

ramoll/ir [ramɔlir] *vt, — se r.* to soften. ◆—**i** *a* soft; (*personne*) soft-headed.

ramon/er [ramɔne] *vt* (*cheminée*) to sweep. ◆—**age** *nm* (chimney) sweeping. ◆—**eur** *nm* (chimney)sweep.

rampe [rɑ̃p] *nf* **1** (*pente*) ramp, slope; **r. de lancement** (*de fusées etc*) launch(ing) pad. **2** (*d'escalier*) banister(s). **3** (*projecteurs*) *Th* footlights.

ramper [rɑ̃pe] *vi* to crawl; (*plante*) to creep; **r. devant** *Fig* to cringe *ou* crawl to.

rancard [rɑ̃kar] *nm Fam* (*rendez-vous*) date; (*renseignement*) tip.

rancart [rɑ̃kar] *nm* **mettre au r.** *Fam* to throw out, scrap.

rance [rɑ̃s] *a* rancid. ◆**rancir** *vi* to turn rancid.

ranch [rɑ̃tʃ] *nm* ranch.

rancœur [rɑ̃kœr] *nf* rancour, resentment.

rançon [rɑ̃sɔ̃] *nf* ransom; **la r. de** (*inconvénient*) the price of (*success, fame etc*). ◆**rançonner** *vt* to hold to ransom.

rancune [rɑ̃kyn] *nf* grudge; **garder r. à qn** to bear s.o. a grudge; **sans r.!** no hard feelings! ◆**rancunier, -ière** *a* vindictive, resentful.

randonnée [rɑ̃dɔne] *nf* (*à pied*) walk, hike; (*en voiture*) drive, ride; (*en vélo*) ride.

rang [rɑ̃] *nm* (*rangée*) row, line; (*condition, grade, classement*) rank; **les rangs** (*hommes*) *Mil* the ranks (**de** of); **les rangs de ses ennemis** (*nombre*) *Fig* the ranks of his enemies; **se mettre en rang(s)** to line up (**par trois**/*etc* in threes/*etc*); **par r. de** in order of. ◆**rangée** *nf* row, line.

rang/er [rɑ̃ʒe] *vt* (*papiers, vaisselle etc*) to put away; (*chambre etc*) to tidy (up); (*chiffres, mots*) to arrange; (*voiture*) to park; **r. parmi** (*auteur etc*) to rank among; — **se r.** *vpr* (*élèves etc*) to line up; (*s'écarter*) to stand aside; (*voiture*) to pull over; (*s'assagir*) to settle down; **se r. à** (*avis de qn*) to fall in with. ◆—**é** *a* (*chambre etc*) tidy; (*personne*) steady; (*bataille*) pitched. ◆—**ement** *nm* putting away; (*de chambre etc*) tidying (up); (*espace*) storage space.

ranimer [ranime] *vt* (*réanimer, revigorer*) to revive; (*encourager*) to spur on; (*feu, querelle*) to rekindle.

rapace [rapas] **1** *a* (*avide*) grasping. **2** *nm* (*oiseau*) bird of prey.

rapatrier [rapatrije] *vt* to repatriate. ◆**rapatriement** *nm* repatriation.

râpe [rɑp] *nf Culin* grater; shredder; (*lime*) rasp. ◆**râp/er** *vt* (*fromage*) to grate; (*carottes etc*) to shred; (*finement*) to grate; (*bois*) to rasp. ◆—**é** **1** *a* (*fromage*) grated; — *nm* grated cheese. **2** *a* (*vêtement*) threadbare.

rapetisser [raptise] *vt* to make (look) smaller; (*vêtement*) to shorten; — *vi* to get smaller; (*au lavage*) to shrink; (*jours*) to get shorter.

râpeux, -euse [rɑpø, -øz] *a* rough.

raphia [rafja] *nm* raffia.

rapide [rapid] *a* fast, quick, rapid; (*pente*) steep; − *nm* (*train*) express (train); (*de fleuve*) rapid. ◆**−ment** *adv* fast, quickly, rapidly. ◆**rapidité** *nf* speed, rapidity.

rapiécer [rapjese] *vt* to patch (up).

rappel [rapɛl] *nm* (*de diplomate etc*) recall; (*évocation, souvenir*) reminder; (*paiement*) back pay; *pl Th* curtain calls; (*vaccination de*) r. *Méd* booster; **r. à l'ordre** call to order. ◆**rappeler** *vt* (*pour faire revenir*) & *Tél* to call back; (*diplomate, souvenir*) to recall; **r. qch à qn** (*redire*) to remind s.o. of sth; − *vi Tél* to call back; − **se r.** *vpr* (*histoire, personne etc*) to remember, recall, recollect.

rappliquer [raplike] *vi* (*arriver*) *Fam* to show up.

rapport [rapɔr] *nm* **1** (*lien*) connection, link; *pl* (*entre personnes*) relations; **rapports** (**sexuels**) (sexual) intercourse; **par r.** à compared to *ou* with; (*envers*) towards; **se mettre en r. avec qn** to get in touch with s.o.; **en r.** avec in keeping with; **sous le r.** de from the point of view of. **2** (*revenu*) *Com* return, yield. **3** (*récit*) report. ◆**rapporter 1** *vt* (*ramener*) to bring *ou* take back; (*ajouter*) to add; − *vi* (*chien*) to retrieve. **2** *vt* (*récit*) to report; (*mot célèbre*) to repeat; − *vi* (*moucharder*) *Fam* to tell tales. **3** *vt* (*profit*) *Com* to bring in, yield; − *vi* (*investissement*) *Com* to bring in a good return. **4** *vt* **r. qch à** (*rattacher*) to relate sth to; **se r. à** to relate to, be connected with; **s'en r. à** to rely on. ◆**rapporteur, -euse 1** *nmf* (*mouchard*) telltale. **2** *nm Jur* reporter. **3** *nm Géom* protractor.

rapproch/er [raproʃe] *vt* to bring closer (*de* to); (*chaise*) to pull up (*de* to); (*réconcilier*) to bring together; (*réunir*) to join; (*comparer*) to compare; − **se r.** *vpr* to come *ou* get closer (*de* to); (*se réconcilier*) to come together, be reconciled; (*ressembler*) to come close (*de* to). ◆**−é** *a* close, near; (*yeux*) close-set; (*fréquent*) frequent. ◆**−ement** *nm* (*réconciliation*) reconciliation; (*rapport*) connection; (*comparaison*) comparison.

rapt [rapt] *nm* (*d'enfant*) abduction.

raquette [rakɛt] *nf* (*de tennis*) racket; (*de ping-pong*) bat.

rare [rar] *a* rare; (*argent, main-d'œuvre etc*) scarce; (*barbe, herbe*) sparse; **il est r. que** (+ *sub*) it's seldom *ou* rare that. ◆**se raréfier** *vpr* (*denrées etc*) to get scarce. ◆**rarement** *adv* rarely, seldom. ◆**rareté** *nf* rarity; scarcity; **une r.** (*objet*) a rarity.

ras [rɑ] *a* (*cheveux*) close-cropped; (*herbe, poil*) short; (*mesure*) full; **en rase campagne**

in (the) open country; **à r.** de very close to; **à r. bord** (*remplir*) to the brim; **en avoir r. le bol** *Fam* to be fed up (**de** with); **pull (au) r. du cou** *ou* **à col r.** crew-neck(ed) pullover; − *adv* short.

ras/er 1 *vt* (*menton, personne*) to shave; (*barbe, moustache*) to shave off; − **se r.** *vpr* to (have a) shave. **2** *vt* (*démolir*) to raze, knock down. **3** *vt* (*frôler*) to skim, brush. **4** *vt* (*ennuyer*) *Fam* to bore. ◆**−ant** *a Fam* boring. ◆**−é** *a* **bien r.** clean-shaven; **mal r.** unshaven. ◆**−age** *nm* shaving. ◆**−eur, -euse** *nmf Fam* bore. ◆**rasoir 1** *nm* shaver. **2** *a inv Fam* boring.

rassasier [rasazje] *vti* to satisfy; **être rassasié** to have had enough (**de** of).

rassembler [rasɑ̃ble] *vt* to gather (together), assemble; (*courage*) to summon up, muster; − **se r.** *vpr* to gather, assemble. ◆**rassemblement** *nm* (*action, gens*) gathering.

rasseoir* (**se**) [səraswar] *vpr* to sit down again.

rassis, f rassie [rasi] *a* (*pain, brioche etc*) stale. ◆**rassir** *vti* to turn stale.

rassur/er [rasyre] *vt* to reassure; **rassure-toi** set your mind at rest, don't worry. ◆**−ant** *a* (*nouvelle*) reassuring, comforting.

rat [ra] *nm* rat; **r. de bibliothèque** *Fig* bookworm.

ratatiner (**se**) [səratatine] *vpr* to shrivel (up); (*vieillard*) to become wizened.

rate [rat] *nf Anat* spleen.

râteau, -x [rɑto] *nm* (*outil*) rake.

râtelier [rɑtəlje] *nm* **1** (*support pour outils, armes etc*) rack. **2** (*dentier*) *Fam* set of false teeth.

rat/er [rate] *vt* (*bus, cible, occasion etc*) to miss; (*gâcher*) to spoil, ruin; (*vie*) to waste; (*examen*) to fail; − *vi* (*projet etc*) to fail; (*pistolet*) to misfire. ◆**−é, -ée 1** *nmf* (*personne*) failure. **2** *nmpl* **avoir des ratés** *Aut* to backfire. ◆**−age** *nm* (*échec*) *Fam* failure.

ratifier [ratifje] *vt* to ratify. ◆**ratification** *nf* ratification.

ration [rɑsjɔ̃] *nf* ration; **r. de** *Fig* share of. ◆**rationn/er** *vt* (*vivres, personne*) to ration. ◆**−ement** *nm* rationing.

rationaliser [rasjɔnalize] *vt* to rationalize. ◆**rationalisation** *nf* rationalization.

rationnel, -elle [rasjɔnɛl] *a* (*pensée, méthode*) rational.

ratisser [ratise] *vt* **1** (*allée etc*) to rake; (*feuilles etc*) to rake up. **2** (*fouiller*) to comb. **3** *vt* **r. qn** (*au jeu*) *Fam* to clean s.o. out.

raton [ratɔ̃] *nm* **r. laveur** rac(c)oon.

rattach/er [rataʃe] *vt* to tie up again; (*in-*

corporer, joindre) to join (à to); (*idée, question*) to link (à to); **r. qn à** (*son pays etc*) to bind s.o. to; **se r. à** to be linked to. ◆—**ement** *nm* (*annexion*) joining (à to).

rattrap/er [ratrape] *vt* to catch; (*prisonnier etc*) to recapture; (*erreur, temps perdu*) to make up for; **r. qn** (*rejoindre*) to catch up with s.o., catch s.o. up; — **se r.** *vpr* to catch up; (*se dédommager, prendre une compensation*) to make up for it; **se r. à** (*branche etc*) to catch hold of. ◆—**age** *nm* **cours de r.** *Scol* remedial classes; **r. des prix/salaires** adjustment of prices/wages (*to the cost of living*).

rature [ratyr] *nf* deletion. ◆**raturer** *vt* to delete, cross out.

rauque [rok] *a* (*voix*) hoarse, raucous.

ravages [ravaʒ] *nmpl* devastation; (*de la maladie, du temps*) ravages; **faire des r.** to wreak havoc. ◆**ravager** *vt* to devastate, ravage.

raval/er [ravale] *vt* **1** (*façade etc*) to clean (and restore). **2** (*salive, sanglots etc*) to swallow. **3** (*avilir*) *Litt* to lower. ◆—**ement** *nm* (*de façade etc*) cleaning (and restoration).

ravi [ravi] *a* delighted (**de** with, **de faire** to do).

ravier [ravje] *nm* hors-d'œuvre dish.

ravigoter [ravigɔte] *vt Fam* to buck up.

ravin [ravɛ̃] *nm* ravine, gully.

ravioli [ravjɔli] *nmpl* ravioli.

rav/ir [ravir] *vt* **1** to delight; **à r.** (*chanter etc*) delightfully. **2** (*emporter*) to snatch (à from). ◆—**issant** *a* delightful, lovely. ◆**ravisseur, -euse** *nmf* kidnapper.

raviser (se) [səravize] *vpr* to change one's mind.

ravitaill/er [ravitaje] *vt* to provide with supplies, supply; (*avion*) to refuel; — **se r.** *vpr* to stock up (with supplies). ◆—**ement** *nm* supplying; refuelling; (*denrées*) supplies; **aller au r.** (*faire des courses*) *Fam* to stock up, get stocks in.

raviver [ravive] *vt* (*feu, sentiment*) to revive; (*couleurs*) to brighten up.

ray/er [reje] *vt* (*érafler*) to scratch; (*mot etc*) to cross out; **r. qn de** (*liste*) to cross *ou* strike s.o. off. ◆—**é** *a* scratched; (*tissu*) striped; (*papier*) lined, ruled. ◆**rayure** *nf* scratch; (*bande*) stripe; **à rayures** striped.

rayon [rɛjɔ̃] *nm* **1** (*de lumière, soleil etc*) *Phys* ray; (*de cercle*) radius; (*de roue*) spoke; (*d'espoir*) *Fig* ray; **r. X** X-ray; **r. d'action** range; **dans un r. de** within a radius of. **2** (*planche*) shelf; (*de magasin*) department. **3** (*de ruche*) honeycomb. ◆**rayonnage** *nm* shelving, shelves.

rayonn/er [rɛjɔne] *vi* to radiate; (*dans une région*) to travel around (*from a central base*); **r. de joie** to beam with joy. ◆—**ant** *a* (*visage etc*) radiant, beaming (**de** with). ◆—**ement** *nm* (*éclat*) radiance; (*influence*) influence; (*radiation*) radiation.

raz-de-marée [radmare] *nm inv* tidal wave; (*bouleversement*) *Fig* upheaval; **r.-de-marée électoral** landslide.

razzia [ra(d)zja] *nf* **faire une r. sur** (*tout enlever sur*) *Fam* to raid.

re- [r(ə)] *préf* re-.

ré- [re] *préf* re-.

réabonn/er (se) [səreabɔne] *vpr* to renew one's subscription (à to). ◆—**ement** *nm* renewal of subscription.

réacteur [reaktœr] *nm* (*d'avion*) jet engine; (*nucléaire*) reactor.

réaction [reaksjɔ̃] *nf* reaction; **r. en chaîne** chain reaction; **avion à r.** jet (aircraft); **moteur à r.** jet engine. ◆**réactionnaire** *a* & *nmf* reactionary.

réadapter [readapte] *vt*, — **se r.** *vpr* to readjust (à to). ◆**réadaptation** *nf* readjustment.

réaffirmer [reafirme] *vt* to reaffirm.

réagir [reaʒir] *vi* to react (**contre** against, **à** to); (*se secouer*) *Fig* to shake oneself out of it.

réalis/er [realize] *vt* (*projet etc*) to carry out, realize; (*ambition, rêve*) to fulfil; (*achat, bénéfice, vente*) to make; (*film*) to direct; (*capital*) *Com* to realize; (*se rendre compte*) to realize (**que** that); — **se r.** *vpr* (*vœu*) to come true; (*projet*) to be carried out; (*personne*) to fulfil oneself. ◆—**able** *a* (*plan*) workable; (*rêve*) attainable. ◆**réalisateur, -trice** *nmf Cin TV* director. ◆**réalisation** *nf* realization; (*de rêve*) fulfilment; *Cin TV* direction; (*œuvre*) achievement.

réalisme [realism] *nm* realism. ◆**réaliste** *a* realistic; — *nmf* realist.

réalité [realite] *nf* reality; **en r.** in (actual) fact, in reality.

réanimer [reanime] *vt Méd* to resuscitate. ◆**réanimation** *nf* resuscitation; (**service de) r.** intensive care unit.

réapparaître [reaparɛtr] *vi* to reappear. ◆**réapparition** *nf* reappearance.

réarmer [rearme] *vt* (*fusil etc*) to reload; — *vi*, — **se r.** *vpr* (*pays*) to rearm. ◆**réarmement** *nm* rearmament.

rébarbatif, -ive [rebarbatif, -iv] *a* forbidding, off-putting.

rebâtir [r(ə)batir] *vt* to rebuild.

rebattu [r(ə)baty] *a* (*sujet*) hackneyed.

rebelle [rəbɛl] a rebellious; (troupes) rebel-; (fièvre) stubborn; (mèche) unruly; **r. à** resistant to; — nmf rebel. **◆se rebeller** vpr to rebel (**contre** against). **◆rébellion** nf rebellion.

rebiffer (se) [sər(ə)bife] vpr Fam to rebel.

rebond [r(ə)bɔ̃] nm bounce; (par ricochet) rebound. **◆rebondir** vi to bounce; to rebound; (faire) **r**. (affaire, discussion etc) to get going again. **◆rebondissement** nm new development (**de** in).

rebondi [r(ə)bɔ̃di] a chubby, rounded.

rebord [r(ə)bɔr] nm edge; (de plat etc) rim; (de vêtement) hem; **r. de (la) fenêtre** windowsill, window ledge.

reboucher [r(ə)buʃe] vt (flacon) to put the top back on.

rebours (à) [ar(ə)bur] adv the wrong way.

rebrousse-poil (à) [arbruspwal] adv prendre qn à r.-poil Fig to rub s.o. up the wrong way.

rebrousser [r(ə)bruse] vt **r. chemin** to turn back.

rebuffade [rəbyfad] nf Litt rebuff.

rébus [rebys] nm inv (jeu) rebus.

rebut [rəby] nm **mettre au r.** to throw out, scrap; **le r. de la société** Péj the dregs of society.

rebut/er [r(ə)byte] vt (décourager) to put off; (choquer) to repel. **◆—ant** a off-putting; (choquant) repellent.

récalcitrant [rekalsitrɑ̃] a recalcitrant.

recaler [r(ə)kale] vt **r. qn** Scol Fam to fail s.o., flunk s.o.; **être recalé, se faire r.** Scol Fam to fail, flunk.

récapituler [rekapityle] vti to recapitulate. **◆récapitulation** nf recapitulation.

recel [rəsɛl] nm receiving stolen goods, fencing; harbouring. **◆receler** vt (mystère, secret etc) to contain; (objet volé) to receive; (malfaiteur) to harbour. **◆receleur, -euse** nmf receiver (of stolen goods), fence.

recens/er [r(ə)sɑ̃se] vt (population) to take a census of; (inventorier) to make an inventory of. **◆—ement** nm census; inventory.

récent [resɑ̃] a recent. **◆récemment** [-amɑ̃] adv recently.

récépissé [resepise] nm (reçu) receipt.

récepteur [resɛptœr] nm Tél Rad receiver. **◆réceptif, -ive** a receptive (**à** to). **◆réception** nf (accueil, soirée) & Rad reception; (de lettre etc) Com receipt; (d'hôtel etc) reception (desk). **◆réceptionniste** nmf receptionist.

récession [resesjɔ̃] nf Écon recession.

recette [r(ə)sɛt] nf **1** Culin & Fig recipe. **2**

(argent, bénéfice) takings; (bureau) tax office; **recettes** (rentrées) Com receipts; **faire r.** Fig to be a success.

recev/oir [rəsvwar] vt to receive; (obtenir) to get, receive; (accueillir) to welcome; (accepter) to accept; **être reçu (à)** (examen) to pass; **être reçu premier** to come first; — vi to receive guests ou visitors ou Méd patients. **◆—able** a (excuse etc) admissible. **◆—eur, -euse** nmf (d'autobus) (bus) conductor, (bus) conductress; (des impôts) tax collector; (des postes) postmaster, postmistress.

rechange (de) [dər(ə)ʃɑ̃ʒ] a (pièce, outil etc) spare; (solution etc) alternative; **vêtements/chaussures de r.** a change of clothes/shoes.

rechapé [r(ə)ʃape] a **pneu r.** retread.

réchapper [reʃape] vi **r. de** ou **à** (accident etc) to come through.

recharge [r(ə)ʃarʒ] nf (de stylo etc) refill. **◆recharger** vt (camion, fusil) to reload; (briquet, stylo etc) to refill; (batterie) to recharge.

réchaud [reʃo] nm (portable) stove.

réchauff/er [reʃofe] vt (personne, aliment etc) to warm up; — **se r.** vpr to warm oneself up; (temps) to get warmer. **◆—é** nm du **r.** Fig Péj old hat. **◆—ement** nm (de température) rise (**de** in).

rêche [rɛʃ] a rough, harsh.

recherche [r(ə)ʃɛrʃ] nf **1** search, quest (**de** for); **à la r. de** in search of. **2 la r., des recherches** (scientifique etc) research (**sur** on, into); **faire des recherches** to research; (enquête) to make investigations. **3** (raffinement) studied elegance; Péj affectation. **◆recherch/er** vt to search ou hunt for; (cause, faveur, perfection) to seek. **◆—é** a **1** (très demandé) in great demand; (rare) much sought-after; **r. pour meurtre** wanted for murder. **2** (élégant) elegant; Péj affected.

rechigner [r(ə)ʃiɲe] vi (renâcler) to jib (**à qch** at sth, **à faire** at doing).

rechute [r(ə)ʃyt] nf Méd relapse. **◆rechuter** vi Méd to (have a) relapse.

récidive [residiv] nf Jur further offence; Méd recurrence (**de** of). **◆récidiver** vi Jur to commit a further offence; (maladie) to recur. **◆récidiviste** nmf Jur further offender.

récif [resif] nm reef.

récipient [resipjɑ̃] nm container, receptacle.

réciproque [resiprɔk] a mutual, reciprocal; — nf (inverse) opposite; **rendre la r. à qn** to get even with s.o. **◆réciprocité** nf reciprocity. ◆**réciproquement** *adv* (*l'un l'autre*) each other; **et r.** and vice versa.

récit [resi] *nm* (*compte rendu*) account; (*histoire*) story.

récital, *pl* **-als** [resital] *nm* Mus recital.

réciter [resite] *vt* to recite. ◆**récitation** *nf* recitation.

réclame [reklam] *nf* advertising; (*annonce*) advertisement; **en r.** Com on (special) offer; **- a** *inv* **prix r.** (special) offer price; **vente r.** (bargain) sale.

réclamer [reklame] *vt* (*demander, nécessiter*) to demand, call for; (*revendiquer*) to claim; **- vi** to complain; **se r. de qn** to invoke s.o.'s authority. ◆**réclamation** *nf* complaint; *pl* (*bureau*) complaints department.

reclasser [r(ə)klase] *vt* (*fiches etc*) to reclassify.

reclus, -use [rəkly, -yz] *a* (*vie*) cloistered; **-** *nmf* recluse.

réclusion [reklyzjɔ̃] *nf* imprisonment (with hard labour); **r. à perpétuité** life imprisonment.

recoiffer (se) [sər(ə)kwafe] *vpr* (*se peigner*) to do *ou* comb one's hair.

recoin [rəkwɛ̃] *nm* nook, recess.

recoller [r(ə)kɔle] *vt* (*objet cassé*) to stick together again; (*enveloppe*) to stick back down.

récolte [rekɔlt] *nf* (*action*) harvest; (*produits*) crop, harvest; (*collection*) Fig crop. ◆**récolter** *vt* to harvest, gather (in); (*recueillir*) Fig to collect, gather; (*coups*) *Fam* to get.

recommand/er [r(ə)kɔmɑ̃de] **1** *vt* (*appuyer, conseiller*) to recommend; **r. à qn de faire** to recommend s.o. to do. **2** *vt* (*lettre etc*) to register. **3** *vt* **r. à** (*âme*) to commend to. **4 se r.** *vpr* **se r. de qn** to invoke s.o.'s authority. ◆**-é** *nm* **en r.** (*envoyer*) by registered post. ◆**-able** *a* **peu r.** not very commendable. ◆**recommandation** *nf* **1** (*appui, conseil, louange*) recommendation. **2** (*de lettre etc*) registration.

recommenc/er [r(ə)kɔmɑ̃se] *vti* to start *ou* begin again. ◆**-ement** *nm* (*reprise*) renewal (**de** of).

récompense [rekɔ̃pɑ̃s] *nf* reward (**de** for); (*prix*) award; **en r. de** in return for. ◆**récompenser** *vt* to reward (**de, pour** for).

réconcilier [rekɔ̃silje] *vt* to reconcile; **- se r.** *vpr* to become reconciled, make it up (**avec** with). ◆**réconciliation** *nf* reconciliation.

reconduire* [r(ə)kɔ̃dɥir] *vt* **1 r. qn** to see *ou*

take s.o. back; (*à la porte*) to show s.o. out. **2** (*mesures etc*) to renew. ◆**reconduction** *nf* renewal.

réconfort [rekɔ̃fɔr] *nm* comfort. ◆**réconfort/er** *vt* to comfort; (*revigorer*) to fortify. ◆**-ant** *a* comforting; (*boisson etc*) fortifying.

reconnaissant [r(ə)kɔnesɑ̃] *a* grateful, thankful (**à qn de qch** to s.o. for sth). ◆**reconnaissance**[1] *nf* (*gratitude*) gratitude.

reconnaître* [r(ə)kɔnɛtr] *vt* to recognize (**à qch** by sth); (*admettre*) to acknowledge, admit (**que** that); (*terrain*) Mil to reconnoitre; **être reconnu coupable** to be found guilty; **- se r.** *vpr* (*s'orienter*) to find one's bearings; **se r. coupable** to admit one's guilt. ◆**reconnu** *a* (*chef, fait*) acknowledged, recognized. ◆**reconnaissable** *a* recognizable (**à qch** by sth). ◆**reconnaissance**[2] *nf* recognition; (*aveu*) acknowledgement; Mil reconnaissance; **r. de dette** IOU.

reconsidérer [r(ə)kɔ̃sidere] *vt* to reconsider.

reconstituant [r(ə)kɔ̃stitɥɑ̃] *adj* (*aliment, régime*) restorative.

reconstituer [r(ə)kɔ̃stitɥe] *vt* (*armée, parti*) to reconstitute; (*crime, quartier*) to reconstruct; (*faits*) to piece together; (*fortune*) to build up again. ◆**reconstitution** *nf* reconstitution; reconstruction.

reconstruire* [r(ə)kɔ̃strɥir] *vt* (*ville, fortune*) to rebuild. ◆**reconstruction** *nf* rebuilding.

reconvertir [r(ə)kɔ̃vertir] **1** *vt* (*bâtiment etc*) to reconvert. **2 se r.** *vpr* to take up a new form of employment. ◆**reconversion** *nf* reconversion.

recopier [r(ə)kɔpje] *vt* to copy out.

record [r(ə)kɔr] *nm & a inv* Sp record.

recoucher (se) [sər(ə)kuʃe] *vpr* to go back to bed.

recoudre* [r(ə)kudr] *vt* (*bouton*) to sew back on.

recoup/er [r(ə)kupe] *vt* (*témoignage etc*) to tally with, confirm; **- se r.** *vpr* to tally, match *ou* tie up. ◆**-ement** *nm* cross-check(ing).

recourbé [r(ə)kurbe] *a* curved; (*nez*) hooked.

recours [r(ə)kur] *nm* recourse (**à** to); Jur appeal; **avoir r. à** to resort to; (*personne*) to turn to; **notre dernier r.** our last resort. ◆**recourir** *vi* **r. à** to resort to; (*personne*) to turn to.

recouvrer [r(ə)kuvre] vt (argent, santé) to recover.

recouvrir* [r(ə)kuvrir] vt (livre, meuble, sol etc) to cover; (de nouveau) to recover; (cacher) Fig to conceal, mask.

récréation [rekreasjɔ̃] nf recreation; (temps) Scol break, playtime.

récriminer [rekrimine] vi to complain bitterly (contre about). ◆**récrimination** nf (bitter) complaint.

récrire [rekrir] vt (lettre etc) to rewrite.

recroqueviller (se) [s(ə)rəkrɔkvije] vpr (papier, personne etc) to curl up.

recrudescence [rəkrydesɑ̃s] nf new outbreak (de of).

recrue [rəkry] nf recruit. ◆**recrut/er** vt to recruit. ◆**—ement** nm recruitment.

rectangle [rɛktɑ̃gl] nm rectangle. ◆**rectangulaire** a rectangular.

rectifier [rɛktifje] vt (erreur etc) to correct, rectify; (ajuster) to adjust. ◆**rectificatif** nm (document) amendment, correction. ◆**rectification** nf correction, rectification.

recto [rɛkto] nm front (of the page).

reçu [r(ə)sy] voir **recevoir**; − a (usages etc) accepted; (idée) conventional, received; (candidat) successful; − nm (écrit) Com receipt.

recueil [r(ə)kœj] nm (ouvrage) collection (de of).

recueill/ir* [r(ə)kœjir] 1 vt to collect, gather; (suffrages) to win, get; (prendre chez soi) to take in. 2 se r. vpr to meditate; (devant un monument) to stand in silence. ◆**—i** − a (air) meditative. ◆**—ement** nm meditation.

recul [r(ə)kyl] nm (d'armée, de négociateur, de maladie) retreat; (éloignement) distance; (déclin) decline; (mouvement de) r. de véhicule) backward movement; avoir un mouvement de r. (personne) to recoil; phare de r. Aut reversing light. ◆**reculade** nf Péj retreat. ◆**recul/er** vi to move ou step back; Aut to reverse; (armée) to retreat; (épidémie, glacier) to recede, retreat; (renoncer) to back down, retreat; (diminuer) to decline; r. devant Fig to recoil ou shrink from; − vt to move ou push back; (différer) to postpone. ◆**—é** a (endroit, temps) remote.

reculons (à) [arkylɔ̃] adv backwards.

récupérer [rekypere] vt to recover, get back; (ferraille etc) to salvage; (heures) to make up; (mouvement, personne etc) Pol Péj to take over, convert; − vi to recuper-

ate, recover. ◆**récupération** nf recovery; salvage; recuperation.

récurer [rekyre] vt (casserole etc) to scour; poudre à r. scouring powder.

récuser [rekyze] vt to challenge; − se r. vpr to decline to give an opinion.

recycl/er [r(ə)sikle] vt (reconvertir) to retrain (s.o.); (matériaux) to recycle; − se r. vpr to retrain. ◆**—age** nm retraining; recycling.

rédacteur, -trice [redaktœr, -tris] nmf writer; (de chronique) Journ editor; (de dictionnaire etc) compiler; r. en chef Journ editor(-in-chief). ◆**rédaction** nf (action) writing; (de contrat) drawing up; (devoir) Scol essay, composition; (rédacteurs) Journ editorial staff; (bureaux) Journ editorial offices.

reddition [redisjɔ̃] nf surrender.

redemander [rədmɑ̃de] vt (pain etc) to ask for more; r. qch à qn to ask s.o. for sth back.

rédemption [redɑ̃psjɔ̃] nf Rel redemption.

redescendre [r(ə)desɑ̃dr] vi (aux être) to come ou go back down; − vt (aux avoir) (objet) to bring ou take back down.

redevable [rədvabl] a être r. de qch à qn (argent) to owe s.o. sth; Fig to be indebted to s.o. for sth.

redevance [rədvɑ̃s] nf (taxe) TV licence fee; Tél rental charge.

redevenir* [rədvənir] vi (aux être) to become again.

rédiger [rediʒe] vt to write; (contrat) to draw up; (dictionnaire etc) to compile.

redire* [r(ə)dir] 1 vt to repeat. 2 vi avoir ou trouver à r. à qch to find fault with sth. ◆**redite** nf (pointless) repetition.

redondant [r(ə)dɔ̃dɑ̃] a (style) redundant.

redonner [r(ə)dɔne] vt to give back; (de nouveau) to give more.

redoubl/er [r(ə)duble] vti 1 to increase; r. de patience/etc to be much more patient/etc; à coups redoublés (frapper) harder and harder. 2 r. (une classe) Scol to repeat a year ou Am a grade. ◆**—ant, -ante** nmf pupil repeating a year ou Am a grade. ◆**—ement** nm increase (de in); repeating a year ou Am a grade.

redout/er [r(ə)dute] vt to dread (de faire doing). ◆**—able** a formidable, fearsome.

redress/er [r(ə)drese] vt to straighten (out); (économie, mât, situation, tort) to right; − se r. vpr (se mettre assis) to sit up; (debout) to stand up; (pays, situation etc) to right itself. ◆**—ement** [-ɛsmɑ̃] nm (essor) recovery.

réduction [redyksjɔ̃] *nf* reduction (**de** in); **en r.** (*copie, modèle etc*) small-scale.

réduire* [redɥir] *vt* to reduce (**à** to, **de** by); **r. qn à** (*contraindre à*) to reduce s.o. to (*silence, inaction etc*); **se r. à** (*se ramener à*) to come down to, amount to; **se r. en cendres***/etc* to be reduced to ashes*/etc*; – *vi* **(faire) r.** (*sauce*) to reduce, boil down. ◆**réduit** 1 *a* (*prix, vitesse*) reduced; (*moyens*) limited; (*à petite échelle*) small-scale. 2 *nm* (*pièce*) *Péj* cubbyhole; (*recoin*) recess.

réécrire [reekrir] *vt* (*texte*) to rewrite.

rééduquer [reedyke] *vt* (*membre*) *Méd* to re-educate; **r. qn** to rehabilitate s.o., re-educate s.o. ◆**rééducation** *nf* re-education; rehabilitation.

réel, -elle [reɛl] *a* real; **r.** reality. ◆**réellement** *adv* really.

réélire [reelir] *vt* to re-elect.

réexpédier [reekspedje] *vt* (*lettre etc*) to forward; (*à l'envoyeur*) to return.

refaire* [r(ə)fɛr] *vt* to do again, redo; (*erreur, voyage*) to make again; (*réparer*) to do up, redo; (*duper*) *Fam* to take in. ◆**réfection** *nf* repair(ing).

réfectoire [refɛktwar] *nm* refectory.

référendum [referɑ̃dɔm] *nm* referendum.

référer [refere] *vi* **en r. à** to refer the matter to; – **se r.** *vpr* **se r. à** to refer to. ◆**référence** *nf* reference.

refermer [r(ə)fɛrme] *vt*, – **se r.** *vpr* to close *ou* shut (again).

refiler [r(ə)file] *vt* (*donner*) *Fam* to palm off (**à** on).

réfléchir [refleʃir] 1 *vt* (*image*) to reflect; – **se r.** *vpr* to be reflected. 2 *vi* (*penser*) to think (**à, sur** about); – *vt* **r. que** to realize that. ◆**–i** *a* (*personne*) thoughtful, reflective; (*action, décision*) carefully thought-out; (*verbe*) *Gram* reflexive. ◆**réflecteur** *nm* reflector. ◆**réflexion** *nf* 1 (*de lumière etc*) reflection. 2 (*méditation*) thought, reflection; (*remarque*) remark; **à la r., r. faite** on second thoughts *ou Am* thought,on reflection.

reflet [r(ə)flɛ] *nm* (*image*) & *Fig* reflection; (*lumière*) glint; (*couleur*) tint. ◆**refléter** *vt* (*image, sentiment etc*) to reflect; – **se r.** *vpr* to be reflected.

réflexe [reflɛks] *nm* & *a* reflex.

refluer [r(ə)flye] *vi* (*eaux*) to ebb, flow back; (*foule*) to surge back. ◆**reflux** *nm* ebb; backward surge.

réforme *nf* 1 (*changement*) reform. 2 (*de soldat*) discharge. ◆**réformateur, -trice** *nmf* reformer. ◆**réformer** 1 *vt* to reform;

– **se r.** *vpr* to mend one's ways. 2 *vt* (*soldat*) to invalid out, discharge.

refoul/er [r(ə)fule] *vt* to force *ou* drive back; (*sentiment*) to repress; (*larmes*) to hold back. ◆**–é** *a* (*personne*) *Psy* repressed. ◆**–ement** *nm Psy* repression.

réfractaire [refrakter] *a* **r. à** resistant to.

refrain [r(ə)frɛ̃] *nm* (*de chanson*) refrain, chorus; (*rengaine*) *Fig* tune.

refréner [r(ə)frene] *vt* to curb, check.

réfrigér/er [refriʒere] *vt* to refrigerate. ◆**–ant** *a* (*accueil, air*) *Fam* icy. ◆**réfrigérateur** *nm* refrigerator. ◆**réfrigération** *nf* refrigeration.

refroid/ir [r(ə)frwadir] *vt* to cool (down); (*décourager*) *Fig* to put off; (*ardeur*) to dampen, cool; – *vi* to get cold, cool down; – **se r.** *vpr Méd* to catch cold; (*temps*) to get cold; (*ardeur*) to cool (off). ◆**–issement** *nm* cooling; (*rhume*) chill; **r. de la température** fall in the temperature.

refuge [r(ə)fyʒ] *nm* refuge; (*pour piétons*) (traffic) island; (*de montagne*) (mountain) hut. ◆**se réfugi/er** *vpr* to take refuge. ◆**–é, -ée** *nmf* refugee.

refus [r(ə)fy] *nm* refusal; **ce n'est pas de r.** *Fam* I won't say no. ◆**refuser** *vt* to refuse (**qch à qn** s.o. sth. ◆**de faire** to do); (*offre, invitation*) to turn down, refuse; (*client*) to turn away, refuse; (*candidat*) to fail; – **se r.** *vpr* (*plaisir etc*) to deny oneself; **se r. à** (*évidence etc*) to refuse to accept, reject; **se r. à croire***/etc* to refuse to believe*/etc*.

réfuter [refyte] *vt* to refute.

regagner [r(ə)gaɲe] *vt* (*récupérer*) to regain; (*revenir à*) to get back to. ◆**regain** *nm* **r. de** (*retour*) renewal of.

régal, *pl* -als [regal] *nm* treat. ◆**régaler** *vt* to treat to a delicious meal; **r. de** to treat to; – **se r.** *vpr* to have a delicious meal.

regard [r(ə)gar] *nm* (*coup d'œil, expression*) look; (*fixe*) stare, gaze; **chercher du r.** to look (a)round for; **attirer les regards** to attract attention; **jeter un r. sur** to glance at. 2 *au r. de* in regard to; **en r. de** compared with. ◆**regard/er** 1 *vt* to look at; (*fixement*) to stare at, gaze at; (*observer*) to watch; (*considérer*) to consider, regard (**comme** as); **r. qn faire** to watch s.o. do; – *vi* to look; to stare, gaze; to watch; **r. à** (*dépense, qualité etc*) to pay attention to; **r. vers** (*maison etc*) to face; – **se r.** *vpr* (*personnes*) to look at each other. 2 *vt* (*concerner*) to concern. ◆**–ant** *a* (*économe*) careful (**with money**).

régates [regat] *nfpl* regatta.

régence [reʒɑ̃s] *nf* regency.

régénérer [reʒenere] *vt* to regenerate.

régenter [reʒɑ̃te] vt to rule over.

régie [reʒi] nf (entreprise) state-owned company; Th stage management; Cin TV production department.

regimber [r(ə)ʒɛ̃be] vi to balk (contre at).

régime [reʒim] nm 1 system; Pol régime. 2 Méd diet; **se mettre au r.** to go on a diet; **suivre un r.** to be on a diet. 3 (de moteur) speed; **à ce r.** Fig at this rate. 4 (de bananes, dattes) bunch.

régiment [reʒimɑ̃] nm Mil regiment; **un r. de** (quantité) Fig a host of.

région [reʒjɔ̃] nf region, area. ◆**régional, -aux** a regional.

régir [reʒir] vt (déterminer) to govern.

régisseur [reʒisœr] nm (de propriété) steward; Th stage manager; Cin assistant director.

registre [rəʒistr] nm register.

règle [rɛgl] 1 nf (principe) rule; **en r.** (papiers d'identité etc) in order; **être/se mettre en r. avec qn** to be/put oneself right with s.o.; **en r. générale** as a (general) rule. 2 nf (instrument) ruler; **r. à calcul** slide rule. 3 nfpl (menstruation) period.

règlement [rɛgləmɑ̃] nm 1 (arrêté) regulation; (règles) regulations. 2 (de conflit, problème etc) settling; (paiement) payment; **r. de comptes** Fig (violent) settling of scores. ◆**réglementaire** a in accordance with the regulations; (tenue) Mil regulation-. ◆**réglementation** nf 1 (action) regulation. 2 (règles) regulations. ◆**réglementer** vt to regulate.

régler [regle] 1 vt (conflit, problème etc) to settle; (mécanisme) to regulate, adjust; (moteur) to tune; (papier) to rule; **se r. sur** to model oneself on. 2 vti (payer) to pay; **r. qn** to settle up with s.o.; **r. son compte à** Fig to settle old scores with s.o. ◆**réglé** a (vie) ordered; (papier) ruled. ◆**réglable** a (siège etc) adjustable. ◆**réglage** nm adjustment; (de moteur) tuning.

réglisse [reglis] nf liquorice, Am licorice.

règne [rɛɲ] nm reign; (animal, minéral, végétal) kingdom. ◆**régner** vi to reign; (prédominer) to prevail; **faire r. l'ordre** to maintain (law and) order.

regorger [r(ə)ɡɔrʒe] vi **r. de** to be overflowing with.

régresser [regrese] vi to regress. ◆**régression** nf regression; **en r.** on the decline.

regret [r(ə)grɛ] nm regret; **à r.** with regret; **avoir la r.** ou **être au r. de faire** to be sorry to do. ◆**regrett/er** vt to regret; **r. qn** to miss s.o.; **je regrette** I'm sorry; **r. que** (+ sub) to

be sorry that, regret that. ◆**—able** a regrettable.

regrouper [r(ə)grupe] vt, **— se r.** vpr to gather together.

régulariser [regylarize] vt (situation) to regularize.

régulation [regylasjɔ̃] nf (action) regulation.

régulier, -ière [regylje, -jɛr] a regular; (progrès, vie, vitesse) steady; (légal) legal; (honnête) honest. ◆**régularité** nf regularity; steadiness; legality. ◆**régulièrement** adv regularly; (normalement) normally.

réhabiliter [reabilite] vt (dans l'estime publique) to rehabilitate.

réhabituer (se) [səreabitɥe] vpr **se r. à qch/à faire qch** to get used to sth/to doing sth again.

rehausser [rəose] vt to raise; (faire valoir) to enhance.

réimpression [reɛ̃presjɔ̃] nf (livre) reprint.

rein [rɛ̃] nm kidney; pl (dos) small of the back; **r. artificiel** Méd kidney machine.

reine [rɛn] nf queen.

reine-claude [rɛnklod] nf greengage.

réintégrer [reɛ̃tegre] vt 1 (fonctionnaire etc) to reinstate. 2 (lieu) to return to. ◆**réintégration** nf reinstatement.

réitérer [reitere] vt to repeat.

rejaillir [r(ə)ʒajir] vi to spurt (up ou out); **r. sur** Fig to rebound on.

rejet [r(ə)ʒɛ] nm 1 (refus) & Méd rejection. 2 Bot shoot. ◆**rejeter** vt to throw back; (épave) to cast up; (vomir) to bring up; (refuser) & Méd to reject; **r. une erreur/etc sur qn** to put the blame for a mistake/etc on s.o.

rejeton [rəʒtɔ̃] nm (enfant) Fam kid.

rejoindre* [r(ə)ʒwɛ̃dr] vt (famille, régiment) to rejoin, get ou go back to; (lieu) to get back to; (route, rue) to join; **r. qn** to join ou meet s.o.; (rattraper) to catch up with s.o.; **— se r.** vpr (personnes) to meet; (routes, rues) to join, meet.

réjou/ir [reʒwir] vt to delight; **— se r.** vpr to be delighted (**de** at, about; **de faire** to do). ◆**—i** a (air) joyful. ◆**—issant** a cheering. ◆**réjouissance** nf rejoicing; pl festivities, rejoicings.

relâche [r(ə)lɑʃ] nf Th Cin (temporary) closure; **faire r.** (théâtre, cinéma) to close; (bateau) to put in (**dans un port** at a port); **sans r.** without a break.

relâch/er [r(ə)lɑʃe] vt 1 **r. qn** to slacken; (discipline, étreinte) to relax; **r. qn** to release s.o.; **— se r.** vpr to slacken; (discipline) to get lax. 2 vi (bateau) to put in. ◆**—é** a lax.

◆**—ement** nm (de corde etc) slackness; (de discipline) slackening.

relais [r(ə)le] nm Él Rad TV relay; (course de) r. Sp (race); **r. routier** transport café, Am truck stop (café); **prendre le r.** to take over (de from).

relance [r(ə)lɑ̃s] nf (reprise) revival. ◆**relancer** vt to throw back; (moteur) to restart; (industrie etc) to put back on its feet; **r. qn** (solliciter) to pester s.o.

relater [r(ə)late] vt to relate (que that).

relatif, -ive [r(ə)latif, -iv] a relative (à to). ◆**relativement** adv relatively; **r. à** compared to, relative to.

relation [r(ə)lasjɔ̃] nf (rapport) relation(ship); (ami) acquaintance; **avoir des relations** (amis influents) to have connections; **entrer/être en relations avec** to come into/be in contact with; **relations internationales/etc** international/etc relations.

relax(e) [rəlaks] a Fam relaxed, informal.

relaxer (se) [sər(ə)lakse] vpr to relax. ◆**relaxation** nf relaxation.

relayer [r(ə)leje] vt to relieve, take over from; (émission) to relay; — **se r.** vpr to take (it in) turns (**pour faire** to do); Sp to take over from one another.

reléguer [r(ə)lege] vt to relegate (à to).

relent [rəlɑ̃] nm stench, smell.

relève [r(ə)lɛv] nf (remplacement) relief; **prendre la r.** to take over (de from).

relev/er [rəlve] vt to raise; (ramasser) to pick up; (chaise etc) to put up straight; (personne tombée) to help up; (col) to turn up; (manches) to roll up; (copier) to note down; (traces) to find; (relayer) to relieve; (rehausser) to enhance; (sauce) to season; (faute) to pick up ou point out; (compteur) to read; (défi) to accept; (économie, pays) to put back on its feet; (mur) to rebuild; **r. qn de** (fonctions) to relieve s.o. of; — vi **r. de** (dépendre de) to come under; (maladie) to get over; — **se r.** vpr (personne) to get up; **se r. de** (malheur) to recover from; (ruines) to rise from. ◆**—é** nm list; (de dépenses) statement; (de compteur) reading; **r. de compte** (bank) statement. ◆**relèvement** nm (d'économie, de pays) recovery.

relief [rəljɛf] nm 1 (forme, ouvrage) relief; **en r.** (cinéma) three-D; (livre) pop-up; **mettre en r.** Fig to highlight. 2 nmpl (de repas) remains.

relier [rəlje] vt to link, connect (à to); (ensemble) to link (together); (livre) to bind.

religion [r(ə)liʒjɔ̃] nf religion; (foi) faith. ◆**religieux, -euse** 1 a religious; **mariage**

r. church wedding; — nm monk; — nf nun. 2 nf Culin cream bun.

reliquat [r(ə)lika] nm (de dette etc) remainder.

relique [r(ə)lik] nf relic.

relire* [r(ə)lir] vt to reread.

reliure [rəljyr] nf (couverture de livre) binding; (art) bookbinding.

reluire [r(ə)lɥir] vi to shine, gleam; **faire r.** (polir) to shine (up). ◆**reluisant** a shiny; **peu r.** Fig far from brilliant.

reluquer [r(ə)lyke] vt Fig to eye (up).

remâcher [r(ə)mɑ̃ʃe] vt Fig to brood over.

remanier [r(ə)manje] vt (texte) to revise; (ministère) to reshuffle. ◆**remaniement** nm revision.

remarier (se) [sər(ə)marje] vpr to remarry.

remarque [r(ə)mark] nf remark; (annotation) note; **je lui en ai fait la r.** I remarked on it to him ou her. ◆**remarquable** a remarkable (par for). ◆**remarquablement** adv remarkably. ◆**remarquer** vt 1 (apercevoir) to notice (que that); **faire r.** to point out (à to, que that); **se faire r.** to attract attention; **remarque!** mind (you)! 2 (dire) to remark (que that).

rembarrer [rɑ̃bare] vt to rebuff, snub.

remblai [rɑ̃ble] nm (terres) embankment. ◆**remblayer** vt (route) to bank up; (trou) to fill in.

rembourr/er [rɑ̃bure] vt (matelas etc) to stuff, pad; (vêtement) to pad. ◆**—age** nm (action, matière) stuffing; padding.

rembourser [rɑ̃burse] vt to pay back, repay; (billet) to refund. ◆**remboursement** nm repayment; refund; **envoi contre r.** cash on delivery.

remède [r(ə)mɛd] nm remedy, cure; (médicament) medicine. ◆**remédier** vi **r. à** to remedy.

remémorer (se) [sər(ə)memɔre] vpr (histoire etc) to recollect, recall.

remercier [r(ə)mɛrsje] vt 1 to thank (**de qch, pour qch,** for sth); **je vous remercie d'être venu** thank you for coming; **je vous remercie** (non merci) no thank you. 2 (congédier) to dismiss. ◆**remerciements** nmpl thanks.

remettre* [r(ə)mɛtr] vt to put back, replace; (vêtement) to put back on; (donner) to hand over (à to); (restituer) to give back (à to); (démission, devoir) to hand in; (différer) to postpone (à until); (ajouter) to add more ou another; (peine) Jur to remit; (guérir) to restore to health; (reconnaître) to place, remember; **r. en cause ou question** to call into question; **r. en état** to repair; **r. ça** Fam to start again; **se r. à** (*activité*) to go back to; **se r. à faire** to start to do again; **se r. de** (*chagrin, maladie*) to recover from, get over; **s'en r. à** to rely on. ◆**remise** *nf* **1** (*de lettre etc*) delivery; (*de peine*) *Jur* remission; (*ajournement*) postponement; **r. en cause** *ou* **question** calling into question; **r. en état** repair(ing). **2** (*rabais*) discount. **3** (*local*) shed; *Aut* garage. ◆**remiser** *vt* to put away.

rèminiscences [reminisɑ̃s] *nfpl* (*vague*) recollections, reminiscences.

rèmission [remisjɔ̃] *nf Jur Rel Mèd* remission; **sans r.** (*travailler etc*) relentlessly.

remmener [rɑ̃mne] *vt* to take back.

remonte-pente [r(ə)mɔ̃tpɑ̃t] *nm* ski lift.

remont/er [r(ə)mɔ̃te] *vi* (*aux être*) to come *ou* go back up; (*niveau, prix*) to rise again, go back up; (*dans le temps*) to go back (à to); **r. dans** (*voiture etc*) to go *ou* get back in(to); (*bus, train*) to go *ou* get back on(to); **r. sur** (*cheval, vèlo*) to remount; – *vt* (*aux avoir*) (*escalier, pente*) to come *ou* go back up; (*porter*) to bring *ou* take back up; (*montre*) to wind; (*relever*) to raise; (*col*) to turn up; (*objet dèmontè*) to reassemble; (*garde-robe etc*) to restock; **r. qn** (*ragaillardir*) to buck s.o. up; **r. le moral à qn** to cheer s.o. up. ◆**—ant** *a* (*boisson*) fortifying; – *nm Mèd* tonic. ◆**—èe** *nf* **1** (*de pente etc*) ascent; (*d'eau, de prix*) rise. **2 r. mècanique** ski lift. ◆**remontoir** *nm* (*de mècanisme, montre*) winder.

remontrance [r(ə)mɔ̃trɑ̃s] *nf* reprimand; **faire des remontrances à** to reprimand, remonstrate with.

remontrer [r(ə)mɔ̃tre] *vi* **en r. à qn** to prove one's superiority over s.o.

remords [r(ə)mɔr] *nm* & *nmpl* remorse; **avoir des r.** to feel remorse.

remorque [r(ə)mɔrk] *nf Aut* trailer; (*câble de*) **r.** towrope; **prendre en r.** to tow; **en r.** on tow. ◆**remorquer** *vt* (*voiture, bateau*) to tow. ◆**remorqueur** *nm* tug(boat).

remous [r(ə)mu] *nm* eddy; (*de foule*) bustle; (*agitation*) *Fig* turmoil.

rempart [rɑ̃par] *nm* rampart.

remplacer [rɑ̃plase] *vt* to replace (**par** with, by); (*succèder à*) to take over from; (*temporairement*) to stand in for. ◆**remplaçant, -ante** *nmf* (*personne*) replacement; (*enseignant*) supply teacher; *Sp* reserve. ◆**remplacement** *nm* (*action*) replacement; **assurer le r. de qn** to stand in for s.o.; **en r. de** in place of.

rempl/ir [rɑ̃plir] *vt* to fill (up) (**de** with); (*fiche etc*) to fill in *ou* out; (*condition, de-*

voir, tâche) to fulfil; (*fonctions*) to perform; – **se r.** *vpr* to fill (up). ◆**—i** *a* full (**de** of). ◆**remplissage** *nm* filling; (*verbiage*) *Pèj* padding.

remporter [rɑ̃pɔrte] *vt* **1** (*objet*) to take back. **2** (*prix, victoire*) to win; (*succès*) to achieve.

remu/er [r(ə)mɥe] *vt* (*dèplacer, èmouvoir*) to move; (*café etc*) to stir; (*terre*) to turn over; (*salade*) to toss; – *vi* to move; (*gigoter*) to fidget; (*se rebeller*) to stir; – **se r.** *vpr* to move; (*se dèmener*) to exert oneself. ◆**—ant** *a* (*enfant*) restless, fidgety. ◆**remue-mènage** *nm inv* commotion.

rèmunèrer [remynere] *vt* (*personne*) to pay; (*travail*) to pay for. ◆**rèmunèrateur, -trice** *a* remunerative. ◆**rèmunèration** *nf* payment (**de** for).

rènâcler [r(ə)nɑkle] *vi* **1** (*cheval*) to snort. **2 r. à** to jib at, balk at.

renaître* [r(ə)nɛtr] *vi* (*fleur*) to grow again; (*espoir, industrie*) to revive. ◆**renaissance** *nf* rebirth, renaissance.

renard [r(ə)nar] *nm* fox.

renchérir [rɑ̃ferir] *vi* **r. sur qn** *ou* **sur ce que qn dit**/*etc* to go further than s.o. in what one says/*etc*.

rencontre [rɑ̃kɔ̃tr] *nf* meeting; (*inattendue*) & *Mil* encounter; *Sp* match, *Am* game; (*de routes*) junction; **aller à la r. de** to go to meet. ◆**rencontrer** *vt* to meet; (*difficultès*) to come up against, encounter; (*trouver*) to come across, find; (*heurter*) to hit; (*èquipe*) *Sp* to play; – **se r.** *vpr* to meet.

rendez-vous [rɑ̃devu] *nm inv* appointment; (*d'amoureux*) date; (*lieu*) meeting place; **donner r.-vous à qn, prendre r.-vous avec qn** to make an appointment with s.o.

rendormir (se) [sərɑ̃dɔrmir] *vpr* to go back to sleep.

rend/re [rɑ̃dr] *vt* (*restituer*) to give back, return; (*hommage*) to pay; (*invitation*) to return; (*santè*) to restore; (*monnaie, son*) to give; (*justice*) to dispense; (*jugement*) to pronounce, give; (*armes*) to surrender; (*exprimer, traduire*) to render; (*vomir*) to bring up; **r. cèlèbre/plus grand/possible**/*etc* to make famous/bigger/possible/*etc*; – *vi* (*arbre, terre*) to yield; (*vomir*) to be sick; – **se r.** *vpr* (*capituler*) to surrender (**à** to); (*aller*) to go (à to); **se r. à** (*èvidence, ordres*) to submit to; **se r. malade/utile**/*etc* to make oneself ill/useful/*etc*. ◆**—u** *a* (*fatiguè*) exhausted; **être r.** (*arrivè*) to have arrived. ◆**rendement** *nm Agr Fin* yield; (*de personne, machine*) output.

rènègat, -ate [rənega, -at] *nmf* renegade.

rênes [rɛn] *nfpl* reins.

renferm/er [rɑ̃fɛrme] *vt* to contain; **— se r.** *vpr* **se r. (en soi-même)** to withdraw into oneself. ◆**—é** *a* (*personne*) withdrawn. **2** *nm* **sentir le r.** (*chambre etc*) to smell stuffy.

renflé [rɑ̃fle] *a* bulging. ◆**renflement** *nm* bulge.

renflouer [rɑ̃flue] *vt* (*navire*) & *Com* to refloat.

renfoncement [rɑ̃fɔ̃smɑ̃] *nm* recess; **dans le r. d'une porte** in a doorway.

renforcer [rɑ̃fɔrse] *vt* to reinforce, strengthen. ◆**renforcement** *nm* reinforcement, strengthening. ◆**renfort** *nm* **des renforts** *Mil* reinforcements; **de r.** (*armée, personnel*) back-up; **à grand r. de** *Fig* with a great deal of.

renfrogn/er (se) [sərɑ̃frɔɲe] *vpr* to scowl. ◆**—é** *a* scowling, sullen.

rengaine [rɑ̃gɛn] *nf* **la même r.** *Fig Péj* the same old song ou story.

rengorger (se) [sərɑ̃gɔrʒe] *vpr* to give oneself airs.

renier [rənje] *vt* (*ami, pays etc*) to disown; (*foi, opinion*) to renounce. ◆**reniement** *nm* disowning; renunciation.

renifler [r(ə)nifle] *vti* to sniff. ◆**reniflement** *nm* sniff.

renne [rɛn] *nm* reindeer.

renom [rənɔ̃] *nm* renown; (*réputation*) reputation (**de** for). ◆**renommé** *a* famous, renowned (**pour** for). ◆**renommée** *nf* fame, renown; (*réputation*) reputation.

renoncer [r(ə)nɔ̃se] *vi* **r. à** to give up, abandon; **r. à faire** to give up (the idea of) doing. ◆**renoncement** *nm*, ◆**renonciation** *nf* renunciation (**à** of).

renouer [rənwe] **1** *vt* (*lacet etc*) to retie. **2** *vt* (*reprendre*) to renew; **— *vi* r. avec qch** (*mode, tradition etc*) to revive sth; **r. avec qn** to take up with s.o. again.

renouveau, -x [r(ə)nuvo] *nm* revival.

renouveler [r(ə)nuvle] *vt* to renew; (*action, erreur, question*) to repeat; **— se r.** *vpr* (*incident*) to recur, happen again; (*cellules, sang*) to be renewed. ◆**renouvelable** *a* renewable. ◆**renouvellement** *nm* renewal.

rénover [renɔve] *vt* (*institution, méthode*) to reform; (*édifice, meuble etc*) to renovate. ◆**rénovation** *nf* reform; renovation.

renseign/er [rɑ̃sɛɲe] *vt* to inform, give information to (**sur** about); **— se r.** *vpr* to inquire, make inquiries, find out (**sur** about). ◆**—ement** *nm* (*piece of*) information; *pl* information; *Tél* directory inquiries, *Am* information; *Mil* intelligence;

prendre ou **demander des renseignements** to make inquiries.

rentable [rɑ̃tabl] *a* profitable. ◆**rentabilité** *nf* profitability.

rente [rɑ̃t] *nf* (*private*) income; (*pension*) pension; **avoir des rentes** to have private means. ◆**rentier, -ière** *nmf* person of private means.

rentr/er [rɑ̃tre] *vi* (*aux* **être**) to go ou come back, return; (*chez soi*) to go ou come (back) home; (*entrer*) to go ou come in; (*entrer de nouveau*) to go ou come back in; (*école*) to start again; (*argent*) to come in; **r. dans** (*entrer dans*) to go ou come into; (*entrer de nouveau dans*) to go ou come back into; (*famille, pays*) to return to; (*ses frais*) to get back; (*catégorie*) to come under; (*heurter*) to crash into; (*s'emboîter dans*) to fit into; **r. (en classe)** to start (school) again; **je lui suis rentré dedans** (*frapper*) *Fam* I laid into him ou her; **— *vt* (*aux* **avoir**) to bring ou take in; (*voiture*) to put away; (*chemise*) to tuck in; (*griffes*) to draw in. ◆**—é** *a* (*colère*) suppressed; (*yeux*) sunken. ◆**—ée** *nf* **1** (*retour*) return; (*de parlement*) reassembly; (*d'acteur*) comeback; **r. (des classes)** beginning of term ou of the school year. **2** (*des foins etc*) bringing in; (*d'impôt*) collection; *pl* (*argent*) receipts.

renverse (à la) [alarɑ̃vɛrs] *adv* (*tomber*) backwards, on one's back.

renvers/er [rɑ̃vɛrse] *vt* (*mettre à l'envers*) to turn upside down; (*faire tomber*) to knock over ou down; (*piéton*) to knock down, run over; (*liquide*) to spill, knock over; (*courant, ordre*) to reverse; (*gouvernement*) to overturn, overthrow; (*projet*) to upset; (*tête*) to tip back; **— se r.** *vpr* (*en arrière*) to lean back; (*bouteille, vase etc*) to fall over. ◆**—ant** *a* (*nouvelle etc*) astounding. ◆**—ement** *nm* (*d'ordre, de situation*) reversal; (*de gouvernement*) overthrow.

renvoi [rɑ̃vwa] *nm* **1** return; dismissal; expulsion; postponement; (*dans un livre*) reference. **2** (*rot*) belch, burp. ◆**renvoyer*** *vt* to send back, return; (*importun*) to send away; (*employé*) to dismiss; (*élève*) to expel; (*balle etc*) to throw back; (*ajourner*) to postpone (**à** until); (*lumière, image etc*) to reflect; **r. qn à** (*adresser à*) to refer s.o. to.

réorganiser [reɔrganize] *vt* to reorganize.

réouverture [reuvɛrtyr] *nf* reopening.

repaire [r(ə)pɛr] *nm* den.

repaître (se) [sərəpɛtr] *vpr* **se r. de** (*sang*) *Fig* to wallow in.

répand/re [repɑ̃dr] *vt* (*liquide*) to spill;

(*idées, joie, nouvelle*) to spread; (*fumée, odeur*) to give off; (*chargement, lumière, larmes, sang*) to shed; (*gravillons etc*) to scatter; (*dons*) to lavish; — **se r.** *vpr* (*nouvelle, peur etc*) to spread; (*liquide*) to spill; **se r. dans** (*fumée, odeur*) to spread through; **se r. en louanges**/*etc* to pour forth praise/*etc*. ◆**—u** *a* (*opinion, usage*) widespread; (*épars*) scattered.

reparaître [r(ə)parɛtr] *vi* to reappear.

réparer [repare] *vt* to repair, mend; (*forces, santé*) to restore; (*faute*) to make amends for; (*perte*) to make good; (*erreur*) to put right. ◆**réparable** *a* (*montre etc*) repairable. ◆**réparateur, -trice** *nmf* repairer; — *a* (*sommeil*) refreshing. ◆**réparation** *nf* repair(ing); (*compensation*) amends, compensation (**de** for); *pl Mil Hist* reparations; **en r.** under repair.

reparler [r(ə)parle] *vi* **r. de** to talk about again.

repartie [reparti] *nf* (*réponse vive*) repartee.

repartir [r(ə)partir] *vi* (*aux être*) to set off again; (*s'en retourner*) to go back; (*reprendre*) to start again; **r. à** *ou* **de zéro** to go back to square one.

répartir [repartir] *vt* to distribute; (*partager*) to share (out); (*classer*) to divide (up); (*étaler dans le temps*) to spread (out) (**sur** over). ◆**répartition** *nf* distribution; sharing; division.

repas [r(ə)pɑ] *nm* meal; **prendre un r.** to have *ou* eat a meal.

repass/er [r(ə)pase] **1** *vi* to come *ou* go back; — *vt* (*traverser*) to go back over; (*examen*) to resist; (*leçon, rôle*) to go over; (*film*) to show again; (*maladie, travail*) to pass on (**à** to). **2** *vt* (*linge*) to iron. **3** *vt* (*couteau*) to sharpen. ◆**—age** *nm* ironing.

repêcher [r(ə)peʃe] *vt* to fish out; (*candidat*) *Fam* to allow to pass.

repenser [r(ə)pɑ̃se] *vt* to rethink.

repentir [r(ə)pɑ̃tir] *nm* repentance. ◆**se repentir** *vpr Rel* to repent (**de** of); **se r. de** (*regretter*) to regret, be sorry for. ◆**repentant** *a*, ◆**repenti** *a* repentant.

répercuter [reperkyte] *vt* (*son*) to echo; — **se r.** *vpr* to echo, reverberate; **se r. sur** *Fig* to have repercussions on. ◆**répercussion** *nf* repercussion.

repère [r(ə)pɛr] *nm* (*guide*) mark; (*jalon*) marker; **point de r.** (*espace, temps*) landmark, point of reference. ◆**repérer** *vt* to locate; (*personnne*) *Fam* to spot; — **se r.** *vpr* to get one's bearings.

répertoire [repertwar] *nm* **1** index; (*carnet*) indexed notebook; **r. d'adresses** address

book. **2** *Th* repertoire. ◆**répertorier** *vt* to index.

répéter [repete] *vti* to repeat; *Th* to rehearse; — **se r.** *vpr* (*radoter*) to repeat oneself; (*se reproduire*) to repeat itself. ◆**répétitif, -ive** *a* repetitive. ◆**répétition** *nf* repetition; *Th* rehearsal; **r. générale** *Th* (final) dress rehearsal.

repiquer [r(ə)pike] *vt* **1** (*plante*) to plant out. **2** (*disque*) to tape, record (on tape).

répit [repi] *nm* rest, respite; **sans r.** ceaselessly.

replacer [r(ə)plase] *vt* to replace, put back.

repli [r(ə)pli] *nm* fold; withdrawal; *pl* (*de l'âme*) recesses. ◆**replier 1** *vt* to fold (up); (*siège*) to fold up; (*couteau, couverture*) to fold back; (*ailes, jambes*) to tuck in; — **se r.** *vpr* (*siège*) to fold up; (*couteau, couverture*) to fold back. **2** *vt*, — **se r.** *vpr Mil* to withdraw; **se r. sur soi-même** to withdraw into oneself.

réplique [replik] *nf* **1** (*réponse*) reply; (*riposte*) retort; *Th* lines; **pas de r.!** no answering back!; **sans r.** (*argument*) irrefutable. **2** (*copie*) replica. ◆**répliquer** *vt* to reply (**que** that); (*riposter*) to retort (**que** that); — *vi* (*être impertinent*) to answer back.

répond/re [repɔ̃dr] *vi* to answer, reply; (*être impertinent*) to answer back; (*réagir*) to respond (**à** to); **r. à qn** to answer s.o., reply to s.o.; (*avec impertinence*) to answer s.o. back; **r. à** (*lettre, objection, question*) to answer, reply to; (*salut*) to return; (*besoin*) to meet, answer; (*correspondre à*) to correspond to; **r. de** (*garantir*) to answer for (*s.o., sth*); — *vt* (*remarque etc*) to answer *ou* reply with; **r. que** to answer *ou* reply that. ◆**—ant, -ante 1** *nmf* guarantor. **2** *nm* **avoir du r.** to have money behind one. ◆**—eur** *nm Tél* answering machine. ◆**réponse** *nf* answer, reply; (*réaction*) response (**à** to); **en r. à** in answer *ou* reply *ou* response to.

reporter[1] [r(ə)pɔrte] *vt* to take back; (*différer*) to postpone, put off (**à** until); (*transcrire, transférer*) to transfer (**sur** to); (*somme*) *Com* to carry forward (**sur** to); **se r. à** (*texte etc*) to refer to; (*en esprit*) to go *ou* think back to. ◆**report** *nm* postponement; transfer; *Com* carrying forward. ◆**reportage** *nm* (*news*) report, article; (*en direct*) commentary; (*métier*) reporting.

reporter[2] [r(ə)pɔrter] *nm* reporter.

repos [r(ə)po] *nm* rest; (*tranquillité*) peace (and quiet); (*de l'esprit*) peace of mind; **r.!** *Mil* at ease!; **jour de r.** day off; **de tout r.** (*situation etc*) safe. ◆**repos/er 1** *vt* (*objet*) to put back down; (*problème, question*) to raise again. **2** vt (délasser) to rest, relax; **r. sa tête sur** (appuyer) to rest one's head on; — vi (être enterré ou étendu) to rest, lie; **r. sur** (bâtiment) to be built on; (théorie etc) to be based on, rest on; **laisser r.** (vin) to allow to settle; — **se r.** vpr to rest; **se r. sur qn** to rely on s.o. ◆—**ant** a relaxing, restful. ◆—**é** a rested, fresh.

repouss/er [r(ə)puse] **1** vt to push back; (écarter) to push away; (attaque, ennemi) to repulse; (importun etc) to turn away, repulse; (dégoûter) to repel; (décliner) to reject; (différer) to put off, postpone. **2** vi (cheveux, feuilles) to grow again. ◆—**ant** a repulsive, repellent.

répréhensible [repreɑ̃sibl] a reprehensible, blameworthy.

reprendre* [r(ə)prɑ̃dr] vt (objet) to take back; (évadé, ville) to recapture; (passer prendre) to pick up again; (souffle) to get back; (activité) to resume, take up again; (texte) to go back over; (vêtement) to alter; (histoire, refrain) to take up; (pièce) Th to put on again; (blâmer) to admonish; (corriger) to correct; **r. de la viande/un œuf/etc** to take (some) more meat/another egg/etc; **r. ses esprits** to come round; **r. des forces** to recover one's strength; — vi (plante) to take again; (recommencer) to resume, start (up) again; (affaires) to pick up; (dire) to go on, continue; — **se r.** vpr (se ressaisir) to take a hold on oneself; (se corriger) to correct oneself; **s'y r. à deux/plusieurs fois** to have another go/several goes (at it).

représailles [r(ə)prezaj] nfpl reprisals, retaliation.

représent/er [r(ə)prezɑ̃te] vt to represent; (jouer) Th to perform; — **se r.** vpr (s'imaginer) to imagine. ◆—**ant, -ante** nmf representative; **r. de commerce** (travelling) salesman ou saleswoman, sales representative. ◆**représentatif, -ive** a representative (**de** of). ◆**représentation** nf representation; Th performance.

répression [represjɔ̃] nf suppression, repression; (mesures de contrôle) Pol repression. ◆**répressif, -ive** a repressive. ◆**réprimer** vt (sentiment, révolte etc) to suppress, repress.

réprimande [reprimɑ̃d] nf reprimand. ◆**réprimander** vt to reprimand.

repris [r(ə)pri] nm **r. de justice** hardened criminal.

reprise [r(ə)priz] nf (de ville) Mil recapture; (recommencement) resumption; (de pièce de théâtre, de coutume) revival; Rad TV repeat; (de tissu) mend, repair; Boxe round;

(essor) Com recovery, revival; (d'un locataire) money for fittings; (de marchandise) taking back; (pour nouvel achat) part exchange, trade-in; pl Aut acceleration; **à plusieurs reprises** on several occasions. ◆**repriser** vt (chaussette etc) to mend, darn.

réprobation [reprɔbasjɔ̃] nf disapproval. ◆**réprobateur, -trice** a disapproving.

reproche [r(ə)prɔʃ] nm reproach; **faire des reproches à qn** to reproach s.o.; **sans r.** beyond reproach. ◆**reprocher** vt **r. qch à qn** to reproach ou blame s.o. for sth; **r. qch à qch** to have sth against sth; **n'avoir rien à se r.** to have nothing to reproach ou blame oneself for.

reproduire* [r(ə)prɔdɥir] **1** vt (son, modèle etc) to reproduce; — **se r.** vpr Biol Bot to reproduce. **2 se r.** vpr (incident etc) to happen again, recur. ◆**reproducteur, -trice** a reproductive. ◆**reproduction** nf (de son etc) & Biol Bot reproduction.

réprouver [repruve] vt to disapprove of, condemn.

reptile [reptil] nm reptile.

repu [rəpy] a (rassasié) satiated.

république [repyblik] nf republic. ◆**républicain, -aine** a & nmf republican.

répudier [repydje] vt to repudiate.

répugnant [repynɑ̃] a repugnant, loathsome. ◆**répugnance** nf repugnance, loathing (**pour** for); (manque d'enthousiasme) reluctance. ◆**répugner** vi **r. à qn** to be repugnant to s.o.; **r. à faire** to be loath to do.

répulsion [repylsjɔ̃] nf repulsion.

réputation [repytasjɔ̃] nf reputation; **avoir la r. d'être franc** to have a reputation for frankness ou for being frank. ◆**réputé** a (célèbre) renowned (**pour** for); **r. pour être** (considéré comme) reputed to be.

requérir [rakerir] vt (nécessiter) to demand, require; (peine) Jur to call for. ◆**requête** nf request; Jur petition. ◆**requis** a required, requisite.

requiem [rekɥijem] nm inv requiem.

requin [r(ə)kɛ̃] nm (poisson) & Fig shark.

réquisition [rekizisjɔ̃] nf requisition. ◆**réquisitionner** vt to requisition, commandeer.

réquisitoire [rekizitwar] nm (critique) indictment (**contre** of).

rescapé, -ée [reskape] a surviving; — nmf survivor.

rescousse (à la) [alareskus] adv to the rescue.

réseau, -x [rezo] *nm* network; **r. d'espionnage** spy ring *ou* network.

réserve [rezɛrv] *nf* **1** (*restriction, doute*) reservation; (*réticence*) reserve; **sans r.** (*admiration etc*) unqualified; **sous r. de** subject to; **sous toutes réserves** without guarantee. **2** (*provision*) reserve; (*entrepôt*) storeroom; (*de bibliothèque*) stacks; **la r.** *Mil* the reserve; **les réserves** (*soldats*) the reserves; **en r.** in reserve. **3** (*de chasse, pêche*) preserve; (*indienne*) reservation; **r. naturelle** nature reserve.

réserv/er [rezɛrve] *vt* to reserve; (*garder*) to keep, save; (*marchandises*) to put aside *ou* by for); (*place, table*) to book, reserve; (*sort, surprise etc*) to hold in store (à for); **se r. pour** to save oneself for; **se r. de faire** to reserve the right to do. ◆**—é** *a* (*personne, place*) reserved; (*prudent*) guarded. ◆**réservation** *nf* reservation, booking. ◆**réservoir** *nm* (*lac*) reservoir; (*citerne, cuve*) tank; **r. d'essence** *Aut* petrol *ou* *Am* gas tank.

résidence [rezidɑ̃s] *nf* residence; **r. secondaire** second home; **r. universitaire** hall of residence. ◆**résident, -ente** *nmf* (*foreign*) resident. ◆**résidentiel, -ielle** *a* (*quartier*) residential. ◆**résider** *vi* to reside, be resident (à, en, dans in); **r. dans** (*consister dans*) to lie in.

résidu [rezidy] *nm* residue.

résigner (se) [s(ə)rezine] *vpr* to resign oneself (à qch to sth, à faire to doing). ◆**résignation** *nf* resignation.

résilier [rezilje] *vt* (*contrat*) to terminate. ◆**résiliation** *nf* termination.

résille [rezij] *nf* (*pour cheveux*) hairnet.

résine [rezin] *nf* resin.

résistance [rezistɑ̃s] *nf* resistance (à to); (*conducteur*) *Él* (*heating*) element; **plat de r.** main dish. ◆**résist/er** *vi* **r. à** to resist; (*chaleur, fatigue, souffrance*) to withstand; (*examen*) to stand up to. ◆**—ant, -ante** *a* tough, strong; **r. à la chaleur** heat-resistant; **r. au choc** shockproof; — *nmf* *Mil Hist* Resistance fighter.

résolu [rezɔly] *voir* **résoudre**; — *a* resolute, determined; **r. à faire** resolved *ou* determined to do. ◆**—ment** *adv* resolutely. ◆**résolution** *nf* (*décision*) resolution; (*fermeté*) determination.

résonance [rezɔnɑ̃s] *nf* resonance.

résonner [rezɔne] *vi* to resound (de with); (*salle, voix*) to echo.

résorber [rezɔrbe] *vt* (*chômage*) to reduce; (*excédent*) to absorb; — **se r.** *vpr* to be re-

duced; to be absorbed. ◆**résorption** *nf* reduction; absorption.

résoudre* [rezudr] *vt* (*problème*) to solve; (*difficulté*) to resolve; **se r. de faire** to decide *ou* resolve to do; **se r. à faire** to decide *ou* resolve to do; (*se résigner*) to bring oneself to do.

respect [rɛspɛ] *nm* respect (**pour, de** for); **mes respects à** my regards *ou* respects to; **tenir qn en r.** to hold s.o. in check. ◆**respectabilité** *nf* respectability. ◆**respectable** *a* (*honorable, important*) respectable. ◆**respecter** *vt* to respect; **qui se respecte** self-respecting. ◆**respectueux, -euse** *a* respectful (**envers, de** of).

respectif, -ive [rɛspɛktif, -iv] *a* respective. ◆**respectivement** *adv* respectively.

respirer [rɛspire] *vi* to breathe; (*reprendre haleine*) to get one's breath (back); (*être soulagé*) to breathe again; — *vt* to breathe (in); (*exprimer*) *Fig* to exude. ◆**respiration** *nf* breathing; (*haleine*) breath; **r. artificielle** *Méd* artificial respiration. ◆**respiratoire** *a* breathing-, respiratory.

resplend/ir [rɛsplɑ̃dir] *vi* to shine; (*visage*) to glow (de with). ◆**—issant** *a* radiant.

responsable [rɛspɔ̃sabl] *a* responsible (**de qch** for sth, **devant qn** to s.o.); — *nmf* (*chef*) person in charge; (*dans une organisation*) official; (*coupable*) person responsible (**de** for). ◆**responsabilité** *nf* responsibility; (*légale*) liability.

resquiller [rɛskije] *vi* (*au cinéma, dans le métro etc*) to avoid paying; (*sans attendre*) to jump the queue, *Am* cut in (line).

ressaisir (se) [s(ə)sezir] *vpr* to pull oneself together.

ressasser [r(ə)sase] *vt* (*ruminer*) to keep going over; (*répéter*) to keep trotting out.

ressemblance [r(ə)sɑ̃blɑ̃s] *nf* resemblance, likeness. ◆**ressembl/er** *vi* **r. à** to resemble, look *ou* be like; **cela ne lui ressemble pas** (*ce n'est pas son genre*) that's not like him *ou* her; — **se r.** *vpr* to look *ou* be alike. ◆**—ant** *a* portrait **r.** good likeness.

ressentiment [r(ə)sɑ̃timɑ̃] *nm* resentment.

ressentir* [r(ə)sɑ̃tir] *vt* to feel; **se r. de** to feel *ou* show the effects of.

resserre [r(ə)sɛr] *nf* storeroom; (*remise*) shed.

resserrer [r(ə)sere] *vt* (*nœud, boulon etc*) to tighten; (*contracter*) to close (up), contract; (*liens*) *Fig* to strengthen; — **se r.** *vpr* to tighten; (*amitié*) to become closer; (*se contracter*) to close (up), contract; (*route etc*) to narrow.

resservir* [r(ə)sɛrvir] **1** *vi* (*outil etc*) to come in useful (again). **2 se r.** *vpr* **se r. de** (*plat etc*) to have another helping of.

ressort [r(ə)sɔr] *nm* **1** *Tech* spring. **2** (*énergie*) spirit. **3 du r. de** within the competence of; **en dernier r.** (*décider etc*) in the last resort, as a last resort.

ressortir[1]* [r(ə)sɔrtir] *vi* (*aux être*) **1** to go *ou* come back out. **2** (*se voir*) to stand out; **faire r.** to bring out; **il ressort de** (*résulte*) it emerges from.

ressortir[2] [r(ə)sɔrtir] *vi* (*conjugated like finir*) **r. à** to fall within the scope of.

ressortissant, -ante [r(ə)sɔrtisɑ̃, -ɑ̃t] *nmf* (*citoyen*) national.

ressource [r(ə)surs] **1** *nfpl* (*moyens*) resources; (*argent*) means, resources. **2** *nf* (*recours*) recourse; (*possibilité*) possibility (**de faire** of doing); **dernière r.** last resort.

ressusciter [resysite] *vi* to rise from the dead; (*malade, pays*) to recover, revive; – *vt* (*mort*) to raise; (*malade, mode*) to revive.

restaurant [rɛstɔrɑ̃] *nm* restaurant.

restaurer [rɛstɔre] **1** *vt* (*réparer, rétablir*) to restore. **2 se r.** *vpr* to (have sth to) eat. ◆**restaurateur, -trice** *nmf* **1** (*de tableaux*) restorer. **2** (*hôtelier, hôtelière*) restaurant owner. ◆**restauration** *nf* **1** restoration. **2** (*hôtellerie*) catering.

reste [rɛst] *nm* rest, remainder (**de** of); *Math* remainder; *pl* remains (**de** of); (*de repas*) leftovers; **un r. de fromage**/*etc* some left-over cheese/*etc*; **au r., du r.** moreover, besides.

rester [rɛste] *vi* (*aux être*) to stay, remain; (*calme, jeune etc*) to keep, stay, remain; (*subsister*) to remain, be left; **il reste du pain**/*etc* there's some bread/*etc* left (over); **il me reste une minute**/*etc* I have one minute/*etc* left; **l'argent qui lui reste** the money he *ou* she has left; **reste à savoir** it remains to be seen; **il me reste deux choses à faire** I still have two things to do; **il me reste à vous remercier** it remains for me to thank you; **en r. à** to stop at; **restons-en là** let's leave it at that. ◆**restant** *a* remaining; **poste restante** poste restante, *Am* general delivery; – *nm* **le r.** the rest, the remainder; **un r. de viande**/*etc* some left-over meat/*etc*.

restituer [rɛstitɥe] *vt* **1** (*rendre*) to return, restore (**à** to). **2** (*son*) to reproduce; (*énergie*) to release. ◆**restitution** *nf* return.

restreindre* [rɛstrɛ̃dr] *vt* to restrict, limit (**à** to); – **se r.** *vpr* to decrease; (*faire des économies*) to cut back *ou* down. ◆**restreint** *a* limited, restricted (**à** to). ◆**restrictif, -ive**

a restrictive. ◆**restriction** *nf* restriction; **sans r.** unreservedly.

résultat [rezylta] *nm* result; (*conséquence*) outcome, result; **avoir qch pour r.** to result in sth. ◆**résulter** *vi* **r. de** to result from.

résum/er [rezyme] *vt* to summarize; (*récapituler*) to sum up; – **se r.** *vpr* (*orateur etc*) to sum up; **se r. à** (*se réduire à*) to boil down to. ◆**-é** *nm* summary; **en r.** in short; (*en récapitulant*) to sum up.

résurrection [rezyrɛksjɔ̃] *nf* resurrection.

rétabl/ir [retablir] *vt* to re-establish, restore; (*fait, vérité*) to re-establish; (*malade*) to restore to health; (*employé*) to reinstate; – **se r.** *vpr* to be restored; (*malade*) to recover. ◆**-issement** *nm* restoring; re-establishment; *Méd* recovery.

retaper [r(ə)tape] *vt* (*maison, voiture etc*) to do up; (*lit*) to straighten; (*malade*) *Fam* to buck up.

retard [r(ə)tar] *nm* lateness; (*sur un programme etc*) delay; (*infériorité*) backwardness; **en r.** late; (*retardé*) backward; **en r. dans qch** behind in sth; **en r. sur qn/qch** behind s.o./sth; **rattraper** *ou* **combler son r.** to catch up; **avoir du r.** to be late; (*sur un programme*) to be behind (schedule); (*montre*) to be slow; **avoir une heure de r.** to be an hour late; **prendre du r.** (*montre*) to lose (time); **sans r.** without delay. ◆**retardataire** *a* (*arrivant*) late; **enfant r.** *Méd* slow learner; – *nmf* latecomer. ◆**retardement** *nm* **à r.** delayed-action-; **bombe à r.** time bomb.

retard/er [r(ə)tarde] *vt* to delay; (*date, départ, montre*) to put back; **r. qn** (*dans une activité*) to put s.o. behind; – *vi* (*montre*) to be slow; **r. de cinq minutes** to be five minutes slow; **r.** (**sur son temps**) (*personne*) to be behind the times. ◆**-é, -ée** *a* (*enfant*) backward; – *nmf* backward child.

retenir* [rətnir] *vt* (*empêcher d'agir, contenir*) to hold back; (*attention, souffle*) to hold; (*réserver*) to book; (*se souvenir de*) to remember; (*fixer*) to hold (in place), secure; (*déduire*) to take off; (*candidature, proposition*) to accept; (*chiffre*) *Math* to carry; (*chaleur, odeur*) to retain; (*invité, suspect etc*) to detain, keep; **r. qn prisonnier** to keep *ou* hold s.o. prisoner; **r. qn de faire** to stop s.o. (from) doing; – **se r.** *vpr* (*se contenir*) to restrain oneself; **se r. de faire** to stop oneself (from) doing; **se r. à** to cling to. ◆**retenue** *nf* **1** (*modération*) restraint. **2** (*de salaire*) deduction, stoppage; (*chiffre*) *Math* figure carried over. **3** *Scol* detention; **en r.** in detention.

retent/ir [r(ə)tãtir] *vi* to ring (out) (**de** with). ◆**—issant** *a* resounding; (*scandale*) major. ◆**—issement** *nm* (*effet*) effect; **avoir un grand r.** (*film etc*) to create a stir.

réticent [retisã] *a* (*réservé*) reticent; (*hésitant*) reluctant. ◆**réticence** *nf* reticence; reluctance.

rétine [retin] *nf Anat* retina.

retir/er [r(ə)tire] *vt* to withdraw; (*sortir*) to take out; (*ôter*) to take off; (*éloigner*) to take away; (*reprendre*) to pick up; (*offre, plainte*) to take back, withdraw; **r. qch à qn** (*permis etc*) to take sth away from s.o.; **r. qch de** (*gagner*) to derive sth from; **— se r.** *vpr* to withdraw, retire (**de** from; (*mer*) to ebb. ◆**—é** *a* (*lieu, vie*) secluded.

retomber [r(ə)tɔ̃be] *vi* to fall; (*de nouveau*) to fall again; (*pendre*) to hang down; (*après un saut etc*) to land; (*intérêt*) to slacken; **r. dans** (*erreur, situation*) to fall ou sink back into; **r. sur qn** (*frais, responsabilité*) to fall on s.o. ◆**retombées** *nfpl* (*radioactives*) fallout.

rétorquer [retɔrke] *vt* **r. que** to retort that.

retors [rətɔr] *a* wily, crafty.

rétorsion [retɔrsjɔ̃] *nf Pol* retaliation; **mesure de r.** reprisal.

retouche [r(ə)tuʃ] *nf* touching up; alteration. ◆**retoucher** *vt* (*photo, tableau*) to touch up, retouch; (*texte, vêtement*) to alter.

retour [r(ə)tur] *nm* return; (*de fortune*) reversal; **être de r.** to be back (**de** from); **en r.** (*en échange*) in return; **par r. (du courrier)** by return (of post), *Am* by return mail; **à mon retour** when I get ou got back (**de** from); **r. en arrière** flashback; **r. de flamme** *Fig* backlash; **match r.** return match ou *Am* game.

retourner [r(ə)turne] *vt* (*aux avoir*) (*tableau etc*) to turn round; (*matelas, steak etc*) to turn over; (*foin, terre etc*) to turn; (*vêtement, sac etc*) to turn inside out; (*maison*) to turn upside down; (*compliment, lettre*) to return; **r. qn** (*bouleverser*) *Fam* to upset s.o., shake s.o.; **r. contre qn** (*argument*) to turn against s.o.; (*arme*) to turn on s.o.; **de quoi il retourne** what it's about; **— (aux être)** to go back, return; **— se r.** *vpr* (*pour regarder*) to turn round, look back; (*sur le dos*) to turn over ou round; (*dans son lit*) to toss and turn; (*voiture*) to overturn; **s'en r.** to go back; **se r. contre** *Fig* to turn against.

retracer [r(ə)trase] *vt* (*histoire etc*) to retrace.

rétracter [retrakte] *vt*, **— se r.** *vpr* to retract. ◆**rétractation** *nf* (*désaveu*) retraction.

retrait [r(ə)trɛ] *nm* withdrawal; (*de bagages, billets*) collection; (*de mer*) ebb(ing); **en r.** (*maison etc*) set back.

retraite [r(ə)trɛt] *nf* **1** (*d'employé*) retirement; (*pension*) retirement pension; (*refuge*) retreat, refuge; **r. anticipée** early retirement; **prendre sa r.** to retire; **à la r.** retired; **mettre à la r.** to pension off. **2** *Mil* retreat; **r. aux flambeaux** torchlight tattoo. ◆**retraité, -ée** *a* retired; **—** *nmf* senior citizen, (old age) pensioner.

retrancher [r(ə)trãʃe] **1** *vt* (*mot, passage etc*) to cut (**de** from); (*argent, quantité*) to deduct (**de** from). **2 se r.** *vpr* (*soldat, gangster etc*) to entrench oneself; **se r. dans/derrière** *Fig* to take refuge in/behind.

retransmettre [r(ə)trãsmɛtr] *vt* to broadcast. ◆**retransmission** *nf* broadcast.

rétréc/ir [retresir] *vt* to narrow; (*vêtement*) to take in; **— vi**, **— se r.** *vpr* (*au lavage*) to shrink; (*rue etc*) to narrow. ◆**—i** *a* (*esprit, rue*) narrow.

rétribuer [retribɥe] *vt* **r.** to pay, remunerate; (*travail*) to pay for. ◆**rétribution** *nf* payment, remuneration.

rétro [retro] *a inv* (*mode etc*) which harks back to the past, retro.

rétro- [retro] *préf* retro-. ◆**rétroactif, -ive** *a* retroactive.

rétrograde [retrograd] *a* retrograde. ◆**rétrograder** *vi* (*reculer*) to move back; (*civilisation etc*) to go backwards; *Aut* to change down; **— vt** (*fonctionnaire, officier*) to demote.

rétrospectif, -ive [retrospɛktif, -iv] *a* (*sentiment etc*) retrospective; **—** *nf* (*de films, tableaux*) retrospective. ◆**rétrospectivement** *adv* in retrospect.

retrousser [r(ə)truse] *vt* (*jupe etc*) to hitch ou tuck up; (*manches*) to roll up ◆**—é** *a* (*nez*) snub, turned-up.

retrouver [r(ə)truve] *vt* to find (again); (*rejoindre*) to meet (again); (*forces, santé*) to regain; (*découvrir*) to rediscover; (*se rappeler*) to recall; **— se r.** *vpr* (*chose*) to be found (again); (*se trouver*) to find oneself (back); (*se rencontrer*) to meet (again); **s'y r.** (*s'orienter*) to find one's bearings ou way. ◆**retrouvailles** *nfpl* reunion.

rétroviseur [retrovizœr] *nm Aut* (rear-view) mirror.

réunion [reynjɔ̃] *nf* (*séance*) meeting; (*d'objets*) collection, gathering; (*d'éléments divers*) combination; (*jonction*) joining. ◆**réunir** *vt* to collect, gather; (*relier*) to join; (*convoquer*) to call together, assemble; (*rapprocher*) to bring together; (*qua-

lités, tendances) to combine. ◆**réunis** *apl* (*éléments*) combined.

réuss/ir [reysir] *vi* to succeed, be successful (à faire in doing); (*plante*) to thrive; r. à (*examen*) to pass; r. à qn to work (out) well for s.o.; (*aliment, climat*) to agree with s.o.; *− vt* to make a success of. ◆**—i** a successful. ◆**réussite** *nf* 1 success. 2 faire des réussites *Cartes* to play patience.

revaloir [r(ə)valwar] *vt* **je vous le revaudrai** (*en bien ou en mal*) I'll pay you back.

revaloriser [r(ə)valɔrize] *vt* (*salaire*) to raise. ◆**revalorisation** *nf* raising.

revanche [r(ə)vɑ̃ʃ] *nf* revenge; *Sp* return game; **en r.** on the other hand.

rêve [rɛv] *nm* dream; **faire un r.** to have a dream; **maison/voiture/etc de r.** dream house/car/etc. ◆**rêvasser** *vi* to daydream.

revêche [rəvɛʃ] *a* bad-tempered, surly.

réveil [revɛj] *nm* waking (up); *Fig* awakening; (*pendule*) alarm (clock). ◆**réveill/er** *vt* (*personne*) to wake (up); (*sentiment, souvenir*) *Fig* to revive, awaken; *− se r.* *vpr* to wake (up); *Fig* to revive, awaken. ◆**—é** a awake. ◆**réveille-matin** *nm inv* alarm (clock).

réveillon [revɛjɔ̃] *nm* (*repas*) midnight supper (*on Christmas Eve or New Year's Eve*). ◆**réveillonner** *vi* to take part in a réveillon.

révéler [revele] *vt* to reveal (que that); *− se r.* to be revealed; **se r. facile/etc** to turn out to be easy/etc. ◆**révélateur, -trice** a revealing; **r. de** indicative of. ◆**révélation** *nf* revelation.

revenant [rəvnɑ̃] *nm* ghost.

revendiquer [r(ə)vɑ̃dike] *vt* to claim; (*exiger*) to demand. ◆**revendicatif, -ive** a (*mouvement etc*) protest-. ◆**revendication** *nf* claim; demand; (*action*) claiming; demanding.

revendre [r(ə)vɑ̃dr] *vt* to resell; **avoir (de) qch à r.** to have sth to spare. ◆**revendeur, -euse** *nmf* retailer; (*d'occasion*) secondhand dealer; **r. (de drogue)** drug pusher; **r. de billets** ticket tout. ◆**revente** *nf* resale.

revenir* [rəvnir] *vi* (*aux être*) to come back, return; (*date*) to come round again; (*mot*) to come ou crop up; (*coûter*) to cost (à qn s.o.); **r. à** (*activité, sujet*) to go back to, return to; (*se ramener à*) to boil down to; **r. à qn** (*forces, mémoire*) to come back to s.o., return to s.o.; (*honneur*) to fall to s.o.; **r. à soi** to come to ou round; **r. de** (*maladie, surprise*) to get over; **r. sur** (*décision, promesse*) to go back on; (*passé, question*)

to go back over; **r. sur ses pas** to retrace one's steps; **faire r.** (*aliment*) to brown.

revenu [rəvny] *nm* income (de from); (*d'un État*) revenue (de from); **déclaration de revenus** tax return.

rêv/er [rɛve] *vi* to dream (de of, de faire of doing); *− vt* to dream (que that); (*désirer*) to dream of. ◆**—é** a ideal.

réverbération [reverberasjɔ̃] *nf* (*de lumière*) reflection; (*de son*) reverberation.

révérence [reverɑ̃s] *nf* reverence; (*salut d'homme*) bow; (*salut de femme*) curts(e)y; **faire une r.** to bow; to curts(e)y. ◆**révérer** *vt* to revere.

révérend, -ende [reverɑ̃, -ɑ̃d] *a & nm Rel* reverend.

rêverie [rɛvri] *nf* daydream; (*activité*) daydreaming.

revers [r(ə)vɛr] *nm* (*côté*) reverse; *Tennis* backhand; (*de veste*) lapel; (*de pantalon*) turn-up, *Am* cuff; (*d'étoffe*) wrong side; (*coup du sort*) setback, reverse; **r. de main** (*coup*) backhander; **le r. de la médaille** *Fig* the other side of the coin.

réversible [reversibl] *a* reversible.

revêtir* [r(ə)vetir] *vt* to cover (de with); (*habit*) to put on; (*caractère, forme*) to assume; (*route*) to surface; **r. qn** (*habiller*) to dress s.o. (de in); **r. de** (*signature*) to provide with. ◆**revêtement** *nm* (*surface*) covering; (*de route*) surface.

rêveur, -euse [rɛvœr, -øz] *a* dreamy; *− nmf* dreamer.

revient [rəvjɛ̃] *nm* **prix de r.** cost price.

revigorer [r(ə)vigɔre] *vt* (*personne*) to revive.

revirement [r(ə)virmɑ̃] *nm* (*changement*) about-turn, *Am* about-face; (*de situation, d'opinion, de politique*) reversal.

réviser [revize] *vt* (*notes, texte*) to revise; (*jugement, règlement etc*) to review; (*machine, voiture*) to overhaul, service. ◆**révision** *nf* revision; review; overhaul, service.

revivre* [r(ə)vivr] *vi* to live again; **faire r.** to revive; *− vt* (*incident etc*) to relive.

révocation [revɔkasjɔ̃] *nf* 1 (*de contrat etc*) revocation. 2 (*de fonctionnaire*) dismissal.

revoici [r(ə)vwasi] *prép* **me r.** here I am again.

revoilà [r(ə)vwala] *prép* **la r.** there she is again.

revoir* [r(ə)vwar] *vt* to see (again); (*texte*) to revise; **au r.** goodbye.

révolte [revɔlt] *nf* revolt. ◆**révolt/er** *vt* to revolt, incense. **2 se r.** *vpr* to revolt, rebel (**contre** against). ◆**—ant** a (*honteux*) revolting. ◆**—é, -ée** *nmf* rebel.

révolu [revɔly] a (*époque*) past; **avoir trente ans révolus** to be over thirty (years of age).

révolution [revɔlysjɔ̃] nf (*changement, rotation*) revolution. ◆**révolutionnaire** a & nmf revolutionary. ◆**révolutionner** vt to revolutionize; (*émouvoir*) Fig to shake up.

revolver [revɔlvɛr] nm revolver, gun.

révoquer [revɔke] vt **1** (*contrat etc*) to revoke. **2** (*fonctionnaire*) to dismiss.

revue [r(ə)vy] nf **1** (*examen*) & Mil review; **passer en r.** to review. **2** (*de music-hall*) variety show. **3** (*magazine*) magazine; (*spécialisée*) journal.

rez-de-chaussée [redʃose] nm inv ground floor, Am first floor.

rhabiller (se) [(sə)rabije] vpr to get dressed again.

rhapsodie [rapsɔdi] nf rhapsody.

rhétorique [retɔrik] nf rhetoric.

Rhin [rɛ̃] nm **le R.** the Rhine.

rhinocéros [rinɔserɔs] nm rhinoceros.

rhododendron [rɔdɔdɛ̃drɔ̃] nm rhododendron.

rhubarbe [rybarb] nf rhubarb.

rhum [rɔm] nm rum.

rhumatisme [rymatism] nm Méd rheumatism; **avoir des rhumatismes** to have rheumatism. ◆**rhumatisant, -ante** a & nmf rheumatic. ◆**rhumatismal, -aux** a (*douleur*) rheumatic.

rhume [rym] nm cold; **r. de cerveau** head cold; **r. des foins** hay fever.

riant [rjɑ̃] a cheerful, smiling.

ricaner [rikane] vi (*sarcastiquement*) to snigger; (*bêtement*) to giggle.

riche [riʃ] a rich; (*personne, pays*) rich, wealthy; **r. en** (*minérai, vitamines etc*) rich in; – nmf riche ou wealthy person; **les riches** the rich. ◆**—ment** adv (*vêtu, illustré etc*) richly. ◆**richesse** nf wealth; (*d'étoffe, de sol, vocabulaire*) richness; pl (*trésor*) riches; (*ressources*) wealth.

ricin [risɛ̃] nm **huile de r.** castor oil.

ricocher [rikɔʃe] vi to ricochet, rebound. ◆**ricochet** nm ricochet, rebound; **par r.** Fig as an indirect result.

rictus [riktys] nm grin, grimace.

ride [rid] nf wrinkle; ripple. ◆**rider** vt (*visage*) to wrinkle; (*eau*) to ripple; – **se r.** vpr to wrinkle.

rideau, -x [rido] nm curtain; (*métallique*) shutter; (*écran*) Fig screen (**de** of); **le r. de fer** Pol the Iron Curtain.

ridicule [ridikyl] a ridiculous, ludicrous; – nm (*moquerie*) ridicule; (*défaut*) absurdity; (*de situation etc*) ridiculousness; **tourner en r.** to ridicule. ◆**ridiculiser** vt to ridicule.

rien [rjɛ̃] pron nothing; **il ne sait r.** he knows nothing, he doesn't know anything; **r. du tout** nothing at all; **r. d'autre/de bon/***etc* nothing else/good/*etc*; **r. de tel** nothing like it; **de r.!** (*je vous en prie*) don't mention it!; **ça ne fait r.** it doesn't matter; **en moins de r.** (*vite*) in no time; **trois fois r.** (*chose insignifiante*) next to nothing; **pour r.** (*à bas prix*) for next to nothing; **il n'en est r.** (*ce n'est pas vrai*) nothing of the kind; **r. que** only, just; – *nm* trifle, (mere) nothing; **un r. de** a hint ou touch of; **en un r. de temps** (*vite*) in no time; **un r. trop petit/***etc* just a bit too small/*etc*.

rieur, -euse [rjœr, -øz] a cheerful.

riflard [riflar] nm Fam brolly, umbrella.

rigide [riʒid] a rigid; (*carton, muscle*) stiff; (*personne*) Fig inflexible; (*éducation*) strict. ◆**rigidité** nf rigidity; stiffness; inflexibility; strictness.

rigole [rigɔl] nf (*conduit*) channel; (*filet d'eau*) rivulet.

rigoler [rigɔle] vi Fam to laugh; (*s'amuser*) to have fun ou a laugh; (*plaisanter*) to joke (**avec** about). ◆**rigolade** nf Fam fun; (*chose ridicule*) joke, farce; **prendre qch à la r.** to make a joke out of sth. ◆**rigolo, -ote** a Fam funny; – nmf Fam joker.

rigueur [rigœr] nf rigour; harshness; strictness; (*précision*) precision; **être de r.** to be the rule; **à la r.** if absolutely necessary, at ou Am in a pinch; **tenir r. à qn de qch** Fig to hold sth against s.o. ◆**rigoureux, -euse** a rigorous; (*climat, punition*) harsh; (*personne, morale, sens*) strict.

rillettes [rijɛt] nfpl potted minced pork.

rime [rim] nf rhyme. ◆**rimer** vi to rhyme (**avec** with); **ça ne rime à rien** it makes no sense.

rincer [rɛ̃se] vt to rinse (out). ◆**rinçage** nm rinsing; (*opération*) rinse.

ring [riŋ] nm (boxing) ring.

ringard [rɛ̃gar] a (*démodé*) Fam unfashionable, fuddy-duddy.

riposte [ripɔst] nf (*réponse*) retort; (*attaque*) counter(attack). ◆**riposter** vi to retort; **r. à** (*attaque*) to counter; (*insulte*) to reply to; – vt **r. que** to retort that.

rire* [rir] vi to laugh (**de** at); (*s'amuser*) to have a good time; (*plaisanter*) to joke; **faire qch pour r.** to do sth for a laugh ou a joke; **se r. de qch** to laugh sth off; – nm laugh; pl laughter; **le r.** (*activité*) laughter. ◆**risée** nf mockery; **être la r. de** to be the laughing stock of. ◆**risible** a laughable.

ris [ri] nm **r. de veau** Culin (calf) sweetbread.

risque [risk] nm risk; **r. du métier** occupational hazard; **au r. de qch/de faire** at the risk of sth/of doing; **à vos risques et périls** at your own risk; **assurance tous risques** comprehensive insurance. ◆**risquer** vt to risk; (question, regard) to venture, hazard; **r. de faire** to stand a good chance of doing; **se r. à faire** to dare to do; **se r. dans** to venture into. ◆**risqué** a risky; (plaisanterie) daring, risqué.

ristourne [risturn] nf discount.

rite [rit] nm rite; (habitude) Fig ritual. ◆**rituel, -elle** a & nm ritual.

rivage [rivaʒ] nm shore.

rival, -ale, -aux [rival, -o] a & nmf rival. ◆**rivaliser** vi to compete (avec with, **de** in). ◆**rivalité** nf rivalry.

rive [riv] nf (de fleuve) bank; (de lac) shore.

rivé [rive] a **r. à** (chaise etc) Fig riveted to; **r. sur** Fig riveted on. ◆**rivet** nm (tige) rivet. ◆**riveter** vt to rivet (together).

riverain, -aine [rivrɛ̃, -ɛn] a riverside; lakeside; — nmf riverside resident; (de lac) lakeside resident; (de rue) resident.

rivière [rivjɛr] nf river.

rixe [riks] nf brawl, scuffle.

riz [ri] nm rice; **r. au lait** rice pudding. ◆**rizière** nf paddy (field), ricefield.

RN abrév = **route nationale**.

robe [rɔb] nf (de femme) dress; (d'ecclésiastique, de juge) robe; (de professeur) gown; (pelage) coat; **r. de soirée ou du soir** evening dress ou gown; **r. de grossesse/de mariée** maternity/wedding dress; **r. de chambre** dressing gown; **r. chasuble** pinafore (dress).

robinet [rɔbinɛ] nm tap, Am faucet; **eau du r.** tap water.

robot [rɔbo] nm robot; **r. ménager** food processor, liquidizer.

robuste [rɔbyst] a robust. ◆**robustesse** nf robustness.

roc [rɔk] nm rock.

rocaille [rɔkaj] nf (terrain) rocky ground; (de jardin) rockery. ◆**rocailleux, -euse** a rocky, stony; (voix) harsh.

rocambolesque [rɔkãbɔlɛsk] a (aventure etc) fantastic.

roche [rɔʃ] nf, **rocher** [rɔʃe] nm (bloc, substance) rock. ◆**rocheux, -euse** a rocky.

rock [rɔk] nm (musique) rock; — a inv (chanteur etc) rock-.

rod/er [rɔde] vt (moteur, voiture) to run in, Am break in; **être rodé** (personne) Fig to have got ou Am gotten the hang of things. ◆**—age** nm running in, Am breaking in.

rôd/er [rode] vi to roam (about); (suspect)

to prowl (about). ◆**—eur, -euse** nmf prowler.

rogne [rɔɲ] nf Fam anger; **en r.** in a temper.

rogner [rɔɲe] vt to trim, clip; (réduire) to cut; — vi **r. sur** (réduire) to cut down on. ◆**rognures** nfpl clippings, trimmings.

rognon [rɔɲɔ̃] nm Culin kidney.

roi [rwa] nm king; **fête ou jour des rois** Twelfth Night.

roitelet [rwatlɛ] nm (oiseau) wren.

rôle [rol] nm role, part; **à tour de r.** in turn.

romain, -aine [rɔmɛ̃, -ɛn] **1** a & nmf Roman. **2** nf (laitue) cos (lettuce), Am romaine.

roman [rɔmã] **1** nm novel; (histoire) Fig story; **r.-fleuve** saga. **2** a (langue) Romance; Archit Romanesque. ◆**romancé** a (histoire) fictional. ◆**romancier, -ière** nmf novelist.

romanesque [rɔmanɛsk] a romantic; (incroyable) fantastic.

romanichel, -elle [rɔmaniʃɛl] nmf gipsy.

romantique [rɔmãtik] a romantic. ◆**romantisme** nm romanticism.

romarin [rɔmarɛ̃] nm Bot Culin rosemary.

romp/re* [rɔ̃pr] vt to break; (pourparlers, relations) to break off; (digue) to burst; — vi to break (Fig avec with); to burst; (fiancés) to break it off; — **se r.** vpr to break; to burst. ◆**—u** a **1** (fatigué) exhausted. **2 r. à** (expérimenté) experienced in.

romsteck [rɔmstɛk] nm rump steak.

ronces [rɔ̃s] nfpl (branches) brambles.

ronchonner [rɔ̃ʃɔne] vi Fam to grouse, grumble.

rond [rɔ̃] a round; (gras) plump; (honnête) straight; (ivre) Fam tight; **dix francs tout r.** ten francs exactly; — adv **tourner r.** (machine etc) to run smoothly; — nm (objet) ring; (cercle) circle; (tranche) slice; Pl (argent) Fam money; **r. de serviette** napkin ring; **en r.** (s'asseoir etc) in a ring ou circle; **tourner en r.** (toupie etc) & Fig to go round and round. ◆**r.-de-cuir** nm (pl ronds-de-cuir) Péj pen pusher. ◆**r.-point** nm (pl ronds-points) Aut roundabout, Am traffic circle. ◆**ronde** nf (tour de surveillance) round; (de policier) beat; (danse) round (dance); (note) Mus semibreve, Am whole note; **à la r.** around; (boire) in turn. ◆**rondelet, -ette** a chubby; (somme) Fig tidy. ◆**rondelle** nf (tranche) slice; Tech washer. ◆**rondement** adv (efficacement) briskly; (franchement) straight. ◆**rondeur** nf roundness; (du corps) plumpness. ◆**rondin** nm log.

ronéotyper [rɔneɔtipe] vt to duplicate, roneo.

ronflant [rɔ̃flɑ̃] a (langage etc) Péj high-flown; (feu) roaring.

ronfler [rɔ̃fle] vi to snore; (moteur) to hum. ◆**ronflement** nm snore, snoring; hum(ming).

rong/er [rɔ̃ʒe] vt to gnaw (at); (ver, mer, rouille) to eat into (sth); r. qn (chagrin, maladie) to consume s.o.; se r. les ongles to bite one's nails; se r. les sangs (s'inquiéter) to worry oneself sick. ◆**-eur** nm (animal) rodent.

ronron [rɔ̃rɔ̃] nm, **ronronnement** [rɔ̃rɔnmɑ̃] nm purr(ing). ◆**ronronner** vi to purr.

roquette [rɔkɛt] nf Mil rocket.

rosbif [rɔsbif] nm du r. (rôti) roast beef; (à rôtir) roasting beef; un r. a joint of roast ou roasting beef.

rose [roz] 1 nf (fleur) rose. 2 a (couleur) pink; (situation, teint) rosy; − nm pink. ◆**rosé** a pinkish; & − a & nm (vin) rosé. ◆**rosette** nf (d'un officier) rosette; (nœud) bow. ◆**rosier** nm rose bush.

roseau, -x [rozo] nm (plante) reed.

rosée [roze] nf dew.

rosse [rɔs] a & nf Fam nasty (person).

ross/er [rɔse] vt Fam to thrash. ◆**-ée** nf Fam thrashing.

rossignol [rɔsiɲɔl] nm 1 (oiseau) nightin-gale. 2 (crochet) picklock.

rot [ro] nm Fam burp, belch. ◆**roter** vi Fam to burp, belch.

rotation [rɔtasjɔ̃] nf rotation; (de stock) turnover. ◆**rotatif, -ive** a rotary; − nf ro-tary press.

rotin [rɔtɛ̃] nm rattan, cane.

rôt/ir [rotir] vti, − se r. vpr to roast; faire r. to roast. ◆**-i** nm du r. roasting meat; (cuit) roast meat; un r. a joint (of) roast of bœuf/de porc (joint of) roast beef/pork. ◆**rôtissoire** nf (roasting) spit.

rotule [rɔtyl] nf kneecap.

roturier, -ière [rɔtyrje, -jɛr] nmf commoner.

rouage [rwaʒ] nm (de montre etc) (working) part; (d'organisation etc) Fig cog.

roublard [rublar] a wily, foxy.

rouble [rubl] nm (monnaie) r(o)uble.

roucouler [rukule] vi (oiseau, amoureux) to coo.

roue [ru] nf wheel; r. (dentée) cog(wheel); faire la r. (paon) to spread its tail; (se pavaner) Fig to strut; faire r. libre Aut to freewheel.

roué, -ée [rwe] a & nmf sly ou calculating (person).

rouer [rwe] vt r. qn de coups to beat s.o. black and blue.

rouet [rwe] nm spinning wheel.

rouge [ruʒ] a (fer) red-hot; − nm (cou-leur) red; (vin) Fam red wine; r. (à lèvres) lipstick; r. (à joues) rouge; le feu est au r. Aut the (traffic) lights are red; − nmf (personne) Pol Red. ◆**r.-gorge** nm (pl rouges-gorges) robin. ◆**rougeâtre** a reddish. ◆**rougeaud** a red-faced. ◆**rougeoyer** vi to glow (red). ◆**rougeur** nf redness; (due à la gêne ou à la honte) blush(ing); pl Méd red spots ou blotches. ◆**rougir** vti to redden, turn red; − vi (de gêne, de honte) to blush (de with); (de colère, de joie) to flush (de with).

rougeole [ruʒɔl] nf measles.

rouget [ruʒɛ] nm (poisson) mullet.

rouille [ruj] nf rust; − a inv (couleur) rust(-coloured). ◆**rouill/er** vi to rust; − se r. vpr to rust; (esprit, sportif etc) Fig to get rusty. ◆**-é** a rusty.

roul/er [rule] vt to roll; (brouette, meuble) to wheel, push; (crêpe, ficelle, manches etc) to roll up; r. qn (duper) Fam to cheat s.o.; − vi to roll; (train, voiture) to go, travel; (con-ducteur) to drive; r. sur (conversation) to turn on; ça roule! Fam everything's fine!; − se r. vpr to roll; se r. dans (couverture etc) to roll oneself (up) in. ◆**-ant** a (es-calier, trottoir) moving; (meuble) on wheels. ◆**-é** nm (gâteau) Swiss roll. ◆**rouleau, -x** nm (outil, vague) roller; (de papier, pellicule etc) roll; r. à pâtisserie roll-ing pin; r. compresseur steamroller. ◆**roulement** nm (bruit) rumbling, rum-ble; (de tambour, de tonnerre, d'yeux) roll; (ordre) rotation; par r. in rotation; r. à bil-les Tech ball bearing. ◆**roulette** nf (de meuble) castor; (de dentiste) drill; (jeu) roulette. ◆**roulis** nm (de navire) roll(ing).

roulotte [rulɔt] nf (de gitan) caravan.

Roumanie [rumani] nf Romania. ◆**rou-main, -aine** a & nmf Romanian; − nm (langue) Romanian.

round [rawnd, rund] nm Boxe round.

roupiller [rupije] vi Fam to kip, sleep.

rouquin, -ine [rukɛ̃, -in] a Fam red-haired; − nmf Fam redhead.

rouspét/er [ruspete] vi Fam to grumble, complain. ◆**-eur, -euse** nmf grumbler.

rousse [rus] voir roux.

rousseur [rusœr] nf redness; tache de r. freckle. ◆**roussir** vt (brûler) to singe, scorch; − vi (feuilles) to turn brown; faire r. Culin to brown.

route [rut] nf road (de to); (itinéraire) way,

route; *(aérienne, maritime)* route; *(chemin)* Fig path, way; **r. nationale/départementale** main/secondary road; **grande r., grand-r.** main road; **code de la r.** Highway Code; **en r.** on the way, en route; **en r.!** let's go!; **par la r.** by road; **sur la bonne r.** Fig on the right track; **mettre en r.** *(voiture etc)* to start (up); **se mettre en r.** to set out *(pour for)*; **une heure de r.** *Aut* an hour's drive; **bonne r.!** *Aut* have a good trip! ◆**routier, -ière** *a (carte etc)* road-; — *nm (camionneur)* (long distance) lorry *ou Am* truck driver; *(restaurant)* transport café, *Am* truck stop.

routine [rutin] *nf* routine; **de r.** *(contrôle etc)* routine-. ◆**routinier, -ière** *a (travail etc)* routine-; *(personne)* addicted to routine.

rouvrir* [ruvrir] *vti*, — **se r.** *vpr* to reopen.

roux, rousse [ru, rus] *a (cheveux)* red, ginger; *(personne)* red-haired; — *nmf* redhead.

royal, -aux [rwajal, -o] *a* royal; *(cadeau, festin etc)* fit for a king; *(salaire)* princely. ◆**royalement** *adv (traiter)* royally. ◆**royaliste** *a* & *nmf* royalist. ◆**royaume** *nm* kingdom. ◆**Royaume-Uni** *nm* United Kingdom. ◆**royauté** *nf (monarchie)* monarchy.

ruade [rɥad] *nf (d'âne etc)* kick.

ruban [rybɑ̃] *nm* ribbon; *(d'acier, de chapeau)* band; **r. adhésif** adhesive *ou* sticky tape.

rubéole [rybeɔl] *nf* German measles, rubella.

rubis [rybi] *nm (pierre)* ruby; *(de montre)* jewel.

rubrique [rybrik] *nf (article)* Journ column; *(catégorie, titre)* heading.

ruche [ryʃ] *nf (bee)hive.

rude [ryd] *a (grossier)* crude; *(rêche)* rough; *(pénible)* tough; *(hiver, voix)* harsh; *(remarquable)* Fam tremendous. ◆**—ment** *adv (parler, traiter)* harshly; *(frapper, tomber)* hard; *(très)* Fam awfully. ◆**rudesse** *nf* harshness. ◆**rudoyer** *vt* to treat harshly.

rudiments [rydimɑ̃] *nmpl* rudiments. ◆**rudimentaire** *a* rudimentary.

rue [ry] *nf* street; **être à la r.** *(sans domicile)* to be on the streets. ◆**ruelle** *nf* alley(way).

ruer [rɥe] **1** *vi (cheval)* to kick (out). **2 se r.** *vpr (foncer)* to rush, fling oneself *(sur* at). ◆**ruée** *nf* rush.

rugby [rygbi] *nm* rugby. ◆**rugbyman**, *pl* **-men** [rygbiman, -men] *nm* rugby player.

rug/ir [ryʒir] *vi* to roar. ◆**—issement** *nm* roar.

rugueux, -euse [rygø, -øz] *a* rough. ◆**rugosité** *nf* roughness; *pl (aspérités)* roughness.

ruine [rɥin] *nf (décombres)* & Fig ruin; **en r.** *(édifice)* in ruins; **tomber en r.** to fall into ruin. ◆**ruiner** *vt* to ruin; — **se r.** *vpr (en dépensant)* to ruin oneself. ◆**ruineux, -euse** *a (goûts, projet)* ruinously expensive; *(dépense)* ruinous.

ruisseau, -x [rɥiso] *nm* stream; *(caniveau)* gutter. ◆**ruisseler** *vi* to stream *(de* with).

rumeur [rymœr] *nf (protestation)* clamour; *(murmure)* murmur; *(nouvelle)* rumour.

ruminer [rymine] *vt (méditer)* to ponder on, ruminate over.

rumsteak [rɔmstɛk] *nm* rump steak.

rupture [ryptyr] *nf* break(ing); *(de fiançailles, relations)* breaking off; *(de pourparlers)* breakdown *(de* in); *(brouille)* break (up), split; *(de contrat)* breach; *(d'organe)* Méd rupture.

rural, -aux [ryral, -o] *a* rural, country-; — *nmpl* country people.

ruse [ryz] *nf (subterfuge)* trick; **la r.** *(habileté)* cunning; *(fourberie)* trickery. ◆**rusé, -ée** *a* & *nmf* crafty *ou* cunning (person). ◆**ruser** *vi* to resort to trickery.

Russie [rysi] *nf* Russia. ◆**russe** *a* & *nmf* Russian; — *nm (langue)* Russian.

rustique [rystik] *a (meuble)* rustic.

rustre [rystr] *nm* lout, churl.

rutabaga [rytabaga] *nm (racine)* swede, *Am* rutabaga.

rutilant [rytilɑ̃] *a* gleaming, glittering.

rythme [ritm] *nm* rhythm; *(de travail)* rate, tempo; *(de la vie)* pace; **au r. de trois par jour** at a *ou* the rate of three a day. ◆**rythmé** *a*, ◆**rythmique** *a* rhythmic(al).

S

S, s [ɛs] *nm* S, s.

s' [s] *voir* **se, si.**

sa [sa] *voir* **son²**.

SA *abrév (société anonyme)* Com plc, *Am* Inc.

sabbat [saba] *nm* (Jewish) Sabbath.

◆**sabbatique** *a* (*année etc*) *Univ* sabbatical.

sable [sabl] *nm* sand; **sables mouvants** quicksand(s). ◆**sabler** *vt* (*route*) to sand. ◆**sableux, -euse** *a* (*eau*) sandy. ◆**sablier** *nm* hourglass; *Culin* egg timer. ◆**sablière** *nf* (*carrière*) sandpit. ◆**sablonneux, -euse** *a* (*terrain*) sandy.

sablé [sable] *nm* shortbread biscuit *ou Am* cookie.

saborder [saborde] *vt* (*navire*) to scuttle; (*entreprise*) *Fig* to shut down.

sabot [sabo] *nm* **1** (*de cheval etc*) hoof. **2** (*chaussure*) clog. **3** (*de frein*) *Aut* shoe; **s. (de Denver)** *Aut* (wheel) clamp.

sabot/er [sabote] *vt* to sabotage; (*bâcler*) to botch. ◆**-age** *nm* sabotage; **un s.** an act of sabotage. ◆**-eur, -euse** *nmf* saboteur.

sabre [sabr] *nm* sabre, sword.

sabrer [sabre] *vt* (*élève, candidat*) *Fam* to give a thoroughly bad mark to.

sac [sak] *nm* **1** bag; (*grand et en toile*) sack; **s. (à main)** handbag; **s. à dos** rucksack. **2** **mettre à s.** (*ville*) *Mil* to sack.

saccade [sakad] *nf* jerk, jolt; **par saccades** jerkily, in fits and starts. ◆**saccadé** *a* (*geste, style*) jerky.

saccager [sakaʒe] *vt* (*ville, région*) *Mil* to sack; (*bouleverser*) *Fig* to turn upside down.

saccharine [sakarin] *nf* saccharin.

sacerdoce [saserdos] *nm* (*fonction*) *Rel* priesthood; *Fig* vocation.

sachet [saʃɛ] *nm* (small) bag; (*de lavande etc*) sachet; **s. de thé** teabag.

sacoche [sakɔʃ] *nf* bag; (*de vélo, moto*) saddlebag; *Scol* satchel.

sacquer [sake] *vt Fam* (*renvoyer*) to sack; (*élève*) to give a thoroughly bad mark to.

sacre [sakr] *nm* (*d'évêque*) consecration; (*de roi*) coronation. ◆**sacrer** *vt* (*évêque*) to consecrate; (*roi*) to crown.

sacré [sakre] *a* (*saint*) sacred; (*maudit*) *Fam* damned. ◆**-ment** *adv Fam* (*très*) damn(ed); (*beaucoup*) a hell of a lot.

sacrement [sakrəmɑ̃] *nm Rel* sacrament.

sacrifice [sakrifis] *nm* sacrifice. ◆**sacrifier** *vt* to sacrifice (**à** to, **pour** for); – *vi* **à** (*mode etc*) to pander to; – **se s.** *vpr* to sacrifice oneself (**à** to, **pour** for).

sacrilège [sakrilɛʒ] *nm* sacrilege; – *a* sacrilegious.

sacristie [sakristi] *nf* vestry.

sacro-saint [sakrosɛ̃] *a Iron* sacrosanct.

sadisme [sadism] *nm* sadism. ◆**sadique** *a* sadistic; – *nmf* sadist.

safari [safari] *nm* safari; **faire un s.** to be *ou* go on safari.

safran [safrɑ̃] *nm* saffron.

sagace [sagas] *a* shrewd, sagacious.

sage [saʒ] *a* wise; (*enfant*) well-behaved, good; (*modéré*) moderate; – *nm* wise man, sage. ◆**sagement** *adv* wisely; (*avec calme*) quietly. ◆**sagesse** *nf* wisdom; good behaviour; moderation.

sage-femme [saʒfam] *nf* (*pl* **sages-femmes**) midwife.

Sagittaire [saʒitɛr] *nm* **le S.** (*signe*) Sagittarius.

Sahara [saara] *nm* **le S.** the Sahara (desert).

saign/er [seɲe] *vti* to bleed. ◆**-ant** [seɲɑ̃] *a* (*viande*) *Culin* rare, underdone. ◆**-ée** *nf* **1** *Méd* bleeding, blood-letting; (*perte*) *Fig* heavy loss. **2 la s. du bras** *Anat* the bend of the arm. ◆**saignement** *nm* bleeding; **s. de nez** nosebleed.

saillant [sajɑ̃] *a* projecting, jutting out; (*trait etc*) *Fig* salient. ◆**saillie** *nf* projection; **en s., faisant s.** projecting.

sain [sɛ̃] *a* healthy; (*moralement*) sane; (*jugement*) sound; (*nourriture*) wholesome, healthy; **s. et sauf** safe and sound, unhurt. ◆**sainement** *adv* (*vivre*) healthily; (*raisonner*) sanely.

saindoux [sɛ̃du] *nm* lard.

saint, sainte [sɛ̃, sɛ̃t] *a* holy; (*personne*) saintly; **s. Jean** Saint John; **sainte nitouche** *Iron* little innocent; **la Sainte Vierge** the Blessed Virgin; – *nmf* saint. ◆**S.-bernard** *nm* (*chien*) St Bernard. ◆**S.-Esprit** *nm* Holy Spirit. ◆**S.-Siège** *nm* Holy See. ◆**S.-Sylvestre** *nf* New Year's Eve.

sais [sɛ] *voir* **savoir**.

saisie [sezi] *nf Jur* seizure; **s. de données** data capture *ou* entry.

sais/ir [sezir] **1** *vt* to grab (hold of), seize; (*occasion*) & *Jur* to seize; (*comprendre*) to understand, grasp; (*frapper*) *Fig* to strike; **se s. de** to grab (hold of), seize. **2** *vt* (*viande*) *Culin* to fry briskly. ◆**-i a s. de** (*joie, peur etc*) overcome by. ◆**-issant** *a* (*film etc*) gripping; (*contraste, ressemblance*) striking. ◆**-issement** *nm* (*émotion*) shock.

saison [sɛzɔ̃] *nf* season; **en/hors s.** in/out of season; **en pleine** *ou* **haute s.** in (the) high season; **en basse s.** in the low season. ◆**saisonnier, -ière** *a* seasonal.

sait [sɛ] *voir* **savoir**.

salade [salad] **1** *nf* (*laitue*) lettuce; **s. (verte)** (green) salad; **s. de fruits/de tomates/etc** fruit/tomato/etc salad. **2** *nf* (*désordre*) *Fam* mess. **3** *nfpl* (*mensonges*) *Fam* stories, nonsense. ◆**saladier** *nm* salad bowl.

salaire [salɛr] nm wage(s), salary.

salaison [salɛzɔ̃] nf Culin salting; pl (denrées) salt(ed) meat ou fish.

salamandre [salamɑ̃dr] nf (animal) salamander.

salami [salami] nm Culin salami.

salarial, -aux [salarjal, -o] a (accord etc) wage-. ◆**salarié, -ée** a wage-earning; – nmf wage earner.

salaud [salo] nm Arg Péj bastard, swine.

sale [sal] a dirty; (dégoûtant) filthy; (mauvais) nasty; (couleur) dingy. ◆**salement** adv (se conduire, manger) disgustingly. ◆**saleté** nf dirtiness; filthiness; (crasse) dirt, filth; (action) dirty trick; (camelote) Fam rubbish, junk; pl (détritus) mess, dirt; (obscénités) filth. ◆**salir** vt to (make) dirty; (réputation) Fig to sully, tarnish; — **se s.** vpr to get dirty. ◆**salissant** a (métier) dirty, messy; (étoffe) easily dirtied. ◆**salissure** nf (tache) dirty mark.

sal/er [sale] vt Culin to salt. ◆**-é a 1** (eau) salt-; (saveur) salty; (denrées) salted; (grivois) Fig spicy. **2** (excessif) Fam steep. ◆**salière** nf saltcellar.

salive [saliv] nf saliva. ◆**saliver** vi to salivate.

salle [sal] nf room; (très grande, publique) hall; Th auditorium; (d'hôpital) ward; (public) Th house, audience; **s. à manger** dining room; **s. d'eau** washroom, shower room; **s. d'exposition** Com showroom; **s. de jeux** (pour enfants) games room; (avec machines à sous) amusement arcade; **s. d'opération** Méd operating theatre.

salon [salɔ̃] nm sitting room, lounge; (exposition) show; **s. de beauté/de coiffure** beauty/hairdressing salon; **s. de thé** tearoom(s).

salope [salɔp] nf (femme) Arg Péj bitch, cow. ◆**saloperie** nf Arg (action) dirty trick; (camelote) rubbish, junk; des saloperies (propos) filth.

salopette [salɔpɛt] nf dungarees; (d'ouvrier) overalls.

salsifis [salsifi] nf Bot Culin salsify.

saltimbanque [saltɛ̃bɑ̃k] nmf (travelling) acrobat.

salubre [salybr] a healthy, salubrious. ◆**salubrité** nf healthiness; **s. publique** public health.

saluer [salɥe] vt to greet; (en partant) to take one's leave; (de la main) to wave to; (de la tête) to nod to; Mil to salute; **s. qn comme** Fig to hail s.o. as. ◆**salut 1** nm greeting; wave; nod; Mil salute; – int Fam hello!, hi!; (au revoir) bye! **2** nm (de peuple etc) salvation; (sauvegarde) safety. ◆**salutation** nf greeting.

salutaire [salytɛr] a salutary.

salve [salv] nf salvo.

samedi [samdi] nm Saturday.

SAMU [samy] nm abrév (service d'assistance médicale d'urgence) emergency medical service.

sanatorium [sanatɔrjɔm] nm sanatorium.

sanctifier [sɑ̃ktifje] vt to sanctify.

sanction [sɑ̃ksjɔ̃] nf (approbation, peine) sanction. ◆**sanctionner** vt (confirmer, approuver) to sanction; (punir) to punish.

sanctuaire [sɑ̃ktɥɛr] nm Rel sanctuary.

sandale [sɑ̃dal] nf sandal.

sandwich [sɑ̃dwitʃ] nm sandwich.

sang [sɑ̃] nm blood; **coup de s.** Méd stroke. ◆**sanglant** a bloody; (critique, reproche) scathing. ◆**sanguin, -ine 1** a (vaisseau etc) blood-; (tempérament) full-blooded. **2** nf (fruit) blood orange. ◆**sanguinaire** a blood-thirsty.

sang-froid [sɑ̃frwa] nm self-control, calm; **avec s.-froid** calmly; **de s.-froid** (tuer) in cold blood.

sangle [sɑ̃gl] nf (de selle, parachute) strap.

sanglier [sɑ̃glije] nm wild boar.

sanglot [sɑ̃glo] nm sob. ◆**sangloter** vi to sob.

sangsue [sɑ̃sy] nf leech.

sanitaire [sanitɛr] a health-; (conditions) sanitary; (personnel) medical; (appareils etc) bathroom-, sanitary.

sans [sɑ̃] ([sɑ̃z] before vowel and mute h) prép without; **s. faire** without doing; **ça va s. dire** that goes without saying; **s. qu'il le sache** without him ou his knowing; **s. cela, s. quoi** otherwise; **s. plus** (but) no more than that; **s. exception/faute** without exception/fail; **s. importance/travail** unimportant/unemployed; **s. argent/manches** penniless/sleeveless. ◆**s.-abri** nmf inv homeless person, les **s.-abri** the homeless. ◆**s.-gêne** a inv inconsiderate; – nm inv inconsiderateness. ◆**s.-travail** nmf inv unemployed person.

santé [sɑ̃te] nf health; **en bonne/mauvaise s.** in good/bad health, well/not well; (à votre) **s.!** (en trinquant) your health!, cheers!; **maison de s.** nursing home.

saoul [su] = soûl.

saper [sape] vt to undermine.

sapeur-pompier [sapœrpɔ̃pje] nm (pl sapeurs-pompiers) fireman.

saphir [safir] nm (pierre) sapphire; (d'électrophone) sapphire, stylus.

sapin [sapɛ̃] *nm* (*arbre, bois*) fir; **s. de Noël** Christmas tree.
sarbacane [sarbakan] *nf* (*jouet*) peashooter.
sarcasme [sarkasm] *nm* sarcasm; **un s.** a piece of sarcasm. ◆**sarcastique** *a* sarcastic.
sarcler [sarkle] *vt* (*jardin etc*) to weed.
Sardaigne [sardɛɲ] *nf* Sardinia.
sardine [sardin] *nf* sardine.
sardonique [sardɔnik] *a* sardonic.
SARL *abrév* (*société à responsabilité limitée*) Ltd, *Am* Inc.
sarment [sarmɑ̃] *nm* vine shoot.
sarrasin [sarazɛ̃] *nm* buckwheat.
sas [sa(s)] *nm* (*pièce étanche*) Nau Av airlock.
Satan [satɑ̃] *nm* Satan. ◆**satané** *a* (*maudit*) blasted. ◆**satanique** *a* satanic.
satellite [satelit] *nm* satellite; **pays s.** Pol satellite (country).
satiété [sasjete] *nf* **à s.** (*boire, manger*) one's fill; (*répéter*) ad nauseam.
satin [satɛ̃] *nm* satin. ◆**satiné** *a* satiny, silky.
satire [satir] *nf* satire (**contre** on). ◆**satirique** *a* satiric(al).
satisfaction [satisfaksjɔ̃] *nf* satisfaction. ◆**satisfaire*** *vt* to satisfy; – *vi* **s. à** (*conditions, engagement etc*) to fulfil. ◆**satisfaisant** *a* (*acceptable*) satisfactory. ◆**satisfait** *a* satisfied, content (**de** with).
saturateur [satyratœr] *nm* (*de radiateur*) humidifier.
saturer [satyre] *vt* to saturate (**de** with).
satyre [satir] *nm* Fam sex fiend.
sauce [sos] *nf* sauce; (*jus de viande*) gravy; **s. tomate** tomato sauce. ◆**saucière** *nf* sauce boat; gravy boat.
saucisse [sosis] *nf* sausage. ◆**saucisson** *nm* (cold) sausage.
sauf[1] [sof] *prép* except (**que** that); **s. avis contraire** unless you hear otherwise; **s. erreur** barring error.
sauf[2], **sauve** [sof, sov] *a* (*honneur*) intact, saved; **avoir la vie sauve** to be unharmed. ◆**sauf-conduit** *nm* (*document*) safeconduct.
sauge [soʒ] *nf* Bot Culin sage.
saugrenu [sogrəny] *a* preposterous.
saule [sol] *nm* willow; **s. pleureur** weeping willow.
saumâtre [somɑtr] *a* (*eau*) briny, brackish.
saumon [somɔ̃] *nm* salmon; – *a inv* (*couleur*) salmon (pink).
saumure [somyr] *nf* (pickling) brine.
sauna [sona] *nm* sauna.

saupoudrer [sopudre] *vt* (*couvrir*) to sprinkle (**de** with).
saur [sɔr] *am* **hareng s.** smoked herring, kipper.
saut [so] *nm* jump, leap; **faire un s.** to jump, leap; **faire un s. chez qn** (*visite*) to pop round to s.o.; **au s. du lit** on getting out of bed; **s. à la corde** skipping, *Am* jumping rope. ◆**sauter** *vi* to jump, leap; (*bombe*) to go off, explode; (*poudrière etc*) to go up, blow up; (*fusible*) to blow; (*se détacher*) to come off; **faire s.** (*détruire*) to blow up; (*arracher*) to tear off; (*casser*) to break; (*renvoyer*) Fam to get rid of, fire; (*fusible*) to blow; *Culin* to sauté; **s. à la corde** to skip, *Am* jump rope; **ça saute aux yeux** it's obvious; – *vt* (*franchir*) to jump (over); (*mot, classe, repas*) to skip. ◆**sautemouton** *nm* (*jeu*) leapfrog. ◆**sautiller** *vi* to hop. ◆**sautoir** *nm* Sp jumping area.
sauté [sote] *a & nm* Culin sauté. ◆**sauteuse** *nf* (shallow) pan.
sauterelle [sotrɛl] *nf* grasshopper.
sautes [sot] *nfpl* (*d'humeur, de température*) sudden changes (**de** in).
sauvage [sovaʒ] *a* (*primitif, cruel*) savage; (*farouche*) unsociable, shy; (*illégal*) unauthorized; – *nmf* unsociable person; (*brute*) savage. ◆**sauvagerie** *nf* unsociability; (*cruauté*) savagery.
sauve [sov] *a voir* **sauf**[2].
sauvegarde [sovgard] *nf* safeguard (**contre** against). ◆**sauvegarder** *vt* to safeguard.
sauver [sove] **1** *vt* to save; (*d'un danger*) to rescue (**de** from); (*matériel*) to salvage; **s. la vie à qn** to save s.o.'s life. **2 se s.** *vpr* (*s'enfuir*) to run away ou off; (*partir*) Fam to get off, go. ◆**sauve-qui-peut** *nm inv* stampede. ◆**sauvetage** *nm* rescue; **canot de s.** lifeboat; **ceinture de s.** life belt; **radeau de s.** life raft. ◆**sauveteur** *nm* rescuer. ◆**sauveur** *nm* saviour.
sauvette (à la) [alasovɛt] *adv* **vendre à la s.** to hawk illicitly (on the streets).
savant [savɑ̃] *a* learned, scholarly; (*manœuvre etc*) masterly, clever; – *nm* scientist. ◆**savamment** *adv* learnedly; (*avec habileté*) cleverly, skilfully.
savate [savat] *nf* old shoe ou slipper.
saveur [savœr] *nf* (*goût*) flavour; (*piment*) Fig savour.
savoir* [savwar] *vt* to know; (*nouvelle*) to know, have heard; **j'ai su la nouvelle** I heard ou got to know the news; **s. lire/nager/etc** (*pouvoir*) to know how to read/swim/etc; **faire s. à qn que** to inform ou tell s.o. that; **à s.** (*c'est-à-dire*) that is,

namely; **je ne saurais pas** I could not, I cannot; **(pas) que je sache** (not) as far as I know; **je n'en sais rien** I have no idea, I don't know; **en s. long sur** to know a lot about; **un je ne sais quoi** a something or other; – nm (culture) learning, knowledge.
◆**s.-faire** nm inv know-how, ability.
◆**s.-vivre** nm inv good manners.

savon [savõ] nm **1** soap; (morceau) bar of soap. **2 passer un s. à qn** (réprimander) Fam to give s.o. a dressing-down ou a talking-to.
◆**savonner** vt to soap. ◆**savonnette** nf bar of soap. ◆**savonneux, -euse** a soapy.

savourer [savure] vt to savour, relish.
◆**savoureux, -euse** a tasty; (histoire etc) Fig juicy.

saxophone [saksofon] nm saxophone.

sbire [sbir] nm (homme de main) Péj henchman.

scabreux, -euse [skabrø, -øz] a obscene.

scalpel [skalpel] nm scalpel.

scandale [skãdal] nm scandal; (tapage) uproar; **faire s.** (livre etc) to scandalize people; **faire un s.** to make a scene.
◆**scandaleux, -euse** a scandalous, outrageous. ◆**scandaleusement** adv outrageously. ◆**scandaliser** vt to scandalize, shock; **— se s.** vpr to be shocked ou scandalized (**de** by, **que** (+ sub) that).

scander [skãde] vt (vers) to scan; (slogan) to chant.

Scandinavie [skãdinavi] nf Scandinavia.
◆**scandinave** a & nmf Scandinavian.

scanner [skaner] nm (appareil) Méd scanner.

scaphandre [skafãdr] nm (de plongeur) diving suit; (de cosmonaute) spacesuit; **s. autonome** aqualung. ◆**scaphandrier** nm diver.

scarabée [skarabe] nm beetle.

scarlatine [skarlatin] nf scarlet fever.

scarole [skarɔl] nf endive.

sceau, -x [so] nm (cachet, cire) seal.
◆**scell/er** vt **1** (document etc) to seal. **2** (fixer) Tech to cement. ◆**—és** nmpl (cachets de cire) seals.

scélérat, -ate [selera, -at] nmf scoundrel.

scel-o-frais® [selofrɛ] nm clingfilm, Am plastic wrap.

scénario [senarjo] nm (déroulement) Fig scenario; (esquisse) Cin scenario; (dialogues etc) screenplay. ◆**scénariste** nmf Cin scriptwriter.

scène [sɛn] nf **1** Th scene; (estrade, art) stage; (action) action; **mettre en s.** (pièce, film) to direct. **2** (dispute) scene; **faire une s.**

(à qn) to make ou create a scene; **s. de ménage** domestic quarrel.

scepticisme [septisism] nm scepticism, Am skepticism. ◆**sceptique** a sceptical, Am skeptical; – nmf sceptic, Am skeptic.

scheik [ʃɛk] nm sheikh.

schéma [ʃema] nm diagram; Fig outline.
◆**schématique** a diagrammatic; (succinct) Péj sketchy. ◆**schématiser** vt to represent diagrammatically; (simplifier) Péj to oversimplify.

schizophrène [skizofrɛn] a & nmf schizophrenic.

sciatique [sjatik] nf Méd sciatica.

scie [si] nf (outil) saw. ◆**scier** vt to saw.
◆**scierie** nf sawmill.

sciemment [sjamã] adv knowingly.

science [sjãs] nf science; (savoir) knowledge; (habileté) skill; **sciences humaines** social science(s); **étudier les sciences** to study science. ◆**s.-fiction** nf science fiction.
◆**scientifique** a scientific; – nmf scientist.

scinder [sɛ̃de] vt, **— se s.** vpr to divide, split.

scintill/er [sɛ̃tije] vi to sparkle, glitter; (étoiles) to twinkle. ◆**—ement** nm sparkling; twinkling.

scission [sisjõ] nf (de parti etc) split (**de** in).

sciure [sjyr] nf sawdust.

sclérose [skleroz] nf Méd sclerosis; Fig ossification; **s. en plaques** multiple sclerosis.
◆**sclérosé** a (société etc) Fig ossified.

scolaire [skɔlɛr] a school-. ◆**scolariser** vt (pays) to provide with schools; (enfant) to send to school, put into school. ◆**scolarité** nf schooling.

scooter [skuter] nm (motor) scooter.

score [skɔr] nm Sp score.

scories [skɔri] nfpl (résidu) slag.

scorpion [skɔrpjõ] nm scorpion; **le S.** (signe) Scorpio.

scotch [skɔtʃ] nm **1** (boisson) Scotch, whisky. **2**® (ruban adhésif) sellotape®, Am scotch (tape)®. ◆**scotcher** vt to sellotape, Am to tape.

scout [skut] a & nm scout. ◆**scoutisme** nm scout movement, scouting.

script [skript] nm (écriture) printing.

scrupule [skrypyl] nm scruple; **sans scrupules** unscrupulous; (agir) unscrupulously. ◆**scrupuleux, -euse** a scrupulous. ◆**scrupuleusement** adv scrupulously.

scruter [skryte] vt to examine, scrutinize.

scrutin [skrytɛ̃] nm (vote) ballot; (opérations électorales) poll(ing).

sculpter [skylte] vt to sculpt(ure), carve.

◆**sculpteur** *nm* sculptor. ◆**sculptural, -aux** *a* (*beauté*) statuesque. ◆**sculpture** *nf* (*art, œuvre*) sculpture; **s. sur bois** wood-carving.

se [s(ə)] (**s'** before vowel or mute h) *pron* 1 (*complément direct*) himself; (*sujet femelle*) herself; (*non humain*) itself; (*indéfini*) oneself; *pl* themselves; **il se lave** he washes himself. 2 (*indirect*) to himself; to herself; to itself; to oneself; **se dire** to say to oneself; **elle se dit** she says to herself. 3 (*réciproque*) (to) each other, (to) one another; **ils s'aiment** they love each other *ou* one another; **ils** *ou* **elles se parlent** they speak to each other *ou* one another. 4 (*passif*) **ça se fait** that is done; **ça se vend bien** it sells well. 5 (*possessif*) **il se lave les mains** he washes his hands.

séance [seãs] *nf* 1 (*d'assemblée etc*) session, sitting; (*de travail etc*) session; **s.** (**de pose**) (*chez un peintre*) sitting. 2 *Cin Th* show, performance. 3 **s. tenante** at once.

séant [seã] 1 *a* (*convenable*) seemly, proper. 2 *nm* **se mettre sur son s.** to sit up.

seau, -x [so] *nm* bucket, pail.

sec, sèche [sɛk, sɛʃ] *a* dry; (*fruits, légumes*) dried; (*ton*) curt, harsh; (*maigre*) spare; (*cœur*) *Fig* hard; **coup s.** sharp blow, tap; **bruit s.** (*rupture*) snap; – *adv* (*frapper, pleuvoir*) hard; (*boire*) neat, straight; – *nm* **à s.** dried up, dry; (*sans argent*) *Fam* broke; **au s.** in a dry place. ◆**séch/er** *vt* to dry; – **se s.** *vpr* to dry oneself. 2 *vt* (*cours*) *Scol Fam* to skip; – *vi* (*ignorer*) *Scol Fam* to be stumped. ◆**—age** *nm* drying. ◆**sécheresse** *nf* dryness; (*de ton*) curtness; *Mét* drought. ◆**séchoir** *nm* (*appareil*) drier; **s. à linge** clotheshorse.

sécateur [sekatœr] *nm* pruning shears, secateurs.

sécession [sesesjõ] *nf* secession; **faire s.** to secede.

sèche [sɛʃ] *voir* **sec**. ◆**sèche-cheveux** *nm inv* hair drier. ◆**sèche-linge** *nm inv* tumble drier.

second, -onde¹ [sgõ, -õd] *a & nmf* second; **de seconde main** second-hand; – *nm* (*adjoint*) second in command; (*étage*) second floor. *Am* third floor; – *nf* *Rail* second class; *Scol* = fifth form, *Am* = eleventh grade; (*vitesse*) *Aut* second (gear). ◆**secondaire** *a* secondary.

seconde² [sgõd] *nf* (*instant*) second.

seconder [sgõde] *vt* to assist.

secouer [s(ə)kwe] *vt* to shake; (*paresse, poussière*) to shake off; **s. qn** (*maladie, nouvelle etc*) to shake s.o. up; **s. qch de qch**

(*enlever*) to shake sth out of sth; – **se s.** *vpr* (*faire un effort*) *Fam* to shake oneself out of it.

secour/ir [skurir] *vt* to assist, help. ◆**—able** *a* (*personne*) helpful. ◆**secourisme** *nm* first aid. ◆**secouriste** *nmf* first-aid worker.

secours [s(ə)kur] *nm* assistance, help; (*aux indigents*) aid, relief; **le s., les s.** *Mil* relief; (**premiers**) **s.** *Méd* first aid; **au s.!** help!; **porter s. à qn** to give s.o. assistance *ou* help; **de s.** (*sortie*) emergency-; (*équipe*) rescue-; (*roue*) spare.

secousse [s(ə)kus] *nf* jolt, jerk; (*psychologique*) shock; *Géol* tremor.

secret, -ète [sɔkrɛ, -ɛt] *a* secret; (*cachottier*) secretive; – *nm* secret; (*discrétion*) secrecy; **en s.** secretly; **dans le s.** (*au courant*) in on the secret.

secrétaire [sɔkretɛr] 1 *nmf* secretary; **s. d'État** Secretary of State; **s. de mairie** town clerk; **s. de rédaction** subeditor. 2 *nm* (*meuble*) writing desk. ◆**secrétariat** *nm* (*bureau*) secretary's office; (*d'organisation internationale*) secretariat; (*métier*) secretarial work; **de s.** (*école, travail*) secretarial.

sécréter [sekrete] *vt* *Méd Biol* to secrete. ◆**sécrétion** *nf* secretion.

secte [sɛkt] *nf* sect. ◆**sectaire** *a & nmf* *Péj* sectarian.

secteur [sɛktœr] *nm* *Mil Com* sector; (*de ville*) district; (*domaine*) *Fig* area; (*de réseau*) *Él* supply area; (*ligne*) *Él* mains.

section [sɛksjõ] *nf* section; (*de ligne d'autobus*) fare stage; *Mil* platoon. ◆**sectionner** *vt* to divide (into sections); (*artère, doigt*) to sever.

séculaire [sekylɛr] *a* (*tradition etc*) age-old.

secundo [sgõdo] *adv* secondly.

sécurité [sekyrite] *nf* (*tranquillité*) security; (*matérielle*) safety; **s. routière** road safety; **s. sociale** = social services *ou* security; **de s.** (*dispositif, ceinture, marge etc*) safety-; **en s.** secure; safe. ◆**sécuriser** *vt* to reassure, make feel (emotionally) secure.

sédatif [sedatif] *nm* sedative.

sédentaire [sedãtɛr] *a* sedentary.

sédiment [sedimã] *nm* sediment.

séditieux, -euse [sedisjø, -øz] *a* seditious. ◆**sédition** *nf* sedition.

séduire* [seduir] *vt* to charm, attract; (*plaire à*) to appeal to; (*abuser de*) to seduce. ◆**séduisant** *a* attractive. ◆**séducteur, -trice** *a* seductive; – *nmf* seducer. ◆**séduction** *nf* attraction.

segment [sɛgmã] *nm* segment.

ségrégation [segregasjõ] *nf* segregation.

seiche [sɛʃ] nf cuttlefish.

seigle [sɛgl] nm rye.

seigneur [sɛɲœr] nm Hist lord; **S.** Rel Lord.

sein [sɛ̃] nm (mamelle, poitrine) breast; Fig bosom; **bout de s.** nipple; **au s. de** (parti etc) within; (bonheur etc) in the midst of.

Seine [sɛn] nf la **S.** the Seine.

séisme [seism] nm earthquake.

seize [sɛz] a & nm sixteen. **◆seizième** a & nmf sixteenth.

séjour [seʒur] nm stay; **(salle de) s.** living room. **◆séjourner** vi to stay.

sel [sɛl] nm salt; (piquant) Fig spice; (humour) wit; Méd (smelling) salts; **sels de bain** bath salts.

sélect [selɛkt] a Fam select.

sélectif, -ive [selɛktif, -iv] a selective. **◆sélection** nf selection. **◆sélectionner** vt to select.

self(-service) [sɛlf(sɛrvis)] nm self-service restaurant ou shop.

selle [sɛl] **1** nf (de cheval) saddle. **2** nfpl **les selles** Méd bowel movements, stools. **◆seller** vt (cheval) to saddle.

sellette [sɛlɛt] nf **sur la s.** (personne) under examination, in the hot seat.

selon [s(ə)lɔ̃] prép according to (que whether); **c'est sa.** Fam it (all) depends.

semailles [s(ə)maj] nfpl (travail) sowing; (période) seedtime.

semaine [s(ə)mɛn] nf week; **en s.** (opposé à week-end) in the week.

sémantique [semɑ̃tik] a semantic; - nf semantics.

sémaphore [semafɔr] nm (appareil) Rail Nau semaphore.

semblable [sɑ̃blabl] a similar (à to); **être semblables** to be alike ou similar; **de semblables propos**/etc (tels) such remarks/etc; - nm fellow (creature); **toi et tes semblables** you and your kind.

semblant [sɑ̃blɑ̃] nm **faire s.** to pretend (de faire to do); **un s. de** a semblance of.

sembler [sɑ̃ble] vi to seem (à to); **il (me) semble vieux** he seems ou looks old (to me); **s. être/faire** to seem to be/to do; - v imp **il semble que** (+ sub ou indic) it seems that, it looks as if; **il me semble que** it seems to me that, I think that.

semelle [s(ə)mɛl] nf (de chaussure) sole; (intérieure) insole.

semer [s(ə)me] vt **1** (graines) to sow; (jeter) Fig to strew; (répandre) to spread; **semé de** Fig strewn with, dotted with. **2** (concurrent, poursuivant) to shake off. **◆semence** nf

seed; (clou) tack. **◆semeur, -euse** nmf sower (**de** of).

semestre [s(ə)mɛstr] nm half-year; Univ semester. **◆semestriel, -ielle** a half-yearly.

semi- [səmi] préf semi-.

séminaire [seminɛr] nm **1** Univ seminar. **2** Rel seminary.

semi-remorque [səmirəmɔrk] nm (camion) articulated lorry, Am semi(trailer).

semis [s(ə)mi] nm sowing; (terrain) seedbed; (plant) seedling.

sémite [semit] a Semitic; - nmf Semite. **◆sémitique** a (langue) Semitic.

semonce [səmɔ̃s] nf reprimand; **coup de s.** Nau warning shot.

semoule [s(ə)mul] nf semolina.

sempiternel, -elle [sɑ̃pitɛrnɛl] a endless, ceaseless.

sénat [sena] nm Pol senate. **◆sénateur** nm Pol senator.

sénile [senil] a senile. **◆sénilité** nf senility.

sens [sɑ̃s] nm **1** (faculté, raison) sense; (signification) meaning, sense; **à mon s.** to my mind; **s. commun** commonsense; **s. de l'humour** sense of humour; **ça n'a pas de s.** that doesn't make sense. **2** (direction) direction; **s. giratoire** Aut roundabout, Am traffic circle, rotary; **s. interdit** ou **unique** (rue) one-way street; **'s. interdit'** 'no entry'; **à s. unique** (rue) one-way; **s. dessus dessous** [sɑ̃dsydsu] upside down; **dans le s./le s. inverse des aiguilles d'une montre** clockwise/anticlockwise, Am counterclockwise.

sensation [sɑ̃sasjɔ̃] nf sensation, feeling; **faire s.** to cause ou create a sensation; **à s.** (film etc) Péj sensational. **◆sensationnel, -elle** a Fig sensational.

sensé [sɑ̃se] a sensible.

sensible [sɑ̃sibl] a sensitive (à to); (douloureux) tender, sore; (perceptible) perceptible; (progrès etc) appreciable. **◆sensiblement** adv (notablement) appreciably; (à peu près) more or less. **◆sensibiliser** vt **s. qn à** (problème etc) to make s.o. alive to ou aware of. **◆sensibilité** nf sensitivity.

sensoriel, -ielle [sɑ̃sɔrjɛl] a sensory.

sensuel, -elle [sɑ̃suɛl] a (sexuel) sensual; (musique, couleur etc) sensuous. **◆sensualité** nf sensuality; sensuousness.

sentence [sɑ̃tɑ̃s] nf **1** Jur sentence. **2** (maxime) maxim.

senteur [sɑ̃tœr] nf (odeur) scent.

sentier [sɑ̃tje] nm path.

sentiment [sɑ̃timɑ̃] nm feeling; **avoir le s. de** (apprécier) to be aware of; **faire du s.** to be sentimental. **◆sentimental, -aux** a sentimental; (*amoureux*) love-. ◆**sentimentalité** *nf* sentimentality.

sentinelle [sɑ̃tinɛl] *nf* sentry.

sentir* [sɑ̃tir] *vt* to feel; (*odeur*) to smell; (*goût*) to taste; (*racisme etc*) to smack of; (*connaître*) to sense, be conscious of; **s. le moisi/la parfum/***etc* to smell musty/of perfume/*etc*; **s. le poisson/***etc* (*avoir le goût de*) to taste of fish/*etc*; **je ne peux pas le s.** (*supporter*) *Fam* I can't bear *ou* stand him; **se faire s.** (*effet etc*) to make itself felt; **se s. fatigué/humilié/***etc* to feel tired/humiliated/*etc*; — *vi* to smell.

séparation [separasjɔ̃] *nf* separation; (*en deux*) division, split; (*départ*) parting. ◆**séparer** *vt* to separate (**de** from); (*diviser en deux*) to divide, split (up); (*cheveux*) to part; — **se s.** *vpr* (*se quitter*) to part; (*adversaires, époux*) to separate; (*assemblée, cortège*) to disperse, break up; (*se détacher*) to split off; **se s. de** (*objet aimé, chien etc*) to part with. ◆**séparé** *a* (*distinct*) separate; (*époux*) separated (**de** from). ◆**séparément** *adv* separately.

sept [sɛt] *a & nm* seven. ◆**septième** *a & nmf* seventh; **un s.** a seventh.

septante [sɛptɑ̃t] *a & nm* (*en Belgique, Suisse*) seventy.

septembre [sɛptɑ̃br] *nm* September.

septennat [sɛptena] *nm Pol* seven-year term (of office).

septentrional, -aux [sɛptɑ̃trijonal, -o] *a* northern.

sépulcre [sepylkr] *nm Rel* sepulchre.

sépulture [sepyltyr] *nf* burial; (*lieu*) burial place.

séquelles [sekɛl] *nfpl* (*de maladie etc*) aftereffects; (*de guerre*) aftermath.

séquence [sekɑ̃s] *nf Mus Cartes Cin* sequence.

séquestrer [sekɛstre] *vt* to confine (illegally), lock up.

sera, serait [s(ə)ra, s(ə)rɛ] *voir* **être**.

serein [sərɛ̃] *a* serene. ◆**sérénité** *nf* serenity.

sérénade [serenad] *nf* serenade.

sergent [sɛrʒɑ̃] *nm Mil* sergeant.

série [seri] *nf* series; (*ensemble*) set; **s. noire** *Fig* string *ou* series of disasters; **de s.** (*article etc*) standard; **fabrication en s.** mass production; **fins de s.** *Com* oddments; **hors s.** *Fig* outstanding.

sérieux, -euse [serjø, -øz] *a* (*personne, maladie, doute etc*) serious; (*de bonne foi*) genuine, serious; (*digne de foi, fiable*) reliable; (*bénéfices*) substantial; **de sérieuses chances de . . .** a good chance of . . . ; —

nm seriousness; (*fiabilité*) reliability; **prendre au s.** to take seriously; **garder son s.** to keep a straight face; **manquer de s.** (*travailleur*) to lack application. ◆**sérieusement** *adv* seriously; (*travailler*) conscientiously.

serin [s(ə)rɛ̃] *nm* canary.

seriner [s(ə)rine] *vt* **s. qch à qn** to repeat sth to s.o. over and over again.

seringue [s(ə)rɛ̃g] *nf* syringe.

serment [sɛrmɑ̃] *nm* (*affirmation solennelle*) oath; (*promesse*) pledge; **prêter s.** to take an oath; **faire le s. de faire** to swear to do; **sous s.** *Jur* on *ou* under oath.

sermon [sɛrmɔ̃] *nm Rel* sermon; (*discours*) *Péj* lecture. ◆**sermonner** *vt* (*faire la morale à*) to lecture.

serpe [sɛrp] *nf* bill(hook).

serpent [sɛrpɑ̃] *nm* snake; **s. à sonnette** rattlesnake.

serpenter [sɛrpɑ̃te] *vi* (*sentier etc*) to meander.

serpentin [sɛrpɑ̃tɛ̃] *nm* (*ruban*) streamer.

serpillière [sɛrpijɛr] *nf* floor cloth.

serre [sɛr] 1 *nf* greenhouse. 2 *nfpl* (*d'oiseau*) claws, talons.

serre-livres [sɛrlivr] *nm inv* bookend. ◆**s.-tête** *nm inv* (*bandeau*) headband.

serr/er [sere] *vt* (*saisir, tenir*) to grip, clasp; (*presser*) to squeeze, press; (*corde, nœud, vis*) to tighten; (*poing*) to clench; (*taille*) to hug; (*pieds*) to pinch; (*frein*) to apply, put on; (*rapprocher*) to close up; (*rangs*) *Mil* to close; **s. la main à** to shake hands with; **s. les dents** *Fig* to grit one's teeth; **s. qn** (*embrasser*) to hug s.o.; (*vêtement*) to be too tight for s.o.; **s. qn de près** (*talonner*) to be close behind s.o.; — *vi* **s. à droite** *Aut* to keep (to the) right; — **se s.** *vpr* (*se rapprocher*) to squeeze up *ou* together; **se s. contre** to squeeze up against. ◆**-é** *a* (*budget, nœud, vêtement*) tight; (*gens*) packed (together); (*mailles, lutte*) close; (*rangs*) serried; (*dense*) dense, thick; (*cœur*) *Fig* heavy; **avoir la gorge serrée** *Fig* to have a lump in one's throat.

serrure [seryr] *nf* lock. ◆**serrurier** *nm* locksmith.

sertir [sɛrtir] *vt* (*diamant etc*) to set.

sérum [serɔm] *nm* serum.

servante [sɛrvɑ̃t] *nf* (*maid*)servant.

serveur, -euse [sɛrvœr, -øz] *nmf* waiter, waitress; (*au bar*) barman, barmaid.

serviable [sɛrvjabl] *a* helpful, obliging. ◆**serviabilité** *nf* helpfulness.

service [sɛrvis] *nm* service; (*fonction, travail*) duty; (*pourboire*) service (charge); (*département*) *Com* department; *Tennis* serve, service; **un s.** (*aide*) a favour; **rendre s.** to be of service (**à qn** to s.o.), help (**à qn** s.o.); **rendre un mauvais s. à qn** to do s.o. a disservice; **ça pourrait rendre s.** *Fam* that might come in useful; **s. (non) compris** service (not) included; **s. après-vente** *Com* aftersales (service); **s. d'ordre** (*policiers*) police; **être de s.** to be on duty; **s. à café/à thé** coffee/tea service *ou* set; **à votre s.!** at your service!

serviette [sɛrvjɛt] *nf* 1 towel; **s. de bain/de toilette** bath/hand towel; **s. hygiénique** sanitary towel; **s. (de table)** serviette, napkin. 2 (*sac*) briefcase.

servile [sɛrvil] *a* servile; (*imitation*) slavish. ◆**servilité** *nf* servility; slavishness.

servir* [sɛrvir] 1 *vt* to serve (**qch à qn** s.o. with sth, sth to s.o.); (*convive*) to wait on; — *vi* to serve; — **se s.** *vpr* (*à table*) to help oneself, it's no good *ou* use (de faire doing). 2 *vi* (*être utile*) to be useful, serve; **s. à qch/à faire** (*objet*) to be used for sth/to do *ou* for doing; **ça ne sert à rien** it's useless, it's no good *ou* use (de faire doing); **à quoi ça sert de protester/etc** what's the use *ou* good of protesting/etc; **s. de qch** (*objet*) to be used for sth, serve as sth; **ça me sert à faire/de qch** I use it to do *ou* for doing/as sth; **s. à qn de guide/etc** to act as a guide/etc to s.o. 3 **se s.** *vpr* **se s. de** (*utiliser*) to use.

serviteur [sɛrvitœr] *nm* servant. ◆**servitude** *nf* (*esclavage*) servitude; (*contrainte*) *Fig* constraint.

ses [se] *voir* **son**².

session [sesjɔ̃] *nf* session.

set [sɛt] *nm* 1 *Tennis* set. 2 **s. (de table)** (*napperon*) place mat.

seuil [sœj] *nm* doorstep; (*entrée*) doorway; (*limite*) *Fig* threshold; **au s. de** *Fig* on the threshold of.

seul, seule [sœl] 1 *a* (*sans compagnie*) alone; **tout s.** all alone, by oneself, on one's own; **se sentir s.** to feel lonely *ou* alone; — *adv* (**tout**) **s.** (*agir, vivre*) by oneself, alone, on one's own; (*parler*) to oneself; **s. à s.** (*parler*) in private. 2 *a* (*unique*) only; **la seule femme/etc** the only *ou* sole woman/etc; **un s. chat/etc** only one cat/etc; **une seule fois** only once; **pas un s. livre/etc** not a single book/etc; **seuls les garçons . . . , les garçons seuls . . .** only the boys . . . ; — *nmf* **le s., la seule** the only one; **un s., une seule** only one, one alone; **pas un s.** not (a single) one. ◆**seulement** *adv* only; **non s. . . . mais . . .** not only . . . but (also) . . . ; **pas s.** (*même*) not even; **sans s. faire** without even doing.

sève [sɛv] *nf* *Bot* & *Fig* sap.

sévère [sever] *a* severe; (*parents, professeur*) strict. ◆**—ment** *adv* severely; (*élever*) strictly. ◆**sévérité** *nf* severity; strictness.

sévices [sevis] *nmpl* brutality.

sévir [sevir] *vi* (*fléau*) *Fig* to rage; **s. contre** to deal severely with.

sevrer [səvre] *vt* (*enfant*) to wean; **s. de** (*priver*) *Fig* to deprive of.

sexe [sɛks] *nm* (*catégorie, sexualité*) sex; (*organes*) genitals; **l'autre s.** the opposite sex. ◆**sexiste** *a* & *nmf* sexist. ◆**sexualité** *nf* sexuality. ◆**sexuel, -elle** *a* sexual; (*éducation, acte etc*) sex-.

sextuor [sɛkstɥɔr] *nm* sextet.

seyant [sɛjɑ̃] *a* (*vêtement*) becoming.

shampooing [ʃɑ̃pwɛ̃] *nm* shampoo; **s. colorant** rinse; **faire un s. à qn** to shampoo s.o.'s hair.

shérif [ʃerif] *nm* *Am* sheriff.

shooter [ʃute] *vti* *Fb* to shoot.

short [ʃɔrt] *nm* (pair of) shorts.

si [si] **1** (= **s'** [s] *before* **il, ils**) *conj* if; **s'il vient** if he comes; **si j'étais roi** if I were *ou* was king; **je me demande si** I wonder whether *ou* if; **si on restait?** (*suggestion*) what if we stayed?; **si je dis ça, c'est que . . .** I say this because . . . ; **si ce n'est** (*sinon*) if not; **si oui** if so. 2 *adv* (*tellement*) so; **pas si riche que toi/que tu crois** not as rich as you/as you think; **un si bon dîner** such a good dinner; **si grand qu'il soit** however big he may be; **si bien que** with the result that. 3 *adv* (*après négative*) yes; **tu ne viens pas? — si!** you're not coming? — yes (I am!)

siamois [sjamwa] *a* Siamese; **frères s., sœurs siamoises** Siamese twins.

Sicile [sisil] *nf* Sicily.

SIDA [sida] *nm* *Méd* AIDS. ◆**sidéen, -enne** *nmf* AIDS sufferer.

sidérer [sidere] *vt* *Fam* to flabbergast.

sidérurgie [sideryrʒi] *nf* iron and steel industry.

siècle [sjɛkl] *nm* century; (*époque*) age.

siège [sjɛʒ] *nm* 1 (*meuble, centre*) & *Pol* seat; (*d'autorité, de parti etc*) headquarters; **s. (social)** (*d'entreprise*) head office. 2 *Mil* siege; **mettre le s. devant** to lay siege to. ◆**siéger** *vi* *Pol* to sit.

sien, sienne [sjɛ̃, sjɛn] *pron poss* **le s., la sienne, les sien(ne)s** his; (*de femme*) hers; (*de chose*) its; **les deux siens** his *ou* her two; — *nmpl* **les siens** (*amis etc*) one's (own) people.

sieste [sjɛst] *nf* siesta; **faire la s.** to have *ou* take a nap.

siffler [sifle] *vi* to whistle; (*avec un sifflet*) to

blow one's whistle; (*gaz, serpent*) to hiss; (*en respirant*) to wheeze; − *vt* (*chanson*) to whistle; (*chien*) to whistle to; (*faute, fin de match Sp*) to blow one's whistle for; (*acteur, pièce*) to boo; (*boisson*) *Fam* to knock back. ◆**sifflement** *nm* whistling, whistle; hiss(ing). ◆**sifflet** *nm* (*instrument*) whistle; *pl Th* booing, boos; **coup de s.** (*son*) whistle. ◆**siffloter** *vti* to whistle.

sigle [sigl] *nm* (*initiales*) abbreviation; (*prononcé comme un mot*) acronym.

signal, -aux [siɲal, -o] *nm* signal; **s. d'alarme** *Rail* communication cord; **signaux routiers** road signs. ◆**signal/er 1** *vt* (*faire remarquer*) to point out (**à qn** to s.o., **que** that); (*annoncer, indiquer*) to indicate, signal; (*dénoncer à la police etc*) to report (**à** to). **2 se s.** *vpr* **se s. par** to distinguish oneself by. ◆**−ement** *nm* (*de personne*) description, particulars. ◆**signalisation** *nf* signalling; *Aut* signposting; **s. (routière)** [*signaux*] road signs.

signature [siɲatyr] *nf* signature; (*action*) signing. ◆**signataire** *nmf* signatory. ◆**signer 1** *vt* to sign. **2 se s.** *vpr Rel* to cross oneself.

signe [siɲ] *nm* (*indice*) sign, indication; **s. particulier/de ponctuation** distinguishing/ punctuation mark; **faire s. à qn** (*geste*) to motion to *ou* beckon s.o. (**de faire** to do); (*contacter*) to get in touch with s.o.; **faire s. que oui** to nod (one's head); **faire s. que non** to shake one's head.

signet [siɲɛ] *nm* bookmark.

signification [siɲifikɑsjɔ̃] *nf* meaning. ◆**significatif, -ive** *a* significant, meaningful; **s. de** indicative of. ◆**signifier** *vt* to mean, signify (**que** that); **s. qch à qn** (*faire connaître*) to make sth known to s.o., signify sth to s.o.

silence [silɑ̃s] *nm* silence; *Mus* rest; **en s.** in silence; **garder le s.** to keep quiet *ou* silent (**sur about**). ◆**silencieux, -euse 1** *a* silent. **2** *nm Aut* silencer, *Am* muffler; (*d'arme*) silencer. ◆**silencieusement** *adv* silently.

silex [silɛks] *nm* (*roche*) flint.

silhouette [silwɛt] *nf* outline; (*en noir*) silhouette; (*ligne du corps*) figure.

silicium [silisjɔm] *nm* silicon. ◆**silicone** *nf* silicone.

sillage [sijaʒ] *nm* (*de bateau*) wake; **dans le s. de** *Fig* in the wake of.

sillon [sijɔ̃] *nm* furrow; (*de disque*) groove.

sillonner [sijɔne] *vt* (*traverser*) to cross; (*en tous sens*) to criss-cross.

silo [silo] *nm* silo.

simagrées [simagre] *nfpl* airs (and graces); (*cérémonies*) fuss.

similaire [similɛr] *a* similar. ◆**similitude** *nf* similarity.

similicuir [similikɥir] *nm* imitation leather.

simple [sɛ̃pl] *a* simple; (*non multiple*) single; (*employé, particulier*) ordinary; − *nmf* **s. d'esprit** simpleton; − *nm Tennis* singles. ◆**simplement** *adv* simply. ◆**simplet, -ette** *a* (*personne*) a bit simple. ◆**simplicité** *nf* simplicity. ◆**simplification** *nf* simplification. ◆**simplifier** *vt* to simplify. ◆**simpliste** *a* simplistic.

simulacre [simylakr] *nm* **un s. de** *Péj* a pretence of.

simuler [simyle] *vt* to simulate; (*feindre*) to feign. ◆**simulateur, -trice 1** *nmf* (*hypocrite*) shammer; (*tire-au-flanc*) & *Mil* malingerer. **2** *nm* (*appareil*) simulator. ◆**simulation** *nf* simulation; feigning.

simultané [simyltane] *a* simultaneous. ◆**−ment** *adv* simultaneously.

sincère [sɛ̃sɛr] *a* sincere. ◆**sincèrement** *adv* sincerely. ◆**sincérité** *nf* sincerity.

sinécure [sinekyr] *nf* sinecure.

singe [sɛ̃ʒ] *nm* monkey, ape. ◆**singer** *vt* (*imiter*) to ape, mimic. ◆**singeries** *nfpl* antics, clowning.

singulariser (se) [səsɛ̃gylarize] *vpr* to draw attention to oneself.

singulier, -ière [sɛ̃gylje, -jɛr] **1** *a* peculiar, odd. **2** *a* & *nm Gram* singular. ◆**singularité** *nf* peculiarity. ◆**singulièrement** *adv* (*notamment*) particularly; (*beaucoup*) extremely.

sinistre [sinistr] **1** *a* (*effrayant*) sinister. **2** *nm* disaster; (*incendie*) fire; (*dommage*) *Jur* damage. ◆**sinistré, -ée** *a* (*population, région*) disaster-stricken; − *nmf* disaster victim.

sinon [sinɔ̃] *conj* (*autrement*) otherwise, or else; (*sauf*) except (**que** that); (*si ce n'est*) if not.

sinueux, -euse [sinɥø, -øz] *a* winding. ◆**sinuosités** *nfpl* twists (and turns).

sinus [sinys] *nm inv Anat* sinus.

siphon [sifɔ̃] *nm* siphon; (*d'évier*) trap, U-bend.

sirène [sirɛn] *nf* **1** (*d'usine etc*) siren. **2** (*femme*) mermaid.

sirop [siro] *nm* syrup; (*à diluer, boisson*) (fruit) cordial; **s. contre la toux** cough mixture *ou* syrup.

siroter [sirɔte] *vt Fam* to sip (at).

sis [si] *a Jur* situated.

sismique [sismik] a seismic; **secousse s.** earth tremor.

site [sit] nm (endroit) site; (environnement) setting; (pittoresque) beauty spot; **s. (touristique)** (monument etc) place of interest.

sitôt [sito] adv **s. que** as soon as; **s. levée, elle partit** as soon as she was up, she left; **s. après** immediately after; **pas de s.** not for some time.

situation [sitɥasjɔ̃] nf situation, position; (emploi) position; **s. de famille** marital status. ◆**situ/er** vt to situate, locate; **— se s.** vpr (se trouver) to be situated; **—é a** (maison etc) situated.

six [sis] ([si] a before consonant, [siz] before vowel) a & nm six. ◆**sixième** a & nmf sixth; **un s.** a sixth.

sketch [skɛtʃ] nm (pl sketches) Th sketch.

ski [ski] nm (objet) ski; (sport) skiing; **faire du s.** to ski; **s. nautique** water skiing. ◆**ski/er** vi to ski. ◆**—eur, -euse** nmf skier.

slalom [slalɔm] nm Sp slalom.

slave [slav] a Slav; (langue) Slavonic; — nmf Slav.

slip [slip] nm (d'homme) briefs, (under)pants; (de femme) panties, pants, knickers; **s. de bain** (swimming) trunks; (d'un bikini) briefs.

slogan [slɔgã] nm slogan.

SMIC [smik] nm abrév (salaire minimum interprofessionnel de croissance) minimum wage.

smoking [smɔkiŋ] nm (veston, costume) dinner jacket, Am tuxedo.

snack(-bar) [snak(bar)] nm snack bar.

SNCF [esensɛef] nf abrév (Société nationale des Chemins de fer français) French railways.

snob [snɔb] nmf snob; — a snobbish. ◆**snober** vt **s. qn** to snub s.o. ◆**snobisme** nm snobbery.

sobre [sɔbr] a sober. ◆**sobriété** nf sobriety.

sobriquet [sɔbrikɛ] nm nickname.

sociable [sɔsjabl] a sociable. ◆**sociabilité** nf sociability.

social, -aux [sɔsjal, -o] a social. ◆**socialisme** nm socialism. ◆**socialiste** a & nmf socialist.

société [sɔsjete] nf society; (compagnie) & Com company; **s. anonyme** Com (public) limited company, Am incorporated company. ◆**sociétaire** nmf (d'une association) member.

sociologie [sɔsjɔlɔʒi] nf sociology.

◆**sociologique** a sociological. ◆**sociologue** nmf sociologist.

socle [sɔkl] nm (de statue, colonne) plinth, pedestal; (de lampe) base.

socquette [sɔkɛt] nf ankle sock.

soda [sɔda] nm (à l'orange etc) fizzy drink, Am soda (pop).

sœur [sœr] nf sister; Rel nun, sister.

sofa [sɔfa] nm sofa, settee.

soi [swa] pron oneself; **chacun pour s.** every man for himself; **en s.** in itself; **cela va de s.** it's self-evident (**que** that); **amour/ conscience de s.** self-love/-awareness. ◆**s.-même** pron oneself.

soi-disant [swadizã] a inv so-called; — adv supposedly.

soie [swa] nf **1** silk. **2** (de porc etc) bristle. ◆**soierie** nf (tissu) silk.

soif [swaf] nf thirst (Fig for); **avoir s.** to be thirsty; **donner s. à qn** to make s.o. thirsty.

soign/er [swaɲe] vt to look after, take care of; (malade) to tend, nurse; (maladie) to treat; (détails, présentation, travail) to take care over; **se faire s.** to have (medical) treatment; **— se s.** vpr to take care of oneself, look after oneself. ◆**—é a** (personne) well-groomed; (vêtement) neat, tidy; (travail) careful. ◆**soigneux, -euse** a careful (**de** with); (propre) tidy, neat. ◆**soigneusement** adv carefully.

soin [swɛ̃] nm care; (ordre) tidiness, neatness; pl care; Méd treatment; **avoir ou prendre s. de qch/de faire** to take care of sth/to do; **les premiers soins** first aid; **soins de beauté** beauty care ou treatment; **aux bons soins de** (sur lettre) care of, c/o; **avec s.** carefully, with care.

soir [swar] nm evening; **le s.** (chaque soir) in the evening; **à neuf heures du s.** at nine in the evening; **du s.** (repas, robe etc) evening-. ◆**soirée** nf evening; (réunion) party; **s. dansante** dance.

soit 1 [swa] voir être. **2** [swa] conj (à savoir) that is (to say); **s. . . . . s. . . .** either . . . or . . . . **3** [swat] adv (oui) very well.

soixante [swasãt] a & nm sixty. ◆**soixantaine** nf **une s. (de)** (nombre) (about) sixty; **avoir la s.** (âge) to be about sixty. ◆**soixante-dix** a & nm seventy. ◆**soixante-dixième** a & nmf seventieth. ◆**soixantième** a & nmf sixtieth.

soja [sɔʒa] nm (plante) soya; **graine de s.** soya bean; **germes ou pousses de s.** beansprouts.

sol [sɔl] nm ground; (plancher) floor; (matière, territoire) soil.

solaire [sɔlɛr] *a* solar; (*chaleur, rayons*) sun's; (*crème, filtre*) sun-; (*lotion, huile*) suntan-.

soldat [sɔlda] *nm* soldier; **simple s.** private.

solde [sɔld] **1** *nm* (*de compte, à payer*) balance. **2** *nm* **en s.** (*acheter*) at sale price, *Am* on sale; (*pl*) (*marchandises*) sale goods; (*vente*) (clearance) sale(s). **3** *nf Mil* pay; **à la s. de** *Fig Péj* in s.o.'s pay. ◆**sold/er 1** *vt* (*articles*) to sell off, clear. **2** *vt* (*compte*) to pay the balance of. **3 se s.** *vpr* **se s. par** (*un échec, une défaite etc*) to end in. ◆—**é -e** *a* (*article etc*) reduced. ◆**solderie** *nf* discount *ou* reject shop.

sole [sɔl] *nf* (*poisson*) sole.

soleil [sɔlɛj] *nm* sun; (*chaleur, lumière*) sunshine; (*fleur*) sunflower; **au s.** in the sun; **il fait (du) s.** it's sunny, the sun's shining; **prendre un bain de s.** to sunbathe; **coup de s.** *Méd* sunburn.

solennel, -elle [sɔlanɛl] *a* solemn. ◆**solennellement** *adv* solemnly. ◆**solennité** [-anite] *nf* solemnity.

solex® [sɔlɛks] *nm* moped.

solfège [sɔlfɛʒ] *nm* rudiments of music.

solidaire [sɔlidɛr] *a* **être s.** (*ouvriers etc*) to be as one, show solidarity (**de** with); (*pièce de machine*) to be interdependent (**de** with). ◆**solidairement** *adv* jointly. ◆**se solidariser** *vpr* to show solidarity (**avec** with). ◆**solidarité** *nf* solidarity; (*d'éléments*) interdependence.

solide [sɔlid] *a* (*voiture, nourriture, caractère etc*) & *Ch* solid; (*argument, qualité, raison*) sound; (*vigoureux*) robust; — *nm Ch* solid. ◆**solidement** *adv* solidly. ◆**se solidifier** *vpr* to solidify. ◆**solidité** *nf* solidity; (*d'argument etc*) soundness.

soliste [sɔlist] *nmf Mus* soloist.

solitaire [sɔlitɛr] *a* solitary; — *nmf* loner; (*ermite*) recluse, hermit; **en s.** on one's own. ◆**solitude** *nf* solitude.

solive [sɔliv] *nf* joist, beam.

solliciter [sɔlisite] *vt* (*audience, emploi etc*) to seek; (*tenter*) to tempt, entice; **s. qn** (*faire appel à*) to appeal to s.o. (**de faire** to do); **être (très) sollicité** (*personne*) to be in (great) demand. ◆**sollicitation** *nf* (*demande*) appeal; (*tentation*) temptation.

sollicitude [sɔlisityd] *nf* solicitude, concern.

solo [sɔlo] *a inv* & *nm Mus* solo.

solstice [sɔlstis] *nm* solstice.

soluble [sɔlybl] *a* (*substance, problème*) soluble; **café s.** instant coffee. ◆**solution** *nf* (*d'un problème etc*) & *Ch* solution (**de** to).

solvable [sɔlvabl] *a Fin* solvent. ◆**solvabilité** *nf Fin* solvency.

solvant [sɔlvɑ̃] *nm Ch* solvent.

sombre [sɔ̃br] *a* dark; (*triste*) sombre, gloomy; **il fait s.** it's dark.

sombrer [sɔ̃bre] *vi* (*bateau*) to sink, founder; **s. dans** (*folie, sommeil etc*) to sink into.

sommaire [sɔmɛr] *a* summary; (*repas, tenue*) scant; — *nm* summary, synopsis.

sommation [sɔmasjɔ̃] *nf Jur* summons; (*de sentinelle etc*) warning.

somme [sɔm] **1** *nf* sum; **faire la s. de** to add up; **en s., s. toute** in short. **2** *nm* (*sommeil*) nap; **faire un s.** to have *ou* take a nap.

sommeil [sɔmɛj] *nm* sleep; (*envie de dormir*) sleepiness, drowsiness; **avoir s.** to be *ou* feel sleepy *ou* drowsy. ◆**sommeiller** *vi* to doze; (*faculté, qualité*) *Fig* to slumber.

sommelier [sɔmalje] *nm* wine waiter.

sommer [sɔme] *vt* **s. qn de faire** (*enjoindre*) & *Jur* to summon s.o. to do.

sommes [sɔm] *voir* **être**.

sommet [sɔmɛ] *nm* top; (*de montagne*) summit, top; (*de la gloire etc*) *Fig* height, summit; **conférence au s.** summit conference.

sommier [sɔmje] *nm* (*de lit*) base; **s. à ressorts** spring base.

sommité [sɔmite] *nf* leading light, top person (**de** in).

somnambule [sɔmnɑ̃byl] *nmf* sleepwalker; **être s.** to sleepwalk. ◆**somnambulisme** *nm* sleepwalking.

somnifère [sɔmnifɛr] *nm* sleeping pill.

somnolence [sɔmnɔlɑ̃s] *nf* drowsiness, sleepiness. ◆**somnolent** *a* drowsy, sleepy. ◆**somnoler** *vi* to doze, drowse.

somptueux, -euse [sɔ̃ptɥø, -øz] *a* sumptuous, magnificent. ◆**somptuosité** *nf* sumptuousness, magnificence.

son¹ [sɔ̃] *nm* **1** (*bruit*) sound. **2** (*de grains*) bran.

son², sa, *pl* **ses** [sɔ̃, sa, se] (*sa becomes* **son** [sɔ̃n] *before a vowel or mute h*) *a poss* his; (*de femme*) her; (*de chose*) its; (*indéfini*) one's; **son père** his *ou* her *ou* one's father; **sa durée** its duration.

sonate [sɔnat] *nf Mus* sonata.

sonde [sɔ̃d] *nf Géol* drill; *Nau* sounding line; *Méd* probe; (*pour l'alimentation*) (feeding) tube; **s. spatiale** *Av* space probe. ◆**sondage** *nm* sounding; drilling; probing; **s. (d'opinion)** opinion poll. ◆**sonder** *vt* (*rivière etc*) to sound; (*terrain*) to drill; *Av* & *Méd* to probe; (*personne, l'opinion*) *Fig* to sound out.

songe [sɔ̃ʒ] *nm* dream.

song/er [sɔ̃ʒe] *vi* **s. à qch/à faire** to think of sth/of doing; — *vt* **s. que** to consider *ou* think that. ◆**—eur, -euse** a thoughtful, pensive.

sonner [sɔne] vi to ring; (cor, cloches etc) to sound; **midi a sonné** it has struck twelve; − vt to ring; (domestique) to ring for; (cor etc) to sound; (l'heure) to strike; (assommer) to knock out. ◆**sonnantes** afpl **à cinq/etc heures s.** on the stroke of five/etc. ◆**sonné** a **1 trois/etc heures sonnées** gone ou past three/etc o'clock. **2** (fou) crazy. ◆**sonnerie** nf (son) ring(ing); (de cor etc) sound; (appareil) bell. ◆**sonnette** nf bell; **s. d'alarme** alarm (bell); **coup de s.** ring.

sonnet [sɔne] nm (poème) sonnet.

sonore [sɔnɔr] a (rire) loud; (salle, voix) resonant; (effet, film, ondes etc) sound-. ◆**sonorisation** nf (matériel) sound equipment ou system. ◆**sonoriser** vt (film) to add sound to; (salle) to wire for sound. ◆**sonorité** nf (de salle) acoustics, resonance; (de violon etc) tone.

sont [sɔ̃] voir **être**.

sophistiqué [sɔfistike] a sophisticated.

soporifique [sɔpɔrifik] a (médicament, discours etc) soporific.

soprano [sɔprano] nmf (personne) Mus soprano; − nm (voix) soprano.

sorbet [sɔrbe] nm Culin water ice, sorbet.

sorcellerie [sɔrselri] nf witchcraft, sorcery. ◆**sorcier** nm sorcerer. ◆**sorcière** nf witch; **chasse aux sorcières** Pol witch-hunt.

sordide [sɔrdid] a (acte, affaire etc) sordid; (maison etc) squalid.

sornettes [sɔrnɛt] nfpl (propos) Péj twaddle.

sort [sɔr] nm **1** (destin, hasard) fate; (condition) lot. **2** (maléfice) spell.

sorte [sɔrt] nf sort, kind (de of); **en quelque s.** as it were, in a way; **de (telle) s. que** so that, in such a way that; **de la s.** (de cette façon) in that way; **faire en s. que** (+ sub) to see to it that.

sortie [sɔrti] nf **1** departure, exit; (porte) exit; (promenade) walk; (porte) exit, way out; (de livre, modèle) Com appearance; (de disque, film) release; (d'ordinateur) output; pl (argent) outgoings; **à la s. de l'école** (moment) when school comes out; **l'heure de la s. de qn** the time at which s.o. leaves; **première s.** (de convalescent etc) first time out. **2 s. de bain** (peignoir) bathrobe.

sortilège [sɔrtilɛʒ] nm (magic) spell.

sort/ir* [sɔrtir] vi (aux **être**) to go out, leave; (venir) to come out; (pour s'amuser) to go out; (film, modèle, bourgeon etc) to come out; (numéro gagnant) to come up; **s. de** (endroit) to leave; (sujet) to stray from; (université) to be a graduate of; (famille, milieu) to come from; (légalité, limites) to go beyond; (compétence) to be outside; (gonds, rails) to come off; **s. de l'ordinaire** to be out of the ordinary; **s. de table** to leave the table; (plante, modèle, fonctions) to come up; **s. indemne** to escape unhurt (de from); − vt (aux **avoir**) to take out (de of); (film, modèle, livre etc) Com to bring out; (dire) Fam to come out with; (expulser) Fam to throw out; **je n'en s., se s. d'affaire** to pull ou come through, get out of trouble. ◆**-ant** a (numéro) winning; (député etc) Pol outgoing. ◆**-able** a (personne) presentable.

sosie [sozi] nm (de personne) double.

sot, sotte [so, sɔt] a foolish; − nmf fool. ◆**sottement** adv foolishly. ◆**sottise** nf foolishness; (action, parole) foolish thing; pl (injures) Fam insults; **faire des sottises** (enfant) to be naughty, misbehave.

sou [su] nm **sous** (argent) money; **elle n'a pas un ou le s.** she's penniless; **pas un s. de** (bon sens etc) not an ounce of; **appareil ou machine à sous** fruit machine, one-armed bandit.

soubresaut [subreso] nm (sursaut) (sudden) start.

souche [suʃ] nf (d'arbre) stump; (de carnet) stub, counterfoil; (de vigne) stock.

souci [susi] nm (inquiétude) worry, concern; (préoccupation) concern; **se faire du s.** to be worried, worry; **ça lui donne du s.** it worries him ou her. ◆**se soucier** vpr **se s. de** to be concerned ou worried about. ◆**soucieux, -euse** a concerned, worried (de qch about sth); **s. de plaire/etc** anxious to please/etc.

soucoupe [sukup] nf saucer; **s. volante** flying saucer.

soudain [sudɛ̃] a sudden; − adv suddenly. ◆**soudainement** adv suddenly. ◆**soudaineté** nf suddenness.

Soudan [sudɑ̃] nm Sudan.

soude [sud] nf Ch soda; **cristaux de s.** washing soda.

souder [sude] vt to solder; (par soudure autogène) to weld; (groupes etc) Fig to unite (closely); − **se s.** vpr (os) to knit (together). ◆**soudure** nf soldering; (métal) solder; **s.** (autogène) welding.

soudoyer [sudwaje] vt to bribe.

souffle [sufl] nm puff, blow; (haleine) breath; (respiration) breathing; (de bombe etc) blast; (inspiration) Fig inspiration; **s. (d'air)** breath of air. ◆**souffler** vi to blow; (haleter) to puff; **laisser s. qn** (reprendre haleine) to let s.o. get his breath back; − vt *(bougie)* to blow out; *(fumée, poussière, verre)* to blow; *(par une explosion)* to blow down, blast; *(chuchoter)* to whisper; *(voler) Fam* to pinch (à from); *(étonner) Fam* to stagger; **s. son rôle à qn** *Th* to prompt s.o.; **ne pas s. mot** not to breathe a word. ◆**souffler** nm **1** *(instrument)* bellows. **2** *(gifle) Litt* slap. ◆**souffleur, -euse** nmf *Th* prompter.

soufflé [sufle] nm *Culin* soufflé.

souffrance [sufrɑ̃s] nf **1** suffering. **2 en s.** *(colis etc)* unclaimed; *(affaire)* in abeyance.

souffreteux, -euse [sufrətø, -øz] a sickly.

souffr/ir* [sufrir] **1** vi to suffer; **s. de** to suffer from; *(gorge, pieds etc)* to have trouble with; **faire s. qn** *(physiquement)* to hurt s.o.; *(moralement)* to make s.o. suffer, hurt s.o. **2** vt *(endurer)* to suffer; **je ne peux pas le s.** I can't bear him. **3** vt *(exception)* to admit of. ◆**—ant** a unwell.

soufre [sufr] nm sulphur, *Am* sulfur.

souhait [swɛ] nm wish; **à vos souhaits!** *(après un éternuement)* bless you!; **à s.** perfectly. ◆**souhait/er** vt *(bonheur etc)* to wish for; **s. qch à qn** to wish s.o. sth; **s. faire** to hope to do; **s. que** (+ *sub*) to hope that. ◆**—able** a desirable.

souiller [suje] vt to soil, dirty; *(déshonorer) Fig* to sully.

soûl [su] **1** a drunk. **2** nm **tout son s.** *(boire etc)* to one's heart's content. ◆**soûler** vt to make drunk; — **se s.** vpr to get drunk.

soulager [sulaʒe] vt to relieve (de of). ◆**soulagement** nm relief.

soulever [sulve] vt to raise, lift (up); *(l'opinion, le peuple)* to stir up; *(poussière, question)* to raise; *(sentiment)* to arouse; **cela me soulève le cœur** it makes me feel sick, it turns my stomach; — **se s.** vpr *(malade etc)* to lift oneself (up); *(se révolter)* to rise (up). ◆**soulèvement** nm *(révolte)* (up)rising.

soulier [sulje] nm shoe.

souligner [suliɲe] vt *(d'un trait)* to underline; *(accentuer, faire remarquer)* to emphasize, underline; **s. que** to emphasize that.

soumettre* [sumɛtr] **1** vt *(pays, rebelles)* to subjugate, subdue; **s. à** *(assujettir)* to subject to; — **se s.** vpr to submit (à to). **2** vt *(présenter)* to submit (à to). ◆**soumis** a *(docile)* submissive; **s. à** subject to. ◆**soumission** nf **1** submission; *(docilité)* submissiveness. **2** *(offre) Com* tender.

soupape [supap] nf valve.

soupçon [supsɔ̃] nm suspicion; **un s. de** *(quantité) Fig* a hint ou touch of. ◆**soupçonner** vt to suspect *(de of, d'avoir fait of* doing, **que** that). ◆**soupçonneux, -euse** a suspicious.

soupe [sup] nf soup. ◆**soupière** nf *(soup)* tureen.

soupente [supɑ̃t] nf *(sous le toit)* loft.

souper [supe] nm supper; — vi to have supper.

soupeser [supəze] vt *(objet dans la main)* to feel the weight of; *(arguments etc) Fig* to weigh up.

soupir [supir] nm sigh. ◆**soupir/er** vi to sigh; **s. après** to yearn for. ◆**—ant** nm *(amoureux)* suitor.

soupirail, -aux [supiraj, -o] nm basement window.

souple [supl] a *(personne, esprit, règlement)* flexible; *(cuir, membre, corps)* supple. ◆**souplesse** nf flexibility; suppleness.

source [surs] nf **1** *(point d'eau)* spring; **eau de s.** spring water; **prendre sa s.** *(rivière)* to rise (à at, dans in). **2** *(origine)* source; **de s. sûre** on good authority.

sourcil [sursi] nm eyebrow. ◆**sourciller** vi **ne pas s.** *Fig* not to bat an eyelid.

sourd, sourde [sur, surd] **1** a deaf *(Fig* à to); — nmf deaf person. **2** a *(bruit, douleur)* dull; *(caché)* secret. ◆**s.-muet** *(pl* **sourds-muets),** ◆**sourde-muette** *(pl* **sourdes-muettes)** a deaf and dumb; — nmf deaf mute.

sourdine [surdin] nf *(dispositif) Mus* mute; **en s.** *Fig* quietly, secretly.

souricière [surisjɛr] nf mousetrap; *Fig* trap.

sourire* [surir] vi to smile (à at); **s. à qn** *(fortune)* to smile on s.o.; — nm smile; **faire un s. à qn** to give s.o. a smile.

souris [suri] nf mouse.

sournois [surnwa] a sly, underhand. ◆**sournoisement** adv slyly. ◆**sournoiserie** nf slyness.

sous [su] prép *(position)* under(neath), beneath; *(rang)* under; **s. la pluie** in the rain; **s. cet angle** from that angle ou point of view; **s. le nom de** under the name of; **s. Charles X** under Charles X; **s. peu** *(bientôt)* shortly.

sous- [su] préf *(subordination, subdivision)* sub-; *(insuffisance)* under-.

sous-alimenté [suzalimɑ̃te] a undernourished. ◆**sous-alimentation** nf undernourishment.

sous-bois [subwa] nm undergrowth.

sous-chef [suʃɛf] nmf second-in-command.

souscrire* [suskrir] vi **s. à** *(payer, approuver)* to subscribe to. ◆**souscription** nf subscription.

sous-développé [sudevlɔpe] *a* (*pays*) underdeveloped.

sous-directeur, -trice [sudirɛktœr, -tris] *nmf* assistant manager, assistant manageress.

sous-entend/re [suzãtãdr] *vt* to imply. ◆**-u** *nm* insinuation.

sous-estimer [suzɛstime] *vt* to underestimate.

sous-jacent [suʒasã] *a* underlying.

sous-louer [sulwe] *vt* (*appartement*) to sublet.

sous-main [sumɛ̃] *nm inv* desk pad.

sous-marin [sumarɛ̃] *a* underwater; **plongée sous-marine** skin diving; – *nm* submarine.

sous-officier [suzɔfisje] *nm* noncommissioned officer.

sous-payer [supeje] *vt* (*ouvrier etc*) to underpay.

sous-produit [suprɔdɥi] *nm* by-product.

soussigné, -ée [susiɲe] *a* & *nmf* undersigned; **je s.** I the undersigned.

sous-sol [susɔl] *nm* basement; *Géol* subsoil.

sous-titre [sutitr] *nm* subtitle. ◆**sous-titrer** *vt* (*film*) to subtitle.

soustraire [sustrɛr] *vt* to remove; *Math* to subtract, take away (**de** from); **s. qn à** (*danger etc*) to shield *ou* protect s.o. from; **se s. à** to escape from; (*devoir, obligation*) to avoid. ◆**soustraction** *nf Math* subtraction.

sous-trait/er [sutrete] *vi Com* to subcontract. ◆**-ant** *nm* subcontractor.

sous-verre [suvɛr] *nm inv* (*encadrement*) (frameless) glass mount.

sous-vêtement [suvɛtmã] *nm* undergarment; *pl* underwear.

soutane [sutan] *nf* (*de prêtre*) cassock.

soute [sut] *nf* (*magasin*) *Nau* hold.

souten/ir [sutnir] *vt* to support, hold up; (*droits, opinion*) to uphold, maintain; (*candidat etc*) to back, support; (*malade*) to sustain; (*effort, intérêt*) to sustain, keep up; (*thèse*) to defend; (*résister à*) to withstand; **s. que** to maintain that; — **se s.** *vpr* (*blessé etc*) to hold oneself up; (*se maintenir, durer*) to be sustained. ◆**-u** *a* (*attention, effort*) sustained; (*style*) lofty. ◆**soutien** *nm* support; (*personne*) supporter; **s. de famille** breadwinner. ◆**soutien-gorge** *nm* (*pl* **soutiens-gorge**) bra.

souterrain [suterɛ̃] *a* underground; – *nm* underground passage.

soutirer [sutire] *vt* **s. qch à qn** to extract *ou* get sth from s.o.

souvenir [suvnir] *nm* memory, recollection;

(*objet*) memento; (*cadeau*) keepsake; (*pour touristes*) souvenir; **en s. de** in memory of; **mon bon s. à** (*give*) my regards to. ◆**se souvenir** *vpr* **se s. de** to remember, recall; **se s. que** to remember *ou* recall that.

souvent [suvã] *adv* often; **peu s.** seldom; **le plus s.** more often than not, most often.

souverain, -aine [suvrɛ̃, -ɛn] *a* sovereign; (*extrême*) supreme; — *nmf* sovereign. ◆**souveraineté** *nf* sovereignty.

soviétique [sɔvjetik] *a* Soviet; **l'Union s.** the Soviet Union; — *nmf* Soviet citizen.

soyeux, -euse [swajø, -øz] *a* silky.

spacieux, -euse [spasjø, -øz] *a* spacious, roomy.

spaghetti(s) [spageti] *nmpl* spaghetti.

sparadrap [sparadra] *nm Méd* sticking plaster, *Am* adhesive tape.

spasme [spasm] *nm* spasm. ◆**spasmodique** *a* spasmodic.

spatial, -aux [spasjal, -o] *a* (*vol etc*) space-; **engin s.** spaceship, spacecraft.

spatule [spatyl] *nf* spatula.

speaker [spikɛr] *nm*, **speakerine** [spikrin] *nf Rad TV* announcer.

spécial, -aux [spesjal, -o] *a* special; (*bizarre*) peculiar. ◆**spécialement** *adv* especially, particularly; (*exprès*) specially.

spécialiser (se) [səspesjalize] *vpr* to specialize (**dans** in). ◆**spécialisation** *nf* specialization. ◆**spécialiste** *nmf* specialist. ◆**spécialité** *nf* speciality, *Am* specialty.

spécifier [spesifje] *vt* to specify (**que** that).

spécifique [spesifik] *a Phys Ch* specific.

spécimen [spesimɛn] *nm* specimen; (*livre etc*) specimen copy.

spectacle [spɛktakl] *nm* **1** (*vue*) spectacle, sight; **se donner en s.** *Péj* to make an exhibition of oneself. **2** (*représentation*) show; **le s.** (*industrie*) show business. ◆**spectateur, -trice** *nmf Sp* spectator; (*témoin*) onlooker, witness; *pl Th Cin* audience.

spectaculaire [spɛktakylɛr] *a* spectacular.

spectre [spɛktr] *nm* **1** (*fantôme*) spectre, ghost. **2** (*solaire*) spectrum.

spéculer [spekyle] *vi Fin Phil* to speculate; **s. sur** (*table tsur*) to bank *ou* rely on. ◆**spéculateur, -trice** *nmf* speculator. ◆**spéculatif, -ive** *a Fin Phil* speculative. ◆**spéculation** *nf Fin Phil* speculation.

spéléologie [speleɔlɔʒi] *nf* (*activité*) potholing, caving, *Am* spelunking. ◆**spéléologue** *nmf* potholer, *Am* spelunker.

sperme [spɛrm] *nm* sperm, semen.

sphère [sfɛr] *nf* (*boule, domaine*) sphere. ◆**sphérique** *a* spherical.

sphinx [sfɛ̃ks] *nm* sphinx.

spirale [spiral] nf spiral.

spirite [spirit] nmf spiritualist. ◆**spiritisme** nm spiritualism.

spirituel, -elle [spirityɛl] a 1 (amusant) witty. 2 (pouvoir, vie etc) spiritual.

spiritueux [spirityø] nmpl (boissons) spirits.

splendide [splãdid] a (merveilleux, riche, beau) splendid. ◆**splendeur** nf splendour.

spongieux, -euse [spɔ̃ʒjø, -øz] a spongy.

spontané [spɔ̃tane] a spontaneous. ◆**spontanéité** nf spontaneity. ◆**spontanément** adv spontaneously.

sporadique [spɔradik] a sporadic.

sport [spɔr] nm sport; **faire du s.** to play sport ou Am sports; **(de) s.** (chaussures, vêtements) casual, sports; **voiture/veste de s.** sports car/jacket. ◆**sportif, -ive** a (attitude, personne) sporting; (association, journal, résultats) sports, sporting; (allure) athletic; – nmf sportsman, sportswoman. ◆**sportivité** nf (esprit) sportsmanship.

spot [spɔt] nm 1 (lampe) spot(light). 2 s. (publicitaire) Rad TV commercial.

sprint [sprint] nm Sp sprint. ◆**sprint/er** vi to sprint; – nm [-œr] sprinter. ◆**-euse** nf sprinter.

square [skwar] nm public garden.

squelette [skəlɛt] nm skeleton. ◆**squelettique** a (personne, maigreur) skeleton-like; (exposé) sketchy.

stable [stabl] a stable. ◆**stabilisateur** nm stabilizer. ◆**stabiliser** vt to stabilize; – **se s.** vpr to stabilize. ◆**stabilité** nf stability.

stade [stad] nm 1 Sp stadium. 2 (phase) stage.

stage [staʒ] nm training period; (cours) (training) course. ◆**stagiaire** a & nmf trainee.

stagner [stagne] vi to stagnate. ◆**stagnant** a stagnant. ◆**stagnation** nf stagnation.

stalle [stal] nf (box) & Rel stall.

stand [stãd] nm (d'exposition etc) stand, stall; **s. de ravitaillement** Sp pit; **s. de tir** (de foire) shooting range; Mil firing range.

standard [stãdar] 1 nm Tél switchboard. 2 a inv (modèle etc) standard. ◆**standardiser** vt to standardize. ◆**standardiste** nmf (switchboard) operator.

standing [stãdiŋ] nm standing, status; **de (grand) s.** (immeuble) luxury-.

starter [starter] nm 1 Aut choke. 2 Sp starter.

station [stasjɔ̃] nf (de métro, d'observation etc) & Rad station; (de ski etc) resort; (d'autobus) stop; **s. de taxis** taxi rank, Am taxi stand; **s. debout** standing (position); **s. (thermale)** spa. ◆**s.-service** nf (pl stations-service) Aut service station.

stationnaire [stasjɔnɛr] vi a stationary.

stationn/er [stasjɔne] vi (se garer) to park; (être garé) to be parked. ◆**-ement** nm parking.

statique [statik] a static.

statistique [statistik] nf (donnée) statistic; **la s.** (techniques) statistics; – a statistical.

statue [staty] nf statue. ◆**statuette** nf statuette.

statuer [statɥe] vi **s. sur** Jur to rule on.

statu quo [statykwo] nm inv status quo.

stature [statyr] nf stature.

statut [staty] nm 1 (position) status. 2 pl (règles) statutes. ◆**statutaire** a statutory.

steak [stɛk] nm steak.

stencil [stɛnsil] nm stencil.

sténo [steno] nf (personne) stenographer; (sténographie) shorthand, stenography; **prendre en s.** to take down in shorthand. ◆**sténodactylo** nf shorthand typist, Am stenographer. ◆**sténographie** nf shorthand, stenography.

stéréo [stereo] nf stereo; – a inv (disque etc) stereo. ◆**stéréophonique** a stereophonic.

stéréotype [stereotip] nm stereotype. ◆**stéréotypé** a stereotyped.

stérile [steril] a sterile; (terre) barren. ◆**stérilisation** nf sterilization. ◆**stériliser** vt to sterilize. ◆**stérilité** nf sterility; (de terre) barrenness.

stérilet [sterilɛ] nm IUD, coil.

stéthoscope [stetɔskɔp] nm stethoscope.

steward [stiwart] nm Av Nau steward.

stigmate [stigmat] nm Fig mark, stigma (de of). ◆**stigmatiser** vt (dénoncer) to stigmatize.

stimul/er [stimyle] vt to stimulate. ◆**-ant** nm Fig stimulus; Méd stimulant. ◆**stimulateur** nm **s. cardiaque** pacemaker. ◆**stimulation** nf stimulation.

stimulus [stimylys] nm (pl stimuli [-li]) (physiologique) stimulus.

stipuler [stipyle] vt to stipulate (que that). ◆**stipulation** nf stipulation.

stock [stɔk] nm Com & Fig stock (de of). ◆**stock/er** vt to (keep in) stock. ◆**-age** nm stocking.

stoïque [stɔik] a stoic(al). ◆**stoïcisme** nm stoicism.

stop [stɔp] 1 int stop; – nm (panneau) Aut stop sign; (feu arrière) Aut brake light. 2 nm **faire du s.** Fam to hitchhike. ◆**stopp/er** 1 vti to stop. 2 vt (vêtement) to mend (invisibly). **—age** nm (invisible) mending.

store [stɔr] nm blind, Am (window) shade; (de magasin) awning.

strabisme [strabism] nm squint.

strapontin [strapɔ̃tɛ̃] nm tip-up seat.

stratagème [strataʒɛm] nm stratagem, ploy.

stratège [strateʒ] nm strategist. **◆stratégie** nf strategy. **◆stratégique** a strategic.

stress [stres] nm inv Méd Psy stress. **◆stressant** a stressful. **◆stressé** a under stress.

strict [strikt] a strict; (langue, tenue, vérité) plain; (droit) basic; **le s. minimum/nécessaire** the bare minimum/necessities. **◆strictement** adv strictly; (vêtu) plainly.

strident [stridã] a strident, shrill.

strie [stri] nf streak; (sillon) groove. **◆strier** vt to streak.

strip-tease [striptiz] nm striptease. **◆strip-teaseuse** nf stripper.

strophe [strɔf] nf stanza, verse.

structure [stryktyr] nf structure. **◆structural, -aux** a structural. **◆structurer** vt to structure.

stuc [styk] nm stucco.

studieux, -euse [stydjø, -øz] a studious; (vacances etc) devoted to study.

studio [stydjo] nm (de peintre) & Cin TV studio; (logement) studio flat ou Am apartment.

stupéfait [stypefe] a amazed, astounded (de at, by). **◆stupéfaction** nf amazement. **◆stupéfi/er** vt to amaze, astound. **◆—ant 1** a amazing, astounding. **2** nm drug, narcotic. **◆stupeur** nf **1** (étonnement) amazement. **2** (inertie) stupor.

stupide [stypid] a stupid. **◆stupidement** adv stupidly. **◆stupidité** nf stupidity; (action, parole) stupid thing.

style [stil] nm style; **de s.** (meuble) period-. **◆stylisé** a stylized. **◆styliste** nmf (de mode etc) designer. **◆stylistique** a stylistic.

stylé [stile] a well-trained.

stylo [stilo] nm pen; **s. à bille** ballpoint (pen), biro®; **s. à encre** fountain pen.

su [sy] voir savoir.

suave [sɥav] a (odeur, voix) sweet.

subalterne [sybaltɛrn] a & nmf subordinate.

subconscient [sypkɔ̃sjɑ̃] a & nm subconscious.

subdiviser [sybdivize] vt to subdivide (en into). **◆subdivision** nf subdivision.

subir [sybir] vt to undergo; (conséquences, défaite, perte, tortures) to suffer; (influence) to be under; **s. qn** (supporter) Fam to put up with s.o.

subit [sybi] a sudden. **◆subitement** adv suddenly.

subjectif, -ive [sybʒɛktif, -iv] a subjective. **◆subjectivement** adv subjectively. **◆subjectivité** nf subjectivity.

subjonctif [sybʒɔ̃ktif] nm Gram subjunctive.

subjuguer [sybʒyge] vt to subjugate; (envoûter) to captivate.

sublime [syblim] a & nm sublime.

sublimer [syblime] vt Psy to sublimate.

submerger [sybmerʒe] vt to submerge; (envahir) Fig to overwhelm; **submergé de** (travail etc) overwhelmed with; **submergé par** (ennemi, foule) swamped by. **◆submersible** nm submarine.

subordonn/er [sybɔrdɔne] vt to subordinate (à to). **◆—é, -ée** a subordinate (à to); **être s. à** (dépendre de) to depend on; — nmf subordinate. **◆subordination** nf subordination.

subreptice [sybreptis] a surreptitious.

subside [sypsid] nm grant, subsidy.

subsidiaire [sybsidjɛr] a subsidiary; **question s.** (de concours) deciding question.

subsister [sybziste] vi (rester) to remain; (vivre) to get by, subsist; (doutes, souvenirs etc) to linger (on), subsist. **◆subsistance** nf subsistence.

substance [sypstɑ̃s] nf substance; **en s.** Fig in essence. **◆substantiel, -ielle** a substantial.

substantif [sypstɑ̃tif] nm Gram noun, substantive.

substituer [sypstitɥe] vt to substitute (à for); **se s. à qn** to take the place of s.o., substitute for s.o.; (représenter) to substitute for s.o. **◆substitution** nf substitution.

subterfuge [sypterfyʒ] nm subterfuge.

subtil [syptil] a subtle. **◆subtilité** nf subtlety.

subtiliser [syptilize] vt (dérober) Fam to make off with.

subvenir* [sybvənir] vi **s. à** (besoins, frais) to meet.

subvention [sybvɑ̃sjɔ̃] nf subsidy. **◆subventionner** vt to subsidize.

subversif, -ive [sybversif, -iv] a subversive. **◆subversion** nf subversion.

suc [syk] nm (gastrique, de fruit) juice; (de plante) sap.

succédané [syksedane] *nm* substitute (*de* for).

succéder [syksede] *vi* s. à qn to succeed s.o.; s. à qch to follow sth, come after sth; **— se s.** *vpr* to succeed one another; to follow one another. **◆successeur** *nm* successor. **◆successif, -ive** *a* successive. **◆successivement** *adv* successively. **◆succession** *nf* 1 succession (*de of, à* to); prendre la s. de qn to succeed s.o. 2 (*patrimoine*) *Jur* inheritance, estate.

succès [sykse] *nm* success; s. de librairie (*livre*) best-seller; avoir du s. to be successful, be a success; à s. (*auteur, film etc*) successful; avec s. successfully.

succinct [syksɛ̃] *a* succinct, brief.

succion [sy(k)sjɔ̃] *nf* suction.

succomber [sykɔ̃be] *vi* 1 (*mourir*) to die. 2 s. à (*céder à*) to succumb to, give in to.

succulent [sykylɑ̃] *a* succulent.

succursale [sykyrsal] *nf* *Com* branch; magasin à succursales multiples chain *ou* multiple store.

sucer [syse] *vt* to suck. **◆sucette** *nf* lollipop; (*tétine*) dummy, comforter, *Am* pacifier.

sucre [sykr] *nm* sugar; (*morceau*) sugar lump; s. cristallisé granulated sugar; s. en morceaux lump sugar; s. en poudre, s. semoule caster sugar, *Am* finely ground sugar; s. d'orge barley sugar. **◆sucr/er** *vt* to sugar, sweeten. **◆-é** *a* sweet, sugary; (*artificiellement*) sweetened; (*doucereux*) *Fig* sugary, syrupy. **◆sucrerie 1** *nf* (*usine*) sugar refinery. **2** *nfpl* (*bonbons*) sweets, *Am* candy. **◆sucrier, -ière** *a* (*industrie*) sugar-; *— nm* (*récipient*) sugar bowl.

sud [syd] *nm* south; au s. de south of; du s. (*vent, direction*) southerly; (*ville*) southern; (*gens*) from *ou* in the south; Amérique/Afrique du S. South America/Africa; l'Europe du S. Southern Europe; *— a inv* (*côte*) south(ern). **◆s.-africain, -aine** *a* & *nmf* South African. **◆s.-américain, -aine** *a* & *nmf* South American. **◆s.-est** *nm* & *a inv* south-east. **◆s.-ouest** *nm* & *a inv* south-west.

Suède [sɥɛd] *nf* Sweden. **◆suédois, -oise** *a* Swedish; *— nmf* Swede; *— nm* (*langue*) Swedish.

suer [sɥe] *vi* (*personne, mur etc*) to sweat; faire s. qn *Fam* to get on s.o.'s nerves; se faire s. *Fam* to be bored stiff; *— vt* (*sang etc*) to sweat. **◆sueur** *nf* sweat; (tout) en s. sweating.

suffire* [syfir] *vi* to be enough *ou* sufficient, suffice (à for); ça suffit! that's enough!; il

suffit de faire one only has to do; il suffit d'une goutte/*etc* pour faire a drop/*etc* is enough to do; il ne me suffit pas de faire I'm not satisfied with doing; **— se s.** *vpr* se s. (à soi-même) to be self-sufficient. **◆suffisant** *a* 1 sufficient, adequate. 2 (*vaniteux*) conceited. **◆suffisamment** *adv* sufficiently; s. de sufficient, enough. **◆suffisance** *nf* (*vanité*) conceit.

suffixe [syfiks] *nm* *Gram* suffix.

suffoquer [syfɔke] *vti* to choke, suffocate. **◆suffocant** *a* stifling, suffocating. **◆suffocation** *nf* suffocation; (*sensation*) feeling of suffocation.

suffrage [syfraʒ] *nm* *Pol* (*voix*) vote; (*droit*) suffrage.

suggérer [sygʒere] *vt* (*proposer*) to suggest (de faire doing, que (+ *sub*) that); (*évoquer*) to suggest. **◆suggestif, -ive** *a* suggestive. **◆suggestion** *nf* suggestion.

suicide [sɥisid] *nm* suicide. **◆suicidaire** *a* suicidal. **◆se suicid/er** *vpr* to commit suicide. **◆-é, -ée** *nmf* suicide (victim).

suie [sɥi] *nf* soot.

suif [sɥif] *nm* tallow.

suinter [sɥɛ̃te] *vi* to ooze, seep. **◆suintement** *nm* oozing, seeping.

suis [sɥi] *voir* être, suivre.

Suisse [sɥis] *nf* Switzerland. **◆suisse** *a* & *nmf* Swiss. **◆Suissesse** *nf* Swiss (woman *ou* girl).

suite [sɥit] *nf* (*reste*) rest; (*continuation*) continuation; (*de film, roman*) sequel; (*série*) series, sequence; (*appartement, escorte*) & *Mus* suite; (*cohérence*) order; *pl* (*résultats*) consequences; (*séquelles*) effects; attendre la s. to wait and see what happens next; donner s. à (*demande etc*) to follow up; faire s. (à) to follow; prendre la s. de qn to take over from s.o.; par la s. afterwards; par s. de as a result of; à la s. one after another; à la s. de (*derrière*) behind; (*événement, maladie etc*) as a result of; de s. in succession.

suiv/re* [sɥivr] *vt* to follow; (*accompagner*) to go with, accompany; (*classe*) *Scol* to attend, go to; (*malade*) to treat; s. (des yeux *ou* du regard) to watch; s. son chemin to go on one's way; se s. to follow each other; *— vi* to follow; faire s. (*courrier*) to forward; 'à s.' 'to be continued'; comme suit as follows. **◆-ant¹, -ante** *a* next, following; (*ci-après*) following; *— nmf* next (one); au s.! next!; the next person! **◆-ant²** *prép* (*selon*) according to. **◆-i** *a* (*régulier*) regular, steady; (*cohérent*) coherent; (*article*)

Com regularly on sale; **peu/très s.** (*cours*) poorly/well attended.

sujet¹, -ette [syʒɛ, -ɛt] *a* **s. à** (*maladie etc*) subject *ou* liable to; **-** *nmf* (*personne*) *Pol* subject.

sujet² [syʒɛ] *nm* **1** (*question*) & *Gram* subject; (*d'examen*) question; **au s. de** about; **à quel s.?** about what? **2** (*raison*) cause; **avoir s. de faire** to have (good) cause *ou* (good) reason to do. **3** *nm* (*individu*) subject; **un mauvais s.** (*garçon*) a rotten egg.

sulfurique [sylfyrik] *a* (*acide*) sulphuric, *Am* sulfuric.

sultan [syltɑ̃] *nm* sultan.

summum [sɔmɔm] *nm* (*comble*) *Fig* height.

super [sypɛr] **1** *a* (*bon*) *Fam* great. **2** *nm* (*supercarburant*) *Fam* four-star (petrol), *Am* premium *ou* hi-test gas.

superbe [sypɛrb] *a* superb.

supercarburant [sypɛrkarbyrɑ̃] *nm* high-octane petrol *ou Am* gasoline.

supercherie [sypɛrʃəri] *nf* deception.

superficie [sypɛrfisi] *nf* surface; (*dimensions*) area. **◆superficiel, -ielle** *a* superficial. **◆superficiellement** *adv* superficially.

superflu [sypɛrfly] *a* superfluous.

super-grand [sypɛrgrɑ̃] *nm* *Pol Fam* superpower.

supérieur, -eure [sypɛrjœr] *a* (*étages, partie etc*) upper; (*qualité, air, ton*) superior; (*études*) higher; **à l'étage s.** on the floor above; **s. à** (*meilleur que*) superior to, better than; (*plus grand que*) above, greater than; **-** *nmf* superior. **◆supériorité** *nf* superiority.

superlatif, -ive [sypɛrlatif, -iv] *a* & *nm* *Gram* superlative.

supermarché [sypɛrmarʃe] *nm* supermarket.

superposer [sypɛrpoze] *vt* (*objets*) to put on top of each other; (*images etc*) to superimpose.

superproduction [sypɛrprɔdyksjɔ̃] *nf* (*film*) blockbuster.

superpuissance [sypɛrpɥisɑ̃s] *nf* *Pol* superpower.

supersonique [sypɛrsɔnik] *a* supersonic.

superstitieux, -euse [sypɛrstisjø, -øz] *a* superstitious. **◆superstition** *nf* superstition.

superviser [sypɛrvize] *vt* to supervise.

supplanter [syplɑ̃te] *vt* to take the place of.

suppléer [syplee] *vt* (*remplacer*) to replace; (*compenser*) to make up for; **-** *vi* **s. à** (*compenser*) to make up for. **◆-ant, -ante**

a & *nmf* (*personne*) substitute, replacement; **(professeur) s.** supply teacher.

supplément [syplemɑ̃] *nm* (*d'argent*) charge, supplement; (*de livre, revue*) supplement; **en s.** extra; **un s. de** (*information, travail etc*) extra, additional. **◆supplémentaire** *a* extra, additional.

supplice [syplis] *nm* torture; **au s.** *Fig* on the rack. **◆supplicier** *vt* to torture.

suppli/er [syplije] *vt* **s. qn de faire** to beg *ou* implore s.o. to do; **je vous en supplie!** I beg *ou* implore you! **◆-ant, -ante** *a* (*regard etc*) imploring. **◆supplication** *nf* plea, entreaty.

support [sypɔr] *nm* **1** support; (*d'instrument etc*) stand. **2** (*moyen*) *Fig* medium; **s. audio-visuel** audio-visual aid.

support/er¹ [sypɔrte] *vt* to bear, endure; (*frais*) to bear; (*affront etc*) to suffer; (*résister à*) to withstand; (*soutenir*) to support. **◆-able** *a* bearable; (*excusable, passable*) tolerable.

supporter² [sypɔrtɛr] *nm* *Sp* supporter.

supposer [sypoze] *vt* to suppose, assume (**que** that); (*impliquer*) to imply (**que** that); **à s.** *ou* **en supposant que** (+ *sub*) supposing (that). **◆supposition** *nf* supposition, assumption.

suppositoire [sypozitwar] *nm* *Méd* suppository.

supprimer [syprime] *vt* to remove, get rid of; (*institution, loi*) to abolish; (*journal etc*) to suppress; (*mot, passage*) to cut, delete; (*train etc*) to cancel; (*tuer*) to do away with; **s. qch à qn** to take sth away from s.o. **◆suppression** *nf* removal; abolition; suppression; cutting; cancellation.

suprématie [sypremasi] *nf* supremacy. **◆suprême** *a* supreme.

sur [syr] *prép* on, upon; (*par-dessus*) over; (*au sujet de*) on, about; **s. les trois heures** at about three o'clock; **six s. dix** six out of ten; **un jour s. deux** every other day; **coup s. coup** blow after *ou* upon blow; **six mètres s. dix** six metres by ten; **mettre/monter/** *etc* **s.** to put/climb/*etc* on (to); **aller/tourner/** *etc* **s.** to go/turn/*etc* towards; **s. ce** after which, and then; (*maintenant*) and now.

sur- [syr] *préf* over-.

sûr [syr] *a* sure, certain (**de** of, **que** that); (*digne de confiance*) reliable; (*avenir*) secure; (*lieu*) safe; (*main*) steady; (*goût*) unerring; (*jugement*) sound; **s. de soi** self-assured; **bien s.!** of course!

surabondant [syrabɔ̃dɑ̃] *a* over-abundant.

suranné [syrane] *a* outmoded.

surboum [syrbum] *nf* *Fam* party.

surcharge [syrʃarʒ] nf **1** overloading; (poids) extra load; **s. de travail** extra work; **en s.** (passagers etc) extra. **2** (correction de texte etc) alteration; (de timbre-poste) surcharge. ◆**surcharger** vt (voiture, personne etc) to overload (**de** with).

surchauffer [syrʃofe] vt to overheat.

surchoix [syrʃwa] a inv Com top-quality.

surclasser [syrklase] vt to outclass.

surcroît [syrkrwa] nm increase (**de** in); **de s., par s.** in addition.

surdité [syrdite] nf deafness.

surdoué, -ée [syrdwe] nmf child who has a genius-level IQ.

surélever [syrelve] vt to raise (the height of).

sûrement [syrmã] adv certainly; (sans danger) safely.

surenchère [syrãʃɛr] nf Com higher bid; **s. électorale** Fig bidding for votes. ◆**surenchérir** vi to bid higher (**sur** than).

surestimer [syrestime] vt to overestimate; (peinture etc) to overvalue.

sûreté [syrte] nf safety; (de l'état) security; (garantie) surety; (de geste) sureness; (de jugement) soundness; **être en s.** to be safe; **mettre en s.** to put in a safe place; **de s.** (épingle, soupape etc) safety-.

surexcité [syreksite] a overexcited.

surf [sœrf] nm Sp surfing; **faire du s.** to surf, go surfing.

surface [syrfas] nf surface; (dimensions) (surface) area; **faire s.** (sous-marin etc) to surface; **(magasin à) grande s.** hypermarket.

surfait [syrfɛ] a overrated.

surgelé [syrʒəle] a (deep-)frozen; **-.** nmpl (deep-)frozen foods.

surgir [syrʒir] vi to appear suddenly (**de** from); (conflit, problème) to arise.

surhomme [syrɔm] nm superman. ◆**surhumain** a superhuman.

sur-le-champ [syrləʃã] adv immediately.

surlendemain [syrlãdəmɛ̃] nm **le s.** two days later; **le s. de** two days after.

surmen/er [syrməne] vt, **— se s.** vpr to overwork. ◆**-age** nm overwork.

surmonter [syrmɔ̃te] vt **1** (obstacle, peur etc) to overcome, get over. **2** (être placé sur) to be on top of, top.

surnager [syrnaʒe] vi to float.

surnaturel, -elle [syrnatyrɛl] a & nm supernatural.

surnom [syrnɔ̃] nm nickname. ◆**surnommer** vt to nickname.

surnombre [syrnɔ̃br] nm **en s.** too many; **je suis en s.** I am one too many.

surpasser [syrpase] vt to surpass (**en** in); **— se s.** vpr to surpass oneself.

surpeuplé [syrpœple] a overpopulated.

surplomb [syrplɔ̃] nm **en s.** overhanging. ◆**surplomber** vti to overhang.

surplus [syrply] nm surplus; pl Com surplus (stock).

surprendre° [syrprãdr] vt (étonner, prendre sur le fait) to surprise; (secret) to discover; (conversation) to overhear; **se s.** à faire to find oneself doing. ◆**surprenant** a surprising. ◆**surpris** a surprised (**de** at, **que** (+ sub) that). ◆**surprise** nf surprise. ◆**surprise-partie** nf (pl surprises-parties) party.

surréaliste [syrealist] a (bizarre) Fam surrealistic.

sursaut [syrso] nm (sudden) start ou jump; **en s.** with a start; **s. de** (énergie etc) burst of. ◆**sursauter** vi to start, jump.

sursis [syrsi] nm Mil deferment; (répit) Fig reprieve; **un an (de prison) avec s.** a one-year suspended sentence.

surtaxe [syrtaks] nf surcharge.

surtout [syrtu] adv especially; (avant tout) above all; **s. pas** certainly not; **s. que** especially as ou since.

surveill/er [syrveje] vt (garder) to watch, keep an eye on; (épier) to watch; (contrôler) to supervise; **s. son langage/sa santé** Fig to watch one's language/health; **— se s.** vpr to watch oneself. ◆**-ant, -ante** nmf (de lycée) supervisor (in charge of discipline); (de prison) warder; (de chantier) supervisor; **s. de plage** lifeguard. ◆**surveillance** nf watch (**sur** over); (de travaux, d'ouvriers) supervision; (de la police) surveillance, observation.

survenir° [syrvənir] vi to occur; (personne) to turn up.

survêtement [syrvɛtmã] nm Sp tracksuit.

survie [syrvi] nf survival. ◆**surviv/re°** vi to survive (**à qch** sth); **s. à qn** to outlive s.o., survive s.o. ◆**-ant, -ante** nmf survivor. ◆**survivance** nf (chose) survival, relic.

survol [syrvɔl] nm **le s. de** flying over; (question) Fig the overview of. ◆**survoler** vt (en avion) to fly over; (question) Fig to go over (quickly).

survolté [syrvɔlte] a (surexcité) worked up.

susceptible [syseptibl] a **1** (ombrageux) touchy, sensitive. **2 s. de** (interprétations etc) open to; **s. de faire** likely ou liable to do; (capable) able to do. ◆**susceptibilité** nf touchiness, sensitiveness.

susciter [sysite] vt (sentiment) to arouse; (ennuis, obstacles etc) to create.

suspect, -ecte [syspε(kt), -εkt] *a* suspicious, suspect; **s. de** suspected of; – *nmf* suspect. ◆**suspecter** *vt* to suspect (**de qch** of sth, **de faire** of doing); (*bonne foi etc*) to question, suspect, doubt.

suspen/dre [syspɑ̃dr] *vt* **1** (*destituer, différer, interrompre*) to suspend. **2** (*fixer*) to hang (up) (**à** on); **se s. à** to hang from. ◆**-u** *a* **s. à** hanging from; **pont s.** suspension bridge. ◆**suspension** *nf* **1** (*d'hostilités, d'employé etc*) & *Aut* suspension; **points de s.** *Gram* dots, suspension points. **2** (*lustre*) hanging lamp.

suspens (en) [ɑ̃syspɑ̃] *adv* **1** (*affaire, travail*) in abeyance. **2** (*dans l'incertitude*) in suspense.

suspense [syspεns] *nm* suspense; **film à s.** thriller, suspense film.

suspicion [syspisjɔ̃] *nf* suspicion.

susurrer [sysyre] *vti* to murmur.

suture [sytyr] *nf* *Méd* stitching; **point de s.** stitch. ◆**suturer** *vt* to stitch up.

svelte [svεlt] *a* slender. ◆**sveltesse** *nf* slenderness.

SVP *abrév* (*s'il vous plaît*) please.

syllabe [silab] *nf* syllable.

symbole [sɛ̃bɔl] *nm* symbol. ◆**symbolique** *a* symbolic; (*salaire*) nominal. ◆**symboliser** *vt* to symbolize. ◆**symbolisme** *nm* symbolism.

symétrie [simetri] *nf* symmetry. ◆**symétrique** *a* symmetrical.

sympa [sɛ̃pa] *a inv* *Fam* = **sympathique**.

sympathie [sɛ̃pati] *nf* liking, affection; (*affinité*) affinity; (*condoléances*) sympathy; **avoir de la s. pour qn** to be fond of s.o. ◆**sympathique** *a* nice, pleasant; (*accueil, geste*) friendly. ◆**sympathis/er** *vi* to get on well (**avec** with). ◆**-ant, -ante** *nmf* *Pol* sympathizer.

symphonie [sɛ̃fɔni] *nf* symphony. ◆**symphonique** *a* symphonic; (*orchestre*) symphony-.

symposium [sɛ̃pozjɔm] *nm* symposium.

symptôme [sɛ̃ptom] *nm* symptom. ◆**symptomatique** *a* symptomatic (**de** of).

synagogue [sinagɔg] *nf* synagogue.

synchroniser [sɛ̃krɔnize] *vt* to synchronize.

syncope [sɛ̃kɔp] *nf* *Méd* blackout; **tomber en s.** to black out.

syndicat [sɛ̃dika] *nm* **1** (*d'employés, d'ouvriers*) (trade) union; (*de patrons etc*) association. **2 s. d'initiative** tourist (information) office. ◆**syndical, -aux** *a* (*réunion etc*) (trade) union-. ◆**syndicalisme** *nm* trade unionism. ◆**syndicaliste** *nmf* trade unionist; – *a* (trade) union-. ◆**syndiqu/er** *vt* to unionize; – **se s.** *vpr* (*adhérer*) to join a (trade) union. ◆**-é, -ée** *nmf* (trade) union member.

syndrome [sɛ̃drom] *nm* *Méd* & *Fig* syndrome.

synode [sinɔd] *nm* *Rel* synod.

synonyme [sinɔnim] *a* synonymous (**de** with); – *nm* synonym.

syntaxe [sɛ̃taks] *nf* *Gram* syntax.

synthèse [sɛ̃tεz] *nf* synthesis. ◆**synthétique** *a* synthetic.

syphilis [sifilis] *nf* syphilis.

Syrie [siri] *nf* Syria. ◆**syrien, -ienne** *a* & *nmf* Syrian.

système [sistεm] *nm* (*structure, réseau etc*) & *Anat* system; **le s. D** *Fam* resourcefulness. ◆**systématique** *a* systematic; (*soutien*) unconditional. ◆**systématiquement** *adv* systematically.

T

T, t [te] *nm* T, t.

t' [t] *voir* **te**.

ta [ta] *voir* **ton** [1].

tabac [taba] **1** *nm* tobacco; (*magasin*) tobacconist's (shop), *Am* tobacco store; **t. (à priser)** snuff. **2** *nm* **passer à t.** to beat up; **passage à t.** beating up. **3** *a inv* (*couleur*) buff. ◆**tabatière** *nf* (*boîte*) snuffbox.

tabasser [tabase] *vt* *Fam* to beat up.

table [tabl] *nf* **1** (*meuble*) table; (*nourriture*) fare; **t. de jeu/de nuit/d'opération** card/bedside/operating table; **t. basse** coffee table; **t. à repasser** ironing board; **t. roulante** (tea) trolley, *Am* (serving) cart; **mettre/débarrasser la t.** to lay out/clear the table; **être à t.** to be sitting at the table; **à t.!** (food's) ready! **faire t. rase** *Fig* to make a clean sweep (**de** of); **mettre sur t. d'écoute** (*téléphone*) to tap. **2** (*liste*) table; **t. des matières** table of contents.

tableau, -x [tablo] *nm* **1** (*peinture*) picture, painting; (*image, description*) picture; *Th* scene; **t. de maître** (*peinture*) old master. **2** (*panneau*) board; *Rail* train-indicator;

(*liste*) list; (*graphique*) chart; **t. (noir)** (black)board; **t. d'affichage** notice board, *Am* bulletin board; **t. de bord** *Aut* dashboard; **t. de contrôle** *Tech* control panel.

tabler [table] *vi* **t. sur** to count *ou* rely on.

tablette [tablet] *nf* (*d'armoire, de lavabo*) shelf; (*de cheminée*) mantelpiece; (*de chocolat*) bar, slab.

tablier [tablije] *nm* **1** (*vêtement*) apron; (*d'écolier*) smock; **rendre son t.** (*démissionner*) to give notice. **2** (*de pont*) roadway.

tabou [tabu] *a* & *nm* taboo.

tabouret [tabure] *nm* stool.

tabulateur [tabylatœr] *nm* (*de machine à écrire etc*) tabulator.

tac [tak] *nm* **répondre du t. au t.** to give tit for tat.

tache [taʃ] *nf* spot, mark; (*salissure*) stain; **faire t.** (*détonner*) *Péj* to jar, stand out; **faire t. d'huile** *Fig* to spread. ◆**tacher** *vt*, **– se t.** *vpr* (*tissu etc*) to stain; **– vi** (*vin etc*) to stain. ◆**tacheté** *a* speckled, spotted.

tâche [taʃ] *nf* task, job; **travailler à la t.** to do piecework.

tâcher [taʃe] *vi* **t. de faire** to try *ou* endeavour to do.

tâcheron [taʃrɔ̃] *nm* drudge.

tacite [tasit] *a* tacit. ◆**–ment** *adv* tacitly.

taciturne [tasityrn] *a* taciturn.

tacot [tako] *nm* (*voiture*) *Fam* (old) wreck, banger.

tact [takt] *nm* tact.

tactile [taktil] *a* tactile.

tactique [taktik] *a* tactical; **– nf la t.** tactics; **une t.** a tactic.

Tahiti [taiti] *nm* Tahiti. ◆**tahitien, -ienne** [taisjɛ̃, -jen] *a* *nmf* Tahitian.

taie [tɛ] *nf* **t. d'oreiller** pillowcase, pillowslip.

taillade [tɑjad] *nf* gash, slash. ◆**taillader** *vt* to gash, slash.

taille¹ [tɑj] *nf* **1** (*stature*) height; (*dimension, mesure commerciale*) size; **de haute t.** (*personne*) tall; **de petite t.** short; **de t. moyenne** (*objet, personne*) medium-sized; **être de t. à faire** *Fig* to be capable of doing; **de t.** (*erreur, objet*) *Fam* enormous. **2** *Anat* waist; **tour de t.** waist measurement.

taille² [tɑj] *nf* cutting; cutting out; trimming; pruning; (*forme*) cut. ◆**tailler 1** *vt* to cut; (*vêtement*) to cut out; (*haie, barbe*) to trim; (*arbre*) to prune; (*crayon*) to sharpen. **2 se t.** *vpr* (*partir*) *Arg* to clear off. ◆**–é a t. en athlète/etc** built like an athlete/etc; **faire t. faire** *Fig* cut out for doing.

taille-crayon(s) [tɑjkrɛjɔ̃] *nm inv* pencilsharpener. ◆**t.-haies** *nm inv* (garden) shears; (*électrique*) hedge trimmer.

tailleur [tɑjœr] *nm* **1** (*personne*) tailor. **2** (*costume féminin*) suit.

taillis [tɑji] *nm* copse, coppice.

tain [tɛ̃] *nm* (*de glace*) silvering; **glace sans t.** two-way mirror.

taire* [tɛr] *vt* to say nothing about; **– vi faire t. qn** to silence s.o. **– se t.** *vpr* (*rester silencieux*) to keep quiet (**sur qch** about sth); (*cesser de parler*) to fall silent, shut up; **tais-toi!** be *ou* keep quiet!, shut up!

talc [talk] *nm* talcum powder.

talent [talɑ̃] *nm* talent; **avoir du t. pour** to have a talent for. ◆**talentueux, -euse** *a* talented.

taler [tale] *vt* (*fruit*) to bruise.

talion [taljɔ̃] *nm* **la loi du t.** (*vengeance*) an eye for an eye.

talisman [talismɑ̃] *nm* talisman.

talkie-walkie [talkiwalki] *nm* (*poste*) walkie-talkie.

taloche [talɔʃ] *nf* (*gifle*) *Fam* clout, smack.

talon [talɔ̃] *nm* **1** heel; (*chaussures à*) **talons hauts** high heels, high-heeled shoes. **2** (*de chèque, carnet*) stub, counterfoil; (*bout de pain*) crust; (*de jambon*) heel. ◆**talonner** *vt* (*fugitif etc*) to follow on the heels of; (*ballon*) *Rugby* to heel; (*harceler*) *Fig* to hound, dog.

talus [taly] *nm* slope, embankment.

tambour [tɑ̃bur] *nm* **1** (*de machine etc*) & *Mus* drum; (*personne*) drummer. **2** (*porte*) revolving door. ◆**tambourin** *nm* tambourine. ◆**tambouriner** *vi* (*avec les doigts etc*) to drum (**sur** on).

tamis [tami] *nm* sieve. ◆**tamiser** *vt* to sift; (*lumière*) to filter, subdue.

Tamise [tamiz] *nf* **la T.** the Thames.

tampon [tɑ̃pɔ̃] *nm* **1** (*bouchon*) plug, stopper; (*d'ouate*) wad, pad; *Méd* swab; **t. hygiénique** *ou* **périodique** tampon; **t. à récurer** scouring pad. **2** (*de train etc*) & *Fig* buffer; **état t.** buffer state. **3** (*marque, instrument*) stamp; **t. buvard** blotter; **t. encreur** ink(ing) pad. ◆**tamponn/er 1** *vt* (*visage etc*) to dab; (*plaie*) to swab. **2** (*train, voiture*) to crash into; **– se t.** *vpr* to crash into each other. **3** *vt* (*lettre, document*) to stamp. ◆**–euses** *afpl* **autos t.** dodgems, bumper cars.

tam-tam [tamtam] *nm* (*tambour*) tom-tom.

tandem [tɑ̃dem] *nm* **1** (*bicyclette*) tandem. **2** (*duo*) *Fig* duo, pair; **en t.** (*travailler etc*) in tandem.

tandis que [tɑ̃dik(ə)] *conj* (*pendant que*) while; (*contraste*) whereas, while.

tangent [tɑ̃ʒɑ̃] *a* **1** *Géom* tangential (**à** to).

2 (*juste*) *Fam* touch and go, close. ◆**tangente** *nf Géom* tangent.

tangible [tãʒibl] *a* tangible.

tango [tãgo] *nm* tango.

tang/uer [tãge] *vi* (*bateau, avion*) to pitch. ◆**—age** *nm* pitching.

tanière [tanjɛr] *n'* den, lair.

tank [tãk] *nm Mil* tank.

tanker [tãkœr] *nm* (*navire*) tanker.

tann/er [tane] *vt* (*cuir*) to tan. ◆**—é** *a* (*visage*) weather-beaten, tanned.

tant [tã] *adv* so much (*que* that); t. de (*pain, temps etc*) so much (*que* that); (*gens, choses etc*) so many (*que* that); t. de fois so often, so many times; **t. que** (*autant que*) as much as; (*aussi fort que*) as hard as; (*aussi longtemps que*) as long as; **t. mieux!** good!, I'm glad!; **t. pis!** too bad!, pity!; **t. soit peu** (*even*) remotely *ou* slightly; **un t. soit peu** somewhat; **t. s'en faut** far from it; **t. bien que mal** more or less, so-so.

tante [tãt] *nf* aunt.

tantinet [tãtinɛ] *nm & adv* **un t.** a tiny bit (*de* of).

tantôt [tãto] *adv* **1 t. ... t.** sometimes ... sometimes, now ... now. **2** (*cet après-midi*) this afternoon.

taon [tã] *nm* horsefly, gadfly.

tapage [tapaʒ] *nm* din, uproar. ◆**tapageur, -euse** *a* **1** (*bruyant*) rowdy. **2** (*criard*) flashy.

tape [tap] *nf* slap. ◆**tap/er** *vt* (*enfant, cuisse*) to slap; (*table*) to bang; **t. qn** (*emprunter de l'argent à qn*) *Fam* to touch s.o., tap s.o. (*de* for); *– vi* (*soleil*) to beat down; **t. sur qch** to bang on sth; **t. à la porte** to bang on the door; **t. sur qn** (*critiquer*) *Fam* to run s.o. down, knock s.o.; **t. sur les nerfs de qn** *Fam* to get on s.o.'s nerves; **t. dans** (*provisions etc*) to dig into; **t. du pied** to stamp one's foot; **t. dans l'œil à qn** *Fam* to take s.o.'s fancy; **– se t.** *vpr* (*travail*) *Fam* to do, take on; (*repas, vin*) *Fam* to put away. **2** *vti* (*écrire à la machine*) to type. ◆**—ant** *a* **à midi t.** at twelve sharp; **à huit heures tapant(es)** at eight sharp. ◆**—eur, -euse** *nmf Fam* person who borrows money.

tape-à-l'œil [tapalœj] *a inv* flashy, gaudy.

tapée [tape] *nf* **une t. de** *Fam* a load of.

tapioca [tapjɔka] *nm* tapioca.

tapir (se) [sətapir] *vpr* to crouch (down). ◆**tapi** *a* crouching, crouched.

tapis [tapi] *nm* carpet; **t. de bain** bathmat; **t. roulant** (*pour marchandises*) conveyor belt; (*pour personnes*) moving pavement *ou Am*

sidewalk; **t. de sol** groundsheet; **t. de table** table cover; **envoyer qn au t.** (*abattre*) to floor s.o.; **mettre sur le t.** (*sujet*) to bring up for discussion. ◆**t.-brosse** *nm* doormat.

tapisser [tapise] *vt* (*mur*) to (wall)paper; to hang with tapestry; (*recouvrir*) *Fig* to cover. ◆**tapisserie** *nf* (*tenture*) tapestry; (*papier peint*) wallpaper. ◆**tapissier, -ière** *nmf* (*qui pose des tissus etc*) upholsterer; **t.(-décorateur)** interior decorator.

tapoter [tapɔte] *vt* to tap; (*joue*) to pat; *– vi* **t. sur** to tap (on).

taquin, -ine [takɛ̃, -in] *a* (fond of) teasing; *– nmf* tease(r). ◆**taquiner** *vt* to tease; (*inquiéter, agacer*) to bother. ◆**taquinerie(s)** *nf(pl)* teasing.

tarabiscoté [tarabiskɔte] *a* over-elaborate.

tarabuster [tarabyste] *vt* (*idée etc*) to trouble (*s.o.*).

tard [tar] *adv* late; **plus t.** later (on); **au plus t.** at the latest; **sur le t.** late in life. ◆**tarder** *vi* (*lettre, saison*) to be a long time coming; **t. à faire** to take one's time doing; (*différer*) to delay (in) doing; **ne tardez pas** (*agissez tout de suite*) don't delay; **elle ne va pas t.** she won't be long; **sans t.** without delay; **il me tarde de faire** I long to do. ◆**tardif, -ive** *a* late; (*regrets*) belated. ◆**tardivement** *adv* late.

tare [tar] *nf* **1** (*poids*) tare. **2** (*défaut*) *Fig* defect. ◆**taré** *a* (*corrompu*) corrupt; *Méd* defective; (*fou*) *Fam* mad, idiotic.

targuer (se) [sətarge] *vpr* **se t. de qch/de faire** to boast about sth/about doing.

tarif [tarif] *nm* (*prix*) rate; *Aut Rail* fare; (*tableau*) price list, tariff. ◆**tarification** *nf* (*price*) fixing.

tarir [tarir] *vti*, **– se t.** *vpr* (*fleuve etc*) & *Fig* to dry up; **ne pas t. d'éloges sur qn** to rave about s.o.

tartare [tartar] *a* **sauce t.** tartar sauce.

tarte [tart] *nf* **1** *nf* tart, flan, *Am* (open) pie. **2** *a inv Fam* (*sot*) silly; (*laid*) ugly. ◆**tartelette** *nf* (small) tart.

tartine [tartin] *nf* slice of bread; **t. de beurre/de confiture** slice of bread and butter/jam. ◆**tartiner** *vt* (*beurre*) to spread; **fromage à t.** cheese spread.

tartre [tartr] *nm* (*de bouilloire*) scale, fur; (*de dents*) tartar.

tas [tɑ] *nm* pile, heap; **un** *ou* **des t. de** (*beaucoup*) *Fam* lots of; **mettre en t.** to pile *ou* heap up; **former qn sur le t.** (*au travail*) to train s.o. on the job.

tasse [tɑs] *nf* cup; **t. à café** coffee cup; **t. à thé** teacup; **boire la t.** *Fam* to swallow a mouthful (*when swimming*).

tasser [tɑse] vt to pack, squeeze (**dans** into); (terre) to pack down; **un café**/etc **bien tassé** (fort) a good strong coffee/etc; **— se t.** vpr (se voûter) to become bowed; (se serrer) to squeeze up; (sol) to sink, collapse; **ça va se t.** (s'arranger) Fam things will pan out (all right).

tâter [tɑte] vt to feel; (sonder) Fig to sound out; **— vi t. de** (métier, prison) to have a taste of, experience; **— se t.** vpr (hésiter) to be in ou of two minds. ◆**tâtonn/er** vi to grope about, feel one's way. ◆**—ement** nm **par t.** (procéder) by trial and error. ◆**tâtons (à)** adv **avancer à t.** to feel one's way (along); **chercher à t.** to grope for.

tatillon, -onne [tatijɔ̃, -ɔn] a finicky.

tatou/er [tatwe] vt (corps, dessin) to tattoo. ◆**—age** nm (dessin) tattoo; (action) tattooing.

taudis [todi] nm slum, hovel.

taule [tol] nf (prison) Fam nick, jug, Am can.

taupe [top] nf (animal, espion) mole. ◆**taupinière** nf molehill.

taureau, -x [tɔro] nm bull; **le T.** (signe) Taurus. ◆**tauromachie** nf bull-fighting.

taux [to] nm rate; **t. d'alcool/de cholestérol**/etc alcohol/cholesterol/etc level.

taverne [tavɛrn] nf tavern.

taxe [taks] nf (prix) official price; (impôt) tax; (douanière) duty; **t. de séjour** tourist tax; **t. à la valeur ajoutée** value-added tax. ◆**taxation** nf fixing of the price (**de** of); taxation (**de** of). ◆**taxer** vt **1** (produit) to fix the price of; (objet de luxe etc) to tax. **2 t. qn de** to accuse s.o. of.

taxi [taksi] nm taxi.

taxiphone [taksifɔn] nm pay phone.

Tchécoslovaquie [tʃekɔslɔvaki] nf Czechoslovakia. ◆**tchèque** a & nmf Czech; **— nm** (langue) Czech.

te [t(ə)] (**t'** before vowel or mute h) pron **1** (complément direct) you; **je te vois** I see you. **2** (indirect) (to) you; **il te parle** he speaks to you; **elle te l'a dit** she told you. **3** (réfléchi) yourself; **tu te laves** you wash yourself.

technicien, -ienne [tɛknisjɛ̃, -jɛn] nmf technician. ◆**technique** a technical; **— nf** technique. ◆**techniquement** adv technically. ◆**technocrate** nm technocrat. ◆**technologie** nf technology. ◆**technologique** a technological.

teck [tɛk] nm (bois) teak.

teckel [tekɛl] nm (chien) dachshund.

tee-shirt* [tiʃœrt] nm tee-shirt.

teindre* [tɛ̃dr] vt to dye; **— se t.** vpr to dye

one's hair. ◆**teinture** nf dyeing; (produit) dye. ◆**teinturerie** nf (boutique) (dry) cleaner's. ◆**teinturier, -ière** nmf dry cleaner.

teint [tɛ̃] nm **1** (de visage) complexion. **2 bon ou grand t.** (tissu) colourfast; **bon t.** (catholique etc) Fig staunch.

teinte [tɛ̃t] nf shade, tint; **une t. de** (dose) Fig a tinge of. ◆**teinter** vt to tint; (bois) to stain; **se t. de** (remarque, ciel) Fig to be tinged with.

tel, telle [tɛl] a such; **un t. homme/livre**/etc such a man/book/etc; **un t. intérêt**/etc such interest/etc; **de tels mots**/etc such words/etc; **t. que** such as, like; **t. que je l'ai laissé** just as I left it; **laissez-le t. quel** leave it just as it is; **en tant que t., comme t.** as such; **t. ou t.** such and such; **rien de t. que** . . . (there's) nothing like . . . ; **rien de t.** nothing like it; **Monsieur Un t.** Mr So-and-so; **t. père t. fils** like father like son.

télé [tele] nf (téléviseur) Fam TV, telly; **à la t.** on TV, on the telly; **regarder la t.** to watch TV ou the telly.

télé- [tele] préf tele-.

télébenne [teleben] nf, **télécabine** [telekabin] nf (cabine, système) cable car.

télécommande [telekɔmɑ̃d] nf remote control. ◆**télécommander** vt to operate by remote control.

télécommunications [telekɔmynikasjɔ̃] nfpl telecommunications.

téléfilm [telefilm] nm TV film.

télégramme [telegram] nm telegram.

télégraphe [telegraf] nm telegraph. ◆**télégraphie** nf telegraphy. ◆**télégraphier** vt (message) to wire, cable (**que** that). ◆**télégraphique** a (fil, poteau) telegraph-; (style) Fig telegraphic. ◆**télégraphiste** nm (messager) telegraph boy.

téléguid/er [telegide] vt to radio-control. ◆**—age** nm radio-control.

télématique [telematik] nf telematics, computer communications.

télépathie [telepati] nf telepathy.

téléphérique [teleferik] nm (système) cable car, cableway.

téléphone [telefɔn] nm (tele)phone; **coup de t.** (phone) call; **passer un coup de t. à qn** to give s.o. a call ou a ring; **au t.** on the (tele)phone; **avoir le t.** to be on the (tele)phone; **par le t. arabe** Fig on the grapevine. ◆**téléphoner** vt (nouvelle etc) to (tele)phone (**à** to); **— vi** to (tele)phone; **t. à qn** to (tele)phone s.o., call s.o. (up). ◆**téléphonique** a (appel etc) (tele)phone-. ◆**téléphoniste** nmf operator, telephonist.

télescope [telɛskɔp] nm telescope. ◆**télescopique** a telescopic.

télescop/er [teleskɔpe] vt Aut Rail to smash into; **se t.** to smash into each other. ◆**—age** nm smash.

téléscripteur [teleskriptœr] nm (appareil) teleprinter.

télésiège [telesjɛʒ] nm chair lift.

téléski [teleski] nm ski tow.

téléspectateur, -trice [telespɛktatœr, -tris] nmf (television) viewer.

téléviser [televize] vt to televise; **journal télévisé** television news. ◆**téléviseur** nm television (set). ◆**télévision** nf television; **à la t.** on (the) television; **regarder la t.** to watch (the) television; **de t.** (programme etc) television-.

télex [telɛks] nm (service, message) telex.

telle [tɛl] voir tel.

tellement [tɛlmɑ̃] adv (si) so; (tant) so much; **t. grand/etc que** so big/etc that; **crier/etc t. que** to shout/etc so much that; **t. de** (travail etc) so much; (soucis etc) so many; **personne ne peut le supporter, t. il est bavard** nobody can stand him, he's so talkative; **tu aimes ça? - pas t.** do you like it? - not much ou a lot.

téméraire [temerɛr] a rash, reckless. ◆**témérité** nf rashness, recklessness.

témoign/er [temwaɲe] **1** vi Jur to testify (contre against); **t. de qch** (personne, attitude etc) to testify to sth; — vt **t. que** Jur to testify that. **2** vt (gratitude etc) to show (à qn (to) s.o.). ◆**—age** nm **1** testimony, evidence; (récit) account; **faux t.** (délit) Jur perjury. **2** (d'affection etc) Fig token, sign (de of); **en t. de** as a token ou sign of.

témoin [temwɛ̃] **1** nm witness; **t. oculaire** eyewitness; **être t. de** (accident etc) to witness; — a **appartement t.** show flat ou Am apartment. **2** nm Sp baton.

tempe [tɑ̃p] nf Anat temple.

tempérament [tɑ̃peramɑ̃] nm **1** (caractère) temperament; (physique) constitution. **2 acheter à t.** to buy on hire purchase ou Am on the installment plan.

tempérance [tɑ̃perɑ̃s] nf temperance.

température [tɑ̃peratyr] nf temperature; **avoir** ou **faire de la t.** Méd to have a temperature.

tempér/er [tɑ̃pere] vt Litt to temper. ◆**—é** a (climat, zone) temperate.

tempête [tɑ̃pɛt] nf storm; **t. de neige** snowstorm, blizzard.

tempêter [tɑ̃pɛte] vi (crier) to storm, rage (contre against).

temple [tɑ̃pl] nm Rel temple; (protestant) church.

tempo [tɛmpo] nm tempo.

temporaire [tɑ̃pɔrɛr] a temporary. ◆**—ment** adv temporarily.

temporel, -elle [tɑ̃pɔrɛl] a temporal.

temporiser [tɑ̃pɔrize] vi to procrastinate, play for time.

temps¹ [tɑ̃] nm (durée, période, moment) time; Gram tense; (étape) stage; **t. d'arrêt** pause, break; **en t. de guerre** in time of war, in wartime; **avoir/trouver le t.** to have/find (the) time (de faire to do); **il est t.** it is time (de faire to do); **il était t.!** it was about time (too)!; **pendant un t.** for a while ou time; **ces derniers t.** lately; **de t. en t.** [dətɑ̃zɑ̃tɑ̃], **de t. à autre** [dətɑ̃zaotr] from time to time, now and again; **en t. utile** [ɑ̃tɑ̃zytil] in good ou due time; **en même t.** at the same time (que as); **à t.** (arriver) in time; **à plein t.** (travailler etc) full-time; **à t. partiel** (travailler etc) part-time; **dans le t.** (autrefois) once, at one time; **avec le t.** (à la longue) in time; **tout le t.** all the time; **de mon t.** in my time; **à quatre t.** (moteur) four-stroke.

temps² [tɑ̃] nm (atmosphérique) weather; **il fait beau/mauvais t.** the weather's fine/bad; **quel t. fait-il?** what's the weather like?

tenable [tənabl] a bearable.

tenace [tənas] a stubborn, tenacious. ◆**ténacité** nf stubbornness, tenacity.

tenailler [tənaje] vt (faim, remords) to rack, torture (s.o.).

tenailles [tənaj] nfpl (outil) pincers.

tenancier, -ière [tənɑ̃sje, -jɛr] nmf (d'hôtel etc) manager, manageress.

tenant, -ante [tənɑ̃, -ɑ̃t] nmf (de titre) Sp holder; **1** (partisan) supporter (de of).

tenants [tənɑ̃] nmpl **les t. et les aboutissants** (d'une question etc) the ins and outs (de of).

tendance [tɑ̃dɑ̃s] nf (penchant) tendency; (évolution) trend (à towards); **avoir t. à faire** to have a tendency to do, tend to do.

tendancieux, -euse [tɑ̃dɑ̃sjø, -øz] a Péj tendentious.

tendeur [tɑ̃dœr] nm (pour arrimer des bagages) elastic strap.

tendon [tɑ̃dɔ̃] nm Anat tendon, sinew.

tend/re¹ [tɑ̃dr] **1** vt to stretch; (main) to hold out (à qn to s.o.); (bras, jambe) to stretch out; (cou) to strain, crane; (muscle) to tense, flex; (arc) to bend; (piège) to lay, set; (filet) to spread; (tapisserie) to hang; **t. qch à qn** to hold out sth to s.o.; **t. l'oreille** Fig to prick up one's ears; — **se t.** vpr (rap-

ports) to become strained. **2** *vi* **t. à** qch/à **faire** to tend towards sth/to do. ◆**–u** *a* (*corde*) tight, taut; (*personne, situation*) tense; (*rapports*) strained; (*main*) outstretched.

tendre² [tãdr] *a* **1** (*viande*) tender; (*peau*) delicate, tender; (*bois, couleur*) soft. **2** (*affectueux*) loving, tender. ◆**–ment** [-amã] *adv* lovingly, tenderly. ◆**tendresse** *nf* (*affection*) affection, tenderness. ◆**tendreté** *nf* (*de viande*) tenderness.

ténèbres [tenɛbr] *nfpl* darkness, gloom. ◆**ténébreux, -euse** *a* dark, gloomy; (*mystérieux*) mysterious.

teneur [tənœr] *nf* (*de lettre etc*) content; **t. en alcool/**etc alcohol/etc content (**de** of).

tenir* [tənir] *vt* (*à la main etc*) to hold; (*pari, promesse*) to keep; (*hôtel*) to run, keep; (*comptes*) Com to keep; (*propos*) to utter; (*rôle*) to play; **t. propre/chaud/**etc to keep clean/hot/etc; **je le tiens!** (*je l'ai attrapé*) I've got him!; **je le tiens de** (*fait etc*) I got it from; (*caractère héréditaire*) I get it from; **t. pour** to regard as; **t. sa droite** *Aut* to keep to the right; **t. la route** (*voiture*) to hold the road; – *vi* (*nœud etc*) to hold; (*coiffure, neige*) to last, hold; (*offre*) to stand; (*résister*) to hold out; **t. à** (*personne, jouet etc*) to be attached to, be fond of; (*la vie*) to value; (*provenir*) to stem from; **t. à faire** to be anxious to do; **t. dans** qch (*être contenu*) to fit into sth; **t. de qn** to take after s.o.; **tenez!** (*prenez*) here (you are)!; **tiens!** (*surprise*) hey!, well!; – *v imp* **il ne tient qu'à vous** it's up to you (**de faire** to do); – **se t.** *vpr* (*rester*) to keep, remain; (*avoir lieu*) to be held; **se t.** (**debout**) to stand (up); **se t. droit** to stand up *ou* sit up straight; **se t. par la main** to hold hands; **se t. à** to hold on to; **se t. bien** to behave oneself; **tout se tient** Fig it all hangs together; **s'en t. à** (*se limiter à*) to stick to; **savoir à quoi s'en t.** to know what's what.

tennis [tenis] *nm* tennis; (*terrain*) (tennis) court; **t. de table** table tennis; – *nfpl* (*chaussures*) plimsolls, pumps, *Am* sneakers.

ténor [tenɔr] *nm* Mus tenor.

tension [tãsjõ] *nf* tension; **t. (artérielle)** blood pressure; **t. d'esprit** concentration; **avoir de la t.** Méd to have high blood pressure.

tentacule [tãtakyl] *nm* tentacle.

tente [tãt] *nf* tent.

tenter¹ [tãte] *vt* (*essayer*) to try; **t. de faire** to try *ou* attempt to do. ◆**tentative** *nf* attempt; **t. de suicide** suicide attempt.

tenter² [tãte] *vt* (*allécher*) to tempt; **tenté de faire** tempted to do. ◆**–ant** *a* tempting. ◆**tentation** *nf* temptation.

tenture [tãtyr] *nf* (wall) hanging; (*de porte*) drape, curtain.

tenu [təny] *voir* **tenir**; – *a* **t. de faire** obliged to do; **bien/mal t.** (*maison etc*) well/badly kept.

ténu [teny] *a* (*fil etc*) fine; (*soupçon, différence*) tenuous; (*voix*) thin.

tenue [təny] *nf* **1** (*vêtements*) clothes, outfit; (*aspect*) appearance; **t. de combat** Mil combat dress; **t. de soirée** (*smoking*) evening dress. **2** (*conduite*) (good) behaviour; (*maintien*) posture; **manquer de t.** to lack (good) manners. **3** (*de maison, hôtel*) running; (*de comptes*) Com keeping. **4 t. de route** *Aut* road-holding.

ter [tɛr] *a* **4 t.** (*numéro*) 4B.

térébenthine [terebãtin] *nf* turpentine.

tergal® [tɛrgal] *nm* Terylene®, *Am* Dacron®.

tergiverser [tɛrʒiverse] *vi* to procrastinate.

terme [tɛrm] *nm* **1** (*mot*) term. **2** (*loyer*) rent; (*jour*) rent day; (*période*) rental period. **3** (*date limite*) time (limit), date; (*fin*) end; **mettre un t. à** to put an end to; **à court/long t.** (*projet etc*) short-/long-term; **être né avant/à t.** to be born prematurely/at (full) term. **4 moyen t.** (*solution*) middle course. **5 en bons/mauvais termes** on good/bad terms (**avec** qn with s.o.).

terminer [tɛrmine] *vt* (*achever*) to finish, complete; (*lettre, phrase, débat, soirée*) to end; – **se t.** *vpr* to end (**par** with, **en** in). ◆**terminaison** *nf* Gram ending. ◆**terminal, -aux** *a* **1** (*phase*) Méd terminal; – *a & nf* (*classe*) **terminale** Scol = sixth form, *Am* = twelfth grade. **2** *nm* (*d'ordinateur, pétrolier*) terminal.

terminologie [tɛrminɔlɔʒi] *nf* terminology.

terminus [tɛrminys] *nm* terminus.

termite [tɛrmit] *nm* (*insecte*) termite.

terne [tɛrn] *a* (*couleur, journée etc*) dull, drab; (*personne*) dull. ◆**ternir** *vt* (*métal, réputation*) to tarnish; (*miroir, meuble*) to dull; – **se t.** *vpr* (*métal*) to tarnish.

terrain [terɛ̃] *nm* (*sol*) A & Fig ground; (*étendue*) land; Mil Géol terrain; (*à bâtir*) plot, site; **un t.** a piece of land; **t. d'aviation** airfield; **t. de camping** campsite; **t. de football/rugby** football/rugby pitch; **t. de golf** golf course; **t. de jeu** playground; **t. de sport** sports ground, playing field; **t. vague** waste ground, *Am* vacant lot; **céder/gagner/perdre du t.** Mil & Fig to give/

lose ground; **tout t., tous terrains** (*véhicule*) all-purpose.

terrasse [teras] *nf* **1** terrace; (*toit*) terrace (roof). **2** (*de café*) pavement *ou Am* sidewalk area; **à la t.** outside.

terrassement [terasmã] *nm* (*travail*) excavation.

terrasser [terase] *vt* (*adversaire*) to floor, knock down; (*accabler*) *Fig* to overcome.

terrassier [terasje] *nm* labourer, navvy.

terre [ter] *nf* (*matière*) earth; (*sol*) ground; (*opposé à mer, étendue*) land; *pl* (*domaine*) land, estate; *El* earth, *Am* ground; **la t.** (*le monde*) the earth; **la T.** (*planète*) Earth; **à** *ou* **par t.** (*poser, tomber*) to the ground; **par t.** (*assis, couché*) on the ground; **aller à t.** *Nau* to go ashore; **sous t.** underground; **t. cuite** (*baked*) clay, earthenware; **en t. cuite** (*poterie*) clay-. ◆**t.-à-terre** *a inv* down-to-earth. ◆**t.-plein** *nm* (*terrace*) platform; (*au milieu de la route*) central reservation, *Am* median strip. ◆**terrestre** *a* (*vie, joies*) earthly; (*animaux, transport*) land-; **la surface t.** the earth's surface; **globe t.** (*terrestrial*) globe. ◆**terreux, -euse** *a* (*goût*) earthy; (*sale*) grubby; (*couleur*) dull; (*teint*) ashen. ◆**terrien, -ienne** *a* land-owning; **propriétaire t.** landowner; — *nmf* (*habitant de la terre*) earth dweller, earthling.

terreau [tero] *nm* compost.

terrer (se) [satere] *vpr* (*fugitif, animal*) to hide, go to ground *ou* earth.

terreur [tercer] *nf* terror; **t. de** fear of. ◆**terrible** *a* terrible; (*formidable*) *Fam* terrific. ◆**terriblement** *adv* (*extrêmement*) terribly. ◆**terrifi/er** *vt* to terrify. ◆**—ant** *a* terrifying; (*extraordinaire*) incredible.

terrier [terje] *nm* **1** (*de lapin etc*) burrow. **2** (*chien*) terrier.

terrine [terin] *nf* (*récipient*) *Culin* terrine; (*pâté*) pâté.

territoire [teritwar] *nm* territory. ◆**territorial, -aux** *a* territorial.

terroir [terwar] *nm* (*sol*) soil; (*région*) region; **du t.** (*accent etc*) rural.

terroriser [terɔrize] *vt* to terrorize. ◆**terrorisme** *nm* terrorism. ◆**terroriste** *a & nmf* terrorist.

tertiaire [tersjer] *a* tertiary.

tertre [tertr] *nm* hillock, mound.

tes [te] *voir* **ton** [^1].

tesson [tesɔ̃] *nm* **t. de bouteille** piece of broken bottle.

test [test] *nm* test. ◆**tester** *vt* (*élève, produit*) to test.

testament [testamã] *nm* **1** *Jur* will; (*œuvre*) *Fig* testament. **2** Ancien/Nouveau T. *Rel* Old/New Testament.

testicule [testikyl] *nm Anat* testicle.

tétanos [tetanos] *nm Méd* tetanus.

têtard [tetar] *nm* tadpole.

tête [tet] *nf* head; (*figure*) face; (*cheveux*) (head of) hair; (*cerveau*) brain; (*cime*) top; (*de clou, cortège, lit*) head; (*de page, liste*) top, head; (*coup*) *Fb* header; **t. nucléaire** nuclear warhead; **tenir t. à** (*s'opposer à*) to stand up to; **t. nue** bare-headed; **tu n'as pas de t.!** you're a scatterbrain!; **faire la t.** (*bouder*) to sulk; **faire une drôle de t.** to have/give a funny look; **perdre la t.** *Fig* to lose one's head; **tomber la t. la première** to fall headlong *ou* head first; **calculer qch de t.** to work sth out in one's head; **se mettre dans la t. de faire** to get it into one's head to do; **à t. reposée** at one's leisure; **à la t. de** (*entreprise, parti*) at the head of; (*classe*) *Scol* at the top of; **de la t. aux pieds** from head *ou* top to toe; **en t.** *Sp* in the lead. ◆**t.-à-queue** *nm inv* **faire un t.-à-queue** *Aut* to spin right round. ◆**t.-à-tête** *adv* (**en**) **t.-à-tête** (*seul*) in private, alone together; — *nm inv* tête-à-tête. ◆**t.-bêche** *adv* head to tail.

tét/er [tete] *vt* (*lait, biberon etc*) to suck; **t. sa mère** (*bébé*) to suck, feed; — *vi* **donner à t.** à to feed, suckle. ◆**—ée** *nf* (*de bébé*) feed. ◆**tétine** *nf* **1** (*de biberon*) teat, *Am* nipple; (*sucette*) dummy, *Am* pacifier. **2** (*de vache*) udder. ◆**téton** *nm Fam* breast.

têtu [tety] *a* stubborn, obstinate.

texte [tekst] *nm* text; *Th* lines, text; (*de voir*) *Scol* subject; (*morceau choisi*) *Littér* passage. ◆**textuel, -elle** *a* (*traduction*) literal.

textile [tekstil] *a & nm* textile.

texture [tekstyr] *nf* texture.

TGV [teʒeve] *abrév* = **train à grande vitesse.**

Thaïlande [tailãd] *nf* Thailand. ◆**thaïlandais, -aise** *a & nmf* Thai.

thé [te] *nm* (*boisson, réunion*) tea. ◆**thélère** *nf* teapot.

théâtre [teatr] *nm* (*art, lieu*) theatre; (*œuvres*) drama; (*d'un crime*) *Fig* scene; (*des opérations*) *Mil* theatre; **faire du t.** to act. ◆**théâtral, -aux** *a* theatrical.

thème [tem] *nm* theme; (*traduction*) *Scol* translation, prose.

théologie [teɔlɔʒi] *nf* theology. ◆**théologien** *nm* theologian. ◆**théologique** *a* theological.

théorème [teɔrɛm] *nm* theorem.

théorie [teɔri] *nf* theory; **en t.** in theory.

◆**théoricien, -ienne** *nmf* theorist, theoretician. ◆**théorique** *a* theoretical. ◆**théoriquement** *adv* theoretically.

thérapeutique [terapøtik] *a* therapeutic; – *nf* (*traitement*) therapy. ◆**thérapie** *nf* Psy therapy.

thermal, -aux [tɛrmal, -o] *a* **station thermale** spa; **eaux thermales** hot springs.

thermique [tɛrmik] *a* (*énergie, unité*) thermal.

thermomètre [tɛrmɔmɛtr] *nm* thermometer.

thermonucléaire [tɛrmonykleɛr] *a* thermonuclear.

thermos® [tɛrmɔs] *nm ou f* Thermos (flask)®, vacuum flask.

thermostat [tɛrmɔsta] *nm* thermostat.

thèse [tɛz] *nf* (*proposition, ouvrage*) thesis.

thon [tɔ̃] *nm* tuna (fish).

thorax [tɔraks] *nm Anat* thorax.

thym [tɛ̃] *nm Bot Culin* thyme.

thyroïde [tiroid] *a & nf Anat* thyroid.

tibia [tibja] *nm* shin bone, tibia.

tic [tik] *nm* (*contraction*) tic, twitch; (*manie*) *Fig* mannerism.

ticket [tikɛ] *nm* ticket; **t. de quai** *Rail* platform ticket.

tic(-)tac [tiktak] *int & nm inv* tick-tock.

tiède [tjɛd] *a* (luke)warm, tepid; (*climat, vent*) mild; (*accueil, partisan*) half-hearted. ◆**tiédeur** *nf* (*luke*)warmness, tepidness; (*accueil*) mildness; half-heartedness. ◆**tiédir** *vt* to cool (down); (*chauffer*) to warm (up); – *vi* to cool (down); to warm up.

tien, tienne [tjɛ̃, tjɛn] *pron poss* **le t., la tienne, les tien(ne)s** yours; **les deux tiens** your two; – *nmpl* **les tiens** (*amis etc*) your (own) people.

tiens, tient [tjɛ̃] *voir* tenir.

tiercé [tjɛrse] *nm* (*pari*) place betting (*on horses*); **gagner au t.** to win on the races.

tiers, tierce [tjɛr, tjɛrs] *a* third; – *nm* (*fraction*) third; (*personne*) third party; **assurance au t.** third-party insurance. ◆**T.-Monde** *nm* Third World.

tige [tiʒ] *nf* (*de plante*) stem, stalk; (*de botte*) leg; (*barre*) rod.

tignasse [tiɲas] *nf* mop (of hair).

tigre [tigr] *nm* tiger. ◆**tigresse** *nf* tigress.

tigré [tigre] *a* (*tacheté*) spotted; (*rayé*) striped.

tilleul [tijœl] *nm* lime (tree), linden (tree); (*infusion*) lime (blossom) tea.

timbale [tɛ̃bal] *nf* **1** (*gobelet*) (metal) tumbler. **2** *Mus* kettledrum.

timbre [tɛ̃br] *nm* **1** (*marque, tampon, vignette*) stamp; (*cachet de la poste*) post-

mark. **2** (*sonnette*) bell. **3** (*d'instrument, de voix*) tone (quality). ◆**t.-poste** *nm* (*pl* timbres-poste*) (postage) stamp. ◆**timbrer** *vt* (*affranchir*) to stamp (*letter*); (*marquer*) to stamp (*document*). ◆**-é** *a* **1** (*voix*) sonorous. **2** (*fou*) *Fam* crazy.

timide [timid] *a* (*gêné*) shy, timid; (*timoré*) timid. ◆**-ment** *adv* shyly; timidly. ◆**timidité** *nf* shyness; timidity.

timonier [timɔnje] *nm Nau* helmsman.

timoré [timɔre] *a* timorous, fearful.

tintamarre [tɛ̃tamar] *nm* din, racket.

tint/er [tɛ̃te] *vi* (*cloche*) to ring, toll; (*clés, monnaie*) to jingle; (*verres*) to chink. ◆**-ement(s)** *nm(pl)* ringing; jingling; chinking.

tique [tik] *nf* (*insecte*) tick.

tiquer [tike] *vi* (*personne*) to wince.

tir [tir] *nm* (*sport*) shooting; (*action*) firing, shooting; (*feu, rafale*) fire; *Fb* shot; **t. (forain), (stand de) t.** shooting *ou* rifle range; **t. à l'arc** archery; **ligne de t.** line of fire.

tirade [tirad] *nf Th & Fig* monologue.

tiraill/er [tirɑje] **1** *vt* to pull (away) at; (*harceler*) *Fig* to pester, plague; **tiraillé entre** (*possibilités etc*) torn between. **2** *vi* (*au fusil*) to shoot wildly. ◆**-ement** *nm* **1** (*conflit*) conflict (**entre** between). **2** (*crampe*) *Méd* cramp.

tire [tir] *nf* **vol à la t.** *Fam* pickpocketing.

tire-au-flanc [tiroflɑ̃] *nm inv* (*paresseux*) shirker. ◆**t.-bouchon** *nm* corkscrew. ◆**t.-d'aile (à)** *adv* swiftly.

tirelire [tirlir] *nf* moneybox, *Am* coin bank.

tir/er [tire] *vt* to pull; (*langue*) to stick out; (*trait, conclusion, rideaux*) to draw; (*chapeau*) to raise; (*balle, canon*) to fire, shoot; (*gibier*) to shoot; *Typ Phot* to print; **t. de** (*sortir*) to take *ou* pull *ou* draw out of; (*obtenir*) to get from; (*nom, origine*) to derive from; (*produit*) to extract from; **t. qn de** (*danger, lit*) to get s.o. out of; – *vi* to pull (*sur on, at*); (*faire feu*) to fire, shoot (*sur* at); *Fb* to shoot; (*cheminée*) to draw; **t. sur** (*couleur*) to verge on; **t. au sort** to draw lots; **t. à sa fin** to draw to a close; – **se t.** *vpr* (*partir*) *Fam* to beat it; **se t. de** (*problème, travail*) to cope with; (*danger, situation*) to get out of; **se t. d'affaire** to get out of trouble; **s'en t.** *Fam* (*en réchapper*) to come *ou* pull through; (*réussir*) to get along. ◆**-é** *a* (*traits, visage*) drawn; **t. par les cheveux** *Fig* far-fetched. ◆**-age** *nm* **1** (*action*) *Typ Phot* printing; (*édition*) edition; (*quantité*) (print) run; (*de journal*) circulation. **2** (*de loterie*) draw; **t. au sort**

drawing of lots. **3** (*de cheminée*) draught. ◆—**eur** *nm* gunman; **t. d'élite** marksman; **un bon/mauvais t.** a good/bad shot. ◆—**euse** *nf* **t. de cartes** fortune-teller.

tiret [tirɛ] *nm* (*trait*) dash.

tiroir [tirwar] *nm* (*de commode etc*) drawer. ◆**t.-caisse** *nm* (*pl* **tiroirs-caisses**) (cash) till.

tisane [tizan] *nf* herb(al) tea.

tison [tizɔ̃] *nm* (fire)brand, ember. ◆**tisonner** *vt* (*feu*) to poke. ◆**tisonnier** *nm* poker.

tiss/er [tise] *vt* to weave. ◆—**age** *nm* (*action*) weaving. ◆**tisserand, -ande** *nmf* weaver.

tissu [tisy] *nm* fabric, material, cloth; *Biol* tissue; **un t. de** (*mensonges etc*) a web of; **le t. social** the fabric of society, the social fabric; **du t.-éponge** (terry) towelling.

titre [titr] *nm* (*nom, qualité*) title; *Com* bond; (*diplôme*) qualification; *pl* (*droits*) claims (à to); (*gros*) *Journ* headline; **t. de propriété** title deed; **t. de transport** ticket; **à quel t.?** (*pour quelle raison*) on what grounds?; **à ce t.** (*en cette qualité*) as such; (*pour cette raison*) therefore; **à aucun t.** on no account; **au même t.** in the same way (**que** as); **à t. d'exemple/d'ami** as an example/friend; **à t. exceptionnel** exceptionally; **à t. privé** in a private capacity; **à juste t.** rightly. ◆**titr/er** *vt* (*film*) to title; *Journ* to run as a headline. ◆—**é** *a* (*personne*) titled. ◆**titulaire** *a* (*professeur*) staff-, full; **être t. de** (*permis etc*) to be the holder of; (*poste*) to hold; — *nmf* (*de permis, poste*) holder (**de** of). ◆**titulariser** *vt* (*fonctionnaire*) to give tenure to.

tituber [titybe] *vi* to reel, stagger.

toast [tost] *nm* **1** (*pain grillé*) piece ou slice of toast. **2** (*allocution*) toast; **porter un t. à** to drink (a toast) to.

toboggan [tɔbɔgɑ̃] *nm* **1** (*pente*) slide; (*traîneau*) toboggan. **2** *Aut* flyover, *Am* overpass.

toc [tɔk] **1** *int* **t. t.!** knock knock! **2** *nm* **du t.** (*camelote*) rubbish, trash; **en t.** (*bijou*) imitation-.

tocsin [tɔksɛ̃] *nm* alarm (bell).

tohu-bohu [tɔybɔy] *nm* (*bruit*) hubbub, commotion; (*confusion*) hurly-burly.

toi [twa] *pron* **1** (*complément*) you; **c'est t.** it's you; **avec t.** with you. **2** (*sujet*) you; **t., tu peux** *you* may. **3** (*réfléchi*) **assieds-t.** sit (yourself) down; **dépêche-t.** hurry up. ◆**t.-même** *pron* yourself.

toile [twal] *nf* **1** cloth; (*à voile*) canvas; (*à draps*) linen; **une t.** a piece of cloth ou canvas ou linen; **t. de jute** hessian; **drap de t.** linen sheet; **t. de fond** *Th* & *Fig* backcloth. **2** (*tableau*) canvas, painting. **3 t. d'araignée** cobweb, (spider's) web.

toilette [twalɛt] *nf* (*action*) wash(ing); (*vêtements*) outfit, clothes; **articles de t.** toiletries; **cabinet de t.** washroom; **eau/savon/trousse de t.** toilet water/soap/bag; **table de t.** dressing table; **faire sa t.** to wash (and dress); **les toilettes** (*W-C*) the toilet(s); **aller aux toilettes** to go to the toilet.

toiser [twaze] *vt* to eye scornfully.

toison [twazɔ̃] *nf* (*de mouton*) fleece.

toit [twa] *nm* roof; **t. ouvrant** *Aut* sunroof. ◆**toiture** *nf* roof(ing).

tôle [tol] *nf* **la t.** sheet metal; **une t.** a steel ou metal sheet; **t. ondulée** corrugated iron.

tolér/er [tɔlere] *vt* (*permettre*) to tolerate, allow; (*supporter*) to tolerate, bear; (*à la douane*) to allow. ◆—**ant** *a* tolerant (**à l'égard de** of). ◆—**able** *a* tolerable. ◆**tolérance** *nf* tolerance; (*à la douane*) allowance.

tollé [tɔle] *nm* outcry.

tomate [tɔmat] *nf* tomato; **sauce t.** tomato sauce.

tombe [tɔ̃b] *nf* grave; (*avec monument*) tomb. ◆**tombale** *af* **pierre t.** gravestone, tombstone. ◆**tombeau, -x** *nm* tomb.

tomb/er [tɔ̃be] *vi* (*aux* être) to fall; (*température*) to drop, fall; (*vent*) to drop (off); (*cheveux, robe*) to hang down; **t. malade** to fall ill; **t. (par terre)** to fall (down); **faire t.** (*personne*) to knock over; (*gouvernement, prix*) to bring down; **laisser t.** (*objet*) to drop; (*personne, projet etc*) *Fig* to drop, give up; **tu m'as laissé t. hier** *Fig* you let me down yesterday; **se laisser t. dans un fauteuil** to drop into an armchair; **tu tombes bien/mal** *Fig* you've come at the right/wrong time; **t. de fatigue** ou **de sommeil** to be ready to drop; **t. un lundi** to fall on a Monday; **t. sur** (*trouver*) to come across. ◆—**ée** *nf* **t. de la nuit** nightfall.

tombereau, -x [tɔ̃bro] *nm* (*charrette*) tip cart.

tombola [tɔ̃bɔla] *nf* raffle.

tome [tɔm] *nm* (*livre*) volume.

ton[1], ta, *pl* **tes** [tɔ̃, ta, te] (*ta* becomes **ton** [tɔ̃n] *before a vowel or mute h*) *a poss* your; **t. père** your father; **ta mère** your mother; **ton ami(e)** your friend.

ton[2] [tɔ̃] *nm* tone; (*de couleur*) shade, tone; (*gamme*) *Mus* key; (*hauteur de son*) & *Ling* pitch; **de bon t.** (*goût*) in good taste; **donner le t.** *Fig* to set the tone. ◆**tonalité** *nf* (*de* *radio etc*) tone; *Tél* dialling tone, *Am* dial tone.

tond/re [tɔ̃dr] *vt* **1** (*mouton*) to shear; (*cheveux*) to clip, crop; (*gazon*) to mow. **2 t. qn** (*escroquer*) *Fam* to fleece s.o. ◆**—euse** *nf* shears; (*à cheveux*) clippers; **t.** (*à gazon*) (lawn)mower.

tonifi/er [tɔnifje] *vt* (*muscles, peau*) to tone up; (*esprit, personne*) to invigorate. ◆**—ant** *a* (*activité, climat etc*) invigorating.

tonique [tɔnik] **1** *a* (*accent*) *Ling* tonic. **2** *a* (*froid, effet, vin*) tonic, invigorating; — *nm Méd* tonic.

tonitruant [tɔnitryɑ̃] *a* (*voix*) *Fam* booming.

tonnage [tɔnaʒ] *nm Nau* tonnage.

tonne [tɔn] *nf* (*poids*) metric ton, tonne; **des tonnes de** (*beaucoup*) *Fam* tons of.

tonneau, -x [tɔno] *nm* **1** (*récipient*) barrel, cask. **2** (*manœuvre*) *Av* roll; **faire un t.** *Aut* to roll over. **3** (*poids*) *Nau* ton. ◆**tonnelet** *nm* keg.

tonnelle [tɔnɛl] *nf* arbour, bower.

tonner [tɔne] *vi* (*canons*) to thunder; (*crier*) *Fig* to thunder, rage (**contre** against); — *v imp* **il tonne** it's thundering. ◆**tonnerre** *nm* thunder; **coup de t.** thunderclap; *Fig* bombshell, thunderbolt; **du t.** (*excellent*) *Fam* terrific.

tonte [tɔ̃t] *nf* (*de moutons*) shearing; (*de gazon*) mowing.

tonton [tɔ̃tɔ̃] *nm Fam* uncle.

tonus [tɔnys] *nm* (*énergie*) energy, vitality.

top [tɔp] *nm* (*signal sonore*) *Rad* stroke.

topaze [tɔpaz] *nf* (*pierre*) topaz.

topinambour [tɔpinɑ̃bur] *nm* Jerusalem artichoke.

topo [tɔpo] *nm* (*exposé*) *Fam* talk, speech.

topographie [tɔpɔgrafi] *nf* topography.

toque [tɔk] *nf* (*de fourrure*) fur hat; (*de juge, jockey*) cap; (*de cuisinier*) hat.

toqu/er (se) [sətɔke] *vpr* **se t. de qn** *Fam* to become infatuated with s.o. ◆**—é** *a* (*fou*) *Fam* crazy. ◆**toquade** *nf Fam* (*pour qch*) craze (**pour** for); (*pour qn*) infatuation (**pour** with).

torche [tɔrʃ] *nf* (*flambeau*) torch; **t. électrique** torch, *Am* flashlight.

torcher [tɔrʃe] *vt* **1** (*travail*) to skimp. **2** (*essuyer*) *Fam* to wipe.

torchon [tɔrʃɔ̃] *nm* (*à vaisselle*) tea towel, *Am* dish towel; (*de ménage*) duster, cloth.

tord/re [tɔrdr] *vt* to twist; (*linge, cou*) to wring; (*barre*) to bend; **se t. la cheville/le pied/le dos** to twist ou sprain one's ankle/foot/back; — **se t.** *vpr* to twist; (*barre*) to bend; **se t. de douleur** to writhe with pain; **se t. (de rire)** to split one's sides

(laughing). ◆**—ant** *a* (*drôle*) *Fam* hilarious. ◆**—u** *a* twisted; (*esprit*) warped.

tornade [tɔrnad] *nf* tornado.

torpeur [tɔrpœr] *nf* lethargy, torpor.

torpille [tɔrpij] *nf* torpedo. ◆**torpill/er** *vt Mil* & *Fig* to torpedo. ◆**—eur** *nm* torpedo boat.

torréfier [tɔrefje] *vt* (*café*) to roast.

torrent [tɔrɑ̃] *nm* (*ruisseau*) torrent; **un t. de** (*injures, larmes*) a flood of; **il pleut à torrents** it's pouring (down). ◆**torrentiel, -ielle** *a* (*pluie*) torrential.

torride [tɔrid] *a* (*chaleur etc*) torrid, scorching.

torsade [tɔrsad] *nf* (*de cheveux*) twist, coil. ◆**torsader** *vt* to twist (together).

torse [tɔrs] *nm Anat* chest; (*statue*) torso.

torsion [tɔrsjɔ̃] *nf* twisting; *Phys Tech* torsion.

tort [tɔr] *nm* (*dommage*) wrong; (*défaut*) fault; **avoir t.** to be wrong (**de faire** to do, in doing); **tu as t. de fumer!** you shouldn't smoke!; **être dans son t.** ou **en t.** to be in the wrong; **donner t. à qn** (*accuser*) to blame s.o.; (*faits etc*) to prove s.o. wrong; **faire du t. à qn** to harm ou wrong s.o.; **à t.** wrongly; **à t. et à travers** wildly, indiscriminately; **à t. ou à raison** rightly or wrongly.

torticolis [tɔrtikɔli] *nm* stiff neck.

tortill/er [tɔrtije] *vt* to twist, twirl; (*moustache*) to twirl; (*tripoter*) to twiddle with; — **se t.** *vpr* (*ver, personne*) to wriggle; (*en dansant, des hanches*) to wiggle. ◆**—ement** *nm* wriggling, wiggling.

tortionnaire [tɔrsjɔner] *nm* torturer.

tortue [tɔrty] *nf* tortoise; (*marine*) turtle; **quelle t.!** *Fig* what a slowcoach ou *Am* slowpoke!

tortueux, -euse [tɔrtɥø, -øz] *a* tortuous.

torture [tɔrtyr] *nf* torture. ◆**torturer** *vt* to torture; **se t. les méninges** to rack one's brains.

tôt [to] *adv* early; **au plus t.** at the earliest; **le plus t. possible** as soon as possible; **t. ou tard** sooner or later; **je n'étais pas plus t. sorti que . . .** no sooner had I gone out than . . . .

total, -aux [tɔtal, -o] *a* & *nm* total; **au t.** all in all, in total; (*somme toute*) all in all. ◆**totalement** *adv* totally, completely. ◆**totaliser** *vt* to total. ◆**totalité** *nf* entirety; **la t. de** all of; **en t.** entirely, totally.

totalitaire [tɔtaliter] *a Pol* totalitarian.

toubib [tubib] *nm* (*médecin*) *Fam* doctor.

touche [tuʃ] *nf* (*de peintre*) touch; *Pêche* bite; (*clavier*) key; **une t. de** (*un peu de*) a touch *ou* hint of; **(ligne de)** t. *Fb Rugby* touchline.

touche-à-tout [tuʃatu] **1** *a & nmf inv (qui touche)* meddlesome (person). **2** *nmf inv (qui se disperse)* dabbler.

touch/er [tuʃe] *vt* to touch; *(paie)* to draw; *(chèque)* to cash; *(cible)* to hit; *(émouvoir)* to touch, move; *(concerner)* to affect; **t. qn** *(contacter)* to get in touch with s.o., reach s.o.; – *vt* **à** to touch; *(sujet)* to touch on; *(but, fin)* to approach; – **se t.** *vpr (lignes etc)* to touch; – *nm (sens)* touch; **au t.** to the touch. ◆—**ant** *a (émouvant)* touching, moving.

touffe [tuf] *nf (de cheveux, d'herbe)* tuft; *(de plantes)* cluster. ◆**touffu** *a (barbe, haie)* thick, bushy; *(livre) Fig* heavy.

toujours [tuʒur] *adv* always; *(encore)* still; **pour t.** for ever; **essaie t.!** *(quand même)* try anyhow!; **t. est-il que ...** the fact remains that ....

toupet [tupɛ] *nm (audace) Fam* cheek, nerve.

toupie [tupi] *nf* (spinning) top.

tour [tur] *nf* **1** *Archit* tower; *(immeuble)* tower block, high-rise. **2** *Échecs* rook, castle.

tour[2] [tur] *nm* **1** *(mouvement, ordre, tournure)* turn; *(artifice)* trick; *(excursion)* trip, outing; *(à pied)* stroll, walk; *(en voiture)* drive; **t. (de phrase)** turn of phrase; **t. (de piste)** *Sp* lap; **t. de cartes** card trick; **t. d'horizon** survey; **t. de poitrine**/*etc* chest/*etc* measurement *ou* size; **de dix mètres de t.** ten metres round; **faire le t. de** to go round; *(question, situation)* to review; **faire un t.** *(à pied)* to go for a stroll *ou* walk; *(en voiture)* to go for a drive; *(en voyage)* to go on a trip; **faire** *ou* **jouer un t. à qn** to play a trick on s.o.; **c'est mon t.** it's my turn; **à qui le tour?** whose turn (is it)?; **à son t.** in (one's) turn; **à t. de rôle** in turn; **t. à t.** in turn, by turns. **2** *Tech* lathe; *(de potier)* wheel.

tourbe [turb] *nf* peat. ◆**tourbière** *nf* peat bog.

tourbillon [turbijɔ̃] *nm (de vent)* whirlwind; *(d'eau)* whirlpool; *(de neige, sable)* eddy; *(tournoiement) Fig* whirl, swirl. ◆**tourbillonner** *vi* to whirl, swirl; to eddy.

tourelle [turɛl] *nf* turret.

tourisme [turism] *nm* tourism; **faire du t.** to do some sightseeing *ou* touring; **agence/office de t.** tourist agency/office. ◆**touriste** *nmf* tourist. ◆**touristique** *a (guide, menu etc)* tourist-; **route t., circuit t.** scenic route.

tourment [turmã] *nm* torment. ◆**tour-**

ment/er *vt* to torment; – **se t.** *vpr* to worry (oneself). ◆—**é** *a (mer, vie)* turbulent, stormy; *(sol)* rough, uneven; *(expression, visage)* anguished.

tourmente [turmãt] *nf (troubles)* turmoil.

tourne-disque [turnədisk] *nm* record player.

tournée [turne] *nf* **1** *(de livreur etc)* round; *(théâtrale)* tour; **faire la t. de** *(magasins etc)* to make the rounds of, go round. **2** *(de boissons)* round.

tourn/er [turne] *vt* to turn; *(film)* to shoot, make; *(difficulté)* to get round; **t. en ridicule** to ridicule; – *vi* to turn; *(tête, toupie)* to spin; *(Terre)* to revolve, turn; *(moteur)* to run, go; *(usine)* to run; *(lait, viande)* to go off; *Cin* to shoot; **t. autour de** *(objet)* to go round; *(maison, personne)* to hang around; *(question)* to centre on; **t. bien/mal** *(évoluer)* to turn out well/badly; **t. au froid** *(temps)* to turn cold; **t. à l'aigre** *(ton, conversation etc)* to turn nasty *ou* sour; **t. de l'œil** *Fam* to faint; – **se t.** *vpr* to turn (**vers** to, towards). ◆—**ant 1** *a* **pont à** swing bridge. **2** *nm (virage)* bend, turning; *(moment) Fig* turning point. ◆—**age** *nm Cin* shooting, filming. ◆—**eur** *nm (ouvrier)* turner. ◆**tournoyer** *vi* to spin (round), whirl. ◆**tournure** *nf (expression)* turn of phrase; **t. d'esprit** way of thinking; **t. des événements** turn of events; **prendre t.** *(forme)* to take shape.

tournesol [turnəsɔl] *nm* sunflower.

tournevis [turnəvis] *nm* screwdriver.

tourniquet [turnikɛ] *nm* **1** *(barrière)* turnstile. **2** *(pour arroser)* sprinkler.

tournoi [turnwa] *nm Sp & Hist* tournament.

tourte [turt] *nf* pie.

tourterelle [turtərɛl] *nf* turtledove.

Toussaint [tusɛ̃] *nf* All Saints' Day.

tousser [tuse] *vi* to cough.

tout, toute, *pl* **tous, toutes** [tu, tut, tu, tut] **1** *a* all; **tous les livres**/*etc* all the books/*etc*; **t. l'argent/le village**/*etc* the whole (of the) money/village/*etc*, all the money/village/*etc*; **toute la nuit** all night, the whole (of the) night; **tous (les) deux** both; **tous (les) trois** all three; **t. un problème** quite a problem. **2** *a (chaque)* every, each; *(n'importe quel)* any; **tous les ans/jours**/*etc* every *ou* each year/day/*etc*; **tous les deux/trois mois**/*etc* every second/third month/*etc*; **tous les cinq mètres** every five metres; **t. homme** [tutɔm] every *ou* any man; **à toute heure** at any time. **3** *pron pl* **(tous** = [tus]) all; **ils sont tous là, tous sont là** they're all there. **4** *pron m sing* **tout** everything;

dépenser t. to spend everything, spend it all; **t. ce que** everything that, all that; **en t.** (au total) in all. **5** adv (tout à fait) quite; (très) very; **t. petit** very small; **t. neuf** brand new; **t. simplement** quite simply; **t. seul** all alone; **t. droit** straight ahead; **t. autour** all around, right round; **t. au début** right at the beginning; **le t. premier** the very first; **t. au moins/plus** at the very least/most; **t. en chantant**/etc while singing/etc; **t. rusé qu'il est** however sly he may be; **t. à coup** suddenly, all of a sudden; **t. à fait** completely, quite; **t. de même** all the same; (indignation) really!; **t. de suite** at once. **6** nm le t. everything, the lot; **un t.** a whole; **le t.** (l'important) the main thing is (que that, de faire to do); **pas du t.** not at all; **rien du t.** nothing at all; **du t. au t.** (changer) entirely, completely. ◆**t.-puissant, toute-puissante** a all-powerful.

tout-à-l'égout [tutalegu] nm inv mains drainage.

toutefois [tutfwa] adv nevertheless, however.

toutou [tutu] nm (chien) Fam doggie.

toux [tu] nf cough.

toxicomane [tɔksikɔman] nmf drug addict. ◆**toxicomanie** nf drug addiction. ◆**toxine** nf toxin. ◆**toxique** a toxic.

trac [trak] nm le t. (peur) the jitters; (de candidat) exam nerves; Th stage fright.

tracas [traka] nm worry. ◆**tracasser** vt, — **se t.** vpr to worry. ◆**tracasseries** nfpl annoyances. ◆**tracassier, -ière** a irksome.

trace [tras] nf (quantité, tache, vestige) trace; (marque) mark; (de fugitif etc) trail; pl (de bête, de pneu) tracks; **traces de pas** footprints; **suivre les traces de qn** Fig to follow in s.o.'s footsteps.

trac/er [trase] vt (dessiner) to draw; (écrire) to trace; **t. une route** to mark out a route; (frayer) to open up a route. ◆**—é** nm (plan) layout; (ligne) line.

trachée [traʃe] nf Anat windpipe.

tract [trakt] nm leaflet.

tractations [traktasjɔ̃] nfpl Péj dealings.

tracter [trakte] vt (caravane etc) to tow. ◆**tracteur** nm (véhicule) tractor.

traction [traksjɔ̃] nf Tech traction; Sp pull-up; **t. arrière/avant** Aut rear-/front-wheel drive.

tradition [tradisjɔ̃] nf tradition. ◆**traditionnel, -elle** a traditional.

traduire* [tradɥir] vt 1 to translate (de from, en into); (exprimer) Fig to express. 2 **t. qn en justice** to bring s.o. before the

courts. ◆**traducteur, -trice** nmf translator. ◆**traduction** nf translation. ◆**traduisible** a translatable.

trafic [trafik] nm 1 Aut Rail etc traffic. 2 Com Péj traffic, trade; **faire du t.** to traffic, trade; **faire le t. de** to traffic in, trade in. ◆**trafiqu/er** vi to traffic, trade. 2 vt (produit) Fam to tamper with. ◆**—ant, -ante** nmf trafficker, dealer; **t. d'armes/de drogue** arms/drug trafficker or dealer.

tragédie [traʒedi] nf Th & Fig tragedy. ◆**tragique** a tragic. ◆**tragiquement** adv tragically.

trahir [trair] vt to betray; (secret etc) to betray, give away; (forces) to fail (s.o.); — **se t.** vpr to give oneself away, betray oneself. ◆**trahison** nf betrayal; (crime) Pol treason.

train [trɛ̃] nm 1 (locomotive, transport, jouet) train; **t. à grande vitesse** high-speed train; **t. couchettes** sleeper; **t. auto-couchettes** (car) sleeper. 2 **en t.** (forme) on form; **se mettre en t.** to get (oneself) into shape. 3 **être en t. de faire** to be (busy) doing; **mettre qch en t.** to get sth going, start sth off. 4 (allure) pace; **t. de vie** life style. 5 (de pneus) set; (de péniches, véhicules) string. 6 **t. d'atterrissage** Av undercarriage.

traîne [trɛn] nf 1 (de robe) train. 2 **à la t.** (en arrière) lagging behind.

traîneau, -x [trɛno] nm sledge, sleigh, Am sled.

traînée [trɛne] nf 1 (de substance) trail, streak; (bande) streak; **se répandre comme une t. de poudre** (vite) to spread like wildfire. 2 (prostituée) Arg tart.

traîner [trɛne] vt to drag; (mots) to drawl; **(faire) t. en longueur** (faire durer) to drag out; — vi (jouets, papiers etc) to lie around; (subsister) to linger on; (s'attarder) to lag behind, dawdle; (errer) to hang around; **t.** **(par terre)** (robe etc) to trail (on the ground); **t.** **(en longueur)** (durer) to drag on; — **se t.** vpr (avancer) to drag oneself (along); (par terre) to crawl; (durer) to drag on. ◆**traînant** a (voix) drawling. ◆**traînailler** vi Fam = **traînasser**. ◆**traînard, -arde** nmf slowcoach, Am slowpoke. ◆**traînasser** vi Fam to dawdle; (errer) to hang around.

train-train [trɛ̃trɛ̃] nm routine.

traire* [trɛr] vt (vache) to milk.

trait [trɛ] nm 1 line; (en dessinant) stroke; (caractéristique) feature, trait; pl (du visage) features; **t. d'union** hyphen; (intermédiaire) Fig link; **d'un t.** (boire) in one gulp, in one go; **à grands traits** in outline; **t. de** (*esprit, génie*) flash of; (*bravoure*) act of; **avoir t. à** (*se rapporter à*) to relate to. **2 cheval de t.** draught horse.

traite [tret] *nf* **1** (*de vache*) milking. **2** *Com* bill, draft. **3 d'une (seule) t.** (*sans interruption*) in one go. **4 t. des Noirs** slave trade; **t. des blanches** white slave trade.

traité [trete] *nm* **1** *Pol* treaty. **2** (*ouvrage*) treatise (**sur** on).

trait/er [trete] *vt* (*se comporter envers*) & *Méd* to treat; (*problème, sujet*) to deal with; (*marché*) *Com* to negotiate; (*matériau, produit*) to treat, process; **t. qn de lâche**/*etc* to call s.o. a coward/*etc*; **-** *vi* to negotiate, deal (**avec** with); **t. de** (*sujet*) to deal with. **◆—ant** [-tɑ̃] *a* **médecin t.** regular doctor. **◆—ement** [-ɛtmɑ̃] *nm* **1** treatment; **mauvais traitements** rough treatment; **t. de données/de texte** data/word processing; **machine de t. de texte** word processor. **2** (*gains*) salary.

traiteur [tretœr] *nm* (*fournisseur*) caterer; **chez le t.** (*magasin*) at the delicatessen.

traître [trɛtr] *nm* traitor; **en t.** treacherously; **- a** (*dangereux*) treacherous; **être t. à** to be a traitor to. **◆traîtrise** *nf* treachery.

trajectoire [traʒɛktwar] *nf* path, trajectory.

trajet [traʒɛ] *nm* journey, trip; (*distance*) distance; (*itinéraire*) route.

trame [tram] *nf* **1** (*de récit etc*) framework. **2** (*de tissu*) weft.

tramer [trame] *vt* (*évasion etc*) to plot; (*complot*) to hatch.

trampoline [trɑ̃polin] *nm* trampoline.

tram(way) [tram(wɛ)] *nm* tram, *Am* streetcar.

tranche [trɑ̃ʃ] *nf* (*morceau coupé*) slice; (*bord*) edge; (*partie*) portion; (*de salaire, impôts*) bracket; **t. d'âge** age bracket.

tranchée [trɑ̃ʃe] *nf* trench.

tranch/er [trɑ̃ʃe] **1** *vt* to cut. **2** *vt* (*difficulté, question*) to settle; **-** *vi* (*décider*) to decide. **3** *vi* (*contraster*) to contrast (**avec, sur** with). **◆—ant 1** *a* (*couteau*) sharp; **-** *nm* (*cutting*) edge. **2** *a* (*péremptoire*) trenchant, cutting. **◆—é** *a* (*couleurs*) distinct; (*opinion*) clear-cut.

tranquille [trɑ̃kil] *a* quiet; (*mer*) calm, still; (*conscience*) clear; (*esprit*) easy; (*enfant, Fam* confident); **je suis t.** (*rassuré*) my mind is at rest; **soyez t.** don't worry; **laisser t.** to leave be *ou* alone. **◆tranquillement** *adv* calmly. **◆tranquillis/er** *vt* to reassure; **tranquillisez-vous** set your mind at rest. **◆—ant** *nm* *Méd* tranquillizer. **◆tranquil-**

lité *nf* (*peace and*) quiet; (*d'esprit*) peace of mind.

trans- [trɑ̃z, trɑ̃s] *préf* trans-.

transaction [trɑ̃zaksjɔ̃] *nf* **1** (*compromis*) compromise. **2** *Com* transaction.

transatlantique [trɑ̃zatlɑ̃tik] *a* transatlantic; **-** *nm* (*paquebot*) transatlantic liner; (*chaise*) deckchair.

transcend/er [trɑ̃sɑ̃de] *vt* to transcend. **◆—ant** *a* transcendent.

transcrire* [trɑ̃skrir] *vt* to transcribe. **◆transcription** *nf* transcription; (*document*) transcript.

transe [trɑ̃s] *nf* **en t.** (*mystique*) in a trance; (*excité*) very exited.

transférer [trɑ̃sfere] *vt* to transfer (**à** to). **◆transfert** *nm* transfer.

transfigurer [trɑ̃sfigyre] *vt* to transform, transfigure.

transformer [trɑ̃sfɔrme] *vt* to transform, change; (*maison, matière première*) to convert; (*robe etc*) to alter; (*essai*) *Rugby* to convert; **t. en** to turn into; **- se t.** *vpr* to change, be transformed (**en** into). **◆transformateur** *nm* *Él* transformer. **◆transformation** *nf* transformation, change; conversion.

transfuge [trɑ̃sfyʒ] *nm* *Mil* renegade; **-** *nmf Pol* renegade.

transfusion [trɑ̃sfyzjɔ̃] *nf* **t.** (*sanguine*) (blood) transfusion.

transgresser [trɑ̃sgrese] *vt* (*loi, ordre*) to disobey.

transi [trɑ̃zi] *a* (*personne*) numb with cold; **t. de peur** paralysed by fear.

transiger [trɑ̃ziʒe] *vi* to compromise.

transistor [trɑ̃zistɔr] *nm* (*dispositif, poste*) transistor. **◆transistorisé** *a* (*téléviseur etc*) transistorized.

transit [trɑ̃zit] *nm* transit; **en t.** in transit. **◆transiter** *vt* (*faire*) **t.** to send in transit; **-** *vi* to be in transit.

transitif, -ive [trɑ̃zitif, -iv] *a* *Gram* transitive.

transition [trɑ̃zisjɔ̃] *nf* transition. **◆transitoire** *a* (*qui passe*) transient; (*provisoire*) transitional.

transmettre* [trɑ̃smɛtr] *vt* (*héritage, message etc*) to pass on (**à** to); *Phys Tech* to transmit; *Rad TV* to broadcast, transmit. **◆transmetteur** *nm* (*appareil*) transmitter, transmitting device. **◆transmission** *nf* transmission; passing on.

transparaître* [trɑ̃sparɛtr] *vi* to show (through).

transparent [trɑ̃sparɑ̃] *a* transparent. **◆transparence** *nf* transparency.

transpercer [trɑ̃spɛrse] vt to pierce, go through.

transpirer [trɑ̃spire] vi (suer) to perspire; (information) Fig to leak out. ◆**transpiration** nf perspiration.

transplanter [trɑ̃splɑ̃te] vt (organe, plante etc) to transplant. ◆**transplantation** nf transplantation; (greffe) Méd transplant.

transport [trɑ̃spɔr] nm 1 (action) transport, transportation (de of); pl (moyens) transport; **moyen de t.** means of transport; **transports en commun** public transport. 2 (émotion) Litt rapture. ◆**transporter** 1 vt (véhicule, train) to transport, convey; (à la main) to carry, take; **t. d'urgence à l'hôpital** to rush to hospital; — **se t.** vpr (aller) to take oneself (à to). 2 vt Litt to enrapture. ◆**transporteur** nm t. (routier) haulier, Am trucker.

transposer [trɑ̃spoze] vt to transpose. ◆**transposition** nf transposition.

transvaser [trɑ̃svaze] vt (vin) to decant.

transversal, -aux [trɑ̃svɛrsal, -o] a (barre, rue etc) cross-, transverse.

trapèze [trapɛz] nm (au cirque) trapeze. ◆**trapéziste** nmf trapeze artist.

trappe [trap] nf (dans le plancher) trap door.

trappeur [trapœr] nm (chasseur) trapper.

trapu [trapy] a 1 (personne) stocky, thickset. 2 (problème etc) Fam tough.

traquenard [traknar] nm trap.

traquer [trake] vt to track ou hunt (down).

traumatis/er [tromatize] vt to traumatize. ◆**-ant** a traumatic. ◆**traumatisme** nm (choc) trauma.

travail, -aux [travaj, -o] nm (activité, lieu) work; (emploi, tâche) job; (façonnage) working (de of); (ouvrage, étude) work, publication; Écon Méd labour; pl work; (dans la rue) roadworks; (aménagement) alterations; **travaux forcés** hard labour; **travaux ménagers** housework; **travaux pratiques** Scol Univ practical work; **travaux publics** public works; **t. au noir** moonlighting; **en t.** (femme) Méd in labour.

travaill/er [travaje] 1 vi to work (à qch at ou on sth); — vt (discipline, rôle, style) to work on; (façonner) to work; (inquiéter) to worry; **t. la terre** to work the land. 2 vi (bois) to warp. ◆**-é** a (style) elaborate. ◆**-eur, -euse** a hard-working; — nmf worker. ◆**travailliste** a Pol Labour-; — nmf Pol member of the Labour party.

travers [travɛr] 1 prep & adv à t. through; **en t.** (de) across. 2 adv de t. (chapeau, nez etc) crooked; (comprendre) badly; (regarder) askance; **aller de t.** Fig to go

wrong; **j'ai avalé de t.** it went down the wrong way. 3 nm (défaut) failing.

traverse [travɛrs] nf 1 Rail sleeper, Am tie. 2 **chemin de t.** short cut.

travers/er [travɛrse] vt to cross, go across; (foule, période, mur) to go through. ◆**-ée** nf (action, trajet) crossing.

traversin [travɛrsɛ̃] nm (coussin) bolster.

travest/ir [travɛstir] vt to disguise; (pensée, vérité) to misrepresent. ◆**-i** nm Th female impersonator; (homosexuel) transvestite. ◆**-issement** nm disguise; misrepresentation.

trébucher [trebyʃe] vi to stumble (sur over); **faire t.** to trip (up).

trèfle [trɛfl] nm 1 (plante) clover. 2 (couleur) Cartes clubs.

treille [trɛj] nf climbing vine.

treillis [treji] nm 1 lattice(work); (en métal) wire mesh. 2 (tenue militaire) combat uniform.

treize [trɛz] a & nm inv thirteen. ◆**treizième** a & nmf thirteenth.

tréma [trema] nm Gram di(a)eresis.

trembl/er [trɑ̃ble] vi to tremble, shake; (de froid, peur) to tremble (de with); (flamme, lumière) to flicker; (voix) to tremble, quaver; (avoir peur) to be afraid (que (+ sub) that, **de faire** to do); **t. pour qn** to fear for s.o. ◆**-ement** nm (action, frisson) trembling; **t. de terre** earthquake. ◆**trembloter** vi to quiver.

trémousser (se) [sətremuse] vpr to wriggle (about).

trempe [trɑ̃p] nf (caractère) stamp; **un homme de sa t.** a man of his stamp.

tremper [trɑ̃pe] 1 vt to soak, drench; (plonger) to dip (dans in); — vi to soak; **faire t.** to soak; — **se t.** vpr (se baigner) to take a dip. 2 vt (acier) to temper. 3 vi **t. dans** (participer) Péj to be mixed up in. ◆**trempette** nf **faire t.** (se baigner) to take a dip.

tremplin [trɑ̃plɛ̃] nm Natation & Fig springboard.

trente [trɑ̃t] a & nm thirty; **un t.-trois tours** (disque) an LP. ◆**trentaine** nf **une t.** (de) (nombre) (about) thirty; **avoir la t.** (âge) to be about thirty. ◆**trentième** a & nmf thirtieth.

trépidant [trepidɑ̃] a (vie etc) hectic.

trépied [trepje] nm tripod.

trépigner [trepiɲe] vi to stamp (one's feet).

très [trɛ] adv (before vowel or mute h) very; **t.** aimé/critiqué/etc much liked/criticized/etc.

trésor [trezɔr] nm treasure; **le T. (public**

tressaillir

294

trompette

(*service*) public revenue (department); (*finances*) public funds; **des trésors de** Fig a treasure house of. ◆**trésorerie** nf (*bureaux d'un club etc*) accounts department; (*capitaux*) funds; (*gestion*) accounting. ◆**trésorier, -ière** nmf treasurer.

tressaill/ir* [tresajir] vi (*sursauter*) to jump, start; (*frémir*) to shake, quiver; (*de joie, peur*) to tremble (**de** with). ◆**—ement** nm start; quiver; trembling.

tressauter [tresote] vi (*sursauter*) to start, jump.

tresse [tres] nf (*cordon*) braid; (*cheveux*) plait, Am braid. ◆**tresser** vt to braid; to plait.

tréteau, -x [treto] nm trestle.

treuil [trœj] nm winch, windlass.

trêve [trev] nf Mil truce; (*répit*) Fig respite.

tri [tri] nm sorting (out); **faire le t. de** to sort (out); (**centre de**) **t.** (*des postes*) sorting office. ◆**triage** nm sorting (out).

triangle [trijɑ̃gl] nm triangle. ◆**triangulaire** a triangular.

tribord [tribɔr] nm Nau Av starboard.

tribu [triby] nf tribe. ◆**tribal, -aux** a tribal.

tribulations [tribylɑsjɔ̃] nfpl tribulations.

tribunal, -aux [tribynal, -o] nm Jur court; (*militaire*) tribunal.

tribune [tribyn] nf **1** (*de salle publique etc*) gallery; (*de stade*) (grand)stand; (*d'orateur*) rostrum. **2 t. libre** (*dans un journal*) open forum.

tribut [triby] nm tribute (**à** to).

tributaire [tribytɛr] a **t. de** Fig dependent on.

tricher [triʃe] vi to cheat. ◆**tricherie** nf cheating, trickery; **une t.** a piece of trickery. ◆**tricheur, -euse** nmf cheat, Am cheater.

tricolore [trikɔlɔr] a **1** (*cocarde etc*) red, white and blue; **le drapeau/l'équipe t.** the French flag/team. **2 feu t.** traffic lights.

tricot [triko] nm (*activité, ouvrage*) knitting; (*chandail*) jumper, sweater; **un t.** (*ouvrage*) a piece of knitting; **en t.** knitted; **t. de corps** vest, Am undershirt. ◆**tricoter** vti to knit.

tricycle [trisikl] nm tricycle.

trier [trije] vt (*séparer*) to sort (out); (*choisir*) to pick ou sort out.

trilogie [trilɔʒi] nf trilogy.

trimbal(l)er [trɛ̃bale] vt Fam to cart about, drag around; **— se t.** vpr Fam to trail around.

trimer [trime] vi Fam to slave (away), toil.

trimestre [trimɛstr] nm (*période*) Com quarter; Scol term. ◆**trimestriel, -ielle** a (*revue*) quarterly; (*bulletin*) Scol end-of-term.

tringle [trɛ̃gl] nf rail, rod; **t. à rideaux** curtain rail ou rod.

Trinité [trinite] nf **la T.** (*fête*) Trinity; (*dogme*) the Trinity.

trinquer [trɛ̃ke] vi to chink glasses; **t. à** to drink to.

trio [trijo] nm (*groupe*) & Mus trio.

triomphe [trijɔ̃f] nm triumph (**sur** over); **porter qn en t.** to carry s.o. shoulder-high. ◆**triomphal, -aux** a triumphal. ◆**triomph/er** vi to triumph (**de** over); (*jubiler*) to be jubilant. ◆**—ant** a triumphant.

tripes [trip] nfpl (*intestins*) Fam guts; Culin tripe. ◆**tripier, -ière** nmf tripe butcher.

triple [tripl] a treble, triple; **— nm le t.** three times as much (**de** as). ◆**tripl/er** vti to treble, triple. ◆**—és, -ées** nmfpl (*enfants*) triplets.

tripot [tripo] nm (*café etc*) Péj gambling den.

tripoter [tripɔte] vt to fiddle about ou mess about with; **— vi** to fiddle ou mess about.

trique [trik] nf cudgel, stick.

triste [trist] a sad; (*couleur, temps, rue*) gloomy, dreary; (*lamentable*) unfortunate, sorry. ◆**tristement** adv sadly. ◆**tristesse** nf sadness; gloom, dreariness.

triturer [trityre] vt (*manipuler*) to manipulate.

trivial, -aux [trivjal, -o] a coarse, vulgar. ◆**trivialité** nf coarseness, vulgarity.

troc [trɔk] nm exchange, barter.

troène [trɔɛn] nm (*arbuste*) privet.

trognon [trɔɲɔ̃] nm (*de pomme, poire*) core; (*de chou*) stump.

trois [trwa] a & nm three. ◆**troisième** a & nmf third. ◆**troisièmement** adv thirdly.

trolley(bus) [trɔlɛ(bys)] nm trolley(bus).

trombe [trɔ̃b] nf **t. d'eau** (*pluie*) rainstorm, downpour; **en t.** (*entrer etc*) Fig like a whirlwind.

trombone [trɔ̃bɔn] nm **1** Mus trombone. **2** (*agrafe*) paper clip.

trompe [trɔ̃p] nf **1** (*d'éléphant*) trunk; (*d'insecte*) proboscis. **2** Mus horn.

tromper [trɔ̃pe] vt to deceive, mislead; (*escroquer*) to cheat; (*échapper à*) to elude; (*être infidèle à*) to be unfaithful to; **— se t.** vpr to be mistaken, make a mistake; **se t. de route/de train/etc** to take the wrong road/train/etc; **se t. de date/de jour/etc** to get the date/day/etc wrong. ◆**tromperie** nf deceit, deception. ◆**trompeur, -euse** a (*apparences etc*) deceptive, misleading; (*personne*) deceitful.

trompette [trɔ̃pɛt] nf trumpet. ◆**trompettiste** nmf trumpet player.

tronc [trɔ̃] nm **1** Bot Anat trunk. **2** Rel collection box.

tronçon [trɔ̃sɔ̃] nm section. **◆tronçonn/er** vt to cut (into sections). **◆-euse** nf chain saw.

trône [tron] nm throne. **◆trôner** vi (vase, personne etc) Fig to occupy the place of honour.

tronquer [trɔ̃ke] vt to truncate; (texte etc) to curtail.

trop [tro] adv too; too much; **t. dur/loin/**etc too hard/far/etc; **t. fatigué** too tired, overtired; **boire/lire/**etc **t.** to drink/read/etc too much; **t. de sel/**etc (quantité) too much salt/etc; **t. de gens/**etc (nombre) too many people/etc; **du fromage/**etc **de** ou **en t.** (quantité) too much cheese/etc; **des œufs/**etc **de** ou **en t.** (nombre) too many eggs/etc; **un franc/verre/**etc **de t.** ou **en t.** one franc/glass/etc too many; **se sentir de t.** Fig to feel in the way.

trophée [trɔfe] nm trophy.

tropique [trɔpik] nm tropic. **◆tropical, -aux** a tropical.

trop-plein [trɔplɛ̃] nm (dispositif, liquide) overflow; (surabondance) Fig excess.

troquer [trɔke] vt to exchange (**contre** for).

trot [tro] nm trot; **aller au t.** to trot; **au t.** (sans retarder) Fam at the double. **◆trott/er** [trɔte] vi (cheval) to trot; (personne) Fig to scurry along.

trotteuse [trɔtøz] nf (de montre) second hand.

trottiner [trɔtine] vi (personne) to patter (along).

trottinette [trɔtinɛt] nf (jouet) scooter.

trottoir [trɔtwar] nm pavement, Am sidewalk; **t. roulant** moving walkway, travelator.

trou [tru] nm hole; (d'aiguille) eye; (manque) Fig gap (**dans** in); (village) Péj hole, dump; **t. d'homme** (ouverture) manhole; **t. de (la) serrure** keyhole; **t. de mémoire** Fig lapse (of memory).

trouble [trubl] **1** a (liquide) cloudy; (image) blurred; (affaire) shady; **voir t.** to see blurred. **2** nm (émoi, émotion) agitation; (désarroi) distress; (désordre) confusion; pl Méd trouble; (révolte) disturbances, troubles. **◆troubl/er** vt to disturb; (liquide) to make cloudy; (projet) to upset; (esprit) to unsettle; (vue) to blur; (inquiéter) to trouble; **— se t.** vpr (liquide) to become cloudy; (candidat etc) to become flustered. **◆-ant** a (détail etc) disquieting. **◆trouble-fête** nmf inv killjoy, spoilsport.

trou/er [true] vt to make a hole ou holes in;

(silence, ténèbres) to cut through. **◆-ée** nf gap; (brèche) Mil breach.

trouille [truj] nf **avoir la t.** Fam to have the jitters, be scared. **◆trouillard** a (poltron) Fam chicken.

troupe [trup] nf Mil troop; (groupe) group; Th company, troupe; **la t., les troupes** (armée) the troops.

troupeau, -x [trupo] nm (de vaches) & Fig Péj herd; (de moutons, d'oies) flock.

trousse [trus] nf **1** (étui) case, kit; (d'écolier) pencil case; **t. à outils** toolkit; **t. à pharmacie** first-aid kit. **2** nfpl **aux trousses de qn** Fig on s.o.'s heels.

trousseau, -x [truso] nm **1** (de clés) bunch. **2** (de mariée) trousseau.

trouver [truve] vt to find; **aller/venir t. qn** to go/come and see s.o.; **je trouve que** (je pense que) I think that; **comment la trouvez-vous?** what do you think of her?; **— se t.** vpr to be; (être situé) to be situated; (se sentir) to feel; (dans une situation) to find oneself; **se t. mal** (s'évanouir) to faint; **il se trouve que** it happens that. **◆trouvaille** nf (lucky) find.

truand [tryɑ̃] nm crook.

truc [tryk] nm **1** (astuce) trick; (moyen) way; **avoir/trouver le t.** to have/get the knack (**pour faire** of doing). **2** (chose) Fam thing. **◆-age** nm = **truquage**.

truchement [tryʃmɑ̃] nm **par le t. de qn** through (the intermediary of) s.o.

truculent [trykylɑ̃] a (langage, personnage) colourful.

truelle [tryɛl] nf trowel.

truffe [tryf] nf **1** (champignon) truffle. **2** (de chien) nose.

truff/er [tryfe] vt (remplir) to stuff (**de** with). **◆-é** a (pâté etc) Culin with truffles.

truie [trɥi] nf (animal) sow.

truite [trɥit] nf trout.

truqu/er [tryke] vt (photo etc) to fake; (élections, match) to rig, fix. **◆-é** a (photo etc) fake-; (élections, match) rigged, fixed; (scène) Cin trick-. **◆-age** nm Cin (special) effect; (action) faking; rigging.

trust [trœst] nm Com (cartel) trust; (entreprise) corporation.

tsar [dzar] nm tsar, czar.

TSF [teɛsɛf] nf abrév (télégraphie sans fil) wireless, radio.

tsigane [tsigan] a & nmf (Hungarian) gipsy.

TSVP [teɛsvepe] abrév (tournez s'il vous plaît) PTO.

TTC [tetese] abrév (toutes taxes comprises) inclusive of tax.

tu[1] [ty] pron you (familiar form of address).

tu [ty] *voir* **taire.**

tuba [tyba] *nm* **1** *Mus* tuba. **2** *Sp* snorkel.

tube [tyb] *nm* **1** tube; (*de canalisation*) pipe. **2** (*chanson, disque*) *Fam* hit. ◆**tubulaire** *a* tubular.

tuberculeux, -euse [tyberkylø, -øz] *a* tubercular; **être t.** to have tuberculosis *ou* TB. ◆**tuberculose** *nf* tuberculosis, TB.

tue-mouches [tymuʃ] *a inv* **papier t.-mouches** flypaper. ◆**t.-tête (à)** *adv* at the top of one's voice.

tu/er [tɥe] *vt* to kill; (*d'un coup de feu*) to shoot (dead), kill; (*épuiser*) *Fig* to wear out; **— se t.** *vpr* to kill oneself; to shoot oneself; (*dans un accident*) to be killed; **se t. à faire** *Fig* to wear oneself out doing. ◆**—ant** *a* (*fatigant*) exhausting. ◆**tuerie** *nf* slaughter. ◆**tueur, -euse** *nmf* killer.

tuile [tɥil] *nf* **1** tile. **2** (*malchance*) *Fam* (stroke of) bad luck.

tulipe [tylip] *nf* tulip.

tuméfié [tymefje] *a* swollen.

tumeur [tymœr] *nf* tumour, growth.

tumulte [tymylt] *nm* commotion; (*désordre*) turmoil. ◆**tumultueux, -euse** *a* turbulent.

tunique [tynik] *nf* tunic.

Tunisie [tynizi] *nf* Tunisia. ◆**tunisien, -ienne** *a & nmf* Tunisian.

tunnel [tynɛl] *nm* tunnel.

turban [tyrbɑ̃] *nm* turban.

turbine [tyrbin] *nf* turbine.

turbulences [tyrbylɑ̃s] *nfpl* *Phys Av* turbulence.

turbulent [tyrbylɑ̃] *a* (*enfant etc*) boisterous, turbulent.

turfiste [tyrfist] *nmf* racegoer, punter.

Turquie [tyrki] *nf* Turkey. ◆**turc, turque** *a* Turkish; **— *nmf* Turk; — *nm* (*langue*) Turkish.

turquoise [tyrkwaz] *a inv* turquoise.

tuteur, -trice [tytœr, -tris] **1** *nmf Jur* guardian. **2** *nm* (*bâton*) stake, prop. ◆**tutelle** *nf Jur* guardianship; *Fig* protection.

tutoyer [tytwaje] *vt* to address familiarly (using *tu*). ◆**tutoiement** *nm* familiar address, use of *tu*.

tutu [tyty] *nm* ballet skirt, tutu.

tuyau, -x [tɥijo] *nm* **1** pipe; **t. d'arrosage** hose(pipe); **t. de cheminée** flue; **t. d'échappement** *Aut* exhaust (pipe). **2** (*renseignement*) *Fam* tip. ◆**tuyauter** *vt* **t. qn** (*conseiller*) *Fam* to give s.o. a tip. ◆**tuyauterie** *nf* (*tuyaux*) piping.

TVA [tevea] *nf abrév* (*taxe à la valeur ajoutée*) VAT.

tympan [tɛ̃pɑ̃] *nm* eardrum.

type [tip] *nm* (*modèle*) type; (*traits*) features; (*individu*) *Fam* fellow, guy, bloke; **le t. même de** *Fig* the very model of; **— *a inv** (*professeur etc*) typical. ◆**typique** *a* typical (de of). ◆**typiquement** *adv* typically.

typhoïde [tifɔid] *nf Méd* typhoid (fever).

typhon [tifɔ̃] *nm* *Mét* typhoon.

typographe [tipɔgraf] *nmf* typographer. ◆**typographie** *nf* typography, printing. ◆**typographique** *a* typographical, printing-.

tyran [tirɑ̃] *nm* tyrant. ◆**tyrannie** *nf* tyranny. ◆**tyrannique** *a* tyrannical. ◆**tyranniser** *vt* to tyrannize.

tzigane [dzigan] *a & nmf* (Hungarian) gipsy.

U

U, u [y] *nm* U, u.

ulcère [ylser] *nm* ulcer, sore.

ulcérer [ylsere] *vt* (*blesser, irriter*) to embitter.

ultérieur [ylterjœr] *a* later. ◆**—ement** *adv* later.

ultimatum [yltimatɔm] *nm* ultimatum.

ultime [yltim] *a* final, last.

ultra- [yltra] *préf* ultra-. ◆**u.-secret, -ète** *a* (*document*) top-secret.

ultramoderne [yltramɔdɛrn] *a* ultramodern.

ultraviolet, -ette [yltravjɔlɛ, -ɛt] *a* ultraviolet.

un, une [œ̃, yn] **1** *art indéf* a, (*devant voyelle*) an; **une page** a page; **un ange** [œ̃nɑ̃ʒ] an angel. **2** *a* one; **la page un** page one; **un kilo** one kilo; **un type** (*un quelconque*) some *ou* a fellow. **3** *pron & nmf* **l'un** one; **les uns** some; **le numéro un** number one; **j'en ai un** I have one; **l'un d'eux** one of them; **la une** *Journ* page one.

unanime [ynanim] *a* unanimous. ◆**unanimité** *nf* unanimity; **à l'u.** unanimously.

uni [yni] a united; (famille etc) close; (surface) smooth; (couleur, étoffe) plain.

unième [ynjɛm] a (après un numéral) (-)first; trente et u. thirty-first; cent u. hundred and first.

unifier [ynifje] vt to unify. ◆unification nf unification.

uniforme [yniform] 1 a (régulier) uniform. 2 nm (vêtement) uniform. ◆uniformément adv uniformly. ◆uniformiser vt to standardize. ◆uniformité nf uniformity.

unijambiste [yniʒɑ̃bist] a & nmf one-legged (man ou woman).

unilatéral, -aux [ynilateral, -o] a unilateral; (stationnement) on one side of the road only.

union [ynjɔ̃] nf union; (association) association; (entente) unity. ◆unir vt to unite, join (together); u. la force au courage/etc to combine strength with courage/etc; — s'u. vpr to unite; (se marier) to be joined together; (se joindre) to join (together).

unique [ynik] a 1 (fille, fils) only; (espoir, souci etc) only, sole; (prix, salaire, voie) single, one; son seul et u. souci his ou her one and only worry. 2 (incomparable) unique. ◆uniquement adv only, solely.

unisexe [ynisɛks] a inv (vêtements etc) unisex.

unisson (à l') [a(l)ynisɔ̃] adv in unison (de with).

unité [ynite] nf (élément, grandeur) & Mil unit; (cohésion, harmonie) unity. ◆unitaire a (prix) per unit.

univers [yniver] nm universe.

universel, -elle [yniversel] a universal. ◆universellement adv universally. ◆universalité nf universality.

université [yniversite] nf university; à l'u. at university. ◆universitaire a university-; — nmf academic.

uranium [yranjɔm] nm uranium.

urbain [yrbɛ̃] a urban, town-, city-. ◆urbaniser vt to urbanize, build up. ◆urbanisme nm town planning, Am city planning. ◆urbaniste nmf town planner, Am city planner.

urgent [yrʒɑ̃] a urgent, pressing. ◆urgence nf (cas) emergency; (de décision, tâche etc) urgency; d'u. (mesures etc) emergency-; état d'u. Pol state of emergency; faire qch d'u. to do sth urgently.

urine [yrin] nf urine. ◆uriner vi to urinate. ◆urinoir nm (public) urinal.

urne [yrn] nf 1 (électorale) ballot box; aller aux urnes to go to the polls. 2 (vase) urn.

URSS [yrs] nf abrév (Union des Républiques Socialistes Soviétiques) USSR.

usage [yzaʒ] nm use; Ling usage; (habitude) custom; faire u. de to make use of; faire de l'u. (vêtement etc) to wear well; d'u. (habituel) customary; à l'u. de for the use of); hors d'u. no longer usable. ◆usagé a worn; (d'occasion) used. ◆usager nm user. ◆us/er vt (vêtement, personne) to wear out; (consommer) to use (up); (santé) to ruin; — vi u. de to use; — s'u. vpr (tissu, machine) to wear out; (personne) to wear oneself out. ◆-é a (tissu etc) worn (out); (sujet etc) well-worn; (personne) worn out.

usine [yzin] nf factory; (à gaz, de métallurgie) works.

usiner [yzine] vt (pièce) Tech to machine.

usité [yzite] a commonly used.

ustensile [ystɑ̃sil] nm utensil.

usuel, -elle [yzɥɛl] a everyday, ordinary; — nmpl (livres) reference books.

usure [yzyr] nf (détérioration) wear (and tear); avoir qn à l'u. Fig to wear s.o. down (in the end).

usurier, -ière [yzyrje, -jɛr] nmf usurer.

usurper [yzyrpe] vt to usurp.

utérus [yterys] nm Anat womb, uterus.

utile [ytil] a useful (à to). ◆utilement adv usefully.

utiliser [ytilize] vt to use, utilize. ◆utilisable a usable. ◆utilisateur, -trice nmf user. ◆utilisation nf use. ◆utilité nf use(fulness); d'une grande u. very useful.

utilitaire [ytiliter] a utilitarian; (véhicule) utility-.

utopie [ytɔpi] nf (idéal) utopia; (projet, idée) utopian plan ou idea. ◆utopique a utopian.

V

V, v [ve] nm V, v.

va [va] voir aller 1.

vacances [vakɑ̃s] nfpl holiday(s), Am vacation; en v. on holiday, Am on vacation; prendre ses v. to take one's holiday(s) ou Am vacation; les grandes v. the summer holidays *ou Am* vacation. ◆**vacancier, -lère** *nmf* holidaymaker, *Am* vacationer.

vacant [vakã] *a* vacant. ◆**vacance** *nf* (*poste*) vacancy.

vacarme [vakarm] *nm* din, uproar.

vaccin [vaksɛ̃] *nm* vaccine; **faire un v. à** to vaccinate. ◆**vaccination** *nf* vaccination. ◆**vacciner** *vt* to vaccinate.

vache [vaʃ] **1** *nf* cow; **v. laitière** dairy cow. **2** *nf* (*peau de*) **v.** (*personne*) *Fam* swine; — *a* (*méchant*) *Fam* nasty. ◆**vachement** *adv Fam* (*très*) damned; (*beaucoup*) a hell of a lot. ◆**vacherie** *nf Fam* (*action, parole*) nasty thing; (*caractère*) nastiness.

vacill/er [vasije] *vi* to sway, wobble; (*flamme, lumière*) to flicker; (*jugement, mémoire etc*) to falter, waver. ◆**—ant** *a* (*démarche, mémoire*) shaky; (*lumière etc*) flickering.

vadrouille [vadruj] *nf* **en v.** *Fam* roaming *ou* wandering about. ◆**vadrouiller** *vi Fam* to roam *ou* wander about.

va-et-vient [vaevjɛ̃] *nm inv* (*mouvement*) movement to and fro; (*de personnes*) comings and goings.

vagabond, -onde [vagabɔ̃, -ɔ̃d] *a* wandering; — *nmf* (*clochard*) vagrant, tramp. ◆**vagabond/er** *vi* to roam *ou* wander about; (*pensée*) to wander. ◆**—age** *nm* wandering; *Jur* vagrancy.

vagin [vaʒɛ̃] *nm* vagina.

vagir [vaʒir] *vi* (*bébé*) to cry, wail.

vague [vag] **1** *a* vague; (*regard*) vacant; (*souvenir*) dim, vague; — *nm* vagueness; **regarder dans le v.** to gaze into space, gaze vacantly; **rester dans le v.** (*être évasif*) to keep it vague. **2** *nf* (*de mer*) & *Fig* wave; **v. de chaleur** heat wave; **v. de froid** cold snap *ou* spell; **v. de fond** (*dans l'opinion*) *Fig* tidal wave. ◆**vaguement** *adv* vaguely.

vaillant [vajã] *a* brave, valiant; (*vigoureux*) healthy. ◆**vaillamment** *adv* bravely, valiantly. ◆**vaillance** *nf* bravery.

vain [vɛ̃] *a* **1** (*futile*) vain, futile; (*promesse*) empty; **en v.** in vain, vainly. **2** (*vaniteux*) vain. ◆**vainement** *adv* in vain, vainly.

vainc/re [vɛ̃kr] *vt* to defeat, beat; (*surmonter*) to overcome. ◆**—u, -ue** *nmf* defeated man *ou* woman; *Sp* loser. ◆**vainqueur** *nm* victor; *Sp* winner; — *am* victorious.

vaisseau, -x [veso] *nm* **1** *Anat Bot* vessel. **2** (*bateau*) ship, vessel; **v. spatial** spaceship.

vaisselle [vesɛl] *nf* crockery; (*à laver*) washing-up; **faire la v.** to do the washing-up, do *ou* wash the dishes.

val, *pl* **vals** *ou* **vaux** [val, vo] *nm* valley.

valable [valabl] *a* (*billet, motif etc*) valid; (*remarquable, rentable*) *Fam* worthwhile.

valet [valɛ] *nm* **1** *Cartes* jack. **2** **v.** (*de chambre*) valet, manservant; **v. de ferme** farmhand.

valeur [valœr] *nf* value; (*mérite*) worth; (*poids*) importance, weight; *pl* (*titres*) *Com* stocks and shares; **la v. de** (*quantité*) the equivalent of; **avoir de la v.** to be valuable; **mettre en v.** (*faire ressortir*) to highlight; **de v.** (*personne*) of merit, able; **objets de v.** valuables.

valide [valid] *a* **1** (*personne*) fit, ablebodied; (*population*) able-bodied. **2** (*billet etc*) valid. ◆**valider** *vt* to validate. ◆**validité** *nf* validity.

valise [valiz] *nf* (suit)case; **v. diplomatique** diplomatic bag *ou Am* pouch; **faire ses valises** to pack (one's bags).

vallée [vale] *nf* valley. ◆**vallon** *nm* (small) valley ◆**vallonné** *a* (*région etc*) undulating.

valoir* [valwar] *vi* to be worth; (*s'appliquer*) to apply (**pour** to); **v. mille francs/cher/etc** to be worth a thousand francs/a lot/*etc*; **un vélo vaut bien une auto** a bicycle is as good as a car; **il vaut mieux rester** it's better to stay; **il vaut mieux que j'attende** I'd better wait; **ça ne vaut rien** it's worthless, it's no good; **ça vaut le coup** *Fam* **ou la peine** it's worthwhile (**de faire** doing); **faire v.** (*faire ressortir*) to highlight, set off; (*argument*) to put forward; (*droit*) to assert; — *vt* **v. qch à qn** to bring *ou* get s.o. sth; — **se v.** *vpr* (*objets, personnes*) to be as good as each other; **ça se vaut** *Fam* it's all the same.

valse [vals] *nf* waltz. ◆**valser** *vi* to waltz.

valve [valv] *nf* (*clapet*) valve. ◆**valvule** *nf* (*du cœur*) valve.

vampire [vɑ̃pir] *nm* vampire.

vandale [vɑ̃dal] *nmf* vandal. ◆**vandalisme** *nm* vandalism.

vanille [vanij] *nf* vanilla; **glace/etc à la v.** vanilla ice cream/*etc*. ◆**vanillé** *a* vanilla-flavoured.

vanité [vanite] *nf* vanity. ◆**vaniteux, -euse** *a* vain, conceited.

vanne [van] *nf* **1** (*d'écluse*) sluice (gate), floodgate. **2** (*remarque*) *Fam* dig, jibe.

vanné [vane] *a* (*fatigué*) *Fam* dead beat.

vannerie [vanri] *nf* (*fabrication, objets*) basketwork, basketry.

vantail, -aux [vɑ̃taj, -o] *nm* (*de porte*) leaf.

vanter [vɑ̃te] *vt* to praise; — **se v.** *vpr* to boast, brag (**de** about, of). ◆**vantard, -arde** *a* boastful; — *nmf* boaster, braggart.

◆**vantardise** nf boastfulness; (*propos*) boast.

va-nu-pieds [vanypje] nmf inv tramp, beggar.

vapeur [vapœr] nf (*brume, émanation*) vapour; v. (**d'eau**) steam; **cuire à la v.** to steam; **bateau à v.** steamship. ◆**vaporeux, -euse** a hazy, misty; (*tissu*) translucent, diaphanous.

vaporiser [vapɔrize] vt to spray. ◆**vaporisateur** nm (*appareil*) spray.

vaquer [vake] vi **v. à** to attend to.

varappe [varap] nf rock-climbing.

varech [varɛk] nm wrack, seaweed.

vareuse [varøz] nf (*d'uniforme*) tunic.

varicelle [varisɛl] nf chicken pox.

varices [varis] nfpl varicose veins.

vari/er [varje] vti to vary (**de** from). ◆**-é** a (*diversifié*) varied; (*divers*) various. ◆**-able** a variable; (*humeur, temps*) changeable. ◆**variante** nf variant. ◆**variation** nf variation. ◆**variété** nf variety; **spectacle de variétés** Th variety show.

variole [varjɔl] nf smallpox.

vas [va] *voir* **aller 1**.

vase [vaz] **1** nm vase. **2** nf (*boue*) silt, mud.

vaseline [vazlin] nf Vaseline®.

vaseux, -euse [vazø, -øz] a **1** (*boueux*) silty, muddy. **2** (*fatigué*) off colour. **3** (*idées etc*) woolly, hazy.

vasistas [vazistas] nm (*dans une porte ou une fenêtre*) hinged panel.

vaste [vast] a vast, huge.

Vatican [vatikā] nm Vatican.

va-tout [vatu] nm inv **jouer son v.-tout** to stake one's all.

vaudeville [vodvil] nm Th light comedy.

vau-l'eau (à) [avolo] adv **aller à v.-l'eau** to go to rack and ruin.

vaurien, -ienne [vorjɛ̃, -jɛn] nmf good-for-nothing.

vautour [votur] nm vulture.

vautrer (se) [savotre] vpr to sprawl; **se v. dans** (*boue, vice*) to wallow in.

va-vite (à la) [alavavit] adv Fam in a hurry.

veau, -x [vo] nm (*animal*) calf; (*viande*) veal; (*cuir*) calf(skin).

vécu [veky] *voir* **vivre**; – a (*histoire etc*) real(-life), true.

vedette [vədɛt] nf **1** Cin Th star; **avoir la v.** (*artiste*) to head the bill; **en v.** (*personne*) in the limelight; (*objet*) in a prominent position. **2** (*canot*) motor boat, launch.

végétal, -aux [veʒetal, -o] a (*huile, règne*) vegetable-; – nm plant. ◆**végétarien,**

-ienne a & nmf vegetarian. ◆**végétation 1** nf vegetation. **2** nfpl Méd adenoids.

végéter [veʒete] vi (*personne*) Péj to vegetate.

véhément [veemā] a vehement. ◆**véhémence** nf vehemence.

véhicule [veikyl] nm vehicle. ◆**véhiculer** vt to convey.

veille [vɛj] nf **1** la v. (**de**) (*jour précédent*) the day before; **à la v. de** (*événement*) on the eve of; **la v. de Noël** Christmas Eve. **2** (*état*) wakefulness; pl vigils.

veill/er [veje] vi to stay on ou awake; (*sentinelle etc*) to be on watch; **v. à qch** to attend to sth, see to sth; **v. à ce que** (+ *sub*) to make sure that; **v. sur qn** to watch over s.o.; – vt (*malade*) to sit with, watch over. ◆**-ée** nf (*soirée*) evening; (*réunion*) evening get-together; (*mortuaire*) vigil. ◆**-eur** nm **v. de nuit** night watchman. ◆**-euse** nf (*lampe*) night light; (*de voiture*) sidelight; (*de réchaud*) pilot light.

veine [vɛn] nf **1** Anat Bot Géol vein. **2** (*chance*) Fam luck; **avoir de la v.** to be lucky; **une v.** a piece ou stroke of luck. ◆**veinard, -arde** nmf Fam lucky devil; – a Fam lucky.

vêler [vele] vi (*vache*) to calve.

vélin [velɛ̃] nm (*papier, peau*) vellum.

velléité [veleite] nf vague desire.

vélo [velo] nm bike, bicycle; (*activité*) cycling; **faire du v.** to cycle, go cycling. ◆**vélodrome** nm Sp velodrome, cycle track. ◆**vélomoteur** nm (lightweight) motorcycle.

velours [v(ə)lur] nm velvet; **v. côtelé** corduroy, cord. ◆**velouté** a soft, velvety; (*au goût*) mellow, smooth; – nm smoothness; **v. d'asperges/etc** (*potage*) cream of asparagus/etc soup.

velu [vəly] a hairy.

venaison [vənɛzɔ̃] nf venison.

vénal, -aux [venal, -o] a mercenary, venal.

vendange(s) [vādāʒ] nf(pl) grape harvest, vintage. ◆**vendanger** vi to pick the grapes. ◆**vendangeur, -euse** nmf grape-picker.

vendetta [vādeta] nf vendetta.

vend/re [vādr] vt to sell; **v. qch à qn** to sell s.o. sth, sell sth to s.o.; **v. qn** (*trahir*) to sell s.o. out; **à v.** (*maison etc*) for sale; – **se v.** vpr to be sold; **ça se vend bien** it sells well. ◆**-eur, -euse** nmf (*de magasin*) sales ou shop assistant, Am sales clerk; (*marchand*) salesman, saleswoman; Jur vendor, seller.

vendredi [vādrədi] nm Friday; **V. saint** Good Friday.

vénéneux, -euse [venenø, -øz] *a* poisonous.

vénérable [venerabl] *a* venerable. ◆**vénérer** *vt* to venerate.

vénérien, -ienne [venerjɛ̃, -jɛn] *a Méd* venereal.

venger [vɑ̃ʒe] *vt* to avenge; **— se v.** *vpr* to take (one's) revenge, avenge oneself (**de qn** on s.o., **de qch** for sth). ◆**vengeance** *nf* revenge, vengeance. ◆**vengeur, -eresse** *a* vengeful; *— nmf* avenger.

venin [vənɛ̃] *nm* (*substance*) & *Fig* venom. ◆**venimeux, -euse** *a* poisonous, venomous; (*haineux*) *Fig* venomous.

venir* [v(ə)nir] *vi* (*aux* **être**) to come (**de** from); **v. faire** to come to do; **viens me voir** come and *ou* to see me; **je viens/venais d'arriver** I've/I'd just arrived; **en v. à** (*conclusion etc*) to come to; **où veux-tu en v.?** what are you driving *ou* getting at?; **d'où vient que ...?** how is it that ...?; **s'il venait à faire** (*éventualité*) if he happened to do; **les jours/etc qui viennent** the coming days/etc; **une idée m'est venue** an idea occurred to me; **faire v.** to send for, get.

vent [vɑ̃] *nm* wind; **il fait** *ou* **il y a du v.** it's windy; **coup de v.** gust of wind; **avoir v. de** (*connaissance de*) to get wind of; **dans le v.** (*à la mode*) *Fam* trendy, with it.

vente [vɑ̃t] *nf* sale; **v. (aux enchères)** auction (sale); **v. de charité** bazaar, charity sale; **en v.** (*disponible*) on sale; **point de v.** sales *ou* retail outlet; **prix de v.** selling price; **salle des ventes** auction room.

ventilateur [vɑ̃tilatœr] *nm* (*électrique*) & *Aut* fan; (*dans un mur*) ventilator. ◆**ventilation** *nf* ventilation. ◆**ventiler** *vt* to ventilate.

ventouse [vɑ̃tuz] *nf* (*pour fixer*) suction grip; **à v.** (*crochet, fléchette etc*) suction-.

ventre [vɑ̃tr] *nm* belly, stomach; (*utérus*) womb; (*de cruche etc*) bulge; **avoir/prendre du v.** to have/get a paunch; **à plat v.** flat on one's face. ◆**ventru** *a* (*personne*) pot-bellied; (*objet*) bulging.

ventriloque [vɑ̃trilɔk] *nmf* ventriloquist.

venu, -ue[1] [v(ə)ny] *voir* **venir**; *— nmf* **nouveau v., nouvelle venue** newcomer; **premier v.** anyone; *— a* **bien v.** (*à propos*) timely; **mal v.** untimely; **être bien/mal v. de faire** to have good grounds/no grounds for doing.

venue[2] [v(ə)ny] *nf* (*arrivée*) coming.

vêpres [vɛpr] *nfpl Rel* vespers.

ver [vɛr] *nm* worm; (*larve*) grub; (*de fruits, fromage etc*) maggot; **v. luisant** glow-worm;

v. à soie silkworm; **v. solitaire** tapeworm; **v. de terre** earthworm.

véracité [verasite] *nf* truthfulness, veracity.

véranda [verɑ̃da] *nf* veranda(h).

verbe [vɛrb] *nm Gram* verb. ◆**verbal, -aux** *a* (*promesse, expression etc*) verbal.

verbeux, -euse [vɛrbø, -øz] *a* verbose. ◆**verbiage** *nm* verbiage.

verdâtre [vɛrdɑtr] *a* greenish.

verdeur [vɛrdœr] *nf* (*de fruit, vin*) tartness; (*de vieillard*) sprightliness; (*de langage*) crudeness.

verdict [vɛrdikt] *nm* verdict.

verdir [vɛrdir] *vti* to turn green. ◆**verdoyant** *a* green, verdant. ◆**verdure** *nf* (*arbres etc*) greenery.

véreux, -euse [verø, -øz] *a* (*fruit etc*) wormy, maggoty; (*malhonnête*) *Fig* dubious, shady.

verge [vɛrʒ] *nf Anat* penis.

verger [vɛrʒe] *nm* orchard.

vergetures [vɛrʒətyr] *nfpl* stretch marks.

verglas [vɛrgla] *nm* (black) ice, *Am* sleet. ◆**verglacé** *a* (*route*) icy.

vergogne (sans) [sɑ̃vɛrgɔɲ] *a* shameless; *— adv* shamelessly.

véridique [veridik] *a* truthful.

vérifier [verifje] *vt* to check, verify; (*confirmer*) to confirm; (*comptes*) to audit. ◆**vérifiable** *a* verifiable. ◆**vérification** *nf* verification; confirmation; audit(ing).

vérité [verite] *nf* truth; (*de personnage, tableau etc*) trueness to life; (*sincérité*) sincerity; **en v.** in fact. ◆**véritable** *a* true, real; (*non imité*) real, genuine; (*exactement nommé*) veritable, real. ◆**véritablement** *adv* really.

vermeil, -eille [vɛrmɛj] *a* bright red, vermilion.

vermicelle(s) [vɛrmisel] *nm*(*pl*) *Culin* vermicelli.

vermine [vɛrmin] *nf* (*insectes, racaille*) vermine.

vermoulu [vɛrmuly] *a* worm-eaten.

vermouth [vɛrmut] *nm* vermouth.

verni [vɛrni] *a* (*chanceux*) *Fam* lucky.

vernir [vɛrnir] *vt* to varnish; (*poterie*) to glaze. ◆**vernis** [vɛrni] *nm* varnish; glaze; (*apparence*) *Fig* veneer; **v. à ongles** nail polish *ou* varnish. ◆**vernissage** *nm* (*d'exposition de peinture*) first day. ◆**vernisser** *vt* (*poterie*) to glaze.

verra, verrait [vɛra, vɛrɛ] *voir* **voir**.

verre [vɛr] *nm* (*substance, récipient*) glass; **boire** *ou* **prendre un v.** to have a drink; **v. à bière/à vin** beer/wine glass; **v. de contact**

contact lens. ◆**verrerie** nf (objets) glass-ware. ◆**verrière** nf (toit) glass roof.

verrou [vɛru] nm bolt; **fermer au v.** to bolt; **sous les verrous** behind bars. ◆**verrouiller** vt to bolt.

verrue [vɛry] nf wart.

vers[1] [vɛr] prép (direction) towards, toward; (approximation) around, about.

vers[2] [vɛr] nm (d'un poème) line; pl (poésie) verse.

versant [vɛrsã] nm slope, side.

versatile [vɛrsatil] a fickle, volatile.

verse (à) [avɛrs] adv in torrents; **pleuvoir à v.** to pour (down).

versé [vɛrse] a (pas mûr) unripe; **en v. dans** (well-)versed in.

Verseau [vɛrso] nm **le V.** (signe) Aquarius.

vers/er [vɛrse] **1** vt to pour; (larmes, sang) to shed. **2** vt (argent) to pay. **3** vti (basculer) to overturn. ◆**—ement** nm payment. ◆**—eur** a bec v. spout.

verset [vɛrsɛ] nm Rel verse.

version [vɛrsjɔ̃] nf version; (traduction) Scol translation, unseen.

verso [vɛrso] nm back (of the page); **'voir au v.'** 'see overleaf'.

vert [vɛr] a green; (pas mûr) unripe; (vin) young; (vieillard) Fig sprightly; — nm green.

vert-de-gris [vɛrdəgri] nm inv verdigris.

vertèbre [vɛrtɛbr] nf vertebra.

vertement [vɛrtəmã] adv (réprimander etc) sharply.

vertical, -ale, -aux [vɛrtikal, -o] a & nf vertical; **à la verticale** vertically. ◆**verticalement** adv vertically.

vertige [vɛrtiʒ] nm (feeling of) dizziness ou giddiness; (peur de tomber dans le vide) vertigo; pl dizzy spells; **avoir le v.** to feel dizzy ou giddy. ◆**vertigineux, -euse** a (hauteur) giddy, dizzy; (très grand) Fig staggering.

vertu [vɛrty] nf virtue; **en v. de** in accordance with. ◆**vertueux, -euse** a virtuous.

verve [vɛrv] nf (d'orateur etc) brilliance.

verveine [vɛrvɛn] nf (plante) verbena.

vésicule [vezikyl] nf v. biliaire gall bladder.

vessie [vesi] nf bladder.

veste [vɛst] nf jacket, coat.

vestiaire [vɛstjɛr] nm cloakroom, Am locker room; (meuble métallique) locker.

vestibule [vɛstibyl] nm (entrance) hall.

vestiges [vɛstiʒ] nmpl (restes, ruines) remains; (traces) traces, vestiges.

vestimentaire [vɛstimãter] a (dépense) clothing-; (détail) of dress.

veston [vɛstɔ̃] nm (suit) jacket.

vêtement [vɛtmã] nm garment, article of

clothing; pl clothes; **du v.** (industrie, commerce) clothing-; **vêtements de sport** sportswear.

vétéran [veterã] nm veteran.

vétérinaire [veterinɛr] a veterinary; — nmf vet, veterinary surgeon, Am veterinarian.

vétille [vetij] nf trifle, triviality.

vêt/ir* [vetir] vt, — **se v.** vpr to dress. ◆**—u** a dressed (**de** in).

veto [veto] nm inv veto; **mettre ou opposer son v. à** to veto.

vétuste [vetyst] a dilapidated.

veuf, veuve [vœf, vœv] a widowed; — nm widower; — nf widow.

veuille [vœj] voir vouloir.

veule [vøl] a feeble. ◆**veulerie** nf feebleness.

veut, veux [vø] voir vouloir.

vex/er [vɛkse] vt to upset, hurt; — **se v.** vpr to be ou get upset (**de** at). ◆**—ant** a hurtful; (contrariant) annoying. ◆**vexation** nf humiliation.

viable [vjabl] a (enfant, entreprise etc) viable. ◆**viabilité** nf viability.

viaduc [vjadyk] nm viaduct.

viager, -ère [vjaʒe, -ɛr] a **rente viagère** life annuity; — nm life annuity.

viande [vjãd] nf meat.

vibrer [vibre] vi to vibrate; (être ému) to thrill (**de** with); **faire v.** (auditoire etc) to thrill. ◆**vibrant** a (émouvant) emotional; (voix, son) resonant, vibrant. ◆**vibration** nf vibration. ◆**vibromasseur** nm (appareil) vibrator.

vicaire [vikɛr] nm curate.

vice [vis] nm vice; (défectuosité) defect.

vice- [vis] préf vice-.

vice versa [vis(e)vɛrsa] adv vice versa.

vicier [visje] vt to taint, pollute.

vicieux, -euse [visjø, -øz] **1** a depraved; — nmf pervert. **2** a **cercle v.** vicious circle.

vicinal, -aux [visinal, -o] a **chemin v.** by-road, minor road.

vicissitudes [visisityd] nfpl vicissitudes.

vicomte [vikɔ̃t] nm viscount. ◆**vicomtesse** nf viscountess.

victime [viktim] nf victim; (d'un accident) casualty; **être v. de** to be the victim of.

victoire [viktwar] nf victory; Sp win. ◆**victorieux, -euse** a victorious; (équipe) winning.

victuailles [viktɥaj] nfpl provisions.

vidange [vidãʒ] nf emptying, draining; Aut oil change; (dispositif) waste outlet. ◆**vidanger** vt to empty, drain.

vide [vid] a empty; — nm emptiness, void; (absence d'air) vacuum; (gouffre etc) drop;

(*trou, manque*) gap; **regarder dans le v.** to stare into space; **emballé sous v.** vacuum-packed; **à v.** empty.

vidéo [video] *a inv* video. ◆**vidéocassette** *nf* video (cassette).

vide-ordures [vidɔrdyr] *nm inv* (refuse) chute. ◆**vide-poches** *nm inv* Aut glove compartment.

vid/er [vide] *vt* to empty; (*lieu*) to vacate; (*poisson, volaille*) Culin to gut; (*querelle*) to settle; **v. qn** Fam (*chasser*) to throw s.o. out; (*épuiser*) to tire s.o. out; **— se v.** *vpr* to empty. ◆**—é** *a* (*fatigué*) Fam exhausted. ◆**—eur** *nm* (*de boîte de nuit*) bouncer.

vie [vi] *nf* life; (*durée*) lifetime; **coût de la v.** cost of living; **gagner sa v.** to earn one's living *ou* livelihood; **en v.** living; **à v., pour la v.** for life; **donner la v. à** to give birth to; **avoir la v. dure** (*préjugés etc*) to die hard; **jamais de la v.!** not on your life!, never!

vieill/ir [vjejir] *vi* to grow old; (*changer*) to age; (*théorie, mot*) to become old-fashioned; **— vt v. qn** (*vêtement etc*) to age s.o. ◆**—i** *a* (*démodé*) Fam old-fashioned. ◆**—issant** *a* ageing. ◆**—issement** *nm* ageing.

viens, vient [vjɛ̃] *voir* venir.

vierge [vjɛrʒ] *nf* virgin; **la V.** (*signe*) Virgo; **— *a* (*femme, neige etc*) virgin; (*feuille de papier, film*) blank; **être v.** (*femme, homme*) to be a virgin.

Viêt-nam [vjetnam] *nm* Vietnam. ◆**vietnamien, -ienne** *a & nmf* Vietnamese.

vieux (*or* **vieil** *before vowel or mute h*), **vieille**, *pl* **vieux, vieilles** (*vjø*) *a* old; **être v. jeu** (*a inv*) to be old-fashioned; **v. garçon** bachelor; **vieille fille** Péj old maid; **— *nm* old man; *pl* old people; **mon v.** (*en cher*) Fam old boy, old man; **— *nf* old woman; **ma vieille** (*ma chère*) Fam old girl. ◆**vieillard** *nm* old man; *pl* old people. ◆**vieillerie** *nf* (*objet*) old thing; (*idée*) old idea. ◆**vieillesse** *nf* old age. ◆**vieillot** *a* antiquated.

vif, vive [vif, viv] *a* (*enfant, mouvement*) lively; (*alerte*) quick, sharp; (*intelligence, intérêt, vent*) keen; (*couleur, lumière*) bright; (*froid*) biting; (*pas*) quick, brisk; (*impression, imagination, style*) vivid; (*parole*) sharp; (*regret, satisfaction, succès etc*) great; (*coléreux*) quick-tempered; **brûler/enterrer qn v.** to burn/bury s.o. alive; **— *nm* **le v. du sujet** the heart of the matter; **à v.** (*plaie*) open; **piqué au v.** (*vexé*) cut to the quick.

vigie [viʒi] *nf* (*matelot*) lookout; (*poste*) lookout post.

vigilant [viʒilɑ̃] *a* vigilant. ◆**vigilance** *nf* vigilance.

vigile [viʒil] *nm* (*gardien*) watchman; (*de nuit*) night watchman.

vigne [viɲ] *nf* (*plante*) vine; (*plantation*) vineyard. ◆**vigneron, -onne** *nmf* wine grower. ◆**vignoble** *nm* vineyard; (*région*) vineyards.

vignette [viɲɛt] *nf* Aut road tax sticker; (*de médicament*) price label (*for reimbursement by Social Security*).

vigueur [vigœr] *nf* vigour; **entrer/être en v.** (*loi*) to come into/be in force. ◆**vigoureux, -euse** *a* (*personne, style etc*) vigorous; (*bras*) sturdy.

vilain [vilɛ̃] *a* (*laid*) ugly; (*mauvais*) nasty; (*enfant*) naughty.

villa [villa] *nf* (detached) house.

village [vilaʒ] *nm* village. ◆**villageois, -oise** *a* village-; **— *nmf* villager.

ville [vil] *nf* town; (*grande*) city; **aller/être en v.** to go into/be in town; **v. d'eaux** spa (town).

villégiature [vileʒjatyr] *nf* **lieu de v.** (holiday) resort.

vin [vɛ̃] *nm* wine; **v. ordinaire** *ou* **de table** table wine; **v. d'honneur** reception (*in honour of s.o.*). ◆**vinicole** *a* (*région*) wine-growing; (*industrie*) wine-.

vinaigre [vinɛgr] *nm* vinegar. ◆**vinaigré** *a* seasoned with vinegar. ◆**vinaigrette** *nf* (*sauce*) vinaigrette, French dressing, Am Italian dressing.

vindicatif, -ive [vɛ̃dikatif, -iv] *a* vindictive.

vingt [vɛ̃] ([vɛ̃t] *before vowel or mute h and in numbers 22–29*) *a & nm* twenty; **v. et un** twenty-one. ◆**vingtaine** *nf* **une v. (de)** (*nombre*) about twenty; **avoir la v.** (*âge*) to be about twenty. ◆**vingtième** *a & nmf* twentieth.

vinyle [vinil] *nm* vinyl.

viol [vjɔl] *nm* rape; (*de loi, lieu*) violation. ◆**violation** *nf* violation. ◆**violenter** *vt* to rape. ◆**violer** *vt* (*femme*) to rape; (*loi, lieu*) to violate. ◆**violeur** *nm* rapist.

violent [vjɔlɑ̃] *a* violent; (*remède*) drastic. ◆**violemment** [-amɑ̃] *adv* violently. ◆**violence** *nf* violence; (*acte*) act of violence.

violet, -ette [vjɔlɛ, -ɛt] **1** *a & nm* (*couleur*) purple, violet. **2** *nf* (*fleur*) violet. ◆**violacé** *a* purplish.

violon [vjɔlɔ̃] *nm* violin. ◆**violoncelle** *nm* cello. ◆**violoncelliste** *nmf* cellist. ◆**violoniste** *nmf* violinist.

vipère [viper] *nf* viper, adder.

virage [viraʒ] *nm* (*de route*) bend; (*de véhicule*) turn; (*revirement*) Fig change of course. ◆**vir/er 1** vi to turn, veer; (sur soi) to turn round; **v. au bleu**/etc to turn blue/etc. **2** vt (expulser) Fam to throw out. **3** vt (somme) Fin to transfer (à to). ◆**-ement** nm Fin (bank ou credit) transfer.

virée [vire] nf Fam trip, outing.

virevolter [virvɔlte] vi to spin round.

virginité [virʒinite] nf virginity.

virgule [virgyl] nf Gram comma; Math (decimal) point; **2 v. 5** 2 point 5.

viril, -e [viril] a virile, manly; (attribut, force) male. ◆**virilité** nf virility, manliness.

virtuel, -elle [virtɥɛl] a potential.

virtuose [virtɥoz] nmf virtuoso. ◆**virtuosité** nf virtuosity.

virulent, -e [virylɑ̃] a virulent. ◆**virulence** nf virulence.

virus [virys] nm virus.

vis[1] [vi] voir **vivre, voir**.

vis[2] [vis] nf screw.

visa [viza] nm (timbre) stamp, stamped signature; (de passeport) visa; **v. de censure** (d'un film) certificate.

visage [vizaʒ] nm face.

vis-à-vis [vizavi] prép **v.-à-vis de** opposite; (à l'égard de) with respect to; (envers) towards; (comparé à) compared to; – nm inv (personne) person opposite; (bois, maison etc) opposite view.

viscères [viser] nmpl intestines. ◆**viscéral, -aux** a (haine etc) Fig deeply felt.

viscosité [viskozite] nf viscosity.

viser [vize] **1** vi to aim (à at); **v. à faire** to aim to do; – vt (cible) to aim at; (concerner) to be aimed at. **2** vt (passeport, document) to stamp. ◆**visées** nfpl (desseins) Fig aims; **avoir des visées sur** to have designs on. ◆**viseur** nm Phot viewfinder; (d'arme) sight.

visible [vizibl] a visible. ◆**visiblement** adv visibly. ◆**visibilité** nf visibility.

visière [vizjer] nf (de casquette) peak; (en plastique etc) eyeshade; (de casque) visor.

vision [vizjɔ̃] nf (conception, image) vision; (sens) (eye)sight, vision; **avoir des visions** Fam to be seeing things. ◆**visionnaire** a & nmf visionary. ◆**visionner** vt Cin to view. ◆**visionneuse** nf (pour diapositives) viewer.

visite [vizit] nf visit; (personne) visitor; (examen) inspection; **rendre v. à, faire une v. à** to visit; **v. (à domicile)** Méd call, visit; **v. (médicale)** medical examination; **v. guidée** guided tour; **de v.** (carte, heures) visiting-. ◆**visiter** vt to visit; (examiner) to inspect. ◆**visiteur, -euse** nmf visitor.

vison [vizɔ̃] nm mink.

visqueux, -euse [viskø, -øz] a viscous; (surface) sticky; (répugnant) Fig slimy.

visser [vise] vt to screw on.

visuel, -elle [vizɥɛl] a visual.

vit [vi] voir **vivre, voir**.

vital, -aux [vital, -o] a vital. ◆**vitalité** nf vitality.

vitamine [vitamin] nf vitamin. ◆**vitaminé** a (biscuits etc) vitamin-enriched.

vite [vit] adv quickly, fast; (tôt) soon; **v.!** quick(ly)! ◆**vitesse** nf speed; (régime) Aut gear; **boîte de vitesses** gearbox; **à toute v.** at top ou full speed; **v. de pointe** top speed; **en v.** quickly.

viticole [vitikɔl] a (région) wine-growing; (industrie) wine-. ◆**viticulteur** nm wine grower. ◆**viticulture** nf wine growing.

vitre [vitr] nf (window)pane; (de véhicule) window. ◆**vitrage** nm (vitres) windows. ◆**vitrail, -aux** nm stained-glass window. ◆**vitré** a glass-, glazed. ◆**vitreux, -euse** a (regard, yeux) Fig glassy. ◆**vitrier** nm glazier.

vitrine [vitrin] nf (de magasin) (shop) window; (meuble) showcase, display cabinet.

vitriol [vitrijɔl] nm Ch & Fig vitriol.

vivable [vivabl] a (personne) easy to live with; (endroit) fit to live in.

vivace [vivas] a (plante) perennial; (haine) Fig inveterate.

vivacité [vivasite] nf liveliness; (de l'air, d'émotion) keenness; (agilité) quickness; (de couleur, d'impression, de style) vividness; (emportement) petulance; **v. d'esprit** quick-wittedness.

vivant, -e [vivɑ̃] a (en vie) alive, living; (être, matière, preuve) living; (conversation, enfant, récit, rue) lively; **langue vivante** modern language; – nm **de son v.** in one's lifetime; **bon v.** jovial fellow; **les vivants** the living.

vivats [viva] nmpl cheers.

vive[1] [viv] voir **vif**.

vive[2] [viv] int **v. le roi**/etc! long live the king!/etc!; **v. les vacances!** hurray for the holidays!

vivement [vivmɑ̃] adv quickly, briskly; (répliquer) sharply; (sentir) keenly; (regretter) deeply; **v. demain!** roll on tomorrow!, I can hardly wait for tomorrow!; **v. que** (+ sub) I'll be glad when.

vivier [vivje] nm fish pond.

vivifier [vivifje] vt to invigorate.

vivisection [vivisɛksjɔ̃] nf vivisection.

vivre* [vivr] **1** vi to live; **elle vit encore** she's still alive ou living; **faire v.** (famille etc) to support; **v. vieux** to live to be old; **difficile/facile à v.** hard/easy to get on with; **manière de v.** way of life; **v. de** (*fruits etc*) to live on; (*travail etc*) to live by; **avoir de quoi v.** to have enough to live on; **vivent les vacances!** hurray for the holidays!; — *vt* (*vie*) to live; (*aventure, époque*) to live through; (*éprouver*) to experience. **2** *nmpl* food, supplies. ◆**vivoter** *vi* to jog along, get by.

vlan! [vlɑ̃] *int* bang!, wham!

vocable [vɔkabl] *nm* term, word.

vocabulaire [vɔkabylɛr] *nm* vocabulary.

vocal, -aux [vɔkal, -o] *a* (*cordes, musique*) vocal.

vocation [vɔkɑsjɔ̃] *nf* vocation, calling.

vociférer [vɔsifere] *vti* to shout angrily. ◆**vociération** *nf* angry shout.

vodka [vɔdka] *nf* vodka.

vœu, -x [vø] *nm* (*souhait*) wish; (*promesse*) vow; **faire le v. de faire** to (make a) vow to do; **tous mes vœux!** (my) best wishes!

vogue [vɔg] *nf* fashion, vogue; **en v.** in fashion, in vogue.

voici [vwasi] *prép* here is, this is; *pl* here are, these are; **me v.** here I am; **me v. triste** I'm sad now; **v. dix ans/***etc* ten years/*etc* ago; **v. dix ans que** it's ten years since.

voie [vwa] *nf* (*route*) road; (*rails*) track, line; (*partie de route*) lane; (*chemin*) way; (*moyen*) means, way; (*de communication*) line; (*diplomatique*) channels; (*quai*) Rail platform; **en v. de** in the process of; **en v. de développement** (*pays*) developing; **v. publique** public highway; **v. navigable** waterway; **v. sans issue** cul-de-sac, dead end; **préparer la v.** Fig to pave the way; **sur la (bonne) v.** on the right track.

voilà [vwala] *prép* there is, that is; *pl* there are, those are; **les v.** there they are; **v., j'arrive!** all right, I'm coming!; **le v. parti** he has left now; **v. dix ans/***etc* ten years/*etc* ago; **v. dix ans que** it's ten years since.

voile¹ [vwal] *nm* (*étoffe qui cache, coiffure etc*) & Fig veil. ◆**voilage** *nm* net curtain. ◆**voil/er**¹ *vt* (*visage, vérité etc*) to veil; — **se v.** *vpr* (*personne*) to wear a veil; (*ciel, regard*) to cloud over. ◆**-é** *a* (*femme, allusion*) veiled; (*terne*) dull; (*photo*) hazy.

voile² [vwal] *nf* (*de bateau*) sail; (*activité*) sailing; **bateau à voiles** sailing boat, *Am* sailboat; **faire de la v.** to sail, go sailing. ◆**voilier** *nm* sailing ship; (*de plaisance*) sailing boat, *Am* sailboat. ◆**voilure** *nf* Nau sails.

voiler² [vwale] *vt*, — **se v.** *vpr* (*roue*) to buckle.

voir* [vwar] *vti* to see; **faire** *ou* **laisser v. qch**

to show sth; **fais v.** let me see, show me; **v. qn faire** to see s.o. do *ou* doing; **voyons!** (*sois raisonnable*) come on!; **y v. clair** (*comprendre*) to see clearly; **je ne peux pas la v.** (*supporter*) Fam I can't stand the (sight of) her; **v. venir** (*attendre*) to wait and see; **on verra bien** (*attendons*) we'll see; **ça n'a rien à v. avec** that's got nothing to do with; — **se v.** *vpr* to see oneself; (*se fréquenter*) to see each other; (*objet, attitude etc*) to be seen; (*reprise, tache*) to show; **ça se voit** that's obvious.

voire [vwar] *adv* indeed.

voirie [vwari] *nf* (*enlèvement des ordures*) refuse collection; (*routes*) public highways.

voisin, -ine [vwazɛ̃, -in] *a* (*pays, village etc*) neighbouring; (*maison, pièce*) next (**de** to); (*idée, état etc*) similar (**de** to); — *nmf* neighbour. ◆**voisinage** *nm* (*quartier, voisins*) neighbourhood; (*proximité*) proximity. ◆**voisiner** *vi* **v. avec** to be side by side with.

voiture [vwatyr] *nf* Aut car; Rail carriage, coach, *Am* car; (*charrette*) cart; **v. (à cheval)** (horse-drawn) carriage; **v. de course/ de tourisme** racing/private car; **v. d'enfant** pram, *Am* baby carriage; **en v.!** Rail all aboard!

voix [vwa] *nf* voice; (*suffrage*) vote; **à v. basse** in a whisper; **à portée de v.** within earshot; **avoir v. au chapitre** Fig to have a say.

vol [vɔl] *nm* **1** (*d'avion, d'oiseau*) flight; (*groupe d'oiseaux*) flock, flight; **v. libre** hang gliding; **v. à voile** gliding. **2** (*délit*) theft; (*hold-up*) robbery; **v. à l'étalage** shoplifting; **c'est du v.!** (*trop cher*) it's daylight robbery!

volage [vɔlaʒ] *a* flighty, fickle.

volaille [vɔlaj] *nf* **la v.** (*oiseaux*) poultry; **une v.** (*oiseau*) a fowl. ◆**volailler** *nm* poulterer.

volatile [vɔlatil] *nm* (*oiseau domestique*) fowl.

volatiliser (se) [səvɔlatilize] *vpr* (*disparaître*) to vanish (into thin air).

vol-au-vent [vɔlovɑ̃] *nm inv* Culin vol-au-vent.

volcan [vɔlkɑ̃] *nm* volcano. ◆**volcanique** *a* volcanic.

voler [vɔle] **1** *vi* (*oiseau, avion etc*) to fly; (*courir*) Fig to rush. **2** *vt* (*dérober*) to steal (**à** from); **v. qn** to rob s.o.; — *vi* to steal. ◆**volant** **1** *a* (*tapis etc*) flying; **feuille volante** loose sheet. **2** *nm* Aut (steering) wheel; (*objet*) Sp shuttlecock; (*de jupe*) flounce. ◆**volée** *nf* flight; (*groupe d'oiseaux*) flock, flight; (*de coups, flèches etc*) volley; (*suite de*

coups) thrashing; **lancer à toute v.** to throw as hard as one can; **sonner à toute v.** to peal *ou* ring out. ◆**voleter** *vi* to flutter.
◆**voleur, -euse** *nmf* thief; **au v.!** stop thief!; – *a* thieving.

volet [vɔlɛ] *nm* **1** (*de fenêtre*) shutter. **2** (*de programme, reportage etc*) section, part.

volière [vɔljɛr] *nf* aviary.

volley(-ball) [vɔlɛ(bol)] *nm* volleyball.
◆**volleyeur, -euse** *nmf* volleyball player.

volonté [vɔlɔ̃te] *nf* (*faculté, intention*) will; (*désir*) wish; *Phil Psy* free will; **elle a de la v.** she has willpower; **bonne v.** goodwill; **mauvaise v.** ill will; **à v.** at will; (*quantité*) as much as desired. ◆**volontaire** *a* (*délibéré, qui agit librement*) voluntary; (*opiniâtre*) wilful, *Am* willful; – *nmf* volunteer.
◆**volontairement** *adv* voluntarily; (*exprès*) deliberately. ◆**volontiers** [-tje] *adv* willingly, gladly; (*habituellement*) readily; **v.!** (*oui*) I'd love to!

volt [vɔlt] *nm* *Él* volt. ◆**voltage** *nm* voltage.

volte-face [vɔltəfas] *nf inv* about turn, *Am* about face; **faire v.-face** to turn round.

voltige [vɔltiʒ] *nf* acrobatics.

voltiger [vɔltiʒe] *vi* to flutter.

volubile [vɔlybil] *a* (*bavard*) loquacious, voluble.

volume [vɔlym] *nm* (*capacité, intensité, tome*) volume. ◆**volumineux, -euse** *a* bulky, voluminous.

volupté [vɔlypte] *nf* sensual pleasure. ◆**voluptueux, -euse** *a* voluptuous.

vom/ir [vɔmir] *vt* to vomit, bring up; (*exécrer*) *Fig* to loathe; – *vi* to vomit, be sick. ◆**—i** *nm* *Fam* vomit. ◆**—issement** *nm* (*action*) vomiting. ◆**vomitif, -ive** *a* *Fam* nauseating.

vont [vɔ̃] *voir* **aller 1.**

vorace [vɔras] *a* (*appétit, lecteur etc*) voracious.

vos [vo] *voir* **votre.**

vote [vɔt] *nm* (*action*) vote, voting; (*suffrage*) vote; (*de loi*) passing; **bureau de v.** polling station. ◆**voter** *vi* to vote; – *vt* (*loi*) to pass; (*crédits*) to vote. ◆**votant, -ante** *nmf* voter.

votre, *pl* **vos** [vɔtr, vo] *a poss* your. ◆**vôtre** *pron poss* **le** *ou* **la v., les vôtres** yours; **à la v.!** (*toast*) cheers!; – *nmpl* **les vôtres** (*parents etc*) your (own) people.

vouer [vwe] *vt* (*promettre*) to vow (**à** to); (*consacrer*) to dedicate (**à** to); (*condamner*) to doom (**à** to); **se v. à** to dedicate oneself to.

vouloir* [vulwar] *vt* to want (**faire** to do); **je veux qu'il parte** I want him to go; **v. dire** to

mean (**que** that); **je voudrais rester** I'd like to stay; **je voudrais un pain** I'd like a loaf of bread; **voulez-vous me suivre** will you follow me; **si tu veux** if you like *ou* wish; **en v. à qn d'avoir fait qch** to hold it against s.o. for doing sth; **l'usage veut que . . .** (+ *sub*) custom requires that . . . ; **v. du bien à qn** to wish s.o. well; **je veux bien** I don't mind (**faire** doing); **que voulez-vous!** (*résignation*) what can you expect!; **sans le v.** unintentionally; **ça ne veut pas bouger** it won't move; **ne pas v. de qch/de qn** not to want sth/s.o.; **veuillez attendre** kindly wait.
◆**voulu** *a* (*requis*) required; (*délibéré*) deliberate, intentional.

vous [vu] *pron* **1** (*sujet, complément direct*) you; **v. êtes** you are; **il v. connaît** he knows you. **2** (*complément indirect*) (to) you; **il v. l'a donné** he gave it to you, he gave you it. **3** (*réfléchi*) yourself, *pl* yourselves; **v. v. lavez** you wash yourself, you wash yourselves. **4** (*réciproque*) each other; **v. v. aimez** you love each other. ◆**v.-même** *pron* yourself. ◆**v.-mêmes** *pron pl* yourselves.

voûte [vut] *nf* (*plafond*) vault; (*porche*) arch(way). ◆**voûté** *a* (*personne*) bent, stooped.

vouvoyer [vuvwaje] *vt* to address formally (*using vous*).

voyage [vwajaʒ] *nm* trip, journey; (*par mer*) voyage; **aimer les voyages** to like travelling; **faire un v., partir en v.** to go on a trip; **être en v.** to be (away) travelling; **de v.** (*compagnon etc*) travelling-; **bon v.!** have a pleasant trip!; **v. de noces** honeymoon; **v. organisé** (package) tour. ◆**voyager** *vi* to travel. ◆**voyageur, -euse** *nmf* traveller; (*passager*) passenger; **v. de commerce** commercial traveller. ◆**voyagiste** *nm* tour operator.

voyant [vwajɑ̃] **1** *a* gaudy, loud. **2** *nm* (*signal*) (warning) light; (*d'appareil électrique*) pilot light.

voyante [vwajɑ̃t] *nf* clairvoyant.

voyelle [vwajɛl] *nf* vowel.

voyeur, -euse [vwajœr, -øz] *nmf* peeping Tom, voyeur.

voyou [vwaju] *nm* hooligan, hoodlum.

vrac (en) [ɑ̃vrak] *adv* (*en désordre*) haphazardly; (*au poids*) loose, unpackaged.

vrai [vrɛ] *a* true; (*réel*) real; (*authentique*) genuine; – *adv* **dire v.** to be right (in what one says); – *nm* (*vérité*) truth. ◆**—ment** *adv* really.

vraisemblable [vrɛsɑ̃blabl] *a* (*probable*) likely, probable; (*plausible*) plausible. ◆**vraisemblablement** *adv* probably.

◆**vraisemblance** *nf* likelihood; plausibility.

vrille [vrij] *nf* **1** (*outil*) gimlet. **2** *Av* (*tail*)spin.

vromb/ir [vrɔ̃bir] *vi* to hum. ◆**—issement** *nm* hum(ming).

vu [vy] **1** *voir* **voir**; — *a* **bien vu** well thought of; **mal vu** frowned upon. **2** *prép* in view of; **vu que** seeing that.

vue [vy] *nf* (*spectacle*) sight; (*sens*) (eye)sight; (*panorama, photo, idée*) view; **en v.** (*proche*) in sight; (*en évidence*) on view; (*personne*) *Fig* in the public eye; **avoir en v.** to have in mind; **à v.** (*tirer*) on sight; (*payable*) at sight; **à première v.** at first sight; **de v.** (*connaître*) by sight; **en v. de faire** with a view to doing.

vulgaire [vylgɛr] *a* (*grossier*) vulgar, coarse; (*ordinaire*) common. ◆**—ment** *adv* vulgarly, coarsely; (*appeler*) commonly. ◆**vulgariser** *vt* to popularize. ◆**vulgarité** *nf* vulgarity, coarseness.

vulnérable [vylnerabl] *a* vulnerable. ◆**vulnérabilité** *nf* vulnerability.

W

W, w [dublǝve] *nm* W, w.

wagon [vagɔ̃] *nm* *Rail* (*de voyageurs*) carriage, coach, *Am* car; (*de marchandises*) wag(g)on, truck, *Am* freight car. ◆**w.-lit** *nm* (*pl* **wagons-lits**) sleeping car, sleeper. ◆**w.-restaurant** *nm* (*pl* **wagons-restaurants**) dining car, diner. ◆**wagonnet** *nm* (small) wagon *ou* truck.

wallon, -onne [walɔ̃, -ɔn] *a* & *nmf* Walloon.

waters [water] *nmpl* toilet.

watt [wat] *nm* *Él* watt.

w-c [(dublǝ)vese] *nmpl* toilet.

week-end [wikɛnd] *nm* weekend.

western [wɛstɛrn] *nm* *Cin* western.

whisky, *pl* **-ies** [wiski] *nm* whisky, *Am* whiskey.

X

X, x [iks] *nm* X, x; **rayon X** X-ray.

xénophobe [ksenɔfɔb] *a* xenophobic; — *nmf* xenophobe. ◆**xénophobie** *nf* xéno-phobia.

xérès [gzeres] *nm* sherry.

xylophone [ksilɔfɔn] *nm* xylophone.

Y

Y, y¹ [igrɛk] *nm* Y, y.

y² [i] **1** *adv* there; (*dedans*) in it; *pl* in them; (*dessus*) on it; *pl* on them; **elle y vivra** she'll live there; **j'y entrai** I entered (it); **allons-y** let's go; **j'y suis!** (*je comprends*) now I get it!; **je n'y suis pour rien** I have nothing to do with it, that's nothing to do with me. **2** *pron* (= *à cela*) **j'y pense** I think of it; **je m'y attendais** I was expecting it; **ça y est!** that's it!

yacht [jɔt] *nm* yacht.

yaourt [jaur(t)] *nm* yog(h)urt.

yeux [jø] *voir* **œil**.

yiddish [(j)idiʃ] *nm* & *a* Yiddish.

yoga [jɔga] *nm* yoga.

yog(h)ourt [jɔgur(t)] *voir* **yaourt**.

Yougoslavie [jugɔslavi] *nf* Yugoslavia. ◆**yougoslave** *a* & *nmf* Yugoslav(ian).

yo-yo [jojo] *nm inv* yoyo.

Z

Z, z [zɛd] *nm* Z, z.
zèbre [zɛbr] *nm* zebra. ◆**zébré** *a* striped, streaked (**de** with).
zèle [zɛl] *nm* zeal; **faire du z.** to overdo it. ◆**zélé** *a* zealous.
zénith [zenit] *nm* zenith.
zéro [zero] *nm* (*chiffre*) nought, zero; (*dans un numéro*) 0 [əu]; (*température*) zero; (*rien*) nothing; (*personne*) *Fig* nobody, nonentity; **deux buts à z.** *Fb* two nil, *Am* two zero; **partir de z.** to start from scratch.
zeste [zɛst] *nm* **un z. de citron** (a piece of) lemon peel.
zézayer [zezeje] *vi* to lisp.
zibeline [ziblin] *nf* (*animal*) sable.

zigzag [zigzag] *nm* zigzag; **en z.** (*route etc*) zigzag(ging); ◆**zigzaguer** *vi* to zigzag.
zinc [zɛg] *nm* (*métal*) zinc; (*comptoir*) *Fam* bar.
zizanie [zizani] *nf* discord.
zodiaque [zɔdjak] *nm* zodiac.
zona [zona] *nm* *Méd* shingles.
zone [zon] *nf* zone, area; (*domaine*) *Fig* sphere; (*faubourgs misérables*) shanty town; **z. bleue** restricted parking zone; **z. industrielle** trading estate, *Am* industrial park.
zoo [zo(o)] *nm* zoo. ◆**zoologie** [zɔɔlɔʒi] *nf* zoology. ◆**zoologique** *a* zoological; **jardin** *ou* **parc z.** zoo.
zoom [zum] *nm* (*objectif*) zoom lens.
zut! [zyt] *int* *Fam* bother!, heck!

French verb conjugations

REGULAR VERBS

	-ER Verbs	-IR Verbs	-RE Verbs
Infinitive	donn/*er*	fin/*ir*	vend/*re*
1 Present	je donne	je finis	je vends
	tu donnes	tu finis	tu vends
	il donne	il finit	il vend
	nous donnons	nous finissons	nous vendons
	vous donnez	vous finissez	vous vendez
	ils donnent	ils finissent	ils vendent
2 Imperfect	je donnais	je finissais	je vendais
	tu donnais	tu finissais	tu vendais
	il donnait	il finissait	il vendait
	nous donnions	nous finissions	nous vendions
	vous donniez	vous finissiez	vous vendiez
	ils donnaient	ils finissaient	ils vendaient
3 Past historic	je donnai	je finis	je vendis
	tu donnas	tu finis	tu vendis
	il donna	il finit	il vendit
	nous donnâmes	nous finîmes	nous vendîmes
	vous donnâtes	vous finîtes	vous vendîtes
	ils donnèrent	ils finirent	ils vendirent
4 Future	je donnerai	je finirai	je vendrai
	tu donneras	tu finiras	tu vendras
	il donnera	il finira	il vendra
	nous donnerons	nous finirons	nous vendrons
	vous donnerez	vous finirez	vous vendrez
	ils donneront	ils finiront	ils vendront
5 Subjunctive	je donne	je finisse	je vende
	tu donnes	tu finisses	tu vendes
	il donne	il finisse	il vende
	nous donnions	nous finissions	nous vendions
	vous donniez	vous finissiez	vous vendiez
	ils donnent	ils finissent	ils vendent
6 Imperative	donne	'inis	vends
	donnons	finissons	vendons
	donnez	finissez	vendez
7 Present participle	donnant	finissant	vendant
8 Past participle	donné	fini	vendu

SPELLING ANOMALIES OF -ER VERBS

Verbs in -**ger** (e.g. **manger**) take an extra e before endings beginning with o or a: *Present* je mange, nous mangeons; *Imperfect* je mangeais, nous mangions; *Past historic* je mangeai, nous mangeâmes; *Present participle* mangeant. Verbs in -**cer** (e.g. **commencer**) change c to ç before endings beginning with o or a: *Present* je commence, nous commençons; *Imperfect* je commençais, nous commencions; *Past historic* je commençai, nous commençâmes; *Present participle* commençant. Verbs containing mute **e** in their penultimate syllable fall into two groups. In the first (e.g. **mener**, **peser**, **lever**), **e** becomes **è** before an unpronounced syllable in the present and subjunctive, and in the future and conditional tenses (e.g. je mène, ils mèneront). The second group contains most verbs ending in **-eler** and **-eter** (e.g. **appeler**, **jeter**). These verbs change **l** to **ll** and **t** to **tt** before an unpronounced syllable (e.g. j'appelle, ils appelleront; je jette, ils jetteront). However, the following verbs in **-eler** and **-eter** fall into the first group in which **e** changes to **è** before mute **e** (e.g. je modèle, ils modèleront; j'achète, ils achèteront): **celer**, **ciseler**, **démanteler**, **geler**, **marteler**, **modeler**, **peler**; **acheter**, **crocheter**, **fureter**, **haleter**. Derived verbs (e.g. **dégeler**, **racheter**) are conjugated in the same way. Verbs with **e** acute in their penultimate syllable change **é** to **è** before the unpronounced endings of the present and subjunctive only (e.g. je cède but je céderai). Verbs in **-yer** (e.g. **essuyer**) change **y** to **i** before an unpronounced syllable in the present and subjunctive, and in the future and conditional tenses (e.g. j'essuie, ils essuieront). In verbs in **-ayer** (e.g. **balayer**), **y** may be retained before mute **e** (e.g. je balaie or balaye, ils balaieront or balayeront).

IRREGULAR VERBS

Listed below are those verbs considered to be the most useful. Forms and tenses not given are fully derivable. Note that the endings of the past historic fall into three categories, the 'a' and 'i' categories shown at **donner**, and at **finir** and **vendre**, and the 'u' category which has the following endings: -us, -ut, -ûmes, -ûtes, -urent. Most of the verbs listed below form their past historic with 'u'. The imperfect may usually be formed by adding -ais, -ait, -ions, -iez, -aient to the stem of the first person plural of the present tense, e.g. 'je buvais' etc may be derived from 'nous buvons' (stem 'buv-' and ending '-ons'); similarly, the present participle may generally be formed by substituting -ant for -ons (e.g. buvant). The future may usually be formed by adding -ai, -as, -a, -ons, -ez, -ont to the infinitive or to an infinitive without final 'e' where the ending is -re (e.g. conduire). The imperative usually has the same forms as the second persons singular and plural and first person plural of the present tense.

1 = Present   2 = Imperfect   3 = Past historic   4 = Future
5 = Subjunctive   6 = Imperative   7 = Present participle
8 = Past participle   n = nous   v = vous   †verbs conjugated with **être** only.

abattre	*like* **battre**
absoudre	1 j'absous, n absolvons 2 j'absolvais 3 j'absolus *(rarely used)* 5 j'absolve 7 absolvant 8 absous, absolute
†s'abstenir	*like* **tenir**
abstraire	1 j'abstrais, n abstrayons 2 j'abstrayais 3 *none* 5 j'abstraie 7 abstrayant 8 abstrait
accourir	*like* **courir**
accroître	*like* **croître** *except* 8 accru
accueillir	*like* **cueillir**
acquérir	1 j'acquiers, n acquérons 2 j'acquérais 3 j'acquis 4 j'acquerrai 5 j'acquière 7 acquérant 8 acquis
adjoindre	*like* **atteindre**
admettre	*like* **mettre**
†aller	1 je vais, tu vas, il va, n allons, v allez, ils vont 4 j'irai 5 j'aille, nous allions, ils aillent 6 va, allons, allez *(but note* vas-y*)*
apercevoir	*like* **recevoir**
apparaître	*like* **connaître**
appartenir	*like* **tenir**
apprendre	*like* **prendre**
asseoir	1 j'assieds, n asseyons, ils asseyent 2 j'asseyais 3 j'assis 4 j'assiérai 5 j'asseye 7 asseyant 8 assis

astreindre	*like* **atteindre**
atteindre	1 j'atteins, n atteignons, ils atteignent 2 j'atteignais
	3 j'atteignis 4 j'atteindrai 5 j'atteigne 7 atteignant
	8 atteint
avoir	1 j'ai, tu as, il a, n avons, v avez, ils ont 2 j'avais 3 j'eus
	4 j'aurai 5 j'aie, il ait, n ayons, ils aient 6 aie, ayons, ayez
	7 ayant 8 eu
battre	1 je bats, n battons 5 je batte
boire	1 je bois, n buvons, ils boivent 2 je buvais 3 je bus
	5 je boive, n buvions 7 buvant 8 bu
bouillir	1 je bous, n bouillons, ils bouillent 2 je bouillais
	3 *not used* 5 je bouille 7 bouillant
braire	(*defective*) 1 il brait, ils braient 4 il braira, ils brairont
combattre	*like* **battre**
commettre	*like* **mettre**
comparaître	*like* **connaître**
comprendre	*like* **prendre**
compromettre	*like* **mettre**
concevoir	*like* **recevoir**
conclure	1 je conclus, n concluons, ils concluent 5 je conclue
concourir	*like* **courir**
conduire	1 je condùis, n conduisons 3 je conduisis 5 je conduise
	8 conduit
connaître	1 je connais, il connaît, n connaissons 3 je connus
	5 je connaisse 7 connaissant 8 connu
conquérir	*like* **acquérir**
consentir	*like* **mentir**
construire	*like* **conduire**
contenir	*like* **tenir**
contraindre	*like* **atteindre**
contredire	*like* **dire** *except* 1 v contredisez
convaincre	*like* **vaincre**
convenir	*like* **tenir**
corrompre	*like* **rompre**
coudre	1 je couds, n cousons, ils cousent 3 je cousis 5 je couse
	7 cousant 8 cousu
courir	1 je cours, n courons 3 je courus 4 je courrai 5 je coure
	8 couru
couvrir	1 je couvre, n couvrons 2 je couvrais 5 je couvre 8 couvert
craindre	*like* **atteindre**
croire	1 je crois, n croyons, ils croient 2 je croyais 3 je crus
	5 je croie, n croyions 7 croyant 8 cru
croître	1 je crois, il croît, n croissons 2 je croissais 3 je crûs
	5 je croisse 7 croissant 8 crû, crue
cueillir	1 je cueille, n cueillons 2 je cueillais 4 je cueillerai
	5 je cueille 7 cueillant
cuire	1 je cuis, n cuisons 2 je cuisais 3 je cuisis 5 je cuise
	7 cuisant 8 cuit
débattre	*like* **battre**
décevoir	*like* **recevoir**
découvrir	*like* **couvrir**
décrire	*like* **écrire**
décroître	*like* **croître** *except* 8 décru
déduire	*like* **conduire**
défaillir	1 je défaille, n défaillons 2 je défaillais 3 je défaillis
	5 je défaille 7 défaillant 8 défailli

défaire	*like* faire
dépeindre	*like* atteindre
déplaire	*like* plaire
déteindre	*like* atteindre
détenir	*like* tenir
détruire	*like* conduire
†devenir	*like* tenir
devoir	1 je dois, n devons, ils doivent 2 je devais 3 je dus 4 je devrai 5 je doive, n devions 6 *not used* 7 devant 8 dû, due, *pl* dus, dues
dire	1 je dis, n disons, v dites 2 je disais 3 je dis 5 je dise 7 disant 8 dit
disparaître	*like* connaître
dissoudre	*like* absoudre
distraire	*like* abstraire
dormir	*like* mentir
†échoir	(*defective*) 1 il échoit 3 il échut, ils échurent 4 il échoira 7 échéant 8 échu
écrire	1 j'écris, n écrivons 2 j'écrivais 3 j'écrivis 5 j'écrive 7 écrivant 8 écrit
élire	*like* lire
émettre	*like* mettre
émouvoir	*like* mouvoir *except* 8 ému
encourir	*like* courir
endormir	*like* mentir
enduire	*like* conduire
enfreindre	*like* atteindre
†s'enfuir	*like* fuir
†s'ensuivre	*like* suivre (*but third person only*)
entreprendre	*like* prendre
entretenir	*like* tenir
entrevoir	*like* voir
entrouvrir	*like* couvrir
envoyer	4 j'enverrai
†s'éprendre	*like* prendre
éteindre	*like* atteindre
être	1 je suis, tu es, il est, n sommes, v êtes, ils sont 2 j'étais 3 je fus 4 je serai 5 je sois, n soyons, ils soient 6 sois, soyons, soyez 7 étant 8 été
exclure	*like* conclure
extraire	*like* abstraire
faillir	(*defective*) 3 je faillis 4 je faillirai 8 failli
faire	1 je fais, n faisons, v faites, ils font 2 je faisais 3 je fis 4 je ferai 5 je fasse 7 faisant 8 fait
falloir	(*impersonal*) 1 il faut 2 il fallait 3 il fallut 4 il faudra 5 il faille 6 *none* 7 *none* 8 fallu
feindre	*like* atteindre
foutre	1 je fous, n foutons 2 je foutais 3 *none* 5 je foute 7 foutant 8 foutu
frire	(*defective*) 1 je fris, tu fris, il frit 4 je frirai (*rare*) 6 fris (*rare*) 8 frit (*for other persons and tenses use* faire frire)
fuir	1 je fuis, n fuyons, ils fuient 2 je fuyais 3 je fuis 5 je fuie 7 fuyant 8 fui
haïr	1 je hais, il hait, n haïssons
inclure	*like* conclure
induire	*like* conduire
inscrire	*like* écrire

(iv)

instruire	*like* **conduire**
interdire	*like* **dire** *except* 1 v interdisez
interrompre	*like* **rompre**
intervenir	*like* **tenir**
introduire	*like* **conduire**
joindre	*like* **atteindre**
lire	1 je lis, n lisons 2 je lisais 3 je lus 5 je lise 7 lisant 8 lu
luire	*like* **nuire**
maintenir	*like* **tenir**
maudire	,1 je maudis, n maudissons 2 je maudissais 3 je maudis 4 je maudirai 5 je maudisse 7 maudissant 8 maudit
méconnaître	*like* **connaître**
médire	*like* **dire** *except* 1 v médisez
mentir	1 je mens, n mentons 2 je mentais 5 je mente 7 mentant
mettre	1 je mets, n mettons 2 je mettais 3 je mis 5 je mette 7 mettant 8 mis
moudre	1 je mouds, n moulons 2 je moulais 3 je moulus 5 je moule 7 moulant 8 moulu
†mourir	1 je meurs, n mourons, ils meurent 2 je mourais 3 je mourus 4 je mourrai 5 je meure, n mourions 7 mourant 8 mort
mouvoir	1 je meus, n mouvons, ils meuvent 2 je mouvais 3 je mus *(rare)* 4 je mouvrai 5 je meuve, n mouvions 8 mû, mue, *pl* mus, mues
†naître	1 je nais, il naît, n naissons 2 je naissais 3 je naquis 4 je naîtrai 5 je naisse 7 naissant 8 né
nuire	1 je nuis, n nuisons 2 je nuisais 3 je nuisis 5 je nuise 7 nuisant 8 nui
obtenir	*like* **tenir**
offrir	*like* **couvrir**
omettre	*like* **mettre**
ouvrir	*like* **couvrir**
paître	*(defective)* 1 il paît 2 il paissait 3 none 4 il paîtra 5 il paisse 7 paissant 8 none
paraître	*like* **connaître**
parcourir	*like* **courir**
†partir	*like* **mentir**
†parvenir	*like* **tenir**
peindre	*like* **atteindre**
percevoir	*like* **recevoir**
permettre	*like* **mettre**
plaindre	*like* **atteindre**
plaire	1 je plais, n plaisons 2 je plaisais 3 je plus 5 je plaise 7 plaisant 8 plu
pleuvoir	*(impersonal)* 1 il pleut 2 il pleuvait 3 il plut 4 il pleuvra 5 il pleuve 6 none 7 pleuvant 8 plu
poursuivre	*like* **suivre**
pourvoir	*like* **voir** *except* 4 je pourvoirai
pouvoir	1 je peux *or* je puis, tu peux, il peut, n pouvons, ils peuvent 2 je pouvais 3 je pus 4 je pourrai 5 je puisse 6 *not used* 7 pouvant 8 pu
prédire	*like* **dire** *except* 1 v prédisez
prendre	1 je prends, n prenons, ils prennent 2 je prenais 3 je pris 5 je prenne 7 prenant 8 pris
prescrire	*like* **écrire**
pressentir	*like* **mentir**

prévenir	*like* tenir
prévoir	*like* voir *except* 4 je prévoirai
produire	*like* conduire
promettre	*like* mettre
promouvoir	*like* mouvoir *except* 8 promu
proscrire	*like* écrire
†provenir	*like* tenir
rabattre	*like* battre
rasseoir	*like* asseoir
recevoir	1 je reçois, n recevons, ils reçoivent 2 je recevais 3 je reçus 4 je recevrai 5 je reçoive, n recevions, ils reçoivent 7 recevant 8 reçu
reconnaître	*like* connaître
reconduire	*like* conduire
reconstruire	*like* conduire
recoudre	*like* coudre
recourir	*like* courir
recouvrir	*like* couvrir
recueillir	*like* cueillir
†redevenir	*like* tenir
redire	*like* dire
réduire	*like* conduire
refaire	*like* faire
rejoindre	*like* atteindre
relire	*like* lire
remettre	*like* mettre
†renaître	*like* naître
rendormir	*like* mentir
renvoyer	*like* envoyer
†repartir	*like* mentir
repentir	*like* mentir
reprendre	*like* prendre
reproduire	*like* conduire
résoudre	1 je résous, n résolvons 2 je résolvais 3 je résolus 5 je résolve 7 résolvant 8 résolu
ressentir	*like* mentir
ressortir	*like* mentir
restreindre	*like* atteindre
retenir	*like* tenir
†trevenir	*like* tenir
revêtir	*like* vêtir
revivre	*like* vivre
revoir	*like* voir
rire	1 je ris, n rions 2 je riais 3 je ris 5 je rie, n riions 7 riant 8 ri
rompre	*regular except* 1 il rompt
rouvrir	*like* couvrir
satisfaire	*like* faire
savoir	1 je sais, n savons, il savent 2 je savais 3 je sus 4 je saurai 5 je sache 6 sache, sachons, sachez 7 sachant 8 su
séduire	*like* conduire
sentir	*like* mentir
servir	*like* mentir
sortir	*like* mentir
souffrir	*like* couvrir
soumettre	*like* mettre
sourire	*like* rire

souscrire	*like* **écrire**
soustraire	*like* **abstraire**
soutenir	*like* **tenir**
†se souvenir	*like* **tenir**
subvenir	*like* **tenir**
suffire	1 je suffis, n suffisons 2 je suffisais 3 je suffis 5 je suffise 7 suffisant 8 suffi
suivre	1 je suis, n suivons 2 je suivais 3 je suivis 5 je suive 7 suivant 8 suivi
surprendre	*like* **prendre**
†survenir	*like* **tenir**
survivre	*like* **vivre**
taire	1 je tais, n taisons 2 je taisais 3 je tus 5 je taise 7 taisant 8 tu
teindre	*like* **atteindre**
tenir	1 je tiens, n tenons, ils tiennent 2 je tenais 3 je tins, tu tins, il tint, n tînmes, v tîntes, ils tinrent 4 je tiendrai 5 je tienne 7 tenant 8 tenu
traduire	*like* **conduire**
traire	*like* **abstraire**
transcrire	*like* **écrire**
transmettre	*like* **mettre**
transparaître	*like* **connaître**
tressaillir	*like* **défaillir**
vaincre	1 je vaincs, il vainc, n vainquons 2 je vainquais 3 je vainquis 5 je vainque 7 vainquant 8 vaincu
valoir	1 je vaux, n valons 2 je valais 3 je valus 4 je vaudrai 5 je vaille 6 *not used* 7 valant 8 valu
†venir	*like* **tenir**
vêtir	1 je vêts, n vêtons 2 je vêtais 5 je vête 7 vêtant 8 vêtu
vivre	1 je vis, n vivons 2 je vivais 3 je vécus 5 je vive 7 vivant 8 vécu
voir	1 je vois, n voyons 2 je voyais 3 je vis 4 je verrai 5 je voie, n voyions 7 voyant 8 vu
vouloir	1 je veux, n voulons, ils veulent 2 je voulais 3 je voulus 4 je voudrai 5 je veuille 6 veuille, veuillons, veuillez 7 voulant 8 voulu

Verbes anglais irréguliers

Infinitif	Prétérit	Participe passé
arise	arose	arisen
be	was, were	been
bear	bore	borne
beat	beat	beaten
become	became	become
begin	began	begun
bend	bent	bent
bet	bet, betted	bet, betted
bid	bade, bid	bidden, bid
bind	bound	bound
bite	bit	bitten
bleed	bled	bled
blow	blew	blown
break	broke	broken
breed	bred	bred

bring	brought	brought
broadcast	broadcast	broadcast
build	built	built
burn	burnt, burned	burnt, burned
burst	burst	burst
buy	bought	bought
cast	cast	cast
catch	caught	caught
choose	chose	chosen
cling	clung	clung
come	came	come
cost	cost	cost
creep	crept	crept
cut	cut	cut
deal	dealt	dealt
dig	dug	dug
dive	dived, *Am* dove	dived
do	did	done
draw	drew	drawn
dream	dreamed, dreamt	dreamed, dreamt
drink	drank	drunk
drive	drove	driven
dwell	dwelt	dwelt
eat	ate [et, *Am* eɪt]	eaten
fall	fell	fallen
feed	fed	fed
feel	felt	felt
fight	fought	fought
find	found	found
fling	flung	flung
fly	flew	flown
forbid	forbad(e)	forbidden
forecast	forecast	forecast
foresee	foresaw	foreseen
forget	forgot	forgotten
forgive	forgave	forgiven
forsake	forsook (*rare*)	forsaken
freeze	froze	frozen
get	got	got, *Am* gotten
give	gave	given
go	went	gone
grind	ground	ground
grow	grew	grown
hang	hung, hanged	hung, hanged
have	had	had
hear	heard	heard
hide	hid	hidden
hit	hit	hit
hold	held	held
hurt	hurt	hurt
keep	kept	kept
kneel	knelt, kneeled	knelt, kneeled
know	knew	known
lay	laid	laid
lead	led	led
lean	leant, leaned	leant, leaned
leap	leapt, leaped	leapt, leaped

learn	learnt, learned	learnt, learned
leave	left	left
lend	lent	lent
let	let	let
lie	lay	lain
light	lit, lighted	lit, lighted
lose	lost	lost
make	made	made
mean	meant	meant
meet	met	met
mislay	mislaid	mislaid
mislead	misled	misled
misunderstand	misunderstood	misunderstood
mow	mowed	mown, mowed
overcome	overcame	overcome
pay	paid	paid
put	put	put
quit	quit, quitted	quit, quitted
read	read [red]	read [red]
rid	rid	rid
ride	rode	ridden
ring	rang	rung
rise	rose	risen
run	ran	run
saw	sawed	sawn, sawed
say	said	said
see	saw	seen
seek	sought	sought
sell	sold	sold
send	sent	sent
set	set	set
sew	sewed	sewn, sewed
shake	shook	shaken
shed	shed	shed
shine	shone ([ʃɒn, *Am* ʃəʊn])	shone ([ʃɒn, *Am* ʃəʊn])
shoot	shot	shot
show	showed	shown, showed
shrink	shrank	shrunk, shrunken
shut	shut	shut
sing	sang	sung
sink	sank	sunk
sit	sat	sat
sleep	slept	slept
slide	slid	slid
sling	slung	slung
slit	slit	slit
smell	smelt, smelled	smelt, smelled
sow	sowed	sown, sowed
speak	spoke	spoken
speed	sped, speeded	sped, speeded
spell	spelt, spelled	spelt, spelled
spend	spent	spent
spill	spilt, spilled	spilt, spilled
spin	spun	spun
spit	spat, spit	spat, spit
split	split	split
spoil	spoilt, spoiled	spoilt, spoiled

spread	spread	spread
spring	sprang	sprung
stand	stood	stood
steal	stole	stolen
stick	stuck	stuck
sting	stung	stung
stink	stank, stunk	stunk
stride	strode	stridden (*rare*)
strike	struck	struck
string	strung	strung
strive	strove	striven
swear	swore	sworn
sweep	swept	swept
swell	swelled	swollen, swelled
swim	swam	swum
swing	swung	swung
take	took	taken
teach	taught	taught
tear	tore	torn
tell	told	told
think	thought	thought
throw	threw	thrown
thrust	thrust	thrust
tread	trod	trodden
undergo	underwent	undergone
understand	understood	understood
undertake	undertook	undertaken
upset	upset	upset
wake	woke	woken
wear	wore	worn
weave	wove	woven
weep	wept	wept
win	won	won
wind	wound	wound
withdraw	withdrew	withdrawn
withhold	withheld	withheld
withstand	withstood	withstood
wring	wrung	wrung
write	wrote	written

Numerals

Les nombres

Cardinal numbers

Les nombres cardinaux

nought	0	zéro
one	1	un
two	2	deux
three	3	trois
four	4	quatre
five	5	cinq
six	6	six
seven	7	sept
eight	8	huit
nine	9	neuf
ten	10	dix

eleven	11	onze
twelve	12	douze
thirteen	13	treize
fourteen	14	quatorze
fifteen	15	quinze
sixteen	16	seize
seventeen	17	dix-sept
eighteen	18	dix-huit
nineteen	19	dix-neuf
twenty	20	vingt
twenty-one	21	vingt et un
twenty-two	22	vingt-deux
thirty	30	trente
forty	40	quarante
fifty	50	cinquante
sixty	60	soixante
seventy	70	soixante-dix
seventy-five	75	soixante-quinze
eighty	80	quatre-vingts
eighty-one	81	quatre-vingt-un
ninety	90	quatre-vingt-dix
ninety-one	91	quatre-vingt-onze
a *or* one hundred	100	cent
a hundred and one	101	cent un
a hundred and two	102	cent deux
a hundred and fifty	150	cent cinquante
two hundred	200	deux cents
two hundred and one	201	deux cent un
two hundred and two	202	deux cent deux
a *or* one thousand	1,000 (1 000)	mille
a thousand and one	1,001 (1 001)	mille un
a thousand and two	1,002 (1 002)	mille deux
two thousand	2,000 (2 000)	deux mille
a *or* one million	1,000,000 (1 000 000)	un million

Ordinal numbers   Les nombres ordinaux

first	1st	1er	premier
second	2nd	2e	deuxième
third	3rd	3e	troisième
fourth	4th	4e	quatrième
fifth	5th	5e	cinquième
sixth	6th	6e	sixième
seventh	7th	7e	septième
eighth	8th	8e	huitième
ninth	9th	9e	neuvième
tenth	10th	10e	dixième
eleventh	11th	11e	onzième
twelfth	12th	12e	douzième
thirteenth	13th	13e	treizième
fourteenth	14th	14e	quatorzième
fifteenth	15th	15e	quinzième
twentieth	20th	20e	vingtième
twenty-first	21st	21e	vingt et unième
twenty-second	22nd	22e	vingt deuxième
thirtieth	30th	30e	trentième

Examples of usage

three (times) out of ten	*trois (fois) sur dix*
ten at a time, in *or* by tens, ten by ten	*dix par dix, dix à dix*
the ten of us/you, we ten/you ten	*nous dix/vous dix*
all ten of them *or* us *or* you	*tous les dix, toutes les dix*
there are ten of us/them	*nous sommes dix/elles sont dix*
(between) the ten of them	*à eux dix, à elles dix*
ten of them came/were living together	*ils sont venus/ils vivaient à dix*
page ten	*page dix*
Charles the Tenth	*Charles Dix*
to live at number ten	*habiter au (numéro) dix*
to be the tenth to arrive/to leave	*arriver/partir le dixième*
to come tenth, be tenth *(in a race)*	*arriver dixième, être dixième*
it's the tenth (today)	*nous sommes le dix (aujourd'hui)*
the tenth of May, May the tenth, *Am* May tenth	*le dix mai*
to arrive/be paid/etc on the tenth	*arriver/être payé/etc le dix*
to arrive/be paid/etc on the tenth of May *or* on May the tenth *or Am* on May tenth	*arriver/être payé/etc le dix mai*
by the tenth, before the tenth	*avant le dix, pour le dix*
it's ten (o'clock)	*il est dix heures*
it's half past ten	*il est dix heures et demie*
ten past ten, *Am* ten after ten	*dix heures dix*
ten to ten	*dix heures moins dix*
by ten (o'clock), before ten (o'clock)	*pour dix heures, avant dix heures*
to be ten (years old)	*avoir dix ans*
a child of ten, a ten-year-old (child)	*un enfant de dix ans*

Days and months

Les jours et les mois

Monday *lundi*; Tuesday *mardi*; Wednesday *mercredi*; Thursday *jeudi*; Friday *vendredi*; Saturday *samedi*; Sunday *dimanche*

January *janvier*; February *février*; March *mars*; April *avril*; May *mai*; June *juin*; July *juillet*; August *août*; September *septembre*; October *octobre*; November *novembre*; December *décembre*

Examples of usage

Exemples d'emplois

on Monday (*e.g.* he arrives on Monday)	*lundi (par exemple il arrive lundi)*
(on) Mondays	*le lundi*
see you on Monday!	*à lundi!*
by Monday, before Monday	*avant lundi, pour lundi*
Monday morning/evening	*lundi matin/soir*
a week/two weeks on Monday, *Am* a week/two weeks from Monday	*lundi en huit/en quinze*
it's Monday (today)	*nous sommes (aujourd'hui) lundi*
Monday the tenth of May, Monday May the tenth, *Am* Monday May tenth	*(le) lundi dix mai*
on Monday the tenth of May, on Monday May the tenth *or Am* May tenth	*le lundi dix mai*
tomorrow is Tuesday	*demain c'est mardi*
in May	*en mai, au mois de mai*
every May, each May	*tous les ans en mai, chaque année en mai*
by May, before May	*avant mai, pour mai*

A

A, a [eɪ] *n* A, a *m*; **5A** (*number*) 5 bis; **A1** (*dinner etc*) *Fam* super, superbe; **to go from A to B** aller du point A au point B.

a [ə, *stressed* eɪ] (*before vowel or mute h an* [ən, *stressed* æn]) *indef art* **1** un, une; **a man** un homme; **an apple** une pomme. **2** (= *def art in Fr*) **six pence a kilo** six pence le kilo; **50 km an hour** 50 km à l'heure; **I have a broken arm** j'ai le bras cassé. **3** (*art omitted in Fr*) **he's a doctor** il est médecin; **Caen, a town in Normandy** Caen, ville de Normandie; **what a man!** quel homme! **4** (*a certain*) **a Mr Smith** un certain M. Smith. **5** (*time*) **twice a month** deux fois par mois. **6** (*some*) **to make a noise/a fuss** faire du bruit/des histoires.

aback [ə'bæk] *adv* **taken a.** déconcerté.

abandon [ə'bændən] **1** *vt* abandonner. **2** *n* (*freedom of manner*) laisser-aller *m*, abandon *m*. ◆**—ment** *n* abandon *m*.

abase [ə'beɪs] *vt* **to a. oneself** s'humilier, s'abaisser.

abashed [ə'bæʃt] *a* confus, gêné.

abate [ə'beɪt] *vi* (*of storm, pain*) se calmer; (*of flood*) baisser; – *vt* diminuer, réduire. ◆**—ment** *n* diminution *f*, réduction *f*.

abbey [æbɪ] *n* abbaye *f*.

abbot ['æbət] *n* abbé *m*. ◆**abbess** *n* abbesse *f*.

abbreviate [ə'briːvɪeɪt] *vt* abréger. ◆**abbrevi'ation** *n* abréviation *f*.

abdicate ['æbdɪkeɪt] *vti* abdiquer. ◆**abdi'cation** *n* abdication *f*.

abdomen ['æbdəmən] *n* abdomen *m*. ◆**ab'dominal** *a* abdominal.

abduct [əb'dʌkt] *vt Jur* enlever. ◆**abduction** *n* enlèvement *m*, rapt *m*.

aberration [æbə'reɪʃ(ə)n] *n* (*folly, lapse*) aberration *f*.

abet [ə'bet] *vt* (**-tt-**) **to aid and a. s.o.** *Jur* être le complice de qn.

abeyance [ə'beɪəns] *n* **in a.** (*matter*) en suspens.

abhor [əb'hɔɪr] *vt* (**-rr-**) avoir horreur de, exécrer. ◆**abhorrent** *a* exécrable. ◆**abhorrence** *n* horreur *f*.

abide [ə'baɪd] **1** *vi* **to a. by** (*promise etc*) rester fidèle à. **2** *vt* supporter; **I can't a. him** je ne peux pas le supporter.

ability [ə'bɪlətɪ] *n* capacité *f* (**to do** pour faire), aptitude *f* (**to do** à faire); **to the best of my a.** de mon mieux.

abject ['æbdʒekt] *a* abject; **a. poverty** la misère.

ablaze [ə'bleɪz] *a* en feu; **a. with** (*light*) resplendissant de; (*anger*) enflammé de.

able ['eɪb(ə)l] *a* (**-er, -est**) capable, compétent; **to be a. to do** être capable de faire, pouvoir faire; **to be a. to swim/drive** savoir nager/conduire. ◆**a.-'bodied** *a* robuste. ◆**ably** *adv* habilement.

ablutions [ə'bluːʃ(ə)nz] *npl* ablutions *fpl*.

abnormal [æb'nɔːm(ə)l] *a* anormal. ◆**abnor'mality** *n* anomalie *f*; (*of body*) difformité *f*. ◆**abnormally** *adv Fig* exceptionnellement.

aboard [ə'bɔːd] *adv Nau* à bord; **all a.** *Rail* en voiture; – *prep* **a. the ship** à bord du navire; **a. the train** dans le train.

abode [ə'bəʊd] *n* (*house*) *Lit* demeure *f*; *Jur* domicile *m*.

abolish [ə'bɒlɪʃ] *vt* supprimer, abolir. ◆**abo'lition** *n* suppression *f*, abolition *f*.

abominable [ə'bɒmɪnəb(ə)l] *a* abominable. ◆**abomi'nation** *n* abomination *f*.

aboriginal [æbə'rɪdʒən(ə)l] *a & n* aborigène (*m*). ◆**aborigines** *npl* aborigènes *mpl*.

abort [ə'bɔːt] *vt Med* faire avorter; (*space flight, computer program*) abandonner; – *vi Med & Fig* avorter. ◆**abortion** *n* avortement *m*; **to have an a.** se faire avorter. ◆**abortive** *a* (*plan etc*) manqué, avorté.

abound [ə'baʊnd] *vi* abonder (**in, with** en).

about [ə'baʊt] *adv* **1** (*approximately*) à peu près, environ; (**at**) **a. two o'clock** vers deux heures. **2** (*here and there*) çà et là, ici et là; (*ideas, flu*) *Fig* dans l'air; (*rumour*) en circulation; **to look a.** regarder autour; **to follow a.** suivre partout; **to bustle a.** s'affairer; **there are lots a.** il en existe beaucoup; (**out and**) **a.** (*after illness*) sur pied, guéri; (**up and**) **a.** (*out of bed*) levé, debout; **a turn, a. face** *Mil* demi-tour *m*; *Fig* volte-face *f inv*; – *prep* **1** (*around*) **a. the garden** autour du jardin; **a. the streets** par ou dans les rues. **2** (*near to*) **a. here** par ici. **3** (*concerning*) au sujet de; **to talk a.** parler de; **a book a.** un livre sur; **what's it (all) a.?** de quoi s'agit-il?; **while you're a. it** pendant que vous y êtes; **what** or **how a. me?** et moi alors?; **what** or **how a. a drink?** que dirais-tu de prendre un verre? **4** (+ *inf*) **a. to do** sur le point de faire; **I was a. to say** j'étais sur le point de dire, j'allais dire.

above [ə'bʌv] *adv* au-dessus; (*in book*) ci-dessus; **from a.** d'en haut; **floor a.** étage *m* supérieur or du dessus; – *prep* au-dessus de; **a. all** par-dessus tout, surtout; **a. the bridge** (*on river*) en amont du pont; **he's a. me** (*in rank*) c'est mon supérieur; **a. lying** incapable de mentir; **a. asking** trop fier pour demander. ◆**a.-'mentioned** *a* susmentionné. ◆**aboveboard** *a* ouvert, honnête; – *adv* sans tricherie, cartes sur table.

abrasion [ə'breɪʒ(ə)n] *n* frottement *m*; *Med* écorchure *f*. ◆**abrasive** *a* (*substance*) abrasif; (*rough*) *Fig* rude, dur; (*irritating*) agaçant; – *n* abrasif *m*.

abreast [ə'brest] *adv* côte à côte, de front; **four a.** par rangs de quatre; **to keep a.** of or **with** se tenir au courant de.

abridge [ə'brɪdʒ] *vt* (*book etc*) abréger. ◆**abridge(e)ment** *n* abrégement *m* (of de); (*abridged version*) abrégé *m*.

abroad [ə'brɔːd] *adv* **1** (*in* or *to a foreign country*) à l'étranger; **from a.** de l'étranger. **2** (*over a wide area*) de tous côtés; **rumour a.** bruit *m* qui court.

abrogate ['æbrəgeɪt] *vt* abroger.

abrupt [ə'brʌpt] *a* (*sudden*) brusque; (*person*) brusque, abrupt; (*slope, style*) abrupt. ◆**-ly** *adv* (*suddenly*) brusquement; (*rudely*) avec brusquerie.

abscess ['æbses] *n* abcès *m*.

abscond [əb'skɒnd] *vi* *Jur* s'enfuir.

absence ['æbsəns] *n* absence *f*; **in the a.** of **sth** à défaut de qch, faute de qch; **a. of mind** distraction *f*.

absent ['æbsənt] *a* absent (**from** de); (*look*) distrait; – [æb'sent] *vt* **to a. oneself** s'absenter. ◆**a.-'minded** *a* distrait. ◆**a.-'mindedness** *n* distraction *f*. ◆**absen'tee** *n* absent, -ente *mf*. ◆**absen'teeism** *n* absentéisme *m*.

absolute ['æbsəluːt] *a* absolu; (*proof etc*) indiscutable; (*coward etc*) parfait, véritable. ◆**-ly** *adv* absolument; (*forbidden*) formellement.

absolve [əb'zɒlv] *vt* *Rel Jur* absoudre; **to a. from** (*vow*) libérer de. ◆**absolution** [æbsə'luːʃ(ə)n] *n* absolution *f*.

absorb [əb'zɔːb] *vt* absorber; (*shock*) amortir; **to become absorbed in** (*work*) s'absorber dans. ◆**-ing** *a* (*work*)

absorbant; (*book, film*) prenant. ◆**absorbent** *a* & *n* absorbant (*m*); **a. cotton** *Am* coton *m* hydrophile. ◆**absorber** *n* **shock a.** *Aut* amortisseur *m*. ◆**absorption** *n* absorption *f*.

abstain [əb'steɪn] *vi* s'abstenir (**from** de). ◆**abstemious** *a* sobre, frugal. ◆**abstention** *n* abstention *f*. ◆**'abstinence** *n* abstinence *f*.

abstract ['æbstrækt] *a* **1** *a* & *n* abstrait (*m*). **2** *n* (*summary*) résumé *m*. **3** [əb'strækt] *vt* (*remove*) retirer; (*notion*) abstraire. ◆**ab'straction** *n* (*idea*) abstraction *f*; (*absent-mindedness*) distraction *f*.

abstruse [əb'struːs] *a* obscur.

absurd [əb'sɜːd] *a* absurde, ridicule. ◆**absurdity** *n* absurdité *f*. ◆**absurdly** *adv* absurdement.

abundant [ə'bʌndənt] *a* abondant. ◆**abundance** *n* abondance *f*. ◆**abundantly** *adv* **a. clear** tout à fait clair.

abuse [ə'bjuːs] *n* (*abusing*) abus *m* (of de); (*curses*) injures *fpl*; – [ə'bjuːz] *vt* (*misuse*) abuser de; (*malign*) dire du mal de; (*insult*) injurier. ◆**abusive** [ə'bjuːsɪv] *a* injurieux.

abysmal [ə'bɪzm(ə)l] *a* (*bad*) *Fam* désastreux, exécrable.

abyss [ə'bɪs] *n* abîme *m*.

acacia [ə'keɪʃə] *n* (*tree*) acacia *m*.

academic [ækə'demɪk] *a* universitaire; (*scholarly*) érudit, intellectuel; (*issue etc*) *Pej* théorique; (*style, art*) académique; – *n* (*teacher*) *Univ* universitaire *mf*. ◆**academy** [ə'kædəmɪ] *n* (*society*) académie *f*; *Mil Mus* école *f*. ◆**acade'mician** *n* académicien, -ienne *mf*.

accede [ək'siːd] *vi* **to a. to** (*request, throne, position*) accéder à.

accelerate [ək'seləreɪt] *vt* accélérer; – *vi* s'accélérer; *Aut* accélérer. ◆**acceleration** *n* accélération *f*. ◆**accelerator** *n* *Aut* accélérateur *m*.

accent ['æksənt] *n* accent *m*; – [æk'sent] *vt* accentuer. ◆**accentuate** [æk'sentʃʊeɪt] *vt* accentuer.

accept [ək'sept] *vt* accepter. ◆**-ed** *a* (*opinion etc*) reçu, admis. ◆**acceptable** *a* (*worth accepting, tolerable*) acceptable. ◆**acceptance** *n* acceptation *f*; (*approval, favour*) accueil *m* favorable.

access ['ækses] *n* accès *m* (**to sth** à qch, **to s.o.** auprès de qn). ◆**ac'cessible** *a* accessible.

accession [æk'seʃ(ə)n] *n* accession *f* (**to** à); (*increase*) augmentation *f*; (*sth added*) nouvelle acquisition *f*.

accessory [ək'sesəri] **1** n (person) Jur complice mf. **2** npl (objects) accessoires mpl.

accident ['æksɪdənt] n accident m; **by a.** (by chance) par accident; (unintentionally) accidentellement, sans le vouloir. ◆**a.-prone** a prédisposé aux accidents. ◆**acci'dental** a accidentel, fortuit. ◆**acci'dentally** adv accidentellement, par mégarde; (by chance) par accident.

acclaim [ə'kleɪm] vt acclamer; **to a. king** proclamer roi. ◆**accla'mation** n acclamation(s) f(pl), louange(s) f(pl).

acclimate ['æklɪmeɪt] vti Am = acclimatize. ◆**a'cclimatize** vt acclimater; – vi s'acclimater. ◆**accli'mation** n Am, ◆**acclimati'zation** n acclimatisation f.

accolade ['ækəleɪd] n (praise) Fig louange f.

accommodat/e [ə'kɒmədeɪt] vt (of house) loger, recevoir; (have room for) avoir de la place pour (mettre); (adapt) adapter (to à); (supply) fournir (s.o. with sth qch à qn); (oblige) rendre service à; (reconcile) concilier; **to a. oneself to** s'accomoder à. ◆**—ing** a accommodant, obligeant. ◆**accommo'dation** n **1** (lodging) logement m; (rented room or rooms) chambre(s) f(pl); pl (in hotel) chambres f(pl). **2** (compromise) compromis m, accommodement m.

accompany [ə'kʌmpəni] vt accompagner. ◆**accompaniment** n accompagnement m. ◆**accompanist** n Mus accompagnateur, -trice mf.

accomplice [ə'kʌmplɪs] n complice mf.

accomplish [ə'kʌmplɪʃ] vt (task, duty) accomplir; (aim) réaliser. ◆**—ed** a accompli. ◆**—ment** n accomplissement m; (of aim) réalisation f; (thing achieved) réalisation f; pl (skills) talents mpl.

accord [ə'kɔːd] **1** n accord m; **of my own a.** volontairement, de mon plein gré; – vi concorder. **2** vt (grant) accorder. ◆**accordance** n **in a. with** conformément à.

according to [ə'kɔːdɪŋtuː] prep selon, d'après, suivant. ◆**accordingly** adv en conséquence.

accordion [ə'kɔːdɪən] n accordéon m.

accost [ə'kɒst] vt accoster, aborder.

account [ə'kaʊnt] **1** n Com compte m; pl comptabilité f, comptes mpl, **accounts department** comptabilité f; **to take into a.** tenir compte de; **ten pounds on a.** un acompte de dix livres; **of some a.** d'une certaine importance; **on a. of** à cause de; **on**

no a. en aucun cas. **2** n (report) compte rendu m, récit m; (explanation) explication f; **by all accounts** au dire de tous; **to give a good a. of oneself** s'en tirer à son avantage; – vi **to a. for** (explain) expliquer; (give reckoning of) rendre compte de. **3** vt **to a. oneself lucky/etc** (consider) se considérer heureux/etc. ◆**accountable** a responsable (for de, to devant); (explainable) explicable.

accountant [ə'kaʊntənt] n comptable mf. ◆**accountancy** n comptabilité f.

accoutrements [ə'kuːtrəmənts] (Am **accouterments** [ə'kuːtərmənts]) npl équipement m.

accredit [ə'kredɪt] vt (ambassador) accréditer; **to a. s.o. with sth** attribuer qch à qn.

accrue [ə'kruː] vi (of interest) Fin s'accumuler; **to a. to** (of advantage etc) revenir à.

accumulate [ə'kjuːmjʊleɪt] vt accumuler, amasser; – vi s'accumuler. ◆**accumu-'lation** n accumulation f; (mass) amas m. ◆**accumulator** n El accumulateur m.

accurate ['ækjʊrət] a exact, précis. ◆**accuracy** n exactitude f, précision f. ◆**accurately** adv avec précision.

accursed [ə'kɜːsɪd] a maudit, exécrable.

accus/e [ə'kjuːz] vt accuser (of de). ◆**—ed** n **the a.** Jur l'inculpé, -ée mf, l'accusé, -ée mf. ◆**—ing** a accusateur. ◆**accu'sation** n accusation f.

accustom [ə'kʌstəm] vt habituer, accoutumer. ◆**—ed** a habitué (to sth à qch, to doing à faire); **to get a. to** s'habituer à, s'accoutumer à.

ace [eɪs] n (card, person) as m.

acetate ['æsɪteɪt] n acétate m.

acetic [ə'siːtɪk] a acétique.

ache [eɪk] n douleur f, mal m; **to have an a. in one's arm** avoir mal au bras; – vi faire mal; **my head aches** ma tête me fait mal; **it makes my heart a.** cela me serre le cœur; **to be aching to do** brûler de faire. ◆**aching** a douloureux.

achieve [ə'tʃiːv] vt accomplir, réaliser; (success, aim) atteindre; (victory) remporter. ◆**—ment** n accomplissement m, réalisation f (of de); (feat) réalisation f, exploit m.

acid ['æsɪd] a & n acide (m). ◆**a'cidity** n acidité f.

acknowledge [ək'nɒlɪdʒ] vt reconnaître (as pour), (greeting) répondre à; **to a. (receipt of)** accuser réception de; **to a. defeat** s'avouer vaincu. ◆**—ment** n reconnaissance f; (of letter) accusé m de réception; (receipt) reçu m, récépissé m.

acme ['ækmɪ] n sommet m, comble m.

acne ['æknɪ] n acné f.

acorn ['eɪkɔːn] n Bot gland m.

acoustic [ə'kuːstɪk] a acoustique; – npl acoustique f.

acquaint [ə'kweɪnt] vt to a. s.o. with sth informer qn de qch; to be acquainted with (person) connaître; (fact) savoir; we are acquainted on se connaît. ◆**acquaintance** n (person, knowledge) connaissance f.

acquiesce [ækwɪ'es] vi acquiescer (in à). ◆**acquiescence** n acquiescement m.

acquire [ə'kwaɪər] vt acquérir; (taste) prendre (for à); (friends) se faire; aquired taste goût m qui s'acquiert. ◆**acqui'sition** n acquisition f. ◆**acquisitive** a avide, cupide.

acquit [ə'kwɪt] vt (-tt-) to a. s.o. of (of a crime) acquitter qn. ◆**acquittal** n acquittement m.

acre ['eɪkər] n acre f (= 0.4 hectare). ◆**acreage** n superficie f.

acrid ['ækrɪd] a (smell, manner etc) âcre.

acrimonious [ækrɪ'məʊnɪəs] a acerbe.

acrobat ['ækrəbæt] n acrobate mf. ◆**acro-'batic** a acrobatique; – npl acrobatie(s) f(pl).

acronym ['ækrənɪm] n sigle m.

across [ə'krɒs] adv & prep (from side to side (of)) d'un côté à l'autre (de); (on the other side (of)) de l'autre côté (de); (crossways) en travers (de); to be a kilometre/etc a. (wide) avoir un kilomètre/etc de large; to walk or go a. (street etc) traverser; to come a. (person) rencontrer (par hasard), tomber sur; (thing) trouver (par hasard); to get sth a. to s.o. faire comprendre qch à qn.

acrostic [ə'krɒstɪk] n acrostiche m.

acrylic [ə'krɪlɪk] a & n acrylique (m).

act [ækt] 1 n (deed) acte m; a. (of parliament) loi f; caught in the a. pris sur le fait; a. of walking action f de marcher; an a. of folly une folie. 2 n (of play) Th acte m; (turn) Th numéro m; in on the a. Fam dans le coup; to put on an a. Fam jouer la comédie; – vt (part) Th jouer; to a. the fool faire l'idiot; – vi Th Cin jouer; (pretend) jouer la comédie. 3 vi (do sth, behave) agir; to a. as (secretary etc) faire office de; (of object) servir de; to a. (up)on (affect) agir sur; (advice) suivre; to a. on behalf of représenter; to a. up (of person, machine) Fam faire des siennes. ◆**—ing 1** a (manager etc) intérimaire, provisoire. **2** n (of play) représentation f; (actor's art) jeu m; (career) théâtre m.

action ['ækʃ(ə)n] n action f; Mil combat m; Jur procès m, action f; to take a. prendre des mesures; to put into a. (plan) exécuter; out of a. hors d'usage, hors (de) service; (person) hors de combat; killed in a. mort au champ d'honneur; to take industrial a. se mettre en grève.

active ['æktɪv] a actif; (interest) vif; (volcano) en activité. ◆**activate** vt Ch activer; (mechanism) actionner. ◆**activist** n activiste mf. ◆**ac'tivity** n activité f; (in street) mouvement m.

actor ['æktər] n acteur m. ◆**actress** n actrice f.

actual ['æktʃuəl] a réel, véritable; (example) concret; the a. book le livre même; in a. fact en réalité, effectivement. ◆**—ly** adv (truly) réellement; (in fact) en réalité, en fait.

actuary ['æktʃuərɪ] n actuaire mf.

actuate ['æktʃueɪt] vt (person) animer; (machine) actionner.

acumen ['ækjumen, Am ə'kjuːmən] n perspicacité f, finesse f.

acupuncture ['ækjupʌŋktʃər] n acupuncture f.

acute [ə'kjuːt] a aigu; (anxiety, emotion) vif, profond; (observer) perspicace; (shortage) grave. ◆**—ly** adv (to suffer, feel) vivement, profondément. ◆**—ness** n acuité f; perspicacité f.

ad [æd] n Fam pub f; (private, in newspaper) annonce f; small ad petite annonce.

AD [eɪ'diː] abbr (anno Domini) après Jésus-Christ.

adage ['ædɪdʒ] n adage m.

Adam ['ædəm] n A.'s apple pomme f d'Adam.

adamant ['ædəmənt] a inflexible.

adapt [ə'dæpt] vt adapter (to à); to a. (oneself) s'adapter. ◆**adaptable** a (person) capable de s'adapter, adaptable. ◆**adaptor** n (device) adaptateur m; (plug) prise f multiple. ◆**adap'tation** n adaptation f.

add [æd] vt ajouter (to à, that que); to a. (up or together) (total) additionner; to a. in inclure; – vi to a. to (increase) augmenter; to a. up to (total) s'élever à; (mean) signifier; it all adds up Fam ça s'explique. ◆**a'ddendum**, pl -da n supplément m. ◆**adding machine** n machine f à calculer. ◆**a'ddition** n addition f; augmentation f; in a. de plus; in a. to en plus de. ◆**a'dditional** a supplémentaire. ◆**a'dditionally** adv de plus. ◆**additive** n additif m.

adder ['ædər] n vipère f.

addict ['ædɪkt] *n* intoxiqué, -ée *mf*; **jazz/sport a.** fanatique *mf* du jazz/du sport; **drug a.** drogué, -ée *mf*. ◆**a'dicted** *a* **to be a.** to (*study, drink*) s'adonner à; (*music*) se passionner pour; (*to have the habit of*) avoir la manie de; **a. to cigarettes** drogué par la cigarette. ◆**a'diction** *n* (*habit*) manie *f*; (*dependency*) Med dépendance *f*; **drug a.** toxicomanie *f*. ◆**a'ddictive** *a* qui crée une dépendance.

address [ə'dres, *Am* 'ædres] *n* (*on letter etc*) adresse *f*; (*speech*) allocution *f*; **form of a.** formule *f* de politesse; – [ə'dres] *vt* (*person*) s'adresser à; (*audience*) parler devant; (*words, speech*) adresser (**to** à); (*letter*) mettre l'adresse sur; **to a. to s.o.** (*send, intend for*) adresser à qn. ◆**addressee** [ædre'si:] *n* destinataire *mf*.

adenoids ['ædɪnɔɪdz] *npl* végétations *fpl* (adénoïdes).

adept ['ædept, *Am* ə'dept] *a* expert (**in, at** à).

adequate ['ædɪkwət] *a* (*quantity*) suffisant; (*acceptable*) convenable; (*person, performance*) compétent. ◆**adequacy** *n* (*of person*) compétence *f*; **to doubt the a. of sth** douter que qch soit suffisant. ◆**adequately** *adv* suffisamment; convenablement.

adhere [əd'hɪər] *vi* **to a. to** adhérer à; (*decision*) s'en tenir à; (*rule*) respecter. ◆**adherence** *n*, ◆**adhesion** *n* (*grip*) adhérence *f*; (*support*) Fig adhésion *f*. ◆**adhesive** *a* & *n* adhésif (*m*).

ad infinitum [ædɪnfɪ'naɪtəm] *adv* à l'infini.

adjacent [ə'dʒeɪsənt] *a* (*house, angle etc*) adjacent (**to** à).

adjective ['ædʒɪktɪv] *n* adjectif *m*.

adjoin [ə'dʒɔɪn] *vt* avoisiner. ◆**—ing** *a* avoisinant, voisin.

adjourn [ə'dʒɜːn] *vt* (*postpone*) ajourner; (*session*) lever, suspendre; – *vi* lever la séance; **to a. to** (*go*) passer à. ◆**—ment** *n* ajournement *m*; suspension *f* (de séance), levée *f* de séance.

adjudicate [ə'dʒuːdɪkeɪt] *vti* juger. ◆**adjudi'cation** *n* jugement *m*. ◆**adjudicator** *n* juge *m*, arbitre *m*.

adjust [ə'dʒʌst] *vt* Tech régler, ajuster; (*prices*) (r)ajuster; (*arrange*) arranger; **to a.** (**oneself**) **to** s'adapter à. ◆**—able** *a* réglable. ◆**—ment** *n* Tech réglage *m*; (*of person*) adaptation *f*; (*of prices*) (r)ajustement *m*.

ad-lib [æd'lɪb] *vi* (**-bb-**) improviser; – *a* (*joke etc*) improvisé.

administer [əd'mɪnɪstər] **1** *vt* (*manage, dispense*) administrer (**to** à). **2** *vi* **to a. to** pourvoir à. ◆**admini'stration** *n* administration *f*; (*ministry*) gouvernement *m*. ◆**administrative** *a* administratif. ◆**administrator** *n* administrateur, -trice *mf*.

admiral ['ædmərəl] *n* amiral *m*.

admir/e [əd'maɪər] *vt* admirer. ◆**—ing** *a* admiratif. ◆**—er** *n* admirateur, -trice *mf*. ◆**admirable** *a* admirable. ◆**admiration** *n* admiration *f*.

admit [əd'mɪt] *vt* (**-tt-**) (*let in*) laisser entrer; (*accept*) admettre; (*acknowledge*) reconnaître, avouer; – *vi* **a. to sth** (*confess*) avouer qch; **a. of** permettre. ◆**admittedly** *adv* c'est vrai (que). ◆**admissible** *a* admissible. ◆**admission** *n* (*entry to theatre etc*) entrée *f* (**to** à, de); (*to club, school*) admission *f*; (*acknowledgement*) aveu *m*; **a. (charge)** (prix *m* d')entrée *f*. ◆**admittance** *n* entrée *f*; **'no a.'** 'entrée interdite'.

admonish [əd'mɒnɪʃ] *vt* (*reprove*) réprimander; (*warn*) avertir.

ado [ə'duː] *n* **without further a.** sans (faire) plus de façons.

adolescent [ædə'lesənt] *n* adolescent, -ente *mf*. ◆**adolescence** *n* adolescence *f*.

adopt [ə'dɒpt] *vt* (*child, method, attitude etc*) adopter; (*candidate*) Pol choisir. ◆**—ed** *a* (*child*) adoptif; (*country*) d'adoption. ◆**adoption** *n* adoption *f*. ◆**adoptive** *a* (*parent*) adoptif.

adore [ə'dɔːr] *vt* adorer; **he adores being flattered** il adore qu'on le flatte. ◆**adorable** *a* adorable. ◆**ado'ration** *n* adoration *f*.

adorn [ə'dɔːn] *vt* (*room, book*) orner; (*person, dress*) parer. ◆**—ment** *n* ornement *m*; parure *f*.

adrenalin(e) [ə'drenəlɪn] *n* adrénaline *f*.

Adriatic [eɪdrɪ'ætɪk] *n* **the A.** l'Adriatique *f*.

adrift [ə'drɪft] *a* & *adv* Nau à la dérive; **to come a.** (*of rope, collar etc*) se détacher; **to turn s.o. a.** Fig abandonner qn à son sort.

adroit [ə'drɔɪt] *a* adroit, habile.

adulation [ædju'leɪʃ(ə)n] *n* adulation *f*.

adult ['ædʌlt] *a* & *n* adulte (*mf*). ◆**adulthood** *n* âge *m* adulte.

adulterate [ə'dʌltəreɪt] *vt* (*food*) altérer.

adultery [ə'dʌltərɪ] *n* adultère *m*. ◆**adulterous** *a* adultère.

advanc/e [əd'vɑːns] *n* (*movement, money*) avance *f*; (*of science*) progrès *mpl*; *pl* (*of friendship, love*) avances *fpl*; **in a.** à l'avance, d'avance; (*to arrive*) en avance; **in a. of s.o.** avant qn; – *a* (*payment*) anticipé; **a. booking** réservation *f*; **a. guard** avant-garde *f*; – *vt* (*put forward, lend*)

avancer; (*science, work*) faire avancer; – *vi*
(*go forward, progress*) avancer; (*towards
s.o.*) s'avancer, avancer; (*studies*) supérieur; **a. in years** âgé.
◆**—ed** *a* avancé; (*studies*) supérieur; **a. in years** âgé.
◆**—ement** *n* (*progress, promotion*)
avancement *m*.

advantage [əd'vɑːntɪdʒ] *n* avantage *m* (**over**
sur); **to take a. of** profiter de; (*person*)
tromper, exploiter; (*woman*) séduire; **to
show (off) to a.** faire valoir. ◆**advan-
'tageous** *a* avantageux (**to**, pour), profitable.

advent ['ædvent] *n* arrivée *f*, avènement *m*;
A. *Rel* l'Avent *m*.

adventure [əd'ventʃər] *n* aventure *f*; – *a*
(*film etc*) d'aventures. ◆**adventurer** *n*
aventurier, -ière *mf*. ◆**adventurous** *a*
aventureux.

adverb ['ædvɜːb] *n* adverbe *m*.

adversary ['ædvəsəri] *n* adversaire *mf*.

adverse ['ædvɜːs] *a* hostile, défavorable.
◆**ad'versity** *n* adversité *f*.

advert ['ædvɜːt] *n Fam* pub *f*; (*private, in
newspaper*) annonce *f*.

advertis/e ['ædvətaɪz] *vt* (*goods*) faire de la
publicité pour; (*make known*) annoncer; –
vi faire de la publicité; **to a. (for s.o.)** mettre
une annonce (pour chercher qn). ◆**—er** *n*
annonceur *m*. ◆**—ement** [əd'vɜːtɪsmənt,
Am ædvə'taɪzmənt] *n* publicité *f*; (*private
or classified in newspaper*) annonce *f*;
(*poster*) affiche *f*; **classified a.** petite
annonce; **the advertisements** *TV* la publicité.

advice [əd'vaɪs] *n* conseil(s) *m(pl)*; *Com*
avis *m*; **a piece of a.** un conseil.

advis/e [əd'vaɪz] *vt* (*counsel*) conseiller;
(*recommend*) recommander; (*notify*)
informer; **to a. s.o. to do** conseiller à qn de
faire; **to a. against** déconseiller. ◆**—ed** *a*
well-a. (*action*) prudent. ◆**—able** *a* (*wise*)
prudent (to do de faire); (*act*) à conseiller.
◆**—edly** [-ɪdlɪ] *adv* après réflexion. ◆**—er**
n conseiller, -ère *mf*. ◆**advisory** *a*
consultatif.

advocate 1 ['ædvəkət] *n* (*of cause*) défenseur *m*, avocat, -ate *mf*; *Jur* avocat *m*. **2**
['ædvəkeɪt] *vt* préconiser, recommander.

aegis ['iːdʒɪs] *n* **under the a. of** sous l'égide
de.

aeon ['iːən] *n* éternité *f*.

aerial ['eərɪəl] *n* antenne *f*; – *a* aérien.

aerobatics [eərə'bætɪks] *npl* acrobatie *f*
aérienne. ◆**ae'robics** *npl* aérobic *f*.
◆**'aerodrome** *n* aérodrome *m*. ◆**aer-
ody'namic** *a* aérodynamique. ◆**aero'-
nautics** *npl* aéronautique *f*. ◆**'aeroplane**

n avion *m*. ◆**'aerosol** *n* aérosol *m*.
◆**'aerospace** *a* (*industry*) aérospatial.

aesthetic [iːs'θetɪk, *Am* es'θetɪk] *a* esthétique.

afar [ə'fɑːr] *adv* **from a.** de loin.

affable ['æfəb(ə)l] *a* affable, aimable.

affair [ə'feər] *n* (*matter, concern*) affaire *f*;
(*love*) **a.** liaison *f*; **state of affairs** état *m* de
choses.

affect [ə'fekt] *vt* (*move, feign*) affecter;
(*concern*) toucher, affecter; (*harm*) nuire à;
(*be fond of*) affectionner. ◆**—ed** *a*
(*manner*) affecté; (*by disease*) atteint.
◆**affec'tation** *n* affectation *f*.

affection [ə'fekʃ(ə)n] *n* affection *f* (**for**
pour). ◆**affectionate** *a* affectueux,
aimant. ◆**affectionately** *adv* affectueuse-
ment.

affiliate [ə'fɪlɪeɪt] *vt* affilier; **to be affiliated**
s'affilier (**to** à); **affiliated company** filiale *f*.
◆**affili'ation** *n* affiliation *f*; *pl* (*political*)
attaches *fpl*.

affinity [ə'fɪnɪtɪ] *n* affinité *f*.

affirm [ə'fɜːm] *vt* affirmer. ◆**affir'mation**
n affirmation *f*. ◆**affirmative** *a* affirmatif; –
n affirmative *f*.

affix [ə'fɪks] *vt* apposer.

afflict [ə'flɪkt] *vt* affliger (**with** de). ◆**affliction** *n* (*misery*) affliction *f*; (*disorder*)
infirmité *f*.

affluent ['æfluənt] *a* riche; **a. society** société
f d'abondance. ◆**affluence** *n* richesse *f*.

afford [ə'fɔːd] *vt* **1** (*pay for*) avoir les moyens
d'acheter, pouvoir se payer; (*time*) pouvoir
trouver; **I can a. to wait** je peux me permettre d'attendre. **2** (*provide*) fournir, donner;
to a. s.o. sth fournir qch à qn.

affray [ə'freɪ] *n Jur* rixe *f*, bagarre *f*.

affront [ə'frʌnt] *n* affront *m*; – *vt* faire un
affront à.

Afghanistan [æf'gænɪstɑːn] *n* Afghanistan
m. ◆**'Afghan** *a* & *n* afghan, -ane (*mf*).

afield [ə'fiːld] *adv* **further a.** plus loin; **too far
a.** trop loin.

afloat [ə'fləʊt] *adv* (*ship, swimmer, business*)
à flot; (*awash*) submergé; **life a.** la vie sur
l'eau.

afoot [ə'fʊt] *adv* **there's sth a.** il se trame
qch; **there's a plan a. to** on prépare un
projet pour.

aforementioned [ə'fɔːmenʃənd] *a* susmentionné.

afraid [ə'freɪd] *a* **to be a.** avoir peur (**of, to**
that; **que**); **to make s.o. afraid** faire peur
à qn; **he's a. (that) she may be ill** il a peur
qu'elle (ne) soit malade; **I'm a. he's out** (*I
regret to say*) je regrette, il est sorti.

afresh [ə'freʃ] *adv* de nouveau.

Africa ['æfrɪkə] *n* Afrique *f*. ◆**African** *a & n* africain, -aine (*mf*).

after ['ɑːftər] *adv* après; *the month a.* le mois suivant, le mois d'après; – *prep* après; *a. all* après tout; *a. eating* après avoir mangé; *day a. day* jour après jour; *page a. page* page sur page; *time a. time* bien des fois; *a. you!* je vous en prie!; *ten a. four Am* quatre heures dix; *to be a. sth/s.o.* (*seek*) chercher qch/qn; – *conj* après que; *a. he saw you* après qu'il t'a vu. ◆**aftercare** *n Med* soins *mpl* postopératoires; *Jur* surveillance *f*. ◆**aftereffects** *npl* suites *fpl*, séquelles *fpl*. ◆**afterlife** *n* vie *f* future. ◆**aftermath** [-mɑːθ] *n* suites *fpl*. ◆**after'noon** *n* après-midi *m or f inv*; *in the a.* l'après-midi; *good a.!* (*hello*) bonjour!; (*goodbye*) au revoir! ◆**after'noons** *adv Am* l'après midi. ◆**aftersales** (**service**) *n* service *m* après-vente. ◆**aftershave** (**lotion**) *n* lotion *f* après-rasage. ◆**aftertaste** *n* arrière-goût *m*. ◆**afterthought** *n* réflexion *f* après coup. ◆**afterward(s)** *adv* après, plus tard.

afters ['ɑːftəz] *npl Fam* dessert *m*.

again [ə'gen, ə'geɪn] *adv* de nouveau, encore une fois; (*furthermore*) en outre; *to do a.* refaire; *to go down/up a.* redescendre/remonter; *never a.* plus jamais; *half as much a.* moitié plus; *a. and a., time and* (*time*) *a.* maintes fois; *what's his name a.?* comment s'appelle-t-il déjà?

against [ə'genst, ə'geɪnst] *prep* contre; *to go or be a.* s'opposer à; *a law a. drinking* une loi qui interdit de boire; *his age is a. him* son âge lui est défavorable; *a. a background of* sur (un) fond de; *a. the light* à contre-jour; *a. the law* illégal; *a. the rules* interdit, contraire aux règlements.

age [eɪdʒ] *n* (*lifespan, period*) âge *m*; (*old*) *a.* vieillesse *f*; *the Middle Ages* le moyen âge; *what a. are you?, what's your a.?* quel âge as-tu?; *five years of a.* âgé de cinq ans; *to be of a.* être majeur; *under a.* trop jeune, mineur; *to wait* (*for*) *ages Fam* attendre une éternité; *a group* tranche *f* d'âge; – *vti* (*pres p* ag(e)ing) vieillir. ◆**a.-old** *a* séculaire. ◆**aged** *a* [eɪdʒd] *a.* *ten* âgé de dix ans; ['eɪdʒɪd] vieux, âgé; *the a.* les personnes *fpl* âgées. ◆**ageless** *a* toujours jeune.

agenda [ə'dʒendə] *n* ordre *m* du jour.

agent ['eɪdʒənt] *n* agent *m*; (*dealer*) Com concessionnaire *mf*. ◆**agency** *n* **1** (*office*) agence *f*. **2** *through the a. of s.o.* par l'intermédiaire de qn.

agglomeration [əglɒmə'reɪʃ(ə)n] *n* agglomération *f*.

aggravate ['ægrəveɪt] *vt* (*make worse*) aggraver; *to s.o.* *Fam* exaspérer qn. ◆**aggra'vation** *n* aggravation *f*; *Fam* exaspération *f*; (*bother*) *Fam* ennui(s) *m*(*pl*).

aggregate ['ægrɪgət] *a* global; – *n* (*total*) ensemble *m*.

aggression [ə'greʃ(ə)n] *n* agression *f*. ◆**aggressive** *a* agressif. ◆**aggressiveness** *n* agressivité *f*. ◆**aggressor** *n* agresseur *m*.

aggrieved [ə'griːvd] *a* (*offended*) blessé, froissé; (*tone*) peiné.

aghast [ə'gɑːst] *a* consterné, horrifié.

agile ['ædʒaɪl, *Am* 'ædʒ(ə)l] *a* agile. ◆**a'gility** *n* agilité *f*.

agitate ['ædʒɪteɪt] *vt* (*worry, shake*) agiter; – *vi to a. for Pol* faire campagne pour. ◆**agi'tation** *n* (*anxiety, unrest*) agitation *f*. ◆**agitator** *n* agitateur, -trice *mf*.

aglow [ə'gləʊ] *a to be a.* briller (*with* de).

agnostic [æg'nɒstɪk] *a & n* agnostique (*mf*).

ago [ə'gəʊ] *adv a year a.* il y a un an; *how long a.?* il y a combien de (cela)?; *as long a. as 1800* (déjà) en 1800.

agog [ə'gɒg] *a* (*excited*) en émoi; (*eager*) impatient.

agony ['ægənɪ] *n* (*pain*) douleur *f* atroce; (*anguish*) angoisse *f*; *to be in a.* souffrir horriblement; *a. column* *Journ* courrier *m* du cœur. ◆**agonize** *vi* se faire beaucoup de souci. ◆**agonized** *a* (*look*) angoissé; (*cry*) de douleur. ◆**agonizing** *a* (*pain*) atroce; (*situation*) angoissant.

agree [ə'griː] *vi* (*come to terms*) se mettre d'accord, s'accorder; (*be in agreement*) être d'accord, s'accorder (*with* avec); (*of facts, dates etc*) concorder; *Gram* s'accorder; *to a. upon* (*decide*) convenir de; *to a. to sth/to doing* consentir à qch/à faire; *it doesn't a. with me* (*food, climate*) ça ne me réussit pas; – *vt* (*figures*) faire concorder; (*accounts*) *Com* approuver; *to a. to do* accepter de faire; *to a. that* (*admit*) admettre que. ◆**agreed** *a* (*time, place*) convenu; *we a.* nous sommes d'accord; *a.!* entendu! ◆**agreeable** *a* **1** (*pleasant*) agréable. **2** *to be a.* (*agree*) être d'accord; *to be a. to sth* consentir à qch. ◆**agreement** *n* accord *m*; *Pol Com* convention *f*, accord *m*; *in a. with* d'accord avec.

agriculture ['ægrɪkʌltʃər] *n* agriculture *f*. ◆**agri'cultural** *a* agricole.

aground [ə'graʊnd] *adv to run a.* *Nau* (s')échouer.

ah! [ɑː] *int* ah!

ahead [əˈhed] *adv* (*in space*) en avant; (*leading*) en tête; (*in the future*) dans l'avenir; **a.** (**of time or of schedule**) en avance (sur l'horaire); **one hour/etc a.** une heure/*etc* d'avance (**of** sur); **a. of** (*space*) devant; (*time, progress*) en avance sur; **to go a.** (*advance*) avancer; (*continue*) continuer; (*start*) commencer; **go a.!** allez-y!; **to go a. with** (*task*) poursuivre; **to get a.** prendre de l'avance; (*succeed*) réussir; **to think a.** penser à l'avenir; **straight a.** tout droit.

aid [eɪd] *n* (*help*) aide *f*; (*apparatus*) support *m*, moyen *m*; **with the a. of** (*a stick etc*) à l'aide de; **in a. of** (*charity etc*) au profit de; **what's this in a. of?** *Fam* quel est le but de tout ça?, ça sert à quoi?; − *vt* aider (**to do** à faire).

aide [eɪd] *n Pol* aide *mf*.

AIDS [eɪdz] *n Med* SIDA *m*.

ail [eɪl] *vt* **what ails you?** de quoi souffrez-vous? **◆−ing** *a* souffrant, malade. **◆−ment** *n* maladie *f*.

aim [eɪm] *n* but *m*; **to take a.** viser; **with the a. of** dans le but de; − *vt* (*gun*) braquer, diriger (**at** sur); (*lamp*) diriger (**at** vers); (*stone*) lancer (**at** à, vers); (*blow, remark*) décocher (**at** à); − *vi* viser; **to a. at s.o.** viser qn; **to a. to do or at doing** avoir l'intention de faire. **◆−less** *a*, **◆−lessly** *adv* sans but.

air [eər] **1** *n* air *m*; **in the open a.** en plein air; **by a.** (*to travel*) en or par avion; (*letter, freight*) par avion; **to be or go on the a.** (*person*) passer à l'antenne; (*programme*) être diffusé; (**up**) **in the a.** (*to throw*) en l'air; (*plan*) incertain, en l'air; **there's sth in the a.** *Fig* il se prépare qch; − *a* (*raid, base etc*) aérien; **a. force/hostess** armée *f*/hôtesse *f* de l'air; **a. terminal** aérogare *f*; − *vt* aérer; (*views*) exposer; **airing cupboard** armoire *f* sèche-linge. **2** *n* (*appearance, tune*) air *m*; **to put on airs** se donner des airs; **with an a. of sadness/etc** d'un air triste/*etc*.

airborne [ˈeəbɔːn] *a* en (cours de) vol; (*troops*) aéroporté; **to become a.** (*of aircraft*) décoller. **◆airbridge** *n* pont *m* aérien. **◆air-conditioned** *a* climatisé. **◆air-conditioner** *n* climatiseur *m*. **◆aircraft** *n inv* avion(s) *m(pl)*; **a. carrier** porte-avions *m inv*. **◆aircrew** *n Av* équipage *m*. **◆airfield** *n* terrain *m* d'aviation. **◆airgun** *n* carabine *f* à air comprimé. **◆airletter** *n* aérogramme *m*. **◆airlift** *n* pont *m* aérien; − *vt* transporter par avion. **◆airline** *n* ligne *f* aérienne. **◆airliner** *n*

avion *m* de ligne. **◆airlock** *n* (*chamber*) *Nau Av* sas *m*; (*in pipe*) bouchon *m*. **◆airmail** *n* poste *f* aérienne; **by a.** par avion. **◆airman** *n* (*pl* **-men**) aviateur *m*. **◆airplane** *n Am* avion *m*. **◆airpocket** *n* trou *m* d'air. **◆airport** *n* aéroport *m*. **◆airship** *n* dirigeable *m*. **◆airsickness** *n* mal *m* de l'air. **◆airstrip** *n* terrain *m* d'atterrissage. **◆airtight** *a* hermétique. **◆airway** *n* (*route*) couloir *m* aérien. **◆airworthy** *a* en état de navigation.

airy [ˈeərɪ] *a* (**-ier, -iest**) (*room*) bien aéré; (*promise*) vain; (*step*) léger. **◆a.-fairy** *a Fam* farfelu. **◆airily** *adv* (*not seriously*) d'un ton léger.

aisle [aɪl] *n* couloir *m*; (*of church*) nef *f* latérale.

aitch [eɪtʃ] *n* (*letter*) h *m*.

ajar [əˈdʒɑːr] *a & adv* (*door*) entrouvert.

akin [əˈkɪn] *a* **a.** (**to**) apparenté (à).

alabaster [ˈæləbɑːstər] *n* albâtre *m*.

alacrity [əˈlækrɪtɪ] *n* empressement *m*.

à la mode [æləˈməʊd] *a Culin Am* avec de la crème glacée.

alarm [əˈlɑːm] *n* (*warning, fear*) alarme *f*; (*apparatus*) sonnerie *f* (d'alarme); **false a.** fausse alerte *f*; **a.** (*clock*) réveil *m*, réveille-matin *m inv*; − *vt* (*frighten*) alarmer. **◆alarmist** *n* alarmiste *mf*.

alas! [əˈlæs] *int* hélas!

albatross [ˈælbətrɒs] *n* albatros *m*.

albeit [ɔːlˈbiːɪt] *conj Lit* quoique.

albino [ælˈbiːnəʊ, *Am* ælˈbaɪnəʊ] *n* (*pl* **-os**) albinos *mf*.

album [ˈælbəm] *n* (*book, record*) album *m*.

alchemy [ˈælkəmɪ] *n* alchimie *f*. **◆alchemist** *n* alchimiste *m*.

alcohol [ˈælkəhɒl] *n* alcool *m*. **◆alco'holic** *a* (*person*) alcoolique; (*drink*) alcoolisé; − *n* (*person*) alcoolique *mf*. **◆alcoholism** *n* alcoolisme *m*.

alcove [ˈælkəʊv] *n* alcôve *f*.

alderman [ˈɔːldəmən] *n* (*pl* **-men**) conseiller, -ère *mf* municipal(e).

ale [eɪl] *n* bière *f*.

alert [əˈlɜːt] *a* (*watchful*) vigilant; (*sharp, awake*) éveillé; − *n* alerte *f*; **on the a.** sur le qui-vive; − *vt* alerter. **◆−ness** *n* vigilance *f*.

alfalfa [ælˈfælfə] *n Am* luzerne *f*.

algebra [ˈældʒɪbrə] *n* algèbre *f*. **◆alge'braic** *a* algébrique.

Algeria [ælˈdʒɪərɪə] *n* Algérie *f*. **◆Algerian** *a & n* algérien, -ienne (*mf*).

alias [ˈeɪlɪəs] *adv* alias; − *n* nom *m* d'emprunt.

alibi [ˈælɪbaɪ] *n* alibi *m*.

alien ['eɪlɪən] *a* étranger (**to** à); – *n* étranger, -ère *mf*. ◆**alienate** *vt* aliéner; **to a. s.o.** (*make unfriendly*) s'aliéner qn.

alight [ə'laɪt] **1** *a* (*fire*) allumé; (*building*) en feu; (*face*) éclairé; **to set a.** mettre le feu à. **2** *vi* descendre (**from** de); (*of bird*) se poser.

align [ə'laɪn] *vt* aligner. ◆**—ment** *n* alignement *m*.

alike [ə'laɪk] **1** *a* (*people, things*) semblables, pareils; **to look** or **be a.** se ressembler. **2** *adv* de la même manière; **summer and winter a.** été comme hiver.

alimony ['ælɪmənɪ, *Am* 'ælɪməʊnɪ] *n Jur* pension *f* alimentaire.

alive [ə'laɪv] *a* vivant, en vie; **a. to** conscient de; **a. with** grouillant de; **burnt a.** brûlé vif; **anyone a.** n'importe qui; **to keep a.** (*custom, memory*) entretenir, perpétuer; **a. and kicking** *Fam* plein de vie; **look a.!** *Fam* (*be unfriendly*) s'activer!

all [ɔːl] *a* tout, toute, *pl* tous, toutes; **a. day** toute la journée; **a. (the) men** tous les hommes; **with a. speed** à toute vitesse; **for a. her wealth** malgré toute sa fortune; – *pron* tous *mpl*, toutes *fpl*; (*everything*) tout; **a. will die** tous mourront; **my sisters are a. here** toutes mes sœurs sont ici; **he ate it a.,** **he ate a. of it** il a tout mangé; **a. (that) he has** tout ce qu'il a; **a. in all** à tout prendre; **in a., a. told** en tout; **a. but impossible/***etc* presque impossible/*etc*; **anything at a.** quoi que ce soit; **if he comes at a.** s'il vient effectivement; **if there's any wind at a.** s'il y a le moindre vent; **not at a.** pas du tout; (*after* 'thank you') il n'y a pas de quoi; **a. of us** nous tous; **take a. of it** prends (le) tout; – *adv* tout; **a. alone** tout seul; **a. bad** entièrement mauvais; **a. over** (*everywhere*) partout; (*finished*) fini; **a. right** (très) bien; **he's a. right** (*not harmed*) il est sain et sauf; (*healthy*) il va bien; **a. too soon** bien trop tôt; **six a.** *Fb* six buts partout; **a. there** *Fam* éveillé, intelligent; **not a. there** *Fam* simple d'esprit; **in a.** *Fam* épuisé; **a.-in price** prix global; – *n* **my a.** tout ce que j'ai; – *adv* tout. ◆**a.-'clear** *n Mil* fin d'alerte. ◆**a.-night** *a* (*party*) qui dure toute la nuit; (*shop*) ouvert toute la nuit. ◆**a.-out** *a* (*effort*) violent; (*war, strike*) tous azimuts. ◆**a.-'powerful** *a* tout-puissant. ◆**a.-purpose** *a* (*tool*) universel. ◆**a.-round** *a* complet. ◆**a.-'rounder** *n* personne *f* qui fait de tout. ◆**a.-time** *a* (*record*) jamais atteint; **to reach an a.-time low/high** arriver au point le plus bas/le plus haut.

allay [ə'leɪ] *vt* calmer, apaiser.

alleg/e [ə'ledʒ] *vt* prétendre. ◆**—ed** *a* (*so-called*) prétendu; (*author, culprit*) présumé; **he is a. to be** on prétend qu'il est. ◆**—edly** [-ɪdlɪ] *adv* d'après ce qu'on dit. ◆**alle'gation** *n* allégation *f*.

allegiance [ə'liːdʒəns] *n* fidélité *f* (**to** à).

allegory ['ælɪɡərɪ, *Am* 'ælɪɡɔːrɪ] *n* allégorie *f*. ◆**alle'gorical** *a* allégorique.

allergy ['ælədʒɪ] *n* allergie *f*. ◆**a'llergic** *a* allergique (**to** à).

alleviate [ə'liːvɪeɪt] *vt* alléger.

alley ['ælɪ] *n* ruelle *f*; (*in park*) allée *f*; **blind a.** impasse *f*; **that's up my a.** *Fam* c'est mon truc. ◆**alleyway** *n* ruelle *f*.

alliance [ə'laɪəns] *n* alliance *f*.

allied ['ælaɪd] *a* (*country*) allié; (*matters*) connexe.

alligator ['ælɪɡeɪtər] *n* alligator *m*.

allocate ['æləkeɪt] *vt* (*assign*) attribuer, allouer (**to** à); (*distribute*) répartir. ◆**allo-'cation** *n* attribution *f*.

allot [ə'lɒt] *vt* (**-tt-**) (*assign*) attribuer; (*distribute*) répartir. ◆**—ment** *n* attribution *f*; (*share*) partage *m*; (*land*) lopin *m* de terre (*loué pour la culture*).

allow [ə'laʊ] **1** *vt* permettre; (*grant*) accorder; (*a request*) accéder à; (*deduct*) *Com* déduire; (*add*) *Com* ajouter; **to a. s.o. to do** permettre à qn de faire, autoriser qn à faire; **a. me!** permettez-moi!; **not allowed** interdit; **you're not allowed to go** on vous interdit de partir. **2** *vi* **to a. for** tenir compte de. ◆**—able** *a* (*acceptable*) admissible; (*expense*) déductible.

allowance [ə'laʊəns] *n* allocation *f*; (*for travel, housing, food*) indemnité *f*; (*for duty-free goods*) tolérance *f*; (*tax-free amount*) abattement *m*; **to make allowance(s) for** (*person*) être indulgent envers; (*thing*) tenir compte de.

alloy ['ælɔɪ] *n* alliage *m*.

allude [ə'luːd] *vi* **to a. to** faire allusion à. ◆**allusion** *n* allusion *f*.

allure [ə'lʊər] *n* attrait *m*.

ally ['ælaɪ] *n* allié, -ée *mf*; – [ə'laɪ] *vt* (*country, person*) allier.

almanac ['ɔːlmənæk] *n* almanach *m*.

almighty [ɔːl'maɪtɪ] **1** *a* tout-puissant; **the A.** le Tout-Puissant. **2** *a* (*great*) *Fam* terrible, formidable.

almond ['ɑːmənd] *n* amande *f*.

almost ['ɔːlməʊst] *adv* presque; **he a. fell/***etc* il a failli tomber/*etc*.

alms [ɑːmz] *npl* aumône *f*.

alone [ə'ləʊn] *a & adv* seul; **an expert a. can ... seul un expert peut ... ;** **I did it (all) a.** je l'ai fait à moi (tout) seul, je l'ai fait (tout) seul; **to leave** or **let a.** (*person*) laisser tranquille or en paix; (*thing*) ne pas toucher à.

along [ə'lɒŋ] *prep* (**all**) **a.** (*tout*) le long de; **to go** or **walk a.** (*street*) passer par; **a. here** par ici; **a. with** avec; – *adv* **all a.** d'un bout à l'autre; (*time*) dès le début; **come a.!** venez!; **move a.!** avancez!

alongside [əlɒŋ'saɪd] *prep* & *adv* à côté (de); **to come a.** *Nau* accoster; **a. the kerb** le long du trottoir.

aloof [ə'luːf] *a* distant; – *adv* à distance; **to keep a.** garder ses distances (**from** par rapport à). ◆**-ness** *n* réserve *f*.

aloud [ə'laʊd] *adv* à haute voix.

alphabet ['ælfəbet] *n* alphabet *m*. ◆**alpha'betical** *a* alphabétique.

Alps [ælps] *npl* **the A.** les Alpes *fpl*. ◆**alpine** *a* (*club, range etc*) alpin; (*scenery*) alpestre.

already [ɔːl'redɪ] *adv* déjà.

alright [ɔːl'raɪt] *adv* Fam = **all right**.

Alsatian [æl'seɪʃ(ə)n] *n* (*dog*) berger *m* allemand, chien-loup *m*.

also ['ɔːlsəʊ] *adv* aussi, également. ◆**a.-ran** *n* (*person*) Fig perdant, -ante *mf*.

altar ['ɔːltər] *n* autel *m*.

alter ['ɔːltər] *vt* changer, modifier; (*clothing*) retoucher; – *vi* changer. ◆**alte'ration** *n* changement *m*, modification *f*; retouche *f*.

altercation [ɔːltə'keɪʃ(ə)n] *n* altercation *f*.

alternate [ɔːl'tɜːnət] *a* alterné; **on a. days** tous les deux jours; **a. laughter and tears** des rires et des larmes qui se succèdent; – ['ɔːltəneɪt] *vi* alterner (**with** avec); –*vt* faire alterner. ◆**-ing** *a* (*current*) *El* alternatif. ◆**-ely** *adv* alternativement. ◆**alter'nation** *n* alternance *f*.

alternative [ɔːl'tɜːnətɪv] *a* **an a. way**/*etc* une autre façon/*etc*; **a. answers**/*etc* d'autres réponses/*etc* (différentes); – *n* (*choice*) alternative *f*. ◆**-ly** *adv* comme alternative; **or a.** (*or else*) ou bien.

although [ɔːl'ðəʊ] *adv* bien que, quoique (+ *sub*).

altitude ['æltɪtjuːd] *n* altitude *f*.

altogether [ɔːltə'geðər] *adv* (*completely*) tout à fait; (*on the whole*) somme toute; **how much a.?** combien en tout?

aluminium [ælju'mɪnjəm] (*Am* **aluminum** [ə'luːmɪnəm]) *n* aluminium *m*.

alumnus, *pl* **-ni** [ə'lʌmnəs, -naɪ] *n Am* ancien(ne) élève *mf*, ancien(ne) étudiant, -ante *mf*.

always ['ɔːlweɪz] *adv* toujours; **he's a. criticizing** il est toujours à critiquer.

am [æm, *unstressed* əm] *see* **be**.

a.m. [eɪ'em] *adv* du matin.

amalgam [ə'mælgəm] *n* amalgame *m*. ◆**a'malgamate** *vt* amalgamer; (*society*) *Com* fusionner; – *vi* s'amalgamer; fusionner.

amass [ə'mæs] *vt* (*riches*) amasser.

amateur ['æmətər] *n* amateur *m*; – *a* (*interest, sports*) d'amateur; **a. painter**/*etc* peintre/*etc* amateur. ◆**amateurish** *a* (*work*) *Pej* d'amateur; (*person*) *Pej* maladroit, malhabile. ◆**amateurism** *n* amateurisme *m*.

amaze [ə'meɪz] *vt* stupéfier, étonner. ◆**-ed** *a* stupéfait (**at sth** de qch), étonné (**at sth** par or de qch); **a. at seeing**/*etc* stupéfait or étonné de voir/*etc*. ◆**-ing** *a* stupéfiant; *Fam* extraordinaire. ◆**-ingly** *adv* extraordinairement; (*miraculously*) par miracle. ◆**amazement** *n* stupéfaction *f*.

ambassador [æm'bæsədər] *n* ambassadeur *m*; (*woman*) ambassadrice *f*.

amber ['æmbər] *n* ambre *m*; **a.** (**light**) *Aut* (feu *m*) orange *m*.

ambidextrous [æmbɪ'dekstrəs] *a* ambidextre.

ambiguous [æm'bɪgjʊəs] *a* ambigu. ◆**ambi'guity** *n* ambiguïté *f*.

ambition [æm'bɪʃ(ə)n] *n* ambition *f*. ◆**ambitious** *a* ambitieux.

ambivalent [æm'bɪvələnt] *a* ambigu, équivoque.

amble ['æmb(ə)l] *vi* marcher d'un pas tranquille.

ambulance ['æmbjʊləns] *n* ambulance *f*; **a. man** ambulancier *m*.

ambush ['æmbʊʃ] *n* guet-apens *m*, embuscade *f*; – *vt* prendre en embuscade.

amen [ɑː'men, eɪ'men] *int* amen.

amenable [ə'miːnəb(ə)l] *a* docile; **a. to** (*responsive to*) sensible à; **a. to reason** raisonnable.

amend [ə'mend] *vt* (*text*) modifier; (*conduct*) corriger; *Pol* amender. ◆**-ment** *n Pol* amendement *m*.

amends [ə'mendz] *npl* **to make a. for** réparer; **to make a.** réparer son erreur.

amenities [ə'miːnɪtɪz, *Am* ə'menɪtɪz] *npl* (*pleasant things*) agréments *mpl*; (*of sports club etc*) équipement *m*; (*of town*) aménagements *mpl*.

America [ə'merɪkə] *n* Amérique *f*; **North/South A.** Amérique du Nord/du Sud. ◆**American** *a* & *n* américain, -aine (*mf*). ◆**Americanism** *n* américanisme *m*.

amethyst ['æmɪθɪst] *n* améthyste *f*.

amiable ['eɪmɪəb(ə)l] *a* aimable.

amicab/le ['æmɪkəb(ə)l] *a* amical. ◆**-ly** *adv* amicalement; *Jur* à l'amiable.

amid(st) [ə'mɪd(st)] *prep* au milieu de, parmi.

amiss [ə'mɪs] *adv* & *a* mal (à propos); **sth is a.** (*wrong*) qch ne va pas; **that wouldn't come a.** ça ne ferait pas de mal; **to take a.** prendre en mauvaise part.

ammonia [ə'məʊnjə] *n* (*gas*) ammoniac *m*; (*liquid*) ammoniaque *f*.

ammunition [æmjʊ'nɪʃ(ə)n] *n* munitions *fpl*.

amnesia [æm'niːzjə] *n* amnésie *f*.

amnesty ['æmnəstɪ] *n* amnistie *f*.

amok [ə'mɒk] *adv* **to run a.** se déchaîner, s'emballer.

among(st) [ə'mʌŋ(st)] *prep* parmi, entre; **a. themselves/friends** entre eux/amis; **a. the French/***etc* (*group*) chez les Français/*etc*; **a. the crowd** dans *or* parmi la foule.

amoral [eɪ'mɒrəl] *a* amoral.

amorous ['æmərəs] *a* amoureux.

amount [ə'maʊnt] **1** *n* quantité *f*; (*sum of money*) somme *f*; (*total of bill etc*) montant *m*; (*scope, size*) importance *f*. **2** *vi* **to a.** s'élever à; (*mean*) *Fig* signifier; **it amounts to the same thing** ça revient au même.

amp(ere) ['æmp(eər)] *n El* ampère *m*.

amphibian [æm'fɪbɪən] *n* & *a* amphibie (*m*). ◆**amphibious** *a* amphibie.

amphitheatre ['æmfɪθɪətər] *n* amphithéâtre *m*.

ample ['æmp(ə)l] *a* (*roomy*) ample; (*enough*) largement assez de; (*reasons, means*) solides; **you have a. time** tu as largement le temps. ◆**amply** *adv* largement, amplement.

amplify ['æmplɪfaɪ] *vt* amplifier. ◆**amplifier** *n El* amplificateur *m*.

amputate ['æmpjʊteɪt] *vt* amputer. ◆**ampu'tation** *n* amputation *f*.

amuck [ə'mʌk] *adv* see **amok.**

amulet ['æmjʊlət] *n* amulette *f*.

amus/e [ə'mjuːz] *vt* amuser, divertir; **to keep s.o. amused** amuser qn. ◆**—ing** *a* amusant. ◆**—ement** *n* amusement *m*, divertissement *m*; (*pastime*) distraction *f*; **a. arcade** salle *f* de jeux.

an [æn, *unstressed* ən] see **a.**

anachronism [ə'nækrənɪz(ə)m] *n* anachronisme *m*.

an(a)emia [ə'niːmɪə] *n* anémie *f*. ◆**an(a)emic** *a* anémique.

an(a)esthesia [ænɪs'θiːzɪə] *n* anesthésie *f*. ◆**an(a)esthetic** [ænɪs'θetɪk] *n* (*substance*) anesthésique *m*; **under the a.** sous anesthésie; **general/local a.** anesthésie *f* générale/locale. ◆**an(a)esthetize** [ə'niːsθɪtaɪz] *vt* anesthésier.

anagram ['ænəgræm] *n* anagramme *f*.

analogy [ə'nælədʒɪ] *n* analogie *f*. ◆**analogous** *a* analogue (**to** à).

analyse ['ænəlaɪz] *vt* analyser. ◆**analysis**, *pl* **-yses** [ə'næləsɪs, -ɪsiːz] *n* analyse *f*. ◆**analyst** *n* analyste *mf*. ◆**ana'lytical** *a* analytique.

anarchy ['ænəkɪ] *n* anarchie *f*. ◆**a'narchic** *a* anarchique. ◆**anarchist** *n* anarchiste *mf*.

anathema [ə'næθəmə] *n Rel* anathème *m*; **it is (an) a. to me** j'ai une sainte horreur de cela.

anatomy [ə'nætəmɪ] *n* anatomie *f*. ◆**ana'tomical** *a* anatomique.

ancestor ['ænsestər] *n* ancêtre *m*. ◆**an'cestral** *a* ancestral. ◆**ancestry** *n* (*lineage*) ascendance *f*; (*ancestors*) ancêtres *mpl*.

anchor ['æŋkər] **1** *n* ancre *f*; **to weigh a.** lever l'ancre; *– vt* (*ship*) mettre à l'ancre; *– vi* jeter l'ancre, mouiller. ◆**—ed** *a* à l'ancre. ◆**—age** *n* mouillage *m*.

anchovy ['æntʃəvɪ, *Am* æn'tʃəʊvɪ] *n* anchois *m*.

ancient ['eɪnʃənt] *a* ancien; (*pre-medieval*) antique; (*person*) *Hum* vétuste.

ancillary [æn'sɪlərɪ] *a* auxiliaire.

and [ænd, *unstressed* ən(d)] *conj* et; **a table and a. fork** un couteau et une fourchette; **two hundred a. two** deux cent deux; **better a. better** de mieux en mieux; **go a. see** va voir.

anecdote ['ænɪkdəʊt] *n* anecdote *f*.

anemone [ə'nemənɪ] *n* anémone *f*.

anew [ə'njuː] *adv Lit* de *or* à nouveau.

angel ['eɪndʒəl] *n* ange *m*. ◆**an'gelic** *a* angélique.

anger ['æŋgər] *n* colère *f*; **in a., out of a.** sous le coup de la colère; *– vt* mettre en colère, fâcher.

angl/e ['æŋg(ə)l] **1** *n* angle *m*; **at an a.** en biais. **2** *vi* (*to fish*) pêcher à la ligne; **to a. for** *Fig* quêter. ◆**—er** *n* pêcheur, -euse *mf* à la ligne. ◆**—ing** *n* pêche *f* à la ligne.

Anglican ['æŋglɪkən] *a* & *n* anglican, -ane (*mf*).

anglicism ['æŋglɪsɪz(ə)m] *n* anglicisme *m*.

Anglo- ['æŋgləʊ] *pref* anglo-. ◆**Anglo-'Saxon** *a* & *n* anglo-saxon, -onne (*mf*).

angora [æŋ'gɔːrə] *n* (*wool*) angora *m*.

angry ['æŋgrɪ] *a* (**-ier, -iest**) (*person, look*) fâché; (*letter*) indigné; **to get a.** se fâcher, se mettre en colère (**with** contre). ◆**angrily** *adv* en colère; (*to speak*) avec colère.

anguish ['æŋgwɪʃ] *n* angoisse *f*. ◆**—ed** *a* angoissé.

angular ['æŋgjʊlər] *a* (*face*) anguleux.

animal ['ænɪməl] a animal; — n animal m, bête f.

animate ['ænɪmeɪt] vt animer; to become animated s'animer; — ['ænɪmət] a (alive) animé. ◆ani'mation n animation f.

animosity [ænɪ'mɒsɪtɪ] n animosité f.

aniseed ['ænɪsiːd] n Culin anis m.

ankle ['æŋk(ə)l] n cheville f; a. sock socquette f.

annals ['æn(ə)lz] npl annales fpl.

annex(e) ['æneks] n (building) annexe f. ◆annex'ation n annexion f.

annex ['æneks] vt annexer.

annihilate [ə'naɪəleɪt] vt anéantir, annihiler. ◆annihi'lation n anéantissement m.

anniversary [ænɪ'vɜːsərɪ] n (of event) anniversaire m, commémoration f.

annotate ['ænəteɪt] vt annoter. ◆anno'tation n annotation f.

announce [ə'naʊns] vt annoncer; (birth, marriage) faire part de. ◆—ement n annonce f; (of birth, marriage) avis m; (private letter) faire-part m inv. ◆—er n TV speaker m, speakerine f.

annoy [ə'nɔɪ] vt (inconvenience) ennuyer, gêner; (irritate) agacer, contrarier. ◆—ed a contrarié, fâché; to get a. se fâcher (with contre). ◆—ing a ennuyeux, contrariant. ◆annoyance n contrariété f, ennui m.

annual ['ænjʊəl] a annuel; — n (book) annuaire m. ◆—ly adv annuellement.

annuity [ə'njuːɪtɪ] n (of retired person) pension f viagère.

annul [ə'nʌl] vt (-ll-) annuler. ◆—ment n annulation f.

anoint [ə'nɔɪnt] vt oindre (with de). ◆—ed a oint.

anomalous [ə'nɒmələs] a anormal. ◆anomaly n anomalie f.

anon [ə'nɒn] adv Hum tout à l'heure.

anonymous [ə'nɒnɪməs] a anonyme; to remain a. garder l'anonymat. ◆ano'nymity n anonymat m.

anorak ['ænəræk] n anorak m.

anorexia [ænə'reksɪə] n anorexie f.

another [ə'nʌðər] a & pron un(e) autre; a. man un autre homme; a. month (additional) encore un mois, un autre mois; a. ten encore dix; one a. l'un(e) l'autre, pl les un(e)s les autres; they love one a. ils s'aiment (l'un l'autre).

answer ['ɑːnsər] n réponse f; (to problem) solution f (to de); (reason) explication f; — vt (person, question, phone etc) répondre à; (word) répondre; (problem) résoudre; (prayer, wish) exaucer; to a. the bell or the door ouvrir la porte; — vi répondre; to a.

back répliquer, répondre; to a. for (s.o., sth) répondre de. ◆—able a responsable (for sth de qch, to s.o. devant qn).

ant [ænt] n fourmi f. ◆anthill n fourmilière f.

antagonism [æn'tægənɪz(ə)m] n antagonisme m; (hostility) hostilité f. ◆antagonist n antagoniste m. ◆antago'nistic a antagoniste; (hostile) hostile. ◆antagonize vt provoquer (l'hostilité de).

antarctic [æn'tɑːktɪk] a antarctique; — n the A. l'Antarctique m.

antecedent [æntɪ'siːd(ə)nt] n antécédent m.

antechamber ['æntɪtʃeɪmbər] n antichambre f.

antedate ['æntɪdeɪt] vt (letter) antidater.

antelope ['æntɪləʊp] n antilope f.

antenatal [æntɪ'neɪt(ə)l] a prénatal.

antenna¹ [æn'tenə], pl -ae [æn'tenə, -iː] n (of insect etc) antenne f.

antenna² [æn'tenə] n (pl -as) (aerial) Am antenne f.

anteroom ['æntɪrʊm] n antichambre f.

anthem ['ænθəm] n national a. hymne m national.

anthology [æn'θɒlədʒɪ] n anthologie f.

anthropology [ænθrə'pɒlədʒɪ] n anthropologie f.

anti- ['æntɪ, Am 'æntaɪ] pref anti-; to be a. sth Fam être contre qch. ◆anti'aircraft a antiaérien. ◆antibi'otic a & n antibiotique (m). ◆antibody n anticorps m. ◆anti'climax n chute f dans l'ordinaire; (let-down) déception f. ◆anti'clockwise adv dans le sens inverse des aiguilles d'une montre. ◆anti'cyclone n anticyclone m. ◆antidote n antidote m. ◆antifreeze n Aut antigel m. ◆anti'histamine n Med antihistaminique m. ◆anti'perspirant n antisudoral m. ◆anti-Se'mitic a antisémite. ◆anti-'Semitism n antisémitisme m. ◆anti'septic a & n antiseptique (m). ◆anti'social a (misfit) asocial; (measure, principles) antisocial; (unsociable) insociable.

anticipate [æn'tɪsɪpeɪt] vt (foresee) prévoir; (forestall) devancer; (expect) s'attendre à; (the future) anticiper sur. ◆antici'pation n prévision f; (expectation) attente f; in a. of en prévision de, dans l'attente de; (to thank s.o., pay etc) d'avance.

antics ['æntɪks] npl bouffonneries fpl.

antipathy [æn'tɪpəθɪ] n antipathie f.

antipodes [æn'tɪpədiːz] npl antipodes mpl.

antiquarian [æntɪ'kweərɪən] a a. bookseller

libraire *mf* spécialisé(e) dans le livre ancien.

antiquated ['æntɪkweɪtɪd] *a* vieilli; (*person*) vieux jeu *inv*.

antique [æn'tiːk] *a* (*furniture etc*) ancien; (*of Greek etc antiquity*) antique; **a. dealer** antiquaire *mf*; **a. shop** magasin *m* d'antiquités; – *n* objet *m* ancien or d'époque, antiquité *f*. ◆**antiquity** *n* (*period etc*) antiquité *f*.

antithesis, *pl* -eses [æn'tɪθəsɪs, -ɪsiːz] *n* antithèse *f*.

antler ['æntlər] *n* (*tine*) andouiller *m*; *pl* bois *mpl*.

antonym ['æntənɪm] *n* antonyme *m*.

Antwerp ['æntwɜːp] *n* Anvers *m* or *f*.

anus ['eɪnəs] *n* anus *m*.

anvil ['ænvɪl] *n* enclume *f*.

anxiety [æŋ'zaɪətɪ] *n* (*worry*) inquiétude *f* (about au sujet de); (*fear*) anxiété *f*; (*eagerness*) impatience *f* (**for** de).

anxious ['æŋkʃəs] *a* (*worried*) inquiet (**about** de, pour); (*troubled*) anxieux; (*causing worry*) inquiétant; (*eager*) impatient (**to do** de faire); **I'm a.** (**that**) **he should go** je tiens beaucoup à ce qu'il parte. ◆—**ly** *adv* avec inquiétude; (*to wait etc*) impatiemment.

any ['enɪ] *a* **1** (*interrogative*) du, de la, des; **have you a. milk/tickets?** avez-vous du lait/des billets?; **is there a. man** (*at all*) **who** ...? y a-t-il un homme (quelconque) qui ...? **2** (*negative*) de; (*not any at all*) aucun; **he hasn't a. milk/tickets** il n'a pas de lait/de billets; **there isn't a. proof** il n'y a aucune preuve. **3** (*no matter which*) n'importe quel. **4** (*every*) tout; **at a. hour** à toute heure; **in a. case, at a. rate** de toute façon; – *pron* **1** (*no matter which one*) n'importe lequel; (*somebody*) quelqu'un; **if a. of you** si l'un d'entre vous, si quelqu'un parmi vous; **more than a.** plus qu'aucun. **2** (*quantity*) en; **have you a.?** en as-tu?; **I don't see a.** je n'en vois pas; – *adv* (*usually not translated*) (**not**) **a. further/happier/etc** (**pas**) plus loin/plus heureux/etc; **I don't see her a. more** je ne la vois plus; **a. more tea?** (*a little*) encore un peu de thé?; **a. better?** (*un peu*) mieux?

anybody ['enɪbɒdɪ] *pron* **1** (*somebody*) quelqu'un; **do you see a.?** vois-tu quelqu'un?; **more than a.** plus qu'aucun. **2** (*negative*) personne; **he doesn't know a.** il ne connaît personne. **3** (*no matter who*) n'importe qui; **a. would think that** ... on croirait que ....

anyhow ['enɪhaʊ] *adv* (*at any rate*) de toute façon; (*badly*) n'importe comment; **to**

leave sth a. (*in confusion*) laisser qch sens dessus dessous.

anyone ['enɪwʌn] *pron* = **anybody**.

anyplace ['enɪpleɪs] *adv Am* = **anywhere**.

anything ['enɪθɪŋ] *pron* **1** (*something*) quelque chose; **can you see a.?** voyez-vous quelque chose? **2** (*negative*) rien; **he doesn't do a.** il ne fait rien; **without a.** sans rien. **3** (*everything*) tout; **a. you like** (tout) ce que tu veux; **like a.** (*to work etc*) *Fam* comme un fou. **4** (*no matter what*) **a. (at all)** n'importe quoi.

anyway ['enɪweɪ] *adv* (*at any rate*) de toute façon.

anywhere ['enɪweər] *adv* **1** (*no matter where*) n'importe où. **2** (*everywhere*) partout; **a. you go** partout où vous allez, où que vous alliez; **a. you like** là où tu veux. **3** (*somewhere*) quelque part; **is he going a.?** va-t-il quelque part? **4** (*negative*) nulle part; **he doesn't go a.** il ne va nulle part; **without a. to put it** sans un endroit où le mettre.

apace [ə'peɪs] *adv* rapidement.

apart [ə'pɑːt] *adv* (*to or at one side*) à part; **to tear a.** (*to pieces*) mettre en pièces; **we kept them a.** (*separate*) on les tenait séparés; **with legs (wide) a.** les jambes écartées; **they are a metre a.** ils se trouvent à un mètre l'un de l'autre; **a. from** (*except for*) à part; **to take a.** démonter; **to come a.** (*of two objects*) se séparer; (*of knot etc*) se défaire; **to tell a.** distinguer entre; **worlds a.** (*very different*) diamétralement opposé.

apartheid [ə'pɑːteɪt] *n* apartheid *m*.

apartment [ə'pɑːtmənt] *n* (*flat*) *Am* appartement *m*; (*room*) chambre *f*; **a. house** *Am* immeuble *m* (d'habitation).

apathy ['æpəθɪ] *n* apathie *f*. ◆**apa'thetic** *a* apathique.

ape [eɪp] *n* singe; – *vt* (*imitate*) singer.

aperitif [ə'perətɪf] *n* apéritif *m*.

aperture ['æpətʃʊər] *n* ouverture *f*.

apex ['eɪpeks] *n Geom & Fig* sommet *m*.

aphorism ['æfərɪz(ə)m] *n* aphorisme *m*.

aphrodisiac [æfrə'dɪzɪæk] *a & n* aphrodisiaque (*m*).

apiece [ə'piːs] *adv* chacun; **a pound a.** une livre (la) pièce or chacun.

apish ['eɪpɪʃ] *a* simiesque; (*imitative*) imitateur.

apocalypse [ə'pɒkəlɪps] *n* apocalypse *f*. ◆**apoca'lyptic** *a* apocalyptique.

apocryphal [ə'pɒkrɪfəl] *a* apocryphe.

apogee ['æpədʒiː] *n* apogée *m*.

apologetic [əpɒlə'dʒetɪk] *a* (*letter*) plein d'excuses; **to be a. about** s'excuser de. ◆**apologetically** *adv* en s'excusant.

apology [ə'pɒlədʒɪ] n excuses fpl; **an a. for a dinner** Fam Pej un dîner minable. ◆**apologist** n apologiste mf. ◆**apologize** vi s'excuser (for de); **to a. to s.o.** faire ses excuses à qn (**for** pour).

apoplexy [æp'əpleksɪ] n apoplexie f. ◆**apo'plectic** a & n apoplectique (mf).

apostle [ə'pɒs(ə)l] n apôtre m.

apostrophe [ə'pɒstrəfɪ] n apostrophe f.

appal [ə'pɔːl] (Am **appall**) vt (-ll-) épouvanter. ◆**appalling** a épouvantable.

apparatus [æpə'reɪtəs, Am -'rætəs] n (equipment, organization) appareil m; (in gym) agrès mpl.

apparel [ə'pærəl] n habit m, habillement m.

apparent [ə'pærənt] a (obvious, seeming) apparent; **it's a. that** il est évident que. ◆**-ly** adv apparemment.

apparition [æpə'rɪʃ(ə)n] n apparition f.

appeal [ə'piːl] n (call) appel m; (entreaty) supplication f; (charm) attrait m; (interest) intérêt m; Jur appel m; — vt **to a.** (s.o., s.o.'s kindness) faire appel à; **to a. to s.o.** (attract) plaire à qn, séduire qn; (interest) intéresser qn; **to a. to s.o. for sth** demander qch à qn; **to a. to s.o. to do** supplier qn de faire; — vi Jur faire appel. ◆**-ing** a (begging) suppliant; (attractive) séduisant.

appear [ə'pɪər] vi (become visible) apparaître; (present oneself) se présenter; (seem, be published) paraître; (act) Th jouer; Jur comparaître; **it appears that** (it seems) il semble que (+ sub or indic); (it is rumoured) il paraîtrait que (+ indic). ◆**appearance** n (act) apparition f; (look) apparence f, aspect m; (of book) parution f; **to put in an a.** faire acte de présence.

appease [ə'piːz] vt apaiser; (curiosity) satisfaire.

append [ə'pend] vt joindre, ajouter (**to** à). ◆**-age** n Anat appendice m.

appendix, pl **-ixes** or **-ices** [ə'pendɪks, -ɪksɪz, -ɪsiːz] n (of book) & Anat appendice m. ◆**appendicitis** [əpendɪ'saɪtɪs] n appendicite f.

appertain [æpə'teɪn] vi **to a. to** se rapporter à.

appetite ['æpɪtaɪt] n appétit m; **to take away s.o.'s a.** couper l'appétit à qn. ◆**appetizer** n (drink) apéritif m; (food) amuse-gueule m inv. ◆**appetizing** a appétissant.

applaud [ə'plɔːd] vt (clap) applaudir; (approve of) approuver, applaudir à; — vi applaudir. ◆**applause** n applaudissements mpl.

apple ['æp(ə)l] n pomme f; **stewed apples, a. sauce** compote f de pommes; **eating/**

cooking **a.** pomme f à couteau/à cuire; **a. pie** tarte f aux pommes; **a. core** trognon m de pomme; **a. tree** pommier m.

appliance [ə'plaɪəns] n appareil m.

apply [ə'plaɪ] **1** vt (put, carry out etc) appliquer; (brake) Aut appuyer sur; **to a. oneself to** s'appliquer à. **2** vi (be relevant) s'appliquer (**to** à); **to a. for** (job) poser sa candidature à, postuler; **to a. to s.o.** (ask) s'adresser à qn (**for** pour). ◆**applied** a (maths etc) appliqué. ◆**applicable** a applicable (**to** à). ◆'**applicant** n candidat, -ate mf (**for** pour). ◆**appli'cation** n application f; (request) demande f; (for job) candidature f; (for membership) demande f d'adhésion or d'inscription; **a.** (form) (job) formulaire m de candidature; (club) formulaire m d'inscription or d'adhésion.

appoint [ə'pɔɪnt] vt (person) nommer (**to sth** à qch, **to do** pour faire); (time etc) désigner, fixer; **at the appointed time** à l'heure dite; **well-appointed** bien équipé. ◆**-ment** n nomination f; (meeting) rendez-vous m inv; (post) place f, situation f.

apportion [ə'pɔːʃ(ə)n] vt répartir.

apposite ['æpəzɪt] a juste, à propos.

appraise [ə'preɪz] vt évaluer. ◆**appraisal** n évaluation f.

appreciate [ə'priːʃɪeɪt] **1** vt (enjoy, value, assess) apprécier; (understand) comprendre; (be grateful for) être reconnaissant de. **2** vi prendre de la valeur. ◆**appreciable** a appréciable, sensible. ◆**appreci'ation** n **1** (judgement) appréciation f; (gratitude) reconnaissance f. **2** (rise in value) plus-value f. ◆**appreciative** a (grateful) reconnaissant (**of** de); (laudatory) élogieux; **to be a. of** (enjoy) apprécier.

apprehend [æprɪ'hend] vt (seize, arrest) appréhender. ◆**apprehension** n (fear) appréhension f. ◆**apprehensive** a inquiet (**about** de, au sujet de); **to be a. of** redouter.

apprentice [ə'prentɪs] n apprenti, -ie mf; — vt mettre en apprentissage (**to** chez). ◆**apprenticeship** n apprentissage m.

approach [ə'prəʊtʃ] vt (draw near to) s'approcher de (qn, feu, porte etc); (age, result, town) approcher de; (subject) aborder; (accost) accoster (qn); **to a. s.o. about** parler à qn de; — vi (of person, vehicle) s'approcher; (of date etc) approcher; — n approche f; (method) façon f de s'y prendre; (path) voie f d'accès m; **a.** to (question) manière f d'aborder; **to make approaches to** faire des avances à

◆—able a (place) accessible; (person) abordable.

appropriate 1 [ə'prəupriət] a (place, tools, clothes etc) approprié, adéquat; (remark, time) opportun; a. to or for propre à, approprié à. 2 [ə'prəuprieit] vt (set aside) affecter; (steal) s'approprier. ◆—ly adv convenablement.

approv/e [ə'pruːv] vt approuver; to a. of sth approuver qch; I don't a. of him il ne me plaît pas, je ne l'apprécie pas; I a. of his going je trouve bon qu'il y aille; I a. of her having accepted je l'approuve d'avoir accepté. ◆—ing a approbateur. ◆approval n approbation f; on a. (goods) Com à l'essai.

approximate 1 [ə'prɒksimət] a approximatif; — [ə'prɒksimeit] vi to a. to se rapprocher de. ◆—ly adv à peu près, approximativement. ◆approxi'mation n approximation f.

apricot ['eiprikɒt] n abricot m.

April ['eiprəl] n avril m; to make an A. fool of faire un poisson d'avril à.

apron ['eiprən] n (garment) tablier m.

apse [æps] n (of church) abside f.

apt [æpt] a (suitable) convenable; (remark, reply) juste; (word, name) bien choisi; (student) doué, intelligent; to be a. to avoir tendance à; a. at sth habile à qch. ◆aptitude n aptitude f (for à, pour). ◆aptly adv convenablement. ◆a. named qui porte bien son nom.

aqualung ['ækwəlʌŋ] n scaphandre m autonome.

aquarium [ə'kweəriəm] n aquarium m.

Aquarius [ə'kweəriəs] n (sign) le Verseau.

aquatic [ə'kwætik] a (plant etc) aquatique; (sport) nautique.

aqueduct ['ækwidʌkt] n aqueduc m.

aquiline ['ækwilain] a (nose, profile) aquilin.

Arab ['ærəb] a & n arabe (mf). ◆Arabian [ə'reibiən] a arabe. ◆Arabic a & n (language) arabe (m); A. numerals chiffres mpl arabes.

arabesque [ærə'besk] n (decoration) arabesque f.

arable ['ærəb(ə)l] a (land) arable.

arbiter ['ɑːbitər] n arbitre m. ◆arbitrate vti arbitrer. ◆arbi'tration n arbitrage m; to go to a. soumettre la question à l'arbitrage. ◆arbitrator n (in dispute) médiateur, -trice mf.

arbitrary ['ɑːbitrəri] a arbitraire.

arbour ['ɑːbər] n tonnelle f, charmille f.

arc [ɑːk] n (of circle) arc m.

arcade [ɑː'keid] n (market) passage m couvert.

arch [ɑːtʃ] n (of bridge) arche f; Archit voûte f, arc m; (of foot) cambrure f; — vt (one's back etc) arquer, courber. ◆archway n passage m voûté, voûte f.

arch- [ɑːtʃ] pref (villain etc) achevé; a. enemy ennemi m numéro un.

arch(a)eology [ɑːki'ɒlədʒi] n archéologie f. ◆arch(a)eologist n archéologue mf.

archaic [ɑː'keiik] a archaïque.

archangel ['ɑːkeindʒəl] n archange m.

archbishop [ɑːtʃ'biʃəp] n archevêque m.

archer ['ɑːtʃər] n archer m. ◆archery n tir m à l'arc.

archetype ['ɑːkitaip] n archétype m.

archipelago [ɑːki'peləgəu] n (pl -oes or -os) archipel m.

architect ['ɑːkitekt] n architecte m. ◆architecture n architecture f.

archives ['ɑːkaivz] npl archives fpl. ◆archivist n archiviste mf.

arctic ['ɑːktik] a arctique; (weather) polaire, glacial; — n the A. l'Arctique m.

ardent ['ɑːdənt] a ardent. ◆—ly adv ardemment. ◆ardour n ardeur f.

arduous ['ɑːdjuəs] a ardu.

are [ɑːr] see be.

area ['eəriə] n Math superficie f; Geog région f; (of town) quartier m; Mil zone f; (domain) Fig domaine m, secteur m, terrain m; built-up a. agglomération f; parking a. aire f de stationnement; a. code Tel Am indicatif m.

arena [ə'riːnə] n Hist & Fig arène f.

Argentina [ɑːdʒən'tiːnə] n Argentine f. ◆Argentine ['ɑːdʒəntain] a & n, ◆Argentinian a & n argentin, -ine (mf).

argu/e ['ɑːgjuː] vi (quarrel) se disputer (with avec, about an sujet de); (reason) raisonner (with avec, about sur); to a. in favour of plaider pour; — vt (matter) discuter; to a. that (maintain) soutenir que. ◆—able ['ɑːguəb(ə)l] a discutable. ◆—ably adv on pourrait soutenir que. ◆—ment n (quarrel) dispute f; (reasoning) argument m; (debate) discussion f; to have an a. se disputer. ◆argu'mentative a raisonneur.

aria ['ɑːriə] n Mus air m (d'opéra).

arid ['ærid] a aride.

Aries ['eəriːz] n (sign) le Bélier.

arise [ə'raiz] vi (pt arose, pp arisen) (of problem, opportunity etc) se présenter; (of cry, objection) s'élever; (result) résulter (from de); (get up) Lit se lever.

aristocracy [æri'stɒkrəsi] n aristocratie f. ◆aristocrat ['æristəkræt, Am ə'ristəkræt] *n* aristocrate *mf.* ◆**aristo'cratic** *a* aristocratique.

arithmetic [ə'rıθmətık] *n* arithmétique *f.*

ark [ɑːk] *n* Noah's a. l'arche *f* de Noé.

arm [ɑːm] **1** *n* bras *m*; a. in a. bras dessus bras dessous; **with open arms** à bras ouverts. **2** *n* (weapon) arme *f*; **arms race** course *f* aux armements; − *vt* armer (with de). ◆**armament** *n* armement *m.* ◆**armband** *n* brassard *m.* ◆**armchair** *n* fauteuil *m.* ◆**armful** *n* brassée *f.* ◆**armhole** *n* emmanchure *f.* ◆**armpit** *n* aisselle *f.* ◆**armrest** *n* accoudoir *m.*

armadillo [ɑːmə'dıləʊ] *n* (*pl* -os) tatou *m.*

armistice ['ɑːmɪstɪs] *n* armistice *m.*

armour ['ɑːmər] *n* (of knight etc) armure *f*; (of tank etc) blindage *m.* ◆**armoured** *a,* ◆**armour-plated** *a* blindé. ◆**armoury** *n* arsenal *m.*

army ['ɑːmɪ] *n* armée *f*; − *a* (uniform etc) militaire; **to join the a.** s'engager; **regular a.** armée *f* active.

aroma [ə'rəʊmə] *n* arôme *m.* ◆**aro'matic** *a* aromatique.

arose [ə'rəʊz] *see* arise.

around [ə'raʊnd] *prep* autour de; (approximately) environ, autour de; **to go a. the world** faire le tour du monde; − *adv* autour; **all a.** tout autour; **to follow a.** suivre partout; **to rush a.** courir çà et là; a. **here** par ici; **he's still a.** il est encore là; **there's a lot of flu a.** il y a pas mal de grippes dans l'air; **up and a.** (after illness) Am sur pied, guéri.

arouse [ə'raʊz] *vt* éveiller, susciter; (sexually) exciter; **to a. from sleep** tirer du sommeil.

arrange [ə'reɪndʒ] *vt* arranger; (time, meeting) fixer; **it was arranged that** il était convenu que; **to a. to do** s'arranger pour faire. · ◆**-ment** *n* (layout, agreement) arrangement *m*; *pl* (preparations) préparatifs *mpl*; (plans) projets *mpl*; **to make arrangements to** s'arranger pour.

array [ə'reɪ] *n* (display) étalage *m.* ◆**arrayed** *a* (dressed) Lit (re)vêtu (in de).

arrears [ə'rɪəz] *npl* (payment) arriéré *m*; **to be in a.** avoir des arriérés.

arrest [ə'rest] *vt* arrêter; − *n* Jur arrestation *f*; **under a.** en état d'arrestation; **cardiac a.** arrêt *m* du cœur. ◆**-ing** *a* (striking) Fig frappant.

arrive [ə'raɪv] *vi* arriver. ◆**arrival** *n* arrivée *f*; **new a.** nouveau venu *m*, nouvelle venue *f*; (baby) nouveau-né, -ée *mf.*

arrogant ['ærəgənt] *a* arrogant. ◆**arro-**

gance *n* arrogance *f.* ◆**arrogantly** *adv* avec arrogance.

arrow ['ærəʊ] *n* flèche *f.*

arsenal ['ɑːsən(ə)l] *n* arsenal *m.*

arsenic ['ɑːsnɪk] *n* arsenic *m.*

arson ['ɑːs(ə)n] *n* incendie *m* volontaire. ◆**arsonist** *n* incendiaire *mf.*

art [ɑːt] *n* art *m*; (cunning) artifice *m*; **work of a.** œuvre *f* d'art; **fine arts** beaux-arts *mpl*; **faculty of arts** Univ faculté *f* des lettres; **a. school** école *f* des beaux-arts.

artefact ['ɑːtɪfækt] *n* objet *m* fabriqué.

artery ['ɑːtərɪ] *n* Anat Aut artère *f.* ◆**ar'terial** *a* Anat artériel; **a. road** route *f* principale.

artful ['ɑːtfəl] *a* rusé, astucieux. ◆**-ly** *adv* astucieusement.

arthritis [ɑː'θraɪtɪs] *n* arthrite *f.*

artichoke ['ɑːtɪtʃəʊk] *n* (globe) a. artichaut *m*; **Jerusalem a.** topinambour *m.*

article ['ɑːtɪk(ə)l] *n* (object, clause) & Journ Gram article *m*; **a. of clothing** vêtement *m*; **articles of value** objets *mpl* de valeur; **leading a.** Journ éditorial *m.*

articulat/e [ɑː'tɪkjʊlət] *a* (sound) net, distinct; (person) qui s'exprime clairement; − [ɑː'tɪkjʊleɪt] *vti* (speak) articuler. ◆**-ed** *a* **a. lorry** semi-remorque *m.* ◆**articu-'lation** *n* articulation *f.*

artifact ['ɑːtɪfækt] *n* objet *m* fabriqué.

artifice ['ɑːtɪfɪs] *n* artifice *m.*

artificial [ɑːtɪ'fɪʃ(ə)l] *a* artificiel. ◆**artifici-'ality** *n* caractère *m* artificiel. ◆**artificially** *adv* artificiellement.

artillery [ɑː'tɪlərɪ] *n* artillerie *f.*

artisan ['ɑːtɪzæn] *n* artisan *m.*

artist ['ɑːtɪst] *n* (actor, painter etc) artiste *mf.* ◆**artiste** [ɑː'tiːst] *n* Th Mus artiste *mf.* ◆**ar'tistic** *a* (sense, treasure etc) artistique; (person) artiste. ◆**artistry** *n* art *m.*

artless ['ɑːtləs] *a* naturel, naïf.

arty ['ɑːtɪ] *a* Pej du genre artiste.

as [æz, unstressed əz] *adv* & *conj* **1** (manner etc) comme; **as you like** comme tu veux; **such as** comme, tel que; **as much or as hard as I can** (autant que je peux); **as it is** (this being the case) les choses étant ainsi; (to leave sth) comme ça, tel quel; **it's late as it is** il est déjà tard; **as if, as though** comme si. **2** (comparison) **as tall as you** aussi grand que vous; **is he as tall as you?** est-il aussi or si grand que vous?; **as white as a sheet** blanc comme un linge; **as much or as hard as you** autant que vous; **the same as** le même que; **twice as big as** deux fois plus grand que. **3** (concessive) **(as) clever as he is** si or aussi intelligent qu'il soit. **4** (capacity) **as a**

teacher comme professeur, en tant que *or* en qualité de professeur; **to act as a father** agir en père. **5** (*reason*) puisque, comme; **as it's late** puisqu'il est tard, comme il est tard. **6** (*time*) **as I left** comme je partais; **as one grows older** à mesure que l'on vieillit; **as he slept** pendant qu'il dormait; **one day as . . .** un jour que . . .; **as from, as of** (*time*) à partir de. **7** (*concerning*) **as for that, as to** that quant à cela. **8** (+ *inf*) **so as to** de manière à; **so stupid as to** assez bête pour.

asbestos [æs'bestəs] *n* amiante *f.*

ascend [ə'send] *vi* monter; – *vt* (*throne*) monter sur; (*stairs*) monter; (*mountain*) faire l'ascension de. **◆ascent** *n* ascension *f* (**of** de); (*slope*) côte *f.*

ascertain [æsə'tein] *vt* (*discover*) découvrir; (*check*) s'assurer de.

ascetic [ə'setik] *a* ascétique; – *n* ascète *mf.*

ascribe [ə'skraib] *vt* attribuer (**to** à).

ash [æʃ] *n* **1** (*of cigarette etc*) cendre *f*; **A. Wednesday** mercredi *m* des Cendres. **2** (*tree*) frêne *m*. **◆ashen** *a* (*pale grey*) cendré; (*face*) pâle. **◆ashcan** *n Am* poubelle *f.* **◆ashtray** *n* cendrier *m.*

ashamed [ə'ʃeimd] *a* honteux; **to be a. of** avoir honte de; **to be a. (of oneself)** avoir honte.

ashore [ə'ʃɔːr] *adv* **to go a.** débarquer; **to put s.o. a.** débarquer qn.

Asia ['eiʃə] *n* Asie *f.* **◆Asian** *a* asiatique; – *n* Asiatique *mf*, Asiate *mf.*

aside [ə'said] **1** *adv* de côté; **to draw a.** (*curtain*) écarter; **to take** *or* **draw s.o. a.** prendre qn à part; **to step a.** s'écarter; **a. from** en dehors de. **2** *n Th* aparté *m.*

asinine ['æsinain] *a* stupide, idiot.

ask [ɑːsk] *vt* demander; (*a question*) poser; (*invite*) inviter; **to a. s.o. (for)** sth demander qch à qn; **to a. s.o. to do** demander à qn de faire; – *vi* demander; **to a. for sth/s.o.** demander qch/qn; **to a. for sth back** redemander qch; **to a. about sth** se renseigner sur qch; **to a. after** *or* **about s.o.** demander des nouvelles de qn; **to a. s.o. about** interroger qn sur; **asking price** prix *m* demandé.

askance [ə'skɑːns] *adv* **to look a.** at regarder avec méfiance.

askew [ə'skjuː] *adv* de biais, de travers.

aslant [ə'slɑːnt] *adv* de travers.

asleep [ə'sliːp] *a* endormi; (*arm, leg*) engourdi; **to be a.** dormir; **to fall a.** s'endormir.

asp [æsp] *n* (*snake*) aspic *m.*

asparagus [ə'spærəgəs] *n* (*plant*) asperge *f*; (*shoots*) *Culin* asperges *fpl.*

aspect ['æspekt] *n* aspect *m*; (*of house*) orientation *f.*

aspersions [ə'spɜːʃ(ə)nz] *npl* **to cast a. on** dénigrer.

asphalt ['æsfælt, *Am* 'æsfɔːlt] *n* asphalte *m*; – *vt* asphalter.

asphyxia [əs'fiksiə] *n* asphyxie *f.* **◆asphyxiate** *vt* asphyxier. **◆asphyxi-'ation** *n* asphyxie *f.*

aspire [ə'spaiər] *vi* **to a.** to aspirer à. **◆aspi-'ration** *n* aspiration *f.*

aspirin ['æsprin] *n* aspirine *f.*

ass [æs] *n* **1** (*animal*) âne *m*; (*person*) *Fam* imbécile *mf*, âne *m*; **she-a.** ânesse *f.*

assail [ə'seil] *vt* assaillir (**with** de). **◆assal-lant** *n* agresseur *m.*

assassin [ə'sæsin] *n Pol* assassin *m.* **◆assassinate** *vt Pol* assassiner. **◆assassi-'nation** *n Pol* assassinat *m.*

assault [ə'sɔːlt] *n Mil* assaut *m*; *Jur* agression *f*; – *vt Jur* agresser; (*woman*) violenter.

assemble [ə'semb(ə)l] *vt* (*objects, ideas*) assembler; (*people*) rassembler; (*machine*) monter; – *vi* se rassembler. **◆assembly** *n* (*meeting*) assemblée *f*; *Tech* montage *m*, assemblage *m*; *Sch* rassemblement *m*; **a. line** (*in factory*) chaîne *f* de montage.

assent [ə'sent] *n* assentiment *m*; – *vi* consentir (**to** à).

assert [ə'sɜːt] *vt* affirmer (**that** que); (*rights*) revendiquer; **to a. oneself** s'affirmer. **◆assertion** *n* affirmation *f*; revendication *f.* **◆assertive** *a* affirmatif; *Pej* autoritaire.

assess [ə'ses] *vt* (*estimate, evaluate*) évaluer; (*decide amount of*) fixer le montant de; (*person*) juger. **◆—ment** *n* évaluation *f*; jugement *m.* **◆assessor** *n* (*valuer*) expert *m.*

asset ['æset] *n* atout *m*, avantage *m*; *pl Com* biens *mpl*, avoir *m.*

assiduous [ə'sidjuəs] *a* assidu.

assign [ə'sain] *vt* (*allocate*) assigner; (*day etc*) fixer; (*appoint*) nommer (**to** à). **◆—ment** *n* (*task*) mission *f*; *Sch* devoirs *mpl.*

assimilate [ə'simileit] *vt* assimiler; – *vi* s'assimiler. **◆assimi'lation** *n* assimilation *f.*

assist [ə'sist] *vti* aider (**in doing, to do** à faire). **◆assistance** *n* aide *f*; **to be of a. to s.o.** aider qn. **◆assistant** *n* assistant, -ante *mf*; (*in shop*) vendeur, -euse *mf*; – *a* adjoint.

assizes [ə'saiziz] *npl Jur* assises *fpl.*

associate [ə'səuʃieit] *vt* associer (**with** à, avec); – *vi* **to a. with s.o.** fréquenter qn; **to**

a. (oneself) with (in business venture) s'associer à or avec; – [ə'səʊʃɪət] n & a associé, -ée (mf). ◆associ'ation n association f; pl (memories) souvenirs mpl.

assort/ed [ə'sɔːtɪd] a (different) variés; (foods) assortis; well-a. bien assorti. ◆—ment n assortiment m.

assuage [ə'sweɪdʒ] vt apaiser, adoucir.

assum/e [ə'sjuːm] vt 1 (take on) prendre; (responsibility, role) assumer; (attitude, name) adopter. 2 (suppose) présumer (that que). ◆—ed a (feigned) faux; a. name nom m d'emprunt. ◆assumption n (supposition) supposition f.

assur/e [ə'ʃʊər] vt assurer. ◆—edly [-ɪdlɪ] adv assurément. ◆assurance n assurance f.

asterisk ['æstərɪsk] n astérisque m.

astern [ə'stɜːn] adv Nau à l'arrière.

asthma ['æsmə] n asthme m. ◆asth'matic a & n asthmatique (mf).

astir [ə'stɜːr] a (excited) en émoi; (out of bed) debout.

astonish [ə'stɒnɪʃ] vt étonner; to be astonished s'étonner (at sth de qch). ◆—ing a étonnant. ◆—ingly adv étonnamment. ◆—ment n étonnement m.

astound [ə'staʊnd] vt stupéfier, étonner. ◆—ing a stupéfiant.

astray [ə'streɪ] adv to go a. s'égarer; to lead a. égarer.

astride [ə'straɪd] adv à califourchon; – prep à cheval sur.

astringent [ə'strɪndʒənt] a (harsh) sévère.

astrology [ə'strɒlədʒɪ] n astrologie f. ◆astrologer n astrologue m.

astronaut ['æstrənɔːt] n astronaute mf.

astronomy [ə'strɒnəmɪ] n astronomie f. ◆astronomer n astronome m. ◆astro'nomical a astronomique.

astute [ə'stjuːt] a (crafty) rusé; (clever) astucieux.

asunder [ə'sʌndər] adv (to pieces) en pièces; (in two) en deux.

asylum [ə'saɪləm] n asile m; lunatic a. Pej maison f de fous, asile m d'aliénés.

at [æt, unstressed ət] prep 1 à; at the end à la fin; at work au travail; at six (o'clock) à six heures. 2 chez; at the doctor's chez le médecin; at home chez soi, à la maison. ◆at-home n réception f. 3 en; at sea en mer; at war en guerre; good at (geography etc) fort en. 4 contre; angry at fâché contre. 5 sur; to shoot at tirer sur; at my request sur ma demande. 6 de; to laugh at rire de; surprised at surpris de. 7 (au)près de; at the window (au)près de la fenêtre. 8 par; to

come in at the door entrer par la porte; six at a time six par six. 9 at night la nuit; to look at regarder; not at all pas du tout; (after 'thank you') pas de quoi!; nothing at all rien du tout; to be (hard) at it être très occupé, travailler dur; he's always (on) at me Fam il est toujours après moi.

ate [et, Am eɪt] see eat.

atheism ['eɪθɪz(ə)m] n athéisme m. ◆atheist n athée mf.

Athens ['æθɪnz] n Athènes m or f.

athlete ['æθliːt] n athlète mf; a.'s foot Med mycose f. ◆ath'letic a athlétique; a. meeting réunion f sportive. ◆ath'letics npl athlétisme m.

atishoo! [ə'tɪʃuː] (Am atchoo [ə'tʃuː]) int atchoum!

Atlantic [ət'læntɪk] a atlantique; – n the A. l'Atlantique m.

atlas ['ætləs] n atlas m.

atmosphere ['ætməsfɪər] n atmosphère f. ◆atmos'pheric a atmosphérique.

atom ['ætəm] n atome m; a. bomb bombe f atomique. ◆a'tomic a atomique. ◆atomizer n atomiseur m.

atone [ə'təʊn] vi to a. for expier. ◆—ment n expiation f (for de).

atrocious [ə'trəʊʃəs] a atroce. ◆atrocity n atrocité f.

atrophy ['ætrəfɪ] vi s'atrophier.

attach [ə'tætʃ] vt attacher (to à); (document) joindre (to à); attached to (fond of) attaché à. ◆—ment n (affection) attachement m; (fastener) attache f; (tool) accessoire m.

attaché [ə'tæʃeɪ] n 1 Pol attaché, -ée mf. 2 a. case attaché-case m.

attack [ə'tæk] n Mil Med & Fig attaque f; (of fever) accès m; (on s.o.'s life) attentat m; heart a. crise f cardiaque; – vt attaquer; (problem, plan) s'attaquer à; – vi attaquer. ◆—er n agresseur m.

attain [ə'teɪn] vt parvenir à, atteindre, réaliser. ◆—able a accessible. ◆—ment n (of ambition, aim etc) réalisation f (of de); pl (skills) talents mpl.

attempt [ə'tempt] n tentative f; to make an a. to essayer or tenter de; a. on (record) tentative pour battre; a. on s.o.'s life attentat m contre qn; – vt tenter; (task) entreprendre; to a. to do essayer or tenter de faire; attempted murder tentative de meurtre.

attend [ə'tend] vt (match etc) assister à; (course) suivre; (school, church) aller à; (wait on, serve) servir; (escort) accompagner; (patient) soigner; – vi assister; to a. to (pay attention to) prêter attention à;

(take care of) s'occuper de. ◆—ed *a* well-a. *(course)* très suivi; *(meeting)* où il y a du monde. ◆attendance *n* présence *f* (at à); *(people)* assistance *f*; school a. scolarité *f*; in a. de service. ◆attendant 1 *n* employé, -ée *mf*; *(in museum)* gardien, -ienne *mf*; *pl (of prince, king etc)* suite *f*. 2 *a (fact)* concomitant.

attention [ə'tenʃ(ə)n] *n* attention *f*; to pay a. prêter or faire attention (to à); a.! *Mil* garde-à-vous!; to stand at a. *Mil* être au garde-à-vous; a. to detail minutie *f*. ◆attentive *a (heedful)* attentif (to à); *(thoughtful)* attentionné (to pour). ◆attentively *adv* avec attention, attentivement.

attenuate [ə'tenjʊeɪt] *vt* atténuer.

attest [ə'test] *vti* to a. (to) témoigner de.

attic ['ætɪk] *n* grenier *m*.

attire [ə'taɪər] *n Lit* vêtements *mpl*.

attitude ['ætɪtjuːd] *n* attitude *f*.

attorney [ə'tɜːnɪ] *n (lawyer) Am* avocat *m*; district a. *Am* = procureur *m* (de la République).

attract [ə'trækt] *vt* attirer. ◆attraction *n* attraction *f*; *(charm, appeal)* attrait *m*. ◆attractive *a (price etc)* intéressant; *(girl)* belle, jolie; *(boy)* beau; *(manners)* attrayant.

attribut/e 1 ['ætrɪbjuːt] *n (quality)* attribut *m*. 2 [ə'trɪbjuːt] *vt (ascribe)* attribuer (to à). ◆—able *a* attribuable (to à).

attrition [ə'trɪʃ(ə)n] *n* war of a. guerre *f* d'usure.

attuned [ə'tjuːnd] *a* a. to *(of ideas, trends etc)* en accord avec; *(used to)* habitué à.

atypical [eɪ'tɪpɪk(ə)l] *a* peu typique.

aubergine ['əʊbəʒiːn] *n* aubergine *f*.

auburn ['ɔːbən] *a (hair)* châtain roux.

auction ['ɔːkʃən] *n* vente *f* (aux enchères); — *vt* to a. (off) vendre (aux enchères). ◆auctio'neer *n* commissaire-priseur *m*, adjudicateur, -trice *mf*.

audacious [ɔː'deɪʃəs] *a* audacieux. ◆audacity *n* audace *f*.

audib/le ['ɔːdɪb(ə)l] *a* perceptible, audible. ◆—ly *adv* distinctement.

audience ['ɔːdɪəns] *n* assistance *f*, public *m*; *(of speaker, musician)* auditoire *m*; *Th Cin* spectateurs *mpl*; *Rad* auditeurs *mpl*; *(interview)* audience *f*.

audio ['ɔːdɪəʊ] *a (cassette, system etc)* audio *inv*. ◆audiotypist *n* dactylo *f* au magnétophone, audiotypiste *mf*. ◆audio-'visual *a* audio-visuel.

audit ['ɔːdɪt] *vt (accounts)* vérifier; — *n* vérifi-

cation *f* *(des comptes)*. ◆auditor *n* commissaire *m* aux comptes.

audition [ɔː'dɪʃ(ə)n] *n* audition *f*; — *vti* auditionner.

auditorium [ɔːdɪ'tɔːrɪəm] *n* salle *f* *(de spectacle, concert etc)*.

augment [ɔːg'ment] *vt* augmenter (with, by de).

augur ['ɔːgər] *vt* présager; — *vi* to a. well être de bon augure.

august [ɔː'gʌst] *a* auguste.

August ['ɔːgəst] *n* août *m*.

aunt [ɑːnt] *n* tante *f*. ◆auntie or aunty *n Fam* tata *f*.

au pair [əʊ'peər] *adv* au pair; — *n* au p. (girl) jeune fille *f* au pair.

aura ['ɔːrə] *n* émanation *f*, aura *f*; *(of place)* atmosphère *f*.

auspices ['ɔːspɪsɪz] *npl* auspices *mpl*.

auspicious [ɔː'spɪʃəs] *a* favorable.

austere [ɔː'stɪər] *a* austère. ◆austerity *n* austérité *f*.

Australia [ɒ'streɪlɪə] *n* Australie *f*. ◆Australian *a & n* australien, -ienne *(mf)*.

Austria ['ɒstrɪə] *n* Autriche *f*. ◆Austrian *a & n* autrichien, -ienne *(mf)*.

authentic [ɔː'θentɪk] *a* authentique. ◆authenticate *vt* authentifier. ◆authen'ticity *n* authenticité *f*.

author ['ɔːθər] *n* auteur *m*. ◆authoress *n* femme *f* auteur. ◆authorship *n (of book etc)* paternité *f*.

authority [ɔː'θɒrɪtɪ] *n* autorité *f*; *(permission)* autorisation *f* (to do de faire); to be in a. (in charge) être responsable. ◆authori'tarian *a & n* autoritaire *(mf)*. ◆authoritative *a (report)* autorisé; *(tone, person)* autoritaire.

authorize ['ɔːθəraɪz] *vt* autoriser (to do à faire). ◆authori'zation *n* autorisation *f*.

autistic [ɔː'tɪstɪk] *a* autiste, autistique.

autobiography [ɔːtəbaɪ'ɒgrəfɪ] *n* autobiographie *f*.

autocrat ['ɔːtəkræt] *n* autocrate *m*. ◆auto'cratic *a* autocratique.

autograph ['ɔːtəgrɑːf] *n* autographe *m*; — *vt* dédicacer (for à).

automat ['ɔːtəmæt] *n Am* cafétéria *f* à distributeurs automatiques.

automate ['ɔːtəmeɪt] *vt* automatiser. ◆auto'mation *n* automatisation *f*, automation *f*.

automatic [ɔːtə'mætɪk] *a* automatique. ◆automatically *adv* automatiquement.

automaton [ɔː'tɒmətən] *n* automate *m*.

automobile ['ɔːtəməbiːl] *n Am* auto(mobile) *f*.

autonomous [ɔː'tɒnəməs] *a* autonome.
◆**autonomy** *n* autonomie *f*.

autopsy ['ɔːtɒpsɪ] *n* autopsie *f*.

autumn ['ɔːtəm] *n* automne *m*. ◆**autumnal** [ɔː'tʌmnəl] *a* automnal.

auxiliary [ɔːg'zɪljərɪ] *a & n* auxiliaire (*mf*); **a.** (**verb**) (verbe) *m* auxiliaire *m*.

avail [ə'veɪl] **1** *vt* **to a. oneself of** profiter de, tirer parti de. **2** *n* **to no a.** en vain; **of no a.** inutile.

available [ə'veɪləb(ə)l] *a* (*thing, means etc*) disponible; (*person*) libre, disponible; (*valid*) valable; **a. to all** (*goal etc*) accessible à tous. ◆**availa'bility** *n* disponibilité *f*; validité *f*; accessibilité *f*.

avalanche ['ævəlɑːnʃ] *n* avalanche *f*.

avarice ['ævərɪs] *n* avarice *f*. ◆**ava'ricious** *a* avare.

avenge [ə'vendʒ] *vt* venger; **to a. oneself** se venger (on de).

avenue ['ævənjuː] *n* avenue *f*; (*way to a result*) *Fig* voie *f*.

average ['ævərɪdʒ] *n* moyenne *f*; **on a.** en moyenne; – *a* moyen; – *vt* (*do*) faire en moyenne; (*reach*) atteindre la moyenne de; (*figures*) faire la moyenne de.

averse [ə'vɜːs] *a* **to be a. to doing** répugner à faire. ◆**aversion** *n* (*dislike*) aversion *f*, répugnance *f*.

avert [ə'vɜːt] *vt* (*prevent*) éviter; (*turn away*) détourner (from de).

aviary ['eɪvɪərɪ] *n* volière *f*.

aviation [eɪvɪ'eɪʃ(ə)n] *n* aviation *f*. ◆'**aviator** *n* aviateur, -trice *mf*.

avid ['ævɪd] *a* avide (for de).

avocado [ævə'kɑːdəʊ] *n* (*pl* -os) **a. (pear)** avocat *m*.

avoid [ə'vɔɪd] *vt* éviter; **to a. doing** éviter de faire. ◆**-able** *a* évitable. ◆**avoidance** *n* **his a. of** (*danger etc*) son désir *m* d'éviter; **tax a.** évasion *f* fiscale.

avowed [ə'vaʊd] *a* (*enemy*) déclaré, avoué.

await [ə'weɪt] *vt* attendre.

awake [ə'weɪk] *vi* (*pt* **awoke**, *pp* **awoken**) s'éveiller; – *vt* (*person, hope etc*) éveiller; – *a* réveillé, éveillé; (**wide-**)**a.** éveillé; **to keep s.o. a.** empêcher qn de dormir, tenir qn éveillé; **he's (still) a.** il ne dort pas (encore); **a. to** (*conscious of*) conscient de. ◆**awaken 1** *vti* = **awake. 2** *vt* **to a. s.o. to sth** faire prendre conscience de qch à qn. ◆**awakening** *n* réveil *m*.

award [ə'wɔːd] *vt* (*money*) attribuer; (*prize*) décerner, attribuer; (*damages*) accorder; – *n* (*prize*) prix *m*, récompense *f*; (*scholarship*) bourse *f*.

aware [ə'weər] *a* avisé, informé; **a. of** (*conscious*) conscient de; (*informed*) au courant de; **to become a. of** prendre conscience de. ◆**-ness** *n* conscience *f*.

awash [ə'wɒʃ] *a* inondé (with de).

away [ə'weɪ] *adv* **1** (*distant*) loin; (**far**) **a.** au loin, très loin; **5 km a.** à 5 km (de distance). **2** (*absent*) parti, absent; **a. with you!** va-t-en!; **to drive a.** partir (en voiture); **to look a.** détourner les yeux; **to work/talk/** *etc* **a.** travailler/parler/*etc* sans relâche; **to fade/melt a.** disparaître/fondre complètement. **3** **to play a.** *Sp* jouer à l'extérieur.

awe [ɔː] *n* crainte *f* (mêlée de respect); **to be in a. of s.o.** éprouver de la crainte envers qn. ◆**a.-inspiring** *a*, ◆**awesome** *a* (*impressive*) imposant; (*frightening*) effrayant.

awful ['ɔːfəl] *a* affreux; (*terrifying*) épouvantable; (*ill*) malade; **an a. lot of** *Fam* un nombre incroyable de; **I feel a.** (**about it**) j'ai vraiment honte. ◆**-ly** *adv* affreusement; (*very*) *Fam* terriblement; **thanks a.** merci infiniment.

awhile [ə'waɪl] *adv* quelque temps; (*to stay, wait*) un peu.

awkward ['ɔːkwəd] *a* **1** (*clumsy*) maladroit; (*age*) ingrat. **2** (*difficult*) difficile; (*cumbersome*) gênant; (*tool*) peu commode; (*time*) inopportun; (*silence*) gêné. ◆**-ly** *adv* maladroitement; (*speak*) d'un ton gêné; (*placed*) à un endroit difficile. ◆**-ness** *n* maladresse *f*; difficulté *f*; (*discomfort*) gêne *f*.

awning ['ɔːnɪŋ] *n* auvent *m*; (*over shop*) store *m*; (*glass canopy*) marquise *f*.

awoke(n) [ə'wəʊk(ən)] *see* **awake.**

awry [ə'raɪ] *adv* **to go a.** (*of plan etc*) mal tourner.

axe [æks] (*Am* **ax**) *n* hache *f*; (*reduction*) *Fig* coupe *f* sombre; – *vt* réduire; (*eliminate*) supprimer.

axiom ['æksɪəm] *n* axiome *m*.

axis, pl axes ['æksɪs, 'æksiːz] *n* axe *m*.

axle ['æks(ə)l] *n* essieu *m*.

ay(e) [aɪ] **1** *adv* oui. **2** *n* **the ayes** (*votes*) voix *fpl* pour.

azalea [ə'zeɪlɪə] *n* (*plant*) azalée *f*.

B

B, b [bi:] *n* B, b *m*; **2B** (*number*) 2 ter.
BA *abbr* = **Bachelor of Arts.**
babble ['bæb(ə)l] *vi* (*of baby, stream*) gazouiller; (*mumble*) bredouiller; – *vt* **to b. (out)** bredouiller; – *n inv* gazouillement *m*, gazouillis *m*; (*of voices*) rumeur *f*.
babe [beɪb] *n* **1** petit(e) enfant *mf*, bébé *m*. **2** (*girl*) *Sl* pépée *f*.
baboon [bə'bu:n] *n* babouin *m*.
baby ['beɪbɪ] *n* bébé *m*; – *a* (*clothes etc*) de bébé; **b. boy** petit garçon *m*; **b. girl** petite fille *f*; **b. carriage** *Am* voiture *f* d'enfant; **b. sling** kangourou® *m*, porte-bébé *m*; **b. tiger/etc** bébé-tigre/etc *m*; **b. face** visage *m* poupin. **2** *n Sl* (*girl*) pépée *f*; (*girlfriend*) copine *f*. **3** *vt Fam* dorloter. ◆**b.-batterer** *n* bourreau *m* d'enfants. ◆**b.-minder** *n* gardien, -ienne *mf* d'enfants. ◆**b.-sit** *vi* (*pt & pp* -sat, *pres p* -sitting) garder les enfants, faire du baby-sitting. ◆**b.-sitter** *n* baby-sitter *mf*. ◆**b.-snatching** *n* rapt *m* d'enfant. ◆**b.-walker** *n* trotteur *m*, youpala® *m*.
babyish ['beɪbɪɪʃ] *a Pej* de bébé; (*puerile*) enfantin.
bachelor ['bætʃələr] *n* **1** célibataire *m*; **b. flat** garçonnière *f*. **2** B. **of Arts/of Science** licencié -ée *mf* ès lettres/ès sciences.
back [bæk] *n* (*of person, animal*) dos *m*; (*of chair*) dossier *m*; (*of hand*) revers *m*; (*of house*) derrière *m*, arrière *m*; (*of room*) fond *m*; (*of page*) verso *m*, (*of fabric*) envers *m*; *Fb* arrière *m*; **at the b. of** (*book*) à la fin de; (*car*) à l'arrière de; **at the b. of one's mind** derrière la tête; **b. to front** devant derrière, à l'envers; **to get s.o.'s b. up** *Fam* irriter qn; **in b. of** *Am* derrière; – *a* arrière *inv*, de derrière; (*taxes*) arriéré; **b. door** porte *f* de derrière; **b. room** pièce *f* du fond; **b. end** (*of bus*) arrière *m*; **b. street** rue *f* écartée; **b. number** vieux numéro *m*; **b. pay** rappel *m* de salaire; **b. tooth** molaire *f*; – *adv* en arrière; **b. there** là derrière; **far b.** loin derrière; **b. in the past** à une époque reculée; **to stand b.** (*of house*) être en retrait (**from** par rapport à); **to go b. and forth** aller et venir; **to come b.** revenir; **he's b.** il est de retour, il est rentré or revenu; **a month b.** il y a un mois; **the trip there and b.** le voyage aller et retour; – *vt Com* financer; (*horse etc*) parier sur, jouer;

(*car*) faire reculer; (*wall*) renforcer; **to b. s.o (up)** (*support*) appuyer qn; – *vi* (*move backwards*) reculer; **to b. down** se dégonfler; **to b. out** (*withdraw*) se retirer; *Aut* sortir en marche arrière; **to b. on to** (*of window etc*) donner par derrière sur; **to b. up** *Aut* faire marche arrière. ◆**—ing** *n* (*aid*) soutien *m*; (*material*) support *m*, renfort *m*. ◆**—er** *n* (*supporter*) partisan *m*; *Sp* parieur, -euse *mf*; *Fin* bailleur *m* de fonds.
backache ['bækeɪk] *n* mal *m* aux reins. ◆**back'bencher** *n Pol* membre *m* sans portefeuille. ◆**backbiting** *n* médisance *f*. ◆**backbreaking** *a* éreintant. ◆**back-cloth** *n* toile *f* de fond. ◆**backchat** *n* impertinence *f*. ◆**back'date** *vt* (*cheque*) antidater. ◆**back'handed** *a* (*compliment*) équivoque. ◆**backhander** *n* revers *m*; (*bribe*) *Fam* pot-de-vin *m*. ◆**backrest** *n* dossier *m*. ◆**backside** *n* (*buttocks*) *Fam* derrière *m*. ◆**back'stage** *adv* dans les coulisses. ◆**backstroke** *n Sp* dos *m* crawlé. ◆**backtrack** *vi* rebrousser chemin. ◆**backup** *n* appui *m*; (*tailback*) *Am* embouteillage *m*; **b. lights** *Aut* feux *mpl* de recul. ◆**backwater** *n* (*place*) trou *m* perdu. ◆**backwoods** *npl* forêts *f* vierges. ◆**back'yard** *n* arrière-cour *f*; *Am* jardin *m* (à l'arrière d'une maison).
backbone ['bækbəʊn] *n* colonne *f* vertébrale; (*of fish*) grande arête *f*; (*main support*) soutien *m*, pivot *m*.
backfire [bæk'faɪər] *vi Aut* pétarader; (*of plot etc*) *Fig* échouer.
backgammon ['bækgæmən] *n* trictrac *m*.
background ['bækgraʊnd] *n* fond *m*, arrière-plan *m*; (*events*) *Fig* antécédents *mpl*; (*education*) formation *f*; (*environment*) milieu *m*; (*conditions*) *Pol* climat *m*, contexte *m*; **to keep s.o. in the b.** tenir qn à l'écart; **b. music** musique *f* de fond.
backlash ['bæklæʃ] *n* choc *m* en retour, retour *m* de flamme.
backlog ['bæklɒg] *n* (*of work*) arriéré *m*.
backward ['bækwəd] *a* (*glance etc*) en arrière; (*retarded*) enfant *m*; **b. in** doing lent à faire; – *adv* = **backwards.** ◆**—ness** *n* (*of country etc*) retard *m*. ◆**backwards** *adv* en arrière; (*to walk*) à reculons; (*to fall*) à la

renverse; **to move b.** reculer; **to go b. and forwards** aller et venir.

bacon ['beɪkən] n lard m; (in rashers) bacon m; **b. and eggs** œufs mpl au jambon.

bacteria [bæk'tɪərɪə] npl bactéries fpl.

bad [bæd] a (**worse, worst**) mauvais; (wicked) méchant; (sad) triste; (accident, wound etc) grave; (tooth) carié; (arm, leg) malade; (pain) violent; (air) vicié; **b. language** gros mots mpl; **it's b. to think that . . .** ce n'est pas bien de penser que . . .; **to feel b.** Med se sentir mal; **I feel b. about it** ça m'a chagriné; **things are b.** ça va mal; **she's not b.!** elle n'est pas mal!; **to go b.** se gâter; (of milk) tourner; **in a b. way** mal en point; (ill) très mal; (in trouble) dans le pétrin; **too b.!** tant pis! **◆b.-'mannered** a mal élevé. **◆b.-'tempered** a grincheux. **◆badly** adv mal; (hurt) grièvement; **b. affected/shaken** très touché/bouleversé; **to be b. mistaken** se tromper lourdement; **b. off** dans la gêne; **to be b. off for** manquer de; **to want b.** avoir grande envie de.

badge [bædʒ] n insigne m; (of postman etc) plaque f; (bearing slogan or joke) badge m.

badger ['bædʒər] **1** n (animal) blaireau m. **2** vt importuner.

badminton ['bædmɪntən] n badminton m.

baffle ['bæf(ə)l] vt (person) déconcerter, dérouter.

bag [bæg] **1** n sac m; pl (luggage) valises fpl, bagages mpl; (under the eyes) poches fpl; **bags of** Fam (lots of) beaucoup de; **an old b.** une vieille taupe; **in the b.** Fam dans la poche. **2** vt (**-gg-**) (take, steal) Fam piquer, s'adjuger; (animal) Sp tuer.

baggage ['bægɪdʒ] n bagages mpl; Mil équipement m; **b. car** Am fourgon m; **b. room** Am consigne f.

baggy ['bægɪ] a (**-ier, -iest**) (clothing) trop ample; (trousers) faisant des poches.

bagpipes ['bægpaɪps] npl cornemuse f.

Bahamas [bə'hɑːməz] npl **the B.** les Bahamas fpl.

bail [beɪl] **1** n Jur caution f; **on b.** en liberté provisoire; – vt **to b. (out)** fournir une caution pour; **to b. out** (ship) écoper; (person, company) Fig tirer d'embarras. **2** vi **to b. out** Am Av sauter (en parachute).

bailiff ['beɪlɪf] n Jur huissier m; (of land-owner) régisseur m.

bait [beɪt] **1** n amorce f, appât m; – vt (fishing hook) amorcer. **2** vt (annoy) asticoter, tourmenter.

baize [beɪz] n green **b.** (on card table etc) tapis m vert.

bak/e [beɪk] vt (faire) cuire (au four); – vi

(of cook) faire de la pâtisserie or du pain; (of cake etc) cuire (au four); **we're** or **it's baking (hot)** Fam on cuit. **◆—ed** a (potatoes) au four; **b. beans** haricots mpl blancs (à la tomate). **◆—ing** n cuisson f; **b. powder** levure f (chimique). **◆—er** n boulanger, -ère mf. **◆bakery** n boulangerie f.

balaclava [bælə'klɑːvə] n **b. (helmet)** passe-montagne m.

balance ['bæləns] n (scales) & Econ Pol Com balance f; (equilibrium) équilibre m; (of account) Com solde m; (remainder) reste m; **to strike a b.** trouver le juste milieu; **sense of b.** sens de la mesure; **in the b.** incertain; **on b.** à tout prendre; **b. sheet** bilan m; – vt tenir or mettre en équilibre (on sur); (budget, account) équilibrer; (compare) mettre en balance, peser; **to b. (out)** (compensate for) compenser; **to b. (oneself)** se tenir en équilibre; – vi (of accounts) être en équilibre, s'équilibrer.

balcony ['bælkənɪ] n balcon m.

bald [bɔːld] a (**-er, -est**) chauve; (statement) brutal; (tyre) lisse; **b. patch** or **spot** tonsure f. **◆b.-'headed** a chauve. **◆balding** a to be **b.** perdre ses cheveux. **◆baldness** n calvitie f.

balderdash ['bɔːldədæʃ] n balivernes fpl.

bale [beɪl] **1** n (of cotton etc) balle f. **2** vi **to b. out** Av sauter en parachute.

baleful ['beɪlfʊl] a sinistre, funeste.

balk [bɔːk] vi reculer (**at** devant), regimber (at contre).

ball¹ [bɔːl] n balle f; (inflated) Fb Rugby etc ballon m; Billiards bille f; (of string, wool) pelote f; (sphere) boule f; (of meat or fish) Culin boulette f; **on the b.** (alert) Fam éveillé; **he's on the b.** (efficient, knowledge-able) Fam il connaît son affaire, il est au point; **b. bearing** roulement m à billes f. **b. game** Am partie f de baseball; **it's a whole new b. game** or **a different b. game** Fig c'est une tout autre affaire. **◆ballcock** n robinet m à flotteur. **◆ballpoint** n stylo m à bille.

ball² [bɔːl] n (dance) bal m. **◆ballroom** n salle f de danse.

ballad ['bæləd] n Liter ballade f; Mus romance f.

ballast ['bæləst] n lest m; – vt lester.

ballet ['bæleɪ] n ballet m. **◆balle'rina** n ballerine f.

ballistic [bə'lɪstɪk] a **b. missile** engin m balistique.

balloon [bə'luːn] n ballon m; Met ballon-sonde m.

ballot ['bælət] n (voting) scrutin m; **b. (paper)** bulletin m de vote; **b. box** urne f; – vt (members) consulter (par un scrutin).

ballyhoo [bælɪ'huː] n Fam battage m (publicitaire).

balm [bɑːm] n (liquid, comfort) baume m. ◆**balmy** a (-ier, -iest) **1** (air) Lit embaumé. **2** (crazy) Fam dingue, timbré.

baloney [bə'ləʊnɪ] n Sl foutaises fpl.

Baltic ['bɔːltɪk] n the **B.** la Baltique.

balustrade ['bæləstreɪd] n balustrade f.

bamboo [bæm'buː] n bambou m.

bamboozle [bæm'buːz(ə)l] vt (cheat) Fam embobiner.

ban [bæn] n interdiction f; – vt (-nn-) interdire; **to b. from** (club etc) exclure de; **to ban s.o. from doing** interdire à qn de faire.

banal [bə'nɑːl, Am 'beɪn(ə)l] a banal. ◆**ba'nality** n banalité f.

banana [bə'nɑːnə] n banane f.

band [bænd] **1** n (strip) bande f; (of hat) ruban m; **rubber** or **elastic b.** élastique m. **2** n (group) bande f; Mus (petit) orchestre m; Mil fanfare f; – vi **to b. together** former une bande, se grouper. ◆**bandstand** n kiosque m à musique. ◆**bandwagon** n to **jump on the b.** Fig suivre le mouvement.

bandage ['bændɪdʒ] n (strip) bande f; (for wound) pansement m; (for holding in place) bandage m; – vt to **b. (up)** (arm, leg) bander; (wound) mettre un pansement sur.

Band-Aid® ['bændeɪd] n pansement m adhésif.

bandit ['bændɪt] n bandit m. ◆**banditry** n banditisme m.

bandy ['bændɪ] **1** a (-ier, -iest) (person) bancal; (legs) arqué. ◆**b.-'legged** a bancal. **2** vt to **b. about** (story etc) faire circuler, propager.

bane [beɪn] n Lit fléau m, funeste. ◆**baneful** a funeste.

bang [bæŋ] n (hit, noise) coup m (violent); (of gun etc) détonation f; (of door) claquement m; – vt cogner, frapper; (door) (faire) claquer; to **b. one's head** se cogner la tête; – vi cogner, frapper; (of door) claquer; (of gun) détoner; (of firework) éclater; to **b. down** (lid) rabattre (violemment); to **b. into** sth heurter qch; – int vlan!, pan!; to go **(off) b.** éclater. **2** adv (exactly) Fam exactement; **b. in the middle** en plein milieu; **b. on** six à six heures tapantes.

banger ['bæŋər] n **1** Culin Fam saucisse f. **2** (firecracker) pétard m. **3** old **b.** (car) Fam tacot m, guimbarde f.

bangle ['bæŋg(ə)l] n bracelet m (rigide).

bangs [bæŋz] npl (of hair) Am frange f.

banish ['bænɪʃ] vt bannir.

banister ['bænɪstər] n **banister(s)** rampe f (d'escalier).

banjo ['bændʒəʊ] n (pl -os or -oes) banjo m.

bank [bæŋk] **1** n (of river) bord m, rive f; (raised) berge f; (of earth) talus m; (of sand) banc m; **the Left B.** (in Paris) la Rive gauche; – vt to **b. (up)** (earth etc) amonceler; (fire) couvrir. **2** n Com banque f; **b. account** compte m en banque; **b. card** carte f d'identité bancaire; **b. holiday** jour m férié; **b. note** billet m de banque; **b. rate** taux m d'escompte; – vt (money) Com mettre en banque; – vi avoir un compte en banque (with à). **3** vi Av virer. **4** vi to **b. on s.o./sth** (rely on) compter sur qn/qch. ◆**-ing** n (activity, profession) la banque. ◆**-er** n banquier m.

bankrupt ['bæŋkrʌpt] a to go **b.** faire faillite; **b. of** (ideas) Fig dénué de; – vt mettre en faillite. ◆**bankruptcy** n faillite f.

banner ['bænər] n (at rallies etc) banderole f; (flag) & Fig bannière f.

banns [bænz] npl bans mpl.

banquet ['bæŋkwɪt] n banquet m.

banter ['bæntər] vti plaisanter; – n plaisanterie f. ◆**-ing** a (tone, air) plaisantin.

baptism ['bæptɪzəm] n baptême m. ◆**bap'tize** vt baptiser.

bar [bɑːr] **1** n barre f; (of gold) lingot m; (of chocolate) tablette f; (on window) & Jur barreau m; **b. of soap** savonnette f; **behind bars** Jur sous les verrous; to **be a b. to** Fig faire obstacle à. **2** n (pub) bar m; (counter) comptoir m. **3** n (group of notes) Mus mesure f. **4** vt (-rr-) (way etc) bloquer, barrer; (window) griller. **5** vt (prohibit) interdire (s.o. from doing à qn de faire); (exclude) exclure (from à). **6** prep sauf.
◆**barmaid** n serveuse f de bar. ◆**barman** n, ◆**bartender** n barman m.

Barbados [bɑː'beɪdɒs] n Barbade f.

barbarian [bɑː'beərɪən] n barbare mf. ◆**barbaric** a barbare. ◆**barbarity** n barbarie f.

barbecue ['bɑːbɪkjuː] n barbecue m; – vt griller (au barbecue).

barbed [bɑːbd] a **b. wire** fil m de fer barbelé; (fence) barbelés mpl.

barber ['bɑːbər] n coiffeur m (pour hommes).

barbiturate [bɑː'bɪtjʊrət] n barbiturique m.

bare [beər] a (-er, -est) nu; (tree, hill etc) dénudé; (cupboard) vide; (mere) simple; **the b. necessities** le strict nécessaire; **with his b. hands** à mains nues; – vt mettre à nu.

◆—ness n (of person) nudité f. **◆bareback** adv **to ride b.** monter à cru. **◆barefaced** a (lie) éhonté. **◆barefoot** adv nu-pieds; – a aux pieds nus. **◆bare-'headed** a à nu-tête inv.

barely ['beəlɪ] adv (scarcely) à peine, tout juste.

bargain ['bɑːgɪn] n (deal) marché m, affaire f; **a (good) b.** (cheap buy) une occasion, une bonne affaire; **it's a b.!** (agreed) c'est entendu!; **into the b.** par-dessus le marché; **b. price** prix m exceptionnel; **b. counter** rayon m des soldes; – vi (negotiate) négocier; (haggle) marchander; **to b. for** or **on sth** Fig s'attendre à qch. **◆—ing** n négociations fpl; marchandage m.

barge [bɑːdʒ] 1 n chaland m, péniche f. 2 vi **to b. in** (enter a room) faire irruption; (interrupt) interrompre; **to b. into** (hit) se cogner contre.

baritone ['bærɪtəʊn] n (voice, singer) baryton m.

bark [bɑːk] 1 n (of tree) écorce f. 2 vi (of dog etc) aboyer; – n aboiement m. **◆—ing** n aboiements mpl.

barley ['bɑːlɪ] n orge f; **b. sugar** sucre m d'orge.

barmy ['bɑːmɪ] a (-ier, -iest) Fam dingue, timbré.

barn [bɑːn] n (for crops etc) grange f; (for horses) écurie f; (for cattle) étable f. **◆barnyard** n basse-cour f.

barometer [bə'rɒmɪtər] n baromètre m.

baron ['bærən] n baron m; (industrialist) Fig magnat m. **◆baroness** n baronne f.

baroque [bə'rɒk, Am bə'rəʊk] a & n Archit Mus etc baroque (m).

barracks ['bærəks] npl caserne f.

barrage ['bærɑːʒ, Am bə'rɑːʒ] n (barrier) barrage m; **a b. of** (questions etc) un feu roulant de.

barrel ['bærəl] n 1 (cask) tonneau m; (of oil) baril m. 2 (of gun) canon m. 3 **b. organ** orgue m de Barbarie.

barren ['bærən] a stérile; (style) Fig aride.

barrette [bə'ret] n (hair slide) Am barrette f.

barricade ['bærɪkeɪd] n barricade f; – vt barricader; **to b. oneself (in)** se barricader.

barrier ['bærɪər] n barrière f; Fig obstacle m, barrière f; (ticket) **b.** Rail portillon m; **sound b.** mur m du son.

barring ['bɑːrɪŋ] prep sauf, excepté.

barrister ['bærɪstər] n avocat m.

barrow ['bærəʊ] n charrette f or voiture f à bras; (wheelbarrow) brouette f.

barter ['bɑːtər] vt troquer, échanger (for contre); – n troc m, échange m.

base [beɪs] 1 n (bottom, main ingredient) base f; (of tree, lamp) pied m. 2 n Mil base f. 3 vt baser, fonder (on sur); **based in** or **on London** basé à Londres. 4 a (dishonourable) bas, ignoble; (metal) vil. **◆—less** a sans fondement. **◆—ness** n bassesse f. **◆baseball** n base-ball m. **◆baseboard** n Am plinthe f.

basement ['beɪsmənt] n sous-sol m.

bash [bæʃ] n Fam (bang) coup m; **to have a b.** (try) essayer un coup; – vt Fam (hit) cogner; **to b. (about)** (ill-treat) malmener; **to b. s.o. up** tabasser qn; **to b. in** or **down** (door etc) défoncer. **◆—ing** n (thrashing) Fam raclée f.

bashful ['bæʃfəl] a timide.

basic ['beɪsɪk] a fondamental; (pay etc) de base; – n **the basics** Fam l'essentiel m. **◆—ally** [-klɪ] adv au fond.

basil ['bæz(ə)l] n Bot Culin basilic m.

basilica [bə'zɪlɪkə] n basilique f.

basin ['beɪs(ə)n] n (for water) bassin m, bassine f; (for soup, food) bol m; (of river) bassin m; (portable washbasin) cuvette f; (sink) lavabo m.

basis, pl **-ses** ['beɪsɪs, -siːz] n base f; **on the b. of** d'après; **on that b.** dans ces conditions; **on a weekly/etc b.** chaque semaine/etc.

bask [bɑːsk] vi se chauffer.

basket ['bɑːskɪt] n panier m; (for bread, laundry, litter) corbeille f. **◆basketball** n basket(-ball) m.

Basque [bæsk] a & n basque (mf).

bass [beɪs] n Mus basse f; – a (note, voice) bas.

bass [bæs] n (sea fish) bar m; (fresh-water) perche f.

bassinet [bæsɪ'net] n (cradle) Am couffin m.

bastard ['bɑːstəd] 1 n & a bâtard, -arde (mf). 2 n Pej Sl salaud m, salope f.

baste [beɪst] vt 1 (fabric) bâtir. 2 Culin arroser.

bastion ['bæstɪən] n bastion m.

bat [bæt] 1 n (animal) chauve-souris f. 2 n Cricket batte f; Table Tennis raquette f; **off my own b.** de ma propre initiative; – vt (-tt-) (ball) frapper. 3 vt **she didn't b. an eyelid** elle n'a pas sourcillé.

batch [bætʃ] n (of people) groupe m; (of letters) paquet m; (of books) lot m; (of loaves) fournée f; (of papers) liasse f.

bated ['beɪtɪd] a **with b. breath** en retenant son souffle.

bath [bɑːθ] n (pl **-s** [bɑːðz]) bain m; (tub) baignoire f; **swimming baths** piscine f; – vt baigner; – vi prendre un bain.

◆**bathrobe** n peignoir m (de bain); *Am* robe f de chambre. ◆**bathroom** n salle f de bain(s); *(toilet) Am* toilettes *fpl*. ◆**bathtub** n baignoire f.

bath/e [beɪð] vt baigner; *(wound)* laver; – vi se baigner; *Am* prendre un bain; – n bain m (de mer), baignade f. ◆—**ing** n baignade(s) f(pl); **b. costume** or **suit** maillot m de bain.

baton ['bætən, *Am* bə'tɒn] n *Mus Mil* bâton m; *(truncheon)* matraque f.

battalion [bə'tæljən] n bataillon m.

batter ['bætər] **1** n pâte f à frire. **2** vt battre, frapper; *(baby)* martyriser; *Mil* pilonner; **to b. down** *(door)* défoncer. ◆—**ed** a *(car, hat)* cabossé; *(house)* délabré; *(face)* meurtri; *(wife)* battu. ◆—**ing** n **to take a b.** *Fig* souffrir beaucoup.

battery ['bætərɪ] n *Mil Aut Agr* batterie f; *(in radio etc)* pile f.

battle ['bæt(ə)l] n bataille f; *(struggle) Fig* lutte f; **that's half the b.** *Fam* c'est ça le secret de la victoire; **b. dress** tenue f de campagne; – vi se battre, lutter. ◆**battlefield** n champ m de bataille. ◆**battleship** n cuirassé m.

battlements ['bæt(ə)lmənts] *npl (indentations)* créneaux *mpl*; *(wall)* remparts *mpl*.

batty ['bætɪ] a *(-ier, -iest) Sl* dingue, toqué.

baulk [bɔːk] vi reculer (at devant), regimber (at contre).

bawdy ['bɔːdɪ] a *(-ier, -iest)* paillard, grossier.

bawl [bɔːl] vti **to b. (out)** beugler, brailler; **to b. s.o. out** *Am Sl* engueuler qn.

bay [beɪ] **1** n *Geog Archit* baie f. **2** n *Bot* laurier m. **3** n *(for loading etc)* aire f. **4** n *(of dog)* aboiement m; **at b.** aux abois; **to hold at b.** tenir à distance; – vi aboyer. **5** a *(horse)* bai.

bayonet ['beɪənɪt] n baïonnette f.

bazaar [bə'zɑːr] n *(market, shop)* bazar m; *(charity sale)* vente f de charité.

bazooka [bə'zuːkə] n bazooka m.

BC [biː'siː] *abbr (before Christ)* avant Jésus-Christ.

be [biː] vi *(pres t* am, are, is; *pt* was, were; *pp* been; *pres p* being) **1** être; **it's green/small** c'est vert/petit; **she's a doctor** elle est médecin; **he's an Englishman** c'est un Anglais; **it's 3 (o'clock)** il est trois heures; **it's the sixth of May** c'est *or* nous sommes le six mai. **2** avoir; **to be hot/right/lucky** avoir chaud/raison/de la chance; **my feet are cold** j'ai froid aux pieds; **he's 20** *(age)* il a 20 ans; **to be 2 metres high** avoir 2 mètres de haut; **to be 6 feet tall** mesurer 1,80 m. **3**

(health) aller; **how are you?** comment vas-tu? **4** *(place, situation)* se trouver, être; **she's in York** elle se trouve *or* elle est à York. **5** *(exist)* être; **the best painter there is** le meilleur peintre qui soit; **leave me be** laissez-moi *(tranquille)*; **that may be** cela se peut. **6** *(go, come)* **I've been to see her** je suis allé *or* j'ai été la voir; **he's (already) been** il est (déjà) venu. **7** *(weather)* & *Math* faire; **it's fine** il fait beau; **2 and 2 are 4** 2 et 2 font 4. **8** *(cost)* coûter, faire; **it's 20 pence** ça coûte 20 pence; **how much is it?** ça fait combien?, c'est combien? **9** *(auxiliary)* **I am/was doing** je fais/faisais; **I'm listening to the radio** *(in the process of)* je suis en train d'écouter la radio; **she's been there some time** elle est là depuis longtemps; **he was killed** il a été tué, on l'a tué; **I've been waiting (for) two hours** j'attends depuis deux heures; **it's said on dit; to be pitied** à plaindre; **isn't it?, aren't you?** *etc* n'est-ce pas?, non?; **I am!, he is!** *etc* oui! **10** (+ *inf)* **he is to come** *(must)* il doit venir; **he's shortly to go** *(intends to)* il va bientôt partir. **11 there is** or **are** il y a; *(pointing)* voilà; **here is** *or* **are** voici.

beach [biːtʃ] n plage f. ◆**beachcomber** n *(person)* ramasseur, -euse mf d'épaves.

beacon ['biːkən] n *Nau Av* balise f; *(lighthouse)* phare m.

bead [biːd] n *(small sphere, drop of liquid)* perle f; *(of rosary)* grain m; *(of sweat)* goutte f; *(string of)* **beads** collier m.

beak [biːk] n bec m.

beaker ['biːkər] n gobelet m.

beam [biːm] **1** n *(of wood)* poutre f. **2** n *(of light)* rayon m; *(of headlight, torch)* faisceau m (lumineux); – vi rayonner; *(of person) Fig* sourire largement. **3** vt *Rad* diffuser. ◆—**ing** a *(radiant)* radieux.

bean [biːn] n haricot m; *(of coffee)* grain m; **(broad) b.** fève f; **to be full of beans** *Fam* déborder d'entrain. ◆**beanshoots** *npl*, ◆**beansprouts** *npl* germes *mpl* de soja.

bear¹ [beər] n *(animal)* ours m.

bear² [beər] vt *(pt* bore, *pp* borne) *(carry, show)* porter; *(endure)* supporter; *(resemblance)* offrir; *(comparison)* soutenir; *(responsibility)* assumer; *(child)* donner naissance à; **to b. in mind** tenir compte de; **to b. out** corroborer; – vi **to b. left/**etc *(turn)* tourner à gauche/etc; **to b. north/**etc *(go)* aller en direction du nord/etc; **to b. (up)on** *(relate to)* se rapporter à; **to b. heavily on** *(of burden) Fig* peser sur; **to b. with** être indulgent envers, être patient avec; **to bring to b.** *(one's energies)* consacrer (on à);

(*pressure*) exercer (**on** sur); **to b. up** ne pas se décourager, tenir le coup; **b. up!** du courage! ◆**—ing** n (*posture, conduct*) maintien m; (*relationship, relevance*) relation f (**on** avec); *Nau Av* position f; **to get one's bearings** s'orienter. ◆**—able** a supportable. ◆**—er** n porteur, -euse m f.

beard [bɪəd] n barbe f. ◆**bearded** a barbu.

beast [biːst] n bête f, animal m; (*person*) *Pej* brute f. ◆**beastly** a *Fam* (*bad*) vilain, infect; (*spiteful*) méchant; — adv *Fam* terriblement.

beat [biːt] n (*of heart, drum*) battement m; (*of policeman*) ronde f; *Mus* mesure f, rythme m; — vt (*pt* beat, *pp* beaten) (*defeat*) vaincre, battre; **to b. a drum** battre du tambour; **that beats me** *Fam* ça me dépasse; **to b.s.o. to it** devancer qn; **b. it!** *Sl* fichez le camp!; **to b. back** *or* **off** repousser; **to b. down** (*price*) faire baisser; **to b. in** *or* **down** (*door*) défoncer; **to b. out** (*rhythm*) marquer; (*tune*) jouer; **to b.s.o. up** tabasser qn; — vi battre; (*at door*) frapper (**at** à); **to b. about** *or* **around the bush** *Fam* tourner autour du pot; **to b. down** (*of rain*) tomber à verse; (*of sun*) taper. ◆**—ing** n (*blows, defeat*) raclée f. ◆**—er** n (*for eggs*) batteur m.

beauty [bjuːtɪ] n (*quality, woman*) beauté f; **it's a b.!** c'est une merveille!; **the b. of it is ...** le plus beau, c'est que ...; **b. parlour** institut m de beauté; **b. spot** (*on skin*) grain m de beauté; (*in countryside*) site m pittoresque. ◆**beau'tician** n esthéticienne f. ◆**beautiful** a (très) beau; (*superb*) merveilleux. ◆**beautifully** adv merveilleusement.

beaver ['biːvər] n castor m; — vi **to b. away** travailler dur (**at sth** à qch).

because [bɪ'kɒz] conj parce que; **b. of** à cause de.

beck [bek] n **at s.o.'s b. and call** aux ordres de qn.

beckon ['bekən] vti **to b. (to) s.o.** faire signe à qn (**to do** de faire).

becom/e [bɪ'kʌm] **1** vi (*pt* became, *pp* become) devenir; **to b. a painter** devenir peintre; **to b. thin** maigrir; **to b. worried** commencer à s'inquiéter; **what has b. of her?** qu'est-elle devenue? **2** vt that hat **becomes her** ce chapeau lui sied *or* lui va. ◆**—ing** a (*clothes*) seyant; (*modesty*) bienséant.

bed [bed] n lit m; *Geol* couche f; (*of vegetables*) carré m; (*of sea*) fond m; (*flower bed*) parterre m; **to go to b.** (aller) se coucher; **in b.** couché; **to get out of b.** se lever; **b. and**

breakfast (*in hotel etc*) chambre f avec petit déjeuner; **b. settee** (*canapé m*) convertible m; **air b.** matelas m pneumatique; — vt (**-dd-**) **to b. (out)** (*plant*) repiquer; — vi **b. down** se coucher. ◆**bedding** n literie f. ◆**bedbug** n punaise f. ◆**bedclothes** npl couvertures fpl et draps mpl. ◆**bedridden** a alité. ◆**bedroom** n chambre f à coucher. ◆**bedside** n chevet m; — a (*lamp, book, table*) de chevet. ◆**bed'sitter** n, *Fam* ◆**bedsit** n chambre f meublée. ◆**bedspread** n dessus-de-lit m inv. ◆**bedtime** n heure f du coucher.

bedeck [bɪ'dek] vt orner (**with** de).

bedevil [bɪ'dev(ə)l] vt (**-ll-**, *Am* **-l-**) (*plague*) tourmenter; (*confuse*) embrouiller; **bedevilled by** (*problems etc*) perturbé par, empoisonné par.

bedlam ['bedləm] n (*noise*) *Fam* chahut m.

bedraggled [bɪ'dræg(ə)ld] a (*clothes, person*) débraillé.

bee [biː] n abeille f. ◆**beehive** n ruche f. ◆**beekeeping** n apiculture f. ◆**beeline** n **to make a b. for** aller droit vers.

beech [biːtʃ] n (*tree, wood*) hêtre m.

beef [biːf] n **1** bœuf m. **2** vi (*complain*) *Sl* rouspéter. ◆**beefburger** n hamburger m. ◆**beefy** a (**-ier, -iest**) *Fam* musclé, costaud.

beer [bɪər] n bière f; **b. glass** chope f. ◆**beery** a (*room, person*) qui sent la bière.

beet [biːt] n betterave f (à sucre); *Am* = **beetroot.** ◆**beetroot** n betterave f (*potagère*).

beetle ['biːt(ə)l] n **1** cafard m, scarabée m. **2** vi **to b. off** *Fam* se sauver.

befall [bɪ'fɔːl] vt (*pt* befell, *pp* befallen) arriver à.

befit [bɪ'fɪt] vt (**-tt-**) convenir à.

before [bɪ'fɔːr] adv avant; (*already*) déjà; (*in front*) devant; **the month b.** le mois d'avant *or* précédent; **the day b.** la veille; **I've never done it b.** je ne l'ai jamais (encore) fait; — prep (*time*) avant; (*place*) devant; **the year b. last** il y a deux ans; — conj avant que (+ ne + *sub*), avant de (+ *inf*); **b. he goes** avant qu'il (ne) parte; **b. going** avant de partir. ◆**beforehand** adv à l'avance, avant.

befriend [bɪ'frend] vt offrir son amitié à, aider.

befuddled [bɪ'fʌd(ə)ld] a (*drunk*) ivre.

beg [beg] vt (**-gg-**) **to b. (for)** solliciter, demander; (*bread, money*) mendier; **to b. s.o. to do** prier *or* supplier qn de faire; **I b. to** je me permets de; **to b. the question** esquiver la question; — vi mendier;

(*entreat*) supplier; **to go begging** (*of food, articles*) ne pas trouver d'amateurs. ◆**beggar** n mendiant, -ante mf; (*person*) Sl individu m; **lucky b.** veinard, -arde mf. ◆**beggarly** a misérable.

beget [br'get] vt (*pt* begot, *pp* begotten, *pres p* begetting) engendrer.

begin [br'gin] vt (*pt* began, *pp* begun, *pres p* beginning) commencer; (*fashion, campaign*) lancer; (*bottle, sandwich*) entamer; (*conversation*) engager; **to b. doing** *or* **to do** commencer *or* se mettre à faire; – vi commencer (**with** par, **by doing** par faire); **to b. on sth** commencer qch; **beginning from** à partir de; **to b. with** (*first*) d'abord. ◆**—ning** n commencement m, début m. ◆**—ner** n débutant, -ante mf.

begrudge [br'grʌdʒ] vt (*give unwillingly*) donner à contrecœur; (*envy*) envier (**s.o. sth** qch à qn); (*reproach*) reprocher (**s.o. sth** qch à qn); **to b. doing** faire à contrecœur.

behalf [br'hɑːf] n **on b. of** pour, au nom de, de la part de; (*in the interest of*) en faveur de, pour.

behave [br'herv] vi se conduire; (*of machine*) fonctionner; **to b. (oneself)** se tenir bien; (*of child*) être sage. ◆**behaviour** n conduite f, comportement m; **to be on one's best b.** se conduire de son mieux.

behead [br'hed] vt décapiter.

behest [br'hest] n Lit ordre m.

behind [br'haɪnd] **1** prep derrière; (*more backward than, late according to*) en retard sur; – adv derrière; (*late*) en retard (**with**, in dans). **2** n (*buttocks*) Fam derrière m. ◆**behindhand** adv en retard.

beholden [br'həʊldən] a redevable (**to** à, **for** de).

beige [beɪʒ] a & n beige (m).

being [ˈbiːɪŋ] n (*person, life*) être m; **to come into b.** naître, être créé.

belated [br'leɪtɪd] a tardif.

belch [beltʃ] **1** vi (*of person*) faire un renvoi, éructer; – n renvoi m. **2** vt **to b. (out)** (*smoke*) vomir.

beleaguered [br'liːgəd] a (*besieged*) assiégé.

belfry ['belfrɪ] n beffroi m, clocher m.

Belgium ['beldʒəm] n Belgique f. ◆**Belgian** ['beldʒən] a & n belge (mf).

belle [bel] n dénantir.

belief [br'liːf] n (*believing, thing believed*) croyance f (**in** s.o. en qn, **in sth** à *or* en qch); (*trust*) confiance f, foi f; (*faith*) Rel foi f (**in** en).

believ/e [br'liːv] vti croire (**in sth** à qch, **in God/s.o.** en Dieu/qn); **I b. so** je crois que oui; **I b. I'm right** je crois avoir raison; **to b.**

in doing croire qu'il faut faire; **he doesn't b. in smoking** il désapprouve que l'on fume. ◆**—able** a croyable. ◆**—er** n Rel croyant, -ante mf; **b. in** (*supporter*) partisan, -ane mf de.

belittle [br'lɪt(ə)l] vt déprécier.

bell [bel] n cloche f; (*small*) clochette f; (*in phone*) sonnerie f; (*on door, bicycle*) sonnette f; (*on dog*) grelot m. ◆**bellboy** n, ◆**bellhop** n Am groom m.

belle [bel] n (*woman*) beauté f, belle f.

belligerent [br'lɪdʒərənt] a & n belligérant, -ante (mf).

bellow ['beləʊ] vi beugler, mugir.

bellows ['beləʊz] npl (*pair of*) b. soufflet m.

belly ['belɪ] n ventre m; **b. button** Sl nombril m. ◆**bellyache** n mal m au ventre; – vi Sl rouspéter. ◆**bellyful** n to have a b. Sl en avoir plein le dos.

belong [br'lɒŋ] vi appartenir (**to** à); **to b. to** (*club*) être membre de; **the cup belongs here** la tasse se range ici. ◆**—ings** npl affaires fpl.

beloved [br'lʌvɪd] a & n bien-aimé, -ée (mf).

below [br'ləʊ] prep (*lower than*) au-dessous de; (*under*) sous, au-dessous de; (*unworthy of*) Fig indigne de; – adv en dessous; **b.** (*in book etc*) voir ci-dessous.

belt [belt] **1** n ceinture f; (*area*) zone f, région f; Tech courroie f. **2** vt (*hit*) Sl rosser. **3** vi **to b. (along)** (*rush*) Sl filer à toute allure; **b. up!** (*shut up*) Sl boucle-la!

bemoan [br'məʊn] vt déplorer.

bench [bentʃ] n (*seat*) banc m; (*work table*) établi m, banc m; **the B.** Jur la magistrature (assise); (*court*) le tribunal.

bend [bend] n courbe f; (*in river, pipe*) coude m; (*in road*) Aut virage m; (*of arm, knee*) pli m; **round the b.** (*mad*) Sl tordu; – vt (*pt & pp* bent) courber; (*leg, arm*) plier; (*direct*) diriger; **to b. the rules** faire une entorse au règlement; – vi (*of branch*) plier, être courbé; (*of road*) tourner; **to b. (down)** se courber; **to b. (over** *or* **forward)** se pencher; **to b. to** (*s.o.'s will*) se soumettre à.

beneath [br'niːθ] prep au-dessous de, sous; (*unworthy of*) indigne de; – adv (au-)dessous.

benediction [benɪˈdɪkʃ(ə)n] n bénédiction f.

benefactor ['benɪfæktər] n bienfaiteur m. ◆**benefactress** n bienfaitrice f.

beneficial [benɪˈfɪʃəl] a bénéfique.

beneficiary [benɪˈfɪʃərɪ] n bénéficiaire mf.

benefit ['benɪfɪt] n (*advantage*) avantage m; (*money*) allocation f; pl (*of science, education etc*) bienfaits mpl; **to s.o.'s b.** dans l'intérêt de qn; **for your (own) b.** pour vous, pour votre bien; **to be of b.** faire du bien (to à); **to give s.o. the b. of the doubt** accorder à qn le bénéfice du doute; **b. concert**/*etc* concert/*etc m* de bienfaisance; – *vt* faire du bien à; (*be useful to*) profiter à; – *vi* gagner (*from doing* à faire); **you'll b. from** or **by the rest** le repos vous fera du bien.

Benelux ['benilʌks] *n* Bénélux *m*.

benevolent [bi'nevələnt] *a* bienveillant.
◆**benevolence** *n* bienveillance *f*.

benign [bi'naɪn] *a* bienveillant, bénin; (*climate*) doux; (*tumour*) bénin.

bent [bent] 1 *a* (*nail, mind*) tordu; (*dishonest*) *Sl* corrompu; **b. on doing** résolu à faire. **2** *n* (*talent*) aptitude *f* (for pour); (*inclination, liking*) penchant *m*, goût *m* (for pour).

bequeath [bi'kwi:ð] *vt* léguer (to à). ◆**bequest** *n* legs *m*.

bereaved [bi'ri:vd] *a* endeuillé; – *n* **the b.** la famille, la femme *etc* du disparu. ◆**bereavement** *n* deuil *m*.

bereft [bi'reft] *a* **b. of** dénué de.

beret ['berei, *Am* bə'rei] *n* béret *m*.

berk [bɜːk] *n* *Sl* imbécile *mf*.

Bermuda [bə'mjuːdə] *n* Bermudes *fpl*.

berry ['beri] *n* baie *f*.

berserk [bə'zɜːk] *a* **to go b.** devenir fou, se déchaîner.

berth [bɜːθ] *n* (*in ship, train*) couchette *f*; (*anchorage*) mouillage *m*; – *vi* (*of ship*) mouiller.

beseech [bi'siːtʃ] *vt* (*pt & pp* **besought** *or* **beseeched**) *Lit* implorer (**to do** de faire).

beset [bi'set] *vt* (*pt & pp* **beset**, *pres p* **besetting**) assaillir (qn); **b. with obstacles**/*etc* semé *or* hérissé d'obstacles/*etc*.

beside [bi'saɪd] *prep* à côté de; **that's b. the point** ça n'a rien à voir; **b. oneself** (*angry, excited*) hors de soi.

besides [bi'saɪdz] *prep* (*in addition to*) en plus de; (*except*) excepté; **there are ten of us b.** Paul nous sommes dix sans compter Paul; – *adv* (*in addition*) de plus; (*moreover*) d'ailleurs.

besiege [bi'siːdʒ] *vt* (*of soldiers, crowd*) assiéger; (*annoy*) *Fig* assaillir (**with** de).

besotted [bi'sɒtɪd] *a* (*drunk*) abruti; **b. with** (*infatuated*) entiché de.

bespatter [bi'spætər] *vt* éclabousser (**with** de).

bespectacled [bi'spektɪk(ə)ld] *a* à lunettes.

bespoke [bi'spəʊk] *a* (*tailor*) à façon.

best [best] *a* meilleur; **the b. page in the book** la meilleure page du livre; **the b. part of** (*most*) la plus grande partie de; **the b. thing is** le mieux; **b. man** (*at wedding*) témoin *m*, garçon *m* d'honneur; – *n* **the b.** (one) le

meilleur, la meilleure; **it's for the b.** c'est pour le mieux; **at b.** au mieux; **to do one's b.** faire de son mieux; **to look one's b.**, be at **one's b.** être à son avantage; **to the b. of my knowledge** autant que je sache; **to make the b. of** (*accept*) s'accommoder de; **to get the b. of it** avoir le dessus; **in one's Sunday b.** endimanché; **all the b.!** portez-vous bien!; (*in letter*) amicalement; – *adv* (**the**) **b.** (*to play etc*) le mieux; **the b. loved** le plus aimé; **to think it b.** to juger prudent de. ◆**b.-'seller** *n* (*book*) best-seller *m*.

bestow [bi'stəʊ] *vt* accorder, conférer (**on** à).

bet [bet] *n* pari *m*; – *vti* (*pt & pp* **bet** *or* **betted**, *pres p* **betting**) parier (**on** sur, **that** que); **you b.!** *Fam* (*of course*) tu paries! ◆**betting** *n* pari(s) *m*(*pl*); **b. shop** *or* **office** bureau *m* du pari mutuel.

betoken [bi'təʊkən] *vt Lit* annoncer.

betray [bi'treɪ] *vt* trahir; **to b. to s.o.** (*give away to*) livrer à qn. ◆**betrayal** *n* (*disloyalty*) trahison *f*; (*disclosure*) révélation *f*.

better ['betər] *a* meilleur (**than** que); **she's** (**much**) **b.** *Med* elle va (bien) mieux; **he's b. than** (*at games*) il joue mieux que; (*at maths etc*) il est plus fort que; **that's b.** tant mieux; **to get b.** (*recover*) se remettre; (*improve*) s'améliorer; **it's b. to go** il vaut mieux partir; **the b. part of** (*most*) la plus grande partie de; – *adv* mieux; **I had b. go** il vaut mieux que je parte; **so much the b.,** **all the b.** tant mieux (**for** pour); – *n* **to get the b. of s.o.** l'emporter sur qn; **change for the b.** amélioration *f*; **one's betters** ses supérieurs *mpl*; – *vt* (*improve*) améliorer; (*outdo*) dépasser; **to b. oneself** améliorer sa condition. ◆**—ment** *n* amélioration *f*.

between [bi'twiːn] *prep* entre; **we did it b.** (**the two of**) **us** nous l'avons fait à nous deux; **b. you and me** entre nous; **in b.** entre; – *adv* **in b.** (*space*) au milieu, entre les deux; (*time*) dans l'intervalle.

bevel ['bevl] *n* (*edge*) biseau *m*.

beverage [bevərɪdʒ] *n* boisson *f*.

bevy ['bevi] *n* (*of girls*) essaim *m*, bande *f*.

beware [bi'weər] *vi* **to b. of** (*s.o., sth*) se méfier de, prendre garde à; **b.!** méfiez-vous!, prenez garde!; **b. of falling**/*etc* prenez garde de (ne pas) tomber/*etc*; **'b. of the trains'** 'attention aux trains'.

bewilder [bi'wɪldər] *vt* dérouter, rendre perplexe. ◆**—ment** *n* confusion *f*.

bewitch [bi'wɪtʃ] *vt* enchanter. ◆**—ing** *a* enchanteur.

beyond [bi'jɒnd] *prep* (*further than*) au-delà

de; (*reach, doubt*) hors de; (*except*) sauf; **b. a year**/*etc* (*longer than*) plus d'un an/*etc*; **b. belief** incroyable; **b. his** *or* **her means** au-dessus de ses moyens; **it's b. me** ça me dépasse; – *adv* (*further*) au-delà.

bias ['baɪəs] **1** *n* penchant *m* (**towards** pour); (*prejudice*) préjugé *m*, parti pris *m*; – *vt* (**-ss-** *or* **-s-**) influencer. **2** *n* **cut on the b.** (*fabric*) coupé dans le biais. ◆**bias(s)ed** *a* partial; **to be b. against** avoir des préjugés contre.

bib [bɪb] *n* (*baby's*) bavoir *m*.

bible ['baɪb(ə)l] *n* bible *f*; **the B.** la Bible. ◆**biblical** ['bɪblɪk(ə)l] *a* biblique.

bibliography [bɪblɪ'ɒgrəfɪ] *n* bibliographie *f*.

bicarbonate [baɪ'kɑːbənət] *n* bicarbonate *m*.

bicentenary [baɪsen'tiːnərɪ] *n*, ◆**bicentennial** *n* bicentenaire *m*.

biceps ['baɪseps] *n Anat* biceps *m*.

bicker ['bɪkər] *vi* se chamailler. ◆**-ing** *n* chamailleries *fpl*.

bicycle ['baɪsɪk(ə)l] *n* bicyclette *f*; – *vi* faire de la bicyclette.

bid¹ [bɪd] *vt* (*pt & pp* **bid**, *pres p* **bidding**) offrir, faire une offre de; – *vi* faire une offre (**for** pour); **to b. for** *Fig* tenter d'obtenir; – *n* (*at auction*) offre *f*, enchère *f*; (*tender*) *Com* soumission *f*; (*attempt*) tentative *f*. ◆**-ding¹** *n* enchères *fpl*. ◆**-der** *n* enchérisseur *m*; soumissionnaire *mf*; **to the highest b.** au plus offrant.

bid² [bɪd] *vt* (*pt* **bade** [bæd], *pp* **bidden** *or* **bid**, *pres p* **bidding**) (*command*) commander (**s.o. to do** à qn de faire); (*say*) dire. ◆**-ding²** *n* ordre(s) *m(pl)*.

bide [baɪd] *vt* **to b. one's time** attendre le bon moment.

bier [bɪər] *n* (*for coffin*) brancards *mpl*.

bifocals [baɪ'fəʊkəlz] *npl* verres *mpl* à double foyer.

big [bɪg] *a* (**bigger, biggest**) grand, gros; (*in age, generous*) grand; (*in bulk, amount*) gros; **b. deal!** *Am Fam* (bon) et alors!; **b. mouth** *Fam* grande gueule *f*; **b. toe** gros orteil *m*; – *adv* **to do things b.** *Fam* faire grand; **to talk b.** fanfaronner. ◆**bighead** *n*, ◆**big'headed** *a Fam* prétentieux, -euse (*mf*). ◆**big-'hearted** *a* généreux. ◆**big-shot** *n*, ◆**bigwig** *n Fam* gros bonnet *m*. ◆**big-time** *a Fam* important.

bigamy ['bɪgəmɪ] *n* bigamie *f*. ◆**bigamist** *n* bigame *mf*. ◆**bigamous** *a* bigame.

bigot ['bɪgət] *n* fanatique *mf*; *Rel* bigot, -ote *mf*. ◆**bigoted** *a* fanatique; *Rel* bigot.

bike [baɪk] *n Fam* vélo *m*; – *vi Fam* aller à vélo.

bikini [bɪ'kiːnɪ] *n* bikini *m*.

bilberry ['bɪlbərɪ] *n* myrtille *f*.

bile [baɪl] *n* bile *f*. ◆**bilious** ['bɪlɪəs] *a* bilieux.

bilge [bɪldʒ] *n* (*nonsense*) *Sl* foutaises *fpl*.

bilingual [baɪ'lɪŋgwəl] *a* bilingue.

bill [bɪl] **1** *n* (*of bird*) bec *m*. **2** *n* (*invoice*) facture *f*, note *f*; (*in restaurant*) addition *f*; (*in hotel*) note *f*; (*draft*) *Com* effet *m*; (*of sale*) acte *m*; (*banknote*) *Am* billet *m*; (*law*) *Pol* projet *m* de loi; (*poster*) affiche *f*; **b. of fare** menu *m*; **b. of rights** déclaration *f* des droits; – *vt Th* mettre à l'affiche, annoncer; **to b. s.o.** *Com* envoyer la facture à qn. ◆**billboard** *n* panneau *m* d'affichage. ◆**billfold** *n Am* portefeuille *m*.

billet ['bɪlɪt] *vt Mil* cantonner; – *n* cantonnement *m*.

billiard ['bɪljəd] *a* (*table etc*) de billard. ◆**billiards** *npl* (*jeu m* de) billard *m*.

billion ['bɪljən] *n* billion *m*; *Am* milliard *m*.

billow ['bɪləʊ] *n* flot *m*; – *vi* (*of sea*) se soulever; (*of smoke*) tourbillonner.

billy-goat ['bɪlɪgəʊt] *n* bouc *m*.

bimonthly [baɪ'mʌnθlɪ] *a* (*fortnightly*) bimensuel; (*every two months*) bimestriel.

bin [bɪn] *n* boîte *f*; (*for bread*) coffre *m*, huche *f*; (*for litter*) boîte *f* à ordures, poubelle *f*.

binary ['baɪnərɪ] *a* binaire.

bind [baɪnd] **1** *vt* (*pt & pp* **bound**) lier; (*fasten*) attacher, lier; (*book*) relier; (*fabric, hem*) border; **to b. s.o. to do** *Jur* obliger *or* astreindre qn à faire. **2** *n* (*bore*) *Fam* plaie *f*. ◆**-ing** *n* (*a contract*) irrévocable; **to be b. on s.o.** *Jur* lier qn. **2** *n* (*of book*) reliure *f*. ◆**-er** *n* (*for papers*) classeur *m*.

binge [bɪndʒ] *n* **to go on a b.** *Sl* faire la bringue.

bingo ['bɪŋgəʊ] *n* loto *m*.

binoculars [bɪ'nɒkjʊləz] *npl* jumelles *fpl*.

biochemistry [baɪəʊ'kemɪstrɪ] *n* biochimie *f*.

biodegradable [baɪəʊdɪ'greɪdəb(ə)l] *a* biodégradable.

biography [baɪ'ɒgrəfɪ] *n* biographie *f*. ◆**biographer** *n* biographe *mf*.

biology [baɪ'ɒlədʒɪ] *n* biologie *f*. ◆**bio'logical** *a* biologique.

biped ['baɪped] *n* bipède *m*.

birch [bɜːtʃ] *n* **1** (*tree*) bouleau *m*. **2** (*whip*) verge *f*; – *vt* fouetter.

bird [bɜːd] *n* oiseau *m*; (*fowl*) *Culin* volaille *f*; (*girl*) *Sl* poulette *f*, nana *f*; **b.'s-eye view**

perspective f à vol d'oiseau; Fig vue f d'ensemble. ◆birdseed n grains mpl de millet.

biro® ['baɪərəʊ] n (pl -os) stylo m à bille, bic® m.

birth [bɜːθ] n naissance f; to give b. to donner naissance à; b. certificate acte m de naissance; b. control limitation f des naissances. ◆birthday n anniversaire m; happy b.! bon anniversaire! ◆birthplace n lieu m de naissance; (house) maison f natale. ◆birthrate n (taux m de) natalité f. ◆birthright n droit m (qu'on a dès sa naissance), patrimoine m.

biscuit ['bɪskɪt] n biscuit m, gâteau m sec; Am petit pain m au lait.

bishop ['bɪʃəp] n évêque m; (in chess) fou m.

bison ['baɪs(ə)n] n inv bison m.

bit¹ [bɪt] n 1 morceau m, (of string, time) bout m; a b. (a little) un peu; a tiny b. un tout petit peu; quite a b. (very) très; (much) beaucoup; not a b. pas du tout; a b. of luck une chance; b. by b. petit à petit; in bits (and pieces) en morceaux; to come to bits se démonter. 2 (coin) pièce f. 3 (of horse) mors m. 4 (of drill) mèche f. 5 (computer information) bit m.

bit² [bɪt] see bite.

bitch [bɪtʃ] 1 n chienne f; (woman) Pej Fam garce f. 2 vi (complain) Fam râler. ◆bitchy a (-ier, -iest) Fam vache.

bit/e [baɪt] n 1 (wound) morsure f; (from insect) piqûre f; Fishing touche f; (mouthful) bouchée f; (of style etc) Fig mordant m; a b. to eat un morceau à manger; – vti (pt bit, pp bitten) mordre; (of insect) piquer, mordre; to b. one's nails se ronger les ongles; to b. on sth mordre qch; to b. sth off arracher qch d'un coup de dent(s). ◆—ing a mordant; (wind) cinglant.

bitter ['bɪtər] 1 a (person, taste, irony etc) amer; (cold, wind) glacial, âpre; (criticism) acerbe; (shock, fate) cruel; (conflict) violent. 2 n bière f (pression). ◆—ness n amertume f; âpreté f; violence f. ◆bitter-'sweet a aigre-doux.

bivouac ['bɪvʊæk] n Mil bivouac m; – vi (-ck-) bivouaquer.

bizarre [bɪ'zɑːr] a bizarre.

blab [blæb] vi (-bb-) jaser. ◆blabber vi jaser. ◆blabbermouth n jaseur, -euse mf.

black [blæk] a (-er, -est) noir; b. eye œil m au beurre noir; to give s.o. a b. eye pocher l'œil à qn; b. and blue (bruised) couvert de bleus; b. sheep Fig brebis f galeuse; b. ice verglas m; b. pudding boudin m; – n (colour) noir m; (Negro) Noir, -e mf; – vt

noircir; (refuse to deal with) boycotter; – to b. out (faint) s'évanouir. ◆blacken vti noircir. ◆blackish a noirâtre. ◆blackness n (of night) obscurité f.

blackberry ['blækbərɪ] n mûre f. ◆blackbird n merle m. ◆blackboard n tableau m (noir). ◆black'currant n cassis m. ◆blackleg n (strike breaker) jaune m. ◆blacklist n liste f noire; – vt mettre sur la liste noire. ◆blackmail n chantage m; – vt faire chanter. ◆blackmailer n maître chanteur m. ◆blackout n panne f d'électricité; (during war) Mil black-out m; Med syncope f; (news) b. black-out m. ◆blacksmith n forgeron m.

blackguard ['blægɑːd, -gəd] n canaille f.

bladder ['blædər] n vessie f.

blade [bleɪd] n lame f; (of grass) brin m; (of windscreen wiper) caoutchouc m.

blame [bleɪm] vt accuser; (censure) blâmer; to b. sth on s.o. or sth rejeter la responsabilité de qch sur qn; to b. s.o. for sth (reproach) reprocher qch à qn; you're to b. c'est ta faute; – n faute f; (censure) blâme m. ◆—less a irréprochable.

blanch [blɑːntʃ] vt (vegetables) blanchir; – vi (turn pale with fear etc) blêmir.

blancmange [blə'mɒnʒ] n blanc-manger m.

bland [blænd] a (-er, -est) doux; (food) fade.

blank [blæŋk] a (paper, page) blanc, vierge; (cheque) en blanc; (look, mind) vide; (puzzled) ébahi; (refusal) absolu; – a & n b. (space) blanc m; b. (cartridge) cartouche f à blanc; my mind's a b. j'ai la tête vide. ◆blankly adv sans expression.

blanket ['blæŋkɪt] 1 n couverture f; (of snow etc) Fig couche f; – vt (cover) Fig recouvrir. 2 a (term etc) général. ◆—ing n (blankets) couvertures fpl.

blare [bleər] n (noise) beuglement m; (of trumpet) sonnerie f; – vi b. (out) (of radio) beugler; (of music, car horn) retentir.

blarney ['blɑːnɪ] n Fam boniment(s) m(pl).

blasé ['blɑːzeɪ] a blasé.

blaspheme [blæs'fiːm] vti blasphémer. ◆'blasphemous a blasphématoire; (person) blasphémateur. ◆'blasphemy n blasphème m.

blast [blɑːst] 1 n explosion f; (air from explosion) souffle m; (of wind) rafale f; coup m; (of trumpet) sonnerie f; (at) full b. (loud) à plein volume; (fast) à pleine vitesse; b. furnace haut fourneau m; – vt (blow up) faire sauter; (hopes) Fig détruire; to b. s.o. Fam réprimander qn. 2 int zut!, merde! ◆—ed a Fam fichu. ◆blast-off n (of spacecraft) mise f à feu.

blatant ['blettant] a (obvious) flagrant, criant; (shameless) éhonté.

blaz/e [bleɪz] 1 n (fire) flamme f, feu m; (conflagration) incendie m; (splendour) Fig éclat m; b. of light torrent m de lumière; – vi (of fire) flamber; (of sun, colour, eyes) flamboyer. 2 vt to b. a trail marquer la voie. ◆—ing a (burning) en feu; (sun) brûlant; (argument) Fig violent.

blazer ['bleɪzər] n blazer m.

bleach [bliːtʃ] n décolorant m; (household detergent) eau f de Javel; – vt (hair) décolorer, oxygéner; (linen) blanchir.

bleak [bliːk] a (-er, -est) (appearance, future etc) morne; (countryside) désolé.

bleary ['blɪərɪ] a (eyes) troubles, voilés.

bleat [bliːt] vi bêler.

bleed [bliːd] vti (pt & pp bled) saigner; to b. to death perdre tout son sang. ◆—ing a (wound) saignant; (bloody) Sl foutu.

bleep [bliːp] n signal m, bip m; – vt appeler au bip-bip. ◆bleeper n bip-bip m.

blemish ['blemɪʃ] n (fault) défaut m; (on fruit, reputation) tache f; – vt (reputation) ternir.

blend [blend] n mélange m; – vt mélanger; – vi se mélanger; (go together) se marier (with avec). ◆—er n Culin mixer m.

bless [bles] vt bénir; to be blessed with avoir le bonheur de posséder; b. you! (sneezing) à vos souhaits! ◆—ed [-ɪd] a saint, béni; (happy) Rel bienheureux; (blasted) Fam fichu, sacré. ◆—ing n bénédiction f; (divine favour) grâce f; (benefit) bienfait m; what a b. that . . . . quelle chance que . . . .

blew [bluː] see blow[1].

blight [blaɪt] n (on plants) rouille f; (scourge) Fig fléau m; to be or cast a b. on avoir une influence néfaste sur; urban b. (area) quartier m délabré; (condition) délabrement m (de quartier). ◆blighter n Pej Fam type m.

blimey! ['blaɪmɪ] int Fam zut!, mince!

blimp [blɪmp] n dirigeable m.

blind [blaɪnd] 1 a aveugle; b. person aveugle mf; b. in one eye borgne; he's b. to (fault) il ne voit pas; to turn a b. eye to fermer les yeux sur; b. alley impasse f; – n the b. les aveugles mpl; – vt aveugler. 2 n (on window) store m; (deception) feinte f. ◆—ly adv aveuglément. ◆—ness n cécité f; Fig aveuglement m. ◆blinders npl Am œillères fpl. ◆blindfold n bandeau m; – vt bander les yeux à; – adv les yeux bandés.

blink [blɪŋk] vi cligner des yeux; (of eyes)

cligner; (of light) clignoter; – vt to b. one's eyes cligner des yeux; – n clignement m; on the b. (machine) Fam détraqué. ◆—ing a (bloody) Fam sacré. ◆blinkers npl (for horse) œillères fpl; (indicators) Aut clignotants mpl.

bliss [blɪs] n félicité f. ◆blissful a (happy) très joyeux; (wonderful) merveilleux. ◆blissfully adv (happy, unaware) parfaitement.

blister ['blɪstər] n (on skin) ampoule f; – vi se couvrir d'ampoules.

blithe [blaɪð] a joyeux.

blitz [blɪts] n (attack) Av raid m éclair; (bombing) bombardement m aérien; Fig Fam offensive f; – vt bombarder.

blizzard ['blɪzəd] n tempête f de neige.

bloat [bləʊt] vt gonfler.

bloater ['bləʊtər] n hareng m saur.

blob [blɒb] n (of water) (grosse) goutte f; (of ink, colour) tache f.

bloc [blɒk] n Pol bloc m.

block [blɒk] 1 n (of stone etc) bloc m; (of buildings) pâté m (de maisons); (in pipe) obstruction f; (mental) blocage m; b. of flats immeuble m; a b. away Am une rue plus loin; school b. groupe m scolaire; b. capitals or letters majuscules fpl. 2 vt (obstruct) bloquer; (pipe) boucher, bloquer; (one's view) boucher; to b. off (road) barrer; (light) intercepter; to b. up (pipe, hole) bloquer. ◆blo'ckade n blocus m; – vt bloquer. ◆blockage n obstruction f. ◆blockbuster n Cin super-production f, film m à grand spectacle. ◆blockhead n imbécile mf.

bloke [bləʊk] n Fam type m.

blond [blɒnd] a & n blond (m). ◆blonde a & n blonde (f).

blood [blʌd] n sang m; – a (group, orange etc) sanguin; (donor, bath etc) de sang; (poisoning etc) du sang; b. pressure tension f (artérielle); high b. pressure (hyper)tension f. ◆bloodcurdling a à vous tourner le sang. ◆bloodhound n (dog, detective) limier m. ◆bloodletting n saignée f. ◆bloodshed n effusion f de sang. ◆bloodshot a (eye) injecté de sang. ◆bloodsucker n (insect, person) sangsue f. ◆bloodthirsty a sanguinaire.

bloody ['blʌdɪ] 1 a (-ier, -iest) sanglant. 2 a (blasted) Fam sacré; – adv Fam vachement. ◆b.-'minded a hargneux, pas commode.

bloom [bluːm] n fleur f; in b. en fleur(s); – vi fleurir; (of person) Fig s'épanouir. ◆—ing *a* **1** (*in bloom*) en fleur(s); (*thriving*) florissant. **2** (*blinking*) Fam fichu.

bloomer ['bluːmər] *n* Fam (mistake) gaffe *f*.

blossom ['blɒsəm] *n* fleur(s) *f* (*pl*); – *vi* fleurir; to b. (out) (*of person*) s'épanouir; to b. (out) into devenir.

blot [blɒt] *n* tache *f*; – *vt* (-tt-) tacher; (*dry*) sécher; to b. out (*word*) rayer; (*memory*) effacer. ◆**blotting** *a* b. paper (papier *m*) buvard *m*. ◆**blotter** *n* buvard *m*.

blotch [blɒtʃ] *n* tache *f*. ◆**blotchy** *a* (-ier, -iest) couvert de taches; (*face*) marbré.

blouse [blauz, *Am* blaus] *n* chemisier *m*.

blow[1] [bləu] *vt* (*pt* blew, *pp* blown) (*of wind*) pousser (*un navire etc*), chasser (*la pluie etc*); (*smoke, glass*) souffler; (*bubbles*) faire; (*trumpet*) souffler dans; (*fuse*) faire sauter; (*kiss*) envoyer (to à); (*money*) Fam claquer; to b. one's nose se moucher; to b. a whistle siffler; to b. away (*of wind*) emporter; to b. down (*chimney etc*) faire tomber; to b. off (*hat etc*) emporter; (*arm*) arracher; to b. out (*candle*) souffler; (*cheeks*) gonfler; to b. up (*building etc*) faire sauter; (*tyre*) gonfler; (*photo*) agrandir; – *vi* (*of wind, person*) souffler; (*of fuse*) sauter; (*of papers etc*) s'éparpiller; b.! Fam zut!; to b. down (*fall*) tomber; to b. off or away s'envoler; to b. out (*of light*) s'éteindre; to b. over (*pass*) passer; to b. up (*explode*) exploser. ◆**-er** *n* (*telephone*) Fam bigophone *m*. ◆**blow-dry** *n* brushing *m*. ◆**blowlamp** *n* chalumeau *m*. ◆**blowout** *n* (*of tyre*) éclatement *m*; (*meal*) *Sl* gueuleton *m*. ◆**blowtorch** *n Am* chalumeau *m*. ◆**blow-up** *n Phot* agrandissement *m*.

blow[2] [bləu] *n* coup *m*; to come to blows en venir aux mains.

blowy ['bləuɪ] *a* it's b. Fam il y a du vent.

blowzy ['blauzɪ] *a* b. woman (*slovenly*) Fam femme *f* débraillée.

blubber ['blʌbər] *n* graisse *f* (de baleine).

bludgeon ['blʌdʒən] *n* gourdin *m*; – *vt* matraquer.

blue [bluː] *a* (bluer, bluest) bleu; to feel b. Fam avoir le cafard; b. film Fam film *m* porno; – *n* bleu *m*; the blues (*depression*) Fam le cafard; *Mus* le blues. ◆**bluebell** *n* jacinthe *f* des bois. ◆**blueberry** *n* airelle *f*. ◆**bluebottle** *n* mouche *f* à viande. ◆**blueprint** *n Fig* plan *m* (de travail).

bluff [blʌf] **1** *a* (*a person*) brusque, direct. **2** *vti* bluffer; – *n* bluff *m*.

blunder ['blʌndər] *n* **1** (*mistake*) bévue *f*, gaffe *f*; – *vi* faire une bévue. **2** *vi* (*move awkwardly*) avancer à tâtons. ◆**-ing** *a* maladroit; – *n* maladresse *f*.

blunt [blʌnt] *a* (-er, -est) (*edge*) émoussé; (*pencil*) épointé; (*person*) brusque; (*speech*) franc; – *vt* émousser; épointer. ◆**-ly** *adv* carrément. ◆**-ness** *n Fig* brusquerie *f*; (*of speech*) franchise *f*.

blur [bləːr] *n* tache *f* floue, contour *m* imprécis; – *vt* (-rr-) estomper, rendre flou; (*judgment*) *Fig* troubler. ◆**blurred** *a* (*image*) flou, estompé.

blurb [bləːb] *n Fam* résumé *m* publicitaire, laïus *m*.

blurt [bləːt] *vt* to b. (out) laisser échapper, lâcher.

blush [blʌʃ] *vi* rougir (at, with de); – *n* rougeur *f*; with a b. en rougissant.

bluster ['blʌstər] *vi* (*of person*) tempêter; (*of wind*) faire rage. ◆**blustery** *a* (*weather*) de grand vent, à bourrasques.

boa ['bəuə] *n* (*snake*) boa *m*.

boar [bɔːr] *n* (wild) b. sanglier *m*.

board[1] [bɔːd] **1** *n* (*piece of wood*) planche *f*; (*for notices, games etc*) tableau *m*; (*cardboard*) carton *m*; (*committee*) conseil *m*, commission *f*; b. (of directors) conseil *m* d'administration; on b. *Nau Av* à bord (de); B. of Trade *Br Pol* ministère *m* du Commerce; across the b. (*pay rise*) général; to go by the b. (*of plan*) être abandonné. **2** *vt Nau Av* monter à bord de; (*bus, train*) monter dans; to b. up (*door*) boucher. ◆**-ing** *n Nau Av* embarquement *m*. ◆**boardwalk** *n Am* promenade *f*.

board[2] [bɔːd] *n* (*food*) pension *f*; b. and lodging, bed and b. (chambre *f* avec) pension *f*; – *vi* (*lodge*) être en pension (with chez); boarding house pension *f* (de famille); boarding school pensionnat *m*. ◆**-er** *n* pensionnaire *mf*.

boast [bəust] *vi* se vanter (about, of de); – *vt* se glorifier de; to b. that one can do ... se vanter de (pouvoir) faire ...; – *n* vantardise *f*. ◆**-ing** *n* vantardise *f*. ◆**boastful** *a* vantard. ◆**boastfully** *adv* en se vantant.

boat [bəut] *n* bateau *m*; (*small*) barque *f*, canot *m*; (*liner*) paquebot *m*; in the same b. *Fig* logé à la même enseigne; b. race course *f* d'aviron. ◆**-ing** *n* canotage *m*; b. trip excursion *f* en bateau.

boatswain ['bəus(ə)n] *n* maître *m* d'équipage.

bob [bɒb] *vi* (-bb-) to b. (up and down) (*on water*) danser sur l'eau.

bobbin ['bɒbɪn] *n* bobine *f*.

bobby ['bɒbɪ] *n* **1** (*policeman*) Fam flic *m*, agent *m*. **2** b. pin *Am* pince *f* à cheveux.

bode [bəʊd] *vi* to b. well/ill être de bon/mauvais augure.

bodice ['bɒdɪs] *n* corsage *m*.

body ['bɒdɪ] *n* corps *m*; (*of vehicle*) carrosserie *f*; (*quantity*) masse *f*; (*institution*) organisme *m*; the main b. of le gros de; b. building culturisme *m*. ◆**bodily** *a* physique; (*need*) matériel; – *adv* physiquement; (*as a whole*) tout entier. ◆**bodyguard** *n* garde *m* du corps, gorille *m*. ◆**bodywork** *n* carrosserie *f*.

boffin ['bɒfɪn] *n Fam* chercheur, -euse *mf* scientifique.

bog [bɒg] *n* marécage *m*; – *vt* to get bogged down s'enliser. ◆**boggy** *a* (-ier, -iest) marécageux.

bogey ['bəʊgɪ] *n* spectre *m*; b. man croque-mitaine *m*.

boggle ['bɒg(ə)l] *vi* the mind boggles cela confond l'imagination.

bogus ['bəʊgəs] *a* faux.

bohemian [bəʊ'hiːmɪən] *a* & *n* (*artist etc*) bohème (*mf*).

boil [bɔɪl] **1** *n Med* furoncle *m*, clou *m*. **2** *vi* bouillir; to b. away (*until dry*) s'évaporer; (*on and on*) bouillir sans arrêt; to b. down to *Fig* se ramener à; to b. over (*of milk, emotions etc*) déborder; – *vt* to b. (up) faire bouillir; – *n* to be on the b., come to the b. bouillir; to bring to the b. amener à ébullition. ◆**-ed** *a* (*beef*) bouilli; (*potato*) cuit à l'eau; b. egg œuf *m* à la coque. ◆**-ing** *n* ébullition *f*; at b. point à ébullition; – *a* & *adv* b. (hot) bouillant; it's b. (hot) (*weather*) il fait une chaleur infernale. ◆**-er** *n* chaudière *f*; b. suit bleu *m* de travail.

boisterous ['bɔɪstərəs] *a* (*noisy*) tapageur; (*child*) turbulent; (*meeting*) houleux.

bold [bəʊld] *a* (-er, -est) hardi; b. type caractères *mpl* gras. ◆**-ness** *n* hardiesse *f*.

Bolivia [bə'lɪvɪə] *n* Bolivie *f*. ◆**Bolivian** *a* & *n* bolivien, -ienne (*mf*).

bollard ['bɒləd, 'bɒlɑːd] *n Aut* borne *f*.

boloney [bə'ləʊnɪ] *n Sl* foutaises *fpl*.

bolster ['bəʊlstər] **1** *n* (*pillow*) traversin *m*, polochon *m*. **2** *vt* to b. (up) (*support*) soutenir.

bolt [bəʊlt] **1** *n* (*on door etc*) verrou *m*; (*for nut*) boulon *m*; – *vt* (*door*) verrouiller. **2** *n* (*dash*) fuite *f*, ruée *f*; – *vi* (*dash*) se précipiter; (*flee*) détaler; (*of horse*) s'emballer. **3** *n* b. (of lightning) éclair *m*. **4** *vt* (*food*) engloutir. **5** *adv* b. upright tout droit.

bomb [bɒm] *n* bombe *f*; letter b. lettre *f* piégée; b. disposal désamorçage *m*; – *vt* bombarder. ◆**-ing** *n* bombardement *m*.

◆**-er** *n* (*aircraft*) bombardier *m*; (*terrorist*) plastiqueur *m*. ◆**bombshell** *n* to come as a b. tomber comme une bombe. ◆**bombsite** *n* terrain *m* vague, lieu *m* bombardé.

bombard [bɒm'bɑːd] *vt* bombarder (with de). ◆**-ment** *n* bombardement *m*.

bona fide [bəʊnə'faɪdɪ, *Am* -'faɪd] *a* sérieux, de bonne foi.

bonanza [bə'nænzə] *n Fig* mine *f* d'or.

bond [bɒnd] **1** *n* (*agreement, promise*) engagement *m*; (*link*) lien *m*; *Com* bon *m*, obligation *f*; (*adhesion*) adhérence *f*. **2** *vt* (*goods*) entreposer.

bondage ['bɒndɪdʒ] *n* esclavage *m*.

bone [bəʊn] **1** *n* os *m*; (*of fish*) arête *f*; b. of contention pomme *f* de discorde; b. china porcelaine *f* tendre; – *vt* (*meat etc*) désosser. **2** *vi* to b. up on (*subject*) *Am Fam* bûcher. ◆**bony** *a* (-ier, -iest) (*thin*) osseux, maigre; (*fish*) plein d'arêtes.

bone-dry [bəʊn'draɪ] *a* tout à fait sec. ◆**b.-idle** *a* paresseux comme une couleuvre.

bonfire ['bɒnfaɪər] *n* (*for celebration*) feu *m* de joie; (*for dead leaves*) feu *m* (de jardin).

bonkers ['bɒŋkəz] *a* (*crazy*) *Fam* dingue.

bonnet ['bɒnɪt] *n* (*hat*) bonnet *m*; *Aut* capot *m*.

bonus ['bəʊnəs] *n* prime *f*; no claims b. *Aut* bonus *m*.

boo [buː] **1** *int* hou! **2** *vti* huer; – *npl* huées *fpl*.

boob [buːb] *n* (*mistake*) gaffe *f*; – *vi Sl* gaffer.

booby-trap ['buːbɪtræp] *n* engin *m* piégé; – *vt* (-pp-) piéger.

book [bʊk] **1** *n* livre *m*; (*of tickets*) carnet *m*; (*record*) registre *m*; *pl* (*accounts*) comptes *mpl*; (*exercise*) b. cahier *m*. **2** *vt* to b. (up) (*seat etc*) réserver, retenir; to b. s.o. *Jur* donner un procès-verbal à qn; to b. (down) inscrire; (fully) booked (up) (*hotel, concert*) complet; (*person*) pris; – *vi* to b. (up) réserver des places; to b. in (*in hotel*) signer le registre. ◆**-ing** *n* réservation *f*; b. clerk guichetier, -ière *mf*; b. office bureau *m* de location, guichet *m*. ◆**-able** *a* (*seat*) qu'on peut réserver. ◆**bookish** *a* (*word, theory*) livresque; (*person*) studieux.

bookbinding ['bʊkbaɪndɪŋ] *n* reliure *f*. ◆**bookcase** *n* bibliothèque *f*. ◆**bookend** *n* serre-livres *m inv*. ◆**bookkeeper** *n* comptable *mf*. ◆**bookkeeping** *n* comptabilité *f*. ◆**booklet** *n* brochure *f*. ◆**book-lover** *n* bibliophile *mf*. ◆**bookmaker** *n* bookmaker *m*. ◆**bookmark** *n* marque f. ◆**bookseller** n libraire mf. ◆**bookshelf** n rayon m. ◆**bookshop** n, Am ◆**bookstore** n librairie f. ◆**bookstall** n kiosque m (à journaux). ◆**bookworm** n rat m de bibliothèque.

boom [buːm] 1 vi (of thunder, gun etc) gronder; – n grondement m; **sonic b.** bang m. 2 n Econ expansion f; essor m, boom m. ◆**boomerang** ['buːməræŋ] n boomerang m.

boon [buːn] n aubaine f, avantage m.

boor [buər] n rustre. ◆**boorish** a rustre.

boost [buːst] vt (push) donner une poussée à; (increase) augmenter; (product) faire de la réclame pour; (economy) stimuler; (morale) remonter; – n to give a b. to = to boost. ◆**-er** n b. (injection) piqûre f de rappel.

boot [buːt] 1 n (shoe) botte f; (ankle) b. bottillon m; (knee) b. bottine f; to get the b. Fam être mis à la porte; b. polish cirage m; – vt (kick) donner un coup or des coups de pied à; to b. out mettre à la porte. 2 n Aut coffre m. 3 n to b. en plus. ◆**bootblack** n cireur m. ◆**boo'tee** n (of baby) chausson m.

booth [buːð, buːθ] n Tel cabine f; (at fair) baraque f.

booty ['buːtɪ] n (stolen goods) butin m.

booz/e [buːz] n Fam alcool m, boisson(s) f(pl); (drinking bout) beuverie f; – vi Fam boire (beaucoup). ◆**-er** n Fam (person) buveur, -euse mf; (place) bistrot m.

border ['bɔːdər] n (of country) & Fig frontière f; (edge) bord m; (of garden etc) bordure f; – a (town) frontière inv; (incident) de frontière; – vt (street) border; to b. (on) (country) toucher à; to b. (up)on (resemble) être voisin de. ◆**borderland** n pays m frontière. ◆**borderline** n frontière f; b. case cas m limite.

bor/e¹ [bɔːr] 1 vt (weary) ennuyer; to be bored s'ennuyer; – n (person) raseur, -euse mf; (thing) ennui m. 2 vt Tech forer, creuser; (hole) percer; – vi forer. 3 n (of gun) calibre m. ◆**-ing** a ennuyeux. ◆**boredom** n ennui m.

bore² [bɔːr] see **bear²**.

born [bɔːn] a né; to be b. naître; he was b. il est né.

borne [bɔːn] see **bear²**.

borough ['bʌrə] n (town) municipalité f; (part of town) arrondissement m.

borrow ['bɒrəu] vt emprunter (from à). ◆**-ing** n emprunt m.

Borstal ['bɔːst(ə)l] n maison f d'éducation surveillée.

bosom ['buzəm] n (chest) & Fig sein m; b. friend ami, -ie mf intime.

boss [bɒs] n Fam patron, -onne mf, chef m; – vt Fam diriger; to b. s.o. around or about régenter qn. ◆**bossy** a (-ier, -iest) Fam autoritaire.

boss-eyed ['bɒsaɪd] a to be b.-eyed loucher.

bosun ['bəus(ə)n] n maître m d'équipage.

botany ['bɒtənɪ] n botanique f. ◆**bo'tanical** a botanique. ◆**botanist** n botaniste mf.

botch [bɒtʃ] vt to b. (up) (spoil) bâcler; (repair) rafistoler.

both [bəuθ] a les deux, l'un(e) et l'autre; – pron tous or toutes (les) deux, l'un(e) et l'autre; b. of us nous deux; – adv (at the same time) à la fois; b. you and I vous et moi.

bother ['bɒðər] vt (annoy, worry) ennuyer; (disturb) déranger; (pester) importuner; I can't be bothered! je n'en ai pas envie!, ça m'embête!; – vi to b. about (worry about) se préoccuper de; (deal with) s'occuper de; to b. doing or to do se donner la peine de faire; – n (trouble) ennui m; (effort) peine f; (inconvenience) dérangement m; (oh) b.! zut alors!

bottle ['bɒt(ə)l] n bouteille f; (small) flacon m; (wide-mouthed) bocal m; (for baby) biberon m; (hot-water) b. bouillotte f; b. opener ouvre-bouteilles m inv; – vt mettre en bouteille; to b. up (feeling) contenir. ◆**b.-feed** vt (pt & pp -fed) nourrir au biberon. ◆**bottleneck** n (in road) goulot m d'étranglement; (traffic holdup) bouchon m.

bottom ['bɒtəm] n (of sea, box, etc) fond m; (of page, hill etc) bas m; (of table) bout m; (buttocks) Fam derrière m; (at the) b. of the class être le dernier de la classe; – a (part, shelf) inférieur, du bas; b. floor rez-de-chaussée m; b. gear première vitesse f. ◆**-less** a insondable.

bough [bau] n Lit rameau m.

bought [bɔːt] see **buy**.

boulder ['bəuldər] n rocher m.

boulevard ['buːləvɑːd] n boulevard m.

bounc/e [bauns] 1 vi (of ball) rebondir; (of person) faire des bonds; to b. into bondir dans; – vt faire rebondir; – n (re)bond m. 2 vi (of cheque) Fam être sans provision, être en bois. ◆**-ing** a (baby) robuste. ◆**-er** n (at club etc) Fam videur m.

bound¹ [baund] 1 a b. to do (obliged) obligé de faire; (certain) sûr de faire; it's b. to happen ça arrivera sûrement; to be b. for être en route pour. **2** n (leap) bond m; – vi bondir.

bound [2] [baund] see **bind 1**; – a b. up with (connected) lié à.

bounds [baundz] npl limites fpl; **out of b.** (place) interdit. ◆**boundary** n limite f. ◆**bounded** a b. by limité par. ◆**boundless** a sans bornes.

bountiful ['bauntiful] a généreux.

bounty ['baunti] n (reward) prime f.

bouquet [bəu'kei] n (of flowers, wine) bouquet m.

bourbon ['bɜːbən] n (whisky) Am bourbon m.

bout [baut] n période f; Med accès m, crise f; Boxing combat m; (session) séance f.

boutique [bu:'tiːk] n boutique f (de mode).

bow [1] [bəu] n (weapon) arc m; Mus archet m; (knot) nœud m; **b. tie** nœud m papillon. ◆**b.-'legged** a aux jambes arquées.

bow [2] [bau] **1** n révérence f; (nod) salut m; – vt courber, incliner; – vi s'incliner (to devant); (nod) incliner la tête; **to b. down** (submit) s'incliner. **2** n Nau proue f.

bowels ['bauəlz] npl intestins mpl; (of earth) Fig entrailles fpl.

bowl [bəul] **1** n (for food) bol m; (basin) & Geog cuvette f; (for sugar) sucrier m; (for salad) saladier m; (for fruit) corbeille f, coupe f. **2** npl Sp boules fpl. **3** vi Cricket lancer la balle; **to b. along** Aut rouler vite; – vt (ball) Cricket servir; **to b. s.o. over** (knock down) renverser qn; (astound) bouleverser qn. ◆**-ing** n (tenpin) b. bowling m; **b. alley** bowling m. ◆**-er** [1] n Cricket lanceur m, -euse mf.

bowler [2] ['bəulər] n b. (hat) (chapeau m) melon m.

box [bɒks] **1** n boîte f; (large) caisse f; (of cardboard) carton m; Th loge f; Jur barre f, banc m; (for horse) box m; TV Fam télé f; **b. office** bureau m de location, guichet m; **b. room** (lumber room) débarras m; (bedroom) petite chambre f (carrée); – vt to **b. (up)** mettre en boîte; **to b. in** (enclose) enfermer. **2** vti Boxing boxer; **to b. s.o.'s ears** gifler qn. ◆**-ing** n **1** boxe f; **b. ring** ring m. **2 B. Day** le lendemain de Noël. ◆**-er** n boxeur m. ◆**boxcar** n Rail Am wagon m couvert. ◆**boxwood** n buis m.

boy [bɔi] n garçon m; **English b.** jeune Anglais m; **old b.** Sch ancien élève m; **yes, old b.!** oui, mon vieux!; **the boys** (pals) Fam les copains mpl; **my dear b.** mon cher ami; **oh b.!** Am mon Dieu! ◆**boyfriend** n petit ami m. ◆**boyhood** n enfance f. ◆**boyish** a de garçon; Pej puéril.

boycott ['bɔikɒt] vt boycotter; – n boycottage m.

bra [brɑː] n soutien-gorge m.

brac/e [breis] n (for fastening) attache f; (dental) appareil m; pl (trouser straps) bretelles fpl; – vt (fix) attacher; (press) appuyer; **to b. oneself for** (news, shock) se préparer à. ◆**-ing** a (air etc) fortifiant.

bracelet ['breislit] n bracelet m.

bracken ['brækən] n fougère f.

bracket ['brækit] n Tech support m, tasseau m; (round sign) Typ parenthèse f; (square) Typ crochet m; Fig groupe m, tranche f; – vt mettre entre parenthèses or crochets; **to b. together** Fig mettre dans le même groupe.

bradawl ['brædɔːl] n poinçon m.

brag [bræg] vi (-gg-) se vanter (about, of de). ◆**-ging** n vantardise f. ◆**braggart** n vantard, -arde mf.

braid [breid] vt (hair) tresser; (trim) galonner; – n tresse f; galon m.

Braille [breil] n braille m.

brain [brein] n cerveau m; (of bird etc) & Pej cervelle f; – a (operation, death) cérébral; – vt Fam assommer; **to have brains** (sense) avoir de l'intelligence; **b. drain** fuite f des cerveaux. ◆**brainchild** n invention f personnelle. ◆**brainstorm** n Psy Fig aberration f; Am idée f géniale. ◆**brainwash** vt faire un lavage de cerveau à. ◆**brainwave** n idée f géniale.

brainy ['breini] a (-ier, -iest) Fam intelligent.

braise [breiz] vt Culin braiser.

brak/e [breik] vi freiner; – n frein m; **b. light** Aut stop m. ◆**-ing** n freinage m.

bramble ['bræmb(ə)l] n ronce f.

bran [bræn] n Bot son m.

branch [brɑːntʃ] n branche f; (of road) embranchement m; (of store etc) succursale f; **b. office** succursale f; – vi to **b. off** (of road) bifurquer; **to b. out** (of family, tree) se ramifier; Fig étendre ses activités.

brand [brænd] n (trademark, stigma & on cattle) marque f; – vt (mark) marquer; (stigmatize) flétrir; **to be branded as** avoir la réputation de.

brandish ['brændiʃ] vt brandir.

brand-new [brænd'njuː] a tout neuf, flambant neuf.

brandy ['brændi] n cognac m; (made with pears etc) eau-de-vie f.

brash [bræʃ] a effronté, fougueux.

brass [brɑːs] n cuivre m; (instruments) Mus cuivres mpl; **the top b.** (officers, executives) Fam les huiles fpl; **b. band** fanfare f.

brassiere ['bræzɪər, *Am* brə'zɪər] *n* soutien-gorge *m*.

brat [bræt] *n Pej* môme *mf*, gosse *mf*; (*badly behaved*) galopin *m*.

bravado [brə'vɑːdəʊ] *n* bravade *f*.

brave [breɪv] *a* (**-er, -est**) courageux, brave; – *n* (*Red Indian*) guerrier *m* (indien), brave *m*; – *vt* braver. ◆**bravery** *n* courage *m*.

bravo! ['brɑːvəʊ] *int* bravo!

brawl [brɔːl] *n* (*fight*) bagarre *f*; – *vi* se bagarrer. ◆**—ing** *a* bagarreur.

brawn [brɔːn] *n* muscles *mpl*. ◆**brawny** *a* (**-ier, -est**) musclé.

bray [breɪ] *vi* (*of ass*) braire.

brazen ['breɪz(ə)n] *a* (*shameless*) effronté; – *vt* **to b. it out** payer d'audace, faire front.

Brazil [brə'zɪl] *n* Brésil *m*. ◆**Brazilian** *a & n* brésilien, -ienne (*mf*).

breach [briːtʃ] **1** *n* violation *f*, infraction *f*; (*of contract*) rupture *f*; (*of trust*) abus *m*; – *vt* (*law, code*) violer. **2** *n* (*gap*) brèche *f*; – *vt* (*wall etc*) ouvrir une brèche dans.

bread [bred] *n inv* pain *m*; (*money*) *Sl* blé *m*, fric *m*; **loaf of b.** pain *m*; (*slice or piece of*) **b. and butter** tartine *f*; **b. and butter** (*job*) *Fig* gagne-pain *m*. ◆**breadbin** *n*, *Am* ◆**breadbox** *n* coffre *m* à pain. ◆**breadboard** *n* planche *f* à pain. ◆**breadcrumb** *n* miette *f* de pain; *pl Culin* chapelure *f*. ◆**breadline** *n* **on the b.** indigent. ◆**breadwinner** *n* soutien *m* de famille.

breadth [bretθ] *n* largeur *f*.

break [breɪk] *vt* (*pt* **broke**, *pp* **broken**) casser; (*into pieces*) briser; (*silence, vow etc*) rompre; (*strike, heart, ice etc*) briser; (*record*) *Sp* battre; (*law*) violer; (*one's word*) manquer à; (*journey*) interrompre; (*sound barrier*) franchir; (*a fall*) amortir; (*news*) révéler (**to** à); **to b.** (**oneself of**) (*habit*) se débarrasser de; **to b. open** (*safe*) percer; **to b. new ground** innover; – *vi* (*se*) casser; se briser; se rompre; (*of boy's voice*) s'altérer; (*of weather*) se gâter; (*of news*) éclater; (*of day*) se lever; (*of wave*) déferler; **to b. free** se libérer; **to b. loose** s'échapper; **to b. with s.o.** rompre avec qn; – *n* cassure *f*; (*in relationship, continuity etc*) rupture *f*; (*in journey*) interruption *f*; (*rest*) repos *m*; (*for tea*) pause *f*; *Sch* récréation *f*; (*change*) *Met* changement *m*; **a lucky b.** *Fam* une chance. ◆**b. point** *Tech* point *m* de rupture; **at b. point** (*patience*) à bout; (*person*) sur le point de craquer, à bout. ◆**—able** *a* cassable. ◆**—age** *n* casse *f*; *pl* (*things broken*) la casse. ◆**—er** *n* (*wave*) brisant *m*; (*dealer*)

Aut casseur *m*. ■ **to b. away** *vi* se détacher; – *vt* détacher. ◆**breakaway** *a* (*group*) dissident; – *n* (*resistance*) briser; (*analyse*) analyser; – *vi* *Aut Tech* tomber en panne; (*of negotiations etc*) échouer; (*collapse*) s'effondrer. ◆**breakdown** *n* panne *f*; analyse *f*; (*in talks*) rupture *f*; (*nervous*) dépression *f*; – *a* (*service*) *Aut* de dépannage; **b. lorry** dépanneuse *f*; **to b. in** *vi* interrompre; (*of burglar*) entrer par effraction; – *vt* (*door*) enfoncer; (*horse*) dresser; (*vehicle*) *Am* roder. ◆**break-in** *n* cambriolage *m*; **to b. into** *vt* (*safe*) forcer; (*start*) entamer; **to b. off** *vt* détacher; (*relations*) rompre; – *vi* se détacher; (*stop*) s'arrêter; **to b. off with** rompre avec; **to b. out** *vi* (*escape*) s'échapper; **to b. out in** (*pimples*) avoir une poussée de; **to b. through** *vi* (*of sun*) & *Mil* percer; – *vt* (*defences*) percer. ◆**breakthrough** *n Fig* percée *f*, découverte *f*; **to b. up** *vt* mettre en morceaux; (*marriage*) briser; (*fight*) mettre fin à; – *vi* (*end*) prendre fin; (*of group*) se disperser; (*of marriage*) se briser; *Sch* partir en vacances. ◆**breakup** *n* fin *f*; (*in friendship, marriage*) rupture *f*.

breakfast ['brekfəst] *n* petit déjeuner *m*.

breakwater ['breɪkwɔːtər] *n* brise-lames *m inv*.

breast [brest] *n* sein *m*; (*chest*) poitrine *f*. ◆**b.-feed** *vt* (*pt & pp* **-fed**) allaiter. ◆**breaststroke** *n* (*swimming*) brasse *f*.

breath [breθ] *n* haleine *f*, souffle *m*; (*of air*) souffle *m*; **under one's b.** tout bas; **one's last b.** son dernier soupir; **out of b.** à bout de souffle; **to get a b. of air** prendre l'air; **to take a deep b.** respirer profondément. ◆**breathalyser®** *n* alcootest® *m*. ◆**breathless** *a* haletant. ◆**breathtaking** *a* sensationnel.

breath/e [briːð] *vti* respirer; **to b. in** aspirer; **to b. out** expirer; **to b. in or into sth** souffler dans qch; – *vt* (*a sigh*) pousser; (*a word*) dire. ◆**—ing** *n* respiration *f*; **b. space** moment *m* de repos. ◆**—er** *n Fam* moment *m* de repos; **to go for a b.** sortir prendre l'air.

bred [bred] *see* **breed 1**; – *a* **well-b.** bien élevé.

breeches ['brɪtʃɪz] *npl* culotte *f*.

breed [briːd] **1** *vt* (*pt & pp* **bred**) (*animals*) élever; (*cause*) *Fig* engendrer; – *vi* (*of animals*) se reproduire. **2** *n* race *f*, espèce *f*. ◆**—ing** *n* élevage *m*; reproduction *f*; *Fig* éducation *f*. ◆**—er** *n* éleveur, -euse *mf*.

breeze [briːz] *n* brise *f*. ◆**breezy** *a* (**-ier,**

-iest) 1 (*weather, day*) frais, venteux. **2** (*cheerful*) jovial; (*relaxed*) décontracté.

breezeblock ['briːzblɒk] *n* parpaing *m*, briquette *f*.

brevity ['brevɪtɪ] *n* brièveté *f*.

brew [bruː] *vt* (*beer*) brasser; (*trouble, plot*) préparer; **to b. tea** préparer du thé; (*infuse*) (faire) infuser du thé; – *vi* (*of beer*) fermenter; (*of tea*) infuser; (*of storm, trouble*) se préparer; – *n* (*drink*) breuvage *m*; (*of tea*) infusion *f*. ◆**–er** *n* brasseur *m*. ◆**brewery** *n* brasserie *f*.

bribe [braɪb] *n* pot-de-vin *m*; – *vt* soudoyer, corrompre. ◆**bribery** *n* corruption *f*.

brick [brɪk] *n* brique *f*; (*child's*) cube *m*; **to drop a b.** *Fam* faire une gaffe; – *vt* **to b. up** (*gap, door*) murer. ◆**bricklayer** *n* maçon *m*. ◆**brickwork** *n* ouvrage *m* en briques; (*bricks*) briques *fpl*.

bridal ['braɪd(ə)l] *a* (*ceremony*) nuptial; **b. gown** robe *f* de mariée.

bride [braɪd] *n* mariée *f*; **the b. and groom** les mariés *mpl*. ◆**bridegroom** *n* marié *m*. ◆**bridesmaid** *n* demoiselle *f* d'honneur.

bridge [brɪdʒ] **1** *n* pont *m*; (*on ship*) passerelle *f*; (*of nose*) arête *f*; (*false tooth*) bridge *m*; – *vt* **to b. a gap** combler une lacune. **2** *n* *Cards* bridge *m*.

bridle ['braɪd(ə)l] *n* (*for horse*) bride *f*; – *vt* (*horse, instinct etc*) brider; **b. path** allée *f* cavalière.

brief [briːf] **1** *a* (*-er, -est*) bref; **in b.** en résumé. **2** *n* *Jur* dossier *m*; (*instructions*) *Mil Pol* instructions *fpl*; *Fig* tâche *f*, fonctions *fpl*; – *vt* donner des instructions à; (*inform*) mettre au courant (**on** de). **3** *npl* (*underpants*) slip *m*. ◆**–ing** *n* *Mil Pol* instructions *fpl*; *Av* briefing *m*. ◆**–ly** *adv* (*quickly*) en vitesse; (*to say*) brièvement.

brigade [brɪ'geɪd] *n* brigade *f*. ◆**briga'dier** *n* général *m* de brigade.

bright [braɪt] *a* (*-er, -est*) brillant, vif; (*weather, room*) clair; (*clever*) intelligent; (*happy*) joyeux; (*future*) brillant, prometteur; (*idea*) génial; **b. interval** *Met* éclaircie *f*; – *adv* **b. and early** (*to get up*) de bonne heure. ◆**–ly** *adv* brillamment. ◆**–ness** *n* éclat *m*; (*of person*) intelligence *f*. ◆**brighten** *vt* **to b. up** (*person, room*) égayer; – *vi* **to b. up** (*of weather*) s'éclaircir; (*of face*) s'éclairer.

brilliant ['brɪljənt] *a* (*light*) éclatant; (*very clever*) brillant. ◆**brilliance** *n* éclat *m*; (*of person*) grande intelligence *f*.

brim [brɪm] *n* bord *m*; – *vi* (*-mm-*) **to b. over** déborder (**with** de).

brine [braɪn] *n* *Culin* saumure *f*.

bring [brɪŋ] *vt* (*pt & pp* **brought**) (*person, vehicle etc*) amener; (*thing*) apporter; (*to cause*) amener; (*action*) Jur intenter; **to b. along** *or* **over** *or* **round** amener; apporter; **to b. back** ramener; apporter; (*memories*) rappeler; **to b. sth up/down** monter/descendre qch; **to b. sth in/out** rentrer/sortir qch; **to b. sth to** (*perfection, a peak etc*) porter qch à; **to b. to an end** mettre fin à; **to b. to mind** rappeler; **to b. sth on oneself** s'attirer qch; **to b. oneself to do** **sth** se résoudre à faire; **to b. about** provoquer, amener; **to b. down** (*overthrow*) faire tomber; (*reduce*) réduire; (*shoot down*) abattre; **to b. forward** (*in time or space*) avancer; (*witness*) produire; **to b. in** (*person*) faire entrer *or* venir; (*introduce*) introduire; (*income*) Com rapporter; **to b. off** (*task*) mener à bien; **to b. out** (*person*) faire sortir; (*meaning*) faire ressortir; (*book*) publier; (*product*) lancer; **to b. over** (*convert to*) convertir à; **to b. round** *Med* ranimer; (*convert*) convertir (**to** à); **to b. s.o. to** *Med* ranimer qn; **to b. together** mettre en contact; (*reconcile*) réconcilier; **to b. up** (*child etc*) élever; (*question*) soulever; (*subject*) mentionner; (*vomit*) vomir.

brink [brɪŋk] *n* bord *m*.

brisk [brɪsk] *a* (*-er, -est*) vif; (*trade*) actif; **at a b. pace** d'un bon pas. ◆**–ly** *adv* vivement; (*to walk*) d'un bon pas. ◆**–ness** *n* vivacité *f*.

bristl/e ['brɪs(ə)l] *n* poil *m*; – *vi* se hérisser. ◆**–ing** *a* **b. with** (*difficulties*) hérissé de.

Britain ['brɪt(ə)n] *n* Grande-Bretagne *f*. ◆**British** *a* britannique; – *n* **the B.** les Britanniques *mpl*. ◆**Briton** *n* Britannique *mf*.

Brittany ['brɪtənɪ] *n* Bretagne *f*.

brittle ['brɪt(ə)l] *a* cassant, fragile.

broach [brəʊtʃ] *vt* (*topic*) entamer.

broad¹ [brɔːd] *a* (*-er, -est*) (*wide*) large; (*outline*) grand, général; (*accent*) prononcé; **in b. daylight** au grand jour; **b. bean** fève *f*; **b. jump** *Sp* Am saut *m* en longueur. ◆**b.-'minded** *a* à l'esprit large. ◆**b.-'shouldered** *a* large d'épaules. ◆**broaden** *vt* élargir; – *vi* s'élargir. ◆**broadly** *adv* **b.** (*speaking*) en gros, grosso modo.

broad² [brɔːd] *n* (*woman*) Am Sl nana *f*.

broadcast ['brɔːdkɑːst] *vt* (*pt & pp* **broadcast**) *Rad & Fig* diffuser; *TV* téléviser; – *vi* (*of station*) émettre; (*of person*) parler à la radio *or* à la télévision; – *a* (*radio*) diffusé; télévisé; – *n* émission *f*. ◆**–ing** *n* radiodiffusion *f*; télévision *f*.

broccoli ['brɒkəlɪ] n inv brocoli m.

brochure ['brəʊʃər] n brochure f, dépliant m.

brogue [brəʊg] n Ling accent m irlandais.

broil [brɔɪl] vti griller. ◆—**er** n poulet m (à rôtir); (apparatus) gril m.

broke [brəʊk] **1** see break. **2** a (penniless) fauché. ◆**broken** see break. — a (ground) accidenté; (spirit) abattu; (man, voice, line) brisé; **b. English** mauvais anglais m; **b. home** foyer m brisé. ◆**broken-'down** a (machine etc) (tout) déglingué, détraqué. ◆**broken-'down** a (machine etc) (tout) déglingué, détraqué.

brolly ['brɒlɪ] n (umbrella) Fam pépin m.

bronchitis [brɒŋ'kaɪtɪs] n bronchite f.

bronze [brɒnz] n bronze m; — a (statue etc) en bronze.

brooch [brəʊtʃ] n (ornament) broche f.

brood [bruːd] **1** n couvée f, nichée f; — vi (of bird) couver. **2** vi méditer tristement (**over**, on sur); to **b. over** (a plan) ruminer. ◆**broody** a (-ier, -iest) (person) maussade, rêveur; (woman) Fam qui a envie d'avoir un enfant.

brook [brʊk] **1** n ruisseau m. **2** vt souffrir, tolérer.

broom [bruːm] n **1** (for sweeping) balai m. **2** Bot genêt m. ◆**broomstick** n manche m à balai.

Bros abbr (Brothers) Frères mpl.

broth [brɒθ] n bouillon m.

brothel ['brɒθ(ə)l] n maison f close, bordel m.

brother ['brʌðər] n frère m. ◆**b.-in-law** n (pl brothers-in-law) beau-frère m. ◆**brotherhood** n fraternité f. ◆**brotherly** a fraternel.

brow [braʊ] n (forehead) front m; (of hill) sommet m.

browbeat ['braʊbiːt] vt (pt -beat, pp -beaten) intimider.

brown [braʊn] a (-er, -est) brun; (reddish) marron; (hair) châtain; (tanned) bronzé; — n brun m; marron m; — vt brunir; Culin faire dorer; to **be browned off** Fam en avoir marre. ◆**brownish** a brunâtre.

Brownie ['braʊnɪ] n **1** (girl scout) jeannette f. **2 b.** Culin Am petit gâteau m au chocolat.

browse [braʊz] vi (in shop) regarder; (in bookshop) feuilleter des livres; (of animal) brouter; to **b. through** (book) feuilleter.

bruis/e [bruːz] vt contusionner, meurtrir; (fruit, heart) meurtrir; — n bleu m, contusion f. ◆—**ed** a couvert de bleus.

brunch [brʌntʃ] n repas m mixte (petit déjeuner pris comme déjeuner).

brunette [bruː'net] n brunette f.

brunt [brʌnt] n to **bear the b. of** (attack etc) subir le plus gros de.

brush [brʌʃ] n brosse f; (for shaving) blaireau m; (little broom) balayette f; (action) coup m de brosse; (fight) accrochage m; — vt (teeth, hair etc) brosser; (clothes) donner un coup de brosse à; to **b. aside** écarter; to **b. away** or **off** enlever; to **b. up (on)** (language) se remettre à; — vi to **b. against** effleurer. ◆**b.-off** n Fam to **give s.o. the b.-off** envoyer promener qn. ◆**b.-up** n coup m de brosse. ◆**brushwood** n broussailles fpl.

brusque [bruːsk] a brusque.

Brussels ['brʌs(ə)lz] n Bruxelles m or f; **B. sprouts** choux mpl de Bruxelles.

brutal ['bruːt(ə)l] a brutal. ◆**bru'tality** n brutalité f.

brute [bruːt] n (animal, person) brute f; — a **by b. force** par la force.

BSc, Am **BS** abbr = **Bachelor of Science.**

bubble ['bʌb(ə)l] n (of air, soap etc) bulle f; (in boiling liquid) bouillon m; **b. and squeak** Fam friture f de purée et de viande réchauffées; **b. bath** bain m moussant; **b. gum** chewing-gum m; — vi bouillonner; to **b. over** déborder (**with** de). ◆**bubbly** n Hum Fam champagne m.

buck [bʌk] **1** n Am Fam dollar m. **2** n (animal) mâle m. **3** vt to **b. up** remonter le moral à; — vi to **b. up** prendre courage; (hurry) se grouiller. ◆**buckshot** n inv du gros plomb m. ◆**buck'tooth** n (pl -teeth) dent f saillante.

bucket ['bʌkɪt] n seau m.

buckle ['bʌk(ə)l] **1** n boucle f; — vt boucler. **2** vti (warp) voiler, gauchir. **3** vi to **b. down to** (task) s'atteler à.

bud [bʌd] n (of tree) bourgeon m; (of flower) bouton m; — vi (-dd-) bourgeonner; pousser des boutons. ◆**budding** a (talent) naissant; (doctor etc) en herbe.

Buddhist ['bʊdɪst] a & n bouddhiste (mf).

buddy ['bʌdɪ] n Am Fam copain m, pote m.

budge [bʌdʒ] vi bouger; — vt faire bouger.

budgerigar ['bʌdʒərɪgɑːr] n perruche f.

budget ['bʌdʒɪt] n budget m; — vi dresser un budget; to **b. for** inscrire au budget. ◆**budgetary** a budgétaire.

budgie ['bʌdʒɪ] n Fam perruche f.

buff [bʌf] **1** a **b.(-coloured)** chamois inv. **2** n jazz/etc **b.** Fam fana(tique) mf du jazz/etc. **3** n **in the b.** Fam tout nu.

buffalo ['bʌfələʊ] n (pl -oes or -o) buffle m; (American) b. bison m.

buffer ['bʌfər] n (on train) tampon m; (at end of track) butoir m; **b. state** état m tampon.

buffet 1 ['bʌfɪt] vt frapper; (of waves) battre; (of wind, rain) cingler (qn). **2** ['bufeɪ] n (table, meal, café) buffet m; **cold b.** viandes fpl froides.

buffoon [bə'fuːn] n bouffon m.

bug 1 [bʌg] **1** n punaise f; (any insect) Fam bestiole f; Med Fam microbe m, virus m; **the travel b.** (urge) le désir de voyager. **2** n (in machine) défaut m; (in computer program) erreur f. **3** n (apparatus) Fam micro m; – vt (-gg-) (room) Fam installer des micros dans.

bug 2 [bʌg] vt (-gg-) (annoy) Am Fam embêter.

bugbear ['bʌgbeər] n (worry) cauchemar m.

buggy ['bʌgɪ] n (baby) b. (pushchair) poussette f; (folding) poussette-canne f; (pram) Am landau m.

bugle ['bjuːg(ə)l] n clairon m. ◆**bugler** n (person) clairon m.

build [bɪld] **1** n (of person) carrure f. **2** vt (pt & pp built) construire; (house, town) construire, bâtir; **to b. in** (cupboard etc) encastrer; – vi bâtir, construire. ◆**built-in** a (cupboard etc) encastré; (element of machine etc) incorporé; (innate) Fig inné. **3 to b. up** vt (reputation) bâtir; (increase) augmenter; (accumulate) accumuler; (business) monter; (speed, one's strength) prendre; – vi augmenter, monter; s'accumuler. ◆**build-up** n montée f; accumulation f; Mil concentration f; Journ publicité f. ◆**built-up** a urbanisé; **b.-up area** agglomération f.

builder ['bɪldər] n maçon m; (contractor) entrepreneur m; (of cars etc) constructeur m; (labourer) ouvrier m.

building ['bɪldɪŋ] n bâtiment m; (flats, offices) immeuble m; (action) construction f; **b. society** caisse f d'épargne-logement, = société f de crédit immobilier.

bulb [bʌlb] n Bot bulbe m, oignon m; El ampoule f. ◆**bulbous** a bulbeux.

Bulgaria [bʌl'geərɪə] n Bulgarie f. ◆**Bulgarian** a & n bulgare (mf).

bulg/e [bʌldʒ] vi **to b. (out)** se renfler, bomber; (of eyes) sortir de la tête; – n renflement m; (increase) Fam augmentation f. ◆**—ing** a renflé, bombé; (eyes) protubérant; (bag) gonflé (**with** de).

bulk [bʌlk] n inv grosseur f, volume m; **the b. of** (most) la majeure partie de; **in b.** (to buy, sell) en gros. ◆**bulky** a (-ier, -iest) gros, volumineux.

bull [bul] n **1** taureau m. **2** (nonsense) Fam foutaises fpl. ◆**bullfight** n corrida f.

◆**bullfighter** n matador m. ◆**bullring** n arène f.

bulldog ['buldɒg] n bouledogue m; **b. clip** pince f (à dessin).

bulldoz/e ['buldəuz] vt passer au bulldozer. ◆**—er** n bulldozer m, bouteur m.

bullet ['bulɪt] n balle f. ◆**bulletproof** a (jacket, Am vest) pare-balles inv; (car) blindé.

bulletin ['bulɪtɪn] n bulletin m.

bullion ['buljən] n or m or argent m en lingots.

bullock ['bulək] n bœuf m.

bull's-eye ['bulzaɪ] n (of target) centre m; **to hit the b.-eye** faire mouche.

bully ['bulɪ] n (grosse) brute f, tyran m; – vt brutaliser; (persecute) tyranniser; **to b. into doing** forcer à faire.

bulwark ['bulwək] n rempart m.

bum [bʌm] **1** n (loafer) Am Fam clochard m; – vi (-mm-) **to b. (around)** se balader. **2** vt (-mm-) **to b. sth off s.o.** (cadge) Am Fam taper qn de qch. **3** n (buttocks) Fam derrière m.

bumblebee ['bʌmb(ə)lbiː] n bourdon m.

bumf [bʌmf] n Pej Sl paperasses fpl.

bump [bʌmp] vt (of car etc) heurter; **to b. one's head/knee** se cogner la tête/le genou; **to b. into** se cogner contre; (of car) rentrer dans; (meet) Fam tomber sur; **to b. off** (kill) Sl liquider; **to b. up** Fam augmenter; – vi **to b. along** (on rough road) Aut cahoter; – n (impact) choc m; (jerk) cahot m; (on road, body) bosse f. ◆**—er** n (of car etc) pare-chocs m inv; – a (crop etc) exceptionnel; **b. cars** autos fpl tamponneuses. ◆**bumpy** a (-ier, -iest) (road, ride) cahoteux.

bumpkin ['bʌmpkɪn] n rustre m.

bumptious ['bʌmpʃəs] a prétentieux.

bun [bʌn] n **1** Culin petit pain m au lait. **2** (of hair) chignon m.

bunch [bʌntʃ] n (of flowers) bouquet m; (of keys) trousseau m; (of bananas) régime m; (of people) bande f; **b. of grapes** grappe f de raisin; **a b. of** (mass) Fam un tas de.

bundle ['bʌnd(ə)l] n **1** paquet m; (of papers) liasse f; (of firewood) fagot m. **2** vt (put) fourrer; (push) pousser (**into** dans); **to b. (up)** mettre en paquet; **to b. s.o. off** expédier qn; – vi **to b. (oneself) up** se couvrir (bien).

bung [bʌŋ] **1** n (stopper) bonde f; – vt **to b. up** (stop up) boucher. **2** vt (toss) Fam balancer, jeter.

bungalow ['bʌŋgələu] n bungalow m.

bungl/e ['bʌŋg(ə)l] vt gâcher; – vi travailler

mal. ◆**-ing** n gâchis m; – a (clumsy) maladroit.

bunion ['bʌnjən] n (on toe) oignon m.

bunk [bʌŋk] n **1** Rail Nau couchette f; **b. beds** lits mpl superposés. **2** Sl = **bunkum.** ◆**bunkum** n Sl foutaises fpl.

bunker ['bʌŋkər] n Mil Golf bunker m; (coalstore in garden) coffre m.

bunny ['bʌnɪ] n Fam Jeannot m lapin.

buoy [bɔɪ] n bouée f; – vt to **b. up** (support) Fig soutenir.

buoyant ['bɔɪənt] a Fig gai, optimiste; (market) Fin ferme.

burden ['bɜːd(ə)n] n fardeau m; (of tax) poids m; – vt charger, accabler (**with** de).

bureau, pl **-eaux** ['bjʊərəʊ, -əʊz] n (office) bureau m; (desk) secrétaire m. ◆**bureaucracy** [bjʊə'rɒkrəsɪ] n bureaucratie f. ◆**bureaucrat** ['bjʊərəkræt] n bureaucrate m.

burger ['bɜːgər] n Fam hamburger m.

burglar ['bɜːglər] n cambrioleur, -euse mf; **b. alarm** sonnerie f d'alarme. ◆**burglarize** vt Am cambrioler. ◆**burglary** n cambriolage m. ◆**burgle** vt cambrioler.

burial ['berɪəl] n enterrement m; – a (service) funèbre; **b. ground** cimetière m.

burlap ['bɜːlæp] n (sacking) Am toile f à sac.

burlesque [bɜː'lesk] n parodie f; Th Am revue f.

burly ['bɜːlɪ] a (-ier, -iest) costaud.

Burma ['bɜːmə] n Birmanie f. ◆**Bur'mese** a & n birman, -ane (mf).

burn [bɜːn] n brûlure f; – vt (pt & pp **burned** or **burnt**) brûler; **to b. down** or **off** or **up** brûler; **burnt alive** brûlé vif; – vi brûler; **to b. down** (of house) brûler (complètement), être réduit en cendres; **to b. out** (of fire) s'éteindre; (of fuse) sauter. ◆**-ing** a en feu; (fire) allumé; (topic, fever etc) Fig brûlant; – n smell of b. odeur f de brûlé. ◆**-er** n (of stove) brûleur m.

burp [bɜːp] n Fam rot m; – vi Fam roter.

burrow ['bʌrəʊ] n (hole) terrier m; – vti creuser.

bursar ['bɜːsər] n (in school) intendant, -ante mf.

bursary ['bɜːsərɪ] n (grant) bourse f.

burst [bɜːst] n éclatement m, explosion f; (of laughter) éclat m; (of applause) salve f; (of thunder) coup m; (surge) élan m; (fit) accès m; (burst water pipe) Fam tuyau m crevé; – vi (pt & pp **burst**) (of bomb etc) éclater; (of bubble, tyre, cloud etc) crever; (with rage) Fig crever (de); **to b. in** (enter room) faire irruption dans; **to b. into tears** fondre en larmes; **to b. into flames** prendre feu, s'embraser; **to b. open** s'ouvrir avec

force; **to b. out laughing** éclater de rire; – vt crever, faire éclater; (rupture) rompre; **to b. open** ouvrir avec force. ◆**-ing** a (full) plein à craquer (**with** de); **b. with** (joy) débordant de; **to be b. to do** mourir d'envie de faire.

bury ['berɪ] vt (dead person) enterrer; (hide) enfouir; (plunge, absorb) plonger.

bus [bʌs] n (auto)bus m; (long-distance) (auto)car m; – a (driver, ticket etc) d'autobus; d'autocar; **b. shelter** abribus m; **b. station** gare f routière; **b. stop** arrêt m d'autobus; – vt (**-ss-**) (children) transporter (en bus) à l'école. ◆**bussing** n Sch ramassage m scolaire.

bush [bʊʃ] n buisson m; (of hair) tignasse f; **the b.** (land) la brousse. ◆**bushy** a (-ier, -iest) (hair, tail etc) broussailleux.

bushed [bʊʃt] a (tired) Fam crevé.

business ['bɪznɪs] n affaires fpl, commerce m; (shop) commerce m; (task, concern, matter) affaire f; **the textile b.** le commerce du textile; **big b.** Fam les grosses entreprises fpl commerciales; **on b.** (to travel) pour affaires; **it's your b. to . . .** c'est à vous de . . . ; **you have no b. to . . .** vous n'avez pas le droit de . . . ; **that's none of your b.!** ça ne vous regarde pas!; **to mean b.** Fam ne pas plaisanter; – a commercial; (meeting, trip) d'affaires; **b. hours** (office) heures fpl de travail; (shop) heures fpl d'ouverture. ◆**businesslike** a sérieux, pratique. ◆**businessman** n (pl **-men**) homme m d'affaires. ◆**businesswoman** n (pl **-women**) femme f d'affaires.

busker ['bʌskər] n musicien, -ienne mf des rues.

bust [bʌst] **1** n (sculpture) buste m; (woman's breasts) poitrine f. **2** a (broken) Fam fichu; **to go b.** (bankrupt) faire faillite; – vt (pt & pp **bust** or **busted**) Fam = **to burst** & **to break.** ◆**b.-up** n Fam (quarrel) engueulade f; (breakup) rupture f.

bustl/e ['bʌs(ə)l] vi **to b. (about)** s'affairer; – n activité f, branle-bas m. ◆**-ing** a (street) bruyant.

bus/y ['bɪzɪ] a (-ier, -iest) occupé (**doing** à faire); (active) actif; (day) chargé; (street) animé; (line) Tel Am occupé; **to be b. doing** (in the process of) être en train de faire; – vt **to b. oneself** s'occuper (**with sth** à qch, **doing** à faire). ◆**-ily** adv activement. ◆**busybody** n to be a b. faire la mouche du coche.

but [bʌt, unstressed bət] **1** conj mais. **2** prep (except) sauf; **b. for that** sans cela; **b. for him** sans lui; **no one b. you** personne d'autre que toi. **3** *adv* (*only*) ne ... que, seulement.

butane ['bjuːteɪn] *n* (*gas*) butane *m*.

butcher ['bʊtʃər] *n* boucher *m*; **b.'s shop** boucherie *f*; – *vt* (*people*) massacrer; (*animal*) abattre. ◆**butchery** *n* massacre *m* (**of** de).

butler ['bʌtlər] *n* maître *m* d'hôtel.

butt [bʌt] **1** *n* (*of cigarette*) mégot *m*; (*of gun*) crosse *f*; (*buttocks*) *Am Fam* derrière *m*; **b. for ridicule** objet *m* de risée. **2** *vi* **to b. in** interrompre, intervenir.

butter ['bʌtər] *n* beurre *m*; **b. bean** haricot *m* blanc; **b. dish** beurrier *m*; – *vt* beurrer; **to b. s.o. up** *Fam* flatter qn. ◆**buttercup** *n* bouton-d'or *m*. ◆**buttermilk** *n* lait *m* de beurre.

butterfly ['bʌtəflaɪ] *n* papillon *m*; **to have butterflies** (*flying b.*) *Fam* avoir le trac; **b. stroke** *Swimming* brasse *f* papillon.

buttock ['bʌtək] *n* fesse *f*.

button ['bʌtən] *n* bouton *m*; – *vt* **to b. (up)** boutonner; – *vi* **to b. up** (*of garment*) se boutonner. ◆**buttonhole** *n* boutonnière *f*; (*flower*) fleur *f*. **2** *vt* (*person*) *Fam* accrocher.

buttress ['bʌtrɪs] *n* *Archit* contrefort *m*; *Fig* soutien *m*; (**flying b.**) arc-boutant *m*; – *vt* (*support*) *Archit* & *Fig* soutenir.

buxom ['bʌksəm] *a* (*woman*) bien en chair.

buy [baɪ] *vt* (*pt & pp* **bought**) acheter (**from s.o.** à qn, **for s.o.** à *or* pour qn); (*story etc*) *Am Fam* avaler, croire; **to b. back** racheter; **to b. over** (*bribe*) corrompre; **to b. up** acheter en bloc; – *n* **a good b.** une bonne affaire. ◆**-er** *n* acheteur, -euse *mf*.

buzz [bʌz] **1** *vi* bourdonner; **to b. off** *Fam* décamper; – *n* bourdonnement *m*. **2** *vt* (*building etc*) *Av* raser. **3** *vt* **to b. s.o.** *Tel*

appeler qn; – *n* *Tel Fam* coup *m* de fil. ◆**-er** *n* interphone *m*; (*of bell, clock*) sonnerie *f*; (*hooter*) sirène *f*.

by [baɪ] *prep* **1** (*agent, manner*) par; **hit/chosen/etc** by frappé/choisi/*etc* par; **surrounded/followed/etc** by entouré/suivi/*etc* de; **by doing** en faisant; **by sea** par mer; **by mistake** par erreur; **by car** en voiture; **by bicycle** à bicyclette; **by moonlight** au clair de lune; **one by one** un à un; **day by day** de jour en jour; **by sight/day/far** de vue/jour/loin; **by the door** (*through*) par la porte; (**all**) **by oneself** tout seul. **2** (*next to*) à côté de; (*near*) près de; **by the lake/sea** au bord du lac/de la mer; **to pass by the bank** passer devant la banque. **3** (*before in time*) avant; **by Monday** avant lundi, d'ici lundi; **by now** à cette heure-ci, déjà; **by yesterday** (dès) hier. **4** (*amount, measurement*) à; **by the kilo** au kilo; **taller by a metre** plus grand d'un mètre; **paid by the hour** payé à l'heure. **5** (*according to*) d'après; – *adv* **close by** tout près; **to go by, pass by** passer; **to put by** mettre de côté; **by and by** bientôt; **by and large** en gros. ◆**by-election** *n* élection *f* partielle. ◆**by-law** *n* (*of organization*) *Am* statut *m*. ◆**by-product** *n* sous-produit *m*. ◆**by-road** *n* chemin *m* de traverse.

bye(-bye)! [baɪ('baɪ)] *int* *Fam* salut!, au revoir!

bygone ['baɪgɒn] *a* **in b. days** jadis.

bypass ['baɪpɑːs] *n* déviation *f* (routière), dérivation *f*; – *vt* contourner; (*ignore*) *Fig* éviter de passer par.

bystander ['baɪstændər] *n* spectateur, -trice *mf*; (*in street*) badaud, -aude *mf*.

byword ['baɪwɜːd] *n* **a b. for** *Pej* un synonyme de.

C

C, c [siː] *n* C, c *m*.

c *abbr* = **cent.**

cab [kæb] *n* taxi *m*; (*horse-drawn*) *Hist* fiacre *m*; (*of train driver etc*) cabine *f*. ◆**cabby** *n* *Fam* (*chauffeur m de*) taxi *m*; *Hist* cocher *m*.

cabaret ['kæbəreɪ] *n* (*show*) spectacle *m*; (*place*) cabaret *m*.

cabbage ['kæbɪdʒ] *n* chou *m*.

cabin ['kæbɪn] *n* *Nau Rail* cabine *f*; (*hut*) cabane *f*, case *f*; **c. boy** mousse *m*.

cabinet ['kæbɪnɪt] **1** *n* (*cupboard*) armoire *f*; (*for display*) vitrine *f*; (**filing**) **c.** classeur *m* (de bureau). **2** *n* *Pol* cabinet *m*; – a ministériel; **c. minister** ministre *m*. ◆**c.-maker** *n* ébéniste *m*.

cable ['keɪb(ə)l] *n* câble *m*; **c. car** (*with overhead cable*) téléphérique *m*; *Rail* funiculaire *m*; **c. television** la télévision par câble; **to have c.** *Fam* avoir le câble; – *vt* (*message etc*) câbler (**to** à).

caboose [kə'buːs] n Rail Am fourgon m (de queue).

cache [kæʃ] n (place) cachette f; **an arms' c.** des armes cachées, une cache d'armes.

cachet ['kæʃeɪ] n (mark, character etc) cachet m.

cackle ['kæk(ə)l] vi (of hen) caqueter; (laugh) glousser; – n caquet m; gloussement m.

cacophony [kə'kɒfənɪ] n cacophonie f.

cactus, pl **-ti** or **-tuses** ['kæktəs, -taɪ, -təsɪz] n cactus m.

cad [kæd] n Old-fashioned Pej goujat m.

cadaverous [kə'dævərəs] a cadavérique.

caddie ['kædɪ] n Golf caddie m.

caddy ['kædɪ] n (tea) c. boîte f à thé.

cadence ['keɪdəns] n Mus cadence f.

cadet [kə'det] n Mil élève m officier.

cadge [kædʒ] vi (beg) Pej quémander; – vt (meal) se faire payer (off s.o. par qn); **to c. money from** or **off s.o.** taper qn.

Caesarean [sɪ'zeərɪən] n c. **(section)** Med césarienne f.

café ['kæfeɪ] n café(-restaurant) m. ◆**cafeteria** [kæfɪ'tɪərɪə] n cafétéria f.

caffeine ['kæfiːn] n caféine f.

cage [keɪdʒ] n cage f; – vt **to c. (up)** mettre en cage.

cagey ['keɪdʒɪ] a Fam peu communicatif (about à l'égard de).

cahoots [kə'huːts] n **in c.** Sl de mèche, en cheville (with avec).

cajole [kə'dʒəʊl] vt amadouer, enjôler.

cak/e [keɪk] n 1 gâteau m; (small) pâtisserie f; **c. of soap** savonnette f. 2 vi (harden) durcir; – vt (cover) couvrir (with de). ◆**–ed** a (mud) séché.

calamine ['kæləmaɪn] n c. **(lotion)** lotion f apaisante (à la calamine).

calamity [kə'læmɪtɪ] n calamité f. ◆**calamitous** a désastreux.

calcium ['kælsɪəm] n calcium m.

calculat/e ['kælkjʊleɪt] vti calculer; **to c. that** Fam supposer que; **to c. on** compter sur. ◆**–ing** a (shrewd) calculateur. ◆**calcu'lation** n calcul m. ◆**calculator** n (desk computer) calculatrice f; (pocket) c. calculatrice (de poche). ◆**calculus** n Math Med calcul m.

calendar ['kælɪndər] n calendrier m; (directory) annuaire m.

calf [kɑːf] n 1 (pl calves) **1** (animal) veau m. 2 Anat mollet m.

calibre ['kælɪbər] n calibre m. ◆**calibrate** vt calibrer.

calico ['kælɪkəʊ] n (pl **-oes** or **-os**) (fabric) calicot m; (printed) Am indienne f.

call [kɔːl] n appel m; (shout) cri m; (vocation) vocation f; (visit) visite f; (telephone) c. communication f, appel m téléphonique; **to make a c.** Tel téléphoner (**to** à); **on c.** de garde; **no c. to do** aucune raison de faire; **there's no c. for that article** Com cet article n'est pas très demandé; **c. box** cabine f (téléphonique); – vt appeler; (wake up) réveiller; (person to meeting) convoquer (**to** à); (attention) attirer (**to** sur); (truce) demander; (consider) considérer; **he's called David** il s'appelle David; **to c. a meeting** convoquer une assemblée; **to c. s.o. a liar/etc** qualifier or traiter qn de menteur/etc; **to c. into question** mettre en question; **let's c. it a day** Fam on va s'arrêter là, ça suffit; **to c. sth (out)** (shout) crier qch; – vi appeler; **to c. (out)** (cry out) crier; **to c. (in** or **round** or **by** or **over)** (visit) passer. ■ **to c. back** vti rappeler; **to c. for** vt (require) demander; (summon) appeler; (collect) passer prendre; **to c. in** vt faire venir or entrer; (police) appeler; (recall) rappeler, faire rentrer; – vi **to c. in on** s.o. passer chez qn. ◆**call-in** a (programme) Rad à ligne ouverte; **to c. off** vt (cancel) annuler; (dog) rappeler; **to c. out** vt (doctor) appeler; (workers) donner une consigne de grève à; – vi **to c. out for** demander à haute voix; **to c. up** vt Mil Tel appeler; (memories) évoquer. ◆**call-up** n Mil appel m, mobilisation f; **to c. (up)on** vi (visit) passer voir, passer chez; (invoke) invoquer; **to c. (up)on s.o. to do** inviter qn à faire; (urge) sommer qn de faire. ◆**calling** n vocation f; **c. card** Am carte f de visite. ◆**caller** n visiteur, -euse mf; Tel correspondant, -ante mf.

calligraphy [kə'lɪgrəfɪ] n calligraphie f.

callous ['kæləs] a **1** cruel, insensible. **2** (skin) calleux. ◆**callus** n durillon m, cal m.

callow ['kæləʊ] a inexpérimenté.

calm [kɑːm] a (-er, -est) calme, tranquille; **keep c.!** (don't panic) du calme!; – n calme m; – vt **to c. (down)** calmer; – vi **to c. down** se calmer. ◆**–ly** adv calmement. ◆**–ness** n calme m.

calorie ['kælərɪ] n calorie f.

calumny ['kæləmnɪ] n calomnie f.

calvary ['kælvərɪ] n Rel calvaire m.

calve [kɑːv] vi (of cow) vêler.

camber ['kæmbər] n (in road) bombement m.

came [keɪm] see come.

camel ['kæməl] n chameau m.

camellia [kə'miːlɪə] n Bot camélia m.

cameo ['kæmɪəʊ] n camée m.

camera ['kæmrə] n appareil(-photo) m; TV Cin caméra f. ◆**cameraman** n (pl -men) caméraman m.

camomile ['kæməmaɪl] n Bot camomille f.

camouflage ['kæməflɑːʒ] n camouflage m; – vt camoufler.

camp[1] [kæmp] n camp m, campement m; **c. bed** lit m de camp; – vi **to c. (out)** camper. ◆**—ing** n Sp camping m; **c. site** (terrain m de) camping m. ◆**—er** n (person) campeur, -euse mf; (vehicle) camping-car m. ◆**campfire** n feu m de camp. ◆**camp-site** n camping m.

camp[2] [kæmp] a (affected) affecté, exagéré (de façon à provoquer le rire).

campaign [kæm'peɪn] n Pol Mil Journ etc campagne f; – vi faire campagne. ◆**—er** n militant, -ante mf (for pour).

campus ['kæmpəs] n Univ campus m.

can[1] [kæn, unstressed kən] v aux (pres t can; pt could) (be able to) pouvoir; (know how to) savoir; **if I c.** si je peux; **she c. swim** elle sait nager; **if I could swim** si je savais nager; **he could do it tomorrow** il pourrait le faire demain; **he couldn't help me** il ne pouvait pas m'aider; **he could have done it** il aurait pu le faire; **you could be wrong** (possibility) tu as peut-être tort; **he can't be old** (probability) il ne doit pas être vieux; **c. I come in?** (permission) puis-je entrer?; **you can't** or **c. not come** tu ne peux pas venir; **I c. see** je vois.

can[2] [kæn] n (for water etc) bidon m; (tin for food) boîte f; – vt (-nn-) mettre en boîte. ◆**canned** a en boîte, en conserve; **c. food** conserves fpl. ◆**can-opener** n ouvre-boîtes m inv.

Canada ['kænədə] n Canada m. ◆**Canadian** [kə'neɪdɪən] a & n canadien, -ienne mf.

canal [kə'næl] n canal m.

canary [kə'neərɪ] n canari m, serin m.

cancan ['kænkæn] n french-cancan m.

cancel ['kænsəl] vt (-ll-, Am -l-) annuler; (goods, taxi, appointment) décommander; (word, paragraph etc) biffer; (train) supprimer; (stamp) oblitérer; **to c. a ticket** (with date) composter un billet; (punch) poinçonner un billet; **to c. each other out** s'annuler. ◆**cance'llation** n annulation f; suppression f; oblitération f.

cancer ['kænsər] n cancer m; **C.** (sign) le Cancer; **c. patient** cancéreux, -euse mf. ◆**cancerous** a cancéreux.

candelabra [kændɪ'lɑːbrə] n candélabre m.

candid ['kændɪd] a franc, sincère. ◆**candour** n franchise f, sincérité f.

candidate ['kændɪdeɪt] n candidat, -ate mf. ◆**candidacy** n, ◆**candidature** n candidature f.

candle ['kænd(ə)l] n bougie f; (tallow) chandelle f; Rel cierge m; **c. grease** suif m. ◆**candlelight** n by c. à la (lueur d'une) bougie; **to have dinner by c.** dîner aux chandelles. ◆**candlestick** n bougeoir m; (tall) chandelier m.

candy ['kændɪ] n Am bonbon(s) m(pl); (sugar) sucre m candi; **c. store** Am confiserie f. ◆**candied** a (fruit) confit, glacé. ◆**candyfloss** n barbe f à papa.

cane [keɪn] n canne f; (for basket) rotin m; Sch baguette f; – vt (punish) Sch fouetter.

canine ['keɪnaɪn] **1** a canin. **2** n (tooth) canine f.

canister ['kænɪstər] n boîte f (en métal).

canker ['kænkər] n (in disease) & Fig chancre m.

cannabis ['kænəbɪs] n (plant) chanvre m indien; (drug) haschisch m.

cannibal ['kænɪbəl] n & a cannibale (mf).

cannon ['kænən] n (pl -s or inv) canon m. ◆**cannonball** n boulet m (de canon).

cannot ['kænɒt] = **can not**.

canny ['kænɪ] a (-ier, -iest) rusé, malin.

canoe [kə'nuː] n canoë m, kayak m; – vi faire du canoë or du kayak. ◆**—ing** n to go c. Sp faire du canoë or du kayak. ◆**canoeist** n canoëiste mf.

canon ['kænən] n (law) canon m; (clergyman) chanoine m. ◆**canonize** vt Rel canoniser.

canopy ['kænəpɪ] n (over bed, altar etc) dais m; (hood of pram) capote f; (awning) auvent m; (made of glass) marquise f; (of sky) Fig voûte f.

cant [kænt] n (jargon) jargon m.

can't [kɑːnt] = **can not**.

cantaloup(e) ['kæntəluːp, Am -ləʊp] n (melon) cantaloup m.

cantankerous [kæn'tæŋkərəs] a grincheux, acariâtre.

cantata [kæn'tɑːtə] n Mus cantate f.

canteen [kæn'tiːn] n (place) cantine f; (flask) gourde f; **c. of cutlery** ménagère f.

canter ['kæntər] n petit galop m; – vi aller au petit galop.

cantor ['kæntər] n Rel chantre m, maître m de chapelle.

canvas ['kænvəs] n (grosse) toile f; (for embroidery) canevas m.

canvass ['kænvəs] vt (an area) faire du démarchage dans; (opinions) sonder; **to c.**

s.o. *Pol* solliciter des voix de qn; *Com* solliciter des commandes de qn. ◆**—ing** *n Com* démarchage *m*, prospection *f*; *Pol* démarchage *m* (électoral). ◆**—er** *n Pol* agent *m* électoral; *Com* démarcheur, -euse *mf.*

canyon ['kænjən] *n* cañon *m*, canyon *m.*

cap¹ [kæp] *n* **1** (*hat*) casquette *f*; (*for shower etc*) & *Nau* bonnet *m*; *Mil* képi *m*. **2** (*of bottle, tube, valve*) bouchon *m*; (*of milk or beer bottle*) capsule *f*; (*of pen*) capuchon *m*. **3** (*of child's gun*) amorce *f*, capsule *f*. **4** (**Dutch**) **c.** (*contraceptive*) diaphragme *m.*

cap² [kæp] *vt* (**-pp-**) (*outdo*) surpasser; **to c. it all** pour comble; **capped with** (*covered*) coiffé de.

capable ['keɪpəb(ə)l] *a* (*person*) capable (**of** sth de qch, **of doing** de faire), compétent; **c. of** (*thing*) susceptible de. ◆**capa'bility** *n* capacité *f*. ◆**capably** *adv* avec compétence.

capacity [kə'pæsətɪ] *n* (*of container*) capacité *f*, contenance *f*; (*ability*) aptitude *f*, capacité *f*; (*output*) rendement *m*; **in my c. as** en ma qualité de; **in an advisory/etc c.** à titre consultatif/*etc*; **filled to c.** absolument plein, comble; **c. audience** salle *f* comble.

cape [keɪp] *n* **1** (*cloak*) cape *f*; (*of cyclist*) pèlerine *f*. **2** *Geog* cap *m*; **C. Town** Le Cap.

caper ['keɪpər] **1** *vi* (*jump about*) gambader. **2** *n* (*activity*) *Sl* affaire *f*; (*prank*) *Fam* farce *f*; (*trip*) *Fam* virée *f*. **3** *n Bot Culin* câpre *f.*

capital ['kæpɪtəl] **1** *a* (*punishment, letter, importance*) capital; **– n c. (city)** capitale *f*; **c. (letter)** majuscule *f*, capitale *f*. **2** *n* (*money*) capital *m*, capitaux *mpl*. ◆**capitalism** *n* capitalisme *m*. ◆**capitalist** *a* & *n* capitaliste (*mf*). ◆**capitalize** *vi* **to c.** on tirer parti de.

capitulate [kə'pɪtʃuleɪt] *vi* capituler. ◆**capitu'lation** *n* capitulation *f.*

caprice [kə'priːs] *n* caprice *m*. ◆**capricious** [kə'prɪʃəs] *a* capricieux.

Capricorn ['kæprɪkɔːn] *n* (*sign*) le Capricorne.

capsize [kæp'saɪz] *vi Nau* chavirer; – *vt* (*faire*) chavirer.

capsule ['kæpsəl, 'kæpsjuːl] *n* (*medicine, of spaceship etc*) capsule *f.*

captain ['kæptɪn] *n* capitaine *m*; – *vt Nau* commander; *Sp* être le capitaine de.

caption ['kæpʃ(ə)n] *n Cin Journ* sous-titre *m*; (*under illustration*) légende *f.*

captivate ['kæptɪveɪt] *vt* captiver.

captive ['kæptɪv] *n* captif, -ive *mf*, prisonnier, -ière *mf*. ◆**cap'tivity** *n* captivité *f.*

capture ['kæptʃər] *n* capture *f*; – *vt* (*person, animal*) prendre, capturer; (*town*) prendre; (*attention*) capter; (*represent in words, on film etc*) rendre, reproduire.

car [kɑːr] *n* voiture *f*, auto(mobile) *f*; *Rail* wagon *m*; – *a* (*industry*) automobile; **c. ferry** ferry-boat *m*; **c. park** parking *m*; **c. radio** autoradio *m*; **c. wash** (*action*) lavage *m* automatique; (*machine*) lave-auto *m*. ◆**carfare** *n Am* frais *mpl* de voyage. ◆**carport** *n* auvent *m* (pour voiture). ◆**carsick** *a* **to be c.** être malade en voiture.

carafe [kə'ræf] *n* carafe *f.*

caramel ['kærəməl] *n* (*flavouring, toffee*) caramel *m.*

carat ['kærət] *n* carat *m.*

caravan ['kærəvæn] *n* (*in desert*) & *Aut* caravane *f*; (*horse-drawn*) roulotte *f*; **c. site** camping *m* pour caravanes.

caraway ['kærəweɪ] *n Bot Culin* cumin *m*, carvi *m.*

carbohydrates [kɑːbəʊ'haɪdreɪts] *npl* (*in diet*) féculents *mpl.*

carbon ['kɑːbən] *n* carbone *m*; **c. copy** double *m* (au carbone); *Fig* réplique *f*, double *m*; **c. paper** (papier *m*) carbone *m.*

carbuncle ['kɑːbʌŋk(ə)l] *n Med* furoncle *m*, clou *m.*

carburettor [kɑːbjʊ'retər] (*Am* **carburetor** ['kɑːbəreɪtər]) *n* carburateur *m.*

carcass ['kɑːkəs] *n* (*body, framework*) carcasse *f.*

carcinogenic [kɑːsɪnə'dʒenɪk] *a* cancérigène.

card [kɑːd] *n* carte *f*; (*cardboard*) carton *m*; (*index*) c. fiche *f*; **c. index** fichier *m*; **c. table** table *f* de jeu; **to play cards** jouer aux cartes; **on** *or Am* **in the cards** *Fam* très vraisemblable; **to get one's cards** (*be dismissed*) *Fam* être renvoyé. ◆**cardboard** *n* carton *m*. ◆**cardsharp** *n* tricheur, -euse *mf.*

cardiac ['kɑːdɪæk] *a* cardiaque.

cardigan ['kɑːdɪgən] *n* cardigan *m*, gilet *m.*

cardinal ['kɑːdɪn(ə)l] **1** *a* (*number etc*) cardinal. **2** *n* (*priest*) cardinal *m.*

care [keər] **1** *vi* **to c. about** (*feel concern about*) se soucier de, s'intéresser à; **I don't c.** ça m'est égal; **I couldn't c. less** *Fam* je m'en fiche; **who cares?** qu'est-ce que ça fait? **2** *vi* (*like*) aimer, vouloir; **would you c. to try?** voulez-vous essayer?, aimeriez-vous essayer?; **I don't c. for it** (*music etc*) je n'aime pas tellement ça; **to c. for** (*a drink, a change etc*) avoir envie de; **to c. about** *or* **for s.o.** avoir de la sympathie pour qn; **to c. for**

(*look after*) s'occuper de; (*sick person*) soigner. **3** *n* (*application, heed*) soin(s) *m*(*pl*), attention *f*; (*charge, protection*) garde *f*, soin *m*; (*anxiety*) souci *m*; **to take c. not to do** faire attention à ne pas faire; **take c. to put everything back** veillez à tout ranger; **to take c. of** s'occuper de; **to take c. of itself** (*of matter*) s'arranger; **to take c. of oneself** (*manage*) se débrouiller; (*keep healthy*) faire attention à sa santé. ◆**carefree** *a* insouciant. ◆**caretaker** *n* gardien, -ienne *mf*, concierge *mf*.

career [kə'rɪər] **1** *n* carrière *f*; – *a* (*diplomat etc*) de carrière. **2** *vi* **to c. along** aller à toute vitesse.

careful ['keəf(ə)l] *a* (*diligent*) soigneux (*about, of* de); (*cautious*) prudent; **c. (with money)** regardant; **to be c. of** *or* **with** (*heed*) faire attention à. ◆**—ly** *adv* avec soin; prudemment. ◆**careless** *a* négligent; (*thoughtless*) irréfléchi; (*inattentive*) inattentif (*of* à). ◆**carelessness** *n* négligence *f*, manque *m* de soin.

caress [kə'res] *n* caresse *f*; – *vt* (*stroke*) caresser; (*kiss*) embrasser.

cargo ['kɑːgəʊ] *n* (*pl* -oes, *Am* -os) cargaison *f*; **c. boat** cargo *m*.

Caribbean [kærɪ'biːən, *Am* kə'rɪbɪən] *a* caraïbe; – *the* **C. (Islands)** les Antilles *fpl*.

caricature ['kærɪkətʃʊər] *n* caricature *f*; – *vt* caricaturer.

caring ['keərɪŋ] *a* (*loving*) aimant; (*understanding*) compréhensif; – *n* affection *f*.

carnage ['kɑːnɪdʒ] *n* carnage *m*.

carnal ['kɑːnəl] *a* charnel, sexuel.

carnation [kɑː'neɪʃən] *n* œillet *m*.

carnival ['kɑːnɪvəl] *n* carnaval *m*.

carnivore ['kɑːnɪvɔːr] *n* carnivore *m*. ◆**carnivorous** *a* carnivore.

carol ['kærəl] *n* chant *m* (de Noël).

carouse [kə'raʊz] *vi* faire la fête.

carp [kɑːp] **1** *n* (*fish*) carpe *f*. **2** *vi* critiquer; **to c. at** critiquer.

carpenter ['kɑːpɪntər] *n* (*for house building*) charpentier *m*; (*light woodwork*) menuisier *m*. ◆**carpentry** *n* charpenterie *f*; menuiserie *f*.

carpet ['kɑːpɪt] *n* tapis *m*; (*fitted*) moquette *f*; **c. sweeper** balai *m* mécanique; – *vt* recouvrir d'un tapis *or* d'une moquette; (*of snow etc*) *Fig* tapisser. ◆**—ing** *n* (*carpets*) tapis *mpl*, moquette *f*.

carriage ['kærɪdʒ] *n* (*horse-drawn*) voiture *f*, équipage *m*; *Rail* voiture *f*; *Com* transport *m*; (*bearing of person*) port *m*; (*of typewriter*) chariot *m*; **c. paid** port payé. ◆**carriageway** *n* (*of road*) chaussée *f*.

carrier ['kærɪər] *n Com* entreprise *f* de transports; *Med* porteur, -euse *mf*; **c. (bag)** sac *m* (en plastique); **c. pigeon** pigeon *m* voyageur.

carrion ['kærɪən] *n* charogne *f*.

carrot ['kærət] *n* carotte *f*.

carry ['kærɪ] *vt* porter; (*goods*) transporter; (*by wind*) emporter; (*involve*) comporter; (*interest*) *Com* produire; (*extend*) faire passer; (*win*) remporter; (*authority*) avoir; (*child*) *Med* attendre; (*motion*) *Pol* faire passer, voter; (*sell*) stocker; *Math* retenir; **to c. too far** pousser trop loin; **to c.** oneself **se** comporter; – *vi* (*of sound*) porter. ■ **to c. away** *vt* emporter; *Fig* transporter; **to be** *or* **get carried away** (*excited*) s'emballer; **to c. back** *vt* (*thing*) rapporter; (*person*) ramener; (*in thought*) reporter; **to c. off** *vt* emporter; (*kidnap*) enlever; (*prize*) remporter; **to c. it off** réussir; **to c. on** *vt* continuer; (*conduct*) diriger, mener; (*sustain*) soutenir; – *vi* continuer (*doing* à faire); (*behave*) *Pej* se conduire (mal); (*complain*) se plaindre; **to c. on with sth** continuer qch; **to c. on about** (*talk*) causer de. ◆**carryings-'on** *npl Pej* activités *fpl*; (*behaviour*) *Pej* façons *fpl*; **to c. out** *vt* (*plan etc*) exécuter, réaliser; (*repair etc*) effectuer; (*duty*) accomplir; *Am* emporter; **to c. through** *vt* (*plan etc*) mener à bonne fin.

carryall ['kærɪɔːl] *n Am* fourre-tout *m inv*. ◆**carrycot** *n* (nacelle *f*) porte-bébé *m*.

cart [kɑːt] **1** *n* charrette *f*; (*handcart*) voiture *f* à bras. **2** *vt* (*goods, people*) transporter; **to c. (around)** *Fam* trimbal(l)er; **to c. away** emporter. ◆**carthorse** *n* cheval *m* de trait.

cartel [kɑː'tel] *n Econ* cartel *m*.

cartilage ['kɑːtɪlɪdʒ] *n* cartilage *m*.

carton ['kɑːtən] *n* (*box*) carton *m*; (*of milk, fruit juice etc*) brick *m*, pack *m*; (*of cigarettes*) cartouche *f*; (*of cream*) pot *m*.

cartoon [kɑː'tuːn] *n Journ* dessin *m* (humoristique); *Cin* dessin *m* animé; (*strip*) **c.** bande *f* dessinée. ◆**cartoonist** *n Journ* dessinateur, -trice *mf* (humoristique).

cartridge ['kɑːtrɪdʒ] *n* (*of firearm, pen, camera, tape deck*) cartouche *f*; (*of record player*) cellule *f*; **c. belt** cartouchière *f*.

carve [kɑːv] *vt* (*cut*) tailler (*out of* dans); (*sculpt*) sculpter; (*initials etc*) graver; **to c. (up)** (*meat*) découper; **to c. up** (*country*) dépecer, morceler; **to c.** oneself **se tailler qch. ◆—ing** *n* (*wood*) **c.** sculpture *f* (sur bois).

cascade [kæs'keɪd] *n* (*of rocks*) chute *f*; (*of*

blows) déluge *m; (of lace)* flot *m; – vi* tomber; *(hang)* pendre.

case [keɪs] *n* **1** *(instance)* & *Med* cas *m; Jur* affaire *f; Phil* arguments *mpl;* **in any c.** en tout cas; **in c. it rains** au cas où il pleuvrait; **in c. of** en cas de; **(just) in c.** à tout hasard. **2** *(bag)* valise *f; (crate)* caisse *f; (for pen, glasses, camera, violin, cigarettes)* étui *m; (for jewels)* coffret *m.* ◆**casing** *n (covering)* enveloppe *f.*

cash [kæʃ] *n* argent *m;* **to pay (in) c.** *(not by cheque)* payer en espèces *or* en liquide; **to pay c. (down)** payer comptant; **c. price** prix *m* (au) comptant; **c. box** caisse *f;* **c. desk** caisse *f;* **c. register** caisse *f* enregistreuse; – *vt (banknote)* changer; **to c. a cheque** *(of person)* encaisser un chèque; *(of bank)* payer un chèque; **to c. in on** *Fam* profiter de. ◆**ca'shier 1** *n* caissier, -ière *mf.* **2** *vt (dismiss) Mil* casser.

cashew [ˈkæʃuː] *n (nut)* cajou *m.*

cashmere [ˈkæʃmɪər] *n* cachemire *m.*

casino [kəˈsiːnəʊ] *n (pl -os)* casino *m.*

cask [kɑːsk] *n* fût *m,* tonneau *m.* ◆**casket** *n (box)* coffret *m; (coffin)* cercueil *m.*

casserole [ˈkæsərəʊl] *n (covered dish)* cocotte *f; (stew)* ragoût *m* en cocotte.

cassette [kəˈset] *n* cassette *f; Phot* cartouche *f;* **c. player** lecteur *m* de cassettes; **c. recorder** magnétophone *m* à cassettes.

cassock [ˈkæsək] *n* soutane *f.*

cast [kɑːst] **1** *n Th* acteurs *mpl; (list) Th* distribution *f; (mould)* moulage *m; (of dice)* coup *m; Med* plâtre *m; (squint)* léger strabisme *m;* **c. of mind** tournure *f* d'esprit. **2** *vt (pt & pp* cast) *(throw)* jeter; *(light, shadow)* projeter; *(blame)* rejeter; *(glance)* jeter; *(doubt)* exprimer; *(lose)* perdre; *(metal)* couler; *(role) Th* distribuer; *(actor)* donner un rôle à; **to c. one's mind back** se reporter en arrière; **to c. a vote** voter; **to c. aside** rejeter; **to c. off** *(chains etc)* se libérer de; *(shed, lose)* se dépouiller de; *Fig* abandonner. **3** *vi* **to c. off** *Nau* appareiller. **4** *n* **c. iron** fonte *f.* ◆**c.-'iron** *a (pan etc)* en fonte; *(will etc) Fig* de fer, solide.

castaway [ˈkɑːstəweɪ] *n* naufragé, -ée *mf.*

caste [kɑːst] *n* caste *f.*

caster [ˈkɑːstər] *n (wheel)* roulette *f;* **c. sugar** sucre *m* en poudre.

castle [ˈkɑːs(ə)l] *n* château *m; (in chess)* tour *f.*

castoffs [ˈkɑːstɒfs] *npl* vieux vêtements *mpl.*

castor [ˈkɑːstər] *n (wheel)* roulette *f;* **c. oil** huile *f* de ricin; **c. sugar** sucre *m* en poudre.

castrate [kæˈstreɪt] *vt* châtrer. ◆**castration** *n* castration *f.*

casual [ˈkæʒjʊəl] *a (meeting)* fortuit; *(remark)* fait en passant; *(stroll)* sans but; *(offhand)* désinvolte, insouciant; *(worker)* temporaire; *(work)* irrégulier; **c. clothes** vêtements *mpl* sport; **a c. acquaintance** quelqu'un que l'on connaît un peu. ◆**—ly** *adv* par hasard; *(informally)* avec désinvolture; *(to remark)* en passant.

casualty [ˈkæʒjʊəltɪ] *n (dead)* mort *m,* morte *f; (wounded)* blessé, -ée *mf; (accident victim)* accidenté, -ée *mf;* **casualties** morts et blessés *mpl; Mil* pertes *fpl;* **c. department** *Med* service *m* des accidentés.

cat [kæt] *n* chat *m,* chatte *f;* **c. burglar** monte-en-l'air *m inv;* **c.'s eyes**® cataphotes® *mpl,* clous *mpl.* ◆**catcall** *n* sifflet *m,* huée *f.*

cataclysm [ˈkætəklɪzəm] *n* cataclysme *m.*

catalogue [ˈkætəlɒg] *(Am* catalog) *n* catalogue *m; – vt* cataloguer.

catalyst [ˈkætəlɪst] *n Ch* & *Fig* catalyseur *m.*

catapult [ˈkætəpʌlt] *n* lance-pierres *m inv; Hist Av* catapulte *f; – vt* catapulter.

cataract [ˈkætərækt] *n (waterfall)* & *Med* cataracte *f.*

catarrh [kəˈtɑːr] *n* catarrhe *m,* rhume *m.*

catastrophe [kəˈtæstrəfɪ] *n* catastrophe *f.* ◆**cata'strophic** *a* catastrophique.

catch [kætʃ] *vt (pt & pp* caught) *(ball, thief, illness etc)* attraper; *(grab)* prendre, saisir; *(surprise)* (sur)prendre; *(understand)* saisir; *(train etc)* attraper, *(réussir à)* prendre; *(attention)* attirer; *(of nail etc)* accrocher; *(finger etc)* se prendre *(in dans);* **to c. sight of** apercevoir; **to c. fire** prendre feu; **to c. s.o. (in)** *Fam* trouver qn *(chez soi);* **to c. one's breath** *(rest a while)* reprendre haleine; *(stop breathing)* retenir son souffle; **she didn't c. the train/etc** j'ai manqué le train/*etc;* **to c. s.o. out** prendre qn en défaut; **to c. s.o. up** rattraper qn; – *vi (of fire)* prendre; **her skirt (got) caught in the door** sa jupe s'est prise *or* coincée dans la porte; **to c. on** prendre, devenir populaire; *(understand)* saisir; **to c. up** se rattraper; **to c. up with s.o.** rattraper qn; – *n* capture *f,* prise *f; (trick, snare)* piège *m; (on door)* loquet *m.* ◆**—ing** *a* contagieux. ◆**catchphrase** *n,* ◆**catchword** *n* slogan *m.*

catchy [ˈkætʃɪ] *a (-ier, -iest) (tune) Fam* facile à retenir.

catechism [ˈkætɪkɪzəm] *n Rel* catéchisme *m.*

category [ˈkætɪgərɪ] *n* catégorie *f.* ◆**cate-**

'gorical *a* catégorique. ◆**categorize** *vt* classer (par catégories).

cater ['keɪtər] *vi* s'occuper de la nourriture; **to c. for** *or* **to** (*need, taste*) satisfaire; (*readership*) *Journ* s'adresser à. ◆**—ing** *n* restauration *f.* ◆**—er** *n* traiteur *m.*

caterpillar ['kætəpɪlər] *n* chenille *f.*

catgut ['kætgʌt] *n* (*cord*) boyau *m.*

cathedral [kə'θiːdrəl] *n* cathédrale *f.*

catholic ['kæθlɪk] **1** *a* **&** *n* **C.** catholique (*mf*). **2** *a* (*taste*) universel; (*view*) libéral. ◆**Ca'tholicism** *n* catholicisme *m.*

cattle ['kæt(ə)l] *npl* bétail *m*, bestiaux *mpl.*

catty ['kætɪ] *a* (-ier, -iest) *Fam* rosse, méchant.

caucus ['kɔːkəs] *n Pol Am* comité *m* électoral.

caught [kɔːt] *see* catch.

cauldron ['kɔːldrən] *n* chaudron *m.*

cauliflower ['kɒlɪflaʊər] *n* chou-fleur *m.*

cause [kɔːz] *n* cause *f*; (*reason*) raison *f*; **c. for complaint** sujet *m* de plainte; — *vt* causer, occasionner; (*trouble*) créer, susciter (for à); **to c. sth to move/etc** faire bouger/*etc* qch.

causeway ['kɔːzweɪ] *n* chaussée *f.*

caustic ['kɔːstɪk] *a* (*remark, substance*) caustique.

cauterize ['kɔːtəraɪz] *vt Med* cautériser.

caution ['kɔːʃ(ə)n] *n* (*care*) prudence *f*, précaution *f*; (*warning*) avertissement *m*; — *vt* (*warn*) avertir; **to c. s.o. against sth** mettre qn en garde contre qch. ◆**cautionary** *a* (*tale*) moral. ◆**cautious** *a* prudent, circonspect. ◆**cautiously** *adv* prudemment.

cavalcade ['kævəlkeɪd] *n* (*procession*) cavalcade *f.*

cavalier [kævə'lɪər] **1** *a* (*selfish*) cavalier. **2** *n* (*horseman, knight*) *Hist* cavalier *m.*

cavalry ['kævəlrɪ] *n* cavalerie *f.*

cave [keɪv] **1** *n* caverne *f*, grotte *f.* **2** *vi* **to c. in** (*fall in*) s'effondrer. ◆**caveman** *n* (*pl* -men) homme *m* des cavernes. ◆**cavern** ['kævən] *n* caverne *f.*

caviar(e) ['kævɪɑːr] *n* caviar *m.*

cavity ['kævɪtɪ] *n* cavité *f.*

cavort [kə'vɔːt] *vi Fam* cabrioler; **to c. naked/etc** se balader tout nu/*etc.*

cease [siːs] *vti* cesser (doing de faire). ◆**c.-fire** *n* cessez-le-feu *m inv.* ◆**ceaseless** *a* incessant. ◆**ceaselessly** *adv* sans cesse.

cedar ['siːdər] *n* (*tree, wood*) cèdre *m.*

cedilla [sɪ'dɪlə] *n Gram* cédille *f.*

ceiling ['siːlɪŋ] *n* (*of room, on wages etc*) plafond *m.*

celebrate ['selɪbreɪt] *vt* (*event*) fêter; (*mass, s.o.'s merits etc*) célébrer; — *vi* faire la fête; **we should c. (that)!** il faut fêter ça! ◆**—ed** *a* célèbre. ◆**cele'bration** *n* fête *f*; **the c. of** (*marriage etc*) la célébration de. ◆**ce'lebrity** *n* (*person*) célébrité *f.*

celery ['selərɪ] *n* céleri *m.*

celibate ['selɪbət] *a* (*abstaining from sex*) célibataire; (*monk etc*) abstinent. ◆**celibacy** *n* (*of young person etc*) célibat *m*; (*of monk etc*) abstinence *f.*

cell [sel] *n* cellule *f*; *El* élément *m.* ◆**cellular** *a* cellulaire; **c. blanket** couverture *f* en cellular.

cellar ['selər] *n* cave *f.*

cello ['tʃeləʊ] *n* (*pl* -os) violoncelle *m.* ◆**cellist** *n* violoncelliste *mf.*

cellophane® ['seləfeɪn] *n* cellophane® *f.*

celluloid ['seljʊlɔɪd] *n* celluloïd *m.*

cellulose ['seljʊləʊs] *n* cellulose *f.*

Celsius ['selsɪəs] *a* Celsius *inv.*

Celt [kelt] *n* Celte *mf.* ◆**Celtic** *a* celtique, celte.

cement [sɪ'ment] *n* ciment *m*; **c. mixer** bétonnière *f*; — *vt* cimenter.

cemetery ['semɪtrɪ, *Am* 'semətərɪ] *n* cimetière *m.*

cenotaph ['senətɑːf] *n* cénotaphe *m.*

censor ['sensər] *n* censeur *m*; — *vt* (*film etc*) censurer. ◆**censorship** *n* censure *f.*

censure ['senʃər] *vt* blâmer; *Pol* censurer; — *n* blâme *m*; **c. motion, vote of c.** motion *f* de censure.

census ['sensəs] *n* recensement *m.*

cent [sent] *n* (*coin*) cent *m*; **per c.** pour cent.

centenary [sen'tiːnərɪ, *Am* sen'tenərɪ] *n* centenaire *m.*

centigrade ['sentɪgreɪd] *a* centigrade.

centimetre ['sentɪmiːtər] *n* centimètre *m.*

centipede ['sentɪpiːd] *n* mille-pattes *m inv.*

centre ['sentər] *n* centre *m*; **c. forward** *Fb* avant-centre *m*; — *vt* centrer; **to c. on** (*of thoughts*) se concentrer sur; (*of question*) tourner autour de. ◆**central** *a* central. ◆**centralize** *vt* centraliser. ◆**centrifugal** [sen'trɪfjʊgəl] *a* centrifuge.

century ['sentʃərɪ] *n* siècle *m*; (*score*) *Sp* cent points *mpl.*

ceramic [sə'ræmɪk] *a* (*tile etc*) de *or* en céramique; — *npl* (*objects*) céramiques *fpl*; (*art*) céramique *f.*

cereal ['sɪərɪəl] *n* céréale *f.*

cerebral ['serɪbrəl, *Am* sə'riːbrəl] *a* cérébral.

ceremony ['serɪmənɪ] *n* (*event*) cérémonie *f*; **to stand on c.** faire des cérémonies *or* des façons. ◆**cere'monial** *a* de cérémonie; —

n cérémonial *m*. ◆**cere'monious** *a* cérémonieux.

certain ['sɜːtən] *a* (*particular, some*) certain; (*sure*) sûr, certain; **she's c. to come, she'll come for c.** c'est certain *or* sûr qu'elle viendra; **I'm not c. what to do** je ne sais pas très bien ce qu'il faut faire; **to be c. of sth/that** être certain de qch/que; **for c.** (*to say, know*) avec certitude; **be c. to go!** vas-y sans faute!; **to make c. of** (*fact*) s'assurer de; (*seat etc*) s'assurer. ◆**—ly** *adv* certainement; (*yes*) bien sûr; (*without fail*) sans faute; (*without any doubt*) sans aucun doute. ◆**certainty** *n* certitude *f*.

certificate [sə'tɪfɪkɪt] *n* certificat *m*; *Univ* diplôme *m*.

certify ['sɜːtɪfaɪ] *vt* certifier; **to c.** (*insane*) déclarer dément; – *vi* **to c. to sth** attester qch.

cervix ['sɜːvɪks] *n* col *m* de l'utérus.

cesspool ['sespuːl] *n* fosse *f* d'aisances; *Fig* cloaque *f*.

chafe [tʃeɪf] *vt* (*skin*) *Lit* frotter.

chaff [tʃæf] *vt* (*tease*) taquiner.

chaffinch ['tʃæfɪntʃ] *n* (*bird*) pinson *m*.

chagrin ['ʃægrɪn, *Am* ʃə'grɪn] *n* contrariété *f*; – *vt* contrarier.

chain [tʃeɪn] *n* (*of rings, mountains*) chaîne *f*; (*of ideas, events*) enchaînement *m*, suite *f*; (*of lavatory*) chasse *f* d'eau; **c. reaction** réaction *f* en chaîne; **to be a c.-smoker**, to **c.-smoke** fumer cigarette sur cigarette, fumer comme un pompier; **c. saw** tronçonneuse *f*; **c. store** magasin *m* à succursales multiples; – *vt* (*down*) enchaîner; **to c.** (**up**) (*dog*) mettre à l'attache.

chair [tʃeər] *n* chaise *f*; (*armchair*) fauteuil *m*; *Univ* chaire *f*; **the c.** (*office*) la présidence; **c. lift** télésiège *m*; – *vt* (*meeting*) présider. ◆**chairman** *n* (*pl* **-men**) président, -ente *mf*. ◆**chairmanship** *n* présidence *f*.

chalet ['ʃæleɪ] *n* chalet *m*.

chalk [tʃɔːk] *n* craie *f*; **not by a long c.** loin de là, tant s'en faut; – *vt* marquer *or* écrire à la craie; **to c. up** (*success*) *Fig* remporter. ◆**chalky** *a* (**-ier, -iest**) crayeux.

challeng/e ['tʃælɪndʒ] *n* défi *m*; (*task*) gageure *f*; *Mil* sommation *f*; **c. for** (*bid*) tentative *f* d'obtenir; – *vt* défier (**s.o. to do** qn de faire); (*dispute*) contester; **to c. s.o. to a game** inviter qn à jouer; **to c. s.o. to a duel** provoquer qn en duel. ◆**—ing** *a* (*job*) exigeant; (*book*) stimulant. ◆**—er** *n* *Sp* challenger *m*.

chamber ['tʃeɪmbər] *n* chambre *f*; (*of judge*) cabinet *m*; – *a* (*music, orchestra*) de cham-

bre; **c. pot** pot *m* de chambre. ◆**chambermaid** *n* femme *f* de chambre.

chameleon [kə'miːlɪən] *n* (*reptile*) caméléon *m*.

chamois ['ʃæmɪ] *n* **c.** (**leather**) peau *f* de chamois.

champagne [ʃæm'peɪn] *n* champagne *m*.

champion ['tʃæmpɪən] *n* champion, -onne *mf*; **c. skier** champion, -onne du ski; – *vt* (*support*) se faire le champion de. ◆**championship** *n* *Sp* championnat *m*.

chance [tʃɑːns] *n* (*luck*) hasard *m*; (*possibility*) chances *fpl*, possibilité *f*; (*opportunity*) occasion *f*; (*risk*) risque *m*; **by c.** par hasard; **by any c.** (*possibly*) par hasard; **on the off c.** (**that**) **you could help me** au cas où tu pourrais m'aider; – *a* (*remark*) fait au hasard; (*occurrence*) accidentel; – *vt* **to c. doing** prendre le risque de faire; **to c. to find**/*etc* trouver/*etc* par hasard; **to c. it** risquer le coup; – *v imp* **it chanced that** (*happened*) il s'est trouvé que.

chancel ['tʃɑːnsəl] *n* (*in church*) chœur *m*.

chancellor ['tʃɑːnsələr] *n* *Pol Jur* chancelier *m*. ◆**chancellery** *n* chancellerie *f*.

chandelier [ʃændə'lɪər] *n* lustre *m*.

chang/e [tʃeɪndʒ] *n* changement *m*; (*money*) monnaie *f*; **for a c.** pour changer; **it makes a c. from** ça change de; **to have a c. of heart** changer d'avis; **a c. of clothes** des vêtements de rechange; – *vt* (*modify*) changer; (*exchange*) échanger (**for** contre); (*money*) changer; (*transform*) transformer (**into** en); **to c. trains/one's skirt**/*etc* changer de train/de jupe/*etc*; **to c. gear** *Aut* changer de vitesse; **to c. the subject** changer de sujet; – *vi* (*alter*) changer; (*change clothes*) se changer; **to c. over** passer. ◆**—ing** *n* (*of guard*) relève *f*; **c. room** vestiaire *m*. ◆**changeable** *a* (*weather, mood etc*) changeant, variable. ◆**changeless** *a* immuable. ◆**changeover** *n* passage *m* (**from** de, **to** à).

channel ['tʃæn(ə)l] *n* (*navigable*) chenal *m*; *TV* chaîne *f*, canal *m*; (*groove*) rainure *f*; *Fig* direction *f*; **through the c. of** par le canal de; **the C.** *Geog* la Manche; **the C. Islands** les îles anglo-normandes; – *vt* (**-ll-**, *Am* **-l-**) (*energies, crowd etc*) canaliser (**into** vers).

chant [tʃɑːnt] *n* (*of demonstrators*) chant *m* scandé; *Rel* psalmodie *f*; – *vt* (*slogan*) scander; – *vi* scander des slogans.

chaos ['keɪɒs] *n* chaos *m*. ◆**cha'otic** *a* chaotique.

chap [tʃæp] **1** *n* (*fellow*) *Fam* type *m*; **old c.!**

mon vieux! **2** n (on skin) gerçure f; – vi
(-pp-) se gercer; – vt gercer.

chapel ['tʃæp(ə)l] n chapelle f; (nonconformist church) temple m.

chaperon(e) ['ʃæpərəun] n chaperon m; –
vt chaperonner.

chaplain ['tʃæplɪn] n aumônier m.

chapter ['tʃæptər] n chapitre m.

char [tʃɑːr] **1** vt (-rr-) (convert to carbon)
carboniser; (scorch) brûler légèrement. **2** n
Fam femme f de ménage; – vi **to go char-
ring** Fam faire des ménages. **3** n (tea) Sl thé
m.

character ['kærɪktər] n (of person, place etc)
& Typ caractère m; (in book, film) personnage m; (strange person) numéro m; **c.
actor** acteur m de genre. ◆**characte-
'ristic** a & n caractéristique (f).
◆**characte'ristically** adv typiquement.
◆**characterize** vt caractériser.

charade [ʃəˈrɑːd] n (game) charade f
(mimée); (travesty) parodie f, comédie f.

charcoal ['tʃɑːkəul] n charbon m (de bois);
(crayon) fusain m, charbon m.

charge [tʃɑːdʒ] n (in battle) Mil charge f;
Jur accusation f; (cost) prix m; (responsibility) responsabilité f, charge f; (care) garde
f; pl (expenses) frais mpl; **there's a c.** (for it)
c'est payant; **free of c.** gratuit; **extra c.**
supplément m; **to take c. of** prendre en
charge; **to be in c. of** (child etc) avoir la
garde de; (office etc) être responsable de;
the person in c. le or la responsable; **who's
in c. here?** qui commande ici?; – vt Mil En
charger; Jur accuser, inculper; **to c. s.o.
Com** faire payer qn; **to c. (up) to Com**
mettre sur le compte de; **how much do you
c.?** combien demandez-vous?; – vi (rush)
se précipiter; vt Mil chargez! ◆**—able** a (to
c.** to) aux frais de; – vt ◆**charger** n (for battery)
chargeur m.

chariot ['tʃærɪət] n Mil char m.

charisma [kəˈrɪzmə] n magnétisme m.

charity ['tʃærɪtɪ] n (kindness, alms) charité f;
(society) fondation f or œuvre f charitable;
to give to c. faire la charité. ◆**charitable** a
charitable.

charlady ['tʃɑːleɪdɪ] n femme f de ménage.

charlatan ['ʃɑːlətən] n charlatan m.

charm [tʃɑːm] n (attractiveness, spell)
charme m; (trinket) amulette f; – vt
charmer. ◆**—ing** a charmant. ◆**—ingly**
adv d'une façon charmante.

chart [tʃɑːt] n (map) carte f; (graph)
graphique m, tableau m; **(pop) charts**
hit-parade m; **flow c.** organigramme m; –

vt (route) porter sur la carte; (figures) faire
le graphique de; (of graph) montrer.

charter ['tʃɑːtər] n (document) charte f;
(aircraft) charter m, **the c. of** (hiring)
l'affrètement m de; **c. flight** charter m; – vt
(aircraft etc) affréter. ◆**—ed** a **c. accountant** expert-comptable m.

charwoman ['tʃɑːwumən] n (pl -women)
femme f de ménage.

chary ['tʃeərɪ] a (-ier, -iest) (cautious) prudent.

chase [tʃeɪs] n poursuite f, chasse f; **to give
c.** se lancer à la poursuite (to de); – vt
poursuivre; **to c. away** or **off** chasser; **to c.
sth up** Fam essayer d'obtenir qch,
rechercher qch; – vi **to c. after** courir après.

chasm ['kæzəm] n abîme m, gouffre m.

chassis ['ʃæsɪ, Am 'tʃæsɪ] n Aut châssis m.

chaste [tʃeɪst] a chaste. ◆**chastity** n chasteté f.

chasten ['tʃeɪs(ə)n] vt (punish) châtier;
(cause to improve) faire se corriger, assagir.
◆**—ing** a (experience) instructif.

chastise [tʃæˈstaɪz] vt punir.

chat [tʃæt] n causette f; **to have a c.**
bavarder; – vi (-tt-) causer, bavarder; – vt
to c. up Fam baratiner, draguer. ◆**chatty** a
(-ier, -iest) (person) bavard; (style)
familier; (text) plein de bavardages.

chatter ['tʃætər] vi bavarder; (of birds,
monkeys) jacasser; **his teeth are chattering**
il claque des dents; – n bavardage m;
jacassement m. ◆**chatterbox** n bavard,
-arde mf.

chauffeur ['ʃəufər] n chauffeur m (de
maître).

chauvinist ['ʃəuvɪnɪst] n & a chauvin, -ine
(mf); **male c.** Pej phallocrate m.

cheap [tʃiːp] a (-er, -est) bon marché inv,
pas cher; (rate etc) réduit; (worthless) sans
valeur; (superficial) facile; (mean, petty)
mesquin; **cheaper** moins cher, meilleur
marché; – adv (to buy) (à) bon marché, à
rabais; (to feel) humilié. ◆**cheapen** vt Fig
déprécier. ◆**cheaply** adv (à) bon marché.
◆**cheapness** n bas prix m; Fig
mesquinerie f.

cheat [tʃiːt] vt (deceive) tromper; (defraud)
frauder; **to c. s.o. out of sth** escroquer qch à
qn; **to c. on** (wife, husband) faire une infidélité or des infidélités à; – vi tricher;
(defraud) frauder; – n (at games etc)
tricheur, -euse mf; (crook) escroc m.
◆**—ing** n (deceit) tromperie f; (trickery)
tricherie f. ◆**—er** n Am = cheat.

check[1] [tʃek] vt (examine) vérifier; (inspect)
contrôler; (tick) cocher, pointer; (stop)

arrêter, enrayer; *(restrain)* contenir, maîtriser; *(rebuke)* réprimander; *(baggage) Am* mettre à la consigne; **to c. in** *(luggage) Av* enregistrer; **to c. sth out** confirmer qch; *– vi* vérifier; **to c. in** *(at hotel etc)* signer le registre; *(arrive at hotel)* arriver; *(at airport)* se présenter (à l'enregistrement), enregistrer ses bagages; **to c. out** *(at hotel etc)* régler sa note; **to c. up** vérifier, se renseigner; *– n* vérification *f*; contrôle *m*; *(halt)* arrêt *m*; *Chess* échec *m*; *(curb)* frein *m*; *(tick)* = croix *f*; *(receipt) Am* reçu *m*; *(bill in restaurant etc) Am* addition *f*; *(cheque) Am* chèque *m*. ◆**c.-in** *n Av* enregistrement *m* (des bagages). ◆**checking account** *n Am* compte *m* courant. ◆**checkmate** *n Chess* échec et mat *m*. ◆**checkout** *n (in supermarket)* caisse *f*. ◆**checkpoint** *n* contrôle *m*. ◆**checkroom** *n Am* vestiaire *m*; *(left-luggage office) Am* consigne *f*. ◆**checkup** *n* bilan *m* de santé.

check² [tʃek] *n (pattern)* carreaux *mpl*; *– a* à carreaux. ◆**checked** *a* à carreaux.

checkered ['tʃekəd] *a Am* = **chequered**.

checkers ['tʃekəz] *npl Am* jeu *m* de dames.

cheddar ['tʃedər] *n (cheese)* cheddar *m*.

cheek [tʃiːk] *n* joue *f*; *(impudence) Fig* culot *m*. ◆**cheekbone** *n* pommette *f*. ◆**cheeky** *a* (**-ier, -iest**) *(person, reply etc)* effronté.

cheep [tʃiːp] *vi (of bird)* piauler.

cheer¹ [tʃiər] *n* cheers *(shouts)* acclamations *fpl*; **cheers!** *Fam* à votre santé! *– vt (applaud)* acclamer; **to c. on** encourager; **to c. (up)** donner du courage à; *(amuse)* égayer; *– vi* applaudir; **to c. up** prendre courage; s'égayer; **c. up!** (du) courage! ◆**—ing** *n (shouts)* acclamations *fpl*; *– a (encouraging)* réjouissant.

cheer² [tʃiər] *n (gaiety)* joie *f*; **good c.** *(food)* la bonne chère. ◆**cheerful** *a* gai. ◆**cheerfully** *adv* gaiement. ◆**cheerless** *a* morne.

cheerio! [tʃiəri'əʊ] *int* salut!, au revoir!

cheese [tʃiːz] *n* fromage *m*. ◆**cheeseburger** *n* cheeseburger *m*. ◆**cheesecake** *n* tarte *f* au fromage blanc. ◆**cheesed** *a* **to be c. (off)** *Fam* en avoir marre (with de). ◆**cheesy** *a* (**-ier, -iest**) *(shabby, bad) Am Fam* miteux.

cheetah ['tʃiːtə] *n* guépard *m*.

chef [ʃef] *n Culin* chef *m*.

chemistry ['kemɪstrɪ] *n* chimie *f*. ◆**chemical** *a* chimique; *– n* produit *m* chimique. ◆**chemist** *n (dispensing)* pharmacien,

-ienne *mf*; *(scientist)* chimiste *mf*; **chemist('s)** *(shop)* pharmacie *f*.

cheque [tʃek] *n* chèque *m*. ◆**chequebook** *n* carnet *m* de chèques.

chequered ['tʃekəd] *a (pattern)* à carreaux; *(career etc)* qui connaît des hauts et des bas.

cherish ['tʃerɪʃ] *vt (person)* chérir; *(hope)* nourrir, caresser.

cherry ['tʃerɪ] *n* cerise *f*; *– a* cerise *inv*; **c. brandy** cherry *m*.

chess [tʃes] *n* échecs *mpl*. ◆**chessboard** *n* échiquier *m*.

chest [tʃest] *n* **1** *Anat* poitrine *f*. **2** *(box)* coffre *m*; **c. of drawers** commode *f*.

chestnut ['tʃesnʌt] *n* châtaigne *f*, marron *m*; *– a (hair)* châtain; **c. tree** châtaignier *m*.

chew [tʃuː] *vt* **to c. (up)** mâcher; **to c. over** *Fig* ruminer; *– vi* mastiquer; **chewing gum** chewing-gum *m*.

chick [tʃik] *n* poussin *m*; *(girl) Fam* nana *f*. ◆**chicken** **1** *n* poulet *m*; *(pl poultry)* volaille *f*; **it's c. feed** *Fam* c'est deux fois rien, c'est une bagatelle. **2** *a Fam* froussard; *– vi* **to c. out** *Fam* se dégonfler. ◆**chickenpox** *n* varicelle *f*.

chickpea ['tʃikpiː] *n* pois *m* chiche.

chicory ['tʃikərɪ] *n (in coffee etc)* chicorée *f*; *(for salad)* endive *f*.

chide [tʃaɪd] *vt* gronder.

chief [tʃiːf] *n* chef *m*; *(boss) Fam* patron *m*, chef *m*; **in c.** *(commander, editor)* en chef; *– a (main, highest in rank)* principal. ◆**—ly** *adv* principalement, surtout. ◆**chieftain** *n (of clan etc)* chef *m*.

chilblain ['tʃilbleɪn] *n* engelure *f*.

child, *pl* **children** [tʃaɪld, 'tʃildrən] *n* enfant *mf*; **c. care** *or* **welfare** protection *f* de l'enfance; **child's play** *Fig* jeu d'enfant; **c. minder** gardien, -ienne *mf* d'enfants. ◆**childbearing** *n (act)* accouchement *m*; *(motherhood)* maternité *f*. ◆**childbirth** *n* accouchement *m*, couches *fpl*. ◆**childhood** *n* enfance *f*. ◆**childish** *a* puéril, enfantin. ◆**childishness** *n* puérilité *f*. ◆**childlike** *a* naïf, innocent.

chill [tʃil] *n* froid *m*; *(coldness in feelings)* froideur *f*; *Med* refroidissement *m*; **to catch a c.** prendre froid; *– vt (wine, melon)* faire rafraîchir; *(meat, food)* réfrigérer; **to c. s.o.** *(with fear, cold etc)* faire frissonner qn (with de); **to be chilled to the bone** être transi. ◆**—ed** *a (wine)* frais. ◆**chilly** *a* (**-ier, -iest**) froid; *(sensitive to cold)* frileux; **it's c.** il fait (un peu) froid.

chilli ['tʃilɪ] *n* (*pl* -ies) piment *m* (de Cayenne).

chime [tʃaɪm] vi (*of bell*) carillonner; (*of clock*) sonner; **to c. in** (*interrupt*) interrompre; – n carillon m; sonnerie f.

chimney ['tʃɪmnɪ] n cheminée f. ◆**chimneypot** n tuyau m de cheminée. ◆**chimneysweep** n ramoneur m.

chimpanzee [tʃɪmpæn'ziː] n chimpanzé m.

chin [tʃɪn] n menton m.

china ['tʃaɪnə] n inv porcelaine f; – a en porcelaine. ◆**chinaware** n (*objects*) porcelaine f.

China ['tʃaɪnə] n Chine f. ◆**Chi'nese** a & n chinois, -oise (mf); – n (*language*) chinois m.

chink [tʃɪŋk] 1 n (*slit*) fente f. 2 vi tinter; – vt faire tinter; – n tintement m.

chip [tʃɪp] vt (-pp-) (*cup etc*) ébrécher; (*table etc*) écorner; (*paint*) écailler; (*cut*) tailler; – vi **to c. in** Fam contribuer; – n (*splinter*) éclat m; (*break*) ébréchure f; écornure f; (*microchip*) puce f; (*counter*) jeton m; pl (*French fries*) frites fpl; (*crisps*) Am chips mpl. ◆**chipboard** n (*bois m*) aggloméré m. ◆**chippings** npl road or loose c. gravillons mpl.

chiropodist [kɪ'rɒpədɪst] n pédicure mf.

chirp [tʃɜːp] vi (*of bird*) pépier; – n pépiement m.

chirpy ['tʃɜːpɪ] a (-ier, -iest) gai, plein d'entrain.

chisel ['tʃɪz(ə)l] n ciseau m; – vt (-ll-, Am -l-) ciseler.

chit [tʃɪt] n (*paper*) note f, billet m.

chitchat ['tʃɪttʃæt] n bavardage m.

chivalry ['ʃɪvəlrɪ] n (*practices etc*) chevalerie f; (*courtesy*) galanterie f. ◆**chivalrous** a (*man*) galant.

chives [tʃaɪvz] npl ciboulette f.

chloride ['klɔːraɪd] n chlorure m. ◆**chlorine** n chlore m. ◆**chloroform** n chloroforme m.

choc-ice ['tʃɒkaɪs] n (*ice cream*) esquimau m.

chock [tʃɒk] n (*wedge*) cale f; – vt caler. ◆**chock-a-block** [tʃɒkə'blɒk] a, **◆c.-'full** a Fam archiplein.

chocolate ['tʃɒklɪt] n chocolat m; **milk c.** chocolat au lait; **plain** or Am **bittersweet c.** chocolat à croquer; – a (*cake*) au chocolat; (*colour*) chocolat inv.

choice [tʃɔɪs] n choix m; **from c., out of c.** de son propre choix; – a (*goods*) de choix.

choir ['kwaɪər] n chœur m. ◆**choirboy** n jeune choriste m.

choke [tʃəʊk] 1 vt (*person*) étrangler, étouffer; (*clog*) boucher, engorger; **to c. back** (*sobs etc*) étouffer; – vi s'étrangler,

étouffer; **to c. on** (*fish bone etc*) s'étrangler avec. 2 n Aut starter m. ◆**—er** n (*scarf*) foulard m; (*necklace*) collier m (de chien).

cholera ['kɒlərə] n choléra m.

cholesterol [kə'lestərɒl] n cholestérol m.

choose [tʃuːz] vt (pt **chose**, pp **chosen**) choisir (**to do** de faire); **to c. to do** (*decide*) juger bon de faire; – vi choisir; **as I/you/etc c.** comme il me/vous/etc plaît. ◆**choos(e)y** a (-sier, -siest) difficile (*about* sur).

chop [tʃɒp] 1 n (*of lamb, pork*) côtelette f; **to lick one's chops** Fig s'en lécher les babines; **to get the c.** Sl être flanqué à la porte. 2 vt (-pp-) couper (à la hache); (*food*) hacher; **to c. down** (*tree*) abattre; **to c. off** trancher; **to c. up** hacher. 3 vti (-pp-) **to c. and change** changer constamment d'idées, et projets etc. ◆**chopper** n hachoir m; Sl hélicoptère m. ◆**choppy** a (*sea*) agité.

chopsticks ['tʃɒpstɪks] npl Culin baguettes fpl.

choral ['kɔːrəl] a choral; **c. society** chorale f. ◆**chorister** ['kɒrɪstər] n choriste mf.

chord [kɔːd] n Mus accord m.

chore [tʃɔːr] n travail m (routinier); (*unpleasant*) corvée f; pl (*domestic*) travaux mpl du ménage.

choreographer [kɒrɪ'ɒɡrəfər] n chorégraphe mf.

chortle ['tʃɔːt(ə)l] vi glousser; – n gloussement m.

chorus ['kɔːrəs] n chœur m; (*dancers*) Th troupe f; (*of song*) refrain m; **c. girl** girl f.

chose, chosen [tʃəʊz, 'tʃəʊz(ə)n] see choose.

chowder ['tʃaʊdər] n Am soupe f aux poissons.

Christ [kraɪst] n Christ m. ◆**Christian** ['krɪstʃən] a & n chrétien, -ienne (mf); **C. name** prénom m. ◆**Christi'anity** n christianisme m.

christen ['krɪs(ə)n] vt (*name*) & Rel baptiser. ◆**—ing** n baptême m.

Christmas ['krɪsməs] n Noël m; **at C.** (time) à (la) Noël; **Merry C.** Joyeux Noël; **Father C.** le père Noël; – a (*tree, card, day, party etc*) de Noël; **C. box** étrennes fpl.

chrome [krəʊm] n, ◆**chromium** n chrome m.

chromosome ['krəʊməsəʊm] n chromosome m.

chronic ['krɒnɪk] a (*disease, state etc*) chronique; (*bad*) Sl atroce.

chronicle ['krɒnɪk(ə)l] n chronique f; – vt faire la chronique de.

chronology [krə'nɒlədʒɪ] *n* chronologie *f*. ◆**chrono'logical** *a* chronologique.

chronometer [krə'nɒmɪtər] *n* chronomètre *m*.

chrysanthemum [krɪ'sænθəməm] *n* chrysanthème *m*.

chubby ['tʃʌbɪ] *a* (**-ier, -iest**) (*body*) dodu; (*cheeks*) rebondi. ◆**c.-'cheeked** *a* joufflu.

chuck [tʃʌk] *vt Fam* jeter, lancer; **to c. (in)** *or* (**up**) (*give up*) *Fam* laisser tomber; **to c. away** *Fam* balancer; (*money*) gaspiller; **to c. out** *Fam* balancer.

chuckle ['tʃʌk(ə)l] *vi* glousser, rire; – *n* gloussement *m*.

chuffed [tʃʌft] *a Sl* bien content; (*displeased*) *Iron Sl* pas heureux.

chug [tʃʌɡ] *vi* (**-gg-**) **to c. along** (*of vehicle*) avancer lentement (*en faisant teuf-teuf*).

chum [tʃʌm] *n Fam* copain *m*. ◆**chummy** *a* (**-ier, -iest**) *Fam* amical; **c. with** copain avec.

chump [tʃʌmp] *n* (*fool*) crétin, -ine *mf*.

chunk [tʃʌŋk] *n* (gros) morceau *m*. ◆**chunky** *a* (**-ier, -iest**) (*person*) *Fam* trapu; (*coat, material etc*) de grosse laine.

church [tʃɜːtʃ] *n* église *f*; (*Catholic*) messe *f*; **c. hall** salle *f* paroissiale. ◆**churchgoer** *n* pratiquant, -ante *mf*. ◆**churchyard** *n* cimetière *m*.

churlish ['tʃɜːlɪʃ] *a* (*rude*) grossier; (*bad-tempered*) hargneux.

churn [tʃɜːn] **1** *n* (*for making butter*) baratte *f*; (*milk can*) bidon *m*. **2** *vt* **to c. out** *Pej* produire (*en série*).

chute [ʃuːt] *n* glissière *f*; (*in playground, pool*) toboggan *m*; (*for refuse*) vide-ordures *m inv*.

chutney ['tʃʌtnɪ] *n* condiment *m* épicé (*à base de fruits*).

cider ['saɪdər] *n* cidre *m*.

cigar [sɪ'ɡɑːr] *n* cigare *m*. ◆**ciga'rette** *n* cigarette *f*; **c. end** mégot *m*; **c. holder** fume-cigarette *m inv*; **c. lighter** briquet *m*.

cinch [sɪntʃ] *n* **it's a c.** *Fam* (*easy*) c'est facile; (*sure*) c'est (sûr et) certain.

cinder ['sɪndər] *n* cendre *f*; **c. track** *Sp* cendrée *f*.

Cinderella [sɪndə'relə] *n Liter* Cendrillon *f*; *Fig* parent *m* pauvre.

cine-camera ['sɪnɪkæmrə] *n* caméra *f*.

cinema ['sɪnəmə] *n* cinéma *m*. ◆**cinemagoer** *n* cinéphile *mf*. ◆**cinemascope** *n* cinémascope *m*.

cinnamon ['sɪnəmən] *n Bot Culin* cannelle *f*.

cipher ['saɪfər] *n* (*code, number*) chiffre *m*; (*zero, person*) *Fig* zéro *m*.

circle ['sɜːk(ə)l] *n* (*shape, group, range etc*)

cercle *m*; (*around eyes*) cerne *m*; *Th* balcon *m*; *pl* (*milieux*) milieux *mpl*; – *vt* (*move round*) faire le tour de; (*word etc*) entourer d'un cercle; – *vi* (*of aircraft, bird*) décrire des cercles. ◆**circular** *a* circulaire; – *n* (*letter*) circulaire *f*; (*advertisement*) prospectus *m*. ◆**circulate** *vi* circuler; – *vt* faire circuler. ◆**circu'lation** *n* circulation *f*; *Journ* tirage *m*; **in c.** (*person*) *Fam* dans le circuit.

circuit ['sɜːkɪt] *n* circuit *m*; *Jur Th* tournée *f*; **c. breaker** *El* disjoncteur *m*. ◆**circuitous** [sɜː'kjuːɪtəs] *a* (*route, means*) indirect. ◆**circuitry** *n* *El* circuits *mpl*.

circumcised ['sɜːkəmsaɪzd] *a* circoncis. ◆**circum'cision** *n* circoncision *f*.

circumference [sɜː'kʌmfərəns] *n* circonférence *f*.

circumflex ['sɜːkəmfleks] *n* circonflexe *m*.

circumscribe ['sɜːkəmskraɪb] *vt* circonscrire.

circumspect ['sɜːkəmspekt] *a* circonspect.

circumstance ['sɜːkəmstæns] *n* circonstance *f*; *pl Com* situation *f* financière; **in** *or* **under no circumstances** en aucun cas. ◆**circum'stantial** *a* (*evidence*) *Jur* indirect.

circus ['sɜːkəs] *n Th Hist* cirque *m*.

cirrhosis [sɪ'rəʊsɪs] *n Med* cirrhose *f*.

cistern ['sɪstən] *n* (*in house*) réservoir *m* (d'eau).

citadel ['sɪtəd(ə)l] *n* citadelle *f*.

cite [saɪt] *vt* citer. ◆**citation** [saɪ'teɪʃ(ə)n] *n* citation *f*.

citizen ['sɪtɪz(ə)n] *n Pol Jur* citoyen, -enne *mf*; (*of town*) habitant, -ante *mf*; **Citizens' Band** *Rad* la CB. ◆**citizenship** *n* citoyenneté *f*.

citrus ['sɪtrəs] *a* **c. fruit(s)** agrumes *mpl*.

city ['sɪtɪ] *n* (grande) ville *f*, cité *f*; **c. dweller** citadin, -ine *mf*; **c. centre** centre-ville *m inv*; **c. hall** *Am* hôtel *m* de ville; **c. page** *Journ* rubrique *f* financière.

civic ['sɪvɪk] *a* (*duty*) civique; (*centre*) administratif; (*authorities*) municipal; – *npl* (*social science*) instruction *f* civique.

civil ['sɪv(ə)l] *a* **1** (*rights, war, marriage etc*) civil; **c. defence** défense *f* passive; **c. servant** fonctionnaire *mf*; **c. service** fonction *f* publique. **2** (*polite*) civil. ◆**ci'vilian** *a & n* civil, -ile (*mf*). ◆**ci'vility** *n* civilité *f*.

civilize ['sɪvɪlaɪz] *vt* civiliser. ◆**civili'zation** *n* civilisation *f*.

civvies ['sɪvɪz] *npl* **in c.** *Sl* (habillé) en civil.

clad [klæd] *a* vêtu (**in** de).

claim [kleɪm] *vt* (*one's due etc*) revendiquer, réclamer; (*require*) réclamer; **to c. that**

(*assert*) prétendre que; – *n* (*demand*) prétention *f*, revendication *f*; (*statement*) affirmation *f*, (*complaint*) réclamation *f*; (*right*) droit *m*; (*land*) concession *f*; (**insurance**) **c.** demande *f* d'indemnité; **to lay c.** to prétendre à. ◆**claimant** *n* allocataire *mf*.

clairvoyant [kleə'vɔɪənt] *n* voyant, -ante *mf*.

clam [klæm] *n* (*shellfish*) praire *f*.

clamber ['klæmbər] *vi* **to c. (up)** grimper; **to c. up** (*stairs*) grimper; (*mountain*) gravir.

clammy ['klæmɪ] *a* (*hands etc*) moite (et froid).

clamour ['klæmər] *n* clameur *f*; – *vi* vociférer (**against** contre); **to c. for** demander à grands cris.

clamp [klæmp] *n* crampon *m*; *Carp* serre-joint(s) *m*; (**wheel**) c. *Aut* sabot *m* (de Denver); – *vt* serrer; – *vi* **to c. down** *Fam* sévir (**on** contre). ◆**clampdown** *n* (*limitation*) *Fam* coup *m* d'arrêt, restriction *f*.

clan [klæn] *n* clan *m*.

clandestine [klæn'destɪn] *a* clandestin.

clang [klæŋ] *n* son *m* métallique. ◆**clanger** *n Sl* gaffe *f*; **to drop a c.** faire une gaffe.

clap [klæp] **1** *vti* (**-pp-**) (*applaud*) applaudir; **to c. (one's hands)** battre des mains; – *n* battement *m* (des mains); (*on back*) tape *f*; (*of thunder*) coup *m*. **2** *vt* (**-pp-**) (*put*) *Fam* fourrer. ◆**clapped-'out** *a* (*car, person*) *Sl* crevé. ◆**clapping** *n* applaudissements *mpl*. ◆**claptrap** *n* (*nonsense*) *Fam* boniment *m*.

claret ['klærət] *n* (*wine*) bordeaux *m* rouge.

clarify ['klærɪfaɪ] *vt* clarifier. ◆**clarification** *n* clarification *f*.

clarinet [klærɪ'net] *n* clarinette *f*.

clarity ['klærətɪ] *n* (*of water, expression etc*) clarté *f*.

clash [klæʃ] *vi* (*of plates, pans*) s'entrechoquer; (*of interests, armies*) se heurter; (*of colours*) jurer (**with** avec); (*of people*) se bagarrer; (*coincide*) tomber en même temps (**with** que); – *n* (*noise, of armies*) choc *m*, heurt *m*; (*of interests*) conflit *m*; (*of events*) coïncidence *f*.

clasp [klɑːsp] *vt* (*hold*) serrer; **to c. one's hands** joindre les mains; – *n* (*fastener*) fermoir *m*; (*of belt*) boucle *f*.

class [klɑːs] *n* classe *f*; (*lesson*) cours *m*; (*grade*) *Univ* mention *f*; **the c. of 1987** *Am* la promotion de 1987; – *vt* classer. ◆**classmate** *n* camarade *mf* de classe. ◆**classroom** *n* (*salle f de*) classe *f*.

classic ['klæsɪk] *a* classique; – *n* (*writer, work etc*) classique *m*; **to study classics**

étudier les humanités *fpl*. ◆**classical** *a* classique. ◆**classicism** *n* classicisme *m*.

classify ['klæsɪfaɪ] *vt* classer, classifier. ◆**-ied** *a* (*information*) secret. ◆**classification** *n* classification *f*.

classy ['klɑːsɪ] *a* (**-ier, -iest**) *Fam* chic *inv*.

clatter ['klætər] *n* bruit *m*, fracas *m*.

clause [klɔːz] *n Jur* clause *f*; *Gram* proposition *f*.

claustrophobia [klɔːstrə'fəʊbɪə] *n* claustrophobie *f*. ◆**claustrophobic** *a* claustrophobe.

claw [klɔː] *n* (*of cat, sparrow etc*) griffe *f*; (*of eagle*) serre *f*; (*of lobster*) pince *f*; – *vt* (*scratch*) griffer; **to c. back** (*money etc*) *Pej Fam* repiquer, récupérer.

clay [kleɪ] *n* argile *f*.

clean [kliːn] *a* (**-er, -est**) propre; (*clear-cut*) net; (*fair*) *Sp* loyal; (*joke*) non paillard; (*record*) *Jur* vierge; **c. living** vie *f* saine; **to make a c. breast of it** tout avouer; – *adv* (*utterly*) complètement, carrément; **to break c.** se casser net; **to cut c.** couper net; – *n* **to give sth a c.** nettoyer qch; – *vt* nettoyer; (*wash*) laver; (*wipe*) essuyer; **to c. one's teeth** se brosser *or* se laver les dents; **to c. out** nettoyer; (*empty*) *Fig* vider; **to c. up** nettoyer; (*reform*) *Fig* épurer; – *vi* **to c. (up)** faire le nettoyage. ◆**-ing** *n* nettoyage *m*; (*housework*) ménage *m*; **c. woman** femme *f* de ménage. ◆**-er** *n* (*woman*) femme *f* de ménage; (**dry**) **c.** teinturier, -ière *mf*. ◆**-ly** *adv* (*to break, cut*) net. ◆**-ness** *n* propreté *f*. ◆**clean-'cut** *a* net. ◆**clean-'living** *a* honnête, chaste. ◆**clean-'shaven** *a* rasé (de près). ◆**clean-up** *n Fig* épuration *f*.

cleanliness ['klenlɪnɪs] *n* propreté *f*.

cleanse [klenz] *vt* nettoyer; (*soul, person etc*) *Fig* purifier. ◆**-ing** *a* **c. cream** crème *f* démaquillante. ◆**-er** *n* (*cream, lotion*) démaquillant *m*.

clear [klɪər] *a* (**-er, -est**) (*water, sound etc*) clair; (*glass*) transparent; (*outline, photo*) net, clair; (*mind*) lucide; (*road*) libre, dégagé; (*profit*) net; (*obvious*) évident, clair; (*certain*) certain; (*complete*) entier; **to be c.** (*free of*) être libre de; (*out of*) être hors de; **to make oneself c.** se faire comprendre; **c. conscience** conscience *f* nette *or* tranquille; – *adv* (*quite*) complètement; **c. of** (*away from*) à l'écart de; **to keep** *or* **steer c. of** se tenir à l'écart de; **to get c. of** (*away from*) s'éloigner de; – *vt* (*path, place, table*) débarrasser, dégager; (*land*) défricher; (*fence*) franchir (sans toucher); (*obstacle*) éviter; (*person*) *Jur* disculper;

(*cheque*) compenser; (*goods, debts*) liquider; (*through customs*) dédouaner; (*for security etc*) autoriser; **to c. s.o. of** (*suspicion*) laver qn de; **to c. one's throat** s'éclaircir la gorge; – *vi* **to c. (up)** (*of weather*) s'éclaircir; (*of fog*) se dissiper. ■ **to c. away** *vt* (*remove*) enlever; – *vi* (*of fog*) se dissiper; **to c. off** *vi* (*leave*) *Fam* filer; – *vt* (*table*) débarrasser; **to c. out** *vt* (*empty*) vider; (*clean*) nettoyer; (*remove*) enlever; **to c. up** *vt* (*mystery etc*) éclaircir; – *vti* (*tidy*) ranger. ◆–**ing** *n* (*in woods*) clairière *f*. ◆–**ly** *adv* clairement; (*to understand*) bien, clairement; (*obviously*) évidemment. ◆–**ness** *n* (*of sound*) clarté *f*, netteté *f*; (*of mind*) lucidité *f*. ◆**clearance** *n* (*sale*) soldes *mpl*; (*space*) dégagement *m*; (*permission*) autorisation *f*; (*of cheque*) compensation *f*. ◆**clear-'cut** *a* net. ◆**clear-'headed** *a* lucide.

clearway ['kliɔwei] *n* route *f* à stationnement interdit.

cleavage ['kliːvidʒ] *n* (*split*) clivage *m*; (*of woman*) *Fam* naissance *f* des seins.

cleft [kleft] *a* (*palate*) fendu; (*stick*) fourchu; – *n* fissure *f*.

clement ['klemənt] *a* clément. ◆**clemency** *n* clémence *f*.

clementine ['klemıntaın] *n* clémentine *f*.

clench [klentʃ] *vt* (*press*) serrer.

clergy ['kləːdʒı] *n* clergé *m*. ◆**clergyman** (*pl* **-men**) ecclésiastique *m*.

cleric ['klerık] *n Rel* clerc *m*. ◆**clerical** *a* (*job*) d'employé; (*work*) de bureau; (*error*) d'écriture; *Rel* clérical.

clerk [klɔːk, *Am* klɜːk] *n* employé, -ée *mf* (*de* bureau); *Jur* clerc *m*; (*in store*) *Am* vendeur, -euse *mf*; **c. of the court** *Jur* greffier *m*.

clever ['klevər] *a* (**-er, -est**) intelligent; (*smart, shrewd*) astucieux; (*skilful*) habile (**at sth** à qch, **at doing** à faire); (*ingenious*) ingénieux; (*gifted*) doué; **c. at** (*English etc*) fort en; **c. with one's hands** habile or adroit de ses mains. ◆–**ly** *adv* intelligemment; astucieusement; habilement. ◆–**ness** *n* intelligence *f*; astuce *f*; habileté *f*.

cliché ['kliːʃeı] *n* (*idea*) cliché *m*.

click [klık] **1** *n* déclic *m*, bruit *m* sec; – *vi* faire un déclic; (*of lovers etc*) *Fam* se plaire du premier coup; **it clicked** (*I realized*) *Fam* j'ai compris tout à coup. **2** *vt* **to c. one's heels** *Mil* claquer des talons.

client ['klaıənt] *n* client, -ente *mf*. ◆**clientele** [kliːɑn'tel] *n* clientèle *f*.

cliff [klıf] *n* falaise *f*.

climate ['klaımıt] *n Met* & *Fig* climat *m*; **c.**

of opinion opinion *f* générale. ◆**cli'matic** *a* climatique.

climax ['klaımæks] *n* point *m* culminant; (*sexual*) orgasme *m*; – *vi* atteindre son point culminant.

climb [klaım] *vt* **to c. (up)** (*steps*) monter, gravir; (*hill, mountain*) gravir, faire l'ascension de; (*tree, ladder*) monter à, grimper à; **to c. (over)** (*wall*) escalader; **to c. down (from)** descendre de; – *vi* **to c. (up)** monter; (*of plant*) grimper; **to c. down** descendre; (*back down*) *Fig* en rabattre; – *n* montée *f*. ◆–**ing** *n* montée *f*; (*mountain*) **c.** alpinisme *m*. ◆–**er** *n* grimpeur, -euse *mf*; *Sp* alpiniste *mf*; *Bot* plante *f* grimpante; **social c.** arriviste *mf*.

clinch [klıntʃ] *vt* (*deal, bargain*) conclure; (*argument*) consolider.

cling [klıŋ] *vi* (*pt & pp* **clung**) se cramponner, s'accrocher (**to** à); (*stick*) adhérer (**to** à). ◆–**ing** *a* (*clothes*) collant. ◆**clingfilm** *n* scel-o-frais®*m*, film *m* étirable.

clinic ['klınık] *n* (*private*) clinique *f*; (*health centre*) centre *m* médical. ◆**clinical** *a Med* clinique; *Fig* scientifique, objectif.

clink [klıŋk] *vi* tinter; – *vt* faire tinter; – *n* tintement *m*.

clip [klıp] **1** *vt* (**-pp-**) (*cut*) couper; (*sheep*) tondre; (*hedge*) tailler; (*ticket*) poinçonner; **to c. sth out of** (*newspaper etc*) découper qch dans. **2** *n* (*for paper*) attache *f*, trombone *m*; (*of brooch, of cyclist, for hair*) pince *f*; – *vt* (**-pp-**) **to c. (on)** attacher. **3** *n* (*of film*) extrait *m*; (*blow*) *Fam* taloche *f*. ◆**clipping** *n Journ* coupure *f*. ◆**clippers** *npl* (*for hair*) tondeuse *f*; (*for nails*) pince *f* à ongles; (*pocket-sized, for finger nails*) coupe-ongles *m inv*.

clique [kliːk] *n Pej* clique *f*. ◆**cliquey** *a Pej* exclusif.

cloak [kləuk] *n* (grande) cape *f*; *Fig* manteau *m*; **c. and dagger** (*film etc*) d'espionnage. ◆**cloakroom** *n* vestiaire *m*; (*for luggage*) *Rail* consigne *f*; (*lavatory*) toilettes *fpl*.

clobber ['klɒbər] **1** *vt* (*hit*) *Sl* rosser. **2** *n* (*clothes*) *Sl* affaires *fpl*.

clock [klɒk] *n* (*large*) horloge *f*; (*small*) pendule *f*; *Aut* compteur *m*; **against the c.** *Fig* contre la montre; **round the c.** *Fig* vingt-quatre heures sur vingt-quatre; **c. tower** clocher *m*; – *vt Sp* chronométrer; **to c. up** (*miles*) *Aut Fam* faire; – *vi* **to c. in** or **out** (*of worker*) pointer. ◆**clockwise** *adv* dans le sens des aiguilles d'une montre. ◆**clockwork** *a* mécanique; *Fig* régulier;

– *n* to go like a c. aller comme sur des roulettes.

clod [klɒd] *n* **1** (*of earth*) motte *f*. **2** (*oaf*) *Fam* balourd, -ourde *mf*.

clog [klɒg] **1** *n* (*in shoe*) sabot *m*. **2** *vt* (-**gg**-) to c. (up) (*obstruct*) boucher.

cloister ['klɔɪstər] *n* cloître *m*; – *vt* cloîtrer.

close¹ [kləʊs] *a* (-er, -est) (*place, relative etc*) proche (**to** de); (*collaboration, resemblance, connection*) étroit; (*friend etc*) intime; (*order, contest*) serré; (*study*) rigoureux; (*atmosphere*) Met lourd; (*vowel*) fermé; **c. to** (*near*) près de, proche de; **to c. tears** au bord des larmes; **to have a c. shave** *or* **call** l'échapper belle; – *adv* **c. (by), c. at hand** (tout) près; **c. to** près de; **c. behind** juste derrière; **c. on** (*almost*) Fam pas loin de; **c. together** (*to stand*) serrés; **to follow c.** suivre de près; – *n* (*enclosed area*) enceinte *f*. ◆**c.-'cropped** *a* (*hair*) (coupé) ras. ◆**c.-'knit** *a* très uni. ◆**c.-up** *n* gros plan *m*.

close² [kləʊz] *n* fin *f*, conclusion *f*; **to bring to a c.** mettre fin à; **to draw to a c.** tirer à sa fin; – *vt* fermer; (*discussion*) terminer, clore; (*opening*) boucher; (*road*) barrer; (*gap*) réduire; (*deal*) conclure; **to c. the meeting** lever la séance; **to c. ranks** serrer les rangs; **to c. in** (*enclose*) enfermer; **to c. up** fermer; – *vi* se fermer; (*end*) (se) terminer; **to c. (up)** (*of shop*) fermer; (*of wound*) se refermer; **to c. in** (*approach*) approcher; **to c. in on s.o.** se rapprocher de qn. ∎ **to c. down** *vti* (*close for good*) fermer (définitivement); – *vi* TV terminer les émissions. ◆**c.-down** *n* fermeture *f* (définitive); TV fin *f* (des émissions). ◆**closing** *n* fermeture *f*; (*of session*) clôture *f*; – *a* final; **c. time** heure *f* de fermeture. ◆**closure** ['kləʊʒər] *n* fermeture *f*.

closely ['kləʊslɪ] *adv* (*to link, guard*) étroitement; (*to follow*) de près; (*to listen*) attentivement; **c. contested** très disputé; **to hold s.o. c.** tenir qn contre soi. ◆**closeness** *n* proximité *f*; (*of collaboration etc*) étroitesse *f*; (*of friendship*) intimité *f*; (*of weather*) lourdeur *f*.

closet ['klɒzɪt] *n* (*cupboard*) Am placard *m*; (*wardrobe*) Am penderie *f*.

clot [klɒt] **1** *n* (*of blood*) caillot *m*; – *vt* (-**tt**-) (*blood*) coaguler; – *vi* (*of blood*) se coaguler. **2** *n* (*person*) Fam imbécile mf.

cloth [klɒθ] *n* tissu *m*, étoffe *f*; (*of linen*) toile *f*; (*of wool*) drap *m*; (*for dusting*) chiffon *m*; (*for dishes*) torchon *m*; (*tablecloth*) nappe *f*.

cloth/e [kləʊð] *vt* habiller, vêtir (**in** de).

◆**-ing** *n* habillement *m*; (*clothes*) vêtements *mpl*; **an article of c.** un vêtement.

clothes [kləʊðz] *npl* vêtements *mpl*; **to put one's c. on** s'habiller; **c. shop** magasin *m* d'habillement; **c. brush** brosse *f* à habits; **c. peg,** Am **c. pin** pince *f* à linge; **c. line** corde *f* à linge.

cloud [klaʊd] *n* nuage *m*; (*of arrows, insects*) Fig nuée *f*; – *vt* (*mind, issue*) obscurcir; (*window*) embuer; – *vi* **to c. (over)** (*of sky*) se couvrir. ◆**cloudburst** *n* averse *f*. ◆**cloudy** *a* (-ier, -iest) (*weather*) couvert, nuageux; (*liquid*) trouble.

clout [klaʊt] **1** *n* (*blow*) Fam taloche *f*; – *vt* Fam flanquer une taloche à, talocher. **2** *n* Pol Fam influence *f*, pouvoir *m*.

clove [kləʊv] *n* clou *m* de girofle; **c. of garlic** gousse *f* d'ail.

clover ['kləʊvər] *n* trèfle *m*.

clown [klaʊn] *n* clown *m*; – *vi* **to c. (around)** faire le clown.

cloying ['klɔɪɪŋ] *a* écœurant.

club [klʌb] **1** *n* (*weapon*) matraque *f*, massue *f*; (*golf*) **c.** (*stick*) club *m*; – *vt* (-**bb**-) matraquer. **2** *n* (*society*) club *m*, cercle *m*; – *vi* (-**bb**-) **to c. together** se cotiser (**to buy** pour acheter). **3** *n* & *npl* Cards trèfle *m*. ◆**clubhouse** *n* pavillon *m*.

clubfoot ['klʌbfʊt] *n* pied *m* bot. ◆**club-'footed** *a* pied bot *inv*.

cluck [klʌk] *vi* (*of hen*) glousser.

clue [kluː] *n* indice *m*; (*of crossword*) définition *f*; (*to mystery*) clef *f*; **I don't have a c.** Fam je n'en ai pas la moindre idée. ◆**clueless** *a* Fam stupide.

clump [klʌmp] *n* (*of flowers, trees*) massif *m*.

clumsy ['klʌmzɪ] *a* (-ier, -iest) maladroit; (*shape*) lourd; (*tool*) peu commode. ◆**clumsily** *adv* maladroitement. ◆**clumsiness** *n* maladresse *f*.

clung [klʌŋ] *see* cling.

cluster ['klʌstər] *n* groupe *m*; (*of flowers*) grappe *f*; (*of stars*) amas *m*; – *vi* se grouper.

clutch [klʌtʃ] **1** *vt* (*hold tight*) serrer, étreindre; (*cling to*) se cramponner à; (*grasp*) saisir; – *vi* **to c. at** essayer de saisir; – *n* étreinte *f*. **2** *n* (*apparatus*) Aut embrayage *m*; (*pedal*) pédale *f* d'embrayage. **3** *npl* **s.o.'s clutches** (*power*) les griffes *fpl* de qn.

clutter ['klʌtər] *n* (*objects*) fouillis *m*, désordre *m*; – *vt* **to c. (up)** encombrer (**with** de).

cm *abbr* (*centimetre*) cm.

co- [kəʊ] *pref* co-.

Co *abbr* (*company*) Cie.

coach [kəʊtʃ] **1** *n* (*horse-drawn*) carrosse *m*; Rail voiture *f*, wagon *m*; Aut autocar *m*. **2** *n* (*person*) Sch répétiteur, -trice *mf*; Sp entraîneur m; - vt (pupil) donner des leçons (particulières) à; (sportsman etc) entraîner; **to c. s.o. for** (exam) préparer qn à. ◆**coachman** n (pl -men) cocher m.

coagulate [kəʊˈægjʊleɪt] vi (of blood) se coaguler; - vt coaguler.

coal [kəʊl] n charbon m; Geol houille f; - a (basin etc) houiller; (merchant, fire) de charbon; (cellar, bucket) à charbon. ◆**coalfield** n bassin m houiller. ◆**coalmine** n mine f de charbon.

coalition [kəʊəˈlɪʃ(ə)n] n coalition f.

coarse [kɔːs] a (-er, -est) (person, manners) grossier, vulgaire; (surface) rude; (fabric) grossier; (salt) gros; (accent) commun, vulgaire. ◆**-ness** n grossièreté f; vulgarité f.

coast [kəʊst] **1** n côte f. **2** vi **to c.** (**down** or **along**) (of vehicle etc) descendre en roue libre. ◆**coastal** a côtier. ◆**coaster** n (ship) caboteur m; (for glass etc) dessous m de verre, rond m. ◆**coastguard** n (person) garde m maritime, garde-côte m. ◆**coastline** n littoral m.

coat [kəʊt] n manteau m; (overcoat) pardessus m; (jacket) veste f; (of animal) pelage m; (of paint) couche f; **c. of arms** blason m, armoiries fpl; **c. hanger** cintre m; - vt couvrir, enduire (**with de**); (with chocolate) enrober (**with de**). ◆**-ed** a **c. tongue** langue f chargée. ◆**-ing** n couche f.

coax [kəʊks] vt amadouer, cajoler; **to c. s.o. to do** or **into doing** amadouer qn pour qu'il fasse. ◆**-ing** n cajoleries fpl.

cob [kɒb] n **corn on the c.** épi m de maïs.

cobble [ˈkɒb(ə)l] n pavé m; - vt **to c. together** (text etc) Fam bricoler. ◆**cobbled** a pavé. ◆**cobblestone** n pavé m.

cobbler [ˈkɒblər] n cordonnier m.

cobra [ˈkəʊbrə] n (snake) cobra m.

cobweb [ˈkɒbweb] n toile f d'araignée.

cocaine [kəˈkeɪn] n cocaïne f.

cock [kɒk] **1** n (rooster) coq m; (male bird) (oiseau m) mâle m. **2** vt (gun) armer; **to c.** (**up**) (ears) dresser. ◆**c.-a-doodle-'doo** n & int cocorico (m). ◆**c.-and-'bull story** n histoire f à dormir debout.

cockatoo [kɒkəˈtuː] n (bird) cacatoès m.

cocker [ˈkɒkər] n **c.** (**spaniel**) cocker m.

cockerel [ˈkɒkərəl] n jeune coq m, coquelet m.

cock-eyed [kɒkˈaɪd] a Fam **1** (cross-eyed) bigleux. **2** (crooked) de travers. **3** (crazy) absurde, stupide.

cockle [ˈkɒk(ə)l] n (shellfish) coque f.

cockney [ˈkɒknɪ] a & n cockney (mf).

cockpit [ˈkɒkpɪt] n Av poste m de pilotage.

cockroach [ˈkɒkrəʊtʃ] n (beetle) cafard m.

cocksure [kɒkˈʃʊər] a Fam trop sûr de soi.

cocktail [ˈkɒkteɪl] n (drink) cocktail m; (fruit) **c.** macédoine f (de fruits); **c. party** cocktail m; **prawn c.** crevettes fpl à la mayonnaise.

cocky [ˈkɒkɪ] a (-ier, -iest) Fam trop sûr de soi, arrogant.

cocoa [ˈkəʊkəʊ] n cacao m.

coconut [ˈkəʊkənʌt] n noix f de coco; **c. palm** cocotier m.

cocoon [kəˈkuːn] n cocon m.

cod [kɒd] n morue f; (bought fresh) cabillaud m. ◆**c.-liver 'oil** n huile f de foie de morue.

COD [siːəʊˈdiː] abbr (cash on delivery) livraison f contre remboursement.

coddle [ˈkɒd(ə)l] vt dorloter.

cod/e [kəʊd] n code m; - vt coder. ◆**-ing** n codage m. ◆**codify** vt codifier.

co-educational [kəʊedjuˈkeɪʃən(ə)l] a (school, teaching) mixte.

coefficient [kəʊɪˈfɪʃənt] n Math coefficient m.

coerce [kəʊˈɜːs] vt contraindre. ◆**coercion** n contrainte f.

coexist [kəʊɪɡˈzɪst] vi coexister. ◆**coexistence** n coexistence f.

coffee [ˈkɒfɪ] n café m; **white c.** café m au lait; (ordered in restaurant etc) (café m) crème m; **black c.** café m noir, café nature; **c. bar, c. house** café m, cafétéria f; **c. break** pause-café f; **c. table** table f basse. ◆**coffeepot** n cafetière f.

coffers [ˈkɒfəz] npl (funds) coffres mpl.

coffin [ˈkɒfɪn] n cercueil m.

cog [kɒg] n Tech dent f; (person) Fig rouage m.

cogent [ˈkəʊdʒənt] a (reason, argument) puissant, convaincant.

cogitate [ˈkɒdʒɪteɪt] vi Iron cogiter.

cognac [ˈkɒnjæk] n cognac m.

cohabit [kəʊˈhæbɪt] vi (of unmarried people) vivre en concubinage.

coherent [kəʊˈhɪərənt] a cohérent; (speech) compréhensible. ◆**cohesion** n cohésion f. ◆**cohesive** a cohésif.

cohort [ˈkəʊhɔːt] n (group) cohorte f.

coil [kɔɪl] n (of wire etc) rouleau m; El bobine f; (contraceptive) stérilet m; - vt (rope, hair) enrouler; - vi (of snake etc) s'enrouler.

coin [kɔɪn] n pièce f (de monnaie); (currency) monnaie f; - vt (money) frapper; (word) Fig inventer, forger; **to c. a phrase** pour ainsi dire. ◆**c.-operated**

automatique. ◆**coinage** n (coins) monnaie f; Fig invention f.

coincide [kəʊɪn'saɪd] vi coïncider (with avec). ◆**co'incidence** n coïncidence f. ◆**coinci'dental** a fortuit; **it's c.** c'est une coïncidence.

coke [kəʊk] n **1** (fuel) coke m. **2** (Coca-Cola®) coca m.

colander ['kʌləndər] n (for vegetables etc) passoire f.

cold [kəʊld] n froid m; Med rhume m; **to catch c.** prendre froid; **out in the c.** Fig abandonné, en carafe; – a (-er, -est) froid; **to be** or **feel c.** (of person) avoir froid; **my hands are c.** j'ai les mains froides; **it's c.** (of weather) il fait froid; **to get c.** (of weather) se refroidir; (of food) refroidir; **to get c. feet** Fam se dégonfler; **in c. blood** de sang-froid; **c. cream** crème f de beauté; **c. meats,** Am **c. cuts** Culin assiette f anglaise. ◆**c.-'blooded** a (person) cruel, insensible; (act) de sang-froid. ◆**c.-'shoulder** vt snober. ◆**coldly** adv avec froideur. ◆**coldness** n froideur f.

coleslaw ['kəʊlslɔː] n salade f de chou cru.

colic ['kɒlɪk] n Med coliques fpl.

collaborate [kə'læbəreɪt] vi collaborer (on à). ◆**collabo'ration** n collaboration f. ◆**collaborator** n collaborateur, -trice mf.

collage ['kɒlɑːʒ] n (picture) collage m.

collapse [kə'læps] vi (fall) s'effondrer, s'écrouler; (of government) tomber; (faint) Med se trouver mal; – n effondrement m, écroulement m; (of government) chute f. ◆**collapsible** a (chair etc) pliant.

collar ['kɒlər] n (on garment) col m; (of dog) collier m; **to seize by the c.** saisir au collet; – vt Fam saisir (qn) au collet; Fig Fam retenir (qn); (take, steal) Sl piquer. ◆**collarbone** n clavicule f.

collate [kə'leɪt] vt collationner, comparer (with avec).

colleague ['kɒliːg] n collègue mf, confrère m.

collect [kə'lekt] vt (pick up) ramasser; (gather) rassembler, recueillir; (taxes) percevoir; (rent, money) encaisser; (stamps etc as hobby) collectionner; (fetch, call for) (passer) prendre; – vi (of dust) s'accumuler; (of people) se rassembler; **to c. for** (in street, church) quêter pour; – adv **to call** or **phone c.** Am téléphoner en PCV. ◆**collection** [kə'lekʃ(ə)n] n ramassage m; (of taxes) perception f; (of objects) collection f; (of poems etc) recueil m; (of money in church etc) quête f; (of mail) levée f. ◆**collective** a collectif. ◆**collectively** adv

collectivement. ◆**collector** n (of stamps etc) collectionneur, -euse mf.

college ['kɒlɪdʒ] n Pol Rel Sch collège m; (university) université f; Mus conservatoire m; **teachers' training c.** école f normale; **art c.** école f des beaux-arts; **agricultural c.** institut m d'agronomie, lycée m agricole.

collide [kə'laɪd] vi entrer en collision (with avec), se heurter (with à). ◆**collision** n collision f; Fig conflit m, collision f.

colliery ['kɒlɪərɪ] n houillère f.

colloquial [kə'ləʊkwɪəl] a (word etc) familier. ◆**colloquialism** n expression f familière.

collusion [kə'luːʒ(ə)n] n collusion f.

collywobbles ['kɒlɪwɒb(ə)lz] npl **to have the c.** (feel nervous) Fam avoir la frousse.

cologne [kə'ləʊn] n eau f de Cologne.

colon ['kəʊlən] n **1** Gram deux-points m inv. **2** Anat côlon m.

colonel ['kɜːn(ə)l] n colonel m.

colony ['kɒlənɪ] n colonie f. ◆**colonial** [kə'ləʊnɪəl] a colonial. ◆**coloni'zation** n colonisation f. ◆**colonize** vt coloniser.

colossal [kə'lɒs(ə)l] a colossal.

colour ['kʌlər] n couleur f; – a (photo, television) en couleurs; (television set) couleur inv; (problem) racial; **c. supplement** Journ supplément m illustré; **off c.** (not well) mal fichu; (improper) scabreux; – vt colorer; **to c. (in)** (drawing) colorier. ◆**c.-blind** a (person, pencil) de couleur; (glass, water) coloré. ◆**—ed** a (person, pencil) de couleur; (glass, water) coloré. ◆**—ing** n coloration f; (with crayons) coloriage m; (hue, effect) coloris m; (matter) colorant m. ◆**colour-blind** a daltonien. ◆**colourful** a (crowd, story) coloré; (person) pittoresque.

colt [kəʊlt] n (horse) poulain m.

column ['kɒləm] n colonne f. ◆**columnist** n Journ chroniqueur m; **gossip c.** échotier, -ière mf.

coma ['kəʊmə] n coma m; **in a c.** dans le coma.

comb [kəʊm] n peigne m; – vt peigner; (search) fouiller; **to c. one's hair** se peigner; **to c. out** (hair) démêler.

combat ['kɒmbæt] n combat m; – vti combattre (for pour). ◆**'combatant** n combattant, -ante mf.

combin/e [kəm'baɪn] vt unir, joindre (with à); (elements, sounds) combiner; (qualities, efforts) allier, joindre; – vi s'unir; **everything combined to...** tout s'est ligué pour .... ◆**—ed** a (effort) conjugué; **c. wealth**/etc (put together) richesses/etc fpl réunies; **c. forces** Mil forces fpl alliées. ◆**combi'nation** n combinaison f; (of

qualities) réunion *f*; (*of events*) concours *m*;
in c. with en association avec.

combine² [ˈkɒmbaɪn] *n Com* cartel *m*; **c. harvester** *Agr* moissonneuse-batteuse *f*.

combustion [kəmˈbʌstʃ(ə)n] *n* combustion *f*.

come [kʌm] *vi* (*pt* **came**, *pp* **come**) venir (**from de**, **to** à); (*arrive*) arriver, venir; (*happen*) arriver; **c. and see me** viens me voir; **I've just c. from** j'arrive de; **to c. for** venir chercher; **to c. home** rentrer; **coming!** j'arrive!; **c. now!** voyons!; **to c. as a surprise (to)** surprendre; **to c. near** *or* **close to doing** faillir faire; **to c. on page 2** se trouver à la page 2; **nothing came of it** ça n'a abouti à rien; **to c. to** (*understand etc*) en venir à; (*a decision*) parvenir à; **to c. to an end** toucher à sa fin; **to c. true** se réaliser; **c. May/etc** *Fam* en mai/*etc*; **the life to c.** la vie future; **how c. that ...?** *Fam* comment se fait-il que ...? ■ **to c. about** *vi* (*happen*) se faire, arriver; **to c. across** *vi* (*of speech*) faire de l'effet; (*of feelings*) se montrer; – *vt* (*thing, person*) tomber sur; **to c. along** *vi* venir (**with** avec); (*progress*) avancer; **c. along!** allons!; **to c. at** *vt* (*attack*) attaquer; **to c. away** *vi* (*leave, come off*) partir; **to c. back** *vi* revenir; (*return home*) rentrer. ◆**come-back** *n* retour *m*; *Th Pol* rentrée *f*; (*retort*) réplique *f*; **to c. by** *vt* (*obtain*) obtenir; (*find*) trouver; **to c. down** *vi* descendre; (*of rain, price*) tomber. ◆**comedown** *n Fam* humiliation *f*. **to c. forward** *vi* (*make oneself known, volunteer*) se présenter; **to c. forward with** offrir, suggérer; **to c. in** *vi* entrer; (*of tide*) monter; (*of train, athlete*) arriver; *Pol* arriver au pouvoir; (*of clothes*) devenir à la mode, se faire beaucoup; (*of money*) rentrer; **to c. in for** recevoir; **to c. into** (*money*) hériter de; **to c. off** *vi* se détacher, partir; (*succeed*) réussir; (*happen*) avoir lieu; (*fare, manage*) s'en tirer; – *vt* (*fall from*) tomber de; (*get down from*) descendre de; **to c. on** *vi* (*follow*) suivre; (*progress*) avancer; (*start*) commencer; (*arrive*) arriver; (*of play*) être joué; **c. on!** allez!; **to c. out** *vi* sortir; (*of sun, book*) paraître; (*of stain*) s'enlever, partir; (*of secret*) être révélé; (*of photo*) réussir; **to c. out on strike** se mettre en grève; **to c. over** *vi* (*visit*) venir, passer; **to c. over funny** *or* **peculiar** se trouver mal; – *vt* (*take hold of*) saisir (*qn*), prendre (*qn*); **to c. round** *vi* (*visit*) venir, passer; (*regain consciousness*) revenir à soi; **to c. through** *vi* (*survive*) s'en tirer; – *vt* se tirer indemne de; **to c. to** *vi* (*regain consciousness*) revenir

à soi; (*amount to*) *Com* revenir à, faire; **to c. under** *vi* être classé sous; (*s.o.'s influence*) tomber sous; **to c. up** *vi* (*rise*) monter; (*of plant*) sortir; (*of question, job*) se présenter; **to c. up to** (*reach*) arriver jusqu'à; (*one's hopes*) répondre à; **to c. up against** (*wall, problem*) se heurter à; **to c. up with** (*idea, money*) trouver; **to c. upon** *vt* (*book, reference etc*) tomber sur. ◆**coming** *a* (*future*) à venir; – *n Rel* avènement *m*; **comings and goings** allées *fpl* et venues.

comedy [ˈkɒmɪdɪ] *n* comédie *f*. ◆**co'median** *n* (*actor m*) comique *m*, actrice *f* comique.

comet [ˈkɒmɪt] *n* comète *f*.

comeuppance [kʌmˈʌpəns] *n* **he got his c.** *Pej Fam* il n'a eu que ce qu'il mérite.

comfort [ˈkʌmfət] *n* confort *m*; (*consolation*) réconfort *m*, consolation *f*; (*peace of mind*) tranquillité *f* d'esprit; **to like one's comforts** aimer ses aises *fpl*; **c. station** *Am* toilettes *fpl*; – *vt* consoler; (*cheer*) réconforter. ◆**—able** *a* (*chair, house etc*) confortable; (*rich*) aisé; **he's c.** (*in chair etc*) il est à l'aise, il est bien; **make yourself c.** mets-toi à l'aise. ◆**—ably** *adv* **c.** **off** (*rich*) à l'aise. ◆**—er** *n* (*baby's dummy*) sucette *f*; (*quilt*) *Am* édredon *m*. ◆**comfy** *a* (*-ier, -iest*) (*chair etc*) *Fam* confortable; **I'm c.** je suis bien.

comic [ˈkɒmɪk] *a* comique; – *n* (*actor*) comique *m*; (*actress*) actrice *f* comique; (*magazine*) illustré *m*; **c. strip** bande *f* dessinée. ◆**comical** *a* comique, drôle.

comma [ˈkɒmə] *n Gram* virgule *f*.

command [kəˈmɑːnd] *vt* (*order*) commander (**s.o. to do** à qn de faire); (*control, dominate*) commander (*régiment, vallée etc*); (*be able to use*) disposer de; (*respect*) imposer (**from** à); (*require*) exiger; – *vi* commander; – *n* ordre *m*; (*power*) commandement *m*; (*troops*) troupes *fpl*; (*mastery*) maîtrise *f* (**of** de); **at one's c.** (*disposal*) à sa disposition; **to be in c. (of)** (*ship, army etc*) commander; (*situation*) être maître de (*de*). ◆**—ing** *a* (*authoritative*) imposant; (*position*) dominant; **c. officer** commandant *m*. ◆**—er** *n* chef *m*; *Mil* commandant *m*. ◆**—ment** *n Rel* commandement *m*.

commandant [ˈkɒməndænt] *n Mil* commandant *m* (*d'un camp etc*). ◆**comman'deer** *vt* réquisitionner.

commando [kəˈmɑːndəʊ] *n* (*pl* *-os* *or* *-oes*) *Mil* commando *m*.

commemorate [kəˈmeməreɪt] *vt* commémorer. ◆**commemo'ration** *n* commémoration f. ◆**commemorative** a commémoratif.

commence [kə'mens] vti commencer (**doing** à faire). ◆**—ment** n commencement m; Univ Am remise f des diplômes.

commend [kə'mend] vt (praise) louer; (recommend) recommander; (entrust) confier (**to** à). ◆**—able** a louable. ◆**commen'dation** n éloge m.

commensurate [kə'menʃərət] a proportionné (**to, with** à).

comment ['kɒment] n commentaire m, remarque f; – vi faire des commentaires or des remarques (**on** sur); **to c. on** (text, event, news item) commenter; **to c. that** remarquer que. ◆**commentary** n commentaire m; (**live**) c. TV Rad reportage m. ◆**commentate** vi TV Rad faire un reportage (**on** sur). ◆**commentator** n TV Rad reporter m, commentateur, -trice mf.

commerce ['kɒmɜːs] n commerce mf. ◆**co'mmercial 1** a commercial; (street) commerçant; (traveller) de commerce. **2** n (advertisement) TV publicité f; **the commercials** TV la publicité. ◆**co'mmercialize** vt (event) Pej transformer en une affaire de gros sous.

commiserate [kə'mɪzəreɪt] vi **to c. with** s.o. s'apitoyer sur (le sort de) qn. ◆**commise-'ration** n commisération f.

commission [kə'mɪʃ(ə)n] n (fee, group) commission f; (order for work) commande f; **out of c.** hors service; **to get one's c.** Mil être nommé officier; – vt (artist) passer une commande à; (book) commander; Mil nommer (qn) officier; **to c. to do** charger de faire. ◆**commissio'naire** n (in hotel etc) commissionnaire m. ◆**commissioner** n Pol commissaire m; (police) c. préfet m (de police).

commit [kə'mɪt] vt (-tt-) (crime) commettre; (entrust) confier (**to** à); **to c. suicide** se suicider; **to c. to memory** apprendre par cœur; **to c. to prison** incarcérer; **to c. oneself** s'engager (**to** à); (compromise oneself) se compromettre. ◆**—ment** n obligation f; (promise) engagement m.

committee [kə'mɪtɪ] n comité m.

commodity [kə'mɒdɪtɪ] n produit m, article m.

common ['kɒmən] 1 a (-er, -est) (shared, vulgar) commun; (frequent) courant, fréquent, commun; **the c. man** l'homme m du commun; **in c.** (shared) en commun (**with** avec); **to have nothing in c.** n'avoir rien de commun (**with** avec); **in c. with** (like) comme; **c. law** droit m coutumier; C.

Market Marché m commun; **c. room** salle f commune; **c. or garden** ordinaire. 2 n (land) terrain m communal; **House of Commons** Pol Chambre f des Communes; **the Commons** Pol les Communes fpl. ◆**—er** n roturier, -ière mf. ◆**—ly** adv (generally) communément; (vulgarly) d'une façon commune. ◆**—ness** n fréquence f; – n banalité f. ◆**commonplace** a banal; – n banalité f. ◆**common'sense** n sens m commun; – a sensé.

Commonwealth ['kɒmənwelθ] n **the C.** le Commonwealth.

commotion [kə'məʊʃ(ə)n] n agitation f.

communal [kə'mjuːn(ə)l] a (of the community) communautaire; (shared) commun. ◆**—ly** adv en commun; (to live) en communauté.

commune 1 ['kɒmjuːn] n (district) commune f; (group) communauté f. 2 [kə'mjuːn] vi Rel & Fig communier (**with** avec). ◆**co'mmunion** n communion f; (Holy) C. communion f.

communicate [kə'mjuːnɪkeɪt] vt communiquer; (illness) transmettre; – vi (of person, rooms etc) communiquer. ◆**communi-'cation** n communication f; **c. cord** Rail signal m d'alarme. ◆**communicative** a communicatif. ◆**communiqué** n Pol communiqué m.

communism ['kɒmjʊnɪz(ə)m] n communisme m. ◆**communist** a & n communiste (mf).

community [kə'mjuːnɪtɪ] n communauté f; – a (rights, life etc) communautaire; **the student** c. les étudiants mpl; **c. centre** centre m socio-culturel; **c. worker** animateur, -trice mf socio-culturel(le).

commut/e [kə'mjuːt] 1 vt Jur commuer (**to** en). 2 vi (travel) faire la navette (**to work** pour se rendre à son travail). ◆**—ing** n trajets mpl journaliers. ◆**—er** n banlieusard, -arde mf; **c. train** train m de banlieue.

compact 1 [kəm'pækt] a (car, crowd, substance) compact; (style) condensé; **c. disc** ['kɒmpækt] disque m compact. 2 ['kɒmpækt] n (for face powder) poudrier m.

companion [kəm'pænjən] n (person) compagnon m, compagne f; (handbook) manuel m. ◆**companionship** n camaraderie f.

company ['kʌmpənɪ] n (fellowship, firm) compagnie f; (guests) invités, amis mpl; **to keep s.o. c.** tenir compagnie à qn; **to keep good c.** avoir de bonnes fréquentations; **he's good c.** c'est un bon compagnon.

compar/e [kəm'peər] vt comparer; **compared to** or **with** en comparaison de; − vi être comparable, se comparer (**with** à). **◆−able** ['kɒmpərəb(ə)l] a comparable. **◆comparative** a comparatif; (relative) relatif. **◆comparatively** adv relativement. **◆comparison** n comparaison f (**between** entre; **with** à, avec).

compartment [kəm'pɑːtmənt] n compartiment m. **◆compart'mentalize** vt compartimenter.

compass ['kʌmpəs] n **1** (for navigation) boussole f; Nau compas m; (range) Fig portée f. **2** (for measuring etc) Am compas m; (**pair of**) **compasses** compas m.

compassion [kəm'pæʃ(ə)n] n compassion f. **◆compassionate** a compatissant; **on c. grounds** pour raisons de famille.

compatible [kəm'pætɪb(ə)l] a compatible. **◆compati'bility** n compatibilité f.

compatriot [kəm'pætrɪət, kəm'peɪtrɪət] n compatriote mf.

compel [kəm'pel] vt (-ll-) contraindre (**to do** à faire); (respect etc) imposer (**from** à); **compelled to do** contraint de faire. **◆compelling** a irrésistible.

compendium [kəm'pendɪəm] n abrégé m.

compensate ['kɒmpənseɪt] vt **to c. s.o.** (with payment, recompense) dédommager qn (**for** de); **to c. for sth** (make up for) compenser qch; − vi compenser. **◆compen'sation** n (financial) dédommagement m; (consolation) compensation f, dédommagement m; **in c. for** en compensation de.

compère ['kɒmpeər] n TV Rad animateur, -trice mf, présentateur, -trice mf; − vt (a show) animer, présenter.

compete [kəm'piːt] vi prendre part (**in** à), concourir (**in** à); (vie) rivaliser (**with** avec); Com faire concurrence (**with** à); **to c. for** (prize etc) concourir pour; **to c. in a rally** courir dans un rallye.

competent ['kɒmpɪtənt] a (capable) compétent (**to do** pour faire); (sufficient) suffisant. **◆−ly** adv avec compétence. **◆competence** n compétence f.

competition [kɒmpə'tɪʃ(ə)n] n (rivalry) compétition f, concurrence f; **a c.** (contest) un concours; Sp une compétition. **◆com'petitive** a (price, market) compétitif; (selection) par concours; (person) aimant la compétition; **c. exam(ination)** concours m. **◆com'petitor** n concurrent, -ente mf.

compil/e [kəm'paɪl] vt (dictionary) rédiger; (list) dresser; (documents) compiler. **◆−er** n rédacteur, -trice mf.

complacent [kəm'pleɪsənt] a content de soi. **◆complacence** n, **◆complacency** n autosatisfaction f, contentement m de soi.

complain [kəm'pleɪn] vi se plaindre (**of, about de; that** que). **◆complaint** n plainte f; Com réclamation f; Med maladie f; (**cause for**) **c.** sujet m de plainte.

complement ['kɒmplɪmənt] n complément m; − ['kɒmplɪment] vt compléter. **◆comple'mentary** a complémentaire.

complete [kəm'pliːt] a (total) complet; (finished) achevé; (downright) Pej parfait; − vt (add sth missing) compléter; (finish) achever; (a form) remplir. **◆−ly** adv complètement. **◆completion** n achèvement m, réalisation f.

complex ['kɒmpleks] **1** a complexe. **2** n (feeling, buildings) complexe m; **housing c.** grand ensemble m. **◆com'plexity** n complexité f.

complexion [kəm'plekʃ(ə)n] n (of the face) teint m; Fig caractère m.

compliance [kəm'plaɪəns] n (agreement) conformité f (**with** avec).

complicat/e ['kɒmplɪkeɪt] vt compliquer. **◆−ed** a compliqué. **◆compli'cation** n complication f.

complicity [kəm'plɪsɪti] n complicité f.

compliment ['kɒmplɪmənt] n compliment m; pl (of author) hommages mpl; **compliments of the season** meilleurs vœux pour Noël et la nouvelle année; − ['kɒmplɪment] vt complimenter. **◆compli'mentary** a **1** (flattering) flatteur. **2** (free) à titre gracieux; (ticket) de faveur.

comply [kəm'plaɪ] vi obéir (**with** à); (request) accéder à.

component [kəm'pəunənt] a (part) constituant; − n (chemical, electronic) composant m; Tech pièce f; (element) Fig composante f.

compos/e [kəm'pəuz] vt composer; **to c. oneself** se calmer. **◆−ed** a calme. **◆−er** n Mus compositeur, -trice mf. **◆compo-'sition** n Mus Liter Ch composition f; Sch rédaction f. **◆composure** n calme m, sang-froid m.

compost ['kɒmpɒst, Am 'kɒmpəust] n compost m.

compound 1 ['kɒmpaund] n (substance, word) composé m; (area) enclos m; − a Ch composé; (sentence, number) complexe. **2** [kəm'paund] vt Ch composer; (increase) Fig aggraver.

comprehend [kɒmprɪ'hend] vt comprendre. **◆comprehensible** a compréhensible. **◆comprehension** n compréhension

f. ◆**comprehensive** a complet; (*knowledge*) étendu; (*view, measure*) d'ensemble; (*insurance*) tous-risques *inv*; – a & n c. (**school**) – collège m d'enseignement secondaire.

compress [kəm'pres] *vt* comprimer; (*ideas etc*) *Fig* condenser. ◆**compression** *n* compression *f*; condensation *f*.

comprise [kəm'praɪz] *vt* comprendre, englober.

compromise ['kɒmprəmaɪz] *vt* compromettre; – *vi* accepter un compromis; – *n* compromis *m*; – a (*solution*) de compromis.

compulsion [kəm'pʌlʃ(ə)n] *n* contrainte *f*. ◆**compulsive** a (*behaviour*) *Psy* compulsif; (*smoker, gambler*) invétéré; **c. liar** mythomane *mf*.

compulsory [kəm'pʌlsərɪ] a obligatoire.

compunction [kəm'pʌŋkʃ(ə)n] *n* scrupule *m*.

comput/e [kəm'pjuːt] *vt* calculer. ◆**—ing** *n* informatique *f*. ◆**computer** *n* ordinateur *m*; – a (*system*) informatique; (*course*) d'informatique; **c. operator** opérateur, -trice *mf* sur ordinateur; **c. science** informatique *f*; **c. scientist** informaticien, -ienne *mf*. ◆**computerize** *vt* informatiser.

comrade ['kɒmreɪd] *n* camarade *mf*. ◆**comradeship** *n* camaraderie *f*.

con [kɒn] *vt* (**-nn-**) *Sl* rouler, escroquer; **to be conned** se faire avoir *or* rouler; – *n Sl* escroquerie *f*; **c. man** escroc *m*.

concave ['kɒnkeɪv] a concave.

conceal [kən'siːl] *vt* (*hide*) dissimuler (**from** s.o. à qn); (*plan etc*) tenir secret. ◆**—ment** *n* dissimulation *f*.

concede [kən'siːd] *vt* concéder (**to** à, **that** que); – *vi* céder.

conceit [kən'siːt] *n* vanité *f*. ◆**conceited** a vaniteux. ◆**conceitedly** *adv* avec vanité.

conceiv/e [kən'siːv] *vt* (*idea, child etc*) concevoir; – *vi* (*of woman*) concevoir; **to c. of** concevoir. ◆**—able** a concevable, envisageable. ◆**—ably** *adv* yes, c. oui, c'est concevable.

concentrate ['kɒnsəntreɪt] *vt* concentrer; – *vi* se concentrer (**on** sur); **to c. on doing** s'appliquer à faire. ◆**concen'tration** *n* concentration *f*; **c. camp** camp *m* de concentration.

concentric [kən'sentrɪk] a concentrique.

concept ['kɒnsept] *n* concept *m*. ◆**con'ception** *n* (*idea*) & *Med* conception *f*.

concern [kən'sɜːn] *vt* concerner; **to c. oneself with, be concerned with** s'occuper de; **to be concerned about** s'inquiéter de; –

n (*matter*) affaire *f*; (*anxiety*) inquiétude *f*; (*share*) *Com* intérêt(s) *m(pl)* (**in** dans); (*business*) c. entreprise *f*. ◆**—ed** a (*anxious*) inquiet; **the department** c. le service compétent; **the main person c.** le principal intéressé. ◆**—ing** *prep* en ce qui concerne.

concert ['kɒnsət] *n* concert *m*; **in c.** (*together*) de concert (**with** avec). ◆**c.-goer** n habitué, -ée *mf* des concerts. ◆**con'certed** a (*effort*) concerté.

concertina [kɒnsə'tiːnə] *n* concertina *m*; **c. crash** *Aut* carambolage *m*.

concession [kən'seʃ(ə)n] *n* concession *f* (**to** à).

conciliate [kən'sɪlɪeɪt] *vt* **to c. s.o.** (*win over*) se concilier qn; (*soothe*) apaiser qn. ◆**concili'ation** *n* conciliation *f*; apaisement *m*. ◆**conciliatory** [kən'sɪlɪətərɪ, *Am* -tɔːrɪ] a conciliant.

concise [kən'saɪs] a concis. ◆**—ly** *adv* avec concision. ◆**—ness**, ◆**concision** a concision *f*.

conclud/e [kən'kluːd] *vt* (*end, settle*) conclure; **to c. that** (*infer*) conclure que; – *vi* (*of event etc*) se terminer (**with** par); (*of speaker*) conclure. ◆**—ing** a final. ◆**conclusion** *n* conclusion *f*; **in c.** pour conclure. ◆**conclusive** a concluant. ◆**conclusively** *adv* de manière concluante.

concoct [kən'kɒkt] *vt* *Culin Pej* concocter, confectionner; (*scheme*) *Fig* combiner. ◆**concoction** *n* (*substance*) *Pej* mixture *f*; (*act*) confection *f*; *Fig* combinaison *f*.

concord ['kɒŋkɔːd] *n* concorde *f*.

concourse ['kɒŋkɔːs] *n* (*hall*) *Am* hall *m*; *Rail* hall *m*, salle *f* des pas perdus.

concrete ['kɒŋkriːt] **1** a (*real, positive*) concret. **2** n béton *m*; – a en béton; **c. mixer** bétonnière *f*, bétonneuse *f*.

concur [kən'kɜːr] *vi* (**-rr-**) **1** (*agree*) être d'accord (**with** avec). **2** **to c. to** (*contribute*) concourir à.

concurrent [kən'kʌrənt] a simultané. ◆**—ly** *adv* simultanément.

concussion [kən'kʌʃ(ə)n] *n* *Med* commotion *f* (cérébrale).

condemn [kən'dem] *vt* condamner; (*building*) déclarer inhabitable. ◆**condem'nation** *n* condamnation *f*.

condense [kən'dens] *vt* condenser; – *vi* se condenser. ◆**conden'sation** *n* condensation *f* (**of** de); (*mist*) buée *f*.

condescend [kɒndɪ'send] *vi* condescendre (**to do** à faire). ◆**condescension** *n* condescendance *f*.

condiment ['kɒndɪmənt] *n* condiment *m*.

condition [kənˈdɪʃ(ə)n] **1** n (stipulation, circumstance, rank) condition f; (state) état m, condition f; **on c. that** one does à condition de faire, à condition que l'on fasse; **in/out of c.** en bonne/mauvaise forme. **2** vt (action etc) déterminer, conditionner; **to c. s.o.** Psy conditionner qn (**into doing** à faire). ◆**conditional** a conditionnel; **to be c. upon** dépendre de. ◆**conditioner** n (hair) n après-shampooing m.

condo [ˈkɒndəʊ] n abbr (pl -os) Am = **condominium**.

condolences [kənˈdəʊlənsɪz] npl condoléances fpl.

condom [ˈkɒndəm] n préservatif m, capote f (anglaise).

condominium [kɒndəˈmɪnɪəm] n Am (building) (immeuble m en) copropriété f; (apartment) appartement m dans une copropriété.

condone [kənˈdəʊn] vt (forgive) pardonner; (overlook) fermer les yeux sur.

conducive [kənˈdjuːsɪv] a **c. to** favorable à.

conduct [ˈkɒndʌkt] n (behaviour, directing) conduite f; — [kənˈdʌkt] vt (lead) conduire, mener; (orchestra) diriger; (electricity etc) conduire; **to c. oneself** se conduire. ◆**-ed** a (visit) guidé; **c. tour** excursion f accompagnée. ◆**conductor** n Mus chef m d'orchestre; (on bus) receveur m; Rail Am chef m de train; (metal, cable etc) conducteur m. ◆**conductress** n (on bus) receveuse f.

cone [kəʊn] n cône m; (of ice cream) cornet m; (paper) c. cornet m (de papier); **traffic c.** cône m de chantier.

confectioner [kənˈfekʃənər] n (of sweets) confiseur, -euse mf; (of cakes) pâtissier, -ière mf. ◆**confectionery** n (sweets) confiserie f; (cakes) pâtisserie f.

confederate [kənˈfedərət] a confédéré; — n (accomplice) complice mf, acolyte m. ◆**confederacy** n, ◆**confede'ration** n confédération f.

confer [kənˈfɜːr] **1** vt (**-rr-**) (grant) conférer (**on** à); (degree) Univ remettre. **2** vi (**-rr-**) (talk together) conférer, se consulter.

conference [ˈkɒnfərəns] n conférence f; (scientific etc) congrès m.

confess [kənˈfes] **1** vt avouer, confesser (that que, to à); — vi avouer; **to c. to** (crime etc) avouer, confesser. **2** vt Rel confesser; — vi se confesser. ◆**confession** n aveu m, confession f; Rel confession f. ◆**confessional** n Rel confessional m.

confetti [kənˈfetɪ] n confettis mpl.

confide [kənˈfaɪd] vt confier (**to** à, that que);

— vi **to c. in** (talk to) se confier à. ◆**'confidant, -ante** [-ænt] n confident, -ente mf. ◆**'confidence** n (trust) confiance f; (secret) confidence f; (self-)c. confiance f en soi; **in c.** en confidence; **motion of no c.** Pol motion f de censure; **c. trick** escroquerie f; **c. trickster** escroc m. ◆**'confident** a sûr, assuré; (self-)c. sûr de soi. ◆**confi'dential** a confidentiel; (secretary) particulier. ◆**confi'dentially** adv en confidence. ◆**'confidently** adv avec confiance.

configuration [kənfɪgjʊˈreɪʃ(ə)n] n configuration f.

confine [kənˈfaɪn] vt enfermer, confiner (**to, in** dans); (limit) limiter (**to** à); **to c. oneself to doing** se limiter à faire. ◆**-ed** a (atmosphere) confiné; (space) réduit; **c. to bed** obligé de garder le lit. ◆**-ement** n Med couches fpl; Jur emprisonnement m. ◆**'confines** npl limites fpl, confins mpl.

confirm [kənˈfɜːm] vt confirmer (that que); (strengthen) raffermir. ◆**-ed** a (bachelor) endurci; (smoker, habit) invétéré. ◆**confir'mation** n confirmation f; raffermissement m.

confiscate [ˈkɒnfɪskeɪt] vt confisquer (**from s.o.** à qn). ◆**confis'cation** n confiscation f.

conflagration [kɒnfləˈgreɪʃ(ə)n] n (grand) incendie m, brasier m.

conflict [ˈkɒnflɪkt] n conflit m; — [kənˈflɪkt] vi être en contradiction, être incompatible (**with** avec); (of dates, events, TV programmes) tomber en même temps (**with** que). ◆**-ing** a (views, theories etc) contradictoires; (dates) incompatibles.

confluence [ˈkɒnflʊəns] n (of rivers) confluent m.

conform [kənˈfɔːm] vi se conformer (**to, with** à); (of ideas etc) être en conformité. ◆**conformist** a & n conformiste (mf). ◆**conformity** n (likeness) conformité f; Pej conformisme m.

confound [kənˈfaʊnd] vt confondre; **c. him!** que le diable l'emporte! ◆**-ed** a (damned) Fam sacré.

confront [kənˈfrʌnt] vt (danger) affronter; (problems) faire face à; **to c. s.o.** (be face to face with) se trouver en face de qn; (oppose) s'opposer à qn; **to c. s.o. with** (person) confronter qn avec; (thing) mettre qn en présence de. ◆**confron'tation** n confrontation f.

confus/e [kənˈfjuːz] vt (perplex) confondre; (muddle) embrouiller; **to c. with** (mistake for) confondre avec. ◆**-ed** a (situation, *noises etc*) confus; **to be c.** (*of person*) s'y perdre; **to get c.** s'embrouiller. ◆**—ing** a difficile à comprendre, déroutant. ◆**con-fusion** n confusion f; **in c.** en désordre.

congeal [kən'dʒiːl] vt figer; – vi (se) figer.

congenial [kən'dʒiːnɪəl] a sympathique.

congenital [kən'dʒenɪtl] a congénital.

congested [kən'dʒestɪd] a (*street*) encombré; (*town*) surpeuplé; *Med* congestionné. ◆**congestion** n (*traffic*) encombrement(s) m(pl); (*overcrowding*) surpeuplement m; *Med* congestion f.

Congo ['kɒŋgəʊ] n Congo m.

congratulate [kən'grætʃuleɪt] vt féliciter (s.o. on sth qn de qch). ◆**congratu-'lations** npl félicitations fpl (on pour). ◆**congratu'latory** a (*telegram etc*) de félicitations.

congregate ['kɒŋgrɪgeɪt] vi se rassembler. ◆**congre'gation** n (*worshippers*) assemblée f, fidèles mfpl.

congress ['kɒŋgres] n congrès m; **C.** *Pol Am* le Congrès. ◆**Congressman** n (pl -men) *Am* membre du Congrès. ◆**Con-'gressional** a *Am* du Congrès.

conic(al) ['kɒnɪk(əl)] a conique.

conifer ['kɒnɪfər] n (*tree*) conifère m.

conjecture [kən'dʒektʃər] n conjecture f; – vt conjecturer; – vi faire des conjectures. ◆**conjectural** a conjectural.

conjugal ['kɒndʒʊgəl] a conjugal.

conjugate ['kɒndʒʊgeɪt] vt (*verb*) conjuguer. ◆**conju'gation** n *Gram* conjugaison f.

conjunction [kən'dʒʌŋkʃ(ə)n] n *Gram* conjonction f; **in c. with** conjointement avec.

conjur/e ['kʌndʒər] vt **to c. up** (*by magic*) faire apparaître; **to c. up** (*memories etc*) *Fig* évoquer. ◆**—ing** n prestidigitation f. ◆**—er** n prestidigitateur, -trice mf.

conk [kɒŋk] **1** n (*nose*) *Sl* pif m. **2** vi **to c. out** (*break down*) *Fam* claquer, tomber en panne.

conker ['kɒŋkər] n (*horse-chestnut fruit*) *Fam* marron m (d'Inde).

connect [kə'nekt] vt relier (with, to à); (*telephone, stove etc*) brancher; **to c. with** *Tel* mettre en communication avec; (*in memory*) associer avec; – vi (*be connected*) être relié; **to c. with** (*of train, bus*) assurer la correspondance avec. ◆**—ed** a (*facts etc*) lié, connexe; (*speech*) suivi; **to be c. with** (*have dealings with*) être lié à; (*have to do with, relate to*) avoir rapport à; (*by marriage*) être allié à. ◆**connection** n (*link*) rapport m, relation f (with avec;

(*train, bus etc*) correspondance f; (*phone call*) communication f; (*between pipes etc*) *Tech* raccord m; pl (*contacts*) relations fpl; **in c. with** à propos de.

connive [kə'naɪv] vi **to c.** at fermer les yeux sur; **to c. to do** se mettre de connivence pour faire (with avec); **to c. together** agir en complicité. ◆**connivance** n connivence f.

connoisseur [kɒnə'sɜːr] n connaisseur m.

connotation [kɒnə'teɪʃ(ə)n] n connotation f.

conquer ['kɒŋkər] vt (*country, freedom etc*) conquérir; (*enemy, habit*) vaincre. ◆**—ing** a victorieux. ◆**conqueror** n conquérant, -ante mf, vainqueur m. ◆**conquest** n conquête f.

cons [kɒnz] npl the pros and (the) **c.** le pour et le contre.

conscience ['kɒnʃəns] n conscience f. ◆**c.-stricken** a pris de remords.

conscientious [kɒnʃɪ'enʃəs] a consciencieux; **c. objector** objecteur m de conscience. ◆**—ness** n application f, sérieux m.

conscious ['kɒnʃəs] a conscient (of sth de qch); (*intentional*) délibéré; *Med* conscient; **to be c. of doing** avoir conscience de faire. ◆**—ly** adv (*knowingly*) consciemment. ◆**—ness** n conscience f (of de); *Med* connaissance f.

conscript ['kɒnskrɪpt] n *Mil* conscrit m; – [kən'skrɪpt] vt enrôler (par conscription). ◆**con'scription** n conscription f.

consecrate ['kɒnsɪkreɪt] vt (*church etc*) *Rel* consacrer. ◆**conse'cration** n consécration f.

consecutive [kən'sekjʊtɪv] a consécutif. ◆**—ly** adv consécutivement.

consensus [kən'sensəs] n consensus m, accord m (général).

consent [kən'sent] vi consentir (to à); – n consentement m; **by common c.** de l'aveu de tous; **by mutual c.** d'un commun accord.

consequence ['kɒnsɪkwəns] n (*result*) conséquence f; (*importance*) importance f, conséquence f. ◆**consequently** adv par conséquent.

conservative [kən'sɜːvətɪv] **1** a (*estimate*) modeste; (*view*) traditionnel. **2** a & n **C.** *Pol* conservateur, -trice (mf). ◆**conservatism** n (*in behaviour*) & *Pol Rel* conservatisme m.

conservatoire [kən'sɜːvətwɑːr] n *Mus* conservatoire m.

conservatory [kən'sɜːvətrɪ] n (*greenhouse*) serre f.

conserve [kən'sɜːv] vt préserver, conserver;

(*one's strength*) ménager; **to c. energy** faire des économies d'énergie. ◆**conser-** **'vation** n (*energy-saving*) économies fpl d'énergie; (*of nature*) protection f de l'environnement; *Phys* conservation f.

consider [kən'sɪdər] vt considérer; (*take into account*) tenir compte de; **I'll c. it** j'y réfléchirai; **to c. doing** envisager de faire; **to c. that** estimer *or* considérer que; **he's** *or* **she's being considered (for the job)** sa candidature est à l'étude; **all things considered** en fin de compte. ◆**—ing** prep étant donné, vu. ◆**—able** a (*large*) considérable; (*much*) beaucoup de. ◆**—ably** adv beaucoup, considérablement. ◆**conside-** **'ration** n (*thought, thoughtfulness, reason*) considération f; **under c.** à l'étude; **out of c. for** par égard pour; **to take into c.** prendre en considération.

considerate [kən'sɪdərət] a plein d'égards (**to** pour), attentionné (**to** à l'égard de).

consign [kən'saɪn] vt (*send*) expédier; (*give, entrust*) confier (**to** à). ◆**—ment** n (*act*) expédition f; (*goods*) arrivage m.

consist [kən'sɪst] vi consister (**of** en, **in** dans, **in doing** à faire).

consistent [kən'sɪstənt] a logique, conséquent; (*coherent*) cohérent; (*friend*) fidèle; **c. with** compatible avec, conforme à. ◆**—ly** adv (*logically*) avec logique; (*always*) constamment. ◆**consistency** n 1 logique f; cohérence f. 2 (*of liquid etc*) consistance f.

console[1] [kən'səʊl] vt consoler. ◆**conso-** **'lation** n consolation f; **c. prize** prix m de consolation.

console[2] ['kɒnsəʊl] n (*control desk*) *Tech* console f.

consolidate [kən'sɒlɪdeɪt] vt consolider; — vi se consolider. ◆**consoli'dation** n consolidation f.

consonant ['kɒnsənənt] n consonne f.

consort 1 ['kɒnsɔːt] n époux m, épouse f; **prince c.** prince m consort. **2** [kən'sɔːt] vi **to c. with** *Pej* fréquenter.

consortium [kən'sɔːtɪəm] n *Com* consortium m.

conspicuous [kən'spɪkjʊəs] a visible, en évidence; (*striking*) remarquable, manifeste; (*showy*) voyant; **to be c. by one's absence** briller par son absence; **to make oneself c.** se faire remarquer. ◆**—ly** adv visiblement.

conspire [kən'spaɪər] **1** vi (*plot*) conspirer (**against** contre); **to c. to do** comploter de faire. **2** vt **to c. to do** (*of events*) conspirer à faire. ◆**conspiracy** n conspiration f.

constable ['kʌnstəb(ə)l] n (*police*) **c. agent** m (de police). ◆**con'stabulary** n la police.

constant ['kɒnstənt] a (*frequent*) incessant; (*unchanging*) constant; (*faithful*) fidèle. ◆**constancy** n constance f. ◆**constantly** adv constamment, sans cesse.

constellation [kɒnstə'leɪʃ(ə)n] n constellation f.

consternation [kɒnstə'neɪʃ(ə)n] n consternation f.

constipate ['kɒnstɪpeɪt] vt constiper. ◆**consti'pation** n constipation f.

constituent [kən'stɪtjʊənt] **1** a (*element etc*) constituant, constitutif. **2** n *Pol* électeur, -trice mf. ◆**constituency** n circonscription f électorale; (*voters*) électeurs mpl.

constitute ['kɒnstɪtjuːt] vt constituer. ◆**consti'tution** n (*of person etc*) & *Pol* constitution f. ◆**consti'tutional** a *Pol* constitutionnel.

constrain [kən'streɪn] vt contraindre.

constrict [kən'strɪkt] vt (*tighten, narrow*) resserrer; (*movement*) gêner. ◆**con-** **'striction** n resserrement m.

construct [kən'strʌkt] vt construire. ◆**con-** **struction** n construction f; **under c.** en construction. ◆**constructive** a constructif.

construe [kən'struː] vt interpréter, comprendre.

consul ['kɒnsəl] n consul m. ◆**consular** a consulaire. ◆**consulate** n consulat m.

consult [kən'sʌlt] vt consulter; – vi **to c. with** discuter avec, conférer avec. ◆**—ing** a (*room*) *Med* de consultation; (*physician*) consultant. ◆**consultancy** n **c. (firm)** *Com* cabinet m d'experts-conseils; **c. fee** honoraires mpl de conseils. ◆**consultant** n conseiller, -ère mf; *Med* spécialiste mf; (*financial, legal*) conseil m, expert-conseil m; – a (*engineer etc*) consultant. ◆**consul'tation** n consultation f. ◆**con-** **sultative** a consultatif.

consum/e [kən'sjuːm] vt (*food, supplies etc*) consommer; (*of fire, grief, hate*) consumer. ◆**—ing** a (*ambition*) brûlant. ◆**—er** n consommateur, -trice mf; **c. goods/society** biens mpl/société f de consommation. ◆**con'sumption** n consommation f (**of** de).

consummate ['kɒnsəmət] a (*perfect*) consommé.

contact ['kɒntækt] n contact m; (*person*) relation f; **in c. with** en contact avec; **c. lenses** lentilles fpl *or* verres mpl de contact; – vt se mettre en contact avec, contacter.

contagious [kənˈteɪdʒəs] *a* contagieux.
contain [kənˈteɪn] *vt* (*enclose, hold back*) contenir; **to c. oneself** se contenir. ◆**—er** *n* récipient *m*; (*for transporting freight*) conteneur *m*, container *m*.
contaminate [kənˈtæmɪneɪt] *vt* contaminer. ◆**contamiˈnation** *n* contamination *f*.
contemplate [ˈkɒntəmpleɪt] *vt* (*look at*) contempler; (*consider*) envisager (**doing** de faire). ◆**contemˈplation** *n* contemplation *f*; **in c. of** en prévision de.
contemporary [kənˈtemprərɪ] *a* contemporain (**with** de); − *n* (*person*) contemporain, -aine *mf*.
contempt [kənˈtempt] *n* mépris *m*; **to hold in c.** mépriser. ◆**contemptible** *a* méprisable. ◆**contemptuous** *a* dédaigneux (**of** de).
contend [kənˈtend] **1** *vi* **to c. with** (*problem*) faire face à; (*person*) avoir affaire à; (*compete*) rivaliser avec; (*struggle*) se battre avec. **2** *vt* **to c. that** (*claim*) soutenir que. ◆**—er** *n* concurrent, -ente *mf*. ◆**contention** *n* **1** (*argument*) dispute *f*. **2** (*claim*) affirmation *f*. ◆**contentious** *a* (*issue*) litigieux.
content[1] [kənˈtent] *a* satisfait (**with** de); **he's c. to do** il ne demande pas mieux que de faire. ◆**—ed** *a* satisfait. ◆**—ment** *n* contentement *m*.
content[2] [ˈkɒntent] *n* (*of text, film etc*) contenu *m*; *pl* (*of container*) contenu *m*; (**table of**) **contents** (*of book*) table *f* des matières; **alcoholic/iron/etc c.** teneur *f* en alcool/fer/*etc*.
contest [kənˈtest] *vt* (*dispute*) contester; (*fight for*) disputer; − *n* [ˈkɒntest] (*in competition*) concours *m*; (*fight*) lutte *f*; *Boxing* combat *m*. ◆**conˈtestant** *n* concurrent, -ente *mf*; (*in fight*) adversaire *mf*.
context [ˈkɒntekst] *n* contexte *m*.
continent [ˈkɒntɪnənt] *n* continent *m*; **the C.** l'Europe *f* (continentale). ◆**contiˈnental** *a* continental; européen; **c. breakfast** petit déjeuner *m* à la française.
contingent [kənˈtɪndʒənt] **1** *a* (*accidental*) contingent; **to be c. upon** dépendre de. **2** *nm Mil* contingent *m*. ◆**contingency** *n* éventualité *f*; **c. plan** plan *m* d'urgence.
continu/e [kənˈtɪnjuː] *vt* continuer (**to do** or **doing** à or de faire); (*resume*) reprendre; **to c. (with)** (*work, speech etc*) poursuivre, continuer; − *vi* continuer; (*resume*) reprendre; **to c. in** (*job*) garder. ◆**—ed** *a* (*interest, attention etc*) soutenu, assidu; (*presence*) continu(el); **to be c.** (*of story*) à suivre. ◆**continual** *a* continuel. ◆**continually**

adv continuellement. ◆**continuance** *n* continuation *f*. ◆**continuˈation** *n* continuation *f*; (*resumption*) reprise *f*; (*new episode*) suite *f*. ◆**continuity** [kɒntɪˈnjuːɪtɪ] *n* continuité *f*. ◆**continuous** *a* continu; **c. performance** *Cin* spectacle *m* permanent. ◆**continuously** *adv* sans interruption.
contort [kənˈtɔːt] *vt* (*twist*) tordre; **to c. oneself** se contorsionner. ◆**contortion** *n* contorsion *f*. ◆**contortionist** *n* (*acrobat*) contorsionniste *mf*.
contour [ˈkɒntʊər] *n* contour *m*.
contraband [ˈkɒntrəbænd] *n* contrebande *f*.
contraception [kɒntrəˈsepʃ(ə)n] *n* contraception *f*. ◆**contraceptive** *a* & *n* contraceptif (*m*).
contract **1** [ˈkɒntrækt] *n* contrat *m*; **c. work** travail *m* en sous-traitance; − *vi* **to c. out of** (*agreement etc*) se dégager de. **2** [kənˈtrækt] *vt* (*habit, debt, muscle etc*) contracter; − *vi* (*of heart etc*) se contracter. ◆**conˈtraction** *n* (*of muscle, word*) contraction *f*. ◆**conˈtractor** *n* entrepreneur *m*.
contradict [kɒntrəˈdɪkt] *vt* contredire; (*belie*) démentir. ◆**contradiction** *n* contradiction *f*. ◆**contradictory** *a* contradictoire.
contralto [kənˈtræltəʊ] *n* (*pl* -os) contralto *m*.
contraption [kənˈtræpʃ(ə)n] *n Fam* machin *m*, engin *m*.
contrary **1** [ˈkɒntrərɪ] *a* contraire (**to** à); − *adv* **c. to** contrairement à; − *n* contraire *m*; **on the c.** au contraire; **unless you, I** *etc* **hear to the c.** sauf avis contraire; **she said nothing to the c.** elle n'a rien dit contre. **2** [kənˈtreərɪ] *a* (*obstinate*) entêté, difficile.
contrast **1** [ˈkɒntrɑːst] *n* contraste *m*; **in c. to** par opposition à. **2** [kənˈtrɑːst] *vi* contraster (**with** avec); − *vt* faire contraster, mettre en contraste. ◆**—ing** *a* (*colours etc*) opposés.
contravene [kɒntrəˈviːn] *vt* (*law*) enfreindre. ◆**contravention** *n* **in c. of** en contravention de.
contribute [kənˈtrɪbjuːt] *vt* donner, fournir (**to** à); (*article*) écrire (**to** pour); **to c. money to** contribuer à, verser de l'argent à; − *vi* **to c. to** contribuer à; (*publication*) collaborer à. ◆**contriˈbution** *n* contribution *f*; (*to pension fund etc*) cotisation(s) *f*(*pl*); *Journ* article *m*. ◆**contributor** *n Journ* collaborateur, -trice *mf*; (*of money*) donateur, -trice *mf*. ◆**contributory** *a* **a c. factor** un facteur qui a contribué (**in** à).
contrite [kənˈtraɪt] *a* contrit. ◆**contrition** *n* contrition *f*.
contriv/e [kənˈtraɪv] *vt* inventer; **to c. to do**

trouver moyen de faire. ◆—ed a artificiel.
◆contrivance n (device) dispositif m;
(scheme) invention f.

control [kən'trəʊl] vt (-ll-) (business, organization) diriger; (traffic) régler; (prices, quality) contrôler; (emotion, reaction) maîtriser, contrôler; (disease) enrayer; (situation) être maître de; to c. oneself se contrôler; − n (authority) autorité f (over sur); (of traffic) réglementation f; (of prices etc) contrôle m; (of emotion etc) maîtrise f; pl (of plane etc) commandes fpl; (knobs) TV Rad boutons mpl; the c. of (fires etc) la lutte contre; (self-)c. le contrôle de soi-même; to keep s.o. under c. tenir qn; everything is under c. tout est en ordre; in c. of maître de; to lose c. of (situation, vehicle) perdre le contrôle de; out of c. (situation, crowd) difficilement maîtrisable; c. tower Av tour f de contrôle. ◆controller n air traffic c. aiguilleur m du ciel.

controversy ['kɒntrəvɜːsɪ] n controverse f.
◆contro'versial a (book, author) contesté, discuté; (doubtful) discutable.

conundrum [kə'nʌndrəm] n devinette f,
énigme f; (mystery) énigme f.

conurbation [kɒnɜː'beɪʃ(ə)n] n agglomération f, conurbation f.

convalesce [kɒnvə'les] vi être en convalescence. ◆convalescence n convalescence f. ◆convalescent n convalescent, -ente mf; c. home maison f de convalescence.

convector [kən'vektər] n radiateur m à convection.

convene [kən'viːn] vt convoquer; − vi se réunir.

convenient [kən'viːnɪənt] a commode, pratique; (well-situated) bien situé (for the shops/etc par rapport aux magasins/etc); (moment) opportun, opportun; to be c. (for) (suit) convenir (à). ◆—ly adv (to arrive) à propos; c. situated bien situé.
◆convenience n commodité f; (comfort) confort m; (advantage) avantage m; to or at one's c. à sa convenance; c. food(s) plats mpl or aliments mpl minute; (public) conveniences toilettes fpl.

convent ['kɒnvənt] n couvent m.

convention [kən'venʃ(ə)n] n (agreement) & Am Pol convention f; (custom) usage m, convention f; (meeting) Pol assemblée f.
◆conventional a conventionnel.

converg/e [kən'vɜːdʒ] vi converger.
◆—ing a convergent. ◆convergence n convergence f.

conversant [kən'vɜːsənt] a to be c. with

(custom etc) connaître; (fact) savoir; (cars etc) s'y connaître en.

conversation [kɒnvə'seɪʃ(ə)n] n conversation f. ◆conversational a (tone) de la conversation; (person) loquace. ◆conversationalist n causeur, -euse mf.

converse 1 [kən'vɜːs] vi s'entretenir (with avec). 2 ['kɒnvɜːs] a & n inverse (m).
◆con'versely adv inversement.

convert [kən'vɜːt] vt (change) convertir (into en); (building) aménager (into en); to c. s.o. convertir qn (to à); − ['kɒnvɜːt] n converti, -ie mf. ◆con'version n conversion f; aménagement m. ◆con'vertible a convertible; − n (car) (voiture f) décapotable f.

convex ['kɒnveks] a convexe.

convey [kən'veɪ] vt (goods, people) transporter; (sound, message, order) transmettre; (idea) communiquer; (evoke) évoquer; (water etc through pipes) amener. ◆conveyance n transport m; Aut véhicule m.
◆conveyor n c. belt tapis m roulant.

convict ['kɒnvɪkt] n forçat m; [kən'vɪkt] vt déclarer coupable, condamner. ◆conviction n Jur condamnation f; (belief) conviction f; to carry c. (of argument etc) être convaincant.

convinc/e [kən'vɪns] vt convaincre, persuader. ◆—ing a convaincant. ◆—ingly adv de façon convaincante.

convivial [kən'vɪvɪəl] a joyeux, gai; (person) bon vivant.

convoke [kən'vəʊk] vt (meeting etc) convoquer.

convoluted [kɒnvə'luːtɪd] a (argument, style) compliqué, tarabiscoté.

convoy ['kɒnvɔɪ] n (ships, cars, people) convoi m.

convulse [kən'vʌls] vt bouleverser, ébranler; (face) convulser. ◆convulsion n convulsion f. ◆convulsive a convulsif.

coo [kuː] vi (of dove) roucouler.

cook [kʊk] vt (faire) cuire; (accounts) Fam truquer; to c. up Fam inventer; − vi (of food) cuire; (of person) faire la cuisine; what's cooking? Fam qu'est-ce qui se passe?; − n (person) cuisinier, -ière mf.
◆—ing n cuisine f; c. apple pomme f à cuire. ◆—er n (stove) cuisinière f; (apple) pomme f à cuire. ◆cookbook n livre m de cuisine. ◆cookery n cuisine f; c. book livre m de cuisine.

cookie ['kʊkɪ] n Am biscuit m, gâteau m sec.

cool [kuːl] a (-er, -est) (weather, place etc) frais; (manner, person) calme; (reception etc) froid; (impertinent) insolent; I feel

c. j'ai (un peu) froid; **a c. drink** une boisson fraîche; **a c. £50** la coquette somme de 50 livres; – *n* (*of evening*) fraîcheur *f*; **to keep (in the) c.** tenir au frais; **to keep/lose one's c.** garder/perdre son sang-froid; – *vi* **to c. (down)** refroidir, rafraîchir; – *vi* **to c. (down or off)** (*of enthusiasm*) se refroidir; (*of anger, angry person*) se calmer; (*of hot liquid*) refroidir; **to c. off** (*refresh oneself by drinking, bathing etc*) se rafraîchir; **to c. (off) towards s.o.** se refroidir envers qn. ◆**—ing** *n* (*of air, passion etc*) refroidissement *m*. ◆**—er** (*for food*) glacière *f*. ◆**—ly** *adv* calmement; (*to welcome*) froidement; (*boldly*) effrontément. ◆**—ness** *n* fraîcheur *f*; (*unfriendliness*) froideur *f*. ◆**cool-'headed** *a* calme.

coop [kuːp] **1** *n* (*for chickens*) poulailler *m*. **2** *vt* **to c. up** (*person*) enfermer.

co-op ['kəʊɒp] *n Am* appartement *m* en copropriété.

co-operate [kəʊ'ɒpəreɪt] *vi* coopérer (**in** à, **with** avec). ◆**co-ope'ration** *n* coopération *f*. ◆**co-operative** *a* coopératif; – *n* coopérative *f*.

co-opt [kəʊ'ɒpt] *vt* coopter.

co-ordinate [kəʊ'ɔːdɪneɪt] *vt* coordonner. ◆**co-ordinates** [kəʊ'ɔːdɪnəts] *npl Math* coordonnées *fpl*; (*clothes*) coordonnés *mpl*. ◆**co-ordi'nation** *n* coordination *f*.

cop [kɒp] **1** *n* (*policeman*) *Fam* flic *m*. **2** *vt* (**-pp-**) (*catch*) *Sl* piquer. **3** *vi* (**-pp-**) **to c. out** *Sl* se défiler, éviter ses responsabilités.

cope [kəʊp] *vi* **to c. with** s'occuper de; (*problem*) faire face à; (**to be able) to c.** (*savoir*) se débrouiller.

co-pilot ['kəʊpaɪlət] *n* copilote *m*.

copious ['kəʊpɪəs] *a* copieux.

copper ['kɒpər] *n* **1** cuivre *m*; *pl* (*coins*) petite monnaie *f*. **2** (*policeman*) *Fam* flic *m*.

coppice ['kɒpɪs] *n*, ◆**copse** [kɒps] *n* taillis *m*.

copulate ['kɒpjʊleɪt] *vi* s'accoupler. ◆**copu'lation** *n* copulation *f*.

copy ['kɒpɪ] *n* copie *f*; (*of book etc*) exemplaire *m*; *Phot* épreuve *f*; – *vti* copier; – *vti* **to c. out** *or* **down** (re)copier. ◆**copyright** *n* copyright *m*.

coral ['kɒrəl] *n* corail *m*; **c. reef** récif *m* de corail.

cord [kɔːd] **1** *n* (*of curtain, pyjamas etc*) cordon *m*; *El* cordon *m* électrique; **vocal cords** cordes *fpl* vocales. **2** *npl Fam* velours *m*, pantalon *m* en velours (côtelé).

cordial ['kɔːdɪəl] **1** *a* (*friendly*) cordial. **2** *n* (*fruit*) **c.** sirop *m*.

cordon ['kɔːdən] *n* cordon *m*; – *vt* **to c. off** (*place*) boucler, interdire l'accès à.

corduroy ['kɔːdərɔɪ] *n* (*fabric*) velours *m* côtelé; *pl* pantalon *m* en velours (côtelé), velours *m*.

core [kɔːr] *n* (*of fruit*) trognon *m*; (*of problem*) cœur *m*; (*group of people*) & *Geol* El noyau *m*; – *vt* (*apple*) vider. ◆**corer** *n* vide-pomme *m*.

cork [kɔːk] *n* liège *m*; (*for bottle*) bouchon *m*; – *vt* **to c. (up)** (*bottle*) boucher. ◆**corkscrew** *n* tire-bouchon *m*.

corn [kɔːn] *n* **1** (*wheat*) blé *m*; (*maize*) *Am* maïs *m*; (*seed*) grain *m*; **c. on the cob** épi *m* de maïs. **2** (*hard skin*) cor *m*. ◆**corned** *a* **c. beef** corned-beef *m*, singe *m*. ◆**cornflakes** *npl* céréales *fpl*. ◆**cornflour** *n* farine *f* de maïs, maïzena® *f*. ◆**cornflower** *n* bleuet *m*. ◆**cornstarch** *n Am* = cornflour.

cornea ['kɔːnɪə] *n Anat* cornée *f*.

corner ['kɔːnər] *n* **1** coin *m*; (*of street, room*) coin *m*, angle *m*; (*bend in road*) virage *m*; *Fb* corner *m*; **in a (tight) c.** dans une situation difficile. **2** *vt* (*animal, enemy etc*) acculer; (*person in corridor etc*) *Fig* coincer, accrocher; (*market Com*) accaparer; – *vi Aut* prendre un virage. ◆**cornerstone** *n* pierre *f* angulaire.

cornet ['kɔːnɪt] *n* (*of ice cream etc*) & *Mus* cornet *m*.

Cornwall ['kɔːnwəl] *n* Cornouailles *fpl*. ◆**Cornish** *a* de Cornouailles.

corny ['kɔːnɪ] *a* (**-ier, -iest**) (*joke etc*) rebattu.

corollary [kə'rɒlərɪ, *Am* 'kɒrələrɪ] *n* corollaire *m*.

coronary ['kɒrənərɪ] *n Med* infarctus *m*.

coronation [kɒrə'neɪʃ(ə)n] *n* couronnement *m*, sacre *m*.

coroner ['kɒrənər] *n Jur* coroner *m*.

corporal ['kɔːpərəl] **1** *n Mil* caporal(-chef) *m*. **2** *a* **c. punishment** châtiment *m* corporel.

corporation [kɔːpə'reɪʃ(ə)n] *n* (*business*) société *f* commerciale; (*of town*) conseil *m* municipal. ◆**'corporate** *a* collectif; **c. body** corps *m* constitué.

corps [kɔːr, *pl* kɔːz] *n Mil Pol* corps *m*.

corpse [kɔːps] *n* cadavre *m*.

corpulent ['kɔːpjʊlənt] *a* corpulent. ◆**corpulence** *n* corpulence *f*.

corpus ['kɔːpəs] *n Ling* corpus *m*.

corpuscle ['kɔːpʌs(ə)l] *n Med* globule *m*.

corral [kə'rɑːl] *n Am* corral *m*.

correct [kə'rekt] *a* (*right, accurate*) exact, correct; (*proper*) correct; **he's c.** il a raison; – *vt* corriger. ◆**—ly** *adv* correctement.

◆—ness n (accuracy, propriety) correction f. ◆correction n correction f. ◆corrective a (act, measure) rectificatif.

correlate ['kɒrəleɪt] vi correspondre (with à); – vt faire correspondre. ◆corre'lation n corrélation f.

correspond [kɒrɪ'spɒnd] vi 1 (agree, be similar) correspondre (to à, with avec). 2 (by letter) correspondre (with avec). ◆—ing a (matching) correspondant; (similar) semblable. ◆correspondence n correspondance f; c. course cours m par correspondance. ◆correspondent n correspondant, -ante mf; Journ envoyé, -ée mf.

corridor ['kɒrɪdɔːr] n couloir m, corridor m.

corroborate [kə'rɒbəreɪt] vt corroborer.

corrode [kə'rəud] vt ronger, corroder; – vi se corroder. ◆corrosion n corrosion f. ◆corrosive a corrosif.

corrugated ['kɒrəgeɪtɪd] a (cardboard) ondulé; c. iron tôle f ondulée.

corrupt [kə'rʌpt] vt corrompre; – a corrompu. ◆corruption n corruption f.

corset ['kɔːsɪt] n (boned) corset m; (elasticated) gaine f.

Corsica ['kɔːsɪkə] n Corse f.

cos [kɒs] n c. (lettuce) (laitue f) romaine f.

cosh [kɒʃ] n matraque f; – vt matraquer.

cosiness ['kəʊzɪnəs] n intimité f, confort m.

cosmetic [kɒz'metɪk] n produit m de beauté; – a esthétique; Fig superficiel.

cosmopolitan [kɒzmə'pɒlɪtən] a & n cosmopolite (mf).

cosmos ['kɒzmɒs] n cosmos m. ◆cosmic a cosmique. ◆cosmonaut n cosmonaute mf.

Cossack ['kɒsæk] n cosaque m.

cosset ['kɒsɪt] vt choyer.

cost [kɒst] vti (pt & pp cost) coûter; how much does it c.? ça coûte or ça vaut combien?; to c. the earth Fam coûter les yeux de la tête; – n coût m, prix m; at great c. à grands frais; to my c. à mes dépens; at any c., at all costs à tout prix; at c. price au prix coûtant. ◆c.-effective a rentable. ◆costly a (-ier, -iest) (expensive) coûteux; (valuable) précieux.

co-star ['kəʊstɑːr] n Cin Th partenaire mf.

costume ['kɒstjuːm] n costume m; (woman's suit) tailleur m; (swimming) c. maillot m (de bain); c. jewellery bijoux mpl de fantaisie.

cosy ['kəʊzɪ] 1 a (-ier, -iest) douillet, intime; make yourself (nice and) c. mets-toi à l'aise; we're c. on est bien ici. 2 n (tea) c. couvre-théière m.

cot [kɒt] n lit m d'enfant; (camp bed) Am lit m de camp.

cottage ['kɒtɪdʒ] n petite maison f de campagne; (thatched) c. chaumière f; c. cheese fromage m blanc (maigre); c. industry travail m à domicile (activité artisanale).

cotton ['kɒtən] 1 n coton m; (yarn) fil m (de coton); absorbent c. Am, c. wool coton m hydrophile, ouate f; c. candy Am barbe f à papa. 2 vi to c. on to Sl piger.

couch [kaʊtʃ] 1 n canapé m. 2 vt (express) formuler.

couchette [kuː'ʃet] n Rail couchette f.

cough [kɒf] 1 n toux f; c. mixture sirop m contre la toux; – vi tousser; – vt to c. up (blood) cracher. 2 vt to c. up (money) Sl cracher; – vi to c. up Sl payer, casquer.

could [kʊd, unstressed kəd] see can¹.

couldn't ['kʊd(ə)nt] = could not.

council ['kaʊns(ə)l] n conseil m; c. flat/house appartement m/maison f loué(e) à la municipalité, HLM m or f. ◆councillor n conseiller, -ère mf; (town) c. conseiller m municipal.

counsel ['kaʊnsəl] n (advice) conseil m; Jur avocat, -ate mf; – vt (-ll-, Am -l-) conseiller (s.o. to do à qn de faire). ◆counsellor n conseiller, -ère mf.

count¹ [kaʊnt] vt (find number of, include) compter; (deem) considérer; not counting Paul sans compter Paul; to c. in (include) inclure; to c. out exclure; (money) compter; – vi (calculate, be important) compter; to c. against s.o. être un désavantage pour qn, jouer contre qn; to c. on s.o. (rely on) compter sur qn; to c. on doing compter faire; – n compte m; Jur chef m (d'accusation); he's lost c. of the books he has il ne sait plus combien il a de livres. ◆countdown n compte m à rebours.

count² [kaʊnt] n (title) comte m.

countenance ['kaʊntɪnəns] 1 n (face) mine f, expression f. 2 vt (allow) tolérer; (approve) approuver.

counter ['kaʊntər] 1 n (in shop, bar etc) comptoir m; (in bank etc) guichet m; under the c. Fig clandestinement, au marché noir; over the c. (to obtain medicine) sans ordonnance. 2 n (in games) jeton m. 3 n Tech compteur m. 4 adv c. to à l'encontre de. 5 vt (plan) contrarier; (insult) riposter à; (blow) parer; – vi riposter (with par).

counter- ['kaʊntər] pref contre-.

counterattack ['kaʊntərətæk] n contre-attaque f; – vti contre-attaquer.

counterbalance ['kaʊntəbæləns] n contre-poids m; – vt contrebalancer.

counterclockwise [kauntə'klɒkwaız] *a* & *adv Am* dans le sens inverse des aiguilles d'une montre.

counterfeit ['kauntəfıt] *a* faux; − *n* contrefaçon *f*, faux *m*; − *vt* contrefaire.

counterfoil ['kauntəfɔıl] *n* souche *f*.

counterpart ['kauntəpɑːt] *n* (*thing*) équivalent *m*; (*person*) homologue *mf*.

counterpoint ['kauntəpɔınt] *n Mus* contrepoint *m*.

counterproductive [kauntəprə'dʌktıv] *a* (*action*) inefficace, qui produit l'effet contraire.

countersign ['kauntəsaın] *vt* contresigner.

countess ['kauntıs] *n* comtesse *f*.

countless ['kauntləs] *a* innombrable.

countrified ['kʌntrıfaıd] *a* rustique.

country ['kʌntrı] *n* pays *m*; (*region*) région *f*, pays *m*; (*homeland*) patrie *f*; (*opposed to town*) campagne *f*; − *a* (*house etc*) de campagne; **c. dancing** danse folklorique. ◆**countryman** *n* (*pl* -men) (*fellow*) *c.* compatriote *m*. ◆**countryside** *n* campagne *f*.

county ['kauntı] *n* comté *m*; **c. seat** *Am*, **c. town** chef-lieu *m*.

coup [kuː, *pl* kuːz] *n Pol* coup *m* d'État.

couple ['kʌp(ə)l] **1** *n* (*of people, animals*) couple *m*; **a c.** (*of*) deux ou trois; (*a few*) quelques. **2** *vt* (*connect*) accoupler. **3** *vi* (*mate*) s'accoupler.

coupon ['kuːpɒn] *n* (*voucher*) bon *m*; (*ticket*) coupon *m*.

courage ['kʌrıdʒ] *n* courage *m*. ◆**courageous** [kə'reıdʒəs] *a* courageux.

courgette [kuə'ʒet] *n* courgette *f*.

courier ['kurıər] *n* **1** (*for tourists*) guide *m*; (*messenger*) messager *m*; **c. service** service *m* de messagerie.

course [kɔːs] *n* **1** (*duration, movement*) cours *m*; (*of ship*) route *f*; (*of river*) cours *m*; (*way*) *Fig* voie *f*, chemin *m*; (*means*) moyen *m*; **c.** (*of action*) ligne *f* de conduite; (*option*) parti *m*; **your best c. is to** . . . le mieux c'est de . . . ; **as a matter of c.** normalement; **in (the) c. of time** le temps, à la longue; **in due c.** en temps utile. **2** *Sch Univ* cours *m*; **c. of lectures** série *f* de conférences; (*of treatment*) *Med* traitement *m*. **3** *Culin* plat *m*; **first c.** entrée *f*. **4** *n* (*racecourse*) champ *m* de courses; (*golf*) **c.** terrain *m* (de golf). **5** *adv* of c.! bien sûr!, mais oui!; **of c. not!** bien sûr que non!

court [kɔːt] **1** *n* (*of monarch*) cour *f*; *Jur* cour *f*, tribunal *m*; *Tennis* court *m*; **c. of enquiry** commission *f* d'enquête; **high c.** cour *f* suprême; **to take to c.** poursuivre en

justice; **c. shoe** escarpin *m*. **2** *vt* (*woman*) faire la cour à; (*danger, support*) rechercher; − *vi* (*couple*) d'amoureux; **they are c.** ils sortent ensemble. ◆**−ing** *a* (*couple*) faire la cour. ◆**courthouse** *n* palais *m* de justice. ◆**courtier** *n Hist* courtisan *m*. ◆**courtroom** *n* salle *f* du tribunal. ◆**courtship** *n* (*act, period of time*) cour *f*. ◆**courtyard** *n* cour *f*.

courteous ['kɜːtıəs] *a* poli, courtois. ◆**courtesy** *n* politesse *f*, courtoisie *f*.

court-martial [kɔːt'mɑːʃəl] *n* conseil *m* de guerre; − *vt* (**-ll-**) faire passer en conseil de guerre.

cousin ['kʌz(ə)n] *n* cousin *m*, -ine *mf*.

cove [kəuv] *n* (*bay*) *Geog* anse *f*.

covenant ['kʌvənənt] *n Jur* convention *f*; *Rel* alliance *f*.

Coventry ['kɒvəntrı] *n* **to send s.o. to C.** *Fig* mettre qn en quarantaine.

cover ['kʌvər] *n* (*lid*) couvercle *m*; (*of book*) & *Fin* couverture *f*; (*for furniture, typewriter*) housse *f*; (*bedspread*) dessus-de-lit *m*; **the covers** (*blankets*) les couvertures *fpl*; **to take c.** se mettre à l'abri; **c. charge** (*in restaurant*) couvert *m*; **c. note** certificat *m* provisoire d'assurance; **under separate c.** (*letter*) sous pli séparé; − *vt* couvrir; (*protect*) protéger, couvrir; (*distance*) parcourir, couvrir; (*include*) englober, recouvrir; (*treat*) traiter; (*event*) *Journ TV Rad* couvrir le reportage de; (*aim gun at*) tenir en joue; (*insure*) assurer; **to c. over** recouvrir; **to c. up** recouvrir; (*truth, tracks*) dissimuler; (*scandal*) étouffer, camoufler; − *vi* **to c.** (*oneself*) se couvrir; **to c. up for s.o.** couvrir qn. ◆**c.-up** *n* tentative *f* pour étouffer *or* camoufler une affaire. ◆**covering** *n* (*wrapping*) enveloppe *f*; (*layer*) couche *f*; **c. letter** lettre *f* jointe (à un document).

coveralls ['kʌvərɔːlz] *npl Am* bleus *mpl* de travail.

covert ['kəuvət, 'kʌvət] *a* secret.

covet ['kʌvıt] *vt* convoiter. ◆**covetous** *a* avide.

cow [kau] **1** *n* vache *f*; (*of elephant etc*) femelle *f*; (*nasty woman*) *Fam* chameau *m*. **2** *vt* (*person*) intimider. ◆**cowboy** *n* cow-boy *m*. ◆**cowhand** *n* vacher, -ère *mf*. ◆**cowshed** *n* étable *f*.

coward ['kauəd] *n* lâche *mf*. ◆**−ly** *a* lâche. ◆**cowardice** *n* lâcheté *f*.

cower ['kauər] *vi* (*crouch*) se tapir; (*with fear*) *Fig* reculer (par peur).

cowslip ['kauslıp] *n Bot* coucou *m*.

cox [kɒks] vt Nau barrer; – n barreur, -euse mf.

coy [kɔɪ] a (-er, -est) qui fait son or sa timide. ◆**coyness** n timidité f feinte.

coyote [kɔɪˈəʊtɪ] n (wolf) Am coyote m.

cozy [ˈkəʊzɪ] Am = cosy.

crab [kræb] 1 n crabe m. 2 n c. apple pomme f sauvage. 3 vi (-bb-) (complain) Fam rouspéter. ◆**crabbed** a (person) grincheux.

crack¹ [kræk] n (fissure) fente f; (in glass etc) fêlure f; (in skin) crevasse f; (snapping noise) craquement m; (of whip) claquement m; (blow) coup m; (joke) plaisanterie f (at aux dépens de); **to have a c. at doing** Fam essayer de faire; **at the c. of dawn** au point du jour; – vt (glass, ice) fêler; (nut) casser; (ground, skin) crevasser; (whip) faire claquer; (joke) lancer; (problem) résoudre; (code) déchiffrer; (safe) percer; **it's not as hard as it's cracked up to be** ce n'est pas aussi dur qu'on le dit; – vi se fêler; se crevasser, (of branch, wood) craquer; **to get cracking** (get to work) Fam s'y mettre; (hurry) Fam se grouiller; **to c. down on** sévir contre; **to c. up** (mentally) Fam craquer. ◆**c.-up** n Fam dépression f nerveuse; (crash) Am Fam accident m. ◆**cracked** a (crazy) Fam fou. ◆**cracker** n (cake) biscuit m (salé). 2 (firework) pétard m; Christmas c. diablotin m. 3 **she's a c.** Fam elle est sensationnelle. ◆**crackers** a (mad) Sl cinglé. ◆**crackpot** a Fam fou; – n fou m, folle f.

crack² [kræk] a (first-rate) de premier ordre; **c. shot** tireur m d'élite.

crackle [ˈkræk(ə)l] vi crépiter; (of sth frying) Culin grésiller; – n crépitement m; grésillement m.

cradle [ˈkreɪd(ə)l] n berceau m; – vt bercer.

craft [krɑːft] 1 n (skill) art m; (job) métier m (artisanal); – vt façonner. 2 n (cunning) ruse f. 3 n inv (boat) bateau m. ◆**craftsman** n (pl -men) artisan m. ◆**craftsmanship** n (skill) art m; **a piece of c.** un beau travail, une belle pièce. ◆**crafty** a (-ier, -iest) astucieux, Pej rusé.

crag [kræg] n rocher m à pic. ◆**craggy** a (rock) à pic; (face) rude.

cram [kræm] vt (-mm-) **to c. into** (force) fourrer dans; **to c. with** (fill) bourrer de; – vi **to c. into** (of people) s'entasser dans; **to c.** (for an exam) bachoter.

cramp [kræmp] n Med crampe f (in à). ◆**cramped** a (in a room or one's clothes) à l'étroit; **in c. conditions** à l'étroit.

cranberry [ˈkrænbərɪ] n Bot canneberge f.

crane [kreɪn] 1 n (bird) & Tech grue f. 2 vt **to c. one's neck** tendre le cou.

crank [kræŋk] 1 n (person) Fam excentrique mf; (fanatic) fanatique mf. 2 n (handle) Tech manivelle f; – vt **to c. (up)** (vehicle) faire démarrer à la manivelle. ◆**cranky** a (-ier, -iest) excentrique; (bad-tempered) Am grincheux.

crannies [ˈkrænɪz] npl **nooks and c.** coins et recoins mpl.

craps [kræps] n **to shoot c.** Am jouer aux dés.

crash [kræʃ] n accident m; (of firm) faillite f; (noise) fracas m; (of thunder) coup m; **c. course/diet** cours m/régime m intensif; **c. helmet** casque m (anti-choc); **c. landing** atterrissage m en catastrophe; – int (of fallen object) patatras!; – vt (car) avoir un accident avec; **to c. one's car into** faire rentrer sa voiture dans; – vi Aut Av s'écraser; **to c. into** rentrer dans; **the cars crashed (into each other)** les voitures se sont percutées or carambolées; **to c. (down)** tomber; (break) se casser; (of roof) s'effondrer. ◆**c.-land** vi atterrir en catastrophe.

crass [kræs] a grossier; (stupidity) crasse.

crate [kreɪt] n caisse f, cageot m.

crater [ˈkreɪtər] n cratère m; (bomb) entonnoir m.

cravat [krəˈvæt] n foulard m (autour du cou).

crav/e [kreɪv] vt **to c. (for)** éprouver un grand besoin de; (mercy) implorer. ◆**—ing** n désir m, grand besoin m (for de).

craven [ˈkreɪvən] a Pej lâche.

crawl [krɔːl] vi ramper; (of child) se traîner (à quatre pattes); Aut avancer au pas; **to be crawling with** grouiller de; – n Swimming crawl m; **to move at a c.** Aut avancer au pas.

crayfish [ˈkreɪfɪʃ] n inv écrevisse f.

crayon [ˈkreɪən] n crayon m, pastel m.

craze [kreɪz] n manie f (for de), engouement m (for pour). ◆**crazed** a affolé.

crazy [ˈkreɪzɪ] a (-ier, -iest) fou; **c. about sth** fana de qch; **c. about s.o.** fou de qn; **c. paving** dallage m irrégulier. ◆**craziness** n folie f.

creak [kriːk] vi (of hinge) grincer; (of timber) craquer. ◆**creaky** a grinçant; qui craque.

cream [kriːm] n crème f; (élite) Fig crème f, gratin m; – a (cake) à la crème; **c.(-coloured)** crème inv; **c. cheese** fromage m blanc; – vt (milk) écrémer; **to c. off** Fig écrémer. ◆**creamy** a (-ier, -iest) crémeux.

crease [kriːs] vt froisser, plisser; – vi se froisser; – n pli m; (accidental) (faux) pli m. ◆**c.-resistant** a infroissable.

create [kri'eɪt] vt créer; (impression, noise) faire. ◆**creation** n création f. ◆**creative** a créateur, créatif. ◆**creativeness** n créativité f. ◆**crea'tivity** n créativité f. ◆**creator** n créateur, -trice mf.

creature ['kriːtʃər] n animal m, bête f; (person) créature f; **one's c. comforts** ses aises fpl.

crèche [kreʃ] n (nursery) crèche f; (manger) Rel Am crèche f.

credence ['kriːdəns] n **to give** or **lend c. to** ajouter foi à.

credentials [krɪ'denʃəlz] npl références fpl; (identity) pièces fpl d'identité; (of diplomat) lettres fpl de créance.

credible ['kredɪb(ə)l] a croyable; (politician, information) crédible. ◆**credi'bility** n crédibilité f.

credit ['kredɪt] n (influence, belief) & Fin crédit m; (merit) mérite m; Univ unité f de valeur; pl Cin générique m; **to give c. to** (person) Fin faire crédit à; Fig reconnaître le mérite de; (statement) ajouter foi à; **to be a c. to** faire honneur à; **on c.** à crédit; **in c.** (account) créditeur; **to one's c.** Fig à son actif; − a (balance) créditeur; **c. card** carte f de crédit; **c. facilities** facilités fpl de paiement; − vt (believe) croire; Fin créditer (s.o. with sth qn de qch); **to c. s.o. with** (qualities) attribuer à qn. ◆**creditable** a honorable. ◆**creditor** n créancier, -ière mf. ◆**creditworthy** a solvable.

credulous ['kredjʊləs] a crédule.

creed [kriːd] n credo m.

creek [kriːk] n (bay) crique f; (stream) Am ruisseau m; **up the c.** (in trouble) Sl dans le pétrin.

creep [kriːp] vi (pt & pp crept) ramper; (silently) se glisser (furtivement); (slowly) avancer lentement; **it makes my flesh c.** ça me donne la chair de poule. **2** n (person) Sl salaud m; **it gives me the creeps** Fam ça me fait froid dans le dos. ◆**creepy** a (-ier, -iest) Fam terrifiant; (nasty) Fam vilain. ◆**creepy-'crawly** n Fam, Am ◆**creepy-'crawler** n Fam bestiole f.

cremate [krɪ'meɪt] vt incinérer. ◆**cremation** n crémation f. ◆**crema'torium** n crématorium m. ◆**'crematory** n Am crématorium m.

Creole ['kriːəʊl] n créole mf; Ling créole m.

crêpe [kreɪp] n (fabric) crêpe m; **c.** (rubber) crêpe m; **c. paper** papier m crêpon.

crept [krept] see creep 1.

crescendo [krɪ'ʃendəʊ] n (pl -os) crescendo m inv.

crescent ['kres(ə)nt] n croissant m; (street) Fig rue f (en demi-lune).

cress [kres] n cresson m.

crest [krest] n (of bird, wave, mountain) crête f; (of hill) sommet m; (on seal, letters etc) armoiries fpl.

Crete [kriːt] n Crète f.

cretin ['kretɪn, Am 'kriːt(ə)n] n crétin, -ine mf. ◆**cretinous** a crétin.

crevasse [krɪ'væs] n (in ice) Geol crevasse f.

crevice ['krevɪs] n (crack) crevasse f, fente f.

crew [kruː] n Nau & Av équipage m; (gang) équipe f; **c. cut** (coupe f en) brosse f. ◆**c.-neck(ed)** a à col ras.

crib [krɪb] **1** n (cradle) berceau m; (cot) Am lit m d'enfant; Rel crèche f. **2** n (copy) plagiat m; Sch traduction f; (list of answers) Sch pompe f anti-sèche; − vti (-bb-) copier.

crick [krɪk] n **c. in the neck** torticolis m; **c. in the back** tour m de reins.

cricket ['krɪkɪt] n **1** (game) cricket m. **2** (insect) grillon m. ◆**cricketer** n joueur, -euse mf de cricket.

crikey! ['kraɪkɪ] int Sl zut (alors)!

crime [kraɪm] n crime m; (not serious) délit m; (criminal practice) criminalité f. ◆**criminal** a & n criminel, -elle (mf).

crimson ['krɪmz(ə)n] a & n cramoisi (m).

cringe [krɪndʒ] vi reculer (from devant); Fig s'humilier (**to, before** devant). ◆**-ing** a Fig servile.

crinkle ['krɪŋk(ə)l] vt froisser; − vi se froisser; − n fronce f. ◆**crinkly** a froissé; (hair) frisé.

crippl/e ['krɪpəl] n (lame) estropié, -ée mf; (disabled) infirme mf; − vt estropier; (disable) rendre infirme; (nation etc) Fig paralyser. ◆**-ed** a estropié; infirme; (ship) désemparé; **c. with** (rheumatism, pains) perclus de. ◆**-ing** a (tax) écrasant.

crisis ['kraɪsɪs, pl -siːz] n crise f.

crisp [krɪsp] **1** a (-er, -est) (biscuit) croustillant; (apple etc) croquant; (snow) craquant; (air, style) vif. **2** npl (potato) crisps (pommes fpl) chips mpl. ◆**crispbread** n pain m suédois.

criss-cross ['krɪskrɒs] a (lines) entrecroisés; (muddled) enchevêtrés; − vi s'entrecroiser; − vt sillonner (en tous sens).

criterion, pl -ia [kraɪ'tɪərɪən, -ɪə] n critère m.

critic ['krɪtɪk] n critique m. ◆**critical** a critique. ◆**critically** adv (to examine etc) en critique; (harshly) sévèrement; (ill) gravement. ◆**criticism** n critique f. ◆**criticize** vti critiquer. ◆**cri'tique** n (essay etc) critique f.

croak [krəʊk] vi (of frog) croasser; – n croassement m.

crochet ['krəʊʃeɪ] vt faire au crochet; – vi faire du crochet; – n (travail m au) crochet m; **c. hook** crochet m.

crock [krɒk] n a c., **an** (old) c. Fam (person) un croulant; (car) un tacot.

crockery ['krɒkərɪ] n (cups etc) vaisselle f.

crocodile ['krɒkədaɪl] n crocodile m.

crocus ['krəʊkəs] n crocus m.

crony ['krəʊnɪ] n Pej Fam copain m, copine f.

crook [krʊk] n **1** (thief) escroc m. **2** (shepherd's stick) houlette f.

crooked ['krʊkɪd] a courbé; (path) tortueux; (hat, picture) de travers; (deal, person) malhonnête; – adv de travers. ◆**-ly** adv de travers.

croon [kruːn] vti chanter (à voix basse).

crop [krɒp] n **1** (harvest) récolte f; (produce) culture f; (of questions etc) Fig série f; (of people) groupe m. **2** vt (-pp-) (hair) couper (ras); – n c. of hair chevelure f. **3** vi (-pp-) to c. up se présenter, survenir. ◆**cropper** n to come a c. Sl (fall) ramasser une pelle; (fail) échouer.

croquet ['krəʊkeɪ] n (game) croquet m.

croquette [krəʊ'ket] n Culin croquette f.

cross[1] [krɒs] **1** n croix f. **2** a c. between (animal) un croisement entre or de. **2** vt traverser; (threshold, barrier) franchir; (legs, animals) croiser; (thwart) contrecarrer; (cheque) barrer; to c. off or out rayer; **it never crossed my mind that ...** il ne m'est pas venu à l'esprit que ...; **crossed lines** Tel lignes fpl embrouillées; – vi (of paths) se croiser; to c. (over) traverser. ◆**-ing** n Nau traversée f; (pedestrian) passage m clouté. ◆**cross-breed** n métis, -isse mf, hybride m. ◆**c.-'country** a à travers champs; **c.-country race** cross-(country) m. ◆**c.-exami'nation** n contre-interrogatoire m. ◆**c.-e'xamine** vt interroger. ◆**c.-eyed** a qui louche. ◆**c.-'legged** a & adv les jambes croisées. ◆**c.-'purposes** npl to be at c.-purposes se comprendre mal. ◆**c.-'reference** n renvoi m. ◆**c.-section** n coupe f transversale; Fig échantillon m.

cross[2] [krɒs] a (angry) fâché (with contre). ◆**-ly** adv d'un air fâché.

crossbow ['krɒsbəʊ] n arbalète f.

crosscheck [krɒs'tʃek] n contre-épreuve f; – vt vérifier.

crossfire ['krɒsfaɪər] n feux mpl croisés.

crossroads ['krɒsrəʊdz] n carrefour m.

crosswalk ['krɒswɔːk] n Am passage m clouté.

crossword ['krɒswɜːd] n c. (puzzle) mots mpl croisés.

crotch [krɒtʃ] n (of garment) entre-jambes m inv.

crotchet ['krɒtʃɪt] n Mus noire f.

crotchety ['krɒtʃɪtɪ] a grincheux.

crouch [kraʊtʃ] vi to c. (down) s'accroupir, se tapir. ◆**-ing** a accroupi, tapi.

croupier ['kruːpɪər] n (in casino) croupier m.

crow [krəʊ] **1** n corbeau m, corneille f; **as the c. flies** à vol d'oiseau; **c.'s nest** Nau nid m de pie. **2** vi (of cock) chanter; (boast) Fig se vanter (about de). ◆**crowbar** n levier m.

crowd [kraʊd] n foule f; (particular group) bande f; (of things) Fam masse f; **quite a c.** beaucoup de monde; – vi **to c. into** (of people) s'entasser dans; **to c. round s.o.** se presser autour de qn; **to c. together** se serrer; – vt (fill) remplir; **to c. into** (press) entasser dans; **don't c. me!** Fam ne me bouscule pas! ◆**-ed** a plein (with de); (train etc) bondé, plein; (city) encombré; **it's very c.!** il y a beaucoup de monde!

crown [kraʊn] n (of king, tooth) couronne f; (of head, hill) sommet m; **c. court** cour f d'assises; **C. jewels**, joyaux mpl de la Couronne; – vt couronner. ◆**-ing** a (glory etc) suprême; **c. achievement** couronnement m.

crucial ['kruːʃəl] a crucial.

crucify ['kruːsɪfaɪ] vt crucifier. ◆**crucifix** ['kruːsɪfɪks] n crucifix m. ◆**cruci'fixion** n crucifixion f.

crude [kruːd] a (-er, -est) (oil, fact) brut; (manners, person) grossier; (language, light) cru; (painting, work) rudimentaire. ◆**-ly** adv (to say, order etc) crûment. ◆**-ness** n grossièreté f; crudité f; état m rudimentaire.

cruel [krʊəl] a (crueller, cruellest) cruel. ◆**cruelty** n cruauté f; **an act of c.** une cruauté.

cruet ['kruːɪt] n c. (stand) salière f, poivrière f et huilier m.

cruis/e [kruːz] vi Nau croiser; Aut rouler; Av voler; (of taxi) marauder; (of tourists) faire une croisière; – n croisière f. ◆**-ing** a c. speed Nau Av & Fig vitesse f de croisière. ◆**-er** n Nau croiseur m.

crumb [krʌm] n miette f; (of comfort) Fig brin m; **crumbs!** Hum Fam zut!

crumble ['krʌmb(ə)l] vt (bread) émietter; – vi (collapse) s'effondrer; **to c. (away)** (in small pieces) & Fig s'effriter. ◆**crumbly** a friable.

crummy ['krʌmɪ] a (-ier, -iest) Fam moche, minable.

crumpet ['krʌmpɪt] n Culin petite crêpe f grillée (servie beurrée).

crumple ['krʌmp(ə)l] vt froisser; – vi se froisser.

crunch [krʌntʃ] 1 vt (food) croquer; – vi (of snow) craquer. 2 n the c. Fam le moment critique. ◆**crunchy** a (-ier, -iest) (apple etc) croquant.

crusade [kruːˈseɪd] n Hist & Fig croisade f; – vi faire une croisade. ◆**crusader** n Hist croisé m; Fig militant, -ante m f.

crush [krʌʃ] 1 n (crowd) cohue f; (rush) bousculade f; to have a c. on s.o. Fam avoir le béguin pour qn. 2 vt écraser; (hope) détruire; (clothes) froisser; (cram) entasser (into dans). ◆—ing a (defeat) écrasant.

crust [krʌst] n croûte f. ◆**crusty** a (-ier, -iest) (bread) croustillant.

crutch [krʌtʃ] n 1 Med béquille f. 2 (crotch) entre-jambes m inv.

crux [krʌks] n the c. of (problem, matter) le nœud de.

cry [kraɪ] n (shout) cri m; to have a c. Fam pleurer; – vi (weep) pleurer; to c. (out) pousser un cri, crier; (exclaim) s'écrier; to c. (out) for demander (à grands cris); to be crying out for avoir grand besoin de; to c. off (withdraw) abandonner; to c. off (sth) se désintéresser (de qch); to c. over pleurer (sur); – vt (shout) crier. ◆—ing a (need etc) très grand; a c. shame une véritable honte; – n cris mpl; (weeping) pleurs mpl.

crypt [krɪpt] n crypte f.

cryptic ['krɪptɪk] a secret, énigmatique.

crystal ['krɪst(ə)l] n cristal m. ◆**c.-'clear** a (water, sound) cristallin; Fig clair comme le jour ou l'eau de roche. ◆**crystallize** vt cristalliser; – vi (se) cristalliser.

cub [kʌb] n 1 (of animal) petit m. 2 (scout) louveteau m.

Cuba ['kjuːbə] n Cuba m. ◆**Cuban** a & n cubain, -aine (m f).

cubbyhole ['kʌbɪhəʊl] n cagibi m.

cube [kjuːb] n cube m; (of meat etc) dé m. ◆**cubic** a (shape) cubique; (metre etc) cube; c. capacity volume m; Aut cylindrée f.

cubicle ['kjuːbɪk(ə)l] n (for changing) cabine f; (in hospital) box m.

cuckoo ['kʊkuː] 1 n (bird) coucou m; c. clock coucou m. 2 a (stupid) Sl cinglé.

cucumber ['kjuːkʌmbər] n concombre m.

cuddle ['kʌd(ə)l] vt (hug) serrer (dans les bras); (caress) câliner; – vi (of lovers) se serrer; to (kiss and) c. s'embrasser; to c. up to (huddle) se serrer ou se blottir contre; – n

caresse f. ◆**cuddly** a (-ier, -iest) a câlin, caressant; (toy) doux, en peluche.

cudgel ['kʌdʒəl] n trique f, gourdin m.

cue [kjuː] n 1 Th réplique f; (signal) signal m. 2 (billiard) c. queue f (de billard).

cuff [kʌf] 1 n (of shirt etc) poignet m, manchette f; (of trousers) Am revers m; off the c. Fig impromptu. 2 vt (strike) gifler. ◆**c. link** bouton m de manchette.

cul-de-sac ['kʌldəsæk] n impasse f, cul-de-sac m.

culinary ['kʌlɪnərɪ] a culinaire.

cull [kʌl] vt choisir; (animals) abattre sélectivement.

culminate ['kʌlmɪneɪt] vi to c. in finir par. ◆**culmi'nation** n point m culminant.

culprit ['kʌlprɪt] n coupable m f.

cult [kʌlt] n culte m.

cultivate ['kʌltɪveɪt] vt (land, mind etc) cultiver. ◆—**ed** a cultivé. ◆**culti'vation** n culture f; land or fields under c. cultures fpl.

culture ['kʌltʃər] n culture f. ◆**cultural** a culturel. ◆**cultured** a cultivé.

cumbersome ['kʌmbəsəm] a encombrant.

cumulative ['kjuːmjʊlətɪv] a cumulatif; c. effect (long-term) effet m ou résultat m à long terme.

cunning ['kʌnɪŋ] a astucieux; Pej rusé; – n astuce f; ruse f. ◆—**ly** adv avec astuce; avec ruse.

cup [kʌp] n tasse f; (goblet, prize) coupe f; that's my c. of tea Fam c'est à mon goût; c. final Fb finale f de la coupe. ◆**c.-tie** n Fb match m éliminatoire. ◆**cupful** n tasse f.

cupboard ['kʌbəd] n armoire f; (built-in) placard m.

Cupid ['kjuːpɪd] n Cupidon m.

cupola ['kjuːpələ] n Archit coupole f.

cuppa ['kʌpə] n Fam tasse f de thé.

curate ['kjʊərɪt] n vicaire m.

curator [kjʊəˈreɪtər] n (of museum) conservateur m.

curb [kɜːb] 1 n (kerb) Am bord m du trottoir. 2 vt (feelings) refréner, freiner; (ambitions) modérer; (expenses) limiter; – n frein m; to put a c. on mettre un frein à.

curdle ['kɜːd(ə)l] vt cailler; – vi se cailler; (of blood) Fig se figer.

curds [kɜːdz] npl lait m caillé. ◆**curd cheese** n fromage m blanc (maigre).

cure [kjʊər] 1 vt guérir (of de); (poverty) Fig éliminer; – n remède m (for contre); (recovery) guérison f; rest c. cure f de repos. 2 vt Culin (smoke) fumer; (salt) saler; (dry) sécher. ◆**curable** a guérissable, curable. ◆**curative** a curatif.

curfew ['kɜːfjuː] n couvre-feu m.

curio ['kjʊərɪəʊ] *n* (*pl* -os) bibelot *m*, curiosité *f*.

curious ['kjʊərɪəs] *a* (*odd*) curieux; (*inquisitive*) curieux (**about** de); **c. to know** curieux de savoir. ◆—**ly** *adv* (*oddly*) curieusement. ◆**curi'osity** *n* curiosité *f*.

curl [kɜːl] **1** *vti* (*hair*) boucler, friser; – *n* boucle *f*; (*of smoke*) Fig spirale *f*. **2** *vi* **to c. up** (*shrivel*) se racornir; **to c. oneself up** (*into a ball*) se pelotonner. ◆—**er** *n* bigoudi *m*. ◆**curly** *a* (-ier, -iest) bouclé, frisé.

currant ['kʌrənt] *n* (*fruit*) groseille *f*; (*dried grape*) raisin *m* de Corinthe.

currency ['kʌrənsɪ] *n* (*money*) monnaie *f*; (*acceptance*) Fig cours *m*; (**foreign**) **c.** devises *fpl* (étrangères).

current ['kʌrənt] **1** *a* (*fashion, trend etc*) actuel; (*opinion, use, phrase*) courant; (*year, month*) en cours, courant; **c. affairs** questions *fpl* d'actualité; **c. events** actualité *f*; **the c. issue** (*of magazine etc*) le dernier numéro. **2** *n* (*of river, air*) & *El* courant *m*. ◆—**ly** *adv* actuellement, à présent.

curriculum, *pl* -la [kə'rɪkjʊləm, -lə] *n* programme *m* (scolaire); **c. (vitae)** curriculum (vitae) *m inv*.

curry ['kʌrɪ] **1** *n* Culin curry *m*, cari *m*. **2** *vt* **to c. favour** with s'insinuer dans les bonnes grâces de.

curs/e [kɜːs] *n* malédiction *f*; (*swearword*) juron *m*; (*bane*) Fig fléau *m*; – *vt* maudire; (*swear*) jurer. ◆—**ed** [-ɪd] *a* Fam maudit.

cursor ['kɜːsər] *n* (*on computer screen*) curseur *m*.

cursory ['kɜːsərɪ] *a* (*trop*) rapide, superficiel.

curt [kɜːt] *a* brusque. ◆—**ly** *adv* d'un ton brusque. ◆—**ness** *n* brusquerie *f*.

curtail [kɜː'teɪl] *vt* écourter, raccourcir; (*expenses*) réduire. ◆—**ment** *n* raccourcissement *m*; réduction *f*.

curtain ['kɜːt(ə)n] *n* rideau *m*; **c. call** *Th* rappel *m*.

curts(e)y ['kɜːtsɪ] *n* révérence *f*; – *vi* faire une révérence.

curve [kɜːv] *n* courbe *f*; (*in road*) *Am* virage *m*; *pl* (*of woman*) Fam rondeurs *fpl*; – *vt* courber; – *vi* se courber; (*of road*) tourner, faire une courbe.

cushion ['kʊʃən] *n* coussin *m*; – *vt* (*shock*) Fig amortir. ◆**cushioned** *a* (*seat*) rembourré; **c. against** Fig protégé contre.

cushy ['kʊʃɪ] *a* (-ier, -iest) (*job, life*) Fam pépère, facile.

custard ['kʌstəd] *n* crème *f* anglaise; (*when set*) crème *f* renversée.

custodian [kʌ'stəʊdɪən] *n* gardien, -ienne *mf*.

custody ['kʌstədɪ] *n* (*care*) garde *f*; **to take into c.** *Jur* mettre en détention préventive. ◆**cu'stodial** *a* **c. sentence** peine *f* de prison.

custom ['kʌstəm] *n* coutume *f*; (*patronage*) *Com* clientèle *f*. ◆**customary** *a* habituel, coutumier; **it is c. to** il est d'usage de. ◆**custom-built** *a*, ◆**customized** *a* (*car etc*) (fait) sur commande.

customer ['kʌstəmər] *n* client, -ente *mf*; Pej individu *m*.

customs ['kʌstəmz] *n* & *npl* (**the**) **c.** la douane; **c. (duties)** droits *mpl* de douane; **c. officer** douanier *m*; **c. union** union *f* douanière.

cut [kʌt] *n* coupure *f*; (*stroke*) coup *m*; (*of clothes, hair*) coupe *f*; (*in salary*) réduction *f*; (*of meat*) morceau *m*; – *vt* (*pt & pp* **cut**, *pres p* **cutting**) couper; (*meat*) découper; (*glass, tree*) tailler; (*record*) graver; (*hay*) faucher; (*profits, prices etc*) réduire; (*tooth*) percer; (*corner*) *Aut* prendre à la corde; **to c. open** ouvrir (*au couteau etc*); **to c. short** (*visit*) abréger; – *vi* (*of person, scissors*) couper; (*of material*) se couper; **to c. in** (*cake*) entamer. ■ **to c. away** *vt* (*remove*) enlever; **to c. back** (**on**) *vti* réduire. ◆**cutback** *n* réduction *f*. **to c. down** *vt* (*tree*) abattre, couper; **to c. down** (**on**) *vti* réduire; **to c. in** *vti* interrompre; *Aut* faire une queue de poisson (**on s.o.** à qn); **to c. off** *vt* couper; (*isolate*) isoler; **to c. out** *vi* (*of engine*) *Aut* caler; – *vt* (*article*) découper; (*garment*) tailler; (*remove*) enlever; (*leave out, get rid of*) Fam supprimer; **to c. out drinking** (*stop*) Fam s'arrêter de boire; **c. it out!** Fam ça suffit!; **c. out to be a doctor**/*etc* fait pour être médecin/*etc*. ◆**cutout** *n* (*picture*) découpage *m*; *El* coupe-circuit *m inv*; **to c. up** *vt* couper (en morceaux); (*meat*) découper; **c. up about** démoralisé par. ◆**cutting** *n* coupe *f*; (*of diamond*) taille *f*; (*article*) *Journ* coupure *f*; (*plant*) bouture *f*; *Cin* montage *m*; – *a* (*wind, word*) cinglant; **c. edge** tranchant *m*.

cute [kjuːt] *a* (-er, -est) Fam (*pretty*) mignon; (*shrewd*) astucieux.

cuticle ['kjuːtɪk(ə)l] *n* petites peaux *fpl* (de l'ongle).

cutlery ['kʌtlərɪ] *n* couverts *mpl*.

cutlet ['kʌtlɪt] *n* (*of veal etc*) côtelette *f*.

cut-price ['kʌtpraɪs] *a* à prix réduit.

cutthroat ['kʌtθrəʊt] *n* assassin *m*; – *a* (*competition*) impitoyable.

cv [si'vi:] *n abbr* curriculum (vitae) *m inv.*

cyanide ['saɪənaɪd] *n* cyanure *m.*

cybernetics [saɪbə'netɪks] *n* cybernétique *f.*

cycle ['saɪk(ə)l] **1** *n* bicyclette *f*, vélo *m*; – *a* (*path, track*) cyclable; (*race*) cycliste; – *vi* aller à bicyclette (**to** à); *Sp* faire de la bicyclette. **2** *n* (*series, period*) cycle *m.* ◆**cycling** *n* cyclisme *m*; – *a* (*champion*) cycliste. ◆**cyclist** *n* cycliste *mf.* ◆**cyclic(al)** ['sɪklɪk(ə)l] *a* cyclique.

cyclone ['saɪkləʊn] *n* cyclone *m.*

cylinder ['sɪlɪndər] *n* cylindre *m.* ◆**cy-'lindrical** *a* cylindrique.

cymbal ['sɪmbəl] *n* cymbale *f.*

cynic ['sɪnɪk] *n* cynique *mf.* ◆**cynical** *a* cynique. ◆**cynicism** *n* cynisme *m.*

cypress ['saɪprəs] *n* (*tree*) cyprès *m.*

Cyprus ['saɪprəs] *n* Chypre *f.* ◆**Cypriot** ['sɪprɪət] *a & n* cypriote (*mf*).

cyst [sɪst] *n Med* kyste *m.*

czar [zɑːr] *n* tsar *m.*

Czech [tʃek] *a & n* tchèque (*mf*). ◆**Czecho'slovak** *a & n* tchécoslovaque (*mf*). ◆**Czechoslo'vakia** *n* Tchécoslovaquie *f.* ◆**Czechoslo'vakian** *a & n* tchécoslovaque (*mf*).

D

D, d [di:] *n* D, d *m.* ◆**D.-day** *n* le jour J.

dab [dæb] *n a* **d. of** un petit peu de; – *vt* (**-bb-**) (*wound, brow etc*) tamponner; **to d. sth on sth** appliquer qch (à petits coups) sur qch.

dabble ['dæb(ə)l] *vi* **to d. in** s'occuper *or se* mêler un peu de.

dad [dæd] *n Fam* papa *m.* ◆**daddy** *n Fam* papa *m*; **d. longlegs** (*cranefly*) tipule *f*; (*spider*) *Am* faucheur *m.*

daffodil ['dæfədɪl] *n* jonquille *f.*

daft [dɑːft] *a* (**-er, -est**) *Fam* idiot, bête.

dagger ['dægər] *n* poignard *m*; **at daggers drawn** à couteaux tirés (**with** avec).

dahlia ['deɪljə, *Am* 'dæljə] *n* dahlia *m.*

daily ['deɪlɪ] *a* quotidien, journalier; (*wage*) journalier; – *adv* quotidiennement; – *n* **d.** (*paper*) quotidien *m*; **d. (help)** (*cleaning woman*) femme *f* de ménage.

dainty ['deɪntɪ] *a* (**-ier, -iest**) délicat; (*pretty*) mignon; (*tasteful*) élégant. ◆**daintily** *adv* délicatement; élégamment.

dairy ['deərɪ] *n* (*on farm*) laiterie *f*; (*shop*) crémerie *f*; – *a* (*produce, cow etc*) laitier. ◆**dairyman** *n* (*pl* **-men**) (*dealer*) laitier *m.* ◆**dairywoman** *n* (*pl* **-women**) laitière *f.*

daisy ['deɪzɪ] *n* pâquerette *f.*

dale [deɪl] *n Geog Lit* vallée *f.*

dally ['dælɪ] *vi* musarder, lanterner.

dam [dæm] *n* (*wall*) barrage *m*; – *vt* (**-mm-**) (*river*) endiguer.

damage ['dæmɪdʒ] *n* dégâts *mpl*, dommages *mpl*; (*harm*) *Fig* préjudice *m*; *pl Jur* dommages-intérêts *mpl*; – *vt* (*spoil*) abîmer; (*material object*) endommager, abîmer; (*harm*) *Fig* nuire à. ◆**—ing** *a* préjudiciable (**to** à).

dame [deɪm] *n Lit* dame *f*; *Am Sl* nana *f*, fille *f.*

damn [dæm] *vt* (*condemn, doom*) condamner; *Rel* damner; (*curse*) maudire; **d. him!** *Fam* qu'il aille au diable!; – *int* **d. (it)!** *Fam* zut!, merde!; – **n he** doesn't care **a d.** *Fam* il s'en fiche pas mal; – *a Fam* fichu, sacré; – *adv Fam* sacrément; **d.** all rien du tout. ◆**—ed 1** *a* (*soul*) damné. **2** *Fam* = **damn** *a & adv.* ◆**—ing** *a* (*evidence etc*) accablant. ◆**dam'nation** *n* damnation *f.*

damp [dæmp] *a* (**-er, -est**) humide; (*skin*) moite; – *n* humidité *f.* ◆**damp(en)** *vt* humecter; **to d. (down)** (*zeal*) refroidir; (*ambition*) étouffer. ◆**damper** *n* **to put a d.** on jeter un froid sur. ◆**dampness** *n* humidité *f.*

damsel ['dæmzəl] *n Lit & Hum* demoiselle *f.*

damson ['dæmzən] *n* prune *f* de Damas.

danc/e [dɑːns] *n* danse *f*; (*social event*) bal *m*; **d. hall** dancing *m*; – *vi* danser; **to d. for joy** sauter de joie; – *vt* (*polka etc*) danser. ◆**—ing** *n* danse *f*; **d. partner** cavalier, -ière *mf.* ◆**—er** *n* danseur, -euse *mf.*

dandelion ['dændɪlaɪən] *n* pissenlit *m.*

dandruff ['dændrʌf] *n* pellicules *fpl.*

dandy ['dændɪ] **1** *n* dandy *m.* **2** *a* (*very good*) *Am Fam* formidable.

Dane [deɪn] *n* Danois, -oise *mf.*

danger ['deɪndʒər] *n* (*peril*) danger *m* (**to** pour); (*risk*) risque *m*; **in d.** en danger; **in d. of** (*threatened by*) menacé de; **to be in d. of falling**/*etc* risquer de tomber/*etc*; **on the d. list** *Med* dans un état critique; **d. signal** signal *m* d'alarme; **d. zone** zone *f* dangereuse. ◆**dangerous** *a* (*place, illness,*

person etc) dangereux (**to** pour).
◆**dangerously** *adv* dangereusement; (*ill*) gravement.

dangle ['dæŋg(ə)l] *vt* balancer; (*prospect*) *Fig* faire miroiter (**before s.o.** aux yeux de qn); − *vi* (*hang*) pendre; (*swing*) se balancer.

Danish ['deɪnɪʃ] *a* danois; − *n* (*language*) danois *m*.

dank [dæŋk] *a* (*-er, -est*) humide (et froid).

dapper ['dæpər] *a* pimpant, fringant.

dappled ['dæp(ə)ld] *a* pommelé, tacheté.

dar/e [deər] *vt* oser (**do** faire); **she d. not come** elle n'ose pas venir; **he doesn't d.** (**to**) **go** il n'ose pas y aller; **if you d.** (**to**) si tu l'oses, si tu oses le faire; **I d. say he tried** il a sans doute essayé, je suppose qu'il a essayé; **to d. s.o. to do** défier qn de faire. ◆**−ing** *a* audacieux; − *n* audace *f*.
◆**daredevil** *n* casse-cou *m inv*, risque-tout *m inv*.

dark [dɑːk] *a* (*-er, -est*) obscur, noir, sombre; (*colour*) foncé, sombre; (*skin*) brun, foncé; (*hair*) brun, noir, foncé; (*eyes*) foncé; (*gloomy*) sombre; **it's d.** il fait nuit or noir; **to keep sth d.** tenir qch secret; **d. glasses** lunettes *fpl* noires; − *n* noir *m*, obscurité *f*; **after d.** après la tombée de la nuit; **to keep s.o. in the d.** laisser qn dans l'ignorance (**about** de). ◆**d.-'haired** *a* aux cheveux bruns. ◆**d.-'skinned** *a* brun; (*race*) de couleur. ◆**darken** *vt* assombrir, obscurcir; (*colour*) foncer; − *vi* s'assombrir; (*of colour*) foncer. ◆**darkness** *n* obscurité *f*, noir *m*.

darkroom ['dɑːkruːm] *n Phot* chambre *f* noire.

darling ['dɑːlɪŋ] *n* (*favourite*) chouchou, -oute *mf*; (**my) d.** (mon) chéri, (ma) chérie; **he's a d.** c'est un amour; **be a d.!** sois un ange!; − *a* (*delightful*) *Fam* adorable.

darn [dɑːn] **1** *vt* (*socks*) repriser. **2** *int* **d. it!** bon sang! ◆**−ing** *n* reprise *f*; − *a* (*needle, wool*) à repriser.

dart [dɑːt] **1** *vi* se précipiter, s'élancer (**for** vers); − *n* **to make a d.** se précipiter (**for** vers). **2** *n Sp* fléchette *f*; *pl* (*game*) fléchettes *fpl*. ◆**dartboard** *n Sp* cible *f*.

dash [dæʃ] **1** *n* (*run, rush*) ruée *f*; **to make a d.** se précipiter (**for** vers); − *vi* se précipiter; (*of waves*) se briser (**against** contre); **to d. off** *or* **away** partir *or* filer en vitesse; − *vt* jeter (*avec force*); (*hopes*) briser; (*shatter*) briser; **d. (it)!** *Fam* zut!; **to d. off** (*letter*) faire en vitesse. **2** *n* **a d. of** un (petit) peu de; **a d. of milk** une goutte *or* un nuage de lait. **3** *n* (*stroke*) trait

m; *Typ* tiret *m*. ◆**−ing** *a* (*person*) sémillant.

dashboard ['dæʃbɔːd] *n Aut* tableau *m* de bord.

data ['deɪtə] *npl* données *fpl*; **d. processing** informatique *f*.

date¹ [deɪt] *n* date *f*; (*on coin*) millésime *m*; (*meeting*) *Fam* rendez-vous *m*; (*person*) *Fam* copain, -ine *mf* (*avec qui on a un rendez-vous*); **up to d.** moderne; (*information*) à jour; (*well-informed*) au courant (**on** de); **out of d.** (*old-fashioned*) démodé; (*expired*) périmé; **to d.** à ce jour, jusqu'ici; **d. stamp** (*object*) (tampon *m*) dateur *m*; (*mark*) cachet *m*; − *vt* (*letter etc*) dater; (*girl, boy*) *Fam* sortir avec; − *vi* (*become out of date*) dater; **to d. back to, d. from** dater de. ◆**dated** *a* démodé.

date² [deɪt] *n Bot* datte *f*.

datebook ['deɪtbuk] *n Am* agenda *m*.

daub [dɔːb] *vt* barbouiller (**with** de).

daughter ['dɔːtər] *n* fille *f*. ◆**d.-in-law** *n* (*pl* **daughters-in-law**) belle-fille *f*, bru *f*.

daunt [dɔːnt] *vt* décourager, rebuter. ◆**−less** *a* intrépide.

dawdl/e ['dɔːd(ə)l] *vi* traîner, lambiner. ◆**−er** *n* traînard, -arde *mf*.

dawn [dɔːn] *n* aube *f*, aurore *f*; − *vi* (*of day*) poindre; (*of new era, idea*) naître, voir le jour; **it dawned upon him that . . .** il lui est venu à l'esprit que . . . ◆**−ing** *a* naissant.

day [deɪ] *n* jour *m*; (*working period, whole day long*) journée *f*; *pl* (*period*) époque *f*, temps *mpl*; **all d.** (**long**) toute la journée; **what d. is it?** quel jour sommes-nous?; **the following** *or* **next d.** le lendemain; **the d. before** la veille; **the d. before yesterday** avant-hier; **the d. after tomorrow** après-demain; **to the d.** jour pour jour; **d. boarder** demi-pensionnaire *mf*. ◆**d.-to-'d.** *a* journalier; **on a d.-to-day basis** (*every day*) journellement. ◆**daybreak** *n* point *m* du jour. ◆**daydream** *n* rêverie *f*; − *vi* rêvasser. ◆**daylight** *n* (lumière *f* du) jour *m*; (*dawn*) point *m* du jour; **it's d.** il fait jour. ◆**daytime** *n* journée *f*, jour *m*.

daze [deɪz] *vt* (*with drugs etc*) hébéter; (*by blow*) étourdir; − *n* **in a d.** étourdi; hébété.

dazzle ['dæz(ə)l] *vt* éblouir; − *n* éblouissement *m*.

deacon ['diːkən] *n Rel* diacre *m*.

dead [ded] *a* mort; (*numb*) engourdi; (*party etc*) qui manque de vie, mortel; (*telephone*) sans tonalité; **in (the) d. centre** au beau milieu; **to be a d. loss** (*person*) *Fam* n'être bon à rien; **it's a d. loss** *Fam* ça ne vaut rien; **d. silence** un silence de mort; **d. stop** un arrêt complet; **d. end** (*street*) & *Fig* impasse *f*; **a d.-end job** un travail sans avenir; – *adv* (*completely*) absolument; (*very*) très; **d. beat** *Fam* éreinté; **d. drunk** *Fam* ivre mort; **to stop d.** s'arrêter net; – *n* **the d.** les morts *mpl*; **in the d. of** (*night, winter*) au cœur de. ◆**-ly** *a* (-ier, -iest) (*enemy, silence, paleness*) mortel; (*weapon*) meurtrier; **d. sins** péchés *mpl* capitaux; – *adv* mortellement. ◆**deadbeat** *n Am Fam* parasite *m*. ◆**deadline** *n* date *f* limite; (*hour*) heure *f* limite. ◆**deadlock** *n Fig* impasse *f*. ◆**deadpan** *a* (*face*) figé, impassible.

deaden ['ded(ə)n] *vt* (*shock*) amortir; (*pain*) calmer; (*feeling*) émousser.

deaf [def] *a* sourd (**to** à); **d. and dumb** sourd-muet; **d. in one ear** sourd d'une oreille; **the d.** les sourds *mpl*. ◆**d.-aid** *n* audiophone *m*, prothèse *f* auditive. ◆**deafen** *vt* assourdir. ◆**deafness** *n* surdité *f*.

deal [di:l] **1** *n* **a good** or **great d.** beaucoup (**of** de). **2** *n Com* marché *m*, affaire *f*; *Cards* donne *f*; **fair d.** traitement *m* or arrangement *m* équitable; **it's a d.** d'accord; **big d.!** *Iron* la belle affaire! **3** *vt* (*pt* & *pp* **dealt** [delt]) (*blow*) porter; **to d.** (**out**) (*cards*) donner; (*money*) distribuer. **4** *vi* (*trade*) traiter (**with** s.o. avec qn); **to d. in** faire le commerce de; **to d. with** (*take care of*) s'occuper de; (*concern*) traiter de, parler de; **I can d. with him** (*handle*) je sais m'y prendre avec lui. ◆**-ings** *npl* relations *fpl* (**with** avec); *Com* transactions *fpl*. ◆**-er** *n* marchand, -ande *mf* (**in** de); (*agent*) dépositaire *mf*; (*for cars*) concessionnaire *mf*; (*in drugs*) *Sl* revendeur, -euse *mf* de drogues; *Cards* donneur, -euse *mf*.

deal² [di:l] *n* (*wood*) sapin *m*.

dean [di:n] *n Rel Univ* doyen *m*.

dear [diər] *a* (-er, -est) (*loved, precious, expensive*) cher; (*price*) élevé; **D. Sir** (*in letter*) *Com* Monsieur; **D. Uncle** (*mon*) cher oncle; **oh d.!** oh là là!, oh mon Dieu!; – *n* (my) **d.** (*darling*) (mon) chéri, (ma) chérie; (*friend*) mon cher, ma chère; **she's a d.** c'est un amour; **be a d.!** sois un ange!; – *adv* (*to cost, pay*) cher. ◆**-ly** *adv* tendrement; (*very much*) beaucoup; **to pay d. for sth** payer qch cher.

dearth [dɜːθ] *n* manque *m*, pénurie *f*.

death [deθ] *n* mort *f*; **to put to d.** mettre à mort; **to be bored to d.** s'ennuyer à mourir;

to be burnt to d. mourir carbonisé; **to be sick to d.** en avoir vraiment marre; **many deaths** (*people killed*) de nombreux morts *mpl*; – *a* (*march*) funèbre; (*mask*) mortuaire; **d. certificate** acte *m* de décès; **d. duty** droits *mpl* de succession; **d. penalty** or **sentence** peine *f* de mort; **d. rate** mortalité *f*; **it's a d. trap** il y a danger de mort. ◆**deathbed** *n* lit *m* de mort. ◆**death-blow** *n* coup *m* mortel. ◆**deathly** *a* mortel, de mort; – *adv* **d. pale** d'une pâleur mortelle.

debar [di'bɑːr] *vt* (-rr-) exclure; **to d. from doing** interdire de faire.

debase [di'beis] *vt* (*person*) avilir; (*reputation, talents*) galvauder; (*coinage*) altérer.

debat/e [di'beit] *vti* discuter; **to d.** (**with oneself**) **whether to leave**/*etc* se demander si on doit partir/*etc*; – *n* débat *m*, discussion *f*. ◆**-able** *a* discutable, contestable.

debauch [di'bɔːtʃ] *vt* corrompre, débaucher. ◆**debauchery** *n* débauche *f*.

debilitate [di'biliteit] *vt* débiliter. ◆**debility** *n* faiblesse *f*, débilité *f*.

debit ['debit] *n* débit *m*; **in d.** (*account*) débiteur; – *a* **d. balance** Fin débiteur; – *vt* débiter (**s.o. with sth** qn de qch).

debonair [debə'neər] *a* jovial, (*charming*) charmant; (*polite*) poli.

debris ['debri] *n* débris *mpl*.

debt [det] *n* dette *f*; **to be in d.** avoir des dettes; **to be £50 in d.** devoir 50 livres; **to run** or **get into d.** faire des dettes. ◆**debtor** *n* débiteur, -trice *mf*.

debunk [di'bʌŋk] *vt Fam* démystifier.

debut ['deibjuː] *n* Th début *m*.

decade ['dekeid] *n* décennie *f*.

decadent ['dekədənt] *a* décadent. ◆**decadence** *n* décadence *f*.

decaffeinated [di'kæfineitid] *a* décaféiné.

decal ['diːkæl] *n Am* décalcomanie *f*.

decant [di'kænt] *vt* (*wine*) décanter. ◆**-er** *n* carafe *f*.

decapitate [di'kæpiteit] *vt* décapiter.

decathlon [di'kæθlɒn] *n Sp* décathlon *m*.

decay [di'kei] *vi* (*go bad*) se gâter; (*rot*) pourrir; (*of tooth*) se carier, se gâter; (*of building*) tomber en ruine; (*decline*) Fig décliner; – *n* pourriture *f*; *Archit* délabrement *m*; (*of tooth*) carie(s) *f*(*pl*); (*of nation*) décadence *f*; **to fall into d.** (*of building*) tomber en ruine. ◆**-ing** *a* (*nation*) décadent; (*meat, fruit etc*) pourrissant.

deceased [di'siːst] *a* décédé, défunt; – *n* **the d.** le défunt, la défunte; *pl* les défunt(e)s.

deceit [di'siːt] *n* tromperie *f*. ◆**deceitful** *a*

trompeur. ◆**deceitfully** adv avec duplicité.
deceive [dɪ'siːv] vti tromper; **to d. oneself** se
faire des illusions.
December [dɪ'sembər] n décembre m.
decent ['diːsənt] a (respectable) convenable,
décent; (good) Fam bon; (kind) Fam
gentil; **that was d. (of you)** c'était chic de ta
part. ◆**decency** n décence f; (kindness)
Fam gentillesse f. ◆**decently** adv décemment.
decentralize [diː'sentrəlaɪz] vt décentraliser. ◆**decentrali'zation** n décentralisation f.
deception [dɪ'sepʃ(ə)n] n tromperie f.
◆**deceptive** a trompeur.
decibel ['desɪbel] n décibel m.
decid/e [dɪ'saɪd] vt (question etc) régler,
décider; (s.o.'s career, fate etc) décider de;
to d. to do décider de faire; **to d. that**
décider que; **to d. s.o. to do** décider qn à
faire; – vi (make decisions) décider; (make
up one's mind) se décider (**on doing** à faire);
to d. on sth décider de qch, se décider à
qch; (choose) se décider pour qch. ◆**—ed** a
(firm) décidé, résolu; (clear) net. ◆**—edly**
adv résolument; nettement. ◆**—ing** a
(factor etc) décisif.
decimal ['desɪml] a décimal; **d. point**
virgule f; – n décimale f. ◆**decimali-**
'zation n décimalisation f.
decimate ['desɪmeɪt] vt décimer.
decipher [dɪ'saɪfər] vt déchiffrer.
decision [dɪ'sɪʒ(ə)n] n décision f. ◆**deci-**
sive [dɪ'saɪsɪv] a (defeat, tone etc) décisif;
(victory) net, incontestable. ◆**decisively**
adv (to state) avec décision; (to win) nettement, incontestablement.
deck [dek] **1** n Nau pont m; **top d.** (of bus)
impériale f. **2** n **d. of cards** jeu m de cartes. **3**
n (of record player) platine f. **4** vt **to d.** (out)
(adorn) orner. ◆**deckchair** n chaise f
longue.
declare [dɪ'kleər] vt déclarer (**that** que);
(verdict, result) proclamer. ◆**decla'ration**
n déclaration f; proclamation f.
declin/e [dɪ'klaɪn] **1** vi (deteriorate) baisser;
(of birthrate, price etc) baisser; **to**
d. in importance perdre de l'importance; –
n déclin m; (fall) baisse f. **2** vt refuser,
décliner; **to d. to do** refuser de faire.
◆**—ing** a one's d. years ses dernières
années.
decode [diː'kəʊd] vt (message) décoder.
decompose [diːkəm'pəʊz] vt décomposer;
– vi se décomposer. ◆**decompo'sition** n
décomposition f.

decompression [diːkəm'preʃ(ə)n] n
décompression f.
decontaminate [diːkən'tæmɪneɪt] vt décontaminer.
decor ['deɪkɔːr] n décor m.
decorat/e ['dekəreɪt] vt (cake, house,
soldier) décorer (**with** de); (paint etc) peindre (et tapisser); (hat, skirt etc) orner (**with**
de). ◆**—ing** n interior d. décoration f
d'intérieurs. ◆**deco'ration** n décoration
f. ◆**decorative** a décoratif. ◆**decorator**
n (house painter etc) peintre m décorateur;
(interior) d. ensemblier m, décorateur,
-trice mf.
decorum [dɪ'kɔːrəm] n bienséances fpl.
decoy ['diːkɔɪ] n (artificial bird) appeau m;
(police) policier m en civil.
decreas/e [dɪ'kriːs] vti diminuer; –
['diːkriːs] n diminution f (**in** de). ◆**—ing** a
(number etc) décroissant. ◆**—ingly** adv de
moins en moins.
decree [dɪ'kriː] n Pol Rel décret m; Jur jugement m; (municipal) arrêté m; – vt (pt &
pp **decreed**) décréter.
decrepit [dɪ'krepɪt] a (building) en ruine;
(person) décrépit.
decry [dɪ'kraɪ] vt décrier.
dedicat/e ['dedɪkeɪt] vt (devote) consacrer
(**to** à); (book) dédier (**to** à); **to d. oneself to**
se consacrer à. ◆**dedi'cation** n (in book)
dédicace f; (devotion) dévouement m.
deduce [dɪ'djuːs] vt (conclude) déduire (**from**
de, **that** que).
deduct [dɪ'dʌkt] vt (subtract) déduire,
retrancher (**from** de); (from wage, account)
prélever (**from** sur). ◆**deductible** a à
déduire (**from** de); (expenses) déductible.
◆**deduction** n (inference) & Com déduction f.
deed [diːd] n action f, acte m; (feat) exploit
m; Jur acte m (notarié).
deem [diːm] vt juger, estimer.
deep [diːp] a (-er, -est) profond; (snow)
épais; (voice) grave; note Mus bas;
(person) insondable; **to be six metres/etc d.**
avoir six mètres/etc de profondeur; **d. in**
thought absorbé ou plongé dans ses
pensées; **the d. end** (in swimming pool) le
grand bain; **d. red** rouge foncé; – adv (to
breathe) profondément; **d. into the night**
tard dans la nuit; – n the d. l'océan m.
◆**—ly** adv (grateful, to regret etc)
profondément. ◆**deep-'freeze** vt surgeler; – n congélateur m. ◆**d.-'fryer** n
friteuse f. ◆**d.-'rooted** a, ◆**d.-'seated** a
bien ancré, profond. ◆**d.-'set** a (eyes)
enfoncés.

deepen [ˈdiːpən] vt approfondir; (increase) augmenter; – vi devenir plus profond; (of mystery) s'épaissir. ◆**—ing** a grandissant.

deer [dɪər] n inv cerf m.

deface [dɪˈfeɪs] vt (damage) dégrader; (daub) barbouiller.

defamation [defəˈmeɪʃ(ə)n] n diffamation f. ◆**deˈfamatory** a diffamatoire.

default [dɪˈfɔːlt] n **by d.** Jur par défaut; **to win by d.** gagner par forfait; – vi Jur faire défaut; **to d. on one's payments** Fin être en rupture de paiement.

defeat [dɪˈfiːt] vt battre, vaincre; (plan) faire échouer; – n défaite f; (of plan) échec m. ◆**defeatism** n défaitisme m.

defect 1 [ˈdiːfekt] n défaut m. **2** [dɪˈfekt] vi Pol déserter, faire défection; **to d. to** (the West, the enemy) passer à. ◆**deˈfection** n défection f. ◆**deˈfective** a défectueux; Med déficient. ◆**deˈfector** n transfuge mf.

defence [dɪˈfens] (Am **defense**) n défense f; **the body's defences** la défense de l'organisme (against contre); **in his d.** Jur à sa décharge, pour le défendre. ◆**defenceless** a sans défense. ◆**defensible** a défendable. ◆**defensive** a défensif; – n **on the d.** sur la défensive.

defend [dɪˈfend] vt défendre. ◆**defendant** n (accused) Jur prévenu, -ue mf. ◆**defender** n défenseur m; (of title) Sp détenteur, -trice mf.

defer [dɪˈfɜːr] **1** vt (-rr-) (postpone) différer, reporter. **2** vi (-rr-) **to d. to** (yield) déférer à. ◆**—ment** n report m.

deference [ˈdefərəns] n déférence f. ◆**defeˈrential** a déférent, plein de déférence.

defiant [dɪˈfaɪənt] a (tone etc) de défi; (person) rebelle. ◆**defiance** n (resistance) défi m (of à); **in d. of** (contempt) au mépris de. ◆**defiantly** adv d'un air de défi.

deficient [dɪˈfɪʃənt] a insuffisant; Med déficient; **to be d. in** manquer de. ◆**deficiency** n manque m; (flaw) défaut m; Med carence f; (mental) déficience f.

deficit [ˈdefɪsɪt] n déficit m.

defile [dɪˈfaɪl] vt souiller, salir.

define [dɪˈfaɪn] vt définir. ◆**defiˈnition** n définition f.

definite [ˈdefɪnɪt] a (date, plan) précis, déterminé; (obvious) net, évident; (firm) ferme; (certain) certain; **d. article** Gram article m défini. ◆**—ly** adv certainement; (appreciably) nettement; (to say) catégoriquement.

definitive [dɪˈfɪnɪtɪv] a définitif.

deflate [dɪˈfleɪt] vt (tyre) dégonfler. ◆**deflation** n dégonflement m; Econ déflation f.

deflect [dɪˈflekt] vt faire dévier; – vi dévier.

deform [dɪˈfɔːm] vt déformer. ◆**—ed** a (body) difforme. ◆**deformity** n difformité f.

defraud [dɪˈfrɔːd] vt (customs, State etc) frauder; **to d. s.o. of sth** escroquer qch à qn.

defray [dɪˈfreɪ] vt (expenses) payer.

defrost [diːˈfrɒst] vt (fridge) dégivrer; (food) décongeler.

deft [deft] a adroit (with de). ◆**—ness** n adresse f.

defunct [dɪˈfʌŋkt] a défunt.

defuse [diːˈfjuːz] vt (bomb, conflict) désamorcer.

defy [dɪˈfaɪ] vt (person, death etc) défier; (effort, description) résister à; **to d. s.o. to do** défier qn de faire.

degenerate [dɪˈdʒenəreɪt] vi dégénérer (into en); – [dɪˈdʒenərət] a & n dégénéré, -ée (mf). ◆**degeneˈration** n dégénérescence f.

degrade [dɪˈgreɪd] vt dégrader. ◆**degradation** [degrəˈdeɪʃ(ə)n] n Mil Ch dégradation f; (of person) déchéance f.

degree [dɪˈgriː] n **1** degré m; **not in the slightest d.** pas du tout; **to such a d.** à tel point (that que). **2** Univ diplôme m; (Bachelor's) licence f; (Master's) maîtrise f; (PhD) doctorat m.

dehumanize [diːˈhjuːmənaɪz] vt déshumaniser.

dehydrate [diːhaɪˈdreɪt] vt déshydrater.

de-ice [diːˈaɪs] vt Av Aut dégivrer.

deign [deɪn] vt daigner (to do faire).

deity [ˈdiːɪtɪ] n dieu m.

dejected [dɪˈdʒektɪd] a abattu, découragé. ◆**dejection** n abattement m.

dekko [ˈdekəʊ] n Sl coup m d'œil.

delay [dɪˈleɪ] vt retarder; (payment) différer; – vi (be slow) tarder (doing à faire); (linger) s'attarder; – n (lateness) retard m; (waiting period) délai m; **without d.** sans tarder. ◆**delayed-ˈaction** a (bomb) à retardement. ◆**delaying** a **d. tactics** moyens mpl dilatoires.

delectable [dɪˈlektəb(ə)l] a délectable.

delegate 1 [ˈdelɪget] vt déléguer (to à). **2** [ˈdelɪget] n délégué, -ée mf. ◆**deleˈgation** n délégation f.

delete [dɪˈliːt] vt rayer, supprimer. ◆**deletion** n (thing deleted) rature f; (act) suppression f.

deleterious [delɪˈtɪərɪəs] a néfaste.

deliberate 1 [dɪˈlɪbəreɪt] vi délibérer; – vt délibérer sur.

deliberate 2 [dɪˈlɪbərət] a (intentional) délibéré; (cautious) réfléchi; (slow) mesuré.

◆—ly adv (intentionally) exprès, délibérément; (to walk) avec mesure. ◆deliberation f.

delicate ['delɪkɪt] a délicat. ◆delicacy n délicatesse f; Culin mets m délicat, gourmandise f. ◆delicately adv délicatement. ◆delica'tessen n (shop) épicerie f fine, traiteur m.

delicious [dɪ'lɪʃəs] a délicieux.

delight [dɪ'laɪt] n délice m, grand plaisir m, joie f; pl (pleasures, things) délices fpl; to be the d. of faire les délices de; to take d. in sth/in doing se délecter de qch/à faire; – vt réjouir; – vi se délecter (in doing à faire). ◆—ed a ravi, enchanté (with sth de qch, to do de faire, that que). ◆delightful a charmant; (meal, perfume, sensation) délicieux. ◆delightfully adv avec beaucoup de charme; (wonderfully) merveilleusement.

delineate [dɪ'lɪnɪeɪt] vt (outline) esquisser; (portray) décrire.

delinquent [dɪ'lɪŋkwənt] a & n délinquant, -ante (mf). ◆delinquency n délinquance f.

delirious [dɪ'lɪərɪəs] a délirant; to be d. avoir le délire, délirer. ◆delirium n Med délire m.

deliver [dɪ'lɪvər] vt 1 (goods, milk etc) livrer; (letters) distribuer; (hand over) remettre (to à). 2 (rescue) délivrer (from de). 3 (give birth to) mettre au monde, accoucher de; to d. a woman('s baby) accoucher une femme. 4 (speech) prononcer; (ultimatum, warning) lancer; (blow) porter. ◆deliverance n délivrance f. ◆delivery n 1 livraison f; distribution f; remise f. 2 Med accouchement m. 3 (speaking) débit m. ◆deliveryman n (pl -men) livreur m.

delta ['deltə] n (of river) delta m.

delude [dɪ'luːd] vt tromper; to d. oneself se faire des illusions. ◆delusion n illusion f; Psy aberration f mentale.

deluge ['deljuːdʒ] n (of water, questions etc) déluge m; – vt inonder (with de).

de luxe [dɪ'lʌks] a de luxe.

delve [delv] vi to d. into (question, past) fouiller; (books) fouiller dans.

demagogue ['deməgɒg] n démagogue mf.

demand [dɪ'mɑːnd] vt exiger (sth from s.o. qch de qn), réclamer (sth from s.o. qch à qn); (rights, more pay) revendiquer; to d. that exiger que; to d. to know insister pour savoir; – n exigence f; (claim) revendication f, réclamation f; (request) & Econ demande f; in great d. très demandé; to

make demands on s.o. exiger beaucoup de qn. ◆—ing a exigeant.

demarcation [diːmɑːˈkeɪʃ(ə)n] n démarcation f.

demean [dɪ'miːn] vt to d. oneself s'abaisser, s'avilir.

demeanour [dɪ'miːnər] n (behaviour) comportement m.

demented [dɪ'mentɪd] a dément.

demerara [deməˈreərə] n d. (sugar) cassonade f, sucre m roux.

demise [dɪ'maɪz] n (death) décès m; Fig disparition f.

demo ['deməʊ] n (pl -os) (demonstration) Fam manif f.

demobilize [dɪ'məʊbɪlaɪz] vt démobiliser.

democracy [dɪ'mɒkrəsɪ] n démocratie f. ◆democrat ['deməkræt] n démocrate mf. ◆demo'cratic a démocratique; (person) démocrate.

demography [dɪ'mɒgrəfɪ] n démographie f.

demolish [dɪ'mɒlɪʃ] vt démolir. ◆demo'lition n démolition f.

demon ['diːmən] n démon m.

demonstrate ['demənstreɪt] vt démontrer; (machine) faire une démonstration de; – vi Pol manifester. ◆demon'stration n démonstration f; Pol manifestation f. ◆de'monstrative a démonstratif. ◆demonstrator n Pol manifestant, -ante mf; (in shop etc) démonstrateur, -trice mf.

demoralize [dɪ'mɒrəlaɪz] vt démoraliser.

demote [dɪ'məʊt] vt rétrograder.

demure [dɪ'mjʊər] a sage, réservé.

den [den] n antre m, tanière f.

denationalize [diːˈnæʃ(ə)nəlaɪz] vt dénationaliser.

denial [dɪ'naɪəl] n (of truth etc) dénégation f; (of rumour) démenti m; (of authority) rejet m; to issue a d. publier un démenti.

denigrate ['denɪgreɪt] vt dénigrer.

denim ['denɪm] n (toile f de) coton m; pl (jeans) (blue-)jean m.

denizen ['denɪz(ə)n] n habitant, -ante mf.

Denmark ['denmɑːk] n Danemark m.

denomination [dɪnɒmɪˈneɪʃ(ə)n] n confession f, religion f; (sect) secte m; (of coin, banknote) valeur f; Math unité f. ◆denominational a (school) confessionnel.

denote [dɪ'nəʊt] vt dénoter.

denounce [dɪ'naʊns] vt (person, injustice etc) dénoncer (to à); to d. s.o. as a spy/etc accuser qn publiquement d'être un espion/etc. ◆denunci'ation n dénonciation f; accusation f publique.

dense [dens] a (-er, -est) dense; (stupid)

Fam lourd, bête. ◆**—ly** *adv* d. populated/*etc* très peuplé/*etc*. ◆**density** *n* densité *f*.

dent [dent] *n* (*in metal*) bosselure *f*; (*in car*) bosse *f*, gnon *m*; **full of dents** (*car*) cabossé; **to make a d. in one's savings** taper dans ses économies; *— vt* cabosser, bosseler.

dental ['dent(ə)l] *a* dentaire; **d. surgeon** chirurgien *m* dentiste. ◆**dentist** *n* dentiste *mf*. ◆**dentistry** *n* médecine *f* dentaire; **school of d.** école *f* dentaire. ◆**dentures** *npl* dentier *m*.

deny [dɪ'naɪ] *vt* nier (**doing** avoir fait, **that** que); (*rumour*) démentir; (*authority*) rejeter; (*disown*) renier; **to d. s.o. sth** refuser qch à qn.

deodorant [di:'əudərənt] *n* déodorant *m*.

depart [dɪ'pɑːt] *vi* partir; (*deviate*) s'écarter (**from** de); *— vt* **to d. this world** *Lit* quitter ce monde. ◆**—ed** *a & n* (*dead*) défunt, -unte (*mf*). ◆**departure** *n* départ *m*; **a d. from** (*custom, rule*) un écart par rapport à, une entorse à; **to be a new d. for** constituer une nouvelle voie pour.

department [dɪ'pɑːtmənt] *n* département *m*; (*in office*) service *m*; (*in shop*) rayon *m*; *Univ* section *f*, département *m*; **that's your d.** (*sphere*) c'est ton rayon; **d. store** grand magasin *m*. ◆**depart'mental** *a* **d. manager** (*office*) chef *m* de service; (*shop*) chef *m* de rayon.

depend [dɪ'pend] *vi* dépendre (**on, upon** de); **to d.** (**up**)**on** (*rely on*) compter sur (**for sth** pour qch); **you can d. on it!** tu peux en être sûr! ◆**—able** *a* (*person, information etc*) sûr; (*machine*) fiable, sûr. ◆**dependant** *n* personne *f* à charge. ◆**dependence** *n* dépendance *f*. ◆**dependency** *n* (*country*) dépendance *f*. ◆**dependent** *a* dépendant (**on, upon** de); (*relative*) à charge; **to be d.** (**up**)**on** dépendre de.

depict [dɪ'pɪkt] *vt* (*describe*) dépeindre; (*pictorially*) représenter. ◆**depiction** *n* peinture *f*, représentation *f*.

deplete [dɪ'pliːt] *vt* (*use up*) épuiser; (*reduce*) réduire. ◆**depletion** *n* épuisement *m*; réduction *f*.

deplor/e [dɪ'plɔːr] *vt* déplorer. ◆**—able** *a* déplorable.

deploy [dɪ'plɔɪ] *vt* (*troops etc*) déployer.

depopulate [diː'pɒpjuleɪt] *vt* dépeupler. ◆**depopu'lation** *n* dépeuplement *m*.

deport [dɪ'pɔːt] *vt* *Pol Jur* expulser; (*to concentration camp etc*) *Hist* déporter. ◆**depor'tation** *n* expulsion *f*; déportation *f*.

deportment [dɪ'pɔːtmənt] *n* maintien *m*.

depose [dɪ'pəuz] *vt* (*king etc*) déposer.

deposit [dɪ'pɒzɪt] *vt* (*object, money etc*) déposer; *— n* (*in bank, wine*) & *Ch* dépôt *m*; (*part payment*) acompte *m*; (*against damage*) caution *f*; (*on bottle*) consigne *f*; **d. account** *Fin* compte *m* d'épargne. ◆**—or** *n* déposant, -ante *mf*, épargnant, -ante *mf*.

depot ['depəu, *Am* 'diːpəu] *n* dépôt *m*; (*station*) *Rail Am* gare *f*; (*bus*) **d.** *Am* gare *f* routière.

deprave [dɪ'preɪv] *vt* dépraver. ◆**depravity** *n* dépravation *f*.

deprecate ['deprɪkeɪt] *vt* désapprouver.

depreciate [dɪ'priːʃɪeɪt] *vt* (*reduce in value*) déprécier; *— vi* se déprécier. ◆**depreci-'ation** *n* dépréciation *f*.

depress [dɪ'pres] *vt* (*discourage*) déprimer; (*push down*) appuyer sur. ◆**—ed** *a* déprimé; (*in decline*) en déclin; (*in crisis*) en crise; **to get d.** se décourager. ◆**depression** *n* dépression *f*.

depriv/e [dɪ'praɪv] *vt* priver (**of** de). ◆**—ed** *a* (*child etc*) déshérité. ◆**depri'vation** *n* privation *f*; (*loss*) perte *f*.

depth [depθ] *n* profondeur *f*; (*of snow*) épaisseur *f*; (*of interest*) intensité *f*; **in the depths of** (*forest, despair*) au plus profond de; (*winter*) au cœur de; **to get out of one's d.** *Fig* perdre pied, nager; **in d.** en profondeur.

deputize ['depjutaɪz] *vi* assurer l'intérim (**for** de); *— vt* députer (**s.o. to do** qn pour faire). ◆**depu'tation** *n* députation *f*. ◆**deputy** *n* (*replacement*) suppléant, -ante *mf*; (*assistant*) adjoint, -ointe *mf*; **d.** (*sher-iff*) *Am* shérif *m* adjoint; **d. chairman** vice-président, -ente *mf*.

derailed [dɪ'reɪld] *a* **to be d.** (*of train*) dérailler. ◆**derailment** *n* déraillement *m*.

deranged [dɪ'reɪndʒd] *a* (*person, mind*) dérangé.

derelict ['derɪlɪkt] *a* à l'abandon, abandonné.

deride [dɪ'raɪd] *vt* tourner en dérision. ◆**derision** *n* dérision *f*. ◆**derisive** *a* (*laughter etc*) moqueur; (*amount*) dérisoire. ◆**derisory** *a* dérisoire.

derive [dɪ'raɪv] *vt* **to d. from** (*pleasure, profit etc*) tirer de; *Ling* dériver de; **to be derived from** dériver de, provenir de; *— vi* **to d. from** dériver de. ◆**deri'vation** *n* *Ling* dérivation *f*. ◆**derivative** *a & n* *Ling Ch* dérivé (*m*).

dermatology [dɜːmə'tɒlədʒɪ] *n* dermatologie *f*.

derogatory [dɪ'rɒgət(ə)rɪ] *a* (*word*) péjoratif; (*remark*) désobligeant (**to** pour).

derrick ['derɪk] n (over oil well) derrick m.
derv [dɜːv] n gazole m, gas-oil m.

descend [dɪ'send] vi descendre (from de); (of rain) tomber; **to d. upon** (attack) faire une descente sur, tomber sur; (of tourists) envahir; – vt (stairs) descendre; **to be descended from** descendre de. ◆**—ing** a (order) décroissant. ◆**descendant** n descendant, -ante mf. ◆**descent** n 1 descente f; (into crime) chute f. 2 (ancestry) souche f, origine f.

describe [dɪ'skraɪb] vt décrire. ◆**description** n description f; (on passport) signalement m; **of every d.** de toutes sortes. ◆**descriptive** a descriptif.

desecrate ['desɪkreɪt] vt profaner. ◆**desecration** n profanation f.

desegregate [diː'segrɪgeɪt] vt supprimer la ségrégation raciale dans. ◆**desegregation** n déségrégation f.

desert[1] ['dezət] n désert m; – a désertique; **d. island** île f déserte.

desert[2] [dɪ'zɜːt] vt déserter, abandonner; **to d. s.o.** (of luck etc) abandonner qn; – vi Mil déserter. ◆**—ed** a (place) désert. ◆**—er** n Mil déserteur m. ◆**desertion** n désertion f; (by spouse) abandon m (du domicile conjugal).

deserts [dɪ'zɜːts] n one's just d. ce qu'on mérite.

deserv/e [dɪ'zɜːv] vt mériter (**to do** de faire). ◆**—ing** a (person) méritant; (act, cause) louable, méritoire; **d. of** digne de. ◆**—edly** [-ɪdlɪ] adv à juste titre.

desiccated ['desɪkeɪtɪd] a (des)séché.

design [dɪ'zaɪn] vt (car, furniture etc) dessiner; (dress) créer, dessiner; (devise) concevoir (**for s.o.** pour qn, **to do** pour faire); **well designed** bien conçu; – n (aim) dessein m, intention f; (sketch) plan m, dessin m; (of dress, car) modèle m; (planning) conception f, création f; (pattern) motif m, dessin m; **industrial d.** dessin m industriel; **by d.** intentionnellement; **to have designs on** avoir des desseins sur. ◆**—er** n dessinateur, -trice mf; **d. clothes** vêtements mpl griffés.

designate ['dezɪgneɪt] vt désigner. ◆**designation** n désignation f.

desir/e [dɪ'zaɪər] n désir m; **I've no d.** to je n'ai aucune envie de; – vt désirer (**to do** faire). ◆**—able** a désirable; **d. property/etc** (in advertising) (très) belle propriété/etc.

desk [desk] n Sch pupitre m; (in office) bureau m; (in shop) caisse f; (reception) **d.** réception f; **the news d.** Journ le service des informations; – a (job) de bureau; **d. clerk** (in hotel) Am réceptionniste mf.

desolate ['desələt] a (deserted) désolé; (in ruins) dévasté; (dreary, bleak) morne, triste. ◆**deso'lation** n (ruin) dévastation f; (emptiness) solitude f.

despair [dɪ'speər] n désespoir m; **to drive s.o. to d.** désespérer qn; in d. au désespoir; – vi désespérer (**of s.o.** de qn, **of doing** de faire). ◆**—ing** a désespéré. ◆**desperate** a désespéré; (criminal) capable de tout; (serious) grave; **to be d. for** (money, love etc) avoir désespérément besoin de; (a cigarette, baby etc) mourir d'envie de. ◆**desperately** adv (ill) gravement; (in love) éperdument. ◆**despe'ration** n désespoir m; in d. (as a last resort) en désespoir de cause.

despatch [dɪ'spætʃ] see dispatch.

desperado [despə'rɑːdəʊ] n (pl -oes or -os) criminel m.

despise [dɪ'spaɪz] vt mépriser. ◆**despicable** a ignoble, méprisable.

despite [dɪ'spaɪt] prep malgré.

despondent [dɪ'spɒndənt] a découragé. ◆**despondency** n découragement m.

despot ['despɒt] n despote m. ◆**despotism** n despotisme m.

dessert [dɪ'zɜːt] n dessert m. ◆**dessertspoon** n cuiller f à dessert.

destabilize [diː'steɪbəlaɪz] vt déstabiliser.

destination [destɪ'neɪʃ(ə)n] n destination f.

destine ['destɪn] vt destiner (**for** à, **to do** à faire); **it was destined to happen** ça devait arriver. ◆**destiny** n destin m; (fate of individual) destinée f.

destitute ['destɪtjuːt] a (poor) indigent; **d. of** (lacking in) dénué de. ◆**desti'tution** n dénuement m.

destroy [dɪ'strɔɪ] vt détruire; (horse etc) abattre. ◆**—er** n (person) destructeur, -trice mf; (ship) contre-torpilleur m. ◆**destruct** vt Mil détruire. ◆**destruction** n destruction f. ◆**destructive** a (person, war) destructeur; (power) destructif.

detach [dɪ'tætʃ] vt détacher (**from** de). ◆**—ed** a (indifferent) détaché; (view) désintéressé; **d. house** maison f individuelle. ◆**—able** a (lining) amovible. ◆**—ment** n (attitude) & Mil détachement m; **the d. of** (action) la séparation de.

detail [dittell, Am də'teɪl] n 1 détail m; **in d.** en détail; – vt raconter ou exposer en détail ou par le menu, détailler; (troops) Mil détacher (**to do** pour faire); – n détachement m. ◆**—ed** a (account etc) détaillé.

detain [dɪ'teɪn] vt retenir; (imprison) détenir.

◆detai'nee n Pol Jur détenu, -ue mf.
◆detention n Jur détention f; Sch retenue f.

detect [dɪ'tekt] vt découvrir; (perceive) distinguer; (identify) identifier; (mine) détecter; (illness) dépister. ◆detection n découverte f; identification f; détection f; dépistage m. ◆detector n détecteur m.

detective [dɪ'tektɪv] n agent m de la Sûreté, policier m (en civil); (private) détective m; – a (film etc) policier; d. story roman m policier; d. constable = inspecteur m de police.

deter [dɪ'tɜːr] vt (-rr-) to d. s.o. dissuader or décourager qn (from doing de faire, from sth de qch).

detergent [dɪ'tɜːdʒənt] n détergent m.

deteriorate [dɪ'tɪərɪəreɪt] vi se détériorer; (of morals) dégénérer. ◆deterio'ration n détérioration f; dégénérescence f.

determin/e [dɪ'tɜːmɪn] vt déterminer; (price) fixer; to d. s.o. to do décider qn à faire; to d. that décider que; to d. to do se déterminer à faire. ◆—ed a (look, quantity) déterminé; d. to do or on doing décidé à faire; I'm d. she'll succeed je suis bien décidé à ce qu'elle réussisse.

deterrent [dɪ'terənt, Am dɪ'tɜːrənt] n Mil force f de dissuasion; to be a d. Fig être dissuasif.

detest [dɪ'test] vt détester (doing faire). ◆—able a détestable.

detonate ['detəneɪt] vt faire détoner or exploser; – vi détoner. ◆deto'nation n détonation f. ◆detonator n détonateur m.

detour ['diːtʊər] n détour m.

detract [dɪ'trækt] vi to d. from (make less) diminuer. ◆detractor n détracteur, -trice mf.

detriment ['detrɪmənt] n détriment m. ◆detri'mental a préjudiciable (to à).

devalue [diː'væljuː] vt (money) & Fig dévaluer. ◆devalu'ation n dévaluation f.

devastat/e ['devəsteɪt] vt (lay waste) dévaster; (opponent) anéantir; (person) Fig foudroyer. ◆—ing a (storm etc) dévastateur; (overwhelming) confondant, accablant; (charm) irrésistible.

develop [dɪ'veləp] vt développer; (area, land) mettre en valeur; (habit, illness) contracter; (talent) manifester; Phot développer; to d. a liking for prendre goût à; – vi se développer; (of event) se produire; to d. into devenir. ◆—ing a (country) en voie de développement; – n Phot développement m. ◆—er n (property) d. promoteur m (de construction).

◆—ment n développement m; (of land) mise f en valeur; (housing) d. lotissement m; (large) grand ensemble m; a (new) d. (in situation) un fait nouveau.

deviate ['diːvɪeɪt] vi dévier (from de); to d. from the norm s'écarter de la norme. ◆deviant a anormal. ◆devi'ation n déviation f.

device [dɪ'vaɪs] n dispositif m, engin m; (scheme) procédé m; left to one's own devices livré à soi-même.

devil ['dev(ə)l] n diable m; a or the d. of a problem Fam un problème épouvantable; a or the d. of a noise Fam un bruit infernal; I had a or the d. of a job Fam j'ai eu un mal fou (doing, to do à faire); what/where/why the d.? Fam que/où/pourquoi diable?; like the d. (to run etc) comme un fou. ◆devil-ish a diabolique. ◆devilry n (mischief) diablerie f.

devious ['diːvɪəs] a (mind, behaviour) tortueux; he's d. il a l'esprit tortueux. ◆—ness n (of person) esprit m tortueux.

devise [dɪ'vaɪz] vt (plan) combiner; (plot) tramer; (invent) inventer.

devitalize [diː'vaɪtəlaɪz] vt rendre exsangue, affaiblir.

devoid [dɪ'vɔɪd] a d. of dénué or dépourvu de; (guilt) exempt de.

devolution [diːvə'luːʃ(ə)n] n Pol décentralisation f; the d. of (power) la délégation de.

devolve [dɪ'vɒlv] vi to d. upon incomber à.

devot/e [dɪ'vəʊt] vt consacrer (to à). ◆—ed a dévoué; (admirer) fervent. ◆—edly adv avec dévouement. ◆devo'tee n Sp Mus passionné, -ée mf. ◆devotion n dévouement m; (religious) dévotion f; pl (prayers) dévotions fpl.

devour [dɪ'vaʊər] vt (eat, engulf, read etc) dévorer.

devout [dɪ'vaʊt] a dévot, pieux; (supporter, prayer) fervent.

dew [djuː] n rosée f. ◆dewdrop n goutte f de rosée.

dext(e)rous ['dekst(ə)rəs] a adroit, habile. ◆dex'terity n adresse f, dextérité f.

diabetes [daɪə'biːtiːz] n Med diabète m. ◆diabetic a & n diabétique (mf).

diabolical [daɪə'bɒlɪk(ə)l] a diabolique; (bad) épouvantable.

diadem ['daɪədem] n diadème m.

diagnosis, pl -oses [daɪəg'nəʊsɪs, -əʊsiːz] n diagnostic m. ◆'diagnose vt diagnostiquer.

diagonal [daɪ'ægən(ə)l] a diagonal; – n (line) diagonale f. ◆—ly adv en diagonale.

diagram ['daɪəgræm] n schéma m,

diagramme *m*; *Geom* figure *f.* ◆**dia-gra'mmatic** *a* schématique.

dial ['daɪəl] *n* cadran *m*; — *vt* (**-ll-**, *Am* **-l-**) (*number*) *Tel* faire, composer; (*person*) appeler; **to d. s.o. direct** appeler qn par l'automatique; **d. tone** *Am* tonalité *f.* ◆**dialling** *a* **d. code** indicatif *m*; **d. tone** tonalité *f.*

dialect ['daɪəlekt] *n* (*regional*) dialecte *m*; (*rural*) patois *m.*

dialogue ['daɪəlɒg] (*Am* **dialog**) *n* dialogue *m.*

dialysis, *pl* **-yses** [daɪ'ælɪsɪs, -ɪsiːz] *n Med* dialyse *f.*

diameter [daɪ'æmɪtər] *n* diamètre *m.* ◆**dia-'metrically** *adv* (*opposed*) diamétralement.

diamond ['daɪəmənd] **1** *n* (*stone*) diamant *m*; (*shape*) losange *m*; (*baseball*) *d. Am* terrain *m* de baseball; **d. necklace**/*etc* rivière *f*/*etc* de diamants. **2** *n & npl Cards* carreau *m.*

diaper ['daɪəpər] *n* (*for baby*) *Am* couche *f.*

diaphragm ['daɪəfræm] *n* diaphragme *m.*

diarrh(o)ea [daɪə'riːə] *n* diarrhée *f.*

diary ['daɪərɪ] *n* (*calendar*) agenda *m*; (*private*) journal *m* (intime).

dice [daɪs] *n inv* dé *m* (à jouer); — *vt Culin* couper en dés.

dicey ['daɪsɪ] *a* (**-ier, -iest**) *Fam* risqué.

dichotomy [daɪ'kɒtəmɪ] *n* dichotomie *f.*

dickens ['dɪkɪnz] *n* **where**/*why*/*what* **the d.?** *Fam* où/pourquoi/que diable?

dictate [dɪk'teɪt] *vt* dicter (**to** à); — *vi* dicter; **to d. to s.o.** (*order around*) régenter qn. ◆**dictation** *n* dictée *f.* ◆**'dictaphone**® *n* dictaphone® *m.*

dictates ['dɪkteɪts] *npl* préceptes *mpl*; **the d. of conscience** la voix de la conscience.

dictator [dɪk'teɪtər] *n* dictateur *m.* ◆**dicta-'torial** *a* dictatorial. ◆**dictatorship** *n* dictature *f.*

diction ['dɪkʃ(ə)n] *n* langage *m*; (*way of speaking*) diction *f.*

dictionary ['dɪkʃənərɪ] *n* dictionnaire *m.*

dictum ['dɪktəm] *n* dicton *m.*

did [dɪd] *see* **do.**

diddle ['dɪd(ə)l] *vt Sl* rouler; **to d. s.o. out of sth** carotter qch à qn; **to get diddled out of sth** se faire refaire de qch.

die [daɪ] **1** *vi* (*pt & pp* **died**, *pres p* **dying**) mourir (**of**, **from** de); **to be dying to do** *Fam* mourir d'envie de faire; **to be dying for sth** *Fam* avoir une envie folle de qch; **to d. away** (*of noise*) mourir; **to d. down** (*of fire*) mourir; (*of storm*) se calmer; **to d. off** mourir (les uns après les autres); **to d. out** (*of custom*) mourir. **2** *n* (*in engraving*) coin

m; *Tech* matrice *f*; **the d. is cast** *Fig* les dés sont jetés.

diehard ['daɪhɑːd] *n* réactionnaire *mf.*

diesel ['diːzl] *a & n* **d. (engine)** (moteur *m*) diesel *m*; **d. (oil)** gazole *m.*

diet ['daɪət] *n* (*for slimming etc*) régime *m*; (*usual food*) alimentation *f*; **to go on a d.** faire un régime; — *vi* suivre un régime. ◆**dietary** *a* diététique; **d. fibre** fibre(s) *f*(*pl*) alimentaire(s). ◆**die'tician** *n* diététicien, -ienne *mf.*

differ ['dɪfər] *vi* différer (**from** de); (*disagree*) ne pas être d'accord (**from** avec). ◆**differ-ence** *n* différence *f* (**in** de); (*in age, weight etc*) écart *m*, différence *f*; **d. (of opinion)** différend *m*; **it makes no d.** ça n'a pas d'importance; **it makes no d. to me** ça m'est égal; **to make a d. in** changer qch. ◆**diff-erent** *a* différent (**from, to** de); (*another*) autre; (*various*) différents, divers. ◆**diffe-'rential** *a* différentiel; — *npl Econ* écarts *mpl* salariaux. ◆**diffe'rentiate** *vt* différencier (**from** de); — *vi* **to d.** (**between**) faire la différence entre. ◆**differently** *adv* différemment (**from, to** de), autrement (**from, to** que).

difficult ['dɪfɪkəlt] *a* difficile (**to do** à faire); **it's d. for us to . . .** il nous est difficile de . . . ; **the d. thing is to . . .** le plus difficile est de . . . . ◆**difficulty** *n* difficulté *f*; **to have d. doing** avoir du mal à faire; **to be in d.** avoir des difficultés; **d. with** des ennuis *mpl* avec.

diffident ['dɪfɪdənt] *a* (*person*) qui manque d'assurance; (*smile, tone*) mal assuré. ◆**diffidence** *n* manque *m* d'assurance.

diffuse [dɪ'fjuːz] *vt* (*spread*) diffuser; — [dɪ'fjuːs] *a* (*spread out, wordy*) diffus. ◆**dif-fusion** *n* diffusion *f.*

dig [dɪg] *vt* (*pt & pp* **dug**, *pres p* **digging**) (*ground*) bêcher; (*hole, grave etc*) creuser; (*understand*) *Sl* piger; (*appreciate*) *Sl* aimer; **to d. sth into** (*thrust*) enfoncer qch dans; **to d. out** (*animal, fact*) déterrer; (*accident victim*) dégager; (*find*) *Fam* dénicher; **to d. up** déterrer; (*weed*) arracher; (*earth*) retourner; (*street*) piocher; — *vi* creuser; (*of pig*) fouiller; **to d.** (**oneself**) **in** *Mil* se retrancher; **to d. in** (*eat*) *Fam* manger; **to d. into** (*s.o.'s past*) fouiller dans; (*meal*) *Fam* attaquer; — *n* (*with spade*) coup *m* de bêche; (*push*) coup *m* de poing *or* de coude; (*remark*) *Fam* coup *m* de griffe. ◆**digger** *n* (*machine*) pelleteuse *f.*

digest [daɪ'dʒest] *vti* digérer; — ['daɪdʒest] *n Journ* condensé *m.* ◆**digestible** *a* digeste.

◆**digestion** n digestion f. ◆**digestive** a digestif.

digit ['dɪdʒɪt] n (number) chiffre m. ◆**digital** a (watch, keyboard etc) numérique.

dignified ['dɪgnɪfaɪd] a digne, qui a de la dignité. ◆**dignify** vt donner de la dignité à; **to d. with the name of** honorer du nom de. ◆**dignitary** n dignitaire m. ◆**dignity** n dignité f.

digress [daɪ'gres] vi faire une digression; **to d. from** s'écarter de. ◆**digression** n digression f.

digs [dɪgz] npl Fam chambre f (meublée), logement m.

dilapidated [dɪ'læpɪdeɪtɪd] a (house) délabré. ◆**dilapi'dation** n délabrement m.

dilate [daɪ'leɪt] vt dilater; − vi se dilater. ◆**dilation** n dilatation f.

dilemma [daɪ'lemə] n dilemme m.

dilettante [dɪlɪ'tænti] n dilettante mf.

diligent ['dɪlɪdʒənt] a assidu, appliqué; **to be d. in doing sth** faire qch avec zèle. ◆**diligence** n zèle m, assiduité f.

dilly-dally [dɪlɪ'dælɪ] vi Fam (dawdle) lambiner, lanterner; (hesitate) tergiverser.

dilute [daɪ'luːt] vt diluer; − a dilué.

dim [dɪm] a (dimmer, dimmest) (feeble) faible; (colour) terne; (room) sombre; (memory, outline) vague; (person) stupide; − vt (-mm-) (light) baisser, réduire; (glory) ternir; (memory) estomper. ◆**—ly** adv faiblement; (vaguely) vaguement. ◆**—ness** n faiblesse f; (of memory etc) vague m; (of room) pénombre f. ◆**dimwit** n idiot, -ote mf. ◆**dim'witted** a idiot.

dime [daɪm] n (US & Can coin) (pièce f de) dix cents mpl; **a d. store** = un Prisunic®, un Monoprix®.

dimension [daɪ'menʃ(ə)n] n dimension f; (extent) Fig étendue f. ◆**dimensional** a **two-d.** à deux dimensions.

diminish [dɪ'mɪnɪʃ] vti diminuer. ◆**—ing** a qui diminue.

diminutive [dɪ'mɪnjutɪv] **1** a (tiny) minuscule. **2** a & n Gram diminutif (m).

dimple ['dɪmp(ə)l] n fossette f. ◆**dimpled** a (chin, cheek) à fossettes.

din [dɪn] **1** n (noise) vacarme m. **2** vt (-nn-) **to d. into s.o. that** rabâcher à qn que.

din/e [daɪn] vi dîner (off, on de); **to d. out** dîner en ville. ◆**—ing** a d. **car** Rail wagon-restaurant m; **d. room** salle f à manger. ◆**—er** n dîneur, -euse mf; Rail wagon-restaurant m; (short-order restaurant) Am petit restaurant m.

ding(dong)! ['dɪŋ(dɒŋ)] int (of bell) dring!, ding (dong)!

dinghy ['dɪŋgɪ] n petit canot m, youyou m; **(rubber) d.** canot m pneumatique.

dingy ['dɪndʒɪ] a (-ier, -iest) (dirty) malpropre; (colour) terne. ◆**dinginess** n malpropreté f.

dinner ['dɪnər] n (evening meal) dîner m; (lunch) déjeuner m; (for dog, cat) pâtée f; **to have d.** dîner; **to have s.o. to d.** avoir qn à dîner; **d. dance** dîner-dansant m; **d. jacket** smoking m; **d. party** dîner m (à la maison); **d. plate** grande assiette f; **d. service, d. set** service m de table.

dinosaur ['daɪnəsɔːr] n dinosaure m.

dint [dɪnt] n **by d. of** à force de.

diocese ['daɪəsɪs] n Rel diocèse m.

dip [dɪp] vt (-pp-) plonger; (into liquid) tremper, plonger; **to d. one's headlights** se mettre en code; − vi (of sun etc) baisser; (of road) plonger; **to d. into** (pocket, savings) puiser dans; (book) feuilleter; − n (in road) déclivité f; **to go for a d.** faire trempette.

diphtheria [dɪp'θɪərɪə] n diphtérie f.

diphthong ['dɪfθɒŋ] n Ling diphtongue f.

diploma [dɪ'pləʊmə] n diplôme m.

diplomacy [dɪ'pləʊməsɪ] n (tact) & Pol diplomatie f. ◆**'diplomat** n diplomate mf. ◆**diplo'matic** a diplomatique; **to be d.** (tactful) Fig être diplomate.

dipper ['dɪpər] n **the big d.** (at fairground) les montagnes fpl russes.

dire ['daɪər] a affreux; (poverty, need) extrême.

direct [daɪ'rekt] **1** a (result, flight, person etc) direct; (danger) immédiat; − adv directement. **2** vt (work, one's steps, one's attention) diriger; (letter, remark) adresser (to à); (efforts) orienter (to, towards vers); (film) réaliser; (play) mettre en scène; **to d. s.o. to** (place) indiquer à qn le chemin de; **to d. s.o. to do** charger qn de faire. ◆**direction** n direction f, sens m; (management) direction f; (of film) réalisation f; (of play) mise f en scène; pl (orders) indications fpl; **directions (for use)** mode m d'emploi; **in the opposite d.** en sens inverse. ◆**directive** [daɪ'rektɪv] n directive f. ◆**directly** adv (without detour) directement; (at once) tout de suite; (to speak) franchement; − conj Fam aussitôt que. ◆**directness** n (of reply) franchise f. ◆**director** n directeur, -trice mf; (of film) réalisateur, -trice mf; (of play) metteur m en scène. ◆**directorship** n Com poste m de directeur.

directory [daɪ'rektərɪ] n Tel annuaire m; (of

streets) guide *m*; (*of addresses*) répertoire *m*; **d. enquiries** *Tel* renseignements *mpl*.

dirge [dɜːdʒ] *n* chant *m* funèbre.

dirt [dɜːt] *n* saleté *f*; (*filth*) ordure *f*; (*mud*) boue *f*; (*earth*) terre *f*; (*talk*) *Fig* obscénité(s) *f*(*pl*); **d. cheap** *Fam* très bon marché; **d. road** chemin *m* de terre; **d. track** *Sp* cendrée *f*. ◆**dirty** *a* (**-ier, -iest**) sale; (*job*) salissant; (*obscene, unpleasant*) sale; (*word*) grossier, obscène; **to get d.** se salir; **to get sth d.** salir qch; **a d. joke** une histoire cochonne; **a d. trick** un sale tour; **a d. old man** un vieux cochon; – *adv* (*to fight*) déloyalement; – *vt* salir; (*machine*) encrasser; – *vi* se salir.

disabl/e [dɪˈseɪb(ə)l] *vt* rendre infirme; (*maim*) mutiler. ◆**—ed** *a* infirme, handicapé; (*maimed*) mutilé; – *n* **the d.** les infirmes *mpl*, les handicapés *mpl*. ◆**disa-'bility** *n* infirmité *f*; *Fig* désavantage *m*.

disadvantage [dɪsədˈvɑːntɪdʒ] *n* désavantage *m*; – *vt* désavantager.

disaffected [dɪsəˈfektɪd] *a* mécontent. ◆**disaffection** *n* désaffection *f* (**for** pour).

disagree [dɪsəˈgriː] *vi* ne pas être d'accord, être en désaccord (**with** avec); (*of figures*) ne pas concorder; **to d. with** (*of food etc*) ne pas réussir à. ◆**—able** *a* désagréable. ◆**—ment** *n* désaccord *m*; (*quarrel*) différend *m*.

disallow [dɪsəˈlaʊ] *vt* rejeter.

disappear [dɪsəˈpɪər] *vi* disparaître. ◆**disappearance** *n* disparition *f*.

disappoint [dɪsəˈpɔɪnt] *vt* décevoir; **I'm disappointed with it** ça m'a déçu. ◆**—ing** *a* décevant. ◆**—ment** *n* déception *f*.

disapprov/e [dɪsəˈpruːv] *vi* **to d. of s.o./sth** désapprouver qn/qch; **I d.** je suis contre. ◆**—ing** *a* (*look etc*) désapprobateur. ◆**disapproval** *n* désapprobation *f*.

disarm [dɪsˈɑːm] *vti* désarmer. ◆**disarmament** *n* désarmement *m*.

disarray [dɪsəˈreɪ] *n* (*disorder*) désordre *m*; (*distress*) désarroi *m*.

disaster [dɪˈzɑːstər] *n* désastre *m*, catastrophe *f*; **d. area** région *f* sinistrée. ◆**d.-stricken** *a* sinistré. ◆**disastrous** *a* désastreux.

disband [dɪsˈbænd] *vt* disperser; – *vi* se disperser.

disbelief [dɪsbəˈliːf] *n* incrédulité *f*.

disc [dɪsk] (*Am* **disk**) *n* disque *m*; **identity d.** plaque *f* d'identité; **d. jockey** animateur, -trice *mf* (de variétés etc), disc-jockey *m*.

discard [dɪsˈkɑːd] *vt* (*get rid of*) se débarrasser de; (*plan, hope etc*) *Fig* abandonner.

discern [dɪˈsɜːn] *vt* discerner. ◆**—ing** *a*

(*person*) averti, sagace. ◆**—ible** *a* perceptible. ◆**—ment** *n* discernement *m*.

discharge [dɪsˈtʃɑːdʒ] *vt* (*gun, accused person*) décharger; (*liquid*) déverser; (*patient, employee*) renvoyer; (*soldier*) libérer; (*unfit soldier*) réformer; (*one's duty*) accomplir; – *vi* (*of wound*) suppurer; – ['dɪstʃɑːdʒ] *n* (*of gun*) & *El* décharge *f*; (*of liquid*) & *Med* écoulement *m*; (*dismissal*) renvoi *m*; (*freeing*) libération *f*; (*of unfit soldier*) réforme *f*.

disciple [dɪˈsaɪp(ə)l] *n* disciple *m*.

discipline [ˈdɪsɪplɪn] *n* (*behaviour, subject*) discipline *f*; – *vt* (*control*) discipliner; (*punish*) punir. ◆**discipli'narian** *n* partisan, -ane *mf* de la discipline; **to be a (strict) d.** être très à cheval sur la discipline. ◆**disci'plinary** *a* disciplinaire.

disclaim [dɪsˈkleɪm] *vt* désavouer; (*responsibility*) (dé)nier.

disclose [dɪsˈkləʊz] *vt* révéler, divulguer. ◆**disclosure** *n* révélation *f*.

disco [ˈdɪskəʊ] *n* (*pl* **-os**) *Fam* disco(thèque) *f*.

discolour [dɪsˈkʌlər] *vt* décolorer; (*teeth*) jaunir; – *vi* se décolorer; jaunir. ◆**disco-lo(u)ration** *n* décoloration *f*; jaunissement *m*.

discomfort [dɪsˈkʌmfət] *n* (*physical, mental*) malaise *m*, gêne *f*; (*hardship*) inconvénient *m*.

disconcert [dɪskənˈsɜːt] *vt* déconcerter.

disconnect [dɪskəˈnekt] *vt* (*unfasten etc*) détacher; (*unplug*) débrancher; (*wires*) *El* déconnecter; (*gas, telephone etc*) couper. ◆**—ed** *a* (*speech*) décousu.

discontent [dɪskənˈtent] *n* mécontentement *m*. ◆**discontented** *a* mécontent.

discontinu/e [dɪskənˈtɪnjuː] *vt* cesser, interrompre. ◆**—ed** *a* (*article*) *Com* qui ne se fait plus.

discord [ˈdɪskɔːd] *n* discorde *f*; *Mus* dissonance *f*.

discotheque [ˈdɪskətek] *n* (*club*) discothèque *f*.

discount 1 [ˈdɪskaʊnt] *n* (*on article*) remise *f*; (*on account paid early*) escompte *m*; **at à d.** (*to buy, sell*) au rabais; **d. store** solderie *f*. **2** [dɪsˈkaʊnt] *vt* (*story etc*) ne pas tenir compte de.

discourage [dɪsˈkʌrɪdʒ] *vt* décourager; **to get discouraged** se décourager. ◆**—ment** *n* découragement *m*.

discourse [ˈdɪskɔːs] *n* discours *m*.

discourteous [dɪsˈkɜːtɪəs] *a* impoli, discourtois. ◆**discourtesy** *n* impolitesse *f*.

discover [dɪsˈkʌvər] *vt* découvrir. ◆**discovery** *n* découverte *f*.

discredit [dɪs'kredɪt] vt (cast slur on) discréditer; (refuse to believe) ne pas croire; – n discrédit m. ◆**-able** a indigne.

discreet [dɪs'kriːt] a (careful) prudent, avisé; (unassuming, reserved etc) discret. ◆**discretion** n prudence f; discrétion f; **I'll use my own d.** je ferai comme bon me semblera. ◆**discretionary** a discrétionnaire.

discrepancy [dɪs'krepənsɪ] n divergence f, contradiction f (**between** entre).

discriminat/e [dɪs'krɪmɪneɪt] vi **to d. between** distinguer entre; **to d. against** établir une discrimination contre; – vt **to d. sth/s.o. from** distinguer qch/qn de. ◆**-ing** a (person) averti, sagace; (ear) fin. ◆**discrimi'nation** n (judgement) discernement m; (distinction) distinction f; (partiality) discrimination f. ◆**discriminatory** [-ətərɪ] a discriminatoire.

discus ['dɪskəs] n Sp disque m.

discuss [dɪs'kʌs] vt (talk about) discuter de; (examine in detail) discuter. ◆**discussion** n discussion f; **under d.** (matter etc) en question, en discussion.

disdain [dɪs'deɪn] vt dédaigner; – n dédain m. ◆**disdainful** a dédaigneux; **to be d. of** dédaigner.

disease [dɪ'ziːz] n maladie f. ◆**diseased** a malade.

disembark [dɪsɪm'bɑːk] vti débarquer. ◆**disembar'kation** n débarquement m.

disembodied [dɪsɪm'bɒdɪd] a désincarné.

disembowel [dɪsɪm'baʊəl] vt (-ll-, Am -l-) éventrer.

disenchant [dɪsɪn'tʃɑːnt] vt désenchanter. ◆**-ment** n désenchantement m.

disengage [dɪsɪn'geɪdʒ] vt (object) dégager; (troops) désengager.

disentangle [dɪsɪn'tæŋg(ə)l] vt démêler; **to d. oneself from** se dégager de.

disfavour [dɪs'feɪvər] n défaveur f.

disfigure [dɪs'fɪgər] vt défigurer. ◆**-ment** n défigurement m.

disgorge [dɪs'gɔːdʒ] vt (food) vomir.

disgrac/e [dɪs'greɪs] n (shame) honte f (**to** à); (disfavour) disgrâce f; – vt déshonorer, faire honte à. ◆**-ed** a (politician etc) disgracié. ◆**disgraceful** a honteux (**of s.o.** de la part de qn). ◆**disgracefully** adv honteusement.

disgruntled [dɪs'grʌnt(ə)ld] a mécontent.

disguise [dɪs'gaɪz] vt déguiser (as en); – n déguisement m; **in d.** déguisé.

disgust [dɪs'gʌst] n dégoût m (**for, at, with** de); **in d.** dégoûté; – vt dégoûter, écœurer. ◆**-ed** a dégoûté (**at, by, with** de); **to be d. with s.o.** (annoyed) être fâché contre qn; **d.**

to hear that . . . indigné d'apprendre que . . . . ◆**-ing** a dégoûtant, écœurant. ◆**-ingly** adv d'une façon dégoûtante.

dish [dɪʃ] n 1 (container) plat m; (food) mets m, plat m; **the dishes** la vaisselle; **she's a (real) d.** Sl c'est un beau brin de fille. **2** vt **to d. out** distribuer; **to d. out** or **up** (food) servir. ◆**dishcloth** n (for washing) lavette f; (for drying) torchon m. ◆**dishpan** n Am bassine f (à vaisselle). ◆**dishwasher** n lave-vaisselle m inv.

disharmony [dɪs'hɑːmənɪ] n désaccord m; Mus dissonance f.

dishearten [dɪs'hɑːt(ə)n] vt décourager.

dishevelled [dɪ'ʃevəld] a hirsute, échevelé.

dishonest [dɪs'ɒnɪst] a malhonnête; (insincere) de mauvaise foi. ◆**dishonesty** n malhonnêteté f; mauvaise foi f.

dishonour [dɪs'ɒnər] n déshonneur m; – vt déshonorer; (cheque) refuser d'honorer. ◆**-able** a peu honorable. ◆**-ably** adv avec déshonneur.

dishy ['dɪʃɪ] a (-ier, -iest) (woman, man) Sl beau, sexy, qui a du chien.

disillusion [dɪsɪ'luːʒ(ə)n] vt désillusionner; – n désillusion f. ◆**-ment** n désillusion f.

disincentive [dɪsɪn'sentɪv] n mesure f dissuasive; **to be a d. to s.o.** décourager qn; **it's a d. to work/invest/etc** cela n'encourage pas à travailler/investir/etc.

disinclined [dɪsɪn'klaɪnd] a peu disposé (**to** à). ◆**disincli'nation** n répugnance f.

disinfect [dɪsɪn'fekt] vt désinfecter. ◆**disinfectant** a & n désinfectant (m). ◆**disinfection** n désinfection f.

disinherit [dɪsɪn'herɪt] vt déshériter.

disintegrate [dɪs'ɪntɪgreɪt] vi se désintégrer; – vt désintégrer. ◆**disinte'gration** n désintégration f.

disinterested [dɪs'ɪntrɪstɪd] a (impartial) désintéressé; (uninterested) Fam indifférent (**in** à).

disjointed [dɪs'dʒɔɪntɪd] a décousu.

disk [dɪsk] n 1 Am = **disc. 2 (magnetic) d.** (of computer) disque m (magnétique).

dislike [dɪs'laɪk] vt ne pas aimer (doing faire); **he doesn't d. it** ça ne lui déplaît pas; – n aversion f (**for, of** pour); **to take a d. to** (person, thing) prendre en grippe; **our likes and dislikes** nos goûts et dégoûts mpl.

dislocate ['dɪsləkeɪt] vt (limb) disloquer; Fig désorganiser. ◆**dislo'cation** n dislocation f.

dislodge [dɪs'lɒdʒ] vt faire bouger, déplacer; (enemy) déloger.

disloyal [dɪs'lɔɪəl] a déloyal. ◆**disloyalty** n déloyauté f.

dismal ['dɪzməl] *a* morne, triste. ◆**─ly** *adv* (*to fail, behave*) lamentablement.

dismantle [dɪs'mænt(ə)l] *vt* (*machine etc*) démonter; (*organization*) démanteler.

dismay [dɪs'meɪ] *vt* consterner; — *n* consternation *f.*

dismember [dɪs'membər] *vt* (*country etc*) démembrer.

dismiss [dɪs'mɪs] *vt* congédier, renvoyer (**from** de); (*official etc*) destituer; (*appeal*) Jur rejeter; (*thought etc*) Fig écarter; **d.!** Mil rompez!; (*class*) d.! Sch vous pouvez partir. ◆**dismissal** *n* renvoi *m*; destitution *f.*

dismount [dɪs'maʊnt] *vi* descendre (**from** de); — *vt* (*rider*) démonter, désarçonner.

disobey [dɪsə'beɪ] *vt* désobéir à; — *vi* désobéir. ◆**disobedience** *n* désobéissance *f.* ◆**disobedient** *a* désobéissant.

disorder [dɪs'ɔːdər] *n* (*confusion*) désordre *m*; (*riots*) désordres *mpl*; (*illness*) Med troubles *mpl.* ◆**disorderly** *a* (*meeting etc*) désordonné.

disorganize [dɪs'ɔːgənaɪz] *vt* désorganiser.

disorientate [dɪs'ɔːrɪənteɪt] (*Am* **disorient** [dɪs'ɔːrɪənt]) *vt* désorienter.

disown [dɪs'əʊn] *vt* désavouer, renier.

disparage [dɪs'pærɪdʒ] *vt* dénigrer. ◆**─ing** *a* peu flatteur.

disparate ['dɪspərət] *a* disparate. ◆**disparity** *n* disparité *f* (**between** entre, de).

dispassionate [dɪs'pæʃənət] *a* (*unemotional*) calme; (*not biased*) impartial.

dispatch [dɪs'pætʃ] *vt* (*letter, work*) expédier; (*troops, messenger*) envoyer; — *n* expédition *f* (**of** de); Journ Mil dépêche *f*; **d. rider** Mil etc courrier *m.*

dispel [dɪs'pel] *vt* (**-ll-**) dissiper.

dispensary [dɪs'pensərɪ] *n* (*in hospital*) pharmacie *f*; (*in chemist's shop*) officine *f.*

dispense [dɪs'pens] **1** *vt* (*give out*) distribuer; (*justice*) administrer; (*medicine*) préparer. **2** *vi* **to d. with** (*do without*) se passer de; **to d. with the need for** rendre superflu. ◆**dispen'sation** *n* distribution *f*; **special d.** (*exemption*) dérogation *f.* ◆**dispenser** *n* (*device*) distributeur *m*; **cash d.** distributeur *m* de billets.

disperse [dɪs'pɜːs] *vt* disperser; — *vi* se disperser. ◆**dispersal** *n*, ◆**dispersion** *n* dispersion *f.*

dispirited [dɪs'pɪrɪtɪd] *a* découragé.

displace [dɪs'pleɪs] *vt* (*bone, furniture, refugees*) déplacer; (*replace*) supplanter.

display [dɪs'pleɪ] *vt* montrer; (*notice, electronic data etc*) afficher; (*painting, goods*) exposer; (*courage etc*) faire preuve de; — *n* (*in shop*) étalage *m*; (*of force*) déploiement *m*; (*of anger etc*) manifestation *f*; (*of paintings*) exposition *f*; (*of luxury*) étalage *m*; Mil parade *f*; (*of electronic data*) affichage *m*; **d.** (**unit**) (*of computer*) moniteur *m*; **on d.** exposé; **air d.** fête *f* aéronautique.

displeas/e [dɪs'pliːz] *vt* déplaire à. ◆**─ed** *a* mécontent (**with** de). ◆**─ing** *a* désagréable. ◆**displeasure** *n* mécontentement *m.*

dispos/e [dɪs'pəʊz] *vt* disposer (**s.o. to do** qn à faire); — *vi* **to d. of** (*get rid of*) se débarrasser de; (*one's time, money*) disposer de; (*sell*) vendre; (*matter*) expédier, liquider; (*kill*) liquider. ◆**─ed** *a* disposé (**to do** à faire); **well-d. towards** bien disposé envers. ◆**─able** *a* (*plate etc*) à jeter, jetable; (*income*) disponible. ◆**disposal** *n* (*sale*) vente *f*; (*of waste*) évacuation *f*; **at the d. of** à la disposition de. ◆**dispo'sition** *n* (*placing*) disposition *f*; (*character*) naturel *m*; (*readiness*) inclination *f.*

dispossess [dɪspə'zes] *vt* déposséder (**of** de).

disproportion [dɪsprə'pɔːʃ(ə)n] *n* disproportion *f.* ◆**disproportionate** *a* disproportionné.

disprove [dɪs'pruːv] *vt* réfuter.

dispute [dɪs'pjuːt] *n* discussion *f*; (*quarrel*) dispute *f*; Pol conflit *m*; Jur litige *m*; **beyond d.** incontestable; **in d.** (*matter*) en litige; (*territory*) contesté; — *vt* (*claim etc*) contester; (*discuss*) discuter.

disqualify [dɪs'kwɒlɪfaɪ] *vt* (*make unfit*) rendre inapte (**from** à); Sp disqualifier; **to d. from driving** retirer le permis à. ◆**disqualifi'cation** *n* Sp disqualification *f.*

disquiet [dɪs'kwaɪət] *n* inquiétude *f*; — *vt* inquiéter.

disregard [dɪsrɪ'gɑːd] *vt* ne tenir aucun compte de; — *n* indifférence *f* (**for** à); (*law*) désobéissance *f* (**for** à).

disrepair [dɪsrɪ'peər] *n* **in** (**a state of**) **d.** en mauvais état.

disreputable [dɪs'repjʊtəb(ə)l] *a* peu recommandable; (*behaviour*) honteux.

disrepute [dɪsrɪ'pjuːt] *n* discrédit *m*; **to bring into d.** jeter le discrédit sur.

disrespect [dɪsrɪ'spekt] *n* manque *m* de respect. ◆**disrespectful** *a* irrespectueux (**to** envers).

disrupt [dɪs'rʌpt] *vt* perturber; (*communications*) interrompre; (*plan*) déranger. ◆**disruption** *n* perturbation *f*; interruption *f*;

dérangement m. ◆**disruptive** a (element etc) perturbateur.

dissatisfied [dɪ'sætɪsfaɪd] a mécontent (with de). ◆**dissatis'faction** n mécontentement m.

dissect [daɪ'sekt] vt disséquer. ◆**dissection** n dissection f.

disseminate [dɪ'semɪneɪt] vt disséminer.

dissension [dɪ'senʃ(ə)n] n dissension f.

dissent [dɪ'sent] vi différer (d'opinion) (from sth à l'égard de qch); – n dissentiment m. ◆**–ing** a dissident.

dissertation [dɪsə'teɪʃ(ə)n] n Univ mémoire m.

dissident ['dɪsɪdənt] a & n dissident, -ente (mf). ◆**dissidence** n dissidence f.

dissimilar [dɪ'sɪmɪlər] a dissemblable (to à).

dissipate ['dɪsɪpeɪt] vt dissiper; (energy) gaspiller. ◆**dissi'pation** n dissipation f; gaspillage m.

dissociate [dɪ'səʊʃɪeɪt] vt dissocier (from de).

dissolute ['dɪsəlʊt] a (life, person) dissolu.

dissolve [dɪ'zɒlv] vt dissoudre; – vi se dissoudre. ◆**disso'lution** n dissolution f.

dissuade [dɪ'sweɪd] vt dissuader (from doing de faire); to d. s.o. from sth détourner qn de qch. ◆**dissuasion** n dissuasion f.

distance ['dɪstəns] n distance f; in the d. au loin; from a d. de loin; at a d. à quelque distance; it's within walking d. on peut y aller à pied; to keep one's d. garder ses distances. ◆**distant** a éloigné, lointain; (relative) éloigné; (reserved) distant; 5 km d. from a (une distance de) 5 km de. ◆**distantly** adv we're d. related nous sommes parents éloignés.

distaste [dɪs'teɪst] n aversion f (for pour). ◆**distasteful** a désagréable, déplaisant.

distemper [dɪs'tempər] 1 n (paint) badigeon m; – vt badigeonner. 2 n (in dogs) maladie f.

distend [dɪs'tend] vt distendre; – vi se distendre.

distil [dɪs'tɪl] vt (-ll-) distiller. ◆**distillation** n distillation f. ◆**distillery** n distillerie f.

distinct [dɪs'tɪŋkt] a 1 (voice, light etc) distinct; (definite, marked) net, marqué; (promise) formel. 2 (different) distinct (from de). ◆**distinction** n distinction f; Univ mention f très bien; of d. (singer, writer etc) de marque. ◆**distinctive** a distinctif. ◆**distinctively** adv distinctement; (to stipulate, forbid) formellement; (noticeably) nettement, sensiblement; d. possible tout à fait possible.

distinguish [dɪs'tɪŋgwɪʃ] vti distinguer (from de, between entre); to d. oneself se distinguer (as en tant que). ◆**–ed** a distingué. ◆**–ing** d. mark signe m particulier. ◆**–able** a qu'on peut distinguer; (discernible) visible.

distort [dɪs'tɔːt] vt déformer. ◆**–ed** a (false) faux. ◆**distortion** n El Med distorsion f; (of truth) déformation f.

distract [dɪs'trækt] vt distraire (from de). ◆**–ed** a (troubled) préoccupé; (mad with worry) éperdu. ◆**–ing** a (noise etc) gênant. ◆**distraction** n (lack of attention, amusement) distraction f; to drive to d. rendre fou.

distraught [dɪs'trɔːt] a éperdu, affolé.

distress [dɪs'tres] n (pain) douleur f; (anguish) chagrin m; (misfortune, danger) détresse f; in d. (ship, soul) en détresse; in (great) d. (poverty) dans la détresse; – vt affliger, peiner. ◆**–ing** a affligeant, pénible.

distribute [dɪs'trɪbjʊt] vt distribuer; (spread evenly) répartir. ◆**distri'bution** n distribution f; répartition f. ◆**distributor** n Aut Cin distributeur m; (of goods) Com concessionnaire mf.

district ['dɪstrɪkt] n région f; (of town) quartier m; (administrative) arrondissement m; d. attorney Am = procureur m (de la République); d. nurse infirmière f visiteuse.

distrust [dɪs'trʌst] vt se méfier de; – n méfiance f (of de). ◆**distrustful** a méfiant; to be d. of se méfier de.

disturb [dɪs'tɜːb] vt (sleep, water) troubler; (papers, belongings) déranger; to d. s.o. (bother) déranger qn; (alarm, worry) troubler qn. ◆**–ed** a (person etc) Psy troublé. ◆**–ing** a (worrying) inquiétant; (annoying, irksome) gênant. ◆**disturbance** n (noise) tapage m; pl Pol troubles mpl.

disunity [dɪs'juːnɪtɪ] n désunion f.

disuse [dɪs'juːs] n to fall into d. tomber en désuétude. ◆**disused** [-'juːzd] a désaffecté.

ditch [dɪtʃ] 1 n fossé m. 2 vt Fam se débarrasser de.

dither ['dɪðər] vi Fam hésiter, tergiverser; to d. (around) (waste time) tourner en rond.

ditto ['dɪtəʊ] adv idem.

divan [dɪ'væn] n divan m.

div/e [daɪv] 1 vi (pt dived, Am dove [dəʊv]) plonger; (rush) se précipiter, se jeter; to d. for (pearls) pêcher; – n plongeon m; (of submarine) plongée f; (of aircraft) piqué m. 2 n (bar, club) Pej boui-boui m. ◆**–ing** a (*underwater*) plongée *f* sous-marine; **d. suit** scaphandre *m*; **d. board** plongeoir *m.* ◆**—er** *n* plongeur, -euse *mf*; (*in suit*) scaphandrier *m.*

diverge [daɪˈvɜːdʒ] *vi* diverger (**from** de). ◆**divergence** *n* divergence *f.* ◆**divergent** *a* divergent.

diverse [daɪˈvɜːs] *a* divers. ◆**diversify** *vt* diversifier; – *vi Econ* se diversifier. ◆**diversity** *n* diversité *f.*

divert [daɪˈvɜːt] *vt* détourner (**from** de); (*traffic*) dévier; (*aircraft*) dérouter; (*amuse*) divertir. ◆**diversion** *n Aut* déviation *f*; (*amusement*) divertissement *m*; *Mil* diversion *f.*

divest [daɪˈvest] *vt* **to d. of** (*power, rights*) priver de.

divid/e [dɪˈvaɪd] *vt* diviser (**into** en); **to d.** (**off**) **from** séparer de; **to d. up** (*money*) partager; **to d. one's time between** partager son temps entre; – *vi* se diviser. ◆**—ed** *a* (*opinion*) partagé. ◆**—ing** *a* **d. line** ligne *f* de démarcation.

dividend [ˈdɪvɪdend] *n Math Fin* dividende *m.*

divine [dɪˈvaɪn] *a* divin. ◆**divinity** *n* (*quality, deity*) divinité *f*; (*study*) théologie *f.*

division [dɪˈvɪʒ(ə)n] *n* division *f*; (*dividing object*) séparation *f.* ◆**divisible** *a* divisible. ◆**divisive** [-ˈvaɪsɪv] *a* qui sème la zizanie.

divorc/e [dɪˈvɔːs] *n* divorce *m*; – *vt* (*spouse*) divorcer d'avec; *Fig* séparer; – *vi* divorcer. ◆**—ed** *a* divorcé (**from** d'avec); **to get d.** divorcer. ◆**divorcee** [dɪvɔːˈsiː, *Am* dɪvɔːˈseɪ] *n* divorcé, -ée *mf.*

divulge [daɪˈvʌldʒ] *vt* divulguer.

DIY [diːaɪˈwaɪ] *n abbr* (*do-it-yourself*) bricolage *m.*

dizzy [ˈdɪzɪ] *a* (**-ier, -iest**) (*heights*) vertigineux; **to feel d.** avoir le vertige; **to make s.o.** (**feel**) **d.** donner le vertige à qn. ◆**dizziness** *n* vertige *m.*

DJ [diːˈdʒeɪ] *abbr* = **disc jockey.**

do [duː] **1** *v aux* (*3rd person sing pres t* **does**; *pt* **did**; *pp* **done**; *pres p* **doing**) **do you know?** savez-vous?; **he does not** *or* **doesn't know** il ne sait pas; **don't you want any?** tu n'en veux pas?; **I do insist** je tiens à insister; **you know him, don't you?** tu le connais, n'est-ce pas?; **better than I do** mieux que je ne le fais; **neither do I** moi non plus; **so do I** moi aussi; **oh, does he?** (*surprise*) ah oui?; **don't!** non! **2** *vt fare*; **to do nothing but sleep** ne faire que dormir; **what does she do?** (*in general*), **what is she doing?** (*now*) qu'est-ce qu'elle fait?, que

fait-elle?; **what have you done (with)...?** qu'as-tu fait (de)...?; **well done** (*congratulations*) bravo!; *Culin* bien cuit; **it's over and done (with)** c'est fini; **that'll do me** (*suit*) ça fera mon affaire; **I've been done** (*cheated*) *Fam* je me suis fait avoir; **I'll do you!** *Fam* je t'aurai!; **to do s.o. out of sth** escroquer qch à qn; **he's hard done by** on le traite durement; **I'm done (in)** (*tired*) *Sl* je suis claqué *or* vanné; **he's done for** *Fam* il est fichu; **to do in** (*kill*) *Sl* supprimer; **to do out** (*clean*) nettoyer; **to do over** (*redecorate*) refaire; **to do up** (*coat, button*) boutonner; (*zip*) fermer; (*house*) refaire; (*goods*) emballer; **do yourself up (well)!** (*wrap up*) couvre-toi (bien)! **3** *vi* (*get along*) aller, marcher; (*suit*) faire l'affaire, convenir; (*be enough*) suffire; (*finish*) finir; **how do you do?** (*introduction*) enchanté; (*greeting*) bonjour; **he did well** *or* **right to leave** il a bien fait de partir; **do as I do** fais comme moi; **to make do** se débrouiller; **to do away with sth/s.o.** supprimer qch/qn; **I could do with** (*need, want*) j'aimerais bien (avoir *or* prendre); **to do without sth/s.o.** se passer de qch/qn; **to have to do with** (*relate to*) avoir à voir avec; (*concern*) concerner; **anything doing?** *Fam* est-ce qu'il se passe quelque chose? **4** *n* (*pl* **dos** *or* **do's**) (*party*) soirée *f*, fête *f*; **the do's and don'ts** ce qu'il faut faire ou ne pas faire.

docile [ˈdəʊsaɪl] *a* docile.

dock [dɒk] **1** *n Nau* dock *m*; – *vi* (*in port*) relâcher; (*at quayside*) se mettre à quai; (*of spacecraft*) s'arrimer. **2** *n Jur* banc *m* des accusés. **3** *vt* (*wages*) rogner; **to d. sth from** (*wages*) retenir qch sur. ◆**—er** *n* docker *m.* ◆**dockyard** *n* chantier *m* naval.

docket [ˈdɒkɪt] *n* fiche *f*, bordereau *m.*

doctor [ˈdɒktər] **1** *n Med* médecin *m*, docteur *m*; *Univ* docteur *m.* **2** *vt* (*text, food*) altérer; (*cat*) *Fam* châtrer. ◆**doctorate** *n* doctorat *m* (**in** en).

doctrine [ˈdɒktrɪn] *n* doctrine *f.* ◆**doctrinaire** *a* & *n Pej* doctrinaire (*mf*).

document [ˈdɒkjumənt] *n* document *m*; – [ˈdɒkjument] *vt* (*inform*) documenter; (*report in detail*) *TV* accorder une large place à. ◆**docu'mentary** *a* & *n* documentaire (*m*).

doddering [ˈdɒdərɪŋ] *a* (*senile*) gâteux; (*shaky*) branlant.

dodge [dɒdʒ] *vt* (*question, acquaintance etc*) esquiver; (*pursuer*) échapper à; (*tax*) éviter de payer; – *vi* faire un saut (de côté); **to d. out of sight** s'esquiver; **to d. through**

(crowd) se faufiler dans; — n mouvement m de côté; (trick) Fig truc m, tour m.

dodgems ['dɒdʒəmz] npl autos fpl tamponneuses.

dodgy ['dɒdʒɪ] a (-ier, -iest) Fam (tricky) délicat; (dubious) douteux; (unreliable) peu sûr.

doe [dəʊ] n (deer) biche f.

doer ['duːər] n Fam personne f dynamique.

does [dʌz] see do.

dog [dɒg] 1 n chien m; (person) Pej type m; **d. biscuit** biscuit m or croquette f pour chien; **d. collar** Fam col m de pasteur; **d. days** canicule f. 2 vt (-gg-) (follow) poursuivre. ◆**d.-eared** a (page etc) écorné. ◆**d.-'tired** a Fam claqué, crevé. ◆**doggy** n Fam toutou m; **d. bag** (in restaurant) Am petit sac m pour emporter les restes.

dogged ['dɒgɪd] a obstiné. ◆**—ly** adv obstinément.

dogma ['dɒgmə] n dogme m. ◆**dog'matic** a dogmatique. ◆**dogmatism** n dogmatisme m.

dogsbody ['dɒgzbɒdɪ] n Pej factotum m, sous-fifre m.

doily ['dɔɪlɪ] n napperon m.

doing ['duːɪŋ] n **that's your d.** c'est toi qui as fait ça; **doings** Fam activités fpl, occupations fpl.

do-it-yourself [duːɪtjə'self] n bricolage m; — a (store, book) de bricolage.

doldrums ['dɒldrəmz] npl **to be in the d.** (of person) avoir le cafard; (of business) être en plein marasme.

dole [dəʊl] 1 n **d.** (money) allocation f de chômage; **to go on the d.** s'inscrire au chômage. 2 vt **to d. out** distribuer au compte-gouttes.

doleful ['dəʊlful] a morne, triste.

doll [dɒl] 1 n poupée f; (girl) Fam nana f; **doll's house**, Am **dollhouse** maison f de poupée. 2 vt **to d. up** Fam bichonner.

dollar ['dɒlər] n dollar m.

dollop ['dɒləp] n (of food) Pej gros morceau m.

dolphin ['dɒlfɪn] n (sea animal) dauphin m.

domain [dəʊ'meɪn] n (land, sphere) domaine m.

dome [dəʊm] n dôme m, coupole f.

domestic [də'mestɪk] a familial, domestique; (animal) domestique; (trade, flight) intérieur; (product) national; **d. science** arts mpl ménagers; **d. servant** domestique mf. ◆**domesticated** a habitué à la vie du foyer; (animal) domestique.

domicile ['dɒmɪsaɪl] n domicile m.

dominant ['dɒmɪnənt] a dominant;

(person) dominateur. ◆**dominance** n prédominance f. ◆**dominate** vti dominer. ◆**domi'nation** n domination f. ◆**domi-'neering** a dominateur.

dominion [də'mɪnjən] n domination f; (land) territoire m; Br Pol dominion m.

domino ['dɒmɪnəʊ] n (pl -oes) domino m; pl (game) dominos mpl.

don [dɒn] 1 n Br Univ professeur m. 2 vt (-nn-) revêtir.

donate [dəʊ'neɪt] vt faire don de; (blood) donner; — vi donner. ◆**donation** n don m.

done [dʌn] see do.

donkey ['dɒŋkɪ] n âne m; **for d.'s years** Fam depuis belle lurette, depuis un siècle; **d. work** travail m ingrat.

donor ['dəʊnər] n (of blood, organ) donneur, -euse mf.

doodle ['duːd(ə)l] vi griffonner.

doom [duːm] n ruine f; (fate) destin m; (gloom) Fam tristesse f; — vt condamner, destiner (to à); **to be doomed (to failure)** être voué à l'échec.

door [dɔːr] n porte f; (of vehicle, train) portière f, porte f; **out of doors** dehors; **d.-to-door salesman** démarcheur m. ◆**doorbell** n sonnette f. ◆**doorknob** n poignée f de porte. ◆**doorknocker** n marteau m. ◆**doorman** n (pl -men) (of hotel etc) portier m, concierge m. ◆**doormat** n paillasson m. ◆**doorstep** n seuil m. ◆**doorstop(per)** n butoir m (de porte). ◆**doorway** n **in the d.** dans l'encadrement de la porte.

dope [dəʊp] 1 n Fam drogue f; (for horse, athlete) doping m; — vt doper. 2 n (information) Fam tuyaux mpl. 3 n (idiot) imbécile mf. ◆**dopey** a (-ier, -iest) Fam (stupid) abruti; (sleepy) endormi; (drugged) drogué, camé.

dormant ['dɔːmənt] a (volcano, matter) en sommeil; (passion) endormi.

dormer ['dɔːmər] n **d.** (window) lucarne f.

dormitory ['dɔːmɪtrɪ, Am 'dɔːmɪtɔːrɪ] n dortoir m; Am résidence f (universitaire).

dormouse, pl **-mice** ['dɔːmaʊs, -maɪs] n loir m.

dos/e [dəʊs] n dose f; (of hard work) Fig période f; (of illness) attaque f; — vt **to d. oneself (up)** se bourrer de médicaments. ◆**—age** n (amount) dose f.

dosshouse ['dɒshaʊs] n Sl asile m (de nuit).

dossier ['dɒsɪeɪ] n (papers) dossier m.

dot [dɒt] n point m; **polka d.** pois m; **on the d.** Fam à l'heure pile; — vt (-tt-) (an i) mettre un point sur. ◆**dotted** *a* d. line pointillé *m*; d. **with** parsemé de.

dot/e [dəʊt] *vt* to d. on être gaga de. ◆**—ing** *a* affectueux; her d. **husband**/**father** son mari/père qui lui passe tout.

dotty ['dɒtɪ] *a* (-ier, -iest) *Fam* cinglé, toqué.

double ['dʌb(ə)l] *a* double; **a** d. **bed** un grand lit; **a** d. **room** une chambre pour deux personnes; d. **'s'** deux 's'; d. **six** deux fois six; d. **three four two** (*phone number*) trente-trois quarante-deux; – *adv* deux fois; (*to fold*) en deux; **he earns** d. **what** I **earn** il gagne le double de moi ou deux fois plus que moi; **to see** d. voir double; – *n* double *m*; (*person*) double *m*, sosie *m*; (*stand-in*) *Cin* doublure *f*; **on** *or* **at the** d. au pas de course; – *vt* doubler; **to** d. **back** *or* **over** replier; – *vi* doubler; **to** d. **back** (*of person*) revenir en arrière; **to** d. **up** (*with pain, laughter*) être plié en deux. ◆**d.-'barrelled** *a* (*gun*) à deux canons; (*name*) à rallonges. ◆**d.-'bass** *n* *Mus* contrebasse *f*. ◆**d.-'breasted** *a* (*jacket*) croisé. ◆**d.-'cross** *vt* tromper. ◆**d.-'dealing** *n* double jeu *m*. ◆**d.-'decker (bus)** *n* autobus *m* à impériale. ◆**d.-'door** *n* porte *f* à deux battants. ◆**d.-'dutch** *n* *Fam* baragouin *m*. ◆**d.-'glazing** *n* (*window*) double vitrage *m*, double(s) fenêtre(s) *f(pl)*. ◆**d.-'parking** *n* stationnement *m* en double file. ◆**d.-'quick** *adv* en vitesse.

doubly ['dʌblɪ] *adv* doublement.

doubt [daʊt] *n* doute *m*; **to be in** d. **about** avoir des doutes sur; **I have no** d. **about it** je n'en doute pas; **no** d. (*probably*) sans doute; **in** d. (*result, career etc*) dans la balance; – *vt* douter de; **to** d. **whether** *or* **that** *or* **if** douter que (+ *sub*). ◆**doubtful** *a* douteux; **it's** d. **whether** *or* **that** il est douteux que (+ *sub*). ◆**doubtless** *adv* sans doute.

dough [dəʊ] *n* pâte *f*; (*money*) *Fam* fric *m*, blé *m*. ◆**doughnut** *n* beignet *m* (rond).

dour ['dʊər] *a* austère.

douse [daʊs] *vt* arroser, tremper; (*light*) *Fam* éteindre.

dove[1] [dʌv] *n* colombe *f*. ◆**dovecote** [-kɒt] *n* colombier *m*.

dove[2] [dəʊv] *Am see* **dive 1**.

Dover ['dəʊvər] *n* Douvres *m* or *f*.

dovetail ['dʌvteɪl] **1** *n* *Carp* queue *f* d'aronde. **2** *vi* (*fit*) *Fig* concorder.

dowdy ['daʊdɪ] *a* (-ier, -iest) peu élégant, sans chic.

down[1] [daʊn] *adv* en bas; (*to the ground*) par terre, à terre; (*of sun*) couché; (*of blind,*

temperature) baissé; (*out of bed*) descendu; (*of tyre*) dégonflé, (*worn*) usé; d. (*in writing*) inscrit; (**lie) d.!** (*to dog*) couché!; **to come** *or* **go** d. descendre; **to come** d. **from** (*place*) arriver de; **to fall** d. tomber (par terre); d. **there** *or* **here** en bas; d. **with traitors**/*etc*! à bas les traîtres/*etc*!; d. **with (the) flu** grippé; **to feel** d. (*depressed*) *Fam* avoir le cafard; d. **to** (*in series, numbers, dates etc*) jusqu'à; d. **payment** acompte *m*; d. **under** aux antipodes, en Australie; d. **at heel**, *Am* d. **at the heels** miteux; – *prep* (*at bottom of*) en bas de; (*from top to bottom of*) du haut en bas de; (*along*) le long de; **to go** d. (*hill etc*) descendre; **to live** d. **the street** habiter plus loin dans la rue; – *vt* (*shoot down*) abattre; (*knock down*) terrasser; **to** d. **a drink** vider un verre. ◆**down-and-'out** *a* sur le pavé; – *n* clochard, -arde *mf*. ◆**downbeat** *a* (*gloomy*) *Fam* pessimiste. ◆**downcast** *a* découragé. ◆**downfall** *n* chute *f*. ◆**downgrade** *vt* (*job etc*) déclasser; (*person*) rétrograder. ◆**down-'hearted** *a* découragé. ◆**down-'hill** *adv* en pente; **to go** d. descendre; *Fig* être sur le déclin. ◆**downmarket** *a* *Com* bas de gamme. ◆**downpour** *n* averse *f*, pluie *f* torrentielle. ◆**downright** *a* (*rogue etc*) véritable; (*refusal etc*) catégorique; **a** d. **nerve** *or* **cheek** un sacré culot; – *adv* (*rude etc*) franchement. ◆**'downstairs** *a* (*room, neighbours*) d'en bas; (*on the ground floor*) du rez-de-chaussée; – [daʊn'steəz] *adv* en bas; au rez-de-chaussée; **to come** *or* **go** d. descendre l'escalier. ◆**down'stream** *adv* en aval. ◆**down-to-'earth** *a* terre-à-terre *inv*. ◆**down'town** *adv* en ville; d. **Chicago**/*etc* le centre de Chicago/*etc*. ◆**downtrodden** *a* opprimé. ◆**downward** *a* vers le bas; (*path*) qui descend; (*trend*) à la baisse. ◆**downward(s)** *adv* vers le bas.

down[2] [daʊn] *n* (*on bird, person etc*) duvet *m*.

downs [daʊnz] *npl* collines *fpl*.

dowry ['daʊərɪ] *n* dot *f*.

doze [dəʊz] *n* petit somme *m*; – *vi* sommeiller; **to** d. **off** s'assoupir. ◆**dozy** *a* (-ier, -iest) assoupi; (*silly*) *Fam* bête, gourde.

dozen ['dʌz(ə)n] *n* douzaine *f*; **a** d. (*eggs, books etc*) une douzaine de; **dozens of** *Fig* des dizaines de.

Dr (*Doctor*) Docteur.

drab [dræb] *a* terne; (*weather*) gris. ◆**—ness** *n* caractère *m* terne; (*of weather*) grisaille *f*.

draconian [drəˈkəʊnɪən] *a* draconien.

draft [drɑːft] **1** n (outline) ébauche f; (of letter etc) brouillon m; (bill) Com traite f; − vt **to d. (out)** (sketch out) faire le brouillon de; (write out) rédiger. **2** n Mil Am conscription f; (men) contingent m; − vt (conscript) appeler (sous les drapeaux). **3** n Am = **draught**.

draftsman [drɑːftsmən] n = **draughtsman**.

drag [dræg] vt (-gg-) traîner, tirer; (river) draguer; **to d. sth from s.o.** (confession etc) arracher qch à qn; **to d. along** (en)traîner; **to d. s.o. away from** entraîner qn de; **to d. s.o. into** entraîner qn dans; − vi traîner; **to d. on** or **out** (last a long time) se prolonger; − n Fam (tedium) corvée f; (person) raseur, -euse mf; (on cigarette) bouffée f (on de); **in d.** (clothing) en travesti.

dragon [drægən] n dragon m. ◆**dragonfly** n libellule f.

drain [dreɪn] n (sewer) égout m; (pipe, channel) canal m; (outside house) puisard m; (in street) bouche f d'égout; **it's (gone) down the d.** (wasted) Fam c'est fichu; **to be a d. on** (resources, patience) épuiser; − vt (land) drainer; (glass, tank) vider; (vegetables) égoutter; (resources) épuiser; **to d. (off)** (liquid) faire écouler; **to d. of** (deprive of) priver de; − vi **to d. (off)** (of liquid) s'écouler; **to d. away** (of strength) s'épuiser; **draining board** paillasse f. ◆**—age** n (act) drainage m; (sewers) système m d'égouts. ◆**—er** n (board) paillasse f; (rack, basket) égouttoir m. ◆**drainboard** n Am paillasse f. ◆**drainpipe** n tuyau m d'évacuation.

drake [dreɪk] n canard m (mâle).

dram [dræm] n (drink) Fam goutte f.

drama [drɑːmə] n (event) drame m; (dramatic art) théâtre m; **d. critic** critique m dramatique. ◆**dra'matic** a dramatique; (very great, striking) spectaculaire. ◆**dra-'matically** adv (to change, drop etc) de façon spectaculaire. ◆**dra'matics** n théâtre m. ◆**dramatist** [dræmətɪst] n dramaturge m. ◆**dramatize** vt (exaggerate) dramatiser; (novel etc) adapter (pour la scène or l'écran).

drank [dræŋk] see **drink**.

drap/e [dreɪp] vt draper (with de); (wall) tapisser (de tentures); (heavy curtains) Am rideaux mpl. ◆**—er** n marchand, -ande f de nouveautés.

drastic [dræstɪk] a radical, sévère; (reduction) massif. ◆**drastically** adv radicalement.

draught [drɑːft] n courant m d'air; (for fire) tirage m; pl (game) dames fpl. − a (horse) de trait; (beer) (à la) pression; **d.** excluder

bourrelet m (de porte, de fenêtre). ◆**draughtboard** n damier m. ◆**draughty** a (-ier, -iest) (room) plein de courants d'air.

draughtsman [drɑːftsmən] n (pl **-men**) dessinateur, -trice mf (industriel(le) or technique).

draw [drɔː] n (of lottery) tirage m au sort; Sp match m nul; (attraction) attraction f; − vt (pt **drew**, pp **drawn**) (pull) tirer; (pass) passer (over sur, into dans); (prize) gagner; (applause) provoquer; (money from bank) retirer (from, out of de); (salary) toucher; (attract) attirer; (well-water, comfort) puiser (from dans); **to d. a smile** faire sourire (from s.o. qn); **to d. a bath** faire couler un bain; **to d. sth to a close** mettre fin à qch; **to d. a match** Sp faire match nul; **to d. in** (claws) rentrer; **to d. out** (money) retirer; (meeting) prolonger; **to d. up** (chair) approcher; (contract, list, plan) dresser, rédiger; **to d. (up)on** (savings) puiser dans; − vi (enter) entrer (into dans); (arrive) arriver; **to d. near** (to) s'approcher (de); (of time) approcher (de); **to d. to a close** tirer à sa fin; **to d. aside** (step aside) s'écarter; **to d. away** (go away) s'éloigner; **to d. back** (recoil) reculer; **to d. in** (of days) diminuer; **to d. on** (of time) s'avancer; **to d. up** (of vehicle) s'arrêter. ◆**drawback** n inconvénient m. ◆**drawbridge** n pont-levis m.

draw [drɔː] vt (pt **drew**, pp **drawn**) (picture) dessiner; (circle) tracer; (parallel, distinction) Fig faire (between entre); − vi (as artist) dessiner. ◆**—ing** n dessin m; **d. board** planche f à dessin; **d. pin** punaise f; **d. room** salon m.

drawer [drɔːr] **1** n (in furniture) tiroir m. **2** npl (women's knickers) culotte f.

drawl [drɔːl] vi parler d'une voix traînante; − n voix f traînante.

drawn [drɔːn] see **draw** [1,2]; − a (face) tiré, crispé; **d. match** or **game** match m nul.

dread [dred] vt redouter (doing de faire); − n crainte f, terreur f. ◆**dreadful** a épouvantable; (child) insupportable; (ill) malade; **I feel d. about it)** j'ai vraiment honte. ◆**dreadfully** adv terriblement; **to be** or **feel d. sorry** regretter infiniment.

dream [driːm] vti (pt & pp **dreamed** or **dreamt** [dremt]) rêver; (imagine) songer (of à, that que); **I wouldn't d. of it!** (il n'en est pas question!; **to d. sth up** imaginer qch; − n rêve m; (wonderful thing or person) Fam merveille f; **to have a d.** faire un rêve (about de); **to have dreams of** rêver de; **a d. house/**etc une maison/etc de rêve; **a d.**

world un monde imaginaire. ◆—er n rêveur, -euse mf. ◆dreamy a (-ier, -iest) rêveur.

dreary ['drɪərɪ] a (-ier, -iest) (gloomy) morne; (monotonous) monotone; (boring) ennuyeux.

dredg/e [dredʒ] vt (river etc) draguer; — n drague f. ◆—er n 1 (ship) dragueur m. 2 Culin saupoudreuse f.

dregs [dregz] npl the d. (in liquid, of society) la lie.

drench [drentʃ] vt tremper; **to get drenched** se faire tremper (jusqu'aux os).

dress [dres] n 1 (woman's garment) robe f; (style of dressing) tenue f; **d. circle** Th (premier) balcon m; **d. designer** dessinateur, -trice mf de mode; (well-known) couturier m; **d. rehearsal** (répétition f) générale f; **d. shirt** chemise f de soirée. 2 vt (clothe) habiller; (adorn) orner; (salad) assaisonner; (wound) panser; (skins, chicken) préparer; **to get dressed** s'habiller; **dressed for tennis/etc** en tenue de tennis/etc; **to d. up** (smartly) bien s'habiller; (in disguise) se déguiser (as en). ◆—ing n Med pansement m; (seasoning) Culin assaisonnement m; **to give s.o. a d.-down** passer un savon à qn; **d. gown** robe f de chambre; (of boxer) peignoir m; **d. room** Th loge f; **d. table** coiffeuse f. ◆—er n 1 (furniture) vaisselier m; **Am** coiffeuse f. 2 **she's a good d.** elle s'habille toujours bien. ◆dressmaker n couturière f. ◆dressmaking n couture f.

dressy ['dresɪ] a (-ier, -iest) (smart) chic inv; (too) a. trop habillé.

drew [druː] see draw [1,2].

dribble ['drɪb(ə)l] vi (of baby) baver; (of liquid) tomber goutte à goutte; Sp dribbler; — vt laisser tomber goutte à goutte; (ball) Sp dribbler.

dribs [drɪbz] npl **in d. and drabs** par petites quantités; (to arrive) par petits groupes.

dried [draɪd] a (fruit) sec; (milk) en poudre; (flowers) séché.

drier ['draɪər] n = dryer.

drift [drɪft] vi être emporté par le vent or le courant; (of ship) dériver; Fig aller à la dérive; (of snow) s'amonceler; **to d. about** (aimlessly) se promener sans but, traînailler; **to d. apart** (of husband and wife) devenir des étrangers l'un pour l'autre; **to d. into/towards** glisser dans/vers; — n mouvement m; (direction) sens m; (of events) cours m; (of snow) amoncellement m, congère f; (meaning) sens m général.

◆—er n (aimless person) paumé, -ée mf. ◆driftwood n bois m flotté.

drill [drɪl] n 1 (tool) perceuse f; (bit) mèche f; (for rock) foreuse f; (for tooth) fraise f; (pneumatic) marteau m pneumatique; — vt percer; (tooth) fraiser; (oil well) forer; — vi **to d. for oil** faire de la recherche pétrolière. 2 n Mil Sch exercice(s) m(pl); (procedure) Fig marche f à suivre; — vi faire l'exercice; — vt faire faire l'exercice à.

drink [drɪŋk] n boisson f; (glass of sth) verre m; **to give s.o. a d.** donner (quelque chose) à boire à qn; — vt (pt drank, pp drunk) boire; **to d. oneself to death** se tuer à force de boire; **to d. down** or **up** boire; — vi boire (out of dans); **to d. up** finir son verre; **to d. to** boire à la santé de. ◆—ing n (of water) potable; (song) à boire; **d. bout** beuverie f; **d. fountain** fontaine f publique, borne-fontaine f; **d. trough** abreuvoir m. ◆—able a (fit for drinking) potable; (palatable) buvable. ◆—er n buveur, -euse mf.

drip [drɪp] vi (-pp-) dégouliner, dégoutter; (of washing, vegetables) s'égoutter; (of tap) fuir; — vt (paint etc) laisser couler; — n (drop) goutte f; (sound) bruit m de goutte; (fool) Fam nouille f. ◆d.-dry a (shirt etc) sans repassage. ◆dripping n (Am drippings) Culin graisse f; — a & adv (wet) dégoulinant.

driv/e [draɪv] n promenade f en voiture; (energy) énergie f; Psy instinct m; Pol campagne f; (road to private house) allée f; **an hour's d.** une heure de voiture; **left-hand** d. Aut (véhicule m à) conduite f à gauche; **front-wheel d.** Aut traction f avant; — vt (pt drove, pp driven) (vehicle, train, passenger) conduire; (machine) actionner; **to d. (away** or **out)** (chase away) chasser; **to d. s.o. to do** pousser qn à faire; **to d. s.o. to despair** réduire au désespoir; **to d. mad** or **crazy** rendre fou; **to d. the rain/smoke against** (of wind) rabattre la pluie/fumée contre; **to d. back** (enemy etc) repousser; (passenger) Aut ramener (en voiture); **to d. in** (thrust) enfoncer; **to d. s.o. hard** surmener qn; **he drives a Ford** il a une Ford; — vi (drive a car) conduire; **to d. (along)** (go, run) Aut rouler; **to d. on the left** rouler à gauche; **to d. away** or **off** Aut partir; **to d. back** Aut revenir; **to d. on** Aut continuer; **to d. to** Aut aller (en voiture) à; **to d. up** Aut arriver; **what are you driving at?** Fig où veux-tu en venir? ◆—ing 1 n conduite f; **d. lesson** leçon f de conduite; **d. licence, d. test** permis m de conduire; **d. school** auto-école *f*. **2** *a* (*forceful*) **d.** force *f* agissante; **d. rain** pluie *f* battante. ◆**—er** *n* (*of car*) conducteur, -trice *mf*; (*of taxi, lorry*) chauffeur *m*, conducteur, -trice *mf*; (**train**) *d.* mécanicien *m*; **she's a good d.** elle conduit bien; **driver's license** *Am* permis *m* de conduire.

drivel ['drɪv(ə)l] *vi* (**-ll-**, *Am* **-l-**) radoter; – *n* radotage *m*.

drizzle ['drɪz(ə)l] *n* bruine *f*, crachin *m*; – *vi* bruiner. ◆**drizzly** *a* (*weather*) de bruine; **it's d.** il bruine.

droll [drəʊl] *a* drôle, comique.

dromedary ['drɒmədərɪ, *Am* 'drɒmɪderɪ] *n* dromadaire *m*.

drone [drəʊn] **1** *n* (*bee*) abeille *f* mâle. **2** *n* (*hum*) bourdonnement *m*; (*purr*) ronronnement *m*; *Fig* débit *m* monotone; – *vi* (*of bee*) bourdonner; (*of engine*) ronronner; **to d. (on)** *Fig* parler d'une voix monotone.

drool [druːl] *vi* (*slaver*) baver; *Fig* radoter; **to d. over** *Fig* s'extasier devant.

droop [druːp] *vi* (*of head*) pencher; (*of eyelid*) tomber; (*of flower*) se faner.

drop [drɒp] **1** *n* (*of liquid*) goutte *f*. **2** *n* (*fall*) baisse *f*, chute *f* (**in** de); (*slope*) descente *f*; (*distance of fall*) hauteur *f* (de chute); (*jump*) *Av* saut *m*; – *vt* (**-pp-**) laisser tomber; (*price, voice*) baisser; (*bomb*) larguer; (*passenger, goods*) *Aut* déposer; *Nau* débarquer; (*letter*) envoyer (**to** à); (*put*) mettre; (*omit*) omettre; (*remark*) laisser échapper; (*get rid of*) supprimer; (*habit*) abandonner; (*team member*) *Sp* écarter; **to d. s.o. off** *Aut* déposer qn; **to d. a line** écrire un petit mot (**to** à); **to d. a hint** faire une allusion; **to d. a hint that** laisser entendre que; **to d. one's h's** ne pas aspirer les h; **to d. a word in s.o.'s ear** glisser un mot à l'oreille de qn; – *vi* (*fall*) tomber; (*of person*) se laisser tomber; (*of price*) baisser; (*of conversation*) cesser; **he's ready to d.** *Fam* il tombe de fatigue; **let it d.!** *Fam* laisse tomber! **to d. across** *or* **in** passer (chez qn); **to d. away** (*diminish*) diminuer; **to d. back** *or* **behind** rester en arrière, se laisser distancer; **to d. off** (*fall asleep*) s'endormir; (*fall off*) tomber; (*of interest, sales etc*) diminuer. ◆**d.-off** *n* (*decrease*) diminution *f* (**in** de); **to d. out** (*fall out*) tomber; (*withdraw*) se retirer; (*socially*) se mettre en marge de la société; *Sch Univ* laisser tomber ses études. ◆**d.-out** *n* marginal, -ale *mf*; *Univ* étudiant, -ante *mf* qui abandonne ses études. ◆**droppings** *npl* (*of animal*) crottes *fpl*; (*of bird*) fiente *f*.

dross [drɒs] *n* déchets *mpl*.

drought [draʊt] *n* sécheresse *f*.

drove [drəʊv] *see* **drive**.

droves [drəʊvz] *npl* (*of people*) foules *fpl*; **in d.** en foule.

drown [draʊn] *vi* se noyer; – *vt* noyer; **to d. oneself, be drowned** se noyer. ◆**—ing** *a* qui se noie; – *n* (*death*) noyade *f*.

drowse [draʊz] *vi* somnoler. ◆**drows/y** *a* (**-ier, -iest**) somnolent; **to feel d.** avoir sommeil; **to make s.o. (feel) d.** assoupir qn. ◆**—ily** *adv* d'un air somnolent. ◆**—iness** *n* somnolence *f*.

drubbing ['drʌbɪŋ] *n* (*beating*) raclée *f*.

drudge [drʌdʒ] *n* bête *f* de somme, esclave *mf* du travail; – *vi* trimer. ◆**drudgery** *n* corvée(s) *f*(*pl*), travail *m* ingrat.

drug [drʌg] *n* *Med* médicament *m*, drogue *f*; (*narcotic*) stupéfiant *m*, drogue *f*; *Fig* drogue *f*; **drugs** (*dope in general*) la drogue; **to be on drugs, take drugs** se droguer; **d. addict** drogué, -ée *mf*; **d. addiction** toxicomanie *f*; **d. taking** usage *m* de la drogue; – *vt* (**-gg-**) droguer; (*drink*) mêler un somnifère à. ◆**druggist** *n* *Am* pharmacien, -ienne *mf*, droguiste *mf*. ◆**drugstore** *n* *Am* drugstore *m*.

drum [drʌm] *n* *Mus* tambour *m*; (*for oil*) bidon *m*; **the big d.** *Mus* la grosse caisse; **the drums** *Mus* la batterie; – *vi* (**-mm-**) *Mil* battre du tambour; (*with fingers*) tambouriner; – *vt* **to d. sth into s.o.** *Fig* rabâcher qch à qn; **to d. up** (*support, interest*) susciter; **to d. up business** *or* **custom** attirer les clients. ◆**drummer** *n* (*joueur, -euse mf* de) tambour *m*; (*in pop or jazz group*) batteur *m*. ◆**drumstick** *n* *Mus* baguette *f* de tambour; (*of chicken*) pilon *m*, cuisse *f*.

drunk [drʌŋk] *see* **drink**; – *a* ivre; **d. with** *Fig* ivre de; **to get d.** s'enivrer. – *n* ivrogne *mf*, pochard, -arde *mf*. ◆**drunkard** *n* ivrogne *mf*. ◆**drunken** *a* (*quarrel*) d'ivrogne; (*person*) ivrogne; (*driver*) ivre; **d. driving** conduite *f* en état d'ivresse. ◆**drunkenness** *n* (*state*) ivresse *f*; (*habit*) ivrognerie *f*.

dry [draɪ] *a* (**drier, driest**) sec; (*well, river*) à sec; (*day*) sans pluie; (*toast*) sans beurre; (*wit*) caustique; (*subject, book*) aride; **on d. land** sur la terre ferme; **to keep sth d.** tenir qch au sec; **to wipe d.** essuyer; **to run d.** se tarir; **to feel** *or* **be d.** *Fam* avoir soif; **d. dock** cale *f* sèche; **d. goods store** *Am* magasin *m* de nouveautés; – *vt* sécher; (*dishes etc*) essuyer; **to d. up** *or* **off** sécher; – *vi* sécher; **to d. off** sécher; **to d. up** sécher; (*run dry*) se tarir; **d. up!** *Fam* tais-toi! ◆**—ing** *n* séchage *m*; essuyage *m*. ◆**—er** *n* (*for hair,* *clothes*) séchoir *m*; (*helmet-style for hair*) casque *m*. ◆—**ness** *n* sécheresse *f*; (*of wit*) causticité *f*; (*of book etc*) aridité *f*. ◆**dry-'clean** *vt* nettoyer à sec. ◆**dry-'cleaner** *n* teinturier, -ière *mf*.

dual ['djuːəl] *a* double; **d. carriageway** route *f* à deux voies (séparées). ◆**du'ality** *n* dualité *f*.

dub [dʌb] *vt* (-**bb**-) **1** (*film*) doubler. **2** (*nickname*) surnommer. ◆**dubbing** *n* Cin doublage *m*.

dubious ['djuːbɪəs] *a* (*offer, person etc*) douteux; **I'm d. about going** *or* **whether to go** je me demande si je dois y aller; **to be d. about sth** douter de qch.

duchess ['dʌtʃɪs] *n* duchesse *f*. ◆**duchy** *n* duché *m*.

duck [dʌk] **1** *n* canard *m*. **2** *vi* se baisser (vivement); – *vt* (*head*) baisser; **to d. s.o.** plonger qn dans l'eau. ◆—**ing** *n* bain *m* forcé. ◆**duckling** *n* caneton *m*.

duct [dʌkt] *n* Anat Tech conduit *m*.

dud [dʌd] *a* Fam (*bomb*) non éclaté; (*coin*) faux; (*cheque*) en bois; (*watch etc*) qui ne marche pas; – *n* (*person*) zéro *m*, type *m* nul.

dude [duːd] *n* Am Fam dandy *m*; **d. ranch** ranch(-hôtel) *m*.

due[1] [djuː] *a* (*money, sum*) dû (**to** à); (*rent, bill*) à payer; (*respect*) qu'on doit (**to** à); (*fitting*) qui convient; **to fall d.** échoir; **she's d. for** (*a rise etc*) elle doit *or* devrait recevoir; **he's d.** (**to arrive**) (*is awaited*) il doit arriver, il est attendu; **I'm d. there** je dois être là-bas; **in d. course** (*at proper time*) en temps utile; (*finally*) à la longue; **d. to** (*attributable to*) dû à; (*because of*) à cause de; (*thanks to*) grâce à; – *n* dû *m*; *pl* (*of club*) cotisation *f*; (*official charges*) droits *mpl*; **to give s.o. his d.** admettre que qn a raison.

due[2] [djuː] *adv* (*tout*) droit; **d. north/south** plein nord/sud.

duel ['djuːəl] *n* duel *m*; – *vi* (-**ll-**, *Am* -**l-**) se battre en duel.

duet [djuː'et] *n* duo *m*.

duffel, duffle ['dʌf(ə)l] *a* **d. bag** sac *m* de marin; **d. coat** duffel-coat *m*.

dug [dʌg] *see* **dig.** ◆**dugout** *n* **1** Mil abri *m* souterrain. **2** (*canoe*) pirogue *f*.

duke [djuːk] *n* duc *m*.

dull [dʌl] *a* (-**er**, -**est**) (*boring*) ennuyeux; (*colour, character*) terne; (*weather*) maussade; (*mind*) lourd, borné; (*sound, ache*) sourd; (*edge, blade*) émoussé; (*hearing, sight*) faible; – *vt* (*senses*) émousser; (*sound, pain*) amortir; (*colour*) ternir;

(*mind*) engourdir. ◆—**ness** *n* (*of mind*) lourdeur *f* d'esprit; (*tedium*) monotonie *f*; (*of colour*) manque *m* d'éclat.

duly ['djuːlɪ] *adv* (*properly*) comme il convient (convenait etc); (*in fact*) en effet; (*in due time*) en temps utile.

dumb [dʌm] *a* (-**er**, -**est**) muet; (*stupid*) Fam idiot, bête. ◆—**ness** *n* mutisme *m*; bêtise *f*. ◆**dumbbell** *n* (*weight*) haltère *m*. ◆**dumbwaiter** *n* (*lift for food*) monte-plats *m inv.*

dumbfound [dʌm'faʊnd] *vt* sidérer, ahurir.

dummy ['dʌmɪ] **1** *n* (*of baby*) sucette *f*; (*of dressmaker*) mannequin *m*; (*of book*) maquette *f*; (*of ventriloquist*) pantin *m*; (*fool*) Fam idiot, -ote *mf*. **2** *a* factice, faux; **d. run** (*on car etc*) essai *m*.

dump [dʌmp] *vt* (*rubbish*) déposer; **to d.** (**down**) déposer; **to d. s.o.** (*ditch*) Fam plaquer qn; – *n* (*for ammunition*) Mil dépôt *m*; (*dirty or dull town*) Fam trou *m*; (*house, slum*) Fam baraque *f*; (*rubbish*) dépôt *m* d'ordures, (*place*) dépôt *m* d'ordures, décharge *f*; **to be** (**down**) **in the dumps** Fam avoir le cafard; **d. truck** = **dumper.** ◆—**er** *n* **d.** (**truck**) camion *m* à benne basculante.

dumpling ['dʌmplɪŋ] *n* Culin boulette *f* (de pâte).

dumpy ['dʌmpɪ] *a* (-**ier**, -**iest**) (*person*) boulot, gros et court.

dunce [dʌns] *n* cancre *m*, âne *m*.

dune [djuːn] *n* dune *f*.

dung [dʌŋ] *n* crotte *f*; (*of cattle*) bouse *f*; (*manure*) fumier *m*.

dungarees [dʌŋɡə'riːz] *npl* (*of child, workman*) salopette *f*; (*jeans*) *Am* jean *m*.

dungeon ['dʌndʒən] *n* cachot *m*.

dunk [dʌŋk] *vt* (*bread, biscuit etc*) tremper.

dupe [djuːp] *vt* duper; – *n* dupe *f*.

duplex ['duːpleks] *n* (*apartment*) *Am* duplex *m*.

duplicate ['djuːplɪkeɪt] *vt* (*key, map*) faire un double de; (*on machine*) polycopier; – ['djuːplɪkət] *n* double *m*; **in d.** en deux exemplaires; **a d. copy/etc** une copie/etc en double; **a d. key** un double de la clef. ◆**dupli'cation** *n* (*on machine*) polycopie *f*; (*of effort*) répétition *f*. ◆**duplicator** *n* duplicateur *m*.

duplicity [djuː'plɪsɪtɪ] *n* duplicité *f*.

durable ['djʊərəb(ə)l] *a* (*shoes etc*) résistant; (*friendship, love*) durable. ◆**dura'bility** *n* résistance *f*; durabilité *f*.

duration [djʊə'reɪʃ(ə)n] *n* durée *f*.

duress [djʊ'res] *n* **under d.** sous la contrainte.

during ['djʊərɪŋ] *prep* pendant, durant.

dusk [dʌsk] n (twilight) crépuscule m.
dusky ['dʌskɪ] a (-ier, -iest) (complexion) foncé.
dust [dʌst] n poussière f; **d. cover** (for furniture) housse f; (for book) jaquette f; **d. jacket** jaquette f; – vt épousseter; (sprinkle) saupoudrer (**with** de). ◆—**er** n chiffon m. ◆**dustbin** n poubelle f. ◆**dustcart** n camion-benne m. ◆**dustman** n (pl -men) éboueur m, boueux m. ◆**dustpan** n petite pelle f (à poussière).
dusty ['dʌstɪ] a (-ier, -iest) poussiéreux.
Dutch [dʌtʃ] a néerlandais, hollandais; **D. cheese** hollande f; **to go D.** partager les frais (**with** avec); – n (language) hollandais m. ◆**Dutchman** n (pl -men) Hollandais m. ◆**Dutchwoman** n (pl -women) Hollandaise f.
duty ['djuːtɪ] n devoir m; (tax) droit m; pl (responsibilities) fonctions fpl; **on d.** Mil de service; (doctor etc) de garde; Sch de permanence; **off d.** libre. ◆**d.-'free** a (goods, shop) hors-taxe inv. ◆**dutiful** a respectueux, obéissant; (worker) consciencieux.
dwarf [dwɔːf] n nain m, naine f; – vt (of building, person etc) rapetisser, écraser.

dwell [dwel] vi (pt & pp **dwelt**) demeurer; **to d. (up)on** (think about) penser sans cesse à; (speak about) parler sans cesse de, s'étendre sur; (insist on) appuyer sur. ◆—**ing** n habitation f. ◆—**er** n habitant, -ante mf.
dwindl/e ['dwɪnd(ə)l] vi diminuer (peu à peu). ◆—**ing** a (interest etc) décroissant.
dye [daɪ] n teinture f; – vt teindre; **to d. green/etc** teindre en vert/etc. ◆**dyeing** n teinture f; (industry) teinturerie f. ◆**dyer** n teinturier, -ière mf.
dying ['daɪɪŋ] see **die 1**; – a mourant, moribond; (custom) qui se perd; (day, words) dernier; – n (death) mort f.
dyke [daɪk] n (wall) digue f; (ditch) fossé m.
dynamic [daɪ'næmɪk] a dynamique. ◆'**dynamism** n dynamisme m.
dynamite ['daɪnəmaɪt] n dynamite f; – vt dynamiter.
dynamo ['daɪnəməʊ] n (pl -os) dynamo f.
dynasty ['dɪnəstɪ, Am 'daɪnəstɪ] n dynastie f.
dysentery ['dɪsəntrɪ] n Med dysenterie f.
dyslexic [dɪs'leksɪk] a & n dyslexique (mf).

E

E, e [iː] n E, e m.
each [iːtʃ] a chaque; – pron chacun, -une; **e. one** chacun, -une; **e. other** l'un(e) l'autre, pl les un(e)s les autres; **to see e. other** se voir (l'un(e) l'autre); **e. of us** chacun, -une d'entre nous.
eager ['iːgər] a impatient (**to do** de faire); (enthusiastic) ardent, passionné; **to be e. for** désirer vivement; **e. for** (money) avide de; **e. to help** empressé à (aider); **to be e. to do** (want) avoir envie de faire. ◆—**ly** adv (to await) avec impatience; (to work, serve) avec empressement. ◆—**ness** n impatience f (**to do** de faire); (zeal) empressement m (**to do** à faire); (greed) avidité f.
eagle ['iːg(ə)l] n aigle m. ◆**e.-'eyed** a au regard d'aigle.
ear¹ [ɪər] n oreille f; **all ears** Fam tout ouïe; **up to one's ears in work** débordé de travail; **to play it by e.** Fam agir selon la situation; **thick e.** Fam gifle f. ◆**earache** n mal m d'oreille. ◆**eardrum** n tympan m. ◆**earmuffs** npl serre-tête m inv (pour

protéger les oreilles), protège-oreilles m inv. ◆**earphones** npl casque m. ◆**earpiece** n écouteur m. ◆**earplug** n (to keep out noise) boule f Quiès®. ◆**earring** n boucle f d'oreille. ◆**earshot** n **within e.** à portée de voix. ◆**ear-splitting** a assourdissant.
ear² [ɪər] n (of corn) épi m.
earl [ɜːl] n comte m.
early ['ɜːlɪ] a (-ier, -iest) (first) premier; (fruit, season) précoce; (death) prématuré; (age) jeune; (painting, work) de jeunesse; (reply) rapide; (return, retirement) anticipé; (ancient) ancien; **it's e.** (looking at time) il est tôt; (referring to appointment etc) c'est tôt; **it's too e. to** get up/etc il est trop tôt pour se lever/etc; **to be e.** (ahead of time) arriver de bonne heure or tôt, être en avance; (in getting up) être matinal; **in e. times** jadis; **in e. summer** au début de l'été; **one's e. life** sa jeunesse; – adv tôt, de bonne heure; (ahead of time) en avance; (to die) prématurément; **as e. as possible** le plus tôt possible; **earlier (on)** plus tôt; **at**

the **earliest** au plus tôt; **as e. as yesterday** déjà hier. ◆**e.-'warning system** n dispositif m de première alerte.

earmark ['ɪəmɑːk] vt (funds) assigner (**for** à).

earn [ɜːn] vt gagner; (interest) Fin rapporter. ◆**-ings** npl (wages) rémunérations fpl; (profits) bénéfices mpl.

earnest ['ɜːnɪst] a sérieux; (sincere) sincère; – n **in e.** sérieusement; **it's raining in e.** il pleut pour de bon; **he's in e.** il est sérieux. ◆**-ness** n sérieux m; sincérité f.

earth [ɜːθ] n (world, ground) terre f; El terre f, masse f; **to fall to e.** tomber à or par terre; **nothing/nobody on e.** rien/personne au monde; **where/what on e.?** où/que diable? ◆**earthly** a (possessions etc) terrestre; **not an e. chance** Fam pas la moindre chance; **for no e. reason** Fam sans la moindre raison. ◆**earthy** a terreux; (person) Fig terre-à-terre inv. ◆**earthquake** n tremblement m de terre. ◆**earthworks** npl (excavations) terrassements mpl. ◆**earthworm** n ver m de terre.

earthenware ['ɜːθənweər] n faïence f; – a en faïence.

earwig ['ɪəwɪg] n (insect) perce-oreille m.

ease [iːz] n **1** (physical) bien-être m; (mental) tranquillité f; (facility) facilité f; **(ill) at e.** (in situation) (mal) à l'aise; **at e.** (of mind) tranquille; **(stand) at e.!** Mil repos!; **with e.** facilement. **2** vt (pain) soulager; (mind) calmer; (tension) diminuer; (loosen) relâcher; **to e. off/along** enlever/déplacer doucement; **to e. oneself through** se glisser par; – vi **to e. (off** or **up)** (of situation) se détendre; (of pressure) diminuer; (of demand) baisser; (of pain) se calmer; (not work so hard) se relâcher. ◆**easily** adv facilement; **e. the best/etc** de loin le meilleur/etc; **that could e. be** ça pourrait bien être. ◆**easiness** n aisance f.

easel ['iːz(ə)l] n chevalet m.

east [iːst] n est m; **Middle/Far E.** Moyen-/Extrême-Orient m; – a (coast) est inv; (wind) d'est; **E. Africa** Afrique f orientale; **E. Germany** Allemagne f de l'Est; – adv à l'est, vers l'est. ◆**eastbound** a (carriageway) est inv; (traffic) en direction de l'est. ◆**easterly** a (point) est inv; (direction) de l'est; (wind) d'est. ◆**eastern** a (coast) est inv; **E. France** l'Est m de la France; **E. Europe** Europe f de l'Est. ◆**easterner** n habitant, -ante mf de l'Est. ◆**eastward(s)** a & adv vers l'est.

Easter ['iːstər] n Pâques m sing or fpl; **E. week** semaine f pascale; **Happy E.!** joyeuses Pâques!

easy ['iːzɪ] a (**-ier, -iest**) facile; (manners) naturel; (life) tranquille; (pace) modéré; **to feel e. in one's mind** être tranquille; **to be an e. first** Sp être bon premier; **I'm e.** Fam ça m'est égal; **e. chair** fauteuil m (rembourré); – adv doucement; **go e. on** (sugar etc) vas-y doucement or mollo avec; (person) ne sois pas trop dur avec or envers; **take it e.** (rest) repose-toi; (work less) ne te fatigue pas; (calm down) calme-toi; (go slow) ne te presse pas. ◆**easy'going** a (carefree) insouciant; (easy to get on with) traitable.

eat [iːt] vt (pt **ate** [et, Am eɪt], pp **eaten** ['iːt(ə)n] manger; (one's words) Fig ravaler; **to e. breakfast** or **lunch** déjeuner; **what's eating you?** Sl qu'est-ce qui te tracasse?; **to e. up** (finish) finir; **eaten up with** (envy) dévoré de; – vi manger; **to e. into** (of acid) ronger; **to e. out** (lunch) déjeuner dehors; (dinner) dîner dehors. ◆**-ing** a **e. apple** pomme f à couteau; **e. place** restaurant m. ◆**-able** a mangeable. ◆**-er** n **big e.** gros mangeur m, grosse mangeuse f.

eau de Cologne [əʊdəkə'ləʊn] n eau f de Cologne.

eaves [iːvz] npl avant-toit m. ◆**eavesdrop** vt (**-pp-**) **to e. (on)** écouter (de façon indiscrète). ◆**eavesdropper** n oreille f indiscrète.

ebb [eb] n reflux m; **e. and flow** le flux et le reflux; **e. tide** marée f descendante; **at a low e.** Fig très bas; – vi refluer; **to e. (away)** (of strength etc) Fig décliner.

ebony ['ebənɪ] n (wood) ébène f.

ebullient [ɪ'bʌlɪənt] a exubérant.

eccentric [ɪk'sentrɪk] a & n excentrique (mf). ◆**eccen'tricity** n excentricité f.

ecclesiastic [ɪkliːzɪ'æstɪk] a & n ecclésiastique (m). ◆**ecclesiastical** a ecclésiastique.

echelon ['eʃəlɒn] n (of organization) échelon m.

echo ['ekəʊ] n (pl **-oes**) écho m; – vt (sound) répercuter; (repeat) Fig répéter; – vi the explosion/etc echoed l'écho de l'explosion/etc se répercuta; **to e. with the sound** of résonner de l'écho de.

éclair [eɪ'kleər] n (cake) éclair m.

eclectic [ɪ'klektɪk] a éclectique.

eclipse [ɪ'klɪps] n (of sun etc) & Fig éclipse f; – vt éclipser.

ecology [ɪ'kɒlədʒɪ] n écologie f. ◆**eco-'logical** a écologique.

economic [iːkə'nɒmɪk] a économique; (profitable) rentable. ◆**economical** a économique; (*thrifty*) économe. ◆**economically** *adv* économiquement. ◆**economics** *n* (*science f*) économique *f*; (*profitability*) aspect *m* financier.

economy ['ɪkɒnəmɪ] *n* (*saving, system, thrift*) économie *f*; **e. class** *Av* classe *f* touriste. ◆**economist** *n* économiste *mf*. ◆**economize** *vti* économiser (**on** sur).

ecstasy ['ekstəsɪ] *n* extase *f*. ◆**ec'static** *a* extasié; **to be e. about** s'extasier sur. ◆**ec'statically** *adv* avec extase.

ecumenical [iːkjuːˈmenɪk(ə)l] *a* œcuménique.

eczema ['eksɪmə] *n Med* eczéma *m*.

eddy ['edɪ] *n* tourbillon *m*, remous *m*.

edg/e [edʒ] *n* bord *m*; (*of forest*) lisière *f*; (*of town*) abords *mpl*; (*of page*) marge *f*; (*of knife etc*) tranchant *m*, fil *m*; **on e.** (*person*) énervé; (*nerves*) tendu; **to set s.o.'s teeth on e.** (*irritate s.o.*) crisper qn, faire grincer les dents à qn; **to have the e.** *or* **a slight e.** *Fig* être légèrement supérieur (**over, on** à); – *vt* (*clothing etc*) border (**with** de); – *vti* **to e.** (**oneself**) **into** (*move*) se glisser dans; **to e.** (**oneself**) **forward** avancer doucement. ◆**—ing** *n* (*border*) bordure *f*. ◆**edgeways** *adv* de côté; **to get a word in e.** *Fam* placer un mot.

edgy ['edʒɪ] *a* (**-ier, -iest**) énervé. ◆**edginess** *n* nervosité *f*.

edible ['edɪb(ə)l] *a* (*mushroom, berry etc*) comestible; (*meal, food*) mangeable.

edict ['iːdɪkt] *n* décret *m*; *Hist* édit *m*.

edifice ['edɪfɪs] *n* (*building, organization*) édifice *m*.

edify ['edɪfaɪ] *vt* (*improve the mind of*) édifier.

Edinburgh ['edɪnb(ə)rə] *n* Édimbourg *m or f*.

edit ['edɪt] *vt* (*newspaper etc*) diriger; (*article etc*) mettre au point; (*film*) monter; (*annotate*) éditer; (*compile*) rédiger; **to e.** (**out**) (*cut out*) couper. ◆**editor** *n* (*of review*) directeur, -trice *mf*; (*compiler*) rédacteur, -trice *mf*; *TV Rad* réalisateur, -trice *mf*; **sports e.** *Journ* rédacteur *m* sportif, rédactrice *f* sportive; **the e.** (**in chief**) (*of newspaper*) le rédacteur *m* en chef. ◆**edi'torial** *a* de la rédaction; **e. staff** rédaction *f*; – *n* éditorial *m*.

edition [ɪˈdɪʃ(ə)n] *n* édition *f*.

educat/e ['edjukeɪt] *vt* (*family, children*) éduquer; (*pupil*) instruire; (*mind*) former, éduquer; **to be educated at** faire ses études à. ◆**—ed** *a* (*voice*) cultivé; (**well-**)**e.** (*person*) instruit. ◆**edu'cation** *n* éducation *f*; (*teaching*) instruction *f*, enseigne-

ment *m*; (*training*) formation *f*; (*subject*) *Univ* pédagogie *f*. ◆**edu'cational** *a* (*establishment*) d'enseignement; (*method*) pédagogique; (*game*) éducatif; (*supplies*) scolaire. ◆**edu'cationally** *adv* du point de vue de l'éducation. ◆**educator** *n* éducateur, -trice *mf*.

EEC [iːtiːˈsiː] *n abbr* (*European Economic Community*) CEE *f*.

eel [iːl] *n* anguille *f*.

eerie ['ɪərɪ] *a* (**-ier, -iest**) sinistre, étrange.

efface [ɪˈfeɪs] *vt* effacer.

effect [ɪˈfekt] **1** *n* (*result, impression*) effet *m* (**on** sur); *pl* (*goods*) biens *mpl*; **to no e.** en vain; **in e.** en fait; **to put into e.** mettre en application, faire entrer en vigueur; **to come into e., take e.** entrer en vigueur; **to take e.** (*of drug etc*) agir; **to have an e.** (*of medicine etc*) faire de l'effet; **to have no e.** rester sans effet; **to this e.** (*in this meaning*) dans ce sens; **to the e. that** (*saying that*) comme quoi. **2** *vt* (*carry out*) effectuer, réaliser.

effective [ɪˈfektɪv] *a* (*efficient*) efficace; (*actual*) effectif; (*striking*) frappant; **to become e.** (*of law*) prendre effet. ◆**—ly** *adv* efficacement; (*in effect*) effectivement. ◆**—ness** *n* efficacité *f*; (*quality*) effet *m*.

effeminate [ɪˈfemɪnɪt] *a* efféminé.

effervescent [efəˈves(ə)nt] *a* (*mixture, youth*) effervescent; (*drink*) gazeux. ◆**effervesce** *vi* (*of drink*) pétiller. ◆**effervescence** *n* (*excitement*) & *Ch* effervescence *f*; pétillement *m*.

effete [ɪˈfiːt] *a* (*feeble*) mou, faible; (*decadent*) décadent.

efficient [ɪˈfɪʃ(ə)nt] *a* (*method*) efficace; (*person*) compétent, efficace; (*organization*) efficace, performant; (*machine*) performant, à haut rendement. ◆**efficiency** *n* efficacité *f*; compétence *f*; performances *fpl*. ◆**efficiently** *adv* efficacement; avec compétence; **to work e.** (*of machine*) bien fonctionner.

effigy ['efɪdʒɪ] *n* effigie *f*.

effort ['efət] *n* effort *m*; **to make an e.** faire un effort (**to** pour); **it isn't worth the e.** ça ne *or* n'en vaut pas la peine; **his** *or* **her latest e.** *Fam* ses dernières tentatives. ◆**—less** *a* (*victory etc*) facile. ◆**—lessly** *adv* facilement, sans effort.

effrontery [ɪˈfrʌntərɪ] *n* effronterie *f*.

effusive [ɪˈfjuːsɪv] *a* (*person*) expansif; (*thanks, excuses*) sans fin. ◆**—ly** *adv* avec effusion.

e.g. [iɪ'dʒiɪ] *abbr* (*exempli gratia*) par exemple.

egalitarian [ɪgælɪ'teərɪən] *a* (*society etc*) égalitaire.

egg¹ [eg] *n* œuf *m*; **e. timer** sablier *m*; **e. whisk** fouet *m* (à œufs). ◆**eggcup** *n* coquetier *m*. ◆**egghead** *n Pej* intellectuel, -elle *mf*. ◆**eggplant** *n* aubergine *f*. ◆**eggshell** *n* coquille *f*.

egg² [eg] *vt* **to e. on** (*encourage*) inciter (to do à faire).

ego ['iɪgəʊ] *n* (*pl* **-os**) **the e.** *Psy* le moi. ◆**ego'centric** *a* égocentrique. ◆**egoism** *n* égoïsme *m*. ◆**egoist** *n* égoïste *mf*. ◆**ego'istic(al)** *a* égoïste. ◆**egotism** *n* égotisme *m*.

Egypt ['iɪdʒɪpt] *n* Égypte *f*. ◆**E'gyptian** *a* & *n* égyptien, -ienne (*mf*).

eh? [eɪ] *int Fam* hein?

eiderdown ['aɪdədaʊn] *n* édredon *m*.

eight [eɪt] *a* & *n* huit (*m*). ◆**eigh'teen** *a* & *n* dix-huit (*m*). ◆**eigh'teenth** *a* & *n* dix-huitième (*mf*). ◆**eighth** *a* & *n* huitième (*mf*); **an e.** un huitième. ◆**eightieth** *a* & *n* quatre-vingtième (*mf*). ◆**eighty** *a* & *n* quatre-vingts (*m*); **e.-one** quatre-vingt-un.

Eire ['eərə] *n* République *f* d'Irlande.

either ['aɪðər] **1** *a* & *pron* (*one or other*) l'un(e) ou l'autre; (*with negative*) ni l'un(e) ni l'autre; (*each*) chaque; on the **e. side of** chaque côté, des deux côtés. **2** *adv* **she can't swim e.** elle ne sait pas nager non plus; **I don't e.** (ni) moi non plus; **not so far off e.** (*moreover*) pas si loin d'ailleurs. **3** *conj* **e. ... or** ou (bien) ... ou (bien), soit ... soit; (*with negative*) ni ... ni.

eject [ɪ'dʒekt] *vt* expulser; *Tech* éjecter. ◆**ejector** *a* **e. seat** *Av* siège *m* éjectable.

eke [iɪk] *vt* **to e. out** (*income etc*) faire durer; **to e. out a living** gagner (difficilement) sa vie.

elaborate [ɪ'læbərət] *a* compliqué, détaillé; (*preparation*) minutieux; (*style*) recherché; (*meal*) raffiné; – [ɪ'læbəreɪt] *vt* (*theory etc*) élaborer; – *vi* entrer dans les détails (**on** de). ◆**-ly** *adv* (*to plan*) minutieusement; (*to decorate*) avec recherche. ◆**elabo'ration** *n* élaboration *f*.

elapse [ɪ'læps] *vi* s'écouler.

elastic [ɪ'læstɪk] *a* (*object, character*) élastique; **e. band** élastique *m*; – *n* (*fabric*) élastique *m*. ◆**ela'sticity** *n* élasticité *f*.

elated [ɪ'leɪtɪd] *a* transporté de joie. ◆**elation** *n* exaltation *f*.

elbow ['elbəʊ] *n* coude *m*; **e. grease** *Fam* huile *f* de coude; **to have enough e. room**

avoir assez de place; – *vt* **to e. one's way** se frayer un chemin (à coups de coude) (**through** à travers).

elder¹ ['eldər] *a* & *n* (*of two people*) aîné, -ée (*mf*). ◆**elderly** *a* assez âgé, entre deux âges. ◆**eldest** *a* & *n* aîné, -ée (*mf*); **his** *or* **her e.** brother l'aîné de ses frères.

elder² ['eldər] *n* (*tree*) sureau *m*.

elect [ɪ'lekt] *vt Pol* élire (**to** à); **to e. to do** choisir de faire; – *a* **the president/*etc* e.** le président/*etc* désigné. ◆**election** *n* élection *f*; **general e.** élections *fpl* législatives; – *a* (*campaign*) électoral; (*day, results*) du scrutin, des élections. ◆**electio'neering** *n* campagne *f* électorale. ◆**elective** *a* (*course*) *Am* facultatif. ◆**electoral** *a* électoral. ◆**electorate** *n* électorat *m*.

electric [ɪ'lektrɪk] *a* électrique; **e. blanket** couverture *f* chauffante; **e. shock** décharge *f* électrique; **e. shock treatment** électrochoc *m*. ◆**electrical** *a* électrique; **e. engineer** ingénieur *m* électricien. ◆**elec'trician** *n* électricien *m*. ◆**elec'tricity** *n* électricité *f*. ◆**electrify** *vt Rail* électrifier; (*excite*) *Fig* électriser. ◆**electrocute** *vt* électrocuter.

electrode [ɪ'lektrəʊd] *n El* électrode *f*.

electron [ɪ'lektrɒn] *n* électron *m*; – *a* (*microscope*) électronique. ◆**elec'tronic** *a* électronique. ◆**elec'tronics** *n* électronique *f*.

elegant ['elɪgənt] *a* élégant. ◆**elegance** *n* élégance *f*. ◆**elegantly** *adv* avec élégance, élégamment.

elegy ['elədʒɪ] *n* élégie *f*.

element ['elɪmənt] *n* (*component, environment*) élément *m*; (*of heater*) résistance *f*; **an e. of truth** un grain *or* une part de vérité; **the human/chance** le facteur humain/chance; **in one's e.** dans son élément. ◆**ele'mental** *a* élémentaire. ◆**ele'mentary** *a* élémentaire; (*school*) *Am* primaire; **e. courtesy** la courtoisie la plus élémentaire.

elephant ['elɪfənt] *n* éléphant *m*. ◆**ele'phantine** [elɪ'fæntaɪn] *a* (*large*) éléphantesque; (*clumsy*) gauche.

elevate ['elɪveɪt] *vt* élever (**to** à). ◆**ele'vation** *n* élévation *f* (**of** de); (*height*) altitude *f*. ◆**elevator** *n Am* ascenseur *m*.

eleven [ɪ'lev(ə)n] *a* & *n* onze (*m*). ◆**elevenses** [ɪ'lev(ə)nzɪz] *n Fam* pause-café *f* (*vers onze heures du matin*). ◆**eleventh** *a* & *n* onzième (*mf*).

elf [elf] *n* (*pl* **elves**) lutin *m*.

elicit [ɪ'lɪsɪt] *vt* tirer, obtenir (**from** de).

elide [ɪ'laɪd] *vt Ling* élider. ◆**elision** *n* élision *f*.

eligible ['elɪdʒəb(ə)l] a (for post etc) admissible (**for** à); (for political office) éligible (**for** à); **to be e. for** (entitled to) avoir droit à; **an e. young man** (suitable as husband) un beau parti. ◆**eligi'bility** n admissibilité f; Pol éligibilité f.

eliminate [ɪ'lɪmɪneɪt] vt éliminer (**from** de). ◆**elimi'nation** n élimination f.

elite [eɪ'liːt] n élite f (**of** de).

elk [elk] n (animal) élan m.

ellipse [ɪ'lɪps] n Geom ellipse f. ◆**elliptical** a elliptique.

elm [elm] n (tree, wood) orme m.

elocution [elə'kjuːʃ(ə)n] n élocution f.

elongate ['iːlɒŋgeɪt] vt allonger. ◆**elon'gation** n allongement m.

elope [ɪ'ləʊp] vi (of lovers) s'enfuir (**with** avec). ◆**—ment** n fugue f (amoureuse).

eloquent ['eləkwənt] a éloquent. ◆**eloquence** n éloquence f.

else [els] adv d'autre; **someone e.** quelqu'un d'autre; **everybody e.** tout le monde à part moi, vous etc; tous les autres; **nobody/nothing e.** personne/rien d'autre; **something e.** autre chose; **something or anything e.?** encore quelque chose?; **somewhere e.** ailleurs, autre part; **who e.?** qui encore?, qui d'autre?; **how e.?** de quelle autre façon?; **or e.** ou bien, sinon. ◆**elsewhere** adv ailleurs; **e. in the town** dans une autre partie de la ville.

elucidate [ɪ'luːsɪdeɪt] vt élucider.

elude [ɪ'luːd] vt (enemy) échapper à; (question) éluder; (obligation) se dérober à; (blow) esquiver. ◆**elusive** a (enemy, aims) insaisissable; (reply) évasif.

emaciated [ɪ'meɪsɪeɪtɪd] a émacié.

emanate ['eməneɪt] vi émaner (**from** de).

emancipate [ɪ'mænsɪpeɪt] vt (women) émanciper. ◆**emanci'pation** n émancipation f.

embalm [ɪm'bɑːm] vt (dead body) embaumer.

embankment [ɪm'bæŋkmənt] n (of path etc) talus m; (of river) berge f.

embargo [ɪm'bɑːgəʊ] n (pl -oes) embargo m.

embark [ɪm'bɑːk] vt embarquer; – vi (s')embarquer; **to e. on** (start) commencer, entamer; (launch into) se lancer dans, s'embarquer dans. ◆**embar'kation** n embarquement m.

embarrass [ɪm'bærəs] vt embarrasser, gêner. ◆**—ing** a (question etc) embarrassant. ◆**—ment** n embarras m, gêne f; (financial) embarras mpl.

embassy ['embəsɪ] n ambassade f.

embattled [ɪm'bæt(ə)ld] a (political party, person etc) assiégé de toutes parts; (attitude) belliqueux.

embedded [ɪm'bedɪd] a (stick, bullet) enfoncé; (jewel) & Ling enchâssé; (in one's memory) gravé; (in stone) scellé.

embellish [ɪm'belɪʃ] vt embellir. ◆**—ment** n embellissement m.

embers ['embəz] npl braise f, charbons mpl ardents.

embezzl/e [ɪm'bez(ə)l] vt (money) détourner. ◆**—ement** n détournement m de fonds. ◆**—er** n escroc m, voleur m.

embitter [ɪm'bɪtər] vt (person) aigrir; (situation) envenimer.

emblem ['embləm] n emblème m.

embody [ɪm'bɒdɪ] vt (express) exprimer; (represent) incarner; (include) réunir. ◆**embodiment** n incarnation f (**of** de).

emboss [ɪm'bɒs] vt (metal) emboutir; (paper) gaufrer, emboutir. ◆**—ed** a en relief.

embrace [ɪm'breɪs] vt étreindre, embrasser; (include, adopt) embrasser; – vi s'étreindre, s'embrasser; – n étreinte f.

embroider [ɪm'brɔɪdər] vt (cloth) broder; (story, facts) Fig enjoliver. ◆**embroidery** n broderie f.

embroil [ɪm'brɔɪl] vt **to e. s.o.** in mêler qn à.

embryo ['embrɪəʊ] n (pl -os) embryon m. ◆**embry'onic** a Med & Fig embryonnaire.

emcee [em'siː] n Am présentateur, -trice mf.

emend [ɪ'mend] vt (text) corriger.

emerald ['emərəld] n émeraude f.

emerge [ɪ'mɜːdʒ] vi apparaître (**from** de); (from hole etc) sortir; (of truth, from water) émerger; (of nation) naître; **it emerges that** il apparaît que. ◆**emergence** n apparition f.

emergency [ɪ'mɜːdʒənsɪ] n (case) urgence f; (crisis) crise f; (contingency) éventualité f; **in an e.** en cas d'urgence; – a (measure etc) d'urgence; (exit, brake) de secours; (ward, services) Med des urgences; **e. landing** atterrissage m forcé; **e. powers** Pol pouvoirs mpl extraordinaires.

emery ['emərɪ] a **e. cloth** toile f (d')émeri.

emigrant ['emɪgrənt] n émigrant, -ante mf. ◆**emigrate** vi émigrer. ◆**emi'gration** n émigration f.

eminent ['emɪnənt] a éminent. ◆**eminence** n distinction f; **his E.** Rel son Éminence f. ◆**eminently** adv hautement, remarquablement.

emissary ['emɪsərɪ] n émissaire m.

emit [ɪ'mɪt] vt (-tt-) (light, heat etc) émettre;

(smell) dégager. ◆**emission** n émission f; dégagement m.

emotion [ɪ'məʊʃ(ə)n] n (strength of feeling) émotion f; (joy, love etc) sentiment m. ◆**emotional** a (person, reaction) émotif; (story, speech) émouvant; (moment) d'émotion intense; (state) Psy émotionnel. ◆**emotionally** adv (to say) avec émotion; to be e. unstable avoir des troubles émotifs. ◆**emotive** a (person) émotif; (word) affectif; an e. issue une question sensible.

emperor ['empərər] n empereur m.

emphasize ['emfəsaɪz] vt souligner (that que); (word, fact) appuyer or insister sur, souligner. ◆**emphasis** n Ling accent m (tonique); (insistence) insistance f; to lay or put e. on mettre l'accent sur. ◆em'**phatic** a (person, refusal) catégorique; (forceful) énergique; to be e. about insister sur. ◆em'**phatically** adv catégoriquement; énergiquement; e. no! absolument pas!

empire ['empaɪər] n empire m.

empirical [em'pɪrɪk(ə)l] a empirique. ◆**empiricism** n empirisme m.

employ [ɪm'plɔɪ] vt (person, means) employer; – n the e. of employé par. ◆**employee** [ɪm'plɔiɪ, emplɔi'iː] n employé, -ée mf. ◆**employer** n patron, -onne mf. ◆**employment** n emploi m; place of e. lieu m de travail; in the e. of employé par; e. agency bureau m de placement.

empower [ɪm'paʊər] vt autoriser (to do à faire).

empress ['emprɪs] n impératrice f.

empty ['emptɪ] a (-ier, -iest) vide; (threat, promise etc) vain; (stomach) creux; on an e. stomach à jeun; to return/etc e.-handed revenir/etc les mains vides; – npl (bottles) bouteilles fpl vides; – vt to e. (out) (box, pocket, liquid etc) vider; (vehicle) décharger; (objects in box etc) sortir (from, out of de); – vi se vider; (of river) se jeter (into dans). ◆—**iness** n vide m.

emulate ['emjʊleɪt] vt imiter. ◆**emu'lation** n émulation f.

emulsion [ɪ'mʌlʃ(ə)n] n (paint) peinture f (mate); Phot émulsion f.

enable [ɪ'neɪb(ə)l] vt to e. s.o. to do permettre à qn de faire.

enact [ɪn'ækt] vt (law) promulguer; (part of play) jouer.

enamel [ɪ'næm(ə)l] n émail m; – a en émail; – vt (-ll-, Am -l-) émailler.

enamoured [ɪn'æməd] a e. of (thing) séduit par; (person) amoureux de.

encamp [ɪn'kæmp] vi camper. ◆—**ment** n campement m.

encapsulate [ɪn'kæpsjʊleɪt] vt Fig résumer.

encase [ɪn'keɪs] vt recouvrir (in de).

enchant [ɪn'tʃɑːnt] vt enchanter. ◆—**ing** a enchanteur. ◆—**ment** n enchantement m.

encircle [ɪn'sɜːk(ə)l] vt entourer; Mil encercler. ◆—**ment** n encerclement m.

enclave ['enkleɪv] n enclave f.

enclos/e [ɪn'kləʊz] vt (send with letter) joindre (in, with à); (fence off) clôturer; to e. with (a fence, wall) entourer de. ◆—**ed** a (space) clos; (cheque etc) ci-joint; (market) couvert. ◆**enclosure** n Com pièce f jointe; (fence, place) enceinte f.

encompass [ɪn'kʌmpəs] vt (surround) entourer; (include) inclure.

encore ['ɒŋkɔːr] int & n bis (m); – vt bisser.

encounter [ɪn'kaʊntər] vt rencontrer; – n rencontre f.

encourage [ɪn'kʌrɪdʒ] vt encourager (to do à faire). ◆—**ment** n encouragement m.

encroach [ɪn'krəʊtʃ] vi empiéter (on, upon sur); to e. on the land (of sea) gagner du terrain. ◆—**ment** n empiétement m.

encumber [ɪn'kʌmbər] vt encombrer (with de). ◆**encum'brance** n embarras m.

encyclical [ɪn'sɪklɪk(ə)l] n Rel encyclique f.

encyclop(a)edia [ɪnsaɪklə'piːdɪə] n encyclopédie f. ◆**encyclop(a)edic** a encyclopédique.

end [end] n (of street, object etc) bout m, extrémité f; (of time, meeting, book etc) fin f; (purpose) fin f, but m; at an e. (discussion etc) fini; (period) écoulé; (patience) à bout; in the e. à la fin; to come to an e. prendre fin; to put an e. to, bring to an e. mettre fin à; there's no e. to it ça n'en finit plus; no e. of Fam beaucoup de; six days on e. six jours d'affilée; for days on e. pendant des jours (et des jours); (standing) on e. (box etc) debout; (hair) hérissé; – a (row, house) dernier; e. product Com produit m fini; Fig résultat m; – vt finir, terminer, achever (with par); (rumour, speculation) mettre fin à; – vi finir, se terminer, s'achever; to e. in failure se solder par un échec; to e. in a point finir en pointe; to e. up doing finir par faire; to e. up in (London etc) se retrouver à; he ended up in prison/a doctor il a fini en prison/par devenir médecin.

endanger [ɪn'deɪndʒər] vt mettre en danger.

endear [ɪn'dɪər] vt faire aimer or apprécier (to de); that's what endears him to me c'est cela qui me plaît en lui. ◆—**ing** a attachant, sympathique. ◆—**ment** n parole *f* tendre; **term of e.** terme *m* d'affection.

endeavour [ɪn'devər] *vi* s'efforcer **(to do de** faire); *n* effort *m* **(to do** pour faire).

ending ['endɪŋ] *n* fin *f*; *(outcome)* issue *f*; **Ling** terminaison *f*. ◆**endless** *a (speech, series etc)* interminable; *(patience)* infini; *(countless)* innombrable. ◆**endlessly** *adv* interminablement.

endive ['endɪv, *Am* 'endaɪv] *n Bot* Culin *(curly)* chicorée *f*; *(smooth)* endive *f*.

endorse [ɪn'dɔːs] *vt (cheque etc)* endosser; *(action)* approuver; *(claim)* appuyer. ◆**—ment** *n (on driving licence)* contravention *f*.

endow [ɪn'dau] *vt (institution)* doter **(with** de); *(chair, hospital bed)* fonder; **endowed with** *(person) Fig* doté de. ◆**—ment** *n* dotation *f*; fondation *f*.

endur/e [ɪn'djuər] **1** *vt (bear)* supporter **(doing** de faire). **2** *vi (last)* durer. ◆**—ing** *a* durable. ◆**—able** *a* supportable. ◆**endurance** *n* endurance *f*; résistance *f*.

enemy ['enəmɪ] *n* ennemi, -ie *mf*; – *a (army, tank etc)* ennemi.

energy ['enədʒɪ] *n* énergie *f*; – *a (crisis, resources etc)* énergétique. ◆**ener'getic** *a* énergique; **to feel e.** se sentir en pleine forme. ◆**ener'getically** *adv* énergiquement.

enforc/e [ɪn'fɔːs] *vt (law)* faire respecter; *(discipline)* imposer **(on** à). ◆**—ed** *a (rest, silence etc)* forcé.

engag/e [ɪn'geɪdʒ] *vt (take on)* engager, prendre; **to e. s.o. in conversation** engager la conversation avec qn; **to e. the clutch** *Aut* embrayer; – *vi* **to e. in** *(launch into)* se lancer dans; *(be involved in)* être mêlé à. ◆**—ed** *a* **1** *(person, toilet)* & *Tel* occupé; **in doing** occupé à faire; **to be e. in busi-ness**/*etc* être dans les affaires/*etc*. **2** *(betrothed)* fiancé; **to get e.** se fiancer. ◆**—ing** *a (smile)* engageant. ◆**—ement** *n (agreement to marry)* fiançailles *fpl*; *(meet-ing)* rendez-vous *m inv*; *(undertaking)* engagement *m*; **to have a prior e.** *(be busy)* être déjà pris, ne pas être libre; **e. ring** bague *f* de fiançailles.

engender [ɪn'dʒendər] *vt (produce)* engen-drer.

engine ['endʒɪn] *n Aut* moteur *m*; *Rail* loco-motive *f*; *Nau* machine *f*; **e. driver** mécanicien *m*.

engineer [endʒɪ'nɪər] **1** *n* ingénieur *m*; *(repairer)* dépanneur *m*; *Rail Am* mécanicien *m*; **civil e.** ingénieur *m* des travaux publics; **mechanical e.** ingénieur *m*

mécanicien. **2** *vt (arrange secretly)* machiner. ◆**—ing** *n* ingénierie *f*; **(civil) e.** génie *m* civil, travaux *mpl* publics; **(mechanical) e.** mécanique *f*; **e. factory** atelier *m* de construction mécanique.

England ['ɪŋglənd] *n* Angleterre *f*. ◆**English** *a* anglais; **the E. Channel** la Manche; **the E. les Anglais** *mpl*; – *n (language)* anglais *m*. ◆**Englishman** *n (pl* **-men)** Anglais *m*. ◆**English-speaking** *a* anglophone. ◆**Englishwoman** *n (pl* **-women)** Anglaise *f*.

engrav/e [ɪn'greɪv] *vt* graver. ◆**—ing** *n* gravure *f*. ◆**—er** *n* graveur *m*.

engrossed [ɪn'grəust] *a* absorbé **(in** par).

engulf [ɪn'gʌlf] *vt* engloutir.

enhance [ɪn'hɑːns] *vt (beauty etc)* rehausser; *(value)* augmenter.

enigma [ɪ'nɪgmə] *n* énigme *f*. ◆**enig'matic** *a* énigmatique.

enjoy [ɪn'dʒɔɪ] *vt* aimer **(doing** faire); *(meal)* apprécier; *(income, standard of living etc)* jouir de; **to e. the evening** passer une bonne soirée; **to e. oneself** s'amuser; **to e. being in London**/*etc* se plaire à Londres/*etc*. ◆**—able** *a* agréable. ◆**—ably** *adv* agréa-blement. ◆**—ment** *n* plaisir *m*.

enlarge [ɪn'lɑːdʒ] *vt* agrandir; – *vi* s'agrandir; **to e. (up)on** *(say more about)* s'étendre sur. ◆**—ment** *n* agrandissement *m*.

enlighten [ɪn'laɪt(ə)n] *vt* éclairer **(s.o. on or about sth** qn sur qch). ◆**—ing** *a* instructif. ◆**—ment** *n (explanations)* éclaircisse-ments *mpl*; **an age of e.** une époque éclairée.

enlist [ɪn'lɪst] *vi (in the army etc)* s'engager; – *vt (recruit)* engager; *(supporter)* recruter; *(support)* obtenir. ◆**—ment** *n* engagement *m*; recrutement *m*.

enliven [ɪn'laɪv(ə)n] *vt (meeting, people etc)* égayer, animer.

enmeshed [ɪn'meʃt] *a* empêtré **(in** dans).

enmity ['enmɪtɪ] *n* inimitié *f* **(between** entre).

enormous [ɪ'nɔːməs] *a* énorme; *(explosion)* terrible; *(success)* fou. ◆**enormity** *n (vast-ness, extent)* énormité *f*; *(atrocity)* atrocité *f*. ◆**enormously** *adv (very much)* énormé-ment; *(very)* extrêmement.

enough [ɪ'nʌf] *a* & *n* assez (de); **e. time/cups**/*etc* assez de temps/de tasses/*etc*; **to have e. to live on** avoir de quoi vivre; **to have e. to drink** avoir assez à boire; **to have had e. of** *Pej* en avoir assez de; **it's e. for me to see that . . .** il me suffit de voir que . . . ; **that's e.** ça suffit, c'est assez; – *adv* assez, suffisamment (to pour); **strangely e.**, he left chose curieuse, il est parti.

enquire [ɪnˈkwaɪər] *vi* = **inquire.**

enquiry [ɪnˈkwaɪərɪ] *n* = **inquiry.**

enrage [ɪnˈreɪdʒ] *vt* mettre en rage.

enrapture [ɪnˈræptʃər] *vt* ravir.

enrich [ɪnˈrɪtʃ] *vt* enrichir; (*soil*) fertiliser. ◆—**ment** *n* enrichissement *m*.

enrol [ɪnˈrəʊl] (*Am* **enroll**) *vi* (**-ll-**) s'inscrire (**in, for** à); – *vt* inscrire. ◆—**ment** *n* inscription *f*; (*people enrolled*) effectif *m*.

ensconced [ɪnˈskɒnst] *a* bien installé (**in** dans).

ensemble [ɒnˈsɒmb(ə)l] *n* (*clothes*) & *Mus* ensemble *m*.

ensign [ˈensən] *n* (*flag*) pavillon *m*; (*rank*) *Am Nau* enseigne *m* de vaisseau.

enslave [ɪnˈsleɪv] *vt* asservir.

ensu/e [ɪnˈsjuː] *vi* s'ensuivre. ◆—**ing** *a* (*day, year* etc) suivant; (*event*) qui s'ensuit.

ensure [ɪnˈʃʊər] *vt* assurer; **to e. that** (*make sure*) s'assurer que.

entail [ɪnˈteɪl] *vt* (*imply, involve*) entraîner, impliquer.

entangle [ɪnˈtæŋg(ə)l] *vt* emmêler, enchevêtrer; **to get entangled** s'empêtrer. ◆—**ment** *n* enchevêtrement *m*; **an e. with** (*police*) des démêlés *mpl* avec.

enter [ˈentər] *vt* (*room, vehicle, army* etc) entrer dans; (*road*) s'engager dans; (*university*) s'inscrire à; (*write down*) inscrire (**in** dans, **on** sur); (*in ledger*) porter (**in** sur); **to e. s.o. for** (*exam*) présenter qn à; **to e. a painting**/etc **in** (*competition*) présenter un tableau/etc à; **it didn't e. my head** ça ne m'est pas venu à l'esprit (**that** que); – *vi* entrer; **to e. for** (*race, exam*) s'inscrire pour; **to e. into** (*plans*) entrer dans; (*conversation, relations*) entrer en; **you don't e. into it** tu n'y es pour rien; **to e. into** or **upon** (*career*) entrer dans; (*negotiations*) entamer; (*agreement*) conclure.

enterpris/e [ˈentəpraɪz] *n* (*undertaking, firm*) entreprise *f*; (*spirit*) *Fig* initiative *f*. ◆—**ing** *a* (*person*) plein d'initiative; (*attempt*) hardi.

entertain [entəˈteɪn] *vt* amuser, distraire; (*guest*) recevoir; (*idea, possibility*) envisager; (*hope*) chérir; **to e. s.o. to a meal** recevoir qn à dîner; – *vi* (*receive guests*) recevoir. ◆—**ing** *a* amusant. ◆—**er** *n* artiste *mf*. ◆—**ment** *n* amusement *m*, distraction *f*; (*show*) spectacle *m*.

enthral(l) [ɪnˈθrɔːl] *vt* (**-ll-**) (*delight*) captiver.

enthuse [ɪnˈθjuːz] *vi* **to e. over** *Fam* s'emballer pour. ◆**enthusiasm** *n* enthousiasme *m*. ◆**enthusiast** *n* enthousiaste

mf; **jazz**/etc **e.** passionné, -ée *mf* du jazz/etc. ◆**enthusi'astic** *a* enthousiaste; (*golfer* etc) passionné; **to be e. about** (*hobby*) être passionné de; **he was e. about** or **over** (*gift* etc) il a été emballé par; **to get e.** s'emballer (**about** pour). ◆**enthusi-'astically** *adv* avec enthousiasme.

entic/e [ɪnˈtaɪs] *vt* attirer (par la ruse); **to e. to do** entraîner (par la ruse) à faire. ◆—**ing** *a* séduisant, alléchant. ◆—**ement** *n* (*bait*) attrait *m*.

entire [ɪnˈtaɪər] *a* entier. ◆—**ly** *adv* tout à fait, entièrement. ◆**entirety** [ɪnˈtaɪərətɪ] *n* intégralité *f*; **in its e.** en entier.

entitl/e [ɪnˈtaɪt(ə)l] *vt* **to e. s.o. to do** donner à qn le droit de faire; **to e. s.o. to sth** donner à qn (le) droit à qch; **that entitles me to believe that ...** ça m'autorise à croire que .... ◆—**ed** *a* (*book*) intitulé; **to be e. to do** avoir le droit de faire; **to be e. to sth** avoir droit à qch. ◆—**ement** *n* **one's e.** son dû.

entity [ˈentɪtɪ] *n* entité *f*.

entourage [ˈɒntʊrɑːʒ] *n* entourage *m*.

entrails [ˈentreɪlz] *npl* entrailles *fpl*.

entrance 1 [ˈentrəns] *n* entrée *f* (**to** de); (*to university* etc) admission *f* (**to** à); **e. examination** examen *m* d'entrée. **2** [ɪnˈtrɑːns] *vt* *Fig* transporter, ravir.

entrant [ˈentrənt] *n* (*in race*) concurrent, -ente *mf*; (*for exam*) candidat, -ate *mf*.

entreat [ɪnˈtriːt] *vt* supplier, implorer (**to do** de faire). ◆**entreaty** *n* supplication *f*.

entrée [ˈɒntreɪ] *n* *Culin* entrée *f*; (*main dish*) *Am* plat *m* principal.

entrench [ɪnˈtrentʃ] *vt* **to e. oneself** *Mil* & *Fig* se retrancher.

entrust [ɪnˈtrʌst] *vt* confier (**to** à); **to e. s.o. with sth** confier qch à qn.

entry [ˈentrɪ] *n* (*way in, action*) entrée *f*; (*in ledger*) écriture *f*; (*term in dictionary or logbook*) entrée *f*; (*competitor*) *Sp* concurrent, -ente *mf*; (*thing to be judged in competition*) objet *m* (or œuvre *f* or projet *m*) soumis à un jury; **e. form** feuille *f* d'inscription; **'no e.'** (*on door* etc) 'entrée interdite'; (*road sign*) 'sens interdit'.

entwine [ɪnˈtwaɪn] *vt* entrelacer.

enumerate [ɪˈnjuːməreɪt] *vt* énumérer. ◆**enume'ration** *n* énumération *f*.

enunciate [ɪˈnʌnsɪeɪt] *vt* (*word*) articuler; (*theory*) énoncer. ◆**enunci'ation** *n* articulation *f*; énonciation *f*.

envelop [ɪnˈveləp] *vt* envelopper (**in** fog/mystery/etc de brouillard/mystère/etc).

envelope [ˈenvələʊp] *n* enveloppe *f*.

envious [ˈenvɪəs] *a* envieux (**of sth** de qch).

e. of s.o. jaloux de qn. ◆**enviable** a enviable. ◆**enviously** adv avec envie.

environment [ɪnˈvaɪərənmənt] n milieu m; (cultural, natural) environnement m. ◆**environ'mental** a du milieu; de l'environnement. ◆**environ'mentalist** n écologiste mf.

envisage [ɪnˈvɪzɪdʒ] vt (imagine) envisager; (foresee) prévoir.

envision [ɪnˈvɪʒ(ə)n] vt Am = envisage.

envoy [ˈenvɔɪ] n Pol envoyé, -ée mf.

envy [ˈenvɪ] n envie f; – vt envier (s.o. sth qch à qn).

ephemeral [ɪˈfemərəl] a éphémère.

epic [ˈepɪk] a épique; – n épopée f; (screen) e. film m à grand spectacle.

epidemic [epɪˈdemɪk] n épidémie f; – a épidémique.

epilepsy [ˈepɪlepsɪ] n épilepsie f. ◆**epileptic** a & n épileptique (mf).

epilogue [ˈepɪlɒg] n épilogue m.

episode [ˈepɪsəʊd] n épisode m. ◆**episodic** [epɪˈsɒdɪk] a épisodique.

epistle [ɪˈpɪs(ə)l] n épître f.

epitaph [ˈepɪtɑːf] n épitaphe f.

epithet [ˈepɪθet] n épithète f.

epitome [ɪˈpɪtəmɪ] n the e. of l'exemple même de, l'incarnation de. ◆**epitomize** vt incarner.

epoch [ˈiːpɒk] n époque f. ◆**e.-making** a (event) qui fait date.

equal [ˈiːkwəl] a égal (to à); with e. hostility avec la même hostilité; on an e. footing sur un pied d'égalité (with avec); to be e. to égaler; e. to (task, situation) Fig à la hauteur de; – n égal, -ale mf; to treat s.o. as an e. traiter qn en égal or d'égal à égal; he doesn't have his e. il n'a pas son pareil; – vt (-ll-, Am -l-) égaler (in beauty/etc en beauté/etc); equals sign Math signe m d'égalité. ◆**e'quality** n égalité f. ◆**equalize** vt égaliser; – vi Sp égaliser. ◆**equally** adv (to an equal degree, also) également; (to divide) en parts égales; he's e. stupid (just as) il est tout aussi bête.

equanimity [ekwəˈnɪmɪtɪ] n égalité f d'humeur.

equate [ɪˈkweɪt] vt mettre sur le même pied (with que), assimiler (with à).

equation [ɪˈkweɪʒ(ə)n] n Math équation f.

equator [ɪˈkweɪtər] n équateur m; at or on the e. sous l'équateur. ◆**equatorial** [ekwəˈtɔːrɪəl] a équatorial.

equestrian [ɪˈkwestrɪən] a équestre.

equilibrium [iːkwɪˈlɪbrɪəm] n équilibre m.

equinox [ˈiːkwɪnɒks] n équinoxe m.

equip [ɪˈkwɪp] vt (-pp-) équiper (with de);

(well-)equipped with pourvu de; (well-)equipped to do compétent pour faire. ◆**—ment** n équipement m, matériel m.

equity [ˈekwɪtɪ] n (fairness) équité f; pl Com actions fpl. ◆**equitable** a équitable.

equivalent [ɪˈkwɪvələnt] a & n équivalent (m). ◆**equivalence** n équivalence f.

equivocal [ɪˈkwɪvək(ə)l] a équivoque.

era [ˈɪərə, Am ˈerə] n époque f; (historical, geological) ère f.

eradicate [ɪˈrædɪkeɪt] vt supprimer; (evil, prejudice) extirper.

erase [ɪˈreɪz, Am ɪˈreɪs] vt effacer. ◆**eraser** n (rubber) gomme f. ◆**erasure** n rature f.

erect [ɪˈrekt] 1 a (upright) (bien) droit. 2 vt (build) construire; (statue, monument) ériger; (scaffolding) monter; (tent) dresser. ◆**erection** n construction f; érection f; montage m; dressage m.

ermine [ˈɜːmɪn] n (animal, fur) hermine f.

erode [ɪˈrəʊd] vt éroder; (confidence etc) Fig miner, ronger. ◆**erosion** n érosion f.

erotic [ɪˈrɒtɪk] a érotique. ◆**eroticism** n érotisme m.

err [ɜːr] vi (be wrong) se tromper; (sin) pécher.

errand [ˈerənd] n commission f, course f; e. boy garçon m de courses.

erratic [ɪˈrætɪk] a (conduct etc) irrégulier; (person) lunatique.

error [ˈerər] n (mistake) erreur f, faute f; (wrongdoing) erreur f; in e. par erreur. ◆**erroneous** [ɪˈrəʊnɪəs] a erroné.

erudite [ˈerʊdaɪt, Am ˈerjʊdaɪt] a érudit, savant. ◆**eru'dition** n érudition f.

erupt [ɪˈrʌpt] vi (of volcano) entrer en éruption; (of pimples) apparaître; (of war, violence) éclater. ◆**eruption** n (of volcano, pimples, anger) éruption f (of de); (of violence) flambée f.

escalate [ˈeskəleɪt] vi (of war, violence) s'intensifier; (of prices) monter en flèche; – vt intensifier. ◆**esca'lation** n escalade f.

escalator [ˈeskəleɪtər] n escalier m roulant.

escapade [ˈeskəpeɪd] n (prank) frasque f.

escape [ɪˈskeɪp] vi (of gas, animal etc) s'échapper; (of prisoner) s'évader, s'échapper; to e. from (person) échapper à; (place, object) s'échapper de; escaped prisoner évadé, -ée mf; – vt (death) échapper à; (punishment) éviter; that name escapes me ce nom m'échappe; to e. notice passer inaperçu; – n (of gas etc) fuite f; (of person) évasion f, fuite f; to have a lucky or narrow e. l'échapper belle. ◆**escapism** n évasion f (hors de la réalité). ◆**escapist** a (film etc) d'évasion.

eschew [ɪs'tʃuː] *vt* éviter, fuir.

escort ['eskɔːt] *n Mil Nau* escorte *f*; *(of woman)* cavalier *m*; – [ɪs'kɔːt] *vt* escorter.

Eskimo ['eskɪməʊ] *n (pl -os)* Esquimau, -aude *mf*; – *a* esquimau.

esoteric [esəʊ'terɪk] *a* obscur, ésotérique.

especial [ɪs'peʃəl] *a* particulier. ◆**-ly** *adv (in particular)* particulièrement; *(for particular purpose)* (tout) exprès; **e. as** d'autant plus que.

espionage ['espɪənɑːʒ] *n* espionnage *m*.

esplanade ['espləneɪd] *n* esplanade *f*.

espouse [ɪ'spaʊz] *vt (a cause)* épouser.

espresso [e'spresəʊ] *n (pl -os)* (café *m*) express *m*.

Esq [ɪ'skwaɪər] *abbr (esquire)* **J. Smith Esq** *(on envelope)* Monsieur J. Smith.

essay ['eseɪ] *n (attempt)* & *Liter* essai *m*; *Sch* rédaction *f*; *Univ* dissertation *f*.

essence ['esəns] *n Phil Ch* essence *f*; *Culin* extrait *m*, essence *f*; *(main point)* essentiel *m* (of de); **in e.** essentiellement.

essential [ɪ'senʃ(ə)l] *a (principal)* essentiel; *(necessary)* indispensable, essentiel; **it's e.** **that** il est indispensable que (+ *sub*); – *npl* **the essentials** l'essentiel *m* (of de); *(of grammar)* les éléments *mpl*. ◆**-ly** *adv* essentiellement.

establish [ɪ'stæblɪʃ] *vt* établir; *(state, society)* fonder. ◆**-ed** *a* (well-)e. *(firm)* solide; *(fact)* reconnu; *(reputation)* établi; **she's (well-)e.** elle a une réputation établie. ◆**-ment** *n (institution, firm)* établissement *m*; **the e. of** l'établissement de; **la fondation de; the E.** les classes *fpl* dirigeantes.

estate [ɪ'steɪt] *n (land)* terre(s) *f(pl)*, propriété *f*; *(possessions)* Jur fortune *f*; *(of deceased person)* succession *f*; **housing e.** lotissement *m*; *(workers')* cité *f* (ouvrière); **industrial e.** complexe *m* industriel; **e. agency** agence *f* immobilière; **e. agent** agent *m* immobilier; **e. car** break *m*; **e. tax** *Am* droits *mpl* de succession.

esteem [ɪ'stiːm] *vt* estimer; **highly esteemed** très estimé; – *n* estime *f*.

esthetic [es'θetɪk] *a Am* esthétique.

estimate ['estɪmeɪt] *vt (value)* estimer, évaluer; *(consider)* estimer (that que); – ['estɪmət] *n (assessment)* évaluation *f*, estimation *f*; *(judgement)* évaluation *f*; *(price for work to be done)* devis *m*; **rough e.** chiffre *m* approximatif. ◆**esti'mation** *n* jugement *m*; *(esteem)* estime *f*; **in my e.** à mon avis.

estranged [ɪ'streɪndʒd] *a* **to become e.** *(of couple)* se séparer.

estuary ['estjʊərɪ] *n* estuaire *m*.

etc [et'setərə] *adv* etc.

etch [etʃ] *vti* graver à l'eau forte. ◆**-ing** *n (picture)* eau-forte *f*.

eternal [ɪ'tɜːn(ə)l] *a* éternel. ◆**eternally** *adv* éternellement. ◆**eternity** *n* éternité *f*.

ether ['iːθər] *n* éther *m*. ◆**e'thereal** *a* éthéré.

ethic ['eθɪk] *n* éthique *f*. ◆**ethics** *n (moral standards)* moralité *f*; *(study) Phil* éthique *f*. ◆**ethical** *a* moral, éthique.

Ethiopia [iːθɪ'əʊpɪə] *n* Éthiopie *f*. ◆**Ethiopian** *a* & *n* éthiopien, -ienne *(mf)*.

ethnic ['eθnɪk] *a* ethnique.

ethos ['iːθɒs] *n* génie *m*.

etiquette ['etɪket] *n (rules)* bienséances *fpl*; **(diplomatic) e.** protocole *m*, étiquette *f*; **professional e.** déontologie *f*.

etymology [etɪ'mɒlədʒɪ] *n* étymologie *f*.

eucalyptus [juːkə'lɪptəs] *n (tree)* eucalyptus *m*.

eulogy ['juːlədʒɪ] *n* panégyrique *m*, éloge *m*.

euphemism ['juːfɪmɪz(ə)m] *n* euphémisme *m*.

euphoria [juː'fɔːrɪə] *n* euphorie *f*. ◆**euphoric** *a* euphorique.

Euro- ['jʊərəʊ] *pref* euro-.

Europe ['jʊərəp] *n* Europe *f*. ◆**Euro'pean** *a* & *n* européen, -éenne *(mf)*.

euthanasia [juːθə'neɪzɪə] *n* euthanasie *f*.

evacuate [ɪ'vækjʊeɪt] *vt* évacuer. ◆**evacu'ation** *n* évacuation *f*.

evade [ɪ'veɪd] *vt* éviter, esquiver; *(pursuer, tax)* échapper à; *(law, question)* éluder.

evaluate [ɪ'væljʊeɪt] *vt* évaluer (at à). ◆**evalu'ation** *n* évaluation *f*.

evangelical [iːvæn'dʒelɪk(ə)l] *a Rel* évangélique.

evaporate [ɪ'væpəreɪt] *vi* s'évaporer; *(of hopes)* s'évanouir. ◆**-ed** *a* **e. milk** lait *m* concentré. ◆**evapo'ration** *n* évaporation *f*.

evasion [ɪ'veɪʒ(ə)n] *n* **e.** of *(pursuer etc)* fuite *f* devant; *(question)* esquive *f* de; **tax e.** évasion *f* fiscale. ◆**evasive** *a* évasif.

eve [iːv] *n* **the e. of** la veille de.

even [ˈiːv(ə)n] **1** *a (flat)* uni, égal, lisse; *(equal)* égal; *(regular)* régulier; *(number)* pair; **to get e. with** se venger de; **I'll get even with him (for that)** je lui revaudrai ça; **we're e.** *(quits)* nous sommes quittes; *(in score)* nous sommes à égalité; **to break e.** *Fin* s'y retrouver; – *vt* **to e.** (out *or* up) égaliser. **2** *adv* même; **e. better/more** encore mieux/plus; **e. if** *or* **though** même si; so quand même. ◆**-ly** *adv* de manière égale; *(regularly)* régulièrement. ◆**-ness** *n (of* *surface, temper)* égalité f; *(of movement etc)* régularité f. ◆**even-'tempered** a de caractère égal.

evening ['iːvnɪŋ] n soir m; *(duration of evening, event)* soirée f; **in the e.**, *Am* **evenings** le soir; **at seven in the e.** à sept heures du soir; **every Tuesday e.** tous les mardis soir; **all e. (long)** toute la soirée; – a *(newspaper etc)* du soir; **e. performance** *Th* soirée f; **e. dress** tenue f de soirée; *(of woman)* robe f du soir or de soirée.

event [ɪ'vent] n événement m; *Sp* épreuve f; **in the e. of death** en cas de décès; **in any e.** en tout cas; **after the e.** après coup. ◆**eventful** a *(journey etc)* mouvementé; *(occasion)* mémorable.

eventual [ɪ'ventʃʊəl] a final, définitif. ◆**eventu'ality** n éventualité f. ◆**eventually** adv finalement, en fin de compte; *(some day or other)* un jour ou l'autre; *(after all)* en fin de compte.

ever ['evər] adv jamais; **has he e. seen it?** l'a-t-il jamais vu?; **more than e.** plus que jamais; **nothing e.** jamais rien; **hardly e.** presque jamais; **e. ready** toujours prêt; **the first e.** le tout premier; **e. since** *(that event etc)* depuis; **e. since then** depuis lors, dès lors; **for e.** *(for always)* pour toujours; *(continually)* sans cesse; **the best son e.** le meilleur fils du monde; **e. so sorry/ happy**/*etc Fam* vraiment désolé/heureux/ *etc*; **thank you e. so much** *Fam* merci mille fois; **it's e. such a pity** *Fam* c'est vraiment dommage; **why e. not?** pourquoi donc? ◆**evergreen** n arbre m à feuilles persistantes. ◆**ever'lasting** a éternel. ◆**ever'more** adv **for e.** à (tout) jamais.

every ['evrɪ] a chaque; **e. child** chaque enfant, tous les enfants; **e. time** chaque fois (that que); **e. one** chacun; **e. single one** (sans exception); **to have e. confidence in** avoir pleine confiance en; **e. second** or **other day** tous les deux jours; **her e. gesture** ses moindres gestes; **e. bit as big** tout aussi grand (as que); **e. so often**, **e. now and then** de temps en temps. ◆**everybody** pron tout le monde; **e. in turn** chacun à son tour. ◆**everyday** a *(happening, life etc)* de tous les jours; *(banal)* banal; **in e. use** d'usage courant. ◆**everyone** pron = **everybody**. ◆**everyplace** adv *Am* = **everywhere**. ◆**everything** pron tout; **e. I have** tout ce que j'ai. ◆**everywhere** adv partout; **e. she goes** où qu'elle aille, partout où elle va.

evict [ɪ'vɪkt] vt expulser (from de). ◆**eviction** n expulsion f.

evidence ['evɪdəns] n *(proof)* preuve(s)

f(pl); *(testimony)* témoignage m; *(obviousness)* évidence f; **to give e.** témoigner (against contre); **e. of** *(wear etc)* des signes mpl de; **in e.** *(noticeable)* (bien) en vue. ◆**evident** a évident (that que); **it is e. from . . .** il apparaît de . . . (that que). ◆**evidently** adv *(obviously)* évidemment; *(apparently)* apparemment.

evil ['iːv(ə)l] a *(spell, influence, person)* malfaisant; *(deed, advice, system)* mauvais; *(consequence)* funeste; – n mal m; **to speak e.** dire du mal (of de).

evince [ɪ'vɪns] vt manifester.

evoke [ɪ'vəʊk] vt *(recall, conjure up)* évoquer; *(admiration)* susciter. ◆**evocative** a évocateur.

evolution [iːvə'luːʃ(ə)n] n évolution f. ◆**evolve** vi *(of society, idea etc)* évoluer; *(of plan)* se développer; – vt *(system etc)* développer.

ewe [juː] n brebis f.

ex [eks] n *(former spouse)* Fam ex mf.

ex- [eks] pref ex-; **ex-wife** ex-femme f.

exacerbate [ɪk'sæsəbeɪt] vt *(pain)* exacerber.

exact [ɪg'zækt] **1** a *(accurate, precise etc)* exact; **to be (more) e. about** préciser. **2** vt *(demand)* exiger (from de); *(money)* extorquer (from à). ◆**-ing** a exigeant. ◆**-ly** adv exactement; **it's e. 5 o'clock** il est 5 heures juste. ◆**-ness** n exactitude f.

exaggerate [ɪg'zædʒəreɪt] vt exagérer; *(in one's own mind)* s'exagérer; – vi exagérer. ◆**exagge'ration** n exagération f.

exalt [ɪg'zɔːlt] vt *(praise)* exalter. ◆**-ed** a *(position, rank)* élevé. ◆**exal'tation** n exaltation f.

exam [ɪg'zæm] n *Univ Sch Fam* examen m.

examine [ɪg'zæmɪn] vt examiner; *(accounts, luggage)* vérifier; *(passport)* contrôler; *(orally)* interroger *(témoin, élève)*. ◆**exami'nation** n *(inspection)* & *Univ Sch* examen m; *(of accounts etc)* vérification f; *(of passport)* contrôle m; **class e.** *Sch* composition f. ◆**examiner** n *Sch* examinateur, -trice mf.

example [ɪg'zɑːmp(ə)l] n exemple m; **for e.** par exemple; **to set a good/bad e.** donner le bon/mauvais exemple (to à); **to make an e. of** punir pour l'exemple.

exasperate [ɪg'zɑːspəreɪt] vt exaspérer; **to get exasperated** s'exaspérer (at de). ◆**exaspe'ration** n exaspération f.

excavate ['ekskəveɪt] vt *(dig)* creuser; *(for relics etc)* fouiller; *(uncover)* déterrer. ◆**exca'vation** n *Tech* creusement m; *(archeological)* fouille f.

exceed [ɪk'siːd] vt dépasser, excéder.
◆**—ingly** adv extrêmement.

excel [ɪk'sel] vi (**-ll-**) exceller (**in sth** en qch, **in doing** à faire); – vt surpasser.

Excellency [ˈeksələnsɪ] n (title) Excellence f.

excellent [ˈeksələnt] a excellent. ◆**excellence** n excellence f. ◆**excellently** adv parfaitement, admirablement.

except [ɪk'sept] prep sauf, excepté; **e. for** à part; **e. that** il faut le fait que, sauf que; **e.** if sauf si; **to do nothing e.** wait ne rien faire sinon attendre; – vt excepter. ◆**exception** n exception f; **with the e. of** à l'exception de; **to take e. to** (object to) désapprouver; (be hurt by) s'offenser de. ◆**exceptional** a exceptionnel. ◆**exceptionally** adv exceptionnellement.

excerpt [ˈeksɜːpt] n (from film, book etc) extrait m.

excess [ˈekses] n excès m; (surplus) Com excédent m; **one's excesses** ses excès mpl; **to e.** à l'excès; **an e. of** (details) un luxe de; – a (weight etc) excédentaire, en trop; **e. fare** supplément m (de billet); **e. luggage** excédent m de bagages. ◆**ex'cessive** a excessif. ◆**ex'cessively** adv (too, too much) excessivement; (very) extrêmement.

exchange [ɪks'tʃeɪndʒ] vt (addresses, blows etc) échanger (**for** contre); – n échange m; Fin change m; (telephone) **e.** central m (téléphonique); **in e.** en échange (**for** de).

Exchequer [ɪks'tʃekər] n **Chancellor of the E.** = ministre des Finances.

excise [ˈeksaɪz] n taxe f (**on** sur).

excit/e [ɪk'saɪt] vt (agitate, provoke, stimulate) exciter; (enthuse) passionner, exciter. ◆**—ed** a excité; (laughter) énervé; **to get e.** (nervous, angry, enthusiastic) s'exciter; **to be e. about** (new car, news) se réjouir de; **to be e. about the holidays** être surexcité à l'idée de partir en vacances. ◆**—ing** a (book, adventure) passionnant. ◆**—able** a excitable. ◆**—edly** adv avec agitation; (to wait, jump about) dans un état de surexcitation. ◆**—ement** n agitation f, excitation f, fièvre f; (emotion) vive émotion f; (adventure) aventure f; **great e.** surexcitation f.

exclaim [ɪk'skleɪm] vti s'exclamer, s'écrier (**that** que). ◆**excla'mation** n exclamation f; **e. mark** or Am **point** point m d'exclamation.

exclude [ɪks'kluːd] vt exclure (**from** de); (name from list) écarter (**from** de). ◆**exclusion** n exclusion f. ◆**exclusive** a (right, interest, design) exclusif; (club, group) fermé; (interview) en exclusivité; **e.**

of wine/etc vin/etc non compris. ◆**exclusively** adv exclusivement.

excommunicate [ekskəˈmjuːnɪkeɪt] vt excommunier.

excrement [ˈekskrəmənt] n excrément(s) m(pl).

excruciating [ɪk'skruːʃɪeɪtɪŋ] a insupportable, atroce.

excursion [ɪk'skɜːʃ(ə)n] n excursion f.

excuse [ɪk'skjuːz] vt (justify, forgive) excuser (**s.o. for doing** qn d'avoir fait, qn de faire); (exempt) dispenser (**from** de); **e. me** **for asking** permettez-moi de demander; **e. me!** excusez-moi!, pardon!; **you're excused** tu peux t'en aller or sortir; – [ɪk'skjuːs] n excuse f; **it was an e. for** cela a servi de prétexte à.

ex-directory [eksdaɪˈrektərɪ] a Tel sur la liste rouge.

execute [ˈeksɪkjuːt] vt (criminal, order, plan etc) exécuter. ◆**exe'cution** n exécution f. ◆**exe'cutioner** n bourreau m.

executive [ɪg'zekjutɪv] a (power) exécutif; (ability) d'exécution; (job) de cadre; (car, plane) de direction; – n (person) cadre m; (board, committee) bureau m; **the e.** Pol l'exécutif m; (senior) **e.** cadre m supérieur; **junior e.** jeune cadre m; **business e.** directeur m commercial.

exemplary [ɪg'zemplərɪ] a exemplaire. ◆**exemplify** vt illustrer.

exempt [ɪg'zempt] a exempt (**from** de); – vt exempter (**from** de). ◆**exemption** n exemption f.

exercise [ˈeksəsaɪz] n (of power etc) & Sch Sp Mil exercice m; pl Univ Am cérémonies fpl; **e. book** cahier m; – vt exercer; (troops) faire faire l'exercice à; (dog, horse etc) promener; (tact, judgement etc) faire preuve de; (rights) faire valoir, exercer; – vi (take exercise) prendre de l'exercice.

exert [ɪg'zɜːt] vt exercer; (force) employer; **to e. oneself** (physically) se dépenser; **he never exerts himself** (takes the trouble) il ne se fatigue jamais; **to e. oneself to do** (try hard) s'efforcer de faire. ◆**exertion** n effort m; (of force) emploi m.

exhale [eks'heɪl] vt (breathe out) expirer; (give off) exhaler; – vi expirer.

exhaust [ɪg'zɔːst] **1** vt (use up, tire) épuiser; **to become exhausted** s'épuiser. **2** n (pipe) Aut pot m or tuyau m d'échappement. ◆**—ing** a épuisant. ◆**exhaustion** n épuisement m. ◆**exhaustive** a (study etc) complet; (research) approfondi.

exhibit [ɪg'zɪbɪt] vt (put on display) exposer; (ticket, courage etc) montrer; – n objet m exposé; *Jur* pièce *f* à conviction. ◆**exhi-'bition** *n* exposition *f*; **an e. of** (*display*) une démonstration de; **to make an e. of oneself** se donner en spectacle. ◆**exhi'bitionist** *n* exhibitionniste *mf*. ◆**exhibitor** *n* exposant, -ante *f*.

exhilarate [ɪgˈzɪləreɪt] *vt* stimuler; (*of air*) vivifier; (*elate*) rendre fou de joie. ◆**exhila'ration** *n* liesse *f*, joie *f*.

exhort [ɪgˈzɔːt] *vt* exhorter (**to do** à faire, **to sth** à qch).

exhume [eksˈhjuːm] *vt* exhumer.

exile [ˈegzaɪl] *vt* exiler; – *n* (*absence*) exil *m*; (*person*) exilé, -ée *mf*.

exist [ɪgˈzɪst] *vi* exister; (*live*) vivre (**on** de); (**to continue**) **to e.** subsister; **the notion exists that** ... il existe une notion selon laquelle .... ◆**-ing** *a* (*law*) existant; (*circumstances*) actuel. ◆**existence** *n* existence *f*; **to come into e.** être créé; **to be in e.** exister. ◆**exi'stentialism** *n* existentialisme *m*.

exit [ˈeksɪt, ˈegzɪt] *n* (*action*) sortie *f*; (*door, window*) sortie *f*, issue *f*; – *vi Th* sortir.

exodus [ˈeksədəs] *n inv* exode *m*.

exonerate [ɪgˈzɒnəreɪt] *vt* (*from blame*) disculper (**from** de).

exorbitant [ɪgˈzɔːbɪtənt] *a* exorbitant. ◆**-ly** *adv* démesurément.

exorcize [ˈeksɔːsaɪz] *vt* exorciser. ◆**exorcism** *n* exorcisme *m*.

exotic [ɪgˈzɒtɪk] *a* exotique.

expand [ɪkˈspænd] *vt* (*one's fortune, knowledge etc*) étendre; (*trade, ideas*) développer; (*production*) augmenter; (*gas, metal*) dilater; – *vi* s'étendre; se développer; augmenter; se dilater; **to e. on** développer ses idées sur; (*fast or rapidly*) **expanding sector/etc** *Com* secteur/*etc* en (pleine) expansion. ◆**expansion** *n Com Phys Pol* expansion *f*; développement *m*; augmentation *f*. ◆**expansionism** *n* expansionnisme *m*.

expanse [ɪkˈspæns] *n* étendue *f*.

expansive [ɪkˈspænsɪv] *a* expansif. ◆**-ly** *adv* avec effusion.

expatriate [eksˈpætrɪət, *Am* eksˈpeɪtrɪət] *a* & *n* expatrié, -ée (*mf*).

expect [ɪkˈspekt] *vt* (*anticipate*) s'attendre à, attendre, escompter; (*think*) penser (**that** que); (*suppose*) supposer (**that** que); (*await*) attendre; **to e. sth from s.o./sth** attendre qch de qn/qch; **to e. to do** compter faire; **to e. that** (*anticipate*) s'attendre à ce que (+ *sub*); **I e. you to come** (*want*) je te demande de venir; **it was expected** c'était prévu (**that** que); **she's expecting a baby** elle attend un

bébé. ◆**expectancy** *n* attente *f*; **life e.** espérance *f* de vie. ◆**expectant** *a* (*crowd*) qui attend; **e. mother** future mère *f*. ◆**expec'tation** *n* attente *f*; **to come up to s.o.'s expectations** répondre à l'attente de qn.

expedient [ɪksˈpiːdɪənt] *a* avantageux; (*suitable*) opportun; – *n* (*resource*) expédient *m*.

expedite [ˈekspɪdaɪt] *vt* (*hasten*) accélérer; (*task*) expédier.

expedition [ekspɪˈdɪʃ(ə)n] *n* expédition *f*.

expel [ɪkˈspel] *vt* (-**ll**-) expulser (**from** de); (*from school*) renvoyer; (*enemy*) chasser.

expend [ɪkˈspend] *vt* (*energy, money*) dépenser; (*resources*) épuiser. ◆**-able** *a* (*object*) remplaçable; (*soldiers*) sacrifiable. ◆**expenditure** *n* (*money spent*) dépenses *fpl*; **an e. of** (*time, money*) une dépense de.

expense [ɪkˈspens] *n* frais *mpl*, dépense *f*; *pl Fin* frais *mpl*; **business/travelling expenses** frais *mpl* généraux/de déplacement; **to go to some e.** faire des frais; **at s.o.'s e.** aux dépens de qn; **an or one's e. account** une or sa note de frais (professionnels).

expensive [ɪkˈspensɪv] *a* (*goods etc*) cher, coûteux; (*hotel etc*) cher; (*tastes*) dispendieux; **to be e.** coûter cher; **an e. mistake** une faute qui coûte cher. ◆**-ly** *adv* à grands frais.

experienc/e [ɪkˈspɪərɪəns] *n* (*knowledge, skill, event*) expérience *f*; **from or by e.** par expérience; **he's had e. of** (*work etc*) il a déjà fait; (*grief etc*) il a déjà éprouvé; **I've had e. of driving** j'ai déjà conduit; **terrible experiences** de rudes épreuves *fpl*; **unforgettable e.** moment *m* inoubliable; – *vt* (*undergo*) connaître, subir; (*remorse, difficulty*) éprouver; (*joy*) ressentir. ◆**-ed** *a* (*person*) expérimenté; (*eye, ear*) exercé; **to be e. in** s'y connaître en (matière de).

experiment [ɪkˈsperɪmənt] *n* expérience *f*; – [ɪkˈsperɪment] *vi* faire une expérience or des expériences; **to e. with sth** *Phys Ch* expérimenter qch. ◆**experi'mental** *a* expérimental; **e. period** période *f* d'expérimentation.

expert [ˈekspɜːt] *n* expert *m* (**on, in** en), spécialiste *mf* (**on, in** de); – *a* expert (**in sth** en qch, **in** *or* **at doing** à faire); (*advice*) d'un expert, d'expert; (*eye*) connaisseur; **e. touch** doigté *m*, grande habileté *f*. ◆**exper'tise** *n* compétence *f* (**in** en). ◆**expertly** *adv* habilement.

expiate [ˈekspɪeɪt] *vt* (*sins*) expier.

expir/e [ɪkˈspaɪər] *vi* expirer. ◆**-ed** *a*

(ticket, passport etc) périmé. ◆expi'ration n Am. ◆expiry n expiration f.

explain [ik'splein] vt expliquer (to s.o. that que); (reasons) exposer; (mystery) éclaircir; e. yourself! explique-toi!; to e. away justifier. ◆—able a explicable. ◆expla'nation n explication f. ◆explanatory a explicatif.

expletive [ik'splitiv, Am 'eksplətiv] n (oath) juron m.

explicit [ik'splisit] a explicite. ◆—ly adv explicitement.

explode [ik'sploud] vi exploser; to e. with laughter Fig éclater de rire; – vt faire exploser; (theory) Fig démythifier, discréditer.

exploit 1 [ik'sploit] vt (person, land etc) exploiter. 2 ['eksploit] n (feat) exploit m. ◆exploi'tation n exploitation f.

explore [ik'splor] vt explorer; (possibilities) examiner. ◆explo'ration n exploration f. ◆exploratory a d'exploration; (talks, step etc) préliminaire, exploratoire; e. operation Med sondage m. ◆explorer n explorateur, -trice mf.

explosion [ik'splouʒ(ə)n] n explosion f. ◆explosive a (weapon, question) explosif; (mixture, gas) détonant; – n explosif m.

exponent [ik'spounant] n (of opinion, theory etc) interprète m (of de).

export ['eksport] n exportation f; – a (goods etc) d'exportation; – [ik'sport] vt exporter (to vers, from de). ◆expor'tation n exportation f. ◆ex'porter n exportateur, -trice mf; (country) pays m exportateur.

expose [ik'spouz] vt (leave uncovered, describe) & Phot exposer; (wire) dénuder; (plot, scandal etc) révéler, dévoiler; (crook etc) démasquer; to e. to (subject to) exposer à; to e. oneself Jur commettre un attentat à la pudeur. ◆expo'sition n exposition f.

exposure [ik'spouʒər] n exposition f (to à); (of plot etc) révélation f; (of house etc) exposition f; Phot pose f; to die of e. mourir de froid.

expound [ik'spaund] vt (theory etc) exposer.

express [ik'spres] 1 vt exprimer; (proposition) énoncer; to e. oneself s'exprimer. 2 a (order) exprès, formel; (intention) exprès; (purpose) seul; (letter, delivery) exprès inv; (train) rapide, express inv; – adv (to send) par exprès; – n (train) rapide m, express m inv. ◆expression n (phrase, look etc) expression f; an e. of (gratitude, affection etc) un témoignage de. ◆expressive a expressif. ◆expressly adv expressément. ◆expressway n Am autoroute f.

expulsion [ik'spʌlʃ(ə)n] n expulsion f; (from school) renvoi m.

expurgate ['ekspəgeit] vt expurger.

exquisite [ik'skwizit] a exquis. ◆—ly adv d'une façon exquise.

ex-serviceman [eks'sɜːvismən] n (pl -men) ancien combattant m.

extant [ek'stænt] a existant.

extend [ik'stend] vt (arm, business) étendre; (line, visit, meeting) prolonger (by de); (hand) tendre (to s.o. à qn); (house) agrandir; (knowledge) étendre; (time limit) reculer; (help, thanks) offrir (to à); to e. an invitation to faire une invitation à; – vi (of wall, plain etc) s'étendre (to jusqu'à); (in time) se prolonger; to e. to s.o. (of joy etc) gagner qn. ◆extension n (in space) prolongement m; (in time) prolongation f; (of powers, measure, meaning, strike) extension f; (for table, wire) rallonge f; (to building) agrandissement(s) m(pl); (of telephone) appareil m supplémentaire; (of office telephone) poste m; an e. (of time) un délai. ◆extensive a étendu, vaste; (repairs, damage) important; (use) courant. ◆extensively adv (very much) beaucoup, considérablement; e. used largement répandu.

extent [ik'stent] n (scope) étendue f; (size) importance f; (degree) mesure f; to a large/certain e. dans une large/certaine mesure; to such an e. that à tel point que.

extenuating [ik'stenjueitiŋ] a e. circumstances circonstances fpl atténuantes.

exterior [ik'stiəriər] a & n extérieur (m).

exterminate [ik'stɜːmineit] vt (people etc) exterminer; (disease) supprimer; (evil) extirper. ◆extermi'nation n extermination f; suppression f.

external [ek'stɜːn(ə)l] a (influence, trade etc) extérieur; for e. use (medicine) à usage externe; e. affairs Pol affaires fpl étrangères. ◆—ly adv extérieurement.

extinct [ik'stiŋkt] a (volcano, love) éteint; (species, animal) disparu. ◆extinction n extinction f; disparition f.

extinguish [ik'stiŋgwiʃ] vt éteindre. ◆—er n (fire) e. extincteur m.

extol [ik'stəul] vt (-ll-) exalter, louer.

extort [ik'stɔːt] vt (money) extorquer (from à); (consent) arracher (from à). ◆extortion n Jur extorsion f de fonds; it's (sheer) e.! c'est du vol! ◆extortionate a exorbitant.

extra ['ekstrə] a (additional) supplémentaire; one e. glass un verre de or en plus, encore un verre; (any) e. bread?

encore du pain?; **to be e.** (*spare*) être en trop; (*cost more*) être en supplément; (*of postage*) être en sus; **wine is 3 francs e.** il y a un supplément de 3F pour le vin; **e. care** un soin tout particulier; **e. charge** *or* **portion** supplément *m*; **e. time** *Fb* prolongation *f*; – *adv* **e. big**/*etc* plus grand/*etc* que d'habitude; – *n* (*perk*) à-côté *m*; *Cin Th* figurant, -ante *mf*; *pl* (*expenses*) frais *mpl* supplémentaires; **an optional e.** (*for car etc*) un accessoire en option.

extra- ['ekstrə] *pref* extra-. **◆e.-'dry** *a* (*champagne*) brut. **◆e.-'fine** *a* extra-fin. **◆e.-'strong** *a* extra-fort.

extract [ik'strækt] *vt* extraire (**from** de); (*tooth*) arracher, extraire; (*promise*) arracher, soutirer (**from** à); (*money*) soutirer (**from** à); – ['ekstrækt] *n* (*of book etc*) & *Culin Ch* extrait *m*. **◆ex'traction** *n* extraction *f*; arrachement *m*; (*descent*) origine *f*.

extra-curricular [ekstrəkə'rikjulər] *a* (*activities etc*) en dehors des heures de cours, extrascolaire.

extradite ['ekstrədait] *vt* extrader. **◆extra-'dition** *n* extradition *f*.

extramarital [ekstrə'mærit(ə)l] *a* en dehors du mariage, extra-conjugal.

extramural [ekstrə'mjuərəl] *a* (*studies*) hors faculté.

extraneous [ik'streiniəs] *a* (*detail etc*) accessoire.

extraordinary [ik'strɔːdən(ə)ri] *a* (*strange, exceptional*) extraordinaire.

extra-special [ekstrə'speʃəl] *a* (*occasion*) très spécial; (*care*) tout particulier.

extravagant [ik'strævəgənt] *a* (*behaviour, idea etc*) extravagant; (*claim*) exagéré; (*wasteful with money*) dépensier, prodigue. **◆extravagance** *n* extravagance *f*; prodigalité *f*; (*thing bought*) folle dépense *f*.

extravaganza [ikstrævə'gænzə] *n* *Mus Liter & Fig* fantaisie *f*.

extreme [ik'striːm] *a* (*exceptional, furthest*) extrême; (*danger, poverty*) très grand; (*praise*) outré; **at the e. end** à l'extrémité; **of**

e. importance de première importance; – *n* (*furthest degree*) extrême *m*; **to carry** *or* **take to extremes** pousser à l'extrême; **extremes of temperature** températures *fpl* extrêmes; **extremes of climate** excès *mpl* du climat. **◆extremely** *adv* extrêmement. **◆extremist** *a & n* extrémiste (*mf*). **◆extremity** [ik'stremiti] *n* extrémité *f*.

extricate ['ekstrikeit] *vt* dégager (**from** de); **to e. oneself from** (*difficulty*) se tirer de.

extrovert ['ekstrəvɜːt] *n* extraverti, -ie *mf*.

exuberant [ig'z(j)uːbərənt] *a* exubérant. **◆exuberance** *n* exubérance *f*.

exude [ig'zjuːd] *vt* (*charm, honesty etc*) *Fig* respirer.

exultation [egzʌl'teiʃ(ə)n] *n* exultation *f*.

eye[1] [ai] *n* œil *m* (*pl* yeux); **before my very eyes** sous mes yeux; **to be all eyes** être tout yeux; **as far as the e. can see** à perte de vue; **up to one's eyes in debt** endetté jusqu'au cou; **up to one's eyes in work** débordé de travail; **to have an e. on** (*house, car*) avoir en vue; **to keep an e. on** surveiller; **to make eyes at** *Fam* faire de l'œil à; **to lay** *or* **set eyes on** voir, apercevoir; **to take one's eyes off s.o./sth** quitter qn/qch des yeux; **to catch the e.** attirer l'œil, accrocher le regard; **keep an e. out!, keep your eyes open!** ouvre l'œil!, sois vigilant!; **we don't see e. to e.** nous n'avons pas le même point de vue; **e. shadow** fard *m* à paupières; **to be an e.-opener for s.o.** *Fam* être une révélation pour qn. **◆eyeball** *n* globe *m* oculaire. **◆eyebrow** *n* sourcil *m*. **◆eyecatching** *a* (*title etc*) accrocheur. **◆eyeglass** *n* monocle *m*. **◆eyeglasses** *npl* (*spectacles*) *Am* lunettes *fpl*. **◆eyelash** *n* cil *m*. **◆eyelid** *n* paupière *f*. **◆eyeliner** *n* eye-liner *m*. **◆eyesight** *n* vue *f*. **◆eyesore** *n* (*building etc*) horreur *f*. **◆eyestrain** *n* **to have e.** avoir les yeux qui tirent. **◆eyewash** *n* (*nonsense*) *Fam* sottises *fpl*. **◆eyewitness** *n* témoin *m* oculaire.

eye[2] [ai] *vt* reluquer, regarder.

F

F, f [ef] *n* F, f *m*.
fable ['feib(ə)l] *n* fable *f*.
fabric ['fæbrik] *n* (*cloth*) tissu *m*, étoffe *f*; (*of building*) structure *f*; **the f. of society** le tissu

social.
fabricate ['fæbrikeit] *vt* (*invent, make*) fabriquer. **◆fabri'cation** *n* fabrication *f*.

fabulous ['fæbjʊləs] a (incredible, legendary) fabuleux; (wonderful) Fam formidable.

façade [fə'sɑːd] n Archit & Fig façade f.

face [feɪs] n visage m, figure f; (expression) mine f; (of clock) cadran m; (of building) façade f; (of cliff) paroi f; (of the earth) surface f; **she laughed in my f.** elle m'a ri au nez; **to show one's f.** se montrer; **f. down(wards)** (person) face contre terre; (thing) tournée à l'envers; **f. to f.** face à face; **in the f. of** devant; (despite) en dépit de; **to save/lose f.** sauver/perdre la face; **to make** or **pull faces** faire des grimaces; **to tell s.o. sth to his f.** dire qch à qn tout cru; **f. powder** poudre f de riz; **f. value** (of stamp etc) valeur f; **to take sth at f. value** prendre qch au pied de la lettre; – vt (danger, enemy etc) faire face à; (accept) accepter; (look in the face) regarder (qn) bien en face; **to f., be facing** (the opposite) être en face de; (of window etc) donner sur; **faced with** (prospect, problem) face à, devant; (defeat) menacé par; (bill) contraint à payer; **he can't f. leaving** il n'a pas le courage de partir; – vi (of house) être orienté (**north**/etc au nord/etc; (of person) se tourner (**towards** vers); **to f. up to** (danger) faire face à; (fact) accepter; **about f.!** Am Mil demi-tour! ◆**facecloth** n gant m de toilette. ◆**facelift** n Med lifting m; (of building) ravalement m.

faceless ['feɪsləs] a anonyme.

facet ['fæsɪt] n (of problem, diamond etc) facette f.

facetious [fə'siːʃəs] a (person) facétieux; (remark) plaisant.

facial ['feɪʃ(ə)l] a du visage; Med facial; – n soin m du visage.

facile ['fæsaɪl, Am 'fæs(ə)l] a facile, superficiel.

facilitate [fə'sɪlɪteɪt] vt faciliter. ◆**facility** n (ease) facilité f; pl (possibilities) facilités fpl; (for sports) équipements mpl; (in harbour, airport etc) installations fpl; (means) moyens mpl, ressources fpl; **special facilities** (conditions) conditions fpl spéciales (**for** pour).

facing ['feɪsɪŋ] n (of dress etc) parement m.

fact [fækt] n fait m; **as a matter of f.**, **in f.** en fait; **the facts of life** les choses fpl de la vie; **is that a f.?** c'est vrai?; **f. and fiction** le réel et l'imaginaire.

faction ['fækʃ(ə)n] n (group) Pol faction f.

factor ['fæktər] n (element) facteur m.

factory ['fækt(ə)rɪ] n (large) usine f; (small) fabrique f; **arms**/**porcelain f.** manufacture f d'armes/de porcelaine.

factual ['fæktʃʊəl] a objectif, basé sur les faits, factuel; (error) de fait.

faculty ['fækəltɪ] n (aptitude) & Univ faculté f.

fad [fæd] n (personal habit) marotte f; (fashion) folie f, mode f (**for** de).

fade [feɪd] vi (of flower) se faner; (of light) baisser; (of colour) passer; (of fabric) se décolorer; **to f. (away)** (of memory, smile) s'effacer; (of sound) s'affaiblir; (of person) dépérir; – vt (fabric) décolorer.

fag [fæg] n 1 (cigarette) Fam clope m, tige f; **f. end** mégot m. 2 (male homosexual) Am Sl pédé m.

fagged [fægd] a **f. (out)** (tired) Sl claqué.

faggot ['fægət] n 1 Culin boulette f (de viande). 2 (male homosexual) Am Sl pédé m.

fail [feɪl] vi (of person, plan etc) échouer; (of business) faire faillite; (of light, health, sight) baisser; (of memory, strength) défaillir; (of brakes) Aut lâcher; (run short) manquer; (of gas, electricity) être coupé; (of engine) tomber en panne; **to f.** (**in one's duty**) manquer à; (exam) échouer à; – vt (exam) échouer à; (candidate) refuser, recaler; **to f. s.o.** (let down) laisser tomber qn, décevoir qn; (of words) manquer à qn, faire défaut à qn; **to f. to do** (omit) manquer de faire; (not be able) ne pas arriver à faire; **I f. to see** je ne vois pas; – n **without f.** à coup sûr, sans faute. ◆**-ed** a (attempt, poet) manqué. ◆**-ing** n (fault) défaut m; – prep à défaut de; **f. this, f. that** à défaut. ◆**failure** n échec m; (of business) faillite f; (of engine, machine) panne f; (of gas etc) coupure f, panne f; (person) raté, -ée mf; **f. to do** (inability) incapacité f de faire; **her f. to leave** le fait qu'elle n'est pas partie; **to end in f.** se solder par un échec; **heart f.** arrêt m du cœur.

faint [feɪnt] 1 a (-er, -est) léger; (voice) faible; (colour) pâle; (idea) vague; **I haven't the faintest idea** je n'en ai pas la moindre idée. 2 a Med défaillant (**with** de); **to feel f.** se trouver mal, défaillir; – vi s'évanouir (**from** de); **fainting fit** évanouissement m. ◆**-ly** adv (weakly) faiblement; (slightly) légèrement. ◆**-ness** n légèreté f; faiblesse f. ◆**faint-'hearted** a timoré, timide.

fair¹ [feər] n foire f; (for charity) fête f; (funfair) fête f foraine; (larger) parc m d'attractions. ◆**fairground** n champ m de foire.

fair² [feər] **1** *a* (*-er, -est*) (*equitable*) juste, équitable; (*game, fight*) loyal; **f.** (**and square**) honnête(ment); **f. play** fair-play *m inv*; **that's not f. play!** ce n'est pas du jeu!; **that's not f. to him** ce n'est pas juste pour lui; **f. enough!** très bien!; – *adv* (*to play*) loyalement. **2** *a* (*rather good*) passable, assez bon; (*amount, warning*) raisonnable; **a f. amount (of)** pas mal (de); **f. copy** copie *f* au propre. **3** *a* (*wind*) favorable; (*weather*) beau. ◆**-ly** *adv* **1** (*to treat*) équitablement; (*to get*) loyalement. **2** (*rather*) assez, plutôt; **f. sure** presque sûr. ◆**-ness¹** *n* justice *f*; (*of decision*) équité *f*; **in all f.** en toute justice. ◆**fair-'minded** *a* impartial. ◆**fair-'sized** *a* assez grand.

fair³ [feər] *a* (*hair, person*) blond; (*complexion, skin*) clair. ◆**-ness²** *n* (*of hair*) blond *m*; (*of skin*) blancheur *f*. ◆**fair-'haired** *a* blond. ◆**fair-'skinned** *a* à la peau claire.

fairy [feərɪ] *n* fée *f*; **f. lights** guirlande *f* multicolore; **f. tale** conte *m* de fées.

faith [feɪθ] *n* foi *f*; **to have f. in s.o.** avoir confiance en qn; **to put one's f. in** (*justice, medicine etc*) se fier à; **in good/bad f.** de bonne/mauvaise foi; **f. healer** guérisseur, -euse *mf*. ◆**faithful** *a* fidèle. ◆**faithfully** *adv* fidèlement; **yours f.** (*in letter*) Com veuillez agréer l'expression de mes salutations distinguées. ◆**faithfulness** *n* fidélité *f*. ◆**faithless** *a* déloyal, infidèle.

fake [feɪk] *n* (*painting, document etc*) faux *m*; (*person*) imposteur *m*; – *vt* (*document, signature etc*) falsifier, maquiller; (*election*) truquer; **to f. death** faire semblant d'être mort; – *vi* (*pretend*) faire semblant; – *a* faux; (*elections*) truqué.

falcon [fɔːlkən] *n* faucon *m*.

fall [fɔːl] *n* chute *f*; (*in price, demand etc*) baisse *f*; *pl* (*waterfall*) chutes *fpl* (d'eau); **the f.** *Am* l'automne *m*; – *vi* (*pt* **fell**, *pp* **fallen**) tomber; (*of building*) s'effondrer; **her face fell** *Fig* son visage se rembrunit; **f. into** tomber dans; (*habit*) *Fig* prendre; **to f. off a bicycle/etc** tomber d'une bicyclette/etc; **to f. off** *or* **down a ladder** tomber (en bas) d'une échelle; **to fall on s.o.** (*of onus*) retomber sur qn; **to f. on a Monday/etc** (*of event*) tomber un lundi/etc; **to f. over sth** tomber en butant contre qch; **to f. short of** (*expectation*) ne pas répondre à; **to f. short of being** être loin d'être; **to f. victim** devenir victime (to de); **to f. asleep** s'endormir; **to f. ill** tomber malade; **to f. due** échoir. ■ **to f. apart** (*of mechanism*) tomber en morceaux; *Fig* se désagréger; **to f. away** (*come off*) se détacher, tomber; (*of numbers*) diminuer; **to f. back on** (*as last resort*) se rabattre sur; **to f. behind** rester en arrière; (*in work*) prendre du retard; **to f. down** tomber; (*of building*) s'effondrer; **to f. for** *Fam* (*person*) tomber amoureux de; (*trick*) se laisser prendre à; **to f. in** (*collapse*) s'écrouler; **to f. in with** (*tally with*) cadrer avec; (*agree to*) accepter; **to f. off** (*come off*) se détacher, tomber; (*of numbers*) diminuer. ◆**falling-'off** *n* diminution *f*; **to f. out with** (*quarrel with*) se brouiller avec; **to f. over** tomber; (*of table, vase*) se renverser; **to f. through** (*of plan*) tomber à l'eau, échouer. ◆**fallen** *a* tombé; (*angel, woman*) déchu; **f. leaf** feuille *f* morte. ◆**fallout** *n* (*radioactive*) retombées *fpl*.

fallacious [fəˈleɪʃəs] *a* faux. ◆**fallacy** [ˈfæləsɪ] *n* erreur *f*; *Phil* faux raisonnement *m*.

fallible [ˈfæləb(ə)l] *a* faillible.

fallow [ˈfæləʊ] *a* (*land*) en jachère.

false [fɔːls] *a* faux; **a f. bottom** un double fond. ◆**falsehood** *n* mensonge *m*; **truth and f.** le vrai et le faux. ◆**falseness** *n* fausseté *f*. ◆**falsify** *vt* falsifier.

falter [ˈfɔːltər] *vi* (*of step, resolution*) chanceler; (*of voice, speaker*) hésiter; (*of courage*) vaciller.

fame [feɪm] *n* renommée *f*; (*glory*) gloire *f*. ◆**famed** *a* renommé.

familiar [fəˈmɪljər] *a* (*task, atmosphere etc*) familier; (*event*) habituel; **f. with s.o.** (*too friendly*) familier avec qn; **to be f. with** (*know*) connaître; **I'm f. with her voice** je connais bien sa voix, sa voix m'est familière; **to make oneself f. with** se familiariser avec; **he looks f. (to me)** je l'ai déjà vu (quelque part). ◆**famili'arity** *n* familiarité *f* (**with** avec); (*of event, sight etc*) caractère *m* familier. ◆**familiarize** *vt* familiariser (**with** avec); **to f. oneself with** se familiariser avec.

family [ˈfæmɪlɪ] *n* famille *f*; – *a* (*name, doctor etc*) de famille; (*planning, problem*) familial; (*tree*) généalogique; **f. man** père *m* de famille.

famine [ˈfæmɪn] *n* famine *f*.

famished [ˈfæmɪʃt] *a* affamé.

famous [ˈfeɪməs] *a* célèbre (**for** par, pour). ◆**-ly** *adv* (*very well*) *Fam* rudement bien.

fan [fæn] **1** *n* (*hand-held*) éventail *m*; (*mechanical*) ventilateur *m*; **f. heater** radiateur *m* soufflant; – *vt* (**-nn-**) (*person etc*) éventer; (*fire, quarrel*) attiser. **2** *n* (*of person*) admirateur, -trice *mf*, fan *m*; *Sp* supporter *m*; **to be a jazz/sports f.** être passionné *or* mordu de jazz/de sport.

fanatic [fə'nætɪk] *n* fanatique *mf*. ◆**fanatical** *a* fanatique. ◆**fanaticism** *n* fanatisme *m*.

fancy ['fænsɪ] **1** *n* (*whim, imagination*) fantaisie *f*; (*liking*) goût *m*; **to take a f. to s.o.** se prendre d'affection pour qn; **I took a f. to it, it took my f.** j'en ai eu envie; **when the f. takes me** quand ça me chante; – *a* (*hat, button etc*) fantaisie *inv*; (*idea*) fantaisiste; (*price*) exorbitant; (*car*) de luxe; (*house, restaurant*) chic; **f. dress** (*costume*) travesti *m*; **f.-dress ball** bal *m* masqué. **2** *vt* (*imagine*) se figurer (that que); (*think*) croire (**that** que); (*want*) avoir envie de; (*like*) aimer; **f. that!** tiens (donc)!; **he fancies her** *Fam* elle lui plaît; **to f. oneself** as se prendre pour qn; **she fancies herself!** elle se prend pour qn! ◆**fancier** *n* **horse**/*etc* **f.** amateur *m* de chevaux/*etc*. ◆**fanciful** *a* fantaisiste.

fanfare ['fænfeər] *n* (*of trumpets*) fanfare *f*.

fang [fæŋ] *n* (*of dog etc*) croc *m*; (*of snake*) crochet *m*.

fantastic [fæn'tæstɪk] *a* fantastique; **a f. idea** (*absurd*) une idée aberrante.

fantasy ['fæntəsɪ] *n* (*imagination*) fantaisie *f*; *Psy* fantasme *m*. ◆**fantasize** *vi* fantasmer (**about** sur).

far [fɑːr] *adv* (**farther** *or* **further**, **farthest** *or* **furthest**) (*distance*) loin; **f. bigger/more expensive**/*etc* (*much*) beaucoup plus grand/plus cher/*etc* (**than** que); **f. more beaucoup plus; **f. advanced** très avancé; **how f. is it to** ... ? combien y a-t-il d'ici à ... ?; **is it f. to** ... ? sommes-nous, suis-je *etc* loin de ... ?; **how f. are you going?** jusqu'où vas-tu?; **how f. has he got with?** (*plans, work etc*) où en est-il de?; **so f.** (*time*) jusqu'ici; (*place*) jusque-là; **as f.** (*place*) jusqu'à; **as f.** *or* **so f. as I know** autant que je sache; **as f.** *or* **so f. as I'm concerned** en ce qui me concerne; **as f. back as 1820** dès 1820; **f. from doing** loin de faire; **f. from it!** loin de là!; **f. away** *or* **off** au loin; **to be (too) f. away** être (trop) loin (**from** de); **f. and wide** partout; **by f.** loin; **f. into the night** très avant dans la nuit; – *a* (*side, end*) autre; **it's a f. cry from** on est loin de. ◆**faraway** *a* lointain; (*look*) distrait, dans le vague. ◆**far-'fetched** *a* forcé, exagéré. ◆**f.-'flung** *a* (*widespread*) vaste. ◆**f.-'off** *a* lointain. ◆**f.-'reaching** *a* de grande portée. ◆**f.-'sighted** *a* clairvoyant.

farce [fɑːs] *n* farce *f*. ◆**farcical** *a* grotesque, ridicule.

fare [feər] **1** *n* (*price*) prix *m* du billet; (*ticket*) billet *m*; (*taxi passenger*) client, -ente *mf*. **2** *n* (*food*) chère *f*, nourriture *f*; **prison f.** régime *m* de prison; **bill of f.** menu *m*. **3** *vi* (*manage*) se débrouiller; **how did she f.?** comment ça s'est passé (pour elle)?

farewell [feə'wel] *n* & *int* adieu (*m*); – *a* (*party etc*) d'adieu.

farm [fɑːm] *n* ferme *f*; – *a* (*worker, produce etc*) agricole; **f. land** terres *fpl* cultivées; – *vt* cultiver; – *vi* être agriculteur. ◆**-ing** *n* agriculture *f*; (*breeding*) élevage *m*; **dairy f.** industrie *f* laitière. ◆**-er** *n* fermier, -ière *mf*, agriculteur *m*. ◆**farmhand** *n* ouvrier, -ière *mf* agricole. ◆**farmhouse** *n* ferme *f*. ◆**farmyard** *n* basse-cour *f*.

farther ['fɑːðər] *adv* plus loin; **nothing is f. from** (*my mind, the truth etc*) rien n'est plus éloigné de; **f. forward** plus avancé; **to get f. away** s'éloigner; – *a* (*end*) autre. ◆**farthest** *a* le plus éloigné; – *adv* le plus loin.

fascinate ['fæsɪneɪt] *vt* fasciner. ◆**fasci-'nation** *n* fascination *f*.

fascism ['fæʃɪz(ə)m] *n* fascisme *m*. ◆**fascist** *a* & *n* fasciste (*mf*).

fashion ['fæʃ(ə)n] **1** *n* (*style in clothes etc*) mode *f*; **in f.** à la mode; **out of f.** démodé; **f. designer** (grand) couturier *m*; **f. house** maison *f* de couture; **f. show** présentation *f* de collections. **2** *n* (*manner*) façon *f*; (*custom*) habitude *f*; **after a f.** tant bien que mal, plus au moins. **3** *vt* (*make*) façonner. ◆**-able** *a* à la mode; (*place*) chic *inv*; **it's f. to do** il est de bon ton de faire. ◆**-ably** *adv* (*dressed etc*) à la mode.

fast [fɑːst] **1** *a* (**-er, -est**) rapide; **to be f.** (*of clock*) avancer (**by** de); **f. colour** couleur *f* grand teint *inv*; **f. living** vie *f* dissolue; – *adv* (*quickly*) vite; (*firmly*) ferme, bien; **how f.?** à quelle vitesse?; **f. asleep** profondément endormi. **2** *vi* (*go without food*) jeûner; – *n* jeûne *m*.

fasten ['fɑːs(ə)n] *vt* attacher (**to** à); (*door, window*) fermer (bien); **to f. down** *or* **up** attacher; – *vi* (*of dress etc*) s'attacher; (*of door, window*) se fermer. ◆**-ing** *n* (*clip*) attache *f*; (*of garment*) fermeture *f*; (*hook*) agrafe *f*.

fastidious [fə'stɪdɪəs] *a* difficile (à contenter), exigeant.

fat [fæt] *n* graisse *f*; (*on meat*) gras *m*; **vegetable f.** huile *f* végétale. **2** *a* (**fatter, fattest**) gras; (*cheek, salary, volume*) gros; **to get f.** grossir; **that's a f. lot of good** *or* **use!** *Iron**

Fam ça va vraiment servir (à quelque chose)! ◆**fathead** *n* imbécile *mf.*

fatal ['feɪt(ə)l] *a* mortel; (*error, blow etc*) *Fig* fatal. ◆**-ly** *adv* (*wounded*) mortellement.

fatality [fə'tælɪtɪ] *n* **1** (*person killed*) victime *f.* **2** (*of event*) fatalité *f.*

fate [feɪt] *n* destin *m*, sort *m*; one's f. son sort. ◆**fated** *a* f. to do destiné à faire; our meeting/his death/*etc* was f. notre rencontre/sa mort/*etc* devait arriver. ◆**fateful** *a* (*important*) fatal, décisif; (*prophetic*) fatidique; (*disastrous*) néfaste.

father ['fɑːðər] *n* père *m*; – *vt* engendrer; (*idea*) *Fig* inventer. ◆**f.-in-law** *n* (*pl* fathers-in-law) beau-père *m*. ◆**fatherhood** *n* paternité *f.* ◆**fatherland** *n* patrie *f.* ◆**fatherly** *a* paternel.

fathom ['fæðəm] **1** *n Nau* brasse *f* (= 1,8 m). **2** *vt to* f. (out) (*understand*) comprendre.

fatigue [fə'tiːg] **1** *n* fatigue *f*; – *vt* fatiguer. **2** *n* f. (duty) *Mil* corvée *f.*

fatness ['fætnɪs] *n* corpulence *f.* ◆**fatten** *vt* engraisser. ◆**fattening** *a* qui fait grossir. ◆**fatty** *a* (-ier, -iest) (*food*) gras; (*tissue*) *Med* adipeux; – *n* (*person*) *Fam* gros lard *m.*

fatuous ['fætjʊəs] *a* stupide.

faucet ['fɔːsɪt] *n* (*tap*) *Am* robinet *m.*

fault [fɔːlt] *n* (*blame*) faute *f*; (*failing, defect*) défaut *m*; (*mistake*) erreur *f*; *Geol* faille *f*; to find f. (with) critiquer; he's at f. c'est sa faute, il est fautif; his *or* her memory is at f. sa mémoire lui fait défaut; – *vt* to f. s.o./sth trouver des défauts chez qn/à qch. ◆**f.-finding** *a* critique, chicanier. ◆**faultless** *a* irréprochable. ◆**faulty** *a* (-ier, -iest) défectueux.

fauna ['fɔːnə] *n* (*animals*) faune *f.*

favour ['feɪvər] *n* (*approval, advantage*) faveur *f*; (*act of kindness*) service *m*; to do s.o. a f. rendre service à qn; in f. (*person*) bien vu; (*fashion*) en vogue; it's in her f. to do elle a intérêt à faire; in f. of (*for the sake of*) au profit de, en faveur de; to be in f. of (*support*) être pour, être partisan de; (*prefer*) préférer; – *vt* (*encourage*) favoriser; (*support*) être partisan de; (*prefer*) préférer; he favoured me with a visit il a eu la gentillesse de me rendre visite. ◆**-able** *a* favorable (to à). ◆**favourite** *a* favori, préféré; – *n* favori, -ite *mf.* ◆**favouritism** *n* favoritisme *m.*

fawn [fɔːn] **1** *n* (*deer*) faon *m*; – *a* & *n* (*colour*) fauve (*m*). **2** *vi* to f. (up)on flatter, flagorner.

fear [fɪər] *n* crainte *f*, peur *f*; for f. of de peur de; for f. that de peur que (+ *ne* + *sub*);

there's no f. of his going il ne risque pas d'y aller; there are fears (that) he might leave on craint qu'il ne parte; – *vt* craindre; I f. (that) he might leave je crains qu'il ne parte; to f. for (*one's life etc*) craindre pour. ◆**fearful** *a* (*frightful*) affreux; (*timid*) peureux. ◆**fearless** *a* intrépide. ◆**fearlessness** *n* intrépidité *f.* ◆**fearsome** *a* redoutable.

feasible ['fiːzəb(ə)l] *a* (*practicable*) faisable; (*theory, explanation etc*) plausible. ◆**feasibility** *n* possibilité *f* (of doing de faire); plausibilité *f.*

feast [fiːst] *n* festin *m*, banquet *m*; *Rel* fête *f*; – *vi* banqueter; to f. on (*cakes etc*) se régaler de.

feat [fiːt] *n* exploit *m*, tour *m* de force; f. of skill tour *m* d'adresse.

feather ['feðər] **1** *n* plume *f*; f. duster plumeau *m.* **2** *vt* to f. one's nest (*enrich oneself*) faire sa pelote.

feature ['fiːtʃər] **1** *n* (*of face, person*) trait *m*; (*of thing, place, machine*) caractéristique *f*; f. (article) article *m* de fond; f. (film) grand film *m*; to be a regular f. (*in newspaper*) paraître régulièrement. **2** *vt* représenter (as comme); *Journ Cin* présenter; a film featuring Chaplin un film avec Charlot en vedette; – *vi* (*appear*) figurer (in dans).

February ['februərɪ] *n* février *m.*

fed [fed] *see* **feed**; – *a* to be f. up *Fam* en avoir marre (with de).

federal ['fedərəl] *a* fédéral. ◆**federate** *vt* fédérer. ◆**federation** *n* fédération *f.*

fee [fiː] *n* (*price*) prix *m*; (*sum*) somme *f*; fee(s) (*professional*) honoraires *mpl*; (*of artist*) cachet *m*; (*for registration*) droits *mpl*; tuition fees frais *mpl* de scolarité; entrance f. droit *m* d'entrée; membership fee(s) cotisation *f*; f.-paying school école *f* privée.

feeble ['fiːb(ə)l] *a* (-er, -est) faible; (*excuse*) pauvre. ◆**f.-'minded** *a* imbécile.

feed [fiːd] *n* (*food*) nourriture *f*; (*baby's breast feed*) tétée *f*; (*baby's bottle feed*) biberon *m*; – *vt* (*pt & pp* fed) donner à manger à, nourrir; (*breast-feed*) allaiter (*un bébé*); (*bottle-feed*) donner le biberon à (*un bébé*); (*machine*) *Fig* alimenter; – *vi* (*eat*) manger; to f. on se nourrir de. ◆**-ing** *n* alimentation *f.* ◆**feedback** *n* réaction(s) *f(pl)*.

feel [fiːl] *n* (*touch*) toucher *m*; (*sensation*) sensation *f*; – *vt* (*pt & pp* felt) (*be aware of*) sentir; (*experience*) éprouver, ressentir; (*touch*) tâter, palper; (*think*) avoir l'impression (that que); to f. one's way avancer à tâtons; – vi (tired, old etc) se sentir; to f. (about) (grope) tâtonner; (in pocket etc) fouiller; it feels hard (au toucher); I f. sure je suis sûr (that que); I f. hot/sleepy/hungry j'ai chaud/sommeil/faim; she feels better elle va mieux; to f. like (want) avoir envie de; to f. as if avoir l'impression de; it feels like cotton on dirait du coton; what do you f. about . . . ? que pensez-vous de . . . ?; I f. bad about it ça m'ennuie, ça me fait de la peine; what does it f. like? quelle impression ça (te) fait?; to f. for (look for) chercher; (pity) éprouver de la pitié pour; to f. up to doing être (assez) en forme pour faire. ◆—ing n (emotion, impression) sentiment m; (physical) sensation f; a f. for (person) de la sympathie pour; (music) une appréciation de; bad f. animosité f. ◆—er n (of snail etc) antenne f; to put out a f. lancer un ballon d'essai.

feet [fiːt] see foot[1].

feign [feɪn] vt feindre, simuler.

feint [feɪnt] n Mil Boxing feinte f.

feisty ['faɪstɪ] a (-ier, -iest) (lively) Am Fam plein d'entrain.

felicitous [fə'lɪsɪtəs] a heureux.

feline ['fiːlaɪn] a félin.

fell [fel] 1 see fall. 2 vt (tree etc) abattre.

fellow ['feləʊ] n 1 (man, boy) garçon m, type m; an old f. un vieux; poor f.! pauvre malheureux! 2 (comrade) compagnon m, compagne f; f. being or man semblable m; f. countryman, f. countrywoman compatriote mf; f. passenger compagnon m de voyage, compagne f de voyage. 3 (of society) membre m. ◆fellowship n camaraderie f; (group) association f; (membership) qualité f de membre; (grant) bourse f universitaire.

felony ['felənɪ] n crime m.

felt[1] [felt] see feel.

felt[2] [felt] n feutre m; f.-tip(ped) pen crayon m feutre.

female ['fiːmeɪl] a (animal etc) femelle; (quality, name, voice etc) féminin; (vote) des femmes; f. student étudiante f. – n (woman) femme f; (animal) femelle f.

feminine ['femɪnɪn] a féminin. ◆femi-'ninity n féminité f. ◆feminist a & n féministe (mf).

fenc/e [fens] 1 n barrière f, clôture f; Sp obstacle m; – vt to f. (in) clôturer. 2 vi (with sword) Sp faire de l'escrime. 3 n (criminal) Fam receleur, -euse mf. ◆—ing n Sp escrime f.

fend [fend] 1 vi to f. for oneself se débrouil-

ler. 2 vt to f. off (blow etc) parer, éviter.
◆—er n 1 (for fire) garde-feu m inv. 2 (on car) Am aile f.

fennel ['fenəl] n Bot Culin fenouil m.

ferment ['fɜːment] n ferment m; Fig effervescence f; – [fə'ment] vi fermenter. ◆fermen'tation n fermentation f.

fern [fɜːn] n fougère f.

ferocious [fə'rəʊʃəs] a féroce. ◆ferocity n férocité f.

ferret ['ferɪt] n (animal) furet m; – vi to f. about (pry) fureter; – vt to f. out dénicher.

Ferris wheel ['ferɪswiːl] n (at funfair) grande roue f.

ferry ['ferɪ] n ferry-boat m; (small, for river) bac m; – vt transporter.

fertile ['fɜːtaɪl, Am 'fɜːt(ə)l] a (land, imagination) fertile; (person, creature) fécond. ◆fer'tility n fertilité f; fécondité f. ◆fertilize vt (land) fertiliser; (egg, animal etc) féconder. ◆fertilizer n engrais m.

fervent ['fɜːv(ə)nt] a fervent. ◆fervour n ferveur f.

fester ['festər] vi (of wound) suppurer; (of anger etc) Fig couver.

festival ['festɪv(ə)l] n Mus Cin festival m; Rel fête f. ◆festive a (atmosphere, clothes) de fête; (mood) joyeux; f. season période f des fêtes. ◆fe'stivities npl réjouissances fpl, festivités fpl.

festoon [fe'stuːn] vt to f. with orner de.

fetch [fetʃ] vt 1 (person) amener; (object) apporter; to (go and) f. aller chercher; to f. in rentrer; to f. out sortir. 2 (be sold for) rapporter (ten pounds/etc dix livres/etc); (price) atteindre. ◆—ing a (smile etc) charmant, séduisant.

fête [feɪt] n fête f; – vt fêter.

fetid ['fetɪd] a fétide.

fetish ['fetɪʃ] n (magical object) fétiche m; to make a f. of Fig être obsédé par.

fetter ['fetər] vt (hinder) entraver.

fettle ['fet(ə)l] n in fine f. en pleine forme.

fetus ['fiːtəs] n Am fœtus m.

feud [fjuːd] n querelle f, dissension f.

feudal ['fjuːd(ə)l] a féodal.

fever ['fiːvər] n fièvre f; to have a f. (temperature) avoir de la fièvre. ◆feverish a (person, activity) fiévreux.

few [fjuː] a & pron peu (de); f. towns/etc peu de villes/etc; a f. towns/etc quelques villes/etc; f. of them peu entre eux; a f. quelques-un(e)s (of de); a f. of us quelques-uns d'entre nous; one of the f. books l'un des rares livres; quite a f., a good f. bon nombre (de); a f. more books/etc encore quelques livres/etc; f. and far between rares (et espacés); **f. came** peu sont venus; **to be f.** être peu nombreux; **every f. days** tous les trois ou quatre jours. ◆**fewer** a & pron moins (de) (**than** que); **to be f.** être moins nombreux (**than** que); **no f. than** pas moins de. ◆**fewest** a & pron le moins (de).

fiancé(e) [fɪˈɒnseɪ] n fiancé, -ée mf.

fiasco [fɪˈæskəʊ] n (pl -os, Am -oes) fiasco m.

fib [fɪb] n Fam blague f, bobard m; – vi (-bb-) Fam raconter des blagues. ◆**fibber** n Fam blagueur, -euse mf.

fibre [ˈfaɪbər] n fibre f; Fig caractère m. ◆**fibreglass** n fibre f de verre.

fickle [ˈfɪk(ə)l] a inconstant.

fiction [ˈfɪkʃ(ə)n] n fiction f; (**works of**) **f.** romans mpl. ◆**fictional** a, ◆**fic'titious** a fictif.

fiddl/e [ˈfɪd(ə)l] **1** n (violin) Fam violon m; – vi Fam jouer du violon. **2** vi Fam **to f. about** (waste time) traînailler, glandouiller; **to f. (about) with** (watch, pen etc) tripoter; (cars etc) bricoler. **3** n (dishonesty) Fam combine f, fraude f; – vi (swindle) Fam faire de la fraude; – vt (accounts etc) Fam falsifier. ◆**-ing** a (petty) insignifiant. ◆**-er** n **1** Fam joueur, -euse mf de violon. **2** (swindler) Sl combinard, -arde mf. ◆**fiddly** a (task) délicat.

fidelity [fɪˈdelɪtɪ] n fidélité f (**to** à).

fidget [ˈfɪdʒɪt] vi **to f. (about)** gigoter, se trémousser; **to f. (about) with** tripoter; – n personne f qui ne tient pas en place. ◆**fidgety** a agité, remuant.

field [fiːld] n champ m; Sp terrain m; (sphere) domaine m; **to have a f. day** (a good day) s'en donner à cœur joie; **f. glasses** jumelles fpl; **f. marshal** maréchal m.

fiend [fiːnd] n démon m; **a jazz/etc f.** Fam un(e) passionné, -ée de jazz/etc; (sex) Fam satyre m. ◆**fiendish** a diabolique.

fierce [fɪəs] a (-er, -est) féroce; (wind, attack) furieux. ◆**-ness** n férocité f, fureur f.

fiery [ˈfaɪərɪ] a (-ier, -iest) (person, speech) fougueux; (sun, eyes) ardent.

fiesta [fɪˈestə] n fiesta f.

fifteen [fɪfˈtiːn] a & n quinze (m). ◆**fifteenth** a & n quinzième (mf). ◆**fifth** a & n cinquième (mf); **a f.** un cinquième. ◆**fiftieth** a & n cinquantième (mf). ◆**fifty** a & n cinquante (m).

fig [fɪg] n figue f; **f. tree** figuier m.

fight [faɪt] n bagarre f, rixe f; Mil Boxing combat m; (struggle) lutte f; (quarrel) dispute f; (spirit) combativité f; **to put up a (good) f.** bien se défendre; – vi (pt & pp fought) se battre (**against** contre); Mil se battre, combattre; (struggle) lutter; (quarrel) se disputer; **to f.** se défendre; **to f. over sth** se disputer qch; – vt se battre avec (s.o. qn); (evil) lutter contre, combattre; **to f. a battle** livrer bataille; **to f. back** (tears) refouler; **to f. off** (attacker, attack) repousser; (illness) lutter contre; **to f. it out** se bagarrer. ◆**-ing** n Mil combat(s) m(pl); – a (person) combatif; (troops) de combat. ◆**-er** n combattant, -ante mf; Boxing boxeur m; Fig battant m, lutteur, -euse mf; (aircraft) chasseur m.

figment [ˈfɪgmənt] n **a f. of one's imagination** une création de son esprit.

figurative [ˈfɪgjʊrətɪv] a (meaning) figuré; (art) figuratif. ◆**-ly** adv au figuré.

figure¹ [ˈfɪgər, Am ˈfɪgjər] n **1** (numeral) chiffre m; (price) prix m; pl (arithmetic) calcul m. **2** (shape) forme f; (outlined shape) silhouette f; (of woman) ligne f; **she has a nice f.** elle est bien faite. **3** (diagram) & Liter figure f; **a f. of speech** une figure de rhétorique; Fig une façon de parler; **f. of eight**, Am **f. eight** huit m; **f. skating** patinage m artistique. **4** (important person) figure f, personnage m. ◆**figurehead** n Nau figure f de proue; (person) Fig potiche f.

figure² [ˈfɪgər, Am ˈfɪgjər] **1** vt (imagine) (s')imaginer; (guess) penser (**that** que); **to f. out** arriver à comprendre; (problem) résoudre; – vi (make sense) s'expliquer; **to f. on doing** Am compter faire. **2** vi (appear) figurer (on sur).

filament [ˈfɪləmənt] n filament m.

filch [fɪltʃ] vt (steal) voler (**from** à).

fil/e [faɪl] **1** n (tool) lime f; – vt **to f. (down)** limer. **2** n (folder, information) dossier m; (loose-leaf) classeur m; (for card index, computer data) fichier m; – vt (claim, application) déposer; **to f. (away)** classer. **3** n **in single f.** en file; – vi **to f. in/out** entrer/sortir à la queue leu leu; **to f. past** (coffin etc) défiler devant. ◆**-ing 1** a **f. clerk** documentaliste mf; **f. cabinet** classeur m. **2** npl (particles) limaille f.

fill [fɪl] vt remplir (**with** de); (tooth) plomber; (sail) gonfler; (need) répondre à; **to f. in** (form) remplir; (hole) combler; (door) condamner; **to f. s.o. in on** Fam mettre qn au courant de; **to f. up** (glass etc) remplir; **to f. up or out** (form) remplir; – vi **to f. (up)** se remplir; **to f. out** (get fatter) grossir; **to f. up** Aut faire le plein; – n **to eat one's f.** manger à sa faim; **to have had one's f. of** Pej en avoir assez de. ◆**-ing** a *(meal etc)* substantiel, nourrissant; − *n (in tooth)* plombage *m*; *Culin* garniture *f*; **f. station** poste *m* d'essence. ◆**−er** *n (for cracks in wood)* mastic *m*.

fillet ['fɪlɪt, *Am* fɪ'leɪ] *n Culin* filet *m*; − *vt (pt & pp Am* [fɪ'leɪd]*) (fish)* découper en filets; *(meat)* désosser.

fillip ['fɪlɪp] *n (stimulus)* coup *m* de fouet.

filly ['fɪlɪ] *n (horse)* pouliche *f*.

film [fɪlm] *n* film *m*; *(layer)* pellicule *f*; − *a (festival)* du film; *(studio, technician, critic)* de cinéma; **f. fan** *or* **buff** cinéphile *mf*; **f. library** cinémathèque *f*; **f. star** vedette *f* (de cinéma); − *vt* filmer.

filter ['fɪltər] *n* filtre *m*; *(traffic sign)* flèche *f*; **f. lane** *Aut* couloir *m* (pour tourner); **f. tip** (bout *m*) filtre *m*; **f.-tipped cigarette** cigarette *f* (à bout) filtre; − *vt* filtrer; − *vi* filtrer **(through sth** à travers qch); **to f. through** filtrer.

filth [fɪlθ] *n* saleté *f*; *(obscenities) Fig* saletés *fpl*. ◆**filthy** *a* (**-ier, -iest**) *(hands etc)* sale; *(language)* obscène; *(habit)* dégoûtant; **f. weather** un temps infect, un sale temps.

fin [fɪn] *n (of fish, seal)* nageoire *f*; *(of shark)* aileron *m*.

final ['faɪn(ə)l] *a* dernier; *(decision)* définitif; *(cause)* final: − *n Sp* finale *f*; *pl Univ* examens *mpl* de dernière année. ◆**finalist** *n Sp* finaliste *mf*. ◆**finalize** *vt (plan)* mettre au point; *(date)* fixer (définitivement). ◆**finally** *adv (lastly)* enfin, en dernier lieu; *(eventually)* finalement, enfin; *(once and for all)* définitivement.

finale [fɪ'nɑːlɪ] *n Mus* finale *m*.

finance ['faɪnæns] *n* finance *f*; − *a (company, page)* financier; − *vt* financer. ◆**fi'nancial** *a* financier; **f. year** année *f* budgétaire. ◆**fi'nancially** *adv* financièrement. ◆**fi'nancier** *n (grand)* financier *m*.

find [faɪnd] *n (discovery)* trouvaille *f*; − *vt (pt & pp* **found***)* trouver; *(sth or s.o. lost)* retrouver; *(difficulty)* éprouver, trouver (in doing à faire); **I f. that** je trouve que; **£20 all found** 20 livres logé et nourri; **to f. s.o. guilty** *Jur* prononcer qn coupable; **to f. one's feet** *(settle in)* s'adapter; **to f. oneself** *(to be)* se trouver. ■ **to f. out** *vt (information etc)* découvrir; *(person)* démasquer; − *vi (enquire)* se renseigner (about sur); **to f. out about** *(discover)* découvrir. ◆**−ings** *npl* conclusions *fpl*.

fine [faɪn] *n (money)* amende *f*; *Aut* contravention *f*; − *vt* **to f. s.o.** (**£10/**etc) infliger une amende de (dix livres/etc) à qn.

fine [faɪn] 1 *a* (**-er, -est**) *(thin, small, not coarse)* fin; *(gold)* pur; *(feeling)* délicat;

(distinction) subtil; − *adv (to cut, write)* menu. **2** *a* (**-er, -est**) *(beautiful)* beau; *(good)* bon; *(excellent)* excellent; **to be f.** *(in good health)* aller bien; − *adv (well)* très bien. ◆**−ly** *adv (dressed)* magnifiquement; *(chopped)* menu; *(embroidered, ground)* finement.

finery ['faɪnərɪ] *n (clothes)* parure *f*, belle toilette *f*.

finesse [fɪ'nes] *n (skill, tact)* doigté *m*; *(refinement)* finesse *f*.

finger ['fɪŋgər] *n* doigt *m*; **little f.** auriculaire *m*, petit doigt *m*; **middle f.** majeur *m*; **f. mark** trace *f* de doigt; − *vt* toucher (des doigts), palper. ◆**−ing** *n Mus* doigté *m*. ◆**fingernail** *n* ongle *m*. ◆**fingerprint** *n* empreinte *f* digitale. ◆**fingerstall** *n* doigtier *m*. ◆**fingertip** *n* bout *m* du doigt.

finicky ['fɪnɪkɪ] *a (precise)* méticuleux; *(difficult)* difficile (about sur).

finish ['fɪnɪʃ] *n (end)* fin *f*; *Sp* arrivée *f*; *(of article, car etc)* finition *f*; **paint with a matt f.** peinture *f* mate; − *vt* **to f.** (**off** *or* **up**) finir, terminer; **to f. doing** finir de faire; **to f. s.o. off** *(kill)* achever qn; − *vi (of meeting etc)* finir, se terminer; *(of person)* finir, terminer; **to f. first** terminer premier; *(in race)* arriver premier; **to have finished with** *(object)* ne plus avoir besoin de; *(situation, person)* en avoir fini avec; **to f. off** *or* **up** *(of person)* finir, terminer; **to f. up in** *(end up in)* se retrouver à; **to f. up doing** finir par faire; **finishing school** institution *f* pour jeunes filles; **finishing touch** touche *f* finale. ◆**−ed** *a (ended, done for)* fini.

finite ['faɪnaɪt] *a* fini.

Finland ['fɪnlənd] *n* Finlande *f*. ◆**Finn** *n* Finlandais, -aise *mf*, Finnois, -oise *mf*. ◆**Finnish** *a* finlandais, finnois; − *n (language)* finnois *m*.

fir [fɜːr] *n (tree, wood)* sapin *m*.

fire [faɪər] *n* feu *m*; *(accidental)* incendie *m*; *(electric)* radiateur *m*; **on f.** en feu; **(there's a) f.!** au feu!; **f.!** *Mil* feu!; **f. alarm** avertisseur *m* d'incendie; **f. brigade,** *Am* **f. department** pompiers *mpl*; **f. engine** *(vehicle)* voiture *f* de pompiers; *(machine)* pompe *f* à incendie; **f. escape** escalier *m* de secours; **f. station** caserne *f* de pompiers. ◆**firearm** *n* arme *f* à feu. ◆**firebug** *n* pyromane *mf*. ◆**firecracker** *n Am* pétard *m*. ◆**fireguard** *n* garde-feu *m inv*. ◆**fireman** *n (pl* **-men***)* (sapeur-)pompier *m*. ◆**fireplace** *n* cheminée *f*. ◆**fireproof** *a (door)* ignifugé, anti-incendie. ◆**fireside** *n* coin *m* du feu; **f. chair** fauteuil *m*. ◆**firewood** *n* bois *m* de chauffage.

◆**firework** n feu m d'artifice; a f. display, fireworks, un feu d'artifice.

fire² ['faɪər] vt (cannon) tirer; (pottery) cuire; (imagination) enflammer; to f. a gun tirer un coup de fusil; to f. questions at bombarder de questions; to f. s.o. (dismiss) Fam renvoyer qn; – vi tirer (at sur). f. away! Fam vas-y, parle!; firing squad peloton m d'exécution; in or Am on the firing line en train de subir aux attaques.

firm [fɜːm] 1 n Com maison f, firme f. 2 a (-er, -est) (earth, decision etc) ferme; (strict) ferme (with avec); (faith) solide; (character) résolu. ◆**–ly** adv fermement; (to speak) d'une voix ferme. ◆**–ness** n fermeté f; (of faith) solidité f.

first [fɜːst] a premier; I'll do it f. thing in the morning je le ferai dès le matin, sans faute; f. cousin cousin, -ine mf germain(e); – adv d'abord, premièrement; (for the first time) pour la première fois; f. of all tout d'abord; at f. d'abord; to come f. (in race) arriver premier; (in exam) être le premier; – n premier, -ière mf; Univ = licence f avec mention très bien; from the f. dès le début; f. aid premiers soins mpl or secours mpl; f. (gear) Aut première f. ◆**f.-'class** a (ticket etc) de première (classe); (mail) ordinaire; – adv (to travel) en première. ◆**f.-'hand** a & adv de première main; to have (had) f.-hand experience of avoir fait l'expérience personnelle de. ◆**f.-'rate** a excellent. ◆**firstly** adv premièrement.

fiscal ['fɪsk(ə)l] a fiscal.

fish [fɪʃ] n (pl inv or -es [-ɪz]) poisson m; f. market marché aux poissons; f. bone arête f; f. bowl bocal m; f. fingers, Am f. sticks Culin bâtonnets mpl de poisson; f. shop poissonnerie f; – vi pêcher; to f. for (salmon etc) pêcher; (compliment etc) Fig chercher; – vt pêcher; f. out (from water) repêcher; (from pocket etc) Fig sortir. ◆**–ing** n pêche f; to go f. aller à la pêche; f. net (of fisherman) filet m (de pêche); (of angler) épuisette f; f. rod canne f à pêche. ◆**fisherman** n (pl -men) pêcheur m. ◆**fishmonger** n poissonnier, -ière mf. ◆**fishy** a (-ier, -iest) (smell) de poisson; Fig Pej louche.

fission ['fɪʃ(ə)n] n Phys fission f.

fissure ['fɪʃər] n fissure f.

fist [fɪst] n poing m. ◆**fistful** n poignée f.

fit¹ [fɪt] a (fitter, fittest) (suited) propre, bon (for à); (fitting) convenable; (worthy) digne (for de); (able) capable (for de, to do à faire); (healthy) en bonne santé; f. to eat bon à manger, mangeable; to see f. to do

juger à propos de faire; as you see f. comme bon vous semble; f. to drop Fam prêt à tomber; to keep f. se maintenir en forme. 2 vt (-tt-) (of coat etc) aller (bien) à (qn); être à la taille de (qn); (match) répondre à; (equal) égaler; to f. sth on to sth (put) poser qch sur qch; (adjust) adapter qch à qch; (fix) fixer qch à qch; to f. (out or up) with (house, ship etc) équiper de; to f. (in) (window) poser; to f. in (object) faire entrer; (patient, customer) prendre; to f. (in) (go in) entrer, aller; (of facts, plans) s'accorder, cadrer (with avec); he doesn't f. in il ne peut pas s'intégrer; – n a good f. (dress etc) à la bonne taille; a close or tight f. ajusté. ◆**fitted** a (cupboard) encastré; (garment) ajusté; f. carpet moquette f; f. (kitchen) units éléments mpl de cuisine. ◆**fitting 1** a (suitable) convenable. 2 n (of clothes) essayage m; f. room salon m d'essayage; (booth) cabine f d'essayage. 3 npl (in house etc) installations fpl. ◆**fitment** n (furniture) meuble m encastré; (accessory) Tech accessoire m. ◆**fitness** n (of remark etc) à-propos m; (for job) aptitudes fpl (for pour); Med santé f. ◆**fitter** n Tech monteur, -euse mf.

fit² [fɪt] n Med & Fig accès m, crise f; in fits and starts par à-coups. ◆**fitful** a (sleep) agité.

five [faɪv] a & n cinq (m). ◆**fiver** n Fam billet m de cinq livres.

fix [fɪks] 1 vt (make firm, decide) fixer; (tie with rope) attacher; (mend) réparer; (deal with) arranger; (prepare, cook) Am préparer, faire; (in s.o.'s mind) graver (in dans); (conduct fraudulently) Fam truquer; (bribe) Fam acheter; (hopes, ambitions) mettre (on en); to f. s.o. (punish) Fam régler son compte à qn; to f. (on) (lid etc) mettre en place; to f. up arranger; to f. s.o. up with sth (job etc) procurer qch à qn. 2 n Av Nau position f; (injection) Sl piqûre f; in a f. Fam dans le pétrin. ◆**–ed** a (idea, price etc) fixe; (resolution) inébranlable; how's he f. for ...? Fam (cash etc) a-t-il assez de ...?; (tomorrow etc) qu'est-ce qu'il fait pour ...? ◆**fixings** npl Culin Am garniture f. ◆**fix'ation** n fixation f. ◆**fixer** n (schemer) Fam combinard, -arde mf. ◆**fixture 1** n Sp match m (prévu). 2 npl (in house) meubles mpl fixes, installations fpl.

fizz [fɪz] vi (of champagne) pétiller; (of gas) siffler. ◆**fizzy** a (-ier, -iest) pétillant.

fizzle ['fɪz(ə)l] vi (hiss) siffler; (of liquid) pétiller; **to f. out** (of firework) rater, faire long feu; (of plan) Fig tomber à l'eau; (of custom) disparaître.

flabbergasted ['flæbəgɑːstɪd] a Fam sidéré.

flabby ['flæbɪ] a (-ier, -iest) (skin, character, person) mou, flasque.

flag [flæg] **1** n drapeau m; Nau pavillon m; (for charity) insigne m; **f. stop** Am arrêt m facultatif; (-gg-) **to f. down** (taxi) faire signe à. **2** vi (-gg-) (of plant) dépérir; (of conversation) languir; (of worker) fléchir. ◆**flagpole** n mât m.

flagrant ['fleɪgrənt] a flagrant.

flagstone ['flægstəʊn] n dalle f.

flair [fleər] n (intuition) flair m; **to have a f. for** (natural talent) avoir un don pour.

flake [fleɪk] n (of snow etc) flocon m; (of metal, soap) paillette f; – vi **to f. (off)** (of paint) s'écailler. ◆**flaky** a **f. pastry** pâte f feuilletée.

flamboyant [flæm'bɔɪənt] a (person, manner) extravagant.

flam/e [fleɪm] n flamme f; **to go up in flames** s'enflammer; – vi **to f. (up)** (of fire, house) flamber. ◆**—ing** a **1** (sun) flamboyant. **2** (damn) Fam fichu.

flamingo [flə'mɪŋgəʊ] n (pl -os or -oes) (bird) flamant m.

flammable ['flæməb(ə)l] a inflammable.

flan [flæn] n tarte f.

flank [flæŋk] n flanc m; – vt flanquer (with de).

flannel ['flænəl] n (cloth) flanelle f; (face) f. gant m de toilette, carré-éponge m. ◆**flanne'lette** n pilou m, finette f.

flap [flæp] **1** vi (-pp-) (of wings, sail, shutter etc) battre; – vt **to f. its wings** (of bird) battre des ailes; – n battement m. **2** n (of pocket, envelope) rabat m; (of table) abattant m; (of door) battant m.

flare [fleər] n (light) éclat m; (for signalling) éclairante f; (for runway) balise f; – vi (blaze) flamber; (shine) briller; **to f. up** (of fire) s'enflammer; (of region) Fig s'embraser; (of war) éclater; (get angry) s'emporter. ◆**f.-up** n (of violence, fire) flambée f; (of region) embrasement m. ◆**flared** a (skirt) évasé; (trousers) à pattes d'éléphant.

flash [flæʃ] n (of light) éclat m; (of anger, genius) éclair m; Phot flash m; **f. of lightning** éclair m; **news f.** flash m; **in a f.** en un clin d'œil; – vi (shine) briller; (on and off) clignoter; **to f. past** (rush) Fig passer

comme un éclair; – vt (aim) diriger (on, at sur); (a light) projeter; (a glance) jeter; **to f. (around)** (flaunt) étaler; **to f. one's head-lights** faire un appel de phares. ◆**flashback** n retour m en arrière. ◆**flashlight** n lampe f électrique or de poche; Phot flash m.

flashy ['flæʃɪ] a (-ier, -iest) a voyant, tape-à-l'œil inv.

flask [flɑːsk] n thermos® m or f inv; Ch flacon m; (phial) fiole f.

flat[1] [flæt] a (flatter, flattest) plat; (tyre, battery) à plat; (nose) aplati; (beer) éventé; (refusal) net; (rate, fare) fixe; (voice) Mus faux; (razed to the ground) rasé; **to put sth (down) f.** mettre qch à plat; **f. (on one's face)** à plat ventre; **to fall f.** Fig tomber à plat; **to be f.-footed** avoir les pieds plats; – adv (to say) carrément; (to sing) faux; **f. broke** Fam complètement fauché; **in two minutes f.** en deux minutes pile; **f. out** (to work) d'arrache-pied; (to run) à toute vitesse; – n (of hand) plat m; (puncture) Aut crevaison f; Mus bémol m. ◆**—ly** adv (to deny etc) catégoriquement. ◆**—ness** n (of surface) égalité f. ◆**flatten** vt (crops) coucher; (town) raser; **to f. (out)** (metal etc) aplatir.

flat[2] [flæt] n (rooms) appartement m.

flatter ['flætər] vt flatter; (of clothes) avantager (qn). ◆**—ing** a (flatterer; (of clothes) avantageux. ◆**—er** n flatteur, -euse mf. ◆**flattery** n flatterie f.

flatulence ['flætjʊləns] n **to have f.** avoir des gaz.

flaunt [flɔːnt] vt (show off) faire étalage de; (defy) Am narguer, défier.

flautist ['flɔːtɪst] n flûtiste mf.

flavour ['fleɪvər] n (taste) goût m, saveur f; (of ice cream, sweet etc) parfum m; – vt (food) assaisonner; (sauce) relever; (ice cream etc) parfumer (with à). ◆**—ing** n assaisonnement m; (in cake) parfum m.

flaw [flɔː] n défaut m. ◆**flawed** a imparfait. ◆**flawless** a parfait.

flax [flæks] n lin m. ◆**flaxen** a de lin.

flay [fleɪ] vt (animal) écorcher; (criticize) Fig éreinter.

flea [fliː] n puce f; **f. market** marché m aux puces. ◆**fleapit** n Fam cinéma m miteux.

fleck [flek] n (mark) petite tache f.

fledgling ['fledʒlɪŋ] n (novice) blanc-bec m.

flee [fliː] vi (pt & pp fled) fuir, s'enfuir, se sauver; – vt (place) s'enfuir de; (danger etc) fuir.

fleece [fliːs] **1** n (sheep's coat) toison f. **2** vt (rob) voler.

fleet [fliːt] *n* (*of ships*) flotte *f*; **a f. of cars** un parc automobile.

fleeting ['fliːtiŋ] *a* (*visit, moment*) bref; (*beauty*) éphémère.

Flemish ['flemiʃ] *a* flamand; – *n* (*language*) flamand *m*.

flesh [fleʃ] *n* chair *f*; **her** (**own**) **f. and blood** la chair de sa chair; **in the f.** en chair et en os; **f. wound** blessure *f* superficielle. ◆**fleshy** *a* (**-ier, -iest**) charnu.

flew [fluː] *see* **fly** [2].

flex [fleks] **1** *vt* (*limb*) fléchir; (*muscle*) faire jouer, bander. **2** *n* (*wire*) fil *m* (souple); (*for telephone*) cordon *m*.

flexible ['fleksib(ə)l] *a* flexible, souple. ◆**flexi'bility** *n* flexibilité *f*.

flick [flik] *vt* donner un petit coup à; **to f. off** (*remove*) enlever (d'une chiquenaude); – *vi* **to f. over** *or* **through** (*pages*) feuilleter; – *n* petit coup *m*; (*with finger*) chiquenaude *f*; **f. knife** couteau *m* à cran d'arrêt.

flicker ['flikər] *vi* (*of flame, light*) vaciller; (*of needle*) osciller; – *n* vacillement *m*; **f. of light** lueur *f*.

flier ['flaiər] *n* **1** (*person*) aviateur, -trice *mf*. **2** (*handbill*) *Am* prospectus *m*, *Pol* tract *m*.

flies [flaiz] *npl* (*on trousers*) braguette *f*.

flight [flait] *n* **1** (*of bird, aircraft etc*) vol *m*; (*of bullet*) trajectoire *f*; (*of imagination*) élan *m*; (*floor, storey*) étage *m*; **f. of stairs** escalier *m*; **f. deck** cabine *f* de pilotage. **2** (*fleeing*) fuite *f* (**from** de); **to take f.** prendre la fuite.

flighty ['flaiti] *a* (**-ier, -iest**) inconstant, volage.

flimsy ['flimzi] *a* (**-ier, -iest**) (*cloth, structure etc*) (trop) léger *or* mince; (*excuse*) mince, frivole.

flinch [flintʃ] *vi* (*with pain*) tressaillir; **to f. from** (*duty etc*) se dérober à; **without flinching** (*complaining*) sans broncher.

fling [fliŋ] **1** *vt* (*pt & pp* **flung**) jeter, lancer; **to f. open** (*door etc*) ouvrir brutalement. **2** *n* **to have one's** *or* **a f.** (*indulge oneself*) s'en donner à cœur joie.

flint [flint] *n* silex *m*; (*for cigarette lighter*) pierre *f*.

flip [flip] **1** *vt* (**-pp-**) (*with finger*) donner une chiquenaude à; – *vi* **to f. through** (*book etc*) feuilleter; – *n* chiquenaude *f*; **the f. side** (*of record*) la face deux. **2** *a* (*cheeky*) *Am Fam* effronté.

flip-flops ['flipflops] *npl* tongs *fpl*.

flippant ['flipənt] *a* irrévérencieux; (*off-hand*) désinvolte.

flipper ['flipər] *n* (*of seal*) nageoire *f*; (*of swimmer*) palme *f*.

flipping ['flipiŋ] *a Fam* sacré; – *adv Fam* sacrément, bougrement.

flirt [fləːt] *vi* flirter (**with** avec); – *n* flirteur, -euse *mf*. ◆**flir'tation** *n* flirt *m*. ◆**flir'tatious** *a* flirteur.

flit [flit] *vi* (**-tt-**) (*fly*) voltiger; **to f. in and out** (*of person*) *Fig* entrer et sortir (rapidement).

float [fləut] *n Fishing* flotteur *m*; (*in parade*) char *m*; – *vi* flotter (**on** sur); **to f. down the river** descendre la rivière; – *vt* (*boat, currency*) faire flotter; (*loan*) *Com* émettre. ◆**—ing** *a* (*wood, debt etc*) flottant; (*population*) instable; (*voters*) indécis.

flock [flok] *n* (*of sheep etc*) troupeau *m*; (*of birds*) volée *f*; *Rel Hum* ouailles *fpl*; (*of tourists etc*) foule *f*; – *vi* venir en foule; **to f. round s.o.** s'attrouper autour de qn.

floe [fləu] *n* (**ice**) **f.** banquise *f*.

flog [flog] *vt* (**-gg-**) **1** (*beat*) flageller. **2** (*sell*) *Sl* vendre. ◆**flogging** *n* flagellation *f*.

flood [flʌd] *n* inondation *f*; (*of letters, tears etc*) *Fig* flot *m*, déluge *m*, torrent *m*; – *vt* (*field etc*) inonder (**with** de); (*river*) faire déborder; **to f. (out)** (*house*) inonder; – *vi* (*of building*) être inondé; (*of river*) déborder; (*of people, money*) affluer; **to f. into** (*of tourists etc*) envahir. ◆**—ing** *n* inondation *f*. ◆**floodgate** *n* (*in water*) vanne *f*.

floodlight ['flʌdlait] *n* projecteur *m*; – *vt* (*pt & pp* **floodlit**) illuminer; **floodlit match** *Sp* (match *m* en) nocturne *m*.

floor [flɔːr] **1** *n* (*ground*) sol *m*; (*wooden etc in building*) plancher *m*; (*storey*) étage *m*; (*dance*) piste *f* (de danse); **on the f.** par terre; **first f.** premier étage *m*; (*ground floor*) *Am* rez-de-chaussée *m inv*; **f. polish** encaustique *f*; **f. show** spectacle *m* (de cabaret). **2** *vt* (*knock down*) terrasser; (*puzzle*) stupéfier. ◆**floorboard** *n* planche *f*.

flop [flop] **1** *vi* (**-pp-**) **to f. down** (*collapse*) s'effondrer; **to f. about** s'agiter mollement. **2** *vi* (**-pp-**) *Fam* échouer; (*of play, film etc*) faire un four; – *n Fam* échec *m*, fiasco *m*; *Th Cin* four *m*.

floppy ['flopi] *a* (**-ier, -iest**) (*soft*) mou; (*clothes*) (trop) large; (*ears*) pendant; **f. disk** (*of computer*) disquette *f*.

flora ['flɔːrə] *n* (*plants*) flore *f*. ◆**floral** *a* floral; (*material*) à fleurs.

florid ['florid] *a* (*style*) fleuri; (*complexion*) rougeaud, fleuri.

florist ['florist] *n* fleuriste *mf*.

floss [flos] *n* (**dental**) **f.** fil *m* (de soie) dentaire.

flotilla [flə'tilə] *n Nau* flottille *f*.

flounce [flauns] *n* (*frill on dress etc*) volant *m*.

flounder ['flaundər] **1** *vi* (*in water etc*) patauger (avec effort), se débattre; (*in speech*) hésiter, patauger. **2** *n* (*fish*) carrelet *m*.

flour ['flauər] *n* farine *f*.

flourish ['flʌrɪʃ] **1** *vi* (*of person, business, plant etc*) prospérer; (*of the arts*) fleurir. **2** *vt* (*wave*) brandir. **3** *n* (*decoration*) fioriture *f*; *Mus* fanfare *f*. ◆**—ing** *a* prospère, florissant.

flout [flaut] *vt* narguer, braver.

flow [fləu] *vi* couler; (*of current*) El circuler; (*of hair, clothes*) flotter; (*of traffic*) s'écouler; **to f. in** (*of people, money*) affluer; **to f. back** refluer; **to f. into the sea** se jeter dans la mer; – *n* (*of river*) courant *m*; (*of tide*) flux *m*; (*of blood*) & El circulation *f*; (*of traffic, liquid*) écoulement *m*; (*of words*) *Fig* flot *m*. ◆**—ing** *a* (*movement*) gracieux; (*style*) coulant; (*beard*) flottant.

flower ['flauər] *n* fleur *f*; **f. bed** plate-bande *f*; **f. shop** (boutique *f* de) fleuriste *m*; **f. show** floralies *fpl*; – *vi* fleurir. ◆**—ed** *a* (*dress*) à fleurs. ◆**—ing** *n* floraison *f*; – *a* (*in bloom*) en fleurs; (*plant*) à fleurs. ◆**flowery** *a* (*style etc*) fleuri; (*material*) à fleurs.

flown [fləun] *see* fly[2].

flu [flu:] *n* (*influenza*) *Fam* grippe *f*.

fluctuate ['flʌktjueɪt] *vi* varier. ◆**fluctu-ation(s)** *n(pl)* (*in prices etc*) fluctuations *fpl* (in *de*).

flue [flu:] *n* (*of chimney*) conduit *m*.

fluent ['flu:ənt] *a* (*style*) aisé; **to be f., be a f. speaker** s'exprimer avec facilité; **he's f. in Russian, his Russian is f.** il parle couramment le russe. ◆**fluency** *n* facilité *f*. ◆**fluently** *adv* avec facilité; (*to speak*) *Ling* couramment.

fluff [flʌf] **1** *n* (*down*) duvet *m*; (*of material*) peluche(s) *f(pl)*; (*on floor*) moutons *mpl*. **2** *vt* (*bungle*) *Fam* rater. ◆**fluffy** *a* (-ier, -iest) (*bird etc*) duveteux; (*material*) pelucheux; (*toy*) en peluche; (*hair*) bouffant.

fluid ['flu:ɪd] *a* fluide; (*plans*) flexible, non arrêté; – *n* fluide *m*, liquide *m*.

fluke [flu:k] *n* *Fam* coup *m* de chance; **by a f.** par raccroc.

flummox ['flʌməks] *vt* *Fam* désorienter, dérouter.

flung [flʌŋ] *see* fling 1.

flunk [flʌŋk] *vi* (*in exam*) *Am* *Fam* être collé; – *vt* *Am* *Fam* (*pupil*) coller; (*exam*) être collé à; (*school*) laisser tomber.

flunk(e)y ['flʌŋkɪ] *n* *Pej* larbin *m*.

fluorescent [fluə'res(ə)nt] *a* fluorescent.

fluoride ['fluəraɪd] *n* (*in water, toothpaste*) fluor *m*.

flurry ['flʌrɪ] *n* **1** (*of activity*) poussée *f*. **2** (*of snow*) rafale *f*.

flush [flʌʃ] **1** *n* (*of blood*) flux *m*; (*blush*) rougeur *f*; (*of youth, beauty*) éclat *m*; (*of victory*) ivresse *f*; – *vi* (*blush*) rougir. **2** *vt* **to f. (out)** (*clean*) nettoyer à grande eau; **to f. the pan** *or* **the toilet** tirer la chasse d'eau; **to f. s.o. out** (*chase away*) faire sortir qn (from *de*). **3** *a* (*level*) de niveau (with *avec*). **f. (with money)** *Fam* bourré de fric. ◆**—ed** *a* (*cheeks etc*) rouge; **f. with** (*success*) ivre de.

fluster ['flʌstər] *vt* énerver; **to get flustered** s'énerver.

flute [flu:t] *n* flûte *f*. ◆**flutist** *n* *Am* flûtiste *mf*.

flutter ['flʌtər] **1** *vi* voltiger; (*of wing*) battre; (*of flag*) flotter (mollement); (*of heart*) palpiter; **to f. about** (*of person*) papillonner; – *vt* **to f. its wings** battre des ailes. **2** *n* **to have a f.** (*bet*) *Fam* parier.

flux [flʌks] *n* changement *m* continuel.

fly[1] [flaɪ] *n* (*insect*) mouche *f*; **f. swatter** (*instrument*) tapette *f*. ◆**flypaper** *n* papier *m* tue-mouches.

fly[2] [flaɪ] *vi* (*pt* **flew**, *pp* **flown**) (*of bird, aircraft etc*) voler; (*of passenger*) aller en avion; (*of time*) passer vite; (*of flag*) flotter; (*flee*) fuir; **to f. away** *or* **off** s'envoler; **to f. out** *Av* partir en avion; (*from home*) sortir à toute vitesse; **I must f.!** il faut que je file!; **to f. at s.o.** (*attack*) sauter sur qn; – *vt* (*aircraft*) piloter; (*passengers*) transporter (par avion); (*airline*) voyager par; (*flag*) arborer; (*kite*) faire voler; **to f. the French flag** battre pavillon français; **to f. across** *or* **over** survoler. ◆**—ing** *n* (*flight*) vol *m*; (*air travel*) aviation *f*; **to like to f.** aimer l'avion; – *a* (*personnel, saucer etc*) volant; (*visit*) éclair *inv*; **with f. colours** (*to succeed*) haut la main; **a f. start** un très bon départ; **f. time** (*length*) *Av* durée *f* du vol; **ten hours'/etc f. time** dix heures/etc de vol. ◆**—er** *n* = flier. ◆**flyby** *n* *Av* *Am* défilé *m* aérien. ◆**fly-by-night** *a* (*firm*) véreux. ◆**flyover** *n* (*bridge*) toboggan *m*. ◆**flypast** *n* *Av* défilé *m* aérien.

fly[3] [flaɪ] *n* (*on trousers*) braguette *f*.

foal [fəul] *n* poulain *m*.

foam [fəum] *n* (*on sea, mouth*) écume *f*; (*on beer*) mousse *f*; **f. rubber** caoutchouc *m* mousse; **f. (rubber) mattress/etc** matelas *m/etc* mousse; – *vi* (*of sea, mouth*) écumer; (*of beer, soap*) mousser.

fob [fɒb] vt (-bb-) to f. sth off on s.o., f. s.o. off with sth, refiler qch à qn.

focal ['fəʊk(ə)l] a focal; **f. point** point m central. ◆**focus** n foyer m; (of attention, interest) centre m; **in f.** au point; — vt Phot mettre au point; (light) faire converger; (efforts, attention) concentrer (on sur); — vi (converge) converger (on sur); **to f. (one's eyes) on** fixer les yeux sur; **to f. on** (direct one's attention to) se concentrer sur.

fodder ['fɒdər] n fourrage m.

foe [fəʊ] n ennemi, -ie mf.

foetus ['fiːtəs] n fœtus m.

fog [fɒg] n brouillard m, brume f; — vt (-gg-) (issue) Fig embrouiller. ◆**fogbound** a bloqué par le brouillard. ◆**foghorn** n corne f de brume; (voice) Pej voix f toni-truante. ◆**foglamp** n (phare m) anti-brouillard m. ◆**foggy** a (-ier, -iest) (day) de brouillard; **it's f.** il fait du brouillard; **f. weather** brouillard m; **she hasn't the foggiest (idea)** Fam elle n'en a pas la moindre idée.

fog(e)y ['fəʊgɪ] n **old f.** vieille baderne f.

foible ['fɔɪb(ə)l] n petit défaut m.

foil [fɔɪl] n 1 feuille f de métal; Culin papier m alu(minium). **2** n (contrasting person) repoussoir m. **3** vt (plans etc) déjouer.

foist [fɔɪst] vt **to f. sth on s.o.** (fob off) refiler qch à qn; **to f. oneself on s.o.** s'imposer à qn.

fold [fəʊld] 1 n pli m; — vt plier; (wrap) envelopper (in dans); **to f. away** or **down** or **up** plier; **to f. back** or **over** replier; **to f. one's arms** (se) croiser les bras; — vi (of chair etc) se plier; (of business) Fam s'écrouler; **to f. away** or **down** or **up** (of chair etc) se plier; **to f. back** or **over** (of blanket etc) se replier. ◆**—ing** a (chair etc) pliant. ◆**—er** n (file holder) chemise f; (pamphlet) dépliant m.

fold [fəʊld] n (for sheep) parc m à moutons; Rel Fig bercail m.

-fold [fəʊld] suffix **tenfold** a par dix; — adv dix fois.

foliage ['fəʊlɪɪdʒ] n feuillage m.

folk [fəʊk] n gens mpl or fpl; pl gens mpl or fpl; (parents) Fam parents mpl; **hello folks!** Fam salut tout le monde!; **old f.** like it les vieux l'apprécient. **2** a (dance etc) folklorique; **f. music** (contemporary) (musique f) folk m. ◆**folklore** n folklore m.

follow ['fɒləʊ] vt suivre; (career) pour-suivre; **followed by** suivi de; **to f. suit** Fig en faire autant; **to f. s.o. around** suivre qn partout; **to f. through** (idea etc) poursuivre jusqu'au bout; **to f. up** (suggestion, case) suivre; (advantage) exploiter; (letter) donner suite à; (remark) faire suivre (with de); — vi **to f. (on)** suivre; **it follows that** il s'ensuit que; **that doesn't f.** ce n'est pas logique. ◆**—ing 1** a suivant; — prep à la suite de. **2** n (supporters) partisans mpl; **to have a large f.** avoir de nombreux partisans; (of serial, fashion) être très suivi. ◆**—er** n partisan m. ◆**follow-up** n suite f; (letter) rappel m.

folly ['fɒlɪ] n folie f, sottise f.

foment [fəʊ'ment] vt (revolt etc) fomenter.

fond [fɒnd] a (-er, -est) (loving) tendre, affectueux; (doting) indulgent; (wish, ambi-tion) naïf; **to be (very) f. of** aimer (beaucoup). ◆**—ly** adv tendrement. ◆**—ness** n (for things) prédilection f (for pour); (for people) affection f (for pour).

fondle ['fɒnd(ə)l] vt caresser.

food [fuːd] n nourriture f; (particular substance) aliment m; (cooking) cuisine f; (for cats, pigs) pâtée f; (for plants) engrais m; pl (foodstuffs) aliments mpl; — a (needs etc) alimentaire; **a fast f. shop** un fast-food; **f. poisoning** intoxication f alimentaire; **f. value** valeur f nutritive. ◆**foodstuffs** npl denrées fpl or produits mpl alimentaires.

fool [fuːl] n imbécile mf, idiot, -ote mf; (you silly f.) espèce d'imbécile!; **to make a f. of** (ridicule) ridiculiser; (trick) duper; **to be f. enough to do** être assez stupide pour faire; **to play the f.** faire l'imbécile; — vt (trick) duper; — vi **to f. (about** or **around)** faire l'imbécile; (waste time) perdre son temps; **to f. around** (make love) Am Fam faire l'amour (with avec). ◆**foolish** a bête, idiot. ◆**foolishly** adv bêtement. ◆**foolishness** n bêtise f, sottise f. ◆**foolproof** a (scheme etc) infaillible.

foolhardy ['fuːlhɑːdɪ] a téméraire. ◆**foolhardiness** n témérité f.

foot [fʊt], pl **feet** [fʊt, fiːt] n pied m; (of animal) patte f; (measure) pied m (= 30,48 cm), at **the f. of** (page, stairs) au bas de; (table) au bout de; **on f.** à pied; **on one's feet** (stand-ing) debout; (recovered) Med sur pied; **f. brake** Aut frein m au plancher; **f.-and-mouth disease** fièvre f aphteuse. ◆**footbridge** n passerelle f. ◆**foothills** npl contreforts mpl. ◆**foothold** n prise f (de pied); Fig position f; **to gain a f.** prendre pied. ◆**footlights** npl Th rampe f. ◆**footloose** a libre de toute attache. ◆**footman** n (pl **-men**) valet m de pied. ◆**footmark** n empreinte f (de pied). ◆**footnote** n note f au bas de la page; Fig post-scriptum m. ◆**footpath** n sentier m; (at roadside) chemin m (piétonnier). ◆**footstep** n pas m; **to follow in s.o.'s footsteps** suivre les traces de qn. ◆**footwear** n chaussures fpl.

foot² [fut] vt (bill) payer.

football ['futbɔːl] n (game) football m; (ball) ballon m. ◆**footballer** n joueur, -euse mf de football.

footing ['futiŋ] n prise f (de pied); Fig position f; **on a war f.** sur le pied de guerre; **on an equal f.** sur un pied d'égalité.

for [fɔr, unstressed fər] **1** prep pour; (in exchange for) contre; (for a distance of) pendant; (in spite of) malgré; **f. you/me/etc** pour toi/moi/etc; **what f.?** pourquoi?; **what is it f.?** ça sert à quoi?; **f. example** par exemple; **f. love** par amour; **f. sale** à vendre; **to swim f.** (towards) nager vers; **a train f.** un train à destination de or en direction de; **the road f. London** la route (en direction) de Londres; **fit f. eating** bon à manger; **eager f.** avide de; **to look f.** chercher; **to come f. dinner** venir dîner; **to sell f. £7** vendre sept livres; **what's the Russian f. 'book'?** comment dit-on 'livre' en russe?; **but f. her** sans elle; **he was away f. a month** (throughout) il a été absent pendant un mois; **he won't be back f. a month** il ne sera pas de retour avant un mois; **he's been here f. a month** (he's still here) il est ici depuis un mois; **I haven't seen him f. ten years** voilà dix ans que je ne l'ai vu; **it's easy f. her to do it** il lui est facile de le faire; **it's f. you to say** c'est à toi de dire; **f. that to be done** pour que ça soit fait. **2** conj (because) car.

forage ['fɔridʒ] vi **to f.** (about) fourrager (for pour trouver).

foray ['fɔrei] n incursion f.

forbearance [fɔːˈbeərəns] n patience f.

forbid [fəˈbid] vt (pt forbad(e), pp forbidden, pres p forbidding) interdire, défendre (s.o. to do à qn de faire); **to f. s.o. sth** interdire or défendre qch à qn. ◆**forbidden** a (fruit etc) défendu; **she is f. to leave** il lui est interdit de partir. ◆**forbidding** a menaçant, sinistre.

force [fɔːs] n force f; **the (armed) forces** Mil les forces armées; **by (sheer) f.** de force; **in f.** (rule) en vigueur; (in great numbers) en grand nombre, en force; — vt contraindre, forcer (**to do** à faire); (impose) imposer (**on** à); (push) pousser; (lock) forcer; (confession) arracher (**from** à); **to f. back** (enemy etc) faire reculer; (repress) refouler; **to f. down** (aircraft) forcer à atterrir; **to f. out**

faire sortir de force. ◆**forced** a forcé (**to do** de faire); **a f. smile** un sourire forcé. ◆**force-feed** vt (pt & pp f.-fed) nourrir de force. ◆**forceful** a énergique, puissant. ◆**forcefully** adv avec force, énergiquement. ◆**forcible** a de force; (forceful) énergique. ◆**forcibly** adv (by force) de force.

forceps ['fɔːseps] n forceps m.

ford [fɔːd] n gué m; — vt (river etc) passer à gué.

fore [fɔːr] n **to come to the f.** se mettre en évidence.

forearm ['fɔːrɑːm] n avant-bras m inv.

forebod/e [fɔːˈbəud] vt (be a warning of) présager. ◆**—ing** n (feeling) pressentiment m.

forecast ['fɔːkɑːst] vt (pt & pp forecast) prévoir; — n prévision f; Met prévisions fpl; Sp pronostic m.

forecourt ['fɔːkɔːt] n avant-cour f; (of filling station) aire f (de service), devant m.

forefathers ['fɔːfɑːðəz] npl aïeux mpl.

forefinger ['fɔːfiŋgər] n index m.

forefront ['fɔːfrʌnt] n **in the f.** of au premier rang de.

forego [fɔːˈgəu] vt (pp foregone) renoncer à. ◆**'foregone** a **it's a f. conclusion** c'est couru d'avance.

foreground ['fɔːgraund] n premier plan m.

forehead ['fɔrid, 'fɔːhed] n (brow) front m.

foreign ['fɔrən] a étranger; (trade) extérieur; (travel, correspondent) à l'étranger; (produce) de l'étranger; **F. Minister** ministre m des Affaires étrangères. ◆**foreigner** n étranger, -ère mf.

foreman ['fɔːmən] n (pl -men) (worker) contremaître m; (of jury) président m.

foremost ['fɔːməust] **1** a principal. **2** adv **first and f.** tout d'abord.

forensic [fəˈrensik] a (medicine) légal; (laboratory) médico-légal.

forerunner ['fɔːrʌnər] n précurseur m.

foresee [fɔːˈsiː] vt (pt foresaw, pp foreseen) prévoir. ◆**—able** a prévisible.

foreshadow [fɔːˈʃædəu] vt présager.

foresight ['fɔːsait] n prévoyance f.

forest ['fɔrist] n forêt f. ◆**forester** n (garde m) forestier m.

forestall [fɔːˈstɔːl] vt prévenir.

foretaste ['fɔːteist] n avant-goût m.

foretell [fɔːˈtel] vt (pt & pp foretold) prédire.

forethought ['fɔːθɔːt] n prévoyance f.

forever [fəˈrevər] adv (for always) pour toujours; (continually) sans cesse.

forewarn [fɔːˈwɔːn] vt avertir.

foreword ['fɔːwɜːd] n avant-propos m inv.

forfeit ['fɔːfɪt] vt (lose) perdre; – n (penalty) peine f; (in game) gage m.

forg/e [fɔːdʒ] **1** vt (signature, money) contrefaire; (document) falsifier. **2** vt (friendship, bond) forger. **3** vi to f. ahead (progress) aller de l'avant. **4** vt (metal) forger; – n forge f. ◆**—er** n (of banknotes etc) faussaire m. ◆**forgery** n faux m, contrefaçon f.

forget [fə'get] vt (pt forgot, pp forgotten, pres p forgetting) oublier (to do de faire); f. it! Fam (when thanked) pas de quoi!; (it doesn't matter) peu importe!; to f. oneself s'oublier; – vi oublier; to f. about oublier. ◆**f.-me-not** n Bot myosotis m. ◆**forgetful** a to be f. (of) oublier, être oublieux (de). ◆**forgetfulness** n manque m de mémoire; (carelessness) négligence f; in a moment of f. dans un moment d'oubli.

forgiv/e [fə'gɪv] vt (pt forgave, pp forgiven) pardonner (s.o. sth qch à qn). ◆**—ing** a indulgent. ◆**forgiveness** n pardon m; (compassion) clémence f.

forgo [fɔː'gəʊ] vt (pp forgone) renoncer à.

fork [fɔːk] **1** n (for eating) fourchette f; (for garden etc) fourche f. **2** vi (of road) bifurquer; to f. left (in vehicle) prendre à gauche; – n bifurcation f, fourche f. **3** vt to f. out (money) Fam allonger; – vi to f. out (pay) Fam casquer. ◆**—ed** a fourchu. ◆**forklift truck** n chariot m élévateur.

forlorn [fə'lɔːn] a (forsaken) abandonné; (unhappy) triste, affligé.

form [fɔːm] n (shape, type, style) forme f; (document) formulaire m; Sch classe f; it's good f. c'est ce qui se fait; in the f. of en forme de; a f. of speech une façon de parler; on f., in good f. en (pleine) forme; – vt (group, character etc) former; (clay) façonner; (habit) contracter; (an opinion) se former; (constitute) constituer, former; to f. part of faire partie de; – vi (appear) se former. ◆**for'mation** n formation f. ◆**formative** a formateur.

formal ['fɔːm(ə)l] a (person, tone etc) cérémonieux; (stuffy) Pej compassé; (official) officiel; (in due form) en bonne et due forme; (denial, structure, logic) formel; (resemblance) extérieur; f. dress tenue f or habit m de cérémonie; f. education éducation f scolaire. ◆**for'mality** n cérémonie f; (requirement) formalité f. ◆**formally** adv (to declare etc) officiellement; f. dressed en tenue de cérémonie.

format ['fɔːmæt] n format m.

former ['fɔːmər] **1** a (previous) ancien; (situ-

ation) antérieur; her f. husband son ex-mari m; in f. days autrefois. **2** a (of two) premier; – pron the f. celui-là, celle-là, le premier, la première. ◆**—ly** adv autrefois.

formidable ['fɔːmɪdəb(ə)l] a effroyable, terrible.

formula ['fɔːmjʊlə] n (1 (pl -as or -ae [-iː]) formule f. **2** (pl -as) (baby's feed) Am mélange m lacté. ◆**formulate** vt formuler. ◆**formu'lation** n formulation f.

forsake [fə'seɪk] vt (pt forsook, pp forsaken) abandonner.

fort [fɔːt] n Hist Mil fort m; to hold the f. (in s.o.'s absence) Fam prendre la relève.

forte ['fɔːteɪ, Am fɔːt] n (strong point) fort m.

forth [fɔːθ] adv en avant; from this day f. désormais; and so f. et ainsi de suite.

forthcoming [fɔːθ'kʌmɪŋ] a **1** (event) à venir; (book, film) qui va sortir; my f. book mon prochain livre. **2** (available) disponible. **3** (open) communicatif; (helpful) serviable.

forthright ['fɔːθraɪt] a direct, franc.

forthwith [fɔːθ'wɪθ] adv sur-le-champ.

fortieth ['fɔːtɪəθ] a & n quarantième (mf).

fortify ['fɔːtɪfaɪ] vt (strengthen) fortifier; to f. s.o. (of food, drink) réconforter qn, remonter qn. ◆**fortifi'cation** n fortification f.

fortitude ['fɔːtɪtjuːd] n courage m (moral).

fortnight ['fɔːtnaɪt] n quinze jours mpl, quinzaine f. ◆**—ly** adv bimensuel; – adv tous les quinze jours.

fortress ['fɔːtrɪs] n forteresse f.

fortuitous [fɔː'tjuːɪtəs] a fortuit.

fortunate ['fɔːtʃənɪt] a (choice, event etc) heureux; to be f. (of person) avoir de la chance; it's f. (for her) that c'est heureux (pour elle) que. ◆**—ly** adv heureusement.

fortune ['fɔːtʃuːn] n (wealth) fortune f; (luck) chance f; (chance) sort, hasard m, fortune f; to have the good f. to avoir la chance or le bonheur de; to tell s.o.'s f. dire la bonne aventure à qn; to make one's f. faire fortune. ◆**f.-teller** n diseur, -euse mf de bonne aventure.

forty ['fɔːtɪ] a & n quarante (m).

forum ['fɔːrəm] n forum m.

forward ['fɔːwəd] adv forward(s) en avant; to go f. avancer; from this time f. désormais; – a (movement) en avant; (gears) Aut avant inv; (child) Fig précoce; (pert) effronté; – n Fb avant m; – vt (letter) faire suivre; (goods) expédier. ◆**—ness** n précocité f; effronterie f. ◆**forward-looking** a tourné vers l'avenir.

fossil ['fɒs(ə)l] n & a fossile (m).

foster ['fɒstər] 1 *vt* encourager; *(hope)* nourrir. 2 *vt (child)* élever; – *a (child, family)* adoptif.

fought [fɔːt] *see* fight.

foul [faul] 1 *a* (-er, -est) infect; *(air)* vicié; *(breath)* fétide; *(language)* grossier; *(action, place)* immonde; **to be f.-mouthed** avoir un langage grossier. 2 *n Sp* coup *m* irrégulier; Fb faute *f*; – a **f. play** Sp jeu *m* irrégulier; Jur acte *m* criminel. 3 *vt* to **f.** (up) salir; *(air)* vicier; *(drain)* encrasser; **to f. up** *(life, plans)* Fam gâcher. ◆**f.-up** *n (in system)* Fam raté *m*.

found[1] [faund] *see* find.

found[2] [faund] *vt (town, opinion etc)* fonder (on sur). ◆**—er**[1] *n* fondateur, -trice *mf*. ◆**foun'dation** *n* fondation *f*; *(basis)* Fig base *f*, fondement *m*; **without f.** sans fondement; **f. cream** fond *m* de teint.

founder[2] ['faundər] *vi (of ship)* sombrer.

foundry ['faundri] *n* fonderie *f*.

fountain ['fauntin] *n* fontaine *f*; **f. pen** stylo(-plume) *m*.

four [fɔːr] *a & n* quatre (*m*); **on all fours** à quatre pattes; **the Big F.** Pol les quatre Grands; **f.-letter word** = mot *m* de cinq lettres. ◆**fourfold** *a* quadruple; – *adv* au quadruple. ◆**foursome** *n* deux couples *mpl*. ◆**four'teen** *a & n* quatorze (*m*). ◆**fourth** *a & n* quatrième (*mf*).

fowl [faul] *n (hens)* volaille *f*; **a f.** une volaille.

fox [fɒks] 1 *n* renard *m*. 2 *vt (puzzle)* mystifier; *(trick)* tromper. ◆**foxy** *a (sly)* rusé, futé.

foxglove ['fɒksglʌv] *n* Bot digitale *f*.

foyer ['fɔɪeɪ] *n* Th foyer *m*; *(in hotel)* hall *m*.

fraction ['frækʃ(ə)n] *n* fraction *f*. ◆**fractionally** *adv* un tout petit peu.

fractious ['frækʃəs] *a* grincheux.

fracture ['fræktʃər] *n* fracture *f*; – *vt* fracturer; **to f. one's leg/etc** se fracturer la jambe/*etc*; – *vi* se fracturer.

fragile ['frædʒaɪl, *Am* 'frædʒ(ə)l] *a* fragile. ◆**fra'gility** *n* fragilité *f*.

fragment ['frægmənt] *n* fragment *m*, morceau *m*. ◆**frag'mented** *a*, ◆**fragmentary** *a* fragmentaire.

fragrant ['freɪgrənt] *a* parfumé. ◆**fragrance** *n* parfum *m*.

frail [freɪl] *a* (-er, -est) *(person)* frêle, fragile; *(hope, health)* fragile. ◆**frailty** *n* fragilité *f*.

frame [freɪm] 1 *n (of person, building)* charpente *f*; *(of picture, bicycle)* cadre *m*; *(of window, car)* châssis *m*; *(of spectacles)* monture *f*; **f. of mind** humeur *f*; – *vt (picture)* encadrer; *(proposals etc)* Fig

formuler. 2 *vt* **to f. s.o.** Fam monter un coup contre qn. ◆**f.-up** *n* Fam coup *m* monté. ◆**framework** *n* structure *f*; **(with)in the f. of** *(context)* dans le cadre de.

franc [fræŋk] *n* franc *m*.

France [frɑːns] *n* France *f*.

franchise ['fræntʃaɪz] *n* 1 Pol droit *m* de vote. 2 *(right to sell product)* Com franchise *f*.

Franco- ['fræŋkəʊ] *pref* franco-.

frank [fræŋk] 1 *a* (-er, -est) *(honest)* franc. 2 *vt (letter)* affranchir. ◆**-ly** *adv* franchement. ◆**-ness** *n* franchise *f*.

frankfurter ['fræŋkfɜːtər] *n* saucisse *f* de Francfort.

frantic ['fræntɪk] *a (activity, shout)* frénétique; *(rush, desire)* effréné; *(person)* hors de soi; **f. with joy** fou de joie. ◆**frantically** *adv* comme un fou.

fraternal [frə'tɜːn(ə)l] *a* fraternel. ◆**fraternity** *n (bond)* fraternité *f*; *(society)* & Univ *Am* confrérie *f*. ◆**fraternize** ['frætənaɪz] *vi* fraterniser (with avec).

fraud [frɔːd] *n* 1 Jur fraude *f*. 2 *(person)* imposteur *m*. ◆**fraudulent** *a* frauduleux.

fraught [frɔːt] *a* **f. with** plein de, chargé de; **to be f.** *(of situation)* être tendu; *(of person)* Fam être contrarié.

fray [freɪ] 1 *vt (garment)* effilocher; *(rope)* user; – *vi* s'effilocher; s'user. 2 *n (fight)* rixe *f*. ◆**-ed** *a (nerves)* Fig tendu.

freak [friːk] *n (person)* phénomène *m*, monstre *m*; **a jazz/etc f.** Fam un(e) fana de jazz/*etc*; – *a (result, weather etc)* anormal. ◆**freakish** *a* anormal.

freckle ['frek(ə)l] *n* tache *f* de rousseur. ◆**freckled** *a* couvert de taches de rousseur.

free [friː] *a* (freer, freest) *(at liberty, not occupied)* libre; *(gratis)* gratuit; *(lavish)* généreux (with de); **to get f.** se libérer; **f. to do** libre de faire; **to let s.o. go f.** relâcher qn; **f. of charge** gratuit; **f. of** *(without)* sans; **f. of s.o.** *(rid of)* débarrassé de qn; **to have a f. hand** Fig avoir carte blanche (**to do** pour faire); **f. and easy** décontracté; **f. trade** libre-échange *m*; **f. speech** liberté *f* d'expression; **f. kick** Fb coup *m* franc; **f.-range egg** œuf *m* de ferme; – *adv* **f.** (of charge) gratuitement; – *vt (pt & pp* freed) *(prisoner etc)* libérer; *(trapped person, road)* dégager; *(country)* affranchir, libérer; *(untie)* détacher. ◆**Freefone**® Tel = numéro *m* vert. ◆**free-for-'all** *n* mêlée *f* générale. ◆**freehold** *n* propriété *f* foncière libre. ◆**freelance** *a* indépendant; – *n* collaborateur, -trice *mf* indépendant(e). ◆**freeloader** n (sponger) Am parasite m. ◆**Freemason** n franc-maçon m. ◆**Freemasonry** n franc-maçonnerie f. ◆**freestyle** n Swimming nage f libre. ◆**free'thinker** n libre penseur, -euse mf. ◆**freeway** n Am autoroute f.

freedom ['fri:dəm] n liberté f; f. from (worry, responsibility) absence f de.

freely ['fri:li] adv (to speak, circulate etc) librement; (to give) libéralement.

freez/e [fri:z] vi (pt froze, pp frozen) geler; (of value) Fig se figer; Culin se congeler; to f. to death mourir de froid; to f. up or over geler; (of windscreen) se givrer; – vt Culin congeler, surgeler; (credits, river) geler; (prices, wages) bloquer; **frozen food** surgelés mpl; – n Met gel m; (of prices etc) blocage m. ◆**—ing** a (weather etc) glacial; (hands, person) gelé; **it's f. on gèle**; – n below f. au-dessous de zéro. ◆**—er** n (deep-freeze) congélateur m; (in fridge) freezer m.

freight [freit] n (goods, price) fret m; (transport) transport m; **f. train** Am train m de marchandises; – vt (ship) affréter. ◆**—er** n (ship) cargo m.

French [frentʃ] a français; (teacher) de français; (embassy) de France; **F. fries** Am frites fpl; **the F. les Français** mpl; – n (language) français m. ◆**Frenchman** n (pl -men) Français m. ◆**French-speaking** a francophone. ◆**Frenchwoman** n (pl -women) Française f.

frenzy ['frenzi] n frénésie f. ◆**frenzied** a (shouts etc) frénétique; (person) effréné; (attack) violent.

frequent [ˈfriːkwənt] a fréquent; **f. visitor** habitué, -ée mf (to de); – [friˈkwent] vt fréquenter. ◆**frequency** n fréquence f. ◆**frequently** adv fréquemment.

fresco [ˈfreskəʊ] n (pl -oes or -os) fresque f.

fresh [freʃ] 1 a (-er, -est) frais; (new) nouveau; (impudent) Fam culotté; **to get some f. air** prendre le frais; **f. water** eau f douce. 2 adv **f. from** fraîchement arrivé de; **f. out of** or **f. from** (university) frais émoulu de. ◆**freshen** 1 vi (of wind) fraîchir. 2 vi to **f. up** faire un brin de toilette; – vt to **f. up** (house etc) retaper; to **f. s.o. up** (of bath) rafraîchir qn. ◆**freshener** n air f. désodorisant m. ◆**freshman** n (pl -men) étudiant, -ante mf de première année. ◆**freshness** n fraîcheur f; (cheek) Fam culot m.

fret [fret] vi (-tt-) (worry) se faire du souci, s'en faire; (of baby) pleurer. ◆**fretful** a (baby etc) grognon.

friar [ˈfraɪər] n frère m, moine m.

friction [ˈfrɪkʃ(ə)n] n friction f.

Friday [ˈfraɪdɪ] n vendredi m.

fridge [frɪdʒ] n Fam frigo m.

fried [fraɪd] pt & pp of **fry** 1; – a (fish etc) frit; **f. egg** œuf m sur le plat. ◆**frier** n (pan) friteuse f.

friend [frend] n ami, -ie mf; (from school, work) camarade mf; **to be friends with** être ami avec; **to make friends** se lier (with avec). ◆**friendly** a (-ier, -iest) amical; (child, animal) gentil, affectueux; (kind) gentil; **some f. advice** un conseil d'ami; **to be f. with** être ami avec. ◆**friendship** n amitié f.

frieze [fri:z] n Archit frise f.

frigate [ˈfrɪgət] n (ship) frégate f.

fright [fraɪt] n peur f; (person, hat etc) Fig Fam horreur f; **to have a f.** avoir peur; **to give s.o. a f.** faire peur à qn. ◆**frighten** vt effrayer, faire peur à; **to f. away** or **off** (animal) effaroucher; (person) chasser. ◆**frightened** a effrayé; **to be f.** avoir peur (of de). ◆**frightening** a effrayant. ◆**frightful** a affreux. ◆**frightfully** adv (ugly, late) affreusement; (kind, glad) terriblement.

frigid [ˈfrɪdʒɪd] a (air, greeting etc) froid; Psy frigide.

frill [frɪl] n Tex volant m; pl (fuss) Fig manières fpl, chichis mpl; (useless embellishments) fioritures fpl, superflu m; **no frills** (spartan) spartiate.

fringe [frɪndʒ] 1 n (of hair, clothes etc) frange f. 2 n (of forest) lisière f; **on the fringe(s) of society** en marge de la société; – a (group, theatre) marginal; **f. benefits** avantages mpl divers.

frisk [frɪsk] 1 vt (search) fouiller (au corps). 2 vi to f. (about) gambader. ◆**frisky** a (-ier, -iest) a vif.

fritter [ˈfrɪtər] 1 vt to **f. away** (waste) gaspiller. 2 n Culin beignet m.

frivolous [ˈfrɪvələs] a frivole. ◆**fri'volity** n frivolité f.

frizzy [ˈfrɪzɪ] a (hair) crépu.

fro [frəʊ] adv **to go to and f.** aller et venir.

frock [frɒk] n (dress) robe f; (of monk) froc m.

frog [frɒg] n grenouille f; **a f. in one's throat** Fig un chat dans la gorge. ◆**frogman** n (pl -men) homme-grenouille m.

frolic [ˈfrɒlɪk] vi (pt & pp frolicked) to f. (about) gambader; – npl (capers) ébats mpl; (pranks) gamineries fpl.

from [frɒm, unstressed frəm] prep 1 de; a letter f. une lettre de; **to suffer f.** souffrir de;

where are you f.? d'où êtes-vous?; **a train f.** un train en provenance de; **to be ten metres (away) f. the house** être à dix mètres de la maison. **2** (time onwards) à partir de, dès, depuis; **f. today (on), as f. today** à partir d'aujourd'hui, dès aujourd'hui; **f. her childhood** dès or depuis son enfance. **3** (numbers, prices onwards) à partir de; **f. five francs** à partir de cinq francs. **4** (away from) à; **to take/hide/borrow f.** prendre/cacher/emprunter à. **5** (out of) dans; sur; **to take f.** (box) prendre dans; (table) prendre sur; **to drink f. a cup**/etc boire dans une tasse/etc; **to drink (straight) f. the bottle** boire à (même) la bouteille. **6** (according to) d'après; **f. what I saw** d'après ce que j'ai vu. **7** (cause) par; **f. conviction/habit**/etc par conviction/habitude/ etc. **8** (on the part of, on behalf of) de la part de; **tell her f. me** dis-lui de ma part.

front [frʌnt] n (of garment, building) devant m; (of boat, car) avant m; (of crowd) premier rang m; (of book) début m; Mil Pol Met front m; (beach) front m de mer; (appearance) Fig façade f; **in f. (of)** devant; **in f.** (ahead) en avant; Sp en tête; **in the f.** (of vehicle) à l'avant; (of house) devant; **– a** (tooth etc) de devant; (part, wheel, car seat) avant inv; (row, page) premier; (view) de face; **f. door** porte f d'entrée; **f. line** Mil front m; **f. room** (lounge) salon m; **f. runner** Fig favori, -ite mf; **f.-wheel drive** (on vehicle) traction f avant; **– vi to f. on to** (of windows etc) donner sur. **◆frontage** n façade f. **◆frontal** a (attack) de front.

frontier ['frʌntɪər] n frontière f; **– a** (town, post) frontière inv.

frost [frɒst] n gel m, gelée f; (frozen drops on glass, grass etc) gelée f blanche, givre m; **– vi to f. up** (of windscreen etc) se givrer. **◆frostbite** n gelure f. **◆frostbitten** a gelé. **◆frosty** a (-ier, -iest) glacial; (window) givré; **it's f.** il gèle.

frosted ['frɒstɪd] a (glass) dépoli.

frosting ['frɒstɪŋ] n (icing) Culin glaçage m.

froth [frɒθ] n mousse f; **– vi** mousser. **◆frothy** a (-ier, -iest) (beer etc) mousseux.

frown [fraʊn] n froncement m de sourcils; **– vi** froncer les sourcils; **to f. (up)on** Fig désapprouver.

froze, frozen [frəʊz, 'frəʊz(ə)n] see **freeze**.

frugal ['fruːg(ə)l] a (meal) frugal; (thrifty) parcimonieux. **◆–ly** adv parcimonieusement.

fruit [fruːt] n fruit m; (some) (one item) un fruit; (more than one) des fruits; **– a**

(basket) à fruits; (drink) aux fruits; (salad) de fruits; **f. tree** arbre m fruitier. **◆fruit-cake** n cake m. **◆fruiterer** n fruitier, -ière mf. **◆fruitful** a (meeting, career etc) fructueux, fécond. **◆fruitless** a stérile. **◆fruity** a (-ier, -iest) a fruité, de fruit; (joke) Fig Fam corsé.

fruition [fruːˈɪʃ(ə)n] n **to come to f.** se réaliser.

frumpish ['frʌmpɪʃ] a, **frumpy** ['frʌmpɪ] a Fam (mal) fagoté.

frustrat/e [frʌˈstreɪt] vt (person) frustrer; (plans) faire échouer. **◆–ed** a (mentally, sexually) frustré; (effort) vain. **◆–ing** a irritant. **◆fru'stration** n frustration f; (disappointment) déception f.

fry [fraɪ] **1** vt (faire) frire; **– vi** frire. **2** n small f. menu fretin m. **◆–ing** n friture f; **f. pan** poêle f (à frire). **◆–er** n (pan) friteuse f.

ft abbr (measure) = **foot, feet.**

fuddled ['fʌd(ə)ld] a (drunk) gris; (confused) embrouillé.

fuddy-duddy ['fʌdɪdʌdɪ] n **he's an old f.-duddy** Fam il est vieux jeu.

fudge [fʌdʒ] **1** n (sweet) caramel m mou. **2** vt **to f. the issue** refuser d'aborder le problème.

fuel [fjuəl] n combustible m; Aut carburant m; **f. (oil)** mazout m; **– vt** (-ll-, Am -l-) (stove) alimenter; (ship) ravitailler (en combustible); (s.o.'s anger etc) attiser.

fugitive ['fjuːdʒɪtɪv] n fugitif, -ive mf.

fugue [fjuːg] n Mus fugue f.

fulfil, Am fulfill [fʊlˈfɪl] vt (-ll-) (ambition, dream) accomplir, réaliser; (condition, duty) remplir; (desire) satisfaire; **to f. oneself** s'épanouir. **◆fulfilling** a satisfaisant. **◆fulfilment, Am ◆fulfillment** n accomplissement m, réalisation f; (feeling) satisfaction f.

full [fʊl] a (-er, -est) plein (of de); (bus, theatre, meal) complet; (life, day) bien rempli; (skirt) ample; (hour) entier; (member) à part entière; **the f. price** le prix fort; **to pay (the) f.** fare payer plein tarif; **to be f. (up)** (of person) Culin n'avoir plus faim; (of hotel) être complet; **the f. facts** tous les faits; **at f. speed** à toute vitesse; **f. name** (on form) nom et prénom; **f. stop** Gram point m; **– adv to know f. well** savoir fort bien; **f. in the face** (to hit etc) en pleine figure; **– n in f.** (text) intégral; (to publish, read) intégralement; (to write one's name) en toutes lettres; **to the f.** (completely) tout à fait. **◆fullness** n (of details) abondance *f;* (*of dress*) ampleur *f.* ◆**fully** *adv* entièrement; (*at least*) au moins.

full-back ['fulbæk] *n* Fb arrière *m.* ◆**f.-'grown** *a* adulte; (*foetus*) arrivé à terme. ◆**f.-'length** *a* (*film*) de long métrage; (*portrait*) en pied; (*dress*) long. ◆**f.-'scale** *a* (*model etc*) grandeur nature *inv;* (*operation etc*) Fig de grande envergure. ◆**f.-'sized** *a* (*model*) grandeur nature *inv.* ◆**f.-'time** *a & adv* à plein temps.

fully-fledged, Am **full-fledged** [ful(i)'fledʒd] *a* (*engineer etc*) diplômé; (*member*) à part entière. ◆**f.-formed** *a* (*baby etc*) formé. ◆**f.-grown** *a* = **full-grown.**

fulsome ['fulsəm] *a* (*praise etc*) excessif.

fumble ['fʌmb(ə)l] *vi* to f. (about) (*grope*) tâtonner; (*search*) fouiller (for pour trouver); to f. (about) with tripoter.

fume [fjuːm] *vi* (*give off fumes*) fumer; (*of person*) Fig rager; — *npl* émanations *fpl;* (*from car exhaust*) gaz *m inv.*

fumigate ['fjuːmɪgeɪt] *vt* désinfecter (par fumigation).

fun [fʌn] *n* amusement *m;* to be (good) f. être très amusant; to have (some) f. s'amuser; to make f. of, poke f. at se moquer de; for f., for the f. of it pour le plaisir.

function ['fʌŋkʃ(ə)n] **1** *n* (*role, duty*) & Math fonction *f;* (*meeting*) réunion *f;* (*ceremony*) cérémonie *f* (publique). **2** *vi* (*work*) fonctionner. ◆**functional** *a* fonctionnel.

fund [fʌnd] *n* (*for pension, relief etc*) Fin caisse *f;* (*of knowledge etc*) Fig fond *m;* pl (*money resources*) fonds *mpl;* (*for special purpose*) crédits *mpl;* — *vt* (*with money*) fournir des fonds or des crédits à.

fundamental [fʌndə'ment(ə)l] *a* fondamental; — *npl* principes *mpl* essentiels.

funeral ['fjuːnərəl] *n* enterrement *m;* (*grandiose*) funérailles *fpl;* — *a* (*service, march*) funèbre; (*expenses, parlour*) funéraire.

funfair ['fʌnfeər] *n* fête *f* foraine; (*larger*) parc *m* d'attractions.

fungus, *pl* -**gi** ['fʌŋgəs, -gaɪ] *n* Bot champignon *m;* (*mould*) moisissure *f.*

funicular [fjuː'nɪkjulər] *n* funiculaire *m.*

funk [fʌŋk] *n* to be in a f. (*afraid*) Fam avoir la frousse; (*depressed, sulking*) Am Fam faire la gueule.

funnel ['fʌn(ə)l] *n* **1** (*of ship*) cheminée *f.* **2** (*tube for pouring*) entonnoir *m.*

funny ['fʌnɪ] *a* (-**ier,** -**iest**) (*amusing*) drôle; (*strange*) bizarre; a f. idea une drôle d'idée; there's some f. business going on il y a quelque chose de louche; to feel f. ne pas se

sentir très bien. ◆**funnily** *adv* drôlement; bizarrement; f. enough . . . chose bizarre . . .

fur [fɜːr] **1** *n* (*of animal*) poil *m,* pelage *m;* (*for wearing etc*) fourrure *f.* **2** *n* (*in kettle*) dépôt *m* (de tartre); — *vi* (-rr-) to f. (up) s'entartrer.

furious ['fjuərɪəs] *a* (*violent, angry*) furieux (with, at contre); (*pace, speed*) fou. ◆—**ly** *adv* furieusement; (*to drive, rush*) à une allure folle.

furnace ['fɜːnɪs] *n* (*forge*) fourneau *m;* (*room etc*) Fig fournaise *f.*

furnish ['fɜːnɪʃ] *vt* **1** (*room*) meubler. **2** (*supply*) fournir (s.o. with qch à qn). ◆—**ings** *npl* ameublement *m.*

furniture ['fɜːnɪtʃər] *n* meubles *mpl;* a piece of f. un meuble.

furrier ['fʌrɪər] *n* fourreur *m.*

furrow ['fʌrəu] *n* (*on brow*) & Agr sillon *m.*

furry ['fɜːrɪ] *a* (*animal*) à poil; (*toy*) en peluche.

further ['fɜːðər] **1** *adv & a* = **farther. 2** *adv* (*more*) davantage, plus; (*besides*) en outre; — *a* (*additional*) supplémentaire; (*education etc*) post-scolaire; f. details de plus amples détails; a f. case/*etc* (*another*) un autre cas/*etc;* without f. delay sans plus attendre. **3** *vt* (*cause, research etc*) promouvoir. ◆**furthermore** *adv* en outre. ◆**furthest** *a & adv* = **farthest.**

furtive ['fɜːtɪv] *a* furtif.

fury ['fjuərɪ] *n* (*violence, anger*) fureur *f.*

fuse [fjuːz] **1** *vti* (*melt*) Tech fondre; Fig fusionner. **2** *vt* to f. the lights *etc* faire sauter les plombs; — *vi* the lights *etc* have fused les plombs ont sauté; — *n* (*wire*) El fusible *m,* plomb *m.* **3** *n* (*of bomb*) amorce *f.* ◆**fused** *a* (*plug*) El avec fusible incorporé. ◆**fusion** *n* (*union*) & Phys Biol fusion *f.*

fuselage ['fjuːzəlɑːʒ] *n* Av fuselage *m.*

fuss [fʌs] *n* façons *fpl,* histoires *fpl,* chichis *mpl;* (*noise*) agitation *f;* what a (lot of) f.! quelle histoire!; to kick up or make a f. faire des histoires; to make a f. of (*over*) être aux petits soins pour; — *vi* faire des chichis; (*worry*) se tracasser (about pour); (*rush about*) s'agiter; to f. over s.o. être aux petits soins pour qn. ◆**fusspot** *n,* Am **fussbudget** *n* Fam enquiquineur, -euse *mf.* ◆**fussy** *a* (-**ier,** -**iest**) méticuleux; (*difficult*) difficile (about sur).

fusty ['fʌstɪ] *a* (-**ier,** -**iest**) (*smell*) de renfermé.

futile ['fjuːtaɪl, Am 'fjuːt(ə)l] *a* futile, vain. ◆**fu'tility** *n* futilité *f.*

future ['fjuːtʃər] n avenir m; Gram futur m; **in f.** (from now on) à l'avenir; **in the f.** (one day) un jour (futur); – a futur, à venir; (date) ultérieur.

fuzz [fʌz] n **1** (down) Fam duvet m. **2 the f.** (police) Sl les flics mpl. ◆**fuzzy** a (-ier, -iest) (hair) crépu; (picture, idea) flou.

G

G, g [dʒiː] n G, g m. ◆**G.-string** n (cloth) cache-sexe m inv.

gab [gæb] n **to have the gift of the g.** Fam avoir du bagou(t).

gabardine ['gæbədiːn] n (material, coat) gabardine f.

gabble ['gæb(ə)l] vi (chatter) jacasser; (indistinctly) bredouiller; – n baragouin m.

gable ['geɪb(ə)l] n Archit pignon m.

gad [gæd] vi (-dd-) **to g. about** se balader, vadrouiller.

gadget ['gædʒɪt] n gadget m.

Gaelic ['geɪlɪk, 'gælɪk] a & n gaélique (m).

gaffe [gæf] n (blunder) gaffe f, bévue f.

gag [gæg] n **1** (over mouth) bâillon m; – vt (-gg-) (victim, press etc) bâillonner. **2** n (joke) plaisanterie f; Cin Th gag m. **3** vi (-gg-) (choke) Am s'étouffer (on avec).

gaggle ['gæg(ə)l] n (of geese) troupeau m.

gaiety ['geɪətɪ] n gaieté f; (of colour) éclat m. ◆**gaily** adv gaiement.

gain [geɪn] vt (obtain, win) gagner; (experience, reputation) acquérir; (popularity) gagner en; **to g. speed/weight** prendre de la vitesse/du poids; – vi (of watch) avancer; **to g. in strength** gagner en force; **to g. on** (catch up with) rattraper; – n (increase) augmentation f (**in** de); (profit) Com bénéfice m, gain m; Fig avantage m. ◆**gainful** a profitable; (employment) rémunéré.

gainsay [geɪn'seɪ] vt (pt & pp **gainsaid** [-sed]) (person) contredire; (facts) nier.

gait [geɪt] n (walk) démarche f.

gala ['gɑːlə, 'geɪlə] n gala m, fête f; **swimming g.** concours m de natation.

galaxy ['gæləksɪ] n galaxie f.

gale [geɪl] n grand vent m, rafale f (de vent).

gall [gɔːl] **1** n Med bile f; (bitterness) Fig fiel m; (cheek) Fam effronterie f; **g. bladder** vésicule f biliaire. **2** vt (vex) blesser, froisser.

gallant ['gælənt] a (brave) courageux; (splendid) magnifique; (chivalrous) galant. ◆**gallantry** n (bravery) courage m.

galleon ['gælɪən] n (ship) Hist galion m.

gallery ['gælərɪ] n (room etc) galerie f; (for public, press) tribune f; **art g.** (private) galerie f d'art; (public) musée m d'art.

galley ['gælɪ] n (ship) Hist galère f; (kitchen) Nau Av cuisine f.

Gallic ['gælɪk] a (French) français. ◆**gallicism** n (word etc) gallicisme m.

gallivant ['gælɪvænt] vi **to g. (about)** Fam courir, vadrouiller.

gallon ['gælən] n gallon m (Br = 4,5 litres, Am = 3,8 litres).

gallop ['gæləp] n galop m; – vi galoper; **to g. away** (rush) Fig partir au galop or en vitesse. ◆**-ing** a (inflation etc) Fig galopant.

gallows ['gæləuz] npl potence f.

gallstone ['gɔːlstəun] n Med calcul m biliaire.

galore [gə'lɔːr] adv à gogo, en abondance.

galoshes [gə'lɒʃɪz] npl (shoes) caoutchoucs mpl.

galvanize ['gælvənaɪz] vt (metal) & Fig galvaniser.

gambit ['gæmbɪt] n **opening g.** Fig manœuvre f stratégique.

gambl/e ['gæmb(ə)l] vi jouer (**on** sur, **with** avec); **to g. on** (count on) miser sur; – vt (wager) jouer; **to g. (away)** (lose) perdre (au jeu); – n (bet) & Fig coup m risqué. ◆**-ing** n jeu m. ◆**-er** n joueur, -euse mf.

game [geɪm] n **1** n jeu m; (of football, cricket etc) match m; (of tennis, chess, cards) partie f; **to have a g. of** jouer un match de; faire une partie de; **games** Sch le sport; **games teacher** professeur m d'éducation physique. **2** n (animals, birds) gibier m; **to be fair g. for** Fig être une proie idéale pour. **3** a (brave) courageux; **to be g. for** (willing) prêt à. **4** a (leg) estropié; **to have a g. leg** être boiteux. ◆**gamekeeper** n garde-chasse m.

gammon ['gæmən] n (ham) jambon m fumé.

gammy ['gæmɪ] a Fam = **game 4.**

gamut ['gæmət] n Mus & Fig gamme f.

gang [gæŋ] n bande f; (of workers) équipe f; (of crooks) gang m; – vi **to g. up on** or

against se liguer contre. ◆**gangster** n gangster m.

gangling ['gæŋglɪŋ] a dégingandé.

gangrene ['gæŋgri:n] n gangrène f.

gangway ['gæŋweɪ] n passage m; (in train) couloir m; (in bus, cinema, theatre) allée f; (footbridge) Av Nau passerelle f; g.! dégagez!

gaol [dʒeɪl] n & vt = **jail**.

gap [gæp] n (empty space) trou m, vide m; (breach) trou m; (in time) intervalle m; (in knowledge) lacune f; **the g. between** (divergence) l'écart m entre.

gap/e [geɪp] vi (stare) rester or être bouche bée; **to g. at** regarder bouche bée. ◆—ing a (chasm, wound) béant.

garage ['gæra:(d)ʒ, 'gærɪdʒ, Am gə'ra:ʒ] n garage m; — vt mettre au garage.

garb [ga:b] n (clothes) costume m.

garbage ['ga:bɪdʒ] n ordures fpl; **g. can** Am poubelle f; **g. collector** or **man** Am éboueur m; **g. truck** Am camion-benne m.

garble ['ga:b(ə)l] vt (words etc) déformer, embrouiller.

garden ['ga:d(ə)n] n jardin m; **the gardens** (park) le parc; **g. centre** (store) jardinerie f; (nursery) pépinière f; **g. party** garden-party f; **g. produce** produits mpl maraîchers; — vi **to be gardening** jardiner. ◆—ing n jardinage m. ◆—er n jardinier, -ière f.

gargle ['ga:g(ə)l] vi se gargariser; — n gargarisme m.

gargoyle ['ga:gɔɪl] n Archit gargouille f.

garish ['geərɪʃ, Am 'gærɪʃ] a voyant, criard.

garland ['ga:lənd] n guirlande f.

garlic ['ga:lɪk] n ail m; **g. sausage** saucisson m à l'ail.

garment ['ga:mənt] n vêtement m.

garnish ['ga:nɪʃ] vt garnir (with de); — n garniture f.

garret ['gærət] n mansarde f.

garrison ['gærɪsən] n Mil garnison f.

garrulous ['gærələs] a (talkative) loquace.

garter ['ga:tər] n (round leg) jarretière f; (attached to belt) Am jarretelle f; (for men) fixe-chaussette m.

gas [gæs] **1** n gaz m inv; (gasoline) Am essence f; Med Fam anesthésie f au masque; – a (meter, mask, chamber) à gaz; (pipe) de gaz; (industry) du gaz; (heating) au gaz; **g. fire** or **heater** appareil m de chauffage à gaz; **g. station** Am poste m d'essence; **g. stove** (portable) réchaud m à gaz; (large) cuisinière f à gaz; – vt (-ss-) (poison) asphyxier; Mil gazer. **2** vi (-ss-) (talk) Fam bavarder; – n **for a g.** (fun) Am Fam pour rire. ◆**gasbag** n Fam commère

f. ◆**gasman** n (pl -men) employé m du gaz. ◆**gasoline** n Am essence f. ◆**gasworks** n usine f à gaz.

gash [gæʃ] n entaille f; – vt entailler.

gasp [ga:sp] **1** vi **to g.** (for breath) haleter; – n halètement m. **2** vi **to g. with** or **in surprise**/etc avoir le souffle coupé de surprise/etc; – vt (say gasping) hoqueter; – n a **g. of surprise**/etc un hoquet de surprise/etc.

gassy ['gæsɪ] a (-ier, -iest) (drink) gazeux.

gastric ['gæstrɪk] a (juices, ulcer) gastrique.

gastronomy [gæs'trɒnəmɪ] n gastronomie f.

gate [geɪt] n (of castle, airport etc) porte f; (at level crossing, field etc) barrière f; (metal) grille f; (in Paris Metro) portillon m. ◆**gateway** n **the g. to success**/etc le chemin du succès/etc.

gâteau, pl **-eaux** ['gætəʊ, -əʊz] n Culin gros gâteau m à la crème.

gatecrash ['geɪtkræʃ] vti **to g. (a party)** s'inviter de force (à une réception).

gather ['gæðər] vt (people, objects) rassembler; (pick up) ramasser; (flowers) cueillir; (information) recueillir; (understand) comprendre; (skirt, material) froncer; **I g. that . . .** (infer) je crois comprendre que . . . ; **to g. speed** prendre de la vitesse; **to g. in** (crops, harvest) rentrer; (essays, exam papers) ramasser; **to g. up** (strength) rassembler; (papers) ramasser; – vi (of people) se rassembler, s'assembler, s'amasser; (of clouds) se former; (of dust) s'accumuler; **to g. round** s'approcher; **to g. round s.o.** entourer qn. ◆—ing n (group) réunion f.

gaudy ['gɔ:dɪ] a (-ier, -iest) voyant, criard.

gauge [geɪdʒ] n (instrument) jauge f, indicateur m; Rail écartement m; **to be a g. of sth** Fig permettre de jauger qch; – vt (measure) mesurer; (estimate) évaluer, jauger.

gaunt [gɔ:nt] a (thin) décharné.

gauntlet ['gɔ:ntlɪt] n gant m; **to run the g. of** Fig essuyer (le feu de).

gauze [gɔ:z] n (fabric) gaze f.

gave [geɪv] see **give**.

gawk [gɔ:k] vi **to g. (at)** regarder bouche bée.

gawp [gɔ:p] vi = **gawk**.

gay [geɪ] a (-er, -est) **1** (cheerful) gai, joyeux; (colour) vif, gai. **2** Fam homo(sexuel), gay inv.

gaze [geɪz] n regard m (fixe); – vi regarder; **to g. at** regarder (fixement).

gazelle [gə'zel] n (animal) gazelle f.

gazette [gə'zet] n journal m officiel.

GB [dʒiːˈbiː] abbr (Great Britain) Grande-Bretagne f.

GCSE [dʒiːsiːesˈiː] abbr (General Certificate of Secondary Education) = baccalauréat m.

gear [gɪər] 1 n matériel m, équipement m; (belongings) affaires fpl; (clothes) Fam vêtements mpl (à la mode); (toothed wheels) Tech engrenage m; (speed) Aut vitesse f; **in g.** Aut en prise; **not in g.** Aut au point mort; **g. lever,** Am **g. shift** levier m de (changement de) vitesse. 2 vt (adapt) adapter (to à); **geared (up) to do** prêt à faire; **to g. oneself up for** se préparer pour. ◆**gearbox** n boîte f de vitesses.

gee! [dʒiː] int Am Fam ça alors!

geese [giːs] see **goose.**

geezer [ˈgiːzər] n Hum Sl type m.

Geiger counter [ˈgaɪgəkaʊntər] n compteur m Geiger.

gel [dʒel] n (substance) gel m.

gelatin(e) [ˈdʒelətɪn, Am -tiːn] n gélatine f.

gelignite [ˈdʒelɪgnaɪt] n dynamite f (au nitrate de soude).

gem [dʒem] n pierre f précieuse; (person or thing of value) Fig perle f; (error) Iron perle f.

Gemini [ˈdʒemɪnaɪ] n (sign) les Gémeaux mpl.

gen [dʒen] n (information) Sl coordonnées fpl; – vi (-nn-) **to g. up on** Sl se rancarder sur.

gender [ˈdʒendər] n Gram genre m; (of person) sexe m.

gene [dʒiːn] n Biol gène m.

genealogy [dʒiːnɪˈælədʒɪ] n généalogie f.

general [ˈdʒenərəl] 1 a général; **in g.** en général; **the g. public** le (grand) public; **for g. use** à l'usage du public; **a g. favourite** aimé ou apprécié de tous; **g. delivery** Am poste f restante; **to be g.** (widespread) être très répandu. 2 n (officer) Mil général m. ◆**gene'rality** n généralité f. ◆**generali'zation** n généralisation f. ◆**generalize** vti généraliser. ◆**generally** adv généralement; **g. speaking** en général, généralement parlant.

generate [ˈdʒenəreɪt] vt (heat) produire; (fear, hope etc) & Ling engendrer. ◆**gene'ration** n génération f; **the g. of** (heat) la production de; **g. gap** conflit m des générations. ◆**generator** n El groupe m électrogène, génératrice f.

generous [ˈdʒenərəs] a généreux (with de); (helping, meal etc) copieux. ◆**gene'rosity** n générosité f. ◆**generously** adv généreusement; (to serve s.o.) copieusement.

genesis [ˈdʒenəsɪs] n genèse f.

genetic [dʒɪˈnetɪk] a génétique. ◆**genetics** n génétique f.

Geneva [dʒɪˈniːvə] n Genève m or f.

genial [ˈdʒiːnɪəl] a (kind) affable; (cheerful) jovial.

genie [ˈdʒiːnɪ] n (goblin) génie m.

genital [ˈdʒenɪt(ə)l] a génital; – npl organes mpl génitaux.

genius [ˈdʒiːnɪəs] n (ability, person) génie m; **to have a g. for doing/for sth** avoir le génie pour faire/de qch.

genocide [ˈdʒenəsaɪd] n génocide m.

gent [dʒent] n Fam monsieur m; **gents' shoes** Com chaussures fpl pour hommes; **the gents** Fam les toilettes fpl (pour hommes).

genteel [dʒenˈtiːl] a Iron distingué.

gentle [ˈdʒent(ə)l] a (-er, -est) (person, sound, slope etc) doux; (hint, reminder) discret; (touch) léger; (pace) mesuré; (exercise, progress) modéré; (birth) noble. ◆**gentleman** n (pl -men) monsieur m; (well-bred) gentleman m, monsieur m bien élevé. ◆**gentlemanly** a distingué, bien élevé. ◆**gentleness** n douceur f. ◆**gently** adv doucement; (to remind) discrètement; (smoothly) en douceur.

genuine [ˈdʒenjuɪn] a (authentic) véritable, authentique; (sincere) sincère, vrai. ◆**–ly** adv authentiquement; sincèrement. ◆**–ness** n authenticité f; sincérité f.

geography [dʒɪˈɒgrəfɪ] n géographie f. ◆**geo'graphical** a géographique.

geology [dʒɪˈɒlədʒɪ] n géologie f. ◆**geo-'logical** a géologique. ◆**geologist** n géologue mf.

geometry [dʒɪˈɒmɪtrɪ] n géométrie f. ◆**geo'metric(al)** a géométrique.

geranium [dʒɪˈreɪnɪəm] n Bot géranium m.

geriatric [dʒerɪˈætrɪk] a (hospital) du troisième âge; **g. ward** service m de gériatrie.

germ [dʒɜːm] n Biol & Fig germe m; Med microbe m; **g. warfare** guerre f bactériologique.

German [ˈdʒɜːmən] a & n allemand, -ande (mf); **G. measles** Med rubéole f; **G. shepherd** (dog) Am berger m allemand; – n (language) allemand m. ◆**Ger'manic** a germanique.

Germany [ˈdʒɜːmənɪ] n Allemagne f; **West G.** Allemagne de l'Ouest.

germinate [ˈdʒɜːmɪneɪt] vi Bot & Fig germer.

gestation [dʒeˈsteɪʃ(ə)n] n gestation f.

gesture [ˈdʒestʃər] n geste m; – vi **to g. to**

s.o. to do faire signe à qn de faire.
◆ge'sticulate *vi* gesticuler.

get [get] 1 *vt* (*pt & pp* got, *pp Am* gotten, *pres p* getting) (*obtain*) obtenir, avoir; (*find*) trouver; (*buy*) acheter, prendre; (*receive*) recevoir, avoir; (*catch*) attraper, prendre; (*seize*) prendre, saisir; (*fetch*) aller chercher (*qn, qch*); (*put*) mettre; (*derive*) tirer (from *de*); (*understand*) comprendre, saisir; (*prepare*) préparer; (*lead*) mener; (*target*) atteindre, avoir; (*reputation*) se faire; (*annoy*) *Fam* ennuyer; **I have got,** *Am* **I have gotten** j'ai; **to g. s.o. to do** sth faire faire qch à qn; **to g. sth built/etc** faire construire/etc qch; **to g. things going or started** faire démarrer les choses. **2** *vi* (*go*) aller; (*arrive*) arriver (to à); (*become*) devenir, se faire; **to g. caught/run over/etc** se faire prendre/écraser/etc; **to g. married** se marier; **to g. dressed/washed** s'habiller/se laver; **where have you got or** *Am* **gotten to?** où en es-tu?; **you've got to stay** (*must*) tu dois rester; **to g. to do** (*succeed in doing*) parvenir à faire; **to g. working** se mettre à travailler. ▪ **to g. about** **or (a)round** *vi* se déplacer; (*of news*) circuler; **to g. across** *vt* (*road*) traverser; (*person*) faire traverser; (*message*) communiquer; – *vi* traverser; (*of speaker*) se faire comprendre (to à); **to g. across to s.o. that** faire comprendre à qn que; **to g. along** *vi* (*leave*) se sauver; (*manage*) se débrouiller; (*progress*) avancer; (*be on good terms*) s'entendre (with *avec*); **to g. at** *vt* (*reach*) parvenir à, atteindre; (*taunt*) s'en prendre à; **what is he getting at?** où veut-il en venir?; **to g. away** *vi* (*leave*) partir, s'en aller; (*escape*) s'échapper; **there's no getting away from it** il faut le reconnaître, c'est comme ça. ◆**getaway** *n* (*escape*) fuite *f*; **to g. back** *vi* (*recover*) récupérer; (*replace*) remettre; – *vi* (*return*) revenir, retourner; **to g. back at,** **g. one's own back at** (*punish*) se venger de; **g. back!** (*move back*) reculez!; **to g. by** *vi* (*pass*) passer; (*manage*) se débrouiller; **to g. down** *vi* (*go down*) descendre (from *de*); – *vt* (*bring down*) descendre (from *de*); (*write*) noter; (*depress*) *Fam* déprimer; **to g. down to** (*task, work*) se mettre à; **to g. in** *vt* (*bicycle, washing etc*) rentrer; (*buy*) acheter; (*summon*) faire venir; **to g. in a car/etc** monter dans une voiture/etc; – *vi* (*enter*) entrer; (*come home*) rentrer; (*enter vehicle or train*) monter; (*of plane, train*) arriver; (*of candidate*) *Pol* être élu; **to g. into** *vt* entrer dans; (*vehicle, train*) monter dans;

(*habit*) prendre; **to g. into bed/a rage** se mettre au lit/en colère; **to g. into trouble** avoir des ennuis; **to g. off** *vi* (*leave*) partir; (*from vehicle or train*) descendre (from *de*); (*escape*) s'en tirer; (*finish work*) sortir; (*be acquitted*) *Jur* être acquitté; – *vt* (*remove*) enlever; (*despatch*) expédier; *Jur* faire acquitter (*qn*); **to g. off (from) a chair** se lever d'une chaise; **to g. off doing** *Fam* se dispenser de faire; **to g. on** *vt* (*shoes, clothes*) mettre; (*bus, train*) monter dans; – *vi* (*progress*) marcher, avancer; (*continue*) continuer; (*succeed*) réussir; (*enter bus or train*) monter; (*be on good terms*) s'entendre (with *avec*); **how are you getting on?** comment ça va?; **to g. on to s.o.** (*telephone*) toucher qn, contacter qn; **to g. on with** (*task*) continuer; **to g. out** *vi* sortir; (*from vehicle or train*) descendre (from *de*); – *vt* (*remove*) enlever; (*bring out*) sortir (qch), faire sortir (*qn*); **to g. over** *vt* (*road*) traverser; (*obstacle*) surmonter, (*fence*) franchir; (*illness*) se remettre de; (*surprise*) revenir de; (*ideas*) communiquer; **let's g. it over with** finissons-en; – *vi* (*cross*) traverser; **to g. round** *vt* (*obstacle*) contourner; (*person*) entortiller; – *vi* **to g. round to doing** en venir à faire; **to g. through** *vt* (*pass*) passer; (*finish*) finir; (*pass exam*) être reçu à; – *vi* (*pass*) passer; **to g. through to s.o.** se faire comprendre de qn; (*on the telephone*) contacter qn; – *vt* (*hole etc*) passer par; (*task, meal*) venir à bout de; (*exam*) être reçu à; **g. me through to your boss** (*on the telephone*) passe-moi ton patron; **to g. together** *vi* (*of people*) se rassembler. ◆**g.-together** *n* réunion *f*; **to g. up** *vi* (*rise*) se lever (from *de*); **to g. up to** (*in book*) en arriver à; (*mischief, trouble etc*) faire; – *vt* (*ladder, stairs etc*) monter; (*party, group*) organiser; **to g. sth up** (*bring up*) monter qch. ◆**g.-up** *n* (*clothes*) *Fam* accoutrement *m*.

geyser ['giːzər] *n* **1** (*water heater*) chauffe-eau *m inv.* **2** *Geol* geyser *m*.

Ghana ['gɑːnə] *n* Ghana *m*.

ghastly ['gɑːstlɪ] *a* (*-ier, -iest*) (*pale*) blême, pâle; (*horrible*) affreux.

gherkin ['gɜːkɪn] *n* cornichon *m*.

ghetto ['getəʊ] *n* (*pl* -os) ghetto *m*.

ghost [gəʊst] *n* fantôme *m*; **not the g. of a chance** pas l'ombre d'une chance; – *a* (*story*) de fantômes; (*ship*) fantôme; (*town*) mort. ◆**—ly** *a* spectral.

ghoulish ['guːlɪʃ] *a* morbide.

giant ['dʒaɪənt] *n* géant *m*; – *a* géant, gigantesque; (*steps*) de géant; (*packet etc*) Com géant.

gibberish ['dʒɪbərɪʃ] *n* baragouin *m*.

gibe [dʒaɪb] *vi* railler; **to g. at** railler; – *n* raillerie *f*.

giblets ['dʒɪblɪts] *npl* (*of fowl*) abats *mpl*.

giddy ['gɪdɪ] *a* (**-ier, -iest**) (*heights*) vertigineux; **to feel g.** avoir le vertige; **to make g.** donner le vertige à. ◆**giddiness** *n* vertige *m*.

gift [gɪft] *n* cadeau *m*; (*talent*) & *Jur* don *m*; **g. voucher** chèque-cadeau *m*. ◆**gifted** *a* doué (**with** de, **for** pour). ◆**giftwrapped** *a* en paquet-cadeau.

gig [gɪg] *n* Mus Fam engagement *m*, séance *f*.

gigantic [dʒaɪˈgæntɪk] *a* gigantesque.

giggle ['gɪg(ə)l] *vi* rire (sottement); – *n* petit rire *m* sot; **to have the giggles** avoir le fou rire.

gild [gɪld] *vt* dorer. ◆**gilt** *a* doré; – *n* dorure *f*.

gills [gɪlz] *npl* (*of fish*) ouïes *fpl*.

gimmick ['gɪmɪk] *n* (*trick, object*) truc *m*.

gin [dʒɪn] *n* (*drink*) gin *m*.

ginger ['dʒɪndʒər] **1** *a* (*hair*) roux. **2** *n* Bot Culin gingembre *m*; **g. beer** boisson *f* gazeuse au gingembre. ◆**gingerbread** *n* pain *m* d'épice.

gingerly ['dʒɪndʒəlɪ] *adv* avec précaution.

gipsy ['dʒɪpsɪ] *n* bohémien, -ienne *mf*; (*Central European*) Tsigane *mf*; – *a* (*music*) tsigane.

giraffe [dʒɪˈrɑːf, dʒɪˈræf] *n* girafe *f*.

girder ['gɜːdər] *n* (*metal beam*) poutre *f*.

girdle ['gɜːd(ə)l] *n* (*belt*) ceinture *f*; (*corset*) gaine *f*.

girl [gɜːl] *n* (jeune) fille *f*; (*daughter*) fille *f*; (*servant*) bonne *f*; (*sweetheart*) Fam petite amie *f*; **English g.** jeune Anglaise *f*; **g. guide** éclaireuse *f*. ◆**girlfriend** *n* amie *f*; (*of boy*) petite amie *f*. ◆**girlish** *a* de (jeune) fille.

girth [gɜːθ] *n* (*measure*) circonférence *f*; (*of waist*) tour *m*.

gist [dʒɪst] *n* **to get the g. of** comprendre l'essentiel de.

give [gɪv] *vt* (*pt* **gave**, *pp* **given**) donner (**to** à); (*help, support*) prêter; (*gesture, pleasure*) faire; (*a sigh*) pousser; (*a look*) jeter; (*a blow*) porter; **g. me York 234** passez-moi le 234 à York; **she doesn't g. a damn** Fam elle s'en fiche; **to g. way** (*yield, break*) céder (**to** à); (*collapse*) s'effondrer; Aut céder la priorité (**to** à); – *n* (*in fabric etc*) élasticité *f*. ■ **to g. away** *vt* (*prize*) distribuer; (*money*) donner; (*facts*) révéler; (*betray*) trahir (*qn*);

to g. back *vt* (*return*) rendre; **to g. in** *vi* (*surrender*) céder (**to** à); – *vt* (*hand in*) remettre; **to g. off** *vt* (*smell, heat*) dégager; **to g. out** *vt* distribuer; – *vi* (*of supplies, patience*) s'épuiser; (*of engine*) rendre l'âme; **to g. over** *vt* (*devote*) donner, consacrer (**to** à); **to g. oneself over to** s'adonner à; – *vi* **g. over!** (*stop*) Fam arrête!; **to g. up** *vi* abandonner, renoncer; – *vt* abandonner, renoncer à; (*seat*) céder (**to** à); (*prisoner*) livrer (**to** à); (*patient*) condamner; **to g. up smoking** cesser de fumer. ◆**given** *a* (*fixed*) donné; **to be g. to doing** (*prone to do*) avoir l'habitude de faire; **g. your age** (*in view of*) étant donné votre âge; **g. that** étant donné que. ◆**giver** *n* donateur, -trice *mf*.

glacier ['glæsɪər, Am 'gleɪʃər] *n* glacier *m*.

glad [glæd] *a* (*person*) content (**of, about** de). ◆**gladden** *vt* réjouir. ◆**gladly** *adv* (*willingly*) volontiers.

glade [gleɪd] *n* clairière *f*.

gladiolus, *pl* **-i** [glædɪˈəʊləs, -aɪ] *n* Bot glaïeul *m*.

glamour ['glæmər] *n* (*charm*) enchantement *m*; (*splendour*) éclat *m*. ◆**glamorize** *vt* montrer sous un jour séduisant. ◆**glamorous** *a* séduisant.

glance [glɑːns] **1** *n* coup *m* d'œil; – *vi* jeter un coup d'œil (**at** à, sur). **2** *vt* **to g. off sth** (*of bullet*) ricocher sur qch.

gland [glænd] *n* glande *f*. ◆**glandular** *a* **g. fever** Med mononucléose *f* infectieuse.

glar/e [gleər] **1** *vi* **to g. at s.o.** foudroyer qn (du regard); – *n* regard *m* furieux. **2** *vi* (*of sun*) briller d'un éclat aveuglant; – *n* éclat *m* aveuglant. ◆**-ing** *a* (*sun*) aveuglant; (*eyes, injustice*) flagrant; **a g. mistake** une faute grossière.

glass [glɑːs] *n* verre *m*; (*mirror*) miroir *m*, glace *f*; *pl* (*spectacles*) lunettes *fpl*; **a pane of g.** une vitre, un carreau; – *a* (*door*) vitré; (*industry*) du verre. ◆**glassful** *n* (plein) verre *m*.

glaze [gleɪz] *vt* (*door*) vitrer; (*pottery*) vernisser; (*paper*) glacer; – *n* (*on pottery*) vernis *m*; (*on paper*) glacé *m*. ◆**glazier** *n* vitrier *m*.

gleam [gliːm] *n* lueur *f*; – *vi* (re)luire.

glean [gliːn] *vt* (*grain, information etc*) glaner.

glee [gliː] *n* joie *f*. ◆**gleeful** *a* joyeux.

glen [glen] *n* vallon *m*.

glib [glɪb] *a* (*person*) qui a la parole facile; (*speech*) facile, peu sincère. ◆**-ly** *adv* (*say*) peu sincèrement.

glid/e [glaɪd] *vi* glisser; (*of vehicle*) avancer

silencieusement; (*of aircraft, bird*) planer.
◆—**ing** n Av Sp vol m à voile. ◆—**er** n Av
planeur m.

glimmer ['glɪmər] vi luire (faiblement); – n
(*light, of hope etc*) (faible) lueur f.

glimpse [glɪmps] n aperçu m; **to catch** or **get
a g. of** entrevoir.

glint [glɪnt] vi (*shine with flashes*) briller; – n
éclair m; (*in eye*) étincelle f.

glisten ['glɪs(ə)n] vi (*of wet surface*) briller;
(*of water*) miroiter.

glitter ['glɪtər] vi scintiller, briller; – n scintillement m.

gloat [gləʊt] vi jubiler (**over** à la vue de).

globe [gləʊb] n globe m. ◆**global** a
(*comprehensive*) global; (*universal*) universel, mondial.

gloom [gluːm] n (*darkness*) obscurité f;
(*sadness*) Fig tristesse f. ◆**gloomy** a (**-ier,
-iest**) (*dark, dismal*) sombre, triste; (*sad*)
Fig triste; (*pessimistic*) pessimiste.

glory ['glɔːrɪ] n gloire f; **in all one's g.**
dans toute sa splendeur; **to be in one's g.**
(*very happy*) Fam être à son affaire; – vi **to
g. in** se glorifier de. ◆**glorify** vt (*praise*)
glorifier; **it's a glorified barn**/etc ce n'est
guère plus qu'une grange/etc. ◆**glorious**
a (*full of glory*) glorieux; (*splendid, enjoya-
ble*) magnifique.

gloss [glɒs] 1 n (*shine*) brillant m; **g. paint**
peinture f brillante; **g. finish** brillant m. 2 n
(*note*) glose f, commentaire m. 3 vt **to g.
over** (*minimize*) glisser sur; (*conceal*)
dissimuler. ◆**glossy** a (**-ier, -iest**) brillant;
(*paper*) glacé; (*magazine*) de luxe.

glossary ['glɒsərɪ] n glossaire m.

glove [glʌv] n gant m; **g. compartment** Aut
(*shelf*) vide-poches m inv; (*enclosed*) boîte f
à gants. ◆**gloved** a a **g. hand** une main
gantée.

glow [gləʊ] vi (*of sky, fire*) rougeoyer; (*of
lamp*) luire; (*of eyes, person*) Fig rayonner
(**with** de); – n rougeoiement m; (*of colour*)
éclat m; (*of lamp*) lueur f. ◆—**ing** a
(*account, terms etc*) très favorable, enthousiaste. ◆**glow-worm** n ver m luisant.

glucose ['gluːkəʊs] n glucose m.

glue [gluː] n colle f; – vt coller (**to, on** à).
◆**glued** a **g. to** (*eyes*) Fam fixés or rivés
sur; **to be g. to** (*television*) Fam être cloué
devant.

glum [glʌm] a (*glummer, glummest*) triste.

glut [glʌt] vt (-**tt**-) (*overfill*) rassasier;
(*market*) inonder (**with** de); – n (*of
produce, oil etc*) Com surplus m (**of** de).

glutton ['glʌt(ə)n] n glouton, -onne mf; **g.
for work** bourreau m de travail; **g. for**

punishment masochiste mf. ◆**gluttony** n
gloutonnerie f.

glycerin(e) ['glɪsəriːn] n glycérine f.

GMT [dʒiːem'tiː] abbr (*Greenwich Mean
Time*) GMT.

gnarled [nɑːld] a noueux.

gnash [næʃ] vt **to g. one's teeth** grincer des
dents.

gnat [næt] n (*insect*) cousin m.

gnaw [nɔː] vti **to g. (at)** ronger.

gnome [nəʊm] n (*little man*) gnome m.

go [gəʊ] **1** vi (*3rd person sing pres* t **goes**; pt
went; pp **gone**; pres p **going**) aller (**to** à, **from**
de); (*depart*) partir, s'en aller; (*disappear*)
disparaître; (*be sold*) se vendre; (*function*)
marcher, fonctionner; (*progress*) aller,
marcher; (*become*) devenir; (*be*) être; (*of
time*) passer; (*of hearing, strength*) baisser;
(*of rope*) céder; (*of fuse*) sauter; (*of material*) s'user; **to go well**/badly (*of event*) se
passer bien/mal; **she's going to do** (*is about
to, intends to*) elle va faire; **it's all gone**
(*finished*) il n'y en a plus; **to go and get**
(*fetch*) aller chercher; **to go and see** aller
voir; **to go riding**/sailing/**on a trip**/etc faire
du cheval/de la voile/un voyage/etc; **to let
go of** lâcher; **to go to** (*doctor, lawyer etc*)
aller voir; **to get things going** faire démarrer les choses; **is there any beer going?**
(*available*) y a-t-il de la bière?; **it goes to
show that . . .** ça sert à montrer que . . . ;
two hours/etc **to go** (*still left*) encore deux
heures/etc. **2** n (*pl* **goes**) (*energy*) dynamisme m; (*attempt*) coup m; **to have a go at
(doing) sth** essayer (de faire) qch; **at one go**
d'un seul coup; **on the go** en mouvement,
actif; **to make a go of** (*make a success of*)
réussir. ■ **to go about** or (**a)round** vi se
déplacer; (*of news, rumour*) circuler; **to go
about** or (*one's duties etc*) s'occuper de; **to
know how to go about it** savoir s'y prendre;
to go across vt traverser; – vi (*cross*) traverser; (*go*) aller (**to** à); **to go across to
s.o.('s)** faire un saut chez qn; **to go after** vt
(*follow*) suivre; (*job*) viser; **to go against** vt
(*of result*) être défavorable à; (*s.o.'s wishes*)
aller contre; (*harm*) nuire à; **to go ahead** vi
aller de l'avant; **to go ahead with** (*plan etc*)
poursuivre; **go ahead!** allez-y! ◆**go-
ahead** a dynamique; – n **to get the
go-ahead** avoir le feu vert; **to go along** vi
aller, avancer; **to go along with** (*agree*) être
d'accord avec; **to go away** vi partir, s'en
aller; **to go back** vi retourner, revenir; (*in
time*) remonter; (*retreat, step back*) reculer;
to go back on (*promise*) revenir sur; **to go
by** vi passer; – vt (*act according to*) se

fonder sur; (*judge from*) juger d'après; (*instruction*) suivre; **to go down** *vi* descendre; (*fall down*) tomber; (*of ship*) couler; (*of sun*) se coucher; (*of storm*) s'apaiser; (*of temperature, price etc*) baisser; (*of tyre*) se dégonfler; **to go down well** (*of speech etc*) être bien reçu; **to go down with** (*illness*) attraper; − *vt* **to go down the stairs/street** descendre l'escalier/la rue; **to go for** *vt* (*fetch*) aller chercher; (*attack*) attaquer; (*like*) *Fam* aimer beaucoup; **to go forward(s)** *vi* avancer; **to go in** *vi* (r)entrer; (*of sun*) se cacher; **to go in for** (*exam*) se présenter à; (*hobby, sport*) faire; (*career*) entrer dans; (*like*) *Fam* aimer beaucoup; − *vt* **to go in a room**/*etc* entrer dans une pièce/*etc*; **to go into** *vt* (*room etc*) entrer dans; (*question*) examiner; **to go off** *vi* (*leave*) partir; (*go bad*) se gâter; (*of effect*) passer; (*of alarm*) se déclencher; (*of event*) se passer; − *vt* (*one's food*) perdre le goût de; **to go on** *vi* continuer (**doing** à faire); (*travel*) poursuivre sa route; (*happen*) se passer; (*last*) durer; (*of time*) passer; **to go on at** (*nag*) *Fam* s'en prendre à; **to go on about** *Fam* parler sans cesse de; **to go out** *vi* sortir; (*of light, fire*) s'éteindre; (*of tide*) descendre; (*of newspaper, product*) être distribué (**to** à); (*depart*) partir; **to go out to work** travailler (au dehors); **to go over** *vi* (*go*) aller (**to** à); (*cross over*) traverser; (*to enemy*) passer (**to** à); **to go over to s.o.('s)** faire un saut chez qn; − *vt* examiner; (*speech*) revoir; (*in one's mind*) repasser; (*touch up*) retoucher; (*overhaul*) réviser (*véhicule, montre*); **to go round** *vi* (*turn*) tourner; (*make a detour*) faire le tour; (*be sufficient*) suffire; **to go round to s.o.('s)** passer chez qn, faire un saut chez qn; **enough to go round** assez pour tout le monde; − *vt* **to go round a corner** tourner un coin; **to go through** *vi* passer; (*of deal*) être conclu; − *vt* (*undergo, endure*) subir; (*examine*) examiner; (*search*) fouiller; (*spend*) dépenser; (*wear out*) user; (*perform*) accomplir; **to go through with** (*carry out*) réaliser, aller jusqu'au bout de; **to go under** *vi* (*of ship, person, firm*) couler; **to go up** *vi* monter; (*explode*) sauter; − *vt* **to go up the stairs/street** monter l'escalier/la rue; **to go without** *vi* se passer de.

goad [gəʊd] *n* aiguillon *m*; − *vt* **to g. (on)** aiguillonner.

goal [gəʊl] *n* but *m*. ◆**goalkeeper** *n* Fb gardien *m* de but, goal *m*. ◆**goalpost** *n* Fb poteau *m* de but.

goat [gəʊt] *n* chèvre *f*; **to get s.o.'s g.** *Fam*

énerver qn. ◆**goa'tee** *n* (*beard*) barbiche *f*.

gobble ['gɒb(ə)l] *vt* **to g. (up)** engloutir, engouffrer.

go-between ['gəʊbɪtwiːn] *n* intermédiaire *mf*.

goblet ['gɒblɪt] *n* verre *m* à pied.

goblin ['gɒblɪn] *n* (*evil spirit*) lutin *m*.

god [gɒd] *n* dieu *m*; **G.** Dieu *m*; **the gods** *Th Fam* le poulailler. ◆**g.-fearing** *a* croyant. ◆**g.-forsaken** *a* (*place*) perdu, misérable. ◆**goddess** *n* déesse *f*. ◆**g.-'eyed** *a* dévot. ◆**godchild** *n* (*pl* **-children**) filleul, -eule *mf*. ◆**goddaughter** *n* filleule *f*. ◆**godfather** *n* parrain *m*. ◆**godmother** *n* marraine *f*. ◆**godson** *n* filleul *m*.

goddam(n) ['gɒdæm] *a* Am Fam foutu.

godsend ['gɒdsend] *n* aubaine *f*.

goes [gəʊz] *see* **go** 1.

goggle ['gɒg(ə)l] **1** *vi* **to g. at** regarder en roulant de gros yeux. **2** *npl* (*spectacles*) lunettes *fpl* (*protectrices*). ◆**g.-'eyed** *a* aux yeux saillants.

going ['gəʊɪŋ] **1** *n* (*departure*) départ *m*; (*speed*) allure *f*; (*conditions*) conditions *fpl*; **it's hard g.** c'est difficile. **2** *a* **the g. price** le prix pratiqué (**for** pour); **a g. concern** une entreprise qui marche bien. ◆**goings-'on** *npl Pej* activités *fpl*.

go-kart ['gəʊkɑːt] *n* Sp kart *m*.

gold [gəʊld] *n* or *m*; − *a* (*watch etc*) en or; (*coin, dust*) d'or. ◆**golden** *a* (*made of gold*) d'or; (*in colour*) doré, d'or; (*opportunity*) excellent. ◆**goldmine** *n* mine *f* d'or. ◆**gold-'plated** *a* plaqué or. ◆**goldsmith** *n* orfèvre *m*.

goldfinch ['gəʊldfɪntʃ] *n* (*bird*) chardonneret *m*.

goldfish ['gəʊldfɪʃ] *n* poisson *m* rouge.

golf [gɒlf] *n* golf *m*. ◆**golfer** *n* golfeur, -euse *mf*.

golly! ['gɒlɪ] *int* (**by**) **g.!** *Fam* mince (alors)!

gondola ['gɒndələ] *n* (*boat*) gondole *f*. ◆**gondo'lier** *n* gondolier *m*.

gone [gɒn] *see* **go** 1; − *a* **it's g. two** *Fam* il est plus de deux heures. ◆**goner** *n* **to be a g.** *Sl* être fichu.

gong [gɒŋ] *n* gong *m*.

good [gʊd] *a* (**better, best**) bon; (*kind*) gentil; (*weather*) beau; (*pleasant*) bon, agréable; (*well-behaved*) sage; **be g. enough to ...** ayez la gentillesse de ...; **my g. friend** mon cher ami; **a g. chap** *or* **fellow** un brave type; **a g. and strong** bien fort; **a g. (long) walk** une bonne promenade; **very g.!** (*all right*) très bien!; **that's g. of you** c'est gentil de ta part; **to feel g.** se sentir bien;

that isn't g. enough (bad) ça ne va pas; (not sufficient) ça ne suffit pas; it's g. for us ça nous fait du bien; g. at (French etc) Sch bon or fort en; to be g. with (children) savoir s'y prendre avec; it's a g. thing (that) . . . heureusement que . . . ; a g. many, a g. deal (of) beaucoup (de); as g. as (almost) pratiquement; g. afternoon, g. morning bonjour; (on leaving someone) au revoir; g. evening bonsoir; g. night bonsoir; (before going to bed) bonne nuit; to make g. vi (succeed) réussir; – vt (loss) compenser; (damage) réparer; G. Friday Vendredi m Saint; – n (virtue) bien m; for her g. pour son bien; there's some g. in him il a du bon; it's no g. crying/shouting/etc ça ne sert à rien de pleurer/crier/etc; that's no g. (worthless) ça ne vaut rien; (bad) ça ne va pas; what's the g.? à quoi bon?; for g. (to leave, give up etc) pour de bon. ◆g.-for-'nothing a & n propre à rien (mf). ◆g.-'humoured a de bonne humeur. ◆g.-'looking a beau. ◆goodness n bonté f; my g.! mon Dieu! ◆good'will n bonne volonté f; (zeal) zèle m.

goodbye [gud'bai] int & n au revoir (m inv).

goodly ['gudli] a (size, number) grand.

goods [gudz] npl marchandises fpl; (articles for sale) articles mpl.

gooey ['guːi] a Fam gluant, poisseux.

goof [guːf] vi to g. (up) (blunder) Am faire une gaffe.

goon [guːn] n Fam idiot, -ote mf.

goose, pl geese [guːs, giːs] n oie f; g. pimples or bumps chair f de poule. ◆gooseflesh n chair f de poule.

gooseberry ['guzbəri, Am 'guːsbəri] n groseille f à maquereau.

gorge [gɔːdʒ] 1 n (ravine) gorge f. 2 vt (food) engloutir; to g. oneself s'empiffrer (on de).

gorgeous ['gɔːdʒəs] a magnifique.

gorilla [gə'rilə] n gorille m.

gormless ['gɔːmləs] a Fam stupide.

gorse [gɔːs] n inv ajonc(s) m(pl).

gory ['gɔːri] a (-ier, -iest) (bloody) sanglant; (details) Fig horrible.

gosh! [gɒʃ] int Fam mince (alors)!

go-slow [gəu'sləu] n (strike) grève f perlée.

gospel ['gɒspəl] n évangile m.

gossip ['gɒsip] n (talk) bavardage(s) m(pl); (malicious) cancan(s) m(pl); (person) commère f; g. column Journ échos mpl; – vi bavarder; (maliciously) cancaner. ◆–ing n, ◆–gossipy a bavard, cancanier.

got, Am gotten [gɒt, 'gɒt(ə)n] see get.

Gothic ['gɒθik] a & n gothique (m).

gouge [gaudʒ] vt to g. out (eye) crever.

goulash ['guːlæʃ] n Culin goulasch f.

gourmet ['guəmei] n gourmet m.

gout [gaut] n Med goutte f.

govern ['gʌvən] vt (rule) gouverner; (city) administrer; (business) gérer; (emotion) maîtriser, gouverner; (influence) déterminer; – vi Pol gouverner; governing body conseil m d'administration. ◆governess n gouvernante f. ◆government n gouvernement m; (local) administration f; – a (department, policy etc) gouvernemental; (loan) d'État. ◆govern'mental a gouvernemental. ◆governor n gouverneur m; (of school) administrateur, -trice mf; (of prison) directeur, -trice mf.

gown [gaun] n (dress) robe f; (of judge, lecturer) toge f.

GP [dʒiː'piː] n abbr (general practitioner) (médecin m) généraliste m.

GPO [dʒiːpiː'əu] abbr (General Post Office) = PTT fpl.

grab [græb] vt (-bb-) to g. (hold of) saisir, agripper; to g. sth from s.o. arracher qch à qn.

grace [greis] 1 n (charm, goodwill etc) Rel grâce f; (extension of time) délai m de grâce; to say g. dire le bénédicité. 2 vt (adorn) orner; (honour) honorer (with de). ◆graceful a gracieux. ◆gracious a (kind) aimable, gracieux (to envers); (elegant) élégant; good g.! Fam bonté divine!

gradation [grə'deiʃ(ə)n, Am grei'deiʃ(ə)n] n gradation f.

grade [greid] n catégorie f; Mil Math grade m; (of milk) qualité f; (of eggs) calibre m; (level) niveau m; (mark) Sch Univ note f; (class) Am Sch classe f; g. school Am école f primaire; g. crossing Am passage m à niveau; – vt (classify) classer; (colours etc) graduer; (paper) Sch Univ noter.

gradient ['greidiənt] n (slope) inclinaison f.

gradual ['grædjuəl] a progressif, graduel; (slope) doux. ◆–ly adv progressivement, peu à peu.

graduat/e ['grædjueit] vi Univ obtenir son diplôme; Am Sch obtenir son baccalauréat; to g. from sortir de; – vt (mark with degrees) graduer; – ['grædjuət] n diplômé, -ée mf, licencié, -ée mf. ◆–ed a (tube etc) gradué; to be g. Am Sch Univ = to graduate vi. ◆gradu'ation n Univ remise f des diplômes.

graffiti [grə'fiːti] npl graffiti mpl.

graft [grɑːft] n Med Bot greffe f; – vt greffer (on to à).

grain [grein] n (seed, particle) grain m;

(*seeds*) grain(s) *m*(*pl*); (*in cloth*) fil *m*; (*in wood*) fibre *f*; (*in leather, paper*) grain *m*; (*of truth*) Fig once *f*.

gram(me) ['græm] *n* gramme *m*.

grammar ['græmər] *n* grammaire *f*; **g. school** lycée *m*. ◆**gra'mmatical** *a* grammatical.

gramophone ['græməfəʊn] *n* phonographe *m*.

granary ['grænərɪ] *n* Agr grenier *m*; **g. loaf** pain *m* complet.

grand [grænd] **1** *a* (**-er, -est**) magnifique, grand; (*style*) grandiose; (*concert, duke*) grand; (*piano*) à queue; (*wonderful*) Fam magnifique. **2** *n inv* Am Sl mille dollars *mpl*; Br Sl mille livres *fpl*. ◆**grandeur** ['grændʒər] *n* magnificence *f*; (*of person, country*) grandeur *f*.

grandchild ['græntʃaɪld] *n* (*pl* **-children**) petit(e)-enfant *mf*. ◆**grand(d)ad** *n* Fam pépé *m*, papi *m*. ◆**granddaughter** *n* petite-fille *f*. ◆**grandfather** *n* grand-père *m*. ◆**grandmother** *n* grand-mère *f*. ◆**grandparents** *npl* grands-parents *mpl*. ◆**grandson** *n* petit-fils *m*.

grandstand ['grændstænd] *n* Sp tribune *f*.

grange [greɪndʒ] *n* (*house*) manoir *m*.

granite ['grænɪt] *n* granit(e) *m*.

granny ['grænɪ] *n* Fam mamie *f*.

grant [grɑːnt] **1** *vt* accorder (**to** à); (*request*) accéder à; (*prayer*) exaucer; (*admit*) admettre (**that** que); **to take for granted** (*event*) considérer comme allant de soi; (*person*) considérer comme faisant partie du décor; **I take (it) for granted that** . . . je présume que . . . . **2** *n* subvention *f*, allocation *f*; Univ bourse *f*.

granule ['grænjuːl] *n* granule *m*. ◆**granulated** *a* **g. sugar** sucre *m* cristallisé.

grape [greɪp] *n* grain *m* de raisin; *pl* le raisin, les raisins *mpl*; **to eat grapes** manger du raisin *or* des raisins; **g. harvest** vendange *f*. ◆**grapefruit** *n* pamplemousse *m*. ◆**grapevine** *n* **on the g.** Fig par le téléphone arabe.

graph [græf, grɑːf] *n* graphique *m*, courbe *f*; **g. paper** papier *m* millimétré.

graphic ['græfɪk] *a* graphique; (*description*) Fig explicite, vivant. ◆**graphically** *adv* (*to describe*) explicitement.

grapple ['græp(ə)l] *vi* **to g. with** (*person, problem etc*) se colleter avec.

grasp [grɑːsp] *vt* (*seize, understand*) saisir; – *n* (*firm hold*) prise *f*; (*understanding*) compréhension *f*; (*knowledge*) connaissance *f*; **to have a strong g.** (*strength of hand*) avoir de la poigne; **within s.o.'s g.**

(*reach*) à la portée de qn. ◆**—ing** *a* (*greedy*) rapace.

grass [grɑːs] *n* herbe *f*; (*lawn*) gazon *m*; **the g. roots** Pol la base. ◆**grasshopper** *n* sauterelle *f*. ◆**grassland** *n* prairie *f*. ◆**grassy** *a* herbeux.

grat/e [greɪt] **1** *n* (*for fireplace*) grille *f* de foyer. **2** *vt* Culin râper. **3** *vi* (*of sound*) grincer (**on** sur); **to g. on the ears** écorcher les oreilles; **to g. on s.o.'s nerves** taper sur les nerfs de qn. ◆**—ing 1** *a* (*sound*) grinçant; Fig irritant. **2** *n* (*bars*) grille *f*. ◆**—er** *n* Culin râpe *f*.

grateful ['greɪtfʊl] *a* reconnaissant (**to** à, **for** de); (*words, letter*) de remerciement; (*friend, attitude*) plein de reconnaissance; **I'm g. (to you) for your help** je vous suis reconnaissant de votre aide; **I'd be g. if you'd be quieter** j'aimerais bien que tu fasses moins de bruit; **g. thanks** mes sincères remerciements. ◆**—ly** *adv* avec reconnaissance.

gratif/y ['grætɪfaɪ] *vt* (*whim*) satisfaire; **to g. s.o.** faire plaisir à qn. ◆**—ied** *a* très content (**with** *or* **at** sth de qch, **to do** de faire). ◆**—ying** *a* très satisfaisant; **it's g. to . . .** ça fait plaisir de . . . . ◆**gratifi'cation** *n* satisfaction *f*.

gratis ['grætɪs, 'greɪtɪs] *adv* gratis.

gratitude ['grætɪtjuːd] *n* reconnaissance *f*, gratitude *f* (**for** de).

gratuitous [grə'tjuːɪtəs] *a* (*act etc*) gratuit.

gratuity [grə'tjuːɪtɪ] *n* (*tip*) pourboire *m*.

grave [greɪv] *n* tombe *f*; **g. digger** fossoyeur *m*. ◆**gravestone** *n* pierre *f* tombale. ◆**graveyard** *n* cimetière *m*; **auto g.** Am Fam cimetière *m* de voitures.

grave [greɪv] *a* (**-er, -est**) (*serious*) grave. ◆**—ly** *adv* gravement; (*concerned, displeased*) extrêmement.

gravel ['græv(ə)l] *n* gravier *m*.

gravitate ['grævɪteɪt] *vi* **to g. towards** (*be drawn towards*) être attiré vers; (*move towards*) se diriger vers. ◆**gravi'tation** *n* gravitation *f*.

gravity ['grævɪtɪ] *n* **1** (*seriousness*) gravité *f*. **2** Phys pesanteur *f*, gravité *f*.

gravy ['greɪvɪ] *n* jus *m* de viande.

gray [greɪ] Am = **grey**.

graze [greɪz] **1** *vi* (*of cattle*) paître. **2** *vt* (*scrape*) écorcher; (*touch lightly*) frôler, effleurer; – *n* (*wound*) écorchure *f*.

grease [griːs] *n* graisse *f*; – *vt* graisser. ◆**greaseproof** *a* **&** *n* **g.** (**paper**) papier *m* sulfurisé. ◆**greasy** *a* (**-ier, -iest**) graisseux; (*hair*) gras; (*road*) glissant.

great [greɪt] *a* (**-er, -est**) grand; (*effort, heat,* *parcel*) gros, grand; (*excellent*) magnifique, merveilleux; **g. at** (*English, tennis etc*) doué pour; **a g. deal** *or* **number (of)**, a g. many beaucoup (*de*); **a g. opinion of** une haute opinion de; **a very g. age** un âge très avancé; **the greatest team**/*etc* (*best*) la meilleure équipe/*etc*; **Greater London** le grand Londres. ◆**g.-'grandfather** *n* arrière-grand-père *m*. ◆**g.-'grandmother** *n* arrière-grand-mère *f*. ◆**greatly** *adv* (*much*) beaucoup; (*very*) très, bien; **I g. prefer** je préfère de beaucoup. ◆**greatness** *n* (*in size, importance*) grandeur *f*; (*in degree*) intensité *f*.

Great Britain [greɪt'brɪt(ə)n] *n* Grande-Bretagne *f*.

Greece [griːs] *n* Grèce *f*. ◆**Greek** *a* grec; – *n* Grec *m*, Grecque *f*; (*language*) grec *m*.

greed [griːd] *n* avidité *f* (**for** de); (*for food*) gourmandise *f*. ◆**greed/y** *a* (**-ier**, **-iest**) avide (**for** de); (*for food*) glouton, gourmand. ◆**—ily** *adv* avidement; (*to eat*) gloutonnement. ◆**—iness** *n* = greed.

green [griːn] *a* (**-er**, **-est**) vert; (*pale*) blême, vert; (*immature*) *Fig* inexpérimenté, naïf; **to turn** *or* **go g.** verdir; **the g. belt** (*land*) la ceinture verte; **the g. light** *Fig* le (feu) vert; **to have g. fingers** *or* *Am* **a g. thumb** avoir la main verte; **g. with envy** *Fig* vert de jalousie; – *n* (*colour*) vert *m*; (*lawn*) pelouse *f*; (*village square*) place *f* gazonnée; *pl Culin* légumes *mpl* verts. ◆**greenery** *n* (*plants, leaves*) verdure *f*. ◆**greenfly** *n* puceron *m* (*des plantes*). ◆**greengrocer** *n* marchand, -ande *mf* de légumes. ◆**greenhouse** *n* serre *f*. ◆**greenish** *a* verdâtre. ◆**greenness** *n* (*colour*) vert *m*; (*greenery*) verdure *f*.

greengage ['griːngeɪdʒ] *n* (*plum*) reine-claude *f*.

Greenland ['griːnlənd] *n* Groenland *m*.

greet [griːt] *vt* saluer, accueillir; **to g. s.o.** (*of sight*) s'offrir aux regards de qn. ◆**—ing** *n* salutation *f*; (*welcome*) accueil *m*; *pl* (*for birthday, festival*) vœux *mpl*; **send my greetings to . . .** envoie mon bon souvenir à . . . ; **greetings card** carte *f* de vœux.

gregarious [grɪ'geərɪəs] *a* (*person*) sociable; (*instinct*) grégaire.

gremlin ['gremlɪn] *n* *Fam* petit diable *m*.

grenade [grə'neɪd] *n* (*bomb*) grenade *f*.

grew [gruː] *see* grow.

grey [greɪ] *a* (**-er**, **-est**) gris; (*outlook*) *Fig* sombre; **to be going g.** grisonner; – *vi* to be greying être grisonnant. ◆**g.-'haired** *a* aux cheveux gris. ◆**greyhound** *n* lévrier *m*. ◆**greyish** *a* grisâtre.

grid [grɪd] *n* (*grating*) grille *f*; (*system*) *El* réseau *m*; *Culin* gril *m*. ◆**gridiron** *n* *Culin* gril *m*.

griddle ['grɪd(ə)l] *n* (*on stove*) plaque *f* à griller.

grief [griːf] *n* chagrin *m*, douleur *f*; **to come to g.** avoir des ennuis; (*of driver, pilot etc*) avoir un accident; (*of plan*) échouer; **good g.!** ciel!, bon sang!

grieve [griːv] *vt* peiner, affliger; – *vi* s'affliger (**over** de); **to g. for s.o.** pleurer qn. ◆**grievance** *n* grief *m*; *pl* (*complaints*) doléances *fpl*.

grievous ['griːvəs] *a* (*serious*) très grave.

grill [grɪl] **1** *n* (*utensil*) gril *m*; (*dish*) grillade *f*; – *vti* griller. **2** *vt* (*question*) *Fam* cuisiner.

grille [grɪl] *n* (*metal bars*) grille *f*; (*radiator*) g. *Aut* calandre *f*.

grim [grɪm] *a* (**grimmer**, **grimmest**) sinistre; (*face*) sévère; (*truth*) brutal; (*bad*) *Fam* (*plutôt*) affreux; **a g. determination** une volonté inflexible. ◆**—ly** *adv* (*to look at*) sévèrement.

grimace ['grɪməs] *n* grimace *f*; – *vi* grimacer.

grime [graɪm] *n* saleté *f*. ◆**grimy** *a* (**-ier**, **-iest**) sale.

grin [grɪn] *vi* (**-nn-**) avoir un large sourire; (*with pain*) avoir un rictus; – *n* large sourire *m*; rictus *m*.

grind [graɪnd] **1** *vt* (*pt & pp* **ground**) moudre; (*blade, tool*) aiguiser; (*handle*) tourner; (*oppress*) *Fig* écraser; **to g. one's teeth** grincer des dents; – *vi* **to g. to a halt** s'arrêter (*progressivement*). **2** *n* *Fam* corvée *f*, travail *m* long et monotone. ◆**—ing** *a* **g. poverty** la misère noire. ◆**—er** *n* **coffee g.** moulin *m* à café.

grip [grɪp] *vt* (**-pp-**) (*seize*) saisir; (*hold*) tenir serré; (*of story*) *Fig* empoigner (qn); **to g. the road** (*of tyres*) adhérer à la route; – *vi* (*of brakes*) mordre; – *n* (*hold*) prise *f*; (*hand clasp*) poigne *f*; **get a g. on yourself!** secoue-toi!; **to get to grips with** (*problem*) s'attaquer à; **in the g. of** en proie à. ◆**gripping** *a* (*book, film etc*) prenant.

gripe [graɪp] *vi* (*complain*) *Sl* rouspéter.

grisly ['grɪzlɪ] *a* (*gruesome*) horrible.

gristle ['grɪs(ə)l] *n* *Culin* cartilage *m*.

grit [grɪt] **1** *n* (*sand*) sable *m*; (*gravel*) gravillon *m*; – *vt* (**-tt-**) (*road*) sabler. **2** *n* (*pluck*) *Fam* cran *m*. **3** *vt* (**-tt-**) **to g. one's teeth** serrer les dents.

grizzle ['grɪz(ə)l] *vi* *Fam* pleurnicher. ◆**grizzly** *a* **1** (*child*) *Fam* pleurnicheur. **2** (*bear*) gris.

groan [grəʊn] *vi* (*with pain*) gémir;

grocer ['grəusə] *n* épicier, -ière *mf*; **grocer's (shop)** épicerie *f*. ◆**grocery** *n* (*shop*) épicerie *f*; *pl* (*food*) épicerie *f*.

grog [grɒg] *n* (*drink*) grog *m*.

groggy ['grɒgɪ] *a* (**-ier, -iest**) (*weak*) faible; (*shaky on one's feet*) pas solide sur les jambes.

groin [grɔɪn] *n Anat* aine *f*.

groom [grum] **1** *n* (*bridegroom*) marié *m*. **2** *n* (*for horses*) lad *m*; – *vt* (*horse*) panser; **to g. s.o. for** (*job*) *Fig* préparer qn pour; **well groomed** (*person*) très soigné.

groove [gruːv] *n* (*for sliding door etc*) rainure *f*; (*in record*) sillon *m*.

grope [grəup] *vi* **to g. (about)** tâtonner; **to g. for** chercher à tâtons.

gross [grəus] **1** *a* (**-er, -est**) (*coarse*) grossier; (*error*) gros, grossier; (*injustice*) flagrant. **2** *a* (*weight, income*) Com brut; – *vt* faire une recette brute de. **3** *n* (*number*) grosse *f*. ◆—**ly** *adv* grossièrement; (*very*) énormément, extrêmement.

grotesque [grəu'tesk] *a* (*ludicrous, strange*) grotesque; (*frightening*) monstrueux.

grotto ['grɒtəu] *n* (*pl* **-oes** *or* **-os**) grotte *f*.

grotty ['grɒtɪ] *a* (**-ier, -iest**) *Fam* affreux, moche.

ground[1] [graund] **1** *n* terre *f*, sol *m*; (*area for camping, football etc*) & *Fig* terrain *m*; (*estate*) terres *fpl*; (*earth*) El *Am* terre *f*, masse *f*; (*background*) fond *m*; *pl* (*reasons*) raisons *fpl*, motifs *mpl*; (*gardens*) parc *m*; **on the g.** (*lying etc*) par terre; **to lose g.** perdre du terrain; **g. floor** rez-de-chaussée *m inv*; **g. frost** gelée *f* blanche. **2** *vt* (*aircraft*) bloquer *or* retenir au sol. ◆—**ing** *n* connaissances *fpl* (de fond) (**in** en). ◆**groundless** *a* sans fondement. ◆**groundnut** *n* arachide *f*. ◆**groundsheet** *n* tapis *m* de sol. ◆**groundswell** *n* lame *f* de fond. ◆**groundwork** *n* préparation *f*.

ground[2] [graund] *see* **grind 1**; – *a* (*coffee*) moulu; – *npl* (*coffee*) **grounds** marc *m* (de café).

group [gruːp] *n* groupe *m*; – *vt* **to g.** (**together**) grouper; – *vi* se grouper. ◆—**ing** *n* (*group*) groupe *m*.

grouse [graus] **1** *n inv* (*bird*) coq *m* de bruyère. **2** *n* (*complain*) *Fam* rouspéter.

grove [grəuv] *n* bocage *m*.

grovel ['grɒv(ə)l] *vi* (**-ll-,** *Am* **-l-**) *Pej* ramper, s'aplatir (**to s.o.** devant qn).

grow [grəu] *vi* (*pt* **grew**, *pp* **grown**) (*of person*) grandir; (*of plant, hair*) pousser;

(*increase*) augmenter, grandir, croître; (*expand*) s'agrandir; **to g. fat(ter)** grossir; **to g. to like** finir par aimer; **to g. into** devenir; **to g. on s.o.** (*of book, music etc*) plaire progressivement à qn; **to g. out of** (*one's clothes*) devenir trop grand pour; (*a habit*) perdre; **to g. up** devenir adulte; **when I g. up** quand je serai grand; – *vt* (*plant, crops*) cultiver, faire pousser; (*beard, hair*) laisser pousser. ◆—**ing** *a* (*child*) qui grandit; (*number*) grandissant. ◆**grown** *a* (*full-grown*) adulte. ◆**grown-up** *n* grande personne *f*, adulte *mf*; – *a* (*ideas etc*) d'adulte. ◆**grower** *n* (*person*) cultivateur, -trice *mf*.

growl [graul] *vi* grogner (**at** contre); – *n* grognement *m*.

growth [grəuθ] *n* croissance *f*; (*increase*) augmentation *f* (**in** de); (*of hair*) pousse *f*; (*beard*) barbe *f*; *Med* tumeur *f* (**on** à).

grub [grʌb] *n* (*food*) *Fam* bouffe *f*.

grubby ['grʌbɪ] *a* (**-ier, -iest**) sale.

grudg/e [grʌdʒ] **1** *vt* (*give*) donner à contrecœur; (*reproach*) reprocher (**s.o. sth** qch à qn); **to g. doing** faire à contrecœur. **2** *n* rancune *f*; **to have a g. against** en vouloir à. ◆—**ing** *a* peu généreux. ◆—**ingly** *adv* (*to give etc*) à contrecœur.

gruelling, *Am* **grueling** ['gruːəlɪŋ] *a* (*day, detail etc*) éprouvant, atroce.

gruesome ['gruːsəm] *a* horrible.

gruff [grʌf] *a* (**-er, -est**) (*voice, person*) bourru.

grumble ['grʌmb(ə)l] *vi* (*complain*) grogner (**about, at** contre), se plaindre (**about, at** de).

grumpy ['grʌmpɪ] *a* (**-ier, -iest**) grincheux.

grunt [grʌnt] *vti* grogner; – *n* grognement *m*.

guarantee [gærən'tiː] *n* garantie *f*; – *vt* garantir (**against** contre); (*vouch for*) se porter garant de; **to g.** (**s.o.**) **that** certifier *or* garantir (à qn) que. ◆**guarantor** *n* garant, -ante *mf*.

guard [gɑːd] *n* (*vigilance, group of soldiers etc*) garde *f*; (*individual person*) garde *m*; *Rail* chef *m* de train; **to keep a g. on** surveiller; **under g.** sous surveillance; **on one's g.** sur ses gardes; **to catch s.o. off his g.** prendre qn au dépourvu; **on g.** (*duty*) de garde; **to stand g.** monter la garde; – *vt* (*protect*) protéger (**against** contre); (*watch over*) surveiller, garder; – *vi* **to g. against** (*protect oneself*) se prémunir contre; (*prevent*) empêcher; **to g. against doing** se garder de faire. ◆—**ed** *a* (*cautious*) prudent.

◆**guardian** n gardien, -ienne mf; (of child) Jur tuteur, -trice mf.

guerrilla [gə'rɪlə] n (person) guérillero m; g. **warfare** guérilla f.

guess [ges] n conjecture f; (intuition) intuition f; (estimate) estimation f; to make a g. (essayer de) deviner; **an educated or informed g.** une conjecture fondée; **at a g.** au jugé, à vue de nez; – vt deviner (that que); (estimate) estimer; (suppose) Am supposer (that que); (think) Am croire (that que); – vi deviner; **I g. (so)** Am je suppose; je crois. ◆**guesswork** n hypothèse f; **by g.** au jugé.

guest [gest] n invité, -ée mf; (in hotel) client, -ente mf; (at meal) convive mf; – a (speaker, singer etc) invité. ◆**guesthouse** n pension f de famille. ◆**guestroom** n chambre f d'ami.

guffaw [gə'fɔ:] vi rire bruyamment.

guidance ['gaɪdəns] n (advice) conseils mpl.

guid/e [gaɪd] n (person, book etc) guide m; (indication) indication f; (girl) g. éclaireuse f; **g. dog** chien m d'aveugle; **g. book** guide m; – vt (lead) guider. ◆**-ed** a (missile, rocket) téléguidé; **g. tour** visite f guidée. ◆**-ing** a (principle) directeur. ◆**guidelines** npl lignes fpl directrices, indications fpl à suivre.

guild [gɪld] n association f; Hist corporation f.

guile [gaɪl] n (deceit) ruse f.

guillotine ['gɪlətiːn] n guillotine f; (for paper) massicot m.

guilt [gɪlt] n culpabilité f. ◆**guilty** a (-ier, -iest) coupable; **g. person** coupable mf; **to find s.o. g.** déclarer qn coupable.

guinea pig ['gɪnɪpɪg] n (animal) & Fig cobaye m.

guise [gaɪz] n **under the g. of** sous l'apparence de.

guitar [gɪ'tɑ:r] n guitare f. ◆**guitarist** n guitariste m.

gulf [gʌlf] n (in sea) golfe m; (chasm) gouffre m; **a g. between** Fig un abîme entre.

gull [gʌl] n (bird) mouette f.

gullet ['gʌlɪt] n gosier m.

gullible ['gʌlɪb(ə)l] a crédule.

gully ['gʌlɪ] n (valley) ravine f; (drain) rigole f.

gulp [gʌlp] **1** vt **to g. (down)** avaler (vite); – n (of drink) gorgée f, lampée f; **in or at one**

g. d'une seule gorgée. 2 vi (with emotion) avoir la gorge serrée; – n serrement m de gorge.

gum[1] [gʌm] n Anat gencive f. ◆**gumboil** n abcès m (dentaire).

gum[2] [gʌm] **1** n (glue from tree) gomme f; (any glue) colle f; – vt (-mm-) coller. **2** n (for chewing) chewing-gum m.

gumption ['gʌmpʃ(ə)n] n Fam (courage) initiative f; (commonsense) jugeote f.

gun [gʌn] n pistolet m, revolver m; (cannon) canon m; – vt (-nn-) **to g. down** abattre. ◆**gunfight** n échange m de coups de feu. ◆**gunfire** n coups mpl de feu; Mil tir m d'artillerie. ◆**gunman** n (pl -men) bandit m armé. ◆**gunner** n Mil artilleur m. ◆**gunpoint** n **at g.** sous la menace d'un pistolet or d'une arme. ◆**gunpowder** n poudre f à canon. ◆**gunshot** n coup m de feu; **g. wound** blessure f par balle.

gurgle ['gɜːg(ə)l] vi (of water) glouglouter; – n glouglou m.

guru ['gʊruː] n (leader) Fam gourou m.

gush [gʌʃ] vi jaillir (out of de); – n jaillissement m.

gust [gʌst] n (of smoke) bouffée f; **g. (of wind)** rafale f (de vent). ◆**gusty** a (-ier, -iest) (weather) venteux; (day) de vent.

gusto ['gʌstəʊ] n **with g.** avec entrain.

gut [gʌt] **1** n Anat intestin m; (catgut) boyau m; pl Fam (innards) tripes fpl, tripes fpl; (pluck) cran m, tripes fpl; **he hates your guts** Fam il ne peut pas te sentir. **2** vt (-tt-) (of fire) dévaster.

gutter ['gʌtər] n (on roof) gouttière f; (in street) caniveau m.

guttural ['gʌtərəl] a guttural.

guy [gaɪ] n (fellow) Fam type m.

guzzle ['gʌz(ə)l] vi (eat) bâfrer; – vt (eat) engloutir; (drink) siffler.

gym [dʒɪm] n gym(nastique) f; (gymnasium) gymnase m; **g. shoes** tennis fpl. ◆**gym-'nasium** n gymnase m. ◆**gymnast** n gymnaste mf. ◆**gym'nastics** n gymnastique f.

gynaecology, Am **gynecology** [gaɪnɪ'kɒlədʒɪ] n gynécologie f. ◆**gynae-cologist** n, Am ◆**gynecologist** n gynécologue mf.

gypsy ['dʒɪpsɪ] = **gipsy.**

gyrate [dʒaɪ'reɪt] vi tournoyer.

H

H, h [eɪtʃ] *n* H, h *m*; **H bomb** bombe *f* H.

haberdasher ['hæbədæʃər] *n* mercier, -ière *mf*; *(men's outfitter) Am* chemisier *m*. ◆**haberdashery** *n* mercerie *f*; *Am* chemiserie *f*.

habit ['hæbɪt] *n* **1** habitude *f*; **to be in/get into the h. of doing** avoir/prendre l'habitude de faire; **to make a h. of doing** avoir pour habitude de faire. **2** *(addiction) Med* accoutumance *f*; **a h.-forming drug** une drogue qui crée une accoutumance. **3** *(costume) Rel* habit *m*. ◆**ha'bitual** *a* habituel; *(smoker, drinker etc)* invétéré. ◆**ha'bitually** *adv* habituellement.

habitable ['hæbɪtəb(ə)l] *a* habitable. ◆**habitat** *n (of animal, plant)* habitat *m*. ◆**habi'tation** *n* habitation *f*; **fit for h.** habitable.

hack [hæk] **1** *vt (cut)* tailler, hacher. **2** *n (old horse)* rosse *f*; *(hired)* cheval *m* de louage; **h.** *(writer) Pej* écrivaillon *m*.

hackney ['hæknɪ] *a* **h. carriage** *Hist* fiacre *m*. ◆**hackneyed** ['hæknɪd] *a (saying)* rebattu, banal.

had [hæd] *see* have.

haddock ['hædək] *n (fish)* aiglefin *m*; **smoked h.** haddock *m*.

haemorrhage ['hemərɪdʒ] *n Med* hémorragie *f*.

haemorrhoids ['hemərɔɪdz] *npl* hémorroïdes *fpl*.

hag [hæg] *n (woman) Pej* (vieille) sorcière *f*.

haggard ['hægəd] *a (person, face)* hâve, émacié.

haggl/e ['hæg(ə)l] *vi* marchander; **to h. over** *(thing)* marchander; *(price)* débattre, discuter. ◆**—ing** *n* marchandage *m*.

Hague (The) [ðə'heɪg] *n* La Haye.

ha-ha! [hɑːhɑː] *int (laughter)* ha, ha!

hail[1] [heɪl] *n Met & Fig* grêle *f*; *– v imp Met* grêler; **it's hailing** il grêle. ◆**hailstone** *n* grêlon *m*.

hail[2] [heɪl] **1** *vt (greet)* saluer; *(taxi)* héler. **2** *vi* **to h. from** *(of person)* être originaire de; *(of ship etc)* être en provenance de.

hair [heər] *n (on head)* cheveux *mpl*; *(on body, of animal)* poils *mpl*; **a h.** *(on head)* un cheveu; *(on body, of animal)* un poil; **by a hair's breadth** de justesse; **long-/red-/etc haired** aux cheveux longs/roux/etc; **h.**

cream brillantine *f*; **h. dryer** sèche-cheveux *m inv*; **h. spray** (bombe *f* de) laque *f*. ◆**hairbrush** *n* brosse *f* à cheveux. ◆**haircut** *n* coupe *f* de cheveux; **to have a h.** se faire couper les cheveux. ◆**hairdo** *n (pl -dos) Fam* coiffure *f*. ◆**hairdresser** *n* coiffeur, -euse *mf*. ◆**hairgrip** *n* pince *f* à cheveux. ◆**hairnet** *n* résille *f*. ◆**hairpiece** *n* postiche *m*. ◆**hairpin** *n* épingle *f* à cheveux; **h. bend** *Aut* virage *m* en épingle à cheveux. ◆**hair-raising** *a* à faire dresser les cheveux sur la tête. ◆**hair-splitting** *n* ergotage *m*. ◆**hairstyle** *n* coiffure *f*.

hairy ['heərɪ] *a (-ier, -iest) (person, animal, body)* poilu; *(unpleasant, frightening) Fam* effroyable.

hake [heɪk] *n (fish)* colin *m*.

hale [heɪl] *a* **h. and hearty** vigoureux.

half [hɑːf] *n (pl halves)* moitié *f*, demi, -ie *mf*; *(of match) Sp* mi-temps *f*; **h. (of) the apple/etc** la moitié de la pomme/etc; **ten and a h.** dix et demi; **ten and a h. weeks** dix semaines et demie; **to cut in h.** couper en deux; **to go halves with** partager les frais avec; *– a* demi; **h. a day, a h.-day** une demi-journée; **at h. price** à moitié prix; **h. man h. beast** mi-homme mi-bête; **h. sleeves** manches *fpl* mi-longues; *– adv (dressed, full etc)* à demi, à moitié; *(almost)* presque; **h. asleep** à moitié endormi; **h. past one** une heure et demie; **he isn't h. lazy/etc** *Fam* il est rudement paresseux/etc; **h. as much as** moitié moins que; **h. as much again** moitié plus.

half-back ['hɑːfbæk] *n Fb* demi *m*. ◆**h.-'baked** *a (idea) Fam* à la manque, à la noix. ◆**h.-breed** *n*, ◆**h.-caste** *n Pej* métis, -isse *mf*. ◆**h.-(a-)'dozen** *n* demi-douzaine *f*. ◆**h.-'hearted** *a (person, manner)* peu enthousiaste; *(effort)* timide. ◆**h.-'hour** *n* demi-heure *f*. ◆**h.-light** *n* demi-jour *m*. ◆**h.-'mast** *n* **at h.-mast** *(flag)* en berne. ◆**h.-'open** *a* entrouvert. ◆**h.-'term** *n Sch* petites vacances *fpl*, congé *m* de demi-trimestre. ◆**h.-'time** *n Sp* mi-temps *f*. ◆**half'way** *adv (between places)* à mi-chemin (between entre); **to fill/etc h.** remplir/etc à moitié; **h. through**

(*book*) à la moitié de. ◆**h.-wit** *n*, ◆**h.-'witted** *a* imbécile (*mf*).

halibut ['hælɪbət] *n* (*fish*) flétan *m*.

hall [hɔːl] *n* (*room*) salle *f*; (*house entrance*) entrée *f*, vestibule *m*; (*of hotel*) hall *m*; (*mansion*) manoir *m*; (*for meals*) *Univ* réfectoire *m*; **h. of residence** *Univ* pavillon *m* universitaire; **halls of residence** cité *f* universitaire; **lecture h.** *Univ* amphithéâtre *m*. ◆**hallmark** *n* (*on silver or gold*) poinçon *m*; *Fig* sceau *m*. ◆**hallstand** *n* portemanteau *m*. ◆**hallway** *n* entrée *f*, vestibule *m*.

hallelujah [hælɪˈluːjə] *n* & *int* alléluia (*m*).

hallo! [həˈləʊ] *int* (*greeting*) bonjour!; *Tel* allô!; (*surprise*) tiens!

hallow ['hæləʊ] *vt* sanctifier.

Hallowe'en [hæləʊˈiːn] *n* la veille de la Toussaint.

hallucination [həluːsɪˈneɪʃ(ə)n] *n* hallucination *f*.

halo ['heɪləʊ] *n* (*pl* -oes *or* -os) auréole *f*, halo *m*.

halt [hɔːlt] *n* halte *f*; **to call a h.** to mettre fin à; **to come to a h.** s'arrêter; – *vi* faire halte; – *int Mil* halte! ◆—**ing** *a* (*voice*) hésitant.

halve [hɑːv] *vt* (*time, expense*) réduire de moitié; (*cake, number etc*) diviser en deux.

ham [hæm] **1** *n* jambon *m*; **h. and eggs** œufs *mpl* au jambon. **2** (*actor*) *Th Pej* cabotin, -ine *mf*. ◆**h.-'fisted** *a Fam* maladroit.

hamburger ['hæmbɜːɡər] *n* hamburger *m*.

hamlet ['hæmlɪt] *n* hameau *m*.

hammer ['hæmər] *n* marteau *m*; – *vt* (*metal, table*) marteler; (*nail*) enfoncer (**into** dans); (*defeat*) *Fam* battre à plate(s) couture(s); (*criticize*) *Fam* démolir; **to h. out** (*agreement*) mettre au point; – *vi* frapper (au marteau). ◆—**ing** *n* (*defeat*) *Fam* raclée *f*, défaite *f*.

hammock ['hæmək] *n* hamac *m*.

hamper ['hæmpər] **1** *vt* gêner. **2** *n* (*basket*) panier *m*; (*laundry basket*) *Am* panier *m* à linge.

hamster ['hæmstər] *n* hamster *m*.

hand¹ [hænd] **1** *n* main *f*; **to hold in one's h.** tenir à la main; **by h.** (*to deliver etc*) à la main; **at** *or* **to h.** (*within reach*) sous la main, à portée de la main; (*close*) **at h.** (*person etc*) tout près; (*day etc*) proche; **in h.** (*situation*) bien en main; (*matter*) en question; (*money*) disponible; **on h.** (*ready for use*) disponible; **to have s.o. on one's hands** *Fig* avoir qn sur les bras; **on the right h.** du côté droit (**of** de); **on the one h.** . . . d'une part . . . ; **on the other h.** . . . d'autre part . . . ; **hands up!** (*in attack*) haut les mains!; *Sch* levez la main!; **hands off!** pas touche!, bas les pattes!; **my hands are full** *Fig* je suis très occupé; **to give s.o. a** (*helping*) **h.** donner un coup de main à qn; **to get out of h.** (*of person*) devenir impossible; (*of situation*) devenir incontrôlable; **h. in h.** la main dans la main; **h. in h. with** (*together with*) *Fig* de pair avec; **at first h.** de première main; **to win hands down** gagner haut la main; – *a* (*luggage etc*) à main. **2** *n* (*worker*) ouvrier, -ière *mf*; (*of clock*) aiguille *f*; *Cards* jeu *m*; (*writing*) écriture *f*. ◆**handbag** *n* sac *m* à main. ◆**handbook** *n* (*manual*) manuel *m*; (*guide*) guide *m*. ◆**handbrake** *n* frein *m* à main. ◆**handbrush** *n* balayette *f*. ◆**handcuff** *vt* passer les menottes à. ◆**handcuffs** *npl* menottes *fpl*. ◆**hand'made** *a* fait à la main. ◆**hand'picked** *a Fig* trié sur le volet. ◆**handrail** *n* (*on stairs*) rampe *f*. ◆**handshake** *n* poignée *f* de main. ◆**handwriting** *n* écriture *f*. ◆**hand'written** *a* écrit à la main.

hand² [hænd] *vt* (*give*) donner (**to** à); **to h. down** (*bring down*) descendre; (*knowledge, heirloom*) transmettre (**to** à); **to h. in** remettre; **to h. out** distribuer; **to h. over** remettre; (*power*) transmettre; **to h. round** (*cakes*) passer. ◆**handout** *n* (*leaflet*) prospectus *m*; (*money*) aumône *f*.

handful ['hændfʊl] *n* (*bunch, group*) poignée *f*; (*quite*) **a h.** (*difficult*) *Fig* difficile.

handicap ['hændɪkæp] *n* (*disadvantage*) & *Sp* handicap *m*; – *vt* (**-pp-**) handicaper. ◆**handicapped** *a* (*disabled*) handicapé.

handicraft ['hændɪkrɑːft] *n* artisanat *m* d'art. ◆**handiwork** *n* artisanat *m* d'art; (*action*) *Fig* ouvrage *m*.

handkerchief ['hæŋkətʃɪf] *n* (*pl* -fs) mouchoir *m*; (*for neck*) foulard *m*.

handle ['hænd(ə)l] *n* (*of door*) poignée *f*; (*of knife*) manche *m*; (*of bucket*) anse *f*; (*of saucepan*) queue *f*; (*of pump*) bras *m*. **2** *vt* (*manipulate*) manier; (*touch*) toucher à; (*ship, vehicle*) manœuvrer; (*deal with*) s'occuper de; (*difficult child etc*) s'y prendre avec; – *vi* **to h. well** (*of machine*) être facile à manier.

handlebars ['hænd(ə)lbɑːz] *npl* guidon *m*.

handsome ['hænsəm] *a* (*person, building etc*) beau; (*gift*) généreux; (*profit, sum*) considérable. ◆—**ly** *adv* (*generously*) généreusement.

handy ['hændɪ] *a* (**-ier, -iest**) (*convenient, practical*) commode, pratique; (*skilful*) habile (**at doing** à faire); (*useful*) utile; (*near*) proche, accessible; **to come in h.** se révéler utile; **to keep h.** avoir sous la main. ◆**handyman** n (pl -men) (DIY enthusiast) bricoleur m.

hang¹ [hæŋ] **1** vt (pt & pp hung) suspendre (**on, from** à); (on hook) accrocher (**on, from** à); suspendre; (wallpaper) poser; (let dangle) laisser pendre (**from, out of** de); **to h. with** (decorate with) orner de; **to h. out** (washing) étendre; (flag) arborer; **to h. up** (picture etc) accrocher; — vi (of threat) planer; (of fog, smoke) flotter; **to h. about** (loiter) traîner, rôder; (wait) Fam attendre; **to h. down** (dangle) pendre; (of hair) tomber; **to h. on** (hold out) résister; (wait) Fam attendre; **to h. on to** (cling to) ne pas lâcher; (keep) garder; **to h. out** (of tongue, shirt) pendre; (live) Sl crécher; **to h. together** (of facts) se tenir; (of plan) tenir debout; **to h. up** Tél raccrocher. **2** n **to get the h. of sth** Fam arriver à comprendre qch; **to get the h. of doing** Fam trouver le truc pour faire. ◆**—ing¹** n suspension f; — a suspendu (**from** à); (leg, arm) pendant; **h. on** (wall) accroché à. ◆**hang-glider** n delta-plane® m. ◆**hang-gliding** n vol m libre. ◆**hangnail** n petites peaux fpl. ◆**hangover** n Fam gueule f de bois. ◆**hangup** n Fam complexe m.

hang² [hæŋ] vt (pt & pp hanged) (criminal) pendre (**for** pour); — vi (of criminal) être pendu. ◆**—ing²** n Jur pendaison f. ◆**hangman** n (pl -men) bourreau m.

hangar ['hæŋər] n Av hangar m.

hanger ['hæŋər] n (coat) h. cintre m. ◆**hanger-'on** n (pl hangers-on) (person) Pej parasite m.

hanker ['hæŋkər] vi **to h. after** or **for** avoir envie de. ◆**—ing** n (forte) envie f, (vif) désir m.

hankie, hanky ['hæŋkı] n Fam mouchoir m.

hanky-panky ['hæŋkı'pæŋkı] n inv Fam (deceit) manigances fpl, magouilles fpl; (sexual behaviour) papouilles fpl, pelotage m.

haphazard [hæp'hæzəd] a au hasard, au petit bonheur; (selection, arrangement) aléatoire. ◆**—ly** adv au hasard.

hapless ['hæplıs] a Lit infortuné.

happen ['hæpən] vi arriver, se passer, se produire; **to h. to s.o./sth** arriver à qn/qch; **it (so) happens that I know, I h. to know** it se trouve que je le sais; **do you h. to have . . . ?** est-ce que par hasard vous avez . . . ?; **whatever happens** quoi qu'il arrive. ◆**—ing** n événement m.

happy ['hæpı] a (-ier, -iest) heureux (**to do** de faire, **about sth** de qch); **I'm not (too** or **very) h. about (doing) it** ça ne me plaît pas beaucoup (de le faire); **H. New Year!** bonne année!; **H. Christmas!** joyeux Noël! ◆**h.-go-'lucky** a insouciant. ◆**happily** adv (contentedly) tranquillement; (joyously) joyeusement; (fortunately) heureusement. ◆**happiness** n bonheur m.

harass ['hærəs, Am hə'ræs] vt harceler. ◆**—ment** n harcèlement m.

harbour ['hɑːbər] **1** n port m. **2** vt (shelter) héberger; (criminal) cacher, abriter; (fear, secret) nourrir.

hard [hɑːd] a (-er, -est) (not soft, severe) dur; (difficult) difficile, dur; (study) assidu; (fact) brutal; (drink) alcoolisé; (water) calcaire; **h. drinker/worker** gros buveur m/travailleur m; **a h. frost** une forte gelée; **to be h. on** or **to s.o.** être dur avec qn; **to find it h. to sleep/etc** avoir du mal à dormir/etc; **h. labour** Jur travaux mpl forcés; **h. cash** espèces fpl; **h. core** (group) noyau m; **h. of hearing** malentendant; **h. up** (broke) Fam fauché; **to be h. up for** manquer de; — adv (-er, -est) (to work) dur; (to pull) fort; (to hit, freeze) dur, fort; (to study) assidûment; (to think) sérieusement; (to rain) à verse; (badly) mal; **h. by** tout près; **h. done by** traité injustement. ◆**hard-and-fast** [hɑːdən(d)'fɑːst] a (rule) strict. ◆**'hardback** n livre m relié. ◆**'hardboard** n Isorel® m. ◆**hard-'boiled** a (egg) dur. ◆**hard-'core** a (rigid) Pej inflexible. ◆**hard-'headed** a réaliste. ◆**hard'wearing** a résistant. ◆**hard-'working** a travailleur.

harden ['hɑːd(ə)n] vti durcir; **to h. oneself to** s'endurcir à. ◆**—ed** a (criminal) endurci.

hardly ['hɑːdlı] adv à peine; **he h. talks** il parle à peine, il ne parle guère; **h. ever** presque jamais.

hardness ['hɑːdnıs] n dureté f.

hardship ['hɑːdʃıp] n (ordeal) épreuve(s) f(pl); (deprivation) privation(s) f(pl).

hardware ['hɑːdweər] n inv quincaillerie f; (of computer) & Mil matériel m.

hardy ['hɑːdı] a (-ier, -iest) (person, plant) résistant.

hare [heər] n lièvre m. ◆**h.-brained** a (person) écervelé; (scheme) insensé.

harem [hɑːˈriːm] n harem m.

hark [hɑːk] vi Lit écouter; **to h. back to** (subject etc) Fam revenir sur.

harm [hɑːm] n (hurt) mal m; (prejudice) tort m; **he means no h.** il ne nous veut pas de mal; **she'll come to no h.** il ne lui arrivera rien; — vt (hurt) faire du mal à; (prejudice) nuire à, faire du tort à; (object) endommager, abîmer. ◆**harmful** a nuisible. ◆**harmless** a (person, treatment) inoffensif; (hobby, act) innocent; (gas, fumes etc) qui n'est pas nuisible, inoffensif.

harmonica [hɑːˈmɒnɪkə] n harmonica m.

harmony [ˈhɑːmənɪ] n harmonie f. ◆**harmonic** a & n Mus harmonique (m). ◆**harmonious** a harmonieux. ◆**harmonium** n Mus harmonium m. ◆**harmonize** vt harmoniser; — vi s'harmoniser.

harness [ˈhɑːnɪs] n (for horse, baby) harnais m; — vt (horse) harnacher; (energy etc) Fig exploiter.

harp [hɑːp] 1 n Mus harpe f. 2 vt to h. on (about) sth Fam rabâcher qch. ◆**harpist** n harpiste m.

harpoon [hɑːˈpuːn] n harpon m; — vt (whale) harponner.

harpsichord [ˈhɑːpsɪkɔːd] n Mus clavecin m.

harrowing [ˈhærəʊɪŋ] a (tale, memory) poignant; (cry, sight) déchirant.

harsh [hɑːʃ] a (-er, -est) (severe) dur, sévère; (sound, taste) âpre; (surface) rugueux; (fabric) rêche. ◆**-ly** adv durement, sévèrement. ◆**-ness** n dureté f, sévérité f; âpreté f; rugosité f.

harvest [ˈhɑːvɪst] n moisson f, récolte f; (of people, objects) Fig ribambelle f; — vt moissonner, récolter.

has [hæz] see **have**. ◆**has-been** n Fam personne f finie.

hash [hæʃ] 1 n Culin hachis m; — vt to h. (up) hacher. 2 n (mess) Fam gâchis m. 3 n (hashish) Sl hasch m, H m.

hashish [ˈhæʃiːʃ] n haschisch m.

hassle [ˈhæs(ə)l] n Fam (trouble) histoires fpl; (bother) mal m, peine f.

haste [heɪst] n hâte f; in h. à la hâte; to make h. se hâter. ◆**hasten** vi se hâter (to do faire); — vt hâter. ◆**hasty** a (-ier, -iest) (sudden) précipité; (visit) rapide; (decision, work) hâtif. ◆**hastily** adv (quickly) en hâte; (too quickly) hâtivement.

hat [hæt] n chapeau m; that's old h. Fam (old-fashioned) c'est vieux jeu; (stale) c'est vieux comme les rues; to score or get a h. trick Sp réussir trois coups consécutifs.

hatch [hætʃ] 1 vi (of chick, egg) éclore; — vt faire éclore; (plot) Fig tramer. 2 n (in kitchen wall) passe-plats m inv.

hatchback [ˈhætʃbæk] n (door) hayon m; (car) trois-portes f inv, cinq-portes f inv.

hatchet [ˈhætʃɪt] n hachette f.

hate [heɪt] vt détester, haïr; to h. doing or to

do détester faire; I h. to say it ça me gêne de le dire; — n haine f; pet h. Fam bête f noire. ◆**hateful** a haïssable. ◆**hatred** n haine f.

haughty [ˈhɔːtɪ] a (-ier, -iest) hautain. ◆**haughtily** adv avec hauteur.

haul [hɔːl] 1 vt (pull) tirer, traîner; (goods) camionner. 2 n (fish) prise f; (of thief) butin m; a long h. (trip) un long voyage. ◆**haulage** n camionnage m. ◆**hauler** n Am, ◆**haulier** n transporteur m routier.

haunt [hɔːnt] 1 vt hanter. 2 n endroit m favori; (of criminal) repaire m. ◆**-ing** a (music, memory) obsédant.

have [hæv] 1 (3rd person sing pres t has; pt & pp had; pres p having) vt avoir; (get) recevoir, avoir; (meal, shower etc) prendre; he has got, he has à; to h. a walk/ dream/etc faire une promenade/un rêve/ etc; to h. a drink prendre or boire un verre; to h. a wash se laver; to h. a holiday (spend) passer des vacances; will you h. ...? (a cake, some tea etc) est-ce que tu veux...?; to let s.o. h. sth donner qch à qn; to h. it from s.o. that tenir de qn que; he had me by the hair il me tenait par les cheveux; I won't h. this (allow) je ne tolérerai pas ça; you've had it! Fam tu es fichu!; to h. on (clothes) porter; to have sth on (be busy) être pris; to h. s.o. over inviter qn chez soi. 2 v aux avoir; (with monter, sortir etc & pronominal verbs) être; to h. decided/been avoir décidé/été; to h. gone être allé; to h. cut oneself s'être coupé; I've just done it je viens de le faire; to h. to do (must) devoir faire; I've got to go, I h. to go je dois partir, je suis obligé de partir, il faut que je parte; I don't h. to go je ne suis pas obligé de partir; to h. sth done (get sth done) faire faire qch; he's had his suitcase brought up il a fait monter sa valise; I've had my car stolen on m'a volé mon auto; she's had her hair cut elle s'est fait couper les cheveux; I've been doing it for months je le fais depuis des mois; haven't I?, hasn't she? etc n'est-ce pas?; no I haven't! non!; yes I h.! si!; after he had eaten, he left après avoir mangé, il partit. 3 npl the haves and (the) have-nots les riches mpl et les pauvres mpl.

haven [ˈheɪv(ə)n] n refuge m, havre m.

haversack [ˈhævəsæk] n (shoulder bag) musette f.

havoc [ˈhævək] n ravages mpl.

hawk [hɔːk] 1 n (bird) & Pol faucon m. 2 vt (goods) colporter. ◆**-er** n colporteur, -euse mf.

hawthorn [ˈhɔːθɔːn] n aubépine f.

hay [heɪ] *n* foin *m*; **h. fever** rhume *m* des foins. ◆**haystack** *n* meule *f* de foin.

haywire ['heɪwaɪər] *a* **to go h.** (*of machine*) se détraquer; (*of scheme, plan*) mal tourner.

hazard ['hæzəd] *n* risque *m*; **health h.** risque *m* pour la santé; **it's a fire h.** ça risque de provoquer un incendie; — *vt* (*guess, remark etc*) hasarder, risquer. ◆**hazardous** *a* hasardeux.

haze [heɪz] *n* brume *f*; **in a h.** (*person*) Fig dans le brouillard. ◆**hazy** *a* (**-ier, -iest**) (*weather*) brumeux; (*sun*) voilé; (*photo, idea*) flou; **I'm h. about my plans** je ne suis pas sûr de mes projets.

hazel ['heɪz(ə)l] *n* (*bush*) noisetier *m*; — *a* (*eyes*) noisette *inv.* ◆**hazelnut** *n* noisette *f*.

he [hiː] *pron* il; (*stressed*) lui; **he wants it** il veut; **he's a happy man** c'est un homme heureux; **if I were he** si j'étais lui; **he and I** lui et moi; — *n* mâle *m*; **he-bear** ours *m* mâle.

head [hed] **1** *n* (*of person, hammer etc*) tête *f*; (*of page*) haut *m*; (*of bed*) chevet *m*, tête *f*; (*of arrow*) pointe *f*; (*of beer*) mousse *f*; (*leader*) chef *m*; (*subject heading*) rubrique *f*; **h. of hair** chevelure *f*; **h. cold** rhume *m* de cerveau; **it didn't enter my h.** ça ne m'est pas venu à l'esprit (**that** que); **to take it into one's h. to do** se mettre en tête de faire; **the h.** *Sch* = **the headmaster**; = **the headmistress**; **to shout one's h. off** *Fam* crier à tue-tête; **to have a good h. for business** avoir le sens des affaires; **at the h. of** (*in charge of*) à la tête de; **at the h. of the table** au haut bout de la table; **at the h. of the list** en tête de liste; **it's above my h.** ça me dépasse; **to keep one's h.** garder son sang-froid; **to go off one's h.** devenir fou; **it's coming to a h.** (*of situation*) ça devient critique; **heads or tails?** pile ou face?; **per h., a h.** (*each*) par personne. **2** *a* principal; (*gardener*) en chef; **h. waiter** maître *m* d'hôtel; **a h. start** une grosse avance. **3** *vt* (*group, firm*) être à la tête de; (*list, poll*) être en tête de; (*vehicle*) diriger (**towards** vers); **to h. the ball** *Fb* faire une tête; **to h. off** (*person*) détourner de son chemin; (*prevent*) empêcher; **to be headed for** *Am* = **to h. for**; — *vi* **to h. for, be heading for** (*place*) se diriger vers; (*ruin etc*) Fig aller à. ◆**—ed** *a* (*paper*) à en-tête. ◆**—ing** *n* (*of chapter, page etc*) titre *m*; (*of subject*) rubrique *f*; (*printed on letter etc*) en-tête *m*. ◆**—er** *n* *Fb* coup *m* de tête.

headache ['hedeɪk] *n* mal *m* de tête; (*difficulty, person*) Fig problème *m*. ◆**headdress** *n* (*ornamental*) coiffe *f*.

◆**headlamp** *n*, ◆**headlight** *n* Aut phare *m.* ◆**headline** *n* (*of newspaper*) manchette *f*; *pl* (*gros*) titres *mpl*; Rad TV (*grands*) titres *mpl.* ◆**headlong** *adv* (*to fall*) la tête la première; (*to rush*) tête baissée. ◆**head-master** *n* Sch directeur *m*; (*of lycée*) proviseur *m.* ◆**headmistress** *n* Sch directrice *f*; (*of lycée*) proviseur *m.* ◆**head-on** *adv* & *a* (*to collide, collision*) de plein fouet. ◆**headphones** *npl* casque *m* (à écouteurs). ◆**headquarters** *npl* Com Pol siège *m* (central); Mil quartier *m* général. ◆**headrest** *n* appuie-tête *m inv.* ◆**headscarf** *n* (*pl* **-scarves**) foulard *m.* ◆**headstrong** *a* têtu. ◆**headway** *n* progrès *mpl.*

heady ['hedɪ] *a* (**-ier, -iest**) (*wine etc*) capiteux; (*action, speech*) emporté.

heal [hiːl] *vi* **to h. (up)** (*of wound*) se cicatriser; — *vt* (*wound*) cicatriser, guérir; (*person, sorrow*) guérir. ◆**—er** *n* guérisseur, -euse *mf.*

health [helθ] *n* santé *f*; **h. food** aliment *m* naturel; **h. food shop** *or* Am **store** magasin *m* diététique; **h. resort** station *f* climatique; **the H. Service** = la Sécurité Sociale. ◆**healthful** *a* (*climate*) sain. ◆**healthy** *a* (**-ier, -iest**) (*person*) en bonne santé, sain; (*food, attitude etc*) sain; (*appetite*) bon, robuste.

heap [hiːp] *n* tas *m*; **heaps of** (*books etc*) des tas de; **to have heaps of time** *Fam* avoir largement le temps; — *vt* entasser, empiler; **to h. on s.o.** (*gifts, praise*) couvrir qn de; (*work*) accabler qn de. ◆**—ed** *a* **h. spoonful** grosse cuillerée *f*. ◆**—ing** *a* **h. spoonful** *Am* grosse cuillerée *f*.

hear [hɪər] *vt* (*pt* & *pp* **heard** [hɜːd]) entendre; (*listen to*) écouter; (*learn*) apprendre (**that** que); **I heard him coming** je l'ai entendu venir; **to h. it said that** entendre dire que; **have you heard the news?** connais-tu la nouvelle?; **I've heard that ...** on m'a dit que ..., j'ai appris que ...; **to h. out** écouter jusqu'au bout; **h., h.!** bravo!; — *vi* entendre; (*get news*) recevoir *or* avoir des nouvelles (**from** de); **I've heard of** *or* **about him** j'ai entendu parler de lui; **she wouldn't h. of it** elle ne voulait pas en entendre parler; **I wouldn't h. of it!** pas question! ◆**—ing** *n* (*sense*) ouïe *f*; Jur audition *f*; **h. aid** appareil *m* auditif. ◆**hearsay** *n* ouï-dire *m inv.*

hearse [hɜːs] *n* corbillard *m.*

heart [hɑːt] *n* cœur *m*; *pl* Cards cœur *m*; (**off**) **by h.** par cœur; **to lose h.** perdre courage; **to one's h.'s content** tout son saoul or content; **at h.** au fond; **his h. is set on it** il le veut à tout prix, il y tient; **his h. is set on doing it** il veut le faire à tout prix, il tient à le faire; **h. disease** maladie *f* de cœur; **h. attack** crise *f* cardiaque. ◆**heartache** *n* chagrin *m*. ◆**heartbeat** *n* battement *m* de cœur. ◆**heartbreaking** *a* navrant. ◆**heartbroken** *a* navré, au cœur brisé. ◆**heartburn** *n* Med brûlures *fpl* d'estomac. ◆**heartthrob** *n* (*man*) Fam idole *f*.

hearten ['hɑːt(ə)n] *vt* encourager. ◆**—ing** *a* encourageant.

hearth [hɑːθ] *n* foyer *m*.

hearty ['hɑːtɪ] *a* (**-ier, -iest**) (*meal, appetite*) gros. ◆**heartily** *adv* (*to eat*) avec appétit; (*to laugh*) de tout son cœur; (*absolutely*) absolument.

heat [hiːt] **1** *n* chaleur *f*; (*of oven*) température *f*; (*heating*) chauffage *m*; **in the h. of** (*argument etc*) dans le feu de; (*the day*) au plus chaud de; **at low h., on a low h.** Culin à feu doux; **h. wave** vague *f* de chaleur; – *vti* **to h. (up)** chauffer. **2** *n* (*in race, competition*) éliminatoire *f*; **it was a dead h.** ils sont arrivés ex aequo. ◆**—ed** *a* (*swimming pool*) chauffé; (*argument*) passionné. ◆**—edly** *adv* avec passion. ◆**—ing** *n* chauffage *m*. ◆**—er** *n* radiateur *m*, appareil *m* de chauffage; **water h.** chauffe-eau *m inv*.

heath [hiːθ] *n* (*place, land*) lande *f*.

heathen ['hiːð(ə)n] *a & n* païen, -enne (*mf*).

heather ['heðər] *n* (*plant*) bruyère *f*.

heave [hiːv] *vt* (*lift*) soulever; (*pull*) tirer; (*drag*) traîner; (*throw*) Fam lancer; (*a sigh*) pousser; – *vi* (*of stomach, chest*) se soulever; (*retch*) Fam avoir des haut-le-cœur; – *n* (*effort*) effort *m* (*pour soulever etc*).

heaven ['hev(ə)n] *n* ciel *m*, paradis *m*; **h. knows when** Fam Dieu sait quand; **good heavens!** mon Dieu!; **it was h.** Fam c'était divin. ◆**—ly** *a* céleste; (*pleasing*) Fam divin.

heavy ['hevɪ] *a* (**-ier, -iest**) lourd; (*weight etc*) lourd, pesant; (*work, cold etc*) gros; (*blow*) violent; (*concentration, rain*) fort; (*traffic*) dense; (*smoker, drinker*) grand; (*film, text*) difficile; **a h. day** une journée chargée; **h. casualties** de nombreuses victimes; **to be h. on petrol** *or* Am **gas** Aut consommer beaucoup; **it's h. going** c'est difficile. ◆**heavily** *adv* (*to walk, tax etc*) lourdement; (*to breathe*) péniblement; (*to smoke, drink*) beaucoup; (*underlined*) fortement; (*involved*) très; **to rain h.** pleuvoir à verse. ◆**heaviness** *n* pesanteur *f*, lourdeur *f*.

◆**heavyweight** *n* Boxing poids *m* lourd; Fig personnage *m* important.

Hebrew ['hiːbruː] *a* hébreu (*m only*), hébraïque; – *n* (*language*) hébreu *m*.

heck [hek] *int* Fam zut!; – *n* = **hell** in expressions.

heckl/e ['hek(ə)l] *vt* interpeller, interrompre. ◆**—ing** *n* interpellations *fpl*. ◆**—er** *n* interpellateur, -trice *mf*.

hectic ['hektɪk] *a* (*activity*) fiévreux; (*period*) très agité; (*trip*) mouvementé; **h. life** vie *f* trépidante.

hedge [hedʒ] **1** *n* Bot haie *f*. **2** *vi* (*answer evasively*) ne pas se mouiller, éviter de se compromettre. ◆**hedgerow** *n* Bot haie *f*.

hedgehog ['hedʒhɒg] *n* (*animal*) hérisson *m*.

heed [hiːd] *vt* faire attention à; – *n* **to pay h.** to faire attention à. ◆**—less** *a* **h. of** (*danger etc*) inattentif à.

heel [hiːl] *n* **1** talon *m*; **down at h.,** Am **down at the heels** (*shabby*) miteux; **h. bar** cordonnerie *f* express; (*on sign*) 'talon minute'. **2** (*person*) Am Fam salaud *m*.

hefty ['heftɪ] *a* (**-ier, -iest**) (*large, heavy*) gros; (*person*) costaud.

heifer ['hefər] *n* (*cow*) génisse *f*.

height [haɪt] *n* hauteur *f*; (*of person*) taille *f*; (*of mountain*) altitude *f*; **the h. of** (*glory, success, fame*) le sommet de, l'apogée *m* de; (*folly, pain*) le comble de; **at the h. of** (*summer, storm*) au cœur de. ◆**heighten** *vt* (*raise*) rehausser; (*tension, interest*) Fig augmenter.

heinous ['heɪnəs] *a* (*crime etc*) atroce.

heir [eər] *n* héritier *m*. ◆**heiress** *n* héritière *f*. ◆**heirloom** *n* héritage *m*, bijou *m* or meuble *m* de famille.

heist [haɪst] *n* Am Sl hold-up *m inv*.

held [held] *see* **hold**.

helicopter ['helɪkɒptər] *n* hélicoptère *m*. ◆**heliport** *n* héliport *m*.

hell [hel] *n* enfer *m*; **a h. of a lot** (*very much*) Fam énormément, vachement; **a h. of a lot of** (*very many, very much*) Fam énormément de; **a h. of a nice guy** Fam un type super; **what the h. are you doing?** Fam qu'est-ce que tu fous?; **to h. with him** Fam qu'il aille se faire voir; **h.!** Fam zut!; **to be h.-bent on** Fam être acharné à. ◆**hellish** *a* diabolique.

hello! [hə'ləʊ] *int* = **hallo**.

helm [helm] *n* Nau barre *f*.

helmet ['helmɪt] *n* casque *m*.

help [help] *n* aide *f*, secours *m*; (*cleaning woman*) femme *f* de ménage; (*office or shop workers*) employés, -ées *mfpl*; **with the h. of**

(stick etc) à l'aide de; **to cry** or **shout for h.**
crier au secours; **h.!** au secours!; — vt aider
(**to, to do** à faire); **to h. s.o.** to soup/etc
(serve) servir du potage/etc à qn; **to h. out**
aider; **to h. up** aider à monter; **to h. oneself**
se servir (**to do**); **I can't h. laughing**/etc je ne
peux m'empêcher de rire/etc; **he can't h.
being blind**/etc ce n'est pas sa faute s'il est
aveugle/etc; **it can't be helped** on n'y peut
rien; — vi to h. (out) aider. ◆—ing n (serving) portion f. ◆—er n assistant, -ante mf.
◆helpful a (useful: advice) utile; (obliging)
serviable. ◆helpless a (powerless) impuissant; (baby) désarmé; (disabled) impotent. ◆helplessly adv (to struggle) en
vain.

helter-skelter [heltə'skeltər] **1** adv à la
débandade. **2** n (slide) toboggan m.

hem [hem] n ourlet m; — vt (-mm-)
(garment) ourler; **to h. in** Fig enfermer,
cerner.

hemisphere ['hemisfiər] n hémisphère m.

hemorrhage ['hemərɪdʒ] n Med hémorragie
f.

hemorrhoids ['hemərɔɪdz] npl hémorroïdes
fpl.

hemp [hemp] n chanvre m.

hen [hen] n poule f; **h. bird** oiseau m femelle.
◆**henpecked** a (husband) harcelé or
dominé par sa femme.

hence [hens] adv **1** (therefore) d'où. **2** (from
now) **ten years**/etc **h.** d'ici dix ans/etc.
◆**henceforth** adv désormais.

henchman ['hentʃmən] n (pl -men) Pej
acolyte m.

hepatitis [hepə'taɪtɪs] n hépatite f.

her [hɜːr] **1** pron la, l'; (after prep etc) elle;
(**to**) **h.** (indirect) lui; **I see h.** je la vois; **I saw
h.** je l'ai vue; **I give (to) h.** je lui donne; **with
h.** avec elle. **2** poss a son, sa, pl ses.

herald ['herəld] vt annoncer.

heraldry ['herəldrɪ] n héraldique f.

herb [hɜːb, Am ɜːb] n herbe f; pl Culin fines
herbes fpl. ◆**herbal** a **h. tea** infusion f
(d'herbes).

Hercules ['hɜːkjʊliːz] n (strong man) hercule
m.

herd [hɜːd] n troupeau m; — vti **to h.
together** (se) rassembler (en troupeau).

here [hiər] **1** adv ici; (then) alors; **h. is, h. are**
voici; **h. he is** le voici; **h. she is** la voici; **this
man h.** cet homme-ci; **I won't be h. tomor-
row** je ne serai pas là demain; **h. and there**
çà et là; **h. you are!** (take this) tenez!; **h.'s to
you!** (toast) à la tienne! **2** int (calling s.o.'s
attention) holà!, écoutez!; (giving s.o. sth)
tenez! ◆**herea'bouts** adv par ici. ◆**here-**

'**after** adv après; (in book) ci-après.
◆**here'by** adv (to declare) par le présent
acte. ◆**here'with** adv (with letter) Com
ci-joint.

heredity [hɪ'redɪtɪ] n hérédité f. ◆**hereditary** a héréditaire.

heresy ['herəsɪ] n hérésie f. ◆**heretic** n
hérétique mf. ◆**he'retical** a hérétique.

heritage ['herɪtɪdʒ] n héritage m.

hermetically [hɜː'metɪklɪ] adv hermétique-
ment.

hermit ['hɜːmɪt] n solitaire mf, ermite m.

hernia ['hɜːnɪə] n Med hernie f.

hero ['hɪərəʊ] n (pl -oes) héros m.
◆**he'roic** a héroïque. ◆**he'roics** npl Pej
grandiloquence f. ◆**heroine** ['herəʊɪn] n
héroïne f. ◆**heroism** ['herəʊɪz(ə)m] n
héroïsme m.

heroin ['herəʊɪn] n (drug) héroïne f.

heron ['herən] n (bird) héron m.

herring ['herɪŋ] n hareng m; **a red h.** Fig une
diversion.

hers [hɜːz] poss pron le sien, la sienne, pl les
sien(ne)s; **this hat is h.** ce chapeau est à elle
or est le sien; **a friend of h.** une amie à elle.
◆**her'self** pron elle-même; (reflexive) se,
s'; (after prep) elle; **she cut h.** elle s'est
coupée; **she thinks of h.** elle pense à elle.

hesitate ['hezɪteɪt] vi hésiter (over, about
sur; **to do** à faire). ◆**hesitant** a hésitant.
◆**hesitantly** adv avec hésitation. ◆**hesi-
'tation** n hésitation f.

hessian ['hesɪən] n toile f de jute.

heterogeneous [het(ə)rəʊ'dʒiːnɪəs] a
hétérogène.

het up [het'ʌp] a Fam énervé.

hew [hjuː] vt (pp hewn or hewed) tailler.

hexagon ['heksəgən] n hexagone m. ◆**hex-
'agonal** a hexagonal.

hey! [heɪ] int hé!, holà!

heyday ['heɪdeɪ] n (of person) apogée m,
zénith m; (of thing) âge m d'or.

hi! [haɪ] int Am Fam salut!

hiatus [haɪ'eɪtəs] n (gap) hiatus m.

hibernate ['haɪbəneɪt] vi hiberner. ◆**hiber-
'nation** n hibernation f.

hiccough, hiccup ['hɪkʌp] n hoquet m;
(the) hiccoughs, (the) hiccups le hoquet; —
vi hoqueter.

hick [hɪk] n (peasant) Am Sl Pej plouc mf.

hide[1] [haɪd] vt (pt hid, pp hidden) cacher,
dissimuler (from à); — vi **to h.** (away or out)
se cacher (from de). ◆**h.-and-seek** n
cache-cache m inv. ◆**h.-out** n cachette f.
◆**hiding** n **1** to go into h. se cacher; **h.
place** cachette f. **2 a good h.** (thrashing)
Fam une bonne volée or correction.

hide² [haɪd] n (skin) peau f.

hideous ['hɪdɪəs] a horrible; (person, sight, crime) hideux. ◆**-ly** adv (badly, very) horriblement.

hierarchy ['haɪərɑːkɪ] n hiérarchie f.

hi-fi ['haɪfaɪ] n hi-fi f inv; (system) chaîne f hi-fi; – a hi-fi inv.

high [haɪ] a (-er, -est) haut; (speed) grand; (price) élevé; (fever) fort, gros; (colour, complexion) vif; (idea, number) grand, élevé; (meat, game) faisandé; (on drugs) Fam défoncé; **to be five metres h.** être haut de cinq mètres, avoir cinq mètres de haut; **it is h. time that** il est grand temps que (+ sub); **h. jump** Sp saut m en hauteur; **h. noon** plein midi m; **h. priest** grand prêtre m; **h. school** Am = collège m d'enseignement secondaire; **h. spirits** entrain m; **h. spot** (of visit, day) point m culminant; (of show) clou m; **h. street** grand-rue f; **h. summer** le cœur de l'été; **h. table** table f d'honneur; **h. and mighty** arrogant; **to leave s.o. h. and dry** Fam laisser qn en plan; – adv **h. (up)** (to fly, throw etc) haut; (to aim h.) viser haut; – n en haut; **a new h., an all-time h.** (peak) Fig un nouveau record. ◆**-er** a supérieur (**than** à). ◆**-ly** adv hautement, fortement, (interesting) très; (paid) très bien; (to recommend) chaudement; **to speak h. of** dire beaucoup de bien de; **h. strung** nerveux. ◆**-ness** n H. (title) Altesse f.

highbrow ['haɪbraʊ] a & n intellectuel, -elle (mf).

high-chair ['haɪtʃeər] n chaise f haute. ◆**h.-'class** a (service) de premier ordre; (building) de luxe; (person) raffiné. ◆**h.-'flown** a (language) ampoulé. ◆**h.-'handed** a tyrannique. ◆**h.-'minded** a à l'âme noble. ◆**h.-'pitched** a (sound) aigu. ◆**h.-'powered** a (person) très dynamique. ◆**h.-rise** a **h.-rise flats** tour f. ◆**h.-'speed** a ultra-rapide. ◆**h.-'strung** a Am nerveux. ◆**h.-'up** a (person) haut placé.

highlands ['haɪləndz] npl régions fpl montagneuses.

highlight ['haɪlaɪt] n (of visit, day) point m culminant; (of show) clou m; (in hair) reflet m; – vt souligner.

highroad ['haɪrəʊd] n grand-route f.

highway ['haɪweɪ] n grande route f; Am autoroute f; **public h.** voie f publique; **h. code** code m de la route.

hijack ['haɪdʒæk] vt (aircraft, vehicle) détourner; – n détournement m. ◆**-ing** n (air piracy) piraterie f aérienne; (hijack)

détournement m. ◆**-er** n Av pirate m de l'air.

hik/e [haɪk] **1** n excursion f à pied; – vi marcher à pied. **2** vt (price) Am Fam augmenter; – n Am Fam hausse f. ◆**-er** n excursionniste mf.

hilarious [hɪ'leərɪəs] a (funny) désopilant.

hill [hɪl] n colline f; (small) coteau m; (slope) pente f. ◆**hillbilly** n Am Fam péquenaud, -aude mf. ◆**hillside** n coteau m; **on the h.** à flanc de coteau. ◆**hilly** a (-ier, -iest) accidenté.

hilt [hɪlt] n (of sword) poignée f; **to the h.** Fig au maximum.

him [hɪm] pron le, l'; (after prep etc) lui; (to) **h.** (indirect) lui; **I see h.** je le vois; **I saw h.** je l'ai vu; **I give (to) h.** je lui donne; **with h.** avec lui. ◆**him'self** pron lui-même; (reflexive) se, s'; (after prep) lui; **he cut h.** il s'est coupé; **he thinks of h.** il pense à lui.

hind [haɪnd] a **h.** de derrière, postérieur. ◆**hindquarters** npl arrière-train m.

hinder ['hɪndər] vt (obstruct) gêner; (prevent) empêcher (**from doing** de faire). ◆**hindrance** n gêne f.

hindsight ['haɪndsaɪt] n **with h.** rétrospectivement.

Hindu ['hɪnduː] a & n hindou, -oue (mf).

hing/e [hɪndʒ] **1** n (of box, stamp) charnière f; (of door) gond m, charnière f. **2** vi **to h. on** (depend on) dépendre de. ◆**-ed** a à charnière(s).

hint [hɪnt] n indication f; (insinuation) allusion f; (trace) trace f; pl (advice) conseils mpl; **to drop a h.** faire une allusion; – vt laisser entendre (**that** que); – vi **to h. at** faire allusion à.

hip [hɪp] n Anat hanche f.

hippie ['hɪpɪ] n hippie mf.

hippopotamus [hɪpə'pɒtəməs] n hippopotame m.

hire ['haɪər] vt (vehicle etc) louer; (person) engager; **to h. out** donner en location, louer; – n location f; (of boat, horse) louage m; **for h.** à louer; **on h.** en location; **h. purchase** vente f à crédit, location-vente f; **on h. purchase** à crédit.

his [hɪz] **1** poss a son, sa, pl ses. **2** poss pron le sien, la sienne, pl les sien(ne)s; **this hat is h.** ce chapeau est à lui or est le sien; **a friend of h.** un ami à lui.

Hispanic [hɪs'pænɪk] a & n Am hispano-américain, -aine (mf).

hiss [hɪs] vti siffler; – n sifflement m; pl Th sifflets mpl. ◆**-ing** n sifflement(s) m(pl).

history ['hɪstərɪ] n (study, events) histoire f; **it will make h.** or **go down in h.** ça va faire date; **your medical h.** vos antécédents médicaux. ◆**hi'storian** n historien, -ienne mf. ◆**hi'storic(al)** a historique.

histrionic [hɪstrɪ'ɒnɪk] a Pej théâtral; — npl attitudes fpl théâtrales.

hit [hɪt] vti (pt & pp **hit**, pres p **hitting**) (strike) frapper; (knock against) & Aut heurter; (reach) atteindre; (affect) toucher, affecter; (find) trouver, rencontrer; **to h. the head-lines** Fam faire les gros titres; **to h. back** rendre coup pour coup; (verbally, militarily etc) riposter; **to h. it off** Fam s'entendre bien (with avec); **to h. out (at)** Fam attaquer; **to h. (up)on** (find) tomber sur; — n (blow) coup m; (success) coup m réussi; Th succès m; **h. (song)** chanson f à succès; **to make a h. with** Fam avoir un succès avec; **h.-and-run driver** chauffard m (qui prend la fuite). ◆**h.-or-'miss** a (chancy, random) aléatoire.

hitch [hɪtʃ] 1 n (snag) anicroche f, os m, problème m. 2 vt (fasten) accrocher (to à). 3 vti **to h. (a lift** or a **ride)** Fam faire du stop (to jusqu'à). ◆**hitchhike** vi faire de l'auto-stop (to jusqu'à). ◆**hitchhiking** n auto-stop m. ◆**hitchhiker** n auto-stop-peur, -euse mf.

hitherto [hɪðə'tuː] adv jusqu'ici.

hive [haɪv] 1 n ruche f. 2 vt **to h. off** (industry) dénationaliser.

hoard [hɔːd] n réserve f; (of money) trésor m; — vt amasser. ◆—**ing** n (fence) panneau m d'affichage.

hoarfrost ['hɔːfrɒst] n givre m.

hoarse [hɔːs] a (-er, -est) (person, voice) enroué. ◆—**ness** n enrouement m.

hoax [həʊks] n canular m; — vt faire un canular à, mystifier.

hob [hɒb] n (on stove) plaque f chauffante.

hobble ['hɒb(ə)l] vi (walk) clopiner.

hobby ['hɒbɪ] n passe-temps m inv; **my h.** mon passe-temps favori. ◆**hobbyhorse** n (favourite subject) dada m.

hobnob ['hɒbnɒb] vi (-bb-) **to h. with** frayer avec.

hobo ['həʊbəʊ] n (pl -oes or -os) Am vaga-bond m.

hock [hɒk] vt (pawn) Fam mettre au clou; — n in h. Fam au clou.

hockey ['hɒkɪ] n hockey m; **ice h.** hockey sur glace.

hocus-pocus [həʊkəs'pəʊkəs] n (talk) charabia m; (deception) tromperie f.

hodgepodge ['hɒdʒpɒdʒ] n fatras m.

hoe [həʊ] n binette f, houe f; — vt biner.

hog [hɒg] 1 n (pig) cochon m, porc m; **road h.** Fig chauffard m. 2 n **to go the whole h.**

Fam aller jusqu'au bout. 3 vt (-gg-) Fam monopoliser, garder pour soi.

hoist [hɔɪst] vt hisser; — n Tech palan m.

hold [həʊld] n (grip) prise f; (of ship) cale f; (of aircraft) soute f; **to get h. of** (grab) saisir; (contact) joindre; (find) trouver; **to get a h. of oneself** se maîtriser; — vt (pt & pp **held**) tenir; (breath, interest, heat, atten-tion) retenir; (a post) occuper; (a record) détenir; (weight) supporter; (possess) posséder; (contain) contenir; (maintain, believe) maintenir (that que); (ceremony, mass) célébrer; (keep) garder; **to h. hands** se tenir par la main; **to h. one's own** se débrouiller; (of sick person) se maintenir; **h. the line!** Tel ne quittez pas!; **h. it!** (stay still) ne bouge pas!; **to be held** (of event) avoir lieu; **to h. back** (crowd, tears) contenir; (hide) cacher (from à); **to h. down** (job) occuper; (keep) garder; (person on ground) maintenir au sol; **to h. in** (stomach) rentrer; **to h. off** (enemy) tenir à distance; **to h. on** (keep in place) tenir en place (son chapeau etc); (offer) offrir; (arm) étendre; **to h. over** (postpone) remettre; **to h. together** (nation, group) assurer l'union de; **to h. up** (raise) lever; (support) soutenir; (delay) retarder; (bank) attaquer (à main armée); — vi (of nail, rope) tenir; (of weather) se maintenir; **to h. (good)** (of argu-ment) valoir (for pour); **to h. forth** (talk) Pej disserter; **if the rain holds off** s'il ne pleut pas; **to h. on** (endure) tenir bon; (wait) attendre; **h. on!** Tel ne quittez pas!; **to h. onto** (cling to) tenir bien; (keep) garder; **h. on (tight)!** tenez bon!; **to h. out** (resist) résister; (last) durer. ◆**holdall** n (bag) fourre-tout m inv. ◆**holdup** n (attack) hold-up m inv; (traffic jam) bouchon m; (delay) retard m.

holder ['həʊldər] n (of post, passport) titu-laire mf; (of record, card) détenteur, -trice mf; (container) support m.

holdings ['həʊldɪŋz] npl Fin possessions fpl.

hole [həʊl] n trou m; (job etc) Fam bled m, trou m; (room) Fam baraque f; — vt trouer; — vi **to h. up** (hide) Fam se terrer.

holiday ['hɒlɪdeɪ] n (rest) vacances fpl; holi-day(s) (from work, school etc) vacances fpl; a h. (day off) un congé; a (public or bank) h., Am a legal h. un jour férié; on h. en vacances; holidays with pay congés mpl payés; — a (camp, clothes etc) de vacances; in h. mood d'humeur folâtre. ◆**holiday-maker** n vacancier, -ière mf.

holiness ['həʊlɪnəs] n sainteté f.

Holland ['hɒlənd] n Hollande f.

hollow ['hɒləʊ] *a* creux; (*victory*) faux; (*promise*) vain; – *n* creux *m*; – *vt* **to h. out** creuser.

holly ['hɒlɪ] *n* houx *m*.

holocaust ['hɒləkɔːst] *n* (*massacre*) holocauste *m*.

holster ['həʊlstər] *n* étui *m* de revolver.

holy ['həʊlɪ] *a* (-**ier**, -**iest**) saint; (*bread*, *water*) bénit; (*ground*) sacré.

homage ['hɒmɪdʒ] *n* hommage *m*.

home¹ [həʊm] *n* maison *f*; (*country*) pays *m* (natal); (*for soldiers*) foyer *m*; (**at**) **h.** à la maison, chez soi; **to feel at h.** se sentir à l'aise; **to play at h.** Fb jouer à domicile; **far from h.** loin de chez soi; **a broken h.** un foyer désuni; **a good h.** une bonne famille; **to make one's h.** s'installer à *or* en; **my h. is here** j'habite ici; – *adv* à la maison, chez soi; **to go** *or* **come h.** rentrer; **to be h.** être rentré; **to drive h.** ramener (*qn*) (en voiture); (*nail*) enfoncer; **to bring sth h. to s.o.** Fig faire voir qch à qn; – *a* (*life*, *pleasures etc*) de famille; Pol national; (*cooking*, *help*) familial; (*visit*, *match*) à domicile; **h. economics** économie *f* domestique; **h. town** (*birth place*) ville *f* natale; **h. rule** Pol autonomie *f*; **H. Office** = ministère *m* de l'Intérieur; **H. Secretary** = ministre *m* de l'Intérieur. ◆**homecoming** *n* retour *m* au foyer. ◆**home'grown** *a* Bot du jardin; Pol du pays. ◆**homeland** *n* patrie *f*. ◆**homeloving** *a* casanier. ◆**home'made** *a* (fait à la) maison *inv*. ◆**homework** *n* Sch devoir(s) *m*(*pl*).

home² [həʊm] *vi* **to h. in on** se diriger automatiquement sur.

homeless ['həʊmlɪs] *a* sans abri; – *n* **the h.** les sans-abri *m inv*.

homely ['həʊmlɪ] *a* (-**ier**, -**iest**) (*simple*) simple; (*comfortable*) accueillant; (*ugly*) Am laid.

homesick ['həʊmsɪk] *a* nostalgique; **to be h.** avoir le mal du pays. ◆**–ness** *n* nostalgie *f*, mal *m* du pays.

homeward ['həʊmwəd] *a* (*trip*) de retour; – *adv* **h. bound** sur le chemin de retour.

homey ['həʊmɪ] *a* (-**ier**, -**iest**) Am Fam accueillant.

homicide ['hɒmɪsaɪd] *n* homicide *m*.

homily ['hɒmɪlɪ] *n* homélie *f*.

homogeneous [həʊmə'dʒiːnɪəs] *a* homogène.

homosexual [həʊmə'sekʃʊəl] *a* & *n* homosexuel, -elle (*mf*). ◆**homosexu-'ality** *n* homosexualité *f*.

honest ['ɒnɪst] *a* honnête; (*frank*) franc (**with** avec); (*profit*, *money*) honnêtement

gagné; **the h. truth** la pure vérité; **to be (quite) h.** . . . . pour être franc . . . . ◆**honesty** *n* honnêteté *f*; franchise *f*; (*of report*, *text*) exactitude *f*.

honey ['hʌnɪ] *n* miel *m*; (*person*) Fam chéri, -ie *mf*. ◆**honeycomb** *n* rayon *m* de miel. ◆**honeymoon** *n* (*occasion*) lune *f* de miel; (*trip*) voyage *m* de noces. ◆**honeysuckle** *n* Bot chèvrefeuille *f*.

honk [hɒŋk] *vi* Aut klaxonner; – *n* coup *m* de klaxon®.

honour ['ɒnər] *n* honneur *m*; **in h. of** en l'honneur de; **an honours degree** Univ = une licence; – *vt* honorer (**with** de). ◆**honorary** *a* (*member*) honoraire; (*title*) honorifique. ◆**honourable** *a* honorable.

hood [hʊd] *n* **1** capuchon *m*; (*mask of robber*) cagoule *f*; (*soft car or pram roof*) capote *f*; (*bonnet*) Aut Am capot *m*; (*above stove*) hotte *f*. **2** (*hoodlum*) Am Sl gangster *m*. ◆**hooded** *a* (*person*) encapuchonné; (*coat*) à capuchon.

hoodlum ['huːdləm] *n* Fam (*hooligan*) voyou *m*; (*gangster*) gangster *m*.

hoodwink ['hʊdwɪŋk] *vt* tromper, duper.

hoof, *pl* **-fs, -ves** [huːf, -fs, -vz] (*Am* [huf, -fs, hʊvz]) *n* sabot *m*.

hoo-ha ['huːhɑː] *n* Fam tumulte *m*.

hook [hʊk] *n* crochet *m*; (*on clothes*) agrafe *f*; Fishing hameçon *m*; **off the h.** (*phone*) décroché; **to let** *or* **get s.o. off the h.** tirer qn d'affaire; – *vt* **to h.** (**on** *or* **up**) accrocher (**to** à). ◆**–ed** *a* (*nose*, *beak*) recourbé, crochu; (*end*, *object*) recourbé; **h. on** Fam (*chess etc*) enragé de; (*person*) entiché de; **to be h. on drugs** Fam ne plus pouvoir se passer de la drogue. ◆**–er** *n* Am Sl prostituée *f*.

hook(e)y ['hʊkɪ] *n* **to play h.** Am Fam faire l'école buissonnière.

hooligan ['huːlɪɡən] *n* vandale *m*, voyou *m*. ◆**hooliganism** *n* vandalisme *m*.

hoop [huːp] *n* cerceau *m*; (*of barrel*) cercle *m*.

hoot [huːt] **1** *vi* Aut klaxonner; (*of train*) siffler; (*of owl*) hululer; – *n* Aut coup *m* de klaxon®. **2** *vti* (*jeer*) huer; – *n* huée *f*. ◆**–er** *n* Aut klaxon®·*m*; (*of factory*) sirène *f*.

hoover® ['huːvər] *n* aspirateur *m*; – *vt* Fam passer à l'aspirateur.

hop [hɒp] *vi* (-**pp-**) (*of person*) sauter (à cloche-pied); (*of animal*) sauter; (*of bird*) sautiller; **h. in!** (*in car*) montez!; **to h. on a bus** monter dans un autobus; **to h. on a plane** attraper un vol; – *vt* **h. it!** Fam fiche le camp!; – *n* (*leap*) saut *m*; Av étape *f*.

hope [həʊp] *n* espoir *m*, espérance *f*; – *vi*

espérer; **to h. for** (*desire*) espérer; (*expect*) attendre; **I h. so/not** j'espère que oui/non; – *vt* espérer (**to do** faire, **that** que). ◆**hopeful** *a* (*person*) optimiste, plein d'espoir; (*promising*) prometteur; (*encouraging*) encourageant; **to be h. that** avoir bon espoir que. ◆**hopefully** *adv* avec optimisme; (*one hopes*) on espère (que). ◆**hopeless** *a* désespéré, sans espoir; (*useless, bad*) nul; (*liar*) invétéré. ◆**hopelessly** *adv* sans espoir; (*extremely*) complètement; (*in love*) éperdument.

hops [hɒps] *npl Bot* houblon *m*.

hopscotch ['hɒpskɒtʃ] *n* (*game*) marelle *f*.

horde [hɔːd] *n* horde *f*, foule *f*.

horizon [hə'raɪz(ə)n] *n* horizon *m*; **on the h.** à l'horizon.

horizontal [hɒrɪ'zɒnt(ə)l] *a* horizontal. ◆**–ly** *adv* horizontalement.

hormone ['hɔːməʊn] *n* hormone *f*.

horn [hɔːn] **1** *n* (*of animal*) corne *f*; *Mus* cor *m*; *Aut* klaxon® *m*. **2** *vi* **to h. in** *Am Fam* dire son mot, interrompre.

hornet ['hɔːnɪt] *n* (*insect*) frelon *m*.

horoscope ['hɒrəskəʊp] *n* horoscope *m*.

horror ['hɒrər] *n* horreur *f*; (*little*) **h.** (*child*) *Fam* petit monstre *m*; – *a* (*film etc*) d'épouvante, d'horreur. ◆**ho'rrendous** *a* horrible. ◆**horrible** *a* horrible, affreux. ◆**horribly** *adv* horriblement. ◆**horrid** *a* horrible; (*child*) épouvantable, méchant. ◆**ho'rrific** *a* horrible, horrifiant. ◆**horrify** *vt* horrifier.

hors-d'œuvre [ɔː'dɜːv] *n* hors-d'œuvre *m inv*.

horse [hɔːs] *n* **1** cheval *m*; **to go h. riding** faire du cheval; **h. show** concours *m* hippique. **2 h. chestnut** marron *m* (d'Inde). ◆**horseback** *n* **on h.** à cheval. ◆**horseman** *n* (*pl -men*) cavalier *m*. ◆**horseplay** *n* jeux *mpl* brutaux. ◆**horsepower** *n* cheval *m* (vapeur). ◆**horseracing** *n* courses *fpl*. ◆**horseradish** *n* radis *m* noir, raifort *m*. ◆**horseshoe** *n* fer *m* à cheval. ◆**horsewoman** *n* (*pl -women*) cavalière *f*.

horticulture ['hɔːtɪkʌltʃər] *n* horticulture *f*. ◆**horti'cultural** *a* horticole.

hose [həʊz] *n* (*tube*) tuyau *m*; – *vt* (*garden etc*) arroser. ◆**hosepipe** *n* tuyau *m*.

hosiery ['həʊzɪərɪ, *Am* 'həʊʒərɪ] *n* bonneterie *f*.

hospice ['hɒspɪs] *n* (*for dying people*) hospice *m* (pour incurables).

hospitable [hɒ'spɪtəb(ə)l] *a* hospitalier. ◆**hospitably** *adv* avec hospitalité. ◆**hospi'tality** *n* hospitalité *f*.

hospital ['hɒspɪt(ə)l] *n* hôpital *m*; **in h.,** *Am* **in the h.** à l'hôpital; – *a* (*bed etc*) d'hôpital; (*staff, services*) hospitalier. ◆**hospitalize** *vt* hospitaliser.

host [həʊst] *n* **1** (*man who receives guests*) hôte *m*. **2 a h. of** (*many*) une foule de. **3** *Rel* hostie *f*. ◆**hostess** *n* (*in house, aircraft, nightclub*) hôtesse *f*.

hostage ['hɒstɪdʒ] *n* otage *m*; **to take s.o. h.** prendre qn en otage.

hostel ['hɒst(ə)l] *n* foyer *m*; **youth h.** auberge *f* de jeunesse.

hostile ['hɒstaɪl, *Am* 'hɒst(ə)l] *a* hostile (**to, towards** à). ◆**ho'stility** *n* hostilité *f* (**to, towards** envers); *pl Mil* hostilités *fpl*.

hot[1] [hɒt] *a* (**hotter, hottest**) chaud; (*spice*) fort; (*temperament*) passionné; (*news*) *Fam* dernier; (*favourite*) *Fam* grand favori; **to be** or **feel h.** avoir chaud; **it's h.** il fait chaud; **not so h. at** (*good at*) *Fam* pas très calé en; **not so h.** (*bad*) *Fam* pas fameux; **h. dog** (*sausage*) hot-dog *m*. ◆**hotbed** *n Pej* foyer *m* (**of** de). ◆**hot-'blooded** *a* ardent. ◆**hothead** *n* tête *f* brûlée. ◆**hot'headed** *a* impétueux. ◆**hothouse** *n* serre *f* (chaude). ◆**hotplate** *n* chauffe-plats *m inv*; (*on stove*) plaque *f* chauffante. ◆**hot-'tempered** *a* emporté. ◆**hot-'water bottle** *n* bouillotte *f*.

hot[2] [hɒt] *vi* (**-tt-**) **to h. up** (*increase*) s'intensifier; (*become dangerous or excited*) chauffer.

hotchpotch ['hɒtʃpɒtʃ] *n* fatras *m*.

hotel [həʊ'tel] *n* hôtel *m*; – *a* (*industry*) hôtelier. ◆**hotelier** [həʊ'telɪər] *n* hôtelier, -ière *mf*.

hotly ['hɒtlɪ] *adv* passionnément.

hound [haʊnd] **1** *n* (*dog*) chien *m* courant. **2** *vt* (*pursue*) poursuivre avec acharnement; (*worry*) harceler.

hour ['aʊər] *n* heure *f*; **half an h., a half-h.** une demi-heure; **a quarter of an h.** un quart d'heure; **paid ten francs an h.** payé dix francs (de) l'heure; **ten miles an h.** dix miles à l'heure; **open all hours** ouvert à toute heure; **h. hand** (*of watch, clock*) petite aiguille *f*. ◆**–ly** *a* (*rate, pay*) horaire; **an h. bus/train/***etc* un bus/train/*etc* toutes les heures; – *adv* toutes les heures; **h. paid, paid h.** payé à l'heure.

house[1], *pl* **-ses** [haʊs, -zɪz] *n* maison *f*; (*audience*) *Th* salle *f*, auditoire *m*; (*performance*) *Th* séance *f*; **the H.** *Pol* la Chambre; **the Houses of Parliament** le Parlement; **at** or **to my h.** chez moi; **on the h.** (*free of charge*) aux frais de la maison; **h. prices** prix *mpl* immobiliers. ◆**housebound** *a* confiné chez soi. ◆**house-**

breaking n Jur cambriolage m. ◆**house-broken** a (dog etc) Am propre. ◆**household** n ménage m, maison f, famille f; **h. duties** soins mpl du ménage; **a h. name** un nom très connu. ◆**householder** n (owner) propriétaire mf; (family head) chef m de famille. ◆**housekeeper** n (employee) gouvernante f; (housewife) ménagère f. ◆**housekeeping** n ménage m. ◆**houseman** n (pl -men) interne mf (des hôpitaux). ◆**houseproud** a qui s'occupe méticuleusement de sa maison. ◆**housetrained** a (dog etc) propre. ◆**housewarming** n & a **to have a h.-warming (party)** pendre la crémaillère. ◆**housewife** n (pl -wives) ménagère f. ◆**housework** n (travaux mpl de) ménage m.

hous/e² [hauz] vt loger; (of building) abriter; **it is housed in** (kept) on le garde dans. ◆**—ing** n logement m; (houses) logements mpl; − a (crisis etc) du logement.

hovel ['hɒv(ə)l] n (slum) taudis m.

hover ['hɒvər] vi (of bird, aircraft, danger etc) planer; (of person) rôder, traîner. ◆**hovercraft** n aéroglisseur m.

how [hau] adv (comment; **h.'s that?**, **h. so?**, **h. come?** Fam comment ça?; **h. kind!** comme c'est gentil!; **h. do you do?** (greeting) bonjour; **h. long/high is . . . ?** quelle est la longueur/hauteur de . . . ?; **h. much?**, **h. many?** combien?; **h. much time/etc?** combien de temps/etc?; **h. many apples/etc?** combien de pommes/etc?; **h. about a walk?** si on faisait une promenade?; **h. about some coffee?** (si on prenait) du café?; **h. about me?** et moi?

howdy! ['haudɪ] int Am Fam salut!

however [hau'evər] **1** adv **h. big he may be** quelque or si grand qu'il soit; **h. she may do it** de quelque manière qu'elle le fasse; **h. that may be** quoi qu'il en soit. **2** conj cependant.

howl [haul] vi hurler; (of baby) brailler; (of wind) mugir; − n hurlement m; braillement m; mugissement m; (of laughter) éclat m.

howler ['haulər] n (mistake) Fam gaffe f.

HP [eɪtʃ'piː] abbr = hire purchase.

hp abbr (horsepower) CV.

HQ [eɪtʃ'kjuː] abbr = headquarters.

hub [hʌb] n (of wheel) moyeu m; Fig centre m. ◆**hubcap** n Aut enjoliveur m.

hubbub ['hʌbʌb] n vacarme m.

huckleberry ['hʌk(ə)lbərɪ] n Bot Am myrtille f.

huddle ['hʌd(ə)l] vi **to h. (together)** se blottir (les uns contre les autres).

hue [hjuː] n (colour) teinte f.

huff [hʌf] n **in a h.** (offended) Fam fâché.

hug [hʌg] vt (-gg-) (person) serrer dans ses bras, étreindre; **to h. the kerb/coast** (stay near) serrer le trottoir/la côte; − n (embrace) étreinte f.

huge [hjuːdʒ] a énorme. ◆**-ly** adv énormément. ◆**-ness** n énormité f.

hulk [hʌlk] n (person) lourdaud, -aude mf.

hull [hʌl] n (of ship) coque f.

hullabaloo [hʌləbə'luː] n Fam (noise) vacarme m; (fuss) histoire(s) f(pl).

hullo! [hʌ'ləu] int = hallo.

hum [hʌm] vi (-mm-) (of insect) bourdonner; (of person) fredonner; (of top, radio) ronfler; (of engine) vrombir; − vt (tune) fredonner; − n (of insect) bourdonnement m.

human ['hjuːmən] a humain; **h. being** être m humain; − npl humains mpl. ◆**hu'mane** a (kind) humain. ◆**hu'manely** adv humainement. ◆**humani'tarian** a & n humanitaire (mf). ◆**hu'manity** n (human beings, kindness) humanité f. ◆**humanly** adv (possible etc) humainement.

humble ['hʌmb(ə)l] a humble; − vt humilier. ◆**humbly** adv humblement.

humbug ['hʌmbʌg] n (talk) fumisterie f; (person) fumiste mf.

humdrum ['hʌmdrʌm] a monotone.

humid ['hjuːmɪd] a humide. ◆**hu'midify** vt humidifier. ◆**hu'midity** n humidité f.

humiliate [hjuː'mɪlɪeɪt] vt humilier. ◆**humili'ation** n humiliation f. ◆**humility** n humilité f.

humour ['hjuːmər] **1** n (fun) humour m; (temper) humeur f; **to have a sense of h.** avoir le sens de l'humour; **in a good h.** de bonne humeur. **2** vt **to h. s.o.** faire plaisir à qn, ménager qn. ◆**humorist** n humoriste mf. ◆**humorous** a (book etc) humoristique; (person) plein d'humour. ◆**humorously** adv avec humour.

hump [hʌmp] **1** n (lump, mound) bosse f; − vt (one's back) voûter. **2** n **to have the h.** Fam (depression) avoir le cafard; (bad temper) être en rogne. ◆**humpback** n. **bridge** Aut pont m en dos d'âne.

hunch [hʌntʃ] **1** vt (one's shoulders) voûter. **2** n (idea) Fam intuition f, idée f. ◆**hunchback** n bossu, -ue mf.

hundred ['hʌndrəd] a & n cent (m); **a h. pages** cent pages; **two h. pages** deux cents pages; **hundreds of** des centaines de.

◆**hundredfold** a centuple; – adv au centuple. ◆**hundredth** a & n centième (mf). ◆**hundredweight** n 112 livres (= 50,8 kg); Am 100 livres (= 45,3 kg).

hung [hʌŋ] see hang[1].

Hungary ['hʌŋgərɪ] n Hongrie f. ◆**Hun'garian** a & n hongrois, -oise (mf); – n (language) hongrois m.

hunger ['hʌŋgər] n faim f. ◆**hungry** a (-ier, -iest) to be or feel h. avoir faim; to go h. souffrir de la faim; to make h. donner faim à; h. for (news etc) avide de. ◆**hungrily** adv avidement.

hunk [hʌŋk] n (gros) morceau m.

hunt [hʌnt] n Sp chasse f; (search) recherche f (for de); – vt Sp chasser; (pursue) poursuivre; (seek) chercher; to h. down (fugitive etc) traquer; to h. out (information etc) dénicher; – vi Sp chasser; to h. for sth (re)chercher qch. ◆**—ing** n Sp chasse f. ◆**—er** n (person) chasseur m.

hurdle ['hɜːd(ə)l] n (fence) Sp haie f; Fig obstacle m.

hurl [hɜːl] vt (throw) jeter, lancer; (abuse) lancer; to h. oneself at s.o. se ruer sur qn.

hurly-burly ['hɜːlɪbɜːlɪ] n tumulte m.

hurray! [hʊ'reɪ] int hourra!

hurricane ['hʌrɪkən, Am 'hʌrɪkeɪn] n ouragan m.

hurry ['hʌrɪ] n hâte f; in a h. à la hâte, en hâte; to be in a h. être pressé; to be in a h. to do avoir hâte de faire; there's no h. rien ne presse; – vi se dépêcher, se presser (to do de faire); to h. out sortir à la hâte; to h. along or on or up se dépêcher; – vt (person) bousculer, presser; (pace) presser; to h. one's meal manger à toute vitesse; to h. s.o. out faire sortir qn à la hâte. ◆**hurried** a (steps, decision etc) précipité; (travail) fait à la hâte; (visit) éclair inv; to be h. (in a hurry) être pressé.

hurt [hɜːt] vt (pt & pp hurt) (physically) faire du mal à, blesser; (emotionally) faire de la peine à; (offend) blesser; (prejudice, damage) nuire à; to h. s.o.'s feelings blesser qn; his arm hurts (him) son bras lui fait mal; – vi faire mal; – n mal m; – a (injured) blessé. ◆**hurtful** a (remark) blessant.

hurtle ['hɜːt(ə)l] vi to h. along aller à toute vitesse; to h. down dégringoler.

husband ['hʌzbənd] n mari m.

hush [hʌʃ] int chut!; – n silence m; – vt (person) faire taire; (baby) calmer; to h. up (scandal) Fig étouffer. ◆**—ed** a (voice)

étouffé; (silence) profond. ◆**hush-hush** a Fam ultra-secret.

husk [hʌsk] n (of rice, grain) enveloppe f.

husky ['hʌskɪ] a (-ier, -iest) (voice) enroué, voilé.

hussy ['hʌsɪ] n Pej friponne f, coquine f.

hustings ['hʌstɪŋz] npl campagne f électorale, élections fpl.

hustle ['hʌs(ə)l] 1 vt (shove, rush) bousculer (qn); – vi (work busily) Am se démener (to get sth pour avoir qch). 2 n h. and bustle agitation f, activité f, tourbillon m.

hut [hʌt] n cabane f, hutte f.

hutch [hʌtʃ] n (for rabbit) clapier m.

hyacinth ['haɪəsɪnθ] n jacinthe f.

hybrid ['haɪbrɪd] a & n hybride (m).

hydrangea [haɪ'dreɪndʒə] n (shrub) hortensia m.

hydrant ['haɪdrənt] n (fire) h. bouche f d'incendie.

hydraulic [haɪ'drɔːlɪk] a hydraulique.

hydroelectric [haɪdrəʊɪ'lektrɪk] a hydro-électrique.

hydrogen ['haɪdrədʒən] n Ch hydrogène m.

hyena [haɪ'iːnə] n (animal) hyène f.

hygiene ['haɪdʒiːn] n hygiène f. ◆**hy'gienic** a hygiénique.

hymn [hɪm] n Rel cantique m, hymne m.

hyper- ['haɪpər] pref hyper-.

hypermarket ['haɪpəmɑːkɪt] n hypermarché m.

hyphen ['haɪf(ə)n] n trait m d'union. ◆**hyphenat/e** vt mettre un trait d'union à. ◆**—ed** a (word) à trait d'union.

hypnosis [hɪp'nəʊsɪs] n hypnose f. ◆**hypnotic** a hypnotique. ◆**'hypnotism** n hypnotisme m. ◆**'hypnotist** n hypnotiseur m. ◆**'hypnotize** vt hypnotiser.

hypochondriac [haɪpə'kɒndriæk] n malade mf imaginaire.

hypocrisy [hɪ'pɒkrɪsɪ] n hypocrisie f. ◆**'hypocrite** n hypocrite mf. ◆**hypo'critical** a hypocrite.

hypodermic [haɪpə'dɜːmɪk] a hypodermique.

hypothesis, pl **-eses** [haɪ'pɒθɪsɪs, -ɪsiːz] n hypothèse f. ◆**hypo'thetical** a hypothétique.

hysteria [hɪ'stɪərɪə] n hystérie f. ◆**hysterical** a hystérique; (funny) Fam désopilant; to be or become h. (wildly upset) avoir une crise de nerfs. ◆**hysterically** adv (cry) sans pouvoir s'arrêter; to laugh h. rire aux larmes. ◆**hysterics** npl (tears etc) crise f de nerfs; (laughter) crise f de rire.

I

I, i [aɪ] n I, i m.

I [aɪ] pron je, j'; (stressed) moi; **I want** je veux; **she and I** elle et moi.

ice/e [aɪs] n glace f; (on road) verglas m; **i. (cream)** glace f; **black i.** (on road) verglas m; **i. cube** glaçon m; – vi **to i. (over)** (of lake) geler; (of windscreen) givrer. ◆—**ed** a (tea) glacé. ◆**iceberg** n iceberg m ◆**icebox** n (box) & Fig glacière f; Am réfrigérateur m. ◆**ice-'cold** a glacial; (drink) glacé. ◆**ice-skating** n patinage m (sur glace). ◆**icicle** n glaçon m.

ic/e [aɪs] vt (cake) glacer. ◆—**ing** n (on cake etc) glaçage m.

Iceland ['aɪslənd] n Islande f. ◆**Ice'landic** a islandais.

icon ['aɪkɒn] n Rel icône f.

icy ['aɪsɪ] a (-ier, -iest) (water, hands, room) glacé; (manner, weather) glacial; (road etc) verglacé.

idea [aɪ'dɪə] n idée f (of de); **I have an i. that . . .** j'ai l'impression que . . . ; **that's my i. of rest** c'est ce que j'appelle du repos; **that's the i.!** Fam c'est ça!; **not the slightest** or **foggiest i.** pas la moindre idée.

ideal [aɪ'dɪəl] a idéal; – n (aspiration) idéal m; pl (spiritual etc) idéal m. ◆**idealism** n idéalisme m. ◆**idealist** n idéaliste mf. ◆**idea'listic** a idéaliste. ◆**idealize** vt idéaliser. ◆**ideally** adv idéalement; **i. we should stay** l'idéal, ce serait de rester or que nous restions.

identical [aɪ'dentɪk(ə)l] a identique (**to, with** à). ◆**identifi'cation** n identification f; **I have (some) i.** j'ai une pièce d'identité. ◆**identify** vt identifier; **to i. (oneself) with** s'identifier avec. ◆**identikit** n portrait-robot m ◆**identity** n identité f; **i. card** carte f d'identité.

ideology [aɪdɪ'ɒlədʒɪ] n idéologie f. ◆**ideo-'logical** a idéologique.

idiom ['ɪdɪəm] n expression f idiomatique; (language) idiome m. ◆**idio'matic** a idiomatique.

idiosyncrasy [ɪdɪə'sɪŋkrəsɪ] n particularité f.

idiot ['ɪdɪət] n idiot, -ote mf. ◆**idiocy** n idiotie f. ◆**idi'otic** a idiot, bête. ◆**idi'otically** adv idiotement.

idle ['aɪd(ə)l] a (unoccupied) désœuvré, oisif;

(lazy) paresseux; (unemployed) en chômage; (moment) de loisir; (machine) au repos; (promise) vain; (pleasure, question) futile; (rumour) sans fondement; – vi (laze about) paresser; (of machine, engine) tourner au ralenti; – vt **i. away** (time) gaspiller. ◆—**ness** n oisiveté f; (laziness) paresse f. ◆**idler** n paresseux, -euse mf. ◆**idly** adv paresseusement; (to suggest, say) négligemment.

idol ['aɪd(ə)l] n idole f. ◆**idolize** vt idolâtrer.

idyllic [aɪ'dɪlɪk] a idyllique.

i.e. [aɪ'iː] abbr (id est) c'est-à-dire.

if [ɪf] conj si; **if he comes** s'il vient; **even if** même si; **if so** dans ce cas, si c'est le cas; **if not for pleasure** sinon pour le plaisir; **if only I were rich** si seulement j'étais riche; **if only to look** ne serait-ce que pour regarder; **as if** comme si; **as if nothing had happened** comme si de rien n'était; **as if to say** comme pour dire; **if necessary** s'il le faut.

igloo ['ɪgluː] n igloo m.

ignite [ɪg'naɪt] vt mettre le feu à; – vi prendre feu. ◆**ignition** n Aut allumage m; **to switch on the i.** mettre le contact.

ignominious [ɪgnə'mɪnɪəs] a déshonorant, ignominieux.

ignoramus [ɪgnə'reɪməs] n ignare mf.

ignorance ['ɪgnərəns] n ignorance f (of de). ◆**ignorant** a ignorant (of de). ◆**ignorantly** adv par ignorance.

ignore [ɪg'nɔː] vt ne prêter aucune attention à, ne tenir aucun compte de; (duty) méconnaître; (pretend not to recognize) faire semblant de ne pas reconnaître.

ilk [ɪlk] n of that **i.** (kind) de cet acabit.

ill [ɪl] a (sick) malade; (bad) mauvais; **i. will** malveillance f; – npl (misfortunes) maux mpl, malheurs mpl; – adv mal; **to speak i. of** dire du mal de. ◆**ill-ad'vised** a malavisé, peu judicieux. ◆**ill-'fated** a malheureux. ◆**ill-'gotten** a mal acquis. ◆**ill-in'formed** a mal renseigné. ◆**ill-'mannered** a mal élevé. ◆**ill-'natured** a (mean, unkind) désagréable. ◆**ill-'timed** a inopportun. ◆**ill-'treat** vt maltraiter.

illegal [ɪ'liːg(ə)l] a illégal. ◆**ille'gality** n illégalité f.

illegible [ɪ'ledʒəb(ə)l] a illisible.

illegitimate [ɪlɪ'dʒɪtɪmət] a (child, claim) illégitime. ◆**illegitimacy** n illégitimité f.

illicit [ɪ'lɪsɪt] a illicite.

illiterate [ɪ'lɪtərət] a & n illettré, -ée (mf), analphabète (mf). ◆**illiteracy** n analphabétisme m.

illness ['ɪlnɪs] n maladie f.

illogical [ɪ'lɒdʒɪk(ə)l] a illogique.

illuminate [ɪ'luːmɪneɪt] vt (street, question etc) éclairer; (monument etc for special occasion) illuminer. ◆**illumi'nation** n éclairage m; illumination f.

illusion [ɪ'luːʒ(ə)n] n illusion f (about sur); **I'm not under any i.** je ne me fais aucune illusion (about sur, quant à). ◆**illusive** a, ◆**illusory** a illusoire.

illustrate ['ɪləstreɪt] vt (with pictures, examples) illustrer (with de). ◆**illu'stration** n illustration f. ◆**i'llustrative** a (example) explicatif.

illustrious [ɪ'lʌstrɪəs] a illustre.

image ['ɪmɪdʒ] n image f; (public) i. (of firm etc) image f de marque; **he's the (living** or **spitting** or **very) i. of his brother** c'est (tout) le portrait de son frère. ◆**imagery** n images fpl.

imagin/e [ɪ'mædʒɪn] vt (picture to oneself) (s')imaginer, se figurer (that que); (suppose) imaginer (that que); **i. that . . .** imaginez que . . . ; **you're imagining (things)!** tu te fais des illusions! ◆**-ings** npl (dreams) imaginations fpl. ◆**-able** a imaginable; **the worst thing i.** le pire que l'on puisse imaginer. ◆**imaginary** a imaginaire. ◆**imagi'nation** n imagination f. ◆**imaginative** a plein d'imagination, imaginatif.

imbalance [ɪm'bæləns] n déséquilibre m.

imbecile ['ɪmbəsiːl, Am 'ɪmbəs(ə)l] a & n imbécile (mf). ◆**imbe'cility** n imbécillité f.

imbibe [ɪm'baɪb] vt absorber.

imbued [ɪm'bjuːd] a **i. with** (ideas) imprégné de; (feelings) pénétré de, imbu de.

imitate ['ɪmɪteɪt] vt imiter. ◆**imi'tation** n imitation f; – a (jewels) artificiel; **i. leather** imitation f cuir. ◆**imitative** a imitateur. ◆**imitator** n imitateur, -trice mf.

immaculate [ɪ'mækjʊlət] a (person, appearance, shirt etc) impeccable.

immaterial [ɪmə'tɪərɪəl] a peu important (to pour).

immature [ɪmə'tʃʊər] a (fruit) vert; (animal) jeune; (person) qui manque de maturité.

immeasurable [ɪ'meʒərəb(ə)l] a incommensurable.

immediate [ɪ'miːdɪət] a immédiat. ◆**immediacy** n caractère m immédiat. ◆**immediately** adv (at once) tout de suite, immédiatement; (to concern, affect) directement; – conj (as soon as) dès que.

immense [ɪ'mens] a immense. ◆**immensely** adv (rich etc) immensément; **to enjoy oneself i.** s'amuser énormément. ◆**immensity** n immensité f.

immerse [ɪ'mɜːs] vt plonger, immerger; **immersed in work** plongé dans le travail. ◆**immersion** n immersion f; **i. heater** chauffe-eau m inv électrique.

immigrate ['ɪmɪgreɪt] vi immigrer. ◆**immigrant** n immigrant, -ante mf; (long-established) immigré, -ée mf; – a immigré. ◆**immi'gration** n immigration f.

imminent ['ɪmɪnənt] a imminent. ◆**imminence** n imminence f.

immobile [ɪ'məʊbaɪl, Am ɪ'məʊb(ə)l] a immobile. ◆**immo'bility** n immobilité f. ◆**immobilize** vt immobiliser.

immoderate [ɪ'mɒdərət] a immodéré.

immodest [ɪ'mɒdɪst] a impudique.

immoral [ɪ'mɒrəl] a immoral. ◆**immo'rality** n immoralité f.

immortal [ɪ'mɔːt(ə)l] a immortel. ◆**immor'tality** n immortalité f. ◆**immortalize** vt immortaliser.

immune [ɪ'mjuːn] a Med & Fig immunisé (to, from contre). ◆**immunity** n immunité f. ◆**'immunize** vt immuniser (against contre).

immutable [ɪ'mjuːtəb(ə)l] a immuable.

imp [ɪmp] n diablotin m, lutin m.

impact ['ɪmpækt] n impact m (on sur).

impair [ɪm'peər] vt détériorer; (hearing, health) abîmer.

impale [ɪm'peɪl] vt empaler.

impart [ɪm'pɑːt] vt communiquer (to à).

impartial [ɪm'pɑːʃ(ə)l] a impartial. ◆**imparti'ality** n impartialité f.

impassable [ɪm'pɑːsəb(ə)l] a (road) impraticable; (river) infranchissable.

impasse ['æmpɑːs, Am 'ɪmpæs] n (situation) impasse f.

impassioned [ɪm'pæʃ(ə)nd] a (speech etc) enflammé, passionné.

impassive [ɪm'pæsɪv] a impassible. ◆**-ness** n impassibilité f.

impatient [ɪm'peɪʃ(ə)nt] a impatient (to do de faire); **i. of** or **with** intolérant à l'égard de. ◆**impatience** n impatience f. ◆**impatiently** adv impatiemment.

impeccab/le [ɪm'pekəb(ə)l] a impeccable. ◆**-ly** adv impeccablement.

impecunious [ˌɪmpɪˈkjuːnɪəs] *a Hum* sans le sou, impécunieux.

impede [ɪmˈpiːd] *vt* (*hamper*) gêner; **to i. s.o. from doing** (*prevent*) empêcher qn de faire.

impediment [ɪmˈpedɪmənt] *n* obstacle *m*; (*of speech*) défaut *m* d'élocution.

impel [ɪmˈpel] *vt* (**-ll-**) (*drive*) pousser; (*force*) obliger (**to do** à faire).

impending [ɪmˈpendɪŋ] *a* imminent.

impenetrable [ɪmˈpenɪtrəb(ə)l] *a* (*forest, mystery etc*) impénétrable.

imperative [ɪmˈperətɪv] *a* (*need, tone*) impérieux; (*necessary*) essentiel; **it is i. that you come** il faut absolument que *or* il est indispensable que tu viennes; – *n Gram* impératif *m*.

imperceptible [ɪmpəˈseptəb(ə)l] *a* (*imperceptible* (**to** à).

imperfect [ɪmˈpɜːfɪkt] **1** *a* imparfait; (*goods*) défectueux. **2** *n* (*tense*) *Gram* imparfait *m*. ◆**imper'fection** *n* imperfection *f*.

imperial [ɪmˈpɪərɪəl] *a* impérial; (*majestic*) majestueux; (*measure*) *Br* légal. ◆**imperialism** *n* impérialisme *m*.

imperil [ɪmˈperɪl] *vt* (**-ll-**, *Am* **-l-**) mettre en péril.

imperious [ɪmˈpɪərɪəs] *a* impérieux.

impersonal [ɪmˈpɜːsən(ə)l] *a* impersonnel.

impersonate [ɪmˈpɜːsəneɪt] *vt* (*mimic*) imiter; (*pretend to be*) se faire passer pour. ◆**imperso'nation** *n* imitation *f*. ◆**impersonator** *n* imitateur, -trice *mf*.

impertinent [ɪmˈpɜːtɪnənt] *a* impertinent (**to** envers). ◆**impertinence** *n* impertinence *f*. ◆**impertinently** *adv* avec impertinence.

impervious [ɪmˈpɜːvɪəs] *a* imperméable (**to** à).

impetuous [ɪmˈpetjʊəs] *a* impétueux. ◆**impetu'osity** *n* impétuosité *f*.

impetus [ˈɪmpɪtəs] *n* impulsion *f*.

impinge [ɪmˈpɪndʒ] *vi* **to i. on** (*affect*) affecter; (*encroach on*) empiéter sur.

impish [ˈɪmpɪʃ] *a* (*naughty*) espiègle.

implacable [ɪmˈplækəb(ə)l] *a* implacable.

implant [ɪmˈplɑːnt] *vt* (*ideas*) inculquer (**in** à).

implement¹ [ˈɪmplɪmənt] *n* (*tool*) instrument *m*; (*utensil*) *Culin* ustensile *m*; *pl Agr* matériel *m*.

implement² [ˈɪmplɪment] *vt* (*carry out*) mettre en œuvre, exécuter. ◆**implemen'tation** *n* mise *f* en œuvre, exécution *f*.

implicate [ˈɪmplɪkeɪt] *vt* impliquer (**in** dans). ◆**impli'cation** *n* (*consequence, involvement*) implication *f*; (*innuendo*) insinuation *f*; (*impact*) portée *f*; **by i.** implicitement.

implicit [ɪmˈplɪsɪt] *a* (*implied*) implicite; (*belief, obedience etc*) absolu. ◆**—ly** *adv* implicitement.

implore [ɪmˈplɔːr] *vt* implorer (**s.o. to do** qn de faire).

imply [ɪmˈplaɪ] *vt* (*assume*) impliquer, supposer (**that** que); (*suggest*) laisser entendre (**that** que); (*insinuate*) *Pej* insinuer (**that** que). ◆**implied** *a* implicite.

impolite [ɪmpəˈlaɪt] *a* impoli. ◆**—ness** *n* impolitesse *f*.

import 1 [ɪmˈpɔːt] *vt* (*goods etc*) importer (**from** de); – [ˈɪmpɔːt] *n* (*object, action*) importation *f*. **2** [ˈɪmpɔːt] *n* (*meaning*) sens *m*. ◆**im'porter** *n* importateur, -trice *mf*.

importance [ɪmˈpɔːtəns] *n* importance *f*; **to be of i.** avoir de l'importance; **of no i.** sans importance. ◆**important** *a* (*significant*) important. ◆**importantly** *adv* **more i.** ce qui est plus important.

impose [ɪmˈpəʊz] *vt* imposer (**on** à); (*fine, punishment*) infliger (**on** à); **to i.** (**oneself**) **on s.o.** s'imposer à qn; – *vi* s'imposer. ◆**impo'sition** *n* imposition *f* (**of** de); (*inconvenience*) dérangement *m*.

impossible [ɪmˈpɒsəb(ə)l] *a* impossible (**to do** à faire); **it is i.** (**for us**) **to do** il (nous) est impossible de faire; **it is i. that** il est impossible que (+ *sub*); **to make it i. for s.o. to do** mettre qn dans l'impossibilité de faire; – *n* **to do the i.** faire l'impossible. ◆**impossi'bility** *n* impossibilité *f*. ◆**impossibly** *adv* (*late, hard*) incroyablement.

impostor [ɪmˈpɒstər] *n* imposteur *m*.

impotent [ˈɪmpətənt] *a Med* impuissant. ◆**impotence** *n Med* impuissance *f*.

impound [ɪmˈpaʊnd] *vt* (*of police*) saisir, confisquer; (*vehicle*) emmener à la fourrière.

impoverish [ɪmˈpɒvərɪʃ] *vt* appauvrir.

impracticable [ɪmˈpræktɪkəb(ə)l] *a* irréalisable, impraticable.

impractical [ɪmˈpræktɪk(ə)l] *a* peu réaliste.

imprecise [ɪmprɪˈsaɪs] *a* imprécis.

impregnable [ɪmˈpregnəb(ə)l] *a Mil* imprenable; (*argument*) *Fig* inattaquable.

impregnate [ˈɪmpregneɪt] *vt* (*imbue*) imprégner (**with** de); (*fertilize*) féconder.

impresario [ɪmprɪˈsɑːrɪəʊ] *n* (*pl* **-os**) impresario *m*.

impress [ɪmˈpres] *vt* impressionner (qn); (*mark*) imprimer; **to i. sth on s.o.** faire comprendre qch à qn. ◆**impression** *n* impression *f*; **to be under** *or* **have the i.** that avoir l'impression que; **to make a good i. on s.o.** faire une bonne impression à qn. ◆**impressionable** *a* (*person*) impressionnable; *(age)* où l'on est impressionnable. ◆**impressive** *a* impressionnant.

imprint [ɪm'prɪnt] *vt* imprimer; – ['ɪmprɪnt] *n* empreinte *f*.

imprison [ɪm'prɪz(ə)n] *vt* emprisonner. ◆**—ment** *n* emprisonnement *m*; **life i.** (la prison à vie.

improbable [ɪm'prɒbəb(ə)l] *a* improbable; *(story, excuse)* invraisemblable. ◆**improba'bility** *n* improbabilité *f*; invraisemblance *f*.

impromptu [ɪm'prɒmptjuː] *a & adv* impromptu.

improper [ɪm'prɒpər] *a (indecent)* inconvenant, indécent; *(wrong)* incorrect. ◆**impropriety** [ɪmprə'praɪətɪ] *n* inconvenance *f*; *(wrong use)* Ling impropriété *f*.

improve [ɪm'pruːv] *vt* améliorer; *(mind)* cultiver, développer; **to i. one's English** se perfectionner en anglais; **to i. s.o.'s looks** embellir qn; **to i. oneself** se cultiver; – *vi* s'améliorer; *(of business)* aller de mieux en mieux, reprendre; **to i. on** *(do better than)* faire mieux que. ◆**—ment** *n* amélioration *f*; *(of mind)* développement *m*; *(progress)* progrès *m(pl)*; **there has been some** *or* **an i.** il y a du mieux.

improvise ['ɪmprəvaɪz] *vti* improviser. ◆**improvi'sation** *n* improvisation *f*.

impudent ['ɪmpjʊdənt] *a* impudent. ◆**impudence** *n* impudence *f*.

impulse ['ɪmpʌls] *n* impulsion *f*; **on i.** sur un coup de tête. ◆**im'pulsive** *a (person, act)* impulsif, irréfléchi; *(remark)* irréfléchi. ◆**im'pulsively** *adv* de manière impulsive.

impunity [ɪm'pjuːnɪtɪ] *n* **with i.** impunément.

impure [ɪm'pjʊər] *a* impur. ◆**impurity** *n* impureté *f*.

in [ɪn] *prep* **1** dans; **in the box/the school/***etc* dans la boîte/l'école/*etc*; **in an hour('s time)** dans une heure; **in so far as** dans la mesure où. **2** à; **in school** à l'école; **in the garden** dans le jardin, au jardin; **in Paris** à Paris; **in the USA** aux USA; **in Portugal** au Portugal; **in fashion** à la mode; **in pencil** au crayon; **in my opinion** à mon avis. **3** en; **in summer/winter/French** en été/secret/français; **in Spain** en Espagne; **in May** en mai, au mois de mai; **in season** en saison; **in an hour** *(during the period of an hour)* en une heure; **in doing** en faisant; **dressed in black** habillé en noir; **in all** en tout. **4** de; **in a soft voice** d'une voix douce; **the best in the class** le meilleur de la classe. **5** in the rain sous la pluie; **in the morning** le matin; **he hasn't done it in years** ça fait des années qu'il ne l'a pas fait; **in an hour** *(at the end of*

an hour) au bout d'une heure; **one in ten** un sur dix; **in thousands** par milliers; **in here** ici; **in there** là-dedans. **6** *adv* **to be in** *(home)* être là, être à la maison; *(of train)* être arrivé; *(in fashion)* être en vogue; *(in season)* être en saison; *(in power)* Pol être au pouvoir; **day in day out** jour après jour; **in on** *(a secret)* au courant de; **we're in for some rain/trouble/***etc* on va avoir de la pluie/des ennuis/*etc*; **it's the in thing** *Fam* c'est dans le vent. **7** *npl* **the ins and outs of** les moindres détails de.

inability [ɪnə'bɪlɪtɪ] *n* incapacité *f* **(to do** de faire).

inaccessible [ɪnək'sesɪb(ə)l] *a* inaccessible.

inaccurate [ɪn'ækjʊrət] *a* inexact. ◆**inaccuracy** *n* inexactitude *f*.

inaction [ɪn'ækʃ(ə)n] *n* inaction *f*.

inactive [ɪn'æktɪv] *a* inactif; *(mind)* inerte. ◆**inac'tivity** *n* inactivité *f*, inaction *f*.

inadequate [ɪn'ædɪkwət] *a (quantity)* insuffisant; *(person)* pas à la hauteur, insuffisant; *(work)* médiocre. ◆**inadequacy** *n* insuffisance *f*. ◆**inadequately** *adv* insuffisamment.

inadmissible [ɪnəd'mɪsəb(ə)l] *a* inadmissible.

inadvertently [ɪnəd'vɜːtəntlɪ] *adv* par inadvertance.

inadvisable [ɪnəd'vaɪzəb(ə)l] *a (action)* à déconseiller; **it is i.** to il est déconseillé de.

inane [ɪ'neɪn] *a (absurd)* inepte.

inanimate [ɪn'ænɪmət] *a* inanimé.

inappropriate [ɪnə'prəʊprɪət] *a (unsuitable)* peu approprié, inadéquat; *(untimely)* inopportun.

inarticulate [ɪnɑː'tɪkjʊlət] *a (person)* incapable de s'exprimer; *(sound)* inarticulé.

inasmuch as [ɪnəz'mʌtʃəz] *adv (because)* vu que; *(to the extent that)* en ce sens que.

inattentive [ɪnə'tentɪv] *a* inattentif (**to** à).

inaudible [ɪn'ɔːdəb(ə)l] *a* inaudible.

inaugural [ɪ'nɔːgjʊrəl] *a* inaugural. ◆**inaugurate** *vt (policy, building)* inaugurer; *(official)* installer (dans ses fonctions). ◆**inaugu'ration** *n* inauguration *f*; investiture *f*.

inauspicious [ɪnɔː'spɪʃəs] *a* peu propice.

inborn [ɪn'bɔːn] *a* inné.

inbred [ɪn'bred] *a (quality etc)* inné.

Inc *abbr (Incorporated)* Am Com SA, SARL.

incalculable [ɪn'kælkjʊləb(ə)l] *a* incalculable.

incandescent [ɪnkæn'des(ə)nt] *a* incandescent.

incapable [ɪn'keɪpəb(ə)l] *a* incapable (of

doing de faire; **i. of** (*pity etc*) inaccessible à.

incapacitate [ɪnkə'pæsɪteɪt] *vt Med* rendre incapable (*de travailler etc*). ◆**incapacity** *n* (*inability*) *Med* incapacité *f*.

incarcerate [ɪn'kɑːsəreɪt] *vt* incarcérer. ◆**incarce'ration** *n* incarcération *f*.

incarnate [ɪn'kɑːnət] *a* incarné; – [ɪn'kɑːneɪt] *vt* incarner. ◆**incar'nation** *n* incarnation *f*.

incendiary [ɪn'sendɪərɪ] *a* (*bomb*) incendiaire.

incense 1 [ɪn'sens] *vt* mettre en colère. **2** ['ɪnsens] *n* (*substance*) encens *m*.

incentive [ɪn'sentɪv] *n* encouragement *m*, motivation *f*; **to give s.o. an i. to work**/*etc* encourager qn à travailler/*etc*.

inception [ɪn'sepʃ(ə)n] *n* début *m*.

incessant [ɪn'ses(ə)nt] *a* incessant. ◆**—ly** *adv* sans cesse.

incest ['ɪnsest] *n* inceste *m*. ◆**in'cestuous** *a* incestueux.

inch [ɪntʃ] *n* pouce *m* (= 2,54 cm); (*loosely*) *Fig* centimètre *m*; **within an i. of** (*success*) à deux doigts de; **i. by i.** petit à petit; – *vti* **to i.** (**one's way**) **forward** avancer petit à petit.

incidence ['ɪnsɪdəns] *n* fréquence *f*.

incident ['ɪnsɪdənt] *n* incident *m*; (*in book, film etc*) épisode *m*.

incidental [ɪnsɪ'dent(ə)l] *a* accessoire, secondaire; (*music*) de fond; **i. expenses** frais *mpl* accessoires. ◆**—ly** *adv* accessoirement; (*by the way*) à propos.

incinerate [ɪn'sɪnəreɪt] *vt* (*refuse, leaves etc*) incinérer. ◆**incinerator** *n* incinérateur *m*.

incipient [ɪn'sɪpɪənt] *a* naissant.

incision [ɪn'sɪʒ(ə)n] *n* incision *f*.

incisive [ɪn'saɪsɪv] *a* incisif.

incisor [ɪn'saɪzər] *n* (*tooth*) incisive *f*.

incite [ɪn'saɪt] *vt* inciter (**to do** à faire). ◆**—ment** *n* incitation *f* (**to do** à faire).

incline 1 [ɪn'klaɪn] *vt* (*tilt, bend*) incliner; **to i. s.o. to do** incliner qn à faire; **to be inclined to do** (*feel a wish to*) être enclin à faire; (*tend to*) avoir tendance à faire; – *vi* **to i.** or **be inclined towards** (*indulgence etc*) incliner à. **2** ['ɪnklaɪn] *n* (*slope*) inclinaison *f*. ◆**incli'nation** *n* inclination *f*; **to have no i. to do** n'avoir aucune envie de faire.

includ / e [ɪn'kluːd] *vt* (*contain*) comprendre, englober; (*refer to*) s'appliquer à; **my invitation includes you** mon invitation s'adresse aussi à vous; **to be included** être compris; (*on list*) être inclus. ◆**—ing** *prep* y compris. ◆**i. service** service *m* compris. ◆**inclusion** *n* inclusion *f*. ◆**inclusive** *a* inclus; **from the fourth to the tenth of May**

i. du quatre jusqu'au dix mai inclus(ivement); **to be i. of** comprendre; **i. charge** prix *m* global.

incognito [ɪnkɒg'niːtəʊ] *adv* incognito.

incoherent [ɪnkəʊ'hɪərənt] *a* incohérent. ◆**—ly** *adv* sans cohérence.

income ['ɪŋkʌm] *n* revenu *m*; **private i.** rentes *fpl*; **i. tax** impôt *m* sur le revenu.

incoming ['ɪnkʌmɪŋ] *a* (*tenant, president*) nouveau; **i. tide** marée *f* montante; **i. calls** *Tel* appels *mpl* de l'extérieur.

incommunicado [ɪnkəmjuːnɪ'kɑːdəʊ] *a* (tenu) au secret.

incomparable [ɪn'kɒmpərəb(ə)l] *a* incomparable.

incompatible [ɪnkəm'pætəb(ə)l] *a* incompatible (**with** avec). ◆**incompati'bility** *n* incompatibilité *f*.

incompetent [ɪn'kɒmpɪtənt] *a* incompétent. ◆**incompetence** *n* incompétence *f*.

incomplete [ɪnkəm'pliːt] *a* incomplet.

incomprehensible [ɪnkɒmprɪ'hensəb(ə)l] *a* incompréhensible.

inconceivable [ɪnkən'siːvəb(ə)l] *a* inconcevable.

inconclusive [ɪnkən'kluːsɪv] *a* peu concluant.

incongruous [ɪn'kɒŋgruəs] *a* (*building, colours*) qui jure(nt) (**with** avec); (*remark, attitude*) incongru; (*absurd*) absurde.

inconsequential [ɪnkɒnsɪ'kwenʃ(ə)l] *a* sans importance.

inconsiderate [ɪnkən'sɪdərət] *a* (*action, remark*) irréfléchi, inconsidéré; **to be i.** (*of person*) manquer d'égards (**towards** envers).

inconsistent [ɪnkən'sɪstənt] *a* inconséquent, incohérent; (*reports etc at variance*) contradictoire; **i. with** incompatible avec. ◆**inconsistency** *n* inconséquence *f*, incohérence *f*.

inconsolable [ɪnkən'səʊləb(ə)l] *a* inconsolable.

inconspicuous [ɪnkən'spɪkjʊəs] *a* peu en évidence, qui passe inaperçu. ◆**—ly** *adv* discrètement.

incontinent [ɪn'kɒntɪnənt] *a* incontinent.

inconvenient [ɪnkən'viːnɪənt] *a* (*room, situation*) incommode; (*time*) inopportun; **it's i.** (**for me**) **to ...** ça me dérange de ...; **that's very i.** c'est très gênant. ◆**inconvenience** *n* (*bother*) dérangement *m*; (*disadvantage*) inconvénient *m*; – *vt* déranger, gêner.

incorporate [ɪn'kɔːpəreɪt] *vt* (*introduce*) incorporer (**into** dans); (*contain*) contenir;

incorporated society *Am* société *f* anonyme, société *f* à responsabilité limitée.

incorrect [ɪnkəˈrekt] *a* incorrect, inexact; **you're i.** vous avez tort.

incorrigible [ɪnˈkɒrɪdʒəb(ə)l] *a* incorrigible.

incorruptible [ɪnkəˈrʌptəb(ə)l] *a* incorruptible.

increas/e [ɪnˈkriːs] *vi* augmenter; (*of effort, noise*) s'intensifier; **to i. in weight** prendre du poids; – *vt* augmenter; intensifier; – [ˈɪnkriːs] *n* augmentation *f* (**in, of** de); intensification *f* (**in, of** de); **on the i.** en hausse.
◆**—ing** *a* (*amount etc*) croissant.
◆**—ingly** *adv* de plus en plus.

incredib/le [ɪnˈkredəb(ə)l] *a* incroyable.
◆**—ly** *adv* incroyablement.

incredulous [ɪnˈkredjuləs] *a* incrédule.
◆**incre'dulity** *n* incrédulité *f*.

increment [ˈɪŋkrəmənt] *n* augmentation *f*.

incriminat/e [ɪnˈkrɪmɪneɪt] *vt* incriminer.
◆**—ing** *a* compromettant.

incubate [ˈɪŋkjubeɪt] *vt* (*eggs*) couver.
◆**incu'bation** *n* incubation *f*. ◆**incubator** *n* (*for baby, eggs*) couveuse *f*.

inculcate [ˈɪnkʌlkeɪt] *vt* inculquer (**in** à).

incumbent [ɪnˈkʌmbənt] *a* **it is i. upon him** *or* **her** to il lui incombe de; – *n Rel Pol* titulaire *mf*.

incur [ɪnˈkɜːr] *vt* (**-rr-**) (*debt*) contracter; (*expenses*) faire; (*criticism, danger*) s'attirer.

incurable [ɪnˈkjuərəb(ə)l] *a* incurable.

incursion [ɪnˈkɜːʃ(ə)n] *n* incursion *f* (**into** dans).

indebted [ɪnˈdetɪd] *a* **i. to s.o. for sth/for doing sth** redevable à qn de qch/d'avoir fait qch. ◆**—ness** *n* dette *f*.

indecent [ɪnˈdiːs(ə)nt] *a* (*offensive*) indécent; (*unsuitable*) peu approprié.
◆**indecency** *n* indécence *f*; (*crime*) Jur outrage *m* à la pudeur. ◆**indecently** *adv* indécemment.

indecisive [ɪndɪˈsaɪsɪv] *a* (*person, answer*) indécis. ◆**indecision** *n*, ◆**indecisiveness** *n* indécision *f*.

indeed [ɪnˈdiːd] *adv* en effet; inv; **very good/etc i.** vraiment très bon/*etc*; **yes i.!** bien sûr!; **thank you very much i.!** merci mille fois!

indefensible [ɪndɪˈfensəb(ə)l] *a* indéfendable.

indefinable [ɪndɪˈfaɪnəb(ə)l] *a* indéfinissable.

indefinite [ɪnˈdefɪnət] *a* (*feeling, duration etc*) indéfini; (*plan*) mal déterminé. ◆**—ly** *adv* indéfiniment.

indelible [ɪnˈdeləb(ə)l] *a* (*ink, memory*) indélébile; **i. pencil** crayon *m* à marquer.

indelicate [ɪnˈdelɪkət] *a* (*coarse*) indélicat.

indemnify [ɪnˈdemnɪfaɪ] *vt* indemniser (**for** de). ◆**indemnity** *n* indemnité *f*.

indented [ɪnˈdentɪd] *a* (*edge*) dentelé, découpé; (*line*) *Typ* renfoncé. ◆**inden-'tation** *n* denteleure *f*, découpure *f*; *Typ* renfoncement *m*.

independent [ɪndɪˈpendənt] *a* indépendant (**of** de); (*opinions, reports*) de sources différentes. ◆**independence** *n* indépendance *f*. ◆**independently** *adv* de façon indépendante; **i. of** indépendamment de.

indescribable [ɪndɪˈskraɪbəb(ə)l] *a* indescriptible.

indestructible [ɪndɪˈstrʌktəb(ə)l] *a* indestructible.

indeterminate [ɪndɪˈtɜːmɪnət] *a* indéterminé.

index [ˈɪndeks] *n* (*in book etc*) index *m*; (*in library*) catalogue *m*; (*number, sign*) indice *m*; **i. card** fiche *f*; **i. finger** index *m*; – *vt* (*classify*) classer. ◆**i.-'linked** *a Econ* indexé (**to** sur).

India [ˈɪndɪə] *n* Inde *f*. ◆**Indian** *a & n* indien, -ienne (*mf*).

indicate [ˈɪndɪkeɪt] *vt* indiquer (**that** que); **I was indicating right** *Aut* j'avais mis mon clignotant droit. ◆**indi'cation** *n* (*sign*) indice *m*, indication *f*; (*idea*) idée *f*. ◆**in'dicative** *a* indicatif (**of** de); – *n* (*mood*) *Gram* indicatif *m*. ◆**indicator** *n* (*instrument*) indicateur *m*; (*sign*) indication *f* (**of** de); *Aut* clignotant *m*; (*display board*) tableau *m* (indicateur).

indict [ɪnˈdaɪt] *vt* inculper (**for** de).
◆**—ment** *n* inculpation *f*.

Indies [ˈɪndɪz] *npl* **the West I.** les Antilles *fpl*.

indifferent [ɪnˈdɪf(ə)rənt] *a* indifférent (**to** à); (*mediocre*) *Pej* médiocre. ◆**indifference** *n* indifférence *f* (**to** à). ◆**indifferently** *adv* indifféremment.

indigenous [ɪnˈdɪdʒɪnəs] *a* indigène.

indigestion [ɪndɪˈdʒestʃ(ə)n] *n* dyspepsie *f*; (**an attack of**) **i.** une indigestion, une crise de foie. ◆**indigestible** *a* indigeste.

indignant [ɪnˈdɪgnənt] *a* indigné (**at** de, **with** contre); **to become i.** s'indigner. ◆**indignantly** *adv* avec indignation. ◆**indig'nation** *n* indignation *f*.

indignity [ɪnˈdɪgnɪtɪ] *n* indignité *f*.

indigo [ˈɪndɪgəʊ] *n & a* (*colour*) indigo *m & a inv*.

indirect [ɪndaɪˈrekt] *a* indirect. ◆**—ly** *adv* indirectement.

indiscreet [ɪndɪˈskriːt] *a* indiscret. ◆**indiscretion** *n* indiscrétion *f*.

indiscriminate [ɪndɪˈskrɪmɪnət] *a* (*person*)

qui manque de discernement; (*random*) fait, donné etc au hasard. ◆—**ly** *adv* (*at random*) au hasard; (*without discrimination*) sans discernement.

indispensable [ɪndɪ'spensəb(ə)l] *a* indispensable (**to** à).

indisposed [ɪndɪ'spəʊzd] *a* (*unwell*) indisposé. ◆**indispo'sition** *n* indisposition *f*.

indisputable [ɪndɪ'spjuːtəb(ə)l] *a* incontestable.

indistinct [ɪndɪ'stɪŋkt] *a* indistinct.

indistinguishable [ɪndɪ'stɪŋgwɪʃəb(ə)l] *a* indifférenciable (**from** de).

individual [ɪndɪ'vɪdʒʊəl] *a* individuel; (*unusual, striking*) singulier, particulier; – *n* (*person*) individu *m*. ◆**individualist** *n* individualiste *mf*. ◆**individua'listic** *a* individualiste. ◆**individu'ality** *n* (*distinctiveness*) individualité *f*. ◆**individually** *adv* (*separately*) individuellement; (*unusually*) de façon (très) personnelle.

indivisible [ɪndɪ'vɪzəb(ə)l] *a* indivisible.

Indo-China [ɪndəʊ'tʃaɪnə] *n* Indochine *f*.

indoctrinate [ɪn'dɒktrɪneɪt] *vt Pej* endoctriner. ◆**indoctri'nation** *n* endoctrinement *m*.

indolent ['ɪndələnt] *a* indolent. ◆**indolence** *n* indolence *f*.

indomitable [ɪn'dɒmɪtəb(ə)l] *a* (*will, energy*) indomptable.

Indonesia [ɪndəʊ'niːʒə] *n* Indonésie *f*.

indoor ['ɪndɔːr] *a* (*games, shoes etc*) d'intérieur; (*swimming pool etc*) couvert. ◆**in'doors** *adv* à l'intérieur; **to go** or **come i. rentrer**.

induce [ɪn'djuːs] *vt* (*persuade*) persuader (**to do** de faire); (*cause*) provoquer; **to i. labour** *Med* déclencher le travail. ◆—**ment** *n* encouragement *m* (**to do** à faire).

indulge [ɪn'dʌldʒ] *vt* (*s.o.'s desires*) satisfaire; (*child etc*) gâter, tout passer à; **to i. oneself** se gâter; – *vi* **to i. in** (*action*) s'adonner à; (*ice cream etc*) se permettre. ◆**indulgence** *n* indulgence *f*. ◆**indulgent** *a* indulgent (**to** envers, avec).

industrial [ɪn'dʌstrɪəl] *a* industriel; (*conflict, legislation*) du travail; **i. action** action *f* revendicative; **i. park** *Am* complexe *m* industriel. ◆**industrialist** *n* industriel, -ielle *mf*. ◆**industrialized** *a* industrialisé.

industrious [ɪn'dʌstrɪəs] *a* travailleur.

industry ['ɪndəstrɪ] *n* industrie *f*; (*hard work*) application *f*.

inedible [ɪn'edəb(ə)l] *a* immangeable.

ineffective [ɪnɪ'fektɪv] *a* (*measure etc*) sans effet, inefficace; (*person*) incapable. ◆—**ness** *n* inefficacité *f*.

ineffectual [ɪnɪ'fektʃʊəl] *a* (*measure etc*) inefficace; (*person*) incompétent.

inefficient [ɪnɪ'fɪʃ(ə)nt] *a* (*person, measure etc*) inefficace; (*machine*) peu performant. ◆**inefficiency** *n* inefficacité *f*.

ineligible [ɪn'elɪdʒəb(ə)l] *a* (*candidate*) inéligible; **to be i. for** ne pas avoir droit à.

inept [ɪ'nept] *a* (*foolish*) inepte; (*unskilled*) peu habile (**at sth** à qch); (*incompetent*) incapable, inapte. ◆**ineptitude** *n* (*incapacity*) inaptitude *f*.

inequality [ɪnɪ'kwɒlətɪ] *n* inégalité *f*.

inert [ɪ'nɜːt] *a* inerte. ◆**inertia** [ɪ'nɜːʃə] *n* inertie *f*.

inescapable [ɪnɪ'skeɪpəb(ə)l] *a* inéluctable.

inevitable [ɪn'evɪtəb(ə)l] *a* inévitable. ◆**inevitably** *adv* inévitablement.

inexcusable [ɪnɪk'skjuːzəb(ə)l] *a* inexcusable.

inexhaustible [ɪnɪg'zɔːstəb(ə)l] *a* inépuisable.

inexorable [ɪn'eksərəb(ə)l] *a* inexorable.

inexpensive [ɪnɪk'spensɪv] *a* bon marché *inv*.

inexperience [ɪnɪk'spɪərɪəns] *n* inexpérience *f*. ◆**inexperienced** *a* inexpérimenté.

inexplicable [ɪnɪk'splɪkəb(ə)l] *a* inexplicable.

inexpressible [ɪnɪk'spresəb(ə)l] *a* inexprimable.

inextricable [ɪn'ɪk'strɪkəb(ə)l] *a* inextricable.

infallible [ɪn'fæləb(ə)l] *a* infaillible. ◆**infalli'bility** *n* infaillibilité *f*.

infamous ['ɪnfəməs] *a* (*evil*) infâme. ◆**infamy** *n* infamie *f*.

infant ['ɪnfənt] *n* (*child*) petit(e) enfant *mf*; (*baby*) nourrisson *m*; **i. school** classes *fpl* préparatoires. ◆**infancy** *n* petite enfance *f*; **to be in its i.** (*of art, technique etc*) en être à ses premiers balbutiements. ◆**infantile** *a* (*illness, reaction etc*) infantile.

infantry ['ɪnfəntrɪ] *n* infanterie *f*.

infatuated [ɪn'fætjʊeɪtɪd] *a* amoureux; **i. with** (*person*) amoureux de, engoué de; (*sport etc*) engoué de. ◆**infatu'ation** *n* engouement *m* (**for, with** pour).

infect [ɪn'fekt] *vt* (*contaminate*) *Med* infecter; **to become infected** s'infecter; **to i. s.o. with sth** communiquer qch à qn. ◆**infection** *n* infection *f*. ◆**infectious** *a* (*disease*) infectieux, contagieux; (*person, laughter etc*) contagieux.

infer [ɪn'fɜːr] *vt* (**-rr-**) déduire (**from** de, **that** que). ◆**'inference** *n* déduction *f*, conclusion *f*.

inferior [ɪnˈfɪəriər] *a* inférieur (**to** à); (*goods, work*) de qualité inférieure; − *n* (*person*) Pej inférieur, -eure *mf*. ◆**inferi'ority** *n* infériorité *f*.

infernal [ɪnˈfɜːn(ə)l] *a* infernal. ◆**—ly** *adv Fam* épouvantablement.

inferno [ɪnˈfɜːnəʊ] *n* (*pl -os*) (*blaze*) brasier *m*, incendie *m*; (*hell*) enfer *m*.

infertile [ɪnˈfɜːtaɪl, *Am* ɪnˈfɜːt(ə)l] *a* (*person, land*) stérile.

infest [ɪnˈfest] *vt* infester (**with** de).

infidelity [ɪnfɪˈdelɪtɪ] *n* infidélité *f*.

infighting [ˈɪnfaɪtɪŋ] *n* (*within group*) luttes *fpl* intestines.

infiltrate [ˈɪnfɪltreɪt] *vi* s'infiltrer (**into** dans); − *vt* (*group etc*) s'infiltrer dans. ◆**infil'tration** *n* infiltration *f*; *Pol* noyautage *m*.

infinite [ˈɪnfɪnɪt] *a* & *n* infini *m*. ◆**infinitely** *adv* infiniment. ◆**in'finity** *n Math Phot* infini *m*; **to i.** *Math* à l'infini.

infinitive [ɪnˈfɪnɪtɪv] *n Gram* infinitif *m*.

infirm [ɪnˈfɜːm] *a* infirme. ◆**infirmary** *n* (*sickbay*) infirmerie *f*; (*hospital*) hôpital *m*. ◆**infirmity** *n* (*disability*) infirmité *f*.

inflame [ɪnˈfleɪm] *vt* enflammer. ◆**inflammable** *a* inflammable. ◆**infla'mmation** *n Med* inflammation *f*. ◆**inflammatory** *a* (*remark*) incendiaire.

inflate [ɪnˈfleɪt] *vt* (*tyre, prices etc*) gonfler. ◆**inflatable** *a* gonflable. ◆**inflation** *n Econ* inflation *f*. ◆**inflationary** *a Econ* inflationniste.

inflection [ɪnˈflekʃ(ə)n] *n Gram* flexion *f*; (*of voice*) inflexion *f*.

inflexible [ɪnˈfleksəb(ə)l] *a* inflexible.

inflexion [ɪnˈflekʃ(ə)n] *n* = **inflection**.

inflict [ɪnˈflɪkt] *vt* infliger (**on** à); (*wound*) occasionner (**on** à).

influence [ˈɪnfluəns] *n* influence *f*; **under the i. of** (*anger, drugs*) sous l'effet de; **under the i. of drink** *or* **alcohol** *Jur* en état d'ébriété; − *vt* influencer. ◆**influ'ential** *a* influent.

influenza [ɪnfluˈenzə] *n Med* grippe *f*.

influx [ˈɪnflʌks] *n* flot *m*, afflux *m*.

info [ˈɪnfəʊ] *n Sl* tuyaux *mpl*, renseignements *mpl* (**on** sur).

inform [ɪnˈfɔːm] *vt* informer (**of** de, **that** que); − *vi* **to i. on** dénoncer. ◆**—ed** *a* informé; **to keep s.o. i. of** tenir qn au courant de. ◆**informant** *n* informateur, -trice *mf*. ◆**informative** *a* instructif. ◆**informer** *n* (*police*) i. indicateur, -trice *mf*.

informal [ɪnˈfɔːm(ə)l] *a* (*without fuss*) simple, sans façon; (*occasion*) dénué de formalité; (*tone, expression*) familier; (*announcement*) officieux; (*meeting*) non-officiel. ◆**infor-**

'mality *n* simplicité *f*; (*of tone etc*) familiarité *f*. ◆**informally** *adv* (*without fuss*) sans cérémonie; (*to meet*) officieusement; (*to dress*) simplement.

information [ɪnfəˈmeɪʃ(ə)n] *n* (*facts*) renseignements *mpl* (**about, on** sur); (*knowledge*) & *Math* information *f*; **a piece of i.** un renseignement, une information; **to get some i.** se renseigner.

infrared [ɪnfrəˈred] *a* infrarouge.

infrequent [ɪnˈfriːkwənt] *a* peu fréquent.

infringe [ɪnˈfrɪndʒ] *vt* (*rule*) contrevenir à; − *vi* **to i. upon** (*encroach on*) empiéter sur. ◆**—ment** *n* infraction *f* (**of** à).

infuriat/e [ɪnˈfjʊərɪeɪt] *vt* exaspérer. ◆**—ing** *a* exaspérant.

infuse [ɪnˈfjuːz] *vt* (*tea*) (faire) infuser. ◆**infusion** *n* infusion *f*.

ingenious [ɪnˈdʒiːnɪəs] *a* ingénieux. ◆**inge'nuity** *n* ingéniosité *f*.

ingot [ˈɪŋgət] *n* lingot *m*.

ingrained [ɪnˈgreɪnd] *a* (*prejudice*) enraciné; **i. dirt** crasse *f*.

ingratiat/e [ɪnˈgreɪʃɪeɪt] *vt* **to i. oneself with** s'insinuer dans les bonnes grâces de. ◆**—ing** *a* (*person, smile*) insinuant.

ingratitude [ɪnˈgrætɪtjuːd] *n* ingratitude *f*.

ingredient [ɪnˈgriːdɪənt] *n* ingrédient *m*.

ingrown [ɪnˈgrəʊn] *a* (*nail*) incarné.

inhabit [ɪnˈhæbɪt] *vt* habiter. ◆**—able** *a* habitable. ◆**inhabitant** *n* habitant, -ante *mf*.

inhale [ɪnˈheɪl] *vt* aspirer; **to i. the smoke** (*of smoker*) avaler la fumée. ◆**inha'lation** *n* inhalation *f*. ◆**inhaler** *n Med* inhalateur *m*.

inherent [ɪnˈhɪərənt] *a* inhérent (**in** à). ◆**—ly** *adv* intrinsèquement, en soi.

inherit [ɪnˈherɪt] *vt* hériter (de); (*title*) succéder à. ◆**inheritance** *n* héritage *m*; (*process*) *Jur* succession *f*; (*cultural*) patrimoine *m*.

inhibit [ɪnˈhɪbɪt] *vt* (*hinder*) gêner; (*control*) maîtriser; (*prevent*) empêcher (**from** de); **to be inhibited** être inhibé, avoir des inhibitions. ◆**inhi'bition** *n* inhibition *f*.

inhospitable [ɪnhɒˈspɪtəb(ə)l] *a* inhospitalier.

inhuman [ɪnˈhjuːmən] *a* (*not human, cruel*) inhumain. ◆**inhu'mane** *a* (*not kind*) inhumain. ◆**inhu'manity** *n* brutalité *f*, cruauté *f*.

inimitable [ɪˈnɪmɪtəb(ə)l] *a* inimitable.

iniquitous [ɪˈnɪkwɪtəs] *a* inique. ◆**iniquity** *n* iniquité *f*.

initial [ɪˈnɪʃ(ə)l] *a* initial, premier; − *n* (*letter*) initiale *f*; (*signature*) paraphe *m*; −

vt (**-ll-**, *Am* **-l-**) parapher. ◆**—ly** *adv* initialement, au début.

initiate [ɪ'nɪʃɪeɪt] *vt* (*reforms*) amorcer; (*schemes*) inaugurer; **to i. s.o. into** initier qn à; **the initiated** les initiés *mpl*. ◆**initi'ation** *n* amorce *f*; inauguration *f*; initiation *f*. ◆**initiator** *n* initiateur, -trice *mf*.

initiative [ɪ'nɪʃətɪv] *n* initiative *f*.

inject [ɪn'dʒekt] *vt* injecter (**into**); (*new life etc*) Fig insuffler (**into** à). ◆**injection** *n* Med injection *f*, piqûre *f*.

injunction [ɪn'dʒʌŋkʃ(ə)n] *n* Jur ordonnance *f*.

injur/e ['ɪndʒər] *vt* (*physically*) blesser; (*prejudice, damage*) nuire à; (*one's chances*) compromettre; **to i. one's foot/etc** se blesser au pied/*etc*. ◆**—ed** *a* blessé; — **the i.** les blessés *mpl*. ◆**injury** *n* (*to flesh*) blessure *f*; (*fracture*) fracture *f*; (*sprain*) foulure *f*; (*bruise*) contusion *f*; (*wrong*) Fig préjudice *m*.

injurious [ɪn'dʒʊərɪəs] *a* préjudiciable (**to** à).

injustice [ɪn'dʒʌstɪs] *n* injustice *f*.

ink [ɪŋk] *n* encre *f*; **Indian i.** encre *f* de Chine. ◆**inkpot** *n*, ◆**inkwell** *n* encrier *m*. ◆**inky** *a* couvert d'encre.

inkling ['ɪŋklɪŋ] *n* (petite) idée *f*; **to have some** or **an i. of sth** soupçonner qch, avoir une (petite) idée de qch.

inlaid [ɪn'leɪd] *a* (*marble etc*) incrusté (**with** de); (*wood*) marqueté.

inland ['ɪnlənd, 'ɪnlænd] *a* intérieur; the **I. Revenue** le fisc; — [ɪn'lænd] *adv* à l'intérieur (*des terres*).

in-laws ['ɪnlɔːz] *npl* belle-famille *f*.

inlet ['ɪnlet] *n* (*of sea*) crique *f*; **i. pipe** tuyau *m* d'arrivée.

inmate ['ɪnmeɪt] *n* résident, -ente *mf*; (*of asylum*) interné, -ée *mf*; (*of prison*) détenu, -ue *mf*.

inmost ['ɪnməʊst] *a* le plus profond.

inn [ɪn] *n* auberge *f*. ◆**innkeeper** *n* aubergiste *m*.

innards ['ɪnədz] *npl* Fam entrailles *fpl*.

innate [ɪ'neɪt] *a* inné.

inner ['ɪnər] *a* intérieur; (*ear*) interne; (*feelings*) intime, profond; **the i. city** le cœur de la ville; **an i. circle** (*group of people*) un cercle restreint; **the i. circle** le saint des saints; **i. tube** (*of tyre*) chambre *f* à air. ◆**innermost** *a* le plus profond.

inning ['ɪnɪŋ] *n* Baseball tour *m* de batte. ◆**innings** *n inv* Cricket tour *m* de batte; **a good i.** Fig une vie longue.

innocent ['ɪnəs(ə)nt] *a* innocent. ◆**inno-**

cence *n* innocence *f*. ◆**innocently** *adv* innocemment.

innocuous [ɪ'nɒkjʊəs] *a* inoffensif.

innovate ['ɪnəveɪt] *vi* innover. ◆**inno-'vation** *n* innovation *f*. ◆**innovator** *n* innovateur, -trice *mf*.

innuendo [ɪnjʊ'endəʊ] *n* (*pl* **-oes** or **-os**) insinuation *f*.

innumerable [ɪ'njuːmərəb(ə)l] *a* innombrable.

inoculate [ɪ'nɒkjʊleɪt] *vt* vacciner (**against** contre). ◆**inocu'lation** *n* inoculation *f*.

inoffensive [ɪnə'fensɪv] *a* inoffensif.

inoperative [ɪn'ɒpərətɪv] *a* (*without effect*) inopérant.

inopportune [ɪn'ɒpətjuːn] *a* inopportun.

inordinate [ɪ'nɔːdɪnət] *a* excessif. ◆**—ly** *adv* excessivement.

in-patient ['ɪnpeɪʃ(ə)nt] *n* malade *mf* hospitalisé(e).

input ['ɪnpʊt] *n* (*computer operation*) entrée *f*; (*data*) données *fpl*; (*current*) El énergie *f*.

inquest ['ɪnkwest] *n* enquête *f*.

inquir/e [ɪn'kwaɪər] *vi* se renseigner (**about** sur); **to i. after** s'informer de; **to i. into** examiner, faire une enquête sur; — *vt* demander; **to i. how to get to** demander le chemin de. ◆**—ing** *a* (*mind, look*) curieux. ◆**inquiry** *n* (*question*) question *f*; (*request for information*) demande *f* de renseignements; (*information*) renseignements *mpl*; Jur enquête *f*; **to make inquiries** demander des renseignements; (*of police*) enquêter.

inquisitive [ɪn'kwɪzɪtɪv] *a* curieux. ◆**inquisitively** *adv* avec curiosité. ◆**inqui'sition** *n* (*inquiry* & Rel) inquisition *f*.

inroads ['ɪnrəʊdz] *npl* (*attacks*) incursions *fpl* (**into** dans); **to make i. into** (*start on*) Fig entamer.

insane [ɪn'seɪn] *a* fou, dément. ◆**insanely** *adv* comme un fou. ◆**insanity** *n* folie *f*, démence *f*.

insanitary [ɪn'sænɪt(ə)rɪ] *a* insalubre.

insatiable [ɪn'seɪʃəb(ə)l] *a* insatiable.

inscribe [ɪn'skraɪb] *vt* inscrire; (*book*) dédicacer (**to** à). ◆**inscription** *n* inscription *f*; dédicace *f*.

inscrutable [ɪn'skruːtəb(ə)l] *a* impénétrable.

insect ['ɪnsekt] *n* insecte *m*; — *a* (*powder, spray*) insecticide; **i. repellant** crème *f* anti-insecte. ◆**in'secticide** *n* insecticide *m*.

insecure [ɪnsɪ'kjʊər] *a* (*not fixed*) peu solide; (*furniture, ladder*) branlant, bancal; (*window*) mal fermé; (*uncertain*) incertain;

(*unsafe*) peu sûr; (*person*) qui manque d'assurance. ◆**insecurity** n (*of person, situation*) insécurité f.

insemination [ɪnsemɪ'neɪʃ(ə)n] n Med insémination f.

insensible [ɪn'sensəb(ə)l] a Med inconscient.

insensitive [ɪn'sensɪtɪv] a insensible (**to** à). ◆**insensi'tivity** n insensibilité f.

inseparable [ɪn'sep(ə)rəb(ə)l] a inséparable (**from** de).

insert [ɪn'sɜːt] vt insérer (**in, into** dans). ◆**insertion** n insertion f.

inshore ['ɪnʃɔːr] a côtier.

inside [ɪn'saɪd] adv dedans, à l'intérieur; **come i.!** entrez!; – prep à l'intérieur de, dans; (*time*) en moins de; – n dedans m, intérieur m; pl (*stomach*) Fam ventre m; **on the i.** à l'intérieur (**of** de); **i. out** (*coat, socks etc*) à l'envers; (*to know, study etc*) à fond; **to turn everything i. out** Fig tout chambouler; – a intérieur; (*information*) obtenu à la source; **the i. lane** Aut la voie de gauche, Am la voie de droite.

insidious [ɪn'sɪdɪəs] a insidieux.

insight ['ɪnsaɪt] n perspicacité f; **to give an i. into** (*s.o.'s character*) permettre de comprendre, éclairer; (*question*) donner un aperçu de.

insignia [ɪn'sɪɡnɪə] npl (*of important person*) insignes mpl.

insignificant [ɪnsɪɡ'nɪfɪkənt] a insignifiant. ◆**insignificance** n insignifiance f.

insincere [ɪnsɪn'sɪər] a peu sincère. ◆**insincerity** n manque m de sincérité.

insinuate [ɪn'sɪnjueɪt] vt 1 Pej insinuer (**that** que). **2 to i. oneself into** s'insinuer dans. ◆**insinu'ation** n insinuation f.

insipid [ɪn'sɪpɪd] a insipide.

insist [ɪn'sɪst] vi insister (**on doing** pour faire); **to i. on sth** (*demand*) exiger qch; (*assert*) affirmer qch; – vt (*order*) insister (**that** pour que); (*declare firmly*) affirmer (**that** que); **I i. that you come** or **on your coming** j'insiste pour que tu viennes. ◆**insistence** n insistance f; **her i. on seeing me** l'insistance qu'elle met à vouloir me voir. ◆**insistent** a insistant; **I was i.** (**about it**) j'ai été pressant. ◆**insistently** adv avec insistance.

insolent ['ɪnsələnt] a insolent. ◆**insolence** n insolence f. ◆**insolently** adv insolemment.

insoluble [ɪn'sɒljub(ə)l] a insoluble.

insolvent [ɪn'sɒlvənt] a Fin insolvable.

insomnia [ɪn'sɒmnɪə] n insomnie f. ◆**insomniac** n insomniaque mf.

insomuch as [ɪnsəʊ'mʌtʃəz] adv = **inasmuch as**.

inspect [ɪn'spekt] vt inspecter; (*tickets*) contrôler; (*troops*) passer en revue. ◆**inspection** n inspection f; contrôle m; revue f. ◆**inspector** n inspecteur, -trice mf; (*on bus*) contrôleur, -euse mf.

inspir/e [ɪn'spaɪər] vt inspirer (**s.o. with sth** qch à qn); **to be inspired to do** avoir l'inspiration de faire. ◆**—ed** a inspiré. ◆**—ing** a qui inspire. ◆**inspi'ration** n inspiration f; (*person*) source f d'inspiration.

instability [ɪnstə'bɪlɪtɪ] n instabilité f.

install [ɪn'stɔːl] vt installer. ◆**insta'llation** n installation f.

instalment [ɪn'stɔːlmənt] (*Am* **installment**) n (*of money*) acompte m, versement m (partiel); (*of serial*) épisode m; (*of publication*) fascicule m; **to buy on the i. plan** Am acheter à crédit.

instance ['ɪnstəns] n (*example*) exemple m; (*case*) cas m; (*occasion*) circonstance f; **for i.** par exemple; **in the first i.** en premier lieu.

instant ['ɪnstənt] a immédiat; **i. coffee** café m soluble or instantané, nescafé® m; **of the 3rd i.** (*in letter*) Com du 3 courant; – n (*moment*) instant m; **this (very) i.** (*at once*) à l'instant; **the i. that** (*as soon as*) dès que. ◆**instan'taneous** a instantané. ◆**instantly** adv immédiatement.

instead [ɪn'sted] adv (*as alternative*) au lieu de cela, plutôt; **i. of** au lieu de; **i. of s.o.** à la place de qn; **i. (of him or her)** à sa place.

instep [ɪn'step] n (*of foot*) cou-de-pied m; (*of shoe*) cambrure f.

instigate ['ɪnstɪɡeɪt] vt provoquer. ◆**insti'gation** n instigation f. ◆**instigator** n instigateur, -trice mf.

instil [ɪn'stɪl] vt (**-ll-**) (*idea*) inculquer (**into** à); (*courage*) insuffler (**into** à).

instinct ['ɪnstɪŋkt] n instinct m; **by i.** d'instinct. ◆**in'stinctive** a instinctif. ◆**in'stinctively** adv instinctivement.

institute ['ɪnstɪtjuːt] **1** vt (*rule, practice*) instituer; (*inquiry, proceedings*) Jur entamer, intenter. **2** n institut m. ◆**insti'tution** n (*custom, private or charitable organization etc*) institution f; (*school, hospital*) établissement m; (*home*) Med asile m. ◆**insti'tutional** a institutionnel.

instruct [ɪn'strʌkt] vt (*teach*) enseigner (**s.o. in sth** qch à qn); **to i. s.o. about sth** (*inform*) instruire qn de qch; **to i. s.o. to do** (*order*) charger qn de faire. ◆**instruction** n (*teaching*) instruction f; pl (*orders*) instructions fpl; **instructions (for use)** mode m

d'emploi. ◆**instructive** a instructif.
◆**instructor** n professeur m; Sp moniteur,
-trice mf; Mil instructeur m; Univ Am
maître-assistant, -ante mf; **driving i.**
moniteur, -trice mf de conduite.
instrument ['ɪnstrəmənt] n instrument m.
◆**instru'mental** a Mus instrumental; **to
be i. in sth/in doing sth** contribuer à qch./à
faire qch. ◆**instru'mentalist** n Mus
instrumentaliste mf. ◆**instrumen'tation**
n Mus orchestration f.
insubordinate [ɪnsəˈbɔːdɪnət] a indiscipliné. ◆**insubordi'nation** n indiscipline f.
insubstantial [ɪnsəbˈstænʃ(ə)l] a (argument,
evidence) peu solide.
insufferable [ɪnˈsʌfərəb(ə)l] a intolérable.
insufficient [ɪnsəˈfɪʃənt] a insuffisant.
◆**—ly** adv insuffisamment.
insular ['ɪnsjʊlər] a (climate) insulaire;
(views) Pej étroit, borné.
insulate ['ɪnsjʊleɪt] vt (against cold etc) & El
isoler; (against sound) insonoriser; **to i. s.o.
from** Fig protéger qn de; **insulating tape**
chatterton m. ◆**insu'lation** n isolation f;
insonorisation f; (material) isolant m.
insulin ['ɪnsjʊlɪn] n Med insuline f.
insult [ɪnˈsʌlt] vt insulter; — ['ɪnsʌlt] n insulte
f (to à).
insuperable [ɪnˈsuːpərəb(ə)l] a insurmontable.
insure [ɪnˈʃʊər] vt 1 (protect against damage
etc) assurer (**against** contre). 2 Am =
ensure. ◆**insurance** n assurance f; **i.
company** compagnie f d'assurances; **i.
policy** police f d'assurance.
insurgent [ɪnˈsɜːdʒənt] a & n insurgé, -ée
(mf).
insurmountable [ɪnsəˈmaʊntəb(ə)l] a
insurmontable.
insurrection [ɪnsəˈrekʃ(ə)n] n insurrection
f.
intact [ɪnˈtækt] a intact.
intake ['ɪnteɪk] n (of food) consommation f;
Sch Univ admissions fpl; Tech admission f.
intangible [ɪnˈtændʒəb(ə)l] a intangible.
integral ['ɪntɪgrəl] a intégral; **to be an i. part
of** faire partie intégrante de.
integrate ['ɪntɪgreɪt] vt intégrer (**into** dans);
— vi s'intégrer (**into** dans); (racially) integrated (school etc) Am où se pratique la
déségrégation raciale. ◆**integration** n
intégration f; (racial) i. déségrégation f
raciale.
integrity [ɪnˈtegrɪtɪ] n intégrité f.
intellect ['ɪntɪlekt] n (faculty) intellect m,
intelligence f; (cleverness, person) intelli-

gence f. ◆**inte'llectual** a & n intellectuel,
-elle (mf).
intelligence [ɪnˈtelɪdʒəns] n intelligence f;
Mil renseignements mpl. ◆**intelligent** a
intelligent. ◆**intelligently** adv intelligemment. ◆**intelli'gentsia** n intelligentsia f.
intelligible [ɪnˈtelɪdʒəb(ə)l] a intelligible.
◆**intelligi'bility** n intelligibilité f.
intemperance [ɪnˈtempərəns] n intempérance f.
intend [ɪnˈtend] vt (gift, remark etc) destiner
(**for** à); **to i. to do** avoir l'intention de faire;
I i. you to stay mon intention est que vous
restiez. ◆**—ed** a (deliberate) intentionnel,
voulu; (planned) projeté; **i. to be** (meant)
destiné à être. ◆**intention** n intention f (**of
doing** de faire). ◆**intentional** a intentionnel; **it wasn't i.** ce n'était pas fait exprès.
◆**intentionally** adv intentionnellement,
exprès.
intense [ɪnˈtens] a intense; (interest) vif;
(person) passionné. ◆**intensely** adv intensément; Fig extrêmement. ◆**intensifi-
'cation** n intensification f. ◆**intensify** vt
intensifier; — vi s'intensifier. ◆**intensity** n
intensité f. ◆**intensive** a intensif; **in i.
care** Med en réanimation.
intent [ɪnˈtent] 1 a (look) attentif; **i. on** (task)
absorbé par; **i. on doing** résolu à faire. 2 n
intention f; **to all intents and purposes** en
fait, essentiellement.
inter [ɪnˈtɜːr] vt (-rr-) enterrer.
inter- ['ɪntə(r)] pref inter-.
interact [ɪntəˈrækt] vi (of ideas etc) être
interdépendants; (of people) agir conjointement; Ch interagir. ◆**interaction** n
interaction f.
intercede [ɪntəˈsiːd] vi intercéder (**with**
auprès de).
intercept [ɪntəˈsept] vt intercepter. ◆**interception** n interception f.
interchange ['ɪntətʃeɪndʒ] n Aut échangeur
m. ◆**inter'changeable** a interchangeable.
intercom ['ɪntəkɒm] n interphone m.
interconnect/ed [ɪntəkəˈnektɪd] a (facts
etc) liés. ◆**—ing** a **i. rooms** pièces fpl
communicantes.
intercontinental [ɪntəkɒntɪˈnent(ə)l] a
intercontinental.
intercourse ['ɪntəkɔːs] n (sexual, social)
rapports mpl.
interdependent [ɪntədɪˈpendənt] a interdépendant; (parts of machine) solidaire.
interest ['ɪnt(ə)rɪst, 'ɪntrəst] n intérêt m; Fin
intérêts mpl; **an i. in** (stake) Com des intérêts dans; **his** or **her i. is** (hobby etc) ce qui

l'intéresse c'est; **to take an i.** in s'intéresser
à; **to be of i.** to s.o. intéresser qn; – *vt* intéresser. ◆**—ed** *a (involved)* intéressé; *(look)*
d'intérêt; **to seem i.** sembler intéressé (**in**
par); **to be i.** in sth/s.o. s'intéresser à
qch/qn; **I'm i. in** doing ça m'intéresse de
faire; **are you i.?** ça vous intéresse? ◆**—ing**
a intéressant. ◆**—ingly** *adv* i. (enough),
she . . . curieusement, elle . . . .

interface ['intəfeis] *n Tech* interface *f*.

interfer/e [intə'fiər] *vi* se mêler des affaires
d'autrui; **to i.** in s'ingérer dans; **to i. with**
(upset) déranger; *(touch)* toucher (à).
◆**—ing** *a (person)* importun. ◆**interference** *n* ingérence *f*; *Rad* parasites *mpl*.

interim ['intərim] *n* intérim *m*; **in the i.**
pendant l'intérim; – *a (measure etc)*
provisoire; *(post)* intérimaire.

interior [in'tiəriər] *a* intérieur; – *n* intérieur
m; **Department of the I.** *Am* ministère *m* de
l'Intérieur.

interjection [intə'dʒekʃ(ə)n] *n* interjection *f*.

interlock [intə'lɒk] *vi Tech* s'emboîter.

interloper ['intələupər] *n* intrus, -use *mf*.

interlude ['intəluːd] *n* intervalle *m*; *Th*
intermède *m*; *Mus TV* interlude *m*.

intermarry [intə'mæri] *vi* se marier (entre
eux). ◆**intermarriage** *n* mariage *m (entre
personnes de races etc différentes).*

intermediary [intə'miːdiəri] *a* & *n*
intermédiaire *(mf).*

intermediate [intə'miːdiət] *a* intermédiaire;
(course) *Sch* moyen.

interminable [in'tɜːminəb(ə)l] *a* interminable.

intermingle [intə'miŋg(ə)l] *vi* se mélanger.

intermission [intə'miʃ(ə)n] *n Cin Th*
entracte *m*.

intermittent [intə'mitənt] *a* intermittent.
◆**—ly** *adv* par intermittence.

intern 1 [in'tɜːn] *vt Pol* interner. 2 ['intɜːn] *n*
Med Am interne *mf* (des hôpitaux).
◆**inter'nee** *n* interné, -ée *mf*.
◆**in'ternment** *n Pol* internement *m*.

internal [in'tɜːn(ə)l] *a* interne; *(policy,
flight)* intérieur; **i. combustion engine**
moteur *m* à explosion; **the I. Revenue
Service** *Am* le fisc. ◆**—ly** *adv* intérieurement.

international [intə'næʃ(ə)nəl] *a* international; *(fame, reputation)* mondial; – *n*
(match) rencontre *f* internationale;
(player) international *m*. ◆**—ly** *adv*
(renowned etc) mondialement.

interplanetary [intə'plænit(ə)ri] *a* interplanétaire.

interplay ['intəplei] *n* interaction *f*, jeu *m*.

interpolate [in'tɜːpəleit] *vt* interpoler.

interpret [in'tɜːprit] *vt* interpréter; – *vi Ling*
faire l'interprète. ◆**interpre'tation** *n*
interprétation *f*. ◆**interpreter** *n* interprète
mf.

interrelated [intəri'leitid] *a* en corrélation.
◆**interrelation** *n* corrélation *f*.

interrogate [in'terəgeit] *vt (question closely)*
interroger. ◆**interro'gation** *n* interrogation *f*; *Jur* interrogatoire *m*. ◆**interro-
gator** *n (questioner)* interrogateur, -trice
mf.

interrogative [intə'rɒgətiv] *a* & *n Gram*
interrogatif *(m).*

interrupt [intə'rʌpt] *vt* interrompre.
◆**interruption** *n* interruption *f*.

intersect [intə'sekt] *vt* couper; – *vi*
s'entrecouper, se couper. ◆**intersection** *n*
(crossroads) croisement *m*; *(of lines etc)*
intersection *f*.

intersperse [intə'spɜːs] *vt* parsemer (**with**
de).

intertwine [intə'twain] *vt* entrelacer.

interval ['intəv(ə)l] *n* intervalle *m*; *Th*
entracte *m*; **at intervals** *(time)* de temps à
autre; *(space)* par intervalles; **bright intervals** *Met* éclaircies *fpl.*

intervene [intə'viːn] *vi* intervenir; *(of event)*
survenir; **ten years intervened** dix années
s'écoulèrent; **if nothing intervenes** s'il
n'arrive rien entre-temps. ◆**intervention**
n intervention *f*.

interview ['intəvjuː] *n* entrevue *f*, entretien
m (**with** avec); *Journ TV* interview *f*; **to call
for (an) i.** convoquer; – *vt* avoir une
entrevue avec; *Journ TV* interviewer.
◆**—er** *n Journ TV* interviewer *m*; *Com Pol*
enquêteur, -euse *mf.*

intestine [in'testin] *n* intestin *m*.

intimate 1 ['intimət] *a* intime; *(friendship)*
profond; *(knowledge, analysis)* approfondi.
◆**intimacy** *n* intimité *f*. ◆**intimately** *adv*
intimement.

intimate 2 ['intimeit] *vt (hint)* suggérer (**that**
que). ◆**inti'mation** *n (announcement)*
annonce *f*; *(hint)* suggestion *f*; *(sign)* indication *f.*

intimidate [in'timideit] *vt* intimider.
◆**intimi'dation** *n* intimidation *f.*

into ['intuː, *unstressed* 'intə] *prep* **1** dans; **to
put i.** mettre dans; **to go i.** *(room, detail)*
entrer dans. **2** en; **to translate i.** traduire
en; **to change i.** transformer *or* changer en;
to go i. town aller en ville *(to break
etc)* en morceaux. **3 to be i.** yoga/*etc Fam*
être à fond dans le yoga/*etc.*

intolerable [in'tɒlərəb(ə)l] *a* intolérable

(that que (+ *sub*)). **◆intolerably** *adv* insupportablement. **◆intolerance** *n* intolérance *f*. **◆intolerant** *a* intolérant **(of** de). **◆intolerantly** *adv* avec intolérance.

intonation [ɪntə'neɪʃ(ə)n] *n* Ling intonation *f*.

intoxicate [ɪn'tɒksɪkeɪt] *vt* enivrer. **◆intoxicated** *a* ivre. **◆intoxi'cation** *n* ivresse *f*.

intra- ['ɪntrə] *pref* intra-.

intransigent [ɪn'trænsɪdʒənt] *a* intransigeant. **◆intransigence** *n* intransigeance *f*.

intransitive [ɪn'trænsɪtɪv] *a* & *n* Gram intransitif (*m*).

intravenous [ɪntrə'viːnəs] *a* Med intraveineux.

intrepid [ɪn'trepɪd] *a* intrépide.

intricate [ɪn'trɪkət] *a* complexe, compliqué. **◆intricacy** *n* complexité *f*. **◆intricately** *adv* de façon complexe.

intrigu/e 1 [ɪn'triːg] *vt* (*interest*) intriguer; **I'm intrigued to know . . .** je suis curieux de savoir . . . . **2** ['ɪntriːg] *n* (*plot*) intrigue *f*. **◆—ing** *a* (*news etc*) curieux.

intrinsic [ɪn'trɪnsɪk] *a* intrinsèque. **◆intrinsically** *adv* intrinsèquement.

introduce [ɪntrə'djuːs] *vt* (*insert, bring in*) introduire (**into** dans); (*programme, subject*) présenter; **to i. s.o. to s.o.** présenter qn à qn; **to i. s.o. to Dickens/geography/etc** faire découvrir Dickens/la géographie/etc à qn. **◆introduction** *n* introduction *f*; présentation *f*; (*book title*) initiation *f*; **her i. to** (*life abroad etc*) son premier contact avec. **◆introductory** *a* (*words*) d'introduction; (*speech*) de présentation; (*course*) d'initiation.

introspective [ɪntrə'spektɪv] *a* introspectif. **◆introspection** *n* introspection *f*.

introvert ['ɪntrəvɜːt] *n* introverti, -ie *mf*.

intrude [ɪn'truːd] *vi* (*of person*) s'imposer (**on s.o.** à qn), déranger (**on s.o.** qn); **to i. on** (*s.o.'s time etc*) abuser de. **◆intruder** *n* intrus, -use *mf*. **◆intrusion** *n* intrusion *f* (**into** dans); **forgive my i.** pardonnez-moi de vous avoir dérangé.

intuition [ɪntjʊ'ɪʃ(ə)n] *n* intuition *f*. **◆in'tuitive** *a* intuitif.

inundate ['ɪnʌndeɪt] *vt* inonder (**with** de); **inundated with work** submergé de travail. **◆inun'dation** *n* inondation *f*.

invad/e [ɪn'veɪd] *vt* envahir; (*privacy*) violer. **◆—er** *n* envahisseur, -euse *mf*.

invalid¹ ['ɪnvəlɪd] *a* & *n* malade (*mf*); (*through injury*) infirme (*mf*); **i. car** voiture *f* d'infirme.

invalid² [ɪn'vælɪd] *a* non valable. **◆invalidate** *vt* invalider, annuler.

invaluable [ɪn'væljʊəb(ə)l] *a* (*help etc*) inestimable.

invariab/le [ɪn'veərɪəb(ə)l] *a* invariable. **◆—ly** *adv* invariablement.

invasion [ɪn'veɪʒ(ə)n] *n* invasion *f*; **i. of s.o.'s privacy** intrusion *f* dans la vie privée de qn.

invective [ɪn'vektɪv] *n* invective *f*.

inveigh [ɪn'veɪ] *vi* **to i. against** invectiver contre.

inveigle [ɪn'veɪg(ə)l] *vt* **to i. s.o. into doing** amener qn à faire par la ruse.

invent [ɪn'vent] *vt* inventer. **◆invention** *n* invention *f*. **◆inventive** *a* inventif. **◆inventiveness** *n* esprit *m* d'invention. **◆inventor** *n* inventeur, -trice *mf*.

inventory ['ɪnvənt(ə)rɪ] *n* inventaire *m*.

inverse [ɪn'vɜːs] *a* & *n* Math inverse (*m*).

invert [ɪn'vɜːt] *vt* intervertir; **inverted commas** guillemets *mpl*. **◆inversion** *n* interversion *f*; Gram Anat inversion *f*.

invest [ɪn'vest] *vt* (*funds*) investir (**in** dans); (*money*) placer, investir; (*time, effort*) consacrer (**in** à); **to i. s.o. with** (*endow*) investir qn de; *– vi* **to i. in** (*project*) placer son argent dans; (*firm*) investir dans; (*house, radio etc*) Fig se payer. **◆investiture** *n* (*of bishop etc*) investiture *f*. **◆investment** *n* investissement *m*, placement *m*. **◆investor** *n* (*shareholder*) actionnaire *mf*; (*saver*) épargnant, -ante *mf*.

investigate [ɪn'vestɪgeɪt] *vt* (*examine*) examiner, étudier; (*crime*) enquêter sur. **◆investi'gation** *n* examen *m*, étude *f*; (*by police*) enquête *f* (**of** sur); (*inquiry*) enquête *f*, investigation *f*. **◆investigator** *n* (*detective*) enquêteur, -euse *mf*.

inveterate [ɪn'vetərət] *a* invétéré.

invidious [ɪn'vɪdɪəs] *a* qui suscite la jalousie; (*hurtful*) blessant; (*odious*) odieux.

invigilate [ɪn'vɪdʒɪleɪt] *vi* être de surveillance (**à un examen**). **◆invigilator** *n* surveillant, -ante *mf*.

invigorat/e [ɪn'vɪgəreɪt] *vt* revigorer. **◆—ing** *a* stimulant.

invincible [ɪn'vɪnsəb(ə)l] *a* invincible.

invisible [ɪn'vɪzəb(ə)l] *a* invisible; **i. ink** encre *f* sympathique.

invit/e [ɪn'vaɪt] *vt* inviter (**to do** à faire); (*ask for*) demander; (*lead to, give occasion for*) appeler; (*trouble*) chercher; **to i. out** inviter (à sortir); **to i. over** inviter (à venir); *–* ['ɪnvaɪt] *n Fam* invitation *f*. **◆—ing** *a* engageant, invitant; (*food*) appétissant. **◆invi'tation** *n* invitation *f*.

invoice ['ɪnvɔɪs] *n* facture *f*; *– vt* facturer.

invoke [ɪn'vəʊk] vt invoquer.

involuntar/y [ɪn'vɒləntərɪ] a involontaire. ◆**-ily** adv involontairement.

involv/e [ɪn'vɒlv] vt (include) mêler (qn) (in à), impliquer (qn) (in dans); (associate) associer (qn) (in à); (entail) entraîner; **to i. oneself, get involved** (commit oneself) s'engager (in à); **to i. s.o. in expense** entraîner qn à des dépenses; **the job involves going abroad** le poste nécessite des déplacements à l'étranger. ◆**-ed** a (complicated) compliqué; **the factors/etc i.** (at stake) les facteurs/etc en jeu; **the person i. la** la personne en question; **i. with s.o.** mêlé aux affaires de qn; **personally i.** concerné; **emotionally i. with** amoureux de; **to become i.** (of police) intervenir. ◆**-ement** n participation f (in à), implication f (in dans); (commitment) engagement m (in dans); (problem) difficulté f; **emotional i.** liaison f.

invulnerable [ɪn'vʌln(ə)rəb(ə)l] a invulnérable.

inward ['ɪnwəd] a & adv (movement, to move) vers l'intérieur; - a (inner) intérieur. ◆**i.-looking** a replié sur soi. ◆**inwardly** adv (inside) à l'intérieur; (to laugh, curse etc) intérieurement. ◆**inwards** adv vers l'intérieur.

iodine ['aɪədiːn, Am 'aɪədaɪn] n Med teinture f d'iode.

iota [aɪ'əʊtə] n (of truth etc) grain m; (in text) iota m.

IOU [aɪəʊ'juː] n abbr (I owe you) reconnaissance f de dette.

IQ [aɪ'kjuː] n abbr (intelligence quotient) QI m inv.

Iran [ɪ'rɑːn] n Iran m. ◆**Iranian** [ɪ'reɪnɪən] a & n iranien, -ienne (mf).

Iraq [ɪ'rɑːk] n Irak m. ◆**Iraqi** a & n irakien, -ienne (mf).

irascible [ɪ'ræsəb(ə)l] a irascible.

ire [aɪər] n Lit courroux m. ◆**i'rate** a furieux.

Ireland ['aɪələnd] n Irlande f. ◆**Irish** a irlandais; - n (language) irlandais m. ◆**Irishman** n (pl -men) Irlandais m. ◆**Irishwoman** n (pl -women) Irlandaise f.

iris ['aɪərɪs] n Anat Bot iris m.

irk [ɜːk] vt ennuyer. ◆**irksome** a ennuyeux.

iron ['aɪən] n fer m; (for clothes) fer m (à repasser); **old i., scrap i.** ferraille f; **i. and steel industry** sidérurgie f; **the I. Curtain** Pol le rideau de fer; - vt (clothes) repasser; **to i. out** (difficulties) Fig aplanir. ◆**-ing** n repassage m; **i. board** planche f à repasser. ◆**ironmonger** n quincailler m. ◆**iron-**

mongery n quincaillerie f. ◆**ironwork** n ferronnerie f.

irony ['aɪərənɪ] n ironie f. ◆**i'ronic(al)** a ironique.

irradiate [ɪ'reɪdɪeɪt] vt irradier.

irrational [ɪ'ræʃən(ə)l] a (act) irrationnel; (fear) irraisonné; (person) peu rationnel, illogique.

irreconcilable [ɪrekən'saɪləb(ə)l] a irréconciliable, inconciliable; (views, laws etc) inconciliable.

irrefutable [ɪrɪ'fjuːtəb(ə)l] a irréfutable.

irregular [ɪ'regjʊlər] a irrégulier. ◆**irregu-'larity** n irrégularité f.

irrelevant [ɪ'reləvənt] a (remark) non pertinent; (course) peu utile; **i. to** sans rapport avec; **that's i.** ça n'a rien à voir. ◆**irrelevance** n manque m de rapport.

irreparable [ɪ'rep(ə)rəb(ə)l] a (harm, loss) irréparable.

irreplaceable [ɪrɪ'pleɪsəb(ə)l] a irremplaçable.

irrepressible [ɪrɪ'presəb(ə)l] a (laughter etc) irrépressible.

irresistible [ɪrɪ'zɪstəb(ə)l] a (person, charm etc) irrésistible.

irresolute [ɪ'rezəluːt] a irrésolu, indécis.

irrespective of [ɪrɪ'spektɪvəv] prep sans tenir compte de.

irresponsible [ɪrɪ'spɒnsəb(ə)l] a (act) irréfléchi; (person) irresponsable.

irretrievable [ɪrɪ'triːvəb(ə)l] a irréparable.

irreverent [ɪ'revərənt] a irrévérencieux.

irreversible [ɪrɪ'vɜːsəb(ə)l] a (process) irréversible; (decision) irrévocable.

irrevocable [ɪ'revəkəb(ə)l] a irrévocable.

irrigate ['ɪrɪgeɪt] vt irriguer. ◆**irri'gation** n irrigation f.

irritat/e ['ɪrɪteɪt] vt irriter. ◆**-ing** a irritant. ◆**irritable** a (easily annoyed) irritable. ◆**irritant** n irritant m. ◆**irri'tation** n (anger) & Med irritation f.

is [ɪz] see be.

Islam ['ɪzlɑːm] n islam m. ◆**Islamic** [ɪz'læmɪk] a islamique.

island ['aɪlənd] n île f; **traffic i.** refuge m; - a insulaire. ◆**islander** n insulaire mf. ◆**isle** [aɪl] n île f; **the British Isles** les îles Britanniques.

isolate ['aɪsəleɪt] vt isoler (from de). ◆**isolated** a (remote, unique) isolé. ◆**iso'lation** n isolement m; **in i.** isolément.

Israel ['ɪzreɪl] n Israël m. ◆**Is'raeli** a & n israélien, -ienne (mf).

issue ['ɪʃuː] vt (book etc) publier; (an order) donner; (tickets) distribuer; (passport) délivrer; (stamps, banknotes) émettre;

isthmus ['ɪsməs] *n Geog* isthme *m.*

it [ɪt] *pron* **1** (*subject*) il, elle, l'; **(to) it** (*indirect object*) lui; **it bites** (*dog*) il mord; **I've done it** je l'ai fait. **2** (*impersonal*) il; **it's snowing** il neige; **it's hot** il fait chaud. **3** (*non specific*) ce, cela, ça; **it's good** c'est bon; **it was pleasant** c'était agréable; **who is it?** qui est-ce?; **that's it!** (*I agree*) c'est ça!; (*it's done*) ça y est!; **to consider it wise to do** juger prudent de faire; **it was Paul who . . .** c'est Paul qui . . . ; **she's got it in her to succeed** elle est capable de réussir; **to have it in for s.o.** en vouloir à qn. **4 of it, from it, about it** en; **in it, to it, at it** y; **on it** dessus; **under it** dessous.

italic [ɪ'tælɪk] *a Typ* italique; – *npl* italique *m.*

Italy ['ɪtəlɪ] *n* Italie *f.* ◆**I'talian** *a & n* italien, -ienne (*mf*); – *n* (*language*) italien *m.*

itch [ɪtʃ] *n* démangeaison(s) *f(pl)*; **to have an i. to do** avoir une envie folle de faire; – *vi* démanger; **his arm itches** son bras le *or* lui démange; **I'm itching to do** Fig ça me démange de faire. ◆—**ing** *n* démangeaison(s) *f(pl)*. ◆**itchy** *a* **an i. hand** une main qui me démange.

item ['aɪtəm] *n Com Journ* article *m*; (*matter*) question *f*; (*on entertainment programme*) numéro *m*; **a news i.** une information. ◆**itemize** *vt* détailler.

itinerant [aɪ'tɪnərənt] *a* (*musician, actor*) ambulant; (*judge, preacher*) itinérant.

itinerary [aɪ'tɪnərərɪ] *n* itinéraire *m.*

its [ɪts] *poss a* son, sa, *pl* ses. ◆**it'self** *pron* lui-même, elle-même; (*reflexive*) se, s'; **goodness i.** la bonté même; **by i.** tout seul.

IUD [aɪjuː'diː] *n abbr* (*intrauterine device*) stérilet *m.*

ivory ['aɪvərɪ] *n* ivoire *m.*

ivy ['aɪvɪ] *n* lierre *m.*

J

J, j [dʒeɪ] *n* J, j *m.*

jab [dʒæb] *vt* (**-bb-**) (*thrust*) enfoncer (**into** dans); (*prick*) piquer (*qn*) (**with sth** du bout de qch); – *n* coup *m* (sec); (*injection*) *Med Fam* piqûre *f.*

jabber ['dʒæbər] *vi* bavarder, jaser; – *vt* bredouiller. ◆—**ing** *n* bavardage *m.*

jack [dʒæk] **1** *n Aut* cric *m*; – *vt* **to j. up** soulever (*avec un cric*); (*price*) *Fig* augmenter. **2** *n Cards* valet *m.* **3** *vt* **to j. (in)** (*job etc*) *Fam* plaquer. **4** *n* **j. of all trades** homme *m* à tout faire. ◆**j.-in-the-box** *n* diable *m* (à ressort).

jackal ['dʒæk(ə)l] *n* (*animal*) chacal *m.*

jackass ['dʒækæs] *n* (*fool*) idiot, -ote *mf.*

jackdaw ['dʒækdɔː] *n* (*bird*) choucas *m.*

jacket ['dʒækɪt] *n* (*short coat*) veste *f*; (*of man's suit*) veston *m*; (*of woman*) veste *f*, jaquette *f*; (*bulletproof*) gilet *m*; (*dust*) *j.* (*of book*) jaquette *f*; **in their jackets** (*potatoes*) en robe des champs.

jack-knife ['dʒæknaɪf] **1** *n* couteau *m* de poche. **2** *vi* (*of lorry, truck*) se mettre en travers de la route.

jackpot ['dʒækpɒt] *n* gros lot *m.*

jacks [dʒæks] *npl* (*jeu* m d')osselets *mpl.*

jacuzzi [dʒə'kuːzɪ] *n* (*bath, pool*) jacousi *m.*

jade [dʒeɪd] *n* **1** (*stone*) jade *m.* **2** (*horse*) rosse *f*, canasson *m.*

jaded ['dʒeɪdɪd] *a* blasé.

jagged ['dʒægɪd] *a* déchiqueté.

jaguar ['dʒægjuər] *n* (*animal*) jaguar *m.*

jail [dʒeɪl] *n* prison *f*; – *vt* emprisonner (**for** theft/etc pour vol/etc); **to j. for life** condamner à perpétuité. ◆**jailbreak** *n* évasion *f* (de prison). ◆**jailer** *n* geôlier, -ière *mf.*

jalopy [dʒə'lɒpɪ] *n* (*car*) *Fam* vieux tacot *m.*

jam[1] [dʒæm] *n Culin* confiture *f.* ◆**jamjar** *n* pot *m* à confiture.

jam[2] [dʒæm] **1** *n* (*traffic*) **j.** embouteillage *m*; **in a j.** (*trouble*) *Fig Fam* dans le pétrin. **2** *vt* (**-mm-**) (*squeeze, make stuck*) coincer, bloquer; (*gun*) enrayer; (*street, corridor etc*) encombrer; (*building*) envahir; *Rad* brouiller; **to j. sth into** (*pack, cram*) (en)tasser qch dans; (*thrust, put*) enfoncer *or* fourrer qch dans; **to j. on** (*brakes*) bloquer; – *vi* (*get stuck*) se coincer, se bloquer; (*of gun*) s'enrayer; **to j. into** (*of crowd*) s'entasser dans. ◆**jammed** a (machine etc) coincé, bloqué; (street etc) encombré. ◆**jam-packed** a (hall etc) bourré de monde.

Jamaica [dʒə'meɪkə] n Jamaïque f.

jangl/e ['dʒæŋ(ə)l] vi cliqueter; – n cliquetis m. ◆**-ing** a (noise) discordant.

janitor ['dʒænɪtər] n concierge m.

January ['dʒænjʊəri] n janvier m.

Japan [dʒə'pæn] n Japon m. ◆**Japa'nese** a & n japonais, -aise (mf); – n (language) japonais m.

jar [dʒɑːr] **1** n (vessel) pot m; (large, glass) bocal m. **2** n (jolt) choc m; (-rr-) (shake) ébranler. **3** vi (-rr-) (of noise) grincer; (of note) Mus détonner; (of colours, words) jurer (with avec); **to j. on** (s.o.'s nerves) porter sur; (s.o.'s ears) écorcher. ◆**jarring** a (note) discordant.

jargon ['dʒɑːgən] n jargon m.

jasmine ['dʒæzmɪn] n Bot jasmin m.

jaundice ['dʒɔːndɪs] n Med jaunisse f. ◆**jaundiced** a (bitter) Fig aigri; **to take a j. view of** voir d'un mauvais œil.

jaunt [dʒɔːnt] n (journey) balade f.

jaunt/y ['dʒɔːntɪ] a (-ier, -iest) (carefree) insouciant; (cheerful, lively) allègre; (hat etc) coquet, chic. ◆**-ily** adv avec insouciance; allégrement.

javelin ['dʒævlɪn] n javelot m.

jaw [dʒɔː] **1** n Anat mâchoire f. **2** vi (talk) Pej Fam papoter; – n **to have a j.** Pej Fam tailler une bavette.

jay [dʒeɪ] n (bird) geai m.

jaywalker ['dʒeɪwɔːkər] n piéton m imprudent.

jazz [dʒæz] n jazz m; – vt **to j. up** Fam (music) jazzifier; (enliven) animer; (clothes, room) égayer.

jealous ['dʒeləs] a jaloux (of de). ◆**jealousy** n jalousie f.

jeans [dʒiːnz] npl (blue-)jean m.

jeep [dʒiːp] n jeep f.

jeer [dʒɪər] vti **to j. (at)** (mock) railler; (boo) huer; – n raillerie f; pl (boos) huées fpl. ◆**-ing** a railleur; – n railleries fpl; (of crowd) huées fpl.

jell [dʒel] vi (of ideas etc) Fam prendre tournure.

jello® ['dʒeləʊ] n inv Culin Am gelée f. ◆**jellied** a Culin en gelée. ◆**jelly** n Culin gelée f. ◆**jellyfish** n méduse f.

jeopardy ['dʒepədɪ] n danger m, péril m. ◆**jeopardize** vt mettre en danger or en péril.

jerk [dʒɜːk] **1** vt donner une secousse à (pour tirer, pousser etc); – n secousse f, saccade f. **2** n (person) Pej Fam pauvre type m;

(stupid) j. crétin, -ine mf. ◆**jerk/y** a (-ier, -iest) **1** saccadé. **2** (stupid) Am Fam stupide, bête. ◆**-ily** adv par saccades.

jersey ['dʒɜːzɪ] n (cloth) jersey m; (garment) & Fb maillot m.

Jersey ['dʒɜːzɪ] n Jersey f.

jest [dʒest] n plaisanterie f; **in j.** pour rire; – vi plaisanter. ◆**-er** n Hist bouffon m.

Jesus ['dʒiːzəs] n Jésus m; **J. Christ** Jésus-Christ m.

jet [dʒet] **1** n (of liquid, steam etc) jet m. **2** n Av avion m à réaction; – a (engine) à réaction; **j. lag** fatigue f (due au décalage horaire). ◆**jet-lagged** n Fam qui souffre du décalage horaire.

jet-black [dʒet'blæk] a noir comme (du) jais, (noir) de jais.

jettison ['dʒetɪs(ə)n] vt Nau jeter à la mer; (fuel) Av larguer; Fig abandonner.

jetty ['dʒetɪ] n jetée f; (landing-place) embarcadère m.

Jew [dʒuː] n (man) Juif m; (woman) Juive f. ◆**Jewess** n Juive f. ◆**Jewish** a juif.

jewel ['dʒuːəl] n bijou m; (in watch) rubis m. ◆**jewelled** a orné de bijoux. ◆**jeweller** n bijoutier, -ière mf. ◆**jewellery** n, Am ◆**jewelry** n bijoux mpl.

jib [dʒɪb] vi (-bb-) regimber (at devant); **to j. at doing** se refuser à faire.

jibe [dʒaɪb] vi & n = gibe.

jiffy ['dʒɪfɪ] n Fam instant m.

jig [dʒɪg] n (dance, music) gigue f.

jigsaw ['dʒɪgsɔː] n (j. puzzle) puzzle m.

jilt [dʒɪlt] vt (lover) laisser tomber.

jingle ['dʒɪŋg(ə)l] vi (of keys, bell etc) tinter; – vt faire tinter; – n tintement m.

jinx [dʒɪŋks] n (person, object) porte-malheur m inv; (spell, curse) (mauvais) sort m, poisse f.

jitters ['dʒɪtəz] npl **to have the j.** Fam avoir la frousse. ◆**jittery** a **to be j.** Fam avoir la frousse.

job [dʒɒb] n (task) travail m; (post) poste m, situation f; (crime) Fam coup m; **to have a j. doing** or **to do** (much trouble) avoir du mal à faire; **to have the j. of doing** (unpleasant task) être obligé de faire; (for a living etc) être chargé de faire; **it's a good j. (that)** Fam heureusement que; **that's just the j.** Fam c'est juste ce qu'il faut; **out of a j.** Fam au chômage. ◆**jobcentre** n agence f nationale pour l'emploi. ◆**jobless** a au chômage.

jockey ['dʒɒkɪ] n jockey m; – vi **to j. for** (position, job) manœuvrer pour obtenir.

jocular ['dʒɒkjʊlər] a jovial, amusant.

jog [dʒɒg] **1** n (jolt) secousse f; (nudge) coup

m de coude; – *vt* (**-gg-**) (*shake*) secouer; (*elbow*) pousser; (*memory*) *Fig* rafraîchir. **2** *vi* (**-gg-**) **to j. along** (*of vehicle*) cahoter; (*of work*) aller tant bien que mal; (*of person*) faire son petit bonhomme de chemin. **3** *vi* (**-gg-**) *Sp* faire du jogging. ◆**jogging** *n Sp* jogging *m*.

john [dʒɒn] *n* (*toilet*) *Am Sl* cabinets *mpl*.

join [dʒɔɪn] **1** *vt* (*unite*) joindre, réunir; (*link*) relier; (*wires, pipes*) raccorder; **to j. s.o.** (*catch up with, meet*) rejoindre qn; (*associate oneself with, go with*) se joindre à (**in** doing pour faire); **to j. the sea** (*of river*) rejoindre la mer; **to j. hands** se donner la main; **to j. together** or **up** (*objects*) joindre; – *vi* (*of roads, rivers etc*) se rejoindre; **to j. (together** or **up)** (*of objects*) se joindre (**with** à); **to j. in** participer; **to j. in a game** prendre part à un jeu; – *n* raccord *m*, joint *m*. **2** *vt* (*become a member of*) s'inscrire à (*club, party*); (*army*) s'engager dans; (*queue, line*) se mettre à; – *vi* (*become a member*) devenir membre; **to j. up** *Mil* s'engager.

joiner [ˈdʒɔɪnər] *n* menuisier *m*.

joint [dʒɔɪnt] **1** *n Anat* articulation *f*; *Culin* rôti *m*; *Tech* joint *m*; **out of j.** *Med* démis. **2** *n* (*nightclub etc*) *Sl* boîte *f*. **3** *a* (*account, statement etc*) commun; (*effort*) conjugué; **j. author** coauteur *m*. ◆**-ly** *adv* conjointement.

jok/e [dʒəʊk] *n* plaisanterie *f*; (*trick*) tour *m*; **it's no j.** (*it's unpleasant*) ce n'est pas drôle (**doing** de faire); – *vi* plaisanter (**about** sur). ◆**-er** *n* plaisantin *m*; (*fellow*) *Fam* type *m*; *Cards* joker *m*. ◆**-ingly** *adv* en plaisantant.

jolly [ˈdʒɒlɪ] **1** *a* (**-ier, -iest**) (*happy*) gai; (*drunk*) *Fam* éméché. **2** *adv* (*very*) *Fam* rudement. ◆**jolli'fication** *n* (*merry-making*) réjouissances *fpl*. ◆**jollity** *n* jovialité *f*; (*merry-making*) réjouissances *fpl*.

jolt [dʒəʊlt] *vt* **to j. s.o.** (*of vehicle*) cahoter qn; (*shake*) *Fig* secouer qn; – *vi* **to j. (along)** (*of vehicle*) cahoter; – *n* cahot *m*, secousse *f*; (*shock*) *Fig* secousse *f*.

Jordan [ˈdʒɔːd(ə)n] *n* Jordanie *f*.

jostle [ˈdʒɒs(ə)l] *vt* (*push*) bousculer; – *vi* (*push each other*) se bousculer (**for** pour obtenir); **don't j.!** ne bousculez pas!

jot [dʒɒt] *vt* (**-tt-**) **to j. down** noter. ◆**jotter** *n* (*notepad*) bloc-notes *m*.

journal [ˈdʒɜːn(ə)l] *n* (*periodical*) revue *f*, journal *m*. ◆**journa'lese** *n* jargon *m* journalistique. ◆**journalism** *n* journalisme *m*. ◆**journalist** *n* journaliste *mf*.

journey [ˈdʒɜːnɪ] *n* (*trip*) voyage *m*;

(*distance*) trajet *m*; **to go on a j.** partir en voyage; – *vi* voyager.

jovial [ˈdʒəʊvɪəl] *a* jovial.

joy [dʒɔɪ] *n* joie *f*; *pl* (*of countryside, motherhood etc*) plaisirs *mpl* (**of** de). ◆**joyful** *a*, ◆**joyous** *a* joyeux. ◆**joyride** *n* virée *f* (*dans une voiture volée*).

joystick [ˈdʒɔɪstɪk] *n* (*of aircraft, computer*) manche *m* à balai.

JP [dʒeɪˈpiː] *abbr* = **Justice of the Peace.**

jubilant [ˈdʒuːbɪlənt] *a* **to be j.** jubiler. ◆**jubi'lation** *n* jubilation *f*.

jubilee [ˈdʒuːbɪliː] *n* (*golden*) *j*. jubilé *m*.

Judaism [ˈdʒuːdeɪɪz(ə)m] *n* judaïsme *m*.

judder [ˈdʒʌdər] *vi* (*shake*) vibrer; – *n* vibration *f*.

judg/e [dʒʌdʒ] *n* juge *m*; – *vti* juger; **judging by** à en juger par. ◆**-(e)ment** *n* jugement *m*.

judicial [dʒuːˈdɪʃ(ə)l] *a* judiciaire. ◆**judiciary** *n* magistrature *f*. ◆**judicious** *a* judicieux.

judo [ˈdʒuːdəʊ] *n* judo *m*.

jug [dʒʌg] *n* cruche *f*; (*for milk*) pot *m*.

juggernaut [ˈdʒʌgənɔːt] *n* (*truck*) poids *m* lourd, mastodonte *m*.

juggl/e [ˈdʒʌg(ə)l] *vi* jongler; – *vt* jongler avec. ◆**-er** *n* jongleur, -euse *mf*.

Jugoslavia [juːgəʊˈslɑːvɪə] *n* Yougoslavie *f*. ◆**Jugoslav** *a & n* yougoslave (*mf*).

juice [dʒuːs] *n* jus *m*; (*in stomach*) suc *m*. ◆**juicy** *a* (**-ier, -iest**) (*fruit*) juteux; (*meat*) succulent; (*story*) *Fig* savoureux.

jukebox [ˈdʒuːkbɒks] *n* juke-box *m*.

July [dʒuːˈlaɪ] *n* juillet *m*.

jumble [ˈdʒʌmb(ə)l] *vt* **to j. (up)** (*objects, facts etc*) brouiller, mélanger; – *n* fouillis *m*; **j. sale** (*used clothes etc*) vente *f* de charité.

jumbo [ˈdʒʌmbəʊ] *a* géant; – *a & n* (*pl -os*) **j. (jet)** jumbo-jet *m*, gros-porteur *m*.

jump [dʒʌmp] *n* (*leap*) saut *m*, bond *m*; (*start*) sursaut *m*; (*increase*) hausse *f*; – *vi* sauter (**at** sur); (*start*) sursauter; (*of price, heart*) faire un bond; **to j. about** sautiller; **to j. across sth** traverser qch d'un bond; **to j. to conclusions** tirer des conclusions hâtives; **j. in** or **on!** *Aut* montez!; **to j. on** (*bus*) sauter dans; **to j. off** or **out** sauter; **to j. off sth, j. out of sth** sauter de qch; **to j. out of the window** sauter par la fenêtre; **to j. up** se lever d'un bond; – *vt* sauter; **to j. the lights** *Aut* griller un feu rouge; **to j. the rails** (*of train*) dérailler; **to j. the queue** resquiller.

jumper [ˈdʒʌmpər] *n* pull(-over) *m*; (*dress*) *Am* robe *f* chasuble.

jumpy [ˈdʒʌmpɪ] *a* (**-ier, -iest**) nerveux.

junction ['dʒʌŋkʃ(ə)n] n (joining) jonction f; (crossroads) carrefour m.

juncture ['dʒʌŋktʃər] n **at this j.** (critical point in time) en ce moment même.

June [dʒuːn] n juin m.

jungle ['dʒʌŋg(ə)l] n jungle f.

junior ['dʒuːnɪər] a (younger) plus jeune; (in rank, status etc) subalterne; (teacher, doctor) jeune; **to be j. to s.o.**, **be s.o.'s j.** être plus jeune que qn; (in rank, status) être au-dessous de qn; **Smith j.** Smith fils or junior; **j. school** école f primaire; **j. high school** Am = collège m d'enseignement secondaire; — n cadet, -ette mf; Sch petit, -ite mf, petit(e) élève mf; Sp junior mf, cadet, -ette mf.

junk [dʒʌŋk] **1** n (objects) bric-à-brac m inv; (metal) ferraille f; (goods) Pej camelote f; (film, book etc) Pej idiotie f; (nonsense) idioties fpl; **j. shop** (boutique f de) brocanteur m. **2** vt (get rid of) Am Fam balancer.

junkie ['dʒʌŋkɪ] n Fam drogué, -ée mf.

junta ['dʒʌntə] n Pol junte f.

jurisdiction [dʒuərɪs'dɪkʃ(ə)n] n juridiction f.

jury ['dʒuərɪ] n (in competition) & Jur jury m. ◆**juror** n Jur juré m.

just [dʒʌst] **1** adv (exactly, slightly) juste; (only) juste, seulement; (simply) (tout) simplement; **it's j. as I thought** c'est bien ce que je pensais; **j. at that time** à cet instant même; **she has/had j. left** elle vient/venait de partir; **I've j. come from** j'arrive de; **I'm j. coming!** j'arrive!; **he'll (only) j. catch the bus** il aura son bus de justesse; **he j. missed it** il l'a manqué de peu; **j. as big/light/etc** tout aussi grand/léger/etc (as que); **j. listen!** écoute donc!; **j. a moment!** un instant!; **j. over ten** un peu plus de dix; **j. one** un(e) seul(e) (of de); **j. about** (approximately) à peu près; (almost) presque; **j. about to do** sur le point de faire. **2** a (fair) juste (to envers). ◆**-ly** adv avec justice. ◆**-ness** n (of cause etc) justice f.

justice ['dʒʌstɪs] n justice f; (judge) juge m; **to do j. to** (meal) faire honneur à; **it doesn't do you j.** (hat, photo) cela ne vous avantage pas; (attitude) cela ne vous fait pas honneur; **J. of the Peace** juge m de paix.

justify ['dʒʌstɪfaɪ] vt justifier; **to be justified in doing** (have right) être en droit de faire; (have reason) avoir toutes les bonnes raisons de faire. ◆**justi'fiable** a justifiable. ◆**justi'fiably** adv légitimement. ◆**justifi'cation** n justification f.

jut [dʒʌt] vi (-tt-) **to j. out** faire saillie; **to j. out over sth** (overhang) surplomber qch.

jute [dʒuːt] n (fibre) jute m.

juvenile ['dʒuːvənaɪl] n adolescent, -ente mf; — a (court, book etc) pour enfants; (delinquent) jeune; (behaviour) Pej puéril.

juxtapose [dʒʌkstə'pəuz] vt juxtaposer. ◆**juxtapo'sition** n juxtaposition f.

K

K, k [keɪ] n K, k m.

kaleidoscope [kə'laɪdəskəup] n kaléidoscope m.

kangaroo [kæŋgə'ruː] n kangourou m.

kaput [kə'put] a (broken, ruined) Sl fichu.

karate [kə'rɑːtɪ] n Sp karaté m.

keel [kiːl] n Nau quille f; — vi **to k. over** (of boat) chavirer.

keen [kiːn] a (edge, appetite) aiguisé; (interest, feeling) vif; (mind) pénétrant; (wind) coupant, piquant; (enthusiastic) enthousiaste; **a k. sportsman** un passionné de sport; **to be k. to do** or **on doing** tenir (beaucoup) à faire; **to be k. on** (music, sport etc) être passionné de; **he is k. on** her/the idea elle/l'idée lui plaît beaucoup. ◆**-ly** adv (to work etc) avec enthousiasme; (to feel, interest) vivement. ◆**-ness** n

enthousiasme m; (of mind) pénétration f; (of interest) intensité f; **k. to do** empressement m à faire.

keep¹ [kiːp] vt (pt & pp kept) garder; (shop, car) avoir; (diary, promise) tenir; (family) entretenir; (rule) observer, respecter; (feast day) célébrer; (birthday) fêter; (detain, delay) retenir; (put) mettre; **to k. (on) doing** (continue) continuer à faire; **to k. clean** tenir or garder propre; **to k. from** (conceal) cacher à; **to k. s.o. from doing** (prevent) empêcher qn de faire; **to k. s.o. waiting/working** faire attendre/travailler qn; **to k. sth going** (engine, machine) laisser qch en marche; **to k. s.o. in whisky/etc** fournir qn en whisky/etc; **to k. an appointment** se rendre à un rendez-vous; **to k. back** (withhold, delay) retenir; (conceal) cacher (**from**

à); **to k. down** (*control*) maîtriser; (*restrict*) limiter; (*costs, price*) maintenir bas; **to k. in** empêcher de sortir; (*pupil*) *Sch* consigner; **to k. off** *or* **away** (*person*) éloigner (**from** de); **'k. off the grass'** 'ne pas marcher sur les pelouses'; **k. your hands off!** n'y touche(z) pas!; **to k. on** (*hat, employee*) garder; **to k. out** empêcher d'entrer; **to k. up** (*continue, maintain*) continuer; (*road, building*) entretenir; – *vi* (*continue*) continuer; (*remain*) rester; (*of food*) se garder, se conserver; (*wait*) attendre; **how is he keeping?** comment va-t-il?; **to k. still** rester *or* se tenir tranquille; **to k. from doing** (*refrain*) s'abstenir de faire; **to k. going** (*continue*) continuer; **to k. at it** (*keep doing it*) continuer à le faire; **to k. away** *or* **off** *or* **back** ne pas s'approcher (**from** de); **if the rain keeps off** s'il ne pleut pas; **to k. on at s.o.** harceler qn; **to k. out** rester en dehors (**of** de); **to k. to** (*subject, path*) ne pas s'écarter de; (*room*) garder; **to k. to the left** tenir la gauche; **to k. to oneself** se tenir à l'écart; **to k. up** (*continue*) continuer; (*follow*) suivre; **to k. up with s.o** (*follow*) suivre qn; (*in quality of work etc*) se maintenir à la hauteur de qn; – *n* (*food*) subsistance *f*; **to have one's k.** être logé et nourri; **for keeps** *Fam* pour toujours. ◆**—ing** *n* (*care*) garde *f*; **in k. with** en rapport avec. ◆**—er** *n* gardien, -ienne *mf*.

keep² [kiːp] *n* (*tower*) *Hist* donjon *m*.

keepsake ['kiːpseɪk] *n* (*object*) souvenir *m*.

keg [keg] *n* tonnelet *m*.

kennel ['ken(ə)l] *n* niche *f*; (*for boarding*) chenil *m*.

Kenya ['kiːnjə, 'kenjə] *n* Kenya *m*.

kept [kept] *see* keep¹; – **a well** *or* **nicely k.** (*house etc*) bien tenu.

kerb [kɜːb] *n* bord *m* du trottoir.

kernel ['kɜːn(ə)l] *n* (*of nut*) amande *f*.

kerosene ['kerəsiːn] *n* (*aviation fuel*) kérosène *m*; (*paraffin*) *Am* pétrole *m* (lampant).

ketchup ['ketʃəp] *n* (*sauce*) ketchup *m*.

kettle ['ket(ə)l] *n* bouilloire *f*; **the k. is boiling** l'eau bout.

key [kiː] *n* clef *f*, clé *f*; (*of piano, typewriter, computer*) touche *f*; – *a* (*industry, post etc*) clef (*f inv*), clé (*f inv*); **k. man** pivot *m*; **k. ring** porte-clefs *m inv*. ◆**keyboard** *n* clavier *m*. ◆**keyhole** *n* trou *m* de (la) serrure. ◆**keynote** *n* (*of speech*) note *f* dominante. ◆**keystone** *n* (*of policy etc*) & *Archit* clef *f* de voûte.

keyed [kiːd] *a* **to be k. up** avoir les nerfs tendus.

khaki ['kɑːkɪ] *a* & *n* kaki *a inv* & *m*.

kibbutz [kɪ'bʊts] *n* kibboutz *m*.

kick [kɪk] *n* coup *m* de pied; (*of horse*) ruade *f*; **to get a k. out of doing** (*thrill*) *Fam* prendre un malin plaisir à faire; **for kicks** *Pej Fam* pour le plaisir; – *vt* donner un coup de pied à; (*of horse*) lancer une ruade à; **to k. back** (*ball*) renvoyer (*du pied*); **to k. down** *or* **in** démolir à coups de pied; **to k. out** (*eject*) *Fam* flanquer dehors; **to k. up** (*fuss, row*) *Fam* faire; – *vi* donner des coups de pied; (*of horse*) ruer; **to k. off** *Fb* donner le coup d'envoi; (*start*) *Fig* démarrer. ◆**k.-off** *n Fb* coup d'envoi.

kid [kɪd] **1** *n* (*goat*) chevreau *m*. **2** *n* (*child*) *Fam* gosse *mf*; **his** *or* **her k. brother** *Am Fam* son petit frère. **3** *vti* (*-dd-*) (*joke, tease*) *Fam* blaguer; **to k. oneself** se faire des illusions.

kidnap ['kɪdnæp] *vt* (*-pp-*) kidnapper. ◆**kidnapping** *n* enlèvement *m*. ◆**kidnapper** *n* kidnappeur, -euse *mf*.

kidney ['kɪdnɪ] *n Anat* rein *m*; *Culin* rognon *m*; **on a k. machine** sous rein artificiel; **k. bean** haricot *m* rouge.

kill [kɪl] *vt* tuer; (*bill*) *Pol* repousser, faire échouer; (*chances*) détruire; (*rumour*) étouffer; (*story*) *Fam* supprimer; (*engine*) *Fam* arrêter; **my feet are killing me** *Fam* je ne sens plus mes pieds, j'ai les pieds en compote; **to k. off** (*person etc*) & *Fig* détruire; – *vi* tuer; – *n* mise *f* à mort; (*prey*) animaux *mpl* tués. ◆**—ing 1** *n* (*of person*) meurtre *m*; (*of group*) massacre *m*; (*of animal*) mise *f* à mort; **to make a k.** *Fin* réussir un beau coup. **2** *a* (*tiring*) *Fam* tuant. ◆**—er** *n* tueur, -euse *mf*. ◆**killjoy** *n* rabat-joie *m inv*.

kiln [kɪln] *n* (*for pottery*) four *m*.

kilo [kiːləʊ] *n* (*pl -os*) kilo *m*. ◆**kilogramme** ['kɪləʊɡræm] *n* kilogramme *m*. ◆**kilometre** [kɪ'lɒmɪtər] *n* kilomètre *m*. ◆**kilowatt** ['kɪləʊwɒt] *n* kilowatt *m*.

kilt [kɪlt] *n* kilt *m*.

kimono [kɪ'məʊnəʊ] *n* (*pl -os*) kimono *m*.

kin [kɪn] *n* (*relatives*) parents *mpl*; **one's next of k.** son plus proche parent.

kind [kaɪnd] **1** *n* (*sort, type*) genre *m*; **a k. of** une sorte *or* une espèce *m*; **to pay in k.** payer en nature; **what k. of drink/etc is it?** qu'est-ce que c'est comme boisson/*etc*?; **that's the k. of man he is** il est comme ça; **nothing of the k.!** absolument pas!; **k. of worried/sad/etc** (*somewhat*) *Fam* inquiet/triste/*etc*; **k. of fascinated** (*as if*) *Fam* comme fasciné; **in a k. of way** d'une certaine façon; **it's the only one of its k.,** it's one of a k. c'est unique en son genre; **we are**

two of a k. nous nous ressemblons. 2 *a* (-er, -est) (*helpful, pleasant*) gentil (**to** avec, pour); bon (**to** pour); **that's k. of you** c'est gentil *or* aimable à vous. ◆**k.-'hearted** *a* qui a bon cœur. ◆**kindly** *adv* avec bonté; **k. wait**/*etc* ayez la bonté d'attendre/*etc*; **not to take k. to sth** ne pas apprécier qch; – *a* (*person*) bienveillant. ◆**kindness** *n* bonté *f*, gentillesse *f*.

kindergarten ['kındəgɑːt(ə)n] *n* jardin *m* d'enfants.

kindle ['kınd(ə)l] *vt* allumer; – *vi* s'allumer.

kindred ['kındrıd] *n* (*relationship*) parenté *f*; (*relatives*) parents *mpl*; **k. spirit** semblable *mf*, âme *f* sœur.

king [kıŋ] *n* roi *m*. ◆**k.-size(d)** *a* géant; (*cigarette*) long. ◆**kingdom** *n* royaume *m*; **animal/plant k.** règne *m* animal/végétal. ◆**kingly** *a* royal.

kingfisher ['kıŋfıʃər] *n* (*bird*) martin-pêcheur *m*.

kink [kıŋk] *n* (*in rope*) entortillement *m*.

kinky ['kıŋkı] *a* (-ier, -iest) (*person*) *Psy Pej* vicieux; (*clothes etc*) bizarre.

kinship ['kınʃıp] *n* parenté *f*.

kiosk ['kiːɒsk] *n* kiosque *m*; (**telephone**) **k.** cabine *f* (téléphonique).

kip [kıp] *vi* (-pp-) (*sleep*) *Sl* roupiller.

kipper ['kıpər] *n* (*herring*) kipper *m*.

kiss [kıs] *n* baiser *m*, bise *f*; **the k. of life** *Med* le bouche-à-bouche; – *vt* (*person*) embrasser; **to k. s.o.'s hand** baiser la main de qn; – *vi* s'embrasser.

kit [kıt] *n* équipement *m*, matériel *m*; (*set of articles*) trousse *f*; **gym k.** (*belongings*) affaires *fpl* de gym; **tool k.** trousse *f* à outils; (**do-it-yourself**) **k.** kit *m*; **in k. form** en kit; **k. bag** sac *m* (de soldat *etc*); – *vt* (-tt-) **to k. out** équiper (**with** de).

kitchen ['kıtʃın] *n* cuisine *f*; **k. cabinet** buffet *m* de cuisine; **k. garden** jardin *m* potager; **k. sink** évier *m*. ◆**kitche'nette** *n* kitchenette *f*, coin-cuisine *m*.

kite [kaɪt] *n* (*toy*) cerf-volant *m*.

kith [kıθ] *n* **k. and kin** amis *mpl* et parents *mpl*.

kitten ['kıt(ə)n] *n* chaton *m*, petit chat *m*.

kitty ['kıtı] *n* (*fund*) cagnotte *f*.

km *abbr* (*kilometre*) km.

knack [næk] *n* (*skill*) coup *m* (de main), truc *m* (**of doing** pour faire); **to have a** *or* **the k. of doing** (*aptitude, tendency*) avoir le don de faire.

knackered ['nækəd] *a* (*tired*) *Sl* vanné.

knapsack ['næpsæk] *n* sac *m* à dos.

knead [niːd] *vt* (*dough*) pétrir.

knee [niː] *n* genou *m*; **to go down on one's**

knees se mettre à genoux; **k. pad** *Sp* genouillère *f*. ◆**kneecap** *n* *Anat* rotule *f*. ◆**knees-up** *n* *Sl* soirée *f* dansante, sauterie *f*.

kneel [niːl] *vi* (*pt & pp* knelt *or* kneeled) **to k. (down)** s'agenouiller; **to be kneeling (down)** être à genoux.

knell [nel] *n* glas *m*.

knew [njuː] *see* know.

knickers ['nıkəz] *npl* (*woman's undergarment*) culotte *f*, slip *m*.

knick-knack ['nıknæk] *n* babiole *f*.

knife [naɪf] *n* (*pl* knives) couteau *m*; (*penknife*) canif *m*; – *vt* poignarder.

knight [naɪt] *n* *Hist & Br Univ* chevalier *m*; *Chess* cavalier *m*; – *vt* (*of monarch*) *Br Pol* faire (qn) chevalier. ◆**knighthood** *n* titre *m* de chevalier.

knit [nɪt] *vt* (-tt-) tricoter; **to k. together** *Fig* souder; **to k. one's brow** froncer les sourcils; – *vi* tricoter; **to k. (together)** (*of bones*) se souder. ◆**knitting** *n* tricot *m*; **k. needle** aiguille *f* à tricoter. ◆**knitwear** *n* tricots *mpl*.

knob [nɒb] *n* (*on door etc*) bouton *m*; (*on stick*) pommeau *m*; (*of butter*) noix *f*.

knock [nɒk] *vt* (*strike*) frapper; (*collide with*) heurter; (*criticize*) *Fam* critiquer; **to k. one's head on** se cogner la tête contre; **to k. senseless** (*stun*) assommer; **to k. to the ground** jeter à terre; **to k. about** (*ill-treat*) malmener; **to k. back** (*drink, glass etc*) *Fam* s'envoyer (derrière la cravate), siffler; **to k. down** (*vase, pedestrian etc*) renverser; (*house, tree, wall etc*) abattre; (*price*) baisser, casser; **to k. in** (*nail*) enfoncer; **to k. off** (*person, object*) faire tomber (**from** de); (*do quickly*) *Fam* expédier; (*steal*) *Fam* piquer; **to k. £5 off** (**the price**) baisser le prix de cinq livres, faire cinq livres sur le prix; **to k. out** (*stun*) assommer; (*beat in competition*) éliminer; **to k. oneself out** (*tire*) *Fam* s'esquinter (**doing** à faire); **to k. over** (*pedestrian, vase etc*) renverser; **to k. up** (*meal*) *Fam* préparer à la hâte; – *vi* (*strike*) frapper; **to k. against** *or* **into** (*bump into*) heurter; **to k. about** (*travel*) *Fam* bourlinguer; (*lie around, stand around*) traîner; **to k. off** (*stop work*) *Fam* s'arrêter de travailler; – *n* (*blow*) coup *m*; (*collision*) heurt *m*; **there's a k. at the door** quelqu'un frappe; **I heard a k.** j'ai entendu frapper. ◆**knockdown** *n* **k. price** prix *m* imbattable. ◆**knock-'kneed** *a* cagneux. ◆**knock-out** *n* *Boxing* knock-out *m*; **to be a k.-out** (*of person, film etc*) *Fam* être formidable.

knocker ['nɒkər] n (for door) marteau m.

knot [nɒt] **1** n (in rope etc) nœud m; — vt (-tt-) nouer. **2** n (unit of speed) Nau nœud m. ◆**knotty** a (-ier, -iest) (wood etc) noueux; (problem) Fig épineux.

know [nəʊ] vt (pt knew, pp known) (facts, language etc) savoir; (person, place etc) connaître; (recognize) reconnaître (by à); **to k. that** savoir que; **to k. how to** do savoir faire; **for all I k.** (autant) que je sache; **I'll let you k. that** je te le ferai savoir; **I'll have you k. that** . . . sachez que . . . ; **to k. (a lot) about** (person, event) en savoir long sur; (cars, sewing etc) s'y connaître en; **I've never known him to complain** je ne l'ai jamais vu se plaindre; **to get to k. (about) sth** apprendre qch; **to get to k. s.o.** (meet) faire la connaissance de qn; — vi savoir; **I k.** je (le) sais; **I wouldn't k., I k. nothing about it** je n'en sais rien; **I k. about that** je sais ça, je suis au courant; **to k. of** (have heard of) avoir entendu parler de; **do you k. of?** (a good tailor etc) connais-tu?; **you (should) k. better than to do that** tu es trop intelligent pour faire ça; **you should have known better** tu aurais dû réfléchir; — n **in the k.** Fam au courant. ◆**-ing** a (smile, look) entendu. ◆**-ingly** adv (consciously) sciemment. ◆**known** a connu; **a k. expert** un expert reconnu; **well k.** (bien) connu (that que); **she is k. to be** . . . on sait qu'elle est . . . . ◆**know-all** n, Am ◆**know-it-all** n je-sais-tout m/inv. ◆**know-how** n (skill) compétence f (to do pour faire), savoir-faire m inv.

knowledge ['nɒlɪdʒ] n connaissance f (of de); (learning) connaissances fpl, savoir m; **to (the best of) my k.** à ma connaissance; **without the k. of** à l'insu de; **to have no k. of** ignorer; **general k.** culture f générale. ◆**knowledgeable** a bien informé (about sur).

knuckle ['nʌk(ə)l] **1** n articulation f du doigt. **2** vi **to k. down to** (task) Fam s'atteler à; **to k. under** céder.

Koran [kə'rɑːn] n Rel Coran m.

kosher ['kəʊʃər] a Rel kascher inv.

kowtow [kaʊ'taʊ] vi se prosterner (to devant).

kudos ['kjuːdɒs] n (glory) gloire f.

L

L, l [el] L, l m.

lab [læb] n Fam labo m. ◆**laboratory** [lə'bɒrət(ə)rɪ, Am 'læbrətərɪ] n laboratoire m; **language l.** laboratoire m de langues.

label ['leɪb(ə)l] n étiquette f; — vt (-ll-, Am -l-) (goods, person) étiqueter (as comme).

laborious [lə'bɔːrɪəs] a laborieux.

labour ['leɪbər] n (work, childbirth) travail m; (workers) main-d'œuvre f; L. Br Pol les travaillistes mpl; **in l.** Med au travail; — a (market, situation) du travail; (conflict, dispute) ouvrier; (relations) ouvriers-patronat inv; **l. force** main-d'œuvre f; **l. union** Am syndicat m; — vi (toil) peiner; — vt **to l. a point** insister sur un point. ◆**-ed** a (style) laborieux. ◆**-er** n (on roads etc) manœuvre m; Agr ouvrier m agricole.

laburnum [lə'bɜːnəm] n Bot cytise f.

labyrinth ['læbɪrɪnθ] n labyrinthe m.

lace [leɪs] **1** n (cloth) dentelle f. **2** n (of shoe) lacet m; — vt **to l. (up)** (tie up) lacer. **3** vt (drink) additionner, arroser (with de).

lacerate ['læsəreɪt] vt (flesh etc) lacérer.

lack [læk] n manque m; **for l. of** à défaut de; — vt manquer de; — vi **to be lacking** manquer (in, for de).

lackey ['lækɪ] n Hist & Fig laquais m.

laconic [lə'kɒnɪk] a laconique.

lacquer ['lækər] n laque f; — vt laquer.

lad [læd] n gars m, garçon m; **when I was a l.** quand j'étais gosse.

ladder ['lædər] n échelle f; (in stocking) maille f filée; — vti (stocking) filer.

laden ['leɪd(ə)n] a chargé (with de).

ladle ['leɪd(ə)l] n louche f.

lady ['leɪdɪ] n dame f; **a young l.** une jeune fille; (married) une jeune femme; **the l. of the house** la maîtresse de maison; **Ladies and Gentlemen!** Mesdames, Mesdemoiselles, Messieurs!; **l. doctor** femme f médecin; **l. friend** amie f; **ladies' room** Fig toilettes fpl. ◆**l.-in-'waiting** n (pl ladies-in-waiting) dame f d'honneur. ◆**ladybird** n, Am ◆**ladybug** n coccinelle f. ◆**ladylike** a (manner) distingué; **she's (very) l.** elle est très grande dame.

lag [læg] **1** vi (-gg-) **to l. behind** (in progress, work) avoir du retard; (dawdle) traîner; **to l. behind s.o.** avoir du retard sur qn; — n time l. (*between events*) décalage *m*; (*between countries*) décalage *m* horaire. **2** *vt* (-gg-) caloufuger.

lager ['lɑːgər] *n* bière *f* blonde.

lagoon [ləˈguːn] *n* lagune *f*; (*small, coral*) lagon *m*.

laid [leɪd] *see* lay². ◆l.-'back *a* Fam relax.

lain [leɪn] *see* lie¹.

lair [leər] *n* tanière *f*.

laity ['leɪtɪ] *n* the l. les laïcs *mpl*.

lake [leɪk] *n* lac *m*.

lamb [læm] *n* agneau *m*. ◆lambswool *n* laine *f* d'agneau.

lame [leɪm] *a* (-er, -est) (*person, argument*) boiteux; (*excuse*) piètre; **to be l.** boiter. ◆—**ness** *n* Med claudication *f*; (*of excuse*) Fig faiblesse *f*.

lament [ləˈment] *n* lamentation *f*; – *vt* **to l.** (**over**) se lamenter sur. ◆lamentable *a* lamentable. ◆lamen'tation *n* lamentation *f*.

laminated ['læmɪneɪtɪd] *a* (*metal*) laminé.

lamp [læmp] *n* lampe *f*; (*bulb*) ampoule *f*; Aut feu *m*. ◆lamppost *n* réverbère *m*. ◆lampshade *n* abat-jour *m inv*.

lance [lɑːns] **1** *n* (*weapon*) lance *f*. **2** *vt* Med inciser.

land [lænd] **1** *n* terre *f*; (*country*) pays *m*; (*plot of*) l. terrain *m*; on dry l. sur la terre ferme; no man's l. Mil & Fig no man's land *m inv*; – *a* (*flora, transport etc*) terrestre; (*reform, law*) agraire; (*owner, tax*) foncier. **2** *vi* (*of aircraft*) atterrir, se poser; (*of ship*) mouiller, relâcher; (*of passengers*) débarquer; (*of bomb etc*) (re)tomber; **to l. up** (*end up*) se retrouver; – *vt* (*passengers, cargo*) débarquer; (*aircraft*) poser; (*blow*) Fig flanquer (on à); (*job, prize etc*) Fam décrocher; **to l. s.o. in trouble** Fam mettre-qn dans le pétrin; **to be landed with** Fam (*person*) avoir sur les bras; (*fine*) ramasser, écoper de. ◆—**ed** *a* (*owning land*) terrien. ◆—**ing** *n* **1** Av atterrissage *m*; Nau débarquement *m*; **forced l.** atterrissage *m* forcé; l. **stage** débarcadère *m*. **2** *n* (*at top of stairs*) palier *m*; (*floor*) étage *m*. ◆landlady *n* logeuse *f*, propriétaire *f*. ◆landlocked *a* sans accès à la mer. ◆landlord *n* propriétaire *m*; (*of pub*) patron *m*. ◆landmark *n* point *m* de repère. ◆landslide *n* Geol glissement *m* de terrain, éboulement *m*; Pol raz-de-marée *m inv* électoral.

landscape ['lændskeɪp] *n* paysage *m*.

lane [leɪn] *n* (*in country*) chemin *m*; (*in town*) ruelle *f*; (*division of road*) voie *f*; (*line of*

traffic) file *f*; Av Nau Sp couloir *m*; **bus l.** couloir *m* (*réservé aux autobus*).

language ['læŋgwɪdʒ] *n* (*faculty, style*) langage *m*; (*national tongue*) langue *f*; **computer l.** langage *m* machine; – *a* (*laboratory*) de langues; (*teacher, studies*) de langue(s).

languid ['læŋgwɪd] *a* languissant. ◆languish *vi* languir (for, after après).

lank [læŋk] *a* (*hair*) plat et terne.

lanky ['læŋkɪ] *a* (-ier, -iest) dégingandé.

lantern ['læntən] *n* lanterne *f*; **Chinese l.** lampion *m*.

lap [læp] **1** *n* (*of person*) genoux *mpl*; **the l. of luxury** le plus grand luxe. **2** *n* Sp (*of track*) tour *m* (*de piste*). **3** *vt* (-pp-) **to l. up** (*drink*) laper; (*like very much*) Fam adorer; (*believe*) Fam gober; – *vi* (*of waves*) clapoter. **4** *vi* (-pp-) **to l. over** (*overlap*) se chevaucher.

lapel [ləˈpel] *n* (*of jacket etc*) revers *m*.

lapse [læps] **1** *n* (*fault*) faute *f*; (*weakness*) défaillance *f*; **a l. of memory** un trou de mémoire; **a l. in behaviour** un écart de conduite; – *vi* (*err*) commettre une faute; **to l. into** retomber dans. **2** *n* (*interval*) intervalle *m*; **a l. of time** un intervalle (*between* entre). **3** *vi* (*expire*) se périmer, expirer; (*of subscription*) prendre fin.

larceny ['lɑːsənɪ] *n* vol *m* simple.

lard [lɑːd] *n* saindoux *m*.

larder ['lɑːdər] *n* (*cupboard*) garde-manger *m inv*.

large [lɑːdʒ] *a* (-er, -est) (*in size or extent*) grand; (*in volume, bulkiness*) gros; (*quantity*) grand, important; **to become or grow or get l.** grossir, grandir; **to a l. extent** en grande mesure; **at l.** (*of prisoner, animal*) en liberté; (*as a whole*) en général; **by and l.** dans l'ensemble, généralement. ◆l.-**scale** *a* (*reform*) fait sur une grande échelle. ◆largely *adv* (*to a great extent*) en grande mesure. ◆largeness *n* grandeur *f*; grosseur *f*.

largesse [lɑːˈʒes] *n* largesse *f*.

lark [lɑːk] **1** *n* (*bird*) alouette *f*. **2** *n* (*joke*) Fam rigolade *f*, blague *f*; – *vi* **to l. about** Fam s'amuser.

larva, *pl* -**vae** ['lɑːvə, -viː] *n* (*of insect*) larve *f*.

larynx ['lærɪŋks] *n* Anat larynx *m*. ◆laryn'**gitis** *n* Med laryngite *f*.

lascivious [ləˈsɪvɪəs] *a* lascif.

laser ['leɪzər] *n* laser *m*.

lash¹ [læʃ] *n* (*with whip*) coup *m* de fouet; – *vt* (*strike*) fouetter; (*tie*) attacher (to à); **the dog lashed its tail** le chien donna un coup de queue; – *vi* **to l. out** (*spend wildly*) Fam claquer son argent; **to l. out at** envoyer des coups à; (abuse) Fig invectiver; (criticize) Fig fustiger. ◆—ings npl l. of Culin Fam des masses de, une montagne de.

lash² [læʃ] n (eyelash) cil m.

lass [læs] n jeune fille f.

lassitude [ˈlæsɪtjuːd] n lassitude f.

lasso [læˈsuː] n (pl -os) lasso m; – vt attraper au lasso.

last¹ [lɑːst] a dernier; the l. ten lines les dix dernières lignes; l. night (evening) hier soir; (during night) cette nuit; the day before l. avant-hier; l. night (evening) hier soir; (during night) cette nuit; the day before l. avant-hier; – adv (lastly) en dernier lieu, enfin; (on the last occasion) (pour) la dernière fois; to leave l. sortir le dernier or en dernier; – n (person, object) dernier, -ière mf; (end) fin f; the l. of the beer/etc (remainder) le reste de la bière/etc; at (long) l. enfin. ◆l.-ditch a désespéré. ◆l.-minute a de dernière minute. ◆lastly adv en dernier lieu, enfin.

last² [lɑːst] vi durer; to l. (out) (endure, resist) tenir; (of money, supplies) durer; it lasted me ten years ça m'a duré or fait dix ans. ◆—ing a durable.

latch [lætʃ] **1** n loquet m; the door is on the l. la porte n'est pas fermée à clef. **2** vi to l. on to Fam (grab) s'accrocher à; (understand) saisir.

late¹ [leɪt] a (-er, -est) (not on time) en retard (for à); (former) ancien; (meal, fruit, season, hour) tardif; (stage) avancé; (edition) dernier; to be l. (of person, train etc) être en retard, avoir du retard; to be l. (in) coming arriver en retard; he's an hour l. il a une heure de retard; it's l. il est tard; to make s.o. l. mettre qn en retard; it's l. il est tard; Easter/etc is l. Pâques/etc est tard; in l. June/etc fin juin/etc; a later edition/etc (more recent) une édition/etc plus récente; the latest edition/etc (last) la dernière édition/etc; in later life plus tard dans la vie; to take a later train prendre un train plus tard; at a later date à une date ultérieure; the latest date la date limite; at the latest au plus tard; of l. dernièrement; – adv (in the day, season etc) tard; (not on time) en retard; it's getting l. il se fait tard; later (on) plus tard; not or no later than pas plus tard que. ◆latecomer n retardataire mf. ◆lately adv dernièrement. ◆lateness n (of person, train etc) retard m; constant l. des retards continuels; the l. of the hour l'heure tardive.

late² [leɪt] a the l. Mr Smith/etc (deceased) feu Monsieur Smith/etc; our l. friend notre regretté ami.

latent [ˈleɪtənt] a latent.

lateral [ˈlætərəl] a latéral.

lathe [leɪð] n Tech tour m.

lather [ˈlɑːðər] n mousse f; – vt savonner; – vi mousser.

Latin [ˈlætɪn] a latin; L. America Amérique f latine; L. American d'Amérique latine; – n (person) Latin, -ine mf; (language) latin m.

latitude [ˈlætɪtjuːd] n Geog & Fig latitude f.

latrines [ləˈtriːnz] npl latrines fpl.

latter [ˈlætər] a (later, last-named) dernier; (second) deuxième; – n dernier, -ière mf; second, -onde mf. ◆—ly adv dernièrement; (late in life) sur le tard.

lattice [ˈlætɪs] n treillis m.

laudable [ˈlɔːdəb(ə)l] a louable.

laugh [lɑːf] n rire m; to have a good l. bien rire; – vi rire (at, about de); to l. to oneself rire en soi-même; – vt to l. off tourner en plaisanterie. ◆—ing a riant; it's no l. matter il n'y a pas de quoi rire; to be the l.-stock of être la risée de. ◆—able a ridicule. ◆laughter n rire(s) m(pl); to roar with l. rire aux éclats.

launch [lɔːntʃ] **1** n (motor boat) vedette f; (pleasure boat) bateau m de plaisance. **2** vt (rocket, boat, fashion etc) lancer; – vi to l. (out) into (begin) se lancer dans; – n lancement m. ◆—ing n lancement m.

launder [ˈlɔːndər] vt (clothes) blanchir; (money from drugs etc) Fig blanchir. ◆—ing n blanchissage m. ◆launde'rette n, Am ◆laundromat n laverie f automatique. ◆laundry n (place) blanchisserie f; (clothes) linge m.

laurel [ˈlɒrəl] n Bot laurier m.

lava [ˈlɑːvə] n Geol lave f.

lavatory [ˈlævətrɪ] n cabinets mpl.

lavender [ˈlævɪndər] n lavande f.

lavish [ˈlævɪʃ] a prodigue (with de); (helping, meal) généreux; (decor, house etc) somptueux; (expenditure) excessif; – vt prodiguer (sth on s.o. qch à qn). ◆—ly adv (to give) généreusement; (to furnish) somptueusement.

law [lɔː] n (rule, rules) loi f; (study, profession, system) droit m; court of l., l. court cour f de justice; l. and order l'ordre public. ◆l.-abiding a respectueux des lois. ◆lawful a (action) légal; (child, wife etc) légitime. ◆lawfully adv légalement. ◆lawless a (country) anarchique. ◆lawlessness n anarchie f. ◆lawsuit n procès m.

lawn [lɔːn] n pelouse f, gazon m; l. mower tondeuse f (à gazon); l. tennis tennis m (sur gazon).

lawyer [ˈlɔːjər] n (in court) avocat m; (author,

legal expert) juriste *m*; (*for wills, sales*) notaire *m*.

lax [læks] *a* (*person*) négligent; (*discipline, behaviour*) relâché; **to be l. in doing** faire avec négligence. ◆**laxity** *n*, ◆**laxness** *n* négligence *f*; relâchement *m*.

laxative [ˈlæksətɪv] *n* & *a Med* laxatif (*m*).

lay¹ [leɪ] *a* (*non-religious*) laïque (*non-specialized*) d'un profane; **l. person** profane *mf*. ◆**layman** *n* (*pl* -men) (*non-specialist*) profane *m*.

lay² [leɪ] (*pt & pp* laid) **1** *vt* (*put down, place*) poser; (*table*) mettre; (*blanket*) étendre (**over** sur); (*trap*) tendre; (*money*) miser (**on** sur); (*accusation*) porter; (*ghost*) exorciser; **to l. a bet** parier; **to l. bare** mettre à nu; **to l. waste** ravager; **to l. s.o. open to** exposer qn à; **to l. one's hands on** mettre la main sur; **to l. a hand or a finger on s.o.** lever la main sur qn; **to l. down** poser; (*arms*) déposer; (*condition*) (im)poser; **to l. down the law** faire la loi (**to** à); **to l. s.o. off** (*worker*) licencier qn; **to l. on** (*install*) mettre, installer; (*supply*) fournir; **to l. it on** (thick) *Fam* y aller un peu fort; **to l. out** (*garden*) dessiner; (*house*) concevoir; (*prepare*) préparer; (*display*) disposer; (*money*) *Fam* dépenser (**on** pour); **to be laid up** (*in bed*) *Med* être alité; – *vi* **to l. into** *Fam* attaquer; **to l. off** (*stop*) *Fam* arrêter; **to l. off s.o.** (*leave alone*) *Fam* laisser qn tranquille; **l. off!** (*don't touch*) *Fam* pas touche!; **to l. out** *Fam* payer. **2** *vt* (*egg*) pondre; – *vi* (*of bird etc*) pondre. ◆**layabout** *n Fam* fainéant, -ante *mf*. ◆**lay-by** *n* (*pl* -bys) *Aut* aire *f* de stationnement *or* de repos. ◆**lay-off** *n* (*of worker*) licenciement *m*. **layout** *n* disposition *f*; *Typ* mise *f* en pages. ◆**lay-over** *n Am* halte *f*.

lay³ [leɪ] *see* **lie¹**.

layer [ˈleɪər] *n* couche *f*.

laze [leɪz] *vi* **to l.** (**about** *or* **around**) paresser. ◆**lazy** (-ier, -iest) (*person etc*) paresseux; (*holiday*) passé à ne rien faire. ◆**lazybones** *n Fam* paresseux, -euse *mf*.

lb *abbr* (*libra*) = **pound** (*weight*).

lead¹ [liːd] *vt* (*pt & pp* led) (*conduct*) mener, conduire (**to** à); (*team, government etc*) diriger; (*regiment*) commander; (*life*) mener; **to l. s.o. in/out/etc** faire entrer/sortir/etc qn; **to l. s.o. to do** (*induce*) amener qn à faire; **to l. the way** montrer le chemin; **to l. the world** tenir le premier rang mondial; **easily led** influençable; **to l. away** *or* **off** emmener; **to l. back** ramener; (*in tease*) faire marcher; – *vi* (*of street etc*) mener, conduire (**to** à); (*in match*) mener;

(*in race*) être en tête; (*go ahead*) aller devant; **to l. to** (*result in*) aboutir à; (*cause*) causer, amener; **to l. up to** (*of street*) conduire à, mener à; (*precede*) précéder; (*approach gradually*) en venir à; – *n* (*distance or time ahead*) *Sp* avance *f* (**over** sur); (*example*) exemple *m*, initiative *f*; (*clue*) piste *f*, indice *m*; (*star part*) *Th* rôle *m* principal; (*leash*) laisse *f*; (*wire*) *El* fil *m*; **to take the l.** *Sp* prendre la tête; **to be in the l.** (*in race*) être en tête; (*in match*) mener. ◆**leading** *a* (*main*) principal; (*important*) important; (*front*) de tête; **the l. author** l'auteur principal *or* le plus important; **a l. figure** un personnage marquant; **the l. lady** *Cin* la vedette féminine; **l. article** *Journ* éditorial *m*. ◆**leader** *n* chef *m*; *Pol* dirigeant, -ante *mf*; (*of strike, riot*) meneur, -euse *mf*; (*guide*) guide *m*; (*article*) *Journ* éditorial *m*. ◆**leadership** *n* direction *f*; (*qualities*) qualités *fpl* de chef; (*leaders*) *Pol* dirigeants *mpl*.

lead² [led] *n* (*metal*) plomb *m*; (*of pencil*) mine *f*; **l. pencil** crayon *m* à mine de plomb. ◆**leaden** *a* (*sky*) de plomb.

leaf [liːf] *n* (*pl* leaves) *Bot* feuille *f*; (*of book*) feuillet *m*; (*of table*) rallonge *f*. **2** *vi* **to l. through** (*book*) feuilleter. ◆**leaflet** *n* prospectus *m*; (*containing instructions*) notice *f*. ◆**leafy** *a* (-ier, -iest) (*tree*) feuillu.

league [liːg] *n* **1** (*alliance*) ligue *f*; *Sp* championnat *m*; **in l. with** *Pej* de connivence avec. **2** (*measure*) *Hist* lieue *f*.

leak [liːk] *n* (*in pipe, roof etc*) fuite *f*; (*in boat*) voie *f* d'eau; – *vi* (*of liquid, pipe, tap etc*) fuir; (*of ship*) faire eau; **to l. out** (*of information*) *Fig* être divulgué; – *vt* (*liquid*) répandre; (*information*) *Fig* divulguer. ◆**—age** *n* fuite *f*; (*amount lost*) perte *f*. ◆**leaky** *a* (-ier, -iest) *a* (*kettle etc*) qui fuit.

lean¹ [liːn] *a* (-er, -est) (*thin*) maigre; (*year*) difficile. ◆**—ness** *n* maigreur *f*.

lean² [liːn] *vi* (*pt & pp* leaned *or* leant [lent]) (*of object*) pencher; (*of person*) se pencher; **to l. against/on** (*of person*) s'appuyer contre/sur; **to l. on s.o.** (*influence*) *Fam* faire pression sur qn (**to do** pour faire); **to l. forward** *or* **over** (*of person*) se pencher (en avant); **to l. over** (*of object*) pencher; – *vt* appuyer (**against** contre); **to l. one's head on/out of** pencher la tête sur/par. ◆**—ing** **1** *a* penché; **l. against** (*resting*) appuyé contre. **2** *npl* tendances *fpl* (**towards** à). ◆**lean-to** *n* (*pl* -tos) (*building*) appentis *m*.

leap [liːp] *n* (*jump*) bond *m*, saut *m*; (*change, increase etc*) *Fig* bond *m*; **l. year** année *f* bissextile; **in leaps and bounds** à pas de géant; − *vi* (*pt* & *pp* **leaped** or **leapt** [lept]) bondir, sauter; (*of flames*) jaillir; (*of profits*) faire un bond; **to l. to one's feet, l. up** se lever d'un bond. ◆**leapfrog** *n* saute-mouton *m inv.*

learn [lɜːn] *vt* (*pt* & *pp* **learned** or **learnt**) apprendre (**that** que); (**how to**) do apprendre à faire; − *vi* apprendre; **to l. about** (*study*) étudier; (*hear about*) apprendre. ◆−**ed** [-ɪd] *a* savant. ◆−**ing** *n* érudition *f*, savoir *m*; (*of language*) apprentissage *m* (**of** de). ◆−**er** *n* débutant, -ante *mf.*

lease [liːs] *n Jur* bail *m*; **a new l. of life** or *Am* **on life** un regain de vie, une nouvelle vie; − *vt* (*house etc*) louer à bail. ◆**leasehold** *n* propriété *f* louée à bail.

leash [liːʃ] *n* laisse *f*; **on a l.** en laisse.

least [liːst] *a* **the l.** (*smallest amount of*) le moins de; (*slightest*) le or la moindre; **he has (the) l. talent** il a le moins de talent (**of** all de tous); **the l. effort/noise/**etc le moindre effort/bruit/etc; − *n* **the l.** (to do, eat etc) le moins; (*with quantity*) au moins; **at l. that's what she says** du moins c'est ce qu'elle dit; **not in the l.** pas du tout; − *adv* (*to work, eat etc*) le moins; (*with adjective*) le or la moins; **l. of all** (*especially not*) surtout pas.

leather [ˈleðər] *n* cuir *m*; (*wash*) l. peau *f* de chamois.

leave [liːv] **1** *n* (*holiday*) congé *m*; (*consent*) & *Mil* permission *f*; **l. of absence** congé *m* exceptionnel; **to take (one's) l. of** prendre congé de. **2** *vt* (*pt* & *pp* **left**) (*allow to remain, forget*) laisser; (*depart from*) quitter; (*room*) sortir de, quitter; **to l. the table** sortir de table; **to l. s.o. in charge of s.o./sth** laisser à la garde de qn/qch; **to l. sth with s.o.** (*entrust, give*) laisser qch à qn; **to be left** (*over*) rester; **there's no hope/bread/**etc **left** il ne reste plus d'espoir/de pain/etc; **l. it to me!** laissez-moi faire!; **I'll l. it (up) to you** je m'en remets à toi; **to l. go (of)** (*release*) lâcher; **to l. behind** laisser; (*surpass*) dépasser; (*in race*) *Sp* distancer; **to l. off** (*lid*) ne pas (re)mettre; **to l. off doing** (*stop*) Fam arrêter de faire; **to l. on** (*hat, gloves*) garder; **to l. out** (*forget*) omettre; (*exclude*) exclure; − *vi* (*depart*) partir (**from** de, **for** pour); **to l. off** (*stop*) Fam s'arrêter. ◆**leavings** *npl* restes *mpl.*

Lebanon [ˈlebənən] *n* Liban *m*. ◆**Leba-'nese** *a* & *n* libanais, -aise (*mf*).

lecher [ˈletʃər] *n* débauché *m*. ◆**lecherous** *a* lubrique, luxurieux.

lectern [ˈlektən] *n* (*for giving speeches*) pupitre *m*; *Rel* lutrin *m.*

lecture [ˈlektʃər] **1** *n* (*public speech*) conférence *f*; (*as part of series*) *Univ* cours *m* (magistral); − *vi* faire une conférence or un cours; **I l. in chemistry** je suis professeur de chimie. **2** *vt* (*scold*) *Fig* faire la morale à, sermonner; − *n* (*scolding*) sermon *m.* ◆**lecturer** *n* conférencier, -ière *mf*; *Univ* enseignant, -ante *mf.* ◆**lectureship** *n* poste *m* à l'université.

led [led] *see* **lead**[1].

ledge [ledʒ] *n* rebord *m*; (*on mountain*) saillie *f.*

ledger [ˈledʒər] *n Com* registre *m*, grand livre *m.*

leech [liːtʃ] *n* (*worm, person*) sangsue *f.*

leek [liːk] *n* poireau *m.*

leer [lɪər] *vi* **to l. (at)** lorgner; − *n* regard *m* sournois.

leeway [ˈliːweɪ] *n* (*freedom*) liberté *f* d'action; (*safety margin*) marge *f* de sécurité.

left[1] [left] *see* **leave** 2; − *a* **l. luggage office** consigne *f.* ◆**leftovers** *npl* restes *mpl.*

left[2] [left] *a* (*side, hand etc*) gauche; − *adv* à gauche; − *n* gauche *f*; **on** or **to the l.** à gauche (**of** de). ◆**l.-hand** *a* à *à* or de gauche; **on the l.-hand side** à gauche (**of** de). ◆**l.-'handed** *a* (*person*) gaucher. ◆**l.-wing** *a Pol* de gauche. ◆**leftist** *n* & *a Pol* gauchiste (*mf*).

leg [leg] *n* jambe *f*; (*of bird, dog etc*) patte *f*; (*of lamb*) *Culin* gigot *m*; (*of chicken*) *Culin* cuisse *f*; (*of table*) pied *m*; (*of journey*) étape *f*; **to pull s.o.'s l.** (*make fun of*) mettre qn en boîte; **on its last legs** (*machine etc*) Fam prêt à claquer; **to be on one's last legs** Fam avoir un pied dans la tombe. ◆**l.-room** *n* place *f* pour les jambes. ◆**leggy** *a* (-**ier**, -**iest**) (*person*) aux longues jambes, tout en jambes.

legacy [ˈlegəsɪ] *n Jur* & *Fig* legs *m.*

legal [ˈliːg(ə)l] *a* (*lawful*) légal; (*mind, affairs, adviser*) juridique; (*aid, error*) judiciaire; **l. expert** juriste *m*; **l. proceedings** procès *m.* ◆**le'gality** *n* légalité *f.* ◆**legalize** *vt* légaliser. ◆**legally** *adv* légalement.

legation [lɪˈgeɪʃ(ə)n] *n Pol* légation *f.*

legend [ˈledʒənd] *n* (*story, inscription etc*) légende *f.* ◆**legendary** *a* légendaire.

leggings [ˈlegɪnz] *npl* jambières *fpl.*

legible [ˈledʒəb(ə)l] *a* lisible. ◆**legi'bility** *n* lisibilité *f.* ◆**legibly** *adv* lisiblement.

legion [ˈliːdʒən] *n Mil* & *Fig* légion *f.*

legislate [ˈledʒɪsleɪt] *vi* légiférer. ◆**legis-**

'**lation** n (laws) législation f; (action) élaboration f des lois; (piece of) l. loi f. ◆**legislative** a législatif.

legitimate [lɪˈdʒɪtɪmət] a (reason, child etc) légitime. ◆**legitimacy** n légitimité f.

legless [ˈleɡləs] a (drunk) Fam (complètement) bourré.

leisure [ˈleʒər, Am ˈliːʒər] n l. (time) loisirs mpl; l. activities loisirs mpl; moment of l. moment m de loisir; at (one's) l. à tête reposée. ◆**─ly** a (walk, occupation) peu fatigant; (meal, life) calme; at a l. pace, in a l. way sans se presser.

lemon [ˈlemən] n citron m; l. drink, l. squash citronnade f; l. tea thé m au citron. ◆**lemo'nade** n (fizzy) limonade f; (still) Am citronnade f.

lend [lend] vt (pt & pp lent) prêter (to à); (charm, colour etc) Fig donner (to à); to l. credence to ajouter foi à. ◆**─ing** n prêt m. ◆**─er** n prêteur, -euse mf.

length [leŋθ] n longueur f; (section of pipe etc) morceau m; (of road) tronçon m; (of cloth) métrage m; (of horse, swimming pool) Sp longueur f; (duration) durée f; l. of time temps m; at l. (at last) enfin; (at great) l. (in detail) dans le détail; (for a long time) longuement; to go to great lengths to do beaucoup de mal (to do pour faire). ◆**lengthen** vt allonger; (in time) prolonger. ◆**lengthwise** adv dans le sens de la longueur. ◆**lengthy** a (-ier, -iest) long.

lenient [ˈliːnɪənt] a indulgent (to envers). ◆**leniency** n indulgence f. ◆**leniently** adv avec indulgence.

lens [lenz] n lentille f; (in spectacles) verre m; Phot objectif m.

Lent [lent] n Rel Carême m.

lentil [ˈlentl] n Bot Culin lentille f.

leopard [ˈlepəd] n léopard m.

leotard [ˈliːətɑːd] n collant m (de danse).

leper [ˈlepər] n lépreux, -euse mf. ◆**leprosy** n lèpre f.

lesbian [ˈlezbɪən] n & a lesbienne (f).

lesion [ˈliːʒ(ə)n] n Med lésion f.

less [les] a & n moins de (than que); l. time/etc moins de temps/etc; she has l. (than you) elle en a moins (que toi); l. than a kilo/ten/etc (with quantity, number) moins d'un kilo/de dix/etc; ─ adv (to sleep, know etc) moins (than que); l. (often) souvent; l. and l. de moins en moins; one l. un(e) de moins; ─ prep moins; l. six francs moins six francs. ◆**lessen** vti diminuer. ◆**lessening** n diminution f. ◆**lesser** a moindre; ─ n the l. of le ou la moindre de.

-less [ləs] suffix sans; **childless** sans enfants.

lesson [ˈles(ə)n] n leçon f; an English l. une leçon or un cours d'anglais; **I have lessons now** j'ai cours maintenant.

lest [lest] conj Lit de peur que (+ ne + sub).

let¹ [let] 1 vt (pt & pp let, pres p letting) (allow) laisser (s.o. do qn faire); to l. so. have sth donner qch à qn; to l. away (allow to leave) laisser partir; to l. down (lower) baisser; (hair) dénouer; (dress) rallonger; (tyre) dégonfler; to l. s.o. down (disappoint) décevoir qn; don't l. me down je compte sur toi; the car l. me down la voiture est tombée en panne. ◆**letdown** n déception f; to l. in (person, dog) faire entrer; (noise, light) laisser entrer; to l. s.o. in on sth mettre qn au courant de; to l. oneself in for (expense) se laisser entraîner à; (trouble) s'attirer; to l. off (bomb) faire éclater; (firework, gun) faire partir; to l. s.o. off laisser partir qn; (not punish) ne pas punir qn; (clear) Jur disculper qn; to be l. off with (a fine etc) s'en tirer avec; to l. s.o. off doing dispenser qn de faire; to l. on that Fam (admit) avouer que; (reveal) dire que; to l. out faire or laisser sortir; (prisoner) relâcher; (cry, secret) laisser échapper; (skirt) élargir; to l. s.o. out of the house) ouvrir la porte à qn; to l. out the clutch Aut débrayer; ─ vi not to l. on Fam ne rien dire, garder la bouche cousue; to l. up (of rain, person etc) s'arrêter. ◆**letup** n arrêt m, répit m. 2 v aux l. us eat/go/etc, l.'s eat/go/etc mangeons/partons/etc; l.'s go for a stroll allons nous promener; l. him come qu'il vienne.

let² [let] vt (pt & pp let, pres p letting) to l. (off or out) (house, room etc) louer. ◆**letting** n (of premises) location f.

lethal [ˈliːθ(ə)l] a mortel; (weapon) meurtrier.

lethargy [ˈleθədʒɪ] n léthargie f. ◆**le'thargic** a léthargique.

letter [ˈletər] n (missive, character) lettre f; man of letters homme m de lettres; l. bomb lettre f piégée; l. writer correspondant, -ante mf. ◆**letterbox** n boîte f aux or à lettres. ◆**letterhead** n en-tête m. ◆**lettering** n (letters) lettres fpl; (on tomb) inscription f.

lettuce [ˈletɪs] n laitue f, salade f.

leuk(a)emia [luːˈkiːmɪə] n leucémie f.

level [ˈlev(ə)l] 1 n niveau m; (speed) en palier; ─ a (surface) plat, uni; (object on surface) horizontal; (spoonful) ras; (equal in score) à égalité (with avec); (in height) au même niveau, à la même hauteur (**with** que); **l. crossing** *Rail* passage *m* à niveau; – *vt* (**-ll-,** *Am* **-l-**) (*surface, differences*) niveler, aplanir, (*plane down*) raboter; (*building*) raser; (*gun*) braquer; (*accusation*) lancer (**at** contre); – *vi* to **l. off** *or* **out** (*stabilize*) *Fig* se stabiliser. **2 n on the l.** *Fam* (*honest*) honnête, franc; (*frankly*) honnêtement, franchement; – *vi* – (**-ll-,** *Am* **-l-**) to **l. with** *Fam* être franc avec. ◆**l.-'headed** *a* équilibré.

lever ['liːvər, *Am* 'levər] *n* levier *m*. ◆**lever-age** *n* (*power*) influence *f*.

levity ['leviti] *n* légèreté *f*.

levy ['levi] *vt* (*tax, troops*) lever; – *n* (*tax*) impôt *m*.

lewd [luːd] *a* (**-er, -est**) obscène.

liable ['laɪəb(ə)l] *a.* **to** (*dizziness etc*) sujet à; (*fine, tax*) passible de; **he's l.** to do it est susceptible de faire, il pourrait faire; **l. for** (*responsible*) responsable de. ◆**lia'bility** *n* responsabilité *f* (**for** de); (*disadvantage*) handicap *m*; *pl* (*debts*) dettes *fpl*.

liaise [liˈeɪz] *vi* travailler en liaison (**with** avec). ◆**liaison** *n* (*association*) & *Mil* liaison *f*.

liar ['laɪər] *n* menteur, -euse *mf*.

libel ['laɪb(ə)l] *vt* (**-ll-,** *Am* **-l-**) diffamer (par écrit); – *n* diffamation *f*.

liberal ['lɪbərəl] *a* (*open-minded*) & *Pol* libéral; (*generous*) généreux (**with** de); – *n Pol* libéral, -ale *mf*. ◆**liberalism** *n* libéralisme *m*.

liberate ['lɪbəreɪt] *vt* libérer. ◆**libe'ration** *n* libération *f*. ◆**liberator** *n* libérateur, -trice *mf*.

liberty ['lɪbəti] *n* liberté *f*; **at l. to do** libre de faire; **what a l.!** (*cheek*) *Fam* quel culot!; **to take liberties with s.o.** se permettre des familiarités avec qn.

Libra ['liːbrə] *n* (*sign*) la Balance.

library ['laɪbrəri] *n* bibliothèque *f*. ◆**li'brarian** *n* bibliothécaire *mf*.

libretto [lɪˈbretəʊ] *n* (*pl* **-os**) *Mus* livret *m*.

Libya ['lɪbjə] *n* Libye *f*. ◆**Libyan** *a* & *n* libyen, -enne (*mf*).

lice [laɪs] *see* **louse.**

licence, *Am* **license** ['laɪsəns] *n* **1** permis *m*, autorisation *f*; (*for driving*) permis *m*; *Com* licence *f*; **pilot's l.** brevet *m* de pilote; **l. fee** *Rad TV* redevance *f*; **l. plate/number** *Aut* plaque *f*/numéro *m* d'immatriculation. **2** (*freedom*) licence *f*.

license ['laɪsəns] *vt* accorder une licence à, autoriser; **licensed premises** établissement *m* qui a une licence de débit de boissons.

licit ['lɪsɪt] *a* licite.

lick [lɪk] *vt* lécher; (*defeat*) *Fam* écraser; (*beat physically*) *Fam* rosser; **to be licked** (*by problem etc*) *Fam* être dépassé; – *n* coup *m* de langue; **a l. of paint** un coup de peinture. ◆**—ing** *n Fam* (*defeat*) déculottée *f*; (*beating*) rossée *f*.

licorice ['lɪkərɪʃ, -rɪs] *n Am* réglisse *f*.

lid [lɪd] *n* **1** (*of box etc*) couvercle *m*. **2** (*of eye*) paupière *f*.

lido ['liːdəʊ] *n* (*pl* -os) piscine *f* (*découverte*).

lie [laɪ] *vi* (*pt* **lay,** *pp* **lain,** *pres p* **lying**). (*in flat position*) s'allonger, s'étendre; (*remain*) rester; (*be*) être; (*in grave*) reposer; **to be lying** (*on the grass etc*) être allongé *or* étendu; **he lay asleep** il dormait; **here lies** (*on tomb*) ci-gît; **the problem lies in** le problème réside dans; **to l. heavy on** (*of meal etc*) & *Fig* peser sur; **to l. low** (*hide*) se cacher; (*be inconspicuous*) se faire tout petit; **to l. about** *or* **around** (*of objects, person*) traîner; **to l. down, to have a l.-down** s'allonger, se coucher; **lying down** (*resting*) allongé, couché; **to l. in, to have a l.-in** *Fam* faire la grasse matinée.

lie [laɪ] *vi* (*pt* & *pp* **lied,** *pres p* **lying**) (*tell lies*) mentir; – *n* mensonge *m*; **to give the l. to** (*show as untrue*) démentir.

lieu [luː] *n* **in l. of** au lieu de.

lieutenant [lefˈtenənt, *Am* luːˈtenənt] *n* lieutenant *m*.

life [laɪf] *n* (*pl* **lives**) vie *f*; (*of battery, machine*) durée (*de vie*); **to come to l.** (*of street, party etc*) s'animer; **at your time of l.** à ton âge; **loss of l.** perte *f* en vies humaines; **true to l.** conforme à la réalité; **to take one's (own) l.** se donner la mort; **bird l.** les oiseaux *mpl*; – *a* (*cycle, style*) de vie; (*belt, raft*) de sauvetage; (*force*) vital; **l. annuity** rente *f* viagère; **l. blood** *Fig* âme *f*; **l. insurance** assurance-vie *f*; **l. jacket** gilet *m* de sauvetage; **l. peer** pair *m* à vie. ◆**lifebelt** *n* canot *m* de sauvetage. ◆**lifebuoy** *n* bouée *f* de sauvetage. ◆**lifeguard** *n* maître-nageur *m* sauveteur. ◆**lifeless** *a* sans vie. ◆**lifelike** *a* qui semble vivant. ◆**lifelong** *a* de toute sa vie; (*friend*) de toujours. ◆**lifesaving** *n* sauvetage *m*. ◆**lifesize(d)** *a* grandeur nature *inv.* ◆**lifetime** *n* vie *f*; *Fig* éternité *f*; **in my l.** de mon vivant; **a once-in-a-l. experience/etc** l'expérience/*etc* de votre vie.

lift [lɪft] *vt* lever; (*sth heavy*) (sou)lever; (*ban, siege*) *Fig* lever; (*idea etc*) *Fig* voler, prendre (**from** à); **to l. down** *or* **off** (*take down*) descendre (**from** de); **to l. out** (*take out*) sortir; **to l. up** (*arm, eyes*) lever; (*object*) (sou)lever; – vi (of fog) se lever; **to l. off** (of space vehicle) décoller; – n (elevator) ascenseur m; **to give s.o. a l.** emmener or accompagner qn (en voiture) (**to** à). ◆**l.-off** n Av décollage m.

ligament ['lɪgəmənt] n ligament m.

light¹ [laɪt] **1** n lumière f; (daylight) jour m, lumière f; (on vehicle) feu m, (headlight) phare m; **by the l. of** à la lumière de; **in the l. of** (considering) à la lumière de; **in that l.** Fig sous ce jour or cet éclairage; **against the l.** à contre-jour; **to bring to l.** mettre en lumière; **to come to l.** être découvert; **to throw l. on** (matter) éclaircir; **do you have a l.?** (for cigarette) est-ce que vous avez du feu?; **to set l. to** mettre le feu à; **leading l.** (person) Fig phare m, sommité f, lumière f; **l. bulb** ampoule f (électrique); – vt (pt & pp lit or lighted) (candle etc) allumer; (match) gratter; **to l. (up)** (room) éclairer; – vi **to l. up** (of window) s'allumer. **2** a (bright, not dark) clair; **a l. green jacket** une veste vert clair. ◆**-ing** n El éclairage m; **the l. of** (candle etc) l'allumage m de. ◆**lighten¹** vt (light up) éclairer; (colour, hair) éclaircir. ◆**lighter** n (for cigarettes etc) briquet m; Culin allume-gaz m inv. ◆**lighthouse** n phare m. ◆**lightness¹** n clarté f.

light² [laɪt] a (in weight, quantity, strength etc) léger; (task) facile; **l. rain** pluie f fine; **to travel l.** voyager avec peu de bagages. ◆**l.-'fingered** a chapardeur. ◆**l.-'headed** a (giddy, foolish) étourdi. ◆**l.-'hearted** a gai. ◆**lighten²** vt (a load) alléger. ◆**lightly** adv légèrement. ◆**lightness²** n légèreté f.

light³ [laɪt] vi (pt & pp lit or lighted) **to l. upon** trouver par hasard.

lightning ['laɪtnɪŋ] n Met (light) éclair m; (charge) foudre f; (flash of) l. éclair m; – a (speed) foudroyant; (visit) éclair inv; **l. conductor** paratonnerre m.

lightweight ['laɪtweɪt] a (cloth etc) léger; (not serious) pas sérieux, léger.

like¹ [laɪk] a (alike) semblable, pareil; – prep comme; **l. this** comme ça; **what's he l.?** (physically, as character) comment est-il?; **to be or look l.** ressembler à; **what was the book l.?** comment as-tu trouvé le livre? **I have one l. it** j'en ai un pareil; – adv nothing l. as big/etc loin d'être aussi grand/etc; – conj (as) Fam comme; **it's l.** c'est comme je vous le dis; – n . . . **and the l.** . . . et ainsi de suite; **the l. of which we shan't see again** comme on n'en reverra plus; **the likes of you** des gens de ton acabit.

lik/e² [laɪk] vt aimer (bien) (**to do, doing** faire); **I l. him** je l'aime bien, il me plaît; **she likes it here** elle se plaît ici; **to l. best** préférer; **I'd l. to come** (want) je voudrais (bien) or j'aimerais (bien) venir; **I'd l. a kilo of apples** je voudrais un kilo de pommes; **would you l. a cigar?** voulez-vous un cigare?; **if you l.** si vous voulez; (**how**) **would you l. to come?** ça te plairait or te dirait de venir?; – npl one's likes **mpl.** ◆**-ing** n **a l. for** (person) de la sympathie pour; (thing) du goût pour; **to my l.** à mon goût. ◆**likeable** a sympathique.

likely ['laɪklɪ] a (-ier, -iest) (event, result etc) probable; (excuse) vraisemblable; (place) propice; (candidate) prometteur; **a l. excuse!** Iron belle excuse!; **it's l.** (that) **she'll come** il est probable qu'elle viendra; **he's l. to come** il viendra probablement; **he's not l. to come** il ne risque pas de venir; – adv very l. très probablement; **not l.!** pas question! ◆**likelihood** n probabilité f; **there's little l. that** il y a peu de chances que (+ sub).

liken ['laɪkən] vt comparer (**to** à).

likeness ['laɪknɪs] n ressemblance f; **a family l.** un air de famille; **it's a good l.** c'est très ressemblant.

likewise ['laɪkwaɪz] adv (similarly) de même, pareillement.

lilac ['laɪlək] n lilas m; – a (colour) lilas inv.

Lilo® ['laɪləʊ] n (pl -os) matelas m pneumatique.

lilt [lɪlt] n Mus cadence f.

lily ['lɪlɪ] n lis m, lys m; **l. of the valley** muguet m.

limb [lɪm] n Anat membre m; **to be out on a l.** Fig être le seul de son opinion.

limber ['lɪmbər] vi **to l. up** faire des exercices d'assouplissement.

limbo (in) [ɪn'lɪmbəʊ] adv (uncertain, waiting) dans l'expectative.

lime [laɪm] n **1** (tree) tilleul m. **2** (substance) chaux f. **3** (fruit) lime f, citron m vert; **l. juice** jus m de citron vert.

limelight ['laɪmlaɪt] n **in the l.** (glare of publicity) en vedette.

limit ['lɪmɪt] n limite f; (restriction) limitation f (of de); **that's the l.!** Fam c'est le comble!; **within limits** dans une certaine limite; – vt limiter (**to** à); **to l. oneself to doing** se borner à faire. ◆**-ed** a (restricted) limité; (mind) borné; (edition) à tirage limité; **l. company** Com société f à responsabilité limitée; (**public) l. company** (with shareholders) société f anonyme; **to a**

l. degree jusqu'à un certain point. ◆limi'tation n limitation f. ◆limitless a illimité.

limousine ['lɪməziːn] n (car) limousine f; (airport etc shuttle) Am voiture-navette f.

limp [lɪmp] 1 vi (of person) boiter; (of vehicle etc) Fig avancer tant bien que mal; − n to have a l. boiter. 2 a (-er, -est) (soft) mou; (flabby) flasque; (person, hat) avachi.

limpid ['lɪmpɪd] a (liquid) Lit limpide.

linchpin ['lɪntʃpɪn] n (person) pivot m.

linctus ['lɪŋktəs] n Med sirop m (contre la toux).

line¹ [laɪn] n ligne f; (stroke) trait m, ligne f; (of poem) vers m; (wrinkle) ride f; (track) voie f; (rope) corde f; (row) rangée f, ligne f; (of vehicles) file f; (queue) Am file f, queue f; (family) lignée f; (business) métier m, rayon m; (article) Com article m; one's lines (of actor) son texte m; (in household) Tel speaking) au téléphone; (at other end of line) au bout du fil; to be on the l. (at risk) être en danger; hold the l.! Tel ne quittez pas!; the hot l. Tel le téléphone rouge; to stand in l. Am faire la queue; to step or get out of l. Fig refuser de se conformer; (misbehave) faire une incartade; out of l. with (ideas etc) en désaccord avec; in l. with conforme à; he's in l. for (promotion etc) il doit recevoir; to take a hard l. adopter une attitude ferme; along the same lines (to work, think) de la même façon; sth along those lines qch dans ce genre-là; to drop a l. Fam envoyer un mot (to à); where do we draw the l.? où fixer les limites?; − vt (paper) régler; (face) rider; to l. the street (of trees) border la rue; (of people) faire la haie le long de la rue; to l. up (children, objects) aligner; (arrange) organiser; (get ready) préparer; to have sth lined up (in mind) avoir qch en vue; − vi to l. up s'aligner; (queue) Am faire la queue. ◆l.-up n (row) file f; Pol front m; TV programme(s) n(pl).

line² [laɪn] vt (clothes) doubler; (pockets) Fig se remplir. ◆lining n (of clothes) doublure f; (of brakes) garniture f.

lineage ['lɪnɪɪdʒ] n lignée f.

linear ['lɪnɪər] a linéaire.

linen ['lɪnɪn] n (sheets etc) linge m; (material) (toile f de) lin m, fil m.

liner ['laɪnər] n 1 (ship) paquebot m. 2 (dust)bin l. sac m poubelle.

linesman ['laɪnzmən] n (pl -men) Fb etc juge m de touche.

linger ['lɪŋɡər] vi to l. (on) (of person) s'attarder; (of smell, memory) persister; (of doubt) subsister. ◆-ing a (death) lent.

lingo ['lɪŋɡəʊ] n (pl -os) Hum Fam jargon m.

linguist ['lɪŋɡwɪst] n linguiste mf. ◆lin'guistic a linguistique. ◆lin'guistics n linguistique f.

liniment ['lɪnɪmənt] n onguent m, pommade f.

link [lɪŋk] vt (connect) relier (to à); (relate, associate) lier (to à); to l. up Tel relier; − vi to l. up (of roads) se rejoindre; − n (connection) lien m; (of chain) maillon m; (by road, rail) liaison f. ◆l.-up n TV Rad liaison f; (of spacecraft) jonction f.

lino ['laɪnəʊ] n (pl -os) lino m. ◆linoleum [lɪ'nəʊlɪəm] n linoléum m.

linseed ['lɪnsiːd] n l. oil huile f de lin.

lint [lɪnt] n Med tissu m ouaté; (fluff) peluche(s) f(pl).

lion ['laɪən] n lion m; l. cub lionceau m. ◆lioness n lionne f.

lip [lɪp] n Anat lèvre f; (rim) bord m; (cheek) Sl culot m. ◆l.-read vi (pt & pp -read [red]) lire sur les lèvres. ◆lipstick n (material) rouge m à lèvres; (stick) tube m de rouge.

liqueur [lɪ'kjʊər] n liqueur f.

liquid ['lɪkwɪd] n & a liquide (m). ◆liquefy vt liquéfier; − vi se liquéfier. ◆liquidizer n Culin (for fruit juices) centrifugeuse f; (for purées etc) robot m, moulinette® f.

liquidate ['lɪkwɪdeɪt] vt (debt, person) liquider. ◆liqui'dation n liquidation f.

liquor ['lɪkər] n alcool m, spiritueux m; l. store Am magasin m de vins et de spiritueux.

liquorice ['lɪkərɪʃ, -rɪs] n réglisse f.

lira, pl lire ['lɪərə, 'lɪəreɪ] n (currency) lire f.

lisp [lɪsp] vi zézayer; − n to have a l. zézayer.

list [lɪst] n 1 liste f; − vt (one's possessions etc) faire la liste de; (names) mettre sur la liste; (enumerate) énumérer; (catalogue) cataloguer. 2 vi (of ship) gîter. ◆—ed a (monument etc) classé.

listen ['lɪsən] vi écouter; to l. to écouter; to l. (out) for (telephone, person etc) tendre l'oreille pour, guetter; to l. in (to) Rad écouter. ◆—ing n écoute f (to de). ◆—er n Rad auditeur, -trice mf; to be a good l. (pay attention) savoir écouter.

listless ['lɪstləs] a apathique, indolent. ◆—ness n apathie f.

lit [lɪt] see light¹ 1.

litany ['lɪtənɪ] n Rel litanies fpl.

literal ['lɪtərəl] a littéral; (not exaggerated) réel. ◆—ly adv littéralement; (really) réellement; he took it l. il l'a pris au pied de la lettre.

literate ['lɪtərət] a qui sait lire et écrire;

highly l. (*person*) très instruit. ◆**literacy** *n* capacité *f* de lire et d'écrire; (*of country*) degré *m* d'alphabétisation.

literature ['lɪt(ə)rɪtʃər] *n* littérature *f*; (*pamphlets etc*) documentation *f*. ◆**literary** *a* littéraire.

lithe [laɪð] *a* agile, souple.

litigation [lɪtɪ'geɪʃ(ə)n] *n* Jur litige *m*.

litre ['liːtər] *n* litre *m*.

litter ['lɪtər] **1** *n* (*rubbish*) détritus *m*; (*papers*) papiers *mpl*; (*bedding for animals*) litière *f*; (*confusion*) Fig fouillis *m*; **l. basket** *or* **bin** boîte *f* à ordures; − *vt* **to l. (with papers** *or* **rubbish**) (*street etc*) laisser traîner des papiers *or* des détritus dans; **a street littered with** une rue jonchée de. **2** *n* (*young animals*) portée *f*.

little ['lɪt(ə)l] **1** *a* (*small*) petit; **the l. ones** les petits. **2** *a* & *n* (*not much*) peu (de); **l. time/money/etc** peu de temps/d'argent/*etc*; **I've l. left** il m'en reste peu; **she eats l.** elle mange peu; **to have l. to say** avoir peu de chose à dire; **as l. as possible** le moins possible; **a l. money/time/etc** (*some*) un peu d'argent/de temps/*etc*; **I have a l.** (*some*) j'en ai un peu; **the l. that I have** le peu que j'ai; − *adv* (*somewhat, rather*) peu; **a l. heavy/etc** un peu lourd/*etc*; **to work/etc a l.** travailler/*etc* un peu; **it's l. better** (*hardly*) ce n'est guère mieux; **l. by l.** peu à peu.

liturgy ['lɪtədʒɪ] *n* liturgie *f*.

live¹ [lɪv] *vi* (*reside*) habiter, vivre; **where do you l.?** où habitez-vous?; **to l. in Paris** habiter (à) Paris; **to l. off** *or* **on** (*eat*) vivre de; (*sponge on*) Pej vivre aux crochets *or* aux dépens de (*qn*); **to l. on** (*of memory etc*) survivre, se perpétuer; **to l. through** (*experience*) vivre; (*survive*) survivre à; **to l. up to** (*one's principles*) vivre selon; (*s.o.'s expectations*) se montrer à la hauteur de; − *vt* (*life*) vivre, mener; (*one's faith etc*) vivre pleinement; **to l. down** faire oublier (avec le temps); **to l. it up** Fam mener la grande vie.

live² [laɪv] **1** *a* (*alive, lively*) vivant; (*coal*) ardent; (*bomb*) non explosé; (*ammunition*) réel, de combat; (*wire*) El sous tension; (*switch*) El mal isolé; (*plugged in*) El branché; **a real l. king/etc** un roi/*etc* en chair et en os. **2** *a* & *adv* Rad TV en direct; **a l. broadcast** une émission en direct; **a l. audience** un *or* un public; **a l. recording** un enregistrement public.

livelihood ['laɪvlɪhʊd] *n* moyens *mpl* de subsistance; **my l.** mon gagne-pain; **to earn one's** *or* **a l.** gagner sa vie.

lively ['laɪvlɪ] *a* (**-ier, -iest**) (*person, style*)

vif, vivant; (*street, story*) vivant; (*interest, mind, colour*) vif; (*day*) mouvementé; (*forceful*) vigoureux; (*conversation, discussion*) animé. ◆**−iness** *n* vivacité *f*.

liven ['laɪv(ə)n] *vt* **to l. up** (*person*) égayer; (*party*) animer; − *vi* **to l. up** (*of person, party*) s'animer.

liver ['lɪvər] *n* foie *m*.

livery ['lɪvərɪ] *n* (*uniform*) livrée *f*.

livestock ['laɪvstɒk] *n* bétail *m*.

livid ['lɪvɪd] *a* (*blue-grey*) livide; (*angry*) Fig furieux; **l. with cold** blême de froid.

living ['lɪvɪŋ] **1** *a* (*alive*) vivant; **not a l. soul** (*nobody*) personne, pas âme qui vive; **within l. memory** de mémoire d'homme; **l. or dead** mort ou vif; **the l.** les vivants *mpl*. **2** *n* (*livelihood*) vie *f*; **to make a** *or* **one's l.** gagner sa vie; **to work for a l.** travailler pour vivre; **the cost of l.** le coût de la vie; − *a* (*standard, conditions*) de vie; (*wage*) qui permet de vivre; **l. room** salle *f* de séjour.

lizard ['lɪzəd] *n* lézard *m*.

llama ['lɑːmə] *n* (*animal*) lama *m*.

load [ləʊd] *n* (*object carried, burden*) charge *f*; (*freight*) chargement *m*, charge *f*; (*strain, weight*) poids *m*; **a l. of, loads of** (*people, money etc*) Fam un tas de, énormément de; **to take a l. off s.o.'s mind** ôter un grand poids à qn; − *vt* charger; **to l. down** *or* **up** charger (**with** de); − *vi* **to l. (up)** charger la voiture, le navire *etc*. ◆**−ed** *a* (*gun, vehicle etc*) chargé; (*dice*) pipé; (*rich*) Fam plein aux as; **a l. question** une question piège; **l. (down) with** (*debts*) accablé de.

loaf [ləʊf] **1** *n* (*pl* **loaves**) pain *m*; French **l.** baguette *f*. **2** *vi* **to l. (about)** fainéanter. ◆**−er** *n* fainéant, -ante *mf*.

loam [ləʊm] *n* (*soil*) terreau *m*.

loan [ləʊn] *n* (*money lent*) prêt *m*; (*money borrowed*) emprunt *m*; **on l. from** prêté par; (*out*) **on l.** (*book*) sorti; **may I have the l. of . . . ?** puis-je emprunter . . . ?; − *vt* (*lend*) prêter (**to** à).

loath [ləʊθ] *a* **l. to do** Lit peu disposé à faire.

loath·e [ləʊð] *vt* détester (**doing** faire). ◆**−ing** *n* dégoût *m*. ◆**loathsome** *a* détestable.

lobby ['lɒbɪ] **1** *n* (*of hotel*) vestibule *m*, hall *m*; Th foyer *m*. **2** *n* Pol groupe *m* de pression, lobby *m*; − *vt* faire pression sur.

lobe [ləʊb] *n* Anat lobe *m*.

lobster ['lɒbstər] *n* homard *m*; (*spiny*) langouste *f*.

local ['ləʊk(ə)l] *a* local; (*of the neighbourhood*) du *or* de quartier; (*regional*) du pays; **are you l.?** êtes-vous du coin *or* d'ici?; **the doctor is l.** le médecin est tout près d'ici; **a l. phone call** (*within town*) une communication urbaine; – *n* (*pub*) *Fam* bistrot *m* du coin, pub *m*; **she's a l.** elle est du coin; **the locals** (*people*) les gens du coin. ◆**lo'cality** *n* (*neighbourhood*) environs *mpl*; (*region*) région *f*; (*place*) lieu *m*; (*site*) emplacement *m*. ◆**localize** *vt* (*confine*) localiser. ◆**locally** *adv* dans les environs, dans le coin; (*around here*) par ici; (*in precise place*) localement.

locate [ləʊˈkeɪt] *vt* (*find*) repérer; (*pain, noise, leak*) localiser; (*situate*) situer; (*build*) construire. ◆**location** *n* (*site*) emplacement *m*; (*act*) repérage *m*; localisation *f*; **on l.** *Cin* en extérieur.

lock [lɒk] **1** *vt* **to l. (up)** fermer à clef; **to l. the wheels** *Aut* bloquer les roues; **to l. s.o. in** enfermer qn; **to l. s.o. in sth** enfermer qn dans qch; **to l. s.o. out** (*accidentally*) enfermer qn dehors; **to l. away** *or* **up** (*prisoner*) enfermer; (*jewels etc*) mettre sous clef, enfermer; – *vi* **to l. (up)** fermer à clef; – *n* (*on door, chest etc*) serrure *f*; (*of gun*) cran *m* de sûreté; (*turning circle*) *Aut* rayon *m* de braquage; **(anti-theft) l.** *Aut* antivol *m*; **under l. and key** sous clef. **2** *n* (*on canal*) écluse *f*. **3** *n* (*of hair*) mèche *f*. ◆**locker** *n* casier *m*; (*for luggage*) *Rail* casier *m* de consigne automatique; (*for clothes*) vestiaire *m* (métallique); **l. room** *Sp Am* vestiaire *m*. ◆**lockout** *n* (*industrial*) lock-out *m inv*. ◆**locksmith** *n* serrurier *m*.

locket [ˈlɒkɪt] *n* (*jewel*) médaillon *m*.

loco [ˈləʊkəʊ] *a* *Sl* cinglé, fou.

locomotion [ləʊkəˈməʊʃ(ə)n] *n* locomotion *f*. ◆**locomotive** *n* locomotive *f*.

locum [ˈləʊkəm] *n* (*doctor*) remplaçant, -ante *mf*.

locust [ˈləʊkəst] *n* criquet *m*, sauterelle *f*.

lodge [lɒdʒ] **1** *vt* (*person*) loger; (*valuables*) déposer (**with** chez); **to l. a complaint** porter plainte; – *vi* (*of bullet*) se loger (**in** dans); **to be lodging** (*accommodated*) être logé (**with** chez). **2** *n* (*house*) pavillon *m* de gardien *or* de chasse; (*of porter*) loge *f*. ◆**—ing** *n* (*accommodation*) logement *m*; *pl* (*flat*) logement *m*; (*room*) chambre *f*; **in lodgings** en meublé. ◆**—er** *n* (*room and meals*) pensionnaire *mf*; (*room only*) locataire *mf*.

loft [lɒft] *n* (*attic*) grenier *m*.

loft/y [ˈlɒftɪ] *a* (**-ier, -iest**) (*high, noble*) élevé; (*haughty*) hautain. ◆**—iness** *n* hauteur *f*.

log [lɒg] **1** *n* (*tree trunk*) rondin *m*; (*for fire*) bûche *f*, rondin *m*; **l. fire** feu *m* de bois. **2** *vt* (**-gg-**) (*facts*) noter; **to l. (up)** (*distance*) faire, couvrir. ◆**logbook** *n* *Nau Av* journal *m* de bord.

logarithm [ˈlɒgərɪðəm] *n* logarithme *m*.

loggerheads (at) [ætˈlɒgəhedz] *adv* en désaccord (**with** avec).

logic [ˈlɒdʒɪk] *n* logique *f*. ◆**logical** *a* logique. ◆**logically** *adv* logiquement.

logistics [ləˈdʒɪstɪks] *n* logistique *f*.

logo [ˈləʊgəʊ] *n* (*pl* **-os**) logo *m*.

loin [lɔɪn] *n* (*meat*) filet *m*.

loins [lɔɪnz] *npl* Anat reins *mpl*.

loiter [ˈlɔɪtər] *vi* traîner.

loll [lɒl] *vi* (*in armchair*) se prélasser.

lollipop [ˈlɒlɪpɒp] *n* (*sweet on stick*) sucette *f*; (*ice on stick*) esquimau *m*. ◆**lolly** *n* *Fam* sucette *f*; (*money*) *Sl* fric *m*; **(ice) l.** *Fam* esquimau *m*.

London [ˈlʌndən] *n* Londres *m or f*; – *a* (*taxi etc*) londonien. ◆**Londoner** *n* Londonien, -ienne *mf*.

lone [ləʊn] *a* solitaire; **l. wolf** *Fig* solitaire *mf*. ◆**loneliness** *n* solitude *f*. ◆**lonely** *a* (**-ier, -iest**) (*road, house, life etc*) solitaire; (*person*) seul, solitaire. ◆**loner** *n* solitaire *mf*. ◆**lonesome** *a* solitaire.

long¹ [lɒŋ] **1** *a* (**-er, -est**) long; **to be ten metres l.** être long de dix mètres, avoir dix mètres de long; **to be six weeks l.** durer six semaines; **how l. is ...** quelle est la longueur de ...?; (*time*) quelle est la durée de ...?; **a l. time** longtemps; **in the l. run** à la longue; **a l. face** une grimace; **a l. memory** une bonne mémoire; **l. jump** *Sp* saut *m* en longueur. **2** *adv* (*a long time*) longtemps; **l. before** longtemps avant; **has he been here l.?** il y a longtemps qu'il est ici?, il est ici depuis longtemps?; **how l. (ago)?** (il y a) combien de temps?; **not l. ago** il y a peu de temps; **before l.** sous *or* avant peu; **no longer** ne plus; **she no longer swims** elle ne nage plus; **a bit longer** (*to wait etc*) encore un peu; **I won't be l.** je n'en ai pas pour longtemps; **at the longest** (tout) au plus; **all summer l.** tout l'été; **l. live the queen/etc** vive la reine/*etc*; **as l. as, so l. as** (*provided that*) pourvu que (+ *sub*); **as l. as I live** tant que je vivrai.

long² [lɒŋ] *vi* **to l. for sth** avoir très envie de qch; **to l. for s.o.** languir après qn; **to l. to do** avoir très envie de faire. ◆**—ing** *n* désir *m*, envie *f*.

long-distance [lɒŋˈdɪstəns] *a* (*race*) de fond; (*phone call*) interurbain; (*flight*) long-courrier. ◆**long-drawn-'out** *a* interminable. ◆**long'haired** *a* aux cheveux longs. ◆**longhand** *n* écriture *f* normale. ◆**long-'playing** *a* **l.-playing record** 33 tours *m inv*. ◆**long-range** *a* (*forecast*) à long terme. ◆**long'sighted** *a* *Med* presbyte. ◆**long'standing** a de longue date. ◆**long'suffering** a très patient. ◆**long-'term** a à long terme. ◆**long-'winded** a (speech, speaker) verbeux.

longevity [lɒn'dʒevɪtɪ] n longévité f.

longitude ['lɒndʒɪtjuːd] n longitude f.

longways ['lɒŋweɪz] adv en longueur.

loo [luː] n (toilet) Fam cabinets mpl.

look [lʊk] n regard m; (appearance) air m, allure f; (good) looks la beauté, un beau physique; **to have a l. (at)** jeter un coup d'œil (à), regarder; **to have a l. (for)** chercher; **to have a l. (a)round** regarder; (walk) faire un tour; **let me have a l.** fais voir; **I like the l. of him** il me fait bonne impression, il me plaît; − vti regarder; **to l. s.o. in the face** regarder qn dans les yeux; **to l. tired/happy/etc** (seem) sembler or avoir l'air fatigué/heureux/etc; **to l. pretty/ugly** (be) être joli/laid; **to l. one's age** faire son âge; **l. here!** dites donc!; **you l. like or as if you're tired** tu as l'air fatigué, on dirait que tu es fatigué; **it looks like or as if she won't leave** elle n'a pas l'air de vouloir partir; **it looks like it!** c'est probable; **to l. like a child** avoir l'air d'un enfant; **to l. like an apple** avoir l'air d'être une pomme; **you l. like my brother** (resemble) tu ressembles à mon frère; **it looks like rain (to me)** il me semble or on dirait qu'il va pleuvoir; **what does he l. like?** (describe him) comment est-il?; **to l. well or good** (of person) avoir bonne mine; **you l. good in that hat/etc** ce chapeau/etc te va très bien; **that looks bad** (action etc) ça fait mauvais effet. ■ **to l. after** vt (deal with) s'occuper de; (patient, hair) soigner; (keep safely) garder (**for** s.o. pour qn); **to l. after oneself** (keep healthy) faire bien attention à soi; **I can l. after myself** (cope) je suis assez grand pour me débrouiller; **to l. around** vt (visit) visiter; − vi (have a look) regarder; (walk round) faire un tour; **to l. at** vt regarder; (consider) considérer, voir; (check) vérifier; **to l. away** vi détourner les yeux; **to l. back** vi regarder derrière soi; (in time) regarder en arrière; **to l. down** vi baisser les yeux; (from height) regarder en bas; **to l. down on** (consider scornfully) mépriser, regarder de haut; **to l. for** vt (seek) chercher; **to l. forward to** vt (event) attendre avec impatience; **to l. in** vi regarder (à l'intérieur); **to l. in on s.o.** Fam passer voir qn; **to l. into** vt (examine) examiner; (find out about) se renseigner sur; **to l. on** vi regarder; − vt (consider) considérer; **to l. out** vi (be careful) faire attention (**for** à); **to l. out for** (seek)

chercher; (watch) guetter; **to l. (out) on to** (of window, house etc) donner sur; **to l. over** or **through** vt (examine fully) examiner, regarder de près; (briefly) parcourir; (region, town) parcourir, visiter; **to l. round** vt (visit) visiter; − vi (have a look) regarder; (walk round) faire un tour; (look back) se retourner; **to l. round for** (seek) chercher; **to l. up** vi (of person) lever les yeux; (into the air or sky) regarder en l'air; (improve) s'améliorer; **to l. up to s.o.** Fig respecter qn; − vt (word) chercher; **to l. s.o. up** (visit) passer voir qn. ◆**-looking** suffix pleasant-/tired-/etc à l'air agréable/fatigué/etc. ◆**looking-glass** n glace f, miroir m.

lookout ['lʊkaʊt] n (soldier) guetteur m; (sailor) vigie f; **l. (post)** poste m de guet; (on ship) vigie f; **to be on the l.** faire le guet; **to be on the l. for** guetter.

loom [luːm] **1** vi **to l. (up)** (of mountain etc) apparaître indistinctement; Fig paraître imminent. **2** n Tex métier m à tisser.

loony ['luːnɪ] n & a Sl imbécile (mf).

loop [luːp] n (in river etc) & Av boucle f; (contraceptive device) stérilet m; − vt **to l. the loop** Av boucler la boucle. ◆**loophole** n (in rules) point m faible, lacune f; (way out) échappatoire f.

loose [luːs] a (-er, -est) (screw, belt, knot) desserré; (tooth, stone) branlant; (page) détaché; (animal) libre, (set loose) lâché; (clothes) flottant; (hair) dénoué; (flesh) flasque; (wording, translation) approximatif, vague; (link) vague; (discipline) relâché; (articles) Com en vrac; (cheese, tea etc) Com au poids; (woman) Pej facile; **l. change** petite monnaie f; **l. covers** housses fpl; **l. living** vie f dissolue; **to get l.** (of dog, page) se détacher; **to set** or **turn l.** (dog etc) libérer, lâcher; **he's at a l. end** or Am **at l. ends** il ne sait pas trop quoi faire; − n **on the l.** (prisoner etc) en liberté; − vt (animal) lâcher. ◆**loosely** adv (to hang) lâchement; (to hold, tie) sans serrer; (to translate) librement; (to link) vaguement. ◆**loosen** vt (knot, belt, screw) desserrer; (rope) détendre; (grip) relâcher; − vi **to l. up** Sp faire des exercices d'assouplissement. ◆**looseness** n (of screw, machine parts) jeu m.

loot [luːt] n butin m; (money) Sl fric m; − vt piller. ◆**-ing** n pillage m. ◆**-er** n pillard, -arde mf.

lop [lɒp] vt (-pp-) **to l. (off)** couper.

lop-sided [lɒp'saɪdɪd] a (crooked) de travers; **to walk l.-sided** (limp) se déhancher.

loquacious [ləʊ'kweɪʃəs] a loquace.

lord [lɔːd] *n* seigneur *m*; (*title*) *Br* lord *m*; **good L.!** *Fam* bon sang!; **oh L.!** *Fam* mince!; **the House of Lords** *Pol* la Chambre des Lords; – *vt* **to l. it over s.o.** *Fam* dominer qn. ◆**lordly** *a* digne d'un grand seigneur; (*arrogant*) hautain. ◆**lordship** *n* **Your L.** (*to judge*) Monsieur le juge.

lore [lɔːr] *n* traditions *fpl*.

lorry ['lɒrɪ] *n* camion *m*; (*heavy*) poids *m* lourd; **l. driver** camionneur *m*; **long-distance l. driver** routier *m*.

los/e [luːz] *vt* (*pt & pp* lost) perdre; **to get lost** (*of person*) se perdre; **the ticket/etc got lost** on a perdu le billet/etc; **get lost!** *Fam* fiche le camp!; **to l. s.o. sth** faire perdre qch à qn; **to l. interest in** se désintéresser de; **I've lost my bearings** je suis désorienté; **the clock loses six minutes a day** la pendule retarde de six minutes par jour; – *vi* perdre; **to l. to s.o.** trouver la mort (in dans); – *vi* perdre; **to l. out** être perdant; **to l. to** *Sp* être battu par. ◆**—ing** *a* perdant; **l. battle** *Fig* une bataille perdue d'avance. ◆**—er** *n* perdant, -ante *mf*; (*failure in life*) paumé, -ée *mf*; **to be a good l.** être bon *or* beau joueur.

loss [lɒs] *n* perte *f*; **at a l.** (*confused*) perplexe; **to sell at a l.** *Com* vendre à perte; **at a l. to do** incapable de faire. ◆**lost** *a* perdu; **l. property**, *Am* **l. and found** objets *mpl* trouvés.

lot¹ [lɒt] *n* **1** (*destiny*) sort *m*; (*batch, land*) lot *m*; **to draw lots** tirer au sort; **parking l.** *Am* parking *m*; **a bad l.** (*person*) *Fam* un mauvais sujet. **2 the l.** (*everything*) (le) tout; **the l. of you** vous tous; **a l. of, lots of** beaucoup de; **a l.** beaucoup; **quite a l.** pas mal (**of** de); **such a l.** tellement (**of** de), tant (**of** de); **what a l. of flowers/water/etc!** que de fleurs/d'eau/etc!; **what a l.!** quelle quantité!; **what a l. of flowers/etc you have!** vous avez (beaucoup) de fleurs/etc!

lotion ['ləuʃ(ə)n] *n* lotion *f*.

lottery ['lɒtərɪ] *n* loterie *f*.

lotto ['lɒtəu] *n* (*game*) loto *m*.

loud [laud] *a* (**-er, -est**) bruyant; (*voice, radio*) fort; (*noise, cry*) grand; (*gaudy*) voyant; – *adv* (**of** to shout etc) fort; **out l.** tout haut. ◆**—ly** *adv* (*to speak, laugh etc*) bruyamment, fort; (*to shout*) fort. ◆**—ness** *n* (*of voice etc*) force *f*; (*noise*) bruit *m*. ◆**loud'hailer** *n* mégaphone *m*. ◆**loudmouth** *n* (*person*) *Fam* grande gueule *f*. ◆**loud'speaker** *n* haut-parleur *m*; (*of hi-fi unit*) enceinte *f*.

lounge [laundʒ] *n* **1** salon *m*; **l. suit** complet

m veston. **2** *vi* (*loll*) se prélasser; **to l. about** (*idle*) paresser; (*stroll*) flâner.

louse, *pl* **lice** [laus, laıs] **1** *n* (*insect*) pou *m*. **2** *n* (*person*) *Pej Sl* salaud *m*. **3** *vt* **to l. up** (*mess up*) *Sl* gâcher.

lousy ['lauzɪ] *a* (**-ier, -iest**) (*bad*) *Fam* infect; **l. with** (*crammed, loaded*) *Sl* bourré de.

lout [laut] *n* rustre *m*. ◆**loutish** *a* (*attitude*) de rustre.

love [lʌv] *n* amour *m*; *Tennis* zéro *m*; **in l.** amoureux (**with** de); **they're in l.** ils s'aiment; **art is his** *or* **her l.** l'art est sa passion; **yes, my l.** oui mon amour; – *vt* aimer; (*like very much*) adorer, aimer (**beaucoup**) (**to do, doing** faire); **give him** *or* **her my l.** (*greeting*) dis-lui bien des choses de ma part; **l. affair** liaison *f* (*amoureuse*). ◆**—ing** *a* affectueux, aimant. ◆**—able** *a* adorable. ◆**—er** *n* (*man*) amant *m*; (*woman*) maîtresse *f*; **a l. of** (*art, music etc*) un amateur de; **a nature l.** un amoureux de la nature. ◆**lovesick** *a* amoureux.

lovely ['lʌvlɪ] *a* (**-ier, -iest**) (*pleasing*) agréable, bon; (*excellent*) excellent; (*pretty*) joli; (*charming*) charmant; (*kind*) gentil; **the weather's l.** il fait beau; **l. to see you!** je suis ravi de te voir; **l. and hot/dry/etc** bien chaud/sec/etc.

low¹ [ləu] *a* (**-er, -est**) bas; (*speed, income, intelligence*) faible; (*opinion, quality*) mauvais; **she's l. on** (*money etc*) elle n'a plus beaucoup de; **to feel l.** (*depressed*) être déprimé; – *adv* (**-er, -est**) bas; **to turn** (**down**) **l.** mettre plus bas; **to run l.** (*of supplies*) s'épuiser; – *n Met* dépression *f*; **to reach a new l.** *or* **an all-time l.** (*of prices etc*) atteindre leur niveau le plus bas. ◆**low-'calorie** *a* (*diet*) (à) basses calories. ◆**low-'cost** *a* bon marché *inv*. ◆**low-cut** *a* décolleté. ◆**low-down** *a* méprisable. ◆**lowdown** *n* (*facts*) *Fam* tuyaux *mpl*. ◆**low-'fat** *a* (*milk*) écrémé; (*cheese*) de régime. ◆**low-'key** *a* (*discreet*) discret. ◆**lowland(s)** *n* plaine *f*. ◆**low-level** *a* bas. ◆**low-paid** *a* mal payé. ◆**low-'salt** *a* (*food*) à faible teneur en sel.

low² [ləu] *vi* (*of cattle*) meugler.

lower ['ləuər] *vt* baisser; **to l. s.o./sth** (*by rope*) descendre qn/qch; **to l. oneself** *Fig* s'abaisser. ◆**—ing** *n* (*drop*) baisse *f*.

lowly ['ləulɪ] *a* (**-ier, -iest**) humble.

loyal ['lɔɪəl] *a* loyal (**to** envers), fidèle (**to** à). ◆**loyalty** *n* loyauté *f*, fidélité *f*.

lozenge ['lɒzɪndʒ] *n* (*sweet*) *Med* pastille *f*; (*shape*) *Geom* losange *m*.

LP [el'piː] *abbr* = long-playing record.

L-plates ['elpleɪts] *npl Aut* plaques *fpl* d'apprenti conducteur.

Ltd *abbr (Limited) Com* SARL.

lubricate ['lu:brɪkeɪt] *vt* lubrifier; *Aut* graisser. ◆**lubricant** *n* lubrifiant *m*. ◆**lubri'cation** *n Aut* graissage *m*.

lucid ['lu:sɪd] *a* lucide. ◆**lu'cidity** *n* lucidité *f*.

luck [lʌk] *n (chance)* chance *f; (good fortune)* (bonne) chance *f,* bonheur *m; (fate)* hasard *m,* fortune *f;* **bad l.** malchance *f,* malheur *m;* **hard l.!, tough l.!** pas de chance!; **worse l.** *(unfortunately)* malheureusement. ◆**luckily** *adv* heureusement. ◆**lucky** *a* (-**ier,** -**iest**) *(person)* chanceux, heureux; *(guess, event)* heureux; **to be l.** *(of person)* avoir de la chance (to do de faire); **I've had a l. day** j'ai eu de la chance aujourd'hui; **l. charm** porte-bonheur *m inv;* **l. number**/*etc* chiffre *m/etc* porte-bonheur; **how l.!** quelle chance!

lucrative ['lu:krətɪv] *a* lucratif.

ludicrous ['lu:dɪkrəs] *a* ridicule.

ludo ['lu:dəʊ] *n* jeu *m* des petits chevaux.

lug [lʌg] *vt* (-**gg-**) *(pull)* traîner; **to l. around** trimbaler.

luggage ['lʌgɪdʒ] *n* bagages *mpl.*

lugubrious [lu:'gu:brɪəs] *a* lugubre.

lukewarm ['lu:kwɔ:m] *a* tiède.

lull [lʌl] **1** *n* arrêt *m; (in storm)* accalmie *f.* **2** *vt* (-**ll-**) apaiser; **to l. to sleep** endormir.

lullaby ['lʌləbaɪ] *n* berceuse *f.*

lumbago [lʌm'beɪgəʊ] *n* lumbago *m.*

lumber[1] ['lʌmbər] *n (timber)* bois *m* de charpente; *(junk)* bric-à-brac *m inv.* ◆**lumberjack** *n Am Can* bûcheron *m.* ◆**lumberjacket** *n* blouson *m.* ◆**lumber-room** *n* débarras *m.*

lumber[2] ['lʌmbər] *vt* **to l. s.o. with sth/s.o.** *Fam* coller qch/qn à qn; **he got lumbered with the chore** il s'est appuyé la corvée.

luminous ['lu:mɪnəs] *a (dial etc)* lumineux.

lump [lʌmp] *n* morceau *m; (in soup)* grumeau *m; (bump)* bosse *f; (swelling) Med* grosseur *f;* **l. sum** somme *f* forfaitaire; – *vt* **to l. together** réunir; *Fig Pej* mettre dans le même sac. ◆**lumpy** *a* (-**ier,** -**iest**) *(soup etc)* grumeleux; *(surface)* bosselé.

lunar ['lu:nər] *a* lunaire.

lunatic ['lu:nətɪk] *a* fou, dément; – *n* fou *m,* folle *f.* ◆**lunacy** *n* folie *f,* démence *f.*

lunch [lʌntʃ] *n* déjeuner *m;* **to have l.** déjeuner; **l. break, l. hour, l. time** heure *f* du déjeuner; – *vi* déjeuner (**on, off** de). ◆**luncheon** *n* déjeuner *m;* **l. meat** mortadelle *f,* saucisson *m;* **l. voucher** chèque-déjeuner *m.*

lung [lʌŋ] *n* poumon *m;* **l. cancer** cancer *m* du poumon.

lunge [lʌndʒ] *n* coup *m* en avant; – *vi* **to l. at s.o.** se ruer sur qn.

lurch [lɜ:tʃ] **1** *vi (of person)* tituber; *(of ship)* faire une embardée. **2** *n* **to leave s.o. in the l.** *Fam* laisser qn en plan, laisser tomber qn.

lure [lʊər] *vt* attirer (par la ruse) (**into** dans); – *n (attraction)* attrait *m.*

lurid ['lʊərɪd] *a (horrifying)* horrible, affreux; *(sensational)* à sensation; *(gaudy)* voyant; *(colour, sunset)* sanglant.

lurk [lɜ:k] *vi (hide)* se cacher (**in** dans); *(prowl)* rôder; *(of suspicion, fear etc)* persister.

luscious ['lʌʃəs] *a (food etc)* appétissant.

lush [lʌʃ] **1** *a (vegetation)* luxuriant; *(wealthy) Fam* opulent. **2** *n Am Sl* ivrogne *mf.*

lust [lʌst] *n (for person, object)* convoitise *f* (**for** de); *(for power, knowledge)* soif *f* (**for** de); – *vi* **to l. after** *(object, person)* convoiter; *(power, knowledge)* avoir soif de.

lustre ['lʌstər] *n (gloss)* lustre *m.*

lusty ['lʌstɪ] *a* (-**ier,** -**iest**) vigoureux.

lute [lu:t] *n Mus* luth *m.*

Luxembourg ['lʌksəmbɜ:g] *n* Luxembourg *m.*

luxuriant [lʌg'ʒʊərɪənt] *a* luxuriant. ◆**luxuriate** *vi (laze about)* paresser (**in bed**/*etc* au lit/*etc*).

luxury ['lʌkʃərɪ] *n* luxe *m; – a (goods, flat etc)* de luxe. ◆**luxurious** [lʌg'ʒʊərɪəs] *a* luxueux.

lying ['laɪɪŋ] *see* lie[1,2]; – *n* le mensonge; – *a (account)* mensonger; *(person)* menteur.

lynch [lɪntʃ] *vt* lyncher. ◆**—ing** *n* lynchage *m.*

lynx [lɪŋks] *n (animal)* lynx *m.*

lyre ['laɪər] *n Mus Hist* lyre *f.*

lyric ['lɪrɪk] *a* lyrique; – *npl (of song)* paroles *fpl.* ◆**lyrical** *a (effusive)* lyrique. ◆**lyricism** *n* lyrisme *m.*

M

M, m [em] n M, m m.

m abbr **1** (metre) mètre m. **2** (mile) mile m.

MA abbr = **Master of Arts.**

ma'am [mæm] n madame f.

mac [mæk] n (raincoat) Fam imper m.

macabre [məˈkɑːbrə] a macabre.

macaroni [mækəˈrəʊnɪ] n macaroni(s) m(pl).

macaroon [mækəˈruːn] n (cake) macaron m.

mace [meɪs] n (staff, rod) masse f.

Machiavellian [mækɪəˈvelɪən] a machiavélique.

machination [mækɪˈneɪʃ(ə)n] n machination f.

machine [məˈʃiːn] n (apparatus, car, system etc) machine f. ◆**machinegun** n mitrailleuse f; - vt (-nn-) mitrailler. ◆**machinery** n (machines) machines fpl; (works) mécanisme m; Fig rouages mpl. ◆**machinist** n (on sewing machine) piqueur, -euse mf.

macho [ˈmætʃəʊ] n (pl -os) macho m; - a (attitude etc) macho (f inv).

mackerel [ˈmækrəl] n inv (fish) maquereau m.

mackintosh [ˈmækɪntɒʃ] n imperméable m.

mad [mæd] a (madder, maddest) fou; (dog) enragé; (bull) furieux; **m. (at)** (angry) Fam furieux (contre); **to be m. (keen) on** Fam (person) être fou de; (films etc) se passionner or s'emballer pour; **to drive m. to go** Fam il m'a cassé les pieds pour que j'y aille; like m. comme un fou. ◆**maddening** a exaspérant. ◆**madhouse** n Fam maison f de fous. ◆**madly** adv (in love, to spend money etc) follement; (desperately) désespérément. ◆**madman** n (pl -men) fou m. ◆**madness** n folie f.

Madagascar [mædəˈgæskər] n Madagascar f.

madam [ˈmædəm] n (married) madame f; (unmarried) mademoiselle f.

made [meɪd] see **make.**

Madeira [məˈdɪərə] n (wine) madère m.

madonna [məˈdɒnə] n Rel madone f.

maestro [ˈmaɪstrəʊ] n (pl -os) Mus maestro m.

Mafia [ˈmæfɪə] n maf(f)ia f.

magazine [mægəˈziːn] n (periodical) magazine m, revue f; (of gun, camera) magasin m.

maggot [ˈmægət] n ver m, asticot m. ◆**maggoty** a véreux.

magic [ˈmædʒɪk] n magie f; - a (word, wand) magique. ◆**magical** a (evening etc) magique. ◆**magician** n magicien, -ienne mf.

magistrate [ˈmædʒɪstreɪt] n magistrat m.

magnanimous [mægˈnænɪməs] a magnanime.

magnate [ˈmægneɪt] n (tycoon) magnat m.

magnesium [mægˈniːzɪəm] n magnésium m.

magnet [ˈmægnɪt] n aimant m. ◆**magnetic** a magnétique. ◆**magnetism** n magnétisme m. ◆**magnetize** vt magnétiser.

magnificent [mægˈnɪfɪsənt] a magnifique. ◆**magnificence** n magnificence f. ◆**magnificently** adv magnifiquement.

magnify [ˈmægnɪfaɪ] vt (image) & Fig grossir; (sound) amplifier; **magnifying glass** loupe f. ◆**magnifi'cation** n grossissement m; amplification f. ◆**magnitude** n ampleur f.

magnolia [mægˈnəʊlɪə] n (tree) magnolia m.

magpie [ˈmægpaɪ] n (bird) pie f.

mahogany [məˈhɒgənɪ] n acajou m.

maid [meɪd] n (servant) bonne f; **old m.** Pej vieille fille f. ◆**maiden** n Old-fashioned jeune fille f; - a (speech etc) premier; (flight) inaugural; **m. name** nom m de jeune fille. ◆**maidenly** a virginal.

mail [meɪl] n (system) poste f; (letters) courrier m; - a (van, bag etc) postal; **m. order** vente f par correspondance; - vt mettre à la poste; **mailing list** liste f d'adresses. ◆**mailbox** n Am boîte f à or aux lettres. ◆**mailman** n (pl -men) Am facteur m.

maim [meɪm] vt mutiler, estropier.

main [meɪn] **1** a principal; **the m. thing is to** ... l'essentiel est de...; **m. line** Rail grande ligne f; **m. road** grande route f; **in the m.** (mostly) en gros, dans l'ensemble. **2** n water/gas m. conduite f d'eau/de gaz; **the mains** El le secteur; **a mains radio** une radio secteur. ◆**—ly** adv principalement, surtout. ◆**mainland** n continent m. ◆**main-**

stay n (of family etc) soutien m; (of organization, policy) pilier m. ◆**mainstream** n tendance f dominante.

maintain [meɪnˈteɪn] vt (continue, assert) maintenir (that que); (vehicle, family etc) entretenir; (silence) garder. ◆**maintenance** n (of vehicle, road etc) entretien m; (of prices, order, position etc) maintien m; (alimony) pension f alimentaire.

maisonette [meɪzəˈnet] n duplex m.

maize [meɪz] n (cereal) maïs m.

majesty [ˈmædʒəsti] n majesté f; **Your M.** (title) Votre Majesté. ◆**maˈjestic** a majestueux.

major [ˈmeɪdʒər] **1** a (main, great) & Mus majeur; **a m. road** une grande route. **2** n Mil commandant m; (subject) Univ Am dominante f; – vi to m. in se spécialiser en. ◆**majoˈrette** n (drum) majorette f.

Majorca [məˈjɔːkə] n Majorque f.

majority [məˈdʒɒrɪti] n majorité f (of de); **in the** or **a m.** en majorité, majoritaire; **the m. of people** la plupart des gens; – a (vote etc) majoritaire.

make [meɪk] vt (pt & pp made) faire; (tool, vehicle etc) fabriquer; (decision) prendre; (friends, wage) se faire; (points) Sp marquer; (destination) arriver à; to m. happy/tired/etc rendre heureux/fatigué/etc; **he made ten francs on it** Com ça lui a rapporté dix francs; **she made the train** (did not miss) elle a eu le train; **to m. s.o. do sth** faire qch à qn, obliger qn à faire qch; **to m. oneself heard** se faire entendre; **to m. oneself at home** se mettre à l'aise; **to m. ready** préparer; **to m. yellow** jaunir; **she made him her husband** elle en a fait son mari; **to m. do** (manage) se débrouiller (**with** avec); **to m. do with** (be satisfied with) se contenter de; **to m. it** (arrive) arriver; (succeed) réussir; (say) dire; **I m. it five o'clock** j'ai cinq heures; **what do you m. of it?** qu'en penses-tu? **I can't m. anything of it** je n'y comprends rien; **to m. a living** gagner sa vie; **you're made** (for life) ton avenir est assuré; **to m. believe** (pretend) faire semblant (**that one is** à être); (n) **it's m.-believe** (story etc) c'est pure invention; **to live in a world of m.-believe** se bercer d'illusions; – vi **to m. as if to** (appear to) faire mine de; **to m. for** (go towards) aller vers; – n (brand) marque f; **of French/etc m.** de fabrication française/etc. ■ **to m. off** vi (run away) se sauver; **to m. out** vt (see) distinguer; (understand) comprendre; (decipher) déchiffrer; (draw up) faire (cheque, liste); (claim) prétendre (that que);

you made me out to be silly tu m'as fait passer pour un idiot; – vi (manage) Fam se débrouiller; **to m. over** vt (transfer) céder; (change) transformer (**into** en); **to m. up** vt (story) inventer; (put together) faire (collection, liste, lit etc); (prepare) préparer; (form) former, composer; (loss) compenser; (quantity) compléter; (quarrel) régler; (one's face) maquiller; – vi (of friends) se réconcilier; **to m. up for** (loss, damage, fault) compenser; (lost time, mistake) rattraper. ◆**m.-up** n (of object etc) constitution f; (of person) caractère m; (for face) maquillage m. ◆**making** n (manufacture) fabrication f; (of dress) confection f; **history in the m.** l'histoire en train de se faire; **the makings of** les éléments mpl (essentiels) de; **to have the makings of a pianist**/etc avoir l'étoffe d'un pianiste/etc. ◆**maker** n Com fabricant m. ◆**makeshift** n expédient m; – a (arrangement etc) de fortune, provisoire.

maladjusted [mæləˈdʒʌstɪd] a inadapté.

malaise [mæˈleɪz] n malaise m.

malaria [məˈleərɪə] n malaria f.

Malaysia [məˈleɪzɪə] n Malaisie f.

male [meɪl] a Biol Bot etc mâle; (clothes, sex) masculin; – n (man, animal) mâle m.

malevolent [məˈlevələnt] a malveillant. ◆**malevolence** n malveillance f.

malfunction [mælˈfʌŋkʃ(ə)n] n mauvais fonctionnement m; – vi fonctionner mal.

malice [ˈmælɪs] n méchanceté f; **to bear s.o. m.** vouloir du mal à qn. ◆**maˈlicious** a malveillant. ◆**maˈliciously** adv avec malveillance.

malign [məˈlaɪn] vt (slander) calomnier.

malignant [məˈlɪgnənt] a (person etc) malfaisant; **m. tumour** Med tumeur f maligne. ◆**malignancy** n Med malignité f.

malingerer [məˈlɪŋgərər] n (pretending illness) simulateur, -euse mf.

mall [mɔːl] n (shopping) **m.** (covered) galerie f marchande; (street) rue f piétonnière.

malleable [ˈmælɪəb(ə)l] a malléable.

mallet [ˈmælɪt] n (tool) maillet m.

malnutrition [mælnjuːˈtrɪʃ(ə)n] n malnutrition f, sous-alimentation f.

malpractice [mælˈpræktɪs] n Med Jur faute f professionnelle.

malt [mɔːlt] n malt m.

Malta [ˈmɔːltə] n Malte f. ◆**Malˈtese** a & n maltais, -aise (mf).

mammal [ˈmæm(ə)l] n mammifère m.

mammoth [ˈmæməθ] a (large) immense; – n (extinct animal) mammouth m.

man [mæn] n (pl **men** [men]) homme m; (player) Sp joueur m; (chess piece) pièce f; a golf m. (enthusiast) un amateur de golf; he's a Bristol m. (by birth) il est de Bristol; to be m. and wife être mari et femme; my old m. Fam (father) mon père; (husband) mon homme; yes old m.! Fam oui mon vieux!; the m. in the street l'homme de la rue; – vt (-nn-) (ship) pourvoir d'un équipage; (fortress) armir; (guns) servir; (be on duty at) être de service à; manned spacecraft engin m spatial habité. ◆manhood n (period) âge m d'homme. ◆manhunt n chasse f à l'homme. ◆manlike a (quality) d'homme viril. ◆manly a (-ier, -iest) viril. ◆man-'made a artificiel; (fibre) synthétique. ◆manservant n (pl menservants) domestique m. ◆man-to-'man a & adv d'homme à homme.

manacle ['mænɪk(ə)l] n menotte f.

manag/e ['mænɪdʒ] vt (run) diriger; (affairs etc) Com gérer; (handle) manier; (take) Fam prendre; (eat) Fam manger; (contribute) Fam donner; to m. to do (succeed) réussir or arriver à faire; (contrive) se débrouiller pour faire; I'll m. it j'y arriverai; – vi (succeed) y arriver; (make do) se débrouiller (with avec); to m. without sth se passer de qch. ◆—ing a the m. director directeur m général; the m. director le PDG. ◆—eable a (parcel, person etc) maniable; (feasible) faisable. ◆—ement n direction f; (of property etc) gestion f; (executive staff) cadres mpl. ◆—er n directeur m; (of shop, café) gérant m; (business) m. (of actor, boxer etc) manager m. ◆manage'ress n directrice f; gérante f. ◆managerial [mænə'dʒɪərɪəl] a directorial; the m. class or staff les cadres mpl.

mandarin ['mændərɪn] 1 n (high-ranking official) haut fonctionnaire m; (in political party) bonze m; (in university) Pej mandarin m. 2 a & n m. (orange) mandarine f.

mandate ['mændeɪt] n mandat m. ◆mandatory a obligatoire.

mane [meɪn] n crinière f.

maneuver [mə'nuːvər] n & vti Am = manoeuvre.

mangle ['mæŋg(ə)l] 1 n (for wringing) essoreuse f; – vt (clothes) essorer. 2 vt (damage) mutiler.

mango ['mæŋgəʊ] n (pl -oes or -os) (fruit) mangue f.

mangy ['meɪndʒɪ] a (animal) galeux.

manhandle [mæn'hænd(ə)l] vt maltraiter.

manhole ['mænhəʊl] n trou m d'homme; m. cover plaque f d'égout.

mania ['meɪnɪə] n manie f. ◆maniac n fou m, folle f; Psy Med maniaque mf; sex m. obsédé m sexuel.

manicure ['mænɪkjʊər] n soin m des mains; – vt (person) manucurer; (s.o.'s nails) faire. ◆manicurist n manucure mf.

manifest ['mænɪfest] 1 a (plain) manifeste. 2 vt (show) manifester.

manifesto [mænɪ'festəʊ] n (pl -os or -oes) Pol manifeste m.

manifold ['mænɪfəʊld] a multiple.

manipulate [mə'nɪpjʊleɪt] vt manœuvrer; (facts, electors etc) Pej manipuler. ◆manipu'lation n manœuvre f; Pej manipulation f (of de).

mankind [mæn'kaɪnd] n (humanity) le genre humain.

manner ['mænər] n (way) manière f; (behaviour) attitude f, comportement m; pl (social habits) manières fpl; in this m. (like this) de cette manière; all m. of toutes sortes de. ◆mannered a (affected) maniéré; well-/bad-m. bien/mal élevé. ◆mannerism n Pej tic m.

manoeuvre [mə'nuːvər] n manœuvre f; – vti manœuvrer. ◆manoeuvra'bility n (of vehicle etc) maniabilité f.

manor ['mænər] n m. (house) manoir m.

manpower ['mænpaʊər] n (labour) main-d'œuvre f; Mil effectifs mpl; (effort) force f.

mansion ['mænʃ(ə)n] n hôtel m particulier; (in country) manoir m.

manslaughter ['mænslɔːtər] n Jur homicide m involontaire.

mantelpiece ['mænt(ə)lpiːs] n (shelf) cheminée f.

mantle ['mænt(ə)l] n (cloak) cape f.

manual ['mænjʊəl] 1 a (work etc) manuel. 2 n (book) manuel m.

manufacture [mænjʊ'fæktʃər] vt fabriquer; – n fabrication f. ◆—er n fabricant, -ante mf.

manure [mə'njʊər] n fumier m, engrais m.

manuscript ['mænjʊskrɪpt] n manuscrit m.

many ['menɪ] a & n beaucoup (de); m. things beaucoup de choses; m. came beaucoup sont venus; very m., a good or great m. un très grand nombre (de); (a good or great) m. of un (très) grand nombre de; m. of them un grand nombre d'entre eux; m. times, m. a time bien des fois; m. kinds toutes sortes (de); how m.? combien (de)?; too m. trop (de); one too m. un de trop; there are too m. of them ils sont trop nombreux; so m. tant (de); as m. books/etc

map 500 Marxism

as autant de livres/*etc* que; **as m. as** (*up to*) jusqu'à.

map [mæp] *n* (*of country etc*) carte *f*; (*plan*) plan *m*; − *vt* (**-pp-**) faire la carte *or* le plan de; **to m. out** (*road*) faire le tracé de; (*one's day etc*) *Fig* organiser.

maple ['meip(ə)l] *n* (*tree, wood*) érable *m*.

mar [mɑːr] *vt* (**-rr-**) gâter.

marathon ['mærəθɒn] *n* marathon *m*.

maraud [mə'rɔːd] *vi* piller. ◆**—ing** *a* pillard. ◆**—er** *n* pillard, -arde *mf*.

marble ['mɑːb(ə)l] *n* (*substance*) marbre *m*; (*toy ball*) bille *f*.

march [mɑːtʃ] *n Mil* marche *f*; − *vi Mil* marcher (au pas); **to m. in/out/etc** *Fig* entrer/sortir/*etc* d'un pas décidé; **to m. past** défiler; − *vt* **to m. s.o. off** *or* **away** emmener qn. ◆**m.-past** *n* défilé *m*.

March [mɑːtʃ] *n* mars *m*.

mare [meər] *n* jument *f*.

margarine [mɑːdʒə'riːn] *n* margarine *f*.

margin ['mɑːdʒɪn] *n* (*of page etc*) marge *f*; **by a narrow m.** (*to win*) de justesse. ◆**marginal** *a* marginal; **m. seat** *Pol* siège *m* disputé. ◆**marginally** *adv* très légèrement.

marguerite [mɑːgə'riːt] *n* (*daisy*) marguerite *f*.

marigold ['mærɪgəʊld] *n* (*flower*) souci *m*.

marijuana [mærɪ'wɑːnə] *n* marijuana *f*.

marina [mə'riːnə] *n* marina *f*.

marinate ['mærɪneɪt] *vti Culin* mariner.

marine [mə'riːn] **1** *a* (*life, flora etc*) marin. **2** *n* (*soldier*) fusilier *m* marin, *Am* marine *m*.

marionette [mærɪə'net] *n* marionnette *f*.

marital ['mærɪt(ə)l] *a* matrimonial; (*relations*) conjugal; **m. status** situation *f* de famille.

maritime ['mærɪtaɪm] *a* (*province, climate etc*) maritime.

marjoram ['mɑːdʒərəm] *n* (*spice*) marjolaine *f*.

mark[1] [mɑːk] *n* (*symbol*) marque *f*; (*stain, trace*) trace *f*, tache *f*, marque *f*; (*token, sign*) *Fig* signe *m*; (*for exercise etc*) *Sch* note *f*; (*target*) but *m*; (*model*) *Tech* série *f*; **to make one's m.** *Fig* s'imposer; **up to the m.** (*person, work*) à la hauteur; − *vt* marquer; (*exam etc*) *Sch* corriger, noter; (*pay attention to*) faire attention à; **to m. time** *Mil* marquer le pas; *Fig* piétiner; **m. you . . . !** remarquez que . . . !; **to m. down** (*price*) baisser; **to m. off** (*separate*) séparer; (*on list*) cocher; **to m. out** (*area*) délimiter; **to m. s.o. out for** désigner qn pour; **to m. up** (*increase*) augmenter. ◆**—ed** *a* (*noticeable*) marqué. ◆**—edly** [-ɪdlɪ] *adv* visiblement.

◆**—ing(s)** *n*(*pl*) (*on animal etc*) marques *fpl*; (*on road*) signalisation *f* horizontale. ◆**—er** *n* (*flag etc*) marque *f*; (*pen*) feutre *m*, marqueur *m*.

mark[2] [mɑːk] *n* (*currency*) mark *m*.

market ['mɑːkɪt] *n* marché *m*; **on the open m.** en vente libre; **on the black m.** au marché noir; **the Common M.** le Marché commun; **m. value** valeur *f* marchande; **m. price** prix *m* courant; **m. gardener** maraîcher, -ère *mf*; − *vt* (*sell*) vendre; (*launch*) commercialiser. ◆**—ing** *n* marketing *m*, vente *f*. ◆**—able** *a* vendable.

marksman ['mɑːksmən] *n* (*pl* **-men**) tireur *m* d'élite.

marmalade ['mɑːməleɪd] *n* confiture *f* d'oranges.

maroon [mə'ruːn] *a* (*colour*) bordeaux *inv*.

marooned [mə'ruːnd] *a* abandonné; (*in snowstorm etc*) bloqué (by par).

marquee [mɑːkiː] *n* (*for concerts, garden parties etc*) chapiteau *m*; (*awning*) *Am* marquise *f*.

marquis ['mɑːkwɪs] *n* marquis *m*.

marrow ['mærəʊ] *n* **1** (*of bone*) moelle *f*. **2** (*vegetable*) courge *f*.

marr/y ['mærɪ] *vt* épouser, se marier avec; **to m.** (**off**) (*of priest etc*) marier; − *vi* se marier. ◆**—ied** *a* marié; (*life, state*) conjugal; **m. name** nom *m* de femme mariée; **to get m.** se marier. ◆**marriage** *n* mariage *m*; **to be related by m.** to être parent par alliance de; − *a* (*bond*) conjugal; (*certificate*) *de* mariage; **m. bureau** agence *f* matrimoniale. ◆**marriageable** *a* en état de se marier.

marsh [mɑːʃ] *n* marais *m*, marécage *m*. ◆**marshland** *n* marais *mpl*. ◆**marsh-'mallow** *n Bot Culin* guimauve *f*.

marshal ['mɑːʃ(ə)l] **1** *n* (*in army*) maréchal *m*; (*in airforce*) général *m*; (*at public event*) membre *m* du service d'ordre; *Jur Am* shérif *m*. **2** *vt* (**-ll-**, *Am* **-l-**) (*gather*) rassembler; (*lead*) mener cérémonieusement.

martial ['mɑːʃ(ə)l] *a* martial; **m. law** loi *f* martiale.

Martian ['mɑːʃ(ə)n] *n & a* martien, -ienne (*mf*).

martyr ['mɑːtər] *n* martyr, -yre *mf*; − *vt Rel* martyriser. ◆**martyrdom** *n* martyre *m*.

marvel ['mɑːv(ə)l] *n* (*wonder*) merveille *f*; (*miracle*) miracle *m*; − *vi* (**-ll-**, *Am* **-l-**) s'émerveiller (**at** de); − *vt* **to m. that** s'étonner de ce que (+ *sub or indic*). ◆**marvellous** *a* merveilleux.

Marxism ['mɑːksɪz(ə)m] *n* marxisme *m*. ◆**Marxist** *a & n* marxiste (*mf*).

marzipan ['mɑːzɪpæn] n pâte f d'amandes.

mascara [mæ'skɑːrə] n mascara m.

mascot ['mæskɒt] n mascotte f.

masculine ['mæskjʊlɪn] a masculin.
◆**mascu'linity** n masculinité f.

mash [mæʃ] n (for poultry etc) pâtée f; (potatoes) Culin purée f; – vt to m. (up) (crush) & Culin écraser; **mashed potatoes** purée f de pommes de terre.

mask [mɑːsk] n masque m; – vt (cover, hide) masquer (from à).

masochism ['mæsəkɪz(ə)m] n masochisme m. ◆**masochist** n masochiste mf. ◆**maso'chistic** a masochiste.

mason ['meɪs(ə)n] n maçon m. ◆**masonry** n maçonnerie f.

masquerade [mɑːskə'reɪd] n (gathering, disguise) mascarade f; – vi to m. as se faire passer pour.

mass¹ [mæs] n masse f; a m. of (many) une multitude de; (pile) un tas de, une masse de; **to be a m. of bruises** Fam être couvert de bleus; **masses of** Fam des masses de; **the masses** (people) les masses fpl; – a (education) de masse; (culture, demonstration) de masse; (protests, departure) en masse; (production) en série, en masse; (hysteria) collectif; **m. grave** fosse f commune; **the media** mass media mpl; – vi (of troops, people) se masser.

mass² [mæs] n Rel messe f.

massacre ['mæsəkər] n massacre m; – vt massacrer.

massage ['mæsɑːʒ] n massage m; – vt masser. ◆**ma'sseur** n masseur m.
◆**ma'sseuse** n masseuse f.

massive ['mæsɪv] a (solid) massif; (huge) énorme, considérable. ◆**—ly** adv (to increase, reduce etc) considérablement.

mast [mɑːst] n Nau mât m; Rad TV pylône m.

master ['mɑːstər] n maître m; (in secondary school) professeur m; a **m.'s degree** une maîtrise (in de); **M. of Arts/Science** (person) Univ Maître m ès lettres/sciences; **m. of ceremonies** (presenter) Am animateur, -trice mf; **m. card** carte f maîtresse; **m. stroke** coup m de maître; **m. key** passe-partout m inv; **old m.** (painting) tableau m de maître; **I'm my own m.** je ne dépends que de moi; – vt (control) maîtriser; (subject, situation) dominer; **she has mastered Latin** elle possède le latin. ◆**masterly** a magistral. ◆**mastery** n maîtrise f (of de).

mastermind ['mɑːstəmaɪnd] n (person) cerveau m; – vt organiser.

masterpiece ['mɑːstəpiːs] n chef-d'œuvre m.

mastic ['mæstɪk] n mastic m (silicone).

masturbate ['mæstəbeɪt] vi se masturber. ◆**mastur'bation** n masturbation f.

mat [mæt] 1 n tapis m, natte f; (at door) paillasson m; (table) m. (of fabric) napperon m; (hard) dessous-de-plat m inv; (place) m. set m (de table). 2 a (paint, paper) mat.

match¹ [mætʃ] n allumette f; **book of matches** pochette f d'allumettes. ◆**matchbox** n boîte f à allumettes. ◆**matchstick** n allumette f.

match² [mætʃ] n (game) Sp match m; (equal) égal, -ale mf; (marriage) mariage m; **to be a good m.** (of colours, people etc) être bien assortis; **he's a good m.** (man to marry) c'est un bon parti; – vt (of clothes) aller (bien) avec; **to m. (up to)** (equal) égaler; **to m. (up)** (plates etc) assortir; **to be well-matched** (of colours, people etc) être (bien) assortis, aller (bien) ensemble; – vi (go with each other) être assortis, aller (bien) ensemble. ◆**—ing** a (dress etc) assorti.

mate [meɪt] 1 n (friend) camarade mf; (of animal) mâle m, femelle f; (builder's/electrician's/etc m.) aide-maçon/-électricien/etc m. 2 vt (of animals) s'accoupler (with avec). 3 n Chess mat m; – vt faire ou mettre mat.

material [mə'tɪərɪəl] 1 a matériel; (important) important. 2 n (substance) matière f; (cloth) tissu m; (for book) matériaux mpl; **material(s)** (equipment) matériel m; **building material(s)** matériaux mpl de construction. ◆**materialism** n matérialisme m.
◆**materialist** n matérialiste mf.
◆**materia'listic** a matérialiste. ◆**materialize** vi se matérialiser. ◆**materially** adv matériellement; (well-off etc) sur le plan matériel.

maternal [mə'tɜːn(ə)l] a maternel.
◆**maternity** n maternité f; **m. hospital, m. unit** maternité f; – a (clothes) de grossesse; (allowance, leave) de maternité.

mathematical [mæθə'mætɪk(ə)l] a mathématique; **to have a m. brain** être doué pour les maths. ◆**mathema'tician** n mathématicien, -ienne mf. ◆**mathematics** n mathématiques fpl. ◆**maths**, Am ◆**math** n Fam maths fpl.

matinée ['mætɪneɪ] n Th matinée f.

matriculation [mətrɪkjʊ'leɪʃ(ə)n] *n Univ* inscription *f.*

matrimony ['mætrɪmənɪ] *n* mariage *m.* ◆**matri'monial** *a* matrimonial.

matrix, *pl* **-ices** ['meɪtrɪks, -ɪsɪz] *n Tech* matrice *f.*

matron ['meɪtrən] *n Lit* mère *f* de famille, dame *f* âgée; (*nurse*) infirmière *f* (en) chef. ◆**matronly** *a* (*air etc*) de mère de famille; (*mature*) mûr; (*portly*) corpulent.

matt [mæt] *a* (*paint, paper*) mat.

matted ['mætɪd] *a* m. hair cheveux *mpl* emmêlés.

matter[1] ['mætər] *n* matière *f*; (*affair*) affaire *f*, question *f*; (*thing*) chose *f*; no m.! (*no importance*) peu importe!; no m. what she does quoi qu'elle fasse; no m. where you go où que tu ailles; no m. who you are qui que vous soyez; no m. when quel que soit le moment; what's the m.? qu'est-ce qu'il y a?; what's the m. with you? qu'est-ce que tu as?; there's sth the m. il y a qch qui ne va pas; there's sth the m. with my leg j'ai qch à la jambe; there's nothing the m. with him il n'a rien; – *vi* (*be important*) importer (**to** à); it doesn't m. if/when/who/*etc* peu importe si/quand/qui/*etc*; it doesn't m.! ça ne fait rien!, peu importe! ◆**m.-of-'fact** *a* (*person, manner*) terre à terre; (*voice*) neutre.

matter[2] ['mætər] *n* (*pus*) *Med* pus *m.*

matting ['mætɪŋ] *n* (*material*) nattage *m*; a piece of m., some m. une natte.

mattress ['mætrɪs] *n* matelas *m.*

mature [mə'tʃʊər] *a* mûr; (*cheese*) fait; – *vt* (*person, plan*) (faire) mûrir; – *vi* mûrir; (*of cheese*) se faire. ◆**maturity** *n* maturité *f.*

maul [mɔːl] *vt* (*of animal*) mutiler; (*of person*) *Fig* malmener.

mausoleum [mɔːsə'lɪəm] *n* mausolée *m.*

mauve [məʊv] *a* & *n* (*colour*) mauve (*m*).

maverick ['mævərɪk] *n* & *a Pol* dissident, -ente (*mf*).

mawkish ['mɔːkɪʃ] *a* d'une sensiblerie excessive, mièvre.

maxim ['mæksɪm] *n* maxime *f.*

maximum ['mæksɪməm] *n* (*pl* **-ima** [-ɪmə] *or* **-imums**) maximum *m*; – *a* maximum (*f inv*), maximal. ◆**maximize** *vt* porter au maximum.

may [meɪ] *v aux* (*pt* **might**) **1** (*possibility*) he m. come il peut arriver; he might come il pourrait arriver; I m. or might be wrong il se peut que je me trompe, je me trompe peut-être; you m. or might have to je aurais pu; I m. or might have forgotten it je l'ai peut-être oublié; we m. or might as well go

nous ferions aussi bien de partir; she fears I m. or might get lost elle a peur que je ne me perde. **2** (*permission*) m. I stay? puis-je rester?; m. I? vous permettez?; you m. go tu peux partir. **3** (*wish*) m. you be happy (que tu) sois heureux. ◆**maybe** *adv* peut-être.

May [meɪ] *n* mai *m.*

mayhem ['meɪhem] *n* (*chaos*) pagaïe *f*; (*havoc*) ravages *mpl.*

mayonnaise [meɪə'neɪz] *n* mayonnaise *f.*

mayor [meər] *n* (*man, woman*) maire *m.* ◆**mayoress** *n* femme *f* du maire.

maze [meɪz] *n* labyrinthe *m.*

MC [em'siː] *abbr* = master of ceremonies.

me [miː] *pron* me, m'; (*after prep etc*) moi; (*to*) me (*indirect*) me, m'; she knows me elle me connaît; he helps me il m'aide; he gives (*to*) me il me donne; with me avec moi.

meadow ['medəʊ] *n* pré *m*, prairie *f.*

meagre ['miːgər] *a* maigre.

meal [miːl] *n* **1** (*food*) repas *m.* **2** (*flour*) farine *f.*

mealy-mouthed [miːlɪ'maʊðd] *a* mielleux.

mean[1] [miːn] *vt* (*pt* & *pp* **meant** [ment]) (*signify*) vouloir dire, signifier; (*destine*) destiner (**for** à); (*entail*) entraîner; (*represent*) représenter; (*refer to*) faire allusion à; to m. to do (*intend*) avoir l'intention de faire, vouloir faire; I m. it, I m. what I say je suis sérieux; to m. sth to s.o. (*matter*) avoir de l'importance pour qn; it means much to me (*name, face*) ça me dit qch; I didn't m. to! je ne l'ai pas fait exprès!; you were meant to come vous étiez censé venir. ◆**—ing** *n* sens *m*, signification *f.* ◆**meaningful** *a* significatif. ◆**meaningless** *a* qui n'a pas de sens; (*absurd*) *Fig* insensé.

mean[2] [miːn] *a* (**-er, -est**) (*stingy*) avare, mesquin; (*petty*) mesquin; (*nasty*) méchant; (*inferior*) misérable. ◆**—ness** *n* (*greed*) avarice *f*; (*nastiness*) méchanceté *f.*

mean[3] [miːn] *a* (*distance*) moyen; – *n* (*middle position*) milieu *m*; (*average*) *Math* moyenne *f*; the happy m. le juste milieu.

meander [mɪ'ændər] *vi* (*of river*) faire des méandres.

means [miːnz] *n*(*pl*) (*method*) moyen *m*(*pl*) (to do, of doing de faire); (*wealth*) moyens *mpl*; by m. of (*stick etc*) au moyen de; (*work, concentration*) à force de; by all m.! très certainement!; by no m. nullement; independent *or* private m. fortune *f* personnelle.

meant [ment] *see* **mean**[1].

meantime ['miːntaɪm] *adv* & *n* (in the) m. entre-temps. ◆**meanwhile** *adv* entre-temps.

measles ['miːz(ə)lz] *n* rougeole *f*.

measly ['miːzli] *a* (*contemptible*) *Fam* minable.

measur/e ['meʒər] *n* mesure *f*; (*ruler*) règle *f*; **made to m.** fait sur mesure; – *vt* mesurer; (*strength etc*) Fig estimer, mesurer; (*adjust, adapt*) adapter (**to** à); **to m. up** mesurer; – *vi* **to m. up to** être à la hauteur de. ◆**—ed** *a* (*careful*) mesuré. ◆**—ement** *n* (*of chest, waist etc*) tour *m*; *pl* (*dimensions*) mesures *fpl*; **your hip m.** ton tour de hanches.

meat [miːt] *n* viande *f*; (*of crab, lobster etc*) chair *f*; Fig substance *f*; **m. diet** régime *m* carné. ◆**meaty** *a* (*-ier, -iest*) (*fleshy*) charnu; (*flavour*) de viande; Fig substantiel.

mechanic [mɪ'kænɪk] *n* mécanicien, -ienne *mf*. ◆**mechanical** *a* mécanique; (*reply etc*) Fig machinal. ◆**mechanics** *n* (*science*) mécanique *f*; *pl* (*workings*) mécanisme *m*. ◆'**mechanism** *n* mécanisme *m*. ◆'**mechanize** *vt* mécaniser.

medal ['med(ə)l] *n* médaille *f*. ◆**me-'dallion** *n* (*ornament, jewel*) médaillon *m*. ◆**medallist** *n* médaillé, -ée *mf*; **to be a gold/silver m.** *Sp* être médaille d'or/d'argent.

meddle ['med(ə)l] *vi* (*interfere*) se mêler (**in** de); (*tamper*) toucher (**with** à). ◆**med-dlesome** *a* qui se mêle de tout.

media ['miːdɪə] *npl* **1** (*the (mass*) **m.** les médias *mpl*. **2** *see* **medium 2**.

mediaeval [medɪ'iːv(ə)l] *a* médiéval.

median ['miːdɪən] *a* **m. strip** *Aut Am* bande *f* médiane.

mediate ['miːdɪeɪt] *vi* servir d'intermédiaire (**between** entre). ◆**medi'ation** *n* médiation *f*. ◆**mediator** *n* médiateur, -trice *mf*.

medical [medɪk(ə)l] *a* médical; (*school, studies*) de médecine; (*student*) en médecine; – *n* (*in school, army*) visite *f* médicale; (*private*) examen *m* médical. ◆**medicated** *a* (*shampoo*) médical. ◆**medi'cation** *n* médicaments *mpl*. ◆**me'dicinal** *a* médicinal. ◆**medicine** *n* médecine *f*; (*substance*) médicament *m*; **m. cabinet, m. chest** pharmacie *f*.

medieval [medɪ'iːv(ə)l] *a* médiéval.

mediocre [miːdɪ'əukər] *a* médiocre. ◆**mediocrity** *n* médiocrité *f*.

meditate ['medɪteɪt] *vi* méditer (**on** sur). ◆**medi'tation** *n* méditation *f*. ◆**meditative** *a* méditatif.

Mediterranean [medɪtə'reɪnɪən] *a* méditerranéen; – *n* **the M.** la Méditerranée.

medium ['miːdɪəm] **1** *a* (*average, middle*) moyen. **2** *n* (*pl* **media** ['miːdɪə]) *Phys*

véhicule *m*; *Biol* milieu *m*; (*for conveying data or publicity*) support *m*; **through the m.** **of** par l'intermédiaire de; **the happy m.** le juste milieu. **3** *n* (*person*) médium *m*. ◆**m.-sized** *a* moyen, de taille moyenne.

medley ['medlɪ] *n* mélange *m*; *Mus* pot-pourri *m*.

meek [miːk] *a* (*-er, -est*) doux.

meet [miːt] *vt* (*pt & pp* **met**) (*encounter*) rencontrer; (*see again, join*) retrouver; (*pass in street, road etc*) croiser; (*fetch*) (aller *or* venir) chercher; (*wait for*) attendre; (*debt, enemy, danger*) faire face à; (*need*) combler; (*be introduced to*) faire la connaissance de; **to arrange to m. s.o.** donner rendez-vous à qn; – *vi* (*of people, teams, rivers, looks*) se rencontrer; (*of people by arrangement*) se retrouver; (*be introduced*) se connaître; (*of society*) se réunir; (*of trains, vehicles*) se croiser; **to m.** **up with** rencontrer; (*by arrangement*) retrouver; **to m. up** se rencontrer; se retrouver; **to m. with** (*accident, problem*) avoir; (*loss, refusal*) essuyer; (*obstacle, difficulty*) rencontrer; **to m. with s.o.** *Am* rencontrer qn; retrouver qn; – *n Sp Am* réunion *f*; **to make a m. with** *Fam* donner rendez-vous à. ◆**—ing** *n* réunion *f*; (*large*) assemblée *f*; (*between two people*) rencontre *f*; (*prearranged*) rendez-vous *m inv*; **in a m.** en conférence.

megalomania [megələʊ'meɪnɪə] *n* mégalomanie *f*. ◆**megalomaniac** *n* mégalomane *mf*.

megaphone ['megəfəʊn] *n* porte-voix *m inv*.

melancholy ['melənkəlɪ] *n* mélancolie *f*; – *a* mélancolique.

mellow ['meləʊ] *a* (*-er, -est*) (*fruit*) mûr; (*colour, voice, wine*) moelleux; (*character*) mûri par l'expérience; – *vi* (*of person*) s'adoucir.

melodrama ['melədrɑːmə] *n* mélodrame *m*. ◆**melodra'matic** *a* mélodramatique.

melody ['melədɪ] *n* mélodie *f*. ◆**me'lodic** *a* mélodique. ◆**me'lodious** *a* mélodieux.

melon ['melən] *n* (*fruit*) melon *m*.

melt [melt] *vi* fondre; **to m. into** (*merge*) Fig se fondre dans; – *vt* (*faire*) fondre; **to m.** **down** (*metal object*) fondre; **melting point** point *m* de fusion; **melting pot** Fig creuset *m*.

member ['membər] *n* membre *m*; **M. of** **Parliament** député *m*. ◆**membership** *n* adhésion *f* (**of à**); (*number*) nombre *m* de(s) membres; (*members*) membres *mpl*; **m.** **(fee)** cotisation *f*.

membrane ['membreɪn] n membrane f.

memento [mə'mentəʊ] n (pl -os or -oes) (object) souvenir m.

memo ['meməʊ] n (pl -os) note f; **m. pad** bloc-notes m. ◆**memo'randum** n note f; Pol Com mémorandum m.

memoirs ['memwɑːz] npl (essays) mémoires mpl.

memory ['memərɪ] n mémoire f; (recollection) souvenir m; **to the** or **in m. of** à la mémoire de. ◆**memorable** a mémorable. ◆**me'morial** a (plaque etc) commémoratif; – n monument m, mémorial m. ◆**memorize** vt apprendre par cœur.

men [men] see **man**. ◆**menfolk** n Fam hommes mpl.

menac/e ['menɪs] n danger m; (nuisance) Fam plaie f; (threat) menace f; – vt menacer. ◆**-ingly** adv (to say) d'un ton menaçant; (to do) d'une manière menaçante.

menagerie [mɪ'nædʒərɪ] n ménagerie f.

mend [mend] vt (repair) réparer; (clothes) raccommoder; **to m. one's ways** se corriger, s'amender; – n raccommodage m; **to be on the m.** (after illness) aller mieux.

menial ['miːnɪəl] a inférieur.

meningitis [menɪn'dʒaɪtɪs] n Med méningite f.

menopause ['menəpɔːz] n ménopause f.

menstruation [menstrʊ'eɪʃ(ə)n] n menstruation f.

mental ['ment(ə)l] a mental; (hospital) psychiatrique; (mad) Sl fou; **m. strain** tension f nerveuse. ◆**men'tality** n mentalité f. ◆**mentally** adv mentalement; **he's m. handicapped** c'est un handicapé mental; **she's m. ill** c'est une malade mentale.

mention ['menʃ(ə)n] vt mentionner, faire mention de; **not to m. . . .** sans parler de . . . , sans compter . . . ; **don't m. it!** il n'y a pas de quoi!; **no savings/etc worth mentioning** pratiquement pas d'économies/etc; – n mention f.

mentor ['mentɔː] n (adviser) mentor m.

menu ['menjuː] n menu m.

mercantile ['mɜːkəntaɪl] a (activity etc) commercial; (ship) marchand; (nation) commerçant.

mercenary ['mɜːsɪnərɪ] a & n mercenaire (m).

merchandise ['mɜːtʃəndaɪz] n (articles) marchandises fpl; (total stock) marchandise f.

merchant ['mɜːtʃ(ə)nt] n (trader) Fin négociant, -ante mf; (retail) **m.** commerçant m (en détail); **wine m.** négociant, -ante mf en vins; (shopkeeper) marchand m de

vins; – a (vessel, navy) marchand; (seaman) de la marine marchande; **m. bank** banque f de commerce.

mercury ['mɜːkjʊrɪ] n mercure m.

mercy ['mɜːsɪ] n pitié f; Rel miséricorde f; **to beg for m.** demander grâce; **at the m. of** à la merci de; **it's a m. that . . .** (stroke of luck) c'est une chance que . . . . ◆**merciful** a miséricordieux. ◆**mercifully** adv (fortunately) Fam heureusement. ◆**merciless** a impitoyable.

mere [mɪər] a simple; (only) ne . . . que; **she's a m. child** ce n'est qu'une enfant; **it's a m. kilometre** ça ne fait qu'un kilomètre; **by m. chance** par pur hasard; **the m. sight of** her or him sa seule vue. ◆**-ly** adv (tout) simplement.

merg/e [mɜːdʒ] vi (blend) se mêler (with à); (of roads) se (re)joindre; (of firms) Com fusionner; – vt (unify) Pol unifier; Com fusionner. ◆**-er** n Com fusion f.

meridian [mə'rɪdɪən] n méridien m.

meringue [mə'ræŋ] n (cake) meringue f.

merit ['merɪt] n mérite m; **on its merits** (to consider sth etc) objectivement; – vt mériter.

mermaid ['mɜːmeɪd] n (woman) sirène f.

merry ['merɪ] a (-ier, -iest) gai; (drunk) Fam éméché. ◆**m.-go-round** n (at funfair etc) manège m. ◆**m.-making** n réjouissances fpl. ◆**merrily** adv gaiement. ◆**merriment** n gaieté f, rires mpl.

mesh [meʃ] n (of net etc) maille f; (fabric) tissu m à mailles; (of intrigue etc) Fig réseau m; (of circumstances) Fig engrenage m; **wire m.** grillage m.

mesmerize ['mezmeraɪz] vt hypnotiser.

mess¹ [mes] **1** n (confusion) désordre m, pagaie f; (muddle) gâchis m; (dirt) saleté f; **in a m.** en désordre; (trouble) Fam dans le pétrin; (pitiful state) dans un triste état; **to make a m. of** (spoil) gâcher. **2** vi **to m. s.o. about** (bother, treat badly) Fam déranger qn, embêter qn; **to m. up** (spoil) gâcher; (dirty) salir; (room) mettre en désordre; – vi **to m. about** (have fun, idle) s'amuser; (play the fool) faire l'idiot; **to m. about with** (fiddle with) s'amuser avec. ◆**m.-up** n (disorder) Fam gâchis m. ◆**messy** a (-ier, -iest) (untidy) en désordre; (dirty) sale; (confused) Fig embrouillé, confus.

mess² [mes] n Mil mess m inv.

message ['mesɪdʒ] n message m. ◆**messenger** n messager, -ère mf; (in office, hotel) coursier, -ière mf.

Messiah [mɪ'saɪə] n Messie m.

Messrs ['mesəz] npl M. Brown Messieurs or MM Brown.

met [met] see **meet**.

metal ['met(ə)l] n métal m. ◆**me'tallic** a métallique; (paint) métallisé. ◆**metalwork** n (objects) ferronnerie f; (study, craft) travail m des métaux.

metamorphosis, pl **-oses** [metə'mɔːfəsɪs, -əsiːz] n métamorphose f.

metaphor ['metəfər] n métaphore f. ◆**meta'phorical** a métaphorique.

metaphysical [metə'fɪzɪk(ə)l] a métaphysique.

mete [miːt] vt to m. out (justice) rendre; (punishment) infliger.

meteor ['miːtɪər] n météore m. ◆**mete'oric** a m. rise Fig ascension f fulgurante. ◆**meteorite** n météorite m.

meteorological [miːtɪərə'lɒdʒɪk(ə)l] a météorologique. ◆**meteo'rology** n météorologie f.

meter ['miːtər] n (device) compteur m; (parking) m. parcmètre m; m. maid Aut Fam contractuelle f.

method ['meθəd] n méthode f. ◆**me'thodical** a méthodique.

Methodist ['meθədɪst] a & n Rel méthodiste (mf).

methylated ['meθɪleɪtɪd] a m. spirit(s) alcool m à brûler. ◆**meths** n Fam = methylated spirits.

meticulous [mɪ'tɪkjʊləs] a méticuleux. ◆**—ness** n soin m méticuleux.

metre ['miːtər] n mètre m. ◆**metric** ['metrɪk] a métrique.

metropolis [mə'trɒpəlɪs] n (chief city) métropole f. ◆**metro'politan** a métropolitain.

mettle ['met(ə)l] n courage m, fougue f.

mew [mjuː] vi (of cat) miauler.

mews [mjuːz] n (street) ruelle f; m. flat appartement m chic (aménagé dans une ancienne écurie).

Mexico ['meksɪkəʊ] n Mexique m. ◆**Mexican** a & n mexicain, -aine (mf).

mezzanine ['mezəniːn] n m. (floor) entresol m.

miaow [miːˈaʊ] vi (of cat) miauler; – n miaulement m; – int miaou.

mice [maɪs] see **mouse**.

mickey ['mɪkɪ] n to take the m. out of s.o. Sl charrier qn.

micro- ['maɪkrəʊ] pref micro-.

microbe ['maɪkrəʊb] n microbe m.

microchip ['maɪkrəʊtʃɪp] n puce f.

microcosm ['maɪkrəʊkɒz(ə)m] n microcosme m.

microfilm ['maɪkrəʊfɪlm] n microfilm m.

microphone ['maɪkrəfəʊn] n microphone m.

microscope ['maɪkrəskəʊp] n microscope m. ◆**micro'scopic** a microscopique.

microwave ['maɪkrəʊweɪv] n micro-onde f; m. oven four m à micro-ondes.

mid [mɪd] a (in) m.-June (à) la mi-juin; (in) m. morning au milieu de la matinée; in m. air en plein ciel; to be in one's m.-twenties avoir environ vingt-cinq ans.

midday [mɪd'deɪ] n midi m; – a de midi.

middle ['mɪd(ə)l] n milieu m; (waist) Fam taille f; (right) in the m. of au (beau) milieu de; in the m. of work en plein travail; in the m. of saying/working/etc en train de dire/travailler/etc; – a (central) du milieu; (class, ear, quality) moyen; (name) deuxième. ◆**m.-'aged** a d'un certain âge. ◆**m.-'class** a bourgeois. ◆**m.-of-the-'road** a (politics, views) modéré; (music, tastes) sage.

middling ['mɪdlɪŋ] a moyen, passable.

midge [mɪdʒ] n (fly) moucheron m.

midget ['mɪdʒɪt] n nain m, naine f; – a minuscule.

Midlands ['mɪdləndz] npl the M. les comtés mpl du centre de l'Angleterre.

midnight ['mɪdnaɪt] n minuit f.

midriff ['mɪdrɪf] n Anat diaphragme m; (belly) Fam ventre m.

midst [mɪdst] n in the m. of (middle) au milieu de; in/our/their m. parmi nous/eux.

midsummer [mɪd'sʌmər] n milieu m de l'été; (solstice) solstice m d'été. ◆**midwinter** n milieu m de l'hiver; solstice m d'hiver.

midterm ['mɪdtɜːm] a m. holidays Sch petites vacances fpl.

midway [mɪd'weɪ] a & adv à mi-chemin.

midweek [mɪd'wiːk] n milieu m de la semaine.

midwife ['mɪdwaɪf] n (pl -wives) sage-femme f.

might [maɪt] 1 see **may**. 2 n (strength) force f. ◆**mighty** a (-ier, -iest) puissant; (ocean) vaste; (very great) Fam sacré; – adv (very) Fam rudement.

migraine ['miːgreɪn, 'maɪgreɪn] n Med migraine f.

migrate [maɪ'greɪt] vi émigrer. ◆'**migrant** a & n m. (worker) migrant, -ante (mf). ◆**migration** n migration f.

mike [maɪk] n Fam micro m.

mild [maɪld] a (-er, -est) (person, weather, taste etc) doux; (beer, punishment) léger; (medicine, illness) bénin. ◆**—ly** adv doucement; (*slightly*) légèrement; **to put it m.** pour ne pas dire plus. ◆**-ness** n douceur f; légèreté f; caractère m bénin.

mildew ['mɪldjuː] n (*on cheese etc*) moisissure f.

mile [maɪl] n mile m, mille m (= 1,6 km); pl (*loosely*) = kilomètres mpl; **to walk for miles** marcher pendant des kilomètres; **miles better** (*much*) *Fam* bien mieux. ◆**mileage** n = kilométrage m; (*per gallon*) = consommation f aux cent kilomètres. ◆**milestone** n = borne f kilométrique; *Fig* jalon m.

militant ['mɪlɪtənt] a & n militant, -ante (mf). ◆**military** a militaire; – **the m.** (*soldiers*) les militaires mpl; (*army*) l'armée f. ◆**militate** vi (*of arguments etc*) militer (**in favour of** pour).

militia [mə'lɪʃə] n milice f. ◆**militiaman** n (pl **-men**) milicien m.

milk [mɪlk] A 1 n; **evaporated m.** lait m concentré; – a (*chocolate*) au lait; (*bottle, can*) à lait; (*diet*) lacté; (*produce*) laitier; **m. float** voiture f de laitier; **m. shake** milk-shake m; – vt (*cow*) traire; (*extract*) *Fig* soutirer (**s.o. of sth** qch à qn); (*exploit*) *Fig* exploiter. ◆**-ing** n traite f. ◆**milkman** n (pl **-men**) laitier m. ◆**milky** a (**-ier, -iest**) (*diet*) lacté; (*coffee, tea*) au lait; (*colour*) laiteux; **the M. Way** la Voie lactée.

mill [mɪl] 1 n moulin m; (*factory*) usine f; **cotton m.** filature f de coton; **paper m.** papeterie f; – vt (*grind*) moudre. 2 vi **to m. around** (*of crowd*) grouiller. ◆**miller** n meunier, -ière mf. ◆**millstone** n (*burden*) boulet m (**round one's neck** qu'on traîne).

millennium [mɪ'lenɪəm] n (pl **-nia** [mɪ'lenɪə, -nɪə]) n millénaire m.

millet ['mɪlɪt] n *Bot* millet m.

milli- [mɪlɪ] pref milli-.

millimetre ['mɪlɪmiːtər] n millimètre m.

million ['mɪljən] n million m; **a m. men/etc** un million d'hommes/etc; **two m.** deux millions. ◆**millio'naire** n millionnaire mf. ◆**millionth** a & n millionième (mf).

mime [maɪm] n (*actor*) mime mf; (*art*) mime m; – vti mimer.

mimeograph® ['mɪmɪəgrɑːf] vt polycopier.

mimic ['mɪmɪk] vt (**-ck-**) imiter; – n imitateur, -trice mf. ◆**mimicking** n, ◆**mimicry** n imitation f.

mimosa [mɪ'məʊzə] n *Bot* mimosa m.

minaret [mɪnə'ret] n (*of mosque*) minaret m.

mince [mɪns] n (*meat*) hachis m (de viande); *Am* = **mincemeat**; – vt hacher; **not to m. matters** or **one's words** ne pas mâcher ses

mots. ◆**mincemeat** n (*dried fruit*) mélange m de fruits secs. ◆**mincer** n (*machine*) hachoir m.

mind [maɪnd] 1 n esprit m; (*sanity*) raison f; (*memory*) mémoire f; (*opinion*) avis m, idée f; (*thought*) pensée f; (*head*) tête f; **to change one's m.** changer d'avis; **to my m.** à mon avis; **in two minds** (*undecided*) irrésolu; **to make up one's m.** se décider; **to be on s.o.'s m.** (*worry*) préoccuper qn; **out of one's m.** (*mad*) fou; **to bring to m.** (*recall*) rappeler; **to bear** or **keep in m.** (*remember*) se souvenir de; **to have in m.** (*person, thing*) avoir en vue; **to have a good m. to do** avoir bien envie de faire. 2 vti (*heed*) faire attention à; (*look after*) garder, s'occuper de; (*noise, dirt etc*) être gêné par; (*one's language*) surveiller; **m. you don't fall** (*beware*) prends garde de ne pas tomber; **m. you do it** n'oublie pas de le faire; **do you m. if?** (*I smoke etc*) ça vous gêne si?; (*I leave, help etc*) ça ne vous fait rien si?; **I don't m. the sun** le soleil ne me gêne pas, je ne suis pas gêné par le soleil; **I don't m.** (*care*) ça m'est égal; **I wouldn't m. a cup of tea** (*would like*) j'aimerais bien une tasse de thé; **I m. that . . .** ça m'ennuie or me gêne que . . . ; **never m.!** (*it doesn't matter*) ça ne fait rien!, tant pis!; (*don't worry*) ne vous en faites pas!; **m. (out)!** (*watch out*) attention!; **m. you . . .** remarquez (que) . . . ; **m. your own business!**, **never you m.!** mêlez-vous de ce qui vous regarde! ◆**-ed** suffix **fair-m.** a impartial; **like-m.** a de même opinion. ◆**-er** n (*for children*) gardien, -ienne mf, (*nurse*) nourrice f; (*bodyguard*) *Fam* gorille m. ◆**mind-boggling** a stupéfiant, qui confond l'imagination. ◆**mindful** a **m. of sth/doing** attentif à qch/à faire. ◆**mindless** a stupide.

mine¹ [maɪn] poss pron le mien, la mienne, pl les mien(ne)s; **this hat is m.** ce chapeau est à moi or est le mien; **a friend of m.** un ami à moi.

mine² [maɪn] 1 n (*for coal, gold etc*) & *Fig* mine f; – vt **to m. (for)** (*coal etc*) extraire. 2 n (*explosive*) mine f; – vt (*beach, bridge etc*) miner. ◆**-ing** n exploitation f minière; – a (*industry*) minier. ◆**-er** n mineur m.

mineral ['mɪnərəl] a & n minéral (m).

mingle ['mɪŋg(ə)l] vi se mêler (**with** à); **to m. with** (*socially*) fréquenter.

mingy ['mɪndʒɪ] a (**-ier, -iest**) (*mean*) *Fam* radin.

mini- [mɪnɪ] pref mini-.

miniature ['mɪnɪtʃər] n miniature f; – a (*train etc*) miniature inv; (*tiny*) minuscule.

minibus ['mɪnɪbʌs] n minibus m. ◆**mini-cab** n (radio-)taxi m.

minim ['mɪnɪm] n Mus blanche f.

minimum ['mɪnɪməm] n (pl -ima [-ɪmə] or -imums) minimum m; – a minimum (f inv), minimal. ◆**minimal** a minimal. ◆**minimize** vt minimiser.

minister ['mɪnɪstər] n Pol Rel ministre m. ◆**mini'sterial** a ministériel. ◆**ministry** n ministère m.

mink [mɪŋk] n (animal, fur) vison m.

minor ['maɪnər] a (small) Jur Mus mineur; (detail, operation) petit; – n Jur mineur, -eure mf.

Minorca [mɪ'nɔːkə] n Minorque f.

minority [maɪ'nɒrɪtɪ] n minorité f; in the or a m. en minorité, minoritaire; – a minoritaire.

mint [mɪnt] **1** n (place) Hôtel m de la Monnaie; **a m. (of money)** Fig une petite fortune; – vt (money) frapper; – a (stamp) neuf; **in m. condition** à l'état neuf. **2** n Bot Culin menthe f; (sweet) pastille f de menthe; – a à la menthe.

minus ['maɪnəs] prep Math moins; (without) Fam sans; **it's m. ten (degrees)** il fait moins dix (degrés); – n m. (**sign**) (signe m) moins m.

minute[1] ['mɪnɪt] **1** n minute f; **this (very) m.** (now) à la minute; **any m.** (now) d'une minute à l'autre; **m. hand** (of clock) grande aiguille f. **2** npl (of meeting) procès-verbal m.

minute[2] [maɪ'njuːt] a (tiny) minuscule; (careful, exact) minutieux.

minx [mɪŋks] n (girl) Pej diablesse f, chipie f.

miracle ['mɪrək(ə)l] n miracle m. ◆**mi'raculous** a miraculeux.

mirage ['mɪrɑːʒ] n mirage m.

mire [maɪər] n Lit fange f.

mirror ['mɪrər] n miroir m, glace f; Fig miroir m; (rear view) m. Aut rétroviseur m; – vt refléter.

mirth [mɜːθ] n Lit gaieté f, hilarité f.

misadventure [mɪsəd'ventʃər] n mésaventure f.

misanthropist [mɪ'zænθrəpɪst] n misanthrope mf.

misapprehend [mɪsæprɪ'hend] vt mal comprendre. ◆**misapprehension** n malentendu m.

misappropriate [mɪsə'prəuprɪeɪt] vt (money) détourner.

misbehave [mɪsbɪ'heɪv] vi se conduire mal; (of child) faire des sottises.

miscalculate [mɪs'kælkjuleɪt] vt – vi

calculer; – vi Fig se tromper. ◆**miscalcu-'lation** n erreur f de calcul.

miscarriage [mɪs'kærɪdʒ] n to have a m. Med faire une fausse couche; **m. of justice** erreur f judiciaire. ◆**miscarry** vi Med faire une fausse couche; (of plan) Fig échouer.

miscellaneous [mɪsɪ'leɪnɪəs] a divers.

mischief ['mɪstʃɪf] n espièglerie f; (maliciousness) méchanceté f; **to get into m.** faire des bêtises; **full of m.** = mischievous; **to make m. for** (trouble) créer des ennuis à; **to do s.o. a m.** (harm) faire mal à qn; **a little m.** (child) un petit démon. ◆**mischievous** a (playful, naughty) espiègle, malicieux; (malicious) méchant.

misconception [mɪskən'sepʃ(ə)n] n idée f fausse.

misconduct [mɪs'kɒndʌkt] n mauvaise conduite f; Com mauvaise gestion f.

misconstrue [mɪskən'struː] vt mal interpréter.

misdeed [mɪs'diːd] n méfait m.

misdemeanor [mɪsdɪ'miːnər] n Jur délit m.

misdirect [mɪsdɪ'rekt] vt (letter) mal adresser; (energies) mal diriger; (person) mal renseigner.

miser ['maɪzər] n avare mf. ◆**—ly** a avare.

misery ['mɪzərɪ] n (suffering) souffrances fpl; (sadness) tristesse f; (sad person) Fam grincheux, -euse mf; pl (troubles) misères fpl; **his life is a m.** il est malheureux. ◆**miserable** a (wretched) misérable; (unhappy) malheureux; (awful) affreux; (derisory) dérisoire. ◆**miserably** adv misérablement; (to fail) lamentablement.

misfire [mɪs'faɪər] vi (of engine) avoir des ratés; (of plan) Fig rater.

misfit ['mɪsfɪt] n Pej inadapté, -ée mf.

misfortune [mɪs'fɔːtʃuːn] n malheur m, infortune f.

misgivings [mɪs'gɪvɪŋz] npl (doubts) doutes mpl; (fears) craintes fpl.

misguided [mɪs'gaɪdɪd] a (action etc) imprudent; **to be m.** (of person) se tromper.

mishandle [mɪs'hænd(ə)l] vt (affair, situation) traiter avec maladresse; (person) s'y prendre mal avec.

mishap ['mɪshæp] n (accident) mésaventure f; (hitch) contretemps m.

misinform [mɪsɪn'fɔːm] vt mal renseigner.

misinterpret [mɪsɪn'tɜːprɪt] vt mal interpréter.

misjudge [mɪs'dʒʌdʒ] vt (person, distance etc) mal juger.

mislay [mɪs'leɪ] vt (pt & pp mislaid) égarer.

mislead [mɪs'liːd] vt (pt & pp misled) tromper. ◆**—ing** a trompeur.

mismanage [mɪs'mænɪdʒ] *vt* mal administrer. ◆**—ment** *n* mauvaise administration *f*.

misnomer [mɪs'nəʊmər] *n* (*name*) nom *m* or terme *m* impropre.

misogynist [mɪ'sɒdʒɪnɪst] *n* misogyne *mf*.

misplac/e [mɪs'pleɪs] *vt* (*trust etc*) mal placer; (*lose*) égarer. ◆**—ed** *a* (*remark etc*) déplacé.

misprint [mɪsprɪnt] *n* faute *f* d'impression, coquille *f*.

mispronounce [mɪsprə'naʊns] *vt* mal prononcer.

misquote [mɪs'kwəʊt] *vt* citer inexactement.

misrepresent [mɪsreprɪ'zent] *vt* présenter sous un faux jour.

miss¹ [mɪs] *vt* (*train, target, opportunity etc*) manquer, rater; (*not see*) ne pas voir; (*not understand*) ne pas comprendre; (*one's youth, deceased person etc*) regretter; (*sth just lost*) remarquer l'absence de; **he misses Paris/her** Paris/elle lui manque; **I m. you** tu me manques; **don't m. seeing this play** (*don't fail to*) ne manque pas de voir cette pièce; **to m. out** (*omit*) sauter; – *vi* manquer, rater; **to m. out** (*lose a chance*) rater l'occasion; **to m. out on** (*opportunity etc*) rater, laisser passer; – *n* coup *m* manqué; **that was or we had a near m.** on l'a échappé belle; **I'll give it a m.** *Fam* (*not go*) je n'y irai pas; (*not take or drink or eat*) je n'en prendrai pas. ◆**—ing** *a* (*absent*) absent; (*in war, after disaster*) disparu; (*object*) manquant; **there are two cups/students m.** il manque deux tasses/deux étudiants.

miss² [mɪs] *n* mademoiselle *f*; **Miss Brown** Mademoiselle or Mlle Brown.

misshapen [mɪs'ʃeɪp(ə)n] *a* difforme.

missile ['mɪsaɪl, *Am* 'mɪs(ə)l] *n* (*rocket*) *Mil* missile *m*; (*object thrown*) projectile *m*.

mission [mɪʃ(ə)n] *n* mission *f*. ◆**missionary** *n* missionnaire *m*.

missive [mɪsɪv] *n* (*letter*) missive *f*.

misspell [mɪs'spel] *vt* (*pt & pp* -ed *or* misspelt) mal écrire.

mist [mɪst] *n* (*fog*) brume *f*; (*on glass*) buée *f*; – *vi* to m. over *or* up s'embuer.

mistake [mɪ'steɪk] *n* erreur *f*, faute *f*; **to make a m.** se tromper, faire (une) erreur; **by m.** par erreur; – *vt* (*pt* mistook, *pp* mistaken) (*meaning, intention etc*) se tromper sur; **to m. the date/place/etc** se tromper de date/de lieu/etc; **you can't m., there's no mistaking** (*his face, my car etc*) il est impossible de ne pas reconnaître; **to m.**

s.o./sth for prendre qn/qch pour. ◆**mistaken** *a* (*idea etc*) erroné; **to be m.** se tromper. ◆**mistakenly** *adv* par erreur.

mister ['mɪstər] *n Fam* monsieur *m*.

mistletoe ['mɪs(ə)ltəʊ] *n Bot* gui *m*.

mistreat [mɪs'triːt] *vt* maltraiter.

mistress ['mɪstrɪs] *n* maîtresse *f*; (*in secondary school*) professeur *m*.

mistrust [mɪs'trʌst] *n* méfiance *f*; – *vt* se méfier de. ◆**mistrustful** *a* méfiant.

misty ['mɪstɪ] *a* (*-ier, -iest*) (*foggy*) brumeux; (*glass*) embué.

misunderstand [mɪsʌndə'stænd] *vt* (*pt & pp* -stood) mal comprendre. ◆**misunderstanding** *n* (*disagreement*) malentendu *m*; (*mistake*) erreur *f*. ◆**misunderstood** *a* (*person*) incompris.

misuse [mɪs'juːz] *vt* (*word, tool*) mal employer; (*power etc*) abuser de; – [mɪs'juːs] *n* (*of word*) emploi *m* abusif; (*of tool*) usage *m* abusif; (*of power etc*) abus *m*.

mite [maɪt] *n* **1** (*insect*) mite *f*. **2** (*poor*) m. (*child*) (pauvre) petit, -ite *mf*. **3** a m. (*somewhat*) *Fam* un petit peu.

mitigate ['mɪtɪgeɪt] *vt* atténuer.

mitt(en) [mɪt, 'mɪt(ə)n] *n* (*glove*) moufle *f*.

mix [mɪks] *vt* mélanger, mêler; (*cement, cake*) préparer; (*salad*) remuer; **to m. up** mélanger; (*perplex*) embrouiller (qn); (*confuse, mistake*) confondre (with avec); **to be mixed up with s.o.** (*involved*) être mêlé aux affaires de qn; **to m. up in** (*involve*) mêler à; – *vi* se mêler; (*of colours*) s'allier; **to m. with** (*socially*) fréquenter; **she doesn't m. (in)** elle n'est pas sociable; – *n* (*mixture*) mélange *m*. ◆**—ed** *a* (*school, marriage*) mixte; (*society*) mêlé; (*feelings*) mitigés, mêlés; (*results*) divers; (*nuts, chocolates etc*) assortis; **to be (all) m. up** (*of person*) être désorienté; (*of facts, account etc*) être embrouillé. ◆**—ing** *n* mélange *m*. ◆**—er** *n* *Culin El* mixe(u)r *m*; (*for mortar*) *Tech* malaxeur *m*; **to be a good m.** (*of person*) être sociable. ◆**mixture** *n* mélange *m*; (*for cough*) sirop *m*. ◆**mix-up** *n Fam* confusion *f*.

mm *abbr* (*millimetre*) mm.

moan [məʊn] *vi* (*groan*) gémir; (*complain*) se plaindre (**to** à, **about** de, **that** que); – *n* gémissement *m*; plainte *f*.

moat [məʊt] *n* douve(s) *f*(*pl*).

mob [mɒb] *n* (*crowd*) cohue *f*, foule *f*; (*gang*) bande *f*; **the m.** (*masses*) la populace; (*Mafia*) *Am* la mafia; – *vt* (**-bb-**) assiéger. ◆**mobster** *n Am Sl* gangster *m*.

mobile ['məʊbaɪl, *Am* 'məʊb(ə)l] *a* mobile; (*having a car etc*) *Fam* motorisé; **m. home**

mobil-home *m*; **m. library** bibliobus *m*; *– n* (*Am* ['məubiːl]) (*ornament*) mobile *m*.
◆**mo'bility** *n* mobilité *f*. ◆**mobili'zation** *n* mobilisation *f*. ◆**mobilize** *vti* mobiliser.

moccasin ['mɒkəsɪn] *n* (*shoe*) mocassin *m*.

mocha ['mɒkə] *n* (*coffee*) moka *m*.

mock [mɒk] **1** *vt* se moquer de; (*mimic*) singer; *– vi* se moquer (at de). **2** *a* (*false*) simulé; (*exam*) blanc. ◆**–ing** *n* moquerie *f*; *– a* moqueur. ◆**mockery** *n* (*act*) moquerie *f*; (*parody*) parodie *f*; **to make a m. of** tourner en ridicule.

mock-up ['mɒkʌp] *n* (*model*) maquette *f*.

mod cons [mɒd'kɒnz] *abbr Fam* = **modern conveniences.**

mode [məud] *n* (*manner, way*) mode *m*; (*fashion, vogue*) mode *f*.

model ['mɒd(ə)l] *n* (*example, person etc*) modèle *m*; (*fashion*) **m.** mannequin *m*; (*scale*) **m.** modèle *m* (réduit); *– a* (*behaviour, factory etc*) modèle; (*car, plane*) modèle réduit *inv*; **m. railway** train *m* miniature; *– vt* modeler (**on** sur); (*hats*) présenter (les modèles de); *– vi* (*for fashion*) être mannequin; (*pose for artist*) poser. ◆**modelling** *n* (*of statues etc*) modelage *m*.

moderate[1] ['mɒdərət] *a* modéré; (*in speech*) mesuré; (*result*) passable; *– n Pol* modéré, -ée *mf*. ◆**—ly** *adv* (*in moderation*) modérément; (*averagely*) moyennement.

moderate[2] ['mɒdəreɪt] *vt* (*diminish, tone down*) modérer. ◆**mode'ration** *n* modération *f*; **in m.** avec modération.

modern ['mɒd(ə)n] *a* moderne; **m. languages** langues *fpl* vivantes; **m. conveniences** tout le confort moderne. ◆**modernism** *n* modernisme *m*. ◆**moderni'zation** *n* modernisation *f*. ◆**modernize** *vt* moderniser.

modest ['mɒdɪst] *a* modeste. ◆**modesty** *n* (*quality*) modestie *f*; (*moderation*) modération *f*; (*of salary etc*) modicité *f*.

modicum ['mɒdɪkəm] *n* **a m.** of un soupçon de, un petit peu de.

modify ['mɒdɪfaɪ] *vt* (*alter*) modifier; (*tone down*) modérer. ◆**modifi'cation** *n* modification *f*.

modulate ['mɒdjʊleɪt] *vt* moduler. ◆**modu'lation** *n* modulation *f*.

module ['mɒdjuːl] *n* module *m*.

mogul ['məug(ə)l] *n* magnat *m*, manitou *m*.

mohair ['məuheər] *n* mohair *m*.

moist [mɔɪst] *a* (-**er**, -**est**) humide; (*clammy, sticky*) moite. ◆**moisten** *vt* humecter. ◆**moisture** *n* humidité *f*; (*on glass*) buée *f*.

◆**moisturiz/e** *vt* (*skin*) hydrater. ◆**—er** *n* (*cream*) crème *f* hydratante.

molar ['məulər] *n* (*tooth*) molaire *f*.

molasses [mə'læsɪz] *n* (*treacle*) *Am* mélasse *f*.

mold [məuld] *Am* = **mould.**

mole [məul] *n* **1** (*on skin*) grain *m* de beauté. **2** (*animal, spy*) taupe *f*.

molecule ['mɒlɪkjuːl] *n* molécule *f*.

molest [mə'lest] *vt* (*annoy*) importuner; (*child, woman*) *Jur* attenter à la pudeur de.

mollusc ['mɒləsk] *n* mollusque *m*.

mollycoddle ['mɒlɪkɒd(ə)l] *vt* dorloter.

molt [məult] *Am* = **moult.**

molten ['məult(ə)n] *a* (*metal*) en fusion.

mom [mɒm] *n Am Fam* maman *f*.

moment ['məumənt] *n* moment *m*, instant *m*; **this** (**very**) **m.** (*now*) à l'instant; **the m. she leaves** dès qu'elle partira; **any m.** (**now**) d'un moment *or* d'un instant à l'autre. ◆**momentarily** (*Am* [məumən'terɪlɪ]) *adv* (*temporarily*) momentanément; (*soon*) *Am* tout à l'heure. ◆**momentary** *a* momentané.

momentous [məu'mentəs] *a* important.

momentum [məu'mentəm] *n* (*speed*) élan *m*; **to gather** *or* **gain m.** (*of ideas etc*) *Fig* gagner du terrain.

mommy ['mɒmɪ] *n Am Fam* maman *f*.

Monaco ['mɒnəkəu] *n* Monaco *f*.

monarch ['mɒnək] *n* monarque *m*. ◆**monarchy** *n* monarchie *f*.

monastery ['mɒnəst(ə)rɪ] *n* monastère *m*.

Monday ['mʌndɪ] *n* lundi *m*.

monetary ['mʌnɪt(ə)rɪ] *a* monétaire.

money ['mʌnɪ] *n* argent *m*; **paper m.** papier-monnaie *m*, billets *mpl*; **to get one's m.'s worth** en avoir pour son argent; **he gets** *or* **earns good m.** il gagne bien (sa vie); **to be in the m.** *Fam* rouler sur l'or; **m. order** mandat *m*. ◆**moneybags** *n Pej Fam* richard, -arde *mf*. ◆**moneybox** *n* tirelire *f*. ◆**moneychanger** *n* changeur *m*. ◆**moneylender** *n* prêteur, -euse *mf* sur gages. ◆**moneymaking** *a* lucratif. ◆**money-spinner** *n* (*source of wealth*) *Fam* mine *f* d'or.

mongol ['mɒŋg(ə)l] *n & a Med* mongolien, -ienne (*mf*).

mongrel ['mʌŋgrəl] *n* (*dog*) bâtard *m*.

monitor ['mɒnɪtər] **1** *n* (*pupil*) chef *m* de classe. **2** *n* (*screen*) *Tech* moniteur *m*. **3** *vt* (*a broadcast*) *Rad* écouter; (*check*) *Fig* contrôler.

monk [mʌŋk] *n* moine *m*, religieux *m*.

monkey ['mʌŋkɪ] *n* singe *m*; **little m.** (*child*) *Fam* polisson, -onne *mf*; **m. business** *Fam* singeries *fpl*; – *vi* **to m. about** *Fam* faire l'idiot.

mono ['mɒnəʊ] *a* (*record etc*) mono *inv*.

mono- ['mɒnəʊ] *pref* mono-.

monocle ['mɒnək(ə)l] *n* monocle *m*.

monogram ['mɒnəgræm] *n* monogramme *m*.

monologue ['mɒnəlɒg] *n* monologue *m*.

monopoly [mə'nɒpəlɪ] *n* monopole *m*. ◆**monopolize** *vt* monopoliser.

monosyllable ['mɒnəsɪləb(ə)l] *n* monosyllabe *m*. ◆**monosy'llabic** *a* monosyllabique.

monotone ['mɒnətəʊn] *n* **in a m.** sur un ton monocorde. ◆**monotony** [mə'nɒtənɪ] *n* monotonie *f*. ◆**monotonous** *a* monotone.

monsoon [mɒn'suːn] *n* (*wind, rain*) mousson *f*.

monster ['mɒnstər] *n* monstre *m*. ◆**mon'strosity** *n* (*horror*) monstruosité *f*. ◆**monstrous** *a* (*abominable, enormous*) monstrueux.

month [mʌnθ] *n* mois *m*. ◆**monthly** *a* mensuel; **m. payment** mensualité *f*; – *n* (*periodical*) mensuel *m*; – *adv* (*every month*) mensuellement.

Montreal [mɒntrɪ'ɔːl] *n* Montréal *m or f*.

monument ['mɒnjʊmənt] *n* monument *m*. ◆**monu'mental** *a* monumental; **m. mason** marbrier *m*.

moo [muː] *vi* meugler; – *n* meuglement *m*.

mooch [muːtʃ] **1** *vi* **to m. around** *Fam* flâner. **2** *vt* **to m. sth off s.o.** (*cadge*) *Am Sl* taper qch à qn.

mood [muːd] *n* (*of person*) humeur *f*; (*of country*) état *m* d'esprit; *Gram* mode *m*; **in a good/bad m.** de bonne/mauvaise humeur; **to be in the m. to do** *or* **for doing** être d'humeur à faire, avoir envie de faire. ◆**moody** *a* (-ier, -iest) (*changeable*) d'humeur changeante; (*bad-tempered*) de mauvaise humeur.

moon [muːn] *n* lune *f*; **once in a blue m.** (*rarely*) *Fam* tous les trente-six du mois; **over the m.** (*delighted*) *Fam* ravi (**about** de). ◆**moonlight 1** *n* clair *m* de lune. **2** *vi Fam* travailler au noir. ◆**moonshine** *n* (*talk*) *Fam* balivernes *fpl*.

moor [mʊər] **1** *vt Nau* amarrer; – *vi* mouiller. **2** *n* (*open land*) lande *f*. ◆**—ings** *npl Nau* (*ropes etc*) amarres *fpl*; (*place*) mouillage *m*.

moose [muːs] *n inv* (*animal*) orignac *m*, élan *m*.

moot [muːt] **1** *a* (*point*) discutable. **2** *vt* (*question*) soulever, suggérer.

mop [mɒp] **1** *n* balai *m* (à laver), balai *m* éponge; **dish m.** lavette *f*; **m. of hair** tignasse *f*. **2** *vt* (-pp-) **to m. (up)** (*wipe*) essuyer; **to m. one's brow** s'essuyer le front.

mope [məʊp] *vi* **to m. (about)** être déprimé, avoir le cafard.

moped ['məʊped] *n* cyclomoteur *m*, mobylette® *f*.

moral ['mɒrəl] *a* moral; – *n* (*of story etc*) morale *f*; *pl* (*standards*) moralité *f*, morale *f*. ◆**morale** [mə'rɑːl, *Am* mə'ræl] *n* moral *m*. ◆**moralist** *n* moraliste *mf*. ◆**mo'rality** *n* (*morals*) moralité *f*. ◆**moralize** *vi* moraliser. ◆**morally** *adv* moralement.

morass [mə'ræs] *n* (*land*) marais *m*; (*mess*) *Fig* bourbier *m*.

moratorium [mɒrə'tɔːrɪəm] *n* moratoire *m*.

morbid ['mɔːbɪd] *a* morbide.

more [mɔːr] *a & n* plus (de) (**than** que); (*other*) d'autres; **m. cars/etc** plus de voitures/*etc*; **he has m.** (**than you**) il en a plus (que toi); **a few m. months** encore quelques mois, quelques mois de plus; (*some*) **m. tea**/*etc* encore du thé/*etc*; (*some*) **m. details** d'autres détails; **m. than a kilo/ten**/*etc* (*with quantity, number*) plus d'un kilo/de dix/*etc*; – *adv* (*tired, rapidly etc*) plus (**than** que); **m. and m.** de plus en plus; **m. or less** plus ou moins; **the m. he shouts the m.** hoarse **he gets** plus il crie plus il s'enroue; **she hasn't any m.** elle n'en a plus. ◆**mo'reover** *adv* de plus, d'ailleurs.

moreish ['mɔːrɪʃ] *a Fam* qui a un goût de revenez-y.

mores ['mɔːreɪz] *npl* mœurs *fpl*.

morgue [mɔːg] *n* (*mortuary*) morgue *f*.

moribund ['mɒrɪbʌnd] *a* moribond.

morning ['mɔːnɪŋ] *n* matin *m*; (*duration of morning*) matinée *f*; **in the m.** (*every morning*) le matin; (*during the morning*) pendant la matinée; (*tomorrow*) demain matin; **at seven in the m.** à sept heures du matin; **every Tuesday m.** tous les mardis matin; **in the early m.** au petit matin; – *a* du matin, matinal. ◆**mornings** *adv Am* le matin.

Morocco [mə'rɒkəʊ] *n* Maroc *m*. ◆**Moroccan** *a & n* marocain, -aine (*mf*).

moron ['mɔːrɒn] *n* crétin, -ine *mf*.

morose [mə'rəʊs] *a* morose.

morphine ['mɔːfiːn] *n* morphine *f*.

Morse [mɔːs] *n & a* **M. (code)** morse *m*.

morsel ['mɔːs(ə)l] *n* (*of food*) petite bouchée *f*.

mortal ['mɔːt(ə)l] *a & n* mortel, -elle (*mf*). ◆**mor'tality** *n* (*death rate*) mortalité *f*.

mortar ['mɔːtər] *n* mortier *m*.

mortgage ['mɔːgɪdʒ] n prêt-logement m; − vt (house, future) hypothéquer.

mortician [mɔːˈtɪʃ(ə)n] n Am entrepreneur m de pompes funèbres.

mortify ['mɔːtɪfaɪ] vt mortifier.

mortuary ['mɔːtʃʊərɪ] n morgue f.

mosaic [məʊˈzeɪɪk] n mosaïque f.

Moscow ['mɒskəʊ, Am 'mɒskaʊ] n Moscou m or f.

Moses ['məʊzɪz] n M. basket couffin m.

Moslem ['mɒzlɪm] a & n musulman, -ane (mf).

mosque [mɒsk] n mosquée f.

mosquito [mɒˈskiːtəʊ] n (pl -oes) moustique m; m. net moustiquaire f.

moss [mɒs] n Bot mousse f. ◆**mossy** a moussu.

most [məʊst] a & n the m. (greatest in amount etc) le plus (de); I have (the) m. books j'ai le plus de livres; I have (the) m. j'en ai le plus; m. (of the) books/etc la plupart d'entre eux; m. of it la plus grande partie du gâteau/etc; m. of them la plupart d'entre eux; m. of it la grande partie; at (the very) m. tout au plus; to make the m. of profiter (au maximum) de; − adv (le) plus; (very) fort, très; the m. beautiful le plus beau, la plus belle (in, of de); to talk (the) m. parler le plus; m. of all (especially) surtout. ◆−ly adv surtout, pour la plupart.

motel [məʊˈtel] n motel m.

moth [mɒθ] n papillon m de nuit; (clothes) m. mite f. ◆**m.-eaten** a mité. ◆**mothball** n boule f de naphtaline.

mother ['mʌðər] n mère f; M.'s Day la fête des Mères; m. tongue langue f maternelle; − vt (care for) materner. ◆**motherhood** n maternité f. ◆**motherly** a maternel.

mother-in-law ['mʌðərɪnlɔː] n (pl mothers-in-law) belle-mère f. ◆**m.-of-pearl** n (substance) nacre f. ◆**m.-to-'be** n (pl mothers-to-be) future mère f.

motion ['məʊʃ(ə)n] n mouvement m; Pol motion f; m. picture film m; − vti to m. to s.o. to do faire signe à qn de faire. ◆−**less** a immobile.

motive ['məʊtɪv] n motif m (for, de); Jur mobile m (for de). ◆**motivate** vt (person, decision etc) motiver. ◆**moti'vation** n motivation f; (incentive) encouragement m.

motley ['mɒtlɪ] a (coloured) bigarré; (collection) hétéroclite.

motor ['məʊtər] n (engine) moteur m; (car) Fam auto f; − a (industry, vehicle etc) automobile; (accident) d'auto; m. boat canot m automobile; m. mechanic mécanicien-auto

m; m. mower tondeuse f à moteur; − vi (drive) rouler en auto. ◆−**ing** n Sp automobilisme m; school of m. auto-école f. ◆**motorbike** n Fam moto f. ◆**motorcade** n cortège m (officiel) (de voitures). ◆**motorcar** n automobile f. ◆**motorcycle** n moto f, motocyclette f. ◆**motorcyclist** n motocycliste mf. ◆**motorist** n automobiliste mf. ◆**motorized** a motorisé. ◆**motorway** n autoroute f.

mottled ['mɒt(ə)ld] a tacheté.

motto ['mɒtəʊ] n (pl -oes) devise f.

mould [məʊld] 1 n (shape) moule m; − vt (clay etc) mouler; (statue, character) modeler. 2 n (growth, mildew) moisissure f. ◆**mouldy** a (-ier, -iest) moisi; to go m. moisir.

moult [məʊlt] vi muer. ◆−**ing** n mue f.

mound [maʊnd] n (of earth) tertre m; (pile) Fig monceau m.

mount [maʊnt] 1 n (mountain) Lit mont m. 2 n (horse) monture f; (frame for photo or slide) cadre m; (stamp hinge) charnière f; − vt (horse, hill, jewel, photo, demonstration etc) monter; (ladder, tree etc) monter sur, grimper à; (stamp) coller (dans un album); − vi to m. (up) (on horse) se mettre en selle. 3 vi (increase) monter; to m. up (add up) chiffrer (to à); (accumulate) s'accumuler.

mountain ['maʊntɪn] n montagne f; − a (people, life) montagnard. ◆**mountai-'neer** n alpiniste mf. ◆**mountai'neering** n alpinisme m. ◆**mountainous** a montagneux.

mourn [mɔːn] vti to m. (for) pleurer. ◆−**ing** n deuil m; in m. en deuil. ◆−**er** n parent, -ente mf or ami, -ie mf du défunt or de la défunte. ◆**mournful** a triste.

mouse, pl **mice** [maʊs, maɪs] n souris f. ◆**mousetrap** n souricière f.

mousse [muːs] n Culin mousse f.

moustache [məˈstɑːʃ, Am 'mʌstæʃ] n moustache f.

mousy ['maʊsɪ] a (-ier, -iest) (hair) Pej châtain terne; (shy) Fig timide.

mouth [maʊθ] n (pl -s [maʊðz]) bouche f; (of dog, lion etc) gueule f; (of river) embouchure f; (of cave, harbour) entrée f; − [maʊð] vt Pej dire. ◆**mouthful** n (of food) bouchée f; (of liquid) gorgée f. ◆**mouthorgan** n harmonica m. ◆**mouthpiece** n Mus embouchure f; (spokesman) Fig porte-parole m inv. ◆**mouthwash** n bain m de bouche. ◆**mouth-watering** a appétissant.

mov/e [muːv] n mouvement m; (change of

house etc) déménagement *m*; (*change of job*) changement *m* d'emploi; (*transfer of employee*) mutation *f*; (*in game*) coup *m*, (*one's turn*) tour *m*; (*act*) Fig démarche *f*; (*step*) pas *m*; (*attempt*) tentative *f*; **to make a m.** (*leave*) se préparer à partir; (*act*) Fig passer à l'action; **to get a m. on** *Fam* se dépêcher; **on the m.** en marche; *– vt* déplacer, remuer, bouger; (*arm, leg*) remuer; (*crowd*) faire partir; (*put*) mettre; (*transport*) transporter; (*piece in game*) jouer; (*propose*) Pol proposer; **to m. s.o.** (*incite*) pousser qn (**to do** à faire); (*emotionally*) émouvoir qn; (*transfer in job*) muter qn; **to m. house** déménager; **to m. sth back** reculer qch; **to m. sth down** descendre qch; **to m. sth forward** avancer qch; **to m. sth over** pousser qch; *– vi* bouger, remuer; (*go*) aller (**to** à); (*pass*) passer (**to** à); (*leave*) partir; (*change seats*) changer de place; (*progress*) avancer; (*act*) agir; (*play*) jouer; **to m. (out)** (*of house etc*) déménager; **to m. to** (*a new region etc*) aller habiter; **to m. about** se déplacer; (*fidget*) remuer; **to m. along** *or* **forward** *or* **on** avancer; **to m. away** *or* **off** (*go away*) s'éloigner; **to m. back** (*withdraw*) reculer; (*return*) retourner; **to m. in** (*to house*) emménager; **to m. into** (*house*) emménager dans; **m. on!** circulez!; **to m. over** *or* **up** se pousser. **◆–ing** *a* en mouvement; (*part*) Tech mobile; (*stairs*) mécanique; (*touching*) émouvant. **◆move(e)able** *a* mobile. **◆movement** *n* (*action, group etc*) & *Mus* mouvement *m*.

movie ['muːvɪ] *n Fam* film *m*; **the movies** (*cinema*) le cinéma; **m. camera** caméra *f*. **◆moviegoer** *n* cinéphile *mf*.

mow [məʊ] *vt* (*pp* **mown** *or* **mowed**) (*field*) faucher; **to m. the lawn** tondre le gazon; **to m. down** (*kill etc*) Fig faucher. **◆–er** *n* (**lawn**) **m.** tondeuse *f* (à gazon).

MP [em'piː] *n abbr* (*Member of Parliament*) député *m*.

Mrs ['mɪsɪz] *n* (*married woman*) **Mrs Brown** Madame *or* Mme Brown.

Ms [mɪz] *n* (*married or unmarried woman*) **Ms Brown** Madame *or* Mme Brown.

MSc, *Am* **MS** *abbr* = **Master of Science.**

much [mʌtʃ] *a & n* beaucoup (**de**); **not m. time/money/***etc* pas beaucoup de temps/d'argent/*etc*; **not m.** pas beaucoup; *Fam* **not m. of a** (*good deal of*) une bonne partie de; **as m. as** (*to do, know etc*) autant que; **as m. wine/***etc* **as** autant de vin/*etc* que; **as m. as you like** autant que tu veux; **twice as m.** deux fois plus (**de**); **how m.?** combien (**de**)?; **too m.**

trop (**de**); **so m.** tant (**de**), tellement (**de**); **I know/I shall do this m.** je sais/je ferai ceci (**du moins**); **this m. wine** ça de vin; **it's not m. of a garden** ce n'est pas merveilleux comme jardin; **m. the same** presque le même; *– adv* **very m.** beaucoup; **not (very) m.** pas beaucoup; **she doesn't say very m.** elle ne dit pas grand-chose.

muck [mʌk] **1** *n* (*manure*) fumier *m*; (*filth*) Fig saleté *f*. **2** *vi* **to m. about** *Fam* (*have fun, idle*) s'amuser; (*play the fool*) faire l'idiot; **to m. about with** *Fam* (*fiddle with*) s'amuser avec; (*alter*) changer (*texte etc*); **to m. in** (*join in*) *Fam* participer, contribuer; *– vt* **to m. s.o. about** *Fam* embêter qn, déranger qn; **to m. up** (*spoil*) *Fam* gâcher, ruiner. **◆m.-up** *n Fam* gâchis *m*. **◆mucky** *a* (*-ier, -iest*) sale.

mucus ['mjuːkəs] *n* mucosités *fpl*.

mud [mʌd] *n* boue *f*. **◆muddy** *a* (*-ier, -iest*) (*water*) boueux; (*hands etc*) couvert de boue. **◆mudguard** *n* garde-boue *m inv*.

muddle ['mʌd(ə)l] *n* (*mess*) désordre *m*; (*mix-up*) confusion *f*; **in a m.** (*room etc*) sens dessus dessous, en désordre; (*person*) désorienté; (*mind, ideas*) embrouillé; *– vt* (*person, facts etc*) embrouiller; (*papers*) mélanger; *– vi* **to m. through** *Fam* se débrouiller tant bien que mal.

muff [mʌf] *n* (*for hands*) manchon *m*.

muffin ['mʌfɪn] *n* petit pain *m* brioché.

muffl/e ['mʌf(ə)l] *vt* (*noise*) assourdir. **◆–ed** *a* (*noise*) sourd. **◆–er** *n* (*scarf*) cache-col *m inv*; *Aut Am* silencieux *m*.

mug [mʌg] **1** *n* grande tasse *f*, (*of metal or plastic*) gobelet *m*; (**beer**) **m.** chope *f*. **2** *n* (*face*) *Sl* gueule *f*; **m. shot** *Pej* photo *f* d'identité. **3** *n* (*fool*) *Fam* niais, -aise *mf*. **4** *vt* (-**gg**-) (*attack*) agresser. **◆mugger** *n* agresseur *m*. **◆mugging** *n* agression *f*.

muggy ['mʌgɪ] *a* (*-ier, -iest*) (*weather*) lourd.

mulberry ['mʌlbərɪ] *n* (*fruit*) mûre *f*.

mule [mjuːl] *n* (*male*) mulet *m*; (*female*) mule *f*.

mull [mʌl] **1** *vt* (*wine*) chauffer. **2** *vi* **to m. over** (*think over*) ruminer.

mullet ['mʌlɪt] *n* (*fish*) mulet *m*; (**red**) **m.** rouget *m*.

multi- ['mʌltɪ] *pref* multi-.

multicoloured ['mʌltɪkʌləd] *a* multicolore.

multifarious [mʌltɪ'feərɪəs] *a* divers.

multimillionaire [mʌltɪmɪljə'neər] *n* milliardaire *mf*.

multinational [mʌltɪ'næʃ(ə)nəl] *n* multinationale *f*.

multiple ['mʌltɪp(ə)l] a multiple; – n Math multiple m. ◆**multipli'cation** n multiplication f. ◆**multi'plicity** n multiplicité f. ◆**multiply** vt multiplier; – vi (reproduce) se multiplier.

multistorey [mʌltɪ'stɔːrɪ] (Am **multistoried**) a à étages.

multitude ['mʌltɪtjuːd] n multitude f.

mum [mʌm] **1** n Fam maman f. **2** a to keep m. garder le silence.

mumble ['mʌmb(ə)l] vti marmotter.

mumbo-jumbo [mʌmbəʊ'dʒʌmbəʊ] n (words) charabia m.

mummy ['mʌmɪ] n **1** Fam maman f. **2** (body) momie f.

mumps [mʌmps] n oreillons mpl.

munch [mʌnʃ] vti (chew) mastiquer; to m. (on) (eat) Fam bouffer.

mundane [mʌn'deɪn] a banal.

municipal [mjuː'nɪsɪp(ə)l] a municipal. ◆**munici'pality** n municipalité f.

munitions [mjuː'nɪʃ(ə)nz] npl munitions fpl.

mural ['mjʊərəl] a mural; – n fresque f, peinture f murale.

murder ['mɜːdər] n meurtre m, assassinat m; it's m. (dreadful) Fam c'est affreux; – vt (kill) assassiner; (spoil) Fig massacrer. ◆**—er** n meurtrier, -ière mf, assassin m. ◆**murderous** a meurtrier.

murky ['mɜːkɪ] a (-ier, -iest) obscur; (water, business, past) trouble; (weather) nuageux.

murmur ['mɜːmər] n murmure m; (of traffic) bourdonnement m; – vti murmurer.

muscle ['mʌs(ə)l] n muscle m; – vi to m. in on (group) Sl s'introduire par la force à. ◆**muscular** a (tissue etc) musculaire; (brawny) musclé.

muse [mjuːz] vi méditer (sur).

museum [mjuː'zɪəm] n musée m.

mush [mʌʃ] n (soft mass) bouillie f; Fig sentimentalité f. ◆**mushy** a (-ier, -iest) (food etc) en bouillie; Fig sentimental.

mushroom ['mʌʃrʊm] **1** n champignon m. **2** vi (grow) pousser comme des champignons; (spread) se multiplier.

music ['mjuːzɪk] n musique f; m. centre chaîne f stéréo compacte; m. critic critique m musical; m. hall music-hall m; m. lover mélomane mf; canned m. musique f (de fond) enregistrée. ◆**musical** a musical; (instrument) de musique; to be (very) m. être (très) musicien; – n (film, play)

comédie f musicale. ◆**mu'sician** n musicien, -ienne mf.

musk [mʌsk] n (scent) musc m.

Muslim ['mʊzlɪm] a & n musulman, -ane (mf).

muslin ['mʌzlɪn] n (cotton) mousseline f.

mussel ['mʌs(ə)l] n (mollusc) moule f.

must [mʌst] v aux **1** (necessity) you m. obey tu dois obéir, il faut que tu obéisses. **2** (certainty) **she m. be clever** elle doit être intelligente; **I m. have seen it** j'ai dû le voir; – n **this is a m.** ceci est (absolument) indispensable.

mustache ['mʌstæʃ] n Am moustache f.

mustard ['mʌstəd] n moutarde f.

muster ['mʌstər] vt (gather) rassembler; (sum) réunir; – vi se rassembler.

musty ['mʌstɪ] a (-ier, -iest) (smell) de moisi; **it smells m., it's m.** ça sent le moisi.

mutation [mjuː'teɪʃ(ə)n] n Biol mutation f.

mut/e [mjuːt] a (silent) & Gram muet; – vt (sound, colour) assourdir. ◆**—ed** a (criticism) voilé.

mutilate ['mjuːtɪleɪt] vt mutiler. ◆**muti'lation** n mutilation f.

mutiny ['mjuːtɪnɪ] n mutinerie f; – vi se mutiner. ◆**mutinous** a (troops) mutiné.

mutter ['mʌtər] vti marmonner.

mutton ['mʌt(ə)n] n (meat) mouton m.

mutual ['mjuːtʃʊəl] a (help, love etc) mutuel, réciproque; (common, shared) commun; **m. fund** Fin Am fonds m commun de placement. ◆**—ly** adv mutuellement.

muzzle ['mʌz(ə)l] n (snout) museau m; (device) muselière f; (of gun) gueule f; – vt (animal, press etc) museler.

my [maɪ] poss a mon, ma, pl mes. ◆**my'self** pron moi-même; (reflexive) me, m'; (after prep) moi; **I wash m.** je me lave; **I think of m.** je pense à moi.

mystery ['mɪstərɪ] n mystère m. ◆**my'sterious** a mystérieux.

mystic ['mɪstɪk] a n mystique (mf). ◆**mystical** a mystique. ◆**mysticism** n mysticisme m. ◆**my'stique** n (mystery, power) mystique f (of de).

mystify ['mɪstɪfaɪ] vt (bewilder) laisser perplexe; (fool) mystifier. ◆**mystifi'cation** n (bewilderment) perplexité f.

myth [mɪθ] n mythe m. ◆**mythical** a mythique. ◆**mytho'logical** a mythologique. ◆**my'thology** n mythologie f.

N

N, n [en] *n* N, n *m*; **the nth time** la énième fois.

nab [næb] *vt* (**-bb-**) (*catch, arrest*) *Fam* épingler.

nag [næg] *vti* (**-gg-**) (*criticize*) critiquer; **to n.** (**at**) **s.o.** (*pester*) harceler *or* embêter qn (**to do pour qu'il fasse**). ◆**nagging** *a* (*doubt, headache*) qui subsiste; – *n* critiques *fpl*.

nail [neɪl] **1** *n* (*of finger, toe*) ongle *m*; – *a* (*polish, file etc*) à ongles. **2** *n* (*metal*) clou *m*; – *vt* clouer; **to n. s.o.** (*nab*) *Fam* épingler qn; **to n. down** (*lid etc*) clouer.

naïve [naɪ'iːv] *a* naïf. ◆**naïveté** *n* naïveté *f*.

naked ['neɪkɪd] *a* (*person*) (tout) nu; (*eye, flame*) nu; **to see with the n. eye** voir à l'œil nu. ◆**-ness** *n* nudité *f*.

name [neɪm] *n* nom *m*; (*reputation*) *Fig* réputation *f*; **my n. is ...** je m'appelle ... ; **in the n. of** au nom de; **to put one's n. down for** (*school, course*) s'inscrire à; (*job, house*) demander, faire une demande pour avoir; **to call s.o. names** injurier qn; **first n., given n.** prénom *m*; **last n.** nom *m* de famille; **a good/bad n.** *Fig* une bonne/mauvaise réputation; **n. plate** plaque *f*; – *vt* nommer; (*ship, street*) baptiser; (*designate*) désigner, nommer; (*date, price*) fixer; **he was named after** *or Am* **for ...** il a reçu le nom de ... ◆**-less** *a* sans nom, anonyme. ◆**-ly** *adv* (*that is*) à savoir. ◆**namesake** *n* (*person*) homonyme *m*.

nanny ['nænɪ] *n* nurse *f*, bonne *f* d'enfants; (*grandmother*) *Fam* mamie *f*.

nanny-goat ['nænɪgəʊt] *n* chèvre *f*.

nap [næp] *n* (*sleep*) petit somme *m*; **to have** *or* **take a n.** faire un petit somme; (*after lunch*) faire la sieste; – *vi* (**-pp-**) **to be napping** sommeiller; **to catch napping** *Fig* prendre au dépourvu.

nape [neɪp] *n* n. (**of the neck**) nuque *f*.

napkin ['næpkɪn] *n* (*at table*) serviette *f*; (*for baby*) couche *f*. ◆**nappy** *n* (*for baby*) couche *f*. ◆**nappy-liner** *n* protège-couche *m*.

narcotic [nɑːˈkɒtɪk] *a & n* narcotique (*m*).

narrate [nəˈreɪt] *vt* raconter. ◆**narration** *n*, ◆**narrative** *n* (*story*) récit *m*, narration *f*; (*art, act*) narration *f*. ◆**narrator** *n* narrateur, -trice *mf*.

narrow ['nærəʊ] *a* (**-er, -est**) étroit; (*major-*

ity) faible, petit; – *vi* (*of path*) se rétrécir; **to n. down** (*of choice etc*) se limiter (**to** à); – *vt* **to n.** (**down**) (*limit*) limiter. ◆**-ly** *adv* (*to miss etc*) de justesse; (*strictly*) strictement; **he n. escaped** *or* **missed being killed/etc** il a failli être tué/*etc*. ◆**-ness** *n* étroitesse *f*.

narrow-minded [nærəʊ'maɪndɪd] *a* borné. ◆**-ness** *n* étroitesse *f* (d'esprit).

nasal ['neɪz(ə)l] *a* nasal; (*voice*) nasillard.

nasty ['nɑːstɪ] *a* (**-ier, -iest**) (*bad*) mauvais, vilain; (*spiteful*) méchant, désagréable (**to, towards** avec); **a n. mess** *or* **muddle** un gâchis. ◆**nastily** *adv* (*to act*) méchamment; (*to rain*) horriblement. ◆**nastiness** *n* (*malice*) méchanceté *f*; **the n. of the weather/taste/etc** le mauvais temps/goût/*etc*.

nation ['neɪʃ(ə)n] *n* nation *f*; **the United Nations** les Nations Unies. ◆**n.-wide** *a & adv* dans le pays (tout) entier. ◆**national** *a* national; **n. anthem** hymne *m* national; **N. Health Service** = Sécurité *f* Sociale; **n. insurance** = assurances *fpl* sociales; – *n* (*citizen*) ressortissant, -ante *mf*. ◆**nationalist** *n* nationaliste *mf*. ◆**nationalistic** *a* *Pej* nationaliste. ◆**nationality** *n* nationalité *f*. ◆**nationalize** *vt* nationaliser. ◆**nationally** *adv* (*to travel, be known etc*) dans le pays (tout) entier.

native ['neɪtɪv] *a* (*country*) natal; (*habits, costume*) du pays; (*tribe, plant*) indigène; (*charm, ability*) inné; **n. language** langue *f* maternelle; **to be an English n. speaker** parler l'anglais comme langue maternelle; – *n* (*person*) autochtone *mf*; (*non-European in colony*) indigène *mf*; **to be a n. of** être originaire *or* natif de.

nativity [nəˈtɪvɪtɪ] *n* *Rel* nativité *f*.

NATO ['neɪtəʊ] *n* *abbr* (*North Atlantic Treaty Organization*) OTAN *f*.

natter ['nætər] *vi* *Fam* bavarder; – *n* *Fam* **to have a n.** bavarder.

natural ['nætʃ(ə)rəl] *a* naturel; (*actor, gardener etc*) né; – *n* **to be a n. for** (*job etc*) *Fam* être celui qu'il faut pour, être fait pour. ◆**naturalist** *n* naturaliste *mf*. ◆**naturally** *adv* (*as normal, of course*) naturellement; (*by nature*) de nature; (*with naturalness*) avec naturel. ◆**naturalness** *n* naturel *m*.

naturalize ['nætʃ(ə)rəlaɪz] vt (person) Pol naturaliser. ◆**naturali'zation** n naturalisation f.

nature ['neɪtʃər] n (natural world, basic quality) nature f; (disposition) naturel m; **by n.** de nature; **n. study** sciences fpl naturelles.

naught [nɔːt] n **1** Math zéro m. **2** (nothing) Lit rien m.

naught/y ['nɔːtɪ] a (-ier, -iest) (child) vilain, malicieux; (joke, story) osé, grivois. ◆**-ily** adv (to behave) mal; (to say) avec malice. ◆**-iness** n mauvaise conduite f.

nausea ['nɔːzɪə] n nausée f. ◆**nauseate** vt écœurer. ◆**nauseous** a (smell etc) nauséabond; **to feel n.** Am (sick) avoir envie de vomir; (disgusted) Fig être écœuré.

nautical ['nɔːtɪk(ə)l] a nautique.

naval ['neɪv(ə)l] a naval; (power, hospital) maritime; (officer) de marine.

nave [neɪv] n (of church) nef f.

navel ['neɪv(ə)l] n Anat nombril m.

navigate ['nævɪgeɪt] vi naviguer; – vt (boat) diriger, piloter; (river) naviguer sur. ◆**navigable** a (river) navigable; (seaworthy) en état de naviguer. ◆**navi'gation** n navigation f. ◆**navigator** n Av navigateur m.

navvy ['nævɪ] n (labourer) terrassier m.

navy ['neɪvɪ] n marine f; – a **n. (blue)** bleu marine inv.

Nazi ['nɑːtsɪ] a & n Pol Hist nazi, -ie (mf).

near [nɪər] adv (-er, -est) près; **quite n., n. at hand** tout près; **to draw n.** (s')approcher (to de); (of date) approcher; **n. to** près de; **to come n. to being killed**/etc faillir être tué/etc; **n. enough** (more or less) Fam plus ou moins; – prep (-er, -est) **n.** (to) près de; **n. the bed** près du lit; **to be n.** (to) victory/death frôler la victoire/la mort; **n. the end** vers la fin; **to come n. s.o.** s'approcher de qn; – a (-er, -est) proche; (likeness) fidèle; **the nearest hospital** l'hôpital le plus proche; **the nearest way** la route la plus directe; **in the n. future** dans un avenir proche; **to the nearest franc** (to calculate) à un franc près; (to round up or down) au franc supérieur or inférieur; – side Aut côté m gauche, Am côté m droit; – vt (approach) approcher de; **nearing completion** près d'être achevé. ◆**near'by** adv tout près; ['nɪəbaɪ] a proche. ◆**nearness** n (in space, time) proximité f.

nearly ['nɪəlɪ] adv presque; **she (very) n. fell** elle a failli tomber; **not n. as clever**/etc as loin d'être aussi intelligent/etc que.

neat [niːt] a (-er, -est) (clothes, work) soigné,

propre, net; (room) ordonné, bien rangé; (style) élégant; (pretty) Fam joli, beau; (pleasant) Fam agréable; **to drink one's whisky**/etc **n.** prendre son whisky/etc sec. ◆**-ly** adv avec soin; (skilfully) habilement. ◆**-ness** n netteté f; (of room) ordre m.

necessary ['nesəsərɪ] a nécessaire; **it's n. to do** il est nécessaire de faire, il faut faire; **to make it n. for s.o. to do** mettre qn dans la nécessité de faire; **to do what's n.** or **the n.** Fam faire le nécessaire (for pour); – npl **the necessaries** (food etc) l'indispensable m. ◆**nece'ssarily** adv nécessairement.

necessity [nɪ'sesɪtɪ] n (obligation, need) nécessité f; (poverty) indigence f; **there's no n. for you to do that** tu n'es pas obligé de faire cela; **of n.** nécessairement; **to be a n.** être indispensable; **the (bare) necessities** le (strict) nécessaire. ◆**necessitate** vt nécessiter.

neck [nek] n Anat cou m; (of dress, horse) encolure f; (of bottle) col m; **low n.** (of dress) décolleté m; – **and n.** Sp à égalité. ◆**necklace** n collier m. ◆**neckline** n encolure f. ◆**necktie** n cravate f.

neck [nek] vi (kiss etc) Fam se peloter.

nectarine ['nektərɪn] n (fruit) nectarine f, brugnon m.

née [neɪ] adv **n.** Dupont née Dupont.

need [niːd] n **1** (necessity, want, poverty) besoin m; **in n.** dans le besoin; **to be in n. of** avoir besoin de; **there's no n. (for you) to do** tu n'as pas besoin de faire; **if n. be** si besoin est, s'il le faut; – vt avoir besoin de; **you n. it** tu en as besoin, il te le faut; **it needs an army to do, an army is needed to do** il faut une armée pour faire; **this sport needs patience** ce sport demande de la patience; **her hair needs cutting** il faut qu'elle se fasse couper les cheveux. **2** v aux **n. he wait?** est-il obligé d'attendre?, a-t-il besoin d'attendre?; **I needn't have rushed** ce n'était pas la peine de me presser; **I n. hardly say that** . . . je n'ai guère besoin de dire que . . . . ◆**needless** a inutile. ◆**needlessly** adv inutilement. ◆**needy** a (-ier, -iest) a nécessiteux.

needle ['niːd(ə)l] n **1** aiguille f; (of record player) saphir m. **2** vt (irritate) Fam agacer. ◆**needlework** n couture f, travaux mpl d'aiguille; (object) ouvrage m.

negate [nɪ'geɪt] vt (nullify) annuler; (deny) nier. ◆**negation** n (denial) & Gram négation f.

negative ['negətɪv] a négatif; – n Phot négatif m; (word) Gram négation f; (form)

Gram forme *f* négative; **to answer in the n.** répondre par la négative.

neglect [nɪ'glekt] *vt* (*person, health, work etc*) négliger; (*garden, car etc*) ne pas s'occuper de; (*duty*) manquer à; (*rule*) désobéir à, méconnaître; **to n. to do** négliger de faire; – *n* (*of person*) manque *m* de soins (*of* de); (*of rule*) désobéissance *f* (*of* à); (*of duty*) manquement *m* (*of* à); (*carelessness*) négligence *f*; **in a state of n.** (*garden, house etc*) mal tenu. ◆**neglected** *a* (*appearance, person*) négligé; (*garden, house etc*) mal tenu; **to feel n.** sentir qu'on vous néglige. ◆**neglectful** *a* négligent; **to be n.** of négliger.

negligent ['neglɪdʒənt] *a* négligent. ◆**negligence** *n* négligence *f*. ◆**negligently** *adv* négligemment.

negligible ['neglɪdʒəb(ə)l] *a* négligeable.

negotiate [nɪ'gəʊʃɪeɪt] **1** *vti* Fin Pol négocier. **2** *vt* (*fence, obstacle*) franchir; (*bend*) Aut négocier. ◆**negotiable** *a* Fin négociable. ◆**negoti'ation** *n* négociation *f*; **in n. with** en pourparlers avec. ◆**negotiator** *n* négociateur, -trice *mf*.

Negro ['niːgrəʊ] *n* (*pl* **-oes**) (*man*) Noir *m*; (*woman*) Noire *f*; – *a* noir; (*art, sculpture etc*) nègre. ◆**Negress** *n* Noire *f*.

neigh [neɪ] *vi* (*of horse*) hennir; – *n* hennissement *m*.

neighbour ['neɪbər] *n* voisin, -ine *mf*. ◆**neighbourhood** *n* (*neighbours*) voisinage *m*; (*district*) quartier *m*, voisinage *m*; (*region*) région *f*; **in the n. of ten pounds** dans les dix livres. ◆**neighbouring** *a* avoisinant. ◆**neighbourly** *a* (*feeling etc*) de bon voisinage, amical; **they're n.** (*people*) ils sont bons voisins.

neither ['naɪðər, *Am* 'niːðər] *adv* ni; **n. . . . nor** ni . . . ni; **n. you nor me** ni toi ni moi; **he n. sings nor dances** il ne chante ni ne danse; – *conj* (*not either*) (ne) . . . non plus; **n. shall I go** je n'y irai pas non plus; **n. do I, n. can I** *etc* (ni) moi non plus; – *a n.* **boy** (*came*) aucun des deux garçons (n'est venu); **on n. side** ni d'un côté ni de l'autre; – *pron* **n.** (**of them**) ni l'un(e) ni l'autre, aucun(e) (des deux).

neo- ['niːəʊ] *pref* néo-.

neon ['niːɒn] *n* (*gas*) néon *m*; – *a* (*lighting etc*) au néon.

nephew ['nevjuː, 'nefjuː] *n* neveu *m*.

nepotism ['nepətɪz(ə)m] *n* népotisme *m*.

nerve [nɜːv] *n* nerf *m*; (*courage*) Fig courage *m* (**to do** de faire); (*confidence*) assurance *f*; (*calm*) sang-froid *m*; (*cheek*) Fam culot *m* (**to do** de faire); **you get on my nerves** Fam

tu me portes *or* me tapes sur les nerfs; **to have (an attack of) nerves** (*fear, anxiety*) avoir le trac; **a bundle** *or* **mass** *or* **bag of nerves** (*person*) Fam un paquet de nerfs; **to have bad nerves** être nerveux; – *a* (*cell, centre*) nerveux. ◆**n.-racking** *a* éprouvant pour les nerfs. ◆**nervous** *a* (*tense*) & Anat nerveux; (*worried*) inquiet (**about** de); **to be** *or* **feel n.** (*ill-at-ease*) se sentir mal à l'aise; (*before exam etc*) avoir le trac. ◆**nervously** *adv* nerveusement; (*worriedly*) avec inquiétude. ◆**nervousness** *n* nervosité *f*; (*fear*) trac *m*. ◆**nervy** *a* (**-ier, -iest**) Fam (*anxious*) nerveux; (*brash*) Am culotté.

nest [nest] *n* nid *m*; **n. egg** (*money saved*) pécule *m*; **n. of tables** table *f* gigogne; – *vi* (*of bird*) (se) nicher.

nestle ['nes(ə)l] *vi* se pelotonner (**up to** contre); **a village nestling in** (*forest, valley etc*) un village niché dans.

net [net] **1** *n* filet *m*; **n. curtain** voilage *m*; – *vt* (**-tt-**) (*fish*) prendre au filet. **2** *a* (*profit, weight etc*) net *inv*; – *vt* (**-tt-**) (*of person, firm etc*) gagner net; **this venture netted him** *or* **her . . .** cette entreprise lui a rapporté . . . . ◆**netting** *n* (*nets*) filets *mpl*; (*mesh*) mailles *fpl*; (*fabric*) voile *m*; (*wire*) n. treillis *m*.

Netherlands (the) [ðə'neðələndz] *npl* les Pays-Bas *mpl*.

nettle ['net(ə)l] *n* Bot ortie *f*.

network ['netwɜːk] *n* réseau *m*.

neurosis, *pl* **-oses** [njʊə'rəʊsɪs, -əʊsiːz] *n* névrose *f*. ◆**neurotic** *a* & *n* névrosé, -ée (*mf*).

neuter ['njuːtər] **1** *a* & *n* Gram neutre (*m*). **2** *vt* (*cat etc*) châtrer.

neutral ['njuːtrəl] *a* neutre; (*policy*) de neutralité; – *n* El neutre *m*; (*in gear*) Aut au point mort. ◆**neu'trality** *n* neutralité *f*. ◆**neutralize** *vt* neutraliser.

never ['nevər] *adv* **1** (*not ever*) (ne) . . . jamais; **she n. lies** elle ne ment jamais; **n. in (all) my life** jamais de ma vie; **n. again** plus jamais. **2** (*certainly not*) Fam **I n. did it** je n'ai pas fait. ◆**n.-'ending** *a* interminable.

nevertheless [nevəðə'les] *adv* néanmoins, quand même.

new [njuː] *a* (**-er, -est**) nouveau; (*brand-new*) neuf; **to be n. to** (*job*) être nouveau dans; (*city*) être un nouveau-venu dans, être fraîchement installé dans; **a n. boy** Sch un nouveau; **what's n.?** Fam quoi de neuf?; **a n. glass/pen/**etc (*different*) un autre verre/stylo/*etc*; **to break n. ground** innover. ◆**n. look** style *m* nouveau; **as good as**

n. comme neuf; **a n.-laid egg** un œuf du jour; **a n.-born baby** un nouveau-né, une nouveau-née. ◆**newcomer** n nouveau-venu m, nouvelle-venue f. ◆**new-'fangled** a Péj moderne. ◆**new-found** a nouveau. ◆**newly** adv (recently) nouvellement, fraîchement; **the n.-weds** les nouveaux mariés. ◆**newness** n (condition) état m neuf; (novelty) nouveauté f.

news [njuːz] n nouvelle(s) f(pl); Journ Rad TV informations fpl, actualités fpl; **sports/etc n.** (newspaper column) chronique f ou rubrique f sportive/etc; **a piece of n.,** **some n.** une nouvelle; Journ Rad TV une information; **n. headlines** titres mpl de l'actualité; **n. flash** flash m. ◆**newsagent** n marchand, -ande mf de journaux. ◆**newsboy** n vendeur m de journaux. ◆**newscaster** n présentateur, -trice mf. ◆**newsletter** n (of club, group etc) bulletin m. ◆**newspaper** n journal m. ◆**newsreader** n présentateur, -trice mf. ◆**newsreel** n Cin actualités fpl. ◆**newsworthy** a digne de faire l'objet d'un reportage. ◆**newsy** a (-ier, -iest) Fam plein de nouvelles.

newt [njuːt] n (animal) triton m.

New Zealand [njuːˈziːlənd] n Nouvelle-Zélande f; - a néo-zélandais. ◆**New Zealander** n Néo-Zélandais, -aise mf.

next [nekst] a prochain; (room, house) d'à-côté, voisin; (following) suivant; **n.** **month** (in the future) le mois prochain; **he returned the n. month** (in the past) il revint le mois suivant; **the n. day** le lendemain; **the n. morning** le lendemain matin; **within the n. ten days** d'ici (à) dix jours, dans un délai de dix jours; **(by) this time n. week** d'ici (à) la semaine prochaine; **from one year to the n.** d'une année à l'autre; **you're n.** c'est ton tour; **n. (please)!** (au suivant!; **the n. thing to do is...** ce qu'il faut faire ensuite c'est...; **the n. size (up)** la taille au-dessus; **to live/etc n. door** habiter/etc à côté (to de); **n.-door neighbour/room** voisin m/pièce f d'à-côté; - n (in series etc) suivant, -ante mf; - adv (afterwards) ensuite, après; (now) maintenant; **when you come n.** la prochaine fois que tu viendras; **the n. best solution** la seconde solution; - prep **n. to** (beside) à côté de; **n. to nothing** presque rien.

NHS [enetʃˈes] abbr = National Health Service.

nib [nɪb] n (of pen) plume f, bec m.

nibble [ˈnɪb(ə)l] vti (eat) grignoter; (bite) mordiller.

nice [naɪs] a (-er, -est) (pleasant) agréable; (charming) charmant, gentil; (good) bon; (fine) beau; (pretty) joli; (kind) gentil (to avec); (respectable) bien inv; (subtle) délicat; **it's n. here** c'est bien ici; **n. and easy/warm/etc** (very) bien facile/chaud/etc. ◆**n.-'looking** a beau, joli. ◆**nicely** adv agréablement; (kindly) gentiment; (well) bien. ◆**niceties** [ˈnaɪsətɪz] npl (pleasant things) agréments mpl; (subtleties) subtilités fpl.

niche [niːʃ, nɪtʃ] n 1 (recess) niche f. 2 (job) (bonne) situation f; (direction) voie f; **to make a n. for oneself** faire son trou.

nick [nɪk] 1 n (on skin, wood) entaille f; (in blade, crockery) brèche f. 2 n (prison) Sl taule f; - vt (steal, arrest) Sl piquer. 3 n **in the n. of time** juste à temps; **in good n.** Sl en bon état.

nickel [ˈnɪk(ə)l] n (metal) nickel m; (coin) Am pièce f de cinq cents.

nickname [ˈnɪkneɪm] n (informal name) surnom m; (short form) diminutif m; - vt surnommer.

nicotine [ˈnɪkətiːn] n nicotine f.

niece [niːs] n nièce f.

nifty [ˈnɪftɪ] a (-ier, -iest) (stylish) chic inv; (skilful) habile; (fast) rapide.

Nigeria [naɪˈdʒɪərɪə] n Nigéria m or f. ◆**Nigerian** a & n nigérian, -ane (mf).

niggardly [ˈnɪɡədlɪ] a (person) avare; (amount) mesquin.

niggling [ˈnɪɡlɪŋ] a (trifling) insignifiant; (irksome) irritant; (doubt) persistant.

night [naɪt] n nuit f; (evening) soir m; Th soirée f; **last n.** (evening) hier soir; (night) la nuit dernière; **to have an early/late n.** se coucher tôt/tard; **to have a good n.** (sleep well) bien dormir; **first n.** Th première f; - a (work etc) de nuit; (life) nocturne; **n.** **school** cours mpl du soir; **n. watchman** veilleur m de nuit. ◆**nightcap** n (drink) boisson f (alcoolisée ou chaude prise avant de se coucher). ◆**nightclub** n boîte f de nuit. ◆**nightdress** n, ◆**nightgown** n, Fam ◆**nightie** n (woman's) chemise f de nuit. ◆**nightfall** n at n. à la tombée de la nuit. ◆**nightlight** n veilleuse f. ◆**nighttime** n nuit f.

nightingale [ˈnaɪtɪŋɡeɪl] n rossignol m.

nightly [ˈnaɪtlɪ] adv chaque nuit ou soir; - a de chaque nuit ou soir.

nil [nɪl] n (nothing) & Sp zéro m; **the** **risk/result/etc is n.** le risque/résultat/etc est nul.

nimble [ˈnɪmb(ə)l] a (-er, -est) agile.

nincompoop ['nıŋkəmpuːp] n Fam imbécile mf.

nine [naın] a & n neuf (m). ◆**nine'teen** a & n dix-neuf (m). ◆**nine'teenth** a & n dix-neuvième (mf). ◆**ninetieth** a & n quatre-vingt-dixième (mf). ◆**ninety** a & n quatre-vingt-dix (m); **in one's nineties** dans la quarantaine; **n.** un neuvième.

nip [nıp] 1 vt (-pp-) (pinch, bite) pincer; **to n. in the bud** étouffer dans l'œuf; **there's a n. in the air** ça pince. 2 vi (-pp-) (dash) faire vite; **to n. round to s.o.** courir or faire un saut chez qn; **to n. in/out** entrer/sortir un instant.

nipper ['nıpər] n (child) Fam gosse mf.

nipple ['nıp(ə)l] n bout m de sein, mamelon m; (teat on bottle) Am tétine f.

nippy ['nıpı] a 1 (-ier, -iest) (chilly) frais; **it's n.** (weather) ça pince. 2 **to be n.** (about it) (quick) Fam faire vite.

nit [nıt] n 1 (fool) Fam idiot, -ote mf. 2 (of louse) lente f. ◆**nitwit** n (fool) Fam idiot, -ote mf.

nitrogen ['naıtrədʒən] n azote m.

nitty-gritty [nıtı'grıtı] n **to get down to the n.-gritty** Fam en venir au fond du problème.

no [nəʊ] adv & n non (m inv); **no! no!**; **no more than** ten/a kilo/etc pas plus de dix/d'un kilo/etc; **no more time**/etc plus de temps/etc; **I have no more time** je n'ai plus de temps; **no more than you** pas plus que vous; **you can do no better** tu ne peux pas faire mieux; **the noes** Pol les non; – a aucun(e); pas de; **I've (got)** or **I have no idea** je n'ai aucune idée; **no child** aucun enfant n'est venu; **I've (got)** or **I have no time**/etc je n'ai pas de temps/etc; **of no importance/value**/etc sans importance/valeur/etc; **with no gloves**/etc on sans gants/etc; **there's no knowing . . .** impossible de savoir . . . ; **'no smoking'** 'défense de fumer'; **no way!** Am Fam pas question!; **no one = nobody.**

noble ['nəʊb(ə)l] a (-er, -est) noble; (building) majestueux. ◆**nobleman** n (pl -men) noble m. ◆**noblewoman** n (pl -women) noble f. ◆**no'bility** n (character, class) noblesse f.

nobody ['nəʊbɒdı] pron (no) . . . personne; **n. came** personne n'est venu; **he knows n.** il ne connaît personne; **n.!** personne!; – n a **n.** une nullité.

nocturnal [nɒk'tɜːn(ə)l] a nocturne.

nod [nɒd] 1 vti (-dd-) **to n.** (one's head) incliner la tête, faire un signe de tête; – n

inclination f or signe m de tête. 2 vi (-dd-) **to n. off** (go to sleep) s'assoupir.

noise [nɔız] n bruit m; (of bell, drum) son m; **to make a n.** faire du bruit. ◆**noisily** adv bruyamment. ◆**noisy** a (-ier, -iest) (person, street etc) bruyant.

nomad ['nəʊmæd] n nomade mf. ◆**no'madic** a nomade.

nominal ['nɒmın(ə)l] a (value, fee etc) nominal; (head, ruler) de nom.

nominate ['nɒmıneıt] vt Pol désigner, proposer (for comme candidat à); (appoint) désigner, nommer. ◆**nomi'nation** n désignation f or proposition f de candidat; (appointment) nomination f. ◆**nomi'nee** n (candidate) candidat m.

non- [nɒn] pref non-.

nonchalant ['nɒnʃələnt] a nonchalant.

noncommissioned [nɒnkə'mıʃ(ə)nd] a **n. officer** Mil sous-officier m.

non-committal [nɒnkə'mıt(ə)l] a (answer, person) évasif.

nonconformist [nɒnkən'fɔːmıst] a & n non-conformiste (mf).

nondescript ['nɒndıskrıpt] a indéfinissable; Pej médiocre.

none [nʌn] pron aucun(e) mf; (in filling a form) néant; **n. of them** aucun d'eux; **she has n. (at all)** elle n'en a pas (du tout); **n. (at all) came** pas une(e) seule(e) n'est venu(e); **n. can tell** personne ne peut le dire; **n. of the cake**/etc une seule partie du gâteau/etc; **n. of the trees**/etc aucun arbre/etc, aucun des arbres/etc; **n. of it** or **this** rien (de ceci); – adv **n. too hot**/etc pas tellement chaud/etc; **he's n. the happier/wiser**/etc il n'en est pas plus heureux/sage/etc; **n. the less** néanmoins. ◆**nonethe'less** adv néanmoins.

nonentity [nɒ'nentıtı] n (person) nullité f.

non-existent [nɒnıg'zıstənt] a inexistant.

non-fiction [nɒn'fıkʃ(ə)n] n littérature f non-romanesque; (in library) ouvrages mpl généraux.

non-flammable [nɒn'flæməb(ə)l] a ininflammable.

nonplus [nɒn'plʌs] vt (-ss-) dérouter.

nonsense ['nɒnsəns] n absurdités fpl; **that's n.** c'est absurde. ◆**non'sensical** a absurde.

non-smoker [nɒn'sməʊkər] n (person) non-fumeur, -euse mf; (compartment) Rail compartiment m non-fumeurs.

non-stick [nɒn'stık] a (pan) anti-adhésif, qui n'attache pas.

non-stop [nɒn'stɒp] a sans arrêt; (train,

flight) direct; *– adv (to work etc)* sans arrêt; *(to fly)* sans escale.

noodles ['nuːd(ə)lz] *npl* nouilles *fpl*; *(in soup)* vermicelle(s) *m(pl).*

nook [nuk] *n* coin *m*; **in every n. and cranny** dans tous les coins et recoins.

noon [nuːn] *n* midi *m*; **at n.** à midi; *– a (sun etc)* de midi.

noose [nuːs] *n (loop)* nœud *m* coulant; *(of hangman)* corde *f.*

nor [nɔːr] *conj* ni; **neither you n.** me ni toi ni moi; **she neither drinks n.** smokes elle ne fume ni ne boit; **n. do I, n. can I** *etc* (ni) moi non plus; **n. will I (go)** je n'y irai pas non plus.

norm [nɔːm] *n* norme *f.*

normal ['nɔːm(ə)l] *a* normal; *– n* **above n.** au-dessus de la normale. ◆**nor'mality** *n* normalité *f.* ◆**normalize** *vt* normaliser. ◆**normally** *adv* normalement.

Norman ['nɔːmən] *a* normand.

north [nɔːθ] *n* nord *m*; *– a (coast)* nord *inv*; *(wind)* du nord; **to be n. of** être au nord de; **N. America/Africa** Amérique *f*/Afrique *f* du Nord; **N. American** *a* & *n* nord-américain, -aine *(mf)*; *– adv* au nord, vers le nord. ◆**northbound** *a (carriageway)* nord *inv*; *(traffic)* en direction du nord. ◆**north-'east** *n* & *a* nord-est *m* & *a inv*. ◆**northerly** *a (point)* nord *inv*; *(direction, wind)* du nord. ◆**northern** *a (coast)* nord *inv*; *(town)* du nord; **N. France** le Nord de la France; **N. Europe** Europe *f* du Nord; **N. Ireland** Irlande *f* du Nord. ◆**northerner** *n* habitant, -ante *mf* du Nord. ◆**northward(s)** *a* & *adv* vers le nord. ◆**north-'west** *n* & *a* nord-ouest *m* & *a inv.*

Norway ['nɔːweɪ] *n* Norvège *f.* ◆**Nor'wegian** *a* & *n* norvégien, -ienne *(mf)*; *– n (language)* norvégien *m.*

nose [nəuz] *n* nez *m*; **her n. is bleeding** elle saigne du nez; **to turn one's n. up** *Fig* faire le dégoûté **(at** devant); *– vi* **to n. about** *(pry)* *Fam* fouiner. ◆**nosebleed** *n* saignement *m* de nez. ◆**nosedive** *n* *Av* piqué *m*; *(in prices)* chute *f.*

nos(e)y ['nəuzɪ] *a* (-ier, -iest) fouineur, indiscret; **n. parker** fouineur, -euse *mf.*

nosh [nɒʃ] *vi* *Fam (eat heavily)* bouffer; *(nibble)* grignoter (entre les repas); *– n (food)* *Fam* bouffe *f.*

nostalgia [nɒ'stældʒɪə] *n* nostalgie *f.* ◆**nostalgic** *a* nostalgique.

nostril ['nɒstr(ə)l] *n (of person)* narine *f*; *(of horse)* naseau *m.*

not [nɒt] *adv* **1** (ne) . . . pas; **he's n. there, he** isn't there il n'est pas là; **n. yet** pas encore; **why n.?** pourquoi pas?; **n. one reply/etc** pas une seule réponse/etc; **n. at all** pas du tout; *(after 'thank you')* je vous en prie. **2** non; **I think/hope n.** je pense/j'espère que non; **n. guilty** non coupable; **isn't she?, don't you?** *etc* non?

notable ['nəutəb(ə)l] *a (remarkable)* notable; *– n (person)* notable *m.* ◆**notably** *adv (noticeably)* notablement; *(particularly)* notamment.

notary ['nəutərɪ] *n* notaire *m.*

notation [nəu'teɪʃ(ə)n] *n* notation *f.*

notch [nɒtʃ] **1** *n (in wood etc)* entaille *f*, encoche *f*; *(in belt, wheel)* cran *m*. **2** *vt* **to n. up** *(a score)* marquer; *(a victory)* enregistrer.

note [nəut] *n (written comment, tone etc)* & *Mus* note *f*; *(summary, preface)* notice *f*; *(banknote)* billet *m*; *(piano key)* touche *f*; *(message, letter)* petit mot *m*; **to take (a) n. of, make a n. of** prendre note de; **of n.** *(athlete, actor etc)* éminent; *– vt (take note of)* noter; *(notice)* remarquer, noter; **to n. down** noter. ◆**notebook** *n* carnet *m*; *Sch* cahier *m*; *(pad)* bloc-notes *m.* ◆**notepad** *n* bloc-notes *m.* ◆**notepaper** *n* papier *m* à lettres.

noted ['nəutɪd] *a (author etc)* éminent; **to be n. for** être connu pour.

noteworthy ['nəutwɜːðɪ] *a* notable.

nothing ['nʌθɪŋ] *pron* (ne) . . . rien; **he knows n.** il ne sait rien; **n. to do/eat/etc** rien à faire/manger/etc; **n. big/etc** rien de grand/etc; **n. much** pas grand-chose; **I've got n. to do with it** je n'y suis pour rien; **I can do n. (about it)** je n'y peux rien faire; **to come to n.** *(of effort etc)* ne rien donner; **there's n. like it** il n'y a rien de tel; **for n.** *(in vain, free of charge)* pour rien; *– adv* **to look n. like s.o.** ne ressembler nullement à qn; **n. like as large/etc** loin d'être aussi grand/etc; *– n a* **(mere) n.** *(person)* aussi nullité *f*; *(thing)* un rien. ◆**—ness** *n (void)* néant *m.*

notice ['nəutɪs] *n (notification)* avis *m*; *Journ* annonce *f*; *(sign)* pancarte *f*, écriteau *m*; *(poster)* affiche *f*; *(review of film etc)* critique *f*; *(attention)* attention *f*; *(knowledge)* connaissance *f*; *(advance) n. (of departure etc)* préavis *m*; **n. (to quit), n. (of dismissal)** congé *m*; **to give (in) one's n.** *(resignation)* donner sa démission; **to give s.o. n. of** *(inform of)* avertir qn de; **to take n.** faire attention **(of** à); **to bring sth to s.o.'s n.** porter qch à la connaissance de qn; **until further n.** jusqu'à nouvel ordre; **at short n.** à bref délai; **n. board** tableau *m* d'affichage; **– vt** (*perceive*) remarquer (*qn*); (*fact, trick, danger*) s'apercevoir de, remarquer; **I n. that** je m'aperçois que. ◆**—able** *a* visible, perceptible; **that's n.** ça se voit; **she's n.** elle se fait remarquer.

notify ['nəʊtɪfaɪ] *vt* (*inform*) aviser (**s.o. of sth** qn de qch); (*announce*) notifier (**to** à). ◆**notifi'cation** *n* annonce *f*, avis *m*.

notion ['nəʊʃ(ə)n] **1** *n* (*thought*) idée *f*; (*awareness*) notion *f*; **some n. of** (*knowledge*) quelques notions de. **2** *npl* (*sewing articles*) *Am* mercerie *f*.

notorious [nəʊ'tɔːrɪəs] *a* (*event, person etc*) tristement célèbre; (*stupidity, criminal*) notoire. ◆**notoriety** [-ə'raɪətɪ] *n* (*triste*) notoriété *f*.

notwithstanding [nɒtwɪð'stændɪŋ] *prep* malgré; **–** *adv* tout de même.

nougat ['nuːgɑː, 'nʌgət] *n* nougat *m*.

nought [nɔːt] *n* Math zéro *m*.

noun [naʊn] *n* Gram nom *m*.

nourish ['nʌrɪʃ] *vt* nourrir. ◆**—ing** *a* nourrissant. ◆**—ment** *n* nourriture *f*.

novel ['nɒv(ə)l] **1** *n* Liter roman *m*. **2** *a* (*new*) nouveau, original. ◆**novelist** *n* romancier, -ière *mf*. ◆**novelty** *n* (*newness, object, idea*) nouveauté *f*.

November [nəʊ'vembər] *n* novembre *m*.

novice ['nɒvɪs] *n* novice *mf* (**at** en).

now [naʊ] *adv* maintenant; (*at this very moment*) en ce moment; **I saw her just n.** je l'ai vue à l'instant; **for n.** pour le moment; **even n.** encore maintenant; **from n. on** désormais, à partir de maintenant; **until n., up to n.** jusqu'ici; **before n.** avant; **n. and then** de temps à autre; **n. hot, n. cold** tantôt chaud, tantôt froid; **n. (then)!** bon!, alors!; (*telling s.o. off*) allons!; **it happened that . . .** or **it advint que . . .** **;** **– conj n. (that)** maintenant que. ◆**nowadays** *adv* aujourd'hui, de nos jours.

noway ['nəʊweɪ] *adv Am* nullement.

nowhere ['nəʊweər] *adv* nulle part; **n. else** nulle part ailleurs; **it's n. I know** ce n'est pas un endroit que je connais; **n. near the house** loin de la maison; **n. near enough** loin d'être assez.

nozzle ['nɒz(ə)l] *n* (*of hose*) jet *m*, lance *f* (à eau); (*of syringe, tube*) embout *m*.

nth [enθ] *a* nième.

nuance ['njuːɑːns] *n* (*of meaning, colour etc*) nuance *f*.

nub [nʌb] *n* (*of problem*) cœur *m*.

nuclear ['njuːklɪər] *a* nucléaire; **n. scientist** spécialiste *mf* du nucléaire, atomiste *mf*.

nucleus, pl -clei ['njuːklɪəs, -klɪaɪ] *n* noyau *m*.

nude [njuːd] *a* nu; **–** *n* (*female or male figure*) nu *m*; **in the n.** (tout) nu. ◆**nudism** *n* nudisme *m*, naturisme *m*. ◆**nudist** *n* nudiste *mf*, naturiste *mf*; **–** *a* (*camp*) de nudistes, de naturistes. ◆**nudity** *n* nudité *f*.

nudge [nʌdʒ] *vt* pousser du coude; **–** *n* coup *m* de coude.

nugget ['nʌgɪt] *n* (*of gold etc*) pépite *f*.

nuisance ['njuːs(ə)ns] *n* (*annoyance*) embêtement *m*; (*person*) peste *f*; **that's a n.** c'est embêtant; **he's being a n., he's making a n. of himself** il nous embête, il m'embête *etc*.

null [nʌl] *a* **n. (and void)** nul (et non avenu). ◆**nullify** *vt* infirmer.

numb [nʌm] *a* (*stiff*) engourdi; Fig paralysé; **–** *vt* engourdir; Fig paralyser.

number ['nʌmbər] *n* nombre *m*; (*of page, house, newspaper etc*) numéro *m*; **a dance/song n.** un numéro de danse/de chant; **a/any n. of** un certain/grand nombre de; **n. plate** (*of vehicle*) plaque *f* d'immatriculation; **–** *vt* (*page etc*) numéroter; (*include, count*) compter; **they n. eight** ils sont au nombre de huit. ◆**—ing** *n* numérotage *m*.

numeral ['njuːm(ə)rəl] *n* chiffre *m*; **–** *a* numéral. ◆**nu'merical** *a* numérique. ◆**numerous** *a* nombreux.

numerate ['njuːm(ə)rət] *a* (*person*) qui sait compter.

nun [nʌn] *n* religieuse *f*.

nurs/e [nɜːs] **1** *n* infirmière *f*; (*nanny*) nurse *f*; (*male*) **n.** infirmier *m*. **2** *vt* (*look after*) soigner; (*cradle*) bercer; (*suckle*) nourrir; (*a grudge etc*) Fig nourrir; (*support, encourage*) Fig épauler (*qn*). ◆**—ing** *a* (*mother*) qui allaite; **the n. staff** le personnel infirmier; **–** *n* (*care*) soins *mpl*; (*job*) profession *f* d'infirmière *or* d'infirmier; **n. home** clinique *f*. ◆**nursemaid** *n* bonne *f* d'enfants.

nursery ['nɜːsərɪ] *n* (*room*) chambre *f* d'enfants; (*for plants, trees*) pépinière *f*; (**day**) **n.** (*school etc*) crèche *f*, garderie *f*; **n. rhyme** chanson *f* enfantine; **n. school** école *f* maternelle.

nurture ['nɜːtʃər] *vt* (*educate*) éduquer.

nut¹ [nʌt] *n* (*fruit*) fruit *m* à coque; (*walnut*) noix *f*; (*hazelnut*) noisette *f*; (*peanut*) cacah(o)uète *f*; **Brazil/cashew n.** noix *f* du Brésil/de cajou. ◆**nutcracker(s)** *n*(*pl*) casse-noix *m inv*. ◆**nutshell** *n* coquille *f* de noix; **in a n.** Fig en un mot.

nut² [nʌt] *n* **1** (*for bolt*) Tech écrou *m*. **2**

(head) *Sl* caboche *f*. **3** *(person)* *Sl* cinglé, -ée *mf*; **to be nuts** *Sl* être cinglé. ◆**nutcase** *n* cinglé, -ée *mf*. ◆**nutty** *a* (-ier, -iest) *Sl* cinglé.

nutmeg ['nʌtmeg] *n* muscade *f*.

nutritious [njuː'trɪʃəs] *a* nutritif. ◆**'nutri-**

ent *n* élément *m* nutritif. ◆**nutrition** *n* nutrition *f*.

nylon ['naɪlɒn] *n* nylon *m*; *pl (stockings)* bas *mpl* nylon.

nymph [nɪmf] *n* nymphe *f*. ◆**nympho-'maniac** *n* *Pej* nymphomane *f*.

O

O, o [əʊ] *n* O, o *m*.

oaf [əʊf] *n* rustre *m*. ◆**oafish** *a* (*behaviour*) de rustre.

oak [əʊk] *n* (*tree, wood*) chêne *m*.

OAP [əʊeɪ'piː] *n abbr* (*old age pensioner*) retraité, -ée *mf*.

oar [ɔːr] *n* aviron *m*, rame *f*.

oasis, *pl* oases [əʊ'eɪsɪs, əʊ'eɪsiːz] *n* oasis *f*.

oath [əʊθ] *n* (*pl* -s [əʊðz]) (*promise*) serment *m*; (*profanity*) juron *m*; **to take an o. to do** faire le serment de faire.

oats [əʊts] *npl* avoine *f*. ◆**oatmeal** *n* flocons *mpl* d'avoine.

obedient [ə'biːdɪənt] *a* obéissant. ◆**obedience** *n* obéissance *f* (to à). ◆**obediently** *adv* docilement.

obelisk ['ɒbəlɪsk] *n* (*monument*) obélisque *m*.

obese [əʊ'biːs] *a* obèse. ◆**obesity** *n* obésité *f*.

obey [ə'beɪ] *vt* obéir à; **to be obeyed** être obéi; *– vi* obéir.

obituary [ə'bɪtjʊərɪ] *n* nécrologie *f*.

object¹ ['ɒbdʒɪkt] *n* (*thing*) objet *m*; (*aim*) but *m*, objet *m*; *Gram* complément *m* (d'objet); **with the o. of** dans le but de; **that's no o.** (*no problem*) ça ne pose pas de problème; **price no o.** prix *m* indifférent.

object² [əb'dʒekt] *vi* **to o. to sth/s.o.** désapprouver qch/qn; **I o. to you(r) doing that** ça me gêne que tu fasses ça; **I o.!** je proteste!; **she didn't o. when . . .** elle n'a fait aucune objection quand . . . ; *– vt* **to o. that** objecter que. ◆**objection** *n* objection *f*; **I've got no o.** ça ne me gêne pas, je n'y vois pas d'objection *or* d'inconvénient. ◆**objectionable** *a* très désagréable. ◆**objector** *n* opposant, -ante *mf* (to à); **conscientious o.** objecteur *m* de conscience.

objective [əb'dʒektɪv] **1** *a* (*opinion etc*) objectif. **2** *n* (*aim, target*) objectif *m*. ◆**objectively** *adv* objectivement. ◆**objec'tivity** *n* objectivité *f*.

obligate ['ɒblɪgeɪt] *vt* contraindre (**to do** à faire). ◆**obli'gation** *n* obligation *f*; (*debt*) dette *f*; **under an o. to do** dans l'obligation de faire; **under an o. to s.o.** redevable à qn (**for** de). ◆**o'bligatory** *a* (*compulsory*) obligatoire; (*imposed by custom*) de rigueur.

oblig/e [ə'blaɪdʒ] *vt* **1** (*compel*) obliger (**s.o. to do** qn à faire); **obliged to do** obligé de faire. **2** (*help*) rendre service à, faire plaisir à; **obliged to s.o.** reconnaissant à qn (**for** de); **much obliged!** merci infiniment! ◆**—ing** *a* (*kind*) obligeant. ◆**—ingly** *adv* obligeamment.

oblique [ə'bliːk] *a* oblique; (*reference*) *Fig* indirect.

obliterate [ə'blɪtəreɪt] *vt* effacer. ◆**oblite-'ration** *n* effacement *m*.

oblivion [ə'blɪvɪən] *n* oubli *m*. ◆**oblivious** *a* inconscient (**to, of** de).

oblong ['ɒblɒŋ] *a* (*elongated*) oblong; (*rectangular*) rectangulaire; *– n* rectangle *m*.

obnoxious [əb'nɒkʃəs] *a* odieux; (*smell*) nauséabond.

oboe ['əʊbəʊ] *n* *Mus* hautbois *m*.

obscene [əb'siːn] *a* obscène. ◆**obscenity** *n* obscénité *f*.

obscure [əb'skjʊər] *a* (*reason, word, actor, life etc*) obscur; *– vt* (*hide*) cacher; (*confuse*) embrouiller, obscurcir. ◆**obscurely** *adv* obscurément. ◆**obscurity** *n* obscurité *f*.

obsequious [əb'siːkwɪəs] *a* obséquieux.

observe [əb'zɜːv] *vt* (*notice, watch, respect*) observer; (*say*) (faire) remarquer (**that** que); **to o. the speed limit** respecter la limitation de vitesse. ◆**observance** *n* (*of rule etc*) observation *f*. ◆**observant** *a* observateur. ◆**obser'vation** *n* (*observing, remark*) observation *f*; (*by police*) surveillance *f*; **under o.** (*hospital patient*) en observation. **observatory** n observatoire m. **observer** n observateur, -trice mf.

obsess [əb'ses] vt obséder. **obsession** n obsession f; **to have an o. with** or **about** avoir l'obsession de. **obsessive** a (memory, idea) obsédant; (fear) obsessif; (neurotic) Psy obsessionnel; **to be o. about** avoir l'obsession de.

obsolete ['ɒbsəliːt] a (out of date, superseded) désuet, dépassé; (ticket) périmé; (machinery) archaïque. **obso'lescent** a quelque peu désuet; (word) vieilli.

obstacle ['ɒbstək(ə)l] n obstacle m.

obstetrics [əb'stetrɪks] n Med obstétrique f. **obste'trician** n médecin m accoucheur.

obstinate ['ɒbstɪnət] a (person, resistance etc) obstiné, opiniâtre; (disease, pain) rebelle, opiniâtre. **obstinacy** n obstination f. **obstinately** adv obstinément.

obstreperous [əb'strepərəs] a turbulent.

obstruct [əb'strʌkt] vt (block) boucher; (hinder) entraver; (traffic) entraver, bloquer. **obstruction** n (act, state) & Med Pol Sp obstruction f; (obstacle) obstacle m; (in pipe) bouchon m; (traffic jam) embouteillage m. **obstructive** a to be o. faire de l'obstruction.

obtain [əb'teɪn] **1** vt obtenir. **2** vi (of practice etc) avoir cours. **—able** a (available) disponible; (on sale) en vente.

obtrusive [əb'truːsɪv] a (person) importun; (building etc) trop en évidence.

obtuse [əb'tjuːs] a (angle, mind) obtus.

obviate ['ɒbvɪeɪt] vt (necessity) éviter.

obvious ['ɒbvɪəs] a évident; **he's the o. man to see** c'est évidemment l'homme qu'il faut voir. **—ly** adv (evidently, of course) évidemment; (conspicuously) visiblement.

occasion [ə'keɪʒ(ə)n] **1** n (time, opportunity) occasion f; (event, ceremony) événement m; **on the o. of** à l'occasion de; **on o.** à l'occasion; **on several occasions** à plusieurs reprises or occasions. **2** n (cause) raison f, occasion f; − vt occasionner. **occasional** a (event) qui a lieu de temps en temps; (rain, showers) intermittent; **she drinks the o. whisky** elle boit un whisky de temps en temps. **occasionally** adv de temps en temps; **very o.** très peu souvent, rarement.

occult [ə'kʌlt] a occulte.

occupy ['ɒkjʊpaɪ] vt (house, time, space, post etc) occuper; **to keep oneself occupied** s'occuper (doing à faire). **occupant** n (inhabitant) occupant, -ante mf. **occu'pation** n (activity) occupation f; (job) emploi m; (trade) métier m; (profession) profession f; **the o. of** (action) l'occupation f de; **fit for o.** (house) habitable. **occu'pational** a (hazard) du métier; (disease) du travail. **occupier** n (of house) occupant, -ante mf; Mil occupant m.

occur [ə'kɜːr] vi (-rr-) (happen) avoir lieu; (be found) se rencontrer; (arise) se présenter; **it occurs to me that** . . . il me vient à l'esprit que . . . ; **the idea occurred to her to** . . . l'idée lui est venue de . . . . **occurrence** [ə'kʌrəns] n (event) événement m; (existence) existence f; (of word) Ling occurrence f.

ocean ['əʊʃ(ə)n] n océan m. **oce'anic** a océanique.

o'clock [ə'klɒk] adv (it's) three o'c./etc (il est) trois heures/etc.

octagon ['ɒktəgən] n octogone m. **oc'tagonal** a octogonal.

octave ['ɒktɪv, 'ɒkteɪv] n Mus octave f.

October [ɒk'təʊbər] n octobre m.

octogenarian [ɒktəʊ'dʒɪneərɪən] n octogénaire m f.

octopus ['ɒktəpəs] n pieuvre f.

odd [ɒd] a **1** (strange) bizarre, curieux; **an o. size** une taille peu courante. **2** (number) impair. **3** (left over) **I have an o. penny** il me reste un penny; **a few o. stamps** quelques timbres (qui restent); **the o. man out**, **the o. one out** l'exception f; **sixty et quelques**; **an o. glove/book/etc** un gant/livre/etc dépareillé. **4** (occasional) qu'on fait, voit etc de temps en temps; **to find the o. mistake** trouver de temps en temps une (petite) erreur; **at o. moments** de temps en temps; **o. jobs** (around house) menus travaux mpl; **o. job man** homme m à tout faire. **oddity** n (person) personne f bizarre; (object) curiosité f; pl (of language, situation) bizarreries fpl. **oddly** adv bizarrement; **o. (enough), he was** . . . chose curieuse, il était . . . . **oddment** n Com fin f de série. **oddness** n bizarrerie f.

odds [ɒdz] npl **1** (in betting) cote f; (chances) chances fpl; **we have heavy o. against us** nous avons très peu de chances de réussir. **2** **it makes no o.** (no difference) Fam ça ne fait rien. **3** **at o.** (in disagreement) en désaccord (with avec). **4** **o. and ends** des petites choses.

ode [əʊd] n (poem) ode f.

odious ['əʊdɪəs] a détestable, odieux.

odour ['əʊdər] n odeur f. **—less** a inodore.

oecumenical [iːkjuːr'menɪk(ə)l] a Rel œcuménique.

of [əv, stressed ɒv] prep de; **of the table** de la

table; **of the boy** du garçon; **of the boys** des garçons; **of a book** d'un livre; **of it, of them** en; **she has a lot of it** or **of them** elle en a beaucoup; **a friend of his** un ami à lui; **there are ten of us** nous sommes dix; **that's nice of you** c'est gentil de ta part; **no value/interest/etc** sans valeur/intérêt/etc; **of late** ces derniers temps; **a man of fifty** un homme de cinquante ans; **the fifth of June** le cinq juin.

off [ɒf] **1** adv (absent) absent, parti; (light, gas, radio etc) éteint, fermé; (tap) fermé; (switched off at mains) coupé; (detached) détaché; (removed) enlevé; (cancelled) annulé; (not fit to eat or drink) mauvais; (milk, meat) tourné; **2 km o.** à 2 km (d'ici or de là), éloigné de 2 km; **to be** ou **go o.** (leave) partir; **where are you o. to?** où vas-tu?; **he has his hat o.** il a enlevé son chapeau; **with his, my etc gloves o.** sans gants; **a day o.** (holiday) un jour de congé; **I'm o. today, I have today o.** j'ai congé aujourd'hui; **the strike's o.** il n'y aura pas de grève, la grève est annulée; **5% o.** une réduction de 5%; **on and o., o. and on** (sometimes) de temps à autre; **to be better o.** (wealthier, in a better position) être mieux. **2** prep (from) de; (distant) éloigné de; **to fall/etc o. the** wall/ladder/etc tomber/etc du mur/de l'échelle/etc; **to get o. the** bus/etc descendre du bus/etc; **to take sth o. the** table/etc prendre qch sur la table/etc; **to eat o. a plate** manger dans une assiette; **to keep** or **stay o. the grass** ne pas marcher sur les pelouses; **she's o. her food** elle ne mange plus rien; **o. Dover/etc** Nau au large de Douvres/etc; **o. limits** interdit; **the o. side** Aut le côté droit, Am le côté gauche. ◆**off'beat** a excentrique. ◆**off-'colour** a (ill) patraque; (indecent) scabreux. ◆**off'hand** a désinvolte; – adv impromptu. ◆**off'handedness** n désinvolture f. ◆**off-licence** n magasin m de vins et de spiritueux. ◆**off-'load** vt (vehicle etc) décharger; **to o.-load sth onto s.o.** (task etc) se décharger de qch sur qn. ◆**off-'peak** a (crowds, traffic) aux heures creuses; (rate, price) heures creuses inv; **o.-peak hours** heures creuses fpl. ◆**off-putting** a Fam rebutant. ◆**off'side** a to be o. Fb être hors jeu. ◆**off'stage** a & adv dans les coulisses. ◆**off-'white** a blanc cassé inv.

offal ['ɒf(ə)l] n Culin abats mpl.

offence [ə'fens] n Jur délit m; **to take o.** s'offenser (at de); **to give o.** offenser.

offend [ə'fend] vt froisser, offenser; (eye) Fig

choquer; **to be offended (at)** se froisser (de), s'offenser (de). ◆**—ing** a (object, remark) incriminé. ◆**offender** n Jur délinquant, -ante mf; (habitual) récidiviste mf.

offensive [ə'fensiv] **1** a (unpleasant) choquant, repoussant; (insulting) insultant, offensant; (weapon) offensif. **2** n Mil offensive f.

offer ['ɒfər] n offre f; **on (special) o.** Com en promotion, en réclame; **o. of marriage** demande f en mariage; – vt offrir; (opinion, remark) proposer; **to o. to do sth** offrir or proposer de faire. ◆**—ing** n (gift) offrande f; (act) offre f; **peace o.** cadeau m de réconciliation.

office ['ɒfis] n **1** bureau m; (of doctor) Am cabinet m; (of lawyer) étude f; **head o.** siège m central; **o. block** immeuble m de bureaux; **o. worker** employé, -ée mf de bureau. **2** (post) fonction f; (duty) fonctions fpl; **to be in o.** (of party etc) Pol être au pouvoir. **3** one's good offices (help) ses bons offices mpl.

officer ['ɒfisər] n (in army, navy etc) officier m; (of company) Com directeur, -trice mf; (police) o. agent m (de police).

official [ə'fiʃ(ə)l] a officiel; (uniform) réglementaire; – n (person of authority) officiel m; (civil servant) fonctionnaire mf; (employee) employé, -ée mf. ◆**officialdom** n bureaucratie f. ◆**officially** adv officiellement. ◆**officiate** vi faire fonction d'officiel (at à); (preside) présider; Rel officier.

officious [ə'fiʃəs] a Pej empressé.

offing ['ɒfiŋ] n **in the o.** en perspective.

offset ['ɒfset, ɒf'set] vt (pt & pp offset, pres p offsetting) (compensate for) compenser; (s.o.'s beauty etc by contrast) faire ressortir.

offshoot ['ɒfʃuːt] n (of firm) ramification f; (consequence) conséquence f.

offspring ['ɒfspriŋ] n progéniture f.

often ['ɒf(t)ən] adv souvent; **how o.?** combien de fois?; **how o. do they run?** (trains, buses etc) il y en a tous les combien?; **once too o.** une fois de trop; **every so o.** de temps en temps.

ogle ['əʊg(ə)l] vt Pej reluquer.

ogre ['əʊgər] n ogre m.

oh! [əʊ] int oh!, ah!; (pain) aïe!; **oh yes?** ah oui?, ah bon?

oil [ɔil] n (for machine, in cooking etc) huile f; (mineral) pétrole m; (fuel oil) mazout m; **to paint in oils** faire de la peinture à l'huile; – a (industry, product) pétrolier; (painting, paints) à l'huile; **o. lamp** lampe f à pétrole or à huile; **o. change** Aut vidange f; – vt

graisser, huiler. **◆oilcan** n burette f.
◆oilfield n gisement m pétrolifère. **◆oilfired** a au mazout. **◆oilskin(s)** n(pl)
(garment) ciré m. **◆oily** a (-ier, -iest)
(substance, skin) huileux; (hands) graisseux; (food) gras.

ointment ['ɔɪntmənt] n pommade f.

OK [əʊ'keɪ] int (approval, exasperation) ça
va!; (agreement) d'accord!, entendu!, OK!;
– a (satisfactory) bien en; (unharmed) sain
et sauf; (undamaged) intact; (without
worries) tranquille; **I'm OK now** (fixed) ça
marche maintenant; **I'm OK** (healthy) je
vais bien; – adv (to work etc) bien; – vt (pt
& pp OKed, pres p OKing) approuver.

okay [əʊ'keɪ] a = OK.

old [əʊld] a (-er, -est) vieux; (former)
ancien; **how o. is he?** quel âge a-t-il?; **he's
ten years o.** il a dix ans; **the o. age of ten
ans; he's older than** il est plus âgé que; **an
older son** un fils aîné; **the oldest son** le fils
aîné. **o. enough to do** assez grand pour
faire; **o. enough to marry/vote** en âge de se
marier/de voter; **an o. man** un vieillard, un
vieil homme; **an o. woman** une vieille
(femme); **to get** or **grow old(er)** vieillir; **o.
age** vieillesse f; **the O. Testament** l'Ancien
Testament; **the O. World** l'Ancien Monde;
any o. how Fam n'importe comment; – n
the o. (people) les vieux mpl. **◆o.-
fashioned** a (customs etc) d'autrefois;
(idea, attitude) Pej vieux jeu inv; (person)
de la vieille école, Pej vieux jeu inv.
◆o.-timer n (old man) Fam vieillard m.

olden ['əʊld(ə)n] a in o. days jadis.

olive ['ɒlɪv] n (fruit) olive f; – a o. (green)
(vert) olive inv; **o. oil** huile f d'olive; **o. tree**
olivier m.

Olympic [ə'lɪmpɪk] a olympique.

ombudsman ['ɒmbudzmən] n (pl -men)
Pol médiateur m.

omelet(te) ['ɒmlɪt] n omelette f; **cheese/etc
o.** omelette au fromage/etc.

omen ['əʊmən] n augure m. **◆ominous** a
de mauvais augure; (tone) menaçant;
(noise) sinistre.

omit [əʊ'mɪt] vt (-tt-) omettre (to do or
faire). **◆omission** n omission f.

omni- ['ɒmnɪ] prep omni-. **◆om'nipotent**
a omnipotent.

on [ɒn] prep 1 (position) sur; **on the chair** sur
la chaise; **to put on (to)** mettre sur; **to look
out on to** donner sur. 2 (concerning, about)
sur; **an article on** un article sur; **to speak** or
talk on Dickens/etc parler sur Dickens/etc.
3 (manner, means) à; **on foot** à pied; **on the
blackboard** au tableau; **on the radio** à la

radio; **on the train/plane**/etc dans le
train/avion/etc; **on holiday**, Am **on vacation** en vacances; **to be on** (course) suivre;
(project) travailler à; (salary) toucher;
(team, committee) être membre de, faire
partie de; **to keep** or **stay on** (road, path etc)
suivre; **it's on me!** (I'll pay) Fam c'est moi
qui paie! 4 (time) **on Monday** lundi; **on
Mondays** le lundi; **on May 3rd** le 3 mai; **on
the evening of May 3rd** le 3 mai au soir; **on
my arrival** à mon arrivée. 5 (+ present
participle) en; **on learning that ...** en
apprenant que ...; **on seeing this** en
voyant ceci. 6 adv (ahead) en avant; (in
progress) en cours; (started) commencé;
(lid, brake) mis; (light, radio) allumé; (gas,
tap) ouvert; (machine) en marche; **on and
on** sans cesse; **to play**/etc on continuer à
jouer/etc; **she has her hat** on elle a mis or
elle porte son chapeau; **he has sth/nothing
on** il est habillé/tout nu; **I've got sth on**
(I'm busy) je suis pris; **the strike's on** la
grève aura lieu; **what's on?** TV qu'y a-t-il à
la télé?; Cin Th qu'est-ce qu'on joue?;
there's a film on passe un film; **to be on
at s.o.** (pester) Fam être après qn; **I've been
on to him** Tel je l'ai eu au bout du fil; **to be
on to s.o.** (of police etc) être sur la piste de
qn; **from then on** à partir de là.
◆on-coming a (vehicle) qui vient en sens
inverse. **◆on-going** a (project) en cours.

once [wʌns] adv (on one occasion) une fois;
(formerly) autrefois; **o. a month/etc** une
fois par mois/etc; **o. again**, **o. more** encore
une fois; **at o.** (immediately) tout de suite;
all at o. (suddenly) tout à coup; (at the same
time) à la fois; **o. and for all** une fois pour
toutes; – conj une fois que. **◆o.-over** n **to
give sth the o.-over** (quick look) Fam
regarder qch d'un coup d'œil.

one [wʌn] a 1 un, une; **o. man** un homme; **o.
woman** une femme; **twenty-o.** vingt-et-un.
2 (sole) seul; **my o. (and only) aim** mon seul
(et unique) but. 3 (same) même; **in the o.
bus** dans le même bus; – pron 1 un, une; **do
you want o.?** en veux-tu (un)?; **he's o. of us**
il est des nôtres; **o. of them** l'un or l'une, l'une
d'elles; **a big/small/etc o.** un grand/petit/
etc; **this book is o.** that I've read ce livre est
parmi ceux que j'ai lus; **she's o.** (a teacher,
gardener etc) elle l'est; **this o.** celui-ci,
celle-ci; **that o.** celui-là, celle-là; **the o. who**
or **which** celui or celle qui; **it's Paul's o.** Fam
c'est celui de Paul; **it's o.** à moi; **I for o.** pour
ma part. 2 (impersonal) on; **o. knows** on
sait; **it helps o.** ça nous or vous aide; **one's**

family sa famille. ◆one-'armed a (person) manchot. ◆one-'eyed a borgne. ◆one-'off a, Am one-of-a-'kind a Fam unique, exceptionnel. ◆one-'sided a (judgement etc) partial; (contest) inégal; (decision) unilatéral. ◆one-time a (former) ancien. ◆one-'way a (street) à sens unique; (traffic) en sens unique; (ticket) Am simple.

oneself [wʌn'self] pron soi-même; (reflexive) se, s'; to cut o. se couper.

onion ['ʌnjən] n oignon m.

onlooker ['ɒnlʊkər] n spectateur, -trice mf.

only ['əʊnlɪ] a seul; the o. house/etc la seule maison/etc; the o. one le seul, la seule; an o. son un fils unique; – adv seulement, ne ... que; I have ten, I have ten o. je n'en ai que dix, j'en ai dix seulement; if o. si seulement; not o. non seulement; I have o. just seen it je viens tout juste de le voir; he knows lui seul le sait; – conj (but) Fam seulement; o. I can't seulement je ne peux pas.

onset ['ɒnset] n (of disease) début m; (of old age) approche m.

onslaught ['ɒnslɔːt] n attaque f.

onto ['ɒntʊ] prep = on to.

onus ['əʊnəs] n inv the o. is on you/etc c'est votre/etc responsabilité (to do de faire).

onward(s) ['ɒnwəd(z)] adv en avant; from that time o. à partir de là.

onyx ['ɒnɪks] n (precious stone) onyx m.

ooze [uːz] vi to o. (out) suinter; – vt (blood etc) laisser couler.

opal ['əʊp(ə)l] n (precious stone) opale f.

opaque [əʊ'peɪk] a opaque; (unclear) Fig obscur.

open ['əʊpən] a ouvert; (site, view, road) dégagé; (car) décapoté, découvert; (meeting) public; (competition) ouvert à tous; (post) vacant; (attempt, envy) manifeste; (question) non résolu; (result) indécis; (ticket) Av open inv; with o. arms à bras ouverts; in the o. air en plein air; in (the) o. country en rase campagne; the o. spaces les grands espaces; it's o. to doubt c'est douteux; o. to (criticism, attack) exposé à; (ideas, suggestions) ouvert à; I've got an o. mind on it je n'ai pas d'opinion arrêtée là-dessus; to leave o. (date) ne pas préciser; – n (out) in the o. (outside) en plein air; to sleep (out) in the o. dormir à la belle étoile; to bring (out) into the o. (reveal) divulguer; – vt ouvrir; (conversation) entamer; (legs) écarter; to o. out or up ouvrir; – vi (of flower, eyes etc) s'ouvrir; (of shop, office etc) ouvrir; (of play) débuter; (of film) sortir; the door opens (is

opened) la porte s'ouvre; (can open) la porte ouvre; to o. on to (of window etc) donner sur; to o. out or up s'ouvrir; to o. out (widen) s'élargir; to o. up (open a or the door) ouvrir. ◆—ing n ouverture f; (of flower) éclosion f; (career prospect, trade outlet) débouché m; – a (time, speech) d'ouverture; o. night Th première f. ◆—ly adv (not secretly, frankly) ouvertement; (publicly) publiquement. ◆—ness n (frankness) franchise f; o. of mind ouverture f d'esprit.

open-air [əʊpən'eər] a (pool etc) en plein air. ◆o.-'heart a (operation) Med à cœur ouvert. ◆o.-'necked a (shirt) sans cravate. ◆o.-'plan a Archit sans cloisons.

opera ['ɒprə] n opéra m; o. glasses jumelles fpl de théâtre. ◆ope'ratic a d'opéra. ◆ope'retta n opérette f.

operat/e ['ɒpəreɪt] 1 vi (of machine etc) fonctionner; (proceed) opérer; – vt faire fonctionner; (business) gérer. 2 vi (of surgeon) opérer (on s.o. qn, for de). ◆—ing a o. costs frais mpl d'exploitation; o. theatre, Am o. room Med salle f d'opération; o. wing Med bloc m opératoire. ◆ope'ration n (working) fonctionnement m; Med Mil Math etc opération f; in o. (machine) en service; (plan) Fig en vigueur. ◆ope-'rational a opérationnel. ◆ope-'rative a Med opératoire; (law, measure etc) en vigueur; – n ouvrier, -ière m. ◆operator n Tel standardiste mf; (on machine) opérateur, -trice mf; (criminal) escroc m; tour o. organisateur, -trice mf de voyages, voyagiste m.

opinion [ə'pɪnjən] n opinion f, avis m; in my o. à mon avis. ◆opinionated a dogmatique.

opium ['əʊpɪəm] n opium m.

opponent [ə'pəʊnənt] n adversaire mf.

opportune ['ɒpətjuːn] a opportun. ◆oppor'tunism n opportunisme m.

opportunity [ɒpə'tjuːnɪtɪ] n occasion f (to do de faire); pl (prospects) perspectives fpl; equal opportunities des chances fpl égales.

oppos/e [ə'pəʊz] vt (person, measure etc) s'opposer à; (law, motion) Pol faire opposition à. ◆—ed a opposé (to à); as o. to par opposition à. ◆—ing a (team, interests) opposé. ◆oppo'sition n opposition f (to à); the o. (rival camp) Fam l'adversaire m.

opposite ['ɒpəzɪt] a (side etc) opposé; (house) d'en face; one's o. number (counterpart) son homologue mf; – adv (to sit etc) en face; – prep o. (to) en face de; – n the o. le contraire, l'opposé m.

oppress [ə'pres] vt (tyrannize) opprimer; (of heat, anguish) oppresser; **the oppressed** les opprimés mpl. ◆**oppression** n oppression f. ◆**oppressive** a (ruler etc) oppressif; (heat) oppressant; (régime) tyrannique. ◆**oppressor** n oppresseur m.

opt [ɒpt] vi **to o. for** opter pour; **to o. to do** choisir de faire; **to o. out** Fam refuser de participer (**of** à). ◆**option** n option f; (subject) Sch matière f à option; **she has no o.** elle n'a pas le choix. ◆**optional** a facultatif; **o. extra** (on car etc) option f, accessoire m en option.

optical ['ɒptɪk(ə)l] a (glass) optique; (illusion, instrument etc) d'optique. ◆**op'tician** n opticien, -ienne mf.

optimism ['ɒptɪmɪz(ə)m] n optimisme m. ◆**optimist** n optimiste mf. ◆**opti'mistic** a optimiste. ◆**opti'mistically** adv avec optimisme.

optimum ['ɒptɪməm] a & n optimum (m); **the o. temperature** la température optimum. ◆**optimal** a optimal.

opulent ['ɒpjʊlənt] a opulent. ◆**opulence** n opulence f.

or [ɔːr] conj ou; **one or two** un ou deux; **he doesn't drink or smoke** il ne boit ni ne fume; **ten or so** environ dix.

oracle ['ɒrək(ə)l] n oracle m.

oral ['ɔːrəl] a oral; – n (examination) Sch oral m.

orange ['ɒrɪndʒ] **1** n (fruit) orange f; – a (drink) à l'orange; **o. tree** oranger m. **2** a & n (colour) orange a & m inv. ◆**orangeade** n orangeade f.

orang-outang [ɔːræŋʊ'tæŋ] n orang-ou-tan(g) m.

oration [ɔː'reɪʃ(ə)n] n **funeral o.** oraison f funèbre.

oratory ['ɒrətərɪ] n (words) Pej rhétorique f.

orbit ['ɔːbɪt] n (of planet etc) & Fig orbite f; – vt (sun etc) graviter autour de.

orchard ['ɔːtʃəd] n verger m.

orchestra ['ɔːkɪstrə] n (classical) orchestre m. ◆**or'chestral** a (music) orchestral; (concert) symphonique. ◆**orchestrate** vt (organize) & Mus orchestrer.

orchid ['ɔːkɪd] n orchidée f.

ordain [ɔː'deɪn] vt (priest) ordonner; **to o. that** décréter que.

ordeal [ɔː'diːl] n épreuve f, supplice m.

order ['ɔːdər] n (command, structure, association etc) ordre m; (purchase) Com commande f; **in o.** (drawer, room etc) en ordre; (passport etc) en règle; **in (numerical) o.** dans l'ordre numérique; **in working o.** en état de marche; **in o. of age** par ordre d'âge; **in o. to do** pour faire; **in o. that** pour que (+ sub); **it's in o. to smoke/etc** (allowed) il est permis de fumer/etc; **out of o.** (machine) en panne; (telephone) en dérangement; **to make** or **place an o.** Com passer une commande; **on o.** Com commandé; **money o.** mandat m; **postal o.** mandat m postal; – vt (command) ordonner (**s.o. to do** à qn de faire); (meal, goods etc) commander; (taxi) appeler; **to o. s.o. around** commander qn, régenter qn; – vi (in café etc) commander. ◆**—ly 1** a (tidy) ordonné; (mind) méthodique; (crowd) discipliné. **2** n Mil planton m; (in hospital) garçon m de salle.

ordinal ['ɔːdɪnəl] a (number) ordinal.

ordinary ['ɔːd(ə)nrɪ] a (usual) ordinaire; (average) moyen; (mediocre) médiocre, ordinaire; **an o. individual** un simple particulier; **in o. use** d'usage courant; **in the o. course of events** en temps normal; **in the o. way** normalement; **it's out of the o.** ça sort de l'ordinaire.

ordination [ɔːdɪ'neɪʃ(ə)n] n Rel ordination f.

ordnance ['ɔːdnəns] n (guns) Mil artillerie f.

ore [ɔːr] n minerai m.

organ ['ɔːgən] n **1** Anat & Fig organe m. **2** Mus orgue m, orgues fpl; **barrel o.** orgue m de Barbarie. ◆**organist** n organiste mf.

organic [ɔː'gænɪk] a organique. ◆**organism** n organisme m.

organization [ɔːgənaɪ'zeɪʃ(ə)n] n (arrangement, association) organisation f.

organiz/e ['ɔːgənaɪz] vt organiser. ◆**—ed** a (mind, group etc) organisé. ◆**—er** n organisateur, -trice mf.

orgasm ['ɔːgæz(ə)m] n orgasme m.

orgy ['ɔːdʒɪ] n orgie f.

orient ['ɔːrɪənt] vt Am = orientate. ◆**orientate** vt orienter.

Orient ['ɔːrɪənt] n **the O.** l'Orient m. ◆**ori'ental** a & n oriental, -ale (mf).

orifice ['ɒrɪfɪs] n orifice m.

origin ['ɒrɪdʒɪn] n origine f.

original [ə'rɪdʒɪn(ə)l] a (first) premier, originel, primitif; (novel, unusual) original; (sin) originel; (copy, version) original; – n (document, painting etc) original m. ◆**origi'nality** n originalité f. ◆**originally** adv (at first) à l'origine; (in a novel way) originalement; **she comes o. from** elle est originaire de. ◆**originate** vi (begin) prendre naissance (**in** dans); **to o. from** (of idea etc) émaner de; (of person) être originaire de; – vt être l'auteur de. ◆**originator** n auteur m (of de).

ornament ['ɔːnəmənt] n (decoration) orne-

ment *m*; *pl* (*vases etc*) bibelots *mpl*.
◆orna'mental *a* ornemental. ◆orna-
men'tation *n* ornementation *f*. ◆or'nate
a (*style etc*) (très) orné. ◆or'nately *adv*
(*decorated etc*) de façon surchargée, à
outrance.

orphan ['ɔːf(ə)n] *n* orphelin, -ine *mf*; – *a*
orphelin. ◆orphaned *a* orphelin; he was
o. by the accident l'accident l'a rendu
orphelin. ◆orphanage *n* orphelinat *m*.

orthodox ['ɔːθədɒks] *a* orthodoxe.
◆orthodoxy *n* orthodoxie *f*.

orthop(a)edics [ɔːθə'piːdɪks] *n* orthopédie
f.

Oscar ['ɒskər] *n* Cin oscar *m*.

oscillate ['ɒsɪleɪt] *vi* osciller.

ostensibly [ɒ'stensɪblɪ] *adv* apparemment,
en apparence.

ostentation [ɒsten'teɪʃ(ə)n] *n* ostentation *f*.
◆ostentatious *a* plein d'ostentation,
prétentieux.

ostracism ['ɒstrəsɪz(ə)m] *n* ostracisme *m*.
◆ostracize *vt* proscrire, frapper
d'ostracisme.

ostrich ['ɒstrɪtʃ] *n* autruche *f*.

other ['ʌðər] *a* autre; o. people d'autres; the
o. one l'autre *mf*; I have no o. gloves than
these je n'ai pas d'autres gants que ceux-ci;
– *pron* autre; (some) others d'autres; some
do, others don't les uns le font, les autres ne
le font pas; none o. than, no o. than nul
autre que; – *adv* o. than autrement que.
◆otherwise *adv* autrement; – *a* (*different*) (tout) autre.

otter ['ɒtər] *n* loutre *f*.

ouch! [aʊtʃ] *int* aïe!, ouille!

ought [ɔːt] *v aux* 1 (*obligation, desirability*)
you o. to leave tu devrais partir; I o. to have
done it j'aurais dû le faire; he said he o. to
stay il a dit qu'il devait rester. 2
(*probability*) it o. to be ready ça devrait être
prêt.

ounce [aʊns] *n* (*measure*) & *Fig* once *f* (=
28,35 g).

our [aʊər] *poss a* notre, *pl* nos. ◆ours *pron*
le nôtre, la nôtre, *pl* les nôtres; this book is
o. ce livre est à nous *or* est le nôtre; a friend
of o. un ami à nous. ◆our'selves *pron*
nous-mêmes; (*reflexive & after prep etc*)
nous; we wash o. nous nous lavons.

oust [aʊst] *vt* évincer (from de).

out [aʊt] *adv* (*outside*) dehors; (*not at home
etc*) sorti; (*light, fire*) éteint; (*news, secret*)
connu, révélé; (*flower*) ouvert; (*book*)
publié, sorti; (*finished*) fini; to be *or* go o. a
lot sortir beaucoup; he's o. in Italy il est
(parti) en Italie; o. there là-bas; to have a

day o. sortir pour la journée; 5 km o. Nau à
5 km du rivage; the sun's o. il fait (du)
soleil; the tide's o. la marée est basse;
you're o. (*wrong*) tu t'es trompé; (*in game
etc*) tu es éliminé (of de); the trip *or* journey
o. l'aller *m*; to be o. to win être résolu à
gagner; – *prep* o. of (*outside*) en dehors de;
(*danger, breath, reach, water*) hors de;
(*without*) sans; o. of pity/love/*etc* par
pitié/amour/*etc*; to look/jump/*etc* o. of
(*window etc*) regarder/sauter/*etc* par; to
drink/take/copy o. of boire/prendre/
copier dans; made o. of (*wood etc*) fait en;
to make sth o. of a box/rag/*etc* faire qch
avec une boîte/un chiffon/*etc*; a page o. of
une page de; she's o. of town elle n'est pas
en ville; 5 km o. of (*away from*) à 5 km de;
four o. of five quatre sur cinq; o. of the blue
de manière inattendue; to feel o. of it *or* of
things se sentir hors du coup. ◆'out-and-
out *a* (*cheat, liar etc*) achevé; (*believer*) à
tout crin. ◆o.-of-'date *a* (*expired*)
périmé; (*old-fashioned*) démodé. ◆o.-of-
'doors *adv* dehors. ◆o.-of-the-'way *a*
(*place*) écarté.

outbid [aʊt'bɪd] *vt* (*pt & pp* outbid, *pres p*
outbidding) to o. s.o. (sur)enchérir sur qn.

outboard ['aʊtbɔːd] *a* o. motor Nau moteur
m hors-bord *inv*.

outbreak ['aʊtbreɪk] *n* (*of war*) début *m*; (*of
violence, pimples*) éruption *f*; (*of fever*)
accès *m*; (*of hostilities*) ouverture *f*.

outbuilding ['aʊtbɪldɪŋ] *n* (*of mansion,
farm*) dépendance *f*.

outburst ['aʊtbɜːst] *n* (*of anger, joy*) explosion *f*; (*of violence*) flambée *f*; (*of laughter*)
éclat *m*.

outcast ['aʊtkɑːst] *n* (*social*) o. paria *m*.

outcome ['aʊtkʌm] *n* résultat *m*, issue *f*.

outcry ['aʊtkraɪ] *n* tollé *m*.

outdated [aʊt'deɪtɪd] *a* démodé.

outdistance [aʊt'dɪstəns] *vt* distancer.

outdo [aʊt'duː] *vt* (*pt* outdid, *pp* outdone)
surpasser (in en).

outdoor ['aʊtdɔː] *a* (*game*) de plein air;
(*pool, life*) en plein air; o. clothes tenue *f*
pour sortir. ◆out'doors *adv* dehors.

outer ['aʊtər] *a* extérieur; o. space l'espace
m (cosmique); the o. suburbs la grande
banlieue.

outfit ['aʊtfɪt] *n* équipement *m*; (*kit*) trousse
f; (*toy*) panoplie *f* (*de pompier, cow-boy etc*);
(*clothes*) costume *m*; (*for woman*) toilette *f*;
(*group, gang*) Fam bande *f*; (*firm*) Fam
boîte *f*; sports/ski o. tenue *f* de sport/de
ski. ◆outfitter *n* chemisier *m*.

outgoing ['aʊtɡəʊɪŋ] 1 *a* (*minister etc*)

sortant; (*mail, ship*) en partance. **2** *a* (*sociable*) liant, ouvert. **3** *npl* (*expenses*) dépenses *fpl*.

outgrow [autˈɡrəu] *vt* (*pt* **outgrew**, *pp* **outgrown**) (*clothes*) devenir trop grand pour; (*habit*) perdre (en grandissant); **to o. s.o.** (*grow more than*) grandir plus vite que qn.

outhouse [ˈauthaus] *n* (*of mansion, farm*) dépendance *f*; (*lavatory*) *Am* cabinets *mpl* extérieurs.

outing [ˈautiŋ] *n* sortie *f*, excursion *f*.

outlandish [autˈlændiʃ] *a* (*weird*) bizarre; (*barbaric*) barbare.

outlast [autˈlɑːst] *vt* durer plus longtemps que; (*survive*) survivre à.

outlaw [ˈautlɔː] *n* hors-la-loi *m inv*; – *vt* (*ban*) proscrire.

outlay [ˈautleɪ] *n* (*money*) dépense(s) *f(pl)*.

outlet [ˈautlet] *n* (*for liquid, of tunnel etc*) sortie *f*; *El* prise *f* de courant; (*market for goods*) *Com* débouché *m*; (*for feelings, energy*) moyen *m* d'exprimer, exutoire *m*; **retail o.** *Com* point *m* de vente, magasin *m*.

outline [ˈautlaɪn] *n* (*shape*) contour *m*, profil *m*; (*rough*) **o.** (*of article, plan etc*) esquisse *f*; **the broad** *or* **general** *or* **main outline(s)** (*chief features*) les grandes lignes; – *vt* (*plan, situation*) décrire à grands traits, esquisser; (*book, speech*) résumer; **to be outlined against** (*of tree etc*) se profiler sur.

outlive [autˈlɪv] *vt* survivre à.

outlook [ˈautluk] *n inv* (*for future*) perspective(s) *f(pl)*; (*point of view*) perspective *f* (**on** sur), attitude *f* (**on** à l'égard de); *Met* prévisions *fpl*.

outlying [ˈautlaɪɪŋ] *a* (*remote*) isolé; (*neighbourhood*) périphérique.

outmoded [autˈməudɪd] *a* démodé.

outnumber [autˈnʌmbər] *vt* être plus nombreux que.

outpatient [ˈautpeɪʃ(ə)nt] *n* malade *mf* en consultation externe.

outpost [ˈautpəust] *n* avant-poste *m*.

output [ˈautput] *n* rendement *m*, production *f*; (*computer process*) sortie *f*; (*computer data*) donnée(s) *f(pl)* de sortie.

outrage [ˈautreɪdʒ] *n* atrocité *f*, crime *m*; (*indignity*) indignité *f*; (*scandal*) scandale *m*; (*indignation*) indignation *f*; **bomb o.** attentat *m* à la bombe; – *vt* (*morals*) outrager; **outraged by sth** indigné de qch. ◆**out'rageous** *a* (*atrocious*) atroce; (*shocking*) scandaleux; (*dress, hat etc*) grotesque.

outright [autˈraɪt] *adv* (*completely*) complètement; (*to say, tell*) franchement; (*to be*

killed) sur le coup; **to buy o.** (*for cash*) acheter au comptant; – [ˈautraɪt] *a* (*complete*) complet; (*lie, folly*) total; (*refusal, rejection etc*) catégorique, net; (*winner*) incontesté.

outset [ˈautset] *n* **at the o.** au début; **from the o.** dès le départ.

outside [autˈsaɪd] *adv* (au) dehors, à l'extérieur; **to go o.** sortir; – *prep* à l'extérieur de, en dehors de; (*beyond*) *Fig* en dehors de; **o. my room** *or* **door** à la porte de ma chambre; – *n* extérieur *m*, dehors *m*; – [ˈautsaɪd] *a* extérieur; (*bus or train seat etc*) côté couloir *inv*; (*maximum*) *Fig* maximum; **the o. lane** *Aut* la voie de droite, *Am* la voie de gauche; **an o. chance** une faible chance. ◆**out'sider** *n* (*stranger*) étranger, -ère *mf*; *Sp* outsider *m*.

outsize [ˈautsaɪz] *a* (*clothes*) grande taille *inv*.

outskirts [ˈautskɜːts] *npl* banlieue *f*.

outsmart [autˈsmɑːt] *vt* être plus malin que.

outspoken [autˈspəuk(ə)n] *a* (*frank*) franc.

outstanding [autˈstændɪŋ] *a* remarquable, exceptionnel; (*problem, business*) non réglé, en suspens; (*debt*) impayé; **work o.** travail *m* à faire.

outstay [autˈsteɪ] *vt* **to o. one's welcome** abuser de l'hospitalité de son hôte, s'incruster.

outstretched [autˈstretʃt] *a* (*arm*) tendu.

outstrip [autˈstrɪp] *vt* (-**pp**-) devancer.

outward [ˈautwəd] *a* (*look, movement*) vers l'extérieur; (*sign, appearance*) extérieur; **o. journey** *or* **trip** aller *m*. ◆**outward(s)** *adv* vers l'extérieur.

outweigh [autˈweɪ] *vt* (*be more important than*) l'emporter sur.

outwit [autˈwɪt] *vt* (-**tt**-) être plus malin que.

oval [ˈəuv(ə)l] *a* & *n* ovale (*m*).

ovary [ˈəuvəri] *n* *Anat* ovaire *m*.

ovation [əuˈveɪʃ(ə)n] *n* **(standing) o.** ovation *f*.

oven [ˈʌv(ə)n] *n* four *m*; (*hot place*) *Fig* fournaise *f*; **o. glove** gant *m* isolant.

over [ˈəuvər] *prep* (*on*) sur; (*above*) au-dessus de; (*on the other side of*) de l'autre côté de; **bridge o. the river** pont *m* sur le fleuve; **to jump/look/etc o. sth** sauter/regarder/*etc* par-dessus qch; **to fall o. the balcony/** tomber du balcon/*etc*; **she fell o.** il elle est tombée; **o. it** (*on*) dessus; (*above*) au-dessus de; (*to jump etc*) par-dessus; **to criticize/etc o. sth** (*about*) critiquer/*etc* à propos de qch; **an advantage o.** un avantage sur *or* par rapport à; **o. the radio** (*on*) à la radio; **o. the phone** au télé-

phone; **o. the holidays** (*during*) pendant les vacances; **o. ten days** (*more than*) plus de dix jours; **men o. sixty** les hommes de plus de soixante ans; **o. and above** en plus de; **he's o. his flu** (*recovered from*) il est remis de sa grippe; **all o. Spain** (*everywhere in*) dans toute l'Espagne, partout en Espagne; **all o. the carpet** (*everywhere on*) partout sur le tapis; – *adv* (*above*) (par-)dessus; (*finished*) fini; (*danger*) passé; (*again*) encore; (*too*) trop; **jump o.!** sautez par-dessus!; **o. here** ici; **there là-bas; to be o.** or **come** or **go o.** (*visit*) passer; **he's o. in Italy** il est (parti) en Italie; **she's o. from Paris** elle est venue de Paris; **wet all o.** tout mouillé; **it's (all) o.!** (*finished*) c'est fini!; **she's o.** (*fallen*) elle est tombée; **a kilo o o.** (*more*) un kilo ou plus; **I have ten o.** (*left*) il m'en reste dix; **there's some bread o.** il reste du pain; **o. and o.** (*again*) (*often*) à plusieurs reprises; **to start all o.** (*again*) recommencer à zéro; **o. pleased/etc** trop content/etc.
◆**o.-a'bundant** *a* surabondant. ◆**o.-de'veloped** *a* trop développé. ◆**o.-fa'miliar** *a* trop familier. ◆**o.-in'dulge** *vt* (*one's desires etc*) céder trop facilement à; (*person*) trop gâter. ◆**o.-sub'scribed** *a* (*course*) ayant trop d'inscrits.

overall 1 [əʊvər'ɔːl] *a* (*measurement, length, etc*) total; (*result, effort etc*) global; – *adv* globalement. **2** ['əʊvərɔːl] *n* blouse *f* (de travail); *pl* bleus *mpl* de travail.

overawe [əʊvər'ɔː] *vt* intimider.

overbalance [əʊvə'bæləns] *vi* basculer.

overbearing [əʊvə'beərɪŋ] *a* autoritaire.

overboard [əʊvəbɔːd] *adv* à la mer.

overburden [əʊvə'bɜːd(ə)n] *vt* surcharger.

overcast [əʊvə'kɑːst] *a* (*sky*) couvert.

overcharge [əʊvə'tʃɑːdʒ] *vt* **to o. s.o. for sth** faire payer qch trop cher à qn.

overcoat ['əʊvəkəʊt] *n* pardessus *m*.

overcome [əʊvə'kʌm] *vt* (*pt* **overcame**, *pp* **overcome**) (*enemy, shyness etc*) vaincre; (*disgust, problem*) surmonter; **to be o. by** (*fatigue, grief*) être accablé par; (*fumes, temptation*) succomber à; **he was o. by emotion** l'émotion eut raison de lui.

overcrowded [əʊvə'kraʊdɪd] *a* (*house, country*) surpeuplé; (*bus, train*) bondé. ◆**overcrowding** *n* surpeuplement *m*.

overdo [əʊvə'duː] *vt* (*pt* **overdid**, *pp* **overdone**) exagérer; *Culin* cuire trop; **to o. it** (*exaggerate*) exagérer; (*work too much*) se surmener; *Iron* se fatiguer.

overdose ['əʊvədəʊs] *n* overdose *f*, dose *f* excessive (*de barbituriques etc*).

overdraft ['əʊvədrɑːft] *n Fin* découvert *m*. ◆**over'draw** *vt* (*pt* **overdrew**, *pp* **overdrawn**) (*account*) mettre à découvert.

overdress [əʊvə'dres] *vi* s'habiller avec trop de recherche.

overdue [əʊvə'djuː] *a* (*train etc*) en retard; (*debt*) arriéré; (*apology, thanks*) tardif.

overeat [əʊvər'iːt] *vi* manger trop.

overestimate [əʊvər'estɪmeɪt] *vt* surestimer.

overexcited [əʊvərɪk'saɪtɪd] *a* surexcité.

overfeed [əʊvə'fiːd] *vt* (*pt & pp* **overfed**) suralimenter.

overflow 1 [əʊvə'fləʊ] *n* (*outlet*) trop-plein *m*; (*of people, objects*) *Fig* excédent *m*. **2** [əʊvə'fləʊ] *vi* déborder (**with** de); **to be overflowing with** (*of town, shop, house etc*) regorger de (*visiteurs, livres etc*).

overgrown [əʊvə'grəʊn] *a* envahi par la végétation; **o. with** (*weeds etc*) envahi par; **you're an o. schoolgirl** *Fig Pej* tu as la mentalité d'une écolière.

overhang [əʊvə'hæŋ] *vi* (*pt & pp* **overhung**) faire saillie; – *vt* surplomber.

overhaul [əʊvə'hɔːl] *vt* (*vehicle, doctrine etc*) réviser; – ['əʊvəhɔːl] *n* révision *f*.

overhead [əʊvə'hed] *adv* au-dessus; – ['əʊvəhed] **1** *a* (*railway etc*) aérien. **2** *npl* (*expenses*) frais *mpl* généraux.

overhear [əʊvə'hɪər] *vt* (*pt & pp* **overheard**) surprendre, entendre.

overheat [əʊvə'hiːt] *vt* surchauffer; – *vi* (*of engine*) chauffer.

overjoyed [əʊvə'dʒɔɪd] *a* ravi, enchanté.

overland [əʊvəlænd] *a & adv* par voie de terre.

overlap [əʊvə'læp] *vi* (**-pp-**) se chevaucher; – *vt* chevaucher; – ['əʊvəlæp] *n* chevauchement *m*.

overleaf [əʊvə'liːf] *adv* au verso.

overload [əʊvə'ləʊd] *vt* surcharger.

overlook [əʊvə'lʊk] *vt* **1** (*not notice*) ne pas remarquer; (*forget*) oublier; (*disregard, ignore*) passer sur. **2** (*of window, house etc*) donner sur; (*of tower, fort*) dominer.

overly ['əʊvəlɪ] *adv* excessivement.

overmuch [əʊvə'mʌtʃ] *adv* trop, excessivement.

overnight [əʊvə'naɪt] *adv* (*during the night*) (pendant) la nuit; (*all night*) toute la nuit; (*suddenly*) *Fig* du jour au lendemain; **to stay o.** passer la nuit; – ['əʊvənaɪt] *a* (*stay*) d'une nuit; (*clothes*) pour une nuit; (*trip*) de nuit.

overpass ['əʊvəpæs] *n* (*bridge*) *Am* tobogan *m*.

overpopulated [əʊvəˈpɒpjʊleɪtɪd] *a* sur-peuplé.

overpower [əʊvəˈpaʊər] *vt* (*physically*) maîtriser; (*defeat*) vaincre; *Fig* accabler. **◆—ing** *a* (*charm etc*) irrésistible; (*heat etc*) accablant.

overrat/e [əʊvəˈreɪt] *vt* surestimer. **◆—ed** *a* surfait.

overreach [əʊvəˈriːtʃ] *vt* to o. oneself trop entreprendre.

overreact [əʊvərɪˈækt] *vi* réagir excessive-ment.

overrid/e [əʊvəˈraɪd] *vt* (*pt* **overrode**, *pp* **overridden**) (*invalidate*) annuler; (*take no notice of*) passer outre à; (*be more important than*) l'emporter sur. **◆—ing** *a* (*passion*) prédominant; (*importance*) primordial.

overrule [əʊvəˈruːl] *vt* (*reject*) rejeter.

overrun [əʊvəˈrʌn] *vt* (*pt* **overran**, *pp* **overrun**, *pres p* **overrunning**) **1** (*invade*) envahir. **2** (*go beyond*) aller au-delà de.

overseas [əʊvəˈsiːz] *adv* (*Africa etc*) outre-mer; (*abroad*) à l'étranger; – ['əʊvəsiːz] *a* (*visitor*, *market etc*) d'outre-mer; étranger; (*trade*) extérieur.

overse/e [əʊvəˈsiː] *vt* (*pt* **oversaw**, *pp* **overseen**) surveiller. **◆—er** ['əʊvəsiːər] *n* (*fore-man*) contremaître *m*.

overshadow [əʊvəˈʃædəʊ] *vt* (*make less important*) éclipser; (*make gloomy*) assom-brir.

overshoot [əʊvəˈʃuːt] *vt* (*pt* & *pp* **overshot**) (*of aircraft*) *Fig* dépasser.

oversight ['əʊvəsaɪt] *n* omission *f*, oubli *m*; (*mistake*) erreur *f*.

oversimplify [əʊvəˈsɪmplɪfaɪ] *vti* trop sim-plifier.

oversize(d) ['əʊvəsaɪz(d)] *a* trop grand.

oversleep [əʊvəˈsliːp] *vi* (*pt* & *pp* **overslept**) dormir trop longtemps, oublier de se réveiller.

overspend [əʊvəˈspend] *vi* dépenser trop.

overstaffed [əʊvəˈstɑːft] *a* au personnel pléthorique.

overstay [əʊvəˈsteɪ] *vt* to o. one's welcome abuser de l'hospitalité de son hôte, s'incruster.

overstep [əʊvəˈstep] *vt* (**-pp-**) dépasser.

overt ['əʊvɜːt] *a* manifeste.

overtake [əʊvəˈteɪk] *vt* (*pt* **overtook**, *pp* **overtaken**) dépasser; (*vehicle*) doubler, dépasser; **overtaken by** (*nightfall*, *storm*) surpris par; – *vi Aut* doubler, dépasser.

overtax [əʊvəˈtæks] *vt* **1** (*strength*) excéder; (*brain*) fatiguer. **2** (*taxpayer*) surimposer.

overthrow [əʊvəˈθrəʊ] *vt* (*pt* **overthrew**, *pp* **overthrown**) *Pol* renverser; – ['əʊvəθrəʊ] *n* renversement *m*.

overtime ['əʊvətaɪm] *n* heures *fpl* supplé-mentaires; – *adv* to work o. faire des heures supplémentaires.

overtones ['əʊvətəʊnz] *npl Fig* note *f*, nuance *f* (**of** de).

overture ['əʊvətjʊər] *n Mus* & *Fig* ouver-ture *f*.

overturn [əʊvəˈtɜːn] *vt* (*chair*, *table etc*) renverser; (*car*, *boat*) retourner; (*decision etc*) *Fig* annuler; – *vi* (*of car*, *boat*) se retourner.

overweight [əʊvəˈweɪt] *a* to be o. (*of suitcase etc*) peser trop; (*of person*) avoir des kilos en trop.

overwhelm [əʊvəˈwelm] *vt* (*of feelings*, *heat etc*) accabler; (*defeat*) écraser; (*amaze*) bouleverser. **◆—ed** *a* (*overjoyed*) ravi (**by**, **with** de); **o. with** (*grief*, *work etc*) accablé de; (*offers*) submergé par; **o. by** (*kindness*, *gift etc*) vivement touché par. **◆—ing** *a* (*heat*, *grief etc*) accablant; (*majority*, *defeat*) écrasant; (*desire*) irrésistible; (*impression*) dominant. **◆—ingly** *adv* (*to vote*, *reject etc*) en masse; (*utterly*) carrément.

overwork [əʊvəˈwɜːk] *n* surmenage *m*; – *vi* se surmener; – *vt* surmener.

overwrought [əʊvəˈrɔːt] *a* (*tense*) tendu.

owe [əʊ] *vt* devoir (**to** à); **I'll o. it** (**to**) **you, I'll o. you** (**for**) **it** (*money*) je te le devrai; **to o. it to oneself to do sth** se devoir de faire. **◆owing 1** *a* (*money etc*) dû, qu'on doit. **2** *prep* **o. to** à cause de.

owl [aʊl] *n* hibou *m*.

own [əʊn] **1** *a* propre; **my o. house** ma propre maison; – *pron* **it's my** (**very**) **o.** c'est à moi (tout seul); **a house of his o.** sa propre maison, sa maison à lui; (**all**) **on one's o.** (*alone*) tout seul; **to get one's o. back** prendre sa revanche (**on** sur, **for** de); **to come into one's o.** (*fulfil oneself*) s'épanouir. **2** *vt* (*possess*) posséder; **who owns this ball/etc?** à qui appartient cette balle/*etc*? **3** *vi* **to o. up** (*confess*) avouer; **to o. up to sth** avouer qch. **◆owner** *n* propriétaire *mf*. **◆ownership** *n* posses-sion *f*; **home o.** accession *f* à la propriété; **public o.** *Econ* nationalisation *f*.

ox, *pl* **oxen** [ɒks, ˈɒks(ə)n] *n* bœuf *m*.

oxide ['ɒksaɪd] *n Ch* oxide *m*. **◆oxidize** *vi* s'oxyder; – *vt* oxyder.

oxygen ['ɒksɪdʒ(ə)n] *n* oxygène *m*; – *a* (*mask*, *tent*) à oxygène.

oyster ['ɔɪstər] *n* huître *f*.

P

P, p [piː] n P, p m.
p [piː] abbr = penny, pence.
pa [pɑː] n (father) Fam papa m.
pace [peɪs] n (speed) pas m, allure f; (measure) pas m; **to keep p. with** (follow) suivre; (in work, progress) se maintenir à la hauteur de; – vi **to p. up and down** faire les cent pas; – vt (room etc) arpenter. **◆pacemaker** n (device) stimulateur m cardiaque.
Pacific [pəˈsɪfɪk] a (coast etc) pacifique; – n **the P.** le Pacifique.
pacify [ˈpæsɪfaɪ] vt (country) pacifier; (calm, soothe) apaiser. **◆pacifier** n (dummy) Am sucette f, tétine f. **◆pacifist** n & a pacifiste (mf).
pack [pæk] **1** n (bundle, packet) paquet m; (bale) balle f; (of animal) charge f; (rucksack) sac m (à dos); Mil paquetage m; (of hounds, wolves) meute f; (of runners) Sp peloton m; (of thieves) bande f; (of cards) jeu m; (of lies) tissu m. **2** vt (fill) remplir (**with** de); (excessively) bourrer; (suitcase) faire; (object into box etc) emballer; (object into suitcase) mettre dans sa valise; (make into package) empaqueter; **to p. into** (cram) entasser dans; (put) mettre dans; **to p. away** (tidy away) ranger; **to p.** (**down**) (compress, crush) tasser; **to p. off** (person) Fam expédier; (of thieves) bande f; **to p. up** (put into box) emballer; (put into case) mettre dans sa valise; (give up) Fam laisser tomber; – vi (fill one's bags) faire ses valises; **to p. into** (of people) s'entasser dans; **to p. in or up** (of machine, vehicle) Fam tomber en panne; **to p. up** (stop) Fam s'arrêter; (leave) plier bagage. **◆—ed** a (bus, cinema etc) bourré; **p. lunch** panier-repas m; **p. out** (crowded) Fam bourré. **◆—ing** n (material, action) emballage m; **p. case** caisse f d'emballage.
packag/e [ˈpækɪdʒ] n paquet m; (computer programs) progiciel m; **p. deal** Com contrat m global, train m de propositions; **p. tour** voyage m organisé; – vt emballer, empaqueter. **◆—ing** n (material, action) emballage m.
packet [ˈpækɪt] n paquet m; (of sweets) sachet m, paquet m; **to make/cost a p.** Fam faire/coûter beaucoup d'argent.
pact [pækt] n pacte m.

pad [pæd] n (wad, plug) tampon m; (for writing, notes etc) bloc m; (on leg) Sp jambière f; (on knee) Sp genouillère f; (room) Sl piaule f; **launch(ing) p.** rampe f de lancement; **ink(ing) p.** tampon m encreur; – vt (-dd-) (stuff) rembourrer, matelasser; **to p. out** (speech, text) délayer. **◆padding** n rembourrage m; (of speech, text) délayage m.
paddle [ˈpæd(ə)l] **1** vi (splash about) barboter; (dip one's feet) se mouiller les pieds; – n **to have a (little) p.** se mouiller les pieds. **2** n (pole) pagaie f; **p. boat, p. steamer** bateau m à roues; – vt **to p. a canoe** pagayer.
paddock [ˈpædək] n enclos m; (at racecourse) paddock m.
paddy [ˈpædɪ] n **p. (field)** rizière f.
padlock [ˈpædlɒk] n (on door etc) cadenas m; (on bicycle, moped) antivol m; – vt (door etc) cadenasser.
p(a)ediatrician [piːdɪəˈtrɪʃ(ə)n] n Med pédiatre mf.
pagan [ˈpeɪɡən] a & n païen, -enne (mf). **◆paganism** n paganisme m.
page [peɪdʒ] **1** n (of book etc) page f. **2** n **p. (boy)** (in hotel etc) chasseur m; (at court) Hist page m; – vt **to p. s.o.** faire appeler qn.
pageant [ˈpædʒənt] n grand spectacle m historique. **◆pageantry** n pompe f, apparat m.
pagoda [pəˈɡəʊdə] n pagode f.
paid [peɪd] see **pay**; – a (assassin etc) à gages; **to put p. to** (hopes, plans) anéantir; **to put p. to s.o.** (ruin) couler qn.
pail [peɪl] n seau m.
pain [peɪn] n (physical) douleur f; (grief) peine f; pl (efforts) efforts mpl; **to have a p. in one's arm** avoir mal or une douleur au bras; **to be in p.** souffrir; **to go to or take (great) pains to do** (exert oneself) se donner du mal à faire; **to go to or take (great) pains not to do** (be careful) prendre bien soin de ne pas faire; **to be a p. (in the neck)** (of person) Fam être casse-pieds; – vt (grieve) peiner. **◆p.-killer** n analgésique m, calmant m. **◆painful** a (illness, operation) douloureux; (arm, leg) qui fait mal, douloureux; (distressing) douloureux, pénible; (difficult) pénible; (bad) Fam

affreux. **painless** a sans douleur; (illness, operation) indolore; (easy) Fam facile. **painstaking** a (person) soigneux; (work) soigné.

paint [peɪnt] n peinture f. pl (in box, tube) couleurs fpl; — vt (colour, describe) peindre; to p. blue/etc peindre en bleu/etc; — vi peindre. **-ing** n (activity) peinture f; (picture) tableau m, peinture f. **-er** n peintre m. **paintbrush** n pinceau m. **paintwork** n peinture(s) f(pl).

pair [peər] n paire f; (man and woman) couple m; a p. of shorts un short; the p. of you Fam vous deux; — vi to p. off (of people) former un couple; — vt (marry) marier.

pajama(s) [pəˈdʒɑːmə(z)] a & npl Am = pyjama(s).

Pakistan [pɑːkɪˈstɑːn] n Pakistan m. **Pakistani** a & n pakistanais, -aise (mf).

pal [pæl] n Fam copain m, copine f; — vi (-ll-) to p. up devenir copains; to p. up with devenir copain avec.

palace ['pælɪs] n (building) palais m. **palatial** [pəˈleɪʃ(ə)l] a comme un palais.

palatable ['pælətəb(ə)l] a (food) agréable; (fact, idea etc) acceptable.

palate ['pælɪt] n Anat palais m.

palaver [pəˈlɑːvər] n Fam (fuss) histoire(s) f(pl); (talk) palabres mpl.

pale [peɪl] a (-er, -est) (face, colour etc) pâle; p. ale bière f blonde; — vi pâlir. **-ness** n pâleur f.

palette ['pælɪt] n (of artist) palette f.

paling ['peɪlɪŋ] n (fence) palissade f.

pall [pɔːl] vi devenir insipide or ennuyeux (on four). 2 n (of smoke) voile m.

pallbearer ['pɔːlbeərər] n personne f qui aide à porter un cercueil.

pallid ['pælɪd] a pâle. **pallor** n pâleur f.

pally ['pælɪ] a (-ier, -iest) Fam copain am, copine af (with avec).

palm [pɑːm] 1 n (of hand) paume f. 2 n (symbol) palme f; p. (tree) palmier m; p. (leaf) palme f; P. Sunday les Rameaux mpl. 3 vt Fam to p. sth off (pass off) refiler qch (on à), coller qch (on à); to p. s.o. off on s.o. coller qn à qn.

palmist ['pɑːmɪst] n chiromancien, -ienne mf. **palmistry** n chiromancie f.

palpable ['pælpəb(ə)l] a (obvious) manifeste.

palpitate ['pælpɪteɪt] vi (of heart) palpiter. **palpi'tation** n palpitation f.

paltry ['pɔːltrɪ] a (-ier, -iest) misérable, dérisoire.

pamper ['pæmpər] vt dorloter.

pamphlet ['pæmflɪt] n brochure f.

pan [pæn] 1 n casserole f; (for frying) poêle f (à frire); (of lavatory) cuvette f. 2 vt (-nn-) (criticize) Fam éreinter. 3 vi (-nn-) to p. out (succeed) aboutir.

Pan- [pæn] pref pan-.

panacea [pænəˈsɪə] n panacée f.

panache [pəˈnæʃ] n (showy manner) panache m.

pancake ['pænkeɪk] n crêpe f.

pancreas ['pæŋkrɪəs] n Anat pancréas m.

panda ['pændə] n (animal) panda m; P. car = voiture f pie inv (de la police).

pandemonium [pændɪˈməʊnɪəm] n (chaos) chaos m; (uproar) tumulte m; (place) bazar m.

pander ['pændər] vi to p. to (tastes, fashion etc) sacrifier à; to p. to s.o. or to s.o.'s desires se plier aux désirs de qn.

pane [peɪn] n vitre f, carreau m.

panel ['pæn(ə)l] n 1 (of door etc) panneau m; (control) p. Tech El console f; (instrument) p. Av Aut tableau m de bord. 2 (of judges) jury m; (of experts) groupe m; (of candidates) équipe f; a p. of guests des invités. a p. game TV Rad un jeu par équipes. **panelled** a (room etc) lambrissé. **panelling** n lambris m. **panellist** n TV Rad (guest) invité, -ée mf; (expert) expert m; (candidate) candidat, -ate mf.

pangs [pæŋz] npl p. of conscience remords mpl (de conscience); p. of hunger/death les affres fpl de la faim/de la mort.

panic ['pænɪk] n panique f; to get into a p. paniquer; — vi (-ck-) s'affoler, paniquer. **p.-stricken** a affolé. **panicky** (person) a Fam qui s'affole facilement; to get p. s'affoler.

panorama [pænəˈrɑːmə] n panorama m. **panoramic** a panoramique.

pansy ['pænzɪ] n Bot pensée f.

pant [pænt] vi (gasp) haleter.

panther ['pænθər] n (animal) panthère f.

panties ['pæntɪz] npl (female underwear) slip m.

pantomime ['pæntəmaɪm] n (show) spectacle m de Noël.

pantry ['pæntrɪ] n (larder) garde-manger m inv; (storeroom in hotel etc) office m or f.

pants [pænts] npl (male underwear) slip m; (loose, long) caleçon m; (female underwear) slip m; (trousers) Am pantalon m.

pantyhose ['pæntɪhəʊz] n (tights) Am collant(s) m(pl).

papacy ['peɪpəsɪ] n papauté f. **papal** a papal.

paper ['peɪpər] n papier m; (newspaper) journal m; (wallpaper) papier m peint;

(*exam*) épreuve *f* (écrite); (*student's exercise*) *Sch* copie *f*; (*learned article*) exposé *m*, communication *f*; (*paper*) papier *m* d'emballage; **to put down on p.** mettre par écrit; – *a* (*bag etc*) en papier; (*cup, plate*) en carton; **p. clip** trombone *m*; **p. knife** coupe-papier *m inv*; **p. mill** papeterie *f*; **p. shop** marchand de journaux; – *vt* (*room, wall*) tapisser. ◆**paperback** *n* (*book*) livre *m* de poche. ◆**paperboy** *n* livreur *m* de journaux. ◆**paperweight** *n* presse-papiers *m inv*. ◆**paperwork** *n* *Com* écritures *fpl*; (*red tape*) *Pej* paperasserie *f*.

paprika ['pæprɪkə] *n* paprika *m*.

par [pɑːr] *n* **on a p.** au même niveau (**with** que); **below p.** (*unwell*) *Fam* pas en forme.

para- ['pærə] *pref* para-.

parable ['pærəb(ə)l] *n* (*story*) parabole *f*.

parachute ['pærəʃuːt] *n* parachute *f*; **to drop by p.** (*men, supplies*) parachuter; – *vi* descendre en parachute; – *vt* parachuter. ◆**parachutist** *n* parachutiste *mf*.

parade [pə'reɪd] *n* **1** *Mil* (*ceremony*) parade *f*; (*procession*) défilé *m*; **fashion p.** défilé *m* de mode *or* de mannequins; **p. ground** *Mil* terrain *m* de manœuvres; **to make a p. of** faire étalage de; – *vi* *Mil* défiler; **to p. about** (*walk about*) se balader; – *vt* faire étalage de. **2** (*street*) avenue *f*.

paradise ['pærədaɪs] *n* paradis *m*.

paradox ['pærədɒks] *n* paradoxe *m*. ◆**para'doxically** *adv* paradoxalement.

paraffin ['pærəfɪn] *n* pétrole *m* (lampant); (*wax*) *Am* paraffine *f*; **p. lamp** lampe *f* à pétrole.

paragon ['pærəg(ə)n] *n* **p. of virtue** modèle *m* de vertu.

paragraph ['pærəgrɑːf] *n* paragraphe *m*; '**new p.**' 'à la ligne'.

parakeet ['pærəkiːt] *n* perruche *f*.

parallel ['pærəlel] *a* (*comparable*) & *Math* parallèle (**with, to** à); **to run p. to** *or* **with** être parallèle à; – *n* (*comparison*) & *Geog* parallèle *m*; (*line*) *Math* parallèle *f*; – *vt* être semblable à.

paralysis [pə'ræləsɪs] *n* paralysie *f*. ◆**'paralyse** *vt* (*Am* -**lyze**) paralyser. ◆**para'lytic** *a* & *n* paralytique (*mf*).

parameter [pə'ræmɪtər] *n* paramètre *m*.

paramount ['pærəmaʊnt] *a* **of p. importance** de la plus haute importance.

paranoia [pærə'nɔɪə] *n* paranoïa *f*. ◆**'paranoid** *a* & *n* paranoïaque (*mf*).

parapet ['pærəpɪt] *n* parapet *m*.

paraphernalia [pærəfə'neɪlɪə] *n* attirail *m*.

paraphrase ['pærəfreɪz] *n* paraphrase *f*; – *vt* paraphraser.

parasite ['pærəsaɪt] *n* (*person, organism*) parasite *m*.

parasol ['pærəsɒl] *n* (*over table, on beach*) parasol *m*; (*lady's*) ombrelle *f*.

paratrooper ['pærətruːpər] *n* *Mil* parachutiste *m*. ◆**paratroops** *npl* *Mil* parachutistes *mpl*.

parboil [pɑː'bɔɪl] *vt* *Culin* faire bouillir à demi.

parcel ['pɑːs(ə)l] **1** *n* colis *m*, paquet *m*; **to be part and p. of** faire partie intégrante de. **2** *vt* (-**ll**-, *Am* -**l**-) **to p. out** (*divide*) partager; **to p. up** faire un paquet de.

parch [pɑːtʃ] *vt* dessécher; **to be parched** (*thirsty*) être assoiffé; **to make parched** (*thirsty*) donner très soif à.

parchment ['pɑːtʃmənt] *n* parchemin *m*.

pardon ['pɑːd(ə)n] *n* pardon *m*; *Jur* grâce *f*; **general p.** amnistie *f*; **I beg your p.** (*apologize*) je vous prie de m'excuser; (*not hearing*) vous dites?; **p.?** (*not hearing*) comment?; **p. (me)!** (*sorry*) pardon!; – *vt* pardonner (**s.o. for sth** qch à qn); **to p. s.o.** pardonner (à) qn; *Jur* gracier qn.

pare [peər] *vt* (*trim*) rogner; (*peel*) éplucher; **to p. down** *Fig* réduire, rogner.

parent ['peərənt] *n* père *m*, mère *f*; **one's parents** ses père et mère *mpl*, son père et sa mère; **p. firm, p. company** *Com* maison *f* mère. ◆**parentage** *n* (*origin*) origine *f*. ◆**pa'rental** *a* des parents, parental. ◆**parenthood** *n* paternité *f*, maternité *f*.

parenthesis, *pl* -**eses** [pə'renθəsɪs, -əsiːz] *n* parenthèse *f*.

Paris ['pærɪs] *n* Paris *m or* *f*. ◆**Parisian** [pə'rɪzɪən, *Am* pə'rɪʒən] *a* & *n* parisien, -ienne (*mf*).

parish ['pærɪʃ] *n* *Rel* paroisse *f*; (*civil*) commune *f*; – *a* (*church, register*) paroissial; **p. council** conseil *m* municipal. ◆**pa'rishioner** *n* paroissien, -ienne *mf*.

parity ['pærɪtɪ] *n* parité *f*.

park [pɑːk] **1** *n* (*garden*) parc *m*. **2** *vt* (*vehicle*) garer; (*put*) *Fam* mettre, poser; – *vi* *Aut* se garer; (*remain parked*) stationner. ◆**—ing** *n* stationnement *m*; '**no p.**' 'défense de stationner'; **p. bay** aire *f* de stationnement; **p. lot** *Am* parking *m*; **p. meter** parcmètre *m*; **p. place** endroit *m* pour se garer; **p. ticket** contravention *f*.

parka ['pɑːkə] *n* (*coat*) parka *m*.

parkway ['pɑːkweɪ] *n* *Am* avenue *f*.

parliament ['pɑːləmənt] *n* parlement *m*; **P.** *Br* Parlement *m*. ◆**parlia'mentary** *a* parlementaire *mf* (expérimenté(e)).

parlour ['pɑːlər] *n* (*in mansion*) (petit) salon

m; **ice-cream p.** *Am* salon de glaces; **p. game** jeu *m* de société.

parochial [pə'rəʊkɪəl] *a (mentality, quarrel) Pej* de clocher; *(person) Pej* provincial, borné; *Rel* paroissial.

parody ['pærədɪ] *n* parodie *f*; – *vt* parodier.

parole [pə'rəʊl] *n* **on p.** *Jur* en liberté conditionnelle.

parquet ['pɑːkeɪ] *n* **p. (floor)** parquet *m*.

parrot ['pærət] *n* perroquet *m*; **p. fashion** *Pej* comme un perroquet.

parry ['pærɪ] *vt (blow)* parer; *(question)* éluder; – *n Sp* parade *f*.

parsimonious [pɑːsɪ'məʊnɪəs] *a* parcimonie. ◆—**ly** *adv* avec parcimonie.

parsley ['pɑːslɪ] *n* persil *m*.

parsnip ['pɑːsnɪp] *n* panais *m*.

parson ['pɑːs(ə)n] *n* pasteur *m*; **p.'s nose** *(of chicken)* croupion *m*.

part [pɑːt] **1** *n* partie *f*; *(of machine)* pièce *f*; *(of periodical)* livraison *f*; *(of serial)* épisode *m*; *(in play, film, activity)* rôle *m*; *(division) Culin* mesure *f*; *(in hair) Am* raie *f*; **to take p.** participer (**in à**); **to take s.o.'s p.** *(side)* prendre parti pour qn; **in p.** en partie; **for the most p.** dans l'ensemble; **to be a p. of** faire partie de; **on the p. of** *(on behalf of)* de la part de; **for my p.** pour ma part; **in these parts** dans ces parages; **p. exchange** reprise *f*; **to take in p. exchange** reprendre; **p. owner** copropriétaire *mf*; **p. payment** paiement *m* partiel; – *adv* en partie; **p. American** en partie américain. **2** *vt (separate)* séparer; *(crowd)* diviser; **to p. one's hair** se faire une raie; **to p. company with** *(leave)* quitter; – *vi (of friends etc)* se quitter; *(of married couple)* se séparer; **to p. with** *(get rid of)* se séparer de. ◆—**ing 1** *n* séparation *f*; – *a (gift, words)* d'adieu. **2** *n (in hair)* raie *f*.

partake [pɑː'teɪk] *vi (pt* **partook***, pp* **partaken)** **to p. in** participer à; **to p. of** *(meal, food)* prendre, manger.

partial ['pɑːʃəl] *a* partiel; *(biased)* partial *(towards* envers); **to be p. to** *(fond of) Fam* avoir un faible pour. ◆**parti'ality** *n (bias)* partialité *f*; *(liking)* prédilection *f*.

participate [pɑː'tɪsɪpeɪt] *vi* participer (**in à**). ◆**participant** *n* participant, -ante *mf*. ◆**partici'pation** *n* participation *f*.

participle ['pɑːtɪsɪp(ə)l] *n* participe *m*.

particle ['pɑːtɪk(ə)l] *n (of atom, dust, name)* particule *f*; *(of truth)* grain *m*.

particular [pə'tɪkjʊlər] **1** *a (specific, special)* particulier; *(fastidious, fussy)* difficile **(about** sur); *(meticulous)* méticuleux; **this p. book** ce livre-ci en particulier; **in p.** en

particulier; **to be p. about** faire très attention. **à 2** *n (detail)* détail *m*; **s.o.'s particulars** le nom et l'adresse de qn; *(description)* le signalement de qn. ◆—**ly** *adv* particulièrement.

partisan [pɑːtɪ'zæn, *Am* 'pɑːtɪz(ə)n] *n* partisan *m*.

partition [pɑː'tɪʃ(ə)n] **1** *n (of room)* cloison *f*; – *vt* **to p. off** cloisonner. **2** *n (of country) Pol* partition *f*, partage *m*; – *vt Pol* partager.

partly ['pɑːtlɪ] *adv* en partie; **p. English p. French** moitié anglais moitié français.

partner ['pɑːtnər] *n Com* associé, -ée *mf*; *(lover, spouse)* & *Sp Pol* partenaire *mf*; *(of racing driver etc)* coéquipier, -ière *mf*; *(dancing)* **p.** cavalier, -ière *mf*. ◆**partnership** *n* association *f*; **to take into p.** prendre comme associé(e); **in p. with** en association avec.

partridge ['pɑːtrɪdʒ] *n* perdrix *f*.

part-time [pɑːt'taɪm] *a* & *adv* à temps partiel; *(half-time)* à mi-temps.

party ['pɑːtɪ] *n* **1** *(group)* groupe *m*; *Pol* parti *m*; *(in contract, lawsuit) Jur* partie *f*; *Mil* détachement *m*; *Tel* correspondant, -ante *mf*; **rescue p.** équipe *f* de sauveteurs *or* de secours; **third p.** *Jur* tiers *m*; **innocent p.** innocent, -ente *mf*; **to be (a) p. to** *(crime)* être complice de; **p. line** *Tel* ligne *f* partagée; *Pol* ligne *f* du parti; **p. ticket** billet *m* collectif. **2** *(gathering)* réception *f*; *(informal)* surprise-partie *f*; *(for birthday)* fête *f*; **cocktail p.** cocktail *m*; **dinner p.** dîner *m*; **tea p.** thé *m*.

pass [pɑːs] **1** *n (entry permit)* laissez-passer *m inv*; *(free ticket) Th* billet *m* de faveur; *(season ticket)* carte *f* d'abonnement; *(over mountains) Geog* col *m*; *Fb etc* passe *f*; *(in exam)* mention *f* passable **(in French***/etc* en français*/etc)*; **to make a p. at** faire des avances à; **p. mark** *(in exam)* moyenne *f*, barre *f* d'admissibilité; **p. key** passepartout *m inv*. **2** *vi (go, come, disappear)* passer **(to à, through** par); *(overtake) Aut* dépasser; *(in exam)* être reçu **(in French***/etc* en français*/etc)*; *(take place)* se passer; **that'll p.** *(be acceptable)* ça ira; **he can p. for thirty** on lui donnerait trente ans; **to p. along** *or* **through** passer; **to p. away** *or* **on** *(die)* mourir; **to p. by** passer (à côté); **to p. off** *(happen)* se passer; **to p. on to** *(move on to)* passer à; **to p. out** *(faint)* s'évanouir; – *vt (move, spend, give etc)* passer **(to à);** *(go past)* passer devant; *(exam)* être reçu à; *(candidate)* recevoir; *(judgement, opinion)* prononcer **(on** sur); *(remark)* faire; *(allow)* autoriser; (*bill, law*) *Pol* voter; **to p. (by) s.o.** (*in street*) croiser qn; **to p. by** (*building*) passer devant; **to p. oneself off as** se faire passer pour; **to p. sth off on** (*fob off on*) refiler qch à; **to p. on** (*message, title, illness etc*) transmettre (**to** à); **to p. out** *ou* **round** (*hand out*) distribuer; **to p. over** (*ignore*) passer sur, oublier; **to p. round** (*cigarettes, sweets etc*) faire passer; **to p. up** (*chance etc*) laisser passer. ◆**—ing** *a* (*a vehicle etc*) qui passe; (*beauty*) passager; – *n* (*of visitor, vehicle etc*) passage *m*; (*of time*) écoulement *m*; (*death*) disparition *f*.

passable ['pɑːsəb(ə)l] *a* (*not bad*) passable; (*road*) praticable; (*river*) franchissable.

passage ['pæsɪdʒ] *n* (*passing, way through, of text, of speech etc*) passage *m*; (*of time*) écoulement *m*; (*corridor*) couloir *m*; *Nau* traversée *f*, passage *m*. ◆**passageway** *n* (*way through*) passage *m*; (*corridor*) couloir *m*.

passbook ['pɑːsbʊk] *n* livret *m* de caisse d'épargne.

passenger ['pæsɪndʒər] *n* passager, -ère *mf*; *Rail* voyageur, -euse *mf*.

passer-by [pɑːsə'baɪ] *n* (*pl* **passers-by**) passant, -ante *mf*.

passion ['pæʃ(ə)n] *n* passion *f*; **to have a p. for** (*cars etc*) avoir la passion de, adorer. ◆**passionate** *a* passionné. ◆**passionately** *adv* passionnément.

passive ['pæsɪv] *a* (*not active*) passif; – *n Gram* passif *m*. ◆**—ness** *n* passivité *f*.

Passover ['pɑːsəʊvər] *n Rel* Pâque *f*.

passport ['pɑːspɔːt] *n* passeport *m*.

password ['pɑːswɜːd] *n* mot *m* de passe.

past [pɑːst] **1** *n* (*time, history*) passé *m*; **in the p.** (*formerly*) dans le temps; **it's a thing of the p.** ça n'existe plus; – *a* (*gone by*) passé; (*former*) ancien; **these p. months** ces derniers mois; **that's all p.** c'est du passé; **in the p. tense** *Gram* au passé. **2** *prep* (*in front of*) devant; (*after*) après; (*further than*) plus loin que; (*too old for*) *Fig* trop vieux pour; **p. four o'clock** quatre heures passées, plus de quatre heures; **to be p. fifty** avoir cinquante ans passés; **it's p. belief** c'est incroyable; **I wouldn't put it p. him** ça ne m'étonnerait pas de lui, il en est bien capable; – *adv* devant; **to go p.** passer.

pasta ['pæstə] *n Culin* pâtes *fpl* (alimentaires).

paste [peɪst] **1** *n* (*of meat*) pâté *m*; (*of anchovy etc*) beurre *m*; (*dough*) pâte *f*. **2** *n* (*glue*) colle *f* (blanche); – *vt* coller; **to p. up** (*notice etc*) afficher.

pastel ['pæstəl, *Am* pæ'stel] *n* pastel *m*; – *a* (*shade*) pastel *inv*; (*drawing*) au pastel.

pasteurized ['pæstəraɪzd] *a* (*milk*) pasteurisé.

pastiche [pæ'stiːʃ] *n* pastiche *m*.

pastille ['pæstɪl, *Am* pæ'stiːl] *n* pastille *f*.

pastime ['pɑːstaɪm] *n* passe-temps *m inv*.

pastor ['pɑːstər] *n Rel* pasteur *m*. ◆**pastoral** *a* pastoral.

pastry ['peɪstrɪ] *n* (*dough*) pâte *f*; (*cake*) pâtisserie *f*; **puff p.** pâte *f* feuilletée. ◆**pastrycook** *n* pâtissier, -ière *mf*.

pasture ['pɑːstʃər] *n* pâturage *m*.

pasty 1 ['peɪstɪ] *a* (**-ier, -iest**) (*complexion*) terreux. **2** ['pæstɪ] *n Culin* petit pâté *m* (en croûte).

pat [pæt] **1** *vt* (**-tt-**) (*cheek, table etc*) tapoter; (*animal*) caresser; – *n* petite tape; caresse *f*. **2** *adv* **to answer p.** avoir la réponse toute prête; **to know sth off p.** savoir qch sur le bout du doigt.

patch [pætʃ] *n* (*for clothes*) pièce *f*; (*over eye*) bandeau *m*; (*for bicycle tyre*) rustine® *f*; (*of colour*) tache *f*; (*of sky*) morceau *m*; (*of fog*) nappe *f*; (*of ice*) plaque *f*; **a cabbage/etc p.** un carré de choux/*etc*; **a bad p.** *Fig* une mauvaise passe; **not to be a p. on** (*not as good as*) *Fam* ne pas arriver à la cheville de; – *vt* **to p. up** (*clothing*) rapiécer; **to p. up** (*quarrel*) régler; (*marriage*) replâtrer. ◆**patchwork** *n* patchwork *m*. ◆**patchy** *a* (**-ier, -iest**) inégal.

patent 1 ['peɪtənt] *a* patent, manifeste; **p. leather** cuir *m* verni. **2** ['peɪtənt, 'pætənt] *n* brevet *m* (d'invention); – *vt* (faire) breveter. ◆**—ly** *adv* manifestement.

paternal [pə'tɜːn(ə)l] *a* paternel. ◆**paternity** *n* paternité *f*.

path [pɑːθ] *n* (*pl* **-s** [pɑːðz]) sentier *m*, chemin *m*; (*in park*) allée *f*; (*of river*) cours *m*; (*of bullet, planet*) trajectoire *f*. ◆**pathway** *n* sentier *m*, chemin *m*.

pathetic [pə'θetɪk] *a* pitoyable.

pathology [pə'θɒlədʒɪ] *n* pathologie *f*. ◆**patho'logical** *a* pathologique.

pathos ['peɪθɒs] *n* pathétique *m*.

patient ['peɪʃ(ə)nt] **1** *a* patient. **2** *n* (*in hospital*) malade *mf*, patient, -ente *mf*; (*on doctor's or dentist's list*) patient, -ente *mf*. ◆**patience** *n* patience *f*; **to have p.** prendre patience; **to lose p.** perdre patience; **I have no p. with him** il m'impatiente; **to play p.** *Cards* faire des réussites. ◆**patiently** *adv* patiemment.

patio ['pætɪəʊ] *n* (*pl* **-os**) patio *m*.

patriarch ['peɪtrɪɑːk] *n* patriarche *m*.

patriot ['pætriət, 'peitriət] n patriote mf.
◆**patri'otic** a (views, speech etc) patriotique; (person) patriote. ◆**patriotism** n patriotisme m.

patrol [pə'trəul] n patrouille f; p. boat patrouilleur m; police p. car voiture f de police; p. wagon Am fourgon m cellulaire; − vi (-ll-) patrouiller; − vt patrouiller dans. ◆**patrolman** n (pl -men) Am agent m de police; (repair man) Aut dépanneur m.

patron ['peitrən] n (of artist) protecteur, -trice mf; (customer) Com client, -ente mf; (of cinema, theatre) habitué, -ée mf; p. saint patron, -onne mf. ◆**patronage** n (support) patronage m; (of the arts) protection f; (custom) Com clientèle f. ◆**patroniz/e** ['pætrənaiz, Am 'peitrənaiz] vt 1 Com accorder sa clientèle à. 2 (person) Pej traiter avec condescendance. ◆**−ing** a condescendant.

patter ['pætər] 1 n (of footsteps) petit bruit m; (of rain, hail) crépitement m; − vi (of rain, hail) crépiter, tambouriner. 2 n (talk) baratin m.

pattern ['pæt(ə)n] n dessin m, motif m; (paper model for garment) patron m; (fabric sample) échantillon m; Fig modèle m; (plan) plan m; (method) formule f; (of a crime) scénario m. ◆**patterned** a (dress, cloth) à motifs.

paucity ['pɔːsiti] n pénurie f.

paunch [pɔːntʃ] n panse f, bedon m. ◆**paunchy** a (-ier, -iest) bedonnant.

pauper ['pɔːpər] n pauvre mf, indigent, -ente mf.

pause [pɔːz] n pause f; (in conversation) silence m; − vi (stop) faire une pause; (hesitate) hésiter.

pav/e [peiv] vt paver; to p. the way for Fig ouvrir la voie à. ◆**−ing** n (surface) pavage m, dallage m; p. stone pavé m. ◆**pavement** n trottoir m; (roadway) Am chaussée f; (stone) pavé m.

pavilion [pə'viljən] n (building) pavillon m.

paw [pɔː] 1 n patte f; − vt (of animal) donner des coups de patte à. 2 vt (touch improperly) tripoter.

pawn [pɔːn] 1 n Chess pion m. 2 vt mettre en gage; − n in la p. en gage. ◆**pawnbroker** n prêteur, -euse mf sur gages. ◆**pawnshop** n mont-de-piété m.

pay [pei] n salaire m, (of workman) paie f, salaire m; Mil solde f, paie f; p. phone téléphone m public; p. day jour m de paie; p. slip bulletin m or fiche f de paie; − vt (pt & pp **paid**) (person, sum) payer; (deposit) verser; (yield) Com rapporter; (compli-

ment, attention, visit) faire; to p. s.o. to do or for doing payer qn pour faire; to p. s.o. for sth payer qch à qn; to p. money into one's account or the bank verser de l'argent sur son compte; it pays (one) to be cautious on a intérêt à être prudent; to p. homage or tribute to rendre hommage à; to p. back (creditor, loan etc) rembourser; I'll p. you back for this! je te revaudrai ça!; to p. in (cheque) verser (to one's account sur son compte); to p. off (debt, creditor etc) rembourser; (in instalments) rembourser par acomptes; (staff, worker) licencier; to p. off an old score or a grudge Fig régler un vieux compte; to p. out (spend) dépenser; to p. up payer; − vi payer; to p. for sth payer qch; to p. a lot (for) payer cher; to p. off (be successful) être payant; to p. up payer. ◆**−ing** a (guest) payant; (profitable) rentable. ◆**−able** a (due) payable; a cheque p. to un chèque à l'ordre de. ◆**−ment** n paiement m; (of deposit) versement m; (reward) récompense f; on p. of 20 francs moyennant 20 francs. ◆**payoff** n Fam (reward) récompense f; (revenge) règlement m de comptes. ◆**payroll** n to be on the p. of (firm, factory) être employé par; to have twenty workers on the p. employer vingt ouvriers.

pea [piː] n pois m; garden or green peas petits pois mpl; p. soup soupe f aux pois.

peace [piːs] n paix f; p. of mind tranquillité f d'esprit; in p. en paix; at p. en paix (with avec); to have (some) p. and quiet avoir la paix; to disturb the p. troubler l'ordre public; to hold one's p. garder le silence. ◆**p.-keeping** a (force) de maintien de la paix; (measure) de pacification. ◆**p.-loving** a pacifique. ◆**peaceable** a paisible, pacifique. ◆**peaceful** a paisible, calme; (coexistence, purpose, demonstration) pacifique. ◆**peacefulness** n paix f.

peach [piːtʃ] n (fruit) pêche f; (tree) pêcher m; − a (colour) pêche inv.

peacock ['piːkɒk] n paon m.

peak [piːk] n (mountain top) sommet m; (mountain itself) pic m; (of cap) visière f; (of fame etc) Fig sommet m, apogée m; the traffic has reached or is at its p. la circulation est à son maximum; − a (hours, period) de pointe; (demand, production) maximum; − vi (of sales etc) atteindre son maximum. ◆**peaked** a p. cap casquette f.

peaky ['piːki] a (-ier, -iest) Fam (ill) patraque; (pale) pâlot.

peal [piːl] 1 n (of laughter) éclat m; (of thun-

der) roulement *m.* **2** *n* **p. of bells** carillon *m*; – *vi* **to p. (out)** (*of bells*) carillonner.

peanut ['piːnʌt] *n* cacah(o)uète *f*; (*plant*) arachide *f*; **to earn**/*etc* **peanuts** (*little money*) *Fam* gagner/*etc* des clopinettes.

pear [peər] *n* poire *f*; **p. tree** poirier *m*.

pearl [pɜːl] *n* perle *f*; (*mother-of-pearl*) nacre *f*. ◆**pearly** *a* (-ier, -iest) (*colour*) nacré.

peasant ['pezənt] *n & a* paysan, -anne (*mf*).

peashooter ['piːʃuːtər] *n* sarbacane *f*.

peat [piːt] *n* tourbe *f*.

pebble ['peb(ə)l] *n* (*stone*) caillou *m*; (*on beach*) galet *m*. ◆**pebbly** *a* (*beach*) (couvert) de galets.

pecan ['piːkæn] *n* (*nut*) *Am* pacane *f*.

peck [pek] *vti* **to p. (at)** (*of bird*) picorer (*du pain etc*); (*person*) *Fig* donner un coup de bec à; **to p. at one's food** (*of person*) manger du bout des dents; – *n* coup *m* de bec; (*kiss*) *Fam* bécot *m*.

peckish ['pekiʃ] *a* **to be p.** (*hungry*) *Fam* avoir un petit creux.

peculiar [pɪ'kjuːliər] *a* (*strange*) bizarre; (*characteristic, special*) particulier (**to** à). ◆**peculi'arity** *n* (*feature*) particularité *f*; (*oddity*) bizarrerie *f*. ◆**peculiarly** *adv* bizarrement; (*specially*) particulièrement.

pedal ['ped(ə)l] *n* pédale *f*; **p. boat** pédalo *m*; – *vi* (**-ll-**, *Am* **-l-**) pédaler; – *vt* (*bicycle etc*) actionner les pédales de. ◆**pedalbin** *n* poubelle *f* à pédale.

pedant ['pedənt] *n* pédant, -ante *mf*. ◆**pe'dantic** *a* pédant. ◆**pedantry** *n* pédantisme *m*.

peddl/e ['ped(ə)l] *vt* colporter; (*drugs*) faire le trafic de; – *vi* faire du colportage. ◆**-er** *n Am* (*door-to-door*) colporteur, -euse *mf*; (*in street*) camelot *m*; **drug p.** revendeur, -euse *mf* de drogues.

pedestal ['pedist(ə)l] *n Archit & Fig* piédestal *m*.

pedestrian [pə'destriən] **1** *n* piéton *m*; **p. crossing** passage *m* pour piétons; **p. precinct** zone *f* piétonnière. **2** *a* (*speech, style*) prosaïque. ◆**pedestrianize** *vt* (*street etc*) rendre piétonnier.

pedigree ['pedigriː] *n* (*of dog, horse etc*) pedigree *m*; (*of person*) ascendance *f*; – *a* (*dog, horse etc*) de race.

pedlar ['pedlər] *n* (*door-to-door*) colporteur, -euse *mf*; (*in street*) camelot *m*.

pee [piː] *n* **to go for a p.** *Fam* faire pipi.

peek [piːk] *n* coup *m* d'œil (furtif); – *vi* jeter un coup d'œil (furtif) (**at** à).

peel [piːl] *n* (*of vegetable, fruit*) pelure(s) *f(pl)*, épluchure(s) *f(pl)*; (*of orange skin*) écorce *f*; (*in food, drink*) zeste *m*; **a piece of**

p. une pelure, une épluchure; – *vt* (*fruit, vegetable*) peler, éplucher; **to keep one's eyes peeled** *Fam* être vigilant; **to p. off** (*label etc*) décoller; – *vi* (*of sunburnt skin*) peler; (*of paint*) s'écailler; **to p. easily** (*of fruit*) se peler facilement. ◆**-ings** *npl* pelures *fpl*, épluchures *fpl*. ◆**-er** *n* (*knife etc*) éplucheur *m*.

peep [piːp] **1** *n* coup *m* d'œil (furtif); – *vi* **to p.** (**at**) regarder furtivement; **to p. out** se montrer; **peeping Tom** voyeur, -euse *mf*. **2** *vi* (*of bird*) pépier. ◆**peephole** *n* judas *m*.

peer [piər] **1** *n* (*equal*) pair *m*, égal, -ale *mf*; (*noble*) pair *m*. **2** *vi* **to p.** (**at**) regarder attentivement (*comme pour mieux voir*); **to p. into** (*darkness*) scruter. ◆**peerage** *n* (*rank*) pairie *f*.

peeved [piːvd] *a Fam* irrité.

peevish ['piːviʃ] *a* grincheux, irritable.

peg [peg] **1** *n* (*wooden*) *Tech* cheville *f*; (*metal*) *Tech* fiche *f*; (*for tent*) piquet *m*; (*for clothes*) pince *f* (à linge); (*for coat, hat etc*) patère *f*; **to buy off the p.** acheter en prêt-à-porter. *Fam* prêt à porter. **2** *vt* (-**gg**-) (*prices*) stabiliser.

pejorative [pɪ'dʒɒrətɪv] *a* péjoratif.

pekin(g)ese [piːkɪ'niːz] *n* (*dog*) pékinois *m*.

pelican ['pelɪkən] *n* (*bird*) pélican *m*.

pellet ['pelɪt] *n* (*of paper etc*) boulette *f*; (*for gun*) (grain *m* de) plomb *m*.

pelt [pelt] **1** *n* (*skin*) peau *f*; (*fur*) fourrure *f*. **2** *vt* **to p. s.o. with** (*stones etc*) bombarder qn de. **3** *vi* **it's pelting (down)** (*raining*) il pleut à verse. **4** *vi* **to p.** along (*run, dash*) *Fam* foncer, courir.

pelvis [pelvis] *n Anat* bassin *m*.

pen [pen] **1** *n* (*dipped in ink*) porte-plume *m inv*; (*fountain pen*) stylo *m* (à encre *or* à plume); (*ballpoint*) stylo *m* à bille, stylo(-)bille *m*; **to live by one's p.** *Fig* vivre de sa plume; **p. friend, p. pal** correspondant, -ante *mf*; **p. name** pseudonyme *m*; **p. nib** (bec *m* de) plume *f*; **p. pusher** *Pej* gratte-papier *m inv*; – *vt* (-**nn**-) (*write*) écrire. **2** *n* (*enclosure for baby or sheep or cattle*) parc *m*.

penal ['piːn(ə)l] *a* (*law, code etc*) pénal; (*colony*) pénitentiaire. ◆**penalize** *vt Sp Jur* pénaliser (**for** pour); (*handicap*) désavantager.

penalty ['pen(ə)ltɪ] *n Jur* peine *f*; (*fine*) amende *f*; *Sp* pénalisation *f*; *Fb* penalty *m*; *Rugby* pénalité *f*; **to pay the p.** *Fig* subir les conséquences.

penance ['penəns] *n* pénitence *f*.

pence [pens] *see* **penny**.

pencil ['pens(ə)l] *n* crayon *m*; **in p.** au crayon; **p. box** plumier *m*; **p. sharpener**

taille-crayon(s) *m inv*; – *vt* (**-ll-**, *Am* **-l-**) crayonner; **to p. in** *Fig* noter provisoirement.

pendant ['pendant] *n* pendentif *m*; (*on earring, chandelier*) pendeloque *f*.

pending ['pendɪŋ] **1** *a* (*matter*) en suspens. **2** *prep* (*until*) en attendant.

pendulum ['pendjʊləm] *n* (*of clock*) balancier *m*, pendule *m*; *Fig* pendule *m*.

penetrat/e ['penɪtreɪt] *vt* (*substance, mystery etc*) percer; (*plan, secret etc*) découvrir; – *vti* **to p. (into)** (*forest, group etc*) pénétrer dans. ◆—**ing** *a* (*mind, cold etc*) pénétrant. ◆**pene'tration** *n* pénétration *f*.

penguin ['peŋgwɪn] *n* manchot *m*, pingouin *m*.

penicillin [penɪ'sɪlɪn] *n* pénicilline *f*.

peninsula [pə'nɪnsjʊlə] *n* presqu'île *f*, péninsule *f*. ◆**peninsular** *a* péninsulaire.

penis ['piːnɪs] *n* pénis *m*.

penitent ['penɪtənt] *a & n* pénitent, -ente (*mf*). ◆**penitence** *n* pénitence *f*.

penitentiary [penɪ'tenʃərɪ] *n Am* prison *f* (centrale).

penknife ['pennaɪf] *n* (*pl* -knives) canif *m*.

pennant ['penənt] *n* (*flag*) flamme *f*, banderole *f*.

penny ['penɪ] *n* **1** (*pl* pennies) (*coin*) penny *m*; *Am Can* cent *m*; **I don't have a p.** *Fig* je n'ai pas le sou. **2** (*pl* pence [pens]) (*value, currency*) penny *m*. ◆**p.-pinching** *a* (*miserly*) *Fam* avare. ◆**penniless** *a* sans le sou.

pension ['penʃ(ə)n] *n* pension *f*; **retirement p.** (*pension f de*) retraite *f*; (*private*) retraite *f* complémentaire; – *vt* **to p. off** mettre à la retraite. ◆—**able** *a* (*age*) de la retraite; (*job*) qui donne droit à une retraite. ◆—**er** *n* pensionné, -ée *mf*; (**old age**) **p.** retraité, -ée *mf*.

pensive ['pensɪv] *a* pensif.

pentagon ['pentəgən] *n* **the P.** *Am Pol* le Pentagone.

pentathlon [pen'tæθlən] *n Sp* pentathlon *m*.

Pentecost ['pentɪkɒst] *n* (*Whitsun*) *Am* Pentecôte *f*.

penthouse ['penthaʊs] *n* appartement *m* de luxe (*construit sur le toit d'un immeuble*).

pent-up [pent'ʌp] *a* (*feelings*) refoulé.

penultimate [pɪ'nʌltɪmət] *a* avant-dernier.

peony ['pɪənɪ] *n Bot* pivoine *f*.

people ['piːp(ə)l] *npl* (*in general*) gens *mpl* or *fpl*; (*specific persons*) personnes *fpl*; (*of region, town*) habitants *mpl*, gens *mpl* or *fpl*; **the p.** (*citizens*) *Pol* le peuple; **old p.** les personnes *fpl* âgées; **old people's home**

hospice *m* de vieillards; (*private*) maison *f* de retraite; **two p.** deux personnes; **English p.** les Anglais *mpl*, le peuple anglais; **a lot of p.** beaucoup de monde or de gens; **p. think that . . .** on pense que . . . ; – *n* (*nation*) peuple *m*; – *vt* (*populate*) peupler (**with** de).

pep [pep] *n* entrain *m*; **p. talk** *Fam* petit laïus d'encouragement; – *vt* (**-pp-**) **to p. up** (*perk up*) ragaillardir.

pepper ['pepər] *n* poivre *m*; (*vegetable*) poivron *m*; – *vt* poivrer. ◆**peppercorn** *n* grain *m* de poivre. ◆**peppermint** *n* menthe *f* poivrée; (*sweet*) pastille *f* de menthe. ◆**peppery** *a Culin* poivré.

per [pɜːr] *prep* par; **p. annum** par an; **p. head, p. person** par personne; **p. cent** pour cent; **50 pence p. kilo** 50 pence le kilo; **40 km p. hour** 40 km à l'heure. ◆**per'centage** *n* pourcentage *m*.

perceive [pə'siːv] *vt* (*see, hear*) percevoir; (*notice*) remarquer (**that** que). ◆**perceptible** *a* perceptible. ◆**perception** *n* perception *f* (**of** de); (*intuition*) intuition *f*. ◆**perceptive** *a* (*person*) perspicace; (*study, remark*) pénétrant.

perch [pɜːtʃ] **1** *n* perchoir *m*; – *vi* (*of bird*) (se) percher; (*of person*) *Fig* se percher, se jucher; – *vt* (*put*) percher. **2** *n* (*fish*) perche *f*.

percolate ['pɜːkəleɪt] *vi* (*of liquid*) filtrer, passer (**through** par); – *vt* (*coffee*) faire dans une cafetière; **percolated coffee** du vrai café. ◆**percolator** *n* cafetière *f*; (*in café or restaurant*) percolateur *m*.

percussion [pə'kʌʃ(ə)n] *n Mus* percussion *f*.

peremptory [pə'remptərɪ] *a* péremptoire.

perennial [pə'renɪəl] **1** *a* (*complaint, subject etc*) perpétuel. **2** *a* (*plant*) vivace; – *n* plante *f* vivace.

perfect ['pɜːfɪkt] *a* parfait; – *a & n* **p. (tense)** *Gram* parfait *m*; – [pə'fekt] *vt* (*book, piece of work etc*) parachever, parfaire; (*process, technique*) mettre au point; (*one's French etc*) parfaire ses connaissances en. ◆**per'fection** *n* perfection *f*; (*act*) parachèvement *m* (**of** de); mise *f* au point (**of** de); **to p.** à la perfection. ◆**per'fectionist** *n* perfectionniste *mf*. ◆**'perfectly** *adv* parfaitement.

perfidious [pə'fɪdɪəs] *a Lit* perfide.

perforate ['pɜːfəreɪt] *vt* perforer. ◆**perforation** *n* perforation *f*.

perform [pə'fɔːm] *vt* (*task, miracle*) accomplir; (*a function, one's duty*) remplir; (*rite*) célébrer; (*operation*) *Med* pratiquer (**on**

sur); *(a play, symphony)* jouer; *(sonata)*
interpréter; – *vi (play)* jouer; *(sing)*
chanter; *(dance)* danser; *(of circus animal)*
faire un numéro; *(function)* fonctionner;
(behave) se comporter; **you performed very
well!** tu as très bien fait! ◆—**ing** *a
(animal)* savant. ◆**performance** *n* 1
(show) Th représentation *f*, séance *f*; Cin
Mus séance *f*. 2 *(of athlete, machine etc)*
performance *f*; *(of actor, musician etc)*
interprétation *f*; *(circus act)* numéro *m*;
(fuss) Fam histoire(s) *f(pl)*; **the p. of one's
duties** l'exercice *m* de ses fonctions.
◆**performer** *n* interprète *mf* (**of** de);
(entertainer) artiste *mf*.

perfume ['pɜ:fju:m] *n* parfum *m*; – [pə'fju:m] *vt* parfumer.

perfunctory [pə'fʌŋktəri] *a (action)*
superficiel; *(smile etc)* de commande.

perhaps [pə'hæps] *adv* peut-être; **p. not**
peut-être que non.

peril ['peril] *n* péril *m*, danger *m*; **at your p.** à
vos risques et péril. ◆**perilous** *a* périlleux.

perimeter [pə'rɪmɪtər] *n* périmètre *m*.

period ['pɪərɪəd] 1 *n (length of time, moment
in time)* période *f*; *(historical)* époque *f*;
(time limit) délai *m*; *(lesson)* Sch leçon *f*;
(full stop) Gram point *m*; **in the p. of a
month** en l'espace d'un mois; **I refuse, p.!**
Am je refuse, un point c'est tout!; – *a
(furniture etc)* d'époque; *(costume)* de
l'époque. 2 *n (menstruation)* règles *fpl*.
◆**peri'odic** *a* périodique. ◆**peri'odical**
n (magazine) périodique *m*. ◆**peri-
'odically** *adv* périodiquement.

periphery [pə'rɪfəri] *n* périphérie *f*. ◆**per-
'ipheral** *a (question)* sans rapport direct (**to**
avec); *(interest)* accessoire; *(neighbourhood)* périphérique.

periscope ['periskəup] *n* périscope *m*.

perish ['periʃ] *vi (die)* périr; *(of food,
substance)* se détériorer; **to be perished or
perishing** *(of person)* Fam être frigorifié.
◆—**ing** *a (cold, weather)* Fam glacial.
◆—**able** *a (food)* périssable; – *npl*
denrées *fpl* périssables.

perjure ['pɜ:dʒər] *vt* **to p. oneself** se parjurer.
◆**perjurer** *n (person)* parjure *mf*.
◆**perjury** *n* parjure *m*; **to commit p.** se
parjurer.

perk [pɜ:k] 1 *vi* **to p. up** *(buck up)* se ragaillardir; – *vt* **to p. s.o. up** remonter qn, ragaillardir qn. 2 *n (advantage)* avantage *m*;
(extra profit) à-côté *m*. ◆**perky** *a* (**-ier,
-iest**) *(cheerful)* guilleret, plein d'entrain.

perm [pɜ:m] *n (of hair)* permanente *f*; – *vt* **to**

have one's hair permed se faire faire une
permanente.

permanent ['pɜ:mənənt] *a* permanent;
(address) fixe; **she's p.** elle est ici à titre
permanent. ◆**permanence** *n* permanence *f*. ◆**permanently** *adv* à titre permanent.

permeate ['pɜ:mɪeɪt] *vt (of ideas etc)* se
répandre dans; **to p. (through)** *(of liquid
etc)* pénétrer. ◆**permeable** *a* perméable.

permit [pə'mɪt] *vt* (**-tt-**) permettre *(s.o. to do*
à qn de faire); **weather permitting** si le
temps le permet; – ['pɜ:mɪt] *n (licence)*
permis *m*; *(entrance pass)* laissez-passer *m
inv*. ◆**per'mission** *n* permission *f*, autorisation *f* (**to
do de** faire); **to ask (for)/give p.**
demander/donner la permission. ◆**per-
'missive** *a* (trop) tolérant, laxiste. ◆**per-
'missiveness** *n* laxisme *m*.

permutation [pɜ:mju:'teɪʃ(ə)n] *n* permutation *f*.

pernicious [pə'nɪʃəs] *a (harmful)* & Med
pernicieux.

pernickety [pə'nɪkətɪ] *a* Fam *(precise)* pointilleux; *(demanding)* difficile (**about** sur).

peroxide [pə'rɒksaɪd] *n (bleach)* eau *f*
oxygénée; – *a (hair, blond)* oxygéné.

perpendicular [pɜ:pən'dɪkjulər] *a & n*
perpendiculaire (*f*).

perpetrate ['pɜ:pɪtreɪt] *vt (crime)* perpétrer.
◆**perpetrator** *n* auteur *m*.

perpetual [pə'petʃuəl] *a* perpétuel. ◆**perpetually** *adv* perpétuellement. ◆**perpetuate** *vt* perpétuer. ◆**perpetuity**
[pɜ:pɪ'tju:ɪtɪ] *n* perpétuité *f*.

perplex [pə'pleks] *vt* rendre perplexe,
dérouter. ◆—**ed** *a* perplexe. ◆—**ing** *a*
déroutant. ◆**perplexity** *n* perplexité *f*;
(complexity) complexité *f*.

persecute ['pɜ:sɪkju:t] *vt* persécuter.
◆**perse'cution** *n* persécution *f*.

persevere [pɜ:sɪ'vɪər] *vi* persévérer (**in**
dans). ◆—**ing** *a (persistent)* persévérant.
◆**perseverance** *n* persévérance *f*.

Persian ['pɜ:ʃ(ə)n, 'pɜ:ʒ(ə)n] *a (language,
cat, carpet)* persan; – *n (language)* persan
m.

persist [pə'sɪst] *vi* persister (**in doing** à faire,
in sth dans qch). ◆**persistence** *n* persistance *f*. ◆**persistent** *a (fever, smell etc)*
persistant; *(person)* obstiné; *(attempts,
noise etc)* continuel. ◆**persistently** *adv*
(stubbornly) obstinément; *(continually)*
continuellement.

person ['pɜ:s(ə)n] *n* personne *f*; **in p.** en
personne; **a p. to p. call** Tel une communi-

cation avec préavis. ◆**personable** *a* avenant, qui présente bien.

personal ['pɜːs(ə)l] *a* personnel; *(application)* en personne; *(hygiene, friend)* intime; *(life)* privé; *(indiscreet)* indiscret; **p. assistant**, **p. secretary** secrétaire *m* particulier, secrétaire *f* particulière. ◆**perso'nality** *n (character, famous person)* personnalité *f*; **a television p.** une vedette de la télévision. ◆**personalize** *vt* personnaliser. ◆**personally** *adv* personnellement; *(in person)* en personne.

personify [pə'sɒnɪfaɪ] *vt* personnifier. ◆**personifi'cation** *n* personnification *f*.

personnel [pɜːsə'nel] *n (staff)* personnel *m*; *(department)* service *m* du personnel.

perspective [pə'spektɪv] *n (artistic & viewpoint)* perspective *f*; **in (its true) p.** Fig sous son vrai jour.

perspire [pə'spaɪər] *vi* transpirer. ◆**perspi'ration** *n* transpiration *f*, sueur *f*.

persuade [pə'sweɪd] *vt* persuader (**s.o. to do** qn de faire). ◆**persuasion** *n* persuasion *f*; Rel religion *f*. ◆**persuasive** *a (person, argument etc)* persuasif. ◆**persuasively** *adv* de façon persuasive.

pert [pɜːt] *a (impertinent)* impertinent; *(lively)* gai, plein d'entrain; *(hat etc)* coquet, chic. ◆**—ly** *adv* avec impertinence.

pertain [pə'teɪn] *vi* **to p. to** *(relate)* se rapporter à; *(belong)* appartenir à.

pertinent ['pɜːtɪnənt] *a* pertinent. ◆**—ly** *adv* pertinemment.

perturb [pə'tɜːb] *vt* troubler, perturber.

Peru [pə'ruː] *n* Pérou *m*. ◆**Peruvian** *a & n* péruvien, -ienne *(mf)*.

peruse [pə'ruːz] *vt* lire (attentivement); *(skim through)* parcourir. ◆**perusal** *n* lecture *f*.

pervade [pə'veɪd] *vt* se répandre dans. ◆**pervasive** *a* qui se répand partout, envahissant.

perverse [pə'vɜːs] *a (awkward)* contrariant; *(obstinate)* entêté; *(wicked)* pervers. ◆**perversion** *n* perversion *f*; *(of justice, truth)* travestissement *m*. ◆**perversity** *n* esprit *m* de contradiction; *(obstinacy)* entêtement *m*; *(wickedness)* perversité *f*.

pervert [pə'vɜːt] *vt* pervertir; *(mind)* corrompre; *(justice, truth)* travestir; – ['pɜːvɜːt] *n* perverti, -ie *mf*.

pesky ['peskɪ] *a* (-ier, -iest) *(troublesome)* Am Fam embêtant.

pessimism ['pesɪmɪz(ə)m] *n* pessimisme *m*. ◆**pessimist** *n* pessimiste *mf*. ◆**pessi'mistic** *a* pessimiste. ◆**pessi'mistically** *adv* avec pessimisme.

pest [pest] *n* animal *m or* insecte *m* nuisible; *(person)* Fam casse-pieds *mf inv*, peste *f*. ◆**pesticide** *n* pesticide *m*.

pester ['pestər] *vt (harass)* harceler (**with questions** de questions); **to p. s.o. to do sth/for sth** harceler *or* tarabuster qn pour qu'il fasse qch/jusqu'à ce qu'il donne qch.

pet [pet] **1** *n* animal *m* (domestique); *(favourite person)* chouchou, -oute *mf*; **yes (my) p.** Fam oui mon chou; **to have** *or* **keep a p.** avoir un animal chez soi; – *a (dog etc)* domestique; *(tiger etc)* apprivoisé; *(favourite)* favori; **p. shop** magasin *m* d'animaux; **p. hate** bête *f* noire; **p. name** petit nom *m* (d'amitié); **p. subject** dada *m*. **2** *vt* (-tt-) *(fondle)* caresser; *(sexually)* Fam peloter; – *vi* Fam se peloter.

petal ['pet(ə)l] *n* pétale *m*.

peter ['piːtər] *vi* **to p. out** *(run out)* s'épuiser; *(dry up)* se tarir; *(die out)* mourir; *(disappear)* disparaître.

petite [pə'tiːt] *a (woman)* petite et mince, menue.

petition [pə'tɪʃ(ə)n] *n (signatures)* pétition *f*; *(request)* Jur requête *f*; **p. for divorce** demande *f* en divorce; – *vt* adresser une pétition *or* une requête à (**for sth** pour demander qch).

petrify ['petrɪfaɪ] *vt (frighten)* pétrifier de terreur.

petrol ['petrəl] *n* essence *f*; **I've run out of p.** je suis tombé en panne d'essence; **p. engine** moteur *m* à essence; **p. station** poste *m* d'essence, station-service *f*.

petroleum [pə'trəʊlɪəm] *n* pétrole *m*.

petticoat ['petɪkəʊt] *n* jupon *m*.

petty ['petɪ] *a* (-ier, -iest) *(small)* petit; *(trivial)* insignifiant, menu, petit; *(mean)* mesquin; **p. cash** Com petite caisse *f*, menue monnaie *f*. ◆**pettiness** *n* petitesse *f*; insignifiance *f*, mesquinerie *f*.

petulant ['petjʊlənt] *a* irritable. ◆**petulance** *n* irritabilité *f*.

petunia [pɪ'tjuːnɪə] *n* Bot pétunia *m*.

pew [pjuː] *n* banc *m* d'église; **take a p.!** Hum assieds-toi!

pewter ['pjuːtər] *n* étain *m*.

phallic ['fælɪk] *a* phallique.

phantom ['fæntəm] *n* fantôme *m*.

pharmacy ['fɑːməsɪ] *n* pharmacie *f*. ◆**pharmaceutical** [-'sjuːtɪk(ə)l] *a* pharmaceutique. ◆**pharmacist** *n* pharmacien, -ienne *mf*.

pharynx ['færɪŋks] *n* Anat pharynx *m*. ◆**pharyn'gitis** *n* Med pharyngite *f*.

phase [feɪz] *n (stage)* phase *f*; – *vt* **to p.**

in/out introduire/supprimer progressivement. **◆phased** a (changes etc) progressif.
PhD [piːeɪtʃˈdiː] n abbr (Doctor of Philosophy) (degree) Univ doctorat m.
pheasant [ˈfezənt] n (bird) faisan m.
phenomenon, pl **-ena** [fɪˈnɒmɪnən, -ɪnə] n phénomène m. **◆phenomenal** a phénoménal.
phew! [fjuː] int (relief) ouf!
philanderer [fɪˈlændərər] n coureur m de jupons.
philanthropist [fɪˈlænθrəpɪst] n philanthrope m. **◆philan'thropic** a philanthropique.
philately [fɪˈlætəlɪ] n philatélie. **◆phila'telic** a philatélique. **◆philatelist** n philatéliste mf.
philharmonic [fɪləˈmɒnɪk] a philharmonique.
Philippines [ˈfɪlɪpiːnz] npl the P. les Philippines fpl.
philistine [ˈfɪlɪstaɪn] n béotien, -ienne mf, philistin m.
philosophy [fɪˈlɒsəfɪ] n philosophie f. **◆philosopher** n philosophe mf. **◆philo'sophical** a philosophique; (stoical, resigned) Fig philosophe. **◆philo'sophically** adv (to say etc) avec philosophie. **◆philosophize** vi philosopher.
phlegm [flem] n Med glaires fpl; (calmness) Fig flegme m. **◆phleg'matic** a flegmatique.
phobia [ˈfəʊbɪə] n phobie f.
phone [fəʊn] n téléphone m; **on the p.** (speaking here) au téléphone; (at other end) au bout du fil; **to be on the p.** (as subscriber) avoir le téléphone; **p. call** coup m de fil or de téléphone; **to make a p. call** téléphoner (to à); **p. book** annuaire m; **p. box, p. booth** cabine f téléphonique; **p. number** numéro m de téléphone; — vt (message) téléphoner (to à); **to p. s.o. (up)** téléphoner à qn; — vi **to p. (up)** téléphoner; **to p. back** rappeler. **◆phonecard** n télécarte f.
phonetic [fəˈnetɪk] a (-ier, -iest) Fam (jewels, writer etc) faux; (attack, firm) bidon inv; (attitude) fumiste; — n Fam (impostor) imposteur m; (joker, shirker) fumiste m; it's a p. (jewel, coin etc) c'est du faux.
phonograph [ˈfəʊnəgrɑːf] n Am électrophone m.
phosphate [ˈfɒsfeɪt] n Ch phosphate m.
phosphorus [ˈfɒsfərəs] n Ch phosphore m.
photo [ˈfəʊtəʊ] n (pl -os) photo f; **to have one's p. taken** se faire photographier.

◆photocopier n (machine) photocopieur m. **◆photocopy** n photocopie f; — vt photocopier. **◆photo'genic** a photogénique. **◆photograph** n photographie f; — vt photographier; — vi **to p. well** être photogénique. **◆photographer** [fəˈtɒgrəfər] n photographe mf. **◆photo'graphic** a photographique. **◆photography** [fəˈtɒgrəfɪ] n (activity) photographie f. **◆photostat®** = photocopy.
phrase [freɪz] n (saying) expression f; (idiom) & Gram locution f; — vt (express) exprimer; (letter) rédiger. **—ing** n (wording) termes mpl. **◆phrasebook** n (for tourists) manuel m de conversation.
physical [ˈfɪzɪk(ə)l] a physique; (object, world) matériel; **p. examination** Med examen m médical; **p. education, p. training** éducation f physique. **◆physically** adv physiquement; **p. impossible** matériellement impossible.
physician [fɪˈzɪʃ(ə)n] n médecin m.
physics [ˈfɪzɪks] n (science) physique f. **◆physicist** n physicien, -ienne mf.
physiology [fɪzɪˈɒlədʒɪ] n physiologie f. **◆physio'logical** a physiologique.
physiotherapy [fɪzɪəʊˈθerəpɪ] n kinésithérapie f. **◆physiotherapist** n kinésithérapeute mf.
physique [fɪˈziːk] n (appearance) physique m; (constitution) constitution f.
piano [pɪˈænəʊ] n (pl -os) piano m. **◆'pianist** n pianiste mf.
piazza [pɪˈætsə] n (square) place f; (covered) passage m couvert.
picayune [pɪkəˈjuːn] a (petty) Am Fam mesquin.
pick [pɪk] n (choice) choix m; **the p. of** (best) le meilleur de; **the p. of the bunch** le dessus du panier; **to take one's p.** faire son choix, choisir; — vt (choose) choisir; (flower, fruit etc) cueillir; (hole) faire (in dans); (lock) crocheter; **to p. one's nose** se mettre les doigts dans le nez; **to p. one's teeth** se curer les dents; **to p. a fight** chercher la bagarre (with avec); **to p. holes in** Fig relever les défauts de; **to p. (off)** (remove) enlever; **to p. out** (choose) choisir; (identify) reconnaître, distinguer; **to p. up** (sth dropped) ramasser; (fallen person or chair) relever; (person into air, weight) soulever; (cold, money) Fig ramasser; (habit, accent, speed) prendre; (fetch, collect) (passer) prendre; (find) trouver; (baby) prendre dans ses bras; (programme) Rad capter; (survivor) recueillir; (arrest) arrêter, ramasser; (learn) apprendre; — vi **to p. and choose** choisir

avec soin; **to p. on** (*nag*) harceler; (*blame*) accuser; **why p. on me?** pourquoi moi?; **to p. up** (*improve*) s'améliorer; (*of business, trade*) reprendre; *Med* aller mieux; (*resume*) continuer. ◆—**ing 1** *n* (*choosing*) choix *m* (**of** de); (*of flower, fruit etc*) cueillette *f*. **2** *npl* (*leftovers*) restes *mpl*; *Com* profits *mpl*. ◆**pick-me-up** *n* (*drink*) Fam remontant *m*. ◆**pick-up** *n* (*of record player*) bras *m* de; (*person*) Fam partenaire *mf* de rencontre; **p.-up** (*truck*) pick-up *m*.

pick(axe) (*Am* **-ax**) ['pɪk(æks)] *n* (*tool*) pioche *f*; **ice pick** pic *m* à glace.

picket ['pɪkɪt] **1** *n* (*striker*) gréviste *mf*; **p. (line)** piquet *m* (de grève); — *vt* (*factory*) installer des piquets de grève aux portes de. **2** *n* (*stake*) piquet *m*.

pickle ['pɪk(ə)l] **1** *n* (*brine*) saumure *f*; (*vinegar*) vinaigre *m*; *pl* (*vegetables*) pickles *mpl*; *Am* concombres *mpl*, cornichons *mpl*; — *vt* mariner. **2** *n* **in a p.** (*trouble*) *Fam* dans le pétrin.

pickpocket ['pɪkpɒkɪt] *n* (*thief*) pickpocket *m*.

picky ['pɪkɪ] *a* (**-ier, -iest**) (*choosey*) *Am* difficile.

picnic ['pɪknɪk] *n* pique-nique *m*; — *vi* (**-ck-**) pique-niquer.

pictorial [pɪk'tɔːrɪəl] *a* (*in pictures*) en images; (*periodical*) illustré.

picture ['pɪktʃər] **1** *n* image *f*; (*painting*) tableau *m*, peinture *f*; (*drawing*) dessin *m*; (*photo*) photo *f*; (*film*) film *m*; (*scene*) *Fig* tableau *m*; **the pictures** *Cin* le cinéma; **to put s.o. in the p.** *Fig* mettre qn au courant; **p. frame** cadre *m*. **2** *vt* (*imagine*) s'imaginer (**that** que); (*remember*) revoir; (*depict*) décrire.

picturesque [pɪktʃə'resk] *a* pittoresque.

piddling ['pɪdlɪŋ] *a* *Pej* dérisoire.

pidgin ['pɪdʒɪn] *n* **p. (English)** pidgin *m*.

pie [paɪ] *n* (*of meat, vegetable*) tourte *f*; (*of fruit*) tarte *f*, tourte *f*; (*compact filling*) pâté *m* en croûte; **cottage p.** hachis *m* Parmentier.

piebald ['paɪbɔːld] *a* pie *inv*.

piece [piːs] *n* morceau *m*; (*of bread, paper, chocolate, etc*) bout *m*, morceau *m*; (*of fabric, machine, game, artillery*) pièce *f*; (*coin*) pièce *f*; **bits and pieces** des petites choses; **in pieces** en morceaux, en pièces; **to smash to pieces** briser en morceaux; **to take to pieces** (*machine etc*) démonter; **to come to pieces** se démonter; **to go to pieces** (*of person*) *Fig* craquer; **a p. of luck/news/**etc une chance/nouvelle/etc; **in**

one p. (*object*) intact; (*person*) indemne; — *vt* **to p. together** (*facts*) reconstituer; (*one's life*) refaire. ◆**piecemeal** *adv* petit à petit; — *a* (*unsystematic*) peu méthodique. ◆**piecework** *n* travail *m* à la tâche *or* à la pièce.

pier [pɪər] *n* (*promenade*) jetée *f*; (*for landing*) appontement *m*.

pierc/e [pɪəs] *vt* percer; (*of cold, sword, bullet*) transpercer (*qn*). ◆—**ing** *a* (*voice, look etc*) perçant; (*wind etc*) glacial.

piety ['paɪətɪ] *n* piété *f*.

piffling ['pɪflɪŋ] *a* Fam insignifiant.

pig [pɪg] *n* cochon *m*, porc *m*; (*evil person*) *Pej* cochon, *m*; (*glutton*) *Pej* goinfre. ◆**piggish** *a* *Pej* (*dirty*) sale; (*greedy*) goinfre. ◆**piggy** *a* (*greedy*) *Fam* goinfre. ◆**piggybank** *n* tirelire *f* (*en forme de cochon*).

pigeon ['pɪdʒɪn] *n* pigeon *m*. ◆**pigeonhole** *n* casier *m*; — *vt* classer; (*shelve*) mettre en suspens.

piggyback ['pɪgɪbæk] *n* **to give s.o. a p.** porter qn sur le dos.

pigheaded [pɪg'hedɪd] *a* obstiné.

pigment ['pɪgmənt] *n* pigment *m*. ◆**pigmen'tation** *n* pigmentation *f*.

pigsty ['pɪgstaɪ] *n* porcherie *f*.

pigtail ['pɪgteɪl] *n* (*hair*) natte *f*.

pike [paɪk] *n* **1** (*fish*) brochet *m*. **2** (*weapon*) pique *f*.

pilchard ['pɪltʃəd] *n* pilchard *m*, sardine *f*.

pile¹ [paɪl] *n* pile *f*; (*fortune*) *Fam* fortune *f*; **piles of, a p. of** *Fam* beaucoup de, un tas de; — *vt* **to p. (up)** (*stack up*) empiler; — *vi* **to p. into** (*of people*) s'entasser dans; **to p. up** (*accumulate*) s'accumuler, s'amonceler. ◆**p.-up** *n* *Aut* collision *f* en chaîne, carambolage *m*.

pile² [paɪl] *n* (*of carpet*) poils *mpl*.

piles [paɪlz] *npl* *Med* hémorroïdes *fpl*.

pilfer ['pɪlfər] *vt* (*steal*) chaparder (**from s.o.** à qn). ◆—**ing** *n*, ◆—**age** *n* chapardage *m*.

pilgrim ['pɪlgrɪm] *n* pèlerin *m*. ◆**pilgrimage** *n* pèlerinage *m*.

pill [pɪl] *n* pilule *f*; **to be on the p.** (*of woman*) prendre la pilule; **to go on/off the p.** se mettre à/arrêter la pilule.

pillage ['pɪlɪdʒ] *vti* piller; — *n* pillage *m*.

pillar ['pɪlər] *n* pilier *m*; (*of smoke*) *Fig* colonne *f*. ◆**p.-box** *n* boîte *f* à *or* aux lettres (*située sur le trottoir*).

pillion ['pɪljən] *adv* **to ride p.** (*on motorbike*) monter derrière.

pillory ['pɪlərɪ] *vt* (*ridicule, scorn*) mettre au pilori.

pillow ['piləʊ] n oreiller m. ◆**pillowcase** n, ◆**pillowslip** n taie f d'oreiller.

pilot ['paɪlət] 1 n (of aircraft, ship) pilote m; – vt piloter; – a **p. light** (on appliance) voyant m. 2 a (experimental) (-)pilote; **p. scheme** projet(-)pilote m.

pimento [pɪ'mentəʊ] n (pl -os) piment m.

pimp [pɪmp] n souteneur m.

pimple ['pɪmp(ə)l] n bouton m. ◆**pimply** a (-ier, iest) boutonneux.

pin [pɪn] n épingle f; (drawing pin) punaise f; Tech goupille f, fiche f; **to have pins and needles** Med Fam avoir les fourmis (in dans); **p. money** argent m de poche; – vt (-nn-) **to p.** (on) (attach) épingler (to sur, à); (to wall) punaiser (to, on à); **to p. one's hopes on** mettre tous ses espoirs dans; **to p. on** (to) s.o. (crime, action) accuser qn de; **to p. down** (immobilize) immobiliser; (fix) fixer; (enemy) clouer; **to p. s.o. down** Fig forcer qn à préciser ses idées; **to p. up** (notice) afficher. ◆**pincushion** n pelote f (à épingles). ◆**pinhead** n tête f d'épingle.

pinafore ['pɪnəfɔːr] n (apron) tablier m; (dress) robe f chasuble.

pinball ['pɪnbɔːl] a **p. machine** flipper m.

pincers ['pɪnsəz] npl tenailles fpl.

pinch [pɪntʃ] 1 n (mark) pinçon m; (of salt) pincée f; **to give s.o. a p.** pincer qn; **at a p.**, Am **in a p.** (if necessary) au besoin; **to feel the p.** Fig souffrir (du manque d'argent etc); – vt pincer; – vi (of shoes) faire mal. 2 vt Fam (steal) piquer (from à); (arrest) pincer.

pine [paɪn] 1 n (tree, wood) pin m; **p. forest** pinède f. 2 vi **to p. for** désirer vivement (retrouver), languir après; **to p. away** dépérir.

pineapple ['paɪnæp(ə)l] n ananas m.

ping [pɪŋ] n bruit m métallique. ◆**pinger** n (on appliance) signal m sonore.

ping-pong ['pɪŋpɒŋ] n ping-pong m.

pink [pɪŋk] a & n (colour) rose (m).

pinkie ['pɪŋkɪ] n Am petit doigt m.

pinnacle ['pɪnək(ə)l] n (highest point) Fig apogée m.

pinpoint ['pɪnpɔɪnt] vt (locate) repérer; (define) définir.

pinstripe ['pɪnstraɪp] a (suit) rayé.

pint [paɪnt] n pinte f (Br = 0,57 litre, Am = 0,47 litre); **a p. of beer** = un demi.

pinup ['pɪnʌp] n (girl) pin-up f inv.

pioneer [paɪə'nɪər] n pionnier, -ière mf; – vt (research, study) entreprendre pour la première fois.

pious ['paɪəs] a (person, deed) pieux.

pip [pɪp] 1 n (of fruit) pépin m. 2 n (on

uniform) Mil galon m, sardine f. 3 npl **the pips** (sound) Tel le bip-bip.

pipe/e [paɪp] 1 n tuyau m; (of smoker) pipe f; (instrument) Mus pipeau m, **the pipes** (bagpipes) Mus la cornemuse; (peace) **p.** calumet m de la paix; **to smoke a p.** fumer la pipe; **p. cleaner** cure-pipe m; **p. dream** chimère f; – vt (water etc) transporter par tuyaux or par canalisation; **piped music** musique f (de fond) enregistrée. 2 vi **to p. down** (shut up) Fam la boucler, se taire. ◆**—ing** n (system of pipes) canalisations fpl, tuyaux mpl; **length of p.** tuyau m; – adv **it's p. hot** (soup etc) c'est très chaud. ◆**pipeline** n pipeline m; **it's in the p.** Fig c'est en route.

pirate ['paɪərət] n pirate m; – a (radio, ship) pirate. ◆**piracy** n piraterie f. ◆**pirated** a (book, record etc) pirate.

Pisces ['paɪsiːz] npl (sign) les Poissons mpl.

pistachio [pɪ'stæʃɪəʊ] n (pl -os) (fruit, flavour) pistache f.

pistol ['pɪstəl] n pistolet m.

piston ['pɪst(ə)n] n Aut piston m.

pit [pɪt] 1 n (hole) trou m; (mine) mine f; (quarry) carrière f; (of stomach) creux m; Th orchestre m; Sp Aut stand m de ravitaillement. 2 vt (-tt-) **to p. oneself or one's wits against** se mesurer à. 3 n (stone of fruit) Am noyau m. ◆**pitted** a (face) grêlé; **p. with rust** piqué de rouille. 2 (fruit) Am dénoyauté.

pitch [pɪtʃ] 1 n Sp terrain m; (in market) place f. 2 n (degree) degré m; (of voice) hauteur f; Mus ton m. 3 vt (ball) lancer; (camp) établir; (tent) dresser; **a pitched battle** Mil une bataille rangée; Fig une belle bagarre. 4 vi (of ship) tanguer. 5 vi **to p. in** (cooperate) Fam se mettre de la partie; **to p. into s.o.** attaquer qn.

pitch² [pɪtʃ] n (tar) poix f. ◆**p.-'black** a, ◆**p.-'dark** a noir comme dans un four.

pitcher ['pɪtʃər] n cruche f, broc m.

pitchfork ['pɪtʃfɔːk] n fourche f (à foin).

pitfall ['pɪtfɔːl] n (trap) piège m.

pith [pɪθ] n (of orange) peau f blanche; (essence) Fig moelle f. ◆**pithy** a (-ier, -iest) (remark etc) piquant et concis.

pitiful ['pɪtɪfəl] a pitoyable. ◆**pitiless** a impitoyable.

pittance ['pɪtəns] n (income) revenu m or salaire m misérable; (sum) somme f dérisoire.

pitter-patter ['pɪtəpætər] n = patter 1.

pity ['pɪtɪ] n pitié f; (what) **a p.!** (quel) dommage!; **it's a p.** c'est dommage (that

que (+ *sub*), **to do** de faire); **to have** *or* **take p. on** avoir pitié de; − *vt* plaindre.
pivot ['pɪvət] *n* pivot *m*; − *vi* pivoter.
pixie ['pɪksɪ] *n* (*fairy*) lutin *m*.
pizza ['piːtsə] *n* Pizza *f*.
placard ['plækɑːd] *n* (*notice*) affiche *f*.
placate [plə'keɪt, *Am* 'pleɪkeɪt] *vt* calmer.
place [pleɪs] *n* endroit *m*; (*specific*) lieu *m*; (*house*) maison *f*; (*premises*) locaux *mpl*; (*seat, position, rank*) place *f*; **in the first p.** (*firstly*) en premier lieu; **to take p.** (*happen*) avoir lieu; **p. of work** lieu *m* de travail; **market p.** (*square*) place *f* du marché; **at my p.,** to my p. Fam chez moi; **some p.** (*somewhere*) *Am* quelque part; **no p.** (*nowhere*) *Am* nulle part; **all over the p.** partout; **to lose one's p.** perdre sa place; (*in book etc*) perdre sa page; **p. setting** couvert *m*; **to lay three places** (*at the table*) mettre trois couverts; **to take the p. of** remplacer; **in p.** of à la place de; **out of p.** (*remark, object*) déplacé; (*person*) dépaysé; **to mat** set *m* (de table); − *vt* (*put, situate, invest*) & *Sp* placer; (*an order*) *Com* passer (**with s.o.** à qn); (*remember*) se rappeler; (*identify*) reconnaître. **◆placing** *n* (*of money*) placement *m*.
placid ['plæsɪd] *a* placide.
plagiarize ['pleɪdʒəraɪz] *vt* plagier. **◆plagiarism** *n* plagiat *m*.
plague [pleɪg] *n* **1** (*disease*) peste *f*; (*nuisance*) *Fam* plaie *f*. **2** *vt* (*harass, pester*) harceler (**with** de).
plaice [pleɪs] *n* (*fish*) carrelet *m*, plie *f*.
plaid [plæd] *n* (*fabric*) tissu *m* écossais.
plain[1] [pleɪn] **1** *a* (**-er, -est**) (*clear, obvious*) clair; (*outspoken*) franc; (*simple*) simple; (*not patterned*) uni; (*woman, man*) sans beauté; (*sheer*) pur; **in p. clothes** en civil; **to make it p. to s.o. that** faire comprendre à qn que; **p. speaking** franc-parler *m*; − *adv* (*tired etc*) tout bonnement. **◆−ly** *adv* clairement; franchement. **◆−ness** *n* clarté *f*; simplicité *f*; manque *m* de beauté.
plain[2] [pleɪn] *n* Geog plaine *f*.
plaintiff ['pleɪntɪf] *n* Jur plaignant, -ante *mf*.
plait [plæt] *n* tresse *f*, natte *f*; − *vt* tresser, natter.
plan [plæn] *n* projet *m*; (*elaborate*) plan *m*; (*of house, book etc*) & Pol Econ plan *m*; **the best p. would be to . . .** le mieux serait de . . . ; **according to p.** comme prévu; **to have no plans** (*be free*) n'avoir rien de prévu; **to change one's plans** (*decide differently*) changer d'idée; **master p.** stratégie *f* d'ensemble; − *vt* (**-nn-**) (*envisage, decide on*) prévoir, projeter; (*organize*) organiser;

(*prepare*) préparer; (*design*) concevoir; Econ planifier; **to p. to do** (*intend*) avoir l'intention de faire; **as planned** comme prévu; − *vi* faire des projets; **to p. for** (*rain, disaster*) prévoir. **◆planning** *n* Econ planification *f*; (*industrial, commercial*) planning *m*; **family p.** planning *m* familial; **town p.** urbanisme *m*. **◆planner** *n* **town p.** urbaniste *mf*.
plane [pleɪn] *n* **1** (*aircraft*) avion *m*. **2** Carp rabot *m*. **3** (*tree*) platane *m*. **4** (*level*) & Fig plan *m*.
planet ['plænɪt] *n* planète *f*. **◆plane-'tarium** *n* planétarium *m*. **◆planetary** *a* planétaire.
plank [plæŋk] *n* planche *f*.
plant [plɑːnt] **1** *n* plante *f*; **house p.** plante d'appartement; − *vt* planter (**with** en, de); (*bomb*) Fig (dé)poser; **to p. sth on s.o.** (*hide*) cacher qch sur qn. **2** *n* (*machinery*) matériel *m*; (*fixtures*) installation *f*; (*factory*) usine *f*. **◆plan'tation** *n* (*land, trees etc*) plantation *f*.
plaque [plæk] *n* **1** (*commemorative plate*) plaque *f*. **2** (*on teeth*) plaque *f* dentaire.
plasma ['plæzmə] *n* Med plasma *m*.
plaster ['plɑːstər] *n* (*substance*) plâtre *m*; (*sticking*) **p.** sparadrap *m*; **p. of Paris** plâtre *m* à mouler; **in p.** Med dans le plâtre; **p. cast** Med plâtre *m*; − *vt* plâtrer; **to p. down** (*hair*) plaquer; **to p. with** (*cover*) couvrir de. **◆−er** *n* plâtrier *m*.
plastic ['plæstɪk] *a* (*substance, art*) plastique; (*object*) en plastique; **p. explosive** plastic *m*; **p. surgery** chirurgie *f* esthétique; − *n* plastique *m*, matière *f* plastique.
plasticine® ['plæstɪsiːn] *n* pâte *f* à modeler.
plate [pleɪt] *n* (*dish*) assiette *f*; (*metal sheet on door, on vehicle etc*) plaque *f*; (*book illustration*) gravure *f*; (*dental*) dentier *m*; **gold/silver p.** vaisselle *f* d'or/d'argent; **a lot on one's p.** (*work*) Fig du pain sur la planche; **p. glass** verre *m* à vitre; (*jewellery, metal*) plaquer (**with** de). **◆plateful** *n* assiettée *f*, assiette *f*.
plateau ['plætəʊ] *n* Geog (*pl* **-s** *or* **-x**) plateau *m*.
platform ['plætfɔːm] *n* estrade *f*; (*for speaker*) tribune *f*; (*on bus*) & Pol plate-forme *f*; Rail quai *m*; **p. shoes** chaussures *fpl* à semelles compensées.
platinum ['plætɪnəm] *n* (*metal*) platine *m*; − *a* **p.** *or* **p.-blond(e) hair** cheveux *mpl* platinés.
platitude ['plætɪtjuːd] *n* platitude *f*.
platonic [plə'tɒnɪk] *a* (*love etc*) platonique.
platoon [plə'tuːn] *n* Mil section *f*.

platter ['plætər] n Culin plat m.

plaudits ['plɔːdɪts] npl applaudissements mpl.

plausible ['plɔːzəb(ə)l] a (argument etc) plausible; (speaker etc) convaincant.

play [pleɪ] n (amusement, looseness) jeu m; Th pièce f (de théâtre), spectacle m; **a p. on words** un jeu de mots; **to come into p.** entrer en jeu; **to call into p.** faire entrer en jeu; – vt (card, part, tune etc) (game) jouer à; (instrument) jouer de; (match) disputer (with avec); (team, opponent) jouer contre; (record) passer; (radio) faire marcher; **to p. ball with** Fig coopérer avec; **to p. the fool** faire l'idiot; **to p. a part in doing/in sth** contribuer à faire/à qch; **to p. it cool** Fam garder son sang-froid; **to p. back** (tape) réécouter; **to p. down** minimiser; **to p. s.o. up** Fam (of bad back etc) tracasser qn; (of child etc) faire enrager qn; **played out** Fam (tired) épuisé; (idea, method) périmé, vieux jeu inv; – vi jouer (with avec, at à); (of record player, tape recorder) marcher; **what are you playing at?** Fam qu'est-ce que tu fais?; **to p. about** or **around** jouer, s'amuser; **to p. on** (piano etc) jouer de; (s.o.'s emotions etc) jouer sur; **to p. up** (of child, machine etc) Fam faire des siennes; **to p. up to s.o.** faire de la lèche à qn. ◆—ing n jeu m; **p. card** carte f à jouer; **p. field** terrain m de jeu. ◆—er n Sp joueur, -euse mf; Th acteur m, actrice f; **clarinette/etc p.** joueur, -euse mf de clarinette/etc; **cassette p.** lecteur m de cassettes.

play-act ['pleɪækt] vi jouer la comédie. ◆**playboy** n playboy m. ◆**playgoer** n amateur m de théâtre. ◆**playground** n Sch cour f de récréation. ◆**playgroup** n = **playschool**. ◆**playmate** n camarade mf. ◆**playpen** n parc m (pour enfants). ◆**playroom** n (in house) salle f de jeux. ◆**playschool** n garderie f (d'enfants). ◆**plaything** n (person) Fig jouet m. ◆**playtime** n Sch récréation f. ◆**playwright** n dramaturge mf.

playful ['pleɪfəl] a enjoué; (child) joueur. ◆—ly adv (to say) en badinant. ◆—ness n enjouement m.

plc [piːel'siː] abbr (public limited company) SA.

plea [pliː] n (request) appel m; (excuse) excuse f; **to make a p. of guilty** Jur plaider coupable. ◆**plead** vi Jur plaider; **to p. with s.o. to do** implorer qn de faire; **to p. for** (help etc) implorer; – vt Jur plaider; (as excuse) alléguer. ◆**pleading** n (requests) prières fpl.

pleasant ['plezənt] a agréable; (polite) aimable. ◆—ly adv agréablement. ◆—ness n (charm) charme m; (of person) amabilité f. ◆**pleasantries** npl (jokes) plaisanteries fpl; (polite remarks) civilités fpl.

pleas/e [pliːz] adv s'il vous plaît, s'il te plaît; **p. sit down** asseyez-vous, je vous prie; **p. do!** bien sûr!, je vous en prie!; **'no smoking p.'** 'prière de ne pas fumer'; – vt plaire à; (satisfy) contenter; **hard to p.** difficile (à contenter), exigeant; **p. yourself!** comme tu veux!; – vi plaire; **do as you p.** fais comme tu veux; **as much** or **as many as you p.** autant qu'il vous plaira. ◆—ed a content (with de, that que (+ sub), to do de faire); **p. to meet you!** enchanté!; **I'd be p. to!** avec plaisir! ◆—ing a agréable, plaisant.

pleasure ['pleʒər] n plaisir m; **p. boat** bateau m de plaisance. ◆**pleasurable** a très agréable.

pleat [pliːt] n (fold) pli m; – vt plisser.

plebiscite ['plebɪsɪt, -saɪt] n plébiscite m.

pledge [pledʒ] 1 n (promise) promesse f, engagement m (to do de faire); – vt promettre (to do de faire). 2 n (token, object) gage m; – vt (pawn) engager.

plenty ['plentɪ] n abondance f; **in p.** en abondance; **p. of** beaucoup de; **that's p.** (enough) c'est assez, ça suffit. ◆**plentiful** a abondant.

plethora ['pleθərə] n pléthore f.

pleurisy ['plʊərɪsɪ] n Med pleurésie f.

pliable ['plaɪəb(ə)l] a souple.

pliers ['plaɪəz] npl (tool) pince(s) f(pl).

plight [plaɪt] n (crisis) situation f critique; (sorry) p. triste situation f.

plimsoll ['plɪmsəul] n chaussure f de tennis, tennis f.

plinth [plɪnθ] n socle m.

plod [plɒd] vi (-dd-) **to p. (along)** avancer or travailler laborieusement; **to p. through** (book) lire laborieusement. ◆**plodding** a (slow) lent; (step) pesant. ◆**plodder** n (steady worker) bûcheur, -euse mf.

plonk [plɒŋk] 1 int (splash) plouf! 2 vt **to p. (down)** (drop) Fam poser (bruyamment). 3 n (wine) Pej Sl pinard m.

plot [plɒt] 1 n (conspiracy) complot m (against contre); Cin Th Liter intrigue f; – vti (-tt-) comploter (to do de faire). 2 n **p.** (of land) terrain m; (patch in garden) carré m de terre; **building p.** terrain m à bâtir. 3 vt (-tt-) **to p. (out)** déterminer; (graph, diagram) tracer; (one's position) relever. ◆**plotting** n (conspiracies) complots mpl.

plough [plau] n charrue f; – vt labourer;

p. back into (*money*) *Fig* réinvestir dans; – *vi* labourer; **to p. into** (*crash into*) percuter; **to p. through** (*snow etc*) avancer péniblement dans; (*fence, wall*) défoncer. ◆**ploughman** *n* (*pl* -**men**) laboureur *m*; **p.'s lunch** *Culin* assiette *f* composée (*de crudités et fromage*).

plow [plau] *Am* = **plough**.

ploy [plɔi] *n* stratagème *m*.

pluck [plʌk] **1** *n* courage *m*; – *vt* **to p. up courage** s'armer de courage. **2** *vt* (*fowl*) plumer; (*eyebrows*) épiler; (*string*) *Mus* pincer; (*flower*) cueillir. ◆**plucky** *a* (-**ier**, -**iest**) courageux.

plug [plʌg] **1** *n* (*of cotton wool, wood etc*) tampon *m*, bouchon *m*; (*for sink etc drainage*) bonde *f*; – *vt* (-**gg-**) **to p. (up)** (*stop up*) boucher. **2** *n El* fiche *f*, prise *f* (*mâle*); – *vt* (-**gg-**) **to p. in** brancher. **3** *n Aut* bougie *f*. **4** *n* (*publicity*) *Fam* battage *m* publicitaire; – *vt* (-**gg-**) *Fam* faire du battage publicitaire pour. **5** *vi* (-**gg-**) **to p. away** (*work*) *Fam* bosser (**at** à). ◆**plughole** *n* trou *m* (*du lavabo etc*), vidange *f*.

plum [plʌm] *n* prune *f*; **a p. job** *Fam* un travail en or, un bon fromage.

plumage [ˈpluːmɪdʒ] *n* plumage *m*.

plumb [plʌm] **1** *vt* (*probe, understand*) sonder. **2** *adv* (*crazy etc*) *Am Fam* complètement; **p. in the middle** en plein milieu. ◆**plumber** [ˈplʌmər] *n* plombier *m*. ◆**plumbing** *n* plomberie *f*.

plume [pluːm] *n* (*feather*) plume *f*; (*on hat etc*) plumet *m*; **a p. of smoke** un panache de fumée.

plummet [ˈplʌmɪt] *vi* (*of aircraft etc*) plonger; (*of prices*) dégringoler.

plump [plʌmp] **1** *a* (-**er**, -**est**) (*person*) grassouillet; (*arm, chicken*) dodu; (*cushion, cheek*) rebondi. **2** *vi* **to p. for** (*choose*) se décider pour, choisir. ◆—**ness** *n* rondeur *f*.

plunder [ˈplʌndər] *vt* piller; – *n* (*act*) pillage *m*; (*goods*) butin *m*.

plung/e [plʌndʒ] *vt* (*thrust*) plonger (**into** dans); – *vi* (*dive*) plonger (**into** dans); (*fall*) tomber (**from** de); (*rush*) se lancer; – *n* (*dive*) plongeon *m*; (*fall*) chute *f*; **to take the p.** *Fig* se jeter à l'eau. ◆—**ing** *a* (*neckline*) plongeant. ◆—**er** *n* ventouse *f* (*pour déboucher un tuyau*), débouchoir *m*.

plural [ˈpluərəl] *a* (*form*) pluriel (*noun*) au pluriel; – *n* pluriel *m*; **in the p.** au pluriel.

plus [plʌs] *prep* plus; – *a* (*factor etc*) *El* positif; **twenty p.** vingt et quelques; – *n* **p.**

(*sign*) *Math* (signe *m*) plus *m*; **it's a p.** c'est un (avantage en) plus.

plush [plʌʃ] *a* (-**er**, -**est**) (*splendid*) somptueux.

plutonium [pluːˈtəʊnɪəm] *n* plutonium *m*.

ply [plaɪ] **1** *vt* (*trade*) exercer; (*oar, tool*) *Lit* manier. **2** *vi* **to p. between** (*travel*) faire la navette entre. **3** *vt* **to p. s.o. with** (*whisky etc*) faire boire continuellement à qn; (*questions*) bombarder qn de.

p.m. [piːˈem] *adv* (*afternoon*) de l'après-midi; (*evening*) du soir.

PM [piːˈem] *n abbr* (*Prime Minister*) Premier ministre *m*.

pneumatic [njuːˈmætɪk] *a* **p. drill** marteau-piqueur *m*, marteau *m* pneumatique.

pneumonia [njuːˈməʊnɪə] *n* pneumonie *f*.

poach [pəʊtʃ] **1** *vt* (*egg*) pocher. **2** *vi* (*hunt, steal*) braconner; – *vt* (*employee from rival firm*) débaucher, piquer. ◆—**ing** *n* braconnage *m*. ◆—**er** *n* (*person*) braconnier *m*. **2** (*egg*) *n* pocheuse *f*.

PO Box [piːəʊˈbɒks] *abbr* (*Post Office Box*) BP.

pocket [ˈpɒkɪt] *n* poche *f*; (*area*) *Fig* petite zone *f*; (*of resistance*) poche *f*, îlot *m*; **I'm $5 out of p.** j'ai perdu 5 dollars; – *a* (*money, book etc*) de poche; – *vt* (*gain, steal*) empocher. ◆**pocketbook** *n* (*notebook*) carnet *m*; (*woman's handbag*) *Am* sac *m* à main. ◆**pocketful** *n* **a p. of** une pleine poche de.

pockmarked [ˈpɒkmɑːkt] *a* (*face*) grêlé.

pod [pɒd] *n* cosse *f*.

podgy [ˈpɒdʒɪ] *a* (-**ier**, -**iest**) (*arm etc*) dodu; (*person*) rondelet.

podium [ˈpəʊdɪəm] *n* podium *m*.

poem [ˈpəʊɪm] *n* poème *m*. ◆**poet** *n* poète *m*. ◆**po'etic** *a* poétique. ◆**poetry** *n* poésie *f*.

poignant [ˈpɔɪnjənt] *a* poignant.

point [pɔɪnt] **1** *n* (*of knife etc*) pointe *f*; *pl Rail* aiguillage *m*; (*power*) *El* prise *f* (*de courant*). **2** *n* (*dot, position, question, degree, score etc*) point *m*; (*decimal*) virgule *f*; (*meaning*) *Fig* sens *m*; (*importance*) intérêt *m*; (*remark*) remarque *f*; **p. of view** point *m* de vue; **at this p. in time** en ce moment; **on the p. of doing** sur le point de faire; **what's the p.?** à quoi bon? (*of waiting/etc*) attendre/*etc*); **there's no p. (in) staying**/*etc* ça ne sert à rien de rester/*etc*; **that's not the p.** il ne s'agit pas de ça; **it's beside the p.** c'est à côté de la question; **to the p.** (*relevant*) pertinent; **get to the p.!** au fait!; **to make a p. of doing** prendre garde de faire; **his good**

points ses qualités *fpl*; **his bad points** ses défauts *mpl*. **3** *vt* (*aim*) pointer (**at** sur); (*vehicle*) tourner (**towards** vers); **to p. the way** indiquer le chemin (**to** à); *Fig* montrer la voie (**to** à); **to p. one's finger at** indiquer du doigt, pointer son doigt vers; **to p. out** (*show*) indiquer; (*mention*) signaler (**that** que); − *vi* **to p. (at** *or* **to s.o.)** indiquer (qn) du doigt; **to p. to, be pointing to** (*show*) indiquer; **to p. east** indiquer l'est; **to be pointing** (*of vehicle*) être tourné (**towards** vers); (*of gun*) être braqué (**at** sur). ◆**─ed** *a* pointu; (*beard*) en pointe; (*remark, criticism*) *Fig* pertinent; (*incisive*) mordant. ◆**─edly** *adv* (*to the point*) avec pertinence; (*incisively*) d'un ton mordant. ◆**─er** *n* (*on dial etc*) index *m*; (*advice*) conseil *m*; (*clue*) indice *m*; **to be a p. to** (*possible solution etc*) laisser entrevoir. ◆**─less** *a* inutile, futile. ◆**─lessly** *adv* inutilement.

point-blank [pɔɪnt'blæŋk] *adv & a* (*to shoot, a shot*) à bout portant; (*to refuse, a refusal*) *Fig* (tout) net; (*to request, a request*) de but en blanc.

pois/e [pɔɪz] *n* (*balance*) équilibre *m*; (*of body*) port *m*; (*grace*) grâce *f*; (*confidence*) assurance *f*, calme *m*; − *vt* tenir en équilibre. ◆**─ed** *a* en équilibre; (*hanging*) suspendu; (*composed*) calme; **p. to attack/** *etc* (*ready*) prêt à attaquer/*etc*.

poison ['pɔɪz(ə)n] *n* poison *m*; (*of snake*) venin *m*; **p. gas** gaz *m* toxique; − *vt* empoisonner; **to p. s.o.'s mind** corrompre qn. ◆**poisoning** *n* empoisonnement *m*. ◆**poisonous** *a* (*fumes, substance*) toxique; (*snake*) venimeux; (*plant*) vénéneux.

pok/e [pəʊk] *vt* (*push*) pousser (*avec un bâton etc*); (*touch*) toucher; (*fire*) tisonner; **to p. sth into** (*put, thrust*) fourrer *or* enfoncer qch dans; **to p. one's finger at** pointer son doigt vers; **to p. one's nose into** fourrer le nez dans; **to p. a hole in** faire un trou dans; **to p. one's head out of the window** passer la tête par la fenêtre; **to p. out s.o.'s eye** crever un œil à qn; − *vi* pousser; **to p. about** *or* **around in** fourrer dans; − *n* (*jab*) (petit) coup *m*; (*shove*) poussée *f*, coup *m*. ◆**─er** *n* **1** (*for fire*) tisonnier *m*. **2** *Cards* poker *m*.

poky ['pəʊkɪ] *a* (*-ier, -iest*) (*small*) exigu et misérable, rikiki; (*slow*) *Am* lent.

Poland ['pəʊlənd] *n* Pologne *f*. ◆**Pole** *n* Polonais, -aise *mf*.

polarize ['pəʊləraɪz] *vt* polariser.

pole [pəʊl] *n* **1** (*rod*) perche *f*; (*fixed*) poteau *m*; (*for flag*) mât *m*. **2** *Geog* pôle *m*;

North/South P. pôle Nord/Sud. ◆**polar** *a* polaire; **p. bear** ours *m* blanc.

polemic [pə'lemɪk] *n* polémique *f*. ◆**polemical** *a* polémique.

police [pə'liːs] *n* police *f*; **more** *or* **extra p.** des renforts *mpl* de police; − *a* (*inquiry etc*) de la police; (*state, dog*) policier; **p. cadet** agent *m* de police stagiaire; **p. car** voiture *f* de police; **p. force** police *f*; − *vt* (*city etc*) maintenir l'ordre *or* la paix dans; (*frontier*) contrôler. ◆**policeman** *n* (*pl* **-men**) agent *m* de police. ◆**policewoman** *n* (*pl* **-women**) femme-agent *f*.

policy ['pɒlɪsɪ] *n* **1** *Pol Econ etc* politique *f*; (*individual course of action*) règle *f*, façon *f* d'agir; *pl* (*ways of governing*) *Pol* politique *f*; **matter of p.** question *f* de principe. **2** (*insurance*) **p.** police *f* (d'assurance); **p. holder** assuré, -ée *mf*.

polio(myelitis) ['pəʊlɪəʊ(maɪə'laɪtɪs)] *n* polio(myélite) *f*; **p. victim** polio *mf*.

polish ['pɒlɪʃ] *vt* (*floor, table, shoes etc*) cirer; (*metal*) astiquer; (*rough surface*) polir; (*smooth*) polir; (*style*) *Fig* polir; **to p. up** (*one's French etc*) travailler; **to p. off** (*food, work etc*) *Fam* liquider, finir (en vitesse); − *n* (*for shoes*) cirage *m*; (*for floor, furniture*) cire *f*; (*shine*) vernis *m*; *Fig* raffinement *m*; (*nail*) **p.** vernis *m* (à ongles); **to give sth a p.** faire briller qch.

Polish ['pəʊlɪʃ] *a* polonais; − *n* (*language*) polonais *m*.

polite [pə'laɪt] *a* (*-er, -est*) poli (**to, with** avec); **in p. society** dans la bonne société. ◆**─ly** *adv* poliment. ◆**─ness** *n* politesse *f*.

political [pə'lɪtɪk(ə)l] *a* politique. ◆**politician** *n* homme *m* *or* femme *f* politique. ◆**politicize** *vt* politiser. ◆**'politics** *n* politique *f*.

polka ['pɒlkə, *Am* 'pəʊlkə] *n* (*dance*) polka *f*; **p. dot** pois *m*.

poll [pəʊl] *n* (*voting*) scrutin *m*, élection *f*; (*vote*) vote *m*; (*turnout*) participation *f* électorale; (*list*) liste *f* électorale; **to go to the polls** aller aux urnes; (*opinion*) **p.** sondage *m* (d'opinion); **50% of the p.** 50% des votants; − *vt* (*votes*) obtenir; (*people*) sonder l'opinion de. ◆**─ing** *n* (*election*) élections *fpl*; **p. booth** isoloir *m*; **p. station** bureau *m* de vote.

pollen ['pɒlən] *n* pollen *m*.

pollute [pə'luːt] *vt* polluer. ◆**pollutant** *n* polluant *m*. ◆**pollution** *n* pollution *f*.

polo ['pəʊləʊ] *n* *Sp* polo *m*; **p. neck** (*sweater, neckline*) col *m* roulé.

polyester [pɒlɪ'estər] *n* polyester *m*.

Polynesia [pɒlɪ'niːʒə] n Polynésie f.

polytechnic [pɒlɪ'teknɪk] n institut m universitaire de technologie.

polythene ['pɒlɪθiːn] n polyéthylène m; p. bag sac m en plastique.

pomegranate ['pɒmɪgrænɪt] n (fruit) grenade f.

pomp [pɒmp] n pompe f. ◆**pom'posity** n emphase f, solennité f. ◆**pompous** a pompeux.

pompon ['pɒmpɒn] n (ornament) pompon m.

pond [pɒnd] n étang m; (stagnant) mare f;(artificial) bassin m.

ponder ['pɒndər] vt to p. (over) réfléchir à; – vi réfléchir.

ponderous ['pɒndərəs] a (heavy, slow) pesant.

pong [pɒŋ] n Sl mauvaise odeur f; – vi (stink) Sl schlinguer.

pontificate [pɒn'tɪfɪkeɪt] vi (speak) Pej pontifier (about sur).

pony ['pəʊnɪ] n poney m. ◆**ponytail** n (hair) queue f de cheval.

poodle ['puːd(ə)l] n caniche m.

poof [puːf] n (homosexual) Pej Sl pédé m.

pooh! [puː] int bah!; (bad smell) ça pue!

pooh-pooh [puː'puː] vt (scorn) dédaigner; (dismiss) se moquer de.

pool [puːl] 1 n (puddle) flaque f; (of blood) mare f; (pond) étang m; (for swimming) piscine f. 2 n (of experience, talent) réservoir m; (of advisers etc) équipe f; (kitty) cagnotte f; (football) pools prognostics mpl (sur les matchs de football); – vt (share) mettre en commun; (combine) unir. 3 n Sp billard m américain.

pooped [puːpt] a (exhausted) Am Fam vanné, crevé.

poor [pʊər] a (-er, -est) (not rich, deserving pity) pauvre; (bad) mauvais; (inferior) médiocre; (meagre) maigre; (weak) faible; p. thing! le or la pauvre!; – n the p. les pauvres mpl. ◆**-ly** 1 adv (badly) mal; (clothed, furnished) pauvrement. 2 a (ill) malade.

pop¹ [pɒp] 1 int pan! – n (noise) bruit m sec; to go p. faire pan; (of champagne bottle) faire pop; – vt (-pp-) (balloon etc) crever; (bottle top, button) faire sauter; – vi (burst) crever; (come off) sauter; (of ears) se déboucher. 2 vt (put) Fam mettre; – vi Fam to p. in (go in) entrer (en passant); to p. off (leave) partir; to p. out sortir (un instant); to p. over or round faire un saut (to chez); to p. up (of person) surgir, réapparaître; (of question etc) surgir.

◆**p.-'eyed** a aux yeux exorbités. ◆**p.-up book** n livre m en relief.

pop² [pɒp] 1 n (music) pop m; – a (concert, singer etc) pop inv. 2 n (father) Am Fam papa m. 3 n (soda) p. (drink) Am soda m.

popcorn ['pɒpkɔːn] n pop-corn m.

pope [pəʊp] n pape m; p.'s nose (of chicken) croupion m.

poplar ['pɒplər] n (tree, wood) peuplier m.

poppy ['pɒpɪ] n (cultivated) pavot m; (red, wild) coquelicot m.

poppycock ['pɒpɪkɒk] n Fam fadaises fpl.

popsicle® ['pɒpsɪk(ə)l] n (ice lolly) Am esquimau m.

popular ['pɒpjʊlər] a (a person, song, vote, science etc) populaire; (fashionable) à la mode; to be p. with plaire beaucoup à. ◆**popu'larity** n popularité f (with auprès de). ◆**popularize** vt populariser; (science, knowledge) vulgariser. ◆**popularly** adv communément.

populat/e ['pɒpjʊleɪt] vt peupler. ◆**—ed** a peuplé (with de). ◆**popu'lation** n population f. ◆**populous** a (crowded) populeux.

porcelain ['pɔːsəlɪn] n porcelaine f.

porch [pɔːtʃ] n porche m; (veranda) Am véranda f.

porcupine ['pɔːkjʊpaɪn] n (animal) porc-épic m.

pore [pɔːr] 1 n (of skin) pore m. 2 vi to p. over (book, question etc) étudier de près. ◆**porous** a poreux.

pork [pɔːk] n (meat) porc m; p. butcher charcutier, -ière mf.

pornography [pɔː'nɒgrəfɪ] n (Fam porn) pornographie f. ◆**porno'graphic** a pornographique, porno (f inv).

porpoise ['pɔːpəs] n (sea animal) marsouin m.

porridge ['pɒrɪdʒ] n porridge m; p. oats flocons mpl d'avoine.

port [pɔːt] 1 n (harbour) port m; p. of call escale f; – a (authorities, installations etc) portuaire. 2 n p. (side) (left) Nau Av bâbord m; – a de bâbord. 3 n (wine) porto m.

portable ['pɔːtəb(ə)l] a portatif, portable.

portal ['pɔːt(ə)l] n portail m.

porter ['pɔːtər] n (for luggage) porteur m; (doorman) portier m; (caretaker) concierge m, (of public building) gardien, -ienne mf.

portfolio [pɔːt'fəʊlɪəʊ] n (pl -os) Com Pol portefeuille m.

porthole ['pɔːthəʊl] n Nau Av hublot m.

portico ['pɔːtɪkəʊ] n (pl -oes or -os) Archit portique m; (of house) porche m.

portion ['pɔːʃ(ə)n] n (share, helping) portion

f; *(of train, book etc)* partie *f*; − *vt* **to p. out** répartir.

portly ['pɔːtlɪ] *a* (**-ier, -iest**) corpulent.

portrait ['pɔːtrɪt, 'pɔːtreɪt] *n* portrait *m*; **p. painter** portraitiste *mf*.

portray [pɔː'treɪ] *vt (describe)* représenter. ◆**portrayal** *n* portrait *m*, représentation *f*.

Portugal ['pɔːtjʊg(ə)l] *n* Portugal *m*. ◆**Portu-'guese** *a* & *n* portugais, -aise (*mf*); − *n (language)* portugais *m*.

pose [pəʊz] **1** *n (in art or photography)* & *Fig* pose *f*; − *vi (of model etc)* poser *(for* pour); **to p. as a lawyer/*etc*** se faire passer pour un avocat/*etc*. **2** *vt (question)* poser. ◆**poser** *n* **1** *(question) Fam* colle *f*. **2** = **poseur**. ◆**poseur** [-'zɜːr] *n Pej* poseur, -euse *mf*.

posh [pɒʃ] *a Pej Fam (smart)* chic *inv*; *(snobbish)* snob (*f inv*).

position [pə'zɪʃ(ə)n] *n (place, posture, opinion etc)* position *f*; *(of building, town)* emplacement *m*, position *f*; *(job, circumstances)* situation *f*; *(customer window in bank etc)* guichet *m*; **in a p. to do** en mesure *or* en position de faire; **in a good p. to do** bien placé pour faire; **in p.** en place, en position; − *vt (camera, machine etc)* mettre en position; *(put)* placer.

positive ['pɒzɪtɪv] *a* positif, -ive; *(order)* catégorique; *(progress, change)* réel; *(tone)* assuré; *(sure)* sûr, certain (**of**, **that** que); **a p. genius** *Fam* un vrai génie. ◆**-ly** *adv (for certain)* & *El* positivement; *(undeniably)* indéniablement; *(completely)* complètement; *(categorically)* catégoriquement.

possess [pə'zes] *vt* posséder. ◆**possession** *n* possession *f*; **in p. of** en possession de; **to take p. of** prendre possession de. ◆**possessive** *a (adjective, person etc)* possessif; − *n Gram* possessif *m*. ◆**possessor** *n* possesseur *m*.

possible ['pɒsəb(ə)l] *a* possible (**to do** à faire); **it is p. (for us) to do it** il (nous) est possible de le faire; **it is p. that** il est possible que (+ *sub*); **as far as p.** dans la mesure du possible; **if p.** si possible; **as much** *or* **as many as p.** autant que possible; − *n (person, object) Fam* choix *m* possible. ◆**possi'bility** *n* possibilité *f*; **some p. of** quelques chances *fpl* de; **there's some p. that it** c'est (tout juste) possible que (+ *sub*); **she has possibilities** elle promet; **it's a distinct p.** c'est bien possible. ◆**possibly** *adv* **1** *(with can, could etc)* **if you p. can** si cela t'est possible; **to do all one p. can** faire tout son possible (**to do** faire); **he**

cannot p. stay il ne peut absolument pas rester. **2** *(perhaps)* peut-être.

post¹ [pəʊst] *n (postal system)* poste *f*; *(letters)* courrier *m*; **by p.** par la poste; **to catch/miss the p.** avoir/manquer la levée; − *a (bag, code etc)* postal; **p. office** *(bureau m de)* poste *f*; **P. Office** *(administration)* *(service m des)* postes *fpl*; − *vt (put in postbox)* poster, mettre à la poste; *(send)* envoyer; **to keep s.o. posted** *Fig* tenir qn au courant. ◆**postage** *n* tarif *m* (postal), tarifs *mpl* (postaux) (**to** pour); **p. stamp** timbre-poste *m*. ◆**postal** *a (district etc)* postal; *(inquiries)* par la poste; *(clerk)* des postes; *(vote)* par correspondance. ◆**postbox** *n* boîte *f* à *or* aux lettres. ◆**postcard** *n* carte *f* postale. ◆**postcode** *n* code *m* postal. ◆**post-'free** *adv*, **post'paid** *adv* franco.

post² [pəʊst] *n (job, place)* & *Mil* poste *m*; − *vt (sentry, guard)* poster; *(employee)* affecter (**to** à). ◆**-ing** *n (appointment)* affectation *f*.

post³ [pəʊst] *n (pole)* poteau *m*; *(of bed, door)* montant *m*; **finishing** *or* **winning p.** *Sp* poteau *m* d'arrivée; − *vt* **to p. (up)** *(notice etc)* afficher.

post- [pəʊst] *pref* post-; **p.-1800** après 1800.

postdate [pəʊst'deɪt] *vt* postdater.

poster ['pəʊstər] *n* affiche *f*; *(for decoration)* poster *m*.

posterior [pɒ'stɪərɪər] *n (buttocks) Hum* postérieur *m*.

posterity [pɒ'sterɪtɪ] *n* postérité *f*.

postgraduate [pəʊst'grædʒʊət] *a (studies etc) Univ* de troisième cycle; − *n* étudiant, -ante *mf* de troisième cycle.

posthumous ['pɒstjʊməs] *a* posthume. ◆**-ly** *adv* à titre posthume.

postman ['pəʊstmən] *n (pl* **-men**) facteur *m*. ◆**postmark** *n* cachet *m* de la poste; − *vt* oblitérer. ◆**postmaster** *n* receveur *m* (des postes).

post-mortem [pəʊst'mɔːtəm] *n* **p.-mortem (examination)** autopsie *f* (**on** de).

postpone [pəʊ'spəʊn] *vt* remettre (**for** de), renvoyer (à plus tard). ◆**-ment** *n* remise *f*, renvoi *m*.

postscript ['pəʊstskrɪpt] *n* post-scriptum *m inv*.

postulate ['pɒstjʊleɪt] *vt* postuler.

posture ['pɒstʃər] *n* posture *f*; *Fig* attitude *f*; − *vi (for effect) Pej* poser.

postwar ['pəʊstwɔːr] *a* d'après-guerre.

posy ['pəʊzɪ] *n* petit bouquet *m* (de fleurs).

pot [pɒt] **1** *n* pot *m*; *(for cooking)* marmite *f*; **pots and pans** casseroles *fpl*; **jam p.** pot *m* à confiture; **to take p. luck** tenter sa chance; (*with food*) manger à la fortune du pot; **to go to p.** *Fam* aller à la ruine; **gone to p.** (*person, plans etc*) *Fam* fichu; – *vt* (**-tt-**) mettre en pot. **2** *n* (*marijuana*) *Sl* marie-jeanne *f*; (*hashish*) *Sl* haschisch *m*. ◆**potted** *a* **1** (*plant*) en pot; (*jam, meat*) en bocaux. **2** (*version etc*) abrégé, condensé.

potato [pə'teɪtəʊ] *n* (*pl* **-oes**) pomme de terre; **p. peeler** (*knife*) couteau *m* à éplucher, éplucheur *m*; **p. crisps**, *Am* **p. chips** pommes *fpl* chips.

potbelly ['pɒtbelɪ] *n* bedaine *f*. ◆**potbellied** *a* ventru.

potent ['pəʊtənt] *a* puissant; (*drink*) fort; (*man*) viril. ◆**potency** *n* puissance *f*; (*of man*) virilité *f*.

potential [pə'tenʃ(ə)l] *a* (*danger, resources*) potentiel; (*client, sales*) éventuel; (*leader, hero etc*) en puissance; – *n* potentiel *m*; *Fig* (*perspectives fpl d'*)avenir *m*; **to have p.** avoir de l'avenir. ◆**potenti'ality** *n* potentialité *f*; *pl* Fig (perspectives fpl d')avenir *m*. ◆**potentially** *adv* potentiellement.

pothole ['pɒthəʊl] *n* (*in road*) nid *m* de poules; (*in rock*) gouffre *m*; (*cave*) caverne *f*. ◆**potholing** *n* spéléologie *f*.

potion ['pəʊʃ(ə)n] *n* breuvage *m* magique; *Med* potion *f*.

potshot ['pɒtʃɒt] *n* **to take a p.** faire un carton (**at** sur).

potter ['pɒtər] **1** *n* (*person*) potier *m*. **2** *vi* **to p. (about)** bricoler. ◆**pottery** *n* (*art*) poterie *f*; (*objects*) poteries *fpl*; **a piece of p.** une poterie.

potty ['pɒtɪ] *a* (**-ier, -iest**) (*mad*) *Fam* toqué. **2** *n* pot *m* (de bébé).

pouch [paʊtʃ] *n* petit sac *m*; (*of kangaroo, under eyes*) poche *f*; (*for tobacco*) blague *f*.

pouf(fe) [puːf] *n* (*seat*) pouf *m*.

poultice ['pəʊltɪs] *n* Med cataplasme *m*.

poultry ['pəʊltrɪ] *n* volaille *f*. ◆**poulterer** *n* volailler *m*.

pounce [paʊns] *vi* (*leap*) bondir, sauter (**on** sur); **to p. on** (*idea*) *Fig* sauter sur; – *n* bond *m*.

pound [paʊnd] **1** *n* (*weight*) livre *f* (= 453,6 grammes); **p.** (*sterling*) livre *f* (sterling). **2** *n* (*for cars, dogs*) fourrière *f*. **3** *vt* (*spices, nuts etc*) piler; (*meat*) attendrir; (*bombard*) Mil pilonner; **to p. (on)** (*thump*) *Fig* taper sur, marteler; (*of sea*) battre; – *vi* (*of heart*) battre à tout rompre; (*walk heavily*) marcher à pas pesants.

pour [pɔːr] *vt* (*liquid*) verser; (*wax*) couler; **to p. money into** investir beaucoup d'argent

dans; **to p. away** or **off** (*empty*) vider; **to p. out** verser; (*empty*) vider; (*feelings*) épancher (**to** devant); – *vi* **to p. (out)** (*of liquid*) couler or sortir à flots; **to p. in** (*of liquid, sunshine*) entrer à flots; (*of people, money*) *Fig* affluer; **to p. out** (*of people*) sortir en masse (**from** de); (*of smoke*) s'échapper (**from** de); **it's pouring (down)** il pleut à verse; **pouring rain** pluie *f* torrentielle.

pout [paʊt] *vti* **to p.** (**one's lips**) faire la moue; – *n* moue *f*.

poverty ['pɒvətɪ] *n* pauvreté *f*; (**grinding** or **extreme**) **p.** misère *f*. ◆**p.-stricken** *a* (*person*) indigent; (*conditions*) misérable.

powder ['paʊdər] *n* poudre *f*; **p. keg** (*place*) *Fig* poudrière *f*; **p. puff** houppette *f*; **p. room** toilettes *fpl* (*pour dames*); – *vt* (*hair, skin*) poudrer; **to p. one's face** or **nose** se poudrer. ◆**-ed** *a* (*milk, eggs*) en poudre. ◆**powdery** *a* (*snow*) poudreux; (*face*) couvert de poudre.

power ['paʊər] *n* (*ability, authority*) pouvoir *m*; (*strength, nation*) & Math Tech puissance *f*; (*energy*) Phys Tech énergie *f*; (*current*) El courant *m*; **he's a p. within the firm** c'est un homme de poids au sein de l'entreprise; **in p.** Pol au pouvoir; **in one's p.** en son pouvoir; **the p. of speech** la faculté de la parole; **p. cut** coupure *f* de courant; **p. station**, *Am* **p. plant** El centrale *f* (électrique); – *vt* **to be powered by** être actionné or propulsé par; (*gas, oil etc*) fonctionnant à. ◆**powerful** *a* puissant. ◆**powerfully** *adv* puissamment. ◆**powerless** *a* impuissant (**to do** à faire).

practicable ['præktɪkəb(ə)l] *a* (*project, road etc*) praticable.

practical ['præktɪk(ə)l] *a* (*knowledge, person, tool etc*) pratique; **p. joke** farce *f*. ◆**practi'cality** *n* (*of scheme etc*) aspect *m* pratique; (*of person*) sens *m* pratique; (*detail*) détail *m* pratique.

practically ['præktɪk(ə)lɪ] *adv* (*almost*) pratiquement.

practice ['præktɪs] *n* (*exercise, proceeding*) pratique *f*; (*habit*) habitude *f*; *Sp* entraînement *m*; (*rehearsal*) répétition *f*; (*of profession*) exercice *m* (**of** de); (*clients*) clientèle *f*; **to put into p.** mettre en pratique; **in p.** (*in reality*) en pratique; **to be in p.** (*have skill etc*) être en forme; (*of doctor, lawyer*) exercer; **to be in general p.** (*of doctor*) faire de la médecine générale; **to be out of p.** avoir perdu la pratique. ◆**practis/e** *vt* (*put into practice*) pratiquer; (*medicine, law etc*) exercer; (*flute,* *piano* etc) s'exercer à; (*language*) (s'exercer à) parler (**on** avec); (*work at*) travailler; (*do*) faire; – *vi* *Mus Sp* s'exercer; (*of doctor, lawyer*) exercer; – *n* *Am* = **practice.** ◆—**ed** *a* (*experienced*) chevronné; (*ear, eye*) exercé. ◆—**ing** *a* *Rel* pratiquant; (*doctor, lawyer*) exerçant.

practitioner [præk'tɪʃ(ə)nər] *n* praticien, -ienne *mf*; **general p.** (médecin *m*) généraliste *m*.

pragmatic [præg'mætɪk] *a* pragmatique.

prairie(s) ['preər(z)] *n*(*pl*) (*in North America*) Prairies *fpl*.

praise [preɪz] *vt* louer (**for sth** de qch); **to p. s.o. for doing** *or* **having done** louer qn d'avoir fait; – *n* louange(s) *f*(*pl*), éloge(s) *m*(*pl*); **in p. of** à la louange de. ◆**praiseworthy** *a* digne d'éloges.

pram [præm] *n* landau *m*, voiture *f* d'enfant.

prance [prɑːns] *vi* **to p. about** (*of dancer* etc) caracoler; (*strut*) se pavaner; (*go about*) *Fam* se balader.

prank [præŋk] *n* (*trick*) farce *f*, tour *m*; (*escape*) frasque *f*.

prattle ['præt(ə)l] *vi* jacasser.

prawn [prɔːn] *n* crevette *f* (rose), bouquet *m*.

pray [preɪ] *vt* *Lit* prier (**that** que (+ *sub*)), s.o. **to do** qn de faire); – *vi* *Rel* prier; **to p.** (**to God**) **for** sth prier Dieu pour qu'il nous accorde qch. ◆**prayer** [preər] *n* prière *f*.

pre- [priː] *pref* **p.-1800** avant 1800.

preach [priːtʃ] *vti* prêcher; (*sermon*) faire; **to p. to s.o.** *Rel* & *Fig* prêcher qn. ◆—**ing** *n* prédication *f*. ◆—**er** *n* prédicateur *m*.

preamble [priː'æmb(ə)l] *n* préambule *m*.

prearrange [priːə'reɪndʒ] *vt* arranger à l'avance.

precarious [prɪ'keərɪəs] *a* précaire.

precaution [prɪ'kɔːʃ(ə)n] *n* précaution *f* (**of doing** de faire); **as a p.** par précaution.

preced/e [prɪ'siːd] *vti* précéder; **to p. sth by sth** faire précéder qch de qch. ◆—**ing** *a* précédent.

precedence ['presɪdəns] *n* (*in rank*) préséance *f*; (*importance*) priorité *f*; **to take p. over** avoir la préséance sur; avoir la priorité sur. ◆**precedent** *n* précédent *m*.

precept ['priːsept] *n* précepte *m*.

precinct ['priːsɪŋkt] *n* (*of convent* etc) enceinte *f*; (*boundary*) limite *f*; (*of town*) *Am Pol* circonscription *f*; (*for shopping*) zone *f* (piétonnière).

precious ['preʃəs] **1** *a* précieux; **her p. little bike** *Iron* son cher petit vélo. **2** *adv* **p. few, p. little** *Fam* très peu (de).

precipice ['presɪpɪs] *n* (*sheer face*) *Geog* à-pic *m inv*; (*chasm*) *Fig* précipice *m*.

precipitate [prɪ'sɪpɪteɪt] *vt* (*hasten, throw*) & *Ch* précipiter; (*trouble, reaction* etc) provoquer, déclencher. ◆**precipi'tation** *n* (*haste*) & *Ch* précipitation *f*; (*rainfall*) précipitations *fpl*.

précis ['preɪsiː, *pl* 'preɪsiːz] *n inv* précis *m*.

precise [prɪ'saɪs] *a* précis; (*person*) minutieux. ◆—**ly** *adv* précisément; **at 3 o'clock p.** à 3 heures précises; **p. nothing** absolument rien. ◆**precision** *n* précision *f*.

preclude [prɪ'kluːd] *vt* (*prevent*) empêcher (**from doing** de faire); (*possibility*) exclure.

precocious [prɪ'kəʊʃəs] *a* (*child* etc) précoce. ◆—**ness** *n* précocité *f*.

preconceived [priːkən'siːvd] *a* préconçu. ◆**preconception** *n* préconception *f*.

precondition [priːkən'dɪʃ(ə)n] *n* préalable *m*.

precursor [priː'kɜːsər] *n* précurseur *m*.

predate [priː'deɪt] *vt* (*precede*) précéder; (*cheque* etc) antidater.

predator ['predətər] *n* (*animal*) prédateur *m*. ◆**predatory** *a* (*animal, person*) rapace.

predecessor ['priːdɪsesər] *n* prédécesseur *m*.

predicament [prɪ'dɪkəmənt] *n* situation *f* fâcheuse.

predict [prɪ'dɪkt] *vt* prédire. ◆**predictable** *a* prévisible. ◆**prediction** *n* prédiction *f*.

predispose [priːdɪ'spəʊz] *vt* prédisposer (**to do** à faire). ◆**predispo'sition** *n* prédisposition *f*.

predominant [prɪ'dɒmɪnənt] *a* prédominant. ◆**predominance** *n* prédominance *f*. ◆**predominantly** *adv* (*almost all*) pour la plupart, en majorité. ◆**predominate** *vi* prédominer (**over** sur).

preeminent [priː'emɪnənt] *a* prééminent.

preempt [priː'empt] *vt* (*decision, plans* etc) devancer.

preen [priːn] *vt* (*feathers*) lisser; **she's preening herself** *Fig* elle se bichonne.

prefab ['priːfæb] *n* *Fam* maison *f* préfabriquée. ◆**pre'fabricate** *vt* préfabriquer.

preface ['prefɪs] *n* préface *f*; – *vt* (*speech* etc) faire précéder (**with** de).

prefect ['priːfekt] *n* *Sch* élève *mf* chargé(e) de la discipline; (*French official*) préfet *m*.

prefer [prɪ'fɜːr] *vt* (-**rr**-) préférer (**to** à), aimer mieux (**to** que); **to p. to do** préférer faire, aimer mieux faire; **to p. charges** *Jur* porter plainte (**against** contre). ◆**'preferable** *a* préférable (**to** à). ◆**'preferably** *adv* de préférence. ◆**'preference** *n* préférence *f* (**for** pour); **in p. to** de préférence à. ◆**prefe'rential** *a* préférentiel.

prefix ['priːfɪks] n préfixe m.
pregnant ['pregnənt] a (woman) enceinte; (animal) pleine; **five months p.** enceinte de cinq mois. ◆**pregnancy** n (of woman) grossesse f.
prehistoric [priːhɪ'stɒrɪk] a préhistorique.
prejudge [priː'dʒʌdʒ] vt (question) préjuger de; (person) juger d'avance.
prejudic/e ['predʒədɪs] n (bias) préjugé m, parti m pris; (attitude) préjugés mpl; Jur préjudice m; – vt (person) prévenir (against contre); (success, chances etc) porter préjudice à, nuire à. ◆**—ed** a (idea) partial; **she's p.** elle a des préjugés or un préjugé (against contre); (on an issue) elle est de parti pris. ◆**preju'dicial** a Jur préjudiciable.
preliminary [prɪ'lɪmɪnərɪ] a (initial) initial; (speech, inquiry, exam) préliminaire; – npl préliminaires mpl.
prelude ['preljuːd] n prélude m; – vt préluder à.
premarital [priː'mærɪt(ə)l] a avant le mariage.
premature ['premətʃuər, Am priːmə'tʃuər] a prématuré; **◆—ly** adv prématurément; (born) avant terme.
premeditate [priː'medɪteɪt] vt préméditer. ◆**premedi'tation** n préméditation f.
premier ['premɪər, Am prɪ'mɪər] n Premier ministre m.
première ['premɪeər, Am prɪ'mjeər] n Th Cin première f.
premise ['premɪs] n Phil prémisse f.
premises ['premɪsɪz] npl locaux mpl; **on the p.** sur les lieux; **off the p.** hors des lieux.
premium ['priːmɪəm] n Fin prime f; (insurance) p. prime f (d'assurance); **to be at a p.** (rare) être (une) denrée rare, faire prime; **p. bond** bon m à lots.
premonition [premə'nɪʃ(ə)n, Am priːmə'nɪʃ(ə)n] n prémonition f, pressentiment m.
prenatal [priː'neɪt(ə)l] a Am prénatal.
preoccupy [priː'ɒkjupaɪ] vt (worry) préoccuper (with de). ◆**preoccu'pation** n préoccupation f; **a p. with** (money etc) une obsession de.
prep [prep] a **p. school** école f primaire privée; Am école f secondaire privée; – n (homework) Sch devoirs mpl.
prepaid [priː'peɪd] a (reply) payé.
prepar/e [prɪ'peər] vt préparer (sth for s.o. qch à qn, s.o. for sth qn à qch); **to p. to do** se préparer à faire; – vi to p. for (journey, occasion) faire des préparatifs pour; (get dressed up for) se préparer pour; (exam) préparer. ◆**—ed** a (ready) prêt, disposé (to

do à faire); **to be p. for** (expect) s'attendre à. ◆**prepa'ration** n préparation f; pl préparatifs mpl (for de). ◆**pre'paratory** a préparatoire; **p. school** = prep school.
preposition [prepə'zɪʃ(ə)n] n préposition f.
prepossessing [priːpə'zesɪŋ] a avenant, sympathique.
preposterous [prɪ'pɒstərəs] a absurde.
prerecorded [priːrɪ'kɔːdɪd] a (message etc) enregistré à l'avance; **p. broadcast** Rad TV émission f en différé.
prerequisite [priː'rekwɪzɪt] n (condition f) préalable m.
prerogative [prɪ'rɒgətɪv] n prérogative f.
Presbyterian [prezbɪ'tɪərɪən] a & n Rel presbytérien, -ienne (mf).
preschool ['priːskuːl] a (age etc) préscolaire.
prescrib/e [prɪ'skraɪb] vt prescrire. ◆**—ed** a (textbook) (inscrit) au programme. ◆**prescription** n (order) prescription f; Med ordonnance f; **on p.** sur ordonnance.
presence ['prezəns] n présence f; **in the p. of** en présence de; **p. of mind** présence f d'esprit.
present[1] ['prezənt] **1** a (not absent) présent (at à, in dans); **those p.** les personnes présentes. **2** a (year, state etc) présent, actuel; (being considered) présent; (job, house etc) actuel; – n (time) présent m; **for the p.** pour le moment; **at p.** à présent. **3** n (gift) cadeau m. ◆**—ly** adv (soon) tout à l'heure; (now) à présent. ◆**present-'day** a actuel.
present[2] [prɪ'zent] vt (show, introduce, compere etc) présenter (to à); (concert etc) donner; (proof) fournir; **to p. s.o. with** (gift) offrir à qn; (prize) remettre à qn. ◆**—able** a présentable. ◆**—er** n présentateur, -trice mf. ◆**presen'tation** n présentation f; (of prize) remise f.
preserve [prɪ'zɜːv] vt (keep, maintain) conserver; (fruit etc) Culin mettre en conserve; **to p. from** (protect) préserver de. **2** n (sphere) domaine m. **3** n & npl (fruit etc) Culin confiture f. ◆**preser'vation** n conservation f. ◆**preservative** n (in food) agent m de conservation. ◆**preserver** n life p. Am gilet m de sauvetage.
preside [prɪ'zaɪd] vi présider; **to p. over** or **at** (meeting) présider.
president ['prezɪdənt] n président, -ente mf. ◆**presidency** n présidence f. ◆**presi'dential** a présidentiel.
press[1] [pres] **1** n (newspapers) presse f; (printing firm) imprimerie f; (printing) p. presse f; – a (conference etc) de presse. **2** n

(*machine for trousers, gluing etc*) presse *f*; (*for making wine*) pressoir *m*.

press² [pres] *vt* (*button, doorbell etc*) appuyer sur; (*tube, lemon, creditor*) presser; (*hand*) serrer; (*clothes*) repasser; (*demand, insist on*) insister sur; (*claim*) renouveler; **to p. s.o. to do** (*urge*) presser qn de faire; **to p. down** (*button etc*) appuyer sur; **to p. charges** *Jur* engager des poursuites (**against** contre); – *vi* (*with finger*) appuyer (**on** sur); (*of weight*) faire pression (**on** sur); (*of time*) presser; **to p. for sth** faire des démarches pour obtenir qch; (*insist*) insister pour obtenir qch; **to p. on** (*continue*) continuer (**with sth** qch); – *n* to give sth **a p.** (*trousers etc*) repasser qch. ◆—**ed** *a* (*hard*) (*busy*) débordé; **to be hard p.** (*in difficulties*) être en difficultés; **to be** (**hard**) **p. for** (*time, money*) être à court de. ◆—**ing** 1 *a* (*urgent*) pressant. 2 *n* (*ironing*) repassage *m*.

pressgang ['presgæŋ] *vt* **to p. s.o.** faire pression sur qn (**into doing** pour qu'il fasse). ◆**press-stud** *n* (bouton-)pression *m*. ◆**press-up** *n* *Sp* pompe *f*.

pressure ['preʃər] *n* pression *f*; **the p. of work** le surmenage; **p. cooker** cocotte-minute *f*; **p. group** groupe *m* de pression; **under p.** (*duress*) sous la contrainte; (*hurriedly, forcibly*) sous pression; – *vt* **to p. s.o.** faire pression sur qn (**into doing** pour qu'il fasse). ◆**pressurize** *vt Av* pressuriser; **to p. s.o.** faire pression sur qn (**into doing** pour qu'il fasse).

prestige [pre'sti:ʒ] *n* prestige *m*. ◆**prestigious** [pre'stɪdʒəs, *Am* -'sti:dʒəs] *a* prestigieux.

presume [prɪ'zju:m] *vt* (*suppose*) présumer (**that** que); **to p. to do** se permettre de faire. ◆**presumably** *adv* (*you'll come etc*) je présume que. ◆**presumption** *n* (*supposition, bold attitude*) présomption *f*. ◆**presumptuous** *a* présomptueux.

presuppose [pri:sə'pəʊz] *vt* présupposer (**that** que).

pretence [prɪ'tens] *n* feinte *f*; (*claim, affectation*) prétention *f*; (*pretext*) prétexte *m*; **to make a p. of sth/of doing** feindre qch/de faire; **on** *or* **under false pretences** sous des prétextes fallacieux. ◆**pretend** *vt* (*make believe*) faire semblant (**to do** de faire, **that** que); (*claim, maintain*) prétendre (**to do** faire, **that** que); – *vi* faire semblant; **to p. to** (*throne, title*) prétendre à.

pretension [prɪ'tenʃ(ə)n] *n* (*claim, vanity*) prétention *f*; ◆**pre'tentious** *a* prétentieux.

pretext ['pri:tekst] *n* prétexte *m*; **on the p. of/that** sous prétexte de/que.

pretty ['prɪtɪ] 1 *a* (*-ier, -iest*) joli. 2 *adv Fam* (*rather, quite*) assez; **p. well, p. much, p. nearly** (*almost*) pratiquement, à peu de chose près.

prevail [prɪ'veɪl] *vi* (*be prevalent*) prédominer; (*win*) prévaloir (**against** contre); **to p. (up)on s.o.** (*persuade*) persuader qn (**to do** de faire). ◆—**ing** *a* (*most common*) courant; (*most important*) prédominant; (*situation*) actuel; (*wind*) dominant.

prevalent ['prevələnt] *a* courant, répandu. ◆**prevalence** *n* fréquence *f*; (*predominance*) prédominance *f*.

prevaricate [prɪ'værɪkeɪt] *vi* user de faux-fuyants.

prevent [prɪ'vent] *vt* empêcher (**from doing** de faire). ◆**preventable** *a* évitable. ◆**prevention** *n* prévention *f*. ◆**preventive** *a* préventif.

preview ['pri:vju:] *n* (*of film, painting*) avant-première *f*; (*survey*) *Fig* aperçu *m*.

previous ['pri:vɪəs] *a* précédent, antérieur; (*experience*) préalable; **she's had a p. job** elle a déjà eu un emploi; **p. to** avant. ◆—**ly** *adv* avant, précédemment.

prewar ['pri:wɔ:r] *a* d'avant-guerre.

prey [preɪ] *n* proie *f*; **to be (a) p.** to être en proie à; **bird of p.** rapace *m*, oiseau *m* de proie; – *vi* **to p. on** faire sa proie de; **to p. on s.o.** *or* **s.o.'s mind** *Fig* tracasser qn.

price [praɪs] *n* (*of object, success etc*) prix *m*; **to pay a high p. for sth** payer cher qch; *Fig* payer chèrement qch; **he wouldn't do it at any p.** il ne le ferait à aucun prix; – *a* (*control, war, rise etc*) des prix; **p. list** tarif *m*; – *vt* mettre un prix à; **it's priced at £5** ça coûte cinq livres. ◆**priceless** *a* (*jewel, help etc*) inestimable; (*amusing*) *Fam* impayable. ◆**pricey** *a* (*-ier, -iest*) *Fam* coûteux.

prick [prɪk] *vt* piquer (**with** avec); (*burst*) crever; **to p. up one's ears** dresser l'oreille; – *n* (*act, mark, pain*) piqûre *f*.

prickle ['prɪk(ə)l] *n* (*of animal*) piquant *m*; (*of plant*) épine *f*, piquant *m*. ◆**prickly** *a* (*-ier, -iest*) (*plant*) épineux; (*animal*) hérissé; (*subject*) *Fig* épineux; (*person*) *Fig* irritable.

pride [praɪd] *n* (*satisfaction*) fierté *f*; (*self-esteem*) amour-propre *m*, orgueil *m*; (*arrogance*) orgueil *m*; **to take p. in** (*person, work etc*) être fier de; (*look after*) prendre soin de; **to take p. in doing** mettre (toute) sa fierté à faire; **to be s.o.'s p. and joy** être la fierté de qn; **to have p. of place** avoir la place d'honneur; – *vt* **to p. oneself on** s'enorgueillir de.

priest [priːst] *n* prêtre *m*. ◆**priesthood** *n* (*function*) sacerdoce *m*. ◆**priestly** *a* sacerdotal.

prig [prig] *n* hypocrite *mf*, pharisien, -ienne *mf*. ◆**priggish** *a* hypocrite, suffisant.

prim [prim] *a* (**primmer, primmest**) **p. (and proper)** (*affected*) guindé; (*seemly*) convenable; (*neat*) impeccable.

primacy ['praiməsi] *n* primauté *f*.

primary ['praiməri] *a* Sch Pol Geol etc primaire; (*main, basic*) premier; **of p. importance** de première importance; – *n* (*election*) Am primaire *f*. ◆**primarily** [Am prai'merili] *adv* essentiellement.

prime [praim] **1** *a* (*reason etc*) principal; (*importance*) primordial; (*quality, number*) premier; (*meat*) de premier choix; (*example, condition*) excellent, parfait; **P. Minister** Premier ministre *m*. **2** *n* **the p. of life** la force de l'âge. **3** *vt* (*gun, pump*) amorcer; (*surface*) apprêter. ◆**primer** *n* **1** (*book*) Sch premier livre *m*. **2** (*paint*) apprêt *m*.

primeval [prai'miːv(ə)l] *a* primitif.

primitive ['primitiv] *a* (*art, society, conditions etc*) primitif. ◆**–ly** *adv* (*to live*) dans des conditions primitives.

primrose ['primrəuz] *n* Bot primevère *f* (jaune).

prince [prins] *n* prince *m*. ◆**princely** *a* princier. ◆**prin'cess** *n* princesse *f*. ◆**princi'pality** *n* principauté *f*.

principal ['prinsip(ə)l] **1** *a* (*main*) principal. **2** *n* (*of school*) directeur, -trice *mf*. ◆**–ly** *adv* principalement.

principle ['prinsip(ə)l] *n* principe *m*; **in p.** en principe; **on p.** par principe.

print [print] *n* (*of finger, foot etc*) empreinte *f*; (*letters*) caractères *mpl*; (*engraving*) estampe *f*, gravure *f*; (*fabric, textile design*) imprimé *m*; Phot épreuve *f*; (*ink*) encre *m*; **in p.** (*book*) disponible (en librairie); **out of p.** (*book*) épuisé; – *vt* Typ imprimer; (*write*) écrire en caractères d'imprimerie; **to p. 100 copies of** (*book etc*) tirer à 100 exemplaires; **to p. out** (*of computer*) imprimer. ◆**–ed** *a* imprimé; **p. matter** *or* **papers** imprimés *mpl*; **to have a book p.** publier un livre. ◆**–ing** *n* (*action*) Typ impression *f*; (*technique, art*) Typ imprimerie *f*; Phot tirage *m*; **p. press** Typ presse *f*. ◆**–able** *a* **not p.** (*word etc*) Fig obscène. ◆**–er** *n* (*person*) imprimeur *m*; (*of computer*) imprimante *f*. ◆**print-out** *n* (*of computer*) sortie *f* sur imprimante.

prior ['praiər] *a* précédent, antérieur; (*expe-*

rience) préalable; **p. to sth/to doing** avant qch/de faire.

priority [prai'ɒriti] *n* priorité *f* (**over** sur).

priory ['praiəri] *n* Rel prieuré *m*.

prise [praiz] *vt* **to p. open/off** (*box, lid*) ouvrir/enlever (en faisant levier).

prism ['priz(ə)m] *n* prisme *m*.

prison ['priz(ə)n] *n* prison *f*; **in p.** en prison; – *a* (*system, life etc*) pénitentiaire; (*camp*) de prisonniers; **p. officer** gardien, -ienne *mf* de prison. ◆**prisoner** *n* prisonnier, -ière *mf*; **to take s.o. p.** faire qn prisonnier.

prissy ['prisi] *a* (**-ier, -iest**) bégueule.

pristine ['pristiːn] *a* (*condition*) parfait; (*primitive*) primitif.

privacy ['praivəsi, 'privəsi] *n* intimité *f*, solitude *f*; (*quiet place*) coin *m* retiré; (*secrecy*) secret *m*; **to give s.o. some p.** laisser qn seul. ◆**private 1** *a* privé; (*lesson, car etc*) particulier; (*confidential*) confidentiel; (*personal*) personnel; (*wedding etc*) intime; **a p. citizen** un simple particulier; **p. detective, p. investigator,** Fam **p. eye** détective *m* privé; **p. parts** parties *fpl* génitales; **p. place** coin *m* retiré; **p. tutor** précepteur *m*; **to be a very p. person** aimer la solitude; – *n* **in p.** (*not publicly*) en privé; (*ceremony*) dans l'intimité. **2** *n* Mil (*simple*) soldat *m*. ◆**privately** *adv* en privé; (*inwardly*) intérieurement; (*personally*) à titre personnel; (*to marry, dine etc*) dans l'intimité; **p. owned** appartenant à un particulier.

privet ['privit] *n* (*bush*) troène *m*.

privilege ['privilidʒ] *n* privilège *m*. ◆**privileged** *a* privilégié; **to be p. to do** avoir le privilège de faire.

privy ['privi] *a* **p. to** (*knowledge etc*) au courant de.

prize [1] [praiz] *n* prix *m*; (*in lottery*) lot *m*; **the first p.** (*in lottery*) le gros lot; – *a* (*essay, animal etc*) primé; **a p. fool/etc** Fig Hum un parfait idiot/etc. – *a* (*possession*) de grande distinction *f* des prix. ◆**p.-winner** *n* lauréat, -ate *mf*; (*in lottery*) gagnant, -ante *mf*. ◆**p.-winning** *a* (*essay, animal etc*) primé; (*ticket*) gagnant.

prize [2] [praiz] *vt* (*value*) priser. ◆**–ed** *a* (*possession etc*) précieux.

prize [3] [praiz] *vt* = **prise**.

pro [prəu] *n* (*professional*) Fam pro *mf*.

pro- [prəu] *pref* pro-.

probable ['prɒbəb(ə)l] *a* probable (**that** que); (*plausible*) vraisemblable. ◆**proba'bility** *n* probabilité *f*; **in all p.** selon toute probabilité. ◆**probably** *adv* probablement, vraisemblablement.

probation [prə'beiʃ(ə)n] *n* **on p.** Jur en

liberté surveillée, sous contrôle judiciaire; (in job) à l'essai; **p. officer** responsable *mf* des délinquants mis en liberté surveillée. ◆**probationary** *a (period)* d'essai, *Jur* de liberté surveillée.

prob/e [prəʊb] *n (device)* sonde *f; Journ* enquête *f* (**into** dans); — *vt (investigate)* & *Med* sonder; *(examine)* examiner; — *vi (investigate)* faire des recherches; *Pej* fouiner; **to p. into** *(origins etc)* sonder. ◆**—ing** *a (question etc)* pénétrant.

problem ['prɒbləm] *n* problème *m;* **he's got a drug/a drink p.** c'est un drogué/un alcoolique; **you've got a smoking p.** tu fumes beaucoup trop; **no p.!** *Am Fam* pas de problème!; **to have a p. doing** avoir du mal à faire; — *a (child)* difficile, caractériel. ◆**proble'matic** *a* problématique; **it's p. whether** il est douteux que (+ *sub*).

procedure [prə'siːdʒər] *n* procédure *f.*

proceed [prə'siːd] *vi (go)* avancer, aller; *(act)* procéder; *(continue)* continuer; *(of debate)* se poursuivre; **to p. to** *(next question etc)* passer à; **to p. with** *(task etc)* continuer; **to p. to do** *(start)* se mettre à faire. ◆**—ing** *n (course of action)* procédé *m; pl (events)* évènements *mpl; (meeting)* séance *f; (discussions)* débats *mpl; (minutes)* actes *mpl;* **to take (legal) proceedings** intenter un procès (**against** contre).

proceeds ['prəʊsiːdz] *npl (profits)* produit *m,* bénéfices *mpl.*

process ['prəʊses] **1** *n (operation, action)* processus *m; (method)* procédé *m* (**for** or **of doing** pour faire); **in p.** *(work etc)* en cours; **in the p. of doing** en train de faire. **2** *vt (food, data etc)* traiter; *(examine)* examiner; *Phot* développer; **processed cheese** fromage *m* fondu. ◆**—ing** *n* traitement *m; Phot* développement *m;* **data** *or* **information p.** informatique *f.* ◆**processor** *n (in computer)* processeur *m;* **food p.** robot *m (ménager);* **word p.** machine *f* de traitement de texte.

procession [prə'seʃ(ə)n] *n* cortège *m,* défilé *m.*

proclaim [prə'kleim] *vt* proclamer (**that** que); **to p. king** proclamer roi. ◆**procla-'mation** *n* proclamation *f.*

procrastinate [prə'kræstineit] *vi* temporiser, tergiverser.

procreate ['prəʊkrieit] *vt* procréer. ◆**procre'ation** *n* procréation *f.*

procure [prə'kjʊər] *vt* obtenir; **to p. sth (for oneself)** se procurer qch; **to p. sth for s.o.** procurer qch à qn.

prod [prɒd] *vti* (**-dd-**) **to p. (at)** pousser (du

coude, *avec un bâton etc);* **to p. s.o. into doing** *Fig* pousser qn à faire; — *n (petit)* coup *m; (shove)* poussée *f.*

prodigal ['prɒdig(ə)l] *a (son etc)* prodigue.

prodigious [prə'didʒəs] *a* prodigieux.

prodigy ['prɒdidʒi] *n* prodige *m;* **infant p., child p.** enfant *mf* prodige.

produce [prə'djuːs] *vt (manufacture, yield etc)* produire; *(bring out, show)* sortir *(pistolet, mouchoir etc); (passport, proof)* présenter; *(profit)* rapporter; *(cause)* provoquer, produire; *(publish)* publier; *(play) Th TV* mettre en scène; *(film) Cin* produire; *Rad* réaliser; *(baby)* donner naissance à; **oil-producing country** pays *m* producteur de pétrole; — *vi (of factory etc)* produire; — ['prɒdjuːs] *n (agricultural etc)* produits *mpl.* ◆**pro'ducer** *n (of goods)* & *Cin* producteur, -trice *mf; Th TV* metteur *m* en scène; *Rad* réalisateur, -trice *mf.*

product ['prɒdʌkt] *n* produit *m.*

production [prə'dʌkʃ(ə)n] *n* production *f; Th TV* mise *f* en scène; *Rad* réalisation *f;* **to work on the p. line** travailler à la chaîne. ◆**productive** *a (land, meeting, efforts)* productif. ◆**produc'tivity** *n* productivité *f.*

profane [prə'fein] *a (sacrilegious)* sacrilège; *(secular)* profane; — *vt (dishonour)* profaner. ◆**profanities** *npl (oaths)* blasphèmes *mpl.*

profess [prə'fes] *vt* professer; **to p. to be** prétendre être. ◆**—ed** *a (anarchist etc)* déclaré.

profession [prə'feʃ(ə)n] *n* profession *f;* **by p.** de profession. ◆**professional** *a* professionnel; *(man, woman)* qui exerce une profession libérale; *(army)* de métier; *(diplomat)* de carrière; *(piece of work)* de professionnel; — *n* professionnel, -elle *mf; (executive, lawyer etc)* membre *m* des professions libérales. ◆**professionalism** *n* professionnalisme *m.* ◆**professionally** *adv* professionnellement; *(to perform, play)* en professionnel; *(to meet s.o.)* dans le cadre de son travail.

professor [prə'fesər] *n Univ* professeur *m* (titulaire d'une chaire). ◆**profe'ssorial** *a* professoral.

proffer ['prɒfər] *vt* offrir.

proficient [prə'fiʃ(ə)nt] *a* compétent (**in** en). ◆**proficiency** *n* compétence *f.*

profile ['prəʊfail] *n (of person, object)* profil *m;* **in p.** de profil; **to keep a low p.** *Fig* garder un profil bas. ◆**profiled** *a* **to be p. against** se profiler sur.

profit ['prɒfit] *n* profit *m,* bénéfice *m;* **to sell**

at a p. vendre à profit; **p. margin** marge *f* bénéficiaire; **p. motive** recherche *f* du profit; – *vi* **to p. by** *or* **from** tirer profit de. ◆**p.-making** *a* à but lucratif. ◆**profita-'bility** *n Com* rentabilité *f*. ◆**profitable** *a Com* rentable; (*worthwhile*) *Fig* rentable, profitable. ◆**profitably** *adv* avec profit. ◆**profi'teer** *n Pej* profiteur, -euse *mf*; – *vi Pej* faire des profits malhonnêtes.

profound [prə'faund] *a* (*silence, remark etc*) profond. ◆**profoundly** *adv* profondément. ◆**profundity** *n* profondeur *f*.

profuse [prə'fjuːs] *a* abondant; **p. in** (*praise etc*) prodigue de. ◆**profusely** *adv* (*to flow, grow*) à profusion; (*to bleed*) abondamment; (*to thank*) avec effusion; **to apologize p.** se répandre en excuses. ◆**profusion** *n* profusion *f*; **in p.** à profusion.

progeny ['prɒdʒɪnɪ] *n* progéniture *f*.

program¹ ['prəʊgræm] *n* (*of computer*) programme *m*; – *vt* (**-mm-**) (*computer*) programmer. ◆**programming** *n* programmation *f*. ◆**programmer** *n* (*computer*) **p.** programmeur, -euse *mf*.

programme, *Am* **program²** ['prəʊgræm] *n* programme *m*; (*broadcast*) émission *f*; – *vt* (*arrange*) programmer.

progress ['prəʊgres] *n* progrès *m*(*pl*); **to make (good) p.** faire des progrès; (*in walking, driving etc*) bien avancer; **in p.** en cours; – [prə'gres] *vi* (*advance, improve*) progresser; (*of story, meeting*) se dérouler. ◆**pro'gression** *n* progression *f*. ◆**pro-'gressive** *a* (*gradual*) progressif; (*party*) *Pol* progressiste; (*firm, ideas*) moderniste. ◆**pro'gressively** *adv* progressivement.

prohibit [prə'hɪbɪt] *vt* interdire (**s.o. from doing** à qn de faire); **we're prohibited from leaving/etc** il nous est interdit de partir/etc. ◆**prohi'bition** *n* prohibition *f*. ◆**prohibitive** *a* (*price, measure etc*) prohibitif.

project 1 ['prɒdʒekt] *n* (*plan*) projet *m* (**for sth** pour qch; **to do, for doing** pour faire); (*undertaking*) entreprise *f*; (*study*) étude *f*; (*housing*) **p.** (*for workers*) *Am* cité *f* (ouvrière). **2** [prə'dʒekt] *vt* (*throw, show etc*) projeter; – *vi* (*jut out*) faire saillie. ◆**-ed** *a* (*planned*) prévu. ◆**pro'jection** *n* projection *f*; (*projecting object*) saillie *f*. ◆**pro'jectionist** *n Cin* projectionniste *mf*. ◆**pro'jector** *n Cin* projecteur *m*.

proletarian [prəʊlə'teərɪən] *n* prolétaire *mf*; – *a* (*class*) prolétarien; (*outlook*) de prolétaire. ◆**prole'tariat** *n* prolétariat *m*.

proliferate [prə'lɪfəreɪt] *vi* proliférer. ◆**prolife'ration** *n* prolifération *f*.

prolific [prə'lɪfɪk] *a* prolifique.

prologue ['prəʊlɒg] *n* prologue *m* (**to** de, à).

prolong [prə'lɒŋ] *vt* prolonger.

promenade [prɒmə'nɑːd] *n* (*place, walk*) promenade *f*; (*gallery*) *Th* promenoir *m*.

prominent ['prɒmɪnənt] *a* (*nose*) proéminent; (*chin, tooth*) saillant; (*striking*) *Fig* frappant, remarquable; (*role*) marquant; (*politician*) marquant; (*conspicuous*) (bien) en vue. ◆**prominence** *n* (*importance*) importance *f*. ◆**prominently** *adv* (*displayed, placed*) bien en vue.

promiscuous [prə'mɪskjʊəs] *a* (*person*) de mœurs faciles; (*behaviour*) immoral. ◆**promi'scuity** *n* liberté *f* de mœurs; immoralité *f*.

promise ['prɒmɪs] *n* promesse *f*; **to show great p., be full of p.** (*hope*) être très prometteur; – *vt* promettre (**s.o. sth, sth to s.o.** qch à qn; **to do** de faire; **that** que); – *vi* **I p.!** je te le promets!; **p.?** promis? ◆**-ing** *a* (*start etc*) prometteur; (*person*) qui promet; **that looks p.** ça s'annonce bien.

promote [prə'məʊt] *vt* (*product, research*) promouvoir; (*good health, awareness*) favoriser; **to p. s.o.** promouvoir qn (**to** à); **promoted (to) manager/general/etc** promu directeur/général/etc. ◆**promoter** *n Sp* organisateur, -trice *mf*; (*instigator*) promoteur, -trice *mf*. ◆**promotion** *n* (*of person*) avancement *m*, promotion *f*; (*of sales, research etc*) promotion *f*.

prompt [prɒmpt] **1** *a* (*speedy*) rapide; (*punctual*) à l'heure, ponctuel; **p. to act** prompt à agir; – *adv* **at 8 o'clock p.** à 8 heures pile. **2** *vt* (*urge*) inciter, pousser (**to do** à faire); (*cause*) provoquer. **3** *vt* (*person*) *Th* souffler (son rôle) à. ◆**-ing** *n* (*urging*) incitation *f*. ◆**-er** *n Th* souffleur, -euse *mf*. ◆**-ness** *n* rapidité *f*; (*readiness to act*) promptitude *f*.

prone [prəʊn] *a* **1 p. to sth** (*liable*) prédisposé à qch; **to be p. to do** avoir tendance à faire. **2** (*lying flat*) sur le ventre.

prong [prɒŋ] *n* (*of fork*) dent *f*.

pronoun ['prəʊnaʊn] *n Gram* pronom *m*. ◆**pro'nominal** *a* pronominal.

pronounce [prə'naʊns] *vt* (*articulate, declare*) prononcer; – *vi* (*articulate*) prononcer; (*give judgment*) se prononcer (**on** sur). ◆**pronouncement** *n* déclaration *f*. ◆**pronunci'ation** *n* prononciation *f*.

pronto ['prɒntəʊ] *adv* (*at once*) *Fam* illico.

proof [pruːf] **1** *n* (*evidence*) preuve *f*; (*of book, photo*) épreuve *f*; (*of drink*) teneur *f* en alcool. **2** *a* **p. against** (*material*) à l'épreuve de (*feu, acide etc*). ◆**proof-reader** *n Typ* correcteur, -trice *mf*.

prop [prɒp] **1** *n Archit* support *m*, étai *m*; (*for clothes line*) perche *f*; (*person*) *Fig* soutien *m*; — *vt* (**-pp-**) **to p. up** (*ladder etc*) appuyer (**against** contre); (*one's head*) caler; (*wall*) étayer; (*help*) *Fig* soutenir. **2** *n* **prop(s)** *Th* accessoire(s) *m(pl)*.

propaganda [prɒpə'gændə] *n* propagande *f*. ◆**propagandist** *n* propagandiste *mf*.

propagate ['prɒpəgeɪt] *vt* propager; — *vi* se propager.

propel [prə'pel] *vt* (**-ll-**) (*drive, hurl*) propulser. ◆**propeller** *n Av Nau* hélice *f*.

propensity [prə'pensɪtɪ] *n* propension *f* (**for** sth à qch, **to do** à faire).

proper ['prɒpər] *a* (*suitable, seemly*) convenable; (*correct*) correct; (*right*) bon; (*real, downright*) véritable; (*noun, meaning*) propre; **in the p. way** comme il faut; **the village/etc p.** le village/etc proprement dit. ◆**-ly** *adv* comme il faut, convenablement, correctement; (*completely*) *Fam* vraiment; **very p.** (*quite rightly*) à juste titre.

property ['prɒpətɪ] **1** *n* (*building etc*) propriété *f*; (*possessions*) biens *mpl*, propriété *f*; — *a* (*crisis, market etc*) immobilier; (*owner, tax*) foncier. **2** *n* (*of substance etc*) propriété *f*. ◆**propertied** *a* possédant.

prophecy ['prɒfɪsɪ] *n* prophétie *f*. ◆**prophesy** [-ɪsaɪ] *vti* prophétiser; **to p. that** prédire que.

prophet ['prɒfɪt] *n* prophète *m*. ◆**pro-'phetic** *a* prophétique.

proponent [prə'pəʊnənt] *n* (*of cause etc*) défenseur *m*, partisan, -ane *mf*.

proportion [prə'pɔːʃ(ə)n] *n* (*ratio*) proportion *f*; (*portion*) partie *f*; (*amount*) pourcentage *m*; *pl* (*size*) proportions *fpl*; **in p.** en proportion (**to** de); **out of p.** hors de proportion (**to** avec); — *vt* proportionner (**to** à); **well** *or* **nicely proportioned** bien proportionné. ◆**proportional** *a*, ◆**proportionate** *a* proportionnel (**to** à).

propose [prə'pəʊz] *vt* (*suggest*) proposer (**to** à, **that** que (+ *sub*)); **to p. to do, doing** (*intend*) se proposer de faire; — *vi* faire une demande (**en mariage**) (**to** à). ◆**proposal** *n* proposition *f*; (*of marriage*) demande *f* (**en mariage**). ◆**propo'sition** *n* proposition *f*; (*matter*) *Fig* affaire *f*.

propound [prə'paʊnd] *vt* proposer.

proprietor [prə'praɪətər] *n* propriétaire *mf*. ◆**proprietary** *a* (*article*) *Com* de marque déposée; **p. name** marque *f* déposée.

propriety [prə'praɪətɪ] *n* (*behaviour*) bienséance *f*; (*of conduct, remark*) justesse *f.*

propulsion [prə'pʌlʃ(ə)n] *n* propulsion *f.*

pros [prəʊz] *npl* **the p. and cons** le pour et le contre.

prosaic [prəʊ'zeɪɪk] *a* prosaïque.

proscribe [prəʊ'skraɪb] *vt* proscrire.

prose [prəʊz] *n* prose *f*; (*translation*) *Sch* thème *m*.

prosecute ['prɒsɪkjuːt] *vt* poursuivre (**en justice**) (**for stealing**/*etc* pour vol/*etc*). ◆**prose'cution** *n Jur* poursuites *fpl*; **the p.** (*lawyers*) = le ministère public. ◆**prosecutor** *n* (**public**) **p.** *Jur* procureur *m.*

prospect¹ ['prɒspekt] *n* (*idea, outlook*) perspective *f* (**of doing** de faire); (*possibility*) possibilité *f* (**of sth** de qch); (*future*) **prospects** perspectives *fpl* d'avenir; **it has prospects** c'est prometteur; **she has prospects** elle a de l'avenir. ◆**pro'spective** *a* (*possible*) éventuel; (*future*) futur.

prospect² [prə'spekt] *vt* (*land*) prospecter; — *vi* **to p. for** (*gold etc*) chercher. ◆**-ing** *n* prospection *f*. ◆**prospector** *n* prospecteur, -trice *mf.*

prospectus [prə'spektəs] *n* (*publicity leaflet*) prospectus *m*; *Univ* guide *m* (de l'étudiant).

prosper ['prɒspər] *vi* prospérer. ◆**pro-'sperity** *n* prospérité *f*. ◆**prosperous** *a* (*thriving*) prospère; (*wealthy*) riche, prospère.

prostate ['prɒsteɪt] *n* **p.** (**gland**) *Anat* prostate *f.*

prostitute ['prɒstɪtjuːt] *n* (*woman*) prostituée *f*; — *vt* prostituer. ◆**prosti'tution** *n* prostitution *f.*

prostrate ['prɒstreɪt] *a* (*prone*) sur le ventre; (*worshipper*) prosterné; (*submissive*) soumis; (*exhausted*) prostré; — [prɒ'streɪt] *vt* **to p. oneself** se prosterner (**before** devant).

protagonist [prəʊ'tægənɪst] *n* protagoniste *mf.*

protect [prə'tekt] *vt* protéger (**from** de, **against** contre); (*interests*) sauvegarder. ◆**protection** *n* protection *f*. ◆**protective** *a* (*a tone etc*) & *Econ* protecteur; (*screen, clothes etc*) de protection. ◆**protector** *n* protecteur, -trice *mf.*

protein ['prəʊtiːn] *n* protéine *f.*

protest ['prəʊtest] *n* protestation *f* (**against** contre); **under p.** contre son gré; — [prə'test] *vt* protester (**that** que); (*one's innocence*) protester de; — *vi* protester (**against** contre); (*in the streets etc*) *Pol* contester. ◆**-er** *n Pol* contestataire *mf.*

Protestant ['prɒtəstənt] *a & n* protestant,

-ante (*mf*). ◆**Protestantism** *n* protestantisme *m*.

protocol ['prəutəkɒl] *n* protocole *m*.

prototype ['prəutəutaɪp] *n* prototype *m*.

protract [prə'trækt] *vt* prolonger.

protractor [prə'træktər] *n* (*instrument*) *Geom* rapporteur *m*.

protrud/e [prə'truːd] *vi* dépasser; (*of balcony, cliff etc*) faire saillie; (*of tooth*) avancer. ◆**—ing** *a* saillant; (*of tooth*) qui avance.

proud [praud] *a* (-er, -est) (*honoured, pleased*) fier (of de, to de faire); (*arrogant*) orgueilleux. ◆**—ly** *adv* fièrement; orgueilleusement.

prove [pruːv] *vt* prouver (that que); **to p. oneself** faire ses preuves; — *vi* **to p. (to be) difficult/*etc*** s'avérer difficile/*etc*. ◆**proven** *a* (*method etc*) éprouvé.

proverb ['prɒvɜːb] *n* proverbe *m*. ◆**pro-'verbial** *a* proverbial.

provid/e [prə'vaɪd] *vt* (*supply*) fournir (s.o. with sth qch à qn); (*give*) donner, offrir (to à); **to s.o. with** (*equip*) équiper qn de; **to p. that** *Jur* stipuler que; — *vi* **to p. for s.o.** (*s.o.'s needs*) pourvoir aux besoins de qn; (*s.o.'s future*) assurer l'avenir de qn; **to p. for sth** (*make allowance for*) prévoir qch. ◆**—ed** *conj* **p. (that)** pourvu que (+ *sub*). ◆**—ing** *conj* **p. (that)** pourvu que (+ *sub*).

providence ['prɒvɪdəns] *n* providence *f*.

provident ['prɒvɪdənt] *a* (*society*) de prévoyance; (*person*) prévoyant.

province ['prɒvɪns] *n* province *f*; *Fig* domaine *m*, compétence *f*; **the provinces** la province; **in the provinces** en province. ◆**pro'vincial** *a & n* provincial, -ale (*mf*).

provision [prə'vɪʒ(ə)n] *n* (*supply*) provision *f*; (*clause*) disposition *f*; **the p. of** (*supplying*) la fourniture de; **to make p. for** = **to provide for.**

provisional [prə'vɪʒən(ə)l] *a* provisoire. ◆**—ly** *adv* provisoirement.

proviso [prə'vaɪzəu] *n* (*pl* -os) stipulation *f*.

provok/e [prə'vəuk] *vt* (*rouse, challenge*) provoquer (**to do, into doing** à faire); (*annoy*) agacer; (*cause*) provoquer (*accident, reaction etc*). ◆**—ing** *a* (*annoying*) agaçant. ◆**provo'cation** *n* provocation *f*. ◆**provocative** *a* (*person, remark etc*) provocant; (*thought-provoking*) qui donne à penser.

prow [prau] *n* *Nau* proue *f*.

prowess ['prauɪs] *n* (*bravery*) courage *m*; (*skill*) talent *m*.

prowl [praul] *vi* **to p. (around)** rôder; — *n* **to**

be on the p. rôder. ◆**—er** *n* rôdeur, -euse *mf*.

proximity [prɒk'sɪmɪtɪ] *n* proximité *f*.

proxy ['prɒksɪ] *n* **by p.** par procuration.

prude [pruːd] *n* prude *f*. ◆**prudery** *n* pruderie *f*. ◆**prudish** *a* prude.

prudent ['pruːdənt] *a* prudent. ◆**prudence** *n* prudence *f*. ◆**prudently** *adv* prudemment.

prun/e [pruːn] **1** *n* (*dried plum*) pruneau *m*. **2** *vt* (*cut*) *Bot* tailler, élaguer; (*speech etc*) *Fig* élaguer. ◆**—ing** *n* *Bot* taille *f*.

pry [praɪ] *vi* être indiscret; **to p. into** (*meddle*) se mêler de; (*s.o.'s reasons etc*) chercher à découvrir. **2** *vt* **to p. open** *Am* forcer (en faisant levier). ◆**—ing** *a* indiscret.

PS [piː'es] *abbr* (*postscript*) P.-S.

psalm [sɑːm] *n* psaume *m*.

pseud [sjuːd] *n* *Fam* bêcheur, -euse *mf*.

pseudo- ['sjuːdəu] *pref* pseudo-.

pseudonym ['sjuːdənɪm] *n* pseudonyme *m*.

psychiatry [saɪ'kaɪətrɪ] *n* psychiatrie *f*. ◆**psychi'atric** *a* psychiatrique. ◆**psychiatrist** *n* psychiatre *mf*.

psychic ['saɪkɪk] *a* (méta)psychique; **I'm not p.** *Fam* je ne suis pas devin; — *n* (*person*) médium *m*.

psycho- ['saɪkəu] *pref* psycho-. ◆**psycho-a'nalysis** *n* psychanalyse *f*. ◆**psycho-'analyst** *n* psychanalyste *mf*.

psychology [saɪ'kɒlədʒɪ] *n* psychologie *f*. ◆**psycho'logical** *a* psychologique. ◆**psychologist** *n* psychologue *mf*.

psychopath ['saɪkəupæθ] *n* psychopathe *mf*.

psychosis, *pl* **-oses** [saɪ'kəusɪs, -əusiːz] *n* psychose *f*.

PTO [piːtiː'əu] *abbr* (*please turn over*) TSVP.

pub [pʌb] *n* pub *m*.

puberty ['pjuːbətɪ] *n* puberté *f*.

public ['pʌblɪk] *a* public; (*baths, library*) municipal; **to make a p. protest** protester publiquement; **in the p. eye** très en vue; **p. building** édifice *m* public; **p. company** société *f* par actions; **p. corporation** société *f* nationalisée; **p. figure** personnalité *f* connue; **p. house** pub *m*; **p. life** les affaires *fpl* publiques; **to be p.-spirited** avoir le sens civique; — *n* **the public**; **in p.** en public; **a member of the p.** un simple particulier; **the sporting/*etc* p.** les amateurs *mpl* de sport/*etc*. ◆**—ly** *adv* publiquement; **p. owned** (*nationalized*) *Com* nationalisé.

publican ['pʌblɪk(ə)n] *n* patron, -onne *mf* d'un pub.

publication [pʌblɪ'keɪʃ(ə)n] n (publishing, book etc) publication f.

publicity [pʌb'lɪsɪtɪ] n publicité f. ◆'**publicize** vt rendre public; (advertise) Com faire de la publicité pour.

publish ['pʌblɪʃ] vt publier; (book) éditer, publier; **to p. s.o.** éditer qn; '**published weekly**' 'paraît toutes les semaines'. ◆—**ing** n publication f (of de); (profession) édition f. ◆—**er** n éditeur, -trice mf.

puck [pʌk] n (in ice hockey) palet m.

pucker ['pʌkər] vt to p. (up) (brow, lips) plisser; — vi to p. (up) se plisser.

pudding ['pʊdɪŋ] n dessert m, gâteau m; (plum) pudding m; **rice p.** riz m au lait.

puddle ['pʌd(ə)l] n flaque f (d'eau).

pudgy ['pʌdʒɪ] a (-ier, -iest) = podgy.

puerile ['pjʊəraɪl] a puérile.

puff [pʌf] n (of smoke) bouffée f; (of wind, air) bouffée f, souffle m; **to have run out of p.** Fam être à bout de souffle; — vi (blow, pant) souffler; **to p. at** (cigar) tirer sur; — vt (smoke etc) souffler (into dans); **to p. out** (cheeks etc) gonfler. ◆**puffy** a (-ier, -iest) (swollen) gonflé.

puke [pjuːk] vi (vomit) Sl dégueuler.

pukka ['pʌkə] a Fam authentique.

pull [pʊl] n (attraction) attraction f; (force) force f; (influence) influence f; **to give sth a p.** tirer qch; — vt (draw, tug) tirer; (tooth) arracher; (stopper) enlever; (trigger) appuyer sur; (muscle) se claquer; **to p. apart** or **to bits** or **to pieces** mettre en pièces; **to p. a face** faire la moue; **to (get s.o. to) p. strings** Fig se faire pistonner; — vi (tug) tirer; (go, move) aller; **to p. at** or **on** tirer (sur). ▪ **to p. along** vt (drag) traîner (**to** jusqu'à); **to p. away** vi (move) éloigner; (snatch) arracher (**from** à); — vi Aut démarrer; **to p. away from** s'éloigner de; **to p. back** vi (withdraw) Mil se retirer; — vt retirer; (curtains) ouvrir; **to p. down** vt (lower) baisser; (knock down) faire tomber; (demolish) démolir, abattre; **to p. in** vt (rope) ramener; (drag into room etc) faire entrer; (stomach) rentrer; (crowd) attirer; — vi (arrive) Aut arriver; (stop) Aut se garer; **to p. into the station** (of train) entrer en gare; **to p. off** vt (remove) enlever; (plan, deal) Fig mener à bien; **to p. it off** Fig réussir son coup; **to p. on** vt (boots etc) mettre; **to p. out** vt (extract) arracher (**from** à); (remove) enlever (**from** de); (from pocket, bag etc) tirer, sortir (**from** de); (troops) retirer; — vi (depart) Aut démarrer; (move out) Aut déboîter; **to p. out from** (negotiations etc) se retirer de; **to p. over** vt (drag) traîner (**to**

jusqu'à); (knock down) faire tomber; — vi Aut se ranger (sur le côté); **to p. round** vi Med se remettre; **to p. through** vi s'en tirer; **to p. oneself together** vt se ressaisir; **to p. up** vt (socks, bucket etc) remonter; (haul up) hisser; (uproot) arracher; (stop) arrêter; — vi Aut s'arrêter. ◆**p.-up** n Sp traction f.

pulley ['pʊlɪ] n poulie f.

pullout ['pʊlaʊt] n (in newspaper etc) supplément m détachable.

pullover ['pʊləʊvər] n pull-(over) m.

pulp [pʌlp] n (of fruit etc) pulpe f; (for paper) pâte f à papier; **in a p.** Fig en bouillie.

pulpit ['pʊlpɪt] n Rel chaire f.

pulsate [pʌl'seɪt] vi produire des pulsations, battre. ◆**pulsation** n (heartbeat etc) pulsation f.

pulse [pʌls] n Med pouls m.

pulverize ['pʌlvəraɪz] vt (grind, defeat) pulvériser.

pumice ['pʌmɪs] n p. (stone) pierre f ponce.

pump [pʌmp] **1** n pompe f; (petrol) p. **attendant** pompiste mf; — vt pomper; (blood) Med faire circuler; (money) Fig injecter (**into** dans); **to p. s.o.** (for information) tirer les vers du nez à qn; **to p. in** refouler (à l'aide d'une pompe); **to p. out** pomper (**of** de); **to p. air into, to p. up** (tyre) gonfler; — vi pomper; (of heart) battre. **2** n (for dancing) escarpin m; (plimsoll) tennis f.

pumpkin ['pʌmpkɪn] n potiron m.

pun [pʌn] n calembour m.

punch¹ [pʌntʃ] n (blow) coup m de poing; (force) Fig punch m; **to pack a p.** Boxing & Fig avoir du punch; **p. line** (of joke) astuce f finale; — vt (person) donner un coup de poing à; (ball etc) frapper d'un coup de poing. ◆**p.-up** n Fam bagarre f.

punch² [pʌntʃ] **1** n (for tickets) poinçonneuse f; (for paper) perforeuse f; **p. card** carte f perforée; — vt (ticket) poinçonner, (with date) composter; (card, paper) perforer; **to p. a hole in** faire un trou dans. **2** n (drink) punch m.

punctilious [pʌŋk'tɪlɪəs] a pointilleux.

punctual ['pʌŋktʃʊəl] a (arriving on time) à l'heure; (regularly on time) ponctuel, exact. ◆**punctu'ality** n ponctualité f, exactitude f. ◆**punctually** adv à l'heure; (habitually) ponctuellement.

punctuate ['pʌŋktʃʊeɪt] vt ponctuer (**with** de). ◆**punctu'ation** n ponctuation f; **p. mark** signe m de ponctuation.

puncture ['pʌŋktʃər] n (in tyre) crevaison f;

to have a p. crever; − *vt* (*burst*) crever; (*pierce*) piquer; − *vi* (*of tyre*) crever.

pundit ['pʌndɪt] *n* expert *m*, ponte *m*.

pungent ['pʌndʒənt] *a* âcre, piquant. ◆**pungency** *n* âcreté *f*.

punish ['pʌnɪʃ] *vt* punir (**for sth** de qch, **for doing** *or* **having done** pour avoir fait); (*treat roughly*) *Fig* malmener. ◆**−ing** *n* punition *f*; − *a* (*tiring*) éreintant. ◆**−able** *a* punissable (**by** de). ◆**−ment** *n* punition *f*, châtiment *m*; **capital p.** peine *f* capitale; **to take a (lot of) p.** (*damage*) *Fig* en encaisser.

punitive ['pjuːnɪtɪv] *a* (*measure etc*) punitif.

punk [pʌŋk] **1** *n* (*music*) punk *m*; (*fan*) punk *mf*; − *a* punk *inv*. **2** *n* (*hoodlum*) *Am* Fam voyou *m*.

punt [pʌnt] **1** *n* barque *f* (à fond plat). **2** *vi* (*bet*) Fam parier. ◆**−ing** *n* canotage *m*. ◆**−er** *n* **1** (*gambler*) parieur, -euse *mf*. **2** (*customer*) *Sl* client, -ente *mf*.

puny ['pjuːnɪ] *a* (**-ier, -iest**) (*sickly*) chétif; (*small*) petit; (*effort*) faible.

pup [pʌp] *n* (*dog*) chiot *m*.

pupil ['pjuːp(ə)l] *n* **1** (*person*) élève *mf*. **2** (*of eye*) pupille *f*.

puppet ['pʌpɪt] *n* marionnette *f*; − *a* (*government, leader*) fantoche.

puppy ['pʌpɪ] *n* (*dog*) chiot *m*.

purchas/e ['pɜːtʃɪs] *n* (*bought article, buying*) achat *m*; − *vt* acheter (**from s.o.** à qn, **for s.o.** à *or* pour qn). ◆**−er** *n* acheteur, -euse *mf*.

pure [pjʊər] *a* (**-er, -est**) pur. ◆**purely** *adv* purement. ◆**purifi'cation** *n* purification *f*. ◆**purify** *vt* purifier. ◆**purity** *n* pureté *f*.

purée ['pjʊəreɪ] *n* purée *f*.

purgatory ['pɜːgətrɪ] *n* purgatoire *m*.

purge [pɜːdʒ] *n* Pol Med purge *f*; − *vt* (*rid*) purger (**of** de); (*group*) Pol épurer.

purist ['pjʊərɪst] *n* puriste *m*.

puritan ['pjʊərɪt(ə)n] *n* & *a* puritain, -aine (*mf*). ◆**puri'tanical** *a* puritain.

purl [pɜːl] *n* (*knitting stitch*) maille *f* à l'envers.

purple ['pɜːp(ə)l] *a* & *n* violet (*m*); **to go p.** (*with anger*) devenir pourpre; (*with shame*) devenir cramoisi.

purport [pɜː'pɔːt] *vt* **to p. to be** (*claim*) prétendre être.

purpose ['pɜːpəs] *n* **1** (*aim*) but *m*; **for this p.** dans ce but; **on p.** exprès; **to no p.** inutilement; **to serve no p.** ne servir à rien; **for (the) purposes of** pour les besoins de. **2** (*determination, willpower*) résolution *f*; **to have a sense of p.** être résolu. ◆**p.-'built** *a* construit spécialement. ◆**purposeful** *a* (*determined*) résolu. ◆**purposefully** *adv*

dans un but précis; (*resolutely*) résolument. ◆**purposely** *adv* exprès.

purr [pɜːr] *vi* ronronner; − *n* ronron(nement) *m*.

purse [pɜːs] *n* **1** (*for coins*) porte-monnaie *m inv*; (*handbag*) *Am* sac *m* à main. **2** *vt* **to p. one's lips** pincer les lèvres.

purser ['pɜːsər] *n* Nau commissaire *m* du bord.

pursue [pə'sjuː] *vt* (*chase, hound, seek, continue*) poursuivre; (*fame, pleasure*) rechercher; (*course of action*) suivre. ◆**pursuer** *n* poursuivant, -ante *mf*. ◆**pursuit** *n* (*of person, glory etc*) poursuite *f*; (*activity, pastime*) occupation *f*; **to go in p. of** se mettre à la poursuite de.

purveyor [pə'veɪər] *n* Com fournisseur *m*.

pus [pʌs] *n* pus *m*.

push [pʊʃ] *n* (*shove*) poussée *f*; (*energy*) *Fig* dynamisme *m*; (*help*) coup *m* de pouce; (*campaign*) campagne *f*; **to give s.o./sth a p.** pousser qn/qch; **to give s.o. the p.** (*dismiss*) Fam flanquer qn à la porte; − *vt* pousser (**to, as far as** jusqu'à); (*product*) Com pousser la vente de; (*drugs*) Fam revendre; **to p. (down)** (*button*) appuyer sur; (*lever*) abaisser; **to p. (forward)** (*views etc*) mettre en avant; **to p. sth into/between** (*thrust*) enfoncer *or* fourrer qch dans/entre; **to p. s.o. into doing** (*urge*) pousser qn à faire; **to p. sth off the table** faire tomber qch de la table (en le poussant); **to p. s.o. off a cliff** pousser qn du haut d'une falaise; **to be pushing forty/etc** Fam friser la quarantaine/etc; − *vi* pousser; **to p. for** faire pression pour obtenir. ■ **to p. about** *or* **around** *vt* (*bully*) Fam marcher sur les pieds à; **to p. aside** *vt* (*person, objection etc*) écarter; **to p. away** *or* **back** *vt* repousser; (*curtains*) ouvrir; **to p. in** *vi* (*in queue*) Fam resquiller; **to p. off** *vi* (*leave*) Fam filer; **p. off!** Fam fiche le camp!; **to p. on** *vi* continuer (**with** sth qch); (*in journey*) poursuivre sa route; **to p. over** *vt* (*topple*) renverser; **to p. through** *vt* (*law*) faire adopter; − *vti* **to p. (one's way) through** se frayer un chemin (**a crowd**/etc à travers une foule/etc); **to p. up** *vt* (*lever etc*) relever; (*increase*) Fam augmenter, relever. ◆**pushed** *a* **to be p. (for time)** (*rushed, busy*) être très bousculé. ◆**pusher** *n* (*of drugs*) revendeur, -euse *mf* (de drogue).

pushbike ['pʊʃbaɪk] *n* Fam vélo *m*. ◆**push-button** *n* poussoir *m*; − *a* (*radio etc*) à poussoir. ◆**pushchair** *n* poussette *f* (pliante). ◆**pushover** *n* **to be a p.** (*easy*)

Fam être facile, être du gâteau. ◆**push-up** *n Sp Am* pompe *f.*

pushy ['puʃɪ] *a* (**-ier, -iest**) *Pej* entreprenant; (*in job*) arriviste.

puss(y) ['pus(ɪ)] *n* (*cat*) minet *m,* minou *m.*

put [put] *vt* (*pt & pp* **put,** *pres p* **putting**) mettre; (*savings, money*) placer (**into** dans); (*pressure, mark*) faire (**on** sur); (*problem, argument*) présenter (**to** à); (*question*) poser (**to** à); (*say*) dire; (*estimate*) évaluer (**at** à); **to p. it bluntly** pour parler franc. ■ **to p. across** *vt* (*idea etc*) communiquer (**to** à); **to p. away** *vt* (*in its place*) ranger (*livre, voiture etc*); **to p. s.o. away** (*criminal*) mettre qn en prison; (*insane person*) enfermer qn; **to p. back** *vt* remettre; (*receiver*) *Tel* raccrocher; (*progress, clock*) retarder; **to p. by** *vt* (*money*) mettre de côté; **to p. down** *vt* (*on floor, table etc*) poser; (*passenger*) déposer; (*deposit*) *Fin* verser; (*revolt*) réprimer; (*write down*) inscrire; (*kill*) faire piquer (*chien etc*); (*assign*) attribuer (**to** à); **to p. forward** *vt* (*argument, clock, meeting*) avancer; (*opinion*) exprimer; (*candidate*) proposer (**for** à); **to p. in** *vt* (*insert*) introduire; (*add*) ajouter; (*present*) présenter; (*request, application*) faire; (*enrol*) inscrire (**for** à); (*spend*) passer (*une heure etc*) (**doing** à faire); – *vi* **to p. in for** (*job etc*) faire une demande de; **to p. in at** (*of ship etc*) faire escale à; **to p. off** *vt* (*post-pone*) renvoyer (à plus tard); (*passenger*) déposer; (*gas, radio*) fermer; (*dismay*) déconcerter; **to p. s.o. off** (*dissuade*) dissuader qn (**doing** de faire); **to p. s.o. off doing** (*disgust*) dégoûter qn (*sth de qch*); **to p. s.o. off doing** (*disgust*) ôter à qn l'envie de faire; **to p. on** *vt* (*clothes, shoe etc*) mettre; (*weight, accent*) prendre; (*film*) jouer; (*gas, radio*) mettre, allumer; (*record, cassette*) passer; (*clock*) avancer; **to p. s.o. on** (*tease*) *Am* faire marcher qn; **she p. me on to you** elle m'a donné votre adresse; **p. me on to you him!** *Tel* passez-le-moi!; **to p. out** *vt* (*take*

outside) sortir; (*arm, leg*) étendre; (*hand*) tendre; (*tongue*) tirer; (*gas, light*) éteindre, fermer; (*inconvenience*) déranger; (*upset*) déconcerter; (*issue*) publier; (*dislocate*) démettre; **to p. through** *vt Tel* passer (**to** à); **to p. together** *vt* (*assemble*) assembler; (*compose*) composer; (*prepare*) préparer; (*collection*) faire; **to p. up** *vi* (*lodge*) descendre (**at a hotel** dans un hôtel); **to p. up with** (*tolerate*) supporter; – *vt* (*lift*) lever; (*window*) remonter; (*tent, statue, barrier, ladder*) dresser; (*flag*) hisser; (*building*) construire; (*umbrella*) ouvrir; (*picture, poster*) mettre; (*price, sales, numbers*) augmenter; (*resistance, plea, suggestion*) offrir; (*candidate*) proposer (**for** à); (*guest*) loger; **p.-up job** *Fam* coup *m* monté. ◆**p.-you-up** *n* canapé-lit *m,* convertible *m.*

putrid ['pjuːtrɪd] *a* putride. ◆**putrify** *vi* se putréfier.

putt [pʌt] *n Golf* putt *m.* ◆**putting** *n Golf* putting *m;* **p. green** green *m.*

putter ['pʌtər] *vi* **to p. around** *Am* bricoler.

putty ['pʌtɪ] *n* (*pour fixer une vitre*) mastic *m.*

puzzl/e ['pʌz(ə)l] *n* mystère *m,* énigme *f;* (*game*) casse-tête *m inv;* (*jigsaw*) puzzle *m;* – *vt* laisser perplexe; **to p. out why/when/** *etc* essayer de comprendre pourquoi/quand/*etc;* – *vi* **to p. over** (*problem, event*) se creuser la tête sur. ◆**—ed** *a* perplexe. ◆**—ing** *a* mystérieux, surprenant.

PVC [piːviːˈsiː] *n* (*plastic*) PVC *m.*

pygmy ['pɪgmɪ] *n* pygmée *m.*

pyjama [prˈdʒɑːmə] *a* (*jacket etc*) de pyjama. ◆**pyjamas** *npl* pyjama *m;* **a pair of p.** un pyjama.

pylon ['paɪlən] *n* pylône *m.*

pyramid ['pɪrəmɪd] *n* pyramide *f.*

Pyrenees [pɪrəˈniːz] *npl* **the P.** les Pyrénées *fpl.*

python ['paɪθən] *n* (*snake*) python *m.*

Q

Q, q [kjuː] *n* Q, q *m.*
quack [kwæk] **1** *n* (*of duck*) coin-coin *m inv.* **2** *a & n* **q. (doctor)** charlatan *m.*
quad(rangle) ['kwɒd(ræŋɡ(ə)l)] *n* (*of college*) cour *f.*
quadruped ['kwɒdruped] *n* quadrupède *m.*

quadruple [kwɒˈdruːp(ə)l] *vt* quadrupler.
quadruplets [kwɒˈdruːplɪts] (*Fam* **quads** [kwɒdz]) *npl* quadruplés, -ées *mfpl.*
quaff [kwɒf] *vt* (*drink*) avaler.
quagmire ['kwæɡmaɪər] *n* bourbier *m.*
quail [kweɪl] *n* (*bird*) caille *f.*

quaint [kweɪnt] *a* (**-er, -est**) (*picturesque*) pittoresque; (*antiquated*) vieillot; (*odd*) bizarre. ◆**—ness** *n* pittoresque *m*; caractère *m* vieillot; bizarrerie *f*.

quake [kweɪk] *vi* trembler (**with** de); — *n Fam* tremblement *m* de terre.

Quaker ['kweɪkər] *n* quaker, -eresse *mf*.

qualification [kwɒlɪfɪ'keɪʃ(ə)n] *n* **1** (*competence*) compétence *f* (**for** pour, **to do** pour faire); (*diploma*) diplôme *m*; *pl* (*requirements*) conditions *fpl* requises. **2** (*reservation*) réserve *f*.

qualify ['kwɒlɪfaɪ] **1** *vt* (*make competent*) & *Sp* qualifier (**for sth** pour qch, **to do** pour faire); — *vi* obtenir son diplôme (**as a doctor**/*etc* de médecin/*etc*); *Sp* se qualifier (**for** pour); **to q. for** (*post*) remplir les conditions requises pour. **2** *vt* (*modify*) faire des réserves à; (*opinion*) nuancer; *Gram* qualifier. ◆**qualified** *a* (*able*) qualifié (**to do** pour faire); (*doctor etc*) diplômé; (*success*) limité; (*opinion*) nuancé; (*support*) conditionnel. ◆**qualifying** *a* (*exam*) d'entrée; **q. round** *Sp* (épreuve *f*) éliminatoire *f*.

quality ['kwɒlɪtɪ] *n* qualité *f*; — *a* (*product*) de qualité. ◆**qualitative** *a* qualitatif.

qualms [kwɑːmz] *npl* (*scruples*) scrupules *mpl*; (*anxieties*) inquiétudes *fpl*.

quandary ['kwɒndrɪ] *n* **in a q.** bien embarrassé; **to be in a q. about what to do** ne pas savoir quoi faire.

quantity ['kwɒntɪtɪ] *n* quantité *f*; **in q.** (*to purchase etc*) en grande(s) quantité(s). ◆**quantify** *vt* quantifier. ◆**quantitative** *a* quantitatif.

quarantine ['kwɒrəntiːn] *n Med* quarantaine *f*; — *vt* mettre en quarantaine.

quarrel ['kwɒrəl] *n* querelle *f*, dispute *f*; **to pick a q.** chercher querelle (**with s.o.** à qn); — *vi* (**-ll-, *Am* -l-**) se disputer, se quereller (**with** avec); **to q. with sth** trouver à redire à qch. ◆**quarrelling** *n*, *Am* ◆**quarreling** *n* (*quarrels*) querelles *fpl*. ◆**quarrelsome** *a* querelleur.

quarry ['kwɒrɪ] *n* **1** (*excavation*) carrière *f*. **2** (*prey*) proie *f*.

quart [kwɔːt] *n* litre *m* (*mesure approximative*) (*Br* = 1,14 litres, *Am* = 0,95 litre).

quarter ['kwɔːtər] *n* **1** quart *m*; (*of year*) trimestre *m*; (*money*) *Am Can* quart *m* de dollar; (*of moon, fruit*) quartier *m*; **to divide into quarters** diviser en quatre; **q. (of a) pound** quart *m* de livre; **a q.** *Am* quart *m*; **a q. after nine** neuf heures et *or* un quart; **a q. to nine** neuf heures moins le quart; **from all quarters** de toutes parts. **2** *n* (*district*)

quartier *m*; *pl* (*circles*) milieux *mpl*; (*living*) **quarters** logement(s) *m*(*pl*); *Mil* quartier(s) *m*(*pl*); — *vt* (*troops*) *Mil* cantonner. ◆**-ly** *a* trimestriel; — *adv* trimestriellement; — *n* publication *f* trimestrielle.

quarterfinal [kwɔːtə'faɪn(ə)l] *n Sp* quart *m* de finale.

quartet(te) [kwɔː'tet] *n Mus* quatuor *m*; (*jazz*) quartette *m*.

quartz [kwɔːts] *n* quartz *m*; — *a* (*clock etc*) à quartz.

quash [kwɒʃ] *vt* (*rebellion etc*) réprimer; (*verdict*) *Jur* casser.

quaver ['kweɪvər] **1** *vi* chevroter; — *n* chevrotement *m*. **2** *n Mus* croche *f*.

quay [kiː] *n Nau* quai *m*. ◆**quayside** *n* **on the q.** sur les quais.

queas/y ['kwiːzɪ] *a* (**-ier, -iest**) **to feel** *or* **be q.** avoir mal au cœur. ◆**-iness** *n* mal *m* au cœur.

Quebec [kwɪ'bek] *n* le Québec.

queen [kwiːn] *n* reine *f*; *Chess Cards* dame *f*; **the q. mother** la reine mère.

queer ['kwɪər] *a* (**-er, -est**) (*odd*) bizarre; (*dubious*) louche; (*ill*) *Fam* patraque; — *n* (*homosexual*) *Pej Fam* pédé *m*.

quell [kwel] *vt* (*revolt etc*) réprimer.

quench [kwentʃ] *vt* (*fire*) éteindre; **to q. one's thirst** se désaltérer.

querulous ['kweruləs] *a* (*complaining*) grognon.

query ['kwɪərɪ] *n* question *f*; (*doubt*) doute *m*; — *vt* mettre en question.

quest [kwest] *n* quête *f* (**for** de); **in q. of** en quête de.

question ['kwestʃ(ə)n] *n* question *f*; **there's some q. of it** il en est question; **there's no q. of it, it's out of the q.** il n'en est pas question, c'est hors de question; **without q.** incontestable(ment); **in q.** en question, dont il s'agit; (*doubt*) mettre en question; **q. mark** point *m* d'interrogation; **q. master** *TV Rad* animateur, -trice *mf*; — *vt* interroger (**about** sur); (*doubt*) mettre en question; **to q. whether** douter que (+ *sub*). ◆**-ing** *a* (*look etc*) interrogateur; — *n* interrogation *f*. ◆**-able** *a* douteux. ◆**questio'nnaire** *n* questionnaire *m*.

queue [kjuː] *n* (*of people*) queue *f*; (*of cars*) file *f*; **to stand in a q., form a q.** faire la queue; — *vi* **to q. (up)** faire la queue.

quibbl/e ['kwɪb(ə)l] *vi* ergoter, discuter (**over** sur). ◆**-ing** *n* ergotage *m*.

quiche [kiːʃ] *n* (*tart*) quiche *f*.

quick [kwɪk] **1** *a* (**-er, -est**) rapide; **q. to react** prompt à réagir; **to be q.** faire vite; **to have a q. shave/meal**/*etc* se raser/manger/*etc* en vitesse; **to be a q. worker** travailler vite; — *adv* (**-er, -est**) vite; **as q. as a flash** en un clin d'œil. **2** *n* to cut to the q. blesser au vif. ◆**q.-'tempered** *a* irascible. ◆**q.-'witted** *a* à l'esprit vif. ◆**quicken** *vt* accélérer; — *vi* s'accélérer. ◆**quickie** *n* (*drink*) *Fam* pot *m* (*pris en vitesse*). ◆**quickly** *adv* vite. ◆**quicksands** *npl* sables mouvants.

quid [kwɪd] *n inv Fam* livre *f* (sterling).

quiet [kwaɪət] *a* (**-er, -est**) (*silent, still, peaceful*) tranquille, calme; (*machine, vehicle, temperament*) silencieux; (*gentle*) doux; (*voice*) bas, doux; (*sound*) léger, doux; (*private*) intime; (*colour*) discret; **to be or keep q.** (*shut up*) se taire; (*make no noise*) ne pas faire de bruit; **q.!** silence!; **to keep q. about sth, keep sth q.** ne pas parler de qch; **on the q.** (*secretly*) *Fam* en cachette; — *vt* = **quieten**. ◆**quieten** *vti* to q. (**down**) (se) calmer. ◆**quietly** *adv* tranquillement; (*gently, not loudly*) doucement; (*silently*) silencieusement; (*secretly*) en cachette; (*discreetly*) discrètement. ◆**quietness** *n* tranquillité *f*.

quill [kwɪl] *n* (*pen*) plume *f* (d'oie).

quilt [kwɪlt] *n* édredon *m*; (**continental**) **q.** couette *f*; — *vt* (*stitch*) piquer; (*pad*) matelasser.

quintessence [kwɪn'tesəns] *n* quintessence *f*.

quintet(te) [kwɪn'tet] *n* quintette *m*.

quintuplets [kwɪn'tjuːplɪts] (*Fam* **quins** [kwɪnz]) *npl* quintuplés, -ées *mfpl*.

quip [kwɪp] *n* (*remark*) boutade *f*; — *vi* (**-pp-**) faire des boutades; — *vt* dire sur le ton de la boutade.

quirk [kwɜːk] *n* bizarrerie *f*; (*of fate*) caprice *m*.

quit [kwɪt] *vt* (*pt & pp* **quit** *or* **quitted**, *pres p* **quitting**) (*leave*) quitter; **to q. doing** arrêter de faire; — *vi* (*give up*) abandonner; (*resign*) démissionner.

quite [kwaɪt] *adv* (*entirely*) tout à fait; (*really*) vraiment; (*rather*) assez; **q. another matter** une tout autre affaire *or* question; **q. a genius** un véritable génie; **q. good** (*not bad*) pas mal (du tout); **q. (so)!** exactement!; **I q. understand** je comprends très bien; **q. a lot** pas mal (of qch); **q. a (long) time ago** il y a pas mal de temps.

quits [kwɪts] *a* quitte (**with** envers); **to call it q.** en rester là.

quiver ['kwɪvər] *vi* frémir (**with** de); (*of voice*) trembler, frémir; (*of flame*) vaciller, trembler.

quiz [kwɪz] *n* (*pl* **quizzes**) (*riddle*) devinette *f*; (*test*) test *m*; **q.** (**programme**) *TV Rad* jeu-concours *m*; — *vt* (**-zz-**) questionner. ◆**quizmaster** *n TV Rad* animateur, -trice *mf*.

quizzical ['kwɪzɪk(ə)l] *a* (*mocking*) narquois; (*perplexed*) perplexe.

quorum ['kwɔːrəm] *n* quorum *m*.

quota ['kwəʊtə] *n* quota *m*.

quote [kwəʊt] *vt* citer; (*reference number*) *Com* rappeler; (*price*) indiquer; (*price on Stock Exchange*) coter; — *vi* **to q. from** (*author, book*) citer; — *n Fam* = **quotation**; **in quotes** entre guillemets. ◆**quo'tation** *n* citation *f*; (*estimate*) *Com* devis *m*; (*on Stock Exchange*) cote *f*; **q. marks** guillemets *mpl*; **in q. marks** entre guillemets.

quotient ['kwəʊʃ(ə)nt] *n* quotient *m*.

R

R, r [ɑːr] *n* R, r *m*.

rabbi ['ræbaɪ] *n* rabbin *m*; **chief r.** grand rabbin.

rabbit ['ræbɪt] *n* lapin *m*.

rabble ['ræb(ə)l] *n* (*crowd*) cohue *f*; **the r.** *Pej* la populace.

rabies ['reɪbiːz] *n Med* rage *f*. ◆**rabid** ['ræbɪd] *a* (*dog*) enragé; (*person*) *Fig* fanatique.

raccoon [rə'kuːn] *n* (*animal*) raton *m* laveur.

rac/e[1] [reɪs] *n Sp & Fig* course *f*; — *vt* (*horse*) faire courir; (*engine*) emballer; **to r.** (**against or with**) **s.o.** faire une course avec qn; — *vi* (*run*) courir; (*of engine*) s'emballer; (*of pulse*) battre à tout rompre. ◆**—ing** *n* courses *fpl*; — *a* (*car, bicycle etc*) de course; **r. driver** coureur *m* automobile. ◆**racecourse** *n* champ *m* de courses. ◆**racegoer** *n* turfiste *mf*. ◆**racehorse** *n* cheval *m* de course. ◆**racetrack** *n* piste *f*; (*for horses*) *Am* champ *m* de courses.

race[2] [reɪs] *n* (*group*) race *f*; — *a* (*prejudice etc*) racial; **r. relations** rapports *mpl* entre les races. ◆**racial** a racial. ◆**racialism** n racisme m. ◆**racism** n racisme m. ◆**racist** a & n raciste (mf).

rack [ræk] **1** n (shelf) étagère f; (for bottles etc) casier m; (for drying dishes) égouttoir m; (luggage) r. (on bicycle) porte-bagages m inv; (on bus, train etc) filet m à bagages; (roof) r. (of car) galerie f. **2** vt to r. one's brains se creuser la cervelle. **3** n to go to r. and ruin (of person) aller à la ruine; (of building) tomber en ruine; (of health) se délabrer.

racket ['rækɪt] n **1** (for tennis etc) raquette f. **2** (din) vacarme m. **3** (crime) racket m; (scheme) combine f; the drug(s) r. le trafic m de (la) drogue. ◆**racke'teer** n racketteur m. ◆**racke'teering** n racket m.

racoon [rə'ku:n] n (animal) raton m laveur.

racy ['reɪsɪ] a (-ier, -iest) piquant; (suggestive) osé.

radar ['reɪdɑːr] n radar m; — a (control, trap etc) radar inv; r. operator radariste mf.

radiant ['reɪdɪənt] a (person) rayonnant (with de), radieux. ◆**radiance** n éclat m, rayonnement m. ◆**radiantly** adv (to shine) avec éclat; r. happy rayonnant de joie.

radiate ['reɪdɪeɪt] vt (emit) dégager; (joy) Fig rayonner de; — vi (of heat, lines) rayonner (from de). ◆**radia'tion** n (of heat etc) rayonnement m (of de); (radioactivity) Phys radiation f; (rays) irradiation f; r. sickness mal m des rayons.

radiator ['reɪdɪeɪtər] n radiateur m.

radical ['rædɪk(ə)l] a radical; — n (person) Pol radical, -ale mf.

radio ['reɪdɪəʊ] n (pl -os) radio f; on the r. à la radio; car r. autoradio m; r. set poste m (de) radio; r. operator radio m; r. wave onde f hertzienne; — vt (message) transmettre (par radio) (to à); to r. s.o. appeler qn par radio. ◆**r.-con'trolled** a radioguidé. ◆**radio'active** a radioactif. ◆**radioac'tivity** n radioactivité f.

radiographer [reɪdɪ'ɒgrəfər] n (technician) radiologue m. ◆**radiography** n radiographie f. ◆**radiologist** n (doctor) radiologue mf. ◆**radiology** n radiologie f.

radish ['rædɪʃ] n radis m.

radius, pl **-dii** ['reɪdɪəs, -dɪaɪ] n (of circle) rayon m; within a r. of dans un rayon de.

RAF [ɑːreɪ'ef] n abbr (Royal Air Force) armée f de l'air (britannique).

raffia ['ræfɪə] n raphia m.

raffle ['ræf(ə)l] n tombola f.

raft [rɑːft] n (boat) radeau m.

rafter ['rɑːftər] n (beam) chevron m.

rag [ræg] n **1** (old garment) loque f, haillon m; (for dusting etc) chiffon m; in rags (clothes) en loques; (person) en haillons; r.-and-bone man chiffonnier m. **2** (newspaper) torchon m. **3** (procession) Univ carnaval m (au profit d'œuvres de charité). ◆**ragged** ['rægɪd] a (clothes) en loques; (person) en haillons; (edge) irrégulier. ◆**ragman** n (pl -men) chiffonnier m.

ragamuffin ['rægəmʌfɪn] n va-nu-pieds m inv.

rag/e [reɪdʒ] n rage f; (of sea) furie f; to fly into a r. se mettre en rage; to be all the r. (of fashion etc) faire fureur; — vi (be angry) rager; (of storm, battle) faire rage. ◆**—ing** a (storm, fever) violent; a r. fire un grand incendie; in a r. temper furieux.

raid [reɪd] n Mil raid m; (by police) descente f; (by thieves) hold-up m; air r. raid m aérien, attaque f aérienne; — vt faire un raid or une descente or un hold-up dans; Av attaquer; (larder, fridge etc) Fam dévaliser. ◆**raider** n (criminal) malfaiteur m; pl Mil commando m.

rail [reɪl] **1** n (for train) rail m; by r. (to travel) par le train; (to send) par chemin de fer; to go off the rails (of train) dérailler; — a ferroviaire; (strike) des cheminots. **2** n (rod on balcony) balustrade f; (on stairs, for spotlight) rampe f; (for curtain) tringle f; (towel) r. porte-serviettes m inv. ◆**railing** n (of balcony) balustrade f; pl (fence) grille f. ◆**railroad** n Am = railway; r. track voie f ferrée. ◆**railway** n (system) chemin m de fer; (track) voie f ferrée; — a (ticket) de chemin de fer; (network) ferroviaire; r. line (route) ligne f de chemin de fer; (track) voie f ferrée; r. station gare f. ◆**railwayman** n (pl -men) cheminot m.

rain [reɪn] n pluie f; in the r. sous la pluie; I'll give you a r. check (for invitation) Am Fam j'accepterai volontiers à une date ultérieure; — vi pleuvoir; to r. (down) (of blows, bullets) pleuvoir; it's raining il pleut. ◆**rainbow** n arc-en-ciel m. ◆**raincoat** n imper(méable) m. ◆**raindrop** n goutte f de pluie. ◆**rainfall** n (shower) chute f de pluie; (amount) précipitations fpl. ◆**rainstorm** n trombe f d'eau. ◆**rainwater** n eau f de pluie. ◆**rainy** a (-ier, -iest) pluvieux; the r. season la saison des pluies.

raise [reɪz] vt (lift) lever; (sth heavy) (sou)lever; (child, animal, voice, statue) élever; (crops) cultiver; (salary, price) augmenter, relever; (temperature) faire monter; (question, protest) soulever; (taxes, blockade) lever; to r. a smile/a laugh (in others) faire sourire/rire; to r. s.o.'s hopes faire naître les espérances de qn; **to r. money** réunir des fonds; – *n (pay rise) Am* augmentation *f* (de salaire).

raisin ['reɪz(ə)n] *n* raisin *m* sec.

rake [reɪk] *n* râteau *m*; – *vt (garden)* ratisser; *(search)* fouiller dans; **to r. (up)** *(leaves)* ramasser (avec un râteau); **to r. in** *(money) Fam* ramasser à la pelle; **to r. up** *(the past)* remuer. ◆**r.-off** *n Fam* pot-de-vin *m*, ristourne *f*.

rally ['rælɪ] *vt (unite, win over)* rallier (**to** à); *(one's strength) Fig* reprendre; – *vi* se rallier (**to** à); *(recover)* se remettre (**from** de); **to r. round** *(help)* venir en aide (s.o. à qn); – *n Mil* ralliement *m*; *Pol* rassemblement *m*; *Sp Aut* rallye *m*.

ram [ræm] **1** *n (animal)* bélier *m*. **2** *vt (-mm-)* *(ship)* heurter; *(vehicle)* emboutir; **to r. sth into** *(thrust)* enfoncer qch dans.

rambl/e ['ræmb(ə)l] **1** *n (hike)* randonnée *f*; – *vi* faire une randonnée *or* des randonnées. **2** *vi* **to r. on** *(talk) Pej* discourir. ◆**—ing 1** *a (house)* construit sans plan; *(spread out)* vaste; *(rose etc)* grimpant. **2** *a (speech)* décousu; – *npl* divagations *fpl*. ◆**—er** *n* promeneur, -euse *mf*.

ramification [ræmɪfɪ'keɪʃ(ə)n] *n* ramification *f*.

ramp [ræmp] *n (slope)* rampe *f*; *(in garage)* Tech pont *m* (de graissage); *Av* passerelle *f*; **'r.'** *Aut* 'dénivellation'.

rampage ['ræmpeɪdʒ] *n* **to go on the r.** *(of crowd)* se déchaîner; *(loot)* se livrer au pillage.

rampant ['ræmpənt] *a* **to be r.** *(of crime, disease etc)* sévir.

rampart ['ræmpɑːt] *n* rempart *m*.

ramshackle ['ræmʃæk(ə)l] *a* délabré.

ran [ræn] *see* **run**.

ranch [rɑːntʃ] *n Am* ranch *m*; **r. house** maison *f* genre bungalow (sur sous-sol).

rancid ['rænsɪd] *a* rance.

rancour ['ræŋkər] *n* rancœur *f*.

random ['rændəm] *n* **at r.** au hasard; – *a (choice)* fait au hasard; *(sample)* prélevé au hasard; *(pattern)* irrégulier.

randy ['rændɪ] *a (-ier, -iest) Fam* sensuel, lascif.

rang [ræŋ] *see* **ring²**.

range [reɪndʒ] **1** *n (of gun, voice etc)* portée *f*; *(of aircraft, ship)* rayon *m* d'action; *(series)* gamme *f*; *(choice)* choix *m*; *(of prices)* éventail *m*; *(of voice) Mus* étendue *f*; *(of temperature)* variations *fpl*; *(sphere) Fig* champ *m*, étendue *f*; – *vi (vary)* varier; *(extend)* s'étendre; *(roam)* errer, rôder. **2** *n (of mountains)* chaîne *f*; *(grassland) Am*

prairie *f*. **3** *n (stove) Am* cuisinière *f*. **4** *n (shooting or rifle) r. (at funfair)* stand *m* de tir; *(outdoors)* champ *m* de tir.

ranger ['reɪndʒər] *n (forest) r. Am* garde *m* forestier.

rank [ræŋk] **1** *n (position, class)* rang *m*; *(grade) Mil* grade *m*, rang *m*; **the r. and file** *(workers etc) Pol* la base; **the ranks** *(men in army, numbers)* les rangs *mpl* (**of** de); **taxi r.** station *f* de taxi; – *vt* ranger; *vi* compter parmi. **2** *a (-er, -est) (smell)* fétide; *(vegetation)* luxuriant; *Fig* absolu.

rankle ['ræŋk(ə)l] *vi* **it rankles (with me)** ça me reste sur le cœur.

ransack ['rænsæk] *vt (search)* fouiller; *(plunder)* saccager.

ransom ['ræns(ə)m] *n* rançon *f*; **to hold to r.** rançonner; – *vt (redeem)* racheter.

rant [rænt] *vi* **to r. (and rave)** tempêter (**at** contre).

rap [ræp] *n* petit coup *m* sec; – *vi (-pp-)* frapper (**at** à); – *vt* **to r. s.o. over the knuckles** taper sur les doigts de qn.

rapacious [rə'peɪʃəs] *a (greedy)* rapace.

rape [reɪp] *vt* violer; – *n* viol *m*. ◆**rapist** *n* violeur *m*.

rapid ['ræpɪd] **1** *a* rapide. **2** *n & npl (of river)* rapide(s) *m(pl)*. ◆**ra'pidity** *n* rapidité *f*. ◆**rapidly** *adv* rapidement.

rapport [ræ'pɔːr] *n (understanding)* rapport *m*.

rapt [ræpt] *a (attention)* profond.

rapture ['ræptʃər] *n* extase *f*; **to go into raptures** s'extasier (**about** sur). ◆**rapturous** *a (welcome, applause)* enthousiaste.

rare [reər] *a (-er, -est)* rare; *(meat) Culin* saignant; *(first-rate) Fam* fameux; **it's r. for her to do it** il est rare qu'elle le fasse. ◆**—ly** *adv* rarement. ◆**—ness** *n* rareté *f*. ◆**rarity** *n (quality, object)* rareté *f*.

rarefied ['reərɪfaɪd] *a* raréfié.

raring ['reərɪŋ] *a* **r. to start/etc** impatient de commencer/etc.

rascal ['rɑːsk(ə)l] *n* coquin, -ine *mf*. ◆**rascally** *a (child etc)* coquin; *(habit, trick etc)* de coquin.

rash [ræʃ] **1** *n Med* éruption *f*. **2** *a (-er, -est)* irréfléchi. ◆**—ly** *adv* sans réfléchir. ◆**—ness** *n* irréflexion *f*.

rasher ['ræʃər] *n* tranche *f* de lard.

rasp [rɑːsp] *n (file)* râpe *f*.

raspberry ['rɑːzbərɪ] *n (fruit)* framboise *f*; *(bush)* framboisier *m*.

rasping ['rɑːspɪŋ] *a (voice)* âpre.

rat [ræt] **1** *n* rat *m*; **r. poison** mort-aux-rats *f*; **the r. race** *Fig* la course au bifteck, la jungle. **2** *vi (-tt-)* **to r. on** *(desert)* lâcher;

(*denounce*) cafarder sur; (*promise etc*) manquer à.

rate [reɪt] **1** *n* (*percentage, level*) taux *m*; (*speed*) vitesse *f*; (*price*) tarif *m*; *pl* (*on housing*) impôts *mpl* locaux; **insurance rates** primes *fpl* d'assurance; **r. of flow** débit *m*; **postage** *or* **postal r.** tarif *m* postal; **at the r. of** à une vitesse de; (*amount*) à raison de; **at this r.** (*slow speed*) à ce train-là; **at any r.** en tout cas; **the success r.** (*chances*) les chances *fpl* de succès; (*candidates*) le pourcentage de reçus. **2** *vt* (*evaluate*) évaluer; (*regard*) considérer (**as** comme); (*deserve*) mériter; **to r. highly** apprécier (beaucoup); **to be highly rated** être très apprécié. ◆**rateable** *a* **r. value** valeur *f* locative nette. ◆**ratepayer** *n* contribuable *mf*.

rather [ˈrɑːðər] *adv* (*preferably, fairly*) plutôt; **I'd r. stay** j'aimerais mieux *or* je préférerais rester (**than** que); **I'd r. you came** je préférerais que vous veniez; **r. than leave**/*etc* plutôt que de partir/*etc*; **r. more tired**/*etc* un peu plus fatigué/*etc* (**than** que); **it's r. nice** c'est bien.

ratify [ˈrætɪfaɪ] *vt* ratifier. ◆**ratifi'cation** *n* ratification *f*.

rating [ˈreɪtɪŋ] *n* (*classification*) classement *m*; (*wage etc level*) indice *m*; **credit r.** Fin réputation *f* de solvabilité; **the ratings** TV l'indice *m* d'écoute.

ratio [ˈreɪʃɪəʊ] *n* (*pl* -**os**) proportion *f*.

ration [ˈræʃ(ə)n, Am ˈreɪʃ(ə)n] *n* ration *f*; *pl* (*food*) vivres *mpl*; — *vt* rationner; **I was rationed to ...** ma ration était ....

rational [ˈræʃənəl] *a* (*method, thought etc*) rationnel; (*person*) raisonnable. ◆**rationalize** *vt* (*organize*) rationaliser; (*explain*) justifier. ◆**rationally** *adv* raisonnablement.

rattle [ˈræt(ə)l] **1** *n* (*baby's toy*) hochet *m*; (*of sports fan*) crécelle *f*. **2** *n* petit bruit *m* (sec); cliquetis *m*; crépitement *m*; — *vi* faire du bruit; (*of bottles*) cliqueter; (*of gunfire*) crépiter; (*of window*) trembler; — *vt* (*shake*) agiter; (*window*) faire trembler; (*keys*) faire cliqueter. **3** *vt* **to r. s.o.** (*make nervous*) Fam ébranler qn; — **to r. off** (*poem etc*) Fam débiter (à toute vitesse). ◆**rattlesnake** *n* serpent *m* à sonnette.

ratty [ˈrætɪ] *a* (-**ier, -iest**) **1** (*shabby*) Am Fam minable. **2** **to get r.** (*annoyed*) Fam prendre la mouche.

raucous [ˈrɔːkəs] *a* rauque.

raunchy [ˈrɔːntʃɪ] *a* (-**ier, -iest**) (*joke etc*) Am Fam grivois.

ravage [ˈrævɪdʒ] *vt* ravager; — *npl* **ravages** *mpl*.

rav/e [reɪv] *vi* (*talk nonsense*) divaguer; (*rage*) tempêter (**at** contre); **to r. about** (*enthuse*) ne pas se tarir d'éloges sur; — *a* r. **review** Fam critique *f* dithyrambique. ◆**—ing** *a* **to be r. mad** être fou furieux; — *npl* (*wild talk*) divagations *fpl*.

raven [ˈreɪv(ə)n] *n* corbeau *m*.

ravenous [ˈrævənəs] *a* vorace; **I'm r.** Fam j'ai une faim de loup.

ravine [rəˈviːn] *n* ravin *m*.

ravioli [rævɪˈəʊlɪ] *n* ravioli *mpl*.

ravish [ˈrævɪʃ] *vt* (*rape*) Lit violenter. ◆**—ing** *a* (*beautiful*) ravissant. ◆**—ingly** *adv* **r. beautiful** d'une beauté ravissante.

raw [rɔː] *a* (-**er, -est**) (*vegetable etc*) cru; (*sugar*) brut; (*immature*) inexpérimenté; (*wound*) à vif; (*skin*) écorché; (*weather*) rigoureux; **r. edge** bord *m* coupé; **r. material** matière *f* première; **to get a r. deal** Fam être mal traité.

Rawlplug® [ˈrɔːlplʌg] *n* cheville *f*, tampon *m*.

ray [reɪ] *n* (*of light, sun etc*) & Phys rayon *m*; (*of hope*) Fig lueur *f*.

raze [reɪz] *vt* **to r. (to the ground)** (*destroy*) raser.

razor [ˈreɪzər] *n* rasoir *m*.

re [riː] *prep* Com en référence à.

re- [riː] *pref* ré-, re-, r-.

reach [riːtʃ] *vt* (*place, aim etc*) atteindre, arriver à; (*gain access to*) accéder à; (*of letter*) parvenir à (qn); (*contact*) joindre (qn); **to r. s.o.** (*over*) **sth** (*hand over*) passer qch à qn; **to r. out** (*one's arm*) (é)tendre; — *vi* (*extend*) s'étendre (**to** à); (*of voice*) porter; **to r. (out)** (é)tendre le bras (**for** pour prendre); — *n* portée *f*; Boxing allonge *f*; **within r. of** à portée de; (*near*) à proximité de; **within easy r.** (*object*) à portée de main; (*shops*) facilement accessible.

react [rɪˈækt] *vi* réagir. ◆**reaction** *n* réaction *f*. ◆**reactionary** *a* & *n* réactionnaire (*mf*).

reactor [rɪˈæktər] *n* réacteur *m*.

read [riːd] *vt* (*pt & pp* **read** [red]) lire; (*study*) Univ faire des études de; (*meter*) relever; (*of instrument*) indiquer; **to r. back** *or* **over** relire; **to r. out** lire (à haute voix); **to r. through** (*skim*) parcourir; **to r. up (on)** (*study*) étudier; — *vi* lire; **to r. well** (*of text*) se lire bien; **to have a r.** la lecture à qn; **to r. about** (*s.o., sth*) lire qch sur; **to r. for** (*degree*) Univ préparer; — *n* **to have a r.** Fam faire un peu de lecture; **this book's a**

good r. *Fam* ce livre est agréable à lire.
◆-ing n lecture f; (of meter) relevé m; (by instrument) indication f; (variant) variante f; – a (room) de lecture; **r. matter** choses fpl à lire; **r. lamp** lampe f de bureau or de chevet. **◆-able** a lisible. **◆-er** n lecteur, -trice mf; (book) livre m de lecture. **◆readership** n lecteurs mpl, public m.

readdress [riːəˈdrɛs] vt (letter) faire suivre.

readjust [riːəˈdʒʌst] vt (instrument) régler; (salary) réajuster; – vi se réadapter (**to** à). **◆-ment** n réglage m; réajustement m; réadaptation f.

readily [ˈrɛdɪlɪ] adv (willingly) volontiers; (easily) facilement. **◆readiness** n empressement m (**to do** à faire); **in r. for** prêt pour.

ready [ˈrɛdɪ] a (-ier, -iest) prêt (**to do** à faire, **for sth** à or pour qch); (quick) Fig prompt (**to do** à faire); **to get sth r.** préparer qch; **to get r.** se préparer (**for sth** à qch, **to do** à faire); **r. cash, r. money** argent m liquide; – n **at the r.** tout prêt. **◆r.-'cooked** a tout cuit. **◆r.-'made** a tout fait; **r.-made clothes** prêt-à-porter m inv.

real [rɪəl] a réel, véritable; (life, world etc) réel; **it's the r. thing** Fam c'est du vrai de vrai; **r. estate** Am immobilier m; – adv Fam vraiment; **r. stupid** vraiment bête; – n **for r.** Fam pour de vrai. **◆realism** n réalisme m. **◆realist** n réaliste mf. **◆rea-'listic** a réaliste. **◆rea'listically** adv avec réalisme.

reality [rɪˈælɪtɪ] n réalité f; **in r.** en réalité.

realize [ˈrɪəlaɪz] vt **1** (know) se rendre compte de, réaliser; (understand) comprendre (**that** que); **to r. that** (know) se rendre compte que. **2** (carry out, convert into cash) réaliser; (price) atteindre. **◆reali'zation** n **1** (prise f de) conscience f. **2** (of aim, assets) réalisation f.

really [ˈrɪəlɪ] adv vraiment; **is it r. true?** est-ce bien vrai?

realm [rɛlm] n (kingdom) royaume m; (of dreams etc) Fig monde m.

realtor [ˈrɪəltər] n Am agent m immobilier.

reap [riːp] vt (field, crop) moissonner; Fig récolter.

reappear [riːəˈpɪər] vi réapparaître.

reappraisal [riːəˈpreɪz(ə)l] n réévaluation f.

rear [rɪər] **1** n (back part) arrière m; (of column) queue f; **in** or **at the r.** à l'arrière (de); **from the r.** par derrière; – a arrière inv, de derrière; **r.-view mirror** rétroviseur m. **2** vt (family, animals etc) élever; (one's head) relever. **3** vi **to r. (up)** (of horse) se cabrer. **◆rearguard** n arrière-garde f.

rearrange [riːəˈreɪndʒ] vt réarranger.

reason [ˈriːz(ə)n] n (cause, sense) raison f; **the r. for/why** or **that . . .** la raison de/pour laquelle . . . ; **for no r.** sans raison; **that stands to r.** cela va sans dire, c'est logique; **within r.** avec modération; **to do everything within r. to . . .** faire tout ce qu'il est raisonnable de faire pour . . . ; **to have every r. to believe/etc** avoir tout lieu de croire/etc ; – vi **to r. with s.o.** raisonner qn; – vt **to r. that** calculer que. **◆-ing** n raisonnement m. **◆-able** a raisonnable. **◆-ably** adv raisonnablement; (fairly, rather) assez; **r. fit** en assez bonne forme.

reassure [riːəˈʃʊər] vt rassurer. **◆-ing** a rassurant. **◆reassurance** n réconfort m.

reawaken [riːəˈweɪk(ə)n] vt (interest etc) réveiller. **◆-ing** n réveil m.

rebate [ˈriːbeɪt] n (discount on purchase) ristourne f; (refund) remboursement m (partiel).

rebel [ˈrɛb(ə)l] a & n rebelle (mf); – [rɪˈbɛl] vi (-ll-) se rebeller (**against** contre). **◆re'bellion** n rébellion f. **◆re'bellious** a rebelle.

rebirth [ˈriːbɜːθ] n renaissance f.

rebound [rɪˈbaʊnd] vi (of ball) rebondir; (of stone) ricocher; (of lies, action etc) Fig retomber (**on sur**); – [ˈriːbaʊnd] n rebond m; ricochet m; **on the r.** (to marry s.o. etc) par dépit.

rebuff [rɪˈbʌf] vt repousser; – n rebuffade f.

rebuild [riːˈbɪld] vt (pt & pp rebuilt) reconstruire.

rebuke [rɪˈbjuːk] vt réprimander; – n réprimande f.

rebuttal [rɪˈbʌt(ə)l] n réfutation f.

recalcitrant [rɪˈkælsɪtrənt] a récalcitrant.

recall [rɪˈkɔːl] vt (call back) rappeler; (remember) se rappeler (**that** que, **doing** avoir fait); **to r. sth to s.o.** rappeler qch à qn; – n rappel m; **beyond r.** irrévocable.

recant [rɪˈkænt] vi se rétracter.

recap [riːˈkæp] vti (-pp-) récapituler; – n récapitulation f. **◆reca'pitulate** vti récapituler. **◆recapitu'lation** n récapitulation f.

recapture [riːˈkæptʃər] vt (prisoner etc) reprendre; (rediscover) retrouver; (recreate) recréer; – n (of prisoner) arrestation f.

reced/e [rɪˈsiːd] vi (into the distance) s'éloigner; (of floods) baisser. **◆-ing** a (forehead) fuyant; **his hair(line) is r.** son front se dégarnit.

receipt [rɪˈsiːt] n (for payment) reçu m (for de); (for letter, parcel) récépissé m, accusé *m* de réception; *pl (takings)* recettes *fpl*; **to acknowledge r.** accuser réception (**of** de); **on r. of** dès réception de.

receiv/e [rɪ'siːv] *vt* recevoir; *(stolen goods) Jur* receler. ◆**—ing** *n Jur* recel *m*. ◆**—er** *n Tel* combiné *m*; *Rad* récepteur *m*; *(of stolen goods) Jur* receleur, -euse *mf*; **to pick up or lift the r.** *Tel* décrocher.

recent ['riːsənt] *a* récent; **in r. months** ces mois-ci. ◆**—ly** *adv* récemment; **as r. as** pas plus tard que.

receptacle [rɪ'septək(ə)l] *n* récipient *m*.

reception [rɪ'sepʃ(ə)n] *n (receiving, welcome, party etc)* réception *f*; **r. desk** réception *f*; **r. room** salle *f* de séjour. ◆**receptionist** *n* réceptionniste *mf*. ◆**receptive** *a* réceptif (**to an idea**/*etc* à une idée/*etc*); **r. to s.o.** compréhensif envers qn.

recess [rɪ'ses, 'riːses] *n* **1** *(holiday)* vacances *fpl*; *Sch Am* récréation *f*. **2** *(alcove)* renfoncement *m*; *(nook)* & *Fig* recoin *m*.

recession [rɪ'seʃ(ə)n] *n Econ* récession *f*.

recharge [riː'tʃɑːdʒ] *vt (battery)* recharger.

recipe ['resɪpɪ] *n Culin* & *Fig* recette *f* (**for** de).

recipient [rɪ'sɪpɪənt] *n (of award, honour)* récipiendaire *m*.

reciprocal [rɪ'sɪprək(ə)l] *a* réciproque. ◆**reciprocate** *vt (compliment)* retourner; *(gesture)* faire à son tour; – *vi (do the same)* en faire autant.

recital [rɪ'saɪt(ə)l] *n Mus* récital *m*.

recite [rɪ'saɪt] *vt (poem etc)* réciter; *(list)* énumérer. ◆**reci'tation** *n* récitation *f*.

reckless ['rekləs] *a (rash)* imprudent. ◆**—ly** *adv* imprudemment.

reckon ['rek(ə)n] *vt (count)* compter; *(calculate)* calculer; *(consider)* considérer; *(think) Fam* penser (**that** que); – *vi* compter; calculer; **to r. with** *(take into account)* compter avec; *(deal with)* avoir affaire à; **to r. on/without** compter sur/sans; **to r. on doing** *Fam* compter or penser faire. ◆**—ing** *n* calcul(s) *m(pl)*.

reclaim [rɪ'kleɪm] *vt* **1** *(land)* mettre en valeur; *(from sea)* assécher. **2** *(ask for back)* réclamer; *(luggage at airport)* récupérer.

reclin/e [rɪ'klaɪn] *vi (of person)* être allongé; *(of head)* être appuyé; – *vt (head)* appuyer (**on** sur). ◆**—ing** *a (seat)* à dossier inclinable or réglable.

recluse [rɪ'kluːs] *n* reclus, -use *mf*.

recognize ['rekəgnaɪz] *vt* reconnaître (**by** à, **that** que). ◆**recog'nition** *n* reconnaissance *f*; **to change beyond** or **out of all r.** devenir méconnaissable; **to gain r.** être

reconnu. ◆**recognizable** *a* reconnaissable.

recoil [rɪ'kɔɪl] *vi* reculer (**from doing** à l'idée de faire).

recollect [rekə'lekt] *vt* se souvenir de; **to r. that** se souvenir que; – *vi* se souvenir. ◆**recollection** *n* souvenir *m*.

recommend [rekə'mend] *vt (praise, support, advise)* recommander (**to** à, **for** pour); **to r. s.o. to do** recommander à qn de faire. ◆**recommen'dation** *n* recommandation *f*.

recompense ['rekəmpens] *vt (reward)* récompenser; – *n* récompense *f*.

reconcile ['rekənsaɪl] *vt (person)* réconcilier (**with, to** avec); *(opinion)* concilier (**with** avec); **to r. oneself to sth** se résigner à qch. ◆**reconcili'ation** *n* réconciliation *f*.

reconditioned [riːkən'dɪʃ(ə)nd] *a (engine)* refait (à neuf).

reconnaissance [rɪ'kɒnɪsəns] *n Mil* reconnaissance *f*. ◆**reconnoitre** [rekə'nɔɪtər] *vt Mil* reconnaître.

reconsider [riːkən'sɪdər] *vt* reconsidérer; – *vi* revenir sur sa décision.

reconstruct [riːkən'strʌkt] *vt (crime)* reconstituer.

record **1** ['rekɔːd] *n (disc)* disque *m*; **r. library** discothèque *f*; **r. player** électrophone *m*. **2** *n Sp* & *Fig* record *m*; – *a (attendance, time etc)* record *inv*. **3** *n (report)* rapport *m*; *(register)* registre *m*; *(recording on tape etc)* enregistrement *m*; *(mention)* mention *f*; *(note)* note *f*; *(background)* antécédents *mpl*; *(case history)* dossier *m*; *(police)* **r.** casier *m* judiciaire; *(public)* **records** archives *fpl*; **to make** or **keep a r. of** noter; **on r.** *(fact, event)* attesté; **off the r.** à titre confidentiel; **their safety r.** leurs résultats *mpl* en matière de sécurité. **4** [rɪ'kɔːd] *vt (on tape etc, in register etc)* enregistrer; *(in diary)* noter; *(relate)* rapporter (**that** que); – *vi (on tape etc)* enregistrer. ◆**—ed** *a* enregistré; *(prerecorded) TV* en différé; *(fact)* attesté; **letter sent (by) r. delivery** = lettre *f* avec avis de réception. ◆**—ing** *n* enregistrement *m*. ◆**—er** *n Mus* flûte *f* à bec; *(tape)* **r.** magnétophone *m*.

recount **1** [rɪ'kaʊnt] *vt (relate)* raconter. **2** ['riːkaʊnt] *n Pol* nouveau dépouillement *m* du scrutin.

recoup [rɪ'kuːp] *vt (loss)* récupérer.

recourse [rɪ'kɔːs] *n* recours *m*; **to have r. to** avoir recours à.

recover [rɪ'kʌvər] **1** *vt (get back)* retrouver, récupérer. **2** *vi (from shock etc)* se remettre; *(get better) Med* se remettre (**from** de); *(of* *economy, country*) se redresser; (*of currency*) remonter. ◆**recovery** *n* **1** *Econ* redressement *m*. **2 the r. of sth** (*getting back*) la récupération de qch.

recreate [riːkriˈeɪt] *vt* recréer.

recreation [rekrɪˈeɪʃ(ə)n] *n* récréation *f*. ◆**recreational** (*activity etc*) de loisir.

recrimination [rɪkrɪmɪˈneɪʃ(ə)n] *n Jur* contre-accusation *f*.

recruit [rɪˈkruːt] *n* recrue *f*; – *vt* recruter; **to r. s.o. to do** (*persuade*) *Fig* embaucher qn pour faire. ◆—**ment** *n* recrutement *m*.

rectangle [ˈrektæŋg(ə)l] *n* rectangle *m*. ◆**recˈtangular** *a* rectangulaire.

rectify [ˈrektɪfaɪ] *vt* rectifier. ◆**rectifiˈcation** *n* rectification *f*.

rector [ˈrektər] *n Rel* curé *m*; *Univ* président *m*.

recuperate [rɪˈkuːpəreɪt] *vi* récupérer (ses forces); – *vt* récupérer.

recur [rɪˈkɜːr] *vi* (-**rr**-) (*of theme*) revenir; (*of event*) se reproduire; (*of illness*) réapparaître. ◆**recurrence** [rɪˈkʌrəns] *n* répétition *f*; (*of illness*) réapparition *f*. ◆**recurrent** *a* fréquent.

recycle [riːˈsaɪk(ə)l] *vt* (*material*) recycler.

red [red] *a* (**redder, reddest**) rouge; (*hair*) roux; **to turn** *or* **go r.** rougir; **r. light** (*traffic light*) feu *m* rouge; **R. Cross** Croix-Rouge *f*; **R. Indian** Peau-Rouge *mf*; **r. tape** bureaucratie *f*; – *n* (*colour*) rouge *m*; **R.** (*person*) *Pol* rouge *mf*; **in the r.** (*firm, account*) en déficit; (*person*) à découvert. ◆**r.-ˈfaced** *a Fig* rouge de confusion. ◆**r.-ˈhanded** *adv* **caught r.-handed** pris en flagrant délit. ◆**r.-ˈhot** *a* brûlant. ◆**redden** *vti* rougir. ◆**reddish** *a* rougeâtre; (*hair*) carotte. ◆**redness** *n* rougeur *f*; (*of hair*) rousseur *f*.

redcurrant [redˈkʌrənt] *n* groseille *f*.

redecorate [riːˈdekəreɪt] *vt* (*room etc*) refaire; – *vi* refaire la peinture et les papiers.

redeem [rɪˈdiːm] *vt* (*restore to favour, free, pay off*) racheter; (*convert into cash*) réaliser; **redeeming feature** point *m* favorable. ◆**redemption** *n* rachat *m*; réalisation *f*; *Rel* rédemption *f*.

redeploy [riːdɪˈplɔɪ] *vt* (*staff*) réorganiser; (*troops*) redéployer.

redhead [ˈredhed] *n* roux *m*, rousse *f*.

redirect [riːdaɪˈrekt] *vt* (*mail*) faire suivre.

redo [riːˈduː] *vt* (*pt* **redid**, *pp* **redone**) refaire.

redress [rɪˈdres] *n* **to seek r.** demander réparation; – *vt* **to r. the balance** rétablir l'équilibre; **to r. a wrong** réparer une injustice.

reduce [rɪˈdjuːs] *vt* réduire (**to** à, **by** de); (*temperature*) faire baisser; **at a reduced**

price (*ticket*) à prix réduit; (*goods*) au rabais. ◆**reduction** *n* réduction *f*; (*of temperature*) baisse *f*; (*discount*) rabais *m*.

redundant [rɪˈdʌndənt] *a* (*not needed*) superflu, de trop; **to make r.** (*workers*) mettre en chômage, licencier. ◆**redundancy** *n* (*of workers*) licenciement *m*; **r. pay(ment)** indemnité *f* de licenciement.

re-echo [riːˈekəʊ] *vi* résonner; – *vt* (*sound*) répercuter; *Fig* répéter.

reed [riːd] *n* **1** *Bot* roseau *m*. **2** *Mus* anche *f*; – *a* (*instrument*) à anche.

re-educate [riːˈedjʊkeɪt] *vt* (*criminal, limb*) rééduquer.

reef [riːf] *n* récif *m*, écueil *m*.

reek [riːk] *vi* puer; **to r. of** (*smell*) & *Fig* puer; – *n* puanteur *f*.

reel [riːl] **1** *n* (*of thread, film*) bobine *f*; (*film itself*) Cin bande *f*; (*of hose*) dévidoir *m*; (*for fishing line*) moulinet *m*. **2** *vi* (*stagger*) chanceler; (*of mind*) chavirer; (*of head*) tourner. **3** *vt* **to r. off** (*rattle off*) débiter à toute vitesse.

re-elect [riːɪˈlekt] *vt* réélire.

re-entry [riːˈentrɪ] *n* (*of spacecraft*) rentrée *f*.

re-establish [riːɪˈstæblɪʃ] *vt* rétablir.

ref [ref] *n Sp Fam* arbitre *m*.

refectory [rɪˈfektərɪ] *n* réfectoire *m*.

refer [rɪˈfɜːr] *vt* (-**rr**-) **to r. to** (*allude to*) faire allusion à; (*speak of*) parler de; (*apply to*) s'appliquer à; (*consult*) se reporter à; – *vt* **to r. sth to** (*submit*) soumettre qch à; **to r. s.o. to** (*office, article etc*) renvoyer qn à. ◆**refeˈree** *n Sp* arbitre *m*; (*for job etc*) répondant, -ante *mf*; – *vt Sp* arbitrer. ◆**ˈreference** *n* (*in book, recommendation*) référence *f*; (*allusion*) allusion *f* (**to** à); (*mention*) mention *f* (**to** de); (*connection*) rapport *m* (**to** avec); **in** *or* **with r. to** concernant; *Com* suite à; **terms of r.** (*of person, investigating body*) compétence *f*; (*of law*) étendue *f*; **r. book** livre *m* de référence.

referendum [refəˈrendəm] *n* référendum *m*.

refill [riːˈfɪl] *vt* remplir (à nouveau); (*lighter, pen etc*) recharger; – [ˈriːfɪl] *n* recharge *f*; **a r.** (*drink*) Fam un autre verre.

refine [rɪˈfaɪn] *vt* (*oil, sugar, manners*) raffiner; (*metal, ore*) affiner; (*technique, machine*) perfectionner; – *vi* **to r. upon** raffiner sur. ◆**refinement** *n* (*of person*) raffinement *m*; (*of sugar, oil*) raffinage *m*; (*of technique*) perfectionnement *m*; *pl* (*improvements*) Tech améliorations *fpl*. ◆**refinery** *n* raffinerie *f*.

refit [riːˈfɪt] *vt* (-**tt**-) (*ship*) remettre en état.

reflate [riːˈfleɪt] *vt* (*economy*) relancer.

reflect [rɪˈflekt] **1** vt (light) & Fig refléter; (of mirror) réfléchir, refléter; **to r. sth on s.o.** (credit, honour) faire rejaillir qch sur qn; — vi **to r. on s.o.**, **be reflected on s.o.** (rebound) rejaillir sur qn. **2** vi (think) réfléchir (on à); — vt **to r. that** penser que. ◆**reflection** n (thought, criticism) réflexion (on sur); en r. tout bien réfléchi. **2** (image) & Fig reflet m; (reflecting) réflexion f (of de). ◆**reflector** n réflecteur m. ◆**reflexion** n = **reflection**.
◆**reflexive** a (verb) Gram réfléchi.

reflex [ˈriːfleks] n & a réflexe (m); **r. action** réflexe m.

refloat [riːˈfləʊt] vt (ship) & Com renflouer.

reform [rɪˈfɔːm] n réforme f; — vt réformer; (person, conduct) corriger; — vi (of person) se réformer. ◆—**er** n réformateur, -trice mf.

refrain [rɪˈfreɪn] **1** vi s'abstenir (from doing de faire). **2** n Mus & Fig refrain m.

refresh [rɪˈfreʃ] vt (of bath, drink) rafraîchir; (of sleep, rest) délasser; **to r. oneself** (drink) se rafraîchir; **to r. one's memory** se rafraîchir la mémoire. ◆—**ing** a rafraîchissant; (sleep) réparateur; (pleasant) agréable; (original) nouveau. ◆—**er** a (course) de recyclage. ◆—**ments** npl (drinks) rafraîchissements mpl; (snacks) collation f.

refrigerate [rɪˈfrɪdʒəreɪt] vt réfrigérer.
◆**refrigerator** n réfrigérateur m.

refuel [riːˈfjuːəl] vi (-ll-, Am -l-) Av se ravitailler; — vt Av ravitailler.

refuge [ˈrefjuːdʒ] n refuge m; **to take r.** se réfugier (in dans). ◆**refu'gee** n réfugié, -ée mf.

refund [rɪˈfʌnd] vt rembourser; — [ˈriːfʌnd] n remboursement m.

refurbish [riːˈfɜːbɪʃ] vt remettre à neuf.

refuse¹ [rɪˈfjuːz] vt refuser (s.o. sth qch à qn, to do sth faire); — vi refuser. ◆**refusal** n refus m.

refuse² [ˈrefjuːs] n (rubbish) ordures fpl, détritus m; (waste materials) déchets mpl; **r. collector** éboueur m; **r. dump** dépôt m d'ordures.

refute [rɪˈfjuːt] vt réfuter.

regain [rɪˈgeɪn] vt (favour, lost ground) regagner; (strength) récupérer, retrouver, reprendre; (health, sight) retrouver; (consciousness) reprendre.

regal [ˈriːg(ə)l] a royal, majestueux.

regalia [rɪˈgeɪlɪə] npl insignes mpl (royaux).

regard [rɪˈgɑːd] vt (consider) considérer, regarder; (concern) regarder; **as regards** en ce qui concerne; — n considération f (for pour); **to have (a) great r. for** avoir de l'estime pour; **without r. to** sans égard

pour; **with r. to** en ce qui concerne; **to give** or **send one's regards to** (greetings) faire ses hommages à. ◆—**ing** prep en ce qui concerne. ◆—**less 1** a r. of sans tenir compte de. **2** adv (all the same) Fam quand même.

regatta [rɪˈgætə] n régates fpl.

regency [ˈriːdʒənsɪ] n régence f.

regenerate [rɪˈdʒenəreɪt] vt régénérer.

reggae [ˈregeɪ] n (music) reggae m; — a (group etc) reggae inv.

régime [reɪˈʒiːm] n Pol régime m.

regiment [ˈredʒɪmənt] n régiment m.
◆**regi'mental** a régimentaire, du régiment. ◆**regimen'tation** n discipline f excessive.

region [ˈriːdʒ(ə)n] n région f; **in the r. of** (about) Fig environ; **in the r. of £500** dans les 500 livres. ◆**regional** a régional.

register [ˈredʒɪstər] n registre m; Sch cahier m d'appel; **electoral r.** liste f électorale; — vt (record, note) enregistrer; (birth, death) déclarer; (vehicle) immatriculer; (express) exprimer; (indicate) indiquer; (letter) recommander; (realize) Fam réaliser; — vi (enrol) s'inscrire; (in hotel) signer le registre; **it hasn't registered (with me)** Fam je n'ai pas encore réalisé ça. ◆—**ed** a (member) inscrit; (letter) recommandé; **r. trademark** marque f déposée. ◆**regi'strar** n officier m de l'état civil; Univ secrétaire m général. ◆**regi'stration** n enregistrement m; (enrolment) inscription f; **r. (number)** Aut numéro m d'immatriculation; **r. document** Aut = carte f grise. ◆**registry** a & n **r. (office)** bureau m de l'état civil.

regress [rɪˈgres] vi régresser.

regret [rɪˈgret] vt (-tt-) regretter (doing, to do de faire; **that que** (+ sub)); **I r. to hear that** ... je suis désolé d'apprendre que ...; — n regret m. ◆**regretfully** adv r., I ... à mon grand regret, je .... ◆**regrettable** a regrettable (that que (+ sub)). ◆**regrettably** adv malheureusement; (poor, ill etc) fâcheusement.

regroup [riːˈgruːp] vi se regrouper; — vt regrouper.

regular [ˈregjʊlər] a (steady, even) régulier; (surface) uni; (usual) habituel; (price, size) normal; (reader, listener) fidèle; (staff) permanent; (fool, slave etc) Fam vrai; **a r. guy** Am Fam un chic type; — n (in bar etc) habitué, -ée mf; Mil soldat m. ◆**regu-'larity** n régularité f. ◆**regularly** adv régulièrement.

regulate [ˈregjʊleɪt] vt régler. ◆**regu-**

'lation 1 n (rule) règlement m; – a (uniform etc) réglementaire. 2 n (regulating) réglage m.
rehabilitate [riːhəˈbɪlɪteɪt] vt (in public esteem) réhabiliter; (wounded soldier etc) réadapter.
rehash [riːˈhæʃ] vt (text) Pej remanier; Culin réchauffer; – [ˈriːhæʃ] n a r. Culin & Fig du réchauffé.
rehearse [rɪˈhɜːs] vt Th répéter; (prepare) Fig préparer; – vi Th répéter. ◆**rehearsal** n Th répétition f.
reign [reɪn] n règne m; in or during the r. of sous le règne de; – vi régner (over sur).
reimburse [riːɪmˈbɜːs] vt rembourser (for de). ◆—ment n remboursement m.
rein [reɪn] n reins rênes fpl; to give free r. to Fig donner libre cours à.
reindeer [ˈreɪndɪər] n inv renne m.
reinforce [riːɪnˈfɔːs] vt renforcer (with de); reinforced concrete béton m armé. ◆—ment n renforcement m (of de); pl Mil renforts mpl.
reinstate [riːɪnˈsteɪt] vt réintégrer. ◆—ment n réintégration f.
reissue [riːˈɪʃuː] vt (book) rééditer.
reiterate [riːˈɪtəreɪt] vt (say again) réitérer.
reject [rɪˈdʒekt] vt (refuse to accept) rejeter; (as useless) refuser; – [ˈriːdʒekt] n Com article m de rebut; (article) de deuxième choix; r. shop solderie f. ◆**re'jection** n rejet m; (of candidate etc) refus m.
rejoice [rɪˈdʒɔɪs] vi se réjouir (over or at sth de qch, in doing de faire). ◆—ing(s) n(pl) réjouissance(s) f(pl).
rejoin [rɪˈdʒɔɪn] 1 vt (join up with) rejoindre. 2 vi (retort) répliquer.
rejuvenate [rɪˈdʒuːvəneɪt] vt rajeunir.
rekindle [riːˈkɪnd(ə)l] vt rallumer.
relapse [rɪˈlæps] n Med rechute f; – vi Med rechuter; to r. into Fig retomber dans.
relate [rɪˈleɪt] 1 vt (narrate) raconter (that que); (report) rapporter (that que). 2 vt (connect) établir un rapport entre (faits etc); to r. sth to (link) rattacher qch à; – vi to r. to (apply to) se rapporter à; (get on with) communiquer or s'entendre avec. ◆—ed a (linked) lié (to à); (languages, styles) apparentés; to be r. to (by family) être parent de.
relation [rɪˈleɪʃ(ə)n] n (relative) parent, -ente mf; (relationship) rapport m, relation f (between entre, with avec); what r. are you to him? quel est ton lien de parenté avec lui?; international/etc relations relations fpl internationales/etc. ◆**relationship** n (kinship) lien(s) m(pl) de parenté; (rela-

tions) relations fpl, rapports mpl; (connection) rapport m; in r. to relativement à.
relative [ˈrelətɪv] n (person) parent, -ente mf; – a relatif (to à); (respective) respectif; r. to (compared to) relativement à; to be r. to (depend on) être fonction de. ◆**relatively** adv relativement.
relax [rɪˈlæks] 1 vt (person, mind) détendre; – vi se détendre; r.! (calm down) Fam du calme! 2 vt (grip, pressure etc) relâcher; (restrictions, principles, control) assouplir. ◆—ed a (person, atmosphere) décontracté, détendu. ◆—ing a (bath etc) délassant. ◆**rela'xation** n 1 (rest, recreation) détente f; (of body) décontraction f. 2 (of grip etc) relâchement m; (of restrictions etc) assouplissement m.
relay [ˈriːleɪ] n relais m; r. race course f de relais; – vt (message etc) Rad retransmettre, Fig transmettre (to à).
release [rɪˈliːs] vt (free) libérer (from de); (bomb, s.o.'s hand) lâcher; (spring) déclencher; (brake) desserrer; (film, record) sortir; (news, facts) publier; (smoke, trapped person) dégager; (tension) éliminer; – n libération f; (of film, book) sortie f (of de); (record) nouveau disque m; (film) nouveau film m; (relief) Fig délivrance f; Psy défoulement m; press r. communiqué m de presse; to be on general r. (of film) passer dans toutes les salles.
relegate [ˈrelɪgeɪt] vt reléguer (to à).
relent [rɪˈlent] vi (be swayed) se laisser fléchir (change one's mind) revenir sur sa décision. ◆—less a implacable.
relevant [ˈreləvənt] a (apt) pertinent (to à); (fitting) approprié; (useful) utile; (significant) important; that's not r. ça n'a rien à voir. ◆**relevance** n pertinence f (to à); (significance) intérêt m; (connection) rapport m (to avec).
reliable [rɪˈlaɪəb(ə)l] a (person, information, firm) sérieux, sûr, fiable; (machine) fiable. ◆**relia'bility** n (of person) sérieux m, fiabilité f; (of machine, information, firm) fiabilité f. ◆**reliably** adv to be r. informed that apprendre de source sûre que.
reliance [rɪˈlaɪəns] n (trust) confiance f (on en); (dependence) dépendance f (on de). ◆**reliant** a to be r. on (dependent) dépendre de; (trusting) avoir confiance en.
relic [ˈrelɪk] n relique f; pl (of the past) vestiges mpl.
relief [rɪˈliːf] n (from pain etc) soulagement m (from à); (help, supplies) secours m; (in art) & Geog relief m; tax r. dégrèvement m; to be on r. Am recevoir l'aide sociale; – a

(train etc) supplémentaire; (work etc) de
secours; r. road route f de délestage.
◆relieve vt (pain etc) soulager; (boredom)
dissiper; (situation) remédier à; (take over
from) relayer (qn); (help) secourir, soulager; to r. s.o. of (rid) débarrasser qn de;
to r. s.o. of his post relever qn de ses fonctions; to r. congestion in Aut décongestionner; to r. oneself (go to the lavatory) Hum
Fam se soulager.

religion [rɪ'lɪdʒ(ə)n] n religion f. ◆religious a religieux; (war, book) de religion.
◆religiously adv religieusement.

relinquish [rɪ'lɪŋkwɪʃ] vt (give up) abandonner; (let go) lâcher.

relish ['relɪʃ] n (liking, taste) goût m (for
pour); (pleasure) plaisir m; (seasoning)
assaisonnement m; to eat with r. manger de
bon appétit; − vt (food etc) savourer; (like)
aimer (doing faire).

relocate [riːləʊ'keɪt] vi (move to new place)
déménager; to r. in or to s'installer à.

reluctant [rɪ'lʌktənt] a (greeting, gift, promise) accordé à contrecœur; to be r. to do
être peu disposé à faire; a r. teacher/etc un
professeur/etc malgré lui. ◆reluctance n
répugnance f (to do à faire). ◆reluctantly
adv à contrecœur.

rely [rɪ'laɪ] vi to r. on (count on) compter sur;
(be dependent upon) dépendre de.

remain [rɪ'meɪn] 1 vi rester. 2 npl restes mpl;
mortal r. dépouille f mortelle. ◆−ing a
qui reste(nt). ◆remainder n 1 reste m; the
r. (remaining people) les autres mfpl; the r.
of the girls les autres filles. 2 (book)
invendu m soldé.

remand [rɪ'mɑːnd] vt to r. (in custody) Jur
placer en détention préventive; − n on r. en
détention préventive.

remark [rɪ'mɑːk] n remarque f; − vt to r. on
faire des remarques sur. ◆−able a remarquable (for par). ◆−ably adv remarquablement.

remarry [riː'mærɪ] vi se remarier.

remedial [rɪ'miːdɪəl] a (class) Sch de
rattrapage; (measure) de redressement;
(treatment) Med thérapeutique.

remedy ['remɪdɪ] vt remédier à; − n remède
m (for contre, à, de).

remember [rɪ'membər] vt se souvenir de, se
rappeler; (commemorate) commémorer; to
r. that/doing se rappeler que/d'avoir fait;
to r. to do (not forget to do) penser à faire; r.
me to him or her! rappelle-moi à son bon
souvenir!; − vi se souvenir, se rappeler.
◆remembrance n (memory) souvenir m;
in r. of en souvenir de.

remind [rɪ'maɪnd] vt rappeler (s.o. of sth qch
à qn, s.o. that à qn que); to r. s.o. to do faire
penser à qn à faire; that or which reminds
me! à propos! ◆−er n (of event & letter)
rappel m; (note to do sth) pense-bête m; it's
a r. (for him or her) that . . . c'est pour lui
rappeler que. . . .

reminisce [remɪ'nɪs] vi raconter or se
rappeler ses souvenirs (about de). ◆reminiscences npl réminiscences fpl.
◆reminiscent a r. of qui rappelle.

remiss [rɪ'mɪs] a négligent.

remit [rɪ'mɪt] vt (-tt-) (money) envoyer.
◆remission n Jur remise f (de peine);
Med Rel rémission f. ◆remittance n
(sum) paiement m.

remnant ['remnənt] n (remaining part) reste
m; (trace) vestige m; (of fabric) coupon m;
(oddment) fin f de série.

remodel [riː'mɒd(ə)l] vt (-ll-, Am -l-) remodeler.

remonstrate ['remənstreɪt] vi to r. with s.o.
faire des remontrances à qn.

remorse [rɪ'mɔːs] n remords m(pl) (for
pour); without r. sans pitié. ◆−less a
implacable. ◆−lessly adv (to hit etc)
implacablement.

remote [rɪ'məʊt] a (-er, -est) 1 (far-off)
lointain, éloigné; (isolated) isolé; (aloof)
distant; r. from loin de; r. control télécommande f. 2 (slight) petit, vague; not the
remotest idea pas la moindre idée. ◆−ly
adv (slightly) vaguement, un peu; (situated)
au loin; not r. aware/etc nullement
conscient/etc. ◆−ness n éloignement m;
isolement m; Fig attitude f distante.

remould ['riːməʊld] n pneu m rechapé.

remove [rɪ'muːv] vt (clothes, stain etc)
enlever (from s.o. à qn, from sth de qch);
(withdraw) retirer; (lead away) emmener
(to à); (furniture) déménager; (obstacle,
threat, word) supprimer; (fear, doubt)
dissiper; (employee) renvoyer; (far)
removed from loin de. ◆removable a
(lining etc) amovible. ◆removal n enlèvement m; déménagement m; suppression f;
r. man déménageur m; r. van camion m de
déménagement. ◆remover n (for
make-up) démaquillant m; (for nail polish)
dissolvant m; (for paint) décapant m; (for
stains) détachant m.

remunerate [rɪ'mjuːnəreɪt] vt rémunérer.
◆remune'ration n rémunération f.

renaissance [rə'neɪsəns] n (in art etc)
renaissance f.

rename [riː'neɪm] vt (street etc) rebaptiser.

render ['rendər] vt (give, make) rendre; Mus

interpréter; *(help)* prêter. **◆—ing** *n Mus* interprétation *f*; *(translation)* traduction *f*.

rendez-vous ['rɒndɪvuː, *pl* -vuːz] *n inv* rendez-vous *m inv*.

renegade ['renɪgeɪd] *n* renégat, -ate *mf*.

reneg(u)e [rɪ'niːg] *vi* **to r. on** *(promise etc)* revenir sur.

renew [rɪ'njuː] *vt* renouveler; *(resume)* reprendre; *(library book)* renouveler le prêt de. **◆—ed** *a (efforts)* renouvelés; *(attempt)* nouveau; **with r. vigour**/*etc* avec un regain de vigueur/*etc*. **◆renewable** *a* renouvelable. **◆renewal** *n* renouvellement *m*; *(resumption)* reprise *f*; *(of strength etc)* regain *m*.

renounce [rɪ'naʊns] *vt (give up)* renoncer à; *(disown)* renier.

renovate ['renəveɪt] *vt (house)* rénover, restaurer; *(painting)* restaurer. **◆reno'vation** *n* rénovation *f*; restauration *f*.

renown [rɪ'naʊn] *n* renommée *f*. **◆renowned** *a* renommé (**for** pour).

rent [rent] *n* loyer *m*; *(of television)* (prix *m* de) location *f*; **r. collector** encaisseur *m* de loyers; — *vt* louer; **to r. out** louer; — *vi (of house etc)* se louer. **◆r.-'free** *adv* sans payer de loyer; — *a* gratuit. **◆rental** *n (of television)* (prix *m* de) location *f*; *(of telephone)* abonnement *m*.

renunciation [rɪnʌnsɪ'eɪʃ(ə)n] *n (giving up)* renonciation *f* (**of** à); *(disowning)* reniement *m* (**of** de).

reopen [riː'əʊpən] *vti* rouvrir. **◆—ing** *n* réouverture *f*.

reorganize [riː'ɔːgənaɪz] *vt* réorganiser.

rep [rep] *n Fam* représentant, -ante *mf* de commerce.

repaid [riː'peɪd] *see* **repay.**

repair [rɪ'peər] *vt* réparer; — *n* réparation *f*; **beyond r.** irréparable; **in good/bad r.** en bon/mauvais état; **'road under r.'** *Aut* 'travaux'; **r. man** réparateur *m*; **r. woman** réparatrice *f*.

reparation [repə'reɪʃ(ə)n] *n* réparation *f* (**for** de); *pl Mil Hist* réparations *fpl*.

repartee [repɑː'tiː] *n (sharp reply)* repartie *f*.

repatriate [riː'pætrieɪt] *vt* rapatrier.

repay [riː'peɪ] *vt (pt & pp* **repaid***)* *(pay back)* rembourser; *(kindness)* payer de retour; *(reward)* récompenser (**for** de). **◆—ment** *n* remboursement *m*; récompense *f*.

repeal [rɪ'piːl] *vt (law)* abroger; — *n* abrogation *f*.

repeat [rɪ'piːt] *vt* répéter (**that** que); *(promise, threat)* réitérer; *(class)* *Sch* redoubler; **to r. oneself** *or* **itself** se répéter; — *vi* répéter; **to r. on s.o.** *(of food)* *Fam* revenir à

qn; — *n TV Rad* rediffusion *f*; — *a (performance)* deuxième. **◆—ed** *a* répété; *(efforts)* renouvelés. **◆—edly** *adv* à maintes reprises.

repel [rɪ'pel] *vt* (**-ll-**) repousser. **◆repellent** *a* repoussant; **insect r.** insectifuge *m*.

repent [rɪ'pent] *vi* se repentir (**of** de). **◆repentance** *n* repentir *m*. **◆repentant** *a* repentant.

repercussion [riːpə'kʌʃ(ə)n] *n* répercussion *f*.

repertoire ['repətwɑːr] *n Th & Fig* répertoire *m*. **◆repertory** *n Th & Fig* répertoire *m*; **r. (theatre)** théâtre *m* de répertoire.

repetition [repɪ'tɪʃ(ə)n] *n* répétition *f*. **◆repetitious** *a*, **◆re'petitive** *a (speech etc)* répétitif.

replace [rɪ'pleɪs] *vt (take the place of)* remplacer (**by, with** par); *(put back)* remettre, replacer; *(receiver)* *Tel* raccrocher. **◆—ment** *n* remplacement *m* (**of** de); *(person)* remplaçant, -ante *mf*; *(machine part)* pièce *f* de rechange.

replay ['riːpleɪ] *n Sp* match *m* rejoué; **(instant** *or* **action) r.** *TV* répétition *f* immédiate (au ralenti).

replenish [rɪ'plenɪʃ] *vt (refill)* remplir (de nouveau) (**with** de); *(renew)* renouveler.

replete [rɪ'pliːt] *a* **r. with** rempli de; **r. (with food)** rassasié.

replica ['replɪkə] *n* copie *f* exacte.

reply [rɪ'plaɪ] *vti* répondre; — *n* réponse *f*; **in r.** en réponse (**to** à).

report [rɪ'pɔːt] *n (account)* rapport *m*; *(of meeting)* compte rendu *m*; *Journ TV Rad* reportage *m*; *Pol* enquête *f*; *Sch Met* bulletin *m*; *(rumour)* rumeur *f*; *(of gun)* détonation *f*; — *vt (give account of)* rapporter, rendre compte de; *(announce)* annoncer **(that** que); *(notify)* signaler (**to** à); *(denounce)* dénoncer (**to** à); *(event)* *Journ* faire un reportage sur; — *vi* faire un rapport *or Journ* un reportage (**on** sur); *(go)* se présenter (**to** à, **to s.o.** chez qn, **for work** au travail). **◆—ed** *a (speech)* *Gram* indirect; **it is r.** that on dit que; **r. missing** porté disparu. **◆—edly** *adv* à ce qu'on dit. **◆—ing** *n Journ* reportage *m*. **◆—er** *n* reporter *m*.

repose [rɪ'pəʊz] *n Lit* repos *m*.

repossess [riːpə'zes] *vt Jur* reprendre possession de.

reprehensible [reprɪ'hensəb(ə)l] *a* répréhensible.

represent [reprɪ'zent] *vt* représenter. **◆represen'tation** *n* représentation *f*; *pl (complaints)* remontrances *fpl*. **◆repre-**

sentative *a* représentatif (**of** de); – *n* représentant, -ante *mf*; *Pol Am* député *m*.

repress [rɪ'pres] *vt* réprimer; (*feeling*) refouler. ◆**repressive** *a* répressif.

reprieve [rɪ'priːv] *n Jur* sursis *m*; *Fig* répit *m*, sursis *m*; – *vt* accorder un sursis *m* à *ou Fig* un répit à.

reprimand ['reprɪmɑːnd] *n* réprimande *f*; – *vt* réprimander.

reprint ['riːprɪnt] *n* (*reissue*) réimpression *f*; – *vt* réimprimer.

reprisal [rɪ'praɪz(ə)l] *n* **reprisals** représailles *fpl*; **in r. for** en représailles de.

reproach [rɪ'prəʊtʃ] *n* (*blame*) reproche *m*; (*shame*) honte *f*; **beyond r.** sans reproche; – *vt* reprocher (**s.o. for sth** qch à qn). ◆**reproachful** *a* réprobateur. ◆**reproachfully** *adv* d'un ton *ou* d'un air réprobateur.

reproduce [riːprə'djuːs] *vt* reproduire; – *vi Biol Bot* se reproduire. ◆**reproduction** *n* (*of sound etc*) & *Biol Bot* reproduction *f*. ◆**reproductive** *a* reproducteur.

reptile ['reptaɪl] *n* reptile *m*.

republic [rɪ'pʌblɪk] *n* république *f*. ◆**republican** *a* & *n* républicain, -aine (*mf*).

repudiate [rɪ'pjuːdɪeɪt] *vt* (*offer*) repousser; (*accusation*) rejeter; (*spouse, idea*) répudier.

repugnant [rɪ'pʌgnənt] *a* répugnant; **he's r. to me** il me répugne. ◆**repugnance** *n* répugnance *f* (**for** pour).

repulse [rɪ'pʌls] *vt* repousser. ◆**repulsion** *n* répulsion *f*. ◆**repulsive** *a* repoussant.

reputable ['repjʊtəb(ə)l] *a* de bonne réputation. ◆**re'pute** *n* réputation *f*; **of r.** de bonne réputation. ◆**re'puted** *a* réputé (**to be** pour être). ◆**re'putedly** *adv* à ce qu'on dit.

reputation [repjʊ'teɪʃ(ə)n] *n* réputation *f*; **to have a r. for frankness/***etc* avoir la réputation d'être franc/*etc*.

request [rɪ'kwest] *n* demande *f* (**for** de); **on r.** sur demande; **on s.o.'s r.** à la demande de qn; **by popular r.** à la demande générale; **r. stop** (*for bus*) arrêt *m* facultatif; – *vt* demander (**from** *or* **of s.o.** à qn, **s.o. to do** à qn de faire).

requiem ['rekwɪəm] *n* requiem *m inv*.

requir/e [rɪ'kwaɪər] *vt* (*necessitate*) demander; (*demand*) exiger; (*of person*) avoir besoin de (*qch, qn*); (*staff*) rechercher; **to r. sth of s.o.** (*order*) exiger qch de qn; **to r. s.o. to do** exiger de qn qu'il fasse; (*ask*) demander à qn de faire; **if required** s'il le faut. ◆**–ed** *a* requis, exigé. ◆**–ement** *n*

(*need*) exigence *f*; (*condition*) condition *f* (requise).

requisite ['rekwɪzɪt] **1** *a* nécessaire. **2** *n* (*for travel etc*) article *m*; **toilet requisites** articles *mpl ou* nécessaire *m* de toilette.

requisition [rekwɪ'zɪʃ(ə)n] *vt* réquisitionner; – *n* réquisition *f*.

reroute [riː'ruːt] *vt* (*aircraft etc*) dérouter.

rerun ['riːrʌn] *n Cin* reprise *f*; *TV* rediffusion *f*.

resale ['riːseɪl] *n* revente *f*.

resat [riː'sæt] *see* resit.

rescind [rɪ'sɪnd] *vt Jur* annuler; (*law*) abroger.

rescu/e ['reskjuː] *vt* (*save*) sauver; (*set free*) délivrer (**from** de); – *n* (*action*) sauvetage *m* (**of** de), délivrance *f*; (*help, troops etc*) secours *mpl*; **to go/***etc* **to s.o.'s r.** aller/*etc* au secours de qn; **to the r.** à la rescousse; – *a* (*team, operation*) de sauvetage. ◆**–er** *n* sauveteur *m*.

research [rɪ'sɜːtʃ] *n* recherches *fpl* (**on, into** sur); **some r.** de la recherche; **a piece of r.** (*work*) un travail de recherche; – *vi* faire des recherches (**on, into** sur). ◆**–er** *n* chercheur, -euse *mf*.

resemble [rɪ'zemb(ə)l] *vt* ressembler à. ◆**resemblance** *n* ressemblance *f* (**to** avec).

resent [rɪ'zent] *vt* (*anger*) s'indigner de, ne pas aimer; (*bitterness*) éprouver de l'amertume à l'égard de; **I r. that** ça m'indigne. ◆**resentful** *a* **to be r.** éprouver de l'amertume. ◆**resentment** *n* amertume *f*, ressentiment *m*.

reserv/e [rɪ'zɜːv] **1** *vt* (*room, decision etc*) réserver; (*right*) se réserver; (*one's strength*) ménager; – *n* (*reticence*) réserve *f*. **2** *n* (*stock, land*) réserve *f*; *Sp* (*player*) remplaçant, -ante *mf*; **the r.** *Mil* la réserve; **the reserves** (*troops*) *Mil* les réserves *fpl*; **nature r.** réserve *f* naturelle; **in r.** en réserve; **r. tank** *Av Aut* réservoir *m* de secours. ◆**–ed** *a* (*person, room*) réservé. ◆**reser'vation** *n* **1** (*doubt etc*) réserve *f*; (*booking*) réservation *f*. **2** (*land*) *Am* réserve *f*; **central r.** (*on road*) terre-plein *m*.

reservoir ['rezəvwɑːr] *n* réservoir *m*.

resettle [riː'set(ə)l] *vt* (*refugees*) implanter.

reshape [riː'ʃeɪp] *vt* (*industry etc*) réorganiser.

reshuffle [riː'ʃʌf(ə)l] *n* (**cabinet**) **r.** *Pol* remaniement *m* (ministériel); – *vt Pol* remanier.

reside [rɪ'zaɪd] *vi* résider. ◆**'residence** *n* (*home*) résidence *f*; (*of students*) foyer *m*; **in r.** (*doctor*) sur place; (*students on campus*) sur le campus, (*in halls of residence*) rentrés. ◆'**resident** n habitant, -ante mf; (of hotel) pensionnaire mf; (foreigner) résident, -ente mf; — a résidant, qui habite sur place; (population) fixe; (correspondent) permanent; **to be r. in London** résider à Londres. ◆**resi'dential** a (neighbourhood) résidentiel.

residue ['rezidjuː] n résidu m. ◆**re'sidual** a résiduel.

resign [rɪ'zaɪn] vt (right, claim) abandonner; **to r. (from) one's job** démissionner; **to r. oneself to sth/to doing** se résigner à qch/à faire; — vi démissionner (**from** de). ◆—ed a résigné. ◆**resig'nation** n (from job) démission f; (attitude) résignation f.

resilient [rɪ'zɪlɪənt] a élastique; (person) Fig résistant. ◆**resilience** n élasticité f; Fig résistance f.

resin ['rezin] n résine f.

resist [rɪ'zɪst] vt (attack etc) résister à; **to r. doing sth** s'empêcher de faire qch; **she can't r. cakes** elle ne peut pas résister devant les gâteaux; **he can't r. her** (indulgence) il ne peut rien lui refuser; (charm) il ne peut pas résister à son charme; — vi résister. ◆**resistance** n résistance f (**to** à). ◆**resistant** a résistant (**to** à); **r. to** Med rebelle à.

resit [riː'sɪt] vt (pt & pp resat, pres p resitting) (exam) repasser.

resolute ['rezəluːt] a résolu. ◆—ly adv résolument. ◆**reso'lution** n résolution f.

resolve [rɪ'zɒlv] vt résoudre (**to do** de faire, **that** que); — n résolution f. ◆—ed a résolu (**to do** à faire).

resonant ['rezənənt] a (voice) résonnant; **to be r. with** résonner de. ◆**resonance** n résonance f.

resort [rɪ'zɔːt] **1** n (recourse) recours m (**to** à); **as a last r.** en dernier ressort; — vi **to r. to s.o.** avoir recours à qn; **to r. to doing** en venir à faire; **to r. to drink** se rabattre sur la boisson. **2** n (holiday) r. station f de vacances; **seaside/ski r.** station f balnéaire/de ski.

resound [rɪ'zaʊnd] vi résonner (**with** de); Fig avoir du retentissement. ◆—**ing** a (success, noise) retentissant.

resource [rɪ'sɔːs, rɪ'zɔːs] n (expedient, recourse) ressource f; pl (wealth etc) ressources fpl. ◆**resourceful** a (person, scheme) ingénieux. ◆**resourcefulness** n ingéniosité f, ressource f.

respect [rɪ'spekt] n respect m (**for** pour, de); (aspect) égard m; **in r. of, with r. to** en ce qui concerne; **with all due r.** sans vouloir vous vexer; — vt respecter. ◆**respecta'bility** n

respectabilité f. ◆**respectable** a (honourable, sizeable) respectable; (satisfying) honnête; (clothes, behaviour) convenable. ◆**respectably** adv (to dress etc) convenablement; (rather well) passablement. ◆**respectful** a respectueux (**to** envers, **of** de). ◆**respectfully** adv respectueusement.

respective [rɪ'spektɪv] a respectif. ◆—**ly** adv respectivement.

respiration [respɪ'reɪʃ(ə)n] n respiration f.

respite ['respaɪt] n répit m.

respond [rɪ'spɒnd] vi répondre (**to** à); **to r. to treatment** Med réagir positivement au traitement. ◆**response** n réponse f; **in p. to** en réponse à.

responsible [rɪ'spɒnsəb(ə)l] a responsable (**for** de, **to s.o.** devant qn); (job) à responsabilités; **who's r. for . . . ?** qui est (le) responsable de . . . ? ◆**responsi'bility** n responsabilité f. ◆**responsibly** adv de façon responsable.

responsive [rɪ'spɒnsɪv] a (reacting) qui réagit bien; (alert) éveillé; (attentive) qui fait attention; **r. to** (kindness) sensible à; (suggestion) réceptif à. ◆—**ness** n (bonne) réaction f.

rest¹ [rest] n (repose) repos m; (support) support m; **to have** or **take a r.** se reposer; **to set** or **put s.o.'s mind at r.** tranquilliser qn; **to come to r.** (of ball etc) s'immobiliser; (of bird, eyes) se poser (**on** sur); **r. home** maison f de repos; **r. room** Am toilettes fpl; — vi (relax) se reposer; (be buried) reposer; **to r. on** (of roof, argument) reposer sur; **I won't r. till** je n'aurai de repos que (+ sub); **to be resting on** (of hand etc) être posé sur; **a resting place** un lieu de repos; — vt (eyes etc) reposer; (horse etc) laisser reposer; (lean) poser, appuyer (**on** sur); (base) fonder. ◆**restful** a reposant.

rest² [rest] n (remainder) reste m (**of** de); **the r.** (others) les autres mfpl; **the r. of the men/etc** les autres hommes/etc; — vi (remain) **it rests with you to do** il vous incombe de faire; **r. assured** soyez assuré (**that** que).

restaurant ['restərɒnt] n restaurant m.

restitution [restɪ'tjuːʃ(ə)n] n (for damage) Jur réparation f; **to make r.** of restituer.

restive ['restɪv] a (person, horse) rétif.

restless ['restləs] a agité. ◆—**ly** adv avec agitation. ◆—**ness** n agitation f.

restore [rɪ'stɔːr] vt (give back) rendre (**to** à); (order, right) Jur rétablir; (building, painting) restaurer; (to life or power) ramener (qn) (**to** à).

restrain [rɪ'streɪn] vt (person, emotions) retenir, maîtriser; (crowd) contenir; (limit) limiter; **to r. s.o. from doing** retenir qn de faire; **to r. oneself** se maîtriser. ◆**—ed** a (feelings) contenu; (tone) mesuré. ◆**restraint** n (moderation) retenue f, mesure f; (restriction) contrainte f.

restrict [rɪ'strɪkt] vt limiter, restreindre (**to** à). ◆**—ed** a (space, use) restreint; (sale) contrôlé. ◆**restriction** n restriction f, limitation f. ◆**restrictive** a restrictif.

result [rɪ'zʌlt] n (outcome, success) résultat m; **as a r.** en conséquence; **as a r. of** par suite de; – vi résulter (**from** de); **to r. in** aboutir à.

resume [rɪ'zjuːm] vti (begin or take again) reprendre; **to r. doing** se remettre à faire. ◆**resumption** n reprise f.

résumé ['rezjumeɪ] n (summary) résumé m; Am curriculum vitae m inv.

resurface [riː'sɜːfɪs] vt (road) refaire le revêtement de.

resurgence [rɪ'sɜːdʒəns] n réapparition f.

resurrect [rezə'rekt] vt (custom, hero) Pej ressusciter. ◆**resurrection** n résurrection f.

resuscitate [rɪ'sʌsɪteɪt] vt Med réanimer.

retail ['riːteɪl] n (vente f au) détail m; – a (price, shop etc) de détail; – vi se vendre (au détail); – vt vendre (au détail), détailler; – adv (to sell) au détail. ◆**—er** n détaillant, -ante mf.

retain [rɪ'teɪn] vt (hold back, remember) retenir; (freshness, hope etc) conserver. ◆**retainer** n (fee) avance f, acompte m. ◆**retention** n (memory) mémoire f. ◆**retentive** a (memory) fidèle.

retaliate [rɪ'tælɪeɪt] vi riposter (**against s.o.** contre qn, **against an attack** à une attaque). ◆**retali'ation** n riposte f, représailles fpl; **in r. for** en représailles de.

retarded [rɪ'tɑːdɪd] a (mentally) r. arriéré.

retch [retʃ] vi avoir un or des haut-le-cœur.

rethink [riː'θɪŋk] vt (pt & pp rethought) repenser.

reticent ['retɪsənt] a réticent. ◆**reticence** n réticence f.

retina ['retɪnə] n Anat rétine f.

retir/e [rɪ'taɪə] 1 vi (from work) prendre sa retraite; – vt mettre à la retraite. 2 vi (withdraw) se retirer (**from** de, **to** à); (go to bed) aller se coucher. ◆**—ed** a (having stopped working) retraité. ◆**—ing** a 1 (age) de la retraite. 2 (reserved) réservé. ◆**retirement** n retraite f; **r. age** âge m de la retraite.

retort [rɪ'tɔːt] vt rétorquer; – n réplique f.

retrace [riː'treɪs] vt (past event) se

remémorer, reconstituer; **to r. one's steps** revenir sur ses pas, rebrousser chemin.

retract [rɪ'trækt] vt (statement etc) rétracter; – vi (of person) se rétracter. ◆**retraction** n (of statement) rétractation f.

retrain [riː'treɪn] vi se recycler; – vt recycler. ◆**—ing** n recyclage m.

retread ['riːtred] n pneu m rechapé.

retreat [rɪ'triːt] n (withdrawal) retraite f; (place) refuge m; – vi se retirer (**from** de); Mil battre en retraite.

retrial [riː'traɪəl] n Jur nouveau procès m.

retribution [retrɪ'bjuːʃ(ə)n] n châtiment m.

retrieve [rɪ'triːv] vt (recover) récupérer; (rescue) sauver (**from** de); (loss, error) réparer; (honour) rétablir. ◆**retrieval** n récupération f. **information r.** recherche f documentaire. ◆**retriever** n (dog) chien m d'arrêt.

retro- ['retrəʊ] pref rétro-. ◆**retro'active** a rétroactif.

retrograde ['retrəʊɡreɪd] a rétrograde.

retrospect ['retrəspekt] n **in r.** rétrospectivement. ◆**retro'spective 1** a (law, effect) rétroactif. 2 n (of film director, artist) rétrospective f.

return [rɪ'tɜːn] vi (come back) revenir; (go back) retourner; (go back home) rentrer; **to r. to** (subject) revenir à; – vt (give back) rendre; (put back) remettre; (bring back) & Fin rapporter; (send back) renvoyer; (greeting) répondre à; (candidate) Pol élire; – n retour m; (yield) Fin rapport m; pl (profits) Fin bénéfices mpl; **the r. to school** la rentrée (des classes); **r. (ticket)** (billet m d')aller et retour m; **tax r.** déclaration f de revenus; **many happy returns (of the day)!** bon anniversaire!; **in r.** (exchange) en échange (**for** de); – a (trip, flight etc) (de) retour; **r. match** match m retour. ◆**—able** a (bottle) consigné.

reunion [riː'juːnɪən] n réunion f. ◆**reu'nite** vt réunir.

rev [rev] n Aut Fam tour m; **r. counter** compte-tours m inv; – vt (**-vv-**) **to r. (up)** (engine) Fam faire ronfler.

revamp [riː'væmp] vt (method, play etc) Fam remanier.

reveal [rɪ'viːl] vt (make known) révéler (**that** que); (make visible) laisser voir. ◆**—ing** a (sign etc) révélateur.

revel ['rev(ə)l] vi (**-ll-**) faire la fête; **to r. in sth** se délecter de qch. ◆**revelling** n, ◆**revelry** n festivités fpl. ◆**reveller** n noceur, -euse mf.

revenge [rɪ'vendʒ] n vengeance f; Sp revanche f; **to have** or **get one's r.** se venger

(on s.o. de qn, on s.o. for sth de qch sur qn); in r. pour se venger; – *vt* venger.
revenue ['revǝnju:] *n* revenu *m*.
reverberate [rɪ'vɜːbǝreɪt] *vi (of sound)* se répercuter.
revere [rɪ'vɪǝr] *vt* révérer. ◆'**reverence** *n* révérence *f*. ◆'**reverend** *a (father)* Rel révérend; – *n* **R. Smith** *(Anglican)* le révérend Smith; *(Catholic)* l'abbé *m* Smith; *(Jewish)* le rabbin Smith. ◆'**reverent** *a* respectueux.
reverse [rɪ'vɜːs] *a* contraire *(order, image)* inverse; **r. side** *(of coin etc)* revers *m*; *(of paper)* verso *m*; – *n* contraire *m* *(of coin, fabric etc)* revers *m*; *(of paper)* verso *m*; **r. (gear)** *Aut* en marche arrière; – *vt (situation)* renverser; *(order, policy)* inverser; *(decision)* annuler; *(bucket etc)* retourner; **to r. the charges** *Tel* téléphoner en PCV; – *vti* **to r. (the car)** faire marche arrière; **to r. in/out** rentrer/sortir en marche arrière; **reversing light** phare *m* de recul. ◆**reversal** *n* renversement *m*; *(of policy, situation, opinion)* revirement *m*; *(of fortune)* revers *m*. ◆**reversible** *a (fabric etc)* réversible.
revert [rɪ'vɜːt] *vi* **to r. to** revenir à.
review [rɪ'vjuː] **1** *vt (troops, one's life)* passer en revue; *(situation)* réexaminer; *(book)* faire la critique de; – *n* revue *f*; *(of book)* critique *f*. **2** *n (magazine)* revue *f*. ◆**-er** *n* critique *m*.
revile [rɪ'vaɪl] *vt* injurier.
revise [rɪ'vaɪz] *vt (opinion, notes, text)* réviser; – *vi (for exam)* réviser **(for** pour). ◆**revision** *n* révision *f*.
revitalize [riː'vaɪt(ǝ)laɪz] *vt* revitaliser.
revive [rɪ'vaɪv] *vt (unconscious person, memory, conversation)* ranimer; *(dying person)* réanimer; *(custom, plan, fashion)* ressusciter; *(hope, interest)* faire renaître; – *vi (of unconscious person)* reprendre connaissance; *(of country, dying person)* ressusciter; *(of hope, interest)* renaître. ◆**revival** *n (of custom, business, play)* reprise *f*; *(of country)* essor *m*; *(of faith, fashion, theatre)* renouveau *m*.
revoke [rɪ'vǝuk] *vt (decision)* annuler; *(contract)* Jur révoquer.
revolt [rɪ'vǝult] *n* révolte *f*; – *vt (disgust)* révolter; – *vi (rebel)* se révolter **(against** contre). ◆**-ing** *a* dégoûtant; *(injustice)* révoltant.
revolution [revǝ'luːʃ(ǝ)n] *n* révolution *f*. ◆**revolutionary** *a* & *n* révolutionnaire *(mf).* ◆**revolutionize** *vt* révolutionner.
revolv/e [rɪ'vɒlv] *vi* tourner **(around** autour

de). ◆**-ing** *a* **r. chair** fauteuil *m* pivotant; **r. door(s)** *(porte f à)* tambour *m*.
revolver [rɪ'vɒlvǝr] *n* revolver *m*.
revue [rɪ'vjuː] *n (satirical)* Th revue *f*.
revulsion [rɪ'vʌlʃ(ǝ)n] *n* **1** *(disgust)* dégoût *m*. **2** *(change)* revirement *m*.
reward [rɪ'wɔːd] *n* récompense *f* **(for** de); – *vt* récompenser **(s.o. for sth** qn de *ou* pour qch). ◆**-ing** *a (task)* qui (en) vaut la peine; *(satisfying)* satisfaisant; *(financially)* rémunérateur.
rewind [riː'waɪnd] *vt (pt & pp* rewound) *(tape)* réembobiner.
rewire [riː'waɪǝr] *vt (house)* refaire l'installation électrique de.
rewrite [riː'raɪt] *vt (pt* rewrote, *pp* rewritten) récrire; *(edit)* réécrire.
rhapsody ['ræpsǝdɪ] *n* rhapsodie *f*.
rhetoric ['retǝrɪk] *n* rhétorique *f*. ◆**rhe-'torical** *a (question)* de pure forme.
rheumatism ['ruːmǝtɪz(ǝ)m] *n* Med rhumatisme *m*; **to have r.** avoir des rhumatismes. ◆**rheu'matic** *a (pain)* rhumatismal; *(person)* rhumatisant.
rhinoceros [raɪ'nɒsǝrǝs] *n* rhinocéros *m*.
rhubarb ['ruːbɑːb] *n* rhubarbe *f*.
rhyme [raɪm] *n* rime *f*; *(poem)* vers *mpl*; – *vi* rimer.
rhythm ['rɪð(ǝ)m] *n* rythme *m*. ◆**rhythmic(al)** *a* rythmique.
rib [rɪb] *n* Anat côte *f*.
ribald ['rɪbǝld] *a* Lit grivois.
ribbon ['rɪbǝn] *n* ruban *m*; **to tear to ribbons** mettre en lambeaux.
rice [raɪs] *n* riz *m*. ◆**ricefield** *n* rizière *f*.
rich [rɪtʃ] *a* (-er, -est) riche **(in** en); *(profits)* gros; – *n* **the r. les riches** *mpl*. ◆**riches** *npl* richesses *fpl*. ◆**richly** *adv (dressed, illustrated etc)* richement; *(deserved)* amplement. ◆**richness** *n* richesse *f*.
rick [rɪk] *vt* **to r. one's back** se tordre le dos.
rickety ['rɪkɪtɪ] *a (furniture)* branlant.
ricochet ['rɪkǝʃeɪ] *vi* ricocher; – *n* ricochet *m*.
rid [rɪd] *vt (pt & pp* rid, *pres p* ridding) débarrasser *(of* de); **to get r. of, to rid oneself of** se débarrasser de. ◆**riddance** *n* **good r.!** *Fam* bon débarras!
ridden ['rɪd(ǝ)n] *see* ride.
-ridden ['rɪd(ǝ)n] *suffix* **debt-r.** criblé de dettes; **disease-r.** en proie à la maladie.
riddle ['rɪd(ǝ)l] **1** *n (puzzle)* énigme *f*. **2** *vt* cribler **(with** de); **riddled with** *(bullets, holes, mistakes)* criblé de; *(criminals)* plein de; *(corruption)* en proie à.
rid/e [raɪd] *n (on bicycle, by car etc)* promenade *f*; *(distance)* trajet *m*; *(in taxi)* course

f; (*on merry-go-round*) tour *m;* **to go for a (car) r.** faire une promenade (en voiture); **to give s.o. a r.** *Aut* emmener qn en voiture; **to have a r. on** (*bicycle*) monter sur; **to take s.o. for a r.** *Fam* mener qn en bateau; *– vi* (*pt* rode, *pp* ridden) aller (à bicyclette, à moto, à cheval *etc*) (**to** à); (*on horse*) *Sp* monter (à cheval); **to be riding in a car** être en voiture; **to r. up** (*of skirt*) remonter; *– vt* (*a particular horse*) monter; (*distance*) faire (à cheval *etc*); **to r. a horse or horses** (*go riding*) *Sp* monter à cheval; **I was riding (on) a bike/donkey** j'étais à bicyclette/à dos d'âne; **to know how to r. a bike** savoir faire de la bicyclette; **to r. a bike to** aller à bicyclette à; **may I r. your bike?** puis-je monter sur ta bicyclette?; **to r. s.o.** (*annoy*) *Am Fam* harceler qn. ◆**—ing** *n* (*horse*) r. équitation *f;* **r. boots** bottes *fpl* de cheval. ◆**—er** *n* 1 (*on horse*) cavalier, -ière *mf;* (*cyclist*) cycliste *mf.* 2 (*to document*) *Jur* annexe *f.*

ridge [rɪdʒ] *n* (*of roof, mountain*) arête *f,* crête *f.*

ridicule ['rɪdɪkjuːl] *n* ridicule *m;* **to hold up to r.** tourner en ridicule; **object of r.** objet *m* de risée; *– vt* tourner en ridicule, ridiculiser. ◆**ri'diculous** *a* ridicule.

rife [raɪf] *a* (*widespread*) répandu.

riffraff ['rɪfræf] *n* racaille *f.*

rifle ['raɪf(ə)l] 1 *n* fusil *m,* carabine *f.* 2 *vt* (*drawers, pockets etc*) vider.

rift [rɪft] *n* (*crack*) fissure *f;* (*in party*) *Pol* scission *f;* (*disagreement*) désaccord *m.*

rig [rɪg] 1 *n* (*oil*) **r.** derrick *m;* (*at sea*) plate-forme *f* pétrolière. 2 *vt* (*-gg-*) (*result, election etc*) *Pej* truquer; **to r. up** (*equipment*) installer; (*meeting etc*) *Fam* arranger. 3 *vt* (*-gg-*) **to r. out** (*dress*) *Fam* habiller. ◆**r.-out** *n Fam* tenue *f.*

right [raɪt] 1 *a* (*correct*) bon, exact, juste; (*fair*) juste; (*angle*) droit; **to be r.** (*of person*) avoir raison (**to do** de faire); **it's the r. road** c'est la bonne route, c'est bien la route; **the r. time** l'heure exacte; **the clock's r.** la pendule est à l'heure; **at the r. time** au bon moment; **he's the r. man** c'est l'homme qu'il faut; **the r. thing to do** la meilleure chose à faire; **it's not r. to steal** ce n'est pas bien de voler; **it doesn't look r.** ça ne va pas; **to put r.** (*error*) rectifier; (*fix*) arranger; **to put s.o. r.** (*inform*) éclairer qn, détromper qn; **r. you are!** bien!; **that's r.** c'est ça, c'est exact; *– adv* (*straight*) (tout) droit; (*completely*) tout à fait; (*correctly*) juste; (*well*) bien; **she did r.** elle a bien fait; **r. round** tout autour (**sth** de qch);

r. behind juste derrière; **r. here** ici même; **r. away, r. now** tout de suite; **R. Honourable** *Pol* Très Honorable; *– n* **to be in the r.** avoir raison; **r. and wrong** le bien et le mal; *– vt* (*error, wrong, car*) redresser. 2 **all r.** *a* (*satisfactory*) bien *inv;* (*unharmed*) sain et sauf; (*undamaged*) intact; (*without worries*) tranquille; **it's all r.** ça va; **it's all r. now** (*fixed*) ça marche maintenant; **I'm all r.** (*healthy*) je vais bien, ça va; *– adv* (*well*) bien; **all r.!, r. you are!** (*yes*) d'accord!; **I got your letter all r.** j'ai bien reçu ta lettre. ◆**rightly** *adv* bien, correctement; (*justifiably*) à juste titre; **r. or wrongly** à tort ou à raison.

right [raɪt] *a* (*hand, side etc*) droit; *– adv* à droite; *– n* droite *f;* **on** *or* **to the r.** à droite (**of** de). ◆**r.-hand** *a* à *or* de droite; **on the r.-hand side** à droite (**of** de); **r.-hand man** bras *m* droit. ◆**r.-'handed** *a* (*person*) droitier. ◆**r.-wing** *a Pol* de droite.

right [raɪt] *n* (*claim, entitlement*) droit *m* (**to do** de faire); **to have a r. to sth** avoir droit à qch; **he's famous in his own r.** il est lui-même célèbre; **r. of way** *Aut* priorité *f;* **human rights** les droits de l'homme.

righteous ['raɪtʃəs] *a* (*person*) vertueux; (*cause, indignation*) justifié.

rightful ['raɪtfəl] *a* légitime. ◆**—ly** *adv* légitimement.

rigid ['rɪdʒɪd] *a* rigide. ◆**ri'gidity** *n* rigidité *f.* ◆**rigidly** *adv* (*opposed*) rigoureusement (**to** à).

rigmarole ['rɪgmərəʊl] *n* (*process*) procédure *f* compliquée.

rigour ['rɪgər] *n* rigueur *f.* ◆**rigorous** *a* rigoureux.

rile [raɪl] *vt* (*annoy*) *Fam* agacer.

rim [rɪm] *n* (*of cup etc*) bord *m;* (*of wheel*) jante *f.*

rind [raɪnd] *n* (*of cheese*) croûte *f;* (*of melon, lemon*) écorce *f;* (*of bacon*) couenne *f.*

ring [rɪŋ] *n* anneau *m;* (*on finger*) anneau *m,* (*with stone*) bague *f;* (*of people, chairs*) cercle *m;* (*of smoke, for napkin*) rond *m;* (*gang*) bande *f;* (*at circus*) piste *f;* Boxing ring *m;* (*burner on stove*) brûleur *m;* **diamond r.** bague *f* de diamants; **to have rings under one's eyes** avoir les yeux cernés; **r. road** route *f* de ceinture; (*motorway*) périphérique *m;* *– vt* **to r. (round)** (*surround*) entourer (**with** de); (*item on list etc*) entourer d'un cercle. ◆**ringleader** *n Pej* (*of gang*) chef *m* de bande; (*of rebellion etc*) meneur, -euse *mf.*

ring [rɪŋ] *n* (*sound*) sonnerie *f;* **there's a r.** on sonne; **to give s.o. a r.** (*phone call*) passer un coup de fil à qn; **a r. of** (*truth*) Fig l'accent *m* de; – *vi* (*pt* rang, *pp* rung) (*of bell, person etc*) sonner; (*of sound, words*) retentir; **to r. (up)** Tel téléphoner; **to r. back** Tel rappeler; **to r. for s.o.** sonner qn; **to r. off** Tel raccrocher; **to r. out** (*of bell*) sonner; (*of sound*) retentir; – *vt* sonner; **to r. s.o. (up)** Tel téléphoner à qn; **to r. s.o. back** Tel rappeler qn; **to r. the bell** sonner; **to r. the doorbell** sonner à la porte; **that rings a bell** *Fam* ça me rappelle quelque chose; **to r. in** (*the New Year*) carillonner. ◆**-ing** *a* r. **tone** tonalité *f*; – *n* (*of bell*) sonnerie *f*; **a r. in one's ears** un bourdonnement dans les oreilles.

ringlet ['rɪŋlɪt] *n* (*curl*) anglaise *f*.

rink [rɪŋk] *n* (*ice-skating*) patinoire *f*; (*roller-skating*) skating *m*.

rinse [rɪns] *vt* rincer; **to r. one's hands** se passer les mains à l'eau; (*remove soap*) se rincer les mains; **to r. out** rincer; – *n* rinçage *m*; (*hair colouring*) shampooing *m* colorant; **to give sth a r.** rincer qch.

riot ['raɪət] *n* (*uprising*) émeute *f*; (*demonstration*) manifestation *f* violente; **a r. of colour** Fig une orgie de couleurs; **to run r.** (*of crowd*) se déchaîner; **the r. police** = les CRS *mpl*; – *vi* (*rise up*) faire une émeute; (*fight*) se bagarrer. ◆**-ing** *n* émeutes *fpl*; bagarres *fpl*. ◆**-er** *n* émeutier, -ière *mf*; (*demonstrator*) manifestant, -ante *mf* violent(e). ◆**riotous** *a* (*crowd etc*) tapageur; **r. living** vie *f* dissolue.

rip [rɪp] *vt* (-pp-) déchirer; **to r. off or out** arracher; **to r. off** *Fam* (*deceive*) rouler; (*steal*) *Am* voler; **to r. up** déchirer; – *vi* (*of fabric*) se déchirer; – *n* déchirure *f*; **it's a r.-off** *Fam* c'est du vol organisé.

ripe [raɪp] *a* (-er, -est) mûr; (*cheese*) fait. ◆**ripen** *vti* mûrir. ◆**ripeness** *n* maturité *f*.

ripple ['rɪp(ə)l] *n* (*on water*) ride *f*; (*of laughter*) Fig cascade *f*; – *vi* (*of water*) se rider.

ris/e [raɪz] *vi* (*pt* rose, *pp* risen) (*get up from chair or bed*) se lever; (*of temperature, balloon, price etc*) monter, s'élever; (*in society*) s'élever; (*of hope*) grandir; (*of sun, curtain, wind*) se lever; (*of dough*) lever; **to r. in price** augmenter de prix; **to r. to the surface** remonter à la surface; **the river rises in ...** le fleuve prend sa source dans ... ; **to r. (up)** (*rebel*) se soulever (*against* contre); **to r. to power** accéder au pouvoir; **to r. from the dead** ressusciter; – *n* (*of sun, curtain*) lever *m*; (*in pressure, price etc*) hausse *f* (*in* de); (*in river*) crue *f*; (*of leader*) Fig ascension *f*; (*of industry, technology*)

essor *m*; (*to power*) accession *f*; (*slope in ground*) éminence *f*; (**pay**) r. augmentation *f* (de salaire); **to give r. to** donner lieu à. ◆**-ing** *n* (*of curtain*) lever *m*; (*of river*) crue *f*; (*revolt*) soulèvement *m*; – *a* (*sun*) levant; (*number*) croissant; (*tide*) montant; (*artist etc*) d'avenir; **the r. generation** la nouvelle génération; **r. prices** la hausse des prix. ◆**-er** n early r. lève-tôt *mf inv*; **late r.** lève-tard *mf inv*.

risk [rɪsk] *n* risque *m* (**of doing** de faire); **at r.** (*person*) en danger; (*job*) menacé; **at your own r.** à tes risques et périls; (*of one's life, an accident etc*) risquer; **she won't r. leaving** (*take the risk*) elle ne se risquera pas à partir; **let's r. it** risquons le coup. ◆**riskiness** *n* risques *mpl*. ◆**risky** *a* (-ier, -iest) (*full of risk*) risqué.

rissole ['rɪsəʊl] *n* Culin croquette *f*.

rite [raɪt] *n* rite *m*; **the last rites** Rel les derniers sacrements *mpl*. ◆**ritual** *a* & *n* rituel (*m*).

ritzy ['rɪtsɪ] *a* (-ier, -iest) *Fam* luxueux, classe *inv*.

rival ['raɪv(ə)l] *a* (*firm etc*) rival; (*forces, claim etc*) opposé; – *n* rival, -ale *mf*; – *vt* (-ll-, *Am* -l-) (*compete with*) rivaliser avec (**in** de); (*equal*) égaler (**in** en). ◆**rivalry** *n* rivalité *f* (**between** entre).

river ['rɪvər] *n* (*small*) rivière *f*; (*major, flowing into sea*) & Fig fleuve *m*; **the R.** Thames la Tamise; – *a* (*port etc*) fluvial; **r. bank** rive *f*. ◆**riverside** *a* & *n* (**by the**) r. au bord de l'eau.

rivet ['rɪvɪt] *n* (*pin*) rivet *m*; – *vt* riveter; (*eyes*) Fig fixer. ◆**-ing** *a* (*story etc*) fascinant.

Riviera [rɪvɪ'eərə] *n* **the (French) R.** la Côte d'Azur.

road [rəʊd] *n* route *f* (**to** qui va à); (*small*) chemin *m*; (*in town*) rue *f*; (*roadway*) chaussée *f*; (*path*) Fig voie *f*, chemin *m*, route *f* (**to** de); **the Paris r.** la route de Paris; **across** *or* **over the r.** (*building etc*) en face; **by r.** par la route; **get out of the r.!** ne reste pas sur la chaussée!; – *a* (*map, safety*) routier; (*accident*) de la route; (*sense*) de la conduite; **r. hog** *Fam* chauffard *m*; **r. sign** panneau *m* (routier *or* de signalisation); **r. works** travaux *mpl*. ◆**roadblock** *n* barrage *m* routier. ◆**roadside** *a* & *n* (**by the**) r. au bord de la route. ◆**roadway** *n* chaussée *f*. ◆**roadworthy** *a* (*vehicle*) en état de marche.

roam [rəʊm] *vt* parcourir; – *vi* errer, rôder; **to r. (about) the streets** (*of child etc*) traîner dans les rues.

roar [rɔːr] vi hurler; (of lion, wind, engine) rugir; (of thunder) gronder; **to r. with laughter** éclater de rire; **to r. past** (of truck etc) passer dans un bruit de tonnerre; − vt **to r. (out)** hurler; − n hurlement m; rugissement m; grondement m. ◆**—ing** n = roar n; − a **a r. fire** une belle flambée; **a r. success** un succès fou; **to do a r. trade** vendre beaucoup (in de).

roast [rəʊst] vt rôtir; (coffee) griller; − vi (of meat) rôtir; **we're roasting here** Fam on rôtit ici; − n (meat) rôti m; − a (chicken etc) rôti; **r. beef** rosbif m.

rob [rɒb] vt (-bb-) (person) voler; (bank, house) dévaliser; **to r. s.o. of sth** voler qch à qn; (deprive) priver qn de qch. ◆**robber** n voleur, -euse mf. ◆**robbery** n vol m; **it's daylight r.!** c'est du vol organisé; **armed r.** vol m à main armée.

robe [rəʊb] n (of priest, judge etc) robe f; (dressing gown) peignoir m.

robin ['rɒbɪn] n (bird) rouge-gorge m.

robot ['rəʊbɒt] n robot m.

robust [rəʊ'bʌst] a robuste.

rock[1] [rɒk] **1** vt (baby, boat) bercer, balancer; (cradle, branch) balancer; (violently) secouer; − vi (sway) se balancer; (of building, ground) trembler. **2** n Mus rock m. ◆**—ing** n (horse, chair) à bascule. ◆**rocky**[1] a (-ier, -iest) (furniture etc) branlant.

rock[2] [rɒk] n (substance) roche f; (boulder, rock face) roche m; (stone) Am pierre f; **a stick of r.** (sweet) un bâton de sucre d'orge; **r. face** paroi f rocheuse; **on the rocks** (whisky) avec des glaçons; (marriage) en pleine débâcle. ◆**r.-'bottom** n point m le plus bas; − a (prices) les plus bas, très bas. ◆**r.-climbing** n varappe f. ◆**rockery** n (in garden) rocaille f. ◆**rocky**[2] a (-ier, -iest) (road) rocailleux; (hill) rocheux.

rocket ['rɒkɪt] n fusée f; − vi (of prices) Fig monter en flèche.

rod [rɒd] n (wooden) baguette f; (metal) tige f; (of curtain) tringle f; (for fishing) canne f à pêche.

rode [rəʊd] see ride.

rodent ['rəʊdənt] n (animal) rongeur m.

rodeo ['rəʊdɪəʊ] n (pl -os) Am rodéo m.

roe [rəʊ] n **1** (eggs) œufs mpl de poisson. **2 r.** (deer) chevreuil m.

rogue [rəʊg] n (dishonest) crapule f; (mischievous) coquin, -ine mf. ◆**roguish** a (smile etc) coquin.

role [rəʊl] n rôle m.

roll [rəʊl] n (of paper, film etc) rouleau m; (of bread) petit pain m; (of fat, flesh) bourrelet

m; (of drum, thunder) roulement m; (of ship) roulis m; (list) liste f; **to have a r. call** faire l'appel; **r. neck** (neckline, sweater) col m roulé; − vi (of ball, ship etc) rouler; (of person, animal) se rouler; **to be rolling in money** or **in it** Fam rouler sur l'or; **r. on tonight!** Fam vivement ce soir!; **to r. in** Fam (flow in) affluer; (of person) s'amener; **to r. over** (many times) se rouler; (once) se retourner; **to r. up** (arrive) Fam s'amener; **to r. (up) into a ball** (of animal) se rouler en boule; − vt rouler; **to r. down** (blind) baisser; (slope) descendre (en roulant); **to r. on** (paint, stocking) mettre; **to r. out** (dough) étaler; **to r. up** (map, cloth) rouler; (sleeve, trousers) retrousser. ◆**—ing** a (ground, gait) onduleux; **r. pin** rouleau m à pâtisserie. ◆**—er** n (for hair, painting etc) rouleau m; **r. coaster** (at funfair) montagnes fpl russes. ◆**roller-skate** n patin m à roulettes; − vi faire du patin à roulettes.

rollicking ['rɒlɪkɪŋ] a joyeux (et bruyant).

roly-poly [rəʊlɪ'pəʊlɪ] a Fam grassouillet.

Roman ['rəʊmən] **1** a & n romain, -aine mf. **2 R. Catholic** a & n catholique (mf).

romance [rəʊ'mæns] n **1** (story) histoire f or roman m d'amour; (love) amour m; (affair) aventure f amoureuse; (charm) poésie f. **2** a **R. language** langue f romane. ◆**romantic** a (of love, tenderness etc) romantique; (fanciful, imaginary) romanesque; − n (person) romantique mf. ◆**romantically** adv (to behave) de façon romantique. ◆**romanticism** n romantisme m.

Romania [rəʊ'meɪnɪə] n Roumanie f. ◆**Romanian** a n roumain, -aine mf; − n (language) roumain m.

romp [rɒmp] vi s'ébattre (bruyamment); **to r. through** (exam) Fig avoir les doigts dans le nez; − n ébats mpl.

rompers ['rɒmpəz] npl (for baby) barboteuse f.

roof [ruːf] n (of building, vehicle) toit m; (of tunnel, cave) plafond m; **r. of the mouth** voûte f du palais; **r. rack** (of car) galerie f. ◆**—ing** n toiture f. ◆**rooftop** n toit m.

rook [rʊk] n **1** (bird) corneille f. **2** Chess tour f.

rookie ['rʊkɪ] n (new recruit) Mil Fam bleu m.

room [ruːm, rʊm] n **1** (in house etc) pièce f; (bedroom) chambre f; (large, public) salle f; **one's rooms** son appartement m; **in rooms** en meublé; **men's r., ladies' r.** Am toilettes fpl. **2** (space) place f (for pour); (some) **r.** de la place; **there's r. for doubt** le doute est permis; **no r.** for doubt aucun doute possible. ◆**rooming house** n Am maison f de rapport. ◆**roommate** n camarade mf de chambre. ◆**roomy** a (-ier, -iest) spacieux; (clothes) ample.

roost [ruːst] vi (of bird) percher; – n perchoir m.

rooster ['ruːstər] n coq m.

root [ruːt] **1** n (of plant, person etc) & Math racine f; Fig cause f, origine f; **to pull up by the root(s)** déraciner; **to take r.** (of plant) & Fig prendre racine; **to put down (new) roots** Fig s'enraciner; **r. cause** cause f première; – vt **to r. out** (destroy) extirper. **2** vi (of plant cutting) s'enraciner; **to r. about for** fouiller pour trouver. **3** vi **to r. for** (cheer, support) Fam encourager. ◆**—ed** a **deeply r.** bien enraciné (in dans); **r. to the spot** (immobile) cloué sur place. ◆**—less** a sans racines.

rope [rəup] n corde f; Nau cordage m; **to know the ropes** Fam être au courant; – vt (tie) lier; **to r. s.o. in** (force to help) Fam embrigader qn (**to do** pour faire); **to r. off** séparer (par une corde).

rop(e)y ['rəupɪ] a (-ier, -iest) Fam (thing) minable; (person) patraque.

rosary ['rəuzərɪ] n Rel chapelet m.

rose[1] [rəuz] n **1** (flower) rose f; (colour) rose m; **r. bush** rosier m. **2** (of watering can) pomme f. ◆**ro'sette** n Sp cocarde f; (rose-shaped) rosette f. ◆**rosy** a (-ier, -iest) (pink) rose; (future) Fig tout en rose.

rose[2] [rəuz] see **rise**.

rosé ['rəuzeɪ] n (wine) rosé m.

rosemary ['rəuzmərɪ] n Bot Culin romarin m.

roster ['rɒstər] n (duty) n. liste f (de service).

rostrum ['rɒstrəm] n tribune f; Sp podium m.

rot [rɒt] n pourriture f; (nonsense) Fam inepties fpl; – vti (**-tt-**) **to r. (away)** pourrir.

rota ['rəutə] n liste f (de service).

rotate [rəu'teɪt] vi tourner; – vt faire tourner; (crops) alterner. ◆**'rotary** a rotatif; **r. airer** (washing line) séchoir m parapluie; n (roundabout) Aut Am sens m giratoire. ◆**rotation** n rotation f; **in r.** à tour de rôle.

rote [rəut] n **by r.** machinalement.

rotten ['rɒt(ə)n] a (decayed, corrupt) pourri; (bad) Fam moche; (filthy) Fam sale; **to feel r.** (ill) être mal fichu. ◆**rottenness** n pourriture f. ◆**rotting** a (meat, fruit etc) qui pourrit.

rotund [rəu'tʌnd] a (round) rond; (plump) rondelet.

rouble ['ruːb(ə)l] n (currency) rouble m.

rouge [ruːʒ] n rouge m (à joues).

rough[1] [rʌf] a (-er, -est) (surface, task, manners) rude; (ground) inégal, accidenté; (rocky) rocailleux; (plank, bark) rugueux; (sound) âpre, rude; (coarse) grossier; (brutal) brutal; (weather, neighbourhood) mauvais; (sea) agité; (justice) sommaire; (diamond) brut; **a r. child** (unruly) un enfant dur; **to feel r.** (ill) Fam être mal fichu; **r. and ready** (conditions, solution) grossier (mais adéquat); – adv **to sleep, live**) à la dure; (to play) brutalement; – n (violent man) Fam voyou m; – vt **to r. it** Fam vivre à la dure; **to r. up** (hair) ébouriffer; (person) Fam malmener. ◆**r.-and-'tumble** n (fight) mêlée f; (of s.o.'s life) remue-ménage m inv. ◆**roughen** vt rendre rude. ◆**roughly**[1] adv (not gently) rudement; (coarsely) grossièrement; (brutally) brutalement. ◆**roughness** n rudesse f; inégalité f; grossièreté f; brutalité f.

rough[2] [rʌf] a (-er, -est) (calculation, figure, terms etc) approximatif; **r. copy, r. draft** brouillon m; **r. paper** du papier brouillon; **r. guess, r. estimate** approximation f; **a r. plan** l'ébauche f d'un projet; – vt **to r. out** (plan) ébaucher. ◆**—ly**[2] adv (approximately) à peu de (choses) près.

roughage ['rʌfɪdʒ] n (in food) fibres fpl (alimentaires).

roulette [ruː'let] n roulette f.

round [raund] **1** adv autour; **all r., right r.** tout autour; **to go r. to s.o.** passer chez qn; **to ask r.** inviter chez soi; **he'll be r.** il passera; **r. here** par ici; **the long way r.** le chemin le plus long; – prep autour de; **r. about** (house etc) autour de; (approximately) environ; **r. (about) midday** vers midi; **to go r.** (world) faire le tour de; (corner) tourner. **2** a (-er, -est) rond; **a r. trip** Am un (voyage) aller et retour. **3** n (slice) Culin tranche f; Sp Pol manche f; (of golf) partie f; Boxing round m; (of talks) série f; (of drinks, visits) tournée f; **one's round(s)** (of milkman etc) sa tournée; (of doctor) ses visites fpl; (of policeman) sa ronde; **delivery r.** livraisons fpl, tournée f; **r. of applause** salve f d'applaudissements; **r. of ammunition** cartouche f, balle f; – vt **to r. a corner** (in car) prendre un virage; **to r. off** (finish) terminer; **to r. up** (gather) rassembler; (figure) arrondir au chiffre supérieur. ◆**r.-'shouldered** a voûté, aux épaules rondes. ◆**rounded** a arrondi. ◆**round-**ers npl Sp sorte de baseball. ◆**roundness** n rondeur f. ◆**roundup** n (of criminals) rafle f.

roundabout ['raʊndəbaʊt] **1** *a* indirect, détourné. **2** *n* (*at funfair*) manège *m*; (*junction*) *Aut* rond-point *m* (à sens giratoire).

rous/e [raʊz] *vt* éveiller; **roused (to anger)** en colère; **to r. to action** inciter à agir. **◆—ing** *a* (*welcome*) enthousiaste; (*speech*) vibrant; (*music*) allègre.

rout [raʊt] *n* (*defeat*) déen déroute *f*; — *vt* mettre route.

route 1 [ruːt] *n* itinéraire *m*; (*of aircraft*) route *f*; **sea r.** route *f* maritime; **bus r.** ligne *f* d'autobus; — *vt* (*train etc*) fixer l'itinéraire de. **2** [raʊt] *n* (*delivery round*) *Am* tournée *f*.

routine [ruːˈtiːn] *n* routine *f*; **one's daily r.** (*in office etc*) son travail journalier; **the daily r.** (*monotony*) le train-train quotidien; — *a* (*inquiry, work etc*) de routine; *Pej* routinier.

rov/e [rəʊv] *vi* errer; — *vt* parcourir. **◆—ing** *a* (*life*) nomade; (*ambassador*) itinérant.

row¹ [rəʊ] **1** *n* (*line*) rang *m*, rangée *f*; (*of cars*) file *f*; **two days in a r.** deux jours de suite *or* d'affilée. **2** *vi* (*in boat*) ramer; — *vt* (*boat*) faire aller à la rame; (*person*) transporter en canot; — *n* **to go for a r.** canoter; **r. boat** *Am* bateau *m* à rames. **◆—ing** *n* canotage *m*; *Sp* aviron *m*; **r. boat** bateau *m* à rames.

row² [raʊ] *n* *Fam* (*noise*) vacarme *m*; (*quarrel*) querelle *f*; — *vi* *Fam* se quereller (**with** avec).

rowdy ['raʊdɪ] *a* (**-ier, -iest**) chahuteur (et brutal); — *n* (*person*) *Fam* voyou *m*.

royal ['rɔɪəl] *a* royal; — *npl* **the royals** *Fam* la famille royale. **◆royalist** *a* & *n* royaliste (*mf*). **◆royally** *adv* (*to treat*) royalement. **◆royalty 1** *n* (*persons*) personnages *mpl* royaux. **2** *npl* (*from book*) droits *mpl* d'auteur; (*on oil, from patent*) royalties *fpl*.

rub [rʌb] *vt* (**-bb-**) frotter; (*polish*) astiquer; **to r. shoulders with** *Fig* coudoyer, côtoyer; **to r. away** (*mark*) effacer; (*tears*) essuyer; **to r. down** (*person*) frictionner; (*wood, with sandpaper*) poncer; **to r. in** (*cream*) *Med* faire pénétrer en massant; **to r. it in** *Pej Fam* retourner le couteau dans la plaie; **to r. off** *or* **out** (*mark*) effacer; **rubbing alcohol** *Am* alcool *m* à 90°; — *vi* frotter; **to r. off** (*of mark*) déteindre (**on s.o.** sur qn); — *n* (*massage*) friction *f*; **to give sth a r.** frotter qch; (*polish*) astiquer qch.

rubber ['rʌbər] *n* (*substance*) caoutchouc *m*; (*eraser*) gomme *f*; (*contraceptive*) *Am Sl* capote *f*; **r. stamp** tampon *m*. **◆r.-'stamp** *vt* *Pej* approuver (sans discuter). **◆rubbery** *a* caoutchouteux.

rubbish ['rʌbɪʃ] **1** *n* (*refuse*) ordures *fpl*, détritus *mpl*; (*waste*) déchets *mpl*; (*junk*) saleté(s) *f(pl)*; (*nonsense*) *Fig* absurdités *fpl*; **that's r.** (*absurd*) c'est absurde; (*worthless*) ça ne vaut rien; **r. bin** poubelle *f*; **r. dump** dépôt *m* d'ordures, décharge *f* (publique); (*in garden*) tas *m* d'ordures. **2** *vt* **to r. s.o./sth** (*criticize*) *Fam* dénigrer qn/qch. **◆rubbishy** *a* (*book etc*) sans valeur; (*goods*) de mauvaise qualité.

rubble ['rʌb(ə)l] *n* décombres *mpl*.

ruble ['ruːb(ə)l] *n* (*currency*) rouble *m*.

ruby ['ruːbɪ] *n* (*gem*) rubis *m*.

rucksack ['rʌksæk] *n* sac *m* à dos.

ruckus ['rʌkəs] *n* (*uproar*) *Fam* chahut *m*.

rudder ['rʌdər] *n* gouvernail *m*.

ruddy ['rʌdɪ] *a* (**-ier, -iest**) **1** (*complexion*) coloré. **2** (*bloody*) *Sl* fichu.

rude [ruːd] *a* (**-er, -est**) (*impolite*) impoli (**to** envers); (*coarse*) grossier; (*indecent*) indécent, obscène; (*shock*) violent. **◆—ly** *adv* impoliment; grossièrement. **◆—ness** *n* impolitesse *f*; grossièreté *f*.

rudiments ['ruːdɪmənts] *npl* rudiments *mpl*. **◆rudi'mentary** *a* rudimentaire.

ruffian ['rʌfɪən] *n* voyou *m*.

ruffle ['rʌf(ə)l] **1** *vt* (*hair*) ébouriffer; (*water*) troubler; **to r. s.o.** (*offend*) froisser qn. **2** *n* (*frill*) ruche *f*.

rug [rʌg] *n* carpette *f*, petit tapis *m*; (*over knees*) plaid *m*; (*bedside*) r. descente *f* de lit.

rugby ['rʌgbɪ] *n* **r.** (*football*) rugby *m*. **◆rugger** *n* *Fam* rugby *m*.

rugged ['rʌgɪd] *a* (*surface*) rugueux, rude; (*terrain, coast*) accidenté; (*person, features, manners*) rude; (*determination*) *Fig* farouche.

ruin ['ruːɪn] *n* (*destruction, rubble, building*) ruine *f*; **in ruins** (*building*) en ruine; — *vt* (*health, country, person etc*) ruiner; (*clothes*) abîmer; (*spoil*) gâter. **◆—ed** *a* (*person, country etc*) ruiné; (*building*) en ruine. **◆ruinous** *a* ruineux.

rul/e [ruːl] **1** *n* (*principle*) règle *f*; (*regulation*) règlement *m*; (*custom*) coutume *f*; (*authority*) autorité *f*; *Pol* gouvernement *m*; **against the rules** contraire à la règle; **as a (general) r.** en règle générale; **it's the r.** *or* **a r. that** il est de règle (**+** *sub*); — *vt* (*country*) *Pol* gouverner; (*decide*) *Jur Sp* décider (**that** que); **to r. s.o.** (*dominate*) mener qn; **to r. out** (*exclude*) exclure; — *vi* (*of monarch*) régner (**over** sur); (*of judge*) statuer (**against** contre, **on** sur). **2** *n* (*for measuring*) règle *f*. **◆—ed** *a* (*paper*) réglé, ligné. **◆—ing** *a* (*passion*) dominant;

(*class*) dirigeant; (*party*) *Pol* au pouvoir; − *n Jur Sp* décision *f*. ◆**ruler** *n* **1** (*of country*) *Pol* dirigeant, -ante *mf*; (*sovereign*) souverain, -aine *mf*. **2** (*measure*) règle *f*.

rum [rʌm] *n* rhum *m*.

Rumania [ruːˈmeɪnɪə] *see* **Romania**.

rumble [ˈrʌmb(ə)l] *vi* (*of train, thunder, gun*) gronder; (*of stomach*) gargouiller; − *n* grondement *m*; gargouillement *m*.

ruminate [ˈruːmɪneɪt] *vi* **to r.** (**about**) (*scheme etc*) ruminer.

rummage [ˈrʌmɪdʒ] *vi* **to r. (about)** farfouiller; **r. sale** (*used clothes etc*) *Am* vente *f* de charité.

rumour [ˈruːmər] *n* rumeur *f*, bruit *m*. ◆**rumoured** *a* **it is r. that** on dit que.

rump [rʌmp] *n* (*of horse*) croupe *f*; (*of fowl*) croupion *m*; **r. steak** rumsteck *m*.

rumple [ˈrʌmp(ə)l] *vt* (*clothes*) chiffonner.

run [rʌn] *n* (*running*) course *f*; (*outing*) tour *m*; (*journey*) parcours *m*, trajet *m*; (*series*) série *f*; (*period*) période *f*; *Cards* suite *f*; (*rush*) ruée *f* (**on** sur); (*trend*) tendance *f*; (*for skiing*) piste *f*; (*in cricket*) point *m*; **to go for a r.** courir, faire une course à pied; **on the r.** (*prisoner etc*) en fuite; **to have the r. of** (*house etc*) avoir à sa disposition; **in the long r.** avec le temps, à la longue; **the runs** *Med Fam* la diarrhée; − *vi* (*pt* **ran**, *pp* **run**, *pres p* **running**) courir; (*flee*) fuir; (*of curtain*) glisser; (*of river, nose, pen, tap*) couler; (*of colour in washing*) déteindre; (*of ink*) baver; (*melt*) fondre; (*of play, film*) se jouer; (*of contract*) être valide; (*last*) durer; (*pass*) passer; (*function*) marcher; (*tick over*) *Aut* tourner; (*of stocking*) filer; **to r. down/in/etc** descendre/entrer/etc en courant; **to r. for president** être candidat à la présidence; **to r. with blood** ruisseler de sang; **to r. between** (*of bus*) faire le service entre; **to go running** *Sp* faire du jogging; **the road runs to ...** la route va à ...; **the river runs into the sea** le fleuve se jette dans la mer; **it runs into a hundred pounds** ça va chercher dans les cent livres; **it runs in the family** ça tient de famille; − *vt* (*race, risk*) courir; (*horse*) faire courir; (*temperature, errand*) faire; (*blockade*) forcer; (*machine*) faire fonctionner; (*engine*) *Aut* faire tourner; (*drive*) *Aut* conduire; (*furniture, goods*) transporter (**to** à); (*business, country etc*) diriger; (*courses, events*) organiser; (*film, play*) présenter; (*house*) tenir; (*article*) publier (**on** sur); (*bath*) faire couler; **to r. one's hand over** passer la main sur; **to r. one's eye over** jeter un coup d'œil à *or* sur; **to r. its course** (*of illness etc*) suivre son

cours; **to r. 5 km** *Sp* faire 5 km de course à pied; **to r. a car** avoir une voiture. ■ **to r. about** *vi* courir çà et là; (*gallivant*) se balader; **to r. across** *vt* (*meet*) tomber sur; **to r. along** *vi* **r. along!** filez!; **to r. away** *vi* (*flee*) s'enfuir, se sauver (**from** de); **to r. back** *vt* (*person*) *Aut* ramener (**to** à); **to r. down** *vt* (*pedestrian*) *Aut* renverser; (*belittle*) dénigrer; (*restrict*) limiter peu à peu. ◆**r.-'down** *a* (*weak, tired*) *Med* à plat; (*district etc*) miteux; **to r. in** *vt* (*vehicle*) roder; **to r. s.o. in** (*of police*) *Fam* arrêter qn; **to r. into** *vt* (*meet*) tomber sur; (*crash into*) *Aut* percuter; **to r. into debt** s'endetter; **to r. off** *vt* (*print*) tirer; − *vi* (*flee*) s'enfuir; **to r. out** *vi* (*of stocks*) s'épuiser; (*of lease*) expirer; (*of time*) manquer; **to r. out of** (*time, money*) manquer de; **we've r. out of coffee** on n'a plus de café; − *vt* **to r. s.o. out of** (*chase*) chasser qn de; **to r. over** *vi* (*of liquid*) déborder; − *vt* (*kill pedestrian*) *Aut* écraser; (*knock down pedestrian*) *Aut* renverser; (*notes, text*) revoir; **to r. round** *vt* (*surround*) entourer; **to r. through** *vt* (*recap*) revoir; **to r. up** *vt* (*bill, debts*) laisser s'accumuler. ◆**r.-up** *n* **the r.-up to** (*elections etc*) la période qui précède. ◆**running** *n* course *f*; (*of machine*) fonctionnement *m*; (*of firm, country*) direction *f*; **to be in/out of the r.** être/ne plus être dans la course; − *a* (*commentary*) suivi; (*battle*) continuel; **r. water** eau *f* courante; **six days/etc r.** six jours/etc de suite; **r. costs** (*of factory*) frais *mpl* d'exploitation; (*of car*) dépenses *fpl* courantes. ◆**runner** *n Sp* etc coureur *m*; **r. bean** haricot *m* (grimpant). ◆**runner-'up** *n Sp* second, -onde *mf*. ◆**runny** *a* (**-ier**, **-iest**) *a* liquide; (*nose*) qui coule.

runaway [ˈrʌnəweɪ] *n* fugitif, -ive *mf*; − *a* (*car, horse*) emballé; (*lorry*) fou; (*wedding*) clandestin; (*victory*) qu'on remporte haut la main; (*inflation*) galopant.

rung[1] [rʌŋ] *n* (*of ladder*) barreau *m*.

rung[2] [rʌŋ] *see* **ring**[2].

run-of-the-mill [rʌnəvðəˈmɪl] *a* ordinaire.

runway [ˈrʌnweɪ] *n Av* piste *f*.

rupture [ˈrʌptʃər] *n Med* hernie *f*; **the r. of** (*breaking*) la rupture de; − *vt* rompre; **to r. oneself** se donner une hernie.

rural [ˈrʊərəl] *a* rural.

ruse [ruːz] *n* (*trick*) ruse *f*.

rush[1] [rʌʃ] *vi* (*move fast, throw oneself*) se précipiter, se ruer (**at** sur, **towards** vers); (*of blood*) affluer (**to** à); (*hurry*) se dépêcher (**to do** de faire); (*of vehicle*) foncer; **to r. out** partir en vitesse; − *vt* (*attack*) *Mil* foncer sur; **to r. s.o.** bousculer qn; **to r. s.o. to hospital** transporter qn d'urgence à l'hôpital; **to r. (through) sth** (*job, meal, order etc*) faire, manger, envoyer *etc* qch en vitesse; **to be rushed into** (*decision, answer etc*) être forcé à prendre, donner *etc*; – *n* ruée *f* (**for** vers, on sur); (*confusion*) bousculade *f*; (*hurry*) hâte *f*; (*of orders*) avalanche *f*; **to be in a r.** être pressé (**to do** de faire); **to leave**/*etc* **in a r.** partir/*etc* en vitesse; **the gold r.** la ruée vers l'or; **the r. hour** l'heure *f* d'affluence; **a r. job** un travail d'urgence.

rush² [rʌʃ] *n* (*plant*) jonc *m*.

rusk [rʌsk] *n* biscotte *f*.

russet ['rʌsɪt] *a* roux, roussâtre.

Russia ['rʌʃə] *n* Russie *f*. ◆**Russian** *a & n* russe (*mf*); – *n* (*language*) russe *m*.

rust [rʌst] *n* rouille *f*; – *vi* (se) rouiller. ◆**rustproof** *a* inoxydable. ◆**rusty** *a* (**-ier, -iest**) (*metal, athlete, memory etc*) rouillé.

rustic ['rʌstɪk] *a* rustique.

rustle ['rʌs(ə)l] **1** *vi* (*of leaves*) bruire; (*of skirt*) froufrouter; – *n* bruissement *m*; frou-frou *m*. **2** *vt* **to r. up** *Fam* (*prepare*) préparer; (*find*) trouver.

rut [rʌt] *n* ornière *f*; **to be in a r.** *Fig* être encroûté.

rutabaga [ruːtə'beɪgə] *n* (*swede*) *Am* rutabaga *m*.

ruthless ['ruːθləs] *a* (*attack, person etc*) impitoyable, cruel; (*in taking decisions*) très ferme. ◆**-ness** *n* cruauté *f*.

rye [raɪ] *n* seigle *m*; **r. bread** pain *m* de

S

S, s [es] *n* S, s *m*.

Sabbath ['sæbəθ] *n* (*Jewish*) sabbat *m*; (*Christian*) dimanche *m*. ◆**sa'bbatical** *a* (*year etc*) *Univ* sabbatique.

sabotage ['sæbətɑːʒ] *n* sabotage *m*; – *vt* saboter. ◆**saboteur** [-'tɜːr] *n* saboteur, -euse *mf*.

sabre ['seɪbər] *n* (*sword*) sabre *m*.

saccharin ['sækərɪn] *n* saccharine *f*.

sachet ['sæʃeɪ] *n* (*of lavender etc*) sachet *m*; (*of shampoo*) dosette *f*.

sack [sæk] **1** *n* (*bag*) sac *m*. **2** *vt* (*dismiss*) *Fam* renvoyer, virer; – *n* *Fam* **to get the s.** se faire virer; **to give s.o. the s.** virer qn. **3** *vt* (*town etc*) saccager, mettre à sac. ◆**-ing** *n* **1** (*cloth*) toile *f* à sac. **2** (*dismissal*) *Fam* renvoi *m*.

sacrament ['sækrəmənt] *n* *Rel* sacrement *m*.

sacred ['seɪkrɪd] *a* (*holy*) sacré.

sacrifice ['sækrɪfaɪs] *n* sacrifice *m*; – *vt* sacrifier (**to** à, **for** sth/s.o. pour qch/qn).

sacrilege ['sækrɪlɪdʒ] *n* sacrilège *m*. ◆**sacri'legious** *a* sacrilège.

sacrosanct ['sækrəʊsæŋkt] *a* *Iron* sacro-saint.

sad [sæd] *a* (**sadder, saddest**) triste. ◆**sadden** *vt* attrister. ◆**sadly** *adv* tristement; (*unfortunately*) malheureusement; (*very*) très. ◆**sadness** *n* tristesse *f*.

saddle ['sæd(ə)l] *n* selle *f*; **to be in the s.** (*in control*) *Fig* tenir les rênes; – *vt* (*horse*) seller; **to s. s.o. with** (*chore, person*) *Fam* coller à qn.

sadism ['seɪdɪz(ə)m] *n* sadisme *m*. ◆**sadist** *n* sadique *mf*. ◆**sa'distic** *a* sadique.

sae [eseɪ'iː] *abbr* = **stamped addressed envelope**.

safari [sə'fɑːrɪ] *n* safari *m*; **to be** or **go on s.** faire un safari.

safe¹ [seɪf] *a* (**-er, -est**) (*person*) en sécurité; (*equipment, toy, animal*) sans danger; (*place, investment, method*) sûr; (*bridge, ladder*) solide; (*prudent*) prudent; (*winner*) assuré, garanti; **s. (and sound)** sain et sauf; **it's s. to go out** on peut sortir sans danger; **the safest thing to do is . . .** le plus sûr est de . . . ; **s. from** de l'abri de; **to be on the s. side** pour plus de sûreté; **in s. hands** en mains sûres; **s. journey!** bon voyage! ◆**s.-'conduct** *n* sauf-conduit *m*. ◆**safe-'keeping** *n* **for s.** à garder en sécurité. ◆**safely** *adv* (*without mishap*) sans accident; (*securely*) en sûreté; (*without risk*) sans risque, sans danger. ◆**safety** *n* sécurité *f*; (*solidity*) solidité *f*; (*salvation*) salut *m*; – *a* (*belt, device, screen, margin*) de sécurité; (*pin, razor, chain, valve*) de sûreté; **s. precaution** mesure *f* de sécurité.

safe² [seɪf] *n* (*for money etc*) coffre-fort *m*.

safeguard ['seɪfgɑːd] *n* sauvegarde *f* (**against** contre); – *vt* sauvegarder.

saffron ['sæfrən] n safran m.

sag [sæg] vi (-gg-) (of roof, ground) s'affaisser; (of cheeks) pendre; (of prices, knees) fléchir. ◆**sagging** a (roof, breasts) affaissé.

saga ['saɡ] n Liter saga f; (bad sequence of events) Fig feuilleton m.

sage [seɪdʒ] n 1 Bot Culin sauge f. 2 (wise man) sage m.

Sagittarius [sædʒɪ'teərɪəs] n (sign) le Sagittaire.

sago ['seɪɡəʊ] n (cereal) sagou m.

Sahara [sə'hɑːrə] n the S. (desert) le Sahara.

said [sed] see say.

sail [seɪl] vi (navigate) naviguer; (leave) partir; Sp faire de la voile; (glide) Fig glisser; **to s. into port** entrer au port; **to s. round** (world, island etc) faire le tour de en bateau; **to s. through** (exam etc) Fig réussir haut la main; – vt (boat) piloter; (seas) parcourir; – n voile f; (trip) tour m en bateau; **to set s.** (of boat) partir (**for** à destination de). ◆–**ing** n navigation f; Sp voile f; (departure) départ m; (crossing) traversée f. **s. boat** voilier m. ◆**sailboard** n planche f (à voile). ◆**sailboat** n Am voilier m. ◆**sailor** n marin m, matelot m.

saint [seɪnt] n saint m, sainte f; **S. John** saint Jean; **s.'s day** Rel fête f (de saint). ◆**saintly** a (-ier, -iest) saint.

sake [seɪk] n **for my/your s.** pour moi/toi; **for your father's s.** pour (l'amour de) ton père; **(just) for the s. of eating/etc** simplement pour manger/etc; **for heaven's** or **God's s.** pour l'amour de Dieu.

salacious [sə'leɪʃəs] a obscène.

salad ['sæləd] n (dish of vegetables, fruit etc) salade f; **s. bowl** saladier m; **s. cream** mayonnaise f; **s. dressing** vinaigrette f.

salamander ['sæləmændər] n (lizard) salamandre f.

salami [sə'lɑːmɪ] n salami m.

salary ['sælərɪ] n (professional) traitement m; (wage) salaire m. ◆**salaried** a (person) qui perçoit un traitement.

sale [seɪl] n vente f; **sale(s)** (at reduced prices) Com soldes mpl; **in a** or **the s., Am on s.** (cheaply) en solde; **on s.** (available) en vente; **(up) for s.** à vendre; **to put up for s.** mettre en vente; **s. price** Com prix m de solde; **sales check** or **slip** Am reçu m. ◆**saleable** a Com vendable. ◆**sales-clerk** n Am vendeur, -euse mf. ◆**sales-man** n (pl -men) (in shop) vendeur m; (travelling) s. représentant m (de commerce). ◆**saleswoman** n (pl -women) vendeuse f; représentante f (de commerce).

salient ['seɪlɪənt] a (point, fact) marquant.

saliva [sə'laɪvə] n salive f. ◆**'salivate** vi saliver.

sallow ['sæləʊ] a (-er, -est) jaunâtre.

sally ['sælɪ] n Mil sortie f; – vi **to s. forth** Fig sortir allégrement.

salmon ['sæmən] n saumon m.

salmonella [sælmə'nelə] n (poisoning) salmonellose f.

salon ['sælɒn] n **beauty/hairdressing s.** salon m de beauté/de coiffure.

saloon [sə'luːn] n Nau salon m; (car) berline f; (bar) Am bar m; **s. bar** (of pub) salle f chic.

salt [sɔːlt] n sel m; **bath salts** sels mpl de bain; – a (water, beef etc) salé; (mine) de sel; **s. free** sans sel; – vt saler. ◆**saltcellar** n, Am ◆**saltshaker** n salière f. ◆**salty** a (-ier, -iest) a salé.

salubrious [sə'luːbrɪəs] a salubre.

salutary ['sæljʊtərɪ] a salutaire.

salute [sə'luːt] n Mil salut m; (of guns) salve f; – vt (greet) & Mil saluer; – vi Mil faire un salut.

salvage ['sælvɪdʒ] n sauvetage m (of de); récupération f (of de); (saved goods) objets mpl sauvés; – vt (save) sauver (**from** de); (old iron etc to be used again) récupérer.

salvation [sæl'veɪʃ(ə)n] n salut m.

same [seɪm] a même; **the (very) s. house as** (exactement) la même maison que; – pron **the s. le** même, la même; **the s. (thing)** la même chose; **it's all the s. to me** ça m'est égal; **all** or **just the s.** tout de même; **to do the s.** en faire autant. ◆–**ness** n identité f; Pej monotonie f.

sampl/e ['sɑːmp(ə)l] n échantillon m; (of blood) prélèvement m; – vt (wine, cheese etc) déguster, goûter; (product, recipe etc) essayer; (army life etc) goûter de. ◆–**ing** n (of wine) dégustation f.

sanatorium [sænə'tɔːrɪəm] n sanatorium m.

sanctify ['sæŋktɪfaɪ] vt sanctifier. ◆**sanc-tity** n sainteté f. ◆**sanctuary** n Rel sanc-tuaire m; (refuge) & Pol asile m; (for animals) réserve f.

sanctimonious [sæŋktɪ'məʊnɪəs] a (person, manner) tartufe.

sanction ['sæŋkʃ(ə)n] n (approval, punish-ment) sanction f; – vt (approve) sanction-ner.

sand [sænd] n sable m; **the sands** (beach) la plage; – vt (road) sabler; **to s. (down)** (wood etc) poncer. ◆**sandbag** n sac m de sable. ◆**sandcastle** n château m de sable. ◆**sander** n (machine) ponceuse f. ◆**sandpaper** n papier m de verre; – vt

poncer. ◆**sandstone** n (rock) grès m.
◆**sandy** a (-ier, -iest) (beach) de sable;
(road, ground) sablonneux; (water)
sableux. 2 (hair) blond roux inv.

sandal ['sænd(ə)l] n sandale f.

sandwich ['sænwɪdʒ] 1 n sandwich m;
cheese/etc s. sandwich au fromage/etc. 2 vt
to s. (in) (fit in) intercaler; **sandwiched in
between** (caught) coincé entre.

sane [seɪn] a (-er, -est) (person) sain
(d'esprit); (idea, attitude) raisonnable.

sang [sæŋ] see **sing**.

sanguine ['sæŋgwɪn] a (hopeful) optimiste.

sanitarium [sænɪ'teərɪəm] n Am sanatorium
m.

sanitary ['sænɪtərɪ] a (fittings, conditions)
sanitaire; (clean) hygiénique. ◆**sani-
'tation** n hygiène f (publique); (plumbing
etc) installations fpl sanitaires.

sanity ['sænɪtɪ] n santé f mentale; (reason)
raison f.

sank [sæŋk] see **sink**[2].

Santa Claus ['sæntəklɔːz] n le père Noël.

sap [sæp] 1 n Bot & Fig sève f. 2 vt (-pp-)
(weaken) miner (énergie etc).

sapphire ['sæfaɪər] n (jewel, needle) saphir
m.

sarcasm ['sɑːkæz(ə)m] n sarcasme m.
◆**sar'castic** a sarcastique.

sardine [sɑː'diːn] n sardine f.

Sardinia [sɑː'dɪnɪə] n Sardaigne f.

sardonic [sɑː'dɒnɪk] a sardonique.

sash [sæʃ] n 1 (on dress) ceinture f; (of
mayor etc) écharpe f. 2 **s. window** fenêtre f à
guillotine.

sat [sæt] see **sit**.

Satan ['seɪt(ə)n] n Satan m. ◆**sa'tanic** a
satanique.

satchel ['sætʃ(ə)l] n cartable m.

satellite ['sætəlaɪt] n satellite m; **s. (country)**
Pol pays m satellite.

satiate ['seɪʃɪeɪt] vt rassasier.

satin ['sætɪn] n satin m.

satire ['sætaɪər] n satire f (on contre).
◆**sa'tirical** a satirique. ◆**satirist** n
écrivain m satirique. ◆**satirize** vt faire la
satire de.

satisfaction [sætɪs'fækʃ(ə)n] n satisfaction
f. ◆**satisfactory** a satisfaisant. ◆**'satisfy**
vt satisfaire; (persuade, convince)
persuader (that que); (demand, condition)
satisfaire à; **to s. oneself as to/that**
s'assurer de/que; **satisfied with** satisfait de;
– vi donner satisfaction. ◆**'satisfying** a
satisfaisant; (food, meal) substantiel.

satsuma [sæt'suːmə] n (fruit) mandarine f.

saturate ['sætʃəreɪt] vt (fill) saturer (with

de); (soak) tremper. ◆**satu'ration** n saturation f.

Saturday ['sætədɪ] n samedi m.

sauce [sɔːs] n 1 sauce f; **tomato s.** sauce
tomate; **s. boat** saucière f. 2 (cheek) Fam
toupet m. ◆**saucy** a (-ier, -iest) (cheeky)
impertinent; (smart) Fam coquet.

saucepan ['sɔːspən] n casserole f.

saucer ['sɔːsər] n soucoupe f.

Saudi Arabia [saʊdɪə'reɪbɪə, Am sɔːdɪə-
'reɪbɪə] n Arabie f Séoudite.

sauna ['sɔːnə] n sauna m.

saunter ['sɔːntər] vi flâner.

sausage ['sɒsɪdʒ] n (cooked, for cooking)
saucisse f; (precooked, dried) saucisson m.

sauté ['səʊteɪ] a Culin sauté.

savage ['sævɪdʒ] a (primitive) sauvage;
(fierce) féroce; (brutal, cruel) brutal, sauvage; – n (brute) sauvage mf; – vt (of
animal, critic etc) attaquer (férocement).
◆**savagery** n (cruelty) sauvagerie f.

sav/e [seɪv] 1 vt sauver (from de); (keep)
garder, réserver; (money, time) économiser,
épargner; (stamps) collectionner; (prevent)
empêcher (from de); (problems, trouble)
éviter; **that will s. him or her (the bother of)
going** ça lui évitera d'y aller; **to s. up**
(money) économiser; – vi **to s. (up)** faire
des économies (**for sth, to buy sth** pour
(s')acheter qch); – n Fb arrêt m. 2 prep
(except) sauf. ◆**–ing** n (of time, money)
économie f, épargne f (of de); (rescue)
sauvetage m; (thrifty habit) l'épargne f; pl
(money) économies fpl; **savings bank** caisse
f d'épargne. ◆**saviour** n sauveur m.

saveloy ['sævəlɔɪ] n cervelas m.

savour ['seɪvər] n (taste, interest) saveur f; –
vt savourer. ◆**savoury** a (tasty)
savoureux; (not sweet) Culin salé; **not very
s.** (neighbourhood) Fig peu recommandable.

saw[1] [sɔː] n scie f; – vt (pt sawed, pp sawn or
sawed) scier; **to s. off** scier; **a sawn-off** or
Am **sawed-off shotgun** un fusil à canon scié.
◆**sawdust** n sciure f. ◆**sawmill** n scierie
f.

saw[2] [sɔː] see **see**[1].

saxophone ['sæksəfəʊn] n saxophone m.

say [seɪ] vt (pt & pp said [sed]) dire (**to** à, **that**
que); (prayer) faire, dire; (of dial etc)
marquer; **to s. again** répéter; **it is said that
... on dit que...**; **what do you s. to a
walk?** que dirais-tu d'une promenade?;
(let's) **s. tomorrow** disons demain; **to s. the
least** c'est le moins que l'on puisse dire; **to
s. nothing of ...** sans parler de ...; **that's
to s.** c'est-à-dire; – vi dire; **you don't s.!**

Fam sans blague!; **I s.!** dites donc!; **s.!** *Am Fam* dis donc!; – *n* **to have one's s.** dire ce que l'on a à dire, s'exprimer; **to have a lot of s.** avoir beaucoup d'influence; **to have no s.** ne pas avoir voix au chapitre (**in** pour). ◆—**ing** *n* proverbe *m*.

scab [skæb] *n* **1** *Med* croûte *f*. **2** (*blackleg*) *Fam* jaune *m*.

scaffold ['skæfəld] *n* échafaudage *m*; (*gallows*) échafaud *m*. ◆—**ing** *n* échafaudage *m*.

scald [skɔːld] *vt* (*burn, cleanse*) ébouillanter; (*sterilize*) stériliser; – *n* brûlure *f*.

scale [skeɪl] **1** *n* (*of map, wages etc*) échelle *f*; (*of numbers*) série *f*; *Mus* gamme *f*; **on a small/large s.** sur une petite/grande échelle; – *a* (*drawing*) à l'échelle; **s. model** modèle *m* réduit; – *vt* **to s. down** réduire (proportionnellement). **2** *n* (*on fish*) écaille *f*; (*dead skin*) *Med* squame *f*; (*on teeth*) tartre *m*; – *vt* (*teeth*) détartrer. **3** *vt* (*wall*) escalader.

scales [skeɪlz] *npl* (*for weighing*) balance *f*; (*bathroom*) pèse-personne *m*; (*baby*) pèse-bébé *m*.

scallion ['skæljən] *n* (*onion*) *Am* ciboule *f*.

scallop ['skɒləp] *n* coquille *f* Saint-Jacques.

scalp [skælp] *n* *Med* cuir *m* chevelu; – *vt* (*cut off too much hair from*) *Fig Hum* tondre (*qn*).

scalpel ['skælp(ə)l] *n* bistouri *m*, scalpel *m*.

scam [skæm] *n* (*swindle*) *Am Fam* escroquerie *f*.

scamp [skæmp] *n* coquin, -ine *mf*.

scamper ['skæmpər] *vi* **to s. off** *or* **away** détaler.

scampi ['skæmpɪ] *npl* gambas *fpl*.

scan [skæn] **1** *vt* (-nn-) (*look at briefly*) parcourir (des yeux); (*scrutinize*) scruter; (*poetry*) scander; (*of radar*) balayer. **2** *n* **to have a s.** (*of pregnant woman*) passer une échographie.

scandal ['skænd(ə)l] *n* (*disgrace*) scandale *m*; (*gossip*) médisances *fpl*; **to cause a s.** (*of film, book etc*) causer un scandale; (*of attitude, conduct*) faire (du) scandale. ◆**scandalize** *vt* scandaliser. ◆**scandalous** *a* scandaleux.

Scandinavia [skændɪ'neɪvɪə] *n* Scandinavie *f*. ◆**Scandinavian** *a & n* scandinave (*mf*).

scanner ['skænər] *n* (*device*) *Med* scanner *m*.

scant [skænt] *a* (*meal, amount*) insuffisant; **s. attention/regard** peu d'attention/de cas. ◆**scantily** *adv* insuffisamment; **s. dressed** à peine vêtu. ◆**scanty** *a* (-ier, -iest) insuffisant; (*bikini*) minuscule.

scapegoat ['skeɪpɡəʊt] *n* bouc *m* émissaire.

scar [skɑːr] *n* cicatrice *f*; – *vt* (-rr-) marquer d'une cicatrice; *Fig* marquer.

scarce [skeəs] *a* (-er, -est) (*food, people, book etc*) rare; **to make oneself s.** se tenir à l'écart. ◆**scarcely** *adv* à peine. ◆**scarceness** *n*, ◆**scarcity** *n* (*shortage*) pénurie *f*; (*rarity*) rareté *f*.

scare [skeər] *n* peur *f*; **to give s.o. a s.** faire peur à qn; **bomb s.** alerte *f* à la bombe; – *vt* faire peur à; **to s. off** (*person*) faire fuir; (*animal*) effaroucher. ◆**scared** *a* effrayé; **to be s.** (**stiff**) avoir (très) peur. ◆**scarecrow** *n* épouvantail *m*. ◆**scaremonger** *n* alarmiste *mf*. ◆**scary** *a* (-ier, -iest) *Fam* qui fait peur.

scarf [skɑːf] *n* (*pl* **scarves**) (*long*) écharpe *f*; (*square, for women*) foulard *m*.

scarlet ['skɑːlət] *a* écarlate; **s. fever** scarlatine *f*.

scathing ['skeɪðɪŋ] *a* (*remark etc*) acerbe; **to be s. about** critiquer de façon acerbe.

scatter ['skætər] *vt* (*disperse*) disperser (*foule, nuages etc*); (*dot or throw about*) éparpiller; (*spread*) répandre; – *vi* (*of crowd*) se disperser. ◆—**ing** *n* **a s. of houses**/*etc* quelques maisons/*etc* dispersées. ◆**scatterbrain** *n* écervelé, -ée *mf*. ◆**scatty** *a* (-ier, -iest) *Fam* écervelé, farfelu.

scaveng/e ['skævɪndʒ] *vi* fouiller dans les ordures (**for** pour trouver). ◆—**er** *n* *Pej* clochard, -arde *mf* (*qui fait les poubelles*).

scenario [sɪ'nɑːrɪəʊ] *n* (*pl* -os) *Cin & Fig* scénario *m*.

scene [siːn] *n* (*setting, fuss*) & *Th* scène *f*; (*of crime, accident etc*) lieu *m*; (*situation*) situation *f*; (*incident*) incident *m*; (*view*) vue *f*; **behind the scenes** *Th* & *Fig* dans les coulisses; **on the s.** sur les lieux; **to make** *or* **create a s.** faire une scène (à qn). ◆**scenery** *n* paysage *m*, décor *m*; *Th* décor(s) *m*(*pl*). ◆**scenic** *a* (*beauty etc*) pittoresque.

scent [sent] *n* (*fragrance, perfume*) parfum *m*; (*animal's track*) & *Fig* piste *f*; – *vt* parfumer (**with** de); (*smell, sense*) flairer.

sceptic ['skeptɪk] *a n* sceptique (*mf*). ◆**sceptical** *a* sceptique. ◆**scepticism** *n* scepticisme *m*.

sceptre ['septər] *n* sceptre *m*.

schedul/e ['ʃedjuːl, *Am* 'skedjul] *n* (*of work etc*) programme *m*; (*timetable*) horaire *m*; (*list*) liste *f*; **to be behind s.** (*of person, train*) avoir du retard; **to be on s.** (*on time*) être à l'heure; (*up to date*) être à jour; **ahead of s.** en avance; **according to s.** comme prévu; –

scheme 588 scout

vt (*plan*) prévoir; (*event*) fixer le programme *or* l'horaire de. ◆—ed *a* (*planned*) prévu; (*service, flight*) régulier; she's s. to leave at 8 elle doit partir à 8 h.

schem/e [skiːm] *n* plan *m* (to do pour faire); (*idea*) idée *f*; (*dishonest trick*) combine *f*, manœuvre *f*; (*arrangement*) arrangement *m*; – *vi* manœuvrer. ◆—ing *a* intrigant; – *npl Pej* machinations *fpl*. ◆—er *n* intrigant, -ante *mf*.

schizophrenic [skɪtsəʊˈfrenɪk] *a* & *n* schizophrène (*mf*).

scholar [ˈskɒlər] *n* érudit, -ite *mf*; (*specialist*) spécialiste *mf*; (*grant holder*) boursier, -ière *mf*. ◆scholarly *a* érudit. ◆scholarship *n* érudition *f*; (*grant*) bourse *f* (d'études). ◆scho'lastic *a* scolaire.

school [skuːl] *n* école *f*; (*teaching, lessons*) classe *f*; *Univ Am* faculté *f*; (*within university*) institut *m*, département *m*; in *or* at s. à l'école; secondary s., Am high s. collège *m*, lycée *m*; public s. école *f* privée; Am école publique; s. of motoring auto-école *f*; summer s. cours *mpl* d'été *or* de vacances; – *a* (*year, equipment etc*) scolaire; (*hours*) de classe; s. fees frais *mpl* de scolarité. ◆—ing *n* (*learning*) instruction *f*; (*attendance*) scolarité *f*. ◆schoolboy *n* écolier *m*. ◆—ing *n* (*learning*) ◆schooldays *npl* années *fpl* d'école. ◆schoolgirl *n* écolière *f*. ◆schoolhouse *n* école *f*. ◆school-'leaver *n* jeune *mf* qui a terminé ses études secondaires. ◆schoolmaster *n* (*primary*) instituteur *m*; (*secondary*) professeur *m*. ◆schoolmate *n* camarade *mf* de classe. ◆schoolmistress *n* institutrice *f*; professeur *m*. ◆schoolteacher *n* (*primary*) instituteur, -trice *mf*; (*secondary*) professeur *m*.

schooner [ˈskuːnər] *n Nau* goélette *f*.

science [ˈsaɪəns] *n* science *f*; to study s. étudier les sciences; – *a* (*subject*) scientifique; (*teacher*) de science; s. fiction science-fiction *f*. ◆scien'tific *a* scientifique. ◆scientist *n* scientifique *mf*.

scintillating [ˈsɪntɪleɪtɪŋ] *a* (*conversation, wit*) brillant.

scissors [ˈsɪzəz] *npl* ciseaux *mpl*; a pair of s. une paire de ciseaux.

sclerosis [sklɪˈrəʊsɪs] *n Med* sclérose *f*; multiple s. sclérose en plaques.

scoff [skɒf] **1** *vi* to s. at se moquer de. **2** *vti* (*eat*) *Fam* bouffer.

scold [skəʊld] *vt* gronder, réprimander (for doing pour avoir fait). ◆—ing *n* réprimande *f*.

scone [skɒn, skəʊn] *n* petit pain *m* au lait.

scoop [skuːp] *n* (*shovel*) pelle *f* (à main);

(*spoon-shaped*) *Culin* cuiller *f*; *Journ* exclusivité *f*; at one s. d'un seul coup; – *vt* (*prizes*) rafler; to s. out (*hollow out*) (é)vider; to s. up ramasser (avec une pelle *or* une cuiller).

scoot [skuːt] *vi* (*rush, leave*) *Fam* filer.

scooter [ˈskuːtər] *n* (*child's*) trottinette *f*; (*motorcycle*) scooter *m*.

scope [skəʊp] *n* (*range*) étendue *f*; (*of mind*) envergure *f*; (*competence*) compétence(s) *f*(*pl*); (*limits*) limites *fpl*; s. for sth/for doing (*opportunity*) les possibilités *fpl* de qch/de faire; the s. of one's activity champ *m* de ses activités.

score¹ [skɔːr] *n Sp* score *m*; *Cards* marque *f*; *Mus* partition *f*; (*of film*) musique *f*; a s. to settle *Fig* un compte à régler; on that s. (*in that respect*) à cet égard; – *vt* (*point, goal*) marquer; (*exam mark*) avoir; (*success*) remporter; *Mus* orchestrer; – *vi* marquer un point *or* un but; (*keep score*) marquer les points. ◆scoreboard *n Sp* tableau *m* d'affichage. ◆scorer *n Sp* marqueur *m*.

score² [skɔːr] *n* (*twenty*) vingt; a s. of une vingtaine de; scores of *Fig* un grand nombre de.

score³ [skɔːr] *vt* (*cut*) rayer; (*paper*) marquer.

scorn [skɔːn] *vt* mépriser; – *n* mépris *m*. ◆scornful *a* méprisant; to be s. of mépriser. ◆scornfully *adv* avec mépris.

Scorpio [ˈskɔːpɪəʊ] *n* (*sign*) le Scorpion.

scorpion [ˈskɔːpɪən] *n* scorpion *m*.

Scot [skɒt] *n* Écossais, -aise *mf*. ◆Scotland *n* Écosse *f*. ◆Scotsman *n* (*pl* -men) Écossais *m*. ◆Scotswoman *n* (*pl* -women) Écossaise *f*. ◆Scottish *a* écossais.

scotch [skɒtʃ] **1** *a* s. tape® *Am* scotch® *m*. **2** *vt* (*rumour*) étouffer; (*attempt*) faire échouer.

Scotch [skɒtʃ] *n* (*whisky*) scotch *m*.

scot-free [skɒtˈfriː] *adv* sans être puni.

scoundrel [ˈskaʊndrəl] *n* vaurien *m*.

scour [ˈskaʊər] *vt* (*pan*) récurer; (*streets etc*) *Fig* parcourir (for à la recherche de). ◆—er *n* tampon *m* à récurer.

scourge [skɜːdʒ] *n* fléau *m*.

scout [skaʊt] **1** *n* (*soldier*) éclaireur *m*; (*boy*) s. scout *m*, éclaireur *m*; girl s. *Am* éclaireuse *f*; s. camp camp *m* scout. **2** *vi* to

s. round for (look for) chercher. ◆—**ing** n scoutisme m.

scowl [skaʊl] vi se renfrogner; **to s. at s.o.** regarder qn d'un air mauvais. ◆—**ing** a renfrogné.

scraggy ['skrægɪ] a (-ier, -iest) (bony) osseux, maigrichon; (unkempt) débraillé.

scram [skræm] vi (-mm-) Fam filer.

scramble ['skræmb(ə)l] 1 vi **to s. for** se ruer vers; **to s. up** (climb) grimper; **to s. through** traverser avec difficulté; – n ruée f (for vers). 2 vt (egg, message) brouiller.

scrap [skræp] 1 n (piece) petit morceau m (of de); (of information, news) fragment m; pl (food) restes mpl; **not a s. of** (truth etc) pas un brin de; **s. paper** (papier m) brouillon m. 2 n (metal) ferraille f; **to sell for s.** vendre à la casse; – a (yard, heap) de ferraille; **s. dealer, s. merchant** marchand m de ferraille; **s. iron** ferraille f; **on the s. heap** Fig au rebut; – vt (-pp-) (car) envoyer à la ferraille; (unwanted object, idea, plan) Fig mettre au rancart. 3 n (fight) Fam bagarre f. ◆**scrapbook** n album m (pour collages etc).

scrap/e [skreɪp] vt racler, gratter; (skin) Med érafler; **to s. away** or **off** (mud etc) racler; **to s. together** (money, people) réunir (difficilement); – vi **to s. against** frotter contre; **to s. along** Fig se débrouiller; **to s. through** (in exam) réussir de justesse; – n raclement m; éraflure f; **to get into a s.** Fam s'attirer des ennuis. ◆—**ings** npl raclures fpl. ◆—**er** n racloir m.

scratch [skrætʃ] n (mark, injury) éraflure f; (on glass) rayure f; **to have a s.** (scratch oneself) Fam se gratter; **to start from s.** (re)partir de zéro; **to be/come up to s.** être/se montrer à la hauteur; – vt (to relieve an itch) gratter; (skin, wall etc) érafler; (glass) rayer; (with claw) griffer; (one's name) graver (on sur); – vi (relieve an itch) se gratter; (of cat etc) griffer; (of pen) gratter, accrocher.

scrawl [skrɔːl] vt gribouiller; – n gribouillis m.

scrawny ['skrɔːnɪ] a (-ier, -iest) (bony) osseux, maigrichon.

scream [skriːm] vti crier, hurler; **to s. at s.o.** crier après qn; **to s. with pain/etc** hurler de douleur/etc; – n cri m (perçant).

screech [skriːtʃ] vti crier, hurler; (of brakes) hurler; – n cri m; hurlement m.

screen [skriːn] 1 n écran m; Fig masque m; **(folding) s. paravent** m. 2 vt (hide) cacher (from s.o. à qn); (protect) protéger (from de); (a film) projeter; (visitors, documents)

filtrer; (for cancer etc) Med faire subir un test de dépistage à (qn) (for pour). ◆—**ing** n (of film) projection f; (selection) tri m; (medical examination) (test m de) dépistage m. ◆**screenplay** n Cin scénario m.

screw [skruː] n vis f; – vt visser (**to** à); **to s. down** or **on** visser; **to s. off** dévisser; **to s. up** (paper) chiffonner; (eyes) plisser; (mess up) Sl gâcher; **to s. one's face up** grimacer. ◆**screwball** n & a Am Fam cinglé, -ée (mf). ◆**screwdriver** n tournevis m. ◆**screwy** a (-ier, -iest) (idea, person etc) farfelu.

scribble ['skrɪb(ə)l] vti griffonner; – n griffonnage m.

scribe [skraɪb] n scribe m.

scrimmage ['skrɪmɪdʒ] n Fb Am mêlée f.

script [skrɪpt] n (of film) scénario m; (of play) texte m; (in exam) copie f. ◆**script-writer** n Cin scénariste mf, dialoguiste mf; TV Rad dialoguiste m.

Scripture ['skrɪptʃər] n Rel Écriture f (sainte).

scroll [skrəʊl] n rouleau m (de parchemin); (book) manuscrit m.

scrooge [skruːdʒ] n (miser) harpagon m.

scroung/e [skraʊndʒ] vt (meal) se faire payer (off or from s.o. par qn); (steal) piquer (off or from s.o. à qn); **to s. money off** or **from** taper; – vi vivre en parasite; (beg) quémander; **to s. around for** Pej chercher. ◆—**er** n parasite m.

scrub [skrʌb] 1 vt (-bb-) frotter, nettoyer (à la brosse); (pan) récurer; (cancel) Fig annuler; **to s. out** (erase) Fig effacer; – vi (scrub floors) frotter les planchers; **scrubbing brush** brosse f dure; – n brosse f dure; **s. brush** Am brosse f dure. 2 n (land) broussailles fpl.

scruff [skrʌf] n 1 **by the s. of the neck** par la peau du cou. 2 (person) Fam individu m débraillé. ◆**scruffy** a (-ier, -iest) (untidy) négligé; (dirty) malpropre.

scrum [skrʌm] n Rugby mêlée f.

scrumptious ['skrʌmpʃəs] a Fam super bon, succulent.

scruple ['skruːp(ə)l] n scrupule m. ◆**scrupulous** a scrupuleux. ◆**scrupulously** adv (conscientiously) scrupuleusement; (completely) absolument.

scrutinize ['skruːtɪnaɪz] vt scruter. ◆**scrutiny** n examen m minutieux.

scuba ['skjuːbə, Am 'skuːbə] n scaphandre m autonome; **s. diving** la plongée sous-marine.

scuff [skʌf] vt **to s. (up)** (scrape) érafler.

scuffle ['skʌf(ə)l] n bagarre f.

scullery ['skʌləri] n arrière-cuisine f.
sculpt [skʌlpt] vti sculpter. ◆**sculptor** n
sculpteur m. ◆**sculpture** n (art, object)
sculpture f; – vti sculpter.
scum [skʌm] n 1 (on liquid) écume f. 2 Pej
(people) racaille f; (person) salaud m; the s.
of (society etc) la lie de.
scupper ['skʌpər] vt (plan) Fam saboter.
scurf [skɜːf] n pellicules fpl.
scurrilous ['skʌriləs] a (criticism, attack)
haineux, violent et grossier.
scurry ['skʌri] vi (rush) se précipiter, courir;
to s. off décamper.
scuttle ['skʌt(ə)l] 1 vt (ship) saborder. 2 vi to
s. off filer.
scythe [saɪð] n faux f.
sea [siː] n mer f; (out) at s. en mer; by s. par
mer; by or beside the s. au bord de la mer;
to be all at s. Fig nager complètement; – a
(level, breeze) de la mer; (water, fish) de
mer; (air, salt) marin; (battle, power) naval;
(route) maritime; s. bed, s. floor fond m de
la mer; s. lion (animal) otarie f.
◆**seaboard** n littoral m. ◆**seafarer** n
marin m. ◆**seafood** n fruits mpl de mer.
◆**seafront** n bord m de mer. ◆**seagull** n
mouette f. ◆**seaman** n (pl -men) marin m.
◆**seaplane** n hydravion m. ◆**seaport** n
port m de mer. ◆**seashell** n coquillage m.
◆**seashore** n bord m de la mer. ◆**sea-
sick** a to be s. avoir le mal de mer.
◆**seasickness** n mal m de mer. ◆**seaside** n bord m de la mer; – a (town, holiday) au bord de la mer. ◆**seaway** n route f
maritime. ◆**seaweed** n algue(s) f(pl).
◆**seaworthy** a (ship) en état de naviguer.
seal [siːl] 1 n (animal) phoque m. 2 n (mark,
design) sceau m; (on letter) cachet m (de
cire); (putty for sealing) joint m; – vt (document, container) sceller; (with wax)
cacheter; (stick down) coller; (with putty)
boucher; (s.o.'s fate) Fig décider de; to s.
off (room etc) interdire l'accès de; to s. off a
house/district (of police, troops) boucler
une maison/un quartier.
seam [siːm] n (in cloth etc) couture f; (of
coal, quartz etc) veine f.
seamy ['siːmi] a (-ier, -iest) the s. side le côté
peu reluisant (of de).
séance ['seɪɑːns] n séance f de spiritisme.
search [sɜːtʃ] n (quest) recherche f (for de);
(of person, place) fouille f; in s. of à la
recherche de; s. party équipe f de secours;
– vt (person, place) fouiller (for pour
trouver); (study) examiner (documents etc);
to s. (through) one's papers/etc for sth
chercher qch dans ses papiers/etc; – vi

chercher; to s. for sth chercher qch.
◆**-ing** a (look) pénétrant; (examination)
minutieux. ◆**searchlight** n projecteur m.
season ['siːz(ə)n] 1 n saison f; the festive s.
la période des fêtes; in the peak s., in (the)
high s. en pleine or haute saison; in the low
or off s. en basse saison; a Truffaut s. Cin
une rétrospective Truffaut; s. ticket carte f
d'abonnement. 2 vt (food) assaisonner;
highly seasoned (dish) relevé. ◆**-ed** a
(worker) expérimenté; (soldier) aguerri.
◆**-ing** n Culin assaisonnement m.
◆**seasonable** a (weather) de saison.
◆**seasonal** a saisonnier.
seat [siːt] n (for sitting, centre) & Pol siège
m; (on train, bus) banquette f; Cin Th
fauteuil m; (place) place f; (of trousers)
fond m; to take or have a s. s'asseoir; in the
hot s. (in difficult position) Fig sur la
sellette; s. belt ceinture f de sécurité; – vt
(at table) placer (qn); (on one's lap) asseoir
(qn); the room seats 50 la salle a 50 places
(assises); be seated! asseyez-vous! ◆**-ed**
a (sitting) assis. ◆**-ing** n (room) (seats)
places fpl assises; the s. arrangements la
disposition des places; s. capacity nombre
m de places assises. ◆**-er** a capacity in two-s.
(car) voiture f à deux places.
secateurs [sekə'tɜːz] npl sécateur m.
secede [sɪ'siːd] vi faire sécession. ◆**secession** n sécession f.
secluded [sɪ'kluːtɪd] a (remote) isolé.
◆**seclusion** n solitude f.
second[1] ['sekənd] a deuxième, second;
every s. week une semaine sur deux; in s.
(gear) Aut en seconde; s. to none sans
pareil; s. in command second m; Mil
commandant m en second; – adv (to say)
deuxièmement; to come s. Sp se classer
deuxième; the s. biggest la deuxième en
ordre de grandeur; the s. richest country le
deuxième pays le plus riche; my s. best
(choice) mon deuxième choix; – n (person,
object) deuxième mf, second, -onde mf;
Louis the S. Louis Deux; pl (goods) Com
articles mpl de second choix; – vt (motion)
appuyer. ◆**s.-'class** a (product) de qualité inférieure; (ticket) Rail de seconde
(classe); (mail) non urgent. ◆**s.-'rate** a
médiocre. ◆**secondly** adv deuxièmement.
second[2] ['sekənd] n (unit of time) seconde f;
s. hand (of clock, watch) trotteuse f.
second[3] [sɪ'kɒnd] vt (employee) détacher
(to à). ◆**-ment** n détachement m; on s. en
(position de) détachement (to à).
secondary ['sekəndəri] a secondaire.
secondhand [sekənd'hænd] 1 a & adv (not

new) d'occasion. **2** a (*report, news*) de seconde main.

secret ['siːkrɪt] a secret; – n secret m; **in s.** en secret; **an open s.** le secret de Polichinelle. ◆**secrecy** n (*discretion, silence*) secret m; **in s.** en secret. ◆**secretive** a (*person*) cachottier; (*organization*) qui a le goût du secret; **to be s. about** faire un mystère de; (*organization*) être très discret sur. ◆**secretively** adv en catimini.

secretary ['sekrət(ə)rɪ] n secrétaire f; **Foreign S.,** Am **S. of State** = ministre m des Affaires étrangères. ◆**secre'tarial** a (*work*) de secrétaire, de secrétariat; (*school*) de secrétariat. ◆**secre'tariat** n (*in international organization*) secrétariat m.

secrete [sɪ'kriːt] vt Med Biol sécréter. ◆**sec'retion** n sécrétion f.

sect [sekt] n secte f. ◆**sec'tarian** a & n Pej sectaire (mf).

section ['sekʃ(ə)n] n (*of road, book, wood etc*) section f; (*of town, country*) partie f; (*of machine, furniture*) élément m; (*department*) section f; (*in store*) rayon m; **the sports/etc s.** (*of newspaper*) la page des sports/etc; – vt **to s. off** (*separate*) séparer.

sector ['sektər] n secteur m.

secular ['sekjʊlər] a (*teaching etc*) laïque; (*music, art*) profane.

secure [sɪ'kjʊər] **1** a (*person, valuables*) en sûreté, en sécurité; (*in one's mind*) tranquille; (*place*) sûr; (*solid, firm*) solide; (*door, window*) bien fermé; (*certain*) assuré; **s. from** à l'abri de; (**emotionally**) **s.** sécurisé; – vt (*fasten*) attacher; (*window etc*) bien fermer; (*success, future etc*) assurer; **to s. against** protéger de. **2** vt (*obtain*) procurer (sth for s.o. qch à qn); **to s. sth** (*for oneself*) se procurer qch. ◆**securely** adv (*firmly*) solidement; (*safely*) en sûreté. ◆**security** n sécurité f; (*for loan, bail*) caution f; **s. firm** société f de surveillance; **s. guard** agent m de sécurité; (*transferring money*) convoyeur m de fonds.

sedan [sɪ'dæn] n (*saloon*) Aut Am berline f.

sedate [sɪ'deɪt] **1** a calme. **2** vt mettre sous calmants. ◆**sedation** n **under s.** sous calmants. ◆**'sedative** n calmant m.

sedentary ['sedəntərɪ] a sédentaire.

sediment ['sedɪmənt] n sédiment m.

sedition [sə'dɪʃ(ə)n] n sédition f. ◆**seditious** a séditieux.

seduce [sɪ'djuːs] vt séduire. ◆**seducer** n séducteur, -trice mf. ◆**seduction** n séduc-

tion f. ◆**seductive** a (*person, offer*) séduisant.

see¹ [siː] vti (pt **saw**, pp **seen**) voir; **we'll on verra** (bien); **I s.!** je vois!; **I can s.** (*clearly*) j'y vois clair; **I saw him run(ning)** je l'ai vu courir; **to s. reason** entendre raison; **to s. the joke** comprendre la plaisanterie; **s. who it is** va voir qui c'est; **s. you (later)!** à tout à l'heure!; **s. you (soon)!** à bientôt!; **to s. about** (*deal with*) s'occuper de; (*consider*) songer à; **s. in the New Year** fêter la Nouvelle Année; **to s. s.o. off** accompagner qn (*à la gare etc*); **to s. s.o. out** accompagner qn dehors; **to s. through** (*task*) mener à bonne fin; **to s. s.o. through** (*be enough for*) suffire à qn; **to s. through s.o.** deviner le jeu de qn; **to s. to** (*deal with*) s'occuper de; (*mend*) réparer; **to s. (to it) that** (*attend*) veiller à ce que (+ *sub*); (*check*) s'assurer que; **to s. s.o. to** (*accompany*) raccompagner qn à. ◆**s.-through** a (*dress etc*) transparent.

see² [siː] n (*of bishop*) siège m (épiscopal).

seed [siːd] n Agr graine f; (*in grape*) pépin m; (*source*) Fig germe; Tennis tête f de série; **seed(s)** (*for sowing*) Agr graines fpl; **to go to s.** (*of lettuce etc*) monter en graine. ◆**seedbed** n Bot semis m; (*of rebellion etc*) Fig foyer m (*de*). ◆**seedling** n (*plant*) semis m.

seedy ['siːdɪ] a (-ier, -iest) miteux. ◆**seediness** n aspect m miteux.

seeing ['siːɪŋ] conj **s. (that)** vu que.

seek [siːk] vt (pt & pp **sought**) chercher (**to do** à faire); (*ask for*) demander (from à); **to s. (after)** rechercher; **to s. out** aller trouver.

seem [siːm] vi sembler (**to do** faire); **it seems that...** (*impression*) il semble que... (+ *sub or indic*); (*rumour*) il paraît que...; **it seems to me that...** il me semble que...; **we s. to know each other** il me semble qu'on se connaît; **I can't s. to do it** je n'arrive pas à le faire. ◆**-ing** a apparent. ◆**-ingly** adv apparemment.

seemly ['siːmlɪ] a convenable.

seen [siːn] see **see¹**.

seep [siːp] vi (*ooze*) suinter; **to s. into** s'infiltrer dans. ◆**-age** n suintement m; infiltration(s) f(pl) (*into* dans); (*leak*) fuite f.

seesaw ['siːsɔː] n (*jeu m de*) bascule f.

seethe [siːð] vi **to s. with anger** bouillir de colère; **to s. with people** grouiller de monde.

segment ['segmənt] n segment m; (*of orange*) quartier m.

segregate ['segrɪgeɪt] vt séparer; (**racially**)

segregated (*school*) où se pratique la ségrégation raciale. ◆**segre'gation** *n* ségrégation *f*.

seize [siːz] **1** *vt* saisir; (*power, land*) s'emparer de; – *vi* to s. on (*offer etc*) saisir. **2** *vi* to s. up (*of engine*) (se) gripper. ◆**seizure** [-ʒər] *n* (*of goods etc*) saisie *f*; *Mil* prise *f*; *Med* crise *f*.

seldom ['seldəm] *adv* rarement.

select [sɪ'lekt] *vt* choisir (**from** parmi); (*candidates, pupils etc*) & *Sp* sélectionner; – *a* (*chosen*) choisi; (*exclusive*) sélect, chic *inv*. ◆**selection** *n* sélection *f*. ◆**selective** *a* (*memory, recruitment etc*) sélectif; (*person*) qui opère un choix; (*choosey*) difficile.

self [self] *n* (*pl* **selves**) the s. *Phil* le moi; **he's back to his old s.** *Fam* il est redevenu lui-même. ◆**s.-a'ssurance** *n* assurance *f*. ◆**s.-a'ssured** *a* sûr de soi. ◆**s.-'catering** *a* où l'on fait la cuisine soi-même. ◆**s.-'centred** *a* égocentrique. ◆**s.-'cleaning** *a* (*oven*) autonettoyant. ◆**s.-con'fessed** *a* (*liar*) de son propre aveu. ◆**s.-'confident** *a* sûr de soi. ◆**s.-'conscious** *a* gêné. ◆**s.-'consciousness** *n* gêne *f*. ◆**s.-con'tained** *a* (*flat*) indépendant. ◆**s.-con'trol** *n* maîtrise *f* de soi. ◆**s.-de'feating** *a* qui a un effet contraire à celui qui est recherché. ◆**s.-de'fence** *n* *Jur* légitime défense *f*. ◆**s.-de'nial** *n* abnégation *f*. ◆**s.-determi'nation** *n* autodétermination *f*. ◆**s.-'discipline** *n* autodiscipline *f*. ◆**s.-em'ployed** *a* qui travaille à son compte. ◆**s.-es'teem** *n* amour-propre *m*. ◆**s.-'evident** *a* évident, qui va de soi. ◆**s.-ex'planatory** *a* qui tombe sous le sens, qui se passe d'explication. ◆**s.-'governing** *a* autonome. ◆**s-im'portant** *a* suffisant, qui se croit sorti de la cuisse de Jupiter. ◆**s.-in'dulgent** *a* qui ne se refuse rien. ◆**s.-'interest** *n* intérêt *m* (personnel). ◆**s.-o'pinionated** *a* entêté. ◆**s.-'pity** *n* to feel s.-pity s'apitoyer sur son propre sort. ◆**s.-'portrait** *n* autoportrait *m*. ◆**s.-po'ssessed** *a* assuré. ◆**s.-raising** *a* or *Am* **s.-rising 'flour** *n* farine *f* à levure. ◆**s.-re'liant** *a* indépendant. ◆**s.-re'spect** *n* amour-propre *m*. ◆**s.-re'specting** *a* qui se respecte. ◆**s.-'righteous** *a* pharisaïque. ◆**s.-'sacrifice** *n* abnégation *f*. ◆**s.-'satisfied** *a* content de soi. ◆**s.-'service** *n* & *a* libre-service (*m inv*). ◆**s.-'styled** *a* soi-disant. ◆**s.-su'fficient** *a* indépendant, qui a son indépendance. ◆**s.-sup-**

porting *a* financièrement indépendant. ◆**s.-'taught** *a* autodidacte.

selfish ['selfɪʃ] *a* égoïste; (*motive*) intéressé. ◆**selfless** *a* désintéressé. ◆**selfishness** *n* égoïsme *m*.

selfsame ['selfseɪm] *a* même.

sell [sel] *vt* (*pt* & *pp* **sold**) vendre; (*idea etc*) *Fig* faire accepter; **she sold me it for twenty pounds** elle me l'a vendu vingt livres; **to s. back** revendre; **to s. off** liquider; **to have** *or* **be sold out of** (*cheese etc*) n'avoir plus de; **this book is sold out** ce livre est épuisé; – *vi* se vendre; (*of idea etc*) *Fig* être accepté; **to s. up** vendre sa maison; *Com* vendre son affaire; **selling price** prix *m* de vente. ◆**seller** *n* vendeur, -euse *mf*. ◆**sellout** *n* **1** (*betrayal*) trahison *f*. **2** it was a s. *Th Cin* tous les billets ont été vendus.

sellotape® ['seləteɪp] *n* scotch® *m*; – *vt* scotcher.

semantic [sɪ'mæntɪk] *a* sémantique. ◆**semantics** *n* sémantique *f*.

semaphore ['seməfɔːr] *n* (*device*) *Rail Nau* sémaphore *m*; (*system*) signaux *mpl* à bras.

semblance ['sembləns] *n* semblant *m*.

semen ['siːmən] *n* sperme *m*.

semester [sɪ'mestər] *n* *Univ* semestre *m*.

semi- ['semɪ] *pref* demi-, semi-. ◆**semi-auto'matic** *a* semi-automatique. ◆**semibreve** [-briːv] *n* *Mus* ronde *f*. ◆**semicircle** *n* demi-cercle *m*. ◆**semi'circular** *a* semi-circulaire. ◆**semi'colon** *n* point-virgule *m*. ◆**semi-'conscious** *a* à demi conscient. ◆**semide'tached** *a* s. house maison *f* jumelle. ◆**semi'final** *n* *Sp* demi-finale *f*.

seminar ['semɪnɑːr] *n* *Univ* séminaire *m*.

seminary ['semɪnərɪ] *n* *Rel* séminaire *m*.

Semite ['siːmaɪt, *Am* 'semaɪt] *n* Sémite *mf*. ◆**Se'mitic** *a* sémite; (*language*) sémitique.

semolina [semə'liːnə] *n* semoule *f*.

senate ['senɪt] *n* *Pol* sénat *m*. ◆**senator** *n* *Pol* sénateur *m*.

send [send] *vt* (*pt* & *pp* **sent**) envoyer (to à); **to s. s.o. for sth/s.o.** envoyer qn chercher qch/qn; **to s. s.o. crazy** *or* **mad** rendre qn fou; **to s. s.o. packing** *Fam* envoyer promener qn; **to s. away** *or* **off** envoyer (to à); (*dismiss*) renvoyer; **to s. back** renvoyer; **to s. in** (*form*) envoyer; (*person*) faire entrer; **to s. on** (*letter, luggage*) faire suivre; **to s. out** (*invitation etc*) envoyer; (*heat*) émettre; (*from room etc*) faire sortir (*qn*); **to s. up** (*balloon, rocket*) lancer; (*price, luggage*) faire monter; (*mock*) *Fam* parodier; – *vi* **to s. away** *or* **off for** commander (par courrier); **to s. for** (*doctor etc*) faire venir, envoyer chercher; **to s. (out) for** (*meal, groceries*) envoyer chercher. ◆**s.-off** *n* to give s.o. a s.-off *Fam* faire des adieux chaleureux à qn. ◆**s.-up** *n Fam* parodie *f*. ◆**sender** *n* expéditeur, -trice *mf*.

senile ['si:nail] *a* gâteux, sénile. ◆**se'nility** *n* gâtisme *m*, sénilité *f*.

senior ['si:niər] *a* (*older*) plus âgé; (*position, executive, rank*) supérieur; (*teacher, partner*) principal; **to be s. to s.o., s.o.'s s.** être plus âgé que qn; (*in rank*) être au-dessus de qn; **Brown s.** Brown père; **s. citizen** personne *f* âgée; **s. year** *Sch Univ Am* dernière année *f*; – *n* aîné, -ée *mf*; *Sch* grand, -ande *mf*; *Sch Univ Am* étudiant, -ante *mf* de dernière année; *Sp* senior *mf*. ◆**seni'ority** *n* priorité *f* d'âge; (*in service*) ancienneté *f*; (*in rank*) supériorité *f*.

sensation [sen'seiʃ(ə)n] *n* sensation *f*. ◆**sensational** *a* (*event*) qui fait sensation; (*newspaper, film*) à sensation; (*terrific*) *Fam* sensationnel.

sense [sens] *n* (*faculty, awareness, meaning*) sens *m*; **a s. of hearing** (*the*) l'ouïe *f*; **to have (good) s.** avoir du bon sens; **a s. of** (*physical*) une sensation de (*chaleur etc*); (*mental*) un sentiment de (*honte etc*); **a s. of humour/direction** le sens de l'humour/de l'orientation; **a s. of time** la notion de l'heure; **to bring s.o. to his senses** ramener qn à la raison; **to make s.** (*of story, action etc*) avoir du sens; **to make s. of** comprendre; – *vt* sentir (intuitivement) que; (*have a foreboding of*) pressentir. ◆**—less** *a* (*stupid, meaningless*) insensé; (*unconscious*) sans connaissance. ◆**—lessness** *n* stupidité *f*.

sensibility [sensi'biliti] *n* sensibilité *f*; *pl* (*touchiness*) susceptibilité *f*.

sensible ['sensəb(ə)l] *a* (*wise*) raisonnable, sensé; (*clothes*) pratique.

sensitive ['sensitiv] *a* (*responsive, painful*) sensible (**to** à); (*delicate*) délicat (*peau, question etc*); (*touchy*) susceptible (**about** à propos de). ◆**sensi'tivity** *n* sensibilité *f*; (*touchiness*) susceptibilité *f*.

sensory ['sensəri] *a* sensoriel.

sensual ['sensjuəl] *a* (*bodily, sexual*) sensuel. ◆**sensu'ality** *n* sensualité *f*. ◆**sensuous** *a* (*pleasing, refined*) sensuel. ◆**sensuously** *adv* avec sensualité. ◆**sensuousness** *n* sensualité *f*.

sent [sent] *see* send.

sentence ['sentəns] **1** *n Gram* phrase *f*. **2** *n Jur* condamnation *f*; (*punishment*) peine *f*;

to pass s. prononcer une condamnation (**on s.o.** contre qn); **to serve a s.** purger une peine; – *vt Jur* prononcer une condamnation contre; **to s.** to condamner à.

sentiment ['sentimənt] *n* sentiment *m*. ◆**senti'mental** *a* sentimental. ◆**sentimen'tality** *n* sentimentalité *f*.

sentry ['sentri] *n* sentinelle *f*; **s. box** guérite *f*.

separate ['sepərət] *a* (*distinct*) séparé; (*independent*) indépendant; (*different*) différent; (*individual*) particulier; – ['sepəreit] *vt* séparer (**from** de); – *vi* se séparer (**from** de). ◆**'separately** *adv* séparément. ◆**sepa'ration** *n* séparation *f*.

separates ['sepərəts] *npl* (*garments*) coordonnés *mpl*.

September [sep'tembər] *n* septembre *m*.

septic ['septik] *a* (*wound*) infecté; **s. tank** fosse *f* septique.

sequel ['si:kw(ə)l] *n* suite *f*.

sequence ['si:kwəns] *n* (*order*) ordre *m*; (*series*) succession *f*; *Mus Cards* séquence *f*; **film s.** séquence de film; **in s.** dans l'ordre, successivement.

sequin ['si:kwin] *n* paillette *f*.

serenade [serə'neid] *n* sérénade *f*; – *vt* donner une *or* la sérénade à.

serene [sə'ri:n] *a* serein. ◆**serenity** *n* sérénité *f*.

sergeant ['sɑ:dʒənt] *n Mil* sergent *m*; (*in police force*) brigadier *m*.

serial ['siəriəl] *n* (*story, film*) feuilleton *m*; **s. number** (*of banknote, TV set etc*) numéro de série. ◆**serialize** *vt* publier en feuilleton; *TV Rad* adapter en feuilleton.

series ['siəriːz] *n inv* série *f*; (*book collection*) collection *f*.

serious ['siəriəs] *a* sérieux; (*illness, mistake, tone*) grave, sérieux; (*damage*) important. ◆**—ly** *adv* sérieusement; (*ill, damaged*) gravement; **to take s.** prendre au sérieux. ◆**—ness** *n* sérieux *m*; (*of illness etc*) gravité *f*; (*of damage*) importance *f*; **in all s.** sérieusement.

sermon ['sɜ:mən] *n* sermon *m*.

serpent ['sɜ:pənt] *n* serpent *m*.

serrated [sə'reitid] *a* (*knife*) à dents (de scie).

serum ['siərəm] *n* sérum *m*.

servant ['sɜ:vənt] *n* (*in house etc*) domestique *mf*; (*person who serves*) serviteur *m*; **public s.** fonctionnaire *mf*.

serve [sɜ:v] *vt* servir (**to s.o.** à qn, **s.o. with sth** qch à qn); (*of train, bus etc*) desservir (*un village, un quartier etc*); (*supply*) *El* alimenter; (*apprenticeship*) faire; (*summons*) *Jur* remettre (**on** à); **it serves its**

purpose ça fait l'affaire; **(it) serves you right!** *Fam* ça t'apprendra!; **to s. up** or **out** servir; – *vi* servir **(as de)**; **to s. on** (*jury, committee*) être membre de; **to s. to show**/*etc* servir à montrer/*etc*; – *n Tennis* service *m*.

servic/e ['sɜːvɪs] *n* (*serving*) & *Mil Rel Tennis* service *m*; (*machine or vehicle repair*) révision *f*; **to be of s.** to être utile à, rendre service à; **the (armed) services** les forces *fpl* armées; **s. (charge)** (*tip*) service *m*; **s. department** (*workshop*) atelier *m*; **s. area** (*on motorway*) aire *f* de service; **s. station** station-service *f*; – *vt* (*machine, vehicle*) réviser. ◆—**ing** *n Tech Aut* révision *f*. ◆**serviceable** *a* (*usable*) utilisable, (*useful*) commode; (*durable*) solide. ◆**serviceman** *n* (*pl* **-men**) *n* militaire *m*.

serviette [sɜːvɪ'et] *n* serviette *f* (de table).

servile ['sɜːvaɪl] *a* servile.

session ['seʃ(ə)n] *n* séance *f*; *Jur Pol* session *f*, séance *f*; *Univ* année *f* or trimestre *m* universitaire; *Univ Am* semestre *m* universitaire.

set [set] **1** *n* (*of keys, needles, tools*) jeu *m*; (*of stamps, numbers*) série *f*; (*of people*) groupe *m*; (*of facts*) & *Math* ensemble *m*; (*of books*) collection *f*; (*of plates*) service *m*; (*of tyres*) train *m*; (*kit*) trousse *f*; (*stage*) *Th Cin* plateau *m*; (*scenery*) *Th Cin* décor *m*, scène *f*; (*hairstyle*) mise *f* en plis; *Tennis* set *m*; **television s.** téléviseur *m*; **radio s.** poste *m* de radio; **tea s.** service *m* à thé; **chess s.** (*box*) jeu *m* d'échecs; **a s. of teeth** une rangée de dents, une denture; **the skiing/racing s.** le monde du ski/des courses. **2** *a* (*time etc*) fixe; (*lunch*) à prix fixe; (*book etc*) *Sch* au programme; (*speech*) préparé à l'avance; (*in one's habits*) régulier; (*situated*) situé; **s. phrase** expression *f* consacrée; **a s. purpose** un but déterminé; **the s. menu** le plat du jour; **dead s. against** absolument opposé à; **s. on doing** résolu à faire; **to be s. on sth** vouloir qch à tout prix; **all s.** (*ready*) prêt **(to do** pour faire); **to be s. back from** (*route etc*) être en retrait de (*route etc*). **3** *vt* (*pt & pp* **set**, *pres p.* **setting**) (*put*) mettre, poser; (*date, time etc*) fixer; (*record*) *Sp* établir; (*adjust*) *Tech* régler; (*arm etc in plaster*) *Med* plâtrer; (*task*) donner (**for s.o.** à qn); (*problem*) poser; (*diamond*) monter; (*precedent*) créer; **to have one's hair s.** se faire faire une mise en plis; **to s. (loose)** (*dog*) lâcher (**on** contre); **to s. s.o. (off) crying**/*etc* faire pleurer/*etc* qn; **to s. back** (*in time*) retarder; (*cost*) *Fam* coûter; **to s.**

down déposer; **to s. off** (*bomb*) faire exploser; (*activity, mechanism*) déclencher; (*complexion, beauty*) rehausser; **to s. out** (*display, explain*) exposer (**to** à); (*arrange*) disposer; **to s. up** (*furniture*) installer; (*statue, tent*) dresser; (*school*) fonder; (*government*) établir; (*business*) créer; (*inquiry*) ouvrir; **to s. s.o. up in business** lancer qn dans les affaires; – *vi* (*of sun*) se coucher; (*of jelly*) prendre; (*of bone*) *Med* se ressoude; **to s. about** (*job*) se mettre à; **to s. about doing** se mettre à faire; **to s. in** (*start*) commencer; (*arise*) surgir; **to s. off** or **out** (*leave*) partir; **to s. out to do** entreprendre de faire; **to s. up in business** monter une affaire; **to s. upon** (*attack*) attaquer (*qn*). ◆**setting** *n* (*surroundings*) cadre *m*; (*of sun*) coucher *m*; (*of diamond*) monture *f*. ◆**setter** *n* chien *m* couchant.

setback ['setbæk] *n* revers *m*; *Med* rechute *f*.

setsquare ['setskweər] *n Math* équerre *f*.

settee [se'tiː] *n* canapé *m*.

settle ['set(ə)l] *vt* (*decide, arrange, pay*) régler; (*date*) fixer; (*place in position*) placer; (*person*) installer (*dans son lit etc*); (*nerves*) calmer; (*land*) coloniser; **let's s. things** arrangeons les choses; **that's (all) settled** (*decided*) c'est décidé; – *vi* (*live*) s'installer, s'établir; (*of dust*) se déposer; (*of bird*) se poser; (*of snow*) tenir; **to s. (down) into** (*armchair*) s'installer dans; (*job*) s'habituer à; **to s. (up) with s.o.** régler qn; **to s. for** se contenter de, accepter; **to s. down** (*in chair or house*) s'installer; (*of nerves*) se calmer; (*in one's lifestyle*) se ranger; (*marry*) se caser; **to s. down to** (*get used to*) s'habituer à; (*work, task*) se mettre à. ◆**settled** *a* (*weather, period*) stable; (*habits*) régulier. ◆**settlement** *n* (*of account etc*) règlement *m*; (*agreement*) accord *m*; (*colony*) colonie *f*. ◆**settler** *n* colon *m*.

set-to [set'tuː] *n* (*quarrel*) *Fam* prise *f* de bec.

setup ['setʌp] *n Fam* situation *f*.

seven ['sev(ə)n] *a* & *n* sept (*m*). ◆**seven-'teen** *a* & *n* dix-sept (*m*). ◆**seven'teenth** *a* & *n* dix-septième (*mf*). ◆**seventh** *a* & *n* septième (*mf*). ◆**seventieth** *a* & *n* soixante-dixième (*mf*). ◆**seventy** *a* & *n* soixante-dix (*m*); **s.-one** soixante et onze.

sever ['sevər] *vt* sectionner, couper; (*relations*) *Fig* rompre. ◆**severing** *n*, ◆**sever-ance** *n* (*of relations*) rupture *f*.

several ['sev(ə)rəl] *a* & *pron* plusieurs (**of** d'entre).

severe [sə'vɪər] a (*judge, tone etc*) sévère; (*winter, training*) rigoureux; (*test*) dur; (*injury*) grave; (*blow, pain*) violent; (*cold, frost*) intense; (*overwork*) excessif; **a s. cold** *Med* un gros rhume; **s. to** *or* **with s.o.** sévère envers qn. ◆**severely** *adv* sévèrement; (*wounded*) gravement. ◆**se'verity** *n* sévérité *f*; rigueur *f*; gravité *f*; violence *f*.

sew [səʊ] *vti* (*pt* sewed, *pp* sewn [səʊn] *or* sewed) coudre; **to s. on** (*button*) (re)coudre; **to s. up** (*tear*) (re)coudre. ◆**—ing** *n* couture *f*; **s. machine** machine *f* à coudre.

sewage ['su:ɪdʒ] *n* eaux *fpl* usées *or* d'égout. ◆**sewer** *n* égout *m*.

sewn [səʊn] *see* **sew.**

sex [seks] *n* (*gender, sexuality*) sexe *m*; (*activity*) relations *fpl* sexuelles; **the opposite s.** l'autre sexe; **to have s. with** coucher avec; – *a* (*education, act etc*) sexuel; **s. maniac** obsédé, -ée *mf* sexuel(le). ◆**sexist** *a* & *n* sexiste (*mf*). ◆**sexual** *a* sexuel. ◆**sexu'ality** *n* sexualité *f*. ◆**sexy** *a* (*-ier, -iest*) (*book, garment, person*) sexy *inv*; (*aroused*) qui a envie (de faire l'amour).

sextet [sek'stet] *n* sextuor *m*.

sh! [ʃ] *int* chut!

shabby ['ʃæbɪ] *a* (*-ier, -iest*) (*town, room etc*) miteux; (*person*) pauvrement vêtu; (*mean*) *Fig* mesquin. ◆**shabbily** *adv* (*dressed*) pauvrement. ◆**shabbiness** *n* aspect *m* miteux; mesquinerie *f*.

shack [ʃæk] **1** *n* cabane *f*. **2** *vi* **to s. up with** *Pej Fam* se coller avec.

shackles ['ʃæk(ə)lz] *npl* chaînes *fpl*.

shade [ʃeɪd] *n* ombre *f*; (*of colour*) ton *m*, nuance *f*; (*of opinion, meaning*) nuance *f*; (*of lamp*) abat-jour *m inv*; (*blind*) store *m*; **in the s.** à l'ombre; **a s. faster/taller/etc** (*slightly*) un rien plus vite/plus grand/etc; – *vt* (*of tree*) ombrager; (*protect*) abriter (*from* de); **to s. in** (*drawing*) ombrer. ◆**shady** *a* (*-ier, -iest*) (*place*) ombragé; (*person etc*) *Fig* louche.

shadow ['ʃædəʊ] **1** *n* ombre *f*. **2** *a* (*cabinet*) *Pol* fantôme. **3** *vt* **to s. s.o.** (*follow*) filer qn. ◆**shadowy** *a* (*-ier, -iest*) (*form etc*) obscur, vague.

shaft [ʃɑːft] *n* **1** (*of tool*) manche *m*; (*in machine*) arbre *m*; **s. of light** trait *m* de lumière. **2** (*of mine*) puits *m*; (*of lift*) cage *f*.

shaggy ['ʃægɪ] *a* (*-ier, -iest*) (*hair, beard*) broussailleux; (*dog etc*) à longs poils.

shake [ʃeɪk] *vt* (*pt* shook, *pp* shaken) (*move up and down*) secouer; (*bottle*) agiter; (*belief, resolution etc*) *Fig* ébranler; (*upset*) bouleverser, secouer; **to s. the windows** (*of shock*) ébranler les vitres; **to s. one's head**

(*say no*) secouer la tête; **to s. hands with** serrer la main à; **we shook hands** nous nous sommes serré la main; **to s. off** (*dust etc*) secouer; (*cough, infection, pursuer*) *Fig* se débarrasser de; **to s. s.o. up** (*disturb, rouse*) secouer qn; **to s. sth out of sth** (*remove*) secouer qch de qch; **s. yourself out of it!** secoue-toi!; – *vi* trembler (*with* de); – *n* secousse *f*; **to give sth a s.** secouer qch; **a s. of his** *or* **her head** un secouant la tête; **in two shakes** (*soon*) *Fam* dans une minute. ◆**s.-up** *n* *Fig* réorganisation *f*.

shaky ['ʃeɪkɪ] *a* (*-ier, -iest*) (*trembling*) tremblant; (*ladder etc*) branlant; (*memory, health*) chancelant; (*on one's legs, in a language*) mal assuré.

shall [ʃæl, *unstressed* ʃəl] *v aux* **1** (*future*) **I s. come, I'll come** je viendrai; **we s. not come, we shan't come** nous ne viendrons pas. **2** (*question*) **s. I leave?** veux-tu que je parte?; **s. we leave?** on part? **3** (*order*) **he s. do it if I order it** il devra le faire si je l'ordonne.

shallot [ʃə'lɒt] *n* (*onion*) échalote *f*.

shallow ['ʃæləʊ] *a* (*-er, -est*) peu profond; *Fig Pej* superficiel; – *npl* (*of river*) bas-fond *m*. ◆**—ness** *n* manque *m* de profondeur; *Fig Pej* caractère *m* superficiel.

sham [ʃæm] *n* (*pretence*) comédie *f*, feinte *f*; (*person*) imposteur *m*; (*jewels*) imitation *f*; – *a* (*false*) faux; (*illness, emotion*) feint; – *vt* (*-mm-*) feindre.

shambles ['ʃæmb(ə)lz] *n* désordre *m*, pagaïe *f*; **to be a s.** être en pagaïe; **to make a s. of** gâcher.

shame [ʃeɪm] *n* (*feeling, disgrace*) honte *f*; **it's a s.** c'est dommage (**to do** de faire); **it's a s. (that)** c'est dommage que (+ *sub*); **what a s.!** (quel) dommage!; **to put to s.** faire honte à; – *vt* (*disgrace, make ashamed*) faire honte à. ◆**shamefaced** *a* honteux; (*bashful*) timide. ◆**shameful** *a* honteux. ◆**shamefully** *adv* honteusement. ◆**shameless** *a* (*brazen*) effronté; (*indecent*) impudique.

shammy ['ʃæmɪ] *n* **s.** (*leather*) *Fam* peau *f* de chamois.

shampoo [ʃæm'puː] *n* shampooing *m*; – *vt* (*carpet*) shampooiner; **to s. s.o.'s hair** faire un shampooing à qn.

shandy ['ʃændɪ] *n* (*beer*) panaché *m*.

shan't [ʃɑːnt] = **shall not.**

shanty¹ ['ʃæntɪ] *n* (*hut*) baraque *f*. ◆**shantytown** *n* bidonville *f*.

shanty² ['ʃæntɪ] *n* **sea s.** chanson *f* de marins.

shap/e [ʃeɪp] *n* forme *f*; **in** (**good**) **s.** (*fit*) en forme; **to be in good/bad s.** (*of vehicle,* *house etc*) être en bon/mauvais état; (*of business*) marcher bien/mal; **to take s. prendre forme; in the s. of a pear** en forme de poire; – *vt* (*fashion*) façonner (*into* en); (*one's life*) *Fig* déterminer; – *vi* **to s. up** (*of plans*) prendre (bonne) tournure, s'annoncer bien; (*of pupil, wrongdoer*) s'y mettre, s'appliquer; (*of patient*) faire des progrès. ◆—**ed** *suffix* pear-s./*etc* en forme de poire/*etc.* ◆**shapeless** *a* informe. ◆**shapely** *a* (-ier, -iest) (*woman, legs*) bien tourné.

share [ʃeər] *n* part *f* (**of,** in de); (*in company*) *Fin* action *f*; **one's (fair) s.** de sa part de; **to do one's (fair) s.** fournir sa part d'efforts; **stocks and shares** *Fin* valeurs *fpl* (boursières); – *vt* (*meal, joy, opinion etc*) partager (**with** avec); (*characteristic*) avoir en commun; **to s. out** (*distribute*) partager; – *vi* **to s. (in)** partager. ◆**shareholder** *n Fin* actionnaire *mf*.

shark [ʃɑːk] *n* (*fish*) & *Fig* requin *m*.

sharp [ʃɑːp] **1** *a* (-er, -est) (*knife, blade etc*) tranchant; (*pointed*) pointu; (*point, voice*) aigu; (*pace, mind*) vif; (*pain*) aigu, vif; (*change, bend*) brusque; (*taste*) piquant; (*words, wind, tone*) âpre; (*eyesight, cry*) perçant; (*distinct*) net; (*lawyer etc*) *Pej* peu scrupuleux; **s. practice** *Pej* procédé(s) *m*(*pl*) malhonnête(s); – *adv* (*to stop*) net; **five o'clock**/*etc* **s.** cinq heures/*etc* pile; **s. right/left** tout de suite à droite/à gauche. **2** *n Mus* dièse *m*. ◆**sharpen** *vt* (*knife*) aiguiser; (*pencil*) tailler. ◆**sharpener** *n* (*for pencils*) taille-crayon(s) *m inv*; (*for blades*) aiguisoir *m*. ◆**sharply** *adv* (*suddenly*) brusquement; (*harshly*) vivement; (*clearly*) nettement. ◆**sharpness** *n* (*of blade*) tranchant *m*; (*of picture*) netteté *f*. ◆**sharpshooter** *n* tireur *m* d'élite.

shatter [ʃætər] *vt* (*smash*) fracasser; (*glass*) faire voler en éclats; (*career, health*) briser; (*person, hopes*) anéantir; – *vi* (*smash*) se fracasser; (*of glass*) voler en éclats. ◆—**ed** *a* (*exhausted*) anéanti. ◆—**ing** *a* (*defeat*) accablant; (*news, experience*) bouleversant.

shav/e [ʃeɪv] *vt* (*person, head*) raser; **to s. off one's beard**/*etc* se raser la barbe/*etc.*; – *vi* se raser; – *n* **to have a s.** se raser, se faire la barbe; **to have a close s.** *Fig Fam* l'échapper belle. ◆—**ing** *n* rasage *m*; (*strip of wood*) copeau *m*; **s. brush** blaireau *m*; **s. cream, s. foam** crème *f* à raser. ◆**shaven** *a* rasé (de près). ◆**shaver** *n* rasoir *m* électrique.

shawl [ʃɔːl] *n* châle *m*.

she [ʃiː] *pron* elle; **s.** elle; **s. wants** elle veut; **she's a**

happy woman c'est une femme heureuse; **if I were s.** si j'étais elle; – *n* femelle *f*; **s.-bear** ourse *f.*

sheaf [ʃiːf] *n* (*pl* **sheaves**) (*of corn*) gerbe *f.*

shear [ʃɪər] *vt* tondre; – *npl* cisaille(s) *f*(*pl*); **pruning shears** sécateur *m.* ◆—**ing** *n* tonte *f.*

sheath [ʃiːθ] *n* (*pl* -s [ʃiːðz]) (*container*) gaine *f*, fourreau *m*; (*contraceptive*) préservatif *m.*

shed [ʃed] **1** *n* (*in garden etc*) remise *f*; (*for goods or machines*) hangar *m*. **2** *vt* (*pt & pp* **shed,** *pres p* **shedding**) (*lose*) perdre; (*tears, warmth etc*) répandre; (*get rid of*) se défaire de; (*clothes*) enlever; **to s. light on** *Fig* éclairer.

sheen [ʃiːn] *n* lustre *m.*

sheep [ʃiːp] *n inv* mouton *m.* ◆**sheepdog** *n* chien *m* de berger. ◆**sheepskin** *n* peau *f* de mouton.

sheepish [ʃiːpɪʃ] *a* penaud. ◆—**ly** *adv* d'un air penaud.

sheer [ʃɪər] **1** *a* (*luck, madness etc*) pur; (*impossibility etc*) absolu; **it's s. hard work** ça demande du travail; **by s. determination/hard work** à force de détermination/de travail. **2** *a* (*cliff*) à pic; – *adv* (*to rise*) à pic. **3** *a* (*fabric*) très fin.

sheet [ʃiːt] *n* (*on bed*) drap *m*; (*of paper, wood etc*) feuille *f*; (*of glass, ice*) plaque *f*; (*dust cover*) housse *f*; (*canvas*) bâche *f*; **s. metal** tôle *f.*

sheikh [ʃeɪk] *n* scheik *m*, cheik *m.*

shelf [ʃelf] *n* (*pl* **shelves**) rayon *m*, étagère *f*; (*in shop*) rayon *m*; (*on cliff*) saillie *f*; **to be (left) on the s.** (*not married*) *Fam* être toujours célibataire.

shell [ʃel] **1** *n* coquille *f*; (*of tortoise*) carapace *f*; (*seashell*) coquillage *m*; (*of peas*) cosse *f*; (*of building*) carcasse *f*; – *vt* (*peas*) écosser; (*nut, shrimp*) décortiquer. **2** *n* (*explosive*) *Mil* obus *m*; – *vt* (*town etc*) *Mil* bombarder. ◆—**ing** *n Mil* bombardement *m.* ◆**shellfish** *n inv Culin* (*oysters etc*) fruits *mpl* de mer.

shelter [ʃeltər] *n* (*place, protection*) abri *m*; **to take s.** se mettre à l'abri (**from** de); **to seek s.** chercher un abri; – *vt* abriter (**from** de); (*criminal*) protéger; – *vi* s'abriter. ◆—**ed** *a* (*place*) abrité; (*life*) très protégé.

shelve [ʃelv] *vt* (*postpone*) laisser en suspens.

shelving [ʃelvɪŋ] *n* (*shelves*) rayonnage(s) *m*(*pl*); **s. unit** (*set of shelves*) étagère *f.*

shepherd [ʃepəd] **1** *n* berger *m*; **s.'s pie** hachis *m* Parmentier. **2** *vt* **to s. in** faire entrer; **to s. s.o. around** piloter qn. ◆**shepherdess** n bergère f.

sherbet [ˈʃɜːbət] n (powder) poudre f acidulée; (water ice) Am sorbet m.

sheriff [ˈʃerɪf] n Am shérif m.

sherry [ˈʃerɪ] n xérès m, sherry m.

shh! [ʃ] int chut!

shield [ʃiːld] n bouclier m; (on coat of arms) écu m; (screen) Tech écran m; − vt protéger (**from** de).

shift [ʃɪft] n (change) changement m (of, in de); (period of work) poste m; (workers) équipe f; **gear s.** Aut Am levier m de vitesse; **s. work** travail m en équipe; − vt (move) déplacer, bouger; (limb) bouger; (employee) muter (**to** à); (scenery) Th changer; (blame) rejeter (**on to** sur); **to s. places** changer de place; **to s. gear(s)** Aut Am changer de vitesse; − vi bouger; (of heavy object) se déplacer; (of views) changer; (pass) passer (**to** à); (go) aller (**to** à); **to s. to** (new town) déménager à; **to s. along** avancer; **to s. over** or **up** se pousser. ◆**—ing** a (views) changeant.

shiftless [ˈʃɪftləs] a velléitaire, paresseux.

shifty [ˈʃɪftɪ] a (**-ier, -iest**) (sly) sournois; (dubious) louche.

shilling [ˈʃɪlɪŋ] n shilling m.

shilly-shally [ˈʃɪlɪʃælɪ] vi hésiter, tergiverser.

shimmer [ˈʃɪmər] vi chatoyer, miroiter; − n chatoiement m, miroitement m.

shin [ʃɪn] n tibia m; **s. pad** n Sp jambière f.

shindig [ˈʃɪndɪɡ] n Fam réunion f bruyante.

shin/e [ʃaɪn] vi (pt & pp **shone** [ʃɒn, Am ʃəʊn]) briller; **to s. with** (happiness etc) rayonner de; − vt (polish) faire briller; **to s. a light** or **a torch** éclairer (**on sth** qch); − vi (on shoes, cloth) briller m. ◆**—ing** a (bright, polished) brillant; **a shining example of** un bel exemple de. ◆**shiny** a (**-ier, -iest**) (bright, polished) brillant; (clothes, through wear) lustré.

shingle [ˈʃɪŋɡ(ə)l] n (on beach) galets mpl; (on roof) bardeau m.

shingles [ˈʃɪŋɡ(ə)lz] n Med zona m.

ship [ʃɪp] n navire m, bateau m; **by s.** en bateau; **s. owner** armateur m; − vt (-**pp**-) (send) expédier; (transport) transporter; (load up) embarquer (**on to** sur). ◆**shipping** n (traffic) navigation f; (ships) navires mpl; − a (agent) maritime; **s. line** compagnie f de navigation. ◆**shipbuilding** n construction f navale. ◆**shipmate** n camarade m de bord. ◆**shipment** n (goods) chargement m, cargaison f. ◆**shipshape** a & adv en ordre. ◆**shipwreck** n naufrage m. ◆**ship-**

naufragé; **to be s.** faire naufrage. ◆**shipyard** n chantier m naval.

shirk [ʃɜːk] vt (duty) se dérober à; (work) éviter de faire; − vi tirer au flanc. ◆**—er** n tire-au-flanc m inv.

shirt [ʃɜːt] n chemise f; (of woman) chemisier m. ◆**shirtfront** n plastron m. ◆**shirt-sleeves** npl **in** (one's) **s.** en bras de chemise.

shiver [ˈʃɪvər] vi frissonner (**with** de); − n frisson m.

shoal [ʃəʊl] n (of fish) banc m.

shock [ʃɒk] n (moral blow) choc m; (impact) & Med choc m; (of explosion) secousse f; (electric) s. décharge f (électrique) (**from sth** en touchant qch); **a feeling of s.** un sentiment d'horreur; **suffering from s., in a state of s.** en état de choc; **to come as a s. to s.o.** stupéfier qn; − a (tactics, wave) de choc; (effect, image etc) -choc inv; **s. absorber** amortisseur m; − vt (offend) choquer; (surprise) stupéfier; (disgust) dégoûter. ◆**—ing** a affreux; (outrageous) scandaleux; (indecent) choquant. ◆**—ingly** adv affreusement. ◆**—er** n **to be a s.** Fam être affreux or horrible. ◆**shockproof** a résistant au choc.

shoddy [ˈʃɒdɪ] a (**-ier, -iest**) (goods etc) de mauvaise qualité. ◆**shoddily** adv (made, done) mal.

shoe [ʃuː] n chaussure f, soulier m; (for horse) fer m; (brake) Aut sabot m (de frein); **in your shoes** Fig à ta place; **s. polish** cirage m; − vt (pt & pp **shod**) (horse) ferrer. ◆**shoehorn** n chausse-pied m. ◆**shoelace** n lacet m. ◆**shoemaker** n fabricant m de chaussures; (cobbler) cordonnier m. ◆**shoe-string** n **on a s.** Fig avec peu d'argent (en poche).

shone [ʃɒn, Am ʃəʊn] see **shine**.

shoo [ʃuː] vt **to s.** (**away**) chasser; − int ouste!

shook [ʃʊk] see **shake**.

shoot¹ [ʃuːt] vt (pt & pp **shot**) (kill) tuer (d'un coup de feu), abattre; (wound) blesser (d'un coup de feu); (execute) fusiller; (hunt) chasser; (gun) tirer un coup de; (bullet) tirer; (missile, glance, questions) lancer (**at** à); (film) tourner; (person) Phot prendre; **to s. down** (aircraft) abattre; − vi (with gun, bow etc) tirer (**at** sur); **to s. ahead/off** avancer/partir à toute vitesse; **to s. up** (grow) pousser vite; (rise, spurt) jaillir; (of price) monter en flèche. ◆**—ing** n (gunfire, execution) fusillade f; (shots) coups mpl de feu; (murder) meurtre m; (of *film*) tournage *m*; (*hunting*) chasse *f*. ◆**shoot-out** *n Fam* fusillade *f*.

shoot² [ʃuːt] *n* (*on plant*) pousse *f*.

shop [ʃɒp] **1** *n* magasin *m*; (*small*) boutique *f*; (*workshop*) atelier *m*; **at the baker's s.** à la boulangerie, chez le boulanger; **s. assistant** vendeur, -euse *mf*; **s. floor** (*workers*) ouvriers *mpl*; **s. steward** délégué, -ée *mf* syndical(e); **s. window** vitrine *f*; – *vi* (-pp-) faire ses courses (**at** chez); **to s. around** comparer les prix. **2** *vt* (-pp-) **to s. s.o.** *Fam* dénoncer qn (*à la police etc*). ◆**shopping** *n* (*goods*) achats *mpl*; **s.** faire les courses; **to do one's s.** faire ses courses; – *a* (*street, district*) commerçant; (*bag*) à provisions; **s. centre** centre *m* commercial. ◆**shopper** *n* (*buyer*) acheteur, -euse *mf*; (*customer*) client, -ente *mf*; (*bag*) sac *m* à provisions.

shopkeeper [ˈʃɒpkiːpər] *n* commerçant, -ante *mf*. ◆**shoplifter** *n* voleur, -euse *mf* à l'étalage. ◆**shoplifting** *n* vol *m* à l'étalage. ◆**shopsoiled** *a*, *Am* ◆**shopworn** *a* abîmé.

shore [ʃɔːr] **1** *n* (*of sea, lake*) rivage *m*; (*coast*) côte *f*, bord *m* de (la) mer; (*beach*) plage *f*; **on s.** (*passenger*) *Nau* à terre. **2** *vt* **to s. up** (*prop up*) étayer.

shorn [ʃɔːn] *a* (*head*) tondu; (*stripped of*) *Lit* dénué de.

short [ʃɔːt] *a* (-er, -est) court; (*person, distance*) petit; (*syllable*) bref; (*curt, impatient*) brusque; **a s. time** *or* **while ago** il y a peu de temps; **s. cut** raccourci *m*; **to be s. of money/time** être à court d'argent/de temps; **we're s. of ten men** il nous manque dix hommes; **money/time is s.** l'argent/le temps manque; **not far s. of** pas loin de; **s. of** (*except*) sauf; **to be s. for** (*of name*) être l'abréviation *or* le diminutif de; **in s.** bref; **s. circuit** *El* court-circuit *m*; **s. list** liste *f* de candidats choisis; – *adv* **to cut s.** (*visit etc*) abréger; (*person*) couper la parole à; **to go** *or* **get** *or* **run s. of** manquer de; **to get** *or* **run s.** manquer; **to stop s.** s'arrêter net; – *n El* court-circuit *m*; (**a pair of**) **shorts** un short. ◆**shorten** *vt* (*visit, line, dress etc*) raccourcir. ◆**shortly** *adv* (*soon*) bientôt; **s. after** peu après. ◆**shortness** *n* (*of person*) petitesse *f*; (*of hair, stick, legs*) manque *m* de longueur.

shortage [ˈʃɔːtɪdʒ] *n* manque *m*, pénurie *f*; (*crisis*) crise *f*.

shortbread [ˈʃɔːtbred] *n* sablé *m*. ◆**short-'change** *vt* (*buyer*) ne pas rendre juste à. ◆**short-'circuit** *vt El* & *Fig* court-circuiter. ◆**shortcoming** *n* défaut *m*.

◆**shortfall** *n* manque *m*. ◆**shorthand** *n* sténo *f*; **s. typist** sténodactylo *f*. ◆**short-'handed** *a* à court de personnel. ◆**short-'lived** *a* éphémère; *Fig* imprévoyant. ◆**short-'sighted** *a* myope; *Fig* imprévoyant. ◆**short-'sightedness** *n* myopie *f*; imprévoyance *f*. ◆**short-'sleeved** *a* à manches courtes. ◆**short-'staffed** *a* à court de personnel. ◆**short-'term** *a* à court terme.

shortening [ˈʃɔːt(ə)nɪŋ] *n Culin* matière *f* grasse.

shot [ʃɒt] *see* shoot¹; – *n* coup *m*; (*bullet*) balle *f*; *Cin Phot* prise *f* de vues; (*injection*) *Med* piqûre *f*; **a good s.** (*person*) un bon tireur; **to have a s. at** (*doing*) sth essayer de faire qch; **a long s.** (*attempt*) un coup à tenter; **big s.** *Fam* gros bonnet *m*; **like a s.** (*at once*) tout de suite; **to be s. of** (*rid of*) *Fam* être débarrassé de. ◆**shotgun** *n* fusil *m* de chasse.

should [ʃud, *unstressed* ʃəd] *v aux* **1** (= *ought to*) **you s. do it** vous devriez le faire; **I s. have stayed** j'aurais dû rester; **that s. be Pauline** ça doit être Pauline. **2** (= *would*) **I s. like to** j'aimerais bien; **it's strange she s. say no** il est étrange qu'elle dise non. **3** (*possibility*) **if he s. come** s'il vient; **s. I be free** si je suis libre.

shoulder [ˈʃəʊldər] **1** *n* épaule *f*; **to have round shoulders** avoir le dos voûté, être voûté; (**hard**) **s.** (*of motorway*) accotement *m* stabilisé; **s. bag** sac *m* à bandoulière; **s. blade** omoplate *f*; **s.-length hair** cheveux *mpl* mi-longs. **2** *vt* (*responsibility*) endosser, assumer.

shout [ʃaʊt] *n* cri *m*; **to give s.o. a s.** appeler qn; – *vi* **to s. (out)** crier; **to s. to** *or* **at s.o. to do** crier à qn de faire; **to s. at s.o.** (*scold*) crier après qn; – *vt* **to s. (out)** (*insult etc*) crier; **to s. down** (*speaker*) huer. ◆**-ing** *n* (*shouts*) cris *mpl*.

shove [ʃʌv] *n* poussée *f*; **to give s. a s.** (*to*) pousser; – *vt* pousser; (*put*) *Fam* fourrer; **to s. sth into** (*thrust*) enfoncer *or* fourrer qch dans; **to s. s.o. around** *Fam* régenter qn; – *vi* pousser; **to s. off** (*leave*) *Fam* ficher le camp, filer; **to s. over** (*move over*) *Fam* se pousser.

shovel [ˈʃʌv(ə)l] *n* pelle *f*; – *vt* (-ll-, *Am* -l-) (*grain etc*) pelleter; **to s. up** *or* **away** (*remove*) enlever à la pelle; **to s. sth into** (*thrust*) *Fam* fourrer qch dans.

show [ʃəʊ] *n* (*of joy, force*) démonstration *f* (**of** de); (*semblance*) semblant *m* (**of** de); (*ostentation*) parade *f*; (*sight*) & *Th* spectacle *m*; (*performance*) *Cin* séance *f*; (*exhibition*) exposition *f*; **the Boat/Motor S.** le

Salon de la Navigation/de l'Automobile; horse s. concours *m* hippique; **to give a good s.** *Sp Mus Th* jouer bien; **good s.!** bravo!; **(just) for s.** pour l'effet; **on s.** (*painting etc*) exposé; **s. business** le monde du spectacle; **s. flat** appartement *m* témoin; — *vt* (*pt* **showed**, *pp* **shown**) montrer (**to** à, **that** que); (*exhibit*) exposer; (*film*) passer, donner; (*indicate*) indiquer, montrer; **to s. s.o. to the door** reconduire qn; **it (just) goes to s. that . . .** ça (dé)montre (bien) que . . . ; **I'll s. him *or* her!** *Fam* je lui apprendrai!; — *vi* (*be visible*) se voir; (*of film*) passer; **'now showing'** *Cin* 'à l'affiche' (**at** à). ■ **to s. (a)round** *vt* faire visiter; **he *or* she was shown (a)round the house** on lui a fait visiter la maison; **to s. in** *vt* faire entrer; **to s. off** *vt Pej* étaler; (*highlight*) faire valoir; — *vi Pej* crâner. ◆**s.-off** *n Pej* crâneur, -euse *mf*; **to s. out** (*visitor*) reconduire; **to s. up** *vt* (*fault*) faire ressortir; (*humiliate*) faire honte à; — *vi* ressortir (**against** sur); (*of error*) être visible; (*of person*) *Fam* arriver, s'amener. ◆**showing** *n* (*of film*) projection *f* (**of** de); (*performance*) *Cin* séance *f*; (*of team, player*) performance *f*.

showcase ['ʃəukeis] *n* vitrine *f*. ◆**show-down** *n* confrontation *f*, conflit *m*. ◆**showgirl** *n* (*in chorus etc*) girl *f*. ◆**showjumping** *n Sp* jumping *m*. ◆**showmanship** *n* art *m* de la mise en scène. ◆**showpiece** *n* modèle *m* du genre. ◆**showroom** *n* (*for cars etc*) salle *f* d'exposition.

shower ['ʃauər] *n* (*of rain*) averse *f*; (*of blows*) déluge *m*; (*bath*) douche *f*; (*party*) *Am* réception *f* (*pour la remise de cadeaux*); — *vt* **to s. s.o. with** (*gifts, abuse*) couvrir qn de. ◆**showery** *a* pluvieux.

shown [ʃəun] *see* **show**.

showy ['ʃəui] *a* (**-ier, -iest**) (*colour, hat*) voyant; (*person*) prétentieux.

shrank [ʃræŋk] *see* **shrink 1**.

shrapnel ['ʃræpnəl] *n* éclats *mpl* d'obus.

shred [ʃred] *n* lambeau *m*; (*of truth*) *Fig* grain *m*; **not a s. of evidence** pas la moindre preuve; — *vt* (**-dd-**) mettre en lambeaux; (*cabbage, carrots*) râper. ◆**shredder** *n Culin* râpe *f*.

shrew [ʃru:] *n* (*woman*) *Pej* mégère *f*.

shrewd [ʃru:d] *a* (**-er, -est**) (*person, plan*) astucieux. ◆**-ly** *adv* astucieusement. ◆**-ness** *n* astuce *f*.

shriek [ʃri:k] *n* cri *m* (aigu); — *vti* crier; **to s. with pain/laughter** hurler de douleur/de rire.

shrift [ʃrift] *n* **to get short s.** être traité sans ménagement.

shrill [ʃril] *a* (**-er, -est**) aigu, strident.

shrimp [ʃrimp] *n* crevette *f*; (*person*) *Pej* nabot, -ote *mf*; (*child*) *Pej* puce *f*.

shrine [ʃrain] *n* lieu *m* saint; (*tomb*) châsse *f*.

shrink [ʃriŋk] **1** *vi* (*pt* **shrank**, *pp* **shrunk** *or* **shrunken**) (*of clothes*) rétrécir; (*of aging person*) se tasser; (*of amount, audience etc*) diminuer; **to s. from** reculer devant (doing l'idée de faire); — *vt* rétrécir. **2** *n* (*person*) *Am Hum* psy(chiatre) *m*. ◆**—age** *n* rétrécissement *m*; diminution *f*.

shrivel ['ʃriv(ə)l] *vi* (**-ll-**, *Am* **-l-**) **to s. (up)** se ratatiner; — *vt* **to s. (up)** ratatiner.

shroud [ʃraud] *n* linceul *m*; (*of mystery*) *Fig* voile *m*; — *vt* **shrouded in mist** enseveli *or* enveloppé sous la brume; **shrouded in mystery** enveloppé de mystère.

Shrove Tuesday [ʃrəuv'tju:zdi] *n* Mardi *m* gras.

shrub [ʃrʌb] *n* arbrisseau *m*.

shrug [ʃrʌg] *vt* (**-gg-**) **to s. one's shoulders** hausser les épaules; **to s. off** (*dismiss*) écarter (dédaigneusement); — *n* haussement *m* d'épaules.

shrunk(en) ['ʃrʌŋk(ən)] *see* **shrink 1**.

shudder ['ʃʌdər] *vi* frémir (**with** de); (*of machine etc*) vibrer; — *n* frémissement *m*; vibration *f*.

shuffle ['ʃʌf(ə)l] **1** *vti* **to s. (one's feet)** traîner les pieds. **2** *vt* (*cards*) battre.

shun [ʃʌn] *vt* (**-nn-**) fuir, éviter; **to s. doing** éviter de faire.

shunt [ʃʌnt] *vt* (*train, conversation*) aiguiller (**on to** sur); **we were shunted (to and fro)** *Fam* on nous a baladés (**from office to office/etc** de bureau en bureau/etc).

shush! [ʃuʃ] *int* chut!

shut [ʃʌt] *vt* (*pt & pp* **shut**, *pp* **shutting**) fermer; **to s. one's finger in** (*door etc*) se prendre le doigt dans; **to s. away *or* in** (*lock away or in*) enfermer; **to s. down** fermer; **to s. off** fermer; (*engine*) arrêter; (*isolate*) isoler; **to s. out** (*light*) empêcher d'entrer; (*view*) boucher; (*exclude*) exclure (**of, from** de); **to s. s.o. out** (*lock out accidentally*) enfermer qn dehors; **to s. up** fermer; (*lock up*) enfermer (*personne, objet précieux etc*); (*silence*) *Fam* faire taire; — *vi* (*of door etc*) se fermer; (*of shop, museum etc*) fermer; **the door doesn't s.** la porte ne ferme pas; **to s. down** fermer (définitivement); **to s. up** (*be quiet*) *Fam* se taire. ◆**shutdown** *n* fermeture *f*.

shutter ['ʃʌtər] *n* volet *m*, (*of camera*) obturateur *m*.

shuttle ['ʃʌt(ə)l] *n* (*bus, spacecraft etc*) navette *f*; **s. service** navette *f*; – *vi* faire la navette; – *vt* (*in vehicle etc*) transporter. ◆**shuttlecock** *n* (*in badminton*) volant *m*.

shy [ʃaɪ] *a* (**-er, -est**) timide; **to be s. of doing** avoir peur de faire; – *vi* **to s. away** reculer (**from s.o.** devant qn, **from doing** à l'idée de faire). ◆**—ness** *n* timidité *f*.

Siamese [saɪə'miːz] *a* siamois; **S. twins** frères *mpl* siamois, sœurs *fpl* siamoises.

sibling ['sɪblɪŋ] *n* frère *m*, sœur *f*.

Sicily ['sɪsɪlɪ] *n* Sicile *f*.

sick [sɪk] *a* (**-er, -est**) (*ill*) malade; (*mind*) malsain; (*humour*) noir; (*cruel*) sadique; **to be s.** (*vomit*) vomir; **to be off** *or* **away s., be on s. leave** être en congé de maladie; **to feel s.** avoir mal au cœur; **to be s. (and tired) of** *Fam* en avoir marre de; **he makes me s.** *Fam* il m'écœure; – *n* **the s.** les malades *mpl*; – *vt* (*vomit*) **to s. up** *Fam* vomir; **to s. sth up** *Fam* vomir qch. ◆**sickbay** *n* infirmerie *f*. ◆**sickbed** *n* lit *m* de malade. ◆**sickly** *a* (**-ier, -iest**) maladif; (*pale, faint*) pâle; (*taste*) écœurant. ◆**sickness** *n* maladie *f*; (*vomiting*) vomissement(s) *m(pl)*; **motion s.** *Aut* mal *m* de la route.

sicken ['sɪkən] **1** *vt* écœurer. **2** *vi* **to be sickening for** (*illness*) couver. ◆**—ing** *a* écœurant.

side [saɪd] *n* côté *m*; (*of hill, animal*) flanc *m*; (*of road, river*) bord *m*; (*of beef*) quartier *m*; (*of question*) aspect *m*; (*of character*) facette *f*, aspect *m*; *Sp* équipe *f*; *Pol* parti *m*; **the right s.** (*of fabric*) l'endroit *m*, **the wrong s.** (*of fabric*) l'envers *m*; **by the s. of** (*nearby*) à côté de; **at** *or* **by my s.** à côté de moi, à mes côtés; **by s.** l'un à côté de l'autre; **to move to one s.** s'écarter; **on this s.** de ce côté; **on the other s.** de l'autre côté; **the other s.** *TV Fam* l'autre chaîne *f*; **on the big/etc s.** *Fam* plutôt grand/*etc*; **to take sides with** se ranger du côté de; **on our s.** de notre côté, avec nous; **on the s.** *Fam* (*secretly*) en catimini; (*to make money*) en plus; – *a* (*lateral*) latéral; (*effect, issue*) secondaire; (*glance, view*) de côté; (*street*) transversal; – *vi* **to s. with** se ranger du côté de. ◆**-sided** *suffix* **ten-s.** à dix côtés. ◆**sideboard 1** *n* buffet *m*. **2** *npl* (*hair*) pattes *fpl*. ◆**sideburns** *npl* (*hair*) Am pattes *fpl*. ◆**sidecar** *n* side-car *m*. ◆**sidekick** *n* Fam associé, -ée *mf*. ◆**sidelight** *n* Aut feu *m* de position. ◆**sideline** *n* activité *f* secondaire. ◆**sidesaddle** *adv* (*to ride*) en amazone. ◆**sidestep** *vt* (**-pp-**) éviter. ◆**sidetrack** *vt* **to get sidetracked**

s'écarter du sujet. ◆**sidewalk** *n* Am trottoir *m*. ◆**sideways** *adv* & *a* de côté.

siding ['saɪdɪŋ] *n* Rail voie *f* de garage.

sidle ['saɪd(ə)l] *vi* **to s. up to s.o.** s'approcher furtivement de qn.

siege [siːdʒ] *n* Mil siège *m*.

siesta [sɪ'estə] *n* sieste *f*.

sieve [sɪv] *n* tamis *m*; (*for liquids*) Culin passoire *f*; – *vt* tamiser. ◆**sift** *vt* tamiser; **to s. out** (*truth*) Fig dégager; – *vi* **to s. through** (*papers etc*) examiner (à la loupe).

sigh [saɪ] *n* soupir *m*; – *vti* soupirer.

sight [saɪt] *n* vue *f*; (*spectacle*) spectacle *m*; (*on gun*) mire *f*; **to lose s. of** perdre de vue; **to catch s. of** apercevoir; **to come into s.** apparaître; **at first s.** à première vue; **by s.** de vue; **on** *or* **at s.** à vue; **in s.** (*target, end, date etc*) en vue; **keep out of s.!** ne te montre pas!; **he hates the s. of me** il ne peut pas me voir; **it's a lovely s.** c'est beau à voir; **the (tourist) sights** les attractions *fpl* touristiques; **to set one's sights on** (*job etc*) viser; **a s. longer/etc** *Fam* bien plus long/*etc*; – *vt* (*land*) apercevoir. ◆**-ed** *a* qui voit, clairvoyant. ◆**-ing** *n* **to make a s.** of voir. ◆**sightseer** *n* touriste *mf*. ◆**sightseeing** *n* tourisme *m*.

slightly ['saɪtlɪ] *a* not very s. laid.

sign [saɪn] **1** *n* signe *m*; (*notice*) panneau *m*; (*over shop, inn*) enseigne *f*; **no s. of** aucune trace de; **to use s. language** parler par signes. **2** *vt* (*put signature to*) signer; **to s. away** *or* **over** céder (**to à**); **to s. on** *or* **up** (*worker, soldier*) engager; – *vi* signer; **to s. for** (*letter*) signer le reçu de; **to s. in** signer le registre; **to s. off** dire au revoir; **to s. on** (*on the dole*) s'inscrire au chômage; **to s. on** *or* **up** (*soldier, worker*) s'engager; (*for course*) s'inscrire. ◆**signpost** *n* poteau *m* indicateur; – *vt* flécher.

signal ['sɪgnəl] *n* signal *m*; **traffic signals** feux *mpl* de circulation; **s. box**, *Am* **s. tower** *Rail* poste *m* d'aiguillage; – *vt* (**-ll-**, *Am* **-l-**) (*message*) communiquer (**to à**); (*arrival etc*) signaler (**to à**); – *vi* faire des signaux; **to s.** (**to**) **s.o. to do** faire signe à qn de faire. ◆**signalman** *n* (*pl* **-men**) *Rail* aiguilleur *m*.

signature ['sɪgnətʃər] *n* signature *f*; **s. tune** indicatif *m* (*musical*). ◆**signatory** *n* signataire *mf*.

signet ring ['sɪgnɪtrɪŋ] *n* chevalière *f*.

significant [sɪg'nɪfɪkənt] *a* (*meaningful*) significatif; (*important, large*) important. ◆**significance** *n* (*meaning*) signification *f*; (*importance*) importance *f*. ◆**significantly** *adv* (*appreciably*) sensiblement; **s.,**

he . . . fait significatif, il . . . . ◆**'signify** vt (mean) signifier (**that** que); (make known) indiquer, signifier (**to** à).

silence ['saɪləns] n silence m; **in s.** en silence; – vt faire taire. ◆**silencer** n (on car, gun) silencieux m. ◆**silent** a silencieux (film, anger) muet; **to keep** or **be s.** garder le silence (**about** sur). ◆**silently** adv silencieusement.

silhouette [sɪluː'et] n silhouette f. ◆**silhouetted** a **to be s. against** se profiler contre.

silicon ['sɪlɪkən] n silicium m; **s. chip** puce f de silicium. ◆**silicone** ['sɪlɪkən] n silicone f.

silk [sɪlk] n soie f. ◆**silky** a (-ier, -iest) soyeux.

sill [sɪl] n (of window etc) rebord m.

silly ['sɪlɪ] a (-ier, -iest) idiot, bête; **to do sth s.** faire une bêtise; **s. fool,** Fam **s.** billy idiot, -ote mf; – adv (to act, behave) bêtement.

silo ['saɪləʊ] n (pl -os) silo m.

silt [sɪlt] n vase f.

silver ['sɪlvər] n argent m; (silverware) argenterie f; **£5 in s.** 5 livres en pièces d'argent; – a (spoon etc) en argent, d'argent; (hair, colour) argenté; **s. jubilee** vingt-cinquième anniversaire m (d'un évènement); **s. paper** papier m d'argent; **s. plate** argenterie f. ◆**s.-'plated** a plaqué argent. ◆**silversmith** n orfèvre m. ◆**silverware** n argenterie f. ◆**silvery** a (colour) argenté.

similar ['sɪmɪlər] a semblable (**to** à). ◆**simi-'larity** n ressemblance f (**between** entre, **to** avec). ◆**similarly** adv de la même façon; (likewise) de même.

simile ['sɪmɪlɪ] n Liter comparaison f.

simmer ['sɪmər] n Culin mijoter, cuire à feu doux; (of water) frémir; (of revolt, hatred etc) couver; **to s. with** (rage) bouillir de; **to s. down** (calm down) Fam se calmer; – vt faire cuire à feu doux; (water) laisser frémir.

simper ['sɪmpər] vi minauder.

simple ['sɪmp(ə)l] a (-er, -est) (plain, uncomplicated, basic etc) simple. ◆**s.-'minded** a simple d'esprit. ◆**s.-'mindedness** n simplicité f d'esprit. ◆**simpleton** n nigaud, -aude mf. ◆**sim'plicity** n simplicité f. ◆**simplifi'cation** n simplification f. ◆**simplify** vt simplifier. ◆**simplistic** a simpliste. ◆**simply** adv (plainly, merely) simplement; (absolutely) absolument.

simulate ['sɪmjʊleɪt] vt simuler.

simultaneous [sɪməl'teɪnɪəs, Am saɪməl-

'teɪnɪəs] a simultané. ◆**-ly** adv simultanément.

sin [sɪn] n péché m; – vi (-nn-) pécher.

since [sɪns] **1** prep (in time) depuis; **s. my departure** depuis mon départ; – conj depuis que; **s. she's been here** depuis qu'elle est ici; **it's a year s.** I saw him ça fait un an que je ne l'ai pas vu; – adv (ever) s. depuis. **2** conj (because) puisque.

sincere [sɪn'sɪər] a sincère. ◆**sincerely** adv sincèrement; **yours s.** (in letter) Com veuillez croire à mes sentiments dévoués. ◆**sin'cerity** n sincérité f.

sinew ['sɪnjuː] n Anat tendon m.

sinful ['sɪnfəl] a (guilt-provoking) coupable; (shocking) scandaleux; **he's s.** c'est un pécheur; **that's s.** c'est un péché.

sing [sɪŋ] vti (pt sang, pp sung) chanter; **to s. up** chanter plus fort. ◆**-ing** n (of bird & musical technique) chant m; (way of singing) façon f de chanter; – a (lesson, teacher) de chant. ◆**-er** n chanteur, -euse mf.

singe [sɪndʒ] vt (cloth) roussir; (hair) brûler; **to s. s.o.'s hair** (at hairdresser's) faire un brûlage à qn.

single ['sɪŋg(ə)l] a (only one) seul; (room, bed) pour une personne; (unmarried) célibataire; **s. ticket** billet m simple; **every s. day** tous les jours sans exception; **s. party** Pol parti m unique; – n (ticket) aller m (simple); (record) 45 tours m inv; pl Tennis simples mpl; **singles bar** bar m pour célibataires; – vt **to s. out** (choose) choisir. ◆**s.-'breasted** a (jacket) droit. ◆**s.-'decker** n (bus) autobus m sans impériale. ◆**s.-'handed** a sans aide. ◆**s.-'minded** a (person) résolu, qui n'a qu'une idée en tête. ◆**singly** adv (one by one) un à un.

singlet ['sɪŋglɪt] n (garment) maillot m de corps.

singsong ['sɪŋsɒŋ] n **to get together for a s.** se réunir pour chanter.

singular ['sɪŋgjʊlər] **1** a (unusual) singulier. **2** Gram (form) singulier; (noun) au singulier; – n Gram singulier m; **in the s.** au singulier.

sinister ['sɪnɪstər] a sinistre.

sink¹ [sɪŋk] n (in kitchen) évier m; (washbasin) lavabo m.

sink² [sɪŋk] vi (pt sank, pp sunk) (of ship, person etc) couler; (of sun, price, water level) baisser; (collapse, subside) s'affaisser; **to s. (down) into** (mud etc) s'enfoncer dans; (armchair etc) s'affaler dans; **to s. in** (of ink etc) pénétrer; (of fact etc) Fam rentrer (dans le crâne); **has that sunk in?** *Fam* as-tu compris ça?; – *vt* (*ship*) couler; (*well*) creuser; **to s. into** (*thrust*) enfoncer dans; (*money*) *Com* investir dans; **a sinking feeling** un serrement de cœur.

sinner ['sɪnər] *n* pécheur *m*, pécheresse *f*.

sinuous ['sɪnjʊəs] *a* sinueux.

sinus ['saɪnəs] *n Anat* sinus *m inv*.

sip [sɪp] *vi* (-pp-) boire à petites gorgées; – *n* (*mouthful*) petite gorgée *f*; (*drop*) goutte *f*.

siphon ['saɪfən] *n* siphon *m*; – *vt* **to s. off** (*petrol*) siphonner; (*money*) *Fig* détourner.

sir [sɜːr] *n* monsieur *m*; **S. Walter Raleigh** (*title*) sir Walter Raleigh.

siren ['saɪərən] *n* (*of factory etc*) sirène *f*.

sirloin ['sɜːlɔɪn] *n* (*steak*) faux-filet *m*; (*joint*) aloyau *m*.

sissy ['sɪsɪ] *n* (*boy, man*) *Fam* femmelette *f*.

sister ['sɪstər] *n* sœur *f*; (*nurse*) infirmière *f* en chef. ◆**s.-in-law** *n* (*pl* **sisters-in-law**) belle-sœur *f*. ◆**sisterly** *a* fraternel.

sit [sɪt] *vi* (*pp & pp* **sat**, *pres p* **sitting**) s'asseoir; (*for artist*) poser (**for** pour); (*remain*) rester; (*of assembly etc*) siéger, être en séance; **to be sitting** (*of person, cat etc*) être assis; (*of bird*) être perché; **she sat** *or* **was sitting reading** elle était assise à lire; **to s. around** (*do nothing*) ne rien faire; **to s. back** (*in chair*) se caler; (*rest*) se reposer; (*do nothing*) ne rien faire; **to s. down** s'asseoir; **s.-down strike** grève *f* sur le tas; **to s. in on** (*lecture etc*) assister à; **to s. on** (*jury etc*) être membre de; (*fact etc*) *Fam* garder pour soi; **to s. through** *or* **out** (*film etc*) rester jusqu'au bout de; **to s. up** (*straight*) s'asseoir (bien droit); **to s. up waiting for s.o.** (*at night*) ne pas se coucher en attendant qn; – *vt* (*exam*) se présenter à; **to s. s.o. (for)** (*exam*) se présenter à; **to s. out** (*event, dance*) ne pas prendre part à. ◆**sitting** *n* séance *f*; (*for one's portrait*) séance *f* de pose; (*in restaurant*) service *m*; – *a* (*committee etc*) en séance; **s. duck** *Fam* victime *f* facile; **s. tenant** locataire *m* en possession des lieux. ◆**sitting room** *n* salon *m*.

site [saɪt] *n* emplacement *m*; (*archaeological*) site *m*; (*building*) **s.** chantier *m*; **launching s.** aire *f* de lancement; – *vt* (*building*) placer.

sit-in ['sɪtɪn] *n Pol* sit-in *m inv*.

sitter ['sɪtər] *n* (*for child*) baby-sitter *mf*.

situate ['sɪtjʊeɪt] *vt* situer; **to be situated** être situé. ◆**situ'ation** *n* situation *f*.

six [sɪks] *a & n* six (*m*). ◆**six'teen** *a & n* seize (*m*). ◆**six'teenth** *a & n* seizième (*mf*). ◆**sixth** *a & n* sixième (*mf*); (*lower*) **s.**

form *Sch* = classe *f* de première; (**upper**) **s.**

form *Sch* = classe *f* terminale; **a s.** (*fraction*) un sixième *m*. ◆**sixtieth** *a & n* soixantième (*mf*). ◆**sixty** *a & n* soixante (*m*).

size [saɪz] *n* (*of person, animal, garment etc*) taille *f*; (*measurements*) dimensions *fpl*; (*of egg, packet*) grosseur *f*; (*of book*) grandeur *f*, format *m*; (*of problem, town, damage*) importance *f*, étendue *f*; (*of sum*) montant *m*, importance *f*; (*of shoes, gloves*) pointure *f*; (*of shirt*) encolure *f*; **hip/chest s.** tour *m* de hanches/de poitrine; **it's the s. of** ... c'est grand comme ... **2** *n* (*glue*) colle *f*. **3** *vt* **to s. up** (*person*) jauger; (*situation*) évaluer. ◆**sizeable** *a* assez grand *or* gros.

sizzl/e ['sɪz(ə)l] *vi* grésiller. ◆**-ing** *a* s. (hot) brûlant.

skat/e¹ [skeɪt] *n* patin *m*; – *vi* patiner. ◆**-ing** *n* patinage *m*; **to go s.** faire du patinage; **s. rink** (*ice*) patinoire *f*; (*roller*) skating *m*. ◆**skateboard** *n* skateboard *m*. ◆**skater** *n* patineur, -euse *mf*.

skate² [skeɪt] *n* (*fish*) raie *f*.

skedaddle [skɪ'dæd(ə)l] *vi Fam* déguerpir.

skein [skeɪn] *n* (*of yarn*) écheveau *m*.

skeleton ['skelɪt(ə)n] *n* squelette *m*; – *a* (*crew, staff*) (réduit au) minimum; **s. key** passe-partout *m inv*.

skeptic ['skeptɪk] *Am* = **sceptic**.

sketch [sketʃ] *n* (*drawing*) croquis *m*, esquisse *f*; *Th* sketch *m*; **a rough s. of** (*plan*) *Fig* une esquisse de; – *vt* **to s. (out)** (*view, idea etc*) esquisser; **to s. in** (*details*) ajouter; – *vi* faire un *or* des croquis. ◆**sketchy** *a* (-ier, -iest) incomplet, superficiel.

skew [skjuː] *n* **on the s.** de travers.

skewer ['skjuːər] *n* (*for meat etc*) broche *f*; (*for kebab*) brochette *f*.

ski [skiː] *n* (*pl* **skis**) ski *m*; **s. lift** télésiège *m*; **s. pants** fuseau *m*; **s. run** piste *f* de ski; **s. tow** téléski *m*; – *vi* (*pt* **skied** [skiːd], *pres p* **skiing**) faire du ski. ◆**-ing** *n Sp* ski *m*; – *a* (*school, clothes*) de ski. ◆**-er** *n* skieur, -euse *mf*.

skid [skɪd] *vi* (-dd-) *Aut* déraper; **to s. into** déraper et heurter; – *n* dérapage *m*. **2** *a* **s. row** *Am* quartier *m* de clochards *or* de squats.

skill [skɪl] *n* habileté *f*, adresse *f* (**at** à); (*technique*) technique *f*; **one's skills** (*aptitudes*) ses compétences *fpl*. ◆**skilful** *a*, *Am* ◆**skillful** *a* habile (**at doing** à faire, **at sth** à qch). ◆**skilled** *a* habile (**at doing** à faire, **at sth** à qch); (*worker*) qualifié; (*work*) de spécialiste, de professionnel.

skillet ['skɪlɪt] *n Am* poêle *f* (à frire).

skim [skɪm] **1** *vt* (-mm-) (*milk*) écrémer;

(*soup*) écumer **2** *vti* (**-mm-**) to s. (over)
(*surface*) effleurer; **to s. through** (*book*)
parcourir.

skimp [skɪmp] *vi* (*on fabric, food etc*) lésiner
(on sur). ◆**skimpy** *a* (**-ier, -iest**) (*clothes*)
étriqué; (*meal*) insuffisant.

skin [skɪn] *n* peau *f*; **he has thick s.** Fig c'est
un dur; **s. diving** plongée *f* sous-marine; **s.
test** cuti(-réaction) *f*; – *vt* (**-nn-**) (*animal*)
écorcher; (*fruit*) peler. ◆**s.-'deep** *a*
superficiel. ◆**s.-'tight** *a* moulant, collant.

skinflint ['skɪnflɪnt] *n* avare *mf*.

skinhead ['skɪnhed] *n* skinhead *m*, jeune
voyou *m*.

skinny ['skɪnɪ] *a* (**-ier, -iest**) maigre.

skint [skɪnt] *a* (*penniless*) Fam fauché.

skip¹ [skɪp] **1** *vi* (**-pp-**) (*jump*) sauter; (*hop
about*) sautiller; (*with rope*) sauter à la
corde; **to s. off** (*leave*) Fam filer; **skipping
rope** corde *f* à sauter; – *n* petit saut *m*. **2** *vt*
(**-pp-**) (*omit, miss*) sauter; **to s. classes**
sécher les cours; **s. it!** (*forget it*) Fam laisse
tomber!

skip² [skɪp] *n* (*container for debris*) benne *f*.

skipper ['skɪpər] *n Nau Sp* capitaine *m*.

skirmish ['skɜːmɪʃ] *n* accrochage *m*.

skirt [skɜːt] **1** *n* jupe *f*. **2** *vt* **to s. round**
contourner; **skirting board** (*on wall*)
plinthe *f*.

skit [skɪt] *n Th* pièce *f* satirique; **a s. on** une
parodie de.

skittle ['skɪt(ə)l] *n* quille *f*; *pl* (*game*) jeu *m*
de quilles.

skiv/e [skaɪv] *vi* (*skirk*) Fam tirer au flanc;
to s. off (*slip away*) Fam se défiler. ◆**—er** *n*
Fam tire-au-flanc *m inv*.

skivvy ['skɪvɪ] *n Pej* Fam bonne *f* à tout
faire, bon(n)iche *f*.

skulk [skʌlk] *vi* rôder (furtivement).

skull [skʌl] *n* crâne *m*. ◆**skullcap** *n* calotte
f.

skunk [skʌŋk] *n* (*animal*) mouffette *f*;
(*person*) Pej salaud *m*.

sky [skaɪ] *n* ciel *m*. ◆**skydiving** *n* parachutisme *m* (en chute libre). ◆**sky-'high** *a*
(*prices*) exorbitant. ◆**skylight** *n* lucarne *f*.
◆**skyline** *n* (*outline of buildings*) ligne *f*
d'horizon. ◆**skyrocket** *vi* (*of prices*) Fam
monter en flèche. ◆**skyscraper** *n*
gratte-ciel *m inv*.

slab [slæb] *n* (*of concrete etc*) bloc *m*; (*thin,
flat*) plaque *f*; (*of chocolate*) tablette *f*,
plaque *f*; (*paving stone*) dalle *f*.

slack [slæk] *a* (**-er, -est**) (*knot, spring*) lâche;
(*discipline, security*) relâché, lâche; (*trade,
grip*) faible, mou; (*negligent*) négligent;
(*worker, student*) peu sérieux; **s. periods**

(*weeks etc*) périodes *fpl* creuses; (*hours*)
heures *fpl* creuses; **to be s.** (*of rope*) avoir du
mou; – **to s. off** (*in effort*) se relâcher.
◆**slacken** *vi* **to s. (off)** (*in effort*) se
relâcher; (*of production, speed, zeal*)
diminuer; – *vt* **to s. (off)** (*rope*) relâcher;
(*pace, effort*) ralentir. ◆**slacker** *n*
(*person*) Fam flemmard, -arde *mf*.
◆**slackly** *adv* (*loosely*) lâchement.
◆**slackness** *n* négligence *f*; (*of discipline*)
relâchement *m*; (*of rope*) mou *m*; Com stagnation *f*.

slacks [slæks] *npl* pantalon *m*.

slag [slæg] *n* (*immoral woman*) Sl salope *f*,
traînée *f*.

slagheap ['slæghiːp] *n* terril *m*.

slake [sleɪk] *vt* (*thirst*) Lit étancher.

slalom ['slɑːləm] *n Sp* slalom *m*.

slam [slæm] **1** *vt* (**-mm-**) (*door, lid*) claquer;
(*hit*) frapper violemment; **to s. (down)** (*put
down*) poser violemment; **to s. on the
brakes** écraser le frein, freiner à bloc; – *vi*
(*of door*) claquer; – *n* claquement *m*. **2** *vt*
(**-mm-**) (*criticize*) Fam critiquer (avec virulence).

slander ['slɑːndər] *n* diffamation *f*,
calomnie *f*; – *vt* diffamer, calomnier.

slang [slæŋ] *n* argot *m*; – *a* (*word etc*)
d'argot, argotique. ◆**slanging match** *n*
Fam engueulade *f*.

slant [slɑːnt] *n* inclinaison *f*; (*point of view*)
Fig angle *m* (on sur); (*bias*) Fig parti-pris
m; **on a s.** penché; (*roof*) en pente; – *vi* (*of
writing*) pencher; (*of roof*) être en pente; –
vt (*writing*) faire pencher; (*news*) Fig
présenter de façon partiale. ◆**—ed** *a*,
◆**—ing** *a* penché; (*roof*) en pente.

slap [slæp] **1** *n* tape *f*, claque *f*; (*on face*) gifle
f; – *vt* (**-pp-**) donner une tape à; **to s. s.o.'s
face** gifler qn; **to s. s.o.'s bottom** donner
une fessée à qn. **2** *vt* (**-pp-**) (*put*) mettre,
flanquer; **to s. on** (*apply*) appliquer à la
va-vite; (*add*) ajouter. **3** *adv* **s. in the middle**
Fam en plein milieu. ◆**slapdash** *a*
(*person*) négligent; (*task*) fait à la va-vite;
– *adv* à la va-vite. ◆**slaphappy** *a* Fam
(*carefree*) insouciant; (*negligent*) négligent.
◆**slapstick** *a & n* **s.** (*comedy*) grosse farce
f. ◆**slap-up 'meal** *n* Fam gueuleton *m*.

slash [slæʃ] **1** *vt* (*cut with blade etc*) entailler,
tailler; (*sever*) trancher; – *n* entaille *f*,
taillade *f*. **2** *vt* (*reduce*) réduire radicalement; (*prices*) Com écraser.

slat [slæt] *n* (*in blind*) lamelle *f*.

slate [sleɪt] **1** *n* ardoise *f*. **2** *vt* (*book etc*) Fam
critiquer, démolir.

slaughter ['slɔːtər] *vt* (*people*) massacrer;

(*animal*) abattre; – *n* massacre *m*; abattage *m*. ◆**slaughterhouse** *n* abattoir *m*.

Slav [slɑːv] *a & n* slave (*mf*). ◆**Sla'vonic** *a* (*language*) slave.

slave [sleɪv] *n* esclave *mf*; the s. trade *Hist* la traite des noirs; s. driver *Fig Pej* négrier *m*; – *vi* to s. (away) se crever (au travail), bosser comme une bête; to s. away doing s'escrimer à faire. ◆**slavery** *n* esclavage *m*. ◆**slavish** *a* servile.

slaver ['slævər] *vi* (*dribble*) baver (over sur); – *n* bave *f*.

slay [sleɪ] *vt* (*pt* slew, *pp* slain) *Lit* tuer.

sleazy ['sliːzɪ] *a* (-ier, -iest) *Fam* sordide, immonde.

sledge [sledʒ] (*Am* sled [sled]) *n* luge *f*; (*horse-drawn*) traîneau *m*.

sledgehammer ['sledʒhæmər] *n* masse *f*.

sleek [sliːk] *a* (-er, -est) lisse, brillant; (*manner*) onctueux.

sleep [sliːp] *n* sommeil *m*; to have a s., to get some s. dormir; to send to s. endormir; to go or get to s. s'endormir; to go to s. (*of arm, foot*) *Fam* s'engourdir; – *vi* (*pt & pp* slept) dormir; (*spend the night*) coucher; s. tight *or* well! dors bien!; I'll s. on it *Fig* je déciderai demain, la nuit portera conseil; – *vt* this room sleeps six on peut coucher *or* loger six personnes dans cette chambre; to s. it off *Fam* s. off a hangover cuver son vin. ◆**–ing** *a* (*asleep*) endormi; **s. bag** sac *m* de couchage; **s. car** wagon-lit *m*; **s. pill** somnifère *m*; **s. quarters** chambre(s) *f*(*pl*), dortoir *m*. ◆**sleeper** *n* 1 to be a **light/sound** s. avoir le sommeil léger/lourd. 2 *Rail* (*on track*) traverse *f*; (*berth*) couchette *f*; (*train*) train *m* couchettes. ◆**sleepiness** *n* torpeur *f*. ◆**sleepless** *a* (*hours*) sans sommeil; (*night*) d'insomnie. ◆**sleepwalker** *n* somnambule *mf*. ◆**sleepwalking** *n* somnambulisme *m*. ◆**sleepy** *a* (-ier, -iest) (*town, voice*) endormi; **to be s.** (*of person*) avoir sommeil.

sleet [sliːt] *n* neige *f* fondue; (*sheet of ice*) *Am* verglas *m*; – *vi* it's sleeting il tombe de la neige fondue.

sleeve [sliːv] *n* (*of shirt etc*) manche *f*; (*of record*) pochette *f*; up one's s. (*surprise, idea etc*) *Fig* en réserve; long-/short-sleeved à manches longues/courtes.

sleigh [sleɪ] *n* traîneau *m*.

sleight [slaɪt] *n* s. of hand prestidigitation *f*.

slender ['slendər] *a* (*person*) mince, svelte; (*neck, hand*) fin; (*feeble, small*) *Fig* faible.

slept [slept] *see* sleep.

sleuth [sluːθ] *n* (*detective*) *Hum* (fin) limier *m*.

slew [sluː] *n* a s. of *Am Fam* un tas de, une tapée de.

slice [slaɪs] *n* tranche *f*; (*portion*) *Fig* partie *f*, part *f*; – *vt* to s. (up) couper (en tranches); to s. off (*cut off*) couper.

slick [slɪk] *a* 1 (-er, -est) (*glib*) qui a la parole facile; (*manner*) mielleux; (*cunning*) astucieux; (*smooth, slippery*) lisse. 2 *n* oil s. nappe *f* de pétrole; (*large*) marée *f* noire.

slid/e [slaɪd] *n* (*act*) glissade *f*; (*in value etc*) *Fig* (légère) baisse *f*; (*in playground*) tobog-gan *m*; (*on ice*) glissoire *f*; (*for hair*) barrette *f*; *Phot* diapositive *f*; (*of microscope*) lamelle *f*, lame *f*; s. rule règle *f* à calcul; – *vi* (*pt & pp* slid) glisser; to s. into (*room etc*) se glisser dans; – *vt* (*letter etc*) glisser (into dans), (*table etc*) faire glisser. ◆**–ing** *a* (*door, panel*) à glissière; (*roof*) ouvrant; s. scale *Com* échelle *f* mobile.

slight [slaɪt] 1 *a* (-er, -est) (*slim*) mince; (*frail*) frêle; (*intelligence*) faible; the slight-est thing la moindre chose; not in the slightest pas le moins du monde. 2 *vt* (*offend*) offenser; (*ignore*) bouder; – *n* affront *m* (on à). ◆**–ly** *adv* légèrement, un peu; s. built fluet.

slim [slɪm] *a* (slimmer, slimmest) mince; – *vi* (-mm-) maigrir. ◆**slimming** *a* (*diet*) amaigrissant; (*food*) qui ne fait pas grossir. ◆**slimness** *n* minceur *f*.

slime [slaɪm] *n* boue *f* (visqueuse); (*of snail*) bave *f*. ◆**slimy** *a* (-ier, -iest) (*muddy*) boueux; (*sticky, smarmy*) visqueux.

sling [slɪŋ] 1 *n* (*weapon*) fronde *f*; (*toy*) lance-pierres *m* inv; (*for arm*) *Med* écharpe *f*; in a s. en écharpe. 2 *vt* (*pt & pp* slung) (*throw*) jeter, lancer; (*hang*) suspendre; to s. away *or* out (*throw out*) *Fam* balancer. ◆**slingshot** *n Am* lance-pierres *m* inv.

slip [slɪp] 1 *n* (*mistake*) erreur *f*; (*woman's undergarment*) combinaison *f*; (*of paper for filing*) fiche *f*; a s. of paper (*bit*) un bout de papier; a s. (of the tongue) un lapsus; to give s.o. the s. fausser compagnie à qn; s. road *Aut* bretelle *f*. 2 *vi* (-pp-) glisser; to s. into (*go, get*) se glisser dans; (*habit*) prendre; (*garment*) mettre; to let s. (*chance, oath, secret*) laisser échapper; to s. through (*crowd*) se faufiler parmi; to s. along *or* over to faire un saut chez; to s. away (*escape*) s'esquiver; to s. back/in retourner/entrer furtivement; to s. out sortir furtivement; (*pop out*) sortir (un instant); (*of secret*) s'éventer; to s. past (*guards*) passer sans être vu; to s. up (*make a*) *mistake*) *Fam* gaffer; − *vt* (*slide*) glisser (**to à, into** dans); **it slipped his** *or* **her notice** ça lui a échappé; **it slipped his** *or* **her mind** ça lui est sorti de l'esprit; **to s. off** (*garment etc*) enlever; **to s. on** (*garment etc*) mettre. ◆**s.-up** *n Fam* gaffe *f*, erreur *f*.

slipcover ['slɪpkʌvər] *n Am* housse *f*.

slipper ['slɪpər] *n* pantoufle *f*.

slippery ['slɪpərɪ] *a* glissant.

slipshod ['slɪpʃɒd] *a* (*negligent*) négligent; (*slovenly*) négligé.

slit [slɪt] *n* (*opening*) fente *f*; (*cut*) coupure *f*; − *vt* (*pt & pp* **slit**, *pres p* **slitting**) (*cut*) couper; (*tear*) déchirer; **to s. open** (*sack*) éventrer.

slither ['slɪðər] *vi* glisser; (*of snake*) se couler.

sliver ['slɪvər] *n* (*of apple etc*) lichette *f*; (*of wood*) éclat *m*.

slob [slɒb] *n Fam* malotru *m*, goujat *m*.

slobber ['slɒbər] *vi* (*of dog etc*) baver (**over** sur); − *n* bave *f*.

slog [slɒg] **1** *n* **a** (**hard**) **s.** (*effort*) un gros effort; (*work*) un travail dur; − *vi* (-gg-) **to s.** (**away**) bosser, trimer. **2** *vt* (-gg-) (*hit*) donner un grand coup à.

slogan ['sləʊgən] *n* slogan *m*.

slop [slɒp] *n* **slops** eaux *fpl* sales; − *vi* (-pp-) **to s.** (**over**) (*spill*) se répandre; − *vt* répandre.

slop/e [sləʊp] *n* pente *f*; (*of mountain*) flanc *m*; (*slant*) inclinaison *f*; − *vi* être en pente; (*of handwriting*) pencher; **to s. down** descendre en pente. ◆**—ing** *a* en pente; (*handwriting*) penché.

sloppy ['slɒpɪ] *a* (-ier, -iest) (*work, appearance*) négligé; (*person*) négligent; (*mawkish*) sentimental; (*wet*) détrempé; (*watery*) liquide.

slosh [slɒʃ] *vt* (*pour*) *Fam* répandre. ◆**—ed** *a* (*drunk*) *Fam* bourré.

slot [slɒt] *n* (*slit*) fente *f*; (*groove*) rainure *f*; (*in programme*) *Rad TV* créneau *m*; **s. machine** (*vending*) distributeur *m* automatique; (*gambling*) machine *f* à sous; − *vt* (-tt-) (*insert*) insérer (**into** dans); − *vi* s'insérer (**into** dans).

sloth [sləʊθ] *n Lit* paresse *f*.

slouch [slaʊtʃ] **1** *vi* ne pas se tenir droit; (*have stoop*) avoir le dos voûté; (*in chair*) se vautrer (**in** dans); **slouching over** (*desk etc*) penché sur; − *n* mauvaise tenue *f*; **with a s.** (*to walk*) en se tenant mal; le dos voûté. **2** *n Fam* (*person*) lourdaud, -aude *mf*; (*lazy*) paresseux, -euse *mf*.

slovenly ['slʌvənlɪ] *a* négligé. ◆**slovenli-**

ness *n* (*of dress*) négligé *m*; (*carelessness*) négligence *f*.

slow [sləʊ] *a* (-er, -est) lent; (*business*) calme; (*party, event*) ennuyeux; **at (a) s. speed** à vitesse réduite; **to be a s. walker** marcher lentement; **to be s.** (*of clock, watch*) retarder; **to be five minutes s.** retarder de cinq minutes; **to be s. to act** *or* **in acting** être lent à agir; **in s. motion** au ralenti; − *adv* lentement; − *vt* **to s. down** *or* **up** ralentir; (*delay*) retarder; − *vi* **to s. down** *or* **up** ralentir. ◆**—ly** *adv* lentement; (*bit by bit*) peu à peu. ◆**—ness** *n* lenteur *f*.

slowcoach ['sləʊkəʊtʃ] *n Fam* lambin, -ine *mf*. ◆**slow-down** *n* ralentissement *m*; **s.-down** (*strike*) *Am* grève *f* perlée. ◆**slow-'moving** *a* (*vehicle etc*) lent. ◆**slowpoke** *n Am Fam* lambin, -ine *mf*.

sludge [slʌdʒ] *n* gadoue *f*.

slue [sluː] *n Am Fam* = **slew**.

slug [slʌg] **1** *n* (*mollusc*) limace *f*. **2** *n* (*bullet*) *Am Sl* pruneau *m*. **3** *vt* (-gg-) (*hit*) *Am Fam* frapper; − *n* coup *m*, marron *m*.

sluggish ['slʌgɪʃ] *a* lent, mou.

sluice [sluːs] *n* **s.** (**gate**) vanne *f*.

slum [slʌm] *n* (*house*) taudis *m*; **the slums** les quartiers *mpl* pauvres; − *a* (*district*) pauvre; − *vt* (-mm-) **to s. it** *Fam* manger de la vache enragée. ◆**slummy** *a* (-ier, -iest) sordide, pauvre.

slumber ['slʌmbər] *n Lit* sommeil *m*.

slump [slʌmp] *n* baisse *f* soudaine (**in** de); (*in prices*) effondrement *m*; *Econ* crise *f*; − *vi* (*decrease*) baisser; (*of prices*) s'effondrer; **to s. into** (*armchair etc*) s'affaisser dans.

slung [slʌŋ] *see* **sling 2**.

slur [slɜːr] **1** *vt* (-rr-) prononcer indistinctement; **to s. one's words** manger ses mots. **2** *n* **to cast a s. on** (*reputation etc*) porter atteinte à. ◆**slurred** *a* (*speech*) indistinct.

slush [slʌʃ] *n* (*snow*) neige *f* fondue; (*mud*) gadoue *f*. ◆**slushy** *a* (-ier, -iest) (*road*) couvert de neige fondue.

slut [slʌt] *n Pej* (*immoral*) salope *f*, traînée *f*; (*untidy*) souillon *f*.

sly [slaɪ] *a* (-er, -est) (*deceitful*) sournois; (*crafty*) rusé; − *n* **on the s.** en cachette. ◆**—ly** *adv* sournoisement; (*in secret*) en cachette.

smack [smæk] **1** *n* claque *f*; gifle *f*; fessée *f*; − *vt* donner une claque à; **to s. s.o.'s face** gifler qn; **to s. s.o.'s bottom** donner une fessée à qn. **2** *adv* **s. in the middle** *Fam* en plein milieu. **3** *vi* **to s.** (*be suggestive of*) avoir des relents de. ◆**—ing** *n* fessée *f*.

small [smɔːl] *a* (-er, -est) petit; **in the s. hours** au petit matin; **s. talk** menus propos mpl; − adv (to cut, chop) menu; − n **the s. of the back** le creux m des reins. ◆**−ness** n petitesse f. ◆**smallholding** n petite ferme f. ◆**small-scale** a Fig peu important. ◆**small-time** a (crook, dealer etc) petit, sans grande envergure.

smallpox ['smɔːlpɒks] n petite vérole f.

smarmy ['smɑːmɪ] a (**-ier, -iest**) Pej Fam visqueux, obséquieux.

smart[1] [smɑːt] a (**-er, -est**) (in appearance) élégant; (astute) astucieux; (clever) intelligent; (quick) rapide; **s. aleck** Fam je-sais-tout mf inv. ◆**smarten** vt to s. up (room etc) embellir; − vti to s. (oneself) up (make oneself spruce) se faire beau, s'arranger. ◆**smartly** adv élégamment; (quickly) en vitesse; (astutely) astucieusement. ◆**smartness** n élégance f.

smart[2] [smɑːt] vi (sting) brûler, faire mal.

smash [smæʃ] vt (break) briser; (shatter) fracasser; (enemy) écraser; (record) pulvériser; to s. s.o.'s face (in) Fam casser la gueule à qn; to s. down or in (door) fracasser; to s. up (car) esquinter; (room) démolir; − vi se briser; to s. into (of car) se fracasser contre; − n (noise) fracas m; (blow) coup m; (accident) collision f; s. hit Fam succès m fou. ◆**s.-up** n collision f.

smashing ['smæʃɪŋ] a (wonderful) Fam formidable. ◆**smasher** n to be a (real) s. Fam être formidable.

smattering ['smætərɪŋ] n a s. of (French etc) quelques notions fpl de.

smear [smɪər] vt (coat) enduire (with de); (stain) tacher (with de); (smudge) faire une trace sur; − n (mark) trace f; (stain) tache f; Med frottis m; a s. on (attack) Fig une atteinte à; s. campaign campagne f de diffamation.

smell [smel] n odeur f; (sense of) s. odorat m; − vt (pt & pp smelled or smelt) sentir; (of animal) flairer; − vi (stink) sentir (mauvais); (have smell) avoir une odeur; to s. of smoke/etc sentir la fumée/etc; smelling salts sels mpl. ◆**smelly** a (**-ier, -iest**) to be s. sentir (mauvais).

smelt[1] [smelt] see **smell**.

smelt[2] [smelt] vt (ore) fondre; **smelting works** fonderie f.

smidgen ['smɪdʒən] n a s. (a little) Am Fam un brin (of de).

smil/e [smaɪl] n sourire m; − vi sourire (at s.o. à qn, at sth de qn). ◆**−ing** a souriant.

smirk [smɜːk] n (smug) sourire m suffisant; (scornful) sourire m goguenard.

smith [smɪθ] n (blacksmith) forgeron m.

smithereens [smɪðə'riːnz] npl to smash to s. briser en mille morceaux.

smitten ['smɪt(ə)n] a s. with Hum (desire, remorse) pris de; (in love with) épris de.

smock [smɒk] n blouse f.

smog [smɒg] n brouillard m épais, smog m.

smoke [sməʊk] n fumée f; to have a s. fumer une cigarette etc; − vt (cigarette, salmon etc) fumer; to s. out (room etc) enfumer; − vi fumer; **'no smoking'** 'défense de fumer'; **smoking compartment** Rail compartiment m fumeurs. ◆**smokeless** a s. fuel combustible m non polluant. ◆**smoker** n fumeur, -euse mf; Rail compartiment m fumeurs. ◆**smoky** a (**-ier, -iest**) (air) enfumé; (wall) noirci de fumée; **it's s. here** il y a de la fumée ici.

smooth [smuːð] a (**-er, -est**) (surface, skin etc) lisse; (road) à la surface égale; (movement) régulier, sans à-coups; (flight) agréable; (cream, manners) onctueux; (person) doucereux; (sea) calme; **the s. running** la bonne marche (of de); − vt to s. down or out lisser; to s. out or over (problems etc) Fig aplanir. ◆**−ly** adv (to land, pass off) en douceur. ◆**−ness** n aspect m lisse; (of road) surface f égale.

smother ['smʌðər] vt (stifle) étouffer; to s. with (kisses etc) Fig couvrir de.

smoulder ['sməʊldər] vi (of fire, passion etc) couver.

smudge [smʌdʒ] n tache f, bavure f; − vt (paper etc) faire des taches sur, salir.

smug [smʌg] a (smugger, smuggest) (smile) béat; (person) content de soi, suffisant. ◆**−ly** adv avec suffisance.

smuggl/e ['smʌg(ə)l] vt passer (en fraude); **smuggled goods** contrebande f. ◆**−ing** n contrebande f. ◆**−er** n contrebandier, -ière mf.

smut [smʌt] n inv (obscenity) saleté(s) f(pl). ◆**smutty** a (**-ier, -iest**) (joke etc) cochon.

snack [snæk] n casse-croûte m inv; **s. bar** snack(-bar) m.

snafu [snæ'fuː] n Sl embrouillamini m.

snag [snæg] n 1 (hitch) inconvénient m, os m. 2 (in cloth) accroc m.

snail [sneɪl] n escargot m; **at a s.'s pace** comme une tortue.

snake [sneɪk] n (reptile) serpent m; − vi (of river) serpenter.

snap [snæp] 1 vt (**-pp-**) casser (avec un bruit sec); (fingers, whip) faire claquer; to s. up a bargain sauter sur une occasion; − vi se casser net; (of whip) claquer; (of person) Fig parler sèchement (at à); s. out of it! Fam secoue-toi!; − n claquement m, bruit *m* sec; *Phot* photo *f*; (*fastener*) *Am* bouton-pression *m*; **cold** s. *Met* coup *m* de froid. **2** *a* soudain, brusque; **to make a s. decision** décider sans réfléchir. ◆**snapshot** *n* photo *f*, instantané *m*.

snappy ['snæpɪ] *a* (**-ier**, **-iest**) (*pace*) vif; **make it s.!** *Fam* dépêche-toi!

snare [sneər] *n* piège *m*.

snarl [snɑːl] *vi* gronder (en montrant les dents); – *n* grondement *m*. ◆**s.-up** *n Aut Fam* embouteillage *m*.

snatch [snætʃ] *vt* saisir (*d'un geste vif*); (*some rest etc*) *Fig* (réussir à) prendre; **to s. sth from s.o.** arracher qch à qn; – *n* (*theft*) vol *m* (à l'arraché).

snatches ['snætʃɪz] *npl* (*bits*) fragments *mpl* (of).

snazzy ['snæzɪ] *a* (**-ier**, **-iest**) *Fam* (*flashy*) tapageur; (*smart*) élégant.

sneak [sniːk] **1** *vi* **to s. in/out** entrer/sortir furtivement; **to s. off** s'esquiver; – *a* (*attack*, *visit*) furtif. **2** *n* (*telltale*) *Sch Fam* rapporteur, -euse *mf*; – *vi* **to s. on s.o** *Sch Fam* dénoncer. ◆**sneaking** *a* (*suspicion*) vague; (*desire*) secret. ◆**sneaky** *a* (**-ier**, **-iest**) (*sly*) *Fam* sournois.

sneaker ['sniːkər] *n* (*shoe*) tennis *f*.

sneer [snɪər] *n* ricanement *m*; – *vi* ricaner; **to s. at** se moquer de.

sneeze [sniːz] *n* éternuement *m*; – *vi* éternuer.

snicker ['snɪkər] *n & vi Am* = **snigger**.

snide [snaɪd] *a* (*remark etc*) sarcastique.

sniff [snɪf] *n* reniflement *m*; – *vt* renifler; (*of dog*) flairer, renifler; **to s. out** (*bargain*) *Fig* renifler; – *vi* **to s. (at)** renifler. ◆**sniffle** *vi* renifler; – *n* **a s., the sniffles** *Fam* un petit rhume.

snigger ['snɪgər] *n* (petit) ricanement *m*; – *vi* ricaner. ◆**—ing** *n* ricanement(s) *m(pl)*.

snip [snɪp] *n* (*piece*) petit bout *m* (coupé); (*bargain*) *Fam* bonne affaire *f*; **to make a s. couper**; – *vt* (**-pp-**) couper.

sniper ['snaɪpər] *n Mil* tireur *m* embusqué.

snippet ['snɪpɪt] *n* (*of conversation etc*) bribe *f*.

snivel ['snɪv(ə)l] *vi* (**-ll-**, *Am* **-l-**) pleurnicher. ◆**snivelling** *a* pleurnicheur.

snob [snɒb] *n* snob *mf*. ◆**snobbery** *n* snobisme *m*. ◆**snobbish** *a* snob *inv*.

snook [snuːk] *n* **to cock a s.** faire un pied de nez (at à).

snooker ['snuːkər] *n* snooker *m, sorte de jeu de billard*.

snoop [snuːp] *vi* fourrer son nez partout; **to s. on s.o.** (*spy on*) espionner qn.

snooty ['snuːtɪ] *a* (**-ier**, **-iest**) *Fam* snob *inv*.

snooze [snuːz] *n* petit somme *m*; – *vi* faire un petit somme.

snor/e [snɔːr] *vi* ronfler; – *n* ronflement *m*. ◆**—ing** *n* ronflements *mpl*.

snorkel ['snɔːk(ə)l] *n Sp Nau* tuba *m*.

snort [snɔːt] *vi* (*grunt*) grogner; (*sniff*) renifler; (*of horse*) renâcler; – *n* (*grunt*) grognement *m*.

snot [snɒt] *n Pej Fam* morve *f*. ◆**snotty** *a* (**-ier**, **-iest**) *Fam* (*nose*) qui coule; (*child*) morveux. ◆**snotty-nosed** *a Fam* morveux.

snout [snaʊt] *n* museau *m*.

snow [snəʊ] *n* neige *f*; – *vi* neiger; – *vt* **to be snowed in** être bloqué par la neige; **to be s. under with** (*work etc*) être submergé de. ◆**snowball** *n* boule *f* de neige; – *vi* (*increase*) faire boule de neige. ◆**snowbound** *a* bloqué par la neige. ◆**snow-capped** *a* (*mountain*) enneigé. ◆**snowdrift** *n* congère *f*. ◆**snowdrop** *n Bot* perce-neige *m or f inv*. ◆**snowfall** *n* chute *f* de neige. ◆**snowflake** *n* flocon *m* de neige. ◆**snowman** *n* (*pl* **-men**) bonhomme *m* de neige. ◆**snowmobile** *n* motoneige *f*. ◆**snowplough** *n*, *Am* ◆**snowplow** *n* chasse-neige *m inv*. ◆**snowstorm** *n* tempête *f* de neige. ◆**snowy** *a* (**-ier**, **-iest**) (*weather*, *hills*, *day etc*) neigeux.

snub [snʌb] **1** *n* rebuffade *f*; – *vt* (**-bb-**) (*offer etc*) rejeter; **to s. s.o.** snober qn. **2** *a* (*nose*) retroussé.

snuff [snʌf] **1** *n* tabac *m* à priser. **2** *vt* **to s. (out)** (*candle*) moucher. ◆**snuffbox** *n* tabatière *f*.

snuffle ['snʌf(ə)l] *vi & n* = **sniffle**.

snug [snʌg] *a* (**snugger**, **snuggest**) (*house etc*) confortable, douillet; (*garment*) bien ajusté; **we's.** (*in chair etc*) on est bien; **s. in bed** bien au chaud dans son lit.

snuggle ['snʌg(ə)l] *vi* **to s. up to** se pelotonner contre.

so [səʊ] **1** *adv* (*to such a degree*) si, tellement (**that** que); (*thus*) ainsi, comme ça; **that** (*purpose*) pour que (+ *sub*); (*result*) si bien que; **so as to do** pour faire; **I think so** je le pense, je pense que oui; **do so!** faites-le!; **if so** si oui; **is that so?** c'est vrai?; **so am I, so do I** *etc* moi aussi; **so much** (*to work etc*) tant, tellement (**that** que); **so much courage/etc** tant or tellement de courage/etc (**that** que); **so many** tant, tellement; **so many books/etc** tant or tellement de livres/etc (**that** que); **so very fast/etc** vraiment si vite/etc; **ten or so** environ dix; **so long!** *Fam* au revoir!; **and so on** et ainsi de suite. **2** conj (therefore) donc; (in that case) alors; **so what?** et alors? ◆**So-and-so** n **Mr So-and-so** Monsieur Un tel. ◆**so-'called** a soi-disant inv. ◆**so-so** a Fam comme ci comme ça.

soak [səuk] vt (drench) tremper; (washing, food) faire tremper; **to s. up** absorber; – vi (of washing etc) tremper; **to s. in** (of liquid) s'infiltrer; – n **to give sth a s.** faire tremper qch. ◆**-ed** a s. (through) trempé (jusqu'aux os). ◆**-ing** a & adv s. (wet) trempé; – n trempage m.

soap [səup] n savon m; **s. opera** téléroman m; **s. powder** lessive f; – vt savonner. ◆**soapflakes** npl savon m en paillettes. ◆**soapsuds** npl mousse f de savon. ◆**soapy** a (-ier, -iest) savonneux.

soar [sɔɪr] vi (of bird etc) s'élever; (of price) monter (en flèche); (of hope) Fig grandir.

sob [sɒb] n sanglot m; – vi (-bb-) sangloter. ◆**sobbing** n (sobs) sanglots mpl.

sober ['səubər] **1** a **he's s.** (not drunk) il n'est pas ivre; – vti **to s. up** dessoûler. **2** a (serious) sérieux, sensé; (meal, style) sobre. ◆**-ly** adv sobrement.

soccer ['sɒkər] n football m.

sociable ['səuʃəb(ə)l] a (person) sociable; (evening) amical. ◆**sociably** adv (to act, reply) aimablement.

social ['səuʃəl] a social; (life, gathering) mondain; **s. club** foyer m; **s. science(s)** sciences fpl humaines; **s. security** (aid) aide f sociale; (retirement pension) Am pension f de retraite; **s. services** = sécurité f sociale; **s. worker** assistant m social; – n (gathering) réunion f (amicale). ◆**socialism** n socialisme m. ◆**socialist** a & n socialiste (mf). ◆**socialite** n mondain, -aine mf. ◆**socialize** vi (mix) se mêler aux autres; (talk) bavarder (with avec). ◆**socially** adv socialement; (to meet s.o., behave) en société.

society [sə'saɪətɪ] n (community, club, companionship etc) société f; Univ Sch club m; – a (wedding etc) mondain.

sociology [səusɪ'ɒlədʒɪ] n sociologie f. ◆**socio'logical** a sociologique. ◆**soci'ologist** n sociologue mf.

sock [sɒk] **1** n chaussette f. **2** vt (hit) Sl flanquer un marron à.

socket ['sɒkɪt] n (of bone) cavité f; (of eye) orbite f; (power point) El prise f de courant; (of lamp) douille f.

sod [sɒd] n (turf) Am gazon m.

soda ['səudə] **1** n Ch soude f; **washing s.** cristaux mpl de soude. **2** (water) eau f de Seltz; **s. (pop)** Am soda m.

sodden ['sɒd(ə)n] a (ground) détrempé.

sodium ['səudɪəm] n Ch sodium m.

sofa ['səufə] n canapé m, divan m; **s. bed** canapé-lit m.

soft [sɒft] a (-er, -est) (smooth, gentle, supple) doux; (butter, ground, snow) mou; (wood, heart, paste, colour) tendre; (flabby) flasque, mou; (easy) facile; (indulgent) indulgent; (cowardly) Fam poltron; (stupid) Fam ramolli; **it's too s.** (radio etc) ce n'est pas assez fort; **s. drink** boisson f non alcoolisée. ◆**s.-'boiled** a (egg) à la coque. ◆**soften** ['sɒf(ə)n] vt (object) ramollir; (voice, pain, colour) adoucir; – vi se ramollir; s'adoucir. ◆**softie** n Fam sentimental, -ale mf; (weakling) mauviette f. ◆**softly** adv doucement. ◆**softness** n douceur f; (of butter, ground, snow) mollesse f.

software ['sɒftweər] n inv (of computer) logiciel m.

soggy ['sɒgɪ] a (-ier, -iest) (ground) détrempé; (biscuit, bread) ramolli.

soil [sɔɪl] **1** n (earth) sol m, terre f. **2** vt (dirty) salir; – vi se salir.

solar ['səulər] a solaire.

sold [səuld] see sell.

solder ['sɒldər, Am 'sɒdər] vt souder; – n soudure f.

soldier ['səuldʒər] **1** n soldat m, militaire m. **2** vi **to s. on** persévérer.

sole [səul] **1** n (of shoe) semelle f; (of foot) plante f; – vt ressemeler. **2** a (only) seul, unique; (rights, representative) Com exclusif. **3** n (fish) sole f. ◆**-ly** adv uniquement; **you're s. to blame** tu es seul coupable.

solemn ['sɒləm] a (formal) solennel; (serious) grave. ◆**so'lemnity** n solennité f; gravité f. ◆**solemnly** adv (to promise) solennellement; (to say) gravement.

solicit [sə'lɪsɪt] vt (seek) solliciter; – vi (of prostitute) racoler. ◆**solicitor** n (for wills etc) notaire m.

solid ['sɒlɪd] a (car, character, meal, gold) & Ch solide; (wall, line, ball) plein; (gold, rock) massif; (crowd, mass) compact; **frozen s.** entièrement gelé; **ten days s.** dix jours d'affilée; – n Ch solide m; pl Culin aliments mpl solides. ◆**so'lidify** vi se solidifier. ◆**so'lidity** n solidité f. ◆**solidly** adv (built etc) solidement; (to support, vote) en masse.

solidarity [sɒlɪ'darɪtɪ] n solidarité f (with avec).

soliloquy [sə'lɪləkwɪ] n monologue m.

solitary ['sɒlɪtərɪ] a (lonely, alone) solitaire;

(only) scul, **s. confinement** Jur isolement m (cellulaire). ◆**solitude** n solitude f.

solo ['səʊləʊ] n (pl -os) Mus solo m; – a solo inv; – adv Mus en solo; (to fly) en solitaire. ◆**soloist** n Mus soliste mf.

solstice ['sɒlstɪs] n solstice m.

soluble ['sɒljʊb(ə)l] a (substance, problem) soluble.

solution [sə'lu:ʃ(ə)n] n (to problem etc) & Ch solution f (to à).

solv/e [sɒlv] vt (problem etc) résoudre. ◆**—able** a soluble.

solvent ['sɒlvənt] **1** a (financially) solvable. **2** n Ch (dis)solvant m. ◆**solvency** n Fin solvabilité f.

sombre ['sɒmbər] a sombre, triste.

some [sʌm] a **1** (amount, number) s. wine du vin; s. glue de la colle; s. water de l'eau; s. dogs des chiens; s. pretty flowers de jolies fleurs. **2** (unspecified) un, une; s. man (or other) un homme (quelconque); s. charm (a certain amount of) un certain charme; s. other way quelque autre or un autre moyen; **that's s. book!** Fam ça, c'est un livre! **3** (a few) quelques, certains; (a little) un peu de; – pron **1** (number) quelques-un(e)s, certain(e)s (of de, d'entre). **2** (a certain quantity) en; **I want s.;** j'en veux; **do you have s.?** en as-tu?; **s. of it is over** il en reste un peu ou une partie; – adv (about) quelque; **s. ten years** quelque dix ans.

somebody ['sʌmbɒdɪ] pron = **someone.** ◆**someday** adv un jour. ◆**somehow** adv (in some way) d'une manière ou d'une autre; (for some reason) on ne sait pourquoi. ◆**someone** pron quelqu'un; **at s.'s house** chez qn; s. **small**/etc quelqu'un de petit/etc. ◆**someplace** adv Am quelque part. ◆**something** pron quelque chose; s. **awful**/etc quelque chose d'affreux/etc; s. **of a liar**/etc un peu menteur/etc; – adv **she plays s. like** . . . elle joue un peu comme . . . ; **it was s. awful** c'était vraiment affreux. ◆**sometime** adv un jour; s. **in May**/etc au cours du mois de mai/etc; s. **before his departure** avant son départ. **2** a (former) ancien. ◆**sometimes** adv quelquefois, parfois. ◆**somewhat** adv quelque peu, assez. ◆**somewhere** adv quelque part; s. **about fifteen** (approximately) environ quinze.

somersault ['sʌməsɔ:lt] n culbute f; (in air) saut m périlleux; – vi faire la ou une culbute.

son [sʌn] n fils m. ◆**s.-in-law** n (pl **sons-in-law**) beau-fils m, gendre m.

sonar ['səʊnɑ:r] n sonar m.

sonata [sə'nɑ:tə] n Mus sonate f.

song [sɒŋ] n chanson f; (of bird) chant m. ◆**songbook** n recueil m de chansons.

sonic ['sɒnɪk] a s. **boom** bang m (supersonique).

sonnet ['sɒnɪt] n (poem) sonnet m.

soon [su:n] adv (-er, -est) (in a short time) bientôt; (quickly) vite; (early) tôt; s. **after** peu après; **as s. as she leaves** aussitôt qu'elle partira; **no sooner had he spoken than** à peine avait-il parlé que; **I'd sooner leave** je préférerais partir; **I'd just as s. leave** j'aimerais autant partir; **sooner or later** tôt ou tard.

soot [sʊt] n suie f. ◆**sooty** a (-ier, -iest) couvert de suie.

sooth/e [su:ð] vt (pain, nerves) calmer; Fig rassurer. ◆**—ing** a (ointment, words) calmant.

sophisticated [sə'fɪstɪkeɪtɪd] a (person, taste) raffiné; (machine, method, beauty) sophistiqué.

sophomore ['sɒfəmɔ:r] n Am étudiant, -ante mf de seconde année.

soporific [sɒpə'rɪfɪk] a (substance, speech etc) soporifique.

sopping ['sɒpɪŋ] a & adv s. **(wet)** trempé.

soppy ['sɒpɪ] a (-ier, -iest) Fam (silly) idiot, bête; (sentimental) sentimental.

soprano [sə'prɑ:nəʊ] n (pl -os) Mus (singer) soprano mf; (voice) soprano m.

sorbet ['sɔ:beɪ] n (water ice) sorbet m.

sorcerer ['sɔ:sərər] n sorcier m.

sordid ['sɔ:dɪd] a (act, street etc) sordide.

sore [sɔ:r] a (-er, -est) (painful) douloureux; (angry) Am fâché (at contre); s. **point** Fig un sujet délicat; **she has a s. thumb** elle a mal au pouce; **he's still s.** Med il a encore mal; – n Med plaie f. ◆**—ly** adv (tempted, regretted) très; s. **needed** dont on a grand besoin. ◆**—ness** n (pain) douleur f.

sorrow ['sɒrəʊ] n chagrin m, peine f. ◆**sorrowful** a triste.

sorry ['sɒrɪ] a (-ier, -iest) (sight, state etc) triste; **to be s.** (regret) être désolé, regretter (**to do** de faire); **I'm s. she can't come** je regrette qu'elle ne puisse pas venir; **I'm s. about the delay** je m'excuse pour ce retard; s.! pardon!; **to say s.** demander pardon (**to** à); **to feel** ou **be s. for** plaindre.

sort [sɔ:t] **1** n genre m, espèce f, sorte f; **a s. of** une sorte ou espèce de; **a good s.** (person) Fam un brave type; s. **of sad**/etc plutôt triste/etc. **2** vt (letters) trier; **to s. out** (classify, select) trier; (separate) séparer (**from** de); (arrange) arranger; (tidy) ranger; (problem) régler; **to s. s.o. out** (punish) Fam faire voir à qn; – *vi* to s. through (*letters etc*) trier; **sorting office** centre *m* de tri. ◆**—er** *n* (*person*) trieur, -euse *mf*.

soufflé ['suːfleɪ] *n Culin* soufflé *m*.

sought [sɔːt] *see* seek.

soul [səʊl] *n* âme *f*; **not a living s.** (*nobody*) personne, pas âme qui vive; **a good s.** *Fig* un brave type; **s. mate** âme *f* sœur. ◆**s.-destroying** *a* abrutissant. ◆**s.-searching** *n* examen *m* de conscience.

sound[1] [saʊnd] *n* son *m*; (*noise*) bruit *m*; **I don't like the s. of it** ça ne me plaît pas du tout; – *a* (*wave, film*) sonore; (*engineer*) du son; **s. archives** phonothèque *f*; **s. barrier** mur *m* du son; **s. effects** bruitage *m*; – *vt* (*bell, alarm etc*) sonner; (*bugle*) sonner de; (*letter*) *Gram* prononcer; **to s. one's horn** *Aut* klaxonner; – *vi* retentir, sonner; (*seem*) sembler; **to s. like** sembler être; (*resemble*) ressembler à; **it sounds like** *or* **as if** il semble que (+ *sub or indic*); **to s. off about** *Pej* (*boast*) se vanter de; (*complain*) rouspéter à propos de. ◆**soundproof** *a* insonorisé; – *vt* insonoriser. ◆**soundtrack** *n* (*of film etc*) bande *f* sonore.

sound[2] [saʊnd] *a* (**-er, -est**) (*healthy*) sain; (*sturdy, reliable*) solide; (*instinct*) sûr; (*advice*) sensé; (*beating, sense*) bon; – *adv* **s. asleep** profondément endormi. ◆**—ly** *adv* (*asleep*) profondément; (*reasoned*) solidement; (*beaten*) complètement. ◆**—ness** *n* (*of mind*) santé *f*; (*of argument*) solidité *f*.

sound[3] [saʊnd] *vt* (*test, measure*) sonder; **to s. s.o. out** sonder qn (**about** sur).

soup [suːp] *n* soupe *f*, potage *m*; **in the s.** (*in trouble*) *Fam* dans le pétrin.

sour ['saʊər] *a* (**-er, -est**) aigre; **to turn s.** (*of wine*) s'aigrir; (*of milk*) tourner; (*of friendship*) se détériorer; (*of conversation*) tourner au vinaigre; – *vi* (*of temper*) s'aigrir.

source [sɔːs] *n* (*origin*) source *f*; **s. of energy** source *f* d'énergie.

south [saʊθ] *n* sud *m*; – *a* (*coast*) sud *inv*; (*wind*) du sud; **to be s. of** être au sud de; **S. America/Africa** Amérique *f*/Afrique *f* du Sud; **S. American** *a & n* sud-américain, -aine (*mf*); **S. African** *a & n* sud-africain, -aine (*mf*); – *adv* au sud, vers le sud. ◆**southbound** *a* (*carriageway*) sud; (*traffic*) en direction du sud. ◆**south-'east** *n & a* sud-est *m & a inv*. ◆**southerly** ['sʌðəlɪ] *a* (*point*) sud *inv*; (*direction, wind*) du sud. ◆**southern** ['sʌðən] *a* (*town*) du sud; (*coast*) sud *inv*; **S. Italy** le Sud de

l'Italie; **S. Africa** Afrique *f* australe. ◆**southerner** ['sʌðənər] *n* habitant, -ante *mf* du Sud. ◆**southward(s)** *a & adv* vers le sud. ◆**south-'west** *n & a* sud-ouest *m & a inv*.

souvenir [suːvə'nɪər] *n* (*object*) souvenir *m*.

sovereign ['sɒvrɪn] *n* souverain, -aine *mf*; – *a* (*State, authority*) souverain; (*rights*) de souveraineté. ◆**sovereignty** *n* souveraineté *f*.

Soviet ['səʊvɪət] *a* soviétique; **the S. Union** l'Union *f* soviétique.

sow[1] [saʊ] *n* (*pig*) truie *f*.

sow[2] [səʊ] *vt* (*pt* sowed, *pp* sowed *or* sown) (*seeds, doubt etc*) semer; (*land*) ensemencer (**with** de).

soya ['sɔɪə] *n* **s. (bean)** graine *f* de soja. ◆**soybean** *n Am* graine *f* de soja.

sozzled ['sɒz(ə)ld] *a* (*drunk*) *Sl* bourré.

spa [spɑː] *n* (*town*) station *f* thermale; (*spring*) source *f* minérale.

space [speɪs] *n* (*gap, emptiness*) espace *m*; (*period*) période *f*; **blank s.** espace *m*, blanc *m*; (**outer**) **s.** l'espace (cosmique); **to take up s.** (*room*) prendre de la place; **in the s. of** en l'espace de; – *a* (*voyage etc*) spatial; – *vt* **to s. out** espacer; **double/single spacing** (*on typewriter*) double/simple interligne *m*. ◆**spaceman** *n* (*pl* **-men**) astronaute *m*. ◆**spaceship** *n*, ◆**spacecraft** *n inv* engin *m* spatial. ◆**spacesuit** *n* scaphandre *m* (de cosmonaute).

spacious ['speɪʃəs] *a* spacieux, grand. ◆**—ness** *n* grandeur *f*.

spade [speɪd] *n* **1** (*for garden*) bêche *f*; (*of child*) pelle *f*. **2** *Cards* pique *m*. ◆**spadework** *n Fig* travail *m* préparatoire; (*around problem or case*) débroussaillage *m*.

spaghetti [spə'getɪ] *n* spaghetti(s) *mpl*.

Spain [speɪn] *n* Espagne *f*.

span [spæn] *n* (*of arch*) portée *f*; (*of wings*) envergure *f*; (*of life*) *Fig* durée *f*; – *vt* (**-nn-**) (*of bridge etc*) enjamber (*rivière etc*); *Fig* couvrir, embrasser.

Spaniard ['spænjəd] *n* Espagnol, -ole *mf*. ◆**Spanish** *a* espagnol; – *n* (*language*) espagnol *m*. ◆**Spanish-A'merican** *a* hispano-américain.

spaniel ['spænjəl] *n* épagneul *m*.

spank [spæŋk] *vt* fesser, donner une fessée à; – *n* **to give s.o. a s.** fesser qn. ◆**—ing** *n* fessée *f*.

spanner ['spænər] *n* (*tool*) clé *f* (à écrous); **adjustable s.** clé *f* à molette.

spar/e[1] [speər] **1** *a* (*extra, surplus*) de *or* en trop; (clothes, tyre) de rechange; (wheel) de secours; (available) disponible; (bed, room) d'ami; s. time loisirs mpl; — n s. (part) Tech Aut pièce f détachée. 2 vt (do without) se passer de; (s.o.'s life) épargner; (efforts, s.o.'s feelings) ménager; to s. s.o. (not kill) épargner qn; (grief, details etc) épargner à qn; (time) accorder à qn; (money) donner à qn; I can't s. the time je n'ai pas le temps; five to s. cinq de trop. ◆—ing n (use) modéré; to be s. with (butter etc) ménager.

spare² [spɛər] a (lean) maigre.

spark [spɑːk] 1 n étincelle f. 2 vt to s. off (cause) provoquer. ◆spark(ing) plug n Aut bougie f.

sparkl/e ['spɑːk(ə)l] vi étinceler, scintiller; — n éclat m. ◆—ing a (wine, water) pétillant.

sparrow ['spærəu] n moineau m.

sparse [spɑːs] a clairsemé. ◆—ly adv (populated etc) peu.

spartan ['spɑːtən] a spartiate, austère.

spasm ['spæzəm] n (of muscle) spasme m; (of coughing etc) Fig accès m. ◆spas'modic a (pain etc) spasmodique; Fig irrégulier.

spastic ['spæstik] n handicapé, -ée mf moteur.

spat [spæt] see spit 1.

spate [speit] n a s. of (orders etc) une avalanche de.

spatter ['spætər] vt (clothes, person etc) éclabousser (with de); — vi to s. over s.o. (of mud etc) éclabousser qn.

spatula ['spætjulə] n spatule f.

spawn [spɔːn] n (of fish etc) frai m; — vi frayer; — vt pondre; Fig engendrer.

speak [spiːk] vi (pt spoke, pp spoken) parler; (formally, in assembly) prendre la parole; so to s. pour ainsi dire; that speaks for itself c'est évident; to s. well of dire du bien de; nothing to s. of pas grand-chose; Bob speaking Tel Bob à l'appareil; that's spoken for c'est pris or réservé; to s. out or up (boldly) parler (franchement); to s. up (more loudly) parler plus fort; — vt (language) parler; (say) dire; to s. one's mind dire ce que l'on pense. ◆—ing n public s. art m oratoire; — a to be on s. terms with être parler à; English-/French-speaking anglophone/francophone. ◆—er n (public) orateur m; (in dialogue) interlocuteur, -trice mf; (loudspeaker) El haut-parleur m; (of hi-fi) enceinte f; to be a Spanish/a bad/etc s. parler espagnol/mal/etc.

spear [spiər] n lance f. ◆spearhead vt

(attack) être le fer de lance de; (campaign) mener.

spearmint ['spiəmint] n Bot menthe f (verte); — a à la menthe; (chewing-gum) mentholé.

spec [spek] n on s. (as a gamble) Fam à tout hasard.

special ['speʃ(ə)l] a spécial; (care, attention) (tout) particulier; (measures) Pol extraordinaire; (favourite) préféré; by s. delivery (letter etc) par exprès; — n today's s. (in restaurant) le plat du jour. ◆specialist n spécialiste mf (in de); — a (dictionary, knowledge) technique, spécialisé. ◆speci'ality n spécialité f. ◆specialize vi se spécialiser (in dans). ◆specialized a spécialisé. ◆specially adv (specifically) spécialement; (on purpose) (tout) spécialement. ◆specialty n Am spécialité f.

species ['spiːʃiːz] n inv espèce f.

specific [spə'sifik] a précis, explicite; Phys Ch spécifique. ◆specifically adv (expressly) expressément; (exactly) précisément.

specify ['spesifai] vt spécifier (that que). ◆specifi'cation n spécification f; pl (of car, machine etc) caractéristiques fpl.

specimen ['spesimin] n (example, person) spécimen m; (of blood) prélèvement m; (of urine) échantillon m; s. signature spécimen m de signature; s. copy (of book etc) spécimen m.

specious ['spiːʃəs] a spécieux.

speck [spek] n (stain) petite tache f; (of dust) grain m; (dot) point m.

speckled ['spek(ə)ld] a tacheté.

specs [speks] npl Fam lunettes fpl.

spectacle ['spektək(ə)l] 1 n (sight) spectacle m. 2 npl (glasses) lunettes fpl. ◆spec'tacular a spectaculaire. ◆spec'tator n Sp etc spectateur, -trice mf.

spectre ['spektər] n (menacing image) spectre m (of de).

spectrum, pl -tra ['spektrəm, -trə] n Phys spectre m; (range) Fig gamme f.

speculate ['spekjuleit] vi Fin Phil spéculer; to s. about (s.o.'s motives etc) s'interroger sur; — vt to s. that (guess) conjecturer que. ◆specu'lation n Fin Phil spéculation f; (guessing) conjectures fpl (about sur). ◆speculator n spéculateur, -trice mf. ◆speculative a Fin Phil spéculatif; that's s. (guesswork) c'est (très) hypothétique.

sped [sped] see speed 1.

speech [spiːtʃ] n (talk, address) & Gram discours m (on sur); (faculty) parole f;

(*diction*) élocution *f*; (*of group*) langage *m*; **a short s.** une allocution *f*; **freedom of s.** liberté *f* d'expression; **part of s.** *Gram* catégorie *f* grammaticale. ◆**—less** *a* muet (**with de**).

speed [spiːd] **1** *n* (*rate of movement*) vitesse *f*; (*swiftness*) rapidité *f*; **s. limit** *Aut* limitation *f* de vitesse; — *vt* (*pt & pp* **sped**) **to s. up** accélérer; — *vi* **to s. up** (*of person*) aller plus vite; (*of pace*) s'accélérer; **to s. past** passer à toute vitesse (**sth** devant qch). **2** *vi* (*pt & pp* **speeded**) (*drive too fast*) aller trop vite. ◆**—ing** *n Jur* excès *m* de vitesse. ◆**speedboat** *n* vedette *f*. ◆**spee'd-ometer** *n Aut* compteur *m* (de vitesse). ◆**speedway** *n Sp* piste *f* de vitesse pour motos; *Sp Aut Am* autodrome *m*.

speed/y [spiːdi] *a* (**-ier, -iest**) rapide. ◆**—ily** *adv* rapidement.

spell [spel] *n* (*magic*) charme *m*, sortilège *m*; (*curse*) sort *m*; *Fig* charme *m*; **under a s.** envoûté. ◆**spellbound** *a* (*audience etc*) captivé.

spell [spel] *n* (*period*) (courte) période *f*; (*moment, while*) moment *m*; **s. of duty** tour *m* de service.

spell [spel] *vt* (*pt & pp* **spelled** *or* **spelt**) (*write*) écrire; (*say aloud*) épeler; (*of letters*) former (*mot*); (*mean*) *Fig* signifier; **to be able to s.** savoir l'orthographe; **how is it spelt?** comment cela s'écrit-il?; **to s. out** (*aloud*) épeler; *Fig* expliquer très clairement. ◆**—ing** *n* orthographe *f*.

spend [spend] **1** *vt* (*pt & pp* **spent**) (*money*) dépenser (**on** pour); — *vi* dépenser. **2** *vt* (*pt & pp* **spent**) (*time, holiday etc*) passer (**on** sth sur qch, **doing** à faire); (*energy, care etc*) consacrer (**on** sth à qch, **doing** à faire). ◆**—ing** *n* dépenses *fpl*; — *a* (*money*) de poche. ◆**—er** *n* **to be a big s.** dépenser beaucoup. ◆**spendthrift** *n* **to be a s.** être dépensier.

spent [spent] *see* **spend**; — *a* (*used*) utilisé; (*energy*) épuisé.

sperm [spɜːm] *n* (*pl* **sperm** *or* **sperms**) sperme *m*.

spew [spjuː] *vt* vomir.

sphere [sfɪər] *n* (*of influence, action etc*) & *Geom Pol* sphère *f*; (*of music, poetry etc*) domaine *m*; **the social s.** le domaine social. ◆**spherical** ['sferɪk(ə)l] *a* sphérique.

sphinx [sfɪŋks] *n* sphinx *m*.

spice [spaɪs] *n Culin* épice *f*; (*interest etc*) *Fig* piment *m*; — *vt* épicer. ◆**spicy** *a* (**-ier, -iest**) épicé; (*story*) *Fig* pimenté.

spick-and-span [spɪkən'spæn] *a* (*clean*) impeccable.

spider ['spaɪdər] *n* araignée *f*.

spiel [ʃpiːl] *n Fam* baratin *m*.

spike [spaɪk] *n* (*of metal*) pointe *f*; — *vt* (*pierce*) transpercer. ◆**spiky** *a* (**-ier, -iest**) *a* garni de pointes.

spill [spɪl] *vt* (*pt & pp* **spilled** *or* **spilt**) (*liquid*) répandre, renverser (**on, over** sur); **to s. the beans** *Fam* vendre la mèche; — *vi* **to s. (out)** se répandre; **to s. over** déborder.

spin [spɪn] *n* (*motion*) tour *m*; (*car ride*) petit tour *m*; (*on washing machine*) essorage *m*; **s. dryer** essoreuse *f*; — *vt* (*pt & pp* **spun**, *pres p* **spinning**) (*web, yarn, wool etc*) filer (**into** en); (*wheel, top*) faire tourner; (*washing*) essorer; (*story*) *Fig* débiter; **to s. out** (*speech etc*) faire durer; — *vi* (*of spinner, spider*) filer; **to s. (round)** (*of dancer, top, planet etc*) tourner; (*of head, room*) *Fig* tourner; (*of vehicle*) faire une tête-à-queue. ◆**spinning** *n* (*by hand*) filage *m*; (*process*) *Tech* filature *f*; **s. top** toupie *f*; **s. wheel** rouet *m*. ◆**spin-'dry** *vt* essorer. ◆**spin-off** *n* avantage *m* inattendu; (*of process, book etc*) dérivé *m*.

spinach ['spɪnɪdʒ] *n* (*plant*) épinard *m*; (*leaves*) *Culin* épinards *mpl*.

spindle ['spɪnd(ə)l] *n Tex* fuseau *m*. ◆**spindly** *a* (**-ier, -iest**) (*legs, arms*) grêle.

spine [spaɪn] *n Anat* colonne *f* vertébrale; (*spike of animal or plant*) épine *f*. ◆**spinal** *a* (*column*) vertébral; **s. cord** moelle *f* épinière. ◆**spineless** *a Fig* mou, faible.

spinster ['spɪnstər] *n* célibataire *f*, *Pej* vieille fille *f*.

spiral ['spaɪərəl] **1** *n* spirale *f*; — *a* en spirale; (*staircase*) en colimaçon. **2** *vi* (**-ll-**, *Am* **-l-**) (*of prices*) monter en flèche.

spire [spaɪər] *n* (*of church*) flèche *f*.

spirit ['spɪrɪt] **1** *n* (*soul, ghost etc*) esprit *m*; (*courage*) *Fig* courage *m*, vigueur *f*; *pl* (*drink*) alcool *m*, spiritueux *mpl*; **spirit(s)** (*morale*) moral *m*; *Ch* alcool *m*; **in good spirits** de bonne humeur; **the right s.** l'attitude *f* qu'il faut; — *a* (*lamp*) à alcool; **s. level** niveau *m* à bulle (d'air). **2** *vt* **to s. away** (*person*) faire disparaître mystérieusement; (*steal*) *Hum* subtiliser. ◆**—ed** *a* (*person, remark*) fougueux; (*campaign*) vigoureux.

spiritual ['spɪrɪtʃʊəl] *a Phil Rel* spirituel; — *n* (*Negro*) **s.** (negro-)spiritual *m*. ◆**spiritualism** *n* spiritisme *m*. ◆**spiritualist** *n* spirite *mf*.

spit [spɪt] **1** *n* crachat *m*; — *vi* (*pt & pp* **spat** *or* **spit**, *pres p* **spitting**) cracher; (*splutter*) *Fig* crépiter; — *vt* cracher; **to s. out** (re)cracher; **the spitting image of s.o.** le portrait (tout craché) de qn. **2** n (for meat) broche f.

spite [spaɪt] **1** n in s. of malgré; in s. of the fact that (although) bien que (+ sub). **2** n (dislike) rancune f; − vt (annoy) contrarier. ◆**spiteful** a méchant. ◆**spitefully** adv méchamment.

spittle ['spit(ə)l] n salive f; crachat(s) m(pl).

splash [splæʃ] vt (spatter) éclabousser (with de, over sur); (spill) répandre; − vi (of mud, ink etc) faire des éclaboussures; (of waves) clapoter, déferler; to s. over sth/s.o. éclabousser qch/qn; to s. (about) (in river, mud) patauger; (in bath) barboter; to s. out (spend money) Fam claquer de l'argent; − n (splashing) éclaboussement m; (of colour) Fig tache f; s. (mark) éclaboussure f; s.! plouf!

spleen [spli:n] n Anat rate f.

splendid ['splendɪd] a (wonderful, rich, beautiful) splendide. ◆**splendour** n splendeur f.

splint [splɪnt] n Med éclisse f.

splinter ['splɪntər] n (of wood etc) éclat m; (in finger) écharde f; s. group Pol groupe m dissident.

split [splɪt] n fente f; (tear) déchirure f; (of couple) rupture f; Pol scission f; to do the splits (in gymnastics) faire le grand écart; one's s. (share) Fam sa part; − a a s. second une fraction de seconde; − vt (pt & pp split, pres p splitting) (break apart) fendre; (tear) déchirer; to s. (up) (group) diviser; (money, work) partager (between entre); to s. one's head open s'ouvrir la tête; to s. one's sides (laughing) se tordre (de rire); to s. hairs Fig couper les cheveux en quatre; s.-level apartment duplex m; − vi se fendre; (tear) se déchirer; to s. (up) (of group) éclater; (of couple) rompre, se séparer; to s. off (become loose) se détacher (from de); to s. up (of crowd) se disperser. ◆**splitting** a (head-ache) atroce. ◆**split-up** n (of couple) rupture f.

splodge [splɒdʒ] n, **splotch** [splɒtʃ] n (mark) tache f.

splurge [splɜːdʒ] vi (spend money) Fam claquer de l'argent.

splutter ['splʌtər] vi (of sparks, fat) crépiter; (stammer) bredouiller.

spoil [spɔɪl] vt (pt & pp spoilt or spoiled) (pamper, make unpleasant or less good) gâter; (damage, ruin) abîmer; (pleasure, life) gâcher, gâter. ◆**spoilsport** n rabat-joie m inv.

spoils [spɔɪlz] npl (rewards) butin m.

spoke¹ [spəʊk] n (of wheel) rayon m.

spoke² [spəʊk] see speak. ◆**spoken** see speak; − a (language etc) parlé; softly s. (person) à la voix douce. ◆**spokesman** n (pl -men) porte-parole m inv (for, of de).

sponge [spʌndʒ] **1** n éponge f; s. bag trousse f de toilette; s. cake gâteau m de Savoie; − vt to s. down/off laver/enlever à l'éponge. **2** vi to s. off or on s.o. Fam vivre aux crochets de qn; − vt to s. sth off s.o. Fam taper qn de qch. ◆**sponger** n Fam parasite m. ◆**spongy** a (-ier, -iest) spongieux.

sponsor ['spɒnsər] n (of appeal, advertiser etc) personne f assurant le patronage (of de); (for membership) parrain m, marraine f; Jur garant, -ante mf; Sp sponsor m; − vt (appeal etc) patronner; (member, firm) parrainer. ◆**sponsorship** n patronage m; parrainage m.

spontaneous [spɒn'teɪnɪəs] a spontané. ◆**spontaneity** [spɒntə'neɪɪtɪ] n spontanéité f. ◆**spontaneously** adv spontanément.

spoof [spu:f] n Fam parodie f (on de).

spooky ['spu:kɪ] a (-ier, -iest) Fam qui donne le frisson.

spool [spu:l] n bobine f.

spoon [spu:n] n cuiller f. ◆**spoonfeed** vt (pt & pp spoonfed) (help) Fig mâcher le travail à. ◆**spoonful** n cuillerée f.

sporadic [spə'rædɪk] a sporadique; s. fighting échauffourées fpl. ◆**sporadically** adv sporadiquement.

sport [spɔːt] **1** n sport m; a (good) s. (person) Fam un chic type; to play s. or Am sports faire du sport; sports club club m sportif; sports car/jacket voiture f/veste f de sport; sports results résultats mpl sportifs. **2** vt (wear) arborer. ◆**-ing** a (conduct, attitude, person etc) sportif; that's s. of you Fig c'est chic de ta part. ◆**sportsman** n (pl -men) sportif m. ◆**sportsmanlike** a sportif. ◆**sportsmanship** n sportivité f. ◆**sportswear** n vêtements mpl de sport. ◆**sportswoman** n (pl -women) sportive f.

spot¹ [spɒt] n (stain, mark) tache f; (dot) point m; (polka dot) pois m; (pimple) bouton m; (place) endroit m, coin m; (act) Th numéro m; (drop) goutte f; a s. of (bit) Fam un peu de; a soft s. for un faible pour; on the s. sur place, sur les lieux; (at once) sur le coup; in a (tight) s. (difficulty) dans le pétrin; (accident) black s. Aut point m noir; s. cash argent m comptant; s. check contrôle m au hasard or l'improviste. ◆**spotless** a (clean) impeccable. ◆**spot-**

lessly adv s. clean impeccable. ◆**spotlight** n (lamp) Th projecteur m; (for photography etc) spot m; **in the s.** Th sous le feu des projecteurs. ◆**spot-'on** a Fam tout à fait exact. ◆**spotted** a (fur) tacheté; (dress etc) à pois; (stained) taché. ◆**spotty** a (-ier, -iest) 1 (face etc) boutonneux. 2 (patchy) Am inégal.

spot² [spɒt] vt (-tt-) (notice) apercevoir, remarquer.

spouse [spaus, spauz] n époux m, épouse f.

spout [spaut] 1 n (of jug etc) bec m; **up the s.** (hope etc) Sl fichu. 2 vi **to s. (out)** jaillir. 3 vt (say) Pej débiter.

sprain [sprein] n entorse f, foulure f; **to s. one's ankle/wrist** se fouler la cheville/le poignet.

sprang [spræŋ] see **spring¹**.

sprawl [sprɔːl] vi (of town, person) s'étaler; **to be sprawling** être étalé; – n **the urban s.** les banlieues fpl tentaculaires. ◆**—ing** a (city) tentaculaire.

spray [sprei] 1 n (water drops) (nuage m de) gouttelettes fpl; (from sea) embruns mpl; (can, device) bombe f, vaporisateur m; **hair s.** laque f à cheveux; – vt (liquid, surface) vaporiser; (crops, plant) arroser, traiter; (car etc) peindre à la bombe. 2 n (of flowers) petit bouquet m.

spread [spred] vt (pt & pp spread) (stretch, open out) étendre; (legs, fingers) écarter; (strew) répandre, étaler (over sur); (paint, payment, cards, visits) étaler; (people) disperser; (fear, news) répandre; (illness) propager; **to s. out** étendre; écarter; étaler; – vi (of fire, town, fog) s'étendre; (of news, fear) se répandre; **to s. out** (of people) se disperser; – n (of fire, illness, ideas) propagation f; (of wealth) répartition f; (paste) Culin pâte f (à tartiner); (meal) festin m; **cheese s.** fromage m à tartiner. ◆**s.-'eagled** a bras et jambes écartés.

spree [spriː] n **to go on a spending s.** faire des achats extravagants.

sprig [sprig] n (branch of heather etc) brin m; (of parsley) bouquet m.

sprightl/y ['spraitli] a (-ier, -iest) alerte. ◆**—iness** n vivacité f.

spring¹ [spriŋ] n (metal device) ressort m; (leap) bond m; – vi (pt sprang, pp sprung) (leap) bondir; **to s. to mind** venir à l'esprit; **to s. into action** passer à l'action; **to s. from** (stem from) provenir de; **to s. up** (appear) surgir; – vt (news) annoncer brusquement (on à); (surprise) faire (on à); **to s. a leak** (of boat) commencer à faire eau. ◆**spring-**

board n tremplin m. ◆**springy** a (-ier, -iest) élastique.

spring² [spriŋ] n (season) printemps m; **in (the) s.** au printemps; **s. onion** ciboule f. ◆**s.-'cleaning** n nettoyage m de printemps. ◆**springlike** a printanier. ◆**springtime** n printemps m.

spring³ [spriŋ] n (of water) source f; **s. water** eau f de source.

sprinkl/e ['spriŋk(ə)l] vt (sand etc) répandre (on, over sur); **to s. with water, s. water on** asperger d'eau, arroser; **to s. with** (sugar, salt, flour) saupoudrer de. ◆**—ing** n a s. of (a few) quelques. ◆**—er** n (in garden) arroseur m.

sprint [sprint] n Sp sprint m; – vi sprinter. ◆**—er** n sprinter m, sprinteuse f.

sprite [sprait] n (fairy) lutin m.

sprout [spraut] 1 vi (of seed, bulb etc) germer, pousser; **to s. up** (grow) pousser vite; (appear) surgir; – vt (leaves) pousser; (beard) Fig laisser pousser. 2 n (Brussels) s. chou m de Bruxelles.

spruce [spruːs] a (-er, -est) (neat) pimpant, net; – vt **to s. oneself up** se faire beau.

sprung [sprʌŋ] see **spring¹**; – a (mattress, seat) à ressorts.

spry [sprai] a (spryer, spryest) (old person etc) alerte.

spud [spʌd] n (potato) Fam patate f.

spun [spʌn] see **spin**.

spur [spɜːr] n (of horse rider etc) éperon m; (stimulus) Fig aiguillon m; **on the s. of the moment** sur un coup de tête; – vt (-rr-) **to s. (on)** (urge on) éperonner.

spurious ['spjuəriəs] a faux.

spurn [spɜːn] vt rejeter (avec mépris).

spurt [spɜːt] vi (gush out) jaillir; (rush) foncer; **to s. out** jaillir; – n jaillissement m; (of energy) sursaut m; **to put on a s.** (rush) foncer.

spy [spai] n espion, -onne mf; – a (story etc) d'espionnage; **s. hole** (peephole) judas m; **s. ring** réseau m d'espionnage; – vi espionner; **to s. on s.o.** espionner qn; – vt (notice) Lit apercevoir. ◆**—ing** n espionnage m.

squabbl/e ['skwɒb(ə)l] vi se chamailler (over à propos de); – n chamaillerie f. ◆**—ing** n chamailleries fpl.

squad [skwɒd] n (group) & Mil escouade f; (team) Sp équipe f; **s. car** voiture f de police.

squadron ['skwɒdrən] n Mil escadron m; Nau Av escadrille f.

squalid ['skwɒlid] a sordide. ◆**squalor** n conditions fpl sordides.

squall [skwɔːl] n (of wind) rafale f.

squander ['skwɒndər] *vt (money, time etc)* gaspiller (**on** en).

square ['skweər] *n* carré *m*; *(on chessboard, graph paper)* case *f*; *(in town)* place *f*; *(drawing implement)* Tech équerre *f*; **to be back to s. one** repartir à zéro; – *a* carré; *(in order, settled)* Fig en ordre; *(honest)* honnête; *(meal)* solide; **(all) s.** *(quits)* quitte (**with** envers); – *vt (settle)* mettre en ordre, régler; *(arrange)* arranger; Math carrer; *(reconcile)* faire cadrer; – *vi (tally)* cadrer (**with** avec); **to s. up to s.** faire face à. ◆**—ly** *adv (honestly)* honnêtement; *(exactly)* tout à fait; **s. in the face** bien en face.

squash [skwɒʃ] **1** *vt (crush)* écraser; *(squeeze)* serrer; – *n* lemon/orange **s.** *(concentrated)* sirop *m* de citron/d'orange; *(diluted)* citronnade *f*/orangeade *f*. **2** *n (game)* squash *m*. **3** *n (vegetable)* Am courge *f*. ◆**squashy** *a* (**-ier, -iest**) *(soft)* mou.

squat [skwɒt] **1** *a (short and thick)* trapu. **2** *vi* (**-tt-**) **to s.** (**down**) s'accroupir. **3** *n (house)* squat *m*. ◆**squatting** *a* accroupi. ◆**squatter** *n* squatter *m*.

squawk [skwɔːk] *vi* pousser des cris rauques; – *n* cri *m* rauque.

squeak [skwiːk] *vi (of door)* grincer; *(of shoe)* craquer; *(of mouse)* faire couic; – *n* grincement *m*; craquement *m*; couic *m*. ◆**squeaky** *a* (**-ier, -iest**) *(door)* grinçant; *(shoe)* qui craque.

squeal [skwiːl] *vi* pousser des cris aigus; *(of tyres)* crisser; – *n* cri *m* aigu; crissement *m*. **2** *vi* **to s. on s.o.** *(inform on)* Fam balancer qn.

squeamish ['skwiːmɪʃ] *a* bien délicat, facilement dégoûté.

squeegee ['skwiːdʒiː] *n* raclette *f* (à vitres).

squeez/e [skwiːz] *vt (press)* presser; *(hand, arm)* serrer; **to s. sth out of s.o.** *(information)* soutirer qch à qn; **to s. sth into** faire rentrer qch dans; **to s.** (**out**) *(extract)* exprimer (**from** de); – *vi* **to s. through/into/etc** *(force oneself)* se glisser par/dans/ etc; **to s. in** trouver un peu de place; – *n* pression *f*; **to give sth a s.** presser qch; **it's a tight s.** il y a peu de place; **credit s.** Fin restrictions *fpl* de crédit. ◆**—er** *n* lemon **s.** presse-citron *m inv*.

squelch [skweltʃ] **1** *vi* patauger (*en faisant floc-floc*). **2** *vt (silence)* Fam réduire au silence.

squid [skwɪd] *n (mollusc)* calmar *m*.

squiggle ['skwɪg(ə)l] *n* ligne *f* onduleuse, gribouillis *m*.

squint [skwɪnt] *n* Med strabisme *m*; **to have a s.** loucher; – *vi* loucher; *(in the sunlight etc)* plisser les yeux.

squire ['skwaɪər] *n* propriétaire *m* terrien.

squirm [skwɜːm] *vi (wriggle)* se tortiller; **to s. in pain** se tordre de douleur.

squirrel ['skwɪrəl, Am 'skwɜːrəl] *n* écureuil *m*.

squirt [skwɜːt] **1** *vt (liquid)* faire gicler; – *vi* gicler; – *n* giclée *f*, jet *m*. **2** *n* **little s.** *(person)* Fam petit morveux *m*.

stab [stæb] *vt* (**-bb-**) *(with knife etc)* poignarder; – *n* coup *m* (de couteau ou de poignard). ◆**stabbing** *n* there was a **s.** quelqu'un a été poignardé; – *a (pain)* lancinant.

stable[1] ['steɪb(ə)l] *a* (**-er, -est**) stable; **mentally s.** *(person)* bien équilibré. ◆**stability** *n* stabilité *f*; **mental s.** équilibre *m*. ◆**stabilize** *vt* stabiliser; – *vi* se stabiliser. ◆**stabilizer** *n* stabilisateur *m*.

stable[2] ['steɪb(ə)l] *n* écurie *f*; **s. boy** lad *m*.

stack [stæk] **1** *n (heap)* tas *m*; **stacks of** *(lots of)* Fam un tas de; – *vt* **to s.** (**up**) entasser. **2** *npl (in library)* réserve *f*.

stadium ['steɪdɪəm] *n* Sp stade *m*.

staff [stɑːf] **1** *n* personnel *m*; Sch professeurs *mpl*; Mil état-major *m*; **s. meeting** Sch Univ conseil *m* des professeurs; **s. room** Sch Univ salle *f* des professeurs; – *vt* pourvoir en personnel. **2** *n (stick)* Lit bâton *m*.

stag [stæg] *n* cerf *m*; **s. party** réunion *f* entre hommes.

stage[1] [steɪdʒ] *n (platform)* Th scène *f*; **the s.** *(profession)* le théâtre; **on s.** sur (la) scène; **s. door** entrée *f* des artistes; **s. fright** le trac; – *vt (play)* Th monter; Fig organiser, effectuer; **it was staged** *(not real)* c'était un coup monté. ◆**s.-hand** *n* machiniste *m*. ◆**s.-manager** *n* régisseur *m*.

stage[2] [steɪdʒ] *n (phase)* stade *m*, étape *f*; *(of journey)* étape *f*; *(of track, road)* section *f*; **in (easy) stages** par étapes; **at an early s.** au début.

stagecoach ['steɪdʒkəʊtʃ] *n* Hist diligence *f*.

stagger ['stægər] **1** *vi (reel)* chanceler. **2** *vt (holidays etc)* étaler, échelonner. **3** *vt* **to s. s.o.** *(shock, amaze)* stupéfier qn. ◆**—ing** *a* stupéfiant.

stagnant ['stægnənt] *a* stagnant. ◆**stag'nate** *vi* stagner. ◆**stag'nation** *n* stagnation *f*.

staid [steɪd] *a* posé, sérieux.

stain [steɪn] **1** *vt (mark, dirty)* tacher (**with**

de); – *n* tache *f*. **2** *vt* (*colour*) teinter (*du bois*); **stained glass window** vitrail *m*; – *n* (*colouring for wood*) teinture *f*. ◆**—less** *a* (*steel*) inoxydable; **s.-steel knife**/*etc* couteau *m*/*etc* inoxydable.

stair [steər] *n* **a s.** (*step*) une marche; **the stairs** (*staircase*) l'escalier *m*; – *a* (*carpet etc*) d'escalier. ◆**staircase** *n*, ◆**stairway** *n* escalier *m*.

stake [steɪk] **1** *n* (*post*) pieu *m*; (*for plant*) tuteur *m*; *Hist* bûcher *m*; – *vt* **to s.** (**out**) (*land*) jalonner, délimiter; **to s. one's claim** to revendiquer. **2** *n* (*betting*) enjeu *m*; (*investment*) *Fin* investissement *m*, (*interest*) *Fin* intérêts *mpl*; **at s.** en jeu; – *vt* (*bet*) jouer (*on* sur).

stale [steɪl] *a* (-**er, -est**) (*food*) pas frais; (*bread*) rassis; (*beer*) éventé; (*air*) vicié; (*smell*) de renfermé; (*news*) *Fig* vieux; (*joke*) usé, vieux; (*artist*) manquant d'invention. ◆**—ness** *n* (*of food*) manque *m* de fraîcheur.

stalemate ['steɪlmeɪt] *n* *Chess* pat *m*; *Fig* impasse *f*.

stalk [stɔːk] **1** *n* (*of plant*) tige *f*, queue *f*; (*of fruit*) queue *f*. **2** *vt* (*animal, criminal*) traquer. **3** *vi* **to s. out** (*walk*) partir avec raideur *or* en marchant à grands pas.

stall [stɔːl] **1** *n* (*in market*) étal *m*, éventaire *m*; (*for newspapers, flowers*) kiosque *m*; (*in stable*) stalle *f*; **the stalls** *Cin* l'orchestre *m*. **2** *vti* *Aut* caler. **3** *vi* **to s. (for time)** chercher à gagner du temps.

stallion ['stæljən] *n* (*horse*) étalon *m*.

stalwart ['stɔːlwət] *a* (*supporter*) brave, fidèle; – *n* (*follower*) fidèle *mf*.

stamina ['stæmɪnə] *n* vigueur *f*, résistance *f*.

stammer ['stæmər] *vti* bégayer; – *n* bégaiement *m*; **to have a s.** être bègue.

stamp [stæmp] **1** *n* (*for postage, implement*) timbre *m*; (*mark*) cachet *m*, timbre *m*; **the s. of** *Fig* la marque de; **men of your s.** les hommes de votre trempe; **s. collecting** philatélie *f*; – *vt* (*mark*) tamponner, timbrer; (*letter*) timbrer; (*metal*) estamper; **to s. sth on sth** (*affix*) apposer qch sur qch; **to s. out** (*rebellion, evil*) écraser; (*disease*) supprimer; **stamped addressed envelope** enveloppe *f* timbrée à votre adresse. **2** *vti* **to s.** (**one's feet**) taper *or* frapper des pieds; **stamping ground** *Fam* lieu *m* favori.

stampede [stæm'piːd] *n* fuite *f* précipitée; (*rush*) ruée *f*; – *vi* fuir en désordre; (*rush*) se ruer.

stance [stɑːns] *n* position *f*.

stand [stænd] *n* (*position*) position *f*; (*support*) support *m*; (*at exhibition*) stand

m; (*for spectators*) *Sp* tribune *f*; (*witness*) s. *Jur Am* barre *f*; **to make a s., take one's s.** prendre position (*against* contre); **news**/**flower s.** (*in street*) kiosque *m* à journaux/à fleurs; **hat s.** porte-chapeaux *m inv*; **music s.** pupitre *m* à musique; – *vt* (*pt & pp* **stood**) (*pain, journey, person etc*) supporter; **to s. (up)** (*put straight*) mettre (debout); **to s. s.o. sth** (*pay for*) payer qch à qn; **to s. a chance** avoir une chance; **to s. s.o. up** *Fam* poser un lapin à qn; – *vi* être *or* se tenir (debout); (*rise*) se lever; (*remain*) rester (debout); (*be situated*) se trouver; (*be*) être; (*of object, argument*) reposer (*on* sur); **to leave to s.** (*liquid*) laisser reposer; **to s. to lose** risquer de perdre; **to s. around** (*in street etc*) traîner; **to s. aside** s'écarter; **to s. back** reculer; **to s. by** (*do nothing*) rester là (sans rien faire); (*be ready*) être prêt (à partir *or* à intervenir); (*one's opinion etc*) s'en tenir à; (*friend etc*) rester fidèle à; **to s. down** (*withdraw*) se désister; **to s. for** (*represent*) représenter; *Pol* être candidat à; (*put up with*) supporter; **to s. in for** (*replace*) remplacer; **to s. out** (*be visible or conspicuous*) ressortir (*against* sur); **to s. over s.o.** (*watch closely*) surveiller qn; **to s. up** (*rise*) se lever; **to s. up for** (*defend*) défendre; **to s. up to** (*resist*) résister à. ◆**—ing** *a* debout *inv*; (*committee, offer, army*) permanent; **s. room** places *fpl* debout; **s. joke** plaisanterie *f* classique; – *n* (*reputation*) réputation *f*; (*social, professional*) rang *m*; (*financial*) situation *f*; **of six years' s.** (*duration*) qui dure depuis six ans; **of long s.** de longue date. ◆**standby** *n* (*pl* -**bys**) **on s.** prêt à partir *or* à intervenir; – *a* (*battery etc*) de réserve; (*ticket*) *Av* sans garantie. ◆**stand-in** *n* remplaçant, -ante *mf* (**for** de); *Th* doublure *f* (**for** de).

standard ['stændəd] **1** *n* (*norm*) norme *f*, critère *m*; (*level*) niveau *m*; (*of weight, gold*) étalon *m*; (*morals*) principes *mpl*; **s. of living** niveau *m* de vie; **to be** *or* **come up to s.** (*of person*) être à la hauteur; (*of work etc*) être au niveau; – *a* (*average*) ordinaire, courant; (*model, size*) *Com* standard *inv*; (*weight*) étalon *inv*; (*dictionary, book*) classique. **2** *n* (*flag*) étendard *m*. ◆**standardize** *vt* standardiser.

stand-offish [stænd'ɒfɪʃ] *a* (*person*) distant, froid.

standpoint ['stændpɔɪnt] *n* point *m* de vue.

standstill ['stændstɪl] *n* **to bring to a s.** immobiliser; **to come to a s.** s'immobiliser;

at a s. immobile; (industry, negotiations) paralysé.

stank [stæŋk] see stink.

stanza ['stænzə] n strophe f.

stapl/e ['steɪp(ə)l] 1 a (basic) de base; **s. food** or **diet** nourriture f de base. 2 n (for paper etc) agrafe f; – vt agrafer. ◆—er n (for paper etc) agrafeuse f.

star [stɑːr] n étoile f; (person) Cin vedette f; **shooting s.** étoile f filante; **s. part** rôle m principal; **the Stars and Stripes, the S.-Spangled Banner** Am la bannière étoilée; **two-s.** (petrol) de l'ordinaire m; **four-s.** (petrol) du super; – vi (-rr-) (of actor) être la vedette (**in** de); – vt (of film) avoir pour vedette. ◆**stardom** n célébrité f. ◆**starfish** n étoile f de mer. ◆**starlit** a (night) étoilé.

starboard ['stɑːbəd] n Nau Av tribord m.

starch [stɑːtʃ] n (for stiffening) amidon m; pl (foods) féculents mpl; – vt amidonner. ◆**starchy** a (-ier, -iest) (food) féculent; (formal) Fig guindé.

stare [steər] n regard m (fixe); – vi to s. at fixer (du regard); – vt to s. s.o. in the face dévisager qn.

stark [stɑːk] a (-er, -est) (place) désolé; (austere) austère; (fact, reality) brutal; **the s. truth** la vérité toute nue; – adv s. naked complètement nu. ◆**starkers** a Sl complètement nu, à poil.

starling ['stɑːlɪŋ] n étourneau m.

starry ['stɑːrɪ] a (-ier, -iest) (sky) étoilé. ◆**s.-'eyed** a (naive) ingénu, naïf.

start¹ [stɑːt] n commencement m, début m; (of race) départ m; (lead) Sp & Fig avance f (**on** sur); **to make a s.** commencer; **for a s.** pour commencer; **from the s.** dès le début; – vt commencer; (bottle) entamer; commencer; (fashion) lancer; **to s. a war** provoquer une guerre; **to s. a fire** (in grate) allumer un feu; (accidentally) provoquer un incendie; **to s. s.o. off** (on (career) lancer qn dans; **to s. (up)** (engine, vehicle) mettre en marche; **to s. doing** or **to do** commencer or se mettre à faire; – vi commencer (**with sth** par qch, **by doing** faire); **to s. on sth** commencer qch; **to s. (up)** commencer; (of vehicle) démarrer; **to s. off** or **out** (leave) partir (**for** pour); (in job) débuter; **to s. back** (return) repartir; **to s. with** (firstly) pour commencer. ◆—**ing** n (point, line) de départ; **s. post** Sp ligne f de départ; **s. from** à partir de. ◆—**er** n (runner) partant m; (official) Sp starter m; (device) Aut démarreur m; pl Culin

hors-d'œuvre m inv; **for starters** (first) pour commencer.

start² [stɑːt] vi (be startled, jump) sursauter; – n sursaut m; **to give s.o. a s.** faire sursauter qn.

startle ['stɑːt(ə)l] vt (make jump) faire sursauter; (alarm) Fig alarmer; (surprise) surprendre.

starve [stɑːv] vi (die) mourir de faim; (suffer) souffrir de la faim; **I'm starving** Fig je meurs de faim; – vt (kill) laisser mourir de faim; (make suffer) faire souffrir de la faim; (deprive) Fig priver (**of** de). ◆**star'vation** n faim f; – a (wage, ration) de famine; **on a s. diet** à la diète.

stash [stæʃ] vt **to s. away** (hide) cacher; (save up) mettre de côté.

state¹ [steɪt] 1 n (condition) état m; (pomp) apparat m; **not in a (fit) s.** to, **in no (fit) s.** to hors d'état de; **to lie in s.** (of body) être exposé. 2 n S. (nation etc) État m; **the States** Geog Fam les États-Unis mpl; – a (secret, document) d'État; (control, security) de l'État; (school, education) public; **s. visit** voyage m officiel; **S. Department** Pol Am Département m d'État. ◆**stateless** a apatride; **s. person** apatride mf. ◆**state-'owned** a étatisé. ◆**statesman** n (pl -men) homme m d'État. ◆**statesman-ship** n diplomatie f.

state² [steɪt] vt déclarer (**that** que); (opinion) formuler; (problem) exposer; (time, date) fixer. ◆**statement** n déclaration f; Jur déposition f; **bank s.,** s. **of account** Fin relevé m de compte.

stately ['steɪtlɪ] a (-ier, -iest) majestueux; **s. home** château m.

static ['stætɪk] a statique; – n (noise) Rad parasites mpl.

station ['steɪʃ(ə)n] n Rail gare f; (underground) station f; (polic) & Mil poste m; (social) rang m; (police) **s.** commissariat m or poste m (de police); **space/observation/radio/etc s.** station f spatiale/d'observation/de radio/etc; **bus** or **coach s.** gare f routière; **s. wagon** Aut Am break m; – vt (position) placer, poster. ◆**stationmaster** n Rail chef m de gare.

stationary ['steɪʃ(ə)rɪ] a (motionless) stationnaire; (vehicle) à l'arrêt.

stationer ['steɪʃ(ə)nər] n papetier, -ière mf; **s.'s (shop)** papeterie f. ◆**stationery** n (paper) papier m; (articles) papeterie f.

statistic [stə'tɪstɪk] n (fact) statistique f; pl (science) la statistique. ◆**statistical** a statistique.

statue ['stætʃuː] *n* statue *f.* ◆**statu'esque** *a* (*beauty etc*) sculptural.

stature ['stætʃər] *n* stature *f.*

status ['steɪtəs] *n* (*position*) situation *f*; *Jur* statut *m*; (*prestige*) standing *m*, prestige *m*; **s. symbol** marque *f* de standing; **s. quo** statu quo *m inv.*

statute ['stætʃuːt] *n* (*law*) loi *f*; *pl* (*of club, institution*) statuts *mpl.* ◆**statutory** *a* (*right etc*) statutaire; **s. holiday** fête *f* légale.

staunch [stɔːntʃ] *a* (-er, -est) loyal, fidèle. ◆**-ly** loyalement.

stave [steɪv] **1** *vt* **to s. off** (*danger, disaster*) conjurer; (*hunger*) tromper. **2** *n Mus* portée *f.*

stay [steɪ] **1** *n* (*visit*) séjour *m*; – *vi* (*remain*) rester; (*reside*) loger; (*stand*) séjourner; **to s. put** ne pas bouger; **to s. with** (*plan, idea*) ne pas lâcher; **to s. away** (*keep one's distance*) ne pas s'approcher (**from** de); **to s. away from** (*school, meeting etc*) ne pas aller à; **to s. in** (*at home*) rester à la maison; (*of nail, tooth etc*) tenir; **to s. out** (*outside*) rester dehors; (*not come home*) ne pas rentrer; **to s. out of sth** (*not interfere in*) ne pas se mêler de qch; (*avoid*) éviter qch; **to s. up** (*at night*) ne pas se coucher; (*of fence etc*) tenir; **to s. up late** se coucher tard; **staying power** endurance *f.* **2** *vt* (*hunger*) tromper. ◆**s.-at-home** *n* & *a Pej* casanier, -ière (*mf*).

St Bernard [sənt'bɜːnəd, *Am* seɪntbə'nɑːd] *n* (*dog*) saint-bernard *m.*

stead [sted] *n* **to stand s.o. in good s.** être bien utile à qn; **in s.o.'s s.** à la place de qn.

steadfast ['stedfɑːst] *a* (*intention etc*) ferme.

steady ['stedɪ] *a* (-ier, -iest) (*firm, stable*) stable; (*hand*) sûr, assuré; (*progress, speed, demand*) régulier, constant; (*nerves*) solide; (*staid*) sérieux; **a s. boyfriend** un petit ami; **s.** (**on one's feet**) solide sur ses jambes; – *adv* **to go s. with** *Fam* sortir avec; – *vt* (*chair etc*) maintenir (en place); (*hand*) assurer; (*nerves*) calmer; (*wedge, prop up*) caler; **to s. oneself** (*stop oneself falling*) reprendre son aplomb. ◆**steadily** *adv* (*to walk*) d'un pas assuré; (*regularly*) régulièrement; (*gradually*) progressivement; (*continuously*) sans arrêt. ◆**steadiness** *n* stabilité *f*; régularité *f.*

steak [steɪk] *n* steak *m*, bifteck *m.* ◆**steakhouse** *n* grill(-room) *m.*

steal[1] [stiːl] *vti* (*pt* **stole**, *pp* **stolen**) voler (**from s.o.** à qn).

steal[2] [stiːl] *vi* (*pt* **stole**, *pp* **stolen**) **to s. in/out** entrer/sortir furtivement. ◆**stealth**

[stelθ] *n* **by s.** furtivement. ◆**stealthy** *a* (-ier, -iest) furtif.

steam [stiːm] *n* vapeur *f*; (*on glass*) buée *f*; **to let off s.** (*unwind*) *Fam* se défouler, décompresser; **s. engine/iron** locomotive *f*/fer *m* à vapeur; – *vt Culin* cuire à la vapeur; **to get steamed up** (*of glass*) se couvrir de buée; *Fig Fam* s'énerver; – *vi* (*of kettle etc*) fumer; **to s. up** (*of glass*) se couvrir de buée. ◆**steamer** *n*, ◆**steamship** *n* (*bateau m à*) vapeur *m*; (*liner*) paquebot *m.* ◆**steamroller** *n* rouleau *m* compresseur. ◆**steamy** *a* (-ier, -iest) humide; (*window*) embué; (*love affair etc*) brûlant.

steel [stiːl] *n* acier *m*; **s. industry** sidérurgie *f.* **2** *vt* **to s. oneself** s'endurcir (**against** contre). ◆**steelworks** *n* aciérie *f.*

steep [stiːp] **1** *a* (-er, -est) (*stairs, slope etc*) raide; (*hill*) escarpé; (*price*) *Fig* excessif. **2** *vt* (*soak*) tremper (**in** dans); **steeped in** *Fig* imprégné de. ◆**-ly** *adv* (*to rise*) en pente raide, (*of prices*) *Fig* excessivement.

steeple ['stiːp(ə)l] *n* clocher *m.*

steeplechase ['stiːp(ə)ltʃeɪs] *n* (*race*) steeple(-chase) *m.*

steer [stɪər] *vt* (*vehicle, person*) diriger, piloter; (*ship*) diriger, gouverner; – *vi* (*of person*) *Nau* tenir le gouvernail, gouverner; **to s. towards** faire route vers; **to s. clear of** éviter. ◆**-ing** *n Aut* direction *f*; **s. wheel** volant *m.*

stem [stem] **1** *n* (*of plant etc*) tige *f*; (*of glass*) pied *m.* **2** *vt* (-mm-) **to s.** (**the flow of**) (*stop*) arrêter, contenir. **3** *vi* (-mm-) **to s. from** provenir de.

stench [stentʃ] *n* puanteur *f.*

stencil ['stens(ə)l] *n* (*metal, plastic*) pochoir *m*; (*paper, for typing*) stencil *m*; – *vt* (-ll-, *Am* -l-) (*notes etc*) polycopier.

stenographer [stə'nɒɡrəfər] *n Am* sténodactylo *f.*

step [step] *n* (*movement, sound*) pas *m*; (*stair*) marche *f*; (*on train, bus*) marchepied *m*; (*doorstep*) pas *m* de la porte; (*action*) *Fig* mesure *f*; (*flight of steps*) (*indoors*) escalier *m*; (*outdoors*) perron *m*; (*pair of*) **steps** (*ladder*) escabeau *m*; **s. by s.** pas à pas; **to keep in s.** marcher au pas; **in s. with** *Fig* en accord avec; – *vi* (-pp-) (*walk*) marcher (**on** sur); **s. this way!** (*venez*) par ici!; **to s. aside** s'écarter; **to s. back** reculer; **to s. down** descendre (**from** de); (*withdraw*) *Fig* se retirer; **to s. forward** faire un pas en avant; **to s. in** entrer; (*intervene*) *Fig* intervenir; **to s. into** (*car etc*) monter dans; **to s. off** (*chair etc*) descendre de; **to s. out of** (*car etc*) descendre de; **to s. over** (*obstacle*) enjamber; – *vt* **to s. up** (*increase*) augmenter, intensifier; (*speed up*) activer. ◆**step-ladder** *n* escabeau *m*. ◆**stepping-stone** *n Fig* tremplin *m* (**to** pour arriver à).

stepbrother ['stepbrʌðər] *n* demi-frère *m*. ◆**stepdaughter** *n* belle-fille *f*. ◆**step-father** *n* beau-père *m*. ◆**stepmother** *n* belle-mère *f*. ◆**stepsister** *n* demi-sœur *f*. ◆**stepson** *n* beau-fils *m*.

stereo ['steriəʊ] *n* (*pl* -os) (*sound*) stéréo(phonie) *f*; (*record player*) chaîne *f* (stéréo *inv*); – *a* (*record etc*) stéréo *inv*; (*broadcast*) en stéréo. ◆**stereo'phonic** *a* stéréophonique.

stereotype ['steriətaip] *n* stéréotype *m*. ◆**stereotyped** *a* stéréotypé.

sterile ['sterail, *Am* 'sterəl] *a* stérile. ◆**ste-'rility** *n* stérilité *f*. ◆**sterili'zation** *n* stérilisation *f*. ◆**sterilize** *vt* stériliser.

sterling ['st3:liŋ] *n* (*currency*) livre(s) *f(pl)* sterling *inv*; – *a* (*pound*) sterling *inv*; (*silver*) fin; (*quality, person*) *Fig* sûr.

stern [st3:n] **1** *a* (-**er**, -**est**) sévère. **2** *n* (*of ship*) arrière *m*.

stethoscope ['steθəskəʊp] *n* stéthoscope *m*.

stetson ['stetsən] *n Am* chapeau *m* à larges bords.

stevedore ['sti:vədɔ:r] *n* docker *m*.

stew [stju:] *n* ragoût *m*; **in a s.** *Fig* dans le pétrin; **s. pan, s. pot** cocotte *f*; – *vt* (*meat*) faire *ou* cuire en ragoût; (*fruit*) faire cuire; **stewed fruit** compote *f*; – *vi* cuire. ◆**-ing** *a* (*pears etc*) à cuire.

steward ['stju:əd] *n Av Nau* steward *m*; (*in college, club etc*) intendant *m* (*préposé au ravitaillement*); **shop s.** délégué, -ée *mf* syndical(e). ◆**stewar'dess** *n Av* hôtesse *f*.

stick[1] [stik] *n* (*piece of wood, chalk, dynamite*) bâton *m*; (*branch*) branche *f*; (*for walking*) canne *f*; **the sticks** *Pej Fam* la campagne, la cambrousse; **to give s.o. some s.** (*scold*) *Fam* engueuler qn.

stick[2] [stik] *vt* (*pt & pp* **stuck**) (*glue*) coller; (*put*) *Fam* mettre, planter; (*tolerate*) *Fam* supporter; **to s. sth into** (*thrust*) planter *ou* enfoncer qch dans; **to s. down** (*envelope*) coller; (*put down*) *Fam* poser; **to s. on** (*stamp*) coller; (*hat etc*) mettre, planter; **to s. out** (*tongue*) tirer; (*head*) *Fam* sortir; **to s. it out** (*resist*) *Fam* tenir le coup; **to s. up** (*notice*) afficher; (*hand*) lever; – *vi* coller, adhérer (**to** à); (*of food in pan*) attacher; (*remain*) *Fam* rester; (*of drawer etc*) être bloqué *ou* coincé; **to s. by s.o.** rester fidèle à qn; **to s. to the facts** (*confine oneself to*) s'en tenir aux faits; **to s. around** *Fam*

rester dans les parages; **to s. out** (*of petticoat etc*) dépasser; (*of tooth*) avancer; **to s. up for** (*defend*) défendre; **sticking plaster** sparadrap *m*. ◆**sticker** *n* (*label*) autocollant *m*. ◆**stick-on** *a* (*label*) adhésif. ◆**stick-up** *n Fam* hold-up *m inv*.

stickler ['stiklər] *n* **a s. for** (*rules, discipline, details*) intransigeant sur.

sticky ['stiki] *a* (-**ier**, -**iest**) collant, poisseux; (*label*) adhésif; (*problem*) *Fig* difficile.

stiff [stif] *a* (-**er**, -**est**) raide; (*joint, leg etc*) ankylosé; (*brush, paste*) dur; (*person*) *Fig* froid, guindé; (*difficult*) difficile; (*price*) élevé; (*whisky*) bien tassé; **to have a s. neck** avoir le torticolis; **to feel s.** être courbaturé; **to be bored s.** *Fam* s'ennuyer à mourir; **frozen s.** *Fam* complètement gelé. ◆**stiffen** *vt* raidir; – *vi* se raidir. ◆**stiffly** *adv* (*coldly*) *Fig* froidement. ◆**stiffness** *n* raideur *f*; (*hardness*) dureté *f*.

stifle ['staif(ə)l] *vt* (*feeling, person etc*) étouffer; – *vi* **it's stifling** on étouffe.

stigma ['stigmə] *n* (*moral stain*) flétrissure *f*. ◆**stigmatize** *vt* (*denounce*) stigmatiser.

stile [stail] *n* (*between fields etc*) échalier *m*.

stiletto [sti'letəʊ] *a* **s. heel** talon *m* aiguille.

still[1] [stil] *adv* encore, toujours; (*even*) encore; (*nevertheless*) tout de même; **better s., s.** better encore mieux.

still[2] [stil] *a* (-**er**, -**est**) (*motionless*) immobile; (*calm*) calme, tranquille; (*drink*) non gazeux; **to keep** *ou* **lie** *ou* **stand s.** rester tranquille; **s. life** nature *f* morte; – *n* (*of night*) silence *m*; *Cin* photo *f*. ◆**stillborn** *a* mort-né. ◆**stillness** *n* immobilité *f*; calme *m*.

still[3] [stil] *n* (*for making alcohol*) alambic *m*.

stilt [stilt] *n* (*pole*) échasse *f*.

stilted ['stiltid] *a* guindé.

stimulate ['stimjuleit] *vt* stimuler. ◆**stimulant** *n Med* stimulant *m*. ◆**stimu'lation** *n* stimulation *f*. ◆**stimulus**, *pl* -**li** [-lai] *n* (*encouragement*) stimulant *m*; (*physiological*) stimulus *m*.

sting [stiŋ] *vt* (*pt & pp* **stung**) (*of insect, ointment, wind etc*) piquer; (*of remark*) *Fig* blesser; – *vi* piquer; – *n* piqûre *f*; (*insect's organ*) dard *m*. ◆**-ing** *a* (*pain, remark*) cuisant.

sting/y ['stindʒi] *a* (-**ier**, -**iest**) avare, mesquin; **s. with** (*money, praise*) avare de; (*food, wine*) mesquin sur. ◆**-iness** *n* avarice *f*.

stink [stiŋk] *n* puanteur *f*; **to cause** *or* **make a s.** (*trouble*) *Fam* faire du foin; – *vi* (*pt* **stank** *or* **stunk**, *pp* **stunk**) puer; (*of book, film etc*)

Fam être infect; **to s. of smoke**/*etc* empester la fumée/*etc*; − *vt* **to s. out** (*room etc*) empester. ◆−**er** *n Fam* (*person*) sale type *m*; (*question, task etc*) vacherie *f*.

stint [stɪnt] **1** *n* (*share*) part *f* de travail; (*period*) période *f* de travail. **2** *vi* **to s. on** lésiner sur.

stipend ['staɪpend] *n Rel* traitement *n*.

stipulate ['stɪpjʊleɪt] *vt* stipuler (**that** que). ◆**stipu'lation** *n* stipulation *f*.

stir [stɜːr] *n* agitation *f*; **to give sth a s.** remuer qch; **to cause a s.** Fig faire du bruit; − *vt* (**-rr-**) (*coffee, leaves etc*) remuer; (*excite*) Fig exciter; (*incite*) inciter (**to do** à faire); **to s. oneself** (*make an effort*) se secouer; **to s. up** (*trouble*) provoquer; (*memory*) réveiller; − *vi* remuer, bouger. ◆**stirring** *a* (*speech etc*) excitant, émouvant.

stirrup ['stɪrəp] *n* étrier *m*.

stitch [stɪtʃ] *n* point *m*; (*in knitting*) maille *f*; *Med* point *m* de suture; **a s.** (**in one's side**) (*pain*) un point de côté; **to be in stitches** *Fam* se tordre (de rire); − *vt* **to s.** (**up**) (*sew up*) coudre; *Med* suturer.

stoat [stəʊt] *n* (*animal*) hermine *f*.

stock [stɒk] *n* (*supply*) provision *f*, stock *m*, réserve *f*; (*of knowledge, jokes*) fonds *m*, mine *f*; *Fin* valeurs *fpl*, titres *mpl*; (*descent, family*) souche *f*; (*soup*) bouillon *m*; (*cattle*) bétail *m*; **the stocks** *Hist* le pilori; **in s.** (*goods*) en magasin, disponible; **out of s.** (*goods*) épuisé, non disponible; **to take s.** *Fig* faire le point (**of** de); **s. reply/size** réponse *f*/taille *f* courante; **s. phrase** expression *f* toute faite; **the S. Exchange** *or* **Market** la Bourse; − *vt* (*sell*) vendre; (*keep in store*) stocker; **to s.** (**up**) (*shop, larder*) approvisionner; **well-stocked** bien approvisionné; − *vi* **to s. up** s'approvisionner (**with** de, en). ◆**stockbroker** *n* agent *m* de change. ◆**stockcar** *n* stock-car *m*. ◆**stockholder** *n Fin* actionnaire *mf*. ◆**stockist** *n* dépositaire *mf*, stockiste *m*. ◆**stockpile** *vt* stocker, amasser. ◆**stockroom** *n* réserve *f*, magasin *m*. ◆**stocktaking** *n Com* inventaire *m*.

stocking ['stɒkɪŋ] *n* (*garment*) bas *m*.

stocky ['stɒkɪ] *a* (**-ier, -iest**) trapu.

stodge [stɒdʒ] *n* (*food*) *Fam* étouffe-chrétien *m inv*. ◆**stodgy** *a* (**-ier, -iest**) *Fam* lourd, indigeste; (*person, style*) compassé.

stoic ['stəʊɪk] *a & n* stoïque (*mf*). ◆**stoical** *a* stoïque. ◆**stoicism** *n* stoïcisme *m*.

stoke [stəʊk] *vt* (*fire*) entretenir; (*engine*) chauffer. ◆−**er** *n Rail* chauffeur *m*.

stole[1] [stəʊl] *n* (*shawl*) étole *f*.

stole[2], **stolen** [stəʊl, 'stəʊl(ə)n] *see* steal[1,2].

stolid ['stɒlɪd] *a* (*manner, person*) impassible.

stomach ['stʌmək] **1** *n Anat* estomac *m*; (*abdomen*) ventre *m*; − *vt* (*put up with*) *Fig* supporter. ◆**stomachache** *n* mal *m* de ventre; **to have a s.** avoir mal au ventre.

stone [stəʊn] *n* pierre *f*; (*pebble*) caillou *m*; (*in fruit*) noyau *m*; (*in kidney*) *Med* calcul *m*; (*weight*) = 6,348 kg; **a stone's throw away** *Fig* à deux pas d'ici; − *vt* lancer des pierres sur, lapider; (*fruit*) dénoyauter. ◆**stonemason** *n* tailleur *m* de pierre, maçon *m*. ◆**stony** *a* **1** (**-ier, -iest**) (*path etc*) pierreux, caillouteux. **2 s. broke** (*penniless*) *Sl* fauché.

stone- [stəʊn] *pref* complètement. ◆**s.-'broke** *a Am Sl* fauché. ◆**s.-'cold** *a* complètement froid. ◆**s.-'dead** *a* raide mort. ◆**s.-'deaf** *a* sourd comme un pot.

stoned [stəʊnd] *a* (*high on drugs*) *Fam* camé.

stooge [stuːdʒ] *n* (*actor*) comparse *mf*; (*flunkey*) *Pej* larbin *m*; (*dupe*) *Pej* pigeon *m*.

stood [stʊd] *see* stand.

stool [stuːl] *n* tabouret *m*.

stoop [stuːp] **1** *n* **to have a s.** être voûté; − *vi* se baisser; **to s. to doing**/**to sth** *Fig* s'abaisser à faire/à qch. **2** *n* (*in front of house*) *Am* perron *m*.

stop [stɒp] *n* (*place, halt*) arrêt *m*, halte *f*; *Av Nau* escale *f*; *Gram* point *m*; **bus s.** arrêt *m* d'autobus; **to put a s. to** mettre fin à; **to bring to a s.** arrêter; **to come to a s.** s'arrêter; **without a s.** sans arrêt; **s. light** (*on vehicle*) stop *m*; **s. sign** (*road sign*) stop *m*; − *vt* (**-pp-**) arrêter; (*end*) mettre fin à; (*prevent*) empêcher (**from doing** de faire); (*cheque*) faire opposition à; **to s. up** (*sink, pipe, leak etc*) boucher; − *vi* s'arrêter; (*of pain, conversation etc*) cesser; (*stay*) rester; **to s. eating**/*etc* s'arrêter de manger/*etc*; **to s. snowing**/*etc* cesser de neiger/*etc*; **to s. by** passer (**s.o.'s** chez qn); **to s. off** *or* **over** (*on journey*) s'arrêter. ◆**stoppage** *n* arrêt *m*; (*in pay*) retenue *f*; (*in work*) arrêt *m* de travail; (*strike*) débrayage *m*; (*blockage*) obstruction *f*. ◆**stopper** *n* bouchon *m*.

stopcock ['stɒpkɒk] *n* robinet *m* d'arrêt. ◆**stopgap** *n* bouche-trou *m*; − *a* intérimaire. ◆**stopoff** *n*, ◆**stopover** *n* halte *f*. ◆**stopwatch** *n* chronomètre *m*.

store [stɔːr] n (supply) provision f; (of information, jokes etc) Fig fonds m; (depot, warehouse) entrepôt m; (shop) grand magasin m, Am magasin m; (computer memory) mémoire f; **to have sth in s. for s.o.** (surprise) réserver qch à qn; **to keep in s.** garder en réserve; **to set great s. by** attacher une grande importance à; – vt la s. **(up)** (in warehouse etc) emmagasiner; (for future use) mettre en réserve; **to s. (away)** (furniture) entreposer. ◆**storage** n emmagasinage m; (for future use) mise f en réserve; **s. space** or **room** espace m de rangement. ◆**storekeeper** n magasinier m; (shopkeeper) Am commerçant, -ante mf. ◆**storeroom** n réserve f.

storey ['stɔːri] n étage m.

stork [stɔːk] n cigogne f.

storm [stɔːm] 1 n (weather) & Fig tempête f; (thunderstorm) orage m; **s. cloud** nuage m orageux. 2 vt (attack) Mil prendre d'assaut. 3 vi **to s. out** (angrily) sortir comme une furie. ◆**stormy** a (-ier, -iest) (weather, meeting etc) orageux; (wind) d'orage.

story ['stɔːri] n 1 histoire f; (newspaper article) article m; **s. (line)** Cin Th intrigue f; **short s.** Liter nouvelle f, conte m; **fairy s.** conte m de fées. 2 (storey) Am étage m. ◆**storyteller** n conteur, -euse mf; (liar) Fam menteur, -euse mf.

stout [staʊt] a (-er, -est) (person) gros, corpulent; (stick, volume) gros, épais; (shoes) solide. 2 n (beer) bière f brune. ◆**-ness** n corpulence f.

stove [staʊv] n (for cooking) cuisinière f; (solid fuel) fourneau m; (small) réchaud m; (for heating) poêle m.

stow [staʊ] 1 vt (cargo) arrimer; **to s. away** (put away) ranger. 2 vi **to s. away** Nau voyager clandestinement. ◆**stowaway** n Nau passager, -ère mf clandestin(e).

straddle ['stræd(ə)l] vt (chair, fence) se mettre or être à califourchon sur; (step over, span) enjamber; (line in road) Aut chevaucher.

straggl/e ['stræg(ə)l] vi (stretch) s'étendre (en désordre); (trail) traîner (en désordre); **to s. in** entrer par petits groupes. ◆**-er** n traînard, -arde mf.

straight [streit] a (-er, -est) droit; (hair) raide; (route) direct; (tidy) en ordre; (frank) franc; (refusal) net; (actor, role) sérieux; **I want to get this s.** comprenons-nous bien; **to keep a s. face** garder son sérieux; **to put** or **set s.** (tidy) ranger; – n **the s.** Sp la ligne droite; – adv (to walk etc) droit; (directly) tout droit, directe-

ment; (to drink gin, whisky etc) sec; **s. away** (at once) tout de suite; **s. out, s. off** sans hésiter; **s. opposite** juste en face; **s. ahead** or **on** (to walk etc) tout droit; **s. ahead** (to look) droit devant soi. ◆**straigh'tway** adv tout de suite. ◆**straighten** vt **to s. (up)** redresser; (tie, room) arranger; **to s. things out** Fig arranger les choses. ◆**straight-'forward** a (frank) franc; (easy) simple.

strain [strein] 1 n (tiredness) fatigue f; (stress) Med tension f nerveuse; (effort) effort m; – vt (rope, wire) tendre excessivement; (muscle) Med froisser; (ankle, wrist) fouler; (eyes) fatiguer; (voice) forcer; Fig mettre à l'épreuve; **to s. one's ears** (to hear) tendre l'oreille; **to s. oneself** (hurt oneself) se faire mal; (tire oneself) se fatiguer; – vi fournir un effort (**to do** pour faire). 2 vt (soup etc) passer; (vegetables) égoutter. 3 n (breed) lignée f; (of virus) souche f; (streak) tendance f. 4 npl Mus accents mpl (of de). ◆**-ed** a (relations) tendu; (laugh) forcé; (ankle, wrist) foulé. ◆**-er** n passoire f.

strait [streit] 1 n & npl Geog détroit m. 2 npl **in financial straits** dans l'embarras. ◆**straitjacket** n camisole f de force. ◆**strait'laced** a collet monté inv.

strand [strænd] n (of wool etc) brin m; (of hair) mèche f; (of story) Fig fil m.

stranded ['strændɪd] a (person, vehicle) en rade.

strange [streindʒ] a (-er, -est) (odd) étrange, bizarre; (unknown) inconnu; (new) nouveau; **to feel s.** (in a new place) se sentir dépaysé. ◆**strangely** adv étrangement; **s. (enough) she ...** chose étrange, elle .... ◆**strangeness** n étrangeté f. ◆**stranger** n (unknown) inconnu, -ue mf; (outsider) étranger, -ère mf; **he's a s. here** il n'est pas d'ici; **she's a s. to me** elle m'est inconnue.

strangle ['stræŋg(ə)l] vt étrangler. ◆**strangler** n étrangleur, -euse mf. ◆**stranglehold** n emprise f totale (**on** sur).

strap [stræp] n courroie f, sangle f; (on dress) bretelle f; (on watch) bracelet m; (on sandal) lanière f; – vt (-pp-) **to s. (down** or **in)** attacher (avec une courroie).

strapping ['stræpɪŋ] a (well-built) robuste.

stratagem ['strætədʒəm] n stratagème m.

strategy ['strætədʒɪ] n stratégie f. ◆**stra-'tegic** a stratégique.

stratum, pl **-ta** ['strɑːtəm, -tə] n couche f.

straw [strɔː] n paille f; **a (drinking) s.** une paille; **that's the last s.!** c'est le comble!

strawberry ['strɔːbərɪ] n fraise f; – a

(*flavour, ice cream*) à la fraise; (*jam*) de fraises; (*tart*) aux fraises.

stray [streɪ] *a* (*lost*) perdu; **a s. car**/*etc* une voiture/*etc* isolée; **a few s. cars**/*etc* quelques rares voitures/*etc*; – *n* animal *m* perdu; – *vi* s'égarer; **to s. from** (*subject, path*) s'écarter de.

streak [striːk] *n* (*line*) raie *f*; (*of light*) filet *m*; (*of colour*) strie *f*; (*trace*) Fig trace *f*; (*tendency*) tendance *f*; **grey**/*etc* **streaks** (*in hair*) mèches grises/*etc*; **a mad s.** une tendance à la folie; **my literary s.** ma fibre littéraire. ◆**streaked** *a* (*marked*) strié, zébré; (*stained*) taché (**with** de). ◆**streaky** *a* (**-ier, -iest**) strié; (*bacon*) pas trop maigre.

stream [striːm] *n* (*brook*) ruisseau *m*; (*current*) courant *m*; (*flow*) & Fig flot *m*; Sch classe *f* (*de niveau*); – *vi* ruisseler (**with** de); **to s. in** (*of sunlight, people etc*) Fig entrer à flots.

streamer [striːmər] *n* (*paper*) serpentin *m*; (*banner*) banderole *f*.

streamlin/e [striːmlaɪn] *vt* (*work, method etc*) rationaliser. ◆**—ed** *a* (*shape*) aérodynamique.

street [striːt] *n* rue *f*; **s. door** porte *f* d'entrée; **s. lamp, s. light** réverbère *m*; **s. map, s. plan** plan *m* des rues; **up my s.** Fig Fam dans mes cordes; **streets ahead** Fam très en avance (**of** sur). ◆**streetcar** *n* (*tram*) Am tramway *m*.

strength [streŋθ] *n* force *f*; (*health, energy*) forces *fpl*; (*of wood, fabric*) solidité *f*; **on the s. of** Fig en vertu de; **in full s.** au (grand) complet. ◆**strengthen** *vt* (*building, position etc*) renforcer, consolider; (*body, soul, limb*) fortifier.

strenuous [strenjʊəs] *a* (*effort etc*) vigoureux, énergique; (*work*) ardu; (*active*) actif; (*tiring*) fatigant. ◆**—ly** *adv* énergiquement.

strep [strep] *a* **s. throat** Med Am angine *f*.

stress [stres] *n* (*pressure*) pression *f*; Med Psy tension *f* (*nerveuse*), stress *m*; (*emphasis*) & Gram accent *m*; Tech tension *f*; **under s.** Med Psy sous pression, stressé; – *vt* insister sur; (*word*) accentuer; **to s. that** souligner que. ◆**stressful** *a* stressant.

stretch [stretʃ] *vt* (*rope, neck*) tendre; (*shoe, rubber*) étirer; (*meaning*) Fig forcer; **to s.** (**out**) (*arm, leg*) étendre, allonger; **to s.** (**out**) **one's arm** (*reach out*) tendre le bras (**to take** pour prendre); **to s. one's legs** Fig se dégourdir les jambes; **to s. s.o.** Fig exiger un effort de qn; **to be** (**fully**) **stretched** (*of budget etc*) être tiré au maximum; **to s. out** (*visit*) prolonger; – *vi* (*of person, elastic*)

s'étirer; (*of influence etc*) s'étendre; **to s.** (**out**) (*of rope, plain*) s'étendre; – *n* (*area, duration*) étendue *f*; (*of road*) tronçon *m*, partie *f*; (*route, trip*) trajet *m*; **at a s.** d'une (seule) traite; **ten**/*etc* **hours at a s.** dix/*etc* heures d'affilée; **s. socks**/*etc* chaussettes *fpl*/*etc* extensibles; **s. nylon** nylon *m* stretch *inv*. ◆**stretchmarks** *npl* (*on body*) vergetures *fpl*.

stretcher [stretʃər] *n* brancard *m*.

strew [struː] *vt* (*pt* strewed, *pp* strewed *or* strewn) (*scatter*) répandre; **strewn with** (*covered*) jonché de.

stricken [strɪkən] *a* **s. with** (*illness*) atteint de; (*panic*) frappé de.

strict [strɪkt] *a* (**-er, -est**) (*severe, absolute*) strict. ◆**—ly** *adv* strictement; **s. forbidden** formellement interdit. ◆**—ness** *n* sévérité *f*.

stride [straɪd] *n* (grand) pas *m*, enjambée *f*; **to make great strides** Fig faire de grands progrès; – *vi* (*pt* strode) **to s. across** *or* **over** enjamber; **to s. up and down a room** arpenter une pièce.

strident [straɪdənt] *a* strident.

strife [straɪf] *n inv* conflit(s) *m(pl)*.

strik/e [straɪk] **1** *n* (*attack*) Mil raid *m* (aérien); (*of oil etc*) découverte *f*; – *vt* (*pt & pp* struck) (*hit, impress*) frapper; (*collide with*) heurter; (*beat*) battre; (*a blow*) donner; (*a match*) frotter; (*gold, problem*) trouver; (*coin*) frapper; (*of clock*) sonner; **to s. a bargain** conclure un accord; **to s. a balance** trouver l'équilibre; **to s.** (**off**) (*from list*) rayer (**from** de); **to be struck off** (*of doctor*) être radié; **it strikes me as**/*that* il me semble être/que; **how did it s. you?** quelle impression ça t'a fait?; **to s. down** (*of illness etc*) terrasser (*qn*); **to s. up a friendship** lier amitié (**with** avec); – *vi* **to s.** (**at**) (*attack*) attaquer; **to s. back** (*retaliate*) riposter; **to s. out** donner des coups. **2** *n* (*of workers*) grève *f*; **to go** (**out**) **on s.** se mettre en grève (**for** pour obtenir, **against** pour protester contre); – *vi* (*pt & pp* struck) (*of workers*) faire grève. ◆**—ing** *a* (*impressive*) frappant. ◆**—ingly** *adv* (*beautiful etc*) extraordinairement. ◆**—er** *n* gréviste *mf*; Fb buteur *m*.

string [strɪŋ] *n* ficelle *f*; (*of anorak, apron*) cordon *m*; (*of violin, racket etc*) corde *f*; (*of pearls, beads*) rang *m*; (*of onions, insults*) chapelet *m*; (*of people, vehicles*) file *f*; (*of questions etc*) série *f*; **to pull strings** Fig faire jouer ses relations; – *a* (*instrument, quartet*) Mus à cordes; **s. bean** haricot *m* vert; – *vt* (*pt & pp* strung) (*beads*) enfiler; **to s. up**

(hang up) suspendre; – vi to s. along (with) Fam suivre. ◆—ed a (instrument) Mus à cordes. ◆stringy a (-ier, -iest) (meat etc) filandreux.

stringent ['strɪndʒ(ə)nt] a rigoureux. ◆stringency n rigueur f.

strip [strɪp] 1 n (piece) bande f; (of water) bras m; (thin) s. (of metal etc) lamelle f; landing. piste f or terrain m d'atterrissage; s. cartoon, comic s. bande f dessinée. 2 vt (-pp-) (undress) déshabiller; (bed) défaire; (deprive) dépouiller (of de); to s. (down) (machine) démonter; to s. off (remove) enlever; – vi to s. (off) (undress) se déshabiller. ◆stripper n (woman) strip-teaseuse f; (paint) décapant m. ◆strip-'tease n strip-tease m.

stripe [straɪp] n rayure f; Mil galon m. ◆striped a rayé (with de). ◆stripy a rayé.

strive [straɪv] vi (pt strove, pp striven) s'efforcer (to do de faire, for d'obtenir).

strode [strəʊd] see stride.

stroke [strəʊk] n (movement) coup m; (of pen, genius) trait m; (of brush) touche f; (on clock) coup m; (caress) caresse f; Med coup m de sang; (swimming style) nage f; at a s. d'un coup; a s. of luck un coup de chance; you haven't done a s. (of work) tu n'as rien fait; heat s. (sunstroke) insolation f; – vt (beard, cat etc) caresser.

stroll [strəʊl] n promenade f; – vi se promener, flâner; to s. in/etc entrer/etc sans se presser. ◆—ing a (musician etc) ambulant.

stroller ['strəʊlər] n (pushchair) Am poussette f.

strong [strɒŋ] a (-er, -est) fort; (shoes, nerves) solide; (interest) vif; (measures) énergique; (supporter) ardent; sixty s. au nombre de soixante; – adv to be going s. aller toujours bien. ◆—ly adv (to protest, defend) énergiquement; (to desire, advise, remind) fortement; (to feel) profondément; s. built solide. ◆strongarm a brutal. ◆strongbox n coffre-fort m. ◆stronghold n bastion m. ◆strong-'willed a résolu.

strove [strəʊv] see strive.

struck [strʌk] see strike 1,2.

structure ['strʌktʃər] n structure f; (of building) armature f; (building itself) construction f. ◆structural a structural; (fault) Archit de construction.

struggle ['strʌg(ə)l] n (fight) lutte f (to do pour faire); (effort) effort m; to put up a s.

résister; to have a s. doing or to do avoir du mal à faire; – vi (fight) lutter, se battre (with avec); (resist) résister; (thrash about wildly) se débattre; to s. to do (try hard) s'efforcer de faire; to s. out of sortir péniblement de; to s. along or on se débrouiller; a struggling lawyer/etc un avocat/etc qui a du mal à débuter.

strum [strʌm] vt (-mm-) (guitar etc) gratter de.

strung [strʌŋ] see string; – a s. out (things, people) espacés; (washing) étendu.

strut [strʌt] 1 vi (-tt-) to s. (about or around) se pavaner. 2 n (support) Tech étai m.

stub [stʌb] 1 n (of pencil, cigarette etc) bout m; (counterfoil of cheque etc) talon m; – vt (-bb-) to s. out (cigarette) écraser. 2 vt (-bb-) to s. one's toe se cogner le doigt de pied (on, against contre).

stubble ['stʌb(ə)l] n barbe f de plusieurs jours.

stubborn ['stʌbən] a (person) entêté, opiniâtre; (cough, efforts, manner etc) opiniâtre. ◆—ly adv opiniâtrement. ◆—ness n entêtement m, opiniâtreté f.

stubby ['stʌbɪ] a (-ier, -iest) (finger etc) gros et court, épais; (person) trapu.

stuck [stʌk] see stick²; – a (caught, jammed) coincé; s. in bed/indoors cloué au lit/chez soi; to be s. (unable to do sth) ne pas savoir quoi faire; I'm s. (for an answer) je ne sais pas répondre; to be s. with sth/s.o. se farcir qch/qn. ◆s.-'up a Fam prétentieux, snob inv.

stud [stʌd] n 1 (nail) clou m (à grosse tête); (for collar) bouton m de col. 2 (farm) haras m; (horses) écurie f; (stallion) étalon m; (virile man) Sl mâle m. ◆studded a (boots, tyres) clouté; s. with (covered) Fig constellé de, parsemé de.

student ['stjuːdənt] n Univ étudiant, -ante mf; Sch Am élève mf; music/etc s. étudiant, -ante en musique/etc; – a (life, protest) étudiant; (restaurant, residence, grant) universitaire.

studio ['stjuːdɪəʊ] n (pl -os) (of painter etc) & Cin TV studio m; s. flat or Am apartment studio m.

studious ['stjuːdɪəs] a (person) studieux. ◆—ly adv (carefully) avec soin. ◆—ness n application f.

study ['stʌdɪ] n étude f; (office) bureau m; – vt (learn, observe) étudier; – vi étudier; to s. to be a doctor/etc faire des études pour devenir médecin/etc; to s. for (an exam) préparer. ◆studied a (deliberate) étudié.

stuff [stʌf] 1 n (thing) truc m, chose f;

(*substance*) substance *f*; (*things*) trucs *mpl*, choses *fpl*; (*possessions*) affaires *fpl*; (*nonsense*) sottises *fpl*; **this s.'s good, it's good s.** c'est bon (ça). **2** *vt* (*chair, cushion etc*) rembourrer (**with** avec); (*animal*) empailler; (*cram, fill*) bourrer (**with** de); (*put, thrust*) fourrer (**into** dans); (*chicken etc*) Culin farcir; **to s. (up)** (*hole etc*) colmater; **my nose is stuffed (up)** j'ai le nez bouché. ◆**—ing** *n* (*padding*) bourre *f*; Culin farce *f*.

stuffy ['stʌfɪ] *a* (**-ier, -iest**) (*room etc*) mal aéré; (*formal*) Fig compassé; (*old-fashioned*) vieux jeu *inv*; **it smells s.** ça sent le renfermé.

stumble ['stʌmb(ə)l] *vi* trébucher (**over** sur, **against** contre); **to s. across** *or* **on** (*find*) tomber sur; **stumbling block** pierre *f* d'achoppement.

stump [stʌmp] *n* (*of tree*) souche *f*; (*of limb*) moignon *m*; (*of pencil*) bout *m*; Cricket piquet *m*.

stumped ['stʌmpt] *a* **to be s. by sth** (*baffled*) ne pas savoir que penser de qch.

stun [stʌn] *vt* (**-nn-**) (*daze*) étourdir; (*animal*) assommer; (*amaze*) Fig stupéfier. ◆**stunned** *a* Fig stupéfait (**by** par). ◆**stunning** *a* (*blow*) étourdissant; (*news*) stupéfiant; (*terrific*) Fam sensationnel.

stung [stʌŋ] *see* **sting**.

stunk [stʌŋk] *see* **stink**.

stunt [stʌnt] **1** *n* (*feat*) tour *m* (de force); Cin cascade *f*; (*ruse, trick*) truc *m*; **s. man** Cin cascadeur *m*; **s. woman** Cin cascadeuse *f*. **2** *vt* (*growth*) retarder. ◆**—ed** *a* (*person*) rabougri.

stupefy ['stju:pɪfaɪ] *vt* (*of drink etc*) abrutir; (*amaze*) Fig stupéfier.

stupendous [stju:'pendəs] *a* prodigieux.

stupid ['stju:pɪd] *a* stupide, bête; **a s. thing** une sottise; **s. fool, s. idiot** idiot, -ote *mf*. ◆**stu'pidity** *n* stupidité *f*. ◆**stupidly** *adv* stupidement, bêtement.

stupor ['stju:pər] *n* (*daze*) stupeur *f*.

sturdy ['stɜ:dɪ] *a* (**-ier, -iest**) (*person, shoe etc*) robuste. ◆**sturdiness** *n* robustesse *f*.

sturgeon ['stɜ:dʒ(ə)n] *n* (*fish*) esturgeon *m*.

stutter ['stʌtər] *n* bégaiement *m*; **to have a s.** être bègue; — *vi* bégayer.

sty [staɪ] *n* (*pigsty*) porcherie *f*.

stye(e) [staɪ] *n* (*on eye*) orgelet *m*.

style [staɪl] *n* style *m*; (*fashion*) mode *f*; (*design of dress etc*) modèle *m*; (*of hair*) coiffure *f*; (*sort*) genre *m*; **to have s.** avoir de la classe; **in s.** (*in superior manner*) de la meilleure façon possible; (*to live, travel*) dans le luxe; — *vt* (*design*) créer; **he styles**

himself . . . *Pej* il se fait appeler . . . ; **to s. s.o.'s hair** coiffer qn. ◆**styling** *n* (*cutting of hair*) coupe *f*. ◆**stylish** *a* chic, élégant. ◆**stylishly** *adv* élégamment. ◆**stylist** *n* (*hair*) coiffeur, -euse *mf*. ◆**sty'listic** *a* de style, stylistique. ◆**stylized** *a* stylisé.

stylus ['staɪləs] *n* (*of record player*) pointe *f* de lecture.

suave [swɑːv] *a* (**-er, -est**) (*urbane*) courtois; *Pej* doucereux.

sub- [sʌb] *pref* sous-, sub-.

subconscious [sʌb'kɒnʃəs] *a* & *n* subconscient (*m*). ◆**—ly** *adv* inconsciemment.

subcontract [sʌbkən'trækt] *vt* sous-traiter. ◆**subcontractor** *n* sous-traitant *m*.

subdivide [sʌbdɪ'vaɪd] *vt* subdiviser (**into** en). ◆**subdivision** *n* subdivision *f*.

subdu/e [səb'djuː] *vt* (*country*) asservir; (*feelings*) maîtriser. ◆**—ed** *a* (*light*) atténué; (*voice*) bas; (*reaction*) faible; (*person*) qui manque d'entrain.

subheading ['sʌbhedɪŋ] *n* sous-titre *m*.

subject[1] ['sʌbdʒɪkt] *n* **1** (*matter*) & Gram sujet *m*; Sch Univ matière *f*; **s. matter** (*topic*) sujet *m*; (*content*) contenu *m*. **2** (*citizen*) ressortissant, -ante *mf*; (*of monarch, monarchy*) sujet, -ette *mf*; (*person etc in experiment*) sujet *m*.

subject[2] ['sʌbdʒɪkt] *a* (*tribe etc*) soumis; **s. to** (*prone to*) sujet à (*maladie etc*); (*ruled by*) soumis à (*loi, règle etc*); (*conditional upon*) sous réserve de; **prices are s. to change** les prix peuvent être modifiés; — [səb'dʒɛkt] *vt* soumettre (**to** à); (*expose*) exposer (**to** à). ◆**sub'jection** *n* soumission *f* (**to** à).

subjective [səb'dʒɛktɪv] *a* subjectif. ◆**—ly** *adv* subjectivement. ◆**subjec'tivity** *n* subjectivité *f*.

subjugate ['sʌbdʒʊgeɪt] *vt* subjuguer.

subjunctive [səb'dʒʌŋktɪv] *n* Gram subjonctif *m*.

sublet [sʌb'let] *vt* (*pt* & *pp* **sublet**, *pres p* **subletting**) sous-louer.

sublimate ['sʌblɪmeɪt] *vt* Psy sublimer.

sublime [sə'blaɪm] *a* sublime; (*indifference, stupidity*) suprême; — *n* sublime *m*.

submachine-gun [sʌbmə'ʃiːngʌn] *n* mitraillette *f*.

submarine ['sʌbməriːn] *n* sous-marin *m*.

submerge [səb'mɜːdʒ] *vt* (*flood, overwhelm*) submerger; (*immerse*) immerger (**in** dans); — *vi* (*of submarine*) s'immerger.

submit [səb'mɪt] *vt* (**-tt-**) soumettre (**to** à); **to s. that** *Jur* suggérer que; — *vi* se soumettre (**to** à). ◆**submission** *n* soumission *f* (**to** à). ◆**submissive** *a* soumis. ◆**submissively** *adv* avec soumission.

subnormal [sʌb'nɔːm(ə)l] *a* au-dessous de la normale; (*mentally*) arriéré.

subordinate [sə'bɔːdɪnət] *a* subalterne; *Gram* subordonné; − *n* subordonné, -ée *mf*; − [sə'bɔːdɪneɪt] *vt* subordonner (**to** à). ◆subordi'nation *n* subordination *f* (**to** à).

subpoena [səb'piːnə] *vt Jur* citer; − *n Jur* citation *f*.

subscribe [səb'skraɪb] *vt* (*money*) donner (**to** à); − *vi* cotiser; **to s. to** (*take out subscription*) s'abonner à (*journal etc*); (*be a subscriber*) être abonné à (*journal etc*); (*fund, idea*) souscrire à. ◆subscriber *n Journ Tel* abonné, -ée *mf*. ◆subscription *n* (*to newspaper etc*) abonnement *m*; (*to fund, idea*) & *Fin* souscription *f*; (*to club etc*) cotisation *f*.

subsequent ['sʌbsɪkwənt] *a* postérieur (**to** à); **our s. problems** les problèmes que nous avons eus par la suite; **s. to** (*as a result of*) consécutif à. ◆—**ly** *adv* par la suite.

subservient [səb'sɜːvɪənt] *a* obséquieux; **to be s. to** (*a slave to*) être asservi à.

subside [səb'saɪd] *vi* (*of building, land*) s'affaisser; (*of wind, flood*) baisser. ◆'subsidence *n* affaissement *m*.

subsidiary [səb'sɪdɪəri] *a* accessoire; (*subject*) *Univ* secondaire; (*company*) *Com* filiale *f*.

subsidize ['sʌbsɪdaɪz] *vt* subventionner. ◆subsidy *n* subvention *f*.

subsist [səb'sɪst] *vi* (*of person, doubts etc*) subsister. ◆subsistence *n* subsistance *f*.

substance ['sʌbstəns] *n* substance *f*; (*firmness*) solidité *f*; **a man of s.** un homme riche. ◆substantial [səb'stænʃ(ə)l] *a* important, considérable; (*meal*) substantiel. ◆sub'stantially *adv* considérablement, beaucoup; **s. true**/*etc* (*to a great extent*) en grande partie vrai/*etc*; **s. different** très différent.

substandard [sʌb'stændəd] *a* de qualité inférieure.

substantiate [səb'stænʃɪeɪt] *vt* prouver, justifier.

substitute ['sʌbstɪtjuːt] *n* (*thing*) produit *m* de remplacement; (*person*) remplaçant, -ante *mf* (**for** de); **there's no s. for . . .** rien ne peut remplacer . . . ; − *vt* substituer (**for** à); − *vi* **to s. for** remplacer; (*deputize for in job*) se substituer à. ◆substi'tution *n* substitution *f*.

subtitle ['sʌbtaɪt(ə)l] *n* sous-titre *m*; − *vt* sous-titrer.

subtle ['sʌt(ə)l] *a* (**-er, -est**) subtil. ◆sub-

tlety *n* subtilité *f*. ◆subtly *adv* subtilement.

subtotal [sʌb'təʊt(ə)l] *n* total *m* partiel, sous-total *m*.

subtract [səb'trækt] *vt* soustraire (**from** de). ◆subtraction *n* soustraction *f*.

suburb ['sʌbɜːb] *n* banlieue *f*; **the suburbs** la banlieue; **in the suburbs** en banlieue. ◆su'burban *a* (*train*) de banlieue; (*accent*) de la banlieue. ◆su'burbia *n* la banlieue.

subversive [səb'vɜːsɪv] *a* subversif. ◆subversion *n* subversion *f*. ◆subvert *vt* (*system etc*) bouleverser; (*person*) corrompre.

subway ['sʌbweɪ] *n* passage *m* souterrain; *Rail Am* métro *m*.

succeed [sək'siːd] **1** *vi* réussir (**in doing** à faire, **in sth** dans qch). **2** *vt* **to s. s.o.** (*follow*) succéder à qn; − *vi* **to s. to the throne** succéder à la couronne. ◆—**ing** *a* (*in past*) suivant; (*in future*) futur; (*consecutive*) consécutif.

success [sək'ses] *n* succès *m*, réussite *f*; **to make a s. of sth** réussir qch; **he was a s.** il a eu du succès; **his** *or* **her s. in the exam** sa réussite à l'examen; **s. story** réussite *f* complète *or* exemplaire. ◆successful *a* (*venture etc*) couronné de succès, réussi; (*outcome*) heureux; (*firm*) prospère; (*candidate in exam*) admis, reçu; (*election*) élu; (*writer, film etc*) à succès; **to be s.** réussir (**in** dans, **in an exam** à un examen, **in doing** à faire). ◆successfully *adv* avec succès.

succession [sək'seʃ(ə)n] *n* succession *f*; **in s.** successivement; **ten days in s.** dix jours consécutifs; **in rapid s.** coup sur coup. ◆successive *a* successif; **ten s. days** dix jours consécutifs. ◆successor *n* successeur *m* (**of, to** de).

succinct [sək'sɪŋkt] *a* succinct.

succulent ['sʌkjʊlənt] *a* succulent.

succumb [sə'kʌm] *vi* (*yield*) succomber (**to** à).

such [sʌtʃ] *a* tel; **s. a car**/*etc* une telle voiture/*etc*; **s. happiness**/*etc* (*so much*) tant *or* tellement de bonheur/*etc*; **there's no s. thing** ça n'existe pas; **I said no s. thing** je n'ai rien dit de tel; **s. as** comme, tel que; **and s.** tel *ou* tel; − *adv* (*so very*) si; (*in comparisons*) aussi; **s. a kind woman as you** une femme aussi gentille que vous; **s. long trips** de si longs voyages; **s. a large helping** une si grosse portion; − *pron* **happiness**/*etc* **as s.** le bonheur/*etc* tant que tel; **s. was**

my idea telle était mon idée. ◆**suchlike** n . . . **and s.** Fam . . . et autres.

suck [sʌk] vt sucer; (of baby) téter (lait, biberon etc); **to s. (up)** (with straw, pump) aspirer; **to s. up** or **in** (absorb) absorber; — vi (of baby) téter; **to s. at** sucer. ◆**-er** n **1** (fool) Fam pigeon m, dupe f. **2** (pad) ventouse f.

suckle ['sʌk(ə)l] vt (of woman) allaiter; (of baby) téter.

suction ['sʌk(ʃ)ən] n succion f; **s. disc, s. pad** ventouse f.

Sudan [suːˈdaɪn] n Soudan m.

sudden ['sʌd(ə)n] a soudain, subit; **all of a s.** tout à coup. ◆**-ly** adv subitement. ◆**-ness** n soudaineté f.

suds [sʌdz] npl mousse f de savon.

sue [suː] vt poursuivre (en justice); — vi engager des poursuites (judiciaires).

suede [sweɪd] n daim m; — a de daim.

suet ['suːɪt] n graisse f de rognon.

suffer ['sʌfər] vi souffrir (from de); **to s. from** pimples/the flu avoir des boutons/la grippe; **your work/etc will s.** ton travail/etc s'en ressentira; — vt (attack, loss etc) subir; (pain) ressentir; (tolerate) souffrir. ◆**-ing** n souffrance(s) f(pl). ◆**-er** n Med malade mf; (from misfortune) victime f.

suffice [səˈfaɪs] vi suffire.

sufficient [səˈfɪʃ(ə)nt] a (quantity, number) suffisant; **s. money/etc** (enough) suffisamment d'argent/etc; **to have s.** en avoir suffisamment. ◆**-ly** adv suffisamment.

suffix ['sʌfɪks] n Gram suffixe m.

suffocate ['sʌfəkeɪt] vti étouffer, suffoquer. ◆**suffo'cation** n (of industry, mind etc) & Med étouffement m, asphyxie f.

suffrage ['sʌfrɪdʒ] n (right to vote) Pol suffrage m.

suffused [səˈfjuːzd] a **s. with** (light, tears) baigné de.

sugar ['ʃugər] n sucre m; — a (cane, tongs) à sucre; (industry) sucrier; **s. bowl** sucrier m; — vt sucrer. ◆**sugary** a (taste, tone) sucré.

suggest [səˈdʒest] vt (propose) suggérer, proposer (**to** à, **that** que (+ sub)); (evoke, imply) suggérer; (hint) Pej insinuer. ◆**suggestion** n suggestion f, proposition f; (evocation) suggestion f; Pej insinuation f. ◆**suggestive** a suggestif; **to be s. of** suggérer.

suicide ['suːɪsaɪd] n suicide m; **to commit s.** se suicider. ◆**sui'cidal** a suicidaire.

suit [suːt] n **1** (man's) complet m, costume m; (woman's) tailleur m; (of pilot, diver etc) combinaison f. **2** (lawsuit) Jur procès m. **3** n Cards couleur f. **4** vt (satisfy, be appropri-

ate to) convenir à; (of dress, colour etc) aller (bien) à; (adapt) adapter (**to** à); **it suits me to stay** ça m'arrange de rester; **s. yourself!** comme tu voudras!; **suited to** (made for) fait pour; (appropriate to) approprié à; **well suited** (couple etc) bien assorti. ◆**suita-'bility** n (of remark etc) à-propos m; (of person) aptitudes fpl (**for** pour); **I'm not sure of the s. of it** (date etc) je ne sais pas si ça convient. ◆**suitable** a qui convient (**for** à); (dress, colour) qui va (bien); (example) approprié; (socially) convenable. ◆**suitably** adv convenablement.

suitcase ['suːtkeɪs] n valise f.

suite [swiːt] n (rooms) suite f; (furniture) mobilier m; **bedroom s.** (furniture) chambre f à coucher.

suitor ['suːtər] n soupirant m.

sulfur ['sʌlfər] n Am soufre m.

sulk [sʌlk] vi bouder. ◆**sulky** a (-ier, -iest) boudeur.

sullen ['sʌlən] a maussade. ◆**-ly** adv d'un air maussade.

sully ['sʌlɪ] vt Lit souiller.

sulphur ['sʌlfər] n soufre m.

sultan ['sʌltən] n sultan m.

sultana [sʌlˈtaɪnə] n raisin m de Smyrne.

sultry ['sʌltrɪ] a (-ier, -iest) (heat) étouffant; Fig sensuel.

sum [sʌm] n **1** (amount, total) somme f; Math calcul m; pl (arithmetic) le calcul; **s. total** résultat m. **2** vt (-mm-) **to s. up** (facts etc) récapituler, résumer; (text) résumer; (situation) évaluer; (person) jauger; — vi **to s. up** récapituler. ◆**summing-'up** n (pl summings-up) résumé m.

summarize ['sʌmərazz] vt résumer. ◆**summary** n résumé m; — a (brief) sommaire.

summer ['sʌmər] n été m; **in (the) s.** en été; **Indian s.** été indien or de la Saint-Martin; — a d'été; **s. holidays** grandes vacances fpl. ◆**summerhouse** n pavillon m (de jardin). ◆**summertime** n été m; **in (the) s.** en été. ◆**summery** a (weather etc) estival; (dress) d'été.

summit ['sʌmɪt] n (of mountain, power etc) sommet m; **s. conference/meeting** Pol conférence f/rencontre f au sommet.

summon ['sʌmən] vt (call) appeler; (meeting, s.o. to meeting) convoquer (**to** à); **to s. s.o. to do** sommer qn de faire; **to s. up** (courage, strength) rassembler.

summons ['sʌmənz] n Jur assignation f; — vt Jur assigner.

sumptuous ['sʌmptʃuəs] a somptueux. ◆**-ness** n somptuosité f.

sun [sʌn] n soleil m; **in the s.** au soleil; **the**

sun's shining il fait (du) soleil; – *a* (*cream, filter etc*) solaire; **s. lounge** solarium *m*; – *vt* (**-nn-**) **to s. oneself** se chauffer au soleil. ◆**sunbaked** *a* brûlé par le soleil. ◆**sunbathe** *vi* prendre un bain de soleil. ◆**sunbeam** *n* rayon *m* de soleil. ◆**sunburn** *n* (*tan*) bronzage *m*; *Med* coup *m* de soleil. ◆**sunburnt** *a* bronzé; *Med* brûlé par le soleil. ◆**sundial** *n* cadran *m* solaire. ◆**sundown** *n* coucher *m* du soleil. ◆**sundrenched** *a* brûlé par le soleil. ◆**sunflower** *n* tournesol *m*. ◆**sunglasses** *npl* lunettes *fpl* de soleil. ◆**sunlamp** *n* lampe *f* à rayons ultraviolets. ◆**sunlight** *n* (lumière *f* du) soleil *m*. ◆**sunlit** *a* ensoleillé. ◆**sunrise** *n* lever *m* du soleil. ◆**sunroof** *n* *Aut* toit *m* ouvrant. ◆**sunset** *n* coucher *m* du soleil. ◆**sunshade** *n* (*on table*) parasol *m*; (*portable*) ombrelle *f*. ◆**sunshine** *n* soleil *m*. ◆**sunstroke** *n* insolation *f*. ◆**suntan** *n* bronzage *m*; – *a* (*lotion, oil*) solaire. ◆**suntanned** *a* bronzé. ◆**sunup** *n* *Am* lever *m* du soleil.

sundae ['sʌndeɪ] *n* glace *f* aux fruits.

Sunday ['sʌndɪ] *n* dimanche *m*.

sundry ['sʌndrɪ] *a* divers; **all and s.** tout le monde; – *npl Com* articles *mpl* divers.

sung [sʌŋ] *see* sing.

sunk [sʌŋk] *see* sink[2]; – *a* **I'm s.** *Fam* je suis fichu. ◆**sunken** *a* (*rock etc*) submergé; (*eyes*) cave.

sunny ['sʌnɪ] *a* (**-ier, -iest**) ensoleillé; **it's s.** il fait (du) soleil; **s. period** *Met* éclaircie *f*.

super ['suːpər] *a Fam* sensationnel.

super- ['suːpər] *pref* super-.

superannuation [suːpərænjuˈeɪʃ(ə)n] *n* (*amount*) cotisations *fpl* (pour) la retraite.

superb [suːˈpɜːb] *a* superbe.

supercilious [suːpəˈsɪlɪəs] *a* hautain.

superficial [suːpəˈfɪʃ(ə)l] *a* superficiel. ◆**-ly** *adv* superficiellement.

superfluous [suːˈpɜːflʊəs] *a* superflu.

superhuman [suːpəˈhjuːmən] *a* surhumain.

superimpose [suːpərɪmˈpəʊz] *vt* superposer (**on** à).

superintendent [suːpərɪnˈtendənt] *n* directeur, -trice *mf*; (*police*) **s.** commissaire *m* (de police).

superior [suːˈpɪərɪər] *a* supérieur (**to** à); (*goods*) de qualité supérieure; – *n* (*person*) supérieur, -eure *mf*. ◆**superi'ority** *n* supériorité *f*.

superlative [suːˈpɜːlətɪv] *a* sans pareil; – *a & n Gram* superlatif (*m*).

superman ['suːpəmæn] *n* (*pl* **-men**) surhomme *m*.

supermarket ['suːpəmɑːkɪt] *n* supermarché *m*.

supernatural [suːpəˈnætʃ(ə)rəl] *a & n* surnaturel (*m*).

superpower ['suːpəpaʊər] *n Pol* superpuissance *f*.

supersede [suːpəˈsiːd] *vt* remplacer, supplanter.

supersonic [suːpəˈsɒnɪk] *a* supersonique.

superstition [suːpəˈstɪʃ(ə)n] *n* superstition *f*. ◆**superstitious** *a* superstitieux.

supertanker ['suːpətæŋkər] *n* pétrolier *m* géant.

supervise ['suːpəvaɪz] *vt* (*person, work*) surveiller; (*office, research*) diriger. ◆**super'vision** *n* surveillance *f*; direction *f*. ◆**supervisor** *n* surveillant, -ante *mf*; (*in office*) chef *m* de service; (*shop*) chef *m* de rayon. ◆**super'visory** *a* (*post*) de surveillant(e).

supper ['sʌpər] *n* dîner *m*; (*late-night*) souper *m*.

supple ['sʌp(ə)l] *a* souple. ◆**-ness** *n* souplesse *f*.

supplement ['sʌplɪmənt] *n* (*addition*) & *Journ* supplément *m* (**to** à); – ['sʌplɪment] *vt* compléter; **to s. one's income** arrondir ses fins de mois. ◆**supple'mentary** *a* supplémentaire.

supply [səˈplaɪ] *vt* (*provide*) fournir; (*feed*) alimenter (**with** en); (*equip*) équiper, pourvoir (**with** de); **to s. a need** subvenir à un besoin; **to s. s.o. with sth, s. sth to s.o.** (*facts etc*) fournir qch à qn; – *n* (*stock*) provision *f*, réserve *f*; (*equipment*) matériel *m*; **the s. of** (*act*) la fourniture de; **the s. of gas/electricity to** l'alimentation *f* en gaz/électricité de; (*food*) **supplies** vivres *mpl*; (*office*) **supplies** fournitures *fpl* (de bureau); **s. and demand** l'offre *f* et la demande; **to be in short s.** manquer; – *a* (*ship, train*) ravitailleur; **s. teacher** suppléant, -ante *mf*. ◆**-ing** *n* (*provision*) fourniture *f*; (*feeding*) alimentation *f*. ◆**supplier** *n Com* fournisseur *m*.

support [səˈpɔːt] *vt* (*bear weight of*) soutenir, supporter; (*help, encourage*) soutenir, appuyer; (*theory, idea*) appuyer; (*be in favour of*) être en faveur de; (*family, wife etc*) assurer la subsistance de; (*endure*) supporter; – *n* (*help, encouragement*) appui *m*, soutien *m*; *Tech* support *m*; **means of s.** moyens *mpl* de subsistance; **in s. of** en faveur de; (*evidence, theory*) à l'appui de. ◆**-ing** *a* (*role*) *Th Cin* secondaire; (*actor*) qui a un rôle secondaire. ◆**supporter** *n* partisan, -ane *mf*; *Fb* supporter *m*. ◆**supportive** *a* to be s. prêter son appui (**of**, to à).

suppos/e [sə'pəuz] *vti* supposer (that que); **I'm supposed to work** *or* **be working** (*ought*) je suis censé travailler; **he's s. to be rich** on le dit riche; **I s. (so)** je pense; **I don't s. so, I s. not** je ne pense pas; **you're tired, I s.** vous êtes fatigué, je suppose; **s. or supposing we go** (*suggestion*) si nous partions; **s. or supposing (that) you're right** supposons que tu aies raison. ◆**—ed** *a* soi-disant. ◆**—edly** [-ɪdlɪ] *adv* soi-disant. ◆**supposition** *n* supposition *f*.

suppository [sə'pɒzɪtərɪ] *n Med* suppositoire *m*.

suppress [sə'pres] *vt* (*put an end to*) supprimer; (*feelings*) réprimer; (*scandal, yawn etc*) étouffer. ◆**suppression** *n* suppression *f*; répression *f*. ◆**suppressor** *n El* dispositif *m* antiparasite.

supreme [suː'priːm] *a* suprême. ◆**supremacy** *n* suprématie *f* (**over** sur).

supremo [suː'priːməʊ] *n* (*pl* **-os**) *Fam* grand chef *m*.

surcharge ['sɜːtʃɑːdʒ] *n* (*extra charge*) supplément *m*; (*on stamp*) surcharge *f*; (*tax*) surtaxe *f*.

sure [ʃʊər] *a* (**-er, -est**) sûr (**of** de, **that** que); **she's s. to accept** il est sûr qu'elle acceptera; **it's s. to snow** il va sûrement neiger; **to make s. of** s'assurer de; **for s.** à coup sûr, pour sûr; **s.!**, *Fam* **s. thing!** bien sûr!; **s. enough** (*in effect*) en effet; **it s. is cold** *Am* il fait vraiment froid; **be s. to do it!** ne manquez pas de le faire! ◆**surefire** *a* infaillible. ◆**surely** *adv* (*certainly*) sûrement; **s. he didn't refuse?** (*I think, I hope*) il n'a tout de même pas refusé.

surety ['ʃʊərətɪ] *n* caution *f*.

surf [sɜːf] *n* (*foam*) ressac *m*. ◆**surfboard** *n* planche *f* (de surf). ◆**surfing** *n Sp* surf *m*.

surface ['sɜːfɪs] *n* surface *f*; **s. area** superficie *f*; **s. mail** courrier *m* par voie(s) de surface; **on the s.** (*to all appearances*) *Fig* en apparence; − *vt* (*road*) revêtir; − *vi* (*of swimmer etc*) remonter à la surface; (*of ideas, person etc*) *Fam* apparaître.

surfeit ['sɜːfɪt] *n* (*excess*) excès *m* (**of** de).

surge [sɜːdʒ] *n* (*of sea, enthusiasm*) vague *f*; (*rise*) montée *f*; − *vi* (*of crowd, hatred*) déferler; (*rise*) monter; **to s. forward** se lancer en avant.

surgeon ['sɜːdʒən] *n* chirurgien *m*. ◆**surgery** *n* (*science*) chirurgie *f*; (*doctor's office*) cabinet *m*; (*sitting, period*) consultation *f*; **to undergo s.** subir une intervention.

◆**surgical** *a* chirurgical; (*appliance*) orthopédique; **s. spirit** alcool *m* à 90°.

surly ['sɜːlɪ] *a* (**-ier, -iest**) bourru. ◆**surliness** *n* air *m* bourru.

surmise [sə'maɪz] *vt* conjecturer (**that** que).

surmount [sə'maʊnt] *vt* (*overcome, be on top of*) surmonter.

surname ['sɜːneɪm] *n* nom *m* de famille.

surpass [sə'pɑːs] *vt* surpasser (**in** en).

surplus ['sɜːpləs] *n* surplus *m*; − *a* (*goods*) en surplus; **some s. material/etc** (*left over*) un surplus de tissu/*etc*; **s. stock** surplus *mpl*.

surpris/e [sə'praɪz] *n* surprise *f*; **to give s.o. a s.** faire une surprise à qn; **to take s.o. by s.** prendre qn au dépourvu; − *a* (*visit, result etc*) inattendu; − *vt* (*astonish*) étonner, surprendre; (*come upon*) surprendre. ◆**—ed** *a* surpris (**that** que (+ *sub*), **at sth** de qch, **at seeing/etc** de voir/*etc*); **I'm s. at his** *or* **her stupidity** sa bêtise m'étonne *or* me surprend. ◆**—ing** *a* surprenant. ◆**—ingly** *adv* étonnamment; **s. (enough) he ...** chose étonnante, il ....

surrealistic [səriə'lɪstɪk] *a* (*strange*) *Fig* surréaliste.

surrender [sə'rendər] **1** *vi* (*give oneself up*) se rendre (**to** à); **to s. to** (*police*) se livrer à; − *n Mil* reddition *f*, capitulation *f*. **2** *vt* (*hand over*) remettre, rendre (**to** à); (*right, claim*) renoncer à.

surreptitious [sʌrəp'tɪʃəs] *a* subreptice.

surrogate ['sʌrəgət] *n* substitut *m*; **s. mother** mère *f* porteuse.

surround [sə'raʊnd] *vt* entourer (**with** de); *Mil* encercler; **surrounded by** entouré de. ◆**—ing** *a* environnant. ◆**—ings** *npl* environs *mpl*; (*setting*) cadre *m*.

surveillance [sɜː'veɪləns] *n* (*of prisoner etc*) surveillance *f*.

survey [sə'veɪ] *vt* (*look at*) regarder; (*review*) passer en revue; (*house etc*) inspecter; (*land*) arpenter; − ['sɜːveɪ] *n* (*investigation*) enquête *f*; (*of house etc*) inspection *f*; (*of opinion*) sondage *m*; **a (general) s.** of une vue générale de. ◆**sur'veying** *n* arpentage *m*. ◆**sur'veyor** *n* (arpenteur *m*) géomètre *m*; (*of house etc*) expert *m*.

survive [sə'vaɪv] *vi* (*of person, custom etc*) survivre; − *vt* survivre à. ◆**survival** *n* (*act*) survie *f*; (*relic*) vestige *m*. ◆**survivor** *n* survivant, -ante *mf*.

susceptible [sə'septəb(ə)l] *a* (*sensitive*) sensible (**to** à); **s. to colds/etc** (*prone to*) prédisposé aux rhumes/*etc*. ◆**susceptibility** *n* sensibilité *f*; prédisposition *f*; *pl* susceptibilité *f*.

suspect ['sʌspekt] n & a suspect, -ecte (mf); – [sə'spekt] vt soupçonner (**that** que, **of sth** de qch, **of doing** d'avoir fait); (think questionable) suspecter, douter de; **yes, I s.** oui, j'imagine.

suspend [sə'spend] vt **1** (hang) suspendre (**from à**). **2** (stop, postpone, dismiss) suspendre; (passport etc) retirer (provisoirement); (pupil) Sch renvoyer; **suspended sentence** Jur condamnation f avec sursis. ◆**suspender** n (for stocking) jarretelle f; pl (braces) Am bretelles fpl; **s. belt** porte-jarretelles m inv. ◆**suspension** n **1** (stopping) suspension f; (of passport etc) retrait m (provisoire). **2** (of vehicle etc) suspension f; **s. bridge** pont m suspendu.

suspense [sə'spens] n attente f (angoissée); (in film, book etc) suspense m; **in s.** (person, matter) en suspens.

suspicion [sə'spiʃ(ə)n] n soupçon m; **to arouse s.** éveiller les soupçons; **with s.** (distrust) avec méfiance; **under s.** considéré comme suspect. ◆**suspicious** a (person) soupçonneux, méfiant; (behaviour) suspect; **s.(-looking)** (suspect) suspect; **to be s. of** or **about** (distrust) se méfier de. ◆**suspiciously** adv (to behave etc) d'une manière suspecte; (to consider etc) avec méfiance.

sustain [sə'stein] vt (effort, theory) soutenir; (weight) supporter; (with food) nourrir; (life) maintenir; (damage, attack) subir; (injury) recevoir. ◆**sustenance** n (food) nourriture f; (quality) valeur f nutritive.

swab [swɒb] n (pad) Med tampon m; (specimen) Med prélèvement m.

swagger ['swægər] vi (walk) parader; – n démarche f fanfaronne.

swallow ['swɒləʊ] **1** vt avaler; **to s. down** or **up** avaler; **to s. up** Fig engloutir; – vi avaler. **2** n (bird) hirondelle f.

swam [swæm] see **swim**.

swamp [swɒmp] n marais m, marécage m; – vt (flood, overwhelm) submerger (**with** de). ◆**swampy** a (-ier, -iest) marécageux.

swan [swɒn] n cygne m.

swank [swæŋk] vi (show off) Fam crâner, fanfaronner.

swap [swɒp] n échange m; pl (stamps etc) doubles mpl; – vt (-pp-) échanger (**for** contre); **to s. seats** changer de place; – vi échanger.

swarm [swɔːm] n (of bees, people etc) essaim m; – vi (of streets, insects, people etc) fourmiller (**with** de); **to s. in** (of people) entrer en foule.

swarthy ['swɔːðɪ] a (-ier, -iest) (dark) basané.

swastika ['swɒstɪkə] n (Nazi emblem) croix f gammée.

swat [swɒt] vt (-tt-) (fly etc) écraser.

sway [sweɪ] vi se balancer, osciller; – vt balancer; Fig influencer; – n balancement m; Fig influence f.

swear ['sweər] vt (pt swore, pp sworn) jurer (**to do** de faire, **that** que); **to s. an oath** prêter serment; **to s. s.o. to secrecy** faire jurer le silence à qn; **sworn enemies** ennemis mpl jurés; – vi (take an oath) jurer (**to sth** de qch); (curse) jurer, pester (**at** contre); **she swears by this lotion** elle ne jure que par cette lotion. ◆**swearword** n gros mot m, juron m.

sweat [swet] n sueur f; **s. shirt** sweat-shirt m; – vi (of person, wall etc) suer; (of food) – vt **to s. out** (cold) Med se débarrasser de (en transpirant). ◆**sweater** n (garment) pull m. ◆**sweaty** a (-ier, -iest) (shirt etc) plein de sueur; (hand) moite; (person) (tout) en sueur, (tout) en nage.

swede [swiːd] n (vegetable) rutabaga m.

Swede [swiːd] n Suédois, -oise mf. ◆**Sweden** n Suède f. ◆**Swedish** a suédois; – n (language) suédois m.

sweep [swiːp] n coup m de balai; (movement) Fig large) mouvement m; (curve) courbe f; **to make a clean s.** (removal) faire table rase (**of** de); (victory) remporter une victoire totale; – vt (pt & pp swept) (with broom) balayer; (chimney) ramoner; (river) draguer; **to s. away** or **out** or **up** balayer; **to s. away** or **along** (carry off) emporter; **to s. aside** (dismiss) écarter; – vi **to s.** (**up**) balayer; **to s. in** (of person) Fig entrer rapidement or majestueusement; **to s. through** (of fear etc) saisir (groupe etc); (of disease etc) ravager (pays etc). ◆**—ing** a (gesture) large; (change) radical; (statement) trop général. ◆**sweepstake** n (lottery) sweepstake m.

sweet [swiːt] a (-er, -est) (not sour) doux; (agreeable) agréable, doux; (tea, coffee etc) sucré; (person, house, kitchen) mignon, gentil; **to have a s. tooth** aimer les sucreries; **to be s.-smelling** sentir bon; **s. corn** maïs m; **s. pea** Bot pois m de senteur; **s. potato** patate f douce; **s. shop** confiserie f; **s. talk** Fam cajoleries fpl, douceurs fpl; – n (candy) bonbon m; (dessert) dessert m; **my s.!** (darling) mon ange! ◆**sweeten** vt (tea etc) sucrer; Fig adoucir. ◆**sweetener** n saccharine f. ◆**sweetie** n (darling) Fam chéri, -ie mf. ◆**sweetly** adv (kindly) genti-

ment; (*softly*) doucement. ◆**sweetness** *n*
douceur *f*; (*taste*) goût *m* sucré.

sweetbread ['swiːtbred] *n* ris *m* de veau or
d'agneau.

sweetheart ['swiːthaːt] *n* (*lover*) ami, -ie *mf*;
my s.! (*darling*) mon ange!

swell [swel] **1** *n* (*of sea*) houle *f*. **2** *a* (*very
good*) *Am Fam* formidable. **3** *vi* (*pt* **swelled**,
pp **swollen** *or* **swelled**) se gonfler; (*of river,
numbers*) grossir; **to s. (up)** *Med* enfler,
gonfler; − *vt* (*river, numbers*) grossir.
◆**-ing** *n Med* enflure *f*.

swelter ['sweltər] *vi* étouffer. ◆**-ing** *a*
étouffant; **it's s.** on étouffe.

swept [swept] *see* **sweep.**

swerve [swɜːv] *vi* (*while running etc*) faire un
écart; (*of vehicle*) faire une embardée.

swift [swift] **1** *a* (**-er, -est**) rapide; **s. to act**
prompt à agir. **2** *n* (*bird*) martinet *m*.
◆**-ly** *adv* rapidement. ◆**-ness** *n* rapidité *f*.

swig [swig] *n* (*of beer etc*) lampée *f*.

swill [swil] *vt* **to s. (out** *or* **down)** laver (à
grande eau).

swim [swim] *n* baignade *f*; **to go for a s.** se
baigner, nager; − *vi* (*pt* **swam**, *pp* **swum**,
pres p **swimming**) nager; *Sp* faire de la natation; (*of head, room*) Fig tourner; **to go
swimming** aller nager; **to s. away** se sauver
(à la nage); − *vt* (*river*) traverser à la nage;
(*length, crawl etc*) nager. ◆**swimming** *n*
natation *f*; **s. costume** maillot *m* de bain; **s.
pool, s. baths** piscine *f*; **s. trunks** slip *m* or
caleçon *m* de bain. ◆**swimmer** *n* nageur,
-euse *mf*. ◆**swimsuit** *n* maillot *m* de bain.

swindl/e ['swindəl] *n* escroquerie *f*; − *vt*
escroquer; **to s.o. out of money** escroquer
de l'argent à qn. ◆**-er** *n* escroc *m*.

swine [swain] *n inv* (*person*) *Pej* salaud *m*.

swing [swiŋ] *n* (*seat*) balançoire *f*; (*movement*) balancement *m*; (*of pendulum*) oscillation *f*; (*in opinion*) revirement *m*;
(*rhythm*) rythme *m*; **to be in full s.** battre
son plein; **to be in the s. of things** *Fam* être
dans le bain; **s. door** porte *f* de saloon; − *vi*
(*pt & pp* **swung**) (*sway*) se balancer; (*of
pendulum*) osciller; (*turn*) virer; **to s. round**
(*turn suddenly*) virer, tourner; (*of person*) se
retourner (vivement); (*of vehicle in collision
etc*) faire un tête-à-queue; **to s. into action**
passer à l'action; − *vt* (*arms etc*) balancer;
(*axe*) brandir; (*influence*) *Fam* influencer;
to s. round (*car etc*) faire tourner. ◆**-ing** *a
Fam* (*trendy*) dans le vent; (*lively*) plein de
vie; (*music*) entraînant.

swingeing ['swindʒiŋ] *a* **s. cuts** des réduc-
tions *fpl* draconiennes.

swipe [swaip] *vt Fam* (*hit*) frapper dur;
(*steal*) piquer (**from** s.o. à qn); − *n Fam*
grand coup *m*.

swirl [swɜːl] *n* tourbillon *m*; − *vi* tourbillonner.

swish [swiʃ] **1** *a* (*posh*) *Fam* rupin, chic. **2** *vi*
(*of whip etc*) siffler; (*of fabric*) froufrouter;
− *n* sifflement *m*; froufrou *m*.

Swiss [swis] *a* suisse; − *n inv* Suisse *m*, Suis-
sesse *f*; **the S.** les Suisses *mpl*.

switch [switʃ] *n El* bouton *m* (électrique),
interrupteur *m*; (*change*) changement *m* (in
de); (*reversal*) revirement *m* (in en); − *vt*
(*money, employee etc*) transférer (to à);
(*affection, support*) reporter (**to** sur, **from**
de); (*exchange*) échanger (**for** contre); **to s.
buses**/*etc* changer de bus/*etc*; **to s. places**
or **seats** changer de place; **to s. off** (*lamp,
gas, radio etc*) éteindre; (*engine*) arrêter; **to
s. itself off** (*of heating etc*) s'éteindre tout
seul; **to s. on** (*lamp, gas, radio etc*) mettre,
allumer; (*engine*) mettre en marche; − *vi* **to
s. (over)** (*to* passer à; **to s. off** (*switch off
light, radio etc*) éteindre; **to s. on** (*switch on
light, radio etc*) allumer. ◆**switchback** *n*
(*at funfair*) montagnes *fpl* russes.
◆**switchblade** *n Am* couteau *m* à cran
d'arrêt. ◆**switchboard** *n Tel* standard *m*;
s. operator standardiste *mf*.

Switzerland ['switsələnd] *n* Suisse *f*.

swivel ['swivəl] *vi* (**-ll-,** *Am* **-l-**) **to s. (round)**
(*of chair etc*) pivoter; − *a* **s. chair** fauteuil *m*
pivotant.

swollen ['swəʊl(ə)n] *see* **swell 3;** − *a* (*leg etc*)
enflé.

swoon [swuːn] *vi Lit* se pâmer.

swoop [swuːp] **1** *vi* **to s. (down) on** (*of bird*)
fondre sur. **2** *n* (*of police*) descente *f*; − *vi*
faire une descente (**on** dans).

swop [swɒp] *n, vt & vi* = **swap.**

sword [sɔːd] *n* épée *f*. ◆**swordfish** *n*
espadon *m*.

swore, sworn [swɔːr, swɔːn] *see* **swear.**

swot [swɒt] *vti* (**-tt-**) **to s. (up)** (*study*) *Fam*
potasser; **to s. (up) for** (*exam*) **s. up on**
(*subject*) *Fam* potasser; − *n Pej Fam*
bûcheur, -euse *mf*.

swum [swʌm] *see* **swim.**

swung [swʌŋ] *see* **swing.**

sycamore ['sikəmɔːr] *n* (*maple*) sycomore
m; (*plane*) *Am* platane *m*.

sycophant ['sikəfænt] *n* flagorneur, -euse
mf.

syllable ['siləb(ə)l] *n* syllabe *f*.

syllabus ['siləbəs] *n Sch Univ* programme
m.

symbol ['simb(ə)l] *n* symbole *m*. ◆**sym-**

'bolic *a* symbolique. ◆**symbolism** *n* symbolisme *m*. ◆**symbolize** *vt* symboliser.

symmetry ['sɪmɪtrɪ] *n* symétrie *f*. ◆**sy'mmetrical** *a* symétrique.

sympathy ['sɪmpəθɪ] *n* (*pity*) compassion *f*; (*understanding*) compréhension *f*; (*condolences*) condoléances *fpl*; (*solidarity*) solidarité *f* (**for** avec); **to be in s. with** (*workers in dispute*) être du côté de; (*s.o.'s opinion etc*) comprendre, être en accord avec. ◆**sympa'thetic** *a* (*showing pity*) compatissant; (*understanding*) compréhensif; **s. to** (*favourable*) bien disposé à l'égard de. ◆**sympa'thetically** *adv* avec compassion; avec compréhension. ◆**sympathize** *vi* **I s.** (**with you**) (*pity*) je compatis (à votre sort); (*understanding*) je vous comprends. ◆**sympathizer** *n Pol* sympathisant, -ante *mf*.

symphony ['sɪmfənɪ] *n* symphonie *f*; – *a* (*orchestra, concert*) symphonique. ◆**sym'phonic** *a* symphonique.

symposium [sɪm'pəʊzɪəm] *n* symposium *m*.

symptom ['sɪmptəm] *n* symptôme *m*. ◆**sympto'matic** *a* symptomatique (**of** de).

synagogue ['sɪnəgɒg] *n* synagogue *f*.

synchronize ['sɪŋkrənaɪz] *vt* synchroniser.

syndicate ['sɪndɪkət] *n* (*of businessmen, criminals*) syndicat *m*.

syndrome ['sɪndrəʊm] *n Med & Fig* syndrome *m*.

synod ['sɪnəd] *n Rel* synode *m*.

synonym ['sɪnənɪm] *n* synonyme *m*. ◆**sy'nonymous** *a* synonyme (**with** de).

synopsis, *pl* **-opses** [sɪ'nɒpsɪs, -ɒpsiːz] *n* résumé *m*, synopsis *m*; (*of film*) synopsis *m*.

syntax ['sɪntæks] *n Gram* syntaxe *f*.

synthesis, *pl* **-theses** ['sɪnθəsɪs, -θəsiːz] *n* synthèse *f*.

synthetic [sɪn'θetɪk] *a* synthétique.

syphilis ['sɪfɪlɪs] *n* syphilis *f*.

Syria ['sɪrɪə] *n* Syrie *f*. ◆**Syrian** *a* & *n* syrien, -ienne (*mf*).

syringe [sɪ'rɪndʒ] *n* seringue *f*.

syrup ['sɪrəp] *n* sirop *m*; (**golden**) **s.** (*treacle*) mélasse *f* (raffinée). ◆**syrupy** *a* sirupeux.

system ['sɪstəm] *n* (*structure, plan, network etc*) & *Anat* système *m*; (*human body*) organisme *m*; (*order*) méthode *f*; **systems analyst** analyste-programmeur *mf*. ◆**syste'matic** *a* systématique. ◆**syste'matically** *adv* systématiquement.

T

T, t [tiː] *n* T, t *m*. ◆**T-junction** *n Aut* intersection *f* en T. ◆**T-shirt** *n* tee-shirt *m*, T-shirt *m*.

ta! [tɑː] *int Sl* merci!

tab [tæb] *n* (*label*) étiquette *f*; (*tongue*) patte *f*; (*loop*) attache *f*; (*bill*) *Am* addition *f*; **to keep tabs on** *Fam* surveiller (de près).

tabby ['tæbɪ] *a* **t. cat** chat, chatte *mf* tigré(e).

table¹ ['teɪb(ə)l] *n* **1** (*furniture, list*) table *f*; **bedside/card/operating t.** table de nuit/de jeu/d'opération; **to lay** *or* **set/clear the t.** mettre/débarrasser la table; (**sitting**) **at the t.** à table; **t. top** dessus *m* de table. **2** (*list*) table *f*; **t. of contents** table des matières. ◆**tablecloth** *n* nappe *f*. ◆**tablemat** *n* (*of fabric*) napperon *m*; (*hard*) dessous-de-plat *m inv*. ◆**tablespoon** *n* = cuiller *f* à soupe. ◆**tablespoonful** *n* = cuillerée *f* à soupe.

table² ['teɪb(ə)l] *vt* (*motion etc*) *Pol* présenter; (*postpone*) *Am* ajourner.

tablet ['tæblɪt] *n* **1** (*pill*) *Med* comprimé *m*. **2** (*inscribed stone*) plaque *f*.

tabloid ['tæblɔɪd] *n* (*newspaper*) quotidien *m* populaire.

taboo [tə'buː] *a* & *n* tabou (*m*).

tabulator ['tæbjʊleɪtə] *n* (*of typewriter*) tabulateur *m*.

tacit ['tæsɪt] *a* tacite. ◆**-ly** *adv* tacitement.

taciturn ['tæsɪtɜːn] *a* taciturne.

tack [tæk] *n* **1** (*nail*) semence *f*; (*thumbtack*) *Am* punaise *f*; **to get down to brass tacks** *Fig* en venir aux faits; – *vt* **to t.** (**down**) clouer. **2** *n* (*stitch*) *Tex* point *m* de bâti; – *vt* **to t.** (**down** *or* **on**) bâtir; **to t. on** (*add*) *Fig* (r)ajouter. **3** *vi* (*of ship*) louvoyer; – *n* (*course of action*) *Fig* voie *f*.

tackle ['tæk(ə)l] **1** *n* (*gear*) matériel *m*, équipement *m*. **2** *vt* (*task, problem etc*) s'attaquer à; (*thief etc*) saisir; *Sp* plaquer; – *n Sp* plaquage *m*.

tacky ['tækɪ] *a* (**-ier, -iest**) **1** (*wet, sticky*) collant, pas sec. **2** (*clothes, attitude etc*) *Am* moche.

tact [tækt] *n* tact *m*. ◆**tactful** *a* (*remark etc*) plein de tact, diplomatique; **she's t.** elle a du tact. ◆**tactfully** adv avec tact. ◆**tact-less** a qui manque de tact. ◆**tactlessly** adv sans tact.

tactic ['tæktɪk] n a. une tactique; **tactics** la tactique. ◆**tactical** a tactique.

tactile ['tæktaɪl] a tactile.

tadpole ['tædpəʊl] n têtard m.

taffy ['tæfɪ] n (toffee) Am caramel m (dur).

tag [tæg] **1** n (label) étiquette f; (end piece) bout m; − vt (-gg-) **to t. on** (add) Fam rajouter (to à). **2** vi (-gg-) **to t. along** (follow) suivre.

Tahiti [tɑː'hiːtɪ] n Tahiti m.

tail [teɪl] **1** n (of animal) queue f; (of shirt) pan m; pl (outfit) habit m, queue-de-pie f; **t. end** fin f, bout m; **heads or tails?** pile ou face? **2** vt (follow) suivre, filer. **3** vi **to t. off** (lessen) diminuer. ◆**tailback** n (of traffic) bouchon m. ◆**tailcoat** n queue-de-pie f ◆**taillight** n Aut Am feu m arrière inv.

tailor ['teɪlər] n (person) tailleur m; − vt (garment) façonner; Fig adapter (**to, to suit** à). ◆**t.-'made** a fait sur mesure; **t.-made for** (specially designed) conçu pour; (suited) fait pour.

tainted ['teɪntɪd] a (air) pollué; (food) gâté; Fig souillé.

take [teɪk] vt (pt took, pp taken) prendre; (choice) faire; (prize) remporter; (exam) passer; (contain) contenir; Math soustraire (from de); (tolerate) supporter; (bring) apporter (qch) (to à), (person) amener (to à), (person by car) conduire (to à); (escort) accompagner (to à); (lead away) emmener; (of road) mener (qn); **to t. sth to s.o.** (ap)porter qch à qn; **to t. s.o. (out) to** (theatre etc) emmener qn à; **to t. sth with one** emporter qch; **to t. over or round or along** (object) apporter; (person) amener; **to t. s.o. home** (on foot, by car etc) ramener qn; **it takes an army/courage/etc** (requires) il faut une armée/du courage/etc (to do pour faire); **I took an hour to do it** or **over it** j'ai mis une heure à le faire, ça m'a pris une heure pour le faire; **I t. it that** je présume que; − n Cin prise f de vue(s); − vi (of fire) prendre. ■ **to t. after** vi (be like) ressembler à; **to t. apart** vt (machine) démonter; **to t. away** vt (thing) emmener; (person) emmener; (remove) enlever (from à); Math soustraire (from de). ◆**t.-away** a (meal) à emporter; − n café m or restaurant m qui fait des plats à emporter; (meal) plat m à emporter; **to t. back** vt reprendre; (return) rapporter; (statement) retirer; **to t. down** vt (object) descendre; (notes) prendre; **to t. in** vt (chair, car etc) rentrer; (orphan) recueil-lir; (skirt) reprendre; (include) englober; (distance) couvrir; (understand) comprendre; (deceive) Fam rouler; **to t. off** vt (remove) enlever; (train, bus) supprimer; (lead away) emmener; (mimic) imiter; Math déduire (from de); − vi (of aircraft) décoller. ◆**takeoff** n (of aircraft) décollage m; **to t. on** vt (work, employee, passenger, shape) prendre; **to t. out** vt (from pocket etc) sortir; (stain) enlever; (tooth) arracher; (licence, insurance) prendre; **to t. it out on** Fam passer sa colère sur. ◆**t.-out** a & n Am = **t.-away**; **to t. over** vt (be responsible for the running of) prendre la direction de; (overrun) envahir; (buy out) Com racheter (compagnie); − vt Mil Pol prendre le pouvoir; (relieve) prendre la relève (**from** de); (succeed) prendre la succession (**from** de). ◆**t.-over** n Com rachat m; Pol prise f de pouvoir; **to t. round** vt (distribute) distribuer; (visitor) faire visiter; **to t. to** vi **to t. to doing** se mettre à faire; **I didn't t. to him/it** il/ça ne m'a pas plu; **to t. up** vt (carry up) monter; (hem) raccourcir; (continue) reprendre; (occupy) prendre; (hobby) se mettre à; − vi **to t. up with** se lier avec. ◆**taken** a (seat) pris; (impressed) impressionné (**with**, by par); **to be t. ill** tomber malade. ◆**taking** n (capture) Mil prise f; pl (money) Com recette f.

talcum ['tælkəm] n **a t. powder** talc m.

tale [teɪl] n (story) conte m; (account, report) récit m; (lie) histoire f; **to tell tales** rapporter (on sur).

talent ['tælənt] n talent m; (talented people) talents mpl; **to have a t. for** avoir du talent pour. ◆**talented** a doué, talentueux.

talk [tɔːk] n (words) propos mpl; (gossip) bavardage(s) m(pl); (conversation) conversation f (**about** à propos de); (interview) entretien m; (lecture) exposé m (on sur); (informal) causerie f (on sur); pl (negotiations) pourparlers mpl; **to have a t. with** parler avec; **there's t. of** on parle de; − vi parler (**to** à; **with** avec; **about**, **of** de); (chat) bavarder; **to t. down to s.o.** parler à qn comme à un inférieur; − vt (nonsense) dire; **to t. politics** parler politique; **to t. s.o. into doing/out of doing** persuader qn de faire/de ne pas faire; **to t. over** discuter (de); **to t. s.o. round** persuader qn. ◆**—ing** a (film) parlant; **to give s.o. a talking-to** Fam passer un savon à qn. ◆**talkative** a bavard. ◆**talker** n causeur, -euse mf; **she's a good t.** elle parle bien.

tall [tɔːl] a (-er, -est) (person) grand; (tree,

house etc) haut; **how t. are you?** combien mesures-tu?; a **t. story** Fig une histoire invraisemblable *or* à dormir debout. ◆**tallboy** *n* grande commode *f*. ◆**tallness** *n* (*of person*) grande taille *f*; (*of building etc*) hauteur *f*.

tally ['tælɪ] *vi* correspondre (**with** à).

tambourine [tæmbə'riːn] *n* tambourin *m*.

tame [teɪm] *a* (**-er, -est**) (*animal, bird*) apprivoisé; (*person*) Fig docile; (*book, play*) fade. – *vt* (*animal, bird*) apprivoiser; (*lion, passion*) dompter.

tamper ['tæmpər] *vi* **to t. with** (*lock, car etc*) toucher à; (*text*) altérer.

tampon ['tæmpɒn] *n* tampon *m* hygiénique.

tan [tæn] **1** *n* (*suntan*) bronzage *m*; – *vti* (**-nn-**) bronzer. **2** *a* (*colour*) marron clair *inv*. **3** *vt* (**-nn-**) (*hide*) tanner.

tandem ['tændəm] *n* **1** (*bicycle*) tandem *m*. **2** **in t.** (*to work etc*) en tandem.

tang [tæŋ] *n* (*taste*) saveur *f* piquante; (*smell*) odeur *f* piquante. ◆**tangy** *a* (**-ier, -iest**) piquant.

tangerine [tændʒə'riːn] *n* mandarine *f*.

tangible ['tændʒəb(ə)l] *a* tangible.

tangl/e ['tæŋg(ə)l] *n* enchevêtrement *m*; **to get into a t.** (*of rope*) s'enchevêtrer; (*of hair*) s'emmêler; (*of person*) Fig se mettre dans une situation pas possible. ◆**-ed** *a* enchevêtré; (*hair*) emmêlé; **to get t.** = **to get into a tangle**.

tank [tæŋk] *n* **1** (*for storage of water, fuel etc*) réservoir *m*; (*vat*) cuve *f*; (*fish*) t. aquarium *m*. **2** (*vehicle*) Mil char *m*, tank *m*.

tankard ['tæŋkəd] *n* (*beer mug*) chope *f*.

tanker ['tæŋkər] *n* (*truck*) Aut camion-citerne *m*; (**oil**) **t.** (*ship*) pétrolier *m*.

tantalizing ['tæntəlaɪzɪŋ] *a* (*irrésistiblement*) tentant. ◆**-ly** *adv* d'une manière tentante.

tantamount ['tæntəmaunt] *a* **it's t.** to cela équivaut à.

tantrum ['tæntrəm] *n* accès *m* de colère.

tap [tæp] **1** *n* (*for water*) robinet *m*; **on t.** Fig disponible. **2** *vti* (**-pp-**) frapper légèrement, tapoter; – *n* petit coup *m*; **t. dancing** claquettes *fpl*. **3** *vt* (**-pp-**) (*phone*) placer sur table d'écoute. **4** *vt* (**-pp-**) (*resources*) exploiter.

tape [teɪp] **1** *n* ruban *m*; (**sticky**) **t.** ruban adhésif, **t. measure** mètre *m* (à) ruban; – *vt* (*stick*) coller (*avec du ruban adhésif*). **2** *n* (*for sound recording*) bande *f* (magnétique); (**video**) **t.** bande (vidéo); **t. recorder** magnétophone *m*; – *vt* enregistrer.

taper ['teɪpər] *vi* (*of fingers etc*) s'effiler; **to off** Fig diminuer. **2** *n* (*candle*) Rel cierge

m. ◆**-ed** *a*, ◆**-ing** *a* (*fingers*) fuselé; (*trousers*) à bas étroits.

tapestry ['tæpəstrɪ] *n* tapisserie *f*.

tapioca [tæpɪ'əʊkə] *n* tapioca *m*.

tar [taːr] *n* goudron *m*; – *vt* (**-rr-**) goudronner.

tardy ['taːdɪ] *a* (**-ier, -iest**) (*belated*) tardif; (*slow*) lent.

target ['taːgɪt] *n* cible *f*; Fig objectif *m*; **t. date** date *f* fixée; – *vt* (*aim*) Fig destiner (**at** à); (*aim at*) Fig viser.

tariff ['tærɪf] *n* (*tax*) tarif *m* douanier; (*prices*) tarif *m*.

tarmac ['taːmæk] *n* macadam *m* (goudronné); (*runway*) piste *f*.

tarnish ['taːnɪʃ] *vt* ternir.

tarpaulin [taː'pɔːlɪn] *n* bâche *f* (goudronnée).

tarragon ['tærəgən] *n* Bot Culin estragon *m*.

tarry ['tærɪ] *vi* (*remain*) Lit rester.

tart [taːt] **1** *n* (*pie*) tarte *f*. **2** *a* (**-er, -est**) (*taste, remark*) aigre. **3** *n* (*prostitute*) Pej Fam poule *f*. **4** *vt* **to t. up** Pej Fam (*decorate*) embellir; (*dress*) attifer. ◆**-ness** *n* aigreur *f*.

tartan ['taːt(ə)n] *n* tartan *m*; – *a* écossais.

tartar ['taːtər] *n* **1** (*on teeth*) tartre *m*. **2 t. sauce** sauce *f* tartare.

task [taːsk] *n* tâche *f*; **to take to t.** prendre à partie; **t. force** Mil détachement *m* spécial; Pol commission *f* spéciale.

tassel ['tas(ə)l] *n* (*on clothes etc*) gland *m*.

taste [teɪst] *n* goût *m*; **to get a t. for** prendre goût à; **in good/bad t.** de bon/mauvais goût; **to have a t. of** goûter; goûter à; goûter de; – *vt* (*eat, enjoy*) goûter; (*try, sample*) goûter à; (*make out the taste of*) sentir (le goût de); (*experience*) goûter de; – *vi* **to t. of** *or* **like** avoir un goût de; **to t. delicious**/*etc* avoir un goût délicieux/*etc*; **how does it t.?** comment le trouves-tu?; – *a* **t. bud** papille *f* gustative. ◆**tasteful** *a* de bon goût. ◆**tastefully** *adv* avec goût. ◆**tasteless** *a* (*food etc*) sans goût; (*joke etc*) Fig de mauvais goût. ◆**tasty** *a* (**-ier, -iest**) savoureux.

tat [tæt] *see* **tit 2**.

ta-ta [tæ'taː] *int* Sl au revoir!

tattered ['tætəd] *a* (*clothes*) en lambeaux; (*person*) déguenillé. ◆**tatters** *npl* **in t.** en lambeaux.

tattoo [tæ'tuː] **1** *n* (*pl* **-oos**) (*on body*) tatouage *m*; – *vt* tatouer. **2** *n* (*pl* **-oos**) Mil spectacle *m* militaire.

tatty ['tætɪ] *a* (**-ier, -iest**) (*clothes etc*) Fam miteux.

taught [tɔːt] *see* **teach**.

taunt [tɔːnt] vt railler; – n raillerie f.
◆**—ing** a railleur.

Taurus ['tɔːrəs] n (sign) le Taureau.

taut [tɔːt] a (rope, person etc) tendu.

tavern ['tævən] n taverne f.

tawdry ['tɔːdrɪ] a (-ier, -iest) Pej tape-à-l'œil inv.

tawny ['tɔːnɪ] a (colour) fauve; (port) ambré.

tax¹ [tæks] n taxe f, impôt m; (income) t. impôts mpl (sur le revenu); – a fiscal; t. collector percepteur m; t. relief dégrèvement m (d'impôt); – vt (person, goods) imposer. ◆**taxable** a imposable. ◆**tax-'ation** n (act) imposition f; (taxes) impôts mpl. ◆**tax-free** a exempt d'impôts. ◆**taxman** n (pl -men) Fam percepteur m. ◆**taxpayer** n contribuable mf.

tax² [tæks] vt (patience etc) mettre à l'épreuve; (tire) fatiguer. ◆**—ing** a (journey etc) éprouvant.

taxi ['tæksɪ] **1** n taxi m; t. cab taxi m; t. rank, Am t. stand station f de taxis. **2** vi (of aircraft) rouler au sol.

tea [tiː] n thé m; (snack) goûter m; high t. (afternoon snack) goûter m; to have t. prendre le thé; (afternoon snack) goûter; t. break pause-thé f; t. chest caisse f (à thé); t. cloth (for drying dishes) torchon m; t. set service m à thé; t. towel torchon m; t. teabag n sachet m de thé. ◆**teacup** n tasse f à thé. ◆**tealeaf** n (pl -leaves) feuille f de thé. ◆**teapot** n théière f. ◆**tearoom** n salon m de thé. ◆**teaspoon** n petite cuiller f. ◆**teaspoonful** n cuillerée f à café. ◆**teatime** n l'heure f du thé.

teach [tiːtʃ] vt (pt & pp taught) apprendre (s.o. sth qch à qn, that que); (in school etc) enseigner (s.o. sth qch à qn); to t. s.o. (how) to do apprendre à qn à faire; to t. school Am enseigner; to t. oneself sth apprendre qch tout seul; – vi enseigner. ◆**—ing** n enseignement m; – a (staff) enseignant; (method, material) pédagogique; t. profession enseignement m; (teachers) enseignants mpl; t. qualification diplôme m permettant d'enseigner. ◆**—er** n professeur m; (in primary school) instituteur, -trice mf.

teak [tiːk] n (wood) teck m.

team [tiːm] n Sp équipe f; (of oxen) attelage m; t. mate coéquipier, -ière mf; – vi to t. up faire équipe (with avec). ◆**teamster** n Am routier m. ◆**teamwork** n collaboration f.

tear¹ [teər] n 1 déchirure f; – vt (pt tore, pp torn) (rip) déchirer; (snatch) arracher (from s.o. à qn); torn between Fig tiraillé entre; to t. down (house etc) démolir; to t. away or off

or out (forcefully) arracher; (stub, receipt, stamp etc) détacher; to t. up déchirer; – vi (of cloth etc) se déchirer. **2** vi (pt tore, pp torn) to t. along (rush) aller à toute vitesse.

tear² [tɪər] n larme f; in tears en larmes; close to or near (to) tears au bord des larmes. ◆**tearful** a (eyes, voice) larmoyant; (person) en larmes. ◆**tearfully** adv en pleurant. ◆**teargas** n gaz m lacrymogène.

tearaway ['teərəweɪ] n Fam petit voyou m.

teas/e [tiːz] vt taquiner; (harshly) tourmenter; – n (person) taquin, -ine mf. ◆**—ing** a (remark etc) taquin. ◆**—er** n 1 (person) taquin, -ine mf. **2** (question) Fam colle f.

teat [tiːt] n (of bottle, animal) tétine f.

technical ['teknɪk(ə)l] a technique. ◆**techni'cality** n (detail) détail m technique. ◆**technically** adv techniquement; Fig théoriquement. ◆**tech'nician** n technicien, -ienne mf. ◆**tech'nique** n technique f. ◆**technocrat** n technocrate m. ◆**techno'logical** a technologique. ◆**tech'nology** n technologie f.

teddy ['tedɪ] n t. (bear) ours m (en peluche).

tedious ['tiːdɪəs] a fastidieux. ◆**tediousness** n, ◆**tedium** n ennui m.

teem [tiːm] vi **1** (swarm) grouiller (with de). **2** to t. (with rain) pleuvoir à torrents. ◆**—ing** a **1** (crowd, street etc) grouillant. **2** t. rain pluie f torrentielle.

teenage ['tiːneɪdʒ] a (person, behaviour) adolescent; (fashion) pour adolescents. ◆**teenager** n adolescent, -ente mf. ◆**teens** npl in one's t. adolescent.

teeny (weeny) ['tiːnɪ(wiːnɪ)] a (tiny) Fam minuscule.

tee-shirt ['tiːʃɜːt] n tee-shirt m.

teeter ['tiːtər] vi chanceler.

teeth [tiːθ] see tooth. ◆**teeth/e** [tiːð] vi faire ses dents. ◆**—ing** n dentition f; t. ring anneau m de dentition; t. troubles Fig difficultés fpl de mise en route.

teetotal [tiː'təʊt(ə)l] a, ◆**teetotaller** n (personne f) qui ne boit pas d'alcool.

tele- ['telɪ] pref télé-.

telecommunications [telɪkəmjuːnɪ'keɪʃ(ə)nz] npl télécommunications fpl.

telegram ['telɪgræm] n télégramme m.

telegraph ['telɪgrɑːf] n télégraphe m; – a (wire etc) télégraphique; t. pole poteau m télégraphique.

telepathy [tə'lepəθɪ] n télépathie f.

telephone ['telɪfəʊn] n téléphone m; on the t. (speaking) au téléphone; – a (call, line etc) téléphonique; (directory) du téléphone; (*number*) de téléphone; **t. booth, t. box** cabine *f* téléphonique; – *vi* téléphoner; – *vt* (*message*) téléphoner (**to à**); **to t. s.o.** téléphoner à qn. ◆**te'lephonist** *n* téléphoniste *mf*.

teleprinter ['teliprintər] *n* téléscripteur *m*.

telescope ['teliskəup] *n* télescope *m*. ◆**tele'scopic** *a* (*pictures, aerial, umbrella*) télescopique.

teletypewriter [telɪ'taɪpraɪtər] *n Am* téléscripteur *m*.

televise ['telɪvaɪz] *vt* téléviser. ◆**tele'vision** *n* télévision *f*; (**on** (**the**) **t.** à la télévision; **to watch** (**the**) **t.** regarder la télévision; – *a* (*programme etc*) de télévision; (*serial, report*) télévisé.

telex ['teleks] *n* (*service, message*) télex *m*; – *vt* envoyer par télex.

tell [tel] *vt* (*pt & pp* **told**) dire (**s.o. sth** qch à qn, **that** que); (*story*) raconter; (*future*) prédire; (*distinguish*) distinguer (**from** de); (*know*) savoir; **to t. s.o. to do** dire à qn de faire; **to know how to t. the time** savoir lire l'heure; **to t. the difference** voir la différence (**between** entre); **to t. off** (*scold*) *Fam* gronder; – *vi* dire; (*have an effect*) avoir un effet; (*know*) savoir; **to t. of** *or* **about sth** parler de qch; **to t. on s.o.** *Fam* rapporter sur qn. ◆**-ing** *a* (*smile etc*) révélateur; (*blow*) efficace. ◆**telltale** *n Fam* rapporteur, -euse *mf*.

teller ['telər] *n* (*bank*) **t.** caissier, -ière *mf*.

telly ['telɪ] *n Fam* télé *f*.

temerity [tə'merɪtɪ] *n* témérité *f*.

temp [temp] *n* (*secretary etc*) *Fam* intérimaire *mf*.

temper ['tempər] **1** *n* (*mood, nature*) humeur *f*; (*anger*) colère *f*; **to lose one's t.** se mettre en colère; **in a bad t.** de mauvaise humeur; **to have a** (**bad** *or* **an awful**) **t.** avoir un caractère de cochon. **2** *vt* (*steel*) tremper; *Fig* tempérer.

temperament ['temp(ə)rəmənt] *n* tempérament *m*. ◆**tempera'mental** *a* (*person, machine etc*) capricieux; (*inborn*) inné.

temperance ['temp(ə)rəns] *n* (*in drink*) tempérance *f*.

temperate ['tempərət] *a* (*climate etc*) tempéré.

temperature ['temp(ə)rətʃər] *n* température *f*; **to have a t.** *Med* avoir *or* faire de la température.

tempest ['tempɪst] *n Lit* tempête *f*. ◆**tem'pestuous** *a* (*meeting etc*) orageux.

template ['templət] *n* (*of plastic, metal etc*) *Tex* patron *m*; *Math* trace-courbes *m inv*.

temple ['temp(ə)l] *n* **1** *Rel* temple *m*. **2** *Anat* tempe *f*.

tempo ['tempəʊ] *n* (*pl* -os) tempo *m*.

temporal ['temp(ə)rəl] *a* temporel.

temporary ['temp(ə)rərɪ] *a* provisoire; (*job, worker*) temporaire; (*secretary*) intérimaire.

tempt [tempt] *vt* tenter; **tempted to do** tenté de faire; **to t. s.o. to do** persuader qn de faire. ◆**-ing** *a* tentant. ◆**-ingly** *adv* d'une manière tentante. ◆**temp'tation** *n* tentation *f*.

ten [ten] *a & n* dix (*m*). ◆**tenfold** *a* **t. increase** augmentation *f* par dix; – *adv* **to increase t.** (se) multiplier par dix.

tenable ['tenəb(ə)l] *a* (*argument*) défendable; (*post*) qui peut être occupé.

tenacious [tə'neɪʃəs] *a* tenace. ◆**tenacity** *n* ténacité *f*.

tenant ['tenənt] *n* locataire *nmf*. ◆**tenancy** *n* (*lease*) location *f*; (*period*) occupation *f*.

tend [tend] **1** *vt* (*look after*) s'occuper de. **2** *vi* **to t. to do** avoir tendance à faire; **to t. towards** incliner vers. ◆**tendency** *n* tendance *f* (**to do** à faire).

tendentious [ten'denʃəs] *a Pej* tendancieux.

tender¹ ['tendər] *a* (*delicate, soft, loving*) tendre; (*painful, sore*) sensible. ◆**-ly** *adv* tendrement. ◆**-ness** *n* tendresse *f*; (*soreness*) sensibilité *f*; (*of meat*) tendreté *f*.

tender² ['tendər] **1** *vt* (*offer*) offrir; **to t. one's resignation** donner sa démission. **2** *n* **to be legal t.** (*of money*) avoir cours. **3** *n* (*for services etc*) *Com* soumission *f* (**for** pour).

tendon ['tendən] *n Anat* tendon *m*.

tenement ['tenəmənt] *n* immeuble *m* (de rapport) (*Am dans un quartier pauvre*).

tenet ['tenɪt] *n* principe *m*.

tenner ['tenər] *n Fam* billet *m* de dix livres.

tennis ['tenɪs] *n* tennis *m*; **table t.** tennis de table; **t. court** court *m* (de tennis), tennis *m*.

tenor ['tenər] *n* **1** (*sense, course*) sens *m* général. **2** *Mus* ténor *m*.

tenpin ['tenpɪn] *a* **t. bowling** bowling *m*. ◆**tenpins** *n Am* bowling *m*.

tense [tens] **1** *a* (-er, -est) (*person, muscle, situation*) tendu; – *vt* tendre, crisper; – *vi* **to t. (up)** (*of person, face*) se crisper. **2** *n Gram* temps *m*. ◆**tenseness** *n* tension *f*. ◆**tension** *n* tension *f*.

tent [tent] *n* tente *f*.

tentacle ['tentək(ə)l] *n* tentacule *m*.

tentative ['tentətɪv] *a* (*not definite*) provisoire; (*hesitant*) timide. ◆**-ly** *adv* provisoirement; timidement.

tenterhooks ['tentəhʊks] *npl* **on t.** (*anxious*) sur des charbons ardents.

tenth [tenθ] *a* & *n* dixième (*mf*); **a t.** un dixième.

tenuous ['tenjʊəs] *a* (*link, suspicion etc*) ténu.

tenure ['tenjər] *n* (*in job*) période *f* de jouissance; (*job security*) *Am* titularisation *f*.

tepid ['tepɪd] *a* (*liquid*) & *Fig* tiède.

term [tɜːm] *n* (*word, limit*) terme *m*; (*period*) période *f*; *Sch Univ* trimestre *m*; (*semester*) *Am* semestre *m*; *pl* (*conditions*) conditions *fpl*; (*prices*) *Com* prix *mpl*; **t. (of office)** *Pol* mandat *m*; **easy terms** *Fin* facilités *fpl* de paiement; **on good/bad terms** en bons/mauvais termes (**with s.o.** avec qn); **to be on close terms** être intime (**with** avec); **in terms of** (*speaking of*) sur le plan de; **in real terms** dans la pratique; **to come to terms with** (*person*) tomber d'accord avec; (*situation etc*) *Fig* faire face à; **in the long/short t.** à long/court terme; **at (full) t.** (*baby*) à terme; − *vt* (*name, call*) appeler.

terminal ['tɜːmɪn(ə)l] **1** *n* (*of computer*) terminal *m*; *El* borne *f*; (**air**) **t.** aérogare *f*; (**oil**) **t.** terminal *m* (pétrolier). **2** *a* (*patient, illness*) incurable; (*stage*) terminal. −**ly** *adv* **t. ill** (*patient*) incurable.

terminate ['tɜːmɪneɪt] *vt* mettre fin à; (*contract*) résilier; (*pregnancy*) interrompre; − *vi* se terminer. ◆**termi'nation** *n* fin *f*; résiliation *f*; interruption *f*.

terminology [tɜːmɪ'nɒlədʒɪ] *n* terminologie *f*.

terminus ['tɜːmɪnəs] *n* terminus *m*.

termite ['tɜːmaɪt] *n* (*insect*) termite *m*.

terrace ['terɪs] *n* terrasse *f*; (*houses*) maisons *fpl* en bande; **the terraces** *Sp* les gradins *mpl*. ◆**terraced** *a* **t. house** maison *f* attenante aux maisons voisines.

terracota [terə'kɒtə] *n* terre *f* cuite.

terrain [tə'reɪn] *n* *Mil Geol* terrain *m*.

terrestrial [tə'restrɪəl] *a* terrestre.

terrible ['terəb(ə)l] *a* affreux, terrible. ◆**terribly** *adv* (*badly*) affreusement; (*very*) terriblement.

terrier ['terɪər] *n* (*dog*) terrier *m*.

terrific [tə'rɪfɪk] *a* *Fam* (*extreme*) terrible; (*excellent*) formidable, terrible. ◆**terrifically** *adv* *Fam* (*extremely*) terriblement; (*extremely well*) terriblement bien.

terrify ['terɪfaɪ] *vt* terrifier; **to be terrified of** avoir très peur de. ◆−**ing** *a* terrifiant. ◆−**ingly** *adv* épouvantablement.

territory ['terɪtərɪ] *n* territoire *m*. ◆**terri'torial** *a* territorial.

terror ['terər] *n* terreur *f*; (*child*) *Fam* polisson, -onne *mf*. ◆**terrorism** *n* terrorisme

m. ◆**terrorist** *n* & *a* terroriste (*mf*). ◆**terrorize** *vt* terroriser.

terry(cloth) ['terɪ(klɒθ)] *n* tissu-éponge *m*.

terse [tɜːs] *a* laconique.

tertiary ['tɜːʃərɪ] *a* tertiaire.

Terylene® ['terɪliːn] *n* tergal® *m*.

test [test] *vt* (*try*) essayer; (*examine*) examiner; (*analyse*) analyser; (*product, intelligence*) tester; (*pupil*) *Sch* faire subir une interrogation à; (*nerves, courage etc*) *Fig* éprouver; − *n* (*trial*) test *m*, essai *m*; examen *m*; analyse *f*; *Sch* interrogation *f*, test *m*; (*of courage etc*) *Fig* épreuve *f*; **driving t.** (examen *m* du) permis *m* de conduire; − *a* (*pilot, flight*) d'essai; **t. case** *Jur* affaire-test *f*; **t. match** *Sp* match *m* international; **t. tube** éprouvette *f*; **t. tube baby** bébé *m* éprouvette.

testament ['testəmənt] *n* testament *m*; (*proof, tribute*) témoignage *m*; **Old/New T.** *Rel* Ancien/Nouveau Testament.

testicle ['testɪk(ə)l] *n* *Anat* testicule *m*.

testify ['testɪfaɪ] *vi* *Jur* témoigner (**against** contre); **to t. to sth** (*of person, event etc*) témoigner de qch; − *vt* **to t. that** *Jur* témoigner que. ◆**testi'monial** *n* références *fpl*, recommandation *f*. ◆**testimony** *n* témoignage *m*.

testy ['testɪ] *a* (-ier, -iest) irritable.

tetanus ['tetənəs] *n* *Med* tétanos *m*.

tête-à-tête [teɪtɑː'teɪt] *n* tête-à-tête *m inv*.

tether ['teðər] **1** *vt* (*fasten*) attacher. **2** *n* **at the end of one's t.** à bout de nerfs.

text [tekst] *n* texte *m*. ◆**textbook** *n* manuel *m*.

textile ['tekstaɪl] *a* & *n* textile (*m*).

texture ['tekstʃər] *n* (*of fabric, cake etc*) texture *f*; (*of paper, wood*) grain *m*.

Thames [temz] *n* **the T.** la Tamise *f*.

than [ðæn, *stressed* ðæn] *conj* **1** que; **happier t.** plus heureux que; **he has more t. you** il en a plus que toi; **fewer oranges t. plums** moins d'oranges que de prunes. **2** (*with numbers*) de; **more t. six** plus de six.

thank [θæŋk] *vt* remercier (**for sth** de qch, **for doing** d'avoir fait); **t. you** merci (**for sth** pour *or* de qch, **for doing** d'avoir fait); **no, t. you** (non) merci; **t. God, t. heavens, t. goodness** Dieu merci; − *npl* remerciements *mpl*; **thanks to** (*because of*) grâce à; (**many**) **thanks!** merci (beaucoup)! ◆**thankful** *a* reconnaissant (**for** de); **t. that** bien heureux que (+ *sub*). ◆**thankfully** *adv* (*gratefully*) avec reconnaissance; (*happily*) heureusement. ◆**thankless** *a* ingrat. ◆**Thanksgiving** *n* **T. (day)** (*holiday*) *Am* jour *m* d'action de grâce(s).

that [ðət, stressed ðæt] **1** conj que; **to say t.** dire que. **2** rel pron (subject) qui; (object) que; **the boy t. left** le garçon qui est parti; **the book I read** le livre que j'ai lu; **the carpet I put it on** (with prep) le tapis sur lequel je l'ai mis; **the house t. she told me about** la maison dont elle m'a parlé; **the day/morning t. she arrived** le jour/matin où elle est arrivée. **3** dem a (pl see **those**) ce, cet (before vowel or mute h), cette; (opposed to 'this') ... + -là; **t. day** ce jour-là; **t. man** cet homme; cet homme-là; **t. girl** cette fille; cette fille-là. **4** dem pron (pl see **those**) ça, cela; ce; **t. (one)** celui-là m, celle-là f; **give me t.** donne-moi ça or cela; **I prefer t. (one)** je préfère celui-là; **before t.** avant ça or cela; **t.'s right** c'est juste; **who's t.?** qui est-ce?; **t.'s the house** c'est la maison; (pointing) voilà la maison; **what do you mean by t.?** qu'entends-tu par là; **t. is (to say)** ... c'est-à-dire ... **5** adv (so) Fam si; **not t. good** pas si bon; **t. high** (pointing) haut comme ça; **t. much** (to cost, earn etc) (au)tant que ça.

thatch [θætʃ] n chaume m. ◆**thatched** a (roof) de chaume; **t. cottage** chaumière f.

thaw [θɔː] n dégel m; — vi dégeler; (of snow) fondre; **it's thawing** Met ça dégèle; — **to t. (out)** (of person) Fig se dégeler; — vt (ice) dégeler, faire fondre; (food) faire dégeler; (snow) faire fondre.

the [ðə, before vowel ðɪ, stressed ðiː] def art le, l', la, pl les; **t. roof** le toit; **t. man** l'homme; **t. moon** la lune; **t. orange** l'orange; **t. boxes** les boîtes; **the smallest** le plus petit; **of t., from t.** du, de l', de la, pl des; **to t., at t.** au, à l', à la, pl aux; **Elizabeth t. Second** Élisabeth deux; **all t. better** d'autant mieux.

theatre [ˈθɪətər] n (place, art) & Mil théâtre m. ◆**theatregoer** n amateur m de théâtre. ◆**the'atrical** a théâtral; **t. company** troupe f de théâtre.

theft [θeft] n vol m.

their [ðeər] poss a leur, pl leurs; **t. house** leur maison f. ◆**theirs** [ðeəz] poss pron le leur, la leur, pl les leurs; **this book is t.** ce livre est à eux or est le leur; **a friend of t.** un ami à eux.

them [ðəm, stressed ðem] pron les; (after prep etc) eux mpl, elles fpl; **(to) t.** (indirect) leur; **I see t.** je les vois; **I give (to) t.** je leur donne; **with t.** avec eux, avec elles; **ten of t.** dix d'entre eux, dix d'entre elles; **all of t.** tous, toutes. ◆**them'selves** pron eux-mêmes mpl, elles-mêmes fpl; (reflexive) se, s'; (after prep etc) eux mpl, elles fpl;

they wash t. ils se lavent, elles se lavent; **they think of t.** ils pensent à eux, elles pensent à elles.

theme [θiːm] n thème m; **t. song** or **tune** Cin TV chanson f principale.

then [ðen] **1** adv (at that time) alors, à ce moment-là; (next) ensuite, puis; **from t. on** dès lors; **before t.** avant cela; **until t.** jusque-là, jusqu'alors; — **a the t. mayor/etc** le maire/etc d'alors. **2** conj (therefore) donc, alors.

theology [θɪˈɒlədʒɪ] n théologie f. ◆**theo'logical** a théologique. ◆**theo'logian** n théologien m.

theorem [ˈθɪərəm] n théorème m.

theory [ˈθɪərɪ] n théorie f; **in t.** en théorie. ◆**theo'retical** a théorique. ◆**theo-'retically** adv théoriquement. ◆**theorist** n théoricien, -ienne mf.

therapy [ˈθerəpɪ] n thérapeutique f. ◆**thera'peutic** a thérapeutique.

there [ðeər] adv là; (down or over) là-bas; **on t.** là-dessus; **she'll be t.** elle sera là, elle y sera; **t. is, t. are** il y a; (pointing) voilà; **t. he is** le voilà; **t. she is** la voilà; **t. they are** les voilà; **that man t.** cet homme-là; **t. (you are)!** (take this) tenez!; **t., (t.,) don't cry!** allons, allons, ne pleure pas! ◆**therea-'bout(s)** adv par là; (in amount) à peu près. ◆**there'after** adv après cela. ◆**thereby** adv de ce fait. ◆**therefore** adv donc. ◆**thereu'pon** adv sur ce.

thermal [ˈθɜːm(ə)l] a (energy, unit) thermique; (springs) thermal; (underwear) tribo-électrique, en thermolactyl®.

thermometer [θəˈmɒmɪtər] n thermomètre m.

thermonuclear [θɜːməʊˈnjuːklɪər] a thermonucléaire.

Thermos® [ˈθɜːməs] n **T. (flask)** thermos® m or f.

thermostat [ˈθɜːməstæt] n thermostat m.

thesaurus [θɪˈsɔːrəs] n dictionnaire m de synonymes.

these [ðiːz] **1** dem a (sing see **this**) ces; (opposed to 'those') ... + -ci; **t. men** ces hommes; ces hommes-ci. **2** dem pron (sing see **this**) **t. (ones)** ceux-ci mpl, celles-ci fpl; **t. are my friends** ce sont mes amis.

thesis, pl **theses** [ˈθiːsɪs, ˈθiːsiːz] n thèse f.

they [ðeɪ] pron **1** ils mpl, elles fpl; (stressed) eux mpl, elles fpl; **t. go** ils vont, elles vont; **t. are doctors** ce sont des médecins. **2** (people in general) on; **t. say** on dit.

thick [θɪk] a (-er, -est) épais; (stupid) Fam lourd; **to be t.** (of friends) Fam être très liés; — adv (to grow) dru; (to spread) en couche épaisse; — n **in the t. of** (battle etc) au plus gros de. ◆**thicken** vt épaissir; – vi s'épaissir. ◆**thickly** adv (to grow, fall) dru; (to spread) en couche épaisse; (populated, wooded) très. ◆**thickness** n épaisseur f.

thicket ['θɪkɪt] n (trees) fourré m.

thickset [θɪk'set] a (person) trapu. ◆**thick-skinned** a (person) dur, peu sensible.

thief [θiːf] n (pl thieves) voleur, -euse mf. ◆**thiev/e** vti voler. ◆**-ing** n vol m.

thigh [θaɪ] n cuisse f. ◆**thighbone** n fémur m.

thimble ['θɪmb(ə)l] n dé m (à coudre).

thin [θɪn] a (thinner, thinnest) (slice, paper etc) mince; (person, leg) maigre, mince; (soup) peu épais; (hair, audience) clairsemé; (powder) fin; (excuse, profit) Fig maigre, mince; – adv (to spread) en couche mince; – vt (-nn-) to t. (down) (paint etc) délayer; – vi to t. out (of crowd, mist) s'éclaircir. ◆**-ly** adv (to spread) en couche mince; (populated, wooded) peu; (disguised) à peine. ◆**-ness** n minceur f; maigreur f.

thing [θɪŋ] n chose f; one's things (belongings, clothes) ses affaires fpl; it's a funny t. c'est drôle; poor little t.! pauvre petit!; that's (just) the t. voilà (exactement) ce qu'il faut; how are things?, Fam how's things? comment (ça) va?; I'll think things over j'y réfléchirai; for one t. ..., and for another t. d'abord ... et ensuite; tea things (set) service m à thé; (dishes) vaisselle f. ◆**thingummy** n Fam truc m, machin m.

think [θɪŋk] vi (pt & pp thought) penser (about, of à); to t. (carefully) réfléchir (about, of à); to t. of doing penser or songer à faire; to t. highly of, t. a lot of penser beaucoup de bien de; she doesn't t. much of it ça ne lui dit pas grand-chose; to t. better of it se raviser; I can't t. of it je n'arrive pas à m'en souvenir; – vt penser (that que); I t. so je pense or crois que oui; what do you t. of him? que penses-tu de lui?; I thought it difficult je l'ai trouvé difficile; to t. out or through (reply etc) réfléchir sérieusement à, peser; to t. over réfléchir à; to t. up (invent) inventer, avoir l'idée de; – n to have a t. Fam réfléchir (about à); – a t. tank comité m d'experts. ◆**-ing** a (person) intelligent; – n (opinion) opinion f; to my t. à mon avis. ◆**-er** n penseur, -euse mf.

thin-skinned [θɪn'skɪnd] a (person) susceptible.

third [θɜːd] a troisième; t. person or party tiers m; t.-party insurance assurance f au tiers; T. World Tiers-Monde m; – n

troisième mf; a t. (fraction) un tiers; – adv (in race) troisième. ◆**-ly** adv troisièmement.

third-class [θɜːd'klɑːs] a de troisième classe. ◆**t.-rate** a (très) inférieur.

thirst [θɜːst] n soif f (for de). ◆**thirsty** a (-ier, -iest) a to be or feel t. avoir soif; to make t. donner soif à; t. for (power etc) Fig assoiffé de.

thirteen [θɜː'tiːn] a & n treize (m). ◆**thirteenth** a & n treizième (mf). ◆**'thirtieth** a & n trentième (mf). ◆**'thirty** a & n trente (m).

this [ðɪs] 1 dem a (pl see these) ce, cet (before vowel or mute h), cette; (opposed to 'that') ... + -ci; t. book ce livre; ce livre-ci; t. man cet homme; cet homme-ci; t. photo cette photo; cette photo-ci. 2 dem pron (pl see these) ceci; ce; t. (one) celui-ci m, celle-ci f; give me t. donne-moi ceci; I prefer t. (one) je préfère celui-ci; before t. avant ceci; who's t.? qui est-ce?; t. is Paul c'est Paul; t. is the house voici la maison. 3 adv (so) Fam si, t. high (pointing) haut comme ceci; t. far (until now) jusqu'ici.

thistle ['θɪs(ə)l] n chardon m.

thorn [θɔːn] n épine f. ◆**thorny** a (-ier, -iest) (bush, problem etc) épineux.

thorough ['θʌrə] a (painstaking, careful) minutieux, consciencieux; (knowledge, examination) approfondi; (rogue, liar) fieffé; (disaster) complet; to give sth a t. washing laver qch à fond. ◆**-ly** adv (completely) tout à fait; (painstakingly) avec minutie; (to know, clean, wash) à fond. ◆**-ness** n minutie f; (depth) profondeur f.

thoroughbred ['θʌrəbred] n (horse) pur-sang m inv.

thoroughfare ['θʌrəfeər] n (street) rue f; 'no t.' passage interdit.

those [ðəʊz] 1 dem a (sing see that) ces; (opposed to 'these') ... + -là; t. men ces hommes; ces hommes-là. 2 dem pron (sing see that) t. (ones) ceux-là mpl, celles-là fpl; t. are my friends ce sont mes amis.

though [ðəʊ] 1 conj (even) t. bien que (+ sub); as t. comme si; strange t. it may seem si étrange que cela puisse paraître. 2 adv (nevertheless) cependant, quand même.

thought [θɔːt] see think; – n pensée f; (idea) idée f, pensée f; (reflection) t. réflexion f; without (a) t. for sans penser à; to have second thoughts changer d'avis; on second thoughts, Am on second t. à la réflexion. ◆**thoughtful** a (pensive) pensif; (serious) sérieux; (considerate, kind) gentil, prévenant. ◆**thoughtfully** adv (considerately) gentiment. ◆**thoughtfulness** n gentillesse f, prévenance f. ◆**thoughtless** a (towards others) désinvolte; (careless) étourdi. ◆**thoughtlessly** adv (carelessly) étourdiment; (inconsiderately) avec désinvolture.

thousand ['θaʊzənd] a & n mille a & m inv; a t. pages mille pages; **two t. pages** deux mille pages; **thousands of** des milliers de.

thrash [θræʃ] **1** vt **to t. s.o.** rouer qn de coups; (defeat) écraser qn; **to t. out** (plan etc) élaborer (à force de discussions). **2** vi to t. **about** (struggle) se débattre. ◆**—ing** n (beating) correction f.

thread [θred] n (yarn) & Fig fil m; (of screw) pas m; — vt (needle, beads) enfiler; **to t. one's way** Fig se faufiler (**through** (the crowd/etc parmi la foule/etc). ◆**threadbare** a élimé, râpé.

threat [θret] n menace f (to à). ◆**threaten** vi menacer; — vt menacer (**to do** de faire, with sth de qch). ◆**threatening** a menaçant. ◆**threateningly** adv (to say) d'un ton menaçant.

three [θriː] a & n trois (m); **t.-piece suite** canapé m et deux fauteuils. ◆**threefold** a triple; — adv to increase t. tripler. ◆**three-'wheeler** n (tricycle) tricycle m; (car) voiture f à trois roues.

thresh [θreʃ] vt Agr battre.

threshold ['θreʃhəʊld] n seuil m.

threw [θruː] see throw.

thrift [θrɪft] n (virtue) économie f. ◆**thrifty** a (-ier, -iest) économe.

thrill [θrɪl] n émotion f, frisson m; **to get a t. out of doing** prendre plaisir à faire; — vt (delight) réjouir; (excite) faire frissonner. ◆**—ed** a ravi (with sth de qch, **to do** de faire). ◆**—ing** a passionnant. ◆**—er** n film m or roman m à suspense.

thriv/e [θraɪv] vi (of business, person, plant etc) prospérer; **he or she thrives on hard work** le travail lui profite. ◆**—ing** a prospère, florissant.

throat [θrəʊt] n gorge f; **to have a sore t.** avoir mal à la gorge. ◆**throaty** a (voice) rauque; (of person) à la voix rauque.

throb [θrɒb] vi (-bb-) (of heart) palpiter; (of engine) vrombir; Fig vibrer; **my finger is throbbing** mon doigt me fait des élancements; — n palpitation f; vrombissement m; élancement m.

throes [θrəʊz] npl **in the t. of** au milieu de; (illness, crisis) en proie à; **in the t. of doing** en train de faire.

thrombosis [θrɒm'bəʊsɪs] n (coronary) Med infarctus m.

throne [θrəʊn] n trône m.

throng [θrɒŋ] n foule f; — vi (rush) affluer; — vt (street, station etc) se presser dans; **thronged with people** noir de monde.

throttle ['θrɒt(ə)l] **1** n Aut accélérateur m. **2** vt (strangle) étrangler.

through [θruː] prep (place) à travers; (time) pendant; (means) par; (thanks to) grâce à; **to go or get t.** (forest etc) traverser; (hole etc) passer par; **to let t.** laisser passer; **all or right t.** (to the end) jusqu'au bout; **French t. and t.** français jusqu'au bout des ongles; **to be t.** (finished) Am Fam avoir fini; **we're t.** Am Fam c'est fini entre nous; **I'm t. with the book** Am Fam je n'ai plus besoin du livre; **t. to or till** jusqu'à; **I'll put you t. (to him)** Tel je vous le passe; — a (train, traffic, ticket) direct; **'no t. road'** (no exit) 'voie sans issue'. ◆**through'out** prep **t. the neighbourhood/etc** dans tout le quartier/etc; **t. the day/etc** (time) pendant toute la journée/etc; — adv (everywhere) partout; (all the time) tout le temps. ◆**throughway** n Am autoroute f.

throw [θrəʊ] n (of stone etc) jet m; Sp lancer m; (of dice) coup m; (turn) tour m; — vt (pt threw, pp thrown) jeter (**to, at** à); (stone, ball) lancer, jeter; (hurl) projeter; (of horse) désarçonner (qn); (party, reception) donner; (baffle) Fam dérouter; **to t. away** (discard) jeter; (ruin, waste) Fig gâcher; **to t. back** (ball) renvoyer (**to** à); (one's head) rejeter en arrière; **to t. in** (include as extra) Fam donner en prime; **to t. off** (get rid of) se débarrasser de; **to t. out** (discard) jeter; (suggestion) repousser; (expel) mettre (qn) à la porte; (distort) fausser (calcul etc); **to t. over** abandonner; **to t. up** (job) Fam laisser tomber; — vi **to t. up** (vomit) Sl dégobiller. ◆**throwaway** a (disposable) à jeter, jetable.

thrush [θrʌʃ] n (bird) grive f.

thrust [θrʌst] n (push) poussée f; (stab) coup m; (of argument) poids m; (dynamism) allant m; — vt (pt & pp thrust) (push) pousser; (put) mettre (**into** dans); **to t. sth into sth** (stick, knife, pin) enfoncer qch dans qch; **to t. sth/s.o. upon s.o.** Fig imposer qch/qn à qn.

thud [θʌd] n bruit m sourd.

thug [θʌg] n voyou m.

thumb [θʌm] *n* pouce *m*; **with a t. index** (*book*) à onglets; – *vt* **to t. (through)** (*book etc*) feuilleter; **to t. a lift** *or* **a ride** *Fam* faire du stop. ◆**thumbtack** *n Am* punaise *f*.

thump [θʌmp] *vt* (*person*) frapper, cogner sur; (*table*) taper sur; **to t. one's head** (*on door etc*) se cogner la tête (**on** contre); – *vi* frapper, cogner (**on** sur); (*of heart*) battre à grands coups; – *n* (grand) coup *m*; (*noise*) bruit *m* sourd. ◆–**ing** *a* (*huge, great*) Fam énorme.

thunder ['θʌndər] *n* tonnerre *m*; – *vi* (*of weather, person, guns*) tonner; **it's thundering** Met il tonne; **to t. past** passer (vite) dans un bruit de tonnerre. ◆**thunderbolt** *n* (*event*) Fig coup *m* de tonnerre. ◆**thunderclap** *n* coup *m* de tonnerre. ◆**thunderstorm** *n* orage *m*. ◆**thunderstruck** *a* abasourdi.

Thursday ['θɜːzdɪ] *n* jeudi *m*.

thus [ðʌs] *adv* ainsi.

thwart [θwɔːt] *vt* (*plan, person*) contrecarrer.

thyme [taɪm] *n Bot Culin* thym *m*.

thyroid ['θaɪrɔɪd] *a* & *n Anat* thyroïde (*f*).

tiara [tɪ'ɑːrə] *n* (*of woman*) diadème *m*.

tic [tɪk] *n* (*in face, limbs*) tic *m*.

tick [tɪk] **1** *n* (*of clock*) tic-tac *m*; – *vi* faire tic-tac; **to t. over** (*of engine, factory, business*) tourner au ralenti. **2** *n* (*on list*) coche *f*, trait *m*; – *vt* **to t. (off)** cocher; **to t. off** (*reprimand*) Fam passer un savon à. **3** *n* (*moment*) Fam instant *m*. **4** *n* (*insect*) tique *f*. **5** *adv* **on t.** (*on credit*) Fam à crédit. ◆–**ing** *n* (*of clock*) tic-tac *m*; **to give s.o. a t.-off** Fam passer un savon à qn.

ticket ['tɪkɪt] *n* billet *m*; (*for tube, bus, cloakroom*) ticket *m*; (*for library*) carte *f*; (*fine*) Aut Fam contravention *f*, contredanse *f*; Pol Am liste *f*; (*price*) étiquette *f*; **t. collector** contrôleur, -euse *mf*; **t. holder** personne *f* munie d'un billet; **t. office** guichet *m*.

tickle ['tɪk(ə)l] *vt* chatouiller; (*amuse*) Fig amuser; – *n* chatouillement *m*. ◆**ticklish** *a* (*person*) chatouilleux; (*fabric*) qui chatouille; (*problem*) Fig délicat.

tidbit ['tɪdbɪt] *n* (*food*) Am bon morceau *m*.

tiddlywinks ['tɪdlɪwɪŋks] *n* jeu *m* de puce.

tide [taɪd] **1** *n* marée *f*; **against the t.** Nau & Fig à contre-courant; **the rising t. of discontent** le mécontentement grandissant. **2** *vt* **to t. s.o. over** (*help out*) dépanner qn. ◆**tidal** *a* (*river*) qui a une marée; **t. wave** raz-de-marée *m inv*; (*in public opinion etc*) Fig vague *f* de fond. ◆**tidemark** *n* Fig Hum ligne *f* de crasse.

tidings ['taɪdɪŋz] *npl* Lit nouvelles *fpl*.

tidy ['taɪdɪ] *a* (**-ier, -iest**) (*place, toys etc*) bien rangé; (*clothes, looks*) soigné; (*methodical*) ordonné; (*amount, sum*) Fam joli, bon; **to make t.** ranger; – *vt* **to t. (up** *or* **away)** ranger; **to t. oneself (up)** s'arranger; **to t. out** (*cupboard etc*) vider; – *vi* **to t. up** ranger. ◆**tidily** *adv* avec soin. ◆**tidiness** *n* (bon) ordre *m*; (*care*) soin *m*.

tie [taɪ] *n* (*string, strap etc*) & Fig lien *m*, attache *f*; (*necktie*) cravate *f*; (*sleeper*) Rail Am traverse *f*; Sp égalité *f* de points; (*match*) match *m* nul; – *vt* (*fasten*) attacher, lier (**to** à); (*a knot*) faire (**in** à); (*shoe*) lacer; (*link*) lier (**to** à); **to t. down** attacher; **to t. s.o. down to** (*date, place etc*) obliger qn à accepter; **to t. up** attacher; (*money*) Fig immobiliser; **to be tied up** (*linked*) être lié (**with** avec); (*busy*) Fam être occupé; – *vi* Sp finir à égalité de points; Fb faire match nul; (*in race*) être ex aequo; **to t. in with** (*tally with*) se rapporter à. ◆**t.-up** *n* (*link*) lien *m*; (*traffic jam*) Am Fam bouchon *m*.

tier [tɪər] *n* (*seats*) Sp Th gradin *m*; (*of cake*) étage *m*.

tiff [tɪf] *n* petite querelle *f*.

tiger ['taɪgər] *n* tigre *m*. ◆**tigress** *n* tigresse *f*.

tight [taɪt] *a* (**-er, -est**) (*rope etc*) raide; (*closely-fitting clothing*) ajusté, (*fitting too closely*) (trop) étroit, (trop) serré; (*drawer, lid*) dur; (*control*) strict; (*schedule, credit*) serré; (*drunk*) Fam gris; **a t. spot** *or* **corner** Fam une situation difficile; **it's a t. squeeze** il y a juste la place; **to sit t.** ne pas bouger. – *adv* (*to hold, shut, sleep*) bien; (*to squeeze*) fort; **to squeeze t.** serrer fort. ◆**tighten** *vt* **to t. (up)** (*rope*) tendre; (*bolt etc*) (res)serrer; (*security*) Fig renforcer; – *vi* **to t. up on** se montrer plus strict à l'égard de. ◆**tightly** *adv* (*to hold*) bien; (*to squeeze*) fort; **t. knit** (*close*) très uni. ◆**tightness** *n* (*of garment*) étroitesse *f*; (*of control*) rigueur *f*; (*of rope*) tension *f*.

tight-fitting [taɪt'fɪtɪŋ] *a* (*garment*) ajusté. ◆**tightfisted** *a* avare. ◆'**tightrope** *n* corde *f* raide. ◆'**tightwad** *n* (*miser*) Am Fam grippe-sou *m*.

tights [taɪts] *npl* (*garment*) collant *m*; (*for dancer etc*) justaucorps *m*.

til/e [taɪl] *n* (*on roof*) tuile *f*; (*on wall or floor*) carreau *m*; – *vt* (*wall, floor*) carreler. ◆–**ed** *a* (*roof*) de tuiles; (*wall, floor*) carrelé.

till [tɪl] **1** *prep* & *conj* = **until**. **2** *n* (*for money*) caisse *f* (enregistreuse). **3** *vt* (*land*) Agr cultiver.

tilt [tɪlt] *vti* pencher; – *n* inclinaison *f*; **(at) full t.** à toute vitesse.

timber ['tɪmbər] *n* bois *m* (de construction); (*trees*) arbres *mpl*; – *a* de ou en bois. ◆**timberyard** *n* entrepôt *m* de bois.

time [taɪm] *n* temps *m*; (*point in time*) moment *m*; (*epoch*) époque *f*; (*on clock*) heure *f*; (*occasion*) fois *f*; *Mus* mesure *f*; **in (the course of) t., with (the passage of) t.** avec le temps; **some of the t.** (*not always*) une partie du temps; **most of the t.** la plupart du temps; **in a year's t.** dans un an; **a long t.** longtemps; **a short t.** peu de temps, un petit moment; **full-t.** à plein temps; **part-t.** à temps partiel; **to have a good** *or* **a nice t.** (*fun*) s'amuser (bien); **to have a hard t. doing** avoir du mal à faire; **t. off** du temps libre; **in no t. (at all)** en un rien de temps; **(just) in t.** (*to arrive*) à temps (**for** sth pour qch, **to do** pour faire); **in my t.** (*formerly*) de mon temps; **from t. to t.** de temps en temps; **what t. is it?** quelle heure est-il?; **the right** *or* **exact t.** l'heure *f* exacte; **on t.** à l'heure; **at the same t.** en même temps (**as** que); (*simultaneously*) à la fois; **for the t. being** pour le moment; **at the t.** à ce moment-là; **at the present t.** à l'heure actuelle; **at times** par moments, parfois; **at one t.** à un moment donné; **this t. tomorrow** demain à cette heure-ci; **(the) next t. you come** la prochaine fois que tu viendras; **(the) last t.** la dernière fois; **one at a t.** un à un; **t. and again** maintes fois; **ten times ten** dix fois dix; **t. bomb** bombe *f* à retardement; **t. lag** décalage *m*; **t. limit** délai *m*; **t. zone** fuseau *m* horaire; – *vt* (*sportsman, worker etc*) chronométrer; (*programme, operation*) minuter; (*choose the time of*) choisir le moment de; (*to plan*) prévoir. ◆**timing** *n* chronométrage *m*; minutage *m*; (*judgement of artist etc*) rythme *m*; **the t. of** (*time*) le moment choisi pour. ◆**time-consuming** *a* qui prend du temps. ◆**time-honoured** *a* consacré (par l'usage).

timeless ['taɪmləs] *a* éternel.

timely ['taɪmlɪ] *a* à propos. ◆**timeliness** *n* à-propos *m*.

timer ['taɪmər] *n* *Culin* minuteur *m*, compte-minutes *m inv*; (*sand-filled*) sablier *m*; (*on machine*) minuteur *m*; (*to control lighting*) minuterie *f*.

timetable ['taɪmteɪb(ə)l] *n* horaire *m*; (*in school*) emploi *m* du temps.

timid ['tɪmɪd] *a* (*shy*) timide; (*fearful*) timoré. ◆**-ly** *adv* timidement.

tin [tɪn] *n* étain *m*; (*tinplate*) fer-blanc *m*; (*can*) boîte *f*; (*for baking*) moule *m*; **t. can** boîte *f* (en fer-blanc); **t. opener** ouvre-boîtes *m inv*; **t. soldier** soldat *m* de plomb. ◆**tinfoil** *n* papier *m* d'aluminium, papier alu. ◆**tinned** *a* en boîte. ◆**tinplate** *n* fer-blanc *m*.

tinge [tɪndʒ] *n* teinte *f*. ◆**tinged** *a* **t. with** (*pink etc*) teinté de; (*jealousy etc*) *Fig* empreint de.

tingle ['tɪŋg(ə)l] *vi* picoter; **it's tingling** ça me picote. ◆**tingly** *a* (*feeling*) de picotement.

tinker ['tɪŋkər] *n* – *vi* **t.** (**about**) with bricoler.

tinkle ['tɪŋk(ə)l] *vi* tinter; – *n* tintement *m*; **to give s.o. a t.** (*phone s.o.*) *Fam* passer un coup de fil à qn.

tinny ['tɪnɪ] *a* (*-ier, -iest*) (*sound*) métallique; (*vehicle, machine*) de mauvaise qualité.

tinsel ['tɪns(ə)l] *n* clinquant *m*, guirlandes *fpl* de Noël.

tint [tɪnt] *n* teinte *f*; (*for hair*) shampooing *m* colorant; – *vt* (*paper, glass*) teinter.

tiny ['taɪnɪ] *a* (*-ier, -iest*) tout petit.

tip [tɪp] **1** *n* (*end*) bout *m*; (*pointed*) pointe *f*. **2** *n* (*money*) pourboire *m*; – *vt* (*-pp-*) donner un pourboire à. **3** *n* (*advice*) conseil *m*; (*information*) & *Sp* tuyau *m*; **to get a t.-off** se faire tuyauter; – *vt* (*-pp-*) **t. a horse/etc** donner un cheval/*etc* gagnant; **to t. off** (*police*) prévenir. **4** *n* (*for rubbish*) décharge *f*; – *vt* (*-pp-*) **to t.** (**up** *or* **over**) (*tilt*) incliner, pencher; (*overturn*) faire basculer; **to t.** (**out**) (*liquid, load*) déverser (**into** dans); – *vi* **to t.** (**up** *or* **over**) (*tilt*) pencher; (*overturn*) basculer.

tipped [tɪpt] *a* **t. cigarette** cigarette *f* (à bout) filtre.

tipple ['tɪp(ə)l] *vi* (*drink*) *Fam* picoler.

tipsy ['tɪpsɪ] *a* (*-ier, -iest*) (*drunk*) gai, pompette.

tiptoe ['tɪptəʊ] *n* **on t.** sur la pointe des pieds; – *vi* marcher sur la pointe des pieds.

tiptop ['tɪptɒp] *a* *Fam* excellent.

tirade [taɪ'reɪd] *n* diatribe *f*.

tire¹ [taɪər] *vt* fatiguer; **to t. out** (*exhaust*) épuiser; – *vi* se fatiguer. ◆**-ed** *a* fatigué; **to be t. of sth/s.o./doing** en avoir assez de qch/de qn/de faire; **to get t. of doing** se lasser de faire. ◆**-ing** *a* fatigant. ◆**tiredness** *n* fatigue *f*. ◆**tireless** *a* infatigable. ◆**tiresome** *a* ennuyeux.

tire² [taɪər] *n* *Am* pneu *m*.

tissue ['tɪʃuː] *n* *Biol* tissu *m*; (*handkerchief*) mouchoir *m* en papier, kleenex® *m*; **t. (paper)** papier *m* de soie.

tit [tɪt] *n* **1** (*bird*) mésange *f*. **2** **to give t. for tat** rendre coup pour coup.

titbit ['tɪtbɪt] *n* (*food*) bon morceau *m*.

titillate ['tɪtɪleɪt] vt exciter.

titl/e ['taɪt(ə)l] n (name, claim) & Sp titre m; **t. deed** titre m de propriété; **t. role** Th Cin rôle m principal; − vt (film) intituler, titrer. ◆**−ed** a (person) titré.

titter ['tɪtər] vi rire bêtement.

tittle-tattle ['tɪt(ə)ltæt(ə)l] n Fam commérages mpl.

to [tə, stressed tuː] **1** prep à; (towards) vers; (of feelings, attitude) envers; (right up to) jusqu'à; (of) de; **give it to him** or **her** donne-le-lui; **to town** en ville; **to France** en France; **to Portugal** au Portugal; **to the butcher('s)**/etc chez le boucher/etc; **the road to** la route de; **the train to** le train pour; **well-disposed to** bien disposé envers; **kind to** gentil envers or avec or pour; **from bad to worse** de mal en pis; **ten to one** (proportion) dix contre un; **it's ten (minutes) to one** il est une heure moins dix; **one person to a room** une personne par chambre; **to say/to remember**/etc (with inf) dire/se souvenir/etc; **she tried to** die elle a essayé; **wife/**etc**-to-be** future femme f/etc. **2** adv **to push to** (door) fermer; **to go** or **walk to and fro** aller et venir. ◆**-to-do** [tə'duː] n (fuss) Fam histoire f.

toad [təʊd] n crapaud m.

toadstool ['təʊdstuːl] n champignon m (vénéneux).

toast [təʊst] **1** n Culin pain m grillé, toast m; − vt (bread) (faire) griller. **2** n (drink) toast m; − vt (person) porter un toast à; (success, event) arroser. ◆**toaster** n grille-pain m inv.

tobacco [tə'bækəʊ] n (pl -os) tabac m. ◆**tobacconist** n buraliste mf; **t., tobacconist's (shop)** (bureau m de) tabac m.

toboggan [tə'bɒgən] n luge f, toboggan m.

today [tə'deɪ] adv & n aujourd'hui m.

toddle ['tɒd(ə)l] vi **to t. off** (leave) Hum Fam se sauver.

toddler ['tɒdlər] n petit(e) enfant mf.

toddy ['tɒdɪ] n (hot) **t.** grog m.

toe [təʊ] **1** n orteil m; **on one's toes** Fig vigilant. **2** vt **to t. the line** se conformer; **to t. the party line** respecter la ligne du parti. ◆**toenail** n ongle m du pied.

toffee ['tɒfɪ] n (sweet) caramel m (dur); **t. apple** pomme f d'amour.

together [tə'geðər] adv ensemble; (at the same time) en même temps; **t. with** avec. ◆**−ness** n (of group) camaraderie f; (of husband and wife) intimité f.

togs [tɒgz] npl (clothes) Sl nippes fpl.

toil [tɔɪl] n labeur m; − vi travailler dur.

toilet ['tɔɪlɪt] n (room) toilettes fpl, cabinets mpl; (bowl, seat) cuvette f or siège m des cabinets; **to go to the t.** aller aux toilettes; − **a** (articles) de toilette; **t. paper** papier m hygiénique; **t. roll** rouleau m de papier hygiénique; **t. water** (perfume) eau f de toilette. ◆**toiletries** npl articles mpl de toilette.

token ['təʊkən] n (symbol, sign) témoignage m; (metal disc) jeton m; (voucher) bon m; **gift t.** chèque-cadeau m; **book t.** chèque-livre m; **record t.** chèque-disque m; − a symbolique.

told [təʊld] see **tell**; − adv **all t.** (taken together) en tout.

tolerable ['tɒlərəb(ə)l] a (bearable) tolérable; (fairly good) passable. ◆**tolerably** adv (fairly, fairly well) passablement. ◆**tolerance** n tolérance f. ◆**tolerant** a tolérant (of à l'égard de). ◆**tolerantly** adv avec tolérance. ◆**tolerate** vt tolérer.

toll [təʊl] **1** n péage m; − a (road) à péage. **2** n **the death t.** le nombre de morts, le bilan en vies humaines; **to take a heavy t.** (of accident etc) faire beaucoup de victimes. **3** vi (of bell) sonner. ◆**tollfree** a **t. number** Tel Am numéro m vert.

tomato [tə'mɑːtəʊ, Am tə'meɪtəʊ] n (pl -oes) tomate f.

tomb [tuːm] n tombeau m. ◆**tombstone** n pierre f tombale.

tomboy ['tɒmbɔɪ] n (girl) garçon m manqué.

tomcat ['tɒmkæt] n matou m.

tome [təʊm] n (book) tome m.

tomfoolery [tɒm'fuːlərɪ] n niaiserie(s) f(pl).

tomorrow [tə'mɒrəʊ] adv & n demain (m); **t. morning/evening** demain matin/soir; **the day after t.** après-demain.

ton [tʌn] n tonne f (Br = 1016 kg, Am = 907 kg); **metric t.** tonne f (= 1000 kg); **tons of** (lots of) Fam des tonnes de.

tone [təʊn] n ton m; (of radio, telephone) tonalité f; **in that t.** sur ce ton; **to set the t.** donner le ton; **she's t.-deaf** elle n'a pas d'oreille; − vt **to t. down** atténuer; **to t. up** (muscles, skin) tonifier; − vi **to t. in** s'harmoniser (with avec).

tongs [tɒŋz] npl pinces fpl; (for sugar) pince f; (curling) **t.** fer m à friser.

tongue [tʌŋ] n langue f; **t. in cheek** ironique(ment). ◆**t.-tied** a muet (et gêné).

tonic ['tɒnɪk] a & n tonique (m); **gin and t.** gin-tonic m.

tonight [tə'naɪt] adv & n (this evening) ce soir (m); (during the night) cette nuit (f).

tonne [tʌn] n (metric) tonne f. ◆**tonnage** n tonnage m.

tonsil ['tɒns(ə)l] n amygdale f. ◆**tonsi'l-**

lectomy n opération f des amygdales. ◆**tonsillitis** [tɒnsə'laɪtɪs] n **to have t.** avoir une angine.

too [tuː] adv **1** (excessively) trop; **t. tired to play** trop fatigué pour jouer; **t. hard to solve** trop difficile à résoudre; **it's only t. true** ce n'est que trop vrai. **2** (also) aussi; (moreover) en plus.

took [tʊk] see take.

tool [tuːl] n outil m; **t. bag, t. kit** trousse f à outils.

toot [tuːt] vti **to t. (the horn)** Aut klaxonner.

tooth, pl **teeth** [tuːθ, tiːθ] n dent f; **front t.** dent de devant; **back t.** molaire f; **milk/wisdom t.** dent de lait/de sagesse; **to decay** carie f dentaire; **to have a sweet t.** aimer les sucreries; **long in the t.** (old) Hum chenu, vieux. ◆**toothache** n mal m de dents. ◆**toothbrush** n brosse f à dents. ◆**toothcomb** n peigne m fin. ◆**toothpaste** n dentifrice m. ◆**toothpick** n cure-dent m.

top[1] [tɒp] n (of mountain, tower, tree) sommet m; (of wall, dress, ladder, page) haut m; (of box, table, surface) dessus m; (of list) tête f; (of water) surface f; (of car) toit m; (of bottle, tube) bouchon m; (bottle cap) capsule f; (of saucepan) couvercle m; (of pen) capuchon m; **pyjama t.** veste f de pyjama; **(at the) t. of the class** le premier de la classe; **on t. of** sur; (in addition to) Fig en plus de; **on t.** (in bus etc) en haut; **from t. to bottom** de fond en comble; **the big t.** (circus) le chapiteau; – a (drawer, shelf) du haut, premier; (step, layer, storey) dernier; (upper) supérieur; (in rank, exam) premier; (chief) principal; (best) meilleur; (great, distinguished) éminent; (maximum) maximum; **in t. gear** Aut en quatrième vitesse; **at t. speed** à toute vitesse; **t. hat** (chapeau m) haut-de-forme m. ◆**t.-'heavy** a trop lourd du haut. ◆**t.-level** a (talks etc) au sommet. ◆**t.-'notch** a Fam excellent. ◆**t.-'ranking** a (official) haut placé. ◆**t.-'secret** a ultra-secret.

top[2] [tɒp] vt (-pp-) (exceed) dépasser; **to t. up** (glass etc) remplir (de nouveau); (coffee, oil etc) rajouter; **and to t. it all** ... et pour comble ... ; **topped with** Culin nappé de.

top[3] [tɒp] n (toy) toupie f.

topaz ['təʊpæz] n (gem) topaze f.

topic ['tɒpɪk] n sujet m. ◆**topical** a d'actualité. ◆**topi'cality** n actualité f.

topless ['tɒpləs] a (woman) aux seins nus.

topography [tə'pɒɡrəfɪ] n topographie f.

topple ['tɒp(ə)l] vi **to t. (over)** tomber; – vt **to t. (over)** faire tomber.

topsy-turvy [tɒpsɪ'tɜːvɪ] a & adv sens dessus dessous.

torch [tɔːtʃ] n (burning) torche f, flambeau m; (electric) lampe f électrique. ◆**torchlight** n & a **by t.** à la lumière des flambeaux; **t. procession** retraite f aux flambeaux.

tore [tɔːr] see tear[1].

torment [tɔː'ment] vt (make suffer) tourmenter; (annoy) agacer; – ['tɔːment] n tourment m.

tornado [tɔː'neɪdəʊ] n (pl -oes) tornade f.

torpedo [tɔː'piːdəʊ] n (pl -oes) torpille f; **t. boat** torpilleur m; – vt torpiller.

torrent ['tɒrənt] n torrent m. ◆**torrential** [tə'renʃ(ə)l] a torrentiel.

torrid ['tɒrɪd] a (love affair etc) brûlant, passionné; (climate, weather) torride.

torso ['tɔːsəʊ] n (pl -os) torse m.

tortoise ['tɔːtəs] n tortue f. ◆**tortoiseshell** a (comb etc) en écaille; (spectacles) à monture d'écaille.

tortuous ['tɔːtʃʊəs] a tortueux.

tortur/e ['tɔːtʃər] n torture f; – vt torturer. ◆**-er** n tortionnaire m.

Tory ['tɔːrɪ] n tory m; – a tory inv.

toss [tɒs] vt (throw) jeter, lancer (to à); **to t. s.o.** (about) (of boat, vehicle) ballotter qn; **to t. a coin** jouer à pile ou à face; **to t. back** (one's head) rejeter en arrière; – vi **to t.** (about), **t. and turn** (in one's sleep etc) se tourner et se retourner; **we'll t. (up) for it**, we'll **t. up** on va jouer à pile ou à face; – n **with a t. of the head** d'un mouvement brusque de la tête. ◆**t.-up** n **it's a t.-up whether he leaves or stays** Sl il y a autant de chances pour qu'il parte ou pour qu'il reste.

tot [tɒt] n **1** (tiny) **t.** petit(e) enfant mf. **2** vt (-tt-) **to t. up** (total) Fam additionner.

total ['təʊt(ə)l] a total; **the t. sales** le total des ventes; – n total m; **in t.** au total; – vt (-ll-, Am -l-) (of debt, invoice) s'élever à; **to t. (up)** (find the total of) totaliser; **that totals $9** ça fait neuf dollars en tout. ◆**-ly** adv totalement.

totalitarian [təʊtælɪ'teərɪən] a Pol totalitaire.

tote [təʊt] n **1** Sp Fam pari m mutuel. **2** vt (gun) porter.

totter ['tɒtər] vi chanceler.

touch [tʌtʃ] n (contact) contact m, toucher m; (sense) toucher m; (of painter) & Fb Rugby touche f; – a **t. of** (small amount) un petit peu de, un soupçon de; **the finishing**

touches la dernière touche; **in t.** with (*person*) en contact avec; (*events*) au courant de; **to be out of t. with** ne plus être en contact avec; (*events*) ne plus être au courant de; **to get in t.** se mettre en contact (with avec); **we lost t.** on s'est perdu de vue; – *vt* toucher; (*lay a finger on, tamper with, eat*) toucher à; (*move emotionally*) toucher; (*equal*) *Fig* égaler; **to t. up** retoucher; **I don't t. the stuff** (*beer etc*) je n'en bois jamais; – *vi* (*of lines, ends etc*) se toucher; **don't t.!** n'y *or* ne touche pas!; **he's always touching** c'est un touche-à-tout; **to t. down** (*of aircraft*) atterrir; **to t. on** (*subject*) toucher à. ◆**—ed** *a* (*emotionally*) touché (by de); (*crazy*) *Fam* cinglé. ◆**—ing** *a* (*story etc*) touchant. ◆**touch-and-'go** *a* (*uncertain*) *Fam* douteux. ◆**touchdown** *n Av* atterrissage *m*. ◆**touchline** *n Fb Rugby* (ligne *f* de) touche *f*.

touchy ['tʌtʃɪ] *a* (**-ier, -iest**) (*sensitive*) susceptible (about à propos de).

tough [tʌf] *a* (**-er, -est**) (*hard*) dur; (*meat, businessman*) coriace; (*sturdy*) solide; (*strong*) fort; (*relentless*) acharné; (*difficult*) difficile, dur; **t. guy** dur *m*; **t. luck!** *Fam* pas de chance!, quelle déveine!; – *n* (*tough guy*) *Fam* dur *m*. ◆**toughen** *vt* (*body, person*) endurcir; (*reinforce*) renforcer. ◆**toughness** *n* dureté *f*; solidité *f*; force *f*.

toupee ['tuːpeɪ] *n* postiche *m*.

tour [tʊər] *n* (*journey*) voyage *m*; (*visit*) visite *f*; (*by artist, team etc*) tournée *f*; (*on bicycle, on foot*) randonnée *f*; **on t.** en voyage; en tournée; **a t. of** (*France*) un voyage en; une tournée en; une randonnée en; – *vt* visiter; (*of artist etc*) être en tournée en *or* dans etc. ◆**—ing** *n* tourisme *m*; **to go t.** faire du tourisme. ◆**tourism** *n* tourisme *m*. ◆**tourist** *n* touriste *mf*; – *a* touristique; (*class*) touriste *inv*; **t. office** syndicat *m* d'initiative. ◆**touristy** *a Pej Fam* (*trop*) touristique.

tournament ['tʊənəmənt] *n Sp & Hist* tournoi *m*.

tousled ['tauz(ə)ld] *a* (*hair*) ébouriffé.

tout [taʊt] *vi* racoler; **to t. for** (*customers*) racoler; – *n* racoleur, -euse *mf*; **ticket t.** revendeur, -euse *mf* (en fraude) de billets.

tow [taʊ] *vt* (*car, boat*) remorquer; (*caravan, trailer*) tracter; **to t. away** (*vehicle*) *Jur* emmener à la fourrière; – *n* 'on t.' 'en remorque'; **t. truck** (*breakdown lorry*) *Am* dépanneuse *f*. ◆**towpath** *n* chemin *m* de halage. ◆**towrope** *n* (câble *m* de) remorque *f*.

toward(s) [tə'wɔːd(z), *Am* tɔːd(z)] *prep* vers;

(*of feelings*) envers; **money t.** de l'argent pour (acheter).

towel ['taʊəl] *n* serviette *f* (de toilette); (*for dishes*) torchon *m*; **t. rail** porte-serviettes *m inv*. ◆**towelling** *n, Am* ◆**toweling** *n* tissu-éponge *m*; (*kitchen*) t. *Am* essuie-tout *m inv*.

tower ['taʊər] *n* tour *f*; **t. block** tour *f*, immeuble *m*; **ivory t.** *Fig* tour *f* d'ivoire; – *vi* **to t. above** *or* **over** dominer. ◆**—ing** *a* très haut.

town [taʊn] *n* ville *f*; **in t., (in)to t.** en ville; **out of t.** en province; **country t.** bourg *m*; **t. centre** centre-ville *m*; **t. clerk** secrétaire *mf* de mairie; **t. council** conseil *m* municipal; **t. hall** mairie *f*; **t. planner** urbaniste *mf*; **t. planning** urbanisme *m*. ◆**township** *n* (*in South Africa*) commune *f* (noire).

toxic ['tɒksɪk] *a* toxique. ◆**toxin** *n* toxine *f*.

toy [tɔɪ] *n* jouet *m*; **soft t.** (jouet *m* en) peluche *f*; – *a* (*gun*) d'enfant; (*house, car, train*) miniature; – *vi* **to t. with** jouer avec. ◆**toyshop** *n* magasin *m* de jouets.

trac/e [treɪs] *n* trace *f* (of de); **to vanish** *or* **disappear without (a) t.** disparaître sans laisser de traces; – *vt* (*draw*) tracer; (*with tracing paper*) (dé)calquer; (*locate*) retrouver (la trace de), dépister; (*follow*) suivre (la piste de) (to à); (*relate*) retracer; **to t. (back) to** (*one's family*) faire remonter jusqu'à. ◆**—ing** *n* (*drawing*) calque *m*; **t. paper** papier-calque *m inv*.

track [træk] *n* trace *f*; (*of bullet, rocket*) trajectoire *f*; (*of person, animal, tape recorder*) & *Sp* piste *f*; (*of record*) plage *f*; *Rail* voie *f*; (*path*) piste *f*, chemin *m*; *Sch Am* classe *f* (de niveau); **to keep t.** of suivre; **to lose t. of** (*friend*) perdre de vue; (*argument*) perdre le fil de; **to make tracks** *Fam* se sauver; **the right t.** la bonne voie *or* piste; **t. event** *Sp* épreuve *f* sur piste; **t. record** (*of person, firm etc*) *Fig* antécédents *mpl*; – *vt* **to t. (down)** (*locate*) retrouver, dépister; (*pursue*) traquer. ◆**—er** *a* **t. dog** chien *m* policier. ◆**tracksuit** *n Sp* survêtement *m*.

tract [trækt] *n* (*stretch of land*) étendue *f*.

traction ['trækʃ(ə)n] *n Tech* traction *f*.

tractor ['træktər] *n* tracteur *m*.

trade [treɪd] *n* commerce *m*; (*job*) métier *m*; (*exchange*) échange *m*; – *a* (*fair, balance, route*) commercial; (*price*) de (demi-)gros; (*secret*) de fabrication; (*barrier*) douanier; **t. union** syndicat *m*; **t. unionist** syndicaliste *mf*; – *vi* faire du commerce (with avec); **to t. in** (*sugar etc*) faire le commerce de; – *vt* (*exchange*) échanger (for contre); **to t. sth in** (*old article*) faire reprendre qch. ◆**t.-in** *n*

Com reprise *f.* ◆**t.-off** *n* échange *m*. ◆**trading** *n* commerce *m*; - *a* (*activity, port etc*) commercial; (*nation*) commerçant; **t. estate** zone *f* industrielle. ◆**trader** *n* commerçant, -ante *mf*; (*street*) **t.** vendeur, -euse *mf* de rue. ◆**tradesman** *n* (*pl* -men) commerçant *m*.

trademark ['treɪdmɑːk] *n* marque *f* de fabrique; (**registered**) **t.** marque déposée.

tradition [trə'dɪʃ(ə)n] *n* tradition *f*. ◆**traditional** *a* traditionnel. ◆**traditionally** *adv* traditionnellement.

traffic ['træfɪk] **1** *n* (*on road*) circulation *f*; *Av Nau Rail* trafic *m*; **busy** or **heavy t.** beaucoup de circulation; **heavy t.** (*vehicles*) poids *mpl* lourds; **t. circle** *Am* rond-point *m*; **t. cone** cône *m* de chantier; **t. jam** embouteillage *m*; **t. lights** feux *mpl* (de signalisation); (*when red*) feu *m* rouge; **t. sign** panneau *m* de signalisation. **2** *n* (*trade*) *Pej* trafic *m* (**in** de); - *vi* (-ck-) trafiquer (**in** de). ◆**trafficker** *Pej* trafiquant, -ante *mf*.

tragedy ['trædʒədɪ] *n Th & Fig* tragédie *f*. ◆**tragic** *a* tragique. ◆**tragically** *adv* tragiquement.

trail [treɪl] **1** *n* (*of powder, smoke, blood etc*) traînée *f*; (*track*) piste *f*, trace *f*; (*path*) sentier *m*; **in its t.** (*wake*) dans son sillage; - *vt* (*drag*) traîner; (*caravan*) tracter; (*follow*) suivre (la piste de); - *vi* (*on the ground etc*) traîner; (*of plant*) ramper; **to t. behind** (*lag behind*) traîner. ◆**-er** *n* **1** *Aut* remorque *f*; *Am* caravane *f*. **2** *Cin* bande *f* annonce.

train [treɪn] **1** *n* (*engine, transport, game*) train *m*; (*underground*) rame *f*; (*procession*) *Fig* file *f*; (*of events*) suite *f*; (*of dress*) traîne *f*; **my t. of thought** le fil de ma pensée; **t. set** train *m* électrique. **2** *vt* (*teach, develop*) former (**to do** à faire); *Sp* entraîner; (*animal, child*) dresser (**to do** à faire); (*ear*) exercer; **to t. oneself to do** s'entraîner à faire; **to t. sth on** (*aim*) braquer qch sur; - *vi* recevoir une formation (**as a** *doctor/etc* de médecin/*etc*); *Sp* s'entraîner. ◆**-ed** *a* (*having professional skill*) qualifié; (*nurse etc*) diplômé; (*animal*) dressé; (*ear*) exercé. ◆**-ing** *n* formation *f*; (*of animal*) dressage *m*; *Sp* entraînement *m*; **to be in t.** *Sp* s'entraîner; (*teacher's*) **t. college** école *f* normale. ◆**trai'nee** *n* & *a* stagiaire (*mf*). ◆**trainer** *n* (*of athlete, racehorse*) entraîneur *m*; (*of dog, lion etc*) dresseur *m*; (*running shoe*) jogging *m*, chaussure *f* de sport.

traipse [treɪps] *vi Fam* (*tiredly*) traîner les pieds; **to t.** (**about**) (*wander*) se balader.

trait [treɪt] *n* (*of character*) trait *m*.

traitor ['treɪtər] *n* traître *m*.

trajectory [trə'dʒektərɪ] *n* trajectoire *f*.

tram [træm] *n* tram(way) *m*.

tramp [træmp] **1** *n* (*vagrant*) clochard, -arde *mf*; (*woman*) *Am* traînée *f*. **2** *vi* (*walk*) marcher d'un pas lourd; (*hike*) marcher à pied; - *vt* (*streets etc*) parcourir; - *n* (*sound*) pas lourds *mpl*; (*hike*) randonnée *f*.

trample ['træmp(ə)l] *vti* **to t. sth** (**underfoot**), **t. on sth** piétiner qch.

trampoline [træmpə'liːn] *n* trampoline *m*.

trance [trɑːns] *n* **in a t.** (*mystic*) en transe.

tranquil ['træŋkwɪl] *a* tranquille. ◆**tranquillity** *n* tranquillité *f*. ◆**tranquillizer** *n Med* tranquillisant *m*.

trans- [trænz, trænz] *pref* trans-.

transact [træn'zækt] *vt* (*business*) traiter. ◆**transaction** *n* (*in bank etc*) opération *f*; (*on Stock Market*) transaction *f*; **the t. of** (*business*) la conduite de.

transatlantic [trænzət'læntɪk] *a* transatlantique.

transcend [træn'send] *vt* transcender. ◆**transcendent** *a* transcendant.

transcribe [træn'skraɪb] *vt* transcrire. ◆'**transcript** *n* (*document*) transcription *f*. ◆**transcription** *n* transcription *f*.

transfer [træns'fɜːr] *vt* (-rr-) (*person, goods etc*) transférer (**to** à); (*power*) *Pol* faire passer (**to** à); **to t. the charges** téléphoner en PCV; - *vi* être transféré (**to** à); - ['trænsfɜːr] *n* transfert *m* (**to** à); (*of power*) *Pol* passation *f*; (*image*) décalcomanie *f*; **bank** or **credit t.** virement *m* (bancaire). ◆**trans'ferable** *a* **not t.** (*on ticket*) strictement personnel.

transform [træns'fɔːm] *vt* transformer (**into** en). ◆**transfor'mation** *n* transformation *f*. ◆**transformer** *n El* transformateur *m*.

transfusion [træns'fjuːʒ(ə)n] *n* (*blood*) **t.** transfusion *f* (sanguine).

transient ['trænzɪənt] *a* (*ephemeral*) transitoire.

transistor [træn'zɪstər] *n* (*device*) transistor *m*; **t.** (**radio**) transistor *m*.

transit ['trænzɪt] *n* transit *m*; **in t.** en transit.

transition [træn'zɪʃ(ə)n] *n* transition *f*. ◆**transitional** *a* de transition, transitoire.

transitive ['trænsɪtɪv] *a Gram* transitif.

transitory ['trænzɪtərɪ] *a* transitoire.

translate [træns'leɪt] *vt* traduire (**from** de, **into** en). ◆**translation** *n* traduction *f*; (*into mother tongue*) Sch version *f*; (*from mother tongue*) Sch thème *m*. ◆**translator** *n* traducteur, -trice *mf*.

transmit [trænz'mɪt] *vt* (-tt-) (*send, pass*)

transmettre; – *vti* (*broadcast*) émettre.
◆**transmission** *n* transmission *f*; (*broadcast*) émission *f*. ◆**transmitter** *n Rad TV* émetteur *m*.

transparent [træns'pærənt] *a* transparent. ◆**transparency** *n* transparence *f*; (*slide*) *Phot* diapositive *f*.

transpire [træns'paɪər] *vi* (*of secret etc*) s'ébruiter; (*happen*) *Fam* arriver; **it transpired that** . . . il s'est avéré que . . . .

transplant [træns'plɑːnt] *vt* (*plant*) transplanter; (*organ*) *Med* greffer, transplanter; – ['trænsplɑːnt] *n Med* greffe *f*, transplantation *f*.

transport [træns'pɔːt] *vt* transporter; – ['trænspɔːt] *n* transport *m*; **public t.** les transports en commun; **do you have t.?** es-tu motorisé?; **t. café** routier *m*. ◆**transpor'tation** *n* transport *m*.

transpose [træns'pəʊz] *vt* transposer.

transvestite [trænz'vestaɪt] *n* travesti *m*.

trap [træp] *n* piège *m*; (*mouth*) *Pej Sl* gueule *f*; **t. door** trappe *f*; – *vt* (*-pp-*) (*snare*) prendre (au piège); (*jam, corner*) coincer, bloquer; (*cut off by snow etc*) bloquer (by par); **to t. one's finger** se coincer le doigt. ◆**trapper** *n* (*hunter*) trappeur *m*.

trapeze [trə'piːz] *n* (*in circus*) trapèze *m*; **t. artist** trapéziste *mf*.

trappings ['træpɪŋz] *npl* signes *mpl* extérieurs.

trash [træʃ] *n* (*nonsense*) sottises *fpl*; (*junk*) saleté(s) *f*(*pl*); (*waste*) *Am* ordures *fpl*; (*riffraff*) *Am* racaille *f*. ◆**trashcan** *n Am* poubelle *f*. ◆**trashy** *a* (*-ier, -iest*) (*book etc*) moche, sans valeur; (*goods*) de camelote.

trauma ['trɔːmə, 'traʊmə] *n* (*shock*) traumatisme *m*. ◆**trau'matic** *a* traumatisant. ◆**traumatize** *vt* traumatiser.

travel ['trævəl] *vi* (*-ll-, Am -l-*) voyager; (*move*) aller, se déplacer; – *vt* (*country, distance, road*) parcourir; – *n & npl* voyages *mpl*; **on one's travels** en voyage; – *a* (*agency, book*) de voyages; **t. brochure** dépliant *m* touristique. ◆**travelled** *a* **to be well** *or* **widely t.** avoir beaucoup voyagé. ◆**travelling** *n* voyages *mpl*; – *a* (*bag etc*) de voyage; (*expenses*) de déplacement; (*circus, musician*) ambulant. ◆**traveller** *n* voyageur, -euse *mf*; **traveller's cheque,** *Am* **traveler's check** chèque *m* de voyage. ◆**travelogue** *n, Am* **travelog** *n* (*book*) récit *m* de voyages. ◆**travelsickness** *n* (*in car*) mal *m* de la route; (*in aircraft*) mal *m* de l'air.

travesty ['trævəstɪ] *n* parodie *f*.

travolator ['trævəleɪtər] *n* trottoir *m* roulant.

trawler ['trɔːlər] *n* (*ship*) chalutier *m*.

tray [treɪ] *n* plateau *m*; (*for office correspondence etc*) corbeille *f*.

treacherous ['tretʃ(ə)rəs] *a* (*person, action, road, journey etc*) traître. ◆**treacherously** *adv* traîtreusement; (*dangerously*) dangereusement. ◆**treachery** *n* traîtrise *f*.

treacle ['triːk(ə)l] *n* mélasse *f*.

tread [tred] *vi* (*pt* **trod,** *pp* **trodden**) (*walk*) marcher (on sur); (*proceed*) *Fig* avancer; – *vt* (*path*) parcourir; (*soil*) *Fig* fouler; **to t. sth into a carpet** étaler qch (avec les pieds) sur un tapis; – *n* (*step*) pas *m*; (*of tyre*) chape *f*. ◆**treadmill** *n Pej Fig* routine *f*.

treason ['triːz(ə)n] *n* trahison *f*.

treasure ['treʒər] *n* trésor *m*; **a real t.** (*person*) *Fig* une vraie perle; **t. hunt** chasse *f* au trésor; – *vt* (*value*) tenir à, priser; (*keep*) conserver (précieusement). ◆**treasurer** *n* trésorier, -ière *mf*. ◆**Treasury** *n* the **T.** *Pol* = le ministère des Finances.

treat [triːt] **1** *vt* (*person, product etc*) & *Med* traiter; (*consider*) considérer (as comme); **to t. with care** prendre soin de; **to t. s.o. to sth** offrir qch à qn. **2** *n* (*pleasure*) plaisir *m* (spécial); (*present*) cadeau-surprise *m*; (*meal*) régal *m*; **it was a t. (for me)** to do it ça m'a fait plaisir de le faire. ◆**treatment** *n* (*behaviour*) & *Med* traitement *m*; **his t. of her** la façon dont il la traite; **rough t.** mauvais traitements *mpl*.

treatise ['triːtɪz] *n* (*book*) traité *m* (on de).

treaty ['triːtɪ] *n Pol* traité *m*.

treble ['treb(ə)l] *a* triple; – *vti* tripler; – *n* le triple; **it's t. the price** c'est le triple du prix.

tree [triː] *n* arbre *m*; **Christmas t.** sapin *m* de Noël; **family t.** arbre *m* généalogique. ◆**t.-lined** *a* bordé d'arbres. ◆**t.-top** *n* cime *f* (d'un arbre). ◆**t.-trunk** *n* tronc *m* d'arbre.

trek [trek] *vi* (*-kk-*) cheminer *or* voyager (péniblement); *Sp* marcher à pied; (*go*) *Fam* traîner; – *n* voyage *m* (pénible); *Sp* randonnée *f*; (*distance*) *Fam* tirée *f*.

trellis ['trelɪs] *n* treillage *m*.

tremble ['tremb(ə)l] *vi* trembler (**with** de). ◆**tremor** *n* tremblement *m*; (**earth**) **t.** secousse *f* (sismique).

tremendous [trə'mendəs] *a* (*huge*) énorme; (*dreadful*) terrible; (*wonderful*) formidable, terrible. ◆**—ly** *adv* terriblement.

trench [trentʃ] *n* tranchée *f*.

trend [trend] *n* tendance *f* (**towards** à); **the t.** (*fashion*) la mode; **to set a** *or* **the t.** donner le ton, lancer une *or* la mode. ◆**trendy** *a* (-ier, -iest) (*person, clothes, topic etc*) *Fam* à la mode, dans le vent.

trepidation [trepi'deɪʃ(ə)n] *n* inquiétude *f*.

trespass ['trespəs] *vi* s'introduire sans autorisation (**on, upon** dans); **'no trespassing'** 'entrée interdite'.

tresses ['tresiz] *npl Lit* chevelure *f*.

trestle ['tres(ə)l] *n* tréteau *m*.

trial ['traɪəl] *n Jur* procès *m*; (*test*) essai *m*; (*ordeal*) épreuve *f*; **t. of strength** épreuve de force; **to go** *or* **be on t., stand t.** passer en jugement; **to put s.o. on t.** juger qn; **by t. and error** par tâtonnements; – *a* (*period, flight etc*) d'essai; (*offer*) à l'essai; **t. run** (*of new product etc*) période *f* d'essai.

triangle ['traɪæŋg(ə)l] *n* triangle *m*; (*setsquare*) *Math Am* équerre *f*. ◆**tri'angular** *a* triangulaire.

tribe [traɪb] *n* tribu *f*. ◆**tribal** *a* tribal.

tribulations [tribjʊ'leɪʃ(ə)nz] *npl* (**trials and**) **t.** tribulations *fpl*.

tribunal [traɪ'bjuːn(ə)l] *n* commission *f*, tribunal *m*; *Mil* tribunal *m*.

tributary ['tribjʊtərɪ] *n* affluent *m*.

tribute ['tribjuːt] *n* hommage *m*, tribut *m*; **to pay t. to** rendre hommage à.

trick [trik] *n* (*joke, deception & of conjurer etc*) tour *m*; (*ruse*) astuce *f*; (*habit*) manie *f*; **to play a t. on s.o.** jouer un tour à qn; **card t.** tour *m* de cartes; **that will do the t.** *Fam* ça fera l'affaire; **t. photo** photo *f* truquée; **t. question** question-piège *f*; – *vt* (*deceive*) tromper, attraper; **to t. s.o. into doing sth** amener qn à faire qch par la ruse. ◆**trickery** *n* ruse *f*. ◆**tricky** *a* (-ier, -iest) (*problem etc*) difficile, délicat; (*person*) rusé.

trickle ['trik(ə)l] *n* (*of liquid*) filet *m*; **a t. of** (*letters, people etc*) *Fig* un petit nombre de; – *vi* (*flow*) dégouliner, couler (lentement); **to t. in** (*of letters, people etc*) *Fig* arriver en petit nombre.

tricycle ['traɪsɪk(ə)l] *n* tricycle *m*.

trier ['traɪər] *n* **to be a t.** être persévérant.

trifle ['traɪf(ə)l] *n* (*article, money*) bagatelle *f*; (*dessert*) diplomate *m*; – *adv* **a t. small/too much/etc** un tantinet petit/trop/etc; – *vi* **to t. with** (*s.o.'s feelings*) jouer avec; (*person*) plaisanter avec. ◆**—ing** *a* insignifiant.

trigger ['trigər] *n* (*of gun*) gâchette *f*; – *vt* **to t. (off)** (*start, cause*) déclencher.

trilogy ['trilədʒi] *n* trilogie *f*.

trim [trim] *a* (trimmer, trimmest) (*neat*) soigné, net; (*slim*) svelte; – *n* **in t.** (*fit*) en (bonne) forme. **2** *n* (*cut*) légère coupe *f*; (*haircut*) coupe *f* de rafraîchissement; **to**

have a t. se faire rafraîchir les cheveux; – *vt* (-mm-) couper (légèrement); (*finger nail, edge*) rogner; (*hair*) rafraîchir. **3** *n* (*on garment*) garniture *f*; (*on car*) garnitures *fpl*; – *vt* (-mm-) **to t. with** (*lace etc*) orner de. ◆**trimmings** *npl* garniture(s) *f(pl)*; (*extras*) *Fig* accessoires *mpl*.

Trinity ['triniti] *n* **the T.** (*union*) *Rel* la Trinité.

trinket ['trɪŋkɪt] *n* colifichet *m*.

trio ['triːəʊ] *n* (*pl* -os) (*group*) & *Mus* trio *m*.

trip [trip] **1** *n* (*journey*) voyage *m*; (*outing*) excursion *f*; **to take a t. to** (*cinema, shops etc*) aller à. **2** *n* (*stumble*) faux pas *m*; – *vi* (-pp-) **to t. (over** *or* **up)** trébucher; **to t. over sth** trébucher contre qch; – *vt* **to t. s.o. up** faire trébucher qn. **3** *vi* (-pp-) (*walk gently*) marcher d'un pas léger. ◆**tripper** *n* **day t.** excursionniste *mf*.

tripe [traɪp] *n Culin* tripes *fpl*; (*nonsense*) *Fam* bêtises *fpl*.

triple ['trip(ə)l] *a* triple; – *vti* tripler. ◆**triplets** *npl* (*children*) triplés, -ées *mfpl*.

triplicate ['triplikət] *n* **in t.** en trois exemplaires.

tripod ['traɪpɒd] *n* trépied *m*.

trite [traɪt] *a* banal. ◆**—ness** *n* banalité *f*.

triumph ['traɪəmf] *n* triomphe *m* (**over** sur); – *vi* triompher (**over** de). ◆**tri'umphal** *a* triomphal. ◆**tri'umphant** *a* (*team, army, gesture*) triomphant; (*success, welcome, return*) triomphal. ◆**tri'umphantly** *adv* triomphalement.

trivia ['triviə] *npl* vétilles *fpl*. ◆**trivial** *a* (*unimportant*) insignifiant; (*trite*) banal. ◆**trivi'ality** *n* insignifiance *f*; banalité *f*; *pl* banalités *fpl*.

trod, trodden [trɒd, 'trɒd(ə)n] *see* **tread**.

trolley ['trɒlɪ] *n* (*for luggage*) chariot *m*; (*for shopping*) poussette *f* (de marché); (*in supermarket*) caddie® *m*; (*trolleybus*) trolley *m*; (**tea**) **t. table** *f* roulante; (*for tea urn*) chariot *m*; **t. (car)** *Am* tramway *m*. ◆**trolleybus** *n* trolleybus *m*.

trombone [trɒm'bəʊn] *n Mus* trombone *m*.

troop [truːp] *n* bande *f*; *Mil* troupe *f*; **the troops** (*army, soldiers*) les troupes, la troupe; – *vi* **to t. in/out/etc** entrer/ sortir/etc en masse. ◆**—ing t. the colour** le salut du drapeau. ◆**—er** *n* (*state*) **t.** *Am* membre *m* de la police montée.

trophy ['trəʊfɪ] *n* trophée *m*.

tropic ['trɒpɪk] *n* tropique *m*. ◆**tropical** *a* tropical.

trot [trɒt] *n* (*of horse*) trot *m*; **on the t.** (*one after another*) *Fam* de suite; – *vi* (-tt-) trot-

ter; **to t. off** or **along** (*leave*) Hum Fam se
sauver; – *vt* **to t. out** (*say*) Fam débiter.
troubl/e ['trʌb(ə)l] *n* (*difficulty*) ennui(s)
m(*pl*); (*bother, effort*) peine *f*, mal *m*; **trou-
ble(s)** (*social unrest etc*) & *Med* troubles
mpl; **to be in t.** avoir des ennuis; **to get into
t.** s'attirer des ennuis (**with** avec); **the t.
(with you) is** . . . l'ennui (avec toi) c'est que
. . . ; **to go to the t. of doing, take the t. to do**
se donner la peine *or* le mal de faire; **I
didn't put her to any t.** je ne l'ai pas
dérangée; **to find the t.** trouver le
problème; **a spot of t.** un petit problème; **a
t. spot** *Pol* un point chaud; – *vt* (*inconvenience*) déranger, ennuyer; (*worry, annoy*)
ennuyer; (*hurt*) faire mal à; (*grieve*) peiner;
to t. to do se donner la peine de faire; – *vi*
to t. (*oneself*) se déranger. ◆**–ed**
a (*worried*) inquiet; (*period*) agité.
◆**trouble-free** *a* (*machine, vehicle*) qui
ne tombe jamais en panne, fiable.
◆**troublemaker** *n* fauteur de troubles.
◆**troubleshooter** *n* Tech dépanneur *m*,
expert *m*; *Pol* conciliateur, -trice *mf*.
troublesome ['trʌb(ə)ls(ə)m] *a* ennuyeux,
gênant; (*leg etc*) qui fait mal.

trough [trɒf] *n* (*for drinking*) abreuvoir *m*;
(*for feeding*) auge *f*; **t. of low pressure** Met
dépression *f*.

trounce [trauns] *vt* (*defeat*) écraser.

troupe [truːp] *n* Th troupe *f*.

trousers ['trauzəz] *npl* pantalon *m*; **a pair of
t., some t.** un pantalon; (**short**) **t.** culottes
fpl courtes.

trousseau ['truːsəu] *n* (*of bride*) trousseau
m.

trout [traut] *n* truite *f*.

trowel ['trauəl] *n* (*for cement or plaster*)
truelle *f*; (*for plants*) déplantoir *m*.

truant ['truːənt] *n* (*pupil, shirker*) absentéiste
mf; **to play t.** faire l'école buissonnière.
◆**truancy** *n* Sch absentéisme *m* scolaire.

truce [truːs] *n* Mil trêve *f*.

truck [trʌk] *n* **1** (*lorry*) camion *m*; Rail
wagon *m* plat; **t. driver** camionneur *m*;
(*long-distance*) routier *m*; **t. stop** (*restaurant*) routier *m*. **2 t. farmer** Am maraîcher,
-ère *mf*. ◆**trucker** *n* Am (*haulier*) transporteur *m* routier; (*driver*) camionneur *m*,
routier *m*.

truculent ['trʌkjulənt] *a* agressif.

trudge [trʌdʒ] *vi* marcher d'un pas pesant.

true [truː] *a* (-er, -est) vrai; (*accurate*) exact;
(*genuine*) vrai, véritable; **t.** to (*person,
promise etc*) fidèle à; **t. to life** conforme à la
réalité; **to come t.** se réaliser; **to hold t.** (*of
argument etc*) valoir (**for** pour); **too t.!** Fam

ah, ça oui! ◆**truly** *adv* vraiment; (*faithfully*) fidèlement; **well and t.** bel et bien.

truffle ['trʌf(ə)l] *n* (*mushroom*) truffe *f*.

truism ['truːɪz(ə)m] *n* lapalissade *f*.

trump [trʌmp] **1** *n* Cards atout *m*; **t. card**
(*advantage*) Fig atout *m*. **2** *vt* **t. up**
(*charge, reason*) inventer.

trumpet ['trʌmpɪt] *n* trompette *f*; **t. player**
trompettiste *mf*.

truncate [trʌŋ'keɪt] *vt* tronquer.

truncheon ['trʌntʃ(ə)n] *n* matraque *f*.

trundle ['trʌnd(ə)l] *vti* **t. along** rouler
bruyamment.

trunk [trʌŋk] *n* (*of tree, body*) tronc *m*; (*of
elephant*) trompe *f*; (*case*) malle *f*; (*of vehicle*) Am coffre *m*; *pl* (*for swimming*) slip *m*
or caleçon *m* de bain; **t. call** Tel communication *f* interurbaine; **t. road** route *f*
nationale.

truss [trʌs] *vt* **to t. (up)** (*prisoner*) ligoter.

trust [trʌst] *n* (*faith*) confiance *f* (**in** en);
(*group*) Fin trust *m*; *Jur* fidéicommis *m*; **to
take on t.** accepter de confiance; – *vt*
(*person, judgement*) avoir confiance en, se
fier à; (*instinct, promise*) se fier à; **to t. s.o.
with sth, t. sth to s.o.** confier qch à qn; **to t.
s.o. to do** (*rely on, expect*) compter sur qn
pour faire; **I t. that** (*hope*) j'espère que; – *vi*
to t. in s.o. se fier à qn; **to t. to luck** or
chance se fier au hasard. ◆**–ed** *a* (*friend,
method etc*) éprouvé. ◆**–ing** *a* confiant.
◆**trus'tee** *n* (*of school*) administrateur
-trice *mf*. ◆**trustworthy** *a* sûr, digne de
confiance.

truth [truːθ] *n* (*pl* **-s** [truːðz]) vérité *f*; **there's
some t. in** . . . il y a du vrai dans . . . .
◆**truthful** *a* (*statement etc*) véridique, vrai;
(*person*) sincère. ◆**truthfully** *adv* sincèrement.

try [traɪ] **1** *vt* essayer (**to do, doing** de faire);
(*s.o.'s patience etc*) mettre à l'épreuve; **to t.
one's hand at** s'essayer à; **to t. one's luck**
tenter sa chance; **to t. (out)** (*car, method
etc*) essayer; (*employee etc*) mettre à l'essai;
to t. on (*clothes, shoes*) essayer; – *vi* essayer
(**for sth** d'obtenir qch); **to t. hard** faire un
gros effort; **t. and come!** essaie de venir!; –
n (*attempt*) & *Rugby* essai *m*; **to have a t.**
essayer; **at (the) first t.** du premier coup. **2**
vt (*person*) Jur juger (**for theft**/*etc* pour
vol/*etc*). ◆**–ing** *a* pénible, éprouvant.

tsar [zɑːr] *n* tsar *m*.

tub [tʌb] *n* (*for washing clothes etc*) baquet
m; (*bath*) baignoire *f*; (*for ice cream etc*)
pot *m*.

tuba ['tjuːbə] *n* Mus tuba *m*.

tubby ['tʌbɪ] *a* (-ier, -iest) Fam dodu.

tube [tjuːb] *n* tube *m*; *Rail Fam* métro *m*; (*of tyre*) chambre *f* à air. ◆**tubing** *n* (*tubes*) tubes *mpl*. ◆**tubular** *a* tubulaire.

tuberculosis [tjubɜːkjuˈləʊsɪs] *n* tuberculose *f*.

tuck [tʌk] **1** *n* (*fold in garment*) rempli *m*; − *vt* (*put*) mettre; **to t. away** ranger; (*hide*) cacher; **to t. in** (*shirt*) rentrer; (*person in bed, a blanket*) border; **to t. up** (*skirt*) remonter. **2** *vi* **to t. in** (*eat*) *Fam* manger; **to t. into** (*meal*) *Fam* attaquer; − *n t. shop Sch* boutique *f* à provisions.

Tuesday [ˈtjuːzdɪ] *n* mardi *m*.

tuft [tʌft] *n* (*of hair, grass*) touffe *f*.

tug [tʌg] **1** *vt* (**-gg-**) (*pull*) tirer; − *vi* tirer (**at**, **on** sur); − *n* **to give sth a t.** tirer (sur) qch. **2** *n* (*boat*) remorqueur *m*.

tuition [tjuˈɪʃ(ə)n] *n* (*teaching*) enseignement *m*; (*lessons*) leçons *fpl*; (*fee*) frais *mpl* de scolarité.

tulip [ˈtjuːlɪp] *n* tulipe *f*.

tumble [ˈtʌmb(ə)l] *vi* **to t. (over)** (*fall*) dégringoler; (*backwards*)tomber à la renverse; **to t. to sth** (*understand*) *Sl* réaliser qch; − *n* (*fall*) dégringolade *f*; **t. drier** sèche-linge *m inv*. ◆**tumbledown** [ˈtʌmb(ə)ldaʊn] *a* délabré. ◆**tumbler** [ˈtʌmblər] *n* (*drinking glass*) gobelet *m*.

tummy [ˈtʌmɪ] *n Fam* ventre *m*.

tumour [ˈtjuːmər] *n* tumeur *f*.

tumult [ˈtjuːmʌlt] *n* tumulte *m*. ◆**tu'multuous** *a* tumultueux.

tuna [ˈtjuːnə] *n* **t.** (**fish**) thon *m*.

tun/e [tjuːn] *n* (*melody*) air *m*; **to be** *or* **sing in t./out of t.** chanter juste/faux; **in t.** (*instrument*) accordé; **out of t.** (*instrument*) désaccordé; **in t. with** (*harmony*) *Fig* en accord avec; **to the t. of £50** d'un montant de 50 livres, dans les 50 livres; − *vt* **to t. (up)** *Mus* accorder; *Aut* régler; − *vi* **to t. in (to)** *Rad TV* se mettre à l'écoute (de), écouter. ◆**-ing** *n Aut* réglage *m*; **t. fork** *Mus* diapason *m*. ◆**tuneful** *a* mélodieux.

tunic [ˈtjuːnɪk] *n* tunique *f*.

Tunisia [tjuːˈnɪzɪə] *n* Tunisie *f*. ◆**Tunisian** *a* & *n* tunisien, -ienne (*mf*).

tunnel [ˈtʌn(ə)l] *n* tunnel *m*; (*in mine*) galerie *f*; − *vi* (**-ll-**, *Am* **-l-**) percer un tunnel (**into** dans).

turban [ˈtɜːbən] *n* turban *m*.

turbine [ˈtɜːbaɪn, *Am* ˈtɜːbɪn] *n* turbine *f*.

turbulence [ˈtɜːbjʊləns] *n Phys Av* turbulence *fpl*.

turbulent [ˈtɜːbjʊlənt] *a* (*person etc*) turbulent.

tureen [tjuˈriːn, təˈriːn] *n* (*soup*) **t.** soupière *f*.

turf [tɜːf] **1** *n* (*grass*) gazon *m*; **the t.** *Sp* le turf; **t. accountant** bookmaker *m*. **2** *vt* **to t. out** (*get rid of*) *Fam* jeter dehors.

turgid [ˈtɜːdʒɪd] *a* (*style, language*) boursouflé.

turkey [ˈtɜːkɪ] *n* dindon *m*, dinde *f*; (*as food*) dinde *f*.

Turkey [ˈtɜːkɪ] *n* Turquie *f*. ◆**Turk** *n* Turc *m*, Turque *f*. ◆**Turkish** *a* turc; **T. delight** (*sweet*) loukoum *m*; − *n* (*language*) turc *m*.

turmoil [ˈtɜːmɔɪl] *n* confusion *f*, trouble *m*; **in t.** en ébullition.

turn [tɜːn] *n* (*movement, action & in game etc*) tour *m*; (*in road*) tournant *m*; (*of events, mind*) tournure *f*; *Med* crise *f*; *Psy* choc *m*; (*act*) *Th* numéro *m*; **t. of phrase** tour *m* or tournure *f* (de phrase); **to take turns** se relayer; **in t.** à tour de rôle; **by turns** tour à tour; **in (one's) t.** à son tour; **it's your t. to play** c'est à toi de jouer; **to do s.o. a good t.** rendre service à qn; **the t. of the century** le début du siècle; − *vt* tourner; (*mechanically*) faire tourner; (*mattress, pancake*) retourner; **to t. s.o./sth into** (*change*) changer *or* transformer qn/qch en; **to t. sth red/yellow** rougir/jaunir qch; **to t. sth on s.o.** (*aim*) braquer qch sur qn; **she's turned twenty** elle a vingt ans passés; **it's turned seven** il est sept heures passées; **it turns my stomach** cela me soulève le cœur; − *vt* (*of wheel, driver etc*) tourner; (*turn head or body*) se (re)tourner (**towards** vers); (*become*) devenir; **to t. to** (*question, adviser etc*) se tourner vers; **to t. against** se retourner contre; **to t. into** (*change*) se changer *or* se transformer en. ■ **to t. around** *vi* (*of person*) se retourner; **to t. away** *vt* (*avert*) détourner (**from** de); (*refuse*) renvoyer (*qn*); − *vi* (*stop facing*) détourner les yeux, se détourner; **to t. back** *vt* (*bed sheet, corner of page*) replier; (*person*) renvoyer; (*clock*) reculer (**to** jusqu'à); − *vi* (*return*) retourner (sur ses pas); **to t. down** *vt* (*fold down*) rabattre; (*gas, radio etc*) baisser; (*refuse*) refuser (*qn, offre etc*); **to t. in** *vt* (*hand in*) rendre (**to** à); (*prisoner etc*) *Fam* livrer (à la police); − *vi* (*go to bed*) *Fam* se coucher; **to t. off** *vt* (*light, radio etc*) éteindre; (*tap*) fermer; (*machine*) arrêter; − *vi* (*in vehicle*) tourner; **to t. on** *vt* (*light, radio etc*) mettre, allumer; (*tap*) ouvrir; (*machine*) mettre en marche; **to t. s.o. on** (*sexually*) *Fam* exciter qn; − *vi* **to t. on s.o.** (*attack*) attaquer qn; **to t. out** *vt* (*light*) éteindre; (*contents of box etc*) vider (**from** de); (*produce*) produire; − *vi* (*of crowds*) venir; (*happen*) se passer; **it turns out that il**

s'avère que; **she turned out to be** ... elle s'est révélée être ... ; **to t. over** vt (*page*) tourner; – vi (*of vehicle, person etc*) se retourner; (*of car engine*) tourner au ralenti; **to t. round** vt (*head, object*) tourner; (*vehicle*) faire faire demi-tour à; – vi (*of person*) se retourner; **to t. up** vt (*radio, light etc*) mettre plus fort; (*collar*) remonter; (*unearth, find*) déterrer; **a turned-up nose** un nez retroussé; – vi (*arrive*) arriver; (*be found*) être (re)trouvé. ◆**turning** n (*street*) petite rue f; (*bend in road*) tournant m; **t. circle** Aut rayon m de braquage; **t. point** (*in time*) tournant m. ◆**turner** n (*workman*) tourneur m.

turncoat ['tɜːnkəʊt] n renégat, -ate mf. ◆**turn-off** n (*in road*) embranchement m. ◆**turnout** n (*people*) assistance f; (*at polls*) participation f. ◆**turnover** n (*money*) Com chiffre m d'affaires; (*of stock*) Com rotation f; **staff t.** (*starting and leaving*) la rotation du personnel; **apple t.** chausson m (aux pommes). ◆**turnup** n (*on trousers*) revers m.

turnip ['tɜːnɪp] n navet m.

turnpike ['tɜːnpaɪk] n Am autoroute f à péage.

turnstile ['tɜːnstaɪl] n (*gate*) tourniquet m.

turntable ['tɜːnteɪb(ə)l] n (*of record player*) platine f.

turpentine ['tɜːpəntaɪn] (*Fam* **turps** [tɜːps]) n térébenthine f.

turquoise ['tɜːkwɔɪz] a turquoise inv.

turret ['tʌrɪt] n tourelle f.

turtle ['tɜːt(ə)l] n tortue f de mer; Am tortue f. ◆**turtleneck** (*a sweater*) à col roulé; – n col m roulé.

tusk [tʌsk] n (*of elephant*) défense f.

tussle ['tʌs(ə)l] n bagarre f.

tutor ['tjuːtər] n précepteur, -trice mf; Univ directeur, -trice mf d'études; Univ Am assistant, -ante mf; – vt donner des cours particuliers à. ◆**tu'torial** n Univ travaux mpl dirigés.

tut-tut! ['tʌt'tʌt] int allons donc!

tuxedo [tʌk'siːdəʊ] n (pl -os) Am smoking m.

TV [tiː'viː] n télé f.

twaddle ['twɒd(ə)l] n fadaises fpl.

twang [twæŋ] n son m vibrant; (*nasal*) **t.** nasillement m; – vi (*of wire etc*) vibrer.

twee [twiː] a (*fussy*) maniéré.

tweed [twiːd] n tweed m.

tweezers ['twiːzəz] npl pince f (à épiler).

twelve [twelv] a & n douze (m). ◆**twelfth** a & n douzième (mf).

twenty ['twentɪ] a & n vingt (m). ◆**twentieth** a & n vingtième (mf).

twerp [twɜːp] n Sl crétin, -ine mf.

twice [twaɪs] adv deux fois; **t. as heavy/etc** deux fois plus lourd/etc; **t. a month/etc, t. monthly/etc** deux fois par mois/etc.

twiddle ['twɪd(ə)l] vti **to t. (with) sth** (*pencil, knob etc*) tripoter qch; **to t. one's thumbs** se tourner les pouces.

twig [twɪg] n **1** (*of branch*) brindille f. **2** vti (-gg-) (*understand*) Sl piger.

twilight ['twaɪlaɪt] n crépuscule m; – a crépusculaire.

twin [twɪn] n jumeau m, jumelle f; **identical t.** vrai jumeau; **t. brother** frère m jumeau; **t. beds** lits mpl jumeaux; **t. town** ville f jumelée; – vt (-nn-) (*town*) jumeler. ◆**twinning** n jumelage m.

twine [twaɪn] **1** n (*string*) ficelle f. **2** vi (*twist*) s'enlacer (**round** autour de).

twinge [twɪndʒ] n a **t.** (*of pain*) un élancement; **a t. of remorse** un pincement de remords.

twinkle ['twɪŋk(ə)l] vi (*of star*) scintiller; (*of eye*) pétiller; – n scintillement m; pétillement m.

twirl [twɜːl] vi tournoyer; – vt faire tournoyer; (*moustache*) tortiller.

twist [twɪst] vt (*wine, arm etc*) tordre; (*roll round*) enrouler; (*weave together*) entortiller; (*knob*) tourner; (*truth etc*) Fig déformer; **to t. s.o.'s arm** Fig forcer la main à qn; – vi (*wind*) s'entortiller (**round sth** autour de qch); (*of road, river*) serpenter; – n torsion f; (*turn*) tour m; (*in rope*) entortillement m; (*bend in road*) tournant m; (*in story*) coup m de théâtre; (*in event*) tournure f; (*of lemon*) zeste m; **a road full of twists** une route qui fait des zigzags. ◆**-ed** a (*ankle, wire, mind*) tordu. ◆**-er** n **tongue t.** mot m or expression f imprononçable.

twit [twɪt] n Fam idiot, -ote mf.

twitch [twɪtʃ] **1** n (*nervous*) tic m; – vi (*of person*) avoir un tic; (*of muscle*) se convulser. **2** n (*jerk*) secousse f.

twitter ['twɪtər] vi (*of bird*) gazouiller.

two [tuː] a & n deux (m). ◆**t.-cycle** n Am = **t.-stroke**. ◆**t.-'faced** a Fig hypocrite. ◆**t.-'legged** a bipède. ◆**t.-piece** n (*garment*) deux-pièces m inv. ◆**t.-'seater** n Aut voiture f à deux places. ◆**t.-stroke** n **t.-stroke** (*engine*) deux-temps m inv. ◆**t.-way** a (*traffic*) dans les deux sens; **t.-way radio** émetteur-récepteur m.

twofold ['tuːfəʊld] a double; – adv **to increase t.** doubler.

twosome ['tuːsəm] n couple m.

tycoon [taɪ'kuːn] n magnat m.

type[1] [taɪp] n 1 (example, person) type m; (sort) genre m, sorte f, type m; **blood t.** groupe m sanguin. 2 (print) Typ caractères mpl; **in large t.** en gros caractères. ◆**typesetter** n compositeur, -trice mf.

typ/e[2] [taɪp] vti (write) taper (à la machine). ◆**—ing** n dactylo(graphie) f; **a page of t.** une page dactylographiée; **t. error** faute f de frappe. ◆**typewriter** n machine f à écrire. ◆**typewritten** a dactylographié. ◆**typist** n dactylo f.

typhoid ['taɪfɔɪd] n **t. (fever)** Med typhoïde f.

typhoon [taɪ'fuːn] n Met typhon m.

typical ['tɪpɪk(ə)l] a typique (of de); (customary) habituel; **that's t. (of him)!** c'est bien lui! ◆**typically** adv typiquement; (as usual) comme d'habitude. ◆**typify** vt être typique de; (symbolize) représenter.

tyranny ['tɪrənɪ] n tyrannie f. ◆**ty'rannical** a tyrannique. ◆**tyrant** ['taɪərənt] n tyran m.

tyre ['taɪər] n pneu m.

U

U, u [juː] n U, u, m. ◆**U-turn** n Aut demi-tour m; Fig Pej volte-face f inv.

ubiquitous [juː'bɪkwɪtəs] a omniprésent.

udder ['ʌdər] n (of cow etc) pis m.

ugh! [ɜː(h)] int pouah!

ugly ['ʌglɪ] a (-ier, -iest) laid, vilain. ◆**ugliness** n laideur f.

UK [juː'keɪ] abbr = **United Kingdom.**

ulcer ['ʌlsər] n ulcère m.

ulterior [ʌl'tɪərɪər] a **u. motive** arrière-pensée f.

ultimate ['ʌltɪmət] a (final, last) ultime; (definitive) définitif; (basic) fondamental; (authority) suprême. ◆**—ly** adv (finally) à la fin; (fundamentally) en fin de compte; (subsequently) à une date ultérieure.

ultimatum [ʌltɪ'meɪtəm] n ultimatum m.

ultra- ['ʌltrə] pref ultra-.

ultramodern [ʌltrə'mɒdən] a ultra-moderne.

ultraviolet [ʌltrə'vaɪələt] a ultraviolet.

umbilical [ʌm'bɪlɪk(ə)l] a **u. cord** cordon m ombilical.

umbrage ['ʌmbrɪdʒ] n **to take u.** se froisser (at de).

umbrella [ʌm'brelə] n parapluie m; **u. stand** porte-parapluies m inv.

umpire ['ʌmpaɪər] n Sp arbitre m; – vt arbitrer.

umpteen [ʌmp'tiːn] a (many) Fam je ne sais combien de. ◆**umpteenth** a Fam énième.

un- [ʌn] pref in-, peu, non, sans.

UN [juː'en] abbr = **United Nations.**

unabashed [ʌnə'bæʃt] a nullement déconcerté.

unabated [ʌnə'beɪtɪd] a aussi fort qu'avant.

unable [ʌn'eɪb(ə)l] a **to be u. to do** être incapable de faire; **he's u. to swim** il ne sait pas nager.

unabridged [ʌnə'brɪdʒd] a intégral.

unacceptable [ʌnək'septəb(ə)l] a inacceptable.

unaccompanied [ʌnə'kʌmpənɪd] a (person) non accompagné; (singing) sans accompagnement.

unaccountab/le [ʌnə'kaʊntəb(ə)l] a inexplicable. ◆**—ly** adv inexplicablement.

unaccounted [ʌnə'kaʊntɪd] a **to be (still) u. for** rester introuvable.

unaccustomed [ʌnə'kʌstəmd] a inaccoutumé; **to be u. to sth/to doing** ne pas être habitué à qch/à faire.

unadulterated [ʌn'ədʌltəreɪtɪd] a pur.

unaided [ʌn'eɪdɪd] a sans aide.

unanimity [juːnə'nɪmɪtɪ] n unanimité f. ◆**u'nanimous** a unanime. ◆**u'nanimously** adv à l'unanimité.

unappetizing [ʌn'æpɪtaɪzɪŋ] a peu appétissant.

unapproachable [ʌnə'prəʊtʃəb(ə)l] a (person) inabordable.

unarmed [ʌn'ɑːmd] a (person) non armé; (combat) à mains nues.

unashamed [ʌnə'ʃeɪmd] a éhonté; **she's u. about it** elle n'en a pas honte. ◆**—ly** [-ɪdlɪ] adv sans vergogne.

unassailable [ʌnə'seɪləb(ə)l] a (argument, reputation) inattaquable.

unassuming [ʌnə'sjuːmɪŋ] a modeste.

unattached [ʌnə'tætʃt] a (independent, not married) libre.

unattainable [ʌnə'teɪnəb(ə)l] a (goal, aim) inaccessible.

unattended [ʌnə'tendɪd] a sans surveillance.

unattractive [ʌnə'træktɪv] a (idea, appearance etc) peu attrayant; (character) peu sympathique; (ugly) laid.

unauthorized [ʌn'ɔːθəraɪzd] a non autorisé.

unavailable [ʌnə'veɪləb(ə)l] a (person, funds) indisponible; (article) Com épuisé.

unavoidab/le [ʌnə'vɔɪdəb(ə)l] a inévitable. ◆—ly adv inévitablement; (delayed) pour une raison indépendante de sa volonté.

unaware [ʌnə'weər] a to be u. of ignorer; to be u. that ignorer que. ◆**unawares** adv to catch s.o. u. prendre qn au dépourvu.

unbalanced [ʌn'bælənst] a (mind, person) déséquilibré.

unbearab/le [ʌn'beərəb(ə)l] a insupportable. ◆—ly adv insupportablement.

unbeatable [ʌn'biːtəb(ə)l] a imbattable. ◆**unbeaten** a (player) invaincu; (record) non battu.

unbeknown(st) [ʌnbɪ'nəʊn(st)] a u. to à l'insu de.

unbelievable [ʌnbɪ'liːvəb(ə)l] a incroyable. ◆**unbelieving** a incrédule.

unbend [ʌn'bend] vi (pt & pp unbent) (relax) se détendre. ◆—ing a inflexible.

unbias(s)ed [ʌn'baɪəst] a impartial.

unblock [ʌn'blɒk] vt (sink etc) déboucher.

unborn [ʌn'bɔːn] a (child) à naître.

unbounded [ʌn'baʊndɪd] a illimité.

unbreakable [ʌn'breɪkəb(ə)l] a incassable. ◆**unbroken** a (continuous) continu; (intact) intact; (record) non battu.

unbridled [ʌn'braɪd(ə)ld] a Fig débridé.

unburden [ʌn'bɜːd(ə)n] vt to u. oneself Fig s'épancher (to auprès de, avec).

unbutton [ʌn'bʌt(ə)n] vt déboutonner.

uncalled-for [ʌn'kɔːldfɔːr] a déplacé, injustifié.

uncanny [ʌn'kænɪ] a (-ier, -iest) étrange, mystérieux.

unceasing [ʌn'siːsɪŋ] a incessant. ◆—ly adv sans cesse.

unceremoniously [ʌnserɪ'məʊnɪəslɪ] adv (to treat) sans ménagement; (to show out) brusquement.

uncertain [ʌn'sɜːt(ə)n] a incertain (about, of de); it's or he's u. whether or that il n'est pas certain que (+ sub). ◆**uncertainty** n incertitude f.

unchanged [ʌn'tʃeɪndʒd] a inchangé. ◆**unchanging** a immuable.

uncharitable [ʌn'tʃærɪtəb(ə)l] a peu charitable.

unchecked [ʌn'tʃekt] adv sans opposition.

uncivil [ʌn'sɪv(ə)l] a impoli, incivil.

uncivilized [ʌn'sɪvɪlaɪzd] a barbare.

uncle ['ʌŋk(ə)l] n oncle m.

unclear [ʌn'klɪər] a (meaning) qui n'est pas clair; (result) incertain; it's u. whether ... on ne sait pas très bien si ....

uncomfortable [ʌn'kʌmftəb(ə)l] a (house, chair etc) inconfortable; (heat, experience) désagréable; (feeling) troublant; she is or feels u. (uneasy) elle est mal à l'aise.

uncommon [ʌn'kɒmən] a rare. ◆—ly adv (very) extraordinairement; not u. (fairly often) assez souvent.

uncommunicative [ʌnkə'mjuːnɪkətɪv] a peu communicatif.

uncomplicated [ʌn'kɒmplɪkeɪtɪd] a simple.

uncompromising [ʌn'kɒmprəmaɪzɪŋ] a intransigeant.

unconcerned [ʌnkən'sɜːnd] a (not anxious) imperturbable; (indifferent) indifférent (by, with à).

unconditional [ʌnkən'dɪʃ(ə)nəl] a inconditionnel; (surrender) sans condition.

unconfirmed [ʌnkən'fɜːmd] a non confirmé.

uncongenial [ʌnkən'dʒiːnɪəl] a peu agréable; (person) antipathique.

unconnected [ʌnkə'nektɪd] a (events, facts etc) sans rapport (with avec).

unconscious [ʌn'kɒnʃəs] a Med sans connaissance; (desire) inconscient; u. of (unaware of) inconscient de; – n Psy inconscient m. ◆—ly adv inconsciemment.

uncontrollable [ʌnkən'trəʊləb(ə)l] a (emotion, laughter) irrépressible.

unconventional [ʌnkən'venʃ(ə)nəl] a peu conventionnel.

unconvinced [ʌnkən'vɪnst] a to be or remain u. ne pas être convaincu (of de). ◆**unconvincing** a peu convaincant.

uncooperative [ʌnkəʊ'ɒp(ə)rətɪv] a peu coopératif.

uncork [ʌn'kɔːk] vt (bottle) déboucher.

uncouple [ʌn'kʌp(ə)l] vt (carriages) Rail dételer.

uncouth [ʌn'kuːθ] a grossier.

uncover [ʌn'kʌvər] vt (saucepan, conspiracy etc) découvrir.

unctuous ['ʌŋktjʊəs] a (insincere) onctueux.

uncut [ʌn'kʌt] a (film, play) intégral; (diamond) brut.

undamaged [ʌn'dæmɪdʒd] a (goods) en bon état.

undaunted [ʌn'dɔːntɪd] a nullement découragé.

undecided [ʌndɪ'saɪdɪd] a (person) indécis

(about sur); **I'm u. whether to do it or not** je n'ai pas décidé si je le ferai ou non.

undefeated [ʌndɪ'fiːtɪd] a invaincu.

undeniable [ʌndɪ'naɪəb(ə)l] a incontestable.

under ['ʌndər] prep sous; (less than) moins de; (according to) selon; **children u. nine** les enfants de moins de or enfants au-dessous de neuf ans; **u. the circumstances** dans les circonstances; **u. there** là-dessous; **u. it** dessous; **u. (the command of) s.o.** sous les ordres de qn; **u. age** mineur; **u. discussion/repair** en discussion/réparation; **u. way** (in progress) en cours; (on the way) en route; **to be u. the impression that** avoir l'impression que; – adv au-dessous.

under- ['ʌndər] pref sous-.

undercarriage ['ʌndəkærɪdʒ] n (of aircraft) train m d'atterrissage.

undercharge [ʌndə'tʃɑːdʒ] vt **I undercharged him (for it)** je ne (le) lui ai pas fait payer assez.

underclothes ['ʌndəkləʊðz] npl sous-vêtements mpl.

undercoat ['ʌndəkəʊt] n (of paint) couche f de fond.

undercooked [ʌndə'kʊkt] a pas assez cuit.

undercover [ʌndə'kʌvər] a (agent, operation) secret.

undercurrent ['ʌndəkʌrənt] n (in sea) courant m (sous-marin); **an u. of** Fig un courant profond de .

undercut [ʌndə'kʌt] vt (pt & pp undercut, pres p undercutting) Com vendre moins cher que.

underdeveloped [ʌndədɪ'veləpt] a (country) sous-développé.

underdog ['ʌndədɒg] n (politically, socially) opprimé, -ée mf; (likely loser) perdant, -ante mf probable.

underdone [ʌndə'dʌn] a Culin pas assez cuit; (steak) saignant.

underestimate [ʌndər'estɪmeɪt] vt sous-estimer.

underfed [ʌndə'fed] a sous-alimenté.

underfoot [ʌndə'fʊt] adv sous les pieds.

undergo [ʌndə'gəʊ] vt (pt underwent, pp undergone) subir.

undergraduate [ʌndə'grædʒʊət] n étudiant, -ante mf (qui prépare une licence).

underground ['ʌndəgraʊnd] a souterrain; (secret) Fig clandestin; – n Rail métro m; (organization) Pol résistance f; – [ʌndə-'graʊnd] adv sous terre; **to go u.** (of fugitive etc) Fig passer dans la clandestinité.

undergrowth ['ʌndəgrəʊθ] n sous-bois m inv.

underhand [ʌndə'hænd] a (dishonest) sournois.

underlie [ʌndə'laɪ] vt (pt underlay, pp underlain, pres p underlying) sous-tendre. ◆**underlying** a (basic) fondamental; (hidden) profond.

underline [ʌndə'laɪn] vt (text, idea etc) souligner.

undermanned [ʌndə'mænd] a (office etc) à court de personnel.

undermine [ʌndə'maɪn] vt (building, strength, society etc) miner, saper.

underneath [ʌndə'niːθ] prep sous; – adv (en) dessous; **the book u.** le livre d'en dessous; – n dessous m.

undernourished [ʌndə'nʌrɪʃt] a sous-alimenté.

underpants ['ʌndəpænts] npl (male underwear) slip m; (loose, long) caleçon m.

underpass ['ʌndəpɑːs] n (for cars or pedestrians) passage m souterrain.

underpay [ʌndə'peɪ] vt sous-payer. ◆**underpaid** a sous-payé.

underpriced [ʌndə'praɪst] a **it's u.** le prix est trop bas, c'est bradé.

underprivileged [ʌndə'prɪvɪlɪdʒd] a défavorisé.

underrate [ʌndə'reɪt] vt sous-estimer.

undershirt ['ʌndəʃɜːt] n Am tricot m or maillot m de corps.

underside ['ʌndəsaɪd] n dessous m.

undersigned [ʌndə'saɪnd] a soussigné; **I the u.** je soussigné(e).

undersized [ʌndə'saɪzd] a trop petit.

underskirt ['ʌndəskɜːt] n jupon m.

understaffed [ʌndə'stɑːft] a à court de personnel.

understand [ʌndə'stænd] vti (pt & pp understood) comprendre; **I u. that** (hear) je crois comprendre que, il paraît que; **I've been given to u. that** on m'a fait comprendre que. ◆**—ing** n (act, faculty) compréhension f; (agreement) accord m, entente f; (sympathy) entente f; **on the u. that** à condition que (+ sub); – a (person) compréhensif. ◆**understood** a (agreed) entendu; (implied) sous-entendu. ◆**understandable** a compréhensible. ◆**understandably** adv naturellement.

understatement ['ʌndəsteɪtmənt] n euphémisme m.

understudy ['ʌndəstʌdɪ] n Th doublure f.

undertake [ʌndə'teɪk] vt (pt undertook, pp undertaken) (task) entreprendre; (responsibility) assumer; **to u. to do** se charger de faire. ◆**—ing** n (task) entreprise f; (prom-

ise) promesse *f*; **to give an u.** promettre (**that** que).

undertaker ['ʌndəteɪkər] *n* entrepreneur *m* de pompes funèbres.

undertone ['ʌndətəʊn] *n* **in an u.** à mi-voix; **an u. of** (*criticism, sadness etc*) Fig une note de.

undervalue [ʌndə'væljuː] *vt* sous-évaluer; **it's undervalued at ten pounds** ça vaut plus que dix livres.

underwater [ʌndə'wɔːtər] *a* sous-marin; — *adv* sous l'eau.

underwear ['ʌndəweər] *n* sous-vêtements *mpl.*

underweight [ʌndə'weɪt] *a* (*person*) qui ne pèse pas assez; (*goods*) d'un poids insuffisant.

underworld ['ʌndəwɜːld] *n* **the u.** (*criminals*) le milieu, la pègre.

undesirable [ʌndɪ'zaɪərəb(ə)l] *a* peu souhaitable (**that** que (+ *sub*)); (*person*) indésirable; — *n* (*person*) indésirable *mf.*

undetected [ʌndɪ'tektɪd] *a* non découvert; **to go u.** passer inaperçu.

undies ['ʌndɪz] *npl* (*female underwear*) Fam dessous *mpl.*

undignified [ʌn'dɪgnɪfaɪd] *a* qui manque de dignité.

undisciplined [ʌn'dɪsɪplɪnd] *a* indiscipliné.

undiscovered [ʌndɪ'skʌvəd] *a* **to remain u.** ne pas être découvert.

undisputed [ʌndɪ'spjuːtɪd] *a* incontesté.

undistinguished [ʌndɪ'stɪŋgwɪʃt] *a* médiocre.

undivided [ʌndɪ'vaɪdɪd] *a* **my u. attention** toute mon attention.

undo [ʌn'duː] *vt* (*pt* undid, *pp* undone) défaire; (*bound person, hands*) détacher, délier; (*a wrong*) réparer. ◆**—ing** *n* (*downfall*) perte *f*, ruine *f*. ◆**undone** *a* **to leave u.** (*work etc*) ne pas faire; **to come u.** (*of knot etc*) se défaire.

undoubted [ʌn'daʊtɪd] *a* indubitable. ◆**—ly** *adv* indubitablement.

undreamt-of [ʌn'dremtɒv] *a* insoupçonné.

undress [ʌn'dres] *vi* se déshabiller; — *vt* déshabiller; **to get undressed** se déshabiller.

undue [ʌn'djuː] *a* excessif. ◆**unduly** *adv* excessivement.

undulating ['ʌndjuleɪtɪŋ] *a* (*movement*) onduleux; (*countryside*) vallonné.

undying [ʌn'daɪɪŋ] *a* éternel.

unearned [ʌn'ɜːnd] *a* **u. income** rentes *fpl.*

unearth [ʌn'ɜːθ] *vt* (*from ground*) déterrer; (*discover*) Fig dénicher, déterrer.

unearthly [ʌn'ɜːθlɪ] *a* sinistre, mystérieux; **u. hour** Fam heure *f* indue.

uneasy [ʌn'iːzɪ] *a* (*peace, situation*) précaire; (*silence*) gêné; **to be** or **feel u.** (*ill at ease*) être mal à l'aise, être gêné; (*worried*) être inquiet.

uneconomic(al) [ʌniːkə'nɒmɪk((ə)l)] *a* peu économique.

uneducated [ʌn'edʒʊkeɪtɪd] *a* (*person*) inculte; (*accent*) populaire.

unemployed [ʌnɪm'plɔɪd] *a* sans travail, en chômage; — *n* **the u.** les chômeurs *mpl.* ◆**unemployment** *n* chômage *m.*

unending [ʌn'endɪŋ] *a* interminable.

unenthusiastic [ʌnɪnθjuːzɪ'æstɪk] *a* peu enthousiaste.

unenviable [ʌn'envɪəb(ə)l] *a* peu enviable.

unequal [ʌn'iːkwəl] *a* inégal; **to be u. to** (*task*) ne pas être à la hauteur de. ◆**unequalled** *a* (*incomparable*) inégalé.

unequivocal [ʌnɪ'kwɪvək(ə)l] *a* sans équivoque.

unerring [ʌn'ɜːrɪŋ] *a* infaillible.

unethical [ʌn'eθɪk(ə)l] *a* immoral.

uneven [ʌn'iːv(ə)n] *a* inégal.

uneventful [ʌnɪ'ventfəl] *a* (*journey, life etc*) sans histoires.

unexceptionable [ʌnɪk'sepʃ(ə)nəb(ə)l] *a* irréprochable.

unexpected [ʌnɪk'spektɪd] *a* inattendu. ◆**—ly** *adv* à l'improviste; (*suddenly*) subitement; (*unusually*) exceptionnellement.

unexplained [ʌnɪk'spleɪnd] *a* inexpliqué.

unfailing [ʌn'feɪlɪŋ] *a* (*optimism, courage, support etc*) inébranlable; (*supply*) inépuisable.

unfair [ʌn'feər] *a* injuste (**to s.o.** envers qn); (*competition*) déloyal. ◆**—ly** *adv* injustement. ◆**—ness** *n* injustice *f.*

unfaithful [ʌn'feɪθfəl] *a* infidèle (**to** à).

unfamiliar [ʌnfə'mɪlɪər] *a* inconnu, peu familier; **to be u. with** ne pas connaître.

unfashionable [ʌn'fæʃ(ə)nəb(ə)l] *a* (*subject etc*) démodé; (*district etc*) peu chic *inv*, ringard; **it's u. to do** il n'est pas de bon ton de faire.

unfasten [ʌn'fɑːs(ə)n] *vt* défaire.

unfavourable [ʌn'feɪv(ə)rəb(ə)l] *a* défavorable.

unfeeling [ʌn'fiːlɪŋ] *a* insensible.

unfinished [ʌn'fɪnɪʃt] *a* inachevé; **to have some u. business** avoir une affaire à régler.

unfit [ʌn'fɪt] *a* (*unwell*) mal fichu; (*unsuited*) inapte (**for sth** à qch, **to do** à faire); (*unworthy*) indigne (**for sth** de qch, **to do** de faire).

to be u. to do (*incapable*) ne pas être en état de faire.

unflagging [ʌn'flægɪŋ] *a* (*zeal*) inlassable; (*interest*) soutenu.

unflappable [ʌn'flæpəb(ə)l] *a Fam* imperturbable.

unflattering [ʌn'flæt(ə)rɪŋ] *a* peu flatteur.

unflinching [ʌn'flɪntʃɪŋ] *a* (*fearless*) intrépide.

unfold [ʌn'fəʊld] *vt* déplier; (*wings*) déployer; (*ideas, plan*) *Fig* exposer; — *vi* (*of story, view*) se dérouler.

unforeseeable [ʌnfɔː'siːəb(ə)l] *a* imprévisible. ◆**unforeseen** *a* imprévu.

unforgettable [ʌnfə'getəb(ə)l] *a* inoubliable.

unforgivable [ʌnfə'ɡɪvəb(ə)l] *a* impardonnable.

unfortunate [ʌn'fɔːtʃ(ə)nət] *a* malheureux; (*event*) fâcheux; **you were u.** tu n'as pas eu de chance. ◆**-ly** *adv* malheureusement.

unfounded [ʌn'faʊndɪd] *a* (*rumour etc*) sans fondement.

unfriendly [ʌn'frendlɪ] *a* peu amical, froid. ◆**unfriendliness** *n* froideur *f*.

unfulfilled [ʌnfʊl'fɪld] *a* (*desire*) insatisfait; (*plan*) non réalisé; (*condition*) non rempli.

unfurl [ʌn'fɜːl] *vt* (*flag etc*) déployer.

unfurnished [ʌn'fɜːnɪʃt] *a* non meublé.

ungainly [ʌn'ɡeɪnlɪ] *a* (*clumsy*) gauche.

ungodly [ʌn'ɡɒdlɪ] *a* impie; **u. hour** *Fam* heure *f* indue.

ungrammatical [ʌnɡrə'mætɪk(ə)l] *a* non grammatical.

ungrateful [ʌn'ɡreɪtfəl] *a* ingrat.

unguarded [ʌn'ɡɑːdɪd] *a* **in an u. moment** dans un moment d'inattention.

unhappy [ʌn'hæpɪ] *a* (**-ier, -iest**) (*sad*) malheureux, triste; (*worried*) inquiet; **u. with** (*not pleased*) mécontent de; **he's u. about doing it** ça le dérange de le faire. ◆**unhappily** *adv* (*unfortunately*) malheureusement. ◆**unhappiness** *n* tristesse *f*.

unharmed [ʌn'hɑːmd] *a* indemne, sain et sauf.

unhealthy [ʌn'helθɪ] *a* (**-ier, -iest**) (*person*) en mauvaise santé; (*climate, place, job*) malsain; (*lungs*) malade.

unheard-of [ʌn'hɜːdɒv] *a* (*unprecedented*) inouï.

unheeded [ʌn'hiːdɪd] *a* **it went u.** on n'en a pas tenu compte.

unhelpful [ʌn'helpfəl] *a* (*person*) peu obligeant *or* serviable; (*advice*) peu utile.

unhinge [ʌn'hɪndʒ] *vt* (*person, mind*) déséquilibrer.

unholy [ʌn'həʊlɪ] *a* (**-ier, -iest**) impie; (*din*) *Fam* de tous les diables.

unhook [ʌn'hʊk] *vt* (*picture, curtain*) décrocher; (*dress*) dégrafer.

unhoped-for [ʌn'həʊptfɔːr] *a* inespéré.

unhurried [ʌn'hʌrɪd] *a* (*movement*) lent; (*stroll, journey*) fait sans hâte.

unhurt [ʌn'hɜːt] *a* indemne, sain et sauf.

unhygienic [ʌnhaɪ'dʒiːnɪk] *a* pas très hygiénique.

unicorn [ˈjuːnɪkɔːn] *n* licorne *f*.

uniform [ˈjuːnɪfɔːm] **1** *n* uniforme *m.* **2** *a* (*regular*) uniforme; (*temperature*) constant. ◆**uniformed** *a* en uniforme. ◆**uni'formity** *n* uniformité *f*. ◆**uniformly** *adv* uniformément.

unify [ˈjuːnɪfaɪ] *vt* unifier. ◆**unifi'cation** *n* unification *f*.

unilateral [juːnɪ'læt(ə)rəl] *a* unilatéral.

unimaginable [ʌnɪ'mædʒɪnəb(ə)l] *a* inimaginable. ◆**unimaginative** *a* (*person, plan etc*) qui manque d'imagination.

unimpaired [ʌnɪm'peəd] *a* intact.

unimportant [ʌnɪm'pɔːtənt] *a* peu important.

uninhabitable [ʌnɪn'hæbɪtəb(ə)l] *a* inhabitable. ◆**uninhabited** *a* inhabité.

uninhibited [ʌnɪn'hɪbɪtɪd] *a* (*person*) sans complexes.

uninitiated [ʌnɪ'nɪʃɪeɪtɪd] *n* **the u.** les profanes *mpl*, les non-initiés.

uninjured [ʌn'ɪndʒəd] *a* indemne.

uninspiring [ʌnɪn'spaɪərɪŋ] *a* (*subject etc*) pas très inspirant.

unintelligible [ʌnɪn'telɪdʒəb(ə)l] *a* inintelligible.

unintentional [ʌnɪn'tenʃ(ə)nəl] *a* involontaire.

uninterested [ʌn'ɪntrɪstɪd] *a* indifférent (**in** à). ◆**uninteresting** *a* (*book etc*) inintéressant; (*person*) fastidieux.

uninterrupted [ʌnɪntə'rʌptɪd] *a* ininterrompu.

uninvited [ʌnɪn'vaɪtɪd] *a* (*to arrive*) sans invitation. ◆**uninviting** *a* peu attrayant.

union [ˈjuːnɪən] *n* union *f*; (*trade union*) syndicat *m*; – *a* syndical; (*trade*) **u. member** syndiqué, -ée *mf*; **U. Jack** drapeau *m* britannique. ◆**unionist** *n* **trade u.** syndicaliste *mf*. ◆**unionize** *vt* syndiquer.

unique [juː'niːk] *a* unique. ◆**-ly** *adv* exceptionnellement.

unisex [ˈjuːnɪseks] *a* (*clothes etc*) unisexe *inv*.

unison [ˈjuːnɪs(ə)n] *n* **in u.** à l'unisson (**with** de).

unit [ˈjuːnɪt] *n* unité *f*; (*of furniture etc*) élément *m*; (*system*) bloc *m*; (*group, team*) groupe *m*; **u. trust** *Fin* fonds *m* commun de placement.

unite [ju:'naɪt] *vt* unir; (*country, party*) unifier; **United Kingdom** Royaume-Uni *m*; **United Nations** (Organisation *f* des) Nations unies *fpl*; **United States of America**) États-Unis *mpl* (d'Amérique); – *vi* s'unir. ◆**unity** *n* (*cohesion*) unité *f*; (*harmony*) *Fig* harmonie *f*.

universal [ju:nɪ'vɜːs(ə)l] *a* universel. ◆**-ly** *adv* universellement.

universe ['ju:nɪvɜːs] *n* univers *m*.

university [ju:nɪ'vɜːsɪtɪ] *n* université *f*; at **u.** à l'université; – *a* universitaire; (*student, teacher*) d'université.

unjust [ʌn'dʒʌst] *a* injuste.

unjustified [ʌn'dʒʌstɪfaɪd] *a* injustifié.

unkempt [ʌn'kempt] *a* (*appearance*) négligé; (*hair*) mal peigné.

unkind [ʌn'kaɪnd] *a* peu aimable (**to s.o.** avec qn); (*nasty*) méchant (**to s.o.** avec qn). ◆**-ly** *adv* méchamment.

unknowingly [ʌn'nəʊɪŋlɪ] *adv* inconsciemment.

unknown [ʌn'nəʊn] *a* inconnu; **u. to me,** he'd left il était parti, ce que j'ignorais; – *n* (*person*) inconnu, -ue *mf*; **the u.** *Phil* l'inconnu *m*; **u. (quantity)** *Math* & *Fig* inconnue *f*.

unlawful [ʌn'lɔːf(ə)l] *a* illégal.

unleaded [ʌn'ledɪd] *a* (*gasoline*) *Am* sans plomb.

unleash [ʌn'liːʃ] *vt* (*force etc*) déchaîner.

unless [ʌn'les] *conj* à moins que; **u. she comes** à moins qu'elle ne vienne; **u. you work harder, you'll fail** à moins de travailler plus dur, vous échouerez.

unlike [ʌn'laɪk] *a* différent; – *prep* **u. me, she** . . . à la différence de moi *or* contrairement à moi, elle . . .; **he's very u. his father** il n'est pas du tout comme son père; **that's u. him** ça ne lui ressemble pas.

unlikely [ʌn'laɪklɪ] *a* improbable; (*implausible*) invraisemblable; **she's u. to win** il est peu probable qu'elle gagne. ◆**unlikelihood** *n* improbabilité *f*.

unlimited [ʌn'lɪmɪtɪd] *a* illimité.

unlisted [ʌn'lɪstɪd] *a* (*phone number*) *Am* qui ne figure pas à l'annuaire.

unload [ʌn'ləʊd] *vt* décharger.

unlock [ʌn'lɒk] *vt* ouvrir (*avec une clef*).

unlucky [ʌn'lʌkɪ] *a* (**-ier, -iest**) (*person*) malchanceux; (*colour, number etc*) qui porte malheur; **you're u.** tu n'as pas de chance. ◆**unluckily** *adv* malheureusement.

unmade [ʌn'meɪd] *a* (*bed*) défait.

unmanageable [ʌn'mænɪdʒəb(ə)l] *a* (*child*) difficile; (*hair*) difficile à coiffer; (*packet, size*) peu maniable.

unmanned [ʌn'mænd] *a* (*ship*) sans équipage; (*spacecraft*) inhabité.

unmarked [ʌn'mɑːkt] *a* (*not blemished*) sans marque; **u. police car** voiture *f* banalisée.

unmarried [ʌn'mærɪd] *a* célibataire.

unmask [ʌn'mɑːsk] *vt* démasquer.

unmentionable [ʌn'menʃ(ə)nəb(ə)l] *a* dont il ne faut pas parler; (*unpleasant*) innommable.

unmercifully [ʌn'mɜːsɪf(ə)lɪ] *adv* sans pitié.

unmistakable [ʌnmɪ'steɪkəb(ə)l] *a* (*obvious*) indubitable; (*face, voice etc*) facilement reconnaissable.

unmitigated [ʌn'mɪtɪɡeɪtɪd] *a* (*disaster*) absolu; (*folly*) pur.

unmoved [ʌn'muːvd] *a* **to be u.** (*feel no emotion*) ne pas être ému (**by par**); (*be unconcerned*) être indifférent (**by** à).

unnatural [ʌn'nætʃ(ə)rəl] *a* (*not normal*) pas naturel; (*crime*) contre nature; (*affected*) qui manque de naturel. ◆**-ly** *adv* **not u.** naturellement.

unnecessary [ʌn'nesəs(ə)rɪ] *a* inutile; (*superfluous*) superflu.

unnerve [ʌn'nɜːv] *vt* désarçonner, déconcerter.

unnoticed [ʌn'nəʊtɪst] *a* inaperçu.

unobstructed [ʌnəb'strʌktɪd] *a* (*road, view*) dégagé.

unobtainable [ʌnəb'teɪnəb(ə)l] *a* impossible à obtenir.

unobtrusive [ʌnəb'truːsɪv] *a* discret.

unoccupied [ʌn'ɒkjupaɪd] *a* (*person, house*) inoccupé; (*seat*) libre.

unofficial [ʌnə'fɪʃ(ə)l] *a* officieux; (*visit*) privé; (*strike*) sauvage. ◆**-ly** *adv* à titre officieux.

unorthodox [ʌn'ɔːθədɒks] *a* peu orthodoxe.

unpack [ʌn'pæk] *vt* (*case*) défaire; (*goods, belongings, contents*) déballer; **to u. a comb/etc from** sortir un peigne/etc de; – *vi* défaire sa valise; (*take out goods*) déballer.

unpaid [ʌn'peɪd] *a* (*bill, sum*) impayé; (*work, worker*) bénévole; (*leave*) non payé.

unpalatable [ʌn'pælətəb(ə)l] *a* désagréable, déplaisant.

unparalleled [ʌn'pærəleld] *a* sans égal.

unperturbed [ʌnpə'tɜːbd] *a* nullement déconcerté.

unplanned [ʌn'plænd] *a* (*visit, baby etc*) imprévu.

unpleasant [ʌn'plezənt] *a* désagréable (**to s.o.** avec qn). ◆**-ness** *n* caractère *m* désagréable (**of** de); (*quarrel*) petite querelle *f*.

unplug [ʌn'plʌg] *vt* (**-gg-**) *El* débrancher; (*unblock*) déboucher.

unpopular [ʌn'pɒpjʊlər] *a* impopulaire; **to be u. with** ne pas plaire à.

unprecedented [ʌn'presidentid] *a* sans précédent.

unpredictable [ʌnprɪ'dɪktəb(ə)l] *a* imprévisible; (*weather*) indécis.

unprepared [ʌnprɪ'peəd] *a* non préparé; (*speech*) improvisé; **to be u. for** (*not expect*) ne pas s'attendre à.

unprepossessing [ʌnpriːpə'zesɪŋ] *a* peu avenant.

unpretentious [ʌnprɪ'tenʃəs] *a* sans prétention.

unprincipled [ʌn'prɪnsɪp(ə)ld] *a* sans scrupules.

unprofessional [ʌnprə'feʃ(ə)nəl] *a* (*unethical*) contraire aux règles de sa profession.

unpublished [ʌn'pʌblɪʃt] *a* (*text, writer*) inédit.

unpunished [ʌn'pʌnɪʃt] *a* **to go u.** rester impuni.

unqualified [ʌn'kwɒlɪfaɪd] *a* **1** (*teacher etc*) non diplômé; **he's u. to do** il n'est pas qualifié pour faire. **2** (*support*) sans réserve; (*success, rogue*) parfait.

unquestionab/le [ʌn'kwestʃ(ə)nəb(ə)l] *a* incontestable. ◆**—ly** *adv* incontestablement.

unravel [ʌn'ræv(ə)l] *vt* (**-ll-**, *Am* **-l-**) (*threads etc*) démêler; (*mystery*) *Fig* éclaircir.

unreal [ʌn'rɪəl] *a* irréel. ◆**unrea'listic** *a* peu réaliste.

unreasonable [ʌn'riːz(ə)nəb(ə)l] *a* qui n'est pas raisonnable; (*price*) excessif.

unrecognizable [ʌnrekəg'naɪzəb(ə)l] *a* méconnaissable.

unrelated [ʌnrɪ'leɪtɪd] *a* (*facts etc*) sans rapport (**to** avec); **we're u.** il n'y a aucun lien de parenté entre nous.

unrelenting [ʌnrɪ'lentɪŋ] *a* (*person*) implacable; (*effort*) acharné.

unreliable [ʌnrɪ'laɪəb(ə)l] *a* (*person*) peu sérieux, peu sûr; (*machine*) peu fiable.

unrelieved [ʌnrɪ'liːvd] *a* (*constant*) constant; (*colour*) uniforme.

unremarkable [ʌnrɪ'mɑːkəb(ə)l] *a* médiocre.

unrepeatable [ʌnrɪ'piːtəb(ə)l] *a* (*offer*) unique.

unrepentant [ʌnrɪ'pentənt] *a* impénitent.

unreservedly [ʌnrɪ'zɜːvɪdlɪ] *adv* sans réserve.

unrest [ʌn'rest] *n* troubles *mpl*, agitation *f*.

unrestricted [ʌnrɪ'strɪktɪd] *a* illimité; (*access*) libre.

unrewarding [ʌnrɪ'wɔːdɪŋ] *a* ingrat; (*financially*) peu rémunérateur.

unripe [ʌn'raɪp] *a* (*fruit*) vert, pas mûr.

unroll [ʌn'rəʊl] *vt* dérouler; — *vi* se dérouler.

unruffled [ʌn'rʌf(ə)ld] *a* (*person*) calme.

unruly [ʌn'ruːlɪ] *a* (**-ier, -iest**) indiscipliné.

unsafe [ʌn'seɪf] *a* (*place, machine etc*) dangereux; (*person*) en danger.

unsaid [ʌn'sed] *a* **to leave sth u.** passer qch sous silence.

unsaleable [ʌn'seɪləb(ə)l] *a* invendable.

unsatisfactory [ʌnsætɪs'fækt(ə)rɪ] *a* peu satisfaisant. ◆**un'satisfied** *a* insatisfait; **u. with** peu satisfait de.

unsavoury [ʌn'seɪv(ə)rɪ] *a* (*person, place etc*) répugnant.

unscathed [ʌn'skeɪðd] *a* indemne.

unscrew [ʌn'skruː] *vt* dévisser.

unscrupulous [ʌn'skruːpjʊləs] *a* (*person, act*) peu scrupuleux.

unseemly [ʌn'siːmlɪ] *a* inconvenant.

unseen [ʌn'siːn] **1** *a* inaperçu. **2** *n* (*translation*) *Sch* version *f*.

unselfish [ʌn'selfɪʃ] *a* (*person, motive etc*) désintéressé.

unsettl/e [ʌn'set(ə)l] *vt* (*person*) troubler. ◆**—ed** *a* (*weather, situation*) instable; (*in one's mind*) troublé; (*in a job*) mal à l'aise.

unshakeable [ʌn'feɪkəb(ə)l] *a* (*person, faith*) inébranlable.

unshaven [ʌn'feɪv(ə)n] *a* pas rasé.

unsightly [ʌn'saɪtlɪ] *a* laid, disgracieux.

unskilled [ʌn'skɪld] *a* inexpert; (*work*) de manœuvre; **u. worker** manœuvre *m*, ouvrier, -ière *mf* non qualifié(e).

unsociable [ʌn'səʊʃəb(ə)l] *a* insociable.

unsocial [ʌn'səʊʃəl] *a* **to work u. hours** travailler en dehors des heures de bureau.

unsolved [ʌn'sɒlvd] *a* (*problem*) non résolu; (*mystery*) inexpliqué; (*crime*) dont l'auteur n'est pas connu.

unsophisticated [ʌnsə'fɪstɪkeɪtɪd] *a* simple.

unsound [ʌn'saʊnd] *a* (*construction etc*) peu solide; (*method*) peu sûr; (*decision*) peu judicieux; **he is of u. mind** il n'a pas toute sa raison.

unspeakable [ʌn'spiːkəb(ə)l] *a* (*horrible*) innommable.

unspecified [ʌn'spesɪfaɪd] *a* indéterminé.

unsporting [ʌn'spɔːtɪŋ] *a* déloyal.

unstable [ʌn'steɪb(ə)l] *a* instable.

unsteady [ʌn'stedɪ] *a* (*hand, voice, step etc*) mal assuré; (*table, ladder etc*) instable. ◆**unsteadily** *adv* (*to walk*) d'un pas mal assuré.

unstinting [ʌn'stɪntɪŋ] *a* (*generosity*) sans bornes.

unstoppable [ʌn'stɒpəb(ə)l] *a* qu'on ne peut (pas) arrêter.

unstuck [ʌn'stʌk] *a* **to come u.** (*of stamp etc*) se décoller; (*fail*) *Fam* se planter.

unsuccessful [ʌnsək'sesfəl] *a* (*attempt etc*) infructueux; (*outcome, candidate*) malheureux; (*application*) non retenu; **to be u.** ne pas réussir (**in doing** à faire); (*of book, artist*) ne pas avoir de succès. ◆—**ly** *adv* en vain, sans succès.

unsuitable [ʌn'suːtəb(ə)l] *a* qui ne convient pas (**for** à); (*example*) peu approprié; (*manners, clothes*) peu convenable. ◆**unsuited** *a* **u. to** impropre à; **they're u.** ils ne sont pas compatibles.

unsure [ʌn'ʃʊər] *a* incertain (**of, about** de).

unsuspecting [ʌnsə'spektɪŋ] *a* qui ne se doute de rien.

unswerving [ʌn'swɜːvɪŋ] *a* (*loyalty etc*) inébranlable.

unsympathetic [ʌnsɪmpə'θetɪk] *a* incompréhensif; **u. to** indifférent à.

untangle [ʌn'tæŋg(ə)l] *vt* (*rope etc*) démêler.

untapped [ʌn'tæpt] *a* inexploité.

untenable [ʌn'tenəb(ə)l] *a* (*position*) intenable.

unthinkable [ʌn'θɪŋkəb(ə)l] *a* impensable, inconcevable.

untidy [ʌn'taɪdɪ] *a* (**-ier, -iest**) (*appearance, hair*) peu soigné; (*room*) en désordre; (*unmethodical*) désordonné. ◆**untidily** *adv* sans soin.

untie [ʌn'taɪ] *vt* (*person, hands*) détacher; (*knot, parcel*) défaire.

until [ʌn'tɪl] *prep* jusqu'à; **u. then** jusque-là; **not u. tomorrow**/*etc* (*in the future*) pas avant demain/*etc*; **I didn't come u. Monday** (*in the past*) je ne suis venu que lundi; — *conj* **u. she comes** jusqu'à ce qu'elle vienne, en attendant qu'elle vienne; **nothing u. I come** (*before*) ne fais rien avant que j'arrive.

untimely [ʌn'taɪmlɪ] *a* inopportun; (*death*) prématuré.

untiring [ʌn'taɪə)rɪŋ] *a* infatigable.

untold [ʌn'təʊld] *a* (*quantity, wealth*) incalculable.

untoward [ʌntə'wɔːd] *a* malencontreux.

untranslatable [ʌntræn'leɪtəb(ə)l] *a* intraduisible.

untroubled [ʌn'trʌb(ə)ld] *a* (*calm*) calme.

untrue [ʌn'truː] *a* faux. ◆**untruth** *n* contre-vérité *f*. ◆**untruthful** *a* (*person*) menteur; (*statement*) mensonger.

unused 1 [ʌn'juːzd] *a* (*new*) neuf; (*not in use*) inutilisé. 2 [ʌn'juːst] *a* **u. to sth/to doing** peu habitué à qch/à faire.

unusual [ʌn'juːʒʊəl] *a* exceptionnel, rare; (*strange*) étrange. ◆—**ly** *adv* exceptionnellement.

unveil [ʌn'veɪl] *vt* dévoiler. ◆—**ing** *n* (*ceremony*) inauguration *f*.

unwanted [ʌn'wɒntɪd] *a* (*useless*) superflu, dont on n'a pas besoin; (*child*) non désiré.

unwarranted [ʌn'wɒrəntɪd] *a* injustifié.

unwavering [ʌn'weɪvə)rɪŋ] *a* (*belief etc*) inébranlable.

unwelcome [ʌn'welkəm] *a* (*news, fact*) fâcheux; (*gift, visit*) inopportun; (*person*) importun.

unwell [ʌn'wel] *a* indisposé.

unwieldy [ʌn'wiːldɪ] *a* (*package etc*) encombrant.

unwilling [ʌn'wɪlɪŋ] *a* **he's u. to do it** he ne veut pas faire, il est peu disposé à faire. ◆—**ly** *adv* à contrecœur.

unwind [ʌn'waɪnd] 1 *vt* (*thread etc*) dérouler; — *vi* se dérouler. 2 *vi* (*relax*) *Fam* décompresser.

unwise [ʌn'waɪz] *a* imprudent. ◆—**ly** *adv* imprudemment.

unwitting [ʌn'wɪtɪŋ] *a* involontaire. ◆—**ly** *adv* involontairement.

unworkable [ʌn'wɜːkəb(ə)l] *a* (*idea etc*) impraticable.

unworthy [ʌn'wɜːðɪ] *a* indigne (**of** de).

unwrap [ʌn'ræp] *vt* (**-pp-**) ouvrir, défaire.

unwritten [ʌn'rɪt(ə)n] *a* (*agreement*) verbal, tacite.

unyielding [ʌn'jiːldɪŋ] *a* (*person*) inflexible.

unzip [ʌn'zɪp] *vt* (**-pp-**) ouvrir (la fermeture éclair® de).

up [ʌp] *adv* en haut; (*in the air*) en l'air; (*of sun, hand*) levé; (*out of bed*) levé, debout; (*of road*) en travaux; (*of building*) construit; (*finished*) fini; **to come** *or* **go up** monter; **to be up** (*of price, level etc*) être monté (**by** de); **up there** là-haut; **up above** au-dessus; **up on** (*roof etc*) sur; **further** *or* **higher up** plus haut; **up to** (*as far as*) jusqu'à; (*task*) *Fig* à la hauteur de; **to be up to doing** (*capable*) être de taille à faire; (*in a position to*) être à même de faire; **it's up to you to do** c'est à toi de le faire; **it's up to you** ça dépend de toi; **where are you up to?** (*in book etc*) où en es-tu?; **what are you up to?** *Fam* que fais-tu?; **what's up?** (*what's the matter?*) *Fam* qu'est-ce qu'il y a?; **time's up** c'est l'heure; **halfway up** (*on hill etc*) à mi-chemin; **to walk up and down** marcher de long en large; **to be well up in** (*versed in*) *Fam* s'y connaître en; **to be up against**

(*confront*) être confronté à; **up (with) the workers/etc!** *Fam* vive(nt) les travailleurs/etc!; – *prep* (*a hill*) en haut de; (*a tree*) dans; (*a ladder*) sur; **to go up** (*hill, stairs*) monter; **to live up the street** habiter plus loin dans la rue; – *npl* **to have ups and downs** avoir des hauts et des bas; – *vt* (**-pp-**) (*increase*) *Fam* augmenter. ◆**up-and-'coming** *a* plein d'avenir. ◆**upbeat** *a* (*cheerful*) *Am Fam* optimiste. ◆**upbringing** *n* éducation *f*. ◆**upcoming** *a Am* imminent. ◆**up'date** *vt* mettre à jour. ◆**up'grade** *vt* (*job*) revaloriser; (*person*) promouvoir. ◆**up'hill 1** *adv* to go up **u. monter. 2** ['ʌphil] *a* (*struggle, task*) pénible. ◆**up'hold** *vt* (*pt & pp* **upheld**) maintenir. ◆**upkeep** *n* entretien *m*. ◆**uplift** [ʌp'lɪft] *vt* élever; – ['ʌplɪft] *n* élévation *f* spirituelle. ◆**upmarket** *a Com* haut de gamme. ◆**upright 1** *a & adv* (*erect*) droit; – *n* (*post*) montant *m*. **2** *a* (*honest*) droit. ◆**uprising** *n* insurrection *f*. ◆**up'root** *vt* (*plant, person*) déraciner. ◆**upside 'down** *adv* à l'envers; **to turn u. down** (*room, plans etc*) *Fig* chambouler. ◆**up'stairs** *adv* en haut; to go u. monter (l'escalier); – ['ʌpsteəz] *a* (*people, room*) du dessus. ◆**up'stream** *adv* en amont. ◆**upsurge** *n* (*of interest*) recrudescence *f*; (*of anger*) accès *m*. ◆**uptake** *n* **to be quick on the u.** comprendre vite. ◆**up'tight** *a Fam* (*tense*) crispé; (*angry*) en colère. ◆**up-to-'date** *a* moderne; (*information*) à jour; (*well-informed*) au courant (**on** de). ◆**upturn** *n* (*improvement*) amélioration *f* (**in** de); (*rise*) hausse *f* (**in** de). ◆**up'turned** *a* (*nose*) retroussé. ◆**upward** *a* (*movement*) ascendant; (*path*) qui monte; (*trend*) à la hausse. ◆**upwards** *adv* vers le haut; **from five francs u.** à partir de cinq francs; **u. of fifty** cinquante et plus.

upheaval [ʌp'hiːv(ə)l] *n* bouleversement *m*.

upholster [ʌp'həʊlstər] *vt* (*pad*) rembourrer; (*cover*) recouvrir. ◆**upholsterer** *n* tapissier *m*. ◆**upholstery** *n* (*activity*) réfection *f* de sièges; (*in car*) sièges *mpl*.

upon [ə'pɒn] *prep* sur.

upper ['ʌpər] **1** *a* supérieur; **u. class** aristocratie *f*; **to have/get the u. hand** avoir/prendre le dessus. **2** *n* (*of shoe*) empeigne *f*, dessus *m*. ◆**u.-'class** *a* aristocratique. ◆**uppermost** *a* (*highest*) le plus haut; **to be u.** (*on top*) être en dessus.

uproar ['ʌprɔːr] *n* tumulte *m!*

upset [ʌp'set] *vt* (*pt & pp* **upset**, *pres p* **upsetting**) (*knock over*) renverser; (*plans, stomach, routine etc*) déranger; **to s.o.** (*grieve*)

peiner qn; (*offend*) vexer qn; (*annoy*) contrarier qn; – *a* vexé; contrarié; (*stomach*) dérangé; – ['ʌpset] *n* (*in plans etc*) dérangement *m* (**in** de); (*grief*) peine *f*; **to have a stomach u.** avoir l'estomac dérangé.

upshot ['ʌpʃɒt] *n* résultat *m*.

upstart ['ʌpstɑːt] *n Pej* parvenu, -ue *mf*.

uranium [ju'reiniəm] *n* uranium *m*.

urban ['ɜːbən] *a* urbain.

urbane [ɜː'beɪn] *a* courtois, urbain.

urchin ['ɜːtʃin] *n* polisson, -onne *mf*.

urge [ɜːdʒ] *vt* **to u. s.o. to do** (*advise*) conseiller vivement à qn de faire; **to u.** on (*person, team*) encourager; – *n* forte envie *f*, besoin *m*.

urgency ['ɜːdʒənsi] *n* urgence *f*; (*of request, tone*) insistance *f*. ◆**urgent** *a* urgent, pressant; (*tone*) insistant; (*letter*) urgent. ◆**urgently** *adv* d'urgence; (*insistently*) avec insistance.

urinal [ju'raɪn(ə)l] *n* urinoir *m*.

urine ['ju(ə)rɪn] *n* urine *f*. ◆**urinate** *vi* uriner.

urn [ɜːn] *n* urne *f*; (*for coffee or tea*) fontaine *f*.

us [əs, *stressed* ʌs] *pron* nous; (**to) us** (*indirect*) nous; **she sees us** elle nous voit; **he gives (to) us** il nous donne; **with us** avec nous; **all of us** nous tous; **let's** or **let us eat!** mangeons!

US [juː'es] *abbr* = United States.

USA [juːes'eɪ] *abbr* = United States of America.

usage ['juːsɪdʒ] *n* (*custom*) & *Ling* usage *m*.

use 1 [juːs] *n* usage *m*, emploi *m*; (*way of using*) emploi *m*; **to have the u.** of avoir l'usage de; **to make u.** of se servir de; **in u.** en usage; **out of u.** hors d'usage; **ready for u.** prêt à l'emploi; **to be of u.** servir, être utile; **it's no u. crying/etc** ça ne sert à rien de pleurer/etc; **what's the u.** of worrying/etc? à quoi bon s'inquiéter/etc?, à quoi ça sert de s'inquiéter/etc?; **I have no u.** for it je n'en ai pas l'usage, qu'est-ce que je ferais de ça/etc?; **he's no u.** (*hopeless*) il est nul. – **2** [juːz] *vt* se servir de, utiliser, employer (**as** comme; **to do** pour faire); (*fuel etc*) consommer; (*supplies*) épuiser; (*money*) dépenser. ◆**used 1** [juːzd] *a* (*second-hand*) d'occasion; (*stamp*) oblitéré. ◆**2** [juːst] *v aux* **I u. to do** avant, je faisais; – *a* **to be u. to sth/to doing** (*accustomed*) habitué à qch/à faire; **to get u. to** s'habituer à. ◆**useful** ['juːsfəl] *a* utile; **to**

come in u. être utile; **to make oneself u.** se rendre utile. ◆**usefulness** *n* utilité *f.* ◆**useless** ['juːsləs] *a* inutile; (*unusable*) inutilisable; (*person*) nul, incompétent. ◆**user** [*juːzər*] *n* (*of road, dictionary etc*) usager *m*; (*of machine*) utilisateur, -trice *mf.*

usher ['ʌʃər] *n* (*in church or theatre*) placeur *m*; (*in law court*) huissier *m*; − *vt* **to u. in** faire entrer; (*period etc*) Fig inaugurer. ◆**ushe'rette** *n* Cin ouvreuse *f.*

USSR [juːesesˈɑːr] *n abbr* (*Union of Soviet Socialist Republics*) URSS *f.*

usual ['juːʒʊəl] *a* habituel, normal; **as u.** comme d'habitude; **it's her u. practice** c'est son habitude; − *n* **the u.** (*food, excuse etc*) *Fam* la même chose que d'habitude. ◆**—ly** *adv* d'habitude.

usurer ['juːʒərər] *n* usurier, -ière *mf.*

usurp [juːˈzɜːp] *vt* usurper.

utensil [juːˈtens(ə)l] *n* ustensile *m.*

uterus ['juːt(ə)rəs] *n* Anat utérus *m.*

utilitarian [juːtɪlɪˈteərɪən] *a* utilitaire. ◆**u'tility** *n* (*public*) **u.** service *m* public; − *a* (*goods vehicle*) utilitaire.

utilize ['juːtɪlaɪz] *vt* utiliser. ◆**utili'zation** *n* utilisation *f.*

utmost ['ʌtməʊst] *a* **the u. ease**/*etc* (*greatest*) la plus grande facilité/*etc*; **the u. danger/limit**/*etc* (*extreme*) un danger/une limite/*etc* extrême; − *n* **to do one's u.** faire tout son possible (**to do** pour faire).

utopia [juːˈtəʊpɪə] *n* (*perfect state*) utopie *f.* ◆**utopian** *a* utopique.

utter ['ʌtər] **1** *a* complet, total; (*folly*) pur; (*idiot*) parfait; **it's u. nonsense** c'est complètement absurde. **2** *vt* (*say, express*) proférer; (*a cry, sigh*) pousser. ◆**utterance** *n* (*remark etc*) déclaration *f*; **to give u. to** exprimer. ◆**utterly** *adv* complètement.

V

V, v [viː] *n* V *m*, v *m.* ◆**V.-neck(ed)** *a* (*pullover etc*) à col en V.

vacant ['veɪkənt] *a* (*post*) vacant; (*room, seat*) libre; (*look*) vague, dans le vide. ◆**vacancy** *n* (*post*) poste *m* vacant; (*room*) chambre *f* disponible; **'no vacancies'** (*in hotel*) 'complet'. ◆**vacantly** *adv* **to gaze v.** regarder dans le vide.

vacate [vəˈkeɪt, Am ˈveɪkeɪt] *vt* quitter.

vacation [veɪˈkeɪʃ(ə)n] *n Am* vacances *fpl*; **on v.** en vacances. ◆**—er** *n Am* vacancier, -ière *mf.*

vaccinate ['væksɪneɪt] *vt* vacciner. ◆**vacci'nation** *n* vaccination *f.* ◆**vaccine** [-iːn] *n* vaccin *m.*

vacillate ['væsɪleɪt] *vi* (*hesitate*) hésiter.

vacuum ['vækjʊ(ə)m] *n* vide *m*; **v. cleaner** aspirateur *m*; **v. flask** thermos® *m or f*; − *vt* (*carpet etc*) passer à l'aspirateur. ◆**v.-packed** *a* emballé sous vide.

vagabond ['vægəbɒnd] *n* vagabond, -onde *mf.*

vagary ['veɪɡərɪ] *n* caprice *m.*

vagina [vəˈdʒaɪnə] *n* vagin *m.*

vagrant ['veɪɡrənt] *n Jur* vagabond, -onde *mf.*

vague [veɪɡ] *a* (**-er, -est**) vague; (*memory, outline, photo*) flou; **the vaguest idea** la moindre idée; **he was v. (about it)** il est resté vague. ◆**—ly** *adv* vaguement.

vain [veɪn] *a* (**-er, -est**) **1** (*attempt, hope*) vain; **in v.** en vain; **his** *or* **her efforts were in v.** ses efforts ont été inutiles. **2** (*conceited*) vaniteux. ◆**—ly** *adv* (*in vain*) vainement.

valentine ['væləntaɪn] *n* (*card*) carte *f* de la Saint-Valentin.

valet ['væleɪ, 'vælet] *n* valet *m* de chambre.

valiant ['væljənt] *a* courageux. ◆**valour** *n* bravoure *f.*

valid ['vælɪd] *a* (*ticket, motive etc*) valable. ◆**validate** *vt* valider. ◆**va'lidity** *n* validité *f*; (*of argument*) justesse *f.*

valley ['vælɪ] *n* vallée *f.*

valuable ['væljʊəb(ə)l] *a* (*object*) de (grande) valeur; (*help, time etc*) *Fig* précieux; − *npl* objets *mpl* de valeur.

value ['væljuː] *n* valeur *f*; **to be of great/little v.** (*of object*) valoir cher/peu (cher); **it's good v.** c'est très avantageux; **v. added tax** taxe *f* à la valeur ajoutée; − *vt* (*appraise*) évaluer; (*appreciate*) attacher de la valeur à. ◆**valu'ation** *n* évaluation *f*; (*by expert*) expertise *f.* ◆**valuer** *n* expert *m.*

valve [vælv] *n* (*of machine*) soupape *f*; (*in radio*) lampe *f*; (*of tyre*) valve *f*; (*of heart*) valvule *f.*

vampire ['væmpaɪər] *n* vampire *m.*

van [væn] *n* (*small*) camionnette *f*; (*large*) camion *m*; Rail fourgon *m.*

vandal ['vænd(ə)l] *n* vandale *mf.* ◆**vandal-**

ism n vandalisme m. ◆**vandalize** vt saccager, détériorer.

vanguard ['vængɑːd] n (of army, progress etc) avant-garde f.

vanilla [vəˈnɪlə] n vanille f; – a (ice cream) à la vanille.

vanish ['vænɪʃ] vi disparaître.

vanity ['vænɪtɪ] n vanité f; **v. case** vanity m inv.

vanquish ['væŋkwɪʃ] vt vaincre.

vantage point ['vɑːntɪdʒpɔɪnt] n (place, point of view) (bon) point m de vue.

vapour ['veɪpər] n vapeur f; (on glass) buée f.

variable ['veərɪəb(ə)l] a variable. ◆**variance** n at v. en désaccord (with avec). ◆**variant** a différent; – n variante f. ◆**vari'ation** n variation f.

varicose ['værɪkəus] a v. **veins** varices fpl.

variety [vəˈraɪətɪ] n 1 (diversity) variété f; **a v. of opinions/reasons/**etc (many) diverses opinions/raisons/etc; **a v. of** (articles) Com une gamme de. 2 Th variétés fpl; **v. show** spectacle m de variétés.

various ['veərɪəs] a divers. ◆—**ly** adv diversement.

varnish ['vɑːnɪʃ] vt vernir; – n vernis m.

vary ['veərɪ] vti varier (from de). ◆**varied** a varié. ◆**varying** a variable.

vase [vɑːz, Am veɪs] n vase m.

Vaseline® ['væsəliːn] n vaseline f.

vast [vɑːst] a vaste, immense. ◆—**ly** adv (very) infiniment, extrêmement. ◆—**ness** n immensité f.

vat [væt] n cuve f.

VAT [viːeɪˈtiː, væt] n abbr (value added tax) TVA f.

Vatican ['vætɪkən] n Vatican m.

vaudeville ['vɔːdəvɪl] n Th Am variétés fpl.

vault [vɔːlt] 1 n (cellar) cave f; (tomb) caveau m; (in bank) chambre f forte, coffres mpl; (roof) voûte f. 2 vti (jump) sauter.

veal [viːl] n (meat) veau m.

veer [vɪər] vi (of wind) tourner; (of car, road) virer; **to v. off the road** quitter la route.

vegan ['viːgən] n végétaliste mf.

vegetable ['vedʒtəb(ə)l] n légume m; – a (kingdom, oil) végétal; **v. garden** (jardin m) potager m. ◆**vege'tarian** n a en végétarien, -ienne (mf). ◆**vege'tation** n végétation f.

vegetate ['vedʒɪteɪt] vi (of person) Pej végéter.

vehement ['viːəmənt] a (feeling, speech) véhément; (attack) violent. ◆—**ly** adv avec véhémence, violemment.

vehicle ['viːɪk(ə)l] n véhicule m; **heavy goods v.** (lorry) poids m lourd.

veil [veɪl] n (covering) & Fig voile m; – vt (face, truth etc) voiler.

vein [veɪn] n (in body or rock) veine f; (in leaf) nervure f; (mood) Fig esprit m.

vellum ['veləm] n (paper, skin) vélin m.

velocity [vəˈlɒsɪtɪ] n vélocité f.

velvet ['velvɪt] n velours m; – a de velours. ◆**velvety** a velouté.

vendetta [venˈdetə] n vendetta f.

vending machine ['vendɪŋməʃiːn] n distributeur m automatique.

vendor ['vendər] n vendeur, -euse mf.

veneer [vəˈnɪər] n (wood) placage m; (appearance) Fig vernis m.

venerable ['ven(ə)rəb(ə)l] a vénérable. ◆**venerate** vt vénérer.

venereal [vəˈnɪərɪəl] a (disease etc) vénérien.

venetian [vəˈniːʃ(ə)n] a v. **blind** store m vénitien.

vengeance ['vendʒəns] n vengeance f; **with a v.** (to work, study etc) furieusement; (to rain, catch up etc) pour de bon.

venison ['venɪs(ə)n] n venaison f.

venom ['venəm] n (substance) & Fig venin m. ◆**venomous** a (speech, snake etc) venimeux.

vent [vent] 1 n (hole) orifice m; (for air) bouche f d'aération; (in jacket) fente f. 2 n **to give v. to** (feeling etc) donner libre cours à; – vt (anger) décharger (on sur).

ventilate ['ventɪleɪt] vt ventiler. ◆**venti-'lation** n ventilation f. ◆**ventilator** n (in wall etc) ventilateur m.

ventriloquist [venˈtrɪləkwɪst] n ventriloque mf.

venture ['ventʃər] n entreprise f (risquée); **my v. into** mon incursion f dans; – vt (opinion, fortune) hasarder; **to v. to do** (dare) oser faire; – vi s'aventurer, se risquer (into dans).

venue ['venjuː] n lieu m de rencontre or de rendez-vous.

veranda(h) [vəˈrændə] n véranda f.

verb [vɜːb] n verbe m. ◆**verbal** a (promise, skill etc) verbal. ◆**verbatim** [vɜːˈbeɪtɪm] a & adv mot pour mot.

verbose [vɜːˈbəus] a (wordy) verbeux.

verdict ['vɜːdɪkt] n verdict m.

verdigris ['vɜːdɪgrɪs] n vert-de-gris m inv.

verge [vɜːdʒ] n (of road) accotement m, bord m; **on the v. of** Fig (ruin, tears etc) au bord de; (discovery) à la veille de; **on the v. of doing** sur le point de faire; – vi **to v. on** friser, frôler; (of colour) tirer sur.

verger ['vɜːdʒər] n Rel bedeau m.

verify ['verɪfaɪ] vt vérifier. **◆verifi'cation** n vérification f.

veritable ['verɪtəb(ə)l] a véritable.

vermicelli [vɜːmɪ'selɪ] n Culin vermicelle(s) m(pl).

vermin ['vɜːmɪn] n (animals) animaux mpl nuisibles; (insects, people) vermine f.

vermouth ['vɜːməθ] n vermouth m.

vernacular [və'nækjʊlər] n (of region) dialecte m.

versatile ['vɜːsətaɪl, Am 'vɜːsət(ə)l] a (mind) souple; (material, tool, computer) polyvalent; **he's v.** il a des talents variés, il est polyvalent. **◆versa'tility** n souplesse f; **his v.** la variété de ses talents.

verse [vɜːs] n (stanza) strophe f; (poetry) vers mpl; (of Bible) verset m.

versed [vɜːst] a (well) v. in versé dans.

version ['vɜːʃ(ə)n] n version f.

versus ['vɜːsəs] prep contre.

vertebra ['vɜːtɪbrə], pl -ae ['vɜːtɪbrəː, -iː] n vertèbre f.

vertical ['vɜːtɪk(ə)l] a vertical; – n verticale f. **◆—ly** adv verticalement.

vertigo ['vɜːtɪɡəʊ] n (fear of falling) vertige m.

verve [vɜːv] n fougue f.

very ['verɪ] 1 adv très; **I'm v. hot** j'ai très chaud; **v. much** beaucoup; **the v. first** le tout premier; **at the v. least/most** tout au moins/plus; **at the v. latest** au plus tard. 2 a (actual) même; **his or her v. brother** son frère même; **at the v. end** (of play etc) tout à la fin; **to the v. end** jusqu'au bout.

vespers ['vespəz] npl Rel vêpres fpl.

vessel ['ves(ə)l] n Anat Bot Nau vaisseau m; (receptacle) récipient m.

vest [vest] n tricot m or maillot m de corps; (woman's) chemise f (américaine); (waistcoat) Am gilet m.

vested ['vestɪd] a v. interests Com droits mpl acquis; **she's got a v. interest in** Fig elle est directement intéressée dans.

vestige ['vestɪdʒ] n vestige m; **not a v. of** truth/good sense pas un grain de vérité/de bon sens.

vestry ['vestrɪ] n sacristie f.

vet [vet] 1 n vétérinaire mf. 2 vt (-tt-) (document) examiner de près; (candidate) se renseigner à fond sur. **◆veteri'narian** n Am vétérinaire mf. **◆veterinary** n vétérinaire; **v. surgeon** vétérinaire mf.

veteran ['vet(ə)rən] n vétéran m; (war) v. ancien combattant m; – a v. golfer/etc golfeur/etc expérimenté.

veto ['viːtəʊ] n (pl -oes) (refusal) veto m inv; (power) droit m de veto; – vt mettre or opposer son veto à.

vex [veks] vt contrarier, fâcher; **vexed question** question f controversée.

via ['vaɪə] prep via, par.

viable ['vaɪəb(ə)l] a (baby, firm, plan etc) viable. **◆via'bility** n viabilité f.

viaduct ['vaɪədʌkt] n viaduc m.

vibrate [vaɪ'breɪt] vi vibrer. **◆'vibrant** a vibrant. **◆vibration** n vibration f. **◆vibrator** n vibromasseur m.

vicar ['vɪkər] n (in Church of England) pasteur m. **◆vicarage** n presbytère m.

vicarious [vɪ'keərɪəs] a (emotion) ressenti indirectement. **◆—ly** adv (to experience) indirectement.

vice [vaɪs] n 1 (depravity) vice m; (fault) défaut m; **v. squad** brigade f des mœurs. 2 (tool) étau m.

vice- [vaɪs] pref vice-. **◆v.-'chancellor** n Univ président m.

vice versa [vaɪs(ɪ)'vɜːsə] adv vice versa.

vicinity [və'sɪnɪtɪ] n environs mpl; **in the v. of** (place, amount) aux environs de.

vicious ['vɪʃəs] a (spiteful) méchant; (violent) brutal; **v. circle** cercle m vicieux. **◆—ly** adv méchamment; brutalement. **◆—ness** n méchanceté f; brutalité f.

vicissitudes [vɪ'sɪsɪtjuːdz] npl vicissitudes fpl.

victim ['vɪktɪm] n victime f; **to be the v. of** être victime de. **◆victimize** vt persécuter. **◆victimi'zation** n persécution f.

Victorian [vɪk'tɔːrɪən] a & n victorien, -ienne (mf).

victory ['vɪktərɪ] n victoire f. **◆victor** n vainqueur m. **◆vic'torious** a victorieux.

video ['vɪdɪəʊ] a video inv; – n v. (cassette) vidéocassette f; (recorder) magnétoscope m; **on v.** sur cassette; **to make a v. of** faire une cassette de; – vt (programme) enregistrer au magnétoscope. **◆videotape** n bande f vidéo.

vie [vaɪ] vi (pres p vying) rivaliser (with avec).

Vietnam [vjet'næm, Am -'nɑːm] n Việt-nam m. **◆Vietna'mese** a & n vietnamien, -ienne (mf).

view [vjuː] n vue f; **to come into v.** apparaître; **in full v. of everyone** à la vue de tous; **in my v.** (opinion) à mon avis; **on v.** (exhibit) exposé; **with a v. to** (of considering) dans l'intention de; (the fact that que); **with a v. to doing** afin de faire; – vt (regard) considérer; (house) visiter. **◆—er** n 1 TV téléspectateur, -trice mf. 2 (for slides) visionneuse f. **◆viewfinder** n Phot viseur m. **◆viewpoint** n point m de vue.

vigil ['vɪdʒɪl] *n* veille *f*; (*over sick person or corpse*) veillée *f*.

vigilant ['vɪdʒɪlənt] *a* vigilant. ◆**vigilance** *n* vigilance *f*.

vigilante [vɪdʒɪ'læntɪ] *n* Pej membre *m* d'une milice privée.

vigour ['vɪgər] *n* vigueur *f*. ◆**vigorous** *a* (*person, speech etc*) vigoureux.

vile [vaɪl] *a* (-er, -est) (*base*) infâme, vil; (*unpleasant*) abominable.

vilify ['vɪlɪfaɪ] *vt* diffamer.

villa ['vɪlə] *n* (*in country*) grande maison *f* de campagne.

village ['vɪlɪdʒ] *n* village *m*. ◆**villager** *n* villageois, -oise *mf*.

villain ['vɪlən] *n* scélérat, -ate *mf*; (*in story or play*) traître *m*. ◆**villainy** *n* infamie *f*.

vindicate ['vɪndɪkeɪt] *vt* justifier. ◆**vindi-cation** *n* justification *f*.

vindictive [vɪn'dɪktɪv] *a* vindicatif, rancu-nier.

vine [vaɪn] *n* (*grapevine*) vigne *f*; **v. grower** viticulteur *m*. ◆**vineyard** ['vɪnjəd] *n* vignoble *m*.

vinegar ['vɪnɪgər] *n* vinaigre *m*.

vintage ['vɪntɪdʒ] **1** *n* (*year*) année *f*. **2** *a* (*wine*) de grand cru; (*car*) d'époque; (*film*) classique; (*good*) Fig bon; **v. Shaw**/*etc* du meilleur Shaw/*etc*.

vinyl ['vaɪn(ə)l] *n* vinyle *m*.

viola [vɪ'əʊlə] *n* (*instrument*) Mus alto *m*.

violate ['vaɪəleɪt] *vt* violer. ◆**vio'lation** *n* violation *f*.

violence ['vaɪələns] *n* violence *f*. ◆**violent** *a* violent; **a v. dislike** une aversion vive. ◆**violently** *adv* violemment; **to be v. sick** (*vomit*) vomir.

violet ['vaɪələt] **1** *a* & *n* (*colour*) violet (*m*). **2** *n* (*plant*) violette *f*.

violin [vaɪə'lɪn] *n* violon *m*; – *a* (*concerto etc*) pour violon. ◆**violinist** *n* violoniste *mf*.

VIP [vi:aɪ'pi:] *n abbr* (*very important person*) personnage *m* de marque.

viper ['vaɪpər] *n* vipère *f*.

virgin ['vɜːdʒɪn] *n* vierge *f*; **to be a v.** (*of woman, man*) être vierge; – *a* (*woman, snow etc*) vierge. ◆**vir'ginity** *n* virginité *f*.

Virgo ['vɜːgəʊ] *n* (*sign*) la Vierge.

virile ['vɪraɪl, Am 'vɪrəl] *a* viril. ◆**vi'rility** *n* virilité *f*.

virtual ['vɜːtʃʊəl] *a* **it was a v. failure**/*etc* ce fut en fait un échec/*etc*. ◆**—ly** *adv* (*in fact*) en fait; (*almost*) pratiquement.

virtue ['vɜːtʃuː] *n* **1** (*goodness, chastity*) vertu *f*, (*advantage*) mérite *m*, avantage *m*. **2 by**

or in v. of en raison de. ◆**virtuous** *a* vertueux.

virtuoso, *pl* **-si** [vɜːtʃʊ'əʊsəʊ, -siː] *n* virtuose *mf*. ◆**virtuosity** [-'ɒsɪtɪ] *n* virtuosité *f*.

virulent ['vɪrʊlənt] *a* virulent. ◆**virulence** *n* virulence *f*.

virus ['vaɪ(ə)rəs] *n* virus *m*.

visa ['viːzə] *n* visa *m*.

vis-à-vis [viːzɑː'viː] *prep* vis-à-vis de.

viscount ['vaɪkaʊnt] *n* vicomte *m*. ◆**vis-countess** *n* vicomtesse *f*.

viscous ['vɪskəs] *a* visqueux.

vise [vaɪs] *n* (*tool*) Am étau *m*.

visible ['vɪzəb(ə)l] *a* visible. ◆**visi'bility** *n* visibilité *f*. ◆**visibly** *adv* visiblement.

vision ['vɪʒ(ə)n] *n* vision *f*; **a man/a woman of v.** Fig un homme/une femme qui voit loin. ◆**visionary** *a* & *n* visionnaire (*mf*).

visit ['vɪzɪt] *n* (*call, tour*) visite *f*; (*stay*) séjour *m*; – *vt* (*place*) visiter; **to v. s.o.** (*call on*) rendre visite à qn; (*stay with*) faire un séjour chez qn; – *vi* être en visite (*Am with* chez). ◆**—ing** *a* (*card, hours*) de visite. ◆**visitor** *n* visiteur, -euse *mf*; (*guest*) invité, -ée *mf*; (*in hotel*) client, -ente *mf*.

visor ['vaɪzər] *n* (*of helmet*) visière *f*.

vista ['vɪstə] *n* (*view of place etc*) vue *f*; (*of future*) Fig perspective *f*.

visual ['vɪʒʊəl] *a* visuel; **v. aid** (*in teaching*) support *m* visuel. ◆**visualize** *vt* (*imagine*) se représenter; (*foresee*) envisager.

vital ['vaɪt(ə)l] *a* vital; **of v. importance** d'importance capitale; **v. statistics** (*of woman*) Fam mensurations *fpl*. ◆**—ly** *adv* extrêmement.

vitality [vaɪ'tælɪtɪ] *n* vitalité *f*.

vitamin ['vɪtəmɪn, Am 'vaɪtəmɪn] *n* vitamine *f*.

vitriol ['vɪtrɪəl] *n* Ch Fig vitriol *m*. ◆**vitri-'olic** *a* (*attack, speech etc*) au vitriol.

vivacious [vɪ'veɪʃəs] *a* plein d'entrain.

vivid ['vɪvɪd] *a* (*imagination, recollection etc*) vif; (*description*) vivant. ◆**—ly** *adv* (*to describe*) de façon vivante; **to remember sth v.** avoir un vif souvenir de qch.

vivisection [vɪvɪ'sekʃ(ə)n] *n* vivisection *f*.

vocabulary [və'kæbjʊlərɪ] *n* vocabulaire *m*.

vocal ['vəʊk(ə)l] *a* (*cords, music*) vocal; (*outspoken, noisy, critical*) qui se fait enten-dre. ◆**vocalist** *n* chanteur, -euse *mf*.

vocation [vəʊ'keɪʃ(ə)n] *n* vocation *f*. ◆**vocational** *a* professionnel.

vociferous [və'sɪf(ə)rəs] *a* bruyant.

vodka ['vɒdkə] *n* vodka *f*.

vogue [vəʊg] *n* vogue *f*; **in v.** en vogue.

voice [vɔɪs] *n* voix *f*; **at the top of one's v.** à

tue-tête; — vt (feeling, opinion etc) formuler, exprimer.

void [vɔɪd] **1** n vide m; — a **v. of** (lacking in) dépourvu de. **2** a (not valid) Jur nul.

volatile ['vɒlətaɪl, Am 'vɒlət(ə)l] a (person) versatile, changeant; (situation) explosif.

volcano [vɒl'keɪnəʊ] n (pl -oes) volcan m. ◆**volcanic** [-'kænɪk] a volcanique.

volition [və'lɪʃ(ə)n] n of one's own v. de son propre gré.

volley ['vɒlɪ] n (of blows) volée f; (gunfire) salve f; (of insults) Fig bordée f. ◆**volleyball** n Sp volley(-ball) m.

volt [vəʊlt] n El volt m. ◆**voltage** n voltage m.

volume ['vɒljuːm] n (book, capacity, loudness) volume m. ◆**voluminous** [və'luːmɪnəs] a volumineux.

voluntary ['vɒlənt(ə)rɪ] a volontaire; (unpaid) bénévole. ◆**voluntarily** [Am vɒlən'terɪlɪ] adv volontairement; bénévolement. ◆**volun'teer** n volontaire mf; — vi se proposer (for sth pour qch, to do pour faire); Mil s'engager comme volontaire (for dans); — vt offrir (spontanément).

voluptuous [və'lʌptʃʊəs] a voluptueux, sensuel.

vomit ['vɒmɪt] vti vomir; — n (matter) vomi m.

voracious [və'reɪʃəs] a (appetite, reader etc) vorace.

vot/e [vəʊt] n vote m; (right to vote) droit m de vote; **to win votes** gagner des voix; **v. of censure** or **no confidence** motion f de censure; **v. of thanks** discours m de remerciement; — vt (bill, funds etc) voter; (person) élire; — vi voter; **to v. Conservative** voter conservateur or pour les conservateurs. ◆**—ing** n vote m (of de); (polling) scrutin m. ◆**—er** n Pol électeur, -trice mf.

vouch [vaʊtʃ] vi **to v. for** répondre de.

voucher ['vaʊtʃər] n (for meals etc) bon m, chèque m.

vow [vaʊ] n vœu m; — vt (obedience etc) jurer (to à); **to v. to do** jurer de faire, faire le vœu de faire.

vowel ['vaʊəl] n voyelle f.

voyage ['vɔɪdʒ] n voyage m (par mer).

vulgar ['vʌlɡər] a vulgaire. ◆**vul'garity** n vulgarité f.

vulnerable ['vʌln(ə)rəb(ə)l] a vulnérable. ◆**vulnera'bility** n vulnérabilité f.

vulture ['vʌltʃər] n vautour m.

W

W, w ['dʌb(ə)ljuː] n W, w m.

wacky ['wækɪ] a (-ier, -iest) Am Fam farfelu.

wad [wɒd] n (of banknotes, papers etc) liasse f; (of cotton wool, cloth) tampon m.

waddle ['wɒd(ə)l] vi se dandiner.

wade [weɪd] vi **to w. through** (mud, water etc) patauger dans; (book etc) Fig venir péniblement à bout de; **I'm wading through this book** j'avance péniblement dans ce livre.

wafer ['weɪfər] n (biscuit) gaufrette f; Rel hostie f.

waffle ['wɒf(ə)l] **1** n (talk) Fam verbiage m, blabla m; — vi Fam parler pour ne rien dire, blablater. **2** n (cake) gaufre f.

waft [wɒft] vi (of smell etc) flotter.

wag [wæɡ] **1** vt (-gg-) (tail, finger) agiter, remuer; — vi remuer; **tongues are wagging** Pej on en jase, les langues vont bon train. **2** n (joker) farceur, -euse mf.

wage [weɪdʒ] **1** n **wage(s)** salaire m, paie f; **w. claim** or **demand** revendication f salariale; **w. earner** salarié, -ée mf; (breadwin-

ner) soutien m de famille; **w. freeze** blocage m des salaires; **w. increase** or **rise** augmentation f de salaire. **2** vt (campaign) mener; **to w. war** faire la guerre (on à).

wager ['weɪdʒər] n pari m; — vt parier (that que).

waggle ['wæɡ(ə)l] vti remuer.

wag(g)on ['wæɡən] n (cart) chariot m; Rail wagon m (de marchandises); **on the w.** (abstinent) Fam au régime sec.

waif [weɪf] n enfant mf abandonné(e).

wail [weɪl] vi (cry out, complain) gémir; (of siren) hurler; — n gémissement m; (of siren) hurlement m.

waist [weɪst] n taille f; **stripped to the w.** nu jusqu'à la ceinture. ◆**waistband** n (part of garment) ceinture f. ◆**waistcoat** ['weɪskəʊt] n gilet m. ◆**waistline** n taille f.

wait [weɪt] **1** n attente f; **to lie in w.** (for) guetter; — vi attendre; **to w. for** attendre; **w. until I've gone, w. for me to go** attends que je sois parti; **to keep s.o. waiting** faire attendre qn; **w. and see!** attends voir!; **I can't w.**

to do it j'ai hâte de le faire; **to w. about (for)** attendre; **to w. behind** rester; **to w. up** veiller; **to w. up for** attendre le retour de qn avant de se coucher. **2** *vi* (*serve*) **to w. at table** servir à table; **to w. on s.o.** servir qn. ◆**—ing** *n* attente *f*; **'no w.'** *Aut* 'arrêt interdit'; **–** *a* **w. list/room** liste *f*/salle *f* d'attente. ◆**waiter** *n* garçon *m* (de café), serveur *m*; **w.!** garçon! ◆**waitress** *n* serveuse *f*; **w.!** mademoiselle!

waive [weɪv] *vt* renoncer à, abandonner.

wake¹ [weɪk] *vi* (*pt* woke, *pp* woken) **to w. (up)** se réveiller; **to w. up to** (*fact etc*) Fig prendre conscience de; **–** *vt* **to w. (up)** réveiller; **to spend one's waking hours working/etc** passer ses journées à travailler/*etc*. ◆**waken** *vt* éveiller, réveiller; **–** *vi* s'éveiller, se réveiller.

wake² [weɪk] *n* (*of ship*) & Fig sillage *m*; **in the w. of** Fig dans le sillage de, à la suite de.

Wales [weɪlz] *n* pays *m* de Galles.

walk [wɔːk] *n* promenade *f*; (*short*) (petit) tour *m*; (*gait*) démarche *f*; (*pace*) marche *f*, pas *m*; (*path*) allée *f*, chemin *m*; **to go for a w.** faire une promenade; (*shorter*) faire un (petit) tour; **to take for a w.** (*child etc*) emmener se promener; (*baby, dog*) promener; **five minutes' w. (away)** à cinq minutes à pied; **walks of life** Fig conditions sociales *fpl*; **–** *vi* marcher; (*stroll*) se promener; (*go on foot*) aller à pied; **w.!** (*don't run*) ne cours pas!; **to w. away or off** s'éloigner, partir (**from** de); **to w. away or off with** (*steal*) Fam faucher; **to w. in** entrer; **to w. into** (*tree etc*) rentrer dans; (*trap*) tomber dans; **to w. out** (*leave*) partir; (*of workers*) se mettre en grève; **to w. out on** s.o. (*desert*) Fam laisser tomber qn; **to w. over to** (*go up to*) s'approcher de; **–** *vt* (*distance*) faire à pied; (*streets*) (par)courir; (*take for a walk*) promener (bébé, chien); **to w. s.o. to** (*station etc*) accompagner qn à. ◆**—ing** *n* marche *f* (à pied); **–** *a* **a w. corpse/dictionary** (*person*) Fig un cadavre/dictionnaire ambulant; **at a w. pace** au pas; **w. stick** canne *f*. ◆**walker** *n* marcheur, -euse *mf*; (*for pleasure*) promeneur, -euse *mf*. ◆**walkout** *n* (*strike*) grève *f* surprise; (*from meeting*) départ *m* (en signe de protestation). ◆**walkover** *n* (*in contest etc*) victoire *f* facile. ◆**walkway** *n* **moving w.** trottoir *m* roulant.

walkie-talkie [wɔːkɪˈtɔːkɪ] *n* talkie-walkie *m*.

Walkman® [ˈwɔːkmən] *n* (*pl* **Walkmans**) baladeur *m*.

wall [wɔːl] *n* mur *m*; (*of cabin, tunnel, stomach etc*) paroi *f*; (*of ice*) Fig muraille *f*; (*of smoke*) Fig rideau *m*; **to go to the w.** (*of firm*) Fig faire faillite; **–** *a* mural; **–** *vt* **to w. up** (*door etc*) murer; **walled city** ville *f* fortifiée. ◆**wallflower** *n* Bot giroflée *f*; **to be a w.** (*at dance*) faire tapisserie. ◆**wallpaper** *n* papier *m* peint; **–** *vt* tapisser. ◆**wall-to-wall 'carpet(ing)** *n* moquette *f*.

wallet [ˈwɒlɪt] *n* portefeuille *m*.

wallop [ˈwɒləp] *vt* (*hit*) Fam taper sur; **–** *n* (*blow*) Fam grand coup *m*.

wallow [ˈwɒləʊ] *vi* **to w. in** (*mud, vice etc*) se vautrer dans.

wally [ˈwɒlɪ] *n* (*idiot*) Fam andouille *f*, imbécile *mf*.

walnut [ˈwɔːlnʌt] *n* (*nut*) noix *f*; (*tree, wood*) noyer *m*.

walrus [ˈwɔːlrəs] *n* (*animal*) morse *m*.

waltz [wɔːls, Am wɒls] *n* valse *f*; **–** *vi* valser.

wan [wɒn] *a* (*pale*) Lit pâle.

wand [wɒnd] *n* baguette *f* (magique).

wander [ˈwɒndər] *vi* (*of thoughts*) vagabonder; **to w. (about or around)** (*roam*) errer, vagabonder; (*stroll*) flâner; **to w. from or off** (*path, subject*) s'écarter de; **to w. off** (*go away*) s'éloigner; **my mind's wandering** je suis distrait; **–** *vt* **to w. the streets** errer dans les rues. ◆**—ing** *a* (*life, tribe*) vagabond, nomade; **–** *npl* vagabondages *mpl*. ◆**—er** *n* vagabond, -onde *mf*.

wane [weɪn] *vi* (*of moon, fame, strength etc*) décroître; **–** *n* **to be on the w.** décroître, être en déclin.

wangle [ˈwæŋɡ(ə)l] *vt* Fam (*obtain*) se débrouiller pour obtenir; (*avoiding payment*) carotter (**from** à).

want [wɒnt] *vt* vouloir (**to do** faire); (*ask for*) demander; (*need*) avoir besoin de; **I w. him to go** je veux qu'il parte; **you w. to try** (*should*) tu devrais essayer; **you're wanted on the phone** on vous demande au téléphone; **–** *vi* **not to w. for** (*not lack*) ne pas manquer de; **–** *n* (*lack*) manque *m* (**of** de); (*poverty*) besoin *m*; **for w. of** par manque de; **for w. of money/time** faute d'argent/de temps; **for w. of anything better** faute de mieux; **your wants** (*needs*) tes besoins *mpl*. ◆**—ed** *a* (*man, criminal*) recherché par la police; **to feel w.** sentir qu'on vous aime. ◆**—ing** *a* (*inadequate*) insuffisant; **to be w.** manquer (**in** de).

wanton [ˈwɒntən] *a* (*gratuitous*) gratuit; (*immoral*) impudique.

war [wɔːr] *n* guerre *f*; **at w.** en guerre (**with** avec); **to go to w.** entrer en guerre (**with** avec); **to declare w.** déclarer la guerre (**on** à); **–** *a* (*wound, criminal etc*) de guerre; **w.**

memorial monument *m* aux morts.
◆**warfare** *n* guerre *f*. ◆**warhead** *n* (*of missile*) ogive *f*. ◆**warlike** *a* guerrier.
◆**warmonger** *n* fauteur *m* de guerre.
◆**warpath** *n* **to be on the w.** (*angry*) *Fam* être d'humeur massacrante. ◆**warring** *a* (*countries etc*) en guerre; (*ideologies etc*) *Fig* en conflit. ◆**warship** *n* navire *m* de guerre. ◆**wartime** *n* **in w.** en temps de guerre.

warble ['wɔːb(ə)l] *vi* (*of bird*) gazouiller.

ward [wɔːd] *n* **1** (*in hospital*) salle *f*. **2** (*child*) *Jur* pupille *mf*. **3** (*electoral division*) circonscription *f* électorale.

ward² [wɔːd] *vt* **w. off** (*blow, anger*) détourner; (*danger*) éviter.

warden ['wɔːd(ə)n] *n* (*of institution, Am of prison*) directeur, -trice *mf*; (*of park*) gardien, -ienne *mf*; (*traffic*) **w.** contractuel, -elle *mf*.

warder ['wɔːdər] *n* gardien *m* (de prison).

wardrobe ['wɔːdrəʊb] *n* (*cupboard*) penderie *f*; (*clothes*) garde-robe *f*.

warehouse, *pl* -ses ['weəhaʊs, -zɪz] *n* entrepôt *m*.

wares [weəz] *npl* marchandises *fpl*.

warily ['weərɪlɪ] *adv* avec précaution.

warm [wɔːm] *a* (**-er, -est**) chaud; (*iron, oven*) moyen; (*welcome, thanks etc*) chaleureux; **to be** *or* **feel w.** avoir chaud; **it's (nice and) w.** (*of weather*) il fait (agréablement) chaud; **to get w.** (*of person, room etc*) se réchauffer; (*of weather*) se réchauffer; — *vt* **to w. (up)** (*person, food etc*) réchauffer; — *vi* **to w. up** (*of person, room, engine etc*) se réchauffer; (*of food, water*) chauffer; (*of discussion*) s'échauffer; **to w. to s.o.** *Fig* se prendre de sympathie pour qn. ◆**warm-'hearted** *a* chaleureux. ◆**warmly** *adv* (*to wrap up*) chaudement; (*to welcome, thank etc*) chaleureusement. ◆**warmth** *n* chaleur *f*.

warn [wɔːn] *vt* avertir, prévenir (**that** que); **to w. s.o. against** *or* **off sth** mettre qn en garde contre qch; **to w. s.o. against doing** conseiller à qn de ne pas faire. ◆**—ing** *n* avertissement *m*; (*advance notice*) (pré)avis *m*; *Met* avis *m*; (*alarm*) alerte *f*; **without w.** sans prévenir; **a note** *or* **word of w.** une mise en garde; **w. light** (*on appliance etc*) voyant *m* lumineux; **hazard w. lights** *Aut* feux *mpl* de détresse.

warp [wɔːp] **1** *vt* (*wood etc*) voiler; (*judgment, person etc*) *Fig* pervertir; **a warped mind** un esprit tordu; **a warped account** un récit déformé; — *vi* se voiler. **2** *n Tex* chaîne *f*.

warrant ['wɒrənt] **1** *n Jur* mandat *m*; **a w. for**

your arrest un mandat d'arrêt contre vous.
2 *vt* (*justify*) justifier; **I w. you that . . .** (*declare confidently*) je t'assure que . . . .
◆**warranty** *n Com* garantie *f*.

warren ['wɒrən] *n* (*rabbit*) **w.** garenne *f*.

warrior ['wɒrɪər] *n* guerrier, -ière *mf*.

wart [wɔːt] *n* verrue *f*.

wary ['weərɪ] *a* (**-ier, -iest**) prudent; **to be w. of s.o./sth** se méfier de qn/qch; **to be w. of doing** hésiter beaucoup à faire.

was [wəz, *stressed* wɒz] *see* **be**.

wash [wɒʃ] *n* (*clothes*) lessive *f*; (*of ship*) sillage *m*; **to have a w.** se laver; **to give sth a w.** laver qch; **to do the w.** faire la lessive; **in the w.** à la lessive; — *vt* laver; (*flow over*) baigner; **to w. one's hands** se laver les mains (*Fig of sth* de qch); **to w. (away)** (*of sea etc*) emporter (*qch, qn*); **to w. away** *or* **off** *or* **out** (*stain*) faire partir (en lavant); **to w. down** (*vehicle, deck*) laver à grande eau; (*food*) arroser (**with** de); **to w. out** (*bowl etc*) laver; — *vi* se laver; (*do the dishes*) laver la vaisselle; **to w. away** *or* **off** *or* **out** (*of stain*) partir (au lavage); **to w. up** (*do the dishes*) faire la vaisselle; (*have a wash*) *Am* se laver.
◆**washed-'out** *a* (*tired*) lessivé.
◆**washed-'up** *a* (**all) w.-up** (*person, plan*) *Sl* fichu. ◆**washable** *a* lavable.
◆**washbasin** *n* lavabo *m*. ◆**washcloth** *n* *Am* gant *m* de toilette. ◆**washout** *n* *Sl* (*event etc*) fiasco *m*; (*person*) nullité *f*.
◆**washroom** *n* *Am* toilettes *fpl*.

washer ['wɒʃər] *n* (*ring*) rondelle *f*, joint *m*.

washing ['wɒʃɪŋ] *n* (*act*) lavage *m*; (*clothes*) lessive *f*, linge *m*; **to do the w.** faire la lessive; **w. line** corde *f* à linge; **w. machine** machine *f* à laver; **w. powder** lessive *f*.
◆**w.-'up** *n* vaisselle *f*; **to do the w.-up** faire la vaisselle; **w.-up liquid** produit *m* pour la vaisselle.

wasp [wɒsp] *n* guêpe *f*.

wast/e [weɪst] *n* gaspillage *m*; (*of time*) perte *f*; (*rubbish*) déchets *mpl*; *pl* (*land*) étendue *f* déserte; **w. disposal unit** broyeur *m* d'ordures; — *a* **w. material** *or* **products** déchets *mpl*; **w. land** (*uncultivated*) terres *fpl* incultes; (*in town*) terrain *m* vague; **w. paper** vieux papiers *mpl*; **w. pipe** tuyau *m* d'évacuation; — *vt* (*money, food etc*) gaspiller; (*time, opportunity*) perdre; **to w. one's time on frivolities/***etc* gaspiller son temps en frivolités/*etc*, perdre son temps à des frivolités/*etc*; **to w. one's life away** dépérir. ◆**—ed** *a* (*effort*) inutile; (*body etc*) émacié. ◆**wastage** *n* gaspillage *m*; (*losses*) pertes *fpl*; **some w.** (*of goods, staff etc*) du déchet. ◆**wastebin** *n* (*in kitchen*) poubelle *f.* ◆**wastepaper basket** *n* corbeille *f* (à papier).

wasteful ['weɪstfəl] *a* (*person*) gaspilleur; (*process*) peu économique.

watch [wɒtʃ] **1** *n* (*small clock*) montre *f.* **2** *n* (*over suspect, baby etc*) surveillance *f; Nau* quart *m;* **to keep (a) w.** on *or* over surveiller; **to keep w.** faire le guet; **to be on the w.** (**for**) guetter; – *vt* regarder; (*observe*) observer; (*suspect, baby etc*) surveiller; (*be careful of*) faire attention à; – *vi* regarder; **to w. (out) for** (*be on the lookout for*) guetter; **to w. out** (*take care*) faire attention (**for** à); **w. out!** attention!; **to w. over** surveiller. ◆**watchdog** *n* chien *m* de garde. ◆**watchmaker** *n* horloger, -ère *mf.* ◆**watchman** *n* (*pl* -**men**) night **w.** veilleur *m* de nuit. ◆**watchstrap** *n* bracelet *m* de montre. ◆**watchtower** *n* tour *f* de guet.

watchful ['wɒtʃfəl] *a* vigilant.

water ['wɔːtər] *n* eau *f;* **by w.** en bateau; **under w.** (*road, field etc*) inondé; (*to swim*) sous l'eau; **at high w.** à marée haute; **it doesn't hold w.** (*of theory etc*) *Fig* ça ne tient pas debout; **in hot w.** *Fig* dans le pétrin; **w. cannon** lance *f* à eau; **w. ice** sorbet *m;* **w. lily** nénuphar *m;* **w. pistol** pistolet *m* à eau; **w. polo** *Sp* water-polo *m;* **w. power** énergie *f* hydraulique; **w. rates** taxes *fpl* sur l'eau; **w. skiing** ski *m* nautique; **w. tank** réservoir *m* d'eau; **w. tower** château *m* d'eau; – *vt* (*plant etc*) arroser; **w. down** (*wine etc*) couper (d'eau); (*text etc*) édulcorer; – *vi* (*of eyes*) larmoyer; **it makes his** *or* **her mouth w.** ça lui fait venir l'eau à la bouche. ◆**—ing** *n* (*of plant etc*) arrosage *m;* **w. can** arrosoir *m.* ◆**watery** *a* (*colour*) délavé; (*soup*) *Pej* trop liquide; (*eyes*) larmoyant; **w. tea** *or* **coffee** de la lavasse.

watercolour ['wɔːtəkʌlər] *n* (*picture*) aquarelle *f;* (*paint*) couleur *f* pour aquarelle. ◆**watercress** *n* cresson *m* (de fontaine). ◆**waterfall** *n* chute *f* d'eau. ◆**waterhole** *n* (*in desert*) point *m* d'eau. ◆**waterline** *n* (*on ship*) ligne *f* de flottaison. ◆**waterlogged** *a* délavé. ◆**watermark** *n* (*in paper*) filigrane *m.* ◆**watermelon** *n* pastèque *f.* ◆**waterproof** *a* (*material*) imperméable. ◆**watershed** *n* (*turning point*) tournant *m* (décisif). ◆**watertight** *a* (*container etc*) étanche. ◆**waterway** *n* voie *f* navigable. ◆**waterworks** *n* (*place*) station *f* hydraulique.

watt [wɒt] *n El* watt *m.*

wave [weɪv] *n* (*of sea*) & *Fig* vague *f;* (*in hair*) ondulation *f; Rad* onde *f;* (*sign*) signe *m* (de la main); **long/medium/short w.** *Rad*

ondes *fpl* longues/moyennes/courtes; – *vi* (*with hand*) faire signe (de la main); (*of flag*) flotter; **to w. to** (*greet*) saluer de la main; – *vt* (*arm, flag etc*) agiter; (*hair*) onduler; **to w. s.o. on** faire signe à qn d'avancer; **to w. aside** (*objection etc*) écarter. ◆**waveband** *n Rad* bande *f* de fréquence. ◆**wavelength** *n Rad & Fig* longueur *f* d'ondes.

waver ['weɪvər] *vi* (*of flame, person etc*) vaciller.

wavy ['weɪvɪ] *a* (**-ier, -iest**) (*line*) onduleux; (*hair*) ondulé.

wax [wæks] **1** *n* cire *f;* (*for ski*) fart *m;* – *vt* cirer; (*ski*) farter; (*car*) lustrer; – *a* (*candle, doll etc*) de cire; **w. paper** *Culin Am* papier *m* paraffiné. **2** *vi* (*of moon*) croître. **3** *vi* **to w. lyrical/merry** (*become*) se faire lyrique/gai. ◆**waxworks** *npl* (*place*) musée *m* de cire; (*dummies*) figures *fpl* de cire.

way [weɪ] **1** *n* (*path, road*) chemin *m* (**to** de); (*direction*) sens *m,* direction *f;* (*distance*) distance *f;* **all the w., the whole w.** (*to talk etc*) pendant tout le chemin; **this w.** par ici; **that way** par là; **which w.?** par où?; **to lose one's w.** se perdre; **I'm on my w.** (*coming*) j'arrive; (*going*) je pars; **he made his w. out/home** il est sorti/rentré; **the w. there** l'aller *m;* **the w. back** le retour; **the w. in** l'entrée *f;* **the w. out** la sortie; **a w. out of** (*problem etc*) *Fig* une solution à; **the w. is clear** *Fig* la voie est libre; **across the w.** en face; **on the w.** en route (**to** pour); **by w. of** (*via*) par; (*as*) *Fig* comme; **out of the w.** (*isolated*) isolé; **to go out of one's w. to do** se donner du mal pour faire; **by the w. . . . .** *Fig* à propos . . . ; **to be** *or* **stand in the w.** barrer le passage; **she's in my w.** (*hindrance*) *Fig* elle me gêne; **to get out of the w., make w.** s'écarter; **to give w.** céder; *Aut* céder le passage *or* la priorité; **a long w.** (*away or off*) très loin; **it's the wrong w. up** c'est dans le mauvais sens; **do it the other w. round** fais le contraire; **to get under w.** (*of campaign etc*) démarrer; – *adv* (*behind etc*) très loin; **w. ahead** très en avance (**of** sur). **2** *n* (*manner*) façon *f;* (*means*) moyen *m;* (*condition*) état *m;* (*habit*) habitude *f;* (*particular*) égard *m;* **one's ways** (*behaviour*) ses manières *fpl;* **to get one's own w.** obtenir ce qu'on veut; (**in**) **this w.** de cette façon; **in a way** (*to some extent*) dans un certain sens; **w. of life** façon *f* de vivre, mode *m* de vie; **no w.!** (*certainly not*) *Fam* pas question! ◆**wayfarer** *n* voyageur, -euse *mf.* ◆**way-'out** *a Fam* extraordinaire. ◆**wayside** n by the w. au bord de la route.

waylay [wer'leɪ] vt (pt & pp **-laid**) (attack) attaquer par surprise; (stop) Fig arrêter au passage.

wayward ['werwəd] a rebelle, capricieux.

WC [dʌb(ə)lju:'si:] n w-c mpl, waters mpl.

we [wi:] pron nous; **we go** nous allons; **we teachers** nous autres professeurs; **we never know** (indefinite) on ne sait jamais.

weak [wi:k] a (-er, -est) faible; (tea, coffee) léger; (health, stomach) fragile. ◆**w.-'willed** a faible. ◆**weaken** vt affaiblir; – vi faiblir. ◆**weakling** n (in body) mauviette f; (in character) faible mf. ◆**weakly** adv faiblement. ◆**weakness** n faiblesse f; (of health, stomach) fragilité f; (fault) point m faible; **a w. for** (liking) un faible pour.

weal [wi:l] n (wound on skin) marque f, zébrure f.

wealth [welθ] n (money, natural resources) richesse(s) f(pl); **a w. of** (abundance) Fig une profusion de. ◆**wealthy** a (-ier, -iest) riche; – n the w. les riches mpl.

wean [wi:n] vt (baby) sevrer.

weapon ['wepən] n arme f. ◆**weaponry** n armements mpl.

wear [weər] **1** vt (pt **wore**, pp **worn**) (have on body) porter; (look, smile) avoir; (put on) mettre; **to have nothing to w.** n'avoir rien à se mettre; – n men's/sports w. vêtements mpl pour hommes/de sport; **evening w.** tenue f de soirée. **2** vt (pt **wore**, pp **worn**) **to w.** (away or down or out) (material, patience etc) user; **to w. s.o. out** (exhaust) épuiser qn; **to w. oneself out** s'épuiser (doing à faire); – vi (last) faire de l'usage, durer; **to w. (out)** (of clothes etc) s'user; **to w. off** (of colour, paint etc) disparaître; **to w. on** (of time) passer; **to w. out** (of patience) s'épuiser; – n (use) usage m; **w. (and tear)** usure f. ◆**-ing** a (tiring) épuisant. ◆**-er** n the w. of (hat, glasses etc) la personne qui porte.

weary ['wɪərɪ] a (-ier, -iest) (tired) fatigué, las (of doing de faire); (tiring) fatigant; (look, smile) las; – vi to w. of se lasser de. ◆**wearily** adv avec lassitude. ◆**weariness** n lassitude f.

weasel ['wi:z(ə)l] n belette f.

weather ['weðər] n temps m; **what's the w. like?** quel temps fait-il?; **in (the) hot w.** par temps chaud; **under the w.** (ill) Fig patraque; – a (chart etc) météorologique; **w. forecast, w. report** prévisions fpl météorologiques, météo f; **w. vane** girouette f; –

vt (storm, hurricane) essuyer; (crisis) Fig surmonter. ◆**weather-beaten** a (face, person) tanné, hâlé. ◆**weathercock** n girouette f. ◆**weatherman** n (pl -men) TV Rad Fam monsieur m météo.

weav/e [wi:v] vt (pt **wove**, pp **woven**) (cloth, plot) tisser; (basket, garland) tresser; – vi Tex tisser; **to w. in and out of** (crowd, cars etc) Fig se faufiler entre; – n (style) tissage m. ◆**-ing** n tissage m. ◆**-er** n tisserand, -ande mf.

web [web] n (of spider) toile f; (of lies) Fig tissu m. ◆**webbed** a (foot) palmé. ◆**webbing** n (in chair) sangles fpl.

wed [wed] vt (-dd-) (marry) épouser; (qualities etc) Fig allier (to à); – vi se marier. ◆**wedded** a (bliss, life) conjugal. ◆**wedding** n mariage m; **golden/silver w.** noces fpl d'or/d'argent; – a (cake) de noces; (anniversary, present) de mariage; (dress) de mariée; **his** or **her w. day** le jour de son mariage; **w. ring, Am w. band** alliance f. ◆**wedlock** n born out of w. illégitime.

wedge [wedʒ] n (for splitting) coin m; (under wheel, table etc) cale f; **w. heel** (of shoe) semelle f compensée; – vt (wheel, table etc) caler; (push) enfoncer (into dans); **wedged (in) between** (caught, trapped) coincé entre.

Wednesday ['wenzdɪ] n mercredi m.

wee [wi:] a (tiny) Fam tout petit.

weed [wi:d] n (plant) mauvaise herbe f; (weak person) Fam mauviette f; **w. killer** désherbant m; – vti désherber; – vt to **w. out** Fig éliminer (from de). ◆**weedy** a (-ier, -iest) (person) Fam maigre et chétif.

week [wi:k] n semaine f; **the w. before last** pas la semaine dernière, celle d'avant; **the w. after next** pas la semaine prochaine, celle d'après; **tomorrow w., a w. tomorrow** demain en huit. ◆**weekday** n jour m de semaine. ◆**week'end** n week-end m; **at** or **on** or **over the w.** ce week-end, pendant le week-end. ◆**weekly** a hebdomadaire; – adv toutes les semaines; – n (magazine) hebdomadaire m.

weep [wi:p] vi (pt pp **wept**) pleurer; (of wound) suinter; **to w. for s.o.** pleurer qn; – vt (tears) pleurer; **weeping willow** saule m pleureur.

weft [weft] n Tex trame f.

weigh [weɪ] vt peser; **to w. down** (with load etc) surcharger (with de); (bend) faire plier; **to w. up** (goods, chances etc) peser; – vi peser; **it's weighing on my mind** ça me tracasse; **to w. down on s.o.** (of worries etc)

accabler qn. ◆**weighing-machine** n
balance f.

weight [weɪt] n poids m; **to put on w.** grossir;
to lose w. maigrir; **to carry w.** (of argument
etc) Fig avoir du poids (with pour); **to pull
one's w.** (do one's share) Fig faire sa part du
travail; **w. lifter** haltérophile mf; **w. lifting**
haltérophilie f; – vt **to w. (down)** (light
object) maintenir avec un poids; **w. down
with** (overload) surcharger de.
◆**weightlessness** n apesanteur f.
◆**weighty** a (-ier, -iest) lourd; (argument,
subject) Fig de poids.

weighting [weɪtɪŋ] n (on salary) indemnité f
de résidence.

weir [wɪər] n (across river) barrage m.

weird [wɪəd] a (-er, -est) (odd) bizarɪe;
(eerie) mystérieux.

welcome ['welkəm] a (pleasant) agréable;
(timely) opportun; – to be w. (of person,
people) être le bienvenu or la bienvenue or
les bienvenu(e)s; **w.!** soyez le bienvenu or
la bienvenue or les bienvenu(e)s!; **to make
s.o. feel w.** faire bon accueil à qn; **you're
w.!** (after 'thank you') il n'y a pas de quoi!;
w. to do (free) libre de faire; **you're w. to
(take or use) my bike** mon vélo est à ta
disposition; **you're w. to it!** Iron grand bien
vous fasse!; – n accueil m; to extend a **w. to**
(greet) souhaiter la bienvenue à; – vt
accueillir; (warmly) faire bon accueil à; (be
glad of) se réjouir de; **I w. you!** je vous
souhaite la bienvenue! ◆**welcoming** a
(smile etc) accueillant; (speech, words)
d'accueil.

weld [weld] vt **to w. (together)** souder;
(groups etc) Fig unir; – n (joint) soudure f.
◆**—ing** n soudure f. ◆**—er** n soudeur m.

welfare ['welfeər] n (physical, material)
bien-être m; (spiritual) santé f; (public aid)
aide f sociale; **public w.** le bien public; **the w.
state** (in Great Britain) l'État-providence m;
w. work assistance f sociale.

well¹ [wel] **1** n (for water) puits m; (of stairs,
lift) cage f; (oil) **w.** puits de pétrole. **2** vi **to
w. up** (rise) monter.

well² [wel] adv (better, best) bien; **to do w.**
(succeed) réussir; **you'd do w. to refuse** tu
ferais bien de refuser; **w. done!** bravo!; **I,
you, she** etc **might (just) as w. have left** il
valait mieux partir, autant valait partir; **it's
just as w. that** (lucky) heureusement que
...; **as w. (also)** aussi; **as w. as** aussi bien
que; **as w. as two cats, he has ...** en plus de
deux chats, il a ...; – a bien inv; **she's w.**
(healthy) elle va bien; **not a w. man** un

homme malade; **to get w.** se remettre;
that's all very w., but ... tout ça c'est très
joli, mais ...; – int eh bien!; **w., w.!**
(surprise) tiens, tiens!; **enormous, w., quite
big** énorme, enfin, assez grand.

well-behaved [welbɪ'heɪvd] a sage.
◆**w.-'being** n bien-être m. ◆**w.-'built** a
(person, car) solide. ◆**w.-'founded** a bien
fondé. ◆**w.-'heeled** a (rich) Fam nanti.
◆**w.-in'formed** a (person, newspaper)
bien informé. ◆**w.-'known** a (bien)
connu. ◆**w.-'meaning** a bien intentionné. ◆**w.'nigh** adv presque. ◆**w.-'off**
a aisé, riche. ◆**w.-'read** a instruit.
◆**w.-'spoken** a (person) qui a un accent
cultivé, qui parle bien. ◆**w.-'thought-of** a
hautement considéré. ◆**w.-'timed** a
opportun. ◆**w.-to-'do** a aisé, riche.
◆**w.-'tried** a (method) éprouvé. ◆**w.-
'trodden** a (path) battu. ◆**w.-'wish-
ers** npl admirateurs, -trices mfpl.
◆**w.-'worn** a (clothes, carpet) usé.

wellington [welɪŋtən] n botte f de caoutchouc.

welsh [welʃ] vi **to w. on** (debt, promise) ne
pas honorer.

Welsh [welʃ] a gallois; **W. rabbit** Culin toast
m au fromage; – n (language) gallois m.
◆**Welshman** n (pl -men) Gallois m.
◆**Welshwoman** n (pl -women) Galloise f.

wench [wentʃ] n Hum jeune fille f.

wend [wend] vt **to w. one's way** s'acheminer
(to vers).

went [went] see **go 1.**

wept [wept] see **weep.**

were [wər, stressed wɜːr] see **be.**

werewolf ['weəwulf] n (pl -wolves)
loup-garou m.

west [west] n ouest m; – a (coast) ouest inv;
(wind) d'ouest; **W. Africa** Afrique f
occidentale; **W. Indian** a & n antillais, -aise
(mf); **the W. Indies** les Antilles fpl; – adv à
l'ouest, vers l'ouest. ◆**westbound** a
(carriageway) ouest inv; (traffic) en direction de l'ouest. ◆**westerly** a (point) ouest
inv; (direction) de l'ouest; (wind) d'ouest.
◆**western** a (coast) ouest inv; (culture) Pol
occidental; **W. Europe** Europe f de l'Ouest;
– n (film) western m. ◆**westerner** n habitant, -ante mf de l'Ouest; Pol occidental,
-ale mf. ◆**westernize** vt occidentaliser.
◆**westward(s)** a & adv vers l'ouest.

wet [wet] a (wetter, wettest) mouillé; (damp,
rainy) humide; (day, month) de pluie; **w.
paint/ink** peinture f/encre f fraîche; **w,
through** trempé; **to get w.** se mouiller; **it's
w.** (raining) il pleut; **he's w.** (weak-willed)

Fam c'est une lavette; **w. blanket** *Fig* rabat-joie *m inv*; **w. nurse** nourrice *f*; **w. suit** combinaison *f* de plongée; *– n* **(rain)** la pluie; *(damp)* l'humidité *f*; *– vt* **(-tt-)** mouiller. ◆**—ness** *n* humidité *f*.

whack [wæk] *n (blow)* grand coup *m*; *– vt* donner un grand coup à. ◆**—ed** *a* **w. (out)** *(tired) Fam* claqué. ◆**—ing** *a (big) Fam* énorme.

whale [weɪl] *n* baleine *f*. ◆**whaling** *n* pêche *f* à la baleine.

wham! [wæm] *int* vlan!

wharf [wɔːf] *n (pl* **wharfs** *or* **wharves)** *(for ships)* quai *m*.

what [wɒt] **1** *a* quel, quelle, *pl* quel(le)s; **w. book?** quel livre?; **w. one?** *Fam* lequel?, laquelle?; **w. a fool/etc!** quel idiot/*etc*!; **I know w. book it is** je sais quel livre c'est; **w. (little) she has** le peu qu'elle a. **2** *pron (in questions)* qu'est-ce qui; *(object)* qu'est-ce que; *(after prep)* quoi; **w.'s happening?** qu'est-ce qui se passe?; **w. does he do?** qu'est-ce qu'il fait?, que fait-il?; **w. is it?** qu'est-ce que c'est?; **w.'s that book?** quel est ce livre?; **w.!** *(surprise)* quoi!, comment!; **w.'s it called?** comment ça s'appelle?; **w. for?** pourquoi?; **w. about me/etc?** et moi/*etc*?; **w. about leaving/etc?** si on partait/*etc*? **3** *pron (indirect, relative)* ce qui; *(object)* ce que; **I know w. will happen/w. she'll do** je sais ce qui arrivera/ce qu'elle fera; **w. happens is . . .** ce qui arrive c'est que . . . ; **w. I need** ce dont j'ai besoin. ◆**what'ever** *a* **w. (the) mistake/etc (no matter what)** quelle que soit l'erreur/*etc*; **of w. size** de n'importe quelle taille; **no chance w.** pas la moindre chance; **nothing w.** rien du tout; *– pron (no matter what)* quoi que (+ *sub*); **w. happens** quoi qu'il arrive; **w. you do** quoi que tu fasses; **w. is important** tout ce qui est important; **w. you want** tout ce que tu veux. ◆**what's-it** *n (thing) Fam* machin *m*. ◆**whatso'ever** *a* & *pron* = **whatever.**

wheat [wiːt] *n* blé *m*, froment *m*. ◆**wheatgerm** *n* germes *mpl* de blé.

wheedle ['wiːd(ə)l] *vt* **to w. s.o.** enjôler qn *(into doing pour qu'il fasse)*; **to w. sth out of s.o.** obtenir qch de qn par la flatterie.

wheel [wiːl] **1** *n* roue *f*; **at the w.** *Aut* au volant; *Nau* au gouvernail; *– vt (push)* pousser; *– vi (turn)* tourner. **2** *vi* **to w. and deal** *Fam* faire des combines. ◆**wheelbarrow** *n* brouette *f*. ◆**wheelchair** *n* fauteuil *m* roulant.

wheeze [wiːz] **1** *vi* respirer bruyamment. **2** *n*

(scheme) Fam combine *f*. ◆**wheezy** *a* **(-ier, -iest)** poussif.

whelk [welk] *n (mollusc)* buccin *m*.

when [wen] *adv* quand; *– conj* quand, lorsque; *(whereas)* alors que; **w. I finish, w. I've finished** quand j'aurai fini, **w.** I saw him *or* **w.** I'd seen him, I left après l'avoir vu, je suis parti; **the day/moment w.** le jour/moment où; **I talked when w. . . .** j'ai parlé de l'époque où . . . . ◆**when'ever** *conj (at whatever time)* quand; *(each time that)* chaque fois que.

where [weər] *adv* où; **w. are you from?** d'où êtes-vous?; *– conj* où; *(whereas)* alors que; **that's w. you'll find it** c'est là que tu le trouveras; **I found it w. she'd left it** je l'ai trouvé là où elle l'avait laissé; **I went to w. he was** je suis allé à l'endroit où il était. ◆**whereabouts** *adv* où (donc); *– n* **his w.** l'endroit *m* où il est. ◆**where'as** *conj* alors que. ◆**where'by** *adv* par quoi. ◆**where'upon** *adv* sur quoi. ◆**wher'ever** *conj* **w. you go** *(everywhere)* partout où tu iras, où que tu ailles; **I'll go w. you like** *(anywhere)* j'irai (là) où tu voudras.

whet [wet] *vt* **(-tt-)** *(appetite, desire etc)* aiguiser.

whether ['weðər] *conj* si; **I don't know w. to leave** je ne sais pas si je dois partir; **w. she does it or not** qu'elle le fasse ou non; **w. now or tomorrow** que ce soit maintenant ou demain; **it's doubtful w.** il est douteux que (+ *sub*).

which [wɪtʃ] **1** *a (in questions etc)* quel, quelle, *pl* quel(le)s; **w. hat?** quel chapeau?; **in w. case** auquel cas. **2** *rel pron (subject)* qui; *(after prep)* lequel, laquelle, *pl* lesquel(le)s; **the house w. is . . .** la maison qui est . . . ; **the book w. I like** le livre que j'aime; **the film of w. . . .** le film dont *or* duquel . . . ; **she's ill, w. is sad** elle est malade, ce qui est triste; **he lies, w. I don't like it** ment, ce que je n'aime pas; **after w.** *(whereupon)* après quoi. **3** *pron* **w. (one)** *(in questions)* lequel, laquelle, *pl* lesquel(le)s; **w. (one) of us?** lequel *or* laquelle d'entre nous?; **w. (ones) are the best of these books** quels sont les meilleurs de ces livres? **4** *pron* **w. (one)** *(the one that)* celui qui, celle qui, *pl* ceux qui, celles qui; *(object)* celui *etc* que; **show me w. (one) is red** montrez-moi celui *or* celle qui est rouge; **I know w. (ones) you want** je sais ceux *or* celles que vous désirez. ◆**which'ever** *a* & *pron* **w. book/etc** *or* **w. of the books/etc** you buy quel que soit le livre/*etc* que tu achètes; **take w. books** *or* **w. of the books interest you** prenez les livres qui vous intéressent; **take w. (one)** you like prends celui or celle qui te veux; **w. (ones) remain** ceux or celles qui restent.

whiff [wɪf] n (puff) bouffée f; (smell) odeur f.

while [waɪl] conj (when) pendant que; (although) bien que (+ sub); (as long as) tant que; (whereas) tandis que; **w. doing** (in the course of) en faisant; – n a w. un moment, quelque temps; **all the w.** tout le temps; – vt **to w. away** (time) passer. ◆**whilst** [waɪlst] conj = while.

whim [wɪm] n caprice m.

whimper ['wɪmpər] vi (of dog, person) gémir faiblement; (snivel) Pej pleurnicher; – n faible gémissement m; **without a w.** (complaint) Fig sans se plaindre.

whimsical ['wɪmzɪk(ə)l] a (look, idea) bizarre; (person) fantasque, capricieux.

whine [waɪn] vi gémir; (complain) Fig se plaindre; – n gémissement m; plainte f.

whip [wɪp] n fouet m; – vt (-pp-) (person, cream etc) fouetter; (defeat) Fam dérouiller; **to w. off** (take off) enlever brusquement; **to w. out** (from pocket etc) sortir brusquement (from de); **to w. up** (interest) susciter; (meal) Fam préparer rapidement; – vi (move) aller à toute vitesse; **to w. round to s.o.'s** faire un saut chez qn. ◆**whip-round** n Fam collecte f.

whirl [wɜːl] vi tourbillonner, tournoyer; – vt faire tourbillonner; – n tourbillon m. ◆**whirlpool** n tourbillon m; **w. bath** Am bain m à remous. ◆**whirlwind** n tourbillon m (de vent).

whirr [wɜːr] vi (of engine) vrombir; (of top) ronronner.

whisk [wɪsk] 1 n Culin fouet m; – vt fouetter. 2 vt **to w. away** or **off** (tablecloth etc) enlever rapidement; (person) emmener rapidement; (chase away) chasser.

whiskers ['wɪskəz] npl (of animal) moustaches fpl; (beard) barbe f; (moustache) moustache f; (side) w. favoris mpl.

whisky, Am **whiskey** ['wɪskɪ] n whisky m.

whisper ['wɪspər] vti chuchoter; **w. to me!** chuchote à mon oreille!; – n chuchotement m; (rumour) Fig rumeur f, bruit m.

whistle ['wɪs(ə)l] n sifflement m; (object) sifflet m; **to blow** or **give a w.** siffler; – vti siffler; **to w. at** (girl) siffler; **to w. for** (dog, taxi) siffler.

Whit [wɪt] a **W. Sunday** dimanche m de Pentecôte.

white [waɪt] a (-er, -est) blanc; **to go** or **turn w.** blanchir; **w. coffee** café m au lait; **w. elephant** Fig objet m or projet m etc inutile;

w. lie pieux mensonge m; **w. man** blanc m; **w. woman** blanche f; – n (colour, of egg, of eye) blanc m; (person) blanc m, blanche f. ◆**white-collar 'worker** n employé, -ée mf de bureau. ◆**whiten** vti blanchir. ◆**whiteness** n blancheur f. ◆**whitewash** n (for walls etc) blanc m de chaux; – vt blanchir à la chaux; (person) Fig blanchir; (faults) justifier.

whiting ['waɪtɪŋ] n (fish) merlan m.

Whitsun ['wɪts(ə)n] n la Pentecôte.

whittle ['wɪt(ə)l] vt **to w. down** (wood) tailler; (price etc) Fig rogner.

whizz [wɪz] 1 vi (rush) aller à toute vitesse; **to w. past** passer à toute vitesse; **to w. through the air** fendre l'air. 2 a **w. kid** Fam petit prodige m.

who [huː] pron qui; **w. did it?** qui (est-ce qui) a fait ça?; **the woman w.** la femme qui; **w. did you see** tu as vu qui? ◆**who'ever** pron (no matter who) qui que ce soit qui; (object) qui que ce soit que; **w. has travelled** (anyone who) quiconque a or celui qui a voyagé; **w. you are** qui que vous soyez; **this man, w. he is** cet homme, quel qu'il soit; **w. did that?** qui donc a fait ça?

whodunit [huːˈdʌnɪt] n (detective story) Fam polar m.

whole [həʊl] a entier; (intact) intact; **the w. time** tout le temps; **the w. apple** toute la pomme, la pomme (tout) entière; **the w. truth** toute la vérité; **the w. world** le monde entier; **the w. lot** le tout; **to swallow sth w.** avaler qch tout rond; – n (unit) tout m; (total) totalité f; **the w. of the village** le village (tout) entier, tout le village; **the w. of the night** toute la nuit; **on the w., as a w.** dans l'ensemble. ◆**whole-'hearted** a, ◆**whole-'heartedly** adv sans réserve. ◆**wholemeal** a, Am ◆**wholewheat** a (bread) complet. ◆**wholly** adv entièrement.

wholesale ['həʊlseɪl] n Com gros m; – a (firm) de gros; (destruction etc) Fig en masse; – adv (in bulk) en gros; (to buy or sell one article) au prix de gros; (to destroy etc) Fig en masse. ◆**wholesaler** n grossiste mf.

wholesome ['həʊlsəm] a (food, climate etc) sain.

whom [huːm] pron (object) que; (in questions and after prep) qui; **w. did she see?** qui a-t-elle vu?; **the man w. you know** l'homme que tu connais; **with w.** avec qui; **of w.** dont.

whooping cough ['huːpɪŋkɒf] n coqueluche f.

whoops! [wʊps] int (apology etc) oups!
whopping ['wɒpɪŋ] a (big) Fam énorme. ◆**whopper** n Fam chose f énorme.
whore [hɔːr] n (prostitute) putain f.
whose [huːz] poss pron & a à qui, de qui; w. book is this? à qui est ce livre?; w. daughter are you? de qui es-tu la fille?; the woman w. book I have la femme dont or de qui j'ai le livre; the man w. mother I spoke to l'homme à la mère de qui j'ai parlé.
why [waɪ] 1 adv pourquoi; w. not? pourquoi pas?; − conj the reason w. they ... la raison pour laquelle ils ... ; − npl the whys and wherefores le pourquoi et le comment. 2 int (surprise) eh bien!, tiens!
wick [wɪk] n (of candle, lamp) mèche f.
wicked ['wɪkɪd] a (evil) méchant, vilain; (mischievous) malicieux. ◆**─ly** adv méchamment; malicieusement. ◆**─ness** n méchanceté f.
wicker ['wɪkər] n osier m; − a (chair etc) en osier, d'osier. ◆**wickerwork** n (objects) vannerie f.
wicket ['wɪkɪt] n (cricket stumps) guichet m.
wide [waɪd] a (-er, -est) large; (desert, ocean) vaste; (choice, knowledge, variety) grand; to be three metres w. avoir trois mètres de large; − adv (to fall, shoot) loin du but; (to open) tout grand. ◆**wide-'awake** a (alert, not sleeping) éveillé. ◆**widely** adv (to broadcast, spread) largement; (to travel) beaucoup; w. different très différent; it's w. thought or believed that ... on pense généralement que ... ◆**widen** vt élargir; − vi s'élargir. ◆**wideness** n largeur f.
widespread ['waɪdspred] a (très) répandu.
widow ['wɪdəʊ] n veuve f. ◆**widowed** a (man) veuf; (woman) veuve; to be w. (become a widower or widow) devenir veuf or veuve. ◆**widower** n veuf m.
width [wɪdθ] n largeur f.
wield [wiːld] vt (handle) manier; (brandish) brandir; (power) Fig exercer.
wife [waɪf] n (pl wives) femme f, épouse f.
wig [wɪg] n perruque f.
wiggle ['wɪg(ə)l] vt agiter; to w. one's hips tortiller des hanches; − vi (of worm etc) se tortiller; (of tail) remuer.
wild [waɪld] a (-er, -est) (animal, flower, region etc) sauvage; (enthusiasm, sea) déchaîné; (idea, life) fou; (look) farouche; (angry) furieux (with contre); w. with (joy, anger etc) fou de; I'm not w. about it (plan etc) Fam ça ne m'emballe pas; to be w. about s.o. (very fond of) être dingue de qn; to grow w. (of plant) pousser à l'état sau-

vage; to run w. (of animals) courir en liberté; (of crowd) se déchaîner; the W. West Am le Far West; − npl régions fpl sauvages. ◆**wildcat 'strike** n grève f sauvage. ◆**wild-'goose chase** n fausse piste f. ◆**wildlife** n animaux mpl sauvages, faune f.
wilderness ['wɪldənəs] n désert m.
wildly ['waɪldlɪ] adv (madly) follement; (violently) violemment.
wile [waɪl] n ruse f, artifice m.
wilful ['wɪlfəl] a (Am willful) (intentional, obstinate) volontaire. ◆**─ly** adv volontairement.
will[1] [wɪl] v aux he will come, he'll come (future tense) il viendra (won't he? n'est-ce pas?); you will not come, you won't come tu ne viendras pas (will you? n'est-ce pas?); w. you have a tea? veux-tu prendre un thé?; w. you be quiet! veux-tu te taire!; I w.! (yes) oui!; it won't open ça ne s'ouvre pas, ça ne veut pas s'ouvrir.
will[2] 1 vt (wish, intend) vouloir (that que (+ sub)); to w. oneself to do faire un effort de volonté pour faire; − n volonté f; against one's w. à contrecœur; at w. (to depart etc) quand on veut; (to choose) à volonté. 2 n (legal document) testament m. ◆**willpower** n volonté f.
willing ['wɪlɪŋ] a (helper, worker) de bonne volonté; (help etc) spontané; to be w. to do être disposé or prêt à faire, vouloir bien faire; − n volonté f. faire preuve de bonne volonté. ◆**─ly** adv (with pleasure) volontiers; (voluntarily) volontairement. ◆**─ness** n (goodwill) bonne volonté f; his or her w. to do (enthusiasm) son empressement m à faire.
willow ['wɪləʊ] n (tree, wood) saule m.
willowy a (person) svelte.
willy-nilly [wɪlɪ'nɪlɪ] adv bon gré mal gré, de gré ou de force.
wilt [wɪlt] vi (of plant) dépérir; (of enthusiasm etc) Fig décliner.
wily [waɪlɪ] a (-ier, -iest) rusé.
wimp [wɪmp] n (weakling) Fam mauviette f.
win [wɪn] n (victory) victoire f; − vi (pt & pp won, pres p winning) gagner; − vt (money, race etc) gagner; (victory, prize) remporter; (fame) acquérir; (friends) se faire; to w. s.o. over gagner qn (to à). ◆**winning** a (number, horse etc) gagnant; (team) victorieux; (goal) décisif; (smile) engageant; − npl gains mpl.
wince [wɪns] vi (flinch) tressaillir; (pull a face) grimacer; without wincing sans sourciller.

winch [wɪntʃ] n treuil m; – vt to w. (up) hisser au treuil.

wind¹ [wɪnd] n vent m; (breath) souffle m; **to have w.** Med avoir des gaz; **to get w. of** Fig avoir vent de; **in the w.** Fig dans l'air; **w. instrument** Mus instrument m à vent; – vt **to w. s.o.** (of blow etc) couper le souffle à qn. ◆**windbreak** n (fence, trees) brise-vent m inv. ◆**windcheater** n, Am ◆**windbreaker** n blouson m, coupe-vent m inv. ◆**windfall** n (piece of fruit) fruit m abattu par le vent; (unexpected money) Fig aubaine f. ◆**windmill** n moulin m à vent. ◆**windpipe** n Anat trachée f. ◆**windscreen** n, Am ◆**windshield** n Aut pare-brise m inv; **w. wiper** essuie-glace m inv. ◆**windsurfing** n to go w. faire de la planche à voile. ◆**windswept** a (street etc) balayé par les vents. ◆**windy** a (-ier, -iest) venteux, venté; **it's w.** (of weather) il y a du vent.

wind² [waɪnd] vt (pt & pp wound) (roll) enrouler; **to w.** (up) (clock) remonter; **to w. up** (meeting) terminer; (firm) liquider; – vi (of river, road) serpenter; **to w. down** (relax) se détendre; **to w. up** (end up) finir (doing par faire); **to w. up with sth** se retrouver avec qch. ◆**—ing** a (road etc) sinueux; (staircase) tournant. ◆**—er** n (of watch) remontoir m.

window [wɪndəu] n fenêtre f; (pane) vitre f, carreau m; (in vehicle or train) vitre f; (in shop) vitrine f; (counter) guichet m; **French w. porte-fenêtre** f; **w. box** jardinière f; **w. cleaner** or Am **washer** laveur, -euse mf de carreaux; **w. dresser** étalagiste mf; **w. ledge** = windowsill; **to go w. shopping** faire du lèche-vitrines. ◆**windowpane** n vitre f, carreau m. ◆**windowsill** n (inside) appui m de (la) fenêtre; (outside) rebord m de (la) fenêtre.

wine [waɪn] n vin m; – a (bottle, cask) à vin; **w. cellar** cave f (à vin); **w. grower** viticulteur m; **w. list** carte f des vins; **w. taster** dégustateur, -trice mf de vins; **w. tasting** dégustation f de vins; **w. waiter** sommelier m; – vt **to w. and dine s.o.** offrir à dîner et à boire à qn. ◆**wineglass** n verre m à vin. ◆**wine-growing** a viticole.

wing [wɪŋ] n aile f; **the wings** Th les coulisses fpl; **under one's w.** Fig sous son aile. ◆**winged** a ailé. ◆**winger** n Sp ailier m. ◆**wingspan** n envergure f.

wink [wɪŋk] vi faire un clin d'œil (**at, to** à); (of light) clignoter; – n clin m d'œil.

winkle [wɪŋk(ə)l] n (sea animal) bigorneau m.

winner [wɪnər] n (of contest etc) gagnant, -ante mf; (of argument, fight) vainqueur m; **that idea/etc is a w.** Fam c'est une idée/etc en or.

winter [wɪntər] n hiver m; – a d'hiver; **in (the) w.** en hiver. ◆**wintertime** n hiver m. ◆**wintry** a hivernal.

wip/e [waɪp] vt essuyer; **to w. one's feet/hands** s'essuyer les pieds/les mains; **to w. away** or **off** or **up** (liquid) essuyer; **to w. out** (clean) essuyer; (erase) effacer; (destroy) anéantir; – vi **to w. up** (dry the dishes) essuyer la vaisselle; – n coup m de torchon or d'éponge. ◆**—er** n Aut essuie-glace m inv.

wir/e [waɪər] n fil m; (telegram) télégramme m; **w. netting** grillage m; – vt to w. (house) El faire l'installation électrique de; **to w. s.o.** (telegraph) télégraphier à qn. ◆**—ing** n El installation f électrique. ◆**wirecutters** npl pince f coupante.

wireless [waɪələs] n (set) TSF f, radio f; **by w.** (to send a message) par sans-fil.

wiry [waɪərɪ] a (-ier, -iest) maigre et nerveux.

wisdom [wɪzdəm] n sagesse f.

wise [waɪz] a (-er, -est) (prudent) sage, prudent; (learned) savant; **to put s.o. w./be w. to** Fam mettre qn/être au courant de; **w. guy** Fam gros malin m. ◆**wisecrack** n Fam (joke) astuce f; (sarcastic remark) sarcasme m. ◆**wisely** adv prudemment.

-wise [waɪz] suffix (with regard to) money/etc-**wise** question argent/etc.

wish [wɪʃ] vt souhaiter, vouloir (**to do** faire); **I w.** (that) **you could help me**/etc je voudrais que/j'aurais voulu que vous m'aidiez; **I w. I hadn't done that** je regrette d'avoir fait ça; **if you w.** si tu veux; **I w. you well** or **luck** je vous souhaite bonne chance; **I wished him** or **her (a) happy birthday** je lui ai souhaité bon anniversaire; **I w. I could** si seulement je pouvais; – vi **to w. for sth** souhaiter qch; – n (specific) souhait m, vœu m; (general) désir m; **the w. for sth/to do** le désir de qch/de faire; **best wishes** (on greeting card) meilleurs vœux mpl; (in letter) amitiés fpl, bien amicalement; **send him** or **her my best wishes** fais-lui mes amitiés. ◆**wishbone** n bréchet m. ◆**wishful** a **it's w. thinking (on your part)** tu te fais des illusions, tu prends tes désirs pour la réalité.

wishy-washy [wɪʃɪwɒʃɪ] a (taste, colour) fade.

wisp [wɪsp] n (of smoke) volute f; (of hair)

fine mèche f; a (mere) w. of a girl une fillette toute menue.

wisteria [wɪ'stɪərɪə] n Bot glycine f.

wistful ['wɪstfəl] a mélancolique et rêveur. ◆**-ly** adv avec mélancolie.

wit [wɪt] n **1** (humour) esprit m; (person) homme m or femme f d'esprit. **2** (it's) (intelligence) intelligence f (to do de faire); **to be at one's wits'** or **wit's end** ne plus savoir que faire.

witch [wɪtʃ] n sorcière f. ◆**witchcraft** n sorcellerie f. ◆**witch-hunt** n Pol chasse f aux sorcières.

with [wɪð] prep **1** avec; **come w. me** viens avec moi; **w. no hat** sans chapeau; **I'll be right w. you** je suis à vous dans une minute; **I'm w. you** (I understand) Fam je te suis; **w. it** (up-to-date) Fam dans le vent. **2** (at the house, flat etc of) chez; **she's staying w. me** elle loge chez moi; **it's a habit w. me** c'est une habitude chez moi. **3** (cause) de; **to jump w. joy** sauter de joie. **4** (instrument, means) avec, de; **to write w. a pen** écrire avec un stylo; **to fill w.** remplir de; **satisfied w.** satisfait de; **w. my own eyes** de mes propres yeux. **5** (description) à; **w. blue eyes** aux yeux bleus. **6** (despite) malgré.

withdraw [wɪð'drɔː] vt (pt withdrew, pp withdrawn) retirer (from de); — vi se retirer (from de). ◆**withdrawn** a (person) renfermé. ◆**withdrawal** n retrait m; **to suffer from w. symptoms** (of drug addict etc) être en manque.

wither ['wɪðər] vi (of plant etc) se flétrir; — vt flétrir. ◆**-ed** a (limb) atrophié. ◆**-ing** a (look) foudroyant; (remark) cinglant.

withhold [wɪð'həʊld] vt (pt & pp withheld) (help, permission etc) refuser (from à); (decision) différer; (money) retenir (from de); (information etc) cacher (from à).

within [wɪ'ðɪn] adv à l'intérieur; — prep (place, container etc) à l'intérieur de, dans; **w. a kilometre of** à moins d'un kilomètre de; **w. a month** (to return etc) avant un mois; (to finish sth) en moins d'un mois; (to pay) sous un mois; **w. my means** dans les limites de mes moyens; **w. sight** en vue.

without [wɪ'ðaʊt] prep sans; **w. a tie/etc** sans cravate/etc; **w. doing** sans faire.

withstand [wɪð'stænd] vt (pt & pp withstood) résister à.

witness ['wɪtnɪs] n (person) témoin m; (evidence) Jur témoignage m; **to bear w. to témoigner de;** — vt être (le) témoin de, voir; (document) signer (pour attester l'authenticité de).

witty ['wɪtɪ] a (-ier, -iest) spirituel. ◆**witti**-

cism n bon mot m, mot m d'esprit. ◆**wittiness** n esprit m.

wives [waɪvz] see **wife**.

wizard ['wɪzəd] n magicien m; (genius) Fig génie m, as m.

wizened ['wɪz(ə)nd] a ratatiné.

wobble ['wɒb(ə)l] vi (of chair etc) branler, boiter; (of cyclist, pile etc) osciller; (of jelly, leg) trembler; (of wheel) tourner de façon irrégulière. ◆**wobbly** a (table etc) bancal, boiteux; **to be w.** = to wobble.

woe [wəʊ] n malheur m. ◆**woeful** a triste.

woke, woken [wəʊk, 'wəʊkən] see **wake**[1].

wolf [wʊlf] **1** n (pl wolves) loup m; **w. whistle** sifflement m admiratif. **2** vt **to w. (down)** (food) engloutir.

woman, pl **women** ['wʊmən, 'wɪmɪn] n femme f; **she's a London w.** c'est une Londonienne; **w. doctor** femme f médecin; **women drivers** les femmes fpl au volant; **w. friend** amie f; **w. teacher** professeur m femme; **women's** (attitudes, clothes etc) féminin. ◆**womanhood** n (quality) féminité f; **to reach w.** devenir femme. ◆**womanizer** n Pej coureur m (de femmes or de jupons). ◆**womanly** a féminin.

womb [wuːm] n utérus m.

women ['wɪmɪn] see **woman**.

won [wʌn] see **win**.

wonder ['wʌndər] **1** n (marvel) merveille f, miracle m; (sense, feeling) émerveillement m; **in w.** (to watch etc) émerveillé; **(it's) no w.** ce n'est pas étonnant (that que (+ sub)); — vi (marvel) s'étonner (at de); — v **I w. that** je or ça m'étonne que (+ sub). **2** vt (ask oneself) se demander (if si, why pourquoi); — vi (reflect) songer (about à). ◆**wonderful** a (excellent, astonishing) merveilleux. ◆**wonderfully** adv (beautiful, hot etc) merveilleusement; (to do, work etc) à merveille.

wonky ['wɒŋkɪ] a (-ier, -iest) Fam (table etc) bancal; (hat, picture) de travers.

won't [wəʊnt] = **will not**.

woo [wuː] vt (woman) faire la cour à, courtiser; (try to please) Fig chercher à plaire à.

wood [wʊd] n (material, forest) bois m. ◆**woodcut** n gravure f sur bois. ◆**wooded** a (valley etc) boisé. ◆**wooden** a de or en bois; (manner, dancer etc) Fig raide. ◆**woodland** n région f boisée. ◆**woodpecker** n (bird) pic m. ◆**woodwind** n (instruments) Mus bois mpl. ◆**woodwork** n (craft, objects) menuiserie f. ◆**woodworm** n (larvae) vers mpl (du bois); **it has w.** c'est vermoulu. ◆**woody** a

(-ier, -iest) (*hill etc*) boisé; (*stem etc*) ligneux.

wool [wul] *n* laine *f*; – *a* de laine; (*industry*) lainier. ◆**woollen** *a* de laine; (*industry*) lainier; – *npl* (*garments*) lainages *mpl*. ◆**woolly** *a* (-ier, -iest) laineux; (*unclear*) *Fig* nébuleux; – *n* (*garment*) *Fam* lainage *m*.

word [wɜːd] *n* mot *m*; (*spoken*) parole *f*, mot *m*; (*promise*) parole *f*; (*command*) ordre *m*; *pl* (*of song etc*) paroles *fpl*; **by w. of mouth** de vive voix; **to have a w. with s.o.** (*speak to*) parler à qn; (*advise, lecture*) avoir un mot avec qn; **in other words** autrement dit; **I have no w. from** (*news*) je suis sans nouvelles de; **to send w. that** . . . faire savoir que . . . ; **to leave w. that** . . . dire que . . . ; **the last w. in** (*latest development*) le dernier cri en matière de; **w. processing** traitement *m* de texte; – *vt* (*express*) rédiger, formuler. ◆**wording** *n* termes *mpl*. ◆**wordy** *a* (-ier, -iest) verbeux.

wore [wɔːr] *see* wear 1,2.

work [wɜːk] *n* travail *m*; (*product*) & *Liter* œuvre *f*, ouvrage *m*; (*building or repair work*) travaux *mpl*; **to be at w.** travailler; **farm w.** travaux *mpl* agricoles; **out of w.** au *or* en chômage; **a day off w.** un jour de congé *or* de repos; **he's off w.** il n'est pas allé travailler; **the works** (*mechanism*) le mécanisme; **a gas works** (*factory*) une usine à gaz; **w. force** main-d'œuvre *f*; **a heavy w. load** beaucoup de travail; – *vi* travailler; (*of machine etc*) marcher, fonctionner; (*of drug*) agir; **to w. on** (*book etc*) travailler à; (*principle*) se baser sur; **to w. at** *or* **on sth** (*improve*) travailler qch; **to w. loose** (*of knot, screw*) se desserrer; (*of tooth*) se mettre à branler; **to w. towards** (*result, agreement, aim*) travailler à; **to w. out** (*succeed*) marcher; (*train*) *Sp* s'entraîner; **it works out at £5** ça fait cinq livres; **it works up to** (*climax*) ça tend vers; **to w. up to sth** (*in speech etc*) en venir à qch; – *vt* (*person*) faire travailler; (*machine*) faire marcher; (*mine*) exploiter; (*miracle*) faire; (*metal, wood etc*) travailler; **to get worked up** s'exciter; **to w. in** (*reference, bolt*) introduire; **to w. off** (*debt*) payer en travaillant; (*excess fat*) se débarrasser de (par l'exercice); (*anger*) passer, assouvir; **to w. out** (*solve*) résoudre; (*calculate*) calculer; (*scheme, plan*) élaborer; **to w. up an appetite** s'ouvrir l'appétit; **to w. up enthusiasm** s'enthousiasmer; **to w. one's way up** (*rise socially etc*) faire du chemin. ◆**working** *a* (*day, clothes etc*) de travail; (*population*)

actif; **Monday's a w. day** on travaille le lundi, lundi est un jour ouvré; **w. class** class *f* ouvrière; **in w. order** en état de marche; – *npl* (*mechanism*) mécanisme *m*. ◆**workable** *a* (*plan*) praticable. ◆**worker** *n* travailleur, -euse *mf*; (*manual*) ouvrier, -ière *mf*; (*employee, clerk*) employé, -ée *mf*; **blue-collar w.** col *m* bleu.

workaholic [wɜːkəˈhɒlɪk] *n* *Fam* bourreau *m* de travail. ◆**workbench** *n* établi *m*. ◆**working-'class** *a* ouvrier. ◆**'workman** *n* (*pl* -men) ouvrier *m*. ◆**'workmanship** *n* maîtrise *f*, travail *m*. ◆**'workmate** *n* camarade *mf* de travail. ◆**'workout** *n* *Sp* (*séance f*) d'entraînement *m*. ◆**'workroom** *n* salle *f* de travail. ◆**'workshop** *n* atelier *m*. ◆**'work-shy** *a* peu enclin au travail. ◆**work-to-'rule** *n* grève *f* du zèle.

world [wɜːld] *n* monde *m*; **all over the w.** dans le monde entier; **the richest/etc in the world** le *or* la plus riche/etc du monde; **a w. of** (*a lot of*) énormément de; **to think the w. of** penser énormément de bien de; **why in the w.** . . . ? pourquoi diable . . . ?; **out of this w.** (*wonderful*) *Fam* formidable; – *a* (*war etc*) mondial; (*champion, cup, record*) du monde. ◆**world-'famous** *a* de renommée mondiale. ◆**worldly** *a* (*pleasures*) de ce monde; (*person*) qui a l'expérience du monde. ◆**world'wide** *a* universel.

worm [wɜːm] *n* ver *m*. **2 w. to w. one's way into** s'insinuer dans; **to w. sth out of s.o.** soutirer qch à qn. ◆**worm-eaten** *a* (*wood*) vermoulu; (*fruit*) véreux.

worn [wɔːn] *see* wear 1,2; – *a* (*tyre etc*) usé. ◆**worn-'out** *a* (*object*) complètement usé; (*person*) épuisé.

worry [ˈwʌrɪ] *n* souci *m*; – *vi* s'inquiéter (*about sth* de qch, *about s.o.* pour qn); – *vt* inquiéter; **to be worried** être inquiet; **to be worried sick** se ronger les sangs. ◆—**ing** *a* (*news etc*) inquiétant. ◆**worrier** *n* anxieux, -euse *mf*. ◆**worryguts** *n*, *Am* ◆**worrywart** *n* *Fam* anxieux, -euse *mf*.

worse [wɜːs] *a* pire, plus mauvais (*than* que); **to get w.** se détériorer; **he's getting w.** (*in health*) il va de plus en plus mal; (*in behaviour*) il se conduit de plus en plus mal; – *adv* plus mal (*than* que); **I could do w.** je pourrais faire pire; **to hate/etc w. than** détester/etc plus que; **to be w. off** (*financially*) aller moins bien financièrement; – *n* **there's w. (to come)** il y a pire encore; **a change for the w.** une détérioration. ◆**worsen** *vti* empirer.

worship [ˈwɜːʃɪp] *n* culte *m*; **his W. the Mayor** Monsieur le Maire; – *vt* (-pp-)

(*person*) & *Rel* adorer; (*money etc*) *Pej* avoir le culte de; – *vi Rel* faire ses dévotions (**at** à). ◆**worshipper** *n* adorateur, -trice *mf*; (*in church*) fidèle *mf*.

worst [wɜːst] *a* pire, plus mauvais; – *adv* (**the**) **w.** le plus mal; **to come off w.** (*in struggle etc*) avoir le dessous; – *n* **the w.** (**one**) (*object, person*) le *or* la pire, le *or* la plus mauvais(e); **the w. (thing) is that . . .** le pire c'est que . . . ; **at (the) w.** au pis aller; **at its w.** (*crisis*) à son plus mauvais point *or* moment; **to get the w. of it** (*in struggle etc*) avoir le dessous; **the w. is yet to come** on n'a pas encore vu le pire.

worsted [ˈwʊstɪd] *n* laine *f* peignée.

worth [wɜːθ] *n* valeur *f*; **to buy 50 pence w.** **of chocolates** acheter pour cinquante pence de chocolats; – *a* **to be w.** valoir; **how much** *or* **what is it w.?** ça vaut combien?; **the film's** **w.** seeing le film vaut la peine *or* le coup d'être vu; **it's w. (one's) while** ça (en) vaut la peine *or* le coup; **it's w. (while) waiting** ça vaut la peine d'attendre. ◆**worthless** *a* qui ne vaut rien. ◆**worth'while** *a* (*book,* *film etc*) qui vaut la peine d'être lu, vu *etc*; (*activity*) qui (en) vaut la peine; (*contribution, plan*) valable; (*cause*) louable; (*satisfying*) qui donne des satisfactions.

worthy [ˈwɜːðɪ] *a* (**-ier, -iest**) digne (**of** de); (*laudable*) louable; – *n* (*person*) notable *m*.

would [wʊd, *unstressed* wəd] *v aux* **I w. stay,** **I'd stay** (*conditional tense*) je resterais; **he** **w. have done it** il l'aurait fait; **w. you help me,** **please?** voulez-vous m'aider, s'il vous plaît?; **w. you like some tea?** voudriez-vous (prendre) du thé?; **I w. see her every day** (*used to*) je la voyais chaque jour. ◆**would-be** *a* (*musician etc*) soi-disant.

wound[1] [wuːnd] *vt* (*hurt*) blesser; **the** **wounded** les blessés *mpl*; – *n* blessure *f*.

wound[2] [waʊnd] *see* **wind**[2].

wove, woven [wəʊv, ˈwəʊv(ə)n] *see* **weave**.

wow! [waʊ] *int Fam* (c'est) formidable!

wrangle [ˈræŋg(ə)l] *n* dispute *f*; – *vi* se disputer.

wrap [ræp] *vt* (**-pp-**) **to w. (up)** envelopper; **to w.** (**oneself**) **up** (*dress warmly*) se couvrir; **wrapped up in** (*engrossed*) *Fig* absorbé par; – *n* (*shawl*) châle *m*; (*cape*) pèlerine *f*; **plastic w.** *Am* scel-o-frais® *m*. ◆**wrapping** *n* (*action, material*) emballage *m*; **w. paper** papier *m* d'emballage. ◆**wrapper** *n* (*of* *sweet*) papier *m*; (*of book*) jaquette *f*.

wrath [rɒθ] *n Lit* courroux *m*.

wreak [riːk] *vt* **to w. vengeance on** se venger de; **to w. havoc on** ravager.

wreath [riːθ] *n* (*pl* **-s** [riːðz]) (*on head, for* *funeral*) couronne *f*.

wreck [rek] *n* (*ship*) épave *f*; (*sinking*) naufrage *m*; (*train etc*) train *m etc* accidenté; (*person*) épave *f* (humaine); **to** **be a nervous w.** être à bout de nerfs; – *vt* détruire; (*ship*) provoquer le naufrage de; (*career, hopes etc*) *Fig* briser, détruire. ◆**—age** *n* (*fragments*) débris *mpl*. ◆**—er** *n* (*breakdown truck*) *Am* dépanneuse *f*.

wren [ren] *n* (*bird*) roitelet *m*.

wrench [rentʃ] *vt* (*tug at*) tirer sur; (*twist*) tordre; **to w. sth from s.o.** arracher qch à qn; – *n* mouvement *m* de torsion; (*tool*) clé *f* (à écrous), *Am* clé *f* à mollette; (*distress*) *Fig* déchirement *m*.

wrest [rest] *vt* **to w. sth from s.o.** arracher qch à qn.

wrestl/e [ˈres(ə)l] *vi* lutter (**with s.o.** avec qn); **to w. with** (*problem etc*) *Fig* se débattre avec. ◆**—ing** *n Sp* lutte *f*; (**all-in**) **w. catch** *m*. ◆**—er** *n* lutteur, -euse *mf*; catcheur, -euse *mf*.

wretch [retʃ] *n* (*unfortunate person*) malheureux, -euse *mf*; (*rascal*) misérable *mf*. ◆**wretched** [-ɪd] *a* (*poor, pitiful*) misérable; (*dreadful*) affreux; (*annoying*) maudit.

wriggle [ˈrɪg(ə)l] *vi* **to w. (about)** se tortiller; (*of fish*) frétiller; **to w. out of** (*difficulty, task* *etc*) esquiver; – *vt* (*fingers, toes*) tortiller.

wring [rɪŋ] *vt* (*pt & pp* **wrung**) (*neck*) tordre; **to w. (out)** (*clothes*) essorer; (*water*) faire sortir; **to w. sth out of s.o.** *Fig* arracher qch à qn; **wringing wet** (*trempé*) à tordre.

wrinkle [ˈrɪŋk(ə)l] *n* (*on skin*) ride *f*; (*in cloth* *or paper*) pli *m*; – *vt* (*skin*) rider; (*cloth,* *paper*) plisser; – *vi* se rider; faire des plis.

wrist [rɪst] *n* poignet *m*. ◆**wristwatch** *n* montre-bracelet *f*.

writ [rɪt] *n* acte *m* judiciaire; **to issue a w.** **against s.o.** assigner qn (en justice).

write [raɪt] *vti* (*pt* **wrote,** *pp* **written**) écrire; **to** **w. down** noter; **to w. off** (*debt*) passer aux profits et pertes; **to w. out** (*entire; copy*) recopier; **to w. up** (*from notes*) rédiger; (*diary, notes*) mettre à jour; – *vi* écrire; **to** **w. away** *or* **off** *or* **up for** (*details etc*) écrire pour demander; **to w. back** répondre; **to** **w. in** *Rad TV* écrire (**for information**/*etc* pour demander des renseignements/*etc*). ◆**w.-off** *n* **a (complete) w.-off** (*car*) une véritable épave. ◆**w.-up** *n* (*report*) *Journ* compte rendu *m*. ◆**writing** *n* (*handwriting*) écriture *f*; (*literature*) littérature *f*; **to** **put (down) in w.** mettre par écrit; **some w.** (*on page*) quelque chose d'écrit; **his** *or* **her**

writing(s) (works) ses écrits mpl; **w. desk** secrétaire m; **w. pad** bloc m de papier à lettres; **w. paper** papier m à lettres. ◆**writer** n auteur m (**of** de); (literary) écrivain m.

writhe [raɪð] vi (in pain etc) se tordre.

written ['rɪt(ə)n] see **write**.

wrong [rɒŋ] a (sum, idea etc) faux, erroné; (direction, time etc) mauvais; (unfair) injuste; **to be w.** (of person) avoir tort (**to do** de faire); (mistaken) se tromper; **it's w. to swear/etc** (morally) c'est mal de jurer/etc; **it's the w. road** ce n'est pas la bonne route; **you're the w. man** (for job etc) tu n'es pas l'homme qu'il faut; **the clock's w.** la pendule n'est pas à l'heure; **something's w.** quelque chose ne va pas; **something's w. with the phone** le téléphone ne marche pas bien; **something's w. with her arm** elle a quelque chose au bras; **nothing's w.** tout va

bien; **what's w. with you?** qu'est-ce que tu as?; **the w. way round** or **up** à l'envers; – adv mal; **to go w.** (err) se tromper; (of plan) mal tourner; (of vehicle, machine) tomber en panne; – n (injustice) injustice f; (evil) mal m; **to be in the w.** avoir tort; **right and w.** le bien et le mal; – vt faire (du) tort à. ◆**wrongdoer** n (criminal) malfaiteur m. ◆**wrongful** a injustifié; (arrest) arbitraire. ◆**wrongfully** adv à tort. ◆**wrongly** adv incorrectement; (to inform, translate) mal; (to suspect etc) à tort.

wrote [rəʊt] see **write**.

wrought [rɔːt] a **w. iron** fer m forgé. ◆**w.-'iron** a en fer forgé.

wrung [rʌŋ] see **wring**.

wry [raɪ] a (**wryer**, **wryest**) (comment) ironique; (smile) forcé; **to pull a w. face** grimacer.

X

X, x [eks] n X, x m. ◆**X-ray** n (beam) rayon m X; (photo) radio(graphie) f; **to have an X-ray** passer une radio; **X-ray examination** examen m radioscopique; – vt radiographier.

xenophobia [zenə'fəʊbɪə] n xénophobie f.

Xerox® ['zɪərɒks] n photocopie f; – vt photocopier.

Xmas ['krɪsməs] n Fam Noël m.

xylophone ['zaɪləfəʊn] n xylophone m.

Y

Y, y [waɪ] n Y, y m.

yacht [jɒt] n yacht m. ◆**—ing** n yachting m.

yank [jæŋk] vt Fam tirer d'un coup sec; **to y. off** or **out** arracher; – n coup m sec.

Yank(ee) ['jæŋk(ɪ)] n Fam Ricain, -aine m f, Pej Amerloque m f.

yap [jæp] vi (-pp-) (of dog) japper; (jabber) Fam jacasser.

yard [jɑːd] n **1** (of house etc) cour f; (for storage) dépôt m, chantier m; (garden) Am jardin m (à l'arrière de la maison); **builder's y.** chantier m de construction. **2** (measure) yard m (= 91,44 cm). ◆**yardstick** n (criterion) mesure f.

yarn [jɑːn] n **1** (thread) fil m. **2** (tale) Fam longue histoire f.

yawn [jɔːn] vi bâiller; – n bâillement m. ◆**—ing** a (gulf etc) béant.

yeah [jeə] adv (yes) Fam ouais.

year [jɪər] n an m, année f; (of wine) année f; **school/tax/etc y.** année f scolaire/fiscale/ etc; **this y.** cette année; **in the y. 1990** en (l'an) 1990; **he's ten years old** il a dix ans; **New Y.** Nouvel An, Nouvelle Année; **New Year's Day** le jour de l'An; **New Year's Eve** la Saint-Sylvestre. ◆**yearbook** n annuaire m. ◆**yearly** a annuel; – adv annuellement.

yearn [jɜːn] vi **to y. for s.o.** languir après qn; **to y. for sth** avoir très envie de qch; **to y. to do** avoir très envie de faire. ◆**—ing** n grande envie f (**for** de, **to do** de faire); (nostalgia) nostalgie f.

yeast [jiːst] n levure f.

yell [jel] vti **to y. (out)** hurler; **to y. at s.o.** (scold) crier après qn; – n hurlement m.

yellow ['jeləʊ] **1** a & n (colour) jaune (m); – vi jaunir. **2** a (cowardly) Fam froussard. ◆**yellowish** a jaunâtre.

yelp [jelp] vi (of dog) japper; – n jappement m.

yen [jen] n (desire) grande envie f (for de, to do de faire).

yes [jes] adv oui; (contradicting negative question) si; – n oui m inv.

yesterday ['jestədɪ] adv & n hier (m); y. morning/evening hier matin/soir; **the day before y.** avant-hier.

yet [jet] **1** adv encore; (already) déjà; she hasn't come (as) y. elle n'est pas encore venue; **has he come y.?** est-il déjà arrivé?; **the best y.** le meilleur jusqu'ici; **y. more complicated** (even more) encore plus compliqué; **not (just) y.**, not y. awhile pas pour l'instant. **2** conj (nevertheless) pourtant.

yew [juː] n (tree, wood) if m.

Yiddish ['jɪdɪʃ] n & a yiddish (m).

yield [jiːld] n rendement m; (profit) rapport m; – vt (produce) produire, rendre; (profit) rapporter; (give up) céder (to à); – vi (surrender, give way) céder (to à); (of tree, land etc) rendre; 'y.' (road sign) Am 'cédez la priorité'.

yob(bo) ['jɒb(əʊ)] n (pl yob(bo)s) Sl loubar(d) m.

yoga ['jəʊgə] n yoga m.

yog(h)urt ['jɒgət, Am 'jəʊgɜːt] n yaourt m.

yoke [jəʊk] n (for oxen) & Fig joug m.

yokel ['jəʊk(ə)l] n Pej plouc m.

yolk [jəʊk] n jaune m (d'œuf).

yonder ['jɒndər] adv Lit là-bas.

you [juː] pron **1** (polite form singular) vous; (familiar form singular) tu; (polite and familiar form plural) vous; (object) vous; te, t'; pl vous; (after prep & stressed) vous; toi; pl vous; **(to) y.** (indirect) vous; te, t'; pl

vous; **y. are** vous êtes; tu es; **I see y.** je vous vois; je te vois; **I give it to y.** je vous le donne; je te le donne; **with y.** avec vous; avec toi; **y. teachers** vous autres professeurs; **y. idiot!** espèce d'imbécile! **2** (indefinite) on; (object) vous; te, t'; pl vous; **never know** on ne sait jamais.

young [jʌŋ] a (-er, -est) jeune; **my young(er) brother** mon (frère) cadet; **his or her youngest brother** le cadet de ses frères; **the youngest son** le cadet; – n (of animals) petits mpl; **the y.** (people) les jeunes mpl. ◆**young-looking** a qui a l'air jeune. ◆**youngster** n jeune m/f.

your [jɔːr] poss a (polite form singular, polite and familiar form plural) votre, pl vos; (familiar form singular) ton, ta, pl tes; (one's) son, sa, pl ses. ◆**yours** poss pron le vôtre, la vôtre, pl les vôtres; (familiar form singular) le tien, la tienne, pl les tien(ne)s; **this book is y.** ce livre est à vous ou est le vôtre; ce livre est à toi ou est le tien; **a friend of y.** un ami à vous; un ami à toi. ◆**your-self** pron (polite form) vous-même; (familiar form) toi-même; (reflexive) vous; te, t'; (after prep) vous; toi; **you wash y.** vous vous lavez; tu te laves. ◆**your-selves** pron pl vous-mêmes; (reflexive & after prep) vous.

youth [juːθ] n (pl -s [juːðz]) (age, young people) jeunesse f; (young man) jeune m; **y. club** maison f des jeunes. ◆**youthful** a (person) jeune; (quality, smile etc) juvénile, jeune. ◆**youthfulness** n jeunesse f.

yoyo ['jəʊjəʊ] n (pl -os) yo-yo m inv.

yucky ['jʌkɪ] a Sl dégueulasse.

Yugoslav ['juːgəʊslɑːv] a & n yougoslave (mf). ◆**Yugo'slavia** n Yougoslavie f.

yummy ['jʌmɪ] a (-ier, -iest) Sl délicieux.

yuppie ['jʌpɪ] n jeune cadre m ambitieux, jeune loup m, NAP mf.

Z

Z, z [zed, Am ziː] n Z, z m.

zany ['zeɪnɪ] a (-ier, -iest) farfelu.

zeal [ziːl] n zèle m. ◆**zealous** ['zeləs] a zélé. ◆**zealously** adv avec zèle.

zebra ['ziːbrə, 'zebrə] n zèbre m; **z. crossing** passage m pour piétons.

zenith ['zenɪθ] n zénith m.

zero ['zɪərəʊ] n (pl -os) zéro m; **z. hour** Mil & Fig l'heure H.

zest [zest] n **1** (gusto) entrain m; (spice) Fig piquant m; **z. for living** appétit m de vivre. **2** (of lemon, orange) zeste m.

zigzag ['zɪgzæg] n zigzag m; – a & adv en zigzag; – vi (-gg-) zigzaguer.

zinc [zɪŋk] n (metal) zinc m.

zip [zɪp] **1** n **z. (fastener)** fermeture f éclair®; – vt (-pp-) **to z. (up)** fermer (avec une fermeture éclair®). **2** n (vigour) Fam entrain *m*; − *vi* (**-pp-**) (*go quickly*) aller comme l'éclair. **3** *a* **z. code** *Am* code *m* postal. ◆**zipper** *n Am* fermeture *f* éclair®.

zit [zɪt] *n* (*pimple*) *Am Fam* bouton *m*.

zither ['zɪðər] *n* cithare *f*.

zodiac ['zəʊdɪæk] *n* zodiaque *m*.

zombie ['zɒmbɪ] *n* (*spiritless person*) *Fam* robot *m*, zombie *m*.

zone [zəʊn] *n* zone *f*; (*division of city*) secteur *m*.

zoo [zuː] *n* zoo *m*. ◆**zoological** [zuːə-'lɒdʒɪk(ə)l] *a* zoologique. ◆**zoology** [zuː-'ɒlədʒɪ] *n* zoologie *f*.

zoom [zuːm] **1** *vi* (*rush*) se précipiter; **to z. past** passer comme un éclair. **2** *n* **z. lens** zoom *m*; − *vi* **to z. in** *Cin* faire un zoom, zoomer (**on** sur).

zucchini [zuːˈkiːnɪ] *n* (*pl* **-ni** *or* **-nis**) *Am* courgette *f*.

zwieback ['zwiːbæk] *n* (*rusk*) *Am* biscotte *f*.